POSTCARDS FROM

Frommer's

Europe 2002

W9-AWH-319

Neuschwanstein Castle's gothic turrets rise from the rugged Bavarian Alps. See "The Romantic Road" in chapter 7. © Jeff Hunter/The Image Bank.

The Acropolis in Athens—ancient symbol of "the glory that was Greece." See "Athens" in chapter 8. © Kindra Clineff Photography.

Perched on the cliffs of Santorini, a blue-domed church gleams in the sunshine. See "The Cyclades" in chapter 8. © Ben Davidson/Photo 20-20.

Above: Marie Antoinette played shepherdess at her quaint Hamlet, near the Petit Trianon in Versailles. See "Paris" in chapter 6. © Kindra Clineff. Below: Magnificent Chambord, the largest château in the Loire Valley. See "The Loire Valley Châteaux" in chapter 6. © Kevin Galvin Photography.

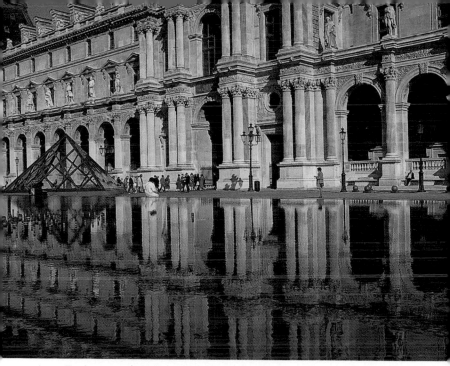

Above: The Louvre and I.M. Pei's controversial glass pyramid reflect the convergence of old and new in Paris. See "Paris" in chapter 6. © Bob Krist Photography. Below: The quieter sidestreets of popular Montmartre are worth seeking out for their views over the Paris rooftops. See "Paris" chapter 6. © Bob Krist Photography.

Above: Walking the cobblestone streets of Stockholm's Gamla Stan (Old Town) at night is a trip back in time. See "Stockholm & Environs" in chapter 17. © Bob Krist Photography.
Below: Restaurant-lined rue des Bouchers in Brussels' historic heart. See "Brussels" in chapter 2. © Kevin Galvin Photography.

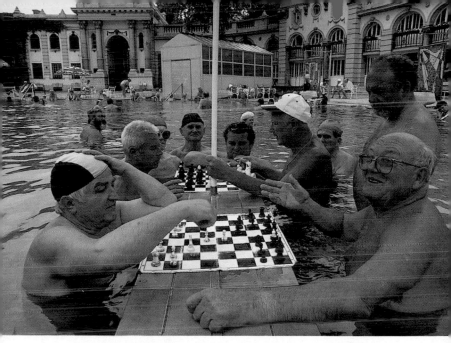

Above: "Checkmate." Men playing chess relax in Budapest's thermal baths. See "Budapest" in chapter 9. © Catherine Karnow Photography. Below: Medieval castles, Gothic cathedrals, cobblestone streets, and tranquil canals hauntingly evoke Bruges' past. See "Bruges & Ghent" in chapter 2. © Kevin Galvin Photography.

Above: The Vltava River winds through historic Prague, one of Europe's most vibrant and beautiful cities. See "Prague & Environs" in chapter 3. © *Anthony Cassidy/Tony Stone Images.*
Below: Baroque Salzburg's alpine setting is on the banks of the Salzach River. See "Salzburg & Environs" in chapter 1. © *Kevin Galvin Photography.*

Left: Amsterdam's graceful cityscape is lined with canals, bridges, and 17th-century townhouses. See "Amsterdam" in chapter 12. © Kevin Galvin Photography.
Below: In Holland, watery expanses are punctuated by scenic windmills. See "Amsterdam" in chapter 12. © Michael Defreitas Photography.

Right: Capped by Brunelleschi's dome—an amazing architectural feat—the Duomo dominates Florence's skyline. See "Florence" in chapter 11. © Kevin Galvin Photography. Below: Olive trees and grapevines dot Tuscany's rolling hills in the heart of Italy. See "Highlights of the Tuscan & Umbrian Countryside" in chapter 11. © Jean Miele/The Stock Market.

The Leaning Tower of Pisa, one of the world's most recognizable buildings, leans about 14 feet from perpendicular. See "Highlights of the Tuscan & Umbrian Countryside" in chapter 11.
© Massimo Mastrorillo/The Stock Market.

The maritime province of the Algarve, often called the "garden of Portugal," is dotted with hundreds of beautiful beaches. See "The Algarve" in chapter 14. © *Bob Krist Photography.*

Above: Hiking the Dingle Peninsula on the lush Emerald Isle. See "Kerry & the Dingle Peninsula" in chapter 10. © M. Timothy O'Keefe Photography. *Below: St. Paul's Cathedral in London is a monument to beauty and tranquility. See "London" in chapter 5.* © Kelly/Mooney Photography.

Above: Rich in history, Edinburgh Castle is one of the highpoints of a visit to Scotland. See "Edinburgh & Environs" in chapter 15. © Kindra Clineff Photography. Below: In Oxford, the towers and spires of one of the world's great universities rise majestically skyward. See "Oxford, the Cotswolds & Stratford-upon-Avon" in chapter 5. © Chris Donaghue Photography.

Segovia's glorious 12th-century Alcázar castle has been the residence of Spanish monarchs since Isabella met Ferdinand here. See "Madrid" in chapter 16. © Paul Hardy/The Stock Market.

Two faces of Europe. Above: The island of Santorini (also known as Thira) is famous for volcanic black sand beaches, dazzling archeological sites, and wonderful restaurants and nightlife. See "The Cyclades" in chapter 8. © Walter Bibikow/The Viesti Collection, Inc. Below: Summer visitors can gaze on fields of sunflowers as they drive through southern France. See "Provence & the Côte d'Azur" in chapter 6. © Bob Krist Photography.

When should I travel to get the best airfare?
Where do I go for answers to my travel questions?
What's the best and easiest way to plan and book my trip?

frommers.travelocity.com

Frommer's, the travel guide leader, has teamed up with **Travelocity.com**, the leader in online travel, to bring you an in-depth, easy-to-use resource designed to help you plan and book your trip online.

At **frommers.travelocity.com**, you'll find free online updates about your destination from the experts at Frommer's plus the outstanding travel planning and purchasing features of Travelocity.com. Travelocity.com provides reservations capabilities for 95 percent of all airline seats sold, more than 47,000 hotels, and over 50 car rental companies. In addition, Travelocity.com offers more than 2,000 exciting vacation and cruise packages. Travelocity.com puts you in complete control of your travel planning with these and other great features:

> **Expert travel guidance from Frommer's** - over 150 writers reporting from around the world!
>
> **Best Fare Finder** - an interactive calendar tells you when to travel to get the best airfare
>
> **Fare Watcher** - we'll track airfare changes to your favorite destinations
>
> **Dream Maps** - a mapping feature that suggests travel opportunities based on your budget
>
> **Shop Safe Guarantee** - 24 hours a day / 7 days a week live customer service, and more!

Whether traveling on a tight budget, looking for a quick weekend getaway, or planning the trip of a lifetime, Frommer's guides and Travelocity.com will make your travel dreams a reality. You've bought the book, now book the trip!

A New Star-Rating System & Other Exciting News from Frommer's!

In our continuing effort to publish the savviest, most up-to-date, and most appealing travel guides available, we've added some great new features.

Frommer's guides now include a new **star-rating system.** Every hotel, restaurant, and attraction is rated from 0 to 3 stars to help you set priorities and organize your time.

We've also added **seven brand-new features** that point you to the great deals, in-the-know advice, and unique experiences that separate travelers from tourists. Throughout the guide look for:

Finds	Special finds—those places only insiders know about
Fun Fact	Fun facts—details that make travelers more informed and their trips more fun
Kids	Best bets for kids—advice for the whole family
Moments	Special moments—those experiences that memories are made of
Overrated	Places or experiences not worth your time or money
Tips	Insider tips—some great ways to save time and money
Value	Great values—where to get the best deals

We've also added a **"What's New"** section in every guide—a timely crash course in what's hot and what's not in every destination we cover.

Other Great Guides for Your Trip:

Frommer's Europe from $70 a Day

Frommer's Gay & Lesbian Europe

Europe For Dummies

Hanging Out in Europe

Frommer's Road Atlas Europe

Frommer's®

Europe

2002

Here's what the critics say about Frommer's:

"Amazingly easy to use. Very portable, very complete."

—*Booklist*

"The only mainstream guide to list specific prices. The Walter Cronkite of guide-books—with all that implies."

—*Travel & Leisure*

"Complete, concise, and filled with useful information."

—*New York Daily News*

"Hotel information is close to encyclopedic."

—*Des Moines Sunday Register*

Hungry Minds™

Best-Selling Books • Digital Downloads • e-Books • Answer Networks •
e-Newsletters • Branded Web Sites • e-Learning
New York, NY • Cleveland, OH • Indianapolis, IN

Published by:

Hungry Minds, Inc.
909 Third Ave.
New York, NY 10022

ISBN 0-7645-6492-7
ISSN 1091-9511

Editors: Ron Boudreau and Matthew X. Kiernan
Production Editor: Jennifer Connolly
Design by Michele Laseau
Cartographer: Roberta Stockwell
Photo Editor: Richard Fox
Production by Hungry Minds Indianapolis Production Services

Front cover photo: Leaning Tower with La Fontana dei Putti in foreground,
Pisa, Italy
Back cover photo: El Alcázar, Segovia, Spain

Special Sales
For general information on Hungry Minds' products and services please contact
our Customer Care department; within the U.S. at 800-762-2974, outside the U.S.
at 317-572-3993 or fax 317-572-4002. For sales inquiries and reseller information,
including discounts, bulk sales, customized editions, and premium sales, please
contact our Customer Care department at 800-434-3422.

Manufactured in the United States of America

5 4 3 2 1

Contents

11 Italy   669

by Darwin Porter & Danforth Prince

12 The Netherlands   772

by George McDonald

13 Norway   805

by Darwin Porter & Danforth Prince

14 Portugal   831

by Darwin Porter & Danforth Prince

15 Scotland   877

by Darwin Porter & Danforth Prince

16 Spain   928

by Darwin Porter & Danforth Prince

17 Sweden   1013

by Darwin Porter & Danforth Prince

18 Switzerland   1038

by Darwin Porter & Danforth Prince

List of Maps

This book is dedicated to Senior Editor Ron Boudreau (1960-2001), whose keen eye and steadfast dedication will be sorely missed.

About the Authors

Darwin Porter, a native of North Carolina, was assigned to write the very first edition of a Frommer's guide devoted solely to one European country. Since then, he has written many best-selling Frommer's guides to all the major European destinations. In 1982, he was joined in his research efforts by **Danforth Prince,** formerly of the Paris bureau of The *New York Times,* who has traveled and written extensively about Europe.

All four of **Joseph S. Lieber**'s grandparents emigrated from Eastern Europe at the turn of the 20th century, settling in New York City, where he was born and raised. Mr. Lieber lived in Hungary for several years in the early 1990s. He presently practices law in Boston and is the coauthor of *Frommer's Budapest & the Best of Hungary* and *Frommer's Europe from $70 a Day.* **Christina Shea** served as a Peace Corps volunteer in Hungary and subsequently directed Peace Corps language-training programs in Lithuania and Kyrghyzstan. She's the author of the novel *Moira's Crossing* (St. Martin's) and a coauthor of *Frommer's Budapest & the Best of Hungary* and *Frommer's Europe from $70 a Day.*

Robert Emmet Meagher, a dual citizen of Ireland and the United States, is professor of humanities at Hampshire College in Amherst, Massachusetts. The author of more than a dozen books, plays, and translations, he has lived and worked in Ireland, twice holding visiting professorships at Trinity College Dublin.

George McDonald has lived in Amsterdam and Brussels as a former editor of the Sabena Belgian World Airlines and deputy editor of the KLM Royal Dutch Airlines in-flight magazines. He is now a freelance journalist and travel writer, and has written extensively about the Netherlands and Belgium for international magazines and guidebooks, such as *Frommer's Amsterdam* and *Frommer's Belgium, Holland & Luxembourg.*

Sherry Marker's love of Greece began when she majored in classical Greek at Harvard. She has studied at the American School of Classical Studies in Athens and studied ancient history at the University of California at Berkeley. Author or coauthor of a number of guides to Greece (such as *Frommer's Greece* and *Frommer's Greek Islands*), she has published articles in The *New York Times, Travel & Leisure,* and *Hampshire Life.* She's also the coauthor of *Frommer's Europe from $70 a Day* and has written books on a variety of subjects, including a history of London for young adults.

Hana Mastrini is a native of the western Czech spa town of Karlovy Vary who became a veteran of the "Velvet Revolution" as a student in Prague in 1989. She began contributing to Frommer's guides while helping her husband, John, better understand his new home in the Czech Republic.

An Invitation to the Reader

In researching this book, we discovered many wonderful places—hotels, restaurants, shops, and more. We're sure you'll find others. Please tell us about them, so we can share the information with your fellow travelers in upcoming editions. If you were disappointed with a recommendation, we'd love to know that, too. Please write to:

Frommer's Europe 2002
Hungry Minds, Inc. • 909 Third Avenue • New York, NY 10022

An Additional Note

Please be advised that travel information is subject to change at any time—and this is especially true of prices. We therefore suggest that you write or call ahead for confirmation when making your travel plans. The authors, editors, and publisher cannot be held responsible for the experiences of readers while traveling. Your safety is important to us, however, so we encourage you to stay alert and be aware of your surroundings. Keep a close eye on cameras, purses, and wallets, all favorite targets of thieves and pickpockets.

New! Frommer's Star Ratings & Icons

Every hotel, restaurant, and attraction listing in this guide has been ranked for quality, value, service, amenities, and special features using a star-rating scale. In country, state, and regional guides, we also rate towns and regions to help you narrow down your choices and budget your time accordingly. Hotels and restaurants in the Very Expensive and Expensive categories are rated on a scale of one (highly recommended) to three stars (exceptional). Those in the Moderate and Inexpensive categories rate from zero (recommended) to two stars (very highly recommended). Attractions, towns, and regions are rated according to the following scale: zero stars (recommended), one star (highly recommended), two stars (very highly recommended), and three stars (must-see).

In addition to the rating system, we also use seven icons to highlight insider information, useful tips, special bargains, hidden gems, memorable experiences, kid-friendly venues, places to avoid, and other useful information:

(*Finds* (*Fun Fact* (*Kids* (*Moments* (*Overrated* (*Tips* (*Value*

The following abbreviations are used for credit cards:

AE	American Express	DISC	Discover	V Visa
DC	Diners Club	MC	MasterCard	

FROMMERS.COM

Now that you have the guidebook to a great trip, visit our website at **www.frommers.com** for travel information on nearly 2,000 destinations. With features updated regularly, we give you instant access to the most current trip-planning information available. At Frommers.com, you'll also find the best prices on air fares, accommodations, and car rentals—and you can even book travel online through our travel booking partners. At Frommers.com you'll also find the following:

- Daily Newsletter highlighting the best travel deals
- Hot Spot of the Month/Vacation Sweepstakes & Travel Photo Contest
- More than 200 Travel Message Boards
- Outspoken Newsletters and Feature Articles on travel bargains, vacation ideas, tips & resources, and more!

What's New in Europe

What's new in Europe? Read on to find out what's recently opened, what's changed, and what's hot for your trip in the year to come.

AUSTRIA **Vienna** Rivaling the long-established Imperial or Bristol, **Ana Grand Hotel Wien,** Kärnter Ring 9, A-1010 Vienna (℘ **01/515-800**), is a seven-story deluxe hotel, only a block from Staatsoper, that's become the new "Grand Hotel" of the Austrian capital. Also in the center, **Das Triest**, Wiedner Hauptstrasse 12, A-1040 Vienna (℘ **01/589-**18), a 5-minute walk from St. Stephan's Cathedral, is an emerging favorite with artists and musicians. A 17th-century building is now a hip hotel, attracting media types.

Dö & Co., in the Haas & Haas, Stephansplatz 4 (℘ **01/512-26-66**), is stylish, upscale, and a delicious venue from one of Austria's most esoteric food stores.

BELGIUM **Brussels** The **Parc de Bruxelles,** rue Royale, between Parliament and the Royal Palace in the center, has been renovated and restored. The Belgian government has decided to legalize possession of small amounts of cannabis for personal consumption.

Bruges The city has been selected as European Capital of Culture for 2002.

THE CZECH REPUBLIC **Prague** Visiting stars Bruce Willis and Italian pop legend Eros Ramazzotti have enjoyed the **Four Seasons Hotel,** Veleslavínova 2a, Praha 1 (℘ **02/2142 7000**), and its view of Prague Castle and Charles Bridge.

Now more than 10 years into the post-Communist transformation, Prague's physical regeneration is gaining pace, while the variety of eating experiences improves by the year. There are so many newly reopened and renovated places to try, along with wholly new haunts. **KOGO,** Havelská 27, Praha 1 (℘ **02/2421 4543**), which brought you some of the best seafood in town, has now opened a light, breezy cafe in the Slovansk_ dům shopping center. **Angel Café,** Opatovická 3, Praha 1 (℘ **02/290 166**), offers tasty sandwiches, in a crisp, modern setting near the National Theater.

The rococo gem **Kinsk_ Palace** (Palác Kinsk_ch), Staroměstské náměstí 12, Praha 1 (℘ **02/2481 0758**), reopened hosting some of the best Czech art collections on Old Town Square. Also, President Havel and Prince Charles have just opened the **Ledeburská, the Small and Great Pálffyovská, Kolowratská** and **Small Furstenberská** gardens below the Prague Castle—beautifully sculpted terraced spaces with stunning views of the city below.

Karlštejn Castle On this most popular day trip from Prague, don't miss the recently reopened **Holy Rood Chapel** featuring early Renaissance paintings by Theodoricus.

DENMARK **Copenhagen** A great new moderately priced hotel has opened here, the **Copenhagen Strand,** Havnegade 37, DK-1058 København K (℘ **33-48-99-00**), dramatically created out of a pair of old brick-and-timber factories.

The big culinary news is Michelin's long-delayed recognition of Copenhagen as one of the dining capitals of Europe—**Era Ora** (Italian), Torvegade 62 (℃ **32-54-06-93**), and **Godt** (international), Gothersgade 38 (℃ **33-15-21-22**), are the two hot new ones. The latest see-and-be-seen place is **Søren K,** on the ground floor of the Royal Library's Black Diamond Wing, 1 Søren Kierkegaards Plads (℃ **33-47-49-49**). It's hot and happening, not like the philosopher for whom it is named.

The two night clubs generating the most local excitement are **Enzo,** Norregade 41 (℃ **33-13-67-88**), which has more bars than any other club—each one different—and **NASA,** Gothersgade 8F, Bolthensgaard (℃ **33-93-74-15**), which features the latest and most avant-garde musical groups.

ENGLAND London In Soho, **Charlotte Street Hotel,** 15 Charlotte St., London W1P 1HB (℃ **800/553-6674** in the U.S.), is creating a sensation, London chic at its finest but with a Los Angeles cutting edge. Also creating shock waves is **Myhotel,** 11–13 Bayley St., Bedford Square, London, WC1B 3HD (℃ **020/7667-6000**). It's designed according to the ancient Chinese art of feng shui. Each traveler is assigned an assistant responsible for one's happiness!

On the restaurant scene, **The Square,** 6–10 Burton St., W1 (℃ **020/7495-7100**), in St. James's is hailed by savvy London foodies as the city's "next great restaurant" thanks to chef Philip Howard.

Oxford In this university city, **Gee's Restaurant,** 61 Banbury Rd. (℃ **01865/553-540**), in a Victorian glass conservatory, has emerged under a new chef as one of Oxford's finest dining choices, with a Mediterranean-inspired cuisine.

FRANCE Paris Small and charming, **Hotel de Jeu de Paume,** 54 rue St-Louis en l'Île, 4e (℃ **01-43-26-14-18**), is chic and hip, formed from a pair of 17th-century town houses. It's an instant success.

In dining, **Georges,** 19 rue Beaubourg, 4e (℃ **01-44-78-47-99**), is a hot new ticket, a restaurant on the top floor of Centre Georges Pompidou. No mere tourist trap, it's a venue for artisty Paris drawn to its refined international cuisine.

GERMANY Berlin Two little hotels are the talk of the town. On the fourth floor of an Art Nouveau building, the aptly named **Art Nouveau Hotel,** Leibnizstrasse 59, D-10629 Berlin (℃ **030/3-27-74-40**), is upmarket, atmospheric, and desirable. Hidden away from the bustle of Berlin, **Bleibtreu Hotel,** Bleibtreustrasse 31 (℃ **030/ 88474-0**), is media hip and trendy, set in the labyrinthine premises of what was originally an Art Nouveau apartment house.

Among Berlin restaurants, **Rockendorf's Gourmet Restaurant,** Passauerstrasse 5–7 (℃ **030/219-92-170**), has moved into the very heart of central Berlin, and the city's serious foodies are flocking to the new location for some grand eating.

Munich It's called merely **Der Tisch,** Maxvorstadt, Nymphenburger Strasse 1 (℃ **089/557-154**), or "the table," but it's one of the best and most fashionable dining venues to have emerged in the Bavarian capital.

GREECE Athens The biggest news these days is the opening of the new **Athens International Airport Eleftherios Venizelos.** But most of the news is about what's *not* open at the airport. Services, access roads, and public transportation are still under construction, so check the airport's status before you land here.

One of Athens's most popular restaurants, **Socrates' Prison,** 17 Robertou Galli St. ((©) **01/922-3434**), has moved from its old location at 20 Mitseon Street just around the corner to a new location with a roof garden at 17 Robertou Galli St.

Wonderful news: the **Benaki Museum,** 1 Odos Koumbari 1 ((©) **01/367-1000**), in Kolonaki, has reopened after a 10-year restoration and renovation project. The new wing doubles the exhibition space of the original 20th-century neoclassical town house that belonged to the wealthy Benaki family. Display cases in the **Syntagma Square Metro station** showcase objects unearthed during the excavations for Athens's new Metro system.

Suddenly **Psirri,** an old warehouse district off Athinas Street, is one of Athens's trendiest neighborhoods. To find out about the bars, cafes, restaurants, theaters, and galleries that are springing up in Psirri, check out www.psirri.gr.

Delphi The **Delphi Archaeology Museum** ((©) **0265/82**-313) at the ancient site should have opened its long-awaited extension and almost doubled the number of objects on view.

Nafplion Everyone's favorite town in the Peloponnese has its first "boutique" hotel: the **Hotel Nafsimedon,** 9 Sideras Merarhias St. ((©) **0752/25-060**), on Kolokotronis Park.

Santorini In Fira, the new **Thera Foundation** ((©) **0286/230-16**) near the cable car station en route to Firostephani has an exhibit of spectacular reproductions and recreations of the frescoes from Akrotiri, sometimes called the "Greek Pompeii."

HUNGARY Budapest The **Gresham Palace,** the once-grand Art Nouveau structure at the head of the Chain Bridge in Pest, is being rescued from its long-time state of woeful disrepair and being converted into a new luxury hotel (of the Four Seasons variety). As anyone who has visited Budapest in the last 30 or 40 years has no doubt noticed, the historic **New York Coffeehouse,** on the Outer Ring at VII. Erzsébet krt. 9–11 ((©) **061/352-1326**), an architectural gem located near Blaha Lujza tér on the Outer Ring, is in awful disrepair. Well, all that is about to change. A Swiss investor group recently won a tender offer to purchase the building and plans to renovate and open a five-star hotel.

Check out the amazing **"Tropicarium"** at a mall in southern Buda called **Campona,** located at XXII. Budapest, Nagytétényi út 37–43 ((©) **061/424-3000**). The Tropicarium features both an aquarium—the largest in Central Europe—and a miniature rain forest, with snakes, alligators, and the like (and rain!).

IRELAND Dublin Visitors seeking a panoramic view of Dublin's skyline will be glad to hear of two new observation towers opened to the public in the past year: For the first time since the 1966 demolition of Nelson's Pillar on O'Connell Street, it's possible to get a close-up look at the rooftop layout of Dublin's city center. The **"gravity bar"** is a glass-walled room perched at the summit of the Guinness Storehouse, James's Gate, a dramatic way to conclude a visit to the new Visitors' Centre ((©) **01/408-4800**). Not quite as lofty but closer to city center is the **Jameson Chimney,** off Arran Quay, part of the elaborate renovation of Dublin's Smithfield district.

ITALY Rome Near Villa Borghese, **Testa Food & Wine,** Via Tirso 30 ((©) **06-8530-0692**), is a real culinary find, attracting disconcerting palates to a decor both classic and elegant. One of Rome's most acclaimed restaurants is **Il Convivio,** Vicolo dei Soldati 31 ((©) **06-686-9432**), attracting *haut*

Roma to its 16th-century site near the Piazza Navona. Another chic, hot dining ticket is **Il Chicco d'Uva,** Corso Rinascimento 70 (℅ **06-686-7983**), also near the Piazza Navona, an emporium of refined Italian and international cuisine.

Florence The landmark *luxe* hotel, **Savoy,** Piazza della Repubblica 7 (℅ **055-27-351**), has returned to give the Excelsior and Grand serious competition in luxury. After a long decline, the hotel has been completely restored.

THE NETHERLANDS Amsterdam Try out the new **All Amsterdam Transport Pass,** which allows unlimited travel for a day by Canal Bus, tram, bus, and metro.

NORWAY Oslo One of Oslo's newest large-scale hotels, **First Hotel Millennium,** Tollbugate 25 (℅ **23-00-30-00**), was successfully created from a 1930s Art Deco office building. Rising nine floors, with a stylish kind of minimalism, it's become an instant hit.

In a warehouse-like building, **Restaurant Huset,** Universitatsgata 26 (℅ **22-41-36-33**), has blossomed as the nightlife center of Oslo, with dance areas, dining rooms (one devoted to Cajun cookery), and discos, with enough bars to drown the navy.

Bergen The hotel scene here has brightened considerably with the opening of the first-class **First Hotel Marin,** Rosenkrantzgaten 8 (℅ **53-05-15-00**), an elegant harbor front choice with more suites than any hotel in town. From fitness center to Turkish bath, it's amenity loaded.

PORTUGAL Lisbon Right in the heart of the city, the **Orion Lisboa Hotel,** 24 Praça dos Restauradores (℅ **21-321-6600**), has been formed

from the old Eden Theater. Now you can rent an apartment at Lisbon's most central location.

The restaurant of the hour, **Notre,** Edificio Nau, Marina Expo '98 (℅ **21-893-1604**), has reincarnated itself in its new location by Expo Marina. Its Portuguese/Continental cuisine is among Lisbon's noblest.

SCOTLAND Edinburgh The **Caledonian Hilton Hotel,** "The Caley," Princes St. (℅ **0131/459-9988**), one of Edinburgh's most enduring landmark hotels, has emerged anew under the Hilton umbrella. At first Edinburghers were shocked at the Americanization of this virtual monument, but they seem to be adjusting.

For dining, the town's most excitement is generated by **The Tower,** Chambers St. (℅ **0131/225-3003**), set on the top floor of the Museum of Scotland. Some of Scotland's tastiest fare, especially seafood, is served at this chic new location.

SPAIN Madrid In the heart of Madrid, **Errota Zar,** Jovellanos 3 (℅ **91-531-25-64**), next to the House of Deputies, has emerged as a serious challenger to all other Basque restaurants.

SWEDEN Stockholm In Gamla Stan, the old town of Stockholm, **Pontus in the Green House,** Österlånggatan 17 (℅ **08/23-85-00**), in a building from the 16th century, is all the rage with its French, Swedish, and Asian fusion cuisine.

SWITZERLAND Geneva In Geneva, **Bal-Esperance,** 1 rue de la Vallée (℅ **022/818-3737**), is an accommodation oddity, set right near the landmark place du Bourg-de-Four. Once owned by the rawbone Salvation Army, it's been turned into a hotel of grace and charm.

Planning Your Trip to Europe

by Darwin Porter & Danforth Prince

Irresistible and intriguing, the ever-changing Europe at the beginning of the new millennium offers you more excitement, experiences, and memories than ever. In compiling this book, we've tried to open the door to Europe's famous cities (their art and architecture, restaurants and theater, hotels and history) and guide you to all the experiences no one would want to miss on even a cursory visit. So though this guide has to skim the highlights, we've also tossed in off-beat destinations and adventurous suggestions leading to surprises and delights around every corner.

As it moves into the 21st century, Europe, or at least the 11-nation "euro zone" (Austria, Belgium, Finland, France, Germany, Ireland, Italy, Luxembourg, the Netherlands, Portugal, Spain) has a dream to steer the continent toward the type of robust growth known in the United States during the Clinton years. During the 1990s, each member nation was burdened with high unemployment, recession, and slow growth, preventing fast economic recovery. Economic reforms, especially in the big three (Germany, Italy, France), are being instigated but face opposition from large segments of the public. By becoming part of the euro zone, these nations have pledged themselves to cut budget deficits and squeeze chronic inflation. And by adopting the euro and yielding to fiercely competitive global pressures, these 11 nations have been sent kicking and screaming into the 2000s whether major political groups in any country wanted it or not.

Of course, you don't visit Europe to fret over economics. The rich culture and histories in each of its myriad countries and regions have always been the lure, and they remain so today. From the splendor of a walled hill town rising above the verdant Tuscan landscape to the majestic snowcapped peaks of the Alps, from the sound of flamenco in a Madrid tablaos to the blasting of a brass band in Munich's Hofbräuhaus—one Europe it may be on the map (and now on the bankbooks), but on the ground it's still a Europe of countless facets and proud, distinct, diverse heritages. There's no other place where you can experience such enormous cultural changes by driving from one mountain valley to the next, where in only a few miles you're likely to encounter not only a different language but also different food, architecture, and culture.

Europe has seen some of the greatest intellectual and artistic developments the world has ever known, and the landscape is dense with museums, cathedrals, palaces, and monuments serving as repositories for much of this past glory. But the good news is that the continent is still in a dynamic creative mode; artistic and cultural ferment are still very much part of the present, and Europe still helps set the trends in fashion, industrial design, cinema, technology, music, literature, and science. The dynamic environment is all about life, innovation, entertainment, and food, which exist side by side with the artistic and cultural grandeur of the past.

Europe

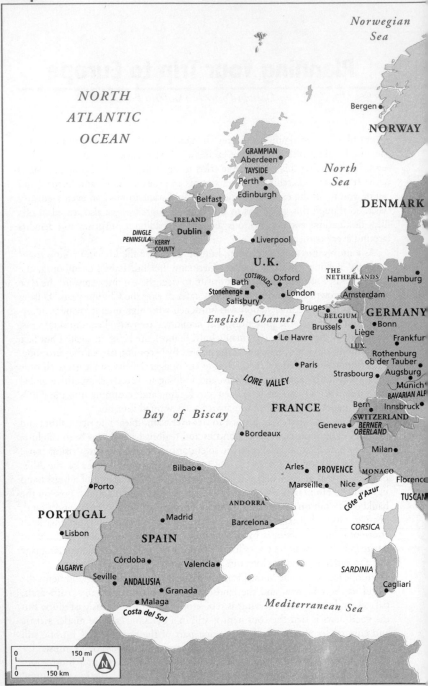

Norwegian Sea

NORTH
ATLANTIC
OCEAN

Bergen●

NORWAY

GRAMPIAN
Aberdeen●
TAYSIDE
Perth●
Edinburgh●

North Sea

Belfast●

DENMARK

IRELAND   **Dublin**●

DINGLE PENINSULA
KERRY COUNTY

Liverpool●

U.K.

COTSWOLDS   Oxford●
Bath●
Stonehenge■   ●London
Salisbury●

THE NETHERLANDS   Hamburg●

Amsterdam●

GERMANY

Bruges●
BELGIUM
Brussels●   Liège●
●Bonn

●Le Havre

LUX.

Frankfur●

Rothenburg
ob der Tauber●

English Channel

●Paris

Strasbourg●   Augsburg●
Munich●
BAVARIAN ALP

LOIRE VALLEY

FRANCE

Bern●   Innsbruck●
SWITZERLAND
Geneva●   *BERNER OBERLAND*

Bay of Biscay

Bordeaux●

Milan●

Bilbao●

Arles●   **PROVENCE**   **MONACO**
Marseille●   Nice●   Florenc●
Côte d'Azur   **TUSCAN**

●Porto

ANDORRA

Madrid●

Barcelona●

CORSICA

PORTUGAL

●Lisbon

SPAIN

Córdoba●   Valencia●

SARDINIA

ALGARVE
Seville●   **ANDALUSIA**
Granada●
●Malaga

Cagliari●

Mediterranean Sea

Costa del Sol

0   150 mi
0   150 km

✆ Number, Please: Calling Europe

To make a phone call **from the United States to Europe**, dial the international access code, **011**, then the **country code** for the country you're calling, then the **city code** for the city you're calling, and then the regular phone number. For an operator-assisted call, dial **01**, then the country code, then the city code, and then the regular phone number; an operator then comes on the line.

The following are the codes for the countries and major cities in this guide. These are the codes you use to call from overseas or from another European country; if you're calling from within the country or within the city, see the "Telephone" entry in the "Fast Facts" section for each city.

European phone systems are undergoing a prolonged change. **Italy, France, Spain, Monaco, Copenhagen, and now Portugal no longer use separate city codes.** The code is now built into all phone numbers, and you must always dial the initial zero or nine (which was previously—and still is in most other countries—added before a city code only when dialing from another city within the country). Also, be aware of these two recent changes: The city codes for London (171 and 181) have been replaced by a new single code, 20, which is then followed by an eight-digit number beginning with either 7 or 8; and the city code for Lisbon has changed from 1 to 21.

Austria	43	Denmark	45
Innsbruck	512	England	44
Salzburg	662	Bath	1225
Vienna	1	London	20
Belgium	32	Oxford	1865
Bruges	50	Stratford-upon-Avon	1789
Brussels	2	France	33
Ghent	9	Germany	49
Czech Republic	420	Berlin	30
Prague	2	Munich	89

Europe is also about people. Europeans have seen the best and the worst of times, and a better-educated, more sophisticated younger generation is waiting to welcome you. They're as diverse and fascinating as the lands they come from, and throughout this book we've noted places not only where you'll meet other visitors, but also where you'll have a chance to meet and chat with the locals, enriching your experience immeasurably.

We've tried to prepare this edition to help you discover where you want to go and what you want to see. This introductory chapter is designed to equip you with what you need to know before you go—the advance-planning tools for an enjoyable and successful trip.

1 Visitor Information

TOURIST OFFICES

Start with the **European tourist offices** in your own country; for a complete list, see below. If you aren't sure which countries you want to visit, send for an information-packed free

Greece	30	Norway	47
Athens	1	Oslo	22
Delphi	265	Portugal	351
Hungary	36	Scotland	44
Budapest	1	Edinburgh	131
Ireland	353	Spain	34
Dublin	1	Sweden	46
Italy	39	Stockholm	8
Monaco	377	Switzerland	41
Netherlands	31	Bern	31
Amsterdam	20	Geneva	22

The easiest and cheapest way to call home from abroad is with a calling card. On the road, you just dial a local access code (almost always free) and then punch in the number you're calling as well as the calling-card number. If you're in a non–Touch-Tone country, just wait for an English-speaking operator to put your call through. The "Telephone" entry in the "Fast Facts" for each city gives the AT&T, MCI, and Sprint access codes for that country (your calling card will probably come with a wallet-sized list of local access numbers). You can also call any one of those companies' numbers to make a collect call as well; just dial it and wait for the operator.

When it comes to dialing direct, calling from the United States to Europe is much cheaper than the other way around, so whenever possible, have friends and family call you at your hotel rather than you calling them. To dial direct back to the United States and Canada from Europe, the international access code is often, but not always, 00; the country code is 1, and then you punch in the area code and number. For Australia and New Zealand, the access code is also 00; the country codes are 61 and 64, respectively.

booklet called *Planning Your Trip to Europe,* revised annually by the 28-nation **European Travel Planner,** P.O. Box 1754, New York, NY 10185 (✆ **800/816-7530;** www.visiteurope. com). Or check out *Europe for Dummies,* available at most bookstores.

AUSTRIAN NATIONAL TOURIST OFFICE
IN THE U.S. P.O. Box 1142, Times Square Station, New York, NY 10108-1142 (✆ **212/944-6880;** fax 212/730-4568).

IN CANADA 1010 Sherbrooke St. W., Suite 1410, Montréal, PQ H3A 2R7 (✆ **514/849-3709;** fax 514/849-9577); 2 Bloor St. E., Suite 3330, Toronto, ON M4W 1A8 (✆ **416/967-3381;** fax 416/967-4101); 200 Granville St., Suite 1380, Vancouver, BC V6C 1S4 (✆ **604/683-5808;** 604/662-8528).

IN THE U.K. 225 Marsh Wall London E14 9FW (✆ **020/7531 0391;** fax 020/7458 0045).

IN AUSTRALIA 36 Carrington St., 1st Floor, Sydney, NSW 2000

(✆ **02/9299-3621;** fax 02/9299-3808).

E-MAIL info@oewnyc.com

WEBSITE www.anto.com

BELGIAN TOURIST OFFICE
IN THE U.S. 780 Third Ave., New York, NY 10017 (✆ **212/758-8130;** fax 212/355-7675).

IN CANADA P.O. Box 760 NDG, Montreal, PQ H4A 382 (✆ **514/489-3594;** fax 514/489-8965).

IN THE U.K. 225 Marsh Wall London E14 9FW **020/7531 0391** fax 020/7458-0045.

E-MAIL info@visitbelgium.com

WEBSITE www.visitbelgium.com

BRITISH TOURIST AUTHORITY
IN THE U.S. 551 Fifth Ave., Suite 701, New York, NY 10176-0799 (✆ **800/462-2748** or 212/986-2200; fax 212/986-1188).

IN CANADA 5915 Airport Rd., Mississaugua, Toronto, ON L4V ITI (✆ **888/VISITUK;** fax 905/405-1835).

IN AUSTRALIA Level 16, Gateway, 1 Macquarie Place, Sydney, NSW 2000 (✆ **02/9377-4400;** fax 02/9377-4499).

IN NEW ZEALAND Fay Richwhite Bld., 17^(th) Floor, 151 Queen St., Auckland 1 (✆ **09/303-1446;** fax 09/377-6965).

E-MAIL travelinfo@bta.org.uk

WEBSITE www.visitbritain.com

CZECH TOURIST AUTHORITY
IN THE U.S. 1109 Madison Ave., New York, NY 10028 (✆ **212/288-0830**).

IN CANADA Simpson Tower 401 Bay St. Suite 1510, Toronto, ON M5H 2Y5. (✆ **416/363-9928,** fax 416/363-0239. cdacanada@iprimus.ca).

IN THE U.K. 95 Great Portland St., London W1N 5RA (✆ **020/7291-9920;** fax 020/7436-1300).

E-MAIL travelczech@pop.net

WEBSITE http://czechcenter.com or www.czech.cz

FRENCH GOVERNMENT TOURIST OFFICE
IN THE U.S. 444 Madison Ave., 16th Floor, New York, NY 10022 (✆ **212/838-7800**); 676 N. Michigan Ave., Suite 3360, Chicago, IL 60611 (✆ **312/751-7800**); 9454 Wilshire Blvd., Suite 715, Beverly Hills, CA 90212 (✆ **310/271-6665;** fax 310/276-2835). To request information at any of these offices call the **France on Call hot line** at ✆ **900/990-0040** (50¢ per minute).

IN CANADA Maison de la France/French Government Tourist Office, 1981 av. McGill College, Suite 490, Montréal, PQ H3A 2W9 (✆ **514/288-4264;** fax 514/845-4868); 30 St. Patrick St., Suite 700, Toronto, ON M5T 3A3 (✆ **416/491-7622;** fax 416/979-7587).

IN THE U.K. Maison de la France/French Government Tourist Office, 178 Piccadilly, London, W1V 0AL (✆ **020/7399-3500;** fax 020/9221-8682).

IN AUSTRALIA French Tourist Bureau, 25 Bligh St., Sydney, NSW 2000 (✆ **02/9231-5244**).

E-MAIL info@francetourism.com

WEBSITE www.francetourism.com

GERMAN NATIONAL TOURIST OFFICE
IN THE U.S. 122 E. 42nd St., 52nd Floor, New York, NY 10168-0072 (✆ **212/661-7200;** fax 212/661-7174).

IN CANADA 175 Bloor St. E., Suite 604, Toronto, ON M4W 3R8 (✆ **877/315-6237;** fax 416/968-1986).

IN THE U.K.   P.O. Box 2695, London W1A 3TN (© **020/7317-0908** or 020/7495-6129).

IN AUSTRALIA   P.O. Box A980, Sydney, NSW 1235 (© **02/9267-8148;** fax 02/9267-9035).

E-MAIL   gntony@aol.com   or germanto @idirect.com

WEBSITE   www.germany-tourism.de

GREEK NATIONAL TOURIST ORGANIZATION
IN THE U.S.   645 Fifth Ave., 5th Floor, New York, NY 10022 (© **212/421-5777;** fax 212/826-6490).

IN CANADA 1300 Bay St., Toronto, ON M5R 3K8 (© **416/968-2220;** fax 416/968-6533).

IN THE U.K.   4 Conduit St., London W1R 0DJ (© **020/7734-5997;** fax 020/7287-1369).

IN AUSTRALIA   51–57 Pitt St., Sydney, NWS 2000 (© **02/9241-1663;** fax 02/9235-2174).

E-MAIL   ento@greektourism.com

WEBSITE   www.gnto.gr

HUNGARIAN NATIONAL TOURIST OFFICE
IN THE U.S. & CANADA   150 E. 58th St., 33rd Floor, New York, NY 10155 (© **212/355-0240;** fax 212/207-4103).

IN THE U.K. ℅ Embassy of the Republic of Hungary, Trade Commission, 46 Eaton Place, London, SW1X 8AL (© **020/7823-1032;** fax 020/7823-1459).

E-MAIL   htnewyork@hungary tourism.hu or htlondon@hungary tourism.hu

WEBSITE   www.hungarytourism.hu

IRISH TOURIST BOARD
IN THE U.S.   345 Park Ave., New York, NY 10154 (© **800/223-6470** or 212/418-0800; fax 212/371-9052).

IN CANADA   160 Bloor St. E., Suite 1150, Toronto, ON M4W 1B9

(© **416/487-3335;** fax 416/929-6783).

IN THE U.K.   150 New Bond St., London W1Y OAQ (© **020/7493-3201;** fax 020/7493-9056).

IN AUSTRALIA   36 Carrington St., 5th Floor, Sydney, NSW 2000 (© **02/9299-6177;** fax 02/9299-6323).

E-MAIL   info@irishtouristboard.com

WEBSITE   www.ireland.travel.ie

ITALIAN GOVERNMENT TOURIST BOARD
IN THE U.S.   630 Fifth Ave., Suite 1565, New York, NY 10111 (© **212/245-4822;** fax 212/586-9249); 500 N. Michigan Ave., Suite 2240, Chicago, IL 60611 (© **312/644-0996;** fax 312/644-3019); 12400 Wilshire Blvd., Suite 550, Beverly Hills, CA 90025 (© **310/820-1898;** fax 310/820-6357).

IN CANADA   175 Bloor St., E., South Tower, Suite 907, Toronto, ON, M4W 3R8 (© **416/925-4882;** fax 416/925-4799).

IN THE U.K.   1 Princes St., London W1R 8AY (© **020/7408-1254;** fax 020/7493-6695).

E-MAIL   enitny@bway.net, 739145@icam.net, or enitlond@globalnct.co.uk

WEBSITE   www.enit.it

MONACO GOVERNMENT TOURIST OFFICE
IN THE U.S. & CANADA   565 Fifth Ave., New York, NY 10017 (© **800/753-9696** or 212/286-3330; fax 212/286-9890).

IN THE U.K.   3–8 Chelsea Garden Market, Chelsea Harbour, London, SW10 0XE (© **020/7352-9962;** fax 020/7352-2103).

E-MAIL   mgto@monaco1.org

WEBSITE   www.monaco-tourism.com or www.monaco.mc

NETHERLANDS BOARD OF TOURISM

IN THE U.S.   355 Lexington Ave., 19th Floor, New York, NY 10017 (© **212/370-7360**); 225 N. Michigan Ave., Suite 1854, Chicago, IL 60601 (© **888/464-6552**).

IN CANADA   Box 1078, Toronto, ON M5C 2K5 (© **888/464-6552**).

IN THE U.K.   18 Buckingham Gate, London, SW1E 6LD (© **020/7802-8108** or 020/7828-7900; fax 020/7828-7941).

E-MAIL   go2holland@aol.com

WEBSITE   www.goholland.com

PORTUGUESE NATIONAL TOURIST OFFICE

IN THE U.S.   590 Fifth Ave., 4th Floor, New York, NY 10036 (© **212/354-4403;** fax 764-6137).

IN CANADA   60 Bloor St. W., Suite 1005, Toronto, ON M4W 3B8 (© **416/921-7376;** fax 416/921-1353).

IN THE U.K.   22-25A Sackville St., 2nd Floor, London W1X 2LY (© **0891/600-370** or 020/7494-1441; fax 020/7494-1868).

E-MAIL   aavila@portugal.org or iceptor@direct.com

WEBSITE   www.portugal.org

SCANDINAVIAN TOURIST BOARDS (DENMARK, NORWAY & SWEDEN)

IN THE U.S. & CANADA   P.O. Box 4649, Grand Central Station, New York, NY 10163-4649 (© **212/885-9700;** fax 212/885-9710).

IN THE U.K.   Danish Tourist Board, 55 Sloane St., London SW1X 95Y (© **020/7259-5959,** fax 020/7259-5955); Norwegian Tourist Board, Charles House, 5 Regent St., London, SW1Y 4LR (© **020/7839-2650;** fax 020/7839-6014); Swedish Travel and Tourism Council, 11 Montagu Pl., London W1H 2AL (© **020/7870-5600;** fax 020/7724-5872).

E-MAIL   usa@nortra.no,   info@gosweden.org, dtb.london@dt.dk, or greatbritain@nortra.no

WEBSITES   www.visitdenmark.com, www.visitnorway.com, or www.gosweden.org

Switzerland Tourism

IN THE U.S.   608 Fifth Ave., New York, NY 10020 (© **212/757-5944;** fax 212/262-6116); 800/974-7795; 877/794-8037.

IN THE U.K.   Swiss Centre, 1 New Coventry St., London, W1V 8EE (© **020/7734-1921;** fax 020/7437-4577).

E-MAIL   stnewyork@switzerland tourism.com or london@switzerland vacation.ch

WEBSITE   www.switzerland tourism.com

TOURIST OFFICE OF SPAIN

IN THE U.S.   666 Fifth Ave., 35th Floor, New York, NY 10103 (© **212/265-8822;** fax 212/265-8864); 845 N. Michigan Ave., Suite 915E, Chicago, IL 60611 (© **312/642-1992;** fax 312/642-9817); 8383 Wilshire Blvd., Suite 960, Beverly Hills, CA 90211 (© **323/658-7188;** fax 213/658-1061); 1221 Brickell Ave., Suite 1850, Miami, FL 33131 (© **305/358-1992;** fax 305/358-8223).

IN CANADA   2 Bloor St. W., 34th Floor, Toronto, ON M5S 1M9 (© **416/961-3131;** fax 416/961-1992).

IN THE U.K.   22–23 Manchester Sq., London W1M 5AP (© **090/6364-0630** or 020/7486-8077; fax 020/7486-8034).

IN AUSTRALIA   203 Castlereagh St., Suite 21A (P.O. Box 675), Sydney, NSW 2000 (© **02/9264-7966**).

E-MAIL   oetny@here-i.com

WEBSITE   www.okspain.org

TRAVEL AGENTS

Travel agents can save you plenty of time and money by hunting down the best airfare for your route and arranging for rail passes and rental cars. For now, most travel agents still charge you nothing for their services—they're paid through commissions from the airlines and other agencies they book for you. However, a number of airlines have begun cutting commissions, and increasingly, agents are finding they have to charge you a fee to hold the bottom line (or else unscrupulous agents will offer you only the travel options that bag them the juiciest commissions). Shop around and ask hard questions.

If you decide to use a travel agent, make sure the agent is a member of the **American Society of Travel Agents (ASTA),** 1101 King St., Alexandria, VA 22314 (© **703/739-8739;** www.astanet.com). If you send them a self-addressed stamped envelope, ASTA will mail you the booklet *Avoiding Travel Problems* for free.

TRAVEL BOOKSTORES

If you live outside a large urban area, you can order maps or travel guides from bookstores specializing in mail- or phone-order service. Some of these are **Book Passage,** 51 Tamal Vista Blvd., Corte Madera, CA 94925 (© **800/321-9785** or 415/927-0960; www.bookpassage.com); and **Forsyth Travel Library,** 1780 E. 131st St., P.O. Box 480800, Kansas City, MO 64148-0800 (© **800/FORSYTH;** www.forsyth.com). And of course there are huge online bookstores at **Amazon** (www.amazon.com) and **Barnes & Noble** (www.barnesandnoble.com).

Canadians can contact **Ulysses Travel Bookshop,** 4176 rue St-Denis, Montréal, PQ H2W 2M5 (© **514/843-9447;** www.ulysses.ca). In London, try **Daunt Books,** 83 Marylebone High St. (© **020/7224-2295**), or any branch of the **Travel Bookshop,** at 13–15 Blenheim Crescent (© **020/7229-5260**), in the USIT Campus office at 52 Grosvenor Gardens (© **0870/240-1010**), or in the British Airways office at 156 Regent St. (© **020/7434-4744**).

2 Entry Requirements & Customs

PASSPORTS

If you don't already have one, you can download a passport application from the websites listed below. Countries covered in this guide do *not* require visas for U.S. or Canadian citizens for stays less than 90 days. Though a valid U.S. state driver's license usually suffices, it's wise to carry an **International Driving Permit** ($12), which you can obtain from any AAA branch if you bring two passport-size photos.

U.S. CITIZENS If applying for a first passport, you need to do it in person at one of 13 passport offices throughout the United States; a federal, state, or probate court; or a major post office (though not all post offices accept applications; call the number below to find ones that do). You need to present a certified birth certificate as proof of citizenship, and it's wise to bring along your driver's license, state or military ID, and Social Security card as well. You also need two identical passport-sized photos (2 in. by 2 in.), taken at any corner photo shop (not one of the strip photos, however, from a photo-vending machine).

For people over 15, a passport is valid for 10 years and costs $60 ($45 plus a $15 handling fee); for those 15 and under, it's valid for 5 years and costs $40. If you're over 15 and have a valid passport that was issued within the past 12 years, you can renew it by mail and bypass the $15 handling fee. Allow plenty of time before your trip to apply; processing normally takes 3 weeks but can take longer during busy periods (especially spring). For general information, call the **National Passport Agency** (© 202/647-0518). To find your regional passport office, contact the **National Passport Information Center** (© 900/225-5674; www.travel.state.gov).

CANADIAN CITIZENS You can pick up a passport application at one of 28 regional passport offices or most travel agencies. The passport is valid for 5 years and costs $60. Children under 16 may be included on a parent's passport but need their own to travel unaccompanied by the parent. Applications, which must be accompanied by two identical passport-sized photographs and proof of Canadian citizenship, are available at travel agencies throughout Canada or from the central **Passport Office, Department of Foreign Affairs and International Trade,** Ottawa, ON K1A 0G3 (© 800/567-6868, 819/994-3500 in the U.S.; www.dfait-maeci.gc.ca). Processing takes 5 to 10 days if you apply in person or about 3 weeks by mail.

U.K. CITIZENS As a member of the European Union (EU), you need only an identity card, not a passport, to travel to other EU countries. However, if you already possess a passport, it's always useful to carry it. To pick up an application for a 10-year passport, visit your nearest passport office, major post office, or travel agency. You can also contact the **London Passport Office** at © 0990/210-410 (www.open.gov.uk or www.ukpa.gov.uk). Passports are £21 for adults and £11 for children under 16.

IRISH CITIZENS You can apply for a 10-year passport, costing IR 45, at the **Passport Office,** Setanta Centre, Molesworth Street, Dublin 2 (© 01/671-1633; www.irlgov.ie/iveagh/foreignaffairs/services). Those under age 18 and over 65 must apply for a IR£10 3-year passport. You can also apply at 1A South Mall, Cork (© 0214/272-525) or over the counter at most main post offices.

AUSTRALIAN CITIZENS Apply at your local post office or passport office or search the government website at **www.dfat.gov.au/passports/**. Passports for adults are A$126 and for those under 18 A$63. Note that Australians now need visas to enter Portugal.

NEW ZEALAND CITIZENS You can pick up a passport application at any travel agency or Link Centre. For more info, contact the **Passport Office,** P.O. Box 805, Wellington (© 0800/225-050). Passports for adults are NZ$80 and for those under 16 NZ$40.

CUSTOMS

U.S. CITIZENS If you've been away 48 hours or more, you're allowed to bring back, once every 30 days, $400 worth of merchandise duty-free. You'll be charged a flat rate of 10% duty on the next $1,000 worth of

---

⁽Tips⁾ Traveler's Tip

Safeguard your passport in an inconspicuous, inaccessible place like a money belt. If you lose it, visit the nearest consulate of your native country as soon as possible for a replacement. Before leaving home, make two photocopy collages of your important documents: the first page of your passport (the page with the photo and identifying info), driver's license, and other ID. Leave one copy at home with a family member or friend and carry the other with you (separate from the originals!).

purchases. Be sure to have your receipts handy. On gifts, the duty-free limit is $100. You can't bring fresh foodstuffs into the United States; tinned foods, however, are allowed. For more information, contact the **U.S. Customs Service,** 1301 Constitution Ave. (P.O. Box 7407), Washington, DC 20044 (℗ **202/927-6724;** www.customs.ustreas.gov), and request the free pamphlet *Know Before You Go.*

U.K. CITIZENS If you're **returning from a European Union (EU) country,** you'll go through a separate Customs Exit ("Blue Exit") especially for EU travelers. In essence, there's no limit on what you can bring back from an EU country, as long as the items are for personal use (this includes gifts) and you've already paid the necessary duty and tax. However, customs law sets out guidance levels. If you bring in more than these levels, you might be asked to prove the goods are for your own use. Guidance levels on goods bought in the EU for your own use are 800 cigarettes, 200 cigars, 1 kilogram smoking tobacco, 10 liters of spirits, 90 liters of wine (of this, not more than 60 liters can be sparkling wine), and 110 liters of beer. For more information, contact **HM Customs & Excise,** Passenger Enquiry Point, 2nd Floor Wayfarer House, Great South West Road, Feltham, Middlesex, TW14 8NP (℗ **020/8910-3744;** www.hmcegov.uk).

If you're **returning from a non-EU country,** you have a customs allowance of 200 cigarettes; 50 cigars; 250 grams of smoking tobacco; 2 liters of still table wine; 1 liter of spirits or strong liqueurs (over 22% volume); 2 liters of fortified wine, sparkling wine, or other liqueurs; 60 cubic centimeters (ml) perfume; 250 cubic centimeters (ml) of toilet water; and £145 worth of all other goods, including gifts and souvenirs. People under 17 can't have the tobacco or alcohol allowance. For more information, contact **HM Customs & Excise,** Passenger Enquiry Point, Wayfarer House, 2nd Floor, Great South West Road, Feltham, Middlesex, TW14 8NP (℗ **020/8910-3744,** or 44/181-910-3744 outside the U.K.; www.hmce.gov.uk).

CANADIAN CITIZENS For a clear summary of rules, write for the booklet *I Declare,* issued by **Revenue Canada,** 2265 St. Laurent Blvd., Ottawa, ON K1G 4KE (℗ **506/636-5064;** www.rc.gc.ca/vco). Canada allows you a $750 exemption, and you're allowed to bring back duty-free 200 cigarettes, 2.2 pounds of tobacco, 40 imperial ounces of liquor, and 50 cigars. In addition, you're allowed to mail gifts to Canada from abroad at the rate of Can$60 a day, provided they're unsolicited and don't contain alcohol or tobacco (write on the package "Unsolicited Gift, Under $60 Value"). All valuables should be declared on the Y-38 form before departure from Canada, including serial numbers of valuables you already own, such as expensive foreign cameras. *Note:* The $500 exemption can be used only once a year and only after an absence of 7 days.

AUSTRALIAN CITIZENS The duty-free allowance is A$400 or, for those under 18, A$200. Personal property mailed back should be marked "Australian Goods Returned" to avoid payment of duty. Upon returning to Australia, you can bring in 250 cigarettes or 250 grams of loose tobacco and 1,125 milliliters of alcohol. If you're returning with valuable goods you already own, such as foreign-made cameras, you should file form B263. A helpful brochure, available from Australian consulates or Customs offices, is *Know Before You Go.* For more information, contact **Australian Customs Services,** GPO

Box 8, Sydney NSW 2001 (© **02/ 9213-2000**).

NEW ZEALAND CITIZENS   The duty-free allowance is NZ$700. Citizens over 17 can bring in 200 cigarettes, 50 cigars, or 250 grams of tobacco (or a mix of all three if their combined weight doesn't exceed 250 grams); plus 4.5 liters of wine and beer or 1.125 liters of liquor. New Zealand currency doesn't carry import or export restrictions. Fill out a certificate of export, listing the valuables you're taking out of the country; that way, you can bring them back without paying duty. Most questions are answered in a free pamphlet available at New Zealand consulates and Customs offices: *New Zealand Customs Guide for Travelers,* Notice no. 4. For more information, contact **New Zealand Customs,** 50 Anzac Ave., P.O. Box 29, Auckland (© **09/359-6655**).

3 Money

Traveler's checks, while still the safest way to carry money, are going the way of the dinosaur. The aggressive evolution of international computerized banking and ATM networks has led to the triumph of plastic in Europe—even if cold cash is still the most trusted currency. Odds are you can saunter up to an ATM in the dinkiest Bavarian village with your bankcard or PIN-enabled Visa and get some local cash out of it. Never rely on credit cards and ATMs alone, however. Though most hotels and many restaurants around Europe accept plastic, smaller towns and cheaper places are still wary, and occasionally the phone lines and computer networks used to verify your card can go down and render your plastic useless. Always carry some local currency and some traveler's checks for insurance.

Although currency conversions in this guide were accurate at press time, European exchange rates fluctuate. For up-to-date rates, look in the business pages or travel section of any major U.S. newspaper, check online at the **Universal Currency Converter** (www. xe.net/currency), or call **Thomas Cook** (see "Traveler's Checks," below).

It's more expensive to purchase foreign currency in your own country than once you've reached your destination. But it's a good idea to arrive in Europe with a bit of the local currency—at least enough to get you from the airport to your hotel, so you can avoid the bad rates you get at airport exchanges. Bring along about $30 to $50 in the local currencies of every European city you'll be visiting (call around to the major branches of local banks in your hometown to find the best rate).

While traveling, either withdraw local currency from an ATM (see below) or convert your cash or traveler's checks at a bank whenever possible—banks invariably give better rates than tourist offices, hotels, travel agencies, or exchange booths. You lose money every time you make a transaction, so it's often better to convert large sums at once (especially in flat-fee transactions). The rates for converting traveler's checks are usually better than those for cash, but you get the best rates by withdrawing money from an ATM with your bank or credit card.

ATMS

Plus, Cirrus, and other networks work on many ATMs in Europe, giving you local currency and drawing it directly from your checking account. This is the fastest, easiest, and least expensive way to change money. You take advantage of the bank's bulk exchange rate (better than anything you'll get on your own exchanging cash or traveler's checks) and, unless your home bank

The World's Greatest Financial Merger: The Euro

The adoption of the single European currency called the **euro** (€) is a contentious move within Europe. Even though most of Western Europe has been closely interconnected as an economic and trade unit for years, the official merger of its national currencies and economies is another matter. Up until the last minute, all the countries involved jockeyed for the best deal for their own nation before the final papers were signed, and even now that the euro is an official currency, they're still fighting over the details of how it will be phased in.

In 1999, the countries that chose to adopt the euro—Austria, Belgium, Finland, France, Germany, Ireland, Italy, Luxembourg, the Netherlands, Portugal, and Spain—officially locked their exchange rates together and switched most business transactions and computer and credit-card banking over to the new single currency—which, after some ups and significant downs, currently seems leveled out just below parity with the dollar ($1 = €1.07). Greece joined the group in 2001. Several countries have opted out from switching over for the time being, including Britain, Denmark, and Sweden (although especially those last two seem to be moving closer to voting it in). The Czech Republic, Hungary, Norway, and Switzerland are not part of the EU.

The euro as physical banknotes and coins will be issued on December 15, 2001 (but not officially to be used until January 1, 2002), and the various national currencies won't be fully withdrawn until February 28— down from the 6 months previously announced. Exceptions: France and Ireland plan to phase out francs and pounds by mid-February, and, oddly, Germany is cutting things extremely close by doing away with deutsche marks on New Year's Eve 2001.

Since you'll still be juggling lire, francs, and pesetas alongside euros until then, the prices in this book are quoted in the old national currencies, the new euros, and dollars: for example, 330F (€50, $47). Note that most Europeans will stilll think in local currencies and settle their prices in round numbers of lire or marks, then merely convert that to the euro amount. Expect when the euro actually exists that the euro price will be the one rounded off. Therefore (just this once!) the rates quoted in this edition may be a little off.

charges you for using a nonproprietary ATM, you won't have to pay a commission. Make sure the PINs on your bank and credit cards will work in Europe; you usually need a four-digit code (six digits often won't work). Keep in mind you're usually able to access only your checking account, not savings, from ATMs abroad.

Both the **Cirrus** (✆ 800/424-7787; www.mastercard.com/atm) and the **Plus** (✆ 800/843-7587; www.visa.com/atms) networks have ATM locators listing the banks in each country that accept your card; alternately, you can just search out any machine with your network's symbol on it. Europe is getting to be like America—a bank on virtually every corner—and most are globally networked. You can also get a cash advance through Visa or MasterCard (contact the issuing bank to enable this feature and get a PIN), but note the credit-card company will begin charging you interest immediately, and many have begun assessing a fee every time. American Express card cash advances are usually available only from AMEX offices, which you'll find in every European city.

CREDIT CARDS

Most middle-bracket and virtually all first-class and deluxe hotels, restaurants, and shops in Europe accept major credit cards—American Express, Diners Club, MasterCard, and Visa (not Discover). Some budget establishments accept plastic; others don't. The most widely accepted cards these days are Visa and MasterCard, but it pays to carry American Express too. Note that you can now often choose to charge credit-card purchases at the price in euros or in the local currency; since most European currencies are now locked together, the dollar amount always comes out the same, but it could help you comparison-shop.

TRAVELER'S CHECKS

Most large banks sell traveler's checks, charging fees of 1% to 2% of the value of the checks. AAA members can buy American Express checks commission-free. Traveler's checks are great travel insurance because if you lose them—and have kept a list of their numbers (and a record of which ones were cashed) in a safe place separate from the checks themselves—you can get them replaced at no charge. Hotels and shops usually accept them, but you get a lousy exchange rate. Use traveler's checks to exchange for local currency at banks or American Express offices. Personal checks are next to useless in Europe.

   American Express (℡ **800/221-7282;** www.americanexpress.com) is one of the largest issuers of traveler's checks, and theirs are the most commonly accepted. They also sell checks to holders of certain types of American Express cards at no commission. **Thomas Cook** (℡ **800/223-7373** in the U.S. and Canada, 020/7480-7226 in London, or 609/987-7300 collect from other parts of the world; www. thomascook.com) issues MasterCard traveler's checks. **Citicorp** (℡ **800/645-6556** in the U.S. and Canada, or 813/623-7300 collect from anywhere else in the world; www.citicorp.com) and many other banks issue checks under their own name or under MasterCard or Visa. Get checks issued in dollar amounts (as opposed to, say, French francs) as they're more widely accepted abroad.

WIRE SERVICES

American Express MoneyGram, Wadsworth St., Englewood, CO 80155 (℡ **800/926-9400**), allows friends back home to wire you money in an emergency in less than 10 minutes. Senders should call AMEX to learn the address of the closest outlet that handles MoneyGrams. Cash, credit card, or the occasional personal check (with ID) are acceptable forms of payment. AMEX's fee is $40 for the first $500 with a sliding scale for larger sums. The service includes a short telex message and a 3-minute phone call from sender to recipient. The beneficiary must present a photo ID at the outlet where the money is received.

VALUE-ADDED TAX (VAT)

All European countries charge a **value-added tax (VAT)** of 15% to 33% on goods and services—it's like a sales tax that's already included in the price. Rates vary from country to country (as does the name—it's called the IVA in Italy and Spain, the TVA in France, and so on), though the goal in EU countries is to arrive at a uniform rate of about 15%. Citizens of non-EU countries can, as they leave the country, get back most of the tax on purchases (not services) if they spend above a designated amount (usually $80–$200) in a single store.

Regulations vary from country to country, so inquire at the tourist office when you arrive to find out the procedure; ask what percentage of the tax is refunded, and if the refund is given to you at the airport or mailed to you later. Look for a **tax free shopping for tourists** sign posted in participating stores. Ask the storekeeper for the necessary forms, and, if possible, keep the purchases in their original packages. Save all your receipts and VAT forms from each EU country to process all of them at the **"Tax Refund"** desk in the airport of the last country you visit before flying home (allow an extra 30 minutes or so at the airport to process forms).

To avoid VAT refund hassles, ask for a Global refund form ("Shopping Checque") at a store where you make a purchase. When leaving a EU country, have it stamped by customs, after which you take it to the Global Refund counter at more than 700 airports and boarder crossings in Europe. Your money is refunded on the spot. For information, contact **Global Refund,** 707 Summer St., Stamford, CT 06901 (ℂ **800/566-9828;** www.globalrefund.com).

4 When to Go

Europe is a continent for all seasons, offering everything from a bikini beach party on the Riviera in summer to the finest skiing in the world in the Alps in winter.

Europe has a continental climate with distinct seasons, but there are great variations in temperature from one part to another. Northern Norway is plunged into Arctic darkness in winter, but in sunny Sicily the climate is usually temperate—though snow can fall even on the Greek Islands in winter, and winter nights are cold anywhere. Europe is north of most of the United States, but along the Mediterranean they see weather patterns more along the lines of the U.S. southern states. In general, however, seasonal changes are less extreme than in most of the United States.

The **high season** lasts from mid-May to mid-September, with the most tourists hitting the continent from mid-June to August. In general, this is the most expensive time to travel, except in Austria and Switzerland, where prices are actually higher in winter during the ski season. And since Scandinavian hotels depend on business clients instead of tourists, lower prices can often be found in the fleeting summer, when business clients vacation and a smaller number of tourists take over.

You'll find smaller crowds, relatively fair weather, and often lower prices at hotels in the **shoulder seasons,** from Easter to mid-May and mid-September to mid-October. **Off-season** (except at ski resorts) is from November to Easter, with the exception of December 25 to January 6. Much of Europe, Italy especially, takes August off, and from August 15 to August 30 is vacation time for many locals, so expect the cities to be devoid of natives but the beaches packed.

WEATHER
BRITAIN & IRELAND Everyone knows it rains a lot in Britain and Ireland. Winters are rainier than summers; August and from September to mid-October are the sunniest months. Summer daytime temperatures average 10 to 20°C (the low to mid-60s ° Fahrenheit), dropping to 5 to 10°C

What Time Is It, Anyway?

Based on U.S. Eastern Standard Time, Britain, Ireland, and Portugal are 5 hours ahead of New York City; Greece is 7 hours ahead of New York. The rest of the countries in this book are 6 hours ahead of New York. For instance, when it's noon in New York, it's 5pm in London and Lisbon; 6pm in Paris, Copenhagen, and Amsterdam; and 7pm in Athens. The European countries now observe daylight saving time. The time change doesn't usually occur on the same day or in the same month as in the United States.

If you plan to travel to Ireland or continental Europe from Britain, keep in mind that the time will be the same in Ireland and Portugal, 2 hours later in Greece, and 1 hour later in the other countries in this guide.

(40s F) on winter nights. Ireland, whose shores are bathed by the Gulf Stream, has a milder climate and the most changeable weather—a dark rainy morning can quickly turn into a sunny afternoon, and vice versa. The Scottish Lowlands have a climate similar to England's, but the Highlands are much colder, with storms and snow in winter.

CENTRAL EUROPE In Vienna and along the Danube Valley the climate is moderate. Summer daytime temperatures average in the low 20s C (70s F), falling at night to the low 10s C (50s F). Winter temperatures are in the 30s and 40s during the day. In Budapest, temperatures can reach 25°C (80°F) in August and dip to 0°C (30°F) in January. Winter is damp and chilly, spring is mild, and May and June are usually wet. The best weather is in the late summer through October. In Prague and Bohemia, summer months have an average temperature of 18°C (65°F) but are the rainiest, while January and February are usually sunny and clear, with temperatures around freezing.

FRANCE & GERMANY The weather in Paris is approximately the same as in the U.S. mid-Atlantic states, but like most of Europe, there's less extreme variation. In summer, the temperature rarely goes above 25°C (mid-70s F). Summers are fair and can be hot along the Riviera. Winters tend to be mild, averaging 5 to 10° C (the 40s F), though it's warmer along the Riviera. Germany's climate ranges from the moderate summers and chilly, damp winters in the north to the mild summers and very cold, sunny winters of the alpine south.

NORTHERN EUROPE In the Netherlands, the weather is never extreme at any time of year. Summer temperatures average around 20°C (67°F) and the winter average is about 5°C (40°F). The climate is rainy, with the driest months from February to May. From Mid-April to mid-May, the tulip fields burst into color. The climate of northern Germany is very similar. Belgium's climate is moderate, varying from 23°C (73°F) in July and August to 5°C (40°F) in December and January. It does rain a lot, but the weather is at its finest in July and August.

SCANDINAVIA Summer temperatures above the Arctic Circle average around 12°C (mid-50s F), dropping to around -10°C (mid-10s F) during the dark winters. In the south, summer temperatures average around 22°C (70°F), dropping to 0 to -5°C (20s F) in winter. Fjords and even the ocean are often warm enough for summer swimming, but rain is frequent. The sun shines 24 hours in midsummer above the Arctic Circle, where winter brings semipermanent twilight. Denmark's climate is relatively mild by comparison, with moderate summer temperatures and winters that can be damp and foggy, with temperatures just above 0°C (mid-30s F).

SOUTHERN EUROPE Summers are hot in Italy, Spain, and Greece, with temperatures around 30°C (high 80s F) or even higher in some parts of Spain. Along the Italian Riviera, summer and winter temperatures are mild, and except in the alpine regions, Italian winter temperatures rarely drop below freezing. The area around Madrid is dry and arid, and summers in Spain are coolest along the Atlantic

coast, with mild temperatures year-round on the Costa del Sol. Seaside Portugal is very rainy but has a temperature of 10 to 25°C (50 to 75°F) year-round. In Greece there's sunshine all year, and winters are usually mild, with temperatures around 10 to 12°C (50 to 55°F). Hot summer temperatures are often helped by cool breezes. The best seasons to visit Greece are from mid-April to June and mid-September to late October, when the wildflowers bloom and the tourists go home.

SWITZERLAND & THE ALPS The alpine climate is shared by Bavaria in southern Germany and the Austrian Tyrol and Italian Dolomites—winters are cold and bright and spring comes late, with snow flurries well into April. Summers are mild and sunny, though the alpine regions can experience dramatic changes in weather any time of year.

5 Active & Other Special-Interest Vacations

CYCLING

Cycling tours are a great way to see Europe at your own pace. Some of the best are conducted by the **Cyclists' Tourist Club,** 69 Meadrow, Godalming, Surrey, England GU7 3HS (© **01483/417-217;** www.ctc. org.uk). **Holland Bicycling Tours, Inc.,** P.O. Box 6485, Thousand Oaks, CA 91359 (© **800/852-3258;** fax 714/593-1710), leads 8-day bicycle tours throughout Europe, and **Experience Plus** (© **800/685-4565;** www. experienceplus.com) runs bike tours across Europe. **Cicilsmo Classico,** 13 Marathon St., Arlington, MA 02174 (© **800/866-7314;** fax 781/641-1512; www.ciclismoclassico.com), is an excellent outfit running tours of Italy, and Florence-based **I Bike Italy** (© **055-234-2371;** www.ibikeitaly. com), offers guided single-day rides in the Tuscan countryside.

HIKING

Wilderness Travel, 1102 9th St., Berkeley, CA 94710 (© **800/368-2794;** www.wildernesstravel.com), specializes in walking tours, treks, and inn-to-inn hiking tours of Europe, as well as less strenuous walking tours. **Sherpa Expeditions,** 131A Heston Rd., Hounslow, Middlesex, England TW5 ORD (© **020/ 8577-2717;** www.sherpa-walking-holidays.co.uk), offers both self-guided and group treks through off-the-beaten-track regions; it's represented in the United States by **Himalayan Travel,** 110 Prospect St., Stamford, CT 06901 (© **800/225-2380;** www.gorp.com/hmtravel.htm). Two somewhat upscale walking tour companies are **Butterfield & Robinson,** 70 Bond St., Suite 300, Toronto, ON M5B 1X3 (© **800/678-1147;** fax 416/864-0541; www.butterfield. com), and **Country Walkers,** P.O.

Box 180, Waterbury, VT 05676-0180 (© **800/464-9255;** fax 802/244-5661; www.countrywalkers.com).

Most European countries have associations geared toward aiding hikers and walkers. In England it's the **Ramblers' Association,** 87–90 Albert Embankment; London SE1 7TW, 2 floor Camelford House (© **020/ 7339-8500;** ww.ramblers.org.uk); Italy, contact the **Club Alpino Italiano,** 7 Via E. Fonseca Pimental, Milan 20127 (© **02-205-7231;** www. cai.it); for Austria, try the **Osterreichischer Alpenverein (Austrian Alpine Club),** Wilhelm-Greil-Strasse 15, Innsbruck, A-6020 (© **0512/ 595470;** www.alpenrerein.at); in Norway, it's the **Norwegian Mountain Touring Association,** Storgata 3, Box 7, Sentrum 0101 Oslo (© **22-82-28-00;** fax 22-82-28-01; www. ONTOA.NO).

HORSEBACK RIDING
One of the best companies is **Equitour,** P.O. Box 807, Dubois, WY 82513 (© **800/545-0019** or 307/ 455-3363; fax 307/455-2354; www. ridingtours.com), with 5- to 7-day rides through many of Europe's most popular areas, such as Tuscany and the Loire Valley.

HOME EXCHANGES
Intervac U.S., P.O. Box 590504, San Francisco, CA 94159 (© **800/756-HOME** or 415/435-3497; www. intervac.com), is part of the largest worldwide home-exchange network, with a special emphasis on Europe. It publishes four catalogs a year, listing homes in more than 36 countries. Members contact each other directly. Depending on your type of membership, fees begin at $87 going up to $148.

EDUCATIONAL TRAVEL
The best (and one of the most expensive) of the escorted tour operators is

IST Cultural Tours (© **800/833-2111;** www.ist-tours.com), whose tours are first class all the way and accompanied by a certified expert in whatever field the trip focuses on. If you missed out on study abroad in college, the brainy **Smithsonian Study Tours** (© **202/357-4700;** www.si.edu/tsa) may be just the ticket, albeit a pricey one. The cheaper alternative is **Smithsonian Odyssey Tours** (© **800/258-5885;** www2.smithsonian mag.51.edu), run by Saga International Holidays (these trips cost less because you stay in three- or four-star hotels rather than deluxe). Also contact your alma mater or local university to see if it offers summer tours open to the public and guided by a professor specialist.

The National Registration Center for Studies Abroad (NRCSA), P.O. Box 1393, Milwaukee, WI 53203 (© **414/278-0631;** www.NRCSA. com), and the American Institute for Foreign Study (AIFS), 102 Greenwich Ave., Greenwich, CT 06830 (© **800/ 727-2437** or 203/399-5000; www. AIFS.com), can both help you arrange study programs and summer programs abroad.

The biggest organization dealing with higher education in Europe is the **Institute of International Education,** with headquarters at 809 United Nations Plaza, New York, NY 10017-3580 (© **800/445-0443** or 212/883-8200; www.iie.org). A few of its booklets are free, but for $39.95, plus $6 postage, you can buy the more definitive *Vacation Study Abroad.* To order publications, check out the IIE's online bookstore at www.iie.org; call © **800/445-0443** or 301/617-7804; fax 301/206-9789; or write to the Institute of International Education, P.O. Box 371, Annapolis Junction, MD 20701-0371.

A clearinghouse for information on European-based language schools is

Lingua Service Worldwide, 75 Prospect St., Suite 4, Huntington, NY 11743 (© **800/394-LEARN** or 631/ 424-0777; www.linguaserviceworld wide.com).

CULINARY SCHOOLS

Cuisine International, P.O. Box 25228, Dallas, TX 75225 (© **214/ 373-1161;** fax 214/373-1162; www.cuisineinternational.com), brings together some of the top independent cooking schools and teachers based in various European countries so you can book your weeklong culinary dream vacation.

Italian Cuisine in Florence, Via Trieste 1, 50139 Firenze (© **055-480041;** mirel@boxl.tin.it), provides several gourmet classes in regional as well as *nouva cucina.* Most courses are 5 days, but short workshops for larger groups are also available. From May to October, the **International Cooking School of Italian Food and Wine,** 201 E. 28th St., New York, NY 10016-8538 (© **212/779-1921;** fax 212/779-3248; www.intl-kitchen. com), offers courses in Bologna, the "gastronomic capital of Italy." **Le Cordon Bleu,** rue Léon-Delhomme 8, 75015 Paris (© **800/457-2433** in the U.S., or 01-53-68-22-50; www. cordonbleu.net), was established in 1895 as a means of spreading the tenets of French cuisine to the world at large. It offers many programs outside its flagship Paris school.

6 Health & Insurance

HEALTH

In most of Europe the tap water is generally safe to drink (except on trains and elsewhere it's marked as nondrinking water), the milk pasteurized, and health services good. You will, however, be eating foods and spices your body isn't used to, so you might want to bring along Pepto-Bismol tablets in case indigestion or diarrhea strikes.

If you worry about getting sick away from home, you may want to consider **medical travel insurance** (see below). In most cases, however, your existing health plan will provide all the coverage you need. Be sure to carry your ID card in your wallet.

If you suffer from a chronic illness, consult your doctor before your departure. For conditions like epilepsy, diabetes, or heart problems, wear a **Medic Alert Identification Tag** (© **800/825-3785;** www. medicalert.org), which immediately alerts doctors to your condition and gives them access to your records through Medic Alert's 24-hour hot line. Membership is $35, plus a $15 annual fee.

Contact the International Association for Medical Assistance to Travelers (IAMAT) (© **716/754-4883** or 519/836-0102; www.sentex. net/~iamat), for tips on travel and health concerns in the countries you'll be visiting and a list of local English-speaking doctors. When you're abroad, any local consulate can provide a list of area doctors who speak English. If you do get sick, you might want to ask the concierge at your hotel to recommend a local doctor.

Many European hospitals are partially socialized, and you'll usually be taken care of speedily, often at no charge for simple ailments. If you have to be admitted, most health insurance plans and HMOs will cover, at least to some extent, out-of-country hospital visits and procedures. However, most make you pay the bills up front at the time of care and reimburse you after you've returned and filed all the paperwork. Members of Blue Cross/Blue Shield can now use their cards at select hospitals in most major cities worldwide (call © **800/810-BLUE** or go to www.bluecares.com for a list of participating hospitals).

> **Tips A Packing Tip**
>
> Pack prescription medications in your carry-on luggage. Carry written prescriptions in generic (not brand-name) form, and dispense all prescription medications from their original labeled vials. This helps foreign pharmacists fill them and customs officials approve them. If you wear contact lenses, pack an extra pair in case you lose one.

INSURANCE

Comprehensive insurance programs, covering basically everything from trip cancellation and lost luggage to medical coverage abroad and accidental death, are offered by **Access America,** 6600 W. Broad St., Richmond, VA 23286-4991 (☎ **800/284-8300**). The following companies sell a variety of travel insurance policies: **Healthcare Abroad (MEDEX),** c/o Wallach & Co., P.O. Box 480 (107 w. Federal St.), Middleburg, VA 20118-0480 (☎ **800/237-6615**) or 540/687-3166; www.wallach.com; **Travelex,** 11717 Burt St., Suite 202, Omaha, NE 68175 (☎ **800/228-9792;** www.travelex-insurance.com; **Travel Guard International,** 1145 Clark Street, Stevens Point, WI 54481 (☎ **800/826-1300** or 715/345-0505; www.noelgroup.com; and **Travel Insured International, Inc.,** P.O. Box 280568 East Hartford, CT 06128-0568 (☎ **800/243-3174** in the U.S. or 860/528-7663 outside the U.S., between 7:45am and 8pm EST; www.travelinsured.com.

Medicare covers only U.S. citizens traveling in Mexico and Canada. Two companies specializing in accident and medical care are **MEDEX International,** P.O. Box 5375, Timonium, MD 21094-5375 (☎ **888/MEDEX-00,** or 410/453-6300 outside the U.S. and Canada; fax 410/453-6301; www.medexassist.com); and **Travel Assistance International** by Worldwide Assistance Services, Inc. 9200 Keystone Crossing, Suite 300, Indianapolis IN 46240 (☎ **800/821-2828** in the U.S., or 202/331-1596; www.specialtyrisk.com), is another option. It offers on-the-spot medical-payment coverage up to $15,000, or $60,000 for emergency care practically anywhere in the world as well as unlimited medical evacuation/repatriation coverage back to the United States if necessary. For an additional fee you can be covered for trip cancellation/disruption, lost/delayed luggage, and accidental death and dismemberment. Fees are based on the length of your trip and the coverage you select. Prices begin at $65 per person ($95 per family) for a 1- to 8-day trip. For information on **car renter's insurance,** see "Getting Around," below.

7 Tips for Travelers with Special Needs

FOR TRAVELERS WITH DISABILITIES

Europe won't win any medals for accessibility for travelers with disabilities, but in the past few years its big cities have made an effort to accommodate travelers with disabilities. *A World of Options,* a 658-page book of resources for travelers with disabilities, covers everything from biking trips to scuba outfitters. It costs $35 ($30 for members) and is available from **Mobility International USA,** P.O. Box 10767, Eugene, OR 97440 (☎ **541/343-1284,** voice and TDD; www.miusa.org); annual membership is $35. In addition, **Twin Peaks Press,** P.O. Box 129, Vancouver, WA 98666 (℃ **360/694-2462**), publishes travel-related books for people with disabilities. The **Moss Rehab Hospital** (℃ **215/456-9600**) has been providing friendly and helpful phone advice and referrals to travelers with disabilities for years through its **Travel Information Service** at ℃ **215/456-9603** (www.mossresourcenet.org).

You can join the Society for the Advancement of Travel for the Handicapped (SATH), 347 Fifth Ave., Suite 610, New York, NY 10016 (℃ **212/ 447-7284;** fax 212-725-8253; www. sath.org), for $45 annually or $30 for seniors/students. It provides info sheets on travel destinations and referrals to tour operators who specialize in traveling with disabilities. Its quarterly magazine, *Open World for Disability and Mature Travel,* is full of good information and resources and costs $13 ($21 outside the U.S.) per year.

You might also want to consider joining a tour catering specifically to travelers with disabilities. One of the best operators is **Flying Wheels Travel,** 143 West Bridge (P.O. Box 382), Owatonna, MN 55060 (℃ **800/535-6790**), offering escorted tours and cruises, with an emphasis on sports, as well as private tours in mini-vans with lifts. Other reputable specialized tour operators are **Access Adventures** (℃ **716/889-9096**), which offers sports-related vacations; **Accessible Journeys** (℃ **800/TIN-GLES** or 610/521-0339), for slow walkers and wheelchair travelers; **The Guided Tour** (℃ **215/782-1370**); **Wilderness Inquiry** (℃ **800/ 728-0719** or 612/379-3858); and **Directions Unlimited** (℃ **800/533-5343**).

You can get a copy of *Air Transportation of Handicapped Persons* by writing to Free Advisory Circular No. AC12032, Distribution Unit, U.S. Department of Transportation, Publications Division, M-4332, Washington, DC 20590. Vision-impaired travelers should contact the **American Foundation for the Blind,** 11 Penn Plaza, Suite 300, New York, NY 10001 (℃ **800/232-5463**), for information on traveling with Seeing Eye dogs.

The Royal Association for Disability and Rehabilitation (RADAR), Unit 12, City Forum, 250 City Rd., London EC1V 8AF (℃ **020/ 7250-3222**), publishes three holiday "fact packs." The first provides general info, including planning and booking a holiday, insurance, finances, and useful organizations and holiday providers; the second outlines transportation and rental equipment options; and the third deals with specialized accommodations. Another good service is the Holiday Care Service, Imperial Building, 2nd Floor, Victoria Road, Horley, Surrey RH6 7PZ (℃ **01293/774-535;** fax 01293/ 784-647), a national charity that advises on accessible accommodations for seniors and persons with disabilities. Annual membership is £30.

FOR FAMILIES

Europeans expect to see families traveling together. It's a multigenerational continent, and you sometimes see the whole clan traveling around. And Europeans tend to love kids. You'll often find a child guarantees you an even warmer reception at hotels and restaurants.

At **restaurants,** ask waiters for a half portion to fit junior's appetite. If you're traveling with small children, three- and four-star hotels may be your best bet—**baby sitters** are on call so you can take the occasional romantic dinner, and such hotels have a better general ability to help you access the city and its services. But even cheaper hotels can usually find you a sitter. Traveling with a pint-sized person usually means pint-sized rates. An

extra cot in the room won't cost more than 30% extra (if anything), and most museums and sights offer **reduced or free admission** for children under a certain age (which can range from 6 to 18). Kids almost always get discounts on plane and train tickets too.

Several books offer tips to help you travel with kids. *Family Travel* (Lanier Publishing International) and *How to Take Great Trips with Your Kids* (Harvard Common Press) are full of good general advice that can apply to travel anywhere. Another reliable tome, with a worldwide focus, is *Adventuring with Children* (Foghorn Press). *Family Travel Times* newsletter cost $40 (online only—www.familytraveltimes.com), and it's updated every 2 weeks. Subscribers also can call in with travel questions but only on Wednesday from 10am to 1pm eastern standard time. Contact Family Travel Times, 40 5th Ave., New York, NY 10011 (© **888/822-4322,** or 212/477-5524).

The University of New Hampshire runs **Familyhostel** (© **800/733-9753**), an intergenerational alternative to standard guided tours. You live on a European college campus for the 2- or 3-week program, attend lectures, seminars, go on lots of field trips, and sightsee—all of it guided by a team of experts and academics. It's designed for children 8 to 15, parents, and grandparents.

FOR GAYS & LESBIANS

Much of Europe has grown to accept same-sex couples over the past few decades, and in most countries homosexual sex acts are legal. To be on the safe side, do a bit of research and test the waters for acceptability in any one city or area. As you might expect, smaller towns tend to be less accepting than cities. Gay centers include London, Paris, Amsterdam, Berlin, Milan, and the Greek Islands (Mykonos). For coverage of the gay scene in Europe's top destinations, consider purchasing a copy of *Frommer's Gay & Lesbian Europe.*

International Gay & Lesbian Travel Association (IGLTA), 4331 N. Federal, Suite 304, Fort Lauderdale, FL 33308 (© **800/448-8550** for voice mail, or 954/776-2626; www.iglta.com, links travelers up with the gay-friendly service organizations or tour specialists. With around 1,200 members, it offers quarterly newsletters, marketing mailings, and a membership directory updated quarterly. Membership is usually gay/lesbian businesses but is open to individuals for $150 yearly, plus a $100 administration fee for new members. Members are kept informed of gay and gay-friendly hoteliers, tour operators, and airline and cruise-line representatives. Contact the IGLTA for a list of its member agencies, who'll be tied into IGLTA's resources.

General gay and lesbian travel agencies include **Above and Beyond Tours** (© 800/397-2681; www.abovebeyond tours.com; mainly gay).

Besides *Frommer's Gay & Lesbian Europe,* two good biannual English-language guidebooks focus on gays but include information for lesbians as well. You can get the *Spartacus* or *Odysseus* guides (and Frommer's guide) from most gay and lesbian bookstores or order them from **Giovanni's Room,** 345 S. 12 St, Philadelphia, PA 19107 (**215/923-2960;** fax 215/023-0813; www.giovannisroom. com). Both lesbians and gays might want to pick up a copy of *Gay Travel A to Z* ($16). The Ferrari Guides (www.q-net.com) is another good series of guidebooks.

The magazine *Our World,* 1104 N. Nova Rd., Suite 251, Daytona Beach, FL 32117 (© **904/441-5367;** www.ourworldmag.com), covers options and bargains for gay and lesbian travel worldwide. It costs $35 for 10 issues. *Out and About, 657 Harrison* St. San Francisco, CA 94107 (📞 **800/929-2268;** 415/229-1793); www.outandabout.com, has been hailed for its "straight" reporting about gay travel. It profiles the best gay or gay-friendly hotels, gyms, clubs, and other places at destinations throughout the world. It costs $49 for 10 information-packed issues.

FOR SENIORS

Don't be shy about asking for discounts but always carry some kind of ID, such as a driver's license, showing your date of birth. Also mention that you're a senior when you first make your travel reservations. Many hotels offer seniors discounts, and in most cities, people over age 60 qualify for reduced admission to theaters, museums, and other attractions as well as discounted fares on public transportation.

The **American Association of Retired Persons (AARP),** 601 E St. NW, Washington, DC 20049 (📞 **800/424-3410** or 202/434-AARP; www.aarp.org), is the best U.S. organization for seniors. It offers discounts on car rentals and hotels. AARP offers members a wide range of special benefits, including *Modern Maturity* magazine and a monthly newsletter.

Grand Circle Travel, 347 Congress St., Suite 3A, Boston, MA 02210 (📞 **800/221-2610** or 617/350-7500; www.gct.com), is also one of the hundreds of travel agencies specializing in vacations for seniors. Many of these packages, however, are of the tour-bus variety, with free trips thrown in for those who organize groups of 10 or more. Seniors seeking more independent travel should consult a regular travel agent. **SAGA International Holidays,** 222 Berkeley St., Boston, MA 02116 (📞 **800/343-0273;** www. sagaholidays.com), offers inclusive tours and cruises for those 50 and older. It also sponsors the more substantial "Road Scholar Tours"

(📞 **800/621-2151**), which are fun-loving but have an educational bent.

If you want something more than the average vacation or guided tour, try **Elderhostel,** 75 Federal St., Boston, MA 02110-1941 (📞 **877/426-8056;** www.elderhostel.org), or the University of New Hampshire's **Interhostel** (📞 **800/733-9753**), both variations on the same theme: educational travel for seniors. These escorted tours are packed with seminars, lectures, field trips, and sightseeing, led by academic experts. Elderhostel arranges study programs for those 55 and over (and a spouse or companion of any age) in the United States and 77 countries around the world. Most courses last about 3 weeks and many include airfare, accommodations in student dorms or modest inns, meals, and tuition. Write or call for a free catalog. Interhostel takes travelers 50 and over (with companions over 40) and offers 2- and 3-week trips, mostly international. The courses in both programs are ungraded, involve no homework, and often focus on the liberal arts. They're not luxury vacations but are fun and fulfilling.

Though these specialty books are U.S.-focused, they do provide general advice and contacts for savvy travelers: *The 50+ Traveler's Guidebook* (St. Martin's Press), *The Seasoned Traveler* (Country Roads Press), and *Unbelievably Good Deals and Great Adventures That You Absolutely Can't Get Unless You're Over 50* (Contemporary Books). Also check out your newsstand for the quarterly magazine *Travel 50 & Beyond.*

FOR STUDENTS

The best resource is the Council on International Educational Exchange (CIEE). It can set you up with an ID card (see below), and its travel branch, Council Travel Service (📞 **888/COUNCIL;** www.counciltravel.com), is the world's biggest student travel agency. It can get you discounts on plane tickets, rail passes, and the like. Ask for a list of CTS offices in major cities so you can keep the discounts flowing (and aid lines open) as you travel.

In Canada, **Travel CUTS,** 200 Ronson St., Suite 320, Toronto, ONT M9W 5Z9 (© **800/667-2887** or 416/614-2887; www.travelcuts.com), offers similar services. **Campus USIT,** 52 Grosvenor Gardens, London SW1W 0AG (© **020/7730-3402;** www.usitcampus.co.uk), opposite Victoria Station, is Britain's leading specialist in student and youth travel.

Other offices of Council Travel are at 844 E. Lancaster Ave., Bryn Mawr, PA 19010 (© **610/527-6272**); 565 Melville, University, City, MO 63130 (© **314/721-7779**), and Franklin House Suite 102, 480 East Broad St., Athens, GA (© **706/543-9600.**

From CIEE you can get the student traveler's best friend, the $20 **International Student Identity Card (ISIC)** (© **212/822-2700**). It's the only officially acceptable form of student ID, good for cut rates on rail passes, plane tickets, and other discounts. It also provides you with basic health and life insurance and a 24-hour help line. If you're no longer a student but are still under 26, you can buy a **Go 25** card from the same people, getting you the insurance and some of the discounts (but not student admission prices in museums).

In Canada, **Travel CUTS**, 200 Ronson St., Suite 320, Toronto, ONT M9W 5Z9 (© **416/614-2887;** www.travelcuts.com, offers similar services. **Campus USIT,** 52 Grosvenor Gardens, London SW1W OAG (© **0870/240-1010;** www.usitcampus.co.uk), opposite Victoria Station, is Britain's leading specialist in student and youth travel.

8 Getting There

FLYING FROM NORTH AMERICA

Most major airlines charge competitive fares to European cities, but price wars break out regularly and fares can change overnight. Tickets tend to be cheaper if you fly midweek or off-season. **High season** on most routes is usually from June to mid-September—the most expensive and most crowded time to travel. **Shoulder season** is from April to May, mid-September to October, and December 15 to 24. **Low season**—with the cheapest fares—is from November to December 14 and December 25 to March.

MAJOR NORTH AMERICAN AIRLINES North American carriers with frequent service and flights to Europe are **Air Canada** (© **800/776-3000;** www.aircanada.ca), **American Airlines** (© **800/433-7300;** www.americanair.com), **Canadian Airlines**

(© **800/426-7000;** www.cdnair.ca), **Continental Airlines** (© **800/525-0280;** www.flycontinental.com), **Delta Airlines** (© **800/221-1212;** www.delta.com)**, Northwest Airlines** (© **800/225-2525;** www.nwa.com), **Tower Air** (© **800/221-2500;** www.towerair.com), **TWA** (© **800/221-2000;** www.twa.com), and **US Airways** (© **800/428-4322;** www.usairways.com).

For the latest on airline websites, check **www.itn.com**.

EUROPEAN NATIONAL AIRLINES Not only will the national carriers of European countries offer the greatest number of direct flights from the United States (and can easily book you through to cities beyond the major hubs), but since their entire U.S. market is to fly you to their home country, they often run more competitive deals than most North American carriers. Major national and country-affiliated European airlines include the following:

- **Austria:** Austrian Airlines. *In the U.S. and Canada:* 800/843-0002. *In the U.K.:* 020/7434-7350. *In Australia:* 800/642-438. www.aua. com.
- **Belgium:** Sabena. *In the U.S. and Canada:* 800/955-2000. *In the U.K.:* 020/7494-2629. www. sabena-usa.com.
- **Czech Republic:** CSA Czech Airlines. *In the U.S. and Canada:* 800/223-2365. *In the U.K.:* 0171/255-1898. *In Australia:* 013/0065-5727. www.csa.cz.
- **France:** Air France. *In the U.S.:* 800/237-2747. *In Canada:* 514/847-1106. *In the U.K.:* 020/8742-6600. *In Australia:* 02/9321-1000. *In New Zealand:* 068/725-8800. www.airfrance.com.
- **Germany:** Lufthansa. *In the U.S.:* 800/645-3880. *In Canada:* 415/360-3600. *In the U.K.:* 0845/773-7747. *In Australia:* 02/9367-3888. *In New Zealand:* 09/303-1529. www.lufthansa.com.
- **Greece:** Olympic Airways. *In the U.S.:* 800/223-1226, or 212/735-0200 in New York State. *In Canada:* 514/878-3891 (Montréal) or 416/914-7137 (Toronto). *In the U.K.:* 020/7399-1500. *In Australia:* 02/9251-2044. www. olympic-airways.gr.com.
- **Hungary:** Malev Hungarian Airlines. *In the U.S.:* 800/223-6884. *In Canada:* 416/9440-093. *In the U.K.:* 020/8745-7093. *In Australia:* 029/244-2111. *In New Zealand:* 09/379-4455. www. malev-airlines.com.
- **Ireland:** Aer Lingus. *In the U.S.:* 800/474-7424. *In the U.K.:* 020/8899-4747. *In Australia:* 02/9244-2123. *In New Zealand:* 09/308-3351. www.aerlingus.ie.

- **Italy:** Alitalia. *In the U.S.:* 800/223-5730. *In Canada:* 514/842-8241 (Montréal) or 416/363-1348 (Toronto). *In the U.K.:* 0870/5448-8259. *In Australia:* 02/9247-1307. *In New Zealand:* 09/308-3357. www.alitalia.com.
- **The Netherlands:** KLM Royal Dutch Airlines. *In the U.S.:* 800/374-7747. *In Canada:* 800/225-2525. *In the U.K.:* 0312/0430-9320. www.klm.nl.
- **Portugal:** TAP Air Portugal. *In the U.S.:* 800/221-7370. *In the U.K.:* 0845/601-0932. www. tap-airportugal.pt.
- **Scandinavia (Denmark, Norway, Sweden):** SAS Scandinavian Airlines. *In the U.S.:* 800/221-2350. *In the U.K.:* 0845/6072-7727. *In Australia:* 02/9299-9800. www.flysas.com.
- **Spain:** Iberia. *In the U.S.:* 800/772-4642. *In Canada:* 800/363-4534. *In the U.K.:* 0845/601-2854. www.iberia.com.
- **Switzerland:** Swissair. *In the U.S. and Canada:* 800/221-4750. *In the U.K.:* 0845/601-0956. www. swissair.com.
- **United Kingdom:** (1) British Airways. *In the U.S. and Canada:* 800/247-9297. *In the U.K.:* 0845/773-3377. *In Australia:* 02/8904-8800. www.britishairways. com. (2) Virgin Atlantic Airways. *In the U.S. and Canada:* 800/862-8621. *In the U.K.:* 01293/747-747. *In Australia:* 02/9244-2747. www.fly.virgin.com.

PACKAGE TOURS Package tours aren't the same thing as escorted tours. They're simply a way of buying your airfare and accommodations at the same time and getting an excellent rate on both. Your trip is your own. In many cases, a package including airfare, hotel, and transportation to and from the airport costs less than the

Tips   Flying for Less: Tips for Getting the Best Airfares

- **Take advantage of APEX fares.** Advance-purchase booking (APEX) fares are often the key to getting the lowest fare. You generally must be willing to make your plans and buy your tickets as far ahead as possible: The **21-day APEX** is seconded only by the **14-day APEX**, with a stay of 7 to 30 days. Since the number of seats allocated to APEX fares is sometimes less than 25% of plane capacity, the early bird gets the low-cost seat. There's often a surcharge for flying on a weekend, and cancellation and refund policies can be strict. A more flexible, but more expensive, option is the regular **economy fare,** allowing for a stay shorter than the 7-day APEX minimum. You're also usually free to make last-minute changes in flight dates and have unrestricted stopovers.

- **Watch for sales.** You'll almost never see them during July and August or the Thanksgiving or Christmas seasons, but at other times you can get great deals. If you already hold a ticket when a sale breaks, it may even pay to exchange it, which usually incurs a $50 to $75 charge.

- **Check out budget travel agencies.** An agency like **Council Travel** (© **888/2-COUNCIL;** www.counciltravel.com), a student travel specialist, always has the scoop on the latest cheap fares, and you don't have to be a student, under 26, or a teacher to use it (though you'll save more if you are). In addition, all specialize in finding the lowest fares. You can often get discounted fares on short notice without all the advance-purchase requirements.

- **Ask if you can secure a cheaper fare by staying an extra day or flying midweek.** If your schedule is flexible, you can definitely save money this way. Many airlines won't volunteer this information.

- **Be aware that consolidators (aka bucket shops) are good places to find low fares.** They buy seats in bulk from airlines and sell them to you at prices below even the airlines' discounted rates. Their small boxed ads usually run in the Sunday travel section. One of the biggest U.S. consolidators is **Travac,** 989 Sixth Ave., New York, NY 10018 (© **800/TRAV-800** or 212/563-3303; www.travac.com). **Council**

hotel alone if you booked it yourself. The downside is that many stick you in large international-style hotels (which in Europe are often outside the historic city center). You do get a good rate for that sort of hotel, but with a little more work (and the hotel reviews in this book), you can easily find on your own a midrange pension or friendly B&B for the same price or less and right in the heart of the action.

All major airlines flying to Europe sell vacation packages (see phone numbers and websites above). The best place to start looking for independent packagers is the travel section of your local Sunday newspaper and national travel magazines. **Central Holidays** (© **800/935-5000;** www.Centralh.com) is one of the best and most reputable package-tour operators. **Liberty Travel** (© **888/271-1584;** www.libertytravel.com) is one

Travel (© 888/COUNCIL; www.counciltravel.com) and **STA Travel** (© 800/781-4040; www.sta.travel.com) cater to young travelers, but their bargains are available to all ages. **Travel Bargains** (© 800/AIR-FARE; www.1800airfare.com) was once owned by TWA but now offers the deepest discounts on many other airlines, with a 4-day advance purchase. Other consolidators are **1-800-FLY-CHEAP** (www.1800flycheap.com); **Cheap Tickets** (© 800/377-1000; www.cheaptickets.com); **1-800/FLY-4-LESS** (www.lowairfare.com); and "rebators" like **Travel Avenue** (© 800/333-3335 or 312/876-1116; www.travelavenue.com). In the United Kingdom, **Trailfinders** (© 020/7937-5400; www.trailfinders.com), is a consolidator offering access to tickets on major European carriers.

- **Book a seat on a charter flight.** Most charter operators advertise and sell their seats through travel agents. Before deciding to take a charter, however, check the ticket restrictions: You may be asked to buy a tour package, pay in advance, be amenable if the departure day is changed, pay a service charge, fly on an airline you're not familiar with (unusual), and pay harsh penalties if you cancel (but be understanding if the charter doesn't fill up and is canceled up to 10 days before departure). Summer charters fill up more quickly than others and are almost sure to fly, but if you decide on a charter, consider cancellation and baggage insurance. **Council Travel,** 205 E. 42nd St., New York, NY 10017 (© 888/COUNCIL; www.counciltravel.com), arranges charter seats on regularly scheduled aircraft. One of the biggest charter operators is **Travac** (see above). For Canadians, good charter deals are offered by **Martinair** (© 800/627-8462; www.martinair.com) and **Travel CUTS** (© 800-667-2887; www.travelcuts.com), which also has an office at 295A Regent St. in London (© 020/7528-6113).

- **Search for deals on the Web.** It's possible to get some great deals on airfare, hotels, and car rentals via the Internet. See **Planning Your Trip Online** at the end of this guide for details on getting the most from the Web.

of the biggest packagers in the Northeast and usually boasts a full-page ad in Sunday papers. **American Express Vacations** (© 800/241-1700; www.americanexpress.com/travel) and **Kemwel** (© 800/678-0678; www.kemwel.com) are both reputable options too.

FLY/DRIVE TOURS Fly/drive vacations, which combine airfare and car rental, are increasing in popularity and are a lot cheaper than booking both airfare and car rental independently. They're available mainly through major European airlines (see above).

ESCORTED GROUP TOURS With a good escorted group tour, you'll know ahead of time what your trip will cost and won't have to worry about transportation, luggage, hotel reservations, communicating in foreign languages, and other basics—an experienced guide will take care of all that and lead you through all the sightseeing. The downside of a guided tour is you trade much of the freedom and personal free time independent travel grants you and often see only the canned postcard-ready side of Europe through the tinted windows of a giant bus. You get to *see* Europe, but rarely do you get the chance to really *know* it. Consult a good travel agent for the latest offerings and advice.

Two of the top escorted tour operators are **American Express Vacations,** with the most comprehensive tours to Europe, and **Kemwel** (for both, see "Package Tours," above). If you want a tour that balances independent-style travel and plenty of free time with all the pluses of a guided tour, try the very popular itineraries offered by **Europe Through the Back Door,** 120 Fourth Ave. N., P.O. Box 2009, Edmonds, WA 98020-2009 (✆ **425/ 771-8303;** www.ricksteves.com), run by Rick Steves, of public TV's *Travels in Europe* fame.

GETTING TO THE CONTINENT FROM THE UNITED KINGDOM

BY TRAIN Many rail passes and discounts are available in the United Kingdom for travel in continental Europe. One of the most complete overviews is available from **Rail Europe Special Services Department,** 10 Leake St., London SE1 7NN (✆ **0990/848-848**) and also from the London Branch of **Campus USIT,** 52 Grosvenor Gardens, London SW1W OAG (✆ **0870/240-1010;** www.usitcampus.co.uk). Both organizations are particularly well-versed in information about discount travel as it applies to persons under 26, full-time or part-time students, and seniors.

The most prevalent option for younger travelers, the **EuroYouth passes,** are available only to travelers under 26 and entitle the pass holder to unlimited second-class rail travel in 26 European countries.

BY CHUNNEL The Eurostar train shuttles between London and both Paris and Brussels; the trip time is less than 3 hours (compared to 10 hours on the traditional train-ferry-train route). **Rail Europe** (✆ **800/361-rail** or 800/848-7245; www.raileurope. com) sells tickets on the Eurostar between London and Paris or Brussels (both $149 one-way).

For Eurostar reservations, call ✆ **0990/300-003** in London, 01-44-51-06-02 in Paris, or 800/ EUROSTAR in the U.S. (www. eurostar.com). Eurostar trains arrive at/depart from Waterloo Station in London, Gare du Nord in Paris, and Central Station in Brussels.

BY FERRY & HOVERCRAFT **Brittany Ferries** (✆ **01705/892-200;** www.brittany-ferries.com) is the largest British ferry/drive outfit, sailing from the southern coast of England to five destinations in Spain and France. From Portsmouth, sailings reach St-Malo and Caen; from Poole, Cherbourg. From Plymouth, sailings go to Santander in Spain. **P&O Stena Lines** (✆ **087/6000-0611;** www.posl. com) operates car and passenger ferries between Portsmouth and Cherbourg (three departures a day; 5–7 hours); between Portsmouth and Le Havre, France (three a day; 5 hours); and between Dover and Calais, France (25 sailings a day; 1¼ hours).

Unless you're interested in a leisurely sea voyage, passengers without cars might be better off using the quicker, and slightly cheaper, **Hoverspeed** (✆ **08705/240-241;** www.hoverspeed.co.uk). Hoverspeeds make the 35-minute crossing between Calais and Dover 7 to 15 times per day, with the more curtailed schedule in winter. Prices are £25 ($38) adults on foot or £14 ($21) children; vehicle fares are £117 to £165 ($176–$248). Prices are one way or 5-day return.

BY CAR Many car-rental companies won't let you rent a car in Britain and take it to the Continent, so always check ahead. There are many "drive-on/drive-off" car-ferry services across the Channel; see "By Ferry & Hovercraft," above. There are also Chunnel trains that run a drive-on/drive-off service every 15 minutes (once an hour at night) for the 35-minute ride between Ashford and Calais.

BY COACH Though travel by coach is considerably slower and less comfortable than travel by train, if you're on a budget you might opt for one of Eurolines's regular departures from London's Victoria Coach Station to destinations throughout Europe. Contact **Eurolines** at 52 Grosvenor Gardens, Victoria, London SW1W OAU (© **0990/143219** or 020/7730-8235; www.eurolines.co.uk).

9 Getting Around

BY TRAIN

In Europe, the shortest and cheapest—distance between two points is lined with rail tracks. European trains are less expensive than those in the United States, far more advanced in many ways, and certainly more extensive. Modern high-speed trains (130 m.p.h.) make the rails faster than the plane for short journeys, and overnight trains get you where you're going without wasting valuable daylight hours—and you save money on lodging to boot.

SOME TRAIN NOTES Many European high-speed trains, including the popular EC (EuroCity), IC (InterCity), and EN (EuroNight), require you to pay a **supplement** in addition to the regular ticket fare. It's included when you buy tickets but not in any rail pass, so check at the ticket window before boarding; otherwise, the conductor will sell you the supplement on the train—along with a fine. **Seat reservations** ($20 to $50 or more, when a meal's included) are required on some high-speed runs—any marked with an *R* on a printed train schedule. You can usually reserve a seat within a few hours of departure, but be on the safe side and book your seat a few days in advance. You need to reserve any sleeping couchette or sleeping berth, too.

With two exceptions, there's no need to buy individual train tickets or make seat reservations **before you leave the United States.** However, on the high-speed Artesia run (Paris-Turin and Milan) you must buy a supplement, on which you can get a substantial discount if you have a rail pass, but only if you buy the supplement in the United States along with the pass. It's also wise to reserve a seat on the Eurostar, as England's frequent "bank holidays" (long weekends) book the train solid with Londoners taking a short vacation to Paris.

The difference between **first class** and **second class** on European trains is minor—a matter of 1 or 2 inches of extra padding and maybe a bit more elbow room. European **train stations** are usually as clean and efficient as the trains, if a bit chaotic at times. In stations you'll find posters showing the track number and timetables for regularly scheduled runs (departures are often on the yellow poster). Many stations also have tourist offices and hotel reservations desks, banks with ATMs, and newsstands where you can buy phone cards, bus and metro tickets, maps, and local English-language event magazines.

You can get many more details about train travel in Europe and automated schedule information by fax by contacting **Rail Europe** (© **800/438-7245;** fax 800/432-1329; www.raileurope.com). If you plan on doing a lot of train travel, consider buying the *Thomas Cook European Timetable* ($27.95 from travel specialty stores or order it at © **800/ FORSYTH**). Each country's national railway website, which includes schedules and fare information, occasionally in English, is hot-listed at **Mercurio** (mercurio.iet.unipi.it).

RAIL PASSES   The greatest value in European travel has always been the **rail pass,** a single ticket allowing you unlimited travel (or travel on a certain number of days) within a set time period. If you plan on going all over Europe by train, buying a rail pass will end up being much less expensive than buying individual tickets. Plus, a rail pass gives you the freedom to hop on a train whenever you feel like it, and there's no waiting in ticket lines. For more focused trips, you might want to look into national or regional passes or just buy individual tickets as you go.

Passes Available in the United States The granddaddy of passes is the **Eurailpass,** covering 17 countries (most of western Europe except Britain). It has been joined by the **Europass,** covering 5 to 12 countries (depending on which version you buy); this pass is mainly for travelers who are going to stay in the heart of western Europe.

Rail passes are available in either **consecutive-day** or **flexipass** versions (in which you have, say, 2 months in which to use 10 days of train travel). Consecutive-day passes are best for those taking the train frequently (every few days), covering a lot of ground, and making many short train hops. Flexipasses are for folks who want to range far and wide, but plan on taking their time over a long trip and intend to stay in each city for a while. If you're under 26, you can opt to buy a regular first-class pass or a second-class youth pass; if you're 26 or over, you're stuck buying a first-class pass. Passes for kids 4 to 11 are half-price, and kids under 4 travel free.

It's best to buy these passes in the United States (they're available from some major European train stations but are up to 10% more expensive). You can get them from most travel agents, but the biggest supplier is **Rail Europe** (© **800/438-7245;** www. raileurope.com), which also sells most national passes, except for a few minor British ones. You can also contact Rick Steve's **Europe Through the Back Door** (© **425/771-8303;** www.rick steves.com), which sells all Europe-wide and national rail passes and sends a free video and guide on how to use rail passes; he doesn't tack on the $10 handling fee all other agencies do.

The rates below are for 2001; they rise each year, usually after press time, so we can't include rates for 2002 here.

- **Eurailpass:**   Consecutive-day Eurailpass at $554 for 15 days, $718 for 21 days, $890 for 1 month, $1,260 for 2 months, or $1,558 for 3 months.
- **Eurail Flexipass:** Good for 2 months of travel at $654 for 10 days (consecutive or not) or $862 for 15 days.
- **Eurail Saverpass:** Good for two-to-five people traveling together at $470 per person for 15 days, $610 for 21 days, $756 for 1 month, $1,072 for 2 months, or $1,324 for 3 months.
- **Eurail Saver Flexipass:** Good for two-to-five people traveling together at $556 per person for 10 days within 2 months or $732 per person for 15 days within 2 months.
- **Eurail Youthpass:** Second-class pass for travelers under 26 at $388 for 15 days, $499 for 21 days, $623 for 1 month, $882 for 2 months, or $1,089 for 3 months.

Countries Honoring Train Passes

Eurail Countries: Austria, Belgium, Denmark, Finland, France, Germany, Greece, Hungary, Ireland, Italy, Luxembourg, the Netherlands, Norway, Portugal, Spain, Sweden, Switzerland.
Europass Core Countries: France, Germany, Switzerland, Italy, Spain.
Europass Add-on "Zones": Austria/Hungary, Belgium/Netherlands/Luxembourg, Greece (including the ferry from Brindisi, Italy), Portugal.
Note: The United Kingdom isn't included in any pass.

- **Eurail Youth Flexipass:** Only for travelers under 26 at $458 for 10 days of travel within 2 months or $599 for 15 days within 2 months.
- **Europass:** For trips focusing on the core of western Europe (France, Germany, Switzerland, Italy, Spain), giving 5, 6, 8, 10, or 15 days of train travel for 2 months. Expand the scope of the pass by buying add-on "zones" (Austria/Hungary; Belgium/Netherlands/Luxembourg; Greece, including the ferry from Brindisi, Portugal). Base pass at $348 for 5 days to $728 for 15 days.
- **Eurail Selectpass:** Travelers can select three countries linked by rail or ferry out of the 17 countries covered by Eurailpass. Passes are available for 5, 6, 8, or 10 days within a 2-month period; prices vary, beginning at $328 for a 5-day pass.
- **Europass Youth:** Second-class pass for travelers under 26 granting 5, 6, 8, 10, or 15 days of unlimited train travel in France, Germany, Italy, Spain, and Switzerland within 2 months. Cost is $233 for 5 days, $253 for 6 days, $313 for 8 days, $363 for 10 days, or $513 for 15 days.
- **EurailDrive Pass:** Mixes train travel and rental cars (through Hertz or Avis) for less money than

it would cost to do them separately (and one of the only ways to get around the high daily car-rental rates in Europe when you rent for less than a week). You get 4 rail days and 2 car days within a 2-month period. Prices (per person for one adult/two adults) vary with the class of the car: $435/$377 economy class, $475/$397 compact, and $495/$407 mid-sized. You can add up to 5 extra rail and/or car days. Extra rail days are $59 each; car days are $61 each for economy class, $80 compact, and $90 midsized. You have to reserve the first car day a week before leaving the United States but can make other reservations as you go (always subject to availability). If there are more than two adults, the extra passengers get the car portion free but must buy the 4-day rail pass for $280.
- **Eurodrive Pass:** A similar deal but good for Europass countries only (and no add-on zones) and for shorter trips. It's good for 3 rail days and 2 car days within a 2-month period. Prices (per person for one adult/two adults) are $345/$284 economy class, $388/$311 compact, and $406/$321 midsized. You can add up to 7 extra rail days at $45 each, and unlimited extra car days for $59 to $89 each, depending on the class of car.

> ## (Tips Train Trip Tips
>
> To make your train travels as pleasant as possible, remember a few general rules:
> - Hold on to your train ticket after it's been marked or punched by the conductor. Some European railroad systems require that you present your ticket when you leave the station platform at your destination.
> - While you sleep—or even nap—be sure your valuables are in a safe place; you might temporarily attach a small bell to each bag to warn you if someone attempts to take it. If you've left bags on a rack in the front or back of the car, consider securing them with a small bicycle chain and lock to deter thieves, who consider trains happy hunting grounds.
> - Few European trains have drinking fountains and the dining car may be closed just when you're at your thirstiest, so take along a bottle of mineral water. As you'll soon discover, the experienced European traveler comes loaded with hampers of food and drink and munches away throughout the trip.
> - If you want to leave bags in a train station locker, don't let anyone help you store them in it. A favorite trick among thieves is feigned helpfulness, then pocketing the key to your locker while passing you the key to an empty one.

There are also **national rail passes** of various kinds and **regional passes** like ScanRail (Scandinavia), BritRail (Great Britain), and the European East Pass (Austria, Czech Republic, Slovakia, Hungary, Poland). Some national passes you have to buy in the United States, some you can get on either side of the Atlantic, and still others you must buy in Europe. Remember: Seniors, students, and youths can usually get discounts on European trains—in some countries just by asking, in others by buying a discount card good for a year (or whatever). Rail Europe or your travel agent can fill you in on all the details.

BritRail (© 888/BRITRAIL; www.britrail.com) specializes in rail passes in Great Britain, and **DER Tours** (© 800/782-2424; www.dertravel.com) is a Germany specialist that also sells other national passes (except French and British ones).

Passes Available in the United Kingdom Many rail passes are available in the United Kingdom for travel in Britain and Europe.

The **InterRail Card** is the most popular rail ticket for anyone who has lived in Europe at least 6 months and is 26 or under (an over-26 version exists but offers discounts in fewer countries). It costs around £279, is valid for 1 month, and entitles you to unlimited second-class travel in 28 European countries. It also gives you a 34% discount on rail travel in Britain and Northern Ireland, plus an up-to-50% discount on the rail portion of travel from London to various continental ports, plus special rates on Eurostar trains. You'll also get a reduction (30% to 50%) on most sailings to Europe and a variety of other shipping services around the Mediterranean and Scandinavia. If you're not planning to travel in 28 countries, you can buy a lower-price card for more limited travel.

Another good option for travelers 26 and under, **Eurotrain** tickets are valid for 2 months and allow you to choose your own route to a final destination and stop off as many times as you like along the way. **Eurotrain "Explorer"** tickets are slightly more expensive but allow you to travel to your final destination along one route and back on another. The price includes round-trip ferry crossing as well as round-trip rail travel from London to the port.

For help in determining the best option for your trip and to buy tickets, stop in London at the **International Rail Centre,** in Victoria Station (© 0990/848-848); or **USIT Campus** (© 0870/240-1010; www.usitcampus.co.uk).

BY CAR

Many rental companies grant discounts if you **reserve in advance** (usually 48 hours) from your home country. Weekly rentals are almost always less expensive than day rentals. Three or more people traveling together can usually get around cheaper by car than by train (even with rail passes).

When you reserve a car, be sure to ask if the price includes the EU value-added tax (VAT), personal accident insurance (PAI), collision-damage waiver (CDW), and any other insurance options. If not, ask what these extras cost, because at the end of your rental, they can make a big difference in your bottom line. The CDW and other insurance might be covered by your credit card if you use the card to pay for the rental; check with the card issuer to be sure.

If your credit card doesn't cover CDW, **Travel Guard International** 1145 Clark St., Stevens Point, WI 54481 (© 800/826-1300 or 715/345-0505; www.noelgroup.com),

offers it for $5 per day. Avis and Hertz, among other companies, require that you purchase a theft-protection policy in Italy.

The main car-rental companies are **Avis** (© 800/331-1034; www.avis.com), **Budget** (© 800/527-0700; www.budgetrentacar.com/), **Europcar** (known as Dollar in the U.S.; © 800/800-6000; www.europcar.com), **Hertz** (© 800/654-3001; www.hertz.com), and **National** (© 800/227-7368; www.nationalcar.com). U.S.-based companies specializing in European rentals are **Auto Europe** (© 800/223-5555; www.autoeurope.com), **Europe by Car** (© 800/223-1516, or 212/581-3040 in New York; www.europebycar.com), and **Kemwel Holiday Auto** (© 800/678-0678; www.kemwel.com). Europe by Car and Kemwel also offer a low-cost alternative to renting for longer than 15 days: **short-term leases** in which you technically buy a fresh-from-the-factory car and then sell it back when you return it. All insurance is included, from liability and theft to personal injury and CDW, with no deductible.

The AAA supplies good maps to its members. **Michelin maps** (© 800/423-0485; www.michelin.com) are made for the tourist. The maps rate cities as "uninteresting" (as a tourist destination); "interesting"; "worth a detour"; or "worth an entire journey." They also highlight particularly scenic stretches of road in green, and have symbols pointing out scenic overlooks, ruins, and other sights along the way.

BY PLANE

Though trains remain the cheapest and easiest way to get around in Europe, air transport options have improved drastically in the past few years. Intense competition with rail and ferry companies has slowly forced airfares into the bargain basement.

British Airways (© 800/AIRWAYS in the U.S., or 0345/222111 in the U.K.; www.britishairways.com) and other scheduled airlines now fly regularly from London to Paris for only £98 to £105 ($167 to $179) round-trip, depending on the season. Lower fares usually apply to midweek flights and carry advance-purchase requirements of 2 weeks or so.

The biggest airline news in Europe is the rise of the **no-frills airline** modeled on American upstarts like Southwest. By keeping their overheads down through electronic ticketing, forgoing meal service, and flying from less popular airports, these airlines are able to offer low fares. Most round-trip tickets are $60 to $160. This means now you can save lots of time, and even money, over long train hauls, especially from, say, London to Venice or from central Europe out to peripheral countries like Greece and Spain. Budget airlines include **EasyJet** (© 870/6-000-000 in England;

www.easyjet.com), and British Airway's subsidiary **Go** (© **1279/666-388**) in England; **Ryanair** (© 087/0333-1231 in England; www.ryanair.com) in Ireland; and **Virgin Express** (© 020/7744-0004; www.virgin-express. com), an offshoot of Virgin Air, in Belgium. Be aware, though, that the names might change because these small airlines are often economically vulnerable and can fail or merge with a big airline. Still, as quickly as one disappears, another will take off.

Lower airfares are also available throughout Europe on **charter flights** rather than regularly scheduled ones. Look in local newspapers to find out about them. Consolidators cluster in cities like London and Athens.

Flying across Europe on regularly scheduled airlines can destroy a budget and be super-expensive. Whenever possible, book your total flight on one ticket before leaving. For example, if you're flying from New York to Rome, but also plan to visit Palermo,

---

✐ The Rules of the Road: Driving in Europe

- First off, know that European drivers tend to be more aggressive than their American counterparts.
- Drive on the right except in England, Scotland, and Ireland, where you drive on the left. And *do not ride* in the left lane on a four-lane highway; it is truly only for passing.
- If someone comes up from behind and flashes his lights at you, it's a signal for you to slow down and drive more on the shoulder so he can pass you more easily (two-lane roads here routinely become three cars wide).
- Except for the German autobahn, most highways do indeed have speed limits of around 60 to 80 miles per hour (100 to 135 kmph).
- Remember that everything's measured in kilometers here (mileage and speed limits). For a rough conversion, 1 kilometer = 0.6 miles.
- Be aware that although gas may look reasonably priced, the price is per liter, and 3.8 liters = 1 gallon—so multiply by four to estimate the equivalent per-gallon price.
- Never leave anything of value in the car overnight and nothing visible any time you leave the car (this goes double in Italy, triple in Naples).

Florence, and Turin, have the total trip written up on one ticket. Don't arrive in Rome and book separate legs of the journey, which costs far more when it's done piecemeal.

Sometimes national carriers offer remarkable deals to non-European residents, which cuts down costs of flying within Europe. For example, **Lufthansa** offers a "Discover Europe" package of three flight coupons, which vary in price, depending on the nation of origin. Another bargain is **Alitalia**'s "Europlus." First, you have to book a transatlantic flight, perhaps from New York to Rome. After that, and for only $299, you can buy a package of three flight coupons entitling you to fly on any three flights anywhere in Europe served by Alitalia (not just Italy). You can also purchase unlimited additional tickets, one way, for another $100 per ticket.

Another fine deal is offered in London by **Go Fly Limited** (℡ **84-56-05-43-21** in London; www.go-fly.com), a subsidiary of British Airways. Go Fly offers 40% off standard round-trip airfares. There is a 2-night minimum stay. Sample round-trip air fares from London are as follows: Edinburgh £48 ($72), Copenhagen £103 ($154.50), Rome £90 ($135), and Lisbon £131 ($196.50).

American citizens can contact **Europe by Air** (℡ **888/387-2479** or 512/404-1291; www.europebyair.com) for their Europe flight pass serving 30 countries, 30 airlines, and 150 European cities. It costs only $99 to travel one way between these cities.

Because discount passes are always changing on air routes within Europe, it's best to check in with **Air Travel Advisory Bureau** in London (℡ **020/7636-5000;** www.atab.co.uk). This bureau offers a free service directory to the public for suppliers of discount airfares from all major U.K. airports.

BY BUS

Bus transportation is readily available throughout Europe; it sometimes is less expensive than train travel and covers a more extensive area but can be slower and much less comfortable. European buses, like the trains, outshine their American counterparts, but they're perhaps best used only to pick up where the extensive train network leaves off. One major bus company serves all the countries of western Europe (no service to Greece): **Eurolines** in London at ℡ **0990/143219,** whose staff can check schedules, make reservations, and quote prices.

10 Planning Your Trip Online

With a mouse, a modem, and a certain do-it-yourself determination, Internet users can tap into the same travel-planning databases that were once accessible only to travel agents. Sites such as **Travelocity, Expedia,** and **Orbitz** allow consumers to comparison shop for airfares, book flights, learn of last-minute bargains, and reserve hotel rooms and rental cars.

But don't fire your travel agent just yet. Although online booking sites offer tips and hard data to help you bargain shop, they cannot endow you with the hard-earned experience that

makes a seasoned, reliable travel agent an invaluable resource, even in the Internet age. And for consumers with a complex itinerary, a trusty travel agent is still the best way to arrange the most direct flights to and from the best airports.

Still, there's no denying the Internet's emergence as a powerful tool in researching and plotting travel time. The benefits of researching your trip online can be well worth the effort:

• **Last-minute specials,** known as "E-savers," such as weekend deals

Europe Online

For country- and city-specific websites, see **"Visitor Information"** sections within each chapter. Also, check individual listings for hotel, restaurant, and attraction websites.

or Internet-only fares, are offered by airlines to fill empty seats. Most of these are announced on Tuesday or Wednesday and must be purchased online. They are only valid for travel that weekend, but some can be booked weeks or months in advance. Sign up for weekly e-mail alerts at airline websites (see page 42) or check megasites that compile comprehensive lists of E-savers, such as Smarter Living (smarterliving. com) or WebFlyer (www.webflyer. com).

- Some sites will send you **e-mail notification** when a cheap fare becomes available to your favorite destination. Some will also tell you when fares to a particular destination are lowest.
- The best of the travel planning sites are now **highly personalized;** they track your frequent-flier miles, and store your seating and meal preferences, tentative itineraries, and credit-card information, letting you plan trips or check agendas quickly.
- All major airlines offer **incentives**—bonus frequent-flier miles, Internet-only discounts, sometimes even free cellphone rentals—when you purchase online or buy an e-ticket.
- Advances in mobile technology provide business travelers and other frequent travelers with **the ability to check flight status, change plans, or get specific directions** from handheld computing devices, mobile phones, and pagers. Some sites will e-mail or page a passenger if a flight is delayed.

TRAVEL PLANNING & BOOKING SITES

The best travel planning and booking sites cast a wide net, offering domestic and international flights, hotel and rental-car bookings, plus news, destination information, and deals on cruises and vacation packages. Keep in mind that free (one-time) registration is often required for booking. Because several airlines are no longer willing to pay commissions on tickets sold by online travel agencies, be aware that these online agencies will either charge a $10 surcharge if you book a ticket on that carrier—or neglect to offer those air carriers' offerings.

The sites in this section are not intended to be a comprehensive list, but rather a discriminating selection to get you started. Recognition is given to sites based on their content value and ease of use and is not paid for—unlike some website rankings, which are based on payment. Remember: This is a press-time snapshot of leading websites—some undoubtedly will have evolved or moved by the time you read this.

- **Travelocity** (www.travelocity.com or www.frommers.travelocity.com) and **Expedia** (www.expedia.com) are the most longstanding and reputable sites, each offering excellent selections and searches for complete vacation packages. Travelers search by destination and dates coupled with how much they are willing to spend.
- The latest buzz in the online travel world is about **Orbitz** (www. orbitz.com), a site launched by

United, Delta, Northwest, American, and Continental airlines. It shows all possible fares for your desired trip, offering fares lower than those available through travel agents. (Stay tuned: At press time, travel-agency associations were waging an antitrust battle against this site.)

- **Qixo** (www.qixo.com) is another powerful search engine that allows you to search for flights and hotel rooms on 20 other travel-planning sites (such as Travelocity) at once. Qixo sorts results by price, after which you can book your travel directly through the site.

SMART E-SHOPPING

The savvy traveler is one armed with good information. Here are a few tips to help you navigate the Internet successfully and safely.

- **Know when sales start.** Last-minute deals may vanish in minutes. If you have a favorite booking site or airline, find out when last-minute deals are released to the public. (For example, Southwest's specials are posted every Tuesday at 12:01am central time.)

- **Shop around.** Compare results from different sites and airlines—and against a travel agent's best fare, if you can. If possible, try a range of times and alternate airports before you make a purchase.
- **Follow the rules of the trade.** Book in advance, and choose an off-peak time and date if possible. Some sites will tell you when fares to a particular destination tend to be cheapest.
- **Stay secure.** Book only through secure sites (some airline sites are not secure). Look for a key icon (Netscape) or a padlock (Internet Explorer) at the bottom of your web browser before you enter credit card information or other personal data.
- **Avoid online auctions.** Sites that auction airline tickets and frequent-flier miles are the number-one perpetrators of Internet fraud, according to the National Consumers League.
- **Maintain a paper trail.** If you book an e-ticket, print out a confirmation, or write down your confirmation number, and keep it safe and accessible—or your trip could be a virtual one!

Frommers.com: The Complete Travel Resource

For an excellent travel planning resource, we highly recommend **Arthur Frommer's Budget Travel Online** (www.frommers.com). We're a little biased, of course, but we guarantee you'll find the travel tips, reviews, monthly vacation giveaways, and online-booking capabilities thoroughly indispensable. Among the special features are: **"Ask the Expert"** bulletin boards, where Frommer's authors answer your questions via online postings; **Arthur Frommer's Daily Newsletter,** for the latest travel bargains and inside travel secrets; and Frommer's **Destinations archive,** where you'll get expert travel tips, hotel and dining recommendations, and advice on the sights to see for more than 200 destinations around the globe. Once your research is done, the **Online Reservation System** (www.frommers.com/booktravelnow) takes you to Frommer's favorite sites for booking your vacation at affordable prices.

ONLINE TRAVELER'S TOOLBOX

Veteran travelers usually carry some essential items to make their trips easier. Following is a selection of online tools to bookmark and use.

- **Visa ATM Locator** (www.visa.com/pd/atm) or **MasterCard ATM Locator** (www.mastercard.com/atm). Find ATMs in hundreds of cities in the U.S. and around the world.
- **Foreign Languages for Travelers** (www.travlang.com). Learn basic terms in more than 70 languages and click on any underlined phrase to hear what it sounds like. *Note:* Audio software and speakers, supplied free, are required.
- **Intellicast** (www.intellicast.com). Weather forecasts for all 50 states and cities around the world. *Note:* temperatures are in Celsius for many international destinations.
- **Mapquest** (www.mapquest.com). This best of the mapping sites lets you choose a specific address or destination, and in seconds, it will return a map and detailed directions.
- **Cybercafes.com** (www.cybercafes.com) or **Net Café Guide** (www.netcafeguide.com/mapindex.htm). Locate Internet cafes at hundreds of locations around the globe. Catch up on your e-mail and log onto the Web for a few dollars per hour.

- **Universal Currency Converter** (www.xe.net/currency). See what your dollar or pound is worth in more than 100 other countries.
- **U.S. State Department Travel Warnings** (www.travel.state.gov/travel_warnings.html). Reports on places where health concerns or unrest might threaten U.S. travelers. It also lists the locations of U.S. embassies around the world.

BY AIR, BUS, OR TRAIN: TRANSPORTATION SITES

Below are the websites for the major airlines, trains, and bus systems operating throughout North America. These sites offer schedules and booking, and most of the airlines have E-saver alerts for weekend deals and late-breaking bargains.

PLANES

- **America West.** www.americawest.com
- **American Airlines.** www.aa.com
- **Continental Airlines.** www.continental.com
- **Delta.** www.delta.com
- **Northwest Airlines.** www.nwa.com
- **Southwest Airlines.** www.iflyswa.com
- **TWA.** www.twa.com
- **United Airlines.** www.ual.com
- **USAirways.** www.usairways.com

11 Tips on Accommodations

Traditional European hotels tend to be simpler than American ones and emphasize cleanliness and friendliness over amenities. For example, even in the cheapest American chain motel, free cable is as standard as indoor plumbing. In Europe, however, few hotels below the moderate level even have in-room TVs.

Unless otherwise noted, all hotel rooms in this book have **private en-suite bathrooms.** However, the standard European hotel bathroom might not look like what you're used to. For example, the European concept of a shower is to stick a nozzle in the bathroom wall and a drain in the floor.

> **Tips A Traveler's Tip**
>
> If you call a hotel from home to reserve a room, *always follow up with a confirmation fax*. Not only is it what most hotels prefer, but it is printed proof you've booked a room. Keep the language simple—state your name, number of people, what kind of room (like "double with bathroom and one bed" or "double with bathroom and two beds"), how many nights you'd like to stay, and the starting date for the first night. Remember that Europeans abbreviate dates day/month/year, not month/day/year.

Shower curtains are optional. In some cramped private bathrooms, you'll have to relocate the toilet paper outside the bathroom before turning on the shower and drenching the whole room. Another interesting fixture is the "half tub," in which there's only room to sit, rather than lie down. The half tub usually sports a shower nozzle that has nowhere to hang—so your knees get very clean and the floor gets very wet. Hot water may be available only once a day and not on demand—this is especially true with shared bathrooms. Heating water is costly, and many smaller hotels do it only once daily, in the morning.

GETTING THE BEST ROOM AT THE BEST RATE

The *rack rate* is the maximum rate a hotel charges for a room—the rate you'd get if you walked in off the street and asked for a room for the night. In our hotel entries, we list these rack rates. Hardly anybody pays these prices, however, and there are many ways around them. Below are some suggestions for getting the most for your money:

- **Don't be afraid to bargain.** Most rack rates include commissions of 10% to 25% or more for travel agents, which many hotels cut if you make your own reservations and haggle a bit. Always ask politely about the availability of a room less expensive than the first one mentioned or whether any special rates apply to you. You may qualify for corporate, student, military, senior, or other discounts. Be sure to mention membership in AAA, AARP, frequent-flyer programs, or trade unions, which could entitle you to special deals, too.

- **You don't have to take the first room they show you.** Unless you really love the first room you're shown, ask to see several. Open and close windows to see how well they shut out noise. Check the firmness of the mattress and the cleanliness of the bathroom. Always ask for a corner room—they're usually larger, quieter, and closer to the elevator and often have more windows and light than standard rooms. When making your reservation, ask if the hotel is renovating; if it is, request a room away from the renovation work and one that has already been redone. Many hotels now offer no-smoking rooms; if smoke bothers you, by all means ask for one. Inquire too about the location of the restaurants, bars, and discos in the hotel—they could all be a source of irritating noise.

- **Rely on a qualified professional.** Certain hotels give travel agents discounts in exchange for steering business their way, so if you're shy about bargaining, an agent may be better equipped to negotiate discounts for you.

- **Dial direct.** When booking a room in a chain hotel, call the hotel's local line and then its toll-free number to see where you get the best deal. A hotel makes nothing on a room that stays empty. The clerk who runs the place is more likely to know about vacancies and often grants deep discounts to fill up.

- **Remember the law of supply and demand.** Resort hotels are most crowded and therefore most expensive on weekends, so discounts are usually available for midweek stays. To the contrary, business hotels in downtown locations are busiest during the week; expect discounts over the weekend. Avoid high-season stays whenever you can: Planning your vacation just a week before or after official peak season can mean big savings.

- **Look into group or long-stay discounts.** If you come as part of a large group, you should be able to negotiate a bargain, since the hotel can then guarantee occupancy in a number of rooms. Likewise, when you're planning a long stay (usually 5 days to a week), you'll qualify for a discount. As a general rule, you get 1 night free after a 7-night stay.

- **Avoid excess charges.** When you book a room, ask whether the hotel charges for parking. Most hotels have free available space, but many urban or beachfront hotels don't. Also find out before you dial whether your hotel imposes a surcharge on local or long-distance calls. A pay phone, however inconvenient, may save you money. And don't open that minibar!

- **Consider a suite.** If you're traveling with your family or another couple, you can pack more people into a suite (which usually comes with a sofa bed), and thereby reduce your per-person rate. Remember that some places charge for extra guests and some don't.

- **Book an efficiency.** A room with a kitchenette allows you to grocery shop and eat some meals in. Especially during long stays with families, you're bound to save money on food this way. And you get the added thrill of shopping in a European food store or (even better) a European street market.

- **Investigate reservation services.** These outfits usually buy up or reserve rooms in bulk and deal them out to you at a profit, garnering special deals at 10% to 50% off; but these discounts apply to rack rates, inflated prices people rarely pay. You're probably better off dealing directly with a hotel, but if you don't like bargaining, this is a viable option. Most offer online reservation services as well. Some of the more reputable providers are **Accommodations Express** (© 800/950-4685; www.accommodationsxpress. com); **Hotel Reservations Network** (© 800/96HOTEL; www. 180096HOTEL.com); **Quibook** (© 800/789-9887, includes fax on demand service; www. quikbook.com); and **Room Exchange** (© 800/846-7000 in the U.S., or 800/486-7000 in Canada). Online, try booking your hotel through **Arthur Frommer's Budget Travel** (www. frommers.com) and save up to 50%. **Microsoft Expedia** (www. expedia.com) features a "Travel Agent" that directs you to affordable lodgings.

HOTEL BOOKING SERVICES

When you arrive in town, you'll find that a desk in the train station or at the tourist office (or both) acts as a central hotel reservations service for the city. Tell them your price range, where you'd like to be in the city, and sometimes even the style of hotel, and they'll use a computer database to find you a room in town.

The advantages of booking services are that they do all the room-finding work for you—for a nominal fee—and always speak English, while individual hoteliers may not. When every hotel in town seems to be booked up (during a convention or festival or just in high season), they can often find space for you at inns not listed in guidebooks or other main sources. On the downside, hotels in many countries often charge higher rates to people booking through such a service.

Austria

by Darwin Porter & Danforth Prince

Austria now stands at the crossroads of Europe, as it did in the heyday of the Austro-Hungarian Empire. Its capital, Vienna, stranded during the postwar years on the edge of Western Europe, is taking its place again as an important international city.

The country offers a lot to do, from exploring historic castles and palaces to skiing on some of the world's finest alpine slopes or hiking in the Danube Valley.

1 Vienna & the Danube Valley

Vienna still retains much of the glory and grandeur of the empire's heady days. Museum treasures from all over Europe, baroque palaces through which Maria Theresa and her brood wandered; Johann Strauss's lively music, Gustav Klimt's paintings, the concert halls, the unparalleled opera—it's all still here, as if the empire were still flourishing.

Tourism is growing as thousands arrive every year to view Vienna's great art and architecture, to feast on lavish Viennese pastries, to explore the Vienna Woods, to sail down the Danube, to attend Vienna's balls, operas, and festivals, and to listen to the "music that never stops."

Visitors today face a newer and brighter Vienna, a city with more joie de vivre and punch than it's had since before the war. There's also a downside: Prices are on the rise—they haven't reached the height of the Ferris wheel at the Prater, but they're climbing there.

ESSENTIALS

GETTING THERE **By Plane** Vienna International Airport (© 01/700-70; http://english.viennaairport.com) is about 19km (12 miles) southeast of the city center. There's regular **bus service** between the airport and the City Air Terminal (Wien Mitte) at the Hotel Hilton. Buses run 24 hours a day every 20 to 60 minutes. There's also service between the airport and two rail stations, the Westbahnhof and the Südbahnhof, with buses leaving every 30 minutes throughout the day (trip time: 20–25 min.). Fares for both services are 70AS (€5.10, $5).

There's also **train** service between the airport and the Wien Nord and Wien Mitte stations daily 5:07am to 9:30pm (trip time: 45 min.). Fares are 38AS (€2.75, $2.55). A one-way **taxi** ride from the airport into the Inner City will likely be 450AS (€32.85, $30).

The branch of the **Vienna Tourist Information Office** in the arrival hall of the airport is open daily 8:30am to 9pm.

By Train Vienna has four principal rail stations, with frequent connections to all Austrian cities and towns and to all major European cities, such as Munich and Milan. For train information for all stations, call © 05/1717.

Wien Westbahnhof, Europaplatz, is for trains arriving from western Austria, western Europe, and many eastern European countries. It has frequent train connections to all major Austrian cities. Trains from Salzburg pull in at the rate of two per hour daily 5:40am to 8:40pm. The **Wien Südbahnhof,** Südtirolerplatz, has train service to southern Austria, Slovenia, Croatia, and Italy. It also has links to Graz, the capital of Styria, and to Klagenfurt, the capital of Carinthia.

Other stations include the **Franz-Josef Bahnhof,** Franz-Josef-Platz, used mainly by local trains, although connections are made here to Prague and Berlin. The **Wien Mitte,** Landstrasser Hauptstrasse 1, is also a terminus of local trains, plus a depot for trains to the Czech Republic and Schwechat Airport.

By Bus   The **City Bus Terminal** is at the Wien Mitte rail station, Landstrasser Hauptstrasse 1. This is the arrival depot for Post buses and Bundesbuses from points all over the country, and also, the arrival point for private buses from various European cities. The terminal has lockers, currency-exchange kiosks, and a ticket counter open daily 6:15am to 6pm. For bus information, call © **05/1717** daily 6am to 9pm.

By Car   You can reach Vienna from all directions via major highways (*Autobahnen*) or by secondary highways. The main artery from the west is Autobahn A-1, coming in from Munich 468km (291 miles), Salzburg 336km (209 miles), and Linz 187km (116 miles). Autobahn A-2 arrives from the south, from Graz 200km (124 miles) and Klagenfurt 309km (192 miles). Autobahn A-4 comes in from the east, connecting with Route E-58, which runs to Bratislava and Prague. Autobahn A-22 takes traffic from the northwest, and Route E-10 connects to the cities and towns of southeastern Austria and Hungary.

VISITOR INFORMATION   **Tourist Office**   The official **Wien Tourist-Information,** Kärntnerstrasse 38 (© **01/513-8892;** http://info.wien.at), is open daily 9am to 7pm. You can make room reservations here. Address postal inquiries to the Vienna Tourist Board, Obere Augartenstrasse 40, A-1025 Vienna (fax 01/211-14-57).

Websites   Besides Wien Tourist-Information (**http://info.wien.at**), go to the Austrian National Tourist Office (**www.anto.com**) for current information on culture and events. The tour finder includes advice for all sorts of vacations, from brewery tours to trips for travelers with disabilities.

CITY LAYOUT   Vienna has evolved into one of the largest metropolises of central Europe, with a surface area covering 415km² (160 sq. miles). It's divided into 23 districts (*Bezirke*), each identified with a Roman numeral.

The size and shape of **Bezirke I,** the **Inner City,** roughly corresponds to the original borders of the medieval city. Other than the Cathedral of St. Stephan, very few medieval (Gothic or medieval) buildings remain—many were reconstructed in the baroque or neoclassical style, whereas others are modern replacements of buildings bombed during World War II. As Austria's commercial and cultural nerve center, the central district contains dozens of streets devoted exclusively to pedestrian traffic. The most famous of these is **Kärntnerstrasse,** which bypasses the Vienna State Opera House during its southward trajectory toward the province of Carinthia (Kärnten).

Ringstrasse, a circular boulevard about 4km (2½ miles) long whose construction between 1859 and 1888 was one of the most ambitious (and controversial) examples of urban restoration in the history of central Europe, surrounds the Inner City. Confusingly, the name of this boulevard changes many times

Vienna

ACCOMMODATIONS ■

Ana Grand Hotel Wien **12**

Astoria **18**

Bristol **13**

Hotel Das Triest **19**

Hotel Post **26**

Imperial **28**

Kaiserin Elisabeth **20**

Kärntnerhof **25**

König von Ungarn **24**

Pension Alstadt Vienna **10**

Royal **21**

Sacher Wien **15**

Wandl **23**

during its encirclement of the Inner City. Names that apply to it carry the suffix *-ring:* for example, Opernring, Schottenring, Burgring, Dr.-Karl-Lueger-Ring, Stubenring, Parkring, Schubertring, and Kärntner Ring.

Surrounding the Ringstrasse are the **inner suburban districts** (Bezirkes II through IX). These contain most of the villas and palaces of Vienna's 18th-century nobility, as well as complexes of modern apartment houses and the 19th-century homes of middle-class entrepreneurs. The **outer suburban districts** embrace a wide range of residential, industrial, and rural settings.

Northeast of the center, beyond the Danube Canal, is the **Second District,** with the famous amusement park, the Prater. East of the center, in the **Third District,** you'll find the art treasures and baroque setting of the Belvedere Palace. West of the center is Schönbrunn Palace.

GETTING AROUND   By Public Transportation   Vienna Transport (*Wiener Verkehrsbetriebe*), with its network of facilities covering hundreds of miles, can take you where you want to go—by U-Bahn (subway), tram (street-car), or bus. Vienna Public Transport has **Information Centers** at Karlsplatz, open from Monday to Friday 7am to 6pm and Saturday, Sunday, and holidays 8:30am to 4pm; on Stephansplatz, open from Monday to Friday 6:30am to 6:30pm and Saturday to Sunday 8:30am to 4pm; and on Praterstern, open from Monday to Friday 7am to 6:30pm. Centers are also at each of the larger Metro stations. For information, call ℭ **01/790-9105.**

Vienna has a **uniform fare,** allowing the same tickets to be used on all means of transportation as well as on the **Schnelbahn (Rapid Transit)** of the Austrian Federal Railways in the Vienna area and on some connecting private bus lines. A single (one-ride) ticket costs 20AS (€1.45, $1.35); that's also the price for two rides by a child. Children under 6 ride free.

It's wise to buy your tickets in advance at a *Tabak-Trafik* (tobacconist shop) or at an advance-sales office in one of the three public transport information centers (see above for locations). All advance-sales offices are open Monday 6am to noon, Tuesday and Wednesday 6:30am to 12:30pm, and Thursday and Friday 12:30 to 6:30pm. Most buses and streetcars don't have conductors, which means you must have the correct change, 20AS (€1.45, $1.35), when you buy your ticket onboard or from a vending machine at the station. A ticket bought from a machine will be stamped with the date and time of purchase. Tickets purchased in advance must be stamped before you start your ride by the machine on conductorless streetcars or at the platform barriers of the underground or

---

𝘝𝘢𝘭𝘶𝘦 The Vienna Card

The **Vienna Card** gives you access to all public modes of transportation (subway, bus, and tram) within Vienna—as well as discounts in city museums, shops, and restaurants—for a single discounted price. A 24-hour network pass costs 50AS (€3.65, $3.35) and is good for a full day of public transport. A 72-hour network pass sells for 130AS (€9.50, $9). For 210AS (€15.35, $14), you can purchase a versatile 3-day strip ticket, which can be used for 3 separate days of travel; a rail attendant punches the ticket each day it's used. Vienna Cards are easy to find throughout the capital, or you can buy one outside Vienna by calling ℭ **01/7984-40028** with a credit card.

Vienna Metro

Stadtbahn. Once a ticket is stamped, it may be used for one trip in one direction, including transfers.

By Bus & U-Bahn (Subway) You can ride directly into the Inner City on the U-Bahn U1 or on city bus 1A, 2A, or 3A. The U-Bahn runs daily 6am to midnight; buses from Monday to Saturday 6am to 10pm and Sunday 6am to 8pm.

By Tram More and more tram routes are being phased out in favor of buses or the U-Bahn, but trams are still in heavy use within the center, especially lines 1 and 2. Trams are also in use between the Westbahnhof and Burgring (line 58), and between the Westbahnhof and the Südbahnhof (line 18). Finally, line D runs between the Südbahnhof and the Ring.

By Taxi Taxi stands are marked by signs, or you can call for a radio cab by phoning ✆ **31300,** 60160, 81400, 91011, or 40100. Fares are indicated on an officially calibrated taximeter. The basic fare is 27AS (€1.95, $1.80), plus 14AS

(€1, 95¢) per kilometer. There's an extra charge of 16AS (€1.15, $1.05) for luggage carried in the trunk. For rides after 11pm, and for trips on Sunday and holidays, there's a surcharge of 10AS (€0.75, 65¢). If you call for a radio cab, additional charges apply.

By Car   Major car-rental companies operating in Vienna include **Avis,** Opernring 3–5 (© **800/654-3001** in the U.S., or 01/587-62-41 in Vienna; U-Bahn: Karlsplatz); **Budget Rent-a-Car,** City/Hilton Air Terminal (© **800/472-3325** in the U.S., or 01/714-6565 in Vienna; U-Bahn: Landstrasse/Wien Mitte); and **Hertz,** Kärntnerring 17 (© **01/512-8677;** U-Bahn: Stephansplatz).

By Bicycle   Vienna has more than 250km (155 miles) of marked bicycle paths within the city limits. In fact, city officials encourage bicycle riding. In July and August, many Viennese leave their cars in the garage and ride bikes. Specially marked cars of the U-Bahn will transport bicycles free in July and August, from Monday to Friday 9am to 3pm and after 6:30pm until the trains stop running, and on weekends from 9am until the trains stop running. All other times, you pay half the regular U-Bahn fare to take a bike on the U-Bahn.

Rental stores abound at such places as the Prater amusement park and along the banks of the Danube Canal, which is the favorite venue for most Viennese to go bicycling. One of the best of the many sites specializing in bike rentals is Copacagrana, Reichsbrücke, on the Donauinsel (© **01/2365-1857;** U-Bahn: Handelskai), open from May to October daily 9am to 9pm. Alternatively, you can rent from a kiosk within the **Westbahnhof** (© **01/2365-1857**), from May to October every day 8am to 10pm. The Vienna Tourist Board can also supply a list of rental shops and more information about bike paths throughout the city. Bike rentals begin at around 200AS (€14.60, $13.40) a day.

© FAST FACTS: Vienna

American Express   The most convenient office is at Kärntnerstrasse 21–23 (© **01/51540-770;** U-Bahn: Stephansplatz), open from Monday to Friday 9am to 6pm and Saturday 9am to noon.

Business Hours   Most shops are open from Monday to Friday 9am to 6pm and Saturday 9am to noon, 12:30pm, or 1pm. On the first Saturday of every month, the custom is for shops to remain open until 4:30 or 5pm. The tradition is called *Langer Samstag.*

Currency   The Austrian currency is the **schilling,** written ASch, AS, ÖS, or simply S. At this writing $1 = 15 schillings, or 1 schilling = 6.7¢ (the rate used in this chapter). The ratio of the British pound to the schilling fluctuates constantly. At press time, £1 = approximately 22AS (or 1AS = 4.3p). The euro rate was currently fixed at 13.69AS (or 1AS = €0.07). The euro will be introduced in the form of cash in January 2002. Until March 1, 2002, Austria will operate under a dual-currency system of both euros and schillings. At that time euros will become the only form of currency, replacing the schilling in Austria.

Currency Exchange   During off-hours you can exchange money at *bureaux de change* (exchange bureaus) throughout the Inner City (there's one at the intersection of Kohlmarkt and the Graben), as well as at travel agencies, train stations, and the airport. There's also a 24-hour exchange service at the Post Office (*Haubtpostamt*) at Fleischmarkt 19.

Dentists/Doctors For dental problems during the night or on Saturday and Sunday, call ☏ **01/512-2078.** If you have a medical emergency during the night, call ☏ **141** daily 7pm to 7am.

Drugstores Called *Apotheke,* they're open from Monday to Friday 8am to noon and 2 to 6pm and Saturday 8am to noon. Each Apotheke posts in its window a list of shops that take turns staying open at night and on Sunday.

Embassies/Consulates The Embassy of the **United States** is at Boltzmann-gasse 16, A-1090 Vienna (☏ **01/31339;** U-Bahn: Stadtpark). The consular section, Gartenbaupromenade 2–4, A-1010 Vienna (☏ **01/31339**), handles lost passports, tourist emergencies, and other matters. Both are open from Monday to Friday 8:30am to noon and 1 to 3:30pm.

The Embassy of **Canada,** Laurenzerberg 2 (☏ **01/531-380;** U-Bahn: Schwedenplatz), is open from Monday to Friday 8:30am to 12:30pm and 1.30 to 3:30pm; the **United Kingdom,** Jauresgasse 12 (☏ **01/7161-0;** tram: 71), is open from Monday to Friday 9:15am to noon and 2 to 4pm; **Australia,** Mattiellistrasse 2–4 (☏ **01/512-8580;** U-Bahn: Karlsplatz), is open from Monday to Friday 8:30am to 1pm and 2 to 5:30pm; **New Zealand,** Springsiedelgasse 28 (☏ **01/318-8505;** bus: 26A, 391, 392, or 590), is open from Monday to Friday 8:30am to 5pm; and **Ireland,** Hilton Center, Land-strasser Hauptstrasse 2 (☏ **01/715-4247;** Tram: 1), is open from Monday to Friday 9 to 11:30am and 1:30 to 4pm.

Emergencies Call ☏ **122** to report a fire, ☏ **133** for the police, or ☏ **144** for an ambulance.

Internet Access In back of the **Amadeus Media Café,** Kärntnerstrasse 19 (☏ **01/514310**), there is free access to the Web. The location is on the fifth floor of Steffi Kaufhaus, one of the leading department stores of Vienna. Hours are from Monday to Friday 9:30am to 7pm and Saturday 9:30am to 5pm. Another location, **Café Stein,** Währingerstrasse 6 (☏ **01/319-72-41**), offers Internet access at the rate of 65AS (€4.75, $4.35) every half hour. This cafe is open daily 5 to 11pm.

Post Office Addresses for these can be found in the telephone directory under "Post." Post offices are generally open for mail services from Monday to Friday 8am to noon and 2 to 6pm. The central post office, the **Hauptpostamt,** at Barbaragasse 2 (☏ **01/515090;** U-Bahn: Schwedenplatz), and most general post offices are open daily 24 hours.

Telephone The **country code** for Austria is **43.** The **city code** for Vienna is **1;** use this code when you're calling from outside Austria. If you're within Austria, use **01.**

A **local call** costs 2AS (€0.15, 15¢) for 1 minute. Hotels add huge surcharges to long-distance calls; go to the post office instead where it costs 31.50AS (€2.30, $2.10) to call the United States for 3 minutes during peak hours from Monday to Friday 8am to 6pm. Otherwise, it is only 28AS (€2.05, $1.90) for 3 minutes. Consider purchasing a **phone card** at any post office for 50AS (€3.65, $3.35), 100AS (€7.30, $6.70), or 200AS (€14.60, $13.40). **International direct dial** numbers include **AT&T** (☏ **022-90-30-11**); **MCI** (☏ **022-90-30-12**); and **Sprint** (☏ **0800-20-02-36**).

WHERE TO STAY
ON OR NEAR KÄRNTNERSTRASSE
Very Expensive

Ana Grand Hotel Wien 𝒜𝒜𝒜   Some of the most discerning hotel guests in Europe, often music lovers, prefer this seven-story deluxe hotel to the more traditional and famous Imperial or Bristol. Only a block from the Staatsoper, it's a honey. You enter a world of beveled mirrors, crystal chandeliers, and a grand staircase. The spacious accommodations are posh, with all the modern amenities such as heated floors, phones in the marble bathrooms, and even "anti-fog" mirrors. The more expensive units have more elaborate furnishings and decoration, including delicate stuccowork.

Kärnter Ring 9, A-1010 Vienna. ℭ **01/515-800.** Fax 01/515-13-12. www.anagrand.com. 205 units. 5,100–5,600AS (€372.30–€408.80, $342–$375) double, 9,000AS (€657, $603) suite. AE, DC, MC, V. U-Bahn: Karlsplatz. **Amenities:** 2 restaurants (Austrian, Japanese), two bars; 24-hour room service; fitness center; business center; baby-sitting; laundry/valet. *In room:* A/C, TV, data port, minibar, coffeemaker, hair dryer, safe, trouser press.

Astoria 𝒜   This landmark is for nostalgia buffs who want to recall the grand life of the closing days of the Austro-Hungarian Empire. A first-class hotel, the Astoria has a desirable location on the shopping mall close to St. Stephan's Cathedral and the State Opera. Decorated in a slightly frayed late 19th-century style, the hotel offers well-appointed and traditionally decorated rooms. The interior rooms tend to be too dark, and singles are just too cramped. It was most recently renovated in 1996, but the old style has been respected. Bathrooms are luxurious with dual basins and heated racks.

Kärntnerstrasse 32–34, A-1015 Vienna. ℭ **01/515770.** Fax 01/515-7782. 118 units. 2,900AS (€211.70, $194) double; 4,000AS (€292, $268) suite. Rates include breakfast. AE, DC, MC, V. Parking 320AS (€23.35, $21). U-Bahn: Stephansplatz. **Amenities:** Restaurant, bar; 24-hour room service; baby-sitting; laundry/dry cleaning. *In room:* TV, minibar, hair dryer.

Bristol 𝒜𝒜𝒜   This six-story landmark is a superb choice—only the Imperial is grander. When it was constructed in 1894 next to the State Opera it was the ultimate in luxury style, but it's been updated to give guests the benefit of black-tile bathrooms and modern conveniences. Rooms are sumptuously appointed. The club floor offers luxurious comfort, enhanced by period furnishings. Every year a different floor of the hotel is completely renovated.

Kärntner Ring 1, A-1015 Vienna. ℭ **888/625-5144** or 01/515-160. Fax 01/515-16-550. www.westin. com/Bristol. 146 units. 3,400–5,600AS (€248.20–€408.80, $228–$375) double; from 7,000–18,000AS (€511–€1,314, $469–$1,206) suite. AE, DC, MC, V. Parking 300AS (€21.90, $20). U-Bahn: Karlsplatz. Tram: 1 or 2. **Amenities:** Elegant Korso restaurant (one of city's best), and more informal Rôtisserie Sirk, 2 bars; 24-hour room service; access to nearby health club; business center; baby-sitting; laundry/valet. *In room:* A/C, TV, minibar, hair dryer, safe.

Hotel Das Triest 𝒜𝒜 *Finds*   The hot new hotel ticket in town is the creation of Sir Terence Conran, famous English architect and designer. He inaugurated this beauty in the center of Vienna, a 5-minute walk from St. Stephan's Cathedral and a short walk from the Ringstrasse. An emerging favorite with artists and musicians, this mid-17th-century structure has been transformed into a hip hotel with such grace notes as a courtyard garden. The building was originally used as a stable for horses pulling stagecoaches between Vienna and Trieste—hence its name, "City of Trieste." Rooms are medium size to spacious, tastefully furnished, and comfortable. Bathrooms come with heated racks and deluxe toiletries.

Wiedner Hauptstrasse 12, A-1040 Vienna. (C) **01/589-18.** Fax 01/589-18-18. www.nethotels.com/das_triest. 73 units. 2,900AS (€211.70, $194) double. AE, DC, MC, V. Rates include buffet breakfast. Parking 200AS (€14.60, $13). U-Bahn: Stephansplatz. **Amenities:** Restaurant (Austrian/Italian), chic bar; 24-hour room service; baby-sitting; laundry/valet. *In room:* A/C, TV, data port, minibar, hair dryer, safe, trouser press.

Imperial ✿✿✿   This hotel is Vienna's grandest and the most "imperial" looking in Austria, 2 blocks from the State Opera and 1 block from the Musikverein. The hotel was built in 1869 as a private residence and was converted into a private hotel in 1873. Everything is outlined against a background of polished marble, crystal chandeliers, Gobelin tapestries, and fine rugs. Some of the royal suites are palatial, but all rooms are soundproof and generally spacious, with deluxe bathrooms.

Kärntner Ring 16, A-1015 Vienna. (C) **800/325-3589** in the U.S., or 01/501100. Fax 01/5011-0410. 160 units. 6,700–9,500AS (€489.10–€693.50, $449–$637) double; from 14,000AS (€1,022, $938) suite. AE, DC, MC, V. Parking 400AS (€29.22, $27). U-Bahn: Karlsplatz. **Amenities:** Fabled turn-of-the-century restaurant, Imperial Café, intimate bar; 24-hour room service; access to health club; business center; baby-sitting. *In room:* A/C, TV, minibar, hair dryer.

Kaiserin Elisabeth ✿   Composers still check into this handsomely maintained inn as did the legends of yesterday—Mozart, Wagner, Liszt, and Grieg. Near the cathedral, it's up to date but reeks of atmosphere, with Oriental carpets, marble and wood floors, gilded mirrors, and classical columns. A portrait of Empress Maria Theresa looks so smug over the fireplace you'll think the Austrian empire is still intact. The soundproof rooms, small to midsize, are modernized as are the private bathrooms with half tubs and showers, vanity mirrors, and in most cases a bidet.

Weihburggasse 3, A-1010 Vienna. (C) **01/515260.** Fax 01/515267. kaiserin@ins.at. 63 units. 2,650AS (€193.45, $178) double; 2,950AS (€215.35, $198) suite. Rates include buffet breakfast. AE, DC, MC, V. Parking 350AS (€25.55, $23). U-Bahn: Stephansplatz. *In room:* TV, minibar, hair dryer.

Sacher Wien ✿✿   Much of the glory of the Hapsburgs is still evoked by the public rooms here, although the hotel is no longer the grandest in Vienna, having lost out to the Bristol or Imperial. The red velvet, crystal chandeliers, and brocaded curtains are reminiscent of Old Vienna. The hotel is popular with groups, however, and the heavy traffic is taking a toll. Demi-suites and chambers with drawing rooms are more expensive. The reception desk is fairly flexible about making arrangements for salons or apartments, or joining two rooms together. Each room comes with an elegantly old-fashioned bathroom.

Philharmonikerstrasse 4, A-1010 Vienna. (C) **01/514560.** Fax 01/512-56-810. www.sacher.com. 106 units. 4,000–9,000AS (€291–€657, $275–$603) double; from 14,000AS (€1,022, $938) suite. AE, DC, MC, V. Parking 390AS (€28.45, $26). U-Bahn: Karlsplatz. **Amenities:** Restaurant (see "Where to Dine," below), bar; 24-hour room service; access to nearby health club baby-sitting; laundry/valet. *In room:* A/C, TV, minibar, hair dryer, safe.

Moderate

König von Ungarn ✿   In a choice site on a narrow street near the cathedral, this hotel has been in the business for more than 4 centuries and is Vienna's oldest continuously operated accommodation. It's an evocative, intimate, and cozy retreat in an early 17th-century building, once a pied-à-terre for Hungarian noble families visiting the Austrian capital. Mozart reportedly lived here in 1791. Midsize guest rooms have Biedermeier accents, classic furniture, often Styrian wood-paneled walls, walk-in closets, and sparkling bathrooms—six without tubs. In spite of frequent renovations, the hotel is committed to preserving its sense of nostalgia. The hotel restaurant is one of Vienna's finest (see "Where to Dine," below).

Schulerstrasse 10, A-1010 Vienna. ℂ 01/515840. Fax 01/515848. www.kvu.at. 33 units. 2,390AS (€174.45, $160) double; 2,790AS (€203.65, $187) apt. Rates include breakfast. AE, DC, MC, V. U-Bahn: Stephansplatz. **Amenities:** Restaurant, bar; room service; baby-sitting; laundry. *In room:* A/C, TV, minibar, hair dryer.

Pension Altstadt Vienna 🅡 This former patrician home is now one of the undiscovered gems of Vienna for those who like their hotels small and charming. The premises were converted from a century-old private home in the mid-1990s by noted connoisseur of modern art Otto Wiesenthal. Although part of the structure remains as a private home, the remainder of the building contains a series of comfortable and cozy rooms that remind you of a stately home in England. Each of the good-size rooms has a quirky personality all its own, but nearly all have high ceilings, antiques, parquet floors, and double glazing. Bathrooms are medium size with a second phone and decent shelf space. About half of the accommodations contain a shower instead of a full tub bath. The suite, however, is hyper-modern, a radical departure from the traditionalism of the other bedrooms.

Kirchengasse 41, A-1070 Vienna. ℂ **01/1526-3399.** Fax 01/523-4901. hotel@altstadt.at. 34 units. 2,180–2,580AS (€159.15–€188.35, $146–$173) double; 2,180AS (€159.15, $146) suite. AE, DC, MC, V. U-Bahn: Volkstheater. *In room:* TV, minibar, hair dryer.

Royal The lobby of this hotel less than a block from St. Stephan's contains the piano where Wagner composed *Die Meistersinger von Nürnberg.* Each good-size room is furnished differently, in a style influenced by 19th-century Italy, with some good reproductions of antiques and an occasional original. The entire facility was built in 1960 and reconstructed in 1982. Try for a room with a balcony and a view of the cathedral. Corner rooms with spacious foyers are also desirable, although those facing the street tend to be noisy. Most bathrooms have both tub and shower.

Singerstrasse 3, A-1010 Vienna. ℂ **01/515680.** Fax 01/513-9696. www.kemslehnen.hotels.or.at. 81 units. 1,650–2,000AS (€120.45–€146, $111–$134) double; 2,800AS (€204.40, $188) suite. Rates include breakfast. AE, DC, MC, V. U-Bahn: Stephansplatz. **Amenities:** 2 restaurants, bar. *In room:* TV, minibar, hair dryer.

Inexpensive

Hotel Post This inn lies in the medieval slaughterhouse district, today an interesting area full of hotels and restaurants. The manager is quick to tell you that both Mozart and Haydn frequently stayed in a former inn at this address, although the structure today is only about a century old. In 1996 and 1997, all the furnishings in the small to midsize rooms were replaced and upgraded. The well-maintained rooms are streamlined and functional, most with a small bathroom.

Fleischmarkt 24, A-1010 Vienna. ℂ **01/51-58-30.** Fax 01/515-83-808. 107 units, 77 with bathroom (shower only). 1,370AS (€100, $92) double without bathroom, 1,480AS (€108.05, $99) double with bathroom; 1,600AS (€116.80, $107) triple without bathroom, 1,830AS (€133.64, $123) triple with bathroom. Rates include buffet breakfast. AE, DC, MC, V. Parking 220AS (€16.05, $15). Tram: 1 or 2. *In room:* TV.

Kärntnerhof 🅡 A 4-minute walk from the cathedral, the Kärntnerhof advertises itself as a *gutbürgerlich* family-oriented hotel. The decor of the public areas is tastefully arranged around Oriental rugs, well-upholstered chairs and couches with cabriole legs, and an occasional 19th-century portrait. The medium-sized rooms are more up-to-date, usually with the original parquet floors and striped or patterned wallpaper set off by curtains. The small private bathrooms have shower stalls.

Grashofgasse 4, A-1011 Vienna. ℂ **01/512-1923.** Fax 01/5132-22833. www.karntnerhof.com. 44 units. 1,270–1,840AS (€92.70–€134.30, $85–$123) double; 2,450–2,950AS (€178.85–€215.35, $164–$198) suite. Rates include buffet breakfast. AE, DC, MC, V. Parking 200AS (€14.60, $13). U-Bahn: Stephansplatz. **Amenities:** None.

Wandl   Despite a discreet 1997 renovation, this hotel still exudes a sense of history—it has been under the same ownership for generations. Built around 1700, the establishment has views of the steeple of St. Stephan's from many of its windows, which often open onto small balconies. Rooms are quite spacious, with small but adequate bathrooms.

Petersplatz 9, A-1010 Vienna. © **01/53-45-50.** Fax 01/53-455-77. reservation@hotelwandl.com. 138 units, 134 with bathroom (shower only). 1,350AS (€98.55, $90) double without bathroom, 1,800–2,200AS (€131.40–€160.60, $121–$147) double with bathroom. Rates include breakfast. AE, DC, MC, V. Parking 250AS (€18.25, $17). U-Bahn: Stephansplatz. **Amenities:** 24-hour room service. *In room:* TV.

WHERE TO DINE
ON OR NEAR KÄRNTNERSTRASSE
Very Expensive

Drei Husaren *Finds* VIENNESE/INTERNATIONAL Just off Karntnerstrasse, this enduring favorite—a Viennese landmark since 1935—serves an inventive and classic Viennese cuisine. To the music of Gypsy melodies, you'll dine on such stellar dishes as freshwater salmon with pike soufflé, mussel soup, breast of guinea fowl, an array of sole dishes, and such long-time favorites as *Tafelspitz* (boiled beef). The chef specializes in veal, including his deliciously flavored *Kalbsbrücken Metternich*. The place is justifiably celebrated for its repertoire of more than 35 hors d'oeuvres, which are rolled around the dining room on four separate carts.

Weihburggasse 4. © **01/512-1092.** Reservations required. Main courses 250–300AS (€18.25–€21.90, $17–$20); tasting menu (6 courses) 920AS (€67.15, $66). 4-course fixed-price business lunch 440AS (€32.10, $30). AE, DC, MC, V. Daily noon–3pm and 6pm–1am. U-Bahn: Stephansplatz.

König von Ungarn (King of Hungary) *Finds* VIENNESE/INTERNATIONAL This beautifully decorated restaurant is inside the famous hotel of the same name. The restaurant has operated since the 1600s, the present management dating from 1979. Food is well prepared but traditional—not at all experimental. You dine under a vaulted ceiling in an atmosphere of crystal, chandeliers, antiques, and marble columns. If you're in doubt about what to order, try the *Tafelspitz*, a savory boiled-beef specialty elegantly dispensed from a cart. Other menu choices, which change seasonally, include venison in a Chinese mushroom sauce, a ragout of fish with fresh mushrooms, grilled sea bass with crabmeat sauce and a spinach-flavored strudel, or tournedos with a mustard-and-horseradish sauce. The service is superb.

In the Hotel König von Ungarn, Schulerstrasse 10. © **01/512-53-19.** Reservations required. Main courses 190–320AS (€13.85–€23.35, $13–$21); fixed-price menu 390AS (€28.45, $26) at lunch, 490AS (€35.75, $33) at dinner. AE, DC, MC, V. Sun–Fri noon–2:30pm and 6–10:30pm. U-Bahn: Stephansplatz.

Sacher Hotel Restaurant *Finds* AUSTRIAN/INTERNATIONAL This is a long-enduring favorite for pre- or post-opera dining. It seems like all celebrities who come to Vienna eventually are seen either in the Red Bar with its adjacent dining room, where live piano music is presented every evening 7 to midnight, or in the brown-and-white Anna Sacher Room, the site of many a high-powered meal. There's no better place in Vienna to sample the restaurant's most famous dish, *Tafelspitz*, the Viennese boiled-beef platter that's fit for an emperor. The chef serves it with a savory, herb-flavored sauce. Other excellent dishes include fish terrine, Styrian-style lamb chops with cream cabbage, veal steak with morels, rib steak with onions, and Viennese fried chicken with potato salad. For dessert, enjoy the world-renowned Sacher torte, said to have been created in 1832 by Franz Sacher while he served as Prince Metternich's apprentice.

Philharmonikerstrasse 4. ✆ 01/514560. Reservations required. Main courses 180–610AS (€13.15–€44.55, $12–$41). AE, DC, MC, V. Daily noon–3pm and 6–11:30pm. U-Bahn: Karlsplatz.

Moderate

Dö & Co ✿ CONTINENTAL/INTERNATIONAL   Stylish, upscale, and rather expensive, this restaurant is owned by one of Austria's most esoteric food stores. Its location is on the seventh floor of the aggressively ultra-modern Haas Haus, which stands in jarring proximity to Vienna's cathedral. You'll navigate your way through somewhat claustrophobic passageways past a vigilant *maître d'hotel,* who will lead you to tables with views of an immaculate "showcase" kitchen on one side, and the city's historic core on the other. Menu items change with the season, but considering the rarefied nature of the organization presenting it, each is appropriately esoteric, rare, and unusual. Examples include Uruguayan beef; Austrian venison; grilled baby turbot from the coast of Norway; deep-fried monkfish; and carpaccio "Parmigiana," as well as traditional Austrian specialties.

In Haas Haus, Stephansplatz 4. ✆ 01/512-26-66. Reservations recommended. Main courses 255–285AS (€18.60–€20.80, $17–$19). V. Daily noon–3pm and 6pm–midnight. U-Bahn: Stephansplatz.

Plachutta ✿ VIENNESE   Few restaurants have built such a culinary shrine around one dish: *Tafelspitz,* the boiled beef dish that was the favorite of Emperor Franz Josef throughout his prolonged reign. Whichever of the 10 versions you order, it will invariably come with sauces and garnishes that perk up what sounds like a dull dish into a delectable culinary traipse through the tastes of yesteryear. The differences between the versions are a function of the cut of beef you request as part of your meal. Two of the ones most often associated with the dish include *Schulterscherzel* (shoulder of beef) or *Beinfleisch* (shank of beef). Regardless of the cut you specify, your meal will be accompanied with hash brown potatoes, chives, and a very appealing version of horseradish and chopped apples.

Wollzeile 10. ✆ 01/512-1577. Reservations recommended. Main courses 200–500AS (€14.60–€36.50, $13–$34). DC, MC, V. Daily 11:30am–11:15pm. U-Bahn: Stubentor.

Inexpensive

Augustinerkeller AUSTRIAN   The beer and wine flow at this Viennese legend. Augustinerkeller, in the basement of the part of the Hofburg complex that shelters the Albertina Collection, has served wine, beer, and food since 1857, although the vaulted ceilings and sense of timelessness evoke an establishment even older than that. It attracts a lively group of patrons from all walks of life, and sometimes they get boisterous, especially when the *Schrammel* music goes late into the night. It's one of the best values for wine tasting in Vienna. Aside from the wine and beer, the establishment serves simple food, including roast chicken on a spit, roast pork shank, schnitzel, and *Tafelspitz.*

Augustinerstrasse 1. ✆ 01/533-1026. Main courses 110–180AS (€8.05–€13.15, $7–$12); glasses of wine 31–35AS (€2.25–€2.55, $2.10–$2.35). AE, DC, MC, V. Daily 11am–midnight. U-Bahn: Stephansplatz.

Buffet Trzesniewski ✿ SANDWICHES   Everyone in Vienna knows about this place, from the most hurried office workers to the city's elite hostesses. Franz Kafka lived next door and used to come in for sandwiches and beer. Its current incarnation is unlike any buffet you may have seen, with six or seven cramped

✏ Coffeehouses & Cafes

The windows of the much-venerated **Café Demel**, Kohlmarkt 14 (✆ **01/533-5516**; U-Bahn: Stephansplatz), are filled with fanciful spun-sugar creations of characters from folk legends. Perhaps Lady Godiva's tresses will shelter a miniature village of Viennese dancers or the Empress Sisi in her royal finery will grace the window. You can definitely expect to see St. Nicholas at Christmastime. Inside is a splendidly baroque Viennese landmark with black marble tables, cream-colored embellished plaster walls, and crystal chandeliers covered with white milk-glass globes. Dozens of pastries are offered every day, including cream-filled horns (*Gugelhupfs*). Coffee costs 52AS (€3.80, $3.55), and those tempting cakes begin at 50AS (€3.65, $3.35). It's open daily 10am to 7pm.

One of the city's most atmospheric cafes, not far from Schönbrunn Palace, **Café Dommayer**, Dommayergasse 1 (✆ **01/877-5465**; U-Bahn: Schönbrunn), is where both Johann Strausses (father and son) played waltzes for members of Vienna's *grande bourgeoisie*. Opened in 1787 by a local writer, the cafe still has an old-world atmosphere, with Biedermeier accessories set amid silver samovars, formally dressed waiters (many of whom are short-tempered), and a stylish and very Viennese clientele. A regular Viennese coffee costs 28AS (€2.05, $1.90). It's open daily 7am to midnight.

One of the Ring's great cafes, **Café Landtmann**, Dr.-Karl-Lueger-Ring 4 (✆ **01/532-0621**; tram: 1, 2, or D), dates from the 1880s. Overlooking the Burgtheater, it has traditionally drawn a mix of politicians, journalists, and actors and was also Freud's favorite. The original chandeliers and the prewar chairs have been refurbished. We highly suggest spending an hour or so here, whether perusing the newspapers, sipping on coffee, or planning the day's itinerary. A large coffee costs 44AS (€3.20, $2.95), and full meals are available. A fixed-price lunch costs 115AS (€8.40, $8). Meals are served daily 11:30am to 3pm and 5 to 11:30pm, but the cafe is open daily 8am to midnight.

tables and a rapidly moving queue of clients who jostle for space next to the glass countertops. You'll indicate to the waitress the kind of sandwich you want, and if you can't read German signs, just point. Most people come here for the delicious finger sandwiches, which include 18 combinations of cream cheese, egg and onion, salami, mushroom, herring, green and red peppers, tomatoes, lobster, and many more.

Dorotheergasse 1. ✆ **01/512-3291**. Reservations not accepted. Sandwiches 10AS (€0.75, 65¢). No credit cards. Mon–Fri 8:30am–7:30pm; Sat 9am–5pm. U-Bahn: Stephansplatz.

East-West ASIAN   Established in 1999, this is the first pan-Asian restaurant to open within the Ring. As such, it's favored by business travelers interested in impressing their Asian clients. It's outfitted in a streamlined, monochromatic, and wood-trimmed design that evokes a blend of contemporary Japanese, Chinese, and Thai architecture. The menu divides its food into dishes deriving from the north, south, west, and east of Asia, with other sections devoted to the mountains of central Asia and traditional Chinese dishes. Examples of unusual, relatively modern dishes include ginger-pepper chicken nuggets in rice wine sauce; "Malaysian triangle" (three different preparations of pork in a satay sauce); the "Golden Age of Siam" (chicken with red and green peppers and red coconut curry); and Marco Polo beef (spicy beef with scallions served on a hot stone).

Seilerstätte 14. ℭ **01/512-9149.** Reservations recommended. Main courses 129–280AS (€9.40–€20.45, $9–$19). AE, DC, MC, V. Daily 11:30am–2:30pm and 5:30–11pm. U-Bahn: Stephansplatz.

Gulaschmuseum 🏵 AUSTRIAN/HUNGARIAN If you thought that *Gulasch* (goulash) was available in only one form, think again. This restaurant celebrates at least 15 varieties of it, each of them an authentic survivor of the culinary traditions of Hungary, and each redolent with the taste of that country's most distinctive spice, paprika. You can order versions of goulash based on roast beef, veal, pork, fried chicken livers, and even all-vegetarian versions made with either potatoes, beans, or mushrooms. Boiled potatoes and rough-textured brown or black bread will usually accompany your choice. An excellent beginning is a dish so firmly associated with Hungary that it's been referred to as the Magyar national crepe, *Hortobágyi Palatschinken,* stuffed with minced beef and paprika-flavored cream sauce.

Schulerstrasse 20. ℭ **01/512-1017.** Reservations recommended. Main courses 80–155AS (€5.85–€11.30, $5–$10). AE, DC, MC, V. Mon–Fri 9am–midnight; Sat–Sun 10am–midnight. U-Bahn: Wollzeile or Stephansplatz.

Hansen MEDITERRANEAN/INTERNATIONAL One of the most intriguing and stylish restaurants in Vienna is a partnership between a time-tested culinary team and the downtown showrooms of one of Austria's most famous horticulturists and gardening stores (Lederleitner, GmbH). You'll find them cheek-by-jowl in the vaulted cellars of Vienna's stock exchange, a beaux-arts pile designed in the 1890s by the restaurant's namesake, Theophile Hansen. Part of the charm of this place involves trekking through masses of plants and elaborate garden ornaments on your way to your dining table. Choose from a small but savory menu that changes every week. Excellent examples include a spicy bean salad with strips of chicken breast served in a summer broth; risotto with cheese and sour cherries; and poached *saibling* (something akin to trout from the cold-water streams of the Austrian alps) with a potato and celery purée and watercress.

In the cellar of the Börsegebäude (Vienna Stock Exchange), Wipplingerstrasse 34 at the Schottenring. ℭ **01/532-05-42.** Reservations recommended. Main courses 85–215AS (€6.20–€15.70, $6–$14). AE, DC, MC, V. Mon–Fri 9am–8pm (last order); Sat 9am–3pm (last order). U-Bahn: Schottenring.

Palmenhaus AUSTRIAN Architectural grace and marvelous food combine for a happy marriage here. Many architectural critics consider the Jugendstil glass canopy of this greenhouse the most beautiful in Austria. Overlooking the formal terraces of the Burggarten, it was built between 1901 and 1904 by the Hapsburg's court architect Friedrich Ohmann as an architectural transition between the Albertina and the National Library. It was restored in 1998 by trend-setting architects Christian Knechtl and Gregor Eichinger. There's a sophisticated menu that changes monthly, and which might include perfectly prepared fresh Austrian goat cheese with stewed peppers and zucchini salad; young herring with sour cream, horseradish, and deep-fried beignets stuffed with apples and cabbage; or breast of chicken layered with goose liver.

In the Burggarten. ℂ **01/533-1033.** Reservations recommended for dinner. Main courses 95–240AS (€6.95–€17.50, $6–$16); pastries 39–48AS (€2.85–€3.50, $2.60–$3.20). AE, DC, MC. V. Daily 10am–2am. U-Bahn: Opera.

Zwölf-Apostelkeller VIENNESE   For those seeking a taste of old Vienna, this is the place. Sections of this old wine tavern's walls predate 1561. Rows of wooden tables stand under vaulted ceilings, with lighting provided partially by streetlights set into the masonry floor. It's so deep that you feel you're entering a dungeon. This place is popular with students, partly because of its low prices and because of its proximity to St. Stephan's. In addition to beer and wine, the establishment serves hearty Austrian fare. Specialties include roast pork with dumplings, Hungarian goulash soup, a limited number of vegetarian dishes, and a *Schlachtplatte* (hot black pudding, liverwurst, pork, and pork sausage with a hot bacon-and-cabbage salad).

Sonnenfelsgasse 3. ℂ **01/512-6777.** Main courses 70–150AS (€5.10–€10.95, $5–$10). AE, DC, MC, V. Daily 4pm–midnight. Closed July. U-Bahn: Stephansplatz.

NEAR FLEISCHMARKT
Moderate
Griechenbeisl AUSTRIAN   This local favorite opened in 1450 and is still one of Vienna's leading restaurants. It has a labyrinthine collection of dining areas on three floors, all with low vaulted ceilings, smoky paneling, wrought-iron chandeliers, and Styrian-vested waiters who scurry around with large trays of food. As you go in, be sure to see the so-called inner sanctum, with signatures of such former patrons as Mozart, Beethoven, and Mark Twain. The food is *gutbürgerlich*—hearty, ample, and solidly bourgeois. Menu items include deer stew, both Hungarian and Viennese goulash, sauerkraut garni, Wiener schnitzel, and venison steak—in other words, all those favorite recipes from Grandmother's kitchen.

Fleischmarkt 11. ℂ **01/533-1941.** Reservations required. Main courses 145–265AS (€10.64–€19.35, $10–$18); fixed-price menu 270–445AS (€19.70–€32.54, $18–$30). AE, DC, MC, V. Daily 11am–1am (last orders at 11:30pm). Tram: N or Z.

Inexpensive
Wein-Comptoir *(Finds* AUSTRIAN/INTERNATIONAL   This is one of the most charming wine-tavern restaurants in the Old Town. You can visit just to sample a wide selection of wines, mostly Austrian, on the street level, or descend into the brick-vaulted cellar, where tables are arranged for meals. Here, waiters serve not only wine but also standard platters of Austrian and international food. Since most dishes are cooked to order, prepare yourself for a long wait. Full meals might include breast of venison in a goose-liver sauce, *Tafelspitz,* or breast of pheasant with bacon, and such vegetarian dishes as spinach dumplings with fresh Parmesan and hot butter sauce.

Bäckerstrasse 6. ℂ **01/512-1760.** Reservations recommended. Main courses 130–250AS (€9.54–€18.25, $9–$17). AE, DC, MC, V. Mon–Sat 5pm–1am (last orders). U-Bahn: Stephansplatz.

IN LANDSTRASSE
Steirereck ✦✦✦ VIENNESE/AUSTRIAN   *Steirereck* means "corner of Styria," which is exactly what Heinz and Margarethe Reitbauer have created in the rustic decor of this intimate restaurant. On the Danube Canal, between Central Station and the Prater, it has been acclaimed by some Viennese as the best in the city. The Reitbauers offer both traditional Viennese dishes and "new Austrian" selections. You might begin with a caviar-semolina dumpling, roasted

turbot with fennel (served as an appetizer), or the most elegant and expensive item of all, goose-liver *Steirereck*. Enticing main courses are asparagus with pigeon and saddle of lamb for two diners. The menu is wisely limited and well prepared, changing daily depending on the fresh produce available at the market.

Rasumofskygasse 2. ☎ 01/713-3168. Reservations required. Main courses 248–395AS (€18.10–€28.85, $17–$26); 3-course fixed-price lunch 425AS (€31.05, $29); 5-course fixed-price dinner 930AS (€67.94, $62). AE, DC, MC, V. Mon–Fri 10:30am–2pm and 7pm–midnight. Closed holidays. Tram: N. Bus: 4.

SEEING THE SIGHTS OF VIENNA

The Inner City (*Innere Stadt*) is the tangle of streets from which Vienna grew in the Middle Ages. Much of your exploration will be confined to this area, encircled by the boulevards of "The Ring" and the Danube Canal. The main street of the Inner City is **Kärntnerstrasse,** most of which is a pedestrian mall. The heart of Vienna is **Stephansplatz,** the square on which St. Stephan's Cathedral sits.

SIGHTSEEING SUGGESTIONS FOR FIRST-TIME VISITORS

If You Have 1 Day Begin at **St. Stephan's Cathedral** and from there branch out for a tour of the enveloping Inner City. But first climb the tower of the cathedral for a panoramic view of the city (you can also take an elevator to the top). Stroll down **Kärntnerstrasse,** the main shopping artery, and enjoy the 11am ritual of coffee in a grand cafe, such as the **Café Imperial.** In the afternoon, visit **Schönbrunn,** seat of the Hapsburg dynasty. Have dinner in a typical Viennese wine tavern.

If You Have 2 Days On the second day, explore other major attractions of Vienna, including the **Hofburg,** the **Imperial Crypts,** and the **Kunsthistorisches Museum.** In the evening, attend an opera performance or some other musical event.

If You Have 3 Days On your third day, try to attend a performance of either the **Spanish Riding School** (from Tuesday to Saturday) or the **Vienna Boys' Choir** (singing at masses on Sunday). Explore the **Belvedere Palace** and its art galleries; stroll through the **Naschmarkt,** the city's major open-air market; and cap the day by a visit to one or more of Vienna's cabarets, wine bars, or beer cellars.

If You Have 4 or 5 Days On day 4, take a tour of the **Vienna Woods** and then visit **Klosterneuburg Abbey,** the major abbey of Austria. Return to Vienna for an evening of fun.

On day 5, "mop up" all the attractions you missed on your first 4 days. These might include a visit to the **Graphische Sammlungen Albertina,** the most important graphic-arts collection in the world; and a walk through the **Stadtpark** at Parkring.

EXPLORING THE HOFBURG PALACE COMPLEX ✦✦✦

The winter palace of the Hapsburgs, known for its vast, impressive courtyards, the Hofburg sits in the heart of Vienna. To reach it (you can hardly miss it), head up Kohlmarkt to Michaelerplatz 1, Burgring (☎ **01/587-5554;** U-Bahn: Herrengasse; tram 1, 2, D, or J to Burgring).

This complex of imperial edifices, the first of which was constructed in 1279, grew and grew as the empire did, so that today the Hofburg Palace is virtually a city within a city. The palace, which has withstood three major sieges and a great fire, is called simply *die Burg*, or "the palace," by Viennese. Of its more than 2,600 rooms, fewer than two dozen are open to the public.

Schatzkammer (Imperial Treasury) 👁️👁️👁️
This is the greatest treasury in the world. It's divided into two sections: the Imperial Profane and the Sacerdotal Treasuries. One part displays the crown jewels and an assortment of imperial riches and the other, of course, ecclesiastical treasures. The most outstanding exhibit is the imperial crown, dating from 962. It's so big that, even though padded, it was likely to slip down over the ears of a Hapsburg at a coronation. Studded with emeralds, sapphires, diamonds, and rubies, this 1,000-year-old symbol of sovereignty is a priceless treasure. Also on display is the imperial crown worn by the Hapsburg rulers from 1804 to the end of the empire. You'll see the saber of Charlemagne and the holy lance. Among great Schatzkammer prizes is the Burgundian Treasure seized in the 15th century, rich in vestments, oil paintings, gems, and robes.

Hofburg, Schweizerhof. ℂ 01/533-7931. Admission 100AS (€7.30, $7) adults; 70AS (€5.10, $5) children, senior citizens, and students; free for children under 6. Wed–Mon 10am–6pm.

Kaiserappartements (Imperial Apartments) 👁️👁️
The Hofburg complex also includes the Kaiserappartements, where the emperors and their wives and children lived, on the first floor. To reach these apartments, enter via the rotunda of Michaelerplatz. The apartments are richly decorated with tapestries, many from Aubusson. The Imperial Silver and Porcelain Collection provides an insight to Hapsburg court etiquette. Most of these pieces are from the 18th and 19th centuries. Leopoldinischer Trakt (Leopold's apartments) date from the 17th century. These Imperial Apartments are more closely associated with Franz Josef than with any other emperor.

Michaeler Platz 1. ℂ 01/533-7570. Admission 95AS (€6.95, $6) adults, 75AS (€5.53, $5) students under 25, 50AS (€3.65, $3.35) children 6–15; free for children 5 and under. Daily 9am–5pm.

Hofburgkapelle (Palace Chapel)
Construction of this Gothic chapel began in 1447 during the reign of Emperor Frederick III, but it was subsequently massively renovated. From 1449, it was the private chapel of the royal family. Today the Burgkapelle is the home of the **Hofmusikkapelle (Court Musicians)** 👁️👁️, an ensemble consisting of the Vienna Boys' Choir and members of the Vienna State Opera chorus and orchestra. Written applications for reserved seats should be sent at least 8 weeks in advance of the time you wish to attend, but send no checks or money. For reservations, write to Verwaltung der Hofmusikkapelle, Hofburg, A-1010 Vienna. If you failed to reserve in advance, you may be lucky enough to secure tickets from a block sold at the Burgkapelle box office every Friday 3 to 5pm, but the queue starts lining up at least half an hour before that. Or you might settle for standing room (it's free).

Burgkapelle 1, Hofburg (entrance on Schweizerhof). ℂ 01/533-9927. Chapel: free admission. Mid-Sept to June Mon–Thurs 11am–3pm, Fri 11am–1pm. Mass with Court Musicians: 70–380AS (€5.10–€27.75, $5–$25). Concerts: 400–550AS (€29.20–€40.15, $27–$37). Mid-Sept to June Sun and Christmas Day 9:15am.

Neue Burg
The last addition to the Hofburg complex was the Neue Burg (New Château). Construction was started in 1881 and continued until work was halted in 1913. The palace was the residence of Archduke Franz Ferdinand,

---

Moments **The Vienna Boys' Choir**

In 1498, the emperor Maximilian I decreed that 12 boys should be included among the official court musicians. Over the next 500 years, this group evolved into the world-renowned Vienna Boys' Choir (Wiener Sängerknaben) 𝕲𝕲. They perform in Vienna at various venues, including the Staatsoper, the Volksoper, and Schönbrunn Palace. The Choir also performs at Sunday and Christmas masses with the Hofmusikkapelle (Court Musicians) at the Hofburgkapelle (see listing for details). For more information on where they are performing and how to get tickets, go to the Choir's website at **www.wsk.at**.

---

the nephew and heir apparent of Franz Josef, whose assassination at Sarajevo set off the chain of events that led to World War I. The **arms and armor collection** 𝕲𝕲 is second only to that of the Metropolitan Museum of Art in New York. It's in the **Hofjagd and Rüstkammer,** on the second floor of the New Château. On display are crossbows, swords, helmets, pistols, and armor. Another section, the **Musikinstrumentensammlung** 𝕲 (℡ 01/52524), is devoted to musical instruments, mainly 17th- and 18th-century. In the **Ephesos-Museum (Museum of Ephesian Sculpture),** Neue Burg 1, Heldenplatz, with an entrance behind the Prince Eugene monument (℡ 01/52524), you'll see the Parthian monument, the most important relief frieze from Roman times ever found in Asia Minor.

Heldenplatz. ℡ **01/525-24-484.** Admission 60AS (€4.43, $4) adults, 40AS (€2.90, $2.70) children. Wed–Mon 10am–6pm.

Albertina 𝕲   The development of graphic arts since the 14th century is explored at this Hofburg museum, named for a son-in-law of Maria Theresa. Slated to reopen in the fall of 2002, it houses one of the world's greatest graphics collections, and the most outstanding treasure is the Dürer collection, though what you'll usually see are copies—the originals are shown only on special occasions. Here, you can see Dürer's *Praying Hands,* which has been reproduced throughout the world.

Albertinaplatz. ℡ **01/53483.** www.albertina.at. Admission 45AS (€3.34, $3) adults, 20AS (€1.45, $1.35) students; free for children under 11. Tues–Sun 10am–5pm.

Augustinerkirche   This church was constructed in the 14th century as part of the Hofburg complex to serve as the parish church of the imperial court. In the latter part of the 18th century it was stripped of its baroque embellishments and returned to the original Gothic features. The Chapel of St. George, dating from 1337, is entered from the right aisle. The royal weddings of Maria Theresa and François of Lorraine (1736), Marie Antoinette and Louis XVI of France (1770), Marie-Louise of Austria to Napoléon (1810, but by proxy—he didn't show up), and Franz Josef and Elizabeth of Bavaria (1854) were all held here.

Augustinerstrasse 3. ℡ **01/533-7099.** Guided tour 10AS (€0.75, 65¢) contribution. Mon and Thurs–Fri 10am–noon; Wed–Sat 10am–6pm. The most convenient, and dramatic, time to visit is Sunday at 11am, when a high mass is celebrated, with choir, soloists, and orchestra.

Spanische Hofreitschule (Spanish Riding School) 𝕲   The Spanish Riding School is in the crystal-chandeliered white ballroom in an 18th-century building of the Hofburg complex. We always marvel at the skill and beauty of the sleek Lippizaner stallions as their adept trainers put them through their paces in a show that hasn't changed in 4 centuries. Reservations for performances must be made in advance, as early as possible. Order your tickets for the Sunday and Wednesday shows in writing to Spanische Reitschule, Hofburg, A-1010 Vienna (fax 43/1/535-0186), or through a travel agency in Vienna. (Tickets for Saturday shows can be ordered only through a travel agency.) Tickets for training sessions with no advance reservations can be purchased at the entrance Innerer Burghof-In der Burg.

Michaelerplatz 1, Hofburg. © **01/533-9032.** www.spanische-reitschule.com. Regular performances, 250–900AS (€18.25–€65.70, $17–$60) seats, 200AS (€14.60, $13) standing room. Classical art of riding with music, 250AS (€18.25, $17). (Children under 3 not admitted, but children 3–6 attend free with adults.) Training session, 100AS (€7.30, $7) adults, 30AS (€2.24, $2) children. Regular shows Mar–June and Sept to mid-Dec, most Suns at 10:45am and some Weds at 7pm. Classical dressage to musical performances Apr–June and Sept, most Sats at 10am. Morning training sessions, Mar–June, first 2 weeks in Sept, and mid-Oct to mid-Dec Tues–Sat 10am–noon. U-Bahn: Stephansplatz.

Lippizaner Museum   The latest attraction at the Hofburg is this museum near the stables of the famous white stallions. The exhibition begins with the historic inception of the Spanish Riding School in the 16th century and extends to the stallions' near destruction in the closing weeks of World War II. Exhibits such as paintings, historic engravings, drawings, photographs, uniforms and bridles, plus video and film presentations, bring to life the history of the Spanish Riding School, offering an insight into the breeding and training of these champion horses. Visitors to the museum are able to see through a window into the stallions' stables while they are being fed and saddled.

Reitschulgasse 2, Stallburg. © **01/533-7811.** Admission 50AS (€3.65, $3.35) adults, 35AS (€2.55, $2.35) children. Daily 9am–6pm. U-Bahn: Stephansplatz.

OTHER TOP ATTRACTIONS IN THE INNER CITY

Dompfarre St. Stephan (St. Stephan's Cathedral) ✧✧✧   A basilica built on the site of a Romanesque sanctuary, the cathedral was founded in the 12th century in what was the town's center. Stephansdom was virtually destroyed in a 1258 fire, and in the early 14th century the ruins of the Romanesque basilica gave way to a Gothic building. The cathedral suffered terribly in the Turkish siege of 1683 and from the Russian bombardments of 1945. Reopened in 1948 after restoration, the cathedral is today one of the greatest Gothic structures in Europe, rich in wood carvings, altars, sculptures, and paintings. The steeple, rising some 135m (450 ft.), has come to symbolize the very spirit of Vienna. You can climb the 343-step south tower, which dominates the Viennese skyline and offers a view of the Vienna Woods. Called Alter Steffl (Old Steve), the tower with its needlelike spire was built between 1350 and 1433. The North Tower (Nordturm), reached by elevator, was never finished, but was crowned in the Renaissance style in 1579. You view a panoramic sweep of the city and the Danube.

Stephansplatz 1. © **01/515-52563.** www.stephansdom.at. Cathedral, free; tour of catacombs, 40AS (€2.90, $2.73) adults, 15AS (€1.10, $1) children under 15. Guided tour of cathedral, 40AS (€2.90, $2.70) adults, 15AS (€1.10, $1) children under 14. North Tower, 40AS (€2.90, $2.70) adults, 15AS (€1.10, $1) children under 15; South Tower, 30AS (€2.240, $2) adults, 20AS (€1.45, $1.35) students, 10AS (€0.75, 65¢) children under 15. Evening tours, including tour of the roof, 130AS (€9.54, $8.70) adults, 50AS (€3.65, $3.35) children under 14. Cathedral, daily 6am–10pm except during services. Tour of catacombs, Mon–Sat at 10, 11, and 11:30am, and 1:30, 2, 2:30, 3:30, 4, and 4:30pm; Sun at 2, 2:30, 3:30, 4, and 4:30pm. North Tower, Oct–Mar daily 8:30am–5pm, Apr–Sept daily 9am–6pm; South Tower, daily 9am–5:30pm. Guided tour of cathedral, Mon–Sat at 10:30am and 3pm; Sun 3pm. Special evening tour Sat 7pm (June–Sept). Bus: 1a, 2a, or 3a. U-Bahn: Stephansplatz.

Gemäldegalerie der Akademie der bildenden 🛦   When in Vienna, visit this painting gallery to see the *Last Judgment* by the incomparable Hieronymus Bosch. In this work, the artist conjured up all the demons of the nether regions for a terrifying view of the suffering and sins of humankind. There are many 15th-century Dutch and Flemish paintings and several works by Lucas Cranach, the Elder. The academy is noted for its 17th-century art by van Dyck, Rembrandt, Botticelli, and a host of others.

Schillerplatz 3. 🕿 **01/58816**. Admission 50AS (€3.65, $3.35) adults and children. Tues–Sun 10am–4pm. U-Bahn: Karlsplatz.

Kunsthistorisches Museum (Museum of Art History) 🛦🛦🛦   Across from the Hofburg, this huge building houses the fabulous art collections gathered by the Hapsburgs. A highlight is the fine collection of ancient Egyptian and Greek art. The museum also has works by many of the greatest European masters, such as Velázquez, Titian, Brueghel the Elder, Rubens, Rembrandt, and Dürer.

Maria-Theresien-Platz, Burgring 5. 🕿 **01/52524-0**. www.khm.at. Admission 102AS (€7.45, $6.85) adults, 80AS (€5.85, $5.35) students and senior citizens, free for children under 6. Daily 10am–6pm; Thurs 10am–9pm. U-Bahn: Mariahilferstrasse. Tram: 52, 58, D, or J.

ATTRACTIONS OUTSIDE THE INNER CITY

Schönbrunn Palace 🛦🛦🛦   A Hapsburg palace of 1,441 rooms, Schönbrunn was designed and built between 1696 and 1712 in a grand baroque style meant to surpass that of Versailles. When Maria Theresa became empress in 1740, she changed the original plans, and the Schönbrunn we see today, with its delicate rococo touches, is her conception. It was the imperial summer palace during Maria Theresa's 40-year reign, the scene of great ceremonial balls and lavish banquets, and the fabulous receptions held here during the Congress of Vienna in 1815. The State Apartments are the most stunning. Much of the interior ornamentation is in 23½-karat gold, and many porcelain tile stoves are in evidence. Of the 40 rooms that you can visit, particularly fascinating is the "Room of Millions," decorated with Indian and Persian miniatures, the grandest rococo salon in the world.

Schönbrunner Schlossstrasse. 🕿 **01/81113**. www.schoenbrunn.at. Admission 125AS (€9.15, $8) adults, 65AS (€4.75, $4.35) children 6–15; free for children under 6. Apartments, Apr–Oct daily 8:30am–5pm; Nov–Mar daily 9am–4:30pm. U-Bahn: Schönbrunn.

Österreichische Galerie Belvedere 🛦🛦   The Belvedere Palace was built as a summer home for Prince Eugene of Savoy and consists of two palatial buildings. The pond reflects the sky and palace buildings, which are made up of a series of interlocking cubes, and the interior is dominated by two great, flowing staircases. The Unteres Belvedere (Lower Belvedere), with its entrance at Rennweg 6A, was constructed from 1714 to 1716 and contains the Gold Salon, one of the palace's most beautiful rooms. It also houses the Barockmuseum (Museum of Baroque Art). The Oberes Belvedere (Upper Belvedere) was started in 1721 and completed in 1723. It contains the Gallery of 19th- and 20th-Century Art, with an outstanding collection of the works of Gustav Klimt, including his extraordinary *Judith*. The Museum of Medieval Austrian Art is in the Orangery.

Prinz-Eugen-Strasse 27. 🕿 **01/79557**. www.belvedere.at. Admission 90AS (€6.55, $6) adults, free for children 16 and under. Tues–Sun 10am–5pm. Tram: D to Schloss Belvedere.

ORGANIZED TOURS

Wiener Rundfahrten (**Vienna Sightseeing Tours**), Stelzhamergasse 4–11 (© **01/7124-6830;** www.viennasightseeingtours.com; U Bahn: Landstrasse/ Wien Mitte), offers some of the best organized tours of Vienna and its surroundings. Tours depart from a signposted area in front of the State Opera (U-Bahn: Karlsplatz) and include running commentary in both German and English.

CITY TOURS   The historical city tour costs 400AS (€29.20, $27) for adults and is free for children 12 and under. It's ideal for visitors who are pressed for time and yet want to be shown the major (and most frequently photographed) monuments of Vienna. It takes you past the historic buildings of Ringstrasse— the State Opera, Hofburg Palace, museums, Parliament, City Hall, Burgtheater, the University, and the Votive Church—into the heart of Vienna. Tours leave from the State Opera daily at 9:30 and 10:30am and at 2:30 and 4:30pm.

The company's "Grand City Tour," a bus tour with commentary that includes an exterior view of the Belvedere Palace and a walk through Schönbrunn Palace, departs daily from the State Opera at 9:15am and 2:15am. April to November, an additional tour is offered at 10:15am. The tour costs 400AS (€29.20, $27) adults and 200AS (€14.60, $13) children under 12.

TOURS OUTSIDE THE CITY   Looking to travel farther afield? Vienna Sightseeing's bus tour to the **"Vienna Woods and Mayerling"** includes a tour of Baden, a spa once favored by the Hapsburg aristocracy, and a stop at Mayerling, site of the still-unexplained sudden death of Crown Prince Rudolf (the only son of Austria's last emperor, Franz Josef) and his mistress, Baroness Maria Vetsera. The tour is long on schmaltz and nostalgia and costs 500AS (€36.50, $24) adults and 200AS (€14.60, $14) children.

THE SHOPPING SCENE

Vienna is known for the excellent quality of its works, including petit point and hand-painted porcelain. Also popular is loden, a boiled and rolled wool fabric made into overcoats, suits, and hats, as well as knitted sweaters. The most famous shopping streets are in the city center (First District), including **Kärntnerstrasse, Graben, Kohlmarkt, and Rotensturmstrasse.** Other shopping streets include Mariahilferstrasse, Favoritenstrasse, and Landstrasser Hauptstrasse.

Albin Denk, Graben 13 (© **01/512-4439;** U-Bahn: Stephanplatz), is the oldest continuously operating porcelain store in Vienna, in business since 1702. You'll see thousands of objects from Meissen, Dresden, and other regions. The state-owned **Dorotheum,** Dorotheergasse 17 (© **01/5156-0449;** U-Bahn: Stephanplatz), the oldest auction house in Europe, was founded in 1707 by Emperor Josef 1 as a place where impoverished aristocrats could fairly (and anonymously) get good value for their heirlooms. Today the Dorotheum is also the scene of many art auctions. If you're interested in what's being auctioned off, you give a small fee to a *sensal,* one of the licensed bidders, and he or she will bid in your name. Auctions are usually conducted every Monday to Saturday at 2pm, though in particularly busy periods, additional auctions might be held at 11am and at 3pm. Viewing of the pieces about to go on the block is possible every Monday to Friday 10am to 6pm and every Saturday 9am to 5pm.

Opened in 1830 by the Plankl family, **Loden Plankl,** Michaelerplatz 6 (© **01/533-8032;** U-Bahn: Stephanplatz), is the oldest and most reputable outlet in Vienna for traditional Austrian clothing. You'll find Austrian loden coats, shoes, trousers, dirndls, jackets, lederhosen, and suits for men, women, and children. The building, opposite the Hofburg, dates from the 17th century. The three-floor **Ö. W. (Österreichische Werkstatten),** Kärntnerstrasse 6 (ℂ **01/ 512-2418;** U-Bahn: Stephanplatz), sells hundreds of handmade art objects from Austria. Some 200 leading artists and craftspeople throughout the country organized this cooperative to showcase their wares. It's easy to find, only half a minute's walk from St. Stephan's Cathedral.

VIENNA AFTER DARK

The best source of information about what's happening on the cultural scene is *Wien Monatsprogramm,* distributed free at tourist information offices and at many hotel reception desks. *Die Presse,* the Viennese daily, publishes a special magazine in its Thursday edition outlining the major cultural events for the coming week. It's in German but might still be helpful.

THE PERFORMING ARTS

OPERA & CLASSICAL MUSIC   Music is at the heart of the cultural life in Vienna. This has been true for a couple of centuries or so, and the city continues to lure composers, musicians, and music lovers. Vienna's opera is still the world's quintessential opera house, one of the three most important in the world.

When the **Staatsoper (State Opera),** Opernring 2 (ℂ **01/5144-42960;** www.wiener-staatsoper.at; U-Bahn: Karlsplatz), was bombed into a shell in World War II, the Viennese made its restoration their top priority, finishing it in time for the country's celebration of independence from occupying forces in 1955. A repertoire of some 40 works is given every season, with the Vienna Philharmonic in the pit and leading stars of the world on the stage. In their day, Gustav Mahler and Richard Strauss worked here as directors. The New Year usually starts off with a gala performance of *Die Fledermaus.* Tickets are 150 to 2,500AS (€10.95 to 182.50, $10 to $168). Tours are offered two to five times daily, 45AS (€3.34, $3) per person; tour times are posted on a board outside the entrance.

When the prestigious **Wiener Philharmoniker (Vienna Philharmonic)** is not traveling throughout the world, its home is the **Musikverein,** Karlsplatz 6 (ℂ **01/505-8190;** www.musikverein-wien.at; U-Bahn: Karlsplatz). Opened in 1870, the concert hall is suitably ornate and is the site of the famous New Year's Day concert, broadcast internationally. Tours are offered Wednesday to Monday at 1:30pm, 70AS (€5.10, $5) adults, 50AS (€3.65, $3.35) children 12 to 16, free for children under 12.

Besides the world-renowned Vienna Philharmonic, Vienna is home to three other major orchestras: the Vienna Symphony, the ÖRF Symphony Orchestra, and the Niederösterreichische Tonkünstler. The Wiener Sympohniker (Vienna Symphony) performs in the **Konzerthaus,** Lothringerstrasse 20 (ℂ **01/ 712-1211;** www.konzerthaus.at; U-Bahn: Stadt-Park), a major concert hall with three auditoriums, also the venue for chamber music and a diversity of programs.

In summer when the state theaters are closed, the Vienna Opera Festival presents performances and movie screenings of highlights from past opera seasons. The venue is the plaza in front of City Hall, and everything is free.

THEATER   For performances in English, head to **Vienna's English Theatre,** Josefsgasse 12 (ℂ **01/402-12600;** www.englishtheatre.at; U-Bahn: Rathaus).

ⓒ Wine Tasting in the *Heurigen*

Heurigen are Viennese wine taverns, celebrated in operettas, films, and song. They are found on the outskirts of Vienna, principally in Grinzing (the most popular district) and in Sievering, Neustift, Nussdorf, or Heiligenstadt. **Grinzing** (tram: 38) lies at the edge of the Vienna Woods, a 15-minute drive northwest of the center.

Only 20 minutes from Vienna, **Weingut Wolff,** Rathstrasse 50, Neustift (ⓒ **01/440-3727;** tram: 41), is one of the most endurable and beloved of Heurigen. Although aficionados claim the best are "deep in the countryside" of Lower Austria, this one comes closest on the borderline of Vienna to offering an authentic experience. In summer, you're welcomed to a flower-decked garden set against a backdrop of ancient vineyards. You can really fill up your platter here, with some of the best wursts (sausages) and roast meats (especially the delectable pork), as well as fresh salads. Find a table under a cluster of grapes and sample the fruity young wines, especially the Chardonnay, Sylvaner, and Gruner Veltliner. The tavern is open from Monday to Saturday 2pm to 1am and Sunday 11am to 1am, with main courses 85 to 240AS (€6.20 to €17.50, $6 to $16).

Altes Presshaus, Cobenzigasse 15 (ⓒ **01/320-0203**), was established in 1527, the oldest continuously operating Heurige in Grinzing, with an authentic cellar you might ask to visit. The place has an authentic, smoked-stained character with wood paneling and antique furniture. The garden terrace blossoms throughout the summer. Meals cost 150 to 350AS (€10.95 to €25.55, $10 to $23), with glasses of wine beginning at 30AS (€2.24, $2). Try such Heurigen-inspired fare as smoked pork shoulder, roast pork shank, sauerkraut, potatoes, and dumplings. Open from March to December daily 4pm to midnight.

The **Burgtheater (National Theater),** Dr. Karl-Lueger-Ring 2 (ⓒ **01/ 5144-4145;** www.burgtheater.at; tram: J; bus: 13A), produces classical and modern plays, and even if you don't understand German, you might want to attend a performance here, especially if a familiar Shakespeare play is being staged. This is one of Europe's premier repertory theaters; it is the dream of every German-speaking actor to appear here. Tickets are 60 to 600AS (€4.43 to €43.80, $4 to $40).

NIGHTCLUBS, CABARETS, BARS & CASINOS

The noteworthy architect Adolf Loos designed the very dark, sometimes mysterious **Loos American Bar,** Kärntnerdurchgang 10 (ⓒ **01/5123283;** U-Bahn: Stephansplatz), in 1908. Today it welcomes singles, couples who tend to be bilingual and very hip, and all manner of clients from the arts and media scene of Vienna. The mixologist's specialties include 15 kinds of martinis, plus 11 kinds of Manhattans. It's open from Monday to Friday noon to 4am and Saturday to Sunday noon to 5am; no cover.

The most famous jazz pub in Austria, **Jazzland,** Franz-Josefs-Kai 29 (ⓒ **01/ 533-2575;** U-Bahn: Schwedenplatz), is noted for the quality of its U.S. and

Central European–based performers. It's in a deep, 200-year-old cellar, of the type the Viennese used to store staples during the city's many sieges. Amid exposed brick walls and dim lighting, you can order drinks or dinner. Platters of Viennese food such as Tafelspitz, Wiener schnitzel, and roulades of beef are served. The place is open nightly 8pm to 1am; cover is 180AS (€13.15, $12). Music begins at 9pm, and every evening, three sets are performed.

Named after the patron saint of wine making, **St. Urbani-Keller,** Am Hof 12 (© **01/533-9102;** U-Bahn: Stephansplatz or Herrengasse), this cellar is one of the most historic in Vienna, having opened in 1906. The cellar has brick vaulting dating from the 13th century and sections of solid Roman walls you can admire while listening to the folk music at night. Open from Monday to Friday 11am to 11pm and Saturday and Sunday 4 to 10pm; no cover. Watch your step on the way up or down.

Volksgarten, entrances from the Heldenplatz and from Burgring 1 (© **01/ 5330-5180;** U-Bahn: Volkstheatre), is the largest and most diverse entertainment complex within the Ring. Established in 1946, it intersperses a series of dining and drinking emporiums within a labyrinth of rooms and outdoor spaces that interconnect into a happy-go-lucky maze. Many visitors prefer the area with the evergreen music, where Tyrolean and Bavarian oom-pah-pah music alternates with classic rock 'n' roll. A restaurant on the premises is open continuously 11am to midnight. Cover is 50AS (€3.65, $3.35) for evergreen music (8pm to 2am nightly), 75 to 140AS (€5.53 to €10.20, $5 to $9) for disco (nightly 11pm to 4am).

Set on the city's main shopping thoroughfare, a 5-minute walk from the Bristol Hotel, **Casino Wien,** Esterházy Palace, Kärntnerstrasse 41 (© **01/512-4836;** tram: 1, 2, or D), is the only casino in Vienna. You'll find gaming tables for French and American roulette, blackjack, poker, a dice game known as 7-11, and chemin de fer, as well as the ever-present slot machines and a bar. Men are encouraged to wear jackets and ties. It's open from Monday to Thursday 9pm to 3am and Friday to Sunday 3pm to 4am; no cover. You'll need to show your passport to enter.

GAY BARS

Alfi's Goldener Spiegel, Linke Wienzeile 46 (entrance on Stiegengasse; © **01/ 586-6608;** U-Bahn: Kettenbrückengasse), is one of the most popular gay havens in Vienna, attracting a lot of foreigners. Food items at the combination restaurant and bar include well-seasoned and well-prepared versions of Wiener schnitzel, served from Wednesday to Monday 7pm to 2am.

Eagle Bar, Blümelgasse 1 (© **01/587-2661;** U-Bahn: Neubaugasse), is the premier leather and denim bar for gay men in Vienna. There's no dancing, but virtually every gay male in town has dropped in at least once or twice for a cruisy look around. Open daily 9pm to 4am.

Frauencafé, Langegasse 11 (© **01/406-3754;** U-Bahn: Rathaus), is exactly what a translation of its name would imply: A politically conscious cafe for lesbian and (to a lesser degree) heterosexual women who appreciate the company of other women. Established in 1977, it has an interior filled with magazines, newspapers, modern paintings, and an international female clientele. Open from Tuesday to Saturday; in summer 8pm to 1am, in winter 7pm to 1am.

DAY TRIPS ALONG THE DANUBE

KLOSTERNEUBURG   On the northwestern outskirts of Vienna, this old market town is the site of **Klosterneuburg Abbey (Stift Klosterneuburg)** ⚜,

The Danube Valley

Stiftsplatz 1 (✆ **02243/411-212**), the most historically significant abbey in Austria. Its art treasures include the world-famous 12th-century **enamel altar** ✛ of Nikolaus of Verdun. The monastery also boasts the largest private library in Austria, with more than 1,250 handwritten books and many antique paintings. You can visit the monastery only as part of 1-hour guided tours daily 9am to noon and 2:30 to 5:30pm, costing 70AS (€5.10, $5). Most tours are conducted in German with occasional brief English translations.

Getting There   By car, follow Route 14 northwest of Vienna along the south bank of the Danube. Otherwise, take the U-Bahn from the Westbahnhof to Heiligenstadt, where you then board a bus marked KLOSTERNEUBURG.

HERZOGENBURG MONASTERY ✛   Founded in the 12th century by a German bishop from Passau, this Augustinian monastery, A-3130 Herzogenburg (✆ **02782/83113**), lies 6km (7 miles) south of Traismauer and 16km (10 miles) south of the Danube. The present complex of buildings comprising the church and the abbey was reconstructed in the baroque style. Outstanding are the high altar and the series of 16th-century paintings on wood. The monastery is known for its library containing more than 80,000 works. Admission is 70AS (€5.10, $5) adults, 40AS (€2.90, $2.70) students, 50AS (€3.65, $3.35) those over 65. You can wander around alone or participate in a guided tour, departing daily at 9am, 10am, 11am, 1pm, 2pm, 3pm, 4pm, and 5pm. The attraction is open only from April to October daily 9am to 6pm. There's a wine tavern in the complex where you can eat platters of Austrian specialties and drink the product of local grapes.

Getting There   By **car,** head west from Vienna via Autobahn A-1, following the signs to Salzburg and Linz, exiting at the signposted turnoff for Heiligenkreuz.

KREMS ⚘   In the eastern part of the Wachau on the left bank of the Danube lies 1,000-year-old Krems. The city today encompasses Stein and Mautern, once separate towns. Krems is a mellow town of courtyards, old churches, and ancient houses in the heart of vineyard country, with some partially preserved town walls. Just as the Viennese flock to Grinzing and other suburbs to sample new wine in Heurigen, so the people of the Wachau come here to taste the vintners' products, which appear in Krems earlier in the year.

The most interesting part of Krems today is what was once the little village of Stein. Narrow streets are terraced above the river, and the single main street, **Steinlanderstrasse,** is flanked with houses, many from the 16th century. The **Grosser Passauerhof,** Steinlanderstrasse 76, is a Gothic structure decorated with an oriel. Another house, at Steinlanderstrasse 84, once the imperial tollhouse, combines Byzantine and Venetian elements.

Pfarrkirche St. Veith (parish church) (℡ 02732/857100) stands in the center of town at the Rathaus, reached by going along either Untere Landstrasse or Obere Landstrasse. Rich with gilt and statuary, it's the town's most visible church and the ecclesiastical centerpiece of the local parish.

Wein Stadt Museum Krems (Historical Museum of Krems), Körnermarkt 14 (℡ **02732/801567**), is in a restored Gothic-style Dominican monastery. It has a gallery displaying the paintings of Martin Johann Schmidt, a noted 18th-century artist better known as Kremser Schmidt. The museum is open from March to November Tuesday to Sunday 1 to 6pm. Admission is 45AS (€3.34, $3) for access to both areas of the museum.

Getting There   Krems is 80km (50 miles) west of Vienna and 29km (18 miles) north of St. Pölten. By **car,** drive north from Vienna along Autobahn A-22 until it splits into three roads near the town of Stockerau. Once here, drive due west along Route 3, following the signs into Krems.

Trains depart from both the Wien Nord Station and the Wien Franz-Josefs Bahnhof for Krems every 2 hours daily 8am until around 2pm. Many are direct, although some will require a transfer in the railway junctions of Absdorf-Hippersdorf or St. Pölten (trip time: 1–1½ hr.). Call ℡ **05/1717** for schedules.

From mid-May to late September, **river cruisers** depart westward from Vienna every Sunday at 8:30am en route to Passau, Germany. They arrive in Tulln around 11:15am, then Krems around 1:40pm. For more information, call the DDSG-Donaureisen Shipping Line in Vienna (℡ **01/588800**) or the tourist office in either Tulln, Albrechtsgasse 32, (℡ **02272/65836**) or Krems, Undstrasse 6, (℡ **02732/82676**).

DÜRNSTEIN ⚘   Less than 8km (5 miles) west of Krems is the loveliest town along the Danube, Dürnstein, which draws throngs of tour groups in summer. Terraced vineyards mark this as a Danube wine town, and the town's fortified walls are partially preserved.

The **ruins of a castle fortress,** 160m (520 ft.) above the town, are a link with the Crusades. Here Richard the Lion-Hearted of England was held prisoner in 1193. You can visit the ruins if you don't mind a vigorous climb (allow an hour).

The castle isn't much, but the view of Dürnstein and the Wachau is more than worth the effort.

The 15th-century **Pfarrkirche (parish church)** also merits a visit. The building was originally an Augustinian monastery, reconstructed in the baroque style; the church tower is the finest baroque example in the whole country.

Getting There   By **car,** take Route 3 west from Krems. **Train** travel to Dürnstein from Vienna requires a transfer in Krems (see above). In Krems, trains depart approximately every 2 hours on routes that parallel the northern bank of the Danube on their way to Linz. These departures connect with trains from Vienna. Call ℭ **05/1717** in Vienna for information.

About eight **buses** a day travel between Krems and Dürnstein, some of which coordinate with the arrival time of one of the many daily trains from Vienna. The bus trip between Krems and Dürnstein takes 20 minutes.

MELK   One of the chief sightseeing goals of every visitor to Austria is Melk. In the words of Empress Maria Theresa, "If I had never come here, I would have regretted it." The reason to visit Melk is the **Melk Abbey** ⌖⌖, Dietmayerstrasse 1 (ℭ **02752/5231-2232**), one of the finest baroque buildings in the world, and the **Stiftskirche (abbey church).**

The rock-strewn bluff where the abbey now stands overlooking the river was the seat of the Babenbergs, who ruled Austria from 976 until the Hapsburgs took over in 1278. The abbey's influence as a center of learning and culture spread all over Austria, a fact familiar to readers of the Umberto Eco's *The Name of the Rose.* Most of the design of the present abbey was by the baroque architect Jakob Prandtauer. The Marmorsaal (marble hall) contains pilasters coated in red marble. Despite all this adornment, the abbey takes second place in lavish glory to the **Stiftskirche,** the golden abbey church, damaged by fire in 1947 but now almost completely restored.

The abbey is open daily, with tours leaving at 15- to 20-minute intervals 9am to 5pm (to 4pm from October to March). Guides make efforts to translate into English a running commentary that is otherwise German. Adults pay 110AS (€8.05, $7) for guided tours and 80AS (€5.85, $5) for unguided tours; children 70AS (€5.10, $5) and 40AS (€2.90, $2.70).

Getting There   By **car,** drive about 88km (55 miles) west of Vienna, along Autobahn A-1, on the right bank of the Danube. Melk marks the western terminus of the Wachau, lying upstream from Krems. **Trains** leave frequently from Vienna's Westbahnhof to Melk, with two brief stops (trip time: 1 hr.).

2 Salzburg & Environs

A baroque city on the banks of the Salzach River, set against a mountain backdrop, Salzburg is the beautiful capital of the state of Salzburg. The city and the river were named after its early residents who earned their living in the salt mines. In this "heart of the heart of Europe," Mozart was born in 1756, and the composer's association with the city beefs up tourism.

The **Old Town** lies on the left bank of the river, where a monastery and bishopric were founded in 700. From that start, Salzburg grew in power and prestige, becoming an archbishopric in 798. In the heyday of the prince-archbishops, the city became known as the "German Rome." Responsible for much of its architectural grandeur are those masters of the baroque, Fischer von Erlach and Lukas von Hildebrandt.

"The City of Mozart," "Silent Night," and *The Sound of Music*—Salzburg lives essentially off its rich past. Site of the world's snobbiest summer musical festival, it is a front-ranking cultural Mecca for classical music year-round. Its natural setting among alpine peaks on both banks of the Salzach River gives it the backdrop needed to perpetuate its romantic image.

One of Europe's greatest tourist capitals, most of Salzburg's day-to-day life spins around promoting its music and its other connections. Although *The Sound of Music* was filmed way back in 1964, this Julie Andrews blockbuster has become a cult attraction and is definitely alive and well in Salzburg. Ironically, Austria was the only country in the world where the musical failed when it first opened. It played for only a single week in Vienna, closing after audiences dwindled.

Salzburg is only a short distance from the Austrian-German frontier, so it's convenient for exploring many of the nearby attractions of Bavaria (see chapter 7). On the northern slopes of the Alps, the city is at the intersection of traditional European trade routes and is well served today by air, autobahn, and rail.

ESSENTIALS

GETTING THERE   By Plane   The **Salzburg Airport–W.A. Mozart,** Innsbrucker Bundesstrasse 95 (© **0662/8580;** www.salzburg-airport.com), lies 3km (2 miles) southwest of the city center. It has regularly scheduled service to all Austrian airports, as well as to Frankfurt, Amsterdam, Brussels, Berlin, Dresden, Düsseldorf, Hamburg, Paris, and Zurich.

Bus 77 runs between the airport and Salzburg's main rail station. The bus departs every 30 minutes during the day, and the trip takes 20 minutes and costs 35AS (€2.55, $2.35) one-way. A taxi takes about 15 minutes, and you're likely to pay from 160 to 200AS (€11.73 to €14.60, $11 to $13).

By Train   Salzburg's main rail station, the **Salzburg Hauptbahnhof,** Südtirolerplatz (© **05/1717**), is on the major rail lines of Europe, with frequent arrivals from all the main cities of Austria and European cities such as Munich. Between 5:05am and 8:05pm, trains arrive every 30 minutes from Vienna (trip time: 3½ hr.). There are eight daily trains from Innsbruck (2 hr.). Trains also arrive every 30 minutes from Munich (2½ hr.).

From the train station, buses depart to various parts of the city, including the Altstadt. Or you can walk to the Altstadt in about 20 minutes. Taxis are also available, and the rail station has a currency exchange and storage lockers.

By Car   Salzburg is 334km (209 miles) southwest of Vienna and 152km (95 miles) east of Munich. It's reached from all directions by good roads, including Autobahn A-8 from the west (Munich), A-1 from the east (Vienna), and A-10 from the south. Route 20 comes into Salzburg from points north and west, and Route 159 serves towns and cities from the southeast.

VISITOR INFORMATION   Tourist Office   The **Salzburg Information Office,** Mozartplatz 5 (© **0662/88987-330;** www.salzburginfo.at; bus: 5, 6, or 51), is open July to September daily 9am to 8pm and off-season from Monday to Saturday 9am to 6pm. The office makes hotel reservations for a 7.2% deposit plus a 30AS (€2.24, $2) booking fee for two people. There's also a tourist information office on Platform 2A of the Hauptbahnhof, Südtirolerplatz (© **0662/ 88987-340**).

Websites   The best information comes from the Salzburg Information Office (**www.salzburginfo.at**) and the Austrian National Tourist Office (**www. anto.com**).

Salzburg

ATTRACTIONS ●
Dom (Salzburg Cathedral) **14**
Festspielhaus (Festival Theater) **9**
Glockenspiel **13**
Hohensalzburg **11**
Mozart Geburtshaus (Mozart Birthplace) **18**
Mozart Wohnhaus (Mozart Residence) **4**
Mozarteum **3**
Museum Carolino Augusteum **6**
Petersfriedhof (St. Peter's Cemetery) **10**
Residenz **15**
Schloss Mirabell **2**
Stiftskirche St. Peter **10**

ACCOMMODATIONS ■
Alstadthotel Wolf-Deitrich **20**
Alstadt Radisson **16**
Auersperg **1**
Blaue Gans **8**
Dr. Wührer's Haus Gastein **21**
Elefant **17**
Goldener Hirsch **7**
Hotel Amadeus **19**
Hotel Restaurant Gablerbräu **22**
Sacher Salzburg **5**
Weisse Taube **12**

Value The Salzburg Card

The **Salzburg Card** not only entitles you to use **public transportation** but also acts as an **admission ticket** to the city's most important cultural sights and institutions. With it, you can visit Mozart's birthplace, the Hohensalzburg fortress, the Residenz gallery, the water fountain gardens at Hellbrunn, the Baroque Museum in the Mirabell Garden, and the gala rooms in the Archbishop's Residence. The card can also be used to take in sights outside town, such as Hellbrunn Zoo, the open-air museum in Grossingmain, the salt mines of the Dürnberg, and a gondola trip at Untersberg. You'll also receive a brochure with maps and sightseeing hints. Cards are valid for 24, 48, and 72 hours and cost 225AS (€16.45, $15), 300AS (€21.90, $20), and 390AS (€28.45, $26), respectively. Children up to 15 receive a 50% discount. You can buy the pass from Salzburg travel agencies, hotels, tobacconists, and municipal offices.

CITY LAYOUT   Most of what visitors come to see lies on the left bank of the Salzach River in the **Altstadt (Old Town).** If you're driving, you must leave your car in the modern part of town—the right bank of the Salzach—and descend on foot to the Altstadt pedestrian zone.

The heart of the inner city is **Residenzplatz,** with the largest and finest baroque fountain this side of the Alps. On the western side of the square stands the **Residenz,** palace of the prince-archbishops, and on the southern side of the square is the **Salzburg Cathedral (Dom).** To the west of the Dom lies **Domplatz,** linked by archways dating from 1658. The squares to the north and south appear totally enclosed.

On the southern side of Max-Reinhardt-Platz and Hofstallgasse, toward **Mönchsberg**—a mountain ridge slightly less than 3km (2 miles) long—stands the **Festspielhaus (Festival Theater).**

GETTING AROUND   By Bus/Tram   A quick, comfortable service is provided by city buses through the center of the city from the Nonntal parking lot to Sigsmundsplatz, the city-center car park. Fares for one ride are 20AS (€1.45, $1.35) adult, 11AS (€0.80, 75¢) children 6 to 15; those 5 and under travel free. *Be warned:* Buses stop running at 11pm.

By Taxi   You'll find taxi stands scattered at key points all over the city center and in the suburbs. To order a taxi in advance, call **Salzburg Funktaxi-Vereinigung (radio taxis),** Rainerstrasse 27 (© 0662/8111). Taxi fares start at 40AS (€2.90, $2.70).

By Car   Driving a car in Salzburg isn't recommended. However, you'll probably want a car for touring around Salzburg, as using public transportation can be time consuming. Arrangements for car rentals are always best if made in advance. Try **Avis** (© 0662/877278) or **Hertz** (© 0662/876674), both at Ferdinand-Porsche-Strasse 7 and open from Monday to Friday 8am to 6pm and Saturday 8am to 1pm. A 21.2% tax is added to car rentals.

By Horse-Drawn Cab   There are horse-drawn cabs (*Fiakers*) at Residenzplatz. Four people usually pay 350AS (€25.55, $23) for 20 minutes or 680AS (€49.65, $46) for 50 minutes. But all fares are subject to negotiation, of course.

By Bicycle   City officials have developed a network of bicycle paths, which are indicated on city maps. From April to November, bicycles can be rented at the **Hauptbahnhof,** Desk 3 (☎ **0662/8887-3163**), on Südtirolerplatz. The cost is about 180AS (€13.15, $12) per day, unless you have a rail ticket; then you pay 120AS (€8.75, $8) per day.

FAST FACTS: Salzburg

American Express   The office at Mozartplatz 5–7 (☎ **0662/8080;** bus: 5 or 6) is open from Monday to Friday 9am to 5:30pm and Saturday 9am to noon.

Baby-Sitters   English-speaking students at the University of Salzburg often baby-sit; call ☎ **0662/8044-6001.** Make arrangements as far in advance as possible.

Business Hours   Most shops and stores are open from Monday to Friday 9am to 6pm and Saturday, usually 9am to noon. Some of the smaller shops shut down at noon for a lunch break. Salzburg observes *langer Samstag,* which means that most stores stay open until 5pm on selected Saturdays.

Currency   See "Fast Facts: Vienna" in section 1.

Currency Exchange   Banks are open from Monday to Friday 8am to noon and 2 to 4:30pm. You can exchange money at the Hauptbahnhof on Südtirolerplatz daily 7am to 10pm and at the airport daily 9am to 4pm.

Dentists   For an English-speaking dentist, call **Dentistenkammer,** Faberstrasse 2 (☎ **0662/87-34-66**).

Doctors   Call **Ärztekammer für Salzburg** (☎ **0662/87-13-27**). For emergencies, the **Medical Emergency Center,** Paris-London-Strasse 8A (☎ **141**), is on duty from 7pm Friday to 7am Monday; it's also open on public holidays.

Drugstores (Apotheke)   They're open from Monday to Friday 8am to 12:30pm and 2:30 to 6pm, and Saturday 8am to noon. For night or Sunday service, shops display a sign giving the address of the nearest open pharmacy. You can also go to **Elisabeth-Apotheke,** Elisabethstrasse 1 (☎ **0662/87-14-84**), near the railway station.

Embassies/Consulates   The Consular Agency of the **United States** at Altermarkt (☎ **0662/84-87-76**) is open from Monday, Wednesday, and Thursday 9am to noon. The Consulate of **Great Britain** at Altermarkt 4 (☎ **0662/ 84-81-33**) is open from Monday to Friday 9am to noon.

Emergencies   Call ☎ **133** for police, ☎ **122** to report a fire, and ☎ **144** for an ambulance.

Internet Access   Visit the **Cybercafe,** Gstättengasse 27 (☎ **0662/84-26-16**), open daily 2 to 11pm. It charges 80AS (€5.85, $5) per hour.

Post Office   The main post office is at Residenzplatz 9 (☎ **0662/844-1210;** bus: 5 or 6), open from Monday to Friday 7am to 7pm and Saturday 8 to 10am. The post office at the main rail station is open 24 hours.

Telephone   The **country code** for Austria is **43.** The **city code** for Salzburg is **662;** use this code when you're calling from outside Austria. If you're within Austria, use **0662.** Phone numbers in Salzburg are undergoing a change. If you can't reach a number we've listed, dial 11181 for information if you're within Austria. If calling from outside Austria, dial 11813 for information.

WHERE TO STAY
ON THE LEFT BANK (ALTSTADT)
Very Expensive

Altstadt Radisson 𝒶𝒶   This is not your typical Radisson property—in fact, it's a radical departure for the chain in style and charm. Dating from 1377, it's a luxuriously and elegantly converted Altstadt hostelry. Its closest rival in town is the old-world Goldener Hirsch, to which it comes in second. The old and new are blended in perfect harmony here, and the historic facade conceals top-rate comforts and amenities. In a structure of this size, rooms naturally vary greatly in size, but all have a certain charm and sparkle and are exceedingly comfortable with some of the city's best beds, plus luxurious bathrooms.

Rudfolkskai 28 & Judengasse 15, A-5020 Salzburg. ℂ **800/333-3333** in the U.S., or 0662/848-571. Fax 0662/848-571-6. www.austria-trend.at. 60 units. 2,900–6,700AS (€211.70–€489.10, $194–$449) double; 5,600–9,900AS (€408.80–€722.70, $375–$663) suite. Rates include buffet breakfast. AE, DC, MC, V. Parking 300AS (€21.90, $20.10). **Amenities:** Restaurant; 24-hour room service; dry cleaning/laundry. *In room:* A/C, TV, minibar, hair dryer.

Goldener Hirsch 𝒶𝒶𝒶   The award for the finest hotel in Salzburg goes to this place, steeped in legend and with a history dating from 1407, though it was last renovated in 1997. Near Mozart's birthplace, the hotel is composed of four medieval townhouses, three of which are joined together in a labyrinth of rustic hallways and staircases. The fourth, called "The Coppersmith's House," is across the street and contains 17 charming spacious rooms. All are beautifully furnished and maintained, with luxurious full-sized bathrooms.

Getreidegasse 37, A-5020 Salzburg. ℂ **800/325-3535** in the U.S., or 0662/8084. Fax 0662/8485-178-45. www.goldenerhirsch.com. 70 units. 3,600–5,900AS (€262.80–€430.70, $241–$395) double; from 7,900AS (€577, $529) suite. Higher rates reflect prices at festival time (1st week of Apr and mid-July to Aug). AE, DC, MC, V. Valet parking 250AS (€18.25, $17). Bus: 55. **Amenities:** 2 restaurants (see "Where to Dine," below), elegant bar; 24-hour room service; baby-sitting; laundry/dry cleaning; car-rental desk. *In room:* A/C, TV, minibar, hair dryer.

Moderate

Blaue Gans   Only a short walk from the much more expensive Goldener Hirsch, the much-renovated "Blue Goose" has been functioning as an inn for more than 400 years. Rooms were renovated between 1995 and 1998. Each is cozy, is comfortable. All have good beds with firm mattresses and a full bathroom. Those facing the courtyard are quieter and much more desirable. Rooms 332 and 336 are the most spacious.

Getreidegasse 41–43, A-5020 Salzburg. ℂ **0662/84-13-17.** Fax 0662/84-13-179. www.blauegans.at. 45 units. 1,250–2,350AS (€91.25–€171.55, $84–$157) double. Rates include breakfast. AE, DC, MC, V. Parking 180AS (€13.15, $12). Bus: 1 or 2. **Amenities:** Historic restaurant and beer hall, bar. *In room:* TV (some rooms).

Elefant   Near the Rathaus in the Old Town, in a quiet alley off Getreidegasse, is this well-established family run hotel. It's one of the most ancient buildings of Salzburg—more than 700 years old—but was last renovated in 1992. One of our favorite rooms is the vaulted Bürgerstüberl, where high wooden banquettes separate the tables. Rooms are well-furnished with high ceilings. Each comes with a tidily maintained bathroom with a shower stall.

Sigmund-Haffner-Gasse 4, A-5020 Salzburg. ℂ **0662/84-33-97.** Fax 0662/84-01-0928. www.elefant.at. 36 units. 1,800–2,300AS (€131.40–€167.90, $121–$154) double. Rates include buffet breakfast. AE, DC, MC, V. Parking 100AS (€7.30, $7). Bus: 1, 5, 6, or 51. **Amenities:** 3 restaurants, including historic 17th-century wine cellar. *In room:* TV, minibar, hair dryer, safe.

Inexpensive
Weisse Taube   "The White Dove" is a few steps from Mozartplatz in the pedestrian zone of the Old Town, but you can drive up to it to unload baggage. Constructed in 1365, the Weisse Taube has been owned by the Haubner family since 1904. The midsize bedrooms were renovated in the 1990s and are comfortably streamlined, with traditional furnishings and full-sized bathrooms, including frequently renewed beds. Some accommodations are reserved for nonsmokers.

Kaigasse 9, A-5020 Salzburg. ② **0662/84-24-04.** Fax 0662/84-17-83. www.weissetaube.at. 31 units. 1,220–1,850AS (€89.12–€135.14, $81–$123) double. Rates include breakfast. AE, DC, MC, V. Parking garage 120AS (€8.75, $8). Bus: 5, 51, or 55. **Amenities:** Bar; TV room. *In room:* TV, minibar.

ON THE RIGHT BANK
Expensive
Sacher Salzburg Osterreichischer Hof 🏵🏵🏵   Only the Goldener Hirsch rivals this charmer. Built as the Hotel d'Autriche in 1866, this hotel has survived the toils of war and has been renovated countless times. A new era began when the Gürtler family, owners of the Hotel Sacher in Vienna, took over in 1988, turning the hotel into a jewel amid the villas on the riverbank. The cheerful rooms are well furnished, quite spacious, and individually decorated, each with a luxurious bathroom. Try to reserve one overlooking the river.

Schwarzstrasse 5–7, A-5020 Salzburg. ② **800/223-6800** in the U.S. and Canada, or 0662/889-77. Fax 0662/889-77-551. www.sacher.com. 120 units. 4,400–6,800AS (€321.20–€496.40, $295–$456) double; from 8,700AS (€635.10, $583) suite. Rates include buffet breakfast. AE, DC, MC, V. Parking 320AS (€23.35, $21). Bus: 1, 5, 29, or 51. **Amenities:** 5 dining rooms, riverside terrace, cafe (serving Austria's most fabled pastry, the original Sacher torte), bar; 24-hour room service; laundry/dry cleaning. *In room:* A/C, TV, minibar, hair dryer, safe.

Moderate
Altstadthotel Wolf-Dietrich 🏵   Two 19th-century townhouses join together to make this select little hotel. The lobby and ground floor reception area have been completely revamped to create a friendly and elegant atmosphere with bright, classical furnishings and often Laura Ashley fabrics. The smallish rooms are comfortably furnished, appealing, and cozy, with excellent beds and tiny but tidy bathrooms with shower stalls.

Wolf-Dietrich-Strasse 7, A-5020 Salzburg. ② **0662/87-12-75.** Fax 0662/88-23-20. www.salzburg-hotel-at. 29 units. 1,500–2,140AS (€109.50–€156.20, $101–$143) double. Rates include breakfast. AE, DC, MC, V. Parking 130AS (€9.50, $9). Closed Feb–Mar 15. Bus: 1, 2, 5, 6, or 51. **Amenities:** Viennese-style cafe, formal restaurant; swimming pool, sauna, solarium, indoor pool. *In room:* TV, minibar.

Auersperg 🏵   With its own sunny gardens, this traditional family-run hotel consists of two buildings, a main structure and a less expensive and less desirable annex. There's an old-fashioned look of charm wherever you go, from the reception hall with its molded ceilings to the antique-filled drawing room. The warm, cozy, and large rooms are especially inviting, with excellent beds and well-equipped bathrooms with tubs and showers.

Auerspergstrasse 61, A-5027 Salzburg. ② **0662/889-44-0.** Fax 0662/889-44-55. www.auesperg.at. 63 units. 1,480–2,100AS (€108.05–€153.30, $99–$141) double; 2,400–3,100AS (€175.20–€226.30, $161–$208) suite. Rates include breakfast. AE, DC, MC, V. Free parking. Bus: 15 from the train station. **Amenities:** Restaurant, bar; sauna, steam bath, fitness center roof terrace. *In room:* TV, minibar, hair dryer.

Dr. Wührer's Haus Gastein   This prosperous-looking Teutonic villa, amid calm scenery on the bank of the Salzach River, was built as a private home in 1953. Guests appreciate the spacious flowering garden, a setting for breakfast or afternoon tea. The interior is sparsely but pleasantly furnished. Rooms—often quite large—contain cozy locally crafted furniture. Many have private balconies, and each comes with a neat little bathroom containing a shower stall.

Ignaz-Rieder-Kai 25, A-5020 Salzburg. ℂ 0662/62-25-65. Fax 0662/62-25-659. www.gastein.at. 13 units. 1,445–2,145AS (€105.54–€156.64, $97–$144) double; 2,200–3,545AS (€160.60–€258.84, $147–$238) suite. Rates include breakfast. MC, V. Parking 300AS (€21.90, $20). Bus: 49. In room: minibar.

Inexpensive
Hotel Amadeus   The walls and foundations of this hotel date from the 15th century, but much of what you'll experience today is a mid-20th-century improvement with lots of country-baroque furnishings and accessories. The quietest rooms are those overlooking the rear, where sight lines encompass the graveyard where the wife of Mozart is buried. Rooms are pleasant, accessible via a cramped elevator. Bathrooms are cramped but well-organized.

Linzer Gasse 43–45, A-5020 Salzburg. ℂ 0662/87-14-01 or 0662/87-61-63. Fax 0662/87-61-63-7. walkets@salzburg.co.at. 30 units, 27 with bathroom (shower only). 700–820AS (€51.10–€59.85, $47–$55) double without bathroom; 1,200–1,800AS (€87.60–€131.40, $80–$121) double with bathroom. Parking 130AS (€9.54, $9). Rates include buffet breakfast. AE, DC, MC, V. Bus 1, 2, 5, 6, or 51 to Makartplatz. **Amenities:** Cafe. In room: TV.

Hotel Restaurant Gablerbräu   This inviting hotel is near the right bank's Makartplatz. The midsize rooms are furnished in a simple, modern style. Beds are frequently renewed, housekeeping is good, and the tiny bathrooms with shower stalls are well kept.

Linzergasse 8, A-5020 Salzburg. ℂ 0662/88-965. Fax 0662/88-965-55. www.gablerbrau.com. 52 units. 1,610–1,960AS (€117.55–€143.130, $108–$131) double. Rates include breakfast. AE, DC, MC, V. Parking 150AS (€10.95, $10). Bus: 51. **Amenities:** 3 restaurants, including a beer hall. In room: TV.

WHERE TO DINE
Two special desserts you'll want to sample while here are the famous *Salzburger Nockerln,* a light mixture of stiff egg whites, as well as the elaborate confection known as the *Mozart-Kugeln,* with bittersweet chocolate, hazelnut nougat, and marzipan. You'll also want to taste the beer in one of the numerous Salzburg breweries.

ON THE LEFT BANK (ALTSTADT)
Very Expensive
Goldener Hirsch ✧✧✧ AUSTRIAN/VIENNESE   The best restaurant in Salzburg's best hotel attracts the brightest luminaries of the international music and business community. It's staffed with a superb team of chefs and waiters who preside over an atmosphere of elegant simplicity. Dishes are impeccably prepared and beautifully served. Specialties include parfait of smoked trout in a mustard-dill sauce, saddle of venison in a cranberry cream sauce, veal in saffron sauce, roast filet of char with dill mustard and asparagus, *Tafelspitz* (boiled beef), and roast duck in its own gravy.

Getreidegasse 37. ℂ 0662/80-84-0. Reservations required. Main courses 290–420AS (€21.15–€30.65, $19–$28); 3-course fixed-price lunch or dinner 490AS (€35.75, $33); 5-course fixed-price dinner 690AS (€50.35, $46). Daily noon–2:30pm and 6:30–9:30pm. Bus: 55.

Purzelbaum ✧ AUSTRIAN/VIENNESE   In a residential neighborhood, this restaurant is near a duck pond at the bottom of a steep incline leading up to Salzburg Castle. Menu items change according to the inspiration of the chef. Look for such well-prepared favorites as venison in red-wine sauce, a delectable sole meunière, beefsteak cooked in a savory casserole or grilled and served with

Cafe Society

Café-Restaurant Glockenspiel, Mozartplatz 2 (℃ 0662/84-14-03-0; bus: 55), is the city's most popular cafe, with about 100 tables with armchairs out front. You might want to spend an afternoon here, particularly when there's live chamber music. Upon entering, you can't miss a glass case filled with every caloric delight west of Vienna. Coffee starts at 35AS (€2.55, $2.35) and comes in many varieties, including Maria Theresa, which contains orange liqueur. Summer hours are daily 9am to midnight (food served to 11pm); the rest of the year hours are daily 9am to 7pm (food served to 6pm). It's closed the second and third weeks of November and January.

Opened in 1705, **Café Tomaselli,** Altermarkt 9 (℃ 0662/84-44-88; bus: 2, 5, 6, 51, or 55), opens onto one of the Altstadt's most charming cobblestone squares. Aside from the outdoor summer chairs, you'll find inside a room with many tables and lots of elegant conversation among the haute bourgeoisie. A waiter brings a pastry tray filled with 40 kinds of cakes. Other menu items include omelets, wursts, ice cream, and a wide range of drinks. Pastries begin at 27AS (€1.95, $1.80), and the most elaborate cakes cost 39AS (€2.85, $2.60). Coffee costs 36AS (€2.65, $2.40) for a mélange. It's open from Monday to Saturday 7am to 9pm, and Sunday and holidays 8am to 9pm (closed 5 days in January).

pepper sauce, and (our favorite) the house specialty, *scampi Grüstl,* composed of fresh shrimp with sliced potatoes and baked with herbs in a casserole.

Zugallistrasse 7. ℃ 0662/84-88-43. Reservations required. Main courses 250–300AS (€18.25–€21.90, $17–$20); 4-course fixed-price menu 620AS (€45.25, $42). AE, DC, MC, V. Mon–Sat noon–2pm and 6–11pm. Closed July 1–14. Bus: 55.

Moderate

Café Winkler INTERNATIONAL   On the rocky Mönchsberg Terrace in an isolated position high above the city, the Winkler was built during the 1950s and has been drawing tourists like a magnet ever since. Ringed with large expanses of glass, it offers the best panoramas in Salzburg. The menu is broad enough to satisfy someone who wants a full Austrian meal or merely a caffeine fix. If you wish to dine, an employee will whip out a tablecloth and silverware, take your order, and provide a standard menu listing dishes that include a gratin of scampi; filet steaks with peppercorns or with mushroom sauce; or saddle of venison with a sauce made from seasonal berries. The food is surprisingly good for such a touristy place.

Mönchsberg Terrace, Mönchsberg. ℃ 0662/847-738. Reservations recommended for meals, not for cafe items. Main courses 220–290AS (€16.05–€21.15, $15–$19); 4-course set menu 400AS (€29.20, $27). AE, DC, MC, V. Tues–Sun noon–2pm and 6–10pm. Limited menu available Tues–Sun 2–6pm. Also open Mon (same hours) during Salzburg Festival. Access via the Mönchsberg elevator.

Zum Eulenspiegel AUSTRIAN/VIENNESE   Opposite Mozart's birthplace, this restaurant sits at one end of a quiet cobblestone square in the Old Town. Inside, guests have a choice of five rooms on three different levels, all rustically but elegantly decorated. A small and rustic bar area on the ground floor is a pleasant place for predinner drinks. Traditional Austrian cuisine is meticulously adhered to here. The menu features such classic dishes as *Tafelspitz* (boiled beef), the famous Wiener schnitzel, braised trout with dill-flavored potatoes, pork cutlets with fresh herbs, filet of pork with warm cabbage salad and bacon, and Salzburger Nockerln or peaches with hot fudge and vanilla ice cream for dessert.

Hagenauerplatz 2. ℂ **0662/84-31-80.** Reservations required. Main courses 79–266AS (€5.75–€19.40, $5–$18). AE, MC, V. Mon–Sat 11am–2pm and 6–10:30pm. Closed Feb 1–Mar 15. Tram: 2. Bus: 2.

Inexpensive

Festungsrestaurant SALZBURG/AUSTRIAN   This pair of solid dining rooms is still going strong ever since the Middle Ages when it opened to dispense food and drink to bishops, priests, servants, soldiers, and wayfarers. The compound is poised 122m (400 ft.) above the Altstadt and the Salzach River, with a panoramic view over the spires and cupolas of the city and its nearby alpine peaks. In warm weather, tables are set up within nearby gardens. The menu presents well-flavored and time-tested cuisine that includes *Salzburger Bierfleische* (goulashlike stew) and a succulent version of *Salzburger Schnitzel* (pork scallop stuffed with mushrooms, bacon, and tomatoes).

Hohensalzburg, Mönchsberg 34. ℂ **0662/84-17-80.** Reservations required July–Aug. Main courses 115–225AS (€8.40–€16.45, $8–$15). MC, V. Apr–May and Oct daily 10am–8pm; June–Sept daily 10am–10pm; Dec–Mar Wed–Sun 10am–5pm. Closed Nov. Funicular from the Old Town.

Krimpelstätter SALZBURG/AUSTRIAN   This is an enduring Salzburg favorite dating from 1548. In summer, the beer garden, full of roses and trellises, attracts up to 300 visitors at a time. If you want a snack, a beer, or a glass of wine, head for the paneled door marked *Gastezimmer* in the entry corridor. If you're looking for a more formal, less visited area, three cozy antique dining rooms sit atop a flight of narrow stone steps. The food is traditional and good tasting, but only for those who like hearty fare and don't fret about calories or cholesterol. The menu offers a hearty Salzburg regional cuisine featuring homemade sausages, spinach noodles, and wild game dishes.

Müllner Hauptstrasse 31. ℂ **0662/43-22-74.** Reservations recommended. Main courses 80–150AS (€5.85–€10.95, $5–$10). No credit cards. Tues–Sat 11am–2pm and 6pm–midnight (and on Mon, May–Sept). Closed 3 weeks in Jan. Bus: 49 or 95.

Sternbräu AUSTRIAN   This place seems big enough to have fed half the Austro-Hungarian army, with a series of rooms that follow one after the other in varying degrees of formality. The Hofbräustübl is a rustic fantasy. You can also eat in the chestnut tree–shaded beer garden, usually packed on a summer's night, or under the weathered arcades of an inner courtyard. Daily specials include typical Austrian dishes such as Wiener and chicken schnitzels, some trout recipes, cold marinated herring, Hungarian goulash, hearty regional soups, and lots of other *gutbürgerlich* selections. You come here for hearty portions—not for refined cuisine.

Griesgasse 23. ℂ **0662/84-21-40.** Main courses 78–215AS (€5.74–€15.70, $5–$14); fixed-price 145–210AS (€10.64–€15.35, $10–$14). AE, DC, MC. Daily 9am–midnight. Bus: 2, 5, 12, 49, or 51.

Stiftskeller St. Peter (Peterskeller) ℝ AUSTRIAN/VIENNESE   Legend has it that Mephistopheles met with Faust in this tavern, which isn't that farfetched, considering it was established by Benedictine monks in A.D. 803. In fact, it's the oldest restaurant in Europe and is housed in the abbey of the church that supposedly brought Christianity to Austria. Aside from a collection of baroque banquet rooms, there's an inner courtyard with rock-cut vaults, a handful of dignified wood-paneled rooms, and a brick-vaulted cellar. In addition to the wine fermented from the abbey's vineyards (*Prelaten*, a young fruity white wine, is the most popular), the tavern serves good home-style Austrian cooking, including braised oxtail with mushrooms and fried polenta, and braised veal knuckle with anchovy sauce. Other menu items include *Tafelspitz* and *Bauernpfandl*, a succulent version of pork filet stuffed with mushrooms and served with spaetzle.

St.-Peter-Bezirk 1–4. ℂ **0662/84-12-680.** Reservations recommended. Main courses 119–265AS (€8.75–€19.35, $8–$18). AE, MC, V. Daily 11am–midnight. Bus: 29.

Trzesniewski ℛ *Value* SANDWICHES   Those great little sandwiches celebrated in Vienna are now being consumed in Salzburg. Around 1900, what eventually became the most famous sandwich shop in the Austro-Hungarian empire opened for business near St. Stephan's cathedral in Vienna. In 1994, it established a branch in Salzburg, within prime real estate on the street level of Mozart's birthplace. How does it work? Select any of 20 different kinds of small sandwiches by pointing to your choices from behind a glass display. You can eat at one of several tables, or better yet, get them for a picnic. Sandwiches here are delicate affairs, not the massive heroes you might be used to. You'll probably want at least four for a real meal.

Getreidegasse 9. ℂ **0662/840-769.** Reservations not accepted. Sandwiches 10AS (€0.75, 65¢) each, or 3 sandwiches plus a small glass of beer 50AS (€3.65, $3.35). No credit cards. Mon–Fri 8am–6pm; Sat 8:30am–5pm; Sun 10:30am–5pm. Bus: 1.

ON THE RIGHT BANK
Moderate
Hotel Stadtkrug Restaurant AUSTRIAN/INTERNATIONAL   Across the river from the Altstadt, on the site of a 14th-century farm, this restaurant occupies a structure rebuilt from an older core in 1458. In the 1960s, a modern hotel was added in back. The old-fashioned dining rooms serve as one of the neighborhood's most popular restaurants. In an antique and artfully rustic setting, you can enjoy hearty, traditional Austrian cuisine, such as cream of potato soup "Old Vienna" style, braised beef with burgundy sauce, or Mozart's favorite roast duckling with bacon dumplings and red cabbage/apple dressing.

Linzer Gasse 20. ℂ **0662/87-35-45.** Reservations recommended. Main courses 175–400AS (€12.83–€29.20, $12–$27). AE, DC, MC, V. Daily noon–2pm and 6–11pm. Bus: 27 or 29.

Inexpensive
Zum Fidelen Affen AUSTRIAN   On the eastern edge of the river near the Staatsbrücke, this is the closest thing in Salzburg to a loud, animated, and jovial pub with food service. It's in one of the city's oldest buildings, from 1407. Management's policy is to allow only three reserved tables on any particular evening; the remainder are given to whomever happens to show up. Menu items are simple, inexpensive, and based on regional culinary traditions. A house specialty is a gratin of green (spinach) noodles in cream sauce with strips of ham. Also justifiably popular are casseroles of seasonal meats and mushrooms, and at least three different kinds of main-course dumplings flavored with meats, cheeses, herbs, and various sauces. Everyone's favorite drink is Trumer pils beer.

Priesterhausgasse 8. ℂ **0662/877-361.** Main courses 105–140AS (€7.65–€10.20, $7–$9). DC, MC, V. Mon–Sat 5pm–midnight. Bus: 1 or 2.

SEEING THE SIGHTS IN THE CITY OF MOZART

The Old Town lies between the left bank of the Salzach River and the ridge known as the **Mönchsberg,** which rises to a height of 500m (1,650 ft.) and is the site of Salzburg's gambling casino. The main street of the Altstadt is **Getreidegasse,** a narrow little thoroughfare lined with five- and six-story burghers' buildings. Most of the houses along the street are from the 17th and 18th centuries. Mozart was born at no. 9 (see below). Many lacy-looking wrought-iron signs are displayed, and a lot of the houses have carved windows.

You might begin your tour at **Mozartplatz,** with its outdoor cafes. From here you can walk to the even more expansive Residenzplatz, where torchlight dancing is staged every year, along with outdoor performances.

SIGHTSEEING SUGGESTIONS FOR FIRST-TIME VISITORS

If You Have 1 Day Start slowly with a cup of coffee at the **Café-Restaurant Glockenspiel** on Mozartplatz. Then from the Altstadt, take the funicular to the **Hohensalzburg Fortress** for a tour. After lunch in an old tavern, visit **Mozart's birthplace** on Getreidegasse, and stroll along the narrow street, most typical in the city. Later, visit the **Residenz.**

If You Have 2 Days In the morning of your second day, explore the **Dom** and the **cemetery of St. Peter's.** Take a walking tour through the **Altstadt.** In the afternoon, explore **Hellbrunn Palace,** 5km (3 miles) south of the city.

If You Have 3 Days On day 3, visit the many attractions of Salzburg you've missed so far: the **Mönchsberg,** the **Mozart Wohnhaus,** and

the **Museum Carolino Augusteum** in the morning. In the afternoon, see the **Mirabell Gardens** and **Mirabell Palace** and at least look at the famous **Festspielhaus (Festival Hall);** tours are sometimes possible.

If You Have 4 or 5 Days On day 4, head for some of the sights in the environs of Salzburg. Go to **Gaisberg** in the morning, which at 1,295m (4,250 ft.) offers a panoramic view of the Salzburg Alps. After lunch, head for **Hallein,** the second-largest town in Land Salzburg, for a look at its salt mines. On day 5, take the *"Sound of Music* **Tour"** (see "Organized Tours," below) and visit the places where this world-famous musical was filmed. Return to Salzburg in time to hear a Mozart concert, if one is featured (as it often is).

THE TOP ATTRACTIONS

Residenz ✿✿ This opulent palace, just north of Domplatz in the pedestrian zone, was the seat of the Salzburg prince-archbishops after they no longer needed the protection of the gloomy Hohensalzburg Fortress of Mönchsberg. The Residenz dates from 1120, but work on its series of palaces, which comprised the ecclesiastical complex of the ruling church princes, began in the late 1500s and continued until about 1796. The 17th-century Residenz fountain is one of the largest and most impressive baroque fountains north of the Alps. The child prodigy Mozart often played in the Conference Room for guests. More than a dozen staterooms, each richly decorated, are open to the public via guided tour. On the second floor you can visit the **Residenzgalerie Salzburg** (✆ **0662/ 84-04-51**), an art gallery containing European paintings from the 16th to the 19th century.

Residenzplatz 1. ℂ **0662/80-42-26-90** or 0662/84-04-51. Admission to Residenz state rooms, 70AS (€5.10, $5) adults, 45AS (€3.34, $3) students 16–18 and senior citizens, 25AS (€1.85, $1.73) children 6–15, free for children 5 and under. Combined ticket to state rooms and gallery, 91AS (€6.65, $6.10). Residenz Gallery, 70AS (€5.10, $5) adults, 25AS (€1.85, $1.73) students 16–18 and senior citizens, free for children under 16. Jan–Apr and Nov Mon–Fri 10am–5pm; May–Oct and Dec daily 10am–4:30pm. Bus: 5 or 6.

Glockenspiel (Carillon)   The celebrated glockenspiel with its 35 bells stands across from the Residenz. You can hear this 18th-century carillon at 7am, 11am, and 6pm. Visits are no longer allowed within the Glockenspiel.

Mozartplatz 1. ℂ **0662/80-42-27-84.**

Dom (Salzburg Cathedral) ⚜   Located where Residenzplatz flows into Domplatz, this cathedral is world renowned for its 4,000-pipe organ. Hailed by some critics as the "most perfect" northern Renaissance building, the cathedral has a marble facade and twin symmetrical towers. The mighty bronze doors were created in 1959. The interior has a rich baroque style with elaborate frescoes, the most important of which, along with the altarpieces, were designed by Mascagni of Florence. In the crypt, traces of the old Romanesque cathedral have been unearthed.

The treasure of the cathedral and the "arts and wonders" the archbishops collected in the 17th century are displayed in the **Dom Museum** entered through the cathedral. The **cathedral excavations** entered around the corner (left of the Dom entrance), show the ruins of the original foundation.

South side of Residenzplatz. ℂ **0662/84-41-89.** Admission to cathedral, free; excavations, 35AS (€2.55, $2.35) adults, 20AS (€1.45, $1.35) children 6–15, free for children 5 and under; museum, 60AS (€4.43, $4) adults, 20AS (€1.45, $1.35) children. Cathedral, daily 8am–8pm (to 6pm in winter); excavations, Easter to mid-Oct, daily 9am–5pm (closed mid-Oct to Easter); museum Wed–Sun 9am–5pm, Sun 1–6pm. Closed Nov–Apr. Bus: 1, 3, or 5.

Stiftskirche St. Peter ⚜⚜   Founded in A.D. 696 by St. Rupert, whose tomb is here, this is the church of St. Peter's Abbey and Benedictine Monastery. Once a Romanesque basilica with three aisles, it was completely overhauled in the 17th and 18th centuries in elegant baroque style. The west door dates from 1240. The church is richly adorned with art treasures including some altar paintings by Kremser Schmidt.

St.-Peter-Bezirk. ℂ **0662/844-578.** Free admission. Daily 9am–6pm.

Petersfriedhof (St. Peter's Cemetery) ⚜⚜   This cemetery lies at the stone wall that merges into the Mönchsberg. Many of the aristocratic families of Salzburg lie buried here as well as many other noted persons, including Nannerl Mozart, sister of Wolfgang Amadeus. You can also see the Romanesque Chapel of the Holy Cross and St. Margaret's Chapel, dating from the 15th century. *Warning:* Tours of the catacombs in theory follow the hours outlined below; however, they may not be offered for almost any reason.

St.-Peter-Bezirk. ℂ **0662/84-45-78-0.** Cemetery, free. Catacombs, 15AS (€1.10, $1) adults, 10AS (€0.75, 65¢) children. May–Sept daily 10am–5pm; Oct–Apr daily 10:30am–4pm. Bus: 1.

Hohensalzburg ⚜⚜   The stronghold of the ruling prince-archbishops before they moved "downtown" to the Residenz, this fortress towers 120m (400 ft.) above the Salzach River on a rocky Dolomite ledge. The massive fortress crowns the Festungsberg and literally dominates Salzburg. Work on Hohensalzburg began in 1077 and wasn't finished until 1681. This is the largest completely preserved castle in central Europe. The elegant state apartments, once the courts of

the prince-archbishops, are on display. The **Burgmuseum** contains a collection of medieval art. Plans and prints tracing the growth of Salzburg are on exhibit, as well as instruments of torture and many Gothic artifacts. The **Rainermuseum** has displays of arms and armor. The beautiful late-Gothic **St. George's Chapel** (1501) is adorned with marble reliefs of the apostles.

Mönchsberg 34. ℭ **0662/84-24-30-11.** Admission (including audio tour and museum) 49AS (€3.63, $3.33) adults, 28AS (€2.05, $1.93) children 6–19; free for children 5 and under free. Family ticket 98AS (€7.15, $7). Fortress and museums Nov–Mar daily 9am–5pm; Apr–June and Oct daily 9am–6pm; July–Sept daily 8am–7pm. The funicular from Festungsgasse (ℭ **0662/84-26-82**) runs every 10 min. during daylight hours and the round-trip costs 69AS (€5.05, $4.60) for adults and 37AS (€2.70, $2.53) for children 6–16; children 5 and under ride free. If you're athletic you can reach the fortress on foot from Kapitelplatz by way of Festungsgasse or from the Mönchsberg via the Schartentor.

MORE ATTRACTIONS

Mozart Gerburtshaus (Mozart's Birthplace) ⚘
The house where Wolfgang Amadeus Mozart was born on January 27, 1756, contains exhibition rooms and the apartment of the Mozart family. The main treasures are the valuable paintings (such as the well-known *Mozart and the Piano*, by Joseph Lange) and the violin Mozart used as a child; his concert violin; and his viola, fortepiano, and clavichord.

Getreidegasse 9. ℭ **0662/84-43-13.** Admission 70AS (€5.10, $5) adults, 55AS (€4, $3.74) students, 25AS (€1.85, $1.73) children. Daily 9am–6pm (last entrance at 5:30pm).

Mozart Wohnhaus (Mozart Residence) ⚘
In 1773, the Mozart family vacated the cramped quarters of Mozart's birthplace, and the young Mozart lived here with his family until 1780. In the rooms of the former Mozart family apartments, a museum documents the history of the house and the life and work of Wolfgang Amadeus. The original house was destroyed by bombing in 1944, rebuilt and reopened on the eve of Mozart's birthday in 1996. A mechanized audio tour in six languages with relevant musical samples accompanies the visitor through the rooms of the museum.

Makartplatz 8. ℭ **0662/84-43-13.** Admission 70AS (€5.10, $5) adults, 55AS (€4, $3.74) students, 25AS (€1.85, $1.73) children 15 and under. June–Sept daily 10am–5pm; Oct–May daily 10am–4pm. Bus: 1 or 5.

Schloss Mirabell (Mirabell Palace) ⚘
This palace and its gardens were built as a luxurious private residence called Altenau. Prince-Archbishop Wolf Dietrich had it constructed in 1606 for his mistress and the mother of his children, Salome Alt. Not much remains of the original grand structure. Lukas von Hildebrandt rebuilt the *Schloss* in the first quarter of the 18th century, and it was modified after a great fire in 1818. The palace, which is like a smaller edition of the Tuileries in Paris, today serves as the official residence of the mayor of Salzburg. The ceremonial marble *Barockstiege-Englesstiege,* "angel staircase," with sculptured cherubs, carved by Raphael Donner in 1726, leads to the Marmorsaal, a marble and gold hall used for concerts and weddings. Chamber music concerts are staged here.

Off Makartplatz. ℭ **0662/8072-0.** Free admission. Staircase: daily 8am–6pm. Marmorsaal: Mon and Wed–Thurs 8am–4pm; Tues and Fri 1–4pm. Bus: 1, 5, 6, or 51.

Museum Carolino Augusteum
Several collections are brought together under one roof in this museum reflecting Salzburg's cultural history. The archaeological collection contains the well-known Dürnberg beaked pitcher, as well as Roman mosaics. Some 15th-century Salzburg art is on view, and there are many paintings from the Romantic period, as well as works by Hans Makart, born in Salzburg in 1840.

Museumsplatz 1. © **0662/841-134-0**. Admission 40AS (€2.90, $2.70) adults; 30AS (€2.24, $2) seniors over 60; 15AS (€1.10, $1) students and children 6–19; free for children 5 and under. Thurs 9am–8pm, Fri–Sun and Tues–Wed 9am–5pm. Bus: 1, 49, or 95.

Mönchsberg ☆☆   This heavily forested ridge extends for some 2km (1½ miles) above the Altstadt and has fortifications dating from the 15th century. A panoramic view of Salzburg is possible from Mönchsberg Terrace just in front of the Grand Café Winkler.

West of the Hohensalzburg Fortress. © **0662/6205-51-180**. Express elevators leave from Gstättengasse 13, daily 9am–11pm; round-trip fare 27AS (€1.95, $1.80) adults, 14AS (€1, 95¢) children 6–15, free for children 5 and under.

Mirabell-Garten (Mirabell Gardens) ☆ are on the right bank of the river off Makartplatz (bus: 1, 5, 6, or 51). Laid out by Fischer von Erlach, these baroque gardens are studded with statuary and reflecting pools, making the gardens a virtual open-air museum. Be sure to visit the bastion with fantastic marble baroque dwarfs and other figures, by the Pegasus Fountains in the lavish garden west of Schloss Mirabell. From the garden you have an excellent view of the Hohensalzburg Fortress. Admission is free, and the gardens are open from June to September daily 7am to 8pm. The rest of the year, hours are daily 7am to dusk.

ORGANIZED TOURS

Bookings may be made at the bus terminal at Mirabellplatz/St. Andrä Kirche (© **0662/87-40-29**). Tour prices are the same for all ages. The best tours are offered by **Salzburg Panorama Tours**, Mirabellplatz (© **0662/88-32-11-0**; www.panoramatours.at). The original *"Sound of Music* **Tour"** combines the city tour with an excursion to the lake district and the places where the film was shot. The English-speaking guide also shows you the historical and architectural landmarks of Salzburg, as well as a part of the Salzkammergut countryside. The 4½-hour tour departs daily at 9:30am and 2pm and costs 440AS (€32.10, $29.53).

You must take your passport along for any of three trips into **Bavaria** in Germany. One of these, called the **"Eagle's Nest Tour,"** takes visitors to Berchtesgaden and on to Obersalzberg, where Hitler and his followers had a vacation retreat. The 4½-hour tour departs daily at 9am, from May 15 to October 31, and costs 590AS (€43.05, $40). Among other tours offered, **"The City & Country Highlights"** takes in historic castles and the surrounding landscape. The 5-hour tour departs daily at 1pm and costs 550AS (€40.15, $37).

THE SHOPPING SCENE

Salzburg obviously doesn't have Vienna's wide range of merchandise. However, if you're not going on to the Austrian capital, you may want to patronize some of the establishments recommended below. Good buys in Salzburg include souvenirs of Salzburg state, dirndls, lederhosen, petit point, and all types of sports gear. **Getreidegasse** is a main shopping thoroughfare, but you'll also find some intriguing little shops on **Residenzplatz.**

Opened in 1871, **Drechslerei Lackner,** Badergasse 2 (© **0662/84-23-85**; bus: 68 or 81), offers both antique and modern country wood furniture. Among the new items are chests, chessboards, angels, cupboards, crèches, candlesticks, and most definitely, chairs. **Musikhaus Pühringer,** Getreidegasse 13 (© **0662/ 84-32-67**; bus: 5, 6, or 55), established in 1910, sells all kinds of classical musical instruments, especially those popular in central Europe, as well as a large selection of electronic instruments (including synthesizers and amplifiers). You'll find classical and folk-music CDs and tapes, plus many classical recordings, especially those by Mozart. The store is only a few buildings away from the composer's birthplace.

Salzburger Heimatwerk, Am Residenzplatz 9 (© **0662/84-41-10;** bus: 5, 6, or 55), is one of the best places in town to buy local Austrian handcrafts and original regional clothing, including Austrian silver and garnet jewelry, painted boxes, candles, wood carvings, copper and brass ceramics, tablecloths, and patterns for cross-stitched samplers in alpine designs. Another section sells dirndls and the rest of the regalia native to the land and still donned during commemorative ceremonies and festivals.

Wiener Porzellanmanufaktur Augarten Gesellschaft, Alter Markt 11 (© **0662/84-07-14;** bus: 68 or 81), might very well tempt you to begin a porcelain collection. The origins of this world-class manufacturer go back 275 years. Today, its product is legendary and its patterns, such as *Wiener Rose, Maria Theresia,* and the highly distinctive *Biedermeier,* are well known. The company also produces such historical pieces as the black-and-white demitasse set created by architect/designer Josef Hoffman.

SALZBURG AFTER DARK
THE PERFORMING ARTS
It's said there's a musical event—often a Mozart concert—staged virtually every night in Salzburg. To find the venue, visit the **Salzburg tourist office,** Mozartplatz 5 (© **0662/88987-330**). Here you'll be given a free copy of *Veranstaltungen,* a frequently updated pamphlet listing all major, and many minor, local cultural events.

The major ticket agency affiliated with the city of Salzburg is located adjacent to Salzburg's main tourist office, at Mozartplatz 5. The **Salzburger Ticket**

Tips   **Getting Tickets to the Salzburg Festival**

One of the premier music attractions of Europe, the **Salzburg Festival** reached its 81st season in 2001. Composer Richard Strauss founded the festival, aided by director Max Reinhardt and writer Hugo von Hofmannsthal. Details on the festival are available by contacting **Salzburg Festival,** Hofstallgasse 1, A-5020 Salzburg, Austria (© **0662/8045-579;** www.salzburgfestival.at).

Festival tickets are in great demand, and there are never enough of them. Don't arrive expecting to get into any of the major events unless you've booked your tickets far ahead. Travel agents can often get tickets for you, and you can also go to branches of the Austrian National Tourist Office at home or abroad.

An annual event is Hofmannsthal's adaptation of the morality play *Everyman,* which is staged (in German) outside the cathedral in Domplatz.

Subject to many exceptions and variations, and excluding ticket agent commissions, drama tickets generally run 300 to 2,500AS (€21.90 to €182.50, $20 to $168). Opera tickets can begin as low as 600AS (€43.80, $40), ranging upward to 4,200AS (€306.60, $281).

Office (℡ **0662/84-03-10**) is open from Monday to Friday 10am to 6pm (to 7pm in midsummer) and Saturday 9am to noon.

If you don't want to pay a ticket agent's commission, you can go directly to the box office of a theater or concert hall. However, many of the best seats may have already been sold, especially those at the Salzburg Festival.

CONCERTS & OTHER ENTERTAINMENT

The rich collection of concerts that combine every summer to form the Salzburg Festival's program are presented in several different concert halls scattered throughout Salzburg. The largest is the **Festspielhaus,** Hofstallgasse 1 (℡ **0662/ 8045;** bus: 1, 5, or 6). Within the Festspielhaus complex you'll find the **Felsenreitschule,** an outdoor auditorium with a makeshift roof. Originally built in 1800 as a riding rink, it's famous as the site where scenes from *The Sound of Music* were filmed. Tickets are 120 to 4,000AS (€8.75 to €292, $8 to $268); average but good seats run 550 to 950AS (€40.15 to €69.35, $37 to $64). Information and tickets are also available through the **Kulturvereiningung** ticket office at Waagplatz 1A, near the tourist office (℡ **0662/84-45-01**); their services are available from Monday to Friday 9:30am to 5pm.

On the right back of the Salzach River, near the Mirabell Gardens, is the **Mozarteum,** Schwarzstrasse 26 and Mirabellplatz 1 (℡ **0662/87-31-54;** bus 1, 5, 6, or 51), the major music and concert hall of Salzburg. All the big orchestra concerts, as well as organ recitals and chamber-music evenings, are offered here. The box office is open from Monday to Thursday 9am to 2pm and Friday 9am to 4pm. Performances are at 11am or 7:30pm. Tickets are 250 to 800AS (€18.25 to €58.40, $17 to $54); the best seats run 1,200 to 2,650AS (€87.60 to €193.45, $80 to $178).

Besides the venues above, you can attend a concert in dramatic surroundings in the Fürstenzimmer (Prince's Chamber) of the **Hohensalzburg Fortress.** Guest musicians of international renown perform on occasion. The box office, at Adlgasser-Weg 22 (℡ **0662/82-58-58**), is open daily 9am to 10pm. Performances are daily from mid-May to mid-October, at either 8 or 8:30pm, and tickets are 360 to 450AS (€26.33 to €32.85, $24 to $30).

BEER GARDENS & THE CASINO

Regardless of the season, you'll have one of your most enjoyable and authentic evenings in Salzburg at **Augustiner Bräustübl,** Augustinergasse 4 (℡ **0662/4 3-12-46;** bus: 27). This Bierstube and Biergarten has been dispensing oceans of beer since it was established in 1622. Depending on the weather, the city's beer-drinking fraternity gathers either within the cavernous interior, where three separate rooms each hold up to 400 people, or in the leafy, chestnut-shaded garden. Brewed on the premises, the beer is excellent and is served from Monday to Friday 3 to 11pm and Saturday and Sunday 2:30 to 11pm. Throughout the year, the staple here is Märzen beer, which sells for 34AS (€2.53, $2.33) for a brimming half-liter mugful.

Immediately below the Hohensalzburg Fortress and established in the early 1800s, part of the **Stiegelkeller,** Festungsgasse 10 (℡ **0662/84-26-81;** bus: 5, 6, or 55), is carved into the rocks of Mönchsberg. To get here, you'll have to negotiate a steep cobblestone street that drops off on one side to reveal a panoramic view of Salzburg. Most of the staff here is preoccupied with supplying large volumes of the local brew (Steigelbräu) and food to enthusiastic locals. If the weather permits, you can head to the leafy garden, or else you'll have to sip your suds in the cavernous interior. Mugs of beer, costing 39AS (€2.85, $2.60) each, are supplemented with small to enormous platters of such traditional Bierkeller food as sausages and schnitzels. It's open from May to September daily 10am to midnight.

Within a separate room, you can participate in folkloric **"Sound of Music"** dinner shows. These are presented from May to September daily 7:30 to 10pm. A three-course meal plus the show costs 520AS (€37.95, $35). If you prefer to skip the dinner, you can show up at 8:15pm and pay 380AS (€27.75, $25), which includes the show, dessert, and coffee.

Casino Salzburg Schloss Klessheim, A-5071 Walzsezenheim (© 0662/ 854-4550), is the only year-round casino in Salzburg state, occupying the Schloss Klessheim, a baroque palace. On the premises is a stylish restaurant, plus bars. Monday night is poker night. You must show a driver's license or a passport, and except during the hottest months of summer, men are encouraged to wear jackets and ties. The complex is open daily 3pm to 3am. The cover of 260AS (€19.03, $17) includes 300AS (€21.90, $20) worth of casino chips. To get here, drive west along Autobahn A-1, exiting at the "Schloss Klessheim" exit, about a mile west of the center of Salzburg. Also, the casino maintains a flotilla of red-sided free shuttle buses that depart from the rocky base of the Mönchsberg every hour on the half-hour, daily 3pm to 3am.

DAY TRIPS FROM SALZBURG

SCHLOSS HELLBRUNN 🍃   This early 17th-century palace was built as a hunting lodge and summer residence for Prince-Archbishop Markus Sittikus. The **Hellbrunn Zoo,** also here, was formerly the palace's deer park. The palace **gardens,** some of the oldest baroque formal gardens in Europe, are known for their trick fountains. As you walk through, take care—you may be showered when you least expect it. Some 265 figures in a mechanical theater are set in motion by a hydraulic movement to the music of an organ, also powered by water. The rooms of the Schloss are furnished and decorated in 18th-century style. See, in particular, the **banquet hall** with its trompe l'oeil painting. The gardens are at Fürstenweg 37, Hellbrunn (© **0662/820-372;** www.hellbrunn.at). Admission is 100AS (€7.30, $7) for adults or 55AS (€4, $3.74) for children. Open July and August daily 9am to 10pm; September and October and April to June daily 9am to 5:30pm. Closed November to March.

Getting There   Bus 55 from Salzburg runs here in 18 minutes.

DÜRNBERG SALT MINES (SALZBERGWERK HALLEIN)   These salt mines (© 06245/83511-0) are the big lure at Hallein, south of Salzburg. An electric mine train takes you deep into the caverns. From here, you go on foot through galleries, changing levels by sliding down polished wooden slides. An underground museum traces the history of salt mining back to remote times.

Tours lasting 1½ hours are conducted from April to October daily 9am to 5pm and from November to March daily 11am to 3pm. Admission is 200AS (€14.60, $13) for adults; 100AS (€7.30, $7) for children between 6 and 15; and 70AS (€5.10, $5) for children between 4 and 6. Free for children under 3.

Getting There   Hallein is connected to Salzburg, 10 miles away, by both train and bus. From Hallein there's a cable railway to Dürnberg. There's also a modern road from Hallein directly to a large parking lot near the ticket office to the mines.

EISRIESENWELT *⚵* One of the region's most unusual geological oddities, Eisriesenwelt lies in the Pongau basin, on the western cliffs of the Hochkogel, towering over the Salzach valley. This is the "World of Ice Giants," the largest known ice caves in the world. The caves stretch for about 42km (26 miles), although only a portion is open to the public. You'll see fantastic ice formations at the entrance, extending for half a mile. The climax of this chilly underworld tour is the spectacular "Ice Palace."

The ice caves are open from May to October and must be visited as part of a tour. Two-hour supervised tours begin at hourly intervals every day between 9:30am and 3:30pm, with more frequent departures offered during July and August when the caves are open until 4:30pm. For more information, call *☎* **06468/5248.** Tours begin at a mountain outpost set 1,567m (5,141 ft.) above sea level. From here, you walk to the nearby entrance to the caves. Tour, with the cable car (see below) included, costs 225AS (€16.45, $15) for adults and 100AS (€7.30, $7) for children 4 to 14.

Getting There To reach the Eisriesenwelt, head for Werfen, a village that's the center for exploring the ice caves. If you go by train to Werfen, 48km (30 miles) south of Salzburg, you can take a taxi bus that's marked EISRIESENWELT, which departs for the ice caves at 15-minute intervals from Werfen's Hauptplatz (main square). Some hardy travelers opt to hike the steep road, a strenuous 3½-mile, uphill trek that rises abruptly from 500 to 1,000m (1,600 to 3,000 ft.). The bus will deposit you at the same point you'll reach if you're traveling in your own car. From the parking lot, a cable car hauls you uphill to the entrance of the caves. Once again, some hardy travelers opt to hike uphill to the entrance of the caves, though this is recommended only if you have lots of time and lots of energy.

BERCHTESGADEN *⚵⚵* Although it lies in Germany, Berchtesgaden is one of the most popular day trips from Salzburg, about 22km (14 miles) south. Berchtesgaden is situated below the many summits of Watzmann Mountain— 2,700m (8,900 ft.) at the highest point. According to legend, these mountain peaks were once a king and his family who were so evil God punished them by turning them into rocks.

Many visitors expect to see one of Hitler's favorite haunts, since the name Berchtesgaden is often linked with the Führer and the Nazi hierarchy. This impression is erroneous. Hitler's playground was actually at Obersalzberg (see below), on a wooded plateau about half a mile up the mountain. Berchtesgaden itself is an old alpine village with ancient winding streets and a medieval marketplace and castle square.

The **Schlossplatz** *⚵* is partially enclosed by the castle and the **Stiftskirche (Abbey Church),** dating from 1122, a Romanesque foundation with Gothic additions. The church interior contains many fine works of art; the high altar has a painting by Zott dating from 1669. The **Königliches Schloss Berchtesgaden** (*☎* **08652/20-85**) is now a museum, and the exhibition is mainly devoted to the royal collection of sacred art, including wood sculptures by the famed artists Veit Stoss and Tilman Riemenschneider. You can also explore a gallery of 19th-century art. Admission is 7DM (€3.65, $3.50) adults and 3DM (€1.55, $1.50) children 6 to 16 (free for children 5 and under). From Easter to September, hours are Sunday to Friday 10am to 1pm. Off-season, hours are from Monday to Friday 10am to 1pm and 2 to 5pm. Tours are conducted at 11am and 2pm.

On the opposite side of the square from the church is a 16th-century arcade that leads to **Marktplatz,** with typical alpine houses and a wooden fountain from 1677 (restored in 1860). Some of Berchtesgaden's oldest inns and houses border this square.

Salzbergwerk Berchtesgaden, Bergwerkstrasse 83 (℗ **08652/60020**), lies at the eastern edge of town. These salt mines have been worked since 1517; the deposits are more than 300m (990 ft.) thick and are still processed today. Older children will especially enjoy the guided tours that begin with a ride into the mine on a small wagonlike train after donning protective miner's clothing. After nearly a half-mile ride, visitors explore the rest of the mine on foot, sliding down a miner's slide and riding on the salt lake in a ferry. The highlight of the tour is the "chapel," a grotto containing unusually shaped salt formations illuminated for an eerie effect. The 1½-hour tour can be taken any time of the year, in any weather. Admission is 21DM (€10.75, $11) adults and 11DM (€5.60, $6) children 4 to 14. The mines are open from May to October 15 daily 9am to 5pm. In the off-season, hours are from Monday to Saturday 11am to 3:30pm.

Getting There   **Trains** run every hour during the day from Salzburg to Berchtesgaden; you'll have to change trains at Freilassing. Frequent **buses** also travel from Salzburg to Berchtesgaden. Motorists take Route 20 south of Salzburg (the route is signposted all the way).

OBERSALZBERG ✶✶   The drive from Berchtesgaden to Obersalzberg at 1,000m (3,300 ft.) is along one of Bavaria's most scenic routes. Here Hitler settled down in a rented cottage while he completed *Mein Kampf.* After he came to power in 1933, he bought Haus Wachenfeld near the hamlet of Hintereck and had it remodeled into his residence, the Berghof. Obersalzberg became the center for holiday living for Nazis leaders who included Martin Bormann and Hermann Göring.

A major point of interest to visitors is the **Kehlstein** ✶✶, or Eagle's Nest, which can be reached only by a thrilling bus ride up a 7km-long (4½-mile-long) mountain road that was blasted out of solid rock, an outstanding feat of construction and engineering when begun in 1937. To reach the spot, you must enter a tunnel and take a 120m- (400-ft.) elevator ride through a shaft to the summit of the Kehlstein Mountain. Here you can enjoy the panoramic view and explore the rooms of the Nazi hierarchy's original teahouse, which includes Eva Braun's living room. Of the many buildings that once comprised the lavish vacation compound favored by Hitler, this is the only one that wasn't bombed into oblivion by Allied troops near the end of the war.

Getting There   For information about trips to Kehlstein, call ℗ **08652/ 54-73.** RVO **buses** (local buses based in Berchtesgaden) run from the Berchtesgaden Post Office 4km (2½ miles) uphill to Obersalzberg-Hintereck; the round-trip journey costs 6.80DM (€3.45, $3.40). From Hintereck, a special mountain bus will carry you another 6km (4 miles) uphill to the Kehlstein parking lot. The bus departs Hintereck every half-hour. The ticket price of 20DM (€10.20, $10) includes the elevator ride from the Kehlstein parking lot up to the teahouse itself.

3 Innsbruck & the Tyrol

Land of ice and mountains, dark forests and alpine meadows full of spring wildflowers, summer holidays and winter sports—that's Tyrol. Those intrepid tourists, the British, discovered its vacation delights and made it a fashionable

Innsbruck

To Hungerburg ↑   ↑ To Alpine Zoo

HÖTTING

SAGGEN

Karl-Kapferer-Strasse
Siebererstrasse

HOFGARTEN

1

Kapuziner-gasse

2

MARIAHILF

Dom-platz

3

4

Universitäts-

8 **9**

7

5 **6**

10
Museumstrasse

11

Rathaus

12 Meraner   Brixner Strasse

15

13 Landhaus-platz   Südtiroler platz   **Hauptbahnhof Autobushof**

Neue Universität Maximilianstrasse

14 Salurnerstrasse

WESTERN CEMETERY

Tivoli-Stadion

Westbahnhof

To Schloss Ambras →

0   1/5 mile
0   200 meters

WILTEN   Pastorstrasse

† Church
ⓘ Information
⊠ Post Office
— Railway

To Bergisel ↓

(A12)

ATTRACTIONS ●

Annasäule
  (St. Anna's Column) **11**
Dom zu St. Jakob
  (Cathedral of St. James) **2**
Goldenes Dachl
  (Golden Roof)
  & Maximilianeum **4**
Herzog-Friedrich-Strasse **5**
Hofburg **3**
Hofkirche **8**

Stadtturm
  (City Tower) **7**
Tiroler Landsmuseum
  Ferdinandeum
  (Ferdinandeum
  Tyrol Museum) **10**
Tiroler Volkskunst Museum
  (Tyrol Museum
  of Popular Art) **9**
Triumphpforte
  (Triumphal Arch) **14**

ACCOMMODATIONS ■

City-Hotel Goldene Krone **13**
Europa Tyrol **15**
Goldener Adler **6**
Maria Theresia **12**
Romantikhotel-Restaurant
  Schwarzer Adler **1**
Weisses Kreuz **5**

destination in the last century. Munich is only a few hours away, and even the Bavarians head for Tyrol when they want a change of scenery. Tyrol is the most frequented winter playground in Austria, and in summer, the extensive network of mountain paths lures visitors.

Skiers flock here in winter for a ski season that runs from mid-December to the end of March. Many prefer its ski slopes to those of Switzerland. It's been a long time since the eyes of the world focused on Innsbruck at the Winter Olympics in 1964 and 1976, but the legacy lives on in the ski conditions and facilities on some of the world's choicest slopes.

INNSBRUCK

Innsbruck is a city with a long imperial past, and even though it is littered with cultural artifacts of a bygone era, most visitors don't come for the history, but for the mountains. Alpine peaks surround Innsbruck, protecting it from the cold winds of the north (we've seen vegetable gardens growing in January).

Innsbruck has a particularly lovely medieval town center, and town planners have protected this historic Altstadt. Visitors can take countless excursions in the environs; at the doorstep of Innsbruck lie some of the most beautiful drives in Europe. Just take your pick: Head in any direction, up any valley, and you'll be treated to mountains and alpine beauty almost unmatched anywhere else, including Switzerland.

ESSENTIALS

GETTING THERE   By Plane   Innsbruck's airport, **Flughafen Innsbruck-Kranebitten,** Fürstenweg 180 (© **0512/22525;** http://tirol-php.highway. telekom.at/innsbruck.flughafen/), is 3km (2 miles) west of the city. It offers regularly scheduled air service from the major airports of Austria and Europe's major cities. From the airport, bus F leads to the center of the city. Tickets cost 21AS (€1.55, $1.40). A taxi ride takes about 10 minutes and costs from 120AS (€8.75, $8).

By Train   Innsbruck is connected with all parts of Europe by international railway links. Arrivals are at the **Hauptbahnhof,** Südtirolerplatz (© **05/1717** for information). Frequent trains pull in here from all major European and Austrian cities. There are at least 10 daily trains from Munich (trip time: 2 hr.) and about a dozen from Salzburg (2–3½ hr.).

By Car   If you're driving down from Salzburg in the northeast, take Autobahn A-8 west, which joins Autobahn A-93 (later it becomes the A-12), heading southwest to Innsbruck. This latter Autobahn (A-93/A-12) is the main artery in from Munich. From the south you can take the Brenner toll motorway.

VISITOR INFORMATION   The **tourist office,** Burggraben 3 (© **0512/ 56-20-00**), is open from Monday to Saturday 8am to 6pm and Sunday 9am to 6pm. It will supply you with a wealth of information, as well as a list of inexpensive private rooms for rent in Innsbruck. On the first floor of the same building is **Innsbruck-Information** (© **0512/59850**), which arranges tours, sells concert tickets, and makes hotel reservations. It's open from Monday to Saturday 8am to 6pm and Sunday 9am to 6pm.

CITY LAYOUT   This historic city is divided by the Inn River into left- and right-bank districts. Two major bridges cross the Inn, the **Universitätsbrücke** and the **Alte Innsbrücke (Old Inn Bridge).** Many of the attractions, including the Hofkirche and the Goldenes Dachl, are on the right bank. If you arrive at the Hauptbahnhof, take Salurner Strasse and Brixener Strasse to Maria-Theresien-Strasse, which will put you into the very heart of Innsbruck.

The **Altstadt** is bounded on the north by the Inn River and on the south by Burggraben and Marktgrabben. The main street of this historic district is **Herzog-Friedrich-Strasse,** which becomes **Maria-Theresien-Strasse,** the axis of the postmedieval new part of town. The Altstadt becomes a pedestrian zone after 10:30am (wear good shoes on the cobblestone streets).

GETTING AROUND   A network of three **tram** and 25 **bus** lines covers all of Innsbruck and its environs. Single tickets in the central area cost 21AS (€1.55, $1.40), and a booklet of four tickets goes for 60AS (€4.43, $4). For information about various routes, call the **Innsbrucker Verkehrsbetriebe** (℡ 0512/58-51-55). You can buy tickets at the Innsbruck tourist office (above), tobacco shops, and vending machines.

Postal buses leave from the Central Bus Station, adjacent to the Hauptbahnhof on Sterzinger Strasse, for all parts of Tyrol. The station is open from Monday to Friday 7am to 5:30pm and Saturday 7am to 1pm. For information about bus schedules, call ℡ **0512/58-51-55.**

Taxi stands are in all parts of town, or you can call a radio car (℡ **0512/ 5311**). You can take a ride in a **horse-drawn cab,** starting in front of Tiroler Landestheater, Rennweg. The cost for a 30-minute ride is 350AS (€25.55, $23).

From April to early November, you can rent **bikes** at the Hauptbahnhof, the main rail station. The cost is 150 to 200AS (€10.95 to €14.60, $10 to $13) per day, although if you carry a Eurail or Interrail pass, the charge is only 100 to 160AS (€7.30 to €11.73, $7 to $11) per day. You can return bikes to any rail station in Austria if you don't plan to come back to Innsbruck.

For exploring Tyrol by car, try either **Avis,** Salurner Strasse 15 (℡ **0512/ 57-17-54**), open from Monday to Friday 8am to 6pm and Saturday and Sunday 9am to noon; or **Hertz,** Südtirolerplatz 1 (℡ **0512/58-29-51**), across from the Hauptbahnhof, open from Monday to Friday 7:30am to 6pm and Saturday 8am to 1pm. Remember that you'll always get a cheaper rental rate if you reserve your car from North America through either company's toll-free reservations networks.

ℓ *FAST FACTS:* Innsbruck

American Express The office at Brixnerstrasse 3 (℡ **0512/58-24-910**; tram: 1 or 3) is open from Monday to Friday 9am to 5:30pm and Saturday 9am to noon.

Currency Exchange Banks are usually open from Monday to Thursday 7:45 am to 12:30pm and 2:30 to 4pm; and Friday 7:45am to 3pm. There are also exchange facilities at Innsbruck's tourist office (see above). The automated currency exchange facilities at the Hauptbahnhof are available 24 hours a day.

Dentists/Doctors The tourist office (above) will supply a list of private English-speaking dentists and doctors in the Innsbruck area. Or you can contact the **University Clinic,** Anichstrasse 35 (℡ **0512/504**; tram: 1 or 3).

Drugstores In the heart of Innsbruck, **St.-Anna Apotheke,** Maria-Theresien-Strasse 4 (℡ **0512/58-58-47**; tram: 1 or 3), is open from Monday to Friday

8am to 12:30pm and 2:30 to 6pm and Saturday 8am to noon; it also posts addresses of other pharmacies open nights and weekends.

Emergencies In case of trouble, call 🕾 **133** for the police, 🕾 **122** for a fire, or 🕾 **144** for an ambulance.

Internet Access You can check e-mail or access the Internet for a fee of 150AS (€10.96, $10) an hour at the **Picasso Internet Café,** Maria-Theresien-Strasse 16 (🕾 **0512/58-48-48;** tram 3). It's open from Monday to Friday 9am to 1am; Saturday 3pm to 1am, and Sunday 5pm to 1am.

Post Office The **Hauptpostamt (Central Post Office),** Maximilianstrasse 2 (🕾 **0512/5000**), is open daily 8am to 9pm. The post office at the **Hauptbahnhof,** Bruneckstrasse 1–3 (🕾 **0512/5000**), is open from Monday to Saturday 6:30am to 9pm.

Telephone The **country code** for Austria is **43.** The **city code** for Innsbruck is **512;** use this code when you're calling from outside Austria. If you're within Austria, use **0512.** For additional information, see "Fast Facts: Vienna," above.

WHERE TO STAY
Very Expensive
Europa Tyrol 🏨🏨   The town's finest and most elegant hotel stands opposite the rail station, inviting you inside its formal lobby. The spacious rooms and suites are handsomely furnished, with all the modern conveniences and Tyrolean or Biedermeier-style decorations. Each tasteful room offers a marble bathroom.

Südtirolerplatz 2, A-6020 Innsbruck. 🕾 **800/223-5652** in the U.S.; or 0512/5931. Fax 0512/58-78-00. www.europatyrol.com. 122 units. 2,200–3,400AS (€160.60–€248.20, $147–$228) double; 3,700–4,800AS (€270.10–€350.40, $248–$322) suite. Rates include breakfast. AE, DC, MC, V. Parking 160AS (€11.73, $11). **Amenities:** The Europastuberl (see "Where to Dine," below); sauna;solarium; 24-hour room service; laundry. *In room:* TV, minibar, hair dryer.

Expensive
Romantikhotel-Restaurant Schwarzer Adler 🏨🏨   This is it for those who like authentic Austrian charm. The hotel's owners, the Ultsch family, have furnished the charming interior with hand-painted regional furniture, antiques, and lots of homey clutter, making for a cozy and inviting ambience. The midsize rooms are virtually one of a kind, each with its special character. Beds are exceedingly comfortable, with some of the thickest mattresses in town and well-stuffed duvets. Bathrooms have dual basins with powerful showerheads.

Kaiserjägerstrasse 2, A-6020 Innsbruck. 🕾 0512/58-71-09. Fax 0512/56-16-97. www.deradler.com. 39 units. 1,950–2,500AS (€142.35–€182.50, $131–$168) double; 3,670–5,400AS (€267.90–€394.20, $246–$362) suite. Rates include breakfast. AE, DC, MC, V. Parking 120AS (€8.75, $8). Tram: 1 or 3. **Amenities:** The original Tiroler Stube, with a history going back 4 centuries, and the award-winning K. u K. (Kaiser und König) Restaurant, an elegant bar; 24-hour room service; baby-sitting; laundry. *In room:* TV, minibar, hair dryer.

Moderate
Goldener Adler 🏨   This is not the best hotel in Innsbruck (the two recommended above are superior), but it is the most famous. In 6 centuries it has hosted everybody from Goethe to Mozart, even the violinist Paganini, who cut his name into the windowpane of his room. The handsomely styled rooms in

this family-run hotel sport travertine floors and ornate carved Tyrolean furniture. The well-maintained bathrooms range from spacious with shower and tub combos to cramped with shower stalls.

Herzog-Friedrich-Strasse 6, A-6020 Innsbruck. © 0512/57-11-11. Fax 0512/58-44-09. www.goldeneradler. com. 37 units. 1,760–2,300AS (€128.53–€167.90, $118–$154) double; from 3,200AS (€233.60, $215)suite. Rates include breakfast. AE, DC, MC, V. Parking 200AS (€14.60, $13). Tram: 1 or 3. **Amenities:** Fine dining room, bar; room service; laundry. *In room:* TV, minibar, safe.

Maria Theresia   This Best Western is on Innsbruck's famous shopping street a few blocks away from the winding alleys of the oldest parts of the city. The helpful staff will do everything possible to make you feel comfortable. All rooms have been recently redecorated. Most are medium-size and each is well appointed with firm mattresses. Bathrooms are tiny.

Maria-Theresien-Strasse 31, A-6020 Innsbruck. © 800/528-1234 in the U.S., or 0512/5933. Fax 0512/57-56-19. www.bestwestern-ce.com/mariatheresia. 107 units. 1,800–2,200AS (€131.40–€160.60, $121–$147) double; 2,500–2,800AS (€182.50–€204.40, $168–$188) suite. Rates include American breakfast. AE, DC, MC, V. Parking 140AS (€10.20, $10). Tram: 1 or 3. **Amenities:** Restaurant, bar; 24-hour room service; babysitting; laundry. *In room:* TV, minibar, hair dryer.

Inexpensive
City-Hotel Goldene Krone *Value*   Near the Triumphal Arch on Innsbruck's main street, this baroque house is one of the best budget bets. All rooms are modern, comfortable, well maintained, and for the most part, spacious with plenty of light. The duvet-covered beds have firm mattress. Bathrooms are small but spotless, with a shower stall.

Maria-Theresien-Strasse 46, A-6020 Innsbruck. © 0512/58-61-60. Fax 0512/580-18-96. www.touringhotels.at. 37 units. 1,150–1,380AS (€83.95–€100.75, $77–$92) double; 1,580–1,790AS (€115.35–€130.65, $106–$120) suite. Rates include breakfast. AE, MC, V. Parking 100AS (€7.30, $7). Tram: 1. Bus: A, H, K, or N. **Amenities:** Viennese inspired coffeehouse/restaurant. *In room:* TV, no phone.

Weisses Kreuz *✦*   This atmospheric and historic inn lies in the center of Innsbruck and has been changed and altered over the years to keep abreast of shifting tastes and requirements. The small rooms have been modernized and updated frequently, with good beds. Most have tidy bathrooms. In 1769, 13-year-old Wolfgang Mozart and his father, Leopold, stayed here.

Herzog-Friedrich-Strasse 31, A-6020 Innsbruck. © 0512/594790. Fax 0512/59-47-990. hotel.weisses. kreuz@eunet.at. 39 units, 30 with bathroom (shower only). 860–900AS (€62.83–€65.70, $58–$60) double without bathroom, 1,240–1,420AS (€90.50–€103.65, $83–$95) double with bathroom. Rates include breakfast. AE, MC, V. Parking 100AS (€7.30, $7). Tram: 1 or 3. **Amenities:** 2 restaurants, bar.

WHERE TO DINE
Expensive
Europastüberl *✦✦* AUSTRIAN/INTERNATIONAL   Traditional regional and creative cookery is the chef's motto at this distinguished restaurant filled with delightful Tyrolean ambience. Fresh Tyrolean trout almost always appears on the menu, and meat dishes range from red deer ragout to saddle of venison to such exotica as fried jelly of calf's head Vienna style with a lamb's tongue salad. Many dishes are served for two people, including roast pikeperch with vegetables and buttery potatoes, and Bresse guinea hen roasted and served with an herb sauce. Smaller appetites appreciate such main course regulars as Tyrolean dumplings stuffed with bacon, spinach, and cheese, and served with sauerkraut. Some seasonal specialties change every 2 weeks.

In the Hotel Europa Tyrol, Brixner Strasse 6. © 0512/5931. Reservations required. Main courses 110–350AS (€8.05–€25.55, $7–$23); fixed-price menus 350–490AS (€25.55–€35.75, $23–$33). AE, DC, MC, V. Daily 11am–2:30pm and 6:30–10pm. Opposite train station; all city buses.

Restaurant Goldener Adler ⭐ AUSTRIAN/TYROLEAN/INTER-NATIONAL   Richly Teutonic and steeped in the decorative traditions of the Tyrolean Alps, this beautifully decorated restaurant with four separate dining rooms enjoys a loyal following among locals. The menu includes good, hearty fare based on cold-weather outdoor life—the chefs aren't into delicate subtleties. The best examples include Tyrolean bacon with horseradish and farmer's bread; carpaccio of filet of beef with Parmesan and olive oil; and *Tyroler Zopfebraten,* a flavor-filled age-old specialty consisting of strips of veal steak served with herb-enriched cream sauce and spinach dumplings. A well-regarded specialty is a platter known as *Adler Tres.* It contains spinach dumplings, stuffed noodles, and cheese dumplings, unified with a brown butter sauce and a gratin of mountain cheese.

Herzog-Friedrich-Strasse 6. ✆ **0512/57-11-11.** Reservations recommended. Main courses 150–275AS (€10.95–€20.13, $10–$18); set-price menus 185–240AS (€13.50–€17.50, $12–$16). AE, DC, MC, V. Daily 11:30am–10:30pm, with a limited menu 2–6pm. Tram: 1 or 3.

Moderate
Altstadtstüberl ⭐ AUSTRIAN/ITALIAN   This is one of the best moderately priced restaurants in Innsbruck. There's a salad buffet and a satisfying roster of dishes that include both international choices (steaks, salads, roast lamb, and pastas) as well as Austrian favorites, including *Tafelspitz* (boiled beef) with horseradish sauce, Wiener schnitzel, rack of lamb, and a frequently changing selection of homemade pastries. Foremost among these are *Kaiserschmarrn,* a doughy crepe filled with a slow-cooked mixture of plum and apricot marmalade enhanced with raisins, cut into bite-sized portions, and served with a compote of apples.

Riesengasse 13. ✆ **0512/58-23-47.** Reservations recommended. Main courses 140–245AS (€10.20–€17.94, $9–$16). AE, DC, MC, V. Mon–Sat 8am–midnight. Tram: 1 or 3.

Hirschen-Stuben AUSTRIAN/ITALIAN   Beneath a vaulted ceiling in a house built in 1631, Hirschen-Stuben is charming and well recommended. Down a short flight of stairs from the street, you'll find brocaded chairs and a warm ambience that is especially attractive in spring, autumn, and winter. The food is well prepared and the staff is helpful, polite, and efficient. On a visit here, we always begin with a steaming bowl of pasta or else the savory fish soup. The monkfish is one of the best items on the menu, and is given added zest with a tomato and basil sauce. The older diners here still prefer their age-old favorite, sliced veal in a cream sauce Zuricher style.

Kiebachgasse 5. ✆ **0512/58-29-79.** Reservations recommended. Main courses 165–260AS (€12.05–€19.03, $11–$17). DC, MC, V. Mon–Sat 11am–2pm and 6–10pm. Tram: 1 or 3.

Inexpensive
Restaurant Ottoburg AUSTRIAN/INTERNATIONAL   This historic restaurant opened around 1745 and occupies two floors of a 13th-century building some historians say is the oldest in Innsbruck. Inside are four intimate and atmospheric dining rooms with a 19th-century neo-Gothic decor. You come here for the hearty, robust food of the Tyrolean people, not a diet spa cuisine. Dig into a venison stew in autumn or else grandmother's mixed grill at any time of the year. We're especially fond of the sautéed trout; and only the largest trenchermen order the veal shank. Most dishes are at the lower end of the price scale.

Herzog-Friedrich-Strasse 1. ✆ **0512/57-46-52.** Reservations recommended. Main courses 100–300AS (€7.30–€21.90, $7–$20). AE, DC, MC, V. Daily 11am–3pm and 5–11pm. Closed Tues Oct–June. Tram: 1 or 3.

Stiegl-Bräu Innsbruck AUSTRIAN/INTERNATIONAL   A Salzburg-based brewery (Stiegl-Bräu) whose product has been brewed nearby since 1492 owns this animated beer hall/restaurant, one of the most atmospheric of the city's cost-conscious restaurants. Besides two crowded and well-used dining rooms there's an outdoor beer garden open in summer. Menu items are described by the hard-working staff as "the people's food," and include rib-sticking versions of braised beef, braised veal, hearty stews, Irish mutton, lamb and pork chops, sausages, and schnitzels that are often accompanied by braised cabbage or sauerkraut and dumplings.

Wilhelm-Greil-Strasse 25. ℂ **0512/58-43-38.** Main courses 100–300AS (€7.30–€21.90, $7–$20). AE, DC, MC, V. Daily 11am–midnight (last orders at 11pm). Tram: 1 or 3.

EXPLORING THE TOWN

The Altstadt and the surrounding alpine countryside are Innsbruck's main attractions. Often it's fascinating just to watch the passersby, who are occasionally attired in Tyrolean regional dress.

Maria-Theresien-Strasse (🎯, which cuts through the heart of the city from north to south, is the main street and a good place to begin to explore the city. Many 17th- and 18th-century houses line this wide street. On the south end of the street, there's a **Triumphpforte (Triumphal Arch),** modeled after those in Rome. Maria Theresa ordered it built in 1765 to honor her son's marriage and to commemorate the death of her beloved husband, Emperor Franz I. From this arch southward the street is called Leopoldstrasse.

Going north from the arch along Maria-Theresien-Strasse, you'll see **Annasäule (St. Anna's Column)** in front of the 19th-century Rathaus (town hall). The column was erected in 1706 to celebrate the withdrawal in 1703 of invading Bavarian armies during the War of the Spanish Succession. Not far north of the Annasäule, the wide street narrows and becomes Herzog-Friedrich-Strasse, running through the heart of the medieval quarter. This street is arcaded and flanked by a number of well-maintained burghers' houses with their jumble of turrets and gables; look for the multitude of dormer windows and oriels.

Hofburg (🎯   The 15th-century imperial palace of Emperor Maximilian I, flanked by a set of domed towers, was rebuilt in rococo style in the 18th century on orders of Maria Theresa. It's a fine example of baroque secular architecture, with four wings and a two-story Riesensaal (Giant's Hall), painted in white and gold and filled with portraits of the Hapsburgs. You can visit the staterooms, the house chapel, the private apartment, and the Riesensaal on a guided tour, lasting about half an hour.

Rennweg 1. ℂ **0512/58-71-86.** Admission 70AS (€5.10, $5) adults, 35AS (€2.55, $2.35) students, 10AS (€0.75, 65¢) children under 10. Daily 9am–5pm. Last admission at 4:30pm. Tram: 1 or 3.

Goldenes Dachl (Golden Roof) & Maximilianeum (🎯

"The Golden Roof," Innsbruck's greatest tourist attraction and its most characteristic land-mark, is a three-story balcony on a house in the Altstadt; the late-Gothic oriels are capped with 2,657 gold-plated tiles. It was constructed for Emperor Maximilian I in the beginning of the 16th century to serve as a royal box where he could sit in luxury and enjoy tournaments in the square below.

In 1996, the city of Innsbruck added a small museum, the **Maximilianeum,** to the second floor of the municipal building attached to the Goldenes Dachl. Inside are exhibits celebrating the life and accomplishments of the Innsbruck-based Hapsburg emperor, Maximilian I, who bridged the gap between the

Middle Ages and the German Renaissance. Look for costumes, silver chalices and coins, portraits, and a video depicting his era and personality.

With the same ticket, you can also visit the **Stadtturm (City Tower),** Herzog-Friedrich-Strasse 21 (✆ **0512/561-5003**). Formerly a prison cell, the tower dates from the mid-1400s and stands adjacent to the Rathaus. Its top affords a panoramic view of the city rooftops and the mountains beyond.

Herzog-Friedrich-Strasse 15. ✆ 0512/581-111. Admission to the Maximilianeum 60AS (€4.43, $4) adults, 50AS (€3.65, $3.35) seniors, 30AS (€2.24, $2) students, 20AS (€1.45, $1.35) children. No charge for views of the Goldenes Dachl, and no restrictions as to when it can be viewed. Museum Tues–Sun 10am–5pm. Tram: 1 or 3.

Museums & Churches

Hofkirche   The most important treasure in the Hofkirche is the cenotaph of Maximilian I, a great feat of German Renaissance style. It has 28 bronze 16th-century statues of Maximilian's real and legendary ancestors surrounding the kneeling emperor, with 24 marble reliefs on the sides depicting scenes from his life.

Universitätsstrasse 2. ✆ 0512/58-43-02. Church admission 30AS (€2.24, $2) adults, 20AS (€1.45, $1.35) students or children under 15. Museum admission 60AS (€4.43, $4) adults, 35AS (€2.55, $2.35) students, 20AS (€1.45, $1.35) children under 15. Combined admission 75AS (€5.53, $5.05) adults, 55AS (€4, $3.74) students, 30AS (€2.24, $2) children under 15. Mon–Sat 9am–5:30pm. Tram: 1 or 3.

Dom zu St. Jakob (Cathedral of St. James)   Designed and rebuilt from 1717 to 1724 by Johann Jakob Herkommer, the Dom has a lavishly embellished baroque interior. A chief treasure is Lucas Cranach the Elder's *Maria Hilf* (*St. Mary of Succor*) on the main altar.

Domplatz 6. ✆ 0512/58-39-02. Free admission. Winter daily 6:30am–6:30pm; summer daily 7am–7pm. Closed Fri noon–3pm. Tram: 1 or 2.

Tiroler Landesmuseum Ferdinandeum (Ferdinandeum Tyrol Museum) 🐾   This museum has a gallery of Flemish and Dutch masters and also traces the development of popular art in the Tyrolean country. You'll also see the original bas-reliefs used in designing the Goldenes Dachl.

Museumstrasse 15. ✆ 0512/59-489. Admission 60AS (€4.43, $4) adults, 40AS (€2.90, $2.70) students, 20AS (€1.45, $1.35) children. May–Sept daily 10am–5pm, Thurs 10am–5pm and 7–9pm. Oct–Apr Tues–Sat 10am–noon and 2–5pm, Sun 10am–1pm. Tram: 1 or 3.

Tiroler Volkskunst Museum (Tyrol Museum of Popular Art) 🐾🐾   This popular art museum is in the Neues Stift (New Abbey) adjoining the Hofkirche on its eastern side. It contains one of the largest and most impressive collections extant of Tyrolean artifacts, ranging from handcrafts, furniture, Christmas cribs, and national costumes to religious and secular popular art.

Universitätsstrasse 2. ✆ 0512/58-43-02. Admission 60AS (€4.43, $4) adults, 35AS (€2.55, $2.35) students, 20AS (€1.45, $1.35) children. Mon–Sat 9am–5pm; Sun 9am–noon. Tram: 1 or 3.

Zoos & Views

Alpenzoo   From this zoo on the southern slope of the Hungerburg plateau, you'll get a panoramic view of Innsbruck and the surrounding mountains. The zoo contains only those animals indigenous to the Alps, plus alpine birds, reptiles, and fish. More than 800 animals belong to more than 140 different and rare species, including otters, eagles, elk, rabbits, vultures, wildcats, bison, and wolves.

Weiherburggasse 37. ✆ 0512/29-23-23. Admission 70AS (€5.10, $5) adults, 50AS (€3.65, $3.35) students, 35AS (€2.55, $2.35) children 6–15, 20AS (€1.45, $1.35) children 4–5. Daily 9am–6pm (to 5pm in winter). Bus: 2 (May 15 to Sept only). Tram: 1 to the Hungerburgbahn (cog railway).

> ### ⓒ The Most Beautiful Spot in the Tyrol
>
> The **Hungerburg mountain plateau** ⚡ (872m/2,860 ft.) is the most beautiful spot in the Tyrol, affording the best view of Innsbruck, especially on summer nights, when much of the city, including fountains and historic buildings, is floodlit. You can drive to the plateau or take a cog railway, the **Hungerburgbahn,** which departs from a point about a half-mile east of the center of Innsbruck, at the corner of Rennweg and Kettenbrücke (take tram 1 or bus C). In summer, the cog railway departs at 15-minute intervals daily 9am to 8pm, then runs at 30-minute intervals until 10:30pm. The rest of the year, it operates at 30-minute intervals daily 8:30am to between 5 and 6pm, depending on the hour of dusk. Round-trip fares on the cog railway cost 55AS (€4, $3.74) adults and 33AS (€2.40, $2.20) children. For schedules and information, call ⓒ 0512/58-61-58.
>
> Once you arrive at the Hungerburg plateau, you can progress even farther into the alpine wilds via the Nordkette cable car. Designed as a skier-friendly gondola suspended high above the rocky terrain, it will carry you up to the Seegrube and the Hafelekar (2,333m/7,655 ft.), for a sweeping view over the Tyrol region's alpine peaks and glaciers. Hill climbers and rock climbers appreciate this route as the debut of a labyrinth of mountain trails; skiers consider it the departure point for dozens of downhill runs. Throughout the year, the Nordkette cable car runs daily, at 20-minute intervals, from 8:30am to 5:30pm. A round-trip between Innsbruck and Hafelekar costs 225AS (€16.45, $15) adults and 120AS (€8.75, $8) students and children under 16.

ENJOYING THE GREAT OUTDOORS

Five sunny, snow-covered, avalanche-free **ski areas** around the Tyrol are served by five cableways, 44 chairlifts, and ski hoists. The area is also known for bobsled and toboggan runs and ice-skating rinks.

In summer you can play tennis at a number of courts, and golf on either a 9- or an 18-hole course; or you can go horseback riding, mountaineering, gliding, swimming, hiking, and shooting.

The **Hofgarten,** a public park containing lakes and many shade trees, lies north of Rennweg.

ORGANIZED TOURS

The best way to get a quick and convenient overview of Innsbruck is to take a 2-hour **bus tour** of the city's major monuments. Tours depart from a clearly marked point in front of the city's main railway station on the Südtirolerplatz and cost 175AS (€12.83, $12) adults or 75AS (€5.53, $5) children under 16. The experience includes multilingual running commentary on the city's history and architectural highlights and a 20-minute walk through the heart of the old city. From April to September, tours depart at 10am, noon, and 2pm; From October to March, one tour a day departs at noon.

If you're really crunched for time, there's a 1-hour bus tour of the city, with no walking, that provides a very basic introduction to the city. Hours vary, according to demand, but since the 1-hour tour costs 140AS (€10.20, $9), almost as much as the 2-hour tour, most visitors opt for the latter. For information on either tour, contact the **Innsbruck Tourist Information Office,** Burggraben 3 (© **0512/56-20-00**).

THE SHOPPING SCENE

You'll find a large selection of Tyrolean specialties and all sorts of skiing and mountain-climbing equipment. Stroll around **Maria-Theresien-Strasse, Herzog-Friedrich-Strasse, and Museumstrasse,** ducking in and making discoveries of your own. Here are some suggestions.

Lodenbaur, Brixner Strasse 4 (© **0512/58-09-11**), is devoted to regional Tyrolean dress, most of which is made in Austria. There's a full array for men, women, and children. **Tiroler Heimatwerk,** Meraner Strasse 2 (© **0512/ 58-23-20**), is one of the best stores in Innsbruck for handcrafted sculpture and pewter, carved chests, and furniture. The store carries textiles, lace, bolts of silk, and dress patterns for those who want to whip up their own dirndl.

Using old molds discovered in abandoned Tyrolean factories, **Zinnreproduktionen Rudolf Boschi,** Kiebachgasse 8 (© **0512/58-92-24**), produces fine reproductions of century-old regional pewter at reasonable prices. Mr. Boschi also reproduces rare pewter objects acquired from auctions throughout Europe. Look for a copy of the 18th-century pewter barometer emblazoned with representations of the sun and the four winds.

INNSBRUCK AFTER DARK

THE PERFORMING ARTS The major venue for the performing arts is the 150-year-old **Landestheater,** Rennweg 2 (© **0512/52074**). The box office is open from Monday to Saturday 8:30am to 8:30pm and Sunday 5:30 to 8:30pm, and performances usually begin at 7:30 or 8pm. Tickets cost 100 to 950AS (€7.30 to €69.35, $7 to $66) for operettas and opera, and 90 to 690AS (€6.55 to €50.35, $6 to $46) for theater. Concerts are often presented at the Kunstpavillon in the Hofgarten in summer.

BARS, CLUBS & FOLK MUSIC In summer, the outdoor bar at **Club Filou,** Stiftsgasse 12 (© **0512/58-02-56**), blossoms with ivy-covered trellises and parasols. Inside you'll find an intimate hangout filled with Victorian settees and pop art. In a separate, very old room is the disco. The cafe is open daily 6pm to 4am; the disco daily 9pm to 4am. Food is available until 3am. Admission to both the cafe and disco is free.

If you want to try an award-winning martini, go to **Sparkling Cocktails,** Innstrasse 45 (© **0512/28-78-80**), where virtually any kind of mixed drink or cocktail, including an almost lethal zombie, can be crafted by the highly experienced staff. Open Monday to Saturday 7pm to 2am.

Young people hang out at **Treibhaus,** Angerzellgasse 8 (© **0512/58-68-74**), a combination cafe, bar, and social club. Within its battered walls, you can attend a changing roster of art exhibitions, cabaret shows, and protest rallies, daily 10am to 1am, with live music presented at erratic intervals. Cover for live performances is 160 to 200AS (€11.73 to €14.60, $11 to $13).

Goethe Stube, Restaurant Goldener Adler, Herzog-Friedrich-Strasse 6 (© **0512/57-11-11**), offers authentic folk music programs throughout the Christmas-New Year's season, Easter, and the winter season. There's no cover, but a one-drink minimum; a large beer costs 40AS (€2.90, $2.70). Open daily 7pm to midnight.

ST. ANTON AM ARLBERG 🐾🐾

A modern resort has grown out of this old village on the Arlberg Pass 99km (62 miles) west of Innsbruck. The Ski Club Arlberg was born here in 1901, and in 1911, the first Arlberg-Kandahar Cup competition was held. At St. Anton (1,288m/4,225 ft.), Hannes Schneider developed modern skiing techniques and began teaching tourists how to ski in 1907. Before his death in 1955, Schneider saw his ski school rated as the world's finest. Today the school is still one of the world's largest and best, with about 300 instructors (most of whom speak English). St. Anton am Arlberg in winter is quite fashionable, popular with the wealthy and occasional royalty—a more conservative segment of the rich and famous than you'll see at other posh ski resorts.

There's so much emphasis on skiing here that few seem to talk of the summertime attractions. In warm weather, St. Anton is tranquil and bucolic, surrounded by meadowland. A riot of wildflowers blooming in the fields announces the beginning of spring.

Essentials

GETTING THERE   By Train   Because of St. Anton's good rail connections to eastern and western Austria, most visitors arrive by train. St. Anton is an express stop on the main lines crossing over the Arlberg Pass between Innsbruck and Bregenz. About one train per hour arrives in St. Anton from both directions. Trip time from Innsbruck is 75 to 85 minutes; from Bregenz, around 85 minutes. For rail information, call ✆ **05/1717.**

By Car   Motorists should take Route 171 west from Innsbruck.

VISITOR INFORMATION   The **tourist office** in the Arlberghaus in the center of town (✆ **05446/22690**) is open from July to mid-September Monday to Friday 8am to noon and 2 to 6pm, Saturday to Sunday 10am to noon; from May to June and mid-September to December Monday to Friday 8am to noon and 2 to 6pm; from January to April Monday to Friday 8am to 6pm, Saturday 9am to noon and 1 to 7pm, Sunday 10am to noon and 2 to 6pm.

WHERE TO STAY

Schwarzer Adler 🐾🐾   Owned and operated by the Tschol family since 1885, this is our preferred stopover at the resort. The beautiful building in the center of St. Anton was constructed as an inn in 1570 and became known for its hospitality to pilgrims crossing the treacherous Arlberg Pass. The 400-year-old frescoes on the exterior were discovered during a restoration. The interior is rustic yet elegant, with blazing fireplaces, painted Tyrolean baroque armoires, and Oriental rugs. There are handsomely furnished and well-equipped rooms in the main hotel, plus 13 slightly less well-furnished (but less expensive) rooms in the annex, which is across the street above the Café Aquila.

A-6580 St. Anton am Arlberg. ✆ **800/528-1234** in the U.S., or 05446/22440. Fax 05446/224462. www.tiscover.com/adler.stanton. 50 units. Winter 2,200–3,900AS (€160.60–€284.70, $147–$261) double. Summer 1,700–2,900AS (€124.10–€211.70, $114–$194) double. Rates include half board. AE, DC, MC, V. Closed May–June and Sept to Dec 5. Free parking. **Amenities:** Restaurant, bar; sauna; fitness center. *In room:* TV.

WHERE TO DINE

Raffl-Stube 🐾 AUSTRIAN   This isn't the most visible or flamboyant restaurant in St. Anton, but it's one of the coziest. Containing only a half-dozen tables, it occupies an enclosed corner off the lobby of one of the resort's most prominent hotels. Because of its small scale and emphasis on well-prepared food, it can

Side Trips to Bavaria

While you're based in Seefeld, it's relatively easy to explore part of Bavaria in Germany. You may or may not get to see little **Wildmoos Lake**. It can, and sometimes does, vanish in a day or so, and then you may find cows grazing on what has become meadowland. However, the lake will suddenly come back again, and if conditions are right, it will become deep enough for swimmers. Wildmoos Lake comes and goes more frequently than Brigadoon.

Wildmoos Lake is a 5-minute drive west from Seefeld (it's signposted from the center of town). Cars are not permitted on the drive until after 5pm. Buses run from the center of Seefeld several times a day. Or it's a 10- to 15-minute walk from the center of town.

The little German town of **Mittenwald** ⚡, one of the highlights of Bavaria, can also be easily explored on a day trip from Seefeld. It's best to take the train, which departs from Seefeld hourly until 9pm (trip time: 1 hr.). Two buses per day also make the trip, although the traffic is so congested the bus trip often takes twice as long as the train. Contact the tourist office for the bus schedule.

get very exclusive. Reservations are essential, especially if you're a nonresident. Overflow diners are offered a seat in a spacious but less special dining room across the hall. The hotel has long enjoyed a reputation for its cuisine, but somehow the food in the stube tastes even better. The kitchen prepares such tempting specialties as roast goose liver with salad, cream of parsley soup with sautéed quail eggs, filet of salmon with wild rice, and trout "prepared as you like it," along with the ever-popular fondue bourguignonne.

In the Hotel St. Antoner Hof, St. Anton am Arlberg. ✆ **05446/2910.** Reservations required. Main courses 200–325AS (€14.60–€23.75, $13–$22); fixed-price menu 800–1,100AS (€58.40–€80.30, $54–$74). AE, DC, MC, V. Daily 11:30am–2pm and 6–10:30pm. Closed mid-Oct to mid-Dec and mid-Apr to mid-June.

MORE DINING   If you're not able to secure a reservation at Raffl-Stube, don't despair. St. Anton has plenty of other less expensive options, usually hotel dining rooms open to nonguests. You can get classic Austrian dishes at the historic **Hotel Alte Post Restaurant** (✆ 05446/25530) and the first-rate **Hotel Kertess Restaurant** (✆ 05446/2005), located high on a slope in the suburb of Oberdorf. For superb international cuisine, head to the medieval **Hotel Schwarzer Adler Restaurant** (✆ 05446/22440). All these hotels are signposted at various places in town, so you should have no trouble finding them.

HITTING THE SLOPES IN ST. ANTON
The snow in this area is perfect for skiers, and the total lack of trees on the slopes makes the situation ideal. The ski fields of St. Anton stretch over a distance of some 15km^2 (6 sq. miles). Beginners stick to the slopes down below, whereas more experienced skiers head to the runs from the Galzig and Valluga peaks. A cableway will take you to **Galzig** (2,090m/6,860 ft.), where there's a self-service restaurant. You go from here to **Vallugagrat** (2,647m/8,685 ft.), the highest station reached. The peak of the **Valluga** (2,810m/9,220 ft.) commands a panoramic view. St. Christoph is the mountain annex of St. Anton.

Other major ski areas include the **Gampen/Kapall,** an advanced-intermediate network of slopes, whose lifts start just behind St. Anton's railway station; and the **Rendl,** a relatively new labyrinth of runs to the south of St. Anton that offers many novice and intermediate slopes.

OTHER ACTIVITIES & ATTRACTIONS

There are many other cold-weather pursuits than just skiing, including ski jumping, mountain tours, curling, skating, tobogganing, and sleigh rides, plus après-ski on the quiet side.

Ski und Heimat Museum (Skiing and Local Museum), in the Arlberg-Kandahar House (© **05446/2475**), traces the development of skiing in the Arlberg, as well as the history of the region from the days of tribal migrations in Roman times. The museum, at the center of the Holiday Park in St. Anton, is open from December to April Monday to Saturday 2:30pm to midnight. From Mid-June to late September, it's open Thursday to Tuesday 10am to 6pm. Admission is 20AS (€1.45, $1.35) adults and 10AS (€0.75, 65¢) children.

SEEFELD ₳₳

Seefeld, 24km (15 miles) northwest of Innsbruck, is a member of Austria's "big three" international rendezvous points for winter-sports crowds (St. Anton and Kitzbühel are the other two). Seefeld hosted the 1964 and 1976 Nordic events for the Olympic Winter Games and the 1985 Nordic Ski World Championships. The fashionable resort lies some 1,050m (3,450 ft.) above sea level on a sunny plateau.

ESSENTIALS

GETTING THERE   By Train   More than a dozen trains per day arrive from Innsbruck (trip time: 40 min.). There's also train service from Munich and Garmisch-Partenkirchen, Germany. For rail information, call © **05/1717.**

By Bus   Buses depart daily from Innsbruck's Hauptbahnhof (trip time: 45 min.). For bus information, call © **0512/58-51-55** in Innsbruck.

By Car   From Innsbruck, head west along Route 171 until you reach the junction with Route 313, at which point turn north.

VISITOR INFORMATION   The **Seefeld tourist office** is at Klosterstrasse 43 (© **05212/2313**) and is open from mid-June to mid-September and mid-December to February Monday to Saturday 8:30am to 6:30pm; from mid-September to mid-December and March to mid-June Monday to Saturday 8:30am to 12:15pm and 3 to 6pm.

WHERE TO STAY

Klosterbräu ₳₳₳   The town's most unusual and elegant hostelry is constructed around a 16th-century cloister. The dramatic entrance is under a thick stucco arch. The interior contains soaring vaults supported by massive columns of the same kind of porous stone that built Salzburg (you can still see prehistoric crustaceans embedded in the stone). The spacious, well-furnished, and elegant rooms are encased in a towering chalet behind the front entrance. Each is equipped with a luxurious bathroom.

Klosterstrasse 30, A-6100 Seefeld. © **05212/26210.** Fax 05212/3885. www.klosterbraeu.com. 120 units. Winter 5,200–7,800AS (€379.60–€569.40, $348–$523) double; from 8,750AS (€638.75, $586) suite. Summer 3,360–3,780AS (€245.33–€275.95, $225–$253) double; from 4,600AS (€336, $308) suite. Rates include breakfast. AE, DC, MC, V. Closed Apr–May and Oct–Nov. Parking 160AS (€11.73, $11). **Amenities:** 3 restaurants, elegant bar, nightclub; indoor and outdoor swimming pools; sauna, health club, solarium; golf, tennis, plus mountain climbing and skiing within walking distance. *In room:* TV, minibar, hair dryer, safe.

WHERE TO DINE

Sir Richard ⚘ AUSTRIAN/ITALIAN   On the southern outskirts of town, this restaurant creates an elegant aura of year-round Christmastime because of its masses of flowers, dozens of burning candles, and immaculately pressed linen. The menu is short and well composed, and everything on it is mouthwatering. You might begin with watercress soup, followed by one of the lamb, veal, or fish dishes, often accompanied by masterful sauces. Even the fresh leafy salads have just the right degree of tartness. For a taste of Italy, try one of the pastas or risottos or even one of the many Italian reds.

Innsbruckerstrasse 162. © 05212/2093. Reservations required. Main courses 200–320AS (€14.60–€23.35, $13–$21). DC, MC, V. Daily 11:30am–2pm and 6:30–10pm. Closed 2 weeks in Nov and Tues in winter.

HITTING THE SLOPES & OTHER ACTIVITIES

SKIING   Skiers are served with one funicular railway, two cable cars, three chairlifts, and 14 drag lifts. The beginner slopes lie directly in the village center. The base stations of the lifts for the main skiing areas (known as **Gschwandtkopt** and **Rosshutte/Seefelder Joch**) are at most half a mile away from the center, and are serviced by free daily nonstop bus service. There are 198km (124 miles) of prepared **cross-country tracks.**

OTHER WINTER ACTIVITIES   Other winter activities offered here include curling, horse-drawn sleigh rides, outdoor skating (ice-skating school, with artificial and natural ice rink), horseback riding, indoor tennis (Swedish tennis school), tube sliding (you slide on rubber inner tubes), indoor golf facilities, parasailing, bowling, squash, hiking (100km/60 miles of cleared paths), fitness studio, swimming, and saunas.

SUMMER ACTIVITIES   Summer visitors can enjoy swimming in three lakes, in a heated open-air swimming pool on Seefeld Lake, or at the Olympia indoor and outdoor pools. Other summer sports include tennis on 18 open-air and eight indoor courts (Swedish tennis school), horseback riding (two stables with indoor schools), and golf on the 18-hole course, which has been rated by golf insiders as one of the 100 most beautiful courses in the world. Hiking on 198km (124 miles) of walks and mountain paths, cycling, minigolf, parasailing, and rafting can also be enjoyed.

THE KITZBÜHEL ALPS ★★★

Hard-core skiers and the rich and famous are attracted to this ski region. The Kitzbühel Alps are covered with such a dense network of lifts that they now form the largest skiing complex in the country, with a series of superlative runs. The action centers on the town of Kitzbühel, but there are many satellite resorts that are much less expensive, including St. Johann in Tyrol.

Kitzbühel is, in a sense, a neighbor of Munich, 130km (81 miles) to the northeast, whose airport is the entry point for most wintertime visitors (see chapter 7).

Edward, prince of Wales (you may remember him better as the duke of Windsor), may have put Kitzbühel on the international map with his 1928 "discovery" of what was then a town of modest guesthouses. Certainly his return a few years later with Mrs. Simpson caused the eyes of the world to focus on this town, and the "upper crust" of England and other countries began flocking here. At the time of this 20th-century renaissance, however, Kitzbühel itself was already some 8 centuries old, and a settlement has been here much, much longer than that.

ESSENTIALS

GETTING THERE **By Train** Kitzbühel sits astride the main train lines between Innsbruck (trip time: 1 hr.) and Salzburg (2½ hr.). For rail information, call ☎ 05/1717.

By Bus Two buses travel daily from Salzburg's main railway station to Kitzbühel (trip time: 2¼ hr.). Nine local bus lines run into and up the surrounding valleys. A bus runs every 30 to 60 minutes between Kitzbühel and St. Johann in Tyrol (25 min.). For information, call ☎ 05356/62715.

By Car Kitzbühel is 99km (62 miles) east of Innsbruck. From Innsbruck, take Autobahn A-12 east to the junction with Route 312 heading to Ellmau. After bypassing Ellmau, continue east to the junction with Route 342, which you take south to Kitzbühel.

VISITOR INFORMATION The tourist office is at Hinterstadt 18 (☎ 05356/62155). In the winter ski season and in July and August it's open from Monday to Friday 8:30am to 6:30pm, Saturday 8:30am to noon and 4 to 6pm, and Sunday 10am to noon and 4 to 6pm. In the off-season, hours are from Monday to Friday 8:30am to 12:30pm and 2:30 to 6pm, and Saturday 8:30am to noon. In winter, call ☎ 182 for snow reports.

WHERE TO STAY

Bruggerhof About a mile west of the town center, near the Schwarzsee, is this countryside chalet with a sun terrace. Originally a 1920s farmhouse, the interior has massive ceiling beams and a corner fireplace. In 1960 it was expanded and enlarged into a three-star hotel that's family oriented and well maintained. Rooms are comfortable and cozy, decorated in an alpine style, with well-maintained bathrooms containing a shower stall.

Reitherstrasse 24, A-6370 Kitzbühel. ☎ 05356/62806. Fax 05356/644-7930. www.bruggerhof.camping.at. 25 units. Winter 1,880–2,050AS (€137.25–€149.65, $126–$137) double. Summer 1,320–1,530AS (€96.35–€111.74, $88–$103) double. Rates includes half board. AE, DC, V. Free parking. Closed Apr to mid-May and mid-Oct to Dec 15. **Amenities:** Restaurant; whirlpool, steam bath, and solarium; tennis and minia-ture golf available in summer. *In room:* TV.

Zur Tenne ♠ This hotel combines Tyrolean *Gemütlichkeit* with urban style and panache. The staff shows genuine concern for their clientele. The hotel was created in the 1950s when three 700-year-old houses were joined into one unit. Accommodations come in a wide range of sizes—each elegantly furnished, with firm mattresses, and often private patios or balconies. Suites have fireplaces, but all rooms come with excellent bathrooms.

Vorderstadt 8–10, A-6370 Kitzbühel. ☎ 05356/644440. Fax 05356/64803-56. www.zurtenne.at. 50 units. Winter 3,500AS (€255.50, $235) double; 4,800AS (€350.40, $322) suite for 3. Summer 1,750–2,530AS (€127.75–€184.74, $117–$170) double, 3,100AS (€226.30, $208) suite for 3. Rates include breakfast. Half board 380AS (€27.75, $25) per person in winter, 310AS (€22.65, $21) in summer. AE, DC, MC, V. Free parking outdoors; 100AS (€7.30, $7) in covered garage nearby. **Amenities:** Superb international restaurant, ele-gant bar; luxurious health complex, hot tubs, sauna. *In room:* TV, minibar, hair dryer.

WHERE TO DINE

Florianistube *Value* INTERNATIONAL/TYROLEAN Named after St. Florian, patron saint of the hearth, this restaurant is in one of the resort's less ostentatious guesthouses, and it welcomes outsiders. The menu might include typical Austrian or Tyrolean dishes, or tournedos with mushroom sauce, spaghetti with clam sauce, or fondue bourguignonne. For something really local, order *Bauernschmaus*, a heaping hot platter of smoked pork, roast pork,

pork sausages, sauerkraut, potatoes, and dumplings. In summer, a lunch or dinner buffet is served outside under the trees of the rear garden.

In the Gasthof Eggerwirt, Gaensbachgasse 12. ℂ **05356/62437.** Reservations recommended. Main courses 125–260AS (€9.15–€19.03, $8–$17). AE, MC, V. Daily 11am–2pm and 6–10pm. Closed Nov 1–Dec 6 and Easter to end of May.

Wirtshaus Unterberger-Stuben 🍴 INTERNATIONAL/TYROLEAN
This celebrity hangout in the 1980s is still going strong today. The movie stars may have disappeared, but the kitchen is as good as ever, and you are likely to be served one of your finest meals in the Tyrolean country. If it's on the menu, try the poppy seed soufflé, or specialties such as terrine of roast chicken liver with a salad of wild mushrooms or filet of pikeperch with mountain herbs and baby vegetables. The establishment is open for snacks, coffee, and drinks 9am to midnight, but meals are only served during lunch and dinner hours.

Wehgasse 2. ℂ **05356/66127.** Reservations recommended. Main courses 190–340AS (€13.85–€24.80, $13–$23); fixed-price menu 820AS (€59.85, $55). V. Daily noon–1:30pm and 6:30–9:30pm. Closed June and Nov and Tues in summer.

SEEING THE SIGHTS IN TOWN

The town has two main streets, both pedestrian walkways, **Vorderstadt** and **Hinterstadt.** Kitzbühel has preserved its traditional style of structure, at least along these streets. You'll see three-story stone houses with oriels and scrollwork around the doors and windows, heavy overhanging eaves, and Gothic gables.

The **Pfarrkirche (parish church)** was built from 1435 to 1506 and reno-vated in the baroque style in the 18th century. The lower part of the **Liebfrauenkirche (Church of Our Lady)** dates from the 13th century, the upper part from 1570. Between these two churches stands the **Ölbergkapelle (Ölberg Chapel)** with a 1450 "lantern of the dead" and frescoes from the latter part of the 16th century.

In the **Heimatmuseum,** Hinterstadt 34 (ℂ **05356/645-88**), you'll see arti-facts from prehistoric European mining eras and the north alpine Bronze Age, a winter-sports section with trophies of Kitzbüheler skiing greats, and exhibits detailing the town's history. The museum is open from Monday to Saturday 9am to 12:30pm; admission is 45AS (€3.34, $3) for adults and 15AS (€1.10, $1) for children and students.

HITTING THE SLOPES & OTHER OUTDOOR ACTIVITIES

SKIING   In winter the emphasis in Kitzbühel, 700m (2,300 ft.) above sea level, is on skiing, and facilities are offered for everyone from novices to experts. The ski season starts just before Christmas and goes until late March. With more than 62 lifts, gondolas (cable cars), and mountain railroads on five different mountains, Kitzbühel has two main ski areas, the **Hahnenkamm** (renovated in 1995) and the **Kitzbüheler Horn.** Cable cars are within easy walking distance, even for those in ski boots.

The linking of the lift systems on the Hahnenkamm has created the cele-brated **Kitzbühel Ski Circus** 🍴🍴🍴, which makes it possible to ski downhill for more than 80km (50 miles), with runs that suit every stage of proficiency. Numerous championship ski events are held here; the World Cup event each January pits the skills of top-flight skiers against the toughest, fastest downhill course in the world, a stretch of the Hahnenkamm especially designed for max-imum speed. Its name, *Die Streif,* is both feared and respected among skiers. A ski pass costing 2,000AS (€146, $134) entitles the holder to use of all the lifts that form the Ski Circus.

Skiing became a fact of life in Kitzbühel as long ago as 1892, when the first pair of skis was imported from Norway and intrepid daredevils began to slide down the snowy slopes at breakneck speeds. Many great names in skiing have since been associated with Kitzbühel, the most renowned being Toni Sailer, a native, who was the triple Olympic champion in the 1956 Winter Games in Cortina.

OTHER WINTER ACTIVITIES   There are many other winter activities: ski-bobbing, ski jumping, ice-skating, tobogganing, hiking on cleared trails, curling, and hang gliding, as well as such indoor activities as tennis, bowling, and swimming. The children's ski school provides training for the very young. And don't forget the lively après-ski scene, with bars, nightclubs, and dance clubs rocking from teatime until the wee hours.

SUMMER ACTIVITIES   Kitzbühel has plenty of summer pastimes too, including walking tours, visits to the **Wild Life Park** at Aurach (about 3km/ 2 miles from Kitzbühel), tennis, horseback riding, golf, squash, brass band concerts in the town center, cycling, and swimming. There's an indoor swimming pool, but we recommend going to the **Schwarzsee** (Black Lake), a peat lake about a 15-minute walk from the center of town. Here you'll find bathing establishments, boats to rent, fishing, windsurfing, a water-ski school, and restaurants.

One of the region's most exotic collections of alpine flora is clustered into the jagged and rocky confines of the **Alpine Flower Garden Kitzbühel,** where various species of edelweiss, gorse, heather, and lichens are found on the sunny slopes of the Kitzbüheler Horn. Set at a height of around 1,800m (6,000 ft.) above sea level, the garden—which the municipality of Kitzbühel owns and maintains as an incentive to midsummer tourism—is open from late May to early September daily 8:30am to 5:30pm. It's at its most impressive from June to August. Admission to the garden is free, and many visitors opt to view it by taking the Kitzbüheler Horn gondola (cable car) to its uppermost station and then descending on foot via the garden's labyrinth of footpaths to the gondola's middle station. The **Kitzbüheler Horn gondola** (© **05356/6951**) departs from the Kitzbühel at 20-minute intervals daily throughout the summer and winter months from 8:30am to 5:30pm; a round-trip ticket is 210AS (€15.35, $14).

Belgium

by George McDonald

Modest little Belgium has never been known to boast of its charms, yet its variety of language, culture, history, and cuisine would do credit to a country many times its size. Belgium's diversity stems from its location at the cultural crossroads of Europe. The boundary between the continent's Germanic north and Latin south cuts clear across the nation's middle, leaving Belgium divided into two major ethnic regions: Dutch-speaking Flanders and French-speaking Wallonia.

Though international attention is focused on Brussels as the "capital of Europe," there's another Belgium of Gothic cathedrals, medieval castles, cobblestone streets, and tranquil canals waiting in the wings. In a country the size of Maryland, the timeless beauty of Bruges and Ghent are accessible, even to the most hurried visitor.

1 Brussels

A city with a notable history, Brussels is carving out a bright future, too. The "capital of Europe" has begun to act like Europe's Washington, D.C., a focus of economic and political power, where decisions are made that affect the lives of people around the world. After centuries of occupation by Spain, Austria, and France, whose power struggles tore Europe apart, the city now hosts the bureaucratic empire trying to bring it all together. Headquarters of the European Union (EU), Brussels both symbolizes the vision of unity and is a bastion of officialdom, a breeding ground for the regulations that govern and often exasperate the rest of Europe.

Bruxellois are more than a little ambivalent about their city's transformation into a power center. At first, the waves of Eurocrats seemed to bring a new cosmopolitan air to a somewhat provincial city, but as old neighborhoods were leveled to make way for office towers, people wondered whether Brussels was losing its soul. After all, Brussels doesn't only mean politics and business. This city inspired surrealism and Art Nouveau, worships comic strips, prides itself on handmade lace and chocolate, and serves each one of its artisanal beers in its own unique glass.

Fortunately, not all of Brussels's individuality has been lost in this transition, and though the urban landscape has suffered from "development," the city's spirit survives in traditional cafes, bars, bistros, and restaurants (its French- and Dutch-speaking residents may have their differences, but they both love a good meal). Whether elegantly Art Nouveau or eccentrically festooned with posters, curios, and knickknacks, such centuries-old establishments provide a warm, convivial ambience that is peculiarly Belgian.

ESSENTIALS

GETTING THERE   By Plane   Brussels Airport (© **0900/70-000** for flight information; www.brusselsairport.be) is 14km (9 miles) northeast of the city. Trains to Brussels's three main stations (Gare du Nord, Gare Centrale, Gare du Midi) depart every 20 minutes or so from the airport's underground train station between 5:43am and 11:14pm (trip time to Gare Centrale: 25 min.). One-way fare is 150BF (€3.75, $3.50) first-class and 100BF (€2.50, $2.35) second. Most trains have wide corridors and extra space for baggage. Taxi fare is around 1,200BF (€30, $28) to the city center. Use only official taxis from the rank outside the Arrivals hall. *Warning:* Turn down any approaches from taxi touts; you are sure to be overcharged for the trip.

By Train   High-speed trains from London, Paris, Amsterdam, and Cologne arrive at Gare du Midi, rue de France, south of the city center. Slower trains arrive at Gare du Midi; Gare Centrale, Carrefour de l'Europe, downtown; and Gare du Nord, rue du Progrès, north of the city center. For international schedule and fare information, call ℂ **0900/10-366;** in Belgium call ℂ 02/555-25-25. All three stations are served by tram, bus, and metro, and have taxi ranks out front.

   Warning: Muggers, attracted by rich pickings from international travelers, haunt the environs of Gare du Midi, which are in the middle of a years-long redevelopment project. Pickpockets and bag-snatchers work the interior. The police seem unable to control the problem. To avoid this threat, do not travel to or leave from the station on foot—take a taxi or public transportation. Inside the station, keep a close eye on your possessions.

By Bus   Eurolines (ℂ 02/203-07-07; www.eurolines.com) coaches from London, Paris, Amsterdam, and other cities arrive at the bus station adjoining Gare du Nord train station.

By Car   Major expressways to Brussels are E19 from Amsterdam and Paris, and E40 from Ostend and Cologne.

By Boat   Car ferries from England arrive at Ostend and Zeebrugge. Both ports have hourly train service to Brussels. In Ostend, the train station is beside the harbor; in Zeebrugge you take the ferry company's bus from the harbor to the train station.

VISITOR INFORMATION   **Tourist Offices**   **Tourist Information Brussels** (T.I.B.) on the ground floor of the Hôtel de Ville (Town Hall), Grand-Place, 1000 Brussels (ℂ **02/513-89-40;** fax 02/514-45-38; www.tib.be; Métro: Centrale), sells a comprehensive visitor booklet, *Brussels Guide & Map,* for 80BF (€2, $1.85); makes same-day hotel reservations; organizes guided walking tours in summer; and has multilingual guides who can be engaged by the hour or day. The office is open from April to December, daily 9am to 6pm; from January to March, Monday to Saturday 9am to 6pm.

   The **Belgian Tourism Center,** rue du Marché-aux-Herbes 63, 1000 Brussels (ℂ **02/504-03-90;** fax 02/504-02-70; www.obt.be; Métro: Centrale), covers the entire country, including Brussels. The office is open from June to September, Monday to Saturday 9am to 7pm, Sunday 9am to 6pm; from October to March, Monday to Saturday 9am to 6pm, Sunday (Apr, May, Oct) 9am to 6pm or (Nov–Mar) 1 to 5pm.

Websites   A good starting point for exploring Brussels and Belgium on the Web is Belgium Tourism (**www.belgique.tourisme.net**). You might also want to check out **www.visitbelgium.com, www.toervl.be,** and **www.art.events.be.** A new site in English that covers Belgian news, weather, tourism, and more is **www.xpats.com.** A good place to research hotels, where you can compare prices and see pictures of the rooms is **www.hotels-belgium.com.**

Brussels

Gare
du Nord

place de
la Reine

place
de l'Yser

place
Rogier

quai au Foin

rue du Canal

place de
Brouckère

place des
Martyrs

Théâtre Royal
de la Monnaie

place
de la
Monnaie

place
de la
Liberté

place de
la Bourse

Grand-
Place

Palais
de la Nation

Gare
Centrale

place
St-Jean

place de
l'Albertine

PARC DE
BRUXELLES

place
Royale

place des
Palais

place du
Grand-Sablon

place de
la Chapelle

place du
Petit-
Sablon

place du
Luxembourg

place
Poelaert

Palais
de Justice

place
Fern. Cocq

✝ Church
ⓘ Information
✉ Post Office
— Railway

113

CITY LAYOUT   Most main attractions are inside the heart-shaped inner ring-road (the *Petite Ceinture*), roughly 2.5km (1.5 miles) in diameter, that follows the line of the old city walls. Small, cobblestone streets cluster around the Grand-Place. Two nearby well-traveled lanes are restaurant-lined rue des Bouchers and petite rue des Bouchers. A block west of the Grand-Place, the classical colonnaded Bourse (Stock Exchange) stands at the center of Brussels's nightlife zone. A few blocks north is the National Opera on place de la Monnaie. The city's busiest shopping street, rue Neuve, runs north for several blocks from Grand-Place.

"Uptown," southeast of the center and literally atop a hill, is where you find the second great square, place du Grand-Sablon, and the Royal Museums of Fine Arts and Royal Palace. Head southwest across boulevard de Waterloo to place Louise, from which a chic shopping street, avenue Louise, extends south, and a slightly less fashionable shopping street, avenue de la Toison d'Or, runs northeast. Both are surrounded by attractive residential side streets, containing typical Belgian architecture. East of this zone, Ixelles district near the Free University has many casual, inexpensive restaurants, bars, and cafes. North of Ixelles, the modern European Union district surrounds place Schuman.

To make navigating challenging, maps list street names within the city limits in both French and Dutch. For consistency and ease, I've used only the French names.

GETTING AROUND   By Public Transportation   Trams, buses and Métro trains run daily 6am to midnight, after which there's a limited night-bus system. You can identify Métro stations by signs with a white letter **M** on a blue background. Trams and buses are yellow; stop them by extending your arm as they approach. Stops are marked with red-and-white signs. Tickets, valid on all urban services, cost 50BF (€1.25, $1.15) for a single (called a *direct*); 240BF (€6, $6) for a five-journey ticket; 350BF (€8.75, $8) for a 10-journey ticket; and 140BF (€3.50, $3.25) for a 1-day ticket. Insert your ticket into the orange machines inside buses and trams and at Métro platforms. Your ticket must be inserted each time you enter a new vehicle, but multiple transfers are permitted within a 1-hour period.

Pocket maps of the network (Métro, tram, bus) are free from the tourist office, main Métro stations, and the S.T.I.B. public transportation company at Galerie de la Toison d'Or 20 (℡ 02/515-20-00). All stations and many bus and tram stops have public transportation maps.

By Taxi   Starting rate is 95BF (€2.50, $2.20) during the day, 170BF (€4.25, $3.95) between 10pm and 6am, increasing by 38BF (€0.95, 90¢) per kilometer inside the city (tariff 1) and 76BF (€1.90, $1.75) per kilometer beyond city limits (tariff 2)—make sure the meter is set to the correct tariff. You can round up the fare if you like, but need not add a tip unless you have received an extra service, such as help with luggage. Taxis cannot be hailed on the street, but there are stands at prominent locations around town. Call **ATR** (℡ 02/241-55-48); **Autolux** (℡ 02/411-12-21); **Taxis Bleus** (℡ 02/268-00-00); **Taxis Oranges** (℡ 02/349-43-43); or **Taxis Verts** (℡ 02/349-49-49).

By Car   Do yourself a favor: Leave the car at a parking garage. Brussels's proximity to the rest of the country, and to France, Germany, and Holland, makes a car an attractive option for continuing on. All the top U.S. firms rent here—including **Hertz,** bd. Maurice-Lemmonier 8 (℡ 02/726-49-50; Métro: Anneesens); **Avis,** rue Américaine 145 (℡ 02/720-09-44; tram: 91, 92); and ggiers, dancers and an assortment of acrobats fill the street.

he shoots you a wide-eyed look as a seven-foot cartoon character approaches.

hat brought you here was wanting the kids

o see something magical while they still believed in magic.

herica Online Keyword: Travel

th 700 airlines, 50,000 hotels and over 5,000 cruise and vaca-

n getaways, you can now go places you've always dreamed of.

Travelocity.com
A Sabre Company
Go Virtually Anywhere.

ORLD'S LEADING TRAVEL WEB SITE, 5 YEARS IN A ROW" WORLD TRAVEL AWARDS

I HAVE TO CALL THE TRAVEL AGENCY AGAIN. DARN, OUT TO LUNCH. NOW HAVE TO CALL THE AIRLINE. I HATE CALLING THE AIRLINES. I GOT PUT ON HOLD AGAIN. "INSTRUMENTAL TOP 40" ... LOVELY. I HATE GETTING PUT ON HOLD. TICKET PRICES ARE ALL OVER THE MAP. HOW DO I DIAL INTERNATIONALLY? OH SHOOT, FORGOT THE RENTAL CAR. I'M STILL ON HOLD. THIS MUSIC IS GIVING ME A HEADACHE. WONDER IF SOMEONE ELSE HAS CHEAPER FLIGHTS. FORGET IT, CAN'T TAKE IT ANYMORE ... I'M HANGING UP

YAHOO! TRAVEL
100% MUZAK-FREE

Booking your trip online at Yahoo! Travel is simple. You compare the best prices. You click. You go have fun. Tickets, hotels, rental cars, cruises & more. Sorry, no muzak.

YAHOO!®
Travel
travel.yahoo.com

Budget, av. Louise 327 (© **02/646-51-30;** Métro: Place Louise). You can also try **Europcar,** rue du Page 29 (© **02/348-92-12;** tram: 81, 82), whose rates may be slightly less. All of these companies have desks at the airport. Rates begin at around 1,800BF (€45, $42) for a small car with unlimited mileage.

ⓒ FAST FACTS: Brussels

American Express The office at bd. du Souverain 100, 1000 Brussels (© **02/676-21-11;** Métro: Horrmann-Debroux) is open from Monday to Friday 9am to 1pm and 2 to 5pm. Call ahead before visiting, as the office is out in the suburbs.

Business Hours Banks are open from Monday to Friday 9am to 1pm and 2 to 4:30 or 5pm. Shopping hours are from Monday to Saturday 9 or 10am to 6 or 7pm. Some stores, such as bakers and news vendors, open earlier, and some open the same hours on Sunday. Many stores stay open on Friday until 8 or 9pm.

Currency From January 1, 2002 the monetary unit in Belgium is the euro, though the old Belgian franc will still be legal tender until March 1. The exchange rate used in this chapter is $1 = 43 Belgian francs (BF) or 1BF = 2.5¢. Also, €1 = 40BF and £1 = 62BF.

Currency Exchange Banks offer the best rates, and exchange offices in train stations come close. Hotels and bureaux de change offer poorer rates and may charge high commissions, but are open evenings and weekends. **Thomas Cook,** Grand-Place 4 (© **02/513-28-45;** Métro: Centrale), has reasonable rates. There are many ATMs around town, connected to Cirrus and Plus, and identified by "Bancontact" and "Mister Cash" logos. You need a four-digit PIN to access ATMs.

Dentists/Doctors For emergency medical service around the clock, call © **02/479-18-18;** ask for an English-speaking doctor. For emergency dental care, call © **02/426-10-26.**

Embassies **U.S.:** bd. du Régent 25–27 (© **02/508-21-11;** Métro: Arts-Loi), open Monday to Friday 9am to noon for visas, 1:30 to 4:30pm for assistance to U.S. citizens. **Canada:** av. de Tervuren 2 (© **02/741-06-11;** Métro: Merode), open from Monday to Friday 9am to noon and Tuesday and Thursday 2 to 4pm. **United Kingdom:** rue Arlon 85 (© **02/287-62-11;** Métro: Maalbeek), open from Monday to Friday 9:30am to noon. **Australia:** rue Guimard 6–8 (© **02/286-05-00;** Métro: Arts-Loi), open from Monday to Friday 9am to 12:30pm and 2 to 4pm. **New Zealand:** Square de Meeûs 1 (© **02/512-10-40;** Métro: Trone), open from Monday to Friday 9am to 1pm and 2 to 3:30pm. **Ireland:** rue Froissart 89 (© **02/230-53-37;** Métro: Schuman), open fom Monday to Friday from 10am to 12:30pm.

Emergencies For an ambulance, call © **100;** for police assistance, © **101;** for fire, © **100.**

Internet Access In the center, the large **easyEverything** store, place de Brouckère 9–13 (© **02/211-08-20;** www.easyeverything.com; Métro: De Brouckère), has 450 PCs. It's open 24 hours a day; access begins at 50BF (€1.25, $1.15).

Post Office The office at Gare du Midi, av. Fonsny 1E/F (*©* **02/538-33-98;** Métro: Midi), is open 24 hours a day. Others are open Monday to Friday 9am to 5pm; the Centre Monnaie office, place de la Monnaie (*©* **02/ 226-21-11;** Métro: De Brouckère), is also open Saturday 9:30am to 3pm.

Telephone Belgium's **country code** is **32.** Brussels's **city code** is **2;** use this code when calling from outside Belgium. In Belgium, use **02** (you always have to dial the area code).

A **local call** costs 15BF (€0.40, 38¢) for 3 minutes. To make international calls, use a Belgacom telecard, available from Belgacom offices and many news vendors for 200BF (€5, $4.65), 500BF (€12.50, $12), and 1,000BF (€25, $23). It costs 100BF (€2.50, $2.35) for a 3-minute call to the United States with a telecard. **International direct dial** numbers include **USA Direct** (*©* **0800/100-10), MCI** (*©* **0800/022-9122), PhoneUSA** (*©* **0800/ 022-0224), Sprint** (*©* **0800/022-9119), Canada Direct** (*©* **0800/022-9116),** and **British Telecom** (*©* **0800/022-9944).**

WHERE TO STAY

The business of Brussels is business, a fact reflected in the cost and nature of available accommodations. Hotels in the upper price range have a wealth of facilities for business travelers—conference rooms, fax machines, and efficient, though impersonal, service. At every level, hotels fill up during the week and empty out on weekends and during July and August. In off-peak periods, rates can drop as much as 50% from those quoted below; be sure to ask for lower rates and that you're quoted the complete rates, which include value added tax (TVA) and service.

The T.I.B. office in the Grand-Place and the Belgian Tourist Office at rue du Marché-aux-Herbes 63 (see "Visitor Information," above) make same-day reservations, if you go in person, for a small fee (deducted by the hotel from its room rate). T.I.B. publishes an annual *Hotel Guide* with listings by price range, and can provide complete information, including space availability, on hostels. **Belgian Tourist Reservations,** bd. Anspach 111, 1000 Brussels (*©* **02/513-74-84;** fax 02/513-92-77), reserves hotel rooms throughout Belgium and often gets substantial discounts.

An alternative to hotels is a bed-and-breakfast. Brussels has several good B&B organizations: **Bed & Brussels,** rue Kindermans 9, 1050 Brussels (*©* **02/ 644-07-37;** fax 02/644-01-14); and **New Windrose,** av. Brugman 11, 1060 Brussels (*©* **02/534-71-91;** fax 02/534-71-92). All will send you a list of host families (the Windrose includes a profile of the families) and rates. Booking fee is 500BF (€12.50, $12) per reservation; rates vary from 1,500BF to 2,200BF (€37.50–€55, $35–$51) for a double.

The **Sheraton Brussels Airport,** Luchthaven Brussel Nationaal (facing Departures), 1930 Zaventem (*©* **800/325-3535** in the U.S. and Canada, or 02/725-10-00; fax 02/710-80-80; www.sheraton.com), couldn't be more convenient to the airport without being on the runway. You have all the comfort you would expect of a top-flight Sheraton. Doubles cost 14,900BF to 15,900BF (€372.50–€397.50, $347–$370) per night. For a cheaper airport option, try the **Holiday Inn Express Brussels Airport,** Berkenlaan 5 (access road opposite NATO HQ), 1831 Diegem (*©* **02/725-33-80;** fax 02/725-38-10). Doubles cost 4,950BF to 7,000BF (€123.75–€175, $115–$163), and frequently are discounted. You can dine at its big brother Holiday Inn next door. There's free parking and an airport shuttle.

VERY EXPENSIVE

Astoria ★★ You're transported to a more elegant age the moment you walk into the belle époque foyer. The Astoria dates from 1909, and its plush interior recalls the panache of that vanished heyday. Rooms are attractively furnished, though not extravagantly so.

Rue Royale 103 (close to Colonne du Congrès), 1000 Brussels. (℗ **800/SOFITEL** in the U.S. and Canada, or 02/227-05-05. Fax 02/217-11-50. www.sofitel.com. 118 units. Mon–Fri 14,000BF (€350, $326) double; from 18,000BF (€450, $419) suite. Weekend double rates include buffet breakfast. AE, DC, MC, V. Valet parking 600BF (€15, $14). Métro: Botanique. **Amenities:** Restaurant (French), lounge; health club & spa; concierge; 24-hour room service; laundry service; same-day dry cleaning. *In room:* A/C, TV w/ pay movies, minibar, coffeemaker, hair dryer, safe.

Métropole ★★ An ornate marble-and-gilt interior distinguishes this 19th-century hotel several blocks from the Grand-Place. The spacious rooms have classic furnishings and modern luxuries, but don't expect the same belle époque glitter that you find in the public spaces. French restaurant L'Alban Chambon caters to the sophisticated diner; belle époque Café Métropole to the sophisticated cafe hound. There's a heated sidewalk terrace, though this has an uninspiring view of a busy street.

Place de Brouckère 31 (close to Centre Monnaie), 1000 Brussels. (℗ **02/217-23-00.** Fax 02/218-02-20. www.metropolehotel.be. 410 units. 12,500–16,500BF (€312.50–€412.50, $291–$384) double; from 18,000BF (€450, $419) suite. Rates include buffet or continental breakfast. AE, DC, MC, V. Parking 500BF (€12.50, $12). Métro: De Brouckère. **Amenities:** Restaurant (French), lounge, sidewalk cafe; health club & spa; concierge; 24-hour room service; laundry service; same-day dry cleaning. *In room:* TV w/ pay movies, minibar, coffeemaker, hair dryer, safe.

Radisson SAS ★★★ Modern, yet in harmony with a refurbished commercial neighborhood just a few blocks from the Grand-Place, this highly regarded hotel incorporates part of the medieval city wall. Large rooms are decorated in a variety of styles, including Scandinavian, Asian, and Italian. The Sea Grill restaurant wins plaudits for its seafood and the Bar Dessinée has a Belgian comic strip theme.

Rue du Fossé-aux-Loups 47 (close to Galeries Royales Saint-Hubert) (℗ **800/333-3333** in the U.S. and Canada, or 02/219-28-28. Fax 02/219-62-62. www.radisson.brussels.be. 281 units. 13,000–15,000BF (€325–€375, $302–$349) double; from 19,000BF (€475, $442) suite. Rates in some doubles include buffet breakfast. AE, DC, MC, V. Parking 800BF (€20, $19). Métro: Centrale. **Amenities:** 3 restaurants (seafood, American), lounge; health club; concierge; 24-hour room service; laundry service; same-day dry cleaning. *In room:* A/C, TV w/ pay movies, minibar, coffeemaker, hair dryer, safe.

EXPENSIVE

Bristol Stephanie ★★★ Every feature of this sleek Norwegian-owned hotel, from its lobby fittings to furnishings in the 16 kitchenette suites, is streamlined, functional, and representative of the best in Nordic design. It's in a pretty section of one of the city's toniest shopping streets, and has an indoor pool. Restaurant Le Chalet d'Odin's international menu is strong on Norwegian specialties.

Av. Louise 91–93, 1050 Brussels. (℗ **02/543-33-11.** Fax 02/538-03-07. www.bristol.be. 142 units. 11,200BF (€280, $260) double; from 20,500BF (€512.50, $477) suite. AE, DC, MC, V. Parking 400BF (€10, $9). Métro: Louise. **Amenities:** Restaurant (international), lounge; heated indoor pool; health club; concierge; 24-hour room service; laundry service; same-day dry cleaning. *In room:* A/C, TV w/ pay movies, minibar, coffeemaker, hair dryer, safe.

L'Amigo 𝒜𝒜𝒜   In Brussels slang, an "amigo" is a prison, and indeed, a prison once stood here, but any resemblance to the former accommodations is purely nominal. Understated old European refinement permeates the stately corridors. Rooms are plushly outfitted. Though the restaurant is unremarkable and fitness buffs have to go elsewhere to exercise, the hotel provides world-class comforts.

Rue de l'Amigo 1–3 (off the Grand-Place), 1000 Brussels. ℭ **02/547-47-47.** Fax 02/513-52-77. www. hotelamigo.com. 185 units. 8,900–11,500BF (€222.50–€287.50, $207–$267) double; from 15,500BF (€387.50, $360) suite. Rates include buffet breakfast. AE, DC, MC, V. Parking 500BF (€12.50, $12). Métro: Bourse. **Amenities:** Restaurant (international), lounge; concierge; 24-hour room service; laundry service; same-day dry cleaning. *In room:* A/C, TV w/ pay movies, minibar, coffeemaker, hair dryer, safe.

MODERATE

Albert Premier 𝒜𝒜   With a fully renovated Art Deco interior behind a 19th-century facade, the Albert, named after Belgium's dashing World War I "Soldier King," has retained a certain cachet despite paralleling the mixed fortunes of the square on which it stands. Once elegant, then seedy, this neighborhood on the edge of the city center has been turned around and is now a thriving business district. Rooms have minimal amenities, yet are modern, comfortable, and attractively decorated.

Place Rogier 20 (beside Gare du Nord), 1210 Brussels. ℭ **02/203-31-25.** Fax 02/203-43-31. 287 units. 3,300–5,800BF (€82.50–€145, $77–$135) double. Rates include buffet breakfast. DC, MC, V. Limited street parking. Métro: Rogier. **Amenities:** Restaurant (international), lounge; concierge; limited room service; laundry service; dry cleaning. *In room:* TV, hair dryer, safe.

Comfort Art Hotel Siru 𝒜𝒜   The owner of this art-gallery-cum-hotel in the middle of a redeveloped business district persuaded 130 Belgian artists, including some of the country's biggest names, to "decorate" each of the coolly modern, well-equipped rooms and the corridors with a work on travel. Given the unpredictable nature of reactions to modern art, some clients apparently reserve the same room time after time; others ask for a room change in the middle of the night. It is not easily forgotten.

Place Rogier 1 (opposite Gare du Nord), 1210 Brussels. ℭ **800/228-3323** in the U.S. and Canada, or 02/ 203-35-80. Fax 02/203-33-03. art.hotel.siru@skynet.be. 101 units. 3,300–6,400BF (€82.50–€160, $77–$149) double. Rates include buffet breakfast. AE, DC, MC, V. Parking 440BF (€11, $10). Métro: Rogier. **Amenities:** Restaurant (international), lounge; concierge; limited room service; laundry service; same-day dry cleaning. *In room:* TV w/ pay movies, minibar, hair dryer, safe.

Le Dixseptième 𝒜𝒜   This graceful, 17th-century house stands close to the Grand-Place in a neighborhood of restored dwellings. Rooms are as big as suites in many hotels, and some have balconies. All are in 18th-century style and are named after Belgian painters from Brueghel to Magritte. Two beautiful lounges are decorated with carved wooden medallions and 18th-century paintings.

Rue de la Madeleine 25, 1000 Brussels (off place de l'Albertine). ℭ 02/502-57-44. Fax 02/502-64-24. www. ledixseptieme.be. 24 units. 6,600BF (€165, $153) studio; 7,200–13,600BF (€180–€340, $167–$316) suite. Rates include buffet breakfast. AE, DC, MC, V. Limited street parking. Métro: Centrale. **Amenities:** Lounge; laundry service; dry cleaning. *In room:* A/C, TV, minibar, hair dryer, safe.

Mozart   Go a flight up from the busy, cheap-eats street level, and guess which famous composer's music wafts through the lobby? Salmon-colored walls, plants, and old paintings create a warm, intimate ambience that's carried into the rooms. Though furnishings are blandly modern, colorful fabrics and exposed beams lend each room a rustic originality. Several are duplexes with a sitting room underneath the loft bedroom. Top rooms have a great view.

Rue du Marché-aux-Fromages 15A, 1000 Brussels (close to Grand-Place). ℂ **02/502-66-61.** Fax 02/502-77-58. www.hotel-mozart.be. 47 units. 3,600BF (€90, $84) double. AE, DC, MC, V. Limited street parking. Métro: Centrale, **Amenities:** Lounge. *In room:* TV.

Sema   This small, modern hotel is warmly inviting. Its cozy lobby is up a flight of stairs, and from there an elevator takes you to your room. Gleaming wood floors, white walls, and bright bedcovers create a cheerful setting in quite large rooms. Windows are double-glazed.

Rue des Harengs 6–8, 1000 Brussels (close to Grand-Place). ℂ **02/514-07-60.** Fax 02/548-90-39. www.grouptorus.com. 11 units. 5,000BF (€125, $116) double. Rates include continental breakfast. AE, DC, MC, V. Limited street parking. Métro: Centrale. *In room:* TV, hair dryer.

INEXPENSIVE

Les Bluets ★★   In a house dating from 1864, you step into a fine old family hotel with a proprietress, Mme Myriam Heller, who considers her guests almost as members of the family. Each room is different, but all have high ceilings and unusual antiques—statuettes, stained glass, paintings—and knickknacks. The effect is more that of a comfortable country house than a hotel. Smoking is forbidden anywhere in the hotel.

Rue Berckmans 124, 1060 Brussels (off av. Louise). ℂ **02/534-39-83.** Fax 02/543-09-70. bluets@euduramail.com. 10 units. 2,000–2,850BF (€50–€71.25, $47–$66) double. Rates include continental breakfast. MC, V. Limited street parking. Métro: Hôtel des Monnaies. *In room:* TV, hair dryer.

Pacific   In a bohemian neighborhood, this hotel is a 5-minute walk from Grand-Place. Most rooms are large, though with plumbing from 80 years ago; front rooms have small balconies. Breakfast is served in a room eclectically decorated with a zebra skin, a Canadian World War II steel helmet, railway signal lamps, copper pots, and a Buddhist prayer wheel. Monks from the Dalai Lama's entourage once stayed here and left mystical symbols in some rooms. Just the place if you prefer atmosphere over comfort.

Rue Antoine Dansaert 57 (2 blocks from the Bourse), 1000 Brussels. ℂ and fax **02/511-84-59.** 15 units, 2 with bathroom (shower only; no toilet). 1,800–2,400BF (€45–€60, $42–$56) double. Showers 100BF (€2.50, $2.35) extra for rooms without bathrooms. Rates include full breakfast. No credit cards. Parking 200BF (€5, $4.65). Métro: Bourse. **Amenities:** none.

Sabina   This small hostelry is like a private residence, presided over by hospitable owners. A grandfather clock in the reception area and polished wood along the restaurant walls give it a warm, homey atmosphere. Rooms vary in size, but all are comfortable and simply yet tastefully done in modern style with twin beds. Three rooms have kitchenettes for 150BF (€3.75, $3.50) extra.

Rue du Nord 78 (close to Colonne du Congrès), 1000 Brussels. ℂ **02/218-26-37.** Fax 02/219-32-39. 24 units. 2,500BF (€62.50, $58) double. Rates include buffet breakfast. AE, DC, MC, V. Limited street parking. Métro: Madou. *In room:* TV.

Welcome ★★★   You'll be hard put to imagine a hotel that leaves you with fonder memories, though the Welcome is the city's smallest hotel. It has such fiercely loyal regulars that it is often fully booked—admittedly not a difficult feat—so you should reserve far ahead. The enthusiastic couple who own it, Michel and Sophie Smeesters, has generated a loyal following with their bright, cheerful rooms and superb attached seafood restaurant, La Truite d'Argent (see "Where to Dine," below).

Rue du Peuplier 5, 1000 Brussels (at the Marché-aux-Poissons). ℂ **02/219-95-46.** Fax 02/217-18-87. www.hotelwelcome.com. 6 units. 2,900–3,600BF (€72.50–€90, $67–$84) double; 4,600BF (€115, $107) suite. DC, MC, V. Free parking. Métro: Ste-Catherine. **Amenities:** Restaurant (seafood/French), lounge. *In room:* A/C, TV, minibar.

WHERE TO DINE

From crisp "French" fries and waffles on the street corner to succulent Flemish and Walloon specialties, it's almost impossible to eat badly in Brussels, and with 2,000 restaurants to choose from you have no problem eating well at a reasonable price.

Most of the city's favorite dishes are based on local products, with the notable exception of its beloved fresh *moules* (mussels), served in multitudinous variations from July through the winter. A steaming bowl of mussels, or a user-friendly *steak-frites* (steak and french fries), always goes down well with Belgian diners.

Belgium is renowned for 400 brands of beer produced by hundreds of small breweries; Belgian chefs use beer in their sauces the way French chefs use wine. Beef, chicken, and fish are often bathed in a savory sauce based on the local *gueuze, faro,* and *kriek* brews. Beer is the perfect accompaniment to the sturdy regional dishes you find on menus around town: *waterzooï,* fish or chicken stew with a parsley-and-cream sauce; *stoemp,* a puree of vegetables and potatoes with sausage, steak, or chop; *paling in 't groen,* eel in a grass-green sauce; *ballekes,* spicy meatballs; *hochepot,* stew; *lapin à la gueuze,* rabbit with a Brussels beer sauce; and *carbonnades à la flamande,* beef stew with a beer sauce. A selection of the country's 300 artisanal cheeses, or waffles and whipped fresh cream, is a good way to finish off.

The main dining-out areas center around the Grand-Place and the Marché-aux-Poissons (Fish Market) in the Center; and in trendy Ixelles and St-Gilles south of the Center. Vegetarian restaurants are thin on the ground, though many places have a vegetarian listing on their menu offering at least a few items. If you are a nonsmoker you're mostly out of luck—get ready to consume a garnish of secondhand smoke with your meal.

Don't fret if service is slow: People take their time dining out here, and just sitting in a good restaurant is part of the pleasure. Service is included in most, but not all, checks, so you usually don't have to do much more than round the total up to the nearest handy amount, unless you're especially pleased with the service, in which case a 10% tip is adequate—even generous by Belgian standards.

VERY EXPENSIVE

Comme Chez Soi 𝒶𝒶𝒶 CLASSIC FRENCH   Looking for unforgettable French cuisine in an Art Nouveau setting? An expedition inside the hallowed portals of "Just Like Home" will surely be the culinary highlight of your trip to Brussels. Though the food is a long way from what most people eat at home, the welcome from master chef Pierre Wynants is warm, and his standards are high enough for the most rigorous taste buds. Ask for a table in the kitchen, where you can watch the master at work. The sautéed lobster with truffles and chanterelles and the roast saddle of lamb are memorable main courses; for dessert, try the soufflé of preserved oranges in Mandarine Napoléon liqueur.

Place Rouppe 23. © **02/512-29-21.** Reservations required for lunch and dinner. Main courses 1,250–3,750BF (€31.25–€93.75, $29–$87); fixed-price menus 2,250–4,950BF (€56.25–€123.75, $52–$115). AE, DC, MC, V. Tues–Sat noon–1:30pm and 7–9:30pm (closed July and Christmas/New Year holidays). Métro: Anneessens.

La Maison du Cygne 𝒶𝒶 CLASSIC FRENCH   This grande dame of Brussels restaurants overlooks the Grand-Place from the former Butchers' Guildhouse. "The House of the Swan's" service, though a tad stuffy, is as elegant as

> **Tips** **On Your Guard in the Ilôt Sacré**
>
> A few restaurants (not reviewed here) in this colorful restaurant district off the Grand-Place take advantage of tourists. Follow these ground rules to ensure you're not one of them:
>
> - An impressive outdoor display of seafood on ice is no guarantee of quality.
> - Be wary if inexpensive menu items, such as the *plat du jour* (plate of the day), are "sold out."
> - Check the price if the waiter proposes "something special."
> - Check the price of both the house wine and house aperitif before ordering. Usually the cheapest options, in a few places they are by far the most expensive.
> - Confirm both the price and the size of a seafood platter before ordering.
> - Be certain of the price of everything you order.
> - Refuse to pay for anything you didn't order or didn't get.
>
> None of this is meant to discourage you. Most visitors leave the Ilôt Sacré with no more serious complaint than an expanded waistline.

the polished walnut walls, bronze wall sconces, and green velvet. Among the classics offered, try the souplike lobster stew, tournedos with green peppercorns, oysters in champagne, or sole mousse. Because of its location, Cygne is usually crowded at lunch, but dinner reservations are likely to be available.

Grand-Place 9 (entrance at rue Charles Buls 2). ℂ 02/511-82-44. Reservations recommended on weekends. Main courses 950–1,600BF (€23.75–€40, $22–$37); *menu du jour* 2,250BF (€56.25, $52). AE, DC, MC, V. Mon–Fri noon–2:15pm and Mon–Sat 7pm–midnight (closed 3 weeks in Aug). Métro: Centrale.

EXPENSIVE

De l'Ogenblik ☆☆ FRENCH/BELGIAN   In the elegant surroundings of the Galeries Royales St-Hubert, this restaurant supplies good taste in a Parisian bistro setting, popular with off-duty actors from the Gallery theater. It often gets busy, but the ambience in the two-level, wood-and-brass dining room, with a sand-strewn floor, is convivial, if a little too tightly packed. Look for garlicky seafood and meat menu dishes, and expect to pay a smidgen more for atmosphere than might be strictly justified by results on the plate.

Galerie des Princes 1. ℂ 02/511-61-51. Main courses 800–1,000BF (€20–€25, $19–$23); *plat du jour* 440BF (€11, $10). AE, DC, MC, V. Mon–Sat noon–2:30pm and 7pm–midnight (Fri–Sat to 12:30am). Métro: Centrale.

La Quincaillerie ☆☆☆ MODERN FRENCH/SEAFOOD   In Ixelles, a part of the city where fine restaurants are as common as streetlights, this spot stands out, even though it may be a little too aware of its own modish good looks and a shade pricey. The setting is a traditional former hardware store, with wood paneling and masses of wooden drawers, designed by students of Art Nouveau master Victor Horta. It's busy enough to get the wait staff harassed and absent-minded, yet they are always friendly. Specialties include salmon in roasted rock salt and baby duck with a crust of honey and lime.

Rue du Page 45 (at rue Américaine). ☎ 02/538-25-53. Main courses 640–960BF (€16–€24, $15–$22); *menu du jour* 1,800BF (€45, $42). AE, DC, MC, V. Mon–Fri noon–2:30pm and 7pm–midnight; Sat–Sun 7pm–midnight. Tram: 81, 82, 91, 92 to chaussée de Charleroi.

La Truite d'Argent 🎭🎭 CLASSIC FRENCH/SEAFOOD   Enthusiastic owners of an 1896 restaurant that once boasted Jacques Brel among its regular customers, Michel and Sophie Smeesters positively insist on delivering savory seafood specialties. *Superb* is the best word to describe the dishes, which include meat choices. All are prepared from fine ingredients, and the presentation is exquisite, so pleasing to the eye you might hesitate to destroy the image by eating it. You can dine on a sidewalk terrace at the Fish Market in good weather.

Quai aux Bois-à-Brûler 23 (at the Marché-aux-Poissons). ☎ 02/219-95-46. Main courses 720–1,080BF (€18–€27, $17–$25); fixed-price menu 1,250BF (€31.25, $29). DC, MC, V. Mon–Fri noon–2:30pm and 7–11:30pm. Métro: Ste-Catherine.

MODERATE

L'Amadeus 🎭🎭 MODERN BELGIAN   The postmodern chic of this restaurant/wine bar/oyster bar in a former sculptor's studio with garden-courtyard terrace makes a refreshing change from traditional Belgian style. Its candlelit interior is so dim you would think they're hiding something, but the cooking is nothing to be ashamed of. The menu includes such vegetarian treats as vegetarian lasagna and ricotta and spinach tortellini, and for meat eaters, caramelized spare ribs and several salmon dishes, all accompanied by delicious homemade nut bread. The Sunday brunch is an all-you-can-eat affair, that includes smoked fish, cheese, eggs, bread, cereal, juice, and coffee.

Rue Veydt 13. ☎ 02/538-34-27. Main courses 575–895BF (€14.40–€22.40, $13–$21); plat du jour (Mon–Fri) 375BF (€9.40, $9); Sun brunch 690BF (€17.25, $16). AE, DC, MC, V. Tues–Fri and Sun noon–2:30pm and 7pm–1am; Mon and Sat 7pm–1am. Métro: Louise.

La Roue d'Or 🎭🎭 TRADITIONAL BELGIAN   This welcoming, Art Nouveau brasserie with lots of dark wood, mirrors, a frescoed ceiling, Magritte images on the walls, and marble-topped tables, has a loyal local following. An extensive menu, ranging from grilled meats to a good selection of cooked salmon and other seafood, and old Belgian favorites like *stoemp,* caters to just about any appetite, and the beer, wine, and spirits list is equally long. Jeff De Gelas, the colorful owner (he also owns 't Kelderke, below), is known locally as the "King of Stoemp."

Rue des Chapeliers 26 (off Grand-Place). ☎ 02/514-25-54. Main courses 495–875BF (€12.40–€21.90, $12–$20); menu du jour 1,450–1,950BF (€36.25–€48.75, $34–$45). AE, DC, MC, V. Daily noon–12:30am; closed mid-July to mid-Aug. Métro: Centrale.

Le Falstaff Gourmand 🎭 *Value* CLASSIC BELGIAN/FRENCH   Le Falstaff cafe across from the Bourse (see "Brussels After Dark," later in this chapter) is widely renowned as a classic Art Nouveau bar and eatery. Around the corner, its sister establishment has a different but equally notable style. Service is attentive, prompt, and friendly. First-class Belgian and French menu dishes include one of the best deals in Brussels: a three-course *menu gourmand,* which includes an aperitif, glass of wine with the starter, and small pitcher of wine with the main course.

Rue des Pierres 38 (near the Bourse). ☎ 02/512-17-61. Main courses 490–750BF (€12.25–€18.75, $11–$17); menu gourmand 1,100BF (€27.50, $26). AE, DC, MC, V. Tues–Sun 11:30am–3pm and 7–11pm (except Sun evening). Métro: Bourse.

Le Joueur de Flûte ★★ MODERN FRENCH/BELGIAN Dining in this tiny Marolles restaurant is nothing if not straightforward. There is only one menu, with a couple of variations for the main course. Don't let that, or the fact that it serves only 16 diners each evening, put you off. Owner/chef Philippe Van Cappelen likes to keep things simple. He changes the decor to suit the changing seasons and cooks whatever he feels like cooking—and it's guaranteed to be delicious.

Rue de l'Epée 26 (beside the Palais de Justice). ℂ 02/513-43-11. Reservations required. Fixed-price menu 1,250BF (€31.25, $29). MC, V. Mon–Fri 8–10pm. Métro: Louise.

Le Marmiton ★★ CLASSIC BELGIAN/FRENCH A welcoming environment, hearty servings, and commitment to satisfying customers are hallmarks at this cozy restaurant, now on two floors. On a menu that emphasizes fish, the seafood cocktail starter is a heap of shellfish and crustaceans substantial enough to be a main course, and the sole is excellent. Meat dishes are available, too. The menu is complemented by an excellent wine list selected by Portuguese/Belgian owner and chef, Antonio Beja da Silva, whose love of his own cooking shows in his waistline and in the attention he devotes to his customers.

Rue des Bouchers 43 (off Grand-Place). ℂ 02/511-79-10. Main courses 480–720BF (€12–€18, $11–$17); menu du jour 395–725BF (€9.90–€18.15, $9–$17). AE, DC, MC, V. Daily noon–3pm and 6–11:30pm (12:30am on weekends). Métro: Centrale.

Shanti VEGETARIAN An exotic look keeps faith with its multicultural menus: lots of greenery and flowers create a gardenlike feel, and crystal lamps, mirrors, and old paintings adorn the walls. Try "Neptune's pleasure," crab with avocado and seaweed, as a starter. For a main course, shrimp Marsala with mixed vegetables and coriander is excellent, as is eggplant with ricotta in a tomato-and-basil sauce. There is also a big choice in fixed-price menus.

Av. Adolphe Buyl 68. ℂ 02/649-40-96. Main courses 300–450BF (€7.50–€11.25, $7–$10); fixed-price menus 450–1,000BF (€11.25–€25, $10–$23). AE, DC, MC, V. Tues–Sat noon–2pm and 6:30–10pm. Bus: 71.

INEXPENSIVE

In 't Spinnekopke ★★ Finds TRADITIONAL BELGIAN A coaching inn from 1762, just far enough off the beaten track downtown to be frequented mainly by "those in the know." Hardy standbys of Belgian cuisine, such as stoemp and waterzooï, are given all the care and attention they deserve, from kitchen staff and diners alike, generally accompanied by an artisanal beer from a list of 500. You dine in a tilting, tiled-floor building, at plain tables, and more likely than not squeezed into a tight space—but getting caught "In the Spider's Web" is well worth it.

Place du Jardin-aux-Fleurs 1 (off rue Van Artevelde). ℂ 02/511-86-95. Main courses 420–780BF (€11–€19.50, $10–$18); plat du jour 325BF (€8.15, $8). AE, DC, MC, V. Mon–Fri noon–3pm and 6–11pm; Sat 6pm–midnight. Métro: Bourse.

L'Auberge des Chapeliers TRADITIONAL BELGIAN Bistro food has been served up in this 17th-century former Hatmakers' Guildhouse for more than a quarter of a century. Popular with locals who live and work in the area, and with tourists fortunate enough to find it, it can be crowded at the height of lunch hour, so it's a good idea to come just before noon or just after 2pm. There are traditional Belgian dishes, many cooked in beer, and mussels on the menu, and servings are more than ample.

Rue des Chapeliers 1–3 (off Grand-Place). ℂ 02/513-73-38. Main courses 320BF–665BF (€8–€16.65, $7–$15); fixed-price menus 625–820BF (€15.65–€20.50, $15–$19). AE, DC, MC, V. Mon–Thurs noon–2pm and 6–11pm; Fri noon–2pm and 6pm–midnight; Sat noon–3pm and 6pm–midnight; Sun noon–3pm and 6–11pm. Métro: Centrale.

La Manufacture 🐾🐾 FRENCH/INTERNATIONAL   Even in its former industrial incarnation, this place was concerned with style—it was the factory of chic leather goods maker Delvaux. Fully refurbished, with parquet floors, polished wood, and stone tables set amid iron pillars and exposed air ducts, it produces trendy world cuisine from a French foundation for a mostly youthful public. It might at first seem disconcerting to find dim sum, sushi, Moroccan couscous, Lyon sausage, and Belgian waterzooï on the same menu, but don't worry—everything is tasty. There's piano music some evenings.

Rue Notre-Dame du Sommeil 12–22 (off place du Jardin-aux-Fleurs). 𝄞 02/502-25-25. Main courses 450–725BF (€11.25–€18.15, $10–$17); menu du jour (lunch only) 545BF (€13.75, $13). AE, DC, MC, V. Mon–Fri noon–2pm and 6–11pm; Sat 6pm–midnight. Métro: Centrale.

't Kelderke 🐾🐾 TRADITIONAL BELGIAN   Despite being on the Grand-Place, this is far from being a tourist trap. As many Bruxellois as tourists throng the long wooden tables in a 17th-century, brick-arched cellar, and all are welcomed with zeal. Memorable traditional Belgian fare, with little in the way of frills, is served up from the open kitchen. It's a great place to try local specialties such as sausage, Flemish beef stew, rabbit in Brussels beer, and big steaming pans piled high with Zeeland mussels.

Grand-Place 15. 𝄞 02/513-7344. Main courses 360–450BF (€9–€11.25, $8–$10); plat du jour 390BF (€9.75, $9). AE, DC, MC, V. Daily noon–2am. Métro: Centrale.

SEEING THE SIGHTS
SIGHTSEEING SUGGESTIONS FOR FIRST-TIME VISITORS

If You Have 1 Day Spend the day exploring the historic Center. Beginning in the magnificent **Grand-Place,** visit the 15th-century Town Hall, Brussels City Museum, and elegant guild houses, before moving on to **Manneken-Pis, St-Michel Cathedral,** and the 19th-century **Royal St Hubert Galleries** for some serious shopping (or window shopping). Buy a bag of chocolates at Wittamer on place du Grand-Sablon and browse the antiques shops around the square before heading over to tranquil **place du Petit-Sablon** for a rest. After a dinner that should include mussels, in season, spend the evening checking out one or more of the city's famed cafes.

If You Have 2 Days On the second day, explore Belgian art and architecture in their many permutations. Begin with Brueghel and Rubens at the **Musée d'Art Ancien,** then move into the 20th century with Magritte and Delvaux at the **Musée d'Art Moderne** next door. While you're in the neighborhood,

take a look at the neoclassical harmony of place Royale and the elegant Royal Palace. At the **Belgian Center for Comic-Strip Art,** follow the adventures of comic-book heroes and admire the Art Nouveau architecture of this restored department store. Continue your Art Nouveau explorations by strolling the side streets off avenue Louise and around square Ambiorix.

If You Have 3 Days On the third day get up early and stop by the flea market in place du Jeu de Balle. Then, head out to **Bruparck,** an attractions park on the city's northern edge that includes Mini-Europe and the Océade water leisure center. Nearby are the giant spheres of the **Atomium** and a panoramic view of the city from its viewing deck. For your last night in Brussels, have dinner or drinks in one of the guild hall restaurants, such as La Maison du Cygne, that overlook the Grand-Place. The illuminated square is even more beautiful at night than during the day.

BRUSSELS'S HISTORIC SQUARES & STREETS

GRAND-PLACE Ornamental gables, medieval banners, gilded facades, sunlight flashing off gold-filigreed rooftop sculptures, a general impression of harmony and timelessness—there's a lot to take in all at once when you first enter the Grand-Place. The Grand-Place has always been the very heart of Brussels. Characterized by Jean Cocteau as "a splendid stage," it's the city's theater of life.

PLACE DU GRAND-SABLON Considered classier than the Grand-Place by the locals, though busy traffic diminishes your enjoyment of its cafe-terraces, the Grand-Sablon is lined with gabled mansions. This is antiques territory, and many of those mansions house antiques shops or private art galleries, with pricey merchandise on display. On Saturday and Sunday an excellent antiques market sets up its stalls in front of Notre-Dame au Sablon Church. Take tram 92, 93, or 94.

PLACE DU PETIT-SABLON Across rue de la Régence, the Grand-Sablon's little cousin is an ornamental garden with a fountain and pool, a magical little retreat from the city bustle. The 48 bronze statuettes adorning the surrounding wrought-iron fence symbolize Brussels's medieval guilds. Take tram 92, 93, or 94.

PLACE ROYALE Meeting point of rue de la Régence and rue Royale, streets on which stand many of the city's premier attractions, the square is graced by an equestrian statue of Duke Godefroi de Bouillon, leader of the First Crusade. Also in place Royale is the neoclassical St-Jacques-sur-Coudenberg Church. Take tram 92, 93, or 94.

MUSEUMS & MONUMENTS

Atomium ✹✹ As the Eiffel Tower is the symbol of Paris, the Atomium is the symbol of Brussels, and, as was Paris's landmark, it was built for a world's fair, the 1958 Brussels World's Fair. Rising 100m (335 ft.) like a giant plaything of the gods that's fallen to earth, the Atomium is an iron crystal molecule magnified 165 billion times. Its metal-clad spheres, representing individual atoms, are connected by enclosed escalators and elevators. Within is an exhibit on human life and medical research. However, it's the topmost atom that attracts most people: a restaurant/observation deck that provides a sweeping panorama.

Bd. du Centenaire, Heysel. ✆ 02/474-89-77. Admission 200BF (€5, $4.65) adults, 150BF (€3.75, $3.50) children 12 and under, free for children under 1.2m (4 ft.). Apr–Aug daily 9am–8pm; Sept–Mar daily 10am–6pm (Panorama to 9:30pm). Métro: Heysel.

Centre Belge de la Bande Dessinée (Belgian Center for Comic-Strip Art) ✹✹✹ Called the "CéBéBéDé" for short, the center displays such popular cartoon characters as Lucky Luke, Thorgal, and, of course, Belgium's own Tintin, complete with red-and-white-checkered moon rocket, yet does not neglect the likes of Superman, Batman, and the Green Lantern. As icing on the cake, it's in a Victor Horta building, the Magasins Waucquez, which was slated for demolition when the center took it over.

Rue des Sables 20. ✆ 02/219-19-80. Admission 250BF (€6.25, $6) adults, 200BF (€5, $4.65) students/seniors, 100BF (€2.50, $2.35) children 11 and under. Tues–Sun 10am–6pm. Métro: Centrale.

Hôtel de Ville (Town Hall) ✹✹✹ The spectacular Gothic Hall chamber is open for visits when Brussels's council of aldermen is not in session. You should begin with the exterior, however, in particular with the sculptures on the facade, many of which are 15th- and 16th-century jokes. Inside are superb 16th- to 18th-century tapestries; one depicts the duke of Alba, whose cruel features

reflect the brutal oppression he and his Council of Blood imposed on Belgium; others are scenes from the life of Clovis, first king of the Franks. The aldermen meet in a plush, mahogany-paneled room surrounded by mirrors—presumably so that each party can see what underhanded maneuvers the others are up to.

Grand-Place. ℂ **02/279-43-55.** Admission 80BF (€2, $1.85) for guided tours only. Apr–Sept Tues 11:30am and 3:15pm, Wed 3:15pm, Sun 12:15pm; Oct–Mar Tues 11:30am and 3:15pm, Wed 3:15pm. Métro: Centrale.

Manneken-Pis 🔎   Brussels's favorite little boy gleefully does what a little boy's gotta do, generally ogled by a throng of admirers snapping pictures. Children especially seem to enjoy his bravura performance. This isn't the original statue, which was prone to theft and anatomical "maltreatment" and was removed for safekeeping. Louis XV of France began the tradition of presenting colorful costumes to "Little Julian" to make amends for Frenchmen having kidnapped the statue in 1747; the outfits are housed in the Musée de la Ville de Bruxelles in the Grand-Place.

Incidentally, Manneken-Pis has a female counterpart called Jeanneke-Pis, located on the dead-end impasse de la Fidélité off rue des Bouchers. The 1987 brainstorm of a local restaurateur who wanted to attract business, its lack of grace is an embarrassment to many Bruxellois.

Corner of rue du Chêne and rue de l'Etuve (2 blocks east of the Grand-Place). Métro: Bourse.

Mini-Europe 🔎🔎 _(Kids)_   Since Brussels is the new capital of Europe, it's fitting the city is home to a miniature rendering of all the continent's most notable architectural sights. Even a few natural wonders and technological developments are represented. Built on a scale of $^1/_{25}$ of the original, Big Ben, the Leaning Tower of Pisa, the Seville bullring, the Channel Tunnel, the Brandenburg Gate, and more exhibit remarkable detail. Though children like Mini-Europe the best, adults certainly find it fun.

In Bruparck, Heysel. ℂ **02/478-05-50.** Admission 420BF (€10.50, $10) adults, 320BF (€8, $7) children 12 and under, free for children under 1.2m (4 ft.). Apr–June and Sept 9:30am–6pm; first 2 weeks of July and last 2 weeks of Aug 9:30am–8pm; mid-July to mid-Aug 9:30am–midnight; Oct–Jan 10am–6pm; closed Feb–Mar. MC, V. Métro: Heysel.

Musées Royaux des Beaux-Arts (Royal Museums of Fine Arts) 🔎🔎🔎 Beyond the main entrance, the Musée d'Art Ancien (Museum of Ancient Art) has Brueghel and Rubens as the stars of the show, but the greater history of Belgian painting is well represented. The collection includes international masters, with works by Van Gogh and the French impressionists. Next-door, the Musée d'Art Moderne (Museum of Modern Art) has an emphasis on underground works—if only because the museum's eight floors are all below ground level. Magritte is well represented; so are Delvaux, De Braekeleer, Dalí, Permeke, and many others.

Rue de la Régence 3 (at place Royale). ℂ **02/508-32-11.** Admission 150BF (€3.75, $3.50) adults, 100BF (€2.50, $2.35) students/seniors, 50BF (€1.25, $1.15) travelers with disabilities and children 12–18, free for children 11 and under. Ancient Art Museum Tues–Sun 10am–noon and 1–5pm; Modern Art Museum Tues–Sun 10am–1pm and 2–5pm. Métro: Parc.

Musée de la Ville de Bruxelles (Brussels City Museum)   In the neo-Gothic Maison du Roi (King's House), the displays cover Brussels through the ages, including its traditional arts and crafts of tapestry and lace making. Among its most fascinating exhibits are old paintings and scale reconstructions of the historic city center, particularly those showing the riverside ambience along the

now-vanished River Senne. Pride of place goes to more than 500 costumes—
including an Elvis costume—belonging to Manneken Pis.

Grand-Place. ℂ **02/279-43-50.** Admission 100BF (€2.50, $2.35) adults, 80BF (€2, $1.85) children 5–15;
free for children under 5. Mon–Thurs 10am–12:30pm and 1:30–5pm (Oct–Mar to 4pm), Sat–Sun 10am–1pm.
Métro: Centrale.

Musée Horta (Horta Museum) *Finds*   Brussels owes much of its rich Art
Nouveau heritage to Victor Horta (1861–1947), a resident architect who led the
development of the style. His home and adjoining studio in St-Gilles are now a
museum. Restored to their original condition, they showcase his use of flowing,
sinuous shapes and colors, in both interior decoration and architecture.

Rue Américaine 25. ℂ **02/543-04-90.** Admission 150BF (€3.75, $3.50) on weekdays; 200BF (€5, $4.65) on
weekends. Tues–Sun 2–5:30pm. Tram: 81, 82, 91, or 92.

Musée du Cinquantenaire (Cinquantenaire Museum) ✪   This vast
museum, which opens half its collection on one day and the other half on the
next, shows off antiques, decorative arts (tapestries, porcelain, silver, and sculptures), and archaeology. Highlights are a tabletop model of imperial Rome in the
fourth century A.D., an Assyrian relief from the ninth century B.C., a Greek vase
from the sixth century B.C., the A.D. 1145 reliquary of Pope Alexander, some
exceptional tapestries, and colossal statues from Easter Island.

Parc du Cinquantenaire. ℂ **02/741-72-11.** Admission 150BF (€3.75, $3.50) adults, 100BF (€2.50, $2.35)
students/seniors, 50BF (€1.25, $1.15) children 12–18, free every first Wed afternoon of the month and for
children 11 and under. Tues–Fri 9:30am–5pm; Sat–Sun and public holidays 10am–5pm. Métro: Mérode.

Musée du Costume et de la Dentelle (Museum of Costume and Lace)
In a city famous for its lace, no visit would be complete without seeing the marvelous antique creations in this museum near the Grand-Place. Besides examples
of historic Belgian lace, the museum displays costumes, including dress from the
16th to the 19th centuries.

Rue de la Violette 6. ℂ **02/512-77-09.** Admission 100BF (€2.50, $2.35) adults, 80BF (€2, $1.85) children
5–16. Mon–Sat 10am–12:30pm and 1:30–5pm (Oct–Mar until 4pm); Sat–Sun 2–4:30pm. Métro: Centrale.

Palais Royal (Royal Palace) ✪   Work on the palace began in 1820, and it
was given a grandiose Louis XVI–style face-lift in 1904. King Albert II has his
offices here and it is used for state receptions, but he and Queen Paola live at the
Royal Palace in suburban Laeken. You can visit the ornate throne room, which
has magnificent chandeliers, and other public rooms.

Place des Palais. ℂ **02/551-20-20.** Free admission. July 22 to late Sept Tues–Sun 10:30am–4:30pm. Métro:
Parc.

CHURCHES
Cathédrale de St-Michel ✪   Victor Hugo considered this magnificent
church to be the "purest flowering of the Gothic style." Begun in 1226, it was
officially dedicated as a cathedral only in 1961. The 16th-century Hapsburg
Emperor Charles V took a personal interest in its decoration, donating the
superb stained-glass windows. In recent years its stonework has undergone
cleaning and restoration, and the dazzlingly bright exterior makes a superb sight.
Inside, spare decoration focuses attention on its soaring columns and arches.

Parvis Ste-Gudule (2 blocks west of Gare Centrale). ℂ **02/217-83-45.** Free admission to church; crypt 40BF
(€1, 95¢). Daily 7am–6pm. Métro: Centrale.

Notre-Dame du Sablon   Between the city park and the Palais de Justice, this
late-Gothic 15th- and 16th-century structure is noted for its four-fold gallery

with brightly colored stained-glass windows, illuminated from the inside at night, in striking contrast with the gray-white Gothic arches and walls. Also worth seeing are the two baroque chapels decorated with funeral symbols in white marble.

3B rue de la Régence (off place du Grand-Sablon). ✆ 02/511-57-41. Free admission. Daily 9am–6pm. Tram: 92, 93, 94.

AN AMUSEMENT PARK

Bruparck 🎠🎠🎠 (Métro: Heysel) is Brussels's amusement park. Built on the site of the 1958 Brussels world's fair, it's home to the Atomium and Mini-Europe (see above), the Kinepolis 26-screen movie complex, Bruparck village, a collection of restaurants and cafes (including a restaurant in a 1930s railway car of the legendary Orient Express), Océade (an indoor/outdoor water-sports pavilion with water slides, pools, and saunas), and a planetarium. Admission to Océade for 4 hours is 470BF (€11.75, $11) adults and 370BF (€9.25, $9) children. Admission to the planetarium is 130BF (€3.25, $3) adults and 100BF (€2.50, $2.35) children 11 and under. Both these attractions are open daily in summer and Tuesday to Sunday the rest of the year. Ask for cheaper combination tickets if you plan to visit more than one Bruparck attraction.

PARKS & GARDENS

The Parc de Bruxelles 🎠🎠 borders rue Royale, between Parliament and the Royal Palace (Métro: Parc). Once a hunting preserve of the dukes of Brabant, it is now a landscaped garden. In 1830, Belgian patriots confronted Dutch troops here during the War of Independence. Though not very big, the park manages to contain everything from carefully trimmed borders to rough patches of trees and bushes, and has fine views along its main paths, which form the outline of Masonic symbols. In 2001, the park was restored to its 18th century look. Diseased chestnut trees have been cut down and lime trees replaced with sturdier specimens; the 1840s bandstand by Jean-Pierre Cluysenaer has been refurbished, with the promise that it will host regular summer concerts.

The city's big public park, the **Bois de la Cambre** 🎠🎠, begins at the top of avenue Louise in the city's southern section (tram: 23, 90, or 93). This is the lung of Brussels, and it gets pretty busy on sunny weekends. Its centerpiece is a small lake with an island in the center reached by an electrically powered pontoon. Some busy roads run through the park and traffic moves fast on them, so be careful with children.

Continuing south from the Bois, the **Forêt de Soignes** 🎠 is no longer a park with playing areas and regularly mown grass, but a forest stretching almost to Waterloo; this is a great place for getting away from it all, particularly in the fall, when the colors are dazzling.

THE EUROPEAN DISTRICT

Home to the European Commission, European Parliament, Council of Ministers, and related institutions, Brussels is packed with 20,000-plus Eurocrats to back up its "capital of Europe" tag. Entire, characterful neighborhoods were swept away to make room for them.

To tour the heartland of European Union governance, take the Métro to Schuman station. Your first sight is the X-shaped **Palais de Berlaymont** (Berlaymont Palace), the Commission's former headquarters, at Rond-Point Schuman. Laced with hazardous asbestos and swathed in a protective covering, it has been evacuated and is undergoing a years-long cleanup.

Across rue de la Loi, the Council of Ministers headquarters, the **Consilium** is instantly recognizable for its facade's lavish complement of rose-colored granite blocks. On its far side, a soothing stroll through little Parc Léopold brings you to the new, post-modern **European Parliament and International Conference Centre** ★ complex, an architectural odyssey in white marble and tinted glass. Take the passageway through the building's middle to place Léopold, an old square that looks lost and forlorn in comparison to its powerful new neighbors.

ORGANIZED TOURS

Three-hour coach tours are available from **De Boeck,** rue de la Colline 8 (✆ 02/ 513-77-44). Each tour costs 840BF (€21, $20) adults and 445BF (€11.15, $10) children. You can book at most hotels, and arrangements can be made for hotel pickup. Regular tours operate throughout the year; private tours can also be arranged.

Chatterbus, rue des Thuyas 12 (✆ 02/673-18-35), operates a daily 3-hour tour, June 15 to September 15, starting at 10am from the Galeries Royales St-Hubert, next to rue du Marché-aux-Herbes 90, a few steps from the Grand-Place. The walking tour covers the historic center, followed by a bus ride through areas most tourists never see. You hear about life in Brussels and get a better feel for the city. The price is 350BF (€8.75, $8).

ARAU, the Workshop for Urban Research and Action, bd. Adolphe Max 55 (✆ 02/219-33-45), is a committee of concerned Brussels residents who give 3-hour themed coach tours, including "Surprising Parks and Squares," "Brussels 1900 Art Nouveau," "Grand-Place and Its Surroundings," and "Alternative Brussels." You are advised to book ahead. Tours cost 600BF (€15, $14) and operate on a rotating basis on Saturdays March to November; private group tours can be arranged throughout the year.

THE SHOPPING SCENE

Don't look for many bargains in Brussels. As a general rule, the upper city around avenues Louise and Porte de Namur is more expensive than the lower city around rue Neuve and the shopping malls on place de la Monnaie and place Brouckère. (For shopping hours, see "Business Hours" under "Fast Facts: Brussels," earlier in this chapter.) A useful source of information is the weekly English-language magazine *The Bulletin,* which keeps tabs on shopping trends, reviews stores, and carries advertising.

Galeries Royales St-Hubert, which claims to be Europe's oldest shopping mall, is a light and airy arcade hosting boutiques, cafe-terraces, and street musicians playing classical music. Opened in 1847, architect Pierre Cluysenaer's Italian neo-Renaissance gallery has a touch of class and is well worth a stroll through, even if you have no intention of shopping. The elegant triple gallery is near the Grand-Place, between rue du Marché-aux-Herbes and rue de l'Ecuyer, and split by rue des Bouchers. There are accesses on each of these streets (Métro: Centrale).

At the **Vieux Marché** (Old Market) flea market on place du Jeu-de-Balle (Métro: Porte de Hal), a large square in the Marolles district, you can find some exceptional decorative items, many recycled from the homes of the "recently deceased," and unusual postcards, clothing, and household goods. Everything from antiques to junk, from North African clothes to Soviet chic, is sold here. The market is held daily 7am to 2pm. Every weekend, place du Grand Sablon hosts a fine **Antiques Market** (Métro: Centrale). Salesmanship is low-key, interest pure, prices not unreasonable, and quality of merchandise—including silverware, pottery, paintings, and jewelry—high. The market is open Saturday 9am to 6pm and Sunday 9am to 2pm.

Manufacture Belge de Dentelle, Galerie de la Reine 6–8 (© **02/511-44-77;** Métro: Centrale), specializes in top-quality handmade Belgian lace. Another good lace store is **Maison Antoine,** Grand-Place 26 (© **02/512-48-59;** Métro: Centrale), in a former guild house where Victor Hugo lived in 1852. The quality is superb, service friendly, and prices reasonable. The Grand-Place has a **Flower Market,** daily 7am to 2pm, and a weekly Bird Market, with many varieties of birds for sale (at press time, the market has been closed down for an unspecified period for animal welfare violations, but it seems likely to start up again once it has cleaned up its act). Nearby, at the top end of rue du Marché-aux-Herbes, in the Agora, the weekend **Crafts Market** has lots of fine little specialized jewelry and other items, most of which are inexpensive.

Forget computer games and Disney stores—if you need to buy a gift for the kids, take home some Tintin mementos from **Boutique de Tintin,** rue de la Colline 13 (© **02/514-45-50;** Métro: Centrale). Visit **De Boe,** rue de Flandre 36 (© **02/511-13-73;** Métro: Ste-Catherine), a small shop near the Fish Market, for the heavenly aromas of roasted and blended coffee, a superb selection of wines in all price categories, and an array of specialty crackers, nuts, spices, teas, and gourmet snacks, many of which come in tins that make them easy to pack.

Among shops selling fashionable clothing and accessories, try **Delvaux,** Galerie de la Reine 31 (© **02/512-71-98;** Métro: Centrale), a local company making and selling some of the best, and priciest, handbags and leather goods in Belgium. **Olivier Strelli,** av. Louise 72 (© **02/511-21-34;** Métro: Louise), is owned by the top-rated Belgian fashion designer, whose line is strong on elegant, ready-to-wear items. For books and magazines in English, visit **Waterstone's,** bd. Adolphe Max 71 (© **02/219-27-08;** Métro: Rogier).

BRUSSELS AFTER DARK

The city offers a full range of evening activities, including dance, opera, classical music, jazz, film, theater, and discos. For an exhaustive listing of events, consult the "What's On" section of the English-language weekly *The Bulletin.*

You can order tickets for all performing-arts venues from the **Central Booking Office** (© **0800/21-221;** open Mon–Fri 9am–7pm and Sat 10am–7pm).

THE PERFORMING ARTS

The main performing-arts season is from September to May, with performances in summer as well. The superb **Théâtre Royal de la Monnaie,** place de

---

Tips Buying Belgian Chocolates & Pastries

Belgian chocolates are rightly famous around the world. You find some of the best handmade confections at **Chocolatier Mary,** rue Royale 73 (© **02/217-45-00;** Métro: Parc), a supplier to the royal court; **Neuhaus,** Galerie de la Reine 25 (© **02/502-59-14;** Métro: Centrale); and **Wittamer,** place du Grand-Sablon 12 (© **02/512-37-42;** tram 92, 93, 94), whose rolls, breads, pastries, and cakes have also been winning fans since 1910. **Dandoy,** rue au Beurre 31 (© **02/511-81-76;** Métro: Bourse), is for cookies-and-cakes fans. Try traditional Belgian specialties such as spicy *speculoos* cookies and *pain à grecque.*

Tips **Legal Highs**

The Belgian government has decided to legalize possession of small amounts of cannabis for personal consumption. At press time, the law had yet to be approved by Parliament, so definite information on the permitted amount and the age limit cannot be given, but there is no intention to legalize the sale of the drug. Readers who intend to take advantage of the new law should first check out the details, because penalties for breaking Belgian drug laws can be severe.

la Monnaie (© 02/229-12-11; Métro: De Brouckère), founded in the 17th century, is home to the Opéra National and the Orchestre Symphonique de la Monnaie. The resident ballet company is Belgian choreographer Anna Theresa de Keersmaeker's Group Rosas. The box office is open from Tuesday to Saturday 11am to 6pm; tickets are 300BF to 3,500BF (€7.50 to €87.50, $7 to $81), but 5 minutes before a show, students 25 and under pay only 200BF (€5, $4.65).

The **Palais des Beaux-Arts,** rue Royale 10 (© 02/507-84-66; Métro: Parc), is home to the Belgian National Orchestra. The box office is open from Monday to Saturday 11am to 6pm, with tickets running 400BF to 3,000BF (€10 to €75, $9 to $70). The **Cirque Royal,** rue de l'Enseignement 81 (© 02/218-20-15; Métro: Parc), formerly a real circus, is used for music, opera, and ballet. The box office is open Tuesday to Saturday 11am to 6pm, with tickets at 300BF to 2,500BF (€7.50–€62.50, $7–$58).

Traditional Bruxellois marionette theater is maintained in an old cafe, the **Théâtre Toone VII,** Impasse Schuddeveld, Petite rue des Bouchers 6 (© 02/217-27-53; Métro: Centrale). Often treating sophisticated subjects, puppet master José Géal presents adaptations of classic tales in the local dialect, Brusseleir, and in English, French, Dutch, and German.

THE CLUB & MUSIC SCENE

Brussels isn't as noted for nightlife as some neighboring capitals—dining out being the most popular activity. However, nightlife is alive and well, and if its range is smaller than that of bigger cities like London and Paris, the quality is not.

CABARETS & DANCE CLUBS   Brussels isn't Paris when it comes to putting on Moulin Rouge–type shows, but **Le Show Point,** place Stéphanie 14 (© 02/511-53-64; Métro: Louise), adopts a similar approach. From 10pm until dawn, showgirls, scantily clad or wearing fanciful costumes, strut their stuff in a variety of fetching choreographies. Drinks cost 1,000BF (€25, $23). No cover. Open from Monday to Saturday 10pm till dawn (show begins at 12:30am). A bit of a hoot, **Chez Flo,** rue au Beurre 25 (© 02/513-31-52; Métro: Bourse), is a popular transvestite cabaret and dinner show that is outrageous and comfortable at the same time. Dinner and floor show are 1,475 to 2,950BF (€36.90 to €73.75, $34 to $69); the highest price includes a half-bottle of champagne per person. Show begins at 8pm.

The disco **Le Sparrow,** rue Duquesnoy 16 (© 02/512-66-22; Métro: Centrale), always seems on the verge of going out of style, yet never quite gets there, even if it has lost the wildness of its younger days. A location off the

Grand-Place helps. So does an up-to-date approach to music—techno, house, trip-hop, garage, whatever. It's open from Thursday to Saturday 10pm to dawn, and cover is 320BF (€8, $7), including a drink. Open from Tuesday to Saturday 10pm to 4 or 5am, **Griffin's Night Club,** in the Royal Windsor Hotel, rue Duquesnoy 5 (© **02/505-55-55;** Métro: Centrale), is a fashionable kind of disco with a varied taste in musical styles and periods. There's no cover.

Le Fuse, rue Blaes 208 (© **02/511-97-89;** bus: 20, 48), is the place if only techno will do. On the first Friday of every month, it reinvents itself as the women-only Pussy Lounge and every Sunday as the men-only La Démence. Cover varies: Saturday techno evenings, Pussy Lounge, and La Démence are free 10 to 11pm, thereafter 300BF (€7.50, $7). It's open from Tuesday to Sunday 10pm to 5am.

JAZZ & BLUES   Jazz has taken a hit in recent years, with some of the city's best-loved spots closing down, but enough remain, and new ones have opened, to feel the city's collective foot tapping.

Very chichi and not the friendliest of scenes, the Art Deco bar **L'Archiduc,** rue Antoine Dansaert 6 (© **02/512-06-52;** Métro: Bourse), serves up a sophisticated program of jazz on weekends, usually beginning at 5pm. A stylish crowd lounges about in the blue light and nods appreciatively at the mellow sounds. Sunday jazz cover is 400 to 500BF (€10 to €12.50, $9 to $12). Open daily from 4pm to 4am. **Marcus Mingus Jazz Spot,** Impasse de la Fidelité 10, off rue des Bouchers (© **02/502-02-97;** Métro: Centrale), is a popular jazz cafe that attracts top local performers and an occasional international name. Concerts begin a couple of hours after opening time. There's a jam session on Thursday. Open from Monday to Saturday 7:30pm to 2am. Cover is 200BF (€5, $4.65) Wednesday, 300BF (€7.50, $7) Friday and Saturday.

THE BAR SCENE

Now you're talking. Bars are where Brussels really dwells. The city's cafes and bars run the gamut from Art Nouveau palaces to convivial local watering holes. Don't leave without lingering a few hours in one, savoring Belgium's incredible variety of beers.

Though its name means "Sudden Death," don't worry. You'll probably survive **A la Mort Subite,** rue Montagne-aux-Herbes-Potagères 7 (© **02/513-13-18;** Métro: Centrale), a fine old cafe, which appeals to an eclectic cross-section of society, from little old ladies to bank managers, dancers and musicians from top cultural venues, and students. Decor consists of stained glass, old photographs, paintings, prints, and plain wooden chairs and tables. Specialties are traditional Brussels beers: gueuze, faro, and kriek, and abbey brews such as Chimay, Maredsous, and Grimbergen. The staff's attitude takes a little getting used to, especially if you need more than 3 seconds to decide what you want. If you can be decisive, you have a friend for life—or at any rate, for the evening.

The decor at **Halloween,** rue des Grands-Carmes 10 (© **02/514-12-56;** Métro: Bourse), is enough to give you the creeps: Gargoyles, devils, and other assorted creatures from the darker recesses of the human mind create a disturbing ambience in what is an unforgettable bar inhabited mostly by the young and the trendy. By contrast, **Le Cirio,** rue de la Bourse 18 (© **02/512-13-95;** Métro: Bourse), is a quiet, refined place to sip your drink in surroundings that make the exercise seem worthwhile. Many customers look like they've made their pile across the road at the Stock Exchange and retired here to a state of genteel splendor.

> ### *Tips* Belgian Brews
>
> Be warned: Belgian beers are stronger than their American counterparts—alcohol content can be as high as 12%. Try a rich, dark Trappist ale brewed by monks from Chimay, Orval, Rochefort, Sint-Benedictus, Westmalle, and Westvleteren monasteries. Brussels is well known for its lambic beers, which use naturally occurring yeast for fermentation, are often flavored with fruit, and come in bottles with champagne-type corks. Unlike any other beer, they're more akin to a sweet sparkling wine. Gueuze, a blend of young and aged lambic beers, is one of the least sweet. If you prefer something sweeter, try raspberry-flavored framboise or cherry-flavored kriek. Faro is a low-alcohol beer, sometimes sweetened or lightly spiced.

Shock and horror reverberated through the city in 1999 when the legendary 1904 Art Nouveau tavern, **Le Falstaff,** rue Henri Maus 17–25 (© 02/511-98-77; Métro: Bourse), went bankrupt and closed. Reopened under new management, it has shed its famously vain wait staff and slipped a few notches on the hip scale as a result. If such considerations don't worry you, there's still the same stunning decor, and reasonably priced brasserie food.

Le Fleur en Papier Doré, rue des Alexiens 53 (© 02/511-16-59; Métro: Bourse), calls itself a "temple of surrealism," but old prints, plates, horns, porcelain, and knickknacks on the walls are more evocative of a cozy hunting lodge than a room Magritte might have painted—though he and other surrealists used to hang out here. Now painters, poets, and an after-theater crowd sip beer, munch on snacks, and enjoy the relaxed atmosphere. On weekend nights, there's an accordion player; poetry readings are held upstairs several times a month.

THE GAY & LESBIAN SCENE
Brussels's gay scene is developing and can claim a substantial clutch of clubs and bars as its own. Lesbians have a harder time of it, with venues thin on the ground.

Rue des Riches-Claires and rue du Marché-au-Charbon, south of the Bourse, host some gay and lesbian bars. **Macho 2,** rue du Marché-au-Charbon 108 (© 02/513-56-67; Métro: Bourse), houses a gay men's sauna, pool, steam room, and cafe. It's open from Monday to Thursday noon to 2am, Friday and Saturday noon to 4am, and Sunday noon to midnight, and admission is 450BF (€11.25, $10), 300BF (€7.50, $7) for men under 25 (on Thurs it's 300BF/€7.50/$7 for everyone); students enter for 200BF (€5, $4.65). Le Fuse and Le Sparrow (above) both have gay and lesbian nights.

For more information, contact **Infor Homo,** av. de Roodebeek 57 (© 02/733-10-24; Métro: Diamant), open from Tuesday to Friday 8am to 6pm. Or stop by the gay and lesbian community center, **Telsquels,** rue du Marché-au-Charbon 81 (© 02/512-45-87; Métro: Bourse), open from Saturday to Thursday 5pm to 2am and Friday 8am to 4am.

A DAY TRIP TO WATERLOO
Europe's Gettysburg, the battle that ended Napoléon's empire, was fought 10km (6 miles) south of Brussels, on a stretch of rolling farmland near Waterloo that remains much as it was on June 18, 1815. Before touring it, you should study a 360° panorama mural and see a short audiovisual presentation of the battle,

including scenes from Sergei Bondarchuk's epic movie *Waterloo,* at the **Centre du Visiteur,** route du Lion 252–254, Braine l'Alleud (ⓒ **02/385-19-12**). To survey the battlefield, climb the nearby Butte du Lion (Lion Mound) monument, a pyramid-like hill behind the center.

These three sites are open daily: from April to September 9:30am to 6:30pm; October 9:30am to 5:30pm; from November to February 10:30am to 4pm; from March 10am to 5pm. The combined ticket costs 385BF (€9.65, $9) adults, 315BF (€7.90, $7) students/seniors, 245BF (€6.15, $6) children ages 6 to 12, free for children 5 and under free. A waxworks museum, and the Hougoumont and La Haie-Sainte farms that played a crucial role in the battle, are only a short stroll from the visitor center.

You can fill in details of the battle at the **Wellington Museum,** chaussée de Bruxelles 147, Waterloo (ⓒ **02/354-78-06**), a former inn that was Wellington's headquarters, and where he wrote his victory dispatch. The museum is open from April to September daily 9:30am to 6:30pm; October to March daily 10:30am to 5pm. Admission is 100BF (€2.50, $2.35) adults, 80BF (€2, $1.85) students/seniors, 40BF (€1, 95¢) children ages 6 to 12, free for children under 6.

Getting There   T.E.C. bus "W" leaves on the half hour and the hour from a bus terminal on avenue de Stalingrad, a block south of place Rouppe, in Brussels. It stops at both the museum in Waterloo and the visitor center at Braine l'Alleud. By car, take the N5 south through the Bois de la Cambre and Forêt de Soignes.

2 Bruges & Ghent

Both Flemish cities are showcases of medieval art and architecture, yet each has a distinctive character that makes visiting them complementary. Walking around Bruges is like taking a step back in time. This almost perfectly preserved medieval city, with graceful squares, such as the Markt and the Burg, is a sight in itself. Ghent is austere but more authentic, with a forbidding castle and three-towered cathedral. Some of the northern Renaissance's most outstanding paintings hang in the cities' museums and churches, most notably in Bruges's Church of Our Lady and Groeninge Museum, and Ghent's St. Bavo's Cathedral. Both cities can be easily seen in day trips from Brussels, but for more thorough inspection, you'll want to stay overnight.

BRUGES (BRUGGE)

From its 13th-century origins as a cloth-manufacturing town to its current incarnation as a tourism magnet, Bruges seems to have changed little. As in a fairy tale, swans glide down the winding canals and the stone houses look like they're made of gingerbread. Even though modern glass-fronted stores have taken over the ground floors of ancient buildings, and the swans scatter before tour boats chugging along the canals, Bruges has managed the transition from medieval to modern with remarkable grace. The town seems revitalized rather than crushed by the tremendous influx of tourists. Even more amazing is the warm welcome that the populace extends to its visitors. Tourism is an economic necessity, of course, but the people of Bruges love their beautiful town and take pride in showing it off.

ESSENTIALS

GETTING THERE   By Train   Trains are frequent from Brussels and Antwerp, via Ghent, and from the nearby ferry ports Ostend (Oostende) and Zeebrugge. From Brussels, the trip is just under an hour.

Bruges

Church
Information
Post Office
Railway

BELGIUM
Bruges
Brussels

ATTRACTIONS ●
Begijnhof **14**
Burg **5**
Groeninge Museum **18**
Gruuthuse Museum **17**
Hallen & Belfort **11**
Heilige-Bloedbasiliek **10**
Kantcentrum **2**
Onze-Lieve-Vrouwekerk **16**
Markt **4**
Stadhuis **9**

ACCOMMODATIONS ■
De Markies **13**
Die Swaene **7**
Duc de Bourgogne **8**
Ensor **12**
Fevery **1**
Het Bourgoensche Cruyce **20**
Lucca **3**
Romantik Pandhotel **21**

> ### *Tips* Cultural Capital
>
> Bruges is Cultural Capital of Europe in 2002. For information on the pro-
> gram of exhibitions, concerts, and other events that have been organized
> to celebrate the city's year as the continent's artistic torch-bearer, contact
> **Brugge 2002,** KBC Huis Ter Beurze, 33 Vlamingstraat, 8000 Brugge
> (*C* **050/44-20-02;** fax 050/33-23-90; www.brugge.be).

Look out for BRUGGE, the town's Dutch name, on destination boards at the
station, on Stationsplein, 1.5km (1 mile) south of the city center. For train information, call *C* **050/38-23-82.** From the train station you can take any bus
labeled CENTRUM (center) and get out at the Markt.

By Bus **Eurolines** (*C* **02/203-07-07;** www.eurolines.com) coaches from
London, Paris, Amsterdam, and other cities arrive at the bus station adjoining
Bruges train station.

By Car   The main expressways to Bruges are E40 from Brussels and Ghent,
E17 and then E40 from Antwerp, and E40 from Ostend.

VISITOR INFORMATION   The tourist office, **Toerisme Brugge,** Burg 11,
8000 Brugge (*C* **050/44-86-86;** fax 050/44-86-00; www.brugge.be), dispenses
brochures that outline walking, coach, canal, and horse-drawn cab tours, and
detailed information on many sightseeing attractions and cultural events. The
office is open from April to September Monday to Friday 9:30am to 6:30pm,
Saturday and Sunday 10am to noon and 2 to 6:30pm; from October to March
Monday to Friday 9:30am to 5pm, Saturday and Sunday 9:30am to 1pm and 2
to 5:30pm.

CITY LAYOUT   Bruges has two hearts, in side-by-side monumental squares
the Markt and the Burg. Narrow streets fan out from these squares, and a network of *reien* (canals) threads its way through every section of this small city. The
center is almost encircled by a canal that opens at its southern end into the Minnewater (Lake of Love), filled with swans and bordered by the Begijnhof and a
park.

GETTING AROUND   Street names and traffic boards are in Dutch; some
transportation information is in English, which in any case is widely spoken, so
you should have no problem getting directions.

By Bus   Most city buses (*C* **059/56-53-53**) depart the bus station beside the
train station, or from the big square called 't Zand, west of the Markt. Several
bus routes pass through the Markt.

By Car   Movement by car through the old center has been tightly restricted.
Leave your car at your hotel parking garage, if it has one. You can use one of the
large, prominently signposted underground parking garages around the center
(these get expensive for long stays), or a free parking zone by the train station,
from where you can take a bus or walk into the heart of the city.

By Taxi   There are taxi ranks at the Markt (*C* **050/33-44-44**) and outside the
train station (*C* 050/38-46-60).

By Bike   You can rent a bike from the train station's Baggage Department
(*C* **050/38-58-71**) for 325BF (€8.15, $8) per day, or 250BF (€6.25, $6) with

a train ticket, plus a deposit. Some hotels and stores rent bikes. Biking is a terrific way to get around town and to the nearby village of Damme, by way of beautiful canal-side roads.

WHERE TO STAY

Bruges's hotels fill up fast. Don't arrive without a reservation, particularly in summer. If you do, the tourist office has a reservation service; you can book in advance here and in tourist offices throughout the country. Accommodations are less heavily booked on weekdays than on weekends.

Expensive

Die Swaene ⭐⭐⭐   This small hotel on the beautiful city-center Groenerei canal has been called one of the most romantic in Europe, thanks in part to the care lavished on it by the Hessels family. The comfortable rooms are elegantly and individually furnished; some are air-conditioned. The lounge, from 1779, was formerly the Tailors' Guild Hall, and there's a sauna and indoor swimming pool. There's an annex across the canal. The restaurant, whose specialty is seafood, has won favorable reviews from guests and critics alike.

Steenhouwersdijk 1, 8000 Brugge. ℂ 050/34-27-98. Fax 050/33-66-74. www.dieswaene-hotel.com. 24 units. 6,500–7,950BF (€162.50–€198.75, $151–$185) double; 11,900BF (€297.50, $277) suite. Rates include buffet breakfast. AE, DC, MC, V. Parking 400BF (€10, $9). **Amenities:** Restaurant (French/Belgian), lounge; heated indoor pool; health club & spa; limited room service. *In room:* TV, minibar, hair dryer.

Romantik Pandhotel ⭐⭐⭐   Close to the Markt, this lovely 18th-century mansion surrounded by plane trees is an oasis of tranquility. Though it provides modern conveniences, its exquisite, old-fashioned furnishings lend special grace to comfortable rooms. Guests praise Mrs. Chris Vanhaecke-Dewaele for her hospitality and attention to detail. There's an Internet-connected computer in the lobby which guests can use to send and receive e-mail.

Pandreitje 16, 8000 Brugge. ℂ 050/34-06-66. Fax 050/34-05-56. www.pandhotel.com. 24 units. 5,490–7,490BF (€137.25–€187.25, $128–$174) double; 10,950–14,450BF (€273.75–€361.25, $255–$336) family rooms and suites. Rates include buffet breakfast. AE, DC, MC, V. Parking 400BF (€10, $9). **Amenities:** Restaurant (French/Belgian), lounge; heated indoor pool; health club & spa; limited room service. *In room:* TV, minibar, hair dryer.

Moderate

De Markies ⭐   For those who want to experience Bruges's old-world charm without surrendering modern comforts or their wallet, this is a good bet. Its position on a corner of the big square, 't Zand, makes it convenient for exploring the old center. The spacious rooms are decorated with modern furnishings.

't Zand 5, 8000 Brugge. ℂ 050/34-83-34. Fax 050/34-87-87. 18 units. 3,100–3,500BF (€77.50–€87.50, $72–$81) double. Rates include continental breakfast. AE, MC, V. Limited street parking. **Amenities:** Restaurant (Belgian), lounge; limited room service. *In room:* TV, hair dryer.

Duc de Bourgogne ⭐⭐   This is an elegant small hotel in a 17th-century canal-side building. Fairly large rooms are luxuriously furnished, with antiques scattered throughout. A good restaurant on the ground floor overlooks the canal (see "Where to Dine," below).

Huidenvettersplein 12, 8000 Brugge. ℂ 050/33-20-38. Fax 050/34-40-37. duc.bourgogne@ssi.be. 10 units. 4,100–5,400BF (€102.50–€135, $95–$126) double. Rates include continental breakfast. AE, DC, MC, V. Limited street parking. **Amenities:** Restaurant (Belgian), lounge; limited room service. *In room:* TV, hair dryer.

Het Bourgoensche Cruyce ⭐⭐   Opening onto a lovely inner courtyard, right in the middle of town, this tiny family-run hotel epitomizes the Bruges experience. Rooms are quite large with contemporary furnishings and modern bathrooms. Best of all is the hospitality of the proprietors, who also oversee one of the best restaurants in town on the ground floor (see "Where to Dine," below).

Wollestraat 41–43, 8000 Brugge. ℂ **050/33-79-26.** Fax 050/34-19-68. bour.cruyce@ssi.be. 5 units. 4,700–5,100BF (€117.50–€127.50, $109–$119) double. Rates include continental breakfast. AE, DC, MC, V. Limited street parking. **Amenities:** Restaurant (Belgian), lounge; limited room service. *In room:* TV, hair dryer.

Inexpensive

Ensor 🌫 If you want to open your window and know right away you're in Bruges, get a room overlooking the canal. Though most rooms are relatively large and neatly furnished and all come with bright modern bathrooms, it's the leafy canal view at a budget price that makes this family hotel a standout. The hotel rents bicycles at 250BF (€6.25, $6).

Speelmansrei 10, 8000 Brugge. ℂ **050/34-25-89.** Fax 050/34-20-18. www.ensorhotel.be. 12 units. 2,100–2,600BF (€52.50–€65, $49–$60) double. Rates include buffet breakfast. AE, MC, V. Parking 250BF (€6.25, $6). **Amenities:** none.

Fevery   Centrally located near the Markt, this small family-owned hotel has comfortable rooms that are beautifully furnished in modern style, with a small table and chairs. There's a downstairs bar and breakfast room, and baby-sitting can be arranged.

Collaert Mansionstraat 3, 8000 Brugge. ℂ **050/33-12-69.** Fax 050/33-17-91. www.hotelfevery.be. 11 units. 2,000–2,650BF (€50–€66.25, $47–$62) double. Rates include buffet breakfast. AE, MC, V. Free parking. *In-room:* TV, hair dryer.

Lucca 🌫🌫   Built in the 14th century by a wealthy merchant from Lucca, Italy, the high ceilings and wide halls of this mansion convey a sense of luxury. Guest rooms are in excellent condition and sport pine furnishings. Rooms with bathrooms also have TV. Breakfast is served in a cozy medieval cellar.

Naaldenstraat 30, 8000 Brugge. ℂ **050/34-20-67.** Fax 050/33-34-64. www.hotellucca.be. 17 units, 14 with bathroom. 2,000BF (€50, $47) double without bathroom; 3,100BF (€77.50, $72) double with bathroom. Rates include buffet breakfast. AE, DC, MC, V. Limited street parking. *In room:* TV (some rooms).

WHERE TO DINE

Bruges isn't short of restaurants. You'll be tripping over the places all the time in the city center. Most are okay, even if some have gotten too complacent about the tourists that are their main market. The restaurants featured below aim to make dining a memory of Bruges that you'll still savor back home.

Very Expensive

De Karmeliet 🌫🌫🌫 BELGIAN/FRENCH   In 1996 chef Geert Van Hecke became the first Flemish chef to be awarded three Michelin stars. He has described his award-winning menu as "international cuisine made with local products" that aims to combine French quality with Flemish quantity. The result is outstanding, and the decor is as elegant as the fine cuisine deserves.

Langestraat 19. ℂ **050/33-82-59.** Reservations required. Main courses 775–1,350BF (€19.40–€33.75, $18–$31); fixed-price menus 2,700–3,300BF (€67.50–€82.50, $63–$77). AE, DC, V. Tues–Sat noon–2pm and 7–9:30pm; Sun 7–9:30pm except June–Sept.

De Snippe 🌫🌫 FLEMISH/FRENCH   In the 18th-century mansion hotel of the same name, this restaurant enjoys a well-earned reputation as one of Bruges's finest regional choices. Try the crayfish creations, scampi, or sliced wild duck.

Nieuwe Gentweg 53. ℂ **050/33-70-70.** Reservations required. Main courses 840–1,360BF (€21–€34, $20–$32). AE, DC, MC, V. Tues–Sat noon–2:30pm; daily 7–10pm.

Expensive

Duc de Bourgogne ☆☆ FRENCH   This splendidly aristocratic dining room, overlooking a canal illuminated at night, is a Bruges classic. The menu is lengthy; the fixed-price lunch menu changes daily, and the fixed-price dinner every 2 weeks. Specialties include veal filets in a port sauce.

Huidenvettersplein 12. ℂ 050/33-20-38. Reservations required. Main courses 950–2,000BF (€23.75–€50, $22–$47); fixed-price menus 1,275–2,150BF (€31.90–€53.75, $30–$50). AE, DC, MC, V. Tues 7–9pm; Wed–Sun noon–2pm and 7–9pm.

't Bourgoensche Cruyce ☆☆ CONTINENTAL   You'd be hard put to find a better location, finer food, or a friendlier welcome. The rustic charm of this small dining room overlooking a canal in the town center is only one intimation of the culinary delights in store. Its regional specialties are perfection, and the menu, reflecting the best ingredients available, includes superb seafood dishes.

Wollestraat 41–43. ℂ 050/33-79-26. Reservations required. Main courses 550–850BF (€13.75–€21.25, $13–$20); 3-course fixed-price meal 1,400BF (€35, $33) lunch, 2,200BF (€55, $51) dinner. AE, DC, MC, V. Thurs–Mon noon–2:30pm and 7–9:30pm.

Moderate

Graaf van Vlaanderen ☆☆ STEAK/SALADS   This reasonably priced restaurant in a small hotel near the train station has an extensive menu and a decor that relies heavily on mirrors and plants. The food is equally simple, featuring minute steak (steak so thin it cooks in a minute) and french fries, spaghetti, and salads.

't Zand 19. ℂ 050/33-31-50. Main courses 375–485BF (€9.40–€12.15, $9–$11). AE, DC, MC, V. Fri–Wed 8am–10pm.

Kasteel Minnewater ☆☆ FRENCH/SEAFOOD   Old paintings on the walls, chandeliers, and fine table linen complement this château/restaurant's location close to the Begijnhof, with a garden terrace on the Minnewater (Lake of Love). It exudes an unstuffy charm, and though its prices are edging up, still provides a good deal considering the setting. Its Belgian specialties include sole Ostendaise, North Sea shrimp, and lamb cutlet with potatoes gratinée.

Minnewater 4. ℂ 050/33-42-54. Main courses 350–980BF (€8.75–€24.50, $8–$23); menu gastronomique 1,200BF (€30, $28). V. Daily 11:30am–2:30pm and 6:30–10pm.

Inexpensive

Brasserie Erasmus ☆ FLEMISH   This small, popular restaurant is a great stop after viewing the cathedral and nearby museums. It serves a large variety of dishes, including a very good waterzooï with fish and rabbit in a beer sauce. About 150 different brands of beer are also offered here.

Wollestraat 35. ℂ 050/33-57-81. Main courses 300–750BF (€7.50–€18.75, $7–$17). AE, MC, V. Tues–Sun 11am–midnight.

't Koffieboontje ☆ SEAFOOD/FLEMISH   The bright, modern interior here strikes a noticeably stylish contrast to the often-dark ambience of many Bruges restaurants. An extensive menu is equally cheery, featuring good, but not fancy, seafood specialties like lobster and salmon, and such Belgian staples as mussels, steak, and sole.

Hallestraat 4. ℂ 050/33-80-27. Main courses 350–650BF (€8.75–€16.25, $8–$15). AE, DC, MC, V. Daily noon–11pm.

EXPLORING HISTORIC BRUGES

Walking is by far the best way to see Bruges, whose town center is traffic-free. Wear good walking shoes, as those charming cobblestones can be hard going.

Begin at the **Markt** ✦✦✦, where a sculpture group depicts two Flemish heroes, butcher Jan Breydel and weaver Pieter de Coninck, who led an uprising in 1302 against the wealthy merchants and nobles who dominated the guilds, and went on to an against-all-odds victory over French knights in the Battle of the Golden Spurs later that same year. The 19th-century neo-Gothic Provinciaal Hof houses the West Flanders provincial government.

An array of beautiful buildings, which form a trip through the history of Bruges architecture, stand in the **Burg** ✦✦✦, a square just steps away from the Markt. Here the Count of Flanders, Baldwin "Iron Arm," built a fortified castle (burg), around which grew the village that developed into Bruges.

Belfort (Belfry) and Hallen (Halls) ✦✦
The 13th- to 16th-century Belfry's octagonal tower soars 84m (272 ft.) and holds a magnificent 47-bell carillon. Climb the 366 steps to the Belfry's summit for a panoramic view all the way to the sea. Much of the city's commerce was conducted in the Hallen in past centuries. Today local art dealers use them for exhibitions. The Belfry and Halls are open daily.

Markt 7. ✆ 050/44-87-11. Admission 100BF (€2.50, $2.35) adults, 50BF (€1.25, $1.15) children. Daily 9:30am–5pm.

Stadhuis (Town Hall) ✦✦
Belgium's oldest town hall is an intricate Gothic structure from the late 1300s. Don't miss the upstairs **Gotische Zaal (Gothic Room)** ✦✦✦, and its ornate wooden vaulted ceiling. Admission includes entry to the neighboring Renaissance Zaal van de Brugse Vrije (Hall of the Liberty of Bruges), which has been restored to its 16th-century condition. It has a superb black marble fireplace decorated with an alabaster frieze and topped by a carved oak chimney-piece with statues of Emperor Charles V and his illustrious grandparents: Emperor Maximilian of Austria, Duchess Mary of Burgundy, King Ferdinand II of Aragon, and Queen Isabella I of Castile.

Burg 11. ✆ 050/44-87-11. Admission 60BF (€1.5, $1.40) adults, 20BF (€0.50E, 45¢) children. Daily 9:30am–5pm.

Heilige-Bloedbasiliek (Holy Blood Basilica) ✦✦
Since 1149, this richly decorated Romanesque church has been the repository of a cloth fragment holding what is said to be the blood of Christ, brought to Bruges after the Second Crusade by the count of Flanders. Every Ascension Day, in the Procession of the Holy Blood, the bishop carries the relic through the streets, accompanied by costumed residents acting out Biblical scenes. The relic is kept in the basilica museum inside a rock-crystal vial, which is in a magnificent gold-and-silver reliquary.

Burg 10. ✆ 050/33-67-92. Admission: basilica free; museum, 40BF (€1, 95¢) adults, 20BF (€0.50, 45¢) children. Apr–Sep daily 9:30am–noon and 2–6pm; Oct–Mar daily 10am–noon and 2–4pm (closed Wed afternoon).

Begijnhof ✦✦
Through the centuries, one of the city's most tranquil spots has been the Begijnhof. *Begijns* were religious women, comparable to nuns, who accepted vows of chastity and obedience but drew the line at poverty. Today, the begijns are no more and the Begijnhof is occupied by Benedictine nuns who keep the begijns' traditions alive. Their tree-sprinkled lawn, surrounded by little whitewashed houses, makes a marvelous place to escape from the hurly-burly of the outside world.

Wijngaardstraat. ✆ 050/33-00-11. Courtyard permanently open and free. Admission to Begijn's House 60BF (€1.5, $1.40) adults, 40BF (€1, 90¢) children. Mar–Nov daily 10am–noon and 1:45–5pm (Apr–Sept to 6pm); Dec–Feb Mon, Tues, Fri 11am–noon, Wed–Thurs 2–4pm.

Onze-Lieve-Vrouwekerk (Church of Our Lady) ✸✸
It took 2 centuries (from the 13th until the 15th) to build this church. Its soaring 122m- (396-ft.) spire can be seen from a wide area around the city. Among its many art treasures are a beautiful marble *Madonna and Child* by Michelangelo (one of his few works to be seen outside Italy); a *Crucifixion* by Anthony Van Dyck; and impressive side-by-side bronze tomb sculptures of Charles the Bold, who died in 1477, and Mary of Burgundy, who died in 1482.

Mariastraat. ✆ 050/34-53-14. Admission to church and Madonna and Child altar free; chapel of Charles and Mary, 60BF (€1.5, $1.40) adults, 30BF (€0.75, 70¢) children. Apr–Sept Mon–Sat 10am–noon and 2–5pm (Sat to 4pm), Sun 2–4pm; Oct–Mar Mon–Sat 10am–noon and 2–4pm, Sun 2–4pm.

Groeninge Museum ✸✸✸
One of Belgium's leading fine arts museums, this collection covers painting in the Low Countries from the 15th to the 20th century. Its Flemish Primitives Gallery holds 30 works by such painters as Jan van Eyck (portrait of his wife, Margerita van Eyck), Rogier van der Weyden, Hieronymus Bosch (*The Last Judgment*), and Hans Memling. Works by Magritte and Delvaux are also on display.

Dijver 12. ✆ 050/44-87-11. Admission 250BF (€6.25, $6) adults, 150BF (€3.75, $3.50) children. Daily 9:30am–5pm.

Gruuthuse Museum ✸
In a courtyard next to the Groeninge is an ornate mansion where Flemish nobleman and herb merchant Louis de Gruuthuse lived in the 1400s. It contains thousands of antiques and antiquities, including paintings, sculptures, tapestries, lace, weapons, glassware, and richly carved furniture.

Dijver 17. ✆ 050/44-87-11. Admission 130BF (€3.25, $3.05) adults, 70BF (€1.75, $1.65) children, 250BF (€6.25, $6) families with children under 18. Apr–Sept daily 9:30am–5pm; Oct–Mar Wed–Mon 9:30am–12:30pm and 2–5pm.

Kantcentrum (Lace Center) ✸
A popular attraction, needless to say, is the Lace Center. Bruges lace is famous the world over, and there's no lack of shops offering you the opportunity to take some home. At the center, in the 15th-century Jerusalem Almshouse founded by the Genoese Adornes merchant family, the ancient art of lace making is passed on to a new generation, while you get a firsthand look at artisans making many of the items sold in the city's lace shops. Lace-making demonstrations are in the afternoon.

Peperstraat 3A. ✆ 050/33-00-72. Admission 60BF (€1.5, $1.40) adults, 40BF (€1, 95¢) children. Mon–Fri 10am–noon and 2–6pm; Sat 10am–5pm.

BOAT TRIPS & OTHER ORGANIZED TOURS
If you'd like a trained, knowledgeable guide to accompany you, the tourist office can provide one for 1,500BF (€37.50, $35) for the first 2 hours, 750BF (€18.75, $19) for each additional hour. In July and August, join a daily guided walking tour at 3pm from the tourist office for 150BF (€3.75, $3.50); free for children under 14.

Make sure you take a **canal boat tour** ✸✸✸; it's a fine way to view the city. Departure points are marked with an anchor icon on tourist office maps. Open-top boats operate from March to November daily 10am to 6pm; from December to February on weekends, school holidays, and public holidays 10am to 6pm (unless the canals are frozen). A half-hour cruise costs 190BF (€4.75, $4.40) adults, 95BF (€2.40, $2.20) children ages 4 to 11, free for children 3 and under. Be sure to wear something warm on cold or windy days.

Sightseeing Line (✆ 050/35-50-24) coach tours (50 min.) depart hourly every day from the Markt; first bus at 10am. Last bus at 7pm July to September;

at 6pm March to June and October, November; at 4pm December to February. Fares are 380BF (€9.50, $9) adults, 250BF (€6.25, $6) children ages 6 to 12, free for children 5 and under.

Another lovely way to tour Bruges is by **horse-drawn carriage.** From March to November, they are stationed in the Burg (Wed in the Markt); a 30-minute ride costs 1,000BF (€25, $23) per cab, and 500BF (€12.50, $12) for each additional 15 minutes. Horse-drawn trams are a cheaper, but no less romantic option: **Den Oekden Peerdentram** (© 050/34-41-82) has 30-minute tours from 't Zand, costing 200BF (€5, $4.65) adults, 100BF (€2.50, $2.35) children ages 4 to 11, free for children 3 and under. **Firmin's Paardentram** (© 050/33-61-36) has 45-minute tours from the Markt, costing 350BF (€8.75, $8) adults, 175BF (€4.40, $4.05) children ages 4 to 11, free for children 3 and under.

Ride through Bruges, and get out of town into the West Flanders countryside on a **Quasimodo Back Road Bikes** bicycle tour (© 050/37-04-70). Call ahead to book; meeting and departure point is the Burg. Tour prices run from 650BF (€16.25, $15), 550BF (€13.75, $13) age 26 and under.

BRUGES AFTER DARK

For what's on information, pick up the tourist office's free monthly brochure *Exit* and free monthly newsletter *Agenda Brugge.*

THE PERFORMING ARTS   The **Koninklijke Stadsschouwburg,** Vlamingstraat 29 (© 050/44-86-86), from 1869, is the city's main opera, classical music, theater, and dance venue. Another important venue is the **Joseph Ryelandtzaal,** Achiel Van Ackerplein (© 050/44-86-86). Smaller-scale events, such as recitals, are held at the **Prinsenhof,** Prinsenhof 8 (© 050/34-50-93), formerly the palace of the dukes of Burgundy, and at Sint-Salvators Kathedraal, Sint-Jacobskerk, and other churches.

The **De Korre Theater,** Sint-Jacobsstraat 36 (© 050/34-47-60), has a puppet theater, **Marionettentheater Brugge,** for this sophisticated, centuries-old local art.

A different kind of theater is on the menu at **Brugge Anno 1468,** Celebration Entertainment, Vlamingstraat 84–86 (© 050/34-75-72). In a former Jesuit church, actors re-enact the wedding of Duke Charles the Bold of Burgundy to Margaret of York while customers pile into a medieval banquet. Performances are 2,095BF to 2,695BF (€52.40–€67.40, $49–$63), and take place from April to October, Thursday to Saturday 7:30 to 10pm; from November to March, Saturday 7:30 to 10pm.

CLUBS & DANCING   The **Cactus Club,** Sint-Jacobsstraat 33 (© 050/33-20-14), presents an eclectic concert schedule Friday and Saturday nights. Try **De Vuurmolen,** Kraanplein 5 (© 050/33-00-79), for a raucous dancing-on-the-tables kind of night; it's open nightly from 10pm until the wee hours.

Ma Rica Rokk, 't Zand 7–8 (© 050/33-83-58), a bar with dancing, attracts a young, techno-oriented crowd nightly 7pm to 4am (9pm–6am on weekends). Gays should visit bar/disco **Ravel,** Karel de Stoutelaan 172 (© 050/31-52-74), open Wednesday and Friday to Monday from 10pm.

Vino Vino, Grauwwerkersstraat 15 (© 050/34-51-15), somehow successfully combines Spanish tapas and the blues. For jazz, from bebop to modern, you won't do better than **De Versteende Nacht,** Langestraat 11 (© 050/34-32-93).

BARS & TAVERNS   Traditional cafe **'t Brugs Beertje,** Kemelstraat 5 (© 050/33-96-16), serves more than 300 kinds of beer. **'t Dreupelhuisje,** Kemelstraat 9 (© 050/34-24-21), does something similar with *jenever* (a gin-like spirit), serving up dozens of craft-produced examples of the deadly art. **Gran Kaffee De Passage,** Dweersstraat 26 (© 050/34-02-32), is a quiet and elegant cafe that does inexpensive meals.

GHENT (GENT)

Tourists often look upon this city at the confluence of the Rivers Scheldt and Leie as a poor relation of Bruges, only to be visited if there was time at the end of a trip. That's no longer true. The old town has been spruced up to attract more visitors, and Ghent has never looked so good. Though it's larger and more citified than Bruges, its center has enough cobblestone streets, meandering canals, and antique Flemish architecture to make it nearly as magical as its more famous sister.

Ghent was the seat of the powerful counts of Flanders, whose great castle, built in 1180, still stands as a gloomy reminder of their dominance.

ESSENTIALS

GETTING THERE   By Train   Ghent is 32 minutes from Brussels; trains depart from the capital every half an hour or so. The main train station, **Gent Sint-Pieters,** Maria Hendrikaplein (© 09/222-44-44), is 1.5km (1 mile) south of the city center. Take tram 1, 10, 11, or 12 to the center.

By Bus   The bus station (© 09/210-94-91) adjoins Sint-Pieters train station.

By Car   You get to Ghent on E40 from Brussels, E17 from Antwerp, and E40 from Bruges and Ostend.

VISITOR INFORMATION   Ghent Tourist Office's **Infokantoor** (Inquiry Desk), in the Raadskelder (Cellar) of the Belfry, Botermarkt 17A, 9000 Gent (© 09/266-52-32; fax 09/225-62-88; www.gent.be), is open April to October daily 9:30am to 6:30pm; from November to March 9:30am to 4:30pm. A helpful "Hotels and Restaurants" booklet is available free.

CITY LAYOUT   Korenmarkt is the city's heart. The most important sights, including the Town Hall, St. Bavo's Cathedral, and Belfry, lie within a short walking distance. The River Leie winds through the center and connects with the River Scheldt and canals that lead to a busy port area. **Citadel Park,** home to the Fine Arts Museum, is close to Sint-Pieters train station.

GETTING AROUND   Ghent has an excellent tram and bus system, with many lines converging at Korenmarkt. Walking is the best way to see the city center and experience at a human pace its effortless combination of history and modernity. Beyond the center, use public transportation. For a taxi, call V-Tax (© 09/222-22-22).

WHERE TO STAY

The tourist office makes hotel reservations for a returnable deposit. Considering its popularity, Ghent has fewer hotels than you might expect, and city-center lodgings are often full at peak times, so try to book ahead.

Very Expensive

Sofitel Gent Belfort ✸✸✸   Ghent's top hotel has an enviable position across from the Town Hall, within easy reach of the main tourist attractions. Its big rooms are furnished in a modern, efficient style. The hotel is bright and modern and has been designed to fit in at least partly with its venerable surroundings.

Hoogpoort 63, 9000 Gent. ✆ **09/233-33-31.** Fax 09/233-11-02. h1673hr@accor_hotels.com. 128 units. 8,500–10,150BF (€212.50–€253.75, $198–$236) double; 15,150BF (€378.75, $352) suite. AE, DC, MC, V. Parking 300BF (€7.50, $7). **Amenities:** Restaurant (French/Belgian), bar; health club & sauna; 24-hour room service. *In room:* A/C, TV w/ pay movies, minibar, hair dryer.

Expensive

Novotel Gent Centrum ✹✹✹   This modern hotel near the Town Hall is within easy walking distance of all the city's major sights. A modern edifice has been designed to fit, more or less, into its ancient surroundings. Rooms are nicely furnished and have individual heating controls. The facilities are all you'd expect from a top hotel, and include light, airy public rooms and a garden terrace.

Goudenleeuwplein 5, 9000 Gent. ✆ **800/221-4542** or 09/224-22-30. Fax 09/224-32-95. www.novotel.com. 117 units. 5,150 (€128.75, $120) double; 6,950BF (€173.75, $162) suite. AE, DC, MC, V. Parking 300BF (€7.50, $7). **Amenities:** Restaurant (French/Belgian), bar; heated indoor pool; health club & sauna; 24-hour room service. *In room:* A/C, TV w/ pay movies, minibar, hair dryer.

Moderate

Erasmus ✹✹   Each room is different in this converted 16th-century house, and all are plush, furnished with antiques and knickknacks. Rooms have high oak-beam ceilings, and bathrooms are luxuriously modern. Some rooms have leaded-glass windows, some overlook a carefully manicured inner garden, and some have elaborate marble fireplaces. Breakfast is served in an impressive room that would have pleased the counts of Flanders.

Poel 25, 9000 Gent. ✆ **09/224-21-95.** Fax 09/233-42-41. 11 units. 3,500–4,200BF (€87.50–€105, $81–$98) double. Rates include buffet breakfast. AE, MC, V. Limited street parking. **Amenities:** Bar. *In room:* TV, coffeemaker, hair dryer.

Sint-Jorishof/Cour St-Georges ✹✹✹   In the city center opposite the town hall, this historical treasure has been a quality inn since 1228. If you stay here you'll be in good company, historically speaking: Mary of Burgundy, Charles V, and Napoléon have all spent the night. Try to get a room in the old building rather than in the modern annex across the street. Decor in the pleasant and comfortable rooms is traditional, and rates are low for such a prime site. Book as far ahead as possible.

Botermarkt 2, 9000 Gent. ✆ **09/224-24-24.** Fax 09/224-26-40. www.hotelbel.com/cour-st-georges.htm. 28 units. 2,900–4,600BF (€72.50–€115, $67–$107) double; 4,920BF (€123, $114) suite. Rates include full breakfast. AE, DC, MC, V. Parking 200BF (€5, $4.65). **Amenities:** Restaurant (French/Belgian), 1 bar; limited room service. *In room:* TV, hair dryer.

Inexpensive

Adoma   Convenient to Sint-Pieters train station, this recently renovated hotel has taken a major leap upward in its style and facilities, without sacrificing its reasonable rates. Spacious rooms, brightly decorated with modern furnishings, add up to a comfortable, though not luxurious, experience.

Sint-Denijslaan 19, 9000 Gent. ✆ **09/222-65-50.** Fax 09/245-09-37. 15 units. 2,100–2,300BF (€52.50–€57.50, $49–$53) double. Rates include continental breakfast. MC, V. Free parking. *In room:* TV.

Eden ✹✹   Not far from the center, this is a nice hotel in its price range. The decor is pleasantly modern, and each room has a tapestry on the wall. Though most bathrooms are small, each has at least a toilet and shower, and some rooms have full bathrooms.

Zuidstationstraat 24, 9000 Gent. ✆ **09/223-51-51.** Fax 09/233-34-57. 28 units. 2,500–3,300BF (€62.50–€82.50, $58–$77) double. Rates include buffet breakfast. MC, V. Free parking. *In room:* TV.

Ghent

0 — 1/5 mile
0 — 200 meters

Burgstraat
Lange Steenstraat
Kraanlei Oudburg
Steendam
Dampoortstraat
Groentenmarkt
Belfortstraat
Nieuwport
Schoolkaai
Eastern Station
Hoogpoort
Koorenlei
Graslei
Nieuw-Brug-Kaai
St. Baafsplein
Lousbergskaai
Slachthuisstraat
Volderstraat
Veldstraat
Recolletenlei
Brauwensplein
Ghent
★ Brussels
BELGIUM
Burg Lippensplein
Keizer-Karelstraat
Brabantdam
Ketelvest
Savaanstraat
President Wilsonplein
Ieperstraat
Lindenlei
Nederkouter
Bagattenstraat
Graf van Vlanderenplein
Tweebruggenstraat
Lange Violettenstraat
Brusselsepoortstraat
Nederschede
Jozef Plateaustraat
St. Pietersnieuwstraat
Opper-Schelde
Pres. Fr. D. Rooseveltlaan
KONING ALBERTPARK
Frère Orbanlaan
Zuidstationlaan
St. Lievenspoortstraat
Leie
To Ghent Sint-Pieters Train Station
St. Amandstraat
Overpoortstraat
Hofstraat
Muinkkaai
MUINKPARK
Gust. Callierlaan
Keizersvest
Burgemeester Charles de Kerchovelaan
van Duyseplein
St. Pietersplein
Bernardstraat
Ter Platen
Tentoonstellingslaan
CITADEL PARK
Kunstlaan

ATTRACTIONS ●
Belfort & Lakenhalle **10**
Graslei **5**
Het Gravensteen **2**
Museum voor Schone Kunsten **15**
Museum voor Volkskunde **3**
Sint-Baafskathedraal **11**
Stadhuis **7**
Vrijdagmarkt **4**

ACCOMMODATIONS ■
Adoma **14**
Eden **12**
Erasmus **1**
Novotel Gent Centrum **6**
Sint-Jorishof
Cour St-Georges **9**
Sofitel Gent Belfort **8**

✝ Church
ⓘ Information
✉ Post Office

WHERE TO DINE

Ghent restaurants keep Flemish culinary traditions alive and well, and prices are generally well below those in Brussels.

Expensive

Jan Breydel ⋘ SEAFOOD/FLEMISH   High honors go to this exquisite restaurant on a quaint street near the Gravensteen. Its interior is a garden delight of greenery, white napery, and light woods. Dishes are as light and airy as the setting, with delicate sauces and seasonings enhancing fresh ingredients. Seafood and regional specialties are all superb.

Jan Breydelstraat 10. ⓒ **09/225-62-87.** Main courses 675–1,150BF (€16.90–€28.75, $16–$27). AE, DC, MC, V. Tues–Sat noon–2pm and 7–10pm; Mon 7–10pm.

't Buikske Vol ⋘⋘ BELGIAN/FRENCH   This is one of the city's gems, thanks to chef Peter Vyncke's insistence on the best ingredients, served in a cozy, intimate atmosphere. You can't go wrong with the salmon in butter sauce, but for more adventure, try the doe steak or the grilled pheasant. It isn't open much, but when it is, it's busy.

Kraanlei 17. ⓒ **09/225-18-80.** Reservations recommended on weekends. Main courses 545–925BF (€13.75–€23.75, $13–$22); fixed-price menus 975–1,800BF (€24.40–€45, $23–$42). AE, V. Mon, Tues, Thurs, Fri noon–2pm and 7–9:30pm; Sat 7–9:30pm.

Moderate

Auberge de Fonteyne ⋘ MUSSELS/FLEMISH   It might seem difficult for the food to equal the extravagant good looks of this Art Deco restaurant, but it comes pretty close. Waterzooï is a favorite here, as are heaps of the big Zeeland mussels that Belgium loses its collective cool over.

Gouden Leeuwplein 7. ⓒ **09/221-69-26.** Main courses 360–720BF (€9–€18, $8–$17). MC, V. Mon–Fri noon–2:30pm and 6pm–midnight; Sat noon–2am; Sun noon–2pm.

Graaf van Egmond ⋘⋘ FRENCH/FLEMISH   In a marvelous 13th-century town house on the River Leie, the restaurant serves Flemish dishes such as beef stew and Flemish-style asparagus, along with French creations. If you can get a window seat, you have a spectacular view of the towers of Ghent.

Sint-Michielsplein 21. ⓒ **09/225-07-27.** Main courses 495–725BF (€12.40–€18.15, $12–$17). AE, DC, MC, V. Tues–Sun noon–2pm and 6:30–10pm.

Guido Meerschaut ⋘⋘ SEAFOOD/FLEMISH   Guido owns a fish shop in the Fish Market, so it's no surprise that his restaurant specializes in seafood. Well-prepared fish fresh from the North Sea is served in a simple yet elegant room painted with scenes from Fish Market history. Dover sole, sole Ostendaise, a variety of cod, herring, and other fish dishes predominate, along with North Sea shrimp, oysters, and mussels prepared in a variety of ways.

Kleine Vismarkt 3. ⓒ **09/223-53-49.** Main courses 340–525BF (€8.50–€13.15, $8–$12); fixed-price menu 880BF (€22, $20). AE, DC, MC, V. Tues–Sat noon–2:30pm and 6–10:30pm.

Inexpensive

Amadeus RIBS/CONTINENTAL   Sure, there are vegetarian and fish plates, but all Ghent comes here for the all-you-can-eat spareribs dinner: a slab of perfectly cooked ribs served on a tray with a choice of delicious sauces and a baked potato. If you're up to it, you can order another and another and another. A bottle of wine is on the table, and you pay for what you drink from it. The decor is sumptuously Art Nouveau with burnished wood, mirrors, and colored glass, and the ambience is fun and relaxed.

ALPS   ASPEN

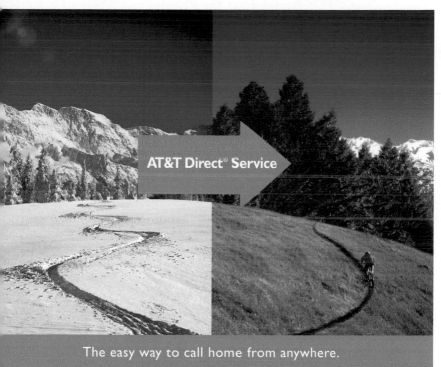

AT&T Direct® Service

The easy way to call home from anywhere.

Global
connection
with the AT&T
Network

AT&T
direct
service

the easy way to call home, take the attached wallet guide.

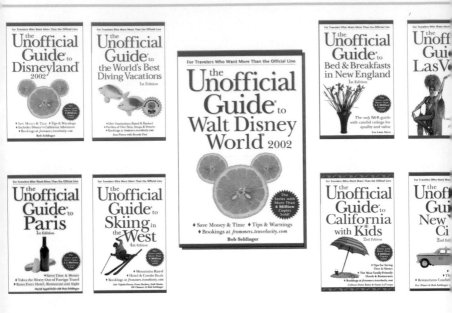

Plotersgracht 8. ✆ **09/225-13-85**. Reservations required. Spareribs dinner 490BF (€12.25, $11). No credit cards. Mon–Thurs 7pm–midnight; Fri–Sat 6pm–midnight; Sun noon–3pm and 6pm–midnight.

EXPLORING HISTORIC GHENT

The city's historic monuments have a solemnity that gives them a somewhat forbidding look. In the case of the Castle of the Counts of Flanders, it was meant to look this way because Ghent's citizens were so often in revolt against their overlord. The "Three Towers of Ghent"—St. Bavo's, the Belfry, and St. Nicholas—form an almost straight line pointing toward St. Michael's Bridge.

A row of gabled **guild houses** 🏠🏠 built along Graslei between the 1200s and 1600s, when the waterway was Ghent's harbor, forms a perfect ensemble of colored facades reflected in the River Leie. To view them as a whole, cross the bridge over the Leie to Korenlei, and walk along the bank past each one. These buildings once housed the craftsmen, tradespeople, and merchants who formed the city's commercial core, and this is an ideal spot to snap a picture that captures the essence of Ghent.

The **Vrijdagmarkt** (Fri Market Square), a popular meeting spot today, was a rallying point in times past. A statue of Jacob Van Arteveld pays tribute to this rebel leader of the 1300s, and its base is adorned by the insignia of some 52 guilds. The square is now a major shopping area and hosts a lively street market every Friday. A short distance away, smaller **Kanonplein** is guarded by a gigantic cannon known as Mad Meg (Dulle Griet), which thundered away in the 1400s in the service of Burgundian armies.

Sint-Baafskathedraal (St. Bavo's Cathedral) 🏠🏠🏠   Within this 14th-century cathedral's plain Gothic exterior lies a splendid baroque interior and some priceless art. A 24-panel altarpiece, *The Adoration of the Mystic Lamb*, completed by Jan van Eyck in 1432, is St. Bavo's showpiece. Other treasures include Rubens's *The Conversion of St. Bavo* (1624), in the Rubens Chapel off the semicircular ambulatory behind the high altar.

Sint-Baafsplein. ✆ **09/225-16-26**. Admission to Cathedral, free; *Mystic Lamb* chapel and Crypt 100BF (€2.50, $2.35) adults (includes audio guide in English), 70BF (€1.75, $1.65) children ages 6–12, free for children 5 and under. Apr–Oct Cathedral daily 8:30am to 6pm; *Mystic Lamb* chapel and Crypt Mon–Sat 10:30am–noon and 2:30–6pm, Sun 2–5pm. Nov–Mar Cathedral daily 8:30am to 5pm; *Mystic Lamb* chapel and Crypt Mon–Sat 10:30am–noon and 2–4pm, Sun 2–5pm.

Belfort (Belfry) and Lakenhalle (Cloth Hall) 🏠🏠   Across the square from St. Bavo's, the Belfry and Cloth Hall form a glorious medieval ensemble. From the 14th-century Belfry, great bells have rung out Ghent's civic pride down through the centuries, and a 54-bell carillon does so today. You can get high in the Belfry with a guide and the aid of an elevator. The 1425 Cloth Hall was the gathering place of medieval wool and cloth merchants.

Sint-Baafsplein. ✆ **09/223-99-22**. Admission 100BF (€2.50, $2.35) adults, 30BF (€0.75, 70¢) children ages 7–16, free for children 6 and under. Tours Tues–Sun hourly 2:10–5:10pm.

Het Gravensteen (Castle of the Counts) 🏠🏠   Crouching like a gray stone lion over the city, grim-looking Gravensteen was clearly designed by the counts of Flanders to send a message to rebellion-inclined Gentenaars: Keep your thoughts to yourself; better still, don't have any at all. Surrounded by the waters of the River Leie, the castle was begun by Count Philip of Alsace, fresh from the Crusades in 1180. If its 2m- (6-ft.-) thick walls, battlements, and turrets failed to intimidate attackers, the counts could turn to the accoutrements of a well-equipped torture chamber, some of which can be seen in a small museum. The view from the ramparts of the central keep, or donjon, is worth the climb. Call ahead if you want a guided tour.

Sint-Veereplein. © **09/225-93-06**. Admission 200BF (€5, $4.65) adults, 50BF (€1.25, $1.15) students/seniors and ages 12–26, free for children 11 and under. Apr–Sept daily 9am–6pm; Oct–Mar daily 9am–5pm.

Stadhuis (Town Hall) 🏚🏚 The Town Hall has what you might call a split personality. A plain Renaissance facade fronts Botermarkt, and a garishly ornamented Gothic side faces Hoogpoort. Work began in 1518 and continued until the 18th century, and the building's many styles reflect the changing tastes of those centuries, and availability or lack of money. In its Pacificatiezaal (Pacification Room), the Pacification of Ghent, signed in 1567, declared the Low Countries' repudiation of Spanish rule and their intention to permit religious freedom.

Botermarkt and Hoogpoort. © **09/223-99-22**. Admission, 100BF (€2.50, $2.35) adults, 30BF (€0.75, 70¢) children. Guided tours, May–Oct Mon–Thurs 2pm from tourist office in Belfry "Raadskelder."

Museum voor Schone Kunsten (Fine Arts Museum) 🏚 This large museum is home to ancient and modern masterpieces, including works by Van der Weyden, Brueghel, Rubens, Van Dyck, and Bosch, along with moderns such as James Ensor and Constant Permeke.

Citadel Park. © **09/222-17-03**. Admission 100BF (€2.50, $2.35) adults, 50BF (€1.25, $1.15) children ages 12–18, free for children 11 and under. Tues–Sun 9:30am–5pm.

Museum voor Volkskunde (Folklore Museum) 🏚 In a group of former almshouses from the 1300s, this museum displays authentic replicas of rooms where crafts skills were practiced around 1900. There is an attached marionette theater (check with the museum for the performance schedule).

Kraanlei 65. © **09/223-13-36**. Admission 100BF (€2.50, $2.35) adults, 50BF (€1.25, $1.15) children ages 14 and under. Tues–Sun 10am–12:30pm and 1:30–5pm.

BOAT RIDES & OTHER ORGANIZED TOURS

A **boat ride** on the canals (© **09/223-88-53**) is an ideal way to see the city's highlights. From April to October, open and covered boats leave every 30 minutes, daily from 10am to 7pm from the Graslei and Korenlei. The narrated trip lasts an hour; the fare is 230BF (€5.75, $5) adults, 120BF (€3, $2.80) children 11 and under.

Qualified guides (© **09/233-07-72**) lead private **walking tours** from the Tourist Office Infokantoor from Monday to Friday at a charge of 1,500BF (€37.50, $35) for the first 2 hours, 600BF (€15, $14) for each additional hour.

Horse-drawn carriages leave from Sint-Baafsplein and Korenlei daily from 10am to 7pm, from Easter to October. A half-hour ride costs 800BF (€20, $19).

GHENT AFTER DARK

THE PERFORMING ARTS Opera is performed in the 19th-century **Vlaamse Opera,** Schouwburgstraat 3 (© **09/225-24-25**), from October to mid-June. For nonpremier performances, tickets are 250 to 2,500BF (€6.25–€62.50, $6–$58). Most performances begin at 8pm, with occasional 3pm matinees. It's best to book ahead.

Ghent venues for puppet shows are the **Museum voor Volkenkunde,** Kraanlei 65 (© **09/223-13-36**); **Taptoe Teater,** Forelstraat 91C (© **09/223-67-58**); and **Magie,** Haspelstraat 39 (© **09/226-42-18**). Performance schedules vary; call ahead or check with the tourist office.

BARS & TAVERNS   In typical Flemish fashion, Ghent's favorite after-dark entertainment is frequenting atmospheric cafes and taverns. You should have a memorable evening in any one you choose. **De Witte Leeuw,** Graslei 6 (℅ **09/ 233-37-33**), has a 17th-century setting and more than 300 varieties of beer. At **Dulle Griet,** Vrijdagmarkt 50 (℅ **09/224-24-55**), you'll be asked to deposit one of your shoes before being given a potent Kwak beer in the too-collectible glass with a wood frame that allows the glass to stand up—you too may need artificial support if you drink too many. The smallest building on Graslei, the former Toll House, is now a nice little tavern called **Het Tolhuisje,** Graslei 10 (℅ **09/ 224-30-90**).

Groentenmarkt, near the Gravensteen, makes for a pretty good pub-crawl in an easily navigable area. Try **Het Waterhuis aan de Bierkant,** Groentenmarkt 9 (℅ **09/225-06-80**), which has more than 100 different Belgian beers, including locally made Stopken. A couple of doors along is **'t Dreupelkot,** Groentenmarkt 12 (℅ **09/224-21-20**), a specialist in deadly little glasses of *jenever* (a stiff spirit similar to gin). Ask owner Paul to recommend one of his 100 or so varieties, or walk straight in and boldly ask for a 64-proof Jonge Hertekamp or a 72-proof Pekèt de Houyeu; if they don't knock you down, you may be up for an 8-year-old 100-proof Filliers Oude Graanjenever or a 104-proof Hoogspanning. Across the tramlines is **'t Galgenhuisje,** Groentenmarkt 5 (℅ **09/233-42-51**), a tiny and, perforce, intimate place popular with students.

3

The Czech Republic

by Hana Mastrini

If you have time to visit only one Eastern European city, the place to go is Prague. The quirky Czech capital, often called a "baroque Disneyland" because of its fairy-tale architecture, is a perfect new cusp-of-the-millennium destination. Here you'll encounter the triumphs and tragedies of the past 10 centuries spiked with the peculiarity of the post-Communist reconstruction.

But Prague isn't the Czech Republic's only draw. Visitors are again flocking to west Bohemia after some of the world's best-known spas were restored to their Victorian-era splendor.

1 Prague & Environs

Almost 75 years after native-son Franz Kafka's death, Prague's mix of the melancholy and the magnificent, the shadows and the fog of everyday life, set against some of Europe's most spectacular architecture, still confounds all who live or visit here. Its tightly wound brick paths have felt the hooves of kings' horses, the jackboots of Hitler's armies, the heaving tracks of Soviet tanks, and the shuffle of students in passive revolt. The 6-centuries-old Charles Bridge is today jammed with visitors and venture capitalists looking for memories or profits from a once-captive city now enjoying yet another renaissance.

A turbulent past and promising future gives Prague its eclectic energy, while its baroque and Renaissance atmosphere provides its gravity.

ESSENTIALS

GETTING THERE **By Plane** Newly rebuilt **Ruzyně Airport** (© **02/2011 1111**) is 19km (12 miles) west of the city center. You'll find a bank for changing money (usually open daily from 7am to 11pm), telephones, and several car-rental offices.

Plenty of taxis line up in front of the airport. CEDAZ operates an airport shuttle bus to náměstí Republiky in central Prague. It leaves the airport daily every 30 minutes from 6am to 9pm and stops near the Náměstí Republiky Metro station (trip time: 30 minutes). Returning, the bus leaves every 30 minutes from 5:30am to 9:30pm. The shuttle costs 90Kč ($2.43). You can also take city bus 119 to the Dejvická Metro station (Line A) for 12Kč (32¢).

By Train Of the two central rail stations, **Hlavní nádražúí,** Wilsonova třída 80, Praha 1 (© **02/2461 4030**), is the grander and more popular; however, it's also seedier. The basement holds a 24-hour luggage-storage counter charging 15Kč (40¢) per bag up to 15kg (33 lbs.) per day (counted from midnight). The nearby lockers aren't secure and should be avoided. Beneath the main hall are surprisingly clean public showers that are a good place to refresh yourself for just 40Kč ($1); they're open from Monday to Friday 6am to 8pm, Saturday 7am to

---

Tips **Traveler's Tip**

Most of Prague's taxi drivers will take advantage of you; getting an hon-
estly metered ride from the airport is close to impossible. The fare from
the airport to Wenceslas Square should be no more than about 600Kč
($16). If you pay only twice this, consider yourself lucky.

7pm, and Sunday 8am to 4pm. On the second floor is the train information
office (marked by a lowercase "i"), open daily from 6am to 10pm. From the
main train station it's a 5-minute stroll to the "top" end of Wenceslas Square or
a 15-minute walk to Old Town Square. Metro Line C connects the station to
the rest of the city. Metro trains depart from the lower level, and city-center no-
transfer tickets, costing 8Kč (21¢), are available at the newsstand near the Metro
entrance. Taxis line up outside the station day and night.

Nádražůí Holešovice, Partyzánská at Vrbenského, Praha 7 (© 02/2422
4200), usually serves trains from Berlin and other points north. Although it isn't
as centrally located as the main station, its more manageable size and position at
the end of Metro Line C make it almost as convenient.

VISITOR INFORMATION   Tourist offices   Those arriving by train at
either of the two primary stations can get information from **AVE Ltd.** (© 02/
2422 3226 or 02/2422 3521; fax 02/5731 2984; www.avetravel.cz), an accommodations agency that also distributes printed information. The two train station offices are open daily from 6am to 10pm.

The city's **Cultural and Information Center,** on the ground floor of the
remodeled Municipal House (Obecní dům), nám. Republiky 5, Praha 1, © 02/
2200 2100; fax 02/2200 2636; Metro: Náměstí Republiky), is a new attempt at
visitor-friendly relations, offering advice, tickets, souvenirs, refreshments, and
rest rooms. It's open daily from 9am to 5pm.

Websites   The city's own information service, PIS, has regularly updated cultural information in English and acts as a gateway to other tourism websites at
www.prague-info.cz. For visa and other consular information, the Foreign
Ministry site is **www.czech.cz.** For the latest local news updates and tourism
info, try the Globe Bookstore's eclectic English-language website **www.globopolis.
com,** the Internet Café supremo Terminal Bar site at **www.terminal.cz** or the
Prague Post at **www.praguepost.cz.** Tom's Travel has developed a fantastic set of
websites, including **www.travel.cz** for general Czech tourist information and
accommodation.

The well-designed **www.czechsite.com** offers tips on getting around, attractions, museums, galleries, and restaurants. You can book your lodging and a
rental car and also find an online message board. The extensive **www.czech-
tourism.com** roundup of links to other websites was pulled together by a Net
veteran who awards a Czech flag icon to sites he considers especially worthy. The
well-organized **www.HotelsCzech.com** shows hotels by the number of stars
bestowed by the government. Click on a hotel to find prices by date and photos
of the buildings and rooms. Reservations aren't instant—after you fill out the
form, an agent is supposed to get back to you within 48 hours.

CITY LAYOUT   The River Vltava bisects Prague. **Staré Město** (Old Town)
and **Nové Město** (New Town) are on the east (right) side of the river, while the

Prague

LETNÁ

Milady Horákové

Korunovační

Veletržní

Milady Horákové

LETENSKÉ SADY

nábř. Edvarda Beneše

HOLEŠOVICE

nábřeží kpt. Jaroše

Farského

Bubenská

VLTAVSKÁ

Bubenské nábřeží

Hlávkův most

Rohanské nábřeží

Vltava

Šermířů most

Čechův most

18

nábř. L. Svobody

Klimentská

Na Františku

U. milosrdných

19

Soukenická

Petrská

Wilsonova

Křižíkova

34

Dušní

Bílkova

Vězeňská

Dlouhá

Revoluční

Kozí

Haštalská

Benediktská

Trutlářská

Na Poříčí

FLORENC

Břehová

nábř.

Pařížská

JOSEFOV

20

21 Široká

STAROMĚSTSKÁ

Kaprova

25

29

30

Old Town Square

32

NÁM. REPUBLIKY

33

Na Florenci

Masaryk Station

Florenc Bus Station

Dvořákovo nábř.

Žatecká

Mánesův most

17. listopadu

Platnéřská

26

Dlouhá

28

27

Celetná

Hybernská

Seifertova

Husitská

31

Karlova

Estates' Theater

35

Karlův most

22

STARÉ MĚSTO

36

Alphonse Mucha Museum

Na Příkopě

Main Train Station

Vltava

MŮSTEK

Jindřišská

37

HLAVNÍ NÁDRAŽÍ

Italská

nábř.

24

Národní

Václavské náměstí

38

Main Post Office

Smetanovo

23

39

Washingtonova

Opletalova

Mezibranská

Wilsonova

most Legií

National Theater

NÁRODNÍ TŘÍDA

40

RIEGROVY SADY

Ostrovní

Myslíkova

Žitná

MUZEUM

41

LOVANSKÝ OSTROV

42

Anglická

Italská

VINOHRADY

Jiráskův most

Resslova

43

Ječná

KARLOVO NÁMĚSTÍ

Dvořák Museum

I.P. PAVLOVA

Rumunská

NÁMĚSTÍ MÍRU

Slezská

Korunní

Masarykovo nábř.

U nemocnice

Na Slupi

NOVÉ MĚSTO

Na bojišti

Sokolská

Legerova

Bělehradská

Londýnská

Belgická

Americká

Francouzská

Palackého most

BOTANICKÁ ZAHRADA

Apolinářská

Ke Karlovu

Záhřebská

Máchova

Koperníkova

Rašínovo nábř.

Svobodova

Albertov

J. Masaryka

VYŠEHRAD

Železniční most

Vnislavova

Sekáninova

0   1/10 mile

0   100 meters

Tips **Reading Maps**

When reading maps or searching for addresses, keep in mind that ulice (abbreviated ul.) means "street," třída means "avenue," náměstí (abbreviated nám.) is a "square" or "plaza," a most is a "bridge," and nábřežûí is a "quay." In Czech, none of these terms are capitalized. In addresses, street numbers follow the street name (like Václavské nám. 25). Each address is followed by a district number, such as Praha 1 (Praha is "Prague" in Czech).

Hradčany (Castle District) and **Malá** Strana (Lesser Town) are on the west (left) bank.

Bridges and squares are the most prominent landmarks. **Charles Bridge,** the oldest and most famous of those spanning the Vltava, is at the epicenter and connects Old Town with Lesser Town and the Castle District. Several important streets radiate from Old Town Square, including fashionable Pařížská to the northwest, historic Celetná to the east, and Melantrichova, connecting to Wenceslas Square (Václavské náměstí) to the southeast. On the west side of Charles Bridge is Mostecká, a 3-block-long connection to Malostranské náměstí, Malá Strana's main square. Hradčany, the Castle District, is just northwest of the square, while a second hill, Petřín, is just southwest.

GETTING AROUND   By Metro, Bus & Tram   Prague's public transport network is a vast—and usually efficient—system of subways, trams, and buses. You can ride a maximum of four stations on the Metro or 15 minutes on a tram or bus, without transfers, for 8Kč (21¢); children 5 and under are free. This is usually enough for trips in the historic districts. Rides of more than four stops on the Metro, or longer tram or bus rides, with unlimited transfers for up to 1 hour after your ticket is validated, cost 12Kč (32¢). You can buy tickets from coin-operated orange machines in Metro stations or at most newsstands marked TABÁK or TRAFIKA. Hold on to your ticket (which you must validate at the orange or yellow stamp clocks in each tram or bus when you get on board or at the entrance to the Metro) during your ride—you'll need it to prove you've paid if a ticket collector asks.

If you're caught without a valid ticket, you have to pay a 400Kč ($11) fine to a plainclothes ticket controller on the spot. Make sure he or she shows you a very official-looking badge. *Warning:* Oversized luggage (larger than carry-on size) requires a single trip ticket for each piece. You may be fined 50Kč ($1.35) for not having tickets for your luggage.

A 1-day pass good for unlimited rides is 70Kč ($1.89); a 3-day pass 200Kč ($5); a 7-day pass 250Kč ($7); and a 15-day pass 280Kč ($8). If you're staying for more than 2 weeks, buy a monthly pass for 420Kč ($11). You can buy the day passes at the "DP" windows at any Metro station, but the photo ID monthly pass is available only at the **Dopravní podnik** (transport department) office on Na bojišti, near the I. P. Pavlova Metro station (© **02/9619 1111**).

Metro trains operate daily from 5am to midnight and run every 3 to 8 minutes. The most convenient stations are Můstek, at the foot of Václavské náměstí (Wenceslas Square); Staroměstská, for Old Town Square and Charles Bridge; and Malostranská, serving Malá Strana and the Castle District.

The electric tram lines run practically everywhere. You never have to hail trams; they make every stop. The most popular, no. 22 (the "tourist tram" or "pickpocket express") and no. 23, run past top sights like the National Theater and Prague Castle. Regular bus and tram service stops at midnight, after which selected routes run reduced schedules, usually only once per hour. If you miss a night connection, expect a long wait for the next.

By Funicular The cog railway makes the scenic run up and down Petřín Hill every 15 minutes or so from 9:15am to 8:45pm, with an intermediate stop at the Nebozízek Restaurant in the middle of the hill overlooking the city. It requires the same 12Kč (32¢) ticket as other public transport. The funicular departs from a small house in the park just above the middle of Újezd in Malá Strana.

By Taxi Avoid taxis! If you must, hail one in the streets or in front of train stations, large hotels, and popular attractions, but be forewarned that many drivers simply gouge tourists. The best fare you can hope for is 17Kč (45¢) per kilometer, but twice or three times that isn't rare. The rates are usually posted on the dashboard, making it too late to haggle once you're in and on your way. Negotiate a price and have it written down before getting in. Better yet, go on foot or by public transport. Somewhat reputable companies with English-speaking dispatchers are **AAA Taxi** (℃ **02/3311 3311** or local phone 1080); **SEDOP** (℃ **02/7172 6666**); and the unfortunately named **ProfiTaxi** (local phone ℃ **1035**). Get a receipt (and send it to the mayor).

By Car   Driving in Prague is not worth the money or effort. The roads are frustrating and slow, and parking is minimal and expensive. If you want to rent a car to explore the environs, try **Europcar,** Pařížůská 28, Praha 1 (℃ **02/2481 0039;** www.europcar.cz; Metro: Staroměstská or at Ruzyně Airport), open daily from 8am to 8pm. Also there's **Hertz,** Karlovo nám. 28, Praha 2 (℃ **02/2223 1010;** www.hertz.com; Metro: Karlovo Náměstí) or Ruzyně Airport or Hotel Diplomat, Praha 6 (Metro: Dejvická). **Budget** is at Ruzyně Airport (℃ **02/2056 0443**) and in the Hotel Inter-Continental, nám. Curieových, Praha 1 (℃ **02/ 2488 9995;** www.budget.cz; Metro: Staroměstská).

Local Czech car-rental companies sometimes offer lower rates than the big international firms. Try **Secco Car,** Přístavní 39, Praha 7 (℃ **02/8387 1031;** www.seccocar.cz; Metro: Nádražůí Holešovice), then tram 12 or 25.

Ⓒ *FAST FACTS:* Prague

American Express For travel arrangements, traveler's checks, currency exchange, and other member services, visit the office at Václavské nám. 56 (Wenceslas Square), Praha 1 (℃ **02/2280 0251;** fax 02/2221 1131; Metro: Můstek), open daily from 9am to 7pm. To report lost or stolen cards, call ℃ 02/2280 0222.

Business Hours Most **banks** are open from Monday to Friday 8am to 6pm. Pubs are usually open daily from 11am to midnight. Most restaurants open for lunch from noon to 3pm and for dinner from 6 to 11pm; only a few stay open later.

Currency The basic unit of currency is the koruna (plural, koruny) or crown, abbreviated Kč. Each koruna is divided into 100 haléřů or hellers. At this writing, $1 = approximately 37Kč and £1 = 55Kč, or 1Kč = 3.70¢.

Currency Exchange Banks generally offer the best exchange rates. Don't hesitate to use a credit or debit card to draw cash for the best rates. **Komerční banka** has three convenient Praha 1 locations with ATMs: Na Příkopě 33, Národní 32, and Václavské nám. 42 (℃ **02/2442 1111** central switchboard for all branches; Metro: Můstek). The exchange offices are open from Monday to Friday 8am to 5pm, but the ATMs are accessible 24 hours.

Doctors/Dentists If you need a doctor or dentist and your condition isn't life-threatening, you can visit the **Polyclinic at Národní,** Národní 9, Praha 1 (℃ **02/2207 5120;** for emergencies, ℃ 02/0600 111; operator 02/140 533; Metro: Můstek), during walk-in hours, from 8am to 5pm. Dr. Stránský is an Ivy League–trained straight-talking physician. For emergency medical aid, call the **Foreigners' Medical Clinic,** Na Homolce Hospital, Roentgenova 2, Praha 5 (℃ **02/5727 2146** or 02/5727 2191 after hours; Metro: Anděl, then bus 167).

Drugstores The most central pharmacy (lékárna) is at Václavské nám. 8, Praha 1 (℃ **02/2422 7532;** Metro: Můstek), open from Monday to Friday 8am to 6pm. The nearest emergency (24-hour) pharmacy is at Palackého 5, Praha 1 (℃ **02/2494 6982;** Metro Můstek). If you're in Praha 2, there's an emergency pharmacy on Belgická 37 (℃ **02/2251 3396;** Metro: Náměstí Míru).

Embassies The **U.S. Embassy** is at Tržůiště 15, Praha 1 (© 02/5753 0663). The **Canadian Embassy** is at Mickiewiczova 6, Praha 6 (© 02/7210 1800). The **U.K. Embassy** is at Thunovská 14, Praha 1 (© 02/5753 0278). The **Australian Honorary Consul** is at Na Ořechovce 38, Praha 6 (© 02/2431 0743). The **Embassy of Ireland** is at Tržůiště 13, Praha 1 (© 02/5753 0061).

Emergencies You can reach Prague's police and fire services by calling © **158** from any phone. For an ambulance, call © **155**.

Hospitals Particularly welcoming to foreigners is **Nemocnice Na Homolce,** Roentgenova 2, Praha 5 (© **02/5727 2146** or 02/5727 2191 after hours; Metro: Anděl, then bus 167). The English-speaking doctors can also make house calls.

Internet Access The best of the cybercafes is **Terminal Bar** at Soukenická 6, 3 blocks from náměstí Republiky on the yellow line (© **02/2187 1115;** Metro: Náměstí Republiky), where about a dozen twin-seater work stations are available for 120Kč ($3.24) an hour for nonmembers (charged by the quarter hour with a 15-minute minimum).

Telephone The country code for the Czech Republic is **420.** The city code for Prague is **2;** use it if you're calling from outside the country. If you're within the Czech Republic but not in Prague, use **02.** If you're calling within Prague, simply leave off the code and dial the regular phone number.

For directory assistance in English, dial (without charge) © **0149.** For information on services and rates, dial 0139. Dial tones are continual high-pitched beeps that sound something like busy signals in America. After dialing a number from a pay phone, you might hear a series of very quick beeps that tell you the line is being connected. Busy signals sound similar to dial tones, only quicker.

There are two kinds of pay phones. One accepts coins and the other operates only with a phone card, available from post offices and news agents in denominations ranging from 50Kč to 500Kč ($1.35 to $14). The minimum cost of a local call is 3Kč (8¢). Coin-op phones, if they work, have displays telling you the minimum price for your call. They don't make change, so don't load more than you have to. You can add more coins as the display gets near zero. The more efficient phone card telephones deduct the price of your call from the card. If you're calling home, get a phone card with plenty of points, as calls run about 42Kč ($1.13) per minute to the United States and 25Kč (45p) to the United Kingdom. Hotels usually add their own surcharge, sometimes as hefty as 100% to 200%, which may surprise you when you're presented with the bill. Ask before placing any call from a hotel. Charging to your phone credit card from a public telephone is often the most economical way to call home.

A fast, convenient way to call home from Europe is via services that bypass the foreign operator and automatically link you to an operator with your long-distance carrier in your home country. The access number in the Czech Republic for **AT&T USA Direct** is © **0042 000 101,** for **MCI World Phone** © **0042 000 112,** and for **Sprint Global One** © **00 420 87187.** Canadians can connect with **Canada Direct** at © **00 420 00151,** and Brits with **BT Direct** at © **00 420 04401** or **Mercury Call UK** at © **00 420 04450.** From a pay phone in the Czech Republic, your local phone card will be debited only for a local call.

Tipping At most restaurants and pubs, locals just round the bill up to the nearest few koruny. When you're given good service at tablecloth places, a 10% tip is proper. Washroom and cloakroom attendants usually demand a couple of koruny, and porters in airports and rail stations usually receive 20Kč (54¢) per bag. Taxi drivers should get about 10%, unless they've already ripped you off.

WHERE TO STAY

Prague's full-service hotels have had to tighten efficiency in the face of heavier international competition, but due to low supply, room rates still top those of many similar or better quality hotels in Western Europe. Pensions with limited services are cheaper than hotels, but compared with similar Western B&Bs, they're pricey. The best budget accommodations are rooms in private homes or apartments.

Expect to pay between 750Kč and 1,500Kč ($20 and $41) for a single and between 1,500Kč and 6,000Kč ($41 and $162) for an apartment for two. All kinds of private housing are offered by several local agencies. The leader now is Prague-based **Tom's Travel,** which offers all types of accommodation at their main site, or you can tap their large pictured database of apartments at www. apartments.cz. Tom's office is near the National Theater at Ostrovní 7 (© **02/ 2499 0983;** fax 02/2499 0999; www.travel.cz; Metro: Národní třída). Another agency, especially for those arriving late by train or air, is **AVE Travel Ltd.** (© **02/2422 3226;** fax 02/5155 6005; www.avetravel.cz). It has outlets at the airport (7am–10pm); at the main train station, Hlavní nádražůí (6am–11pm); and at the north train station, nádražůí Holešovice (7am–9pm).

STARÉ MĚSTO (OLD TOWN) & JOSEFOV
Very Expensive
Four Seasons Hotel ⚜ Prague's most prestigious new residence opened at the dawn of the 21st century. Guests can choose from rooms in the neo-Renaissance house with its towering ceilings, or in the neoclassical wing with suites offering some of the best views of The Bridge and The Castle, or, for an unbelievable splurge, they can book the Presidential Suite in the Baroque wing. The rate of $1,800 to $3,500 per night depends on the season, but no prince or potentate would have a view from a bed as precious as this. The only occasional blight comes from the awful graffiti scrawled on the quay, but the city has vowed to crack down on the vandals.

'Veleslavínova 2a, Praha 1. © 02/2142 7000. Fax 02/2142 6000. www.fourseasons.com. 162 units. Single 8,510–14,060Kč ($230–$380); double 9,065–14,615Kč ($245–$395); from 22,015Kč ($595) suite. Rates exclude breakfast. AE, DC, MC, V. Metro: Staroměstská. **Amenities:** Allegro Restaurant (Northern Italian: Prague's poshest meal), bar and grill. *In room:* A/C, TV, minibar, Internet access, CD player.

Hotel Intercontinental Prague The upper suites have hosted luminaries such as Michael Jackson, Madeleine Albright, and, so legend has it, terrorist Carlos the Jackal. The standard rooms aren't very large but are comfortable, with decent but not exceptional furniture and computer ports. A riverside window might give you a glimpse of the castle or the metronome at the top of Letná park across the river.

Nám. Curieových 43/5, Praha 1. (✆) **02/2488 1111.** Fax 02/2481 0071. www.interconti.com. 364 units. From 10,175Kč ($275) single, 10,545Kč ($285) double, from 13,690Kč ($370) suite. Rates include buffet breakfast. AE, DC, MC, V. Metro: Staroměstská. **Amenities:** Restaurant, fitness center. *In room:* A/C, TV, minibar.

Expensive

Hotel Pařížů ★★   At the edge of náměstí Republiky and across from the Municipal House, the Pařížů provides a rare glimpse back into the gilded First Republic. Each light fixture, etching, and curve at this Art Nouveau landmark recalls the days when Prague was one of the world's richest cities. For a glimpse of the hotel's atmosphere, rent the film *Mission Impossible;* you can see Tom Cruise plotting his revenge from within one of the fine suites. The rooms are some of the most comfortable in Prague, with modern updates of Art Deco accents.

U Obecního domu 1, Praha 1. (✆) **02/2219 5195.** Fax 02/2422 5475. www.hotel-pariz.cz. 93 units. 9,990Kč ($270) double, from 13,320Kč ($360) suite. Rates include breakfast. AE, CB, DC, MC, V. Metro: Nám. Republiky. **Amenities:** Restaurant, sauna, exercise room, concierge, tour-desk, car- rental desk, massage, laundry. *In room:* A/C, TV, dataport, minibar, hair dryer, safe.

Hotel Ungelt *(Kids)*   The Ungelt offers airy, spacious suites. Each contains a living room, a full kitchen, and a bathroom. Rooms have standard-issue beds. One of our editors and his family raved about the location and spaciousness, especially with two small boys in tow.

Štupartská 1, Praha 1. (✆) **02/2482 8686.** Fax 02/2482 8181. www.ungelt.cz. 9 units. 6,330Kč ($171) 1-bedroom suite for 2; 8,640Kč ($233) 2-bedroom suite for 3 or 4. Rates include breakfast. AE, MC, V. Metro: Staroměstská or Nám. Republiky. **Amenities:** Bar. *In room:* TV/VCR, fax, dataport, kitchen, minibar, fridge, coffeemaker, hair dryer, iron.

Moderate

Betlem Club ★★ *(Value)*   This small hotel offers a great location on a cobblestone square across from where Protestant firebrand Jan Hus once preached. Rooms are bland but comfortable and fairly priced. One great advantage is that if you come by car, the Betlem lets you park in front of the hotel, a rarity for this parking-deficient city.

Betlémské nám. 9, Praha 1. (✆) **02/2222 1575.** Fax 02/2222 0580. www.betlemclub.cz. 22 units. 2,700Kč ($73) single, 4,400Kč ($119) double. Rates include breakfast. V, MC. Metro: Národní třída. *In room:* TV, minibar, hair dryer.

Inexpensive

Hotel Cloister Inn/Pension Unitas *(Fun Fact)*   Between Old Town Square and the National Theater, the Cloister Inn/Unitas is half a pension and half a hotel, occupying a building that the secret police converted into holding cells. It sounds ominous, but the Unitas offers sparse, clean accommodations at an unbeatable price for the location. Proprietor Jiří Tlaskal has taken over management from the secret police and the Sisters of Mercy (the nuns, not the rock group). George (in English, as he prefers) has refurbished the hotel side with comfortable Scandinavian furniture. For a bizarre treat in the pension, you might like to stay down in Cell P6, once occupied by dissident playwright Václav Havel, a frequent "guest" of the secret police and now president of the country.

Bartolomějská 9, Praha 1. (✆) **02/232 7700.** Fax 02/232 7709. www.cloister-inn.cz. Pension: 32 units, none with bathroom; 1,020Kč ($28) single, 1,200Kč ($32) double. Hotel: 25 units with ensuite showers; 4,500Kč ($121) double. Both rates include breakfast (a more extensive buffet on the hotel side). AE, MC, V (hotel only). Metro: Národní třída. **Amenities:** Concierge (9am–noon). *In room:* A/C, TV, hair dryer, iron; some rooms only: fax, dataport, minibar, fridge.

NOVÉ MĚSTO (NEW TOWN)
Very Expensive
Hotel Hilton Atrium   The Atrium was built in a galleria style seemingly out of place in Prague, and its rooms are relatively cushy and functional, somewhat like those in a better-than-average U.S. motel. The location of this modern mammoth just outside the central city isn't ideal, but the hotel has overpriced Mercedes ready to take you where you want, and the service is pure Hilton.

Pobřežúní 1, Praha 8. Ⓒ 02/2484 1111. Fax 02/2484 2378. www.hilton.com. 788 units. 8,750Kč ($236) single, 9,139Kč ($247) double; from 9,527Kč ($257) suite. AE, DISC, MC, V. Metro: Florenc. **Amenities:** Restaurant (international); in-door pool; tennis club; health club; casino; concierge; tour-desk; car-rental; limo; massage; laundry. *In room:* A/C; TV; fax and dataport (executive rooms only); kitchen with coffeemaker (suites only); minibar; fridge; hair dryer.

Palace Hotel   Now surpassed in overall comfort by only the Savoy in Hradčany, the Palace is a top, upscale, central-city offering, a block from Wenceslas Square, although if given the choice, the Pařížů has far more character. Rooms are some of the largest and most modern luxury accommodations in Prague. Two rooms for travelers with disabilities are available.

Panská 12, Praha 1. Ⓒ 02/2409 3111. Fax 02/2422 1240. www.palacehotel.cz. 124 units. 9,527Kč ($257) single, 9,990Kč ($270) double; from 11,655Kč ($315) suite. Rates include breakfast. AE, DC, MC, V. Metro: Můstek. **Amenities:** 2 restaurants (international), 2 lounges; concierge with tour-desk; car-rental; limo; room service; baby-sitting; laundry. *In room:* A/C, TV, fax, dataport, minibar, hair dryer, safe.

Expensive
Hotel Esplanade   Located on a side street at the top of the square, the Esplanade began life as a bank and the offices of an Italian insurance company. Rooms are bright and airy, some with standard beds, others with French provincial headboards, and others with extravagant canopies. Number 101 is over-the-top with antique wooden chairs, intricate inlaid tables, and a fascinating embossed wall covering. You might be put off by having the main train station across the street, but an honest-looking doorman says the hotel is safe. Just the same, be advised not to stroll alone in the neighborhood at night.

Washingtonova 19, Praha 1. Ⓒ 800/444-7462 in the U.S.; 800/181-535 in the U.K.; or 02/2421 3696. Fax 02/2422 9306. 74 units. 4,200Kč ($113) single; 5,650Kč ($152) double; from 8,950Kč ($241) suite. Rates include breakfast. AE, MC, V. Metro: Muzeum. **Amenities:** Restaurant (French), cafe, bar; concierge; tour-desk; room service baby-sitting; laundry. *In room:* TV, minibar, safe.

Prague Renaissance   The Renaissance, opened in 1993, has the standard comforts of most top-level business hotels. It's around the corner from the central bank and caters to conferences and entrepreneurs. Suites on the top floor are spacious and have walk-in closets and sizable bathrooms. A few standard rooms are wheelchair accessible.

V Celnici 7, Praha 1. Ⓒ 02/2182 1111. Fax 02/2182 2333. www.renaissancehotel.com. 315 units. 6,800Kč ($200) double; from 11,600Kč ($341) suite. AE, DC, MC, V. Metro: Nám. Republiky. **Amenities:** 3 restaurants (American, Czech, international), cocktail lounge; fitness center with in-door pool; sauna; Jacuzzi; concierge; car-rentals; limo business center with PC and printer; 24-hour room service; baby-sitting; laundry. *In room:* A/C, TV, movies, dataport, minibar, hair dryer, iron, safe.

Moderate
Andante 🏅 (Value   A new addition as the best value choice near Wenceslas Square, the understated Andante is tucked away on a dark side street, about 2 blocks off the top of the square. Despite its less than appealing neighborhood, this is the most comfortable property in the $100 to $125 range. It lacks the character of the old Hotel Evropa, but also the neglect. A close friend of ours, a

young businesswoman, said she enjoyed the stay at the Andante, but she felt safer having her boyfriend with her.

Ve Smečkách 4, Prague 1. ℂ 02/2221 1616. Fax 02/2221 0584. www.andante.cz. 32 units. 3,219Kč ($87) single; 3,922Kč ($106) double; 5,198Kč ($141) suite. Rates, which fluctuate based on the latest crown rate against the German mark because of the crown's volatility, include breakfast. AE, MC, V. Metro: Muzeum. **Amenities:** Restaurant (international), bar; tour-desk; room service. *In room:* TV, minibar; hair dryer, iron available at the reception.

Inexpensive
Hotel Evropa   The statue-studded exterior is still one of the most striking landmarks on Wenceslas Square, but unlike other early 20th-century gems, it hasn't been polished and continues to get duller. Rooms are aging and most don't have baths; some are just plain shabby. The best choice is a room facing the square with a balcony, but all are falling into various levels of disrepair. Still, this is an affordable chance to stay in one of Wenceslas Square's once-grand addresses.

Václavské nám. 25, Praha 1. ℂ 02/2422 8117. Fax 02/2422 4544. 90 units (23 with bathroom). 1,600Kč ($43) single without bathroom, 2,990Kč ($81) single with bathroom; 2,600Kč ($70) double without bathroom, 3,990Kč ($108) double with bathroom; from 4,700Kč ($127) suite. Rates include continental breakfast. AE, MC, V. Metro: Můstek. **Amenities:** Restaurant, cafe. *In room:* None.

MALÁ STRANA (LESSER TOWN)
We used to recommend the **Hotel U červeného lva,** Nerudova 41 (ℂ **02/5753 3832**), as the top pick near the castle, but with ever more tourists walking up Nerudova, the noise has become prohibitive in summer, according to a few Frommer's regulars. Try this place during the colder months when your windows will remain closed.

Expensive
U Krále Karla 🐾   This Castle Hill property does so much to drive home its Renaissance roots, King Charles's heirs should be getting royalties. Replete with period-print open-beamed ceilings and stained-glass windows, the atmosphere is almost Disneyesque in its pretense, but somehow appropriate for this location at the foot of Prague Castle. This is a fun, comfortable choice, with heavy period furniture and colorful angelic accents everywhere.

Nerudova-Úvoz 4, Praha 1. ℂ **02/5753 2869**. Fax 02/5753 3591. www.romantichotels.cz. 19 units. 6,100Kč ($165) single; 6,900Kč ($186) double; 7,900Kč ($213) suite. Rates include breakfast. AE, MC, V. Tram: 22 or 23 to Malostranské nám. **Amenities:** Restaurant (international), cafe, bar; concierge; tour-desk ; car-rental; baby-sitting; laundry. *In room:* TV, minibar, hair dryer.

Moderate
Hotel Kampa   The Kampa has a choice location on a quiet winding alley off the park, giving you quick access to Malá Strana and Charles Bridge. The rooms smack of Communist chintz, but they're comfortable if you don't expect first-class surroundings. The best rooms boast a park view, so request one when booking or checking in.

Všehrdova 16, Praha 1. ℂ **02/5732 0404**. Fax 02/5732 0262. www.euroagentur.cz. 84 units. 3,300Kč ($89) single; 4,460Kč ($121) double. Rates include breakfast. AE, MC, V. Metro: Malostranská, then tram 12, 22, or 23 to Hellichova. **Amenities:** Restaurant (international). *In room:* TV, minibar

HRADČANY
Very Expensive
Hotel Savoy 🐾🐾🐾   Prague's finest new hotel, opened in 1994, belongs to the company that manages the more venerable Palace on Wenceslas Square. Behind

the massive Foreign Ministry and Černín Palace, and a few blocks from the castle, it welcomes you with a tastefully modern lobby. Rooms are richly decorated. Beds are consistently huge, a rejection of the central-European twin-beds-shoved-together look. The pleasant staff provides attention to detail a cut above most hotels here. The Savoy's Hradčany Restaurant is also one of the finest dining rooms in town (see "Where to Dine," below).

Keplerova 6, Praha 1. © 02/2430 2430. Fax 02/2430 2128. www.hotel-savoy.cz. 61 units. From 9,805Kč ($265) double; from 13,505Kč ($365) suite. Rates include breakfast. AE, DC, MC, V. Tram: 22 or 23. **Amenities:** Restaurant (Czech/international), bar; fitness center with sauna; Jacuzzi; concierge; tour-desk; car-rental; business service; laundry; no-smoking floor. *In room:* A/C, TV/VCR, movies, fax, dataport, minibar, hair dryer, safe.

Expensive
Romantik Hotel U raka ✦✦✦ *Finds*   Hidden among the stucco houses and cobblestone streets of a pristine medieval neighborhood on the far side of Prague Castle is this most pleasant surprise. In a ravine below the Foreign Ministry gardens, the old-world farmhouse has been lovingly reconstructed. This is the quietest getaway you could imagine in tightly packed Prague. The rustic rooms have heavy wooden furniture, open-beam ceilings, and exposed brick. The much-sought-after suite has a fireplace and adjoins a private garden, making it a favorite for honeymooners.

Černínská 10, Praha 1. © **02/2051 1100.** Fax 02/2051 0511. www.romantikhotels.com/prag. 6 units. 6,200Kč ($167) double; 7,900Kč ($213) suite. Rates include breakfast. AE, MC, V. Tram: 22 or 23. **Amenities:** Concierge. *In room:* A/C, TV, minibar.

WHERE TO DINE
The true Czech dining experience can be summed up in three native words: *vepřo, knedlo, zelo*—pork, dumplings, cabbage. If that's what you want, try most any *hostinec* (Czech pub). Most offer a hearty *guláš* or pork dish with dumplings and cabbage for about 80Kč to 150Kč ($2 to $4). After you wash it down with Czech beer, you won't care about the taste—or your arteries.

At most restaurants, menu prices include VAT. Tipping has become more commonplace in restaurants where the staff is obviously trying harder; rounding up the bill to about 10% or more is usually adequate.

STARÉ MĚSTO (OLD TOWN) & JOSEFOV
Expensive
Bellevue ✦ INTERNATIONAL/WILD GAME   In short, when in Prague, go to the Bellevue (a great castle view), just a few dozen steps from Charles Bridge on the Old Town side of the river. The intelligent menu boasts choice beef, nouvelle sauces, well-dressed fish and game, delicate pastas, and gorgeous desserts. Poached Norwegian salmon glistens in a light herb sauce, and prawns dance on a piquant garlic glaze. Several wild game options stand out, like fallow deer with oysters and mushrooms. The consistent food and presentation and the pleasant and perfectly timed service make the Bellevue an evening to remember.

Tips **Traveler's Tip**

Beware: Some restaurants gouge customers by charging exorbitant amounts for nuts or other seemingly free premeal snacks left on your table. Ask before you eat.

Smetanovo nábřežúí 18, Praha 1. ℰ 02/2222 1438. Reservations recommended. Main courses 650–990Kč ($17–$26); fixed-price menu 1,200Kč ($32). AE, DC, MC, V. Daily noon–3pm and 5:30–11pm; Sun 11am–3pm (brunch) and 7–11pm. Metro: Staroměstská.

V zátiší ℛ INTERNATIONAL   V zátiší (still life) has a casual elegance, like the living room of a beachfront Mediterranean villa with cushy, upholstered, wrought-iron chairs and plenty of artfully arranged flora. Here, you'll find several fish and game choices, and a scampi that never disappoints. The dessert selections often echo those at the Bellevue, which is run by the same restaurant group, but a flaming vodka-doused Siberian palačinka one snowy Christmas Eve here stands out in our memories. Maybe one of the helpful waiters will convince the chef to do it again.

Liliová 1, Praha 1. ℰ 02/2222 1155. Reservations recommended. Main courses 400–600Kč ($10–$16); fixed-price menu 700–1,500Kč ($19–$40). AE, DC, MC, V. Mon–Sun noon–3pm and 5:30–11pm. Metro: Národní třída.

Moderate

KOGO ℛ *Value* ITALIAN   This ristorante-pizzeria has become very trendy and popular. Fresh and well-prepared specialties are served by an above-average wait-staff in a pleasant atmosphere. The wide selection of salads, pizza, pasta, and main dishes makes you browse through the menu for a while. Beyond the standard and tasty pasta roster, the roasted veal, *vitello al forno a legna*, should be your choice for 250Kč ($7); or try a rare and (for Prague) tasty seafood dish, the mussels in white wine and garlic, *cozze al vino bianco e aglio*, for 290Kč ($8).

Havelská 27, Praha 1. ℰ 02/2421 4543. Reservations recommended. Main courses 130–400Kč ($3.51–$10.81). MC, V. Daily 11am–11pm. Metro: Můstek.

La Provence FRENCH   A French country wine cellar meets urban kitsch. The din of the crowd allows you to discuss private matters without too much eavesdropping. La Provence offers a wide array of French provincial dishes, as well as tangy Italian pastas and the spiciest scampi in Prague. Salads, from Caesar to Niçoise, are large and fresh; they come with fresh French bread and garlic butter. Weekends often attract drag queens from the Banana Cafe upstairs for a funky lip-synch floor show.

Štupartská 9, Praha 1. ℰ 02/232 4801. Reservations recommended. Main courses 300–650Kč ($8–$17). AE, MC, V. Daily 8am–1am. Metro: Nám. Republiky.

Inexpensive

Pivnice Radegast CZECH   The raucous Radegast dishes up Prague's best pub guláš in a single narrow vaulted hall, where the namesake Moravian brew seems to never stop flowing from its taps. Around the corner from a bunch of popular bars, the Radegast attracts a good mix of visitors and locals and a young, upwardly mobile crowd.

Templová 2, Praha 1. ℰ 02/232 8237. Main courses 60–140Kč ($1.62–$3.78). AE, MC, V. Daily 11am–midnight. Metro: Můstek or Nám. Republiky.

Pizzeria Rugantino ℛ *Kids* PIZZA   The wood-fired stoves and handmade dough result in a crisp, delicate crust, a perfect platform for a multitude of cheeses, vegetables, and meats. The Diabolo with fresh garlic bits and very hot chiles goes nicely with a cool iceberg salad and a pull of Krušovice beer. The constant buzz, no-smoking area, and heavy childproof wooden tables make this place a family favorite.

Dušní 4, Praha 1. ℰ 02/231 8172. Individual pizzas 100–300Kč ($2.70–$8). No credit cards. Mon–Sat 10:30am–11pm; Sun 4:30–11pm. Metro: Staroměstská.

U medvídků ♣ CZECH   Bright and noisy, the House at the Little Bears serves a better-than-average vepřo, knedlo, and zelo with two-color cabbage. The pub, on the right after entering, is much cheaper and more lively than the bar to the left. It's a hangout for locals, German tour groups, and foreign journalists in search of the original Czech Budweiser beer, Budvar. In high season, an oompah band plays in the beer wagon.

Na Perštýně 7, Praha 1. ℂ **02/2421 1916.** Main courses 90–250Kč ($2.43–$7). AE, MC, V. Daily 11am–11pm. Metro: Národní třída.

NOVÉ MĚSTO (NEW TOWN)
Moderate
Restaurant U Čížůků ♣ *Value* CZECH   One of the city's first private restaurants, this cozy cellar-cum-hunting lodge on Charles Square can be recognized by the long line of German tour buses outside. The fare is purely Czech, and the massive portions of game, smoked pork, and other meats will stay with you for a while. The traditional *Starý český talíř* (local meat, dumplings, and cabbage) is about as authentic Czech as it gets. The still excellent value earns this pioneer a star.

Karlovo nám. 34, Praha 2. ℂ **02/2223 2257.** Reservations recommended. Main courses 170–320Kč ($5–$9). AE, MC, V. Daily noon–10pm. Metro: Nám. Karlovo.

Inexpensive
Café-Restaurant Louvre CZECH/INTERNATIONAL   This big, breezy upstairs hall, the artsy restaurant formerly known as Gany's, is great for a coffee, an inexpensive pre-theater meal, or an upscale game of pool. A fabulous Art Nouveau interior with huge original chandeliers buzzes with local coffee talk, the shopping crowd, business lunches, and students. Starters include smoked salmon, battered and fried asparagus, and ham au gratin with vegetables. Main dishes range from trout with horseradish to beans with garlic sauce. Avoid the always-overcooked pastas and stick to the basic meats and fish. In the snazzy billiards parlor in back, you can have drinks and light meals served.

Národní třída 20, Praha 1. ℂ **02/2493 0912.** Reservations not accepted. Main courses 100–200Kč ($2.70–$5.40). AE, DC, MC, V. Mon–Fri 8am–11pm; Sat–Sun 9am–11:30pm. Metro: Národní třída.

MALÁ STRANA
Expensive
Ostroff ♣ *Finds* ITALIAN   Nowhere else in Prague is Italian as intricately prepared as at Ostroff, on a river island across from the National Theater. Begin with a flaky vegetable flan laden with goat cheese, a wafer-thin sea bass carpaccio, or oysters on the half shell, then a second plate of tagliatelle in a white bean sauce or a fine minestrone soup. Meat and fresh seafood top the entrees, including a tender grilled rack of lamb or entrecôte on rosemary. The daily three-course lunch special is a great value. Before or after, you can have a cocktail at the riverside bar with a stunning view of the gold-domed National Theater, casting a romantic nighttime glow on the Ostroff and your partner.

Střelecký ostrov 336, Praha 1. ℂ **02/2491 9235.** Reservations recommended. Main courses 500–1,000Kč ($14–$27). AE, MC, V. Open for lunch Mon–Fri noon–2pm, for dinner Mon–Sun 7–10:30pm, for brunch Sun for 590Kč ($16). Tram 22, 23, 9, 6 to Národní divadlo, then walk midway across the bridge (most Legii), down the stairs to the island below (Střelecký ostrov).

U Malířů ♣ FRENCH   The owners of U Malířů have given in to the pressure of competition and are now offering a more affordable chance to sample

Moments Kavárna Society

Cafe life is back in a big way in Prague, now that the Slavia and the Municiple House Kavárna have returned. From dissident blues to high society, these are the places where nonpub Praguers spend their afternoons and evenings, sipping coffee and smoking cigarettes while reading, writing, or talking with friends.

The **Kavárna (Cafe) Slavia** ⚓, Národní at Smetanovo nábřežůí 2, Praha 1 (© **02/2422 0957**; Metro: Národní třída), reopened in 1997, after a half-decade sleep. The restored crisp Art Deco room recalls the Slavia's 100 years as the meeting place for the city's cultural and intellectual crowd. You'll still find a relatively affordable menu of light fare served with the riverfront views of Prague Castle and the National Theater. Open daily 8am to midnight.

The quaint **Café Milena,** Staroměstské nám. 22, Praha 1 (© **02/2163 2609**; Metro: Staroměstská), is managed by the Franz Kafka Society and named for Milena Jesenská, one of the writer's lovers. The draw is a great view of the Orloj, the astronomical clock with the hourly parade of saints on the side of Old Town Square's city hall. It's open daily 10am to 10pm, and no credit cards are accepted.

Of all the beautifully restored spaces in the Municipal House, the **Kavárna Obecní dům** ⚓, nám. Republiky 5, Praha 1 (© **02/2200 2763**; Metro: Náměstí Republiky), might be its most spectacular room. Lofty ceilings, marble accents and tables, an altarlike mantle, huge windows, and period chandeliers provide the awesome setting for coffees, teas, and other drinks, along with pastries and light sandwiches. It's open daily 7:30am to 11pm, and no credit cards are accepted.

A recent addition to the Prague dining scene is **Angel Café**, Opatovická 3, Praha 1 (© **02/290 166**; Metro: Ná rodní třída). In the neighborhood behind the National Theater, this cafe best reflects the light-and-bright 1990s restaurant movement captured by Pret a Manger in Britain. Unlike the cash and carry Pret (in which McDonald's bought a stake last year), you can sit comfortably in the relaxing Angel atmosphere and linger over tasty sandwiches served with quality cheeses, spreads, and vegetables on fresh bread. French pastries highlight the breakfast lineup along with properly stiff espressos. Who needs Starbucks?

the finer attributes of a Parisian kitchen. Surrounded by Romantic-age murals and gorgeously appointed tables in three intimate dining rooms, you're faced with some tough choices. Creamy scallops ragout swim in light vanilla sauce, pike perch comes with truffles, rack of lamb is glazed in tarragon, and an exotic set of quail chicks bathe in Armagnac. If you want a truly Old-World evening of elegant romance and French specialties, U Malířů is finally getting to be worth it.

Maltézské nám. 11, Praha 1. © **02/5753 0000**. Reservations recommended. Main courses 520–1,490Kč ($14–$40); set-price menu 1,190Kč ($32), 1,490Kč ($40), and 2,500Kč ($67). AE, DC, MC, V. Daily noon–10pm. Metro: Malostranská.

Moderate

U modré kachničky CZECH/WILD GAME   The "Blue Duckling," on a narrow Malá Strana street, tries (and often succeeds at) turning traditional Czech food into Bohemian cuisine, but sometimes its results fall short. The menu is loaded with wild game and quirky spins on Czech village favorites. Try the Malá Strana Templar's Sword, a skewer sampling of several domesticated and wild meats.

Nebovidská 6, Praha 1. ℗ **02/5732 0308**. Reservations recommended. Main courses 500–800Kč ($14–$22). No credit cards. Daily noon–4pm and 6:30pm–midnight. Metro: Malostranská.

Inexpensive

Bohemia Bagel *(Value)* BAGELS/SANDWICHES   Bohemia Bagel emerged in 1997 at the base of Petřín Hill as the answer to the lazy-morning bagel-less blues. The roster of golden-brown, hand-rolled, stone-baked bagels is stellar. Plain, cinnamon raisin, garlic, or onion provide a sturdy but tender frame for Scandinavian lox and cream cheese or jalapeño-cheddar cheese (on which you can lop Tex-Mex chili for the Sloppy Bagel). The cushioned wooden booths in an earthy contemporary setting are comfortable.

Újezd 16, Praha 1. ℗ **02/531 002**. bagel@terminal.cz. Bagels and sandwiches 40–150Kč ($1–$4). No credit cards. Mon–Fri 7am–midnight; Sat–Sun 8am–midnight. Tram: 6, 9, 12, 22, or 23 to Újezd.

HRADČANY
Expensive

Hradčany Restaurant 👉 INTERNATIONAL   Matching the crisp English setting of the Savoy Hotel in which it resides, the Hradčany is the most elegant choice this side of the castle. The menu lists a variety of beef, pork, and seafood, including succulent poached salmon and lean sliced veal in herb cream sauce. There are also surprises, such as herb-stuffed tortellini and prawns in avocado mousse. The service sets the standard for Prague, and the new lunch sitting is sure to attract a solid crowd to this jewel beyond the castle gates.

In the Hotel Savoy, Keplerova 8, Praha 1. ℗ **02/2430 2150**. Reservations recommended. Main courses 510–930Kč ($13–$25). AE, MC, V. Daily noon–2pm and 6pm–midnight. Tram: 22 or 23, 2 stops past Prague Castle.

Inexpensive

Saté Indonesian Restaurant INDONESIAN   A lunchtime savior near the castle, the Saté has made quite a business out of its simple Indonesian dishes at simple prices. The unassuming Saté storefront on the same side as the Swedish embassy doesn't scream out to you, so look closely. The pork saté comes in a peanut sauce along with a hearty noodle Migoreng. The casual atmosphere eagerly welcomes foot-dragging visitors in search of a bite and a rest.

Pohořelec 3, Praha 1. ℗ **02/2051 4552**. Main courses 80–200Kč ($2–$5). No credit cards. Daily 11am–10pm. Tram: 22 or 23.

IN VINOHRADY
Moderate

Ponte INTERNATIONAL   Our favorite choice above Wenceslas Square in Vinohrady, Ponte is especially great for shunning the cold of an autumn or winter evening near the roaring fire in the brick cellar dining room. As its name suggests, this place is a bridge between Italian cuisine and other continental foods. Beyond the penne and pesto, you can start with black bean soup with bacon and fresh tomato or tangy spinach salad with chunks of niva cheese. There are several vegetarian and low-calorie, chicken-based selections. Jazz combos play on most nights from a small stage in the corner. Ponte is one of the best values in a full-service restaurant in Prague.

Anglická 15, Praha 2. © **02/2422 1665.** Reservation recommended. Main courses 350–500Kč ($9–$14). AE, MC, V. Daily 11:30am–11pm. Metro: I. P. Pavlova or Nám. Míru.

Inexpensive

Radost FX VEGETARIAN   En vogue and vegetarian, Radost is a clubhouse for hip New Bohemians. The veggie burger is well seasoned and substantial on a grain bun, and the soups, like lentil and onion, are light and full of flavor. The dining area is a dark rec room of upholstered armchairs, chaise lounges, couches from the 1960s, and coffee tables from which you eat.

Bělehradská 120, Praha 2. © **02/2425 4776.** Main courses 100–300Kč ($2.70–$8). MC, V. Daily 11:30am–4am. Metro: I.P. Pavlova.

SEEING THE SIGHTS

In Prague, you'll get the most enjoyment from a slow, aimless wander through the city's heart. Except for the busy main streets, where you may have to dodge traffic, Prague is ideal for walking. Actually, walking is really the only way to explore Prague. Most of the town's oldest areas are walking zones, with motor traffic restricted. If you have the time and energy, absorb the grand architecture of Prague Castle and the Old Town skyline (best from Charles Bridge) at sunrise and then at sunset. You'll see two completely different cities.

SIGHTSEEING SUGGESTIONS FOR FIRST-TIME VISITORS

If You Have 1 Day If you have only 1 day, do what visiting kings and potentates do on a short visit: Walk the **Royal Route** from the top of the Hradčany hill (tram 22 or 23 or a taxi is suggested for the ride up unless you're very fit). Tour **Prague Castle,** and then stroll across Charles Bridge on the way to the winding alleys of **Old Town** (Staré Město).

If You Have 2 Days On day 2, explore the varied sights of **Old Town, Lesser Town** (Malá Strana), and the **Jewish Quarter** (Josefov). Wander and browse through numerous shops and galleries offering the finest Bohemian crystal, porcelain, and modern artwork, as well as top boutiques, cafes, and restaurants.

If You Have 3 Days On day 3, visit the **National Art Gallery** at Šternberk Palace and the **Strahov Monastery** with its ornate libraries, and the **Loreto Palace** with its peculiar artwork.

If You Have 4 or 5 Days Beyond day 3, tour one of the many other museums of galleries. For a great respite from the crowded city, visit the old southern citadel over the Vltava, **Vyšehrad,** where you get a completely different view of the city you've just explored.

PRAGUE CASTLE & CHARLES BRIDGE

Dating from the 14th century, **Charles Bridge** (Karlův most) ⊹, Prague's most celebrated structure, links Prague Castle to Staré Město. For most of its 600 years, the 518m (1,700-ft.) span has been a pedestrian promenade, although for centuries walkers had to share the concourse with horse-drawn vehicles and trolleys. Today, the bridge is filled with hordes walking among folksy artists and street musicians.

The best times to stroll across the bridge are in early morning or around sunset, when the crowds have thinned and the shadows are more mysterious, but you'll be crisscrossing the bridge throughout your stay.

Prague Castle (Pražůský Hrad) *(Moments)* The huge hilltop complex known collectively as Pražůský Hrad encompasses dozens of towers, churches, courtyards, and monuments. A visit could easily take an entire day or more. Still, you can see the top sights—St. Vitus Cathedral, the Royal Palace, St. George's Basilica, the Powder Tower, plus Golden Lane—in the space of a morning or an afternoon.

St. Vitus Cathedral (Chrám sv. Víta), constructed in A.D. 926 as the court church of the Premyslid princes, was named for a wealthy fourth-century Sicilian martyr and has long been the center of Prague's religious and political life. The key part of its Gothic construction took place in the 14th century. In the 18th and 19th centuries, subsequent baroque and neo-Gothic additions were made. In 1997, Pope John Paul II visited Prague to honor the 1,000th anniversary of the death of 10th-century Slavic evangelist St. Vojtěch.

The **Royal Palace (Královský palác)** , in the third courtyard of the castle grounds, served as the residence of kings between the 10th and the 17th centuries. Vaulted Vladislav Hall, the interior's centerpiece, was used for coronations and special occasions. Here Václav Havel was inaugurated president. The adjacent Diet was where the king met with advisers and where the supreme court was held. You'll find a good selection of guidebooks, maps, and other related information at the entrance.

St. George's Basilica (Kostel sv. Jiří), adjacent to the Royal Palace, is Prague's oldest Romanesque structure, dating from the 10th century. It was also Bohemia's first convent, which now houses a museum of historic Czech art.

Golden Lane (Zlatá ulička) is a picturesque, fairy-tale street of tiny 16th-century servants' houses built into the castle fortifications. The houses now contain shops, galleries, and refreshment bars. In 1917, Franz Kafka lived briefly at no. 22.

The **Powder Tower** (Prašná věžů aka Mihulka) forms part of the northern bastion of the castle complex just off the Golden Lane. Originally a gunpowder storehouse and a cannon tower, it was turned into a laboratory for the 17th-century alchemists serving the court of Emperor Rudolf II.

Tickets are sold at the **Prague Castle Information Center** (© **02/2437 3368**), in the second courtyard after passing through the main gate from Hradčanské náměstí. The center also arranges tours in various languages and sells tickets for individual concerts and exhibits.

Hradčanské nám., Hradčany, Praha 1. © **02/2437 3368**. Fax 02/2431 0896. www.hrad.cz. Grounds free. Combination ticket to 4 main attractions (St. Vitus Cathedral, Royal Palace, St. George's Basilica, Powder Tower), 120Kč ($3.24) adults, 60Kč ($1.62) students without guide; 200Kč ($5.40) adults, 140Kč ($3.78) students with English-speaking guide (Tues–Sun 9am–4pm). V. Ticket valid 3 days. Castle daily 9am–5pm (to 4pm Nov–Mar). Metro: Malostranská, then tram 22 or 23, up the hill 2 stops.

THE JEWISH MUSEUM

The Jewish Museum manages all the Jewish landmarks in Josefov, which forms the northwest quarter of Old Town. The museum offers guided package tours as part of a comprehensive admission price, with an English-speaking guide. The package includes the Ceremonial Hall, Old Jewish Cemetery, Pinkas Synagogue, Klaus Synagogue, Maisel Synagogue, and the newly refurbished Spanish Synagogue.

Maisel Synagogue   Maisel Synagogue is used as the exhibition space for the Jewish Museum. Most of Prague's ancient Judaica was destroyed by the Nazis during World War II. Ironically, those same Germans constructed an "exotic museum of an extinct race," thus salvaging thousands of objects, such as the valued Torah covers, books, and silver now displayed at the Maisel Synagogue.

Maiselova 10 (between Široká and Jáchymova 3), Praha 1. ⓒ 02/2481 0099. Fax 02/231 0681. www. jewishmuseum.cz. Admission to museum sites listed above is 280Kč ($8) adults, 200Kč ($5) students. Apr–Oct tours for groups of 10 or more on the hour starting 9am (last tour 5pm). Nov–Apr tours leave whenever enough people gather in same language, open 9am–4:30pm on Sun–Fri. Metro: Staroměstská.

Old-New Synagogue (Staronová synagoga) ⚐   First called the New Synagogue to distinguish it from an even older one that no longer exists, the Old-New Synagogue, built around 1270, is Europe's oldest Jewish house of worship. Jews have prayed here continuously for more than 700 years, carrying on even after a massive 1389 pogrom in Josefov that killed more than 3,000 Jews. It was interrupted only between 1941 and 1945 during the Nazi occupation. The synagogue is also one of Prague's largest Gothic buildings, with vaulted ceilings and Renaissance-era columns.

červená 3. ⓒ 02/2481 0099. Admission 200Kč ($5) adults, 140Kč ($3.78) students. Sun–Thurs 9am–6pm, Fri 9am–5pm. Metro: Staroměstská.

Old Jewish Cemetery (Starý žůidovský hřbitov) ⚐   Dating from the mid-15th century, this is one of Europe's oldest Jewish burial grounds, 1 block from the Old-New Synagogue. Because the local government of the time didn't allow Jews to bury their dead elsewhere, graves were dug deep enough to hold 12 bodies vertically, with each tombstone placed in front of the last. The result is one of the world's most crowded cemeteries: a 1-block area filled with more than 20,000 graves. Among the most famous persons buried here are the celebrated Rabbi Loew (died 1609), who created the legendary Golem (a clay "monster" to protect Prague's Jews). The adjoining Ceremonial Hall at the end of the path is worth a look for the heart-wrenching drawings by children held at the Terezín concentration camp during World War II (see "Day Trips from Prague," below, for more on Terezín).

U Starého hřbitova 3A. ⓒ 02/2481 0099. Fax 02/231 0681. www.jewishmuseum.cz. Admission to all Jewish Museum sites, except Old-New Synagogue, 280Kč ($7.56) adults, 200Kč ($5.40) students. Sun–Fri 9am–6pm. Metro: Staroměstská.

THE NATIONAL GALLERY

The national collection of fine art is grouped for display in the series of venues known collectively as the National Gallery (Národní Galerie). Remember, this term refers to several locations, not just one gallery.

The most extensive collection of classic European works spanning the 14th to 18th centuries is found at the Archbishop's Palace complex in the **Šternberský palác** across from the main gate to Prague Castle. **Veletržní Palace** houses most of the 20th-century art collection, and now also shows the important national revival works from Czech artists of the 19th century. While much of the national collection is shown at **Kinský Palace** on Old Town Square, Gothic pieces may be seen at **St. George's Convent** at Prague Castle, and 19th-century Czech painters and sculptors are shown at **St. Agnes Convent** near the river in Old Town.

Šternberk Palace (Šternberský palác) ⚐   The jewel in the National Gallery crown (also known casually as the European Art Museum), the gallery at Šternberk Palace, adjacent to the main gate of Prague Castle, displays a wide menu of European art throughout the ages. It features 5 centuries of everything from Orthodox icons to Renaissance oils from Dutch masters. Pieces by Rembrandt, El Greco, Goya, and van Dyck are mixed among numerous pieces from Austrian imperial-court painters.

Hradčanské nám. 15, Praha 1. (✆ 02/2051 4599. Admission 90Kč ($2.43) adults, 50Kč ($1.35) students and children. Tues–Sun 10am–6pm. Metro: Malostranská or Hradčanská.

St. Agnes Convent (Klášter sv. Anežůky české)   This complex of early Gothic buildings and churches dates from the 13th century. The convent, tucked in a corner of Staré Město, is scheduled to feature 19th-century Czech painters and sculptors.

U milosrdných 17, Praha 1. (✆ 02/2481 0628. Admission 100Kč ($2.70) adults, 50Kč ($1.35) children. Tues–Sun 10am–6pm. Metro: Staroměstská.

St. George's Convent at Prague Castle (Klášter sv. Jiří na Pražůském hradě)   Dedicated to displaying traditional Czech art, the castle convent is especially packed with Gothic and baroque Bohemian iconography as well as portraits of patron saints. The most famous among the unique collection of Czech Gothic panel paintings are those by the Master of the Hohenfurth Altarpiece and the Master Theodoricus.

Jiřské nám. 33. (✆ 02/5732 0536. Admission 90Kč ($2.43), 50Kč ($1.35) students. Tues–Sun 10am–6pm. Metro: Malostranská or Hradčanská.

Kinský Palace (Palác Kinských) ⭑ (Finds   This rococo palace houses graphic works from the National Gallery collection, including pieces by Georges Braque, André Derain, and other modern masters. Pablo Picasso's 1907 Self-Portrait is here and has virtually been adopted as the National Gallery's logo. The Kinský has been chosen for exhibitions focusing on the glory of baroque in Bohemia, and more special events are expected in the same vein in 2002.

Staroměstské nám., Praha 1. (✆ 02/2481 0758. Admission 80Kč ($2.16), 40Kč ($1.08) students. Tues–Sun 10am–6pm. Metro: Line A to Staroměstská.

Veletržůní Palace   This 1925 constructivist palace, built for trade fairs, holds the bulk of the National Gallery's collection of 20th-century works by Czech and other European artists. Three atrium-lit concourses provide a comfortable setting for some catchy and kitschy Czech sculpture and multimedia works. Alas, the best cubist works from Braque and Picasso, Rodin bronzes, and many other primarily French pieces have been relegated to the second floor. Other displays are devoted to peculiar works from Czech artists that demonstrate how creativity flowed even under the weight of the Iron Curtain.

Veletržůní at Dukelských hrdinů 47, Praha 7. (✆ 02/2430 1111. Admission 150Kč ($4.05), 70Kč ($1.89) students to all 3 floors; first Wed of each month free entrance. Tues–Sun 10am–6pm (Thurs to 9pm). Metro: Vltavská; tram 17.

FAMOUS SQUARES

The most celebrated square, **Old Town Square** (Staroměstské náměstí), is surrounded by baroque buildings and packed with colorful craftspeople, cafes, and entertainers. In ancient days, the site was a major crossroad on central European merchant routes. In its center stands a memorial to Jan Hus, the 15th-century martyr who crusaded against Prague's German-dominated religious and political establishment. Unveiled in 1915, on the 500th anniversary of Hus's execution, the monument's most compelling features are the asymmetry of the composition and the fluidity of the figures.

The **Astronomical Clock** (orloj) at Old Town Hall (Staroměstská radnice) performs a glockenspiel spectacle daily on the hour from 8am to 8pm. Originally constructed in 1410, the clock has long been an important symbol of Prague. Wenceslas Square (Václavské náměstí), a former horse market, has thrice been the focal point of riots and revolutions—in 1918, 1968, and 1989.

MORE ATTRACTIONS

Bertramka (Museum W. A. Mozart)   Mozart loved Prague, and when he visited he often stayed with the family that owned this villa, the Dušeks. Now a museum, the villa contains displays that include his written work and harpsichord. There's also a lock of Mozart's hair, encased in a cube of glass. Much of the Bertramka villa was destroyed by fire in the 1870s, but Mozart's rooms, where he finished composing *Don Giovanni*, miraculously remained untouched.

Mozartova 169, Praha 5. ℂ 02/5731 8461. Admission 90Kč ($2.43) adults, 50Kč ($1.35) students. Daily 9:30am–6pm. Metro: Anděl, then tram 2, 6, 7, 9, 10.

Estates' Theater (Stavovské divadlo) ⚘   The theater was completed in 1783 by the wealthy Count F. A. Nostitz. There are no daily tours, but tickets for performances—and the chance to sit in one of the elegant private boxes—are usually available. Tour events are occasionally scheduled, and you can arrange individual tours by calling the city heritage group of Pražůská informační služůba (PIS) at ℂ **02/2448 2562.**

Ovocný trh 1, Praha 1. ℂ 02/2421 5001. Metro: Můstek.

Strahov Monastery and Library (Strahovský klášter a knihovna) ⚘   The second-oldest monastery in Prague, Strahov was founded high above Malá Strana in 1143 by Vladislav II. It's still home to Premonstratensian monks, a scholarly order closely related to the Jesuits, and their dormitories and refectory are off-limits. What draws visitors are the monastery's ornate libraries, holding more than 125,000 volumes.

Strahovské nádvoří 1, Praha 1. ℂ 02/2051 6671. Admission 50Kč ($1.35) adults, 30Kč (81¢) students. Tues–Sun 9am–noon and 1–5pm. Metro: Malostranská, then tram 22 or 23.

Cathedral of St. Nicholas (Chrám sv. Mikuláše)   This church is critically regarded as one of the best examples of the high baroque north of the Alps. K. I. Dienzenhofer's 1711 design was augmented by his son Kryštof's 80m (260-ft.) dome, which has dominated the Malá Strana skyline since its completion in 1752. Prague's smog has played havoc with the building's exterior, but its gilded interior is stunning. Gold-capped marble-veneered columns frame altars packed with statuary and frescoes.

Malostranské nám., Praha 1. ℂ02/5753 4215. Free admission. Daily 9am–5pm. Metro: Malostranská, then tram 22, 23, or 12 one stop to Malostranské nám.

⌒ Fun Fact   Mozart in Prague

Mozart staged the premier of *Don Giovanni* at the Estates' Theater in 1787 because he felt the conservative patrons in Vienna didn't appreciate him or his passionate and often shocking work. "Praguers understand me," Mozart was quoted as saying. Czech director Miloš Forman returned to his native country to film his Oscar-winning *Amadeus,* shooting the scenes of Mozart in Prague with perfect authenticity at the Estates'.

⌒Value A Special Group Tour

If you're traveling in a large group and really want a unique sightseeing experience, why not rent your own classic trolley? With enough people, it really can be affordable, thanks to the **Historic Tram Tour** (Elektrické dráhy DP), Patočkova 4, Praha 6 (© and fax **02/312 3349**).

If you send a fax with details 1 day ahead, the city transport department can arrange a private tour using one of the century-old wooden trams that once traveled on regular lines through Prague. Up to 24 people can fit in one car, which sports wooden-planked floors, cast-iron conductor's levers, and the "ching-ching" of a proper tram bell.

It costs 3,255Kč ($88) per hour. Up to 60 people can fit into a double car for 4,305Kč ($116) per hour. You can also order a cold smorgasbord with coffee, beer, champagne, a waiter to serve, and an accordion player. You can choose the route the tram takes—the no. 22 route is best.

PARKS & GARDENS

From **Vyšehrad**, Soběslavova 1 (© **02/2491 9939;** tram 3 from Karlovo náměstí to Výtoň south of New Town), legend has it that Princess Libuše looked out over the Vltava valley toward the present-day Prague Castle and predicted the founding of a great state and capital city. Vyšehrad was the seat of the first Czech kings of the Premyslid dynasty before the dawn of this millennium. Today within the confines of the citadel, lush lawns and gardens are crisscrossed by dozens of paths, leading to historic buildings and cemeteries. From here you'll see one of the city's most panoramic views.

The **Royal Garden** (Královská zahrada) at Prague Castle, once the site of the sovereigns' vineyards, was founded in 1534. Dotted with lemon trees and surrounded by 16th-, 17th-, and 18th-century buildings, the park is laid out with abundant shrubbery and fountains. Enter from U Prašného mostu street north of the castle complex.

In Hradčany, the castle's **Garden on the Ramparts** (Zahrada na Valech), below the castle with a gorgeous city panorama, was reopened in spring 1995 after being thoroughly refurbished. The park is open from Tuesday to Sunday 9am to 5pm. Part of the excitement of Waldstein (Wallenstein) Gardens (Valdštejnská zahrada) is its location, behind a 9m (30-ft.) wall on the back streets of Malá Strana. Inside, elegant, leafy gravel paths, dotted by classical bronze statues and gurgling fountains, fan out in every direction Recently refurbished sections include the Ledeburská, the Small and Great Palffyovská, Kolowratská, and Small Furstenberská gardens. All the gardens are open from Tuesday to Sunday 9am to 5pm (or to sundown during winter months).

THE SHOPPING SCENE

Czech porcelain, glass, and cheap but well-constructed clothing draw hoards of day-trippers from Germany. Private retailers have been allowed to operate here only since late 1989, but many top international retailers have already arrived. Shops lining the main route from Old Town Square to Charles Bridge are also great for browsing. For clothing, porcelain, jewelry, garnets, and glass, stroll around Wenceslas Square and Na Příkopě, connecting Wenceslas Square with náměstí Republiky.

For glass and crystal, try **Moser,** at Na Příkopě 12, Praha 1 (℃ **02/2421 1293;** Metro: Můstek), or at Malé nám, 11, Praha 1 (℃ **02/2161 1520;** Metro: Můstek). The Moser family began selling Bohemia's finest crystal in central Prague in 1857, drawing customers from around the world. The dark-wood showroom upstairs at Na Příkopě is worth a look if only to get the feeling of Prague at its most elegant. Open from Monday to Friday 9am to 8pm, Saturday and Sunday 10am to 6pm at Na Příkopě; from Monday to Friday 10am to 7pm, Saturday and Sunday 10am–6pm at Malé nám.

At **Cristallino,** Celetná 12 (Metro: Náměstí Republiky; ℃ **02/2422 5173**), you'll find a good selection of stemware and vases in traditional designs. The shop's central location belies its excellent prices. At **Pavilon,** Vinohradská 50 (℃ **02/2209 7111;** Metro: Jiřího z Poděbrad), a new four-tiered galleria, fashion junkies can browse in stores from Lacoste to Diesel, have their hair done, buy some Timberlands, and bring home a hunk of bacon from the Belgian Butcher.

Havelský trh (Havel's Market), Havelská ulice, Praha 1 (Metro: Můstek), is on a short street running perpendicular to Melantrichova, the main route connecting Staroměstské náměstí with Václavské náměstí. This open-air market (named well before a Havel became president) features dozens of private vendors selling seasonal home-grown fruits and vegetables. Other goods, including flowers and cheese, are also for sale. Since this place is designed primarily for locals, the prices are exceedingly low by Western European standards. The market is open from Monday to Friday 7am to 6pm.

PRAGUE AFTER DARK

Prague's nightlife has changed completely since the Velvet Revolution—for the better if you plan to go clubbing, for the worse if you hope to sample the city's classical offerings. Still, seeing *Don Giovanni* in the Estates' Theater, where Mozart first premiered it, is worth the admission. Ticket prices, while low by Western standards, have become prohibitively high for the average Czech. However, you'll find the exact reverse in the rock and jazz scene. Dozens of clubs have opened, and world-class bands are finally adding Prague to their European tours.

Turn to the *Prague Post* (www.praguepost.cz) for listings of cultural events and nightlife around the city; it's available at most newsstands in Old Town and Malá Strana.

Once in Prague, you can buy tickets at theater box offices or from any one of dozens of agencies throughout the city center. Large, centrally located agencies (take the Metro to Můstek for all) are **Prague Tourist Center,** Rytířská 12, Praha 1 (℃ **02/2421 2209**), open daily from 9am to 8pm; **Bohemia Ticket International,** Na Příkopě 16, Praha 1 (℃ **02/2421 5031**); and **Čedok,** Na Příkopě 18, Praha 1 (℃ **02/2481 1870**).

THE PERFORMING ARTS

Although there's plenty of music year-round, the symphonies and orchestras all come to life during the **Prague Spring Music Festival,** a 3-week series of concerts featuring the country's top performers, as well as noted guest conductors, soloists, and visiting symphony orchestras. The festival runs from May 12 to June 2. Tickets for concerts are 250Kč to 2,000Kč ($7 to $54).

The **Czech Philharmonic** and **Prague Symphony** orchestras usually perform at the **Rudolfinum,** náměstí Jana Palacha, Praha 1 (℃ **02/2489 3352;** Metro:

Staroměstská). The Czech Philharmonic is the traditional voice of the country's national pride, often playing works by Dvořák and Smetana; the Prague Symphony ventures into more eclectic territory. Tickets are 100Kč to 600Kč ($2.70 to $16). Ticket orders and purchases can be made in advance (and you are advised to book well in advance) through the agency **TICKETPRO,** Salvátorská 10, 110 00 Praha 1, Czech Republic (℃ **02/2481 4020;** fax 02/2481 4021; orders@ticketpro.cz). All major credit cards are accepted.

Any remaining tickets are sold at the venues of the performances, which have various opening hours, but usually few seats remain within a month of the festival.

In a city full of spectacularly beautiful theaters, the massive pale-green **Estates' Theater** (Stavovské divadlo), Ovocný trh 1, Praha 1 (℃ **02/2421 5001;** Metro: Můstek), is one of the most awesome. Built in 1783 and site of the premiere of Mozart's *Don Giovanni* (conducted by the composer), the theater now hosts many of the classic productions of European opera and drama. Simultaneous English translation, transmitted via headphone, is available for most plays. Tickets cost 200Kč to 1,000Kč ($5 to $27).

Lavishly constructed in the late-Renaissance style of northern Italy, the gold-crowned **Národní divadlo** (National Theater), Národní třída 2, Praha 1 (℃ **02/ 2490 1448;** Metro: Národní třída), overlooking the Vltava River, is one of Prague's most recognizable landmarks. Completed in 1881, the theater was built to nurture the Czech National Revival—a grassroots movement to replace the dominant German culture with that of native Czechs. Today, classic productions are staged here in a larger setting than at the Estates' Theater, but with about the same ticket prices.

The **National Theater Ballet** performs at the National Theater. The troupe has seen most of its top talent go west since 1989, but it still puts on a good show. Some critics have complained that Prague's top company has been performing virtually the same dances for many years and they're in serious need of refocusing. Choreographer Libor Vaculík has responded with humorous and quirky stagings of off-the-wall ballets such as *Some Like It Hot* and *Psycho.* Tickets cost 200Kč to 600Kč ($5 to $16).

Laterna Magika, Národní třída 4, Praha 1 (℃ **02/2491 4129;** Metro: Národní třída), is a performance-art show in the new wing of the National Theater. The multimedia show, which combines live theater with film and dance, was once considered on the radical edge. The shows are not for those easily offended by nudity. Tickets are 400Kč ($11).

THE CLUB & MUSIC SCENE

Prague's club and music scene is limited but lively. Local acts still have a garage-band sound, but are adding more sophisticated numbers to their gigs. Many venerable jazz groups who toiled in the underground caverns are finding a new audience in visitors who stumble on their clubs. It is no longer a huge shock to see well-known Western bands playing a couple of sets in Prague.

ROCK & DANCE CLUBS   At **Club Lávka,** Novotného lávka 1, Praha 1 (℃ **02/2222 2156;** www.lavka.cz; Metro: Staroměstská), straightforward dance hits attract one of Prague's best-looking young crowds. Because of its location next to the Staré Město foot of Charles Bridge, it also attracts a lot of less well-dressed visitors. Open 24 hours, the club is one of the nicest in town, offering a large bar, a good dance floor, and fantastic outdoor seating in warm months.

Cover is 50Kč to 100Kč ($1.35 to $2.70); ticket prices for performing art are 120Kč to 150Kč ($3.24 to $4).

Popular with a mixed gay and model crowd, **Radost FX,** Bělehradská 120, Praha 2 (© **02/2425 4776;** Metro: I. P. Pavlova), is built in the American mold. In a subterranean labyrinth of nooks and crannies there's a pulsating techno-heavy dance floor with good sight lines for wallflowers. Radost, extremely stylish and self-consciously urban, is open daily from 9pm to 5am. Cover is usually 50Kč ($1.35). No credit cards.

One of the city's most unusual venues, **Roxy Experimental Space,** Dlouhá 33, Praha 1 (© **02/2482 6296;** Metro: Náměstí Republiky), is a subterranean theater with a wraparound balcony overlooking a concrete dance floor. The club is ultra-downscale and extremely popular on Friday and Saturday. Persian rugs and lanterns soften the atmosphere but don't improve the lousy acoustics. Acid jazz, funk, techno, ambient, and other danceable tunes attract an artsy crowd after midnight. Several live acts are also featured here each month, with music ranging from Czech acid jazz to Allanah Miles. Cafe open from noon to midnight; club 8pm to 6am. Cover is 100Kč to 150Kč ($2.70 to $4). No credit cards.

JAZZ CLUBS Upscale by Czech standards, **AghaRTA Jazz Centrum,** Krakovská 5, Praha 1 (© **02/2221 1275;** Metro: Muzeum), regularly features some of the best music in town, from standard acoustic trios to Dixieland, funk, and fusion. Hot Line, the house band led by AghaRTA part-owner and drummer extraordinaire Michael Hejuna, regularly takes the stage with its keyboard-and-sax Crusaders-like sound. Bands usually begin at 9pm. The club is open from Monday to Friday 5pm to 1am and Saturday and Sunday 7pm to 1am. Cover is 60Kč to 100Kč ($1.62 to $2.70). **Reduta Jazz Club,** Národní třída 20, Praha 1 (© **02/2491 2246;** Metro: Národní třída), is a smoky subterranean room that looks exactly like a jazz cellar should. An adventurous booking policy, which even included a saxophone gig with a U.S. president in 1994, means that different bands play almost every night. Music usually starts around 9pm. It's open from 9pm to midnight. Cover is usually 100Kč ($2.70).

PUBS & BARS

You'll experience true Czech entertainment in only one kind of place—a smoky local pub serving some of the world's best beer. Remember to put a cardboard coaster in front of you to show you want a mug, and never wave for service, as the typically surly waiter will just ignore you.

Originally a brewery dating from 1459, **U Fleků,** Křemencova 11, Praha 2 (© **02/2491 5118;** Metro: Národní třída), is Prague's most famous beer hall, and one of the only pubs that still brews its own beer. This huge place has a myriad of timber-lined rooms and a large, loud courtyard where an oompah band performs. Tourists come here by the busload, so U Fleků is avoided by disparaging locals who don't like its German atmosphere anyway. The pub's special dark beer is excellent, however, and not available anywhere else. Open daily from 9am to 11pm.

One of the most famous Czech pubs, **U Zlatého tygra,** Husova 17, Praha 1 (© **02/2222 1111;** Metro: Staroměstská or Můstek), was a favorite watering hole of President Havel and the late writer Bohumil Hrabal. Particularly smoky, and not especially tourist friendly, At the Golden Tiger is a one-stop education in Czech culture. Havel and President Bill Clinton joined Hrabal for a traditional Czech pub evening here during Clinton's 1994 visit to Prague. It's open daily 3pm to 10:30pm.

GAY & LESBIAN BARS

For details on the gay and lesbian community, call the **SOHO Infocentrum** (✆ **02/2422 0327**). For a stylish place to dance, try Radost FX (see "The Club & Music Scene," above). Lesbians should look for the sharply decorated **"A" Klub,** Milíčova 32, Praha 3 (no phone; Metro: Flora, then tram 9), covered with the works of female artists and sporting cushy chairs and couches. Fridays are for women only. Men are allowed on other nights, but only in the company of a woman. There's dancing and relaxed chat here daily from 6pm to 6am. Cover is 25Kč (67¢).

Just across the tracks from the main train station is **Fire Club,** Seifertova 3, Praha 3 (no phone; Metro: Hlavní nádražůí), which used to be the rock palace Alterna Komotovka. It has been transformed into a wild pink-and-neon cavern serving an almost exclusively gay crowd, offering original Budweiser on tap. It's open Friday and Saturday from 9pm until whenever they feel like closing. There's no cover.

CASINOS

Prague has many casinos, most offering blackjack, roulette, and slot machines. House rules are usually similar to those in Las Vegas. **Casino Palais Savarin,** Na Příkopě 10 (✆ **02/2422 1636;** Metro: Můstek), occupying a former rococo palace, is the city's most beautiful game room, open daily from 1pm to 4am. Other recommended casinos are **Casino de France,** in the Hotel Hilton Atrium, Pobřežůní 1 (✆ **02/2484 1111**), open daily from 2pm to 6am; and **Casino U Nováků,** Vodičkova 30 (✆ **02/2422 2098**), open daily from 1pm to 5am. For both, a picture ID or passport is necessary.

DAY TRIPS FROM PRAGUE

KARLŠTEJN CASTLE   By far the most popular day trip from Prague, this medieval castle, 30km (18 miles) southwest of Prague, which has been restored to its original state, was built by Charles IV in the 14th century to safeguard the crown jewels of the Holy Roman Empire. As you approach, little can prepare you for your first view: a spectacular Disneylike castle perched high on a hill, surrounded by lush forests and vineyards. The Holy Rood Chapel is famous for the more than 2,000 precious and semiprecious inlaid gems that adorn its walls, and the Chapel of St. Catherine was King Karel IV's private oratory. Both the Audience Hall and the Imperial Bedroom are impressive, despite being stripped of their original furnishings. To see the Holy Rood Chapel you need to make a reservation (✆ **02/7400 8154;** www.pusc.cz).

Admission for shorter tour is 200Kč ($5) adults and 100Kč ($2.70) students, the longer one with the Holy Rood Chapel is 600Kč ($16) adults, 200Kč ($5) students. It's open daily: May, June, and September from 9am to noon and 12:30 to 5pm; July and August 9am to noon and 12:30 to 6pm; from April and October 9am to noon and 12:30 to 4pm; from January to March 9am to noon and 1pm to 3pm; closed during November and December.

Getting There   The best way to get to Karlštejn is by **train** (there's no bus service). Most trains leave from Prague's Smíchov Station (Metro: Smíchovské nádražůí) hourly throughout the day (trip time: 30 minutes). One-way second-class fare is 30Kč (81¢). You can also **drive:** Leave Prague on Highway 4 southwest in the direction of Strakonice and take the Karlštejn cutoff, following the signs (and traffic!).

KUTNÁ HORA   A medieval town that grew fantastically rich from the silver deposits beneath it, Kutná Hora, 72km (45 miles) east of Prague, is probably the second most popular day trip. The town's ancient heart is quite decayed, making it hard to believe that this was once the second most important city in Bohemia.

Getting There   The **bus** departs from the terminal at Prague's Žželivského Metro station (trip time: 1 hour). To **drive,** take Vinohradská ulice, due east from behind the National Museum at the top of Wenceslas Square, straight to Kutná Hora (trip time: 50 minutes). Once out of the city, the road turns into Highway 333.

Exploring Kutná Hora   The main attraction is the enormous **St. Barbara's Cathedral** (Chrám sv. Barbory) at the southwestern edge of town. Soaring arches, dozens of spires, and intricate designs raise expectations that the interior will be just as impressive—and you won't be disappointed. On entering (from the side, not the front), you see several richly decorated frescoes full of symbols denoting the town's two main industries of mining and minting. Admission is 40Kč ($1) for adults and 20Kč (54¢) for children. It's open from Tuesday to Sunday 9am to noon and 1 to 5pm.

When you leave the cathedral, head down the statue-lined Barborská street, where you'll pass the early **Baroque Jesuit College** built in the late 17th century.

A visit to Kutná Hora isn't complete without a trip to **Kostnice** ⊕, the "bone church." It's located just down the road in Sedlec; those who don't want to walk can board a local bus on Masarykova street; the fare is 8Kč (21¢). From the outside, Kostnice looks like most other Gothic churches. But once you go inside, you know this is no ordinary church. All the decorations, designed by František Rint, are made from human bones. The bones came from victims of the 14th-century plague and the 15th-century Hussite wars; both events left thousands of dead, who were buried in mass graves. As the area developed, the bones were uncovered, and the local monks came up with this idea. Admission is a bargain at 30Kč (81¢) for adults and 15Kč (40¢) for children. It's open July and August, daily 9am to noon and 1 to 5pm; the rest of the year, from Tuesday to Sunday 9am to noon and 1 to 4pm.

TEREZÍN (THERESIENSTADT)   The name Terezín (Theresienstadt in German) occupies a unique place in the atrocious history of Nazism. This former Austro-Hungarian imperial fortress, turned into a concentration camp, 50km (30 miles) northwest of Prague, witnessed no gas chambers, mass machine-gun executions, or medical testing; it was used instead as a transit camp. About 140,000 people passed though Terezín's gates; many died here, and more than half ended up at the death camps of Auschwitz and Treblinka.

Terezín stands as a memorial to the dead and a monument to human depravity. Once inside the **Major Fortress,** you'll immediately be struck by its drab, plain streets. Just off the main square lies the **Museum of the Ghetto,** chronicling the rise of Nazism and life in the camp. English pamphlets describing the exhibits are provided. Admission is 50Kč ($1.35) adults and 25Kč (67¢) children. A ticket to enter both the Major and Minor Fortresses is 100Kč ($2.70) adults and 50Kč ($1.35) children. The Major Fortress is open daily from 9am to 6pm. The **Minor Fortress** is about a 10-minute walk from the Major Fortress over the Ohře River. Just in front of the fortress's main entrance is the **National Cemetery** (Národní hřbitov), where the bodies exhumed from the mass graves were buried. As you enter the main gate, the sign above it, Arbeit Macht Frei

(Work Sets One Free), sets a gloomy tone. You can walk through the prison barracks, execution grounds, workshops, and isolation cells.

Getting There   Terezín is a 45-minute **drive** from Prague, on the main highway north towards Berlin via Dresden. Six **buses** leave daily from Florenc Bus Station (trip time: 1 hour). The Prague-based **AHARON travel** (© **02/3535 3589;** www.aharontravel.cz) organizes an 8-hour tour with guides that includes lunch, a documentary, and transportation, well worth 1,300Kč ($35). The bus leaves daily (except Saturdays and Jewish holidays) at 9:30am from Maiselova 15 and only from April to September.

2 West Bohemia & the Spas

The Czech Republic is composed of two regions: Bohemia and Moravia. The larger of the two, Bohemia, occupying the central and western areas of the country, has for centuries been caught between a rock (Germany) and a hard place (Austria). Bohemia was almost always in the center of regional conflicts, both secular and religious. But the area also flourished, as witnessed by the wealth of castles that dot the countryside and the spa towns that were once the playgrounds of the rich and famous.

Although Bohemia is historically undivided, there are clear-cut distinctions in the region's geography that make going from town to town easier if you "cut" Bohemia into sections. This section focuses on west Bohemia, home to the country's spa towns. It's also one of the few regions in the Czech Republic where a full-blown tourist infrastructure is already in place. Its main towns—Karlovy Vary (Carlsbad), Mariánské Lázně (Marienbad), and to a lesser extent Plzeň and Cheb, offer a wide array of accommodations, restaurants, and services. All are constantly being reconstructed, renovated, and restored.

A relatively inexpensive network of trains and buses covers the region. West Bohemia is generally rougher terrain, so only serious cyclists should consider touring the area on two wheels. For those with a car, the highways can range from top-notch, such as the newly built Prague-Plzeň motorway, to an asphalt horror ride such as the Prague–Karlovy Vary route. Roads generally are much slower than in Western Europe, so leave yourself plenty of time. Gas stations are constantly springing up, so stops for food and fuel are rarely hard to come by. *Note:* If you drive the D-5 (Prague-Plzeň) and D-1 (Prague-Brno) highways, your car must display the country's highway sticker; these stickers, which you can buy at most gas stations and border crossings, cost 800Kč ($22) and save you from being hassled by the police.

Most towns are distant enough that you should drive from one to another. However, if you'd rather stay in one place and make day trips, we'd recommend staying in Karlovy Vary. The **Kur-Info Vřídelní kolonáda,** 360 01 Karlovy Vary (© **017/322 9312** or 017/322 4097; fax 017/246 67), can provide information on bus trips to Mariánské Lázně and other regional sights.

KARLOVY VARY (CARLSBAD)

The discovery of Karlovy Vary (Carlsbad), 120km (75 miles) west of Prague, by Charles IV reads something like a 14th-century episode of *The Beverly Hillbillies.* According to local lore, the king was out huntin' for some food when up from the ground came a-bubblin' water (though discovered by his dogs, not an errant gunshot). Knowing a good thing when he saw it, Charles immediately set to work building a small castle, naming the town that evolved around it Karlovy

Western & Southern Bohemia

Vary (Charles's Boiling Place). The first spa buildings were built in 1522, and before long, notables like Albrecht of Wallenstein, Russian Czar Peter the Great, and later Bach, Beethoven, Freud, and Marx all came to take the waters.

After World War II, East Bloc travelers (following in the footsteps of Marx, no doubt) discovered the town, and Karlovy Vary became a destination for the proletariat. On doctors' orders, most workers enjoyed regular stays of 2 or 3 weeks, letting the mineral waters ranging from 43.5°C to 72°C (110.3°F to 161.6°F) from the town's 12 spas heal their tired and broken bodies. Even now, most spa guests are there by doctor's prescription.

Most of the 40-plus years of communist neglect have been erased by a barrage of renovators who are restoring almost all the spa's former glory. Gone is the statue of Yuri Gagarin, the Russian cosmonaut. Gone are almost all the crumbling building facades that used to line both sides of the river. In their place now stand restored buildings, cherubs, caryatids, and more.

Tips **Warning to Drivers**

Be warned that Highway E-48 from Prague to Karlovy Vary is a popular route for reckless drivers heading to and from the capital. Please take extra care when driving.

Nearly 100,000 people travel annually to the spa resort to sip, bathe, and frolic. Most enjoy the 13th spring, which features a hearty herb-and-mineral liqueur called Becherovka, more than the nonalcoholic versions available at the 12 previous springs. Czechs will tell you that all have medicinal benefits.

ESSENTIALS

GETTING THERE   By Train   At all costs, avoid the train from Prague (trip time: over 4 hours). If you're arriving from another direction, Karlovy Vary's main train station is connected to the town center by bus 11.

By Bus   Frequent express buses make the trip from Prague's Florenc station, platform 21 or 22, to Karlovy Vary (trip time: 2½ hours). Take a 10-minute walk or local bus 4 into Karlovy Vary's center. Note that you must have a ticket to board local transport. You can buy tickets for 8Kč (21¢) at the main station stop, or, if you have no change, the kiosk across the street sells tickets during regular business hours.

By Car   The drive from Prague isn't difficult but can be at times a little hair-raising (trip time: 2 hours). Take Highway E-48 from the western end of the city and follow it straight through to Karlovy Vary. This two-lane highway widens in a few spots to let cars pass slow-moving vehicles on hills.

VISITOR INFORMATION   Kuri-Info, inside the Vřídelní kolonáda (*C* **017/322 9312** or 017/322 4097; fax 017/246 67), is open from Monday to Friday 7am to 5pm, Saturday and Sunday 9am to 3pm. It provides accommodation services, arranges guided tours and spa treatments, and sells tickets for some events. Be sure to pick up the *Cultural Calendar,* a comprehensive collection of events with a small map of the town center.

There are also two privately run **Info-Centrum** booths: one in the train station and the other in a parking lot at the base of Jana Palacha ulice. Both give away free maps and a brochure of current cultural listings and events called *Promenáda.* Info-Centrum also books accommodations in private rooms and sells tours.

SPECIAL EVENTS   The **Karlovy Vary International Film Festival** is one of the few places to see and be seen. Each summer (usually at the beginning of July), film stars and celebrities take part in one of Europe's biggest film festivals. Six venues screen more than 200 films during the 14-day festival.

Karlovy Vary plays host to several other events, including a **jazz festival** and **beer Olympiad** in May, the **Dvořák singing contest** in June, the **Summer Music Festival** in August, and the **Dvořák Autumn Music Festival** in September and October.

For more information on any of the festivals, contact **Kuri-Info,** Vřídelní kolonáda, 360–01 Karlovy Vary (*C* **017/322 9312** or 017/322 4097; fax 017/ 246 67).

WHERE TO STAY

Private rooms used to be the best places to stay in Karlovy Vary for both quality and price, but this is changing as more and more hotels renovate and raise standards—as well as prices. Private accommodations can still provide better value, but it takes a little extra work. If you want to arrange a room, try the Info-Centrum (see "Visitor Information," above). Expect to pay about 500Kč to 1,000Kč ($14 to $27) for a single and 750Kč to 1,200Kč ($20 to $32) for a double.

Some of the town's major spa hotels accommodate only those who are paying for complete treatment, unless their occupancy rates are particularly low. The hotels I've listed below accept guests for stays of any length.

Grandhotel Pupp ✹✹✹   Well known as one of Karlovy Vary's best hotels, the Pupp, built in 1701, is also one of Europe's oldest. While the hotel's public areas ooze with splendor and charm, rooms aren't as consistently enchanting. The best tend to be on the upper floors facing the town center. The Grand Restaurant serves up as grand a dining room as you'll find, with the food to match (see "Where to Dine," below).

Mírové nám. 2, 360 91, Karlovy Vary. ℂ 017/310 9111. Fax 017/322 4032. www.pupp.cz. 110 units. 6,845Kč ($185) double deluxe; from 8,880Kč ($240) suites. Breakfast not included (extra $11). The crown rate for the room fluctuates, based on the latest crown rate against the dollar on the day the payment is made because of the crown's volatility. The dollar rate remains constant for those paying in dollars or by credit card. A daily exchange rate is used for those who want to pay in crowns by cash. AE, DC, MC, V. **Amenities:** 2 restaurants (international), 3 bars, cafe; golf; Roman spa with sauna, Jacuzzi, massages; salon; concierge; room service; car-rental; casino; laundry; dry cleaning. In room: A/C (partly), TV/ w/ movies, minibar, hair dryer, safe.

Hotel Dvořák   Now part of the Vienna International hotel/resort chain, the Dvořák has improved immensely over the past year or two, especially in terms of service. If the Pupp has the history and elegance, the Dvořák has the facilities. However, the rooms, for all their creature comforts, lack the Old World charm found at the Pupp.

Nová Louka 11, 360 21, Karlovy Vary. ℂ **017/310 2111.** Fax 017/310 2119. www.hotel-dvorak.cz. 79 units. 2,465Kč ($66) double; 3,451Kč ($93) suite. A daily exchange rate is used for those who want to pay in crowns by cash. Breakfast is included. AE, DC, MC, V. **Amenities:** Restaurant (Czech/intional), bar, cafe; indoor pool; fitness center; spa treatment with health packages; sauna. In room: A/C, TV w/ movies, minibar, hair dryer.

Hotel Embassy ✹✹   This family-run hotel manages to evoke the turn of the last century with elegantly decorated rooms. Although smaller than those at the Pupp, they're impeccably furnished and overlook the river. The restaurant downstairs is where a lot of movers and shakers at the Karlovy Vary film festival get away from the glitz and get down to business.

Nová Louka 21, 360 01, Karlovy Vary. ℂ **017/322 1161-5.** Fax 017/322 3146. 20 units. 2,788 3,468Kč ($75–$93) double; 3,060–3,740Kč ($82–$101) double deluxe; 3,570–4,420Kč ($97–$119) suite. Rates include breakfast. AE, V. Free parking. **Amenities:** Restaurant (Czech/internaitonal). In room: TV, minibar, hair dryer, safe.

Parkhotel Pupp ✹   This is how the other half live at the Pupp. At four stars, this wing of the Grandhotel Pupp is housed within the same complex as its five-star cousin, but a world apart in terms of frills—and price. Still, rooms are large and all the same facilities are available; the views are just less spectacular.

Mírové nám. 2, 360 91, Karlovy Vary. ℂ **017/310 9111.** Fax 017/322 4032. www.pupp.cz. 255 units. 3,700Kč ($100) double; 4,810Kč ($130) apt. Breakfast $8 extra. AE, DC, MC, V. **Amenities:** Restaurant (international), bar, cafe' golf; fitness center; spa treatment; concierge;salon; room service; car-rental; casino; laundry. In room: TV, minibar, hair dryer.

WHERE TO DINE

Embassy CZECH/CONTINENTAL   On the ground floor of the hotel of
the same name, the Embassy restaurant has a pub on one side and an intimate
dining room on the other. On a cold day the pub works wonders with a hearty
goulash soup. But the dining is the Embassy's hidden treasure. What the meals
lack in flair, they more than make up for with sophistication. Salmon with a delicate dill sauce or beef with a surprisingly light mushroom sauce are two of the
choices that set this restaurant apart.

Nová Louka 21. © 017/322 1161. Reservations recommended. Main courses 145–895Kč ($4–$24). AE, V.
Daily noon–11pm.

Grand Restaurant CONTINENTAL   It's no surprise that the Grandhotel
Pupp has the nicest dining room in town, an elegant affair with tall ceilings,
huge mirrors, and glistening chandeliers. A large menu gives way to larger portions of salmon, chicken, veal, pork, turkey, and beef in a variety of heavy and
heavier sauces. Even the trout with mushrooms is smothered in butter sauce.

In the Grandhotel Pupp, Mírové nám. 2. © 017/310 9111. Reservations recommended. Main courses
240–1,100Kč ($7–$29). AE, V. Daily noon–3pm and 6–11pm.

Hospoda U Švejka CZECH   A new addition to the pub scene, U Švejka
plays on the tried and true Good Soldier Švejk tourist theme. Luckily the tourist
trap goes no further, and once inside, you find a refreshingly nonsmokey
although thoroughly Czech atmosphere. Locals and tourists alike rub elbows
while throwing back some fine lager and standard pub favorites, such as goulash
and beef tenderloin in cream sauce.

Stará Louka 10. © 017/ 323 2276. Main courses 99–214Kč ($2.67–$6); beer 20Kč (54¢). MC, V. Daily
11am–11pm.

Promenáda ✪ CZECH/CONTINENTAL   This intimate spot may not be
as elegant as the Grand, but for Karlovy Vary residents, it has become one of the
places to dine. Across from the Vřídelní kolonáda, the Promenáda serves the best
food around, offering a wide selection of generous portions. The daily menu
usually includes well-prepared wild game, but the mixed grill for two or the
chateaubriand, both flambéed at the table, are the chef's best dishes.

Tržiště 31. © 017/322 5648. Reservations highly recommended. Main courses 139–498Kč ($3.75–$13).
AE, V. Daily noon–11pm.

EXPLORING KARLOVY VARY

The town's slow pace and pedestrian promenades, lined with Art Nouveau
buildings, turn strolling into an art form. Nighttime walks take on an even more
mystical feel as the sewers, river, and many major cracks in the roads emit steam
from the hot springs underneath.

If you're traveling here by train or bus, a good place to start is the **Hotel Thermal** at the north end of the old town's center. The 1970s glass, steel, and concrete Thermal, between the town's eastern hills and the Ohře River, sticks out
like a sore communist thumb amid the 19th-century architecture. Nonetheless,
you'll find three important places here: its outdoor pool with mineral water, the
only centrally located outdoor public pool; its upper terrace, boasting a spectacular view; and its theater, Karlovy Vary's largest, which holds many of the film
festival's premier events. Look at it, and then turn and walk away. Try not to picture it again.

As you enter the heart of the town on the river's west side, you'll see the newly
renovated ornate white wrought-iron **Sadová kolonáda** adorning the beautifully

Moments Spa Cures & Treatments

Most visitors to Karlovy Vary come specifically to get a spa treatment, a therapy that lasts 1 to 3 weeks. After consulting with a spa physician, guests are given a regimen of activities that may include mineral baths, massages, waxings, mud packs, electrotherapy, and pure oxygen inhalation. After spending the morning at a spa or sanatorium, guests are then usually directed to walk the paths of the town's surrounding forest.

The common denominator of all the cures is an ample daily dose of hot mineral water, which bubbles up from 12 springs. This water definitely has a distinct odor and taste. You'll see people chugging it down, but it doesn't necessarily taste very good. Some thermal springs actually taste and smell like rotten eggs. You might want to take a small sip at first.

You'll also notice that almost everyone in town seems to be carrying "the cup," basically a mug with a built-in straw that runs through the handle. Young and old alike parade through town with their mugs, filling and refilling them at each new thermal water tap. You can buy these mugs everywhere for as little as 50Kč ($1.35) or as much as 500Kč ($14); they make a quirky souvenir. *Warning:* None of the mugs can make the hot springs taste any better!

The minimum spa treatment lasts 1 week and must be arranged in advance. A package traditionally includes room, full board, and complete therapy regimen; the cost varies from about $40 to $100 per person per day, depending on the season and facilities. Rates are highest from May to September and lowest from November to February. For information and reservations in Prague, contact **Čedok,** Na Příkopě 18, Praha 1 (© 02/2419 7111; fax 02/2421 0502). Many hotels also offer spa and health treatments, so ask when you book your room. Most will happily arrange a treatment if they don't provide it directly.

Visitors to Karlovy Vary for just a day or two can experience the waters on an "outpatient" basis. The **State Baths III** (© 017/322 5641) welcomes day-trippers with mineral baths, massages, saunas, and a cold pool. It's open for men on Tuesday, Thursday, and Saturday, and for women on Monday, Wednesday, and Friday, 7:45am to 3pm. **Vojenský lázeňský ústav,** Mlýnské nábřežuí 7 (© 017/311 9111), offers similar services and costs about 500Kč ($14) per day.

manicured park **Dvořákovy sady.** Continue following the river, and about 100m (110 yds.) later you'll encounter the **Mlýnská kolonáda,** a long, covered walkway housing several Karlovy Vary springs, which you can sample 24 hours a day. Each spring has a plaque beside it telling which mineral elements are present and the temperature of the water. Bring your own cup or buy one just about anywhere to sip the waters since most are too hot to drink from your hands.

When you hit the river bend, the majestic **Church of St. Mary Magdalene** sits perched atop a hill, overlooking the **Vřídlo,** the hottest spring in town. Built in 1736, the church is the work of Kilian Ignac Dientzenhofer, who also created two of Prague's more notable churches—both named St. Nicholas. Housing Vřídlo, which blasts water some 15m (50 ft.) into the air, is the glass building where the statue of Soviet astronaut Gagarin once stood. (Gagarin's statue has since made a safe landing at the Karlovy Vary airport.) Now called the **Vřídelní kolonáda,** the structure, built in 1974, houses several hot springs you can sample for free. The building also holds the Kuri-Info information center and several kiosks selling postcards, stone roses, and drinking cups.

Heading away from the Vřídelní kolonáda are Stará and Nová Louka streets, which line either side of the river. Along **Stará (Old) Louka** you'll find several fine cafes and glass and crystal shops. **Nová (New) Louka** is lined with hotels and the historic town's main theater, currently under reconstruction.

Both streets lead to the **Grandhotel Pupp.** After a massive reconstruction, the Pupp is once again the crown jewel of the town. Gone are the effects of nearly 50 years of communism (it was temporarily called the Grand Hotel Moskva); once again, splendor radiates from its restored facade. Regardless of capitalism or communism, the Pupp remains what it always was: the grande dame of hotels in the area. Once catering to nobility from all over central Europe, the Pupp still houses one of the town's finest restaurants, the Grand, and its grounds are a favorite with the hiking crowd. The reconstruction has also brought with it a plethora of designer shops catering to those who just don't know what to wear.

If you still have the energy, atop the hill behind the Pupp stands the **Diana Lookout Tower.** Footpaths leading through the forests eventually spit you out at the base of the tower, as if to say, "Ha, the trip is only half over." The five-story climb tests your stamina, but the view of the town is more than worth it. For those who aren't up to the climb just to get to the tower, a cable car runs to the tower every 15 minutes or so.

THE SHOPPING SCENE

Crystal and porcelain are Karlovy Vary's other claims to fame. Dozens of shops throughout town sell everything from plates to chandeliers.

Ludvík Moser founded his first glassware shop in 1857 and soon became one of the country's foremost names in glass. Now his name can be found in almost every store along the river. Many of the stores will pack and ship your purchases, either back to Prague or all the way home. We recommend comparison shopping as prices can sometimes vary greatly for similar items.

ČESKÝ KRUMLOV

If you have time for only one day trip, consider making it Český Krumlov, 155km (96 miles) south of Prague. One of Bohemia's prettiest towns, Krumlov is a living gallery of elegant Renaissance-era buildings housing charming cafes, pubs, restaurants, shops, and galleries. In 1992, UNESCO named Český Krumlov a World Heritage Site for its historic importance and physical beauty.

Tips **Traveler's Tip**

Consider yourself warned: Word has spread about Český Krumlov. Summer season can be unbearable, as thousands of visitors blanket its medieval streets. If possible, try to visit in the off-season—we suggest autumn to take advantage of the colorful surrounding hills—when the crowds recede, the prices decrease, and the town's charm can really shine. Who knows? You might even hear some Czech!

Český Krumlov

Bustling since medieval times, the town, after centuries of embellishment, is exquisitely beautiful. In 1302, the Rožůmberk family inherited the castle and used it as their main residence for nearly 300 years. Looking out from the Lazebnický bridge, with the waters of the Vltava below snaking past the castle's gray stone, you'll feel that time has stopped. At night, with the castle alight, the view becomes even more dramatic.

Few deigned to change the appearance of Český Krumlov over the years, not even the Schwarzenbergs, who usually had an unrestrained flair for opulence. At the turn of the 19th century, several house facades in the town's outer section were built, as were inner courtyards. Thankfully, economic stagnation in the area during communism meant little money for "development," so no glass-and-steel edifices, like the Hotel Thermal in Karlovy Vary, jut out to spoil the architectural beauty. Instead, a medieval impression reigns supreme, now augmented by the many festivals and renovations that keep the town's spirit alive.

ESSENTIALS

GETTING THERE   By Train   The only way to reach Český Krumlov by train from Prague is via České Budějovice, a slow ride that deposits you at a station relatively far from the town center (trip time: 3½ hours); the fare is 170Kč ($4.59) first class or 120Kč ($3.24) second class.

By Bus   The nearly 3-hour bus ride from Prague usually involves a transfer in České Budějovice and costs 125Kč ($3.37). The bus station in Český Krumlov is a 15-minute walk from the town's main square.

By Car   From Prague, it's a 2-hour drive along E-55.

VISITOR INFORMATION   On the main square, the **Information Centrum,** nám. Svornosti 1, 381 00 Český Krumlov (© and fax **0337/711 183**), offers a complete array of services from booking accommodations to ticket reservations for events, as well as a phone and fax service. It's open daily from 9am to 6pm.

SPECIAL EVENTS   After being banned during communism, the **Slavnost pětilisté růžůe** (Festival of the Five-Petaled Rose) has made a triumphant comeback. It's held each year on the summer solstice. Residents of Český Krumlov dress up in Renaissance costume and parade through the streets. Afterward, the streets become a stage with plays, chess games with people dressed as pieces, music, and even duels "to the death."

Český Krumlov also plays host to a 2-week **International Music Festival** every August, attracting performers from all over the world. Performances are held in nine spectacular venues. For information or ticket reservations, contact the information center's ticket hot line at © 0337/711 650.

WHERE TO STAY

Hotels are sprouting up, or are getting a "new" old look; PENSION and ZIMMER FREI signs line Horní and Rooseveltova streets and offer some of the best values in town. For a comprehensive list of area hotels and help with bookings, call or write the Infocentrum listed above.

Moderate

Hotel Růžůe (Rose Hotel)   Once a Jesuit seminary, this stunning Italian Renaissance building has been turned into a well-appointed hotel. Comfortable in a big-city kind of way, it's packed with amenities and is one of the top places to stay in Český Krumlov. But for all of the splendor of the building, you may find the Růžůe a bit of a disappointment. Rooms, although clean and spacious, look as though they were furnished from a Sears warehouse in the U.S. Midwest. The promise of a Renaissance stay dissipates quickly.

Horní 153, 381 01 Český Krumlov. © **0337/772 100.** Fax 0337/713 146. www.hotelruze.cz. 53 units. 3,700Kč ($100) double; 4,500Kč ($121) small suite; 5,700Kč ($154) large suite. Rates include breakfast. AE, MC, V. **Amenities:** Restaurant (Czech/international), bar, Internet cafe; indoor pool; fitness center; sauna; bike-rental; rafting; concierge; guide-tour desk; minibus for transport; salon; limited room service; massages; laundry. *In room:* TV, minibar, hair dryer.

Inexpensive

Hotel Konvice *(Value*   If you can get a room with a view out the back, take it immediately. Rooms themselves are small but clean and comfortable, with nice parquet floors and well-appointed baths. As you overlook the river and the castle on the opposite bank, you'll wonder why anyone would stay at the Růžůe just a few doors up.

Horní ul. 144, 381 01 Český Krumlov. © **0337/711 611.** Fax 0337/711 327. 10 units. 1,300Kč ($35) double; 1,600–2,500Kč ($43–$68) suite. Rates include breakfast. No credit cards. **Amenities:** Restaurant. *In room:* TV.

Pension Anna ✿ Along "pension alley," this is a comfortable and rustic choice. What makes this a favorite is the friendly management and the homey feeling you get as you walk up to your room. Forget hotels—this is the kind of place where you can relax. The owners even let you buy drinks and snacks at the bar downstairs and take them to your room. Suites, with four beds and a living room, are great for families and groups.

Rooseveltova 41, 381 01 Český Krumlov. © **0337/711 692.** 8 units. 1,200Kč ($32) double; 2,100 ($57) suite. Rates include breakfast. No credit cards. **Amenities:** Restaurant-bar with billiard table. *In room:* TV.

Pension Na loužui Smack-dab in the heart of the Inner Town, the small Na loužui, built in 1459 and decorated with early 20th-century wooden furniture, is full of charm. The only drawback is beds with footboards that can be a little short for tall people. Don't worry about the noise—the pub downstairs is not open late!

Kájovská 66, 381 01 Český Krumlov. © and fax **0337/712 880.** 5 units. 1,000Kč ($27) double; 1,200Kč triple ($32). Rates include breakfast. No credit cards. **Amenities:** Czech pub. *In room:* none.

Pension Ve Věžui (In the Tower) ✿✿ A private pension in a renovated medieval tower just a 5-minute walk from the castle, Ve Věžui is one of the most magnificent places to stay in town. It's not the rooms themselves that are so grand—none have a bathroom and all are sparsely decorated—it's the wonderful ancient ambience. Advance reservations are always recommended.

Latrán 28, 381 01 Český Krumlov. © **0337/711 835.** 4 units (none with bathroom). May–Sept 1,400Kč ($37) double; 1,800Kč ($49) quad. Oct–Apr 750Kč ($20) double; 1,200Kč ($32) quad. Rates include breakfast. No credit cards. **Amenities:** None.

WHERE TO DINE

Hospoda Na loužui *Value* CZECH The large wooden tables encourage you to get to know your neighbors in this Inner Town pub, located in a 15th-century house. The atmosphere is fun and the food above average. If no table is available, stand and have a drink; the seating turnover is pretty fast, and the staff is accommodating. In summer, the terrace seats only six, so dash over if a seat becomes empty.

Kájovská 66. © **0337/711 280.** Main courses 49–129Kč ($1.32–$3.48). No credit cards. Daily 10am–10pm.

Restaurant Eggenberg CZECH Located in the former cooling room of the local Eggenberg Brewery, this is one of the few big beer halls in town, with some of the freshest draft anywhere. Traditional meat-and-dumplings–style Czech food is augmented by vegetarian dishes.

Latrán 27. © **0337/711 761.** Main courses 80–195Kč ($2.16–$5). MC, V. Daily 10am–11pm.

Restaurant Na Ostrově (On the island) CZECH In the shadow of the castle and, as the name implies, on an island, this restaurant is best on a sunny day when the terrace overflows with flowers, hearty Czech food with plenty of chicken and fish dishes, and lots of beer. The staff is very friendly and very slow—usually only two waiters work a shift. This is a great place to relax and enjoy the view.

Na Ostrově 171. © **0337/712 532.** Main courses 60–245Kč ($1.62–$7). No credit cards. Daily 11am–11pm.

Rybářská bašta Jakuba Krčína ✿ CZECH One of the town's most celebrated restaurants, this place specializes in freshwater fish from surrounding

lakes. Trout, perch, pike, and eel are sautéed, grilled, baked, and fried in a variety of herbs and spices. Venison, rabbit, and other game are also available, along
with the requisite roast beef and pork cutlet.

Kájovská 54. (✆ **0337/712 692.** Reservations recommended. Main courses 110–340Kč ($3–$9). AE, MC, V.
Daily 7am–11pm.

EXPLORING ČESKÝ KRUMLOV

Bring a good pair of walking shoes and be prepared to wear them out. Český
Krumlov not only lends itself to hours of strolling, but its hills and alleyways
demand it. No cars, thank goodness, are allowed in the historic town, and the
cobblestones keep most other vehicles at bay. The town is split into two parts—
the Inner town and Latrán, which houses the castle. They're best tackled separately, so you won't have to crisscross the bridges several times.

Begin at the **Okresní Muzeum** (Regional Museum) (✆ **0337/711 674**) at
the top of Horní ulice. Once a Jesuit seminary, the three-story museum now
contains artifacts and displays relating to Český Krumlov's 1,000-year history.
The highlight of this mass of folk art, clothing, furniture, and statues is a giant
model of the town that offers a bird's-eye view of the buildings. Admission is
30Kč (81¢), and it's open from Tuesday to Sunday from 10am to 12:30pm and
1 to 6pm.

Across the street is the **Hotel Růžže** (Rose), which was once a Jesuit student
house. Built in the late 16th century, the hotel and the prelature next to it show
the development of architecture; Gothic, Renaissance, and rococo influences are
all present. If you're not staying at the hotel, don't be afraid to walk around and
even ask questions at the reception desk.

Continue down the street to the impressive late Gothic **St. Vitus Cathedral.**
Be sure to climb the church tower, which offers one of the most spectacular
views of both the Inner Town and the castle across the river.

As you continue down the street, you'll come to **náměstí Svornosti.** For such
an impressive town, the main square is a little disappointing, with few buildings
of any character. The **Radnice** (Town Hall), at nám. Svornosti 1, is one of the
few exceptions. Its Gothic arcades and Renaissance vault inside are exceptionally
beautiful in this otherwise run-down area. From the square, streets fan out in all
directions. Take some time just to wander through them. You might want to
grab a light snack before crossing the bridge.

As you cross the bridge and head toward the castle, you'll see immediately to
your right the former **hospital and church of St. Jošt.** Founded at the beginning of the 14th century, it has since been turned into apartments. Feel free to
snoop around, but don't enter the building.

One of Český Krumlov's most famous residents was Austrian-born 20th-
century artist Egon Schiele. He was a bit of an eccentric who, on more than one
occasion, raised the ire of the town's residents (many were distraught with his use
of their young women as his nude models); his stay was cut short when residents'
patience ran out. But the town readopted the artist in 1993, setting up the **Egon
Schiele Foundation** and the **Egon Schiele Centrum** in Inner Town, Široká
70–72, 381 01, Český Krumlov (✆ **0337/711 224;** fax 0337/711 191). Back
across the river from the castle, it documents his life and work, housing a permanent selection of his paintings as well as exhibitions of other 20th-century
artists. Admission depends on the exhibitions being displayed. It's open daily
from 10am to 6pm.

For a different perspective on what the town looks like, take the stairs from the **Městské divadlo** (Town Theater) on Horní ulice down to the riverfront and rent a boat from **Maláček boat rentals** at 40Kč ($1) per hour. Always willing to lend his advice, the affable Pepa Maláček will tell you what to watch out for and where the best fishing is (no matter how many times you say that you don't want to fish!).

SEEING THE ČESKÝ KRUMLOV CHÂTEAU ⟨ℛ⟩

Reputedly the second-largest castle in Bohemia (after Prague Castle), the **Český Krumlov Château** was constructed in the 13th century as part of a private estate. Throughout the ages, it has passed to a variety of private owners, including the Rožůmberk family, Bohemia's largest landholders, and the Schwarzenbergs, the Bohemian equivalent of *Dynasty*'s Carrington family.

From the entrance, by the bear moat, you'll begin the long climb up to the castle. Greeting you is a round 12th-century tower—painstakingly renovated—with its Renaissance balcony. You'll pass over the moat, now occupied by two brown bears. Beyond it is the **Dolní Hrad** (Lower Castle) and then the **Horní Hrad** (Upper Castle).

Perched high atop a rocky hill, the château is open from April to October only, exclusively by guided tour. Visits begin in the rococo **Chapel of St. George,** continue through the portrait-packed **Renaissance Hall,** and end with the **Royal Family Apartments,** outfitted with ornate furnishings that include Flemish wall tapestries and European paintings. Tours last 1 hour and depart frequently. Most are in Czech or German, however. If you want an English-language tour, arrange it ahead of time (✆ **0337/711 465;** fax 0337/711 687; www.castle.ckrumlov.cz).

The tour costs 130Kč ($3.51) adults and 65Kč ($1.75) students. The castle hours are from Tuesday to Sunday: June to August 9am to noon and 1pm to 5pm, May and September 9am to noon and 1pm to 4pm, and April and October 9am to noon and 1pm to 3pm. The last entrance is 1 hour before closing.

Once past the main castle building, you can see one of the more stunning views of Český Krumlov from **Most Na Plášti,** a walkway that doubles as a belvedere over the Inner Town. Even farther up the hill lies the castle's riding school and gardens.

Most visitors don't realize that beyond this part of the castle they can have one of the Czech Republic's finest dining experiences at **Krčma Markéta** ⟨ℛ⟩, Latrán 67 (✆ **0337/711 453**). To get there, walk all the way up the hill through the castle, past the Upper Castle and past the Castle Theater. Walk through the raised walkway and into the Zámecká zahrada (Castle Garden), where you'll eventually find this Renaissance pub. Going inside is like leaving this century. There's no need for plates here, as meals are served on wooden blocks. Drinks come in pewter mugs.

Although owners have come and gone, the atmosphere and good times are still the same. There's no menu—just go up to the spit and see what's roasting; usually there's a wide variety of meat, including succulent pork cutlets, rabbit, chickens, and pork knees, a Czech delicacy. The waiter/cook will bring bread and a slab of spiced pork fat (considered a good base for drinking), but don't worry—refusing to eat it won't raise anyone's ire. Instead, wait until the entree comes. Yes, that obligatory smattering of cabbage is all the vegetables you're going to get. Vegetarians need not apply. Krčma Markéta is open daily from 6 to 11pm. Reservations are recommended. Main courses are 75Kč to 155Kč ($2 to $4). No credit cards are accepted.

MARIÁNSKÉ LÁZNĚ (MARIENBAD)

When Thomas Alva Edison visited Mariánské Lázně in the late 1800s, he proclaimed, "There is no more beautiful spa in all the world." The town is 47km (29 miles) southwest of Karlovy Vary and 160km (100 miles) west of Prague.

While the spa town stands in the shadow of the Czech Republic's most famous spa town, Karlovy Vary, it wasn't always that way. First mentioned in 1528, the town's mineral waters gained prominence at the end of the 18th century and the beginning of the 19th. Nestled among forested hills and packed with romantic and elegant pastel hotels and spa houses, the town, commonly known by its German name, Marienbad, has played host to such luminaries as Goethe (where his love for Ulrika von Levetzow took root); Mark Twain; composers Chopin, Strauss, and Wagner; and Freud and Kafka. England's Edward VII found the spa resort so enchanting he visited nine times and even commissioned the building of the country's first golf club.

ESSENTIALS

GETTING THERE   By Train   The express train from Prague costs 165Kč ($4.45) for first class; 110Kč ($2.97) for second class (trip time: 3 hours). Mariánské Lázně train station, Nádražůní nám. 292 (①), is south of the town center; take bus 5 into town.

By Bus   The 3-hour bus trip from Prague costs 120Kč ($3.24). The Mariánské Lázně bus station is adjacent to the train station on Nádražůní náměstí; take bus 5 into town. Three buses run daily between Prague and Mariánské Lázně. Eight trains run to Mariánské Lázně from Prague every 2 to 3 hours beginning at 6am with the last train leaving Prague just after 10pm.

By Car   Driving from Prague, take E-50 through Plzeň to Stříbro—about 22km (14 miles) past Plzeň—and head northwest on Highway 21. The clearly marked route can take up to 2 hours. From Karlovy Vary, the trip is about 80km (50 miles). Take Highway 20 south and then turn right onto Highway 24 in the town of Bečov.

VISITOR INFORMATION   Along the main strip lies **Infocentrum KaSS,** Dům Chopin, Hlavní 47, 353 01, Mariánské Lázně (① and fax **0165/622 474**). In addition to dispensing advice, the staff sells maps and concert tickets and can arrange accommodations in hotels and private homes. It's open from Monday to Friday 7am to 7pm, Saturday and Sunday 9am to 6pm.

SPECIAL EVENTS   Mariánské Lázně honors one of its frequent visitors, Chopin, with a yearly festival devoted to the Polish composer and his works. The **Chopin Festival** usually runs for 8 to 10 days near the end of August. Tickets range from 70Kč to 1,500Kč ($1.89 to $41).

Each June, the town also plays host to a **classical music festival** featuring many of the Czech Republic's finest musicians, as well as those from around the world. For more information or ticket reservations for either event, contact Infocentrum KaSS (see "Visitor Information," above).

Patriotic Americans can show up on **July 4** for a little down-home fun, including a parade and other flag-waving special events commemorating the town's liberation by U.S. soldiers in World War II.

WHERE TO STAY

The main strip along **Hlavní třída** is lined with hotels, many with rooms facing the colonnade. If you feel comfortable about doing this, I suggest walking the street and shopping around for a room; most hotels charge from 2,000Kč to

3,500Kč ($54 to $95) for a double from May to September. Off-season prices can fall by as much as half.

For private accommodations, try **Palackého ulice,** running south of the main spa area.

Hotel Golf   One of the more luxurious hotels, the Golf isn't actually in town but across from the golf course about 3km (2 miles) down the road leading to Karlovy Vary. This hotel is busy, so reservations are recommended. The English-speaking staff delivers on its pledge to cater to every wish. Rooms are bright and spacious—but sparsely decorated and far from luxurious. Not surprisingly, the staff can help arrange a quick 18 holes across the street. The hotel has also recently opened its own spa center. In the winter, the golf course is used freely by cross-country skiers.

Zádub 55, 353 01 Mariánské Lázně. ℂ 0165/622 651. Fax 0165/622 655. 28 units. 2,479–3,922Kč ($67–$106) double; 4,699–6,068Kč ($127–$164) suite. Rates include breakfast. AE, DC, MC, V. **Amenities:** Excellent restaurant (French); cafe; indoor pool; golf; spa. *In room:* TV, minibar.

Hotel Koliba 🅐   Away from the main strip but still only a 7-minute walk from the colonnade, the Koliba is a rustic hunting lodge set in the hills on Dusíkova, the road leading to the golf course and Karlovy Vary. Rooms are very comfortable. The hotel offers a wide array of spa and health treatments, which cost extra. A small hill directly outside the hotel, serviced by two ski lifts, is per-fect for teaching the children how to ski or for a romantic cross-country skiing weekend. The restaurant is a good choice for lunch or dinner (see "Where to Dine," below).

Dusíkova 592, 353 01 Mariánské Lázně. ℂ 0165/625 169. Fax 0165/763 10. 10 units. 1,295–1,591Kč ($35–$43) double. AE, MC, V. **Amenities:** Restaurant (Czech); spa. *In room:* TV, minibar.

Hotel Palace 🅐🅐   The 1920s Palace is a beautiful Art Nouveau hotel just 90m (300 ft.) from the colonnade. Rooms are not tremendously spacious, but they're comfortable and tastefully, almost regally, decorated with early 20th-century furniture and lavish curtains and chandeliers.

Hlavní třída 67, 353 01 Mariánské Lázně. ℂ 0165/622 222. Fax 0165/624 262. 45 units. 2,331–3,885Kč ($63–$105) double; 3,034–5,550 ($82–$150) suite. AE, DC, MC, V. **Amenities:** Restaurant (Bohemian/French), cafe, wine room, snack bar; Jacuzzi; sauna; salon. *In room:* TV, minibar, hair dryer.

Hotel Villa Butterfly   The Butterfly has upgraded its rather ordinary rooms into 94 first-rate spacious living quarters. Oddly enough, the renovations have had a reverse effect on the hotel's prices, now a good 15% lower. An English-speaking staff and a good selection of foreign-language newspapers at the recep-tion are added bonuses, as is one of the better cups of coffee in town at the ground floor cafe.

Hlavní třída 72, 353 01 Mariánské Lázně. ℂ 0165/626 201. Fax 0165/626 210. villabutterfly@iol.cz. 94 units. 3,300Kč ($89) double; 5,400Kč ($145) suite; 7,200Kč ($194) apt. Rates include breakfast. AE, DC, MC, V. **Amenities:** Restaurant (Czech), cafe, bar fitness center; tour guide; room service; baby-sitting; safe. *In room:* TV, minibar, hair dryer.

Hotel Zvon   Next to the Palace, in a prime spot directly across from the colon-nade, the Zvon lacks a bit of the panache that its smaller neighbor has, but it still ranks as one of the town's nicer hotels. Ask for a room facing the Kolonada. Not only is the view spectacular, rooms on this side tend to be larger and brighter.

Hlavní třída 68, 353 01 Mariánské Lázně. ☎ **0165/622 015.** Fax 0165/623 245. 79 units. 1,720–4,720Kč ($46–$127) double; 2,370–8,460Kč ($64–$228) suite. AE, DC, MC, V. **Amenities:** Cafe restaurant, bar, whisky club; spa treatment. *In room:* TV, minibar.

WHERE TO DINE

Churchill Club Restaurant CZECH   A lively bar atmosphere makes the Churchill one of the few fun places to be after dark. Don't let the name fool you—the food is traditional Czech with few surprises, which is both good and bad. A large selection of beers also sets the Churchill apart from other places along the main strip.

Hlavní třída 121. ☎ **0165/622 705.** Main courses 150–400Kč ($4–$11). AE, MC, V. Daily 11am–11pm.

Hotel Koliba Restaurant ✦ CZECH   Like the hotel it occupies, the Koliba restaurant is a shrine to the outdoors. The rustic dining room, centered on an open fire grill, boasts a hearty rustic atmosphere that goes perfectly with the restaurant's strength: wild game. Check the daily menu to see what's new or choose from the wide assortment of specialties *na roštu* (from the grill), including wild boar and venison. The second room off the dining area makes for a great lunch stop, especially on a cold winter day when the fireplace is roaring.

Dusíkova 592. ☎ **0165/625 169.** Reservations recommended. Main courses 85–385Kč ($2.29–$10). No credit cards. Daily 11am–11pm.

Restaurant Fontaine CZECH/INTERNATIONAL   The restaurant has undergone a major transformation for the better. The dining room is large but remains quiet, although a little too well lit. Bow-tied waiters serve traditional Bohemian specialties, like succulent roast duck, boiled trout, and chateaubriand, as well as some inventive variations such as shark.

In the Villa Butterfly, Hlavní třída 72. ☎ **0165/626 201.** Main courses 90–300Kč ($2.43–$8). AE, DC, MC, V. Daily 6–11pm.

TAKING THE WATERS AT MARIÁNSKÉ LÁZNĚ

When walking through the town, it's almost impossible to miss the **Lázeňská kolonáda,** just off Skalníkovy sady. From Hlavní třída, walk east on Vrchlického ulice. Recently restored to its former glory, the eye-catching cast-iron and glass colonnade is adorned with ceiling frescoes and Corinthian columns. Built in 1889, it connects a half-dozen major springs in the town center; this is the focal point of those partaking in the ritual. Bring a cup to fill or, if you want to fit in with the thousands of guests who are serious about their spa water, buy one of the porcelain mugs with a built-in straw that are offered just about everywhere. Do keep in mind that the waters are used to treat internal disorders, so the minerals may act to cleanse the body thoroughly. You can wander the colonnade any time; water is distributed daily from 6am to noon and 4 to 6pm.

For a relaxing mineral bubble bath or massage, make reservations through the **Spa Information Service,** Mírové nám. 104, 353 29, Mariánské Lázně (☎ **0165/655 555** or 0165/655 550; fax 0165/655 500). Also ask your hotel about spa treatments and massages they offer or can arrange. Treatments cost from 300Kč ($8) and up.

MORE TO SEE & DO

There's not much town history, since Mariánské Lázně officially came into existence only in 1808, but engaging brevity is what makes the two-story **Muzeum města** (City Museum), Goetheovo nám. 11 (☎ **0165/622 740**), recommendable. Chronologically arranged displays include photos and documents of famous visitors. Goethe slept in the upstairs rooms in 1823, when he was 74 years old. If you ask nicely, the museum guards will play an English-language tape that describes the contents of each of the rooms. You can also request to see the museum's English-language film about the town. Admission is 20Kč (54¢), and it's open from Tuesday to Sunday 9am to 4pm.

You can also take a walk in the woods. The surrounding **Slavkovský les** (Slavkov Forest) has about 70km (45 miles) of marked footpaths and trails through the area's gentle hills.

The **Mariánské Lázně Golf Club** (② **0165/624 300**), a 6,195m (6,775-yd.), par-72 championship course, lies on the edge of town. The club takes pay-as-you-play golfers, and a fully equipped pro shop rents clubs. Greens fees are 1,200Kč ($32) and club rental is 500Kč ($14).

ČESKÉ BUDĚJOVICE
This fortress town was born in 1265, when Otakar II decided that the intersection point of the Vltava and Malše rivers would be the perfect site to protect the approaches to southern Bohemia. Although Otakar was killed at the battle of the Moravian Field in 1278, and the town was subsequently ravaged by the rival Vítkovic family, the construction of České Budějovice continued, eventually taking the shape originally envisaged.

Today, České Budějovice, hometown of the original Budweiser brand beer, is more a bastion for the beer drinker than a protector of Bohemia. But its slow pace, relaxed atmosphere, and interesting architecture make it a worthy stop, especially as a base for exploring southern Bohemia or for those heading on to Austria.

ESSENTIALS
GETTING THERE   By Train   Daily express trains from Prague make the trip to české Budějovice in about 2½ hours. The fare is 160Kč ($4.32) first class or 110Kč ($3) second class.

By Bus   Several express buses run from Prague's Florenc station each day, taking 2 hours and costing 109Kč ($3).

By Car   Leave Prague to the south via the main D-1 expressway and take the cutoff for Highway E-55, which runs straight to České Budějovice (trip time: 1½ hours).

VISITOR INFORMATION   Tourist Infocentrum, nám. Přemysla Otakara II 2 (② and fax **038/635 9480**), provides maps and guidebooks and finds lodging.

SPECIAL EVENTS   Each August, České Budějovice hosts the largest **International Agricultural Show,** the country's massive "state fair."

WHERE TO STAY
Several agencies can locate reasonably priced private rooms. Expect to pay about 500Kč ($14) per person, in cash. Tourist Infocentrum (see "Visitor Information," above) can point you toward a wide selection of conveniently located rooms and pensions.

Hotel Malý Pivovar (Small Brewery) 🐸🐸   Around the corner from the Zvon (see below), a renovated 16th-century microbrewery combines the charms of a B&B with the amenities of a modern hotel. Rooms are bright and cheery, with antique-style wooden furniture. Exposed wooden ceiling beams lend a farmhouse feel in the center of town. It's definitely worth consideration if being only 30m (100 feet) from the square isn't a problem.

Moments Keeping Up with the Schwarzenbergs: Visiting a 141-Room English Castle

Only 8km (5 miles) north from České Budějovice lies **Hluboká nad Vltavou** 🎯. The distance is short enough to make a pleasant bike trip from the city or a quick stop on the way to, or coming from, Prague, Třeboň, or Tábor. The castle is open April, May, September, and October from Tuesday to Sunday from 9am to 4:30pm; June from Tuesday to Sunday 9am–5pm; and July and August daily from 9am–5pm. Tours in English run at 11am and 2 and 4pm and cost 80Kč ($2).

Built in the 13th century, Hluboká has undergone many face-lifts over the years, but none that left as lasting an impression as those ordered by the Schwarzenberg family. As a sign of the region's growing wealth and importance in the mid-19th century, the Schwarzenbergs remodeled the 141-room castle in the neo-Gothic style of England's Windsor Castle. Robin Leach would be proud; no expense was spared. The Schwarzenbergs removed the impressive wooden ceiling from their residence at Český Krumlov and reinstalled it in the large dining room. Other rooms are equally garish in their appointments, making a guided tour worth the time, even though only about a third of the rooms are open to the public.

To complete the experience, the **Alšova Jihočeská Galerie** (Art Gallery of South Bohemia), in the riding school at Hluboká, houses the second-largest art collection in Bohemia, including many interesting Gothic sculptures from the area.

If you're driving to Hluboká from České Budějovice, take Highway E-49 north and then Highway 105 just after leaving the outskirts of České Budějovice. For cyclists or drivers who prefer a slower, more scenic route, take the road that runs behind the brewery; it passes through the village of Obora.

Ulice Karla IV 8–10, 370 01 České Budějovice. 🕐 **038/636 0471.** Fax 038/636 0474. budvar.hotel@cbu. pvtnet.cz. 28 units. 1,890–2,450Kč ($51–$66) double; 1,690–2,750Kč ($45–$74) suite. Rates include breakfast. AE, MC, V. **Amenities:** 2 restaurants (traditional Czech), bar, cafe; brewery tours. *In room:* TV, minibar.

Grandhotel Zvon   Location is everything for the city's most elegant hotel, which occupies several historic buildings on the main square. Upper-floor rooms have been renovated and tend to be more expensive, especially those with a view of the square, which aren't only brighter, they're larger and nicer, too. Others are relatively plain and functional. Try to avoid the smaller rooms, usually reserved for tour groups. There's no elevator, but if you don't mind the climb, stay on the fourth floor. One of the biggest changes here in recent years has been the staff, which seems to be learning that guests like respect and quality treatment.

Nám. Přemysla Otakara II 28, 370 42 České Budějovice. 🕐 **038/731 1384.** Fax 038/731 1385. www.hotel-zvon.cz. 75 units. 1,450–2,900Kč ($39–$78) double; 1,800–3,800Kč ($48–$102) suite. AE, DC, MC, V. **Amenities:** 4 restaurants (Czech, international); bar, tour-desk. *In room:* TV, minibar.

WHERE TO DINE

Masné Krámy (Meat Shops) 🌟 CZECH   If you've pledged not to go to any "tourist traps," you might make an exception for this one housed in a historic building. Just northwest of náměstí Přemysla Otakara II, labyrinthine Masné Krámy occupies a series of drinking rooms on either side of a long hall, and is a must for any serious pub-goer. The inexpensive and filling food is pure Bohemia, including several pork, duck, and trout dishes. Come for the boister-ous atmosphere, or for what's possibly the best goulash in the Czech Republic.

Krajinská 29. (℃) **038/633 7957.** Main courses 85–180Kč ($2.29–$4.86). No credit cards. Daily 10am–11pm.

U paní Emy *(Value* CZECH/INTERNATIONAL   Usually crowded, U paní Emy has a good selection on the menu, with reasonable prices for both food and beverages. The chicken and fish dishes are the most popular. The pan-fried trout tastes very light, not oily as most Czech restaurants tend to make it. A wine bar here stays open to the wee hours.

Široká 25. No phone. Main courses 69–200Kč ($1.86–$5). No credit cards. Daily 10am–3am.

EXPLORING THE TOWN

You can comfortably see České Budějovice in a day. At its center is one of cen-tral Europe's largest squares, the cobblestone **náměstí Přemysla Otakara II.** The square contains the ornate **Fountain of Sampson,** an 18th-century water well that was once the town's principal water supply, plus a mishmash of baroque and Renaissance buildings. On the southwest corner is the **town hall,** an elegant baroque structure built by Martinelli between 1727 and 1730. On top of the town hall, the larger-than-life statues by Dietrich represent the civic virtues: justice, bravery, wisdom, and diligence.

One block northwest of the square is the **Černá věžů** (Black Tower), visible from almost every point in the city. Its 360 steps are worth the climb to get a bird's-eye view in all directions. The most famous symbol of České Budějovice, the 70m (232-ft.) 16th-century tower was built as a belfry for the adjacent **St. Nicholas Church.** This 13th-century church, one of the town's most important sights, was a bastion of Roman Catholicism during the 15th-century Hussite rebellion. You shouldn't miss the flamboyant white-and-cream 17th-century baroque interior.

TOURING A BEER SHRINE

On the town's northern edge sits a shrine for those who pray to the gods of the amber nectar. This is where it all began, where **Budějovický Budvar,** the original brewer of Budweiser brand beer, has its one and only factory. Established in 1895, Budvar draws on more than 700 years of Bohemian brewing tradition to produce one of the world's best beers. Contact Budvar n.p., Karolíny Světlé 4, České Budějovice (℃) **038/770 5344;** budvar.hotel@cbu.pvtnet.cz).

Trolley buses 2, 4, 6, and 8 stop by the brewery; this is how it ensures that its workers and visitors reach the plant safely each day. The trolley costs 8Kč (21¢) to the brewery. You can also hop a cab from the town square for about 100Kč to 150Kč ($2.70 to $4).

Tours can be arranged by phoning ahead, but only for groups. If you're travel-ing alone or with only one or two other people, ask a hotel concierge at one of the bigger hotels (we suggest the Zvon) if he or she can put you in with an already scheduled group. Failing that, you might want to take a chance and head up to the brewery, where, if a group has arrived, another person or two won't be noticed.

PLZEŇ (PILSEN)

Some 400 years ago, a group of men formed Plzeň's first beer-drinking guild, and today, beer is probably the only reason you'll want to stop at this industrial town 90km (55 miles) southwest of Prague. Alas, the town's prosperity and architecture were ravaged during World War II, leaving few buildings untouched. The main square, náměstí Republiky, is worth a look, but after that, there's not much to see.

ESSENTIALS

GETTING THERE   By Train   It's more comfortable taking the train to Plzeň than the bus, although a lot slower now that the motorway connects the city to Prague (trip time: 2 hours). Trains between the two cities are plentiful and fit most every schedule. Fare costs 111Kč ($3) first class or 74Kč ($2) second. To get from the train station to town, walk out the main entrance and take Americká street across the river, and then turn right onto Jungmannova, which leads to the main square.

By Bus   The bus from Prague costs 69Kč ($1.86) but tends to be cramped (trip time: 1 hour). If you do take the bus, head back into town along Husova to get to the square.

By Car   A newly finished highway makes the drive between Prague and Plzeň one of the few worry-free trips a motorist can make in the country. Go west from Prague on D-5 (trip time: 40 minutes).

VISITOR INFORMATION   The **City Information Center Plzeň,** nám. Republiky 41, 301 16 Plzeň (© **019/723 6535;** fax 019/722 4473), is packed with literature to answer travelers' questions. A helpful, multilingual staff will also point you in the right direction. Open from Monday to Friday 10am to 5pm, Saturday and Sunday 10am to 3:30pm.

SPECIAL EVENTS   If you're an American, or speak English, being in Plzeň in May is quite an experience. On May 8, Gen. George S. Patton was forced to halt his advance after liberating the area, in accordance with an Allied agreement. The Russians were then allowed to liberate Prague. Forty years of communist oppression, however, means that the town now celebrates May 8 or **Liberation Day** with a vengeance. Although the celebrations have cooled some from the heady days just after the Velvet Revolution of 1989, you'll still be feted and praised into the wee hours, as the city's people give thanks to the forces that ended Nazi occupation.

Anxious to capitalize on its beer heritage and always happy to celebrate, Plzeň has started its own Oktoberfest, called **Pivní slavnosti.**

WHERE TO STAY

For private rooms that are usually outside the town center but a little cheaper, try **Čedok** at Sedláčkova 12 (© **019/723 7419;** fax 019/722 3703), open from Monday to Friday 9am to noon and 1 to 5pm (to 6pm in summer) and Saturday from 9am to noon. Expect to pay about 500Kč to 1,000Kč ($14 to $27) for a double.

Hotel Central   This rather sterile building is across from St. Bartholomew's Church and has generously given itself a four-star rating. The surly staff notwithstanding, it is clean and quiet for such a central location. Rooms are very plain, but beds are surprisingly comfortable. With few choices around, you could do worse than the Central.

Nám. Republiky 33, 305 28 Plzeň. © 019/722 6059. Fax 019/722 6064. 50 units. 1,250Kč ($33) double. AE, MC, V. **Amenities:** Restaurant, garden restaurant; exercise room; sauna. *In room:* TV.

Interhotel Continental ✍   About a block from the old town square, the modern Continental is considered by locals to be one of the best in town, but keep in mind that there's not much to choose from. Rooms are spacious and comfortable.

Zbrojnická 8, 305 34 Plzeň. ✆ **019/723 6479.** Fax 019/722 1746. 55 units (10 with shared shower/bathroom, 20 with private shower only, 25 with private bathroom). 850Kč ($22) double without bathroom; 1,590Kč ($43) double with shower only; 2,150Kč ($58) double with bathroom; 3,700Kč ($100) deluxe double. AE, MC, V. **Amenities:** Restaurant, cafe, nightclub. *In room:* TV.

WHERE TO DINE

Měšťárská Beseda CZECH/CONTINENTAL   The high ceilings and wall murals add a touch of elegance to this large restaurant frequented by the theater crowd. The prices are reasonable for the center, but the meals are unimaginative. It's a great place to stop for a late-evening coffee and some strudel or a nightcap.

Smetanovy sady 13. ✆ **019/723 6667.** Main courses 39–149Kč ($1–$4). MC, V. Sun–Thurs 10am–11pm; Fri–Sat 10am–midnight.

Pilsner Urquell Restaurant CZECH   This isn't a visitor-oriented pub; in the same building that houses the brewery's management, the pub has remained true to its beer suppliers by cooking hearty basic Czech meals, although it has become a little pricey.

U Prazdroje 1 (just outside the brewery gates). No phone. Main courses 65–220Kč ($1.75–$6). AE, MC, V. Mon–Sat 10am–10pm.

Restaurace Na Spilce (At the fermenting cellar) *Value* CZECH   The Na Spilce looks like a 600-seat tourist trap, but the food is quite good and reasonably priced. The standard *řízky* (schnitzels), goulash, and *svíčková na smetaně* (pork tenderloin in cream sauce) are hearty and complement the beer that flows from the brewery. If you've got a big appetite or just can't decide, try the Plzeňská bašta, with ample servings of roasted pork, smoked pork, sausage, sauerkraut, and two kinds of dumplings.

U Prazdroje (just inside the brewery gates). ✆ **019/706 2754.** Main courses 32–195Kč (86¢–$5). AE, MC, V. Mon–Thurs 11am–10pm; Fri–Sat 11am–11pm; Sun 11am–9pm.

EXPLORING PLZEŇ

Founded in 1295 by Přemysl King Václav II, Plzeň was, and remains, western Bohemia's administrative center. Václav's real gift to the town, however, was granting it brewing rights. As a result, more than 200 microbreweries popped up in almost every street-corner basement. Realizing the brews they were drinking had become mostly inferior by the late 1830s, rebellious beer drinkers started demanding quality from their brewers. "Give us what we want in Plzeň, good and cheap beer!" became the battle cry. By 1842, the brewers had combined their expertise to produce a superior brew through what became known as the Pilsner brewing method.

Plzeňský Prazdroj (Pilsner Breweries), at U Prazdroje 7, will interest anyone who wants to learn more about the brewing process. It's actually made up of several breweries, pumping out brands like Pilsner Urquell and Gambrinus, the most widely consumed beer in the Czech Republic. The 1-hour tour of the factory (which has barely changed since its creation) includes a 15-minute film and visits to the fermentation cellars and brewing rooms. The tour is at 12:30pm Monday to Saturday. It costs 100Kč ($2.70); the price includes a dozen beer-oriented postcards and a tasting of some freshly brewed beer (for details on other tours available, call ✆ 019/706 2888 or e-mail visit@pilsner-urquell.com).

If you didn't get your fill of beer facts at the brewery, the **Pivovarské muzeum** (Beer Museum) (© **019/723 4955;** fax 019/723 5574) is 1 block away on Veleslavínova. Inside this former 15th-century house, you'll learn everything there is to know about beer but were afraid to ask. In the first room, once a 19th-century pub, the guard winds up an old German polyphone music box from 1887 that plays the sweet though scratchy strains of Strauss's Blue Danube. Subsequent rooms display a wide collection of pub artifacts, brewing equipment, and mugs. Most displays have English captions, but ask for a more detailed museum description in English when you enter. Admission is 30Kč (81¢), and it's open from Tuesday to Sunday 10am to 6pm.

Now full of more brewing knowledge than you might have wanted, proceed to the main square to see what's hopping (sorry, we couldn't resist). Dominating the center is the Gothic **Cathedral of St. Bartholomew,** boasting the tallest steeple in the Czech Republic at 100m (333 ft.). Inside the church, a beautiful marble Madonna graces the main altar.

You'll see an Italian flair to the first four floors of the 16th-century Town Hall and in the sgrafitto adorning its facade. Later on, more floors were added, as well as a tower, gables, and brass flags, creating the illusion that another building had just fallen on top of the original. In front of the town hall, a 1681 **memorial** commemorates victims of the plague.

Just west of the square on Sady pětatřicátníků lie the shattered dreams of the 2,000 or so Jews who once called Plzeň home. The **Great Synagogue,** the world's third largest, was built in the late 19th century. Sadly, its doors remain locked, although funds are being raised to support urgent repairs.

CHEB (EGER) & FRANTIŠKOVY LÁZNĚ (FRANZENSBAD)

As with Plzeň, few people who travel through **Cheb,** 170km (105 miles) west of Prague and 40km (25 miles) southwest of Karlovy Vary, actually stop and look around. From the outside, that's understandable, but it's too bad. The center of Cheb is one of the more architecturally interesting places in west Bohemia, and its history is fascinating as well.

A former stronghold for the Holy Roman Empire on its eastern flank, Eger, as it was then known, became part of Bohemia in 1322. Cheb stayed under Bohemian rule until it was handed to Germany as part of the 1938 Munich Pact. After World War II, it returned to Czech hands, when most of the area's native Germans, known as Sudeten Germans, were expelled for their open encouragement of the invading Nazis. This bilingual, bicultural heritage can be seen in the town's main square, which could easily sit on either side of the border if it weren't for the Czech writing on the windows. These days, the Germans have returned, but only for a few hours at a time, many for the town's thriving sex trade and cheap alcohol. Don't be surprised to see women around almost every corner looking to ply their trade. Still, Cheb is worth exploring for its melange of architectural styles, the eerie Jewish quarter Špalíček, and the enormous Romanesque Chebský Hrad (Cheb Castle).

Only about 20 minutes up the road from Cheb is the smallest of the three major west Bohemian spa towns, **Františkovy Lázně** (Franzensbad). Although it pales in comparison to Karlovy Vary and Mariánské Lázně, Františkovy Lázně has taken great strides in the past few years to try to erase the decline it experienced under communism. There's not much to see save for the **Spa Museum,** which holds an interesting display of bathing artifacts, but it's a much quieter and cleaner place to spend the night than Cheb.

To get to Františkovy Lázně from Cheb by car, take E-49 (trip time: 20 minutes). You can also take a taxi; just agree with the driver before you get in that the fare won't be more than 250Kč ($7).

ESSENTIALS

GETTING THERE   By Train   Express trains from Prague usually stop in Cheb, as do several trains daily from Karlovy Vary. Cheb is on a main train route, so it's easy to catch many international connections here. The train costs 195Kč ($5) first class and 130Kč ($3.51) second class (trip time: 3½ hours).

By Bus   Cheb is a long bus ride from Prague, and I suggest avoiding it if possible. It's more manageable to take the bus from Karlovy Vary to Cheb.

By Car   Cheb is located on E-48, one of the main highways leading to Germany. If you're driving from Prague, take the same route as you would to Karlovy Vary, which eventually brings you to Cheb (trip time: 2½ hours).

VISITOR INFORMATION   You'll find maps, guidebooks, lodging, and even a currency exchange (at a fairly steep price, so use it only if desperate) at the **Informační Centrum Goetz & Hanzlík,** nám. Přemysla Otakara II 2 (✆ **0166/459 480;** fax 0166/459 291).

WHERE TO STAY

Hotel Hvězda   Overlooking the rather noisy main square, the Hvězda is a lone star in the Cheb hotel universe. Small but clean rooms make it bearable, and the staff tries to make your stay comfortable. If you can't stay in Františkovy Lázně and don't want to drive farther, this is really the only hotel we'd recommend in town.

Nám. Krále Jiřího z Poděbrad 4, 350 01 Cheb. ✆ **0166/422 549.** Fax 0166/422 546. 44 units. 1,150Kč ($31) double. AE, MC, V. **Amenities:** Restaurant (Czech/international). *In room:* TV.

Hotel Tři lilie   In 1808, Goethe stayed here, and he knew what he was doing. The Three Lilies is worth the extra money since it's the only luxury hotel in the area. Cheb needs a nice hotel like this. You can relax here; the spotless, spacious, well-appointed rooms block out any noise. The staff is very attentive and can arrange spa treatments, massages, and other health services.

Jiráskova 17, 351 01 Františkovy Lázně. ✆ **0166/942 350.** Fax 0166/942 970. 32 units. 3,250Kč ($87) double; 4,700Kč ($127) suite. AE, MC, V. **Amenities:** Restaurant, bar. *In room:* TV.

WHERE TO DINE

Restaurace Fortuna CZECH   If you need to have one last schnitzel before leaving, this is as good a place as any. The food is uniformly good but not great, with most Czech specialties accounted for. It's one of the only restaurants open late, and a terrace right on the main square lends to its appeal.

Nám. Krále Jiřího z Poděbrad 29. ✆ **0166/422 110.** Main courses 79–185Kč ($2–$5). No credit cards. Daily 10am–2am.

Staročeská Restaurace CZECH/CHINESE   This restaurant serves much the same fare as all the other restaurants on or around the square, but what caught my eye were the few Chinese meals offered. The kuře kung-pao (kung pao chicken) was a good spicy alternative to the sausages, meat, and dumplings most of the other diners were having.

Kamenná 1. No phone. Main courses 69–190Kč ($2–$5). No credit cards. Daily 10am–10pm.

EXPLORING CHEB

The main square, **náměstí Krále Jiřího z Poděbrad,** attracts most of the attention, and is a good place to begin a tour of the old town. Although it has been overrun with touristy shops and cafes that serve mediocre German fare, the square still shines with Gothic burgher houses and the baroque **old town hall** (Stará radnice). At its south end, the **statue of Kašna Roland,** erected in 1591, is a former symbol of capital punishment, reminding people of the strength justice can wield. At the other end of the square stands the **Kašna Herkules,** a monument to the town's former strength and power. Next to it is a cluster of 11 timber houses, called **Špalíček.** These houses used to be owned by Jews in the early 14th century, but a fervently anti-Semitic clergy in the area incited such hatred against them that they were forced into an alley now called ulička Zavražůděných (Murder Victim's Lane), where they were unceremoniously slaughtered in 1350.

Across from Špalíček is the **Cheb Museum** (© **0166/422 246**), where another murder took place almost 300 years later in 1634—that of Albrecht von Wallenstein, a major player in the Thirty Years' War and hero of a dramatic trilogy by Schiller. On the upper level a display vividly depicts the assassination. The museum's first floor displays many 20th-century paintings from which you can trace the town's slow demise. Admission is 25Kč (67¢), and it's open from Tuesday to Sunday 9am to noon and 1 to 5pm.

The old town of Cheb is also packed with several churches. The most interesting is **St. Nicholas,** around the corner from the museum. It's a hodgepodge of architectural styles: Romanesque tower windows, a Gothic portal, and a baroque interior.

TOURING CHEB CASTLE

An excellent example of Romanesque architecture is **Cheb Castle,** in the northeast part of the old town. Overlooking the Elbe River, the late 12th-century castle is one of central Europe's largest Romanesque structures.

The castle's main draws are its **chapel of Sts. Erhard and Ursala** and the **Černá věžů** (Black Tower). The two-tiered early Gothic chapel has a somber first floor where the proletariat would congregate, while the emperor and his family enjoyed the much cheerier and brighter second floor with its Gothic windows. Alas, there are no tours of the castle, and the English text provided at the entrance does little to inform you. Admission is 50Kč ($1.35). It's open Tuesday to Sunday: from June to August 9am to noon and 1 to 6pm, from May and September 9am to noon and 1 to 5pm, and April and October from 9am to noon and 1 to 4pm.

Across the courtyard from the chapel stands the **Černá věžů** (Black Tower). From its 18m (60-ft.) lookout, you can see the best views of the town. The tower seems dusty and smeared with pollution, but its color isn't from the emissions of the Trabants and Škodas that drive through the streets. Rather, the tower is black because it's actually made from lava rocks taken from the nearby Komorní hůrka volcano (now dormant).

4

Denmark

by Darwin Porter & Danforth Prince

In this chapter, we've concentrated on Copenhagen, Denmark's capital, and added a few important side trips you can take in a day or two. The name for Copenhagen came from the word *københavn,* meaning "merchants' harbor." This city grew in size and importance because of its position on the *øresund* (the Sound) between Denmark and Sweden, guarding the entrance to the Baltic. From its humble beginnings, Copenhagen has become the largest city in Scandinavia, home to 1.5 million people.

In summer 2000, Denmark was linked to Sweden by the 16km (10-mile) Øresund Bridge. The two cities of Copenhagen and Malmö, Sweden, are the hubs of the Øresund Region, northern Europe's largest domestic market, larger than Stockholm and equal in size to Berlin, Hamburg, and Amsterdam. The bridge is the longest combined rail-and-road bridge in the world.

1 Copenhagen

Copenhagen is a city with much charm, as reflected in its canals, narrow streets, and old houses. Its most famous resident was Hans Christian Andersen, whose memory still lives on. Another of Copenhagen's world-renowned inhabitants was Søren Kierkegaard, who used to take long morning strolls in the city, planning his next essay; his completed writings eventually earned him the title "father of existentialism."

But few modern Copenhageners are reading Kierkegaard today, and neither are they as melancholy as Hamlet. Most of them are out having too much fun. Copenhagen epitomizes a Nordic joie de vivre, and the city is filled with a lively atmosphere, good times (none better than at the Tivoli Gardens), sex shows, countless outdoor cafes, and all-night dance clubs. Of course, if you come in winter, the fierce realities of living above the 55th parallel set in. That's when Copenhageners retreat inside their smoky jazz clubs and beer taverns.

Modern Copenhagen still retains some of the characteristics of a village. If you forget the suburbs, you can cover most of the central belt on foot, which makes it a great tourist spot. It's almost as if the city were designed for pedestrians, as reflected by its Strøget (strolling street), Europe's longest and oldest walking street.

ESSENTIALS
GETTING THERE   By Plane   When you arrive at **Kastrup Airport** (© 32-54-17-01; www.cph.dk) 11.5km (7¼ miles) from the center of Copenhagen, you can reduce costs by taking an SAS coach to the city terminal; the fare is 35DKK ($5). A taxi to the city center costs around 130DKK ($16). Even cheaper is local bus 250S, leaving from the international arrivals terminal every

Copenhagen

DENMARK

Copenhagen

✝ Church
ⓘ Information
✉ Post Office
— Railway

Tille Triangel

Dag Hammerskjölds Allé

GARNISONS KIRKEGÅRD

Kristianiagade

Østbanegade

Hovedvej

Østerport Station

Ryesgade

Sortedam Dossering

HOLMENS KIRKEGÅRD

Folke Bernadottes Allé

Sortedams Sø

Øster Søgade

Øster Farimagsgade

Stockholmsgade

Oslo Plads

Forbindelsesvej

⑫

Fredensbro

ØSTER ANLÆG

⑩

Søllerødgade

Store Kongensgade

Grønningen

Suensonsgade

Øster Voldgade

⑪

Gernersgade

Esplanaden

⑬

Øster Farimagsgade

Sølvgade

Rigensgade

Klerkegade

Adelgade

Borgergade

Bredgade

Kunstindustri- museet

⑨

Sølvgade

Kronprinsessegade

⑮

Toldbodgade

⑭

thersgade

⑬⑬

AMALIEHAVN GARDENS

Gothersgade

Store Kongensgade

⑯

Bredgade

Skt. Annae Plads

Pilestræde

⑯

⑲

Krystalgade

⑯⑯

Nyhavn

⑯⑯

Kongens Nytorv

Nyhavn

Østergade

Charlottenborg Palace

Inderhavnen

⑳

University

Amagertorv

Højbro Plads

Det Kongelige Teater

Niels Juelsgade

Holbergsgade

Havnegade

CHRISTIANSHAVN

Vestergade

⑲

Frederiksberggade

Gl. Strand

Holmens Kanal

dhus ads

⑳

Børsen

Strandgade

Overgaden oven Vandet

⑳

SLOTSHOLMEN

Skt. Annae

Prinsessegade

⑳

⑳

Christiansborg Palace

Tøjhusgade

Knippelsbro

Gade

Andersens Boulevard

Vester Voldgade

⑳

Torvegade

Christians Brygge

⑳

Prinsessegade

⑳

Hambrosgade

Langebro

Langebrogade

Sydhavnen

Mitchellsgade

Thorshavnsgade

Stadsgraven

Amager Boulevard

Ved Stadsgraven

Christmas Møllers Plads

Amager Fælled Vej

To Airport

15 to 20 minutes for the Town Hall Square in central Copenhagen and costing 15DKK ($1.90). Air/rail links connect the airport with the Central Railway Station (trip time: 11 min.), costing 16.50DKK ($2). **SAS** (© **800/221-2350;** www.flysas.com) is the major carrier to Copenhagen. **TWA** (© **800/221-2000;** www.twa.com) and **Delta** (© **800/241-4141;** www.delta.com) have daily nonstop flights from New York's JFK airport.

By Train   Trains from the continent arrive at the **Hoved Banegård (Central Railroad Station),** in the very center of Copenhagen, near the Tivoli and the Rådhuspladsen. For **rail information,** call © **33-14-17-01.** The station operates a luggage-checking service but room bookings are available only at the tourist office (see "Visitor Information," below). You can also exchange money at the **Den Danske Bank** (© **33-12-04-11**), open daily 8am to 8pm.

From the Central Railroad Station, you can connect with **S-tog,** the local subway, with trains leaving from platforms in the terminus itself. Ask at the information desk near Tracks 5 and 6 about which train you should board to reach your destination.

By Car   If you're driving from Germany, a car-ferry will take you from Travemünde to Gedser in southern Denmark. From Gedser, get on E-55 north, an express highway that will deliver you to the southern outskirts of Copenhagen. If you're coming from Sweden and crossing at Helsingborg, you'll land on the Danish side at Helsingør. From here, take express highway E-55 south to the northern outskirts of Copenhagen. If you're coming from Malmö, Sweden, you can cross on the Øresund Bridge.

VISITOR INFORMATION   Tourist Office   The **Copenhagen Tourist Information Center,** Bernstorffsgade 1 (© **33-25-38-44;** www.woco.dk), across from Tivoli's main entrance, is open July and August, daily from 8am to 11pm; May, June and September 1 to 15, daily from 9am to 9pm; and from September 16 to April, Monday to Friday 9am to 4:30pm and Saturday 9am to 1:30pm.

Websites   The Copenhagen Tourist Information Center (**www.woco.dk**) takes a while to load but is worth the wait; you'll find all the basics on dining, lodging, and attractions. The Danish Tourist Board (**www.visitdenmark.com**) offers a wide-ranging site where you'll find late news and transportation tips; the accommodation section ranges from "Castles and Manor Houses" to "Farm Holidays."

CITY LAYOUT   The heart of **Old Copenhagen** is a maze of pedestrian streets, formed by Nørreport Station to the north, Town Hall Square (Rådhuspladsen) to the west, and Kongens Nytorv to the east, and the Inderhavnen (Inner Harbor) to the south. One continuous route, **Strøget,** the world's longest pedestrian street, goes east from Town Hall Square to Kongens Nytorv and is made up of five streets: Frederiksberggade, Nygade, Vimmelskaftet, Amagertorv, and Østergade. Strøget is lined with shops, bars, restaurants, and sidewalk cafes in summer. **Pistolstraede,** a narrow street a 3-minute walk west of Kongens Nytorv, is a maze of galleries, restaurants, and boutiques, all housed in restored 18th-century buildings.

Fiolstraede (Violet St.), a dignified street with antique shops and bookshops, cuts through the university (Latin Quarter). If you turn into Rosengaarden at the top of Fiolstraede, you'll come to **Kultorvet** (Coal Sq.) just before you reach Nørreport Station. Here you join the third main pedestrian street, **Købmagergade** (Butcher St.), which winds around and finally meets Strøget on Amagertorv.

At the end of Strøget you approach **Kongens Nytorv** (King's Sq.), the site of the Royal Theater and Magasin, the largest department store. This will put you at the beginning of **Nyhavn,** the former seamen's quarter that has been gentrified into an upmarket area of expensive restaurants, apartments, cafes, and boutiques. The government of Denmark is centered on the small island of **Slotsholmen,** connected to the center by eight bridges. Several museums, notably Christiansborg Castle, are found here.

The center of Copenhagen is **Rådhuspladsen** (Town Hall Sq.). From here it's a short walk to the Tivoli Gardens, the major attraction, and the Central Railroad Station, the main railroad and subway terminus. The wide boulevard, **Vesterbrogade,** passes by Tivoli until it reaches the Central Railroad Station. Another major street is named after Denmark's most famous writer; **H. C. Andersens Boulevard** runs along Rådhuspladsen and the Tivoli Gardens.

GETTING AROUND A joint zone fare system includes Copenhagen Transport buses and State Railway and S-tog trains in Copenhagen and North Zealand, plus some private rail routes in a 40-km (25-mile) radius of the capital, enabling you to transfer from train to bus and vice versa with the same ticket.

A *grundbillet* (basic ticket) for both buses and trains costs 11DKK ($1.40). You can buy 10 tickets for 75DKK ($9). Children under 12 go for half fare; those under 5 travel free on local trains, and those under 7 free on buses. You can purchase a ticket allowing 24-hour bus and train travel through nearly half of Zealand for 70DKK ($9); half price for children 7 to 11; free for children under 7.

Students who have an **International Student Identity Card (ISIC)** are entitled to a number of travel breaks. You can buy a card in the United States at any Council Travel office; for the office nearest you, call ℂ **800/GET-AN-ID.**

For information about low-cost train and plane trips, go to Waastels, Skoubogade 6 (ℂ **33-14-46-33**). Hours are from Monday to Friday 9am to 6pm and Saturday 11am to 3pm. Waastels specializes in inexpensive travel by plane within Europe, and they also are the experts on special youth fares.

Eurailpasses and Nordturist Pass tickets are accepted on local trains.

By Bus Copenhagen's well-maintained buses are the least expensive method of getting around. Most buses leave from Rådhuspladsen. A basic ticket allows 1 hour of travel and unlimited transfers within the zone where you started your trip. For information, call ℂ **36-45-45-45.**

By S-tog (Subway) The S-tog connects heartland Copenhagen with its suburbs. Use of the tickets is the same as on buses (above). You can transfer from a bus line to an S-train on the same ticket. Eurailpass holders generally ride free. For more information, call ℂ **33-14-17-01** at any time.

Tips A Traveler's Tip

The **Copenhagen Card** entitles you to free and unlimited travel by bus and rail throughout the metropolitan area (including North Zealand), 25% to 50% discounts on crossings to and from Sweden, and free admission to many sights and museums. The card is available for 1, 2, or 3 days and costs 155DKK ($19), 255DKK ($32), and 320DKK ($40), respectively. Children 11 and under are given a 50% discount. For more information, contact the Copenhagen Tourist Information Center (see above).

By Car It's best to park your car in any of the dozens of city parking lots, then retrieve it when you're ready to explore the capital's environs. Many parking lots are open 24 hours; a few others tend to close between 1 and 7am. Some close on Saturday afternoon and on Sunday during nonpeak business hours when traffic is presumably lighter. Costs tend to range from 25DKK ($3.15) per hour or 220DKK ($28) per 24 hours. Two of the most central parking lots are Industriens Hus, H. C. Andersens Blvd. 18 (© **33-91-21-75**), open from Monday to Friday 7am to 12:45am and Saturday and Sunday 9am to 12:45am; and the more reasonable Statoil, Israels Plads (© **33-14-37-76**), open 24 hours.

By Taxi Watch for the *fri* (free) sign or green light to hail a taxi. Be sure the taxis are metered. **Københavns Taxa** (© **35-35-35-35**) operates the largest fleet of cabs. Tips are included in the meter price: 25DKK ($3.15) at the drop of the flag and 13DKK ($1.65) per kilometer thereafter, from Monday to Friday 6am to 6pm. From 6pm to 6am and all day and night on Saturday and Sunday, the cost is 14DKK ($1.75) per kilometer. Basic drop-of-the-flag costs remain the same, however. Many drivers speak English.

By Bicycle To reduce pollution from cars, Copenhageners ride bicycles. For 50DKK ($6) per day, you can rent a bike at **Københavns Cykler,** Reventlowsgade 11 (© **33-33-86-13**). Hours are from Monday to Friday 8:30am to 5:30pm, Saturday 9am to 1pm, and Sunday 10am to 1pm.

---

② FAST FACTS: Copenhagen

American Express Amex is represented throughout Denmark by Neiman & Schultz, Norregade 7A (© **33-13-11-81;** bus: 34 or 35), with a branch in Terminal 3 of the Copenhagen Airport. Fulfilling all the functions of mainstream American Express except for foreign exchange services, the main office is open from Monday to Thursday 8:30am to 4:30pm, and Friday 8:30am to 4pm. The airport office remains open till 8:30pm from Monday to Friday.

Business Hours Most **banks** are open from Monday to Friday 9:30am to 4pm (Thurs to 6pm). **Stores** are generally open from Monday to Thursday 9am to 5:30pm, Friday 9am to 7 or 8pm, and Saturday 9am to 2pm; most are closed Sunday.

Currency The Danish currency is the **krone** (crown), or DKK, made up of 100 øre. The rate of exchange used in this chapter is $1 = 8DKK, or 1DKK = 13¢. At press time, £1 = 11.50DKK (or 1DKK = 0.009p). The euro rate is currently fixed at 6.7DKK (or 1DKK = €0.15). Note that though Denmark is part of the EU, it does not plan to switch to the euro at this time.

Currency Exchange Banks are generally your best bet to exchange currency. When banks are closed, you can exchange money at **Forex** (© **33-11-29-05;** S-tog: Central Station) in the Central Railroad Station, open daily 8am to 9pm, or the **Change Group** (© **33-93-04-55;** bus 1, 6, or 9), Østergade 61, open from Monday to Saturday 9am to 10pm and Sunday 9am to 8pm.

Dentists/Doctors For emergency dental treatment, go to **Tandlaegevagten,** Oslo Plads 14 (© **35-38-02-51;** S-tog: Østerport), near Østerport Station and the U.S. Embassy. It's open from Monday to Friday 8am to 9:30pm and

Saturday, Sunday, and holidays 10am to noon. Be prepared to pay in cash. To reach a doctor, dial ☎ **33-93-63-00 from** Monday to Friday 9am to 5pm or ☎ **38-88-60-41** after hours. The doctor's fee is payable in cash. Virtually every doctor speaks English.

Drugstores An *apotek* (pharmacy) open 24 hours a day in central Copenhagen is **Steno Apotek,** Vesterbrogade 6C (☎ **33-14-82-66**; bus: 6).

Embassies The embassy of the **United States** is at Dag Hammarsjölds Allé 24, DK-2100 København (☎ **35-55-31-44**; bus 1 or 6); the embassy of the **United Kingdom,** Kastelsvej 36–40, DK-2100 København (☎ **35-44-52-00**; bus 1 or 6); the embassy of **Canada,** Kristen Berniskowsgadei, DK-1105 København K (☎ **33-48-32-00**; bus 28); the embassy of **Ireland,** Østbanegade 21, DK-2100 København (☎ **35-42-32-33**; S-tog: Østerport); and the embassy of **Australia,** Strandboulevarden, DK-2100 København (☎ **39-29-20-77**; bus 40). There's no New Zealand embassy. Embassies are generally open Monday to Friday 9am to 5pm. Applications for visas and passports are processed generally only in the mornings (9am to noon). Call for more specific hours and services.

Emergencies Dial ☎ **112** for the fire department, the police, or an ambulance, or to report a sea or air accident.

Internet Access To check your e-mail or to send messages, go to **Copenhagen Hovebibliotek,** Krystalgade 15 (☎ **33-73-60-60**; bus: 5, 14, or 16), open from Monday to Friday 10am to 7pm, Saturday 10am to 2pm.

Post Office For information about the Copenhagen post office, call ☎ **33-33-89-00.** The main post office is Tietgensgade 35–39, DK-1704 København (☎ **33-33-89-00**; S-tog: Central Station), open from Monday to Friday 11am to 6pm, Saturday 10am to 1pm. The post office at the Central Railroad Station is open from Monday to Friday 8am to 10pm, Saturday 9am to 4pm, and Sunday 10am to 4pm.

Telephone The **country code** for Denmark is **45,** and this two-digit number will precede any call that's intended for Denmark dialed from another country. Danish phones are fully automatic. Dial just the eight-digit number (there are no city codes).

At public phone booths, use two 50-øre coins or a 1-krone or 5-krone coin only. Don't insert coins until your party answers. You can make more than one call on the same payment if your time hasn't run out. Available at post offices, phone cards cost 30DKK ($3.75), 50DKK ($6), and 100DKK ($13). Remember it can be expensive to phone from your hotel room. Emergency calls are free. To make phone calls or send faxes or telexes, go to the **Telecom Denmark** at the Central Railroad Station, open from Monday to Friday 8am to 10pm and Saturday and Sunday 9am to 9pm. You can reach a U.S. operator with an **AT&T** calling card by dialing ☎ **800-10022.** For **Sprint,** dial ☎ **80-01-08-77**; for **MCI** dial ☎ **80-01-00-22.**

WHERE TO STAY
NEAR KONGENS NYTROV & NYHAVN
Very Expensive
Hotel d'Angleterre ✰✰✰ At the top of Nyhavn, this seven-story hotel, built in 1755 and extensively renovated in the 1980s, is the premier choice for

Denmark (though a bit staid and stodgy). The rooms are beautifully furnished with art objects and the occasional antique. They vary in size, but each has a good bed with a firm mattress; the bathrooms come with phones and scales.

Kongens Nytorv 34, DK-1050 København. ☎ 800/44-UTELL in the U.S., or 33-12-00-95. Fax 33-12-11-18. 124 units. 2,565–3,765DKK ($321–$471) double; from 4,095DKK ($512) suite. AE, DC, MC, V. Parking 175DKK ($22). Bus: 1, 6, or 9. **Amenities:** 2 restaurants (Danish/French); pool; health club; sauna; Turkish bath; solarium; 24-hour room service; laundry. *In room:* A/C, TV, hair dryer, robes.

Phoenix Copenhagen 🏨🏨   More than any other hotel, this top-of-the-line newcomer poses a challenge to the nearby d'Angleterre. Opened in 1991, the Phoenix rose from the ruins of an 18th-century royal house. The spacious rooms are tastefully elegant with discreet interpretations of Louis XVI. Beds are large with firm mattresses. The bathrooms are state-of-the-art. The very best rooms also have faxes, trouser presses, and phones in the bathrooms.

Bredgade 37, DK-1260 København. ☎ **33-95-95-00.** Fax 33-33-98-33. p.remillard@arp-hansen.dk. 212 units. 1,650–2,495DKK ($206–$312) double; 3,000–6,000DKK ($375–$750) suite. AE, DC, MC, V. Parking 95DKK ($12). Bus: 1, 5, 9, or 10. Amenities: Von Plessen restaurant (Danish/French), Murdoch's pub; 24-hour room service; laundry. *In room:* TV, minibar, hair dryer, robes.

Moderate

The Copenhagen Strand 🏨   One of the city's newest hotels, opened in 2000, lies within a pair of former brick-and-timber factories. The savvy architects retained as many of the old-fashioned details as they could. The medium-size rooms are filled with comfortable, contemporary-looking furnishings. The hotel is rated three stars by the Danish government, but frankly, all that it lacks for elevation into a four-star status is a full-fledged restaurant.

Havnegade 37, DK-1058 København. ☎ **33-48-99-00.** Fax 33-48-90-91. www.copenhagenstrand.dk. 174 units. 1,195–1,595DKK ($149–$199) double; 1,795–2,395DKK ($224–$299) suite. AE, DC, MC, V. Tram: 1 or 6. *In room:* TV, minibar, hair dryer.

71 Nyhavn 🏨🏨   On the corner between Copenhagen harbor and Nyhavn Canal, this hotel is a restored old warehouse from 1804, and it was thoroughly renovated in 1997. Most of the rooms have a harbor and canal view. Mattresses are firm but the beds are narrow; bathrooms are rather small; most have a stall shower. The best rooms are also equipped with faxes and robes, and computer plugs are available at the reception desk.

Nyhavn 71, DK-1051 København. ☎ **33-43-62-00.** Fax 33-43-62-01. www.71nyhavnhotelcopenhagen.dk. 126 units. Mon–Thurs 1,450–1,750DKK ($181–$219) double, Fri–Sun 1,065–1,525DKK ($133–$191) double. Mon–Thurs 2,450–2,900DKK ($306–$363) suite, Fri–Sun 2,125–2,550DKK ($266–$319) suite. Rates include breakfast. AE, DC, MC, V. Free parking. Bus: 550-S. **Amenities:** Pakhuskælderen Restaurant; room service 7am–10:30pm; laundry/dry cleaning no-smoking rooms. *In room:* TV, minibar, hair dryer, iron/ironing board.

NEAR RÅDHUSPLADSEN & TIVOLI
Expensive
Sofitel Copenhagen 🏨   This successful overhaul of an older hotel near the rail station combines first-class comfort and antique furnishings. Opposite the Tivoli Gardens, the hotel was commissioned by King Frederik VIII in 1913 and has entertained its share of celebrities and royalty. Rooms vary greatly in size and resemble what you might find in an English country house—but with all the modern amenities. Antiques, double-glazed windows, and views from many rooms make this a good choice. There are some smoke-free accommodations. Bathrooms are generous in size. The Library Bar is one of Copenhagen's most charming.

Bernstorffsgade 4, DK-1577 København. ☎ 800/223-5652 in the U.S., or 33-14-92-62. Fax 33-93-93-62. www.accorhotel.dk. 93 units. 1,695–2,095DKK ($212–$262) double; 3,095–6,495DKK ($387–$812) suite.

AE, DC, MC, V. Parking 120DKK ($15). Bus: 1 or 6. **Amenities:** Flora Danica Restaurant, Library Bar; access to nearby health club; secretarial services; room service 7am to 11pm; dry cleaning; laundry. *In room:* TV, minibar, hair dryer.

Moderate

Ascot Hotel 🍴 On a side street, about a 2-minute walk from Town Hall Square, sits one of Copenhagen's best small hotels. The Ascot was built in 1902 and enlarged and modernized in 1994. The furniture is standard; the firm mattresses are renewed as frequently as needed. The finest rooms open onto the street, though the rooms in the rear get better air circulation and more light. Bathrooms are large and tidily maintained.

Studiestræde 61, DK-1554 København. ✆ **33-12-60-00.** Fax 33-14-60-40. www.ascothotel.dk. 143 units. 1,190–1,390DKK ($149–$174) double; 1,650–2,490DKK ($206–$311) suite. Rates include buffet breakfast. Winter discounts available. AE, DC, MC, V. Free parking. Bus: 14 or 16. **Amenities:** Small gym; bar solarium; laundry/dry cleaning. *In room:* TV, hair dryer.

Grand Hotel 🍴 This landmark hotel—one of the most convenient in the city—is better than ever after a late 20th-century renovation and upgrade. Built in 1880, the hotel's charm was preserved, spacious rooms and bathrooms were updated—each tastefully furnished and well maintained. Singles opening onto the courtyard are more tranquil but don't have views. The corner rooms are the best and most expensive because they have been recently renovated and are larger in size. Bathrooms are quite superior and generous in size.

Vesterbrogade 9A, DK-1620 København. ✆ **33-27-69-00.** Fax 33-27-69-01. www.grandhotelcopenhagen. dk. 151 units. Mon–Thurs 1,495–1,960DKK ($187–$245) double, 2,405DKK ($301) suite. Fri–Sun 1,225–1,600DKK ($153–$200) double, 1,980DKK ($248) suite. Rates include buffet breakfast. AE, DC, MC, V. Bus: 1, 6, 16, 27, 28, or 29. **Amenities:** Restaurant (Danish), Grand Bar (overflowing in summer onto sidewalk); limited room service; laundry/dry cleaning. *In room:* TV, minibar, hair dryer.

Komfort Hotel *Value* In the heart of Copenhagen, close to the Town Hall, the Komfort offers good value. In just 2 minutes you can walk to the Tivoli Gardens. All its medium-size rooms are furnished in a modern Danish design and contain firm mattresses. The overall look, however, including the small but well-maintained bathrooms, is somewhat motel-like. Towels are a bit skimpy, so ask for extras.

Løngangstræde 27, DK-1468 København. ✆ **33-12-65-70.** Fax 33-15-28-99. www.komfort-hotel.dk. 201 units. 1,290DKK ($161) double. Additional bed 225DKK ($28). Rates include buffet breakfast. AE, DC, MC, V. Parking 125DKK ($16). Bus: 1, 5, or 6. **Amenities:** Hattehylden restaurant (Danish), pub; room service; laundry. *In room:* TV.

Kong Arthur 🍴 *Value* An orphanage when it was built in 1882, this good-value hotel sits behind a private courtyard next to the tree-lined Peblinge Lake. A wing with more spacious rooms, including 20 for nonsmokers, was added in 1993. Bathrooms are medium-sized.

Nørre Søgade 11, DK-1370 København. ✆ **33-11-12-12.** Fax 33-32-61-30. www.dk.hotellist.dk/kongarthur.htm. 107 units. 1,280–1,480DKK ($160–$185) double; from 2,900DKK ($363) suite. Rates include buffet breakfast. AE, DC, MC, V. Free parking. Bus: 5, 7, or 16. **Amenities:** 2 restaurants (Danish/French and Japanese); room service; laundry/dry cleaning. *In room:* TV/VCR, minibar, hair dryer, safe.

Inexpensive

Hotel Selandia Solidly built in 1928 behind the railroad station, Hotel Selandia enjoys a new, comfortably modern format today. A longtime favorite of budget-conscious families, it's well maintained and clean. The furnishings are simple, in a modern Scandinavian style, in the small but tidily maintained rooms.

Helgolandsgade 12, DK-1653 København. ℂ **33-31-46-10.** Fax 33-31-46-10. www.hotel-selandia.dk. 87 units, 57 with bathroom (shower only). 540–650DKK ($67.50–$81.25) double without bathroom, 740–950DKK ($92.50–$118.75) double with bathroom. Rates include breakfast. AE, DC, MC, V. Closed Dec 20–Jan 2. Bus: 1, 6, 10, 14, 16, 27, or 28. **Amenities:** Breakfast room; baby-sitting. *In room:* TV, trouser presses.

Missionhotellet Nebo   This hotel near the rail station is a quiet retreat, with clean, up-to-date, although Spartan, rooms. The lounge opens onto a side court-yard. Rooms are small, furnished in a functional, Nordic style. There are bath-rooms on all floors.

Istedgade 6, DK-1650 København. ℂ **33-21-12-17.** Fax 33-23-47-74. www.nebo.dk. 150 units, 72 with bathroom. 650DKK ($81) double without bathroom, 860DKK ($107.50) double with bathroom. Additional bed 240DKK ($30) extra. AE, DC, MC, V. Rates include breakfast. Parking 25DKK ($3.15). Bus: 1, 6, 16, 28, or 41. **Amenities:** Breakfast buffet. *In room:* TV in some units.

Saga Hotel   This is a reasonably priced and solidly acceptable choice among the hotels in this area. The hotel was established in 1947 when a pair of late 19th-century apartment buildings were joined together. Rooms, renovated in 1989, are unusual in that each one has its own unique size and layout. A few have small bathrooms; otherwise, hallway bathrooms are adequate and tidily maintained. This five-story building has no elevator, so hauling luggage upstairs might present a problem for seniors.

Colbjørnsensgade 18–20, DK-1652 København. ℂ **33-24-49-44.** Fax 33-24-60-33. www.sagahotel.dk. 79 units, 24 with bathroom (shower only). 380–580DKK ($48–$73) double without bathroom; 500–870DKK ($63–$109) double with bathroom. Extra bed 150–200DKK ($18.75–$25). Modest winter discounts. Rates include breakfast. AE, DC, MC, V. Bus: 6, 10, 16, 28, or 41. **Amenities:** Breakfast room. *In room:* TV.

A GAY HOTEL
Hotel Jørgensen   No longer a book publishing house as it was in 1906, this hotel is the leading gay hotel of Denmark, and has been since it was founded in 1984. This establishment, located on a busy boulevard in central Copenhagen, obviously appeals to gay men and lesbians, but it also welcomes straight guests. The staff is most helpful. Prices are reasonable, and the rooms are conventional and well organized. The 13 barracks-style dormitories, which accommodate 6 to 14 people each, are segregated according to gender.

Rømersgade 11, DK-1362 København. ℂ **33-13-81-86.** Fax 33-15-51-05. www.hoteljorgensen.dk. 24 units; 13 dormitory rooms (72 beds). TV TEL. 650DKK ($81) double; 115DKK ($14) per person in dormitory. Rates include breakfast. MC, V. Free parking. Bus: 14 or 16. *In room:* TV.

WHERE TO DINE
That national institution, the *smørrebrød* (open-faced sandwich), is introduced at lunch. Literally, this means "bread and butter," but the Danes stack this sand-wich as if it were the Leaning Tower of Pisa—then they throw in a slice of curled cucumber and bits of parsley or perhaps sliced peaches or a mushroom for added color.

NEAR KONGENS NYTORV & NYHAVN
Very Expensive
Kong Hans Kælder 𝒜𝒜𝒜 INTERNATIONAL   This vaulted Gothic cellar is the country's leading restaurant. Its most serious competition comes from Kommandanten, which many discriminating palates hail as the best. On "the oldest corner of Copenhagen," it has been carefully restored and is now a Relais Gourmand. A typical three-course lunch would be smoked salmon from the restaurant's own smokery with aquavit and grain mustard, salmis of mallard

duckling with spätzle, then caramelized vanilla crème with pears. At dinner, you might choose lobster consommé with basil and ravioli, young pigeon with jasmine rice galette, and a selection of Danish and French cheeses, finished with Valrhona chocolate in variations with citrus fruit marmalade.

Vingårdsstræde 6. ℂ **33-11-68-68**. Reservations required. Main courses 285–410DKK ($36–$51); fixed-price menu 595–750DKK ($74–$94). AE, DC, DISC, MC, V. Mon–Sat 6pm–midnight. Closed July 15–Aug 15 and Dec 24–26. Bus: 1, 6, or 9.

Expensive

Era Ora ✿✿ ITALIAN   This reminder of the "Golden Age" is on virtually everyone's list as the best Italian restaurant in Denmark, and one of the consistently best restaurants of any kind within Copenhagen. Established in 1982 by Tuscan-born partners Alessandro and Elvio, it offers an antique-looking dining room. Enjoy a cuisine based on Tuscan and Umbrian models, with sophisticated variations added that are inspired by Denmark's superb array of fresh seafood and produce. Traditional favorites include a platter of ten types of antipasti. All pastas are fresh-made every day. Depending on the season and the inspiration of the chef, main courses include succulent veal dishes, rack of venison with balsamic vinegar and chanterelles, and ultra-fresh fish.

Torvegade 62. ℂ **32-54-06-93**. Reservations required. Set-price menus 495–595DKK ($62–$74). AE, DC, MC, V. Mon–Sat 6pm–midnight. Bus: 2, 8.

Godt ✿ INTERNATIONAL   This small-scale favorite is known to everyone in the neighborhood, including the Queen of Denmark. Despite its fame, there's an appealing lack of pretentiousness here. Food is prepared fresh every day, based on ingredients that are the best at the market. The repertoire served here is splendid and the atmosphere so special it is worth reserving for your final night in Copenhagen. Examples might include crab and rascasse soup with leeks; fried Norwegian redfish with a purée of celery and watercress sauce; and roasted rack of hare with cranberries and chanterelles.

Gothersgade 38. ℂ **33-15-21-22**. Reservations necessary. Set-price menus 385–510DKK ($48–$64). Tues–Sat 5:30–10pm. Closed: July and Dec 23–Jan 3. Bus: 6, 10, and 14.

Kommandanten ✿✿ INTERNATIONAL   Rivaled only by Kong Hans Kælder, this deluxe restaurant is the epitome of Danish chic and charm. The menu offers a mouthwatering array of classical dishes mixed with innovative selections, a medley of strong yet subtle flavors. The finest seasonal ingredients are used, and the menu changes every 2 weeks. You might be offered the grilled catch of the day, breast of duck with port-wine sauce, grilled turbot with spinach sauce, or gratinée of shellfish; or oxtails removed from the bone and served with fried lobster, puree of potatoes and parsley, and a lobster cream sauce.

Ny Adelgade 7. ℂ **33-12-09-90**. Reservations required. Main courses 250–320DKK ($315–$40); fixed-price menu 630DKK ($79). AE, DC, MC, V. Mon–Fri noon–2pm; Mon–Sat 6–10pm. Bus: 1 or 6.

Moderate

Café Lumskebugten DANISH/FRENCH   This restaurant is a well-managed bastion of Danish charm, with an unpretentious elegance. Now-legendary matriarch Karen Marguerita Krog established it in 1854 as a rowdy tavern for sailors. A tastefully gentrified version of the original beef hash is still served. Two glistening-white dining rooms are decorated with antique ships' models, oil paintings, and pinewood floors. The food and service are excellent. Delectable specialties include Danish fish cakes with mustard sauce and minced beets, fried platters of herring, sugar-marinated salmon with mustard-cream sauce, and a symphony of fish with saffron sauce and new potatoes.

Esplanaden 21. © **33-15-60-29.** Reservations recommended. Main courses 168–250DKK ($21–$31); 3 course fixed-price lunch 275DKK ($34); 4-course fixed-price dinner 465DKK ($58). AE, DC, MC, V. Mon–Fri 11am–10:30pm; Sat 5–10:30pm. Bus: 1, 6, or 9.

Inexpensive
Ida Davidsen ☞ SANDWICHES   Denmark is famous for its open-faced sandwiches, and in the capital Ida Davidsen is still known as "queen of the smørrebrød." Flourishing since 1888, the restaurant that began as a modest sandwich shop is now a local legend. This outlet sells a greater variety of open-faced sandwiches (250) than anyone else in Denmark. You'll select your choice by pointing to it within a glass-fronted display case, after which a staff member will carry it to your table. The vast selection includes sandwiches made with salmon, lobster, shrimp, smoked duck with braised cabbage and horseradish, liver pâté, ham, herring, and boiled egg.

Store Kongensgade 70. © **33-91-36-55.** Reservations recommended. Sandwiches 35–250DKK ($4.40–$31). DC, MC, V. Mon–Fri 9am–4pm. Bus: 1, 6, or 9.

NEAR RÅDHUSPLADSEN & TIVOLI
Moderate
Copenhagen Corner SCANDINAVIAN   In the very heart of Copenhagen, this restaurant opens onto Rådhuspladsen, around the corner from the Tivoli Gardens. It offers well-prepared, unpretentious, and reasonably priced meals. The menu features the Danes' favorite dishes, beginning with three kinds of herring or freshly peeled shrimp with dill and lemon. The fish is fresh and beautifully prepared, especially the steamed Norwegian salmon with a "lasagne" of potatoes, and baked halibut with artichokes. Meat and poultry courses, although not always equal to the fish, are tasty and tender, especially the veal liver Provençal.

H. C. Andersens Blvd. 1A. © **33-91-45-45.** Reservations recommended. Main courses 78–250DKK ($10–$31); 3-course fixed-price menu 295DKK ($37). AE, DC, MC, V. Daily 11:30am–11pm. Bus: 1, 6, or 8.

Søren K ☞ INTERNATIONAL   Named after Denmark's most celebrated philosopher, this is an artfully minimalist dining room that's on the ground floor of the newest addition to the Royal Library. Opened in 1999, it has big-windowed views that stretch out over the sea. Menu items change frequently, but might include carpaccio of veal, foie gras, oyster soup, and main courses such as veal chops served with lobster sauce and a half-lobster, and venison roasted with nuts and seasonal berries and a marinade of green tomatoes. The restaurant virtually never cooks with butter, cream, or high-cholesterol cheeses, making a meal here a dietetic as well as a savory experience.

On the ground floor of the Royal Library's Black Diamond Wing, 1 Søren Kierkegaards Plads. © **33-47-49-49.** Reservations recommended. Lunch main courses 65–125DKK ($8–$16); dinner main courses 195–225DKK ($24–$28); set-price 3-course dinner 315DKK ($39). DC, MC, V. Mon–Sat 11am–10:30pm. Bus: 1, 2, 5, 6, 8, or 9.

Inexpensive
Riz Raz *Value* MEDITERRANEAN/VEGETARIAN   Bustling and unpretentious, this decidedly un-Danish hideaway offers the best all-vegetarian buffet. Help yourself from a sprawling network of buffet tables laden with vegetarian specialties of the Mediterranean world, all for a price that by Scandinavian standards is highly reasonable. Carry your selections to a warren of small dining rooms. There's additional seating outdoors during nice weather, or, upstairs.

Expect a medley of virtually every vegetable known to humankind, prepared either au naturel, or as part of a marinated fantasy that might include antipasti of Italy, hummus of Lebanon, or an array of long-simmered casseroles inspired by the cuisines of the Moroccan highlands.

Kompagnistræde 20 (at Knabrostræde). © 33-15-05-75. Vegetarian buffet 59DKK ($7) per person; main courses 82–160DKK ($10–$20). DC, MC, V. Daily 11:30am–midnight. Bus: 5 or 6.

NEAR ROSENBORG SLOT
Very Expensive
Skt. Gertruds Kloster ✦✦ INTERNATIONAL Near Nørreport Station and south of Rosenborg Castle, this is the most romantic restaurant, and it serves some of the finest food, even though nothing to equal the cuisine at Kommandanten or Kong Hans Kaelder. There's no electricity in the labyrinth of 14th-century underground vaults, and the 1,500 flickering candles, open grill, iron sconces, and rough-hewn furniture create an elegant medieval ambience. At dinner, you might start with a pâté of fresh foie gras with a Madeira glacé and duck bacon or king prawn sautéed in parsley butter and served in red curry cream with honey-preserved apples and shallots, then move on to a combination of three kinds of fish with crayfish tails, mild curry jus, and a ratatouille of vegetables and rice. Every flavor is fully focused, each dish balanced to perfection.

Hauser Plads 32. © 33-14-66-30. Reservations required. Main courses 258–310DKK ($32–$39); fixed-price menu 415–625DKK ($52–$78); children's menu 90DKK ($11). AE, DC, MC, V. Daily 4–11pm. Closed Dec 25 to Jan 1. Bus: 4E, 7E, 14, or 16.

AT GRÅBRØDRETORV
Moderate
Bøf & Ost DANISH/FRENCH "Beef & Cheese" is housed in a 1728 building, and its cellars come from a medieval monastery. In summer a pleasant outdoor terrace overlooks Gray Friars Square. Specialties include lobster soup, fresh Danish bay strips, a cheese plate with six selections, and entrecôte with various sauces and butters and a baked potato. Seasonal dishes rotate in and out of the menu, making good use of regional mushrooms, fish, and game. One Danish student summed it up for us: "The food is not worthy of God's own table, but it's so good I come here once a week."

Gråbrødretorv 13. © 33-11-99-11. Reservations required. Main courses 125–179DKK ($16–$22); fixed-price menu 95DKK ($12) at lunch, 235DKK ($29) at dinner. DC, MC, V. Mon–Sat 11:30am–10:30pm. Closed Jan 1 and Dec 24–25. Bus: 5.

Inexpensive
Pasta Basta *Value* ITALIAN/INTERNATIONAL Its main attraction is a loaded table of cold antipasti and salads, which many diners believe is one of the best values in town. The restaurant is divided into half a dozen cozy dining rooms. Menu choices include at least 15 kinds of pasta (all made fresh on the premises), carpaccio with olive oil and basil, a platter with three kinds of Danish caviar (whitefish, speckled trout, and vendace), and fresh mussels cooked in a dry white wine with pasta and creamy saffron sauce. Late nights are often lively, so if you can't sleep and you're hungry, this can be an entertaining option.

Valkendorfsgade 22. © 33-11-21-31. Reservations recommended. Main courses 69–150DKK ($9–$19). No credit cards. Sun–Wed 11:30am–3am; Thurs–Sat 11:30am–5:30am. Bus: 5.

Peder Oxe's Restaurant/Vinkælder Wine Bar *Value* DANISH The building may be from the 18th century, but the crowd is young, fun, and value conscious. The salad bar is 20DKK ($2.50) when accompanied by a main course. It's so tempting that many prefer to enjoy it alone for 56DKK ($7) per person. Dishes include lobster soup, Danish bay shrimp, fresh asparagus, open-faced sandwiches, hamburgers, and fresh fish. The bill of fare, although standard, is well prepared.

Gråbrødretorv 11. ℂ **33-11-00-77.** Reservations recommended. Main courses 78–179DKK ($10–$22); fixed-price lunch 69–108DKK ($9–$14). DC, MC, V. Daily 11:30am–midnight. Bus: 5.

AT CHRISTIANSBORG
Very Expensive
Krogs Fiskerestaurant ✛ SEAFOOD   Classically elegant and opposite the old fish market, this restaurant's premises were built in 1789 as a fish shop, but now it is known as one of the best places to go in Copenhagen for seafood. The canal-side plaza where fishers moored their boats is now the site of the outdoor dining terrace. Converted into a restaurant in 1910, the establishment serves very fresh seafood. The well-chosen menu includes lobster soup, bouillabaisse, natural oysters, mussels steamed in white wine, and sautéed turbot with corn cassoulet. Each dish is impeccably prepared and filled with flavor. A limited selection of meat dishes is also available.

Gammel Strand 38. ℂ **33-15-89-15.** Reservations required. Main courses 258–445DKK ($32–$56); fixed-price menu: 3 courses 445DKK ($56), 5 courses 565DKK ($71). AE, DC, MC, V. Mon–Sat 11:30am–4pm and 5:30–10:30pm. Bus: 1, 2, 10, 16, or 29.

Expensive
Nouvelle ✛ DANISH   Within one of the oldest surviving houses, a prosperous-looking villa built around 1700, this restaurant deserves its fame as a local favorite. Dine in one of three elegantly rustic rooms overlooking a nearby canal. Menu items might include herring in puff pastry with caviar; turbot in a fruity gewürztraminer sauce; filet of veal with truffle sauce; and an unusual starter known as "egg nouvelle," a simple boiled egg with a significant difference (it's stuffed with a mousseline of lobster and accompanied with a dollop of caviar). A gratifying dessert specialty is an assortment of three sherbets: white chocolate, blackberries, and pear.

Gammel Strand 34. ℂ **33-13-50-18.** Reservations required. Main courses 265–310DKK ($33–$39); 3-course fixed-price lunch 465DKK ($58); 4-course fixed-price dinner 595DKK ($74). AE, DC, MC, V. Mon–Fri 11:30am–3pm and 6–10pm; Sat 7:30–9pm. Closed Dec 22 to Jan 6. Bus: 28, 29, or 41.

Moderate
Den Gyldne Fortun DANISH/SEAFOOD   The fish platters here are not the equal of Krogs (see above) but the cuisine is very satisfying. Though the building dates from 1750, Den Gyldne Fortun opened in 1975. The restaurant prides itself on fresh fish from the Mediterranean and the North Atlantic. Warmly nautical in decor, it has a bubbling lobster tank and an ice table displaying the fish of the day. Try the lobster bisque with fish and lobster roe, Danish fish soup, stuffed sole poached in white wine and glazed with hollandaise sauce, fried plaice with potatoes, or fricassee of three types of fish in saffron-flavored bouillon with noodles. Some beef dishes, such as Charolais sirloin, are also served.

Ved Stranden 18. ℂ **33-12-20-11.** Reservations recommended. Main courses 178–248DKK ($22–$31); 3-course fixed-price menu 325DKK ($41) Mon–Sat, 295DKK ($37) Sun. AE, DC, MC, V. Mon–Fri noon–3pm; daily 6–10pm. Bus: 1, 6, or 10.

Inexpensive
Cafeen Nikolaj DANISH   This cafe, which evokes Greenwich Village in the '50s, is on the site where Hans Tausen, a father of the Danish Reformation,

delivered thundering sermons in the 16th century. Today no one is thundering now—they're ordering an array of typical Danish lunches, including a tasty variety of open-faced sandwiches and homemade soups. You can always count on various types of herring. Danish sliced ham on good homemade bread is a perennial favorite, and there is also a selection of Danish cheeses. This is a simple cafe that prepares good-tasting food with fresh ingredients and charges a fair price.

Nikolaj Plads 12. (℃ **70-26-64-64**. Reservations accepted. Main courses 75–155DKK ($10–$19). AE, DC, MC, V. Mon–Sat 11:30am–5pm. Bus: 2, 6, 10, 27, 28, or 29.

IN TIVOLI

Food prices inside Tivoli are about 30% higher than elsewhere. Try skipping dessert at a restaurant and picking up a less expensive treat at one of the many stands. Take bus 1, 6, 8, 16, 29, 30, 32, or 33 to reach the park and either of the following restaurants. *Note:* These restaurants are open only from May to mid-September.

Very Expensive
Divan II ✦✦✦ DANISH/FRENCH   This is the finest restaurant in Tivoli, established in 1843, the same year as Tivoli itself. Despite its designation as Divan II, it's nonetheless older than its nearby competitor, the less formal Divan I. Service is almost unrelentingly impeccable in a garden setting where the cuisine is among the most urbane in the Danish capital. Stellar examples include fried filet of salmon served with a turbot bisque and tomato-and-basil concassé, and monkfish medallions sautéed with veal bacon and served with fricassee of morels. Dinners here are elaborate, memorable, and highly ritualized.

Vesterbrogade 3, Tivoli. (℃ **33-12-51-51**. Reservations recommended. Main courses 290–345DKK ($36–$43); fixed-price menu 345DKK ($43) at lunch. AE, DC, MC, V. Daily 11am–midnight.

Expensive
Færgekroen (*Value*) DANISH   In a cluster of trees at the edge of the lake, this restaurant resembles a pink half-timbered Danish cottage. In warm weather, try to sit on the outside terrace. The menu offers drinks, snacks, and full meals. Meals might include omelets, beef with horseradish, fried plaice with melted butter, pork chops with red cabbage, curried chicken, and fried meatballs. If you like honest and straightforward fare, without fancy trimmings, and don't like to spend a lot of money like you would at Divan II, this is the place for you. A pianist provides sing-along music every evening.

Vesterbrogade 3, Tivoli. (℃ **33-12-94-012**. Main courses 70–170DKK ($9–$21); fixed-price lunch 105DKK ($13). AE, DC, MC, V. Daily 11am–midnight (hot food until 9:45pm).

EXPLORING COPENHAGEN
SIGHTSEEING SUGGESTIONS FOR FIRST-TIME VISITORS

If You Have 1 Day Take a walking tour through the heart of the old city, which will give you time to recover from jet lag. Spend the late afternoon at Christiansborg Palace on Slotsholmen Island, where the queen of Denmark receives guests. Early in the evening, head to the Tivoli.

If You Have 2 Days On day 2, visit Amalienborg Palace, the queen's residence. Try to time your visit to witness the changing of the guard. Continue beyond the palace to *The Little Mermaid* statue. In the afternoon, see the art treasures of Ny Carlsberg Glyptotek. At night, seek out a local tavern.

If You Have 3 Days On the morning of the third day, journey to Rosenborg Castle, summer palace of King Christian IV, then wander through the park and gardens. Have lunch at one of the restaurants lining the canal at Nyhavn, the traditional seamen's quarter of Copenhagen. In the afternoon, go to Rundetårn (Round Tower) for a panoramic view of the city, and if time remains, stop in at the National Museum and Denmark's Fight for Freedom Museum.

If You Have 4 Days Head north to Louisiana, the modern-art museum,

and continue on to Helsingør to visit Kronborg Castle, famously associated with Shakespeare's *Hamlet.* Return by train to Copenhagen in time for a stroll along the Strøget, Europe's longest walking street. For dinner, visit the village of Dragør.

If You Have 5 Days On the fifth day, visit Frilandsmuseet, at Lyngby, a half-hour train ride from Copenhagen. Have lunch at the park. Return to Copenhagen and take a walking tour along its canals. If time remains, tour the Carlsberg brewery. Pay a final visit to the Tivoli to cap your adventure in the Danish capital.

THE TIVOLI GARDENS

Tivoli Gardens ℜℜ   Since it opened in 1843, this 8-hectare (20-acre) garden and amusement park in the center of Copenhagen has been a resounding success, with its thousands of flowers, merry-go-round of tiny Viking ships, games of chance and skill, and Ferris wheel of hot-air balloons and cabin seats. There's even a playground for children. The newest attraction is "The Golden Tower," topped by a shining golden cupola. The ride takes passengers 58m (190 ft.) above ground to enjoy a panoramic view of the city before being dropped to the ground at a blazing speed, even faster than a natural free fall. An Arabian-style fantasy palace, with towers and arches, houses more than two dozen restaurants in all price ranges, from a lakeside inn to a beer garden. Take a walk around the edge of the tiny lake with its ducks, swans, and boats.

A parade of the red-uniformed Tivoli Boys Guard takes place on weekends at 5:20 and 7:20pm, and their regimental band gives concerts Friday at 10pm on the open-air stage. The oldest building at Tivoli, the Chinese-style Pantomime Theater, with its peacock curtain, stages pantomimes in the evening.

Vesterbrogade 3. ⓒ 33-15-10-01. Admission 11am–1pm 49DKK ($6) adults, 25DKK ($3.15) children under 14; 1–9:30pm 45DKK ($6) adults, 20DKK ($2.50) children; 9:30pm–midnight 20DKK ($2.50) for all. Rides 20DKK ($2.50) each. May to mid-Sept daily 11am–midnight. Closed mid-Sept to Apr. Bus: 1, 16, or 29.

THE TOP MUSEUMS

Don't worry about not understanding the explanations in the museums; virtually all have write-ups in English.

Ny Carlsberg Glyptotek ℜℜℜ   The Glyptotek, behind the Tivoli, is one of Scandinavia's most important art museums. Founded by 19th-century art collector Carl Jacobsen, the museum holds modern art and antiquities. The modern section has both French and Danish art, mainly from the 19th century; sculpture, including works by Rodin; and works of the Impressionists and related artists, including van Gogh's *Landscape from St-Rémy.* Antiquities include Egyptian, Greek, Roman, and Etruscan works. The Egyptian collection is outstanding; the prize is a prehistoric rendering of a hippopotamus. A favorite of ours is the Etruscan art display. In 1996, the Ny Glyptotek added a French Masters' wing, where you'll find an extensive collection of masterpieces.

Dantes Plads 7. ⓒ 33-41-81-41. www.glyptoteket.dk. Admission 30DKK ($3.75) adults, free for children; Wed and Sun free for all. Tues–Sun 10am–4pm. Bus: 1, 2, 5, 6, 8, or 10.

Statens Museum for Kunst (Royal Museum of Fine Arts) ⭐⭐ This well-stocked museum, one of the best in Scandinavia, houses painting and sculpture from the 13th century to the present. There are Dutch golden-age landscapes and marine paintings by Rubens, plus portraits by Frans Hals and Rembrandt. Eckersberg, Købke, and Hansen represent the Danish golden age. French 20th-century art includes 20 works by Matisse. In the Royal Print Room are 300,000 drawings, prints, lithographs, and other works by such artists as Dürer, Rembrandt, Matisse, and Picasso.

Sølvgade 48–50. © 33-74-84-94. www.smk.dk. Admission 30–50DKK ($4.35–$7) adults, free for children under 16. Tues and Thurs–Sun 10am–5pm; Wed 10am–8pm. Bus: 10, 14, 43, or 184.

Den Hirschsprungske Samling (The Hirschsprung Collection) This collection of 19th- and early 20th-century Danish art is in Ostre Anlaeg, a park in the city center. Tobacco merchant Heinrich Hirschsprung (1836–1908) created the collection, and it has been growing ever since. The emphasis is on the Danish golden age, with such artists as Eckersberg, Købke, and Lundbye, and on the Skagen painters, P. S. Krøyer, and Anna and Michael Ancher. Some furnishings from the artists' homes are exhibited.

Stockholmsgade 20. © 35-42-03-36. www.hirschsprung.dk. Admission 25DKK ($3.15) adults, 15DKK ($1.90) students, free for children under 16; 40DKK ($5) during special exhibitions. Wed 11am–9pm; Thurs–Mon 11am–4pm. Bus: 10, 14, 42, or 43.

Nationalmuseet (National Museum) ⭐⭐⭐ A gigantic repository of anthropological artifacts, this museum features objects from prehistory, the Middle Ages, and the Renaissance in Denmark, including Viking stones, helmets, and fragments of battle gear. Especially interesting are the "lur" horn, a Bronze Age musical instrument among the oldest in Europe, and the world-famous Sun Chariot, an elegant Bronze Age piece of pagan art. The Royal Collection of Coins and Medals contains various coins from antiquity. There are also outstanding collections of Egyptian and Classical antiquities.

Ny Vestergade 10. © 33-13-44-11. www.natmus.dk. Admission 40DKK ($5) adults, 30DKK ($3.75) students, free for children under 16. Tues–Sun 10am–5pm. Closed Dec 24, 25, and 31. Bus: 1, 2, 5, 6, 8, 10, ot 41.

Frihedsmuseet (Museum of Danish Resistance, 1940–45) The horrors of the Nazi occupation of Denmark live on here. On display are relics of torture

---

⟲ Copenhagen's *Little Mermaid*

The one statue *everybody* wants to see is the life-size bronze of **Den Lille Havfrue** ⭐, inspired by Hans Christian Andersen's "The Little Mermaid," one of the world's most famous fairy tales. The statue, unveiled in 1913, was sculpted by Edvard Eriksen and rests on rocks right off the shore. The mermaid has been attacked more than once, losing an arm in one misadventure, decapitated as recently as January 6, 1998.

All year, there's a 2½-hour Grand Tour of Copenhagen that makes a significant stop at the *Little Mermaid* and costs 175DKK ($22). In summer, a special "Mermaid Bus" leaves from Rådhuspladsen (Vester Voldgade) at 10:30am and then at half-hour intervals until 5:30pm. On the "Langelinie" bus there's a 20-minute stop at *The Little Mermaid.* If you want more time, take bus 1, 6, or 9.

and concentration camps, the equipment used for the wireless and illegal films, British propaganda leaflets, satirical caricatures of Hitler, information about both Danish Jews and Danish Nazis, and the paralyzing nationwide strikes. Also look for an armed car used for drive-by shootings of Danish Nazi informers and collaborators.

Churchillparken. ℂ **33-13-77-14.** www.natmus.dk. Admission 30DKK ($3.75) adults, free for children 16 and under. May to Sept 15 Tues–Sat 10am–4pm, Sun 10am–5pm; Sept 16–Apr Tues–Sat 11am–3pm, Sun 11am–4pm. Bus: 1, 6, or 9.

Frilandsmuseet (Open-Air Museum) 🎇   This reconstructed village in Lyngby, on the fringe of Copenhagen, captures Denmark's one-time rural character. The "museum" is nearly 36 hectares (90 acres); a 3.2-km (2-mile) walk around the compound reveals a dozen authentic buildings—farmsteads, windmills, fishers' cottages. Exhibits include a half-timbered 18th-century farmstead from one of the tiny windswept Danish islands, a primitive longhouse from the remote Faroe Islands, thatched fishers' huts from Jutland, tower windmills, and a mid-19th-century potter's workshop.

Kongevejen 100. ℂ **33-13-44-11.** www.natmus.dk. Admission 30DKK ($3.75) adults, free for children under 16. Easter–Sept, Tues–Sun 10am–5pm; Oct 1–18, Tues–Sun 10am–4pm. Closed Oct 19–Easter. S-tog: Copenhagen Central Station to Sorgenfri (trains leave every 20 min.). Bus: 184 or 194.

Erotica Museum 🎇   This is the only museum in the world where you learn about the sex lives of Freud, Marilyn Monroe, Hugh Hefner, Nietzsche, and Duke Ellington. Founded by Ole Ege, a well-known Danish photographer of nudes, it's within walking distance of the Tivoli and the Central Railroad Station. In addition to revealing a glimpse into the sex lives of the famous, it presents a survey of erotica around the world and through the ages. The exhibits range from Etruscan drawings and Chinese paintings to Greek vases depicting sexual activity.

Købmagergade 24. ℂ **33-12-03-11.** www.museumerotica.dk. Admission 65DKK ($8.15). Those 16–18 must be accompanied by an adult; no one under 16 admitted. May–Sept, daily 10am–11pm; Oct–Apr, Mon–Fri 11am–8pm, Sat 10am–9pm, Sun 10am–8pm. S-tog: Nørreport.

Tøjhusmuseet (Royal Arsenal Museum)   This museum features a fantastic display of weapons used for hunting and warfare. On the ground floor is the Canon Hall, the longest vaulted Renaissance hall in Europe, stocked with artillery equipment from 1500 up to the present day. Above the Canon Hall is the impressive Armory Hall with one of the world's finest collections of small arms, colors, and armor.

Tøjhusgade 3. ℂ **33-11-60-37.** www.thm.dk. Admission 30DKK ($3.75) adults, 10DKK ($1.25) children 6–12, free for children under 6. Tues–Sun noon–4pm. Closed Jan 1, and Dec 24, 25, and 31. Bus: 1, 2, 5, 6, 8, 10, 28, 29, 30, 32, 33, 34, or 35.

Amalienborg Palace 🎇🎇   These four 18th-century French-inspired rococo mansions are the home of the Danish royal family, a position they have held since 1794 when the original royal palace here burned. Visitors flock to witness the changing of the guard at noon when the royal family is in residence. A swallowtail flag at mast signifies that the queen is in Copenhagen. The Royal Life Guard in black bearskin busbies leaves Rosenborg Castle at 11:30am and marches to Amalienborg. After the event, the guard, still accompanied by the band, returns to Rosenborg Castle.

In 1994 some of the official and private rooms in Amalienborg were opened to the public for the first time. The rooms, reconstructed to reflect the period

1863 to 1947, belonged to members of the reigning royal family, the Glücks-borgs, who ascended the throne in 1863. The highlight is the period devoted to the long reign (1863–1906) of King Christian IX and Queen Louise.

Christian VIII's Palace. ℭ **33-12-21-86.** Admission 40DKK ($5) adults, 25DKK ($3.15) students and seniors, 5DKK (65¢) children 5–12, free for children under 5. Jan–Apr, Oct–Dec 13 Tues–Sun 11am–4pm; May, Sept–Oct, Dec 26–30 daily 11am–4pm; June–Aug daily 10am–4pm. Closed Dec 14–Dec 25. Bus: 1, 6, 9, or 10.

Christiansborg Palace ⚐

This granite-and-copper palace on the Slotsholmen—a small island that has been the center of political power in Denmark for more than 800 years—houses the Danish parliament, the Supreme Court, the prime minister's offices, and the Royal Reception Rooms. A guide will lead you through richly decorated rooms, including the Throne Room, banqueting hall, and Queen's Library. Before entering, you'll be asked to put on soft overshoes to protect the floors. Under the palace, visit the well-preserved ruins of the 1167 castle of Bishop Absalon, founder of Copenhagen.

Christiansborg Slotsplads. ℭ **33-92-64-92.** Royal Reception Rooms, 40DKK ($5) adults, 10DKK ($1.25) children; parliament free; castle ruins 20DKK ($2.50) adults, 5DKK (65¢) children. Reception rooms, guided tours June–Aug daily 11am, 1pm, and 3pm; May and Sept Tues–Sun 11am and 3pm; Oct–Apr Tues, Thurs, Sun 11am and 3pm. Parliament, English-language tours daily 11am, 1pm, and 3pm. Ruins, May–Sept Tues–Fri and Sun 9:30am–3:30pm. Closed Oct–Apr. Bus: 1, 2, 6, 8, 9, 42, or 43.

Rosenborg Castle ⚐⚐⚐

This redbrick Renaissance-style castle houses everything from narwhal-tusk and ivory coronation chairs to Frederik VII's baby shoes—all from the Danish royal family. Its biggest draws are the dazzling crown jewels and regalia in the basement Treasury, where a lavishly decorated coronation saddle from 1596 is also shown. Try to see the Knights Hall (Room 21), with its coronation seat, three silver lions, and relics from the 1700s. Room 3 was used by founding father Christian IV, who died in this bedroom decorated with Asian lacquer art and a stucco ceiling.

Øster Voldgade 4A. ℭ **33-15-32-86.** Admission 50DKK ($6.25) adults, 30DKK ($3.75) students and seniors, 10DKK ($1.25) children 5–12. Free ages 4 and under. Palace and treasury (royal jewels), June–Aug daily 10am–4pm; May and Sept to mid-Oct, daily 11am–3pm; mid-Oct to Apr Tues, Fri, Sun 11am–2pm. S-tog: Nørreport. Bus: 5, 10, 14, 16, 31, 42, 43, 184, or 185.

CHURCHES & OTHER ATTRACTIONS

Frederikskirke

This 2-centuries-old church, with its green copper dome—one of the largest in the world—is a short walk from Amalienborg Palace. After an unsuccessful start during the neoclassical revival of the 1750s in Denmark, the church was finally completed in Roman baroque style in 1894. In many ways, it's more impressive than Copenhagen's cathedral.

Frederiksgade 4. ℭ **33-15-01-44.** Admission to church free; to dome, 20DKK ($2.50) adults, 10DKK ($1.25) children. Church: Mon–Tues and Thurs–Fri 11am–2pm, Wed 11am–6pm, Sat 11am–4pm, Sun noon–4pm. Dome: June 15–Sept 1 daily 11am–12:45pm; Oct–May, Sat–Sun 11am–12:45pm. Bus: 1, 6, or 9.

Vor Frue Kirke (Copenhagen Cathedral)

This early 19th-century Greek Revival-style church, near Copenhagen University, features Bertel Thorvaldsen's white marble neoclassical works, including *Christ and the Apostles*. The funeral of H. C. Andersen took place here in 1875, and that of Søren Kierkegaard in 1855.

Nørregade. ℭ **33-14-41-28.** Free admission. Mon–Fri 9am–5pm. Bus: 5.

Rådhus (Town Hall) and World Clock ⚐

Built in 1905, the Town Hall has impressive statues of H. C. Andersen and Niels Bohr, the Nobel Prize–winning physicist. Jens Olsen's famous **World Clock** is open for viewing Monday to

Friday 10am to 4pm and Saturday at noon. The clockwork is so exact that the variation over 300 years is 0.4 seconds. Climb the tower for an impressive view.

Rådhuspladsen. ℭ 33-66-25-82. Rådhus 30DKK ($3.75); clock 10DKK ($1.25) adults, 5DKK (65¢) children. Guided tour: Rådhus, Mon–Fri 3pm, Sat 10am; tower, Mon–Sat noon. Bus: 1, 6, or 8.

Rundetårn (Round Tower) ⚓ This 17th-century public observatory, attached to a church, is visited by thousands who climb the spiral ramp (no steps) for a panoramic view of Copenhagen. The tower is one of the crowning architectural achievements of the Christian IV era. Peter the Great, in Denmark for a state visit, galloped up the ramp on horseback.

Købmagergade 52A. ℭ 33-73-03-73. Admission 15DKK ($1.90) adults, 5DKK (65¢) children. Tower, June–Aug Mon–Sat 10am–8pm, Sun noon–8pm; Sept–May Mon–Sat 10am–5pm, Sun noon–5pm. Observatory, Oct 15–Mar 20, Tues–Wed 7–10pm. Closed Mar 21–Sept 25. Bus: 5, 7E, 14, 16, or 42.

Botanisk Have (Botanical Gardens) Planted from 1871 to 1874, the Botanical Gardens, across from Rosenborg Castle, are on a lake that was once part of the city's defensive moat. Special features include a cactus house and a palm house, all of which appear even more exotic in the far northern country of Denmark. An alpine garden contains mountain plants from all over the world.

Gothersgade 128. ℭ 35-32-22-40. Free admission. May–Sept daily 8:30am–6pm; Oct–Apr daily 8:30am–4pm. S-tog: Nørreport. Bus: 5, 7, 14, 16, 24, 40, or 43.

ORGANIZED TOURS

BUS & BOAT TOURS For orientation, try the 1½-hour **City Tour** (2½ hours with a visit to a brewery) that covers major scenic highlights like *The Little Mermaid,* Rosenborg Castle, and Amalienborg Palace. On workdays, tours also visit the Carlsberg brewery. Tours depart May 30 to September 13 daily at 1pm and cost 130DKK ($16) adults and 20DKK ($2.50) children.

The **City and Harbor Tour,** a 2½-hour trip by launch and bus, departs from Town Hall Square. The boat tours the city's main canals, passing *The Little Mermaid* and the Old Fish Market. It operates from May 30 to September 13 daily at 1pm. Tours cost 175DKK ($22) adults and 90DKK ($11) children under 12.

Shakespeare buffs will be interested in an afternoon excursion to the castles of North Zealand. The 7-hour English-language tour explores the area north of Copenhagen, including visits to Kronborg (Hamlet's Castle), a brief trip to Fredensborg, the queen's residence, and a stopover at Frederiksborg Castle and the National Historical Museum. Tours depart from the Town Hall Square, from May 2 to October 16 Wednesday, Saturday, and Sunday at 10:15am. The cost is 335DKK ($42) adults and 40DKK ($5) children.

One of the most appealing of the guided tours is the **Hans Christian Andersen Tour,** which involves a 10-hour bus trip to the verdant island of Funen. It departs every Wednesday and Sunday from June to September at 8:30am from Rådhusplads. The cost of 550DKK ($69) includes transit from Copenhagen through Zealand, over the recently completed High Bridge spanning the Great Belt, to Odense, birthplace of Hans Christian Andersen. The price of lunch and admission to the various museums and castles visited is extra. Stops along the way include Egeskov Castle, built in 1554, and the house and museum of the fabled storyteller himself. Advance reservations are necessary. For more information about these English-language tours, contact **Copenhagen Excursions** at ℭ **32-54-06-06** or **Vikingbus** at ℭ **32-55-26-00.**

GUIDED WALKS English-language guided walking tours of Copenhagen are offered from May 1 to September 30 at 80DKK ($10) adults and 25DKK

($3.15) children. Tours begin outside the tourist office. Contact the Copenhagen Tourist Information Center, Bernstorffsgade 1 (© **33-25-38-14**).

THE SHOPPING SCENE

Royal Copenhagen, Amagertorv 6 (© **33-13-71-81;** www.royalcopenhagen. com; bus: 1, 2, 6, 8, 28, 29, or 41 for the retail outlet, 1 or 14 for the factory), was founded in 1775. Royal Copenhagen's trademark, three wavy blue lines, has come to symbolize quality in porcelain throughout the world. The factory was a royal possession for a century before passing into private hands in 1868 and has turned out a new plate each year since 1908; most of the motifs depict the Danish countryside in winter.

In the Royal Copenhagen retail center, legendary **Georg Jensen,** Amagertorv 6 (© **33-11-40-80;** www.georgjensen.com; bus: 1, 6, 8, 9, or 10), is known for its fine silver. For the connoisseur, there's no better address—this is the largest and best collection of Jensen hollowware in Europe. Jewelry in traditional and modern design is also featured. One department specializes in seconds produced by various porcelain and glassware manufacturers. In the Royal Copenhagen retail center, **Holmegaards Glasvaerker,** Amagertorv 6 (© **33-12-44-77;** bus: 1, 6, 8, 9, or 10), is the only major producer of glasswork in Denmark. Look for the solidly crafted 1859 Wellington pattern, Holmegaard glasses, and Regiment Bar set.

Customers refer to the two owners of **The Amber Specialist,** Frederiksberggade 28 (© **33-11-88-03;** bus: 28, or 29, or 41), as "The Amber Twins." These blonde-haired ladies specialize in "the gold of the north." This stone—really petrified resin—originated in the large coniferous forests that covered Denmark some 35 million years ago.

A center for modern Scandinavian and Danish design, **Illums Bolighus,** Amagertorv 10, on Strøget (© **33-14-19-41;** bus: 28, 29, or 41), is one of Europe's finest showcases for household furnishings and accessories of every kind. The store also sells fashions and accessories for women and men. There's even a gift shop. At **Sweater Market,** Frederiksberggade 15 (© **33-15-27-73;** bus: 2, 8, or 30), take your pick from Scandinavian and Icelandic top-grade sweaters, hats, and scarves, hand knit in 100% wool. There's also a large selection of Icelandic wool jackets and coats.

One of Denmark's top department stores, **Illum's,** Østergade 52 (© **33-14-40-02;** bus: 1, 6, 9, or 10), is on the Strøget. Take time to browse through its vast world of Scandinavian design. There's a restaurant and a special export cash desk at street level. The elegant **Magasin,** Kongens Nytorv 13 (© **33-11-44-33;** bus: 1, 6, 9, or 10), is the biggest department store in Scandinavia. It offers an assortment of Danish designer fashion, glass and porcelain, and souvenirs. Goods are shipped abroad tax-free.

Established in 1926, **Kunsthallens Kunstauktioner,** Gothersgade 9 (© **33-32-52-00;** bus: 1, 6, 9, or 10), is Europe's leading dealer in the pan-European school of painting known as CoBrA (Copenhagen, Brussels, and Amsterdam). These works, produced from 1948 to 1951, were an important precursor of abstract expressionism. The gallery holds 12 auctions yearly, eight with modern art, others with 19th-century art. **Boghallen,** Rådhuspladsen 37 (© **33-11-85-11;** bus: 2, 8, or 30), is a big store carrying many books in English (including translations of Danish works) as well as a wide selection of travel-related literature, including maps. The shop is at Town Hall Square.

COPENHAGEN AFTER DARK

In Copenhagen, a good night means a late night. On warm weekends hundreds of rowdy revelers crowd Strøget until sunrise, and jazz clubs, traditional beer houses, and wine cellars are routinely packed. The city has a more serious cultural side as well, exemplified by excellent theaters, operas, and ballets. **Half-price tickets** for some concerts and theater productions are available the day of the performance from the ticket kiosk opposite the Nørreport rail station, at Nørrevoldgade and Fiolstræde; it's open from Monday to Friday noon to 7pm and Saturday noon to 3pm. On summer evenings there are outdoor concerts in Fælled Park near the entrance, near Frederik V's Vej; inquire about dates and times at the Copenhagen Tourist Office.

THE PERFORMING ARTS

Det Kongelige Teater (Royal Theater), Kongens Nytorv (℃ **33-69-69-69;** www.kgl-teater.dk; bus: 1, 6, 9, or 10), which dates from 1748, is home to the world-renowned **Royal Danish Ballet** and the **Royal Danish Opera.** Because the arts are state subsidized in Denmark, ticket prices are comparatively low, and some seats may be available at the box office the day before a performance. We recommend making reservations in advance. The season runs from August to May. Tickets are 60 to 600DKK ($8 to $75), half price for seniors 67 and over and those under 26 (1 week before a show begins). The box office is open from Monday to Saturday 1 to 8pm; telephone hours are from Monday to Saturday 1 to 7pm.

NIGHTCLUBS

Across the boulevard from the Tivoli, **Rosie McGee's,** Vesterbrogade 2A (℃ **33-32-19-23;** bus: 250E or 350E), is a funky, American-style nightclub that caters to high-energy Generation X-ers (aged 21–40), whom you may or may not find enchanting. Lots of young people come here to mingle, compare notes, and dance, dance, dance. The simple restaurant serves mostly Mexican food and frothy, foamy drinks. The bar and restaurant open nightly at 5pm, with disco featured every Thursday to Saturday 11:30pm till dawn. Cover is 40DKK ($5) on disco nights only.

Few other night clubs in Copenhagen offer as many bars as **Enzo,** Norregade 41 (℃ **33-13-67-88;** S-tog: Norreport Station). Come here for an all-around introduction to Copenhagen's night owls, then gravitate to either the Couch Lounge; the Cigar Lounge (where you can puff up a storm); a disco bar (where you'll dance between drinks); a Water Bar (where you can, despite the bar's name, still get a drink of whiskey); and the Shot Bar, which boasts a comprehensive collection of tequilas, exotic rums, and vodkas. It's open to the public Friday and Saturday only from 9pm to 5am. The cover is 60DKK ($8).

At **NASA,** Gothersgade 8F, Bolthensgaard (℃ **33-93-74-15;** bus: 1, 6, or 9), a late-night crowd of 25- to 40-year-olds includes many avid fans of whatever musical innovation has just emerged in London or Los Angeles. The decorative theme includes lots of white, lots of mirrors, and lots of artfully directed spotlights. Technically, the site is a private club, but polite and presentable newcomers can usually gain access. It's open from Thursday to Sunday 10pm to 6am. Cover is 100DKK ($13).

LIVE-MUSIC CLUBS

In the very heart of the city, **Den Røde Pimpernel** (the Scarlet Pimpernel), H. C. Andersens Blvd. 7 (℃ **33-12-20-32;** bus: 28 or 30), with its lively atmosphere, is a good place for people watching and dancing to an odd mix of contemporary pop and old-time evergreen ensembles. There's a bit of an attitude; the clientele is admitted only after being inspected through a peephole. The club is open from Tuesday to Saturday 9pm to 5am. There's a 50DKK ($6) cover Friday and Saturday.

Copenhagen JazzHouse, Niels Hammingsensgade 10 (℗ **33-15-26-00;** S-tog: Nørreport), rocks and rolls, offering an all-purpose venue that plays— depending on the night of the week—everything from live jazz concerts to late-night disco. There's dancing to electronically amplified music from Wednesday to Sunday 11pm to at least 3am. The quality and breed of jazz depends entirely on whoever is scheduled to appear on any particular evening. Live music tends to begin around 8:30pm. There's a cafe on the premises and tableside seating for up to 300 jazz fans at a time. Cover is 40 to 70DKK ($5 to $9).

Mojo Blues Bar, Løngangsstraede 21C (℗ **33-11-64-53;** bus: 2, 8, or 30), is one of the leading blues clubs in Scandinavia. Softly lit by candle and globe lamps, Mojo seats about 90 people at wooden tables and chairs and on a long bench along one wall. On weekends, which are often standing room only, up to 125 people cram through the door. Most come for the live blues performed mainly by Danish groups, although German, American, and British bands sometimes take the stage. It's open daily from 8pm to 5am. No cover from Sunday to Thursday, 50DKK ($6) Friday and Saturday.

A DANCE CLUB

Set a short walk from Tivoli, **Baron & Baroness,** Vesterbrøgade 2E (℗ **33-16-01-01;** bus: 250E or 350E), is a relatively upscale nightclub whose decor incorporates faux-medieval crenellations, attracting a crowd that's a bit more prosperous, and a bit more mature, than nearby competitors catering only to teenagers. Full meals cost 150 to 250DKK ($21 to $36), and on nights when there's no disco, you'll find a solo musician playing a fiddle, piano, harmonica, or whatever. The bars are open nightly from 5pm to at least 4:30am, the restaurant from 5 to 11:30pm. Disco, which is featured one floor above the street restaurant, is presented only from Thursday to Saturday, 10pm till dawn. Cover 50DKK ($6) for disco only.

BARS

Det Lille Apotek, Stor Kannikestraede 15 (℗ **33-12-56-06;** bus: 2, 5, 8, or 30), is a good spot for English-speaking foreign students to meet their Danish contemporaries. Though the menu varies, keep an eye out for the prawn cocktail and tenderloin. The main courses run about 88 to 128DKK ($11 to $16) at dinner. The kitchen is open daily from 11:30am to 5pm. The bar is open daily from 11am to midnight.

Frequented by celebrities and royalty, the **Library Bar,** in the Hotel Plaza, Bernstorffsgade 4 (℗ **33-14-15-19;** bus: 6), was rated by the late Malcolm Forbes as one of the top five bars in the world. In a setting of antique books and works of art, you can order everything from a cappuccino to a cocktail. The setting is the lobby level of the landmark Plaza, commissioned in 1913 by King Frederik VIII. The bar was designed and built as the hotel's ballroom, and Oregon pine was used for the paneling. The mural of George Washington and his men dates from 1910. It's open from Monday to Saturday 11:30am to 1am and Sunday 11:30am to midnight.

Nyhavn 17, Nyhavn 17 (© **33-12-54-19;** bus: 1, 6, 27, or 29), is the last of the honky-tonks that used to make up the former sailors' quarter. This cafe is a short walk from the Kongens Nytorv and d'Angleterre hotels. In summer you can sit outside. On Tuesday to Saturday evenings there's free entertainment from a solo guitarist or guitar duet. It's open from Sunday to Thursday 9:30am to 2am and Friday and Saturday until 4am. Built in 1670, **Hvids Vinstue,** Kongens Nytorv 19 (© **33-15-10-64;** bus: 1, 6, 9, or 10), is a wine cellar that's a dimly lit safe haven for an eclectic crowd, many patrons—both theatergoers and actors and dancers—drawn from the Royal Theater across the way. In December only, a combination of red wine and cognac is served. It's open from Monday to Saturday 10am to 2am; closed Sunday in July and August.

GAY & LESBIAN CLUBS

Pan Society, Knabrostræde 3 (© **33-13-19-48** or 33-11-37-84; bus: 28, 29, or 41), is a nationwide organization established in 1948 for the protection and advancement of gay and lesbian rights. Its headquarters is a 19th-century yellow building off the Strøget. A dance club occupies three of its floors, and a modern cafe is situated on the ground floor. Every night is gay night, although a lot of straights come here because the music is good. The cafe is open daily from 8pm to 5am. The dance club is open Wednesday 11pm to 3am, Thursday 10pm to 4am, Friday and Saturday 10pm to 5am, and Sunday 11pm to 3am. Admission to the dance club is 55DKK ($7).

The leading night life venue, popular with gay men and women, is **Sebastian Bar & Café,** Hyskenstraede 10 (© **33-32-22-79;** bus: 6 or 29), which operates a good restaurant serving an international cuisine and also has a cruisy bar. It's an all-around rendezvous point for many of the capital's gay men and women, also attracting a lot of foreign visitors looking for action. The bar and cafe is open daily noon to 2am, the restaurant daily from 5 to 11pm.

A CASINO

At the **Casino Copenhagen,** in the SAS Scandinavia Hotel, Amager Blvd. 70 (© **33-96-59-65;** bus: 5, 11, 30, or 34), gamblers play such popular games as roulette, baccarat, punto banco, blackjack, and slots. The operation is overseen by Casinos of Austria, Europe's largest casino operator. It's open daily 2pm to 4am. Cover is 80DKK ($10). Jackets are required for men and a valid picture ID for all.

DAY TRIPS FROM COPENHAGEN

DRAGØR ☙☙   Visit the past in this old seafaring town on the island of Amager, 5km (3 miles) south of Copenhagen's Kastrup Airport. It's filled with well-preserved, half-timbered, ocher-and-pink 18th-century cottages with steep red-tile or thatch roofs, many of which are under the protection of the National Trust.

Dragør (pronounced *Drah-wer*) was a busy port on the herring-rich Baltic Sea in the early Middle Ages, but when fishing fell off, it became just another sleepy waterfront village. After 1520, Amager Island and its villages—Dragør and Store Magleby—were inhabited by the Dutch, who brought their own customs, Low-German language, and agricultural expertise, especially their love of bulb flowers. In Copenhagen, you still see wooden-shoed Amager selling their hyacinths, tulips, daffodils, and lilies in the streets.

A rich trove of historic treasures is in the **Amager Museum,** Hovedgaden 4–12, Store Magleby (© **32-53-93-07; bus: 30, 33, or 350S), outside Dragør. The exhibits reveal the affluence achieved by the Amager Dutch, with rich textiles, fine embroidery, and amenities like carved silver buckles and buttons. The interiors of a Dutch house are especially interesting. Admission is 20DKK ($2.50) adults, 10DKK ($1.25) children. It's open from April to September Tuesday to Sunday noon to 4pm; from October to March, Wednesday and Sunday noon to 4pm.

The exhibits at the harborfront **Dragør Museum,** Havnepladsen 2–4 (© **32-53-41-06;** bus: 30, 33, or 350S), show how the Amager Dutch lived from prehistoric times to the 20th century. Farming, goose breeding, seafaring, fishing, ship piloting, and ship salvage are delineated through pictures and artifacts. Admission is 20DKK ($2.50) adults, 10DKK ($1.25) children. It's open from May to September Tuesday to Sunday noon to 4pm; closed from October to April.

LOUISIANA   Established in 1958, the **Louisiana Museum of Modern Art** ⋆⋆, Gl. Strandvej 13 (© **49-19-07-19**), is idyllically situated in a 19th-century mansion on the Danish Riviera surrounded by a sculpture park, opening directly onto the Øresund. Paintings and sculptures by modern masters, such as Giacometti and Henry Moore, as well as the best and most controversial works of modern art, are displayed. The museum name came from the estate's first owner, Alexander Brun, who had three wives, each named Louise. Admission is 60DKK ($8) adults, 45DKK ($6) students, 20DKK ($2.50) children 4 to 16, and free for children under 4. It's open daily from 10am to 5pm; closed December 24, 25, and 31.

Getting There   Humlebaek, the nearest town to Louisiana, may be reached by train from Copenhagen (København-Helsingør). Two trains an hour leave from the main station in Copenhagen (trip time: 40 min.). Once you're at Humlebaek, follow signs to the museum, a 15-minute walk.

HELSINGØR (ELSINORE) ⋆   Helsingør is visited chiefly for "Hamlet's Castle." Aside from its literary associations, the town has a certain charm: a quiet market square, medieval lanes, and old half-timbered and brick buildings, remains of its once-prosperous shipping industry. The **Tourist Office,** Havnepladsen 3 (© **49-21-13-33**), is open from Monday to Friday 9:30am to 6pm and Saturday 9am to 4pm.

There's no evidence Shakespeare ever saw this sandstone-and-copper Dutch Renaissance–style castle, full of intriguing secret passages and casemates, but he made **Kronborg Slot** ⋆⋆⋆, Kronborg (© **49-21-30-78**), famous in *Hamlet.* According to 12th-century historian Saxo Grammaticus, though, if Hamlet had really existed, he would've lived centuries before Kronborg was erected (1574–85). Over the years, some famous productions of *Hamlet* have been staged here, the castle's bleak atmosphere providing a good foil to the drama.

During its history, the castle has been looted, bombarded, gutted by fire, and used as a barracks (1785–1922). The starkly furnished Great Hall is the largest in northern Europe. The church with its original oak furnishings and the royal chambers are also worth exploring. Admission to the castle is 40DKK ($5) adults, 10DKK ($1.25) children 6 to 14. From May to September, it's open daily 10:30am to 5pm; October and April, hours are from Tuesday to Sunday

11am to 4pm; from November to March, it's open Tuesday to Sunday 11am to 3pm (closed Christmas). Guided tours are given every half hour from October to April. In summer you can walk around on your own. The castle is 0.8km (½ mile) from the rail station.

Getting There   Once you reach Helsingør, 40km (25 miles) north of Copenhagen, you'll be deposited in the center of town and can cover all the major attractions on foot. There are frequent trains from Copenhagen, taking 50 minutes. Some 30 buses daily leave Copenhagen for the 1-hour trip to Helsingør.

5

England

by Darwin Porter & Danforth Prince

London is the most happening city in Europe—lively, fast paced, and teeming with action. London now touts its fascinating contradictions: It's both an overwhelming jumble of antiquity and a world leader in the latest music, fashion, and food (the cuisine is better than ever). As stimulating as the city is, however, you'll want to tear yourself away from it to visit legendary Stonehenge, Oxford University, and the classic city of Bath.

1 London

Samuel Johnson said, "When a man is tired of London, he is tired of life; for there's in London all that life can afford." We'll survey a segment of that life: ancient monuments, literary shrines, museums, walking tours, Parliament debates, royal castles, waxworks, palaces, cathedrals, and parks.

ESSENTIALS

GETTING THERE   By Plane   For information on all London airports, visit www.baa.co.uk. **Heathrow Airport** (© 0870/000-123) is divided into four terminals, each relatively self-contained. There's an Underground (subway) connection to central London; the 50-minute trip costs £3.50 ($5). Airbuses take about an hour; they cost £7 ($11) adults; up to four children ride free if accompanied by an adult. A taxi usually costs from £35 to £40 ($52.50–$60), but may be higher. For more information about train or bus connections, call © 020/7222-1234.

London-Heathrow Express (© 0845/600-1515) is a 160kph (100 mph) train running every 15 minutes daily 5:10am to 11:40pm to Paddington Station. The 15- to 20-minute trip costs £12 ($18) in economy class or £20 ($30) in first class; children up to 15 ride free. There are special areas for wheelchairs. You can buy tickets on the train or at self-service machines at Heathrow (also available from travel agents).

Gatwick (© 01293/535353 for flight information) is 40km (25 miles) south of London. Trains leave for London every 15 minutes during the day and every hour at night; they cost £10.20 ($15) adults, half price for children aged 5 to 15, and free for under 5. There's also an express Flightline bus (no. 777) from Gatwick to Victoria Station that departs every half hour 6:30am to 8pm and every hour 8 to 11pm; it costs £8 ($12). A taxi from Gatwick to central London usually costs £55 to £65 ($83–$98); however, you must negotiate a fare with the driver before you get into the cab.

By Train   Most trains from Paris traveling through the "Chunnel" pull in at **Waterloo Station.** Visitors from Amsterdam arrive at the **Liverpool Street Station,** and those journeying south by rail from Edinburgh disembark at

King's Cross Station. All are connected to the vast bus and Underground network, and have phones, restaurants, pubs, luggage-storage areas, and London Regional Transport Information Centres.

By Car   If you're taking a car across the channel, you can quickly connect by motorway (superhighway) into London. London is encircled by a ring road. Determine which part of the city you wish to enter and follow the signs. You should confine your driving in London to the *bare minimum;* before you arrive, call your hotel for advice on where to park. Be warned—parking is scarce and expensive. Most important driving tip in England: *Remember to drive on the left.*

VISITOR INFORMATION   Tourist Offices   The **British Visitors Centre,** 1 Regent St., London SW1 4XT (tube: Piccadilly Circus), caters to walk-in visitors. It's often a long wait. On the premises you'll find a British Rail ticket office, a travel agency, theater-ticket agency, hotel-booking service, bookshop, and souvenir shop. It's open from Monday to Friday 9am to 6:30pm and Saturday and Sunday 10am to 4pm, with extended Saturday hours from June to September.

For a full information pack on London, contact the **London Tourist Board,** 26 Grosvenor Gardens, SW1 WODU (www.londontown.com). You can also contact the **British Tourist Authority** (© **800/462-2748** in the U.S.; www.visitbritain.com).

Websites   The British Tourist authority has designed a site expressly for U.S. travelers (**www.usagateway.visitbritain.com**), which lets you order brochures, provides trip planning hints, even allows e-mail questions for prompt answers. The outstanding Automobile Association site (**www.theaa.co.uk**) provides a routing service similar to its U.S. counterpart; it also lays out lodging listings, ranked by price and quality; many accept online bookings. The extensive London Theatre Guide (**www.officiallondontheatre.do.uk**) carries not only information on half-price tickets and what's on but also casting news, impending openings, and "last chances." The official site from the British monarchy (**www.royal.gov.uk/palaces/bp.htm**) offers history, images, and descriptions of the "working palace" and "visitors' palace."

CITY LAYOUT   For our purposes, London begins at **Chelsea,** on the north bank of the Thames, and stretches north through Kensington to **Hampstead,** then east and south to Tower Bridge. Within this area, you'll find all the hotels and restaurants and nearly all the sights that are usually of interest to visitors.

The logical, though not geographical, center of this area is **Trafalgar Square.** Stand here facing the steps of the imposing National Gallery; you're looking northwest. That's the direction of **Piccadilly Circus**—the real core of tourist London—and the maze of streets that makes up **Soho.** Farther north runs **Oxford Street,** London's gift to moderately priced shopping, and still farther northwest lies Regent's Park and the zoo.

At your back (south) runs **Whitehall,** which houses or skirts nearly every British government building, including the official residence of the prime minister at **10 Downing Street.** A bit farther south stand the Houses of Parliament and Westminster Abbey. Flowing southwest from Trafalgar Square is the table-smooth **Mall,** flanked by parks and mansions and leading to Buckingham Palace, the queen's residence. Farther along in the same direction lie **Belgravia** and **Knightsbridge,** the city's plushest residential areas, and south of them is chic **Chelsea** and **King's Road,** an upscale boulevard for shopping.

Due west stretches the superb and high-priced shopping area bordered by **Regent Street** and **Piccadilly.** Farther west lie the equally elegant shops and even more elegant homes of **Mayfair.** Then comes **Park Lane,** with its deluxe hotels. Beyond is **Hyde Park,** the biggest park in central London and one of the largest in the world. **Charing Cross Road** runs north from Trafalgar Square, past **Leicester Square,** and intersects with **Shaftesbury Avenue.** This is London's Theaterland. A bit farther along, Charing Cross Road turns into a browser's paradise, lined with shops selling new and secondhand books. At last, it funnels into **St. Giles Circus.** Beyond is **Bloomsbury,** site of the University of London, the British Museum, and erstwhile stamping ground of the famed "Bloomsbury group," led by Virginia Woolf. Northeast lies **Covent Garden,** known for its Royal Opera House; today it's a major shopping, restaurant, and cafe district.

Follow **The Strand** eastward from Trafalgar Square and you'll come to **Fleet Street.** From the 19th century through most of the 20th century, this area was the most concentrated newspaper district in the world. **Temple Bar** stands where The Strand becomes Fleet Street, and only here do you enter the actual City of London, or "the City." Its focal point and shrine is the Bank of England on **Threadneedle Street,** with the Stock Exchange next door and the Royal Exchange across the street. In the midst of all the hustle and bustle rises **St. Paul's Cathedral,** Sir Christopher Wren's monument to beauty and tranquility. At the far eastern fringe of the City looms the **Tower of London,** shrouded in legend, blood, and history and permanently besieged by battalions of visitors.

GETTING AROUND   By Public Transportation   Both the Underground (subway) and bus systems are operated by **London Transport** (© 020/ **7222-1234;** www.londontransport.co.uk). Travel Information Centres are in the Underground stations at King's Cross, Hammersmith, Oxford Circus, St. James's Park, Liverpool Street Station, and Piccadilly Circus, as well as in the British Rail stations at Euston and Victoria and in each of the terminals at Heathrow Airport. They take reservations for London Transport's guided tours and have free Underground and bus maps and other information.

Travelcards for use on most buses, the Underground, and British Rail inside Greater London can be purchased at Underground ticket offices, Travel Information Centres, and some newsstands. For short stays, a **1-Day Off-Peak Travelcard** can be used from Monday to Friday after 9:30am and any time on weekends and bank holidays. A two-zone card costs £4.50 ($7) adults and £2.80 ($4.20) children 5 to 15; children 4 and under ride free. Travelcards are also available for periods of 7 days. A 7-day Travelcard allowing travel in two zones costs £18.20 ($27) adults and £7.50 ($11) children.

By Underground (Subway)   The Underground is known locally as "the tube"; all stations are clearly marked with a red circle and blue crossbar. Fares are based on zones. The flat fare for one trip within the zone 1 is £1.50 ($2.25). Trips from the zone 1 to destinations in the suburbs generally range from £1.40 to £3.50 ($2.10 to $5). Be sure to keep your ticket, as it must be presented when you exit at your destination.

(Tips A Map Note

See the inside front cover of this guide for a map of the London Underground.

By Bus   The bus system is almost as good as the Underground, and you'll have a better view of the city. To find out about current routes, pick up a free bus map at one of the Travel Information Centres listed above.

A regular fare in zone 1 in the center of London is £1 ($1.50) adults, 40p (60¢) children, with 1-day passes costing £2.40 ($3.60) adults or £1 ($1.50) children. It's also possible to purchase weekly passes, going for £7.50 ($11) adults or £4 ($6) children in zone 1.

By Taxi   For a radio cab, phone © **020/7286-0286.** The minimum fare is £3.80 ($6) for the first half-kilometer (third of a mile) or 1 minute and 51 seconds, with increments of 20p (30¢) thereafter, based on distance or time. Each additional passenger is charged 40p (60¢). Taxis hailed in the streets are much cheaper, with the minimum fare costing £1.40 ($2.10), but rocketing upward real quick. Passengers pay 10p (15¢) for each piece of luggage in the driver's compartment and any other item more than 2 feet long. Surcharges are imposed after 8pm and on weekends and public holidays. All these tariffs include VAT, and fares usually increase annually. It's recommended that you tip 10% to 15% of the fare.

By Car   Rent a car only if you plan to take excursions into the environs. Because of traffic and parking difficulties, it's virtually impossible to see London by car.

By Bicycle   One of the most popular bike rental shops is **On Your Bike,** 52–54 Tooley St., London Bridge, SE1 (© **020/7378-6669;** tube: London Bridge), open from Monday to Friday 9am to 6pm, Saturday 9:30am to 5:30pm, and Sunday 11am to 4pm. The first-class mountain bikes, with high seats and low-slung handlebars, cost £15 ($22.50) per day, £30 ($45) per weekend, or £60 ($90) per week; they require a £200 ($300) deposit on a credit card.

ℰ FAST FACTS: London

American Express   The main office is at 30–31 Haymarket, SW1 (© **020/ 7484-9600;** tube: Piccadilly Circus). Full services are available from Monday to Saturday 9am to 5:30pm; foreign-exchange only is open Sunday 10am to 1pm.

Business Hours   **Banks** are usually open from Monday to Friday 9:30am to 3:30pm. **Pubs and bars** are open from Monday to Saturday 11am to 11pm and Sunday noon to 10:30pm; some pubs close Sunday 3 to 7pm. **Stores** are generally open daily 9am to 5:30pm, to 7pm Wednesday or Thursday. Most central shops close Saturday around 1pm.

Currency   The basic unit of currency is the **pound sterling** (£), which is divided into 100 pence (p). The rate of exchange used in this chapter was £1 = $1.50.

Dentists/Doctors   For dental emergencies, call **Eastman Dental Hospital** (© **020/7915-1000;** tube: King's Cross). Some hotels have doctors on call. **Medical Express,** 117A Harley St., W1 (© **020/7499-1991;** tube: Regent's Park), is a private British clinic that's not part of the free British medical establishment. It's open from Monday to Friday 9am to 6pm and Saturday 9:30am to 2:30pm.

Drugstores In Britain they're called "chemists." **Bliss The Chemist**, 5 Marble Arch, W1 (© 020/7723-6116; tube: Marble Arch), is open daily from 9am to midnight. Every London neighborhood has a branch of **Boots**.

Embassies The **U.S. Embassy** is at 24 Grosvenor St., W1 (© 020/7499-9000; tube: Bond St.). For passport and visa information, go to the U.S. Passport and Citizenship Unit, 55–56 Upper Brook St., London, W1 (© 020/7499-9000, ext. 2563 or 2564; tube: Marble Arch), from Monday to Friday 8:30am to 11:30am and 2 to 4pm (Tuesday the office closes at noon). The **Canadian High Commission,** MacDonald House, 38 Grosvenor St., W1 (© 020/7258-6600; tube: Bond St.), is open from Monday to Friday 8 to 11am. The **Australian High Commission,** Australia House, Strand, WC2 (© 020/7379-4334; tube: Charing Cross or Aldwych), is open from Monday to Friday 9:30am to 3:30pm. The **New Zealand High Commission,** New Zealand House, 80 Haymarket at Pall Mall, SW1 (© 020/7930-8422; tube: Charing Cross or Piccadilly Circus), is open from Monday to Friday 10am to noon and 2 to 4pm. The **Irish Embassy,** 17 Grosvenor Place, SW1 (© 020/7235-2171; tube: Hyde Park Corner), is open from Monday to Friday 9:30am to 1pm and 2:15 to 5pm. The **South African High Commission,** South Africa House, 15 Whitehall, SW1 (© 020/7925-8900; tube: Westminster), is open from Monday to Friday 10am to noon and 2 to 4pm.

Emergencies In London, for police, fire, or an ambulance, dial © **999.**

Hospitals Emergency care 24 hours a day, with the first treatment free under the National Health Service, is offered by Royal Free Hospital, Pond Street, NW10 (© 020/7794-0500; tube: Belsize Park), and University College Hospital, Gower Street, WC1 (© 020/7387-9300; tube: Warren St.).

Internet Access You can send e-mails or check on your messages at **Café Internet,** 22–24 Buckingham Palace Rd., SW1 (© 020/7233-5786; tube: Victoria), open daily from 9am to 9pm.

Post Office The **Main Post Office,** 24 William IV St., WC2N 4DL (© 020/7484-9307; tube: Charing Cross), operates as three separate businesses: inland and international postal service and banking; philatelic postage stamp sales; and the post shop, selling greeting cards and stationery. All are open from Monday to Saturday 8am to 8pm.

Telephone The country code for the United Kingdom is **44.** London's city code is **020.**

To place a local call for 2 minutes costs 10p (15¢), and you can buy phone cards at newsstands for £1 ($1.50), £2 ($3), £5 ($7.50), £10 ($15), and £20 ($30). To make an international call, dial 155 to reach the international operator. To dial direct, dial 00. For the United States, you can reach **AT&T** at © **0800-89-0011, MCI** at © **0800-89-0222,** and **Sprint** at © **0800-89-0877.**

WHERE TO STAY

In most of the places listed, a service charge ranging from 10% to 15% will be added to your bill. Those looking to splurge on very special accommodations may like to stay at Henry VIII's **Hampton Court Palace** for 4 to 7 days (see "Day Trips from London," later in this chapter).

London Accommodations

SHOREDITCH

King's Cross Station Pancras ation

Euston Rd.

York Way

Caledonian Rd.

Pentonville Rd.

King's Cross Rd.

Grav's Inn Rd.

FINSBURY

Goswell Rd.

City Rd.

Shepherdess Walk

New North Rd.

Kingsland Rd.

Hackney Rd.

Bethnal Green

ST. PANCRAS

Coram's Fields

Dickens's House

Lever St.

St. John St.

Old St.

Bath St.

Bunhill Row

East Rd.

City Rd.

Gt. Eastern St.

Commercial St.

Brick Ln.

Judd St.

Bernard St.

Guilford St.

Calthorpe

Farringdon Ave.

Rosebery

Hatton Gdns.

CLERKEN-WELL

Clerkenwell Rd.

Beech St.

The Barbican

Moorgate

Liverpool St. Station

Bishopsgate

Houndsditch

Leman St.

Southampton Row

Theobalds Rd.

Holborn

Holborn

Aldersgate St.

London Wall

Museum of London

THE CITY

British Museum

HOLBORN

High

Kingsway

Fetter Ln.

Via

Farringdon St.

St. Paul's Cathedral

Cheapside

Bank of England

Stock Exchange

Cornhill

Leadenhall St.

Mansell St.

Minories

COVENT GARDEN

Law Courts

Samuel Johnson's House

Cannon St.

Temple of Mithras

Grace Church St.

Dock St.

Leicester Square

29

Aldwych

Courtauld Institute

Strand

Blackfriars Station ⓘ

Upper Thames St.

Cannon Street Station

Lower Thames St.

Byward St.

Tower Hill East

National Gallery

Victoria Embankment

River

Blackfriars Bridge

Millennium Bridge

Thames

Southwark Bridge

London Bridge

ⓘ

Tower of London

THE STRAND

Charing Cross Station

Globe Theatre

Vinopolis

SOUTHWARK

HMS Belfast

Tower Bridge

Charing Cross Rd.

Hungerford Bridge

Waterloo Bridge

Stamford St.

Southwark St.

Southwark Cathedral

Tooley St.

London Bridge Station

falgar uare

Whitehall

Whitehall

Union St.

THE BOROUGH

Jamaica Rd.

Downing Street

York Rd.

Waterloo Rd.

The Cut

Blackfriars Rd.

Borough High St.

Long Ln.

Druid St.

Westminster Bridge

Waterloo Station

Grange Rd.

Houses of Parliament

Lambeth Palace Rd.

Westminster Bridge Rd.

Borough Rd.

Southwark Bridge Rd.

London Rd.

Kennington Causeway

Harper

Great Dover St.

Tower Bridge Rd.

Abbey St.

stminster bey

Lambeth Bridge

St. George's Rd.

NEWINGTON

New Kent Rd.

Old Kent Rd.

WEST-INSTER

Lambeth Rd.

Imperial War Museum

LAMBETH

Kennington Rd.

ELEPHANT & CASTLE

Kennington Park Rd.

Walworth Rd.

ain

Millbank

Albert Embankment

WALWORTH

ridge

Kennington Ln.

KENNINGTON

Harleyford Rd.

VAUXHALL

Clapham Rd.

Brixton Rd.

Lambeth Rd.

Academy Hotel **25**	Durrants Hotel **23**	Myhotel **27**
The Beaufort **14**	Edward Lear Hotel **21**	The Pavilion **19**
Brown's Hotel **1**	Fielding Hotel **29**	Philbeach Hotel **8**
Charlotte Street Hotel **26**	Goring Hotel **5**	Regency Hotel **16**
Claverley Hotel **15**	Hotel Chesterfield **2**	Sheraton Park
Collin House **12**	Ivanhoe Suite Hotel **22**	Lane Hotel **4**
Commodore **17**	James House/	The Sloane **9**
Covent Garden Hotel **28**	Catref House **7**	Tophams Belgravia **6**
Diplomat Hotel **13**	La Gaffe **24**	Wigmore Court **20**
Dukes Hotel **3**	Miller's **18**	Willett Hotel **10**

MAYFAIR
Very Expensive
Brown's Hotel ★★★   This landmark is the quintessential London hotel. It was created by a former butler of Lord Byron and opened in 1837, the year Queen Victoria ascended the throne. Today, Brown's occupies some 14 historic houses on two streets just off Berkeley Square. Bedrooms, many quite small, are furnished traditionally with old-fashioned comfort, just as they were when Teddy Roosevelt honeymooned here.

29–34 Albemarle St., London W1A 4W. © 020/7493-6020. Fax 020/7493-9381. www.brownshotel.com. 118 units. £270–£350 ($405–$525) double, from £420 ($630) suite. AE, DC, MC, V. Tube: Green Park. **Amenities:** Restaurant, bar; health club nearby; business center; 24-hour room service. *In room:* A/C, TV, minibar, hair dryer.

Sheraton Park Lane ★★★   The most traditional of the Park Lane mansions, its silver entrance is an Art Deco marvel and has been used in many films. Some 150 rooms were recently redecorated. The accommodations are luxurious and spacious, and many rooms have marble fireplaces, plus the original marble bathrooms with tub and shower combos. Elegant afternoon tea is served in the fabled 1920s Palm Court.

Piccadilly, London W1Y 8BX. © **800/325-3535** in the U.S., or 020/7499-6321. Fax 020/7499-1965. www.sheraton.com. 307 units. £260 ($390) double; from £395 ($593) suite. AE, DC, MC, V. Parking £26 ($39). Tube: Hyde Park Corner or Green Park. **Amenities:** Restaurant, bar; fitness center; business center; 24-hour room service. *In room:* A/C (in most rooms), TV, minibar, hair dryer.

Expensive
Hotel Chesterfield ★   An air of Victorian respectability and the easy access to Berkeley Square form part of the allure of this Mayfair hotel, once partly the home of the Earl of Chesterfield. The owners take great pride and care in their decorative techniques: Each room contains rich-looking accessories, an antique or two, or some artifact that evokes a stately English home. Each bedroom is equipped with an immaculately kept tiled bathroom with tub and shower combo.

35 Charles St., London W18 LX. © **020/7491-2622.** Fax 020/7491-4793. reservations@chesterfield. viewinn.co.uk. 110 units. £165–£195 ($247.50–$292.50) double; £300 ($450) suite. AE, DC, MC, V. Tube: Green Park. **Amenities:** Restaurant, supper club and bar; conservatory; 24-hour room service. *In room:* A/C, TV, minibar, coffeemaker, hair dryer, iron and ironing board.

Inexpensive
Ivanhoe Suite Hotel   Shopping buffs flock to this little jewel tucked away off Oxford Street, close to the shop-flanked New and Old Bond streets. Above a restaurant, it's on a pedestrian street of boutiques and restaurants. The recently redecorated singles and doubles are attractively furnished, each with a sitting area, entry security video, small bathroom with shower stall, plus a wide selection of videotapes.

1 St. Christopher's Place, Barrett St. Piazza, London W1M 5HB. © **020/7935-1047.** Fax 020/7224-0563. www.scoot.co.uk/ivanhoe-suite-hotel. 8 units. £79 ($118.50) double; £89 ($133.50) triple. Rates include continental breakfast. AE, DC, MC, V. Tube: Bond St. **Amenities:** Breakfast room. *In room:* TV/VCR, fridge, coffeemaker, no phone.

ST. JAMES'S
Expensive
Dukes Hotel ★★★   Dukes provides elegance without ostentation. Since 1908, it has stood in a quiet courtyard off St. James's Street. It attracts the urbane guest who's looking for charm, style, and tradition. Each well-furnished

room is decorated in the style of a particular period, ranging from Regency to Edwardian. All rooms are equipped with luxurious mattresses. The small bathrooms have tub and shower combos.

35 St. James's Place, London SW1A 1NY. ☎ 800/381-4702 in the U.S., or 020/7491-4840. Fax 020/7493-1264. www.dukeshotel.com/co.uk. 81 units. £225 ($338) double; from £350 ($525) suite. AE, DC, MC, V. Parking £32 ($48). Tube: Green Park. **Amenities:** Restaurant, bar; small health spa; 24-hour room service; baby-sitting. *In room:* A/C, TV, minibar, hair dryer.

SOHO
Expensive

Charlotte Street Hotel ⚜   In North Soho, a short walk from the heartbeat of Soho Square, this town house has been luxuriously converted into a high-end hotel that is London chic at its finest, everything from a Los Angeles–style juice bar to a private screening room. The latter has made it a hit with the movie, fashion, and media crowd, many of whom had never ventured to North Soho before. Midsize to spacious rooms have fresh modern English interiors. Bathrooms are state of the art, designed in solid granite and oak with twin basins, walk-in showers, even TVs. Guests relax in the elegant drawing room and library with a log-burning fireplace. The decor evokes memories of the fabled Bloomsbury set of Virginia Woolf.

15 Charlotte St., London W1P 1HB. ☎ 800/553-6674 in the U.S., or 020/7806-2000. Fax 020/7806-2002. www.firmdale.com. 52 units. £195–£255 ($292.50–$382.50) double, from £295 ($442.50) suite. AE, DC, MC, V. Tube: Leicester Square. **Amenities:** Brasserie and bar gym; 24-hour room service. *In room:* A/C, TV, fax, dataport.

BAKER STREET
Inexpensive

Wigmore Court *Value*   A convenient family hotel, this inn lies near the street made famous as the fictional address of Sherlock Holmes. It is close to Marble Arch, Oxford Street, and Madame Tussaud's. A somber Victorian structure, it has been tastefully converted into a fine B&B suitable only for serious stair climbers as there is no elevator. There's traffic outside, so request a room in the rear if you're bothered by the noise. Rooms, many quite spacious, are comfortably furnished. Most contain double or twin beds, plus a small bathroom with shower.

23 Gloucester Place, London W1H 3PB. ☎ 020/7935-0928. Fax 020/7487-4254. www.wigmore-courthotel.com. 18 units. £89–£99 ($134–$149) double, MC, V. Tube: Marble Arch. **Amenities:** Guest kitchen; laundry. *In room:* TV, coffeemaker.

BLOOMSBURY
EXPENSIVE

Myhotel ⚜   Creating shock waves among staid Bloomsbury hoteliers, Myhotel is a London row house on the outside, with Asian modern on its interior. It is designed according to feng shui principles—the ancient Chinese art of placement that analyzes the flow of energy in a space. Tipping is discouraged, and each guest is assigned a personal assistant responsible for one's happiness. A public lounge is dedicated to inner karma. The doorman confided that he even lets people in here who are having a bad hair day. The rooms have mirrors but they're positioned so you don't see yourself when you first wake up—feng shui rule no. 1. Rooms follow simplistic designs but are pockets of comfort and taste, certainly tranquility. Excellent sleep-producing beds are found in all rooms, plus a small bathroom with shower stall.

11–13 Bayley St., Bedford Square, London, WC1B 3HD. ☎ 020/7667-6000. Fax 020/7667-6044. www.holidaycity.com/myhotel-london/. 76 units. £195–£225 ($293–$338) double, from £315 ($473) family room. AE, DC, MC, V. Tube: Tottenham Court Rd. **Amenities:** Restaurant, bar, breakfast cafe; 24-hour room service.

Moderate

Academy Hotel   In the footsteps of Virginia Woolf, this makes a good nest in the heart of London's publishing district. The hotel was substantially upgraded in the 1990s, with a bathroom added to every room—whether there was space or not. Rooms are decorated in a neutral style, but are well cared for.

17–25 Gower St., London WC1E 6HG. ℂ 800/678-3096 in the U.S., or 020/7631-4115. Fax 020/7636-3442. www.etontownhouse.com. 49 units. £145 ($217.50) double; £185 ($277.50) suite. AE, DC, MC, V. Tube: Tottenham Court Rd. or Goodge St. **Amenities:** Restaurant, bar; library; secluded patio garden. *In room:* A/C, TV.

COVENT GARDEN

Expensive

Covent Garden Hotel 🅺🅺   This is Covent Garden's most charming boutique hotel. Soundproof rooms are lushly outfitted in English style. Their decorative trademark? Each contains a clothier's mannequin—a lithe female form draped in the same fabric that went into the composition of that particular room. Marble bathrooms are equipped with deep, soaking tubs.

10 Monmouth St., London WC2H 9HB. ℂ 020/7806-1000. Fax 020/7806-1100. www.firmdale.com. 58 units. £220 ($330) double; £325 ($488) suite. AE, MC, V. Parking: £30 ($45). Tube: Leicester Sq. or Covent Garden. **Amenities:** Brasserie, bar; small gym; 24-hour room service. *In room:* A/C, TV, minibar, hair dryer.

Moderate

Fielding Hotel 🅺   One of London's more eccentric hotels, the Fielding is cramped, quirky, and quaint, but an enduring favorite nonetheless. Almost opposite the Royal Opera House, the hotel is just outside Covent Garden with its pubs, shops, markets, and restaurants. It is named after novelist Henry Fielding of *Tom Jones* fame who lived in Broad Court. Rooms are small, but they are so old-fashioned and traditional they have their devotees. Bathrooms are minuscule with shower stalls. Floors dip and sway, and the furnishings and fabrics have known better times, so be duly warned.

4 Broad Court, Bow St., London WC2B 5QZ. ℂ 020/7836-8305. Fax 020/7497-0064. 24 units. £100–£130 ($150–$195) double. AE, DC, MC, V. Tube: Covent Garden. **Amenities:** Small bar, breakfast room. *In room:* TV, coffeemaker.

VICTORIA

Expensive

Collin House 🅺   This is a good, clean, no-smoking B&B where everything is well maintained. The rooms come in various shapes and sizes, the largest on the lower floors, and there are a number of family rooms. The units at the back are quiet, while those in the front face a lot of traffic noise. Most units come with a small bathroom with a shower stall. The main bus, rail, and tube stations are all about a 5-minute walk from the hotel.

104 Ebury St., London SW1W 9QD. ℂ 020/7730-8031. Fax 020/7730-8031. 13 units, 8 with bathroom. £65 ($98) double without bathroom; £78 ($117) double with bathroom. Rates include English breakfast. No credit cards. Tube: Victoria Station. **Amenities:** Breakfast room. *In room:* No phone.

Goring Hotel 🅺🅺🅺   This is our premier choice for the Victoria area, just behind Buckingham Palace. Built in 1910, this was the first hotel in the world to have central heating and a private bathroom in every bedroom. The charm of a traditional English country home is reflected in the paneled drawing room, where fires burn in ornate fireplaces. All the well-furnished rooms (called apartments) have been refurbished. Rooms vary greatly in size but are maintained in classic style, with the best service of any first-class hotel in London. Bathrooms have extra-long tubs, bidets, and power showerheads. Grand afternoon tea in the drawing room is a London highlight.

15 Beeston Place, Grosvenor Gardens, London SW1W 0JW. © **020/7396-9000**. Fax 020/7834-4393. www. goringhotel.co.uk. 74 units. £195–£235 ($293–$353) double; £250–£320 ($375–$480) suite. AE, DC, MC, V. Parking £21 ($31.50). Tube: Victoria Station. **Amenities:** Restaurant, bar; free use of nearby health club; 24-hour room service; baby-sitting. *In room:* A/C (some units), TV, hair dryer.

James House/Cartref House ⭐   Hailed by many publications as one of the top 10 B&Bs in London, James House and Cartref House (across the street) deserve the accolades. Derek and Sharon James run both properties and are the finest hosts in the area. They're constantly refurbishing, so everything looks state-of-the-art. Each room is individually designed, and some of the large rooms have bunk beds suitable for families. The generous English breakfast means you might skip lunch. Don't worry about which house you're assigned. Each is equally good.

108 Ebury St. and 129 Ebury St., London, SW1W 9QD. © **020/7730-7338** for James House, **020/7730-6176** for Cartref House. Fax 020/7730-7338. www.jamesandcartref.co.uk. 20 units, 11 with bathroom. £65 ($98) double without bathroom, £78 ($117) double with bathroom; £120 ($180) quad with bathroom. AE, MC, V. Tube: Victoria Station. *In room:* TV, no phone.

Tophams Belgravia ⭐   Opened in 1937 and completely renovated in 1997, Tophams retains its country-house flavor, complete with flower-filled window boxes. The finest units have en suite bathrooms and four-poster beds. Other rooms are standard in size but comfortably furnished, each with a small bathroom containing a shower stall. The best feature of this hotel, however, is that it's only a 3-minute walk from Victoria Station.

28 Ebury St., London SW1W 0LU. © **020/7730-8147**. Fax 020/7823-5966. www.tophams.com. 39 units, 38 with bathroom. £110 ($165) double without bathroom, £130–£140 ($195–$210) double with bathroom; £260 ($390) suite. AE, DC, MC, V. Tube: Victoria Station. **Amenities:** Restaurant; access to nearby health club; laundry. *In room:* TV, hair dryer.

KNIGHTSBRIDGE
Expensive
The Beaufort ⭐⭐   This is one of London's finest boutique hotels with an elegant town house atmosphere, offering personal service and the ultimate in tranquility. A short walk from Harrods, it sits behind two Victorian porticoes and an iron fence. Each room features a painting by a London artist, plush carpeting, and a kind of grace throughout. The deluxe and spacious bedrooms open onto the front. Bathrooms are tiled and neatly kept, each with a shower stall.

33 Beaufort Gardens, London SW3 1PP. © **800/888-1199** in the U.S and Canada, or 020/7584-5252. Fax 020/7589-2834. www.thebeaufort.co.uk/index.htm. 28 units. £200 ($300) double; £295 ($443) junior suite for 2. Rates include continental breakfast and afternoon tea. AE, DC, MC, V. Tube: Knightsbridge. **Amenities:** Access to nearby health club; Light meals from room service; 24-hour honor bar; baby-sitting,. *In room:* TV, trouser press.

Moderate
Claverley Hotel ⭐   On a quiet cul-de-sac, this tasteful hotel, one of the neighborhood's very best, is just a few blocks from Harrods. It's a small, cozy place accented with Georgian-era accessories. The lounge evokes a country house. Most rooms have wall-to-wall carpeting and comfortably upholstered armchairs, each coming with a tidy bathroom with a shower stall.

13–14 Beaufort Gardens, London SW3 1PS. © **800/747-0398** in the U.S., or 020/7589-8541. Fax 020/7584-3410. www.claverleyhotel.co.uk. 29 units, 27 with bathroom. £120–£190 ($180–$285) double; £160–£200 ($240–$300) jr. suite. Rates include English breakfast. AE, DC, MC, V. Tube: Knightsbridge. **Amenities:** Breakfast room. *In room:* TV.

BELGRAVIA
Moderate
Diplomat Hotel   This is a small, reasonably priced hotel in an otherwise super-expensive neighborhood. It was built in 1882 by one of the neighborhood's most famous architects, Thomas Cubitt. Rooms are comfortable and many were renovated in 1996. Modern bathrooms are equipped with shower stalls. The staff is very helpful.

2 Chesham St., London SW1X 8DT. (☎ 020/7235-1544. Fax 020/7259-6153. www.btinternet.com/~diplomat.hotel. 26 units. £125–£160 ($188–$240) double. Rates include English breakfast buffet. AE, DC, MC, V. Tube: Sloane Sq. or Knightsbridge. **Amenities:** Light meals in the bar. *In room:* TV, hair dryer.

CHELSEA
Moderate
The Sloane 🐾🐾   Set in a redbrick Victorian-era town house, this hotel combines worthy 19th-century antiques with modern comforts and a desirable Chelsea location near Sloane Square. The rooms come in varying sizes but are opulently furnished, many with four-poster or canopied beds. Each has a small bathroom with a shower and tub combo. The staff is accommodating, pan-European, and tactful. The top-floor bar features a limited menu and a panoramic view.

29 Draycott Place, London SW3 2SH. (☎ 020/7581-5757. Fax 020/7584-1348. 12 units. £150 ($225) double; £240 ($360) suite. AE, DC, MC, V. Tube: Sloane Sq. **Amenities:** Bar; 24-hour room service. *In room:* A/C, TV.

Willett Hotel 🐾 *Value*   On a tree-lined street, leading off Sloane Square, this restored town house lies in the heart of Chelsea. Named for the famous London architect, William Willett, it still evokes the days when King Edward was on the throne; stained glass and chandeliers reflect the opulence of that age. Under a mansard roof, with bay windows projecting, the hotel is just a 5-minute walk from the shopping mecca of King's Road and close to such stores as Peter Jones, Harrods, and Harvey Nichols. Individually decorated bedrooms come in a wide range of sizes. Some are first class with swagged draperies, matching armchairs, and canopied beds. But a few of the standard twins are best left for Tiny Tim and his mate.

32 Sloane Gardens, London SW1 8DJ. (☎ 020/7824-8415. Fax 020/7730-4830. www.eeh.co.uk. 19 units. £105–£170 ($158–$255). Rates include breakfast. AE, DC, MC, V. Tube: Sloane Sq. *In room:* TV, fridge, coffeemaker, hair dryer, trouser press.

SOUTH KENSINGTON
Moderate
Regency Hotel 🐾   This is an unheralded but stellar selection in the increasingly trendy South Kensington area, close to major museums and Knightsbridge. Modernized guest rooms are midsize, tasteful, and elegant with immaculate bathrooms with shower stalls. The suites also have Jacuzzi tubs and iron/ironing boards. To form this hotel, six Victorian terrace houses were converted into one seamless whole.

100 Queen's Gate, London SW7 5AG. (☎ 800/223-5652 in the U.S., or 020/7370-4595. Fax 020/7370-5555. 210 units. £180.95 ($271) double; from £190 ($285) luxury suite. AE, DC, MC, V. Parking: £30 ($45). Tube: South Kensington. **Amenities:** Restaurant, bar; health club; business center; 24-hour room service; babysitting; laundry. *In room:* A/C, TV, minibar, hair dryer, trouser press.

PADDINGTON
Inexpensive
The Pavilion   In the early 1990s, a team of entrepreneurs with inroads to the fashion industry radically redecorated the rooms in a theatrical and often

outrageous decor that's much appreciated by the fashion models and music-industry buffs who make this their temporary home in London. Examples include a "kitsch '70s" room ("Honky-Tonk Afro"); a Chinese bordello theme ("Enter the Dragon") and even some with 19th-century ancestral themes. One Edwardian-style room, a gem of emerald brocade and velvet, is called "Green with Envy." Rooms, regrettably, are rather small, each with a tiled bathroom with a shower stall.

34–36 Sussex Gardens, London W2 1UL. ℂ 020/7262-0905. Fax 020/7262-1324. www.msi.com.mt/pavilion. 27 units. £95 ($143) double. Rates include breakfast. AE, DC, MC, V. Parking £5 ($8). Tube: Edgware Rd. **Amenities:** Breakfast room. *In room:* TV, coffeemaker.

MARYLEBONE
Moderate
Durrants Hotel ⓖ Established in 1789 off Manchester Square, this historic hotel is a snug, cozy, and traditional retreat—almost a poor man's Browns. All rooms are very comfortably furnished. Many contain air-conditioning and mini-bars. Nearly all units contain bathtubs and showers, but are quite cramped.

26–32 George St., London W1H 6BJ. & 020/7935-8131. Fax 020/7487-3510. 92 units. £140 ($210) double; £175 ($263) family room; £275 ($413) suite. AE, MC, V. Tube: Bond St. Amenities: Restaurant, pub; 24-hour room service; baby-sitting; laundry. *In room:* TV.

Inexpensive
Edward Lear Hotel The author, Edward Lear ("The Owl and the Pussycat") used to call it home, but now it's your best budget bet at Marble Arch. This is a noisy area of London, so opt for a room in the rear to escape the sound of traffic. Like the private home it once was, rooms range from most spacious to broom-closet style. Things are a bit tattered here and there, but with this location and price level few can complain, as it's an area of £400 ($600) a night mammoths. That bacon resting on your plate at breakfast came from the same butcher used by the Queen.

28–30 Seymour St., London W1H 5WD. ℂ 020/7402-5401. Fax 020/7706-3766. www.edlear.com. 31 units, 4 with bathroom. £67.50 ($101) double without bathroom; £89.50 ($134) double with bathroom; £92.50 ($139) suite. Rates include English breakfast. MC, V. Tube: Marble Arch. **Amenities:** Breakfast room. *In room:* TV.

Wigmore Court Hotel This small, family-friendly hotel enjoys an enviable location close to Hyde Park, Marble Arch, Oxford Street, and Madame Tussaud's. Personal service and a welcoming atmosphere distinguish it from many others. The owners frequently upgrade, and their well-furnished rooms are comfortable with good, firm beds, plus small bathrooms with shower stalls.

23 Gloucester Place, London, W1N 3PB. ℂ 020/7935-0928. Fax 020/7487-4294. www.wigmore-court hotel.co.uk. 19 units. £89 ($134) double. Rates include English breakfast. MC, V. Tube: Marble Arch. **Amenities:** Breakfast room. *In room:* TV.

BAYSWATER
Moderate
Commodore This quarter-century-old hotel is newly fashionable since the traveling public has rediscovered the charm of its eclectic and somewhat eccentric rooms. About a quarter of the rooms are split-level, with a sleeping gallery set at the top of a short flight of stairs. Others have stained glass, a larger-than-expected closet, or an unexpected layout. Overall, the decor is comfortable and cozy. Each accommodation comes with a small bathroom with shower stall.

50 Lancaster Gate, London W2 3NA. ℂ 020/7402-5291. Fax 020/7262-1088. www.commodore/hotel.com. 90 units. £110–£125 ($165–$188) double; £150 ($225) suite. Rates include breakfast. AE, DC, MC, V. Tube: Lancaster Gate. **Amenities:** Restaurant, bar. *In room:* A/C, TV, minibar.

Miller's ☆ A stay here is like a night spent in the Old Curiosity Shop of Charles Dickens. Others claim the little hotel looks like a set for *La Traviata*. Miller's calls itself an 18th-century rooming house. Regardless of which images come to mind, there's nothing quite like this in London. A roaring log fire blazes in the large book-lined drawing room in winter. The individually designed rooms are named after romantic poets. They vary in shape and size, but all are luxuriously furnished with cushy mattresses, and a small bathroom with a shower stall.

111A Westbourne Grove, London W2 4UW. ℂ 020/7243-1024. Fax 020/7243-1064. www.millersuk.com. 8 units. £160 ($240) double; £180 ($270) suite. Rates include continental breakfast. AE, DISC, MC, V. Tube: Bayswater or Notting Hill Gate. **Amenities:** Breakfast room; laundry; baby-sitting. *In room:* TV.

HAMPSTEAD HEATH
Inexpensive
La Gaffe ☆ A 15-minute tube ride from central London, this little nugget is nestled in exclusive Hampstead Heath. It dates from 1734 and was a shepherd's cottage before being turned into a residential inn. Although relatively small, it offers many of the amenities its large competitors do. The well-furnished rooms are small but cozy, with firm beds, plus small bathrooms with shower stalls. Special rooms include a honeymoon room with a four-poster and a Jacuzzi, plus a triple room with a queen-size four-poster.

107–111 Heath St., Hampstead, London NW3 6SS. ℂ 020/7435-8965. Fax 020/7794-7592. www. lagaffe.co.uk. 18 units. £90 ($135) double; £125 ($188) honeymoon room or triple. Rates include continental breakfast. AE, DISC, MC, V. Tube: Hampstead Heath. **Amenities:** Restaurant (Italian), bar. *In room:* TV.

A GAY HOTEL
Philbeach Hotel One of Europe's largest gay hotels, the Philbeach is a Victorian row house on a wide crescent behind the Earl's Court Exhibition Centre, open to both men and women. It offers standard budget-hotel rooms; the showers are tiny, but the shared bathrooms are clean. Room no. 8A, a double with bathroom, has a balcony overlooking the small back garden.

30–31 Philbeach Gardens, London SW5. ℂ 020/7373-1244. Fax 020/7244-0149. 40 units, 16 with bathroom. £50 ($75) single without bathroom, £60 ($90) single with bathroom; £65 ($98) double without bathroom, £85 ($128) double with bathroom. Rates include continental breakfast. AE, DC, MC, V. Tube: Earl's Court. **Amenities:** Restaurant, bar. *In room:* TV.

AT HEATHROW AIRPORT
Posthouse Heathrow ☆ Once you get past the regrettable 1960s architecture—British critics have compared it to a roll of toilet paper—this is your best bet in the moderate range if you're overnighting at London's major airport. Of course, you can pay a lot more and live more elegantly at all the big chain names here, including Marriott, Sheraton, Radisson, Hilton, Forte, and Renaissance. Having grown tired, the Posthouse has been massively upgraded—ask for one of the new millennium rooms. Rooms are midsize with immaculate bathrooms containing shower stalls; some are no-smoking.

118 Bath Rd., Hayes, Middlesex UB3 5AJ. ℂ 800/225-5843 in the U.S., or 020/400-9040. Fax 020/ 8564-9265. 186 units. Mon–Thurs £109–£129 ($163.50–$193.50) double, Fri–Sun £59–£79 ($88.50–$118.50) double. AE, DC, MC, V. Parking £10 ($15). Hotel Hoppa bus: H2 from Terminals 1 and 3, H12 from Terminal 4. **Amenities:** Bar/restaurant, rotisserie restaurant; room service. *In room:* A/C, TV, minibar, coffeemaker, hair dryer, trouser press.

WHERE TO DINE
All restaurants and cafes in Britain are required to display the prices of their food and drink in a place that the customer can see before entering the eating area.

Charges for service and any minimum charge or cover must also be made clear. Most restaurants add a 10% to 15% service charge to your bill, but if nothing has been added, leave a 12% to 15% tip.

MAYFAIR
Very Expensive

Le Gavroche ✿✿✿ CLASSIC FRENCH   This deluxe citadel has long stood for quality French cuisine, the finest in Britain. It's the creation of two Burgundy-born brothers, Albert and Michel Roux. Service is faultless, the ambience chic and formal without being stuffy. Their wine cellar is among London's most interesting, with many quality Burgundies and Bordeaux. Try, if featured, the soufflé Suissesse, *papillote* of smoked salmon, or *tournedos gratinés aux poivres* (pears).

43 Upper Brook St., W1. ✆ 020/7408-0881. Reservations required, as far in advance as possible. Main courses £23–£37 ($35–$56); fixed-price lunch £38.50 ($58); *menu exceptionnel* £78 ($117). AE, MC, V. Mon–Fri noon–2pm and 7–11pm. Tube: Marble Arch.

The Square ✿✿✿ CONTINENTAL   This is the restaurant to visit on the serious London gastronomic circuit. Savvy London food critics think it will emerge as one of the great London restaurants of the early 21st century. Chef Philip Howard has a magic touch with pasta—it appears as a bulging roll of cannelloni stuffed with shredded trout and green leeks, or as a ravioli of partridge on a pool of creamy game-flavored sauce with finely shredded cabbage. A surprise to the palate awaits in every corner of the menu—for example, risotto of calves' tail with filet of veal and butternut squash. His fish has been called "stunningly fresh," and the Bresse pigeon is as good as it is in its hometown in France.

6–10 Burton St., W1. ✆ 020/7495-7100. Reservations required. Main courses £16.50–£20 ($25–$30). Set-price dinner £45–£65 ($68–$98). AE, DC, MC, V. Mon–Fri noon–2:45pm, Mon–Sat 7–11pm. Tube: Bond St.

Expensive

L'Oranger ✿✿ CONTINENTAL   This bistro-cum-brasserie manages to elevate a Gallic brasserie into an artfully upscale dining experience for a clientele that has been described as "people who have made it." The set-price menus are likely to include foie gras poached in a red Pessac wine sauce and pan-fried filet of sea bass with zucchini, tomatoes, basil, and a black-olive vinaigrette. Other delectable staples might be crispy cod filets with bouillabaisse sauce and new potatoes; and braised leg of rabbit in Madeira sauce with whole cloves of yellow garlic *en confit* and braised cabbage.

5 St. James's St. SW1A. ✆ 020/7839-3774. Reservations recommended. Set-price lunch £23.50 ($35); set-price dinner £39.50 ($59). AE, DC, MC, V. Mon–Fri noon–3pm; Mon–Sat 6–11:15pm. Tube: Green Park.

Petrus ✿✿ MODERN FRENCH   Clubby and not at all stuffy, this is the domain of Marcus Wareing, a former boxer from Lancashire. Here in a sleek, opulent setting, you get reasonably priced food that is prepared with a technical precision but also a touch of whimsy. It's best to order the chef's six-course tasting menu to appreciate his culinary ambitions. You're likely to be dazzled with everything from marinated foie gras to an apple and artichoke salad, from Bresse pigeon in a truffle confit to a Valrhona chocolate fondant. We've delighted in all the dishes sampled here, from the eggplant caviar to crisp roast sea bass paired with caramelized endive and plump oysters that didn't go on a diet.

33 St. James's St., SW1. ✆ 020/7930-4272. Reservations required. Fixed-price menu £26–£45 ($39–$68) for 3 courses, or £55 ($83) for 6-course tasting menu. AE, DC, MC, V. Mon–Fri noon–2:30pm; daily 6:45–10:45pm. Tube: Green Park.

PICCADILLY & LEICESTER SQUARE
Expensive
J. Sheekey ☞ SEAFOOD   British culinary tradition lives on in this restored fish joint, long a favorite of West End actors. The same jellied eels that delighted Laurence Olivier and Vivien Leigh are still here, along with an array of fresh oysters from the coasts of Ireland and Brittany, plus that Victorian favorite, fried whitebait. Sheekey's fish pie is still on the menu, as is a delightful Dover sole, even a Cornish fish stew that's quite savory. The old "mushy" vegetables still appear but the chefs also get experimental and occasionally more daring and offer the likes of steamed organic sea beet. The double chocolate pudding soufflé is a delight, and many old-fashioned favorite puddings remain. But look for something daring every now and then—perhaps fried plum ravioli with yogurt ice cream.

28–32 Martin's Lane, WC2. ⓒ 020/7240-2565. Reservations recommended. Main courses £10.50–£28 ($16–$42). AE, DC, DISC, MC, V. Daily noon–3pm and 7:30pm–midnight. Tube: Charing Cross.

Moderate
Atlantic Bar & Grill ☞ MODERN BRITISH   In a former Art Deco ballroom off Piccadilly Circus, this titanic restaurant draws trendsetters to an untrendy part of London. Classically trained executive chef Richard Sawyer is at the helm, still serving the world's most sublime potato and chive hash, which seems incidental to the accompanying smoked salmon. Try, for example, the delectable Hebridean salmon in a creamy champagne sauce with summer sorrel, the Thai spiced lamb filet with pressed lime and roasted peanuts, or the hickory-smoked Aberdeen Angus beef filet with a green Szechuan peppercorn sauce. The menu changes every 2 months but is always strong on seafood.

20 Glasshouse St., W1. ⓒ 020/7734-4888. Reservations required. Main courses £14–£18 ($21–$27). Set-menu £32 ($48). AE, MC, V. Mon–Fri noon–2:45pm; Mon–Sat 6pm–3am; Sun 6–10:30pm. Tube: Piccadilly Circus.

Criterion Brasserie FRENCH/MEDITERRANEAN   Owned by the "bad boy" of British cookery, this palatial neo-Byzantine mirrored marble hall is the most pulsating restaurant in the heart of London. The Criterion knew its greatest fame in World War II when it was the site of tea dances. The menu is wide ranging, from Paris brasserie food to "nouvelle-classical." The food is excellent but falls just short of sublime. Start with squid ink risotto with roast calamari. The roast skate wing with deep-fried snails is especially delectable, as is the roast saddle of lamb stuffed with mushrooms and spinach.

224 Piccadilly, W1. ⓒ 020/7930-0488. Main courses £11–£15 ($17–$23); fixed-price 2-course lunch £14.95 ($22), fixed-price 3-course lunch £17.95 ($27). AE, MC, V. Daily noon–2:30pm and 6pm–midnight. Tube: Piccadilly Circus.

Incognico ☞☞ FRENCH/MODERN ECLECTIC   A modern brasserie with darkwood paneling and leather banquettes, Incognico offers even better food than the traditional Theaterland favorite, the long-running Ivy. It's ideal for a pre-theater meal. The virtually faultless cuisine makes for a superlative dining experience, especially if you opt for such delights as filet of salmon impregnated with ginger and accompanied by a delicate plum sauce. The chef isn't afraid of the "golden oldies" in his recipe file, as exemplified by marvelous veal kidneys in a mustard sauce. Our favorites are the seared filet of cod and the breast of guinea fowl with lentils. Here is Theaterland's best osso bucco, and you might also enjoy the artichokes with mushrooms and a sensuous hollandaise. One of the most contemporary dishes is open ravioli with goat's cheese.

117 Shaftesbury Ave., WC2. © 020/7836-8866. Reservations required. Lunch or pre-theater menu £12.50 ($19). Main courses £9.50–£16 ($14–$24). AE, MC, V. Mon–Sat noon–3pm and 5:30pm–midnight. Tube: Leicester Sq.

SOHO
Expensive

The Ivy ⚘ ENGLISH/FRENCH   Effervescent and sophisticated, The Ivy has been intimately associated with the West End since it opened in 1911. Meals are served until very late, ideal for after theater. With its ersatz 1930s look, the Ivy is fun and humming. The menu choices appear deceptively simple, but the fresh ingredients are skillfully prepared. Our favorite dishes include white asparagus with sea kale and truffle butter; seared scallops with spinach, sorrel, and bacon; and salmon fish cakes.

1–5 West St., WC2. © 020/7836-4751. Reservations required. Main courses £12–£26 ($18–$39). AE, DC, MC, V. Daily noon–3pm and 5:30pm–midnight (last order). Tube: Leicester Sq.

Mezzo ⚘ CONTINENTAL   This all-out blockbuster is a 750-seat eatery, dubbed the biggest restaurant in Europe. The mammoth space has been split into several separate restaurants, including the Mezzonine upstairs, serving a Thai/Asian cuisine with a European flair. Downstairs is the swankier Mezzo, which evokes an atmosphere of 1930s Hollywood. There's even a Mezzo Café, stocked with sandwiches and drinks. Mezzonine serves dishes such as marinated salmon with ginger, star anise, and shallots; and roast marinated lamb with yogurt and cumin on flat bread. In the basement, the cuisine is more ambitious, with a view of 100 chefs working behind glass. Here a modern British menu includes shoulder of lamb slow-roasted and enlivened with lemon zest and anchovies.

100 Wardour St., W1. © 020/7314-4000. Reservations required for Mezzonine. Mezzonine main courses £15–£20 ($23–$30); Mezzo 3-course dinner £35–£45 ($53–$68). £5 ($8) cover at Mezzo Thurs–Fri after 10:30pm. AE, DC, MC, V. Mezzo: daily noon–2:30pm; Mon–Thurs 6pm–midnight; Fri–Sat 6pm–3am; Sun 6–11:30pm. Mezzonine: daily noon–2:30pm; Mon–Thurs 5:30pm–1am; Fri–Sat 5:30pm–3am; Sun 5:30–11:30pm. Tube: Tottenham Court Rd.

Quo Vadis ⚘ CONTINENTAL   This hyper-trendy restaurant occupies the former apartment house where Karl Marx once lived. He'd never recognize the stylish, postmodern ode to cutting-edge art you'll see today. This is one of the flashiest restaurants in London. And the food? Although competent and highly appealing, cuisine is only secondary to the social blitz of hipdom generated by the clientele, the setting, and the vagaries of fashion.

26–29 Dean St., W1. © 020/7437-9585. Reservations required. Main courses £13.50–£24 ($20–$36); set lunches £14.95–£17.95 ($22–$27). AE, MC, V. Sun–Fri noon–2:30pm; Mon–Sat 5:30–11:30pm. Tube: Leicester Sq. or Tottenham Court Rd.

Moderate

Rasa Samundra ⚘ *Value* INDIAN/KERALAN   Whereas most Indian restaurants in London specialize in the cuisine of the north, Rasa Samundra features the cookery of the southern state of Kerala, whose specialties are plucked from the sea. Try *malslam pattichathu* (king fish cooked in fresh spices, with green chile and coconut paste), *para konju nirachathu* (lobster cooked with black pepper, garlic, and Indian shallots and served with whole lemon and beet root curry), *masala dosa* (paper-thin rice and black graham pancake filled with potato and ginger Masala), and *moru kachlathu* (green bananas and mangoes cooked in a yogurt sauce with turmeric and onions). Rasa also offers a full range of Keralan appetizers, side orders, breads, rices, and desserts. Most dishes are at the lower end of the price scale.

5 Charlotte St., W1. ℂ 020/7637-0222. Reservations required. Main courses £8.50–£30 ($13–$45); fixed-price lunch £10 ($15); set dinner £30 ($45). AE, DC, MC, V. Daily noon–11pm. Tube: Tottenham Court Rd.

Soho Spice SOUTH INDIAN   One of Central London's most stylish Indian restaurants combines a sense of media and fashion hip with the flavors and scents of southern India. You might opt for a drink at the cellar-level bar before heading to the dining room. A staff member will propose choices from a wide array of dishes, including a range of slow-cooked Indian *tikkas* that feature combinations of spices with lamb, chicken, fish, or all-vegetarian fare. The cuisine will satisfy traditionalists but has a nouveau-Soho flair. The presentation takes it a step above typical Indian restaurants, although its chefs fall a bit below the mark of those at Rasa Samundra (see above).

124–126 Wardour St., W1. ℂ 020/7434-0808. Reservations recommended. Main courses £10.50–£20 ($16–$30); set menus £19.95–£24.95 ($30–$37). AE, MC, V. Sun–Wed noon–midnight; Thurs noon–midnight; Fri–Sat noon–3pm. Tube: Tottenham Court Rd.

BLOOMSBURY
Moderate
Townhouse Brasserie ⚲ INTERNATIONAL   Near the British Museum, this old Georgian town house is one of the most up-and-coming restaurants in Bloomsbury. The ground floor is enhanced with contemporary art, and upstairs is a traditional old English dining room, except for an infusion of Peruvian art. The menu is a culinary tour de force, drawing inspiration from around the world. Launch your repast with the cream of leek soup or sweet potato soup with basil. Then it's on to a delectable charcoal-grilled duck breast with an Asian-style salad. Especially pleasing is a fresh seafood pasta flavored with chives, thick cream, and white wine. It's worth it to save up room for one of the tempting desserts, made fresh daily.

24 Coptic St., WC1. ℂ 020/7636-2731. Reservations recommended. Main courses £8.50–£13.95 ($13–$21). AE, DC, MC, V. Mon–Fri 11am–11pm; Sat 4–11pm; Sun 10am–6pm. Tube: Tottenham Court Rd. or Holborn.

Villandry INTERNATIONAL/CONTINENTAL   Food lovers and gourmands flock to this combination food store, florist, delicatessen, and restaurant. The setting is an oversized Edwardian-style storefront north of Oxford Circus. Inside, ingredients change here so frequently the menu is revamped and rewritten twice a day. You're likely to face such perfectly crafted dishes as breast of duck with fresh spinach and a gratin of baby onions; boiled haunch of pork with blood sausages, mashed potatoes, kale, and mustard sauce; filets of black codfish with prosciutto, radicchio, and creamed lentils; and pan-fried turbot with deep-fried celery, artichoke hearts, and hollandaise sauce.

170 Great Portland St., W1. ℂ 020/7631-3131. Reservations recommended. Main courses £12–£15 ($18–$23). AE, MC, V. Mon–Sat 8am–10pm; Sun 11am–4pm. Tube: Great Portland St.

Wagamama JAPANESE   This noodle joint, in a basement just off New Oxford Street, is noisy and overly crowded, and you'll have to wait in line for a table. The fast-serve, fast-out concept calls itself a "non-destination food station" and caters to some 1,200 customers a day. All dishes are built around ramen noodles with your choice of chicken, beef, or salmon served with gyoza, a light pancake filled with vegetables. Vegetarian dishes are available, but skip the so-called Korean-style dishes.

4 Streatham St., WC1. ℗ **020/7323-9223**. Reservations not accepted. Main courses £5–£12 ($8–$18). AE, MC, V. Mon–Sat noon–11pm; Sun 12:30–10pm. Tube: Tottenham Court Rd.

COVENT GARDEN & THE STRAND
Moderate

Rules ⭐ CLASSIC ENGLISH   London's most quintessentially British restaurant opened in 1798 as an oyster bar and is lined with the framed memorabilia of the British Empire at its height. Around the turn of the 19th century, Edward VII, portly future king of England, used to arrive here with his famous mistress, Lillie Langtry. Their signed portraits still embellish the yellowing walls, along with that of Charles Dickens, who crafted several of his novels here. You can order such classic dishes as jugged hare, Greshingham duckling in a bramley apple and five-spice chutney sauce, and game dishes.

35 Malden Lane, WC2. ℗ **020/7836-5314**. Reservations recommended. Main courses £14.95–£18 ($22–$27). AE, DC, MC, V. Daily noon–11:15pm. Tube: Covent Garden.

Sarastro ⭐ TURKISH/CYPRIOT   The setting makes you feel like you're in a prop room of an opera house. This is a fun place, especially after a show in Theaterland. As the manager aptly says, "We're the show after the show." Ten opera boxes adorn three sides of the restaurant. The restaurant takes its name from a character in Mozart's *The Magic Flute*. Live opera performances are staged here from time to time. The cuisine celebrates the bounty of the Mediterranean, especially Turkey and Cyprus. Launch yourself with such delights as asparagus in red wine sauce or fresh grilled sardines. Market-fresh fish is usually the way to go, especially fresh river trout or the grilled halibut. A zesty favorite is lamb Anatolian style (that is, with eggplant and zucchini). We're also fond of the well-seasoned lamb meatballs. A good tasting specialty is chicken Sarastro with walnuts and raisins.

126 Drury Lane, WC2. ℗ **020/7836-0101**. Reservations required. Main courses £12–£50 ($18–$75). Fixed-price menu £19.50 ($29); pre-theater menu £10 ($15). Daily noon–midnight. Tube: Covent Garden.

Inexpensive
Porter's English Restaurant ⭐ *Value* CLASSIC ENGLISH   Porter's specializes in classic English meat pies. Main courses are so generous that the menu eliminates appetizers. The traditional bangers-and-mash plate is featured daily. With whipped cream or custard, the "puddings" come hot or cold, including bread-and-butter pudding or steamed syrup sponge. Although the English call all desserts puddings, at Porter's they're in fact puddings in the American sense.

17 Henrietta St., WC2. ℗ **020/7836-6466**. Reservations recommended. Main courses £8.95–£12.95 ($13–$19); fixed-price menu £17.50 ($26). AE, DC, MC, V. Mon–Sat noon–11:30pm; Sun noon–10:30pm. Tube: Covent Garden or Charing Cross.

FLEET STREET
Inexpensive
Ye Olde Cheshire Cheese CLASSIC ENGLISH   Dating from the 13th century, this is the most famous of the old City chophouses (restaurants) and pubs. It claims to be the spot where Samuel Johnson entertained admirers. Later, many of the ink-stained journalists and scandalmongers of Fleet Street made its four-story premises their "local." Within, you'll find six bars and two dining rooms. The house specialties include "ye famous pudding"—steak, kidney, mushrooms, and game—and Scottish roast beef, with Yorkshire pudding and horseradish sauce.

Wine Office Court, 145 Fleet St., EC4. © 020/7353-6170. Main courses £9.95–£13.25 ($15–$20). AE, DC, MC, V. Mon–Sat noon–9:30pm; Sun noon–3pm. Drinks and bar snacks available daily 11:30am–11pm. Tube: St. Paul's or Blackfriars.

WESTMINSTER
Moderate
Tate Gallery Restaurant ✳ ENGLISH/FRENCH   The restaurant at Tate Britain is particularly attractive to wine fanciers, offering what may be the best bargains for superior wines to be found anywhere in the country. It's especially strong on Bordeaux and Burgundies. Wine connoisseurs frequently come for lunch, regardless of the current exhibitions on view at the museum. The restaurant specializes in French and English cuisine. The menu changes every month and may include such well-prepared selections as duck prepared in a variety of ways or lamb or veal dishes.

Moments **Taking Afternoon Tea in London: Where to Have a Cuppa**

The lounge at **Brown's Hotel,** 29–34 Albemarle St., W1 (© 020/ 7493-6020; tube: Green Park), is decorated with English antiques, oil paintings, and floral chintz, much like an English country estate. Give your name to the concierge upon arrival (reservations aren't accepted); arrangements will be made for you to be seated on clusters of sofas and settees or at low tables. Served daily 3 to 5:45pm, the regular afternoon tea (£18.95/$28) includes a choice of 10 teas, plus sandwiches, scones, and pastries. The teatime rituals at **Claridge's,** Brook Street, W1 (© 020/7629-8860; tube: Bond St.), have managed to persevere through the years with as much pomp and circumstance as the empire itself. A portrait of Lady Claridge gazes beneficently from the paneled walls as a choice of 17 teas is served ever-so-politely. Reservations are recommended, and jackets are required for men. Served daily 3 to 5pm, high tea costs £22 ($33).

A flood of visitors is somehow gracefully herded into the high-volume but nevertheless elegant **Georgian Restaurant,** on the fourth floor of Harrods, 87–135 Brompton Rd., SW1 (© 020/7255-6800; tube: Knightsbridge), in a room so long its staff refers to its shape and size as the "Mississippi River." The list of teas available—at least 50—is sometimes so esoteric the experience might remind you of the choosing among vintages in a sophisticated wine cellar. Served from Monday to Saturday 3:45 to 5:15pm (last order), high tea runs £18 ($27) per person; reservations are recommended. **The Orangery,** in the gardens just north of Kensington Palace, W8 (© 020/7376-0239; tube: Kensington High St. or Queensway), occupies a long and narrow garden pavilion built in 1704 by Queen Anne as a site for her tea parties. Tea is still served amid rows of potted orange trees basking in sunlight from soaring windows. Tea is served daily from April to September 10am to 6pm and from October to March 10am to 4pm. Reservations aren't accepted. A pot of tea is £1.75 ($2.65), and summer cakes and puddings run £1.70 to £3.45 ($2.55 to $5.20).

Millbank, SW1. ℂ 020/7887-8877. Reservations required 2 days in advance. Main courses £10–£16 ($15–$24); 2-course fixed-price lunch £16.75 ($25); 3-course fixed price lunch £19.75 ($30). AE, MC, V. Mon–Sat noon–3pm and Sun noon–4pm; Mon–Sat 3–5pm for afternoon tea. Tube: Pimlico. Bus: 77 or 88.

KNIGHTSBRIDGE
Expensive
Zafferano ☘ MODERN ITALIAN   There's something honest and satisfying about this restaurant, where Margaret Thatcher, Michael Hesseltine, Richard Gere, Princess Margaret, and Eric Clapton have dined. Some of the allure derives from an elegantly modernized interpretation of Italian cuisine, which incorporates such dishes as ravioli of pheasant with black truffles, rabbit with Parma ham and polenta, sea bream with spinach and balsamic vinegar, and monkfish with almonds. The owners pride themselves on one of the most esoteric and well-rounded collections of Italian wine in London.

15 Lowndes St., SW1. ℂ 020/7235-5800. Reservations required. Lunch: £18.50 ($28) for 2-courses or £21.50 ($32) for 3-courses. Dinner: £29.50 ($44) for 2 courses, £35.50 ($53) for 3 courses, £39.50 ($59) for 4 courses. AE, MC, V. Mon–Sat noon–2:30pm and 7–11pm. Tube: Knightsbridge.

Moderate
English Garden ☘ CLASSIC ENGLISH   In this historic Chelsea town house, the Garden Room, with its domed conservatory and banks of plants, is a metropolitan restaurant par excellence. Every component is well prepared and proportioned. Well-crafted old-fashioned dishes include Arbroath smokie fish cake, saddle of venison and "potted" cabbage, and roast rump of lamb with butter beans and bacon. Save room for the mango fool with macaroons or the white chocolate cheesecake, each delectable.

10 Lincoln St., SW3. ℂ 020/7584-7272. Reservations required. Main courses £16–£20 ($24–$30); fixed-price lunch £19.50 ($29). AE, DC, MC, V. Daily 12:30–11:30pm. Closed Dec 25–26. Tube: Sloane Sq.

KENSINGTON
Moderate
Joe's MODERN BRITISH   Joe's is often filled with well-known names from the fashion, music, and entertainment industries. The atmosphere is laid-back, and the food is good but a bit unexciting. You can enjoy such dishes as crab-crusted halibut, breast of duck with roasted root vegetables, charcoal-grilled swordfish with cracked wheat and salsa verde (green sauce), or tiger prawns and monkfish kebabs with sesame balsamic dressing. No one will mind if your meal consists exclusively of appetizers. There's a bar near the entrance, tables for quick meals near the door, and more leisurely (and gossipy) dining a few steps up from the bar. Brunch is served on Sunday, which is the cheapest way to enjoy this place.

126 Draycott Ave., SW3. ℂ 020/7225-2217. Reservations recommended. Main courses £10–£14 ($15–$21). AE, DC, MC, V. Mon–Sun 9am–6pm. Tube: South Kensington.

Pasha MOROCCAN/MEDITERRANEAN   Few ethnic restaurants equal the zest and stylishness of this re-created Marrakech palace. Within a duet of dining rooms outfitted with rich upholsteries, flickering candles, belly dancing music, and artifacts from the sub-Sahara, you'll enjoy regional and time-honored specialties. The best examples include a crispy lamb salad with pomegranate and mint; grilled sea bass with warm hummus and parsley salad; chicken *merguez* (spicy sausage) with a coriander tagine; and charcoal-grilled skewered chicken with green chile salsa. And if you like couscous, you'll have at least three kinds from which to choose.

1 Gloucester Rd., SW7. ✆ 020/7589-7969. Reservations recommended. Main courses £11–£18 ($17–$27). AE, DC, MC, V. Daily noon–3pm and 7–11:30pm. Tube: Gloucester Rd.

SOUTH KENSINGTON
Expensive
Bibendum/Oyster Bar 🏵 MODERN FRENCH/MEDITERRANEAN This fashionable eatery occupies two floors of the former British headquarters of the Michelin tire company. Bibendum is one floor above street level in a white-tiled room whose stained-glass windows, streaming sunlight, and chic clientele make meals extremely pleasant. Menu choices, known for their freshness and simplicity, include roast quail flavored with Marsala and thyme, braised oxtail with prunes and almonds, and *ris de veau* (sweetbreads) with black butter and capers. Simpler meals and cocktails are available on the building's street level, in the Oyster Bar.

81 Fulham Rd., SW3. ✆ 020/7581-5817. Reservations required in Bibendum; not accepted in Oyster Bar. Main courses £19–£27 ($29–$41); 3-course fixed-price lunch £26–£32 ($39–$48); cold seafood platter in Oyster Bar £27.50 ($41) per person. AE, DC, MC, V. Daily noon–2:30pm and 7–11:15pm. Tube: South Kensington.

Hilaire 🏵 MODERN BRITISH This is a jovially cramped restaurant, housed in a Victorian storefront. Chef Bryan Webb prepares a mixture of classical French and cuisine modern; thus, this has become one of London's most stylish restaurants. The menu always reflects the best of the season's offerings. Freshness, clear taste, and first-class ingredients showcase such dishes as rack of lamb with tapenade and wild garlic, saddle of rabbit, or grilled tuna with Provençal vegetables.

68 Old Brompton Rd., SW7. ✆ 020/7584-8993. Reservations recommended. 2-course fixed-price lunch £18.50 ($28); 3-course fixed price lunch £23.50 ($35); 3-course fixed-price dinner £36 ($54); dinner main courses £23.50 ($35). AE, DC, MC, V. Mon–Fri 12:15–2:30pm; Mon–Sat 6:30–11pm. Closed Sun and bank holidays. Tube: South Kensington.

CHELSEA
Inexpensive
Admiral Codrington 🏵 ENGLISH/CONTINENTAL Once a lowly pub, this stylish bar and restaurant is all the rage. The exterior has been maintained, but the old "Cod," as it is affectionately known, has emerged to offer plush dining with a revitalized decor by Nina Campbell and a glass roof that rolls back on sunny days. The bartenders still offer a traditional pint, but the sophisticated menu features such delectable fare as linguine with zucchini, crab, and chile peppers, or rib-eye steak with slow-roasted tomatoes. Opt for the grilled breast of chicken salad with bean sprouts, apple, or cashews, or the perfectly grilled tuna with a couscous salad and eggplant "caviar."

17 Mossop St., SW3. ✆ 020/7581-0005. Reservations recommended. Main courses £3.95–£12.75 ($6–$19). MC, V. Mon–Sat noon–11:30pm; Sun noon–10:30pm. Tube: South Kensington.

MARYLEBONE
Expensive
Orrey 🏵🏵 INTERNATIONAL/CLASSICAL FRENCH With ingredients imported directly from France, this is one of London's classic French restaurants. Our favorites are Bresse pigeon with Savoy cabbage and mushroom ravioli or duckling with an endive tatin and *cèpe* (flap mushrooms) sauce. Where but here can you get a good caramelized calves' sweetbreads salad in a truffle vinaigrette any more? Everything has a brilliant, often whimsical touch as evoked by the sautéed leeks in pumpkin oil. A wild mushroom consommé arrives with a

medley of such fungi as pieds de bleu, pieds de mouton, chanterelles, and trompettes de morte, all from French forests. Skipping the blueberry soufflé, we ended with a cheese plate that featured a Banton goat cheese from Provence so fresh that it oozed onto the plate. Lazy summer evenings are to be enjoyed on a fourth-floor terrace where you can drink and order light fare from the bare menu.

55 Marylebone High St., W1. © 020/7616-8088. Reservations required. Main courses £15.50–£24.50 ($23–$37). Fixed-price 3-course menu £23.50 ($35), 5-course set menu £45 ($68). AE, DC, MC, V. Daily noon–3pm; Mon–Sat 7–1pm; Sun 7–10:30pm. Tube: Baker St.

Moderate

Caldesi TUSCAN   Good food, reasonable prices, fresh ingredients, and authentic Tuscan family recipes attract a never-ending stream to this eatery. The extensive menu includes a wide array of pasta, antipasti, fish, and meat dishes. Start with an excellent insalata Caldesi, made with tomatoes slow roasted in garlic and rosemary oil and served with mozzarella flown in from Tuscany. Pasta dishes include an especially flavor-filled homemade tortelloni stuffed with salmon and ricotta and served with a creamy spinach sauce. Monkfish and prawns are flavored with wild fennel and fresh basil, or you might sample the tender duck breast with fresh peaches, steeped in white wine, honey, thyme, and rosemary.

15–17 Marylebone Lane, W1. © 020/7935-9226. Reservations required. Main courses £6.50–£16 ($10–$24). AE, MC, V. Mon–Fri noon–2:30pm and 6–11pm; Sat 6–11pm. Tube: Bond St.

NOTTING HILL GATE
Moderate

Pharmacy CONTINENTAL/MEDITERRANEAN   This place can be a lot of fun. The "medical chic" restaurant created by Damien Hirst will remind you of a harmless small-town pharmacy or a drug lord's secret stash of mind-altering pills, an ambiguity richly appreciated by the arts-conscious crowd that flocks here. In the bar, a drink menu lists lots of highly palatable martinis as well as a somewhat icky concoction known as a Cough Syrup (cherry liqueur, honey, and vodka). Bottles of pills, aspirin-shaped bar stools, and painted representations of Fire, Water, Air, and Earth decorate the scene. Upstairs in the restaurant the hospital theme is less pronounced. Menu items include such trendy but comforting food items as a carpaccio of sea bass; lamb cooked with celery, spinach, and herb juices; fisherman's pie; home-salted cod and eggplant pie; and roasted duck with white peaches and french fries.

150 Notting Hill Gate, W11. © 020/7221-2442. Reservations required Fri–Sat; otherwise strongly recommended. Main courses £15–£27.50 ($23–$41). MC, V. Daily noon–2:30pm and 6:45pm–midnight. Tube: Notting Hill Gate.

THE CITY
Expensive

Prism MODERN ENGLISH/CONTINENTAL   In the financial district, called "The City," this restaurant attracts London's movers and shakers, at least those with demanding palates. In the former Bank of New York, Harvey Nichols—known for his chic department store in Knightsbridge—took this 1920s neo-Grecian hall and installed Mies van der Rohe chairs in chrome and lipstick red leather. In such a setting, traditional English dishes from the north are given a light touch—try the tempura of Whitby cod or cream of Jerusalem artichoke soup with roasted scallops and truffle oil. For a first course, you might opt for a small seared calf's liver with a mushroom risotto, or else a salad composed of flecks of Parmesan cheese seasoning a Savoy cabbage salad and Parma ham. Unusual for a restaurant, the staff will compose a set menu for each individual table.

147 Leadenhall St., EC3. ⓒ 020/7256-3875. Reservations required. Main courses £16–£20 ($24–$30). Set menus £35–£45 ($53–$68). AE, DISC, DC, MC, V. Mon–Fri noon–3pm and 6–10pm. Tube: Bank.

SEEING THE SIGHTS
LONDON ATTRACTIONS

London isn't a city to visit hurriedly. It is so vast, so stocked with treasures, that it would take a lifetime to explore it thoroughly. But even a quick visit will give you a chance to see what's creating the hottest buzz in shopping and nightlife as well as the city's time-tested treasures.

SIGHTSEEING SUGGESTIONS FOR FIRST-TIME VISITORS

If You Have 1 Day No first-time visitor should leave London without visiting **Westminster Abbey.** See **Big Ben** and the **Houses of Parliament,** then walk over to see the **Changing of the Guard** at Buckingham Palace if it's being held. Have dinner in Covent Garden, perhaps at Porter's English Restaurant. For your nightcap, head over to the **Red Lion,** 2 Duke of York St. (ⓒ **020/7930-2030**), in Mayfair, quite a Victorian pub.

If You Have 2 Days Devote a good part of your second day to exploring the **British Museum,** one of the world's largest and best museums. Spend the afternoon visiting the **Tower of London** and seeing the crown jewels (but expect slow-moving lines). Cap your day by boarding one of the London Launches to experience the city from the river. Go to one of London's landmark restaurants such as Rules, 35 Maiden Lane.

If You Have 3 Days In the morning of your third day, go to the **National Gallery** on Trafalgar

Square. Then enjoy an afternoon at **Madame Tussaud's Waxworks.** Take some time to stroll through **St. James's** and try to catch a cultural performance at the South Bank Centre, site of the Royal Festival Hall, or a play or musical in the West End.

If You Have 4 Days In the morning of your fourth day, head for the **City,** the financial district. Tour **St. Paul's Cathedral.** Spend a few hours strolling the City and visit a few of its many attractions. In the late afternoon, head down **King's Road** in Chelsea to shop the many and varied boutiques.

If You Have 5 Days On your fifth day, explore the **Victoria and Albert Museum** in the morning, then head to the **Tate Gallery** for lunch. Finally, see where history was made during the dark days of World War II in the **Cabinet War Rooms** at Clive Steps, where Churchill directed the British operations against the Nazis. In the evening, attend the theater.

THE TOP ATTRACTIONS

Tower of London ✹✹✹   This ancient fortress continues to pack in visitors because of its macabre associations with all the legendary figures who were imprisoned and/or executed here (Sir Walter Raleigh, Anne Boleyn and her daughter Elizabeth, Lady Jane Grey). The finest structure is the White Tower, begun by William the Conqueror. Here you can view the Royal Armouries collection of armor and weapons. Instruments of torture and execution are on view in Bowyer Tower. In summer, go early in the day to see the **Crown Jewels** because long lines often form. Uniformed Beefeater guides give 1-hour tours at frequent intervals, starting at 9:30am from the Middle Tower near the main entrance. The tour includes the Chapel Royal of St. Peter ad Vincula (St. Peter in Chains). The last guided walk starts about 3:30pm in summer or 2:30pm in winter.

Tower Hill, on the north bank of the Thames, EC3. (C) **020/7709-0765.** Admission £11 ($17) adults, £8.30 ($13) students and senior citizens, £7.30 ($11) children, free for children under 5. Family ticket for 5 members (but no more than 2 adults) £33 ($50). Mar–Oct Mon–Sat 9am–5pm, Sun 10am–5pm; Nov–Feb Sun–Mon 10am–4pm, Tues–Sat 9am–4pm. Closed Dec 24–26 and Jan 1. Tube: Tower Hill. Boats: From Westminster Pier.

Westminster Abbey ★★★

In 1065, the Saxon king, Edward the Confessor, founded a Benedictine abbey on this spot overlooking Parliament Square. The first king crowned in the abbey was Harold in 1066. The coronation tradition has continued to the present day, broken only twice (Edward V and Edward VIII). The abbey is the site of state occasions, including the September 1997 funeral of Diana, Princess of Wales. The Gothic structure existing today owes more to Henry III's plans than to those of any other sovereign, although many architects, including Wren, have contributed to the abbey. Henry VII Chapel is one of the loveliest in Europe, with its fan vaulting, Knights of Bath banners, and Torrigiani designed tomb of the king. You can also visit the most hallowed spot in the abbey, the shrine of Edward the Confessor (canonized in the 12th century). In the saint's chapel is the Coronation Chair, made at the command of Edward I in 1300 to display the Stone of Scone. Another noted spot is the Poets' Corner, to the right of the entrance to the Royal Chapel, with monuments to Chaucer, Shakespeare, "O Rare Ben Johnson" (his name misspelled), Samuel Johnson, the Brontë sisters, Thackeray, Dickens, Tennyson, Kipling, even the American Longfellow.

A guided tour of the abbey lasts about 1½ hours and costs £3 ($4.50) in addition to the entrance fee. For advance bookings, call (C) **020/7222-7110.** Or else enjoy a personal audio tour, an Audioguide renting for £2 ($3).

The cloisters of the abbey are open daily 9am to 6pm, charging no admission. Other attractions to visit on-site are the Chapter House, Pyx Chapter, and the museum of Westminster relics, open daily 10:30am to 4pm, charging £2.50 ($3.75) adults and £1.30 ($1.95) children. The College Garden is open only on Tuesday and Thursday 10am to 6pm. It's free but you're invited to make a donation.

Broad Sanctuary, SW1. (C) **020/7222-7110.** Free admission to cloisters. Abbey, £6 ($9) adults, £3 ($4.50) students, £2 ($3) children 11–18 (free 10 and under). Family ticket (2 adults, 2 children) £12 ($18). Mon–Fri 9:30am–3:45pm; Sat 9:15am–1:45pm and 4–4:45pm. Tube: Westminster or St. James's Park.

Houses of Parliament ★★

These Houses are the stronghold of Britain's democracy. Both Houses (Commons and Lords) are situated in the former royal Palace of Westminster, the king's residence until Henry VIII moved to Whitehall. The present Houses of Parliament were built in 1840, but the Commons chamber was bombed and destroyed by the Luftwaffe in 1941. The 98-m (320-ft.) tower houses Big Ben, the "symbol of London." Except for the Strangers' Galleries, the two Houses of Parliament are closed to tourists. To be admitted to the Strangers' Galleries, join the public line outside the St. Stephen's entrance; often there's a delay before the line is admitted.

London Attractions

King's Cross Station / St. Pancras Station

Euston Rd.

Caledonian Rd.

York Way

Judd

Pentonville Rd.

King's Cross Rd.

Grays Inn Rd.

Shepherdess Walk

New North Rd.

SHOREDITCH

Kingsland Rd.

Hackney Rd.

FINSBURY

Goswell Rd.

City Rd.

St. John St.

Lever St.

Bath St.

Old St.

East Rd.

City Rd.

Bunhill Row

Gt. Eastern St.

Bethnal Green

Commercial St.

Brick Ln.

ST. PANCRAS

Coram's Fields

Dickens's House

Bernard St.

Guilford St.

Theobalds Rd.

Calthorpe

Farringdon Rd.

Rosebury

Grays Inn Rd.

CLERKENWELL

Clerkenwell Rd.

Hatton Gdns.

Aldersgate St.

Beech St.

Moorgate

London Wall

Barbican Centre

Liverpool St. Station

Bishopsgate

Houndsditch

Commercial St.

Leman St.

British Museum

High

Kingsway

Southampton Row

Holborn

HOLBORN

Holborn

Fetter Ln.

Farringdon St.

19 Museum of London

St. Paul's Cathedral

Cheapside

THE CITY

Bank of England

Cornhill

Stock Exchange

Leadenhall St.

Mansell St.

Minories

COVENT GARDEN

Royal Opera House

Leicester Square

National Gallery

Law Courts

Aldwych

Samuel Johnson's House

18

Cannon St.

Blackfriars Station

Temple of Mithras

Cannon Street Station

Lower Thames St.

Byward St.

Tower Hill East

20 Tower of London

THE STRAND

9 Charing Cross Station

Trafalgar Square

Courtauld Institute

Strand

Victoria Embankment

Museum of the Moving Image

River

Blackfriars Bridge

Upper Thames St.

Millennium Bridge

Thames

Southwark Bridge

London Bridge

Lower Thames St.

Tower Bridge

Hungerford Bridge

Globe Theatre

17 Vinopolis

SOUTHWARK

HMS Belfast

Tooley St.

10 Whitehall

10 Downing Street

South Bank Centre

Stamford St.

Southwark St.

Southwark Cathedral

London Bridge Station

11

Westminster Bridge

York Rd.

Waterloo Rd.

The Cut

Blackfriars Rd.

Union St.

Borough High St.

THE BOROUGH

Jamaica Rd.

Druid St.

13 Houses of Parliament

Westminster Abbey

Waterloo Station

Westminster Bridge Rd.

Borough Rd.

London Rd.

Southwark Rd.

Kennington Causeway

Harper Rd.

Long Ln.

Great Dover St.

Tower Bridge

Abbey St.

Grange Rd.

Lambeth Bridge

Lambeth Palace Rd.

Lambeth Rd.

St. George's Rd.

16

LAMBETH

Kennington Rd.

ELEPHANT & CASTLE

Kennington Park Rd.

NEWINGTON

New Kent Rd.

Walworth Rd.

WALWORTH

Old Kent Rd.

Albert Embankment

Millbank

Vauxhall Bridge

Kennington Ln.

KENNINGTON

Harleyford Rd.

VAUXHALL

South Lambeth Rd.

Clapham Rd.

Brixton Rd.

Camberwell New Rd.

Albany Rd.

Camberwell Rd.

0   1/2 mi
0   0.5 km

N

ⓘ Information
— Railway

SCOTLAND

North Sea

Irish Sea

ENGLAND

WALES

London ★

English Channel

0   100 mi
0   100 km

Westminster Palace, Old Palace Yard, SW1. © 020/7219-4272 for the House of Commons, or 020/7219-3107 for the House of Lords. www.parliament.uk (click on V for visit). Free admission. House of Lords, open to the public daily 2:30–10:30pm. House of Commons, open to the public Mon–Tues 2:30–10:30pm; Wed 9:30am–2pm; Thurs 11:30am–7:30pm. Join line at St. Stephen's entrance. Tube: Westminster.

British Museum 𝘳𝘳𝘳   This fabled attraction shelters one of the world's most comprehensive collections of art and artifacts. Even on a cursory first visit, be sure to see the Asian collections (the finest assembly of Islamic pottery outside the Islamic world), the Chinese porcelain, the Indian sculpture, and the Pre-historic and Romano-British collections. The overall storehouse splits into collections of antiquities; prints and drawings; coins and medals; and ethnography. The Assyrian Transept on the ground floor displays the winged and human-headed bulls and lions that once guarded the gateways to the king's palaces. From here, you can continue into the hall of Egyptian sculpture to see the Rosetta stone, whose discovery led to the deciphering of hieroglyphs. Also on the ground floor are the Parthenon Sculptures, which used to be known as the Elgin Marbles. The *Sutton Hoo* Anglo-Saxon burial ship discovered in Suffolk is, in the words of an expert, "the richest treasure ever dug from English soil." The Portland Vase, one of the most celebrated possessions of the British Museum, was found in 1582 outside Rome.

The museum's inner courtyard, hidden for 150 years, has been transformed into the Great Court, a 1-hectare (2-acre) square spanned by a spectacular glass roof. The court houses a center for education, galleries, and more exhibition space. Following the removal of the British Library to St. Pancras, the Reading Room has been restored as a public reference library.

Great Russell St., WC1. © 020/7323-8599, or 020/7636-1555 for recording. www.thebritishmuseum.ac.uk. Free admission. Mon–Sat 10am–5pm; Sun noon–6pm (the galleries start to close 10 min. earlier). Closed Jan 1, Good Friday, and Dec 24–26. Tube: Holborn, Tottenham Court Rd., or Russell Sq.

Buckingham Palace 𝘳𝘳   This massively graceful building is the official residence of the queen. You can tell when Her Majesty is at home by the Royal Standard flying over the palace. The staterooms and picture gallery are usually open to the public for 8 weeks in August and September, when the royal family is away on vacation. The tours include the Throne Room and the grand staircase. The queen's picture gallery has some world-class masterpieces rarely on public view.

Buckingham Palace's most famous spectacle is the **Changing of the Guard.** The new guard, marching behind a band, comes from either the Wellington or Chelsea Barracks and takes over from the old guard in the forecourt of the palace. When this martial ceremony occurs is the subject of mass confusion—*when* it happens, it begins at 11:30am. In theory, that is supposed to be from mid-April to July and on alternate days the rest of the year. It can be canceled in bad weather and during major state events. Call © 020/7414-2497 to see if this world-famous military ritual is likely to be staged during your visit.

At the end of The Mall (the street running from Trafalgar Sq.). © 020/7839-1377. Palace tours £11 ($17) adults to age 60, £7.50 ($11) adults over 60, £5.50 ($8) children under 17. (*Warning:* These ticket prices, or even the possibility of public admission to Buckingham Palace, are subject to change.) Aug–Sept daily 9:30am–4:15pm. Tube: St. James's Park, Green Park, or Victoria.

Madame Tussaud's 𝘳   In 1770, an exhibition of life-size wax figures was opened in Paris by Dr. Curtius. He was soon joined by his niece, Strasbourg-born Marie Tussaud, who learned the secret of making lifelike replicas of the famous and the infamous. During the French Revolution, the head of almost every distinguished victim of the guillotine was molded by Madame Tussaud or her uncle. An enlarged Grand Hall continues to house years of old favorites, as well as many of today's heads of state and political leaders. In the Chamber of Horrors, you can have the vicarious thrill of walking through a Victorian London street where special effects include the shadowy terror of Jack the Ripper. Planetarium shows begin at 10:20am daily and are presented every 40 minutes.

Marylebone Rd., NW1. © 020/7487-0200. www.madame-tussauds.com. Admission £11.50 ($17.25) adults, £9 ($13.50) senior citizens, £8 ($12) children under 16. Combination tickets, including the new planetarium, £13.95 ($21) adults, £10.80 ($16) seniors, £9.50 ($14) children 5–16, free for children under 5. Mon–Sat 10am–5:30pm. Tube: Baker St.

Tate Britain 🌟🌟🌟   What's now known as Tate Britain was known as the Tate Gallery before the modern works in its collection were moved to a new building (see below). Fronting the Thames near Vauxhall bridge in Pimlico, the gallery houses the national collection of British art from the 16th century to the present. The works include some of the best of Gainsborough, Reynolds, Stubbs, Blake, Constable, and Hogarth (particularly his satirical *O the Roast beef of Old England*, known as *The Gate of Calais*). The illustrations of William Blake, the incomparable mystical poet of such works as *The Book of Job*, *The Divine Comedy*, and *Paradise Lost* are here. The collection of works by J. M. W. Turner is its largest by a single artist; Turner himself willed most of the paintings and watercolors here to the nation. Also on display are the works of many major 19th- and 20th-century painters, including Paul Nash.

Millbank, SW1. © 020/7887-8000. www.tate.org.uk. Free admission; special exhibits sometimes £3–£6 ($4.50–$9). Daily 10am–5:50pm. Tube: Pimlico. Bus: 77am, 88, or C10.

Tate Modern 🌟🌟🌟   In a transformed Bankside Power Station in Southwark, this museum, which opened in 2000, draws some two million visitors a year to see the greatest collection of international 20th-century art in Britain. As such it is one of the three or four most important modern art galleries in the world. How would we rate the collection? At the same level of the Pompidou in Paris with a slight edge over New York's Guggenheim. Of course, New York's Museum of Modern Art remains in a class of its own. Tate Modern is also viewer friendly with eye-level hangings. All the big painting stars are here, a whole galaxy ranging from Dalí to Duchamp, from Giacometti to Matisse and Mondrian, from Picasso and Pollock to Rothko and Warhol. The Modern is also a gallery of new and exciting art. Instead of exhibiting art chronologically and by school, the Tate Modern, in a radical break from tradition, takes a thematic approach. This allows displays to cut across movements. You can cross the Millennium Bridge, a pedestrian-only walk from the steps of St. Paul's, over the Thames to the new gallery.

25 Sumner St., SE1. © 020/7887-8000. www.tate.org.uk. Free admission. Sun–Thurs 10am–6pm; Fri–Sat 10am–8pm. Tube: Southwark.

National Gallery 🌟🌟🌟   This museum houses a comprehensive collection of Western paintings, representing all the major schools from the 13th to the early 20th century. Of the early Gothic works, the *Wilton Diptych* is the rarest treasure; it depicts Richard II being introduced to the Madonna and child by John the Baptist and the Saxon king, Edward the Confessor. The 16th-century Venetian masters and the northern European painters are well represented.

Trafalgar Sq., WC2. © 020/7839-3321. www.nationalgallery.org.uk. Free admission. Daily 10am–6pm (Wed 9pm). Closed Jan 1, Good Friday, and Dec 24–26. Tube: Charing Cross, Embankment, or Leicester Sq.

St. Paul's Cathedral 🏵🏵🏵   It was during the Great Fire of 1666 that the old St. Paul's was destroyed, making way for a baroque structure designed by Sir Christopher Wren and built between 1675 and 1710. The dome of St. Paul's dominates the City's square mile. The cathedral houses few art treasures but has many monuments, including a memorial chapel to American service personnel who lost their lives in World War II. Encircling the dome is the Whispering Gallery, where vocal discretion is advised. Wren lies in the crypt, along with the duke of Wellington and Lord Nelson. Of course, this was where Prince Charles married Lady Diana Spencer in 1981.

St. Paul's Churchyard, EC4. ☎ 020/7236-4128. www.stpaulscathedral.org.uk. Cathedral, £5 ($7.50) adults, £2.50 ($3.75) children 6–16. Galleries, £4 ($6) adults, £1.50 ($2.25) children. Guided tours £3.50 ($5.25), recorded tours £3 ($4.50), free for children 5 and under. Sightseeing, Mon–Sat 8:30am–4pm; galleries, Mon–Sat 10am–4:15pm. No sightseeing Sun (services only). Tube: St. Paul's.

Victoria & Albert Museum 🏵🏵🏵   On display here are fine and decorative arts, the world's greatest creation. Medieval holdings include many treasures, such as the Eltenberg Reliquary; the Early English Gloucester Candlestick; the Byzantine Veroli Casket, with its ivory panels based on Greek plays; and the Syon Cope, an English embroidery from the early 14th century. Islamic art includes the 16th-century Persian Ardabil carpet. The V&A has the largest collection of Renaissance sculpture outside Italy, including a Donatello marble relief. Raphael's cartoons for tapestries for the Sistine Chapel, owned by the queen, can also be seen here.

Cromwell Rd., SW7. ☎ 020/7938-8500. www.vam.ac.uk. Admission £5 ($8) adults, £3 ($4.50) students/seniors; free for children under 18. Daily 10am–5:45pm. Tube: South Kensington.

Kensington Palace 🏵   This mansion dates from 1605 but was redesigned by Sir Christopher Wren in 1689. Since the end of the 18th century, it has been home to various members of the royal family, and the State Apartments are open for tours. The palace is now the London home of the ailing Princess Margaret as well as the duke and duchess of Kent. It was once the home of Diana, princess of Wales, and her two sons. Newly restored, the State Apartments and Ceremonial Dress Collection display trompe l'oeil murals by William Kent and ceremonial robes belonging to Queen Mary and George V. Visitors are guided through a series of theme rooms, including a tailor shop stocked with materials used in court dress. Of the 30 rooms, 15, including the restored King's Gallery and the Cupola Room, where Queen Victoria was baptized, are permanently opened to the public. In the northwestern corner of Kensington Gardens (see below), you'll find the new **Princess Diana Memorial Playground.**

The Broad Walk, Kensington Gardens, W8. ☎ 020/8781-9792. Admission £8.50 ($12.75) adults, £6.70 ($10) seniors and students, £6.10 ($9) children, £26.10 ($39) family ticket. June–Sept daily 10am–5pm; off-season daily 10am–4pm. Tube: Queensway or Bayswater on north side of gardens; High St. Kensington on south side.

Whitehall and Cabinet War Rooms 🏵   Whitehall extends south from Trafalgar Square to Parliament Square. Along it you'll find the Home Office, the Old Admiralty Building, and the Ministry of Defense. Visitors today can see the **Cabinet War Rooms,** a bombproof bunker suite of rooms, just as they were left by Winston Churchill at the end of World War II. You can see the Map Room with its huge wall maps; the Atlantic map is a mass of pinholes (each hole represents at least one convoy). Next door is Churchill's bedroom-cum-office, which has two BBC microphones on the desk for his broadcasts of those famous speeches that stirred the nation.

C For Diana Fans

Princess Diana is buried on an island on the Oval Lake at Althorp, the Spencer family estate at Great Brington in Northamptonshire. You won't have access to the gravesite or the island, but you can view the island from across the lake. Admission is £10 ($15) adults, £7.50 ($11) seniors, and £5 ($8) children.

You must book tickets long in advance by calling © **01604/592-020** or writing **Althorp Admissions,** c/o Wayhead, The Hollows, St. James's Street, Nottingham, NG1 6FJ. A special train is operated by Virgin Trains which runs coaches to Althorp daily, costing £12.50 ($19) for a one-day round-trip ticket. For schedules and more information, call **National Rail** at © **0345/484-950.**

At Althorp, Earl Spencer, Diana's brother, opened a $5 million shrine to the late princess, including a museum, a gift shop, and a cafe. The museum contains, among other exhibits, letters she wrote as a schoolgirl, the silk dress she wore as a bride at Westminster Abbey, and the high-fashion outfits she later appeared in. Some exhibits are almost embarrassingly personal, such as a toy rabbit with an ear missing. You can also see poignant films of her as a carefree child dancing in the gardens and later on a ride with her sons, William and Harry. Other relics include the christening robe worn at her baptism in 1961; two bridesmaids' dresses worn at her wedding; Sir Elton John's and Sir George Martin's autographed musical score and parts and Bernie Taupin's hand-written annotated manuscript of *Candle in the Wind '97.* The men in her life—Prince Charles, James Hewitt, and even Dodi al Fayed—are notable only by their absence from the museum.

Clive Steps at the end of King Charles St., SW1, off Whitehall near Big Ben. © 020/7930-6961. Admission £5 ($8) adults, £3.60 ($6) ages 16–18; free for children under 15. Apr–Sept daily 9:30am–6pm (last admission 5:15pm); Oct–Mar daily 10am–5:30pm. Closed Christmas and holidays. Tube: Westminster or St. James's.

MUSEUMS

Imperial War Museum *C* Constructed around 1815 as the Bethlehem Royal Hospital for the Insane (or Bedlam), this large domed building houses collections relating to the two world wars and other military operations. There are four floors of exhibitions, including a vast area showing historical displays, two floors of art galleries, and a dramatic re-creation of London at war during the blitz.

Lambeth Rd., SE1. © 020/7416-5000. www.iwm.org.uk. Admission £5.50 ($85) adults, £4.50 ($7) seniors and students, free for children under 16; free daily 4:30–6pm. Daily 10am–6pm. Closed Dec 24–26. Tube: Lambeth North or Elephant & Castle.

Wellington Museum *C* This former town house of the Iron Duke, the British general (1769–1852) who defeated Napoléon at the Battle of Waterloo and later became prime minister, was opened as a public museum in 1952. The building was designed by Robert Adam and constructed from 1771 to 1778.

Apsley House, Hyde Park Corner, SW1. © 020/7499-5676. Admission £4.50 ($7) adults, free seniors and children under 18. Tues–Sun 11am–5pm. Closed Jan 1, May Day, and Dec 24–26. Tube: Hyde Park Corner.

Museum of London 🎯🎯   In the Barbican near St. Paul's, the museum traces London's history from prehistoric times through relics, costumes, household effects, maps, and models. Anglo-Saxons, Vikings, Normans—they're all here, displayed on two floors around a central courtyard.

150 London Wall, EC2. ℭ 020/7600-3699. www.museum-london.org.uk. Admission £5 ($8) adults, £3 ($4.50) students/seniors, £12 ($18) family ticket; free for 16 and under. Tues–Sat 10am–5:50pm; Sun noon–5:50pm. Tube: St. Paul's, Barbican, or Moorgate.

National Portrait Gallery 🎯🎯   This museum was founded in 1856 to collect the likenesses of famous British men and women. Today the collection is the most comprehensive of its kind in the world and constitutes a unique record of those who created the history and culture of the nation. A few paintings will catch your eye, including Sir Joshua Reynolds's portrait of Samuel Johnson ("a man of most dreadful appearance"). You'll also see a portrait of William Shakespeare, which is claimed to be the most "authentic contemporary likeness" of its subject, and the portrait of the Brontë sisters, painted by their brother Branwell. The most recent addition to the gallery includes portraits of British sports figures, a tribute to athletic icons from the *Chariots of Fire* athletes of the 1920s to the superstars of today.

St. Martin's Place, WC2. ℭ 020/7306-0055. www.npg.org.uk. Free admission. Mon–Sat 10am–6pm; Sun noon–6pm. Tube: Charing Cross or Leicester Sq.

British Airways London Eye 🎯   Opened in early 2000, this extraordinary Ferris wheel is the world's highest observation wheel. Protected from the elements inside 32 high-tech capsules, passengers rise slowly to a height of 135m (450 ft.) and receive a 30-minute slow-moving "flight" over the heart of the capital, complete with commentary and bird's-eye views that are "usually only accessible by helicopter or aircraft."

Jubilee Gardens, SE1. ℭ 020/7654-0864. Admission £9.50 ($14) adults, £7.50 ($11) seniors, £5 ($8) children. Tube: Embankment or Waterloo.

LONDON'S PARKS

London's parklands easily rate as the greatest "green lung" system of any large city. One of the largest is **Hyde Park.** With the adjoining Kensington Gardens, it covers 257 hectares (636 acres) of central London with velvety lawn interspersed with ponds, flowerbeds, and trees. **Kensington Gardens** are home to the celebrated statue of Peter Pan with the bronze rabbits that toddlers are always trying to kidnap. In the northwestern corner of the gardens is the new **Princess Diana Memorial Playground.** East of Hyde Park, across Piccadilly, stretch **Green Park** and **St. James's Park,** forming an almost-unbroken chain of landscaped beauty. This is an ideal area for picnics. You'll find it hard to believe this was once a festering piece of swamp near the leper hospital. **Regent's Park,** north of Baker Street and Marylebone Road, was designed by the 18th-century

---

Fun Fact **To Vent or Not to Vent**

Speakers' Corner in the northeast corner of Hyde Park is one of the most bizarre sights in London. Political activists, evangelists, and every crackpot in Britain who wishes to be heard can hop on a soapbox and speak their minds every Sunday from 11am to dusk. Democracy in action has never been so colorful!

genius John Nash to surround a palace that never materialized. The **open-air theater** and the **London Zoo** are in this most classically beautiful of London's parks.

In July 2000, a 7-mile **walk commemorating the life of Princess Diana** opened. The walk passes through four of London's royal parks—St. James's Park, Green Park, Hyde Park, and Kensington Gardens. Along the way there are 70 plaques pointing out sites associated with Diana, including Kensington Palace (her home for 15 yr.), Buckingham Palace, St. James's Palace (where she once shared an office with Prince Charles), and Spencer House (once her family's mansion and now a museum).

ORGANIZED TOURS

One of the most popular bus tours is called **"The Original London Sightseeing Tour"** (© 020/8877-1722), where London unfolds from a traditional double-decker bus, with live commentary by a guide. The 1½-hour tour costs £12.50 ($19) adults and £6.50 ($10) children under 16. The tour plus Madame Tussaud's costs £21 ($32) adults and £12 ($18) children. You can buy tickets on the bus or from any London Transport or London Tourist Board Information Centre, where you can receive a discount. Departures are from convenient points within the city.

Touring boats operate on the Thames all year and can take you to various places within Greater London and beyond. Main embarkation points are Westminster Pier, Charing Cross Pier, and Tower Pier, a system that enables you, for instance, to take a "water taxi" from the Tower of London to Westminster Abbey, or a more leisurely cruise from Westminster to Hampton Court Palace or Kew Gardens. Several companies operate motor launches offering panoramic views en route. For information and reservations, call the **Westminster/Greenwich** service at © **020/7930-2062, Hampton Court** service at © **020/7930-2062,** and **Tower** service at © **020/7237-5134.** Westminster Pier is on Victoria Embankment, SW1 (tube: Embankment).

The best regularly scheduled walking tours of London are offered by **The Original London Walks** (© **020/7624-3978**). The tours range from ghost walks to one that features sites important in the history of the Beatles. The guides are superb and include prominent actors and actresses and the man many consider to be the foremost authority on Jack the Ripper. Walks cost £5 ($8) adults or £3.50 ($5) students/seniors; free for children under 15. No reservations are needed; call the number above for walk times and starting locations.

THE SHOPPING SCENE
THE TOP SHOPPING STREETS & NEIGHBORHOODS

There are several key streets that offer some of London's best retail stores—or simply one of everything—in a niche or neighborhood, so you can just stroll and shop.

THE WEST END   As a neighborhood, the West End includes Mayfair and is home to the core of London's big-name shopping. Most of the department stores, designer shops, and chain stores have their flagships in this area.

The key streets are **Oxford Street** for affordable shopping (tube: Bond St.), and **Regent Street,** which intersects Oxford Street at Oxford Circus (tube: Oxford Circus). **Marks & Spencer**'s Marble Arch store (on Oxford St.) is their flagship and worth shopping for their high-quality goods. There's a grocery store in the basement and a home furnishings department upstairs. Regent Street has fancier shops—more upscale department stores (including the famed **Liberty of London**), chain stores (**Laura Ashley**), and specialty dealers—and leads all the way to Piccadilly.

In between the two, parallel to Regent Street, is **Bond Street.** Divided into New and Old, Bond Street (tube: Bond St.) also connects Piccadilly with Oxford Street and is synonymous with the luxury trade. Bond Street has had a recent revival and is the hot address for international designers. **Burlington Arcade** (tube: Piccadilly Circus), the famous glass-roofed, Regency-style passage leading off Piccadilly, is lined with intriguing shops and boutiques specializing in fashion, jewelry, Irish linen, cashmere, and more.

Just off Regent Street, **Carnaby Street** (tube: Oxford Circus) might sound like a tired name from the '60s, but it's still alive and flourishing. The area includes surrounding streets as well: Newburg, Ganton, Marlborough Court, Lowndes Court, Marshall, Beak, Kingly, and Foubert's Place. Each of these streets has new and exciting shops along with trendy cafes and bars. New retailers are moving in all the time, including a concept by Levi's to sell its vintage clothing under the label "Red." You can expect the unexpected here, and innovative boutiques come and go virtually every week. The entire district is also a place to hang out at such bars as JUS Cafe, on Foubert's Place, the most fashionable juice bar in London.

For a total contrast, check out **Jermyn Street,** on the far side of Piccadilly, a tiny 2-block-long street devoted to high-end men's haberdashers and toiletries shops; many have been doing business for centuries. Several hold royal warrants, including **Turnball & Asser,** where HRH Prince Charles has his pj's made.

The West End also includes the theater district, so there's two more shopping areas: the still-not-ready-for-prime-time **Soho,** where sex shops are slowly being turned into cutting-edge designer shops; and **Covent Garden,** which is a masterpiece unto itself. The original marketplace has taken over the surrounding neighborhood so that even though the streets run a little higgledy-piggledy and you can easily get lost, it's fun to just wander and shop. Covent Garden is especially mobbed on Sundays (tube: Covent Garden).

KNIGHTSBRIDGE & CHELSEA   This is the second-most famous retail district because it's the home of **Harrods,** 87–135 Brompton Rd., Knightsbridge (© **020/7730-1234;** www.harrods.com; tube: Knightsbridge). Harrods is London's—indeed Europe's—top department store. The sheer range, variety, and quality of merchandise are dazzling; be sure not to miss the delicatessen and food halls. A small street nearby, Sloane Street, is chockablock with designer shops; and another street in the opposite direction, **Cheval Place,** is also lined with designer resale shops.

Walk toward Museum Row and you'll soon find **Beauchamp Place** (pronounced *Bee*-cham). The street is only 1 block long, but it features the kinds of shops where young British aristos buy their clothing. Head out at the **Harvey Nichols** ("Harvey Nicks") end of Knightsbridge, away from Harrods, and shop your way through the designer stores on Sloane Street (**Hermès, Armani, Prada,** and the like), then walk past Sloane Square and you're in an altogether different neighborhood: Chelsea.

King's Road (tube: Sloane Sq.), the main street of Chelsea, which starts at Sloane Square, will forever remain a symbol of London in the Swinging Sixties. More and more, King's Road is a lineup of markets and "multistores," large or small conglomerations of indoor stands, stalls, and booths within one building or enclosure. Chelsea doesn't begin and end with King's Road. If you choose to walk the other direction from Harrods, you connect to a part of Chelsea called **Brompton Cross,** another hip and hot area for designer shops made popular when Michelin House was rehabbed by Sir Terence Conran for **The Conran Shop,** 81 Fulham Rd., SW 3 (© 020/7589-7401).

Also, seek out **Walton Street,** a tiny little snake of a street running off Brompton Cross. About 2 blocks are devoted to fairy-tale shops where a *lady* buys aromatherapy, needlepoint, or costume jewelry, or meets with her interior designer. Finally, don't forget all those museums right there in the corner of the shopping streets. They all have great gift shops.

KENSINGTON & NOTTING HILL   Kensington High Street (tube: High St. Kensington) is the most recent hangout of the classier breed of teen, who has graduated from Carnaby Street and is ready for street chic. While there are a few staples of basic British fashion on this strip, most of the stores feature items that stretch, are very, very short, or are very, very tight.

From Kensington High Street, you can walk up **Kensington Church Street,** which, like Portobello Road, is one of the city's main shopping avenues for antiques. Kensington Church Street dead-ends into the Notting Hill Gate tube station, which is where you would arrive for shopping in **Portobello Road.** The weekend market is 2 blocks beyond.

THE TOP MARKETS

THE WEST END   The most famous market in all of England, **Covent Garden Market** (© 020/7836-9136; tube: Covent Garden), offers several different markets daily from 9am to 5pm (we think it's most fun to come on Sun). **Apple Market** is the fun, bustling market in the courtyard, where traders sell, well, everything. Many of the items are what the English call collectible nostalgia; they include a wide array of glassware and ceramics, leather goods, toys, clothes, hats, and jewelry. Some of the merchandise is truly unusual. This becomes an antiques market on Mondays. Meanwhile, out back is **Jubilee Market** (© 020/7836-2139), which is also an antiques market on Mondays. Every other day of the week, it's sort of a fancy hippie-ish market with cheap clothes and books. Out front there're a few tents of cheap stuff, except again on Monday, when antiques dealers take over here, too.

St. Martin-in-the-Fields Market (tube: Charing Cross) is good for teens and hipsters who don't want to trek all the way to Camden Market (see below) and can be satisfied with imports from India and South America, crafts, and some local football souvenirs. It's near Trafalgar Square and Covent Garden; hours are from Monday to Saturday 11am to 5pm, and Sundays noon to 5pm.

NOTTING HILL   The area has become synonymous with the Julia Roberts and Hugh Grant movie, but Londoners already know, whatever you collect, you'll find it at the **Portobello Market** (tube: Notting Hill Gate). It's mainly a Saturday happening, 6am to 5pm. You needn't be here at the crack of dawn; 9am is fine. You just want to beat the motor-coach crowd. Once known mainly for fruit and vegetables (still sold here throughout the week), Portobello in the past 4 decades has become synonymous with antiques. But don't take the stallholder's word for it that the fiddle he's holding is a genuine Stradivarius left to him in the will of his Italian great-uncle; it might just as well have been nicked from an East End pawnshop.

The market is divided into three major sections. The most crowded is the antiques section, running between Colville Road and Chepstow Villas to the south. (*Warning:* There's a great concentration of pickpockets in this area.)

The second section (and the oldest part) is the "fruit and veg" market, lying between Westway and Colville Road. In the third and final section, there's a flea market, where Londoners sell bric-a-brac and lots of secondhand goods they didn't really want in the first place. But looking around still makes for interesting fun.

NORTH LONDON If it's Wednesday, it's time for **Camden Passage** (© 020/7351-5353; tube: Angel) in Islington, where each Wednesday and Saturday there's a very upscale antiques market. It starts in Camden Passage and then sprawls into the streets behind. It's on Wednesdays 7am to 5:30pm and Saturdays 9am to 5:30pm.

Don't confuse Camden Passage with **Camden Market** (very, very downtown). Camden Market (tube: Camden Town) is for teens and others into body piercing, blue hair (yes, still), and vintage clothing. Serious collectors of vintage may want to explore during the week, when the teen scene isn't quite so overwhelming. Market hours are from 9:30am to 5:30pm daily, with some parts opening at 10am.

LONDON AFTER DARK

Weekly publications such as *Time Out* and *Where,* available at newsstands, give full entertainment listings and contain information on restaurants, nightclubs, and theaters. You'll also find listings in daily newspapers, notably *The Times* and *The Telegraph.*

THE PERFORMING ARTS

If you want to see specific theatrical performances—especially hit ones—purchase your tickets in advance. The best way to do this is to buy your ticket from the theater's box office. Many theaters will accept credit-card bookings by telephone or through their website. You can also make reservations through ticket agents, such as **Keith Prowse/First Call,** 234 W. 44th St., Suite 1000, New York, NY 10036 (© 800/669-8687 or 212/398-1430 in the U.S., or 020/7911-3403 in London). The fee for booking a ticket in the United States is 35%; in London, it's 25%.

THEATER Occupying a prime site on the South Bank of the River Thames is the flagship of British theater, the **Royal National Theatre,** South Bank, SE1 (© 020/7452-3000; www.nationaltheatre.org.uk; tube: Waterloo, Embankment, or Charing Cross). The National houses three theaters. Tickets are £12 to £30 ($18 to $45).

Royal Shakespeare Company (RSC), Barbican Centre, Silk St., Barbican, EC2 (© 020/7638-8891; www.rsc.org.uk; tube: Barbican, Moorgate, or Liverpool St.), is one of the world's finest theater companies. The core of the company's work remains the plays of William Shakespeare, but it also presents a wide-ranging program. There are three different productions each week in the Barbican Theatre, the main auditorium, and the Pit, a small studio space where much of the company's new writing is presented. Barbican Theatre tickets are £8 to £33 ($12 to $50); the Pit, £14 to £18.50 ($21 to $28).

A recent addition to London's theater scene is the replica of Shakespeare's **Globe Theatre,** New Globe Walk, Bankside, SE1 (© 020/7401-9919; www.shakespeares-globe.org; tube: Mansion House). Performances are staged, on the theater's original site, as they were in Elizabethan times: without lighting, scenery, or such luxuries as cushioned seats or a roof over the audience. Tours are £7 ($11) adults, £5 ($8) students and seniors, and £4 ($6) children. Performance tickets and schedules vary; call for details. Tours daily from 9:15am to 12:15pm.

> ### (Tips) Fringe Benefits
>
> Some of the best theater in London is performed on the "fringe"—at the dozens of so-called fringe theaters that usually attempt more adventurous productions than the established West End theaters; they're also dramatically lower in price and staged in more intimate surroundings. Check the weekly listings in *Time Out* for schedules and show times.

Sadler's Wells Theatre, Rosbery Ave., EC1 (© 020/7314-8800; www. sadlers-wells.com; tube: Angel), is London's premier venue for dance. This new theater can change its interior shape, size, mood, and even color for almost any performance. The program for Sadler's for each year will be approximately 25 weeks of dance and 10 to 12 weeks of opera. The remaining time will be a medley of visual theater. Box office is open from Monday to Saturday 10am to 8pm. Tickets are £8.50 to £35 ($13 to $53).

CLASSICAL MUSIC & OPERA   The **Royal Opera** and **Royal Ballet** are back at the newly restored **Royal Opera House,** Bow St., Covent Garden, WC2 (© 020/7212-9123; www.royalopera.org; tube: Covent Garden). New additions include two annexes with shops and restaurants, and rehearsal rooms. Opera performances are usually sung in the original language with English subtitles. The Royal Ballet performs a repertory with a tilt toward the classics, including works by its earlier choreographer-director, Sir Frederick Ashton, and Sir Kenneth MacMillan. Opera tickets are £8 to £150 ($12 to $225), ballet £6 to £63 ($9 to $95).

London Coliseum, St. Martin's Lane, WC2 (© 020/7632-8300; www. eno.org; tube: Leicester Sq.), is London's largest and most splendid theater. **English National Opera** performs a wide range of works in English, from great classics to Gilbert and Sullivan to new and experimental works, staged with flair and imagination. Tickets are £6 to £58 ($9 to $87). About 100 discount balcony tickets are sold on the day of performance.

Royal Albert Hall, Kensington Gore, SW7 (© 020/7589-8212; www. royalalberthall.org.uk; tube: South Kensington), is the annual setting for the BBC Henry Wood Promenade Concerts ("The Proms") from mid-July to mid-September. A British tradition since 1895, the programs are outstanding, often presenting newly commissioned works for the first time. Tickets are £3 to £90 ($4.50 to $135).

Across Waterloo Bridge rises **South Bank Centre,** South Bank, SE1 (© 020/7960-4242; tube: Waterloo or Embankment). Here are three of the most comfortable and acoustically perfect concert halls in the world: Royal Festival Hall, Queen Elizabeth Hall, and the Purcell Room. Within their precincts, more than 1,200 performances a year are presented. Tickets are £5 to £80 ($8 to $120).

THE CLUB & MUSIC SCENE

NIGHTCLUBS & CABARETS   Bagley's Studios, King's Cross Freight Depot, off York Way, N1 (© 020/7278-2777; tube: King's Cross), is vast, echoing, a bit grimy, and very evocative of a munitions warehouse during the dark days of World War II. Set in the bleak industrial landscapes behind King's Cross Station, its interior is radically transformed 3 nights a week into one of London's most animated rave events. It's scattered over two floors, each the size of an American football field, and each divided into a trio of individual rooms, with its own ambience and sound system. You'll be happiest here if you wander from room to room, searching out the site that best corresponds to your energy level at the moment. Guaranteed openings Friday to Sunday 10pm to 7am; otherwise, openings depend on whatever promoter wants to book the space. Cover is £10 to £20 ($15 to $30).

Set in a dingy residential neighborhood in north London, **Barfly Club,** at the Falcon Pub, 234 Royal College St., NW1 (© **020/7482-4884;** tube: Camden Town), is a traditional-looking pub that's distinguished every night by the roster of rock-and-roll bands that come in from throughout the United Kingdom for bouts of beer and high-energy music. A recorded announcement tells fans what to expect on any given night, along with explicit instructions on how to reach it through a warren of narrow streets. You're likely to get virtually anything here—which adds considerably to the sense of fun and adventure. Open nightly from 7:30 to 2 or 3am, with most musical acts beginning at 8:15pm. Cover is £7 to £11 ($11 to $17).

Camden Palace, 1A Camden High St., NW1 (© **020/7387-0428;** tube: Camden Town or Mornington Crescent), is housed inside what was originally a theater built around 1910. It draws an over-18 crowd that flocks there in various costumes and energy levels according to the night of the week. Since it offers a rotating style of music, it's best to phone in advance to see if that evening's musical genre appeals to your taste. Open Tuesday 10am to 2am, Friday 10am to 6am, and Saturday 10am to 7am. Cover is £5 to £20 ($8 to $30).

ROCK   A long-established venue for rock-and-roll, blues, and indie bands, **The Rock Garden,** 6–7 The Piazza, Covent Garden (© **020/7836-4052;** tube: Covent Garden), maintains a bar and a stage in the cellar and a restaurant on the street level. The cellar area, known as The Venue, has hosted such bands as Dire Straits, The Police, and U2 before they became famous. Open daily from 5pm to 2am Sunday to Thursday, 3am Friday and Saturday). Cover is £5 to £10 ($8 to $15); diners enter free. No cover before 8pm, 10pm Friday and Saturday.

Wag Club, 35 Wardour St., W1 (© **020/7437-5534;** tube: Piccadilly Circus or Leicester Sq.), is a popular dance club on two floors, one decorated with Celtic designs in gold with colorful renditions of medieval tarot cards, the other in bright primary colors, with huge black-and-white canvases. White fur fabric sculptures adorn the walls; high-tech lighting illuminates the dance floor. The music policy alternates between live bands and recorded music. Call to see what's happening any given night. Open from Tuesday to Thursday 10pm to 3am, Friday 10pm to 4am, and Sunday 10pm to 5am. Cover is £5 to £10 ($8 to $15).

JAZZ & BLUES   The reasonably priced **100 Club,** 100 Oxford St., W1 (© **020/7636-0933;** tube: Tottenham Court Rd.), is a serious rival to the city's upscale jazz clubs. Its cavalcade of bands includes the best British jazz musicians, as well as many touring Americans. Rock, R&B, and blues are also presented. It's open from Monday to Friday 8:30pm to 3am, Saturday 7:30pm to 1am, and Sunday 7:30 to 11:30pm. Cover is £7 ($11) members, £10 ($15) nonmembers; Sun £6 ($9).

Mention the word *jazz* in London and people immediately think of **Ronnie Scott's,** 47 Frith St., W1 (© **020/7439-0747;** tube: Leicester Sq.), long the citadel of modern jazz in Europe, where the best English and American groups are booked. Featured on almost every bill is an American band, often with a top-notch singer. In the Main Room, you can either stand at the bar to watch the show or sit at a table, where you can order dinner. The Downstairs Bar is more intimate. On weekends, the separate Upstairs Room has a disco called Club Latino. It's open from Monday to Saturday 8:30pm to 3am. Cover is £15 ($23) from Monday to Thursday, £20 ($30) Friday and Saturday.

DANCE CLUBS

Bar Rumba, 26 Shaftesbury Ave., W1 (© 020/7287-2715; tube: Piccadilly Circus), is a Latin bar and club that could be featured in a book on "Underground

---

Moments **The World's Greatest Pub Crawl**

Dropping into the local pub for a pint of real ale or bitter is the best way to soak up the character of the different villages that make up London. You'll hear the accents and slang and see first-hand how far removed upper-crust Kensington is from blue-collar Wapping. Catch the local gossip or football talk—and, of course, enjoy some of the finest ales, stouts, ciders, and malt whiskies in the world.

Central London is awash with wonderful historic pubs as rich and varied as the city itself. The **Cittie of Yorke,** 22 High Holborn, WC1 (© 020/7242-7670; tube: Holborn or Chancery Lane), boasts the longest bar in Britain, rafters ascending to the heavens, and a long row of immense wine vats, all of which give it the air of a great medieval hall—appropriate since a pub has existed at this location since 1430. Samuel Smiths is on tap, and the bar offers novelties like chocolate-orange-flavored vodka. Dickens once hung out in the **Lamb & Flag,** 33 Rose St., off Garrick Street, WC2 (© 020/7497-9504; tube: Leicester Sq.), and the room itself is little changed from the days when he prowled this neighborhood. The pub has an amazing and somewhat scandalous history. John Dryden was almost killed by a band of thugs outside its doors in December 1679; the pub gained the nickname the "Bucket of Blood" during the Regency era (1811–20) because of the routine bare-knuckled prizefights that broke out. Tap beers include Courage Best and Directors, Old Speckled Hen, John Smiths, and Wadworths 6X.

Olde Mitre, Ely Place, EC1 (© 020/7405-4751; tube: Chancery Lane), is the namesake of a working-class inn built here in 1547, when the Bishops of Ely controlled the district. It's a small pub with an odd assortment of customers. Friary Meux, Ind Coope Burton, and Tetleys are on tap. **Seven Stars,** 53 Carey St., WC2 (© 020/7242-8521; tube: Holborn), is tiny and modest except for its collection of toby mugs and law-related art, the latter a tribute to the pub's location at the back of the Law Courts and the large clientele of barristers who drink here. It's a great place to pick up some British legal jargon. Courage Best and Directors are on tap, as well as a selection of single malts.

Black Friar, 174 Queen Victoria St., EC4 (© 020/7236-5474; tube: Blackfriars), will transport you to the Edwardian era. The wedge-shaped pub reeks of marble and bronze Art Nouveau, featuring bas-reliefs of mad monks, a low-vaulted mosaic ceiling, and seating carved out of gold marble recesses. It's especially popular with the city's after-work crowd, and it features Adams, Wadsworth 6X, Tetleys, and Brakspears on tap.

London" in spite of its location on Shaftesbury Avenue. It leans toward radical jazz fusion on some nights, funk on other occasions. It boasts two full bars and a different musical theme every night. Tuesday and Wednesday are the only nights you won't have to queue at the door. Monday's "That's How It Is" showcase features jazz, hip hop, and drum and bass; Friday's "KAT Klub" grooves with soul, R&B, and swing; and Saturday's "Garage City" buzzes with house and garage. On weeknights you have to be 18 or older; on Saturday and Sunday nobody under 21 is allowed in. Cover is £4 to £12 ($6 to $18). Open Wednesday 10pm to 3:30am, Saturday 10pm to 4am, and Sunday 8pm to 1:30am.

Equinox, Leicester Sq., WC2 (© **020/7437-1446;** tube: Leicester Sq.), has nine bars, the largest dance floor in London, and a restaurant modeled along the lines of an American diner from the 1950s. Virtually every kind of dance music, save "rave," is featured here. It's open from Monday to Thursday 9pm to 3am and Friday and Saturday 9pm to 4am. Cover is £5 to £12 ($8 to $18); £3 ($4.50) students. **Hippodrome,** Leicester Sq., WC2 (© **020/7437-4311;** tube: Leicester Sq.), is one of London's greatest discos, an enormous place where light and sound envelop you from all directions. Revolving speakers even descend from the roof to deafen you in patches, and you can watch yourself on closed-circuit video. It's open from Monday to Saturday 9pm to 3am. Cover is £3 to £12 ($4.50 to $18).

Because it's removed from the city center, **Ministry of Sound,** 103 Gaunt St., SE1 (© **020/7378-6528;** tube: Elephant & Castle), is popular with the local set and relatively devoid of tourists. It has a big bar and an even bigger sound system that blasts garage and house music to enthusiastic crowds, who fill the two dance floors or relax in the cinema room. Be warned that entrance to this place isn't particularly cheap and the door policy is selective. Open Friday 10:30pm to 6am, Saturday midnight to 9am. Cover is £10 to £15 ($15 to $23).

Wednesday is one of the most popular nights at **The Office,** 3–5 Rathbone Place, W1 (© **020/7636-1598;** tube: Tottenham Court Rd.), when the "Double Six Club" features easy-listening music and board games from 6pm to 2am. Other nights are devoted to recorded pop, rock, soul, and disco. Come for the fun, not the decor. Open Monday to Friday 11am to 3am, Saturday 9:30pm to 3:30am. Cover is £6 to £9 ($9 to $14).

THE GAY & LESBIAN SCENE

The most reliable source of information on gay clubs and activities is the (always busy) 24-hour **Gay Switchboard** at © **020/7837-7324.** Offering similar help for women is the **Lesbian Line** at © **020/7837-7324,** staffed from Tuesday to Thursday 7 to 10pm and from Monday and Friday 2 to 10pm.

Adjacent to one of Covent Garden's best-known traffic junctions, **The Box,** at Seven Dials, 32–34 Monmouth St., WC2 (© **020/7240-5828;** tube: Covent Garden or Leicester Sq.), is a Mediterranean-style bar. Gay men outnumber lesbians, though the venue is sophisticated and blasé about sexual definitions. Year-round, the place defines itself as a "summer bar," throwing open its doors and windows to a cluster of outdoor tables that attracts a crowd at the slightest hint of warmth. It's open from Monday to Saturday 11:30am to 11pm and Sunday noon to 6pm.

Candy Bar, 4 Carlisle St., London, W1 (© **020/7494-4041;** tube: Tottenham Court Rd.), is a tri-level dance club that's a hot spot for London's lesbian crowd, whether young or of a certain age. The top floor is a lounge with pool tables and comfortable couches. The second floor is a dimly lit bar area. The lower floor is a large dance floor with live DJs playing everything from rock and pop to top 10 R&B, soul, and reggae. The decor is rather plain with more subdued lighting for a more cruisy atmosphere. Providing they appear on the arm of a woman, men are allowed to visit as well. Hours are from Monday to Thursday 5pm to midnight, Friday 5pm to 2am, Saturday 2pm to 2am, and Sunday 5 to 11pm. Cover is £5 ($8) Friday and Saturday.

Few bars in London exemplify tolerance, humor, and sexual sophistication as well as **The Edge,** 11 Soho Sq., W1 (*©* **020/7439-1313;** tube: Tottenham Court Rd.). You'll get the idea the moment you enter; the first two floors are painted in intertwined shades of red and blue, with accessories that change, like the fixtures of an English garden, with the season. The clientele ranges from the ostentatiously gay to "Randy Andy" types slumming on a pub crawl away from the Royal Palace. It's open from Monday to Saturday 11am to 1am and Sunday noon to 10:30pm. **First Out,** 52 St. Giles High St., WC2 (*©* **020/7240-8042;** tube: Tottenham Court Rd.), prides itself on being the first (est. 1986) all-gay coffee shop in London. Set in a 19th-century building whose venerable wood panels have been painted all colors of the rainbow, it maintains two intimate floors (read: not particularly cruisy) where menu items are exclusively vegetarian and invariably priced at £3.80 ($6). Cappuccino and whisky are the preferred drinks, while curry dishes, pot pies in phyllo pastries, and salads are the foods of choice. Don't expect raucousness; some clients have even brought their grandmothers here. Look for the bulletin board, where the leaflets and business cards of gay and gay-friendly entrepreneurs add an aura of resource center to this cozy venue. Open from Monday to Saturday 10am to 11pm and Sunday 11am to 10:30pm.

Heaven, The Arches, Craven St., WC2 (*©* **020/7930-2020;** tube: Charing Cross or Embankment), is a London landmark club within the vaulted cellars of Charing Cross Railway Station. Black inside and reminiscent of a very large air-raid shelter, Heaven is one of England's biggest and best-established gay venues. Its four different areas are connected by a labyrinth of stairs, catwalks, and hallways. The club features different theme nights, where, depending on the night, gay men, gay women, or mostly heterosexuals predominate. Call before you go to learn the latest format. It's open Monday and Wednesday from 10:30pm to 3am, Friday and Saturday from 10:30pm to 6am. Cover is £6 to £12 ($9 to $18).

THE BAR SCENE

At the **American Bar,** in The Savoy, The Strand, WC2 (*©* **020/7836-4343;** tube: Embankment or Covent Garden), still one of the most sophisticated gathering places in London, the bartender is known for such special concoctions as the "Savoy Affair" and the "Prince of Wales," as well as for pouring the best martini in town. The bar is open from Monday to Saturday 11am to 11pm with jazz piano music beginning at 7pm. On Sunday, it's open from noon to 3pm and 7 to 10:30pm.

Rumours, 33 Wellington St., WC2 (*©* **020/7836-0038;** tube: Covent Garden), is the kind of place where you might expect Tom Cruise to turn up as bartender. Set within what functioned a century ago as a wholesale flower market, Rumours combines 1990s sophistication with a flamboyant marine theme. Open from Monday to Saturday 11:30am to 11pm, Sunday noon to 10:30pm.

DAY TRIPS FROM LONDON

HAMPTON COURT PALACE ⋆⋆⋆   On the north side of the Thames, 21km (13 miles) west of London in East Molesey, Surrey, this 16th-century palace of Cardinal Wolsey can teach us a lesson: Don't try to outdo your boss, particularly if he happens to be Henry VIII. The rich cardinal did just that. He eventually lost his fortune, power, and prestige—and he ended up giving his lavish palace to the Tudor monarch. Although the palace enjoyed prestige and pomp in Elizabethan days, it owes much of its present look to William and Mary—or rather to Sir Christopher Wren, who designed and built the Northern or Lion Gates. You can parade through the apartments today, filled as they are with porcelain, furniture, paintings, and tapestries. The Renaissance Gallery is graced with paintings by old masters on loan from Queen Elizabeth II.

The cloisters, courtyards, state apartments, great kitchen, cellars, and Hampton Court exhibition are open from April to October Monday 10:15am to 6pm and from Tuesday to Sunday 9:30am to 6pm. From November to March, hours are Monday 10:15am to 4:30pm and Tuesday to Sunday 9:30am to 4:30pm. The Tudor tennis court and banqueting house are open the same hours as above, but only from mid-March to mid-October. Admission to all these attractions is £10.50 ($16) adults, £8 ($12) students/seniors, £7 ($11) children 5 to 15, and £31.40 ($47) families (two adults and up to three children); free for children under 5. The gardens—including the Great Vine, King's Privy Garden, Great Fountain Gardens, Sunken Gardens, Board Walk, Tiltyard, and Wilderness—are open daily 7am to dusk (but not later than 9pm) and can be visited free.

Landmark Trust, Shootesbrooke, Maidenhead, Berkshire SL6 3SW (© 01628/825-925; www.landmarktrust.co.uk), oversees two palace buildings offering modest self-catering facilities. The Fish Court, sleeping six, was originally the quarters of the pastry chefs; 4-day bookings are £547 ($821) and 7-day bookings £1,591 ($2,387). Sleeping eight, the Georgian House is a former kitchen for the palace with a private garden; 4-night bookings for £595 to £729 ($893 to $1,094) and 7-day bookings £1,950 ($2,925).

You can get to Hampton Court (© 020/8781-9500) by bus, train, boat, or car. Frequent trains from Waterloo Station (Network Southeast) go to Hampton Court Station. London Transport buses 111, 131, 216, 267, and 461 make the trip, as do Green Line Coaches (ask at the nearest London Country Bus office for routes 715, 716, 718, and 726). If you have the time (about 4 hr.), boat service is offered to and from Kingston, Richmond, and Westminster.

WINDSOR CASTLE ✦✦✦   When William the Conqueror ordered a castle built on this spot, he began a legend and a link with English sovereignty that has known many vicissitudes, the most recent being a 1992 fire. The state apartments display many works of art, porcelain, armor, furniture, three Verrio ceilings, and several 17th-century Gibbons carvings. Several works by Rubens adorn the King's Drawing Rooms. Of the apartments, the grand reception room, with its Gobelin tapestries, is the most spectacular.

Queen Mary's Doll's House is a palace in perfect miniature. It was given to Queen Mary in 1923 as a symbol of national goodwill. The house, designed by Sir Edwin Lutyens, was created on a scale of 1 to 12. It took 3 years to complete and involved the work of 1,500 tradesmen and artists.

St. George's Chapel is a gem of the Perpendicular style, sharing the distinction with Westminster Abbey as a pantheon of English monarchs (Victoria is a notable exception). The present St. George's was founded in the late 15th century by Edward IV on the site of the original Chapel of the Order of the Garter (Edward III, 1348).

Admission is £10.50 ($16) adults, £8 ($12) students/seniors, £5 ($8) children 16 and under, £22.50 ($34) families (two adults and two children). The castle at Castle Hill is open from March to October daily 10am to 5pm and from

November to February daily 10am to 4pm. Lying 34km (21 miles) west of London, Windsor Castle (℃ **01753/831118**) can be reached in 50 minutes by train from Paddington Station.

2 Oxford & Stratford-upon-Avon

After visiting London, many move on to visit the ancient university city of Oxford and the country around Shakespeare's birthplace, Stratford-upon-Avon. Both time and tradition beckon you on to these places.

TOWN & GOWN: OXFORD 🏰🏰🏰

Oxford is a city of business and commerce, home to several industries; it's much more of a real city than Cambridge. Oxford isn't entirely dominated by its university, although the college spires are the reason the hordes, including tour buses, flock here. The fast-flowing pedestrian traffic may cause you to think you've been transported back to London instead of delivered to not-so-sleepy Oxford.

At any time of the year, you can tour the colleges, many of which represent a peak in England's architectural kingdom, as well as a valley of Victorian contributions. The Oxford Information Centre (see below) offers guided walking tours daily throughout the year. Just don't mention the other place (Cambridge), and you shouldn't have any trouble. Comparisons between the two universities are inevitable of course, Oxford being better known for the arts and Cambridge more for the sciences.

The city predates the university—in fact, it was a Saxon town in the early part of the 10th century. By the 12th century, Oxford was already growing in reputation as a seat of learning, at the expense of Paris. The first colleges were founded in the 13th century. The story of Oxford is filled with local conflicts: The relationship between town and gown wasn't as peaceful as it is today, and riots often flared over the rights of the university versus the town. Nowadays, the young people of Oxford take out their aggressions in sporting competitions.

Ultimately, the test of a great university lies in the caliber of the people it turns out. Oxford can name-drop a mouthful: Roger Bacon, Sir Walter Raleigh, John Donne, Sir Christopher Wren, Samuel Johnson, William Penn, Lewis Carroll, Harold Macmillan, Graham Greene, T. E. Lawrence, just to name a select few.

ESSENTIALS

GETTING THERE   Oxford is 87km (54 miles) northwest from London.

By Train   Trains from London's Paddington Station depart hourly for Oxford (trip time: 1¼ hr.). A cheap, same-day round-trip ticket costs £28.90 ($43); call **British Rail** at ℃ **0345/484-950** for information.

By Bus   **Oxford Citylink** provides coach service from London's Victoria Station (℃ **020/7824-0056**) to the Oxford bus station. Coaches usually depart about every 20 minutes during the day from gate 10 (trip time: about 1¾ hr.). A same-day round-trip ticket costs £7.50 ($11).

By Car   Take M-40 west from London and follow the signs. Traffic and parking are a disaster in Oxford; you may want to use one of the four "Park and Ride" lots just outside of the city.

VISITOR INFORMATION   The **Oxford Tourist Information Centre,** at The Old School, Gloucester Green (℃ **01865/726871;** www.oxford.gov.uk), sells maps, brochures, and souvenir items, as well as the famous Oxford

University T-shirt. It also provides hotel booking services for £2.50 ($3.75). Guided walking tours leave from the center daily (see below). It's open from Monday to Saturday 9:30am to 5pm and Sunday and bank holidays in summer from 10am to 3:30pm.

GETTING AROUND   Since Oxford is relatively flat, a good way to see the colleges is by bicycle. **Bike Zone,** 6 Lincoln House Market St. (© **01865/ 728877**), rents 15-speed hybrid bicycles for £10 ($15) a day or £20 ($30) for the week with a £100 ($150) refundable deposit. The staff is very friendly and helpful. It's open from Monday to Saturday 9am to 5:30pm.

WHERE TO STAY

Oxford Tourist Information Centre, Gloucester Green, opposite the bus station (© **01865/726871**), operates a year-round room-booking service for a fee of £2.50 ($3.75), plus a refundable deposit. The center has a list of accommodations, maps, and guidebooks.

Expensive

Old Bank Hotel 𝓕𝓕𝓕   Opening in 1999, this is Oxford's first hotel in 135 years, and it immediately surpassed the traditional favorite Randolph in style and amenities. The good-size rooms are comfortably and elegantly appointed, often with views. An understated elegance prevails, and each room comes with a state-of-the-art marble bathroom with tubs and power showers. Throughout the hotel is an array of 20th-century British art.

92–94 High St., Oxford OX1 4BN. © 0186/579-9599. Fax 0186/579-9598. www.oxford-hotels-restaurants. co.uk. 44 units. £160–£170 ($240–$255) double; from £255 ($383) suite. Rates include English breakfast. AE, DC, DISC, MC, V. Bus: 7. **Amenities:** Restaurant, bar; 24-hour room service; baby-sitting; laundry. *In room:* A/C, TV, coffeemaker, hair dryer.

Old Parsonage Hotel 𝓕𝓕   This hotel near St. Giles Church and Keble College is so old (1660) it looks like an extension of one of the ancient colleges. Oscar Wilde once lived here. In 1991 it was completely renovated and transformed into a first-rate hotel. Rooms are individually designed but not large, and the hotel is graced with fireplaces and a roof garden. The bathrooms with tubs and showers have their own phone extensions. The restaurant is the only place in the hotel with air-conditioning. All suites and some rooms have sofa beds.

1 Banbury Rd., Oxford OX2 6NN. © 01865/310210. Fax 01865/311262. www.oxford-hotel.restaurants. co.uk. 30 units. £150–£175 ($225–$263) double; from £200 ($300) suite. Rates include English breakfast and afternoon tea. AE, DC, MC, V. Bus: 7. **Amenities:** Restaurant, bar; laundry. *In room:* TV, minibar, hair dryer.

The Randolph 𝓕   Since 1864 this has been the leading hotel of Oxford, and it's still the largest, even though for sheer class Old Bank has it beat. With its striking arched stone entrance, it overlooks St. Giles, the Ashmolean Museum, and the Cornmarket. The hotel illustrates how historic surroundings can be combined with modern conveniences to make for elegant accommodations. Some rooms are quite large, although others are a bit cramped. The double-glazing on the windows seems inadequate to keep out the midtown traffic noise. All rooms have a tub and shower.

Beaumont St., Oxford, Oxfordshire OX1 2LN. © 800/225-5843 in the U.S. and Canada, or 01865/247481. Fax 01865/791678. 119 units. £155–£375 ($233–$563) double; £225–£375 ($338–$563) suite. AE, DC, MC, V. Parking £10 ($15). Bus: 7. **Amenities:** Restaurant, bar; laundry. *In room:* TV, coffeemaker, hair dryer.

Moderate

Eastgate Hotel   This is the Oxford pacesetter in the moderately priced race. The Eastgate stands opposite the ancient Examination Halls, next to Magdalen

Oxford

SCOTLAND
0   100 mi
0   100 km

North Sea

Irish Sea

ENGLAND

WALES

Oxford   London ★

English Channel

UNIVERSITY PARKS

Walton Cres.

Wellington Sq.

Woodstock Rd.

Banbury Rd.

Keble Rd.

Blackhall Rd.

Richmond Rd.

Worcester Pl.

Walton St.

St. John's St.

Alfred Lane

Pusey St.

St. Giles St.

Museum Rd.

South Parks Rd.

Mansfield Rd.

St. Cross Rd.

River Cherwell

Gloucester St.

Beaumont St.

Magdalen St.

Trinity College

Parks Rd.

Manor Rd.

Green St.

Bus Station

George St.

Broad St.

Jowett Walk

St. Michael's St.

Ship St.

Catte St.

Holywell St.

New College

St. Cross Rd.

New Rd.

Hall Inn

New Inn

Cornmarket St.

Market St.

Turl St.

Radcliff Sq.

Carfax Tower

To Station

Castle St.

St. Ebbe's St.

Queen St.

King Edward St.

Alfred St.

Oriel St.

Magpie Lane

Queen's Lane

High St.

Longwall St.

Path along River Cherwell

Town Hall

ⓘ

Blue Boar St.

University College

Church St.

Old Grey Friars St.

Pembroke St.

Brewer St.

Merton St.

Magdalen College

6

DEER PARK

Christ Church College

Corpus Christi College

Merton College

Rose Lane

BOTANIC GARDEN

Norfolk St.

Littlegate St.

Speedwell St.

St. Aldates St.

MERTON FIELD

CHRIST CHURCH MEADOW

River Thames

ⓘ **Information**

ACCOMMODATIONS
Eastgate **6**
Old Bank Hotel **5**
Old Parsonage **2**
Oxford Moat House **1**
Randolph **3**
River Hotel **4**
Tilbury Lodge Private Hotel **4**

Bridge, within walking distance of Oxford colleges and the city center. Recently refurbished, it offers modern facilities while retaining the atmosphere of an English country house. The comfortably furnished rooms have small bathrooms with shower stalls. The bar is a favorite with undergraduates.

23 Merton St., Oxford, Oxfordshire, OX1 4BE. Ⓒ **01865/248244.** Fax 01865/791681. www.sales-randolph. heritage-hotels.com. 64 units. £145–£155 ($217.50–$232.50) double; from £170 ($255) suite. AE, DC, MC, V. Bus: 7. **Amenities:** Restaurant, bar; laundry. *In room:* TV, coffeemaker.

Oxford Moat House   One of the Queens Moat Houses group, this hostelry emphasizes spacious, glassed-in areas and streamlined rooms. Patronized mainly by motorists, it's at the northern edge of Oxford 3km (2 miles) from the center, hidden from the traffic at the junction of A-40 and A-34. Each refurbished room has a small shower-only bathroom. The 10 no-smoking executive rooms are larger.

Godstow Rd., Wolvercote Roundabout, Oxford, Oxfordshire OX2 8AL. Ⓒ **01865/489988.** Fax 01865/ 310259. 155 units. £120–£151 ($180–$227) double. AE, MC, V. Bus: 60. **Amenities:** Restaurant, bar;

swimming pool; gym; squash courts; sauna; solarium; punt and pitch court (9 holes); snooker (billiards) room; no-smoking rooms. *In room:* TV w/ pay movies, coffeemaker, trouser press, robe.

Inexpensive

River Hotel   Just beyond the railway station west of the center, this hotel charges less than many of its more centrally located competitors. About a quarter of the cozy rooms are across the street, within a comfortable stone-sided annex. Rooms are equipped with small bathrooms containing shower units.

17 Botley Rd., Oxford, Oxfordshire OX2 OAA. ✆ 01865/243475. Fax 01865/724306. 21 units. £70–£81 ($105–$121.50) double. Rates include breakfast. MC, V. Bus: 4C or 52. **Amenities:** Restaurant, bar. *In room:* TV, coffeemaker.

Tilbury Lodge Private Hotel   This small hotel is on a quiet country lane about 3km (2 miles) west of the center, beyond the railway station. Eddie and Eileen Trafford accommodate guests in their well-furnished and comfortable rooms, each with a shower-only bathroom. The most expensive room has a four-poster bed. Children are welcome. If you don't arrive by car, Eddie can pick you up at the train station.

5 Tilbury Lane, Eynsham Rd., Botley, Oxford, Oxfordshire OX2 9NB. ✆ 01865/862138. Fax 01865/863700. 9 units. £70 ($105) double; £75 ($112.50) double with 4-poster bed. Rates include English breakfast. MC, V. Bus: 4A, 4B, or 100. **Amenities:** Jacuzzi. *In room:* TV, coffeemaker.

WHERE TO DINE
Very Expensive

Le Manoir aux Quat' Saisons ᏯᏯᏯ FRENCH   Some 19km (12 miles) southeast of Oxford, Le Manoir aux Quat' Saisons offers the finest cuisine in the Midlands. The stone manor house was originally built by a Norman nobleman in the 1300s. The connection with France has been masterfully revived by the Gallic owner and chef, Raymond Blanc. You can enjoy such highly creative specialties as quail eggs, spinach, Parmesan, and black truffle ravioli in a rosemary jus; light crab bisque with ginger and lemongrass; or braised boned oxtail filled with shallots and wild mushrooms in a Hermitage red-wine sauce with puree of parsnips.

The gabled house was built in the 1500s, improved and enlarged in 1908. Inside, there are 32 luxurious rooms, each decorated boudoir style with radio, TV, and private bathroom; the cost is £230 to £340 ($345 to $510) for a double, £550 ($825) for a suite.

Great Milton, Oxfordshire OX44 7PD. ✆ 01844/278881. Fax 01844/278847. Reservations required. Main courses £32–£37 ($48–$56); lunch menu du jour £45 ($68); lunch or dinner menu gourmand £89 ($134). AE, DC, MC, V. Daily noon–2:15pm and 7:15–10:15pm. Take Exit 7 off M-40 and head along A-329 toward Wallingford; look for signs for Great American Milton Manor about 2km (1 mile) later.

Expensive

Elizabeth Ꮿ FRENCH/CONTINENTAL   Despite the portraits of Elizabeth II that hang near the entrance, this restaurant is named after its original owner, a matriarch who founded the place in the 1930s opposite Christ Church College. The larger of the two dining rooms displays reproductions of paintings by Goya and Velázquez and exudes a restrained kind of dignity; the smaller room is devoted to *Alice in Wonderland* designs inspired by Lewis Carroll. The dishes that show the kitchen at its best include chicken royale; Scottish steaks; several different fish served in white-wine or lemon-butter sauce; and Basque pipérade.

82 St. Aldate's St. ✆ 01865/242230. Reservations recommended. Main courses £13.25–£18.75 ($20–$28); lunch £16 ($24) 3 courses. AE, DC, MC, V. Tues–Sat 12:30–2:30pm and 6:30–11pm; Sun 7–10:30pm. Closed Good Friday and Christmas week. Bus: 7.

Fun Fact **Old School Ties**

Some former owners of the **Bear Inn** developed a prankish and astonishing habit: clipping neckties. Around the lounge bar you'll see the remains of thousands of ties, all labeled with their owners' names. For those who seek to join this legacy of sartorial abuse, the bar patrons will cut a thin stip from the bottom of your tie (with your permission, of course). After this initiation, you may want to take part in some of the informal songfests of the undergraduates.

Moderate

Cherwell Boathouse Restaurant FRENCH   This Oxford landmark on the River Cherwell is owned by Anthony Verdin. The chefs turn out the best roast pheasant in Oxford, and other dishes are delicately handled as well, including one of our favorites, a loin of free-range pork in a creamy tarragon and green peppercorn sauce. There's a very reasonable, even exciting, wine list. In summer, there's service on the terrace.

Bardwell Rd. ℭ **01865/552746.** Reservations recommended. Fixed-price 3-course dinner £20.50 ($31); Sun lunch £19.50 ($30). AE, DC, MC, V. Tues 6–11:30pm; Wed–Sat noon–2pm and 6–11:30pm; Sun noon–2pm. Closed Dec 24–30. Bus: Banbury Rd.

Gee's Restaurant ✦ MEDITERRANEAN/INTERNATIONAL   This restaurant in a spacious Victorian glass conservatory is converted from what for 80 years was the leading florist of Oxford. The owners, the Old Parsonage Hotel (see above), have turned it into one of the most nostalgic and delightful places to dine in the university city. It's been around since 1984 but under a new chef has come into more fashion. From students to professors, clients are mixed, but all enjoy a well-chosen list of offerings that range from succulent pastas to char-grilled steaks, from fresh fish to crisp salads. We recently dug into a tagliatelle with smoked haddock, leeks, pancetta, and a thyme-butter sauce, and found it a delight, our dining partner equally satisfied with duck breast with a sherry sauce. Always reliable is the Scottish prime rib-eye steak with mushrooms and shoestring "chips."

61 Banbury Rd. ℭ **01865/553-540.** Reservations recommended. Set-price lunch £19.50 ($29). Main courses £12–£16 ($18–$24). AE, DC, MC, V. Daily noon–2:30pm and 6–11pm. Bus: 7.

Inexpensive

Bear Inn ENGLISH   A short block from The High, overlooking the north side of Christ Church College, this is the village pub, an Oxford tradition since the 13th century. Its swinging inn sign depicts the bear and ragged staff, old insignia of the earls of Warwick, who were among the early patrons. This is a good place to meet undergraduates who flock here for the good-tasting and inexpensively priced pub grub.

Alfred St. ℭ **01865/728164.** Snacks and bar meals £2–£6 ($3–$9). DC, MC, V. Daily noon–11pm. Bus: 2A or 2B.

Turf Tavern ENGLISH   This 13th-century tavern lies on a very narrow passageway near the Bodleian Library. Thomas Hardy used the place in *Jude the Obscure*. During his student days at Oxford, Bill Clinton was a frequent visitor. At night, the nearby old tower of New College and part of the old city wall are floodlit, and during warm weather you can sit in any of the three gardens that radiate outward from the pub's central core. For wintertime warmth, braziers are lighted in the courtyard and in the gardens. A separate food counter, set behind a glass case, displays the day's good, hearty fare.

4 Bath Place (off Holywell St.). ℭ **01865/243235.** Main dishes £3–£5.50 ($4.50–$8). MC, V. Mon–Sat 11am–11pm; Sun noon–3pm and 7–10:30pm. Bus: 52.

WALKING AROUND THE COLLEGES

The best way to get a running commentary on the important sightseeing attractions is to go to the Oxford Information Centre. Two-hour **walking tours** through the city and the major colleges leave daily at 11am and 2pm, and cost £5.85 ($9) adults and £3 ($4.50) ages 6 to 16. The tours don't include New College or Christ Church.

OVERVIEW   For a bird's-eye view of the city and colleges, climb **Carfax Tower** (ℭ **01865/792653**), in the city center. This structure is distinguished by the clock and figures that strike the quarter hours. Carfax Tower is all that remains of St. Martin's Church, where William Shakespeare once stood as godfather for William Davenant, who also became a successful playwright. A church stood on this site from 1032 until 1896. The tower used to be higher, but after 1340 it was lowered, following complaints from the university to Edward III that townspeople threw stones and fired arrows at students during town-and-gown disputes. Admission is £1.20 ($1.80) adults, 60p (90¢) children. The tower is open from April to October daily 10am to 5:30pm; from November to March it's open from Monday to Saturday 10am to 3:30pm.

CHRIST CHURCH ⋒⋒   Begun by Cardinal Wolsey as Cardinal College in 1525, Christ Church (ℭ **01865/276492**), known as the House, was founded by Henry VIII in 1546. Facing St. Aldate's Street, Christ Church has the largest quadrangle of any college in Oxford. Tom Tower houses Great Tom, the 18,000-pound bell referred to earlier. It rings at 9:05pm nightly, signaling the closing of the college gates. The 101 times it peals originally signified the number of students in residence at the time of the founding of the college.

The college chapel was constructed over a period of centuries, beginning in the 12th century. The cathedral's most distinguishing features are its Norman pillars and the vaulting of the choir, dating from the 15th century. In the center of the great quadrangle is a statue of Mercury mounted in the center of a fishpond. The college and cathedral can be visited daily from 9am to 5:30pm. The entrance fee is £3 ($4.50) adults and £2 ($3) children.

MAGDALEN COLLEGE ⋒⋒   Magdalen (pronounced *Maud*-lin) College, High Street (ℭ **01865/276000**), was founded in 1458 by William of Waynflete, bishop of Winchester and later chancellor of England. Its alumni range from Wolsey to Wilde. Opposite the botanic garden, the oldest in England, is the bell tower, where the choristers sing in Latin at dawn on May Day. The reflection of the 15th-century tower is cast in the waters of the Cherwell below. On a not-so-happy day, Charles I—with his days numbered—watched the oncoming Roundheads from this tower. Visit the 15th-century chapel, in spite of many of its latter-day trappings. Ask when the hall and other places of special interest are open. The grounds of Magdalen are the most extensive of any Oxford college; there's even a deer park. You can visit from Easter to September daily noon to 6pm; off-season, daily from 2 to 6pm. Admission is £2.50 ($3.75), but it's charged only from Easter to September.

MERTON COLLEGE ⋒⋒   Founded in 1264, Merton College, Merton Street (ℭ **01865/276310**), is among the three oldest colleges at the university.

It stands near Corpus Christi College on Merton Street, the sole survivor of Oxford's medieval cobbled streets. Its library, built between 1371 and 1379, is said to be the oldest college library in England. There was once a tradition of keeping some of its most valuable books chained. Now only one book is so secured, to illustrate that historical custom. One treasure of the library is an astrolabe (an astronomical instrument used for measuring the altitude of the sun and stars) thought to have belonged to Chaucer. You pay £1 ($1.50) to visit the ancient library, as well as the Max Beerbohm Room (the satirical English caricaturist who died in 1956). The library and college are open from Monday to Friday 2 to 4pm and Saturday 10am to 4pm (closed for 1 week at Easter and Christmas).

A favorite pastime is to take **Addison's Walk** through the water meadows. The stroll is so named after a former alumnus, Joseph Addison, the 18th-century essayist and playwright noted for his contributions to *The Spectator* and *The Tatler*.

UNIVERSITY COLLEGE   University College, High Street (© **01865/ 276602**), is the oldest one at Oxford and dates back to 1249, when money was donated by an ecclesiastic, William of Durham (the old claim that the real founder was Alfred the Great is more fanciful). The original structures have all disappeared, and what remains today represents essentially 17th-century architecture, with subsequent additions in Victoria's day, as well as in more recent times. The Goodhart Quadrangle was added as late as 1962. The college's most famous alumnus, Shelley, was "sent down" for his part in collaborating on a pamphlet on atheism. However, all is forgiven today, as the romantic poet is honored by a memorial erected in 1894. The hall and chapel of University College can be visited daily during vacations, with special permission from the bursar office, from 2 to 4pm for £1.50 ($2.25) adults, 60p (90¢) children. No paid tours are available. Chapel services are held daily at 4 and 6pm.

NEW COLLEGE   New College, New College Lane, off Queen's Lane (© **01865/279555**), was founded in 1379 by William of Wykeham, bishop of Winchester and later lord chancellor of England. His college at Winchester supplied a constant stream of students. The first quadrangle, dating from before the end of the 14th century, was the initial quadrangle to be built in Oxford and formed the architectural design for the other colleges. In the antechapel is Sir Jacob Epstein's remarkable modern sculpture of *Lazarus* and a fine El Greco painting of St. James. One of the treasures of the college is a crosier (bishop's staff) belonging to the founding father. In the garden, you can stroll among the remains of the old city wall and the mound. The college (entered at New College Lane) can be visited from Easter to September daily

---

Moments **Punting: A Sport & a Pastime**

At **Punt Station,** Cherwell Boathouse, Bardwell Road (© **01865/515978**), you can rent a punt (flat-bottom boat maneuvered by a long pole and a small oar) for £8 to £10 ($12–$15) per hour, plus a £40 to £50 ($60 to $75) deposit. Similar charges are made for punt rentals at Magdalen Bridge Boathouse. Punts are rented from March to mid-June and from late August to October, daily 10am to dusk; from mid-June to late August, when a larger inventory of punts is available, it's open daily 10am to 10pm.

from 11am to 5pm; off-season, daily from 2 to 4pm. Admission is £1.50 ($2.25); after October admission is free.

THE SHOPPING SCENE

In its way, **Alice's Shop,** 83 St. Aldate's (© **01865/723793**), might have played a more important role in English literature than any other shop in Britain. Set in a 15th-century building that has housed some kind of shop since 1820, it functioned as a general store (brooms, hardware, and so on) during the period that Lewis Carroll, at the time a professor of mathematics at Christ Church College, was composing *Alice in Wonderland.* As such, it is believed to have been the model for important settings in the book. Today, the place is a favorite stop of Lewis Carroll fans, who gobble up commemorative pencils, chess sets, party favors, bookmarks, and in rare cases, original editions of some of Carroll's works.

Bodleian Library Shop, Old School's Quadrangle, Radcliffe Square, Broad Street (© **01865/277216**), specializes in Oxford-derived souvenirs. There're more than 2,000 objects inventoried here, including books describing the history of the university and its various colleges, paperweights made of pewter and crystal, and Oxford banners and coffee mugs. **Castell & Son (The Varsity Shop),** 13 Broad St. (© **01865/244000**), is the best outlet for clothing emblazoned with the Oxford logo or heraldic symbol. Objects include both whimsical and dead-on-serious neckties, hats, T-shirts, sweatshirts, pens, bookmarks, beer and coffee mugs, and cuff links. At **The Oxford Collection,** 106 High St. (© **01865/247414**), you'll find Oxford souvenirs such as glass beer steins etched with the university's logo and a wool cardigan-like sweater with brass buttons bearing the university crest.

Magna Gallery, 41 High St. (© **01865/245805**), is one of the best-respected antiquarian galleries in Oxford, with engravings, maps, and prints made between 1550 and 1896. The shop also stocks general topography, botanical prints, caricatures, and maps of Oxford and Oxfordshire.

STRATFORD-UPON-AVON 🔊

Stratford is virtually overrun by visitors in the summer months; the crowds dwindle in winter, allowing you at least to walk on the streets and seek out the places of genuine historic interest. Stratford is 146km (91 miles) northwest of London and 64km (40 miles) northwest of Oxford.

William Shakespeare, of course, was born here. Little is known about his early life, and many of the stories connected with Shakespeare's days in Stratford are largely fanciful, invented to amuse the vast number of literary fans who make the pilgrimage. David Garrick, the actor, really launched the shrine in 1769 when he organized the first of the Bard's commemorative birthday celebrations.

Tourist magnets include the Royal Shakespeare Theatre, where the Royal Shakespeare Company performs for 11 months each year. Visitors often rush back to London after a performance. Despite the crowds, Stratford's literary pilgrimage sights merit your interest. The town today aggressively hustles the Shakespeare connection, a bit suffocatingly so; everybody seems in business to make a buck off the Bard.

ESSENTIALS

GETTING THERE   By Train   Amazingly, considering the demand, there're no direct trains from London to Stratford-upon-Avon. However, from London's Paddington Station you can take the train to Leamington Spa, then change

Calling on Churchill at Blenheim Palace

Just 13km (8 miles) northwest of Oxford stands the extravagantly baroque **Blenheim Palace** ★★★ (© **01993/811325;** www.blenheim-palace.com), England's answer to Versailles. Blenheim is the home of the 11th duke of Marlborough, a descendant of John Churchill, the first duke, who was an on-again, off-again favorite of Queen Anne's. In his day (1650–1722), the first duke became the supreme military figure in Europe. Fighting on the Danube near a village named Blenheim, Churchill defeated the forces of Louis XIV, and the lavish palace of Blenheim was built for the duke as a gift from the queen. It was designed by Sir John Vanbrugh; the landscaping was created by the famous 18th-century landscape gardener, Capability Brown. You may recognize Blenheim because it was used as the setting for Kenneth Branagh's *Hamlet.*

The palace is loaded with riches: antiques, porcelain, oil paintings, tapestries, and chinoiserie. North Americans know Blenheim as the birthplace of Sir Winston Churchill. His birth room is included in the palace tour, as is the Churchill exhibition, four rooms of letters, books, photographs, and other relics. Today the former prime minister lies buried in Bladon Churchyard, near the palace.

Blenheim Palace is open from mid-March to October daily 10:30am to 5:30pm. Admission is £9 ($14) adults, £7 ($11) seniors/children 16 to 17, and £4 ($6) children 5 to 15; free for children 4 and under. If you're driving, take the A-44 from Oxford; otherwise, the no. 20 Gloucester Green bus (© **01865/772250**) leaves Oxford about every 30 minutes during the day for the half-hour trip.

trains for Stratford-upon-Avon (trip time: 3 hr.). The journey costs £22 ($33) round-trip. For information, call © **0345/484950.**

By Bus   Eight **National Express** (© **08705/808080**) coaches a day leave from Victoria Station (trip time: 3¼ hr.). A single-day round-trip ticket costs £16 ($24) except Friday when the price is £17.50 ($26).

By Car   From London, take the M40 toward Oxford and continue on the A34 to Stratford.

VISITOR INFORMATION   The **Tourist Information Centre,** Bridgefoot (© **01789/293127**), will provide any details you might wish about the Shakespeare houses, theater, and other attractions, and will assist you in booking rooms. It's open from March to October Monday to Saturday 9am to 6pm, and Sunday 11am to 5pm. In the off-season, hours are from Monday to Saturday 9am to 5pm.

WHERE TO STAY
Very Expensive
Welcombe Hotel ★★★   For a formal, historic hotel, there's none better in Stratford, and that includes Alveston Manor. One of England's great Jacobean country houses, this hotel is a 10-minute ride from the heart of Stratford. It is surrounded by 64 hectares (157 acres) of grounds. The public areas are heroic in

size, with high windows providing views of the park. Rooms—some big enough for tennis matches—are luxuriously furnished; those in the garden wing, although comfortable, are small. Bathrooms come with a tub and shower combo.

Warwick Rd., Stratford-upon-Avon, Warwickshire CV37 ONR. ℂ **01789/295252.** Fax 01789/414666. www. welcombe.co.uk. 63 units. £175 ($263) double; £260 ($390) suite. Rates include English breakfast. AE, DC, MC, V. Take A-439 2.5km (1½ miles) northeast of the town center. **Amenities:** Restaurant, bar; golf course; tennis courts; 24-hour room service; baby-sitting; laundry/dry cleaning. *In room:* TV, coffeemaker, hair dryer.

Expensive

Alveston Manor Hotel 🐾🐾   This black-and-white timbered manor is perfect for theatergoers. It's just a 2-minute walk from the Avon off B-4066. Whereas the Welcombe is on the outskirts and has cornered the deluxe trade, the Alveston—along with the Shakespeare (see below)—are tied for the most atmospheric choices within the town itself. The hotel has everything from an Elizabethan gazebo to Queen Anne windows. Mentioned in the *Domesday Book,* the building predates the arrival of William the Conqueror. The rooms in the manor house will appeal to those who appreciate old slanted floors, overhead beams, and antique furnishings. Some triples or quads are available in the modern section. The rooms here have built-in pieces. Most of the accommodations have combined tub and shower bathrooms, some shower only.

Clopton Bridge, Stratford-upon-Avon, Warwickshire CV37 7HP. ℂ **800/225-5843** in the U.S. and Canada, or 08704/008181. Fax 01789/414095. www.heritage-hotels.com. 114 units. £140 ($210) double; from £265 ($398) suite. AE, DC, MC, V. **Amenities:** Restaurant, bar; room service; baby-sitting; laundry/dry cleaning; no-smoking rooms. *In room:* TV, coffeemaker, hair dryer.

Shakespeare Hotel 🐾🐾   This is the most historic and traditional hotel in the town center. It even snatched up the premium name in town. The original parts of this hotel date from the 1400s. In the 1880s, the hotel was restored to its original Tudor look. It is rivaled within central Stratford only by Alveston Manor. Residents relax in the post-and-timber-studded public areas with fireplaces and playbills from 19th-century productions of Shakespeare. The rooms are named in honor of noteworthy actors, Shakespeare's plays, or Shakespearean characters. The oldest are capped with hewn timbers, and all have modern comforts. Each room comes with a tiny bathroom with a tub and shower.

Chapel St., Stratford-upon-Avon, Warwickshire CV37 6ER. ℂ **800/225-5843** in the U.S. and Canada, or 01789/294771. Fax 01789/415411. www.heritage-hotels.com. 74 units. £165 ($248) double; £198 ($297) suite. Children up to 12 stay free in parents' room. AE, DC, MC, V. **Amenities:** Restaurant, pub. *In room:* TV.

MODERATE

The Falcon   A blend of the old and the very new, this inn dates back to 25 years after Shakespeare's death. Out front it is half-timbered in the Tudor tradition, but as it grew, a modern extension was built and it's connected to the main structure by a glass-covered passageway. In the heart of Stratford, the inn faces the Guild Chapel and the New Place Gardens. The recently upgraded bedrooms in the mellowed part have oak beams and diamond-shaped windows. The rooms to avoid are those on the street side of the old section, as they are subject to more noise. The bathrooms, although clean, are somewhat hideous with linoleum floors and the like.

Chapel St., Stratford-upon-Avon, Warwickshire CV37 6HA. ℂ **01789/279953.** Fax 01789/414260. 84 units. £105 ($158) double; from £130 ($195) suite. AE, DC, MC, V. **Amenities:** Restaurant, pub. *In room:* TV.

Thistle Stratford-upon-Avon   Across the street from the main entrance of the Royal Shakespeare Theatre, the hotel is the best located of the moderate

Stratford-upon-Avon

† Church
ⓘ Information

ATTRACTIONS ●
Anne Hathaway's Cottage **15**
Cox's Yard/Stratford Tales **10**
Holy Trinity Church **16**
Mary Arden's House & the Shakespeare
   Countryside Museum **1**
New Place/Nash's House **8**
Royal Shakespeare Theatre **11**
Shakespeare's Birthplace **4**
Swan Theatre **13**

ACCOMMODATIONS ■
Alveston Manor Hotel **9**
The Falcon **5**
Hardwick House **2**
Sequoia House **12**
Shakespeare **7**
Stratheden Hotel **6**
Thistle Stratford-upon-Avon **14**
Welcome Hotel **3**

choices. Theatergoers flock here. Its redbrick main section dates from the Regency period. Rooms come in all sizes and shapes here, the most desirable resting under beamed ceilings with vistas over the Avon. Rooms are sometimes graced with a four-poster, and bathrooms, though small, are well equipped, with combo tubs and showers.

44 Waterside, Stratford-upon-Avon, Warwickshire CV37 6BA. © **01789/294949**. Fax 01789/415874. www. stratford-upon-avon.co.uk/arden.htm. 63 units. £139 ($208.50) double. AE, DC, MC, V. **Amenities:** Restaurant, bar. *In room:* TV, coffeemaker, hair dryer, trouser press.

Inexpensive

Hardwick House   Drenaugh and Simen Weetten welcome you to their home on a tree-lined street central to most main attractions, including the Royal Shakespeare Theatre. Their snug retreat has ample rooms, each furnished with comfortable mattresses and modern, tidy pieces, including small, shower-only bathrooms. Breakfast, served in a room so typically English it could be used as a set for a British soap opera, is the only meal offered, but it's a full English one, fit fortification for the day.

1 Avenue Rd., Stratford-upon-Avon, Warwickshire CV37 6UY. © **01789/204307**. Fax 01789/296760. 14 units. £54–£62 ($81–$93) double. AE, MC, V. **Amenities:** Breakfast room. *In room:* TV.

Sequoia House   With its own beautiful garden, this hotel stands across the Avon opposite the theater, convenient for visiting the major Shakespeare properties of the National Trust. Renovation has vastly improved the house, which was created from two late Victorian buildings. Today it offers rooms with comfortable mattresses and neat, shower-only bathrooms. Guests gather in a lounge with a licensed bar and an open Victorian fireplace. The hotel has a private parking area.

51–53 Shipston Rd., Stratford-upon-Avon, Warwickshire CV37 7LN. © **01789/268852**. Fax 01789/414559. 22 units. £69–£89 ($103.50–$133.50) double. Rates include English breakfast. AE, DC, DISC, MC, V. **Amenities:** Bar. *In room:* TV, coffeemaker.

Stratheden Hotel   First mentioned in a property deed in 1333, this hotel lies a short walk north of the Royal Shakespeare Theatre. The Stratheden, built in 1673 (and today the oldest remaining brick building in the town center), has a tiny rear garden and top-floor rooms with slanted, beamed ceilings. It has improved in both decor and comfort. Each room is equipped with a small shower-only bathroom. The breakfast room, with a bay window, has an overscale sideboard that once belonged to the "insanely vain" Marie Corelli, an eccentric novelist, poet, and mystic, and a favorite author of Queen Victoria.

5 Chapel St., Stratford-upon-Avon, Warwickshire CV37 6EP. © **01789/297119**. 9 units. £64–£70 ($96–$105) double. Rates include English breakfast. MC, V. **Amenities:** Breakfast room. *In room:* TV.

WHERE TO DINE

Box Tree Restaurant ⍟ CONTINENTAL/ENGLISH   This restaurant is right in the theater itself, with glass walls providing an unobstructed view of the Avon and its swans. During intermission, there's a snack feast of smoked salmon and champagne. You dine by flickering candlelight. There's a special phone for reservations in the theater lobby. Many dishes are definitely Old English (apple and parsnip soup); others reflect a continental touch. For your main course, you might select Dover sole, salmi of wild boar, pheasant suprême, or roast loin of pork. Homemade desserts are likely to include crème brûlée an old-time favorite at the Box Tree. Better food can be had at other places, such as Hussain's, but none are as convenient for theatergoers.

In the Royal Shakespeare Theatre, Waterside. © **01789/403415.** Reservations required. Matinee lunch £16 ($24); dinner £26.50 ($40). AE, MC, V. Thurs–Sat noon–2:30pm; Mon–Sat 5:45pm–midnight.

Desports ECLECTIC/INTERNATIONAL   At last Stratford has a restaurant worth writing home about. In the town center between the Shakespeare Centre and Market Place, Desports was installed in a 16th-century building. Extremely professional cooking, a vivid use of spices, imaginative menus, and reasonable prices attract a never-ending stream of visitors and locals alike. Is this the Stratford of yore, you ask, as you taste the aromatic pumpkin and Cerny cheese tagliatelle with almond pesto, tomato, and candied eggplant. Grilled vegetables in lemon oil with rosemary chick peas and saffron couscous are followed by cashew nut and herb risotto with wilted rocket and shaved Parmesan. Even such English classics as pan-fried calves' liver, bacon, kidneys, and bubble and squeak (cabbage and potatoes) is given added zest by an orange Dubonnet sauce.

13–14 Meer St. © **01789/269304.** Set-price lunch £15 ($23). Main courses £12–£18 ($18–$27). AE, DC, MC, V. Tues–Sat noon–2pm and 5:45–10:30pm.

Greek Connection GREEK   This restaurant occupies a high-ceilinged building from 1854 that originally served as a Methodist chapel. Today, authentic Greek food is accompanied by live music and dancing nightly. Chefs George and Spiros serve up such favorites as moussaka (freshly minced meat embedded in layers of eggplant, zucchini, and potatoes with a dome of creamy béchamel) and stuffed grape leaves. Many patrons say that ordering the Mezedakia is the best option; you'll get a wide sampling of Greek hors d'oeuvres and won't have to choose only one from the enticing menu.

1 Shakespeare St. © **01789/292214.** Reservations recommended. Main courses £9–£14 ($14–$21). DC, MC, V. Daily noon–2:30pm in summer; daily 5:30pm–12:30am year-round.

Thai Boathouse THAI   The only restaurant set on the Avon, this charming choice is reached by crossing Clopton Bridge toward Oxford and Banbury. The second floor dining room opens onto vistas of the river. This restaurant has brought spice and zest to Stratford's lazy restaurant scene. Seasonal specialties such as wild duck and pheasant are a special feature of the menu. Sample a selection of authentic Thai appetizers before going on to such delectable main courses as fresh sea bass in lemongrass, and lime leaves wrapped in banana leaf and grilled over the charcoal over a salmon stir-fried with curry sauce and coconut cream, enhanced by the use of Thai herbs. One of our favorites is their lamb in a yellow curry with potatoes, onions, and cashew nuts.

Swan's Nest Lane. © **01789/297733.** Reservations recommended. Set menus £19.95–£25 ($30–$38). Main courses £4.50–£15 ($7–$23). MC, V. Daily noon–2:30pm and 5:30–10:30pm.

PUBS
Dirty Duck ("Black Swan") ENGLISH   Since the 18th century, this is the town's most popular hangout for Stratford players. The wall is lined with autographed photos of past patrons, such as Lord Laurence Olivier. The front lounge and bar crackles with intense conversation. In the spring and fall, an open fire blazes. In the Dirty Duck Grill Room, typical English grills, among other dishes, are featured, although no one ever accused the Dirty Duck of serving the best food in Stratford. Main dishes include braised kidneys or oxtails, roast chicken, or honey-roasted duck.

Waterside. © **01789/297312.** Reservations required for dining. Main courses £7–£12.50 ($11–$19); bar snacks £2.90–£8 ($4.35–$12). AE, MC, V (restaurant only). Pub, Mon–Sat 11am–11pm; Sun noon–3pm and 7–10:30pm. Restaurant, Tues–Sun noon–2pm; Mon–Sat 5:30–11:30pm.

Garrick Inn ENGLISH   Near Harvard house, this half-timbered Elizabethan pub with its unpretentious charm dates from 1595. It's named for the great actor, David Garrick. The front bar is decorated with tapestry-covered settles, an old oak refectory table, and an open fireplace that attracts the locals. The back bar has a circular fireplace with a copper hood and mementos of the triumphs of the English stage. The specialty is homemade pies such as steak and ale, steak and kidney, or chicken and mushroom.

25 High St. ⓒ **01789/292186.** Main courses £5–£10 ($8–$15). MC, V. Meals daily noon–9pm. Pub, Mon–Sat 11am–11pm; Sun noon–10:30pm.

THEATER

Royal Shakespeare Company has a major showcase at the Royal Shakespeare Theatre, Waterside, Stratford-upon-Avon CV37 6BB (ⓒ **01789/403403;** www.rsc.org.uk), on the banks of the Avon. Plays, including on average five by Shakespeare each season, are staged at the 1,500-seat Royal Shakespeare and 450-seat Swan theaters as well as 170-seat The Other Place, a smaller, more experimental venue.

It's important to reserve tickets in advance, which you can book by phone or from a travel agent. In New York, try Edwards and Edwards (ⓒ **800/223-6108**) or Keith Prowse (ⓒ **800/669-8687**); a service charge will be added. You can also call the theater box office (payment by major credit card) at the number listed above; it's open from Monday to Saturday 9am to 8pm, closing at 6pm on days with no performances. Seat prices are £75 to £93 ($113 to $140). A small number of tickets are always held for sale on the day of a performance. You can pick up your ticket on the day it is to be used, but you can't cancel once your reservation is made unless 2 full weeks' advance notice is given.

SHAKESPEARE PILGRIMAGE SIGHTS

Besides the attractions on the periphery of Stratford, there are many Elizabethan and Jacobean buildings in town, many of them administered by the Shakespeare Birthplace Trust. The combination ticket costing £12 ($18) adults, £11 ($17) seniors and students, and £6 ($9) children lets you visit the five most important sights. You can buy tickets at any of the Trust properties.

Hall's Croft   It was here Shakespeare's daughter Susanna probably lived with her husband, Dr. John Hall. Furnished in the style of a middle-class home of the time, Hall's Croft is an outstanding Tudor house with a beautiful walled garden. Dr. Hall was widely respected and built up a large medical practice in the area, and exhibits illustrating the theory and practice of medicine in Dr. Hall's time are on view. You're welcome to use the adjoining Hall's Croft Club, which serves morning cofee, lunch, and afternoon tea.

Old Town (near Holy Trinity Church). ⓒ **01789/292107.** Admission £3.50 ($5) adults, £1.70 ($2.55) children; £8.50 ($13) families (2 adults, 3 children) for all 5 Shakespeare-related houses. Mar 20–Oct 19 Mon–Sat 10:30am–5pm, Sun 10am–5pm; off-season Mon–Sat 10am–4pm, Sun 10:30am–4pm. Closed Dec 23–26. To reach Hall's Croft, walk west from High St., which becomes Chapel St. and Church St. At the intersection with Old Town, go left.

Shakespeare's Birthplace ⭐   The son of a glover and whittawer (leather worker), the Bard was born on St. George's Day (Apr 23) in 1564 and died 52 years later on the exact same date. Filled with Shakespeare memorabilia, including a portrait and furnishings of the writer's time, the Trust property is a half-timbered structure, dating from the first part of the 16th century. The house, bought by public donors in 1847, is preserved as a national shrine. You can visit the oak-beamed living room, the bedroom where Shakespeare was probably born, a fully equipped kitchen of the period (look for the "baby-minder"), and a Shakespeare Museum, illustrating his life and times.

Henley St. ☎ **01789/204016.** Admission £5.50 ($8) adults, £2.50 ($3.75) children. Mar 20–Oct 19 Mon–Sat 9am–5pm, Sun 9:30am–5pm; off-season Mon–Sat 9:30am–4pm, Sun 10am–4pm. Closed Dec 23–26. From the center, walk north along Windsor Street, taking a right turn onto Henley Street.

Anne Hathaway's Cottage ⛫

In the hamlet of Shottery, 1.5km (1 mile) from Stratford, is the thatched, wattle-and-daub cottage where Anne Hathaway lived before her marriage to Shakespeare. It's the most interesting of the Trust properties, and the most unchanged. The Hathaways were yeoman farmers, and the cottage provides a rare insight into the life of a family of Shakespeare's day. Many original furnishings, including the courting settle and utensils, are preserved inside the house, which was occupied by descendants of Shakespeare's wife's family until 1892.

Cottage Lane, Shottery. ☎ **01789/292100.** Admission £3.90 ($6) adults, £1.70 ($2.55) children. Mar 20–Oct 19 Mon–Sat 9:30am–5pm, Sun 10am–5pm; off-season Mon–Sat 9:30am–4pm, Sun 10am–4pm. Closed Dec 23–26. You can walk across the meadow to Shottery from Evesham Place in Stratford (pathway marked), or take a bus from Bridge St.

New Place/Nash's House

This is the site where Shakespeare retired in 1610, a prosperous man. He died 6 years later, at the age of 52. Regrettably, his former home was torn down, and only the site remains. You enter the gardens through Nash's House (Thomas Nash married a granddaughter of the poet). The house has 16th-century period rooms and an exhibition illustrating the history of Stratford. The delightful Knott Garden adjoins the site and represents the style of a fashionable Elizabethan garden. New Place has its own great garden, which once belonged to Shakespeare.

Chapel St. ☎ **01789/204016.** Admission £3.50 ($5) adults, £3 ($4.50) seniors and students, £1.70 ($2.55) children. Mar 20–Oct 19 Mon–Sat 9:30am–5pm, Sun 10am–5pm; Oct 20–Mar 19 Mon–Sat 10am–4pm, Sun 10:30am–4pm. Closed Dec 23–26. Walk west down High St.; Chapel St. is a continuation of High St.

Mary Arden's House & the Shakespeare Countryside Museum ⛫

This timber-framed farmhouse with its old stone dovecote and various outbuildings is one of the most intriguing sights outside Stratford, even if local historian Dr. Nat Alcock discovered in 2000 that the actual childhood home of Arden was the dull looking brick-built farmhouse, Glebe Farm, next door. It was all the trick of a tour guide in the 18th century, John Jordan, who decided Glebe Farm was too unimpressive to be the home of the Bard's mother, so he told tourists it was this farmstead instead. Actually the so-called Mary Arden's House, it turns out, wasn't constructed until the late 16th century, a little late to be the home of the Bard's mother. Nonetheless, visit it anyway, as it contains country furniture and domestic utensils. In the barns, stable, cowshed, and farmyard you'll find an extensive collection of farming implements illustrating life and work in the local countryside from Shakespeare's time to the present.

Wilmcote. ☎ **01789/293455.** Admission £5 ($9) adults, £4.5 ($8) students and seniors, £2.5 ($4.25) children. Mar 20–Oct 19 Mon–Sat 9:30am–5pm, Sun 10am–5pm; off-season Mon–Sat 10am–4pm, Sun 10:30am–4pm. Closed Dec 23–26. Take the A-3400 (Birmingham) road for 5.5km (3½ miles).

Cox's Yard/Stratford Tales

The Bedford-based brewery, Charles Wells, leased a former timber yard adjacent to Bancroft Garden in the town center in 1996 and turned it into an array of attractions. Chief among these is the Stratford Tales, which uses elaborate visual and audiovisual displays as well as historic objects to illustrate town stories from the 16th century to the present day. On-site is a microbrewery that brews a variety of cask ales sold in a traditional

Stopping at Warwick Castle

Perched on a rocky cliff above the Avon in the town center, **Warwick Castle** ✦✦✦ is a stately late 17th-century–style mansion surrounded by a magnificent 14th-century fortress. The first significant fortifications were built by Ethelfleda, daughter of Alfred the Great, in 914. Two years after the Norman Conquest in 1068, William the Conqueror ordered the construction of a motte and bailey castle. The mound is all that remains today of the Norman castle.

The Beauchamp family, earls of Warwick, are responsible for the appearance of the castle today, and much of the external structure remains unchanged from the mid-14th century. The staterooms and Great Hall house fine collections of paintings, furniture, arms, and armor. The armory, dungeon, torture chamber, ghost tower, clock tower, and Guy's tower create a vivid picture of the castle's turbulent past and its important role in the history of England.

Sir Walter Scott described Warwick Castle in 1828 as "that fairest monument of ancient and chivalrous splendor which yet remains uninjured by time." Visitors can also see the Victorian rose garden, a recreation of an original design from 1868 by Robert Marnock. On Castle Hill, Warwick Castle (✆ **01926/406600**) is open daily 10am to 5pm. Admission is £9.75 ($15) adults, £5.95 ($9) children 4 to 16, £7 ($11) seniors and students, free for children 3 and under, £28 ($42) family of 4.

Trains run frequently between Stratford and Warwick, and a Midland Red Bus leaves every hour (no. 18 or X16) during the day (trip time: 15–20 min.). Motorists should take A-46 north from Stratford.

English pub where you can enjoy a pint. Other attractions include a restaurant, a gift shop, a tearoom, and even wildlife habitats. Throughout the year, a program of special events also takes place in the yard, including traditional crafts exhibitions.

Cox's Yard. ✆ 01789/404600. Admission £3.95 ($6) adults, £3.25 ($5) seniors and students, £2.50 ($3.75) children. Cox's Yard daily 9am–11pm; Stratford Tales daily 10am–5pm.

ORGANIZED TOURS

Guided tours leave daily from the Guide Friday Tourism Center, Civic Hall, Rother Street (✆ **01789/294466**). In summer, open-top double-decker buses depart every 15 minutes 9:30am to 5:30pm. You can take a 1-hour ride without stops, or you can get off at any or all of the town's five Shakespeare's Properties. Anne Hathaway's Cottage and Mary Arden's House are the two likely stops to make outside the town center. Although the bus stops are clearly marked along the historic route, the most logical starting point is on the sidewalk in front of the Pen & Parchment Pub, at Bridgefoot, at the bottom of Bridge Street. Tour tickets are valid all day, so you can hop on and off the buses wherever you want. The tour price is £8.50 ($13) adults, £7 ($11) seniors or students, and £2.50 ($3.75) children under 12.

THE SHOPPING SCENE

At the **National Trust Shop,** 45 Wood St. (✆ **01789/262197**), you'll find textbooks and guidebooks describing esoteric places in the environs of Stratford, descriptions of National Trust properties throughout England, stationery, books, china, pewter, and toiletries, each inscribed, embossed, or painted with logos that evoke some aspect of English tastes and traditions. Set in an antique house that lies across from the Birthplace, the **Shakespeare Bookshop,** 39 Henley St. (℃ **01789/292176**), is the region's premier source for textbooks and academic treatises on the Bard and his works. It specializes in books conceived for every level of expertise, from picture books for junior high school students to weighty tomes geared toward anyone pursuing a Ph.D. in literature.

Arbour Antiques, Ltd., Poet's Arbour, Sheep St. (℃ **01789/293453**), sells antique weapons, used for both warfare and sport, from Britain, Europe, and in some cases, India and Turkey. If you've always hankered after a full suit of English armor, this place will be able to sell you one. Everything at the **Pickwick Gallery,** 32 Henley St. (℃ **01789/294861**), is a well-crafted work of art produced by copper or steel engraving plates, or printed by means of a carved wooden block. Look for the engravings by William Hogarth showing satirical scenes that lampooned Parliamentary corruption during the late 18th century. More than any other pottery studio in Stratford, **Dianthus,** 1 Centre Craft Yard, off Henley St. (℃ **01789/292252**), benefits from an intimate knowledge of Pacific Rim ceramics, with emphasis on unique creative statements in stoneware. In spacious quarters, three potters display their technique on their potter's wheels.

Scattered over three floors of an Elizabethan House said to have been occupied by one of Shakespeare's daughters as an adult, **Trading Post,** 1 High St. (℃ **01789/267228**), offers a jammed and slightly claustrophobic assortment of gift items that might appeal to your taste for the kitschy and nostalgic. Included in the roster of items are dolls' houses and furnishings, a scattering of small, easy-to-transport antiques, and memorabilia of your visit to the Midlands.

3 Stonehenge & Bath

Many visitors with very limited time head for the West Country, where they explore its two major attractions: Stonehenge—the most important prehistoric monument in Britain—and Bath, England's most elegant city, famed for its architecture and its hot springs. If you have the time, you might also visit Salisbury Cathedral and the other prehistoric sites in the area, at Avebury and Old Sarum.

STONEHENGE ☆☆☆

At the junction of A-303 and A-344/A-360, 3km (2 miles) west of Amesbury and about 15km (9 miles) north of Salisbury, stands the renowned monument of Stonehenge, a stone circle believed to be anywhere from 3,500 to 5,000 years old. This circle of lintels and megalithic pillars is the most important prehistoric monument in Britain.

ESSENTIALS
GETTING THERE   By Car   To reach Stonehenge from London, head in the direction of Salisbury, 145km (90 miles) to the southwest. Take the M-3 to the end of the run, continuing the rest of the way on A-30. Once at Salisbury, after stopping to view its cathedral (see below), head north on Castle Road. At the first roundabout (traffic circle), take the exit toward Amesbury (A-345) and Old Sarum. Continue along this route for 13km (8 miles) and then turn left onto A-303 in the direction of Exeter. Stonehenge is signposted, leading you up the A-344 to the right. In all, it's about 19km (12 miles) from Salisbury.

Tips **A Stonehenge Tip**

We like to visit Stonehenge at twilight, when the last of the photo-snapping bus hordes have departed. Amid relative calm, you can ponder the monument's occult origins. The setting rays of sunshine reflect off the ancient stones and seem to heighten their mystery.

By Train or Bus   A Network Express train departs hourly from Waterloo Station bound for Salisbury (trip time: 2 hr.). Buses also depart four or five times per day from Victoria Station heading for Salisbury (2½ hr.). Once at Salisbury, take a Wilts & Dorset bus (© **01722/336855** for schedules), which runs several vehicles daily, depending on demand, from Salisbury to Stonehenge. This company's buses depart from the train station at Salisbury, heading directly to Stonehenge (30 min.). Round-trip fare is £5 ($8) adults, £2.40 ($3.60) children under 14. Use Salisbury (see below) as a refueling stop.

EXPLORING STONEHENGE

Despite its familiarity, visitors cannot help but be impressed when they first see Stonehenge, an astonishing engineering feat. The boulders, the bluestones in particular, were moved many miles, possibly from as far away as southern Wales, to this site.

The widely held view of the 18th- and 19th-century romantics that Stonehenge was the work of the Druids is without foundation. The boulders, many weighing several tons, are believed to have predated the arrival in Britain of the Celtic Druidic cult. Recent excavations continue to bring new evidence to bear on the origin and purpose of the prehistoric circle; controversy has surrounded the site, especially since the publication of *Stonehenge Decoded* by Gerald S. Hawkins and John B. White, which maintains that Stonehenge was an astronomical observatory—that is, a Neolithic calendar capable of predicting eclipses.

The site is now surrounded by a fence to protect it from vandals and souvenir hunters. Your ticket permits you to go inside the fence, all the way up to a short rope barrier about 15m (50 ft.) from the stones. Spring 1996 saw the start of the full circular tour around Stonehenge; a modular walkway has been introduced to cross the archaeologically important area that runs between the Heel Stone and the main circle of stones. This lets you complete a full circuit of the stones, an excellent addition to the well-received audio tour.

Admission to Stonehenge (© **01980/623108**) is £4 ($6) adults, £3 ($4.50) students and seniors, and £2 ($3) children. It's open from March 16 to May and from September to October 15 daily 9:30am to 6pm; from June to August daily 9am to 7pm; and from October 16 to March 15 daily 9:30am to 4pm.

After visiting Stonehenge, you might wish to move on to Bath. But if you have an extra day or so, you shouldn't miss the other attractions nearby, Avebury and Salisbury.

AVEBURY ☆☆

Avebury, one of Europe's largest prehistoric sites, lies 32km (20 miles) north of Stonehenge on the Kennet River, 11km (7 miles) west of Marlborough. The small village actually lies within the vast stone circle. Unlike Stonehenge, you can walk around the 11-hectare (28-acre) site, winding in and out of the circle of more than 100 stones, some of which weigh up to 50 tons. The stones are made of sarsen, a sandstone found in Wiltshire. Inside this large circle are two smaller ones, each with about 30 stones standing upright. Native Neolithic tribes are believed to have built these circles.

GETTING THERE   Avebury is on A-361 between Swindon and Devizes and 1.5km (1 mile) from the A-4 London-Bath road. The closest rail station is at Swindon, some 19km (12 miles) away, which is served by the main rail line from London to Bath. A limited bus service (no. 49) runs from Swindon to Devizes through Avebury.

You can also reach Avebury by bus from Salisbury by taking one of two buses (no. 5 and 6) run by Wilts & Dorset (☎ **01722/336855**). The buses leave three times a day from Monday to Saturday and twice on Sunday (trip time: 1½ hr.).

AN ARCHAEOLOGICAL MUSEUM

Founded by Alexander Keiller, the **Avebury Museum** (☎ **01672/539250**) houses one of Britain's most important archaeological collections. It began with material from excavations at Windmill Hill and Avebury, and now includes artifacts from other prehistoric digs at West Kennet, Long Barrow, Silbury Hill, West Kennet Avenue, and the Sanctuary. Admission is £1.80 ($2.70) adults, 80p ($1.20) children. Open from April to October daily 10am to 6pm; from November to March daily 10am to 4pm.

SALISBURY ⭒⭒

Long before you enter Salisbury, the spire of the cathedral comes into view, just as John Constable painted it many times. Salisbury lies in the Avon River Valley, and is a fine place to stop for lunch and a look at the cathedral on your way to Stonehenge.

GETTING THERE   For driving directions, see "Stonehenge," above. Salisbury can be reached by bus from the Victoria Coach Station in London. There's also direct rail service from London from Waterloo Station. Call ⓒ **0345/ 484950** for schedules and information.

VISITOR INFORMATION   The **Tourist Information Centre** at Fish Row (ⓒ **01722/334956**) is open from October to April, Monday to Saturday 9:30am to 5pm; in May, from Monday to Saturday 9:30am to 5pm and Sunday 10:30am to 4:30pm; in June and September, from Monday to Saturday 9:30am to 6pm and Sunday 10:30am to 4:30pm; and in July and August, from Monday to Saturday 9:30am to 7pm and Sunday 10:30am to 5pm.

WHERE TO STAY

The Kings Arms Hotel   This former coaching inn features an old pub sign out front and a royalty theme throughout. A special attraction is the William-and-Mary four-poster room. Other rooms are cozy and well kept, with traditional styling. Each is individually decorated, and often full of charm and character. Several contain old-fashioned four-poster beds, and some units are large enough for families. Bathrooms are generally small but tidily maintained.

7A–11 St. Johns St., Salisbury, Wiltshire SP1 2SB. ⓒ 01722/327629. Fax 01722/414246. 17 units. £55–£80 ($94–$136) double. Rates include continental breakfast. AE, MC, V. **Amenities:** Restaurant, bar; baby-sitting; laundry, no-smoking rooms. *In room:* TV, hair dryer.

The Rose and Crown ⭒⭒   This half-timbered, 13th-century gem stands with its feet almost in the River Avon, and beyond is the tall spire of the cathedral. You can easily walk over the arched stone bridge to the center of Salisbury in 10 minutes. The lawns and gardens between the inn and the river are shaded by old trees, and chairs are set out so you can enjoy the view and count the swans. The inn has both a modern wing and a more appealing old wing. Rooms in the main house range from small to medium in size, though those in the new wing are more spacious and better designed. Bathrooms, though small, include a shower and tub combination.

Harnham Rd., Salisbury, Wiltshire SP2 8JQ. ⓒ **01722/399955.** Fax 01722/339816. 28 units. £115–£145 ($196–$247) double; £158 ($269) suite. AE, DC, MC, V. Take A3094 1½ miles from the center of town. **Amenities:** Restaurant, bar; room service; baby-sitting laundry/dry cleaning. *In room:* TV, hair dryer, trouser press.

WHERE TO DINE

Harper's Restaurant ENGLISH   The chef-owner of this place prides himself on specializing in homemade and wholesome "real food." The pleasantly decorated restaurant is on the second floor of a redbrick building at the backside of Salisbury's largest parking lot, in the town center. You can order from two different menus, one featuring cost-conscious bistro-style platters, including beefsteak casserole with "herbey dumplings." A longer menu includes all-vegetarian pasta diavolo or spareribs with french fries and rice.

6–7 Ox Row, Market Sq. ⓒ 01722/333118. Reservations recommended. Main courses £6.50–£12.50 ($10– $19); fixed-price 2-course menu £8.50 ($13). AE, DC, MC, V. Mon–Fri 6–9:30pm; Sat 6–10pm.

Salisbury Haunch of Venison ENGLISH   Right in the heart of Salisbury, this creaky-timbered 1320 restaurant serves excellent dishes, especially English roasts and grills. Stick to what it's known for, and you'll rarely go wrong. Begin perhaps with tasty grilled venison sausages in a Dijon mustard sauce, then follow with the time-honored house specialty: roast haunch of venison with gin and juniper berries. Many other classic English dishes are served, such as a medley of fish and shellfish or else grilled Barnsley lamb chops with "bubble and squeak" (cabbage and potatoes).

1 Minster St. ℂ 01722/322024. Main courses £6.95–£14 ($10–$21); bar platters for lunches, light suppers, and snacks £2.95–£8 ($4.45–$12). AE, MC, V. Daily noon–3pm; Mon–Sat 6:30–9:30pm. Pub, Mon–Sat 11am–11pm; Sun noon–3pm and 7–11pm. Closed Christmas.

Silver Plough ENGLISH   Built as a stone-sided farmhouse 150 years ago, the Silver Plough is a charming country pub with an attached restaurant. Tasty snacks available in the bar include ratatouille au gratin and grilled sardines with garlic butter and freshly baked bread. In the somewhat more formal dining room, the chef prepares such tempting dishes as fresh Dorset mussels in a white wine, garlic, and cream sauce; sliced breast of duck in cracked pepper or orange sauce; and roast guinea fowl in a sharp strawberry sauce. The Silver Plough has known many famous visitors, but the management prefers to stick to its quiet, country atmosphere and concentrate on making its guests feel at home.

White Hill, Pitton, near Salisbury. ℂ 01722/712266. Reservations recommended. Main courses £8–£17 ($12–$26); bar platters £4.50–£7.50 ($7–$11). AE, DC, MC, V. Restaurant, daily noon–2:30pm; Mon–Sat 7–10pm Sun 7–9pm. Pub, Mon–Sat 11am–3pm and 6–11pm; Sun noon–3pm and 7–10.30pm. Closed Dec 25–26 and Jan 1. Take A-30 for 8km (5 miles) east of Salisbury; it's at the southern end of the hamlet of Pitton.

IN & AROUND SALISBURY

Salisbury Cathedral 🏛🏛🏛   You can search all of England, but you'll find no better example of early English or pointed style than Salisbury Cathedral. Construction began as early as 1220 and took 38 years to complete; this was rather fast since it was customary in those days for a cathedral building to require at least 3 centuries. The soaring spire was completed at the end of the 13th century. Despite an ill-conceived attempt at renovation in the 18th century, the architectural integrity of the cathedral has been retained.

The 13th-century octagonal chapter house (note the fine sculpture), which is especially attractive, possesses one of the four surviving original texts of the Magna Carta, along with treasures from the diocese of Salisbury and manuscripts and artifacts belonging to the cathedral. The cloisters enhance the beauty of the cathedral, and the exceptionally large close, with at least 75 buildings in its compound (some from the early 18th century, others earlier), sets off the cathedral most effectively.

The Close. ℂ 01722/555120. Admission £3 ($4.50) adults, £2 ($3) students and seniors, £1 ($1.50) children, or £6 ($9) family of 4. Sept–May daily 7am–6:15pm; June–Aug daily 7am–8:15pm.

Old Sarum   This relic from antiquity is believed to have been an Iron Age fortification. The earthworks were known to the Romans as *Sorbiodunum*. Much later, Saxons also used the fortification. The Normans built a cathedral and a castle here in what was then a Middle Ages walled town. Parts of the old cathedral were taken down to build the city of New Sarum (Salisbury).

Castle Rd. ℂ 01722/335398. Admission £2 ($3) adults, £1.50 ($2.25) senior citizens, £1 ($1.50) children. Apr–Sept daily 10am–6pm; off-season daily 10am–4pm. 3km (2 miles) north of Salisbury off A-345. Bus: 3, 5, 6, 7, 8, and 9 from Salisbury run every 20 minutes.

Wilton House 🏛   One of England's great country estates, Wilton is the home of the earls of Pembroke. The house dates from the 16th century, but has

---

Fun Fact **D-Day at Wilton House**

During World War II, Wilton House was headquarters for the British Army's Southern Command. The Double Cube Room served as the operations room. Preparations for the D-day landings at Normandy were laid out here by General Eisenhower and his advisors, with the silent Van Dyck paintings as witnesses.

---

undergone numerous alterations. Shakespeare's troupe may have entertained here. Celebrated 17th-century architect Inigo Jones designed the staterooms. The house displays paintings by Van Dyck, Rubens, Brueghel, and Reynolds. A dynamic film introduced and narrated by Anna Massey brings to life the history of the family since 1544, the year it was granted the land by Henry VIII. You then visit a reconstructed Tudor kitchen and Victorian laundry plus "The Wareham Bears," a unique collection of some 200 miniature dressed teddy bears.

Giant Cedars of Lebanon grow on the 8.5-hectare (21-acre) estate, the oldest of which were planted in 1630. The Palladian Bridge was built in 1737 by the ninth earl of Pembroke and Roger Morris. There are rose and water gardens, riverside and woodland walks, and a huge adventure playground for children.

Wilton. © **01722/746729.** www.wiltonhouse.com. Admission £6.75 ($10) adults, £4 ($6) children 5–15, free for under 5; grounds only £4.75 ($7) adults, £2.50 ($3.75) children. Daily Apr–Oct 10:30am–5:30pm (last admission at 4:30pm). About 4km (2½ miles) west of Salisbury on A-30. Bus: 60 and 61 from Salisbury run every 10 minutes.

BATH 🐟🐟🐟

The city of Bath has had two lives. Originally, it was a Roman spa known as Aquae Sulis. The foreign legions founded their baths here (which may be visited today) to ease their rheumatism in the curative mineral springs. In 1702 Queen Anne made the trek from London, 185km (115 miles) west to the mineral springs of Bath, thereby launching a fad that was to make the city England's most celebrated spa.

The most famous personage connected with Bath's growing popularity was the 18th-century dandy Beau Nash. The master of ceremonies of Bath, Nash cut a striking figure. In all the plumage of a bird of paradise, he was carted around in a sedan chair, dispensing (at a price) trinkets to courtiers and aspirant gentlemen. This polished arbiter of taste and manners succeeded in making dueling déclassé.

The 18th-century architects John Wood the Elder and his son envisioned a proper backdrop for Nash's activities. They designed a city of honey-colored stone from the nearby hills, a feat so substantial and lasting that Bath today is the most harmoniously laid-out city in England. The city attracted leading political and literary figures, such as Dickens, Thackeray, Nelson, and Pitt, and most important, of course, Jane Austen. Canadians may already know that General Wolfe lived on Trim Street, and Australians may want to visit the house at 19 Bennett St. where their founding father, Admiral Phillip, lived.

Remarkable restoration and careful planning have ensured that Bath retains its handsome look today. It has somewhat of a museum appearance, with the attendant gift shops. Prices, stimulated by massive tourist invasion, tend to be high. But Bath remains one of the high points of the West Country.

Bath

Bath Abbey 7
The Circus 2
Jane Austen Centre 3
North Parade 8
Pulteney Bridge 5
**Pump Room
  & Roman Baths 6**
Queen Square 4
Royal Crescent 1

ESSENTIALS

GETTING THERE   By Train   At least one train an hour leaves London's Paddington Station bound for Bath during the day (trip time: 70–90 min.). For rail schedules and information, call ✆ **0345/484950.**

By Bus   One National Express coach leaves London's Victoria Coach Station every 2 hours during the day (trip time: 2½ hr.). For schedules and information, call ✆ **08705/808080.**

By Car   From London, drive west on M-4 to the junction with A-4, on which you continue west to Bath. From Salisbury take A-36 west to Bath. You'll enter at the southern tier of the city.

VISITOR INFORMATION   The **Bath Tourist Information Centre,** at Abbey Chambers, Abbey Church Yard (✆ **01225/477101;** www.bath.co.uk), opposite the Roman Baths, is open Monday, Tuesday, Friday, and Saturday 9am to 5:30pm, Wednesday and Thursday 9:45am to 5:30pm, and Sunday 10am to 4pm.

SPECIAL EVENTS   For 17 days in late May and early June the city is filled with more than 1,000 performers—orchestras, soloists, and artists from all over the world. The **Bath International Music Festival** focuses on classical music, jazz, new music, and opening night celebrations with fireworks. There's also all the best in walks, tours, and talks, plus free street entertainment. For more information, contact the **Bath Festivals Box Office,** 2 Church St., Abbey Green, Bath BA1 1NL (✆ **01225/463362**).

GETTING AROUND   One of the best ways to explore Bath is by bike. You can rent one from **Somerset Valley Bike Hire** (✆ **01225/442442**), behind the train station. It's open daily from 9am to 5:30pm, charging £14 to £25 ($21 to $38) per day, £9 ($14) per half day, £50 ($75) per week, depending on the type of bike. Deposits range from £20 to £75 ($30 to $113).

WHERE TO STAY
Very Expensive
Bath Priory 🏵🏵   Converted from one of Bath's Georgian houses in 1969, the Priory is set amidst formal and award-winning gardens with manicured lawns and flowerbeds, a swimming pool, and a croquet lawn. The hotel was recently refurbished and improved; if anything, it is more inviting than ever. It's not as overly commercial as the Francis, but is less expensive than the Bath Spa or Royal Crescent, while offering somewhat the same town house aura. Rooms are individually decorated; our personal favorite is Clivia (all rooms are named after flowers or shrubs), a nicely appointed duplex in a circular turret. The 10 rooms in the annex are similar to the main building but are fresher in appearance. Rooms have immaculately kept tub and shower combinations.

Weston Rd., Bath, Somerset BA1 2XT. ✆ **01225/331922.** Fax 01225/448276. www.slh.com/The Priory. 28 units. £230 ($345) standard double; £290 ($435) deluxe room for 2. Rates include English breakfast. AE, DC, MC, V. Free parking. Amenities: Restaurant, bar; indoor and outdoor pools; health club; Jacuzzi; sauna; 24-hour room service; baby-sitting; laundry/dry cleaning. *In room:* TV, hair dryer.

Bath Spa Hotel 🏵🏵🏵   This restored 19th-century mansion, at the end of a tree-lined drive on landscaped grounds, is a 10-minute walk from the center of Bath. It is an even more stunning addition to the Bath hotel scene than the Royal Crescent. The drawing room of what was once an English general's house has been restored, and fireplaces, elaborate moldings, oak paneling, and staircases create a warm country-house charm. Rooms, most quite spacious, are handsomely furnished with the best English furniture. Each comes with a large bathroom with a long tub and a hand-held showerhead.

Sydney Rd., Bath, Somerset BA2 6JF. ✆ **01225/444424.** Fax 01225/444006. www.bathspahotel.com. 98 units. Sun–Thurs £179 ($268.50) double; Fri–Sat £224 ($336) double. Weeklong £254–£354 ($381–$531) suite for 2. AE, DC, MC, V. Free parking. East of the city off A-36. **Amenities:** 2 restaurants; bar; indoor pool; gym; tennis court; health and leisure spa with beauty treatment room. *In room:* TV, minibar, hair dryer, trouser press.

Queensberry Hotel 🏵   Although hardly as grand as the addresses previously considered, this place derives much of its beauty from the many original fireplaces, ornate ceilings, and antiques. The Marquis of Queensberry commissioned John Wood to build this house in 1772. Each room has antique furniture, in keeping with the character of the house. Open since 1988, the Queensberry has become one of Bath's most important hotels. The well-kept bathrooms contain shower units.

Russel St., Bath, Somerset BA1 2QF. ✆ **800/323-5463** in the U.S., or 01225/447928. Fax 01225/446065. 29 units. £120–£210 ($180–$315) double. Rates include continental breakfast. MC, V. Parking £1 ($1.50) per hour. **Amenities:** Olive Tree restaurant (English/Mediterranean; see "Where to Dine," below), bar. *In room:* TV, hair dryer.

Royal Crescent Hotel ✿✿✿ This is both a hotel and a national monument. Standing proudly in the center of the famed Royal Crescent, this Georgian colonnade of town houses was designed by John Wood the Younger in 1767. Before the arrival of the Bath Spa, it was long regarded as Bath's premier hotel. Crystal chandeliers, period furniture, and paintings add to the rich adornment. Rooms, including the Jane Austen Suite, are often lavishly furnished with four-poster beds and Jacuzzis. Bathrooms are also luxurious with tub and shower combos.

16 Royal Crescent, Bath, Somerset BA1 2LS. ✆ **800/457-6000** in the U.S., or 01225/823333. Fax 01225/339401. www.royalcrescent.co.uk. 45 units. £190–£290 ($285–$435) double; from £395 ($592.50) suite. AE, DC, MC, V. Free parking. **Amenities:** 2 restaurants; bar; health club; steam room; Jacuzzi; salon; room service; baby-sitting; laundry/dry cleaning. *In room:* A/C, TV, hair dryer, robes.

Expensive

Francis Hotel ✿ A landmark since 1729, this is no longer the premier address of Bath but it's still going strong in the first of massive competition from such stellar properties as the more regal Royal Crescent. The Francis was opened as a private hotel in 1884 and has offered guests first-class service for more than 100 years, though it seems a bit touristy today. Many of the well-furnished and traditionally styled rooms overlook Queen Square—named in honor of George II's consort, Caroline. Rooms range in size from rather small to medium, with either twin or double beds. Accommodations in the older building have more charm, especially those on the upper floor, than those in the newer section. Bathrooms are small but well equipped, each with a shower unit.

Queen Sq., Bath, Somerset BA1 2HH. ✆ **800/225-5843** in the U.S. and Canada, or 01225/424257. Fax 01225/319715. 94 units. £134–£154 ($201–$231) double; £184–£200 ($276–$300) suite. AE, DC, MC, V. Free parking. **Amenities:** Restaurant, cocktail bar. *In room:* TV, hair dryer.

Moderate

Pratt's Hotel Once the home of Sir Walter Scott, Pratt's, a hotel since 1791, is convenient for sightseeing. Several elegant terraced Georgian town houses were joined together to make a comfortable hotel with individually designed rooms (from small to spacious) containing shower-only bathrooms. Rooms are furnished in a comfortable though utilitarian style.

South Parade, Bath, Somerset BA2 4AB. ✆ **01225/460441.** Fax 01225/448807. 46 units. £100 ($150) double. Rates include English breakfast. Children under 15 stay free in a room shared with 2 adults. AE, DC, MC, V. Parking £8.50 ($13). **Amenities:** Restaurant, bar. *In room:* TV.

Inexpensive

Apsley House Hotel ✿ This charming and stately building, just west of the center of Bath, dates back to 1830 and the reign of William IV. It's set in its own gardens, with a square tower, arched windows, and a walled garden with south views. In 1994, new owners refurbished the hotel, filling it with country-house chintzes and antiques. The rooms are comfortably furnished and filled with attractive accessories, including tidily kept, shower-only private bathrooms.

141 Newbridge Hill, Bath, Somerset BA1 3PT. ✆ **01225/336966.** Fax 01225/425462. www.apsley-house. co.uk. 9 units. £85 ($128) double; £95–£115 ($143–$173) suite. Rates include English breakfast. AE, MC, V. Free parking. Take A-4 to Upper Bristol Rd. and fork right at the traffic signals into Newbridge Hill. *In room:* TV.

Dukes' Hotel A short walk from the heart of Bath, this building dates from 1780. It has been completely restored and rather elegantly furnished and modernized. Many of the original Georgian features have been retained. Rooms, ranging from small to medium, are exceedingly comfortable, and the bath-rooms, a bit tiny, are nonetheless efficiently arranged and contain shower units.

53–54 Great Pulteney St., Bath, Somerset BA2 4DN. ℂ 01225/463512. Fax 01225/483733. 23 units. £72–£103 ($108–$155) double; £125 ($188) family room. Rates include English breakfast. AE, MC, V. Bus: 18. **Amenities:** Cozy bar. *In room:* TV, hair dryer, trouser press.

Laura Place Hotel ⭐   Built in 1789, this hotel won a civic award for the restoration of its stone facade. On the corner of a residential street overlooking a public fountain, it's a 2-minute walk from the Roman Baths and Bath Abbey. The hotel has been skillfully decorated with antique furniture and fabrics evoca-tive of the 18th century, and its medium-size rooms are very cozy in the best tra-dition of an English B&B, each with an immaculately kept, shower-only bathroom.

3 Laura Place, Great Pulteney St., Bath, Somerset BA2 4BH. ℂ 01225/463815. Fax 01225/310222. 8 units. £70–£90 ($105–$135) double; £115 ($173) family suite. Rates include English breakfast. AE, MC, V. Free park-ing. Bus: 18 or 19. *In room:* TV.

Number Ninety Three   This elegant Victorian guesthouse is a traditional British B&B: small but immaculate and well maintained, within easy walking distance from the center and rail and bus stations. Its owner is a mine of local information, who serves a traditional English breakfast. The rooms, small to medium, are very nice, with cozy beds, plus a neat, shower-only bathroom. Parking can be difficult in Bath, but the hotel will advise.

93 Wells Rd., Bath, Somerset BA2 3AN. ℂ 01225/317977. 4 units. £40–£65 ($60–$98) double; £54–£85 ($81–$128) triple. Rates include English breakfast. Bus: 3, 13, 14, 17, 23, or 33. *In room:* TV, no phone.

Paradise House Hotel ⭐ *Finds*   Dating from 1735, this Georgian house—a real find—is set among manicured gardens on the southern slopes of the city, about a 7-minute walk from the center. Join in a game of croquet on the lawns and step back in time. David and Annie Lanz have restored the house to its orig-inal charm, and they offer individually decorated rooms, most often with a romantic decor, as evoked by a garden room with a four-poster. Bedrooms are sumptuous, with neatly tiled bathrooms with shower units. Guests relax and meet each other in the drawing room with its arched windows plus an open fire in winter.

86–88 Holloway, Bath, Somerset BA2 4PX. ℂ 0122/5317723. Fax 01225/482005. www.paradisehouse.co.uk. 10 units. £89 ($133.50) standard double, £89.95 ($134.95) deluxe double. Rates include breakfast. AE, MC, V. **Amenities:** Small bar. *In room:* TV, coffeemaker, hair dryer.

Sydney Gardens Hotel   This spot recalls the letters of Jane Austen, who wrote to friends about the long walks she enjoyed in Sydney Gardens, a public park just outside the city center. In 1852, an Italianate Victorian villa was con-structed here on a lot immediately adjacent to the gardens. Three rooms have twin beds and the other three have 5-foot-wide double beds. Each room is dec-orated with an English country–house charm. Each room comes with a small, shower-only bathroom. There's also a footpath running beside a canal. No smoking.

Sydney Rd., Bath, Somerset BA2 6NT. ℂ 01225/464818. Fax 01225/484347. www.paradisehouse.co.uk. 6 units. Sun–Thurs £69 ($104) double; Fri–Sat £75 ($113) double. Rates include English breakfast. AE, MC, V. Free parking. *In-room:* TV, coffeemaker, hair dryer.

Nearby Places to Stay

Homewood Park ⭐   Overlooking Limpley Stoke Valley, this small, family-run hotel is a large Victorian house with grounds adjoining the 13th-century ruin of Hinton Priory. You can play tennis and croquet in the garden. Riding and golf are available nearby, and beautiful walks in the Limpley Stoke Valley lure guests. Each room is luxuriously decorated and furnished with taste and charm, and adjoins a private bathroom in tile with shower units. Most overlook the gardens and grounds or offer views of the valley.

Hinton Charterhouse, Bath, Somerset BA3 6BB. © **01225/723731.** Fax 01225/723820. 19 units. www.homewoodpark.com. £139–£249 ($209–$374) double; £249 ($374) suite. Rates include English breakfast. AE, DC, MC, V. Free parking. Take A-36 (Bath-Warminster Rd.) 10km (6 miles) south of Bath. **Amenities:** Restaurant. *In room:* TV.

Hunstrete House ★★★
This fine Georgian house, which has earned Relais & Châteaux distinction, is situated on 37 hectares (92 acres) of private parkland. Six units are in the Courtyard House, attached to the main structure and overlooking a paved courtyard with its Italian fountain and flower-filled tubs. Swallow Cottage, which adjoins the main house, has its own private sitting room, double bedroom, and bathroom. Units in the main house are individually decorated, each with a modern bathroom with a tub and shower combo.

Hunstrete, Pensford, near Bristol, Somerset BS39 4NS. © **01761/490490.** Fax 01761/490732. 23 units. £130–£180 ($195–$270) double; £250–£320 ($375–$480) suite. Half board £200–£250 ($300–$375) double; £250 ($375) suite for 2. Rates include English breakfast. AE, DC, MC, V. Free parking. Take A-4 about 6.5km (4 miles) west of Bath, then A-368 another 7km (4½ miles) toward Weston-super-Mare. **Amenities:** Restaurant, swimming pool. *In room:* TV, hair dryer.

Ston Easton Park ★★★
From the moment you pass a group of stone outbuildings and the century-old beeches of the 12-hectare (30-acre) park, you know you've come to a very special place. The mansion was created in the mid-1700s from the shell of an Elizabethan house. In 1977, Peter and Christine Smedley acquired the property and poured money, love, and labor into its restoration. Now it's one of the great country hotels of England. A pair of carved mahogany staircases is ringed with ornate plaster detailing, and the place is replete with antiques. Tasteful, spacious rooms are filled with flowers, and each comes with a luxurious private bathroom with a tub and shower combo. A gardener's cottage comprises two separate suites, and the stateroom is regal with a four-poster bed and a private seating area.

Ston Easton, Somerset BA3 4DF. © **01761/241631.** Fax 01761/241377. 21 units. £190–£395 ($285–$593) double; £225–£470 ($338–$705) suite. AE, DC, MC, V. Free parking. Children under 7 not accepted. Follow A39 south from Bath until you see the signposted turnoff to Ston Easton. **Amenities:** Grand formal dining room, bar. *In room:* TV, hair dryer.

WHERE TO DINE
Expensive
Lettonie Restaurant ★★ FRENCH Moving here from Bristol, this restaurant quickly became the talk of Bath and is the city's best dining choice. In a Georgian house with a lounge bar, it has a terraced garden sloping toward the Avon Valley. Sian and Martin Blunos have won an entire coterie of admirers with their French-inspired cuisine. Main dishes are represented by a delectable medley of deep-fried frogs' legs with a lemon and crumb crust, served with a nettle risotto. If not that, then try the beetroot mousse with seared chicken livers and oak-smoked bacon. Desserts are worth the calories, especially the hot gingerbread tart with poached glazed pear and the to-die-for banana and caramel soufflé with banana ice cream and caramel sauce.

35 Kelston Rd. © **0122/5446676.** Reservations required. Fixed-price dinner £47.50 ($71); fixed-price lunch £15–£25 ($23–$38). AE, DC, MC, V. Tues–Sat noon–2pm and 7–9:30pm.

Moderate
Moon & Sixpence ⊕ *Value* INTERNATIONAL   One of Bath's leading
restaurants and wine bars, the Moon & Sixpence occupies a stone structure just
off Broad Street east of Queen Square, with an extended conservatory and sheltered patio. The food may not be outstanding, but the value is unbeatable. At
lunch, a large cold buffet with a selection of hot dishes is featured in the wine
bar section. In the upstairs restaurant overlooking the bar, full service is offered.
Main courses might include such dishes as filet of lamb with caramelized garlic
or medallions of beef filet with a bacon, red wine, and shallot sauce. Look for
the daily specials.

6A Broad St. ☏ 01225/460962. Reservations recommended. Main courses £11.50–£16 ($17–$24); fixed-
price lunch £9.50–£13.95 ($14–$21); 2-course lunch buffet in the wine bar £8.50 ($13); fixed-price dinner
£26 ($39). AE, MC, V. Daily noon–2:30pm and 5:30–10:30pm (until 11pm Fri–Sat).

Olive Tree MODERN ENGLISH/MEDITERRANEAN   Stephen and
Penny Ross operate one of the most sophisticated little restaurants in Bath.
Game and fish are the specialties. You might begin with a Provençal fish soup
with *rouille* and croutons, or eggplant and mozzarella fritters with a sweet red
pepper sauce—unless the grilled scallops with noodles and pine nuts tempt you
instead. Then you could move on to Gressingham duck breast lightly grilled
with shallots and kumquats, or loin of venison with wild rice and morels delicately flavored with a tarragon sauce. Stephen is also known for his desserts; they
might include a hot chocolate soufflé or an apricot and almond tart.

In the Queensberry Hotel, Russel St. ☏ 01225/447928. Reservations recommended. Main courses
£12.50–£19 ($19–$29); fixed-price 3-course lunch £15.50 ($23); fixed-price 3-course dinner £24 ($36). MC, V.
Mon–Sat noon–2pm and 7–10pm; Sun 7–9:30pm.

Popjoy's Restaurant ⊕ BRITISH/INTERNATIONAL   In this Georgian
home, where Beau Nash and his mistress, Julianna Popjoy, entertained their
friends, two dining rooms are on separate floors. Dishes display inventiveness
and solid technique. The best dishes on the menu are terrine of duck and
chicken liver wrapped in bacon with a tomato coulis; watercress and potato
soup; sautéed lamb kidneys with crispy smoked bacon; braised lamb shoulder
with a sage and garlic stuffing; and a savory tagliatelle with leeks.

Sawclose. ☏ 01225/460494. Reservations recommended. Main courses £14–£20 ($21–$30); fixed-price
3-course lunch £12 ($18). AE, DC, MC, V. Mon–Sat noon–2pm and 6–11pm.

Inexpensive
Beaujolais FRENCH   This is the best-known bistro in Bath, attracting new
admirers every year. Diners are drawn to the good, honest cooking and good
value. Begin perhaps with a salad of warm scallops, or rabbit terrine served with
chutney. You might follow that with an excellent grilled loin of lamb topped
with a crispy julienne of ginger and leeks. House wines are modestly priced. One
area of the restaurant is reserved for nonsmokers; and people with disabilities
(wheelchair access), children (special helpings), and vegetarians will all find
comfort here.

5 Chapel Row, Queen Sq. ☏ 01225/423417. Reservations recommended. Fixed-price 2-course lunch £8.50
($13); fixed-price, 2-course dinner £13.50 ($20); dinner main courses £11–£14.50 ($17–$22). AE, MC, V. Daily
noon–2:30pm and 7–11pm.

Woods ENGLISH/FRENCH/ASIAN   Named after John Wood the Younger,
this restaurant in a Georgian building is run by horse-racing enthusiast David
Price and his French-born wife, Claude. A printed fixed-price menu and a

seasonally changing array of a la carte items noted on a chalkboard detail the choices. Good bets include pear and parsnip soup; smoked chicken salad with Stilton and avocado; pan-fried cod roe; and a perfectly prepared breast of chicken with tomatoes, mushrooms, red wine, and tarragon.

9–13 Alfred St. ℰ 01225/314812. Reservations recommended. Main courses £12–£17 ($18–$26); fixed-price lunches £7 ($11); fixed-price dinners £13.50 ($20). AE, MC, V. Mon–Sat noon–2:30pm and 6–10:30pm; Sun noon–4pm. Closed Dec 25–26.

EXPLORING BATH

In addition to the attractions listed below, you'll want to visit some of the buildings, crescents, and squares in town. John Wood the Elder's **North Parade** (where Oliver Goldsmith lived) and **South Parade** (where English novelist and diarist Frances Burney once resided) are the architectural idealization of harmony. The younger Wood designed the **Royal Crescent,** an elegant half-moon row of town houses. One of the most beautiful squares is **Queen Square,** which displays the work of Wood the Elder. Both Jane Austen and Wordsworth once lived here. Also of interest is **The Circus,** built in 1754, as well as the shop-lined **Pulteney Bridge,** designed by Robert Adam and often compared to the Ponte Vecchio of Florence.

The **Jane Austen Centre,** 40 Gay St. (ℰ **01225/443-000**), is located in a Georgian town house on an elegant street where Miss Austen once lived. Exhibits and a video convey a sense of what life was like in Bath during the Regency period. The center is open Monday to Saturday 10am to 5pm and Sunday 10:30am to 5:30pm. Admission is £7 ($11).

Bath Abbey ⓖ   Built on the site of a much larger Norman cathedral, the present-day abbey is a fine example of the late perpendicular style. When Queen Elizabeth I came to Bath in 1574, she ordered a national fund set up to restore the abbey. The interior and its many windows plainly illustrate why the abbey is called the "Lantern of the West." Note the superb fan vaulting, with its scalloped effect. Beau Nash was buried in the nave and is honored by a simple monument totally out of keeping with his flamboyant character. In 1994 the Bath Abbey Heritage Vaults opened on the south side of the abbey. This subterranean exhibition traces the history of Christianity at the abbey site since Saxon times.

Orange Grove. ℰ 01225/422462. Free admission; donation requested £2 ($3). Heritage Vaults £2 ($3) adults; £1 ($1.50) students, children, and seniors. Abbey, Apr–Oct Mon–Sat 9am–6pm; Nov–Mar Mon–Sat 9am–4:30pm; year-round, Sun 1–2:30pm and 4:30–5:30pm. Heritage Vaults, Mon–Sat 10am–4pm.

Pump Room ⓖ **and Roman Baths** ⓖⓖ   Founded in A.D. 75 by the Romans, the baths were dedicated to the goddess Sulis Minerva; in their day they were an engineering feat. Today, still fed by Britain's most famous hot-spring water, they're among the finest Roman remains in the country. After centuries of decay, the original baths were rediscovered during Queen Victoria's reign. The site of the Temple of Sulis Minerva has been excavated and is now open to view. The museum displays many interesting objects from Victorian and recent digs (look for the head of Minerva). Coffee, lunch, and tea, usually with music from the Pump Room Trio, can be enjoyed in the 18th-century pump room, overlooking the hot springs. There's also a drinking fountain with hot mineral water that tastes horrible, but is supposedly beneficial.

Abbey Church Yard. ℰ 01225/477785. www.romanbaths.co.uk. Admission £6.90 ($10) adults, £4 ($6) children. Oct–Mar Mon–Sat 9:30am–5pm, Sun 10:30am–5pm; Apr–June and Sept daily 9am–6pm; Aug daily 9am–10pm. Last admission 1 hr. before closing.

Two More Magnificent Houses: Longleat House & Stourhead

Between Bath and Salisbury, 6.5km (4 miles) southwest of Warminster and 7km (4½ miles) southeast of Frome on A-362, is **Longleat House** 🏰🏰🏰, Warminster, Wiltshire (℡ **01985/844400**; www.longleat.co.uk), owned by the seventh marquess of Bath. The first view of this Elizabethan house, built in the early Renaissance style, is romantic enough, but the wealth of paintings and furnishings in its lofty rooms is dazzling. From the Elizabethan Great Hall to the library, staterooms and grand staircase, the house is filled with fine tapestries and paintings. The library contains the finest private collection in the country. The Victorian kitchens are open, and various exhibitions are mounted in the stable yard.

Events are staged frequently on the grounds. The Safari Park has a vast array of animals in open parklands, including Britain's only white tiger. The Maze, the longest in the world, was added to the attractions by the current marquess. It has more than 2.5km (1½ miles) of paths; the first part is comparatively easy, but the second is rather more complicated.

Admission is £5 ($) adults, £4 ($6) children; admission to Safari Park is £6 ($9) adults, £4.50 ($7) children. Special exhibitions and rides require separate admission. Passport tickets for all Longleat's attractions cost £13 ($20) adults and £10 ($15) children, including admission to the Butterfly Garden, Simulator Dr. Who Exhibition, Postman Pat's Village, Adventure Castle, and more. It's open daily from mid-March to September 10am to 5pm, from October to Easter 10am to 4pm. The park itself is open daily from mid-March to October 31, 10am to 6pm (last cars are admitted at 5:30pm or sunset).

After a visit to Longleat, you can drive 10km (6 miles) down B-3092 to Stourton, a village just off the highway 5km (3 miles) northwest of Mere (A-303). A Palladian house, **Stourhead** 🏰🏰🏰 (℡ **01747/841152**) was built in the 18th century by the banking family of Hoare. The fabulous gardens, blending art and nature, became known as *le jardin anglais*. Set around an artificial lake, the grounds are decorated with temples, bridges, islands, and grottoes, as well as statuary. The gardens are open daily from 9am to 7pm (or until dusk), and cost £4.60 ($7) adults and £2.60 ($3.90) children from March to October. Off-season tickets cost £3.50 ($5) adults and £1.50 ($2.25) children. The house is open from April 30 to October 30 Saturday to Wednesday noon to 5:30pm. Admission is £4.60 ($7) adults and £2.60 ($3.90) children. A combination ticket to both attractions goes for £8 ($12) adults or £3.80 ($6) children.

No. 1 Royal Crescent 🏰🏰🏰   The interior of this Bath town house has been redecorated and furnished by the Bath Preservation Trust to look as it might have toward the end of the 18th century. The house is at one end of Bath's most magnificent crescent, west of the Circus. Nothing suggests the elegance of 18th-century Bath more than this house at no. 1. The great arc of 30 terrace houses are counterbalanced by 14 gigantic Ionic columns. This was the crowning architectural glory of John Wood in 1767 and to 1774.

1 Royal Crescent. (© 01225/428126. Admission £4 ($6) adults, £3.50 ($5) children; £10 ($15) family ticket. Mar–Oct Tues–Sun 10:30am–5pm; Nov–Dec 1 Tues–Sun 10:30am–4pm (last admission 30 min. before closing). Closed Good Friday.

American Museum   Some 4km (2½ miles) from Bath is the first American museum established outside the United States. In a Greek Revival house (Claverton Manor), the museum sits on extensive grounds high above the Avon valley. Authentic exhibits of pioneer days have been shipped over from the States. On the grounds is a copy of Washington's flower garden at Mount Vernon and an American arboretum. A permanent exhibition in the New Gallery displays the Dallas Pratt Collection of Historical Maps.

Claverton Manor, Bathwick Hill. (© 01225/460503. Admission £5.50 ($8) adults, £5 ($8) students and seniors, £2.50 ($3.75) children. Late Mar to late Oct daily 2–5pm. Bus: 18.

ORGANIZED TOURS

The **Heart of England Tourist Board** (© **01905/360050**) and the **West Country Tourist Board** (© **01392/360050**) have details of numerous guided tours within their regions, and the staff can book you with registered guides for outings ranging from short walks to luxury tours that include accommodations in stately homes.

Free, 1¾-hour walking tours are conducted throughout the year by the Mayor's Honorary Society (© **01225/477786**). Tours depart from outside the Roman Baths from Monday to Friday 10:30am and 2pm; Sunday 2:30pm; and Tuesday, Friday, and Saturday 7pm. A slightly different tour by Bath Parade Tours (© **01225/337111**), costing £4 ($7) per person, leaves Saturday 2:30pm from outside the Roman Baths. Reservations aren't needed for either tour.

Jane Austen Tours take you in the footsteps of the author and her characters. These tours leave Saturday from the Abbey Lace Shop, York Street (© **01225/463030**), and cost £3.50 ($6) per person. You'll be told the time to meet when you make a reservation.

To tour Bath by bus, you can choose among several tour companies; some have open-top buses leaving from the Tourist Information Centre, which supplies details of changing schedules and prices. Among the best bus tours is **Patrick Driscoll/Beau Nash Guides,** Elmsleigh, Bathampton, BA2 6SW (© **01225/462010**); these tours are more personalized than most. Another good outfitter is **Sulis Guides,** 2 Lansdown Terrace, Weston, Bath BA1 4BR (© **01225/429681**).

THE SHOPPING SCENE

Bath has the finest shopping possibilities outside of London. We'll give you a sampling to get you started. The four floors of merchandise at **Rossiter's,** 38–41 Broad St. (© **01225/462227**), might remind you of a very English version of a department store. They'll ship any of the Royal Doulton, Wedgwood, or Spode to anywhere in the world. Look especially for the displays of ginger jars, vases, and clocks manufactured by Moorcroft, and perfumes by London-based Floris.

The most charming and unusual emporium in Bath, **Whittard of Chelsea,** 14 Union Passage (© **01225/483529**), supplies everything you'll need to duplicate the dearly held tea-drinking ritual. If you want a quite exotic tea to wow your friends back home, ask for Monkey-Picked Oolong, a Chinese tea from plants so difficult to reach that leaves can be gathered only by trained monkeys.

Walcot Reclamation, 108 Walcot St. (© **01225/444404**), is a sprawling and dusty storeroom selling 19th-century architectural remnants. The 20,000-square-foot warehouse is just northeast of Bath. Anything can be shipped or altered on-site.

The most important gallery of contemporary art in Bath, **Beaux Arts Gallery,** 13 York St. (© **01225/464850**), specializes in well-known British artists. The gallery occupies a pair of interconnected, stone-fronted Georgian houses, set close to Bath Abbey. The **Bath Stamp & Coin Shop,** 12–13 Pulteney Bridge (© **01225/463073**), is the largest purveyor of antique coins and stamps in Bath, with hundreds of odd or unusual numismatics from throughout England and its former empire. Look also for antique Venetian glass and a scattering of English antiques.

BATH AFTER DARK

Theatre Royal, next to the new Seven Dials development at Sawclose (© **01225/448844;** for credit-card bookings, call 01225/448861), was restored in 1982 and refurbished with plush seats, red carpets, and a painted proscenium and ceiling. Now the most beautiful theater in Britain, it has 940 seats, a small pit, and grand tiers rising to the upper circle. A **studio theater** at the rear of the main building opened in 1996. The theater publishes a list of forthcoming events; its repertoire includes, among other offerings, West End shows. It operates only 6 to 8 weeks a year. Prices vary, but tickets generally begin at £9 ($14).

Beneath the theater, reached from the back of the stalls or by a side door, are the theater vaults, where you will find a bar and a restaurant, serving an array of dishes from soup to light a la carte meals.

France

by Darwin Porter & Danforth Prince

France presents visitors with an embarrassment of riches—no other country concentrates such a diversity of sights and scenery into so compact an area. This chapter explores that diversity: Paris and the Île de France; the Loire Valley in the northwest with its châteaux and vineyards; Provence, in the southwest, with its ancient culture; and the lush semitropical coast of the Mediterranean, the French Riviera, and the Côte d'Azur.

1 Paris

Today, Paris is in many ways less French and more international. Those Parisians who were born and bred in the city and who have French ancestry have accepted the fact that they may one day become a minority in their own hometown, as waves of immigrants from the far stretches of the former empire, including Vietnam and North Africa, flood their gates. And with the millions of visitors pouring in annually from all over the world, you can no longer separate Paris from its visitors—they have virtually become one and the same.

Legendary Paris style and chic are changing, too. Unless you frequent upscale watering holes, you'll see very few Parisians dressed quite as alluringly and formally as they did a few years ago. Many young Parisians have adopted the casual attire of their American counterparts. And while the old haute couture houses have experienced rough times, prêt-a-porter designers are flourishing.

The late president François Mitterrand wanted to leave an architectural legacy to rival or surpass that of the autocratic "Sun King," Louis XIV. Mitterrand's dream was to make Paris the undisputed capital of the European Union. To do that, he virtually painted Paris in gold (well, gilt at least), cleaned the Louvre's facade, spruced up the Champs-Elysées, and ran up a $6 billion tab as he built, restored, and recast. The most famous and controversial of these projects was I. M. Pei's metal-and-glass pyramid entrance for the Louvre, a design selected by Mitterrand himself.

Thanks to Mitterrand, a more glamorous Paris is the stage on which lovers walk arm in arm along the Seine, children scamper about in the Tuileries, cafes fill with animated conversation, and women dance the cancan at the Moulin Rouge.

ESSENTIALS

GETTING THERE   By Plane   Paris has two major international airports: Aéroport d'Orly, 13km (8½ miles) south, and Aéroport Roissy-Charles de Gaulle, 23km (14 miles) northeast of the city. The Air France bus that travels between Orly and Roissy airports departs at 20-minute intervals daily between 6am and 11pm. The trip takes an hour and costs 75F (€11.40, $11).

At **Charles de Gaulle (Roissy) Airport** (© 01-48-62-22-80), foreign carriers use Aérogare (terminal) 1, and Air France flies into Aérogare 2. The two terminals are linked by a shuttle bus (navette). The **free shuttle bus** connecting Aérogare 1 with Aérogare 2 also transports passengers to the Roissy rail station, from which fast RER trains leave every 15 minutes heading to such Métro stations as Gare du Nord, Châtelet, Luxembourg, Port-Royal, and Denfert-Rochereau. A typical train fare from Roissy to any point in central Paris is 49F (€7.45, $7). Passengers arriving on chartered flights from virtually anywhere tend to arrive at Terminal T-9, immediately adjacent to the RER station, a short walk from Aérogare 1.

You can also take an Air France shuttle bus, which departs about every 12 minutes, between 5:40am and 11pm, and costs 60 to 70F (€9.10 to €10.65, $8.70 to $10), to Palais des Congrès (Port e Maillot), then continue on to place de l'Étoile, Gare de Montparnesse, and Gare de Lyon, where Métro lines can carry you to any other point in Paris (trip time: 45–55 min.). Another option is Roissybus, which departs daily from 5:45am to 11pm and costs 45F (€6.85, $7). The bus takes you near the corner of rue Scribe and place de l'Opéra (trip time: 45–50 min.). A more recent service, **Airport Shuttle,** 2 av. Général-Leclerc, 14e (© 04-01-43-21-06-78; Métro: Denfert-Rochereau), will transport you to and from Orly or Charles de Gaulle in a minivan. The cost is 120F (€18.25, $17) per person or else 89F (€13.55, $13) if the van is shared.

A **taxi** from Roissy into the city will cost about 300F (€45.60, $44). From 8pm to 7am, fares are 40% higher. Long queues of both taxis and passengers form outside each of the airport's terminals but are surprisingly orderly.

Orly Airport (© 01-49-75-15-15) also has two terminals—Orly Sud (south) for international flights and Orly Ouest (west) for domestic flights. They're linked by a free shuttle bus. **Air France buses** leave from Exit H of Orly Sud and from Exit D of Orly Ouest every 12 minutes, between 5:45am and 11pm, heading for Gare de Montparnasse and Gare des Invalides. The fare for the trip is 45F (€6.85, $7).

At Exit J arrival level in Orly Ouest and Exit H, Platform 4, in Orly Sud, you can board an **Orly bus** to Denfert-Rochereau in central Paris. Expect to pay 30F (€4.55, $4.35).

An alternative method for reaching central Paris involves taking a monorail (**Orly Val**) to the nearby RER station of Anthony, then the RER train into downtown Paris. The Orly Val makes stops at both the north and the south terminals, then continues at 8-minute intervals for the 10-minute ride to the Anthony RER station. The fare, 57F (€8.65, $8) each way, seems relatively expensive but offsets the horrendous construction costs of a monorail that sails above the congested roadways encircling the airport. At Anthony, RER trains (line B) make the 30-minute ride into the city for 8F (€1.20, $1.15) extra per person.

A taxi from Orly to the center of Paris costs about 225F (€34.20, $33), more at night. Don't take a meterless taxi from Orly Sud or Orly Ouest—it's much safer and usually cheaper to hire a metered cab from the lines, which are under the scrutiny of a police officer.

Returning to the airport, buses leave the Invalides terminal heading either to Orly Sud or Orly Ouest every 15 minutes (trip time: 30 min.).

By Train   There are six major train stations in Paris: **Gare D'Austerlitz,** 55 quai d'Austerlitz, 13e (servicing the southwest with trains to the Loire Valley, the Bordeaux country, and the Pyrénées); **Gare de l'Est,** place du 11-Novembre-1918, 10e (servicing the east, with trains to Strasbourg, Nancy, Reims, and beyond to

Zurich, Basel, Luxembourg, and Austria); **Gare de Lyon,** 20 bd. Diderot, 12e (servicing the southeast with trains to the Côte d'Azur, Provence, and beyond to Geneva, Lausanne, and Italy); **Gare de Montparnasse,** 17 bd. Vaugirard, 15e (servicing the west with trains to Brittany); **Gare du Nord,** 18 rue de Dunkerque, 15e (servicing the north with trains to Holland, Denmark, Belgium, and the north of Germany); and **Gare St-Lazare,** 13 rue d'Amsterdam, 8e (servicing the northwest with trains to Normandy and London).

For **general train information,** or to make reservations, call ✆ **08-36-35-35-35** if your destination takes you from Paris to anywhere else in France or Europe. If your ride will be limited to Paris and its suburbs, call ✆ **01-53-90-20-20** instead.

Buses operate between the stations, and each of these stations has a Métro stop. Taxis are also available at every station at designated stands. *Warning:* The stations and surrounding areas are usually seedy and are frequented by pickpockets, hustlers, hookers, and drug addicts. Be alert, especially at night.

By Bus   Most buses arrive at **Gare Routière Internationale du Paris-Gallieni,** 28 av. du Général-de-Gaulle, Bagnolet (✆ **08-36-69-52-52;** Métro: Gallieni). Bagnolet is a 35-minute Métro ride from central Paris.

By Car   Driving a car in Paris is definitely *not* recommended. Parking is difficult and traffic dense. If you do drive, remember that Paris is encircled by a ring road called the *périphérique.* The major highways into Paris are the **A-1** from the north (Great Britain and Benelux); the **A-13** from Rouen, Normandy, and other points of northwest France; the **A-109** from Spain, the Pyrénées, and the southwest; the **A-7** from the French Alps, the Riviera, and Italy; and the **A-4** from eastern France.

VISITOR INFORMATION   **Tourist Offices**   The city's main **tourist information office** is at 127 av. des Champs-Elysées, 8e (✆ **08-36-68-31-12**), where you can secure information about both Paris and its provinces. The office is open daily April to October, 9am to 8pm (closed May 1); from November to March, it is open 11am to 6pm (closed Dec 25). There's an additional branch in the base of the Eiffel Tower (open only May–Oct, Mon–Sat, 8am–8pm), and within the arrivals hall of the Gare de Lyon (Mon–Sat, 8am–8pm). Any of the above-mentioned tourist offices will give you free copies of English-language leaflets *Time Out* and *Paris Users' Guide.*

Websites   With lots of suggestions for your trip to France—especially Paris—**www.franceway.com** covers dining, lodging, and transportation. The detailed listings of restaurants in Paris don't appear to be paid ads. Take a virtual tour of Paris at **www.paris.cx.** This site has hundreds of photos, maps, links, and a search page for available hotels. Drop in on the chatbox and check out the Q&A on its Paris Forum. Descriptions of lodgings are the strength of this **www.paris.org.** Hotels are organized by arrondissements and price ranges, supplemented with guest reviews. The city guide includes an event calendar, shops, a map of attractions with details about each, and a photo tour.

At **www.bonjour.com** you can pick one of the country's regions and peruse a directory of links to attractions, tour operators, and city visitor bureaus. Check out the hints for getting around Paris. For shopping and vacation packages, go to **www.allthingsfrench.com.**

CITY LAYOUT

Paris is surprisingly compact. Occupying slightly more land space than San Francisco, it's home to more than 10 million people. The River Seine divides Paris into the **Right Bank (Rive Droite)** to the north and the **Left Bank (Rive**

Gauche) to the south. These designations make sense when you stand on a bridge and face downstream, watching the waters flow out toward the sea. Thirty-two bridges link the Right Bank and the Left Bank, some providing access to the two small islands at the heart of the city, **Île de la Cité**—the city's birthplace and site of Notre-Dame—and **Île St-Louis,** an oasis of sober 17th-century mansions.

Between 1860 and 1870, Baron Georges-Eugène Haussmann, at the orders of Napoléon III, forever changed the look of Paris by creating the legendary *grands boulevards:* St-Michel, St-Germain, Haussmann, Sébastopol, Magenta, Voltaire, and Strasbourg.

The "main street" on the Right Bank is the **avenue des Champs-Elysées,** beginning at the Arc de Triomphe and running to **place de la Concorde.** Haussmann also created avenue de l'Opéra and the 12 avenues that radiate starlike from the Arc de Triomphe, giving it its original name, place de l'Étoile (*étoile* means "star"). It was renamed place Charles-de-Gaulle following the general's death; today it's often referred to as **place Charles-de-Gaulle-Étoile.**

ARRONDISSEMENTS IN BRIEF   The heart of medieval Paris was the **Île de la Cité** and the areas immediately surrounding it. As Paris grew it absorbed many of the once-distant villages, and even today each of these *arrondissements* (districts) retains a distinct character. They're numbered 1 to 20 starting at the center and progressing in a clockwise spiral. The key to finding any address in Paris is looking for the arrondissement number, rendered either as a number followed by "e" or "er" (1er, 2e, and so on). If the address is written out more formally, you can tell what arrondissement it's in by looking at the postal code. For example, the address may be written with the street name then "75014 Paris." The last two digits, 14, indicate that the address is in the 14th arrondissement, Montparnasse.

On the Right Bank, the **1er** is home to the Louvre, place Vendôme, rues de Rivoli and St-Honoré, Palais Royal, and Comédie-Française—an area filled with grand institutions and grand stores; at the center of the **2e** is the Bourse (stock exchange), making it the city's financial center; most of the **3e** and the **4e** is referred to as the Marais, the old Jewish quarter that in the 17th century was home to the aristocracy—today it's a trendy area of boutiques and restored mansions as well as the center of Paris's gay and lesbian community. On the Left Bank, the **5e** is known as the Latin Quarter, home to the Sorbonne and associated with the intellectual life that thrived in the 1920s and 1930s; the **6e,** known as St-Germain-des-Prés, stretches from the Seine to boulevard du Montparnasse, and is associated with the 1920s and 1930s as well as being a center for art and antiques; it boasts the Palais and Jardin du Luxembourg within its boundaries. The **7e,** containing both the Tour Eiffel and Hôtel des Invalides, is a residential district for the well heeled.

Back on the Right Bank, the **8e** epitomizes monumental Paris: with the triumphal avenue des Champs-Elysées, the Elysées Palace, and the fashion houses along avenue Montaigne and the Faubourg St-Honoré. The **18e** is home to Sacré-Coeur and Montmartre and all that the name conjures of the bohemian life painted most notably by Toulouse-Lautrec. The **14e** incorporates most of Montparnasse, including its cemetery, whereas the **20e** is where the city's famous lie buried in Père-Lachaise and where today the recent immigrants from North Africa live. Beyond the arrondissements stretch the vast *banlieue,* or suburbs, of Greater Paris, where the majority of Parisians live.

Value Save on Travel

When purchasing Métro tickets, a *carnet* is the best buy—10 tickets for 52F (€7.90, $8). You can also purchase a **Paris-Visite**, a tourist pass valid for 1, 2, 3, or 5 days on the public transportation system, including the Métro, buses, and RER (Réseau Express Régional) trains. (The RER has both first- and second-class compartments, and the pass lets you travel in first class.) As a bonus, the funicular ride to the top of Montmartre is included. A 1-day pass costs 55F (€8.35, $8), a 2-day pass 90F (€13.73, $13), a 3-day pass 175F (€26.60, $25), and a 5-day pass 120F (€18.25, $17). The card is available at RATP (Régie Autonome des Transports Parisiens), tourist offices, or the main Métro stations (ⓒ **01-44-68-20-20** or 08-36-68-77-14).

There are other discount passes as well, though most are available only to French residents with government ID cards and proof of taxpayer status. One available to temporary visitors is **Carte Mobilis**, which allows unlimited travel on all bus, subway, and RER lines during a 1-day period. A 1-day pass costs 32F (€4.85, $4.65). Ask for it at any Métro station. The pass is valid only within the 20 arrondissements.

GETTING AROUND

Paris is a city for strollers whose greatest joy is rambling through unexpected alleys and squares. Given a choice of conveyance, try to make it on your own two feet whenever possible.

BY MÉTRO   The Paris Métro (subway) runs daily from 5:30am to around 1:15am. (Be alert that train arrivals within central Paris stations might be as much as an hour before the end of their run.) The Métro is reasonably safe at any hour, but beware of pickpockets. Transfer stations are known as *correspondances.* Note that some transfers require long walks (Châtelet is the most notorious), but most trips will require only one transfer. On the urban lines, it costs the same to any point. One ticket costs 8F (€1.20, $1.15). See the inside back cover of this guide for a map of the Paris Métro.

BY BUS   Buses are much slower than the Métro. Most run 7am to 8:30pm (a few operate to 12:30am, and 10 operate during the early morning hours). Service is limited on Sundays and holidays. Bus and Métro fares are the same and you can use carnet tickets on both. Most bus rides (including all of those that begin and end within the 20 arrondissements of Paris) require one ticket.

If you intend to use the buses a lot during your stay in Paris, pick up an **RATP bus map** at their office on Place de la Madeleine, 8e, at any tourist information office, or at RATP headquarters, 52–54 quai de la Rapée, 12e (ⓒ **01-44-68-20-20**). For detailed information on bus and Métro routes, call ⓒ **08-36-68-41-14.**

BY TAXI   The flag drops at 14F (€2.15, $2), and you pay 3.36F (€0.50, 50¢) per kilometer. At night, expect to pay 5.45F (€0.85, 80¢) per kilometer. On airport trips you're not required to pay for the driver's empty return ride. Should you get tied up in a traffic jam and have a long wait, a basic charge of 120F (€18.25, $17) per hour will be assessed, or 60F (€9.10, $9) per 30 minutes of waiting time. Tip 12% to 15%—the latter usually elicits a *merci.* For radio cabs, call ⓒ **01-49-36-10-10** or 01-42-70-00-42—note that you'll be charged from the point where the taxi begins the drive to pick you up.

BY CAR   Don't even consider driving in Paris, unless you're a battle-hardened veteran of urban guerilla tactics. The streets are narrow and parking is next to impossible.

BY BICYCLE   **Paris-Vélos,** 2 rue du Fer-à-Moulin, 5e (℃ **01-43-37-59-22;** Métro: Censier-Daubenton), rents by the day, weekend, or week, charging 90 to 160F (€13.70 to €24.30, $13 to $23) per weekday, 160 to 220F (€24.30 to €33.45, $23$32) Saturday and Sunday, and 450 to 600F (€68.40 to €91.20, $65 to $87) for a week. Deposits of 2,000F (€304, $290) are required. Bikes are rented from Monday to Saturday 10am to 12:30pm and 2 to 7pm.

BY BOAT   The **Batobus** (℃ **01-44-11-33-44**), a series of 150-passenger ferry-boats with big windows suitable for viewing the passing riverfronts, operates every day between April and mid-October along the Seine, stopping at five points of tourist interest. You can board at the Eiffel Tower, Musée d'Orsay, Louvre, Notre-Dame, or Hôtel de Ville docks. Transit between each stop costs 20F (€3.05, $2.90), and departures are about every 30 minutes from 10am to 7pm.

FAST FACTS: Paris

American Express   American Express operates a 24-hour-a-day hot line (℃ **01-47-77-70-00**). Day-to-day services, like tours and money changing, are available at 11 rue Scribe, 9e (℃ **01-47-77-77-07;** Métro: Opéra), and 38 av. Wagram, 8e (℃ **01-42-27-58-80;** Métro: Ternes). Both of the branches are open from Monday to Friday 9am to 6:30pm, with money-changing services ending at 4:45pm.

Business Hours   Most **banks** in Paris are open from Monday to Friday 9am to 4:30pm; only a few are open on Saturday. The *grands magasins* (**department stores**) are generally open from Monday to Saturday 9:30am to 6:30pm; **smaller shops** close for lunch and reopen around 2pm, but this has become rarer. Many stores stay open to 7pm in summer; others are closed Monday, especially in the morning. Large **offices** remain open all day, but some also close for lunch.

Currency   The French franc (F) is divided into 100 centimes. At this writing $1 = approximately 6.6F (or 1F = 14½¢), and this is the rate of exchange used to calculate the dollar values in this chapter. At press time, €1 = 6.56F (or 1F = €0.15) and £1 = approximately 10.27F (or 1F = £0.10p). From January 1, 2002 the monetary unit in France is the euro, though the franc will still be legal tender until March 1.

Currency Exchange   American Express (see above) can fill most banking needs. For the best exchange rate, cash your traveler's checks at banks or foreign-exchange offices, not at shops and hotels.

Dentists/Doctors   For emergency dental service, call **S.O.S. Dentaire** at ℃ **01-43-37-51-00** from Monday to Friday 8pm to midnight and Saturday and Sunday 8am to midnight. **American Hospital of Paris,** 63 bd. Victor-Hugo, Neuilly (℃ **01-46-41-25-25;** Métro: Pont de Levallois or Pont de Neuilly; bus: 82), operates a 24-hour medical and dental service.

Drugstores   After regular hours, have your concierge contact the Commis-sariat de Police for the nearest 24-hour *pharmacie.* You'll find the address posted on the doors or windows of all other drugstores. One of the most central all-nighters is **Pharmacie "les Champs,"** in La Galerie Les Champs, 84 av. des Champs-Elysées, 8e (✆ **01-45-62-02-41**; Métro: George V).

Embassies & Consulates Call before you go, as they often keep strange hours and observe both French and home-country holidays. The Embassy of the **United States,** at 2 av. Gabriel, 8e (✆ **01-43-12-22-22**; Métro: Concorde), is open from Monday to Friday 9am to 6pm. Passports are issued (for $55) at its consulate at 2 rue St-Florentin (✆ **01-43-12-22-22**; Métro: Concorde). The Embassy of **Canada,** at 35 av. Montaigne, 8e (✆ **01-44-43-29-00**; Métro: Franklin D. Roosevelt or Alma-Marceau), is open from Monday to Friday 9am to noon and 2 to 4pm. The Embassy of the **United Kingdom,** at 35 rue du Faubourg St-Honoré, 8e (✆ **01-44-51-31-00**; Métro: Concorde or Madeleine), is open from Monday to Friday 9:30am to 12.30pm and 2:30 to 5pm. The consulate is at 16 rue d'Anjou, 8e (✆ **01-44-66-29-79**; Métro: Madeleine), and is open from Monday to Friday 9:30am to 12:30pm and 2:30 to 5pm. The Embassy of **Australia,** at 4 rue Jean-Rey, 15e (✆ **01-40-59-33-00**; Métro: Bir Hakeim), is open from Monday to Friday 9:15am to noon and 2 to 4:30pm. The Embassy of **New Zealand,** at 7 ter rue Léonard-de-Vinci, 16e (✆ **01-45-01-43-43**; Métro: Victor Hugo), is open from Monday to Friday 9am to 1pm and 2:30 to 6pm. The Embassy of **Ireland** is at 4 rue Rude, 16e (✆ **01-44-17-67-00**; Métro: Charles de Gaulle-Étoile). Hours are from Monday to Friday 9:30am to noon. The **Embassy of South Africa** is at 59 quai d'Orsay, 7e (✆ **01-53-59-23-23**; Métro: Invalides). Hours are from Monday to Friday 9am to noon.

Emergencies For the police, call ✆ **17**; to report a fire, call ✆ **18**. For an ambulance, phone the fire department at ✆ **01-45-78-74-52**; a fire vehicle rushes cases to the nearest emergency room. **S.A.M.U** is an independently operated, privately owned ambulance company; call ✆ **15**. For nonemergencies, the police can be reached at 9 bd. du Palais, 4e (✆ **01-53-71-53-71** or 01-53-73-53-73; Métro: Cité).

Internet Access In the Latin Quarter is **Cybercafé Latino,** 13 rue de l'École Polytechnique, 5e (✆ **01-40-51-86-94**; www.cybercafelatino.com; Métro: Maubert-Mutualité), open from Monday to Saturday 10am to 2 am.

Police In an emergency call ✆ **17**. The principal Prefecture is at 9 bd. du Palais, 4e (✆ **01-53-71-53-71**; Métro: Cité).

Post Office The **Bureau de Poste,** 52 rue du Louvre, 75001 Paris (✆ **01-40-28-20-00**; Métro: Louvre-Rivoli), is open 24 hours a day for the sale of stamps and expedition of faxes and telegrams, with limited hours—from 8am to 5pm from Monday to Friday and from 8am to noon on Saturday—for other financial services such as the sale of money orders. Your mail can be sent to this post office *poste restante* (general delivery) for a small fee. Take an ID such as a passport. Airmail letters to North America cost 4.50F (€0.70, 65¢); to other European countries 3F (€0.45, 45¢); to Australia and New Zealand 5.10F (€0.80, 75¢).

Safety Especially beware of child pickpockets. They roam Paris, preying on tourists around such sites as the Louvre, Eiffel Tower, Notre-Dame, and Montmartre, and they especially like to pickpocket in the Métro, often blocking the entrance and exit to the escalator.

Telephones The country code for France is **33**. All phone numbers in France have 10 digits, and this includes the **area code** (or regional prefix). For example, the phone number for the Hôtel Regina, 01-42-60-38-09, contains the area code **(01)** for Paris and the Île de France. To make a **long-distance call within France,** you would just dial this 10-digit number. **When calling from outside France,** dial the international prefix for your country (**011** for the United States and Canada), the country code for France, and then the last 9 digits of the number, dropping the 0 (zero) from the regional prefix.

Public phone booths are in cafes, restaurants, Métro stations, post offices, airports, train stations, and sometimes on the streets. Finding a coin-operated phone in France may be an arduous task; a simpler option is to use the *télécarte,* a prepaid calling card available for purchase at most post offices, Métro stations, and tobacco shops.

From a *télélcabine,* using a *télélcarte,* a 3-minute local call will cost around 2F (€0.30, 30¢); a call to the United States will cost around 3F (€0.45, 45¢) per minute. Note that these rates apply to public phone booths; hotels will add surcharges. Télécartes are sold in denominations of 50 to 200F (€7.60 to €30.40, $7 to $29). Access codes for the major U.S.-based carriers are as follows: To access **ATT,** dial **0800-99-00-11;** to access **MCI,** dial **0800-99-00-19;** to access **Sprint,** dial **0800-99-00-87.**

WHERE TO STAY

Many travelers with an early morning flight at Charles de Gaulle (or those who arrive very late at night) check into the **Hotel Sofitel Paris Aéroport CDG,** Aéroport Charles de Gaulle, Zone Central at Roissy (℃ **800/221-4542** in the U.S. and Canada, or 01-49-19-29-29; fax 01-49-29-00), doubles from 980 to 1,500F (€148.95 to €228, $142 to $218). International food with French overtones is served at a comfortable first-class restaurant and bar on the hotel's ground floor, and other amenities include 24-hour room service and a swimming pool and sauna.

RIGHT BANK: 1ST ARRONDISSEMENT
Very Expensive

Hôtel Costes 𝄐𝄐𝄐 Grand style and a location close to some of the most upscale shops in Paris attract high-style fashion types. The five-story building functioned as a maison bourgeoise for many generations. Today, everything about the town house–style premises evokes the rich days of France's Gilded Age. Although small, rooms are cozy and ornate, with one or two large beds. Bathrooms are fairly spacious. The best rooms are called Grande Chambre, containing sitting areas. For the ultimate luxury, ask for one of the duplex rooms with split-level layouts.

239 rue St-Honoré, 75001 Paris. ℃ **01-42-44-50-50.** Fax 01-42-44-50-01. 83 units. 3,000–3,500F (€456–€532, $435–$508) double; from 7,500F (€1,140, $1,088) suite. AE, DC, MC, V. Métro: Tuileries or Concorde. **Amenities:** Restaurant; bar; pool; gym; car rental; room service; massage; baby-sitting; laundry/dry cleaning. *In room:* A/C, TV, minibar, hair dryer.

Hôtel de Vendôme 𝄐𝄐 Once the home of the Embassy of Texas when the state was a nation, this is an 18th-century jewel box. It opened in summer 1998 at one of the world's most prestigious addresses. It is comparable and almost as good as Costes. Although the sumptuous rooms are only moderate in size, you live in opulent comfort here. Most rooms are decorated in a classic Second Empire style with luxurious beds and mattresses. Bathrooms are equally sumptuous. Security is fantastic, with TV intercoms.

1 Place Vendôme, 75001 Paris. © **01-42-60-32-84.** Fax 01-49-27-97-89. reservations@hoteldevendome. com. 23 units. 2,800–3,200F (€425.60–€486.40, $406–$464) double; 4,500–5,500F (€684–€836, $653–$798) suite. AE, DC, MC, V. Métro: Concorde or Opéra. **Amenities:** Restaurant, bar; room service; laundry. *In room:* A/C, TV, minibar, hair dryer.

Hôtel Ritz 🛇🛇🛇   The Ritz is an enduring symbol of elegance on one of Paris's most beautiful and historic squares. Rooms are individually decorated with thick rugs, tapestries, large mirrors, marble fireplaces, double-glazed windows, and brass beds. The spacious bathrooms are among the city's most luxurious, with scales, private phones, and cords to summon maid and valets.

15 place Vendôme, 75001 Paris. © **800/448-8355** in the U.S. and Canada, or 01-43-16-30-30. Fax 01-43-16-31-78. resa@ritzparis.com. 175 units. 4,000–4,560F (€608–€693.10, $580–$661) double; from 5,415F (€823.10, $785) suite. AE, DC, MC, V. Parking 230F (€34.95, $33). Métro: Opéra, Concorde or Madeleine. **Amenities:** 2 restaurants, 2 bars; pool; health club; boutiques; room service; massage; laundry/dry cleaning. *In room:* A/C, TV, minibar, hair dryer, safe.

Expensive

Hôtel du Louvre 🛇   After a massive overhaul, the hotel is now in a neck-and-neck race with the Regina for neighborhood supremacy. When Napoléon III inaugurated the hotel in 1855, French journalists described it as "a palace of the people, rising adjacent to the palace of kings." In 1897, Camille Pissarro moved into a room with a view that inspired many of his landscapes. Rooms are quintessentially Parisian, filled with souvenirs of the Belle Époque. Most were renovated between 1996 and 1998. Some are small, but most are medium-size to spacious with double-glazed windows and comfortable beds.

Place André-Malraux, 75001 Paris. © **800/888-4747** in the U.S. and Canada, or 01-44-58-38-38. Fax 01-43-36-68. www.hoteldulouvre.com. 195 units. 2,350–5,280F (€357.20–€802.55, $341–$766) double; from 6,000F (€912, $870) suite. Ask about midwinter discounts. AE, DC, MC, V. Parking 120F (€18.25, $17). Métro: Palais Royal or Louvre-Rivoli. **Amenities:** Restaurant, bar; room service; baby-sitting; laundry/dry cleaning. *In room:* A/C, TV, minibar, hair dryer.

Hôtel Regina 🛇   Restored to its old-fashioned grandeur, this hotel stands opposite the Louvre. Rooms are richly decorated in such French styles as Directoire, Louis XVI, or Art Nouveau. There are more grace notes in this hotel than at its closest competitor, Hôtel du Louvre.

2 place des Pyramides, 75001 Paris. © **800/448-8355** in the U.S. and Canada, or 01-42-60-31-10. Fax 01-40-15-95-16. www.regina/hotel.com. 120 units. 2,070–2,900F (€314.65–€440.80, $300–$421) double; from 3,000F (€456, $435) suite. AE, DC, MC, V. Parking 150F (€22.80, $22). Métro: Pyramides or Tuileries. **Amenities:** 2 restaurants, bar; room service; massage; baby-sitting; laundry/dry cleaning. *In room:* A/C, TV, minibar, hair dryer, safe.

Inexpensive

Hôtel Britannique 🛇*Value*   Though the 1st arrondissement has far better hotels, the Britannique is a superior value. Rooms may be small, but they're clean, comfortable, and adequately equipped. Centrally located near Les Halles, the Centre Pompidou, and Notre-Dame, the Britannique was completely renovated in 1998. Bathrooms are small but efficiently organized.

20 av. Victoria, 75001 Paris. © **01-42-33-74-59.** Fax 01-42-33-82-65. 40 units. 920–1,050F (€139.85–€159.60, $133–$152) double. AE, DC, MC, V. Parking 120F (€18.25, $17). Métro: Châtelet. **Amenities:** Room service. *In room:* TV, minibar, safe.

Paris Accommodations

Clos Médicis Hôtel **15**

Grand Hôtel St-Michel **16**

Hôtel Abbatial St-Germain **19**

Hôtel Aviatic **1**

Hôtel Britannique **26**

Hôtel Central **25**

Hôtel Costes **6**

Hôtel des Deux-Iles **20**

Hôtel de Fleurie **13**

Hôtel de l'Académie **11**

Hôtel de Lutéce **22**

Hôtel de la Place des Vosges **24**

Hôtel des Grandes École **18**	Hôtel du Quai-Voltaire **10**	Hôtel St-Louis **23**
	Hôtel Le Ste-Beuve **14**	Hôtel Verneuil **9**
Hôtel de Vendôme **5**	Hôtel Regina **7**	L'Hôtel **12**
Hôtel du Jeu de Paume **21**	Hôtel Ritz **4**	Libertel Quartier Latin **17**
Hôtel du Louvre **8**	Hôtel St-Lazare **3**	Résidence Lord Byron **2**

RIGHT BANK: 3RD, 4TH, & 8TH ARRONDISSEMENTS
Expensive
Hotel de Jeu de Paume ⭐   It's small-scale and charming, with rooms that are a bit larger than those within some of its nearby competitors on the Île St-Louis. It originated as a "clubhouse" used by members of the court of Louis XIII. Rooms are outfitted in a simple and unfrilly version of Art Deco. By mentality and aesthetics, you'll consider yourself more closely aligned with the pervasive ethic of the Marais within this hotel than within the *Quartier Latin* to the south. There's scads of charm from the well-meaning staff.

54 rue St-Louis en l'Isle, 75004 Paris. ℰ **01-43-26-14-18.** Fax 01-40-46-02-76. 30 units. 1,365–1,650F (€207.50–€250.80, $198–$239) suite. AE, DC, MC, V. Parking 120F (€18.25, $17). Métro: Pont-Marie. **Amenities:** Fitness center; sauna; baby-sitting; laundry/dry cleaning. *In room:* TV, minibar, hair dryer, safe.

Moderate
Hotel de la Place des Vosges ⭐ *Value*   Built about 350 years ago, during the same era as the construction of the majestic square it's named after, and which lies less than a 2-minute walk away, this is a well-managed, small-scale property with reasonable prices and lots of charm. Many rooms have are relatively small, but give a sense of cozy, well-ordered efficiency. There are patches of chiseled stone at various parts of the hotel, a decorative touch that helps evoke the era of Louis XIII.

12 rue de Birague, 75004 Paris. ℰ **01-42-72-60-46.** Fax 01-42-72-02-64. hotel.place.des.vosges@gofenet. com. 16 units. 660–690F (€100.30–€104.90, $96–$100) double. MC, V. Métro: Bastille. **Amenities:** Breakfast room. *In room:* TV, hair dryer.

Hôtel de Lutèce   Going into this hotel is much like walking into a country house in Brittany. Each of the individualized rooms is furnished with antiques. The hotel is comparable in style and amenities with Deux-Îles (same ownership). Many of the rooms were renovated in 1998 and plush French mattresses were added. Bathrooms are small.

65 rue St-Louis-en-l'Île, 75004 Paris. ℰ **01-43-26-23-52.** Fax 01-43-29-60-25. 23 units. 890F (€135.30, $129.05) double; 1,000F (€152, $145) triple. AE, MC, V. Parking nearby 110F (€16.70, $16). Métro: Pont Marie. **Amenities:** Breakfast room; room service; laundry/dry cleaning. *In room:* A/C, TV, hair dryer, safe.

Hôtel des Deux-Îles ⭐   This 18th-century hotel is the most appealing on Île St-Louis. The rather small rooms have exposed beams, which lend a sense of old-fashioned charm. In the cellar is a rustic-looking breakfast room whose decor was inspired by a medieval tavern, complete with an open fireplace. Visible from the reception area is a glassed-in courtyard whose landscaping can be admired through glass windows, but not entered.

59 rue St-Louis-en-l'Île, 75004 Paris. ℰ **01-43-26-13-35.** Fax 01-43-29-60-25. 17 units. 870F (€132.25, $126) double. AE, MC, V. Parking nearby 130F (€19.75, $19). Métro: Pont Marie. **Amenities:** Breakfast room; room service; laundry/dry cleaning. *In room:* A/C, TV, hair dryer.

Hotel St-Lazare ⭐   Across from the St-Lazare rail station, this hotel—the area's best—first greeted visitors flocking to the Universal Exposition of 1889. During the late 1990s, rooms were elevated to modern standards of comfort and redecorated. Many rooms (medium-size to quite large) have high ceilings, especially those on the lower floors, which also have double-glazed windows to cut down on the noise. The beds are plush and comfortable.

108 rue St-Lazare, 75008 Paris. ℰ **800/888-4747** in the U.S. outside New York State and Canada, 212/752-3900 in New York State, 0171/630-1704 in London, or 01-40-08-44-44. Fax 01-42-93-01-20. www.concordestlazare-paris.com. 300 units. 2,100–2,350F (€319.20–€357.20, $305–$341) suite. AE, DC, MC, V. Parking 150F (€22.80, $22). Métro: St-Lazare. **Amenities:** Restaurant, bar, cafe; room service; baby-sitting; laundry. *In room:* A/C, TV, minibar, hair dryer.

Hôtel St-Louis *(Value)*   This small hotel occupies a 17th-century town house romantically positioned on Île St-Louis. Guy Record and his wife Andrée maintain a charming family atmosphere that's increasingly hard to find in Paris. Hôtel St-Louis may not be in the same league as its major rivals, Lutéce and Deux-Îles, but it's an even better value. We prefer the rooms on the fifth floor (no elevator), which have the most atmosphere and views over rooftops. A full renovation in 1998 updated the plumbing.

75 rue St-Louis-en-l'Île, 75004 Paris. ℂ **01-46-34-04-80.** Fax 01-46-34-02-13. www.paris-hotel.tm.fr. 21 units. 795–895F (€120.85–€136.05, $115–$130) double. MC, V. Parking nearby 100F (€15.20, $15). Métro: Pont Marie. **Amenities:** Breakfast room; room service; baby-sitting; laundry. *In room:* TV, hair dryer, safe.

Moderate
Résidence Lord Byron   Lord Byron, just off the Champs-Elysées on a curving street, may not be as monumentally grand as other hotels of the 8th, but it's a good price performer. No style setter, it's solid and reliable (and maybe a little stuffy). Owner Françoise Benoit has added many personal touches such as framed prints of butterflies and historic French scenes. Rooms are very *hôtel de charme*, with flowery wallpaper, bedspreads, and curtains. Bathrooms are small with tub/shower combinations (or else only a shower).

5 rue de Chateaubriand, 75008 Paris. ℂ **01-43-59-89-98.** Fax 01-42-89-46-04. www.escapade.paris.com. 31 units. 910–1,015F (€138.30–€154.30, $132–$147) suite. AE, MC, V. Métro: George V. RER: Étoile. **Amenities:** Room service; baby-sitting; dry cleaning. *In room:* A/C, TV, minibar, hair dryer, safe.

LEFT BANK: 5TH ARRONDISSEMENT
Moderate
Grand Hôtel St-Michel   This hotel is larger and more business-like than many of the smaller town house–style inns that lie within the same neighborhood. In 1997, the hotel was renovated and some rooms enlarged, all with quality mattresses. Fifth floor rooms (no elevators) have wrought-iron balconies overlooking the surrounding neighborhood, and sixth floor rooms have interesting views over the surrounding rooftops.

19 rue Cujas, 75005 Paris. ℂ **01-46-33-33-02.** Fax 01-40-46-96-33. www.123.france.com. 46 units. 890F (€135.30, $129) double; 1,290F (€196.10, $187) triple. DC, MC, V. Métro: Cluny–la Sorbonne. RER: Luxembourg. **Amenities:** Bar; baby-sitting; laundry/dry cleaning. *In room:* TV, minibar, hair dryer, safe.

Inexpensive
Hôtel Abbatial St-Germain   From the 17th century such touches remain as dovecotes and massive oaken beams. Rooms are very much French boudoir in style, with many well-crafted decorative touches. Bathrooms are neatly kept and equipped with showers. All rooms are double-glazed, and many on the fifth and sixth floors enjoy views over the cathedral of Notre-Dame. Fifth floor rooms have small balconies.

46 bd. St.-Germain, 75005 Paris. ℂ **01-46-34-02-12.** Fax 01-43-25-47-73. abbatial@hotellerie.net. 43 units. 760–880F (€115.50–€133.75, $110–$128) double. AE, DC, MC, V. Parking nearby 110F (€16.70, $16). Métro: Maubert-Mutualité. **Amenities:** Baby-sitting; laundry/dry cleaning. *In room:* A/C, TV, minibar, hair dryer, safe.

Hotel des Grandes Écoles *(Value)*   Few hotels in the neighborhood offer so much low-key charm at such reasonable prices. With its furniture styled in the time of Louis XV, this trio of high-ceilinged buildings connected by a sheltered courtyard owes its present look to renovations completed in the 1990s. Rooms are artfully old-fashioned with comfortable mattresses. Many offer views of a bucolic garden whose trellises and flowerbeds evoke the countryside. There are dozens of restaurants in the surrounding rue Mouffetard neighborhood, and weather permitting, breakfast is served in the garden.

75 rue de Cardinal Lemoine, 75005 Paris. ✆ **01-43-26-79-23**. Fax 01-43-25-28-15. www.hotel-grandes-Écoles.com. 51 units. 550–720F (€83.60–€109.45, $80–$104) double. MC, V. Parking 100F (€15.20, $15). Métro: Cardinal Lemoine or Place Monge. **Amenities:** Breakfast room. *In room:* Hair dryer.

LEFT BANK: 6TH ARRONDISSEMENT
Expensive
L'Hôtel 🅐   No longer the fleabag where Oscar Wilde died, this is one of the most charming boutique hotels on the Left Bank. Throughout the building is an eclectic collection of antiques. Rooms vary widely in size, style, and price; some are quite small, others are deluxe chambers fit for the occasional celebrity guest. Regardless of size, all rooms have decorative fireplaces. About half of the relatively small bathrooms are tiny tubless nooks.

13 rue des Beaux-Arts, 75006 Paris. ✆ **01-44-41-99-00**. Fax 01-43-25-64-81. www.l-hotel.com. 27 units. 2,500–4,800F (€380–€729.60, $363–$696) double; 5,000–5,300F (€760–€806, $725–$769) suite. AE, DC, MC, V. Métro: St-Germain des Prés or Mabillon. **Amenities:** Breakfast room; room service; baby-sitting; laundry/dry cleaning. *In room:* A/C, TV, minibar, hair dryer.

Moderate
Clos Médicis Hôtel   One of this hotel's major advantages is its location adjacent to the Luxembourg Gardens in the heart of the Latin Quarter. You'll find a verdant garden, a lobby with modern spotlights and simple furniture, and a multilingual staff. The warmly colored rooms are uncomplicated and comfortable. Bathrooms are small but adequate. Breakfast is the only meal served.

56 rue Monsieur-le-Prince, 75006 Paris. ✆ **01-43-29-10-80**. Fax 01-43-54-26-90. clos_medicis@compuserve.com. 38 units. 790–1,140F (€120.10–€173.30, $115–$165) double; 1,400F (€212.80, $203) duplex suite. AE, DC, MC, V. Métro: Odéon. RER: Luxembourg. **Amenities:** Breakfast room; laundry. *In room:* A/C, TV, minibar, hair dryer.

Hôtel Aviatic   The Aviatic is a bit of old Paris—it's been a family-run hotel of character and elegance for a century. The reception lounge provides an attractive traditional setting. There's also a modest inner courtyard. Although it doesn't have the decorative style and flair of some hotels in the 6th, it offers good comfort and a warm ambience. The rather small rooms were renovated in various stages throughout the 1990s.

105 rue de Vaugirard, 75006 Paris. ✆ **01-53-63-25-50**. Fax 01-53-63-25-55. www.aviatic.fr. 43 units. 950F (€144.40, $138) double. AE, DC, MC, V. Parking 120F (€18.25, $17). Métro: Montparnasse-Bienvenue or Saint Placide. **Amenities:** Room service; baby-sitting; laundry/dry cleaning. *In room:* A/C, TV, minibar, hair dryer.

Hôtel de Fleurie 🅐   Just off boulevard St-Germain on a colorful little street, the Fleurie is one of the best of the "new" old hotels. A 1997 renovation upgraded all beds and restored the lobby. Rooms, though generally small, have an 18th-century aura with a mixture of antiques and reproductions. Bathrooms are surprisingly luxurious for a hotel of this rating; seven come only with a shower.

32–34 rue Grégoire-de-Tours, 75006 Paris. ✆ **01-53-73-70-00**. Fax 01-53-73-70-20. www.hotel-de-fleurie. com.fr. 29 units. 1,000–1,300F (€152–€197.60, $145–$189) double. AE, DC, MC, V. Métro: Odéon or St. Germain des Pres. **Amenities:** Breakfast room, bar; car rental; room service; laundry/dry cleaning. *In room:* A/C, TV, minibar, hair dryer, trouser press.

Hotel Le Ste-Beuve 🅐 *(Finds*   The location of this discreet hideaway adds to its charms, on a street that's tucked into a narrow and quiet neighborhood, reeking of bourgeois respectability, near the Luxembourg Garden. The public areas are outfitted with deep leather armchairs and a midwinter fire that blazes merrily on an open hearth. Rooms are not overly large, but all (four to a floor) face the quiet street, noises from which are muffled by double-glazing. Overall, the aura is one of well-managed comfort and respectability.

9 rue Ste-Beuve, 75006 Paris. © 01-45-48-30-07. Fax 01-45-48-33-95. www.paris-hotel-charme.com. 22 units. 780–1,440F (€118.55–€218.90, $113–$209) double; 1,700F (€258.40, $247) suite. Parking 90F (€13.70, $13). Métro: Notre-Dame-des-Champs. **Amenities:** Room service (drinks). *In room:* TV, minibar.

Liberal Quartier Latin   This century-old building in a neighborhood crowded with Quartier Latin color received a radical upgrade in 1997 that transformed the rooms into testimonials to French literature. Proust and Gide used to live here, and the place remains gay friendly. Expect a hardworking and articulate staff and small, cozy rooms. Bathrooms are small but efficiently organized. Breakfast is the only meal served, but many restaurants lie within the area.

9 rue des Écoles, 75006 Paris. © 800/949-7562 or 01-44-27-06-45. Fax 01-43-25-36-70. 29 units. 1,225F (€186.20, $178) double; 1,350F (€205, $196) suite. AE, DC, MC, V. Nearby parking 100F (€15.20, $15) per night. Métro: Jussieu or Cardinal Le Moine. **Amenities:** Breakfast room; room service; baby-sitting; laundry/dry cleaning. *In room:* A/C, TV, minibar, hair dryer, safe.

LEFT BANK: 7TH ARRONDISSEMENT
Moderate
Hôtel de l'Académie ⋆⋆   The exterior walls and old ceiling beams are all that remain of this 17th-century residence of the duc de Rohan's private guards. In 1999, the hotel was completely renovated to include an elegant reception area. The up-to-date rooms have a lush, Île-de-France decor and views over the neighborhood. By American standards the rooms are small, but they're average for Paris. All the bathrooms except eight have a full tub-shower combo.

32 rue des Sts-Pères, 75007 Paris. © 800/246-0041 in the U.S. and Canada, or 01-45-49-80-00. Fax 01-45-44-75-24. www.academiehotel.aol.com. 34 units. 990–1,290F (€150.50–€196.10, $144–$187) double; from 1,590F (€241.70, $231) suite. AE, DC, MC, V. Parking 150F (€22.80, $22). Métro: St-Germain-des-Prés. **Amenities:** Fitness center; massage; baby-sitting. *In room:* A/C, TV, minibar, hair dryer, safe.

Inexpensive
Hôtel du Quai-Voltaire   Built in the 1600s as an abbey, then transformed into a hotel in 1856, Quai-Voltaire is best known for its illustrious guests, who have included Wilde, Baudelaire, and Wagner. Twenty-eight rooms have views over the Seine. Rooms tend to be small, and bathrooms are a bit cramped. Double-glazed windows block out traffic noise. You can have drinks in the small salon, and simple meals can be prepared for those who prefer to eat in.

19 quai Voltaire, 75007 Paris. © 01-42-61-50-91. Fax 01-42-61-62-26. www.hotelduquaivoltaire.com. 33 units. 750–800F (€114–€121.60, $109–$116) double; 870F (€132.25, $126) triple. AE, DC, MC, V. Parking 110F (€16.70, $16) nearby. Métro: Rue du Bac or Musee d'Orsay. **Amenities:** Bar; room service; laundry. *In room:* TV, hair dryer.

Hotel Verneuil ⋆ *Finds*   Small-scale and personalized, this hotel, in the words of a recent critic, combines modernist sympathies with nostalgia for "*la vieille France.*" Within what was built in the 1600s as a town house, it offers a creative and intimate jumble of charm and coziness. Expect a mixture of antique and contemporary furniture, lots of books, and in the rooms, trompe l'oeil ceilings and walls covered in fabric that comes in a rainbow of colors. Some bathrooms offer shower only.

8 rue de Verneuil, 75007 Paris. © 01-42-60-82-14. Fax 01-42-61-40-38. verneuil@cybercable.fr. 26 units. 850–1,100F (€129.20–€167.20, $123–$160) double or suite. AE, DC, MC, V. Parking 120F (€18.25, $17). Métro: St-Germain-des-Prés. **Amenities:** Bar; limited room service; babysitting; laundry/dry cleaning. *In room:* A/C (some rooms), TV, minibar, hair dryer.

A GAY HOTEL

Hôtel Central   This is the most visible gay hotel in Paris. Rooms are on the upper floors of this 18th-century building. If you arrive between 8am and 5pm, you'll find reception one floor above street level; if you arrive at any other time, you'll have to retrieve your key and register at the street-level bar. Accessible via an antique wooden staircase that's as old as the building itself, rooms are simple and serviceable, so aside from a bar, don't expect any in-room amenities.

33 rue Vieille-du-Temple, 75004 Paris. © 01-48-87-99-33. Fax 01-42-77-06-27. 7 units, 1 with bathroom. 535F (€81.30, $78) double with or without bathroom. MC, V. Métro: Hôtel de Ville or Saint Paul. **Amenities:** Bar.

WHERE TO DINE
RIGHT BANK: 1ST ARRONDISSEMENT
Very Expensive
Le Grand Véfour 🦋🦋🦋 FRENCH/TRADITIONAL   Dining here is a great gastronomic experience. Specialties, served on Limoges china, include noisettes of lamb with star anise, and lobster. An exciting dish on a menu of delightful surprises is homemade ravioli stuffed with foie gras and served with an emulsion of truffle-flavored crème fraiche. Desserts are often grand, like the gourmandises au chocolat, a richness of chocolate served with chocolate sorbet.

17 rue de Beaujolais, 1er. © **01-42-96-56-27.** Reservations required. Main courses 290–550F (€44.10–€83.60, $42–$80); set price lunch 415F (€63.10, $60) "Le menu plaisir" (menu of little luxuries). AE, DC, MC, V. Mon–Fri 12:30–2:15pm and 7:30–10pm. Métro: Louvre-Palais Royal.

Moderate
Chez Vong 🦋 CANTONESE   This trendsetter, full of folk from the worlds of entertainment and the arts, is the kind of place you head when you're sick of grand French cuisine and grander culinary pretensions. The decor is steeped in a Chinese colonial ambience. Menu items include shrimps and scallops served with any degree of spiciness you specify, including a superheated version with garlic and red peppers; "joyous beef" that mingles sliced filet with pepper sauce; chicken in puff pastry with ginger; and a tempting array of fresh fish dishes.

10 rue de la Grande-Truanderie, 1er. © 01-40-26-09-36. Reservations recommended. Main courses 250–350F (€38€53.20, $36–$51). Fixed-price lunch 150F (€22.80, $22). AE, DC, MC, V. Mon–Sat noon–2:30pm and 7pm–midnight. Métro: Etienne Marcel.

Le Fumoir 🦋 INTERNATIONAL   Stylish and breezy, a few steps from the Louvre, this upscale brasserie is the most fashionable place to be seen eating or drinking in Paris today. Within a high-ceilinged ambience of warm but somber browns and indirect lighting, you can order salads, pastries, and drinks during the off-hours noted below, and platters of more substantial food during conventional meal times. Examples include filets of codfish with onions and herbs; sliced rack of veal simmered in its own juices with tarragon; calves' liver with onions; a combination platter of lamb chops with grilled tuna steak; and herring in a mustard-flavored cream sauce.

6 rue de l'Amiral Coligny, 1er. © **01-42-92-00-24.** Reservations recommended. Main courses 10–125F (€1.50–€19, $1.45–$18). AE, DC, MC, V. Daily for salads, pastries, and snacks 11am–1am; complete menu daily noon–3pm and 7pm–12:30am. AE, DC, MC, V. Métro: Louvre or Rivoli.

Inexpensive
Lescure 🦋 *Finds* FRENCH/TRADITIONAL   This mini-bistro is a major discovery because reasonably priced restaurants near place de la Concorde are difficult to find. The tables on the sidewalk are tiny and there isn't much room inside, but what this place does have is rustic charm. The kitchen is wide open, and the aroma of drying bay leaves, salami, and garlic hanging from the ceiling

fills the room. Don't expect anything overly thrilling, just hearty fare. House specialties include *confit de canard* (duckling) and salmon in green sauce. A favorite dessert is one of the chef's fruit tarts.

7 rue de Mondovi, 1er. ℂ 01-42-60-18-91. Reservations not accepted. Main courses 50–85F (€7.60–€12.90, $7–$12); set price 4-course menu 110F (€16.70, $16). MC, V. Mon–Fri noon–2:15pm and 7–10:15pm. Closed 3 weeks in Aug. Métro: Concorde.

RIGHT BANK: 3RD ARRONDISSEMENT
Moderate

L'Ambassade d'Auvergne ℱ AUVERGNANT/FRENCH (TRADITIONAL)   In an obscure district, this rustic tavern serves food derivative of the rib-sticking, hearty, savory cuisine associated with Auvergne. You enter through a busy bar; rough wheat bread is stacked in baskets, and rush-seated ladder-back chairs are placed at tables covered with bright cloths, mills to grind your own salt and pepper, and a jug of mustard. Tried-and-true favorites include a parmentier of blood sausage with fried apples; pork sausages served with *aligot* (mashed potatoes with garlic and Cantal cheese); a *potée d'Auvergne* (stewed pork with cabbage, carrots, and white beans); and filet of salmon *à l'Auvergnate* that's prepared with lard, bacon, garlic, and potatoes.

22 rue de Grenier St-Lazare, 3e. ℂ 01-42-72-31-22. Reservations recommended. Main courses 86–120F (€13.05–€18.25, $12–$17); set price menu 170F (€25.85, $25). MC, V. Daily noon–2pm and 7:30–11pm. Métro: Rambuteau.

RIGHT BANK: 4TH ARRONDISSEMENT
Very Expensive

L'Ambroisie ℱ AUVERGNANT/FRENCH (TRADITIONAL & MODERN)   Bernard Pacaud is one of the most talented chefs in Paris. In summer there's outdoor seating. The dishes change seasonally but may include crayfish tails with sesame seeds and curry sauce; filet of turbot braised with celery and celeriac, served with a julienne of black truffles; fricassee of lobster; and one of our favorites, Bresse chicken roasted with black truffles and truffled vegetables.

9 place des Vosges, 4e. ℂ 01-42-78-51-45. Reservations required. Main courses 370–610F (€56.25–€92.70, $54–$88). AE, V. Tues–Sat noon–1:30pm and 8–9:30pm. Métro: St-Paul.

Moderate

Georges ℱ INTERNATIONAL   With the establishment of this restaurant, the Centre Pompidou once again thrusts itself into the public spotlight as the kind of place that artsy Paris is talking about. The venue incorporates a very large space on the top floor of Paris's most comprehensive arts complex, with views through bay windows over most of the city. The decor is minimalist and postmodern, incorporating lots of brushed aluminum and stainless steel. Menu items are mostly continental, with occasional hints of Asia. To access the place, head for the exterior elevator just to the left of the Pompidou Center's main entrance, and know in advance that unless you identify your reservation to the security guard, they might not let you up.

On the uppermost (6th) floor of the Centre Georges Pompidoud, 19 rue Beaubourg, 4e. ℂ 01-44-78-47-99. Reservations imperative for dinner, strongly recommended for lunch. Main courses 45–180F (€6.85–€27.35, $7–$26). AE, DC, MC, V. Wed–Mon noon–6pm and 7pm–2am. Métro: Les Halles.

Inexpensive

Brasserie de l'Île St-Louis ALSATIAN/FRENCH (TRADITIONAL)   This retro-chic brasserie is the perfect place for an impromptu rendezvous. Little about the establishment's patina and paneled decor has changed since it was founded in the 1880s. Menu items are conservative, flavorful, and well prepared;

don't expect cutting-edge culinary fads and trends. Examples include an always-popular version of Alsatian sauerkraut; cassoulet in the old-fashioned style of Toulouse; stingray with a nut and butter sauce; calf's liver; and a succulent version of loin of pork with warm apple marmalade.

55 quai de Bourbon, 4e. (℃) 01-43-54-02-59. No reservations. Main courses 70–120F (€10.65–€18.25, $10–$17). V. Thurs–Tues 11:30am–1am. Métro: Pont Marie or Hotel de Ville.

RIGHT BANK: 8TH ARRONDISSEMENT
Very Expensive

Restaurant Plaza Athénée (Alain Ducasse) ✿✿✿ FRENCH(MODERN & TRADITIONAL)   Few other chefs in the history of French cuisine enjoy the international fame of Alain Ducasse. This five-star Michelin chef divides his time between Paris and Monaco. He seeds his dishes with produce from every corner of France—rare local vegetables, fish from the coasts, and dishes incorporating cardoons, turnips, celery, turbot, cuttlefish, and Bresse fowl. His French cuisine is contemporary and Mediterranean yet not new. Though many dishes are light, Ducasse isn't afraid of lard, as he proves by his thick, oozing slabs of pork grilled to a crisp.

In the Hotel Plaza Athénée, 25 av. Montaigne, 8e (℃) 01-53-67-65-00. Fax 01-53-67-65-12. Reservations required 8 weeks in advance. Main courses 360–558F (€54.70–€84.80, $52–$81); fixed-price menus 985–1,490F (€149.70–€226.50, $143–$216). AE, DC, MC, V. Thurs–Fri noon–2pm; Mon–Fri 8–10:30pm. Closed mid-July to mid-Aug and Dec. 22–30. Métro: FDR or Alma-Marceau.

Moderate

Buddha Bar ✿ PACIFIC RIM/FRENCH (MODERN)   This place is hot, hot, hot—truly the restaurant of the moment in Paris. A location on a chic street near the Champs-Elysées, and allegiance to a fashionable fusion of French, Asian, and California cuisine, almost guarantees a clientele devoted to the whims of fashion. A cutting-edge culinary theme combines Japanese sashimi, Vietnamese spring rolls, lacquered duck, sautéed shrimp with black bean sauce, grilled chicken skewers with orange sauce, sweet-and-sour spareribs, and crackling squab à l'orange. Many come here just for a drink in the carefully lacquered, hip-looking bar, upstairs from the street-level dining room. Others come to enjoy the DJ's music, which begins in the late afternoon.

8 rue Boissy d'Anglas, 8e. (℃) 01-53-05-90-00. Reservations recommended. Main courses 115–260F (€17.50–€39.50, $17–$38). AE, MC, V. Mon–Fri noon–3pm; daily 6pm–2am. Métro: Concorde.

L'Astor ✿✿✿ FRENCH (MODERN)   When culinary guru Joël Robuchon retired from his citadel on avenue Raymond, he started dropping in here as a "culinary consultant." L'Astor's current chef is the well-respected Eric Lecerf, who has created his own specialties, such as roasted and braised rack of lamb and a galette of scallops with sea urchins; but those dishes invented by and forever associated with Robuchon are still on the menu. These include creamy cannelonis with eggplant, Bresse chicken with truffles and macaroni, and a gelée of caviar with cauliflower cream sauce.

In the Hôtel Astor. 11 rue d'Astorg, 8e. (℃) 01-53-05-05-20. Reservations recommended. Main courses 145–290F (€22.05–€44.10, $21–$42); set-price menus 298–540F (€45.30–€82.10, $43–$78). AE, DC, MC, V. Mon–Fri noon–2pm and 7:30–10pm. Métro: St-Augustin.

Shozan ✿ FRENCH (MODERN)/JAPANESE   East and West form a perfect synthesis in this Franco-Japanese alliance. It's not for the traditionalist, but trendy young Paris enjoys the new flavors. For example, the classic foie gras appears as foie gras sushi with sansho pepper, and the roast lamb comes with a green-tea crust. The roast tuna with buckwheat seed and the scampi concoction are delectable. A chef's specialty is lobster with white-sesame sauce spiked with sweet sake. Famous interior designer Christian Liaigre created the stunning setting, dominated by wood and leather.

11 rue de la Trémoille, 8e ☎ **01-47-23-37-32.** Reservations recommended far in advance. Main courses 165–220F (€25.10–€33.45, $24–$32); fixed-price menu 195F (€29.65, $28) at lunch, 395F (€60.05, $57) at dinner. AE, DC, MC, V. Mon–Fri noon–2:30pm; Mon–Sat 7–10:30pm. Closed 15 days in Aug. Métro: Alma-Marceau.

Spoon Food & Wine ✪ INTERNATIONAL   Alain Ducasse's newest restaurant has been both praised and condemned by Parisian food critics. Surreal, a bit absurd, the hypermodern, claustrophobic dining room evokes Paris and California. The cuisine roams the world; there are American classics such as macaroni and cheese (rather bland), and barbecued ribs, as well as dishes from Italy, Latin America, and Asia. Some dishes are more successful than others (try the steamed lobster with mango chutney, a real winner).

In the Marignan-Elysée Hotel, 14 rue Marignan, 8e. ☎ **01-40-76-34-44.** Reservations required. Main courses 135–185F (€20.50–€28.10, $20–$27). Mon–Fri noon–2pm and 7–11pm. AE, DC, MC, V. Métro: Franklin-D-Roosevelt.

RIGHT BANK: 9TH, 10TH & 16TH ARRONDISSEMENTS
Moderate

Au Petit Riche LOIRE VALLEY (ANJOU)   This bistro serves up simple well-prepared food and a sense of nostalgia. You'll be ushered to one of five different "compartments," each of which was crafted for maximum intimacy, with red velour banquettes, ceilings painted with allegorical themes, and accents of brass and frosted glass. The wine list favors Loire Valley vintages that go well with such dishes as *rillettes* and *rillons* (potted fish or meat, especially pork) in an aspic of Vouvray wine; a platter of poached fish with a buttery white-wine sauce; seasonal game dishes; and duck breast with green peppercorns.

25 rue Le Peletier, 9e. ☎ **01-47-70-68-68.** Reservations recommended. Main courses 92–135F (€14–€20.50, $13–$20); set price lunches 165F (€25.10, $24); set price dinner 140–180F (€21.30–€27.35, $20–$26). AE, MC, V. Mon–Sat noon–2:15pm and 7pm–midnight. Métro: Le Peletier or Richelieu-Drouot.

Brasserie Flo ✪ ALSATIAN   This restaurant is remote and a bit hard to find, but once you arrive (after walking through passageway after passageway), you'll see that fin-de-siècle Paris lives on. The restaurant was established in 1860 and has changed its decor very little since. The house specialty is *la formidable choucroute* (a heaping mound of sauerkraut surrounded by boiled ham, bacon, and sausage) for two. It's bountiful in the best tradition of Alsace. The onion soup and sole meunière are always good, as is the warm foie gras and guinea hen with lentils. Look for the *plats du jour* (plates of the day), ranging from roast pigeon to fricassee of veal with sorrel.

7 cour des Petites-Ecuries, 10e. ☎ **01-47-70-13-59.** Reservations recommended. Main courses 90–168F (€13.70–€25.55, $13–$24); set price lunch 138F (€21, $20); set price dinner 189F (€28.75, $27); set price late-night supper (after 10pm) 138F (€21, $20). AE, DC, MC, V. Daily noon–3pm and 7pm–1:30am. Métro: Château d'Eau or Strasbourg–St-Denis.

Relais Gourmand Faugeron ✪✪✪ FRENCH (MODERN)   Henri Faugeron is an inspired chef who many years ago opened this restaurant as an elegant yet unobtrusive backdrop for his superb cuisine, which he calls "revolutionary." Much of the zesty cuisine depends on the season and market. In winter your taste for truffles can be indulged by one of the many dishes expertly prepared, like the brunoise of truffles with asparagus and olive oil and the ravioli stuffed with truffles and foie gras. Roasted leg of milk-fed veal and lamb and crispy-skinned quail are also great choices. If you want something really esoteric, consider the vol-au-vent of lobster, sweetbreads, and morels.

52 rue de Longchamp, 16e. © 01-47-04-24-53. Fax 01-55-73-11-27. Reservations required far in advance. Main courses 250–360F (€38–€54.70, $36–$52); fixed-price menu 320–550F (€48.65–€83.60, $46–$80) at lunch, 550–700F (€83.60–€106.40, $80–$102) at dinner. AE, MC, V. Mon–Fri noon–2pm and 7–10pm (Oct–Apr dinner only, Sat 7–10pm). Closed Aug. Métro: Trocadéro or Boissière.

LEFT BANK: 5TH ARRONDISSEMENT
Very Expensive
La Tour d'Argent 🛠🛠🛠 FRENCH (TRADITIONAL)   From La Tour d'Argent, a national institution, the view over the Seine and the apse of Notre-Dame is panoramic. Although this penthouse restaurant's long-established reputation as "the best" in Paris has long since faded, dining at this temple of gastronomy remains an unsurpassed theatrical event. The restaurant became famous when it was owned by Frédéric Delair, who began issuing certificates to diners who ordered the house specialty, pressed duck (*caneton*)—it's sensational. A new, lighter dish that is divinely refined is asparagus and lobster in puff pastry. You might also try filet of sole cardinal with a mousse of pikeperch and a crayfish sauce; or filet Tour d'Argent with a chive sauce and a slice of warm foie gras resting atop the perfect piece of filet of beef.

15–17 quai de la Tournelle, 5e. © 01-43-54-23-31. Reservations required 2 months in advance. Main courses 500–700F (€76–€106.40, $73–$102); set price lunch 350F (€53.20, $51). AE, DC, MC, V. Tues–Sun noon–1pm and 7:30–9pm. Métro: Maubert-Mutualité or Pont Marie.

Inexpensive
Brasserie Balzar 🛠 FRENCH (TRADITIONAL)   Opened in 1898, this brasserie is a bit battered yet cheerful, with some of the friendliest waiters in Paris. It enjoys an increasing reputation as a hip and desirable brasserie with a scene of retro charm. The menu makes almost no concessions to nouvelle cuisine and includes steak au poivre (pepper steak), sauerkraut garnished with ham and sausage, pigs' feet, and calves' liver. The food is decently prepared, and who wants to come up with anything new when what has been served for more than 40 years is just fine?

49 rue des Écoles, 5e. © 01-43-54-13-67. Reservations required. Main courses 100–120F (€15.20–€18.25, $15–$17). AE, MC, V. Daily noon–11:45am. Métro: Cluny–La Sorbonne.

Coco de Mer 🛠 *(Finds* SEYCHELLE   The theme of this restaurant tugs at the emotions of the thousands of Parisians who have spent their holidays on the legendary beaches of the Seychelles in the Indian Ocean. It contains at least three dining rooms, one of which is outfitted like a beach. Menu items feature such exotic dishes as tartare of tuna flavored with ginger, olive oil, salt and pepper; and smoked swordfish, served either as a carpaccio or in thin slices with mango mousse and a spicy sauce. Main courses focus on fish, including a species of delectable red snapper (*boirzoes*), which is imported from the Seychelles. Dessert might consist of a *crème de banane gratinée*.

34 bd. St-Marcel, 5e © 01-41-07-06-64. Reservations recommended. Main courses 90–110F (€13.70–€16.70, $13–$16). AE, DC, MC, V. Tues–Sat noon–3pm; Mon–Sat 7:30pm–midnight. Métro: Les Gobelins or St-Marcel.

La Petite Hostellerie 🛠 *(Value* FRENCH (TRADITIONAL)   This place has a usually crowded ground-floor dining room and a larger one upstairs. People come for the cozy ambience and decor, decent French country cooking, polite service, and excellent prices. The set price menu might feature favorites like *coq au vin* (chicken cooked in wine), *canard* (duckling) *à l'orange,* or *entrecôte à la moutarde* (steak with mustard sauce). Start with onion soup or stuffed mussels and finish with cheese or salad and peach Melba or apple tart. The menu and everything else remains virtually unchanged year after year.

35 rue de la Harpe (just east of bd. St-Michel), 5e. ℂ **01-43-29-73-57.** All main courses 59F (€8.95, $9), set price menus 59–89F (€8.95–€13.55, $9–$13). AE, DC, MC, V. Mon–Sat noon–2pm and 6:30–10:45pm. Métro: St-Michel or Cluny–La Sorbonne.

LEFT BANK: 6TH ARRONDISSEMENT
Expensive
Jacques Cagna ✰✰✰ FRENCH (TRADITIONAL & MODERN)   Both the food and the clientele in this 17th-century town house are among the grandest in Paris. Menu items are flavorful and creative. Examples include prawns roasted in a lobster sauce with lemon; and snails "surprise-style à la Jacques Cagna" whereby they're removed from their shells and served with butter within a small roasted potato. A particular favorite of ours involves a chicken from Houdan (an Île de France town known for its poultry) that's served as a main course in two separate servings: The first part involves the roasted breast *demi-deuil,* in which truffles have stained the white meat dark. The second combines the roasted thigh with garden vegetables.

14 rue des Grands-Augustins, 6e. ℂ **01-43-26-49-39.** Reservations required. Main courses 200–400F (€30.40–€60.80, $29–$58); set price menu 270F (€41.05, $39) at lunch, 490F (€74.50, $71) at dinner. AE, DC, MC, V. Tues–Fri noon–2pm and Mon–Sat 7:30–10:30pm. Closed 3 weeks in Aug. Métro: St-Michel.

Moderate
Alcazar Bar & Restaurant ✰ FRENCH (MODERN)   One of Paris's newest high-profile, high-style brasseries deluxe is this artfully hi-tech establishment. It features an all-white, futuristic decor within a large, street-level dining room and a busy and hyper-stylish bar one floor above. Especially good dishes include grilled entrecôte with béarnaise sauce and fried potatoes; Charolais duckling with honey and spices; sashimi and sushi with lime; filet of monkfish with saffron in puff pastry; and a comprehensive collection of shellfish and oysters from the waters of Brittany. Wines are stylish and diverse; and the clientele includes lots of trendsetters wearing lots of black.

62 rue Mazarine, 6e. ℂ **01-53-10-19-99.** Reservations recommended. Set price lunches 140–160F (€21.30–€24.30, $20–$23); main courses 90–170F (€13.70–€25.85, $13–$25). AE, DC, MC, V. Daily noon–3pm and 7pm–2am. Métro: Odéon.

Inexpensive
Crémerie-Restaurant Polidor ✰ FRENCH (TRADITIONAL)   Frequented by students and artists, this is one of the Left Bank's most established literary bistros, and has changed little since opening in 1930. Lace curtains and brass hat racks add to the old-fashioned atmosphere. Food is traditional: pumpkin soup, snails from Burgundy, veal in white sauce, confit of duckling, and a supremely old-fashioned holdover from the France of yesterday—roasted guinea fowl with cabbage and ham. The *"crémerie"* of its name refers to its specialty, frosted crème desserts.

41 rue Monsieur-le-Prince, 6e. ℂ **01-43-26-95-34.** Reservations not accepted. Main courses 40–78F (€6.10–€11.85, $6–$11); set price lunch (Mon–Fri) 55–110F (€8.35–€16.70, $8–$16); set price dinner 110F (€16.70, $16). No credit cards. Mon–Sat noon–2:30pm and 7pm–12:30am; Sun noon–2:30pm and 7–12:30am. Métro: Odéon.

LEFT BANK: 7TH ARRONDISSEMENT
Expensive
Le Violon d'Ingres 🌴🌴🌴 FRENCH (TRADITIONAL & MODERN)   For a chance to experience chef/owner Christian Constant's gastronomic master-pieces, you have to reserve a table a minimum of 3 to 4 days in advance. The cleverly artistic dishes range from a starter of pan-fried foie gras with gingerbread and spinach salad to more elegant main courses such as lobster ravioli with crushed vine-ripened tomatoes, roasted veal in a light and creamy milk sauce served with tender spring vegetables, or even a selection from the popular rôtis-serie. Even his familiar dishes seem new at each tasting. Chef Constant keeps a copious and well-chosen selection of wine to accompany his overwhelmingly satisfying meals. The service is charming and discreet.

135 rue St-Dominique, 7e. ℂ 01-45-55-15-05. Fax 01-45-55-48-42. Reservations required. Main courses 190–230F (€28.90–€34.95, $28–$33); fixed-price menu 240–400F (€36.50–€60.80, $35–$58) at lunch, 490F (€74.50, $71) at dinner. AE, MC, V. Tues–Sat noon–2:30pm and 7–11pm. Métro: École Militaire.

Moderate
La Petite Chaise (Value FRENCH (TRADITIONAL)   This is Paris's oldest restaurant, established by the baron de la Chaise in 1680. The only option is a cost-conscious four-course set menu with a large choice of dishes. Choices might include marinated salmon with anise and a creamy mustard sauce; a selection of fresh fish and scallops in saffron sauce with pink potatoes; a salad of leeks and country ham with red-beet vinaigrette; a mignon of pork with figs and honey; and a special dessert of roasted figs with pistachios and vanilla ice cream.

36–38 rue de Grenelle, 7e. ℂ 01-42-22-13-35. Reservations recommended. Set price menus 160–195F (€24.30–€29.65, $23–$28). AE, MC, V. Daily noon–2pm and 7–11pm. Métro: Sèvres-Babylone.

Inexpensive
Chez L'Ami Jean BASQUE/SOUTHWESTERN FRENCH   Ardent fans claim that this is the most authentic Basque restaurant on the Left Bank. You'll dine amid a decor that's as close to an authentic Basque *auberge* (inn) as any other in Paris, with wood panels, sports memorabilia, and red-and-white woven tablecloths. Menu items include cured Bayonne ham; earthy and herb-laden vegetable soups in the style of Béarn; marinated anchovies and fresh duck liver; confit de canard (duckling); and a succulent omelet (*piperade basque*) laden with peppers, tomatoes, and onions.

27 rue Malar, 7e. ℂ 01-47-05-86-89. Reservations recommended. Main courses 180–200F (€27.35–€30.40, $26–$29). Set menu 99F (€15.05, $14). MC, V. Mon–Sat noon–3pm and 7–10:30pm. Closed Aug. Métro: Invalides.

SEEING THE SIGHTS IN THE CITY OF LIGHT
The best way to discover Paris is on foot. Walk along the grand avenue des Champs-Elysées, tour the quays of the Seine, wander around Île de la Cité and Île St-Louis, browse through the countless shops and stalls, wander through the famous squares and parks. Each turn will open a new vista.

SIGHTSEEING SUGGESTIONS FOR FIRST-TIME VISITORS
If You Have 1 Day Get up early and find a little cafe for a typical Parisian breakfast of coffee and crois-sants. If you're a museum and monument junkie, you'll already know that the two most popular museums are the **Louvre** and the **Musée d'Orsay,** and the three most

🅲 Cafe Society

In Paris, cafes are catch-all institutions for social rendezvous, business meetings, letter writing, coffee or wine drinking, snacking, flirting, people-watching, fashion gazing, and so on. Here's our pick of some of the city's most appealing and interesting.

Brasserie Lipp, 151 bd. St-Germain, 6e (🅲 **01-45-48-53-91;** Métro: St-Germain-des-Prés), is known as the "rendezvous for le tout Paris." There's an upstairs dining room, but it's more fashionable to sit in the back room. It's open daily from 9am to 1am, though restaurant service is available only from noon to 1am. Across from the Centre Pompidou, the avant-garde **Café Beaubourg,** 100 rue St-Martin, 4e (🅲 **01-48-87-63-96;** Métro: Rambuteau or Hôtel de Ville), boasts a minimalist decor. In summer, tables are set on the terrace, providing a panoramic view of the neighborhood. It's open from Sunday to Thursday 8am to 1am and Friday and Saturday 8am to 2am.

Fouquet's, 99 av. des Champs-Elysées, 8e (🅲 **01-47-23-70-60;** Métro: George V), is the premier cafe on the Champs-Elysées. The outside tables are separated from the sidewalk by a barricade of potted flowers. Throughout, you'll find a decor of leather banquettes, rattan furniture, and a sense of Champs-Elysées bustle. Fouquet's street level is open as a cafe that serves platters of food, salads, tea, omelets, ice cream, and light platters of food every day from 8am till 2am. One floor above street level is a comfortable and relatively formal restaurant open daily from noon to 3pm and 7pm to 12:30am.

The legendary **Deux Magots,** 6 place St-Germain-des-Prés, 6e (🅲 **01-45-48-55-25;** Métro: St-Germain-des-Prés), is still the hangout for sophisticated neighborhood residents and a tourist favorite in summer. Inside are two large Asian statues that give the cafe its name. It's open daily from 7:30am to 1:30am. At **La Coupole,** 102 bd. Montparnasse, 14e (🅲 **01-43-20-14-20;** Métro: Vavin), the clientele ranges from artists' models to young men dressed like Rasputin. The dining room looks like a rail station but serves surprisingly good food daily from 8:30am to 2am for around 200F (€30.40, $29).

The **Café de la Musique,** 212 av. Jean-Jaurès, 19e (🅲 **01-48-03-15-91;** Métro: Porte de Pantin), lies within the Cité de la Musique—one of the grandest of Mitterrand's *grands travaux.* The site guarantees the presence of a crowd passionately devoted to music. Its modern red-and-green velour setting has a theatricality evocative of a modern opera house. The windows overlook the lions of the modern fountains within nearby place de la Fontaine. They also offer a light menu for 150F (€22.80, $22). It's open daily from 7am to 2am, and there's live jazz every Wednesday from 10pm to 1am.

enduring monuments are the **Eiffel Tower,** the **Arc de Triomphe,** and **Notre-Dame** (which you can save for later in the day). If it's a toss-up

between the Louvre and the d'Orsay, we'd make it the Louvre if you're a first-timer; if it's a toss-up between monuments, we'd make it the Eiffel

Paris Attractions

Musée d'Art Moderne **4**
Musée d'Orsay **9**
Musée du Louvre **10**
Musée National du Moyen
Age/Thermes de Cluny **11**

Musée Picasso **21**
Panthéon **13**
Parc Monceau **6**
Place de la Bastille **15**

Place de la Concorde **7**
Place des Vosges **16**
Sainte-Chapelle **18**
Tour Eiffel **3**

Tower, for the panoramic view of the city. If you feel your day is too short to visit museums, then spend your time strolling—the streets of Paris are live theater. The most elegant place for a walk in Paris is Île St-Louis, filled with 17th-century mansions. On the **Left Bank,** wander St-Germain-des-Prés or the area around place St-Michel, the heart of the student quarter. As the sun sets over Paris, head for **Notre-Dame,** which stands majestically along the banks of the Seine, and watch the shadows fall over Paris and the lights come on for the night.

If You Have 2 Days If you explored the Left Bank on your first day, spend your second day taking in the glories of the Right Bank. Begin at the **Arc de Triomphe** and stroll down the grand **Champs-Elysées,** the main boulevard of Paris, until you reach the Egyptian obelisk at the **place de la Concorde.** The place de la Concorde— where some of France's most notable figures met the guillotine— affords terrific views of the **Madeleine,** the **Palais Bourbon,** the Arc de Triomphe, and the Louvre. After all this walking, we'd suggest a rest stop in the **Jardin de Tuileries,** or a long lunch in a Right Bank bistro. After exploring the heart of elegant, monumental Paris, why not go for a walk on the seedy side? Our favorite is a stroll along rue des Rosiers in the **Marais,** a narrow street that's the heart of the

Jewish community. After a rest back at your hotel, follow Hemingway's footsteps and head down to **Montparnasse** for a lively dinner.

If You Have 3 Days This is the day to follow your special interests. Most visitors will want to select the newly reopened **Centre Pompidou,** which will eat up most of your day. You might save time to explore the **Musée Picasso** as well, along with some of the trendy art galleries of the Marais. At midday, head for lunch to Paris's oldest and most charming square, **place des Vosges.** Reserve the afternoon for the **Île-de-la-Cité,** where you can revisit Notre-Dame and see the **Conciergerie,** where Marie Antoinette and others were held prisoner before beheading, and the **Sainte-Chapelle** in the Palais de Justice with its stunning stained glass. For dinner, we suggest a bistro in Le Marais.

If You Have 4 or 5 Days On your fourth day, go on your own or take an organized tour to **Versailles.** Then head back to the city for dinner and an evening stroll in the **Latin Quarter.** Some of the livelier streets for wandering include the rue de la Huchette and rue Monsieur-le-Prince. On your fifth day, devote at least a morning to **Montmarte,** the former artists' community perched on top of the highest of Paris's seven hills. Visit the **Basilica du Sacré-Coeur,** for the view if nothing else.

THE TOP MUSEUMS

Musée du Louvre ✮✮✮   The Louvre is the world's largest palace and largest museum. You'll have no choice but to miss certain masterpieces since you won't have the time or stamina to see everything—the Louvre's collection is truly staggering. People on one of those "Paris-in-a-day" tours try to break track records to stand with the crowds and see the two most famous ladies here: the *Mona Lisa* and the *Venus de Milo.* Those with an extra 5 minutes go in pursuit of *Winged Victory,* the headless statue discovered at Samothrace and dating from about 200 B.C.

(*Tips*) **Attention Museum Mavens**

Le Pass-Musée (Museum and Monuments Pass) is available at any of the museums that honor it or at any branch of the Paris Tourist Office (see earlier in this chapter). It offers entrance to the permanent collections of 70 monuments and museums in Paris and the Île de France. A 1-day pass is 80F (€12.15, $120), a 3-day pass 160F (€24.30, $23), and a 5-day pass 240F (€36.50, $35).

To enter the Louvre, you pass through the 22-m (71-ft.) I. M. Pei glass pyramid in the courtyard. The collections are divided into departments; those with little time should go on one of the guided tours (in English), lasting about 1½ hours.

Our favorite works include *Ship of Fools* by Hieronymous Bosch (tucked in the Flemish galleries)—no one can depict folly and greed more vividly; *Four Seasons* by Nicolas Poussin, the canonical work of French classicism; Eugène Delacroix's *Liberty Leading the People,* the ultimate endorsement of revolution; and Veronese's gigantic *Wedding Feast at Cana,* showing how stunning colors can be when used by a master. The Richelieu Wing houses northern European and French paintings, along with decorative arts, French sculpture, Asian antiquities (a rich collection of Islamic art), and the grand salons of Napoléon III. The splendid collection of Egyptian artifacts, portrait busts, and sarcophagi, as well as ancient Greek ceramics, is on the ground floor and first floor of the Sully Wing.

Palais de Louvre, 1er. (*C*) **01-40-20-53-17,** or 01-40-20-51-51 for recorded information; advance credit card sales 01-49-87-54-54. www.louvre.fr. Admission 45F (€6.85, $7) before 3pm, 26F (€3.95, $3.75) after 3pm and all day Sun; free for children 17 and under. Free first Sun of every month. Mon and Wed 9am–9:45pm (Mon, short tour only), Thurs–Sun 9am–6pm. 90-minute English-language tours leave Mon and Wed–Sat at various times for 17F (€2.60, $2.45) adults and children alike. Métro: Palais Royal-Musée du Louvre.

Musée d'Orsay *★★★*   The handsome neoclassical Gare d'Orsay rail station has been transformed into a repository of 19th-century art and civilization. The museum houses sculptures and paintings spread across 80 galleries, plus Belle Époque furniture, photographs, objets d'art, architectural models, and even a cinema. One of Renoir's most joyous paintings is here—*Moulin de la Galette* (1876). Another celebrated work is by American James McNeill Whistler—*Arrangement in Grey and Black: Portrait of the Painter's Mother.* The most famous piece in the museum is Manet's 1863 *Déjeuner sur l'herbe (Picnic on the Grass),* which created a scandal when it was first exhibited.

1 rue de Bellechasse or 62 rue de Lille, 7e. (*C*) **01-40-49-48-14.** Admission 40F (€6.10, $6) adults, 30F (€4.55, $4.35) ages 18–24 and seniors, free for children 17 and under. Tues–Wed and Fri–Sat 10am–6pm; Thurs 10am–9:45pm; Sun 9am–6pm. June 20–Sept 20, museum opens 9am. Métro: Solférino. RER: Musée-d'Orsay.

Musée Picasso *★★*   When it opened in the beautifully restored Hôtel Salé, the press hailed it as a "museum for Picasso's Picassos," meaning those he chose not to sell. The greatest Picasso collection in the world, acquired by the state in lieu of $50 million in inheritance taxes, consists of 203 paintings, 158 sculptures, 16 collages, 19 bas-reliefs, 88 ceramics, and more than 1,500 sketches and 1,600 engravings, along with 30 notebooks. These works span 75 years of Picasso's life and changing styles. The range of paintings includes a remarkable 1901 self-portrait and embraces such masterpieces as *Le Baiser (The Kiss).*

painted at Mougins in 1969, and *Reclining Nude* and *The Man with a Guitar*. *Note:* Higher admission prices are charged during special exhibitions.

5 rue de Thorigny, 3e. (℃ **01-42-71-25-21**. Admission 30F (€4.55, $4.35) adults, 20F (€3.05, $2.90) ages 19–24 and over 60, free for ages 18 and under. Apr–Sept Wed–Mon 9:30am–6pm; Oct–Mar Wed–Mon 9:30am–5:30pm. Métro: St-Paul, Filles du Calvaire, Chemin Vert or Châtelet Les Halles.

Centre Pompidou 𝕽𝕽𝕽   Relaunched in January 2000, in what in the 1970s was called "the most avant-garde building in the world," the restored Pompidou Center is packing in the art-loving crowds again. The dream of former president Georges Pompidou, this center for 20th-century art (designed by Renzo Piano) opened in 1977 and immediately became the focus of loud controversy: Its bold exoskeletal architecture and the brightly painted pipes and ducts crisscrossing its transparent facade were jarring in the old Beaubourg neighborhood. Perhaps the detractors were right all along—within 20 years the building began to deteriorate so badly that a major restoration was called for.

The Centre Pompidou encompasses four separate attractions. The **Musée National d'Art Moderne** (National Museum of Modern Art) offers a large collection of 20th-century art. If you want to view some real charmers, see Alexander Calder's 1926 *Josephine Baker,* one of his earliest versions of the mobile. Marcel Duchamps's *Valise* is a collection of miniature reproductions of his fabled Dada sculptures and drawings; they're displayed in a carrying case. And every time we visit Paris we have to see Salvador Dalí's *Portrait of Lenin Dancing on Piano Keys*. In the **Public Information Library** the public has free access to a million French and foreign books, periodicals, films, records, slides, and microfilms in nearly every area of knowledge. The **Center for Industrial Design** emphasizes the contributions made in the fields of architecture, visual communications, publishing, and community planning; and the **Institute for Research and Coordination of Acoustics/Music** brings together musicians and composers interested in furthering the cause of music, both contemporary and traditional. Finally, you can also visit a re-creation of the jazz-age studio of Romanian sculptor Brancusi (**l'Atelier Brancusi**), which is configured as a mini-museum that's slightly separate from the rest of the action.

Place Georges-Pompidou, 4e. (℃ **01-44-78-12-33**. Admission 30F (€4.55, $4.35) adults, 20F (€3.05, $2.90) students, free under 13. Special exhibitions 40F (€6.10, $6) adults, 30F (€4.55, $4.35) students, free for children under 13. Wed–Mon 11am–9pm. Métro: Rambuteau, Hôtel de Ville, or Châtelet-Les-Halles.

ON THE CHAMPS-ELYSÉES

In late 1995, Paris's most prominent triumphal promenade was augmented with several important improvements. The *contre-allées* (side lanes that had always been clogged with parked cars) have been removed, new lighting and underground parking garages added, sidewalks widened, and new trees planted. Now the Grand Promenade truly is grand again.

Tips **More Museum Tips**

Museums require that you check shopping bags and book bags, and sometimes lines for these can be longer than ticket and admission lines. Visitors who value their time should leave these bags behind or do shopping afterward. Ask if a museum has more than one coat line; if so, avoid the main one and go to the less frequented ones.

Arc de Triomphe   At the western end of the Champs-Elysées, the Arc de Triomphe is the world's largest triumphal arch, about 50m (163 ft.) high and 45m (147ft.) wide. Commissioned by Napoléon in 1806 to commemorate his Grande Armée's victories, it wasn't completed until 1836, under Louis-Philippe. Four years later, Napoléon's remains—brought from his grave on St. Helena— passed under the arch on their journey to his tomb at the Invalides. Since then it has become the focal point for state funerals. It's also the site of the tomb of the unknown soldier, where an eternal flame is kept burning.

Place Charles-de-Gaulle–Étoile, 8e. (C) 01-55-37-73-77. Admission 40F (€6.10, $6) adults, 25F (€3.80, $3.65) ages 13–25 and over 60, free for children 12 and under. Free first Sun of every month. Apr–Sept daily 9:30am–11pm; Oct–Mar daily 10am–10:30pm. Métro: Charles de Gaulle-Étoile.

ÎLE DE LA CITÉ: WHERE PARIS WAS BORN

Medieval Paris, that architectural blending of grotesquerie and Gothic beauty, began on this island in the Seine. Explore as much of it as you can, but if you're in a hurry, try to visit at least Notre-Dame, the Sainte-Chapelle, and the Conciergerie.

Cathédrale Notre-Dame ★★★   This is the world's most famous Gothic cathedral. From square Parvis, you can view the trio of 13th-century sculptured portals: On the left, the Portal of the Virgin depicts the signs of the Zodiac and the Virgin's coronation. The restored central Portal of the Last Judgment is divided into three levels: The first shows Vices and Virtues; the second, Christ and his Apostles; the third, Christ in triumph after the Resurrection. On the right is the Portal of St. Anne, depicting such scenes as the Virgin enthroned with Child, the most perfect piece of sculpture in Notre-Dame. Equally interesting (though often missed) is the Portal of the Cloisters around on the left.

The interior is typical Gothic, with slender, graceful columns. Over the central portal is the remarkable rose window, 9m (31 ft.) in diameter. The carved-stone choir screen from the early 14th century depicts such biblical scenes as the Last Supper. Near the altar stands the highly venerated 14th-century Virgin and Child. To visit those grimy gargoyles (immortalized by Victor Hugo as Quasimodo's hangout), you have to scale steps leading to the twin square towers, rising to a height of 69m (225 ft.).

The **crypt** (La crypte archéologique du parvis Notre-Dame), lying under the square in the front of the cathedral, has been turned into an archaeological museum, containing artifacts from previous churches that have stood on this site. There are even artifacts from the Parisians who lived here some 20 centuries ago. Excavations carried out in the 1960s unearthed many of these relics. You can also view the foundations of a Gallo-Roman rampart from the 3rd century and the foundations of the Merovingian church from the 6th century.

6 place du Parvis Notre-Dame, 4e. (C) 01-42-34-56-10. Cathedral, free. Towers 35F (€5.30, $5) adults, 23F (€3.50, $3.35) ages 12–25 and over 60. Free for ages 12 and under. Museum and treasury 15F (€2.30, $2.20) adults, 9F (€1.35, $1.30) ages 12–25 and over 60, free for ages 12 and under. Crypt 33F (€5, $4.84) ages 27–60, free otherwise. Cathedral daily 8am–6:45pm year-round. Towers, Apr–Sept daily 9:30am–6pm; Oct–Mar daily 10am–5:15pm. Museum, Wed and Sat–Sun 2:30–6pm. Treasury, Mon–Sat 9am–noon and 1–5:30pm; Tues–Sun 10am–5:30pm. Métro: Cité or St-Michel. RER: St-Michel-Notre-Dame.

Sainte-Chapelle ★★★   Sainte-Chapelle is Paris's second most important medieval monument after Notre-Dame. It was erected in the flamboyant Gothic style to enshrine relics no longer there, including the Crown of Thorns and two pieces from the True Cross. The walls of the upper chapel consist almost entirely of 15 superb stained-glass windows, and viewed on a bright day with the sun streaming in, they glow with marvelous ruby reds and Chartres blues. The lower level of the chapel is supported by flying buttresses and ornamented with fleurs-de-lis—it was used by the palace servants, the upper chapel by the king and his courtiers.

Palais de Justice, 4 bd. du Palais, 1er. ℂ 01-53-73-78-50. Admission 40F (€6.10, $6) adults, 25F (€3.80, $3.65), students and ages 12–25, free for children under 12. Value ticket for Sainte Chapelle and Conciergerie for 50F (€7.60, $7.25). Apr–Sept daily 9:30am–6:30pm; Oct–Mar daily 10am–5pm. Métro: Cité, St-Michel, or Châtelet.

Conciergerie ⭐⭐   The Conciergerie has been called the most sinister building in France. Though it had a long regal history before the revolution, it's visited today chiefly by those wishing to bask in the Reign of Terror's horrors. You approach the Conciergerie through its landmark twin towers, the Tour d'Argent and Tour de César, but the 14th-century vaulted Guard Room is the actual entrance. Also from the 14th century—and even more interesting—is the vast, dark, foreboding *Salle des Gens d'Armes* (People at Arms), chillingly changed from the days when the king used it as a banqueting hall.

1 quai de l'Horloge, 1er. ℂ 01-53-73-78-50. Admission 35F (€5.30, $5) adults, 23F (€3.50, $3.35) ages 12–25 and over 60, free for children under 12. Apr–Sept daily 9:30am–6:30pm; Oct–Mar daily 10am–5pm. Métro: Cité or Châtelet.

ANOTHER ISLAND IN THE STREAM: ÎLE ST-LOUIS ⭐⭐⭐

As you walk across the iron footbridge from the rear of Notre-Dame, you enter into a world of tree-shaded quays, aristocratic town houses and courtyards, restaurants, and antiques shops.

The sibling island of Île de la Cité, Île St-Louis is primarily residential; its denizens fiercely guard their heritage, privileges, and special position. It was originally two "islets," one named Island of the Heifers. Plaques on the facades make it easier to identify former residents. Madame Curie, for example, lived at 36 quai de Bethune, near ponte de la Tournelle, from 1912 until her death in 1934.

The most exciting mansion is the **Hôtel de Lauzun,** built in 1657, at 17 quai d'Anjou; it's named after a 17th-century rogue, the duc de Lauzun, famous lover and on-again/off-again favorite of Louis XIV. French poet Charles Baudelaire lived here in the 19th century with his "Black Venus," Jeanne Duval. Voltaire resided in the **Hôtel Lambert,** 2 quai d'Anjou, with his mistress, Emilie de Breteuil, the marquise du Châteley (who had an understanding husband).

THE EIFFEL TOWER & ENVIRONS ⭐⭐⭐

From place du Trocadéro, you can step between the two curved wings of the Palais de Chaillot and gaze out on a panoramic view. At your feet lie the Jardins du Trocadéro, centered by fountains. Directly in front of you, the pont d'Iéna spans the Seine, leading to the iron immensity of the Tour Eiffel. And beyond, stretching as far as your eye can see, is the Champ-de-Mars, once a military parade ground but now a garden with arches, grottoes, lakes, and cascades.

Tour Eiffel ⭐⭐⭐   After the Leaning Tower of Pisa, this is the single most recognizable structure in the world—the symbol of Paris. Weighing 10,000 tons but exerting about the same pressure on the ground as an average-size person sitting in a chair, the tower was never meant to be permanent. It was built for the Universal Exhibition of 1889 by Gustave-Alexandre Eiffel, the engineer whose fame rested mainly on his iron bridges. The tower, including its 17-m (55-ft.) TV antenna, is 317m (1,056 ft.) tall. On a clear day, you can see it from some 65km (40 miles) away. An open-framework construction, the tower ushered in the almost-unlimited possibilities of steel construction, paving the way for the

20th century's skyscrapers. You can visit the tower in three stages: Taking the elevator to the first landing, you have a view over the rooftops of Paris; the second landing provides a panoramic look at the city; the third gives the most spectacular view, allowing you to identify monuments and buildings.

Champ-de-Mars, 7e. © **01-44-11-23-23**. www.tour-eiffel.fr. First landing, 27F (€4.10, $3.90); second landing, 43F (€6.55, $6); third landing, 60F (€9.10, $9); stairs to second landing, 15F (€2.35, $2.20). Sept–May daily 9:30am–11pm; June–Aug daily 9am–midnight (in fall and winter the stairs close at 6:15pm). Métro: Bir Hakeim, Trocadéro, or École Militaire. RER: Champ de Mars-Tour Eiffel.

Hôtel des Invalides (Napoléon's Tomb) ★★★   The glory of the French military lives on here in the Musée de l'Armée, the world's greatest army museum. It was the Sun King who decided to build the "hotel" to house soldiers who'd been disabled. Among the collections are Viking swords, Burgundian bacinets, 14th-century blunderbusses, Balkan khandjars, salamander-engraved Renaissance serpentines, and American Browning machine guns. As a sardonic touch, there's even General Daumesnil's wooden leg. To accommodate the Tomb of Napoléon—red porphyry on a green granite base—the architect Visconti had to redesign the high altar in 1842. Surrounding the tomb are a dozen Amazon-like figures representing Napoléon's victories.

At the **Musée des Plans-Reliefs,** you'll find detailed sketches and scale models of the many fortresses of France, beginning with the Middle Ages. It's a subcomponent of the Musée de l'Armée.

129 rue de Grenelle, 7e. © **01-44-42-37-72**. Admission to Musée de l'Armée, Napoléon's Tomb, and Musée des Plans-Reliefs (© **01-45-51-95-05**) 38F (€5.80, $6) adults, 28F (€4.25, $4.05) children 12–18, free for children 11 and under. Oct–Mar daily 10am–6:45pm; Apr–May and Sept daily 10am–6pm; June–Aug daily 10am–9pm. Closed Jan 1, May 1, Nov 1, and Dec 25. Métro: Invalides, Varenne, or Latour-Maubourg.

IN MONTMARTRE ★★★

From the 1880s to just before World War I, Montmartre enjoyed its golden age as the world's best-known art colony. *La Vie de bohème* reigned supreme. Following World War I the pseudoartists flocked here in droves, with camera-snapping tourists hot on their heels. The real artists had long gone to such places as Montparnasse.

Before its discovery and subsequent chic, Montmartre was a sleepy farming community, with windmills dotting the landscape. Since it's at the highest point in the city, if you find it too much of a climb you may want to take the miniature train along the steep streets: **Le Petit Train de Montmartre,** which passes all the major landmarks and seats 55 passengers who can listen to the recorded English-language commentary. Board the train at the bottom of the hill, at Place Blanche (Métro: Blanche), near the Moulin Rouge, and ride it uphill to place du Tertre, within a very short walk of the crest of the hill and its monumental basilica. From June to August, trains run daily from 10am to midnight (at other times to 6pm). The price of 32F (€4.85, $4.65) adults and 10F (€1.50, $1.45) ages 2 to 12 allows you to ascend and descend *la butte* within any of the trains, getting on or off wherever you please en route. Ascents and descents of the hill take about 20 minutes each. For information, contact **Promotrain,** 131 rue de Clignancourt, 18e (© **01-42-62-24-00**).

The simplest way to reach Montmartre is to take the Métro to Anvers, then walk up rue du Steinkerque to the funicular, which runs to the precincts of Sacré-Coeur daily 6am to 11pm.

Basilique du Sacré-Coeur ★★★   De Montmartre's crowning achievement is Sacré-Coeur, though the view of Paris from its precincts takes precedence over the basilica itself. In gleaming white, it towers over Paris—its five bulbous domes suggesting some 12th-century Byzantine church and its campanile inspired by Roman-Byzantine art. After France's defeat by the Prussians in 1870, the basilica was planned as an offering to cure the country's misfortunes. Both rich and poor contributed money to build it. Construction began in 1873, but the church was not consecrated until 1919. On a clear day the vista from the dome can extend for 56km (35 miles).

Place St-Pierre, 18e. ✆ 01-53-41-89-00. Basilica, free; joint ticket to dome and crypt 30F (€4.55, $4.35) adults, 16F (€2.45, $2.30) students and children. Apr–Sept daily 9am–6:45pm; Oct–Mar daily 9am–5:45pm. Métro: Abbesses; then take the elevator to the surface and follow the signs to the funiculaire, which goes up to the church for the price of one Métro ticket.

IN THE LATIN QUARTER 🏰🏰

This is the Left Bank precinct of the **University of Paris** (the **Sorbonne**). Rabelais called it the Quartier Latin, because of the students and professors who spoke Latin in the classrooms and on the streets. The sector teems with belly dancers, exotic restaurants from Vietnamese to Balkan, sidewalk cafes, bookstalls, and caveaux.

A good starting point is **place St-Michel** (Métro: St-Michel), where Balzac used to get water from the fountain when he was a youth. This center was the scene of much Resistance fighting in summer 1944. The quarter centers around **boulevard St-Michel,** to the south (the students call it "Boul Mich").

Musée National du Moyen Age/Thermes de Cluny (Musée de Cluny) 🏰🏰   There are two reasons to go here: The museum houses the world's finest collection of art from the Middle Ages, including jewelry and tapestries, and it's all displayed in a well-preserved manor house built on top of Roman bathrooms. In the cobblestone Court of Honor, you can admire the flamboyant Gothic building with its clinging vines, turreted walls, gargoyles, and dormers with seashell motifs. Along with the Hôtel de Sens in the Marais, this is all that remains in Paris of domestic medieval architecture. Most people come primarily to see the Unicorn Tapestries—all the romance of the age of chivalry lives on in these remarkable yet mysterious tapestries, showing a beautiful princess and her handmaiden, beasts of prey, and just plain pets. They were discovered only a century ago in the Château de Boussac in the Auvergne. Downstairs are the ruins of Roman baths, dating from around A.D. 200. You wander through a display of Gallic and Roman sculptures and an interesting marble bathtub engraved with lions. 6 place Paul-Painlevé, 5e. ✆ 01-53-73-78-00. Admission 30F (€4.55, $4.35) adults, 20F (€3.05, $2.90) ages 18–25, free for age 17 and under and Sun for everyone. Wed–Mon 9:15am–5:45pm. Métro: Cluny-La Sorbonne.

HISTORIC GARDENS & SQUARES

GARDENS   Bordering place de la Concorde, the statue-studded **Jardin des Tuileries** 🏰🏰 (✆ 01-40-20-90-43; Métro: Tuileries) are as much a part of Paris as the Seine. They were designed by Le Nôtre, Louis XIV's gardener and planner of the Versailles grounds. About 100 years before that, Catherine de Médici ordered a palace built here, connected to the Louvre. Twice attacked by enraged Parisians, it was finally burned to the ground in 1871 and never rebuilt.

The **Jardin du Luxembourg** 🏰🏰, 6e (✆ 01-53-35-89-35, Métro: Odéon; RER: Luxembourg), has always been associated with artists, though students from the Sorbonne and children predominate nowadays. The gardens are the best on the Left Bank (if not in all of Paris). Marie de Médici, the much-neglected

---

(Fun Fact **Hemingway in the Luxembourg Gardens**

Hemingway told a friend that the Luxembourg Gardens "kept us from starvation." He related that in his poverty-stricken days in Paris, he wheeled a baby carriage through the gardens because it was known "for the classiness of its pigeons." When the gendarme left to get a glass of wine, the writer would eye his victim, then lure it with corn and snatch it. "We got a little tired of pigeon that year," he confessed, "but they filled many a void."

---

wife and later widow of the roving Henri IV, ordered the Palais du Luxembourg built on this site in 1612.

SQUARES   In **place de la Bastille** 🇫 on July 14, 1789, a mob of Parisians attacked the Bastille and thus sparked the French Revolution. Nothing remains of the historic Bastille, built in 1369. Many prisoners were kept within its walls, the best known being the "Man in the Iron Mask." When the fortress was stormed, only seven prisoners were discovered (the marquis de Sade had been transferred to the madhouse 10 days earlier). Bastille Day is celebrated with great festivity on July 14. In the center of the square is the Colonne de Juillet (July Column), but it doesn't commemorate the revolution. It honors the victims of the 1830 July revolution, which put Louis-Philippe on the throne.

Place des Vosges 🇫🇫🇫, 4e (Métro: St-Paul or Chemin Vert), is Paris's oldest square and was once the most fashionable. In the heart of the Marais, it was called the Palais Royal in the days of Henri IV, who planned to live here—but his assassin, Ravaillac, had other ideas. Henry II was killed while jousting on the square in 1559. Place des Vosges was one of the first planned squares in Europe. Its grand siècle redbrick houses are ornamented with white stone. Its covered arcades allowed people to shop at all times, even in the rain—quite an innovation at the time.

The Champs-Elysées begins at **place de la Concorde** 🇫🇫🇫, an octagonal traffic hub ordered built in 1757 to honor Louis XV and one of the world's grandest squares. The statue of the king was torn down in 1792 and the name of the square changed to place de la Révolution. Floodlit at night, it's dominated now by an Egyptian obelisk from Luxor, the oldest man-made object in Paris; it was carved circa 1200 B.C. and presented to France in 1829 by the viceroy of Egypt. During the Reign of Terror, Dr. Guillotin's little invention was erected on this spot and claimed thousands of lives—everybody from Louis XVI, who died bravely, to Mme du Barry, who went kicking and screaming all the way.

For a spectacular sight, look down the Champs-Elysées—the view is framed by Coustou's Marly horses, which once graced the gardens at Louis XIV's Château de Marly (these are copies—the originals are in the Louvre).

HISTORIC PARKS & A CEMETERY

PARKS   One of the most spectacular parks in Europe is the **Bois de Boulogne** 🇫🇫🇫, Porte Dauphine, 16e (℗ **01-53-92-82-82;** Métro: Les-Sablons, Porte-Maillot, or Porte-D'Autevil). Horse-drawn carriages traverse it, but you can also drive through. Many of its hidden pathways, however, must be discovered by walking. West of Paris, the park was once a forest kept for royal hunts. When Napoléon III gave the grounds to the city in 1852, they were developed by Baron Haussmann. Separating Lac Inférieur from Lac Supérieur is the Carrefour des Cascades (you can stroll under its waterfall). The Lower Lake contains two islands connected by a footbridge.

Parc Monceau 🌟, 17e (☎ **01-43-18-70-70;** Métro: Monceau or Villiers), is ringed with 18th- and 19th-century mansions, some of them evoking Proust's *Remembrance of Things Past.* It was built in 1778 by the Duc de Charties (or Philippe Egalité, as he became known). Parc Monceau was laid out with an Egyptian-style obelisk, a medieval dungeon, a thatched alpine farmhouse, a Chinese pagoda, a Roman temple, an enchanted grotto, various chinoiseries, and a waterfall. The park was opened to the public during Napoléon III's Second Empire.

A CEMETERY The **Cemetière du Père-Lachaise** 🌟🌟, 16 rue de Repos, 20e (☎ **01-43-70-70-33;** Métro: Père-Lachaise), is Paris's largest and contains more illustrious dead than any other. When it comes to name-dropping, this cemetery knows no peer—it's been called the "grandest address in Paris." Everybody from Sarah Bernhardt to Oscar Wilde is buried here. So are Balzac, Delacroix, and Bizet. Colette's body was taken here in 1954, and her pink and black granite slab always sports flowers (legend has it that cats replenish the red roses). In time, the "little sparrow," Edith Piaf, followed. Marcel Proust's black tombstone rarely lacks a tiny bunch of violets. Some tombs are sentimental favorites—Jim Morrison's reportedly draws the most visitors. Another stone is marked Gertrude Stein on one side and Alice B. Toklas on the other. Open from Monday to Friday 8am to 6pm, Saturday 8:30am to 6pm, and Sunday 9am to 6pm (closes at 5:30pm from Nov to early March).

ORGANIZED TOURS

BY BUS A highly visible option for seeing Paris are the get-acquainted tours offered by **Cityrama,** 4 place des Pyramides, 1er (☎ **01-44-55-61-00;** Métro: Palais Royal-Musée du Louvre). The company operates a flotilla of double-decker red-and-yellow buses, each with oversize windows and a series of multi-lingual recorded commentaries that recite an overview of Paris's history and monuments. The most popular tour is a 2-hour affair that departs from the place des Pyramides, adjacent to the rue de Rivoli and the Tuileries Gardens, every day at 9:30am, 10:30am, 1:30pm, and 2:30pm. Throughout the year, there are additional tours every Saturday and Sunday at 11:30am, and between March and October, there are additional tours every day at 3:30 and 4:30pm. The price is 150F (€22.80, $22) per person. Other, more detailed tours are also available. They include a 3½-hour morning tour (Mon, Wed, Fri, and Sat) to the interiors of Notre-Dame and the Louvre, priced at 295F (€44.85, $43) per person. There are 3½-hour morning tours to Versailles at 320F (€48.65, $46) per person, and 3½-hour afternoonz tours to Chartres at 275F (€41.80, $40) per person. If you buy tickets for the tours of Versailles and Chartres simultaneously, you'll pay only 500F (€76, $73) for both. And if you're interested in a night tour of Paris as a means of understanding how the City of Light got its name, tours depart every evening at 10pm in summer and at 7pm in winter at a cost of 150F (€22.80, $22) per person.

BY BOAT A boat tour on the Seine provides sweeping vistas of the riverbanks and some of the best views of Notre-Dame. Many of the boats have open sun decks, bars, and restaurants. **Bateaux-Mouche** cruises (☎ **01-42-25-96-10** for reservations, or 01-40-76-99-99 for schedules; Métro: Alma Marceau) depart from the Right Bank of the Seine, adjacent to pont de l'Alma, and last about 75 minutes each. Tours leave every day at 20- to 30-minute intervals from May to

October, beginning at 10am and ending at 11:30pm. From November to April, there're at least nine departures every day between 11am and 9pm, with a schedule that changes frequently according to demand and the weather. Fares are 40F (€6.10, $6) adults and 20F (€3.05, $2.90) children ages 5 to 15. Dinner cruises depart every evening at 8:30pm, last 2 hours and 15 minutes, and cost between 500 and 800F (€76 and €121.60, $73 and $116), depending on which of the set price menus you order. Aboard dinner cruises, jackets and ties are required for men.

THE SHOPPING SCENE

You don't have to buy anything to appreciate shopping in Paris; just soaking up mass consumerism as the true art form the French have made it is enough. Gawking at the *vitrines* (display windows) will give you a whole new education in style.

THE BEST BUYS

Perfumes and **cosmetics,** including such famous brands as Guerlain, Chanel, Schiaparelli, and Jean Patou, are almost always cheaper in Paris than in the United States. Paris is also a good place to buy Lalique and Baccarat **crystal.** They're expensive but still priced below international market value.

Of course, many people come to Paris just to shop for **fashions.** From Chanel to Yves Saint Laurent, Nina Ricci to Sonia Rykiel, the city overflows with fashion boutiques, ranging from haute couture to the truly outlandish. Fashion accessories, such as Louis Vuitton and Céline, are among the finest in the world. Smart Parisians know how to dress in style without mortgaging their condos: they head for discount and resale shops. One of the most visible of these is **Anna Lowe,** 104 rue du Faubourg St-Honoré, 8e (© **01-42-66-11-32;** Métro: Miromesnil), one of the busiest fashion discounters for women's clothing in Paris, and located within a few steps of the ultra-exclusive Bristol Hotel. Her inventory includes garments by Thierry Mugler, Chanel, Valentino, Givenchy, Ungaro, and Lacroix from the present or previous season, usually sold at wholesale prices. There's also an inventory of fashion accessories such as belts, shawls, and scarves.

Michel Swiss, 16 rue de la Paix, 2e (© **01-42-61-61-11;** Métro: Opéra), looks like the other chic boutiques near place Vendôme. But once you're inside (there's no storefront window), you'll see major brands of luxury perfumes, makeup, leather bags, pens, neckties, accessories, and giftware—all discounted.

Lingerie is another great French export. All the top lingerie designers are represented in boutiques as well as in the major department stores, Galeries Lafayette and Le Printemps.

Chocolate lovers will find much to tempt them in Paris. **Christian Constant,** 37 rue d'Assas, 6e (© **01-53-63-15-15;** Métro: Rennes), produces some of Paris's most sinfully delicious chocolates. Racks and racks of chocolates are

---

(*Value* Paris Shopper's Secret

For bargain cosmetics, try out French dime store (such as **Monoprix** and **Prisunic**) brands. Brands to look for include **Bourjois** (made in the same factories as Chanel cosmetics), **Lierac,** and **Galenic. Vichy,** famous for its water, has a complete skin care and makeup line.

priced individually or by the kilo at **Maison du Chocolat,** 225 rue du Faubourg St-Honoré, 8e (𝒞 **01-42-27-39-44;** Métro: Ternes), though it'll cost you nearly or over 500F ($80) for a kilo. There are five other branches around Paris.

GREAT SHOPPING AREAS

1er & 8e   Because these two adjoin each other and form the heart of what is Paris's best Right Bank shopping, they really function as one shopping neighborhood. This area includes the famed **rue du Faubourg St-Honoré,** where the big designer houses are, and **avenue des Champs-Elysées,** where the mass-market and teen scenes are hot.

At one end of the 1st is the **Palais Royal,** where an arcade of boutiques flanks the garden of the former palace. At the other side of town, at the end of the 8th, lies **avenue Montaigne** (Métro: Franklin D. Roosevelt or Alma Marceau), 2 blocks of the fanciest shops in the world, where you simply float from big name to big name and in a few hours can see everything from **Louis Vuitton** at no. 54 (𝒞 **01-45-62-47-00**) to **Inès de la Fressange** (Chanel model turned retailer) at no. 14 (𝒞 **01-47-23-08-94**). **Ferragamo** (𝒞 **01-47-23-36-37**) is at no. 45 in one of the most beautiful apartment buildings in Paris. In addition, you'll find fabulous perfumes at **Parfums Caron** (𝒞 **01-47-23-40-82**). The shop, which was founded in 1904, can be visited at no. 34.

2e   Right behind the Palais Royal lies the **Garment District (Sentier),** as well as very upscale shopping secrets like **place des Victoires.** This area hosts a few old-fashioned passages, alleys filled with tiny stores, such as **Galerie Vivienne** on rue Vivienne.

3e & 4e   The difference between these two arrondissements gets fuzzy, especially around **place des Vosges**—center stage of Le Marais. Even so, they offer several dramatically different shopping experiences.

On the surface, the shopping includes the real-people stretch of **rue de Rivoli** (which becomes **rue St-Antoine**). Two department stores are in this area: **La Samaritaine,** 19 rue de la Monnaie (𝒞 **01-40-41-20-20;** Métro: Pont Neuf), occupies four architecturally noteworthy buildings erected between 1870 and 1927. Of special interest are the annual sales that go on here during October and November, when much, but not all, of the merchandise is reduced by between 20% and 40%. **BHV (Bazar de l'Hôtel de Ville),** which was first opened in 1856, has seven floors loaded with merchandise. It lies adjacent to Paris's City Hall at 52–64 rue de Rivoli (𝒞 **01-42-74-90-00;** Métro: Hôtel de Ville).

Meanwhile, hidden away in the Marais is a medieval warren of tiny twisting streets chockablock with cutting-edge designers and up-to-the-minute fashions and trends. Start by walking around place des Vosges for art galleries, designer shops, and fabulous little finds, then dive in and get lost in the area leading to the Musée Picasso.

Place de la Bastille—an up-and-coming area for artists and galleries—is in the 4th arrondissement (leading to the 12th), as is the Île St-Louis. One of the newest entries to the retail scene, the **Viaduc des Arts,** begins at Bastille but technically stretches to the 12th arrondissement.

6e & 7e   Whereas the 6th arrondissement is one of the most famous shopping districts—it's the soul of the Left Bank—a lot of the really good stuff is hidden in the zone that becomes the wealthy residential 7th. **Rue du Bac,** stretching from the 6th to the 7th in a few blocks, stands for all that wealth and glamour can buy. The street is jammed with art galleries, home-decorating stores, and gourmet-food shops.

> ### 🏛 Paris's Most Famous Flea Market
>
> The **Marché aux Puces de Clignancourt** (flea market), avenue de la Porte de Clignancourt (Métro: Vanves), has an enormous mixture of vintage bargains and old junk. It's estimated that the complex has 2,500 to 3,000 open stalls. Monday is traditionally the day for bargain hunters, and negotiating is a must (you'll usually be able to find someone who speaks English). Once you arrive at Porte de Clignancourt, turn left and cross boulevard Ney, then walk north on avenue de la Porte de Clignancourt. You'll pass stalls offering cheap clothing, but continue walking until you see the entrances to the first maze of flea-market stalls on the left.

9e To add to the fun of shopping the Right Bank, the 9th arrondissement sneaks in behind the 1st, so if you don't choose to walk toward the Champs-Elysées and the 8th, you can head to the city's big department stores, built in a row along **boulevard Haussmann** in the 9th. These department stores include not only the two mammoth French icons, **Au Printemps,** 64 bd. Haussmann, 9e (© **01-42-82-50-00;** Métro: Havre-Caumartin; RER: Auber), and **Galeries Lafayette,** 40 bd. Haussmann, 9e (© **01-42-82-34-56;** Métro: Chausée d'Antin-La Fayette; RER: Auber), but also a large branch of Britain's **Marks & Spencer** at 35 bd. Haussman, 9e (© **01-47-42-42-91;** Métro: Chausée-d-Antin-La Fayette; RER: Auber).

PARIS AFTER DARK

Parisians tend to do everything later than their Anglo-American counterparts. Once the workday is over, people head straight to the cafe to meet up with friends, and from there they go to a restaurant or bar, and finally to a nightclub.

THE PERFORMING ARTS

Listings of what's playing can be found in *Pariscope,* a weekly entertainment guide, or the English-language *Boulevard.* Performances start later in Paris than in London or New York City—anywhere from 8 to 9pm—and Parisians tend to dine after the theater. There are many ticket agencies in Paris, but most are found near the Right Bank hotels. *Avoid them if possible*—usually, the cheapest tickets can be purchased at the box office.

We do recommend checking a few agencies that sell tickets for cultural events and plays at discounts of up to 50%. One outlet for discount tickets is the **Kiosque Théâtre,** 15 place de la Madeleine, 8e (no phone; Métro: Madeleine), offering leftover tickets for about half price for tickets sold only on the day of a performance. Tickets for evening performances are sold from Tuesday to Friday 12:30 to 8pm and Saturday 2 to 8pm. If you'd like to attend a matinee, buy your ticket Saturday from 12:30 to 2pm or Sunday from 12:30 to 4pm.

For discounts of 20% to 40% on tickets for festivals, concerts, and theater performances, try one of two locations of the **FNAC** department store chain: 136 rue de Rennes, 6e (© **01-49-54-30-00;** Métro: Saint Placide), or in the **Forum des Halles,** 1–7 rue Pierre-Lescot, 1er (© **01-40-41-40-00;** Métro: Châtelet-Les Halles). To obtain discounts on tickets, you must purchase a carte

FNAC, which is valid for 3 years and costs 160F (€24.30, $23) adults or 100F (€15.20, $15) students.

Those with a modest understanding of French can still delight in a sparkling production of Molière at the **Comédie-Française,** 2 rue de Richelieu, 1er (© **01-44-58-15-15;** Métro: Palais Royal-Musée du Louvre), established to keep the classics alive and promote the most important contemporary authors. Nowhere else will you see the works of Molière and Racine so beautifully staged. In 1993, a much-neglected wing of the building was renovated and launched as the Théâtre du Vieux Colombier, specializing in avant-garde productions, with all tickets costing 160F (€24.30, $23). The box office is open daily from 11am to 6pm (closed from July 21 to September 5). Tickets cost 70 to 190F (€10.65 to €28.90, $10 to $28).

Opéra Bastille, place de la Bastille, 120 rue de Lyon, 12e (© **01-43-43-96-96;** www.opera-de-paris.fr; Métro: Bastille), is the home of the **Opera National de Paris.** The main hall is the largest of any French opera house, with 2,700 seats. The building contains two additional concert halls, including an intimate room, usually used for chamber music, with only 250 seats. Both traditional operas and symphony concerts are presented. Several concerts are presented free, in honor of certain French holidays. Write ahead to the above address for tickets, which cost 60 to 680F (€9.10 to €103.35, $9 to $99).

Opéra Garnier (Palais Garnier), place de l'Opéra, 9e (© **01-40-01-17-89;** Métro: Opéra), is the home of the **Ballet National de Paris,** one of the world's great companies, always a leading innovator in the world of dance. This rococo wonder was designed as a contest entry by architect Charles Garnier in the heyday of the empire. Tickets cost 60 to 670F (€9.10 to €101.85, $9 to $97). The box office is open from Monday to Saturday 11am to 6:30pm. Additionally, on evenings when there's a performance, it reopens between 6:45 and 7:30pm.

A particularly charming venue for opera on a smaller scale than those that are the norm within either of Paris's major opera houses is the **Opéra-Comique,** Salle Favart, place Boieldieu, 2e (© **01-42-44-45-46;** Métro: Richelieu-Drouot). Built in the late 1890s in an ornate style reminiscent of the Palais Garnier, it's the site of such operas as *Carmen, Don Giovanni, Tosca,* and *Palleas et Melisande.* There are no performances from mid-July to late August. The box office, however, is open year-round, from Monday to Saturday from 11am to 7pm. Tickets cost 50 to 610F (€7.60 to €92.70, $7 to $88).

Another worthy musical venue in Paris is **Salle Pleyel,** 5 rue du Faubourg St-Honoré, 8e (© **01-45-61-53-00;** Métro: Ternes). Built in 1927 in a conservative Art Deco style, it's the site of appearances by such organizations as the Orchestre de Paris, the Orchestre Philharmonique de Radio-France, and L'Ensemble Orchestrale de Paris. The box office is open from Monday to Saturday from 11am to 6pm. Tickets cost 60 to 320F (€9.10 to €48.65, $9 to $46).

For access to some of the most modern and avant-garde music in France, try the **Radio France Salle Oliver Messian,** 116 av. Président-Kennedy, 16e (© **01-42-30-15-16;** Métro: Passy or Ranelagh), site of many of the performances of the Orchestre Philharmonique de Radio-France. A different organization that performs within the same concert hall is the somewhat more conservative Orchestre National de France. The box office is open from Monday to Saturday 11am to 6pm. Tickets cost 50 to 100F (€7.60 to €15.20, $7 to $15).

Of the half-dozen grands travaux conceived by the Mitterrand administration, the **Cité de la Musique,** 221 av. Jean Jaurès, 19e (© **01-44-84-45-45** or

01-44-84-44-84; Métro: Porte de Pantin), has been the most widely applauded, the least criticized, and the most innovative. Concerts are presented at 4:30pm and 8pm every day except Monday. Tickets cost 80 to 200F (€12.15 to €30.40, $12 to $29).

NIGHTCLUBS & CABARETS

Since it was established in 1951, **Crazy Horse Saloon,** 12 av. Georges-V, 8e (🕐 **01-47-23-32-32;** Métro: Georges V or Alma Marceau), a sophisticated strip joint, has thrived as a staple on the Paris theatrical circuit thanks to good choreography and a sly, often coquettish philosophy that celebrates and exalts the female form. Each of the numbers features gorgeous girls, girls, girls, each outfitted in the kind of costumes that support Paris's image as one of the erotic capitals of Europe. If you opt for dinner as part of the show, it will be a tasteful, well-prepared event served with flair at Chez Francis, a restaurant under separate management a few steps from the cabaret itself. Shows last for 1¾ hours each, and are attended by men, and to a lesser extent, women. Reservations are recommended. Cover is 450 to 560F (€68.40 to €85.10, $65 to $81), including two drinks, at a table; or 290F (€44.10, $42) including two drinks, for standing room at the bar; dinner spectacle (floor show) is 660F (€100.30, $96). Shows are from Sunday to Friday 8:30pm and 11pm; Saturday 7:30pm, 9:45pm, and 11:50pm.

The **Folies-Bergère,** 32 rue Richer, 9e (🕐 **01-44-79-98-98;** Métro: Grand Boulevard or Cadet), is a Paris institution. Since 1886, foreigners have been flocking here for performances, excitement, and scantily clad dancers. Josephine Baker, the African-American singer who used to throw bananas into the audience, became "the toast of Paris" at the Folies-Bergère. The Folies has radically changed its context into a less titillating, more conventional format. It often presents bemused, lighthearted French-language comedies and musicals. Cover is 150 to 350F (€22.80 to €53.20, $22 to $51); dinner and show costs 370 to 550F (€56.25 to €83.60, $54 to $80). Performances are from Tuesday to Saturday 9pm, Sunday 3pm. Restaurant opens at 7pm. Box office is open from Tuesday to Saturday 10am to 6pm, Sunday noon to 6pm.

Moulin Rouge, 82 bd. de Clichy, 18e (🕐 **01-53-09-82-82;** Métro: Blanche), the establishment that Toulouse-Lautrec immortalized in his paintings, is still here. But the artist would probably have a hard time recognizing it today. Try to get a table, as the view is much better on the main floor than from the bar. What's the underlying theme that drives spectators back to the Moulin Rouge generation after generation? It's an ongoing emphasis on the strip routines and saucy sexiness of *La Belle Époque,* and of permissive, promiscuous Paris between the World Wars. Handsome men and girls, girls, girls, virtually all of them topless, contribute to the enduring appeal that survives despite an increasing jadedness on the part of both audiences and staff. Dance finales usually include two-dozen of the belles ripping loose with a topless cancan in a style that might have been appreciated by Gigi herself. Cover including champagne is 560F (€85.10, $81); dinner and show costs from 890 to 990F (€135.30 to €150.50, $129 to $144). Dinner is nightly at 7pm, revues at 9 and 11pm.

JAZZ & ROCK CLUBS

Within a cellar lined with jazz-related paintings, with a large central bar and an ongoing roster of videos showing great jazz moments (Charlie Parker, Miles Davis) of the past, **Baiser Salé,** 58 rue des Lombards, 1er (🕐 **01-42-33-37-71;** Métro: Châtelet), is an appealing and musically varied club. Everything is very mellow and laid-back, with an emphasis on grooving to whatever form of jazz happens to be featured that evening. Genres include Afro-Caribbean, Afro-Latino, salsa, merengue, rhythm and blues, and less frequently, fusion. It's open daily from 6pm to 6am, with music nightly from 10pm to 3am. Entrance is free Monday and Tuesday. Cover is 50 to 100F (€7.60 to €15.20, $7 to $15) from Wednesday to Sunday.

Jazz maniacs come to drink, talk, and dance at **New Morning,** 7–9 rue des Petites-Ecuries, 10e (✆ **01-45-23-51-41;** Métro: Château d'Eau), which is now in the same league as the Village Vanguard in New York's Greenwich Village. The high-ceilinged former newspaper office was turned into a nightclub in 1981. The club remains on the see-and-be-seen circuit. Many styles of music are played and performed. Jazz groups from Central and South Africa are especially popular. Sometimes they're open on Sunday. Cover is 100F (€15.20, $15). Hours are generally Monday to Saturday 8pm to 1:30am. No food is served.

Don't expect any techno, punk, jazz, or blues at **Bus Palladium,** 6 rue Fontaine, 9e (✆ **01-53-21-07-33;** Métro: Blanche or Pigalle). This temple to 1960s-style rock and roll has varnished hardwoods and fabric-covered walls that absorb only some of the reverberations of the nonstop recorded music. Straight singles age 25 to 35 come here. An alcoholic drink will set you back a hefty 80F (€12.15, $12), except on Tuesdays, when women drink free. Cover is 100F (€15.20, $15) for men Tuesday, Friday, and Saturday; 100F (€15.20, $15) for women Friday and Saturday. Open from Tuesday to Saturday 11pm to 6am.

DANCE CLUBS

The chic **Les Bains,** 7 rue du Bourg-l'Abbé, 3e (✆ **01-48-87-01-80;** Métro: Réaumur and Etienne Marcel), has been pronounced "in" and "out" of fashion, but lately it's very "in." The place was formerly a Turkish bath attracting gay clients, none more notable than Marcel Proust. Today, it's predominantly straight, with an emphasis on the young, the trendy, and the fashionable, who usually range in age from 20 to around 45. It can be hard to get in if those at the door don't deem you acceptable. Cover is 120F (€18.25, $17), including the first drink. It's open nightly from 11:30pm to 6am.

A popular nightspot in a former bakery with a vaulted masonry ceiling, **Club Zed,** 2 rue des Anglais, 5e (✆ **01-43-54-93-78;** Métro: Maubert-Mutualité), may surprise you with its mix of musical offerings, including samba, rock, 1960s pop, and jazz. Cover is 5 to 100F (€0.75 to €15.20, 75¢ to $15), including the first drink, and it's open Wednesday and Thursday from 10:30pm to 3am and Friday and Saturday from 11pm to 5:30am.

WINE BARS

The tiny **Au Sauvignon,** 80 rue des Sts-Pères, 7e (✆ **01-45-48-49-02;** Métro: Sèvres-Babylone), has tables overflowing onto a covered terrace. Wines served range from the cheapest Beaujolais to expensive white Bordeaux ranging from 2 to 34F (€0.30 to €5.15, 30¢ to $5) a glass. To go with your wine, choose an Auvergne specialty, such as goat cheese and terrines. Open from Monday to Saturday 8:30am to 10:30pm. Closed August and major religious holidays.

A wide assortment of chic Parisians patronize the increasingly popular **Willi's Wine Bar,** 13 rue des Petits-Champs, 1er (✆ **01-42-61-05-09;** Métro: Pyrimide, Bourse, or Palais Royal-Musée du Louvre), in the center of the financial district. About 250 kinds of wine are offered, including a dozen "wine specials" you can taste by the glass for 17 to 80F (€2.65 to 12.15, $2.45 to $12). Lunch is the busiest time—on quiet evenings you can better enjoy the warm ambience.

Open for meals from Monday to Saturday noon to 2:30pm and 7 to 11pm; the bar is open from Monday to Saturday 11am to midnight.

GAY & LESBIAN CLUBS

Banana Café, 13 rue de la Ferronnerie, 1er (© **01-42-33-35-31;** Métro: Châtelet or Les Halles), is the most popular gay bar in the Marais, a ritualized stopover for European homosexuals (mostly male and to a much lesser extent, female) visiting or doing business in Paris. Occupying two floors of a 19th-century building, it has dim lighting and a well-publicized policy of raising the price of drinks after 10pm, after the joint starts to become really interesting. There's a street-level bar and a dance floor in the cellar featuring a live pianist and recorded music. On many nights, go-go dancers perform from spotlit platforms. It's open daily from 4pm to around 5:30am.

Le Bar Central, 33 rue Vielle-du-Temple, 4e (© **01-48-87-99-33;** Métro: Hôtel de Ville), is one of the leading bars for men in the Marais. Open from Monday to Thursday 4pm to 2am, Friday and Saturday 2pm to 2am. The club has opened a small hotel upstairs. The hotel caters mostly to gay men, less frequently to lesbians. No cover.

Le Pulp, 25 bd. Poissonnière, 2e (© **01-40-26-01-93;** Métro: Grand Blvd.), is one of the most visible and popular lesbian discos in Paris. Outfitted like a burgundy-colored 19th-century French music hall, a new management has made its seedy past a distant memory. Today it's fun, trendy, and chic. It's best to show up before midnight. The venue, as the French like to say, is very cool, with all types of cutting-edge music played in a setting that just happens to discourage the presence of men. Le Pulp is open from Thursday to Saturday midnight to at least 5am. Entrance to Le Pulp is free Wednesday and Thursday, and costs 50F (€7.60, $7) Friday and Saturday.

DAY TRIPS FROM PARIS: THE ÎLE DE FRANCE

VERSAILLES 🎭🎭🎭   Within 50 years the **Château de Versailles** (© **01-39-24-88-88;** www.chateauversailles.fr) was transformed from Louis XIII's simple hunting lodge into an extravagant palace, a monument to the age of absolutism. What you see today is the greatest living museum of a vanished way of life. Begun in 1661, the construction of the château involved 32,000 to 45,000 workmen, some of whom had to drain marshes—often at the cost of their lives—and move forests. Louis XIV set out to create a palace that would awe all Europe, and the result was a symbol of pomp and opulence that was to be copied, yet never quite duplicated, all over Europe and even in America.

The six magnificent **Grands Appartements** 🎭🎭🎭 are in the Louis XIV style; each takes its name from the allegorical painting on its ceiling. The most famous room is the 72-m (236-ft.) **Hall of Mirrors** 🎭🎭🎭. Begun by Mansart in 1678 in the Louis XIV style, it was decorated by Le Brun with 17 large arched windows matched by corresponding beveled mirrors in simulated arcades.

Spread across 100 hectares (250 acres), the **Gardens of Versailles** 🎭 were laid out by the great landscape artist André Le Nôtre. A long walk across the park will take you to the **Grand Trianon** 🎭🎭🎭, in pink-and-white marble, designed by Hardouin-Mansart for Louis XIV in 1687. Traditionally it's been a place where France has lodged important guests. Gabriel, the designer of place de la Concorde in Paris, built the **Petit Trianon** 🎭🎭 in 1768 for Louis XV; its construction was inspired by Mme de Pompadour, who died before it was completed. In time, Marie Antoinette adopted it as her favorite residence.

From May 2 to September 30, the palace is open from Tuesday to Sunday 9am to 6:30pm (to 5:30pm the rest of the year). The grounds are open daily from dawn to dusk. Admission to the palace is 46F (€7, $7) adults, 35F (€5.30, $5) those 18 to 25, free for under 18 and over 60. Admission to the Grand Trianon is 30F (€4.55, $4.35) adults, 20F (€3.05, $2.90) after 3:30 pm for those 18 to 25. Admission to the Grand Trianon and the Petit Trianon is 30F (€4.55, $4.35) adults, 20F (€3.05, $2.90) those 18 to 25, free for those 17 and under. The adult rate is also reduced to 20F (€3.05, $2.90) for all attractions after 3:30pm. Those 18 to 25 pay the reduced rate all day.

Getting There   To get to Versailles, 21km (13 miles) southwest of Paris, catch the RER line C at the Gare d'Austerlitz, St-Michel, Musée d'Orsay, Invalides, Pont-de-l'Alma, Champ-de-Mars, or Javel station and take it to the Versailles Rive Gauche station (trip time: 35–40 min.). From there you can take a shuttle bus or walk to the château. The fare is 35F (€5.30, $5); Eurailpass holders travel free on the train, but pay 20F (€3.05, $2.90) for a ride on the shuttle bus. Regular SNCF trains also make the run from Paris to Versailles: One train departs from the Gare St-Lazare for the Versailles Rive Droite RER station; another departs from the Gare Montparnasse for Versailles Chantiers station. From there it's a 15-minute walk from the château or you can take bus B to the château for 8F (€1.20, $1.15).

If you're driving, take route N-10 and park on the Place d'Armes in front of the château.

FONTAINEBLEAU ✮✮✮   Napoléon joined the grand parade of French rulers who used the **Palais de Fontainebleau** (② 01-64-22-27-40) as a resort, hunting in its magnificent forest. Under François I the hunting lodge was enlarged into a royal palace in the Italian Renaissance style that he admired. Artists from the School of Fontainebleau adorned the 64-m (210-ft.) **Gallery of François I** ✮✮✮.

Fontainebleau found renewed glory under Napoléon. You can wander around much of the palace on your own, but the **Musée Napoléon and the Petits Appartements** ✮ are accessible by guided tour only. Most impressive are his throne room and his bedroom (look for his symbol, a bee). The furnishings in the grand apartments of Napoléon and Joséphine evoke the imperial heyday.

The interior is open from Wednesday to Monday 9:30am to 12:30pm and 2 to 5pm. In July and August, it's open from 9:30am to 6pm. A ticket allowing visits to the Grands Appartements costs 35F (€5.30, 5) adults and 23F (€3.50, $3.35) students 18 to 25; free for under 18. A ticket allowing access to the Petits Appartements and the Musée Napoléon goes for 16F (€2.45, $2.30) adults and 12F (€1.80, $1.75) students 18 to 25; free for under 18.

Getting There   Trains to Fontainebleau, 60km (37 miles) south of Paris, depart from the Gare de Lyon in Paris (trip time: 45–60 min.), and cost 94F (€14.30, $14) round-trip. Fontainebleau's railway station lies 5km (3 miles) from the château, within the suburb of Avon. A local bus marked CHÂTEAU leaves at 15-minute intervals every Monday to Saturday, and at 30-minute intervals every Sunday, for 10F (€1.50, $1.60) each way.

CHARTRES ✮✮✮   The architectural aspirations of the Middle Ages reached their highest expression in the **Cathédrale Notre-Dame de Chartres,** 16 Cloître Notre-Dame (② 02-37-21-56-33). A mystical light seems to stream through this stained glass, which gave the world a new color—Chartres blue. One of the greatest of the world's high Gothic cathedrals, Chartres contains some of the oldest (some of it created as early as the 12th century) and most beautiful medieval stained glass anywhere. It was spared in both world wars; the glass removed painstakingly piece by piece for storage and safekeeping.

The cathedral you see today dates principally from the 13th century. It was the first to use flying buttresses, giving it a higher and lighter construction. French sculpture in the 12th century broke into full bloom when the Royal Portal was added; the sculptured bodies are elongated and formalized in their long flowing robes, but the faces are amazingly lifelike. Admission free, the cathedral is open from Monday to Saturday 7:30am to 7pm and Sunday from 8:30am to 7pm. The crypt can only be visited on a guided tour, costing 11F (€1.65, $1.60) adults or 8F (€1.20, $1.15) for students and children. From April to October, there are five tours daily, curtailed to two per day off-season. Inquire locally about times of tours, as they change frequently.

Getting There   Chartres is 97km (60 miles) southwest of Paris. Direct trains leave from Gare Montparnasse (trip time: 55 min.) and pass through the sea of wheat fields that characterize Beauce, the granary of France.

2 The Loire Valley Châteaux

Bordered by vineyards, the winding Loire Valley cuts through the land of castles deep in France's heart. When royalty and nobility built châteaux throughout this valley during the French Renaissance, sumptuousness was uppermost in their minds. An era of excessive pomp reigned until Henri IV moved his court to Paris, marking the Loire's decline.

The Loire is blessed with abundant attractions—there's even the castle that inspired the fairy tale *Sleeping Beauty*. Tours is the traditional gateway; once here you can explore either east or west, depending on your interests. From Paris, you can reach Tours by autoroute (take A-10 southwest).

In general, Loire Valley **tourist offices** are open from October to March, Monday to Saturday from 9am to 6:30pm and Sunday from 10am to noon; the rest of the year, hours are from Monday to Saturday 9am to 7pm and Sunday from 9:30am to 12:30pm.

TOURS

Tours, 232km (144 miles) southwest of Paris and 113km (70 miles) southwest of Orléans, is at the junction of the Loire and Cher Rivers. The devout en route to Santiago de Compostela in northwest Spain once stopped off here to pay homage at the tomb of St. Martin, the Apostle of Gaul, bishop of Tours in the 4th century. Tours is the traditional place to begin your exploration of the medieval Loire Valley.

ESSENTIALS
GETTING THERE   About 10 **trains** make the run from Paris to Tours every day. At least eight of them are TGVs (*trains à grande vitesse*) from Gare Montparnasse (trip time: 55 min.). TGVs arrive at the railway station in St-Pierre-des-Corps, a hamlet about 3km (2 miles) southeast of Tours, and which is connected to the city's main rail station (La Gare SNCF de Tours, at Place Maréchal Leclerc) by a free shuttle train. If you're coming into Tours on any of the trains that fan out into the Loire Valley, chances are you'll arrive via conventional train at Place Maréchal Leclerc, and thereby avoid the need to make the transfer from the TGV station at St-Pierre-des-Corps. For rail information and schedules in Tours, the Loire Valley, and the rest of France, call © **08-36-35-35-35.**

Once you're in Tours, you can rely on public transport to see much of the Loire; you can also rent a **bike** and tour—the region is relatively flat. Try **Amster'Cycle,** 5 rue des Remparts (℃ **02-47-61-22-23**), which rents both mountain bikes and all-purpose road bikes for 80F (€12.15, $12) per day. A deposit is required in the form of a passport, 1,500F (€228, $218), or a valid credit card. The shop is only 45m (50 yd.) from the rail station.

VISITOR INFORMATION   The **Office de Tourisme** is at 78 rue Bernard-Palissy (℃ **02-47-70-37-37**).

DEPARTING BY CAR   To reach your first major château in the Loire, follow D-7 for 18km (11 miles) west to Villandry.

WHERE TO STAY

Best Western Le Central   Off the main boulevard, this old-fashioned hotel is within walking distance of the river and cathedral, surrounded by gardens, lawns, and trees. Built in 1850, the hotel is a more modest but more economical choice than others in town. The Tremouilles family offers comfortable rooms at reasonable rates. Rooms come in a variety of shapes and sizes; a renovation in 1999 improved them considerably and updated the plumbing in the small bathrooms.

21 rue Berthelot, 37000 Tours. ℃ **800/528-1234** in the U.S., or 02-47-05-46-44. Fax 02-47-66-10-26. www. tour-online.com/central-hotel. 40 units (38 with bathroom). 165F (€25.10, $24) double without bathroom; 400–600F (€60.80–€91.20, $58–$87) double with bathroom. AE, DC, MC, V. Parking 40F (€6.10, $6). Bus: 1, 4, or 5. **Amenities:** Bar; room service; baby-sitting; laundry/dry cleaning. *In room:* A/C, TV, minibar, hair dryer.

Hôtel de l'Univers   This hotel on the main artery of Tours is the oldest in town, erected in 1853. The rooms are beginning to look a bit shopworn, although this remains Tours' favorite traditional hotel. On weekdays, it's filled mainly with business travelers and on weekends it hosts many area brides.

5 bd. Heurteloup, 37000 Tours. ℃ **02-47-05-37-12.** Fax 02-47-61-51-80. 85 units. 880F (€133.75, $128) double. AE, DC, MC, V. Parking 50F (€7.60, $7). Bus 1, 4, or 5. **Amenities:** Restaurant, bar; room service; baby-sitting; laundry/dry cleaning. *In room:* A/C, TV, hair dryer, trouser press.

Hôtel du Manoir   On a quiet street near the train station and many shops and restaurants, this renovated 19th-century residence provides guests with a comfortable place to stay. The cheerful reception area is a good indication of the quality of the rooms. Though small to average in size, all rooms have big windows that let in lots of light and afford views of the residential neighborhood or the hotel's courtyard. Most have simple furnishings and mattresses.

2 rue Traversière, 37000 Tours. ℃ **02-47-05-37-37.** Fax 02-47-05-16-00. 20 units. 270–290F (€41.05–€44.10, $39–$42) double. DC, MC, V. Parking 15F (€2.30, $2) per day. Bus: 3, 70. *In room:* A/C, TV.

WHERE TO DINE

La Rôtisserie Tourangelle   FRENCH (TRADITIONAL)   This is a local favorite, where you can dine on a terrace in summer (though there's not much to see). The ever-changing menu may include homemade foie gras and white fish caught in the Loire served with *beurre blanc* (white butter sauce). Regional ingredients mix well with the local wines, as exemplified by pikeperch with sabayon and *magret de fillet de canard* (duckling) served with a "jam" of red Chinon wine. In summer, strawberry parfait with raspberry coulis is a perfect end to the meal. If only the service were a little better.

23 rue du Commerce Tours. ℃ **02-47-05-71-21.** Reservations required. 3 choices of set price menus 160–240F (€24.30–€36.50, $23–$35) and 300F (€45.60, $44). Tues–Fri 12:15–1:30pm and 7:15–9:30pm. Bus: 1, 4, or 5.

The Loire Valley

Le Relais Buré FRENCH (TRADITIONAL)   A 5-minute walk east of the center, this brasserie specializes in shellfish and regional recipes, though it's somewhat unimaginative. It has a busy bar and a front terrace, with tables scattered inside on the street level and mezzanine. Menu items include six well-flavored versions of sauerkraut; a wide choice of grilled meats, including steak au poivre, foie gras and smoked salmon; and a tempting array of desserts.

1 place de la Résistance. ✆ **02-47-05-67-74.** Main courses 68–115F (€10.35–€17.50, $10–$17); set price menu (Mon–Fri only) 120F (€18.25, $17). AE, DC, MC, V. Daily noon–2pm and 7pm–midnight. Bus: 1 or 5.

Parc de Belmont (Jean Bardet) ✿ FRENCH (MODERN)   Set in three rooms of a 19th-century château and opened in 1987, this fine restaurant is the creation of the famous chef Jean Bardet, who considers all meals here to be "an orchestration of wines, alcohol, food, and cigars." Specialties of spectacular flavor include a lobster ragout, sliced sea bass with a confit of tomatoes and artichoke hearts, and scallops with a puree of shallots and truffle cream. The duck giblets and lobster accompanied by a red wine and orange sauce is reason enough to visit.

The rest of the château has been transformed into a luxury hotel and is the domain of chef Bardet's wife, Sophie. The spacious rooms are individually decorated and have high ceilings, cozy fireplaces, and antique furnishings. Some have private balconies that open onto the gardens. A double room ranges from 750 to 1,500F (€114 to €228, $109 to $218), and suites cost from 1,800 to 2,200F (€273.60 to €334.40, $261 to $319).

57 rue Groison, 37100 Tours. ℭ 02-47-41-41-11. Fax 02-47-51-68-72. Reservations recommended. Main courses 210–380F (€31.90–€57.75, $30–$55); set price menu 250–750F (€38–€114, $36–$109). AE, DC, MC, V. Nov–Mar Tues–Sat noon–2pm and 7:30–9:30pm; Sun noon–2:30pm. Apr–Oct Tues–Sun noon–1:30pm; daily 7:30–9:30pm. Bus: 9.

EXPLORING TOURS

The heart of town is **place Jean-Jaurès. Rue Nationale** is the principal street (the valley's Champs-Elysées), running north to the Loire River. Head along rue du Commerce and rue du Grand-Marché to reach La Vieille Ville, the old town.

Cathédrale St-Gatien   The cathedral's flamboyant Gothic facade is flanked by towers with bases from the 12th century, though the lanterns are Renaissance. The choir is from the 13th century, and each century through the 16th saw new additions. Some of the glorious stained-glass windows are from the 13th century.

5 place de la Cathédrale. ℭ 02-47-70-21-00. Free admission. Daily 9am–7pm. Bus: 3.

Musée de l'Historial de Touraine   A perfect, although a bit kitschy, introduction to the region, this museum features 30 scenes and 165 wax figures tracing 1,000 years of Touraine history.

In the Château Royal, 25 av. André Malraux. ℭ 02-47-61-02-95. Admission 35F (€5.30, $5) adults, 30F (€4.55, $4.35) seniors , 24F (€3.65, $3.50) students, 16F (€2.45, $2.30) children. May 16–June 30 and Sept 1–Oct 31 daily 9am–noon and 2–6pm; July 1–Aug 31 daily 9am–6:30pm; Nov 1–May 15 daily 2–5:30pm. Bus: 3.

Musée des Beaux-Arts   This fine provincial museum is housed in the Palais des Archevêques. It's worth visiting for its lovely rooms and gardens. There are works by Degas, Delacroix, Rembrandt, and Boucher, and sculpture by Houdon and Bourdelle.

18 place François-Sicard. ℭ 02-47-05-68-73. Museum: 30F (€4.55, $4.35) adults, 15F (€2.30, $2.20) students and those over 65; free for 12 and under. Gardens free. Museum Wed–Mon 9am–12:45pm and 2–6pm. Gardens Wed–Mon 7am–8:30pm. Bus: 3.

VILLANDRY ✸✸✸

The extravagant 16th-century–style gardens of the Renaissance **Château de Villandry,** 37510 Joué-les-Tours (ℭ 02-47-50-02-09), are celebrated throughout the Touraine. Forming a trio of superimposed cloisters, with a water garden on the highest level, the gardens were purchased in a decaying state and restored by Spanish doctor/scientist Joachim Carvallo, the present owner's great-grandfather. The grounds contain 17km (10½ miles) of boxwood sculpture, which the gardeners must cut to style in only 2 weeks in September. Every square of the gardens seems like a geometric mosaic. The borders represent the many faces of love: for example, tender, tragic (with daggers), or crazy, the last evoked by a labyrinth that doesn't get you anywhere.

Originally a feudal castle stood at Villandry, but in 1536 Jean Lebreton, the chancellor of François I, built the present château; the buildings form a U and are surrounded by a two-sided moat.

Admission to the gardens with a tour of the château is 45F (€6.85, $7) for adults, 38F (€5.83, $6) for children. Visiting the gardens separately without a guide costs 33F (€5, $4.80) adults, 26F (€3.95, $3.75) children. The château is open from mid-February to mid-November, and guided tours are conducted daily from 9am to 6:30pm. The gardens are open year-round from 9am to 5:30pm. Tours are given in French with leaflets in English.

ESSENTIALS

GETTING THERE   Unfortunately, Villandry doesn't have train or bus service from Tours, 18km (11½ miles) away. Rent a **bike** in Tours (see above) and ride along the Cher or go by car; the ride by bike will take 60 to 90 minutes.

DEPARTING BY CAR   From Villandry, continue west along D-7, then take D-39 south for 11km (7 miles) to Azay-le-Rideau.

WHERE TO STAY & DINE

Le Cheval Rouge   FRENCH (MODERN)   This is a well-known lunch stopover near the château, in spite of a stiff, sometimes unpleasant welcome and difficult staff. Set within a conservatively decorated dining room, about 90m (100 yd.) from the banks of the Cher, it won't be your most memorable meal in the Loire Valley; the food is competent, but not brilliant. Specialties include lobster thermidor, medallions of veal with morels, and turbot with hollandaise sauce. The inn also rents 20 rooms. A double is 270F (€41.05, $39). Parking is free.

Villandry, 37510 Joué-les-Tours. (*C*) **02-47-50-02-07.** Fax 02-47-50-08-77. Reservations recommended. Main courses 95–170F (€14.45–€25.85, $14–$25). Set price menus 95–180F (€14.45–€27.35, $14–$26). MC, V. Tues–Sun noon–2pm and 7:30–9pm. Closed Feb to mid-Mar. Open Sun night and Mon if it's a holiday.

AZAY-LE-RIDEAU ⭐⭐⭐

This château's machicolated towers and blue-slate roof pierced with dormers shimmer in the moat, creating a reflection like a Monet painting. But the defensive medieval look is all for show; the **Château d'Azay-le-Rideau,** 37190 Azay-le-Rideau (*C* **02-47-45-42-04**), was created as a private residence during the Renaissance at an idyllic spot on the Indre River. Gilles Berthelot, François I's finance minister, commissioned the castle, and his spendthrift wife, Philippa, supervised its construction. So elegant was the creation that the chevalier king grew immensely jealous. In time, Berthelot was forced to flee and the château reverted to the king.

Before entering, circle the château, enjoying the perfect proportions of this crowning achievement of the Renaissance in Touraine. Its most fanciful feature is a bay enclosing a grand stairway with a straight flight of steps. The Renaissance interior is a virtual museum. From the second-floor Royal Chamber, look out at the gardens. This bedroom, also known as the Green Room, is believed to have sheltered Louis XIII.

The château is open daily: July to August 9am to 7pm, April to June and October 9:30am to 6pm, and November to March 9:30am to 12:30pm and 2 to 5:30pm. Admission is 35F (€5.30, $5) adults and 23F (€3.50, $3.35) children. May to July, *son et lumière* (sound-and-light) performances are staged at 10:30pm; August at 10pm; and September at 9:30pm. Tickets cost 60F (€9.10, $9) adults and 35F (€5.30, $5) children.

ESSENTIALS

GETTING THERE   Azay-le-Rideau lies astride the railway lines that interconnect Tours with Chinon. The SNCF maintains about seven **trains** or **buses** a day that make the transit from both (trip time: 25 and 30 min.). Trains arrive at the railway station west of Azay's center; buses arrive in the town center. For information about either buses or trains, call (*C*) **02-47-93-11-04** (Chinon railway station) or (*C*) **08-36-35-35-35** (SNCF information throughout France).

VISITOR INFORMATION   The **Syndicat d'Initiative** (tourist office) is at place de l'Europe ((*C*) **02-47-45-44-40**).

DEPARTING BY CAR   After seeing Villandry and Azay-le-Rideau, return to Tours. From Tours, head east for 35km (22 miles) to Amboise. To reach Amboise, take either D-751 on the south bank of the Loire or N-152 on the north bank (both good roads). If you take the northern route, you can follow the signs to Vouvray, which turns out the most famous white wine of the Touraine. Vintners post signs if they allow visits and tastings.

WHERE TO DINE

L'Aigle d'Or FRENCH (TRADITIONAL)   The service is professional, the welcome often charming, and the food the best in Azay. Within a dining room that's accented with a fireplace and pastel colors, you'll enjoy dishes that include a mousseline of scallops with crayfish coulis, and a *blanquette* (stew) of Loire valley whitefish prepared with one of the region's white wines. Desserts are made fresh daily and vary with the chef's moods. In summer, the party expands onto an outdoor terrace.

10 av. Adélaïde-Riché. (℃ **02-47-45-24-58.** Reservations recommended. Main courses 95–120F (€14.45–
€18.25, $14–$17); set price lunch 110–160F (€16.70–€24.30, $16–$23); set price dinner 160–265F
(€24.30–€40.30, $23–$38). V. Thurs–Tues 12:30 2pm; Thurs–Sat and Mon 8:30–9pm. Closed Tues night Oct
and May. Also closed all of Feb and Nov 20–30.

AMBOISE ☆☆☆

On the banks of the Loire, Amboise is in the center of vineyards known as
Touraine-Amboise. Leonardo da Vinci spent his last years in this city. Dominating the town is the **Château d'Amboise** ☆☆ (℃ **02-47-57-00-98**), the first
in France to reflect the Italian Renaissance. A combination of both Gothic and
Renaissance, this 15th-century château is mainly associated with Charles VIII,
who built it on a rocky spur separating the valleys of the Loire and the Amasse.

You enter via a ramp, opening onto a panoramic terrace fronting the river. At
one time, this terrace was surrounded by buildings, and fetes were staged in the
enclosed courtyard. At the time of the revolution, the castle declined and only a
quarter or even less remains of this once-sprawling edifice. First you come to the
flamboyant Gothic Chapelle St-Hubert, distinguished by its lacelike tracery. It
allegedly contains Leonardo's remains; actually the great artist was buried in the
castle's Collegiate Church, which was destroyed between 1806 and 1810. During the Second Empire, excavations here revealed bones "identified" as
Leonardo's.

Today the walls of the château are hung with tapestries and the rooms furnished grandly. The *Logis du Roi* (king's apartment) escaped destruction and can
be visited. The château is open daily, from July and August 9am to 7:30pm,
from April to June 9am to 6:30pm, September and October 9am to 6pm, and
from November to March 9am to noon and 1:30 to 5:30pm. Admission is 40F
(€6.10, $6) adults, 33F (€5, $4.80) students, and 21F (€3.20, $3) children.

You might also wish to visit **Clos-Lucé** ☆, 2 rue de Clos-Lucé (℃ **02-47-
57-00-73**), a 15th-century brick-and-stone manor. In what had been an oratory
for Anne de Bretagne, François I installed "the great master in all forms of art
and science," Leonardo da Vinci. Venerated by the chevalier king, Leonardo
lived here for 3 years, dying at the manor in 1519. (Those paintings of Leonardo
dying in François's arms are symbolic; the king was supposedly away at the
time.) The manor's rooms are well furnished, some with reproductions from
Leonardo's time. Clos-Lucé is open from February to November daily 9am to
7pm; off-season daily from 9am to 6pm. Admission is 39F (€5.95, $6) adults
and 32F (€4.85, $4.65) students, 20F (€3.05, $2.90) ages 6 to 15; free for ages
5 and under.

ESSENTIALS

GETTING THERE   Amboise lies on the main Paris-Blois-Tours rail line, with
14 trains per day arriving from both Tours (trip time: 20 min.) and Blois (trip
time: 15 min.). Five trains arrive daily from Paris (2½ hr.). For train information and schedules, call ℃ **08-36-35-35-35. Tourisme Verney** (℃ **02-47-57-
00-44**) runs five **buses** a day connecting Tours and Amboise (about 30 min.).
The train station is along Boulevard Gambetta, and buses leave from the parking lot adjacent to the tourist office.

VISITOR INFORMATION   The **Office de Tourisme** is on quai du Général-
de-Gaulle (℃ **02-47-57-09-28**).

DEPARTING BY CAR   To reach Blois from Amboise, continue along the
north bank (N-152). Blois is 60km (37 miles) northeast of Tours.

WHERE TO STAY

Belle-Vue   This modest inn lies at the bridge crossing the Loire at the foot of the château. Rooms are furnished in an old-fashioned French style, with low beds and rather thin mattresses. Try to stay in the main building, which has more charm and character than the less convenient annex across the river. Bathrooms are small and have showers. Breakfast is the only meal served.

12 quai Charles-Guinot, 37400 Amboise. ℂ **02-47-57-02-26.** Fax 02-47-30-51-23. 32 units. 420F (€63.85, $61) double. Rates include breakfast. MC, V. Closed Nov 15–Mar 15. **Amenities:** Breakfast room; room service. *In room:* TV.

Hostellerie du Château-de-Pray ⚜   One mile west of the town center, this château from 1224 resembles a tower-flanked castle on the Rhine. Inside, you'll find antlers, hunting trophies, antiques, and a paneled drawing room with a fireplace and a collection of antique oils. Rooms in the thick-walled main building were renovated in 1998 and are stylishly conservative and comfortable. The more spacious chambers are near the ground floor. Bathrooms are small but efficiently organized. Try to avoid the four rooms in the 1990s annex; they're rather impersonally furnished and lack character.

Route de Chargé (D-751), 37400 Amboise. ℂ **02-47-57-23-67.** Fax 02-47-57-32-50. www.chateauxethotels. com. 19 units. 590–1,020F (€89.70–€155.05, $86–$148) double; 990–1,290F (€150.50–€196.10, $144–$187) suite. AE, DC, MC, V. Closed Jan 2–Feb 10. Free parking. **Amenities:** Excellent restaurant; baby-sitting; laundry/dry cleaning. *In room:* TV, hair dryer.

Le Choiseul ⚜⚜⚜   There's no better address in Amboise or any better place for cuisine than this 18th-century hotel, set in the valley between a hillside and the Loire River, close to the château, with a terraced garden on the grounds. Rooms are luxurious; though recently modernized, they've retained their old-world charm. Bathrooms are small. The food is better than that found in Tours or the surrounding area. The formal dining room has a view of the Loire and welcomes nonguests who phone ahead.

36 quai Charles-Guinot, 37400 Amboise. ℂ **02-47-30-45-45.** Fax 02-47-30-46-10. www.choiseul.com. 32 units. 950–1,450F (€144.40–€220.40, $138–$210) double; 1,550–1,950F (€235.60–€296.40, $225–$283) suite. AE, DC, MC, V. Closed Dec 16–Feb 3. **Amenities:** Restaurant; bar; pool; tennis court; room service; baby-sitting; laundry/dry cleaning. *In room:* A/C (half the rooms), TV, minibar, hair dryer.

WHERE TO DINE

Le Manoir St-Thomas ⚜ FRENCH (TRADITIONAL)   The best food in town outside of Le Choiseul is served at this Renaissance house in the shadow of the château. The restaurant is in a pleasant garden, and the elegant dining room is richly decorated with a polychrome ceiling and a massive stone fireplace. Owner/chef François Le Coz's specialties include truffles with foie gras, lamb filet with port, and red mullet filet with cream of sweet pepper sauce. The tender saddle of hare is perfectly flavored. Some special culinary delights are the goose liver pâté wrapped in a combination of truffles and wild black mushrooms, and duck flavored with honey, cinnamon, and ginger.

Place Richelieu. ℂ **02-47-57-22-52.** Reservations required. Main courses 130–150F (€19.75–€22.80, $19–$22). Set price menu 179–305F (€27.20–€46.35, $26–$44). AE, DC, MC, V. Tues 7:15–9:30pm; Wed–Sat 12:15–2:30pm and 7:15–9:30pm; Sun 12:15–2:30pm. Closed Jan 15–Mar 15.

BLOIS ⚜⚜

Blois is the most attractive of the major Loire towns. It rises on the right bank of the Loire, its skyline dominated by its château, where the duc de Guise was assassinated on December 23, 1588, on orders of his archrival, Henri III; it's one of the most famous murders in French history. Several French kings lived here, and the town has a rich architectural history.

The murder of the duc de Guise is only one of the memories evoked by the **Château de Blois** ⭐⭐⭐ (© **02-54-74-16-06**), begun in the 13th century by the comtes de Blois. Charles d'Orléans (son of Louis d'Orléans, assassinated by the Burgundians in 1407) lived at Blois after his release from 25 years of English captivity. He'd married Mary of Cleves and brought a "court of letters" to Blois. In his 70s, Charles became the father of the future Louis XII, who was to marry Anne de Bretagne. Blois was then launched in its new role as a royal château. In time it was to be called the second capital of France, with Blois, the city of kings.

However, Blois soon became a palace of banishment. Louis XIII got rid of his interfering mother, Marie de Médici, by sending her here; but this plump matron escaped by sliding into the moat down a mound of dirt left by the builders. Then in 1626 the king sent his conspiring brother, Gaston d'Orléans, here; he stayed.

If you stand in the courtyard, you'll find the château is like an illustrated storybook of French architecture. The Hall of the Estates-General is a beautiful 13th-century work; the Charles d'Orléans gallery was actually built by Louis XII from 1498 to 1501, as was the Louis XII wing. The Gaston d'Orléans wing was constructed by Mansart between 1635 and 1638. The most remarkable is the François I wing, a masterpiece of the French Renaissance, containing a spiral staircase with elaborately ornamented balustrades and the king's symbol, the salamander.

The château is open daily from mid-October to mid-March from 9am to 12:30pm and 2 to 5:30pm; from mid-March through June and September from 10am to 6:30pm; July and August from 10am to 8pm. Admission is 35F (€5.30, $5) adults, 20F (€3.05, $2.90) students under 25, free for children under 7. A *son et lumière* presentation in French is sponsored nightly from May to September, beginning in most cases at 10:30pm, but in rare instances, including throughout the month of May, at 9:30 or 10:15, depending on the school calendar. Participation in the sound-and-light show costs 60F (€9.10, $9) adults and 30F (€4.55, $4.35) children 7 to 15, free for children under 7.

ESSENTIALS
GETTING THERE   The Paris-Austerlitz line via Orléans delivers eight **trains** per day from Paris (trip time: 2 hr.). From Tours, 10 trains arrive per day (45 min.), and from Amboise, 10 trains per day arrive (20 min.). For train information and schedules, call © **08-36-35-35-35.** The train station is at place de la Gare. If you'd like to explore the area by **bike,** go to **Cycles Le Blond,** 44 levée des Tuileries (© **02-54-74-30-13**), where rentals range from 30 to 120F (€4.55 to €18.25, $4.35 to $17) per day, depending on the model. You have to leave your passport, a credit card, a driver's license, or a deposit of between 500 and 1,500F (€76 and €228, $73 and $218), depending on the value of the bike.

VISITOR INFORMATION   The **Office de Tourisme** is at Pavillon Anne-de-Bretagne, 3 av. Jean-Laigret (© **02-54-90-41-41**).

DEPARTING BY CAR   To reach Chaumont sur-Loire, follow N 152 for 8 miles to Chouzy-Sur-Cisse, then take D114 for 190 yards to Chaumont-sur-Loire.

WHERE TO STAY
Hôtel le Savoie   This modern 1930s era hotel is both inviting and livable, from its courteous staff to the rooms, which though small, are nonetheless quiet

and cozy. They were last renovated in 1999. Bathrooms are small but have sufficient shelf space. In the morning, a breakfast buffet is set up in the bright dining room.

6–8 rue du Docteur-Ducoux, 41000 Blois. ℭ 02-54-74-32-21. Fax 02-54-74-29-58. www.citote.com. 26 units. 250–300F (€38–€45.60, $36–$44) double. MC, V. **Amenities:** Breakfast room. *In room:* TV, hair dryer.

Mercure Centre   This is the newest and best-located hotel in Blois—three stories of reinforced concrete and big windows beside the quays of the Loire, a 5-minute walk from the château. Rooms never rise above their chain format and are very roadside motel in look, but they're roomy and soundproof and equipped with Bordeaux-colored upholsteries and gray walls. Bathrooms are excellent.

28 quai St-Jean, 41000 Blois. ℭ 02-54-56-66-66. Fax 02-54-56-67-00. www.mercure.blois.fr. 96 units. 600–625F (€91.20–€95, $87–$91) double; 660–695F (€100.30–€105.65, $96–$101) suite. AE, DC, MC, V. Parking 40F (€6.10, $6). Bus: Quayside marked PISCINE. **Amenities:** Restaurant, bar; pool; Jacuzzi; sauna; room service; baby-sitting; laundry/dry cleaning. *In room:* A/C, TV, minibar, hairdryer.

WHERE TO DINE

Le Médicis ⟨★⟩ FRENCH (TRADITIONAL)   Christian and Annick Garanger maintain one of the most sophisticated inns in Blois—ideal for a gourmet meal or an overnight stop. Fresh fish is the chef's specialty. Typical main courses are asparagus in mousseline sauce, scampi ravioli with saffron sauce, and supreme of perch with morels. Chocolate in many manifestations is the dessert specialty. In addition, the Garangers rent 12 elegant rooms. The rates are 500 to 700F (€76 to €106.40, $73 to $102) double; there is one suite that goes for 700F (€106.40, $102).

2 allée François-1er, 41000 Blois. ℭ 02-54-43-94-04. Fax 02-54-42-04-05. www.le-medicis.com. Reservations required. Main courses 80–165F (€12.15–€25.10, $12–$24); set price menus 118F (€17.95, $17), 168F (€25.55, $24), 278F (€42.25, $40), and 420F (€63.85, $61). AE, MC, V. Daily noon–2pm and 7–10pm. Closed Jan. Bus: 2.

Rendezvous des Pecheurs ⟨★⟩ FRENCH (TRADITIONAL)   This restaurant occupies a small, 16th-century house a 5-minute walk from the château. The chefs here, the finest in this part of France, continue to maintain their reputation for quality ingredients, generous portions, and creativity. The chef prepares only two or three meat dishes, including roasted chicken with a medley of potatoes and mushrooms and a confit of garlic; and a fricassee of sweetbreads. These appear alongside a much longer roster of fish and seafood dishes, such as a poached filet of zander served with fresh oysters; and filet of sea bass served with a champagne sauce on a bed of sea urchins.

27 rue du Foix. ℭ 02-54-74-67-48. Reservations recommended. Main courses 96–130F (€14.60–€19.75, $14–$19); set price menu 150F (€22.80, $22). MC, V. Mon 7:30–10pm; Tues–Sat noon–2pm and 7:30–10pm. Closed 3 weeks in Aug and 1 week in Feb.

CHAUMONT-SUR-LOIRE

On the morning when Diane de Poitiers crossed the drawbridge, the **Château de Chaumont** ⟨★★⟩ (ℭ 02-54-51-26-26) looked fiercely grim, with its battlements and pepper-pot turrets crowning the towers. Henri II, her lover, had recently died. The king had given her Chenonceau, but his widow, Catherine de Médici, banished her from her favorite château and sent her into exile at Chaumont. Inside, portraits reveal that Diane truly deserved her reputation as forever beautiful. A portrait of Catherine looking like a devout nun invites unfavorable comparisons.

Chaumont (Burning Mount) was built during the reign of Louis XII by Charles d'Amboise, and spans the period between the Middle Ages and the Renaissance. It was privately owned and inhabited until it was acquired by the state in 1938. Its prize exhibit is a rare collection of medallions by the Italian artist, Nini. A guest of the château, he made medallion portraits of kings, queens, and nobles—even Benjamin Franklin, who once visited. In the bedroom once occupied by Catherine de Médici is a rare portrait, painted when she was young.

The château is open daily from January to mid-March and from October to December 10am to 4:30pm; from mid-March to September, it's open daily from 9:30am to 6pm. Admission is 32F (€4.85, $4.65) adults and 21F (€3.20, $3) children 12 to 17, free for children under 12.

ESSENTIALS
GETTING THERE   Seventeen trains per day travel from both Blois (trip time: 15 min.) and Tours (about 45 min.). The train station is in Onzain, 2.5km (1½ miles) north of the château, a pleasant walk. For transportation information, call ℂ **08-36-35-35-35.** From June 15 to September 15, you can take a bus in Blois operated by **Point Bus,** 2 place Victor Hugo (ℂ **02-54-78-15-66**). The bus leaves Blois at 9:10am, returning at 6pm daily.

VISITOR INFORMATION   The **Office de Tourisme** is on rue du Maréchal-Leclerc (ℂ **02-54-20-91-73**).

DEPARTING BY CAR   Blois (above) also makes a perfect launching pad for visiting another important château in the area, that of Chambord, which lies 18km (11 miles) east of Blois along D-33 near Bracieux.

WHERE TO STAY & DINE NEARBY
Domaine des Hauts de Loire   Less than 3km (2 miles) from the Château of Chaumont, on the opposite side of the Loire, this Relais & Châteaux property is a stately manor house built by the prosperous owner of a Paris-based newspaper in 1840 and called, rather coyly at the time, a "hunting lodge." It's the most appealing stopover in the neighborhood, with a roster of intensely decorated rooms each in Louis Philippe or Empire style. About half the rooms lie within the less desirable half-timbered annex that was originally the stables.

The site also offers a restaurant that's open to nonguests who phone in advance. Its well-prepared food served in a stately dining room is a local favorite. Menus include a salad of marinated eel with shallot-flavored vinaigrette; oysters on a layered sheet of sardines; roasted filet of Loire Valley whitefish (sandre) served with parsley-flavored cream sauce and cabbage stuffed with a compote of snails; and the ultimate Loire valley main course, a filet of smoked eel prepared with Vouvray wine.

Route d'Herbault, 41150 Onzain. ℂ **02-54-20-72-57.** Fax 02-54-20-77-32. www.relaischateau.fr/ hauts-loire. 35 units. 700–1,500F (€106.40–€228, $102–$218) double; from 1,850F (€281.20, $268) suite. Closed Dec–Feb. AE, DC, MC, V. **Amenities:** Restaurant, bar. *In room:* TV, minibar, hair dryer.

CHAMBORD
When François I used to say, "Come on up to my place," he meant the **Château de Chambord** 🏰🏰🏰, 41250 Bracieux (ℂ **02-54-50-40-00**), not Fontainebleau or Blois. Some 2,000 workers began to piece together "the pile" in 1519. What emerged after 20 years was the pinnacle of the French Renaissance, the largest château in the Loire Valley. It was ready for the visit of Charles V of Germany, who was welcomed by nymphets in transparent veils gently tossing wildflowers

in his path. French monarchs like Henri II and Catherine de Médici, Louis XIV, and Henri III came and went from Chambord, but none developed an affection for it to match François I's. The state acquired Chambord in 1932.

The château is in a park of more than 5,200 hectares (13,000 acres), enclosed within a wall stretching some 32km (20 miles). Looking out a window in one of the 440 rooms, François is said to have carved these words on a pane with a diamond ring: "A woman is a creature of change; to trust her is to play the fool." Chambord's facade is dominated by four monumental towers. The keep has a spectacular terrace the ladies of the court used to stand on to watch the return of their men from the hunt.

The three-story keep also encloses a corkscrew staircase, superimposed so one person may descend at one end and a second ascend at the other without ever meeting. The apartments of Louis XIV, including his redecorated bedchamber, are also in the keep.

The château is open daily: from January to March and from October to December 9am to 5:15pm; from April to June, it closes at 6:15pm and July and August it closes at 7:15pm. Admission is 40F (€6.10, $6) adults and 25F (€3.80, $3.65) ages 12 to 25, free for children under 12. At the tourist office you can pick up tickets for the *son et lumière* presentation in summer, called *Jours et Siècles* (Days and Centuries), but check the times. A ticket costs 50F (€7.60, $7).

ESSENTIALS

GETTING THERE   It's best to travel to Chambord by car so you can explore the beautiful countryside on the way there and back. You could rent a **bicycle** in Blois (see above) and cycle to Chambord (a trip of 30km/18½ miles lasting 90–120 min.). From June 15 to September 15 **Point Bus,** 2 place Victor Hugo (*©* **02-54-78-15-66**), operates a bus service to Chambord, leaving Blois at 9:10am and again at 1:20pm with a return at 1 and 6:10pm.

VISITOR INFORMATION   The **Office de Tourisme** is on place St-Michel (*©* **02-54-20-34-86**).

DEPARTING BY CAR   Back at the launching pad of Blois, you can strike out in another direction for yet another major château. Cheverny lies 19km (10 miles) south of Blois, reached by taking D-765.

WHERE TO STAY & DINE

Hôtel du Grand-St-Michel   Across from the château, and originally built as a kennel for the hunting hounds of the French Kings, this inn is really the only one of any substance in town. Try for a front room overlooking the château, which is dramatic when floodlit at night. Rooms are plain but comfortable, with provincial decor. Most visitors arrive for lunch, which in summer is served on an awning-shaded terrace. The regional dishes are complemented by a marvelous collection of Loire wines so good they almost overshadow the cooking itself.

103 place St-Michel, 41250 Chambord, near Bracieux. *©* **02-54-20-31-31.** Fax 02-54-20-36-40. 39 units. 290–450F (€44.10–€68.40, $42–$65) double. MC, V. Closed Nov 14–Dec 20. Free parking. **Amenities:** Restaurant, lounges. *In room:* TV.

CHEVERNY

The *haut monde* still come to the Sologne area for the hunt as if the 17th century had never ended. However, 20th-century realities, like taxes, are *formidable* here—hence the **Château de Cheverny** ✶✶✶ (*©* **02-54-79-96-29**) must open some of its rooms for inspection by paying guests. At least that keeps the tax collector at bay and the hounds fed in winter.

Unlike most of the Loire châteaux, Cheverny is actually lived in by the descendants of the original owner, the vicomte de Sigalas. The family's lineage can be traced back to Henri Hurault, the son of the chancellor of Henri III and Henri IV, who built the château here in 1634. Designed in classic Louis XIII style, it boasts square pavilions flanking the central pile.

Inside, the antique furnishings, tapestries, decorations, and objets d'art are quite impressive. A 17th-century French artist, Jean Mosnier, decorated the fireplace with motifs from the legend of Adonis. In the Guards' Room is a collection of medieval armor.

The château is open daily: from November to February 9:30am to noon and 2:15 to 5pm; in March, the last part of September, and October it closes at 5:30pm, in April and May at 6:30pm, and from June to mid-September at 6:45pm. Admission is 35F (€5.30, $5) adults and 17F (€2.60, $2.45) children 7 to 14, free for children under 7.

ESSENTIALS

GETTING THERE   Cheverny is 19km (12 miles) south of Blois, along D-765. It's best reached by car or on an organized **bus tour** from Blois. From the railway station at Blois, there's a bus that departs for Cheverney once a day, at noon, returning to Blois 4 hours later, according to an oft-changing schedule that's dependent on the season and the day of the week. Frankly, most visitors find it a lot easier to take their own car or a taxi from the railway station at Blois.

DEPARTING BY CAR   If after exploring Cheverny you have enthusiasm for one more château, strike out for Valençay. From Cheverny head south on D-102 for 10km (6 miles), crossing the border of the forest of Cheverny. At the town of Contres, connect with the junction of D-956, which traverses the Cher River 19km (12 miles) farther south at Selles-sur-Cher. From here, continue the final signposted 14km (9 miles) to Valençay. The entire ride will take 45 minutes.

WHERE TO STAY & DINE

Les Trois Marchands FRENCH (TRADITIONAL)   This much-renovated coaching inn, more comfortable than Saint-Hubert, has been handed down for many generations. The three-story building sports awnings, a mansard roof, a glassed-in courtyard, and sidewalk tables with bright umbrellas. In the large tavern-style dining room, the menu might include foie gras, lobster salad, frogs' legs, fresh asparagus in mousseline sauce, or fish cooked in a salt crust. The inn also rents 37 well-furnished and comfortable rooms, costing 270 to 360F (€41.05 to €54.70, $39 to $52) for a double with bathroom; 180F (€27.35, $26) without bathroom.

Place de l'Eglise, 41700 Cour-Cheverny. © 02-54-79-96-44. Fax 02-54-79-25-60. Main courses 70–185F (€10.65–€28.10, $10–$27). Set price menus 127–260F (€19.30–€39.50, $18–$38). AE, DC, MC, V. Tues–Sun noon–2:15pm and 7:30–9:15pm. Closed Feb 1–Mar 15.

Saint-Hubert FRENCH (TRADITIONAL)   About 500m (550 yards..) from the side of the château, this roadside inn was built in the 1950s in the old provincial style. The least expensive menu might include terrine of quail, pikeperch with beurre blanc, a selection of cheeses, and a homemade fruit tart. The most expensive menu may offer lobster, an aiguillette of duckling prepared with grapes, salmon braised in local white wine, casserole of seafood with shellfish sauce, and in season, wild boar in cream sauce. The Saint-Hubert offers 19 conservatively decorated rooms with bathroom, charging 250 to 330F (€38 to €50.15, $36 to $48) double.

Route Nationale. 41700 Cour-Cheverny. ✆ **02-54-79-96-60.** Fax 02-54-79-21-17. Main courses 75–110F (€11.40–€16.70, $11–$16); set price menus 80–220F (€12.15–€33.45, $12–$32). AE, MC, V. Daily 12:15–2pm and 7:30–9:30pm. Closed Feb 10 and Sun night in low season.

VALENÇAY

One of the Loire's handsomest Renaissance châteaux, 56km (35 miles) south of Blois, the **Château de Valençay** ✮✮ (✆ **02-54-00-10-66**) was acquired in 1803 by Talleyrand on the orders of Napoléon, who wanted his minister of foreign affairs to receive dignitaries in great style. In 1838 Talleyrand was buried at Valençay, the château passing to his nephew, Louis de Talleyrand-Périgord. Before the Talleyrand ownership, Valençay was built in 1550 by the d'Estampes family. The dungeon and great west tower are of this period, as is the building's main body; other wings were added in the 17th and 18th centuries. The effect is grandiose, almost too much so, with domes, chimneys, and turrets. The private apartments are open to the public; they're sumptuously furnished, mostly in Empire style but with Louis XV and Louis XVI trappings as well.

Admission to the castle, an antique car museum, and the park is 50F (€7.60, $7) adults, 37F (€5.60, $5) seniors, students, and those 17 and under. Price rises to 53F (€8.05, $8) during July and August. It's open daily from April to June and from September to October from 10am to 6pm; daily July and August from 9:30am to 6:30pm; and Saturday, Sunday, and school holidays from November to March from 2 to 5pm.

ESSENTIALS
GETTING THERE   There are frequent SNCF rail connections from Blois. Call ✆ **08-36-35-35-35** for **train** information and schedules. The station is near the village center.

VISITOR INFORMATION   The **Office de Tourisme** is on route de Blois (✆ **02-54-00-04-42**).

DEPARTING BY CAR   To continue château-hopping, drive north from Valençay until you come to Selles-sur-Cher at the river. This time head west in the direction of Amboise, taking N-76 along the south bank. Chenonceaux lies 16km (10 miles) south of Amboise.

WHERE TO STAY & DINE
Hôtel d'Espagne   This former coaching inn provides an old-world ambience. The unique rooms are named after different ancestral manor houses in the region. Bathrooms are exceedingly well maintained. Lunch is served in the dining room or gardens Tuesday to Sunday. Specialties include noisettes of lamb with tarragon and sweetbreads with morels. Within the hotel's dining room, set price menus range from 180 to 260F (€27.35 to €39.50, $26 to $38).

9 rue du Château, 36600 Valençay. ✆ **02-54-00-00-02.** Fax 02-54-00-12-63. 16 units. 450–650F (€68.40–€98.80, $65–$94) double; 900F (€136.80, $131) suite. AE, DC, MC, V. Parking 25F (€3.80, $3.65). Closed Feb. **Amenities:** Restaurant. *In room:* TV, hair dryer.

CHENONCEAUX

A Renaissance masterpiece, the **Château de Chenonceau** ✮✮✮ (✆ **02-47-23-90-07**) is best known for the *dames de Chenonceau* who have occupied it. (Note that the town is spelled with a final x, but the château is not.) Originally it was owned by the Marqués family, whose members were far too extravagant. Deviously, Thomas Bohier, the comptroller-general of finances in Normandy, began buying up land around the château. The Marqués family was forced to sell to Bohier, who tore down Chenonceau, preserving only the keep and building the rest in the emerging Renaissance style.

Many of the château's walls are covered with Gobelin tapestries, including one depicting a woman pouring water over the back of an angry dragon, another of a three-headed dog and a seven-headed monster. The chapel contains a delicate marble *Virgin and Child,* plus portraits of Catherine de Médici in her traditional black and white. There's even a portrait of the stern Catherine in the former bedroom of her rival, Diane de Poitiers. In François I's Renaissance bedchamber, the most interesting portrait is that of Diane de Poitiers as the huntress Diana.

The history of Chenonceau is related in 15 tableaux in the wax museum, which charges 10F (€1.50, $1.45). Diane de Poitiers, who, among other accomplishments, introduced the artichoke to France, is depicted in three tableaux. One portrays Catherine de Médici tossing out her husband's mistress.

The château is open daily from mid-March to mid-September 9am to 7pm; the rest of the year it closes between 4:30 and 6pm. Admission is 50F (€7.60, $7) adults and 35F (€5.30, $5) children 7 to 15; free for children under 7. A *son et lumière* spectacle, *The Era of the Ladies of Chenonceaux,* is staged daily in summer at 10:15pm; admission is 50F (€7.60, $7) adults and 35F (€5.30, $5) children.

ESSENTIALS

GETTING THERE   There are three daily **trains** from Tours to Chenonceaux (trip time: 45 min.). The train deposits you near the base of the château. Call ☎ **08-36-35-35-35** for train information and schedules.

VISITOR INFORMATION   The **Syndicat d'Initiative** (tourist office) is at rue Bretonneau (☎ **02-47-23-94-45**), open from Easter to September.

DEPARTING BY CAR   Continue back to Tours on the N-76, branching out this time for the best of the châteaux in the west. The first stop is Ussé, of *Sleeping Beauty* fame. Follow the directions to the previously visited Azay-le-Rideau. From Tours, it's a short ride down the Indre Valley on D-17 and then D-7 to Ussé.

WHERE TO STAY

Hôtel du Bon-Laboureur et du Château 🕏🕏   This country inn is within walking distance of the château and is your best bet for a comfortable night's sleep and some of the best cuisine in the Loire Valley. The rear garden has a little guesthouse, plus formally planted roses. Founded in 1786, the hotel maintains the flavor of that era, thanks to thick walls, solid masonry, and a scattering of antiques. Most rooms are small, especially those on the upper floors. The place is noted for its restaurant, which receives notably fewer bus groups than many of its competitors within the region. In fair weather, tables are set up within the courtyard, amid trees and flowering shrubs. Set-price menus in the restaurant cost 170 to 370F (€25.85 to €56.25, $25 to $54) each.

6 rue du Dr. Bretonneau, Chenonceaux, 37150 Bléré. ☎ **02-47-23-90-02.** Fax 02-47-23-82-01. bon-laboureur.fr@lemel.fr. 29 units. 420–850F (€63.85–€129.20, $61–$123) double; 850–1,000F (€129.20–€152, $123–$145) suite. AE, DC, MC, V. **Amenities:** Restaurant, bar; pool; room service; babysitting; laundry/dry cleaning. *In room:* A/C, TV, kitchenette, hair dryer.

La Roseraie 🕏 *(Value* La Roseraie is the most charming and appealing hotel in Chenonceaux. The inviting rooms are individually decorated. Well-kept gardens dominate the property. Some of the finest meals in town are served at lunch and dinner in the hotel's restaurant, which is open to the public. Our favorite dishes include house-style foie gras; magret of duckling with pears and cherries; and an unusual and very delicious invention—*emincée* (a dish made with braised meat) of rump steak with wine-marinated pears.

7 rue du Dr. Bretonneau, Chenonceaux, 37150 Bléré. ℂ **02-47-23-90-09.** Fax 02-47-23-91-59. 16 units. 280–800F (€42.55–€121.60, $41–$116) double. AE, DC, MC, V. Closed Dec to mid-Feb. **Amenities:** Restaurant, bar; pool; laundry/dry cleaning. *In room:* TV, hair dryer.

WHERE TO DINE
Au Gateau Breton FRENCH (TRADITIONAL)   The sun terrace in back of this Breton-type inn, a short walk from the château, is a refreshing place for dinner or tea. Gravel paths run among beds of pink geraniums and lilacs, and the red tables have bright canopies and umbrellas. The chef provides home cooking and cherry liqueur—a specialty of the region. In cool months meals are served in rustic dining rooms. Specialties are small chitterling sausages of Tours, chicken with Armagnac sauce, and *coq au vin* (chicken cooked in wine). The medallions of veal with mushroom-cream sauce are excellent. Tasty pastries are sold in the front room.

16 rue du Dr. Bretonneau. ℂ **02-47-23-90-14.** Fax 02-47-23-92-57. Reservations required July–Aug. Set price menus 60–115F (€9.10–€17.50, $9–$17). MC, V. May–Sept Tues 7–9:30pm; Wed 11:30am–2pm; Thurs–Mon 11:30am–2pm and 7–9:30pm. Oct–Apr Thurs–Tues 11:30am–2:30pm and 7–9:30pm.

USSÉ
At the edge of the hauntingly dark forest of Chinon, the **Château d'Ussé** ⌖ (ℂ **02-47-95-54-05**) was the inspiration behind Perrault's legend of *Sleeping Beauty* (*La Belle au bois dormant*). On a hill overlooking the Indre River, it's a complex of steeples, turrets, towers, chimneys, and dormers. Conceived as a medieval fortress, Ussé was erected at the dawn of the Renaissance. Two powerful families, the Bueil and d'Espinay, lived here in the 15th and 16th centuries. The terraces, laden with orange trees, were laid out in the 18th century.

The guided tour begins in the Renaissance chapel, with its sculptured portal and handsome stalls. Then you proceed to the royal apartments, furnished with tapestries and antiques. One gallery displays an extensive collection of swords and rifles. A spiral stairway leads to a tower with a waxwork Sleeping Beauty, and a panoramic view of the river.

The château is open daily from February to October 9am to 6:30pm; it's closed from November to January. Admission is 59F (€8.95, $9) adults and 19F (€2.90, $2.75) ages 8 to 16, free for children under 8.

ESSENTIALS
GETTING THERE   From Tours, motorists can follow N152 to D7 into Ussé, 28km (25 miles) away. The nearest rail station, Langeais, is 12km (7½ miles) away; from Langeais you have to take a taxi.

DEPARTING BY CAR   Chinon is easily reached from Ussé via D-7 and D-16. You approach this ancient town with its rock-of-ages castle looming on the horizon.

CHINON ⌖
In the film *Joan of Arc,* Ingrid Bergman sought out the dauphin as he tried to conceal himself among his courtiers—an action whose real-life equivalent took place at the Château de Chinon, one of the oldest fortress-châteaux in France. Charles VII, mockingly known as the King of Bourges, centered his government at Chinon from 1429 to 1450. In 1429, with the English besieging Orléans, the Maid of Orléans, that "messenger from God," prevailed on the weak dauphin to

give her an army. The rest is history. The seat of French power stayed at Chinon until the Hundred Years' War ended.

Chinon retains a medieval atmosphere. It consists of winding streets and turreted houses, many built in the 15th and 16th centuries in the heyday of the court. For the best view, drive across the river, turning right onto quai Danton. From that vantage point, you'll have the best perspective, seeing the castle in relation to the village and the river. The gables and towers make Chinon look like a toy village. The most typical street is **rue Voltaire**, lined with 15th- and 16th-century town houses. At no. 44, Richard the Lion-Hearted died on April 6, 1199, after being mortally wounded while besieging Chalus in Limousin. In the heart of Chinon, the **Grand Carroi** was the crossroads of the Middle Ages.

The most famous son of Chinon, François Rabelais, the earthy and often bawdy Renaissance writer, lived on the rue de la Lamproie where today a plaque marks the spot where his father practiced law and maintained a prestigious and prosperous home and office. The isolated cottage 6km (3½ miles) west of Chinon where he was born is the site of the **Musée François Rabelais,** La Devinière, 37500 Seuilly (② **02-47-95-91-18**). Entrance costs 24F (€3.65, $3.50) adults, and 17F (€2.60, $2.45) students and those under 24, and it's open as follows: from January 1 to March 13 and from October 1 to December 31, daily from 9:30am to 12:30pm and 2 to 5pm; from March 14 to April 30, daily from 9:30am to 12:30pm and 2 to 6pm; from May 1 to September 14, daily from 10am to 7pm. To reach it from Chinon, follow the road signs pointing to Saumur and the D-17. Along the way make a stop at the Church of Notre Dame in Rivière; admission is free (② **02-47-93-07-53**).

Château de Chinon ②② (② 02-47-93-13-45) is three separate strongholds, once badly ruined, but today at least two of the buildings, the Château du Milieu and the Château du Coudray, have been entirely restored, with the exception of their still nonexistent roofs. Some of the grim walls from other dilapidated edifices remain, though many of the buildings—including the Great Hall where Joan of Arc sought out the dauphin—have been torn down. Some of the most destructive owners were the heirs of Cardinal Richelieu. Now gone, the Château de St Georges was built by Henry II of England, who died here in 1189. The Château du Milieu dates from the 11th to the 15th century, containing the keep and the clock tower, where the Musée Jeanne d'Arc has been installed. Separated from the latter by a moat, the Château du Coudray contains the Tour du Coudray, where Joan of Arc stayed during her time at Chinon. In the 14th century the Knights Templar were imprisoned here before meeting their violent deaths.

The château is open daily from January 2 to March 14, 9am to noon and 2 to 5pm; from March 15 to June 30 and all of September, from 9am to 6pm; from July to August, 9am to 7pm; and October, from 9am to 5pm. Admission is 28F (€4.25, $4) adults and 19F (€2.90, $2.75) children.

ESSENTIALS
GETTING THERE   There are three **trains** daily from Tours (trip time: 1 hr.). Call ② **08-36-35-35-35** for information and schedules. The train station lies at the edge of this very small town. Once leaving it, you walk along quai Jeanne d'Arc, taking a right at the Café de la Paix to get to place de l'Hôtel de Ville, the town hall, and the tourist office. There are three **buses** a day from Tours (1½ hr.).

VISITOR INFORMATION   The **Office de Tourisme** is at Hofheim (② 02-47-93-17-85).

DEPARTING BY CAR   Angers is generally considered the western end of the Loire Valley, though the Loire River continues for another 130km (80 miles) before reaching Nantes. To reach Angers, continue north from Chinon toward the river. The D-7 connects to the N-152 heading west all the way to Saumur. Once at Saumur, the D-952 continues west into Angers, a distance of 51km (32 miles).

WHERE TO STAY

Chris' Hôtel   This well-run hotel is housed in a 19th-century building near the town's historic district. Many of the rooms are small but offer views of the castle and river. Most are furnished in a Louis XV style and all have modern amenities. Bathrooms are quite cramped. Breakfast is the only meal served.

12 place Jeanne-d'Arc, 37500 Chinon. © **02-47-93-36-92.** Fax 02-47-98-48-92. Chrishotel@wanadoo.fr. 32 units. 260–430F (€39.50–€65.35, $38–$62) double. AE, DC, MC, V. Free parking. **Amenities:** Breakfast room, bar; room service. *In room:* A/C, TV.

WHERE TO DINE

Au Plaisir Gourmand FRENCH (TRADITIONAL)   This is the premier restaurant in the area, owned by Jean-Claude Rigollet, who used to direct the chefs at the fabled Les Templiers in Les Bézards. His restaurant offers an intimate dining room with a limited number of tables in a charming 18th-century building. Menu items are likely to include roast rabbit in aspic with foie-gras sauce, oxtail in a Chinon red-wine sauce, zander in beurre blanc, and sautéed crayfish with a spicy salad. For dessert, try the prunes stuffed in puff pastry.

2 rue Parmentier. © **02-47-93-20-48.** Reservations required. Main courses 80–150F (€12.15–€22.80, $12–$22); set price menus 175–340F (€26.60–€51.70, $26–$49). AE, V. Tues–Sat noon–2pm and 7:30–9:30pm; Sun noon–2pm. Closed Feb.

ANGERS

Once the capital of Anjou, Angers straddles the Maine River. Although it suffered extensive damage in World War II, it has been considerably restored, somehow blending provincial charm with the suggestion of sophistication. The town is often used as a base for exploring the château district to the west.

The moated **Château d'Angers** (© **02-41-87-43-47**) from the 9th century was once the home of the comtes d'Anjou. After the castle was destroyed, it was reconstructed by St. Louis. From 1230 to 1238 the outer walls and 17 massive towers were built, creating a formidable fortress well prepared to withstand invaders. The château was favored by Good King René; until he was forced to surrender Anjou to Louis XI, a brilliant court life flourished here. Louis XIV turned the château into a prison, dispatching his finance minister, Fouquet, to one of its cells. In the 19th century, the castle was also used as a prison, and during World War II, it was used by the Nazis as a munitions depot. Allied planes bombed it in 1944.

The castle displays the **Apocalypse Tapestries** , masterpieces of medieval art. (This series of tapestries wasn't always so highly regarded; they once served as a canopy for orange trees to protect the fruit from unfavorable weather and at another time to cover the damaged walls of a church.) The tapestries were created by Nicolas Bataille, master weaver, perhaps in the Parisian workshop of Robert Poinçon based on cartoons by Hennequin of Bruges. The series illustrates the book of St. John in 77 pieces that stretch 102m (335 ft.). One scene is called *La Grande Prostituée,* and another shows Babylon invaded by demons; yet another is a peace scene with two multiheaded monsters holding up a fleur-de-lis.

You can tour the fortress, including the courtyard of the nobles, prison cells, ramparts, windmill tower, 15th-century chapel, and royal apartments. The château is open daily from June to September 15, 9:30am to 7pm; and from September 16 to May, 10am to 5pm. Admission is 35F (€5.30, $5) adults, 23F (€3.50, $3.35) ages 13 to 25, free for children under 13.

Cathédrale St-Maurice 𝕲𝕲, place Monsigneur Shappoulie (𝄢 **02-41-87-58-45**), is mostly from the 12th and 13th centuries; the main tower, however, dates from the 16th century. The statues on the portal represent everybody from the Queen of Sheba to David at the harp. On the tympanum is depicted Christ Enthroned; the symbols, such as the lion for St. Mark, represent the Evangelists. The stained-glass windows from the 12th through the 16th century have made the cathedral famous. The oldest one illustrates the martyrdom of St. Vincent (the most unusual is of former St. Christopher with the head of a dog). Once all the Apocalypse Tapestries were shown here; now only a few remain, and they are mainly exhibited in summer. The 12th-century nave is a landmark in cathedral architecture, a clear, coherent plan that's a work of harmonious beauty, the start of the Plantagenet architecture. It's open daily from 9am to 7pm.

ESSENTIALS
GETTING THERE   **Trains** arrive from Saumur (trip time: 30 min.), Tours (trip time: 1 hr.), and Paris-Montparnasse (1½ hr.). The station at place de la Gare in Angers is a convenient walk from the château. For information and schedules, call 𝄢 **08-36-35-35-35.** There are three bus connections a day from Saumur, from Monday to Saturday (1½ hr.). Buses depart and arrive at place de la République. Call 𝄢 **02-41-88-59-25** for schedules and information.

VISITOR INFORMATION   The **Office de Tourisme** is on place Kennedy (𝄢 **02-41-23-51-11**).

WHERE TO STAY
Hôtel d'Anjou   Situated next to a large park, this hotel is the best choice for overnighting in the area. Although comparable in price to the Hôtel de France, it has more upscale appointments and amenities, and a better restaurant. The high-ceilinged and more spacious rooms are closer to the ground. All rooms and the small bathrooms were overhauled in 1998.

1 bd. Foch, 49100 Angers. 𝄢 **800/528-1234** in the U.S., or 02-41-88-24-82. Fax 02-41-87-22-21. 53 units. 405–905F (€61.55–€137.55, $59–$131) double. AE, DC, MC, V. Parking 50F (€7.60, $7). **Amenities:** Good restaurant, bar; laundry/dry cleaning. *In room:* Minibar.

Quality Hôtel de France   This 19th-century hotel, one of the most respected in town, has been run by the Bouyers since 1893. It's the best choice near the rail station. Rooms are soundproof. Many rooms were renovated in the late 1990s. Bathrooms are very small with a shower stall.

8 place de la Gare, 49100 Angers. 𝄢 02-41-88-49-42. Fax 02-41-86-76-70. hotel.de.france.anjou@wanadoo.fr. 55 units. 450–650F (€68.40–€98.80, $65–$94) double. AE, DC, MC, V. Parking 40F (€6.10, $6). **Amenities:** 2 restaurants, bar; room service; laundry/dry cleaning. *In room:* A/C, TV, minibar, hair dryer, iron.

WHERE TO DINE
Hôtel d'Anjou (see above) boasts the town's best restaurant.

Provence Caffè   PROVENÇAL. This restaurant celebrates the herbs, spices, and seafood of Provence. The decor includes bundles of herbs, bright colors, and souvenirs of the Mediterranean; the ambience is casual and sunny. Recommended dishes include a risotto served with asparagus and basil or with snails, grilled salmon with Provençal herbs, and a ballotine of chicken with ratatouille. The chef here continues to delight, perhaps with carpaccio of foie gras or sea wolf grilled with mushrooms and sprinkled with virgin olive oil.

9 place du Ralliement. (C) 02-41-87-44-15. Reservations recommended. All main courses 85F (€12.90, $12.35); set price menus 98–155F (€14.90–€23.55, $14–$22). AE, MC, V. Tues–Sat noon–2pm and 7–10pm. Closed in Aug.

3 Provence & the Côte d'Azur

Provence has been called a bridge between the past and present, where yesterday blends with today in a quiet, often melancholy way. Peter Mayle's best-selling *A Year in Provence* and *Toujours Provence* (as well as his other books about the area) have played no small part in the burgeoning popularity that this sunny corner of southern France has enjoyed during recent years.

The Greeks and Romans filled the landscape with cities boasting theaters, bathrooms, amphitheaters, and triumphal arches. Romanesque fortresses and Gothic cathedrals followed in the Middle Ages. In the 19th century, Provence's light and landscapes attracted illustrious painters like Cézanne and van Gogh to Aix and Arles and other towns.

Provence has its own language and customs. The region is bounded on the north by the Dauphine, the west by the Rhône, the east by the Alps, and the south by the Mediterranean. We cover the northern area of this region, what's traditionally thought of as Provence, and then head down to the southern part, what's known as the glittering Côte d'Azur, or French Riviera.

The Riviera has been called the world's most exciting stretch of beach and "a sunny place for shady people." Each resort on the Riviera—be it Beaulieu by the sea or eagle's-nest Eze—has a unique flavor and special merits. Glitterati and eccentrics have always been drawn to this narrow strip of fabled real estate. A trail of modern artists, attracted to the brilliant light, have left a rich heritage: Matisse in his chapel at Vence, Cocteau at Menton and Villefranche, Picasso at Antibes and seemingly everywhere else, Léger at Biot, Renoir at Cagnes, and Bonnard at Le Cannet. The best art collection of all is at the Maeght Foundation in St-Paul-de-Vence.

The Riviera's high season used to be winter and spring only. However, with changing tastes, July and August have become the most crowded months, and reservations are imperative. The average summer temperature is 24ºC (75ºF); the average winter temperature, 10ºC (49ºF).

The Corniches of the Riviera, depicted in countless films, stretch from Nice to Menton. The Alps drop into the Mediterranean and roads were carved along the way. The lower road, about 32km (20 miles) long, is the **Corniche Inférieure.** Along this road are the ports of Villefranche, Cap-Ferrat, Beaulieu, and Cap-Martin. Built between World War I and the beginning of World War II, the **Moyenne Corniche** (Middle Road), 30km (19 miles) long, also runs from Nice to Menton, winding spectacularly in and out of tunnels and through mountains. The highlight is at mountaintop Eze. The **Grande Corniche**—the most panoramic—was ordered built by Napoléon in 1806. La Turbie and Le Vistaero are the principal towns along the 32-km (20-mile) stretch, which reaches more than 488m (1,600 ft.) high at Col d'Eze.

In general, **tourist offices** in Provence are open from April to September, Monday to Friday 9am to 1pm and 2 to 6pm, and Saturday and Sunday 9am to 1pm and 2 to 5pm (closed Sun the rest of the year).

Our tour begins in Avignon, 684km (425 miles) south of Paris, 80km (50 miles) northwest of Aix-en-Provence, and 106km (66 miles) northwest of Marseille. Most motorists approach the city from Lyon in the north, taking the autoroute (A-7) south. If you haven't arranged for a rental before leaving home, you can head to the following offices in Avignon: **Budget** at the airport (✆ **04-90-27-94-95**) and at 2 av. de Montclair-Gare (✆ 04-90-27-94-95); **Hertz** at the airport (✆ **04-90-14-26-90**) and at 2 av. Montclair (✆ 04-90-82-37-67); and **Avis** at the airport (✆ **04-90-87-17-75**) and at 160 bis av. Pierre-Senmard (✆ 04-90-87-17-75).

AVIGNON ☆☆☆
In the 14th century, Avignon was the capital of Christendom; the popes lived here during what was called "the Babylonian Captivity." The legacy left by that "court of splendor and magnificence" makes Avignon one of the most interesting and beautiful of Europe's medieval cities.

ESSENTIALS

GETTING THERE   Avignon is a junction for bus routes throughout the region. For information, call 📞 **04-90-82-07-35;** you'll find the depot on boulevard St-Roch. Train service from other towns is also frequent. The TGV **trains** from Paris arrive 13 times per day (trip time: 4 hr.), and 17 trains per day arrive from Marseille (1½ hr.). For train information and schedules, call 📞 **08-36-35-35-35;** the station is at porte de la Rèpublique. If you'd like to explore the area by **bike,** go to **Cycles Peugeot,** 80 rue Guillaume-Puy (📞 **04-90-86-32-49**), which rents all sorts of bikes for 60F (€9.10, $9) per day, including 10-speed road bikes and mountain bikes. A deposit of 1,000F (€152, $145) is required, either in the form of cash or a credit-card imprint.

VISITOR INFORMATION   The **Office de Tourisme** is at 41 cours Jean-Jaurès (📞 **04-90-82-65-11**).

DEPARTING BY CAR   From Avignon, D-571 continues south to St-Rémy-de-Provence.

WHERE TO STAY

Hôtel d'Angleterre *(Value)*   In the heart of Avignon, this classical structure, originally built in 1929, is the city's best budget hotel. Small rooms are comfortably but basically furnished; bathrooms are also small and shower-only. Breakfast is the only meal served.

29 bd. Raspail, 84000 Avignon. 📞 **04-90-86-34-31.** Fax 04-90-86-86-74. www.hoteldangleterre.fr. 40 units. 320–450F (€48.65–€68.40, $46–$65) double with bathroom. MC, V. Free parking. Closed Dec 20–Jan 20. **Amenities:** Laundry/dry cleaning. *In room:* TV, hair dryer.

La Mirande *(ΛΛΛ)*   This restored 700-year-old town house in the heart of Avignon is one of France's grand little luxuries, far better than anything else in town. The individually designed rooms, most of which are quite spacious, have bedside controls, antiques, and art. Bathrooms are sumptuous. The restaurant earns its one star in Michelin and is among the finest in Avignon.

4 place Amirande, 84000 Avignon. 📞 **04-90-85-93-93.** Fax 04-90-86-26-85. mirande@la-mirande.fr. 20 units. 1,700–2,600F (€258.40–€395.20, $247–$377) double; 3,700F (€562.40, $537) suite. AE, DC, MC V. Parking 80F (€12.15, $12). **Amenities:** Excellent restaurant, bar; room service; baby-sitting; laundry/dry cleaning. *In room:* A/C, TV, minibar, hair dryer, safe.

Mercure Palais-des-Papes *(Value)*   This chain hotel is one of the best in Avignon, and is a good value for what it offers. It lies within the city walls, at the foot of the Palace of the Popes. Rooms are well furnished yet functional; what they lack in style they make up for in comfort. Bathrooms are small, but often contain a tub/shower combination. Breakfast is the only meal served.

Quartier de la Balance, rue Ferruce, 84000 Avignon. 📞 **04-90-80-93-93.** Fax 04-90-89-93-94. ho549@accor-hotels.com. 87 units. 580–680F (€88.15–€103.35, $84–$99) double. Children under 16 stay free in parents' room. AE, DC, MC, V. Parking 47F (€7.15, $7). Bus: 11. **Amenities:** Bar; room service; baby-sitting; laundry/dry cleaning. *In room:* A/C, TV, minibar, hair dryer.

WHERE TO DINE

Christian Etienne *(ΛΛΛ)* FRENCH (TRADITIONAL & MODERN)   This restaurant serves the best food in Avignon. The dining room contains very old ceiling and wall frescoes honoring the marriage of Anne de Bretagne to the French king in 1491. Several of the set price menus present specific themes, from vegetarian to lobster. A la carte specialties include a filet of red snapper with a coulis of black olives; roasted pigeon with a truffle-enhanced sauce; and a dessert specialty of fennel-flavored sorbet with saffron-flavored English cream sauce.

Avignon

10 rue Mons. ✆ **04-90-86-16-50.** Fax 04-90-86-67-09. Reservations recommended. Main courses 170–210F (€25.85–€31.90, $25–$30); set price lunch (Mon–Fri) 170F (€25.85, $25); set price dinners 320F (€48.65, $46), 430F (€65.35, $62), 530F (€80.55, $77). AE, DC, MC, V. July daily 12:30–1:30pm and 7:30–9:30pm; the rest of the year, Tues–Fri noon–2:30pm and 8–10:30p, Sat–Sun 8–10:30pm.

La Fourchette FRENCH (TRADITIONAL). This bistro offers creative cooking at a moderate price. There are two dining rooms, one like a summerhouse with walls of glass, the other more like a tavern with oak beams. You might begin with fresh sardines flavored with coriander, ravioli filled with haddock, or parfait of chicken liver with a spinach flan and confiture of onions. Grilled lambs' liver with raisins is a main course specialty.

7 rue Racine. ✆ **04-90-85-20-93.** Set price lunch 100–150F (€15.20–€22.80, $15–$22); set price dinner 150F (€22.80, $22). MC, V. Mon–Fri 12:30–2pm and 7:30–9:30pm. Closed Aug 5–29. Bus: 11.

EXPLORING THE TOWN

Even more famous than the papal residency is the ditty "*Sur le pont d'Avignon, l'on y danse, l'on y danse,*" echoing through every French nursery and around the world. Ironically, **pont St-Bénézet** (✆ **04-90-85-60-16**) was far too narrow for the danse of the rhyme, inspired, according to legend, by a vision a shepherd named Bénézet had while tending his flock. Spanning the Rhône and connecting Avignon with Villeneuve-lèz-Avignon, the bridge is now only a fragmented ruin. Built between 1177 and 1185, it suffered various disasters from then on; in 1669 half of it toppled into the river. On one of the piers is the two-story Chapelle St-Nicolas—one story in Romanesque style, the other Gothic. The bridge is open daily from 9am to 6pm. Admission is 15F (€2.30, $2.20) adults and 7F (€1.05, $1) students, children, and seniors.

Dominating Avignon from a hill is the **Palais des Papes,** place du Palais-des-Papes (© **04-90-27-50-00**). You're shown through on a guided tour, usually lasting 50 minutes. Most of the rooms have been stripped of their finery; the exception is the Chapelle St-Jean, known for its beautiful frescoes of scenes from the life of John the Baptist and John the Evangelist, attributed to the school of Matteo Giovanetti and painted between 1345 and 1348. The Grand Tinel, or banquet hall, is about 41m (135 ft.) long and 9m (30 ft.) wide, and the pope's table stood on the southern side. The pope's bedroom is on the first floor of the Tour des Anges. It's open daily from November to March, 9:30am to 5:45pm; from April to June and from August to October, 9am to 7pm; July, 9am to 8pm. Admission is 45F (€6.85, $7) adults and 36F (€5.45, $5) students, children, and seniors. A guided tour, via either a trained staff member or a prerecorded cassette, is included in the price.

Near the palace is the 12th-century **Cathédrale Notre-Dame,** place du Palais-des-Papes (© **04-90-86-81-01**), containing the flamboyant Gothic tomb of Pope John XXII, who died at age 90. Benedict XII is also buried here. The cathedral's hours vary, but generally it's open daily from 9am to 6pm and admission is free. From the cathedral, enter the promenade du Rocher-des-Doms to stroll through its garden and enjoy the view across the Rhône to Villeneuve-lèz-Avignon.

THE SHOPPING SCENE

Véronique Pichon, 21 place Crillon (© **04-90-85-89-00**), is the newest branch of a porcelain manufacturer whose colorful products have been a

---

Tips **Shopping for Provençal Fabric**

The Avignon branch of **Les Olivades,** 28 rue Lafayette (© **04-90-92-00-80**), is one of the most visible of a chain of outlets associated in the States with Pierre Deux. Look for fabrics by the yard, bedcovers, slipcovers, draperies, and tablecloths. Fabrics, printed often by hand in a factory only 10km (6 miles) from Avignon, tend to feature intricate designs in colors inspired by 19th-century models or, to a somewhat lesser extent, Creole designs with butterflies, pineapples, bananas, and flowers.

The vision that launched **Les Indiens de Nîmes,** 4 rue Joseph-vernet (© **04-90-86-32-05**), in the early 1980s involved the duplication of 18th- and 19th-century Provençal fabric patterns. They're sold as fabric by the meter as well as clothing for men, women, and children. Kitchenware and a selection of furniture inspired by originals from Provence and the steamy wetlands west of Marseille are also sold.

All the clothing at **Souleiado,** 2 Ave Résistance (© **04-90-92-45-90**), derives from a Provençal model, and even the Provençal name (which translates as "first ray of sunshine after a storm") evokes a spirit on which the owners want to capitalize. Most, but not all, of the clothing is designed for women; there are some garments—shirts mostly—for men. Fabrics are also sold by the meter.

regional fixture since the 1700s. Manufactured in the nearby town of Uzès, the tableware, decorative urns, statues, and lamps are cost-effective enough to be shipped virtually anywhere.

ST-RÉMY-DE-PROVENCE 🦚

Nostradamus, the French physician/astrologer and author of more than 600 obscure verses, was born here in 1503. In 1922 Gertrude Stein and Alice B. Toklas found St-Rémy after "wandering around everywhere a bit," as Stein once wrote to Cocteau. But mainly St-Rémy is associated with van Gogh, who committed himself to an asylum here in 1889 after cutting off his left ear. Between moods of despair, he painted such works as *Olive Trees* and *Cypresses* here. The town lies 26km (16 miles) northeast of Arles and 13km (8 miles) north of Les Baux.

ESSENTIALS

GETTING THERE   There are local **buses** (no trains) from Avignon, which will let you off in the center of town (trip time: 45 min.); between four to nine buses run per day. Call ✆ **04-90-82-07-35** in Avignon for information and schedules.

VISITOR INFORMATION   The **Office de Tourisme** is at place Jean-Jaurès (✆ **04-90-92-05-22**).

DEPARTING BY CAR   From St-Rémy-de-Provence, head south for 13km (8 miles) along the winding D-5 until you reach Les Baux.

WHERE TO STAY

Les Antiques 🦚   This stylish 19th-century villa is in a 3-hectare (7-acre) park. It contains an elegant reception lounge, which opens onto several salons, and Napoléon III furnishings. Handsomely furnished rooms come in a variety of styles and shapes. Those in the modern pavilion are more comfortable, larger, and have direct access to the garden, but they don't have as much character as those in the main building. Bathrooms are small. In summer you're served breakfast (the only meal) in the former Orangerie.

15 av. Pasteur, 13210 St-Rémy-de-Provence. ✆ 04-90-92-03-02. Fax 04-90-92-50-40. 27 units. 370–750F (€56.25–€114, $54–$109) double. AE, DC, MC, V. Closed Oct 20–Apr 7. **Amenities:** Breakfast room, lounge; pool; baby-sitting laundry/dry cleaning. *In room:* minibar, hair dryer.

WHERE TO DINE

La Maison Jaune 🦚 FRENCH/PROVENÇAL   One of the most enduringly popular restaurants in St-Rémy is found in a pair of dining rooms scattered over two floors of the yellow-fronted building. Meals are prepared and served with flair. An additional 34 seats are available in nice weather on an outdoor terrace. Good choices include pigeon roasted in wine from Les Baux; grilled sardines with candied lemon and raw fennel; artichoke hearts marinated in white wine; and a succulent roasted rack of lamb served with a black olive and anchovy tapenade.

15 rue Carnot. ✆ 04-90-92-56-14. Reservations recommended. www.franceweb.org/lamaisonjaune. Set price lunches 120–305F (€18.25–€46.35, $17–$44); set price dinners 180–305F (€27.35–€46.35, $26–$44). MC, V. June–Sept Wed–Sun noon–2pm; Tues–Sun 7:30–9:30pm. Oct–May Tues–Sat noon–2pm; Mon–Sat 7:30–9:30pm.

EXPLORING ST-RÉMY & ENVIRONS

One interesting activity is visiting the cloisters of the asylum van Gogh made famous in his paintings at the 12th-century **Monastère de St-Paul-de-Mausolée.** Now a psychiatric hospital, the former monastery is east of D-5, a short drive north of Glanum (see below). You can't visit the cell in which van Gogh was confined, but it's still worth coming to explore the Romanesque chapel and cloisters with their circular arches and columns, which have beautifully carved capitals. The cloisters are open from Tuesday to Sunday 9:30am to 6:30pm between June and September; and from Tuesday to Friday 11am to 5pm, from October to May. On your way to the church, you'll see a bust of van Gogh. Admission costs 15F (€2.30, $2.20) adults, 10F (€1.50, $1.45) ages 12 to 16, free for children under 12. There's no number that's available to the public within the monastery, but you can call the nearby clinic (© **04-90-92-77-00**) for information.

In the center of St-Rémy, **Musée Archéologique,** in the Hôtel de Sade, rue du Parage (© **04-90-92-64-04**), displays both sculptures and bronzes excavated at Glanum. It's open daily from April to September, 10am to noon and 2 to 7pm; from October to March, 10am to noon and 2 to 5pm. Admission is 15F (€2.30, $2.20) adults and 16F (€2.45, $2.30) students, free for children under 12.

Just south of St-Rémy on D-5 is **Ruines de Glanum** 𝒜, avenue Vincent-van-Gogh (© **04-90-92-23-79**), a Gallo-Roman city (follow the signs to Les Antiques). Its historical monuments include an Arc Municipal, a triumphal arch dating from the time of Julius Caesar, and a cenotaph called the Mausolée des Jules. Garlanded with sculptured fruits and flowers, the arch dates from 20 B.C. and is the oldest in Provence. The mausoleum was raised to honor the grandsons of Augustus and is the only extant monument of its type. In the area are entire streets and foundations of private residences from the 1st-century town. Some remains are from an even earlier Gallo-Greek town dating from the 2nd century B.C. Admission is 36F (€5.45, $5) adults, 25F (€3.80, $3.65) ages 12 to 25, free for children under 12. The excavations are open daily from April to September, from 9am to 7pm; from October to March, from 9am to noon and 2 to 5pm.

LES BAUX 𝒜𝒜𝒜

What Cardinal Richelieu called "a nesting place for eagles" lies 19km (12 miles) north of Arles and 80km (50 miles) north of Marseille and the Mediterranean. Once it was the citadel of the powerful seigneurs of Les Baux; today, in its lonely position high on a windswept plateau overlooking the southern Alpilles, Les Baux is a ghost of its former self. Still, there is no more dramatically situated town in Provence than this one nestled in a valley surrounded by mysterious, shadowy rock formations.

ESSENTIALS

GETTING THERE   There's no railway station in Les Baux, so consequently most rail passengers get off at Arles. From Arles, there're four **buses** daily that stop at Les Baux (trip time: 25 min.), and an additional four or five that stop in the nearby hamlet of Maussane-les-Alpilles, 4km (2½ miles) to the south. The frequency of the bus service is reduced by about half between November and March. For information about buses, call © **04-90-49-38-01** in Arles for information and schedules.

VISITOR INFORMATION   The **Office de Tourisme** is on Ilôt Post Tenebras Lux (© **04-90-54-34-39**); fax 04-90-54-51-15.

DEPARTING BY CAR   From Les Baux continue southwest on D-17 for 19km (12 miles) to Arles.

WHERE TO STAY & DINE
La Riboto de Taven *★★★* FRENCH(MODERN)   This 1835 farmhouse outside the medieval section of town serves food filled with brawny flavors and the heady perfumes of Provençal herbs. In summer, you can sit out at the beautifully laid tables (one of which is a millstone). Menu items may include sea bass in olive oil, fricassee of mussels flavored with basil, and lamb en croute with olives—plus homemade desserts. It's also possible to rent seven double rooms so large they're like suites, for 900 to 1,100F (€136.80 to €167.20, $131 to $160), breakfast included.

Le Val d'Enfer, 13520 Valo fontaine. © 04-90-54-34-23. Fax 04-90-54-38-88. Reservations required. Main courses 150–190F (€22.80–€28.90, $22–$28); set price lunch 220F (€33.45, $32); set price dinners 300–450F (€45.60–€68.40, $44–$65). AE, DC, MC, V. Thurs–Mon noon–1:30pm and 7:30–9pm. Closed Jan 15–Mar 1.

EXPLORING LES BAUX
Some one million visitors a year flock here to wander the feudal ruins, inspect the foundation of a demolished castle, and explore the facades of gracefully restored Renaissance homes. The **Château des Baux** (© 04-90-54-55-56) is carved out of the rocky mountain peak; the site of this former castle covers an area at least five times that of Les Baux itself below. As you stand here, you can look out over the **Valley of Hell** (Val d'Enfer). (Later, you might be tempted to drive through its bleak and rugged scenery—access is from the D27 and D78G). At the castle you can enjoy panoramas from Tour Paravel and Tour Sarascenes. The site is open daily, July and August from 9am to 8:30pm; from September to February 9am to 5pm; from March to June 9am to 6pm. Admission is 40F (€6.10, $6) adults, 30F (€4.55, $4.35) students, and 21F (€3.20, $3) ages 7 to 17, free for children under 7.

ARLES *★★★*
Arles, 35km (22 miles) southwest of Avignon and 88km (55 miles) northwest of Marseille, has been called "the soul of Provence," and art lovers, archaeologists, and historians alike are attracted to this town on the Rhône. Van Gogh left Paris for Arles in 1888 and painted some of his most celebrated works here—*Starry Night, The Bridge at Arles, Sunflowers,* and *L'Arlésienne* among others. Many of these luminous scenes remain to delight visitors today.

Arles isn't quite as charming as Aix-en-Provence, but it has first-rate museums, excellent restaurants, and summer festivals, such as an international photography festival in early June. Though not as lovely as it was when Picasso came here, Arles has enough antique Provençal flavor to keep the appeal alive.

ESSENTIALS
GETTING THERE   Arles lies on the Paris-Marseille and Bordeaux-St-Raphaël rail lines, so it has frequent connections from most French cities. Ten **trains** arrive daily from Avignon (trip time: 20 min.) and 10 per day from Marseille (1 hr.). From Aix-en-Provence, 10 trains arrive per day (1¾ hr.). Call © 08-36-35-35-35 for details. There are about five **buses** per day from Aix-en-Provence (1¾ hr.). Call © 04-90-49-38-01 for information and schedules. The bus station is adjacent to the railway station, a 10-minute walk from the center.

VISITOR INFORMATION   The **Office de Tourisme,** where you can buy a *Billet Globale* (see below), is on the esplanade des Lices (© 04-90-18-41-20). If you'd like to get around by bicycle, head for the newspaper kiosk immediately adjacent to the town's tourist information office, a site that doubles as a bike rental outfit: **Europbike,** Kiosk à Journaux Le Provençal, Esplanade Charles de Gaulle (✆ **04-90-49-54-69**). A six-speed road bike—all that this emporium stocks—rents for 70F (€10.65, $10) per day, and requires a deposit of 1,000F (€152, $145). **Cycles Peugeot,** 15 rue du Pont (✆ **04-90-96-03-77**), rents bikes at comparable rates.

DEPARTING BY CAR   From Arles, head east toward Aix-en-Provence on N-113. Once at Salon-de-Provence, take the autoroute southeast for 37km (23 miles) to Aix-en-Provence, the conclusion of your driving tour of Provence. After that, it's south to the French Riviera.

WHERE TO STAY

Hôtel d'Arlatan ✿   In the former residence of the comtes d'Arlatan de Beaumont, near place du Forum, this hotel has been managed by the same family since 1920. It was built in the 15th century on the ruins of an old palace. Rooms are furnished with authentic Provençal antiques and walls covered by tapestries. Try to get a room overlooking the garden. Those on the ground floor are largest.

26 rue du Sauvage, 13100 Arles. ✆ **04-90-93-56-66.** Fax 04-90-49-68-45. hotel-arlatan@provenet.fr. 48 units. 500–850F (€76–€129.20, $73–$123) double; 1,050–1,450F (€159.60–€220.40, $152–$210) suite. AE, DC, MC, V. Parking 70F (€10.65, $10). **Amenities:** Dining room, laundry. *In room:* A/C, TV, minibar, hair dryer.

Hôtel Jules César et Restaurant Lou Marquès ✿✿✿   In the town center, this 17th-century former Carmelite convent is now a stately hotel with the best restaurant in Arles. Though this is a noisy neighborhood, most rooms face the quiet, unspoiled cloister. You wake to the scent of roses and the sounds of birds singing. Interior rooms are the most tranquil, but also the darkest. Most downstairs rooms are spacious; those upstairs have certain old-world charm that offsets their smaller size. Rooms in the modern extensions, though large and comfortable, lack character.

The restaurant, Lou Marques, has tables outside on the front terrace. The food is extremely fresh. From the a la carte menu, we recommend bourride à la Provençale or Arles lamb. A la carte dinners average 240 to 550F (€36.50 to €83.60, $35 to $80).

9 bd. des Lices, 13200 Arles. ✆ **04-90-52-52-52.** Fax 04-90-52-52-53. www.julescesar.fr. 58 units. 900–1,250F (€136.80–€190, $131–$181) double; from 1,600–2,200F (€243.20–€334.40, $232–$319) suite. AE, DC, MC, V. Parking 65F (€9.95, $9). Closed Nov 12–Dec 23. **Amenities:** Restaurant, bar; pool; room service; baby-sitting; laundry/dry cleaning. *In room:* A/C, TV, minibar, hair dryer, safe.

WHERE TO DINE

L'Olivier ✿ PROVENÇAL/FRENCH   One of the most genuinely charming restaurants in Arles occupies a solidly built house on the western edge of the old town. Inside, you'll find a warren of small-scale dining rooms with beamed ceilings, fireplaces, and antique terra-cotta tiles. Menu items vary with the season, but the best examples include fresh local asparagus garnished with sweetbreads settled on a bed of roasted tomatoes; fava-bean soup with garlic croutons and saffron-flavored rouille; codfish steak served with a bouillon of garlic and fresh herbs and camarguais wild rice; and filet of bull served with a concassé of black pepper, anchovy butter, capers, and olives. Also baby pigeon roasted with foie gras-flavored butter and asparagus tips roasted in Parmesan.

1 bis rue Réattu. ✆ **04-90-49-64-88.** Reservations recommended. Main courses 98–170F (€14.90–€25.85, $14–$25); set menus 178–368F (€27.05–€55.95, $26–$53). MC, V. Daily noon–1:15pm and 7:30–9:15pm.

EXPLORING ARLES

At the tourist office you can purchase a Billets Global, the all-inclusive pass that admits you to the town's museums, Roman monuments, and major attractions; it costs 50F (€7.60, $7) adults and 35F (€5.30, $5) children.

The town is full of Roman monuments. The general vicinity of the old Roman forum is occupied by **place du Forum,** shaded by plane trees. Once the Café de Nuit, immortalized by van Gogh, stood on this square. Two Corinthian columns and pediment fragments from a temple can be seen at the corner of the Hôtel Nord-Pinus. South of here is **place de la République** (also known as the place de l'Hôtel de Ville), the principal plaza, dominated by a 15-m (50-ft.) blue porphyry obelisk. On the north is the impressive Hôtel-de-Ville (town hall) from 1673, built to Mansart's plans and surmounted by a Renaissance belfry.

On the east side of the square is the **Fglise St-Trophime** ✵ (© 04-90-96-07-38), noted for its 12th-century portal, one of the finest achievements of southern Romanesque style. In the pediment Christ is surrounded by the symbols of the Evangelists. The cloister, in both the Gothic and Romanesque styles, is noted for its medieval carvings. Admission is free. The church is open from Monday to Saturday 8:30am to 6:30pm, Sunday from 8:30am to 6pm. The cloister's hours are from Monday to Saturday 9am to noon and 2:30 to 6pm. Admission is 15F (€2.30, $2.20) adults and 9F (€1.35, $1.30) students and children under 12.

Museon Arlaten (© 04-90-93-58-11) is entered at 29 rue de la République (its name is written in old Provençal style). It was founded by Frédéric Mistral, the Provençal poet and leader of a movement to establish Modern Provençal as a literary language, using the money from his Nobel Prize for literature in 1904. This is really a folklore museum, with regional costumes, portraits, furniture, dolls, a music salon, and one room devoted to mementos of Mistral. The museum is open from April to October daily from 9am to noon and 2 to 6pm (until 6:30pm in July and Aug); from November to March Tuesday to Sunday from 9:30am to 12:30pm and 2 to 5pm. Admission is 25F (€3.80, $3.65) adults and 20F (€3.05, $2.90) ages 12 to 18, free for children under 12.

The city's two great classical monuments are the **Théâtre Antique,** rue du Cloître (© 04-90-96-93-30), and the Amphitheater. The Roman theater begun by Augustus in the 1st century was mostly destroyed and only two Corinthian columns remain. Now rebuilt, the theater is the setting for an annual drama festival in July. The theater was where the Venus of Arles was discovered in 1651. Take rue de la Calade from the town hall. The theater is open daily from March to November 10am to noon and 2 to 4:30pm; off-season from 10 to 11:30am and 2 to 4pm. Admission is 15F (€2.30, $2.20) adults, 9F (€1.35, $1.30) children.

Nearby, the **Amphitheater** ✵✵, Rond-Pont des Arènes (© 04-90-49-36-36), also built in the 1st century, seats almost 25,000 and still hosts bullfights in summer. The government warns you to visit the old monument at your own risk because of the worn and uneven masonry. For a good view, you can climb the three towers that remain from medieval times, when the amphitheater was turned into a fortress. Hours are daily from March to November 10am to noon and 2 to 4:30pm; off-season from 10 to 11:30am and 2 to 4pm. Admission is 15F (€2.33, $2.20) adults and 9F (€1.35, $1.30) ages 16 and under.

The most memorable sight in Arles is **Nécropoledes Alyscamps** ✵, rue Pierre-Renaudel (© 04-90-49-36-36), once a necropolis established by the Romans, converted into a Christian burial ground in the 4th century. As the latter, it became a setting for legends in epic medieval poetry and was even mentioned in Dante's *Inferno*. Today, it's lined with poplars and the remaining sarcophagi; a cool oasis in hot weather. Open daily from June to September 8:30am to 7pm, October and from March to May 9am to noon and 2 to 4:30pm, and from November to February 10 to 11:30am and 2 to 4pm. Admission is 15F (€2.30, 2.20) adults and 9F (€1.35, $1.30) children. Another ancient monument is the **Thermes de Constantin,** rue Dominique-Maisto, near the banks of the Rhône. Today, only the bathrooms (*thermae*) remain of a once-grand imperial palace. Visiting hours and admission prices are the same as at Les Alyscamps.

AIX-EN-PROVENCE 🟢🟢
Founded in 122 B.C. by Roman general Caius Sextius Calvinus, who named it Aquae Sextiae after himself, Aix evolved from a Roman military outpost to a provincial administrative capital, the seat of an archbishop, and the official residence of the medieval comtes de Provence.

The celebrated son of this old capital city of Provence is Paul Cézanne, who immortalized the countryside nearby. Montagne Ste-Victoire looms over the town today just as it did in Cézanne's time, though a string of high-rises has cropped up. This faded university town, Provence's most charming center, was once a seat of aristocracy, its streets walked by counts and kings. It's 80km (50 miles) southeast of Avignon and 32km (20 miles) north of Marseille.

ESSENTIALS
GETTING THERE   As a rail and highway junction, the city is easily accessible, with **trains** arriving hourly from Marseille (trip time: 40 min.) at the station off rue Gustave Desplace at the end of avenue Victor Hugo. For details, call 📞 **08-36-35-35-35.** There's frequent **bus** service in and out of Aix's **Gare Routière** (📞 **04-42-91-26-80** for information), including four a day to and from Avignon (1½ hr.). Buses arrive at the station on rue Lapierre at intervals of between 15 and 30 minutes throughout the day from Marseille.

If you'd like to explore the region by bike, contact **Cycles Naddeo,** 54 av. de Lattre-de-Tassigny (📞 **04-42-21-06-93**), which rents 10-speeds for 80F (€12.15, $12) per day or mountain bikes for 100F (€15.20, $15) per day. Either a passport or some form of currency representing between 1,000 and 2,500F (€152 and €380, $145 and $363), depending on the value of the bike, is required at the time of rental. The shop lies in the heart of town, midway between town hall and the town's main police station.

VISITOR INFORMATION   The **Office de Tourisme** is at 2 place du Général-de-Gaulle (📞 **04-42-16-11-61**). Fax 04-42-16-11-62.

DEPARTING BY CAR   From Aix-en-Provence, the best way to reach St-Tropez is to take the autoroute (A-8) southeast to the junction with Route 25, then cut south to Ste-Maximin. Once at Ste-Maximin, follow N-555 then D125 to St-Tropez, at which point you connect with N-98/D98A going east via Maleribes for the final lap to St-Tropez.

WHERE TO STAY
Hôtel Cardinal *Value*   Not everything is state of the art, but to many, the Cardinal is still the best value in Aix. Lying on the other side of the Cours in the Mazarin quarter, it is distinguished by a lingering air of fragility and nostalgia. Guests stay in simply furnished rooms either in the main building or in the 18th-century annex up the street, site of most of the hotel's suites. Bathrooms tend to be small but each has a good shower.

22–24 rue Cardinale, 13100 Aix-en-Provence. ☎ **04-42-38-32-30.** Fax 04-42-26-39-05. 29 units. 350–380F (€53.20–€57.75, $51–$55) double; 450–480F (€68.40–€72.95, $65–$70) suite. MC, V. *In room:* A/C, TV, kitchenette, hair dryer.

Villa Gallici ✩✩✩   This elegant inn set within an 18th-century villa in the heart of town is the most stylishly decorated in Aix. Each large room has a king-size bed, often canopied. Some rooms boast a private terrace or garden. Bathrooms are large with modern amenities. The villa sits in a large enclosed garden, close to one of the best restaurants, Le Clos de la Violette. The hotel restaurant serves an a la carte menu only to hotel residents and their guests. On the premises are limited spa facilities.

Av. de la Violette (impasse des Grands Pins), 13100 Aix-en-Provence. ☎ **04-42-23-29-23.** Fax 04-42-96-30-45. villagallici@relaischateaux.fr. 22 units. 1,400–3,300F (€212.80–€501.60, $203–$479) double; 3,000–3,300F (€456–€501.60, $435–$479) suite. AE, DC, MC, V. **Amenities:** Restaurant, bar; pool; room service; baby-sitting; laundry/dry cleaning. *In room:* A/C, TV, minibar, hair dryer, safe.

WHERE TO DINE
Le Bistro Latin   FRENCH PROVENÇAL. This is the best little bistro in Aix for the price. Provençal music plays in two intimate, antiques-decorated dining rooms, and the staff is young and enthusiastic. Try the chartreuse of mussels, one of the meat dishes with spinach-and-saffron cream sauce, or crepe of hare with basil sauce. We've enjoyed the classic cuisine, particularly the scampi risotto, on all our visits.

18 rue de la Couronne. ☎ **04-42-38-22-88.** Reservations recommended. Set price lunch 75–95F (€11.40–€14.45, $11–$14); set price dinner 139–159F (€21.15–€24.15, $20–$23) and 185F (€28.10, $27). MC, V. Mon 7–10:30pm; Tues–Sat noon–2pm and 7–10:30pm. Bus: 27, 42, or 51.

Le Clos de la Violette ✩✩✩   FRENCH (MODERN)   In an elegant residential neighborhood, which most visitors reach by taxi, this is the most innovative restaurant in town. The food produced by Jean-Marc and Brigitte Banzo has been called a "song of Provence." Typical dishes—though they change every 3 months—are an upside-down tart of snails with parsley juice, slow-cooked lamb with brown sauce, scallops with artichoke hearts, and a sumptuous array of desserts.

10 av. de la Violette. ☎ **04-42-23-30-71.** Fax 04-42-21-93-03. Reservations required. Main courses 185–210F (€28.10–€31.90, $27–$31); set price lunch 300–600F (€45.60–€91.20, $44–$87); set price dinner 600F (€91.20, $87). AE, V. Mon 7:30–9:30pm, Tues–Sat noon–1:30pm and 7:30–9:30pm. Closed 2 weeks in Nov and 1 week in Feb. Bus: 27, 42, or 51.

EXPLORING THE CITY
Cours Mirabeau ✩✩, the main street, is one of the most beautiful in Europe. Plane trees act like umbrellas, shading the street from the hot Provençal sun and filtering the light into shadows that play on the rococo fountains. On one side are shops and sidewalk cafes, on the other richly embellished sandstone *hôtels particuliers* (mansions) from the 17th and 18th centuries. The street, which honors Mirabeau, the revolutionary and statesman, begins at the 1860 landmark fountain on place de la Libération.

Cathédrale St-Sauveur, place des Martyrs de la Résistance (☎ **04-42-23-45-65**), is dedicated to Christ under the title St-Sauveur (Holy Savior). Its baptistery dates from the 4th and 5th centuries, but the architectural complex as a whole has seen many additions. It contains a brilliant Nicolas Froment triptych, *The Burning Bush,* from the 15th century. One side depicts the Virgin and Child, the other Good King René and his second wife, Jeanne de Laval. It's open daily from 7:30am to noon and 2 to 6pm; masses are Sunday at 9am, 10:30am, and 7pm.

Nearby in a former archbishop's palace is the **Musée des Tapisseries,** 28 place des Martyrs de la Résistance (© **04-42-23-09-91**). Lining its gilded walls are three series of tapestries from the 17th and 18th centuries collected by the archbishops to decorate the palace: *The History of Don Quixote* by Natoire, *The Russian Games* by Leprince, and *The Grotesques* by Monnoyer. In addition, the museum exhibits rare furnishings from the 17th and 18th centuries as well as contemporary exhibitions. It's open from Wednesday to Monday 10am to noon and 2 to 5:45pm; admission is 15F (€2.30, $2.20) adults, 9F (€1.35, $1.30) students.

Up rue Cardinale is the **Musée Granet** ⍟, place St-Jean-de-Malte (© **04-42-38-14-70**), which owns a not-very-typical collection of Cézannes. Matisse donated a nude in 1941. Housed in the former center of the Knights of Malta, the fine-arts gallery contains work by Van Dyck, Van Loo, and Rigaud; portraits by Pierre and François Puget; and (the most interesting) a Jupiter and Thetis by Ingres. Ingres also did an 1807 portrait of the museum's namesake, François Marius Granet. Granet's own works abound. On the grounds they also include a branch of archaeological finds with the vestiges of Aix-en Provence during the Roman empire. The museum is open from Wednesday to Monday 10am to noon and 2 to 6pm; closed January. Admission is 18F (€2.75, $2.60) adults, 10F (€1.50, $1.45) students.

Outside town, at 9 av. Paul-Cézanne, is the **Atelier de Cézanne** (© **04-42-21-06-53**), the studio of the painter who was the major forerunner of cubism. Surrounded by a wall, the house was restored by American admirers. Repaired again in 1970, it remains much as Cézanne left it in 1906. It's open daily from 10am to noon and from 2 to 6pm (till 5pm Oct–May). Admission costs 18F (€2.75, $2.60) adults and 10F (€1.50, $1.45) students and seniors, free for children under 13.

THE SHOPPING SCENE

Founded in 1934 and set on a busy boulevard just outside the center of Aix, the showroom and factory of **Santons Fouque,** 65 cours Gambetta (Route de Nice, RN7) (© **04-42-26-33-38**), stocks the largest assortment of *santons* in Aix. More than 1,800 figurines are cast in terra-cotta, finished by hand, then painted according to 18th-century models. Each of the trades practiced in medieval Provence is represented, including grizzled but awestruck shoemakers, barrel makers, copper- and ironsmiths, and rope makers, each poised to welcome the newborn Jesus. Depending on their size and complexity, figurines range from 22 to 5,600F (€3.35 to €851.20, $3.20 to $812). At **Girault,** 35 rue Bedarrides (© **04-42-27-17-35**), another outlet for *santons,* a faithful allegiance to the models of long ago is extremely important. Prices are competitive with those charged by Santons Foque, above.

Few boutiques carry so many *santons* (carved Nativity figurines), locally woven textiles and carvings, and an assortment of *calissons* (sugared confections made with almonds and a *confit* of melon) as **La Boutique du Pays d'Aix,** 2 place du Général-de-Gaulle, in the Aix-en-Provence Tourist Information Office (© **04-42-16-11-61**). Established a century ago and a standard stop for anyone planning a dinner party in and around Aix, **Bechard,** 12 cours Mirabeau (© **04-42-26-06-78**), is the most famous bakery in town. It takes its work so seriously that it refers to its underground kitchens as a *laboratoire* (laboratory). The pastries are truly gorgeous, in most cases made fresh every day.

ST-TROPEZ 𝄞𝄞

Sun-kissed lasciviousness is rampant in this carnival town, 76km (47 miles) southwest of Cannes, but the true Tropezian resents the fact that the port has such a bad reputation. "We can be classy, too," one native insisted. Creative people in the arts and ordinary folk create a compelling mixture.

Colette lived here for many years. Diarist Anaïs Nin, confidante of Henry Miller, posed on the beach in 1939 in a Dorothy Lamour bathing suit. Earlier, St-Tropez was known to Guy de Maupassant, Matisse, and Bonnard. Today, artists, composers, novelists, and the film colony come to St-Tropez in summer. Trailing them is a line of humanity unmatched anywhere else on the Riviera for sheer flamboyance.

ESSENTIALS

GETTING THERE The nearest rail station is in St-Raphaël, a neighboring resort; at the Vieux Port, four or five boats per day leave the **Gare Maritime de St-Raphaël**, rue Pierre Auble (© **04-94-95-17-46**), for St-Tropez (trip time: 50 min.). Some 15 **Sodetrav buses** per day leave from the **Gare Routière** in St-Raphaël (© **04-94-95-24-82**) for St-Tropez (1½-2¼ hr.). Buses also run directly to St-Tropez from its nearest airport at Toulon-Hyères, 56km (35 miles) away. If you drive, be aware that parking in St-Tropez is extremely difficult, especially in summer, when the carnival atmosphere virtually guarantees a shortage of parking spots. In 1998, some of the situation was relieved with the construction of a multistoried parking lot beneath the Place des Lices, **Parc des Lices** (© **04-94-97-34-46**), whose entrance is on the avenue Paul Roussel. Designed for 471 cars, it charges between 8 to 13F (€1.20 to €2, $1.15 to $1.90) for the first hour, and between 8 to 12F (€1.20 to €1.80, $1.15 to $1.75) for each subsequent hour, depending on the season. Many visitors with expensive cars prefer this site, as it's more carefully supervised and guarded than other parking lots in St-Tropez.

VISITOR INFORMATION The **Office de Tourisme** is on quai Jean-Jaurès (© **04-94-97-45-21**).

DEPARTING BY CAR After leaving St-Tropez, take the D-98A northwest again (the same route you traveled to get here), and link up with D-559 at the junction, heading east to Ste-Maxime. This route, which becomes N-98, will take you all the way to Cannes.

WHERE TO STAY

Hôtel Byblos 𝄞𝄞𝄞 This deluxe complex on a hill over the harbor resembles a palace in Beirut with salons decorated with Phoenician gold statues from 3000 B.C. Rooms are imaginative—for example, with a fireplace on a raised hearth with beds recessed on a dais. Le Hameau contains 10 duplex apartments built around a small courtyard with an outdoor spa. Some rooms have balconies overlooking an inner courtyard; others open onto a terrace of flowers. About 10 rooms are completely rejuvenated every season. Bathrooms are well equipped.

Av. Paul-Signac, 83990 St-Tropez. © **800/223-6800** in the U.S., or 04-94-56-68-00. Fax 04-94-56-68-01. www.byblos.com. 98 units. 1,580–3,800F (€240.15–€577.60, $229–$551) double; from 2,800–9,000F (€425.60–€1,368, $406–$1,305) suite. AE, DC, MC, V. Parking 170F (€25.85, $25). Closed Oct 15–Apr 12. **Amenities:** 2 restaurants; bar; pool; gym; sauna; room service; baby-sitting; laundry/dry cleaning. *In room:* A/C, TV, minibar, hair dryer, safe, robes.

Hôtel Ermitage Attractively isolated amid the rocky heights of St-Tropez, this hotel dates from in the 19th century when it was a private villa. A walled garden is illuminated at night, and a cozy corner bar near a wood-burning fire-place takes the chill off blustery evenings. Rooms, although a bit small, offer good value for St-Tropez, and have an efficiently organized and well-maintained bathroom with a shower. The staff can be charming. Breakfast is the only meal served.

Av. Paul-Signac, 83990 St-Tropez. ℭ 04-94-97-52-33. Fax 04-94-97-10-43. 26 units. 490–990F (€74.50–€150.50, $71–$144) double. AE, DC, MC, V. **Amenities:** Bar; room service; baby-sitting; laundry/dry cleaning. *In room:* TV, hair dryer.

Hôtel la Tartane   This cozy, small-scale hotel built in the 1980s lies midway between the center of St-Tropez and the Plage des Salins, about a 3-minute drive from each. There's a stone-rimmed pool set into the garden, and an attentive management that works hard to keep everything pulled together. Rooms are well-furnished bungalows centered around the pool, but the bathrooms are on the small side. Breakfasts are elaborate and attractive; bouillabaisse and fresh fish from the Mediterranean are the specialties in the hotel restaurant ranging from 150 to 200F (€22.80 to €30.40, $22 to $29).

Route des Salins, 83990 St-Tropez. ℭ 04-94-97-21-23. Fax 04-94-97-09-16. 16 units. 450–1,000F (€68.40–€152, $65–$145) double. AE, DC, V. Closed Oct 15–March 30. **Amenities:** Restaurant; bar; pool; baby-sitting; laundry/dry cleaning. *In room:* A/C, TV, minibar, safe.

WHERE TO DINE
Bistrot des Lices ⭐ PROVENÇAL   Don't let the "bistrot" in the name fool you. This is a first-class restaurant, with the most celebrated cuisine in St-Tropez, a glamorous clientele, a world-class inventory of cigars, dessert wines, and after-dinner drinks, and an amused and bemused staff. Chef Christophe Jourdren is known for his creative use of local produce at its most fresh. Examples include a risotto of fresh vegetables served with an essence of parsley; codfish served in a basil-flavored crust, with essence of tomatoes and fresh garlic; leg of lamb *en confit* served with Provençal vegetables; and filets of young rabbit served with spice bread.

3 place des Lices. ℭ 04-94-55-82-82. Reservations required in summer. Main courses 139–250F (€21.15–€8, $20–$36); fixed price menus 99F (€15.05, $14) at lunch, 139–380F (€21.15–€57.75, $20–$55) at dinner. AE, MC, V. Daily noon–2pm and 7:30–11pm (to 2am July–Aug).

La Ramade PROVENÇAL   We consider this courtyard-style restaurant an appealing antidote to St-Tropez's congestion and commercialism. It's designed for maximum exposure to the Provençal night, thanks to tables arranged beneath the trees of the garden. Despite the charming albeit a bit disorganized service, you'll genuinely appreciate the seafood-based specialties that emerge amid clouds of herb-infused steam from the tiny kitchens. Examples include savory versions of both *bourrides* and bouillabaisses; as well as a platter of sea wolf that's slow-roasted over charcoal flames.

3 rue du Temple. ℭ 04-94-97-00-15. Reservations recommended. Main courses 120–290F (€18.25–€44.10, $17–$42). AE, DC, MC, V. Daily 8pm–midnight. Closed mid-Oct to Easter.

L'Echalotte FRENCH (PROVENÇAL)   This charming restaurant, with a tiny garden, serves consistently good food for moderate prices. You can enjoy lunch on the veranda or dinner indoors. The food is solidly bourgeois, including grilled veal kidneys, crayfish with drawn-butter sauce, and filet of turbot with truffles. The major specialty is several kinds of fish, like sea bass and daurade royale cooked in a salt crust.

The French Riviera

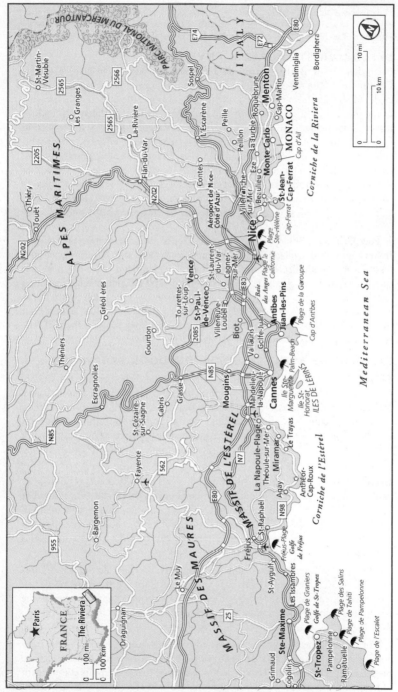

PARC NATIONAL DU MERCANTOUR

ITALY

E74
E72
E80

St-Martin-
Vésubie

2565

2566

Les Granges

Sospel

2565

La-Rivière

L'Escarène

Peille

Peillon

Menton
Roquebrune
La Turbie
MONACO
Monte-Carlo
Cap-Martin
Cap-d'Ail

Ventimiglia

Bordighera

2205

N202

Thiéry

Touët

Flan-du-Var

Contes

Èze

St-Jean-
Cap-Ferrat

Corniche de la Riviera

ALPES MARITIMES

N202

Aéroport de Nice-
Côte d'Azur

Beaulieu

Villefranche-
sur-Mer

Cap-Ferrat

Vence

St-Laurent-
du-Var

Cagnes-
sur-Mer

Nice

Plage
Ste-Hélène

Gréolières

Tourrettes-
sur-Loup

St-Paul-
de-Vence

Villeneuve-
Loubet

Biot

E83

Plage
des Anges Plage le
Californie

Baie

Théniers

2085

Gourdon

Val'auris

Golfe-Juan

Antibes

Juan-les-Pins

Plage de la Garoupe

Cap d'Antibes

Escragnolles

N85

Grasse

Mougins

Plage
Palm-Beach

Mediterranean Sea

St-Cézaire-
sur-Siagne

Cabris

Mandelieu-
la-Napoule

Cannes

Île Ste-
Marguerite
Île St-
Honorat
ÎLES DE LÉRINS

N85

Fayence

562

La Napoule-Plage

Théoule-sur-Mer

Le Trayas

Corniche de l'Estérel

Bargemon

E80

Miramar

Agay

Anthéor-
Cap-Roux

N7

MASSIF DE L'ESTÉREL

955

N98

St-Raphaël

Fréjus

Le Muy

Fréjus-Plage
Golfe
de Fréjus

Draguignan

St-Aygulf

Grimaud

25

Les Issambres

Ste-Maxime

Plage de Graniers
Golfe de St-Tropez

Pampelonne

Plage des Salins

Plage de Tahiti

Cogolin

St-Tropez

Ramatuelle

Plage de Pampelonne

MASSIF DES MAURES

Plage de l'Escalet

FRANCE

★ Paris

The Riviera

0   100 mi
0   100 km

0   10 mi
0   10 km

377

35 rue Général Allard. ✆ **04-94-54-83-26.** Reservations recommended in summer. Main courses 80–140F (€12.15–€21.30, $12–$20); set price menus 105–160F (€15.95–€24.30, $15–$23). AE, MC, V. Thurs 8–11:30pm; Fri–Wed 12:30–2pm and 8–11:30pm. Closed Nov 15–Dec 15.

EXPLORING ST-TROPEZ & ENVIRONS

Near the harbor is the **Musée de l'Annonciade Musée** at place Georges-Grammont (✆ **04-94-97-04-01**), installed in the former chapel of the Annonciade. As a legacy from the artists who loved St-Tropez, the museum shelters one of the finest modern art collections on the Riviera. Many of the artists, including Paul Signac, depicted the port of St-Tropez. Opened in 1955, the collection includes such works as Van Dongen's yellow-faced *Women of the Balustrade* and paintings and sculpture by Bonnard, Matisse, Braque, Utrillo, Seurat, Derain, Maillol, and Van Dongen. The museum is open from June to September Wednesday to Monday from 10am to noon and 3 to 7pm; from October to May Wednesday to Monday from 10am to noon and 2 to 6pm (closed in Nov). Admission is 30F (€4.55, $4.35) adults and 15F (€2.30, $2.20) students, seniors, and those under 16.

Port Grimaud, 3km (2 miles) from St-Tropez, makes an interesting outing. If you approach the village at dusk, when it's softly bathed in Riviera pastels, it'll look like an old hamlet. But this is a mirage. Port Grimaud is the dream fulfillment of its promoter, François Spoerry, who carved it out of marshland and dug canals. Flanking these canals, fingers of land extend from the main square to the sea. The homes are Provençal style, many with Italianate window arches. Boat owners can anchor right at their doorsteps. One newspaper called the port "the most magnificent fake since Disneyland."

HITTING THE BEACH & OTHER OUTDOOR ACTIVITIES

BEACHES St-Tropez has the Riviera's best beaches. The best for families are those closest to the town center, including the amusingly named **Bouillabaisse** and **Plage des Graniers.** The more daring beaches are the 10-km (6-mile) sandy crescents at **Plage des Salins** and **Plage de Pampellone,** beginning some 4km (2 miles) from the town center and best reached by bike (see below) if you're not driving. If you ever wanted to go topless, bottomless, or wear a truly daring bikini, this is the place!

BICYCLING The largest outfitter for bikes and motor scooters is Louis Mas, Multiple Activité Service 3 rue Josef-Quaranta (✆ **04-94-97-00-60**). Bikes rent for 48F (€7.30, $7) and up per hour; motor scooters go for 190 to 275F (€28.90€41.80, $28 to $40) per hour, depending on the size. A deposit of 1,000F (€152, $145), payable with American Express, MasterCard, or Visa, is also required.

BOATING We recommend **Suncap Company,** 15 Quai de Suffren (✆ **04-94-97-11-23**), which rents boats that range from 5.5m (18 ft.) to 12m (40 ft.). The smallest can be rented to qualified sailors without a captain, whereas the larger ones come with a captain at the helm. Daily rates start at 3,000F (€456, $435).

GOLF The nearest golf course, at the edge of Ste-Maxime, across the bay from St-Tropez, is the **Golf Club de Beauvallon,** bd. des Collines, Grimaud, 83120 Ste-Maxime (✆ **04-94-96-16-98**), a popular course that brought its complement of holes up to 18 after a massive improvement and enlargement in 1996. No golf carts are available. Greens fees range from 250 to 300F (€38 to €45.60, $36 to $44) for 18 holes, and a set of golf clubs rents for 100F (€15.20, $15) per set.

Sprawling over a rocky, vertiginous landscape that requires a golf cart and a lot of physical labor is the Don Harradine–designed **Golf de Ste-Maxime-Plaza,** Route de Débarquement, B.P. 1, 83120 Ste-Maxime (© **04-94-55-02-02**). Built in 1991 and associated with the four-star Plaza de Ste-Maxime, it also welcomes nonguests; phone to reserve tee times. Greens fees for 18 holes are 250 to 300F (€38–€45.60, $36–$44) per person; renting a cart for two golfers and their equipment costs 125F (€19, $18) per 18 holes.

SCUBA DIVING A team of dive enthusiasts who are ready, willing, and able to show you the azure depths off the coast of St-Tropez operate from the *Octopussy I* and *II,* based year-round in St-Tropez's Nouveau Port. Experienced divers pay 180F (€27.35, $26) for a one-tank exploration dive, and novices are charged 280F (€42.55, $41) for a *baptême,* which includes one-on-one supervision from a monitor and a descent to a depth of around 5m (15 ft.). For reservations and information, call or write **Les Octopussys,** Quartier de Berteau, Gassin, 83990 St-Tropez (© **04-94-56-53-10;** fax 04-94-56-46-59).

TENNIS Anyone who phones in advance can use the eight courts (both artificial grass and "Quick," a form of concrete) at the **Tennis-Club de St-Tropez,** Route des Plages, in St-Tropez's industrial neighborhood of St-Claude (© **04-94-97-15-52**), about one-half mile from the resort's center. The courts are open year-round and rent for 100F (€15.20, $15) per hour until 5pm and 130F (€19.75, $19) per hour after 5pm.

THE SHOPPING SCENE

In a resort that's increasingly loaded with purveyors of suntan lotion, touristy souvenirs, and T-shirts, **Jacqueline Thienot,** 12 rue Georges-Clemenceau (© **04-94-97-05-70**), maintains an inventory of Provençal antiques, prized by dealers from as far away as Paris. The one-room shop is housed in a late-18th-century building that shows the 18th- and 19th-century antiques to their best advantage.

Although better stocked than the norm, **Choses,** Quai Jean-Jaurès (© **04-94-97-03-44**), is a women's clothing store typical of the hundreds of middle-bracket, whimsically nonchalant emporiums that thrive throughout the Riviera. Its specialty includes clingy and often provocative T-shirt dresses. **Galeries Tropéziennes,** 56 rue Gambetta (© **04-94-97-02-21**), crowds hundreds of unusual gift items, some worthwhile, some rather silly, and textiles into its rambling showrooms near place des Lices. The inspiration is Mediterranean, breezy, and sophisticated.

ST-TROPEZ AFTER DARK

Located on the lobby level of the hyperexpensive, hyperelegant Hôtel Byblos, **Les Caves du Roy,** av. Paul-Signac (© **04-94-97-16-02**), is the most prestigious and most self-consciously chic nightclub in St-Tropez. Entrance is free, but drinks cost a whopping 120F (€18.25, $17) each. It's open nightly from 11:30pm till dawn, but only from Easter to late September.

Le Papagayo, in the Residence du Nouveau Port, rue Gambetta (© **04-94-97-07-56**), is one of the largest nightclubs in St-Tropez, with two floors, three bars, and lots of attractive women and men from throughout the Mediterranean eager to pursue their bait. The decor is neopsychedelic, and the clientele is youthful and high-energy. From Easter to late September, it's open nightly from 11:30pm till dawn. The rest of the year, it's open only on preselected weekends, usually as part of the celebrations of local charities and sports clubs, events to which the public is welcome. Cover is 110F (€16.70, $16) and includes one drink.

Most of the socializing at the largely gay **Le Pigeonnier,** 13 rue de la Ponche (© **04-94-97-84-26**), revolves around the long and narrow bar, where drinks cost around 80F (€12.15, $12). The crowd is composed of some lesbians, but mostly gay men in their 20s or early 30s from all over Europe. There's also a dance floor. No cover.

CANNES ☆☆☆
When Coco Chanel came here and got a suntan, returning to Paris bronzed, she startled the milk-white ladies of society. But they quickly began copying her. Today the bronzed bodies—in nearly nonexistent swimsuits—still line the sandy beaches of this chic resort.

Popular with celebrities, Cannes is at its most frenzied during the **International Film Festival** at the Palais des Festivals on promenade de la Croisette, held in April or May. On the seafront boulevards, cameras flash as the stars emerge. International regattas, galas, concours d'élégance, even a Mimosa Festival in February—something is always happening at Cannes, except in November, traditionally a dead month.

Cannes, sheltered by hills, lies 26km (16 miles) southwest of Nice. For many it consists of only one street, **promenade de la Croisette,** curving along the coast and split by islands of palms and flowers. A port of call for cruise liners, the seafront is lined with hotels, apartment houses, and chic boutiques. Many of the bigger hotels claim part of the beaches for the private use of their guests. But there are also public areas.

ESSENTIALS
GETTING THERE   Cannes lies on the major coastal rail line along the Riviera, with **trains** arriving at the station at 1 rue Jean-Jaurès from Antibes (trip time: 15 min.) and Nice (35 min.). The TGV from Paris going via Marseille (4½ hr.) also services Cannes. For information and schedules, call © **08-36-35-35-35. Bus** service is available from the Nice airport to Cannes every hour during the day (35 min.). For bus information about Cannes routes, call © **04-93-45-20-08;** the station is at place de l'Hôtel de Ville. There's also one bus every half-hour from Antibes. The international airport at Nice is only 20 minutes northeast of Cannes.

VISITOR INFORMATION   The **Office de Tourisme** is in the Palais des Festivals, Esplanade Georges Pompidou (© **04-93-39-24-53**); fax 04-92-99-84-23.

DEPARTING BY CAR   From Cannes, N-7 heads directly east to the resort of Juan-les-Pins, a distance of 10km (6 miles).

WHERE TO STAY
Although hotels in Cannes might elect to have their own e-mail address, there is a shared and collective e-mail address for all hotels in the city: infos@ cannes.hotel.com.

Very Expensive
Hôtel Carlton Inter-Continental ☆☆☆   Today, except for the Cannes Film Festival, you are more likely to see conventions and groups than the stars and royalty of past years. Even so, this remains a bastion of Riviera luxury, style, glitter, and glamour. Rooms feature double-glazed windows and big bathrooms.

The most spacious rooms are in the west wing, and many on the upper floors open onto balconies fronting the sea.

58 bd. de la Croisette, 06414 Cannes. © 800/327-0200 in the U.S., or 04-93-06-40-06. Fax 04-93-06-40-25. www.interconti.com. 338 units. 2,140–4,775F (€325.30–€725.80, $310–$692) double; from 6,815F (€1,035.90, $988) suite. AE, DC, MC, V. Parking 180F (€27.35, $26). Bus: 11. **Amenities:** 4 restaurants, 2 bars; pool; health center; sauna salon; room service; baby-sitting; laundry/dry cleaning. *In room:* A/C, TV, minibar, hair dryer, safe.

Expensive

Hôtel Gray-d'Albion 𝒦𝒦   Because it offers a luxurious setting on a scale smaller than the Carlton and the Majestic, we count the Gray d'Albion among the Riviera's more desirable hotels. Built in a nine-story format in 1980, it has rooms that are fairly standard, with private safes and bedside controls. Each has a balcony; those on the eighth and ninth floors have views of the Mediterranean; otherwise, the views aren't notable. Bathrooms are well equipped.

38 rue des Serbes, 06400 Cannes. © 04-92-99-79-79. Fax 04-93-99-26-10. www.graydalbion@ lucienbarriere.com. 189 units. 1,070–2,170F (€162.65–€329.85, $155–$315) double; from 3,170F (€481.85, $460) suite. AE, DC, MC, V. Bus: 1. **Amenities:** Restaurant, bar; sauna; room service; baby-sitting; laundry/dry cleaning. *In room:* A/C, TV, minibar, hair dryer, safe.

Moderate

Hôtel le Fouquet's 𝒦 *Finds*   This is an intimate hotel drawing a discreet clientele, often from Paris, who'd never think of patronizing the grand palace hotels. Very "Riviera French" in design and decor, it's several blocks from the beach. Each attractive, airy room contains a loggia and a dressing room. Bathrooms, although small, are efficiently organized, with shower.

2 rond-point Duboys-d'Angers, 06400 Cannes. © 04-92-59-25-00. Fax 04-92-98-03-39. 10 units. 550–990F (€83.60–€150.50, $80–$144) double. AE, DC, MC, V. Closed Oct to late Mar. Parking 80F (€12.15, $12). Bus 1. **Amenities:** Room service, laundry/dry cleaning. *In room:* A/C, TV, minibar, hair dryer, safe.

Inexpensive

Hôtel de Provence   This inn stands in its own walled garden of palms and flowering shrubs on a quiet inner street. Most rooms have private balconies and many overlook the garden. Small bathrooms have showers. In warm weather, breakfast is served under the vines and flowers of an arbor.

9 rue Molière, 06400 Cannes. © 04-93-38-44-35. Fax 04-93-39-63-14. 30 units. 490–630F (€74.50–€95.75, $71–$91) double. AE, DC, MC, V. Parking 65F (€9.90, $9). Bus: 1. **Amenities:** Breakfast room, bar. *In room:* A/C, TV, minibar, hair dryer, safe.

Hôtel Le Florian   This hotel is set on a busy but narrow, densely commercial street that leads directly into La Croisette, near both the beach and the city's largest convention hall, Palais des Festivals. It has been maintained by three different generations of the Giordano family since the 1950s. Basic, but comfortable, most rooms are rather small but have fine mattresses. Bathrooms are compact with a shower. No meals are served other than breakfast.

8 rue Commandant-André, 06400 Cannes. © 04-93-39-24-82. Fax 04-92-99-18-30. 28 units. 300–400F (€45.60–€60.80, $44–$58) double. AE, MC, V. Parking 45F (€6.85, $7) per night in a nearby public facility. Closed Nov 1–Jan 15. Bus 1. **Amenities:** Breakfast room. *In room:* A/C, TV, hair dryer.

WHERE TO DINE
Expensive

Gaston-Gastounette   FRENCH (PROVENÇAL). This is the best restaurant to offer views of the marina. Located in the old port, it has a stucco exterior with oak moldings and big windows and a sidewalk terrace surrounded by flowers. Inside you'll be served a delectable bouillabaisse, breast of duckling in garlic-cream sauce, *pot-au-feu de la mer* (seafood stew), and perfectly prepared fish platters such as turbot and sole.

7 quai St-Pierre. ℂ **04-93-39-47-92.** Reservations required. Main courses 160–300F (€24.30–€45.60, $23–$44); set price lunch 125–170F (€19–€25.85, $18–$25); set price dinner 200F (€30.40, $29). AE, DC, MC, V. Daily noon–2pm and 7–11pm. Closed Nov 30–Dec 19. Bus: 1.

La Palme d'Or ✫✫✫ FRENCH (MODERN) This light wood-paneled, Art Deco marvel overlooking a pool and La Croisette is the creation of the Taittinger family of Champagne fame. Chef Christian Willer has worked at some of France's greatest restaurants. Here his sublime specialties include warm foie gras with fondue of rhubarb, filets of fried red mullet in an olive-cream sauce with zucchini and a beignet of potatoes, or a medley of crayfish, clams, and squid marinated in peppered citrus sauce.

In the Hôtel Martinez, 73 bd. de la Croisette. ℂ **04-92-98-74-14.** Reservations required. Main courses 250–480F (€38–€72.95, $36–$70); set price lunch 295F (€44.85, $43); set price dinner 390–820F (€59.30–€124.65, $57–$119). AE, DC, MC, V. Wed–Sun 12:30–2pm and 7:30–10:30pm. Also Tues 7:30–10:30pm mid-June to mid-Sept. Closed Nov 15–Dec 20. Bus: 1.

Moderate

La Mère Besson ✫ PROVENÇAL The references here are Provençal, set within a venue that's as authentic and nostalgic as you're likely to find anywhere in Cannes. The most appealing of the menu items are the Provençal dishes like a savory *bourride* made from monkfish and court bouillon that's featured on Wednesday; and a savory kettle of fish made from a medley of steamed vegetables, mussels, and assorted fish that's offered every Friday with a creamy garlic sauce. There's also an *estouffade Provençal* made with braised beef, red wine, and a rich stock flavored with garlic, onions, herbs, and mushrooms, that's the featured dish every Monday. Come with an appetite and a sense of conviviality.

13 rue des Frères-Pradignac. ℂ **04-93-39-59-24.** Reservations required. Lunch 100F (€15.20, $15). Main courses 75–120F (€11.40–€18.25, $11–$17); set price dinners 140–170F (€21.30–€25.85, $20–$25). AE, DC, MC, V. Apr–Oct Tues–Fri 12:15–2pm and 7:30–10:30pm, Mon and Sat 7:30–10:30pm (open Sun in summer). Nov–Mar Mon–Sat 7:30–10:30pm. Bus: 1.

EXPLORING CANNES

Above the harbor, the old town of Cannes sits on Suquet Hill, where you'll see a 14th-century tower, which the English dubbed the **Lord's Tower.**

Nearby is the **Musée de la Castre,** in the Château de la Castre, Le Suquet (ℂ **04-93-38-55-26**), containing fine and ethnographic arts. The latter includes relics and objects from everywhere from the Pacific islands to Southeast Asia, including both Peruvian and Mayan pottery. There's also a gallery with relics of ancient Mediterranean civilizations. Five rooms are devoted to 19th-century paintings. The museum is open from April to June Wednesday to Monday from 10am to noon and 2 to 6pm; from July to September 10am to noon and 3 to 7pm; from October to March 10am to noon and 2 to 5pm (closed in Jan). Admission is 10F (€1.50, $1.45) adults, and free for children under 16.

Another museum of note, the **Musée de la Mer,** Fort Royal (ℂ **04-93-38-55-26**), displays artifacts from Ligurian, Roman, and Arab civilizations, including paintings, mosaics, and ceramics. You can also see the jail where the "Man in the Iron Mask" was incarcerated. Temporary exhibitions of photography are also shown. It's open from July to September 10:30am to 12:15pm and 2:15 to 6:30pm; from October to June it closes at sundown (4:30–5:30pm). Admission is 10F (€1.50, $1.45) adults and students, free for children under 13.

HITTING THE BEACH & OTHER OUTDOOR PURSUITS

BEACHES   The best beach is **Plage du Midi,** west of the old harborfront, with the best sun in the afternoon. **Plage Gazagnaire,** another good beach, is east of the new port, ideal in the morning. Between these two public beaches are many private ones where you can gain entrance by paying a fee that includes a mattress and sun umbrella. Waiters at these private beach clubs come by to take your lunch order.

BICYCLING & MOTOR SCOOTERING   Despite the roaring traffic, the flat landscapes between Cannes and such satellite resorts as La Napoule are well suited for riding a bike or motor scooter. **Cannes Location Deux Roues,** 11 rue Hélène-Vagliano (© **04-93-39-46-15**), across from the Gray d'Albion, rents pedal bikes for 62F (€9.40, $9) per day and requires a 1,000F (€152, $145) deposit (payable with American Express, MasterCard, or Visa). Motor scooters cost 160 to 200F (€24.30 to €30.40, $23 to $29) per day and require a deposit of 4,000 to 10,000F (€608 to €1,520, $580 to $1,450), depending on their value. A worthwhile competitor for the rentals of bikes and motor scooters is **Cycles Daniel,** 2 rue du Pont Romain (© **04-93-99-90-30**), where *vélos tout terrain* (mountain bikes) cost 70F (€10.65, $10) a day. At both of the establishments recommended above, renters of motorized bikes and scooters will pay 200F (€30.40, $29) per day and must be at least 14 years old. For the larger of the scooters, potential renters must present a valid driver's license.

BOATING   Several companies can rent you a boat of any size, with or without a crew, for a day, a week, or a month, depending on your priorities, your bankroll, and your schedule. An outfit known for its short-term rentals of small craft, including motorboats, sailboats, and canoes, is **Elco Marine,** 110 Bd. Du Midi (© **04-93-47-12-62**). Two others that provide access to larger boats, including motor-driven and sailing yachts and craft suitable for deep-sea fishing, include **MS Yachts,** 57 La Croisette (© **04-93-99-03-51**); and **Mediterranée Courtage** (Agence Y.P.), 22 quai Port Marseille (© **04-93-38-30-40**).

GOLF   The dry and rolling landscapes of Provence contribute to memorable golfing. One of the region's most challenging and interesting courses, **Country-Club de Cannes-Mougins,** 175 rte. d'Antibes, Mougins (© **04-93-75-79-13**), 6km (4 miles) north of Cannes, was a 1976 reconfiguration by Dye & Ellis of an outmoded, under-accessorized course laid out in the 1920s. Noted for olive trees and cypresses that adorn a relatively flat terrain, the par-72 course has many water traps and a deceptively tricky layout loaded with technical challenges. It's the host of the Royal Mougins Open, an important stop on the PGA European Tour. The course is open to anyone with proof of his or her handicap—24 for men, 28 for women—willing to pay greens fees of 400 to 500F (€60.80 to €76, $58 to $73), depending on the day of the week. An electric golf cart rents for 280F (€42.55, $41) and golf clubs can be rented for 150F (€22.80, $22) per set. Reservations are recommended.

SWIMMING   Most of the larger hotels in Cannes have their own pools. In addition to the tennis courts described below, the **Complexe Sportif Montfleury,** 23 av. Beauséjour (© **04-93-38-75-78**), boasts a large modern pool. Entrance fee is 25F (€3.80, $3.65) adults, 20F (€3.05, $2.90) those under 16.

TENNIS   **Complexe Sportif Montfleury,** 23 av. Beauséjour (© **04-93-38-75-78**), has eight hard-surfaced courts that rent for 80F (€12.15, $12) per hour, and two clay-surfaced courts that rent for 100F (€15.20, $15) per hour.

THE SHOPPING SCENE

You're likely to find branch outlets of virtually every stylish Paris retailer in Cannes. Most of the big names in designer fashion line **La Croisette.** The best names are closest to the high-rise **Gray-d'Albion,** 17 La Croisette, which is both a mall and a hotel.

At the edge of the Quartier Suquet, **Marché Forville** is the town's primary fruit, flower, and vegetable market. On Monday it's a flea market. There's a somewhat disorganized and invariably busy outdoor flea market every Saturday along the edges of the allée de la Liberté, across from the Palais des Festivals.

The distinctive and charmingly old-fashioned **Cannolive,** 16–20 rue Vénizelos (☎ 04-93-39-08-19), owned by the Raynaud family, who founded the place in 1880, sells Provençal olives and all of their by-products—purées (tapenades) that connoisseurs refer to as "Provençal caviar," black "olives de Nice," and green "olives de Provence," as well as three grades of olive oil from several regional producers. Oils and food products are dispensed from no. 16, but gift items (fabrics, porcelain, and Provençal souvenirs) are sold next door.

Maiffret, 31 rue d'Antibes (☎ 04-93-39-08-29), specializes in chocolates and candied fruit, made by culinary processes that must be seen to be fully appreciated. Pâtés and confits of fruit, some of which decorate cakes and tarts, are also sold as desirable confections in their own right. Look for the Provençal national confection, *calissons,* crafted from almonds, a confit of melon, and sugar. Richly stocked with books and periodicals from virtually every English-speaking country in the world, **Cannes English Bookshop,** 11 rue Bivouac Napoléon (☎ 04-93-99-40-08), near the main post office, has attracted readers since 1984.

CANNES AFTER DARK

CASINOS The largest and most legendary casino in Cannes is the **Casino Croisette,** in the Palais des Festivals, 1 jetée Albert-Edouard, near promenade de la Croisette (☎ 04-92-98-78-00). Within its glittering confines you'll find all the gaming tables you'd expect. A small subdivision of the casino opens daily at 10am for access to slot machines. The main areas, including the ones with the roulette and baccarat tables, open every day at 7:30pm and close down at 5am. The Palais des Festivals also contains one of the best nightclubs in town, **Jimmy's de Regine** (☎ 04-93-68-00-07), outfitted in shades of red. Jimmy's is open from Thursday to Sunday 11pm to dawn. You must present your passport to enter the gambling room. Admission is 70F (€10.65, $10) and includes a drink.

Considerably smaller than its major competitor, **Le Carlton Casino Club,** in the Carlton Inter-Continental, 58 bd. de la Croisette (☎ 04-92-99-51-00), nonetheless draws its share of devotees. Jackets are required for men, and a passport or government-issued identity card is necessary for admission. It's open daily from 8pm to 4am. Admission is 70F (€10.65, $10).

CLUBS **Jane's,** in the cellar of the Gray d'Albion, 38 rue des Serbes (☎ 04-92-99-79-79), is a stylish and appealing nightclub with an undercurrent of coy permissiveness. The well-dressed crowd (many of the men in jacket and tie) is made up of all ages. The cover ranges from 50 to 100F (€7.60 to €15.20, $7 to $15), depending on business; on some slow nights women enter for free. Open from Thursday to Sunday 11pm to 5am.

JUAN-LES-PINS ⚬

This suburb of Antibes is a resort that was developed in the 1920s by Frank Jay Gould. At that time, people flocked to "John of the Pines" to escape the "crassness" of nearby Cannes. In the 1930s, Juan-les-Pins drew a chic crowd during winter. Today, it's often called a honky-tonk town or the "Coney Island of the Riviera." One newspaper writer labeled it "a pop-art Monte Carlo, with burlesque shows and nude beaches"—a description much too provocative for such a middle-class resort.

The town has some of the best nightlife on the Riviera, and the action reaches its frenzied height during the **Festival International de Jazz** in July. Many revelers stay up all night in the smoky jazz joints, then sleep the next day on the beach. For more information on the festival, contact the tourist office. The **casino,** in the town center, offers cabaret entertainment, often until daybreak. During the day, skin-diving and water-skiing predominate. The pines sweep down to a good beach, crowded with summer sunbathers, most often in skimpy swimwear.

ESSENTIALS

GETTING THERE Juan-les-Pins is connected by rail and bus to most other coastal resorts. Frequent **trains** arrive from Nice throughout the day (trip time: 30 min.). For more information and schedules, call ℂ **08-36-35-35-35.** The station is on avenue l'Esterel. A **bus** leaves from Antibes at place Guynemer (ℂ **04-93-34-37-60**), daily every 20 minutes and costs 7.50F (€1.15, $1.10) one-way (10 min.).

VISITOR INFORMATION The **Office de Tourisme** is at 51 bd. Charles-Guillaumont (ℂ **04-92-90-53-05**).

DEPARTING BY CAR After Juan-les-Pins, ignore the "Direct to Antibes" signs and follow D-2559 around the cape. You'll come first to Cap d'Antibes before approaching the old city of Antibes itself.

WHERE TO STAY

Belles-Rives �につ This is one of the fabled addresses on the Riviera. Over the years it has hosted such illustrious guests as Zelda and F. Scott Fitzgerald, the duke and duchess of Windsor, and Edith Piaf. A certain 1930s aura still lingers, and the sea views of the sea and Esterel mountains are as enchanting as ever. Rooms range from small to spacious, all with luxurious mattresses. The lower terraces are devoted to garden dining rooms and a waterside aquatic club with a jetty extending into the water. Also on the premises are a private beach and a landing dock.

Bd. Baudoin, 06160 Juan-les-Pins. ℂ 04-93-61-02-79. Fax 04-93-67-43-51. belles.rives@atsat.com. 45 units. 1,150–2,900F (€174.80–€440.80, $167–$421) double; from 3,200F (€486.40, $464) suite. AE, MC, V. Closed mid-Oct to Mar. **Amenities:** 2 restaurants, 2 bars; aquatic club; room service; baby-sitting; laundry/dry cleaning. *In room:* A/C, TV, minibar, hair dryer, safe.

Hôtel Juana �につ This balconied Art Deco building is separated from the sea by a park of pines. The hotel has a private swimming club where guests can rent a "parasol and pad" on the sandy beach. The hotel is constantly being refurbished, and the very attractive rooms come complete with mahogany pieces and large bathrooms. Some have balconies. Also on the premises is a private beach.

La Pinède, av. Gallice, 06160 Juan-les-Pins. ℂ 04-93-61-08-70. Fax 04-93-61-76-60. www.hotel-juana.com. 50 units. 1,150–2,550F (€174.80–€387.60, $167–$370) double; from 2,800F (€425.60, $406) suite. AE, MC, V. Parking 50F (€7.60, $7). Closed Nov–Mar. **Amenities:** Restaurant, bar; 2 pools; room service; baby-sitting; laundry/dry cleaning. *In room:* A/C, TV, minibar, hair dryer.

WHERE TO DINE

La Terrasse �につ FRENCH/MEDITERRANEAN The cuisine here is the best in Juan-les-Pins, and among the finest along the entire Riviera. Bill Cosby is such a fan he's been known to fly chef Christian Morisset to the States to prepare dinner for him. The ideal place to dine in summer is the terrace, among a lively, sophisticated crowd. His saddle of lamb is cooked to your taste and served with a rosemary jus, stuffed zucchini flowers, and fresh white beans. Or try the limousine filet of beef—tender and juicy and straight from the charcoal grill. The seafood, including red mullet and sea bass, is caught fresh daily.

In the Hôtel Juana, La Pinède, av. Gallice. ✆ **04-93-61-20-37**. Reservations required. Main courses 240–390F (€36.50–€59.30, $35–$57); set price lunch 290F (€44.10, $42); set price dinners 490–660F (€74.50–€100.30, $71–$96). AE, MC, V. July–Aug daily 12:30–2pm and 7:30–10:30pm; Apr–June and Sept–Oct Tues and Thurs–Sun 12:30–2pm, Thurs–Mon 7:30–10:30pm. Closed Nov–Mar.

ANTIBES & CAP D'ANTIBES ✺✺

On the other side of the Bay of Angels, 21km (13 miles) southwest of Nice, is the port of Antibes. This old Mediterranean town has a quiet charm, unusual for the Côte d'Azur. Its little harbor is filled with fishing boats, the marketplaces with flowers, mostly roses and carnations. If you're in Antibes in the evening, you can watch fishers playing the popular Riviera game of *boule*.

Spiritually, Antibes is totally divorced from Cap d'Antibes, a peninsula studded with the villas and pools of the *haut monde*. In *Tender Is the Night*, F. Scott Fitzgerald described it as a place where "old villas rotted like water lilies among the massed pines."

ESSENTIALS
GETTING THERE   **Trains** from Cannes arrive every 30 minutes (trip time: 16 min.); trains from Nice also pull in every 30 minutes (18 min.). For rail information, call ✆ **08-36-35-35-35**. The station is on avenue Robert Soleau.

VISITOR INFORMATION   The **Office de Tourisme** is at 11 place du Général-de-Gaulle (✆ **04-92-90-53-00**); fax 04-92-90-53-01.

DEPARTING BY CAR   After leaving Antibes, you can take an excursion to the most famous hill towns on the French Riviera: St-Paul-de-Vence and Vence. Follow N7 to Cagnes-sur-Mer, where you can connect with D36 heading first to St-Paul-de-Vence, then continuing north to Vence.

WHERE TO STAY
Auberge de la Gardiole ✺ *(Value)*   M. and Mme Courtot run this country inn with a delightful personal touch. The large villa, surrounded by gardens and pergola, is in an area of private estates. The charming rooms, on the upper floors of the inn and in the little buildings in the garden, are a pleasant stay. The cheerful dining room has a fireplace and hanging pots and pans, and in good weather, you can dine under a wisteria-covered trellis.

74 Chemin de la Garoupe, 06600 Cap d'Antibes. ✆ **04-93-61-35-03**. Fax 04-93-67-61-87. 17 units. 590–790F (€89.70–€120.10, $86–$115) double; from 790F (€120.10, $115) suite. AE, MC, V. Free parking. Closed Nov–Mar. Bus: A2. **Amenities:** Restaurant; bar; pool; room service; laundry. *In room:* A/C, TV, minibar, hair dryer.

Hôtel du Cap–Eden Roc ✺✺✺   This Second Empire hotel, opened in 1870, just after the Franco-Prussian war is surrounded by 9 hectares (22 acres) of splendid gardens. It's like a great country estate, with spacious public areas, marble fireplaces, scenic paneling, and richly upholstered armchairs. Rooms are among the most sumptuous on the Riviera. Bathrooms are roomy. The staff is famed for its snobbery.

Bd. J-F-Kennedy, 06601 Cap d'Antibes. ✆ **04-93-61-39-01**. Fax 04-93-67-76-04. edenroc-hotel@wanadoo.fr. 140 units. 2,500–4,400F (€380–€668.80, $363–$638) double; from 6,500F (€988, $943) suite.

No credit cards. Free parking. Closed mid-Oct to mid-Apr. Bus: A2. **Amenities:** Restaurant, 2 bars; pool; gym; sauna; room service; baby-sitting; laundry/dry cleaning. *In room:* A/C, TV, hair dryer, safe.

Hotel Imperial Garoupe ★★   One of the Riviera's newest upscale hotels is a charming pocket of posh that's a bit less intimidating than the more monumental Hôtel du Cap. The one-story building is designed around a landscaped patio with architectural elements that evoke both Tudor England and the deserts of Morocco, with a gorgeous view. The large, luxurious rooms are filled with oversize furniture. Bathrooms have plenty of shelf space. Set within 45m (50 yd.) of the beach, the hotel is the centerpiece of a 1.5-hectare (3 1/2-acre) park whose rows of pines block some of the views of the sea.

770 Chemin de la Garoupe, 06600 Antibes. € 800/525-4800 in the U.S., or 04-92-93-31-61. Fax 04-92-93-31-62. www.imperial-garoupe.com. 34 units. 3,200–6,400F (€486.40–€972.80, $464–$928) double; 2,800–5,200F (€426.60–€790.40, $406–$754) suite. AE, DC, MC, V. Free parking. Closed Nov–Mar. Bus A2. **Amenities:** Restaurant, bar; pool; room service; baby-sitting; laundry/dry cleaning. *In room:* A/C, TV, minibar, hair dryer.

WHERE TO DINE

La Bonne Auberge FRENCH (TRADITIONAL)   For many years after its 1975 opening, this was one of the most famous restaurants on the French Riviera. In 1992, following the death of its famous founder, Jo Rostang, his culinary heir Philippe Rostang wisely limited its scope and transformed it into a worthwhile but less ambitious restaurant. The set price menu offers a wide selection. Choices vary but may include Basque-inspired pipérade with poached eggs, savory swordfish tart, chicken with vinegar and garlic, and perchpike dumplings Jo Rostang. Dessert might be an enchanting peach soufflé.

Quartier de Brague, route N-7. € 04-93-33-36-65. Reservations required. Set price menu 210F (€31.90, $30). MC, V. Tues–Sun noon–2pm and 7–10pm. Closed mid-Nov to mid-Dec. Take the coastal highway (N-7) 2 1/2 miles from Antibes.

Restaurant de Bacon ★★★ SEAFOOD   Bouillabaisse aficionados claim, and we agree, that Bacon's offers France's best version. In its deluxe version, saltwater crayfish float atop the savory brew; we prefer the simple version—a waiter adds the finishing touches at your table. You can also try a fish soup with the traditional garlic-laden rouille sauce; or try fish terrine, sea bass, John Dory, or one of the exotic fish, such as sar, pageot, or denti, unknown in North America. The venue evokes the chic 1950s, within a low, sprawling, big-windowed building set within a rocky landscape across the coastal highway from the sea.

Bd. de Bacon Cap d Antibes. € 04-93-61-50-02. Reservations required. Set price menus 280–450F (€42.55–€68.40, $41–$65). A la carte 350–850F (€53.20–€129.20, $51–$123). AE, DC, MC, V. Tues–Sun noon–2pm and 8–10pm (open Mon dinner in July–Aug). Closed Nov–Jan.

TWO MUSEUMS WORTH VISITING

On the ramparts above the port is the Château Grimaldi, place Mariejol, which contains the **Musée Picasso** (€ **04-92-90-54-26,** or 04-92-90-54-20 for a recorded message). Once the home of the princes of Antibes of the Grimaldi family, who ruled the city from 1385 to 1608, today it houses one of the greatest Picasso collections in the world. Picasso came to the small town after his bitter war years in Paris and stayed in a hotel at Golfe-Juan until the museum director at Antibes invited him to work and live at the museum. Picasso then spent 1946 painting at the museum. When he departed he gave the museum all the work he'd done that year—two dozen paintings, nearly 80 pieces of ceramics, 44 drawings, 32 lithographs, 11 oils on paper, two sculptures, and five tapestries. In addition, a gallery of contemporary art exhibits Léger, Miro, Ernst, and Calder, among others. The museum is open from Tuesday to Sunday 10am to noon and 2 to 6pm, except from June to September, 10am to 6pm. The museum is closed from October 1 to May 30. Admission costs 20F (€3.05, $2.90) adults, 10F (€1.50, $1.45) students 15 to 24 and people over 60, free for children under 15.

Cap d'Antibes has the **Musée Naval et Napoléonien,** Batterie du Grillon, boulevard J-F-Kennedy (© **04-93-61-45-32**). This ancient military tower contains an interesting collection of Napoleonic memorabilia, naval models, paintings, and mementos. It's open from Monday to Friday 9:30am to noon and 2:15 to 6pm and Saturday from 9:30am to noon. Admission is 20F (€3.05, $2.90), 10F (€1.50, $1.45) students and seniors.

ST-PAUL-DE-VENCE & VENCE 🎭🎭🎭

Of all the perched villages of the Riviera, St-Paul-de-Vence, 27km (17 miles) east of Cannes and 30km (19 miles) north of Nice, is the best known. It was popularized in the 1920s when many noted artists occupied the 16th-century houses flanking the narrow cobblestone streets. The feudal hamlet grew up on a bastion of rock, almost blending into it. Its ramparts—allow about 30 minutes to encircle them—overlook a peaceful setting of flowers and olive and orange trees. As you make your way through the warren of streets, you'll pass endless souvenir shops, a charming old fountain carved in the form of an urn, and a 13th-century Gothic church. St-Paul-de-Vence and Vence itself are most often visited as a day trip from either Cannes or Nice; allow at least an afternoon for this jaunt.

ESSENTIALS

GETTING THERE   Some 20 **buses** per day leave from Nice's gare routière to drop you in the town center (trip time: 50 min.).

VISITOR INFORMATION   The **Office de Tourisme** is at Maison Tours, rue Grande (© **04-93-58-06-38**).

DEPARTING BY CAR   To reach Nice, take the N-202 south to the junction with the N-7; follow the N-7 east to Nice.

EXPLORING ST-PAUL-DE VENCE & VENCE

The **Fondation Maeght** 🎭🎭🎭 (© **04-93-32-81-63**) is one of the most modern art museums in Europe. On a hill in pine-studded woods, the Maeght Foundation is like a Shangri-la. Not only is the architecture avant-garde, but the building houses one of the finest collections of contemporary art on the Riviera. Natural and human creations blend harmoniously in this unique achievement of architect José Luís Sert. Its white concrete arcs give the impression of a giant pagoda.

A stark Calder rises like some futuristic monster on the grassy lawns. In a courtyard, the elongated bronze works of Giacometti form a surrealistic garden, creating a hallucinatory mood. Sculpture is also displayed inside, but it's at its best in a natural setting of surrounding terraces and gardens.

A library, cinema, and cafeteria (open July–Sept only) are also here. In one showroom, original lithographs by artists like Chagal and Giacometti and limited-edition prints are for sale. It's open daily from July to September 10am to 7pm and from October to June 10am to 12:30pm and 2:30 to 6pm. Admission is 50F (€7.60, $7) adults, 40F (€6.10, $6) students and children 12 to 18; free for children under 12.

North of St-Paul, you can visit the sleepy old town of Vence, with its **Vieille Ville** (Old Town). If you're wearing solid, comfortable shoes, the narrow, steep streets are worth exploring. The **cathedral** on place Godeau is unremarkable except for some 15th-century choir stalls. If it's a Tuesday or Thursday, however, most visitors pass quickly through the narrow gates of this once-fortified walled town on their way to the **Chapelle du Rosaire** *⟨⟨*, 466 av. Henri-Matisse (ℂ **04-93-58-03-26**), created by Henri Matisse. Matisse was 77 when, after a turbulent time of introspection, he set out to create this masterpiece, in his own words, "the culmination of a whole life dedicated to the search for truth." From the front you might find the chapel of the Dominican nuns of Monteils unremarkable—until you spot a 40-foot crescent-adorned cross rising from a blue-tile roof. The light inside picks up the subtle coloring in the simply rendered leaf forms and abstract patterns: sapphire blue, aquamarine, and lemon yellow. In black-and-white ceramics, St. Dominic is depicted in a few lines. The Stations of the Cross are also black-and-white tile, with Matisse's self-styled "tormented and passionate" figures. From October and December to June, it's open Tuesday and Thursday 10am to 11:30am and 2:30 to 5:30pm; from July to September it's also open on Wednesday, Friday, and Saturday 2:30 to 5:30pm. Closed in November. Admission is 13F (€2, $1.90) adults, 5F (€0.75, 75¢) children under 13; donations are welcomed.

NICE *⟨⟨⟨*

The Victorian upper class and czarist aristocrats loved Nice in the 19th century, but it's solidly middle class today. Of all the major resorts, from Deauville to Biarritz to Cannes, Nice is the least expensive. It's also the best excursion center on the Riviera, especially if you're dependent on public transportation. From the Nice airport, the second largest in France, you can travel by bus along the entire coast to resorts like Juan-les-Pins and Cannes, the latter only 32km (20 miles) to the west.

Nice is the capital of the Riviera, the largest city between Genoa and Marseille (also one of the most ancient, having been founded by the Greeks, who called it Nike, or Victory). Because of its brilliant sunshine and relaxed living, Nice has attracted artists and writers, among them Matisse, Dumas, Nietzsche, Apollinaire, Flaubert, Hugo, Stendhal, and Mistral.

ESSENTIALS

GETTING THERE   You can take an airport bus (no. 23) that travels at 20-minute intervals throughout the day and evening between the **Aéroport Nice-Côte d'Azur** (ℂ **04-93-21-30-30**) and the city's **Gare Routière,** promenade du Paillon (ℂ **04-93-85-61-81**), in the city center. Buses run daily from 6am to 10:30pm, and cost 8F (€1.20, $1.15) per person. A somewhat more luxurious mode of transport involves a specially conceived navette de l'aéroport (airport shuttle bus) that charges 21F (€3.20, $3) for a ride from the airport to Nice's main railway station. A taxi ride into the city center will cost at least 150 to 200F (€22.80 to €30.40, $22 to $29) for a carload of up to four passengers. **Trains** arrive at **Gare Nice–Ville,** avenue Thiers (ℂ **08-36-35-35-35**). From here you can take frequent trains to Cannes, Monaco, and Antibes, among other destinations.

VISITOR INFORMATION   Thanks to its status as the tourist centerpiece of the Côte d'Azur, Nice maintains three tourist information offices, the largest and most central of which is at 5 promenade des Anglais (ℂ **04-92-14-48-00;**

fax 04-93-16-85-16), near the place Massena. Additional tourist offices are in the arrivals hall of the **Aéroport Nice–Côte d'Azur** (℡ **04-93-21-44-11**); and at the railway station on avenue Thiers (℡ **04-93-87-07-07**). Any of the three can make you a hotel reservation (but only for the night of the day you happen to show up), charging a modest fee that varies according to the classification of the hotel you book.

You can rent bicycles and mopeds from **Nicea Rent,** 9 av. Thiers (℡ **04-93-82-42-71**), or from a competitor, **Cycles Arnaud,** 4 place Grimaldi (℡ **04-93-87-88-55**). Both are open daily from 9am to noon, and 2 to 7pm (closed Sun Oct–Apr). Rentals begin at around 100F (€15.20, $15) per day, plus a deposit of at least 2,000F (€304, $290) or more, depending on the value of the machine you rent. If you want to rent a car here, try the following: **Budget** at the airport (℡ 04-93-21-36-50) and at 12 Av. Thiers, near the rail station (℡ 04-97-03-28-00); **Hertz** at the airport (℡ 04-93-21-36-72) and at 9 Av. Thiers (℡ 04-97-03-01-20); and **Avis** at the airport (℡ 04-93-21-42-80) and at 2 av. des Phocéens (℡ 04-93-80-63-52).

DEPARTING BY CAR   Leaving Nice, drive east along the Corniche Inférieure until reaching Villefranche; turn right onto D-25, which takes you in a very short distance to the wooded peninsula of St-Jean-Cap-Ferrat, 10km (6 miles) east of Nice.

WHERE TO STAY
Very Expensive
Hôtel Négresco ⭐⭐⭐   This Victorian wedding-cake hotel is one of the many super-glamorous hotels along the French Riviera. It was built on the seafront, in the French château style, with a mansard roof and domed tower, and its interior design was inspired by the country's châteaux. Rooms contain antiques, tapestries, paintings, and art and come in the widest range of styles and shapes of any hotel in town. Least desirable are the street-side units on the ground floors, where, in spite of double-glazed windows, you can still hear traffic. The most expensive rooms contain balconies and face the Mediterranean. Bathrooms are spacious.

37 promenade des Anglais, 06007 Nice CEDEX. ℡ **04-93-16-64-00**. Fax 04-93-88-35-68. negresco@ nicematin.fr. 158 units. 1,750–2,750F (€266–€418, $254–$399) double; from 3,400F (€516.80, $493) suite. AE, DC, MC, V. Parking 160F (€24.30, $23). Bus: 8, 9, 10, or 11. **Amenities:** 2 restaurants; bar; fitness center; room service; baby-sitting; laundry/dry cleaning. *In room:* A/C, TV, minibar, hair dryer.

Expensive
Chateau des Ollières ⭐⭐   The most appealing and unusual hotel to open in Nice in many years lies within a 5-minute walk from the Negresco and the promenade des Anglais, within an 8-hectare (20-acre) park. Formerly the property of Prince Lobolnov-Rostowsky, its centerpiece is a beaux-arts villa built in the 1870s. Rooms are outfitted in the same high-ceilinged, richly ornate style as the public areas, and have supremely comfortable mattresses and the kind of decorative porcelain and accessories you'd expect in an impeccably upscale private home. Bathrooms are quite luxurious.

39 av. des Baumettes, 06000 Nice. ℡ **04-92-15-77-99**. Fax 04-92-15-77-98. www.chateaudesollieres.com. 8 units. 850–2,200F (€129.20–€334.40, $123–$319) double; 1,150–3,000F (€174.80–€456, $167–$435) suite. AE, MC, V. Bus: 38. **Amenities:** Restaurant; bar; room service; baby-sitting; laundry/dry cleaning. *In room:* A/C, TV, minibar, hair dryer.

Moderate
Grand Hôtel Aston *Value*   One of the most alluring in its price bracket is this elegantly detailed 19th-century hotel. Rooms have comfortable mattresses and

Nice

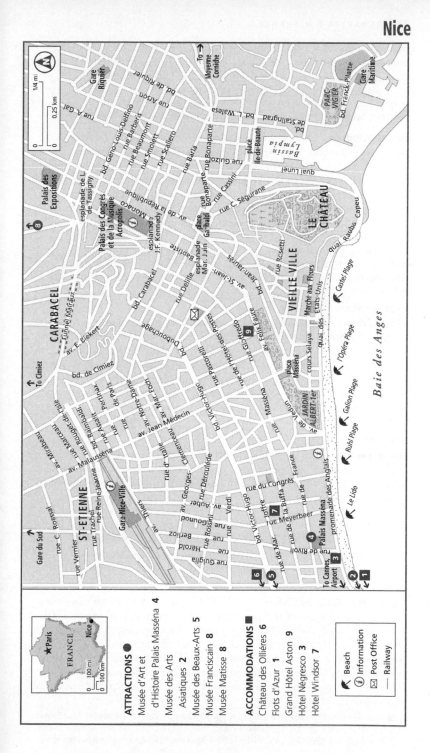

price scales that vary according to their views over the street, the splashing fountains of the place Massena, or the panorama over the coastline from the uppermost floor. The hotel is associated with Holland's Golden Tulip chain.

12 av. Félix-Faure, 06000 Nice. ℂ **04-92-17-53-00.** Fax 04-93-80-53-11. 160 units. 750–1,650F (€114–€250.80, $109–$239) double. AE, DC, MC, V. Parking 100F (€15.20, $15). Bus: 12. **Amenities:** Restaurant, bar; pool; room service; baby-sitting; laundry/dry cleaning. *In room:* A/C, TV, minibar, hair dryer.

Hotel Windsor   One of the most arts-conscious hotels in Provence is set within what was built by disciples of Gustav Eiffel as a maison bourgeoise, near the Hotel Negresco and the promenade des Anglais, in 1895. Inside, you'll find an artsy, somewhat claustrophobic environment that nonetheless is very appealing to artists or those with ties to the artistic community. Rooms have good mattresses, and small, tidy bathrooms. High points include a one-of-a-kind series of frescoes that adorn each of the 57 rooms. The dining room is open only to residents of the hotel.

11 rue Dalpozzo, 06000 Nice. ℂ **04-93-88-59-35.** Fax 04-93-88-94-57. www.windsor@webstore.fr. 560–760F (€85.10–€115.50, $81–$110) double. AE, DC, MC, V. Parking 60F (€9.10, $9). Bus: 9, 10, or 22. **Amenities:** Restaurant, bar; pool; gym; sauna; garden; room service; baby-sitting; laundry/dry cleaning. *In room:* A/C, TV, minibar, safe.

Inexpensive

Flots d'Azur   This villa-hotel, built around 1890, is located next to the sea, a short walk from the more elaborate and costlier promenade hotels. While the rooms vary in size and decor, all have good views and sea breezes. Double-glazed windows were recently added to cut down on the noise. There's a small sitting room and sun terrace in front, where a continental breakfast is served.

101 promenade des Anglais, 06000 Nice. ℂ **04-93-86-51-25.** Fax 04-93-97-22-07. 20 units. 300–550F (€45.60–€83.60, $44–$80) double. AE, MC, DC, V. Bus: 8. **Amenities:** Laundry/dry cleaning. *In room:* A/C, TV, minibar, safe.

WHERE TO DINE

Brasserie Flo FRENCH PROVENÇAL   In 1991, a France-based restaurant chain (Jean-Paul Bucher group), noted for its skill at restoring historic brasseries, bought the premises of a faded but historic century-old theatre near place Masséna and injected it with new life. It's now a stylish, reasonably priced, and fun place, where patrons dine beneath the high ceilings that are covered with frescoes. Menu items include an array of grilled fish, *choucroute* (sauerkraut) in the Alsatian style, steaks with brandied pepper sauce, and fresh oysters and shellfish.

2–4 rue Sacha-Guitry. ℂ **04-93-13-38-38.** Reservations recommended. Main courses 90–140F (€13.70–€21.30, $13–$20). Set price menus 119F (€18.10, $17) served only at lunch and after 10:30pm; 175F (€26.60, $25) served anytime. Open year-round. AE, DC, MC, V. Daily noon–3pm and 7pm–midnight. Bus: 1, 2, or 5.

Chantecler 𝕽𝕽𝕽 FRENCH (MODERN)   This restaurant, with its beautifully restored setting—the wall panels are from a château in Puilly-Fusse—is the most prestigious in Nice, and chef Alain Llorca offers the most sophisticated and creative dishes. Menu items change almost weekly, but may include filet of turbot served with a puree of broad beans, sun-dried tomatoes, and fresh asparagus; roasted suckling lamb served with beignets of fresh vegetables and ricotta-stuffed ravioli; and a melt-in-your-mouth fantasy of marbled hot chocolate drenched in an almond-flavored cream sauce.

In the Hôtel Négresco, 37 promenade des Anglais. ℂ **04-93-16-64-00.** Reservations required. Main courses 210–350F (€31.90–€53.20, $30–$51); set price lunch 300F (€45.60, $44); set price dinner 430–620F (€65.35–€94.25, $62–$90). AE, DC, MC, V. Daily 12:30–2:30pm and 7:30–10:30pm. Closed mid-Nov to mid-Dec. Bus: 8, 9, 10, or 11.

Chez Michel (Le Grand Pavois) ⨕ SEAFOOD   Chez Michel is nestled under an Art Deco apartment building near the water. One of the partners, Jacques Marquise, is from Golfe-Juan, where for 25 years he managed the famous fish restaurant Chez Tétou. His bouillabaisse has been widely celebrated. Other recommended specialties are baked sea bass in white wine, herbs, and lemon sauce and grilled flambé lobster.

11 rue Meyerbeer. ⓒ **04-93-88-77-42.** Reservations required. Main courses 145–400F (€22.05–€60.80, $21–$58); bouillabaisse from 350F (€53.20, $51); set price menus 195–255F (€29.65–€38.75, $28–$37); menu gastronomique 300F (€45.60, $44); set lunch 130F (€19.75, $19). AE, DC, MC, V. Daily noon–2:30pm and 7–11pm. Bus: 8.

Le Safari PROVENÇAL/NIÇOISE   The decor couldn't be simpler, outfitted as it is with a black ceiling, white walls, and an old-fashioned terra-cotta floor, and the youthful staff is mellow. Expect mobs of clients here, many of whom prefer the outdoor terrace overlooking the nearby *Marché aux Fleurs,* and all of whom appreciate the earthy, unpretentious, reasonably priced, and generously proportioned meals. Examples include a pungent *bagna cauda,* where vegetables are immersed in a sizzling brew of hot oil and anchovy paste; *daube* (stew) of beef Provençale; fresh pasta with basil; and the unfortunately named *merda de can* (dog shit), which is gnocchi stuffed with spinach—it's a lot more appetizing than it sounds.

1 Cours Saleya. ⓒ **04-93-80-18-44.** Reservations recommended. Main courses 80–150F (€12.15–€22.80, $12–$22); set menu 150F (€22.80, $22). AE, DC, MC, V. Daily noon–2:30pm and 7–11:30pm. Bus: 1, 2, or 5.

IN & AROUND NICE

The wide **boulevard des Anglais** fronts the bay. Split by "islands" of palms and flowers, it stretches for about 6km (4 miles). Fronting the beach are rows of grand cafes, the Musée Masséna, villas, and hotels—some good, others decaying.

In the east, the promenade becomes **quai des Etats-Unis,** the original boulevard, lined with some of the best restaurants in Nice, each specializing in bouillabaisse. Rising sharply on a rock is the site known as **Le Château,** the spot where the ducs de Savoie built their castle, which was torn down in 1706. The steep hill has been turned into a garden of pines and exotic flowers. To reach the site, many prefer to take an elevator; actually, many prefer to take the elevator up, then walk down. The park is open daily from 8am to 7:30pm.

The center of Nice is **place Masséna,** with pink buildings in the 17th-century Genoese style and the **Fontaine du Soleil** (Fountain of the Sun) by Janoit. Stretching from the main square to the promenade is the **Jardin Albert-Ier,** with an open-air terrace and a Triton Fountain. Palms and exotic flowers make this the most relaxing oasis at the resort.

A TRIO OF MUSEUMS WORTH A LOOK

Musée d'Art et d'Histoire Palais Masséna   The fabulous villa housing this museum was built in 1900 in the style of the First Empire as a residence for Victor Masséna, the prince of Essling and grandson of Napoléon's marshal. The

---

Nice Beach?

Some of the world's most attractive (and skimpily dressed) people cross the boulevard des Anglais heading for the beach, or "on the rocks," as it's called here. Tough on tender feet, the beach is shingled with rocks, one of the least attractive (and least publicized) aspects of this cosmopolitan resort. Many bathhouses provide mattresses for a charge.

city of Nice has converted the villa, next door to the Négresco, into a museum of local history and decorative art. A remarkably opulent drawing room, with mahogany-veneer pieces and ormolu mounts, is on the ground floor. At press time the museum was closed for extensive renovations; check its status at the time of your visit.

65 rue de France. ℰ **04-93-88-11-34**. Admission 25F (€3.80, $3.65) adults, 15F (€2.30, $2.20) children. Free first Sun every month. May 2–Sept 30 Tues–Sun 11am–noon and 3–6pm; Oct 1–Apr 30 Tues–Sun 2–5pm. Bus: 3, 7, 8, 9, 10, 12, 14, or 22.

Musée des Beaux-Arts Housed in the former residence of Ukrainian Princess Kotchubey, this museum has an important gallery devoted to the masters of the Second Empire and belle époque. The gallery of sculptures includes works by J. B. Carpeaux, Rude, and Rodin. Note the important collection by a dynasty of painters, the Dutch Van Loo family. A fine collection of 19th- and 20th-century art is displayed, including works by Ziem, Raffaelli, Boudin, Renoir, Monet, Guillaumin, and Sisley.

33 av. des Baumettes. ℰ **04-92-15-28-28**. Admission 25F (€3.80, $3.65) adults, 15F (€2.30, $2.20) students. Free for those under 18. Tues–Sun 10am–noon and 2–6pm. Bus: 9, 12, 22, 23, or 38.

Musée des Arts Asiatiques Set very close to Nice's airport, this museum opened in 1998 as a tribute to the sculpture and paintings of Cambodia, China, India, Tibet, and Japan. Inside are some of the best ceramics and devotional carvings ever found, many of them hauled back to France by colonials during the 19th and early 20th centuries. Of special interest are the accoutrements associated with Japan's tea-drinking ceremony, and several monumental representations of Buddha.

405 promenade des Anglais. ℰ **04-92-29-37-00**. Admission 35F (€5.30, $5.10) adults, 25F (€3.80, $3.65) children and students. Free for ages 6 and under. Mid-Apr to mid-Oct, Wed–Mon 10am–6pm. Mid-Oct to mid-Apr, Wed–Mon 10am–5pm.

EXPLORING NEARBY CIMIEZ 𝕽𝕽

Founded by the Romans, who called it Cemenelum, Cimiez, a hilltop suburb, was the capital of the Maritime Alps province. Recent excavations have uncovered the ruins of a Roman town, and you can wander around the digs. Take bus 15 or 17 from place Masséna.

Monastère de Cimiez (Cimiez Convent), place du Monastère (ℰ **04-93-81-00-04**), embraces a church that owns three of the most important works from the primitive painting school of Nice by the Bréa brothers. The most stunning is a 1475 Pietà to the right of the entrance as you come in. A Crucifixion on the left in the choir is a later work dating from 1512. Finally, in the third chapel, is a Deposition. In addition, note the huge altarpiece, half in the Renaissance style, half in the baroque, carved in wood and decorated with gold leaf screens. In a restored part of the convent where some Franciscan friars still live, **Musée Franciscain** is decorated with 17th-century frescoes. Some 350 documents and works of art from the 15th to the 18th century are displayed, and a monk's cell has been re-created.

In the gardens, you can get a panoramic view of Nice and the Bay of Angels. Matisse and Dufy are buried in the cemetery. The museum is open from Monday to Saturday 10am to noon and 3 to 6pm; the church is open daily from 8:30am to 12:30pm and 2 to 7:30pm. There is no admission charge.

Musée Matisse 𝕽𝕽, in the Villa des Arènes-de-Cimiez, 164 av. des Arènes-de-Cimiez (ℰ **04-93-53-40-53**), honors the great artist who spent the last years of his life in Nice; he died here in 1954. The museum has several permanent collections, many donated by Matisse and his heirs. These include *Nude in an Armchair with a Green Plant* (1937), *Nymph in the Forest* (1935/1942), and a chronologically arranged series of paintings from 1890 to 1919. The most famous of these is *Portrait of Madame Matisse* (1905), usually displayed near another portrait of the artist's wife, by Marquet, painted in 1900. The museum is open from Wednesday to Monday 10am to 6pm (closes at 5pm off-season, including all of Nov). Admission is 25F (€3.80, $3.65) adults, 15F (€2.30, $2.20) students, free for children under 19; free for everyone the first Sunday of every month.

THE SHOPPING SCENE

You might want to begin with a stroll through the streets and alleys of Nice's historic core. The densest concentrations of boutiques are along **rue Masséna, place Magenta,** and **rue Paradis,** as well as on the streets funneling into and around them. Nice is also known for its colorful street markets. The **flower market,** Marché aux Fleurs, cours Saleya, is open from 6am to 5:30pm except Monday and Sunday afternoon. The main Nice **flea market,** Marché à la Brocante, also at cours Saleya, takes place every Monday. There's another flea market on the port, Les Puces de Nice, place Robilante, open from Tuesday to Saturday 10am to 6pm.

If you're thinking of indulging in a Provençal picnic, you'll find everything you need at **Nicola Alziari,** 14 rue St-François de Paule (*C* **04-93-44-45-12**), from olives, anchovies, and pistous to aïolis and tapenades. It's one of the oldest stores of its kind in Nice. The house brand of olive oil comes in two strengths, a light version that aficionados claim is vaguely perfumed with Provence and a stronger version well suited to the earthy flavors and robust ingredients of a Provençal winter. Also, look for a range of objects crafted from olive wood.

One of the oldest chocolatiers in Nice, **Confiserie/Salon de Thé Auer,** 7 rue St-François-de-Paule (*C* **04-93-85-77-98**), was established five generations ago, in 1820, in a position near the opera house. Since then, few of the original decorative accessories have been changed, allowing tea drinkers to wax nostalgic for an era when taking tea was an integral part of the Niçois afternoon ritual. Today, tea is served from Tuesday to Sunday 8am to 12:30pm and 2:30 to 6pm. Hot chocolate is made the old-fashioned way, by melting bars of chocolate directly into hot milk; and the array of *confits de fruits* is almost comprehensive.

Established in 1949 by the grandfather, Georges Fuchs, of the present English-speaking owners, **Confiserie Florian du Vieux-Nice,** 14 quai Papacino (*C* **04-93-55-43-50**), near the historic center's Old Port, specializes in glazed fruits crystallized in sugar or artfully arranged into chocolates. Look for exotic jams (rose-petal preserves or mandarin marmalade) as well as candied violets, verbena leaves, and rosebuds.

Façonnable, 7–9 rue Paradis (*C* **04-93-87-88-80**), is the site that sparked the creation of what is today several hundred Façonnable menswear stores around the world. Here you'll find one of the largest Façonnable stores, with a wide range of men's suits, raincoats, overcoats, sportswear, and jeans. The look is youthful and conservatively stylish.

HITTING THE LINKS & OTHER OUTDOOR PURSUITS

GOLF   The oldest golf course on the Riviera is about 16km (10 miles) from Nice: **Golf Bastide du Roi** (also known as the Golf de Biot), 1379 rte. Antiber, Biot (*C* **04-93-65-08-48**). This is a flat, not particularly challenging, and much-used sea-fronting course. Open daily throughout the year, tee-off times begin at 8am and continue until 6pm, with the understanding that players then continue their rounds as long as the daylight allows. Reservations aren't necessary, though on weekends you should expect a delay. Greens fees are 240F (€36.50, $35) for 18 holes, and clubs can be rented for 80F (€12.15, $12). No carts are available.

SCUBA DIVING   The best-respected underwater outfitter is the **Centre International de Plongée de Nice,** 2 Ruelle des Moulins (℗ **04-93-55-59-50;** www.cip-nice.com). Adjacent to the city's old port, it lies midway between quai des Docks and boulevard Stalingrad. A *baptème* (initiatory dive for first-timers) costs 200F (€30.40, $29), and a one-tank dive for experienced divers, with all equipment included, is 190F (€28.90, $28). This outfitter is open only from mid-March to mid-November.

TENNIS   The oldest tennis club in Nice is the **Nice Lawn Tennis Club,** Parc Impérial, 5 av. Suzanne-Lenglen (℗ **04-92-15-58-00**), located near the rail station. It's open daily from 9am to 9pm (8pm from mid-Oct to mid-Apr), and charges 120F (€18.25, $17) per person for two noncontiguous hours of court time, or a reduced rate of 300F (€45.60, $44) per person for unlimited access to the courts for a 1-week period. The club has a cooperative staff, 13 clay courts, and six hard-surfaced courts. Reservations should be made the evening before.

NICE AFTER DARK

Nice has some of the most active nightlife along the Riviera; pick up a copy of *La Semaine de Spectacles,* which outlines the week's nighttime diversions, for clues on what's hot. The major cultural center along the Riviera is the **Opéra de Nice,** 9 rue terrasse (℗ **04-92-17-40-40;** bus: 15), with a busy season in winter. A full repertoire is presented, including both operas and the popular French Opéra Comique. In one season you might see *La Bohème, Tristan und Isolde,* and *Carmen,* as well as a *saison symphonique,* dominated by the Orchestre Philharmonique de Nice. The opera hall is also the major venue for concerts and recitals. The box office is open Tuesday to Saturday 10am to 5:30pm, with tickets ranging from 40 to 800F (€6.10 to €121.60, $6 to $116), depending on the event.

Le Cabaret du Casino Ruhl, in the Casino Ruhl, 1 promenade des Anglais (℗ **04-97-03-12-77;** airport bus), is Nice's answer to the cabaret glitter that appears in more ostentatious forms in Monte Carlo and Las Vegas. It includes just enough flesh to titillate; lots of spangles, feathers, and sequins; a medley of cross-cultural jokes and nostalgia for the good old days of French *chanson;* and an acrobat or juggler. The cover of 100F (€15.20, $15) includes the first drink; dinner and the show, complete with a bottle of wine per person, cost 300F (€45.60, $44). Shows are presented every Friday and Saturday at 10pm.

The casino contains an area devoted exclusively to slot machines, open daily from noon to 4 or 5am, entrance is free. A more formal gaming room, replete with blackjack, baccarat, chemin de fer, and 21 tables, is open nightly, at a fee of 75F (€11.40, $11) per person, every Monday to Friday 8pm to 4am, and every Saturday and Sunday 5pm to 5am. Bring your passport.

Near the Négresco and the promenade des Anglais, **Le Blue Boy,** 9 rue Jean Baptiste Spinetta (℗ **04-93-44-68-24;** bus: 15), is the oldest gay disco on the Riviera. With two bars and two floors, it's a vital nocturnal stopover for passengers aboard the dozens of all-gay cruises that make regular stops at Nice. Cover is 60F (€9.10, $9) on Saturday or 30F (€4.55, $4.35) otherwise. Ask the tourist office for a free copy of two of their periodicals, **L'X** and **L'Exces,** that list the entertainment and nightlife options for gay travelers in Nice.

ST-JEAN-CAP-FERRAT ⟨⟩

This has been called Paradise Found. Of all the oases along the Côte d'Azur, no place has the snob appeal of Cap-Ferrat. It's a 14-km (9-mile) promontory sprinkled with luxurious villas, outlined by sheltered bays, beaches, and coves. The vegetation is lush. In the port of St-Jean, the harbor accommodates yachts and fishing boats.

The Italianate **Musée Île-de-France,** avenue Denis-Séméria (✆ **04-93-01-33-09**), allows you to visit one of the most legendary villas along the Côte d'Azur, built by the Baronne Ephrussi de Rothschild. She died in 1934, leaving the building and its magnificent gardens to the Institut de France on behalf of the Académie des Beaux-Arts. The collection includes 18th-century furniture; Tiepolo ceilings; Savonnerie carpets; screens and panels from the Far East; tapestries from Gobelins, Aubusson, and Beauvais; Fragonard drawings; Renoirs, Sisleys, and Bouchers; rare Sèvres porcelain; and more. Covering 5 hectares (12 acres), the gardens contain fragments of statuary from churches, monasteries, and torn-down palaces.

From Mid-February to October, the museum and its gardens are open daily 10am to 6pm. From November to mid-February, they're open from Monday to Friday 2pm to 6pm and Saturday and Sunday 10am to 6pm. The entrance fee is 49F (€7.45, $7) adults and 37F (€5.60, $5) children and students 18 to 24. Guided tours conducted in English every day at 11:30am, 2:30pm, 3:30pm, and 4:30pm are offered for 14F (€2.15, $2).

ESSENTIALS

GETTING THERE   Most visitors drive or take the hourly bus (trip time: 25 min.) or a taxi from the rail station at nearby Beaulieu. There's also **bus service** from Nice (no. 111). For bus information and schedules, call ✆ **04-93-85-61-81.** Buses pull into the center of town, but there's no station.

VISITOR INFORMATION   The **Office de Tourisme** is at 59 av. Denis-Séméria (✆ **04-93-76-08-90**).

DEPARTING BY CAR   From St-Jean-Cap-Ferrat, you can head east toward Monaco by taking D-25 along the coast to the resort of Beaulieu, which is almost as chic as Cap-Ferrat. Continue along N-98 for about 11km (7 miles) into Monaco.

WHERE TO STAY

Grand Hôtel du Cap-Ferrat ⟨★★★⟩   Opened in 1909, this century-old palace is at the tip of the peninsula in the midst of a 6-hectare (14-acre) garden of semitropical trees and manicured lawns. Parts of the exterior have open loggias and big arched windows, and guests enjoy the views from the elaborate flowering terrace over the sea. Most rooms are quite spacious, and elegantly appointed. Each comes with a sumptuously fitted bed containing the town's most comfortable mattresses. Bathrooms feature power showerheads.

Bd. du Général-de-Gaulle, 06230 St-Jean-Cap-Ferrat. ✆ **04-93-76-50-50.** Fax 04-93-76-04-52. www.grand-hotel-cap-ferrat.com. 53 units. 1,400–5,700F (€212.80–€866.40, $203–$827) double; 5,000–18,800F (€760–€2,857.60, $725–$2,726) suite. AE, DC, MC, V. Indoor parking 500F (€76, $73), outdoor parking free. **Amenities:** 2 restaurants, 2 bars; pool; 2 tennis courts; sauna; room service; baby-sitting; laundry/dry cleaning. *In room:* A/C, TV, minibar, hair dryer, safe, robes.

Hotel Clair Logis ⟨Value⟩   Within an otherwise pricey resort strip of deluxe hotels and homes, this B&B was created by the grandmother of the present owners when she added two outbuildings to the spacious grounds of her century-old villa, about a 10-minute walk from the beach. The pleasantly old-fashioned rooms are scattered among three different stucco-covered buildings, with the most romantic and spacious of the lot within the main building. Rooms in the annexes (ca. 1960) are the most modern, but have the least character.

12 av. Centrale, 06230 St.Jean-Cap-Ferrat. ℭ **04-93-76-04-57.** Fax 04-93-76-51-82. www.hotel-clair-logis.fr. 18 units. 490–790F (€74.50–€120.10, $71–$115) double. AE, DC, MC, V. Free parking. Closed Jan 10 to mid-Mar and Nov to Dec 15. **Amenities:** Lounge. *In room:* TV, minibar, hair dryer.

WHERE TO DINE
Le Provençal FRENCH PROVENÇAL   This restaurant, one of the finest in the area, occupies what was a 2-century-old stone-sided farmhouse above the center of St-Jean-Cap Ferrat. You can enjoy marinated artichoke hearts with half a lobster; a *tart fine* of potatoes served with deliberately undercooked foie gras; rack of lamb with local herbs and tarragon sauce; and crayfish served with asparagus and black olive tapenade. A dessert sampler, "*les cinq desserts du Provençal,*" includes five luscious sweets, such as macaroons with chocolate or crème brûlée. The food is solemnly served, as if part of a grand ritual.

2 av. Denis-Séméria. ℭ **04-93-76-03-97.** Reservations required. Main courses 250–350F (€38–€53.20, $36–$51). Set price menus 350F (€53.20, $51). AE, MC, V. Apr–Sept daily noon–2:30pm and 7:30–11pm. Oct–Mar Tues–Sat noon–2:30pm and 7:30–11pm.

MONACO ✸✸✸
Monaco—or rather its capital, Monte Carlo—has for a century been a symbol of glamour. Its legend was further enhanced by the 1956 marriage of the man who was at that time the world's most eligible bachelor, Prince Rainier III, to American actress Grace Kelly. Although not always happy in her role, Princess Grace soon won the respect and adoration of her people. The Monégasques still mourn her death in a 1982 car accident.

Monaco became a property of the Grimaldi clan, a Genoese family, as early as 1297. With shifting loyalties, it has maintained something resembling independence ever since. In a fit of impatience, the French annexed it in 1793, but the ruling family recovered it in 1814, though the prince at the time couldn't bear to tear himself away from the pleasures of Paris for "dreary old Monaco."

ESSENTIALS
GETTING THERE   Monaco has rail, bus, and highway connections from other coastal cities, especially Nice. There are no border formalities for anyone entering Monaco from mainland France. **Trains** arrive at the station on avenue Prince Pierre every 30 minutes from Cannes, Nice, Menton, and Antibes. For rail information and schedules, call ℭ **08-36-35-35-35.** For **bus** information call ℭ **377/93-50-62-41.** Most buses leave from place du Casino (no station).

Tips Phone Tips
On June 21, 1996, Monaco's phone system underwent drastic changes. It's now a separate entity from France, which means that calls to and from such nearby places as Nice are long-distance. If you're calling Monaco from France, dial **00** followed by Monaco's new country prefix, **377,** then the 8-digit local phone number. To call from the United States, use the international access code, **011,** then 377 plus the 8-digit local number.

Monaco

Jardin Exotique **2**
Musée d'Anthropologie Préhistorique **1**
Musée de l'Océanographie **4**
Palais du Prince **3**

✝ Church   ⓘ Information   ✉ Post Office   — Railway

VISITOR INFORMATION   The **Direction du Tourisme** is at 2A bd. des Moulins (ⓒ **377/92-16-61-16**).

WHERE TO STAY
Hôtel Alexandra   This hotel, originally built around 1900 and renovated several times since, is in the center of the business district, on a busy and often noisy street corner. Its comfortably furnished rooms aren't that exciting, but they're reliable and respectable. The Alexandra knows it can't compete with the giants of Monaco and doesn't even try, but if you want to visit the principality without spending a fortune, it's a good deal.

35 bd. Princesse-Charlotte, 98000 Monaco. ⓒ **377/93-50-63-13.** Fax 377/92-16-06-48. 56 units. 760–910F (€115.50–€138.30, $110–$132) double. AE, DC, MC, V. Parking 45F (€6.85, $7). **Amenities:** Baby-sitting, laundry/dry cleaning. *In room:* A/C, TV, minibar, hair dryer.

Hôtel Cosmopolite   This century-old three-story hotel is down a set of steps from the train station. Madame Gay Angèle, the English-speaking owner, is proud of her "Old Monaco" establishment. Her more expensive rooms have showers, but the cheapest way to stay here is to request a room without shower—there are adequate facilities in the hall.

4 rue de la Turbie, 98000 Monaco. ✆ **377/93-30-16-95.** Fax 377/93-30-23-05. 24 units, 5 with bathroom. 228–258F (€34.65–€39.20, $33–$37) double without bathroom; 314–338F (€47.75–€51.45, $46–$49) double with bathroom. Rates include laundry/dry cleaning. **Amenities:** None.

Hôtel de Paris ✧✧✧ On the main plaza, this is one of the most famous hotels in the world and the choicest address in Monaco. The hotel is furnished with a dazzling decor of marble pillars, statues, crystal chandeliers, sumptuous carpets, Louis XVI chairs, and a wall-size fin-de-siècle mural. Rooms are, in many cases, sumptuous, each with an elaborate period decor or a stylish contemporary one. Bathrooms are large. On top of the Hôtel de Paris, Le Grill has an impressive sliding roof. The elegant Le Louis XV is recommended under "Where to Dine, below." Thermes Marins spa, connected to the hotel, offers complete cures of thalassotherapy under medical supervision.

Place du Casino, 98000 Monaco. ✆ **377/92-16-30-00.** Fax 377/92-16-38-50. www.montecarloresort.com. 197 units. 2,330–3,900F (€354.15–€592.80, $338–$566) double; 4,362F (€663, $633) suite. AE, DC, MC, V. Parking 130F (€19.75, $19). **Amenities:** 3 restaurants, bar; pool; sauna; room service; baby-sitting; laundry/dry cleaning. *In room:* A/C, TV, minibar, hair dryer, safe, robes.

Hôtel Mirabeau ✧✧ In the heart of Monte Carlo, next to the casino, the contemporary Mirabeau combines modern design with refined atmosphere. Large mirrors, spacious lighted closets, and sumptuous beds with luxurious mattresses make living here idyllic; many rooms also have terraces with romantic views overlooking the Mediterranean. Although the newest rooms are as fine as those in the main building, many prefer older ones for their old-fashioned French decor and street-front exposures. Bathrooms are roomy and well appointed.

1 av. Princesse-Grace, MC 98000 Monaco. ✆ **377/92-16-65-65.** Fax 377/93-50-84-85. www.montecarloresort. com. 103 units. 1,570–2,600F (€238.65–€395.20, $228–$377) double; from 3,250F (€494, $471) suite. AE, DC, MC, V. Parking 125F (€19, $18). **Amenities:** Restaurant, bar; pool; room service; baby-sitting; laundry/dry cleaning. *In room:* A/C, TV, minibar, hair dryer, safe, robes.

WHERE TO DINE
Café de Paris INTERNATIONAL This is the best positioned cafe and restaurant in Monaco, very close to both the casino and the Hôtel de Paris, and so close to the tourist center of things that you might get more of a dose of Las Vegas than you might care for. But why not revel in the crowds and the hurly-burly? This site provides a front-row seat to the never-ending spectacle of Monte Carlo even though the cafe itself evokes an early 20th-century French brasserie. Food is professional and well-prepared: About a half-dozen *plats du jour* are available, including fried trout with almonds, pepper steak, osso buco, and turbot with hollandaise.

Place du Casino. ✆ **377/92-16-20-20.** Reservations recommended. Main courses 110–220F (€16.70–€33.45, $16–$32); set price menus 200–450F (€30.40–€68.40, $29–$65). AE, DC, MC, V. Daily 8am–4am.

Le Louis XV ✧✧✧ FRENCH/ITALIAN Le Louis XV offers what one critic called "down-home Riviera cooking within a Fabergé egg." In these regal trappings, the chef, Alain Ducasse, creates a cuisine that is light and attuned to the seasons. Ducasse commands the finest ingredients in Europe, and his menu is ever changing to take advantage of what is best in any season. A new and very earthly dish, reflecting the sometimes gruesome but delicious nature of traditional French cuisine, is roasted breast of pigeon served with grilled foie gras, new potatoes, and *jus* composed of the pigeon's organs (offal) with sage. The service is superb.

In the Hôtel de Paris, place du Casino. ℂ 377/92-16-30-01. Reservations recommended. Jacket/tie for men. Main courses 355–535F (€53.95–€81.30, $52–$78); set price dinner 90–1,050F (€13.70–€159.60, $13–$152). Set lunch 500F (€76, $73). AE, DC, MC, V. Thurs–Mon noon–3pm and 8–10pm. Between mid-June and Aug, it's also open Wed 8–10pm. Closed Feb 2–17 and Nov 28–Dec 28.

EXPLORING MONACO

The second-smallest state in Europe (Vatican City is the tiniest), Monaco consists of four parts: The old town, **Monaco-Ville,** is on a promontory, The Rock, 60m (200 ft.) high, and is the seat of the royal palace and the government building, as well as the home of the Oceanographic Museum. To the west of the bay, **La Condamine,** the 19th-century home of the Monégasques, is at the foot of the old town, forming its harbor and port sector. Up from the port (walking is steep in Monaco) is **Monte Carlo,** once the playground of European royalty and still the center for wintering wealthy, the setting for the casino and its gardens and the deluxe hotels. The fourth part, **Fontvieille,** is a neat industrial suburb.

Ironically, **Monte-Carlo Beach,** at the far frontier, is on French soil. It attracts a chic crowd, including movie stars. The resort has a freshwater pool, an artificial beach, and a sea-bathing establishment.

The Italianate home of Monaco's royal family, the **Palais du Prince** 𝒢, dominates the principality from "The Rock." When touring Les Grands Appartements du Palais, place du Palais (ℂ **377/93-25-18-31**), you're shown the Throne Room and allowed to see some of the art collection, including Brueghels and Holbeins, as well as Princess Grace's stunning state portrait. The palace was built in the 13th century and part of it is from the Renaissance. The ideal time to arrive is 11:55am to watch the 10-minute changing of the guard. The palace is open daily from June to September 9:30am to 6:30pm and October from 10am to 5pm. Admission is 30F (€4.55, $4.35) adults, 15F (€2.30, $2.20) children ages 8 to 14, free for children under 8.

Jardin Exotique 𝒢𝒢, boulevard du Jardin-Exotique Moneghetti (ℂ **377/93-15-29-80**), was built on the side of a rock and is known for its cactus collection. The gardens were begun by Prince Albert I in 1933; he was both a naturalist and a scientist. He spotted some succulents growing in the palace gardens, and knowing that these plants were normally found only in Central America or Africa, he created the garden from them. You can also explore the grottoes here, as well as the **Musée d'Anthropologie Préhistorique** (ℂ **377/93-15-80-06**). The view of the principality is splendid. The site is open daily from June to September 9am to 7pm and from October to May 9am to 6pm. Admission is 39F (€5.95, $6) adults and 18F (€2.75, $2.60) children 6 to 18; free for children under 6.

Musée de l'Océanographie 𝒢𝒢𝒢, avenue St-Martin (ℂ **377/93-15-36-00**), was founded by Albert I, great-grandfather of the present prince. In the main rotunda is a statue of Albert dressed as a sea captain. Displayed are specimens he collected during 30 years of expeditions aboard his oceanographic boats. The aquarium, one of the finest in Europe, contains more than 90 tanks. The museum is open daily July and August from 9am to 8pm; from April to June and September 9am to 7pm; from March and October 9:30am to 7pm; and from November to February 10am to 6pm. Admission is 60F (€9.10, $9) adults, 30F (€4.55, $4.35) students and children 6 to 18, free for children under 6.

TWO SHOPS WORTH A LOOK

Rising costs and an increase in crime have changed women's tastes in jewelry. **Bijoux Cascio,** Les Galeries du Metropole, 207 av. des Spélugues (℡ 377/93-50-17-57), sells imitation gemstones, copies of the real ones sold by Cartier and Van Cleef & Arpels. Made in Italy of gold-plated silver, cubic zirconia, and glittering chunks of Austrian-made Swarovski crystal, the fake jewelry costs many thousands of francs less than the authentic gems.

Boutique du Rocher, 1 av. de la Madone (℡ 377/93-30-91-17), a short walk from place du Casino, is the larger of two roughly equivalent boutiques opened in 1966 by Princess Grace as the official retail outlets of the charitable foundation that was established by the Grimaldis in her name. The organization merchandises Monégasque and Provençal handcrafts, including carved frames; gift items crafted from porcelain, textiles, and wood; children's toys; and dolls. On the premises are workshops where local artisans produce the goods you'll find for sale.

TAKING A DIP & OTHER OUTDOOR ACTIVITIES

BEACHES/SWIMMING   Monaco, in its role as the quintessential kingdom by the sea, offers sea bathing at its most popular beach, **La Plage de Larvetto,** off avenue du Princesse-Grace (℡ 377/93-15-28-76). There's no charge for bathing on this strip of beach, which is frequently replenished with sand hauled in by barge. The beach is open to public access at all hours.

If a pool is more to your tastes, most of the large hotels in town boast pools, but the dowager empress, across the border in neighboring France, is **Le Monte Carlo Beach Club,** av. Princesse-Grace, Roquebrune-St-Roman (℡ 04-93-28-66-66). Founded in 1929, it's one of the most famous beach, pool, and social clubs on the Riviera. Some privileges and perks are reserved for members, but nonmembers who pay 200F (€30.40, $29) can use the facilities on a day pass. An additional 1,000F (€152, $145) will get you a striped private cabana. Most of the socializing occurs around the edges of the Olympic-size pool. On the premises are bars and three restaurants. From April to October, windsurfing and water-skiing are popular diversions that are conducted from the stony beach of this club.

GOLF   The **Monte Carlo Golf Club,** Route N-7, La Turbie (℡ 04-93-41-09-11), lying within France, is an 18-hole, par-71 golf course with equal parts prestige, scenic panoramas, and local history. Certain perks, including use of electric golf buggies, are reserved exclusively for members. Before they're allowed to play, nonmembers will be asked to show proof of membership in another golf club and provide evidence of their handicap ratings. Greens fees for 18 holes are 400F (€60.80, $58) from Monday to Friday and 500F (€76, $73) Saturday and Sunday. Clubs can be rented for 80F (€12.15, $12). The course is open daily from 8am to sunset.

TENNIS & SQUASH   In addition to 13 tennis courts (21 clay and 11 concrete), the **Monte Carlo Country Club,** av. Princesse-Grace, Roquebrune-St-Roman (℡ 04-93-41-30-15), has enough other warm-weather distractions to keep you amused for a week. An entrance fee of 220F (€33.45, $32) gets you access to a restaurant, a health club with Jacuzzi and sauna, a putting green, a beach, squash courts, and the above-mentioned roster of well-maintained tennis courts. Residents of the hotels administered by the Societé des Bains de Mer (the Hotel de Paris, the Hermitage, the Mirabeau, and the Monte Carlo Beach Club) pay half-price. It's open daily from 8am to 8 or 9pm, depending on the season.

GAMBLING & OTHER AFTER-DARK DIVERSIONS

The **Sun Casino,** in the Monte Carlo Grand Hotel, 12 av. des Spélugues (© **377/93-50-65-00**), is a huge room filled with the one-armed bandits. It also features blackjack, craps, and American roulette. Additional slot machines are available on the roof starting at 11am—for those who want to gamble with a wider view of the sea. It's open daily 5pm to 4am (until 5am for slot machines). Admission is free. Bring your passport.

A speculator, François Blanc, made the **Monte Carlo Casino,** place du Casino (© **377/92-16-21-21**), the most famous in the world, attracting Sarah Bernhardt, Mata Hari, King Farouk, and Aly Khan (Onassis used to own a part-interest). The architect of Paris's Opéra Garnier, Charles Garnier, built the oldest part of the casino, and it remains an extravagant example of period architecture.

The **Salle Américaine,** containing only Vegas-style slot machines, opens at noon, as do doors for roulette and trente-quarente. A section for roulette and chemin-de-fer opens at 3pm. Everything heats up at 4pm when the full casino swings into action with more roulette, craps, and blackjack. Gambling continues until very late, and closing time depends on the crowd. To enter the casino, you must be at least 21 and have a passport, driver's license, or identity card. Admission to private rooms is 50 to 100F (€7.60 to €15.20, $7 to $15).

The foremost winter establishment, under the same ownership, is the **Cabaret** in the Casino Gardens (© **377/92-16-36-36** for reservations), where you can dance to the music of a smooth orchestra. A good cabaret with feathers, glitter, and Riviera-style semi-nudity is presented at 10pm Wednesday to Monday mid-September to June. From 9pm you can enjoy dinner for 450F (€68.40, $65). Drinks ordered separately begin at 150F (€22.80, $22).

In the **Salle Garnier** of the casino, concerts are held periodically; for information, contact the tourist office (earlier in this chapter). The music is usually classical, featuring the Orchestre Philharmonique de Monte Carlo.

The casino also contains the **Opéra de Monte-Carlo,** whose patron is Prince Rainier. This world-famous house, opened in 1879 by Sarah Bernhardt, presents a winter and spring repertoire that traditionally includes Puccini, Mozart, and Verdi. The famed Ballets Russes de Monte-Carlo, starring Nijinsky and Karsavina, was created in 1918 by Sergei Diaghilev. The national orchestra and ballet company of Monaco appear here. Tickets may be hard to come by; your best bet is to ask your hotel concierge. You can make inquiries about tickets on your own at the **Atrium du Casino** (© **377/92-16-22-99**), open from Tuesday to Sunday 10am to 12:15pm and 2 to 5pm. Standard tickets generally cost 150 to 800F (€22.80 to €121.60, $22 to $116).

7

Germany

by Darwin Porter & Danforth Prince

At long last Berlin moves into the millennium as the capital of a unified Germany. The rebuilding of the city for the 21st century continues at a rapid pace. What was once the city's biggest tourist attraction, the Berlin Wall, is now a bicycle path where Berliners push baby strollers. Restored baroque Munich, in the south, known as Germany's "secret capital," is the gateway to the Bavarian Alps and the colorful alpine villages. For a taste of medieval Germany, explore the untouched towns of the Romantic Road and Ludwig II's fairy-tale castle of Neuschwanstein.

1 Berlin

When Heinrich Heine arrived in Berlin in 1819, he exclaimed, "Isn't the present splendid!" Were he to arrive today, he might make the same remark. Visitors who come by plane to Berlin see a splendid panorama. Few metropolitan areas are blessed with as many lakes, woodlands, and parks—these cover one-third of the city's area, and small farms with fields and meadows still exist within the city limits.

Berlin today is an almost completely modern city. Regrettably, Berlin is hardly the architectural gem that old-time visitors remember from the pre-Nazi era; it wasn't rebuilt with the same kind of care lavished on Munich and Cologne. But in spite of its decades-long "quadripartite status," it's a vibrant city, always receptive to new ideas, a major economic and cultural center, and a leader in development and research. Because of its excellent facilities, it is a favored site for trade fairs, congresses, and conventions, attracting six million visitors a year.

Since the Berlin Wall came down, change within the city has been so rapid that the government has resorted to painting a red line through its central district so that baffled visitors can tell where it stood. The city still seems to have two of everything—two zoos, two opera companies, two major international airports, to name a few. However, there're also new problems for the reunited Berlin. Economic devastation has affected the eastern sector, and panhandling and crime on the streets have become major problems in some areas of the city.

ESSENTIALS
GETTING THERE **By Plane** **Tegel Airport** is the city's busiest, serving most flights from the west. Historic **Tempelhof Airport,** made famous as the city's lifeline during the Berlin Airlift, has declined in importance. **Schönefeld,** the airport in the eastern sector, is used primarily by Russian and Eastern European airlines. Private bus shuttles among the three airports operate constantly so you can make connecting flights at a different airport. Buses from each airport will also take you into the center. For information on all three airports, call ✆ **0180/500-01-86** or contact www.berlin-airport.de.

By Train   Frankfurt and Hamburg, among other cities, have good rail connections to Berlin. From Frankfurt to Berlin takes about 7 hours. Eurailpass and GermanRail passes are valid. Most arrivals from western European and western German cities are at the **Bahnhof Zoologischer Garten** (© 0810/599-66-33), the main train station, called "Bahnhof Zoo," in western Berlin. In the center of the city, close to the Kurfürstendamm, it's well connected for public transportation. Facilities include a tourist information counter dispensing free maps and tourist brochures open daily from 5am to 11pm. The staff will also make same-day hotel reservations for 5DM (€2.55, $2.50).

Berlin has two other train stations, the **Berlin Hauptbahnhof** and **Berlin Lichtenberg.** Call the main station at (© 0810/599-66-33) for information.

By Bus   The operations center for several independent bus operators is headquartered within a central arrivals and departures point, the **ZOB Omnibusbahnhof am Funkturm,** Messedamm 8 (© 030/301-03-80). Call for departure times and fare information for routes to and from other parts of Europe.

By Car   From Frankfurt, take A-66 to Bad Herzfeld, and either go east on A-4 to pick up A-9 to Berlin, or continue on A-7 to Braunschweig and east on A-2 toward Berlin. North of Nürnberg, A-9 leads to Berlin. From Leipzig take A-14 in the direction of Halle; at the intersection of A-9, head northeast into Berlin. From Dresden, head northeast on A-13 into Berlin. Expect heavy traffic delays on *Autobahnen,* especially on weekends and sunny days when everybody is out touring.

VISITOR INFORMATION   Tourist Office   For tourist information and hotel bookings, head for the **Berlin Tourist Information Center,** in the Europa-Center near the Memorial Church, entrance on the Budapesterstrasse side (© 030/25-00-25; www.berlin-tourism.de), open from Monday to Saturday 8am to 10pm and Sunday 9am to 9pm.

Websites   Come to **www.berlin-info.de** for a virtual tour of Berlin's sights, but be aware that some of the links go to German-only pages The informative **www.us.germany-tourism.de** includes basics on lodging, getting around, links, and upcoming events, such as the celebrations commemorating the 250th anniversary of the death of Bach. The site **www.hotelstravel.com/germany.html** not only provides detailed listings for hotels in Germany but also has links to related sites, like Ritz-Carlton and Relais & Châteaux, that offer lodging and general travel info. The definitive dining guide **www.eat-germany.net** lets you search the site or view its Top 10 for each city. The restaurants are selected by users who rate them, giving an aura of objectivity. With lots of detail about type of food, hours, locations, and kinds of patrons, searches can be narrowed by nation, state, or city.

CITY LAYOUT   The center of activity in the western part of Berlin is the 3-km- (2-mile-) long **Kurfürstendamm,** called the Ku'damm by Berliners. Along

---

Value **The Welcome Card**

If you're going to be in Berlin for 3 days, you can purchase a **Welcome-Card** for 32DM (€16.35, $16), entitling holders to 72 free hours on public transportation in Berlin and Brandenburg. You also get free admission or price reductions up to 50% on sightseeing tours, museums, and other attractions. Reductions of 25% are granted at 10 of the city's theaters as well. It's valid for one adult and up to three children 13 or younger.

Western Berlin

0   1/4 mi
0   0.25 km

Mierendorff-platz
Kaiserin- Augusta-Allee
Mierendorffstrasse
Quedlinburgstrasse
Spree
Alt-Moabit
Gotzkowsky Bridge
Levetzowstrasse
Helmholtzstrasse
Franklinstrasse
SCHLOSSGARTEN CHARLOTTENBURG
Schloss Bridge
Spandauer-Damm
Luisen-platz
Dove Bridge
Dove-strasse
Salzufer
Einsteinufer
Christstrasse
Otto-Suhr-Allee
Cauerstrasse
March-strasse
Landwehrkanal
Bachstr.
Danckelmannstrasse
Schlossstrasse
Zillestrasse
Rich.-Wagner-Strasse
Deutsche Oper Berlin
Bismarckstrasse
Strasse des 17. Juni
TIER-GARTEN
Kaiserdamm
Kaiser-Friedrich-Strasse
Wilmersdorfer
Krumme Strasse
Schillerstrasse
Goethestrasse
Pestalozzistrasse
Schlüterstr.
Knesebeckstr.
Hardenbergstrasse
BAHNHOF ZOOLOGISCHER GARTEN
Harden-bergpla
Kantstrasse
CHARLOTTEN-BURG
Lewishamstr.
Savignyplatz
Kantstrasse
Joachimstaler-strasse
Rönnestrasse
Sybelstrasse
Leibnizstr.
SAVIGNYPLATZ
Kurfürstendamm
Uhlandstr.
Ranke-platz
WESTKREUZ
Damasch-kestrasse
Brandenburgische
Konstanzerstr.
Lietzenburgerstr.
Fasanenstrasse
Bundesallee
Kurfürstendamm
Seesener Strasse
Pauls-bornerstrasse
Westfälische Strasse
Pariser Strasse
Düsseldorfer Strasse
Sächsische Strasse
Hohenzollern-strasse
Hohenzollern-platz
Nachod-strasse
To Dahlem

ATTRACTIONS

Ägyptisches Museum **6**
Brandenburger Tor (Gate) **24**
Bröhan Museum **3**
Die Sammlung Berggruen **4**
Gemäldegalerie (Picture Gallery) **28**
Kaiser-Wilhelm Gedächtniskirche
  (Kaiser Wilhelm Memorial Church) **18**

Käthe-Kollwitz Museum **10**
Kunstgewerbe Museum **25**
Museum für Gegenwart **22**
Neue Nationalgalerie **27**
Reichstag **23**
Schloss Charlottenburg **5**
Story of Berlin **11**

ACCOMMODATIONS ■

Art Nouveau **7**
Bleibtreu Hotel **9**
Brandenburger Hof Relais & Châteux **17**
Grand Hotel Esplanade **29**
Hecker's Hotel **12**
Hotel-Pension Bregenz **8**

Hotel Sylter Hof Berlin **19**
Kempinski Hotel Bristol Berlin **15**
Palace Hotel **20**
Pension Munchen **1**
Savoy **14**
Sorat Art'otel **16**

Berlin U-Bahn & S-Bahn

U1 Krumme Lanke/
Warschauer Str.

U2 Ruhleben/
Vinetastr.

U4 Innsbrucker Platz/
Nollendorf-platz

U5 Alexanderplatz/
Hönow

U6 Alt- Mariendorf/
Alt-Tegel

U7 Rudow/
Rathaus Spandau

U8 Hermannstr./
Paracelsus-Bad

U9 Rathaus Steglitz/
Osloer Str.

U12 Ruhleben/
Warschauer Str.

U15 Uhlandstr./
Warschauer Str.

S1 Wannsee/ Oranienburg

S2 Blankenfelde/ Waidmannslust

S3 Westkreuz/ Erkner

S4 Westhafen/ Bernau (b Berlin)

S5 Spandau/ Strausberg Nord

S6 Zeuthen/ Warschauer Str.

S7 Potsdam Stadt/ Ahrenfelde

S8 Blankenburg/ Grünau

S9 Flughafen Berlin-Schönefeld/Westkreuz

S10 Birkenwerder (b Bln)/ Spindlerfeld

S45 Westend/Flughafen Berlin-Schönefeld/

S46 Westend/Königs Wusterhausen

S75 Spandau/ Wartenberg

this wide boulevard you'll find the best hotels, restaurants, theaters, cafes, night-clubs, shops, and department stores. The huge **Tiergarten,** the city's largest park, is crossed by Strasse des 17 Juni, which leads to the famed **Brandenburger Tor (Gate);** just north is the Reichstag. On the southwestern fringe of the Tier-garten is the **Berlin Zoo** (Zoologischer Garten). From the Ku'damm you can take Hardenbergstrasse, crossing Bismarckstrasse and traversing Otto-Suhr-Allee, which leads to **Schloss Charlottenburg** and museums, one of your major sightseeing goals. The Dahlem Museums are on the southwestern fringe, often reached by going along Hohenzollerndamm.

The **Brandenburger Tor** is the start of Berlin's most celebrated street, **Unter den Linden,** the cultural heart of Berlin before World War II. The famous street runs from west to east, cutting a path through the city. It leads to **Museumsin-sel** (Museum Island), where the most outstanding museums of eastern Berlin, including the Pergamon, are situated. As it courses along, Unter den Linden crosses another major Berlin artery, **Friedrichstrasse.** If you continue south along Friedrichstrasse, you'll reach the former location of **Checkpoint Charlie,** the famous border-crossing site of the cold war days.

Unter den Linden continues east until it reaches **Alexanderplatz,** the center of eastern Berlin, with its TV tower (Fernsehturm). A short walk away is the restored **Nikolai Quarter** (Nikolaiviertel), a neighborhood of bars, restaurants, and shops that evoke life in the prewar days.

GETTING AROUND   By Public Transportation   The Berlin transport system consists of buses, trams, and U-Bahn and S-Bahn trains. The network is run by the **BVG** (© 030/1-94-49), which operates an information booth out-side the Bahnhof Zoo on Hardenbergplatz, open daily from 8am to 10pm. The staff will provide details about which U-Bahn (underground) or S-Bahn (ele-vated railway) line to take to various locations and the ticket options possible. You can also purchase tickets, including discount cards.

The **BVG standard ticket** (Einzelfahrschein) is 4DM (€2.05, $2) and is valid for 2 hours of transportation in all directions, transfers included. Also available at counters and vending machines is a 24-hour ticket; the price is 8.70DM (€4.45, $4.35). On buses, only standard tickets can be purchased, and tram tickets must be purchased in advance. Tickets should be kept until the end of the journey; otherwise, you'll be liable for a fine of 60DM (€30.65, $30).

By Taxi   Taxis are available throughout Berlin. The meter starts at 6DM (€3.05, $3), plus 2.20DM (€1.10, $1.10) per kilometer after that. Visitors can flag down taxis that have a T-sign illuminated. For a taxi, call © **21-02-02,** 6-90-22, or 26-10-26.

By Car   Touring Berlin by car isn't recommended. Free parking places are dif-ficult to come by.

FAST FACTS: Berlin

American Express   Reiseland American Express offices at Alte Potsdamer Strasse 7 (© **030/25-29-74-74;** U-Bahn: Hüttenweg), Am Borsigturm 2 (© **030/43-40-20-60;** U-Bahn: Borischverger), Bayreuthstrasse 37–38 (© **030/ 21-49-83-63;** U-Bahn: Wittenbergplatz), and Friedrichstrasse 172 (© **030/ 20-17-40-12;** U-bahn: Friedrichstrasse), are all open from Monday to Friday 9am to 5pm.

Business Hours Most **banks** are open from Monday to Friday 9am to 1 or 3pm. Most other **businesses** and **stores** are open from Monday to Friday 9 or 10am to 6 or 6:30pm and Saturday 9am to 2pm. On *langer Samstag,* the first Saturday of the month, shops stay open until 4 or 6pm. Some stores observe late closing on Thursday, usually at 8:30pm.

Currency During the life of this 2002 edition, the long-standing German mark (called *deutsche mark* or DM) will give way to the euro. Officially, the euro in both physical banknotes and coins will be issued after January 1, 2002, as the deutsche mark is phased out. The phase-out of the German mark will occur on March 1, 2002.

The German monetary unit is the **deutsch mark (DM),** which is divided into 100 pfenning. The rate of exchange for the deutsche mark used throughout this chapter was $1 = 2DM, or 1DM = 50¢. Like the dollar, the ratio of the British pound to the mark fluctuates constantly. At press time, £1 = 3.13DM, or 1DM = 32p. The euro is currently fixed at €1 = 1.955DM (i.e., 1DM = €0.511).

Currency Exchange You can exchange money at all airports, major department stores, any bank, and the American Express offices (above).

Dentists/Doctors The Berlin tourist office in the Europa-Center (see "Visitor Information," above) keeps a list of English-speaking dentists and doctors in Berlin. In case of a medical emergency, call ✆ **030/31-00-31.**

Drugstores If you need a pharmacy (*Apotheke*) at night, go to one on any corner. There you'll find a sign in the window giving the address of the nearest drugstore open at night; such posting is required by law. A central pharmacy is **Europa-Apotheke,** Tauentzienstrasse 9–12 (✆ **030/2-61-41-42;** U-Bahn: Kurfürstendamm), by the Europa-Center. It's open from Monday to Friday 9am to 8pm and Saturday to 4pm.

Embassies & Consulates The embassy of the **United States** is at Neustaedtische Kirchstrasse 4–5 (✆ **030/2-38-51-74;** U-Bahn: Friedrichstrasse), and a consulate at Clayallee 170 (✆ **030/8-32-92-33;** U-Bahn: Hüttenweg). Hours are Monday to Friday 8:30am to 5:30pm. The **British Embassy** is at Unter den Linden 32–34 (✆ **030/20-18-40;** U-Bahn: Friedrichstrasse). Hours are Monday to Friday 9am to noon and 2 to 4pm. The embassy of **Australia** is on Kempinski Plaza, at Uhlandstrasse 181–183 (✆ **030/8-80-08-80;** U-Bahn: Uhlandstrasse). Hours are Monday to Thursday 9am to 5pm, Friday 9am to 4pm. **Canada** maintains a consulate at Friedrichstrasse 95 (✆ **030/20-31-20;** U-Bahn: Friedrichstrasse). Hours are Monday to Friday 8:30am to 12:30m and 1:30 to 5pm. The embassy of **New Zealand** is at Friedrichstrasse 60 (✆ **030/20-62-10;** U-Bahn: Fredrichstrasse). Hours are Monday to Friday 9am to 1pm and 2 to 5:30pm. The consulate of **Ireland** is at Ernst-Reuter-Platz 10 (✆ **030/34-80-08-22;** U-Bahn: Tiergarten). Hours are Monday to Friday 9:30am to noon and 2:30 to 4:45pm.

Emergencies Call the police at ✆ **110;** dial ✆ **112** to report a fire or to call an ambulance.

Internet Access If you're feeling out of touch, visit **Webtimes,** Chausseestrasse 8 (✆ **030/280-49-890;** U-Bahn: Oranienburger Tor), open Monday to Friday 9am to midnight, Saturday and Sunday 10am to midnight.

Post Office The post office at the Bahnhof Zoo is open from Monday to Saturday 6am to midnight and Sunday 8am to midnight. If you have mail sent here, have it marked Hauptpostlagernd, Postamt 120, Bahnhof Zoo, D-10612, Berlin. There's also a post office at Hauptbahnhof, open from Monday to Friday 7am to 8pm and Saturday 8am to 1pm. For postal information, call ℂ **030/311-00-20.** You can make long-distance calls at post offices at far cheaper rates than at hotels.

Telephone The **country code** for Germany is **49;** the **city code** for Berlin is **30** for calls from outside Germany or **030** if you're calling within the country.

If you're going to make a lot of phone calls or wish to make an international call from a phone booth, you'll probably want to purchase a **telephone card.** Phone cards are sold at post offices and newsstands. The 12DM (€6.15, $6) card offers about 40 minutes, and the 50DM (€25.55, $25) card is useful for long-distance calls. Simply insert them into the telephone slot. Phone cards are becoming so popular in Germany that many public phones no longer accept coins.

To make a **collect or calling card call,** dial one of the following access numbers to reach an operator or an English-language voice prompt: **AT&T** (ℂ **0130-0010), MCI** (ℂ **0130-0012),** or **Sprint** (ℂ **0130-0013).** To call the U.S. direct, dial **001** followed by the area code and phone number.

WHERE TO STAY
ON OR NEAR THE KURFÜRSTENDAMM
Very Expensive

Grand Hotel Esplanade 𝕲𝕲𝕲   The Esplanade rivals the Kempinski for supremacy in Berlin. Rooms are spacious, bright, and cheerfully decorated, with sound insulation. Beds are large with quality mattresses and duvets. Bathrooms are among the city's most luxurious. When reserving, ask for one of the corner rooms, as they're the biggest and have the best views.

Lützowufer 15, D-10785 Berlin. ℂ 030/25-47-80. Fax 030/265-11-71. www.esplanade.de. 400 units. 350DM–590DM (€178.85–€301.54, $175–$295) double; from 750DM (€383.25, $375) suite. AE, DC, MC, V. Parking 30DM (€15.35, $15). U-Bahn: Kurfürstenstrasse, Nollendorfplatz, or Wittenbergplatz. **Amenities:** Harlekin restaurant (see "Where to Dine," below), 2 bars (the elegant Harry's New York Bar, plus the traditional German EckKneipe); indoor pool; whirlpool; solarium; sauna; room service; baby-sitting; laundry/dry cleaning; no-smoking rooms. *In room:* A/C, TV/VCR, minibar, hair dryer, robes.

Kempinski Hotel Bristol Berlin 𝕲𝕲𝕲   The legendary Kempinski, or "Kempi," is matched in style only by the Grand Hotel Esplanade. Rooms range in size from medium to spacious. Furnishings are elegant and the mattresses firm. The cheapest (and smallest) rooms are called the Berlin rooms. The high category Bristol rooms are larger and better appointed, and the finest accommodations of all are refined Kempinski rooms. Each room has a spacious bathroom with dual basins, scales, shoehorns, and deluxe toiletries.

Kurfürstendamm 27, D-10719 Berlin. ℂ 800/426-3135 in the U.S., or 030/88-43-40. Fax 030/88-360-75. www.kempinskiberlin.de. 315 units. 425DM–482DM (€217.25–€246.30, $213–$241) double; from 610DM (€311.70, $305) suite. AE, DC, MC, V. Parking 35DM (€17.94, $18). U-Bahn: Kurfürstendamm. **Amenities:** 3 restaurants indoor pool; fitness center; sauna; solarium; room service; massage; baby-sitting; laundry/dry cleaning. *In room:* A/C, TV, minibar, hair dryer.

Expensive

Brandenburger Hof Relais & Châteaux ☆☆☆ Rooms at this white-fronted classic, though perhaps too severe and minimalist for some tastes, are among the most stylish in the city. This is authentic Bauhaus—torchiere lamps, black leather upholstery, and platform beds with deluxe mattresses. French doors open to small balconies, but not on the top floors. Baths are spacious, with large combination tub and showers. Housekeeping is among the finest in Berlin, and there's state-of-the-art security.

Eislebener Strasse 14, D-10789 Berlin. ℂ 030/21-40-50. Fax 030/21-40-51-00. www.brandenburger-hof. com. 82 units. 345DM–465DM (€176.30–€237.60, $173–$233) double; from 745DM (€380.70, $373) suite. Rates include breakfast buffet. AE, DC, MC, V. Parking 25DM (€12.83, $13). U-Bahn: Kurfürstendamm or Augsburger Strasse. S-Bahn: Zoologischer Garten. **Amenities:** 2 restaurants (formal, elegant Die Quadriga, plus a Wintergarten), lively piano bar; room service; baby-sitting; laundry/valet. *In room:* A/C, TV, minibar, hair dryer.

Savoy ☆ If you don't demand the full-service facilities of the grander choices, this is the hotel for you. In general, rooms are a bit small but they are comfortable nonetheless, with such amenities as double-glazed windows and quality mattresses. Bathrooms are decent size, are maintained spotlessly, and contain a shower and tub combination.

Fasanenstrasse 9–10, D-10623 Berlin. ℂ 800/223-5652 in the U.S. and Canada, or 030/3-11-0-30. Fax 030/ 3-11-03-333. www.hotelsavoy.com. 130 units. 306DM–390DM (€156.35–€199.34, $153–$195) double; 445DM–850DM (€227.40–€434.35, $223–$425) suite. Children under 12 stay free in parents' room. AE, DC, MC, V. Parking 18DM (€9.20, $9). U-Bahn: Kurfürstendamm. **Amenities:** Belle Époque restaurant, cozy Times Bar; fitness club; sauna; room service; baby-sitting; laundry. *In room:* TV, minibar, hair dryer, safe, trouser press.

Moderate

Art Nouveau On the fourth floor of an Art Nouveau apartment house, this little-known hotel is an atmospheric choice. Even the elevator is a historic gem of the upmarket and desirable neighborhood. Art Nouveau was fully renovated in 1998. The comfortable midsize rooms are pleasantly decorated and high-ceilinged, with excellent beds and bathrooms with shower units. Rooms in the rear are more tranquil except when the schoolyard is full of children. There's an honesty bar in the lobby where guests keep track of their own drinks. A generous breakfast is the only meal served.

Leibnizstrasse 59, D-10629 Berlin. ℂ 030/3-27-74-40. Fax 030/327-744-40. www.hotelartnouveau.de. 15 units. 210DM (€107.30, $105) double; 350DM (€178.85, $175) suite. U-Bahn: Adenauerplatz. *In room:* TV, hair dryer.

Bleibtreu Hotel ☆ Hidden away from the bustle of Berlin, this is a trend-conscious choice. Its tiny lobby is accessible via an alleyway that leads past a garden and a big-windowed set of dining and drinking facilities. The setting is the labyrinthine premises of what was built long ago as a Jugendstil-era apartment house. Rooms are small, minimalist, and furnished in carefully chosen natural materials. Bathrooms are cramped but well-designed.

Bleibtreustrasse 31, D-10707 Berlin (1 block south of the Kurfürstendamm). ℂ 030/88474-0 or 800/ 223-5652 for reservations in the U.S. and Canada. Fax 030/88474-444. www.savoy-hotels.com. 60 units. 295DM–400DM (€150.75–€204.40, $148–$200) double. Rates include breakfast. AE, MC, V. U-Bahn: Kurfürstendamm. **Amenities:** Restaurant (vegetarian and organic), bar. *In room:* TV, minibar, hair dryer.

Inexpensive

Hotel-Pension Bregenz This dignified pension occupies the fourth and sunniest floor of a four-story turn-of-the-19th-century apartment building, accessible by elevator. The owner, Mr. Zimmermann, works hard to maintain the cleanliness and charm of his comfortably furnished, relatively large rooms. Double doors help to minimize noise from the public corridors outside. A continental breakfast is served each morning in a small dining area. The staff gladly assists guests in reserving tickets for shows and tours.

Bregenzer Strasse 5, D-10707 Berlin. © 030/8-81-43-07. Fax 030/8-82-40-09. 14 units, 10 with bathroom (shower only). 115DM (€58.75, $58) double without bathroom, 170DM (€86.85, $85) double with bathroom. Rates include breakfast. MC, V. Parking 5DM (€2.55, $2.50). S-Bahn: Savignyplatz. U-Bahn: Adenauerplatz. *In room:* TV, minibar.

Pension München   This pension occupies only part of the third floor of a massive four-story building (with an elevator) erected as an apartment house in 1908. It offers a simple but tasteful decor of modern furnishings accented with fresh flowers. The small rooms are clean and color-coordinated, with contemporary furniture and prints and engravings by local artists. Look for sculptures by the owner, an artist, in some of the public areas as well. Note that if there are no rooms available at this place, you're likely to be recommended to a similar pension.

Guntzelstrasse 62 (close to Bayerischer Platz), 10717 Berlin. © 030/8-57-91-20. Fax 030/85-79-12-22. hotel-pension.muenchen@arcormail.de. 8 units, 4 with bathroom. 95DM (€48.55, $48) double without bathroom, 130DM (€66.45, $65) double with bathroom. AE, DC, MC, V. Parking is available on the street. U-Bahn: Guntzelstrasse. *In room:* TV.

NEAR THE MEMORIAL CHURCH & ZOO
Expensive
Palace Berlin 🏰   The stylish and comfortable Palace is much improved over recent years. However, in some rooms, the double-glazing on the windows is unable to deafen the noise from the adjacent Europa-Center. Rooms range from medium to spacious, each with deluxe bed. The best are in the more recent Casino Wing. Bathrooms are medium size, most often with combination tub and shower (sometimes with shower only).

In the Europa-Center, Budapesterstrasse 41, D-10789 Berlin. © 800/457-4000 in the U.S., or 030/2-50-20. Fax 030/2502-1161. www.palace.de. 282 units. 460DM–570DM (€235.05–€291.25, $230–$285) double; from 810DM (€413.90, $405) suite. AE, DC, MC, V. Parking 30DM (€15.35, $15). U-Bahn: Zoologischer Garten. **Amenities:** 3 restaurants (see First Floor, "Where to Dine," below), 1 bar; large health club; no-smoking rooms. *In room:* A/C, TV, minibar, hair dryer, trouser press.

Sorat Art'otel 🏰   Those partial to the more famous and highly regarded Brandenburger Hof (above) also like this tasteful, discreet hotel. Chic and avant-garde, the Sorat is unlike any other hotel in Berlin. Rooms, all medium size, are minimalist, with a touch of industrial design. Although they will not please clients seeking a traditional Berlin hotel, modernists will be at home with the pedestal tables evoking cable spools and chrome-legged furnishings, and everyone will appreciate the deluxe mattresses on the large beds. Bathrooms are generously proportioned.

Joachimstalerstrasse 29, D-10719 Berlin. © 030/88-44-70. Fax 030/88-44-77-00. www.sorathotels.com. 133 units. 405DM–455DM (€206.95–€232.50, $203–$228) double. Rates include buffet breakfast. AE, DC, MC, V. U-Bahn: Kurfürstendamm. **Amenities:** Restaurant (Greek/international); room service; laundry. *In room:* TV, minibar, hair dryer, safe.

Moderate
Hecker's Hotel   This hotel is near the Ku'damm and the many bars, cafes, and restaurants around the Savignyplatz. Rooms range from small to medium, but are fairly routine despite good beds and frequently renewed mattresses. There's a sterility here but also up-to-date comfort and top-notch maintenance. Bathrooms are small, with shower units.

Grolmanstrasse 35, D-10623 Berlin. © **030/8-89-00**. Fax 030/8-89-02-60. www.heckers-hotel.com. 72 units. 280DM–380DM (€143.15–€194.25, $140–$190) double; 350DM–420DM (€178.85–€214.60, $175–$210) suite. Rates include breakfast on weekends. AE, DC, MC, V. Parking 20DM (€10.20, $10). U-Bahn: Uhlandstrasse. Bus: 109 from Tegel Airport to Uhlandstrasse or 119. **Amenities:** Small restaurant, bar (roof dining in summer); room service; baby-sitting; dry cleaning/laundry; no-smoking rooms. *In room:* TV, minibar, hair dryer.

Hotel Sylter Hof Berlin

This hotel offers rich trappings at good prices. The main lounges are warmly decorated in old-world style. The well-maintained rooms, most of which are singles, may be too small for most tastes, but the staff pay special attention to your comfort. Bathrooms are cramped but efficiently arranged, each with a shower.

Kurfürstenstrasse 116, D-10787 Berlin. © **030/2-12-00**. Fax 030/214-28-26. www.sylterhofberlin.de. 161 units. 282DM (€144.10, $141) double; from 360DM (€183.95, $180) suite. Rates include buffet breakfast. AE, DC, MC, V. Parking 16DM (€8.25, $8) U-Bahn: Wittenbergplatz. Bus: 119, 129, 146, or 185. **Amenities:** Restaurant, bar, coffee bar, night club. *In room:* TV, minibar.

IN BERLIN-MITTE
Very Expensive
Hotel Adlon ★★★

Only steps from the Brandenburg Gate, this hotel is one of Berlin's premier addresses and is famous among celebrities. The large, beautifully appointed rooms contain king-size or twin beds with luxury mattresses. Bathrooms are spacious with deluxe toiletries and a phone.

Unter den Linden 77, D-10117 Berlin. © **800/426-3135** in the U.S., or 030/22-61-0. Fax 030/22-61-11-16. www.hotel-adlon.de. 337 units. 540DM–690DM (€275.95–€352.65, $270–$345) double; from 820DM (€419, $410) suite. AE, DC, MC, V. Parking 40DM (€20.45, $20). S-Bahn: Unter den Linden. **Amenities:** 2 restaurants, 2 bars, coffee shop; health club; spa; room service; baby-sitting; laundry/dry cleaning. *In room:* A/C, TV, CD player, fax, minibar, hair dryer.

The Westin Grand ★★★

Many hotels call themselves grand—this one truly is, rivaled only by the Kempinski. Since taking over, Westin has spent a fortune in making the rooms among the finest in the city. All are spacious and tastefully decorated, with deluxe mattresses. Bathrooms are also large and state-of-the-art with deluxe toiletries.

Friedrichstrasse 158–164, D-10117 Berlin. © **800/843-3311** in the U.S., or 030/2-02-70. Fax 030/20-27-33-62. www.westin-grand.com. 358 units. 540DM–570DM (€275.95–€291.25, $270–$285) double; from 750DM (€383.25, $375) jr. suite; from 1,400DM (€715.40, $700) apt suite. AE, DC, MC, V. Parking 40DM (€20.45, $20). U-Bahn: Französische Strasse. S-Bahn: Friedrichstrasse. **Amenities:** Restaurant (German), bar; pool; fitness club; solarium; sauna; 24-hour room service. *In room:* A/C, TV, minibar, hair dryer.

Expensive
Four Seasons ★★★

One of Berlin's most opulent hotels was built in 1996 on the site of a bombed-out parking lot about a block from the Gendarmenmarkt. From the look of things, you'd never realize the venue is new, as everything about the place evokes Versailles and an undeniable sense of well-established and very plush prosperity. Rooms are furnished with timeless taste and elegance, with very large bathrooms, with walk-in showers, deep tubs, and a selection of toiletries.

Charlottenstrasse 49, 10117 Berlin. © **800/332-3442** in the U.S., or 030/2-03-38. Fax 030/203-36-009. www.fourseasons.com. 204 units. 440DM–560DM (€224.85–€286.15, $220–$280) double; from 640DM (€327.05, $320) suite. AE, MC, V. Parking 40DM (€20.45, $20). U-Bahn: Französischestrasse. **Amenities:** Posh restaurant, bar; health club; 24-hour room service; dry cleaning/laundry. *In room:* A/C, TV, minibar, hair dryer.

Moderate
Hotel Hackescher Markt ★

You'd never know this nugget of charm had been newly built in 1998, as everything about it evokes a late 19th-century landmark. Rooms are soothing, partially oak-paneled, and outfitted with comfortable and practical furniture. Standard singles tend to be just a bit small—a better bet might be one of the more upscale doubles. Bathrooms have heated floors. Some guests appreciate the romantic overtones of bedrooms on the uppermost floor, whose walls are angled thanks to the building's mansard roof.

Grosse Präsidentenstrasse 8, D-10178 Berlin. ℭ **030/28-00-30.** Fax 030/28-00-31-11. www. hackescher-maket.de. 31 units. 260DM–330DM (€132.85–€168.65, $130–$165) double; 290DM–340DM (€148.24–173.75, $145–$170) suite. AE, MC, V. U-Bahn: Hackescher Markt. *In room:* TV, minibar.

Hotel Luisenhof ⍟ One of the most desirable small hotels in Berlin's eastern district, the Luisenhof occupies a dignified 1822 house. Five floors of high-ceilinged rooms will appeal to those desiring to escape modern Berlin's sterility. Rooms range greatly in size, but each is equipped with good queen or twin beds and firm mattresses. Bathrooms, though small, are beautifully appointed, with shower stalls (often with a large tub).

Köpenicker Strasse 92, 10179 Berlin. ℭ **030/2-41-59-06.** Fax 030/2-79-29-83. www.luisenhof.de. 27 units. 265DM (€135.40, $133) double; from 380DM (€194.25, $190) suite. Rates include breakfast. AE, DC, MC, V. U-Bahn: Märkisches Museum. **Amenities:** Restaurant; room service (6am–midnight); laundry/dry cleaning. *In room:* TV, minibar, hair dryer.

WHERE TO DINE

For food on the run, try one of the dozens of kebab stalls (*Imbisse*) that dot the streets. Some 200,000 Turks live in Berlin and the food that they've introduced—meat- or *Scharfskäse*- (sheep's cheese, virtually identical to feta) stuffed pitas—make a filling, cheap meal—but watch out for the cascades of cabbage. Good sit-down Turkish restaurants are harder to find, but one of the best is **Hitit,** Knobelsdorffstrasse 35 (ℭ **030/322-45-57**), near Charlottenburg Schloss, with a full array of Turkish specialties, some 150 dishes in all. It's open from Monday to Saturday 5pm to midnight, Sunday from noon to midnight.

ON OR NEAR THE KURFÜRSTENDAMM
Very Expensive
Bamberger Reiter ⍟⍟⍟ CONTINENTAL This is the city's best restaurant, serving French, German, and Austrian dishes. Only Rockendorf's or Alt-Luxemburg can pretend to have better fare. Excellent in its forthright approach to fresh ingredients and meticulous in its preparation and service, the restaurant enjoys a loyal following among Berlin's business elite. The decor evokes old Germany, with lots of mirrors and fresh flowers. The menu changes daily but might include such delights as a roulade of quail, bass with Riesling sauce, lamb with beans and potato croutons, and a date strudel with almond ice cream.

Regensburgerstrasse 7. ℭ **030/218-42-82.** Reservations required. Main courses 52DM–60DM (€26.55–€30.65, $26–$30); 6- or 7-course fixed-price menu 165DM–195DM (€84.30–€99.65, $83–$98). AE, DC, MC, V. Tues–Sat 6pm–1am (last order). U-Bahn: Spichernstrasse.

Rockendorf's Gourmet Restaurant ⍟⍟⍟ CONTINENTAL After 25 years in a villa in north Berlin, Rockendorf's, one of the best known of all the city's restaurants, has moved to newer and central quarters behind KaDeWe, near the Europa Center. This new 35- to 40-seat Art Deco restaurant mounts a serious challenge to Bamberger Reiter and Alt-Luxemburg, the front-runners. Chef Siegfried Rockendorf achieves a happy wedding between nouvelle cuisine and classic specialties. Perhaps you'll try his memorable fresh jellied aspic with cucumber sauce. Other enticing standbys include a filet of turbot in Ricard sauce, and goose-meat pâté in Sauterne with cranberries. The service is exquisitely refined—attentive without being cloying. Some of Germany's most visible names in show biz, journalism, and politics come here.

Passauerstrasse 5–7. ℂ 030/219-92-170. Reservations required. Main courses 45DM–75DM (€23–€38.35, $23–$38). AE, DC, MC, V. Mon–Sat noon–2pm and 7–10pm. Closed last 2 weeks in July. U-Bahn: Wittenbergplatz.

Expensive

Harlekin ⓕⓕ FRENCH/INTERNATIONAL   Chefs at traditional favorites like the Kempinski were chagrined at this restaurant's success. The menu is perfectly balanced between tradition and innovation. Appetizers are likely to include such dishes as calves' consommé with crayfish or osso buco consommé with lobster spätzle. For your main course, you might be won over by the saddle of lamb baked in a spring roll or turbot roasted with mixed root vegetables.

In the Grand Hotel Esplanade, Lützowufer. ℂ 030/254-78-858. Reservations recommended. Main courses 45DM–50DM (€23–€25.55, $23–$25); 4- to 6-course fixed-price menu 130DM–165DM (€66.45–€84.30, $65–$83). AE, DC, MC, V. Tues–Sat 6:30–11pm. Closed 3¹/₂ weeks in July (dates vary). U-Bahn: Nollendorfplatz or Wittenbergplatz.

Mensa ⓕ CONTINENTAL   Mensa ("table" in Latin) has quickly moved to the cutting edge in Berlin, attracting chic models, rising politicians, visiting stars, and new money. Established in 1999, the bright, airy restaurant has a Mediterranean decor and a helpful, hip staff. The cuisine is perfectly seasoned and cooked, and you can sample such delights as lobster salad with wild herbs in a dressing of sauterne and shallots, roasted goose liver with vanilla stalk and salsify (oyster plant), and filet of sea bass with a braised eel ragout and a parsnip-cream sauce.

Am Lützowplatz. ℂ 030/579-93-33. Reservations required. Main courses 47DM–50DM (€24–€25.55, $24–$25); 4-course menu 99DM (€50.64, $50), 6-course menu 150DM (€76.65, $75). AE, MC, V. Mon–Fri 11:15am–2:30pm; Mon–Sat 6–10:30pm. U-Bahn: Nollendorfplatz.

Paris Bar ⓕ FRENCH   This French bistro has been a local favorite since the postwar years, when two Frenchmen established the restaurant to bring a little Parisian cheer to the dismal gray of bombed-out Berlin. The place is just as crowded with elbow-to-elbow tables as a Montmartre tourist trap, but you'll find it a genuinely pleasing little eatery. It's a true restaurant on the see-and-be-seen circuit between Savignyplatz and Gedächtniskiche. The food is invariably fresh and well prepared but not particularly innovative.

Kantstrasse 152. ℂ 030/313-80-52. Reservations recommended. Main courses 36DM–55DM (€18.40–€28.10, $18–$28). AE. Daily noon–1am. U-Bahn: Uhlandstrasse.

Moderate

Istanbul TURKISH   Vegetarians patronize Berlin's oldest Turkish restaurant for its selection of hot and cold appetizers. The dark and lavishly decorated interior evokes old Constantinople (as do the belly dancers performing in a back room). Try the stuffed grape leaves or the hummus (chickpeas with garlic), or the meat-topped Turkish pizza. Shish kebab is the most popular item, and there's a wide array of succulent lamb dishes. A chef's specialty is veal grilled on a roasting spit.

Knesebeckstrasse 77. ℂ 030/883-27-77. Main courses 20DM–40DM (€10.20–€20.45, $10–$20). AE, DC, MC, V. Daily noon–midnight. S-Bahn: Savignyplatz.

Marjellchen ⓕ EAST PRUSSIAN   This is the only restaurant in Berlin specializing in the cuisine of Germany's long-lost province of East Prussia, along with the cuisines of Pomerania and Silesia. Amid a Bismarckian ambience of still lifes, vested waiters, and oil lamps, you can enjoy a savory version of red-beet soup with strips of beef, East Prussian potato soup with crabmeat and bacon, *falscher Gänsebraten* (pork spareribs stuffed with prunes and bread crumbs), and *mecklenburger Kümmelfleisch* (lamb with chives and onions).

Mommsenstrasse 9. ℂ 030/883-26-76. Reservations required. Main courses 20DM–49DM (€10.20–€25.05, $10–$25). AE, DC, MC, V. Mon–Sat 5pm–midnight. Closed Dec 23, 24, and 31. U-Bahn: Adenauerplatz or Uhlandstrasse. Bus: 109, 119, or 129.

Restaurant Mario NORTHERN ITALIAN   Named for its owner, this restaurant serves some of the most imaginative northern Italian food in Berlin. It was created by an East Berliner who'd never been to Italy but wanted to "cook Italian," nevertheless. Today the chefs are fully grounded in the repertoire of Italy. The innovative and refreshing dishes might include platters of the most delectable antipasti in town or else carpaccio. At least two different kinds of pastas are offered nightly, including a favorite made with a green pepper pesto. Savory ravioli and rigatoni appear several different ways.

Carmerstrasse 2. ℂ 030/312-31-15. Reservations recommended. Main courses 20DM–35DM (€10.20–€17.94, $10–$18); fixed-price menus 25DM–65DM (€12.83.0–€33.20, $13–$33). AE, DC, MC, V. Mon–Fri noon–midnight; Sat 4pm–1am. S-Bahn: Savignyplatz.

Inexpensive

Hard Rock Cafe AMERICAN   This is the local branch of the familiar worldwide chain that mingles rock 'n' roll nostalgia with American food. Menu choices range from a veggie burger to a "pig" sandwich (hickory smoked pork barbecue) that you might find in rural Georgia. The food is unexceptional, but service is friendly.

Meinekestrasse 21. ℂ 030/88-46-20. Reservations accepted for groups of 10 or more. Main courses 16DM–34DM (€8.25–€17.35, $8–$17). AE, MC, V. Sun–Thurs noon–midnight; Fri–Sat noon–2am. U-Bahn: Kurfürstendamm.

Lubitsch CONTINENTAL   Its conservative chic reputation was enhanced in 1999 when Chancellor Schröder dropped in for lunch and a photo-op, causing ripples of energy to reverberate through the neighborhood. Menu items include

---

ℂ Cafe Society

At the turn of the last century, the **Café Adlon,** Kurfürstendamm 69 (ℂ 030/883-76-82; U-Bahn: Adenauerplatz), was one of the most prestigious cafes in its neighborhood. It still offers charming summer vistas from its sidewalk tables and a view of Berlin kitsch from its interior. You'll find a huge selection of cakes. Open daily from 8am to 11pm.

   The family-owned **Café/Bistro Leysieffer,** Kurfürstendamm 218 (ℂ 030/885-74-80; U-Bahn: Kurfürstendamm), opened in the early 1980s within what had been the Chinese embassy. The street level contains a pastry and candy shop, but most clients climb the flight of stairs to a marble- and wood-sheathed cafe with a balcony overlooking the busy Ku'damm. The breakfast menu is one of the most elegant in town: Parma ham, smoked salmon, a fresh baguette, French butter, and—to round it off—champagne. Open from Sunday to Thursday 10am to 8pm, Friday and Saturday 10am to 10pm, and Sunday 10am to 8pm.

lots of cafe drinks and steaming pots of afternoon tea, but if you drop in for a meal, expect platters of chicken curry salad with roasted potatoes; Berlin-style potato soup; braised chicken with salad and fresh vegetables; a roulade of suckling pig; and Nürnberger-style wursts. Expect brusque service, a black and white decor with Thonet-style chairs, and a somewhat arrogant environment that despite its drawbacks, is very, very *Berliner*.

Bleibtreustrasse 47. ℂ 030/882-37-56. Reservations not necessary. Main courses 12.50DM–34DM (€6.44–€17.35, $6–$17). AE, DC, MC, V. Daily 9:30am–midnight. U-Bahn: Kurfürstendamm.

NEAR THE MEMORIAL CHURCH & ZOO
Very Expensive
First Floor 🖝🖝 REGIONAL GERMAN/FRENCH   This is the showcase restaurant within one of the most spectacular hotels ever built near the Tier garten. Set one floor above street level, it features a perfectly orchestrated service and setting that revolves around the cuisine of a master chef. Winning our praise are such dishes as a terrine of veal with arugula-flavored butter; sophisticated variations of Bresse chicken; guinea fowl stuffed with foie gras and served with a truffle vinaigrette sauce; a cassoulet of lobster and broad beans in a style vaguely influenced by the culinary precepts of southwestern France; filet of sole with champagne sauce; and a mascarpone mousse with lavender-scented honey.

In the Palace Berlin, Budapesterstrasse 42. ℂ 030/25-02-10-20. Reservations recommended. Main courses 46DM–75DM (€23.50–€38.35, $23–$38). Set menus 80DM (€40.93, $40) at lunch only; and 130DM–158DM (€66.45–€80.75, $65–$79) at lunch and dinner. AE, DC, MC, V. Daily noon–2pm and 8–11pm. U-Bahn: Zoologischer Garten.

TIERGARTEN
Inexpensive
Paris-Moskau INTERNATIONAL   The grand days of the 19th century are alive and well at this restaurant in the beautiful Tiergarten area, where good dining spots are scarce. Menu items are both classic and more cutting-edge. The fresh tomato soup is excellent. Some of the dishes are mundane—the grilled filet of beef in mushroom sauce comes to mind—but other, lighter dishes with delicate seasonings are delightful. We recommend the grilled North Sea salmon with herbs accompanied by basil-flavored noodles. The chef should market his recipe for saffron sauce, which accompanies several dishes. You'll receive attentive service from the formally dressed staff.

Alt-Moabit 141. ℂ 030/3-94-20-81. Reservations recommended. Main courses 34DM–43DM (€17.35–€21.95, $17–$22); fixed-price menus 90DM–140DM (€46.04–€71.55, $45–$70). No credit cards. Daily 6–11:30pm. S-Bahn: Bellevue.

IN & AROUND CHARLOTTENBURG
Expensive
Alt-Luxemburg 🖝🖝 CONTINENTAL   Bamberger Reiter may be the leader among Berlin restaurants, but the Alt-Luxemburg is nipping at its heels. Chef Karl Wannemacher is one of the most outstanding chefs in eastern Germany. Known for his quality and market-fresh ingredients, he prepares a seductively sensual plate. Everything shows his flawless technique, especially the stuffed and stewed oxtail or the saddle of venison with elderberry sauce. Taste his excellent lacquered duck breast with honey sauce or saddle of lamb with stewed peppers. Alt-Luxemburg offers a finely balanced wine list, and service is both unpretentious and gracious.

Windscheidstrasse 31. ✆ 030/323-87-30. Reservations required. Fixed-price 3-course menu 95DM (€48.55, $48); fixed-price 4-course menu 125DM (€63.93, $63); fixed-price 5-course menu 139DM (€71.05, $70). AE, DC, MC, V. Mon–Sun 7–11pm. U-Bahn: Sophie-Charlotteplatz.

Moderate

Bierhaus Luisen-Bräu GERMAN Luisen-Bräu brewery established this restaurant in 1987. The decor includes enormous stainless-steel vats of the fermenting brew, from which the waiters refill your mug. There's no subtlety of cuisine here; it's robust and hearty fare. You serve yourself from a long buffet table. The seating is indoor or outdoor, depending on the season, at long picnic tables that encourage a sense of beer-hall *Bruderschaft* (camaraderie).

Luisenplatz 1, Charlottenburg (close to Charlottenburg Castle). ✆ 030/3-41-93-88. Reservations recommended on weekends. Main courses 10DM–25DM (€5.10–€12.83, $5–$13). AE, MC, V. Sun–Thurs 9am–1am; Fri–Sat 9am–2am. U-Bahn: Richard-Wagner-Platz.

Ernst August FRENCH/INTERNATIONAL Although outclassed by dozens of grander establishments, this restaurant still maintains a special niche. It's the type of place to which a local might take a friend from out of town. The setting is quiet and unobtrusive. Antique bric-a-brac adorns the walls. The chef might prepare one of two variations of hare, a longtime German favorite in which he takes a special pride. Even a simple rump steak gets care and attention here.

Sybelstrasse 16. ✆ 030/3-24-55-76. Reservations required. Main courses 23DM–34DM (€11.75–€17.35, $12–$17). No credit cards. Wed–Sun 6:30pm–1am (kitchen stops serving hot food at midnight). Closed July 15–Aug 15. U-Bahn: Adenauerplatz.

IN BERLIN-MITTE
Expensive

Langhans 🐿🐿 MODERN INTERNATIONAL Few other Berlin restaurants combine the culinary traditions of Italy and Japan with such skill and style. Named after the 18th-century designer of the Brandenburg Gate, and created by Detlef Bernhardt, a German-born long-time resident of Japan, it's in a grand building that flanks the Gendarmenmarkt. Downstairs is a convivial and hip bar, serving Spanish-inspired tapas. Upstairs, there's a long, gracefully minimalist dining room. Here, a team of international craftspersons produces dishes whose flavors are as intriguing as they are delicious. Our favorites are carpaccio of veal with sesame and arugula, braised dorado with green curry and mango, and a superb version of free-range hen with ginger-flavored risotto and sukiyaki sauce.

Charlottenstrasse 59. ✆ 030/20-94-50-70. Reservations recommended. Main courses 28DM–45DM (€14.30–€23, $14–$23); set-price menus 80DM–90DM (€40.93–€46.04, $40–$45). AE, MC, V. Daily noon–11:30pm. U-Bahn: Gendarmenmarkt.

Restaurant Vau 🐿🐿 GERMAN This restaurant is the culinary showcase of master chef Kolja Kleeberg. Choices include terrine of salmon and morels with rocket salad; aspic of suckling pig with sauerkraut; salad with marinated red mullet, mint, and almonds; crisp-fried duck with marjoram; ribs of suckling lamb with thyme-flavored polenta; and desserts such as woodruff soup with champagne-flavored ice cream. The wine list is international and well chosen.

Jägerstrasse 54 (near the Four Seasons Hotel and the Gendamenmarkt). ✆ 030/202-9730. Reservations recommended. Main courses 48DM–65DM (€24.55–€33.20, $24–$33). Set-price lunches 120DM (€61.30, $60); set-price dinners 135DM–229DM (€69.04–€117, $68–$115). AE, DC, MC, V. Mon–Sat noon–3pm and 7–10:30pm. S-Bahn: Hausvoigteiplatz.

Moderate

Guy _✦_ INTERNATIONAL   Few other top-notch restaurants in Berlin were designed with as strong a sense of gastronomy as theater. Proceed to any of three separate balconies, each supporting at least one row of artfully decorated tables. The overall effect can be compared to the balconies and private boxes of an old-fashioned opera house. The cuisine is very _haute_, even to the point of seeming experimental. Examples change frequently, but might include a medley of marinated quail and goose liver; mussels served on a purée of arugula; lobster and sweetbreads cooked in puff pastry with tarragon-flavored cream sauce; and braised breast of goose with a roulade of potatoes and herbs.

Jägerstrasse 59–60. _℃_ **030/20-94-26-00.** Reservations recommended. Main courses 36DM–49DM (€18.40–€25.05, $18–$25). Set-price lunches 34DM–44DM (€17.35–€22.53, $17–$22); set-price dinners 98DM 138DM (€50.13–€70.50, $49–$69). AE, DC, MC, V. U-Bahn: Stadtmitte or Französischer Strasse.

Restaurant Borchardt FRENCH/INTERNATIONAL   This restaurant is elegant, lighthearted, and fashionable among the city's artistic movers and shakers. You can order anything from a simple salad (as supermodel Claudia Schiffer often does) to the more substantial cream of potato soup with bacon and croutons; filet of carp prepared with Riesling and herbs and finished with champagne; foie gras served with caramelized apples; chicken stuffed with morels and served with cream-and-herb sauce; and a pistachio mousse garnished with essence of fresh fruit.

Französische Strasse 47. _℃_ **030/2038-7110.** Reservations recommended. Daily specials 20DM (€10.20, $10); main courses 30DM–55DM (€15.35–€28.10, $15–$28). AE, V. Daily 11:30am–2am (kitchen closes at midnight). U-Bahn: Französische Strasse.

Inexpensive

Boon's CONTINENTAL   It's crowded, it's hip, and its decor evokes the 1930s allure of what might have been a coffee plantation in the highlands of Africa. Many clients come here just for its bar scene, but if you're hungry, the food is firmly based on what's cooking in the area that stretches between North Germany and southern Austria, and served in generous portions. Come here for a chance to meet unattached residents of the surrounding neighborhood, a dialogue with a hip Berliner or two, and good-tasting food items that include beef filet with braised arugula; all manner of fresh fish; homemade salmon with apples, roasted potatoes, and horseradish; and drinks that include raspberry daiquiris.

Monbijouplatz 11–12. _℃_ **030/28-53-98-90.** Reservations recommended. Main courses 22.50DM–34DM (€11.50–€17.35, $11–$17). AE, MC, V. Mon–Sat 5pm–midnight; Sun 2pm–midnight. U-Bahn: Hackescher Markt.

Dressler CONTINENTAL   No other bistro along Unter den Linden so successfully re-creates Berlin's pre-war decor and style. Designed to resemble an arts conscious bistro of the sort that might have amused and entertained tuxedo-clad clients in the 1920s, it's set behind a wine-colored facade, and outfitted with leather banquettes, tile floors, mirrors, and film memorabilia from the great days of early German cinema. Waiters scurry around, carrying trays of everything from caviar to strudel, as well as three kinds of oysters and hefty portions of lobster salad. Substantial menu items include perfectly prepared turbot with champagne vinaigrette; pheasant breast with Riesling sauce; local salmon trout with white- wine sauce and braised endive; stuffed breast of veal; and calf's liver with apples.

Unter den Linden 39. ☎ **030/204-44-22.** Reservations recommended. Main courses 12.50DM–35DM (€6.44–€17.94, $6–$18). AE, DC, MC, V. Daily 8am–midnight. S-Bahn: Unter den Linden.

Mutter Hoppe GERMAN   This cozy, wood-paneled restaurant still serves the solid Teutonic cuisine favored by a quasi-legendary matriarch (Mother Hoppe) who used to churn out vast amounts of *gütbergerlich* cuisine to members of her extended family and entourage. Within a quartet of old-fashioned dining rooms, you'll enjoy heaping portions of such rib-sticking fare as sauerbraten with roasted potatoes; creamy goulash with wild mushrooms; filets of zander with dill-flavored cream sauce; and braised filets of pork in mushroom-flavored cream sauce. Wine is available, but most guests opt for at least one foaming mug of beer.

Rathausstrasse 21, Nikolaiviertel. ☎ **030/241-56-25.** Reservations recommended. Main courses 19DM–30DM (€9.70–€15.35, $10–$15). MC, V. Daily 11:30am–11pm. U- and S-Bahn: Alexanderplatz.

SEEING THE SIGHTS
SIGHTSEEING SUGGESTIONS FOR FIRST-TIME VISITORS

If You Have 1 Day Get up early and visit the **Brandenburg Gate,** symbol of Berlin, then walk down **Unter den Linden** and have coffee and pastry at the Operncafé. Visit the **Gemäldegalerie** to see some of the world's greatest masterpieces. Afterward, go to **Charlottenburg Palace** and its museums to view the celebrated bust of Queen Nefertiti in the **Egyptian Museum.** In the evening, walk along the Kurfürstendamm, visit the **Kaiser Wilhelm Memorial Church,** and dine in a local restaurant.

If You Have 2 Days On day 2, visit the **Pergamon Museum** on Museum Island, seeing the Pergamon Altar. Explore the **National Gallery** and the **Bode Museum,** then head for Alexanderplatz. Take the elevator up for a view from its TV tower, before exploring the **Nikolai Quarter** on foot.

If You Have 3 Days On day 3, go to **Potsdam** (see "Day Trips from Berlin," later in this chapter").

If You Have 4 or 5 Days On day 4, visit the museums of **Dahlem,** especially the **Sculpture Gallery** and **Ethnographical Museum.** In the afternoon return to Charlottenburg Palace and explore the **Historical Apartments,** and in the evening visit the **Europa-Center** for drinks and dinner. On day 5, see some of the sights you might have missed. Take some walks through Berlin and stop at the Cold War's **Checkpoint Charlie,** with its museum. If time remains, visit the **Berlin Zoo,** stroll through the **Tiergarten,** and attend a cabaret in the evening.

THE TOP MUSEUMS
In the Tiergarten
Gemäldegalerie ✫✫✫   Opening in its new home in 1998, this is one of Germany's greatest paintings galleries. Several rooms are devoted to early German masters, with altarpieces dating from the 13th to 15th centuries. Note the panel of *The Virgin Enthroned with Child* (1350), surrounded by angels that resemble the demons so popular in the later works of Hieronymus Bosch. Eight paintings make up the Dürer collection in adjacent rooms.

Another gallery is given over to Italian painting. Here are five Raphael Madonnas; and works by Titian (*The Girl with a Bowl of Fruit*), Fra Filippo

Lippi, Botticelli, and Correggio (*Leda with the Swan*). There're also early Nether-landish paintings from the 15th and 16th centuries (Van Eyck, Van der Weyden, Bosch, and Bruegel). Several galleries are devoted to Flemish and Dutch masters of the 17th century, with no fewer than 20 works by Rembrandt, including the *Head of Christ.*

Mattäiskirchplatz 4. (℃ 030/20-90-55-55. Admission 8DM (€4.14, $4) adults, 4DM (€2.05, $2) children. Tues–Fri 10am–5pm (Thurs to 10pm), Sat–Sun 11am–6pm. U-Bahn: Kurfürstenstrasse, then bus 148. Bus 129 from Ku'damm (plus a 4-minute walk).

Neue Nationalgalerie (New National Galerie) 🎨
In its modern glass-and-steel home designed by Ludwig Mies van der Rohe, the Neue Nationalga-lerie is a sequel of sorts to the art at Dahlem. It contains a continually growing collection of modern European and American art. Here you'll find works of 19th-century artists, with a stellar concentration on French Impressionists. Ger-man art starts with Adolph von Menzel's paintings from about 1850. The 20th-century collection includes works by Max Beckmann, Edvard Munch, and E.L. Kirchner (*Brandenburger Tor*), as well as a few paintings by "the usual suspects," Bacon, Picasso, Ernst, Klee, and American artists such as Barnett Newman. There's food service in the cafe on the ground floor. Hot meals are served from 10:30am to 5:30pm.

Potsdamerstrasse 50 (just south of the Tiergarten). (℃ 030/2-66-26-62. Permanent collection, 8DM (€4.14, $4) adults, 4DM (€2.05, $2) children; temporary exhibitions, 4DM (€2.05, $2). Tues–Fri 10am–6pm; Sat–Sun 11am–6pm. Closed Jan 1, Dec 24–25 and 31, and the Tues after Easter and Whitsunday. U-Bahn: Kurfürstenstrasse. S-Bahn: Potsdamer Platz.

Museumsinsel (Museum Island)

Pergamon Museum 🎨🎨🎨
The Pergamon Museum houses several depart-ments, but if you have time for only one exhibit, go to the central hall of the U-shaped building to see the **Pergamon Altar** 🎨🎨🎨. This Greek altar (180–160 B.C.) has a huge room all to itself. Some 27 steps lead up to the colonnade. Most fascinating is the frieze around the base, tediously pieced together over a 20-year period. Depicting the struggle of the Olympian gods against the Titans as told

---

Moments New Meets Old

On the Kurfürstendamm in the western part of the city, Berliners often glance at a sobering reminder of less happy days. At the end of the street stands the **Kaiser-Wilhelm-Gedächtniskirche (Kaiser Wilhelm Memorial Church),** Breitscheidplatz (℃ 030/218-5023), with only the shell of its neo-Romanesque bell tower (1895) remaining. (You can wander through the ruins from Mon–Sat 10am–4:30pm. Admission is free.) In striking contrast is the new church, constructed west of the old tower in 1961, and nicknamed "lipstick and powder box" by Berlin-ers. Its octagonal hall is lit solely by thousands of colored-glass win-dows set into the honeycomb framework. Ten-minute services are held in the church daily at 5:30 and 6pm for those going home from work. There's a Saturday concert at 6pm, and an English-language service is held daily at 9am from June to August. The church is open daily from 9am to 7pm. This remarkable combination of old and new is what Berlin, which was almost flattened in World War II, is all about.

in Hesiod's *Theogony,* the relief is strikingly alive, with figures projecting as much as a foot from the background. This, however, is only part of the collection of Greek and Roman antiquities, housed in the north and east wings. You'll also find a Roman market gate discovered in Miletus, and sculptures from many Greek and Roman cities, including a statue of a goddess holding a pomegranate (575 B.C.), found in southern Attica. The **Near East Museum** ⊙, in the south wing, contains one of the largest collections anywhere of antiquities discovered in the lands of ancient Babylonia, Persia, and Assyria. Among the exhibits is the Processional Way of Babylon with the Ishtar Gate (580 B.C.).

Kupfergraben, Museumsinsel. © 030/2090-50. Admission 8DM (€4.14, $4) adults, 4DM (€2.05, $2) children; free the first Sun of the month. Tues–Sun 10am–6pm. U-Bahn/S-Bahn: Friedrichstrasse. Tram: 1, 2, 3, 4, 5, 13, 15, or 53.

Altes Museum ⊙ Karl Friedrich Schinkel, the city's greatest architect, designed this structure, which resembles a Greek Corinthian temple, in 1822. On its main floor is the **Antikensammlung** or Museum of Greek and Roman Antiquities. This great collection of world-famous works of antique decorative art was inaugurated in 1960. It's rich in pottery; Greek, Etruscan, and Roman bronze statuettes and implements; ivory carvings, glassware, objects in precious stone, and jewelry of the Mediterranean region, as well as gold and silver treasures; mummy portraits from Roman Egypt; wood and stone sarcophagi; and a few marble sculptures. The collection includes some of the finest Greek vases of the black- and red-figures style dating from the 6th to the 4th century B.C. The best known is a large Athenian wine jar (amphora) found in Vulci, Etruria, dating from 490 B.C., which shows a satyr with a lyre and the god Hermes.

Bodestrasse 13, Museumsinsel. © 030/20-90-5801. Admission 8DM (€4.14, $4) adults, 4DM (€2.05, $2) children. Tues–Sun 9am–5pm (Thurs until 10pm). U-Bahn/S-Bahn: Friedrichstrasse. Bus: 100 to Lustgarten.

In Charlottenburg

Charlottenburg is the quarter of Berlin just west of the Tiergarten. In addition to viewing the exhaustive collections in Charlottenburg Palace, you can enjoy a relaxing ramble through Schlossgarten Charlottenburg. The gardens have been restored and landscaped much as they were in the days of Friedrich Wilhelm II.

Schloss Charlottenburg (Charlottenburg Palace) ⊙⊙ Napoléon exaggerated a bit in comparing Schloss Charlottenburg to Versailles when he invaded Berlin in 1806, but in its heyday this palace was the most elegant residence for Prussian rulers outside the castle in Potsdam. Begun in 1695 as a summer palace for the Electress Sophie Charlotte, patron of philosophy and the arts and wife of King Frederick I (Elector Frederick III), the little residence got out of hand until it grew into the massive structure you see today. The main wing contains the apartments of Frederick I and his "philosopher queen." The **new wing,** known as the Knobelsdorff-Flügel and built from 1740 to 1746, shelters the apartments of Frederick the Great, which now houses a collection of paintings, many of which were either collected or commissioned by the king.

Luisenplatz. © 030/320-91-275. Combined ticket for all buildings and historical rooms 15DM (€7.65, $8) adults, 10DM (€5.10, $5) children under 14 and students. Palace, Tues–Sat 10am–5pm, Sun 10am–4pm; Museum, Tues–Fri 10am–6pm; Gardens (free admission) daily 6:30am–8pm. U-Bahn: Sophie-Charlotte-Platz or Richard-Wagner-Platz. Bus: 109, 121, 245, or 204.

Ägyptisches Museum (Egyptian Museum) ⊙ The western Berlin branch of the Egyptian Museum is housed in the east guardhouse built for the king's bodyguard. It's worth the trip just to see the famous colored bust of **Queen Nefertiti** ⊙⊙⊙, dating from about 1340 B.C. The bust, stunning in every way, is all by itself in a dark first-floor room, illuminated by a spotlight. It is believed that the bust never left the studio in which it was created but served as a model for other portraits of the queen. The left eye was never drawn in. In addition, look for the head of Queen Tiy and the world-famous head of a priest in green stone. The monumental Kalabasha Gateway was built by Emperor Augustus around 30 B.C. Other displays feature jewelry, papyrus, tools, and weapons, as well as objects relating to the Egyptian belief in the afterlife.

Schlossstrasse 70. © **030/32-09-11.** Admission 8DM (€4.14, $4) adults, 4DM (€2.05, $2) children; free admission 1st Sun of each month. Tues–Fri 10am–6pm; Sat–Sun 11am–6pm. U-Bahn: Sophie-Charlotte-Platz or Richard-Wagner-Platz. Bus: 109, 110, or 145.

Die Sammlung Berggruen: Picasso und Seine Zeit (The Berggruen Collection: Picasso and his Era) *Finds* One of the most unusual private museums in Berlin has accumulated the awesome collection of respected art and antiques dealer Heinz Berggruen. A native of Berlin who fled the Nazis in 1936, he later established antiques dealerships in Paris and California before returning, with his collection, to his native home in 1996. The setting is a renovated former army barracks designed by noted architect August Stüler in 1859. Although most of the collection is devoted to Picasso, there're also works by Cézanne, Braque, Klee, and van Gogh. Some 60 or more works in all, the Picasso collection alone is worth the trip, ranging from his teenage efforts to all of his major periods.

Schlossstrasse 1. 𝄢 **030/326-9580.** Admission 8DM (€4.14, $4) adults, 4DM (€2.05, $2) students and children. Tues–Fri 10am–6pm; Sat–Sun 11am–6pm. U-Bahn: Richard-Wagner-Platz, followed by a 10-minute walk. Bus: 21, 109, 110, or 145.

Bröhan Museum   This wonderful museum specializes in decorative objects of the Art Nouveau (*Jugendstil* in German) and Art Deco periods (1889–1939), with exquisite vases, glass, furniture, silver, paintings of artists belonging to the Berlin Secession, and other works of art arranged in drawing-room fashion, including an outstanding porcelain collection.

Schlossstrasse 1a. 𝄢 **030/3269-0600.** Admission 6DM (€3.05, $3) adults, 3DM (€1.55, $1.50) students/children. Tues–Sun 10am–6pm. U-Bahn: Sophie-Charlotte-Platz. Bus: 109 or 145 to Luisenplatz/Schloss Charlottenburg.

OTHER MUSEUMS
Deutsche Guggenheim Berlin 🛝   Opened in autumn 1997, this state-of-the-art museum is devoted to organizing and presenting exhibitions of modern and contemporary art. The Guggenheim Foundation conceives, organizes, and installs several exhibitions annually, and also presents exhibitions of newly commissioned works created specifically for this space by world-renowned artists. In addition to contemporary artists, exhibitions in the past have ranged from Picasso and Cézanne to Andy Warhol.

Unter den Linden 13–15. 𝄢 **030/2020-930.** Admission 8DM (€4.14, $4) adults, 5DM (€2.55, $2.50) children. Free on Mon. Daily 11am–8pm. S-Bahn: Unter den Linden.

Käthe-Kollwitz Museum 🛝   More than any other museum in Germany, this one reflects the individual sorrow of the artist whose work it contains. Some visitors call it a personalized revolt against the agonies of war, as well as a welcome change from the commercialism of the nearby Ku'damm. Established in 1986, it was inspired by Berlin-born Käthe Kollwitz, an ardent socialist, feminist, and pacifist whose stormy social commentary led to the eventual banning of her works by the Nazis. Many Kollwitz works show the agonies of wartime separation of mother and child, inspired in part by her loss of a son in Flanders during World War I and a grandson during World War II.

Fasanenstrasse 24. 𝄢 **030/882-52-10.** Admission 8DM (€4.14, $4) adults, 4DM (€2.05, $2) children and students. Wed–Mon 11am–6pm. U-Bahn: Uhlandstrasse or Kurfürstendamm. Bus: 109, 119, 129, 219, or 249.

(*Tips*   **Museum Preview of Coming Attractions**

Expect the inevitable delays, but a trio of Berlin museums are being readied for opening, perhaps late in 2001. These include the **Alte Nationalgalerie,** the old national gallery of 19th-century art at Bodestrasse 1–3 (𝄢 **030/20-90-55-55);** the **Judisches Museum,** Lindenstrasse 9–14 (𝄢 **030/25-99-33);** and the **Deutsches Historisches Museum,** Under den Linden 2 (𝄢 **030-20-30-40),** the last not expected to open until sometime in 2002.

To East Side Gallery ↗

(S) S-BAHN STOP

1/5 mile

200 meters

To Berlin Wall Documentation Center ↗

ATTRACTIONS ●

Alte Nationalgalerie **7**
Altes Museum **24**
Berliner Dom **25**
Berliner Rathaus **11**
Bodesmuseum **5**

Brandenburger Tor **2**
Deutsche Staatsbibliothek **19**
Deutscher Dom **15**
Deutsche Guggenheim Berlin **18**
Deutsches Historisches Museum **23**
Fernsehturm **9**

Französicher Dom **28**
Humboldt-Universität **21**
Marienkirche **10**
Märkisches Museum **13**
Museum Haus am
   Checkpoint Charlie **16**

Neu Wache **22**
Nikolaikirche **12**
Nikolaiviertel **13**
Pergamon Museum **6**
Reichstag **3**
St -Hedwigs-Kath-edrae **27**

ACCOMMODATIONS ■

Four Seasons **1**
Hotel Adlon **4**
Hotel Hackescher Markt **8**
Hotel Luisenhof **14**
Westin Grand **17**

427

Märkisches Museum   The full cultural history of Berlin is displayed in one of the most prominent buildings on the banks of the Spree; 42 rooms contain collections of artifacts from excavations, plus such art treasures as Slav silver items and Bronze Age finds. You can learn about Berlin's theaters and literature, the arts in Berlin and Brandenburg, and the life and work of Berlin artists. Most visitors like the array of mechanical musical instruments that can be played Wednesday from 3 to 4pm and Sunday from 11am to noon, for an extra 2DM (€1, $1).

Am Köllnischen Park 5. ℂ 030/30-86-60. Admission 8DM (€4.14, $4) adults, 4DM (€2.05, $2) children. Tues–Sun 10am–6pm. U-Bahn: Märkisches Museum. Bus: 147, 240, or 265.

Museum für Gegenwart   This Museum of Contemporary Art opened in 1996 north of the Spree in the old Hamburger Bahnhof. The structure was the terminus for trains from Hamburg. Today, the station no longer receives trains but is a premier storehouse of postwar art, a sort of Musée d'Orsay of Berlin. Traces of its former function are still evident in the building, including the high roof designed for steam engines. The modern art on display is some of the finest in Germany, the nucleus of the collection a donation from the Berlin collector Erich Marx (no relation to Karl Marx). A multimedia event, you can view everything from Andy Warhol's now legendary *Mao* to an audiovisual Joseph Beuys archive. The museum houses one of the best collections of Cy Twombly. Other works on display are by Rauschenberg, Lichtenstein, and Dan Flavin. The conceptual artist Beuys is also represented by 450 drawings.

Invalidenstrasse 50–51. ℂ 030/20-90-55-55. Admission 8DM (€4.14, $4) adults, 4DM (€2.05, $2) children. Tues–Wed and Fri 10am–6pm; Thurs 10am–8pm; Sat–Sun 11am–6pm. U-Bahn: Zinnowitzer Strasse. Bus: 157, 245, 248, or 340.

Museum Haus am Checkpoint Charlie   This small building houses exhibits depicting the tragic events leading up to and following the erection of the former Berlin Wall. You can see some of the instruments of escape used by East Germans. Photos document the construction of the wall, escape tunnels, and the postwar history of both parts of Berlin from 1945 until today, including the airlift of 1948 to 1949. One of the most moving exhibits is the display on the staircase of drawings by schoolchildren who, in 1961 to 1962, were asked to depict both halves of Germany in one picture.

Friedrichstrasse 44. ℂ 030/253-72-50. Admission 10DM (€5.10, $5) adults, 5DM (€2.55, $2.50) children. Daily 9am–10pm. U-Bahn: Kochstrasse or Stadtmitte. Bus: 129.

Kunstgewerbe Museum (Museum of Applied Arts)   This museum, next to the Gemäldegalerie in a modern redbrick edifice built for the collection, is devoted to European applied arts from the early Middle Ages to the present, including the Renaissance, baroque, rococo, Jugendstil (German Art Nouveau), and Art Deco periods. Displayed are glassware, porcelain, silver, furniture, jewelry, and clothing. The collection of medieval goldsmiths' works is outstanding, as are the displays of Venetian glass, early Meissen and KPM porcelain, and Jugendstil vases, porcelain, furniture, and objects.

Matthäikirchplatz. ℂ 030/2662-902. Admission 4DM (€2.05, $2) adults, 2DM (€1, $1) students/children. Tues–Fri 10am–6pm; Sat–Sun 11am–6pm. U-Bahn/S-Bahn: Potsdamer Platz. Bus: 129 from Ku'damm to Potsdamer Brücke.

The Story of Berlin   This multimedia extravaganza portrays 8 centuries of the city's history through photos, films, sounds, and colorful displays. Beginning with the founding of Berlin in 1237, it chronicles the plague, the Thirty Years'

War, Frederick the Great's reign, military life, the Industrial Revolution and the working poor, the Golden 1920s, World War II, divided Berlin during the Cold War, and the fall of the Wall. Lights flash in a media blitz as you enter the display on the fall of the Wall, making you feel like one of the first East Berliners to wonderingly cross to the West. Conclude your tour on the 14th floor with a panoramic view over today's Berlin. Though the displays are a bit jarring and the historical information is too jumbled to be truly educational, the museum does leave a lasting impression. Allow at least 2 hours.

Ku'damm-Karree, Kurfürstendamm 207–208 (at the corner of Uhlandstrasse). ✆ 01805/99-20-10. Admission 18DM (€9.20, $9) adults, 14DM (€7.15, $7) students/children, 40DM (€20.45, $20) families. Daily 10am–8pm (you must enter by 6pm). S-Bahn: Uhlandstrasse.

HIGHLIGHTS OF BERLIN-MITTE

Reichstag (Parliament)   On the night of February 17, 1933, a fire broke out in the seat of the German parliament, the Reichstag. It was obviously set by the Nazis, but the German Communist Party was blamed. That was all the excuse Hitler's troops needed to begin mass arrests of "dissidents and enemies of the lawful government." During World War II, the Reichstag faced massive Allied bombardment. Today it's once again the home of Germany's parliament. A new glass dome, designed by English architect Sir Norman Foster, now crowns the neo-Renaissance structure originally built in 1894. You can go through the west gate for an elevator ride up to the dome, where a sweeping vista of Berlin opens before you. There's both an observation platform and a rooftop restaurant (the view is better than the food).

Platz der Republik 1. ✆ 030/2273-2152. Free admission. Daily 8am–midnight (last entrance at 10pm). Bus: 100. S-Bahn: Unter den Linden.

The Brandenburg Gate (Brandenburger Tor) 🐾🐾   This triumphal arch stood for many years next to the Wall, symbolizing the divided city. Today it represents the reunited German capital. Six Doric columns hold up an entablature inspired by the Propylaea of the Parthenon at Athens. Surrounded by the famous and much photographed Quadriga of Gottfried Schadow from 1793, the gate was designed by Carl Gotthard Langhans in 1789. Napoleon liked the original Quadriga so much he ordered them taken down and shipped to Paris, but they were returned to Berlin in 1814. In Berlin's heyday before World War II, the gate marked the grand western extremity of the "main street," Unter den Linden. In the Room of Silence, visitors still gather to meditate and reflect on Germany's past.

Unter den Linden. Free admission. Room of Silence daily 11am–6pm. Bus: 100. S-Bahn: Unter den Linden.

A PARK & A ZOO

Tiergarten 🐾   Tiergarten, the largest green space in central Berlin, covers just under 2.5km^2 (1 sq. mile), with more than 23km (14 miles) of meandering walkways. Late in the 19th century, partially to placate growing civic unrest, it was opened to the public, with a layout formalized by one of the leading landscape architects of the era, Peter Josef Lenné. The park was devastated during World War II, and the few trees that remained were chopped down for fuel as Berlin shuddered through the winter of 1945 to 1946. Beginning in 1955, trees were replanted and alleyways, canals, ponds, and flowerbeds rearranged in their original patterns through the cooperative efforts of many landscape architects.

The park's largest monuments include the Berlin Zoo, described below, and the **Siegessäule** (Victory Column), which perches atop a soaring red-granite pedestal from a position in the center of the wide boulevard (Strasse des 17 Juni) that neatly bisects the Tiergarten into roughly equivalent sections.

From the Bahnhof Zoo to the Brandenburger Tor. Bus: 100, 141, or 341 to Grosser Stern.

Zoologischer Garten Berlin (Berlin Zoo) 🐾 *Kids*   Occupying most of the southwest corner of Tiergarten is Germany's oldest and finest zoo. Founded in 1844, it's a short walk north from the Ku'damm. Until World War II, the zoo boasted thousands of animals of every imaginable species and description— many familiar to Berliners by nicknames. The tragedy of the war struck here as well, and by the end of 1945, only 91 animals remained. Since the war, the city has been rebuilding its large and unique collection; today more than 13,000 animals are housed here. The zoo has Europe's most modern birdhouse, with more than 550 species. The most valuable inhabitants here are giant pandas.

Hardenbergplatz 8. ℂ 030/25-40-10. Zoo, 14DM (€7.15, $7) adults, 7DM (€3.65, $3.50) children. Aquarium, 14DM (€7.15, $7) adults, 7DM (€3.65, $3.50) children. Combined ticket 22.50DM (€11.50, $11) adults, 11DM (€5.60, $6) children. Zoo, Apr–Oct daily 9am–6pm; Nov–Mar daily 9am–5pm. Aquarium, year-round, daily 9am–6pm. S-Bahn/U-Bahn: Zoologischer Garten.

ORGANIZED TOURS

BUS & BOAT TOURS   Some of the best tours are operated by **Severin + Kühn,** Kurfürstendamm 216 (ℂ **030/880-41-90**), which offers half a dozen tours of Berlin and its environs. Their 2-hour **"12 Stops City Tour"** departs at 30-minute intervals from November to April daily 10am and 3pm, from May to October 10am and 4pm. Priced at 33DM (€16.85, $17) per person, the tour passes most of the important attractions using buses equipped with taped commentaries in eight languages. Among the attractions visited are the Europa-Center, the Brandenburg Gate, and Unter den Linden.

You can supplement this bus tour with a 3-hour boat ride on the Spree, which will carry you past the riverbanks and among some of the backwater harbors that are difficult to access except by water. The boat-tour supplement is available only from May to October, with departures 10:30am to 1pm daily for 47DM (€24, $24) each. The Severin & Kühn drivers and staff, at the end of the bus tour portion of the experience, will deposit you at the appropriate quays (either adjacent to the Berliner Dom or in the Nicolaiviertel, depending on the day of your visit) in time for the boat's departure.

More appealing and personalized is the 3-hour **"Big Berlin Tour,"** which departs from 10am and 2pm daily, costs around 39DM (€19.95, $20) per person, and—depending on the itinerary—usually incorporates sights not included on the shorter tour. Among the attractions is a section of the Grünewald Forest.

One interesting tour lasts 4 hours and visits Potsdam and Sans Souci Palace, former residence of Frederick the Great. The price is 65DM (€33.20, $33) per person. Departures are from Tuesday to Sunday 10am; from May and October, there are additional departures Friday, Saturday, and Sunday at 2:15pm.

THE SHOPPING SCENE

The central shopping destinations are **Kurfürstendamm, Tauentzienstrasse, Am Zoo,** and **Kantstrasse.** You might also want to walk up streets that intersect with Tauentzienstrasse: Marburger, Ranke, and Nürnberger. Most stores are open from Monday to Friday 9 or 10am to 6 or 6:30pm. Many stores stay open late on Thursday evening, usually until about 8:30pm. Saturday hours for most stores are from 9 or 10am to 2pm.

Berlin's largest indoor shopping center, topped by the Mercedes-Benz logo, is the **Europa-Center,** Breitscheidplatz Tauentzienstrasse (ℂ **030/348-0088;**

U-Bahn: Kurfürstendamm), in the heart of the western city. You'll find the Berlin casino and a number of restaurants and cafes, in addition to an array of shops offering wide-ranging merchandise.

THREE STORES WORTH A LOOK

Known popularly as KaDeWe (pronounced kah-*day*-vay), **Kaufhaus des Westens,** Wittenbergplatz (© 030/21-21-0; www.kadewe.com; U-Bahn: Kurfürstendamm), is about 2 blocks from the Kurfürstendamm. The huge luxury store, whose name means "department store of the west," was established some 75 years ago. Displaying extravagant items, it's known mainly for its sixth-floor food department. It's been called the greatest food emporium in the world. More than 1,000 varieties of German sausages are displayed, and delicacies from all over the world are shipped in.

Despite its abbreviated name, **KPM,** Kurfürstendamm 26A (© 030/88-67-21-10; U-Bahn: Kurfürstendamm), is one of Europe's most prestigious emporiums of luxury dinnerware. Königliche Porzellan Manufaktur was founded in 1763 when Frederick the Great invested his personal funds in a lackluster porcelain factory and elevated it to royal status. Each item is hand painted, hand decorated, and hand packed in almost unbreakable formats that can be shipped virtually anywhere.

In the heart of the city near the Europa-Center, **Wertheim,** Kurfürstendamm 231 (© 030/8800-3206; U-Bahn: Kurfürstendamm), is a good all-around store for travel aids and general basics. It sells a number of perfumes, clothing for the entire family, jewelry, electrical devices, household goods, photography supplies, and souvenirs. It also has a shoe-repair section. Shoppers can fuel up at a large restaurant with a grand view over half the city.

BERLIN'S MARKETS

Berliner Antik & Flohmarkt, in the Friedrichstrasse S-Bahn station (© 030/208-2645), is one of Berlin's largest flea markets. Some 100 vendors try to tempt buyers with porcelain, brassware, and assorted bric-a-brac. Some have new or used clothing and others may even be selling World War II mementos. The market is open Monday and Wednesday to Sunday 11am to 6pm. The **Turkish Bazaar** (U-Bahn: Kottbusser Tor, then a 5-min. walk) is held on the bank of the Maybachufer in Kreuzberg. This area adjacent to the Maybachufer Canal has been converted by Germany's "guest workers." Although much of the merchandise involves food, especially grilled kebabs, there's also a good selection of jewelry, glassware, onyx, and copper items. The market is open from Tuesday and Friday noon to 6:30pm. The Friday market is busier and is the best time to attend if you have a choice.

BERLIN AFTER DARK

The German *Zitty* and *Tip* include some listings in English, and keep you informed about various nightlife and cultural venues. Both *Berlin Programm* and *Kultur!news* also contain theater listings and other diversions. Performance arts are also covered in *Berlin,* a quarterly published in both English and German. These pamphlets and magazines are available at news kiosks.

THE PERFORMING ARTS

The **Berliner Philharmonisches Orchester** (Berlin Philharmonic) is one of the world's premier orchestras. Its home, **the Philharmonie,** Matthäikirchstrasse 1 (© 030/254-88-0; www.berlin-philharmonic.com; bus: 129 or 148), is a significant piece of modern architecture; you may want to visit even if you do not attend a performance. None of the 2,218 seats are more than 100 feet from the rostrum. The box office is open from Monday to Friday 3:30 to 6pm and Saturday and Sunday from 11am to 2pm. You can't place orders by phone. If you're staying in a first-class or deluxe hotel, you can usually get the concierge to obtain seats for you. Check their website for advance purchase options. Tickets are 26DM to 90DM (€13.34 to €46.04, $13 to $45); special concerts 40DM to 250DM (€20.45 to €127.75, $20 to $125).

Because of the east-west split, Berlin has two famous opera companies. The famed **Deutsche Oper Berlin** (Berlin Opera), Bismarckstrasse 35 (✆ **030/34-384-01;** www.deutsche-oper.berlin.de; U-Bahn: Deutsche Oper; S-Bahn: Charlottenburg), performs in one of the world's great opera houses, built on the site of the prewar opera house in Charlottenburg. A ballet company performs once a week. Concerts, including Lieder evenings, are also presented on the opera stage. Tickets are 26DM to 190DM (€13.34 to €97.14, $13 to $95).

Deutsche Staatsoper (German State Opera), Unter den Linden 7 (✆ **030/20-35-45-55;** www.staatsoper-berlin.org; U-Bahn: Französische Strasse), presents some of the finest opera in the world, along with a regular repertoire of ballet and concerts. Its home was rebuilt within the walls of the original 1740s Staatsoper, destroyed in World War II. The box office generally sells tickets from Monday to Friday 10am to 6pm and Saturday and Sunday noon to 6pm. Tickets for concerts are 13DM to 120DM (€6.65 to €61.30, $7 to $60), opera are 16DM to 160DM (€8.23 to €81.75, $8 to $80). The opera closes from late June to the end of August.

Komische Oper Berlin, Behrensstrasse 55–57 (✆ **030/20-26-00;** www.komische-oper-berlin.de; U-Bahn: Französische Strasse; S-Bahn: Friedrichstrasse or Unter den Linden), lies in the middle of the city near Brandenburger Tor. Over the years, it has become one of the most innovative theater ensembles in Europe, presenting many avant-garde productions. The box office is open from Monday to Saturday 11am to 7pm and Sunday from 1pm until 1½ hours before the performance. Tickets are 14DM to 106DM (€7.15 to €54.15, $7 to $53).

LIVE-MUSIC CLUBS

A-Trane, Pestalozzistrasse 105 (✆ **030/313-25-50;** S-Bahn: Savignyplatz), is a small and smoky jazz house where virtually everyone seems to have a working familiarity with great names from the jazz world's past and present. The name is a hybrid of the old Duke Ellington standard, "Take the 'A' Train," with the 'e' derived from the legendary John Coltrane. It's open daily at 9pm; music begins around 10pm. Closing hours vary. Cover is 15DM to 25DM (€7.65 to €12.85, $8 to $13), depending on who's playing.

With its kitschy knickknacks, colored lights, and wine-red walls, **Wild at Heart,** Wienerstrasse 20 (✆ **030-6-11-70-10;** U-Bahn: Görlitzer Bahnhof), is dedicated to the rowdier side of rock. Hard-core punk, rock, and rockabilly bands from Germany and elsewhere are featured. Live performances take place from Wednesday to Saturday nights. It's open from Monday to Friday 8pm to 4am, and Saturday and Sunday from 8pm to 10am (yes, you may miss breakfast). Cover is 7DM (€3.65, $3.50).

Hyper trendy, **Oxymoron,** in the courtyard at Rosenthaler Strasse 40–41 (✆ **030/283-91-88-6;** S-Bahn: Hackenschen Höfe), is a lot of fun on most nights. The setting is a high-ceilinged room with old-fashioned proportions and enough battered kitsch to remind you of a century-old coffeehouse in

Moments   Come to the Cabaret!

If you know how to sing "Life is a cabaret, old chum," in German no less, you may enjoy an evening in this postwar "Porcupine." Like its namesake, **Die Stachelschweine,** Tauentzienstrasse and Budapester Strasse (in the basement of the Europa-Center; ✆ **030/261-47-95; U-Bahn: Kurfürstendamm**), pokes prickly fun at both German and often American politicians. Get a ticket early, because the Berliners love this one. The box office is open from Tuesday to Friday 10am to 2pm and 3 to 7:30pm, and Saturday 10am to 2pm and 3 to 8:45pm. Shows are presented from Tuesday to Friday at 7:30pm and Saturday at 6 and 9pm. Cover is 20DM to 40DM (€10.20 to €20.45, $10 to $20). The cabaret is closed during July.

Opened in 1893 as one of the most popular purveyors of vaudeville in Europe, the **Wintergarten,** Potsdamer Strasse 96 (✆ **030/230-88-230; U-Bahn: Kurfürstenstrasse**), operated in fits and starts throughout the war years, until it was demolished in 1944 by Allied bombers. In 1992, a modernized design reopened. Today, it's the largest and most nostalgic Berlin cabaret, laden with schmaltzy reminders of yesteryear and staffed with chorus girls; magicians from America, Britain, and countries of the former Soviet bloc; circus acrobats; political satirists; and musician/dancer combos. Shows begin from Monday to Friday at 8pm, Saturday at 6pm, and Sunday at 6 and 10pm. Shows last around 2¼ hours. The box office is open daily from 7pm to midnight. Cover Friday and Saturday is 59DM to 99DM (€30.15 to €50.64, $30 to $50), from Sunday to Thursday 35DM to 82DM (€17.94 to €41.90, $18 to $41), depending on the seat. Price includes first drink.

Franz-Josef's Vienna. Local wits refer to it as a *Gesamtkunstwerk*—a self-obsessed, self-sustaining work of art that might have been appreciated by Wagner. Most nights after around 11pm, a slightly claustrophobic, much-used annex room—all black with ghostly flares of neon—opens as a disco, usually with a clientele that's about 75% hetero and 100% iconoclastic. If live bands appear at all, it will usually be on Thursday. Open daily from 11am to midnight. Cover is 14DM to 20DM (€7.15 to €10.20, $7 to $10).

Large and artfully drab, **Far Out,** Kurfürstendamm 156 (✆ **030/320-00-717; U-Bahn: Adenauerplatz**), plays danceable rock from the '70s to the '90s that manages to get hundreds of high-energy dancers up and out on the floors. Clientele includes lots of students and artists, who dress up in artfully bizarre clothing that has lots of punk-rock overtones. It occasionally imports celebrity DJs from other disco-crazed cities of Europe. The place only really comes alive after midnight. Open from Tuesday to Sunday 10pm to between 4 and 6am, depending on the crowd. Cover is 5DM to 10DM (€2.55 to €5.10, $2.50 to $5). **Knaack-Klub,** Greifswalderstrasse 224 (✆ **030/442-7060; S-Bahn: Alexanderplatz**), features a live music venue, two floors of dancing, and a floor dedicated to games. There're usually four live rock shows a week, with a fairly even split between German and international touring bands. The music ranges from techno to hip-hop to '80s. Disco music is played on Wednesday, Friday, and Saturday nights. Open nightly from 10pm. Cover is 5DM to 10DM (€2.55 to €5.10, $2.50 to $5).

The premises that contain **Opernschänke,** in the Opernpalais, Unter den Linden 5 (© **030/20-26-83;** U-Bahn: Friedrichstrasse), were built in 1762, a fact that seems to add a certain importance to a setting that's undeniably historic, and to the artists who perform their music live. For the most part, this is a restaurant serving Continental food every day from 9am to midnight, with the last order accepted at 11:30pm. Main courses cost 20DM to 30DM (€10.20 to €15.35, $10 to $15). The food is augmented with live music, usually jazz, Thursday, Friday, and Saturday nights between 6pm and 1am, as well as Sunday afternoons between 11am and 2pm as part of set-price "Jazz Brunch" costing 49DM (€25.05, $25). After the end of the jazz brunch, the restaurant remains open till 7pm for food and drink.

DANCE CLUBS

Gays, straights, and everybody in between show up at **SO 36,** Oranienstrasse 190 (© **030/61-40-13-06;** U-Bahn: Görlitzer Bahnhof), for wild action and frantic dancing into the wee hours. A young, vibrant Kreuzberg crowd is attracted to this joint where the scene changes nightly. On Wednesday it's strictly gay and lesbian disco. On Friday and Saturday the parties "get really wild, man," as the bartender accurately promised. Some nights are devoted to themes such as James Bond where you can show up looking like a Cold War spy. Wednesdays and Sundays are generally all gay. Open from Wednesday to Saturday 11pm until "we feel like closing," and Sunday from 5 to 11pm. Cover is 12DM to 24DM (€6.15 to €12.25, $6 to $12).

Metropole, Nollendorfplatz 5, Schöneberg (© **030/217-36-80;** U-Bahn: Nollendorfplatz), one of the leading dance clubs in Berlin, opens only on weekends and attracts patrons ages 18 to 38. Built as a theater around a century ago, Metropole hosts live concerts and special events for gay people. It is open from Tuesday to Saturday 9pm to 6am. Cover is 15DM (€7.65, $8).

One of Berlin's most rocking techno venues, **Tresor Globus,** Leipzigerstrasse 126A (© **030/229-06-11;** U-Bahn: Mohrenstrasse), has been packing 'em in since 1991. The building was once part of Globus Bank. Downstairs there's a bunkerlike atmosphere with prison-type metal bars and harsh acoustics. The spacious dance floor upstairs has lighter house sounds. There's also a bar in the back when you want to chill out. In summer, tables are placed outside, with lights strung among the shrubbery. The club is open from Wednesday to Sunday at 11pm; it often closes at 6am. Cover on Wednesday is 5DM (€2.55, $2.50), Friday 10DM (€5.10, $5), Saturday and Sunday 15DM to 20DM (€7.65 to €10.20, $8 to $10).

GAY & LESBIAN BERLIN

Andreas Kneipe, Ansbacher Strasse 29 (© **030/218-32-57;** U-Bahn: Wittenbergplatz), is as warm, cozy, and convivial as many of the other traditional bars scattered throughout Berlin, with a distinct appeal for the many gay men and women who consider it their neighborhood hangout. It's been in business since 1938, making it the oldest gay bar in Berlin. Few of the clients dance, and there's no food served, so this is a place just to talk and drink in a convivial setting. Open daily from 11am to 4am. The **Begine Café-und-Kulturzentrum für Frauen,** Potsdamerstrasse 139 (© **030/215-43-25;** U-Bahn: Bülowstrasse), established in 1986, is one of Berlin's most visible headquarters for feminists and

> **Moments**   **A One-stop Night Out**
>
> In the heart of old East Berlin, a complex of about 30 bars, shops, and restaurants, called **Die Hackeschen Höfe** (S-Bahn: Hackescher Markt), is one of the best places to drink in the evening. The stylish and hip minimall attracts counterculture denizens. You can wander through the galleries, boutiques, and cafes; the most happening spot is **Oxymoron** (see above).

the most obvious place for women seeking to meet other women. Within its inner sanctums is a changing array of art exhibitions, poetry readings, music venues, German-language discussions, comedy showcases, lectures, and social events. You can phone in advance for the schedule. The premises are occasionally transformed into a disco. Open daily from 5pm to 1am.

Both gays and straights are welcomed at **Kumpelnest 3000,** Lützowstrasse 23 (© **030/2616-918;** U-Bahn: Kurfürstenstrasse). All that's asked is that you enjoy a kinky nightclubbing good time in what used to be a Berlin brothel. It's really a bar but there's dancing to disco classics. Berliners often show up here for early morning fun after they've exhausted the action at the other hot spots. It's crowded and chaotic. Open daily 5pm to 5am, but if the house crowd merits it, they'll stay open even later on weekends. **Tom's Bar,** Motzstrasse 19 (© **030/2-13-45-70;** U-Bahn: Nollendorfplatz), becomes crowded after 11pm with young gay men. Upstairs, the porno action is merely on the screen; downstairs it's real. The back room is hot, hot, and hotter. Monday nights feature two-for-one drinks. There's a cover charge for special occasions only. Open daily 10pm to 6am.

DAY TRIPS FROM BERLIN

POTSDAM ⟲⟲⟲   Of all the tours possible from Berlin, the best attraction is the baroque town of Potsdam, 24km (15 miles) southwest of Berlin on the Havel River, often called Germany's Versailles. From the beginning of the 18th century it was the residence and garrison town of the Prussian kings. World attention focused on Potsdam from July 17 to August 2, 1945, when the Potsdam Conference shaped postwar Europe.

West of the historic core lies **Sans Souci Park,** with its palaces and gardens. Northwest of Sans Souci is the New Garden and the Cecilienhof Palace, on the Heiliger See.

Getting There   There're 29 daily connections by rail from Bahnhof Zoo (trip time: 23 min.) and Berliner Hauptbahnhof (54 min.). For rail information in Potsdam, call © **018/05-99-66-33.** Potsdam can also be reached by S-Bahn (30 min.). Car access is via the E-30 autobahn east and west or the E-53 north and south.

Visitor Information   Potsdam-Information,   Friedrich-Ebert-Strasse 5 (© **0331/275580**), is open from April to October Monday to Friday from 9am to 8pm, Saturday 10am to 6pm, and Sunday 10am to 4pm; from November to March Monday to Friday from 10am to 6pm, Saturday 10am to 4pm, and Sunday 10am to 2pm.

Exploring Potsdam   With its palaces and gardens, **Sans Souci Park** ⟲⟲⟲, Zur historischen Mühle (© **0331/96-94-202;** tram 94 or 95; bus 612, 614, 631, 632, 692, or 695), was the work of many architects and sculptors. The park covers an area of about a square mile. Once at Potsdam, a complete tour costs

60DM (€30.65, $30). For information on English-speaking tours, call
℗ **0331/96-94-200.**

Frederick II ("the Great") chose Potsdam rather than Berlin as his permanent
residence. The style of the buildings he ordered erected is called Potsdam rococo,
an achievement primarily of Georg Wenzeslaus von Knobelsdorff. Knobelsdorff
built **Sans Souci Palace** 🔎🔎🔎, with its terraces and gardens, as a summer residence for Frederick II. The palace, inaugurated in 1747, is a long one-story
building crowned by a dome and flanked by round pavilions. The music salon
is the supreme example of the rococo style, and the elliptical Marble Hall is the
largest in the palace. As a guest of the king, Voltaire visited in 1750. Sans Souci
is open from April to October 9am to 5pm; from November to March 9am to
4pm; closed Mondays. Admission is 10DM (€5.10, $5) adults and 5DM
(€2.55, $2.50) children.

Schloss Charlottenhof 🔎, south of Okonomieweg (℗ **0331/969-42-00;**
tram: 1 or 4), was designed by Karl Friedrich Schinkel, the great neoclassical
master, and built between 1826 and 1829. He erected the palace in the style of
a villa and designed most of the furniture inside. It's open daily from May to
October 10am to 5pm; also daily from November to April Tuesday to Sunday
9am to 4pm. Admission is 10DM (€5.10, $5) adults and 5DM (€2.55, $2.50)
children.

North of the 80-hectare (200-acre) park, the **Cecilienhof Palace** 🔎, Im
Neuer Garten (℗ **0331/969-42-44;** bus: 694), was built in the style of an
English country house by Kaiser Wilhelm II between 1913 and 1917. The 176-
room mansion became the new residence of Crown Prince Wilhelm of Hohen-
zollern. It was occupied as a royal residence until March 1945, when the crown
prince and his family fled to the West, taking many of their possessions.
Cecilienhof was the headquarters of the 1945 Potsdam Conference. It's open
from April to October daily 9am to 5pm, from November to March Tuesday to
Sunday 9am to 4:30pm. A self-guided tour is 6DM (€3.05, $3) adults, 4DM
(€2.05, $2) children; a guided tour is 8DM (€4.14, $4) adults, 6DM (€3.05,
$3) children (visits must be guided from Nov–Mar).

THE SPREEWALD 🔎   This landmass southeast of Berlin is flat and
water-soaked—but celebrated for its eerie beauty. For at least 1,000 years, residents of the region have channeled the marshlands here into a network of canals,
streams, lakes, and irrigation channels and built unusual clusters of houses,
barns, and chapels on the high points of otherwise marshy ground. Ethnologists
consider it one of central Europe's most distinctive adaptations of humans to an
unlikely landscape, and botanists appreciate the wide diversity of bird and animal life that flourishes, according to the seasons, on its lush and fertile terrain.
And legends of the spirits that inhabit the thick forests of the Spreewald abound.

Many of the people you'll meet here belong to a linguistic subdivision of the
German-speaking people, the Sorbs, descendants of Slavic tribes who settled in
the region around 600 B.C. Most modern-day Sorbs remain fiercely proud of
their dialect and traditions and continue to till the soil of the Spreewald using
labor-intensive methods, producing crops of mostly cucumbers and radishes.

The Spreewald is at its most appealing in early spring and autumn, when the
crowds of sightseers depart and a spooky chill descends with the fog over these
primeval forests and shallow medieval canals.

Getting There   The Spreewald lies 97km (60 miles) southeast of Berlin, and
the best gateway is Lübben, 60 minutes by **train** from Berlin-Lichtenberg station. At the Lübben station, head straight out the front exit and walk in the

> **Tips   A Fabulous Place to Dine in Potsdam**
>
> In 1878, a courtier in the service of the Prussian monarch built an elegant villa on the shore of the Heiliger See. During the 1920s, author Bernhardt Kellerman wrote some of his best work here. After a Cold War stint as a base for Russian officers, it now functions as the most talked-about restaurant in Potsdam: **Villa Kellerman,** Mangerstrasse 33–36 (© **0331/29-15-72;** bus: 695). The classical Italian cuisine might include marinated carpaccio of whitefish; a mixed platter of antipasti; spaghetti with scampi, herbs, and garlic; or John Dory in butter-and-caper sauce. Reservations are recommended. American Express and Visa are accepted. It's open from Monday to Thursday 4 to 11pm, Friday and Sunday from noon to midnight.

same direction on a tree-lined street leading into the center of town. Once here, follow the signs directing you to *Kahfahrten* (boat rides) or *Paddlebooten* (paddleboats) and you're off to discover Spreewald.

Visitor Information   The **tourist office** in Lübben, Ernst von Huwald Damm 16 (© **03546/3090**), is the main point of departure for most Spreewald cruises. A secondary point of departure for Spreewald tours, 10km (6 miles) away, is the tourist office in the hamlet of Lübbenau, Ehm-Welk-Strasse 15 (© **03542/ 3668**). It's open from Monday to Friday 9am to 6pm, Saturday 10am to 2pm.

Exploring the Spreewald   The shallow, nutrient-rich waters of the Spreewald seem ideally suited to boat tours along its timeless surface. If you're interested, several companies offer tours from the piers in the hamlet of Lübben. Each charges equivalent rates of 10DM (€5.10, $5) for a 3-hour tour. Your best bet involves wandering down to the piers near the hamlet's center and hopping aboard the next departure, as virtually no one will speak English. Each of the companies operates only from April to October, with departures scheduled every day between 9am and 4pm. If you're interested in renting a canoe or rowboat and paddling around the Spreewald on your own, head for **Bootsverleih Gebauer,** Lindenstrasse (© **03546/7194**), where canoes can be rented for 8DM (€4.15, $4) per person hourly, 5DM (€2.55, $2.50) each additional hour.

2 Munich & the Bavarian Alps

Sprawling Munich, home of some 1.3 million people and such industrial giants as Siemens and BMW, is the pulsating capital and cultural center of Bavaria. One of Germany's most festive cities, Munich exudes a hearty Bavarian *Gemütlichkeit.*

Longtime resident Thomas Mann wrote: "Munich sparkles." Although the city he described was swept away by some of the most severe bombing of World War II, Munich continues to sparkle, as it introduces itself to thousands of new visitors annually.

The Munich cliché as a beer-drinking town of folkloric charm is marketed by the city itself. Despite a roaring gross national product, Munich likes to present itself as a large, agrarian village peopled by jolly beer drinkers who cling to rustic origins despite the presence on all sides of symbols of the computer age, high-tech industries, a sophisticated business scene, a good deal of Hollywood-style glamour, and fairly hip night action. Bavarians themselves are a minority in Munich—more than two-thirds of the population comes from other parts of the

Munich

Legend:
- ✝ Church
- ⓘ Information
- ✉ Post Office
- —○— S-Bahn
- —□— U-Bahn

NYMPHENBURG

14 Kleiner See

15

Nymphenburger Kanal

Schloss **16**

17

SCHLOSSPARK

18

Grosser See

19

Zuccalistrasse

Richildenstrasse

Schackstrasse

Adalbertstrasse

Blütenstrasse

Türkenstrasse

Schellingstrasse

Veterinärstr.

University

Prof.- Huberplatz

Amalienstrasse

Theresienstrasse

Ludwigstrasse

Keubachstrasse

20

Königin Strasse

Türkenstrasse

Schoenfeldstrasse

Oskar- von- Miller- Ring

Von-der-Tann Strasse

ENGLISCHER GARTEN

Brinnerstrasse

Galeriestrasse

Theater- museum

22

Prinzregentenstrasse

Leichenfeld strasse

Oettingenstrasse

Odeons- platz

HOFGARTEN

24

Hofgartenstrasse

Unsöldstrasse

21

Promenade- platz

25

Wagmüllerstr.

Karl-Faulhaber-Strasse

Theatinerstrasse

Residenz- strasse

Residenz

Cuvilliès Theater

Christophstrasse

St.-Anna-Platzstr.

Liebigstrasse

Thierschstrasse

Steinstrasse

Reitmorstrasse

Widenmayer- strasse

Isar

Frauen- platz

Max Joseph- Platz

26 Nationaltheater

Marstallstrasse

23

27

Weinstrasse

28

Pfisterstrasse

33

Am Kosttor- Platz

34

Bürkleinstr.

ufingerstrasse

Diener- strasse

31

Judisches Museum München

35 Maximilianstrasse

Maximilians- brücke

36

Marien- platz

32 Im Tal

Knöbelstrasse

Th.-Wimmer-Ring

30

K. Scharnagl - Ring

29

Viktualienmarkt

Westenriederstrasse

Isartor- platz

Kanalstrasse

Frauenstrasse

Rumfordstr.

Zweibrücken strasse

Thierschstrasse

Steinsdorfstrasse

Isar

Corneliusstrasse

Blumenstrasse

Müllerstr.

Baader- platz

Morassistrasse

Ludwigs- brücke

Innere Weiner Strasse

Kellerstrasse

Gärtner- platz

Baaderstrasse

Erhardtstrasse

Deutsches Museum

Rosenheimerstrasse

Klenzestrasse

Reichenbachstrasse

Fraunhofer

38

37

Isar

Zeppelinstrasse

Lillienstrasse

Hochstrasse

| 0 | 1/5 mile |
| 0 | 200 meters |

N

(Value A Money-Saving Tip
Munich's S-Bahn is covered by Eurail, so if you have a railpass, don't buy a separate ticket.

country or from outside Germany—but everybody buys into the folkloric charm and schmaltz.

ESSENTIALS

GETTING THERE   By Plane   The **Munich International Airport** (℡ **089/97-52-13-13;** www.munich-airport.de) lies 27km (17 miles) northeast of central Munich at Erdinger Moos.

S-Bahn (℡ **089/41-42-43-44**) trains connect the airport with the Hauptbahnhof (main railroad station) in downtown Munich, with departures every 20 minutes for the 40-minute trip. The fare is 14DM (€7.15, $7); Eurailpass holders ride free. A taxi into the center costs about 100DM to 120DM (€51.10 to €61.30, $50 to $60). Airport buses also run between the airport and the center.

By Train   Munich's main rail station, the **Hauptbahnhof,** on Bahnhofplatz, is one of Europe's largest. Near the city center, it contains a hotel, restaurants, shopping, car parking, and banking facilities. All major German cities are connected to this station, most with service every hour. For information about long-distance trains, call ℡ **01805/99-66-33.**

By Bus   Munich is a focal point for bus service that fans out across Bavaria and the rest of Germany. The West-wing-Starnberger Bahnhof, on Arnulfstrasse within the Hauptbahnhof, is the point of arrivals and departures for most of the bus lines servicing the city. For schedules, information, and reservations, call ℡ **089/545-8700.**

VISITOR INFORMATION   Tourist Office   The main tourist office, **Fremdenverkehrsamt** (℡ **089/23-33-02-72;** www.munchen-tourism.de), is at the Hauptbahnhof at the south exit opening onto Bayerstrasse. Open from Monday to Saturday 9am to 8pm and Sunday 10am to 6pm, it offers a free map of Munich and will reserve hotel rooms. Tourist information can also be obtained at the airport (℡ **089/233-03-00**) from Monday to Thursday 9am to 5pm, Friday to Sunday from 9am to 3pm.

Websites   Updated for each year's Oktoberfest, **www.munich-tourist.de** from the Munich Tourist Office includes a program of events, a guide to various beer tents, and images from past festivals. Descriptions of hotel packages and discount voucher packages are added. All things Bavarian are touched on at **www.bavaria.com**, such as Mad King Ludwig's castle and an Oktoberfest beer and music raft ride down the river Isar. There's advice on shopping, getting around, and enjoying the Alps, among many other nuggets.

CITY LAYOUT   Munich's Hauptbahnhof lies just west of the town center and opens onto Bahnhofplatz. From the square, you can take Schützenstrasse to **Karlsplatz** (nicknamed Stachus), one of the major centers of Munich. Many tramlines converge on this square. From Karlsplatz, you can continue east along the pedestrians-only Neuhauserstrasse and Kaufingerstrasse until you reach Marienplatz, where you'll be deep in the Altstadt (old town) of Munich.

From **Marienplatz,** the center and heart of the city, you can head north on Dienerstrasse, which will lead you to Residenzstrasse and finally to **Max-Joseph-**

Munich U-Bahn & S-Bahn

441

Platz, a landmark square, with the National Theater and the former royal palace, the Residenz. East of this square runs **Maximilianstrasse,** the most fashionable shopping and dining street of Munich. Between Marienplatz and the National theater is the **Platzl** quarter, where you'll want to head for night-time diversions, as it's the seat of some of the finest (and some of the worst) restaurants in Munich, along with the landmark Hofbräuhaus, the most famous beer hall in Europe.

North of the old town is **Schwabing,** the university and former Bohemian section whose main street is Leopoldstrasse. The large, sprawling municipal park grounds, the Englischer Garten, are found due east of Schwabing.

GETTING AROUND   By Public Transportation   The city's efficient rapid-transit system is the **U-Bahn,** or Untergrundbahn, one of the most modern subway systems in Europe. The **S-Bahn** rapid-transit system, a 420-km (260-mile) network of tracks, provides service to various city districts and outlying suburbs. The city is also served by a network of **trams** and **buses.** The same ticket entitles you to ride the U-Bahn, the S-Bahn, trams, and buses. For more information, call ℂ **089/41-42-43-44.**

A single-journey ticket for a ride within the city's central zone—a large area that few tourists ever leave—costs 3.80DM (€1.95, $1.90). If you go to the outermost zones of the subway system, your ride could cost as much as 18DM (€9.20, $9). One of the best things about Munich's transit system is that you can make as many free transfers between subways, buses, and trams as you need to reach your destination.

More economical than single-journey tickets is the *Streifencarte,* a strip-ticket that contains 11 units, two of which are annulled for each zone of the system you travel through. A Streifencarte costs 16DM (€8.23, $8). Children ages 6 to 14 can purchase a *Kinderstreifencarte* for 6.50DM (€3.30, $3.25). With this type of ticket, you can travel in one continuous direction during any 2-hour time period with unlimited transfers. You can also use it for multiple passengers (for two people to ride two zones, simply stamp four strips).

An even better deal may be the **Tageskarte (Day Ticket),** which for 9DM (€4.60, $4.50) gives you unlimited access within the central zone for a full day. Double the price for access to all of Greater Munich—an 80-km (50-mile) radius.

By Taxi   Cabs are relatively expensive—you'll pay 5DM (€2.55, $2.50) when you get inside, plus 2.40DM (€1.25, $1.20) per kilometer; add 2DM (€1, $1) if you call for pickup. In an emergency, call ℂ **089/2161-0** or 089/194-10 for a radio-dispatched taxi.

By Car   Driving in the city, which has an excellent public transportation system, is not advised. The streets around Marienplatz in the Altstadt are pedestrian only. If you are interested in renting a car locally, try **Sixt Autovermietung,** Einsteinstrasse 106 (ℂ **089/550-24-47**), or look under *Autovermietung* in the Munich yellow pages.

On Foot & By Bicycle   Of course, the best way to explore Munich is on foot, since it has a vast pedestrian zone in the center. Many of its attractions can, in fact, be reached only on foot. Pick up a good map and set out.

The tourist office also sells a pamphlet that outlines itineraries for touring Munich by bicycle called *Radl-Touren für unsere Gäste,* costing 0.75DM (€0.43E, 43¢). One of the most convenient places to rent a bike is **Radius Bikes** (ℂ **089/59-61-13**), at the far end of the Hauptbahnhof, near lockers opposite tracks 30 and 31. The charge is 12DM (€6.15, $6) per 2 hours, or else 25DM (€12.83, $13) from 10am to 6pm. Mountain bikes are rented for about 25% more. A deposit of 100DM (€51.10, $50) is assessed; students and Eurail-pass holders are granted a 10% discount. Open from April to early October daily 10am to 6pm, closed from November to March.

 ## FAST FACTS: Munich

American Express The American Express Foreign Exchange Service, Kaufingerstrasse 24 (℡ **089/228-013-87**), is open Monday to Friday 9am to 5pm. Reiesland American Express, Promenadeplatz 6 (℡ **089/290-900;** U-Bahn: Marienplatz), is open for mail pickup and check cashing from Monday to Friday 9am to 5pm.

Business Hours Most **banks** are open from Monday to Friday 8:30am to 12:30pm and 1:30 to 3:30pm (many stay open until 5:30pm on Thurs). Most **businesses** and **stores** are open from Monday to Friday 9am to 6pm and Saturday 9am to 2pm. On *langer Samstag* (first Sat of the month) stores remain open until 6pm. Many observe an 8 or 9pm closing on Thursday.

Consulates There's a **United States** consulate at Königstrasse 5 (℡ **089/ 288-80;** U-Bahn: Unlversltäl); hours are Monday to Friday 8am to 1pm. The Consulate General Office for the **United Kingdom** at Bürkleinstrasse 10 (℡ **089/21-10-90;** U-Bahn: Isartor) is open Monday to Friday 8:30am to noon and 1 to 5pm.The consulate of **Ireland** at Mauerkircherstrasse 1a (℡ **089/98-57-23;** bus: 87) is open Monday to Friday 9am to noon. The con-sulate of **Canada** at Tal Strasse 29 (℡ **089/219-95-70;** U-Bahn: Marienplatz) is open Monday to Thursday 9am to noon and 2 to 5pm, Friday 9am to noon and 2:30 to 3:30pm. The governments of Australia and New Zealand do not maintain offices in Munich.

Currency See "Fast Facts: Berlin."

Currency Exchange You can get a better rate at a bank than at your hotel. On weekends or at night, you can exchange money at the Haupt-bahnhof exchange, open daily from 6am to 11:30pm.

Dentists/Doctors For an English-speaking dentist, go to **Klinik und Poliklinik für Kieferchirurgie der Universität München,** Lindwurmstrasse 2A (℡ **089/51-60-0;** U-Bahn: Goetheplatz); it deals with emergency cases and is always open. The American, British, and Canadian consulates keep a list of recommended English-speaking physicians. For dental or medical emergencies, call **Notfallpraxis,** Elisenstrasse (℡ **089/59-44-75;** bus: 69). It's open Monday, Tuesday, and Thursday from 7pm to midnight; Wednesday and Friday from 2pm to midnight, and Saturday, Sunday, and holidays from 7pm to midnight.

Drugstores For an international drugstore where English is spoken, go to **Bahnhof Apotheke,** Bahnhofplatz (℡ **089/59-41-19;** U-Bahn/S-Bahn: Hauptbahnhof), open from Monday to Friday 8am to 6:30pm and Satur-day 8am to 2pm. If you need a prescription filled in off-hours, call ℡ **089/ 55-76-61** for information about what's open. The information is recorded and in German only, so you may need to get someone from your hotel staff to assist you.

Emergencies For emergency medical aid, phone ℂ **089/59-44-75.** Call the police at ℂ **110.**

Internet Access You can send e-mails or check your messages at the **Internet-Café,** Bayer-Strasse 10A (ℂ **089/55-08-800;** bus: 2, 19, 20, or 29). This is also the site of a cafe, bar, disco, bistro, pastry shop, and pizzeria. Open daily from 11am to 1am.

Post Office A central post office is at Arnulfstrasse 32 (ℂ **089/16-39-80;** U-Bahn: Briennerstrasse), north of the Hauptbahnhof, open from Monday to Friday 8am to 8pm. You can have your mail sent here Poste Restante (general delivery), but include the zip code D-80335. You'll need a passport to reclaim mail.

Telephone The **country code** for Germany is **49.** The **city code** for Munich is **89.** Use this code when you're calling from outside Germany; if you're within Germany, use **089.** For more information on making calls from Germany, see "Fast Facts: Berlin."

WHERE TO STAY
VERY EXPENSIVE
Bayerischer Hof & Palais Montgelas ✶✶✶   A Bavarian version of New York's Waldorf-Astoria, this hotel is in a swank location, opening onto a little tree-filled square. Rooms range from medium to extremely spacious, each with plush duvets topping firm mattresses; many beds are four-posters. Decor ranges from Bavarian provincial to British country house chintz. The large bathrooms have private phones and state-of-the-art amenities.

Promenadeplatz 2–6, D-80333 München. ℂ **800/223-6800** in the U.S., or 089/2-12-00. Fax 089/21-20-906. www.bayerischerhof.de. 495 units. 511DM–605DM (€261.10–€309.15, $256–$303) double; from 1,130DM (€577.45, $565) suite. AE, DC, MC, V. Free parking. Tram: 19. **Amenities:** 2 restaurants (German, Polynesian), bar; rooftop pool and garden; gym; sun terrace; sauna; room service; massage; baby-sitting; laundry. *In room:* TV, minibar, hair dryer.

Hotel Vier Jahreszeiten München ✶✶✶   This grand hotel, with a tradition dating from 1858, is the most elegant place to stay in Munich. Rooms range from medium to very spacious. Bedside controls, luxury mattresses, and Oriental rugs, plus spacious bathrooms, will keep any guest comfortable.

Maximilianstrasse 17, D-80539 München. ℂ **800/426-3135** in the U.S., or 089/2125-0. Fax 089/2125-2777. www.kempinski-vierjahreszeiten.de. 366 units. 540DM–870DM (€275.95–€444.55, $270–$435) double; from 2,000DM (€1,022, $1,000) suite. AE, DC, MC, V. Parking 30DM (€15.35, $15). Tram: 19. **Amenities:** Restaurant (one of the grand dining rooms of Germany), bistro; indoor pool; sun terrace; sauna; solarium; room service; baby-sitting; laundry. *In room:* A/C, TV, minibar, hair dryer, robes.

EXPENSIVE
Eden-Hotel-Wolff ✶   If you must stay near the train station, this is your best bet. With some exceptions, most rooms are spacious, their styles ranging from modern to rustic Bavarian. Rooms have luxurious mattresses and double-glazed windows; and the large bathrooms have tub and shower combos. Some rooms are hypoallergenic with special beds and a private ventilation system.

Arnulfstrasse 4–8, D-80335 München. ℂ **089/55-11-50.** Fax 089/551-15-555. www.ehw.de. 210 units. 235DM–370DM (€120.140–€189.05, $118–$185) double; 400DM–670DM (€204.40–€342.35, $200–$335) suite. One child up to age 6 stays free in parents' room. Rates include buffet breakfast. AE, DC, MC, V. Parking 25DM (€12.85, $13). U-Bahn/S-Bahn: Hauptbahnhof. **Amenities:** Restaurant, bar; room service; baby-sitting; laundry. *In room:* TV, minibar, hair dryer, safe.

MODERATE

Advocat Hotel   This hotel occupies a 1930s apartment house. Its streamlined interior borrows in discreet ways from Bauhaus and minimalist models. The rooms look as if Philippe Starck had gone on a shopping binge at Ikea. The result is an aggressively simple, clean-lined, and artfully Spartan hotel with very few amenities and facilities.

Baaderstrasse 1, 80469 München. (℃) **089/21-63-10.** Fax 089/21-63-190. www.hoteladvocat.de. 50 units. 270DM (€137.95, $135). AE, DC, MC, V. S-Bahn: Isartor. *In room:* TV, minibar.

An der Oper ⋐   Just off Maximilianstrasse, near Marienplatz, this is a superb choice for sightseeing or shopping in the traffic-free malls, just steps from the Bavarian National Theater. Built in the 1970s, it's one of the best-run hotels in this price category. Recently renovated rooms, which range from small to medium, have such amenities as double-glazed windows, firm beds, a small sitting area, and a table for those who want breakfast in their rooms. Bathrooms are medium in size and beautifully maintained, with shower units.

Falkenturmstrasse 11, D-80331 München. (℃) **089/290-02-70.** Fax 089/290-02-729. www.hotel-an-der-opera-munchen.de. 68 units. 270DM–340DM (€137.95–€173.75, $135–$170) double. Rates include buffet breakfast. AE, MC, V. Tram: 19. *In room:* TV.

Gästehaus Englischer Garten ⋐   This oasis of charm and tranquility, close to the Englischer Garten, is one of our preferred stopovers. The decor of the rooms might be termed "Bavarian grandmother." Bathrooms are small and not one of the hotel's stronger features. In an annex across the street are 15 small apartments, each with bathroom and a tiny kitchenette. Try for room nos. 16, 23, 26, or especially 20; all are more spacious, better furnished, and have better views. In fair weather, breakfast is served in a rear garden.

Liebergesellstrasse 8, D-80802 München-Schwabing. (℃) **089/38-39-41-0.** Fax 089/38-39-41-33. 25 units, 19 with bathroom. 140DM (€71.55, $70) double without bathroom; 179DM–195DM (€91.45–€99.65, $90–$98) double with bathroom; from 220DM (€112.40, $110) apt. AE, DC, MC, V. Parking 10DM (€5.10, $5). U-Bahn: Münchner Freiheit. *In room:* TV, minibar.

Hotel Mark *(Value)*   This hotel near the Hauptbahnhof's south exit is known for comfort and moderate prices. The rooms are functionally furnished, although a bit cramped, and mattresses were recently renewed, so you should sleep in peace. Bathrooms are small but tidily maintained, each with a shower unit. Breakfast is the only meal served.

Senefelderstrasse 12, D-80336 München. (℃) **089/55-98-20.** Fax 089/559-82-333. www.heh.de. 90 units. 220DM–460DM (€112.40–€235.05, $110–$230) double. Rates include buffet breakfast. AE, DC, MC, V. Parking 15DM (€7.65, $8). U-Bahn/S-Bahn: Hauptbahnhof. *In room:* TV, minibar.

Hotel Opera ⋐   This charming little gem (not to be confused with the An der Oper) is filled with comfort and an authentic Bavarian atmosphere so lacking in many postwar Munich hotels. Each midsize bedroom is beautifully and individually decorated, often with antiques from the countryside. Rooms are thoughtfully laid out; some contain French doors leading to small balconies. Bathrooms are relatively small but well-maintained, each with a shower unit. The rooms at the rear on the third and fourth floors are more tranquil, although they're slightly smaller than those fronting the street.

St-Anna Strasse 10, 80538 München. (℃) **089/22-55-33.** Fax 089/21-04-09-77. www.hotel-opera.de. 25 units. 320DM–360DM (€163.50–€183.95, $160–$180) double; 500DM (€255.50, $250) suite. Rates include breakfast. AE, MC, V. Parking 45DM (€23, $23) nearby. U-Bahn: U5 to Lehel. **Amenities:** Bar; roof garden; garden terrace; 24-hour room service; dry cleaning. *In room:* TV, hair dryer.

Splendid   This is one of the most attractive old-world hotels in Munich, with antiques, Oriental rugs, and chandeliers decorating the public rooms. Room size ranges from small (usually singles) to quite spacious. You'll be comfortable on the firm beds. Bathrooms are medium-size. You can order breakfast, the only meal served, in your room if you wish, or sit on a trellised patio.

Maximilianstrasse 54, D-80538 München. ✆ **089/29-66-06.** Fax 089/29-131-76. 36 units, 30 with bathroom (shower only). 130DM (€66.45, $65) double without bathroom; 210DM–290DM (€107.30–€148.240, $105–$145) double with bathroom. AE, DC, MC, V. U-Bahn: 4 or 5. Tram: 17 or 19. *In room:* TV.

INEXPENSIVE
Am Markt   This popular but basic Bavarian hotel stands in the heart of the older section. You're likely to find yourself surrounded by opera and concert artists who stay here to be close to where they perform. The rooms are trim, neat, and small—space to store your stuff is at a minimum. Mattresses are well worn, but with enough life for comfort. Private bathrooms are also small, and corridor bathrooms are kept quite fresh.

Heiliggeiststrasse 6, D-80331 München. ✆ **089/22-50-14.** Fax 089/22-40-17. 32 units, 12 with bathroom (shower only). 120DM–170DM (€61.30–€86.85, $60–$85) double without bathroom; 160DM–270DM (€81.75–€137.95, $80–$135) double with bathroom. Rates include continental breakfast. No credit cards. Parking 15DM (€7.65, $8). U-Bahn/S-Bahn: Marienplatz. *In room:* TV.

Hotel Jedermann *Value*   This pleasant spot's central location and value make it a good choice. It's especially good for families, as both cribs and cots are available. Rooms are generally small and old fashioned, but are cozy and comfortable, with firm mattresses. Private bathrooms are also small; corridor bathrooms are numerous enough so you don't usually have to wait in line. A generous breakfast buffet is served in a charming room.

Bayerstrasse 95, D-80335 München. ✆ **089/54-32-40.** Fax 089/54-32-41-11. www.hotel-jedermann.de. 55 units, 34 with bathroom (shower only). 110DM–130DM (€56.20–€66.45, $55–$65) double without bathroom; 180DM–250DM (€92.030–€127.75, $90–$125) double with bathroom; 185DM–210DM (€94.55–€107.30, $93–$105) triple without bathroom; 195DM–310DM (€99.65–€158.40, $98–$155) triple with bathroom. Rates include buffet breakfast. MC, V. Parking 15DM (€7.65, $8). U-Bahn/S-Bahn: Hauptbahnhof. *In room:* TV, hair dryer, private safe (in most units).

Pension Westfalia   Facing the meadow where the annual Oktoberfest takes place, this town house near Goetheplatz is another of Munich's top pensions. Rooms range from small to medium, but the owner takes great pride in seeing that they are well maintained and comfortable, renewing mattresses as needed. Private bathrooms are small, and corridor bathrooms are well maintained and do the job just as well.

Mozartstrasse 23, D-80336 München. ✆ **089/53-03-77.** Fax 089/54-39-120. pension-westfalia@t-online.de. 19 units, 11 with bathroom (shower only). 95DM–105DM (€48.55–€53.65, $48–$53) double without bathroom; 135DM–140DM (€69.05–€71.55, $68–$70) double with bathroom. Rates include buffet breakfast. Credit cards only for reservations. Parking, when available, is free on the street. U-Bahn: Goetheplatz. Bus: 58. *In room:* TV, no phone.

Uhland Garni   In a residential area, just a 10-minute walk from the Hauptbahnhof, the Uhland could easily become your home in Munich. It offers friendly, personal service. The stately town mansion, built in Art Nouveau style, stands in its own small garden. Its rooms are soundproof, snug, traditional, and cozy. The bathrooms contain shower units. Only breakfast is served.

Uhlandstrasse 1, 80336 München. ✆ **089/54-33-50.** Fax 089/54-33-52-50. www.hotel-uhland.de. 30 units. 170DM–201DM (€86.85–€102.70, $85–$101) double. Rates include buffet breakfast. AE, DC, MC, V. Free parking. Bus: 58. *In room:* TV, minibar, hair dryer.

WHERE TO DINE

For beer halls serving plenty of low-priced food, see the box "What's Brewing at the Beer Halls?" later in this chapter.

VERY EXPENSIVE

Boettner's ⭐ INTERNATIONAL   The restaurant today is housed in Orlandohaus, a Renaissance structure in the very heart of Munich. Culinary fans from yesterday will recognize its wood-paneled interior, which was dismantled from a previous site and moved here. The cookery is lighter and more refined, and seems better than ever. Try the lobster stew in a cream sauce and almost any dish with white truffles. Pike balls appear delectably in a Chablis herb sauce, and succulent lamb or venison also appears enticingly in a woodsy morel sauce. Desserts are as sumptuous as ever. The French influence is very evident, as are many traditional Bavarian recipes.

Pfisterstrasse 9. ✆ **089/22-12-10.** Reservations required. Main courses 48DM–70DM (€24.55–€35.75, $24–$35). AE, DC, MC, V. Summer Mon–Sat 11:30am–3pm and 6–10pm. Oct–May Mon–Sat 11:30am–10pm. U-Bahn/S-Bahn: Marienplatz.

Gasthaus Glockenbach ⭐⭐⭐ MODERN CONTINENTAL   The setting is a 200-year-old building, close to a tributary (the Glockenbach) of the Isar. The dignified country-baroque interior is accented with vivid modern paintings and the most elegant table settings in town. Cuisine changes with the season. Examples include imaginative preparations of venison and pheasant in autumn, lamb and veal dishes in springtime, preparations of whatever shellfish is seasonal at the time, and a medley of ultrafresh vegetables and exotica imported from local farms and from sophisticated purveyors throughout Europe and the world.

Kapuzinerstrasse 29, corner of Maistrasse. ✆ **089/53-40-43.** Reservations recommended. Main courses 40DM–55DM (€20.45–€28.10, $20–$28); fixed-price menus 90DM–140DM (€46.040–€71.55, $45–$70). AE, MC, V. Tues–Fri noon–1:30pm (last order); Tues–Sat 7–9:30pm (last order). Closed for 2 weeks in Aug, 1 week at Christmas. U-Bahn: Goetheplatz.

Restaurant Königshof ⭐⭐ INTERNATIONAL   On the top floor of this deluxe hotel, this is Munich's best shot at hotel dining. You're rewarded not only with a fine cuisine, but with a view of the city. Appetizers are sometimes pleasantly startling in their originality, as exemplified by the delicately diminutive rib and loin chops, liver, and rolled duck in a sweet and sour ice wine, the flavor enhanced by a pumpkin vinaigrette. Instead of the typical lasagna, you get a pasta layered with morels and crayfish, a real delicacy. The city's best veal dishes are served here, including veal sweetbreads resting on a bed of fresh vegetables, including beets and green beans. The wine list is one of the finest in Germany, though it may take you a good hour just to read it.

In the Hotel Königshof, Karlsplatz 25 (Am Stachus). ✆ **089/55-13-60.** Reservations required. Main courses 48DM–70DM (€24.55–€35.75, $24–$35); fixed-price menus 120DM–170DM (€61.30–€86.85, $60–$85). AE, DC, MC, V. Daily noon–2:30pm and 7–10pm. S-Bahn: Karlsplatz. Tram: 19, 20, or 21.

Tantris ⭐⭐⭐ FRENCH/INTERNATIONAL   Tantris serves Munich's finest cuisine. Hans Haas was voted the top chef in Germany in 1994, and, if anything, he has refined and sharpened his culinary technique since. Once inside, you're transported into an ultramodern atmosphere with fine service. The food is a treat to the eye as well as to the palate. You might begin with a terrine of smoked fish served with green cucumber sauce, then follow with classic roast duck on mustard-seed sauce, or perhaps a delightful concoction of lobster medallions on black noodles. These dishes show a refinement and attention to detail that you find nowhere else in Munich. And just when you think you've had the perfect meal, the dessert arrives, and you're hungry again as you sample the gingerbread soufflé with chestnut sorbet.

Johann-Fichte-Strasse 7, Schwabing. © 089/3-61-95-90. Reservations required. Fixed-price 5-course lunch 189DM (€96.63, $95); fixed-price dinner 198DM (€101.23, $99) for 4 courses, 245DM (€125.20, $123) for 8 courses. AE, DC, MC, V. Tues–Sat noon–3pm and 6:30pm–1am (last order 11pm). Closed public holidays; annual holidays in Jan and May. U-Bahn: Dietlindenstrasse.

EXPENSIVE
Alois Dallmayr ✦ CONTINENTAL   Munich's most famous restaurant traces its history back to 1700. Near the Rathaus, it is the best-known delicatessen in all of Germany. The upstairs dining room serves a subtle German version of continental cuisine, owing a heavy debt to France. The food array is dazzling, ranging from the best herring and sausages we've ever tasted to such rare treats as perfectly vine-ripened tomatoes flown in from Morocco, and papayas from Brazil. Also shipped in is the famous French *poulet de Bresse*, believed by many gourmets to be the world's finest.

Dienerstrasse 14–15. © 089/213-51-00. Reservations required. Main courses 27DM–45DM (€13.80–€23, $14–$23). AE, DC, MC, V. Mon–Wed 9:30am–7pm; Thurs–Fri 9:30am–8pm; Sat 9am–4pm. Tram: 19.

Spatenhaus ✦ BAVARIAN/INTERNATIONAL   One of Munich's best-known beer restaurants has wide windows overlooking the opera house on Max-Joseph-Platz. Of course, to be loyal, you should accompany your meal with the restaurant's own beer, Spaten-Franziskaner-Bier. You can sit in an intimate, semiprivate dining nook or at a big table. The Spatenhaus has old traditions, offers typical Bavarian food, and is known for generous portions and reasonable prices. If you want to know what all this fabled Bavarian gluttony is all about, order the "Bavarian plate," which is loaded down with various meats, including lots of pork and sausages.

Residenzstrasse 12. © 089/290-70-60. Reservations recommended. Main courses 25DM–49DM (€12.83–€25.05, $13–$25). AE, MC, V. Daily 11:30am–2:30pm and 5:30–11:30pm. U-Bahn: Odeonsplatz or Marienplatz.

MODERATE
Buon Gusto (Talamonti) ✦ ITALIAN   Some of Munich's best Italian food is served here in the rustic-looking bistro, or the more formal and more upscale-looking dining room. Menu items and prices are identical in both. Owned and managed by an extended family, the Talamontis, the restaurant emphasizes fresh ingredients, strong and savory flavors, and food items inspired by the Italian Marches and Tuscany. Stellar examples include ravioli stuffed with mushrooms and herbs, roasted lamb with potatoes, lots of scaloppinis, and fresh fish that seems to taste best when served simply, with oil or butter and lemon. Especially appealing are the array of risottos whose ingredients change with the seasons. During Oktoberfest and trade fairs, the place is mobbed.

Hochbruckenstrasse 3. © 089/296-383. Reservations recommended. Main courses 22DM–50DM (€11.25–€25.55, $11–$25). AE, MC, V. Mon–Sat 11am–11pm. Closed Dec 24–Jan 15. U-Bahn/S-Bahn: Marienplatz.

Der Tisch ✦ INTERNATIONAL   Its minimalist name, "the table," doesn't suggest the allure of this bistro, one of the best and most fashionable in Munich. You can stop in for a pre-dinner beer at the Münchener Lowenbrau brewery and beer hall across the street before heading to this 36-seat dining room. Presented on a clipboard, the daily-changing menu is eclectic and well chosen. The cookery is resolutely contemporary—start with the eggplant mousse with a perfectly balanced tomato vinaigrette or something simpler: tuna flavored with tomato sauce and accompanied by olives and capers. The main courses are always imaginative and satisfying, especially the pikeperch on a mound of cabbage, sprinkled with a beet-flavored pink sauce. In autumn, opt for venison in a red-wine sauce.

Maxvorstadt, Nymphenburger Strasse 1. ℭ 089/557-154. Reservations required. Main courses 25DM–48DM (€12.83–eu]24.55, $13–$24). AE DC, MC, V. Mon–Fri 11:30am–3pm and 6pm–midnight. U-Bahn: Stiglmeier Platz.

Hunsiger's Pacific ℛ INTERNATIONAL   Despite the name, don't expect the menu to be devoted exclusively to Pacific Rim cuisine. Fish is the premier item here. Preparation is based on classic French-inspired methods, but the innovative flavors come from Malaysia (coconut milk), Japan (wasabi), Thailand (lemongrass), and India (curry). You could begin with a tuna carpaccio with sliced plum, fresh ginger, and lime. Main courses include a succulent version of bouillabaisse with aïoli, which you might follow with cold melon soup garnished with a dollop of tarragon-flavored granita. Fried monkfish in the Malaysian style and turbot in chile and ginger sauce are evocative of Hawaii. Prices here are relatively low compared to those of its competitors.

Maximiliansplatz 5 (entrance is on the Max-Joseph-Strasse). ℭ 089/5502-9741. Main courses 26DM–49DM (€13.34–€25.05, $13–$25). AE, DC, MC, V. Mon–Fri noon–3pm; daily 6–11pm. Closed Sun May–Sept. U-Bahn: Stachus/Odeonsplatz.

Pfistermühle BAVARIAN   The country comes right into the heart of Munich at this authentic and old-fashioned place. A warm welcome and a refreshing cuisine await you here. Many of the dishes would be familiar to your Bavarian grandmother, and portions are generous and most satisfying. Come here for some of the most perfectly prepared roasts in the city. You can also opt for a fine array of fresh fish from the lakes and rivers of Bavaria, especially the delectable salmon trout or brown trout. Most fish dishes come with chive-flecked sour cream and a potato pancake. The fish is also simply prepared, such as pikeperch sautéed in butter. Finish with a pyramid of vanilla custard served with a fresh berry sauce followed by a glass of wild cherry schnapps.

In the Platz Hotel, Pfistermühle 4. ℭ 089/2370-3865. Reservations recommended. Main courses 26DM–38DM (€13.34–€19.40, $13–$19); set menus 55DM–60DM (€28.10–€30.65, $28–$30). AE, DC, MC, V. Mon–Sat noon–2pm and 6–10pm. U-Bahn: Marienplatz.

Ratskeller München BAVARIAN   Go here for the old Bavarian ambience at one of the best town hall cellars in the country. The decor is typical: lots of dark wood and carved chairs. The most interesting tables, the ones staked out by in-the-know locals, are the semiprivate dining nooks in the rear, under the vaulted painted ceilings. Bavarian music adds to the ambience. The menu, a showcase of regional fare, includes many vegetarian choices, which is unusual for a rathskeller. Some of the dishes are a little heavy and too porky, but you can find lighter fare if you search the menu.

Im Rathaus, Marienplatz 8. ℭ 089/219-98-90. Reservations required. Main courses 15DM–32DM (€7.65–€16.35, $8–$16). AE, MC, V. Daily 10am–midnight. U-Bahn/S-Bahn: Marienplatz.

INEXPENSIVE

Andechser am Dom GERMAN   Set on two floors of a postwar building erected adjacent to the back side of the Frauenkirche, this restaurant and beer hall serves copious amounts of a beer brewed in a monastery near Munich (Andechser) as well as generous portions of German food. Order a snack, a full meal, or just a beer, and enjoy the frothy fun of it all. Menu items include such dishes as veal schnitzels, steaks, turkey croquettes, roasted lamb, fish, and several kinds of sausages that taste best with tangy mustard. During clement weather, tables are set up on the building's roof and on the sidewalk in front, both of which overlook the back of one of the city's most evocative churches.

Weinstrasse 7A. ℂ **089/29-84-81.** Reservations recommended. Main courses 17.50DM–29DM (€8.95–€14.80, $9–$15). AE, DC, MC, V. Daily 10am–1am. U-Bahn/S-Bahn: Marienplatz.

Donisl ⓖ BAVARIAN/INTERNATIONAL   This is one of Munich's oldest beer halls, dating from 1715. The seating capacity of this relaxed and comfortable restaurant is about 550, and in summer you can enjoy the hum and bustle of Marienplatz while dining in the garden area out front. The standard menu offers traditional Bavarian food, as well as a weekly changing specials menu. The little white sausages, Weisswürst, are a decades-long tradition here.

Weinstrasse 1. ℂ **089/22-01-84.** Reservations recommended. Main courses 12DM–17DM (€6.15–€8.74, $6–$9). AE, DC, MC, V. Daily 9am–11:30pm. U-Bahn/S-Bahn: Marienplatz.

Hundskugel BAVARIAN   The city's oldest tavern, Hundskugel dates back to 1440, and apparently serves the same food as it did back then. If it was good a long time ago, why mess with the menu? Built in an alpine style, it's within easy walking distance of Marienplatz. Perhaps half the residents of Munich have at one time or another made their way here to enjoy the honest Bavarian cookery that has no pretensions. Although the chef specializes in *Spanferkel* (roast suckling pig with potato noodles), you might prefer *Tafelspitz* (boiled beef) in dill sauce, or roast veal stuffed with goose liver.

Hotterstrasse 18. ℂ **089/26-42-72.** Reservations required. Main courses 15DM–40DM (€7.65–€20.45, $8–$20). No credit cards. Daily 10am–midnight. U-Bahn/S-Bahn: Marienplatz.

Nürnberger Bratwurst Glöckl Am Dom BAVARIAN   In the coziest and warmest of Munich's local restaurants, the chairs look as if they were made by some Black Forest woodcarver, and the place is full of memorabilia—pictures, prints, pewter, and beer steins. Upstairs through a hidden stairway is a dining room decorated with reproductions of Dürer prints. The restaurant has a strict policy of shared tables, and service is on tin plates. The homesick Nürnberger comes here just for one dish: *Nürnberger Schweinwurstl mit Kraut* (little sausages with kraut). Last food orders go in at midnight.

Frauenplatz 9. ℂ **089/29-52-64.** Reservations recommended. Main courses 20DM–30DM (€10.20–€15.35, $10–$15). No credit cards. Daily 9am–1am. U-Bahn/S-Bahn: Marienplatz.

SEEING THE SIGHTS
SIGHTSEEING SUGGESTIONS FOR FIRST-TIME VISITORS

If You Have 1 Day Local tourist tradition calls for a morning breakfast of Weisswürst; head for Donisl (see "Where to Dine, above"). A true Münchener downs them with a mug of beer. Then walk to **Marienplatz,** with its glockenspiel and **Altes Rathaus** (old town hall). Later, stroll along **Maximilianstrasse,** one of Europe's great shopping streets. In the afternoon,

visit the **Neue Pinakothek** and see at least some exhibits at the **Deutsches Museum.** Cap the evening with a night of Bavarian food, beer, and music at the **Hofbräuhaus am Platzl.**

If You Have 2 Days In the morning of day 2, visit the **Bayerisches Nationalmuseum (Bavarian National Museum),** with three vast floors devoted to Bavaria's artistic and historical riches. If the weather's right, plan a lunch in one of the beer gardens of the **Englischer Garten.** In the afternoon, visit the **Nymphenburg Palace,** summer residence of the Wittelsbach dynasty, longtime rulers of Bavaria.

If You Have 3 Days Pass your third day exploring the sights you've missed so far: the **Residenz,** the **Antikensammlungen (Museum of Antiquities),** and the **Glyptothek.** If you have any more time, return to the Deutsches Museum. Enjoy

dinner or at least a drink at **Olympiapark,** enjoying a panoramic view of the Alps.

If You Have 4 or More Days As fascinating as Munich is, tear yourself away on day 4 for a excursion to the **Royal Castles** once occupied by the "mad king" Ludwig II (see "Organized Tours" and "The Romantic Road"). On day 5, take an excursion to **Dachau,** the notorious World War II concentration camp, and in the afternoon visit **Mittenwald** for a taste of the Bavarian Alps.

EXPLORING THE ALTSTADT (OLD TOWN)

Marienplatz, dedicated to the patron of the city whose statue stands on a huge column in the center of the square, is the heart of the Altstadt. On its north side is the **Neues Rathaus** (New City Hall) built in 19th-century Gothic style. Each day at 11am, and also at noon and 5pm in the summer, the **Glockenspiel** on the facade performs a miniature tournament, with enameled copper figures moving in and out of the archways. Since you're already at the Rathaus, you may wish to climb the 55 steps to the top of its tower (an elevator is available if you're conserving energy) for a good overall view of the city center. The **Altes Rathaus** (Old City Hall), with its plain Gothic tower, is to the right. It was reconstructed in the 15th century, after being destroyed by fire.

MUSEUMS & PALACES

Munich's newest museum, the **Pinakothek der Moderne,** may open in 2002, although plans, as of this writing, were not definite. This museum, when it does open on Barenstrasse, beside the Alte Pinakothek, will display some of the leading painters of the 20th century, including works by Ernst, Kirchner, Picasso, Jasper Johns, Braque, and Matisse. If you're interested, call © **089/2380-5296** during your stay in Munich and check on its status.

Alte Pinakothek ✦✦✦   This is one of the most significant art museums in Europe. The paintings represent the greatest European artists of the 14th through the 18th centuries. Begun as a small court collection by the royal Wittelsbach family in the early 1500s, the collection has grown and grown. There are two floors with exhibits, but the museum is immense. Albrecht Altdorfer, landscape painter par excellence of the Danube school, is represented by no fewer than six monumental works. Albrecht Dürer's works include his greatest—and final—*Self-Portrait* (1500). Here the artist has portrayed himself with almost Christ-like solemnity. Also displayed is the last great painting by the artist, his two-paneled work called *The Four Apostles* (1526).

Barer Strasse 27. © 089/238-050. Admission 7DM (€3.63, $3.50) adults, 4DM (€2.05, $2) students, free for children 15 and under. Combination ticket to Neue Pinakothek, Alte Pinakothek, and State Gallery of Modern Art, 12DM (€6.15, $6) adults, 6DM (€3.05, $3) students and seniors, free for children 15 and under. Wed and Fri–Sun 10am–5pm, Tues and Thurs 10am–8pm. U-Bahn: Theresienstrasse. Tram: 27. Bus: 53.

Antikensammlungen (Museum of Antiquities) ✦   On the south side of Königsplatz, five main-floor halls house more than 650 Greek vases. The oldest

452 CHAPTER 7 · GERMANY

piece is "the goddess from Aegina" from 3000 B.C. This pre-Mycenaean figure, carved from a mussel shell, is on display with the Mycenaean pottery exhibits in Room I. Take the stairs down to the lower level to see the collection of Greek, Roman, and Etruscan jewelry. The collection of Etruscan jewelry itself is reason enough to visit the museum, as necklaces, fibula, and rings compete with each other in delicacy and craftsmanship.

Königsplatz 1. ℭ 089/59-83-59. Admission 8DM (€4.14, $4) adults, 4DM (€2.05, $2) students and children. Combination ticket to the Museum of Antiquities and the Glyptothek, 12DM (€6.15, $6) adults, 6DM (€3.05, $3) students and children. Tues and Thurs–Sun 10am–5pm; Wed 10am–8pm. U-Bahn: Königsplatz.

Bayerisches Nationalmuseum (Bavarian National Museum) 🀄🀄

Three vast floors of sculpture, painting, folk art, ceramics, furniture, textiles, and scientific instruments demonstrate Bavaria's artistic and historical riches. Entering the museum, turn to the right and go into the first large gallery, called the **Wessobrunn Room.** Devoted to early church art from the fifth to the 13th centuries, this room holds some of the oldest and most valuable works. The desk case contains ancient and medieval ivories, including the so-called Munich ivory, from about A.D. 400. The **Riemenschneider Room** is devoted to the works of the great sculptor Tilman Riemenschneider (ca. 1460–1531) and his contemporaries. The second floor contains a fine collection of stained and painted glass—an art in which medieval Germany excelled—baroque ivory carvings, Meissen porcelain, and ceramics.

Prinzregentenstrasse 3. ℭ 089/211-2401. Admission 5DM (€2.55, $2.50) adults, 3DM (€1.55, $1.50) students and seniors, free for children under 15. Free on Sun. Tues–Sun 9:30am–5pm. U-Bahn: Lehel. Tram: 17. Bus: 53.

Deutsches Museum (German Museum of Masterpieces of Science and Technology) 🀄🀄🀄

On an island in the Isar River is the largest technological museum of its kind in the world. Its huge collection of priceless artifacts and historic originals includes the first electric dynamo (Siemens, 1866), the first automobile (Benz, 1886), the first diesel engine (1897), and the laboratory bench at which the atom was first split (Hahn, Strassmann, 1938). There are hundreds of buttons to push, levers to crank, and gears to turn, as well as a knowledgeable staff to answer questions and demonstrate how steam engines, pumps, or historical musical instruments work. Among the most popular displays are those on mining, with a series of model coal, salt, and iron mines, as well as the electrical power hall, with high-voltage displays that actually produce lightning. There are many other exhibits, covering the whole range of science and technology.

Museuminsel 1. ℭ 089/2-17-91. Admission 12DM (€6.15, $6) adults, 8DM (€4.140, $4) seniors, 5DM (€2.55, $2.50) students; free for children 6 and under . Daily 9am–5pm (closes at 2pm the second Wed in Dec). Closed major holidays. S-Bahn: Isartor. Tram: 18.

Glyptothek 🀄

The Glyptothek supplements the pottery and smaller pieces of the main museum with an excellent collection of ancient Greek and Roman sculpture. Included are the famous pediments from the temple of Aegina, two marvelous statues of *kouroi* (youths) from the sixth century B.C., the colossal figure of a *Sleeping Satyr* from the Hellenistic period, and a splendid collection of Roman portraits.

Königsplatz 3. ℭ 089/28-61-00. Admission 7DM (€3.63, $3.50) adults, 4DM (€2.05, $2) students and seniors, 2DM (€1, $1) children. Combination ticket to the Museum of Antiquities and the Glyptothek, 10DM (€5.10, $5) adults, 5DM (€2.55, $2.50) for students and children, free for children under 14. Tues–Sun 10am–5pm. U-Bahn: Königsplatz.

Neue Pinakothek ⭐ This gallery is a showcase of Munich's most valuable 18th- and 19th-century art, an artistic period that was hardly the Renaissance but has its artistic devotees nonetheless. Across Theresienstrasse from the Alte Pinakothek, the museum has paintings by Gainsborough, Goya, David, Manet, van Gogh, and Monet. Among the more popular German artists represented are Wilhelm Leibl and Gustav Klimt. Note particularly the genre paintings by Carl Spitzweg.

Barer Strasse 29. ℰ **089/23-80-51-95.** Admission 7DM (€3.63, $3.50) adults, 4DM (€2.05, $2) students and seniors, free for children 15 and under. Combination ticket to Neue Pinakothek, Alte Pinakothek, and State Gallery of Modern Art, 12DM (€6.15, $6) adults, 6DM (€3.05, $3) students and seniors, free for children 15 and under. Tues 10am–8pm; Wed–Sun 10am–5pm. U-Bahn: Theresienstrasse. Tram: 27. Bus: 53.

Residenz ⭐ The official residence of Bavaria's rulers from 1385 to 1918, the complex is a conglomerate of various styles of art and architecture. Depending on how you approach the Residenz, you might first see a German Renaissance hall (the western facade), a Palladian palace (on the north), or a Florentine Renaissance palace (on the south facing Max-Joseph-Platz). The Residenz has been completely restored since its almost total destruction in World War II and now houses the Residenz Museum, a concert hall, the Cuvilliés Theater, and the Residenz Treasure House.

Residenzmuseum comprises the southwestern section of the palace, some 120 rooms of art and furnishings collected by centuries of Wittelsbachs. There are two guided tours, one in the morning and the other in the afternoon, or you may visit the rooms on your own.

If you have time to view only one item in the **Schatzkammer (Treasure House)** ⭐⭐, make it the 16th-century Renaissance statue of *St. George Slaying the Dragon*. The equestrian statue is made of gold, but you can barely see the precious metal for the thousands of diamonds, rubies, emeralds, sapphires, and semiprecious stones embedded in it.

From the Brunnenhof, you can visit the **Cuvilliés Theater** ⭐, whose rococo tiers of boxes are supported by seven bacchants. The huge box, where the family sat, is in the center. In summer, this theater is the scene of frequent concert and opera performances. Mozart's *Idomeneo* was first performed here in 1781.

Max-Joseph-Platz 3. ℰ **089/29-06-71.** Combination ticket for Residenzmuseum and Schatzkammer 14DM (€7.15, $7) adults, 8DM (€4.15, $4) students/seniors, free for ages 15 and under. Ticket for either Schatzkammer or Residenzmuseum 8DM (€4.15, $4) adults, 5DM (€2.55, $2.50) seniors/students, free for ages 16 and under. Museum and Treasury, daily 10am–4pm; Theater, Mon–Sat 2–5pm, Sun 10am–5pm. U-Bahn: Odeonsplatz.

Schloss Nymphenburg ⭐⭐ In summer, the Wittelsbachs would pack up their bags and head for their country house, Schloss Nymphenburg. A more complete, more sophisticated palace than the Residenz, it was begun in 1664 in Italian villa style and went through several architectural changes before completion.

The main building's great hall, decorated in rococo colors and stuccos with frescoes by Zimmermann (1756), was used for both banquets and concerts. Concerts are still presented here in summer. From the main building, turn left and head for the arcaded gallery connecting the northern pavilions. The first room in the arcade is the Great Gallery of Beauties. More provocative, however, is Ludwig I's Gallery of Beauties in the south pavilion (the apartments of Queen Caroline). Ludwig commissioned no fewer than 36 portraits of the most beautiful women of his day. The paintings by J. Stieler include the *Schöne Münchnerin* (*Lovely Munich Girl*) and a portrait of Lola Montez, the dancer whose "friendship" with Ludwig I caused a scandal that factored into the Revolution of 1848.

To the south of the palace buildings, in the rectangular block of low structures that once housed the court stables, is the **Marstallmuseum.** In the first hall, look for the glass coronation coach of Elector Karl Albrecht, built in Paris in 1740. From the same period comes the elaborate hunting sleigh of Electress Amalia, adorned with a statue of Diana, goddess of the hunt; even the sleigh's runners are decorated with shellwork and hunting trophies. The coaches and sleighs of Ludwig II are displayed in the third hall.

One of Nymphenburg's greatest attractions is the **park**. Stretching for 200 hectares (500 acres) in front of the palace, it's divided into two sections by the canal that runs from the pool at the foot of the staircase to the cascade at the far end of the English-style gardens.

Within the park are a number of pavilions. The guided tour begins with **Amalienburg**, whose plain exterior belies the rococo decoration inside. Built as a hunting lodge for Electress Amalia (in 1734), the pavilion carries the hunting theme through the first few rooms and then bursts into salons of flamboyant colors, rich carvings, and wall paintings. The most impressive room is the Hall of Mirrors, a symphony of silver ornaments on a faint blue background.

Other attractions include the **Porzellansammlung,** or museum of porcelain, which is above the stables of the Marstallmuseum. Some of the finest pieces of porcelain in the world, executed in the 18th century, are displayed here, along with an absolute gem—extraordinarily detailed miniature porcelain reproductions of some of the grand masterpieces in the Old Pinakothek, each commissioned by Ludwig I.

The Botanical Gardens or Botanischer Garten is among the most richly planted in Europe. It's worth a spring trip to Munich for garden lovers to see this great mass of vegetation burst into bloom.

Schloss Nymphenburg 1. © **089/17-908-668.** Admission to all attractions 15DM (€7.65, $8) adults, free for children 15 and under. Separate admissions: 7DM (€3.63, $3.50) Schloss Nymphenburg or 5DM (€2.55, $2.50) to either Marstallmuseum, Amalienburg, or Porzellansammlung porcelain. Free for children 15 and under. Apr–Sept daily 10am–5pm; Oct–Mar daily 10am–4pm. Parking beside the Marstallmuseum. U-Bahn: Rotkreuzplatz, then tram 17 to Amalienburgstrasse. Bus: 41.

CHURCHES

When the smoke cleared from the 1945 bombings, only a fragile shell remained of Munich's largest church, the **Frauenkirche (Cathedral of Our Lady)**, Frauenplatz 1 (U-Bahn/S-Bahn: Marienplatz). Workers and architects who restored the 15th-century Gothic cathedral used whatever remains they could find in the rubble, along with modern innovations. The overall effect of the rebuilt Frauenkirche is strikingly simple yet dignified. The twin towers, which remained intact, have been a city landmark since 1525. Instead of the typical flying buttresses, huge props on the inside that separate the side chapels support the edifice. The Gothic vaulting over the nave and chancel is borne by 22 simple octagonal pillars. Except for the tall chancel window, when you enter the main doors at the west end, you don't notice windows; they're hidden by the enormous pillars. According to legend, the devil laughed at the notion of hidden windows and stamped in glee at the stupidity of the architect—you can still see the strange footlike mark called "the devil's step" in the entrance hall.

Peterskirche (St. Peter's Church), Rindermarkt 1 (© **089/260-48-28;** U-Bahn/S-Bahn: Marienplatz), is Munich's oldest church (1180). Its tall steeple is worth the climb in clear weather for a view as far as the Alps. In its gilded baroque interior are murals by Johann Baptist Zimmermann. The **Asam kirche** (★, Sendlinger Strasse (U-Bahn/S-Bahn: Sendlingertor), is a remarkable example of rococo, designed by the Asam brothers, Cosmas Damian and Edgar Quirin, in 1733 to 1746. The **Michaelskirche,** Neuhauser Strasse 52 (U-Bahn/S-Bahn: Karlsplatz), has the distinction of being the largest Renaissance church north of the Alps. The lovely **Theatinerkirche,** Theatinerstrasse 22 (U-Bahn/S-Bahn: Odeonsplatz), with its graceful fluted columns and arched ceilings, is the work of the court architect, François Cuvilliés and his son.

ORGANIZED TOURS

The easiest, and fastest, ways to gain an overview of Munich is on a guided tour. One of the largest organizers of these tours is **Panorama Tours** (an affiliate of Gray Line), Arnulfstrasse 8 (© **089/550-28995;** U-Bahn/S-Bahn: Hauptbahnhof), just north of the Hauptbahnhof. At least a half-dozen touring options are available, ranging from a quickie 1-hour overview of the city to full-day excursions to such outlying sites as Berchtesgaden, Oberammergau, and Hohenschwangau, site of three of Bavaria's most stunning palaces.

City tours encompass aspects of both modern and medieval Munich, and depart from the main railway station aboard blue-sided buses. Departures, depending on the season and the tour, occur between two and eight times a day, and tours are conducted in both German and English. Most tours don't last more than 2½ hours, with the exception of a scientific odyssey that focuses on the technological triumphs of Munich as witnessed by various museums that include the Deutsches Museum. That experience usually lasts for a minimum of 4 hours, plus whatever time you spend wandering through museums at the end of your tour.

Depending on the tour, adults pay 19DM to 39DM (€9.70 to €19.95, $10 to $20); children under 12 pay 9DM to 20DM (€4.60 to €10.20, $4.50 to $10). Advance reservations for most city tours aren't required, and you can buy your ticket from the bus driver at the time you board.

If you want to participate in any tour that covers attractions outside the city limits, advance reservations are required, especially if you want the bus to pick you up at any of Munich's hotels. Travel agents in Munich, as well as the concierge or reception staff at your hotel, can book any of these tours, but if you want to contact Panorama Tours directly, they're open from May and October, daily 7:30am to 6pm; from November to April, Tuesday, Thursday, and Saturday from 7:30am to 6pm, and Monday, Wednesday, and Friday from 9am to 6pm.

Pedal pushers will want to try Mike Lasher's **Mike's Bike Tour** (© **089/ 651-4275**). His bike rentals for 35DM (€17.94, $18) include maps and locks, child and infant seats, and helmets at no extra charge. English and bilingual tours of central Munich run from March through November, leaving daily at 12:30pm (call to confirm). The cost of the tour is included in rental fee.

THE SHOPPING SCENE

The most interesting shops are concentrated on Munich's pedestrians-only streets between **Karlsplatz** and **Marienplatz.**

Handmade crafts can be found on the fourth floor of Munich's major department store, **Ludwig Beck am Rathauseck,** Am Marienplatz 11 (© **089/236-91-00;** U-Bahn/S-Bahn: Marienplatz). **Wallach,** Residenzstrasse 3 (© **089/22-08-71;** U-Bahn/S-Bahn: Odeonplatz), is a fine place to obtain handcrafts and folk art, both new and antique. Shop here for a memorable object to remind you of your trip. You'll find antique churns, old hand-painted wooden boxes and trays, painted porcelain clocks, and many other items.

Dirndl-Ecke, Am Platzl 1/Sparkassenstrasse 10 (© **089/22-01-63;** U-Bahn/ S-Bahn: Marienplatz), 1 block up from the famed Hofbräuhaus, gets our unreserved recommendation as a stylish place specializing in dirndls, feathered alpine hats, and all the clothing associated with the alpine regions. Everything is of the best quality—there's no tourist junk. Bavarian clothing for children is also available.

The founders of **Hemmerle,** Maximilianstrasse 14 (© **089/24-22-600**), made their fortune designing bejeweled fantasies for the Royal Bavarian Court of the fairy-tale king, Ludwig II. Today, all pieces are limited editions, designed and made in-house by Bavarian craftspeople.

On the grounds of Schloss Nymphenburg at Nördliches Schlossrondell 8, you'll find **Nymphenburger Porzellan-manufaktur** (© **089/17-91-970;** U-Bahn: Rotkreuzplatz, then tram no. 17 toward Amalienburgstrasse; bus: 41), one of Germany's most famous porcelain makers. You can visit the exhibition and sales rooms; shipments can be arranged if you make purchases. There's also a branch in Munich's center, at Odeonsplatz 1 (© **089/28-24-28;** U-Bahn/ S-Bahn: Odeonplatz).

MUNICH AFTER DARK

To find out what's happening in the Bavarian capital, go to the tourist office and buy a copy of *Monats-programm.* This pamphlet contains complete information about what's going on in Munich and how to purchase tickets.

THE PERFORMING ARTS

Nowhere else in Europe, other than London and Paris, will you find so many musical and theatrical performances. And the good news is the low cost of the seats—you'll get good tickets if you're willing to pay anywhere from 15DM to 75DM (€7.65 to 38.35, $8 to $38).

A part of the Residenz (see "Museums & Palaces," above), **Altes Residenztheater** (Cuvilliés Theater), Residenzstrasse 1 (© **089/2185-19-40;** U-Bahn: Odeonsplatz), is a sightseeing attraction in its own right, and Germany's most outstanding example of a rococo tier-boxed theater. During World War II, the interior was dismantled and stored. You can tour it from Tuesday to Friday 2 to 4pm and Sunday from 11am to 5pm. The **Bavarian State Opera** and the **Bayerisches Staatsschauspiel (State Theater Company)** perform smaller works here in keeping with the tiny theater's intimate character. Box-office hours are from Monday to Friday 10am to 6pm, plus 1 hour before performances; Saturday from 10am to 1pm only. Opera tickets are 30DM to 255DM (€15.35 to €130.30, $15 to $128); theater tickets, 20DM to 80DM (€10.20 to €40.93, $10 to $40); building tours 5DM (€2.55, $2.50).

The regular season of the **Deutsches Theater,** Schwanthalerstrasse 13 (© **089/552-34-444;** U-Bahn: Karlsplatz/Stachus), lasts year-round. Musicals, operettas, ballets, and international shows are performed here. During carnival season (from Jan–Feb) the theater becomes a ballroom for more than 2,000 guests. Tickets are 40DM to 99DM (€20.45 to €50.64, $20 to $50), higher for special events.

The **Gasteig München GmbH,** Rosenheimer Strasse 5 (© **089/48-09-80;** S-Bahn: Rosenheimerplatz; www.muenchnerphilharmoniker.de; tram: 18; bus: 51), is the home of the **Münchner Philharmoniker** (Munich Philharmonic), founded in 1893. Its present home opened in 1985 and shelters the Richard

Strauss Conservatory and the Munich Municipal Library. The orchestra performs in Philharmonic Hall. Purchase tickets from Monday to Friday 9am to 6pm, Saturday from 9am to 2pm. The Philharmonic season runs from mid-September to July. Tickets are 17DM to 99DM (€8.74 to€50.64, $9 to $50).

Practically any night of the year, except from August to mid-September, you'll find a performance at the **Nationaltheater,** Max-Joseph-Platz 2 (ℂ **089/ 2185-1920;** www.staatstheater.bayern.de; U-Bahn/S-Bahn: Marienplatz or Odeonsplatz), home of the **Bavarian State Opera,** one of the world's great opera companies. The productions are beautifully mounted and presented, and sung by famous singers. Hard-to-get tickets may be purchased from Monday to Friday 10am to 6pm, plus 1 hour before performance; Saturday from 10am to 1pm. The Nationaltheater is also home to the **Bavarian State Ballet.** Opera tickets are 20DM to 200DM (€10.20 to €102.20, $10 to $100); ballet tickets, 10DM to 130DM (€5.10 to €66.45, $5 to $65).

THE CLUB & MUSIC SCENE

You'll find some of Munich's most sophisticated entertainment at **Bayerischer Hof Night Club,** in the Hotel Bayerischer Hof, Promenadeplatz 2–6 (ℂ **089/ 212-09-94;** tram: 19). Within one very large room is a piano bar where a musician plays melodies every night except from Monday 7 to 10pm. Behind a partition that disappears at 10pm, there's a bandstand for live orchestras, which play to a crowd of dancing patrons until 3 or 4am. The piano bar is free, but there's a nightclub cover charge of 18DM to 28DM (€9.20 to €14.30, $9 to $14). Daily happy hour is from 7 to 8:30pm in the piano bar.

Jazzclub Unterfahrt, Einstienstrasse 42 (ℂ **089/448-27-94;** U-Bahn/ S-Bahn: Ostbahnhof), is Munich's leading jazz club, lying near the Ostbahnhof in the Haidhausen district. The club presents live music from Tuesday to Sunday 8:30pm to 1am (it opens at 8pm). Wine, small snacks, beer, and drinks are sold as well. Sunday night there's a special jam session for improvisation. Cover from Tuesday to Saturday is 18DM to 28DM (€9.20 to €14.30, $9 to $14), Sunday jam session 30DM (€15.35, $15). Club members pay half the regular cover. Small, dark, and popular with blues and jazz aficionados, **Mister B's,** Herzog-Heinrichstrasse 38 (ℂ **089/534901;** U-Bahn: Goetheplatz), hosts a slightly older, mellower crowd than the rock and dance clubs. It's open from Tuesday to Sunday 8pm to 3am. Blues, jazz, and rhythm-and-blues combos take the stage Thursday to Saturday. Cover is 8DM to 12DM (€4.14 to €6.15, $4 to $6).

Set in a huge factory warehouse, **Nachtwerk,** Landesbergerstrasse 185 (ℂ **089/578-3800;** S-Bahn: Donnersbergerbrücke), is a mostly straight dance club that also books bands. It's a festive place that's not nearly as pretentious as other more "exclusive" discos (the doorman won't send you away for wearing the wrong shoes or pants). Open Thursday from 10pm to 4am; Friday and Saturday from 10:30pm. Cover is 10DM (€5.10, $5).

Parkcafé, Sophienstrasse 7 (ℂ **089/59-83-13;** U-Bahn: Lebachplatz), contains five lively bars, two of them outfitted like the inside of a ship. Who'd ever guess this home to chic freaks was a Nazi hangout in the 1930s? Many nights are themed, ranging from "Black Beat" music on Wednesday to "gay Sundays." It's open from Wednesday to Sunday 11pm to 4am. It's also open the first Tuesday of every month from 11pm to 4am. Cover is 10DM (€5.10, $5).

THE BAR & CAFE SCENE

Once a literary cafe, **Alter Simpl,** Türkenstrasse 57 (ℂ **089/272-30-83;** U-Bahn: University), attracts a diverse crowd of locals, including young people.

What's Brewing at the Beer Halls?

The world's most famous beer hall, **Hofbraühaus am Platzl,** Am Platzl 9 (© **089/22-16-76;** U-Bahn/S-Bahn: Marienplatz), is a legend. Visitors with only 1 night in Munich usually target the Hofbräuhaus as their top nighttime destination. Owned by the state, the present Hofbräuhaus was built at the end of the 19th century, but the tradition of a beer house on this spot dates from 1589. In the 19th century it attracted artists, students, and civil servants and was known as the Blue Hall because of its dim lights and smoky atmosphere. When it grew too small to contain everybody, architects designed another in 1897. This one was the 1920 setting for the notorious meeting of Hitler's newly launched German Workers Party. Today, 4,500 beer drinkers can crowd in on a given night. Several rooms are spread over three floors, including a top-floor room for dancing. The ground floor, with its brass band (which starts playing at 11am), is exactly what you expect of a beer hall—here it's eternal Oktoberfest. It's open daily from 9:30am to midnight.

In a century-old house northwest of Schwabing at the edge of Luitpold Park, **Bamberger Haus,** Brunnerstrasse 2 (© **089/308-89-66;** U-Bahn: Scheidplatz), is named after the city most noted for the quantity of beer its residents drink. Bavarian and international specialties served in the street-level restaurant include well-seasoned soups, grilled steak, veal, pork, and sausages. If you only want to drink, visit the rowdier and less expensive beer hall in the cellar, where a large beer is 5.50DM to 6.50DM (€2.80 to €3.30, $2.75 to $3.25). The restaurant is open daily from noon to midnight and the beer hall daily from 5pm to

The real fun begins after 11pm, when the iconoclastic artistic ferment becomes more reminiscent of Berlin than Bavaria. Open from Sunday to Thursday 11am to 3am, Friday and Saturday from 11am to 4am.

Nachtcafé, Maximilianplatz 5 (© **089/59-59-00;** tram: 19), hums, thrives, and captures the nocturnal imagination of everyone—no other nightspot in Munich attracts such an array of soccer stars, film celebrities, literary figures, and, as one employee put it, "ordinary people, but only the most sympathetically crazy ones." Waves of patrons appear at different times of the evening: at 11pm, when live concerts begin; at 2am, when the restaurants close; and at 4am, when die-hard revelers seek a final drink in the predawn hours. The music is jazz, blues, funk, and soul, and the decor is updated 1950s. There's a cover only rarely and for special entertainment. Open daily from 9pm to 6am.

Schumann's, Maximilianstrasse 36 (© **089/22-90-60;** tram: 19), doesn't waste any money on decor—it depends on the local *beau monde* to keep it looking chic. In warm weather the terrace spills out onto the street. Schumann's is known as a "thinking man's bar." Charles Schumann, author of three bar books, wanted a bar that would be an artistic, literary, and communicative social focus of the metropolis. Popular with the film, advertising, and publishing worlds, his place is said to have contributed to a remarkable renaissance of bar culture in the city. Open Sunday from 6pm to 3am, from Monday to Friday 5pm to 3am, closed Saturday.

1am; in summer, weather permitting, a beer garden is open daily from 11am to 11pm.

Englischer Garten, the park between the Isar River and Schwabing, is the biggest city-owned park in Europe. It has a main restaurant and several beer gardens, of which the **Biergärten Chinesischer Turm,** Englischer Garten 3 (℡ **089/38-38-730;** U-Bahn: Giselastrasse), is our favorite. It takes its name from its location at the foot of a pagoda-like tower. Plenty of beer and cheap Bavarian food are what you get here. A large glass or mug of beer (ask for *ein mass Bier*), enough to bathe in, costs 11DM (€5.60, $6). Homemade dumplings are a specialty, as are all kinds of tasty sausage. Oompah bands often play. It's open daily from 10am to 11pm (closed from Jan 11–Feb 5).

On the principal pedestrian-only street of Munich, **Augustinerbrau,** Neuhäuserstrasse 27 (℡ **089/231-83-257;** U-Bahn/S-Bahn: Stachus), offers generous helpings of food, good beer, and a mellow atmosphere. It's been around for a little less than a century, but beer was first brewed on this spot in 1328. The cuisine is not for dieters: It's hearty, heavy, and starchy, but it sure soaks up that beer. Hours are daily from 9:30am to midnight. **Waldwirtschaft Grosshesslohe,** George-Kalb-Strasse 3 (℡ **089/74-99-4030;** tram: 7), is a popular summertime rendezvous seating some 2,000 drinkers. The gardens are open daily from 11am to 11pm (they have to close early because neighborhood residents complain). Music ranges from Dixieland to English jazz to Polish bands. Entrance is free and you bring your own food. It's above the Isar River in the vicinity of the zoo.

GAY & LESBIAN CLUBS

Much of Munich's gay and lesbian scene takes place in the blocks between the Viktualienmarkt and Gärtnerplatz, particularly on Hans-Sachs-Strasse.

A virtual communications center of gay and lesbian Munich, the **Stadtcafe,** St. Jakobsplatz 1 (℡ **089/266-949;** U-Bahn: Marienplatz), attracts creative people, often in the arts. By Munich nightlife standards, it closes relatively early; night owls drift on to other late-night venues. Expect lots of chitchat from table to table, and there's sure to be someone scribbling away at his or her unfinished story (or unfinished novel). It's open from Sunday to Thursday 11am to midnight and Friday and Saturday from 11am to 1am. **Soul City,** Maximilianplatz 5 (℡ **089/595272;** U-Bahn: Karlsplatz), is *the* gay dance club in Munich. Scattered nooks allow conversation sheltered from one of the best sound systems in the city, as well as offer a brief respite from the throng on the dance floor and at the bar. The 10DM (€5.10, $5) cover charge on Thursday and Friday includes free drinks, and on Saturday you get discounted drink coupons. Open from Sunday to Thursday 10pm to 4am, and Friday and Saturday from 11pm to 6am.

Teddy Bar, Hans-Sachsstrasse 1 (℡ **089/260-33-59;** U-Bahn: Sendlingertor), is a small, cozy gay bar decorated with teddy bears. It draws a congenial crowd, both foreign and domestic. There's no cover. From October to April, there's a Sunday brunch 11am to 3pm. Open daily from 6pm to 3am. Other hot spots include **Mylord,** Ickstattstrasse 2A ((ℭ **089/260-44-98;** U-Bahn: Sendlinger-torplatz; tram: 17), for 3 decades a lesbian hangout, although it draws a mixed crowd these days, often actors, writers, and musicians, even transvestites and transsexuals. It has a cozy living room atmosphere. Open from Sunday to Thursday 6pm to 1am, Friday and Saturday from 6pm to 3am.

It is said that if Rick (that is, Bogie of *Casblanca*) were alive today, he'd be operating **Club Morizz,** Klenzestrasse 43 (ℭ **089/2-01-67-76;** U-Bahn: Fraunhoferstrasse), a stylish gay bar ringed with mirrors. Relax with drinks or food in red leather armchairs clustered around marble-topped tables. The eclectic menu includes well-prepared Thai dishes, as well as European specialties. Open from Sunday to Thursday 7pm to 2am, Friday and Saturday from 7pm to 3am.

DAY TRIPS FROM MUNICH

DACHAU   In 1933, what had once been a quiet little artists' community just 16km (10 miles) from Munich became a tragic symbol of the Nazi era. In March, shortly after Hitler became chancellor, Himmler and the SS set up the first German concentration camp on the grounds of a former ammunition factory. Countless prisoners arrived at Dachau between 1933 and 1945. Although the files show a registry of more than 206,000, the exact number of people imprisoned here is unknown.

Entering the camp, **KZ-Gedenkstätte Dachau,** Alte-Römar-Strasse 75 (ℭ **08131/1741**), you are faced by three memorial chapels—Catholic, Protestant, and Jewish. Immediately behind the Catholic chapel is the Lagerstrasse, the main camp road lined with poplar trees, once flanked by 32 barracks, each housing 208 prisoners. Two barracks have been rebuilt to give visitors insight into the conditions endured by the prisoners.

The **museum** is housed in the large building that once contained the kitchen, laundry, and shower bathrooms where the SS often brought prisoners for torture. Photographs, documents, and exhibits depict the rise of the Nazi regime and the history of the camp.

Getting There   Take the frequent S-Bahn S2 train (direction: Petershausen) from the Hauptbahnhof to the Dachau station, and then bus 724 or 726 from the station to the camp. Admission is free; the camp is open from Tuesday to Sunday 9am to 5pm. The English version of a documentary film, *KZ-Dachau,* is shown at 11:30am, 2:30, and 3:30pm.

HERRENCHIEMSEE *ℜ* **& NEUES SCHLOSS** *ℜℜ*   Known as the "Bavarian Sea," Chiemsee is one of the Bavarian Alps' most beautiful lakes in a serene landscape. Its main attraction lies on the island of Herrenchiemsee where "Mad" King Ludwig II built one of his fantastic castles.

Neues Schloss, begun in 1878, was never completed because of the king's death in 1886. The castle was to have been a replica of the grand palace of Versailles that Ludwig so admired. One of the architects was Julius Hofmann, whom the king had also employed for the construction of his alpine castle, Neuschwanstein. When work was halted in 1886, only the center of the enormous palace had been completed. The palace and its formal gardens remain one of the most fascinating of Ludwig's adventures, in spite of their unfinished state.

The splendid Great Hall of Mirrors most authentically replicates Versailles. The 17 door panels contain enormous mirrors reflecting the 33 crystal chandeliers and the 44 gilded candelabra. The vaulted ceiling is covered with 25 paintings depicting the life of Louis XIV. The dining room is a popular attraction

The Bavarian Alps

because of "the little table that lays itself." A mechanism in the floor permitted the table to go down to the room below to be cleared and relaid between courses.

You can visit Herrenchiemsee at any time of the year. From April to September, tours are given daily from 9am to 5pm; off-season, from 10am to 4pm. Admission—in addition to the 10DM (€5.10, $5) for the round-trip boat fare—is 11DM (€5.60, $6) adults, 7DM (€3.63, $3.50) students, and free for children under 17.

Getting There   Take the train to Prien am Chiemsee (trip time: 1 hr.). For information, call © **08051/99-66-33.** There's also regional bus service offered by **RVO Regionalver-kehr Oberbayern** (© **08021/948274**). Access by car is via A-8 Autobahn.

From Prien, lake steamers make the trip to Herrenchiemsee. They are operated by **Chiemsee-Schiffahrt Ludwig Fessler** (© **08051/60-90**). The round-trip fare is 10DM (€5.10, $5). For visitor information, contact the **Kur und Verkehrsamt,** Alte Rathausstrasse 11, in Prien am Chiemsee (© **08051/69050**), open from Monday to Friday 8:30am to 6pm. From March to September the office is also open on Saturday from 8:30am to 6pm.

In spite of its urban flair, Garmisch-Partenkirchen, Germany's top alpine resort, has maintained the charm of an ancient village. Even today, you occasionally see country folk in traditional costumes, and you may be held up in traffic while the cattle are led from their mountain grazing grounds down through the streets of town. Garmisch is about 88km (55 miles) southwest of Munich.

ESSENTIALS
GETTING THERE   By Train   The **Garmisch-Partenkirchen Bahnhof** lies on the major Munich-Weilheim-Garmisch-Mittenwald-Innsbruck rail line with frequent connections in all directions. Twenty trains per day arrive from Munich (trip time: 1 hr. 22 min.). For rail information and schedules, call © **01805/99-66-33.**

By Bus   Both long-distance and regional buses through the Bavarian Alps are provided by **RVO Regionalverkehr Oberbayern** in Garmisch-Partenkirchen (© **08821/948-274** for information).

By Car   Access is via A-95 Autobahn from Munich; exit at Eschenlohe.

VISITOR INFORMATION   For tourist information, contact the **Kurverwaltung und Verkehrsamt,** Richard-Strauss-Platz (© **08821/18-06**), open from Monday to Saturday 8am to 6pm, Sunday from 10am to noon.

GETTING AROUND   An unnumbered municipal bus services the town, depositing passengers at Marienplatz or the Bahnhof, from where you can walk to all central hotels. This free bus runs every 15 minutes.

WHERE TO STAY
Gästehaus Trenkler   For a number of years, Frau Trenkler has made travelers feel well cared for in her quiet, centrally located guesthouse. She rents five doubles with showers and toilets and five doubles with hot and cold running water. Each duvet-covered bed is equipped with a good mattress. Rooms range from small to medium, and corridor bathrooms are adequate and tidily maintained.

Kreuzstrasse 20, D-82467 Garmisch-Partenkirchen. © **08821/34-39.** Fax 08821/15-67. 10 units, 5 with shower. 95DM–105DM (€48.55–€53.65, $48–$53) double without shower, 110DM–115DM (€56.20–€58.75, $55–$58) double with shower. Rates include continental breakfast. No credit cards. Free parking. Closed Nov to Dec 26.Bus: Eibsee no. 1. **Amenities:** Breakfast is the only meal served. *In room:* No phone.

Post-Hotel Partenkirchen 𝒢 This is one of the town's most prestigious hotels, especially with the added asset of its unusually fine restaurant (see "Where to Dine," below). The U-shaped and handsomely furnished rooms are generally medium size. Duvets rest on comfortable beds with firm mattresses, mostly doubles or twins. Bathrooms are handsomely maintained with deluxe toiletries. The balconies overlook a garden and offer a view of the Alps.

Ludwigstrasse 49, D-82467 Garmisch-Partenkirchen. ℂ **08821/9363-0.** Fax 08821/9363-2222. www. post-hotel.de. 59 units. 250DM–280DM (€127.75–€143.130, $125–$140) double. Rates include buffet breakfast. AE, DC, MC, V. Closed Oct 15–Dec 2. **Amenities:** 2 dining rooms, bar; room service; laundry; nearby golf, tennis, swimming, and mountain climbing. *In room:* TV, minibar, hair dryer.

Reindl's Partenkirchner Hof 𝒢𝒢 This special Bavarian retreat maintains a high level of luxury and hospitality. The annexes have balconies and the main building has wraparound verandas, giving each room an unobstructed view of the mountains and town. All rooms have a cozy charm. The best are suites opening onto panoramic views of mountains or the garden. Rustic pine furniture and excellent mattresses add to the allure of this place. Bathrooms are spacious with a tub and shower combo.

Bahnhofstrasse 15, D-82467 Garmisch-Partenkirchen. ℂ **08821/5-80-25.** Fax 08821/73-401. www.garmisch-partenkirchen.de/reindl. 65 units. 170DM–282DM (€86.85–€144.10, $85–$141) double; 280DM–300DM (€143.15–€153.30, $140–$150) suite. AE, DC, MC, V. Parking 15DM (€7.65, $8). Closed Nov 10–Dec 15. **Amenities:** Restaurant (see "Where to Dine," below); health club; covered pool; sauna; sunroom; open terrace; two gardens; room service; laundry. *In room:* TV, minibar, hair dryer.

Romantik-Hotel Clausing's Posthotel 𝒢 This hotel in the heart of town was originally built in 1512 as a tavern and has retained its *gemütlich* antique charm. In the early 1990s, it was radically upgraded. Rooms range from rather small and cozy Bavarian nests to spacious. The owners have installed state-of-the-art German mattresses. Bathrooms are beautifully kept and have shower and tub combos.

Marienplatz 12, D-82467 Garmisch-Partenkirchen. ℂ **08821/7090.** Fax 08821/70-92-05. www.clausings-posthotel.de. 43 units. 250DM–290DM (€127.75–€148.25, $125–$145) double. DC, MC, V. Free parking. **Amenities:** 2 restaurants, historic Stüberl or tavern, bar (live music); room service; laundry. *In room:* TV, minibar, hair dryer.

WHERE TO DINE

Flösserstuben INTERNATIONAL Regardless of the season, a bit of the Bavarian Alps always seems to flower amid the wood-trimmed nostalgia of this intimate restaurant close to the town center. You can select a seat at a colorful wooden table or on an ox yoke–inspired stool in front of the spliced saplings that decorate the bar. Moussaka and souvlaki, as well as sauerbraten and all kinds of Bavarian dishes, are abundantly available. You can also order Mexican tacos and tortillas or even *Tafelspitz* (boiled beef) from the Austrian kitchen. The menu isn't imaginative but is soul satisfying, especially on a cold night.

Schmiedstrasse 2. ℂ **08821/28-88.** Reservations recommended. Main courses 15DM–32DM (€7.65–€16.35, $8–$16). AE, MC, V. Daily 11:30am–3:30pm and 5–10:30pm. Town bus.

Post-Hotel Partenkirchen 𝒢 CONTINENTAL This hotel dining room is renowned for its distinguished cuisine. The interior rooms are rustic, with lots of mellow, old-fashioned atmosphere. You could imagine meeting Dürer here. Everything seems comfortably subdued, including the guests. The best way to dine is to order one of the fixed-price menus, which change daily, depending on the availability of seasonal produce. The a la carte menu is extensive, featuring

⟲ Outdoors in the Bavarian Alps

The Bavarian Alps are both a winter wonderland and a summer playground.

HITTING THE SLOPES & OTHER WINTER ACTIVITIES   The winter **skiing** here is the best in Germany. A regular winter snowfall in January and February measures 30 to 50cm (12–20 in.), which in practical terms means about 1.8m (6 ft.) of snow in the areas served by ski lifts. The great **Zugspitzplatt** snowfield can be reached in spring or autumn by a rack railway. The Zugspitze at 2,960m (9,720 ft.) above sea level is the tallest mountain peak in Germany. Ski slopes begin at a height of 2,650m (8,700 ft.).

The second great ski district is **Berchtesgadener Land,** with alpine skiing centered on Jenner, Rossfeld, Götschen, and Hochschwarzeck, and consistently good snow conditions until March. Here you'll find a cross-country skiing center and many miles of tracks kept in first-class condition, natural toboggan runs, one artificial toboggan and skibob run, artificial ice skating, and ice-curling rinks. Call the local "Snow-Telefon" at ℂ **08652/967-297** for current snow conditions.

From October to February, you can use the world-class **ice-skating** rink in Berchtesgaden (the Eisstadion). Less reliable, but more evocative of Bavaria's wild open spaces, it involves skating on the surface of the Hintersee Lake once it's sufficiently frozen. Rarer is an ice-skating experience on the Königsee, whose surface freezes to the degree where you can skate on average only once every 10 winters. A particularly cozy way to spend a winter's night is to huddle with a companion in the back of a **horse-drawn sled.** For a fee of 50DM to 70DM (€25.55 to €35.75, $25 to $35) per hour, this can be arranged by calling ℂ **08652/1760.**

HIKING & OTHER SUMMER ACTIVITIES   In summer, **alpine hiking** is a major attraction—climbing mountains, enjoying nature, watching animals in the forest. Hikers are able at times to observe endangered species firsthand. One of the best areas for hiking is the 1,237-m (4,060-ft.) **Eckbauer,** lying on the southern fringe of Partenkirchen (the tourist office at Garmisch-Partenkirchen will supply maps and details). Many visitors come to the Alps in summer just to hike through the **Berchtesgaden National Park,** bordering the Austrian province of Salzburg. The 2,466-m (8,091-ft.) Watzmann Mountain, the Königssee (Germany's cleanest, clearest lake), and parts of the Jenner—the pride of Berchtesgaden's four ski areas—are within the boundaries of the national park, which has well-mapped trails cut through protected areas, leading the hiker along spectacular flora and fauna. Information about hiking in the park is provided by the **Nationale Parkverwaltung,** Franciscanalplatz 7, D-83471 Berchtesgaden (ℂ **08652/64343**). Open from Monday to Saturday 9am to 5:30pm.

From Garmisch-Partenkirchen, serious hikers can embark on full-day or, if they're more ambitious, overnight alpine treks, following clearly marked footpaths and staying in isolated mountain huts maintained by the German Alpine Association (Deutscher Alpenverein/DAV). Some huts are staffed and serve meals. For the truly remote unsupervised huts, you'll be provided with information on how to gain access, and your responsibility in leaving them tidy after your visit. For information, inquire at the local tourist office or write to the **German Alpine Association,** Am Franciscanalplatz 7, D-83471, Berchtesgaden (© 08652/64343). At the same address and phone number, you'll also be routed to staff members of a privately owned tour operator, the **Summit Club,** an outfit devoted to the organization of high-altitude expeditions throughout Europe and the world.

In addition to hill climbing and rock climbing, summertime activities include **ballooning,** which, weather permitting, can be arranged through **Outdoor Club Berchtesgaden,** Am Gmundberg (© 08652/50-01), open from Monday to Friday 8am to 6pm. Local enthusiasts warn that ballooning is not a sport for the timid or anyone who suffers unduly in the cold: Warm thermal currents that prevail around Berchtesgaden in summer limit the sport to the cold-weather months, mainly December to February. A local variation of **curling** (*Eisstock*) that makes use of wooden, rather than stone, instruments can usually be arranged even when ice and snows have melted on the surrounding slopes at the town's biggest ice rink, **Berchtesgaden Eisstadion,** An der Schiessstätte (© 08652/61405). If you opted not to carry your ice skates within your luggage during your transatlantic flight, don't worry: A kiosk (© 08652/3384) within the ice stadium rents a wide spectrum of ice skates in all sizes for around 6DM (€3.05, $3) adults, 5DM (€2.55, $2.50) children per hour.

Cycling and **mountain biking,** available through the rental facilities of **Full Stall,** Maximilianstrasse 16 (© 08652/948450), give outdoor enthusiasts an opportunity to enjoy the outdoors and exercise their leg muscles simultaneously. Open from Monday to Friday 9am to 12:30pm and 2 to 6pm, Saturday from 9am to 12:30pm.

Anglers will find plenty of **fishing** opportunities (especially salmon, pikeperch, and trout) at Lake Hintersee and the rivers Ramsauer Ache and Königseer Ache, although in most cases it's best to obtain a fishing permit. To acquire one, contact the Kurdirektion (tourist office) at Berchtesgaden, which will direct you to any of four different authorities, based on where you want to fish. For fishing specifically within the Hintersee, contact officials at the **Kurverwaltung,** Im Tal 2 (© 08657/98-89-20) at Ramsau, 12km (7½ miles) from Berchtesgaden.

Despite its obvious dangers, **hang gliding** or **para gliding** from the vertiginous slopes of Mount Jenner can be thrilling. To arrange it, contact the previously recommended Full Stall (see above), or Full Stall's competitor, **Para-Taxi,** Maximilianstrasse 15 (© 08652/948450). The headquarters for a loosely allied group of parasailing enthusiasts, the **Berchtesgaden Gleitschirmflieger** (© 08652/23-63) sometimes arranges communal paragliding excursions to which qualified newcomers are invited. Practice your **kayaking** or **white-water rafting** techniques on one of the many rivers in the area, such as the Ramsauer, Königisser, Bischofswiesener, and Berchtesgadener Aches. For information and options, contact the above-mentioned **Outdoor Club Berchtesgaden.**

game in the autumn. The Wiener schnitzel served with a large salad is the best we've had in the resort.

Ludwigstrasse 49. ⓒ 08821/5-10-67. Reservations required. Main courses 25DM–50DM (€12.83–€25.55, $13–$25); fixed-price menus 38DM–65DM (€19.40–€33.20, $19–$33). AE, DC, MC, V. Daily noon–2pm and 6–9:30pm. Closed Oct 15–Dec 2.

Reindl's Restaurant ⓕ CONTINENTAL   Reindl's is first class all the way. The seasonal menu comprises *cuisine moderne* as well as regional Bavarian dishes. Among main dishes, we recommend *coq au Riesling* (chicken with wine) with noodles, or a perfect veal roasted with *Steinpilzen,* a special mushroom from the Bavarian mountains. For dessert, try the spectacular Grand Marnier sabayon with strawberry and vanilla ice cream or a *Salzburger Nockerln* (a feathery light soufflé made of eggs, flour, butter, and sugar) for two.

In the Partenkirchner Hof, Bahnhofstrasse 15. ⓒ 08821/5-80-25. Reservations required. Main courses 27DM–45DM (€13.80–€23, $14–$23); fixed-price menus 42DM–56DM (€21.45–€28.60, $21–$28). AE, DC, MC, V. Daily noon–2pm and 6:30–9:30pm. Closed Nov 10–Dec 15.

SEEING THE SIGHTS IN TOWN

The symbol of the city's growth and modernity is the **Olympic Ice Stadium,** built for the 1936 Winter Olympics and capable of holding nearly 12,000 people. On the slopes at the edge of town is the much larger **Ski Stadium,** with two ski jumps and a slalom course. In 1936 more than 100,000 people watched the events in this stadium. Today it's still an integral part of winter life in Garmisch—the World Cup Ski Jump is held here every New Year.

Garmisch-Partenkirchen is a center for winter sports, summer hiking, and mountain climbing. In addition, the town environs offer some of the most panoramic views and colorful buildings in Bavaria. The **Philosopher's Walk** in the park surrounding the pink and silver 18th-century pilgrimage **Chapel of St. Anton** is a delightful spot to enjoy the views of the mountains around the low-lying town.

Exploring the Environs

One of the most beautiful of the alpine regions around Garmisch is the **Alpspitz region,** which hikers and hill climbers consider uplifting and healing for both body and soul. Here, you'll find alpine meadows, masses of seasonal wildflowers, and a rocky and primordial geology whose savage panoramas might strike you as Wagnererian. Ranging in altitude from 1,200m to 1,800m (4,000–6,000 ft.) above sea level, the Alps around Garmisch-Partenkirchen are accessible via more than 30 ski lifts and funiculars, many of which run throughout the year.

The most appealing and panoramic of the lot includes the Alpspitz (Osterfelderkopf) cable car that runs uphill from the center of Garmisch to the top of the Osterfelderkopf peak, at a height of 1,980m (6,500 ft.). It makes its 9-minute ascent at least every hour, year-round, 8am to 5pm. The round-trip cost is 40DM (€20.45, $20) adults, 22DM (€11.25, $11) children ages 4 to 15, and 28DM (€14.30, $14) persons aged 16 to 18. After admiring the view at the top, you can either return directly to Garmisch, or continue your journey into the mountains via other cable cars. If you opt to continue, take the Hochalm cable car across the high-altitude plateaus above Garmisch. At its terminus, you'll have two options, both across clearly marked alpine trails. The 20-minute trek will take you to the uppermost station of the Kreuzbergbahn, which will carry you back to Garmisch. The 75-minute trek will carry you to the upper terminus of the Hausbergbahn, which will also carry you back to Garmisch.

Another of the many cable car options within Garmisch involves an eastward ascent from the center of Partenkirchen to the top of the 1,780-m (5,850-ft.) Wank via the Wankbahn, for a round-trip price of 30DM (€15.35, $15) for adults, 21DM (€10.75, $11) for persons ages 16 to 18, and 16DM (€8.23, $8) for children. From here, you'll get a sweeping view of the plateau upon which the twin villages of Garmisch and Partenkirchen sit. In winter, the top of the Wank is a favorite departure point for many downhill ski runs. It's also, however, a favorite with the patrons of Garmisch's spa facilities because the plentiful sunshine makes it ideal for the *Liegekur* (deck-chair cure).

If you plan on pursuing any of these options, it's to your advantage to invest in a day pass, the **Classic Garmisch Pass,** with which you'll be able to ride most of the cable cars in the region (including those to the above-recommended Alpspitz, Kreuzeck, and Wank, as well as several others that fan out over the Eckbauer and the Ausberg) as many times as you like within the same day. Priced at 63DM (€32.24, $32) per person, the pass is available from any of the town's cable car stations. For information on all the cable car schedules and itineraries within the region, call ℂ **08821/7970.**

Another option for exploring the environs of Garmisch involves an ascent to the top of the **Zugspitze,** at 2,960m (9,720 ft.) the tallest mountain in Germany, with a base set astride the Austrian frontier. Ski slopes begin at 2,650m (8,700 ft.). For a panoramic view over both the Bavarian and Tyrolean Alps, go to the summit. The first stage begins in the center of Garmisch by taking the cog railway to an intermediary alpine plateau (Zugspitzplatz). Trains depart hourly throughout the year from 7:39am to 2:39pm, although we recommend that you begin by 1:39pm (and preferably earlier) and not wait until the cog railway's final ascent from Garmisch. At Zugspitzplatz, you can continue uphill on the same cog railway to the debut of a high-speed, 4-minute ride aboard the Gletscherbahn cable car, the high-altitude conveyance you'll ride to the top of the Zugspitz peak. (The distance between Zugspitzplatz and debut of the Gletscherbahn can also be transited aboard a secondary cable car—the Eibsee-Seilbahn, but this will require that you walk uphill for part of the route). Regardless of the exact route you follow, round-trip transit between the center of Garmisch and the top of the Zugspitz costs 79DM (€40.35, $40) for adults, 56DM (€28.60, $28) for persons 16 to 17, and 46DM (€23.50, $23) for children 5 to 15. Children under 4 ride free. Note that the price of the ascent to the Zugspitz is not included in the above-mentioned Classic Garmisch Pass, as it forms part of an independent network of cable cars that's not associated with the other cable cars within the region. For more information, call the tourist office or ℂ **08821/1806.**

MITTENWALD ⌀

Seeming straight out of *The Sound of Music,* the year-round resort of Mittenwald lies in a pass in the Karwendel Range, 18km (11 miles) southeast of Garmisch-Partenkirchen. Especially noteworthy and photogenic are the painted Bavarian houses with overhanging eaves. Even the baroque church tower is covered with frescoes. On the square stands a monument to Mathias Klotz, who introduced violin making to Mittenwald in 1684. The town is a major international center for this highly specialized craft.

ESSENTIALS

GETTING THERE   By Train   Mittenwald lies on the express rail line between Munich and Innsbruck and can be reached by almost hourly train service from Munich (trip time: 1½–2 hr.). Call ✆ **01805/99-66-33** for information.

By Bus   Regional bus service from Garmisch-Partenkirchen and nearby towns is frequent; call **RVO Regionalverkehr Oberbayern** at Garmisch (✆ **08821/ 94-82-74** for information).

By Car   Access by car is via A-95 Autobahn from Munich.

VISITOR INFORMATION   Contact the **Kurverwaltung und Verkehrsamt,** Dammkarstrasse 3 (✆ **08823/3-39-81**), open from Monday to Friday 8am to noon and 1 to 5pm, Saturday 10am to noon.

WHERE TO STAY
Alpenrose   In the village center at the foot of a rugged mountain, this inn is covered with decorative designs and window boxes holding flowering vines. The main building, a former 14th-century monastery, is much more desirable than the more functionally furnished annex, the Bichlerhof. Rooms in the main building are very charming with their old-fashioned farmhouse cupboards and dark wood paneling. The private bathrooms are well kept but a bit small, with shower stalls.

Obermarkt 1, D-82481 Mittenwald. ✆ **08823/92-700.** Fax 08823/37-20. alpenrose-mittenwald@online.de. 18 units. 142DM–166DM (€72.55–€84.85, $71–$83) double; 170DM–199DM (€86.85–€101.75, $85–$100) suite. Rates include buffet breakfast. AE, DC, DISC, MC, V. Free parking. *In room:* None.

Gästehaus Franziska *Value*   The Kufler family labors to make this the most personalized guesthouse in town. Each small room is comfortably furnished and beautifully maintained—first-rate beds feature crisp linen duvets and fine mattresses. All have balconies with mountain views. Bathrooms are a bit small but inviting and tidy, with shower stalls. Breakfast is the only meal served. It's extremely difficult to obtain bookings from June 20 to October 2.

Innsbrucker-Strasse 24, D-82481 Mittenwald. ✆ **08823/92030.** Fax 08823/3893. www.franziskatourism.de. 19 units. 150DM (€76.65, $75) double; from 188DM (€96.05, $94) suite. Rates include buffet breakfast. AE, V. Free parking. Closed Nov to Dec 1. *In room:* TV, minibar, tea/coffeemaker (suites only), safe (suites only).

Hotel Post ✦   Dating from 1632, this hotel remains Mittenwald's finest address. A delightful breakfast is served on the sun terrace, with a view of the Alps; in cool weather you can enjoy a beer in the snug lounge-bar with its open fireplace. Rooms are comfortable but standard. Beds (twin or double) and mattresses are among the best in town. Bathrooms are small and contain shower stalls. The maids are especially helpful if you need something extra.

Obermarkt 9, D-82481 Mittenwald. ✆ **08823/10-94.** Fax 08823/10-96. posthotel-mittenwald@online.de. 81 units. 190DM–220DM (€97.15–€112.40, $95–$110) double; 270DM–340DM (€137.95–€173.75, $135–$170) suite. Rates include buffet breakfast. MC, V. Parking 8DM (€4.140, $4). **Amenities:** Wine tavern/restaurant (Bavarian), bar/lounge; indoor pool; sauna; massage. *In room:* TV, hair dryer.

WHERE TO DINE
Restaurant Arnspitze BAVARIAN   Housed in a modern chalet hotel on the outskirts, this is the finest dining room in town. The restaurant is decorated in the old style; the cuisine is solid, satisfying, and wholesome. You might order sole with homemade noodles or veal steak in creamy smooth sauce, then finish with one of the freshly made desserts. There's an excellent fixed-price lunch.

Innsbruckerstrasse 68. ✆ **08823/24-25.** Reservations required. Main courses 29DM–43DM (€14.80–€21.95, $15–$22); fixed-price lunch 45DM (€23, $23); fixed-price dinner 85DM–99DM (€43.45–€50.64, $43–$50). AE. Thurs noon–2pm; daily 6–9pm; closed Tues all day and Wed for lunch. Closed Oct 25–Dec 15. Bus: RVO.

SEEING THE SIGHTS

The town's museum, with a workshop, has exhibits devoted to the evolution of violins and other string instruments. The **Geigenbau-und Heimatmuseum,** Ballenhausgasse 3 (© **08823/25-11**), is open from Monday to Friday 10am to noon and 2 to 5pm, Saturday and Sunday from 10am to noon. Admission is 3DM (€1.55, $1.50) adults and 1DM (€0.50, 50¢) children. The museum is closed from November 1 to December 20.

In the countryside, you are constantly exposed to the changing scenery of the Wetterstein and Karwendel ranges. Horse and carriage trips are available as well as coach tours from Mittenwald to nearby villages. In the evening there's typical Bavarian entertainment, often consisting of folk dancing and singing, zither playing, and yodeling, but you also have your choice of concerts, dance bands, discos, and bars. Mittenwald has good spa facilities, in large gardens landscaped with tree-lined streams and trout pools. Concerts during the summer are held in the music pavilion.

OUTDOOR ACTIVITIES

In winter, the town is a skiing center, but it remains equally active throughout the summer. Some 130km (80 miles) of paths wind up and down the mountains around the village, with chairlifts making the hiking trails readily accessible. Of course, where there are trails, there's mountain biking. A biking map is available from the tourist office (see above), and mountain climbing expeditions are also available. You can always go swimming to cool off on a hot summer's day—the Lautersee and Ferchensee are brisk waters that, even in summer, might be forfeited by the fainthearted for the heated adventure pool in Mittenwald.

OBERAMMERGAU 🛱

A visit to Oberammergau, 19km (12 miles) north of Garmisch-Partenkirchen, is ideal in summer or winter. It stands in a wide valley surrounded by forests and mountains, with sunny slopes and meadows. The world-famous **passion play** is presented here, usually every 10 years; the next one is scheduled for 2010. It has also long been known for the skill of its wood-carvers. Here in this village right under the Kofel, farms are still intact, and tradition prevails.

ESSENTIALS

GETTING THERE   By Train   The Oberammergau Bahnhof is on the Murnau-Bad Kohlgrum-Oberammergau rail line, with frequent connections in all directions. Murnau has connections to all major German cities. Daily trains from Munich take 2 hours. For information, call © **01805/99-66-33.**

By Bus   Regional bus service to nearby towns is offered by **RVO Regionalverkehr Oberbayern** in Garmisch-Partenkirchen (© **08821/948-274**). An unnumbered bus travels between Oberammergau and Garmisch-Partenkirchen.

By Car   Take A-95 Munich-Garmisch-Partenkirchen Autobahn and exit at Eschenlohe (trip time: 1½ hr.).

VISITOR INFORMATION   Contact the **Oberammergau Tourist Information Office,** Eugen-Papst-Strasse 9A (© **08822/92310**), open from Monday to Friday 8am to 6pm, Saturday from 8am to noon.

SEEING THE SIGHTS

Oberammergau's most respected citizens include an unusual group, the wood-carvers, many of whom have been trained in the village's wood-carver's school. In the **Pilatushaus,** Ludwigthomstrasse (© **08822/1682**), you can watch local artists at work, including wood-carvers, painters, sculptors, and potters. Hours are from May to October, Monday to Friday 1 to 6pm. You'll see many examples of these art forms throughout the town, on the painted cottages and inns and in the churchyard. Also worth seeing when strolling through the village are the houses with 18th-century frescoes by Franz Zwink that are named after fairy-tale characters, such as "Hansel and Gretel House" and the "Little Red Riding Hood House."

Heimatmuseum, Dorfstrasse 8 ((©) 08822/94136), has a notable collection of Christmas crêches, all hand carved and painted, and dating from the 18th through the 20th century. It's open from mid-April to mid-October, Tuesday to Saturday 2 to 6pm; off-season, only on Saturday from 2 to 6pm. Admission is 4DM (€2.05, $2) adults and 1.50DM (€0.75, 75¢) children.

NEARBY ATTRACTIONS   The Ammer Valley, with Oberammergau in the (almost) center, offers easy access to many nearby attractions. **Schloss Linderhof** 🎖🎖 ((©) 08822/92030), designed as a French rococo palace, the smallest of Ludwig II's constructions, is open year-round. This is in many ways the most successful of his palaces. The gardens and smaller buildings here are even more elaborate than the two-story main structure. Especially outstanding is a Hall of Mirrors, set in white and gold panels, decorated with gilded woodcarvings. The king's bedchamber overlooks a Fountain of Neptune and the cascades of the garden. The palace is open daily from April to September 9am to 5pm, from October to March 10am to 4pm. Admission is 8DM (€4.14, $4), free for children under 15 . Buses arrive from Garmisch-Partenkirchen throughout the day. Motorists can leave Oberammergau following the road signs to Ettal, 5km (3 miles) away. From Ettal, follow the signs for another 5km (3 miles) to Draswang, at which point the road into Schloss Linderhof is signposted.

OUTDOOR ACTIVITIES
Numerous **hiking trails** lead through the mountains around Oberammergau to hikers' inns such as the **Kolbenalm** and the **Romanshohe.** You can, however, simply go up to the mountaintops on the Laber cable railway or the Kolben chairlift. Oberammergau also offers opportunities to tennis buffs, minigolf players, cyclists, swimmers, hang-gliding enthusiasts, and canoeists. The recreation center **Wellenberg,** with its large alpine swimming complex with open-air pools, hot water and fountains, sauna, solarium, and restaurant, is one of the Alps' most beautiful recreation centers.

WHERE TO STAY & DINE
Alte Post   This provincial inn in the village center with a wide overhanging roof, green-shuttered windows, and tables set on a sidewalk under a long awning, is the village social hub. The interior has storybook charm, with a ceiling-high green ceramic stove, alpine chairs, and shelves of pewter plates. Most of the rustic rooms have views. Wide comfortable beds with giant posts range in size from cozy to spacious. Bathrooms are medium size with a shower stall. Nonresidents are welcome to the thriving and excellent restaurant.

Dorfstrasse 19, D-82487 Oberammergau. (©) 08822/91-00. Fax 08822/910-100. www. oberammergau.de/altepost. 32 units. 125DM–155DM (€63.93–€79.20, $63–$78) double. Rates include buffet breakfast. AE, DC, MC, V. Parking 6DM (€3.05, $3). Closed Oct 29–Dec 17. Bus: 30. **Amenities:** Restaurant (Bavarian), bar. *In room:* TV.

Hotel Café-Restaurant Friedenshöhe *Value*   This 1906 villa enjoys a beautiful location and is among the town's best bargains. Well-maintained rooms range from rather small singles to spacious doubles. Corner rooms are bigger, but bathrooms tend to be small, each with a shower stall. Even nonresidents join the townspeople who head for one of the four dining rooms, with both indoor and outdoor terraces opening onto panoramic views.

König-Ludwig-Strasse 31, D-82487 Oberammergau. © **08822/35-98**. Fax 08822/43-45. www. friedenshöhe.com. 17 units. 120DM–170DM (€61.30–€86.85, $60–$85) double. Rates include buffet breakfast. AE, DC, MC, V. Closed Nov to Dec 14. **Amenities:** Restaurant (Bavarian/international), intimate bar. *In room:* TV on request.

Hotel Restaurant Böld   A stone's throw from the river, this well-designed chalet hotel is one of the town's premier choices. Rooms in both the main building and the annex have equally good beds, usually doubles or twins, each with a firm German mattress. Most rooms open onto balconies. The spotless bathrooms are medium size with shower stalls. A tranquil atmosphere and attentive service await you here.

König-Ludwig-Strasse 10, D-82487 Oberammergau. © **08822/91-20**. Fax 08822/71-02. www.hotel-bold.de. 57 units. 180DM–238DM (€92.05–€121.60, $90–$119) double. Rates include continental breakfast. AE, MC, V. Free outside parking; 10DM (€5.10, $5) in the garage. **Amenities:** Restaurant (Bavarian/international), popular bar; sauna; solarium; whirlpool. *In room:* TV.

3 The Romantic Road

No area of Germany is more aptly named than the Romantische Strasse. Stretching 290km (180 miles) from Würzburg to Füssen in the foothills of the Bavarian Alps, it passes through untouched medieval villages and 2,000-year-old towns.

The best way to see the Romantic Road is by car, stopping whenever the mood strikes you and then driving on through vineyards and over streams until you arrive at the alpine passes in the south. Frankfurt and Munich are convenient gateways. Access is by A-7 Autobahn from north and south, or A-3 Autobahn from east and west; A-81 Autobahn has links from the southwest. You can also explore the Romantic Road by train or bus, or by organized tour.

ROTHENBURG OB DER TAUBER ✸✸✸

This city was first mentioned in written records in 804 as Rotinbure, a settlement above (*ob*) the Tauber River that grew to be a free imperial city, reaching its apex of prosperity under a famous Burgermeister, Heinrich Toppler, in the 14th century.

The place is such a gem and so well known that its popularity is its chief disadvantage—tourist hordes march through here, especially in summer, and the concomitant souvenir peddlers hawk kitsch. Even so, if your time is limited and you can visit only one town on the Romantic Road, make it Rothenburg.

Contemporary life and industry have made an impact, and if you arrive at the railroad station, the first things you'll see are factories and office buildings. But don't be discouraged. Inside those undamaged 13th-century city walls is a completely preserved medieval town, relatively untouched by the passage of time.

ESSENTIALS
GETTING THERE   By Train   Rothenburg lies on the Steinach-Rothenburg rail line, with frequent connections to all major German cities, including Nürnberg and Stuttgart. Daily trains arrive from Frankfurt (trip time: 3 hr.), Hamburg (5½ hr.), or Berlin (7 hr.). For information, call © **01805/99-66-33**.

By Bus   The bus that traverses the length of the Romantic Road is EB189 or EB189E, operated by **Deutsche Touring Frankfurt** (© **069/790-3281**). Two buses operate along this route every day, but only from April to October. Know in advance that although you'll see a lot of romantic color en route, travel time to Rothenburg from Frankfurt via these buses is 6½ hours because of frequent stops en route. Any travel agent in Germany or abroad can book you a seat on any of these buses, each of which stops at Würzburg, Augsburg, Füssen, and Munich.

Regional bus service that's limited to towns and hamlets within the vicinity of Rothenburg and the rest of the Romantic Road is provided by **OVF Omnibusverkehr Franken GmbH,** Kopernikusplatz 5, 90159 Nürnberg (© **0911/43-90-60**).

VISITOR INFORMATION Contact **Stadt Verkehrsamt,** Marktplatz (© **09861/40-492**), open from Monday to Friday 9am to 1pm and 2 to 6pm, Saturday and Sunday from 10am to 3pm (from Nov–Mar it closes at 5pm weekdays).

WHERE TO STAY
Expensive
Burg Hotel ✿ This old-fashioned timbered house at the end of a cul-de-sac is out of the Brothers Grimm. Its Tauber Valley view, picket fences, and window boxes exude German charm. Rooms are spread across three floors (no elevator). Mattresses are deluxe; extras include safes and spacious bathrooms with combination shower and tub, and large mirrors. Any room is likely to please, but if you want a view, ask for nos. 7, 12, or 25.

Klostergasse 1–3, D-91541 Rothenburg o.d.T. © **09861/94-89-0**. Fax 09861/94-89-40. www.burghotel.rothenburg.de. 15 units. 210DM–250DM (€107.30–€127.75, $105–$125) double; from 280DM (€143.15, $140) suite. Rates include buffet breakfast. V. Parking 10DM (€5.10, $5). *In room:* TV, minibar, hair dryer.

Eisenhut ✿✿ The most celebrated inn on the Romantic Road, Eisenhut is also one of the finest small hotels in Germany. Four medieval patrician houses were joined to make this distinctive inn. Demand for rooms is great, and the staff appears forever overworked. No two rooms are alike—yours may contain hand-carved, monumental pieces or have a 1940s Hollywood touch with a tufted satin headboard. All are enhanced by comforters and pillows piled high on state-of-the-art German mattresses. Extras include bedside controls, and spacious bathrooms outfitted with twin basins. The three-story galleried dining hall is one of the most distinctive in Germany, with a multi-tiered flagstone terrace on the Tauber.

Herrngasse 3–5, D-91541 Rothenburg o.d.T. © **09861/70-50**. Fax 09861/70-545. www.eisenhut.com. 70 units. 300DM–395DM (€153.30–€201.85, $150–$198) double; 540DM–660DM (€275.95–€337.25, $270–$330) suite. AE, DC, MC, V. Parking 15DM (€7.65, $8). **Amenities:** Restaurant, piano bar, Bavarian beer garden; room service; dry cleaning/laundry. *In room:* TV, minibar, hair dryer, safe.

Hotel Tilman Riemenschneider ✿ This hotel's half-timbered facade rises directly above one of Rothenburg's busy historic streets. Its rear courtyard, adorned with geraniums, offers a cool and calm oasis from the heavy pedestrian traffic in front. Most rooms are medium size though a few are small. All have exceedingly comfortable mattresses.

Georgengasse 11–13, D-91541, Rothenburg o.d.T. © **09861/9790**. Fax 09861/29-79. www.tilman-riemenschneider.de. 65 units. 240DM–300DM (€122.65–€153.30, $120–$150) double. Rates include buffet breakfast. AE, DC, MC, V. Parking 10DM (€5.10, $5). **Amenities:** Restaurant (see "Where to Dine," below), bar; fitness center; solarium; two whirlpools; room service; laundry/dry cleaning. *In room:* TV, hair dryer.

The Romantic Road

Romantik Hotel Markusturm ★★   This is one of the charming nuggets of Rothenburg, without the facilities and physical plant of the Eisenut, but a winner in its own right. When this hotel was constructed in 1264, one of Rothenburg's defensive walls was incorporated into the building. Some rooms have four-poster beds; all have high-quality firm mattresses. About half the bathrooms have tubs and showers. Many guests request room 30, a cozy attic retreat. The hotel employs one of the most helpful staffs in town.

Rödergasse 1, D-91541 Rothenburg o.d.T. ℭ **09861/9-42-80.** Fax 09861/9-42-81-13. www.markusturm. 25 units. 180DM–350DM (€92.05–€178.85, $90–$175) double. Rates include buffet breakfast. AE, DC, MC, V. Free parking. **Amenities:** Restaurant (Bavarian, closed mid-Jan to mid-Feb); tennis court; room service; baby-sitting; dry cleaning/laundry. *In room:* TV, hair dryer.

Moderate

Hotel Gasthof Glocke *Value*   South of the town center off Wenggasse, this hotel does not have the charm and style of the premier inns, but it's a good choice for those who want plain, simple, affordable rooms, a family atmosphere, and good food. The small rooms, though a bit institutional, are nonetheless comfortable and a good value for pricey Rothenburg. Mattresses are generally thin but adequate. Bathrooms are exceedingly small, each with a shower stall.

Am Plönlein 1, D-91541 Rothenburg o.d.T. ℭ **09861/95899-0.** Fax 09861/95899-22. www.ringshotels.de. 24 units. 174DM–194DM (€88.90–€99.15, $87–$97) double. Rates include continental breakfast. AE, DC, MC, V. Parking 8.50DM (€4.35, $4.25). Closed Dec 24–Jan 11. **Amenities:** Restaurant (see "Where to Dine," below). *In room:* TV.

Hotel Reichs-Küchenmeister ★   We consider this hotel, one of Rothenburg's oldest structures, near St. Jakobskirche, comparable with Tilman Riemenschneider and the Goldener Hirsch. The owners take special care with the guests' comfort. Rooms are nicely furnished with painted wooden furniture and frequently renewed firm mattresses. Bathrooms are a bit small, each with a shower stall. An extra 17 rooms are available in the duller annex across the street.

Kirchplatz 8, D-91541 Rothenburg o.d.T. ℭ **09861/9700.** Fax 09861/86-965. hotel@reichskuechenmeister.de. 48 units. 160DM–200DM (€81.75–€102.20, $80–$100) double; 230DM (€117.55, $115) suite for 2; 330DM (€168.65, $165) suite for 5. Rates include buffet breakfast. AE, DC, MC, V. Parking 8DM (€4.15, $4) in lot, 12DM (€6.15, $6) in garage. **Amenities:** Restaurant (see "Where to Dine," below); whirlpool; sauna; Turkish bath. *In room:* TV.

Inexpensive

Bayerischer Hof   This little place, midway between the Bahnhof and the medieval walled city, doesn't even try to compete with the grand inns. And why should it? It's found a niche as a B&B, and although the outside looks rather sterile, many cozy warm Bavarian touches grace the interior. Beds are comfortable though mattresses are a bit thin. Rooms are small, as are the bathrooms with shower stalls, but housekeeping is excellent and the staff is most hospitable.

Ansbacherstrasse 21, D-91541 Rothenburg o.d.T. ℭ **09861/60-63.** Fax 09861/86-56-1. bayerischer. rothenburg@online.de. 9 units. 130DM–160DM (€66.45–€81.75, $65–$80) double. Rates include breakfast. MC, V. Free parking. Closed Jan. **Amenities:** Restaurant/bar (Bavarian/international). *In room:* TV.

Gasthof Goldener Greifen ★   This is one of the very best B&Bs in town if you want Bavarian home-style warmth. Fine mattresses, tidy housekeeping, and a willing staff make this patrician 1374 house off Marktplatz extremely comfortable. Corridor bathrooms are adequate, and generally spruced up after use. Those in rooms with private bathrooms will find them small but well maintained. You can order your morning coffee in the garden amid roses and geraniums.

Obere Schmiedgasse 5, D-91541 Rothenburg o.d.T. ℂ 09861/22-81. Fax 09861/86-374. www.gasthofgreifen. rothenburg.de. 21 units (20 with bathroom). 74DM (€37.80, $37) double without bathroom; 138DM (€70.50, $69) double with shower or bathroom. Rates include buffet breakfast. AE, MC, V. Closed Aug 22–Sept 2 and Dec 22–Feb. *In room:* No phone.

WHERE TO DINE
Expensive
Louvre ✹ NEW GERMAN   Chef Berhard Reiseer is a man of multiple talents, and he has brought a lighter touch to the kitchens of Rothenburg with his *Neuer Küche* (new cuisine) style of cookery. His appetizers are dazzling, especially the goose liver terrine with huckleberries and white port or our favorite, consommé of crayfish with ravioli. For a main course, try the perfectly cooked halibut with a potato sauce or else the roulade of guinea fowl with herb infused cabbage and white-flour dumplings. The elegant cuisine is served against a mainly black decor with high-tech lighting and paintings on display. The wine list, for the most part, is good and fairly priced.

Klingengasse 15. ℂ 09861/87809. Reservations required. Main courses 39DM–48DM (€19.95–€24.55, $20–$24); fixed-price menu 57DM–145DM (€29.15–€74.10, $29–$73). AE, MC, V. Daily 6–11pm.

Moderate
Baumeisterhaus ✹ FRANCONIAN   Right off Marktplatz, the Baumeisterhaus is housed in an ancient patrician residence, built in 1596. It has Rothenburg's most beautiful courtyard (which only guests can visit), with colorful murals, serenely draped by vines. Frankly, although the menu is good, the romantic setting is better. The food, for the most part, is rib-sticking fare beloved of Bavarians, including roast suckling pig with potato dumplings, and one of the chef's best dishes, *sauerbraten* (braised beef marinated in vinegar), served with *spätzle* (small flour dumplings).

Obere Schmiedgasse 3. ℂ 09861/94-700. Reservations required for courtyard tables. Main courses 14DM–40DM (€7.15–€20.45, $7–$20). AE, DC, MC, V. Daily 9am–9pm.

Ratsstube FRANCONIAN   This restaurant enjoys a position right on the market square, one of the most photographed spots in Germany. It's a bustling center of activity throughout the day—a day that begins when practically every Rothenburger stops by for coffee. Inside, a true tavern atmosphere prevails with hardwood chairs and tables, vaulted ceilings, and pierced copper lanterns. The a la carte menu of Franconian wines and dishes includes sauerbraten and venison, both served with fresh vegetables and potatoes. For dessert, you can order homemade Italian ice cream and espresso. This is a longtime favorite of those who prefer typical Franconian cookery without a lot of fuss and bother. If you arrive at 9am, the staff will serve you an American breakfast.

Marktplatz 6. ℂ 09861/55-11. Reservations recommended. Main courses 18DM–40DM (€9.20–€20.45, $9–$20). AE, MC, V. Mon–Sat 9am–10pm; Sun noon–6pm. Closed Jan 7 to Feb.

Reichs-Küchenmeister FRANCONIAN   The main dishes served here are the type Bavarians have loved for years, including sauerbraten, or pork tenderloin; white herring and broiled salmon are also available. The *Lebensknodel* (liver dumpling) or goulash soup is perfect for cold days. The chef makes one of the best Wiener schnitzels in town. The restaurant is near St. Jakobskirche and has a typical Weinstube decor, along with a garden terrace and a *Konditorei* (cake shop). Service is warm and efficient.

Kirchplatz 8. ℂ 09861/9700. Reservations required. Main courses 19.50DM–47DM (€9.95–€24, $10–$24). AE, DC, MC, V. Daily 9:30am–9:30pm.

Inexpensive

Hotel Gasthof Glocke FRANCONIAN   This traditional hotel and guest-house serves good-tasting regional specialties along with a vast selection of local wine. Meals emphasize seasonal dishes and range from a simple vegetarian plate to lobster. If your expectations aren't too high, you'll probably enjoy this good regional cookery. Service is polite and attentive.

Am Plönlein 1. (℃) 09861/958-990. Reservations recommended. Main courses 16DM–40DM (€8.25–€20.45, $8–$20). AE, DC, MC, V. Daily 11am–2pm; Mon–Sat 6–9pm. Closed Dec 24–Jan 6.

Tilman Riemenschneider FRANCONIAN   This traditional old Weinstube is housed in one of Rothenburg's finest hotels. The old-fashioned cookery is served in generous portions. You might begin with air-dried beef or smoked filet of trout, then follow it with poached eel, halibut steak, or loin of pork. Everything is served in generous portions with good results.

Georgengasse 11. (℃) 09861/9790. Main courses 18.50DM–40DM (€9.45–€20.45, $9.25–$20); fixed-price menu 35DM–45DM (€17.94–€23, $18–$23). AE, DC, MC, V. Daily 11:30am–2pm and 6–9pm.

EXPLORING THE MEDIEVAL TOWN

The **Rathaus (Town Hall)** ℛ on the Marktplatz ((℃) **09861/404-92**) and the Jakobskirche are the outstanding attractions, along with the medieval walls. The town hall consists of two sections: The older, Gothic section dates from 1240. From the 50-m (165-ft.) tower of the Gothic hall, you get an overview of the town. The belfry has quite a history—in 1501, fire destroyed part of the building, and after that the belfry became a fire watchtower. Guards had to ring the bell every quarter hour to prove they were awake and on the job. The newer Renaissance section, built in 1572, is decorated with intricate friezes, an oriel extending the building's full height, and a large stone portico opening onto the square. The octagonal tower at the center of the side facing the square contains a grand staircase leading to the upper hall. On the main floor is the large courtroom.

Admission to the tower is 1DM (€0.50, 50¢) adults, 0.50DM (€0.25, 25¢) children. The Rathaus is open from Monday to Friday 8am to 6pm; the tower is open from April to October, daily 9:30am to 12:30pm and 1 to 5pm; from November to March, Saturday, Sunday, and holidays only from noon to 3pm.

St. Jakobskirche (Church of St. James), Klostergasse 15 ((℃) **09861/ 70-06-20**), contains the famous *Altar of the Holy Blood* ℛℛ (west gallery), a masterpiece of the Würzburg sculptor and wood-carver Tilman Riemenschneider (1460–1531). The Rothenburg Council commissioned the work in 1499 to provide a worthy setting for the *Reliquary of the Holy Blood.* The relic is contained in a rock-crystal capsule set in the reliquary cross (about 1270) in the center of the shrine, and beneath it the scene of the *Last Supper* makes an immediate impact on the viewer—Jesus is giving Judas the morsel of bread, marking him as the traitor. The altar wings show (left) the *Entry of Christ into Jerusalem* and (right) *Christ Praying in the Garden of Gethsemane.*

The vertical Gothic church has three naves. The choir, dating from 1336, is the oldest section and has fine late Gothic painted-glass windows. To the left is the tabernacle (1390–1400), which was recognized as a "free place," a sanctuary for condemned criminals where they could not be touched. It's open from April to October Monday to Saturday 9am to 5:30pm, Sunday 11am to 5:30pm. In December, it's open daily from 10am to 5pm. And during November and from January to March, it's open daily from 10am to noon and from 2 to 4pm.

Admission costs 2.50DM (€1.33, $1.25) for adults, and 1DM (€0.50, 50¢) for children under 6 and for students of any age.

Also of interest is the **Reichsstadtmuseum** 𝕰, Klosterhof 5 (℗ **09861/ 939-043**). This is Rothenburg's historical collection, housed in a 13th-century Dominican nunnery with well-preserved cloisters. You'll find on display here an enormous tankard that holds 3.5 liters (3½ qt.) whose story has echoes all over the city. In 1631, during the Thirty Years' War, the Protestant city of Rothenburg was captured by General Tilly, commander of the armies of the Catholic League. He promised to spare the town from destruction if one of the town burghers would drink the huge tankard full of wine in one draught. Burgermeister Nusch accepted the challenge and succeeded, and so saved Rothenburg. There's a festival every spring at Whitsuntide to celebrate this event. Among the exhibits is the 1494 *Rothenburg Passion* series, 12 pictures by Martinus Schwartz, and works by English painter Arthur Wasse (1854–1930), whose pictures managed to capture in a romantic way the many moods of the city. Admission to the museum is 5DM (€2.55, $2.50) adults, 3DM (€1.55, $1.50) children; a family card costs 10DM (€5.10, $5). It's open daily from April to October, 9:30am to 5:30pm; from November to March, 1 to 4pm.

Kriminal Museum, Burggasse 3 (℗ **09861/53-59**), is the only one of its kind in Europe. The museum's four floors display 10 centuries of legal history and provide insight into the life, laws, and punishments of medieval days. You'll see chastity belts, shame masks, a shame flute for bad musicians, and a cage for bakers who baked bread too small or too light. It's open daily from April to October, 9:30am to 6pm; November and from January to March, 2 to 4pm; and December, from 10am to 4pm. Admission is 6DM (€3.05, $3) adults and 3DM (€1.55, $1.50) children under 13.

DINKELSBÜHL 𝕰

Still surrounded by medieval walls and towers, Dinkelsbühl is straight out of a Brothers Grimm story, even down to the gingerbread, which is one of its main products. Behind the ancient 10th-century walls is a town that retains its quiet, provincial ambience in spite of the many tourists who come here. The cobblestone streets are lined with fine 16th-century houses, many with carvings and paintings depicting biblical and mythological themes. In the center of town, on Marktplatz, is the late Gothic **Georgenkirche** (1448–99). It contains a carved Holy Cross Altar and pillar sculptures.

ESSENTIALS

GETTING THERE By Train The nearest train station is in Ansbach, which has several trains arriving daily from Munich and Frankfurt (trip time: 2½–3 hr.), Nürnberg, and Stuttgart. From Ansbach, Dinkelsbühl can be reached by bus. For information, call ℗ **01805/99-66-33.**

By Bus For long-distance bus service along the Romantic Road, see "Rothenburg," earlier in this chapter. Regional buses link Dinkelsbühl with local towns. There're three to five buses a day to Rothenburg and five or six to Nördlingen.

By Car Take B-25 south from Rothenburg.

VISITOR INFORMATION Contact **Stadt Verkehrsamt,** Marktplatz (℗ **09851/9-02-40**). From April to October, hours are Monday to Friday 9am to noon and 2 to 6pm, Saturday 10am to 1pm and 2 to 4pm, and Sunday 10am to 1pm. From November to March, it's open only on Saturday from 10am to 1pm.

SPECIAL EVENTS   The **Kinderzeche (Children's Festival),** held for 10 days in July, commemorates the saving of the village by its children in 1632. According to the story, the children pleaded with conquering Swedish troops to leave their town without pillaging and destroying it—and got their wish. The pageant includes concerts given by the local boys' band dressed in historic military costumes.

WHERE TO STAY & DINE

Blauer Hecht   The inn is the best of a lackluster lot. The elegant ocher 17th-century building was once a brewery tavern, and the owners still brew in the backyard. The midsize rooms are tranquil and sunny. The mattresses are the newest and finest in town, and most rooms have bedside controls. Bathrooms are routine but well maintained, each with a shower stall. Good regional meals are served in the hotel restaurant/bar open to nonresidents.

Schweinemarkt 1, D-91150 Dinkelsbühl. ℭ 09851/5810. Fax 09851/581170. 44 units. 158DM–180DM (€80.75–€92.05, $79–$90) double. Rates include continental breakfast. AE, DC, MC, V. Free parking. Closed Jan. **Amenities:** Restaurant/bar. *In room:* TV.

Deutsches Haus   The facade of Deutsches Haus, which dates from 1440, is rich in painted designs and festive woodcarvings. Rooms are unique; you may find yourself in one with a ceramic stove or in another with a Biedermeier desk. For the tradition-minded, there're no finer rooms in town. Bathrooms are spotless, often with a shower and tub combination. The Altdeutsches Restaurant, one of the finest in Dinkelsbühl, is an attractive rendezvous, intimate and convivial.

Weinmarkt 3, D-91550 Dinkelsbühl. ℭ **09851/60-58.** Fax 09851/79-11. deutsches.haus@online.de. 15 units. 150DM–210DM (€76.65–€107.30, $75–$105) double; 240DM (€122.65, $120) suite. Rates include continental breakfast. AE, DC, MC, V. Parking 15DM (€7.65, $8). Closed Dec 23–Jan 6. **Amenities:** Restaurant (Franconian/regional). *In room:* TV.

Eisenkrug   This is a hit or miss choice, letting you stay in traditional style or sterile modernity. The stylish rooms are filled with engaging old furniture. A newer wing contains the most contemporary rooms, all rather standard and modern, each medium in size. The older rooms offer more charm, although some tend to be smaller. Some beds are canopied, and all have first-class German mattresses. Housekeeping and maintenance are top-notch. Bathrooms vary from small to spacious; all but one have a shower instead of a tub. Consider Mediterrano for your dining choice even if a nonresident. The chef invents his own recipes and carefully selects ingredients that go into his market-fresh cuisine. His is an indigenous Franconian-Swabian approach, with many innovative touches. The superior wine cellar has some really unusual vintages.

Dr.-Martin-Luther-Strasse 1, D-91550 Dinkelsbühl. ℭ **09851/57700.** Fax 09851/577070. www.eisenkrughotel-de.com. 23 units. 190DM–210DM (€97.15–€107.30, $95–$105) double. Rates include continental breakfast. MC, V. Parking 10DM (€5.10, $5). **Amenities:** Restaurant (international). *In room:* TV, minibar.

Goldene Rose *(Value)*   A landmark in the heart of this village since 1450, the intricately timbered Goldene Rose rises three stories, with a steeply pitched roof and overflowing window boxes. Although it doesn't match the impressive standards of the Eisenkrug, it is one of Dinkelsbühl's best values. The small to medium-size rooms have been modernized in a style more institutional and functional than traditional Bavarian. The more expensive rooms offer more charm. Bathrooms are rather small, but 10 have full tub and shower. The dining rooms are country-inn style. The a la carte menu (in English) offers such tempting items as tenderloin of wild hare flavored with hazelnuts, and rump steak. This is another good choice to consider even if you're a nonresident.

Marktplatz 4, D-91550 Dinkelsbühl. (C) **09851/57-750.** Fax 09851/57-75-75. hotel-goldene-rose@ t-online.de, 34 units. 145DM–230DM (€74.10–€117.55, $73–$115) double. Rates include continental breakfast. AE, DC, MC, V. Parking 6DM (€3.05, $3) in lot, 15DM (€7.65, $8) in garage. **Amenities:** Restaurant (international). *In room:* TV, minibar.

NÖRDLINGEN

One of the most irresistible and perfectly preserved medieval towns along the Romantic Road, Nördlingen is still completely encircled by its well-preserved 14th- to 15th-century **city fortifications.** You can walk around the town on the covered parapet, which passes 11 towers and five fortified gates set into the walls.

Things are rather peaceful around Nördlingen today, and the city still employs sentries to sound the message, *"So G'sell so"* ("All is well"), as they did in the Middle Ages. However, events around here weren't always so peaceful. The valley sits in a gigantic crater, the Ries. Once thought to be the crater of an extinct volcano, it is now known that a large meteorite was responsible. It hit the ground at more than 100,000 miles per hour, the impact having the destructive force of 250,000 atomic bombs. Debris was hurled as far as Slovakia, and all plant and animal life within a radius of 160km (100 miles) was destroyed. This momentous event took place some 15 million years ago. Today it is the best-preserved and most scientifically researched meteorite crater on earth. The American Apollo 14 and 17 astronauts had their field training in the Ries in 1970.

ESSENTIALS

GETTING THERE   By Train   Nördlingen lies on the main Nördlingen-Aalen-Stuttgart line, with frequent connections in all directions (trip time: 2 hr. from Stuttgart and Nürnberg, 1 hr. from Augsburg). Call (C) **01805/99-66-33** for information.

By Bus   The long-distance bus that operates along the Romantic Road includes Nördlingen; see "Rothenburg," earlier in this chapter.

By Car   Take B-25 south from Dinkelsbühl.

VISITOR INFORMATION   Contact the **Verkehrsamt,** Marktplatz 2 ((C) **09081/43-80**). The office is open from Easter to October, Monday to Thursday 9am to 5pm, and Friday from 9am to 3:30pm. The rest of the year, hours are from Monday to Thursday 9am to 6pm, Friday from 9am to 4:30pm, Saturday from 9:30am to 1pm.

WHERE TO STAY

Astron Hotel Klösterle   This is the best place to stay in town. In 1991, this 13th-century former monastery was renovated, a new wing added, and the entire complex transformed into the town's most luxurious hotel. Rated four stars, it offers elevator access and a hardworking, polite staff. Rooms have excellent mattresses, lots of electronic extras, and large bathrooms with deluxe toiletries.

Am Klösterle 1, D-86720 Nördlingen. (C) **09081/88-054.** Fax 09081/22-740. www.astron-hotels.de. 90 units. 265DM (€135.40, $133) double; from 256DM (€$138) suite. Rates include breakfast. AE, DC, MC, V. Parking 15DM (€7.65, $8). **Amenities:** Restaurant, bar; fitness center; sauna. *In room:* TV, minibar, hair dryer.

Kaiser Hotel Sonne   Next to the cathedral and the Rathaus is the Sonne, an inn since 1405. Among its guests have been Frederick III, Maximilian I, Charles V, and, in more recent times, the American Apollo astronauts. Many of the midsize rooms contain hand-painted four-posters to bring out the romantic in you. Others are regular doubles or twins, but each has a firm mattress. Goethe may have complained of the lack of comfort he found here, but you'll fare well. Bathrooms are fresh and immaculate, with tub and shower combos.

Marktplatz 3, D-86720 Nördlingen. (℅ **09081/50-67.** Fax 09081/23-999. kaiserhofhotelsonnet@online.de. 43 units (35 with bathroom). 150DM (€76.65, $75) double without bathroom; 185DM (€94.55, $93) double with bathroom; 230DM (€117.55, $115) suite. Rates include breakfast and parking. AE, DC, MC, V. **Amenities:** Restaurant, cozy bar; room service' baby-sitting; laundry/dry cleaning. *In room:* TV, minibar, hair dryer.

WHERE TO DINE
Meyer's Keller CONTINENTAL   The conservative, modern decor here seems a suitable setting for the restrained *neue Küche* of talented chef and owner Joachim Kaiser, adroit with both rustic and refined cuisine. The menu changes according to availability of ingredients and the chef's inspiration; typical selections are likely to include roulade of sea wolf and salmon with baby spinach and wild rice, or—a perfect delight—John Dory with champagne-flavored tomato sauce. The wine list is impressive, with many bottles quite reasonably priced.

Marienhöhe 8. (℅ **09081/44-93.** Reservations required. Main courses 25DM–40DM (€12.83–€20.45, $13–$20); fixed-price meals 55DM–110DM (€28.10–€56.20, $28–$55). AE, MC, V. Wed–Sun noon–2pm; Tues–Sun 6–10pm. Local bus to Marktplatz.

SEEING THE SIGHTS
At the center of the circular Altstadt within the walls is **Rübenmarkt.** If you stand in this square on market day, you'll be swept into a world of the past—the country people have preserved many traditional customs and costumes here, which, along with the ancient houses, create a living medieval city. Around the square stand a number of buildings, including the Gothic **Rathaus.** An antiquities collection is displayed in the **Stadtmuseum,** Vordere Gerbergasse 1 (℅ **09081/2738230**), open from Tuesday to Sunday 1:30 to 4:30pm; closed from November to February. Admission is 5DM (€2.55, $2.50) adults and 3DM (€1.55, $1.50) children.

The 15th-century Hallenkirche, the **Church of St. George,** on the square's northern side, is the town's most interesting sight and one of its oldest buildings. Plaques and epitaphs commemorating the town's more illustrious 16th- and 17th-century residents decorate the fan-vaulted interior. Although the original Gothic altarpiece by Friedrich Herlin (1470) is now in the Reichsstadt Museum, a portion of it, depicting the crucifixion, remains in the church. Above the high altar today stands a more elaborate baroque altarpiece. The church's most prominent feature, however, is the 90-m (295-ft.) French Gothic tower, called the "Daniel." At night, the town watchman calls out from the steeple, his voice ringing through the streets. The tower is open daily from April to October 9am to 8pm. Admission is 3DM (€1.55, $1.50) adults and 2DM (€1, $1) children.

Rieskrater-Museum, Hintere Gerbergasse (℅ **09081/273-8220**), documents the impact of the stone meteorite that created the Ries. Examine fossils from Ries Lake deposits and learn about the fascinating evolution of this geological wonder. Hours are from Tuesday to Sunday 10am to 4pm. Admission is 5DM (€2.55, $2.50) adults and 2.50DM (€1.33, $1.25) students, seniors, and large groups. Tours of the crater are possible through the museum.

EN ROUTE TO AUGSBURG
After Nördlingen, B-25 heads south to Augsburg. After a 19-km (12-mile) ride you can stop to visit **Schloss Harburg** ⚔ (it's signposted), one of the best-preserved medieval castles in Germany. It once belonged to the Hohenstaufen emperors and contains treasures collected by the family over the centuries. It is

open from mid-March to September, Tuesday to Sunday 10am to 5pm; October, from Tuesday to Sunday 10am to 4pm. Admission is 6DM (€3.05, $3) adults and 4DM (€2.05, $2) children, including a guided tour. For information call © **09080/969930.**

After exploring the castle, continue 11km (7 miles) south to the walled town of **Donauwörth** ✿, where you can stop to walk through the oldest part of the town, on an island in the river, connected by a wooden bridge. Here the Danube is only a narrow, placid stream. The town's original walls overlook its second river, the Woernitz.

After a brief stopover, continue your southward trek for 48km (30 miles) to Augsburg, the largest city on the Romantic Road.

AUGSBURG ✿✿

Augsburg is near the center of the Romantic Road and the gateway to the Alps and the south. Founded 2,000 years ago by the Roman emperor Augustus, for whom it was named, it once was the richest city in Europe. Little remains from the early Roman period. However, the wealth of Renaissance art and architecture is staggering. Over the years, Augsburg has boasted an array of famous native sons, including painters Hans Holbein the Elder and Hans Holbein the Younger, and playwright Bertolt Brecht. It was here in 1518 that Martin Luther was summoned to recant his 95 theses before a papal emissary. Only 15% of the city was left standing after World War II, but there's still much here to intrigue. Today, Augsburg is an important industrial center on the Frankfurt-Salzburg autobahn, and Bavaria's third largest city after Munich and Nürnberg.

ESSENTIALS

GETTING THERE   By Train   About 90 Euro and InterCity trains arrive here daily from all major German cities. For information, call © **01805/ 99-66-33.** There are 60 trains a day from Munich (trip time: 30–50 min.), and 35 from Frankfurt (3–4½ hr.).

By Bus   Long-distance buses (lines EB190 and 190A, plus line 189) service the Romantic Road. The buses are operated by **Deutsche Touring GmbH** at Am Römerhof in Frankfurt (© **069/790-32-56** for reservations and information).

VISITOR INFORMATION   Contact **Tourist-Information,** Bahnhofstrasse (© **0821/50-20-70**), from Monday to Friday 9am to 6pm, Saturday at Rathausplatz 10am to 4pm, closed Sunday.

GETTING AROUND   The public transportation system in Augsburg consists of four tram and 31 bus lines covering the inner city and reaching into the suburbs. Public transportation operates daily from 5am to midnight.

WHERE TO STAY
Very Expensive
Steigenberger Drei Mohren ✿✿   This is one of the premier choices for a stopover along the Romantic Road and one of the top inns if you didn't book into the Eisenhut at Rothenburg. The original hotel, dating from 1723, was renowned in Germany before its destruction in an air raid. In 1956, it was rebuilt in a modern style. Decorators worked hard to create a decor that was both comfortable and inviting, with thick carpets, subdued lighting, and double-glazing at the windows. Rooms vary in size and appointments, however, ranging from some economy specials that are a bit small with narrow twin beds and showers (no tubs) to spacious, luxurious rooms with full shower and tub.

Each has a good mattress, however. Many rooms are smoke free, and most bathrooms are fairly spacious.

Maximilianstrasse 40, D-86150 Augsburg. © **800/223-5652** in the U.S. and Canada, or 0821/5-03-60. Fax 0821/15-78-64. www.Augsburg-steigenberger.de. 107 units. 329DM–379DM (€168.10–€193.65, $165–$190) double; 550DM–700DM (€281.05–€357.70, $275–$350) suite. Rates include buffet breakfast. AE, DC, MC, V. Parking 25DM (€12.85, $13). Tram: 1. **Amenities:** First-class restaurant (international), cozy bar; the staff can arrange golf; room service; baby-sitting; laundry/dry cleaning. *In room:* TV, minibar, hair dryer, safe, trouser press.

Moderate
Dom Hotel   Although it may not have the decorative flair of the more expensive hotels such as Drei Mohren, the low rates and an indoor pool make this one of the most appealing choices in town. The hotel is a half-timbered structure, next to Augsburg's famous cathedral, and was built in the 15th century. Rooms on most floors are medium size and nicely appointed, although we prefer the smaller attic accommodations where you can rest under a beamed ceiling and enjoy a panoramic sweep of the rooftops of the city. All rooms have good beds with firm mattresses. Bathrooms are small, with tub and shower combos. Breakfast only is served but it's a treat in a garden beside the town's medieval fortifications.

Frauentorstrasse 8, D-86152 Augsburg. © **0821/34-39-30.** Fax 0821/34-39-32-00. www.domhotel-augsburg.de. 43 units. 160DM–200DM (€81.75–€102.20, $80–$100) double. Rates include buffet breakfast. AE, DC, MC, V. Free parking or 10DM (€5.10, $5) garage. Tram: 2. *In room:* TV.

Hotel Am Rathaus *(Value*   Many repeat guests consider this hotel's location just behind the town hall to be its best asset. Built in a three-story contemporary format in 1986, it offers comfortable, midsize rooms but small bathrooms with tidy maintenance. It may be short on style but it's long on value.

Am Hinteren Perlachberg 1, D-86150 Augsburg. © **0821/34-64-90.** Fax 0821/346-49-99. 32 units. 210DM (€107.30, $105) double. Rates include breakfast. AE, DC, MC, V. Parking 15DM (€7.65, $8). Tram: 1. **Amenities:** Generous breakfast buffet. *In room:* TV, minibar.

Romantik Hotel Augsburger Hof 🌟🌟   Its main competitor, the Drei Mohren, still has more flair, but this hotel enjoys a comfortable runner-up slot. Originally built in 1767 in a solid, thick-walled design with exposed beams and timbers, this hotel was carefully restored in 1988. In the town center, it's a favorite for its traditional atmosphere and its excellent food. In spite of the Renaissance interior, the rooms are completely up to date and not as romantic as the name of the hotel suggests. They range from cozy to spacious, each with a fine bed and quality mattress. Those overlooking the calm inner courtyard are more expensive than ones facing the street. Some bathrooms seemed crowded in as an afterthought, but each is beautifully maintained, containing a tub and shower combo.

Auf dem Kreuz 2, D-86152 Augsburg. © **0821/34-30-50.** Fax 0821/343-0555. www.romantichotels.de/augsburger. 36 units. 175DM–280DM (€89.45–€143.13, $88–$140) double. Rates include buffet breakfast. AE, DC, MC, V. Parking 10DM (€5.10, $5). Tram: 1. **Amenities:** Restaurant (German/international), bar; room service; baby-sitting; dry cleaning/laundry. *In room:* TV, minibar, hair dryer.

Inexpensive
Hotel Garni Weinberger   One of the best budget accommodations in the area lies about 3km (2 miles) from the center along Augsburgerstrasse in the western sector. Rooms are small but well kept with good beds and firm mattresses. The bathrooms are rather cramped with shower stalls, but housekeeping is excellent. The place is well patronized by bargain-hunting Germans.

Bismarckstrasse 55, D-86391 Stadtbergen. ℭ **0821/24-39-10.** Fax 0821/43-88-31. 31 units. 150DM (€76.65, $75) double. Rates include buffet breakfast. No credit cards. Closed Aug 15–30. Tram: 3. **Amenities:** Popular cafe and bar. *In room:* No phone.

WHERE TO DINE

Die Ecke ⊛ FRENCH/SWABIAN   Dripping with atmosphere, this place seemingly dates from the Last Supper. Well, almost. At least it was founded in the year Columbus sighted the New World, and its guests have included Hans Holbein the Elder, Wolfgang Amadeus Mozart, and, in more contemporary times, Bertolt Brecht, whose sharp-tongued irreverence tended to irritate diners of more conservative political leanings. The Weinstube ambience belies the skilled cuisine of the chef, which wins us over year after year. Breast of duckling might be preceded by pâté, and the filet of sole in Riesling is deservedly a classic. Venison dishes in season are a specialty—the best in town.

Elias-Holl-Platz 2. ℭ **0821/51-06-00.** Reservations required. Main courses 26DM–55DM (€13.34–€28.10, $13–$28); fixed-price dinner 75DM (€38.35, $38) for 4 courses, 115DM (€58.75, $58) for 6 courses. AE, DC, MC, V. Daily 11:30am–2pm and 5:30pm–1am. Tram: 2.

Fuggerei Stube GERMAN/SWABIAN   Not as atmospheric as Die Ecke, this is nonetheless a local and enduring favorite with good food and decent prices. The large dining room, suitable for 60 persons, has welcomed diners since 1946, with very little change in the menu, the decor, or the ambience. Expect generous portions of well-prepared food such as sauerbraten, roasted pork, pork schnitzel; game dishes such as venison, pheasant, and rabbit; and fish such as filet of sole served with boiled potatoes and parsley. The beer foaming out of the taps here is Storchenbräu, and most visitors find that it goes wonderfully with the conservative German specialties.

Jakoberstrasse 26. ℭ **0821/3-08-70.** Reservations recommended. Main courses 20DM–30DM (€10.20–€15.35, $10–$15); set price menu 40DM (€20.45, $20). AE, MC, V. Tues–Sun 11:30am–2pm; Tues–Sat 6:30pm–1:30am.

Oblinger ⊛ CONTINENTAL   Near the cathedral, in the heart of the historic section, Oblinger is the best restaurant within the city. It's a charming, intimate 20-seat choice offering a changing array of seasonal specialties. The surroundings are unpretentious, the waiters attentive, and there's a superb collection of wine. You can savor the goose-liver terrine with mushrooms and cabbage, going on to an equally well-prepared sole roulade with crepes. The turbot with chanterelles and the stuffed Bresse pigeon are also successes—quite simply, the cuisine has personality.

Pfäarrle 14. ℭ **0821/345-83-92.** Reservations required. Main courses 22DM–42DM (€11.25–€21.45, $11–$21). AE, DC, MC, V. Daily 11am–2pm; Tues–Sat 6–11pm. Closed Aug 1–19. Tram: 12.

SEEING THE SIGHTS IN TOWN

Rathaus   In 1805 and 1809, Napoléon visited the Rathaus, built by Elias Holl in 1620. Regrettably, it was also visited by an air raid in 1944, leaving a mere shell of the building that had once been a palatial eight-story monument to the glory of the Renaissance. Its celebrated "golden chamber" was left in shambles. Now, after costly restoration, the Rathaus is open to the public.

Am Rathausplatz 2. ℭ **0821/3241.** Admission 4DM (€2.05, $2) adults, 2DM (€1, $1) children 7–14. Daily 10am–6pm. Tram: 1.

Dom St. Maria   The cathedral of Augsburg has the distinction of containing the oldest stained-glass windows in the world. Those in the south transept,

Tips **Exploring the Fuggerei**

Throughout its history, Augsburg has been an important city, but during the 15th and 16th centuries it was one of Europe's wealthiest communities, mainly because of its textile industry and the political and financial clout of its two banking families, the Welsers and the Fuggers. The Welsers, who once owned nearly all of Venezuela, have long since faded from the minds of Augsburgers. But the founders of the powerful Fugger family have established themselves forever in the hearts of townsfolk by an unusual legacy, the **Fuggerei** ⟨*, created in 1519 to house poorer Augsburgers. A master mason fallen on hard times, Franz Mozart (great-grandfather of Wolfgang Amadeus Mozart), once lived at Mittlere Gasse 14. The quarter consists of several streets lined with well-maintained Renaissance houses, as well as a church and administrative offices, all enclosed within walls. The Fugger Foundation still owns the Fuggerei.

The house at Mittlere Gasse 13, next to the one once occupied by Mozart's ancestor, is now the Fuggerei's **museum** (⟨ **0821/3198810**). The rough 16th- and 17th-century furniture, wood-paneled ceilings and walls, and cast-iron stove, as well as other objects of everyday life, show what it was like to live there in earlier times. Admission is 1DM (€0.50, 50¢). It's open from March to October, daily from 9am to 6pm. Take tram no. 1.

dating from the 12th century, depict Old Testament prophets in a severe but colorful style. They are younger than the cathedral itself, which was begun in 944. You'll find the ruins of the original basilica in the crypt beneath the west chancel. Partially Gothicized in the 14th century, the church stands on the edge of the park, which also fronts the **Episcopal Palace,** where the basic Lutheran creed was presented at the Diet of Augsburg in 1530. The 11th-century bronze doors, leading into the three-aisle nave, are adorned with bas-reliefs of biblical and mythological characters. The cathedral's interior, restored in 1934, contains side altars with altarpieces by Hans Holbein the Elder and Christoph Amberger.
Hoher Weg. ⟨ 0821/31-66-353. Free admission. Mon–Sat 7am–6pm; Sun noon–6pm. Tram: 1.

Church of St. Ulrich and St. Afra ⟨* This is the most attractive church in Augsburg. It was constructed between 1476 and 1500 on the site of a Roman temple. The church and the dom, one Protestant, one Catholic, stand side by side, a tribute to the 1555 Peace of Augsburg, which recognized the two denominations, Roman Catholic and Lutheran. Many of the church's furnishings, including the three altars representing the birth and resurrection of Christ and the baptism of the church by the Holy Spirit, are baroque. In the crypt are the tombs of the Swabian saints, Ulrich and Afra.
Ulrichplatz 19. ⟨ 0821/34-55-60. Free admission. Daily 9am–6pm. Tram: 1.

Schaezlerpalais Facing the Hercules Fountain is the Schaezlerpalais, home to the city's art galleries. Constructed as a 60-room mansion between 1765 and 1770, it was willed to Augsburg after World War II. Most of the paintings are Renaissance and baroque. One of the most famous is Dürer's portrait of Jakob

Fugger the Rich, founder of the dynasty that was once powerful enough to influence the elections of the Holy Roman emperors. Other works are by local artists Hans Burgkmair and Hans Holbein the Elder; Rubens, Veronese, and Tiepolo are also represented.

Maximilianstrasse 46. ℂ 0821/3244125. Admission 4DM (€2.05, $2) adults, 2DM (€1, $1) children. Wed–Sun 10am–4pm. Tram: 1.

NEUSCHWANSTEIN ✸✸✸ & HOHENSCHWANGAU ✸✸: THE ROYAL CASTLES

The 19th century saw a great classical revival in Germany, especially in Bavaria, mainly because of the enthusiasm of Bavarian kings for ancient art forms. Beginning with Ludwig I (1786–1868), who was responsible for many Greek Revival buildings in Munich, this royal house ran the gamut of ancient architecture in just 3 short decades. It culminated in the remarkable flights of fancy of "Mad" King Ludwig II, who died under mysterious circumstances in 1886. In spite of his rather lonely life and controversial alliances, both personal and political, he was a great patron of the arts.

Although the name "Royal Castles" is limited to Hohenschwangau (built by Ludwig's father, Maximilian II) and Neuschwanstein, the extravagant king was responsible for the creation of two other magnificent castles, Linderhof (near Oberammergau) and Herrenchiemsee (on an island in Chiemsee).

In 1868, after a visit to the great castle of Wartburg, Ludwig wrote to his good friend, composer Richard Wagner: "I have the intention to rebuild the ancient castle ruins of Hohenschwangau in the true style of the ancient German knight's castle." The following year, construction began on the first of a series of fantastic edifices, a series that stopped only with Ludwig's death in 1886, only 5 days after he was deposed because of alleged insanity.

The nearest towns to the castles are **Füssen,** 3km (2 miles) away at the very end of the Romantic Road, and **Schwangau,** where accommodations can be found.

ESSENTIALS
GETTING THERE   By Train   There're frequent trains from Munich (trip time: 2½ hr.) and Augsburg (3 hr.) to Füssen. For information, call ℂ **01805/ 99-66-33.** Frequent buses travel to the castles.

By Bus   Long-distance bus service into Füssen from other parts of the Romantic Road, including Würzburg, Augsburg, and Munich, is provided by the **Deutsche Touring GmbH** bus EB189 or EB189E. For information and reservations, call ℂ **069/790-3281** in Frankfurt. Regional service to villages around Füssen is provided by **RVA Regionalverkehr Allgau GmbH** in Füssen (ℂ **08362/37771**). Its most important routing, at least for visitors to Füssen, includes about 14 orange, yellow, or white-sided buses that depart every day from Füssen's railway station for the village of Hohenschwangau, site of both Hohenschwangau Palace and Neuschwanstein Palace, a 10-minute ride. The cost of a one-way ticket to the village or to either of the two palaces is 4DM (€2.05, $2). For more information, contact the Füssen Tourist office.

By Car   Take B-17 south to Füssen, then head east from Füssen on B-17.

VISITOR INFORMATION   For information about the castles and the region in general, contact the **Kurverwaltung,** Kaiser-Maximilian-Platz 1, Füssen (ℂ **08362/938-50**), open from Monday to Friday 8am to noon and 2 to 5pm, Saturday from 10am to noon. Information is also available at the **Kurverwaltung,**

Rathaus, Münchenerstrasse 2, Schwangau (© **08362/8-19-80**). It's open from Monday to Friday 8am to 5pm.

WHERE TO STAY
In Hohenschwangau
Hotel Lisl and Jägerhaus   This graciously styled villa and its annex across the street sit in a narrow valley, surrounded by their own gardens. Most rooms have a view of at least one of the two royal castles, and some rooms open onto views of both. We prefer the rooms in the main building to the more sterile annex, but all are comfortable and have good, firm mattresses. Bathrooms, though small, are adequate, with shower stalls.

Neuschwansteinstrasse 1–3, D-87645 Hohenschwangau. © **08362/88-70**. Fax 08362/81-107. www.lisl.de. 47 units. 290DM (€148.25, $145) double. AE, DC, MC, V. Free parking. Closed Christmas and New Year's. **Amenities:** Good restaurant (Bavarian/international), cozy bar. *In room:* TV.

Hotel Müller Hohenschwangau   As if the yellow walls, green shutters, and gabled alpine detailing of this hospitable inn weren't incentive enough, its location near the foundation of Neuschwanstein Castle makes it even more alluring. Midsize rooms are inviting and have a bit of Bavarian charm, each with a good bed. The shower-only bathrooms are spotless. Nature lovers usually enjoy hiking the short distance to nearby Hohenschwangau Castle.

Alpseestrasse 16, D-87645 Hohenschwangau. © **08362/8-19-90**. Fax 08362/81-99-13. www. hotel-mueller.de. 43 units. 240DM–300DM (€122.65–€153.30, $120–$150) double; 420DM–600DM (€214.60–€306.60, $210–$300) suite. Rates include buffet breakfast. DC, MC, V. Free parking. Closed Jan–Feb. **Amenities:** 2 pleasant restaurants (Bavarian). *In room:* TV.

In or Near Füssen
AlstadHotel Zum Hechten   Family owners have maintained this impeccable guesthouse for generations—it's one of the oldest (and most comfortable) in town. In spring, you'll open your window to a flower box of geraniums, and feel like Gretel (or Hansel) getting ready to milk the cows. Rooms are small to medium size; the bathrooms are spotless but a bit cramped, containing shower stalls. Corridor bathrooms are adequate and well maintained.

Ritterstrasse 6, D-87629 Füssen. © **08362/91-600**. Fax 08362/91-6099. www.hotel-hechten.com. 35 units, 29 with bathroom. 110DM–140DM (€56.20–€71.55, $55–$70) double without bathroom; 130DM–150DM (€66.45–€76.65, $65–$75) double with bathroom. Rates include buffet breakfast. AE, V. Free outside parking, 5DM (€2.55, $2.50) garage. **Amenities:** 2 restaurants (Bavarian/Swabian). *In room:* TV.

Hotel Christine   The Christine, 5 minutes by taxi from the train station in Füssen, is one of the best local choices for accommodation. The staff spends the winter months refurbishing the rooms so they'll be fresh and sparkling for spring visitors. A Bavarian charm pervades the hotel, and rooms are cozy, though hardly fit for King Ludwig. Each is well maintained and supplied with firm German mattresses. The shower-only bathrooms are a bit cramped. Breakfast, the only meal offered, is served on beautiful regional china as classical music plays in the background.

Weidachstrasse 31, D-87629 Füssen. © **08362/72-29**. Fax 08362/940554. 13 units. 170DM–230DM (€86.85–€117.55, $85–$115) double. Rates include breakfast. No credit cards. Closed Jan 15–Feb 15. *In room:* TV.

Seegasthof Weissensee   The hotel is good but the view is better. The paneled rooms at this hotel have sliding glass doors opening onto a balcony overlooking the lake, 6.5km (4 miles) from central Füssen on B-310. Each room has a minibar stocked with beer, wine, and champagne. Owners are extra careful about the comfort of their guests, maintaining quality mattresses in the small but very well-maintained rooms. Bathrooms, also small, are well kept with shower stalls. Breakfast is an appetizing and generous meal of cheese, cold cuts, bread, pastry, eggs, and beverages.

An der B-310, D-87629 Füssen-Weissensee. ℂ 08362/91780. Fax 08362/917888. 19 units. 136DM (€69.50, $68) double. Rates include breakfast. No credit cards. Free parking. **Amenities:** Restaurant. *In room:* TV, minibar.

Steig Mühle ⟨*Value* Owners and hosts Gunter and Nedwig Buhmann like things to be cozy, and their chaletlike guesthouse is almost a cliché of Bavarian charm. The rooms open onto a view of the lake or mountains, and many have their own balconies. Each room has been outfitted with double or twin beds and firm mattresses. Private bathrooms (shower only) are well kept. There aren't a lot of frills, but the place offers one of the most exceptional hotel values in the area.

Alte Steige 3, D-87629 Weissensee-Oberkirch. ℂ 08362/91-76-0. Fax 08362/31-48. 13 units. 110DM–120DM (€56.20–€61.30, $55–$60) double. Rates include buffet breakfast. No credit cards. Free outside parking, 4.50DM (€2.30, $2.25) in garage. From Füssen, take Route B310 north toward Kempten, a 5-minute drive. *In room:* None.

WHERE TO DINE
Fischerhütte SEAFOOD   In the hamlet of Hopfen am See, at the edge of the lake within sight of dramatic mountain scenery 5km (3 miles) northwest of Füssen, lie four old-fashioned dining rooms, plus a terrace in summer. As the name "Fisherman's Cottage" suggests, the establishment specializes in an array of international fish dishes: half an Alaskan salmon (for two); a garlicky version of French bouillabaisse; fresh alpine trout, pan-fried or with aromatic herbs in the style of Provence; North Atlantic lobster; and grilled halibut. A few meat dishes are also offered, as well as tempting desserts. The food is well-prepared and top rate.

Uferstrasse 16, Hopfen am See. ℂ 08362/91-97-0. Reservations recommended. Main courses 30DM–45DM (€15.35–€23, $15–$23). AE, DC, MC, V. Daily 11am–2pm and 6–10pm. Closed Tues in Jan–Mar.

Zum Schwanen SWABIAN/BAVARIAN   This small, old-fashioned restaurant serves a conservative yet flavor-filled blend of Swabian and Bavarian specialties. Good-tasting and hearty specialties include homemade sausage, roast pork, lamb, and venison. Expect robust flavors and a crowd of cheery diners who don't believe in the Weight Watchers packaged dinner.

Brotmarkt 4, Füssen. ℂ 08362/61-74. Reservations required. Main courses 15DM–35DM (€7.65–€17.94, $8–$18). AE, DC, V. Tues–Sun noon–2pm; Tues–Sat 6:30–10pm. Closed Nov.

VISITING THE ROYAL CASTLES
There are often very long lines in summer, especially August. With 25,000 people a day visiting, the wait in peak summer months can be as long as 4 or 5 hours for a 20-minute tour. The telephone number for Neuschwanstein is ℂ **08362/8-10-35,** for Hohenschwangau, ℂ **08362/8-11-27.**

Neuschwanstein ✮✮✮
This is the fairy-tale castle of Ludwig II. Construction went on for 17 years, until the king's death, when all work stopped, leaving a part of the interior uncompleted. Ludwig lived here on and off for about 6 months from 1884 to 1886.

The doorway off the left side of the vestibule leads to the king's apartments. The study, like most of the rooms, is decorated with wall paintings showing scenes from the Nordic legends (which inspired Wagner's operas). The theme of the study is the Tannhäuser saga, painted by J. Aigner. The curtains and chair coverings are in hand-embroidered silk, designed with the Bavarian coat of arms.

From the vestibule, you enter the throne room through the doorway at the opposite end. This hall, designed in Byzantine style by J. Hofmann, was never completed. The floor, a mosaic design, depicts the animals of the world. The columns in the main hall are the deep copper red of porphyry.

The king's bedroom is the most richly carved and decorated in the entire castle—it took 4½ years to complete. Aside from the mural showing the legend of Tristan and Isolde, the walls are decorated with panels carved to look like Gothic windows. In the center is a large wooden pillar completely encircled with gilded brass sconces. The ornate bed is on a raised platform with an elaborately carved canopy.

The fourth floor of the castle is almost entirely given over to the **Singer's Hall,** the pride of Ludwig II and all of Bavaria. Modeled after the hall at Wartburg, where the legendary song contest of Tannhäuser supposedly took place, this hall is decorated with marble columns and elaborately painted designs interspersed with frescoes depicting the life of Parsifal.

The castle is open year-round, and in September, visitors have the additional treat of hearing Wagnerian concerts and other music in the Singer's Hall. For information and reservations, contact the tourist office in Schwangau, **Verkehrsamt,** at the Rathaus (℅ **08362/8-19-80**). The castle, which is seen by guided tour, is open daily from April to September 9am to 5:30pm, from October to March 10am to 4pm. Admission is 14DM (€7.15, $7) for adults, 9DM (€4.60, $4.50) for students and seniors over 65; children 13 and under enter free.

Reaching Neuschwanstein involves a steep 0.8-km (half-mile) climb from the parking lot of Hohenschwangau Castle, about a 25-minute walk for the energetic, an eternity for anybody else. To cut down on the climb, you can take a bus to Marienbrücke, a bridge that crosses over the Pollat Gorge at a height of 93m (305 ft.). From that vantage you, like Ludwig, can stand and meditate on the glories of the castle and its panoramic surroundings. If you want to photograph the castle, don't wait until you reach the top, where you'll be too close. It costs 4DM (€2.05, $2) for the bus ride up to the bridge or 2DM (€1, $1) if you'd like to take the bus back down the hill. From the Marienbrücke Bridge it's a 10-minute walk to Neuschwanstein over a very steep footpath that is not easy to negotiate for anyone who has trouble walking up or down precipitous hills.

The most colorful way to reach Neuschwanstein is by horse-drawn carriage, costing 10DM (€5.10, $5) for the ascent, 5DM (€2.55, $2.50) for the descent. However, some readers have objected to the rides, complaining that too many people are crowded in.

Hohenschwangau ✴✴

Not as glamorous or spectacular as Neuschwanstein, the neo-Gothic Hohenschwangau Castle nevertheless has a much richer history. The original structure dates back to the 12th-century knights of Schwangau. When the knights faded away, the castle began to do so too, helped along by the Napoleonic Wars. When Ludwig II's father, Crown Prince Maximilian (later Maximilian II), saw the castle in 1832, he purchased it and 4 years later had completely restored it. Ludwig II spent the first 17 years of his life here and later received Richard Wagner in its chambers, although Wagner never visited Neuschwanstein on the hill above.

The rooms of Hohenschwangau are styled and furnished in a much heavier Gothic mode than those in Ludwig's castle and are typical of the halls of medieval knights' castles. Also unlike Neuschwanstein, this castle has a comfortable look about it, as if it actually were a home, not just a museum. The small chapel, once a reception hall, still hosts Sunday Mass. The suits of armor and the Gothic arches set the stage. Among the most attractive chambers is the **Hall of the Swan Knight,** named for the wall paintings that tell the saga of Lohengrin.

Hohenschwangau is open daily from March 15 to mid-October 8:30am to 5:30pm, off-season from 9:30am to 4pm. Admission is 14DM (€7.15, $7) adults and 9DM (€4.60, $4.50) children 12 to 15 and seniors over 65; free for children 11 and under . Several parking lots nearby enable you to leave your car while visiting both castles.

OUTDOOR ACTIVITIES IN THE AREA

Most visitors come to Füssen for views of its magnificent Bavarian castles, testimonials to the megalomania of a demented king. But if you want to get away from the grandeur of his dreams, nearby Forggensee and Hopfensee provide lots of opportunities for windsurfing, swimming, and sailing. The focal points for all of these include the Forggensee's **Yachtschule Forggensee,** Seestrasse 10, 87669 Rieden (*C* **08367/471**), and the Hopfensee's **Selbach Bootsvermietung,** Höhenstrasse 51, 87629 Hopfen (*C* **08362/1487**). At both of these sites, instruction for, and rentals of, windsurfers and sailboats are available.

There's also a limited amount of midwinter skiing available in the area, at lower altitudes and with less reliable snowfall, than that which prevails at more visible resorts such as Garmisch. About 6.5km (4 miles) from Füssen, the **Schigebiet Tegelberg,** near the hamlet of Schwangau (*C* **08362/98-36-0**), provides a half-dozen lifts and a cable car that ascend the slopes of the Tegelberg.

Frankly, your best bet for recreation, diversion, and distraction will probably involve hiking and hill climbing in the foothills around Füssen and Schwangau. Maps, guide services, and hiking-related information of all kinds are available from the local tourist offices.

A SIDE TRIP TO WIESKIRCHE

A fascinating excursion is to the **Wieskirche** *R* (*C* **08861/8173**), one of the most extravagant and flamboyant rococo buildings in the world, a masterpiece of Dominikus Zimmermann. On the slopes of the Ammergau Alps, between Ammer and Lech, the Wieskirche is a noted pilgrimage church, drawing visitors from all over the globe. It's in an alpine meadow just off the Romantic Road near Steingaden. Ask at the tourist office for a map and the exact location before setting out. The church, which in German means "in the meadows," was built to honor the memory of Jesus Scourged. With the help of his brother, Johann Baptist, Zimmermann worked on the building from 1746 to 1754. Around the choir, the church has "upside-down" arches, and its ceiling is richly frescoed. Hours are daily from 8am to 7pm. A bus heading for the church leaves Füssen from Monday to Saturday at 11:15am and on Sunday at 1:05pm. You can return on the 3:50pm bus from the church. The trip takes an hour and costs 18DM (€9.20, $9) round-trip.

8

Greece

by Sherry Marker

The "glory that was Greece" continues to lure visitors to see the Acropolis in Athens; Olympia, where the games began; Delphi, with the magnificent temple of Apollo; Mycenae, where Agamemnon met his bloody death when he returned home from Troy; and Epidauros, with its astonishingly well-preserved ancient theater. There's also a profusion of less well-known ancient sites—such as Nemea, home to a newly restored stadium—as well as a wealth of Byzantine monuments, including the churches of Daphni and Osios Loukas. Greece is the quintessential land of mountains and seashore, where you can laze the day away on a perfect beach before dancing the night away on Mykonos or Santorini or one of the other breathtakingly beautiful "isles of Greece."

1 Athens

Athens is the city that Greeks love to hate, complaining that it's too expensive, too crowded, and too polluted. Some 40% of Greece's population lives here, and with five million inhabitants, a rumored 17,000 taxis, and streets so congested you'll suspect that each of those five million Athenians has a car, the city is bursting at the seams. Work on the Metro proceeds at a snail's pace, with the tunneling disrupting traffic in much of central Athens. So, why are you here? Because you, too, will probably soon develop a love-hate relationship with Athens, snarling at the traffic and gasping in wonder at the Acropolis, fuming at the taxi driver who tries to overcharge you, and marveling at the stranger who realizes that you're lost and walks several blocks out of his way to take you where you're going.

Allow yourself some time to make haste slowly in Athens. Your best moments may come at a small cafe, sipping a tiny cup of the sweet sludge that Greeks call coffee, or getting hopelessly lost in the Plaka—only to find yourself in the shady courtyard of an old church. With only a little planning, you should find a good hotel, eat well in convivial restaurants, and leave Athens expecting to return, as the Greeks say, *Tou Chronou:* next year.

ESSENTIALS

GETTING THERE   By Plane   The new **Athens International Airport Eleftherios Venizelos** (✆ **01/353-0000;** www.aia.gr), 27 kilometers (17 miles) northeast of Athens at Spata, opened in 2001. At press time, it was unclear to what extent the new airport would be fully operational, and major problems have beset virtually every aspect of the airport. The airport's website and official publications cannot be relied on for accurate information. Until the direct six-lane link road and Metro link are completed, hopefully by the summer Olympics in 2004, expect a journey of at least an hour on traffic-clogged secondary roads into Athens. A taxi into central Athens can cost 5,000 to 8,000Dr

(€14.70 to €23.50, $14 to $23). Bus service to Syntagma Square or to Piraeus costs 1,000Dr (€2.95, $2.90). Officially, there is one bus to Syntagma and one to Piraeus every hour. *Note:* If you decide to take a taxi, ask an airline official or a policeman what the fare should be, and let the taxi driver know that you have been told the official rate before you begin your journey. If you are taking a taxi to the airport, try to have the desk clerk at your hotel order it for you well in advance of your departure. Many taxis refuse to go to the airport, fearing that they will have a long wait before they get a return fare.

Most flights arrive at the Main Terminal, which has both an "A" and "B" area, but some flights arrive and depart from Spata's first of a projected cluster of satellite terminals. When planning your carry-on luggage, keep in mind that you may have quite a trek from your arrival point to the baggage claim area. Tourist information, currency exchange, post office, baggage storage (left luggage), and car rentals are available at the Arrivals level of the Main Terminal. ATMs, telephones, toilets, and luggage carts are available at the baggage claim area. There are also several free phones from which you can call for a porter. *Note:* porter's fees are highly negotiable.

There have been frequent complaints that adequate information on arrivals, departures, cancellations, delays, and gate changes is not always posted on the flight information screens. Nonetheless, it is important to check these screens, and at the information desks, as there are *no* flight announcements.

By Train   Trains from the west, including Eurail connections via Patra, arrive at the **Peloponnese Station (Stathmos Peloponnissou),** about 1.5km (1 mile) northwest of Omonia Square. Trains from the north arrive 3 blocks north at the **Larissa Station (Stathmos Larissis),** on the opposite side of the tracks from the Peloponnese Station. If you are making connections from one station to the other, allow 10 to 15 minutes for the walk. Both stations have currency-exchange offices that are usually open daily from 8am to 9pm and a luggage-storage office usually open from 6am to 9pm that charges 500Dr (€1.47, $1.45) per bag per day. A taxi into the center of town from either station should cost about 1,000Dr (€2.95, $2.90).

By Boat   Athens's main seaport, **Piraeus,** 11km (7 miles) southwest of Athens, is a 15-minute subway ride from Monastiraki and Omonia squares. The subway runs from about 5am to midnight and costs 250Dr (€0.75, 75¢).

VISITOR INFORMATION   Tourist Office   The Greek National Tourist Organization (EOT, also known as the Hellenic Tourism Organization) has its central office on the ground floor at 2 Amerikis St. (© **01/331-0437** or 01/331-0562), 2 blocks west of Syntagma Square between Stadiou and Venizelou. It's open weekdays from 9am to 7pm and Saturday 9:30am to 2pm (closed holidays). No sign identifies the building as an EOT office, but there's a

Athens

EXARCHIA

Tossitsa

Patission (28 Octobriou)

Stournari

Solomou

Kapodistriou

Marni

Tritis Septembriou

Veranzerou

Omonia
Square

Themistokleous

Benaki

Zoodochou Pighis

Navarinou

Aladimias

Panepistimiou (Eleftheriou Venizelou)

National Library

University

Academy of
Arts & Letters

Stadiou

Eolou (Aiolou)

Stadiou

Itiadou

Praxitelous

Kolokotroni

Perikleos

Lekka

Karayioryi Servias

Ermou

Ermou

Mitropoleos

Apollonos

Voulis

Nikis

Filellinon

Nikodimou

Adrianou

PLAKA

Kidathineon

Tripodon

Dedalou

Thespidos

Lysikratous

Vyronos

Amalias

Vas. Olgas

ZAPPION
PARK

Temple of
Olympian Zeus

Methonis

Aressou

Dervenakiou

Arachevis

Kallidromiou

Strefi
Hill

Vatatzi

Voulgaroktonou

Tsimiski

Issauron

Smolenski

NEAPOLIS

Trikoupi

Mavromihali

Ippokratous

N. Ouranou

Dafnomilis

Chersonos

Sarantapichou

Tsimiski

Mount Likavitos
(Lycabettus)

Askilepiou

Skoufa

Massalias

Sina

Solonos

Omirou

Didotou

Amerikis

Dimokritou

Navarinou

Voukourestiou

Pindarou

Skoufa

Anagnostopoulou

Aristippou

KOLONAKI

Pat. Ioakim

Iroditou

Alopekis

Karneadou

Ypsilantou

Kanari

Merlin

Kolonaki
Square

SYNTAGMA

Syntagma
Square

Parliament

Vas. Sofias

Vas. Sofias

NATIONAL GARDEN

Presidential
Palace

Vas. Konstandinou

493

round sign with an I above the door. Information about Athens, free city maps, transportation schedules, hotel lists, and other booklets on many regions of Greece are available in Greek, English, French, and German—although many publications on popular sites seem to be perpetually out of print.

Websites   You can also get information on Greece from the Internet. Some of the most useful websites for general information on Greece include **www.phantis. com**, **www.in.gr**, **www.iboom.com**, **www.greece.gr**, and **www.culture.gr**. For information on ancient Greece and antiquities, try www.perseus.tufts.edu or www.ancientgreece.com. For what's going on in Athens and most of Greece, check out **http://athensnews.dolnet.gr**, the site of the English language newspaper the *Athens News*. As yet, **www.gnto.gr**, the website of the Greek National Tourist Organization, is a disappointment.

CITY LAYOUT   If you, like the Greek mathematician Euclid, find it easy to imagine geometric forms, it will help you to think of Central Athens as an almost perfect equilateral triangle, with its points at **Syntagma (Constitution) Square, Omonia (Harmony) Square,** and **Monastiraki (Little Monastery) Square,** near the **Acropolis.** In government jargon, the area bounded by Syntagma, Omonia, and Monastiraki squares is defined as the commercial center, from which cars are banned (in theory, if not in practice) except for several cross streets. Most Greeks consider Omonia the city center, but visitors usually get their bearings from Syntagma, where the House of Parliament is. Omonia and Syntagma squares are connected by the parallel **Stadiou Street** and **Panepistimiou Street,** also called Eleftheriou Venizelou. West from Syntagma Square, ancient **Ermou Street** and broader **Mitropoleos Street** lead slightly downhill to Monastiraki Square. Here you'll find the **flea market,** the **Ancient Agora (Market)** below the Acropolis, and the **Plaka,** the oldest neighborhood, with many street names and a scattering of monuments from antiquity. From Monastiraki Square, **Athinas Street** leads north past the modern Market (the Central Market) to Omonia Square. Bustling with shoppers in the daytime, Athinas Street is best avoided at night, when prostitutes and drug dealers tend to hang out here.

In general, finding your way around Athens is relatively easy, except in the Plaka, at the foot of the Acropolis. This labyrinth of narrow, winding streets can challenge even the best navigators. Don't panic: The area is small enough that you can't go far astray, and its side streets, with small houses and neighborhood churches, are so charming that you won't mind being lost. One excellent map may help: the Greek Archaeological Service's **Historical Map of Athens,** which has maps of the Plaka and of the city center showing the major archaeological sites. The map costs about 1,200Dr (€3.55, $3.50) and is sold at many bookstores, museums, ancient sites, and newspaper kiosks.

GETTING AROUND   By Public Transportation   The **blue-and-white buses** run regular routes in Athens and its suburbs every 15 minutes from 5am to midnight. (For the more distant suburbs, you may need to change buses at a transfer station.) The **orange electric trolley buses** serve areas in the city center from 5am to midnight. The **green buses** run between the city center and Piraeus every 20 minutes from 6am to midnight, then hourly until 6am. Tickets cost 150Dr (€0.45, 45¢) and must be purchased in advance, usually in groups of 10, from any news kiosk or special bus ticket kiosks at the main stations.

When you board, validate your ticket in the automatic machine. Hold on to your ticket: Uniformed and plainclothes inspectors periodically check tickets and can levy a basic fine of 1,500Dr (€4.40, $4.30), or a more punitive fine of 6,000Dr (€17.60, $17) on the spot.

The **Athens map** distributed by the Greek National Tourist Organization indicates major public transportation stops and routes. Keep in mind that the buses are usually very crowded and their schedules are erratic.

The original **Metro** line links Piraeus, Athens's seaport; central Athens; and Kifissia, an upscale northern suburb. A second line, with its main station in Syntagma Square, links the Defense Ministry on Mesogheion Avenue with central Athens and the northwest suburb of Sepolia.

In the city center, the trains run underground, and the main stops are **Syntagma, Monastiraki, Omonia,** and **Viktorias (Victoria).** Trains run about every 5 to 15 minutes daily from 5am to midnight, with tickets at 250Dr (€0.75, 75¢). Validate your ticket in the machine as you enter the waiting platform or risk a fine. Metro and bus tickets aren't interchangeable.

By Taxi   Supposedly there're 17,000 taxis in Athens, but finding one empty is almost never easy. Especially if you have travel connections to make, it's a good idea to reserve a radio taxi.

When you get into a taxi, check to see that the meter is turned on and set on "1" rather than "2"; it should be set on "2" (double fare) only between midnight and 5am or if you take a taxi outside the city limits. (If you plan to do this, try to negotiate a flat rate in advance.) Unless your cab is caught in very heavy traffic, a trip to the center of town from the airport between 5am and midnight should not cost more than 3,000Dr (€8.80, $9). Don't be surprised if your driver picks up other passengers en route; he will work out everyone's share, and probably the worst that will happen is that you'll get less of a break than you would if you spoke Greek.

At press time, the minimum fare is 200DR (€0.60, 60¢), and the "1" meter rate is 62DR (€0.18, 18¢) per kilometer, with a surcharge of 150DR (€0.45, 45¢) for service from a port or rail or bus station, 300DR (€0.90, 90¢) for service from the airport, and a luggage fee of 100DR (€0.30, 30¢) for every bag over 10 kilograms (22 lb.). These prices will almost certainly be higher by the time you visit Greece.

There're about 15 radio taxi companies, including **Athina** (© 01/921-7942), **Express** (© 01/993-4812), **Parthenon** (© 01/581-4711), and **Piraeus** (© 01/418-2333-5). If you're trying to make travel connections or traveling during rush hours, the service will be well worth the 300Dr (€0.90, 90¢) surcharge.

If you suspect you've been overcharged, ask for help at your hotel or other destination before you pay the fare. Keep in mind that your driver may have difficulty understanding your pronunciation of your destination. If you are taking a taxi from your hotel, a staff member can tell the driver your destination or write down the address for you to show to the driver. If you carry a business card from your hotel, you can show it to the driver when you return. Most restaurants will

---

⟨Tips A Taxi Warning

There're increasing numbers of unlicensed cab drivers in Athens and Piraeus. Usually, these pirate cabbies (many from Eastern Europe) drive not the standard gray Athens taxi, but a gray car you might mistake for an Athens cab. It's always a good idea to make sure your cab driver has a meter and a photo ID.

also call for a taxi at no charge. The Hellenic Tourism Organization's pamphlet **"Helpful Hints for Taxi Users"** has information on fares as well as a complaint form.

On Foot Most of what you probably want to see and do in Athens is in the city center, allowing you to sightsee mostly on foot. All visitors should keep in mind that a red traffic light or stop sign is no guarantee that cars will stop for pedestrians. The pedestrian zones in sections of the Plaka, the commercial center, and Kolonaki make strolling, window-shopping, and sightseeing infinitely more pleasant than on other, traffic-clogged streets. Don't relax completely even on pedestrianized streets, though: Athens's multitude of kamikaze motorcycles seldom respects the rules.

By Car Parking is so difficult and traffic so heavy in Athens that you should use a car only for trips outside the city. Keep in mind that on any day trip (to Sounion or Daphni, for example) you'll spend at least several hours leaving and reentering central Athens.

Car-rental agencies in the Syntagma Square area include **Avis,** 48 Amalias Ave. (© **800/331-1084** in the U.S., or 01/322-4951); **AutoEurope,** 29 Hatzihristou St., right off Syngrou (© **01/924-2206; 800/223-5555** in the U.S.); **Budget,** 8 Syngrou Ave. (© **01/921-4711; 800/527-0700** in the U.S.). Prices for 1-day rentals range from 15,000 to 30,000Dr (€44.05–€88.05, $43–$86) and usually include unlimited mileage but not full insurance, which I strongly recommend. You can usually reduce the price considerably by booking from outside Greece; sometimes, especially in the off-season, on-the-spot bargaining is effective.

Warning: Most companies add, and do not always mention, the hefty surcharge for picking up or dropping off your car at the airport. And be sure to take full insurance; if you are renting with a credit card, check with your company to see exactly what, if any, insurance it provides.

FAST FACTS: Athens

American Express The office at 2 Ermou St., near the southwest corner of Syntagma Square (© **01/324-4975;** fax 01/322-7893), offers currency exchange and other services weekdays from 8:30am to 4pm and Saturday from 8:30am to 1:30pm.

Business Hours **Banks** are generally open from Monday to Thursday 8am to 2pm and Friday from 8am to 1:30pm. In winter, **shops** are generally open Monday and Wednesday from 9am to 5pm; Tuesday, Thursday, and Friday from 10am to 7pm; and Saturday 8:30am to 3:30pm. In summer, shops are generally open Monday, Wednesday, and Saturday from 8am to 3pm; and Tuesday, Thursday, and Friday from 8am to 1:30pm and 5:30 to 10pm. Note that many shops geared to visitors keep especially long hours, but some close from about 2 to 5pm. Most **food stores** and the **Central Market** are open Monday and Wednesday from 9am to 4:30pm, Tuesday 9am to 6pm, Thursday 9:30am to 6:30pm, Friday 9:30am to 7pm, and Saturday 8:30am to 4:30pm.

Currency The **drachma (Dr)** is the Greek national currency. The rate of exchange used to calculate the dollar values given in this chapter is $1 = about 350Dr. Amounts over $5 have been rounded to the nearest dollar. At press time, €1 = 340.75Dr and £1 = about 530Dr. Note that exchange rates fluctuate and may not be the same when you travel to Greece. Greece is scheduled to switch to using the euro on January 1, 2002. Until the change takes place, you will often see prices in both drachmas and in euros.

Currency Exchange Most banks have currency-exchange counters that use the rates set daily by the government, which are usually more favorable than those offered at unofficial exchange bureaus. It's worth doing a little comparison shopping for the best rate of exchange; for example, many hotels offer rates (usually only for cash) that are better than the official bank rates. ATM cash dispensers are increasingly common in Athens, and the National Bank of Greece operates a 24-hour ATM next to the tourist information office on Syntagma Square. It's not a good idea to rely on using ATMs exclusively in Athens because the machines are often out of service when you need them most: on holidays or during bank strikes.

Dentists & Doctors If you need an English-speaking doctor or dentist, call your embassy for advice; or try **SOS Doctor** (© 01/331-0310 or 01/331-0311). The English-language *Athens News* lists some American- and British-trained doctors and hospitals offering emergency services. Most of the larger hotels have doctors whom they can call for you in an emergency.

Drugstores Pharmakia, identified by green crosses, are scattered throughout Athens. Hours are usually from 8am to 2pm weekdays. In the evening and on weekends most are closed, but they usually post a notice listing the names and addresses of pharmacies that are open or will open in an emergency. The *Athens News* lists pharmacies open outside regular hours.

Embassies/Consulates **United States,** Leoforos Vas. Sofias 91 (© 01/721-2951; emergency number 01/729-4301); **Canada,** Odos Ioannou Yenadiou 4 (© 01/727-3400 or 01/725-4011); **United Kingdom,** Odos Ploutarchou 1 (© 01/723-6211); **Ireland,** Vas. Konstantinou 7 (© 01/723-2771); **Australia,** Leoforos Dimitriou Soutsou 37 (© 01/645-0404-5); **New Zealand,** Xenias 24, Ambelokipi (© 01/771-0112); **South Africa,** Kifissias 60, Maroussi (© 01/680-6645). Be sure to phone ahead before you go to any embassy; most are only open for business Monday to Friday 9am to noon and are usually closed on their own as well as Greek holidays.

Emergencies In an emergency, dial © **100** for fast **police** assistance and © **171** for the **Tourist Police.** Dial © **199** to report a **fire** and © **166** for an **ambulance** and **hospital.**

Internet Access Most cybercafes charge about 1,500Dr (€4.40, $4.30) an hour. The very efficient **Sofokleous.com Internet C@fe** , Stadiou 5, a block off Syntagma Square (© and fax **01/324-8105;** www.sofokleous.com), is open daily from 10am to 10pm. The **Astor Internet Cafe,** Odos Patission 27, a block off Omonia Square (© **01/523-8546**), is open from Monday to Saturday 10am to 10pm and Sunday 10am to 4pm. Across from the National Archaeological Museum is the **Museum Internet Cafe,** Odos Octobriou 28, also called Odos Patission (© **01/883-3418;** www.museumcafe.gr), open daily from 9am to 11pm.

Post Office The main **post offices** in central Athens are at 100 Eolou St., just south of Omonia Square, and in Syntagma Square on the corner of

Mitropoleos Street. They're open from Monday to Friday 7:30am to 8pm, Saturday 7:30am to 2pm, and Sunday 9am to 1pm. All the post offices can accept small parcels. The **parcel post office,** 4 Stadiou St., inside the arcade (✆ **01/322-8940**), is open from Monday to Friday 7:30am to 8pm. Parcels must be open for inspection before you seal them (bring your own tape and string) at the post office.

Telephone/Telegrams/Telefaxes The country code for Greece is **30.** The city code for Athens is **1;** use this code when you're calling from outside Greece. If you're within Greece, use **01.**

Many of the city's public phones now accept only **phone cards,** available at newsstands and OTE offices in several denominations starting at 1,700Dr (€5.02, $4.90). The card works for 100 short local calls (or briefer long distance or international calls). Some kiosks still have **metered phones;** you pay what the meter records. Local phone calls cost 20Dr (€0.06, 6¢). North Americans can phone home directly by contacting **AT&T** at ✆ **00-800-1311, MCI** at ✆ **00-800-1211,** or **Sprint** at ✆ **00-800-1411;** calls can be collect or billed to your phone charge card. You can send a telegram or fax from offices of the **Telecommunications Organization of Greece (OTE).** At press time, the OTE office at 15 Stadiou, near Syntagma, was temporarily closed, leaving the Omonia Square OTE office and the Victoria Square Office at 85 Patission St. as Athens's most central OTE offices.

Tipping Restaurants include a service charge in the bill, but many visitors add a 10% tip. Most Greeks don't give a percentage tip to taxi drivers but often round the fare out to the nearest 100Dr unit, add an extra 100Dr to a fare over 1000Dr, and add a bit more on a higher fare.

WHERE TO STAY

Warning: Hotel prices were accurate at press time, but price increases of 10% to 15% are rumored. Virtually all Greek hotels are clean and comfortable; few are charming or elegant. If shower and tub facilities are important to you, be sure to have a look at the bathroom: Many Greek tubs are tiny, and the showers hand held. Don't assume that just because a hotel says it has air-conditioning, the air-conditioning is working—and check to see if there's functioning central heating in the winter. And keep in mind that very few Greek hotel rooms have hair dryers or coffee- and tea-making facilities.

The area south and west of Syntagma Square and the neighborhoods of Plaka, Kolonaki, Koukaki, **Makriyanni,** and **Monastiraki** offer the most convenient and comfortable choices. For pure convenience, the **Syntagma** hotels and those in the lively **Plaka** area can't be beat. **Kolonaki** is an upscale neighborhood on the slopes of Mount Likavitos—but you'll have an uphill walk to your hotel. The **Koukaki** district, near Philopappos Hill and off the non-Acropolis side of Dionysiou Areopayitou Avenue, offers quiet residential back streets and the feeling of a real Greek neighborhood. From Koukaki, almost everything you want to do, including buying an English-language newspaper, involves extra walking.

IN PLAKA
Expensive
Electra Palace ✦   The Electra, just a few blocks southwest of Syntagma Square, is the most modern and stylish Plaka hotel; it even has a decent restaurant, and the

> ## *Tips* Planning Ahead
>
> If you're visiting Athens in the summer, **write or fax ahead of time for reservations** because the best-value hotels tend to be full then. If you arrive without a reservation, you can try to book a room at the tourist information booth at the airport, run by a private tourist agency and open from 7am to 1am; the agency charges a small fee. If you visit Athens in the off-season, especially in the winter, you may be pleasantly surprised at the not-always-publicized low rates available in even the most expensive hotels.

rooftop pool is a real bonus. Rooms are good size and have balconies. The top floors are where you want to be, both for the Acropolis view and to escape traffic noise. And that's the problem: the Electra won't guarantee you a top-floor room when you reserve, and if you sit on your balcony on one of the lower floors, you'll inhale lots of fumes, hear lots of traffic noise—and have a view of the building across the street. Still, you can always retreat to the rooftop pool and take in the Acropolis view there.

18 Nikodimou St., Plaka, 105 57 Athens. ☎ **01/324-1401** or 01/324-1407. Fax 01/324-1875. 106 units. 40,000–50,000Dr (€117.40–€146.80, $114–$143) double. Rates include breakfast. AE, DC, MC, V. **Amenities:** Restaurant, bar; rooftop pool. *In room:* A/C, TV, minibar, hair dryer.

Moderate

Acropolis House Hotel   Try to get room 401 or 402 for an Acropolis view in this small hotel in a renovated 150-year-old villa. The relatively quiet pedestrianized Plaka side street is a real plus, although motorcycles can be a problem. The newer wing (only 65 years old) isn't architecturally special, but the toilets (one for each room but across the hall) are fully tiled and modern. There's a washing machine (for a small fee; free after a 4-day stay). If the Acropolis House is full, try the less appealing Adonis or (still less appealing) Kouros.

6–8 Kodrou St., 105 58 Athens. ☎ **01/322-2344.** Fax 01/324-4143. 25 units, 15 with bathroom. 16,100 Dr (€47.25, $46) double without bathroom; 21,640Dr (€63.40, $59) double with bathroom. 4,000Dr (€11.75, $11) surcharge for A/C. Rates include continental breakfast. V. Walk 2 blocks out of Syntagma Sq. on Mitropoleos St. and turn left on Voulis, which becomes pedestrianized Kodrou. **Amenities:** Breakfast room. *In room:* A/C.

Byron Hotel   There's one real plus here: the relatively quiet central Plaka location just off recently pedestrianized Dionysiou Areopayitou Street. The price is fair (and often negotiable). That said, if you don't remember the dingy Byron before its remodeling last year, the new decor, which lacks charm, may not impress you. We've also had reports that the new air-conditioning is temperamental at best. Unfortunately, the same can be said for the service, which is usually haphazard and sometimes curt.

19 Vyronos St., 105 58 Athens. ☎ **01/325-3554.** Fax 01/323-0327. 20 units. 25,000Dr (€73.40, $72) double. Rates include breakfast. No credit cards. From Syntagma Sq., walk south on Amalias Ave. past Hadrian's Arch, stay right, and turn right on Dionysiou Areopayitou St.; Vyronos (Byron in Greek) is 2nd street on right, and hotel (with a portrait of Lord Byron by the door) is on right. **Amenities:** Breakfast room, bar. *In room:* A/C.

Hotel Nefeli ⋌   The charming little Nefeli, just steps from the main Plaka shopping and restaurant streets, was completely redecorated in 1998, with new beds and furniture. Rooms are small but comfortable, the quietest overlooking pedestrianized Angelikis Hatzimihali Street (although illegal motorcycle traffic can be a real problem at night). I have found the staff courteous and helpful, and friends who have stayed here say the same. We were, therefore, surprised by one reader's recent report of curt service, a noisy tour group, and a grubby bathroom, and look forward to hearing from other visitors here.

16 Iperidou St., 105 58 Athens. ℂ 01/322-8044. Fax 01/322-5800. 18 units. 15,000Dr (€44.05, $43) single; 21,200Dr (€62.25, $61) double. Rates include continental breakfast. AE, V. Walk 2 blocks west from Syntagma Sq. on Mitropoleos St., turn left on Voulis, cross Nikodimou St., and turn right on Iperidou. **Amenities:** Breakfast room. *In room:* A/C or ceiling fan.

Hotel Plaka ☆   This 10-year-old hotel—popular with Greeks, who prefer its modern conveniences to the old-fashioned charms of most other hotels in the Plaka area, as well as with gays—has a terrific location and fair prices. Many rooms have balconies. Fifth- and sixth-floor rooms in the rear (where it's usually quieter) have views of the Plaka and the Acropolis, also splendidly visible from the roof garden. Friends who stayed here recently weren't charmed by the service but found it adequate.

Mitropoleos and 7 Kapnikareas St., 105 56 Athens. ℂ **01/322-2096.** Fax 01/322-2412. plaka@tourhotel.gr. 67 units. 35,000Dr (€102.75, $100) double. AE, MC, V. Rates include breakfast. Follow Mitropoleos St. out of Syntagma Sq. past cathedral and turn left onto Kapnikareas. **Amenities:** Breakfast room, bar; roof garden. *In room:* A/C, TV.

NEAR MONASTIRAKI SQUARE
Moderate
Attalos Hotel ☆   One of the pleasures of staying at the Attalos is taking in the frenzied street life of the nearby Central Market. The nighttime scene is equally lively, but less attractive, with streetwalkers and drug dealers in evidence. Rooms are plain, but 44 have balconies. The roof garden offers fine views of the city and the Acropolis. The Attalos often gives a 10% discount to Frommer's readers.

29 Athinas St., 105 54 Athens. ℂ **01/321-2801.** Fax 01/324-3124. atthot@hol.gr. 80 units. 14,000Dr (€41.10, $40) single; 23,000Dr (€67.50, $66) double. Rates include buffet breakfast. AE, V. From Monastiraki Sq., walk about 1½ blocks north on Athinas St. **Amenities:** Breakfast room; free luggage storage. *In room:* A/C, TV, hair dryer (some rooms).

Jason Inn Hotel ☆☆   If you don't mind walking a few extra blocks to Syntagma, this is one of the best values in Athens, with an eager-to-help staff. You're just out of the Plaka, around the corner from the newly fashionable Psirri district, and steps from bustling Athinas Street. The recently renovated inn (admittedly on a very dull stretch of street) features attractive rooms with modern amenities and double-paned windows. If it's full, the staff may be able to find you a room in one of its other hotels: the similarly priced **Adrian,** in the Plaka, or the slightly less expensive **King Jason** or **Jason,** both a few blocks from Omonia Square.

12 Ayion Assomaton St., 105 53 Athens. ℂ **01/325-1106.** Fax 01/324-3123 or 01/523-4786. Douros@ hotelnet.gr. 57 units. 27,000Dr (€79.25, $77) double. Rates include American buffet breakfast. AE, MC, V. From Monastiraki Sq., head west on Ermou, turn right at Thisio Metro station, pass small below-ground-level church and bear left. **Amenities:** Breakfast room. *In room:* A/C, TV, minibar.

ON & AROUND SYNTAGMA SQUARE
Very Expensive
Hotel Grande Bretagne ☆☆   This venerable 1864 hotel with elegant beaux arts decor is an Athens landmark. Political and social movers and shakers pass through the lobby, with its ornately carved wood paneling, soaring ceilings, and polished marble floors, for power lunches at the popular GB Corner. (So, increasingly, do the tour groups staying here, which doesn't help the ambience.)

Be sure to avoid the courtyard rooms, most of which look the worse for wear and utterly lack the elegance of the front rooms, which have marvelous views over Syntagma Square and toward the National Gardens and Acropolis. If you go, check to see if the rumored renovations are underway, which will be nice in the long run, but disruptive while work goes on.

Syntagma Sq., 105 63 Athens. & 01/321-5555. Fax 01/322-0211. In the U.S. you can make reservations through Sheraton Hotels at & 800/325-3535. gbhotel@otenet.gr. 365 units, 33 suites. 52,500–121,500Dr (†153.80–†353.50, $150–$347) double; from 200,000Dr (†580.70, $572) suite. AE, DC, MC, V. Across from the Parliament Building in Syntagma Sq. Amenities: 2 restaurants, bar; concierge; business center; salon; 24-hour in-room service; same day dry cleaning/laundry. *In room:* A/C, TV, minibar.

N.J.V. Athens Plaza 🏵 The Athens Plaza, managed by the Grecotel group, reopened its glitzy doors in March 1998 after a complete remodeling. Many of the bedrooms—most with two king size beds, arm chairs, a desk, and table—are larger than our own living room, and many have balconies overlooking Syntagma Square. In short, a modern, up-to-date hotel with a superb location. Hardly a place where you'd expect bare wires dangling from the ceiling in your bathroom, or a bedside table with a small hole cut out of its side and covered in aluminum foil. Mysterious.

Syntagma Sq., 105 64 Athens. ✆ **01/325-5301**. Fax 01/323-5856. 207 units. 112,000–120,000Dr (€328.80–€352.20, $320–$345) double. AE, DC, MC, V. **Amenities:** 2 restaurants, 2 bars; exercise room; concierge; business center; 24-hour room service, same-day dry cleaning/laundry. *In room:* A/C, TV, minibar, hair dryer.

Expensive
Electra Hotel 🏵 *Value* If Ermou Street remains pedestrianized and the Electra sticks to its present rates, this hotel is excellent value, with a location that's both central (steps from Syntagma Square) and quiet (despite the presence of lots of tour groups). Most rooms, although not large, come with comfortable armchairs, large windows, and modern bathrooms; about half have balconies. The front desk is sometimes understaffed, but the service is generally acceptable. Off-season prices are usually considerably lower.

5 Ermou St., 105 63 Athens. ✆ **01/322-3223**. Fax 01/322-0310. electrahotel@ath.forthnet.gr. 110 units. 48,400Dr (€140.90, $138) double. Rates include buffet breakfast. AE, DC, MC, V. The Electra is about 2 blocks down on the left as you walk along Ermou with Syntagma Sq. behind you. **Amenities:** Restaurant, bar. *In room:* A/C, TV, minibar, hair dryer.

Moderate
Athens Cypria 🏵🏵 After extensive renovations, the former Diomia Hotel was reborn in 2000 as the Athens Cypria. Gone are the Diomia's gloomy lobby and rooms, but the very convenient central location on a street with (usually) no traffic and the splendid Acropolis views from nos. 603 to 607 remain. The halls and rooms have been painted bright white, the units have cheerful floral bedspreads and curtains, and the bathrooms are freshly tiled with all new fixtures. The breakfast buffet offers hot and cold dishes from 7 to 10am. The Cypria promises to be an excellent addition to Athens's moderately priced hotels in a neighborhood where most hotels cost more.

5 Diomias St., 105 62 Athens. ✆ **01/323-8034**. Fax 01/324-8792. 71 units. 29,000Dr (€85.10, $83) double. Reductions possible off-season. Rates include breakfast. AE, MC, V. Take Karagiorgi Servias out of Syntagma Sq.; Diomias St. is on the left, after Lekka St. **Amenities:** Breakfast room, bar, snackbar; luggage storage. *In room:* A/C, TV, minibar, hair dryer.

Hotel Achilleas The Achilleas (Achilles) has a great location on a relatively quiet side street steps from Syntagma Square, and was completely renovated in 2000. Rooms are good-size and light; some rear ones have small balconies.

Breakfast is served in the first-floor breakfast room, which has lots of green plants. The Achilleas's very central location and fair prices make it a good choice, but don't expect to be charmed by the service.

Odos Lekka 21, 105 62 Athens. (C) **01/323-3197.** Fax 01/322-2412. achilleas@tourhotel.gr. 34 units. 28,000Dr (€82.20, $80) double. Rates include breakfast. AE, DC, MC, V. With Hotel Grande Bretagne on your right, walk 2 blocks out of Syntagma Sq. on Karayioryi Servias and turn right into Lekka. **Amenities:** Breakfast room, snack bar, bar. *In room:* A/C, TV, minibar.

Inexpensive
Hotel Carolina (🌟 *(Value)* The Carolina, a 5-minute walk from Syntagma Square, has undertaken some badly needed renovations (including new firm mattresses and up-to-date bathrooms with constant hot water) which make it appealing for the young-in-heart, who will appreciate the low prices and house party atmosphere here that have made the place popular with generations of students. Bring your guitar—or ear plugs—and let us know what you think of the Carolina: this seems to be a place that people either love or hate.

Odos Kolokotroni 55, 105 60 Athens. (C) **01/324-3551.** Fax 01/324-3350. 31 units, 15 with shower and toilet. 14,000Dr (€41.10, $40) double without shower and toilet; 17,500–21,000Dr (€50.35–€61.65, $50–60) double with shower and toilet. AE, MC, V. Take Stadiou St. out of Syntagma Sq. to Kolokotroni St (on left). **Amenities:** Breakfast room.

IN KOLONAKI
Very Expensive
Saint George Lycabettus Hotel (🌟   As yet, the Saint George Lycabettus does not get many tour groups, which contributes to the tranquil tone here. The rooftop pool is a real plus, and the hotel is just steps from the chic Kolonaki restaurants and shops—but keep in mind that when you head back to the hotel, those steps are steeply uphill. The nicely appointed rooms look toward Mount Likavitos or a small park (some have views of both Likavitos and the Acropolis), although the surrounding street traffic keeps this from being a real oasis of calm.

2 Kleomenous St., 106 75 Athens. (C) **01/729-0711.** Fax 01/721-0439. www.sglycabettus.gr. 167 units. 58,500–83,300Dr (€171.40–€245.50, $168–$238) double. AE, DC, MC, V. From Kolonaki Sq., take Patriarchou Ioachim to Loukianou; follow Loukianou uphill to Kleomenous; turn left on Kleomenous; the hotel overlooks Dexamini Park. **Amenities:** Restaurant, bar; pool; concierge; 24-hour room service. *In room:* A/C, TV, minibar.

Moderate
Athenian Inn (🌟   Kolonaki is a fashionable residential and shopping neighborhood northeast of Syntagma at the foot of Mount Likavitos. The Athenian Inn is on a relatively quiet side street 3 blocks from Kolonaki Square, with its cafes, restaurants, and shops. The Inn has a loyal following, including many teachers, despite its small rooms (many of which do have small balconies). Between stays, I tend to forget how small the rooms are here, which suggests to me that the staff is doing a good job of making guests feel comfortable. A quote from the guest book: "At last the ideal Athens hotel, good and modest in scale but perfect in service and goodwill." Breakfast is served in the small ground-floor lounge, which has a fireplace, piano, and TV. Keep in mind that if you stay here, you will be doing a good deal of walking (some of it fairly steeply uphill) to get to and from the central attractions. Neighborhood doves coo vigorously at night, a sound you will probably find either soothing, or infuriating.

22 Haritos St., Kolonaki, 106 75 Athens. (C) **01/723-8097.** Fax 01/724-2268. 28 units. 38,000Dr (€111.55, $109) double. Rates include breakfast. AE, DC, V. From Syntagma Sq., go east on Vasilissis Sofias Ave. to Loukianou; turn left on Loukianou and take it 6 blocks uphill to Haritos. **Amenities:** Breakfast room. *In room:* A/C.

IN THE EMBASSY DISTRICT
Very Expensive
Andromeda Hotel ☆☆   The city's only boutique hotel is easily the most charming in Athens, with a staff that makes you feel that this is your home away from home. Rooms are large and elegantly decorated. This very quiet hotel overlooks the garden of the American ambassador's home, and has marvelous breakfasts and snacks (at present there is no restaurant). The only drawbacks: It's a serious hike (20–30 min.) or 10-minute taxi ride to Syntagma, and there are few restaurants in this residential neighborhood, although the superb Vlassis is just around the corner. If you're planning a long stay in Athens, check out the Andromeda's new (and very lovely) service apartments just across the street.

Odos Timoleontos Vassou 22 (off Plateia Mavili), 115 21 Athens. © 01/643 7302. Fax 01/646-6361. 42 units. 91,000–122,500Dr (€267.60–€360, $260–$350) double. Special rates sometimes available. AE, DC, MC, V. Amenities: Breakfast room, bar. In room: A/C, TV, minibar, hair dryer.

Athens Hilton ☆☆   The Athens Hilton, near the U.S. Embassy, is a brisk 10-minute walk from Syntagma Square. It's something of an Athenian institution, where businesspeople and diplomats meet for a drink or a meal. Rooms (looking toward either the hills outside Athens or the Acropolis) have large marble bathrooms and are decorated in the generic but comfortable international Hilton style. The Plaza Executive floor of rooms and suites offers a separate business center and higher level of service. The Hilton often runs promotions, so check about special rates before booking.

Leoforos Vas. Sofias 46, 11528 Athens. & 800/445-8667 in the U.S., or 01/728-1000. Fax 01/728-1111. Reservations: Athens@Hilton.com. www.hilton.com. 446 units. 129,500–156,000Dr (†378.50–†458, $370–$446) double. AE, DC, MC, V. Amenities: 3 restaurants, 3 bars; large pool; health club; concierge; executive business services; 24-hour room service; same day dry cleaning/laundry. In room: A/C, TV, minibar, hair dryer.

NEAR THE ACROPOLIS (MAKRIYANNI & KOUKAKI DISTRICTS)
Very Expensive
Divani-Palace Acropolis ☆☆   Just 3 blocks south of the Acropolis, in a quiet residential neighborhood (there's a handy Veropoulos SPAR supermarket a block away at 4 Parthenos St., as well as a shop at 7 Parthenos that sells American and English newspapers), the Divani Palace Acropolis does a brisk tour business, but is welcoming to independent travelers. The blandly decorated rooms are large and comfortable with generous-size bathrooms. (The breakfast buffet is more than generous.) A section of Athens's 5th-century B.C. defense wall is preserved behind glass in the basement. The same hotel group operates the **Divani Caravel Hotel,** near the National Art Gallery and Hilton Hotel at 2 Vas. Alexandrou Ave. (© **01/725-3725;** fax 01-725-3770).

19–25 Parthenonos St., Makriyanni, 117 42 Athens. & 01/92-22-2945. Fax 01/92-14-993. acropol@ otenet.gr. 253 units. 70,000–87,500Dr (†205.50–†250.50, $200–$250) double. AE, DC, MC, V. From Syntagma Square take Amalias Ave. to pedestrianized Dionysiou Areopagitou; turn left into Parthenonos; the hotel is on your left after about 3 blocks. Amenities: Restaurant, 2 bars; roof garden; small pool; concierge; business center; 24-hour room service. In room: A/C, TV, minibar, hair dryer.

Moderate
Acropolis View Hotel ☆   This nicely maintained hotel with a helpful staff is on a residential side street off Rovertou Galli, not far from the Herodes Atticus theater. The usually quiet neighborhood, at the base of Philopappos Hill, is a 10- to 15-minute walk from the heart of the Plaka. Rooms (most freshly painted each year) are small but clean and pleasant, with good bathrooms; 16 have balconies. Some, like no. 405, overlook Philopappos Hill, and others, like no. 407, face the Acropolis.

Rovertou Galli and 10 Webster St., 117 42 Athens. ☎ **01/921-7303.** Fax 01/923-0705. 32 units. 33,000Dr (€96.85, $95) double. Rates include generous buffet breakfast. Substantial reductions Nov–Apr 1. AE, MC, V. From Syntagma Sq. take Amalias Ave. to Dion. Areopagitou; head west past Herodes Atticus theater to Rovertou Galli St. Webster (Gouemster on some maps) is the little street intersecting Rovertou Galli St. between Propilion and Garabaldi. **Amenities:** Breakfast room, bar. *In room:* A/C, TV, minibar.

Art Gallery Hotel   As you might expect, this small hotel—in a half-century-old house that has been home to several artists—has an artistic flair (and a nice old-fashioned cage elevator). Customers tend to be loyal, with many on repeat visits. Rooms are small and plain, but comfortable. There's a nice Victorian-style breakfast room on the fourth floor.

Odos Erechthiou 5, Koukaki, 117 42 Athens. ☎ **01/923-8376.** Fax 01/923-3025. ecotec@otenet.gr. 22 units. 18,000Dr (€52.85, $52) double. Breakfast 1,700Dr (€5.02, $4.90). Hotel sometimes closed Nov–Mar; when open, prices reduced. AE, MC, V. **Amenities:** Breakfast room. *In room:* A/C, TV, ceiling fan.

Austria Hotel ⭐   This well-maintained hotel at the base of wooded Philopappos Hill is operated by a Greek-Austrian family, who will exchange your foreign money into drachmas, and can point you to the convenient neighborhood laundry. The Austria's rooms and bathrooms are rather spartan (the linoleum floors aren't enchanting) but tidy. There's a great view over Athens and out to sea (I could see the island of Aegina) from the rooftop, where you can sun or sit under an awning.

7 Mousson St., Filopappou, 117 42 Athens. ☎ **01/923-5151.** Fax 01/924-7350. austriahotel.com. 37 units, 9 with shower only. 30,000Dr (€88.05, $86) double with or without full bathroom. Rates include breakfast. AE, DC, MC, V. Follow Dionysiou Areopagitou St. around south side of Acropolis to where it meets Roverto Galli St.; take Garibaldi around base of Filopappou Hill until reaching Mousson St. **Amenities:** Breakfast room; rooftop terrace. *In room:* A/C, fax.

Inexpensive

Marble House Pension ⭐   Named for its marble facade, usually covered by bougainvillea, this small hotel, whose front rooms offer balconies overlooking quiet Zinni Street, is famous among budget travelers (including many teachers) for its friendly staff. When I visited in 2000, the hotel was being remodeled, and the owner said it would have all new bathrooms and bedroom furniture and minibars by the time you arrive. If you're spending more than a few days in Athens and don't mind being out of the center, this is a homey base. There's a satellite TV in the library/lounge.

35 A. Zinni St., Koukaki, 117 41 Athens. ☎ **01/923-4058.** Fax 01/922-6461. 17 units, 12 with bathroom. 14,000Dr (€41.10, $40) double with bathroom. Monthly rate 100,000Dr (€293.60, $285) Oct–March. No credit cards. From Syntagma Sq. take Amalias Ave. into Syngrou Ave; turn right into Zinni; the hotel is in the cul de sac beside the small church. **Amenities:** Luggage storage. *In room:* A/C, TV, minibar.

WHERE TO DINE

Athens has an astonishing number of restaurants and tavernas (and a growing number of fast-food joints) offering everything from good, cheap Greek food in plain surroundings to fine Greek, French, Asian, and other international cuisines served in luxurious surroundings. ***Warning:*** **Many Athenian restaurants do not accept credit cards.** If you want to pay with a credit card, double-check to make sure the restaurant will accept your card.

Most restaurants have menus in Greek and English, but many don't keep their printed (or handwritten) menus up to date. If a menu is not in English, there's almost always someone working at the restaurant who will either translate or rattle off suggestions for you in English. That may mean you'll be offered some fairly repetitive suggestions because restaurant staff members tend to suggest what most tourists request. In Athens, that means **moussaka** (baked eggplant casserole, usually with ground meat), **souvlakia** (chunks of beef, chicken, pork, or lamb grilled on a skewer), **pastitsio** (baked pasta, usually with ground meat and béchamel sauce), or **dolmadakia** (grape leaves, stuffed usually with rice and ground meat). Although all these dishes can be delicious, all too often restaurants catering to tourists serve profoundly dull moussaka and unpleasantly chewy souvlakia.

Mezedes (appetizers served with bread) are one of the great delights of Greek cuisine, and often can be enjoyed in lieu of a main course. Some perennial favorites include **tzatziki** (garlic, cucumber, dill, and yogurt dip), **melitzanosalata** (eggplant dip), **skordalia** (garlic sauce), **taramosalata** (fish roe dip), **keftedes** (crispy meatballs), **kalamaria** (squid), **gigantes** (large white beans in tomato sauce), **loukanika** (little sausages), and **oktopodi** (octopus).

If you're wondering what to use to wash all this down with, the most popular Greek table wine is **retsina.** It's usually white, although sometime rosé or red, and flavored with pine resin. In theory, the European Union now controls the amount of resin added, so you're less likely to come across the harsh retsina that some compare to turpentine. If you don't like the taste of retsina, try **aretsinato** (wine without resin).

If you want to find out more about Greek wine, pick up a copy of Dimitri Hadjinicolaou's *The A to Z Guide of Greek Wines* (Oenos O Agapitos Publisher). This handy pocket-sized Greek/English guide has illustrations of labels and information on vintages, and sells for about 2,400Dr (€7, $8).

When it comes time for dessert or a midafternoon infusion of sugar, Greeks usually head to a **zaharoplastion** (sweet shop). Consequently, most restaurants don't offer a wide variety of desserts. Almost all do serve fruit (stewed in winter, fresh in season), and increasingly, many serve sweets such as **baklava** (pastry and ground nuts with honey), **halva** (sesame, chopped nuts, and honey), and **kataifi** (shredded wheat with chopped nuts and lots of honey). All these sweets are seriously sweet. If you want **coffee** with your dessert, keep in mind that for Greeks, regular coffee usually includes a mere teaspoon of sugar. Sweet coffee seems to be about a fifty-fifty mixture of coffee and sugar. Watch out for the grounds in the bottom of the cup.

Greek **brandy** is a popular after-dinner drink (although—you guessed it—a bit sweet for non-Greek tastes), but the most popular Greek hard drink is **ouzo.** The anise-flavored liqueur is taken either straight or with water, which turns it cloudy white. You may see Greek men drinking quarter- and even half-bottles of ouzo with their lunch; if you do the same, you'll find out why the after-lunch siesta is so popular. There're many cafes (*ouzeri*) where ouzo, wine, and a selection of mezedes are served from breakfast to bedtime.

Tips **Eating Well**

To avoid the ubiquitous favorites-for-foreigners, you might prefer to tell your waiter you'd like to have a look at the food display case, often positioned just outside the kitchen, and then point out what you'd like to order. Many restaurants are perfectly happy to have you take a look in the kitchen itself, but it's not a good idea to do this without checking first. Not surprisingly, you'll get the best value and the tastiest food at establishments serving a predominantly Greek, rather than a transient tourist, clientele.

IN PLAKA

Some of the most charming old restaurants in Athens are in Plaka—as are some of the worst tourist traps. Here are a few things to keep in mind when you head off for a meal.

Some Plaka restaurants station waiters outside who don't just urge you to come in and sit down, but virtually pursue you down the street with an unrelenting sales pitch. The hard sell is almost always a giveaway that the place caters to tourists.

In general, it's a good idea to avoid places with floor shows; many charge outrageous amounts (and levy surcharges not always openly stated on menus) for drinks and food. If you get burned, stand your ground, phone the **Tourist Police** (✆ 171), and pay nothing before they arrive. Often the mere threat of calling the Tourist Police has the miraculous effect of causing a bill to be lowered.

Expensive

Daphne's ⍟⍟⍟ ELEGANT GREEK/NOUVELLE   There're frescoes on the walls of this neoclassical 1830s former home, a shady garden with bits of ancient marble found when the restaurant was built, and sophisticated Athenians at many tables. The cuisine here gives you all the old favorites (try the zesty eggplant salad) with new distinction, and combines familiar ingredients in innovative ways (delicious hot pepper and feta cheese dip). I could cheerfully just eat the hors d'oeuvres all night, but have also enjoyed the *stifado* (stew) of rabbit in *mavrodaphne* (sweet wine) sauce and the tasty prawns with toasted almonds. Most nights, there's a pair of strolling musicians, whose repertoire ranges from Greek favorites to "My Darling Clementine."

4 Lysikratous St. ✆ and fax **01-322-7971.** Main courses 4,500–8,500Dr (€13.20–€25, $13–$24), with some fish priced by the kilo. Daily 8pm–1am. Closed Dec 20–Jan 15. AE, DC, MC, V. From Syntagma Sq, head south on Amalias to Lysikratous (across from Hadrian's Gate).

Moderate

Eden Vegetarian Restaurant ⍟ VEGETARIAN   You can find vegetarian dishes at almost every Greek restaurant, but if you want to experience organically grown products, soy (rather than eggplant) moussaka, mushroom pie with a whole-wheat crust, freshly squeezed juices, and salads with bean sprouts, join the young Athenians and Europeans who patronize the Eden. The prices are reasonable if not cheap, and the decor is engaging, with 1920s-style prints and mirrors and wrought-iron lamps.

12 Lissiou St. ✆/fax **01/324-8858.** Main courses 1,800–2,900Dr (€5.29–€8.55, $5–$8). AE, DC, MC, V. Daily noon–midnight. From Syntagma Sq., head south on Filellinon or Nikis St. to Kidathineon, which intersects Adrianou St.; turn right on Adrianou and take Mnissikleos up 2 blocks toward the Acropolis to Lissiou.

Platanos Taverna ⍟⍟ TRADITIONAL GREEK   This taverna on a quiet pedestrian square has tables outdoors in good weather beneath a spreading plane tree ("Platanos" means plane tree). Inside, where locals usually congregate to escape the summer sun at midday and the tourists in the evening, you can enjoy looking at the old paintings and photos on the walls. The Platanos has been serving good *spitiko fageto* (home cooking) since 1932 and has managed to keep steady customers happy while enchanting visitors. If artichokes or spinach with lamb are on the menu, you're in luck: They're delicious. The house wine is tasty, and there's a wide choice of bottled wines from many regions of Greece.

4 Dioyenous St. ✆ **01/322-0666.** Fax 01/322-8624. Main courses 2,800–4,300Dr (€ 8.25–€12.65, $8–$12). No credit cards. Mon–Sat noon–4:30pm and 8pm–midnight. From Syntagma Sq., head south on Filellinon or Nikis St. to Kidathineon; turn right on Adrianou St., and take Mnissikleos up 1 block toward the Acropolis and turn right on Dioyenous.

Taverna Xinos ⭐ TRADITIONAL GREEK   Despite the forgivable spelling lapse, Xinos's business card says it best: "In the heart of old Athens there is still a flace [sic] where the traditional Greek way of cooking is upheld." In summer, there are tables in the courtyard; in winter, you can warm yourself by the coal-burning stove. While the strolling musicians may not be as good as the Three Tenors, they do sing wonderful Greek golden oldies, accompanying themselves on the guitar and bouzouki. (If you're serenaded, you may want to give the musicians a tip. If you want to hear the theme from *Never on Sunday,* ask for "Ena Zorbas.") Most evenings, tourists predominate until after 10pm, when locals begin to arrive.

4 Agelou Geronta St. ☎ 01/322-1065. Main courses 2,000–4,000Dr (€5.90–€11.75, $6–$11). No credit cards. Daily 8pm–anywhere from 11pm to 1am; sometimes closed Sun, usually closed part of July and Aug. From Syntagma Sq., head south on Filellinon or Nikis St. to Kidathineon; turn right on Angelou Geronta and look for the sign for Xinos in the cul de sac.

Inexpensive

Damigos (The Bakaliarakia) ⭐⭐⭐ GREEK/CODFISH   Since 1865, Damigos has been serving delicious deep-fried codfish and eggplant, as well as chops and stews for inveterate meat-eaters. This basement taverna serves wine from family vineyards. (If you like it, you can usually buy a bottle to take away.) There are few pleasures greater than sipping the white or rosé retsina while watching the cook turn out unending meals in his absurdly small kitchen. Don't miss the delicious *skordalia* (garlic sauce), equally good with cod, eggplant, bread—well, you get the idea.

41 Kidathineon St. ☎ 01/322-5084. Main courses 1,200–2,900Dr (€3.53–€8.55, $3.45–$8). No credit cards. Daily 7pm–anywhere from 11pm to 1am. Usually closed July–Sept. From Syntagma Sq., head south on Filellinon or Nikis St. to Kidathineon; Damigos is downstairs on left just before Adrianou St.

Kouklis Ouzeri (To Yerani) ⭐ GREEK/MEZEDES   Besides Kouklis Ouzeri and To Yerani, Greeks call this popular old favorite with its winding staircase to the second floor the "Skolario" because of the nearby school. Sit down at one of the small tables and a waiter will present a large tray with about a dozen plates of *mezedes*—appetizer portions of fried fish, beans, grilled eggplant, taramosalata, cucumber-and-tomato salad, olives, fried cheese, sausages, and other seasonal specialties. Accept the ones that appeal. If you don't order all 12, you can enjoy a tasty and inexpensive meal, washed down with the house krasi (wine). No prices are posted, but the waiter will tell you what everything costs if you ask. Now if only the staff could be just a bit more patient when foreigners are trying to decide what to order.

14 Tripodon St. ☎ 01/324-7605. Appetizers 600–1,500Dr (€1.78–€4.40, $1.75–$5.15). No credit cards. Daily 11am–2am. From Syntagma Sq., head south on Filellinon or Nikis St. to Kidathineon; take Kidathineon across Adrianou to Thespidos and climb toward the Acropolis; Tripodon is 1st street on right after Adrianou.

NEAR MONASTIRAKI SQUARE
Moderate

Abyssinia Cafe ⭐ GREEK   This small cafe in a ramshackle building has a nicely restored interior featuring lots of gleaming dark wood and polished copper. It faces a lopsided square where furniture restorers ply their trade. You can sit indoors or outside and have just a coffee, but it's tempting to snack on Cheese Abyssinia (feta cheese scrambled with spices and garlic), mussels and rice pilaf, or *keftedes* (meatballs).

Plateia Abyssinia, Monastiraki. ☎ 01/321-7047. Appetizers and main courses 1,000–2,500Dr (€2.95–€7.35, $2.90–$7). No credit cards. Tues–Sun 10:30am–2pm; often open evenings as well. Closed Mon. Usually closed for a week at Christmas and Easter, sometimes closed part of Jan and Feb. Abyssinia Sq. is just off Ifaistou (Hephaistos) St. across from the entrance to the Ancient Agora on Adrianou.

Tips Quick Bites

In general, the Syntagma Square area is not known for its food, but it has a number of places to get a snack. The **Apollonion Bakery,** 10 Nikis St., and the **Elleniki Gonia,** 10 Karayioryis Servias St., make sandwiches to order and sell croissants, both stuffed and plain. **Ariston** is a small chain of *zaharoplastia* (confectioners), with a branch at the corner of Karayioryis tis Servias and Voulis streets (just off the square) that sells snacks as well as pastries. **Floca** is another excellent chain of pastry shops, with 14 branches; there's one in the arcade on Panepistimiou Street near Syntagma Square and another just south of the Center for Acropolis Studies, at Makriyanni and Hatzihristou streets. As always, you pay extra to be served at a table.

For the quintessential Greek sweet loukoumades—round doughnut-centerlike pastries deep-fried and then drenched with honey and topped with powdered sugar and cinnamon—nothing beats **Doris,** 30 Praxiteles St. (a continuation of Lekka Street), a few blocks from Syntagma Square. If you're still hungry, Doris serves hearty stews and pasta dishes for absurdly low prices from Monday to Saturday until 3:30pm. **Aigaion,** 46 Panepistimiou St., is a good place to stop on the way to or from the National Archaeological Museum for some louk-oumades or creamy rice pudding. **Everest** is another chain worth try-ing; there's a branch 1 block north of Kolonaki Square at Tsakalof and Iraklitou streets. Also in Kolonaki Square, **To Kotopolo** ("the Chicken Place") serves succulent grilled chicken to take out or eat in. In Plaka, you'll find excellent coffee and sweets at the **K. Kotsolis Pastry Shop,** 112 Adrianou St., an oasis of old-fashioned charm in the midst of the souvenir shops. The **Orea Ellada** (Beautiful Greece) cafe is at the Cen-ter of Hellenic Tradition, opening onto 36 Pandrossou St. and 59 Mitropoleos St. near the flea market. You can revive yourself with a cappuccino and snack on pastries while you enjoy a spectacular view of the Acropolis.

Taverna Sigalas ⋆ TRADITIONAL GREEK   This longtime Plaka taverna, housed in a vintage 1879 commercial building with a newer outdoor pavilion, boasts that it is open 365 days a year. Its lively interior has huge old retsina kegs in the back and dozens of black-and-white photos of Greek movie stars on the walls. After 8pm nightly, there's Greek muzak. At all hours, Greeks and tourists wolf down large portions of stews, moussaka, grilled meatballs, baked toma-toes, gyros, and other hearty dishes, washed down with the house red and white retsinas.

Plateia Monastiraki 2. ⓒ 01/321-3036. Main courses 1,800–3,000Dr (€5.29–€8.80, $5.15–$9). No credit cards. Daily 7am–2am. Sigalas is across Monastiraki Square from the Metro station.

Inexpensive
Diporto GREEK   This little place, sandwiched between olive shops, serves up salads, stews, and delicious *revithia* (chickpeas), a Greek winter dish popular among stall owners, shoppers, and Athenians who make their way to the mar-ket for cheap and delicious food. If you like Diporto, try Papandreou, also in the

Central Market; the tripe soup here is reputed to cure all ailments, especially hangovers.

Athens Central Market. No phone. Main courses 900–2,500Dr (€2.65[nd€7.35, $2.60–$7). No credit cards. Mon–Sat 6am–6pm. From Syntagma Sq, follow Hermou to Athinas St; the Central Market is on the right side of the street.

Thanasis 𝒻𝒻 *Finds* GREEK/SOUVLAKIA   Thanasis serves souvlakia and pita and exceptionally good fries, both to go and at its outdoor and indoor tables; as always, the prices are higher if you sit down. On weekends, it often takes the strength and determination of an Olympic athlete to get through the door and place an order. It's worth the effort: This is both a great budget choice and a great place to take in the local scene, which often includes a fair sprinkling of gypsies, including some cute and very determined child beggars.

69 Mitropoleos St. ☎ 01/324-4705. Main courses 500–3,000Dr (€1.47–€8.80, $1.45–$9). No credit cards. Daily 9am–2am. Thanasis is on northeast corner of Monastiraki Sq. Hermou St. leads directly from Syntagma Sq. to Monastiraki Sq.

NEAR SYNTAGMA SQUARE
Moderate
Gerofinikas GREEK/INTERNATIONAL   For years, this was the place to go for a special lunch or dinner, and the food is still very good—which is why tour groups have, alas, discovered it. Still, it's always pleasant to walk down the passageway into Gerofinikas (the name means "the old palm tree"), look at the long display cases of tempting dishes, and try to decide between shrimp with feta cheese, rabbit stew with onions, and the tasty eggplant dishes—all the while keeping room for one of the rich desserts.

10 Pindar St. ☎ 01/363-6710. Reservations strongly recommended. Main courses 3,000–6,000Dr (€9.80–€17.60, $9–$17). Fixed-price menu 8,500Dr (€25, $24), not including beverage. AE, DC, MC, V. Daily usually noon–2pm and 7pm–midnight.

Inexpensive
Neon 𝒻 GREEK/INTERNATIONAL   This recent addition to the Neon chain is convenient, although not as charming as the original on Omonia Square. There is also a Neon a block north of Kolonaki Square at Tsakalof and Iraklitou. You're sure to find something to your taste—maybe a Mexican omelet, spaghetti Bolognese, the salad bar, or sweets ranging from Black Forest cake to tiramisu. If you're tired of practicing your restaurant Greek, the Neon restaurants are a good place to eat, since most things are self-service.

3 Mitropoleos St. (on the southwest corner of Syntagma Sq.). ☎ 01/322-8155. Snacks 200–700Dr (€0.60–€2.05, 45¢–$1.90); sandwiches 700–1,400Dr (€2.05–€4.10, $2–$4); main courses 1,000–4,200Dr (€2.95–€12.35, $2.90–$12). No credit cards. Daily 9am–midnight.

IN KOLONAKI
Expensive
To Kafeneio 𝒻𝒻 GREEK/INTERNATIONAL   This is hardly a typical *kafeneio* (coffee shop/cafe). If you relax, you can easily run up a substantial tab ($50 for lunch or dinner for two is easy), but you can also eat more modestly and equally elegantly. If you have something light, like the artichokes à la polita, leeks in crème fraîche, or onion pie, washed down with draft beer or the house wine, you can finish with profiteroles and not put too big a dent in your budget. I've always found this an especially congenial spot when I'm eating alone (perhaps because I love people-watching and profiteroles).

26 Loukianou St. ℂ **01/722-9056.** Main courses 2,000–7,000Dr (€5.90–€20.55, $6–$20). No credit cards. Mon–Sat 11am–midnight or later. Closed Sun and most of Aug. From Kolonaki Sq., follow Patriarkou Ioakim St. several blocks uphill to Loukianou and turn right to Kafeneio.

Moderate

Dimokritos GREEK   Overlooking the Church of Ayios Dionysios, this cozy taverna serves good food to lots of steady customers. The large menu features grilled veal, rabbit, fish, and lamb, and usually has excellent swordfish souvlaki. A variety of Greek salads and hors d'oeuvres are usually on display in a case by the entrance, and you can usually point out what you want for starters on your way to your table.

Odos Dimokritou 23 and Tsakalof. ℂ **01/361-3588.** Fax 01/361-9293. Main courses 4,700–5,500Dr (€13.80–€16.15, $14–$16). No credit cards. Mon–Sat 1–5pm and 8pm–1am. From Syntagma Sq. take Vas. Sofias Ave. to Akadamias Ave.; take Akadamias Ave. to Dimokritou; turn right into Dimokritou and climb until you see the Church of Ayios Dionysios. The restaurant is marked only by the word TAVERNA on the doors.

Rhodia ⌗ TRADITIONAL GREEK   This long-time taverna in a hand-some old Kolonaki house has tables in its small garden in good weather—although the interior, with its tile floor and old prints, is so charming that you might be tempted to eat indoors. The Rhodia is a favorite of visiting archaeologists from the nearby British and American Schools of Classical Studies, as well as of Kolonaki residents. It may not sound like just what you'd always hoped to have for dinner, but the octopus in mustard sauce is terrific, as are the veal and dolmades (stuffed grape leaves) in egg-lemon sauce. The house wine is excellent, as is the halva, which manages to be both creamy and crunchy.

Odos Aristipou 44. ℂ **01/722-9883.** Main courses 2,000–4,200Dr (€5.90–€12.35, $6–$12). No credit cards. Mon–Sat 8pm–2am. From Kolonaki Sq. take Patriarkou Ioakim uphill to Loukianou; turn left on Loukianou and climb steeply uphill to Aristipou; turn right on Aristipou.

To Ouzadiko ⌗⌗ GREEK/MEZEDES   This ouzo bar has at least 40 kinds of ouzo and as many mezedes, including fluffy *keftedes* (meatballs) that make all others taste leaden. This place is very popular with Athenians young and old who come to see and be seen while having a snack or a full meal, often after con-certs and plays. A serious foodie friend of mine goes here especially for the wide variety of *horta* (greens), which she says are the best she's ever tasted. If you see something you want and aren't sure of the name, let your waiter know, and it will appear for you.

Odos Karneadou 25–29 (in the Lemos International Shopping Center), Kolonaki. ℂ **01/729/5484.** Reserva-tions recommended. Mezedes and main courses 2,300–5,000Dr (€6.75–€14.70, $7–$14). No credit cards. Mon–Sat 9pm–12:30am. From Kolonaki Sq. take Kapsali St. across Irodotou St. into Karneadou St. The Lemos Center is the miniskyscraper on your left.

To Prytaneion GREEK/INTERNATIONAL.   The trendy bare stone walls here are decorated with movie posters and illuminated by baby spotlights. Wait-ers dressed mostly in black serve customers, glued to cellular phones; plates of some of Athens's most expensive and eclectic mezedes, including beef carpaccio, smoked salmon, bruschetta, and shrimps in fresh cream, as well as Greek olives and that international favorite, the hamburger. The decibel level here (conversa-tion, music) is often seriously high.

7 Milioni, Kolonaki. ℂ **01-364-3353-4.** Mezedes and snacks 2,000–7,000Dr (€5.90–€20.55, $6–$20). No credit cards. Mon–Sat 10am–3am.

AROUND OMONIA SQUARE & THE NATIONAL ARCHAEOLOGICAL MUSEUM

Expensive

Restaurant Kostoyannis ★★ *Finds* GREEK/SEAFOOD   It's not easy to simply walk into Kostoyannis and sit down: Just inside the entrance is a show-stopping display of shrimp, mussels, fresh fish, seemingly endless appetizers, tempting stews (*stifada*) in ceramic pots, and yards of chops that could almost make a dedicated vegetarian fall off the wagon. You can choose the items you'd like to sample, or you could make an entire meal just from the mezedes (appetizers), which I think are even better than the entrees. Don't be put off by this restaurant's slightly out-of-the-way location on a rather uninteresting street: It's well worth the trip.

37 Odos Zaimi ☎ 01/822-0624. Main courses 2,500–8,000Dr (€7.35 €23.50, $7–$23). No credit cards. Mon–Sat 8pm–2am. From Omonia Sq. take Patission (28 Oktovriou) toward the National Museum to Tositsa; turn right on Tositsa and then left on Zaimi.

Moderate

Athinaikon ★★ GREEK/OUZERIE   Not many tourists come to this favorite haunt of lawyers and businesspeople working in the Omonia Square area. You can have just some appetizers (technically, this is an ouzeri) or a full meal. Obviously, the way to have a reasonably priced snack is to stick to the appetizers, including delicious *loukanika* (sausages) and *keftedes* (meatballs) and pass on the more pricey grilled shrimp or seafood casserole. Whatever you have, you'll enjoy taking in the old photos on the walls, the handsome tiled floor, the marble-topped tables and bentwood chairs, and the regular customers, who combine serious eating with animated conversation.

2 Themistokleous St. ☎ 01/383-8485. Main courses 1,000–4,000Dr (€2.95–€11.75, $2.90–$11). No credit cards. Mon–Sat 11am–midnight. Closed Aug. From Omonia Sq., take Panepistimou St. a block to Themistokleous St.; the Athinaikon is almost immediately on your right.

Inexpensive

Taygetos *Value* GREEK/SOUVLAKIA   This is a great place to stop for a quick meal on your way to/from the National Archaeological Museum. The service is swift, and the souvlakia and fried potatoes are excellent, as are the grilled lamb and chicken (priced by the kilo). The menu sometimes also includes delicious *kokoretsi* (grilled entrails). The Ellinikon Restaurant next door is also a good value.

4 Satovriandou St. ☎ 01/523-5352. Main courses 1,500–3,000Dr (€4.40–€8.80, $4.30–$9). No credit cards. Mon–Sat 9am–1am. From Omonia Sq. take Patision (28 Oktovriou) toward the National Museum; Satovriandou is 3rd major turning on your left.

NEAR THE OLYMPIC STADIUM

Very Expensive

Bajazzo ★★ INTERNATIONAL   Bajazzo put Greek cuisine on the map when it won its Michelin star in 1998. Chef Klaus Feuerbach rightly says that two can eat here for $150, but I have friends who have eaten at Bajazzo and cheerfully spent almost twice that on the fine food and wine. Specialties include the feta tart, langostino souvlaki, kid with Peloponnesian herbs, and sea bass with mustard sauce. The menu changes from night to night.

1 Tyrteou and 14 Anapafseos sts., Mets. ☎/fax **01/921-3013**. Reservations required Fri–Sat, and always a good idea. Dinner for 2 from 52,500Dr (€154.15, $150). AE, DC, MC, V. Mon–Sat 8pm–1am. Take a taxi to this hard-to-find restaurant, off Ardittou St., south of the Temple of Olympian Zeus.

NEAR THE ACROPOLIS
Moderate
Socrates' Prison ☆ GREEK/CONTINENTAL   This long-time favorite has moved around the corner to a new location, where it remains an excellent place to head when you want good food near the Plaka, but want to avoid the frenzy of the central Plaka. The new place has a roof garden, a real plus for summer evenings. Greeks, as well as American and European expats living in Athens, love this place, with its tables outdoors in good weather and in the pleasant indoor rooms year-round. The food is somewhat more imaginative than average Greek fare (try the veggie croquettes) and includes continental dishes like salade Niçoise and vegetable-stuffed pork roll. The retsina is excellent, and there's a wide choice of bottled wines and beers.

17 Robertou Galli St. ☎ 01/922-3434. Main courses 3,000–4,500Dr (€8.80–€13.20, $9–$13). AE, DC, MC, V. Mon–Sat 11am–4pm and 7pm–1am. Closed Aug. From Syntagma Sq., take Amalias Ave. to pedestrianized Dionysiou Areopayitou St., walk away from Temple of Zeus on the side of Dionysiou Areopagitou across from the Acropolis, and turn left onto Mitseon and right into Rovertou Galli.

WORTH A (SHORT) TRIP
Expensive
Varoulko ☆☆☆ SEAFOOD/NOUVELLE   In an unlikely location on a side street in Piraeus, chef-owner Lefteris Lazarou has created what many consider not just the finest seafood restaurant, but the finest restaurant in the greater Athens area. I had one of the best meals in my life here—smoked eel; artichokes with fish roe; crayfish with sun-dried tomatoes; monkfish livers with soy sauce, honey, and balsamic vinegar—and the best sea bass and monkfish I have ever eaten. Everything is beautifully presented, and everything is delicious.

14 Deligeorgi, Piraeus. ☎ 01/411-2043. Fax 01/422-1283. Reservations necessary (arrange several days in advance). Dinner for 2 from 35,000Dr (€102.75, $100); fish priced by the kilo. No credit cards. Mon–Sat about 8pm–midnight. Closed Sun and most of June–Sept, when it often relocates outdoors at the Peace and Friendship Stadium. We recommend taking a taxi to this restaurant, which is hard to find and not in central Piraeus.

Vitrina ☆ NOUVELLE GREEK/INTERNATIONAL   This drop-dead-fashionable restaurant is one of several new hot spots in the old warehouse district of Psirri off Ermou Street. The walls are pale gold, the tablecloths and chairs are pale gray, and many of the young waiters and waitresses are aspiring actors and writers. The kitchen seems to try too hard with some dishes (shrimp in Muscatel and lavender sauce, for example), but the food is usually both delicious and beautifully presented, and there's a serious wine list. The fashion accessory of choice is a cellular phone—so useful for calling people at the next table—and almost no one arrives before 10pm.

7 Odos Navarchou Apostoli, in the Psirri district. ☎ 01/321-1200. Reservations necessary. Main courses 5,000–9,000Dr (€14.70–€26.40, $14–$26). No credit cards. Oct–May Tues–Sat about noon–4pm and about 8pm–midnight; Sun about noon–4pm; closed rest of year. We suggest that you take a cab here, as it's a good hike from Syntagma Sq. If you want to walk, from Syntagma Sq. take Ermou to Navarchou Apostoli.

Moderate
Vlassis ☆☆☆ TRADITIONAL GREEK   Greeks call this kind of food paradisiako—traditional, but paradisiacal is just as good a description. This very reasonably priced food is fit for the gods: delicious fluffy vegetable croquettes, eggplant salad that tastes like no other, hauntingly tender lamb in egg-lemon sauce. It's a sign of Vlassis's popularity with Athenians—each time I eat here, I seem to be the only obvious foreigner—that there's not even a discreet sign announcing its presence in a small apartment building on hard-to-find Paster. Figure the price of a taxi (no more than $10) into your meal tab; you may

feel so giddy with delight after eating you won't mind the half-hour walk back to Syntagma.

8 Paster St. (off Plateia Mavili). *(C)* **01/646-3060.** Main courses 2,000–5,000Dr (€5.90–€14.70, $6–$14). No credit cards. Mon–Sat 8pm–1am. Closed much of June–Sept. Since Vlassis is not easy to find, we suggest that you take a cab. If you want to walk, from Syntagma Sq., take Vas. Sophias Ave. to Plateia Mavili; follow D. Soustou out of Plateia Mavili to Chatzikosta; Paster is the cul de sac on left after you turn right into Chatzikosta.

Zeidoron ✫✫ GREEK/MEZEDES   This *mezedopolio* (hors d'oeuvres place) is one of a number of restaurants springing up in the old warehouse district of Psirri, now on the verge of being reclaimed. There are lots of delicious mezedes to choose from, including vegetable croquettes, several eggplant dishes, and some heartier meat dishes, like pork in mustard. You can have a varied and delicious meal—and keep the price tab reasonable—by avoiding the more expensive mezedes like shrimp. There's a wide variety of wines, beers, and ouzos. And, you can take in the passing scene, which gets more and more lively as the night wears on and Athens' young beautiful people hit the street with their cell phones and Prada gear.

10 Taki and Ayios Anaryiron. *(C)* **01/321-5368.** www.psirri.gr/zeidoron. Main courses 2,000–5,000Dr (€5.90–€14.70, $6–$14). No credit cards. Mon–Sat 11am to at least midnight. Closed Aug. We suggest that you take a cab, as Zeidoron is not easy to find. If you do walk, from Syntagma Sq. take Ermou to Navarchou Apostoli, which runs into Taki, which intersects Ayios Anayiron.

SEEING THE SIGHTS
SIGHTSEEING SUGGESTIONS FOR FIRST-TIME VISITORS

If You Have 1 Day Try to be at the **Acropolis** as soon as it opens so that you can take in the site and enjoy seeing the **Parthenon** and the Acropolis Museum before the crowds arrive. Afterward, walk downhill to visit the **Ancient Agora** and then head into **Monastiraki** and **Plaka,** where you can window-shop and relax over lunch or dinner. Keep an eye out for the **Plaka tram.** The half-hour ride begins in Palia Agora Square, loops through the Plaka, and then heads past the Acropolis on Dionissiou Areopayitou Boulevard before heading back into Plaka (from 10am to 10pm in summer; 1,000Dr/€2.95/$2.60). This is a great (and relaxing) way to get a sense of what you may want to explore on foot in the Plaka.

If You Have 2 Days It's worth spending several hours of day 2 at the **National Archaeological Museum** (again, try to arrive the minute it opens to beat the crowds). Then, visit some of Athens's smaller museums—or, if you need a change of pace, head up **Mount Likavitos** on the funicular that leaves from the top of Ploutarchou Street (500Dr/€1.47/$1.45), 10am to midnight, about every 20 minutes in summer). If the *nefos* (smog) isn't too bad, you'll have a wonderful view of Athens, Piraeus, and the Saronic Gulf. If you have an extra hour, take one of the paths from the summit and stroll down Likavitos, enjoying the scent of the pine trees and the changing views of the city.

If You Have 3 Days or More For the rest of your stay, visit more of the museums listed below, or consider a day trip to one of the great sights of antiquity, such as **Delphi** or **Sounion;** or a day excursion to **Corinth, Mycenae,** and **Epidaurus** (best done on a bus tour). If you don't want to go home without seeing one of the "isles of Greece," take a day trip by boat from Piraeus to one of the islands of the Saronic Gulf. **Aegina (Egina), Poros,** and **Hydra (Idra)** are all feasible day trips—but best not done the day before you leave Athens, lest bad weather strands you on an island. Whatever else you do, be sure to give yourself time to sit in cafes and watch the world go by.

THE TREASURES OF ANTIQUITY

The Acropolis 🅐🅐🅐   When you climb up the Acropolis—the heights above the city—you'll realize why people seem to have lived here as long ago as 5000 B.C. The sheer sides of the Acropolis make it a superb natural defense, just the place to avoid enemies and to be able to see invaders coming across the sea or the plains of Attica. And, of course, it helped that in antiquity there was a spring here, ensuring a steady supply of water.

In classical times, when Athens's population had grown to around 250,000, people lived on the slopes below the Acropolis, which had become the city's most important religious center. Athens's civic and business center, the Agora, and its cultural center, with several theaters and concert halls, bracketed the Acropolis; when you peer over the sides of the Acropolis at the houses in Plaka and the remains of the ancient Agora and the Theater of Dionysos, you'll see the layout of the ancient city. Syntagma and Omonia squares, the heart of today's Athens, were well out of the ancient city center.

Even the Acropolis's height couldn't protect it from the Persian invasion of 480 B.C., when most of its monuments were burned and destroyed. You may notice some immense column drums built into the Acropolis's walls. When the great Athenian statesman Pericles ordered the monuments rebuilt, he had the drums from the destroyed Parthenon built into the walls lest Athenians forget what had happened—and so they would remember that they had rebuilt what they had lost. Pericles's rebuilding program began about 448 B.C.; the new Parthenon was dedicated 10 years later, but work on other monuments continued for a century.

The **Parthenon** 🅐🅐🅐—dedicated to Athena Parthenos (the Virgin), patron goddess of Athens—was the most important religious monument, but there were shrines to many other gods and goddesses on the Acropolis's broad summit. As you climb up, you pass through first the **Beule Gate,** built by the Romans, and now known by the name of the French archaeologist who discovered it in 1852. Next comes the **Propylaia** 🅐, the monumental 5th-century B.C. entranceway. You'll notice the little **Temple of Athena Nike (Athena of Victory)** 🅐 perched above the Propylaia; the beautifully proportioned Ionic temple was built in 424 B.C. and restored in the 1930s. Off to the left of the Parthenon is the **Erechtheion** 🅐🅐, which the Athenians honored as the tomb of Erechtheus, a legendary king of Athens. A hole in the ceiling and floor of the

---

**Tips** **Strike!**

Strikes that close museums and archaeological sites can occur without warning. Decide what you most want to see, and go there as soon as possible after your arrival. The fact that something is open today says nothing about tomorrow. If you're visiting in the off-season, check with the **Greek National Tourist Organization (© 01/331-0437)** for the abbreviated winter hours of sites and museums.

---

northern porch indicates the spot where Poseidon's trident struck to make a spring (symbolizing control of the sea) gush forth during his contest with Athena to be the city's chief deity. Athena countered with an olive tree (symbolizing control of the rich Attic plain); the olive tree planted beside the Erechtheion reminds visitors of her victory. Give yourself a little time to enjoy the delicate carving on the Erechtheion, and be sure to see the original Caryatids (the monumental female figures who served as columns on the Erechtheion's porch) in the Acropolis Museum.

However charmed you are by these elegant little temples, you're probably still heading resolutely toward the **Parthenon,** and you may be disappointed to realize that visitors are not allowed inside, both to protect the monument and to allow ongoing restoration work to proceed safely. If you find this frustrating, keep in mind that in antiquity only priests and honored visitors were allowed in to see the monumental—some 11-m- (36-ft.-) tall statue of Athena designed by the great Phidias, who supervised Pericles's building program. Nothing of the

---

Value **Combination Ticket**

Be sure to check when you visit Athens as to whether a projected discounted ticket allowing 1-day entrance to the Acropolis, Acropolis
Museum, Theater of Dionysos, Ancient Agora, and National Archaeological Museum has been instituted. If it has, and you get it, brace yourself
for a long day!

---

huge gold-and-ivory statue remains, but there's a small Roman copy in the
National Archaeological Museum—and horrific renditions on souvenirs ranging
from T-shirts to ouzo bottles.

The Parthenon's entire roof and much of the interior were blown to
smithereens in 1687, when a party of Venetians attempted to take the Acropolis from the Turks. A shell fired from nearby Mouseion Hill struck the
Parthenon—where the Turks were storing gunpowder and munitions—and
caused appalling damage to the building and its sculptures. Most of the remaining sculptures were carted off to London by Lord Elgin in the first decade of the
19th century. Those surviving sculptures—long known as the **Elgin Marbles**—
are on display in the British Museum, causing ongoing pain to generations of
Greeks, who continue to press for their return.

The Parthenon originally had sculpture in both its pediments, as well as a frieze
running around the entire temple. Alternating **triglyphs** (panels with three incised
grooves) and **metopes** (sculptured panels) made up the frieze. The message of
most of this sculpture was the triumph of knowledge and civilization (read:
Athens) over the forces of darkness and barbarians. An interior frieze showed
scenes from the Panathenaic Festival each August, when citizens processed through
the streets, bringing a new *peplos* (tunic) for the statue of Athena. Only a few fragments of any of the sculptures remain in place, and every visitor will have to decide
whether it's a good or a bad thing that Lord Elgin removed so much before the
smog spread over Athens and ate away at the remaining sculpture.

If you're lucky enough to visit the Acropolis on a smog-free and sunny day,
you'll see the golden and cream tones of the Parthenon's handsome Pentelic marble at their most subtle. It may come as something of a shock to realize that the
Parthenon, like most other monuments here, was painted in antiquity, with gay
colors that have since faded, revealing the tones of the marble.

The **Acropolis Archaeological Museum** ★★ hugs the ground to detract as
little as possible from the ancient monuments. Inside, you'll see the four original **Caryatids** from the Erechtheion that are still in Athens (one disappeared
during the Ottoman occupation, and one is in the British Museum). Other
delights here include sculpture from the Parthenon burnt by the Persians, statues of **korai** (maidens) dedicated to Athena, figures of **kouroi** (young men), and
a wide range of finds from the Acropolis.

Those interested in learning more about the Acropolis should check to see if the
Center for Acropolis Studies, on Makriyanni Street just southeast of the Acropolis (© **01/923-9381**), has reopened. If so, it should be open daily from 9am to
2:30pm; admission is free. On display are artifacts, reconstructions, photographs,
drawings, and plaster casts of the Elgin Marbles. A museum is being built here to
house the marbles themselves when (if) they're returned to Athens. Construction
has been slowed by the discovery of important Byzantine remains here.

You'll probably want to spend half a day on the Acropolis.

Dionysiou Areopayitou St. ℂ **01/321-0219.** Admission 2,000Dr (€5.90, $6) adults. Free Sun. Admission includes entrance to Acropolis Museum, which sometimes closes earlier than the site. Summer daily 8am–7pm; winter daily 8:30am–2:30pm. From Syntagma Sq., take Amalias Ave. into pedestrianized Dionysiou Areopayitou St., and follow marble path up to the Acropolis. The ticket booth, along with a small post office and a snack bar, are slightly below the Acropolis entrance.

Ancient Agora 𝕣𝕣   The Agora was Athens's commercial and civic center, with buildings used for a wide range of political, educational, philosophical, theatrical, and athletic purposes—which may be why what remains seems such a jumble. This is a nice place to wander and enjoy the views up toward the Acropolis; take in the herb garden and flowers planted around the 5th century B.C. **Temple of Hephaistos (the Theseion);** peek into the heavily restored 11th-century church of Ayii Apostoli (Holy Apostles); and admire the 2nd-century B.C. **Stoa of Attalos,** totally reconstructed in the 1950s.

The **museum** in the Stoa's ground floor has finds from 5,000 years of Athenian history, including sculpture and pottery, as well as a voting machine and a child's potty seat, all with labels in English. The museum (which has excellent toilet facilities) closes 15 minutes before the site.

You'll want to spend at least 3 hours here.

Below the Acropolis on the edge of Monastiraki (entrance on Adrianou St., near Ayiou Philippou Sq., east of Monastiraki Sq.). ℂ **01/321-0185.** Admission (includes museum) 1,200Dr (€3.55, $3.50) adults, 900Dr (€2.65, $2.60) seniors, 600Dr (€1.78, $1.75) students. Tues–Sun 8:30am–3pm.

Cemetery of Keramikos   This ancient cemetery, where Pericles gave his famous funeral oration, is a short walk from the Ancient Agora and not far from the presumed site of Plato's Academy. There're a number of well-preserved funerary monuments and the remains of the colossal **Dipylon Gate,** the main entrance to the ancient city of Athens. You can also see substantial remains of the 5th-century B.C. fortifications known as the "Long Walls" that ran from Athens to Piraeus. The Keramikos can be a pleasant spot to sit and read because it's seldom crowded. If you like cemeteries, be sure to take in Athens's enormous **First Cemetery,** near the Athens Stadium, where notables such as former Prime Minister George Panandreou are buried beneath elaborate monuments. Both are pleasant spots in which to spend a few hours.

148 Ermou St. ℂ **01/346-3552.** Admission 500Dr (€1.47, $1.45) adults, 400Dr (€1.17, $1.15) seniors, 300Dr (€0.90, 90¢) students. Tues–Sun 8:30am–3pm. Walk west from Monastiraki Sq. on Ermou St. past Thisio Metro station; cemetery is on the right.

THE TOP MUSEUMS

National Archaeological Museum 𝕣𝕣𝕣   This is an enormous and enormously popular museum; try to arrive as soon as it opens so you can see the exhibits and not just the other visitors' backs. Early arrival should give you at least an hour before most tour groups turn up. Don't miss the stunning gold

---

Tips **A National Archaeological Museum Update**

The second floor of the National Archaeological Museum has been closed since an earthquake shook Athens in 1999. At press time, this floor hadn't reopened, and there were plans to move the restored 3500 B.C. Thira frescoes (on that floor) back to the island of Thira (Santorini). In addition, a number of splendid marble statues on the ground floor are still under protective wraps.

masks, cups, dishes, and jewelry unearthed from the site of Mycenae by Hein-rich Schliemann in 1876, on display in the first room, and the elegant marble Cycladic figurines (ca. 2000 B.C.) in the adjacent room. The museum's extensive collection of black-and-red figure vases are on the museum's second floor, which may not have reopened when you visit. Frustratingly, the museum shop displays a wide range of excellent reproductions—almost none of which are in stock. You'll probably want to spend a minimum of 3 hours here.

44 Patission St. ✆ 01/821-7717. Fax 01/821-3573. protocol@eam.culture.gr. Admission 2,000Dr (€5.90, $6) adults. Summer daily 8am–7pm; winter 8am–3pm. (Be sure to double-check that these hours are in effect when you visit. Budget considerations may force the museum to revert to its former closing time of 5pm in winter, 3pm on Sun and holidays, and its midday opening on Mon.) Walk 10 minutes—about ½ km (⅓ mile)—north of Omonia Sq. on the road officially named 28 Oktobriou Ave. but usually called Patission.

N.P. Goulandris Foundation Museum of Cycladic Art 🏛🏛   This hand-some new museum houses the largest collection of Cycladic art outside the National Archaeological Museum. See if you agree with those who have com-pared the faces of the Cycladic figurines to the work of the Italian painter, Modigliani. Be sure to go through the courtyard into the museum's newest acquisition: an elegant 19th-century house with some of its original furnishings and visiting exhibits. The museum shop has a wide variety of books and reproductions—and wildly unhelpful staff. You'll want at least 3 hours here; be sure to give yourself a break in the garden or in the cafe.

4 Neophytou Douka St. ✆ 01/722-8321. Admission 1,000Dr (€ 2.95, $2.90) adults, 500Dr (€1.47, $1.45) students. Mon and Wed–Fri 10am–4pm; Sat 10am–3pm. From Syntagma Sq., walk 7 blocks east along Vasilis-sis Sofias Ave., then half a block north on Neophytou Douka.

Benaki Museum 🏛🏛   This stunning private collection includes treasures from the Neolithic era to the 20th century. The folk art collection (including magnificent costumes and icons) is superb, as are the two entire rooms from 18th-century northern Greek mansions, the ancient Greek bronzes, gold cups, Fayum portraits, and rare early Christian textiles. A new wing doubles the exhi-bition space of the original 20th-century neoclassical town house that belonged to the wealthy Benaki family. The museum shop is excellent, the cafe has a spec-tacular view over Athens, and new galleries will house special exhibitions. A very pleasant place to spend several hours.

1 Odos Koumbari 1 (at Leoforos Vas. Sofias, Kolonaki, 5 blocks east of Syntagma Sq.). ✆ 01/367-1000. Admission 2,000Dr (€5.90, $6); free Thurs. Mon, Wed, Fri, Sat 9am–5pm; Thurs 9am–midnight; Sun 9am–3pm; closed Tues.

Byzantine Museum 🏛   If you love icons (paintings, usually of saints, usually on wood) or want to find out about them, this is the place to go. As its name makes clear, this museum, in a 19th-century Florentine-style villa, is devoted to the art and history of the Byzantine era (roughly the 4th to the 15th century A.D.). Selections from Greece's most important collection of icons and religious art—along with sculptures, altars, mosaics, religious vestments, Bibles, and a small-scale reconstruction of an early Christian basilica—are exhibited on sev-eral floors around a courtyard. Allow at least an hour for your visit.

22 Vasilissis Sofias Ave. ✆ 01/723-1570 or 01/721-1027. Admission 500Dr (€1.47, $1.45) adults, 250Dr (€0.75, 75¢) students. Tues–Sun 8:30am–3pm. From Syntagma Sq., walk along Queen Sophias Ave. (aka Venizelou Ave.) for about 15 min. The museum is on your right.

Greek Folk Art Museum 🏛🏛 *Kids*   This endearing small museum has daz-zling embroideries and costumes, carved wood furniture and tools, and ceramic and copper utensils from all over the country, plus a small room with zany frescoes of gods and heroes done by eccentric artist Theofilos Hadjimichael, who painted in the early part of the 20th century. Lots of Greek school children visit here, and there are sometimes puppet shows and special exhibits. A great place to spend several hours.

17 Kidathineon St., Plaka. (C) 01/322-9031. Admission 500Dr (€1.47, $1.45) adults, 400Dr (€1.17, $1.15) seniors, 300Dr (€0.90, 90¢) students. Tues–Sun 10am–2pm. From Syntagma, take Filellinon St. to Kidathineon.

GALLERIES

One of the great (usually free) pleasures of visiting Athens is browsing in its small art galleries. Very occasionally a gallery will have an admission fee for a special exhibit, but usually there is no charge. This is a wonderful way to get a sense of the contemporary Greek art scene— and possibly buy something to take home. Openings are usually not by invitation only, so if you see a notice of an opening, feel free to stop by. Here are some galleries to keep an eye out for in central Athens. The **Epistrofi Gallery,** 6 Taki (C) **01/321-8640**), in trendy Psirri, has occasional concerts as well as shows; the **Epikentro Gallery,** 10 Armodiou ((C) **01/331-2187**), stages frequent exhibits in its improbable location in the Athens Central Market; the **Rebecca Kamhi Gallery,** Sophokleous 23 ((C) **01/321-0448**), not far from the Central Market, and one of Athens's best known galleries, is open by appointment only in August; **Bernier/Eliades** Gallery, 11 Eptachalkou, Theseion ((C) **01/341-3935**), stages group exhibitions, as does **Kappatos,** Agias Irenes 6 ((C) **01/321-7931**). There are also frequent shows at the **Melina Mercouri Cultural Center,** Iraklidon and Thessalonikis 66 ((C) **01/345-2150**), not far from the Theseion and at the **Melina Mercouri Foundation,** Polygnotou 9–11 ((C) **01/331-5601**), in Plaka. The fashionable Kolonaki district is chock-a-block with galleries: the **Athens Art Center,** 4 Glyconos, Dexameni, Kolonaki ((C) **01/721-3938**); **Photohoros,** Tsakalof 44 ((C) **01/321-0448**); and **Medussa,** Xenokratous 7 ((C) **01/724-4552**), are three to look for. The **Athens Arts and Technology School** ((C) **01/381-3700**) usually stages shows around Athens in July and August when many galleries close or move out of town. One just-out-of-town suburban gallery that's open year-round and well worth a visit (in part for its great cafe and shop) is **The Deste Foundation for Contemporary Art,** Omirou 8, Nea Psychico ((C) **01/672-9460;** www.deste.gr), a 20-minute cab ride from Syntagma.

ORGANIZED TOURS

You can book tours of Athens through most hotels or any travel agency. A half-day tour of city highlights should cost about 17,500Dr (€50.35, $50). Night tours can include a sound-and-light show, Greek folk dancing at the Dora Stratou Dance Theater, or dinner and Greek dancing; they range from 17,500Dr to 35,000Dr (€50.35–€102.75, $50–$100). Since many Athenian nightclubs are clip joints, the safety-in-numbers aspect of a visit with a tour group may appeal to you.

   Educational Tours & Cruises, 9 Irving St., Medford, MA 02111 ((C) **800/275-4109;** edtours@ars.nep.gr), and 1 Artemídos St., Glyfáda 16674, Athens ((C) **01/898-1741**), can arrange tours in Athens and throughout Greece, including individual tours with an emphasis on Greek culture. **CHAT Tours,** 4 Stadiou St. ((C) **01/322-3137**); **GO Tours,** 31–33 Voulis St. ((C) **01/322-5951**); and **Key Tours,** 4 Kaliroïs St. ((C) **01/923-3166**), are all reliable, established companies that offer tours of Athens and various day trips. Destinations include the temple of Apollo at Sounion, Delphi, and the Peloponnese (usually taking in Corinth, Mycenae, and Epidauros).

THE SHOPPING SCENE

If you want to pick up retro clothes or old copper, try the **flea market,** a daily spectacle between Plaka and Monastiraki Square. It's most lively on Sunday, but you can find the usual touristy trinkets, copies of ancient artifacts, jewelry, sandals, and various handmade goods, including embroideries, any day. Keep in mind that not everything sold as an antique is genuine, and that it's illegal to take antiquities and icons more than 100 years old out of the country without a hard-to-obtain export license.

In the Plaka-Monastiraki area, several shops with nicer-than-usual arts and crafts and fair prices include **Stavros Melissinos,** the Poet-Sandalmaker of Athens, 89 Pandrossou St. (© 01/321-9247); **Iphanta,** the weaving workshop, 6 Selleu St. (© 01/322-3628); **Emanuel Masmanidis' Gold Rose Jewelry** shop, 85 Pandrossou St. (© 01/321-5662); and the **Center of Hellenic Tradition,** 59 Mitropoleos and 36 Pandrossou sts. (© 01/321-3023), which sells arts and crafts. At the **Hellenic Folk-Art Gallery,** 6 Ipatias and Apollonos sts., Plaka (© 01/324-0017), a portion of the proceeds from everything sold (including handsome woven and embroidered carpets), goes to the National Welfare Organization, which encourages traditional crafts. Finally, don't forget that most museums have excellent shops.

The biggest **foreign-language bookstore** in Athens is **Eleftheroudakis,** which has a branch at 4 Nikis St. (© 01/322-2255) and a new headquarters at 17 Panepistimiou St. (© 01/331-4480). The new store has eight stories filled with a full range of subjects, plus a cafe and a music shop, and stages a series of small concerts and readings by local authors.

Compendium, 28 Nikis St. (© 01/322-1248), on the edge of Plaka near Syntagma Square, is a good English-language bookstore, selling new and used fiction and nonfiction, plus magazines and maps. **Reymondos,** 18 Voukourestiou St., a pedestrianized street just off Syntagma Square (© 01/364-8189), has a good selection in English, including some dazzling photo books on Greece, and is often open after usual shop hours.

On your way there, you can ogle the window displays at **Zolotas,** 10 Panepistimiou St. (© 01/361-3782), and **Lalaounis,** 6 Panepistimiou St. (© 01/362-1371), Greece's two finest jewelers, which have branches at the foot of Voukourestiou Street.

ATHENS AFTER DARK

Greeks enjoy their nightlife so much that they take an afternoon nap to rest up for it. The evening often begins with a leisurely *volta* (stroll); you'll see it in most neighborhoods, including Plaka and Kolonaki Square. Most Greeks don't think of dinner until at least 9pm—when there's still no hurry. Around midnight the party may move on to a club for music and dancing. Feel free to try places on your own, although you may feel like the odd man out because Greeks seldom go anywhere alone. If you're a woman on your own and want to be left alone, you'll probably find hitting the bars and dance clubs uncongenial.

Check the daily Kathimerini insert in the *International Herald-Tribune* or the *Athens News,* both sold at most major newsstands, for current cultural and entertainment events, including films, lectures, theater, music, and dance. The weekly *Hellenic Times* and *Athenscope* and the monthly *Now in Athens* list nightspots, restaurants, movies, theater, and much else. The weekly Greek publication *Athinorama* has comprehensive listings of events.

Best of all, if you have a Greek friend, ask for pointers on what's currently on. If you ask a taxi driver, he's likely to take you to either his cousin George's joint or the place that gives him a kickback for bringing you. Be especially wary of heading out of the city to the places that spring up each summer on the airport road; these spots are usually over-priced and often unsavory. That said, the **Asteria Club** (© 01/894-4558) and the **Bio-Bio Club** (© 01/894-1300) in Glyfada were both popular during the summer of 2000, as was **Riba's** (© 01/965-5555) in Varkiza. Expect to pay at least 6000Dr (€17.60, $17) per drink after paying an entrance charge of perhaps 20,000Dr (€58.70, $57) at all these live music joints.

THE PERFORMING ARTS

The **Athens Festival** at the Odeon of Herodes Atticus has famous Greek and foreign artists performing music, plays, opera, and ballet from the beginning of June to the beginning of October in a beautiful open-air setting. Find out what's being presented through the English-language press or at the **Athens Festival Office,** 4 Stadiou St. ((© 01/322-1459, 01/322-3111, or 01/322-3110, ext. 137). The office is open from Monday to Saturday 8:30am to 2pm and 5 to 7pm, and Sunday 10am to 1pm. If available—and that's a big "if"—tickets, which range from about 3,500 to 10,500Dr (€10.30 to €30.80, $10 to $30), can also be purchased at the **Odeon** (© 01/323-2771) several hours before a performance.

The acoustically marvelous new **Megaron Mousikis Concert Hall,** 89 Vasilissis Sofias Ave. (© 01/729-0391 or 01/728-2333), hosts a wide range of classical music programs that include chamber music, operas in concert, symphonic concerts, and recitals. The box office is open weekdays from 10am to 6pm, Saturday 10am to 2pm, and Sunday 6 to 10:30pm on performance nights only. Tickets, costing about 1,000Dr to 20,000Dr (€2.95–€58.70, $2.90–$57), are also sold weekdays from 10am to 5pm in the Megaron's convenient downtown kiosk in the Spiromillios Arcade, 4 Stadiou St. The Megaron has a limited summer season but is in full swing the rest of the year.

Most major jazz and rock concerts, as well as some classical performances, take place at the **Pallas Theater,** 1 Voukourestiou St. (© 01/322-8275).

English-language theater and American-style music are performed at the **Hellenic American Union Auditorium,** 22 Massalias St., between Kolonaki and Omonia squares (© 01/362-9886); you can usually get a ticket for around 3,000Dr (€8.80, $9). Arrive early and check out the art show or photo exhibition at the adjacent gallery. The **Greek National Opera** performs at the Olympia Theater, 59 Akadimias St., at Mavromihali (© 01/361-2461).

The **Dora Stratou Folk Dance Theater,** which performs on Philopappos Hill, is the best known of the traditional dance troupes. Regional dances are performed in costume with appropriate musical accompaniment nightly at 10:15pm, with additional shows at 8:15pm on Wednesday and Sunday. You can buy tickets (3,000Dr–5,200Dr/€8.80–€15.30/$9–$15) from 8am to 2pm at the box office, 8 Scholio St., Plaka (© 01/924-4395, or 01/921-4650 after 5:30pm).

Sound-and-light Shows, seen from the Pnyx, the hill across Dionysiou Areopayitou Street from the Acropolis, illuminate (sorry) Athens's history by focusing on the history of the Acropolis. Try to sit away from the (very) loud speakers, so you won't be deafened by the booming historical narrative and all-too-stirring music and can concentrate instead on the play of lights on the monuments of the Acropolis. Shows are held from April to October. Performances in English begin at 9pm and last 45 minutes. Tickets can be purchased at the **Athens Festival Office,** 4 Stadiou St. (© 01/322-7944), or at the entrance to the Sound and Light (© **01/922-6210**), which is signposted on the Pnyx. Tickets are 2,000Dr (€5.90, $6) for adults and 600Dr (€1.78, $1.75) for students.

LIVE-MUSIC CLUBS

Walk the streets of the Plaka on any night and you'll find lots of tavernas offering pseudo-traditional live music (usually at clip-joint prices) and a few offering the real thing. **Taverna Mostrou,** 22 Mnissikleos St. (© **01/324-2441**), is one of the largest, oldest, and best known for traditional Greek music and dancing. Shows begin about 11pm and usually last to 2am. The 5,000Dr (€14.70, $14) cover includes a fixed-price supper; a la carte fare is available but expensive. Nearby, **Palia Taverna Kritikou,** 24 Odos Mnissikleos (© **01/322-2809**), is another lively open-air taverna with music and dancing. Other reliable tavernas with live traditional music are **Nefeli,** 24 Panos St. (© **01/321-2475**); **Dioyenis,** 3 Sellei St. (© **01/324-7933**); **Stamatopoulou,** 26 Lissiou St. (© **01/322-8722**); and **Xinos,** 4 Agelou Geronta St. (© **01/322-1065**).

For Greek pop music, try **Zoom,** 37 Kidathineon St., in the heart of the Plaka (© **01/322-5920**). Performers, who are likely to have current hit albums, are showered with carnations by adoring fans. The minimum drink order is 5,000Dr (€14.70, $14). If you want to check out the local rock and blues scene along with small doses of metal, Athenian popsters play at **Memphis,** 5 Ventiri St., near the Hilton Hotel east of Syntagma (© **01/722-4104**); it's open from Tuesday to Friday 10:30pm to 2:30am.

Those interested in authentic *rebetika* (music of the urban poor and dispossessed) should consult their hotel receptionist or the current issue of *Athenscope* or *Athinorama* (in Greek) to see which clubs are featuring the best performers. Shows usually don't start until nearly midnight, and although there's usually no cover, a 5,000Dr ($14) charge per drink isn't uncommon. Most clubs are closed in summer, and many are far from the town center, so budget another 2,500Dr to 5,000Dr (€7.35–€14.70, $7–$14) for round-trip taxi fare.

One of the more central clubs is the **Stoa Athanaton,** 19 Sofokleous, in the Central Meat Market (© **01/321-4362**), which has live rebetika Monday to Saturday 3 to 6pm and after midnight and serves good food; the minimum is 3,500Dr (€10.30, $10). **Taximi,** 29 Odos Isavron, Exarchia (© **01/363-9919**), is consistently popular, with drinks costing 3,500Dr (€10.30, $10). It's closed Sunday and July and August. **Frangosyriani,** 57 Odos Arachovis, Exarchia (© **01/360-0693**), specializes in the music of rebetika legend Markos Vamvakaris; it's closed Tuesday and Wednesday. The downscale, smoke-filled **Rebetiki Istoria,** in a neoclassical building at 181 Ippokratous St. (© **01/642-4937**), features old-style rebetika music, played to a mixed crowd of older regulars and younger students and intellectuals. The music usually starts at 11pm, but arrive earlier to get a seat. The legendary Maryo I Thessaloniki (Maryo from Thessaloniki), sometimes described as the Bessie Smith of Greece, sometimes sings rebetika at **Perivoli t'Ouranou,** 19 Lysikratous St. in the Plaka ([tel **01/323-5517** or 01/322-2048); admission is around 12,000Dr (€35.25, $34).

A number of clubs and cafes specialize in jazz but also offer everything from Indian sitar music to rock and punk. The **Café Asante,** 78 Damareos in Pangrati (© **01/756-0102**), has music most nights from 11pm; admission varies, but count on spending around 12,000Dr (€35.25, $34) if you have a couple of drinks. The very popular **Half Note Jazz Club,** 17 Trivonianou St., Mets (© **01/921-3310**), offers up everything from medieval music to jazz nightly; performance times vary from 8 to 11pm and later; admission is usually 4,000Dr to 7,000Dr (€11.75–€20.55, $11–$20). At **The House of Art,** 4 Sahtouri and

---

> ### Tips   Open in August
>
> Many popular after-dark spots close in August, when Athenians flee the summer heat and head to the country. You'll find that a number of bars, cafes, ouzeries, and tavernas on the pedestrianized **Irakleidon** walkway off Apostolos Pauvlos Street across from the Theseion stay open in August: **Stavlos,** the restaurant/bar/disco popular with all ages, remains open on August weekends. A few doors away, the **Berlin Club,** which caters to a young crowd and specializes in rock, is open most nights, and **Ambibagio** has quite genuine Greek music. The sweet shop **Aistisis** offers great views of the Acropolis and stays open as late as the nearby bars.

Sari, Psirri (© **01/321-7678**), and **Pinakothiki,** 5 Agias Theklas (© **01/324-7741**), both in newly fashionable Psyrri, you can often hear jazz from 11pm; admission is around 7,000Dr (€20.55, $20), including the first drink. **The Rodon Club,** 24 Marni St., west of Omonia Square (© **01/523-6293**), also has jazz and pop concerts many nights from 10pm; admission is from 7,000Dr (€20.55, $20).

GAY & LESBIAN BARS

The gay scene is fairly low-key; get-togethers are sometimes advertised in the English-language press. Information is also available from the Greek national gay and lesbian organization **AKOE-AMPHI,** P.O. Box 26002, 10022 Athens.

The friendliest bar is **Aleko's Island,** 42 Tsakalof St., Kolonaki (no phone), a fun place where you can actually have a conversation. **Granazi,** 20 Lebesi St. (© **01/325-3979**), attracts a loud and lively young crowd. The disco **Lambda,** 15 Lembessi St. and 9 Syngrou Ave. (© **01/922-4202**), is hip and trendy with the young locals. In Kolonaki, **Alexander's,** 44 Anagnostopoulou, Kolonaki (© **01/364-6660**), is more sedate, with more variety. And **Porta,** 10 Phalirou St. (© **01/924-3858**), is the only true lesbian bar in town. There's usually a lively nighttime transvestite cruising scene along Syngrou Avenue in Makriyanni. **Koukles,** at Zan. Moreas and Syngrou Avenue, Koukaki (no phone), has drag shows most evenings.

DANCE CLUBS

Hidden on the outskirts of the Plaka, **Booze,** 57 Kolokotroni St., second floor (© **01/324-0944**), blasts danceable rock to a hip student crowd. There's art on every wall, jelled stage lights, and two bars. Admission is 1,800Dr (€5.29, $5.15), plus 1,500Dr (€4.40, $4.30) per drink. If it's disco you're craving, head east to **Absolut,** 23 Filellinon St. (no phone); **Q Base,** 49 Evripidou, Omonia (© **01/321-8256**); or **R-Load,** 161 Ermou (© **01/345-6187**). If you feel a bit too old there, head north to Panepistimiou Street, where the **Wild Rose,** in the arcade at 10 Panepistimiou (© **01/364-2160**); and **Mercedes Rex,** at 48 Panepistimiou (© **01/361-4591**), usually have varied programs.

DAY TRIPS FROM ATHENS
PIRAEUS

You probably won't fall in love with Piraeus, but if you have some time to kill—or want to escape Athens's summer heat—you can find lots to enjoy.

Piraeus has been the port of Athens since antiquity and is still where you catch most island boats and cruise ships. Keep in mind that there are three harbors:

the **main harbor (Megas Limani),** where you'll see everything from tankers to island boats and cruise ships; **Zea Marina** (also called Zea Limani), the port for most of the swift hydrofoils; and **Little Harbor** (Microlimani, also called Turkolimani, or Turkish Harbor), the location of many fish restaurants. As in antiquity, today's Piraeus has the seamier side of a sailors' port of call and the color and bustle of an active harbor—both aspects, somewhat sanitized, were portrayed in the film *Never on Sunday.* There're a number of fish restaurants, but many are overpriced and serve fish that is not as fresh as the bread.

GETTING THERE   The fastest and easiest way to Piraeus is to take the Metro from Omonia Square or Monastiraki to the last stop. It costs 250Dr (€0.73, 75¢) and leaves you 1 block from the principal domestic port. You can also take bus 40 from the corner of Filellinon Street at Syntagma Square; it leaves you 1 block from the international port, about a 10-minute walk along the water from the domestic port. From the airport, bus 91 goes to Piraeus. The fare is 300Dr (€0.90, 90¢). A taxi from Syntagma Square or the airport costs about 3,000Dr (€8.80, $9). When tourists headed back to Athens disembark, taxi drivers usually offer flat fees that are wildly out of line. Either insist on the metered rate, or walk away from the harbor and try again.

FERRIES TO THE ISLANDS   The boats to the islands are opposite the Metro station. Boats to the **Saronic Gulf** and hydrofoils (Flying Dolphins) to **Aegina** are opposite and to the left of the station; the hydrofoils leave from the foot of Gounari Street. Boats to the other islands are around to the right and away from the station. Boats to **Italy** and **Turkey** are a mile or so to the left. Hydrofoils to other destinations leave from Zea Marina, a separate harbor some distance from the Metro station. Very few signs point the way, so try to arrive early.

Ferry **tickets** can be purchased at a ticket office up to 1 hour before departure; after that they can be bought on the boat. To book **first-class cabins** or purchase **advance tickets,** see one of the harborside travel agents around Karaiskaki Square by the domestic ferries and along Akti Miaouli, opposite the Crete ferries. Most open at 6am, and some will hold your baggage for the day (but there's no security). The Greek National Tourist Organization (EOT) publishes a list of weekly sailings, and the **Tourist Police** (© 171) or the **Port Authority** (© 01/451-1311) can provide schedule information. Keep in mind that all such schedules are tentative.

SEEING THE SIGHTS ON LAND   The **Maritime Museum** at Akti Themistokleous (© 01/451-6264), near the departure pier for the Flying Dolphin hydrofoils, has handsome models of ancient, medieval, and modern ships. The museum is open from Tuesday to Saturday 9am to 2pm; admission is 500Dr (€ 1.47, $1.45). The nearby **Archaeological Museum,** 32 Harilaou Trikoupi St. (© 01/452-1598), is open from Tuesday to Sunday 8:30am to 3pm, and also costs 500Dr (€1.47, $1.45). The stars of the museum are the

---

Tips Traveler's Tip

Whatever your destination from Piraeus, don't be too surprised if your boat leaves late. Schedules depend on the weather, and sailings are often delayed or canceled. It's not a good idea to plan to arrive back in Athens less than 24 hours before your flight home, lest bad weather strands you on an island.

three superb monumental bronzes of a youth, the goddess Artemis, and the goddess Athena. If you have time for only one museum, you'll probably find the Maritime Museum a pleasant departure from what you've seen in other archaeological museums.

WHERE TO DINE   Piraeus has some good restaurants, but the places to eat along the harbor are generally mediocre. If you decide to try one of the seafood restaurants in central Piraeus or Microlimani, make sure you know the price before ordering; if the final tab seems out of line, insist on a receipt, and phone the Tourist Police. In addition to our suggestions here, don't forget **Varoulko** *✪* at 14 Deligeorgi, Piraeus, which serves the best fish in Greece (see "Where to Dine—Worth a (Short) Trip," earlier in this chapter).

Dourambeis SEAFOOD   This taverna near the Delphinario theater in Piraeus is where locals go when they want to splurge on a good fish dinner. The decor is simple, the food excellent. The crayfish soup alone is excellent, as is the grilled fish.

29A Dilaveri St., Piraeus. *©* **01/412-2092.** Reservations suggested. Fish prices (by the kilo) change daily, ranging from about 10,000–15,000Dr (€29.35–€44.05, $29–$43). No credit cards. Mon–Sat noon–5pm and 8pm–1am. Take a cab from the Metro station, as this place is hard to find.

Vassilenas *✪* SEAFOOD/GREEK   There's no menu at this restaurant in an old grocery store in a suburb just north of Piraeus; for a flat fee of 6,000Dr (€17.60, $20) per person, you're presented with a steady flow of more than 15 dishes. Even if you come here hungry, you probably won't be able to eat everything set before you. There's plenty of seafood, plus good Greek dishes.

72 Etolikou 72, Ayia Sofia. *©* **01/461-2457.** Reservations recommended Fri–Sat. Meals 6,000Dr (€17.60, $17). No credit cards. Mon–Sat 8pm–midnight. Closed Aug 1–25. Take a cab from the Metro station, as this place is hard to find.

PICNICKING AT THE TEMPLE OF POSEIDON *✪✪*
One of the most popular, and easiest, day trips from Athens is to the 5th-century B.C. **Temple of Poseidon** at **Cape Sounion** (*©* **0292/39-363**), about 2 hours by bus outside Athens. The temple, which was built at about the same time as the Parthenon, occupies a dramatic position on a cliff high above the sea. In antiquity, as today, sailors knew they were nearing Athens when they caught sight of the temple's slender Doric columns. Fifteen of them remain; try to find the spot on one where Lord Byron carved his name. Then you can swim in the sea below and grab a snack at one of the overpriced restaurants. (Better yet, bring a picnic.) This is a good place not to go on the weekend, when it's very crowded and the traffic to and from beaches outside Athens is very heavy.

The archaeological site is open daily from 10am to sunset. Admission is 800Dr (€2.35, $2.30) adults, 600Dr (€1.78, $1.75) seniors, and 400Dr (€1.17, $1.15) students.

GETTING THERE   Buses to Sounion leave hourly on the half-hour 6:30am to 6:30pm from the **station** at 14 Mavromateon St. (*©* **01/821-3203**), at the southwest corner of Areos Park, well north of Omonia Square—best reached by taxi.

2 Delphi and the Northern Peloponnese

With the exception of the Acropolis in Athens, the most famous and beautiful ancient sites in Greece bracket the Gulf of Corinth. Apollo's sanctuary at Delphi is on the mainland north of the gulf, and Agamemnon's palace at Mycenae, the Mycenaean fortress of Tiryns, the spectacular 4th century B.C. theater of

Epidauros and the birthplace of the Olympic Games at Olympia, are south of the gulf in the northern Peloponnese.

EXPLORING THE REGION BY CAR   Thanks to the excellent road linking Athens and the Peloponnese at Corinth, and the frequent ferry service across the Gulf of Corinth between Rio and Anti-Rio, it's easy to combine a visit to Delphi with a tour of the most important ancient sites in the Peloponnese. Try to allow at least 4 days (spending 2 nights at Nafplion and 1 night each at Olympia and Delphi).

If traffic is light (and it almost never is), you can drive the 88km (55 miles) from Athens to Corinth on the National Road in an hour. After you take a look at the Corinth Canal and the sprawling site of ancient Corinth, an hour's drive (less if you take the new National Road to Argos and double back) through the farmland of Corinthia and Argolis will take you to Mycenae, 114km (71 miles) southwest of Athens. From Mycenae, it's less than an hour to Nafplion, 145km (90 miles) southwest of Athens. Generally considered the prettiest town in the Peloponnese, Nafplion is the perfect spot to spend the night before visiting Epidauros.

Although it's only 32km (20 miles) from Nafplion to Epidauros, the road is usually clogged with tour buses, especially when there are performances at the ancient theater; allow at least an hour for the drive. From Nafplion and Epicauros, two routes lead across the Peloponnese to Olympia. You can return to Corinth and join the National Road, which runs as far as Patras, where you take the good coast road on to Olympia. (Although there're signs in Patras pointing you toward Olympia, the heavy traffic in Patras means that you can easily spend an hour getting across town.)

If you want to avoid Patras, you can join the new National Road at Argos and drive through the Arcadian mountains via Tripolis to Olympia, 320km (199 miles) west of Athens. Either way, expect to spend at least 4 hours en route— and try to spend more, so that you can enjoy the coastal scenery or the mountain villages of Arcadia. Then, to reach Delphi from Olympia, simply head to Rio, just north of Patras, and catch one of the frequent ferries across the gulf to Anti-Rio, where a new road runs all the way to Delphi, 177km (110 miles) west of Athens. Allow at least 5 hours for the trip from Olympia to Delphi, and 3 hours to get from Delphi to Athens.

THE NORTHERN PELOPONNESE & THE CLASSICAL SITES

One of the delights of visiting the northern Peloponnese is that it's relatively uncrowded when many of the Aegean islands are sagging under the weight of tourists each summer. That doesn't mean you'll have famous spots like Mycenae,

---

Tips Driving Times

Keep in mind that although most Greek roads are quite good, much of your journey to and around the Peloponnese will be on beautiful, but sometimes vertiginous, winding mountain and coastal roads that make distances deceptive. Therefore, I've indicated how long you should expect each part of the trip to take, rather than giving you a false sense of how quickly you can travel by just telling you how much distance you'll cover. Also keep in mind that only Portugal has more traffic fatalities each year than Greece: buckle up and be careful out there!

Central Greece & the Northern Peloponnese

Epidauros, and Olympia to yourself if you arrive at high noon in August. It does mean that if you arrive just as they open or just before they close, you may have an hour under the pine trees at Olympia or Epidauros virtually alone, and be able to stand in Mycenae's Treasury of Atreus with swallows as your only companions.

Because even the most avid tourists do not live by culture alone, it's good to know that one of the great delights of spending time in the northern Peloponnese comes from quiet hours in shady *plateias* (squares), watching fishers mend their nets while local families settle down for a leisurely meal. An hour in a seaside cafe watching the locals watching you watch them is the ideal way to unwind after a day's sightseeing. By the way, if you visit here in the winter, make sure your hotel has functioning heating.

CORINTH

Corinth exported its pottery around the Mediterranean and dominated trade in Greece for much of the 8th and 7th centuries B.C. It experienced a second golden age under the Romans in the 2nd century A.D. Today, as in antiquity, Corinth and Patras are the two major gateways to the Peloponnese. As you pause here, you'll want to leave the main highway (look for the turnoff for the Canal Tourist Area) to take a look at the Corinth Canal and visit ancient Corinth before heading deeper into the northern Peloponnese.

Essentials

GETTING THERE   By Train   Several trains a day run from Athens's Stath-mos Peloponnisou to the Corinth station off Odos Demokratias (℗ **0741/ 22-522**). The trains are almost invariably late, often taking 3 hours or more. Refreshments sometimes are available on board. For information on schedules and fares, call ℗ **01/512-4913** in Athens.

By Bus   At least 15 buses a day run to Corinth from the Stathmos Leoforia Pelo-ponnisou, 100 Odos Kifissou in Athens. For schedule and fare information, call ℗ **01/512-8233** in Athens. Buses to and from Athens come and go from the bus station at Ermou and Koliatsou streets (℗ **0741/25-645**). Buses for ancient Corinth sometimes leave from this station and sometimes leave from another bus stop on Odos Koliatsou. Inquire upon arrival and allow 20 minutes for the bus ride to Archaia Korinthos (Ancient Corinth); buses usually run once an hour from about 8am to 8pm. Buses from Corinth for the Peloponnese leave from the sta-tion at the corner of Konstantinou and Aratou streets (℗ **0741/24-403**).

By Car   Corinth is 88km (55 miles) west of Athens on the National Highway; the toll is 500Dr (€1.47, $1.45). The highway continues past the Corinth Canal; just after the canal, you'll see signs for Ancient Corinth (the splendid archaeo-logical site) and Corinth (the architecturally uninteresting modern town).

FAST FACTS   The telephone **area code** for Corinth is **0741**. The **police sta-tion** is on Ermou Street (℗ **0741/22-143**).

The Corinth Canal

When the main road ran directly past the restaurants and cafes on either side of the canal, almost everyone used to stop here for a coffee, a souvlaki, and a look at the canal that separates the Peloponnese from the mainland. Now buses, trucks, and most cars stay on the new highway, but you can still take the exit for the Canal and Tourist Area to see the canal and have a snack. There's a small post office at the canal and a kiosk with postcards and English-language newspapers. Most of the large souvlaki places have surprisingly clean toilet facilities (and very tough souvlaki). One word of warning that's necessary here and almost nowhere else in Greece: Be sure to lock your car door. This is a popular spot for thieves to prey on unwary tourists.

The French engineers who built the Corinth Canal between 1881 and 1893 used lots of dynamite, blasting through 87m (285 ft.) of sheer rock to make this 6-km- (4-mile-) long, 27-m- (30-yd.-) wide passageway. The canal utterly revo-lutionized shipping in the Mediterranean; vessels that previously had spent days making their way around Cape Matapan, at the southern tip of the Peloponnese, could dart through the canal in hours.

Exploring Ancient Corinth

To reach Ancient Corinth, follow the signs after the Corinth Canal for Ancient and Old Corinth. It's a 20-minute bus ride from the train station or 10 minutes by taxi.

Ancient Corinth 🗲🗲   Although Corinth's greatest period of prosperity was between the 8th and 5th centuries B.C., most of the ancient remains here are from the Roman period. Razed and destroyed when the Romans conquered Greece in 146 B.C., Corinth was refounded by Julius Caesar in 44 B.C. and began a second period of wealth and prosperity. When St. Paul visited here in A.D. 52, he found Corinth all too sophisticated and chastised the Corinthians for their wanton ways.

By the 2nd century A.D., Corinth was much larger and more powerful than Athens. During the next hundred years, a series of barbarian invasions and attacks undermined Corinth's prosperity. Thereafter, although the long series of invaders fought for control of the strategic citadel of Acrocorinth, Corinth itself was a provincial backwater with a glorious past.

The most conspicuous—and the most handsome—surviving building at Ancient Corinth is clearly the 6th-century B.C. **Temple of Apollo,** which stands on a low hill overlooking the extensive remains of the **Roman Agora** (market-place). Only seven of the temple's 38 monolithic Doric columns are standing, the others having long since been toppled by earthquakes.

Ancient Corinth's main drag, the 12-m- (40-ft.-) wide marble-paved road that ran from the port of Lechaion into the heart of the marketplace, is clearly visible from the temple. Along the road, and throughout the Agora, are the foundations of hundreds of the stores that once stocked everything from spices imported from Asia Minor to jugs of wine made from Corinth's excellent grapes.

Two spots in the Agora are especially famous—the **Fountain of Peirene** and the **Bema.** In the 2nd century A.D., the famous Roman traveler, Philhellene, and benefactor Herodes Atticus encased the modest Greek fountain in the elaborate two-story building with arches, arcades, and the 5m^2 (50-sq.-ft.) courtyard whose remains you see today. Peirene was a woman who wept so hard when her son died that she dissolved into the spring that still flows here. The Bema (public platform) was where St. Paul had to plead his case when the Corinthians, irritated by his constant criticisms, hauled him in front of the Roman governor Gallo in A.D. 52.

Old Corinth. ℭ **0741/31-207.** Admission to archaeological site and museum 1,200Dr (€3.55, $3.50). Summer, Mon–Fri 8am–7pm; Sat–Sun 8am–3pm. Winter, Mon–Fri 8:45am–3pm; Sat–Sun 8:30am–3pm.

Archaeological Museum 𝕬   As you'd expect, this museum just inside the site entrance has a particularly fine collection of the famous Corinthian pottery, which is often decorated with charming red and black figures of birds and animals. There're also a number of statues of Roman worthies and several mosaics, including one in which Pan is shown piping away to a clutch of cows. The museum courtyard is a shady spot to sit and read up on the ancient site, which has virtually no shade.

Ancient Corinth, in the town of Old Corinth. ℭ **0741/31-207.** Admission to museum and archaeological site 1,200Dr (€3.55, $3.50). Summer, Mon–Fri 8am–7pm; Sat–Sun 8am–3pm. Winter, Mon–Fri 8:45am–3pm; Sat–Sun 8:30am–3pm.

Acrocorinth 𝕬𝕬 *Moments*   It's hard to say what's more impressive here: the superb fortifications or the spectacular view across the plain of Corinth to the Gulf and beyond into Central Greece. A winding dirt road runs from the site of Ancient Corinth to the summit of Acrocorinth, the rugged limestone sugarloaf mountain topped by centuries of fortifications that dominates the plain of Corinth. A superb natural acropolis, Acrocorinth was fortified first by the Greeks and later by the Byzantines, Franks, Venetians, and Turks. Extensive remains of the centuries of walls, turrets, and towers built here still remain. After you roam around enjoying the seemingly endless view over the rich plain below, you can relax at the small cafe just outside the site entrance.

Old Corinth. Free. Summer, daily 8am–7pm; winter, daily 8am–5pm.

NAFPLION 𝕬𝕬

With two hilltop Venetian fortresses, shady parks, an interesting assortment of small museums, and better-than-average hotels, restaurants, and shops—and even a miniature castle (the Bourtzi) in the harbor—this port town on the northeast coast of the Gulf of Argos is almost everyone's first choice as the most charming town in the Peloponnese. A good deal of Nafplion's appeal comes from the fact that for several years after the Greek War of Independence (1821–28), this was the country's first capital. Although the palace of Greece's young King Otto—a mail-order monarch from Bavaria—burnt down in the 19th century, an impressive number of handsome neoclassical civic buildings and private houses have survived, as have a scattering of Turkish fountains and several mosques.

Essentials

GETTING THERE   By Bus   At least a dozen buses a day run to Nafplion from the **Stathmos Leoforia Peloponnisou,** 100 Odos Kifissou (© **01/ 513-4110** or 01/513-4588), Athens. The trip takes about 4 hours because the bus goes into Corinth and Argos before reaching Nafplion.

By Boat   Flying Dolphin hydrofoil service runs from Marina Zea, Piraeus, to Nafplion, from Monday to Saturday, weather permitting. The hydrofoil makes a number of stops and takes almost as long as the bus to reach Nafplion. For fare and schedule information, call © **01/324-2281** or 01/453-6107 in Athens.

By Car   From Athens, head south to the Corinth Canal. Take the new Corinth-Tripolis road to the Argos exit and follow signs into Argos and Nafplion. You'll almost certainly get lost at least once in Argos, which has an abysmal system of directional signs. Allow at least 3 hours for the drive from Athens to Nafplion. When you reach Nafplion, park in the large, free municipal lot by the harbor. If you want to stop at Mycenae or Nemea, take the winding old road to Nafplion. If you want to stop at Epidauros, take the sign-posted turn for Epidauros just after the canal.

VISITOR INFORMATION   The **Greek National Tourist Organization (EOT)** office is at 16 Photomara St. (© **0752/28-131**), catercorner from the bus station in Plateia Nikitara. It's usually open weekdays from 9am to 2pm, but seems to have frequent unscheduled closings. The helpful brochure "Nafplion Day and Night" is sometimes available here, sometimes in shops and hotels.

FAST FACTS   The telephone **area code** for Nafplion is **0752.** The **post office** is open weekdays from 8am to 2pm, and the **OTE telephone and telegraph** office is open weekdays from 8am to 7pm. Both are signposted from the bus station. The **National Bank of Greece** has a branch on the main square, Syntagma Square. There're a number of **travel agencies** in Nafplion, including Staikos Travel, by the harbor (© **0752/27-950**). The best place to swim is at the **beach** beneath the Palamidi, a 15-minute walk (with the sea on your right) from the harborside cafes.

Where to Stay

Byron Hotel ⚔   This pleasant small hotel is in a quiet, breezy location overlooking the Church of Agiou Spiridona, a short, steep hike up from the main plateia. There're a number of nice bits of Victoriana in the sitting rooms and bedrooms (some of which are quite small for two), as well as modern conveniences. Word has gotten out about the Byron's charm, and it's almost impossible to stay here in July or August without a reservation.

Plateia Agiou Spiridona, Nafplion 21100. © **0752/22-351.** Fax 0752-26-338. byronhotel@otenet.gr. 17 units. 21,000Dr (€61.65, $60) double. AE, MC, V. **Amenities:** Breakfast room; terrace. *In room:* A/C, TV, minibar, hair dryer.

Epidauros Hotel   Rooms here are small but pleasant, with good, firm beds, small bathroom, and large hanging cupboard. The location, on a quiet street just off the main square, is excellent; the staff is neither wildly welcoming nor noticeably efficient. The Epidauros has an annex across the street, as well as nearby pension quarters at 8,800Dr (€25.85, $25) for a double.

2 Kokkinou St. (beside the Commercial Bank), Nafplion 21100. ℭ/fax **0752/27-541.** 15 units. 15,000Dr (€44.05, $43) double. No credit cards. **Amenities:** Restaurant, bar, breakfast room.

Hotel Nafsimedon ☆   This "boutique" hotel in a handsome mid-19th-century neoclassical house is a welcome addition to Nafplion's hotels. The hotel is set back from the street and overlooks relatively quiet Kolokotronis Park. The exterior is a warm peach color, and the interior walls are peach and apricot (sponge painted, of course). Rooms are attractively furnished, some with four-poster beds; most are larger than those in most Greek hotels. The service was rather casual for a "boutique" hotel when we visited.

9 Sideras Merarhias St. (on Kolokotronis Park), Nafplion 21100. ℭ **0752/25-060.** Fax 0752/26-913. 13 units. 30,000Dr (€88.05, $86) double. No credit cards. **Amenities:** Breakfast room, bar; terrace. *In room:* A/C, TV.

Nafplia Palace (former **Xenia Palace Hotel**)   When the Xenia Palace was built in the 1970s, its disco, minibars and in-bathroom telephones made it relentlessly modern. For some years now, it has been sadly down at the heels. At press time, it was closed for a thorough renovation. If the renovations are successful, this hotel, with its splendid views of the harbor and Bourtzi, may once again be the place to stay in Nafplion. (Information on the renovations may be available from helios@helioshotels.gr.)

Acronafplia, 21000 Nafplion. ℭ **0752/28-981.** Fax 0752/28-783. 51 units, 54 bungalow units. 60,000Dr (€176.10, $172) double, 50,000Dr (€146.80, $144) bungalow (projected rates). Off-season reductions possible. Rates include breakfast. AE, DC, MC, V. **Amenities:** Restaurant, bar; pool. *In room:* A/C, TV, minibar.

Omorfi Poli Pension ☆☆   What a lovely place! This small pension/hotel above the charming cafe by the same name (Beautiful City) has gone all out, giving guests the sense that they're staying in a Nafplion home—but with their own privacy. There's nothing to fault here—the beds are good, and the tile floors and prints on the walls are nice. This makes a very pleasant base for touring the area. Families will like the rooms with fridges and sleeping lofts for children (25,000Dr/€73.40/$72 for three), and the breakfasts with freshly baked bread. The cafe on the ground floor is very charming.

Odos Sofroni 5, 21100 Nafplion. ℭ **0752/21-565.** 9 units, all with shower only. 17,000Dr (€49.90, $49) double; 25,000Dr (€73.40, $72) family suite for up to 5. Rates include breakfast. Sometimes closed off-season. **Amenities:** Cafe. *In room:* A/C, TV.

Where to Dine

Oddly enough, the restaurants in and just off Syntagma Square are not the tourist traps you'd expect. Furthermore, you'll see a good number of Greeks at the big harborside cafes on Akti Miaoulis. In short, Nafplion has lots of good restaurants, and any number of ice-cream parlors selling elaborate gooey confections.

Benetsianiko SNACKS   The Benetsianiko (Venetian) has taken over the old Pharos restaurant, which specialized in *mezedes* (hors d'oeuvre), and added charcoal grills and an expanded menu of fresh fish to its original offerings.

Akti Miaoulis (by the playground). ℭ **0752/23-598.** Ouzo and standard mezedes from 900Dr (€2.65, $2.60); ouzo and meal of mezedes from 3,500Dr (€10.30, $10); fish by the kilo. No credit cards. Daily 10am–midnight.

Hellas Restaurant ✿ GREEK   Kostas, the omnipresent host of the Hellas, says that there's been a restaurant here for more than 100 years. Shady trees and awnings make this a cool spot to eat outdoors; there's also an inside dining room, where locals tend to congregate year-round. Excellent dolmades with egg-lemon sauce are usually on the menu, as well as stuffed tomatoes and peppers in season. Just about everyone in town passes through Syntagma Square, so this is a great spot to people-watch.

Syntagma Sq. ✆ 0752/27-278. Main courses 1,800–3,600Dr (€5.29–€10.60, $5.15–$9). AE, MC, V. Daily 9am–midnight.

Karamanlis GREEK   This simple harborfront taverna several blocks east of the cluster of harborfront cafes tends to get fewer tourists than most of the places in town. It serves good grills and several kinds of meatballs (*keftedes, sousoutakia,* and *yiouvarlakia*). If you like the food here, you'll probably also enjoy the **Kanares Taverna** and the **Hundalos Taverna,** both also on Bouboulinas.

1 Leoforos Bouboulinas. ✆ 0752/27-668. Main courses 1,500–3,000Dr (€4.40–€8.80, $4.30–$9); fish priced daily by the kilo. AE, MC, V. Daily 11am–midnight.

Noufara ✿ ITALIAN/GREEK   If you're not sure you can face another stuffed tomato, head for the Noufara, which has a wide range of Italian dishes as well as the usual Greek favorites. You can sit under the umbrellas and have a cool drink or a full meal—or you can retreat inside to the air-conditioned dining room. The Noufara also has a branch with the same menu (but a wider offering of fish) just outside Nafplion on the shore in Nea Chios (✆ 0752/52-314).

Plateia Syntagma, Nafplion. ✆ 0752/23-648. Fax 0752/23-945. Main courses 1,500–5,200Dr (€4.40–€15.30, $4.30–$15). MC, V. Daily about 8am–1am.

Savouras Psarotaverna ✿ SEAFOOD   This harborside restaurant has been here more than 20 years, and its fresh fish attracts Greek day-trippers from Tripolis and even Athens. What you eat depends on what was caught that day—and it's always a good idea to check the price before ordering. Expect to pay $50 (and easily more) for two fish dinners, a salad, and some house wine. On summer weekends this restaurant can be terribly crowded.

79 Leoforos Bouboulinas. ✆ 0752/27-704. Fish priced daily by the kilo. AE, MC, V. Daily noon–11pm.

Sokaki CREPES/SWEETS/BREAKFASTS/COFFEES   In the morning, tourists tuck into the full American breakfast here, while locals toy with a tiny cup of Greek coffee. In the evening, young men lounge here, some eyeing the women who pass by, others eyeing the men. A nice place to take a break and watch people watching people.

Corner of Eth. Antistaseos and Nafpleo sts. ✆ 0752/26-032. Drinks and snacks from 600–2,500Dr (€1.78–€7.35, $1.75–$7). Daily 9am–midnight (about 8pm in winter).

Stathmos Cafe ✿ *Moments* DRINKS/SNACKS   This is a nice shady spot to sit and take a break from touring Nafplion, perhaps after visiting the Museum of Childhood next door. The old train station is decorated with a splendid painting of an old steam engine, and has elaborate wooden gingerbread trim, comfortable chairs under shady trees, and a cozy inside room for cold weather.

The old railroad station, Kapodistras Park. No phone. Coca-Cola 600Dr (€1.78, $1.75); mezedes from 1,000Dr (€2.95, $2.90). No credit cards. Daily from about 9am–midnight.

Exploring the Town
Nafplion is a stroller's delight, and one of the great pleasures here is simply walking through the parks, up and down the stepped side streets, and along the

harbor. Don't make the mistake of stopping your harborside stroll when you come to the last of the large seaside cafes by the Hotel Agamemnon. If you continue, you can watch fishing boats putting in at the pier and explore several cliffside chapels. Nafplion is so small that you can't get seriously lost, so have fun exploring. Here are some suggestions on how to take in the official sights after you've had your initial stroll.

ACRONAFPLIA & THE PALAMIDI   Nafplion's two massive fortresses, Acronafplia and the Palamidi, dominate the skyline. There's no charge to visit the cliffs known as **Acronafplia,** where there are considerable remains of Greek, Frankish, and Venetian fortresses, as well as two modern hotels, undergoing renovations at press time (see the Nafplia Palace, above). This is not an easy walk if it is hot, and you may prefer to take a taxi up and walk down (1,500Dr/ €4.40/$4.30). If you do walk up, follow signs in the lower town to the **Church of Saint Spyridon,** one of whose walls has the mark left by one of the bullets that killed Ianni Kapodistria, the first governor of modern Greece. From Saint Spyridon, follow the signs farther uphill to the **Catholic Church of the Metamorphosis.**

This church is as good a symbol as any for Nafplion's vexed history. Built by the Venetians, it was converted into a mosque by the Turks, and then reconsecrated as a church after the War of Independence. Inside, an ornamental doorway has an inscription listing Philhellenes who died for Greece, including nephews of Lord Byron and George Washington. As you continue to climb to Acronafplia, keep an eye out for several carvings of the winged lion that was the symbol of St. Mark, the patron saint of Venice.

Similarly, if you're not in the mood to climb the 800-plus steps to the summit of the **Palamidi** ⚓, you can take a taxi up and then walk down. The Venetians spent 3 years building the Palamidi, only to have it conquered the next year (1715) by the Turks. You'll enter the fortress the way the Turkish attackers did, through the main gate to the east. Once inside, you can trace the course of the massive wall that encircled the entire summit and wander through the considerable remains of the five fortresses that failed to stop the Turkish attack. In June, there're sometimes concerts here in the evening. The Palamidi is open weekdays 8am to 7pm in summer, 8:30am to 5pm in winter. Admission is 800Dr (€2.35, $2.30).

NAFPLION'S MUSEUMS   All four of Nafplion's museums are within easy walking distance of one another. Almost as soon as it opened in 1981, the **Folk Art Museum** ⚓⚓ (1 Odos V. Alexandros; © **0752/28-947;** fax 0752/27-960; pff@otenet.gr), with its superb collection of Greek costumes, won the European Museum of the Year Award. The display highlights "The Best of the Peloponnesian Folk Foundation," with exhibits from its more than 25,000-object collection, which includes coins, ceramics, furniture, and farm implements as well as all those costumes. The museum occupies three floors in an elegant 18th-century house with a shady courtyard and a welcome snack bar. Throughout, labels are in English as well as Greek and a number of dioramas (my favorite shows nine elegant matrons in a 19th-century parlor) help visitors to imagine life in Greece, especially during the 19th century when the Western world impinged on the Greek world. The small gift shop is excellent, with fine ceramic and copper reproductions. This is a wonderful place to get an idea of life in Greece in the "good old days"—which still exist in many villages. It's open from Wednesday to Monday 9am to 3pm; closed Tuesdays and the month of February. Admission is 1,000Dr (€2.95, $2.90).

The **Museum of Childhood,** Stathmos, Kolokotronis Park, an offshoot of the Folk Art Museum, has an eclectic collection of dolls, baby clothes, and toys. In theory, it's open year-round, weekdays from 4 to 8pm and Saturday 9am to 1pm, but there are frequent unscheduled closings. Admission is 400Dr (€1.17, $1.15).

The **Archaeological Museum,** Syntagma Square (© 0752/27-502), is housed in the handsome 18th-century Venetian arsenal that dominates Syntagma Square. The thick walls make it a deliciously cool place to visit on even the hottest day. Displays are from sites in the area and include pottery, jewelry, and some horrific Mycenaean terra-cotta idols, as well as a handsome bronze Mycenaean suit of armor. Open from Tuesday to Sunday 8:30am to 1pm; admission is 500Dr (€1.47, $1.45).

If you like old prints and old photographs, not to mention muskets, you'll enjoy strolling through the exhibits at the **Military Museum,** on Leoforos Amalias (© 0752/25-591). It covers Greek wars from the War of Independence to World War II. Open from Tuesday to Sunday 9am to 2pm; admission is free.

The Shopping Scene

Nafplion has not escaped the invasion of T-shirt and mass-produced–souvenir shops that threatens to overwhelm Greece, but there're some genuinely fine shops. Many are on or just off Odos Spiliadou, the street immediately above Plateia Syntagma. As in most Greek towns heavily dependent on tourism, many of the shops are closed in the winter.

There're lots of jewelry shops in Nafplion, but one that stands out is **Preludio,** 2 Vas. Constantinou (just off Syntagma Square), Nafplion (© 0752/25-277). Preludio has a surprisingly wide range of handsome earrings, necklaces, bracelets, and rings. Some designs are modern, some traditional, others are replicas of ancient and Byzantine styles (including some nice rings and necklaces with good reproductions of ancient coins). The staff speaks excellent English and is very helpful.

In her shop near the waterfront, **Helene Papadopoulou,** 5 Odos Spiliadou (© 0752/25-842), sells traditional weavings and dolls made from brightly painted gourds. Prices start at 10,000Dr (€29.35, $29). Next door, her husband has a wide collection of excellent-quality Greek costume dolls (from 14,000Dr/€41.10/$40), as well as some nice ceramic jewelry of Greek ships and flowers from 1,800Dr (€5.29, $5.15).

Konstantine Beselmes, 6 Athan Siokou St. (© 0752/27-274), sells his own magical paintings of village scenes, sailing ships, idyllic landscapes, and family groups. Although new, the paintings are done on weathered boards, which gives them a pleasantly aged look. Prices begin at around 15,000Dr (€44.05, $43). The **Komboloi Museum,** 25 Staikopoulou St., Nafplion (© and fax 0752/21-618), is a fascinating shop with its own museum of komboloi, usually referred to as "worry beads." Both the shop and museum have examples of Muslim prayer beads, Catholic rosaries, and the secular Greek worry bead. Prices range from a few dollars into the thousands. Some of the antique amber beads are as smooth as silk. Admission is 500Dr (€1.47, $1.45).

The Corner, Staikopoulou and Koletti, just off Syntagma Square (© 0752/21-359), often has old photographs, prints, wood and copper, and, sometimes, handsome old embroidered aprons and vests from traditional costumes. **The Wine Shop,** 5 Amalias, Nafplion (© and fax 0752/24-446), is one of the best wine shops in the Peloponnese and an excellent place to head if you want to browse and learn about Greek wines. Owner Dimitris Karonis is usually happy to talk to browsers about his wide selection of Greek wines, and he also stocks wines and spirits from Europe and North America. The **Odyssey** bookshop, Syntagma Square (no phone), has a wide selection of newspapers, magazines, and books in English, as well as a collection of startling pornographic drink coasters.

Day Trips from Nafplion

TIRYNS The **archaeological site** of Tiryns is 5km (3 miles) outside Nafplion on the Argos road. (Before you visit here, check with the GNTO to make sure that the site is open. It has had several unscheduled closings recently due to damage from several recent earthquakes.) From the moment you see it, you'll understand why Homer called this **citadel,** which may have been Mycenae's port, "well walled." Tiryns stands on a rocky outcropping 27m (87 ft.) high and about 302m (990 ft.) long, girdled by the massive walls that so impressed Homer— but that didn't keep Tiryns from being destroyed around 1200 B.C. Later Greeks thought that only the giants known as Cyclopes could have hefted the 14-ton red limestone blocks into place for the walls that archaeologists still call "cyclopean." Even today, Tiryns's walls stand more than 9m (30 ft.) high; originally, they were twice as tall—and as much as 17m (57 ft.) thick. The citadel is crowned by the palace, whose **megaron (great hall)** has a well-preserved circular hearth and the base of a throne. This room would have been gaily decorated with frescoes (the surviving frescoes are now in the National Archaeological Museum in Athens).

The site is officially open daily, from 8am to 7pm in the summer, 8am to 5pm in the winter. Admission is 500Dr (€1.47, $1.45). Visitors without cars can reach Tiryns from Nafplion by taxi (expect to pay about 7,000Dr/€20.01/$20 for a 1-hour round-trip) or the frequent (about every half-hour) Nafplion-Argos-Nafplion bus (about 700Dr/€2.05/$2; tell the driver you want to get off at Tiryns).

NEMEA 𝓰𝓰 Nemea is signposted on the both the old and new highways from Corinth into the Peloponnese. Throughout antiquity, panhellenic games were held every 4 years at Olympia and Delphi and every 2 years at Isthmia (near Corinth) and Nemea, in a gentle valley in the eastern foothills of the Arcadian mountains. Thanks to the Society for the Revival of the Nemean Games, games were held again at Nemea in 1996 and 2000. The stadium you visit here is not only the place where athletes once contended, but the site of the new Nemean Games.

The **Nemea Museum,** set on an uncharacteristically green Greek lawn, is one of the most charming small museums in Greece, with helpful labels in English. Two excellent site guides are on sale here: "Nemea" and "The Ancient Stadium of Nemea," 500Dr (€1.47, $1.45) each. When you're in the museum, be sure to peer out one of the large picture windows that overlook the shaded ancient site where the coins, vases, athletic gear, and architectural fragments on display were found. A raised stone path tactfully suggests the route from the museum to the site. It passes a carefully preserved early Christian **tomb** and skirts a large Christian **basilica** and Hellenistic bath before arriving at the **Temple of Zeus,** where three of the 32 original Doric columns still stand.

The stadium is signposted across the road from the site. Athletes would have stripped down in the locker room, whose foundations are visible just outside the stadium, and then oiled their bodies with olive oil before sprinting into the stadium through the vaulted tunnel. In the stadium, spectators sprawled on earthen benches carved out of the hillside and watched the athletes take their places at the well-preserved stone starting line.

Tips **Traveler's Tip**

There's almost no shade at Mycenae, where the terrain is alternately rough and slippery. Be sure to wear a hat, sunscreen, and good shoes.

The site is open year-round, from Tuesday to Sunday 8:30am to 3pm. Admission to the museum and the ancient site is 500Dr (€1.47, $1.45), plus another 500Dr (€1.47, $1.45) for the stadium.

MYCENAE ✫✫✫

Greek legend and the poet Homer tell us that King Agamemnon of Mycenae was the most powerful leader in Greece at the time of the Trojan War. In about 1250 B.C., Homer says, Agamemnon led the Greeks from Mycenae to Troy, where they fought for 10 years to reclaim fair Helen, the wife of Agamemnon's brother Menelaus, from the Trojan prince Paris. The German archaeologist Heinrich Schliemann, who found and excavated Troy, began to excavate at Mycenae in 1874. Did Schliemann's excavations here prove that what Homer wrote was based on an actual event, not myth and legend? Scholars are suspicious, although most admit that Mycenae could have been built to order from Homer's descriptions of its palaces.

Essentials

GETTING THERE   By Bus   Buses run frequently from Athens's **Stathmos Leoforia Peloponnisou,** 100 Odos Kifissou (© **01/513-4100**), to Corinth, Argos, and Nafplion. Allow 3 to 4 hours. From any of those places, allow an hour for the trip to Mycenae.

By Car   Mycenae is 114km (71 miles) southwest of Athens and 50km (31 miles) south of Corinth. From Corinth, take the old Corinth–Argos highway south for about 48km (30 miles), and then take the left turn to Mycenae, which is about 8km (5 miles) down the road. From Nafplion, take the road out of town toward Argos. When you reach the Corinth–Argos highway, turn right and then, after about 16km (10 miles), turn right again at the sign for Mycenae. If you're going to Nafplion when you leave Mycenae, try the pleasant back road that runs through villages and rich farmland. You'll see the sign for Nafplion on your left shortly after you leave Mycenae.

FAST FACTS   The telephone **area code** for the modern village of Mycenae is **0751.** You can buy stamps and change money at the mobile **post office** at the ancient site weekdays from 8am to 2pm. This office is sometimes open on weekends and after 2pm, but don't count on it.

Where to Stay & Dine

Most of the restaurants specialize in serving set-price meals to groups. If you eat at one of the big, impersonal roadside restaurants, you're likely to be served a bland, lukewarm "European-style" meal of overcooked roast veal, underripe tomatoes, and, even in summer, canned vegetables. You'll have better luck at the smaller restaurants at the hotels listed below.

La Belle Helene   The real reason to stay here is to add your name to those of Schliemann and other luminaries in the guest book. Tradition aside, this small hotel is usually quiet, and the simple rooms are clean and comfortable. If you stay here, be sure to drive or walk up to the ancient site at night, especially if it's a full moon—it's magical.

Mycenae, 212 00 Argolis. ⓒ **0751/76-225.** Fax 0751/76-179. 8 units, none with bathroom. 12,500–21,000Dr (€36.70–€61.65, $36–$60) double. Rates include breakfast. Off-season discounts sometimes available. DC, V. On the main road to Mycenae, on the left as you approach the site. **Amenities:** Restaurant.

La Petite Planete   The bright, good-size rooms would make this a nice place to stay even without its swimming pool, which is irresistible after a hot day's trek around Mycenae. We've usually found it quieter here than at La Belle Helene, and friends who stayed here recently praised the restaurant (in the evening, not lunch, which is aimed at tour groups) and enjoyed the view over the hills from their window.

Mycenae, 212 00 Argolis. ⓒ **0751/76-240.** Fax 0751/76-610. 30 units. 22,600Dr (€66.35, $65) double. Rates include breakfast. Off-season discounts sometimes available. AE, V. On the main road to Mycenae, on the left as you approach the site. **Amenities:** Restaurant, pool.

Exploring Ancient Mycenae

The Citadel & the Treasury of Atreus 🏛🏛🏛   Just as when you visit the Acropolis in Athens, when you walk uphill to Mycenae, you begin to get an idea of why people settled here as long ago as 5000 B.C. Mycenae straddles a low bluff between two protecting mountains and is a superb natural citadel overlooking one of the richest plains in Greece. By the time of the classical era, almost all memory of the Mycenaeans had been lost, and Greeks speculated that places like Mycenae and Tiryns had been built by the Cyclopes. Only such enormous giants, people reasoned, could have moved the huge rocks used to build the ancient citadels' defense walls.

You enter Mycenae through just such a wall, passing under the massive **Lion Gate,** whose two lions probably symbolized Mycenae's strength. The door itself (missing, like the lions' heads) probably was made of wood, covered with bronze for additional protection; cuttings for the doorjambs and pivots are clearly visible in the lintel. Soldiers stationed in the round **tower** on your right would have shot arrows down at any attackers who tried to storm the citadel.

One of the most famous spots at Mycenae is immediately ahead of the Lion Gate—the so-called **Grave Circle A,** where Schliemann found the gold jewelry now on display at the National Archaeological Museum in Athens. When Schliemann opened the tombs and found some 14kg (30 lb.) of gold here, including several solid-gold face masks, he concluded he had found the grave of Agamemnon himself. However, recent scholars have concluded that Schliemann was wrong, and that the kings buried here died long before Agamemnon was born.

From the grave circle, head uphill past the low remains of a number of houses. Mycenae was not merely a palace, but a small village, with administrative buildings and homes on the slopes below the palace. The **palace** had reception rooms, bedrooms, a throne room, and a large megaron (ceremonial hall). You can see the imprint of the four columns that held up the roof in the megaron, as well as the outline of a circular altar on the floor.

If you're not claustrophobic, head to the northeast corner of the citadel and climb down the flight of stairs to have a look at Mycenae's enormous **cistern.** (You may find someone here selling candles, but it's a good idea to bring your own flashlight.) Along with Mycenae's great walls, this cistern, which held a water supply channeled from a spring 450m (500 yd.) away, helped to make the citadel impregnable for several centuries.

There's one more thing to see before you leave Mycenae. The massive tomb known as the **Treasury of Atreus** is the largest of the tholos tombs found here. You'll see signs for the Treasury of Atreus on your right as you head down the modern road away from Mycenae. The Treasury of Atreus may have been built around 1300 B.C., at about the same time as the Lion Gate, in the last century of Mycenae's real greatness. The enormous tomb, with its 118-ton lintel, is 13m (43 ft.) high and 14m (47 ft.) wide. To build the tomb, workers first cut the 35-m (115-ft.) passageway into the hill and faced it with stone blocks. Then the tholos chamber itself was built, by placing slightly overlapping courses of stone one on top of the other until a capstone could close the final course. As you look up toward the ceiling of the tomb, you'll see why these are called "beehive tombs." Once your eyes get accustomed to the poor light, you can make out the bronze nails that once held hundreds of bronze rosettes in place in the ceiling. This tomb was robbed even in antiquity, so we'll never know what it contained, although the contents of Grave Circle A give an idea of what riches must have been here. If this was the family vault of Atreus, it's entirely possible that Agamemnon himself was buried here.

There's a good deal of up-and-down walking here, much on slippery terrain; give yourself at least 3 hours to absorb this magnificent and mysterious site.

No phone. Admission 1,500Dr (€4.40, $4.30). Summer, Mon–Fri 8am–7:30pm; Sat–Sun 8am–3pm. Winter, Mon–Fri 8am–5pm; Sat–Sun 8:30am–3pm.

EPIDAUROS ✸✸

Epidauros, dedicated to the healing god Asclepios, was one of the most famous shrines in ancient Greece. Greeks came to the shrine of Asclepios in antiquity as they go to the shrine of the Virgin on the island of Tinos today, to give thanks for good health and in hopes of finding cures for their ailments. While at Epidauros, patients and their families could "take the waters" at any one of a number of healing springs and in the superb baths. Visitors could also take in a performance in the theater, just as you can today.

Essentials

GETTING THERE   By Bus   Two buses a day run from the **Stathmos Leoforia Peloponnisou,** 100 Odos Kifissou, Athens (✆ 01/513-4100). The trip takes about 3 hours. There're three buses a day to Epidauros from the Nafplion bus station, off Plateia Kapodistrias (✆ 0752/27-323), with extra buses when there are performances at the Theater of Epidauros. The trip takes about an hour.

By Car   Epidauros is 63km (39 miles) south of Corinth and 32km (20 miles) east of Nafplion. If you're coming from Athens or Corinth, turn left at the sign for Epidauros immediately after the Corinth Canal and take the coast road to the Theatro (ancient theater), not to Nea Epidauvos or Palaia Epidauros. From Nafplion, follow the signs for Epidauros. If you drive to Epidauros from Nafplion for a performance, be alert; the road will be clogged with tour buses and other tourists who are driving the road for the first time.

THEATER PERFORMANCES   There are usually performances at the ancient theater on Saturday and Sunday June to September. Many are given by the National Theater of Greece, some by foreign companies. For information and ticket prices, contact the **Athens Festival Office,** 4 Odos Stadiou (✆ 01/322-1459). Most of the travel agencies in Nafplion sell tickets, as does the theater itself, from 5pm on the day of a performance. The performance starts around 9pm. The ancient tragedies are usually performed in classical or modern Greek; programs cost 1,000Dr (€ 2.95, $2.90) and usually have a full translation or a full synopsis of the play. The excellent Odyssey bookstore on Syntagma Square in Nafplion often has English translations of the plays being performed at Epidauros.

Where to Stay & Dine

Epidauros Xenia Hotel   The best place to stay overnight at Epidauros is here, at the site itself. Once everyone leaves, this is a lovely, quiet spot, in a pine grove beside the ancient site. The bungalow-like units (which could use some serious sprucing up and redecoration) go quickly, so reserve well in advance if you plan to be here the night of a performance. The restaurant serves bland but acceptable food, so you may want to try the **Leonidas Restaurant** (© 0752/ 22-115) in the village of Epidauros; this restaurant is usually packed (often with actors) after performances at the ancient theater.

Ligourio, Nafplias, Peloponnese. © 0753/22-003-5. 26 units, 12 with bathroom. 22,500Dr (€66.05, $64) double. Rates include breakfast. Off-season discounts sometimes available. No credit cards.

Exploring the Ancient Site

The **excavation museum** at the entrance to the site helps put some flesh on the bones of the confusing remains of the Sanctuary of Asclepios. The museum has an extensive collection of architectural fragments from the sanctuary, including lovely acanthus flowers from the mysterious tholos, which you'll see when you visit the site. Also on view are an impressive number of votive offerings that pilgrims dedicated: The terra-cotta body parts show precisely what part of the anatomy was cured. The display of surgical implements will send you away grateful that you didn't have to go under the knife here, although hundreds of inscriptions record the gratitude of satisfied patients.

It's pleasant to wander through the shady **Sanctuary of Asclepios,** but it's not at all easy to decipher the scant remains. The Asklepion had accommodations for visitors, several large bathhouses, civic buildings, a stadium and gymnasium, and several temples and shrines. The remains are so meager that you might have to take this on faith. Try to find the round tholos, which you'll pass about halfway into the sanctuary. The famous 4th-century B.C. architect Polykleitos, who built similar round buildings at Olympia and Delphi, was the designer here. If you wonder why the inner foundations of the tholos are so convoluted and labyrinthine, you're in good company—scholars still aren't sure what went on here, although some suspect that Asclepios's healing serpents lived in the labyrinth.

The museum and archaeological site are open in summer, weekdays 8am to 7pm and Saturday and Sunday 8:30am to 3:15pm; in winter, weekdays 8am to 5pm and Saturday and Sunday 8:30am to 3:15pm. Admission (also covering the theater; see below) is 1,500Dr (€4.40, $4.30). There're several kiosks selling snacks and cold drinks near the ticket booth.

The Theater

If you found the remains of the ancient sanctuary a bit of a letdown, don't worry—the **Theater of Epidauros** is one of the most impressive sights in Greece. Probably built in the 4th century B.C., possibly by Polykleitos, the architect of the tholos, the theater seats some 14,000 spectators. Unlike so many ancient buildings, and almost everything at the Sanctuary of Asclepios, the theater was not pillaged for building blocks in antiquity. As a result, it's astonishingly well preserved; restorations have been minimal and tactful.

If you climb to the top, you can look down over the seats, divided into a lower section of 34 rows and an upper section with 21 rows. The upper seats were added when the original theater was enlarged in the 2nd century B.C. The theater's acoustics are famous; you'll almost certainly see someone demonstrating that a whisper can be heard all the way from the orchestra to the topmost row of seats. Just as the stadium at Olympia brings out the sprinter in many visitors, the theater at Epidauros tempts many to step center stage and recite poetry, declaim the opening of the Gettysburg Address, or burst into song. It's always a magical moment when a performance begins, as the sun sinks behind the orchestra and the first actor steps onto the stage.

Admission to the museum and archaeological site (see above) includes the theater; they keep the same hours.

OLYMPIA 𝖆𝖆𝖆

With its shady groves of pine, olive, and oak trees, the considerable remains of two temples, and the stadium where the first Olympic races were run in 776 B.C., Olympia is the most beautiful major site in the Peloponnese. When you realize that the archaeological museum is one of the finest in Greece, you'll see why you can easily spend a full day or more here. The straggling modern village of Olympia (confusingly known as Ancient Olympia) is bisected by its one main street, Leoforos Kondili. The town has the usual assortment of tourist shops as well as more than a dozen hotels and restaurants.

The ancient site of Olympia lies a 15-minute walk south of the modern village, but if you have a car, you might as well drive; the road teems with tour buses, and the walk is less than relaxing.

Essentials

GETTING THERE   By Train   Several trains a day run from Athens to Pirgos, where you change to the train for Olympia. Information on schedules and fares is available from the **Stathmos Peloponnisou (Railroad Station for the Peloponnese)** in Athens (𝄐 **01/513-1601**).

By Bus   Three buses a day run to Olympia from the Stathmos Leoforia Peloponnisou, 100 Odos Kifissou, Athens (𝄐 **01/513-4110**). There're also frequent buses from Patras to Pirgos, with connecting service to Olympia. In Patras, **KTEL** buses leave from the intersection of Zaimi and Othonos streets (𝄐 **061/ 273-694**).

By Car   Olympia, 320km (199 miles) from Athens, is at least a 6-hour drive whether you take the coast road that links Athens to Corinth, Patras, and Olympia or head inland to Tripolis and Olympia on the new Corinth-Tripolis road. Heavy traffic in Patras, 159km (99 miles) south, means that the drive from Patras to Olympia can easily take 2 hours.

VISITOR INFORMATION   The office of the **Greek National Tourist Organization (EOT)** is on the way to the ancient site near the south end of Leoforos Kondili, the main street (𝄐 **0624/23-100** or 0624/23-125). It's usually open daily, from 9am to 10pm in the summer and from 11am to 6pm in the winter.

FAST FACTS   The telephone **area code** for Olympia is **0624.** The **OTE telephone and telegraph** office on Odos Praxitelous is open weekdays from 7:30am to 10pm. The **train station** is at the north end of town, one street off Leoforos Kondili. You can call 𝄐 **0624/22-580** for a taxi.

Where to Stay

Olympia has more than 20 hotels, which means you can almost always find a room, although if you arrive without a reservation in July or August, you might not get your first choice. In the winter, many hotels are closed.

Hotel Europa 𝖆𝖆   The Europa is clearly the best hotel in town—and one of the best in the entire Peloponnese. Part of the Best Western chain, it's a few minutes' drive out of town on a hill overlooking both the modern village and the ancient site. Most rooms overlook a large pool and garden, and several have views of the ancient site. Rooms are large, with extra-firm mattresses and sliding glass doors opening onto generous balconies. One drawback: although there is an elevator, you have to use the stairs to get to the pool and the breakfast room.

270 65 Ancient Olympia, Peloponnese. © **800/528-1234** in the U.S., 0624/22-650, or 0624/22-700. Fax 0624/23-166. 118 units. 35,000Dr (€102.75, $100) double. Considerable reductions off-season. Rates include breakfast. AE, DC, MC, V. **Amenities:** Restaurant, bar; pool. *In room:* A/C, TV, minibar, hair dryer.

Hotel Neda   With a pleasant rooftop cafe, a comfortable lobby, a serviceable restaurant, and a distinctive red-and-white facade, the Neda (off the noisy main drag) offers good value. Rooms are large, with good bedside reading lamps. Some of the doubles have double beds, but most have twins, so specify which you want. Each room has a good-size balcony, and the bathrooms are better than those usually found in hotels in this price category (thanks to the presence of shower curtains, which help you to avoid spraying the entire room). Rooms here are usually quieter than those at hotels on the main street.

Odos Praxiteles, 270 65 Ancient Olympia, Peloponnese. © **0624/22-563.** Fax 0624/22-206. 43 units. 15,500Dr (€45.50, $44) double. AE, V. **Amenities:** Restaurant, rooftop cafe bar, breakfast room.

Hotel Praxiteles   Just one street back from Olympia's main street, Odos Spiliopoulou, this hotel has a nice neighborhood feel and is the best bargain in town—if you don't mind a no-frills approach. (Someone may, or may not, be on duty at the front desk and there's neither air-conditioning nor central heating.) Rooms are small and spare, with narrow beds; those in front have balconies. If you want to avoid the sounds of conversation from the hotel's excellent restaurant on the sidewalk below the balconies, ask for a room at the back (and hope that the neighborhood dogs don't bark too much).

7 Odos Spiliopoulou, 270 65 Ancient Olympia, Peloponnese. © **0624/22-592.** 10 units. 10,500Dr (€30.80, $30) double. AE, V. **Amenities:** Restaurant.

Where to Dine

There're almost as many restaurants as hotels in Olympia. The ones on and just off the main street with large signs in English and German tend to have indifferent food and service, although it's possible to get good snacks of yogurt or *tiropites* (cheese pies) in most of the cafes.

Taverna Ambrosia GREEK   This large restaurant with a pleasant outside veranda continues to attract locals, although it does a brisk business with tour groups. You'll find the usual grilled chops and souvlakia here, and the vegetable dishes are unusually good, as is the lamb stew with lots of garlic and oregano.

Behind the train station. © **0624/23-414.** Main courses 1,800–3,500Dr (€4.40–€10.30, $5.15–$10). AE, MC, V. Daily 8–11pm. Lunch served every weekend.

Taverna Kladeos ★★ GREEK   The charming Kladeos, with the best food in town, is at the end of the little paved road that runs steeply downhill past the Ambrosia restaurant. You may not be the only foreigner, but you'll probably find lots of locals here. In good weather, tables are set up under canvas awnings and roofs made of rushes. The menu changes according to what's in season. The lightly grilled green peppers, zucchini, and eggplant are especially delicious. The house wine, a light rosé, is heavenly. If you want to buy a bottle to take with you, give your empty water bottle to your waiter and ask him to fill it with krasi (wine).

Behind the train station in Ancient Olympia. © **0624/23-322.** Main courses 1,800–3,000Dr (€5.29–€8.80, $5.15–$9). MC V. Daily 1:30–3pm and 6pm–1am. Sometimes closed Nov–April.

Taverna Praxiteles *(R* *(value* GREEK   The reputation of the Hotel Praxiteles's excellent and reasonably priced restaurant has spread rapidly. It's packed almost every evening, first with foreigners eating unfashionably early, then with locals, who start showing up around 10pm. Although the entrées are very good— especially the rabbit stew with onions (stifado)—it's easy to make a meal of the delicious and varied appetizers. A sampling of mezedes costs about 1,800Dr (€5.28, $5.15) and may include octopus, eggplant salad, taramosalata and Russian salad, meatballs stuffed with zucchini, fried cheese, and a handful of olives. In good weather, tables are outside on the sidewalk; the rest of the year, meals are in the pine-paneled dining room.

7 Odos Spiliopoulou (in the Hotel Praxiteles), Ancient Olympia. © **0624/23-570** and 0624/22-592. Main courses 1,000–3,500Dr (€2.95–€10.30, $2.60–$10). AE, V. Daily about 11am–3pm and about 7pm–midnight.

The Museums & the Ancient Site *(R(R(R*

Archaeological Museum   Even though you'll be eager to see the ancient site, it's a good idea to begin your visit with the museum, whose collection makes clear Olympia's astonishing wealth and importance in antiquity. Every victorious city and almost every victorious athlete dedicated a bronze or marble statue here. Nothing but the best was good enough for Olympia, and many of the superb works of art found since excavations began here more than 150 years ago are on view in the museum. Most of the exhibits are in galleries on either side of the main entrance and follow a chronological sequence, from severe Neolithic vases to baroque Roman imperial statues. The museum's superstars are in the central galleries directly ahead of the entrance.

The monumental images from the **Temple of Zeus** are probably the finest surviving examples of archaic Greek sculpture. The sculpture from the west pediment shows the battle of the Lapiths and Centaurs raging around the magisterial figure of Apollo. On the east pediment, Zeus oversees the chariot race between Oinomaos, king of Pisa, and Pelops, the legendary figure who wooed and won Oinomaos' daughter by the unsporting expedient of loosening his opponent's chariot pins. On either end of the room, sculptured metopes show scenes from the labors of Hercules, including the one he performed at Olympia: cleaning the Augean stables.

Just beyond the sculpture from the Temple of Zeus are the 5th-century B.C. **winged victory** done by the artist Paionios and the 4th-century B.C. figure of Hermes and the infant Dionysios known as the **Hermes of Praxiteles.** The Hermes has a room to itself—or would, if tourists didn't make a beeline to admire Hermes smiling with amused tolerance at his chubby half-brother Dionysios. In addition to several cases of glorious bronze heads of snarling griffins and the lovely terra-cotta of a resolute Zeus carrying off the youthful Ganymede, the museum has a good deal of **athletic paraphernalia** from the ancient games. You'll see stone and bronze weights used for balance by long jumpers, bronze and stone discuses, and even an enormous stone with an inscription boasting that a weight lifter raised it over his head with only one hand.

Before you leave the museum, have a look at the two excellent **site models** just inside the main entrance. As the models make clear, a low wall divided ancient Olympia into two distinct parts: the Altis, or religious sanctuary, containing temples and shrines, and the civic area, with athletic and municipal buildings. Between festivals, Olympia was crowded only with its thousands of statues. Every 4 years, during the games, so many people thronged here that it was said by the time the games began, not even one more spectator could have wedged himself into the stadium. So if the site is crowded when you visit, just remember it would have been much worse in antiquity. You can easily spend a day at Olympia, wandering back and forth between the site and the museum, with a break for lunch. It's also possible to "do" both site and museum in 3 energetic hours.

ⓒ/fax **0624/22-529.** www.culture.gr. Admission 1,200Dr (€3.55, $3.50). Summer, Mon noon–7pm; Tues–Sun 8am–7pm. Winter, Mon noon–5pm; Tues–Sat 8am–5pm; Sat–Sun 8:30am–5pm. The museum is directly across the road from the Ancient Site (see below).

The Ancient Site   Olympia's setting is magical—pine trees shade the little valley, dominated by the conical Hill of Kronos that lies between the Alphios and Kladeos rivers. The handsome temples and the famous stadium are not at once apparent as you enter the site. Immediately to the left are the unimpressive low walls that are all that remain of the **Roman baths** where athletes and spectators could enjoy hot and cold plunge baths. The considerably more impressive remains with the slender columns on your right mark the **gymnasium** and **palestra,** where athletes practiced their foot racing and boxing skills. The enormous gymnasium had one roofed track, precisely twice the length of the stadium, where athletes could practice in bad weather. Also on the right are the fairly meager remains of a number of structures, including a swimming pool and the large square **Leonidaion,** which served as a hotel for visiting dignitaries until a Roman governor decided it would do nicely as his villa. If you want, you can continue around the outskirts of the site, identifying other civic buildings, but you'll probably want to enter the sanctuary itself.

The **religious sanctuary** is dominated by two shrines: the good-sized Temple of Hera and the massive Temple of Zeus. The **Temple of Hera,** with its three standing columns, is the older of the two, built around 600 B.C. If you look closely, you'll see that the temple's column capitals and drums are not uniform. That's because this temple was originally built with wooden columns, and as each column decayed, it was replaced; inevitably, the new columns had variations. The Hermes of Praxiteles was found here, buried under the mud that covered Olympia for so long, caused by the repeated flooding of the rivers. The **Temple of Zeus,** which once had a veritable thicket of 34 stocky Doric columns, was built around 456 B.C. The entire temple—so austere and gray today—was anything but plain in antiquity. Gold, red, and blue paint was everywhere, and inside the temple stood an enormous gold-and-ivory statue of Zeus seated on an ivory-and-ebony throne. The statue was so ornate that it was considered one of the Seven Wonders of the Ancient World—and so large that people joked that if Zeus stood up, his head would go through the temple's roof. In fact, the antiquarian Philo of Byzantium suggested that Zeus had created elephants simply so that the sculptor Phidias would have the ivory to make his statue.

Not only do we know that Phidias made the 13-m (42-ft.) statue, we know where he made it: The **Workshop of Phidias** was on the site of the well-preserved brick building clearly visible west of the temple just outside the sanctuary. How do we know that this was Phidias's workshop? Because a cup with "I belong to Phidias" on it and artists' tools were found here. Between the Temples of Zeus and Hera you can make out the low foundations of a round building: This is all that remains of the shrine that Philip of Macedon, never modest, built here to pat himself on the back after conquering Greece in 338 B.C. Beyond the two temples, built up against the Hill of Kronos itself, are the curved remains of a

---

Fun Fact **Olympic Traditions**

Ancient tradition makes it clear that the Olympic games began here in 776 B.C. and ended in A.D. 395, but is less clear on why they were held every 4 years. According to one legend, Herakles (Hercules) initiated the games to celebrate completing his 12 labors, one of which took place nearby when the hero diverted the Alphios River to clean the fetid stables that King Augeas had neglected for more than a decade. The stables clean, Herakles paced off the stadium and then ran its entire length—600 Olympic feet (192.27m)—without having to take a single breath.

---

once-elegant **Roman fountain** and the foundations of 11 **treasuries** where Greek cities stored votive offerings and money. In front of the treasuries are the low bases of a series of bronze statues of Zeus dedicated not by victorious athletes but by those caught cheating in the stadium. The statues would have been the last thing competitors saw before they ran through the vaulted tunnel into the stadium.

Admission 1,200Dr (€3.55, $3.50). Summer, Mon–Fri 7:30am–7pm; Sat–Sun 8:30am–3pm. Winter, Mon–Fri 8am–5pm; Sat–Sun 8:30am–3pm.

Museum of the Olympic Games   When you head back to town, try to set aside half an hour or so to visit the Museum of the Olympic Games. Not many tourists come here, and the guards are often glad to show visitors around. Displays include victors' medals, commemorative stamps, and photos of winning athletes, such as former King Constantine of Greece and the great American athlete Jesse Owens. A pleasant place to spend an hour.

Admission 500Dr (€1.47, $1.45). Mon–Sat 8am–3:30pm; Sun and holidays 9am–2:30pm.

DELPHI ✹✹✹

Delphi, which the ancient Greeks believed was the center of the world, is the big enchilada of Greek sites. Even more than Olympia, it has everything: a long and glorious history as the scene of Apollo's famous oracle and the Pythian games; spectacular ancient remains, including the Temple of Apollo and the well-preserved stadium where the ancient games took place; a superb museum; and a heart-achingly beautiful location on the slopes of Mount Parnassus. Look up and you see the cliffs and crags of Parnassus; look down at Greece's most beautiful plain of olive trees stretching as far as the eye can see toward the town of Itea on the Gulf of Corinth.

Many tour groups offer day trips to **Delphi,** stopping at the Byzantine Monastery of Osios Loukas (see "Organized Tours," above). In the summer, tour groups clog Delphi's few streets by day, but many head elsewhere for the night, which means that hotel rooms are usually available—although often all the cheap rooms are gone by midmorning. In the winter, thousands of Greeks head here each weekend, not for the archaeological site, but for the excellent skiing on Mount Parnassus. Getting a room in the once-sleepy nearby hamlet of Arachova is virtually impossible without a reservation on winter weekends, and Delphi itself is often full.

ESSENTIALS

GETTING THERE   By Bus   Depending on the season, as many as five daily buses make the 3-hour trip to Delphi from the Athens station, 260 Liossion St. (© **01/831-7096**), north of Omnia Square.

By Car   Take the Athens–Corinth National Highway 74km (46 miles) west of Athens to the Thebes turnoff and continue 40km (25 miles) west to Levadia. If you want to stop at the monastery of Osios Loukas, take the Distomo turnoff for 9km (5½ miles). Return to Distomo and continue via Arachova for 26km (16 miles) to Delphi or via the seaside town of Itea for 64km (40 miles) to Delphi. The approach from Itea is well worth the time if you aren't in a hurry.

VISITOR INFORMATION   The **GNTO** Office (© **0265/82-900**) in the town hall on the main street (Odos Frederikis) is usually open from 8am to 3pm (sometimes later in summer).

FAST FACTS   The telephone **area code** for Delphi is **0265.** Most services are available on Odos Frederikis Street. The **post office** is usually open from 8am to 4pm, and sometimes also open Sunday 9am to 1pm. The **OTE telephone and telegraph office** is open from Monday to Saturday 7:30am to 3pm and Sunday 9am to 1pm. Both banks on Frederikis Street have ATMs (not always in service).

GETTING AROUND   The village of Delphi, with its handful of long, parallel streets connected by stepped side streets, is small enough that most visitors find it easiest to abandon their cars and explore on foot. If you have to drive to the site rather than make the 5- to 10-minute walk from town, be sure to set off early to get one of the few parking places. Whether you walk or drive, keep an eye out for the enormous tour buses that barrel down the center of the road— and for the not-terribly-well-marked one-way streets in the village.

WHERE TO STAY

There's no shortage of hotels in Delphi, and you can usually get a room even in July and August. Still, if you want a room in a specific price category, or with a view, it's best to make a reservation. Finally, in summer (but not in winter when the skiers take over this hamlet) consider staying in nearby **Arachova,** where the hotels are usually less crowded (see "A Day Trip from Delphi," below). Be sure to check whether your hotel has functioning heating if you visit here in the winter.

Castalia Hotel   The Castalia, a white stucco building with projecting balconies on Delphi's main street, has been here since 1938. Most of the good-sized rooms have hand-loomed rugs, and the rear ones have fine views over the olive plain. In 1999, the Castalia added a wing, the 12-unit Villa Apollonia, whose rooms have air-conditioning and TV. Air-conditioning is almost never needed in Delphi; you can decide if you want to pay about 10% more for a room with TV.

13 Vasileos Pavlou and Frederikis sts., 33054 Delphi. © **0265/82-205.** Fax 0265/82-208. 26 units. 30,000Dr (€88.05, $86) double. Rates include breakfast. AE, DC, V. Usually closed weekdays Jan–Feb. **Amenities:** Restaurant. *In room:* A/C (12 rooms), TV.

Hotel Varonos ☆ *(Value)*   This small, family-owned hotel has very clean, spare rooms with fine views out over the olive plain. If you can, take in the rooftop view. This is a very welcoming place: we once arrived here with an ailing gardenia plant, and the entire family pitched in to make sure that it was well taken care of during our stay. If you want to have an early breakfast, mention it at the desk the night before. Be sure to check out the owners' shop next door, with local produce and crafts.

25 Vasileos Pavlou and Frederikis, 33054 Delphi. ©/fax **0265/82-345.** 9 units, 8 with tub/shower, 1 with shower only. 22,000Dr (€64.60, $63). Rates include breakfast (although room without breakfast sometimes possible). Inquire about the 20% discount often available. AE, V. **Amenities:** Breakfast room, lounge with fireplace. *In room:* A/C, TV.

Hotel Vouzas ⓖ   If you don't mind not having a swimming pool, this is the place to stay. It has a cozy fireplace in the lobby and spectacular views, and is a short walk from everything you've come to see. Rooms and bathrooms are very comfortable, and the balconies have not only a table and chairs, but also, when we stayed there, a welcoming pot of basil. That said, the desk staff was supremely uninterested that our TV did not work—but with the view at Delphi, it's borderline criminal to watch TV.

1 Frederikis St. (at Vasileos Pavlou), 33054 Delphi. ⓒ **0265/82-232.** Fax 0265/82-033. 59 units. 40,500Dr (€118.90, $116) double. AE, DC, MC, V. **Amenities:** Restaurant, bar. *In room:* A/C, TV.

WHERE TO DINE

You won't starve in Delphi, but there's no really outstanding restaurant, so you may prefer to head to the village of Arachova, 10km (6 miles) to the north (see "A Day Trip from Delphi," below). That said, in Delphi you might try **Topiki Gefsi,** Odos Pavlou and Frederikis 19 (ⓒ **0265/82-480**), the **Taverna Vakchos,** 31 Apollonos St. (ⓒ **0265/82-448**), or the family run **Taverna Lekaria,** 33 Apollonos St. (ⓒ **0265/82-864**). Its main street location, periodic live music, and usual fine views probably makes **Topiki Gefsi** the most expensive of the three (about 5,500Dr/€16.15/$16) per person). I've often enjoyed the simple food (and tasty toasted bread, sometimes topped with garlic and cheese) at the Lekaria, but this is not a good place to come if you are in a hurry.

EXPLORING THE SITE

If possible, begin your visit when the site and museum open in the morning (both are sometimes relatively uncrowded in the hour before closing, too). If you begin your visit at the museum, you'll arrive at the site already familiar with many of the works of art that once decorated the sanctuary. As with Olympia, it's easy to spend a day here, taking in the site and museum, with a break for lunch.

Delphi Archaeology Museum ⓖⓖⓖ   Each of the museum's 13 rooms has a specific focus: sculpture from the elegant Sifnian treasury in one room, finds from the Temple of Apollo in two rooms, discoveries from the Roman period (including the Parian marble statue of the epicene youth Antinous, the beloved of the emperor Hadrian) in another. If you're lucky, the museum extension will have opened by the time you visit here and there'll be lots more to see. Just outside the first display room stands a 4th-century B.C. marble egg, a symbol of Delphi's position as the center of the world. According to legend, when Zeus wanted to determine the earth's center, he released two eagles from Mount Olympus. When the eagles met over Delphi, Zeus had his answer. (You can still see eagles in the sky above Delphi, but as often as not, the large birds circling overhead are the less distinguished Egyptian vultures.)

The star of the museum, with a room to himself, is the famous 5th-century B.C. **Charioteer of Delphi,** a larger-than-life bronze figure that was part of a group that originally included a four-horse chariot. It's an irresistible statue—don't miss the handsome youth's delicate eyelashes shading wide enamel and stone eyes or the realistic veins that stand out in his hands and feet.

Although the charioteer is the star of the collection, he's in good company. Delphi was chockablock with superb works of art given by wealthy patrons, such as King Croesus of Lydia, who contributed the massive silver bull that's on display. Many of the finest exhibits are quite small, such as the elegant bronzes in the museum's last room, including one that shows Odysseus clinging to the belly of a ram. According to Homer, this is how the wily hero escaped from the cave of the ferocious (but nearsighted) monster Cyclops.

C **0265/82-313.** Admission (which includes the site) 2,000Dr (€5.90, $6) adults, 900Dr (€2.65, $2.60) seniors, and 600Dr (€1.47, $1.45) students. Summer, Mon noon–5:30pm, Tues–Fri 7:30am–6:30pm, Sat–Sun 8:30am–3pm; winter, usually 8:30am–3pm.

Sanctuary of Apollo, Castalian Spring & Sanctuary of Athena Pronaia

As you enter the **Sanctuary of Apollo,** just past the museum, you'll be on the marble **Sacred Way,** following the route that visitors to Delphi have taken for thousands of years. The Sacred Way twists uphill past the remains of Roman **stoas** and a number of Greek **treasuries** (including the Siphnian and Athenian treasuries, whose sculpture is in the museum). Take a close look at the treasury walls: You'll see not only beautiful dry-wall masonry, but countless inscriptions. The ancient Greeks were never shy about using the walls of their buildings as bulletin boards. Alas, so many contemporary visitors have added their own names to the ancient inscriptions that the Greek archaeological service no longer allows visitors inside the massive 4th-century B.C. **Temple of Apollo,** which was built here after several earlier temples were destroyed.

From the temple, it's a fairly steep uphill climb to the remarkably well-preserved 4th-century B.C. theater and the stadium, extensively remodeled by the Romans. In antiquity, contests in the Pythian festivals took place in both venues. Today the theater and stadium are used most summers for the Festival of Delphi—which, on occasion, has featured exceptionally unclassical pop music.

Keep your ticket as you leave the Sanctuary of Apollo and begin the 10-minute walk along the Arachova-Delphi road to the Sanctuary of Athena (also called the Marmaria, which refers to all the marble found here). En route, you'll pass the famous Castalian Spring, where Apollo planted a laurel. Above are the rose-colored cliffs known as the **Phaedriades (the Bright Ones),** famous for the way they reflect the sun's rays. Drinking from the Castalian Spring has inspired legions of poets; however, poets now have to find their inspiration elsewhere because the spring is off-limits to allow repairs to the Roman fountain facade. Poets, be warned: Once an antiquity is closed in Greece, it often stays closed for quite a while.

A path descends from the main road to the **Sanctuary of Athena,** goddess of wisdom, who shared the honors at Delphi with Apollo. The remains here are quite fragmentary, except for the large 4th-century B.C. gymnasium, and you might choose simply to wander about and enjoy the site without trying too hard to figure out what's what. The round 4th-century B.C. tholos with its three graceful standing Doric columns is easy to spot—but no one knows why the building was constructed, why it was so lavishly decorated, or what went on inside. Again, the oracle is silent.

C **0265/82-313.** Admission (which includes the museum) 2,000Dr (€5.90, $6) adults, 900Dr (€2.65, $2.60) seniors, and 600Dr (€1.78, $1.75) students. Summer, Mon–Fri 7:30am–6:30pm; Sat, Sun, holidays 8:30am–3pm; winter, usually 8:30am–3pm.

(Tips **Insider Tip**

Delphi taxi driver Elias Karatzogles (*C* **0265/82-741;** mobile 093/202-3659) speaks English, drives an air-conditioned taxi, and will whisk you off to see Osios Loukas, Arachova, Mount Parnassos, or just about anywhere you want to go at competitive prices.

A DAY TRIP FROM DELPHI

ARACHOVA   The mountain village of Arachova, 10km (6 miles) north of Delphi, clings to Mount Parnassus some 945m (3,100 ft.) above sea level. Arachova is famous for its hand-loomed tagari shoulder bags, heavy blankets, and fluffy flokakia rugs. When several tour buses stop here during the daytime, the tiny village can be seriously crowded. Don't despair—come in the evening, when the shops are still open and the cafes and restaurants allow you to escape from the tourist world of Delphi to the village world of Greece—except, of course, in winter, when Athenian skiers in full après-ski outfits roam the village. Year-round, in decent weather, there's usually an energetic evening *volta* (stroll) on the main street, and if you climb the steep stairs to the upper town, you'll find yourself on quiet neighborhood streets where children play and families sit in front of their homes.

On main street, have a look at the weavings in Georgia Charitou's shop, **Anemi** (𝄐 **0267/31-701**), which also offers some nice reproductions of antiques. **Katina Panagakou's shop,** on the main street (𝄐 **0267/31-743**), has examples of local crafts, too.

For lunch or dinner, try one of the restaurants strung out along the main street with its lovely fresh water springs and cafes: the **Taverna Karathanassi** (𝄐 **0267/31-360**), the **Taverna Dasargyri** (also known as Barba Iannis; 𝄐 **0267/31-391**), or the **Taverna Kaplanis** (𝄐 **0267/31-891**). The Dasargyri has tasty *loukanika* (sausages) and delicious *kokoretsi,* the stuffed entrails that are not perhaps to every traveler's taste. No credit cards are accepted; all are open daily approximately noon to midnight, but sometimes close from about 4pm to 7pm. Dinner for two costs about 7,000 to 8,600Dr (€20.55–€25.25, $20–$25) at all these restaurants.

If you want to stay in Arachova, the **Xenia Hotel** (𝄐 **0267/31-230;** fax 0267/32-175) in town, with 42 rooms, each with a balcony (but charmless decor), has doubles at 24,000Dr (€70.45, $69). The very pleasant **Best Western Anemolia** (𝄐 **800/528-1234** in the U.S., or 0267/31-640), with 52 rooms, on a hill just outside Arachova above the Delphi road, charges 28,000Dr (€82.20, $80) for a double (prices sometimes are much as $20 higher on the weekend). **The Arachova Inn** (𝄐 **0267/31-353;** fax 0267/31-134; www.arachova.com/arachova-inn), with 42 rooms, charges 28,000Dr (€82.20, $80) all summer and on winter weekdays and 35,000Dr (€102.75, $100) on winter weekends. (All these room prices are somewhat negotiable: in the winter, depending on ski conditions, in summer, depending on how good the tourist season is.)

3 The Cyclades

When most people think of the "Isles of Greece," they're thinking of the Cyclades, the rugged (even barren) chain of Aegean islands whose villages of dazzling white houses look from a distance like so many sugar cubes. The Cyclades got their name from the ancient Greek word meaning "to circle," or surround, because the island chain encircles the sacred island of Delos. Today, especially in the summer, it's the visitors who circle these islands, taking advantage of the swift island boats and hydrofoils that link them.

If you were to describe the best-known Cycladic islands (roughly from north to south), **Tinos** would probably be called the "Lourdes of Greece." Its famous church of the Panagia Evangelistria is Greece's most important pilgrimage destination, especially on the Feast of the Assumption (Aug 15). **Mykonos**'s superior

The Cyclades

ATTICA

0   30 mi
0   30 km

GREECE
★ Athens
The Cyclades

ANDROS
Gavrio • Batsi

Aegean Sea

○ Kea
KEA

Gyaros

TINOS
Koumaros
○ Falatados
○ Tinos

Ayios Stephanos
MYKONOS

Kythnos
SYROS
Ano Syros
Ermoupolis ○
Possidon
DELOS
Platis Yialos

KYTHNOS

Serfopoula

SERIFOS
○ Serifos
○ Livadi

Naxos (Hora)
Apollonas
○ Koronos
DONOUSSA
○ Donoussa

○ Naoussa
Ay. Anna
Ay. Prokopios

SIFNOS
Artemona Parikia ○ Aliki
○ Kastro
Kamares ○ Apollonia
Platis Yialos *Antiparos*
PAROS

NAXOS

Koufonissi
Karos
AMORGOS
Lefkes

Iraklia

Milos ○
○ Apolonia
○ Adamas
MILOS

Yialos
○ Hora
IOS

Folegandros

Ia
SANTORINI (THIRA)
Fira ○
○ Kamari
Emborio Perissa
Anafi

Ferry Route

amenities (you can get a margarita as easily as an ouzo) first made it popular in the '60s, and although the Beautiful People might have moved on, Mykonos remains a favorite, although expensive, island—especially in the summer, when reservations are imperative. The crescent of **Santorini (Thira),** with its black sand beaches and blood-red cliffs, is all that remains of the island that was blown apart in antiquity by a volcano that still steams and hisses today. Santorini's exceptional physical beauty, dazzling relics, and elegant restaurants and boutiques cause people to call it "sophisticated." Unfortunately, Santorini's charms draw so many day-trippers from cruise ships that the island almost sinks under the weight of tourists each summer. **Sifnos,** long popular with Athenians, increasingly draws summer visitors to its handsome whitewashed villages, which many consider to have the finest architecture in all the Cyclades. In the spring it's one of the greenest and most fertile of the islands. Finally, some think of **Paros** as the poor man's Mykonos, with excellent windsurfing and a profusion of restaurants and nightspots less pricey than those on its better-known neighbor.

The islands are crowded and expensive in the high season, roughly mid-June to mid-September—and the season seems to get longer every year. If this doesn't appeal to you, visit the Cyclades in the off-season; the best times are in the autumn (mid-Sept to Oct) or in the spring (May to early June—Apr can still be very cold in these islands). Note that while the restaurant you'd hoped to eat in may be closed, and some of the chic shops shuttered, you'll be able to enjoy the islands without feeling that you're surrounded by other visitors. Should you visit in winter, keep in mind that many island hotels have minimal heating; make sure that your hotel has genuine heat before you check in.

On most of these islands, the capital town has the name of the island itself. It's also sometimes called "Hora," or "Chora," a term meaning "the place" that's commonly used for the most important regional town. The capital of Paros, Parikia, is also called Hora, as is Apollonia, the capital of Sifnos.

One note of explanation: We've dropped our coverage of the island of Ios. Alas, in recent years some visitors have transformed Ios from a lively "party island" into an Aegean Animal House, complete with food fights in the tavernas. Let's hope that things calm down on the once-lovely island so that we can again recommend visiting.

GETTING TO THE CYCLADES

BY AIR   Olympic Airways (℃ 01/926-7593 or 01/966-6666 in Athens) has frequent daily service from Athens to Mykonos, Paros, and Santorini; there's service several times a week from Mykonos or Santorini to Thessaloniki, Iraklio, Crete, and Rhodes. In addition, an increasing number of charter flights from all over Europe fly into the various islands. Several small, private Greek airlines serving the islands have gone in (and out) of business in recent years.

BY SEA   Ferries leave daily from Athens's main port of Piraeus and from Rafina, the port east of Athens; contact the Piraeus Port Authority (℃ 01/451-1310 or 01/451-1311) or the Rafina Port Police (℃ 0294/22-300) for schedules. The speedy Seajet (℃ 01/414-1250) catamaran service also departs from Rafina and zips between Andros, Syros, Tinos, Mykonos, Paros, Naxos, and Santorini (Thira).

Ilio Lines (℃ 01/422-4772 in Athens, or 0294/22-888 in Rafina) offers regular hydrofoil service from Rafina to a number of destinations.

It can take an hour for the 27-km (17-mile) bus ride from Athens to Rafina (the most convenient port for Tinos, Mykonos, and sometimes Paros), but you save about an hour of sailing time and usually about 20% on the fare. Buses leave every 30 minutes from 6am to 10pm from 29 Mavromateon St. (℃ 01/821-0872), near Areos Park north of the National Archaeological Museum (indicated on most city maps).

In the summer there's regular ferry service to Iraklio, Crete, from Piraeus, the port of Athens. There're also ferry and hydrofoil connections three to four times a week in the summer between Paros and Samos, Ikaria, Karpathos, and Rhodes; several times a week between Mykonos and Kos and Rhodes; twice a week between Mykonos and Skyros, Skiathos, and Thessaloniki; and two or three times a week between Syros and the Dodecanese.

GETTING AROUND THE CYCLADES

There's frequent ferry service between most of the islands. Schedules can be erratic, and service diminishes suddenly at the end of the season. Smaller excursion vessels are easily affected by high winds. To further complicate matters, a line will sometimes authorize only one agent to sell tickets or limit the number

> **Tips Traveler's Tip**
>
> The winds frequently complicate sea travel on the Aegean. For this rea-
> son, plan to arrive back in Athens from the islands at least 24 hours
> before you have to make any air or sea connections. In July the strong
> winds known as the *meltemi* usually kick up, often playing havoc with
> hydrofoil schedules. The larger ferries still run—although if you're prone
> to seasickness, take precautions. In the winter the strong north winds
> (*vorias*) frequently make sea travel impossible for days at a time.

of tickets available to an agency, giving other agents little incentive to tout its service. You may want to visit several agents or inquire at the port authority. (For specifics, see "Getting There" under "Essentials" for each island.)

The easiest, most comfortable, and most expensive way to island-hop is on a **chartered yacht cruise;** you don't have to worry about ferry connections, hotel reservations, and most meals. **Viking Star Cruises,** 1 Artemidos St., Glyfada, 166 74 Athens (✆ **01/898-0729;** fax 01/894-0952; vikings@forum.ars.net.gr or bjgh44a@prodigy.com), offers 7-day cruises beginning every Friday, from April to early November. They stop on Tinos, Ios, Santorini, Paros, Naxos, Mykonos, and Delos. Last-minute discount fares are occasionally available.

If you want to cruise around the Cyclades (or elsewhere in Greece) for a week or two, and don't want to travel with strangers, put together your own group and contact **Ari Drivas Yachting** (✆ **01/411-3194;** fax 01/411-4459; drivasy@ath. forthnet.gr). Choose among a stunning array of motor yachts and sailing vessels with from 2 to 24 cabins. Drivas prides itself on its superbly trained crews, which include excellent cooks.

For more information on cruises, contact the **Greek National Tourist Orga-nization** (✆ **212/421-5777** in New York; 020/7734-5997 in London; or 01/331-0437 or 01/331-0562 in Athens) or the **Greek Island Cruise Center** (✆ **800/342-3030** in the U.S.). **Sea Cloud Cruises** (✆ **888/732-2568** in the U.S. or 201/884-0407), uses a four-masted private yacht that takes up to 60 pas-sengers on Aegean cruises.

TINOS

An island of green hills and austere mountains, Tinos (pop. 9,500) is home to the famous icon of the Panagia Evangelistria (Virgin of the Annunciation), housed in the handsome church of the same name. Tinos has some good beaches, and there's good walking through the countryside. The area is dotted with small villages and the distinctive dovecotes (some dating from the Venetian occupation) for which this island, like neighboring Andros, is known.

Keep in mind that almost every Greek visiting here is on a pilgrimage, espe-cially on and around March 25 (Feast of the Annunciation) and August 15 (Feast of the Assumption), the most significant pilgrimage days. Be sure to act and dress respectfully (no halters, shorts, or slacks for women; no shorts or sleeveless shirts for men) when you visit Panagia Evangelistria—or any other church. On Tinos alone there're said to be at least 1,000 chapels to visit—although because of van-dalism and theft, many remain locked except on feast days.

Unless you have firm hotel reservations, don't plan an overnight visit to Tinos on summer weekends or during important religious holidays—unless you're willing to rough it and sleep outside.

ESSENTIALS

GETTING THERE   By Boat   There're several ferries daily from Piraeus and three daily from Rafina; you should confirm schedules with **Tourist Information** in Athens (*C* **143**), the **Piraeus Port Authority** (*C* **01/422-6000** or 01/451-1311), or the **Rafina Port Police** (*C* **0294/22-300** or 0294/25-200). **Ilio Lines** (*C* **01/422-4772** in Athens, or 0294/22-888 in Rafina) runs hydrofoil service from Rafina. In summer, there are connections from Tinos several times daily with nearby Andros, Mykonos, and Syros, and several daily excursions to Mykonos and Delos from about 10,000Dr (€29.35, $29).

There are three piers in Tinos harbor; be sure to find out from which your ship will depart. The **port authority** can be reached at *C* **0283/22-348.**

VISITOR INFORMATION   The small **tourist information office** (*C* **0283/22-255**) is near the waterfront at the corner of Kionion and Vlachaki. There are also several helpful travel agents along the waterfront, including the consistently reliable **Windmills Travel** (*C* **0283/23-398;** tinos@ windmills-travel.com).

FAST FACTS   The telephone **area code** for Tinos is **0283.** The **banks** are on the waterfront. The **police station** (*C* **0283/22-255**) is signposted on the harbor. The **OTE telephone office** (*C* **0283/22-399**) is on Megaloharis Avenue, the main street leading up to the Church of Panagia Evangelistria. It's open from Monday to Friday 8am to midnight. The **post office** (*C* 0283/22-247) is at the southeast end of the waterfront.

GETTING AROUND   The **bus station** is at the harbor; check at the KTEL office there for the schedule (which is erratic) and rates. The **taxi stand** is also nearby on the harbor. Several agencies on the harborfront rent **mopeds** and **cars;** we recommend **Vidalis** (*C* **0283/23-400**), which rents both. Rates for mopeds start at about 5,000Dr (€14.70, $14) a day. Car rates are steep in summer, at about 22,500Dr (€66.05, $64) a day, although the rate can drop to 10,000Dr(€29.35, $29) off-season. *Note:* Make sure the rate includes full insurance.

WHERE TO STAY

If you avoid the religious holidays and summer weekends, you'll have no trouble finding a room. You'll find a place to stay easily in the winter, although some small hotels close down if business is slow. Year-round, people often meet the boats to rent you rooms in their homes. For those planning to stay a week or longer, contact **Windmills Travel** (see "Visitor Information," above), which has houses for rent in several villages—a great way to see more of the island and get a taste for village life. The weekly cost is about 254,000Dr (€740.55, $725) for a one-bedroom house, including car rental.

Alonia Hotel *☆☆*   Half a mile from the beach, a mile out of Tinos town, with a big pool and panoramic views from most rooms over the countryside, this is a pleasant retreat. In season, a minibus shuttles back and forth hourly into Tinos town, but you may find yourself lounging happily by the pool (some rooms overlook the pool and its garden). The in-hotel restaurant (also called the Alonia) draws locals with its excellent inventive Greek/international menu.

Ayia Sophia 84 200, Tinos. *C* **0283/23-541**. Fax 0283/23-544. 34 units. 20,000Dr (€58.70, $58) double. Breakfast 2,500Dr (€7.35, $7) extra. No credit cards. Usually closed Nov–Mar. **Amenities:** Restaurant, bar; pool. *In room:* TV, minibar.

Avra Hotel ⚐ This charming century-old neoclassical hotel has simple, spacious, high-ceilinged rooms. The interior was scheduled for a renovation in 2001. Some rooms have balconies with views of the (noisy) harbor, some overlook the garden courtyard, a pleasant place to relax after sightseeing. This is the place to stay in Tinos town if you do not need all the modern conveniences to be happy in a hotel, and don't mind the sometimes noisy bustle of the harbor.

Tinos town, 842 00 Tinos. ✆ 0283/22-242. Fax 0283/22-176. 17 units. 15,000Dr (€44.05, $43) double. Continental breakfast 1,000Dr (€2.95, $2.90) extra. No credit cards. On the harborfront. **Amenities:** Breakfast room; garden.

Hotel Eleana *Value* This excellent value hotel doesn't have harbor views, doesn't serve breakfast or have a restaurant, but the rooms are large, comfortable, and usually quiet.

Ierarchon Sq., Tinos town, 842 00 Tinos. ✆ 0283/22-561. 17 units. 14,000Dr (€41.10, $40) double. V. Just off the harbor and about 365m (400 yd.) past the conspicuous Hotel Poseidon. *In room:* TV (some rooms).

Tinion If you don't mind not having an elevator and think you'd enjoy sitting on a balcony overlooking the bustling harbor, this is the place to stay. The Tinion has been here since 1925, and has the high-ceilinged rooms, nicely tiled floors, and many of the original solid old furnishings to prove it.

Constantinou Alavanou 1, Tinos town, 842 00 Tinos. ✆ 0283/22-261. Fax 0283/24-754. kchatzi@ath.forth-net.gr. 21 units. 18,000Dr (€52.85, $52) double. Continental breakfast 2,500Dr (€7.35, $7). MC, V. Just off the harbor. **Amenities:** Breakfast room. *In room:* A/C, TV.

Tinos Beach Hotel *Kids* This sprawling 1960s beachfront resort hotel with pools, tennis courts, and a restaurant is a good choice for families (there's a separate children's pool). Rooms, all with balconies, are perfectly utilitarian and comfortable, but could use sprucing up (carpets, furniture, and grounds here have all been neglected).

Kionia (4km/2.5 miles west of Tinos town on the coast road), 84200 Tinos. ✆ 0283/22-626. Fax 0283/23-153. 180 units. 30,000Dr (€88.05, $86) double. Rates include breakfast. AE, DC, MC, V. Usually closed Nov–Mar. **Amenities:** Breakfast room.

WHERE TO DINE

Tinos has a number of good restaurants (probably because most of its customers are Greeks). As in most Greek ports, you should (with one exception) avoid harborfront joints; the food is often inferior and expensive, and the service can be rushed. In addition to the ones we suggest, you might check out the longstanding favorite **Palea Pallada Taverna** (✆ 0285/23-516) and **Metaxi Mas** (✆ 0295/29-545), both just off the harbor in Tinos town. Both usually stay open all winter, and Metaxi Mas serves an interesting combination of traditional hearty dishes (goat in red sauce) and off-beat mezedes (deep-fried sun-dried tomatoes).

Caffe Italia ⚐ ITALIAN This welcome place is run by a Greek-Italian couple, who turn out delectable pasta dishes (and serve some wines and cheeses imported from Italy). A nice place to go when you can't face another moussaka, don't want to splurge on seafood, and want to pretend that you're momentarily in Italy (lots of photos of Italy on the stone walls of this taverna).

New port, Tinos town. ✆ 0283/25-756. Main courses 1,200–3,500Dr (€3.55–€10.30, $3.45–$10). No credit cards. Daily 10am–3pm and 6pm–12:30am.

Lefteris GREEK/SEAFOOD This place is an exception to the rule that waterfront restaurants and/or those that cater to tourists are best avoided. Look for a blue sign on the harbor over an arched entrance that leads to a large court-yard decorated with fish plaques. The menu is large and varied; the grilled sea bass, veal *stifado* (stew), and *dolmades* (stuffed grape leaves) in lemon sauce are tasty. Waiters here sometimes perform Greek dances and urge diners to join in.

Harbor front, Tinos town. ℂ **0283/24-213**. Main courses 1,500–4,200Dr (€4.40–€12.35, $4.30–$12); fish priced daily by the kilo. V. Daily 11am–midnight.

O Kipos GREEK   At this small taverna, the cooking is typical down-home Greek, with the usual dishes, including moussaka and souvlakia. You can have a complete meal with good retsina for around 7,000Dr (€20.55, $20).

Tinos town. ℂ **0283/22-838**. Main courses 900–3,000Dr (€2.65–€8.80,$2.60–$9). No credit cards. Daily noon–midnight. Just off the harbor near the conspicuous Hotel Poseidon.

Peristerionas GREEK   On a small lane uphill behind the Lido Hotel, this restaurant, decorated like one of the island's famous dovecotes, has outdoor tables. You can get good grilled meats and fish here, but also try the delicious fennel pancakes, a house specialty.

12 Paksimadi Fraiskou St., Tinos town. ℂ **0283/23-425**. tonyk@mail.otenet.gr. Main courses 3,000–4,500Dr (€8.80–€13.20, $9–$13). No credit cards. Daily noon–3pm and 7–11:30pm. Closed in winter.

Xinari GREEK   This chic spot serves a combination of traditional dishes with a difference (roast pork—but with plums), nouvelle Greek food (familiar dishes with a less heavy hand pouring out the olive oil), and some Lebanese dishes. Meals aren't cheap, but the food is usually very good and the surroundings charming.

Plateia Evangelistria, Tinos town. ℂ **0283/23-337**. Reservations recommended. Main courses 2,800–7,000Dr (€8.20–€20.55, $8–$20). MC, V. Daily noon–4pm and 8pm–12am. Closed Oct–Apr.

EXPLORING THE ISLAND

Each year, the **Church of Panagia Evangelistria (Our Lady of Good Tidings)** ✸✸ draws thousands of pilgrims seeking the aid of the church's miraculous icon. According to local lore, one night in 1822, a nun named Pelagia dreamed that a miraculous icon was buried nearby. Pelagia led her neighbors to the place she had seen in her dream, and when they began to dig, they discovered the remains of a Byzantine church with the icon. As is the case with many of the most holy icons, the Panagia Evangelistria is believed to be the work of St. Luke. The massive church—made of marble from the islands of Paros and Tinos, with a distinctive bell tower—was built in 1824 to house the icon.

A broad flight of marble stairs flanked by lovely pebble mosaics leads to the church; inside, hundreds of gold and silver hanging lamps illuminate the holy icon of the Virgin and the gifts—many in gold, silver, and precious jewels—dedicated by the faithful. Even those who do not make a lavish gift customarily light one of the many candles burning inside the church. The pilgrims' devotion is manifest in these gifts—and in the piety of the visitors who crawl on their knees to the church from the dock.

The church is open daily, from 8am to 8pm in the summer and noon to 6pm in the winter; the small **museum** is usually open from Tuesday to Sunday 8:30am to 3pm; admission is 500Dr (€1.47, $1.45). To enter the church, men must wear long pants and shirts with sleeves, and women must wear dresses or skirts and blouses with sleeves. If there's a church service while you are here, you will hear the beautiful, resonant chanting that typifies a Greek Orthodox service—but remember that it's not appropriate to explore the church during a service.

The **town** of Tinos is always a pleasant place to explore. There's a lively **flea market** and a great many shops selling religious souvenirs, delicate embroidery, and the special sweet of the island, nougat.

The **Weaving School** on Evangelistria Street sells handsome hand-loomed fabrics made by its students. Several **ceramics shops** on the waterfront, including **Margarita, Bernardo,** and **Manina,** have interesting pottery, jewelry, and copperware at moderate prices. Those interested in contemporary hand-painted icons might ask to be directed to **Maria Vryoni,** off Leoforos Megaloharis, the street from the port to the Panagia Evangelistria. The shop accepts credit cards.

Once you're away from the shops near the harbor, you'll find yourself on quiet residential streets where many of the houses have small gardens—or, at a minimum, some bright geraniums planted in whitewashed metal containers that once held olive oil. The small **Archaeological Museum** (© **0283/22-670**) near the Panagia Evangelistria has finds from the Sanctuary of Poseidon at Kionia. It's usually open from Tuesday to Sunday 8:30 am to 3pm; admission is 500Dr (€ 1.47, $1.45). There's also a **Gallery of Modern Greek Painters** and a **Gallery of Tiniot Artists** near the Panagia Evangelistria.

The famous **Venetian dovecotes** (peristerionas), many dating from the 17th century, are scattered throughout the island. You can see several, as well as the scattered remains of the **Temple of Poseidon,** by taking the coastal road 2km (1¼ miles) west of Tinos to the town of Kionia ("Columns"), a pleasant 30-minute hike past the Hotel Aigli. Another hike, from the village of Xinara, leads 565m (1,850 ft.) steeply uphill to the ruins of the **Venetian Fortress of Exoburgo** (Xombourgo, on some maps). There are terrific views from the fortress of at least 60 of the island's small villages. The less energetic may prefer to enjoy some of the villages, such as **Steni** and **Pirgos.**

Tinos has several good **beaches:** The sand beach at Kionia, about 3km (2 miles) west of Tinos town, and at Kolimbithra, on the north coast, are especially good. About 2.5km (1½ miles) east of Tinos town, the beach at Ayios Fokas has a small hotel; more hotels are rumored to be in the works for Kionia and Kolimbithria.

There's **bus service** (usually four times a day) from Tinos town to Ayios Fokas and farther east to the resort of Porto, which has two beaches and several new hotel complexes.

TINOS AFTER DARK

Tinos is not known for its nightlife, but there's a small enclave of music bars off the harbor, including **Argonautis, Fevgatos, Koutsaros,** the **Sibylla Bar,** and **George's Place,** which features Greek dancing. Things usually get going around 10pm.

MYKONOS

If you haven't been to Mykonos (pop. 15,000) for a number of years, you'll probably wander around muttering "ruined" when you arrive. Then you'll realize that once you're away from the shops, bars, and restaurants along the harbor, you're pleasantly surprised at how familiar many of the twisting back streets seem. You might even admit that it's not half bad to have such a wide choice of restaurants. If this is your first visit, you'll find lots to enjoy—especially if you avoid July and August, when it seems that every one of the island's 800,000 annual visitors is here.

What makes this small, arid island so popular? At least initially, it was the exceptionally handsome Cycladic architecture—and the fact that many on the poor island were more than eager to rent their houses to visitors. First came the jet-setters, artists, and expatriates (including many sophisticated gay visitors), as well as the mainland Greeks who opened many of the chic shops and restaurants—all followed by a curious mixture of jet-set wannabes and back-packers. Now, with cruise ships lined up in the harbor all summer and as many as 10 flights each day from Athens, it's easier to say who doesn't come to Mykonos than who does. That's why it's very important not to arrive here without reservations in the high season, unless you enjoy sleeping outdoors—and don't mind being moved from your sleeping spot by the police, who are not always charmed to find foreigners alfresco.

ESSENTIALS

GETTING THERE   By Air   Olympic Airways has as many as 10 flights daily between Athens and Mykonos. In addition, there's usually one flight daily between Mykonos and Iraklio (Crete), Rhodes, and Santorini, and three flights a week between Mykonos and Ios, Lesvos, and Samos. It's difficult to get a seat on any of these flights, so make reservations early and reconfirm them at the office in Athens (© **01/961-6161** or 01/966-6666) or Mykonos (© **0289/ 22-490** or 0289/22-237).

By Sea   From Piraeus, **Ventouris Lines** (© **01/482-5815**) has departures at least once daily, usually at 8am, with a second on summer afternoons; check schedules in Athens by calling the **Tourist Police** (© **171**). From Rafina, **Strintzis Lines** has daily ferry service; schedules can be checked with the **Port Police** (© **0294/ 22-300**). There're daily ferry connections between Mykonos and Andros, Paros, Syros, and Tinos; five to seven trips a week to Ios; four a week to Iraklio, Crete; several a week to Kos and Rhodes; and two a week to Ikaria, Samos, Skiathos, Sky-ros, and Thessaloniki. **Ilio Lines** (© **01/422-4772** in Athens, or 0294/22-888 in Rafina) offers daily hydrofoil service to Mykonos from Rafina.

On Mykonos, your best bet for getting boat information is to check at individual agents, or to see if either the **tourist police** (© **0289/22-482**) at the north end of the harbor, or the **tourist office** (© **0289/23-990;** fax 0289/ 22-229), also on the harbor, has an up-to-date list of sailings.

Check each travel agent's current schedule because most ferry tickets are not interchangeable. **Sea & Sky Travel,** Taxi Square, Mykonos town (Hora) (© **0289/22-853;** fax 0289/24-753), represents the Strintzis, Ilio, and Agapitos lines, changes money, and offers excursions to Delos. The **Veronis Agency** (© **0289/22-687;** fax 0289/23-763), also on the main square, offers information, luggage facilities, and other services.

Hydrofoil service to Crete, Ios, Paros, and Santorini is often irregular. For information, check at the **Port Authority** in Piraeus (© **01/451-1311**), Rafina (© **0294/23-300**), or Mykonos (© **0289/22-218**).

VISITOR INFORMATION   The **Mykonos Tourist Office** (© **0289/ 23-990;** fax 0289/22-229) is on the west side of the port near the excursion boats to Delos. The **Mykonos Accommodations Center,** at the corner of Enoplon Dhinameon and Malamatenias (© **0289/23-160;** mac@mac.myk. forthnet.gr), as its name implies, helps visitors find accommodations. The excellent **Windmills Travel** (© **0289/26-555;** www.windmills-travel.com) has an office at the south bus station where you can get general information, book accommodations, arrange excursions, and rent a car or moped. Look for the free Mykonos *Summertime* magazine, available in cafes, shops, and hotels throughout the island.

TOWN LAYOUT   Legend has it that the streets of Mykonos town—which locals call Hora—were designed to confuse pirates, so your own confusion will be understandable. As you get off the ferry, you can see the main square south across the harbor beyond the small town beach and a cluster of buildings; we refer to it as **Taxi Square,** although it's officially called Plateia Manto Mavroyennis, after a local heroine. Here you'll find several travel agents, kiosks, snack bars, and of course, the town's taxi stand. The map published by **Stamatis Bozinakis** is sold at most kiosks for 400Dr (€1.17, $1.15) and is quite decent; the excellent **Mykonos Sky Map** is free at some hotels and shops.

The main street, **Matoyanni,** leads south off Taxi Square behind the church; it's narrow, but you can hardly miss the bars, boutiques, and restaurants. Several "blocks" along it you'll find a "major" cross street, **Kaloyera,** and by turning right, you'll find several of the hotels and restaurants we recommend. If you get lost—and you will—remember that in Mykonos that's part of the fun.

GETTING AROUND   On Foot   One of Hora's greatest assets is the government decree that made the town an architectural landmark and prohibited motorized traffic on its streets. If you don't arrive with your donkey or bicycle, you can walk around town. Much of the rest of the island is served by local buses.

By Bus   Mykonos has one of the best bus systems in the Greek islands; the buses run frequently and on schedule. They cost 200 to 800Dr (€0.60–€2.35, 60¢–$2.60) one-way. There're two bus stations in Hora: the **north station,** near the middle of the harbor below the Leto Hotel; and the **south station,** about a 10-minute walk from the harbor, near the Olympic Airways office (follow the helpful blue signs). Schedules are posted, although subject to change. Bus information in English is sometimes available from the **KTEL** office (✆ 0289/23-360).

By Boat   Weather permitting, excursion boats to **Delos** depart every day at 9am from the west side of the harbor near the tourist office. For more information, see "An Excursion to the Island of Delos," below, or consult a travel agent; guided tours are available. Caïques to the beaches of **Super Paradise, Agrari,** and **Elia** depart from the town harbor every morning, weather permitting. Caïques to **Paradise, Super Paradise, Agrari,** and **Elia** also leave from Plati Yialos every morning, weather permitting. (Caïque service is almost continuous during the high season, when boats also depart from Ornos Bay.)

By Car & Moped   Rental cars and Jeeps are available from travel agents for about 17,500Dr (€50.35, $50) per day, including full insurance, during the high season, and substantially less at other times if you bargain. Mopeds can be a fun way to get around if you know how to handle one and can negotiate the sometimes treacherous roads. Mopeds (around 3,500–8,500Dr/€10.30–€24/$10–$25 a day) are available from shops near both bus stations.

Tips **Finding an Address**

Although some shops hand out a map of Mykonos town, you'll probably do better finding restaurants, hotels, and attractions by asking people to point you in the right direction. Many streets do not have their names posted, and the map leaves off lots of small, twisting, streets—and Mykonos has almost nothing but small, twisting, streets!

Note: If you park in town or in a no-parking area, the police will remove your license plates, and you—not the rental office—will have to find the police station and pay a steep fine to get them back.

By Taxi   Getting a taxi in Hora is easy; walk to Taxi Square, near the statue, and get in line; a notice board gives rates for each destination for both high and low seasons. You can also phone (© **0289/22-400,** or 0289/23-700 for late-hours and out-of-town service). You'll be charged the fare from Hora to your pickup point plus the fare to your destination, so before calling, try to find an empty taxi returning to Hora or flag one down along the road. You can also take a moped taxi in Mykonos town—but only if you like to live dangerously.

FAST FACTS   Area Code   The telephone area code for Mykonos is **0289.**

Banks   The Commercial Bank and the National Bank of Greece are on the harbor a couple of blocks west of Taxi Square. Both are open weekdays 8am to 2pm. The ATMs usually (but not always) function after hours. Traveler's checks can be cashed at the post office and at many travel agents and hotels, usually at a less favorable rate than at banks.

Hospital   The **Mykonos Health Center** (© **0289/23-994** or 0289/23-996) handles routine medical complaints; serious cases are usually airlifted to the mainland.

Internet Access   The **Mykonos Cyber Café,** 26 M. Axioti, on the road between the south bus station and the windmills (© **0289/27-684;** www. mykonos-cyber-cafe.com), is usually open daily from 9am to 10pm and charges 6,000Dr (€17.60, $17) per hour or 1,500Dr (€4.40, $4.30) for 15 minutes.

Laundry   The **Ace Laundry** is on Ayios Efthimiou (© **0289/28-389**) near the bus station. A self-service **launderette** is on Ayion Anaryiron Street at Scarpa, behind the Church of Paraportiani. Hotel chambermaids often do laundry for a reasonable fee, which you should agree on in advance.

Police   The **Tourist Police** office (© **0289/22-482**) is on the west side of the port near the ferries to Delos. The **Port Police** office (© **0289/22-218**) is on the east side of the harborfront near the post office. The **local police** office (© **0289/22-235**) is behind the grammar school.

Post Office   The post office (© **0289/22-238**), on the east side of the harbor near the Port Police, is open weekdays from 7:30am to 2pm.

Telephones   The **OTE telephone office** (© **0289/22-499**), on the east side of the harbor beyond the Hotel Leto, is usually open daily from 7:30am to 10pm.

WHERE TO STAY

In summer, if you arrive by ferry, you're met by a throng of people hawking rooms, some in small hotels, others in private homes. If you don't have a hotel reservation, one of these rooms may be very welcome. If you're pretty sure that won't suit your needs, be sure you have reserved a room 1 to 3 months in advance of your visit. Many hotels are fully booked all summer by tour groups or regular patrons. Keep in mind that Mykonos is an easier, more pleasant place to visit in the spring or fall—and off-season hotel rates are sometimes half the quoted high-season rate. Also keep in mind that many small hotels (and restaurants and shops) close in winter, especially if business is slow.

   Mykonos Accommodations Center (MAC), Odos Enoplon Dinameon 10 (© **0289/23-160** or 0289/23-408; fax 0289/24-137; http://mykonos-accommodation.com; mac@mac.myk.forthnet.gr), will correspond, talk by phone, or meet with you to determine the best accommodation for your budget. The service is free when booking hotel stays of 3 nights or longer; shorter stays or bookings of budget accommodations will bring a fee of 7,000Dr (€20.55, $20).

In & Around Hora

Belvedere Hotel ⭐⭐   The spiffy new (1998) Belvedere, on the main road into town, has stunning views over the town and harbor, a few minutes' walk away. Rooms are nicely furnished. This is the place to stay if you want the amenities of Mykonos's beach resorts, but prefer to be within walking distance of Hora. The in-house Remvi restaurant, in a handsomely restored 1850s house that is part of the hotel, is excellent (and pricey). In 1999, the Belvedere added the Campani Lounge, with full conference facilities, including state of the art digital video display and constant Greek stock market reports. In season, there is often massage, hairdresser, and barber service.

Hora (Rohari District), 846 00 Mykonos. ℂ **0289/25-112**. Fax 0289/25-126. www.belvederehotel.com. 47 units. 35,000–100,000Dr (€ 102.75–€290.35, $100–)$286) double. Rates include breakfast. Considerable off-season reductions usually available. AE, MC, V. **Amenities:** Restaurant, bar; pool; Jacuzzi; sauna. *In room:* A/C, TV, dataport (10 rooms), minibar, hair dryer.

Cavo Tagoo ⭐   This elegant hotel set into a cliff is hard to resist—its island-style architecture has won awards, and its gleaming marble floors, nicely crafted wooden furniture and local-style weavings are a genuine pleasure. It's only a 15-minute walk to Hora's harbor, although you may find it hard to budge: A (salt-water) pool and a good restaurant are right here.

Hora, 846 00 Mykonos. ℂ **0289/23-692**, 0289/23-693, or 0289/23-694. Fax 0289/24-923. 72 units. 60,000–70,000Dr (€88.05–€204.50, $177–$200) double. Rates include buffet breakfast. AE, MC, V. Closed Nov–Mar. **Amenities:** Restaurant, bar; pool. *In room:* A/C, TV, minibar, hair dryer.

Matina Hotel ⭐   This small hotel is inside a large garden that makes it especially quiet for its central location. Rooms are small, modern, and comfortable, and the owner has been described by several readers as "very helpful." We agree.

3 Fournakion St., Hora, 846 00 Mykonos. ℂ **0289/22-387**. Fax 0289/24-501. 14 units. 30,000Dr (€88.05, $86) double. Continental breakfast 2,000Dr (€5.90, $6). AE, MC, V. **Amenities:** Breakfast room; garden.

Philippi Hotel   Each room in this homey little hotel in the heart of Mykonos town is different, so you might want to have a look at several before choosing yours. The owner tends a lush garden that often provides flowers for her son's restaurant, the elegant Philippi (see "Where to Dine," below), which can be reached through the garden.

25 Kaloyera St., Hora, 846 00 Mykonos. ℂ **0289/22-294**. Fax 0289/24-680. 13 units. 17,500Dr (€50.35, $50) double. No credit cards. **Amenities:** Restaurant, breakfast room; garden.

AROUND THE ISLAND

Although most visitors prefer to stay in Hora and commute to the beaches, there are hotels near many of the more popular island beaches.

There are private studios and simple pensions at Paradise and Super Paradise beaches, but rooms are almost impossible to get, and prices more than double in July and August. Contact the **Mykonos Accommodations Center** (ℂ **0289/ 23-160**)—or, for Super Paradise, **GATS Travel** (ℂ **0289/22-404**)—for information on the properties they represent. The tavernas at each beach may also have suggestions.

AT KALAFATI   **The Paradise Aphrodite Hotel** (ℂ **0289/71-367**) has a large pool, two restaurants, and 150 rooms. It's a good value in May, June, and October, when a double costs about 30,000Dr (€102.75, $100).

AT ORNOS BAY   Try elegant new **Kivotos Clubhouse,** Ornos Bay, 846 00 Mykonos (ⓒ **800/345-8236** or 0289/25-795; fax 0289/22-844), where most of the 21 units overlook the sea. If you don't like saltwater, head for the freshwater pool, or the Jacuzzi and sauna. Kivotos Clubhouse is small enough to be intimate and tranquil. Small wonder that this is a popular honeymoon destination. If you ever want to leave (there are several restaurants), the hotel minibus will whisk you into town. Doubles run 52,500 to 140,000Dr (€150.30–€410.10, $150–$400).

AT PLATI YIALOS   The 82 units at the **Hotel Petassos Bay,** Plati Yialos, 846 00 Mykonos (ⓒ **0289/23-737;** fax 0289/24-101; www.vacation.forthnet.gr/ petabeac.htm), all have air-conditioning and minibars, and are large and comfortable. Doubles rent for 52,500Dr (€150.30, $150). Each has a balcony overlooking the (relatively secluded) beach, which is less than 36m (40 yd.) away. The hotel has a good-size pool and sun deck, Jacuzzi, gym, and sauna, and offers free round-trip transportation from the harbor or airport, safety boxes, and laundry service. The new seaside restaurant has a great view and serves a big buffet breakfast (not included in room rate).

AT AYIOS STEPHANOS   This popular resort, about 4km (2½ miles) north of Hora, has a number of hotels; the 38-unit **Princess of Mykonos,** Ayios Stephanos beach, 846 00 Mykonos (ⓒ **0289/23-806;** fax 0289/23031), is the most elegant. The Princess has bungalows, a gym, a pool, and an excellent beach; doubles cost from 60,000Dr (€ 176.10, $172). The **Hotel Artemis,** Ayios Stephanos, 846 00 Mykonos (ⓒ **0289/22-345**), near the beach and bus stop, offers 23 units with bathroom for 35,000Dr (€102.75, $100), breakfast included. The small **Hotel Mina,** Ayios Stephanos, 846 00 Mykonos (ⓒ **0289/23-024**), uphill behind the Artemis, has 15 doubles with bathroom that go for 21,000Dr (€61.65, $60). All these hotels are usually closed from November to March.

WHERE TO DINE

Unfortunately, most restaurants here know that you're probably just passing through—hardly an incentive to offer the best in food or service. Restaurants also come and go, so if possible, check with other travelers or locals as to what's new and good.

As usual on the islands, most of the harborside tavernas are expensive and mediocre, although **Kounelas** 𝄞 on the harbor (no phone; no credit cards) is still a good value.

Antonini's GREEK   Antonini's is one of the oldest of Mykonos's restaurants, and it serves consistently decent stews, chops, and mezedes. Locals still eat here, although in summer, they tend to leave the place to tourists.

Plateia Manto, Hora. ⓒ **0289/22-319.** Main courses 3,000–5,000Dr (€8.80–€14.70, $9–$14). No credit cards. Daily noon–3pm and 7pm–1am in summer. Usually closed Nov–Mar.

Edem 𝄞 GREEK/CONTINENTAL   This restaurant beside a pool in a garden has a quiet location—unless you have the bad luck to arrive here, as I once did, just before a raucous tour group occupied all the other tables. If that happens, console yourself with the food: the excellent appetizers, lots of tasty (and very pricey) seafood, and lamb stews with delicate seasonings that visitors have enjoyed here for more than 30 years.

Signposted off Matoyanni St. (near the church). ⓒ **0289/22-855.** Reservations recommended July–Aug. Main courses 3,500–6,500Dr (€10.30–€19.10, $10–$19). AE, DC, MC, V. Daily noon–3pm and 7pm–midnight in summer (hours are flexible; sometimes open in winter).

Philippi ⭐⭐ GREEK/CONTINENTAL   This restaurant in the garden of the Hotel Philippi is a nice place to go to escape the hurly-burly of the harbor. Old Greek favorites share space on the menu with French dishes and a more than usually impressive wine list.

32 Kalogera, off Matoyanni St. ℂ **0289/22-294.** Reservations recommended July–Aug. Main courses 3,000–7,000Dr (€8.80–€20.55, $9–$20). AE, MC, V. Daily 7pm–1am. Walk up the main street, past Kaloyera, and you'll find it on the right.

Sea Satin Market ⭐⭐ GREEK/SEAFOOD   Restaurants open and close on Mykonos, but this new (1999) place on the sea by Hora's famous cluster of windmills looks like a success. First, there's the location: a perfect spot to take in the sunset by the sea. And the food is more than tasty, specializing in fish, grills, and decent salads and vegetables.

On the beach below the windmills, Hora. ℂ **0289/24-676.** Main courses 2,000–10,000Dr (€5.90–€20.35, $6–$29). AE, V. Daily 6:30pm–12:30am.

Sesame Kitchen ⭐ GREEK/INTERNATIONAL/VEGETARIAN   This small, health-conscious taverna draws a big crowd with its spinach, vegetable, cheese, and chicken pies, all baked fresh daily. There's a large variety of salads, brown rice, and soy dishes, including an all-vegetable moussaka, lightly grilled and seasoned meat dishes, and a seafood paella.

Odos Dinameon, Tria Pigadia Sq. ℂ **0289/24-710.** Main courses 1,500–5,000Dr (€4.40–€14.70, $4.30–$14). V. Daily 7pm–12:30am. Walk up the main street, turn right on Enoplon Dinameon, and it's on the right next to the Nautical Museum.

EXPLORING THE ISLAND

Even if you're here for the beaches or to visit the island of Delos, you'll probably want to spend some time exploring Hora and enjoying the twists and turns of the narrow streets—and admiring the harborfront's resident pelican. Try to remember to make haste slowly, and enjoy the unexpected sights you'll see when you (inevitably!) get lost in Hora's maze of streets.

The **Archaeological Museum** (ℂ **0289/22-325**), near the harbor, has finds from Delos; it's open Monday and Wednesday to Saturday from 9am to 3:30pm, Sunday and holidays from 10am to 3pm. Admission is 600Dr (€1.78, $1.75); free on Sunday. The **Nautical Museum of the Aegean** (ℂ **0289/22-700**), across from the park on Enoplon Dinameon Street, has just what you'd expect, including some handsome ship models. It's open daily from 10:30am to 1pm and 7 to 9pm; admission is 300Dr (€0.90, 90¢). The **Museum of Folklore** (ℂ **0289/25-591**), in a 19th-century sea captain's mansion near the quay, has examples of local crafts and furnishings and a re-created 19th-century island kitchen. It's usually open Monday to Saturday 4 to 8pm; admission is free.

Hora also has the remains of a small **Venetian Kastro** (fortress) and the island's most famous church, the **Panagia Paraportiani (Our Lady of the Postern Gate),** a thickly whitewashed asymmetrical edifice made up of four small chapels. Beyond the Panagia Paraportiani is the Alefkanda quarter, better known as **Little Venice** ⭐⭐, for its cluster of homes built overhanging the sea. Many buildings here have been converted into fashionable bars prized for their sunset views; you can sip a margarita and listen to Mozart most nights at the Montparnasse or Kastro bar (see "Mykonos After Dark," below).

Another nearby watering spot is at the famous **Tria Pigadia (Three Wells)** ⭐⭐. Local legend says that if a virgin drinks from all three she is sure to find a husband, but it's probably not a good idea to test this hypothesis by drinking the brackish well water. After you visit the Tria Pigadia, you may want to take in the famous **windmills** of Kato Myli and enjoy the views back toward Little Venice.

Mykonos has a lot of shops, mostly selling overpriced souvenirs, clothing, and jewelry. The finest jewelry shop is **Lalaounis,** 14 Polykandrioti St. (✆ **0289/ 22-444**), associated with the famous Lalaounis museum and shops in Athens. It has superb reproductions of ancient and Byzantine jewelry as well as original designs. If you can't afford Lalaounis, you might have a look at **Delos Dolphins,** Matoyanni at Enoplon Dimameon (✆ **0289/22-765**), which specializes in copies of museum pieces, or **Vildiridis,** 12 Matoyanni St. (✆ **0289/23-245**), which also has designs based on ancient jewelry. If you want to see some serious works of art, try the **Scala Gallery,** 48 Matoyianni (✆ **0289/23-407;** fax 0289/26-993), which represents a wide range of contemporary Greek artists and frequently has exhibitions.

THE BEACHES   If you've come to Mykonos to find a secluded beach, you have made a serious mistake. People come to Mykonos to see and be seen, whether in their best togs at cafes or naked on nudist beaches. If you want to hit the "in" beaches, take a little time to ask around, because beaches go in and out of favor quickly. Then catch the bus or a caïque to the beach of your choice. If you want a quick swim, the closest beach to Hora is **Megali Ammos (Big Sand),** about a 10-minute walk south of town, and usually very crowded. A better but still-crowded beach is 4km (2½ miles) farther north of Megali Ammos at **Ayios Stephanos,** a major resort center with water sports.

Plati Yialos is another favorite. It's served by a bus that runs every 15 minutes from 8am to 8pm, then every 30 minutes until midnight during the summer. If Plati Yialos is too crowded, you can catch a caïque there for the more distant beaches of Paradise, Super Paradise, Agrari, and Elia. **Paradise,** the island's most famous nude beach, remains beautiful, despite the crowds and activity, with especially clear water. Paradise is also easily reached by local bus or taxi.

Super Paradise (Plindri) is accessible only by a very poor road, footpath, or caïque, so it's less crowded. It's predominantly gay and nude, but clothed sunbathing by heterosexuals is tolerated. Farther east across the little peninsula is **Agrari,** a lovely cove sheltered by lush foliage, with a good little taverna.

Elia, a 45-minute caïque ride from Plati Yialos, is one of the island's best and largest beaches, attracting many nudists. It's usually one of the least crowded, although bus service from the north station will probably soon put an end to that. If it gets too crowded, head back west to Agrari.

The next major beach, **Kalo Livadi (Good Pasture),** a beautiful spot in an idyllic farming valley, is accessible by a scramble over the peninsula east from Elia and by bus from the north station in the summer. There's even a nice restaurant.

The last resort area on the southern coast accessible by bus from the north station is at **Kalafati,** a fishing village that was once the port for the ancient citadel of Mykonos. It's now dominated by the large Aphrodite Beach Hotel complex. Several miles farther east, accessible by a fairly good road from Kalafati, is **Lia,** which has fine sand, clear water, bamboo windbreaks, and a small taverna.

MYKONOS AFTER DARK

Mykonos has the liveliest, most abundant (and expensive), and most chameleon-like nightlife—especially gay nightlife—in the Aegean. Don't be surprised if the places we suggest have closed, moved, or changed their name or image.

Watching the sunset is a popular sport at the sophisticated bars in Little Venice. The **Kastro** (✆ **0289/23-070**), near the Paraportiani Church, is famous for classical music and frozen daiquiris. This is a great spot to watch handsome young men flirting with each other. If you find it too crowded or tame, sashay along to **Le Caprice,** which also has a seaside perch. The **Montparnasse** (© **0289/23-719**), on the same lane, is cozier, with classical music and Toulouse-Lautrec posters. The **Veranda** (© **0289/23-290**), in an old mansion overlooking the water with a good view of the windmills, is as relaxing as its name implies.

The decibel level is considerably higher along the harbor, where **Pierro's** (© **0289/22-177**), popular with gay visitors, rocks all night long to American and European music. The **Anchor** plays blues, jazz, and classic rock for its 30-something clients, as does **Argo. Stavros Irish Bar** (© **0298/23-359**), behind the town hall, is among the wildest places on the island. The **Windmill Disco** draws a younger crowd interested in chatting before anything significant happens. And if you'd like to sample some Greek music and dancing, try **Thalami,** a small club underneath the town hall.

The **City Club Disco** has a nightly drag show, and the **Factory,** near the windmills, is the place for gay striptease.

AN EXCURSION TO THE ISLAND OF DELOS ✸✸✸

According to legend, Delos is the spot where Leto gave birth to the twins Artemis and Apollo. Why did Leto pick this tiny—less than 5km² (2 sq. miles)—barren island as her nursery? Because she hoped to escape her lover Zeus's jealous spouse Hera by hiding on the smallest of the Cycladic islands. Although remote and tiny, Delos had an excellent harbor (long since silted up) that made it a vital way station for ancient ships plying the Aegean. The island was also a significant religious shrine in the cult of Apollo, with an oracle second in importance only to Delphi. In addition, the Delian Festival was an important ancient athletic festival. Less endearingly, in Roman times Delos was the most important slave market in the Aegean; there're reports of as many as 10,000 slaves being sold here in a single day. Today, the extensive ruins on Delos make the island rival Delphi and Olympia as one of the most impressive ancient sites in all Greece—although you'll long for the shady pine trees of Delphi and Olympia when you visit virtually shadeless Delos.

GETTING THERE   Delos can be visited only by sea—and many days the sea is too rough for boats to put in here. The site is usually open from 8:30am to 3pm and is always closed on Monday. Most people visit on excursion boats from nearby Mykonos, although there are excursions from other neighboring islands, and Delos is a prominent stop for cruise ships and yachts. Spending the night is not allowed. From Mykonos, organized guided and unguided excursions leave from Tuesday to Sunday from the west end of the harbor; the trip takes about 40 minutes and costs about 3,000Dr (€8.80, $9) round-trip for transportation alone (departure from Mykonos around 8:30am; return to Mykonos around 3pm). **Yiannakis Tours** (© **0289/22-089**) offers guided tours for about 9,000Dr (€26.40, $26) that depart at 9 or 10am and return at 12:30 or 2pm.

High seas can prevent boats going to Delos at any time of the year, so if you want to go here, don't put it off when you visit, as the weather can change unexpectedly. When you go, try to leave as early as possible in the morning, especially in the summer, when both the afternoon heat and the crowds are intense. Be sure to wear sturdy shoes, sunscreen, and a hat, and bring water and a snack. (There's a cafe near the museum, but the prices are high and the quality is poor.)

Exploring the Island

Delos flourished from the earliest days of Greek history through the Roman era, and the remains here attest to its life as the most important religious, maritime, and commercial center in the Aegean. Still, the 3 hours allotted by most excursion boats should be enough for all except the most avid archaeology enthusiasts to explore the site and museum.

Entrance to the site costs 1,500Dr (€4.40, $4.30) unless it was included in your tour; site plans and picture guides are sold at the ticket facility. If you intend to explore the sprawling remains, be sure to get a site plan. If you're energetic enough, climb up **Mount Kythnos,** at 113m (371 ft.) the highest point on the island, for an overview of the site (and a fine view of the neighboring Cyclades).

French archaeologists have been excavating Delos since 1872, and there's a lot to see on and off the **Sacred Way,** the route that runs to the Sanctuary of Apollo. Note that most visitors are more interested in the marble phalluses in the **Sanctuary of Dionysos** than in the remains of houses, stoas, and religious shrines here—although the marble lions along the **Avenue of the Lions** have their admirers. (Some lions may not be in place when you visit, having been taken off-island for restoration work.) If you've never seen ancient mosaics, be sure to take in the handsome pebble mosaics in the **House of the Dolphins,** the **House of the Masks,** and the **House of the Tridents.**

SANTORINI (THIRA) 🟊🟊

Especially if you arrive by sea, you won't confuse Santorini with any of the other Cyclades—although you might be confused to learn that it's also known as Thira. Small ships arrive at Santorini (pop. 8,000; 240km or 130 nautical miles southeast of Piraeus) in Skala, a spectacular harbor that's part of the enormous *caldera* (crater) formed when a volcano blew out the island's center around 1450 B.C. To this day, some scholars speculate that the destruction gave birth to the myth of the lost continent of Atlantis.

Your first choice upon disembarking at Skala will be to decide whether you want to ride the funicular or a donkey 335m (1,100 ft.) up the sheer sides of the caldera to the island's capital, Fira. If you arrive on a large ship, you'll be spared this choice, as you'll dock at the new harbor at Athinios and grab a cab (500Dr/€1.47/$1.45) into Fira. Once there, you may decide to reward yourself with a glass of the island's rosé wine before you explore the shops and restaurants of Fira, swim at the black volcanic beach of Kamari, or visit the dazzling site of Akrotiri, an Aegean Pompeii destroyed when the volcano erupted. In case you were wondering, the volcano is now officially dormant, so you don't have to fret about the plumes of steam you might see around the islands of Kamenes in the harbor.

ESSENTIALS

GETTING THERE   By Air   Olympic Airways has several (six in the high season) daily flights between Athens and the airport at Monolithos (☎ **0286/ 31525**), which also receives European charters. There're also daily connections with Mykonos, three or four a week with Rhodes, two or three a week with Iraklion, Crete, and three a week during the high season with Thessaloniki. For schedule information and reservations, check with the Olympic Airways office on Ayiou Athanassiou Street (☎ **0286/22-493,** or 01/961-6161 or 01/966-6666 in Athens). **Aegean Airlines** (☎ **01/998-2888** in Athens), with an office at the Monolithos airport (☎ **0286/28-500**), also has several flights daily between Athens and Santorini.

By Sea Several companies operate **ferry service** at least twice daily from Piraeus; the trip takes 10 to 12 hours, and costs about 7,000Dr (€20.55, $20) one-way. If you can book a day sailing, you'll pass many of the Cyclades. In summer, there are often daily ferry connections from Santorini to Ios, Mykonos, and Paros. **Excursion boats** go to and from Iraklion, Crete, almost daily. The fare is about 4,000Dr (€11.75, $11) one-way. Because this is an open-sea route, the trip can be an ordeal in bad weather. Check the schedules with the **Tourist Police** in Athens (© 171) or the **Port Authority** in Piraeus (© 01/451-1310) or Santorini (© 0286/22-239).

The high-speed **hydrofoil** Nearchos connects Santorini with Ios, Paros, Mykonos, and Iraklio, Crete, almost daily in the high season and three times weekly in the low season, if the winds aren't too strong.

VISITOR INFORMATION There's no official government tourist office, but there're a number of travel agencies. Several travelers have written of good experiences dealing with **Kamari Tours,** 2 blocks south of the main square on the right (© **0286/22-666;** fax 0286/22-971; kamaritours@santonet.gr). Other agencies include **Joint Travel Service** (© **0286/2 4900;** fax 0286/24992), next to the Olympic Airways Office in Fira; **Nomikos Travel** (© **0286/23-660**), with offices in Fira, Karterados, and Perissa; also, **Damigos Tours,** on the main Fira square (© **0286/22-504;** fax 0286/22-266), often offers excellent guided tours at slightly lower prices than the others. Any of these agencies should be able to help you find accommodations, rent a car, get boat tickets, or book a tour. Expect to pay about 6,800Dr (€20.10, $20) to join a bus tour to Akrotiri or Ancient Thira.

GETTING AROUND **By Bus** Santorini has very good bus service. The island's central bus station is just south of the main square in Fira. Schedules are posted on the wall of the office above it; most routes are serviced every half hour from 7am to 11pm in the summer, less frequently in the off-season.

By Car Most travel agents can help you rent a car. You might find that a local company such as **Zeus** (© **0286/24-013**) offers better prices than the big names, although the quality might be a bit lower. Of the better-known agencies, try **Budget Rent-A-Car,** a block below the bus stop square in Fira (© **0286/ 22-900;** fax 0286/22-887), where a four-seat Fiat Panda should cost about 19,000Dr (€55.75/$54) a day, with unlimited mileage. If you reserve in advance through Budget in the United States (© **800/527-0700**), you should be able to beat that price. The rates are often somewhat lower in Ia; try **Rea Car Rental** (contact Markos Karvounis at © **0286/71-290** or 0286/71-292; mkarvounis@otenet.gr) or **Auto Europe** (© **0286/71-200;** www.vazeos.gr).

By Moped The roads on the island are notoriously treacherous, narrow, and winding; add local drivers who take the roads at high speed and visiting drivers who aren't sure where they're going, and you'll understand the island's high accident rate. If you're determined to use two-wheeled transportation, expect to pay about 3,000 to 6,000Dr (€8.80–€17.60, $9–$17) per day, depending on size and season.

By Taxi The taxi station is just south of the main square. In high season, you should book ahead by phone (© **0286/22-555** or 0286/23-700) if you want a taxi for an excursion; prices are standard from point to point. If you call for a taxi outside Fira, you'll be charged a pickup fee of at least 500Dr (€1.47, $1.45). The maximum fare you should have to pay (from Ia to Akrotiri, for example) is 5,000Dr (€14.70, $14), not including additional charges for luggage, pickup, or late-night travel. If you call for a taxi outside Fira, you're required to pay the fare from there to your pickup point, although you can sometimes find one that has dropped off a passenger. Taxis are not cheap and not always easy to find, so it's a good idea to book one well in advance if you want to plan a trip around the island by taxi. On the other hand, after the bus service shuts down at midnight, taxis (or walking) are your best options for getting around.

FAST FACTS   American Express   The **X-Ray Kilo Travel Service,** near the Tropical Bar at the head of the steps up to Fira from the harbor (🕐 **0286/ 22-624;** fax 0286/23-600), is the American Express representative on Santorini.

Area Code   The telephone area code for Santorini is **0286.**

Banks   The **National Bank** (open weekdays from 8am–2pm; ATM machine) is a block south from the main square on the right near the taxi station. Many travel agents also change money; most are open daily from 8am to 9:30pm.

Hospital   The **health clinic** (🕐 **0286/23-123**) is on the southeast edge of town on Odos Ayiou Athanassiou, immediately below the bus station and the new archaeological museum.

Internet Access   The **PC Club** (🕐 **0286/24-600**) is in Fira. It's usually open from Monday to Saturday 9am to 2pm and 5 to 8pm; 1,500Dr (€4.40, $4.30) per hour for use.

Police   The police station is on Dekigala Street (🕐 **0286/22-649**), several blocks south of the main square, on the left. The **port authority** can be reached at 🕐 **0286/22-239.**

Post Office   The **post office** (🕐 **0286/22-238;** fax 0286/22-698) is off to the right of the bus station. It's open weekdays from 8am to 1pm.

Telephone   The **OTE telephone** office is just off Ypapantis Street, up from the post office. It's usually open from Monday to Friday 8am to 4pm.

WHERE TO STAY

Santorini is packed in July and August, so if you plan a summer visit, make a reservation with a deposit at least 2 months in advance or be prepared to accept potluck. Don't accept rooms offered at the port unless you're exhausted and don't care how remote the village is that you wake up in. If you come between April and mid-June or in September or October, when the island is less crowded and far more pleasant, the rates can be nearly half the high-season rates we quote. Most of the hotels recommended below don't have air-conditioning, but with cool breezes blowing through, you won't need it.

Astra Apartments 🕐🕐🕐   Perched on a cliff-side, with spectacular views, this is one of the nicest places to stay in all of Greece. The Astra Apartments look like a tiny, whitewashed village (flanking an elegant small pool) in still-sleepy Imerovigli. Every detail here is perfect. Best of all, although each unit has its own kitchenette, breakfast is served on your private terrace or balcony, and you can order delicious salads and sandwiches from the bar day and night. Manager George Karayiannis is always at the ready to arrange car rentals, recommend a wonderful beach or restaurant—or even help you plan your wedding and honeymoon here. Our only problem when we stayed here: We didn't want to budge from our terrace, especially at sunset, when the view over the offshore islands is dazzling.

Imerovigli, 847 00 Santorini. ⓒ **0286/23-641.** Fax 0286/24-765. astra-ae@oenet.gr. 18 units. 36,000–100,000Dr (€105.70–€290.35, $103–$285) double. AE, MC, V. **Amenities:** Bar, pool. *In room:* A/C, TV, radio, minibar, hair dryer.

Katikies 🅐🅐   If you find a more spectacular pool anywhere on the island, let us know: This one runs virtually to the side of the caldera, so that you can paddle about and enjoy an endless view. (There's also a smaller pool intended for the use of guests who have suites.) The hotel's island-style architecture incorporates twists and turns, secluded patios, and antiques. If the people in the next room like to sing in the shower, you might hear them—but most people who stay here treasure the tranquility. The top-of-the-line honeymoon suite has its own Jacuzzi, just in case you can't be bothered going to either outdoor pool.

Oia, 847 02 Santorini. ⓒ **800/345-8236** In the U.S., or 0286/71-401. Fax 0286/71-129. katikies@otenet.gr. 22 units. 52,500–105,000Dr (€153.80–€300.80, $150–$300) double. MC, V. **Amenities:** Bar; pool. *In room:* A/C, TV, minibar, hair dryer.

Loucas Hotel 🅐   This is one of the oldest and best hotels on the caldera, with barrel-ceilinged "caves" built to prevent collapse during an earthquake. Rooms are newly renovated; some were enlarged and have arched ceilings and shared patios overlooking the caldera. It's an excellent value for the location, amenities, and view, although it's sufficiently in the heart of things in Fira that it can be noisy here at night.

Fira, 847 00 Santorini. ⓒ **0286/22-480** or 0286/22-680. Fax 0286/24-882. 22 units. 35,000–42,000Dr (€102.75–€123.30, $100–$120) double. Rates include breakfast. MC, V. **Amenities:** Restaurant, bar. *In room:* A/C, TV, minibar.

Youth Hostel Ia   This hostel is both very cheap and very attractive, occupying a cluster of (modern) buildings on the grounds of a 19th-century convent. Lodgings are dorm style, but at these prices, you may not care. You probably won't find better prices than these in season on Santorini—and the garden and breakfast terrace (with sea views) are lovely. You can get snacks most of the day in the cafe. We've had reports that this place is usually reasonably quiet, unlike some hostels, where visitors party through the night.

Oia, 847 02 Santorini. ⓒ/fax **0286/71-465.** 7 units (4-, 6- and 10-person dormitories). 3,500Dr (€10.30, $10) per person. Rates include continental breakfast. No credit cards. Closed Nov–Apr. **Amenities:** Breakfast room, snack bar; garden.

WHERE TO DINE

Camille Stephani GREEK/INTERNATIONAL   Even if you're not staying at Kamari, this restaurant on the north end of the beach, 460m (500 yd.) from the bus stop, will make the trip worthwhile. The house specialty is a tender beef filet with green pepper in Madeira sauce. You can take a moonlight stroll along the beach after dinner.

Kamari Beach. ⓒ **0286/31-716.** Reservations recommended July–Sept. Main courses 4,200–8,600Dr (€12.35–€25.25, $12–$25). AE, DC, MC, V. Daily 1–4pm and 6:30pm–midnight (but often open all day; often closed off-season).

Katina Fish–Taverna 🅐 *Moments* SEAFOOD   One of the best places to eat in Oia isn't in town but down in the port of Ammoudi, which is best reached by donkey (ask in the village about hiring a donkey), or you can walk, or take a taxi. Katina Pagoni is considered one of the very best local cooks, and the setting beside the glittering Aegean is romantic.

Port of Oia (Ammoudi). ⓒ **0286/71-280.** Fish priced daily by the kilo. No credit cards. Daily 11am–1am.

Koukoumavolos ★★ NOUVELLE GREEK   This elegant restaurant was for many years in Oia, but now overlooks the caldera in Fira. There's delicious fresh fish (wonderful monkfish!) and an adventurous menu of "nouvelle Greek" cuisine (dishes are lighter and less oil-saturated than is customary in Greece), and a wide selection of island and off-island wines and cheeses. The view over the caldera is, of course, fantastic—and so is the panacotta with yogurt and cherry sauce.

Fira (Below the Atlantis Hotel). © 0286/23-807. Reservations recommended for dinner. Fish priced daily by the kilo. Main courses 4,000–6,500Dr (€11.75–€19.10, $11–$19). AE, MC, V. Daily noon–3pm and 8pm–midnight.

Selene ★★★ TRADITIONAL GREEK   The best restaurant on Santorini—and one of the best in all Greece—Selene uses local produce to highlight what owners Evelyn and George Hatziyiannakis call the "creative nature of Greek cuisine." The appetizers, including a delicious eggplant salad with octopus and tomato, mushrooms with crabmeat and cheese, and fluffy fava balls with caper sauce, are deservedly famous. Entrees include sea bass grilled with pink peppers, rabbit, quail, and saddle of lamb with yogurt and mint sauce. If you eat only one meal on Santorini, eat it here, in a truly distinguished restaurant with distinctive local architecture—and be sure to try the enormous local capers.

Fira (in the passageway between the Atlantis and Aressana Hotels). © 0286/22-249. Fax 0286/24-395. Reservations recommended. Main courses 4,200–6,800Dr (€12.35–€20.10, $12–$20). AE, MC, V. Mid-Apr to early Oct, Mon–Sat noon–3pm; daily 7pm–midnight. Closed late Oct to early Apr.

EXPLORING THE ISLAND

FIRA   If you're staying overnight on Santorini, take advantage of the fact that almost all the day-trippers from cruise ships leave in the late afternoon, and explore the capital in the evening. As you stroll, you may be surprised to discover that Fira has a Roman Catholic cathedral and convent in addition to the predictable Greek Orthodox cathedral, a legacy from the days when the Venetians controlled much of the Aegean. The name Santorini, in fact, is a Latinate corruption of the Greek for "Saint Irene." The small **Archaeological Museum** (© **0286/22-217**), with both Minoan and classical finds, is near the cable car station in Fira. It's open from Tuesday to Sunday 8:30am to 3pm; admission is 800Dr (€2.35, $2.30). You might find it almost deserted, as most visitors head directly for Thira's shops. Before you do the same, stop at the **Thera Foundation** (© **0286/230-16**), near the cable car station en route to Firostephani, to have a look at the spectacular reproductions and re-creations of the frescoes from Akrotiri. It's usually open from Tuesday to Sunday 8:30am to 3pm; admission is 1,000Dr (€2.95, $2.90).

As to the shops, Fira has a number of nice, small galleries selling watercolors, posters, ceramics, and handcrafted glass—and a great many shops selling jewelry, in addition to the inevitable mass-produced souvenir and T-shirt.

It's a good idea to remember the maxim that all that glitters is not necessarily gold as you scout out Fira's seemingly nonstop jewelry shops. Here, as in virtually every place in the world where cruise ships disgorge eager shoppers, a number of shops sell overpriced fakes.

The best-known (and perhaps the most innovative) jeweler here is probably **Kostas Antoniou,** on Ayiou Ioannou Street (© **0286/22-633;** © and fax 0296/23-557), north of the cable-car station. **Porphyra,** in the Fabrica Shopping Center near the cathedral (© **0286/22-981**), also has some impressive work. Most jewelers will first weigh, then price, what you're interested in—and some will bargain.

VILLAGES Two island villages well worth visiting are **Pirgos (Tower),** the oldest and highest settlement on the island, and **Oia** (also spelled Ia), on a cliff above the caldera. Badly damaged in a massive earthquake in 1956, Oia was virtually a ghost town until it was rebuilt in the 1960s and '70s and resettled. Now its chic shops and gorgeous sunsets make it an increasingly popular place to stay or to visit—especially with those who find Fira too frenetic. If you travel to either village (local buses run there from Fira, or you can take a taxi), keep a lookout for some of the island's cave dwellings (homes hollowed out of Santorini's soft volcanic stone).

BEACHES Santorini does not have the soft sand beaches of Mykonos, but the black volcanic sand and pebble beach make **Kamari** a very nice place to swim, especially in the morning, before the all-day sunbathers arrive (and before the black sand gets seriously hot). On the way to or from Kamari from Fira by local bus or taxi, you can stop at the **Antoniou, Roussos,** or **Boutari** vintners to see how wine is made, have a free sample, and perhaps buy a bottle or two to sample later. Be warned: Vino Santo, Santorini's sweet wine, is very sweet. **Boutari,** Megalohori (© **0286/81-011**), is the island's largest vintner. For 1,800Dr (€5.29, $5.15) you can see the wine press, sample the wines, and snack on mezedes (hors d'oeuvre). The **Antoniou winery** (run by the same family who has the Antoniou jewelry in Fira) is especially charming, with the old wine press and barrels on display.

ANCIENT THIRA & AKROTIRI Above Kamari beach on a rocky promontory are the ruins of **Ancient Thira** (© **0286-22-217** or 0286-22-366), settled in the 9th century B.C., although most of the scattered remains date from the Hellenistic era. At press time, it was open from Tuesday to Friday 8am to 2:30pm, Sunday and holidays 8am to 2:30pm; it was also sometimes open on Saturday 8am to 2:30pm; admission is 1,200Dr (€3.55, $3.50). A good, but alarmingly narrow, road now runs almost to the summit, which can also be reached on foot or by donkey (for hire from some travel agents) by a path. The hilltop site is very fine, but if you have to choose between Ancient Thira and Akrotiri, head for Akrotiri.

The excavations at **Akrotiri,** the Minoan settlement destroyed when the volcano erupted around 1450 B.C., have unearthed buildings three stories tall that were lavishly decorated with frescoes (which are now on view in the National Archaeological Museum in Athens). It's still breathtaking to walk down the streets and peek in the windows of houses in a town whose life was extinguished in a torrent of lava and ash so long ago. The site (© **0286/81-366**) is open from Tuesday to Sunday 8:30am to 3pm; admission is 1,500Dr (€4.40, $4.30). Akrotiri can be reached by public bus or private bus tour; **Damigos Tours,** on the main square (© **0286/22-504**), has knowledgeable and entertaining guides.

SANTORINI AFTER DARK

Most people will want to start the evening with a drink on the caldera watching the sunset. **Franco's** (© **0286/22-881**) is the most famous place for this magic hour, but drinks are expensive; the nearby **Tropical** (no phone) has almost as good a view and charges less. **Archipelago** (© **0286/23-673**) and the **Canava Cafe** (© **0286/22-565**) also have good views. For more reasonable prices and the same fantastic view, continue past the Loucas Hotel to the **Renaissance Bar** (© **0286/22-880**).

Most of the action is north and west of the main square. Underneath the square, the **Kirathira Bar** plays jazz at a level that permits conversation. The

Town Club appeals to clean-cut rockers, while the **Two Brothers** pulls in the biggest, chummiest crowd on the island. For Greek music, find the **Apocalypse Club,** or **Bar 33** for bouzouki. Discos come and go; follow your ears to find them. The **Koo Club** is the biggest, and **Enigma** is popular with those interested in good music. In Oia, **Melissa's Piano Bar** and **Zorba's** are good spots for a drink at sunset.

None of the places recommended above have specific street addresses; it's best just to ask someone for directions. Remember: at virtually all of these places, you'll pay at least 3,000Dr (€8.80, $9) for one drink.

For more sedate entertainment, those visiting in August and September may be able to catch a performance of classical music at the 2-week **Santorini International Music Festival** (© 0286/23-166), when international singers and musicians perform at the Nomikos Centre in Fira. Admission to most events is 5,000Dr (€14.70, $14).

SIFNOS

Sifnos (pop. 2,500) is the most beautiful of the western Cyclades—although the port is bland and uninteresting. Just beyond the port, however, are the island's unusually green hills and valleys, particularly lovely villages. Sifnos also has a reputation for especially good olive oil and distinguished cooking. All this has made the island a favorite summer retreat for Athenians, and now that foreign visitors have discovered Sifnos's charms, the island can be terribly crowded in July (especially around the feast day of the Prophet Elias, the patron saint of the island's most important monastery) and in August. If possible, don't visit then, unless you like your restaurants and beaches very busy—and very noisy.

ESSENTIALS

GETTING THERE   There's at least one boat daily from Piraeus, in addition to daily (twice daily in summer) connections to the other western Cyclades, Serifos and Milos, and less frequently to Kimolos and Kythnos. There are ferry connections four times a week with Santorini; three times a week with Folegandros, Ios, and Sikinos; and once a week with Andros, Crete, Mykonos, Paros, Rafina, Syros, and Tinos. There's a weekly connection with the Dodecanese islands of Karpathos, Kassos, Rhodes, and Symi. Contact the **Port Authority** in Piraeus (© 01/171, 01/451-1130, or 01/322-2545) or in Sifnos (© 0284/31-617) for information.

VISITOR INFORMATION   You can book a room, buy ferry tickets, rent a car or motorbike, arrange excursions, and usually leave your luggage at the **Aegean Thesaurus Travel and Tourism office** on the port (© 0284/32-190; www.travelling.gr/sifnos-aegean-thesaurus), at **Siphanto Travel** (© 0284/32-034;** fax 0284/31-024), or at **Katzoulakis Tourist Agency** (© 0284/32-362) on the port. Check to see if Aegean Thesaurus, which also has an office on the main square in Apollonia (© 028431-151;** fax 0284/332-190), still has its excellent information packet on Sifnos for 400Dr (€1.17, $1.15). At press time, **Ventouris Ferries** (© 0284/31-700) in Kamares had the concession for tickets for most ferry lines, while Aegean Thesaurus handled hydrofoil (flying dolphin) tickets.

FAST FACTS   The telephone **area code** for Sifnos is **0284.** Tourist services are centered around the main square, Plateia Iroon ("Heroes' Square"), in Apollonia, the capital. The **post office** (© 0284/31-329) is open weekdays from 8am to 3pm, and in the summer, Saturday and Sunday 9am to 1:30pm. The **National**

Bank (© **0284/31-317**) is open from Monday to Thursday 8am to 2pm and Friday 8am to 1:30pm. The **OTE telephone office** is open daily from 8am to 3pm, and in summer from 5 to 10pm. The **news kiosk** on the square has a metered phone for after-hours calls. The **police station** (© **0284/31-210**), which also functions as an informal information center, is just east of the square, and a first-aid station is nearby; for **medical emergencies,** phone © **0284/31-315.**

GETTING AROUND   Many visitors come to Sifnos just for the wonderful hiking and mountain trails. A car or moped isn't really necessary, but cars can be rented at **FS** (© **0284/31-795**) and **Aegean Thesaurus** (© **0284/32-190**) in Apollonia, or in Kamares at **Sifnos Car** (© **0284/31-793**). Apollonia has a few moped dealers; try **Yanni's** (© **0284/31-155**), on the main square, or **Easy Rider** (© **0284/31-001**), on the road circling the village. As always, exercise caution if you do decide to rent a car or moped; many drivers, like you, will be unfamiliar with the island roads. The daily rate for an economy car with full insurance is about 18,000Dr (€52.85, $52); a moped rents for about 6,500Dr (€19.10, $20).

By Bus   Apollonia's Heroes' Square (Plateia Iroon) is the central bus stop for the island. The system is fairly efficient; buses run regularly to and from the port at Kamares, north to Artemonas, east to Kastro, and south to Faros and Plati Yialos. A bus schedule is usually posted by the stop in Heroes' Square.

By Taxi   Apollonia's Heroes' Square is also the main taxi stand, although there aren't many of them on the island. Some mobile phone numbers for taxis are © **094/642-680,** 094/444-904, 094/761-210, or 094/936-111.

WHERE TO STAY

Many young Athenians vacation on Sifnos, particularly on summer weekends, when it can be very difficult to find a room. If you plan to be in Kamares during the high season, be sure to make reservations by May. If you're here off-season, many of these hotels are closed, but several remain open year-round. The efficient **Aegean Thesaurus Travel Agency** (see "Visitor Information," above) can place you in a room in a private house with your own bathroom, in a studio with a kitchenette, or in other, more stylish accommodations.

Hotel Anthoussa   This hotel is above the excellent and popular Yerontopoulos cafe and patisserie, on the right past Heroes' Square. Although street-side rooms offer wonderful views over the hills, they overlook the late-night sweet-tooth crowd and can be recommended only to night owls. Back rooms are quieter and overlook a beautiful bower of bougainvillea.

Apollonia, 840 03 Sifnos. © **0284/31-431.** 15 units. 18,500Dr (€54.30, $53) double. Continental breakfast 1,600Dr (€4.71, $4.60). MC, V. **Amenities:** Breakfast room. *In room:* A/C, TV.

Hotel Petali ⚘   This would be a nice place to stay a week, on a relatively quiet side street not far (but all of it uphill) from Apollonia's main square, Plateia Iroon. There are lovely views over Ano Petali (a suburb of Apollonia) to the sea, a large terrace with handsome, comfortable chairs, rooms furnished in Cycladic style, good beds, modern bathrooms, and a small restaurant that serves delicious Sifnian specialties. Although the Hotel Petali does not accept credit cards, its managing office, **Aegean Thesaurus Travel Agency** (© **0284/33-151;** fax 0284/32-190) accepts MasterCard and Visa.

Apollonia, 84003 Sifnos. ©/fax **0284/33-024.** petali@par.forthnet.gr. 10 units. A/C TV TEL. 33,000Dr (€96.85, $95) double. Breakfast 3,000Dr ($9) extra. AE, MC, V. Closed Nov–Mar. **Amenities:** Restaurant, bar. *In room:* A/C, TV.

Hotel Plati Yialos ✫✫   When this hotel was built in the 1970s, it was the island's only beach hotel. Thanks to a recent renovation, it's still the best, standing at the west end of the cove apart from the pack of newer hotels. Ground-floor rooms have private patios, and all rooms have modern bathrooms. There are also a number of suites, which are ideal for families. The Plati Yialos's flagstone sun deck extends from the beach to a dive platform at the end of the cove, with a bar and restaurant sharing the same Aegean views.

Plati Yialos, 84003 Sifnos. ✆ **0284/31-324**, or 0831/22-626 in winter. Fax 0284/31-325, or 0831/55-042 in winter. 29 units. 45,000Dr (€132.10, $129) double; 90,000Dr (€264.15, $257) suite. Rates include breakfast. No credit cards. **Amenities:** Restaurant, bar. *In room:* A/C, TV, minibar.

Hotel Sifnos ✫✫   Many consider this hotel on a quiet pedestrianized street off the Plateia Iroon the best in Apollonia. The hospitable owners have tried hard to make it reflect island taste, using local pottery and weavings in the good-size, bright rooms. It's usually open year-round and has an excellent indoor/outdoor restaurant that attracts locals.

Apollonia, 840 03 Sifnos. ✆ **0284/31-624**. 9 units. 18,000Dr (€52.85, $52) double. AE, MC, V. Usually open in winter. **Amenities:** Restaurant, bar. *In room:* A/C, TV.

WHERE TO DINE
Apostoli's Koutouki Taverna GREEK   There're several tavernas in Apollonia, and this one on the main pedestrian street is generally the best for Greek food. The service is usually leisurely at best. All the vegetable dishes, most made from locally grown produce, are tasty, but portions are on the skimpy side.

Apollonia. ✆ **0284/31-186**. Main courses 1,500–4,500Dr (€4.40–€13.20, $4.30–$13). No credit cards. Daily noon–midnight.

Captain Andreas GREEK/SEAFOOD   This is a typical fish taverna, on the beach, with the catch of the day on the menu, as well as the usual chops and salads. Captain Andreas has many fans, although some find him a bit dour.

Kamares, on the town beach. ✆ **0284/32-356**. Main courses 1,000–2,500Dr (€2.90–€7.35, $2.90–$7); fish priced by the kilo. No credit cards. Daily 1–5pm and 7:30pm–12:30am.

Sifnos Cafe–Restaurant ✫ GREEK   You can start the day here with breakfast, including fresh fruit juice and your choice of a dozen coffees. Stop by later in the day for a snack, light meal, ouzo and mezedes, or dessert. This place often has delicious *rivithia* (chickpeas), a Sifnian specialty, on Sunday.

Apollonia. ✆ **0284/31-624**. Main courses 1,500–5,000Dr (€4.40–€14.70, $4.30–$14). AE, MC, V. Daily 8am–midnight.

To Liotrivi (Manganas) ✫✫ GREEK   One of the island's favorite tavernas is in the pretty village of Artemona, just over a mile's walk from Apollonia. Taste for yourself why the Sifnians consider Yannis Yiorgoulis one of their best cooks. Try his delectable *kaparosalata* (minced caper leaves and onion salad), *povithokeftedes* (croquettes of ground chickpeas), or *ambelofasoula* (crisp local black-eyed peas in the pod). In short, there're lots of vegetarian delights here, but there's also a very tasty beef filet with potatoes baked in foil. This place usually has the excellent Siphnian specialty of chickpeas rivithia on Sundays.

Artemona. ✆ **0284/31-246**. Main courses 1,500–5,000Dr (€4.40–€14.70, $4.30–$14). No credit cards. Daily noon–midnight.

EXPLORING THE ISLAND
Kamares, on the west coast, is the island's port and will be most visitors' introduction to Sifnos—a pity, because it has none of the charm of the capital,

Apollonia, or the inland villages. Still, there's a good **sand beach** at Kamares, and the usual assortment of restaurants and shops, some of which sell the distinctive local pottery, made from island clay.

From Kamares, you can catch a bus for the 5-km (3-mile) trip to **Apollonia** (also called Hora), the largest of the island's seven villages. En route up the hill to Apollonia, you'll begin to get a sense of the island's handsome architecture, especially its stone paths and small, cubical, whitewashed houses, almost all with whitewashed containers of geraniums.

Apollonia's **Heroes' Square (Plateia Iroon)** is the site of a monument to Sifnos's World War II veterans. Home to a number of small cafes, restaurants, and shops, it's the transportation hub of the island, where its vehicular roads converge. There's also a **Museum of Folk Art** on the square. It's usually open from July to mid-September 10am to 1pm and 6pm to 10pm; admission is 500Dr (€1.47, $1.45).

More and more asphalt roads are appearing on Sifnos, but you'll still be able to do most of your walking on the island's distinctive flagstone and marble paths. You'll probably see village women whitewashing the edges of the paving stones, transforming the monochrome paths into elaborate abstract patterns. Apollonia gleams with whitewash, as does the handsome village of Kastro, the former capital, where you can see remains of the walls of the **medieval fortress (kastro).** Throughout the island, you'll see dovecotes, windmills, and small white chapels in amazingly remote spots.

Most connoisseurs rank **Plati Yialos** on the island's south coast as Sifnos's best beach. Don't expect to be alone: A hotel and a campground are on the popular, long crescent beach. There's also good swimming at **Heronissos, Vroulidia,** and **Faros,** a small resort on the east coast with some good budget accommodations and tavernas. **Apokofto** has a good sand beach, and you can often reach the lovely beach at **Vathy** by one of the caïques that leave from Kamares, or by bus on the new road. **Aegean Thesaurus Travel** (see "Visitor Information," above) has caïque excursions to a number of isolated beaches.

SIFNOS AFTER DARK

In Apollonia, the **Argo Bar, Botzi,** and **Volto,** on the main pedestrian street, are good for the latest European and American pop. In summertime the large **Dolphin Pub** becomes a lively nightspot (it closes in mid-Sept). At Kamares, the **Old Captain's Bar, Collage Bar, Mobilize Dance Club,** and more elegant **Follie-Follie,** all on the beach, compete most nights to see who can crank up the volume for disco music the loudest. If this doesn't appeal to you, check to see whether the **Cultural Society of Sifnos** has scheduled any concerts in Artemonas (usually only in summer).

PAROS

You can catch a boat from Paros (pop. 12,000) to most of the Aegean islands, which means that a lot of people pass through here, especially in summer. Some decide to stay: Paros's good beaches, lovely villages, and increasingly sophisticated nightlife, especially in the village of Naoussa and the capital town Parikia (also known as Hora), have earned it a reputation for being a less expensive Mykonos. In addition, Paros has attractions its better-known neighbor lacks, including extensive vineyards, the substantial remains of a Venetian castle, and the finest Byzantine cathedral in the Cyclades. The celebrations here of the Feast of the Assumption (Aug 15) make Paros very crowded in August.

ESSENTIALS

GETTING THERE **By Plane** **Olympic Airways** (www.olympic-airways. gr) has at least two flights daily between Paros and Athens. For schedules and reservations, call ℭ **0284/21-900** in Parikia, **0284/91-257** at the airport, or **01/966-6666** in Athens.

By Sea The main port, Parikia, has ferry service from Piraeus at least once daily and four times daily in the summer (trip time: 6 hr.). Confirm schedules with the **Tourist Police** in Athens (ℭ **171** or 01/322-2545) or the **Port Authority** in Piraeus (ℭ **01/451-1310 or 01/459-3223**). **Strintzis Lines** (ℭ **01/422-5000** in Athens) and **Ventouris Ferries** (ℭ **01/482-8901** in Athens) operate from Piraeus via Syros three or four times a week. **Ilio Lines** (ℭ **01/422-4772** in Athens) has hydrofoil service almost daily from Rafina.

Daily ferry service from Parikia links Paros with Ios, Mykonos, Santorini (Thira), and Tinos. Daily excursion tours link Parikia and Naoussa (the north coast port) with Mykonos. Call the **port authority** (ℭ **0284/21-240**) or check each travel agent's current schedule. Most ferry tickets are not interchangeable.

VISITOR INFORMATION The **Paros Information Bureau** is inside the windmill on the harbor (ℭ **0284/22-078** or 0284/21-673). In theory, it's open from June to September, daily 9am to 11pm; the staff speaks English, provides local schedules, and changes traveler's checks. There is a **visitor information office** on Mavroyenous Square, just behind and to the right of the windmill at the end of the pier. This office is often closed, but there are numerous travel agencies on the seafront, including the helpful **Santorineos Travel** (ℭ **0284/24-245;** fax 0284/23-922; santorinaios-travel@ticketcom.gr), 100m south of the pier (to the right as you get off the boat). Here you can store luggage, buy ferry and airline tickets, rent a car, and exchange money. The island has an excellent website, **www.parosweb.com**, with abundant information for visitors.

GETTING AROUND The capital, Parikia, is best enjoyed by simply strolling about and getting pleasantly lost. Naoussa can also be enjoyed on foot. If you plan to explore the island, however, you may want to rent a car, or take one of the guided tours of the island offered by **Paros Travel** (ℭ **0284/21-582**).

By Bicycle With its rolling, fertile hills, Paros is well suited to exploration by bike, although some of the pebble-and-dirt roads will require strong tires. **Mountain Bike Club Paros,** just off the waterfront (ℭ **0284/23-778**), supplies bikes for their organized tours as well as such essentials as a helmet, insurance, repair kits, and water bottles.

By Bus The **bus station** in Parikia is on the waterfront (ℭ **0284/21-395**), left from the windmill. There's hourly public bus service between Parikia and Naoussa. The other public buses from Parikia run hourly. Schedules are posted at the stations.

By Car There're several agencies along the waterfront, and except in July and August you should be able to bargain. **Rent-A-Car Acropolis,** left from the windmill on the waterfront (ℭ **0284/21-830**), has wildly painted dune buggies or Suzuki jeeps. **Budget Rent-a-Car** (ℭ **0284/22-320**) and **Paros Europcar S.A.** (ℭ **0284/24-408;** fax 0284/22-544 in Parikia) usually have a good selection. Be sure to buy full insurance. You'll probably get the best rate if you reserve in advance through **Budget** in the United States (ℭ **800/527-0700**). Expect to pay at least 17,500Dr (€50.35, $50) per day in the summer.

By Moped There're several moped dealers along the waterfront. Make sure the cycle is in proper condition before you accept it, and be careful on pebble-and-dirt surfaces. Depending on size, mopeds cost 4,000 to 6,000Dr (€11.75–€17.60, $11–$17) per day.

By Taxi Taxis can be booked (© 0284/21-500) or hailed at the windmill taxi stand. Taxi fare to Naoussa with luggage should be 2,500 to 3,000Dr (€7.35–€8.80, $7–$9).

FAST FACTS The **American Express** agent is Santorineos Travel, on the seafront 100m south of the pier (© **0284/24-245;** fax 0284/23-922; santorinaios-travel@ticketcom.gr).

Banks The four banks on Mavroyenous Square (to the right behind the windmill) are open from Monday to Friday 8am to 2pm and Friday 8am to 1:30pm.

Hospital The private **Medical Center of Paros** (© **0284/24-410**) is left (west) of Parikia's central square, across from the post office, a block off the port. The public **Parikia Health Clinic** (© **0284/22-500**) is down the road from the Ekantopyliani Church.

Internet Access Internet access is available on the Wired Network (www.parosweb.com) at eight locations around the island; you can buy a "smart card" that stores your personal settings and provides access at any of these locations. The main office is in Parikia at the Wired Cafe on Market Street (© **0284/22-003**). The fee is 2,500Dr (€7.35, $7).

Police The **police station** is on the central square (© **100** or 0284/23-333). The **Tourist Police** are behind the windmill on the port (© **0284/21-673**). In Marpissa, call © **0284/41-202;** in Naoussa, © **0284/51-202.**

Post Office The **post office** (© **0284/21-236**) is on the waterfront road; it's open from Monday to Friday 7:30am to 2pm, with extended hours in July and August. It offers fax service at 0284/22-449.

Telephone The telephone area code for Paros is **0284.** The **OTE telephone office** (© **0284/22-135**) is to the right of the windmill; it's open from Monday to Friday 7:30am to midnight. (If the front door is closed, go around to the back—wind direction determines which door is open.) There's a branch in Naoussa with similar hours.

WHERE TO STAY

Most hotels require reservations for July and August; it's advisable to book at least a month in advance. If you arrive without a room, you can often get one in a private house from one of the hawkers who meet ships. If you don't like what you're offered, the **Hotelliers Association of Paros** (© **0284/24-555** or 0284/24-556) in Mavroyenous Square may be able to help. Keep in mind that all hotels in Parikia are likely to be noisy in season.

Astir of Paros ★★ The Hotel Astir of Paros, on Kolymbithres Beach across from the village of Naoussa, is one of the glamour spots of the Cyclades. There's just about everything you'd expect here: large, quiet suites and rooms, a freshwater pool, miniature golf for the kiddies—in other words, this is as close to a full resort hotel (built to suggest an island village) as you'll find in the Aegean. That said, rooms are comfortable, but not luxurious (although bathrooms are large and modern). The breakfast buffet is enormous, and delicious.

Kolimbithres Beach, Naoussa, 844 01 Paros. ⓒ **0284/51-976.** Fax 0284/51-985. astir@mail.otenet.gr; 57 units. 60,000Dr (€176.20, $172) double; 70,000–105,000Dr (€205.50–€308.25, $200–$300) suite. AE, DC, MC, V. **Amenities:** Restaurant, bar; pool; miniature golf. *In room:* A/C, TV, minibar, hair dryer.

Hotel Fotilia   Climb to the top of the steps at the end of town, and to the left of the church you'll see a restored windmill behind a stone archway. The Fotilia's large rooms are furnished in tasteful country style and have doors opening to balconies overlooking the old harbor and bay. There're also some studio apartments with simple kitchenettes.

Naoussa, 84401 Paros. ⓒ **0284/52-581** or 0284/52-582. Fax 0284/52-583. 14 units. 22,000Dr (€64.40, $63) double. Breakfast 1,500Dr (€4.40, $4.30) extra. No credit cards. **Amenities:** Breakfast room. *In room:* A/C, TV, minibar.

Lefkes Village Hotel ★★   This handsome new hotel 10km (6 miles) from Parikia is designed to look like a small island village, and is situated in Lefkes, one of Paros's most charming inland villages, with views over the countryside to the sea. Rooms are light and bright, with good bathrooms; some have balconies. There's a small Museum of Popular Aegean Culture and a winery.

P.O. Box 71, Lefkes Village 844 00 Paros. ⓒ **0284/41-827** or 01/251-6497. Fax 0284/41-827 or 01/675-5019. 25 units. In season 52,500Dr (€153.10, $150) double; off-season 30,000Dr (€88.05, $86) double. Rates include buffet breakfast. No credit cards. **Amenities:** Restaurant; pool; Jacuzzi. *In room:* A/C, TV, minibar.

Papadakis Hotel ★   The new Papadakis offers the best views in town— enjoyed from every room as well as from the new pool with Jacuzzi. The large guest rooms were renovated in 1998, with new wardrobes, beds, and desks in dark walnut; several units also have sofa beds. The excellent breakfast includes homemade baked goods prepared by owner Argyro Barbarigou, who happens to be an incredible chef—be sure to visit her new venture, the Papadakis fish taverna (see "Where to Dine," below).

Naoussa (a 5-min. walk uphill from the main square), 84401 Paros. ⓒ **0284/51-643** or 0284/52-504. Fax 0284/51-269. 19 units. 22,000Dr (€64.60, $63) double. Breakfast 2,500Dr (€7.35, $7) extra. No credit cards. **Amenities:** Restaurant, bar; pool. *In room:* A/C, TV, kitchenettes (some rooms), minibar.

WHERE TO DINE
Aligaria Restaurant GREEK   Owner Elizabeth Nikolousou is an excellent cook; her zucchini pie and generous portions of stuffed tomatoes disappear early. There's a good selection of local wines.

Plateia Aligari, Parikia (behind Hotel Kontes). ⓒ **0284/22-026.** Main courses 1,500–4,200Dr (€4.40– €12.35, $4.30–$12). MC, V. Daily noon–3:30pm and 6:30pm–midnight.

Apollon GREEK   With a shady garden with olive trees, whitewashed walls, handsome icons, and pots of flowers everywhere, the Apollon has been a popular place to eat just off the harbor for more than 40 years. Specialties include lamb in zesty lemon sauce and a rich panacotta. The Apollon's business card says, "The place to go—The place to be seen," and from the crowds here most nights, lots of people seem to agree.

Agora (Market St.), Parikia. ⓒ **0284/21-875.** Main courses 2,000–6,000Dr (€5.90–€17.60, $6–$17). AE, MC, V. Daily 6pm–1am.

Barbarossa Ouzeri SNACKS   This authentic ouzeri is right on the port. Wind-burned fishermen sit for hours nursing their milky ouzo in water and their miniportions of grilled octopus and olives. This is a good spot to sit and watch the world go by.

> **Tips Traveler's Warning**
>
> Several places in Paros offer very cheap drinks or "buy one, get one free"
> deals—usually the locally brewed alcohol that the natives call **bomba**.
> If you drink it, you'll know why: intoxication and nausea are virtually
> simultaneous.

On the waterfront, Naoussa. ☎ **0284/51-391.** Mezedes 600–2,000Dr (€1.78–€5.90, $1.75–$6). No credit
cards. Daily 7:30–11:30pm.

Lalula ✿ GREEK/MEDITERRANEAN/VEGETARIAN   A gifted German
restaurateur is responsible for the delicious and distinctive food, subdued decor,
and interesting but unobtrusive music at Lalula. There's a lovely little garden in
the back. The cooking is lighter than typical Greek cuisine; the menu depends
on what's fresh at the market. Regular items include vegetable quiche, sweet-
and-sour chicken with rice and ginger chutney, and fish steamed in herbs. Check
to see if there's a set-price menu; it's usually an excellent value.

Naoussa. ☎ **0284/51-547.** Reservations recommended July–Aug. Main courses 2,000–5,500Dr (€5.90–
€16.15, $6–$16). No credit cards. Daily 7–11:45pm.Take a left at the post office; it's across from the Minoa
Hotel.

Papadakis ✿✿ INNOVATIVE GREEK   The specialty here is fresh fish grilled
to perfection—and lots of very tasty appetizers and desserts. The tzatziki with dill
is delicious and refreshingly different, the traditionally prepared melitzanosalata is
redolent of wood-smoked eggplant. Desserts include *kataifi ekmek,* a confection
conjured from honey, walnuts, cinnamon, custard, and cream.

Naoussa waterfront. ☎ **0284/51047.** Reservations recommended. Main courses 1,800–8,000Dr (€5.29–
€23.50, $5.15–$23). AE, V. Daily 7:30pm–midnight.

Porphyra ✿ GREEK/FISH   The small Porphyra serves the best fish in town.
The nondescript, utilitarian service and decor are typical of your average taverna; the difference here is that the owner farms the shellfish himself, resulting
in an exceptional mussels *Saganaki* (mussels cooked with tomato, feta, and
wine). The tzatziki and other traditional cold appetizers are also very good. The
fish is predictably fresh, and offerings vary with the season.

Paralia. ☎ **0284/22-693.** Main courses 1,500–5,000Dr (€4.40–€14.70, $4.30–$14). AE, V. Daily 6:30pm–
midnight. Closed Jan–Feb. Between the pier and the post office, just back from the waterfront.

EXPLORING THE ISLAND

Parikia, site of the ancient capital, is the main port and largest town on the
island, with a busy harborfront whose best-known landmark is the squat,
whitewashed windmill just off the main pier. Most of what you'll need—banks,
travel agents, several hotels, restaurants, and shops—is clustered nearby in
Mavroyenous Square. Things get more interesting when you head inland to
Parikia's picturesque **Agora (market)** section, a mixture of food markets and
handicraft shops. The nicest part of town is around the 13th-century **Venetian
Kastro (fortress).** Like a number of houses and churches here, the Kastro was
built of the famous Parian marble originally used to build the temples of Apollo
and Demeter.

Today, the churches of Ayios Konstantinos and Ayia Eleni form part of the
Kastro, but Parikia's most famous church is the 6th-century **Panayia Ekaton-
dapyliani (Our Lady of a Hundred Doors).** This hyperbolic name simply

suggests that the church has more than the usual number of doors. The church is usually open daily from 8am to 1pm and 5 to 8pm; admission is free. There's a 500Dr (€1.47, $1.45) fee for the small **Cathedral Museum.** As on Tinos, many pilgrims come here on the feast of the Virgin on August 15, when finding accommodations on Paros is virtually impossible.

Parikia's **Archaeological Museum** (© 0284/21-231) is open from Tuesday to Sunday 8:30am to 2:30pm; admission is 500Dr (€1.47, $1.45). Enter just behind the Panayia Ekatondapyliani. The museum has a lovely statue of a **winged victory** and part of the famous **Parian Chronicle,** a 3rd-century B.C. inscription recording important happenings in the history of ancient Greece.

Paros's best-known and most picturesque fishing village, **Naoussa,** with the remains of a Venetian castle, is in the throes of overdevelopment. Much of the construction is concentrated along the shore, and you can still find pleasant old streets in the village itself, as well as a number of new bars, restaurants, boutiques, and hotels. If you want a quieter spot and like butterflies, head for **Petaloudes** ✁, the **Valley of the Butterflies,** about 6km (4 miles) out of Parikia. You can visit the colorful butterflies—actually moths—daily in season (usually May–July) 9am to 8pm for 400Dr (€1.17, $1.15). (Take the main coast road south out of Parikia; turn left at the sign for the Convent of Christou Dassos, and follow the signs.) The small **Museum of Popular Aegean Culture** (free) in the Lefkes Village Hotel in the village of Lefkes has examples of island pottery, furniture, and farm implements.

If you find Paros too crowded for your tastes, you can take a caïque over to **Antiparos,** a small island with some nice beaches and small tavernas (and rapidly increasing touristic development) half a mile offshore. Spelunkers will want to visit the **Cave of Antiparos,** open daily from 10am to 4pm; admission is 500Dr (€1.47, $1.45).

OUTDOOR ACTIVITIES   The free booklet **Paros Windsurfing Guide** has a good small map of the island, maps of several beaches, and useful information. It's especially good for those interested in water sports. The free publication **Summer Paros/Antiparos** also has a map of the island, a fairly good map of Parikia, and information.

There're **beaches** north along Parikia Bay, but beach seekers will probably want to head east to Naoussa Bay. One of the island's best and most famous beaches, picturesque **Kolymbithres,** where smooth giant rocks divide the golden sand beach into little coves, is an hour's walk or a 10-minute moped ride west from Naoussa. There're several tavernas and hotels nearby.

North of Kolymbithres, by Ayios Ioannis Church, is **Monastery Beach,** where there's some nudism, and the **Monasteri Club,** a bar and restaurant with music and beach service. Most of the other beaches west of Naoussa are overcrowded because of all the new hotels. Sandy **Santa Maria Beach,** on the northeast coast, is particularly popular with windsurfers; the Santa Maria Surf Club rents gear and sometimes gives lessons. There is also a fine beach and windsurfing facilities at **Chrissi Akti (Golden Beach),** half a mile of fine golden sand, which some consider the island's best beach. The frequent stiff winds make it a better spot for windsurfers than for sunbathers. South of the village of Drios, **Lolantonis Beach** is often surprisingly uncrowded. There're small tavernas on all these beaches.

PAROS AFTER DARK
Just behind the windmill is a local landmark, the **Port Cafe,** a basic kafenio lit by bare incandescent bulbs and filled day and night with tourists waiting for a

ferry, bus, taxi, or fellow traveler. The **Saloon d'Or,** south of the port, is another spot for cheap drinks. If you're not in a mood to party, try the **Pebbles Bar,** where you can usually hear tapes of classical music at sunset, or the **Pirate Bar** (© **0284/21-114**), in the Agora, where classical music alternates with jazz and blues. For partiers, there's the **Rendezvous,** where you'll hear rock music, and **Black Bart's** (© **0284/21-802**), with loud music and a boisterous, boozy crowd.

In Naoussa, try **Leonardo's, Agosta,** or the **Sofrano Bar,** all on the harbor, or **Banana Moon,** just off the harbor. In summer, many of these bars impose a cover charge of at least 3,000Dr (€8.80, $9).

Two movie theaters, the **Cine Rex** (© **0284/21-676**) in Parika, and the **Makis** (© **0284/22-221**) in Naoussa, are open all summer, and often have English language films.

9

Hungary

By Joseph S. Lieber & Christina Shea

The dramatic political changes of 1989 have irreversibly altered life in Hungary. Awakened after its long slumber behind the Iron Curtain, Hungary is now one of Europe's hottest destinations. Poised between East and West, both geographically and culturally, it's at the center of the region's rebirth. To best understand and appreciate Hungary, you ought to go beyond its stately capital. Get to know the great river that runs through the country's heart. Take a slow boat (or a fast hydrofoil) up the Danube to the "Bend" towns of Szentendre, Esztergom, or Visegrád. For pure relaxation, you can sample the resorts at Europe's largest inland pond, Lake Balaton.

1 Budapest

Budapest came of age in the 19th century, at the start of which the two towns of Buda and Pest were little more than provincial outposts on the Danube. The dawning of a modern Hungarian identity spawned the city's neoclassical development. The rise of the eclectic style coincided with the great post-1867 boom, creating most of the historic inner city. Indeed, Budapest, notwithstanding its long and tattered history of Roman, Mongol, and Turkish conquest, is very much a late 19th-century city, with its characteristic coffeehouse and music hall culture. The decades after World War I and the fall of the Hapsburg monarchy weren't kind to Hungary's charming capital, and until recently Budapest's glory seemed irretrievably lost. How fitting it is, then, that Budapest's post–Cold War renaissance comes when it does: The city is once again attracting visitors from far and wide as the new century dawns.

Budapest retains an exotic feeling seldom experienced in the better-known capitals of Europe. Take a turn off any of the city's main boulevards and you'll quickly find yourself in a quiet residential neighborhood, where the scent of a hearty *gulyás* wafts from a kitchen window and cigarette smoke fogs the cavelike entry of the corner pub.

ESSENTIALS

GETTING THERE **By Plane** All flights arrive at **Ferihegy II** (© **061/ 296-7155** for general info, © 061/296-5052 for arrivals, © 061/296-5883 for departures), located in the XVIII district in southeastern Pest.

The easiest way into the city is probably the **Airport Minibus** (© **061/ 296-8555** or fax 061/296-8993), a service of the LRI (Budapest Airport Authority). The minibus, leaving every 10 or 15 minutes throughout the day, takes you directly to any city address and costs 1,800Ft ($6). The trip takes 30 minutes to an hour, depending on how many stops are made before your own. The Airport Minibus desk is easily found in the main hall. Minibuses also provide the same efficient service returning to the airports; arrange for your pickup *a full day in advance.*

LRI also runs an **Airport-Centrum** shuttle bus, leaving every half hour (5am to 9pm). Passengers are dropped off at Erzsébet tér, across from the Kempinski Hotel and just off Deák tér, where all three Metro lines converge. The price is 800Ft ($2.65), and tickets are sold aboard the bus (trip time: 30 to 40 minutes).

We strongly *discourage* the use of cabs from the **Airport Taxi** fleet (☎ 061/ 282-2222), which is notoriously overpriced. A ride downtown from one of these cabs might cost as much as twice the fare in a cheaper fleet. Alas, for reasons no one has been able to explain to us with a straight face, cabs from the Airport Taxi fleet are the only cabs permitted to wait for fares on the airport grounds. However, dozens of cabs from the cheaper fleets we recommend are at all times stationed at roadside pullouts just off the airport property, a stone's throw from the terminal, waiting for radio calls from their dispatchers. You can phone from the terminal to any of these fleets and a cab will be there for you in a few minutes. (See "Getting Around" by taxi, below, for phone numbers.) For three or more people traveling together (and maybe even two people), a taxi from a recommended fleet to the city will be cheaper than the combined minibus fares, at about 3,000Ft ($10). A taxi from the airport to downtown takes about 20 to 30 minutes (see "Getting Around," below).

It's also possible (and very cheap) to get to the city by public transportation; the bus-to-Metro-to-town trip takes about 1 hour total. Take the red-lettered **bus 93** to the last stop, Kóbánya-Kispest. From there, the Blue Metro line runs to the Inner City of Pest. The cost is two transit tickets, which is 200Ft (65¢); you can buy tickets from the automated vending machine at the bus stop (coins only) or from any newsstand in the airport.

By Train Budapest has three major train stations: Keleti pályaudvar (Eastern Station), Nyugati pályaudvar (Western Station), and Déli pályaudvar (Southern Station). The stations' names, curiously, correspond neither to their geographical location in the city nor to the origins or destinations of trains serving them. Each has a Metro station beneath it and an array of accommodation offices, currency-exchange booths, and other services.

Most international trains pull into bustling **Keleti Station** (☎ 061/ 314-5010; Metro: Keleti pu.), a classic steel-girdered European train station located in Pest's seedy Baross tér. In addition to the Metro, numerous bus, tram, and trolleybus lines serve Baross tér. Some international trains arrive at **Nyugati Station** (☎ 061/349-0115; Metro: Nyugati pu.), another classic of a station designed by the Eiffel company and built in the 1870s. Numerous tram and bus lines serve busy Nyugati tér. Few international trains arrive at **Déli Station** (☎ 061/375-6293; Metro: Déli pu.), an ugly modern building in central Buda.

Train station phone numbers are good from 8pm to 6am. During the day, obtain **in-land train information** at ☎ 061/461-5400 and **international train information** at ☎ 061/461-5500. Purchase **tickets** at train station ticket windows or from the MÁV Service Office, VI. Andrássy út 35 (☎ 061/322-8082), open Monday to Friday 9am to 5pm. You can access a timetable on the Web at www.elvira.mavinformatika.hu. (As you must conduct your search in Hungarian, it's helpful to know that *honnan* means "from where," *hova* "to where," *ma* "today," *holnap* "tomorrow," and *keres* "ask" or, in this context, "search.")

MÁV operates a **minibus** that'll take you from any of the three stations to any point in the city for 1,100Ft ($3.65) per person, to the airport for 1,500Ft ($5),

Budapest

18

Victor Hugo u.
Csanády u.

Balzac u.
Jédus Gyula u.
Visegrádi u.
Kresz Géza u.
Váci út
Váci út
Lehel u.

19

20

SZÉCHENYI FÜRDŐ

Dózsa György út
Rippl-Rónai u.

Kós Károly sétány

VÁROSLIGET
(CITY PARK)

21

Podmaniczky u.
Munkácsy u.
Bajza u.

Szinyei Merse
Andrássy út

HŐSÖK
TÉRE

NYUGATI
TRAIN STATION

Szív u.
Rózsa Ferenc u.
Isabella u.
Vörösmarty u.

BAJZA UTCA

KODÁLY
KÖRÖND

Bajza u.

Városligeti fasor

Dózsa György út

Ajtósi Dürer

22

Podmaniczky u.
Csengery u.
Eötvös u.
Teréz körút
Nagymező u.
Szív u.

Felső erdősor

Damjanich u.

Bajcsy Zsilinszky út

23

OKTOGON

VÖRÖSMARTY
UTCA

Király

Vörösmarty u.
Csengery u.
Dob u.
Rottenbiller u.
Rózsa Ferenc u.

Dembinszky u.

István út
Petőfi Sándor

Hajós u.

ARANY
JÁNOS U.

Andrássy út
Paulay Ede u.

24

Hungarian State
Opera House
OPERA

Király

Erzsébet körút
Wesselényi u.
Izabella u.
Dohány u.
Hárslta u.

Thököly út

KELETI
TRAIN
STATION

5

Vista Visitor Center
BAJCSY-ZSILINSZKY ÚT
bet tér Bus Station

DEÁK TÉR

Kertész u.
Akácfa u.

Rákóczi út

Kerepesi út

Károly

Dob u.
Wesselényi u.

26

BLAHA
LUJZA TÉR

Fiumei út

Tourinform

27

Dohány u.
Rákóczi út

Népszínház u.

I Kossuth L. u.

ASTORIA

Múzeum krt.

József krt.
Bérkocsis u.

Déri Miksa u.

ERENCIEK
TERE

28

29

Krúdy József u.

30

KÁLVIN
TÉR

Baross u.

József krt.

Baross u.

Vámház krt.

Üllői út

Práter u.

PEST

Szabadság
híd

Danube

FERENC
KÖRÚT

Üllői út

Ferenc körút

583

or between stations for 700Ft ($2.35) per person. To order the minibus, call
℡ **061/353-2722** or 061/357-2617. Often, however, a taxi fare will be cheaper,
especially for groups of two or more travelers.

By Bus   Buses use three terminals, though plans are afoot to close the Erzsébet
tér station and expand the Népstadion station. At the moment, however, buses
to and from Western Europe and points in Hungary west of the Danube call at
the **Erzsébet tér bus station** (℡ **061/317-2966** in-land info and 061/
317-2562 international info; Metro: Deák tér), in central Pest. Buses to and
from Eastern and Central Europe, as well as points in Hungary east of the
Danube, call at the **Népstadion bus station** (℡ **061/252-2995** in-land info
and 061/252-1896 international info; Metro: Népstadion). Buses to/from the
Danube bend and other points north of Budapest call at the **Árpád híd bus station** (℡ **061/320-9229** or 317-9886; Metro: Árpád híd).

By Car   Vienna, 275 kilometers (170 miles) from Budapest, connects to the
Hungarian capital by the Austrian A4 superhighway, which becomes the M1 and
feeds into the city via southern Buda. The border crossings from Austria and Slovakia are generally hassle-free. You may be requested to present your driver's
license, vehicle registration, and proof of insurance (the number plate and symbol indicating country of origin are acceptable proof). Hungary doesn't require
an international driver's license. Cars entering Hungary are required to have a
decal indicating country of registration, a first-aid kit, and an emergency triangle.

By Hydrofoil   The Hungarian state shipping company **MAHART** operates
hydrofoils on the Danube between Vienna and Budapest in spring and summer.
It's an extremely popular route, so book your tickets well in advance; contact
your local Austrian National Tourist Board. In Vienna, contact MAHART, Handelskai 265 (℡ **0043/729-2161;** fax 061/729-2163). The Budapest office of
MAHART is at V. Belgrád rakpart (℡ **0043/318-1704** or 061/318-1880).
Boats and hydrofoils from Vienna arrive at the international boat station next
door to the MAHART office on the **Belgrád rakpart,** which is on the Pest side
of the Danube, between the Szabadság and Erzsébet bridges.

VISITOR INFORMATION   Tourist offices   The city's best info source is
Tourinform, V. Sütő u. 2, just off Deák tér in Pest (℡ **061/317-9800** or
061/317-8992; www.hungarytourism.hu; Metro: Deák tér). It's open daily from
8am to 8pm. Another useful source is the **Vista Visitor Center,** V. Paulay Ede
u. 7 (℡ **061/267-8603;** www.vista.hu; Metro: Deák tér). It's open from Monday to Friday 8am to 10pm and Saturday and Sunday 10am to 10pm.

Websites   U.S.-based **www.gotohungary.com** loads far more quickly than
sites based in Europe and has a wealth of information. Especially useful is the
up-to-date events calendar and special-interest guide, with links, for example,
to spas and thermal baths. Use the extensive collection of links at **www.
hungary.org** as a jumping-off point for learning more about Hungary's history,
culture, cuisine, and more. Come to **www.budapest.com** to view a virtual slide
show, consult the shopping guide, or see what the city looked like a century ago.

CITY LAYOUT   The city of Budapest was founded in 1873 by joining three
cities: Buda, Pest, and Óbuda. Budapest, like Hungary itself, is defined by the
River Danube (Duna), along which many historic sites are found. Eight bridges
join the two banks; five of them are in the city center.

On the right bank lies **Pest,** the commercial and administrative center. Central Pest is that part of the city between the river and the semicircular **Outer
Ring boulevard (Nagykörút),** stretches of which take the names of former

> (Tips **A Note on Addresses**
>
> Budapest is divided into 22 districts called **kerülets** (abbreviated ker.). A Roman numeral followed by a period precedes every written address in Budapest, signifying the kerület; for example, XII. Csörsz utca 9 is in the 12th kerület. Because many street names are repeated in different parts of the city, it's very important to know which kerület a certain address is in.

monarchs: Ferenc, József, Erzsébet, Teréz, and Szent István. The Outer Ring begins at the Pest side of the Petófi Bridge in the south and wraps itself around the center, ending at the Margit Bridge in the north. Several of Pest's busiest squares are along the Outer Ring, and Pest's major east–west avenues bisect it at these squares.

Central Pest proper is defined by the **Inner Ring (Kiskörút).** It starts at Szabadság híd (Freedom Bridge) in the south and is alternately named Vámház körút, Múzeum körút, Károly körút, Bajcsy-Zsilinszky út, and József Attila utca before ending at the Chain Bridge (Széchenyi lánchíd). Inside this ring is the **Belváros,** the historic Inner City of Pest.

Váci utca is a popular pedestrian shopping street between the Inner Ring and the Danube. It spills into **Vörösmarty tér,** one of the best-known squares. The **Dunakorzó (Danube Promenade),** a popular evening stroll, runs along the river in Pest, between the Chain Bridge and the Erzsébet Bridge. The **historic Jewish district** of Pest is in the Erzsébetváros, between the two ring boulevards. **Margaret Island (Margit-sziget)** is in the middle of the Danube. Accessible by the Margaret Bridge or Árpád Bridge, it's a popular park without vehicular traffic.

On the left bank is **Buda;** to its north, beyond the city center, lies Óbuda. Buda is as hilly as Pest is flat. **Castle Hill** is widely considered the most beautiful part of Budapest. A number of steep paths, staircases, and small streets go up to Castle Hill, but no major roads. The easiest access is from **Clark Ádám tér** (at the head of the Chain Bridge) by funicular, or from **Várfok utca** (near Moszkva tér) by foot or bus. Castle Hill consists of the royal palace itself, home to numerous museums, and the so-called **Castle District,** a lovely neighborhood of small, winding streets, centered on the Gothic Matthias Church. Below Castle Hill, along the Danube, is a long, narrow neighborhood, historically populated by fishermen and other river workers, known as the **Víziváros (Watertown). Central Buda** is a collection of low-lying neighborhoods below Castle Hill. The main square is **Moszkva tér,** just north of Castle Hill. Beyond Central Buda, mainly to the east, are the Buda Hills.

Óbuda is on the left bank of the Danube, north of Buda. Although the greater part of Óbuda is modern and drab, it features a beautiful old city center and impressive Roman ruins.

GETTING AROUND

Budapest has an extensive and inexpensive public transportation system. Except for 17 well-traveled bus and tram routes, all forms of transport shut down nightly at around 11:30pm; certain areas of the city, most notably the Buda Hills, are beyond the reach of the limited night service, so you have to take a taxi. Be on the alert for pickpockets when on crowded public transportation. Keep your money and valuables inside your clothing in a money belt.

All forms of public transportation require the self-validation of prepurchased **tickets (*vonaljegy*),** costing 100Ft (33¢) apiece (children under 6 travel free). Single tickets can be bought at Metro ticket windows, newspaper kiosks, and the occasional tobacco shop. There are also automated machines in most Metro stations and at major transportation hubs, but the older ones among these are not too reliable. On weekends and at night it can be rather difficult to find an open ticket window, so buy enough to avoid the trouble of constantly having to replenish your stock. For 950Ft ($3.15) you can get a **10-pack (*tizes csomag*),** and for 1,850Ft ($6), you can get a **20-pack (*huszos csomag*).**

Your best bet is to buy a day pass or multiday pass. Passes are inexpensive and need be validated only once. A pass will probably save you some money too, as you're likely to be getting on and off public transportation all day long. **Day passes (*napijegy*)** cost 800Ft ($2.65) and are valid until midnight of the day of purchase. Buy them from Metro ticket windows; the clerk validates the pass at the time of purchase. A **3-day pass (*turistajegy*)** costs 1,600Ft ($5) and a **7-day pass (*hétibérlet*)** 1,950Ft ($7); these have the same validation procedure as the day pass.

Plainclothes inspectors (who flip out a hidden red armband for ID) frequently come around checking for valid tickets, particularly at the top or bottom of the escalators to Metro platforms. On-the-spot fines (1,500Ft/$5) are assessed to fare dodgers. All public transport operates on rough schedules, posted at bus and tram shelters and in Metro stations. The Budapest Transport Authority (BKV térkép) produces a more detailed transportation map, available at most Metro ticket windows for 250FT (85¢).

By Metro   The Metro is clean and efficient, with trains running every 3 to 5 minutes from about 4:30am until about 11:30pm. The three lines are universally known by color——Yellow, Red, and Blue. Officially they have numbers as well, but all signs are color-coded. All three lines converge at **Deák tér.**

The **Yellow (1) line** is the oldest Metro on the European continent, but was fully renovated in 1996. This easily accessible line, just a few steps underground, runs from Vörösmarty tér in the heart of central Pest, out the length of Andrássy út, past the Városliget (City Park), ending at Mexikói út. Tickets for the Yellow line are validated on the train itself. The **Red (2)** and **Blue (3) lines** are modern Metros, deep underground and accessible by escalator. The Red line runs from eastern Pest, through the center, across the Danube to Déli Station. The Blue line runs from southeastern Pest, through the center, to northern Pest. Tickets should be validated at the automated time-stamp boxes before you descend the escalator. When changing lines at Deák tér, you must validate a new ticket at the orange machines in the hallway between lines.

By Bus   Many parts of the city, most notably the Buda Hills, are best accessed by bus **(*busz*).** Most lines are in service from about 4:30am to about 11:30pm, with less frequent weekend service on some. You must validate your bus ticket on board at the mechanical red box found by each door. Tickets cannot be purchased from the driver. You can board the bus by any door.

Black-numbered local buses constitute the majority of bus lines. Red-numbered are express. If the red number on the bus is followed by an *E,* the bus runs nonstop between terminals (whereas an *É*—with an accent—signifies *észak,* meaning night). A few buses are labeled by something other than a number; one you'll probably use is the **Várbusz (Palace Bus),** a minibus that runs between Várfok utca, off Buda's Moszkva tér, and the Castle District.

Budapest Metro

Újpest-Központ

Blue Line
(Line 3)

Újpest-Városkapu

Gyöngyösi u.

Forgách u.

Árpád hid

Dózsa György út

Yellow Line
(Line 1)

Lehel tér

Mexikói út

Széchenyi fürdő

Hősök tere

Nyugati pu.

Bajza utca

Kodály körönd

Moszkva tér

Batthyány tér

Kossuth L. tér

Vörösmarty utca

Oktogon

Red Line
(Line 2)

Örs vezér tere

Arany János utca

Opera

Bajcsy-Zsilinszky út

Népstadion

Déli pu.

Deák tér

Keleti pu.

Pillangó utca

Blaha L. tér

Vörösmarty tér

Astoria

Ferenciek tere

Kálvin tér

Ferenc körút

Klinikák

Nagyvárad tér

Népliget

Ecseri út

Kőbánya-Kispest

Pöttyös u.

Határ út

By Tram   You'll find Budapest's bright-yellow trams (known as *villamos* in Hungarian) very useful, particularly the **4** and **6,** which travel along the Outer Ring (Nagykörút). You must validate your ticket on board. As with buses, tickets are valid for one ride, not for the line itself. Trams stop at every station, and all doors open, regardless of whether anyone is waiting to get on. The buttons near the tram doors are for emergency stops, not stop requests.

By Trolleybus   There are 14 trolleybus lines in Budapest, all in Pest. Of particular interest to train travelers is no. 73, the fastest route between Keleti Station and Nyugati Station. All the information in the "By Bus" section above on boarding and ticket validation applies to trolleybuses as well.

By HÉV   The HÉV is a suburban railway network that connects Budapest to various points along the city's outskirts. There are four HÉV lines; only one, the **Szentendre line,** is of serious interest to tourists. The terminus for the Szentendre HÉV line is Buda's Batthyány tér, also a station of the Red Metro line. To reach Óbuda's Fó tér (Main Square), get off at the Árpád híd (Árpád Bridge) stop. The HÉV runs regularly between 4am and 11:30pm. For trips within the city limits, you need one transit ticket, available at HÉV ticket windows at the Batthyány tér station or from the conductor on board. These tickets are different from the standard transportation tickets and are punched by conductors on board. If you have a valid day pass, you do not need to buy a ticket for trips within the city limits.

By Taxi   Budapest taxis are unregulated, so fares vary tremendously. Perhaps because there are more taxi drivers than the level of business can support, many drivers are experts at fleecing foreigners. However, if you watch out, taxis are still a bit cheaper than in the West. Several fleet companies have good reputations, honest drivers, and competitive rates. We particularly recommend **Fő Taxi** (© 061/**222-2222**). Other reliable fleets are **Volántaxi** (© **061/466-6666**), **City Taxi** (© **061/211-1111**), **Tele5** (© **061/355-5555**), and **6x6** (© **061/266-6666**).

By Car   We don't recommend using a car for sightseeing in Budapest. You may, however, want to rent one for trips outside the capital. We recommend **Denzel Europcar InterRent,** VIII. Üllői út 60–62 (© **061/477-1080;** fax 061/477-1099), where you can rent a Suzuki Swift for 4,500Ft ($15) per day (insurance included), plus 45Ft (15¢) per kilometer. They also have a rental counter at the airport (© **061/296-6610**), but there you pay an 11% airport tax. You might also try **LRI Airport Rent-A-Car,** with a counter at the airport (© or fax **061/296-5970**); they offer a Volkswagen Polo for $19 per day (insurance included) and 19¢ per kilometer.

Ⓒ *FAST FACTS:* **Budapest**

American Express   Budapest's Amex office is between Vörösmarty tér and Deák tér in central Pest, at V. Deák Ferenc u. 10, 1052 Budapest (© **061/235-4330** or 061/235-4300; fax 061/267-2028; Metro: Deák tér). Summer hours are from Monday to Saturday 9am to 7:30pm and Sunday 9am to 2pm; winter hours are from Monday to Friday 9am to 5:30pm and Saturday 9am to 2pm. There's an ATM on the street in front.

Business Hours **Banks** are usually open from Monday to Thursday 8am to 3pm and Friday 8am to 1pm. Most **stores** are open from Monday to Friday 10am to 6pm and Saturday 9 or 10am to 1 or 2pm. Many shops close for an hour at lunch, and only stores in central tourist areas are open Sunday. Many shops and restaurants close for 2 weeks in August.

Currency The basic unit of currency in Hungary is the **forint (Ft).** The rate of exchange used to calculate the dollar values given in this chapter is $1 = about 300Ft (or 100Ft = 33¢). At press time, the rate of exchange for the British pound was £1 = about 400Ft (or 100Ft = 25p). Note that exchange rates fluctuate from time to time and may not be the same when you travel to Hungary.

Currency Exchange The best official rates for both cash and traveler's checks are obtained at banks. Exchange booths are located throughout the city center, in train stations, and in most luxury hotels, but they almost uniformly offer lower rates than banks. This is particularly true of one chain called Inter Change, which offers a rate up to 20% lower than the going bank rate, depending on the amount you exchange. ATMs (Cirrus and PLUS networks) are found in front of banks throughout the city. *Warning:* On departing Hungary, you're allowed to reexchange only half the amount of forints you originally purchased, so be circumspect in converting your currency and save all exchange receipts.

Doctors We recommend the **American Clinic,** in a modern building across from the Mammut shopping center at I. Hattyu u. 14 (© **061/224-9090;** Metro: Moszkva tér); it's a newly opened private outpatient clinic with two U.S. board–certified physicians and several English-speaking Hungarian doctors. Check with Vista Visitor Center for discount coupons. For dental work, we recommend **Dr. Susan Linder,** II. Vihorlat u. 23 (© **061/ 335-5245;** bus: 5, 29), the dentist for the U.S. and British embassies; she did her postdoctoral work at the University of California at San Francisco and speaks flawless English.

Drugstores The Hungarian word for *drugstore* is *gyógyszertár* or *patika.* Generally, pharmacies carry only prescription drugs. Hotel "drugstores" are just shops with soap, perfume, aspirin, and other nonprescription items. There are a number of 24-hour pharmacies in the city—every pharmacy posts the address of the nearest one in its window.

Embassies The embassy of the **United States** is at V. Szabadság tér 12 (© **061/475-4000;** Metro: Kossuth tér); the embassy of **Canada** at XII. Budakeszi út 32 (© **061/392-3360;** Metro: Moszkva tér, then tram 22); the embassy of the **United Kingdom** at V. Harmincad u. 6 (© **061/266-2888;** Metro: Deák tér); the embassy of **Ireland** at V. Szabadság tér 7 (© **061/ 302-9600;** Metro: Kossuth tér); and the embassy of **Australia** at XII. Királyhágó tér 8–9 (© **061/457-9777;** Metro: Déli pu.). The U.K. embassy handles matters for **New Zealand** citizens.

Emergencies Dial © **104** for an ambulance, © **105** for the fire department, or © **107** for the police.

Internet Access We generally use **Vista Visitor Center,** V. Paulay Ede u. 7 (© **061/267-8603;** Metro: Deák tér), with about 10 terminals costing 11Ft (4¢) per minute; the wait is sometimes pretty long. It's open from Monday to Friday 8am to 10pm and Saturday and Sunday 10am to 10pm. Another option, with less risk of a wait, is the **Internet Café**, V. Kecskeméti u. 5 (© **061/328-0292**; Metro: Kálvin tér), with about 20 terminals costing 700Ft ($2.35) per hour, with pricing by 30-minute intervals (except 10 minutes or less, which costs 150Ft or 50¢).

Post Office The main branch of the Hungarian Postal Service (Magyar Posta) is at V. Petófi Sándor u. 17–19, 1052 Budapest, Hungary (Metro: Deák tér). This rather confusing office is open from Monday to Friday 8am to 8pm and Saturday 8am to 2pm. The post office at VIII. Baross tér 11/c (Metro: Keleti pu.) is open from Monday to Saturday 7am to 9pm. The post office at VI. Teréz krt. 51 (Metro: Nyugati pu.) is open Monday to Saturday 7am to 9pm and Sunday 8am to 8pm. At press time, an airmail postcard costs 100Ft (33¢); an airmail letter 150Ft (50¢) and up.

Safety By U.S. standards, Budapest is a relatively safe city—muggings and violent attacks are rare. Nevertheless, foreigners are always prime targets. Though they're clearly less of a threat now than a few years ago, teams of professional pickpockets still plague Budapest, operating on crowded trams, Metros, and buses. Be particularly careful on bus 26 (Margaret Island) and trams 4 and 6 or in any other crowded setting. The pickpockets' basic trick is to create a distraction to take your attention away from yourself and your own security. Avoid being victimized by wearing a money belt under your clothes instead of wearing a fanny pack or carrying a wallet or purse. No valuables should be kept in the outer pockets of a backpack.

Telephone The **country code** for Hungary is **36**. The **city code** for Budapest is **1**; use this code when you're calling from outside Hungary. If you're within Hungary but not in Budapest, first dial **06**; when you hear a tone, dial the city code and phone number. If you're calling within Budapest, simply leave off the code and dial only the regular seven-digit phone number.

Be aware that Budapest phone numbers are constantly changing as MATÁV continues to upgrade its system. Note, for instance, that any number beginning with a "1" has been changed; try replacing the 1 with a 3 or 4. Usually, if the number you're dialing has changed, you'll get a recording first in Hungarian and than in English, indicating the new number. If further information is needed, dial © **198** for directory assistance.

The Hungarian phone company MATÁV provides much better service than in the past, but it still falls significantly short of Western standards. For best results, dial slowly and don't be too quick to trust a busy signal—try again.

Numbers beginning with 06-20 or 06-30, followed by a seven-digit number, are **mobile phone numbers.** If the mobile number you've been given has only six digits, it's incorrect; add a 9 before the other six digits. Be aware that you pay for a long-distance call when you call a mobile phone. A GTE Hungarian yellow pages phone number search is available in English on the Web at www.gte-yellow-pages.com/2Eng.htm.

Public **pay phones** charge varying amounts for local calls depending on the time of day you place your call. It's apparently cheapest to call late in the evenings and on weekends. Public phones operate with 20Ft coins or with phone cards (in 50 or 120 units) you can buy from post offices, tobacco shops, supermarkets, travel agencies, and any MATÁV customer service office (MATÁV Pont).

You can reach the **AT&T** operator at ℰ **00/800-01111**, the **MCI** operator at ℰ **00/800-01411**, and the **Sprint** operator at ℰ **00/800-01877**.

Tipping Tipping is generally 10%. Among those who welcome tips are waiters, taxi drivers, hotel employees, barbers, cloakroom attendants, toilet attendants, masseuses, and tour guides.

WHERE TO STAY

One of the happy developments of the post-1989 boom in Budapest has been the proliferation of new pensions and small hotels. The better choices among these—and the less expensive—are usually outside the city center, but all the places we list can easily be reached by public transportation. Notwithstanding the arrival of these new places, Budapest retains its reputation as a city without enough guest beds. Indeed, in high season it can be difficult to secure a hotel or pension room or hostel bed, so make reservations and get written confirmation well ahead if possible.

Many hotels and pensions in Budapest list their prices in German marks (DM); a few list them in U.S. dollars. This is done solely as a hedge against forint inflation; all hotels in Budapest accept payment in Hungarian forints as well as foreign currencies. We have converted the DM prices into dollar prices, basing our calculations on an exchange rate of 2DM to $1.

An alternative is a room in a **private apartment.** Typically, you share the bath with the hosts or with other guests. Breakfast isn't officially included, but the host will often offer continental breakfast for 400Ft to 600Ft ($1.35 to $2). You may have limited kitchen privileges (ask in advance). Some hosts will greet you when you arrive, give you a key, and seemingly disappear; others will want to befriend you, show you around, and cook for you. Most rooms are adequate, some even memorable, but any number of reasons may cause you to dislike yours: Noisy neighborhoods, tiny baths, and bad coffee are among the complaints we've heard. The great majority of visitors, though, appear to be satisfied; at the very least, staying in a private room provides a window into everyday Hungarian life you'd otherwise miss.

The most established agencies are the former state-owned travel agents **Ibusz, Cooptourist,** and **Budapest Tourist.** Although newer, private agencies have proliferated, the older ones tend to have the greatest number of rooms listed. There are agencies at the airport, all three major train stations, throughout

---

Hotel Boom

New hotel construction—like construction in general—is a booming business in Budapest, though predictably few of the new buildings can stand up to the architectural quality of old Budapest. This being the case, one of the more interesting developments in the city is the ongoing renovation of several dilapidated but classic Budapest buildings—in particular the **Gresham Palace** and the **New York Coffeehouse**—which will be converted to luxury hotels.

central Pest, and along the main roads into Budapest for travelers arriving by car. The main **Ibusz reservations office** is at Ferenciek tere 10 (© **061/485-2700;** fax 061/318-2805; Metro: Ferenciek tere), open summer from Monday to Friday 8:15am to 6pm; off-season, from Monday to Friday to 5pm. All major credit cards are accepted.

IN THE INNER CITY & CENTRAL PEST
Very Expensive
K & K Hotel Opera ☆   Operated by the Austrian K & K hotel chain, this tasteful, elegant establishment opened in 1994 and expanded in 1997. Directly across the street from the Opera House in central Pest, the hotel blends nicely with its surroundings. The interior is equally pleasing. The staff is uniformly friendly and helpful. Pets are welcome.

VI. Révay u. 24, 1065 Budapest. © **061/269-0222.** Fax 061/269-0230. www.kkhotels.com. 205 units. 280DM ($140) double; 240DM ($120) single. Rates 5% lower in low season. Rates include breakfast. AE, DC, MC, V. Parking 15DM ($7). Metro: Opera. **Amenities:** Restaurant, bar; fitness center; sauna; business center; no-smoking rooms. *In room:* A/C, TV, minibar, safe.

Moderate
King's Hotel   King's Hotel opened for business in 1995 in a beautifully renovated and restored fin de siècle building in the heart of Pest's Jewish district. The reception is uniformly friendly and helpful. Despite the somewhat drab modern furnishings, rooms retain a 19th-century atmosphere, many with small balconies overlooking the quiet residential street. Most, but not all, have a private bathroom. The kosher hotel restaurant is the only one of its kind in Budapest.

VII. Nagydiófa u. 25–27 Budapest. © and fax **061/352-7675.** 80 units. $60–$80 double; $140 suite. Rates include breakfast. AE, DC, MC, V. Parking available on street for $5 per day. Metro: Astoria. **Amenities:** Restaurant (kosher). *In room:* A/C, TV.

Inexpensive
Hotel Cédrus (formerly known as MEDOSZ) *Value*   The location of the Hotel Cédrus on sleepy Jókai tér, in the heart of Pest's theater district and not far from the Opera House, is as good as it gets off the river in central Pest. Although the hotel hasn't been renovated since privatization (it once was a trade-union hotel), it remains a great value given its location, with simple but clean rooms. Next door is one of Budapest's special treats for children: a puppet theater (*bábszínház*). Note that the hotel was until recently called Hotel MEDOSZ, and is still referred to by that former name in its own pamphlets and by travel agents.

VI. Jókai tér 9, 1061 Budapest. © **061/374-3000.** Fax 061/332-4316. 68 units. 71DM ($36) single; 95DM ($48) double. Rates include breakfast. Rates 10% lower in low season. No credit cards. Parking difficult in neighborhood. Metro: Oktogon. **Amenities:** Restaurant, bar, cafe; solarium. *In room:* TV.

Tips Traveler's Tip
Most hotels and pensions in Budapest divide the year into three seasons. **High season** is roughly from March or April to September or October and the week between Christmas and New Year's. **Midseason** is usually considered March, and October and/or November. **Low season** is roughly from November to February, except Christmas week. Some hotels discount as much as 50% in low season, while others offer no winter discount; be sure to inquire.

Peregrinus ELTE Hotel 🕸🕸   This is the guest house of Pest's ELTE University, and its location couldn't be better—in the heart of the Inner City, on a small side street just half a block from the quiet southern end of the popular pedestrians-only Váci utca. Reserve at least a week ahead. The building dates from the early 1900s and was renovated in 1994, when the guesthouse was opened. Rooms are simple but comfortable.

V. Szerb u. 3, 1056 Budapest. ✆ **061/266-4911.** Fax 061/266-4913. 26 units. 150DM ($75) double; 120DM ($60) in low season. Rates include breakfast. Major credit cards accepted. No parking. Metro: Kálvin tér. *In-room:* TV, minibar.

JUST BEYOND CENTRAL PEST
Expensive
Family Hotel 🕸🕸   A charming, elegant little place opened in 1991, the Family Hotel stands 2 blocks from the Danube in a quiet, mostly residential neighborhood in the Újlipótváros (New Leopold Town), just north of the Inner City of Pest. Perhaps the nicest thing about this hotel is the low-key atmosphere. The suites, all duplexes, are among the nicest in the city, with skylights over the upstairs bedrooms and enormous floor-to-ceiling windows. All rooms are spacious, with simple wood furniture and large bathrooms.

XIII. Ipoly u. 8/b, 1133 Budapest. ✆ **061/320-1284.** Fax 061/329-1620. family.hotel@mail.matav.hu. 13 units. 160DM–180DM ($80–90) double; 240DM ($120) suite. Rates include breakfast. Rates 20% less in low season. AE, DC, MC, V. Parking available 1,500Ft ($5) daily. Metro: Keleti pu., then trolleybus 79 to Ipoly utca. **Amenities:** Restaurant (Hungarian/international), bar; sauna; solarium. *In room:* A/C, TV, minibar.

Inexpensive
Radio Inn 🕸🕸🕸   As the official guesthouse of Hungarian National Radio, the Radio Inn houses many visiting dignitaries, and also offers apartments to individual tourists. Reserve well ahead. The inn is in an exclusive embassy neighborhood. Behind the building, there's an enormous private courtyard full of flowers. The huge apartments (all with fully equipped, spacious kitchens) are comfortably furnished and painstakingly clean. Note that the toilets and bathrooms are separate, European style. The management is somewhat old-system (read: begrudging with information, slightly suspicious of foreigners), yet cordial enough.

VI. Benczúr u. 19, 1068 Budapest. ✆ **061/342-8347** or 061/322-8284. Fax 061/322-8284. 33 units. 78DM ($39) one person, 122DM ($61) two persons, 157DM ($79) three persons per apt; Rates 15–20% less in low season. Breakfast 9DM ($4.50). MC, V. Parking available on street. Metro: Bajza utca. **Amenities:** Bar; laundry service. *In room:* TV.

IN CENTRAL BUDA & THE CASTLE DISTRICT
Very Expensive
Hilton Hotel 🕸   One of only two hotels in Buda's elegant Castle District (the other is Hotel Kulturinnov), the Hilton, built in 1977, is widely considered the city's classiest hotel. Its location, on Hess András tér, next door to Matthias Church and the Fisherman's Bastion, is no less than spectacular. The award-winning design incorporates the ruins of a 13th-century Dominican church and the baroque facade of a 17th-century Jesuit college (the main entrance). More expensive rooms have views over the Danube, with a full Pest skyline; rooms on the other side of the hotel overlook the delightful streets of the Castle District.

I. Hess András tér 1–3, 1014 Budapest. ✆ **061/488-6600.** Fax 061/488-6644. www.hilton.com. 322 units. 420DM–510DM ($201–$260) double; 750DM–1,100DM ($375–$550) suite. Children stay free in parents' room. Breakfast 34DM ($17). AE, DC, MC, V. Parking for a fee in garage. Metro Moszkva tér, then bus "Várbusz"; or Deák tér, then bus 16. **Amenities:** 2 restaurants, coffee shop, sushi bar, bar, wine cellar; fitness center. *In room:* A/C, TV, minibar, hair dryer.

Hotel Gellért ⋆   First opened in 1918, this splendid, sprawling Art Nouveau hotel, located in Buda at the base of Gellért Hill on the bank of the Danube, has not seen renovation since 1970. It's pretty run-down, but still one of the most charming hotels in Budapest. The quality and size of the rooms vary greatly—it seems to be hit or miss. Some rooms with balconies offer great views over the Danube, but these can be noisy since the hotel fronts loud and busy Gellért Square. The Gellért Bathrooms are perhaps the most popular of Budapest's thermal baths.

XI. Gellért tér 1, 1111 Budapest. ℂ **061/385-2200.** Fax 061/466-6631. www.danubiusgroup.com/danubius/ gellert.html. 233 units. 350DM–376DM ($175–$188) double; 466DM–500DM ($233–$250) suite. Rates include breakfast. Spa packages available. AE, DC, MC, V. Free parking. Metro: Deák tér, then tram 47 or 49. **Amenities:** Restaurant, coffee shop, bar; indoor and outdoor pools; spa. *In room:* A/C (some rooms), TV, minibar.

Expensive

Hotel Astra Vendégház ⋆⋆⋆   This little gem was opened in 1996 in a renovated 300-year-old building on a quiet side street in Buda's lovely Watertown. Rooms are large, and far more homey and pleasant than most hotel rooms. Indeed, the hotel is tasteful throughout and the staff friendly. Some rooms overlook the inner courtyard, while others face onto the street.

I. Vám u. 6, 1011 Budapest. ℂ **061/214-1906.** Fax 061/214-1907. 12 units. 190DM ($95) double. Rates include breakfast. Rates 10% lower in low season. No credit cards. Parking available on street. Metro: Batthyány tér. **Amenities:** Cellar bar with snookers table. *In room:* A/C, TV, minibar.

Hotel Victoria ⋆⋆   The Hotel Victoria, located in Buda's lovely Watertown district, is separated from the Danube bank by the busy road that runs alongside the river. The narrow building has only three rooms on each of its nine floors. Two-thirds are corner rooms with large double windows providing great views over the river to Pest. Rooms are quite large, with spacious bathrooms. Middle rooms, though smaller than corner ones, also have windows facing the river. Unfortunately, noise from the busy road beneath your window may disturb your rest.

I. Bem rakpart 11, 1011 Budapest. ℂ **061/457-8080.** Fax 061/457-8088. www.victoria.hu. 27 units. 189DM ($95) single; 199DM ($100) double. Rates include breakfast. Rates 25% lower in low season. AE, DC, MC, V. Parking in garage 17DM ($9). Metro: Batthyány tér, then tram 19 to first stop. **Amenities:** Bar; sauna. *In room:* A/C, TV, minibar.

Moderate

Hotel Kulturinnov ⋆   This is the guesthouse of the Hungarian Culture Foundation, dedicated to forging ties with ethnic Hungarians in neighboring countries. It's open to the public, but few travelers know about it. The rooms are small and simple; nothing is modern, but everything works and the bathrooms are clean. One chagrined traveler reported a nocturnal battle with certain tiny insects who live inside mattresses, but that has not been our experience. The hotel can be a bit hard to find; the entrance is unassuming and practically unmarked. Go through the iron grille door and pass through an exhibition hall, continuing up the grand red-carpeted staircase to the right.

I. Szentháromság tér 6, 1014 Budapest. ℂ **061/355-0122** or 061/375-1651. Fax 061/375-1886. 16 units. $60 single; $75 double. Rates include breakfast. AE, DC, MC, V. Parking 2,000Ft ($7). Metro: Moszkva tér, then bus "Várbusz"; or Deák tér, then bus 16. *In room:* None.

Inexpensive

Charles Apartment House ⋆   Owner Károly Szombati has amassed 22 apartments in a building in a dull but convenient Buda neighborhood (near the large luxury Novotel). All are average Budapest apartments with full kitchens. The furnishings are comfortable and clean. Hegyalja út is a very busy street, but only two apartments face onto it; the rest are in the interior or on the side of the building.

I. Hegyalja út 23, 1016 Budapest. ℂ **061/212-9169.** Fax 061/202-2984. charles@mail.matav.hu. 50 units. 89DM–180DM ($45–$90) apt for 1–4 beds. Rates include breakfast. Rates 10%–15% lower in low season. AE, DC, MC, V. Parking 10DM ($3.35) per day or for free on nearby side street. Metro: Keleti pu., then bus 78 to Mészáros utca. **Amenities:** Restaurant. *In room:* TV.

IN THE BUDA HILLS
Moderate

Gizella Panzió ⊛   This fine pension in the Buda Hills is a 10-minute walk from the tram station. Built on the side of a hill, it has a lovely view and a series of terraced gardens leading down to the swimming pool. Rooms are unique but uniformly quaint, sunny, and tasteful. Owner Gizella Varga also rents fully furnished apartments in the center of town for 110DM to 180DM ($55 to $90), depending on the number of people.

XII. Arató u. 42/b, 1121 Budapest. ℂ and fax **061/249-2281.** gazella@mail.matav.hu. 9 units. 110DM ($55) double; 130DM ($65) suite. Rates include breakfast and sauna. Rates lower in low season. MC, V. Free parking. Metro: Moszkva tér, then tram 59 to the last stop. **Amenities:** Bar; pool; fitness room; sauna; solarium. *In-room:* TV, minibar.

WHERE TO DINE

You can get more for your money dining in Budapest than anywhere in Western Europe. The selection of international eateries is wide, and the Hungarian cuisine itself adventurous with spices. In most restaurants, you have to initiate the paying and tipping ritual by summoning the waiter. The bill is then written out on the spot. If you think the bill is incorrect, don't be embarrassed to call it into question; waiters readily correct the bill when challenged. In all but the fanciest restaurants, the waiter stands there waiting patiently for payment after handing over the bill. The tip (generally about 10%) should be included in the amount you give him. State the full amount you are paying (bill plus tip) and the waiter will make change. Hungarians never leave tips on the table.

Étterem is the most common Hungarian word for restaurant and is used for everything from cafeteria-style eateries to first-class restaurants. A *vendéglő*, or guesthouse, is a smaller, more intimate restaurant, often with a Hungarian folk motif; a *csárda* is a countryside vendéglő. An *étkezde* is an informal lunchroom open only in the daytime. *Önkiszolgáló* means self-service cafeteria, typically open only for lunch. Stand-up *bufes* are often found in bus stations and near busy transport hubs. A *cukrászda* or *kávéház* is a classic Central European coffeehouse, where lingering has developed into an art form. A *borozó* is a wine bar, a *söröző* is a beer bar; sandwiches are usually available at both. Finally, a *kocsma* is a sort of roadside tavern; the Buda Hills are filled with them. Most kocsmas serve full (if greasy) dinners, but the kitchens close very early.

IN THE INNER CITY & CENTRAL PEST
Expensive

Légrádi & Társa ⊛ HUNGARIAN   Very small (nine tables) and inconspicuously marked, on a sleepy side street in the southern part of the Inner City, this is one of the city's most elegant and formal restaurants. The food is served on Herend china, the cutlery is sterling, and an excellent string trio livens the atmosphere. We suggest you pass on the initial premenu offer of hors d'oeuvres costing 1,500Ft ($5). If you'd like to try a soup, the cream of asparagus is a fine interpretation of a Hungarian favorite. The chicken paprika served with cheese dumplings seasoned with fresh dill will surpass any you've tried elsewhere, and the veal, smothered in cauliflower-cheese sauce, is delightful.

V. Magyar u. 23. ℂ 061/318-6804. Reservations highly recommended. Soup 600–700Ft ($2–$2.35); main courses 2,000–3,500Ft ($7–$12). AE, MC, V. Mon–Sat 6pm–midnight. Metro: Kálvin tér.

Lou Lou 🟉 FRENCH   Located on a quiet side street not far from Parliament in the financial district, this is a handsome new addition to the Budapest dining scene. The decor is rustic and tasteful, with Roman yellow walls and a vaulted ceiling. They specialize in fresh fish dishes. Lou Lou features an extensive wine list, up to 12,000Ft ($40) a bottle. House wine is also available.

V. Vigyázó F. u. 4. ℂ 061/312-4505. Reservations recommended. Appetizers 900–2,000Ft ($3–$7); main courses 1,500–3,000Ft ($5–$10). AE, MC, V. Mon–Fri noon–3pm and 7pm–midnight; Sat 7pm–midnight. Closed Sun. Metro: Deák tér or Kossuth tér.

Moderate
Marquis de Salade 🟉🟉 RUSSIAN/MIDDLE EASTERN/AFRICAN   Vegetarians will feel right at home here. On the edge of Pest's theater district, this recently renovated restaurant is owned by an Azerbaijan woman and employs eight cooks from various countries (Russia, Bangladesh, East Africa, Hungary, Italy, and the Caucasus Mountains) and turns out an amazing assortment of exceptional dishes from a number of cuisines. The offerings are sophisticated yet earthy. Try the lamb with rice (Azerbaijan) or the borscht soup (Russian). A no-smoking area is available, and tablecloths and tapestries are for sale.

VI. Hajós u. 43. ℂ 061/302-4086. Appetizers 750–2,500Ft ($2.50–$8); main courses 1,200–2,800Ft ($4–$9). V. Daily 11am–midnight. Metro: Arany János u.

Inexpensive
Kádár Étkezde 🟉🟉🟉 HUNGARIAN   By 11:45am, Uncle Kádár's, in the heart of the Jewish district, is filled with regulars—from paint-spattered workers to elderly Jewish couples. Uncle Kádár, a neighborhood legend, personally greets them as they file in. From the outside the only sign of the place is a very small red sign saying "Kádár Étkezde." The place is no more than a lunchroom, but it has a great atmosphere: high ceilings, wood-paneled walls with photos (many

---

🅲 Coffeehouse Culture

Imperial Budapest, like Vienna, was famous for its coffeehouse culture. Literary movements and political circles alike were identified in large part by which coffeehouse they met in. You can still go to several classic coffeehouses, all of which offer delicious pastries, coffee, and more in an atmosphere of splendor. Table sharing is common.

The best are **Gerbeaud's** 🟉🟉🟉, in the Inner City at V. Vörösmarty tér 7 (ℂ 1/429-9000); **Művész Kávéház** 🟉, across the street from the Opera House at VI. Andrássy út 29 (ℂ 1/352-1337; Metro: Opera); the **New York Kávéház**, on the Outer Ring at VII. Erzsébet krt. 9–11 (ℂ 1/352-1326; Metro: Blaha Lujza tér), but avoid the overpriced and mediocre dinners here; **Ruszwurm Cukrászda** 🟉, in the Castle District at I. Szentháromság u. 7 (ℂ 1/375-5284; Várbusz [Castle Bus] from Moszva tér); and **Angelika Cukrászda** 🟉🟉, also in Buda, at I. Batthyány tér 7 (no phone; Metro: Batthyány tér).

autographed) of actors and athletes, and old-fashioned seltzer bottles on every table. The food is simple but hearty and the service friendly. Table sharing is the norm.

VII. Klauzál tér 9. © 061/321-3622. Soup 140Ft (45¢); main courses 360–570Ft ($1.20–$1.90). No credit cards. Tues–Sat 11:30am–3:30pm. Metro: Astoria or Deák tér.

JUST BEYOND CENTRAL PEST
Very Expensive
Gundel 🍴 HUNGARIAN/INTERNATIONAL Budapest's fanciest and most famous historic restaurant, Gundel was reopened in 1992 by the well-known restaurateur George Lang, owner of New York's Café des Artistes. Located in City Park, Gundel has an opulent dining room and a large, carefully groomed garden. Lamb and wild-game entrees are house specialties. The menu highlights fruits and vegetables in season. In late spring, don't miss out on the asparagus served in hollandaise with grilled salmon. Gundel has an extensive wine list, and the waiters are well versed in its offerings. Homemade fruit ice cream served in the shape of the fruit makes for a delectable dessert, as does the famous Gundel torta, a decadently rich chocolate layer cake.

XIV. Állatkerti út 2. © 061/322-1002 or 061/321-3550. Reservations highly recommended. Soup 1,000Ft ($3.35); main courses 3,600–6,900Ft ($12–$23). AE, DC, MC, V. Daily noon–4pm and 7pm–midnight. Metro: Hósök tere.

IN CENTRAL BUDA
Expensive
Kacsa Vendéglő 🍴 HUNGARIAN Kacsa (meaning "duck") is located on the main street of Watertown, the Buda neighborhood that lies between Castle Hill and the Danube. Here you'll find an intimate, elegant, and understated dining atmosphere, though the service seems overly attentive and ceremonious. Enticing main courses include roast duck with Morello cherries, haunch of venison with grapes, and pikeperch Russian style. The vegetarian plate is the best we've had anywhere.

I. Fó u. 75. © 061/201-9992. Reservations recommended. Soup 400–500Ft ($1.35–$1.65); main courses 1,900–3,000Ft ($6–$10). MC, V. Daily 6pm–1am. Metro: Batthyány tér.

Moderate
Le Jardin de Paris 🍴 Finds FRENCH This wonderful little French bistro is in the heart of Buda's Watertown, across from the hideous Institut Français. A cozy cellar space, it's decorated with an eclectic collection of graphic arts, with a jazz trio entertaining diners from 7 to 11pm daily. The menu contains nouvelle French specialties, and the wine list features French as well as Hungarian vintages. The presentation is impeccable and the waiters aren't overbearing. In summer there's outdoor seating in a new garden area.

I. Fó u. 20. © 061/201-0047. Reservations recommended. Soup 590–890Ft ($1.95–$2.95); appetizers 850–2,000Ft ($2.85–$6.65); main courses 1,500–2,500Ft ($5–$8). AE, DC, MC, V. Daily noon–midnight. Metro: Batthyány tér.

Taverna Ressaikos Value GREEK In the heart of Buda's Watertown, next to the Hotel Carlton Budapest, the Ressaikos features generous portions of carefully prepared food at reasonable prices. Try the calamari or the lamb in wine sauce. The menu also features a number of interesting goat dishes. Vegetarians can easily make a meal of the appetizers: stuffed tomatoes, spanakopita, tsatsiki, and the like. The live guitar music (weekends only) can get a bit loud, and the service, while attentive, is definitely slow.

I. Apor Péter u. 1. Ⓒ🆃 061/212-1612. Reservations recommended. Soup and appetizers 300–800Ft ($1–$2.65); main courses 750–1,300Ft ($2.50–$4.35). MC, V. Daily noon–midnight. Metro: Deák tér, then bus 16 to Clark Ádám tér.

IN THE BUDA HILLS
Moderate
Náncsi Néni Vendéglóje 🅡 HUNGARIAN Decorated with photographs of early 1900s Budapest, this popular but remote restaurant is located high in the Buda Hills. There's outdoor garden dining in the summer, with live accordion music at night. The menu features typical Hungarian dishes, prepared with great care.

II. Ördögárok út 80. Ⓒ🆃 061/397-2742. Reservations recommended for dinner. Soup 500Ft ($1.65); main courses 1,200–2,000Ft ($4–$7). MC, V. Daily noon–11pm. Metro: Moszkva tér, then tram 56 to last stop, then bus 63 to Széchenyi utca.

Szép Ilona 🅡🅡 HUNGARIAN This cheerful, unassuming restaurant serves a mostly local crowd. There's a good selection of specialties: Try the *borjúpaprikás galuskával* (veal paprika) served with *galuska* (a typical Central European style of dumpling). There's a small sidewalk garden for summer dining. The Szép Ilona is in a pleasant Buda neighborhood; after your meal, have a stroll through the tree-lined streets.

II. Budakeszi út 1–3. Ⓒ🆃 061/275-1392. Soup 290–610Ft (95¢–$3); main courses 780–2,300Ft ($2.60–$8). No credit cards. Daily 11:30am–10pm. Metro: Moszkva tér, then bus 158 (departs from Csaba utca, at the top of the stairs, near the stop from which the Várbusz departs for the Castle District).

IN NORTHERN BUDA & ÓBUDA
Expensive
Kis Buda Gyöngye 🅡🅡🅡 HUNGARIAN On a quiet side street in a residential Óbuda neighborhood, Kis Buda Gyöngye ("Little Pearl of Buda") is a favorite of Hungarians and visitors, serving standard Hungarian fare. This cheerful place features an interior garden, which sits in the shade of a wonderful old gnarly tree. Inside, an eccentric violinist entertains diners. Consider the goose plate, a rich combination platter including a roast goose leg, goose cracklings, and goose liver.

III. Kenyeres u. 34. Ⓒ🆃 061/368-6402 or 061/368-9246. Reservations highly recommended. Soup 680–780Ft ($2.25–$2.60); main courses 1,800–3,200Ft ($6–$11). AE, DC, MC, V. Mon–Sat noon–midnight. Tram: 17 from Margit híd (Buda side).

SEEING THE SIGHTS
SIGHTSEEING SUGGESTIONS FOR FIRST-TIME VISITORS

If You Have 1 Day Spend a few hours in the morning exploring the **Inner City** and **central Pest.** Stroll along the Danube as far as the neo-Gothic **Parliament,** noting along the way the **Chain Bridge.** In the afternoon, visit the major sites of **Castle Hill** and meander the cobblestone streets of the **Castle District.**

If You Have 2 Days On day 1, head for Buda's **Gellért Hotel** and take a dip in its spa waters. Then hike up the stairs of **Gellért Hill** for an unparalleled panorama. Devote most of day 2 to the **Castle District** and the sites of **Castle Hill** and visit some of the smaller museums. Head back to Pest to see **Heroes' Square** and **City Park,** and in the evening stroll the length of grand **Andrássy út** back to the center of Pest.

If You Have 3 Days Or More On day 3, take a boat up the Danube to visit Szentendre, a charming riverside town. On days 4 and 5, visit some of the central sites you may have missed, and after lunch cross the Chain Bridge to Watertown to explore Buda's historic riverside neighborhood. See St. Anne's Church, the Capuchin Church, and the Király Bathrooms. Check out Pest's indoor market halls and visit Margaret Island.

THE TOP ATTRACTIONS
In Pest

Néprajzi Múzeum (Ethnographical Museum)   Directly across from Parliament, the vast Ethnographical Museum features an ornate interior equal to that of the Opera House. A ceiling fresco of Justitia, the goddess of justice, by artist Károly Lotz, dominates the lobby. Although a third of the museum's holdings are from outside Hungary, most concentrate on the items from Hungarian ethnography. The fascinating permanent exhibition, "From Ancient Times to Civilization," features everything from drinking jugs to razor cases to chairs to clothing.

V. Kossuth tér 12. © 061/473-2440. Admission 500Ft ($1.65). Tues–Sun 10am–6pm. Metro: Kossuth tér.

Nemzeti Múzeum (Hungarian National Museum) ☆☆   This enormous neoclassical structure, built from 1837 to 1847, played a major role in the beginning of the Hungarian Revolution of 1848 and 1849; on its wide steps on March 15, 1848, poet Sándor Petőfi and other young radicals are said to have exhorted the people of Pest to revolt against the Hapsburgs. The two main museum exhibits on view are "The History of the Peoples of Hungary from the Paleolithic Age to the Magyar Conquest" and "The History of the Hungarian People from the Magyar Conquest to 1989." "The Hungarian Royal Insignia" is another permanent exhibit.

VIII. Múzeum krt. 14. © 061/338-2122. Admission 400Ft ($1.35). Tues–Sun 10am–6pm (to 5pm in winter). Metro: Kálvin tér.

In Buda

Budapesti Történeti Múzeum (Budapest History Museum)   This museum, also known as the Castle Museum, is the best place to get a sense of the once-great medieval Buda. It's probably worth splurging for a guided tour; even though the museum's descriptions are written in English, the history of the palace's repeated construction and destruction is so arcane it's difficult to understand what you're really seeing.

I. In Buda Palace, Wing E, on Castle Hill. © 061/225-7815 or 061/355-8849. Admission 500Ft ($1.65). Guided tours by qualified staff in English for serious history buffs, 5,000Ft ($17; open to negotiation), available on advance request. May 15–Sept 15 Wed–Mon 10am–6pm; Sept 16–May 14 Wed–Mon 10am–5pm. Metro: Moszkva tér, then bus "Várbusz"; or Deák tér, then bus 16. Funicular: From Clark Ádám tér to Castle Hill.

Nemzeti Galéria (Hungarian National Gallery) ☆   Hungary has produced some fine artists, particularly in the late 19th century, and this is the place to view their work. The giants of the time are the brilliant but moody Mihály Munkácsy; László Paál, a painter of village scenes; Károly Ferenczy, a master of light; and Pál Szinyei Merse, the plein-air artist and contemporary of the early French impressionists.

I. In Buda Palace, Wings B, C, and D, on Castle Hill. © 061/375-5567. Admission 500Ft ($1.65). Mar 16–Nov 14 Tues–Sun 10am–6pm; Nov 15–Mar 15 Tues–Sun 10am–4pm. Metro: Moszkva tér, then bus "Várbusz"; or Deák tér, then bus 16. Funicular: From Clark Ádám tér to Castle Hill.

MORE ATTRACTIONS

Vidám Park (Amusement Park) *★★★* (Kids)   This is a must if you're traveling with kids, but two rides in particular aren't to be missed. The 100-year-old
Merry-Go-Round (*Körhinta*), constructed almost entirely of wood, was
recently restored to its original grandeur. The riders must actively pump to keep
the horses rocking, and authentic Würlitzer music plays. As the carousel spins
round and round, it creaks mightily. The **Ferris wheel** (*Óriáskerék*) is also wonderful, though it has little in common with rambunctious modern Ferris wheels.
A gangly bright-yellow structure, it rotates at a liltingly slow pace, gently lifting
you high for a remarkable view. The Vidám Park also features Europe's longest
wooden roller-coaster.

XIV. Állatkerti krt. 14–16. ℭ 061/343-0996. Admission 200Ft (65¢) adults, 100Ft (20¢) children; rides 200–
500Ft (65¢–$1.65). Apr–Sept daily 10am–8pm; Oct–Mar 10am–7pm. Metro: Széchenyi fürdő.

Historic Buildings

Magyar Állami Operaház (Hungarian State Opera House) *★*   Completed in 1884, Budapest's Opera House boasts a fantastically ornate interior
featuring frescoes by two of the best-known Hungarian artists of the day, Bertalan Székely and Károly Lotz. Home to both the State Opera and the State Ballet, the Opera House has a rich and evocative history.

VI. Andrássy út 22. ℭ 061/331-2550. Admission (by guided tour only) 700FT ($2.35). Tours daily at 3 and
4pm. Metro: Opera.

Parliament   Budapest's great Parliament, an eclectic design mixing the predominant neo-Gothic style with a neo-Renaissance dome, was completed in
1902. Standing proudly on the Danube bank, visible from almost any riverside
point, it has from the outset been one of Budapest's symbols, though until 1989
a democratically elected government had convened here only once (just after
World War II, before the Communist takeover). The main cupola is decorated
with statues of Hungarian kings. On either side of the cupola are waiting rooms
leading into the respective houses of Parliament. Here the MPs gather during
breaks in the session to smoke and chat. The waiting room on the Senate side
(blue carpet) is adorned with statues of farmers, peasants, tradesmen, and workers. The statues that decorate the waiting room on the representatives' side (red
carpet) are of sailors, soldiers, postal officials, etc. The interior decor is predominantly neo-Gothic. The ceiling frescoes are by Károly Lotz, Hungary's best-
known artist of that genre. Note the purportedly largest handmade carpet in
Europe, from the small Hungarian village of Békésszentandrás.

V. Kossuth tér. ℭ 061/441-4415. Admission (by guided tour only): 30-min tour in English, 1,500Ft ($5)
adults, 750Ft ($2.50) students. Tickets available at gate X, enter at gate XII. Tours year-round Mon–Fri 10am
and 2pm; Sat–Sun 10am. Closed when Parliament is in session. Metro: Kossuth tér.

Churches & Synagogues

Dohány Synagogue *★★*   Built in 1859 and just recently restored, this is said
to be the largest synagogue in Europe and the second largest in the world. The
architecture has striking Moorish elements; the interior is vast and ornate, with
two balconies, and the usual presence of an organ in a neologue synagogue. The
synagogue has a rich but tragic history. There's a Jewish museum next door that
traces the origins of Hungarian Judaism and features exhibits of ceremonial
Judaica throughout the centuries, including Torah covers, scholarly writings,
and documents.

VII. Dohány u. 2–8. ℭ 061/342-8949. Admission by donation. Officially Tues–Thurs 10am–5pm; Fri 10am–
3pm; Sat 10am–1pm. Metro: Astoria or Deák tér.

Bazilika (St. Stephen's Church)   The country's largest church, this basilica took more than 50 years to build (the 1868 collapse of the dome caused significant delay) and was finally completed in 1906. However, during this time Pest underwent radical growth—while the front of the church dominates sleepy Szent István tér, the rear faces out onto the far busier Inner Ring boulevard. In the Chapel of the Holy Right (Szent Jobb Kápolna), you can see Hungarian Catholicism's most cherished—and bizarre—holy relic: the preserved right hand of Hungary's first Christian king, Stephen.

V. Szent István tér 33. ℭ 061/332-0873. Church, free; treasury, 200Ft (65¢); tower, 500Ft ($1.65). Church, daily 7am–7pm, except during services; treasury, daily 9am–5pm (10am–4pm in winter); Szent Jobb Chapel, Mon–Sat 9am–5pm (10am–4pm in winter) and Sun 1–5pm; tower, daily Apr–May 10am–4:30pm, June–Aug 9:30am–6pm, Sept–Oct 10am–5:30pm. Metro: Arany János utca or Bajcsy-Zsilinszky út.

Mátyás Templom (Matthias Church) ✵✵✵   Officially named the Church of Our Lady, this symbol of Buda's Castle District is popularly known as Matthias Church after the 15th-century king who was twice married here. Though it dates from the mid-13th century, like other old churches in Budapest it has an interesting history of destruction and reconstruction, always being refashioned in the architectural style of the time.

I. Szentháromság tér 2. ℭ 061/355-5657. Church free; exhibit rooms beneath altar 200Ft (65¢). Daily 9:30am–6pm (to 5pm in winter). Metro: Moszkva tér, then bus "Várbusz"; or Deák tér, then bus 16. Funicular: From Clark Ádám tér to Castle Hill.

PARKS & PANORAMAS

Gellért Hegy (Gellért Hill), towering 230 meters (750 ft.) above the Danube, offers the city's single best panorama (bus: 27 from Móricz Zsigmond körtér). It's named after the Italian Bishop Gellért, who assisted Hungary's first Christian king, Stephen I, in converting the Magyars. Gellért became a martyr when vengeful pagans, outraged at the forced and violent nature of Stephen's proselytization, rolled him in a barrel to his death from the side of the hill on which his enormous statue now stands. On top of Gellért Hill you'll find the Liberation Monument, built in 1947 to commemorate the Red Army's liberation of Budapest from Nazi occupation. Also atop the hill is the Citadella, built by the Austrians shortly after they crushed the Hungarian War of Independence (1848–49).

Margaret Island (Margit-sziget) ✵✵✵ has been a public park since 1908 (bus: 26 from Nyugati tér; tram: 4 or 6, which stop at the entrance to the island midway across the Margaret Bridge). The long, narrow island, connected to both Buda and Pest by the Margaret and Árpád bridges, is barred to most vehicular traffic. Facilities on the island include the Palatinus Strand open-air baths, which draw upon the famous thermal waters under Margaret Island; the Alfréd Hajós Sport Pool; and the Open Air Theater. Sunbathers line the steep embankments along the river and bicycles are available for rent. Despite all this, Margaret Island is a quiet, tranquil place.

City Park (Városliget) ✵ is an equally popular place to spend a summer day (Metro: Hósök tere/Heroes' Square and Széchenyi Fürdó). Heroes' Square, at the end of Andrássy út, is the most logical starting point for a walk in City Park. The lake behind the square is used for boating in summer and ice-skating in winter. The park's Zoo Boulevard (Állatkerti körút), the favorite street of generations of Hungarian children, is where the **zoo**, the **circus**, and the **amusement park** are all found. **Gundel**, Budapest's most famous restaurant, is also here, as are the **Széchenyi Baths.**

Károly kert (Charles Garden) ✹✹✹, a little enclosed park in the southern half of the Inner City (Metro: Astoria), is the location of what we consider to be Budapest's most charming playground. To enter the park, you must pass through a gigantic wrought-iron gate. The equipment here might not be as modern or as varied as at some of the city's other playgrounds, but the place has a distinct old-world charm and its location in the Inner City makes it a convenient destination.

ORGANIZED TOURS

BUS & BOAT TOURS   Ibusz (☎ 061/318-1139 or 061/318-1043), with decades of experience, sets the standard with organized tours in terms of quality and quantity. It offers 11 boat and bus tours, from basic city tours to special folklore-oriented tours. Ibusz tours operate year-round, with an abbreviated schedule off-season. Bus tours leave from the Erzsébet tér bus station (Metro: Deák tér) and boat tours from the Vigadó tér landing on the Pest waterfront, between the Erzsébet Bridge and the Chain Bridge (Metro: Vörösmarty tér). There's also a free hotel pickup service 30 minutes before departure.

A boat tour is a great way to get your measure of the scope and scale of the Hungarian capital, and you can see a majority of the city's grand sights from the river. The Hungarian state company **MAHART,** V. Belgrád rakpart (☎ **061/ 318-1704** or 061/318-1880), operates daily sightseeing cruises on the Danube. Boats depart frequently from Vigadó tér on weekends and holidays in spring and every day in summer.

WALKING TOURS   We recommend "Walking Tours in Budapest" offered by a company called **Image Advantage** ✹✹ (☎ **06-30/211-8861** [cell phone]; www.budapestours.com). They have three different walks: The Absolute Walk, the Hammer and Sickle Walk, and the Absolute Dark Side and Pub Crawl. Your best bet is The Absolute Walk, with tickets costing 2,990Ft ($10); free for children under 12. Show this book (or the company's flyer, found at many tourist haunts) and you'll get a 500Ft ($2.35) discount. Buy your ticket from the guide at the start of the tour. From Mid-May to September, tours are daily at 9:30am and 13:30pm; from October to mid-December and February to early May, tours are daily at 10:30am. All three tours, conducted by knowledgeable and personable guides, start on the front steps of the Műcsarnok (Metro: Hősök tere) or at Deák tér (Metro: Deák tér), in front of the church. Tours last anywhere from 3½ to 5 hours, depending on the mood of the group, and take you throughout central Pest and central Buda. You get quite a comprehensive introduction to the city, but be aware that it's practically an entire day on your feet.

THE SHOPPING SCENE

Year-round, shoppers fill the pedestrians-only **Váci utca,** from the stately Vörösmarty tér, the center of Pest, across the roaring Kossuth Lajos utca, all the way to Vámház krt (Yellow line). The **Castle District** in Buda, with many folk-art boutiques and galleries, is another popular area for souvenir hunters. Locals (and budget travelers) might window-shop in these two neighborhoods, but they do their serious shopping elsewhere. One popular street is Pest's **Outer Ring (Nagykörút);** another bustling shopping street is Pest's **Kossuth Lajos utca,** off the Erzsébet Bridge, and its continuation **Rákóczi út,** extending all the way out to Keleti Station.

BEST BUYS   Folkloric Objects   Hungary's famous folkloric objects are the most popular souvenirs among foreign visitors. The state-owned Folkart shops

(Népmúvészeti Háziipar) have a great selection of handmade goods. Popular items include pillowcases, pottery, porcelain, dolls, dresses, skirts, and sheepskin vests. The main store, **Folkart Centrum,** is at V. Váci u. 14 (© 061/318-5840), and is open daily from 9:30am to 7pm. One outstanding private shop on Váci utca is **Vali Folklór** 🐾🐾🐾, in the courtyard of Váci u. 23 (© 061/337-6301). This cluttered shop is run by a soft-spoken man named Bálint Ács who travels the villages of Hungary and neighboring countries in search of authentic folk items.

Holló Folkart Gallery, at V. Vitkovics Mihály u. 12 (© 061/317-8103), is an unusual gallery selling handcrafted reproductions of folk-art pieces from various regions of the country.

Porcelain & Pottery   Another popular Hungarian item is porcelain, particularly from the country's two best-known producers, Herend and Zsolnay. Although both brands are available in the West, here you'll find a better selection and prices about 50% lower.

You'll find world-renowned hand-painted Herend porcelain (www.herend. com), first produced in 1826 in the town of Herend near Veszprém in western Hungary, at the **Herend Shop,** V. József nádor tér 11 (© 061/317-2622). This shop has the widest Herend selection in the capital; now they can arrange shipping if you are dealing with them on the premises. There are also two new Herend shops at the following locations: V. Kigyó u. 5 (© 061/318-3439)—this shop offers shipping—and I. Szentháromság u. 5 (© 061/225-1050) in the Castle District. If Herend porcelain isn't within your price range, you'll find lovely pottery at **Herend Village Pottery,** V. Váci u. 23 (© 061/318-2094). This shop sells Herend porcelain as well as a lovely casual "village-style" pottery. There is a second shop at II. Bem rakpart 37 (© 061/356-7899) in Buda's Watertown. Delightfully gaudy Zsolnay porcelain from the southern city of Pécs is Hungary's second-most celebrated brand of porcelain; you'll find it at **Zsolnay Márkabolt** 🐾, V. Kígyó u. 4 (© 061/318-3712).

(Kids   **Tropical Budapest**

The city of Budapest is now awash in huge new Western-style malls. As a general matter, we tend to avoid such malls, but you might want to check out the amazing **"Tropicarium"** at a mall in southern Buda called **Campona,** located at XXII. Budapest, Nagytétényi út 37-43 (© 061/ 424-3000; bus: 3, 14, or 114). The Tropicarium features both an aquarium—the largest in Central Europe—and a miniature rain forest, with snakes, alligators and the like (and rain!). As the *Budapest Sun* puts it, "The aquarium is a particularly pleasant place to stroll around if you can manage to go on a weekday morning. At other times it can get a little hectic, packed with over-excited children trying to catch the monkeys and parrots and harassed pensioners meditating by the shark tank." The *Sun* goes on to note that "the highlight for many visitors is the final glass tunnel which leads under a giant tank where a group of plump sharks circle round and round. . . . As the sharks approach the tunnel, they come so close visitors can look right into their mouths." There's also a bowling alley and an 11-screen multiplex cinema at the mall.

Hungarian Foods   Connoisseurs generally agree that **Pick Salami** ⚜⚜ from the southeastern city of Szeged is the best of world-renowned Hungarian salami, and it's easy to carry home without giving your clothes an unforgettable aroma. Chestnut paste (*gesztenye püré*), found in a tin or block wrapped in foil, is rare abroad and used primarily as a pastry filling, but can also top desserts and ice cream. Paprika paste (*pirosarany*) is also hard to find outside Hungary; it comes in a bright-red tube in hot (*csípós*), deli-style (*csemege*), and sweet (*édes*) varieties. All these can be found in grocery stores (*élelmiszer*) and delicatessens (*csemege*).

Hungarian Wines   Fine, affordable Hungarian wines from the Szekszárd, Villány, Tokaj, and Eger regions are abundant. The most renowned red wines come from the region around Villány, a town to the south of Pécs by the Croatian border. As a result of the aggressive marketing strategy of the former Communist regime, many foreigners are familiar with the red wines from Eger, especially *Egri Bikavér* (Eger Bull's Blood). Eger wines, though rich and fruity, are markedly inferior to Villányi reds. The country's best white wines are generally believed to be those from the Lake Balaton region, though some Hungarians insist that white wines from the Sopron region (by the Austrian border) are better. *Tokaj* wines— *száraz* (dry) or *édes* (sweet)—are popular as aperitifs and dessert wines.

MARKETS   Budapest has a handful of **vintage market halls (vásárcsarnok)** ⚜⚜⚜, wonders of steel and glass, built in the 1890s in the ambitious grandiose style of the time. Three are still in use and provide a measure of local color you won't find in the grocery store. The **Központi Vásárcsarnok (Central Market Hall),** on IX. Vámház körút, is the largest and most spectacular market hall. In the Inner Ring (Kiskörút), on the Pest side of the Szabadság Bridge, this trilevel

---

Moments **Music for a Summer Evening**

During the warm lazy days, you'll find several special venues for classical music. Tickets for them are available at the **National Philharmonic Ticket Office,** V. Vörösmarty tér 1 (✆ **061/318-0281;** Metro: Vörösmarty tér).

The historic outdoor Dominican Courtyard, inside the Castle District's Hilton Hotel, I. Hess András tér 1–3 (✆ **061/488-6600;** Metro: Moszkva tér, then bus "Várbusz"; or Deák tér, then bus 16), is the site for a series of classical recitals during the summer. The District's beautiful **Matthias Church (Mátyás Templom),** next door at I. Szentháromság tér 2, holds a regular Tuesday- and Friday-night series of organ concerts from June to September. Concerts start at 7:30pm. Tickets can be purchased before the performance at the church entry.

Organ concerts are also held Monday evenings at 7pm during July and August at **St. Stephen's Church (Basilica),** Hungary's largest church, V. Szent István tér 33 (✆ **061/332-0873;** Metro: Arany János utca or Bajcsy-Zsilinszky út). You can buy tickets at the church entry before the performance.

The **Dohány Synagogue,** VII. Dohány u. 2–8 (✆ **061/342-8949;** Metro: Astoria or Deák tér), is the venue for occasional concerts from May to September. Concerts begin at 7pm, but days are not regular. For information and tickets, call the **Central Theater Ticket Office** (✆ **061/267-1267;** Metro: Opera).

hall was impeccably reconstructed in 1995. Other vintage market halls include the **Belvárosi Vásárcsarnok (Inner City Market Hall),** on V. Hold utca, behind Szabadság tér in central Pest; and the **Józsefváros Vásárcsarnok,** on VIII. Rákóczi tér. Other active and lively markets are found in unspectacular buildings, such as the **Fehérvári úti Vásárcsarnok,** on XI. Fehérvári út, in front of the Buda Skála department store, just a block from the Móricz Zsigmond körtér transportation hub; and the **Fény utca Piac,** on II. Fény utca, just off Moszkva tér in Buda.

BUDAPEST AFTER DARK

The most complete schedule of mainstream performing arts is found in the free bimonthly *Koncert Kalendárium* at the Central Philharmonic Ticket Office in Vörösmarty tér. The *Budapest Sun* is a good source, as is the new magazine *Scene,* and the *Budapest Week* Web site (www.budapestweek.hu).

The **Central Theater Ticket Office (Színházak Központi Jegyiroda),** VI. Andrássy út 18 (© **061/267-1267;** Metro: Opera), sells tickets to just about everything, from theater and operetta to sports events and rock concerts; it's open from Monday to Friday 10am to 6pm. For **classical performances,** go to the National Philharmonic Ticket Office (Filharmónia Nemzeti Jegyiroda), V. Vörösmarty tér 1 (© **061/318-0281;** Metro: Vörösmarty tér). For **opera and ballet,** go to the Hungarian State Opera Ticket Office (Magyar Állami Opera Jegyiroda), VI. Andrássy út 20 (entrance inside the courtyard; © **061/ 332-7914;** Metro: Opera). For events in the **Spring Festival,** go to the Festival Ticket Service, V. 1081 Rákóczi út 65 (© **061/333-2337;** Red line, Blaha Lujza Tér). For **rock and jazz concert** tickets, try Ticket Express, VI. Jókai u. 40 (© **061/353-0692;** Yellow line, Opera).

THE PERFORMING ARTS

Completed in 1884, the **Magyar Állami Operaház (Hungarian State Opera House)** ✱✱, VI. Andrássy út 22 (© **061/331-2550;** Metro: Opera), is Budapest's most famous performance hall and a tourist attraction in its own right. Hungarians adore opera, and a large percentage of seats are sold on a subscription basis; buy your tickets a few days ahead if possible. The box office is open from Monday to Friday 11am to 6pm. Ticket prices range from 3,200 to 6,600Ft ($11 to $22).

The Great Hall (Nagyterem) of the **Zeneakadémia (Ferenc Liszt Academy of Music)** ✱✱✱, VI. Liszt Ferenc tér 8 (© **061/341-4788;** Metro: Oktogon), is the premier music hall. The Academy was built in the Art Nouveau style of the early 20th century with the best acoustics in the city. Box office hours are from 2pm to show time on the day of performance. Tickets range from 500 to 5,000Ft ($1.65 to $17), except special events.

LIVE-MUSIC CLUBS

The club scene has found fertile ground since 1989's political changes—so much so, in fact, that clubs come in and out of fashion overnight. Check the *Budapest Sun* for up-to-the-minute club listings.

The popular **Made Inn Mine,** VI. Andrássy út 112 (© **061/311-3437;** Metro: Bajza utca), has a subterranean, cavelike atmosphere. Wednesday features a funk dance party, with all drinks half price. For some reason, Thursday is *the* night to be here; you may have to wait in line to enter. It's open daily from 8pm to 5am, with the kitchen open to 3am. Cover is 300Ft ($1), but 500Ft ($1.65) on Thursday. **TRAFO** ✱✱, XI. Liliom u. 41 (© **061/215-1600;** tram: 4 or 6 to Üllöi út), is an old electric power station recently renovated and transformed into a cultural center for young alternative artists. It also hosts the hippest disco in town. *The* night is Tuesday with DJ Palotai, with the party starting at 9pm but you can have a great time on Fridays dancing to the '60s and '70s greatest hits.

The **Fél 10 Jazz Klub** *R*, VIII. Baross u. 30 (no phone; Metro: Kálvin tér), is a classy multilevel club. The place features live jazz performances nightly, while techno-free dance parties get going in the wee hours from Thursday to Saturday. It's open from Monday to Friday noon to 4am and Saturday and Sunday 7pm to 4am. **Old Man's,** VIII. Akácfa u. 13 (© **061/322-7645;** Metro: Blaha Luzja tér), is the place to take in the best jazz and blues in Hungary. The Pege Quartet plays here, as does Hobo and his blues band. This very hip spot is open daily from 3pm to 4am.

BARS

The **Irish Cat Pub** *RR*, V. Múzeum krt. 41 (© **061/266-4085;** Metro: Kálvin tér), is an Irish-style pub with Guinness on tap and a whiskey bar. It's a popular meeting place for expatriates and travelers, serving a full menu, and is open from Monday to Thursday and Sunday 11am to 3am and Friday and Saturday 11am to 5am. **Morrison's Music Pub,** VI. Révay u. 25 (© **061/269-4060;** Metro: Opera), is a casual place packed by an almost-20-something crowd. There's a small dance floor, an eclectic variety of loud live music, and a number of beers on tap. It's open from Wednesday to Saturday 8:30pm to 4am.

An American-style microbrewery on one of Pest's busiest squares, **Chicago Sörgyár,** VII. Erzsébet krt. 2 (© **061/478-0580;** Metro: Blaha Lujza tér)), has a die-hard expatriate crowd that comes not just for the fairly good home-brewed beer but for the hamburgers, nachos, and fries. Happy hour is weekdays from 4 to 6pm, with half-price drinks. It's open from Monday to Saturday noon to midnight, and Sunday noon to 11pm.

HUNGARIAN DANCE HOUSES

Recent years have seen the growth of an urban-centered folk revival movement known as the táncház **(dance house).** This interactive evening of **folk music** and **folk dancing,** held in community centers around town, is one of the best cultural experiences you can have in Hungary. The format usually consists of about an hour of dance-step instruction, followed by several hours of dancing accompanied by a live band, which might include some of Hungary's best folk musicians, in an authentic, casual atmosphere.

The leading Hungarian folk band Muzsikás, whose lead singer is the incomparable Márta Sebestyén, hosts a táncház every Thursday (from September to June only) at 8pm for 350Ft ($1.25) at the **Marczibányi Square Cultural House (Marczibányi tér Művelődésiház)** *RRR*, II. Marczibányi tér 5/a (© **061/212-0803;** Metro: Moszkva tér). If you're in town and have an evening to catch a Muzsikás performance, don't miss it. The **FMH Cultural House (Szakszervezetek Fővárosi Művelődési Háza),** XI. Fehérvári út 47 (© **061/ 203-3868;** Metro: Deák tér, then tram 47), hosts a táncház for kids every Tuesday (except in July and August), from 5 to 6pm, for 150Ft (50¢). Folk bands that perform on traditional instruments play every Thursday evening, from September to May, for 350Ft ($1.15). These Thursdays are the csángó táncház nights, that of the oldest and most authentic type of traditional Hungarian folk dance. The evening kicks off with a táncház hour for kids, at 5pm. Kletzmer bands play on Saturdays, from 7pm to 11pm, for 300Ft ($1).

GAY & LESBIAN BARS

As with the fickle club scene, "in" bars become "out," or even close down, at a moment's notice. See the *Budapest Sun* for additional, and always current, listings.

Angel Bar & Dance Club, VII. Szövetség u. 33 (© **061/351-6490;** Metro: Blaha Lujza tér), is a basement place with a bar, restaurant, and huge dance floor. It has been around for a while now and is presumably here to stay. The club isn't exclusively gay; many straights attend, especially on Friday. On Friday and Sunday, Angel hosts a now-famous transvestite show at 11:45pm. Cover is 600Ft ($2), but there are no shows and no cover on Thursday, the only night without dance. It's open from Thursday to Sunday 10pm to dawn. **Mystery Bar,** V. Nagysándor József u. 3 (© **061/312-1436;** Metro: Arany János utca), is a smaller place, with a larger foreign crowd. It is open from 4pm to 4 am daily. **Eklektika Café** ☆☆, V. Semmelweis u. 21 (© **061/266-3054;** Metro: Deák tér), is a wonderfully appointed place with 1950s socialist realist furnishings; it features live jazz on Wednesday, Friday, and Sunday. An intimate place, Eklektika hosts a women-only night every second Saturday, 10pm. It's open from Monday to Friday 10am to midnight and Saturday and Sunday 5pm to midnight.

DAY TRIPS ALONG THE DANUBE BEND

The delightful towns along the Bend—Szentendre, Esztergom, and Visegrád—are easy day trips from Budapest. The great natural beauty of the area, where forested hills loom over the river, makes it a welcome departure for the city weary.

GETTING THERE   By Boat & Hydrofoil   From April to September, **boats** run between Budapest and the towns of the Danube Bend. All boats leave Budapest's Vigadó tér boat landing, stopping to pick up passengers 5 minutes later at Buda's Batthyány tér landing, before continuing up the river.

Schedules and towns served are complicated, so contact **MAHART,** the state shipping company, at the Vigadó tér landing (© **061/318-1704**) for information. Round-trip prices are 1020Ft ($3.40) to Szentendre, 1,100Ft ($3.65) to Visegrád, and 1,155Ft ($3.85) to Esztergom. Children ages 4 to 14 receive a 50% discount. Travel time is 2 hours to Szentendre, 3½ hours to Visegrád, and 5 hours to Esztergom.

By Train   To Szentendre: The HÉV suburban railroad connects Budapest's Batthyány tér with Szentendre. Trains leave daily, year-round, every 20 minutes or so from 4am to 11:30pm (trip time: 45 minutes). The one-way fare is 300Ft ($1); subtract 100Ft (33¢) if you have a valid Budapest public transportation pass.

To Visegrád: There's no direct train service to Visegrád. Instead, take one of 23 daily trains departing from Nyugati Station for Nagymaros (trip time: 1 hour). From Nagymaros, take a ferry across the river to Visegrád. The ferry dock (RÉV) is a 5-minute walk from the train station. A ferry leaves every hour throughout the day. The train ticket to Nagymaros costs 388Ft ($1.30); the ferry boat ticket to Visegrád costs 150Ft (50¢).

To Esztergom: Nineteen trains daily make the run between Budapest's Nyugati Station and Esztergom (trip time: 1¼ hours). Train tickets cost 388Ft ($1.30).

SZENTENDRE   Peopled in medieval times by Serbian settlers, Szentendre (pronounced *Sen*-ten-dreh), 21 kilometers (13 miles) north of Budapest, counts half a dozen Serbian churches among its rich collection of historical buildings. Since the turn of the century, Szentendre has been home to an artist's colony and has a wealth of museums and galleries. The town is an extremely popular tourist destination.

Visitor Information   The information office **Tourinform** is at Dumtsa Jenó u. 22 (© **26/317-965**), with maps of Szentendre (and the Danube Bend region), as well as concert and exhibition schedules. The office can also provide accommodations information and is open from Monday to Friday 9:30am to 4:30pm and weekends in summer 10am to 2pm. If you arrive by train, you'll come upon this office as you follow the flow of pedestrian traffic into town on Kossuth Lajos utca. If you arrive by boat, you may find the **Ibusz** office sooner, corner of Bogdányi út and Gőzhajó utca (© **26/310-181**). It's open from April to October, Monday to Friday 9am to 5pm and weekends 10am to 2pm; from November to March, weekdays only, 9am to 4pm.

Exploring the Museums & Churches   The **Margit Kovács Museum** 👁👁👁, Vastagh György u. 1 (© **26/310-244**), is a must-see, displaying the exceptional and highly original work of Hungary's best-known ceramic artist. Her sculptures of elderly women and friezes of village life are particularly moving. The museum is open from April to October Tuesday to Sunday 9am to 5pm (from November to March to 4pm). Admission is 300Ft ($1). The **Blagovestenska church** at Fó tér 4 dates from 1752. A rococo iconostasis features paintings of Mihailo Zivkovic—notice that the eyes of all the icons are on you; the effect is extraordinary. Next door at Fó tér 6 (© **26/310-244**) is the **Ferenczy Museum** 👁👁, dedicated to the art of the prodigious Ferenczy family. The paintings of Károly Ferenczy, one of Hungary's leading Impressionists, are featured. It's open from April to October Tuesday to Sunday 10am to 5pm; from November to March Friday to Sunday 10am to 4pm. Admission is 300Ft ($1).

The **Ámos and Anna Muzeum,** Bogdány u. 10 (© **26/310-790**), was the former home of artist couple Imre Ámos and Margit Anna, whose work represents the beginning of expressionist painting in Hungary. Opened after Anna's death in 1991, the collection is Szentendre's best-kept secret. It's open from Tuesday to Sunday 10am to 6pm (in winter 1 to 5pm), and admission is 300Ft ($1).

Where to Dine   If you get hungry, **Aranysárkány Vendégló (Golden Dragon Inn)** 👁, Alkotmány u. 1/a (© **26/301-479**), just east of Fó tér on Hunyadi utca, is always crowded, often with locals (a definite good sign in a tourist town like Szentendre). Choose from such enticing offerings as alpine lamb, roast leg of goose, quail, and venison ragout. A very tasty vegetarian plate is also offered. Various beers are on draft.

If you walk directly south from Fó tér, you'll find **Régimodi,** Fútó u. 3 (© **26/311-105**). This elegant restaurant in a former private home serves Hungarian specialties, with an emphasis on game dishes. The wild-boar stew in red wine is particularly sumptuous. Be sure to stop in at the **Dobos Museum & café** 👁, Dumtsa Jenó u. 7, for a slice of authentic *dobos torta,* a sumptuously rich layer cake named after pastry chef József Dobos, who experimented with butter frostings in the 19th century.

ESZTERGOM   Formerly a Roman settlement, Esztergom (pronounced *Ess*-tair-gome), 46 kilometers (29 miles) northwest of Budapest, was the seat of the Hungarian kingdom for 300 years. Hungary's first king, István I (Stephen I), crowned by the pope in A.D. 1000, converted Hungary to Catholicism, and Esztergom became the country's center of the early church. Although its glory days are long gone, the quiet town remains the seat of the archbishop-primate—the "Hungarian Rome."

Visitor Information   **Gran Tours,** Széchenyi tér 25 (© **33/413-756**), is the best source of information. Summer hours are from Monday to Friday 8am to 6pm and Saturday 9am to noon; winter hours are from Monday to Friday 8am to 4pm.

Exploring the Town   The massive, neoclassical **Esztergom Cathedral,** in Szent István tér on Castle Hill, is Esztergom's most popular attraction and one of Hungary's most impressive buildings. It was built in the last century to replace the cathedral ruined during the Turkish occupation. The cathedral **Treasury (Kincstár)** ⚓ contains a stunning array of ecclesiastical jewels and gold works. Since Cardinal Mindszenty's body was moved to the crypt in 1991 (he died in exile in 1975), it has been a place of pilgrimage for Hungarians. If you brave the ascent of the cupola, you're rewarded at the top with unparalleled views of Esztergom and the surrounding Hungarian and Slovak countryside. The cathedral is open daily, summer from 8am to 8pm, winter from 9am to 3pm. The treasury, crypt, and cupola are open daily, summer from 9am to 5pm, winter from 10am to 3pm. Admission to the cathedral and the crypt are free, but it costs 250Ft (85¢) to see the treasury and 150Ft (50¢) to see the cupola.

It's definitely worth taking a break from the crowds at the cathedral and strolling through the quiet cobblestone streets of **Víziváros** (Watertown). There you'll find the **Keresztény Múzeum (Christian Museum),** Mindszenty tér 2 (© **33/413-880**), in the neoclassical former primate's palace. It houses Hungary's largest collection of religious art and the largest collection of medieval art outside the National Gallery. Hours are from Tuesday to Sunday 10am to 6pm, and admission is 100Ft (35¢).

Where to Dine   The food at **Szalma Csárda** 🐾🐾🐾, Nagy-Duna sétány 2 (© **33/315-336**), is absolutely first-rate, with everything made to order and served piping hot. The excellent house soups—fish soup (*halászlé*), goulash (*gulyásleves*), and bean soup (*babgulyás*)—constitute meals in themselves. It's open daily from 10am to 10pm and doesn't accept credit cards.

VISEGRÁD   Halfway between Szentendre and Esztergom, Visegrád (pronounced *Vee*-sheh-grod) is a sparsely populated, sleepy riverside village, which makes its history all the more fascinating and hard to believe. The Romans built a fort here, which was still extant when Slovak settlers gave the town its present name (meaning "High Castle") in the 9th or 10th century. After the Mongol invasion (1241–42), construction began on both the present ruined hilltop citadel and the former riverside palace. Eventually, Visegrád could boast one of the finest royal palaces ever built in Hungary. Only one king, Charles Robert (1307–42), actually used it as his primary residence, but monarchs from Béla IV, in the 13th century, through Matthias Corvinus, in the late 15th century, spent time in Visegrád and contributed to its development, the latter expanding the palace into a great Renaissance center known throughout Europe.

Visitor Information   **Visegrád Tours,** RÉV u. 15 (© **26/398-160**), is located across the road from the RÉV ferry boat landing (not to be confused with the MAHART boat landing, just down the road). It is open from April to October, daily 9am to 6pm; from November to March, weekdays 10am to 4pm.

Each summer at 6pm on Thursdays in July and August, Visegrád hosts the **International Palace Tournament,** an authentic medieval festival replete with dueling knights on horseback, early music, and dance. For more information, contact Visegrád Tours.

Exploring the Palace & the Citadel   The **Royal Palace** covered much of the area where the MAHART boat landing and Fő utca (Main Street) are now found. Indeed, the entrance to its open-air ruins, called the **King Matthias Museum** 🐾🐾, is at Fő u. 27 (© **26/398-026**). Admission is 200Ft (65ce]). The museum is open daily from 9am to 5pm. The buried ruins of the palace, having achieved a near-mythical status, were not discovered until this century. Almost all of what you see is the result of ongoing reconstruction, which has been rigorous in recent years. Because of the under-construction aspect of the place, you need to keep a close eye on the kids here.

The **Citadel** 🐾🐾🐾 (& **26/398-101**) on the hilltop above Visegrád affords one of the finest views you'll find over the Danube. Admission to the Citadel is 400Ft (85¢). It is open daily from 9am to 6pm. There are three buses a day to the Citadel, departing from the RÉV ferry boat terminal at 9:26am, 12:26pm, and 3:26pm, respectively. Otherwise, "City Bus," a van taxi which awaits passengers outside Visegrad Tours, takes people up the steep hill for the steep fare of 2,000Ft ($6.65) apiece. It's more than a casual walk to the Citadel, suitable for a day hike.

Where to Dine   In keeping with its name, **Renaissance Restaurant,** at Fő u. 11, across the street from the MAHART boat landing (© **26/398-081**), specializes in authentic medieval cuisine. Food is served in clay crockery without silverware (only a wooden spoon) and guests are offered paper crowns to wear. The menu meal is 2,000Ft ($7), but available for groups only. It's open daily, from noon to 10pm. If you're big on the medieval theme, come for dinner on a Thursday (July to August), when a six-course "Royal Feast" is celebrated following a 45-minute duel between knights. No vegetarians, please! Tickets for this special evening are handled by Visegrád Tours. The duel gets underway at 6pm sharp.

Benito Pizzeria ✪, Fő u. 83 (© **26/397-230**), serves very good pizza in a pleasant, relaxed atmosphere. This is a good option if you're traveling with kids. Individual pan-size pizzas cost 550 to 880Ft ($1.85 to $2.95). Try the "Don Vito," a delicious ricotta, garlic, and herb pizza. Beer and wine are served.

2 Lake Balaton

Lake Balaton might not be the Mediterranean, but don't tell that to the Hungarians. Somehow, over the years, they have managed to create their own Central European hybrid variety of a Mediterranean culture along the shores of their long, shallow, milky-white lake, Europe's largest at 80 kilometers (50 miles) long and 15 kilometers (10 miles) wide at its broadest stretch.

Throughout the long summer, swimmers, windsurfers, sailboats, kayaks, and cruisers enjoy the warm and silky-smooth waters; people cast their reels for pike, play tennis, ride horses, and hike in the hills.

The **south shore** towns are as flat as Pest; walk 10 minutes from the lake and you're in farm country. The air here is still and quiet; in summer, the sun hangs heavily in the sky. Teenagers, students, and young travelers tend to congregate in the hedonistic towns of the south shore. Here, huge 1970s-style beachside hotels are filled to capacity all summer long, and disco music pulsates into the early morning hours.

On the more graceful **north shore,** little villages are neatly tucked away in the rolling countryside, where the grapes of the popular Balaton wines ripen in the strong southern sun. Traveling from Budapest, the northern shore of the lake at first appears every bit as built up and crowded as the southern shore. Beyond Balatonfüred, this impression begins to fade. You'll discover the **Tihany Peninsula,** a protected area whose 12 square kilometers (4¾ sq. miles) jut out into the lake like a knob. Stop for a swim—or the night—in a small town like **Szigliget.** Moving westward along the coast, you can make forays inland into the rolling hills of the Balaton wine country. The city of **Keszthely,** sitting at the lake's western edge, marks the end of its northern shore.

Passenger boat travel on Lake Balaton lets you travel across the lake as well as between towns on the same shore. It's both extensive and cheap, but considerably slower than surface transportation. All major towns have a dock with departures and arrivals. Children 3 and under travel free, and those 13 and under get half-price tickets. A single ferry (*komp*) running between Tihany and Szántód lets you transport a car across the width of the lake. Boat and ferry information is available from the **MAHART** office in Siófok (© **84/310-050**). Local tourist offices along the lake also have schedules and information.

Because hotel prices are unusually high in the Balaton region, and because just about every local family rents out a room or two in summer, we especially recommend private rooms. You can reserve a room through a local tourist office, or you can just look for the ubiquitous **szoba kiadó** (or **zimmer frei**) signs along the roads. When you take a room without using a tourist agency as the intermediary, prices are generally negotiable. In the height of the season, you shouldn't

Lake Balaton

have to pay more than 7,000Ft ($23) for a double room within reasonable proximity of the lake.

ESSENTIALS

GETTING THERE   By Train   From Budapest, trains to the various towns along the lake depart from Déli Station. The local (sebes) trains are interminably slow, stopping at each village along the lake. Unless you're going to one of these little villages (sometimes a good idea), try to get on an express (gyors). To Keszthely, the trip takes about 3 ½ hours and costs 1,482Ft ($4.95). To reach Tihany, take a train to Balatonfüred for 1,032Ft ($3.45) (trip time: 2 hours), and then a local bus to Tihany.

By Car   If you're driving from Budapest, take the M-7 motorway south through Székesfehérvár until you hit the lake. Route 71 circles the lake.

VESZPRÉM

On your way to Lake Balaton, you might want to make a stop in this charming town. Just 16 kilometers (10 miles) from Lake Balaton, Veszprém (pronounced *Vess*-praym), 116 kilometers (72 miles) southwest of Budapest, surely ranks as one of Hungary's most vibrant small cities, and is often used as a starting point for trips to that popular resort area. In Veszprém you'll find a harmonious mix of old and new: A delightfully self-contained and well-preserved 18th-century baroque Castle District spills effortlessly into a typically modern city center, itself distinguished by lively wide-open, pedestrian-only plazas.

ESSENTIALS

GETTING THERE   Six daily **trains** depart Budapest's Déli Station for Veszprém (trip time: 1¾ hours). Tickets cost 882Ft ($2.95).

VISITOR INFORMATION   **Tourinform,** Rákóczi u. 3 (© **88/404-548**), is open from Monday to Friday 9am to 5pm, Saturday and Sunday 9am to 4pm (open only weekdays in winter); and **Ibusz,** Kossuth u. 10, in the odd modern structure marked KINIZSI ÜZLETHÁZ (© **88/426-492** or 88/427-604), is open from Monday to Friday 9am to 5pm and Saturday 9am to noon. Both offices provide information, sell city maps, and help with hotel or private-room bookings.

WHERE TO DINE

For fast food, try **Mackó Cukrászda,** at Kossuth u. 6, © **88/426-430.** Open daily from 7:30am to 7:30pm (opening at 9am and closing at 5:30pm on Sunday), this stand-up eatery, which is somewhat grungy yet always bustling, is popular with young locals. Pizza, hot dogs, french fries, fried chicken, and various sweets are served. **Cserhát Étterem** ⓖ (© **88/425-441**), housed in the same structure, is an authentic *önkiszólgáló* (self-service cafeteria). You'll find the restaurant behind the Nike store; go up the winding staircase inside the building. A menu is posted.

For something more upscale, try **Villa Medici Étterem** ⓖⓖ, next to the zoo at Kittenberger u. 11 (© **88/321-273**). Reputedly one of Hungary's best restaurants, it's also relatively expensive. Villa Medici serves Hungarian and continental cuisine. Open daily from 11am to 11pm.

SEEING THE SIGHTS

Most of Veszprém's main sights are clustered along Vár utca, the street that runs the length of the city's small but lovely **Castle District.**

Housed inside the 18th-century canon's house, the **Exhibition of Religious Art,** Vár u. 35, has a fine collection of Roman Catholic art. Admission is 100Ft (35¢). Open daily from 9am to 5pm; closed from October to April. At Vár u. 16, the vaulted **Gizella Chapel,** named for King Stephen's wife, was unearthed during the construction of the adjoining Bishop's Palace in the 18th century. Today it houses a modest collection of ecclesiastical art, but is best known for the 13th-century **frescoes** that, in various states of restoration, decorate its walls. Admission is 40Ft (15¢). Open daily from 9am to 5pm; closed from October to April.

For a wonderful view of the surrounding Bakony region, climb up the steps to the narrow observation deck at the top of the **Fire Tower** 𝒢, at Áváros tér. Although the tower's foundations are medieval, the structure itself was built in the early 19th century. Enter through the courtyard of Vár u. 17, behind Áváros tér. Admission is 150Ft (50¢). Open daily from 10am to 6pm (closed in winter).

THE TIHANY PENINSULA

The Tihany (pronounced *Tee*-hine) Peninsula is a protected area, and building is heavily restricted. Consequently, it maintains a rustic charm that's unusual in the Balaton region. The peninsula also features a lush, protected interior, accessible by a trail from Tihany Village, with several little inland lakes as well as a lookout tower offering views over the Balaton.

ESSENTIALS

GETTING THERE   The rail line that circles Lake Balaton does not serve the Tihany Peninsula. The nearest station is in Aszófó, about 5 kilometers (3 miles) from Tihany Village. A local **bus** comes to Tihany from the nearby town of Balatonfüred. You can also go by **ferry** from Szántód or Balatonföldvár, or by boat from Balatonfüred.

By Car   From Budapest, take M7 south through Székesfehérvár until you hit the lake. Route 71 circles the lake. If you're planning a trip to Lake Balaton for more than a day or two, you should consider renting a car, which will give you much greater mobility. The various towns differ enough from one another that you may want to keep driving until you find the place that's right for you. Without a car, this is obviously more difficult. Also, wherever you go in the region, you'll find private rooms to be both cheaper and easier to get if you travel a few miles off the lake. Driving directly to the lake from Budapest will take about an hour and 15 minutes.

By Train   To reach Tihany, take a train to Balatonfüred for 1,032Ft ($3.45) (trip time: 2 hours), and then a local bus to Tihany. (You can also pick up this bus at Aszófó, halfway between Balatonfüred and Tihany.) Depending on what train you take, it is possible to stop at Balatonfüred, Szántód, or Balatonföldvár, if you are so inclined.

VISITOR INFORMATION   Visitor information is available at **Balatontourist,** Kossuth u. 20 (𝒞 and fax **87/448-519**). The office is open from May to October only, Monday to Friday 8:30am to 7pm and weekends 8:30am to 12:30pm.

SEEING THE SIGHTS

The 18th-century baroque **Abbey Church** ✿✿ is Tihany Village's main attraction. A resident monk carved the exquisite wooden altar and pulpit in the 18th century. The frescoes in the church are by three of Hungary's better-known 19th-century painters: Károly Lotz, Bertalan Székely, and Lajos Deák-Ébner.

Next door to the Abbey Church is the **Tihany Museum** (✆ 87/448-650), housed in an 18th-century baroque structure like the church. The museum features exhibitions on the surrounding region's history and culture. You pay a single entry fee of 250Ft (85¢) for both church and museum. Both are open daily from 9am to 5:30pm.

SZIGLIGET

Halfway between Tihany and Keszthely is the scenic little village of Szigliget (pronounced *Sig*-lee-get), with thatched roof houses, lush vineyards, and a lovely Mediterranean quality. Szigliget is marked by the fantastic ruins of the 13th-century **Szigliget Castle** ✿, which stand above it on **Várhegy (Castle Hill)** ✿✿✿. In the days of the Turkish invasions, the Hungarian Balaton fleet, protected by the high castle, called Szigliget its home. You can hike up to the ruins for a splendid view of the lake and the surrounding countryside; look for the path behind the white 18th-century church that stands on the highest spot in the village. A good place to fortify yourself for the hike is the **Vár Vendéglő** (on the road up to the castle), a casual restaurant with plenty of outdoor seating, serving traditional Hungarian fare.

The lively **beach** at Szigliget provides a striking contrast to the quiet village. In summer, buses from neighboring towns drop off hordes of beach-goers. The beach area is crowded with fried food and beer stands, ice cream vendors, a swing set, and a volleyball net. Admission to the beach is 300Ft ($1). Szigliget

---

✐ Heating Things Up at the Thermal Lake in Hévíz

If you find the water of Lake Balaton warm, just wait until you jump into the lake at **Hévíz** ✿✿✿ (pronounced *Hay*-veez), a town about 8 kilometers (5 miles) northwest of Keszthely.

This is Europe's largest **thermal lake** ✿ (and the second largest in the world). The lake's water temperature seldom dips below 30 to 32°C (85 to 90°F), even in the bitterest storm of winter. Consequently, people swim in the lake year-round. Hévíz has been one of Hungary's leading spa resorts for more than 100 years, and it retains some of the 19th-century character that's more typical of the spas in the Czech Republic than of those in Hungary.

You can easily reach Hévíz by bus from Keszthely. Buses depart every half hour or so from the bus station (conveniently stopping to pick up passengers in front of the church on Fő tér). The entrance to the lake is just opposite the bus station. You'll see a whimsical wooden facade and the words TÓ FÜRDŐ (Bathing Lake) (✆ 83/340-587). Tickets cost 490Ft ($1.65) for up to 3 hours or 990Ft ($3.30) for a day pass (the latter is not available from November to March). Your ticket entitles you to a locker. Keep the ticket until exiting, as the attendant needs to see it to determine whether you've stayed a half-day or a full day.

is also home to the **Eszterházy Wine Cellar** ⟨⋆⟩, the largest wine cellar in the region. After a hike in the hills or a day in the sun, a little wine tasting just might be in order.

Natur Tourist (© 87/461-197), in the village center, is your best (and only) source of information in Szigliget. It's open daily from 9am to 7pm (closing earlier in winter).

KESZTHELY

At the western edge of Lake Balaton, Keszthely (pronounced *Kest*-hay), 188 kilometers (117 miles) southwest of Budapest, is one the largest towns on the lake. Although Keszthely was largely destroyed during the Turkish wars, the town was rebuilt in the 18th century by the Festetics family, an aristocratic family who made Keszthely their home through World War II.

The center of Keszthely's summer scene, just like that of every other settlement on Lake Balaton, is down by the water on the "strand." Keszthely's beachfront is dominated by several large hotels. Regardless of whether you're a guest, you can rent Windsurfers, boats, and other water-related equipment from these hotels.

ESSENTIALS

VISITOR INFORMATION   For visitor information, stop at **Tourinform,** Kossuth u. 28 (© and fax **83/314-144**), open from Monday to Friday 9am to 5pm and Saturday (and Sundays in high season) 10am to 1pm. For private-room bookings, try **Zalatours,** Kossuth u. 1 (© **83/312-560**), or **Ibusz,** Kossuth u. 27 (© **83/314-320**).

A BAROQUE MANSION

The highlight of a visit to Keszthely is the splendid baroque **Festetics Mansion** ⟨⋆⟩, Szabadsag u. 1 (© **83/312-190**), the 18th-century home (with its 19th-century additions) of the Festetics family. Part of the mansion is now open as a museum, the main attraction of which is the ornate library. The museum also features hunting gear and trophies of a bygone era.

The mansion's lovely concert hall is the site of **classical music concerts** ⟨⋆⋆⋆⟩ almost every night throughout the summer (just two or three times a month from September to May). Concerts usually start at 8pm; tickets, at 900Ft ($3) to 5,000Ft ($16.65) apiece, are available at the door or earlier in the day at the museum cashier. Another part of the mansion has in the past served—and, we are informed, may again serve—as a hotel.

Admission is 1,400Ft ($4.65) for foreigners (cheaper for Hungarians). Summer hours are daily from 9am to 6pm; winter: from Tuesday to Sunday 9am to 5pm.

Ireland

by Robert Meagher

If you haven't been to Ireland lately, then you haven't been to Ireland. The scale and pace of change here is dizzying. Once the donkey-cart of the European Union, Ireland is now the pace-setter—a young, turbulent, venturesome nation that's slow to look back and quick to outreach itself. If you look for it, the old Ireland lingers here and there, and, to be sure, Ireland remains a land of breathtaking beauty, whose people possess more than their share of wit and welcoming charm. What's new is that Ireland at the millennium is where "it's" happening—a boom, a renaissance, a revolution. No one knows what to call it, because no one knows where it's going. All the same, six million annual visitors come a long way to see it for themselves.

1 Dublin

"Seedy elegance" may have aptly described much, if not most, of Dublin until quite recently, but no longer. Named by *Fortune* magazine as the number one European city in which to do business, and edging out Rome, Venice, and Prague as the fifth most visited city in Europe, Dublin is no backwater. In fact, at the turn of the millennium Dublin was named by the annual Mercer survey as one of the world's top 10 places to live.

Needless to say Dublin is a great place to visit. The Liffey may never be potable, but otherwise the sky seems to be the limit here. Over 40 new hotels have sprouted up in the past several years alone in what seems a nearly hopeless race to keep up with tourist demand. Dublin is "ground zero" for the new Ireland, the lair of the "Celtic Tiger," and without any contest the hottest spot on the island.

ESSENTIALS

GETTING THERE   By Plane   The **Dublin Airport** (© **01/704-4222;** www.dublin-airport.com) is located 11 kilometers (7 miles) north of the city center. **Dublin Bus** (© **01/873-4222**) provides express coach service from the airport into the city's central bus station, **Busaras,** on Store Street, to **Heuston Rail Station,** or to **O'Connell Street.** Service runs daily, from 7am until 10:45pm (11:10pm Sundays), with departures every 10 to 20 minutes. One-way fare is £3.50 (€4.45, $4.40) adults and £2 (€2.55, $2.50) children under 12. Bus 41 is also available to the city center for £1.15 (€1.50, $1.45). There is also a new private licensed coach service called "AirCoach" operating 60 services a day at 15-minute intervals between 5:30am and 11pm, 7 days a week. Air-Coach runs direct from the airport to Dublin's south side, servicing key hotel and business districts. The one-way fare is £4 (€5.10, $5).

For speed and ease, a **taxi** is the best way to get directly to your hotel or guesthouse. Depending on your destination, fares average between £15 (€19, $19) and £20 (€25, $25). Taxis are lined up at a first-come, first-served taxi stand outside the arrivals terminal.

Dublin

Legend:
- ✝ Church
- ⓘ Information
- ✉ Post Office
- — Railway

Dublin Zoo **1**

PHOENIX PARK **2**

St. Brendan's Hospital

St. Lawrence Hospital

Hospital

Collins **3**

Arbour Hill

Old James Distille...

Montpelier Hill

Conyngham Road

Parkgate Street

Benburb Street

River Liffey

King's Bridge

Wolfe Tone Quay

Victoria's Bridge

Ellis Quay

Queen's Bridge

Arran Quay

Heuston Station

Victoria Quay

Island Street

Usher's Quay

West Hospital

Guinness Brewery

Bonham St.

Whitw... Brid... Coo...

St. John's Road

Military Road

St. Patrick's Hospital

Steven's Lane

Thomas Street West

Cornmarket

6

Kilmainham Lane

St. James's Street

Rainsford St.

THE LIBERTIE...

Old Kilmainham

Basin Street

Bellevue **5**

Earl St. S.

Meath St.

7

St. Patrick's Hospital

Bond St.

Robert St.

Pimlico

South Circular Road

St. Kevin's Hospital

Grand Canal Bank

Marrowbone Lane

Cork Street

Ardee Street

NORTHERN IRELAND

Dublin ★

IRELAND

South Circular Road

Barn Street

Brown Street

Grand Canal

Dolphin Road

Hospital

O'Donovan Road

Dolphin's...

0		1/5 mile
0	200 meters	

ATTRACTIONS ●

Book of Kells **22**
Christchurch Cathedral **15**
Collins Barracks **3**
Dublin Castle **18**
Dublin Writers Museum **9**
Dublin Zoo **1**
Dublinia **16**

GAA Museum **8**
Garden of Remembrance **11**
Guinness Brewery/
   Visitor Centre **5**
Heraldic Museum/
   Genealogical Office **25**
Hugh Lane Municipal Gallery
   of Modern Art **10**

Irish Museum of Modern Art **6**
Irish Traditional Music Centre and
   Jameson Chimey **4**
James Joyce Centre **12**
Kilmainham Gaol Historical
   Museum **7**
National Gallery **24**

By Ferry   Passenger/car ferries from Britain arrive at the **Dublin Ferryport** (✆ 01/ 855-2222), on the eastern end of the North Docks, and at the **Dun Laoghaire Ferryport** (✆ 01/661-0511), about 16 kilometers (10 miles) south of the city center. There is bus and taxi service from both ports.

By Train   Irish Rail (✆ 01/836-6222) operates daily train service into Dublin from Belfast in Northern Ireland and all major cities in the Irish Republic, including Cork, Galway, Limerick, Killarney, Sligo, Wexford, and Waterford. Trains from the south, west, and southwest arrive at **Heuston Station,** Kingsbridge, off St. John's Road; from the north and northwest at **Connolly Station,** Amiens Street; and from the southeast at **Pearse Station,** Westland Row, Tara Street.

By Bus   Bus Eireann (✆ 01/836-6111) operates daily express coach and local bus services from all major cities and towns in Ireland into Dublin's central bus station, Busaras, on Store Street.

By Car   If you are arriving by car from other parts of Ireland or via car ferry from Britain, all main roads lead into the heart of Dublin and are well signposted to An Lar (City Centre). To bypass the city center, the East Link and West Link are signposted, and the M50 circuits the city on three sides.

VISITOR INFORMATION   Tourist offices   Dublin Tourism operates five year-round walk-in visitor centers in greater Dublin. The principal center is at **St. Andrew's Church,** Suffolk Street, Dublin 2, open from June to August Monday to Saturday 9am to 8:30pm, Sunday and bank holidays 10:30am to 2:30pm, and the rest of the year from Monday to Saturday 9am to 5:30pm. For accommodation reservations throughout Ireland by credit card, contact Dublin Tourism (✆ **011 800/668-668-66;** www.visitdublin.com); for other information call Bord Failte (✆ **1850/230330** from within Ireland, or ✆ **066/979-2083;** information@dublintourism.ie). Other services at the Suffolk Street office include a currency exchange counter, a car-rental counter, accommodation reservations, bus and rail information desks, a gift shop, and a cafe. The other four centers are at the Arrivals Hall of **Dublin Airport;** the new ferry terminal, **Dun Laoghaire;** the **Baggot Street Bridge,** Dublin 2; and **The Square,** Tallaght, Dublin 24 (all telephone inquiries should be directed to the numbers listed above). All centers are open year-round with at least the following hours: from Monday to Friday 9am to 5:30pm and Saturday 9am to 1pm.

In addition, an independent center offers details on concerts, exhibits, and other arts events in the **Temple Bar** section at 18 Eustace St., Temple Bar, Dublin 2 (✆ 01/671-5717), open year-round from Monday to Friday 9:30am to 5:30pm, and Saturday 10am to 5:30pm.

At any of these centers you can pick up the free *Tourism News;* or the free *Event Guide,* a biweekly entertainment guide (www.eventguide.ie). *In Dublin,* a biweekly arts-and-entertainment magazine selling for £1.95 (€2.50, $2.45), is available at most newsstands.

Websites   Your first stop should be Dublin Tourism's **www.visitdublin.com**. The breadth of **www.goireland.com** is almost overwhelming: more than 11,000 lodging listings (many with pictures) and thousands of restaurants (some with menus), although in some cases the info is pretty thin. Use the well-designed **www.ireland.travel.ie** for tips on getting around, places to stay, and things to do. Come to **www.shamrock.org** to learn about package vacations and find some special deals, such as off-peak fares on Aer Lingus. Use **www.heritageireland.ie** to get visitor information and view images of historic sites, parks, gardens, and cultural attractions.

CITY LAYOUT   Compared with other European capitals, Dublin is a relatively small metropolis and easy to get to know. The downtown core of the city, identified in Gaelic on bus destination signs as **an lar** (the Center), is shaped somewhat like a pie, with the **River Liffey** cutting across the middle from east to west. The top half of the pie, or north side of the city, is rimmed in a semicircular sweep by the **Royal Canal,** and the bottom half, or south side, is edged in a half-circle shape by the waters of the **Grand Canal.** To the north of the Royal Canal are the suburbs of Drumcondra, Glasnevin, Howth, Clontarf, and Malahide; to the south of the Grand Canal are the suburbs of Ballsbridge, Blackrock, Dun Laoghaire, Dalkey, Killiney, Rathgar, Rathmines, and other residential areas.

GETTING AROUND   By Bus   Dublin Bus operates a fleet of green double-decker buses, frequent single-deck buses, and minibuses throughout the city and its suburbs. Most buses originate on or near **O'Connell Street, Abbey Street,** or **Eden Quay** on the north side, and from **Aston Quay, College Street,** or **Fleet Street** on the south side. Destinations and bus numbers are posted above the front windows; buses destined for the city center are marked with the Gaelic words **an lar.**

Bus service runs daily throughout the city, starting around 6am (10am on Sunday), with the last bus at 11:30pm on most routes; the Nitelink service from city center to the suburbs extends bus hours to 2am or 3am from Monday to Wednesday, and 3:30 or 4:30am on Thursday, Friday, and Saturday. Schedules are posted on revolving notice boards at each bus stop. City bus fares are calculated on the distances traveled and run from a base fare of 60p (€0.80, 75¢) to £1.30 (€1.65, $1.65). The NiteLink fare is a flat £3 (€3.80, $3.75). Tickets should be purchased from a ticket machine as you enter the bus; note that exact change is now required on most buses, and only coins are accepted. One-day, 4-day, and weekly passes are available at reduced rates. For more information, contact **Dublin Bus,** 59 Upper O'Connell St. (© **01/873-4222**). Dublin Bus also operates an information desk at the central Tourist Office on Suffolk Street.

By DART   Although Dublin has no subway in the strict sense, there is an electrified-train rapid-transit system, known as the **DART** (Dublin Area Rapid Transit), Pearse Station, Dublin 2 (© **01/703-3054**). It links the city-center stations at **Tara Street, Pearse Street,** and **Amiens Street (Connelly Station)** with suburbs and seaside communities as far as Howth to the north and Bray to the south. Service operates roughly every 10 to 20 minutes from Monday to Saturday 7am to midnight and Sunday 9:30am to 11pm. The minimum fare is 70p (€0.90, 90¢). One-day, 4-day, and weekly passes, as well as family tickets, are available at reduced rates.

By Taxi   Dublin taxis do not cruise the streets looking for fares; instead, they line up at ranks located outside all the leading hotels, at bus and train stations, and on prime thoroughfares, such as Upper O'Connell Street, College Green, and the north side of St. Stephen's Green. You can also phone for a taxi. Some of the companies that operate a 24-hour radio-call service are **Co-Op** (© **01/677-7777**), **National** (© **01/677-2222**), and **VIP Taxis** (© **01/478-3333**). If you need a wake-up call, **VIP** offers that service, along with especially courteous dependability. Taxi rates are fixed by law and posted in each taxi. At peak times in Dublin's often backed-up traffic, it's the minutes and not the miles that are going to add up. The most costly add-ons are for dispatched pickup and for service from Dublin airport. Some hotel or guesthouse staff, when asked to arrange for a taxi, tack on as much as £4 (€5.10, $5) for their services, although this practice violates city taxi regulations.

By Bicycle   Riding a bike in Dublin isn't recommended. Traffic is very heavy, the streets are narrow, and pedestrians crowd every corner. For those determined to take to the streets on wheels, a good option is **Dublin Bike Tours,** Harding Hotel, Fishamble Street (next to Christchurch) (© **01/679-0899** or 087/284-0799; www.dublinbiketours.com), offering 3-hour tours of the city as well as bike rentals and self-guided tours. The cost is £15 (€19, $19) per person for a guided tour, offered Saturday and Sunday at 10am and 2pm; other days are by request only. Bike rentals are available daily from April to October from 9:30am to 5:30pm; the rate is £10 (€13, $13) per day including lock, helmet, repair kit, and route advice.

By Car   The bottom line here is that you're better off without a car in Dublin, as the city is aggressively discouraging the car as the vehicle of choice for commuters, much less for tourists. The most reliable and safest places to park are at surface parking lots or in multistory car parks in central locations, such as Kildare Street, Lower Abbey Street, Marlborough Street, and St. Stephen's Green West.

On Foot   Small and compact, Dublin is ideal for walking, but be careful to look left and right for oncoming traffic and to obey traffic signals. Each traffic light has timed "walk/don't walk" signals for pedestrians. Pedestrians have the right of way at specially marked, zebra-striped crossings; as a warning, there are usually two flashing lights at these intersections. For some walking-tour suggestions, see "Organized Tours" under "Dublin's Top Attractions," below).

(C) *FAST FACTS:* Dublin

American Express   The Dublin office offers currency exchange, traveler's checks, and (for members) mail-holding. It's located opposite Trinity College, just off College Green, at 41 Nassau St., Dublin 2 (© **01/679-9000**), and is open from Monday to Friday 9am to 5pm. Amex also has a desk at the Dublin Tourism Office on Suffolk Street. In an emergency, traveler's checks can be reported lost or stolen by dialing collect © **1-44-1-273-571-600,** or © **800-626-000** within Ireland.

Business Hours   Most **business offices** are open from 9am to 5pm, Monday to Friday. **Stores and shops** are open from 9am to 5:30pm Monday to Wednesday and Friday to Saturday, and from 9am to 8pm on Thursday. Some bookshops and tourist-oriented stores also open on Sunday 11am or noon to 4 or 5pm. During the peak season (May to September), many gift and souvenir shops post Sunday hours.

Currency   Ireland, as of January 1, 1999, has adopted the single European currency known as the "euro." Scheduled to appear as hard currency on January 1, 2002, it is already the actual medium of exchange in the Republic. The punt or Irish pound is permanently fixed at £1 = €1.269738. Already in shops and elsewhere, prices are cited in both punts and euros; and, before we know it, punts will disappear both from signs and from our pockets. The rate of exchange used in this chapter is: $1 = 80p or Irish £1 = $1.25.

Currency Exchange Currency-exchange services, signposted as BUREAU DE CHANGE, are in all banks and at many branches of the Irish post office system, known as **An Post.** A bureau de change operates daily during flight arrival and departure times at Dublin airport; a foreign currency note-exchanger machine is also available on a 24-hour basis in the main arrivals hall. Many hotels and travel agencies offer bureau de change services, although the best rate of exchange is usually given at banks or, better yet, when you use your credit card for purchases or expenses.

Dentist & Doctor For medical or dental emergencies, contact the **Eastern Health Board Headquarters,** Dr. Steevens Hospital, Dublin 8 (© **01/679-0700).** See also "Dental Surgeons" or "Doctors—Medical" in the Golden Pages (yellow pages) of the telephone book.

Drugstores Centrally located drugstores, known locally as pharmacies or chemist shops, include **Hamilton Long and Co.,** 5 Lower O'Connell St., Dublin 1 (© **01/874-8456);** and **Byrnes Late Night Pharmacy,** 4 Merrion Rd., Dublin 4 (© **01/668-3287).**

Embassies/Consulates The **United States** Embassy is located at 42 Elgin Rd., Ballsbridge, Dublin 4 (© **01/668-8777); Canadian** Embassy, 65/68 St. Stephen's Green, Dublin 2 (© **01/478/1988); British** Embassy, 29 Merrion Rd., Dublin 4 (© **01/205-3700); Australian** Embassy, Fitzwilton House, Wilton Terrace, Dublin 2 (© **01/676-1517);** the **New Zealand consulate** is located at 46 Upper Mount St, Dublin 2 (© 01/660-4233).

Emergencies For the **Garda** (police), fire, or other emergencies, dial © **999.**

Hospitals For emergency care, two of the most modern health-care facilities are **St. Vincent's Hospital,** Elm Park (© **01/269-4533),** on the south side of the city, and **Beaumont Hospital,** Beaumont Road, Dublin 9 (© **01/837-7755** or 01/809-3000), on the north side.

Internet Access In cyber-literate Dublin public access terminals are no longer hard to find, appearing in shopping malls, in hotels, in hostels, and on every street corner in Temple Bar. One of the best of these is **Does Not Compute,** 2 Pudding Row, Essex St. West, Temple Bar, Dublin 8 (© **01/670-4464;** www.doesnotcompute.ie), on a back street between Kinlay House Hostel and Essex Quay. Fifteen minutes online will set you back £1 (€1.27, $1.25); 1 hour is £3.75 (€4.80, $4.70), or £3 (€3.80, $3.75) for students. They also offer photocopying, scanning, and fax service. It's open from Monday to Friday 8am to 11pm and Saturday to Sunday 10am to 11pm. **Planet Cybercafe** has two branches in the city center: 23 South Great Georges St., Dublin 2 (© **01/679-0583),** or 13 St. Andrew St., Dublin 2 (© **01/670-5183),** just around the corner from the Suffolk St. office of Dublin Tourism; 30 minutes online cost £2.75 (€3.50, $3.45).

Post Office The **General Post Office** (GPO) is located on O'Connell Street, Dublin 1 (© **01/705-7000).** Hours are from Monday to Saturday 8am to 8pm, Sunday and holidays 10am to 6pm. Branch offices, identified by the sign OIFIG AN POST/POST OFFICE, are open Monday through Saturday only, 9am to 6pm.

Telephone The **country code** for the Republic of Ireland is **353.** The **city code** for Dublin is **01.** If you're calling from outside Ireland, drop the initial

0 (zero) from the city code. Thus, to call the Georgian Hotel from the United States, you would dial ☏ 011-353-1/661-8832. For direct-dial calls to the United States, dial the international access code (**00** from Ireland), and then the country code (**1**), followed by area code and number. To place a collect call to the United States from Ireland, dial ☏ **1-800/550-000** for USA Direct service. The toll-free international access codes are: **AT&T** ☏**1-800-550-000**, **Sprint** ☏**1-800-552-001**, and **MCI** ☏**1-800-55-1001**.

Ireland has one of Europe's most sophisticated phone systems, and the quality of international connections is exceptional. Throughout the city you can find pay phones that accept coins, both on the street and in pubs; a **local call** costs 20p (€0.25, 25¢). If you want to use one of the many yellow Callcard phones, almost as common as coin phones, you have to buy a **Callcard** (available at post offices, newsstands, and many convenience stores). The Callcard is available in denominations of 10, 20, 50, and 100 units, priced at £2 (€2.55, $2.50), £3.50 (€4.45, $4.40), £8 (€10, $10), and £16 (€20, $20), respectively. There's a local and international phone center at the General Post Office on O'Connell Street. For information on finding a telephone number, dial ☏ **1190.**

WHERE TO STAY
HISTORIC OLD CITY & TEMPLE BAR/ TRINITY COLLEGE AREA
Expensive
Temple Bar Hotel ☞ If you want to be in the heart of the action in the Temple Bar district, then this is a prime place to stay. Opened in summer 1993, this five-story hotel was developed from a row of town houses, and great care was taken to preserve the Georgian brick-front facade with Victorian mansard roof. Rooms are modern with traditional furnishings.

Fleet St., Temple Bar, Dublin 2. ☏ **800/44-UTELL** from the U.S., or 01/677-3333. Fax 01/677-3088. www. towerhotelgroup.ie. 129 units, 13 with shower only. £115–£195 (€146–€248, $144–$244) double. Rates include full breakfast. No service charge. AE, DC, MC, V. DART: Tara St. Station. Bus: 78A or 78B. **Amenities:** Restaurant, bar; access to nearby health club. *In-room:* TV, tea/coffeemaker, hair dryer, trouser press.

Moderate
Blooms Lovers of Irish literature will feel at home at Blooms. Named after Leopold Bloom, a character in James Joyce's *Ulysses,* this hotel is in the heart of Dublin, near Trinity College and on the edge of the artsy Temple Bar district. Rooms are modern and functional. Late-night entertainment is available in the basement-level nightclub, known simply as Club M.

Anglesea St., Dublin 2. ☏ **800/44-UTELL** from the U.S., or 01/671-5622. Fax 01/671-5997. www.blooms.ie. 86 units. £110 (€140, $138) double. Service charge 12.5%. DC, MC, V. No parking provided. DART: Tara St. Station. Bus: 21A, 46A, 46B, 51B, 51C, 68, 69, or 86. **Amenities:** Restaurant, bar/lounge; concierge; 24-hour room service; laundry service. *In room:* TV, hair dryer, trouser press.

Inexpensive
Jurys Christchurch Inn *Value* Across from Christ Church Cathedral, this relatively new hotel was designed in keeping with the area's Georgian/Victorian architecture. Geared to the cost-conscious traveler, it's the first of its kind in the city's historic district, offering quality hotel lodgings at guesthouse prices. Rooms, decorated with contemporary furnishings, can accommodate up to three adults or two adults and two children—all for the same price.

> ## (Tips) Getting the Best Rates
>
> In general, rates for Dublin hotels don't vary as greatly with the seasons as they do in the Irish countryside. Hotels often charge higher prices, however, during special events, such as the Dublin Horse Show. For the best deals, try to reserve a room in Dublin over a weekend, and ask if there's a reduction or a weekend package in effect. Some Dublin hotels cut their rates by as much as 50% on Friday and Saturday nights, when business traffic is low. Also, significant reductions are sometimes available when rooms are booked from the States using the 800 numbers listed in this book.

Christ Church Place, Dublin 8. ℭ **800/44-UTELL** from the U.S., or 01/454-0000. Fax 01/454-0012. www.jurys.com. 182 units. £66–£69 (€84–€88, $83–$86) double. No service charge. AE, DC, MC, V. Public car park nearby. Bus: 21A, 50, 50A, 78, 78A, or 78B. **Amenities:** Restaurant, lounge; laundry/dry-cleaning service; no-smoking rooms. *In room:* A/C, TV, tea/coffeemaker, hair dryer.

ST. STEPHEN'S GREEN/GRAFTON STREET AREA
Very Expensive
Clarion Stephen's Hall ⭐   On the southeast corner of St. Stephen's Green, with a gracious Georgian exterior and entranceway, this is Dublin's first all-suite hotel. It's ideal for visitors who plan an extended stay or want to entertain. Newly renovated and furnished in a contemporary motif, each suite contains a hallway, sitting room, dining area, kitchen, bathroom, and one or two bedrooms with orthopedic beds. The luxury suites on the upper floors offer city views, while the ground-level town house suites have private entrances. Twelve suites have computers.

Earlsfort Centre, 14–17 Lower Leeson St., Dublin 2. ℭ **01/638-1111.** Fax 01/638-1122. www.premgroup.com. 37 units. £190–£290 (€241–€368, $238–$363) double. No service charge. AE, DC, MC, V. DART: Pearse Station. Bus: 14A, 11A, 11B, 13, 46A, 46B, or 86. **Amenities:** Restaurant. *In room:* TV, fax, data port, kitchen, tea/coffeemaker, hair dryer.

Shelbourne ⭐⭐   Built in 1824, this grand hostelry has played a significant role in Irish history (the new nation's constitution was signed in Room 112 in 1921) and has often been host to international leaders, stars of stage and screen, and literary giants. The public areas, replete with glowing fireplaces, Waterford chandeliers, and original art, are popular rendezvous spots for Dubliners. Rooms vary in size, but all offer up-to-date comforts. The front units overlook the bucolic St. Stephen's Green. In 1996, nearly $2.5 million was spent refurbishing the Shelbourne. Needless to say, you don't stay here just for the beds, which represent the Irish preference for a mattress somewhere beyond soft and short of firm.

27 St. Stephen's Green, Dublin 2. ℭ **800/225-5843** from the U.S., or 01/ 676-6471. Fax 01/661-6006. www.shelbourne.ie. 190 units. £230–£255 (€292–€324, $288–$319) double; £380–£950 (€483–€1,207, $475–$1,188) suite. Service charge 15%. AE, DC, MC, V. DART: Pearse Station. Bus: 10, 11A, 11B, 13, or 20B. **Amenities:** 2 restaurants, 2 bars, tea room; pool; health club; Jacuzzi; sauna; salon; 24-hour room service; baby-sitting; laundry service. *In room:* TV, minibar, hair dryer, trouser press.

Expensive
Buswells ⭐   Situated on a quiet street 2 blocks from Trinity College and opposite the National Museum, Library, and Art Gallery and Leinster House, this vintage hotel has long been a meeting point for artists, poets, scholars, and politicians. Originally two Georgian town houses (dating back to 1736), it was

launched as a hotel in 1928. The public areas have period furniture, intricate plasterwork, Wedgwood flourishes, old prints, and memorabilia. Rooms, completely refurbished in 1997, have been updated in a contemporary decor with Victorian touches.

25 Molesworth St., Dublin 2. © **800/473-9527** from the U.S., or 01/614-6500. Fax 01/676-2090. www. quinnhotels.com. 69 units. £169 (€215, $211) double. Rates include full breakfast. No service charge. AE, DC, MC, V. Free overnight (5:30pm–9:30am) parking. DART: Pearse Station. Bus: 10, 11A, 11B, 13, or 20B. **Amenities:** 2 restaurants, bar; concierge; room service; no-smoking rooms. *In room:* TV, tea/coffeemaker, hair dryer, trouser press.

Moderate

Georgian Hotel   Located less than 2 blocks from St. Stephen's Green, this four-story, 200-year-old brick town house sits in the heart of Georgian Dublin, within walking distance of most major attractions. In 1999 nearly 20 new spacious rooms were added in a modern annex at the rear of the original hotel, and the smallish older rooms have been fully renovated. Rooms are bright, with light woods and floral fabrics. The hotel's restaurant, the Celts Banquet, features open log fires and traditional music.

18–22 Lower Baggot St., Dublin 2. © **01/634-5000.** Fax 01/634-5100. hotel@georgianhouse.ie. 65 units. £120–£165 (€152–€210, $150–$206) double. Rates include full breakfast. No service charge. AE, DC, MC, V. Free overnight parking. DART: Pearse Station. Bus: 10. **Amenities:** Restaurant (seafood/Irish), lively bar. *In room:* TV, hair dryer.

FITZWILLIAM/MERRION SQUARE AREA
Very Expensive

Davenport Hotel ⚜   The hotel building incorporates the neoclassical facade of Merrion Hall, an 1863 church. Inside is an impressive domed entranceway, with a six-story atrium lobby. Rooms in a new section have traditional furnishings, orthopedic beds, textured wall coverings, and brass accessories. It's a sister hotel to the Mont Clare, which is across the street and shares valet car-parking arrangements.

Merrion Sq., Dublin 2. © **800/569-9983** from the U.S., or 01/607-3500. Fax 01/661-5663. www. davenporthotel.ie. 116 units. £225–£350 (€286–€445, $281–$438) double. Rates include full breakfast. Service charge 12.5%. AE, DC, MC, V. DART: Pearse Station. Bus: 5, 7A, 8, or 62. **Amenities:** Restaurant, bar; no-smoking rooms. *In-room:* A/C, TV, data port, hair dryer, safe, trouser press.

Expensive

Longfield's ⚜   Created from two 18th-century Georgian town houses, this small, classy hotel is named after Richard Longfield, also known as Viscount Longueville, who originally owned this site and was a member of the Irish Parliament 2 centuries ago. Totally restored and recently refurbished, it combines Georgian decor and reproduction period furnishings of dark woods and brass trim. Like the eye of a storm, Longfield's is in the midst of town but remarkably quiet, an elegant yet unpretentious getaway 5 minutes' walk from St. Stephen's Green.

10 Lower Fitzwilliam St., Dublin 2. © **01/676-1367.** Fax 01/676-1542. www.longfields.ie. 26 units. £140–£180 (€178–€229, $175–$225) double. Rates include full breakfast. No service charge. AE, DC, MC, V. DART: Pearse Station. Bus: 10. **Amenities:** Restaurant, bar; room service. *In room:* TV, data port, coffeemaker, hair dryer.

Moderate

Fitzwilliam Guesthouse ⚜   This guesthouse occupies a meticulously restored 18th-century town house on Fitzwilliam Street, the best-preserved Georgian thoroughfare in Dublin and a convenient location for exploring the city. The entrance parlor has a homey atmosphere, with a carved marble fireplace and antique furnishings. The bright rooms have high ceilings; bathrooms are somewhat small, but impeccably clean. Tea/coffeemakers are available just outside every room. A full Irish breakfast is served in the vaulted basement restaurant.

41 Upper Fitzwilliam St., Dublin 2. **01/662-5155.** Fax 01/676-7488. 12 units. £95 (€121, $119) double. Rates include full breakfast. AE, DC, MC, V. DART: Pearse Station (then a 10-minute walk southeast). Bus: 10. *In-room:* TV, hair dryer.

Kilronan House   Terry Masterson is the proprietor at this comfortable guesthouse, five minutes' walk from St. Stephen's Green and just north of the Royal Canal. The sitting room on the ground floor is small and intimate, with a fire glowing through the cold months of the year. Rooms are very well kept, and those facing the front have commodious bay windows. If you don't like stairs, request a room on the second floor, since there isn't an elevator. The front rooms, facing Adelaide Street, are also preferable to those in back, which face onto office buildings and a parking lot. When you book, ask about a reduction for Frommer's readers.

70 Adelaide Rd., Dublin 2. **01/475-5266.** Fax: 01/478-2841. www.dublinn.com. 15 units, all with shower only. £70–£100 (€89–€127, $88–$125) double. Children under 7 stay free. Rates include full breakfast. AE, MC, V. Bus: 14, 15, 19, 20, or 46A. *In-room:* TV, tea/coffeemaker, hair dryer.

O'CONNELL STREET AREA
Very Expensive

Gresham   Centrally located on the city's main business thoroughfare, this Regency-style hotel is one of Ireland's oldest (1817) and best-known lodgings. Although much of the tourist trade in Dublin has shifted south of the River Liffey in recent years, the Gresham is still synonymous with stylish Irish hospitality and provides easy access to the Abbey and Gate Theatres and other northside attractions. The lobby and public areas are a panorama of marble floors, molded plasterwork, and crystal chandeliers. The newly renovated rooms vary in size and style, with high ceilings, tiled bathrooms, and period furniture. One-of-a-kind luxury terrace suites grace the upper front floors.

23 Upper O'Connell St., Dublin 1. **01/874-6881.** Fax 01/878-7175. 288 units. £230 (€292, $288) double; from £280 (€356, $350) suite. Service charge 12.5%. AE, DC, MC, V. Parking in the multistory car park £5 (€6.35, $6.25) per day. DART: Connolly Station. Bus: 40A, 40B, 40C, or 51A. **Amenities:** Exercise room; babysitting; laundry service. *In room:* A/C, TV.

Moderate

Royal Dublin   Romantically floodlit at night, this modern five-story hotel is positioned near Parnell Square at the north end of Dublin's main thoroughfare, within walking distance of all the main theaters and northside attractions. It combines a contemporary skylit lobby full of Art Deco overtones with adjacent lounge areas that were part of an original building, dating back to 1752, with high Georgian ceilings, ornate cornices, crystal chandeliers, gilt-edged mirrors, and open fireplaces. Rooms are strictly modern, with light woods and three-sided full-length windows that extend over the busy street below.

40 Upper O'Connell St., Dublin 1. **800/528-1234** from the U.S., or 01/873-3666. Fax 01/873-3120. www.fitzwilliamh.com/royal/. 117 units. £126 (€160, $158) double. Rates include full Irish breakfast and service charge. AE, DC, MC, V. Secure car park available nearby. DART: Connolly Station. Bus: 36A, 40A, 40B, 40C, or 51A. **Amenities:** Restaurant, lounge/bar; 24-hour room service; laundry service (same day). *In room:* TV, tea/coffeemaker, hair dryer.

BALLSBRIDGE/EMBASSY ROW AREA

Situated south of the Grand Canal, this is Dublin's most prestigious suburb, yet it is within walking distance of downtown. Although primarily a residential area, it is also the home of some of the city's leading hotels, restaurants, and embassies.

Very Expensive

Berkeley Court The flagship of the Irish-owned Jurys Doyle Hotel group, and the first Irish member of Leading Hotels of the World, the Berkeley Court (pronounced Bark-lay) is nestled in a residential area near the American Embassy. A favorite haunt of diplomats and international business leaders, the hotel is known for its posh lobby decorated with fine antiques, original paintings, and Irish-made carpets and furnishings. Rooms, which aim to convey an air of elegance, have firm half-canopy beds. Suites have Jacuzzis.

Lansdowne Rd., Ballsbridge, Dublin 4. ☏ 01/660-1711. Fax 01/661-7238. www.jurysdoyle.com. 188 units. £225 (€286, $281) double; from £245 (€311, $306) suite. Service charge 15%. AE, DC, MC, V. Free valet parking. DART: Lansdowne Rd. Bus: 7, 8, or 45. **Amenities:** 3 restaurants, bar, lounge; health club; concierge; 24-hour room service; laundry service. *In-room:* TV, data port, minibar, safe, trouser press.

Jurys Hotel and Towers Setting a progressive tone in a city steeped in tradition, this massive hotel, which enjoyed a major refurbishment in 1999, is actually two interconnected hotels in one: a modern high-rise and a new tower with its own check-in desk, separate elevators, and private entrance, as well as full access to all the main hotel's amenities. The Towers section is an exclusive wing of oversize concierge-style rooms with bay windows. Towers guests also enjoy exclusive use of a private hospitality lounge with library, board room, and access to complimentary continental breakfast, daily newspapers, and coffee/tea service throughout the day. The casual Coffee Dock is one of Dublin's few late-night eateries.

Pembroke Rd., Ballsbridge, Dublin 4. ☏ 800/843-3311 from the U.S., or 01/660-5000. Fax 01/667-5471. www.jurys.com. 390 units. Main hotel £195 (€248, $244) double; Towers wing (with continental breakfast) £220 (€279, $275) double. Service charge 12.5%. AE, DC, MC, V. DART: Lansdowne Rd. Station. Bus: 5, 7, 7A, or 8. 260 free parking spaces on a first-come, first-served basis. **Amenities:** 2 restaurants, pub/lounge; pool; health club; sauna; business center; salon; 24-hour room service; same-day laundry/dry-cleaning; concierge-style rooms. *In room:* AC, TV, data port, minibar, tea/coffeemaker, hair dryer, trouser press.

Expensive

Butlers Town House This beautifully restored and expanded Victorian town house has a formal yet welcoming elegance—class without the starched collar. Rooms are richly furnished and equipped with climate control, activated from a hand-held remote. It's hard to elude comfort here, and the staff are especially solicitous. The gem, in our opinion, is the Glendalough Room, which can be requested if you book early. There is also one room equipped for travelers with disabilities. You'll find that there isn't much Helen Finnegan, the manager, has overlooked here.

44 Lansdowne Rd., Ballsbridge, Dublin 4. ☏1-800-44-UTELL from the U.S., or 01/667-4022. Fax 01/667-3960. info@butlers-hotel.com. 20 units, 1 with shower only. £150 (€191, $188) double. Rates include full breakfast. AE, DC, MC, V. DART: Lansdowne Rd. Station. Bus: 7, 7A, 8, 45. **Amenities:** Restaurant (breakfast, tea, and high tea); room service; baby-sitting; laundry/dry cleaning service. *In room:* A/C, TV, data port, tea/coffeemaker, hair dryer.

Moderate

Ariel House In the age of the generic, Ariel House remains a bastion of distinction and quality. For Dublin guesthouses, this one sets the standard. Michael and Maurice O'Brien are warm and consummate hosts. Guests are welcome to relax in the Victorian-style drawing room with its Waterford glass chandeliers, open fireplace, and delicately carved cornices. Rooms are individually decorated, with period furniture, fine paintings and watercolors, and crisp Irish linens, as well as an array of modern extras.

50–52 Lansdowne Rd., Ballsbridge, Dublin 4. ✆ **01/668-5512.** Fax 01/668-5845. www.ariel-house.com. 40 units. £100–£169 (€127–€215, $125–$211) double (rates vary seasonally). Service charge 10%. Full Irish breakfast £8.50 (€11, $11). MC, V. Private car park. DART: Lansdowne Rd. Station. Bus: 7, 7A, 8, or 45. **Amenities:** Restaurant (breakfast, tea, and high tea), wine bar. *In room:* TV, tea/coffeemaker.

Mount Herbert Hotel 🄥*Value*   This hotel offers simple, comfortable accommodation for a reasonable price. Over 40 years ago, the Loughran family welcomed their first guests to what had once been the family home of Lord Robinson. Rooms are simply furnished and moderate in size; bathrooms are moderate to small. The primary disadvantage here is the view: most rooms face the parking lot or an adjacent wing of the hotel. There are two wheelchair-friendly rooms on the ground floor. During the winter of 2001 a third of the rooms underwent a substantial (and much needed) renovation; the rest of the rooms should be renovated by 2003. The hotel grounds are thoughtfully planted, and a small garden and children's playground are in the back.

7 Herbert Rd., Ballsbridge, Dublin 4. ✆ **01/668-4321.** Fax 01/660-7077. www.mountherberthotel.ie. 180 units. £70–£99 (€89–€126, $88–$124) double. Rates include full breakfast. No service charge. AE, DC, MC, V. Secure parking for 100 cars. DART: Lansdowne Rd. Station. Bus: 3, 5, 7, 7A, 8, 18, or 45. **Amenities:** Restaurant, wine bar, cafe; sauna; gift shop; room service (7am to 11:30pm). *In room:* TV, data port (some rooms), tea/coffeemaker, hair dryer, trouser press.

Inexpensive
Bewley's Hotel 🄖 🄥*Value*   The new Bewley's Hotel, located in a fashionable suburb south of city center, occupies an elegant 19th-century brick Masonic school building adjacent to the R.D.S. showgrounds and next to the British Embassy. A new wing harmonizes well with the old structure, and is indistinguishable on the interior. Rooms are spacious and generously furnished—all have a writing desk, armchair, and either a king bed or a double and a twin bed. Bathrooms are moderate in size. The suites include an additional room with fold-out couch, table (seats six), tiny kitchen/bar cleverly hidden in a cabinet, and additional bathroom (shower only). The *per room* rate makes this hotel excellent value for families and groups; the only downside is its location outside city center, a small obstacle given the frequent bus and DART service.

Merrion Rd., Ballsbridge, Dublin 4. ✆ **01/668-1111.** Fax: 01/668-1999. www.bewleyshotels.com. 220 units. £69 (€88, $86) per room (sleeps up to 3 adults). AE, DC, MC, V. DART: Sandymount (5-minute walk). Bus: 7, 7A, 7X, 8, 45. **Amenities:** Very good restaurant, tearoom. *In room:* TV, tea/coffeemaker, trouser press.

Self-Catering
Lansdowne Village   Lansdowne Village is a modest and appealing residential development on the banks of the River Dodder. Within this community, Trident Holiday Homes offers fully equipped two- and three-bedroom rental units, each with an additional pull-out double-bed sofa in the living room. They are bright and comfortable, trim and well-maintained so that everything really works. The location is ideal. Not only are you a 5-minute walk from the DART and less than a half-hour's walk from St. Stephen's Green, but the Sandymount Strand, a favorite walking spot for Dubliners, is only 10 minutes away on foot for a pleasant after-dinner stroll. Shops and supermarkets are also nearby, so you can manage here quite well without a car, feeling apart from the city's frenzy and yet not at all cut off. The smaller units are perfect for couples, perhaps with one

child; the considerably more spacious three-bedroom units are recommended for larger families or for more than one couple.

Newbridge Ave. off Lansdowne Rd., Ballsbridge, Dublin 4. © **01/668-3534.** Fax 01/660-6465. 19 units (2- or 3-bedroom). £550–£700 (€699–€889, $688–$875) per week, depending on size of apt and season. Shorter periods available at reduced rates Oct–Mar. MC, V. DART: Lansdowne Rd. Station. Bus: 2, 3, 5, 7, 7A, 8, 18, 45. *In-room:* TV, kitchen.

WHERE TO DINE
HISTORIC OLD CITY & TEMPLE BAR/ TRINITY COLLEGE AREA
Expensive
Les Frères Jacques ☆ FRENCH   Well situated between Crampton Court and Sycamore Street opposite Dublin Castle, this restaurant brings a touch of haute cuisine to the lower edge of the trendy Temple Bar district. The menu offers such creative main courses as filet of beef in red wine and bone marrow sauce; duck suprême on a sweet corn pancake in tangy ginger sauce; rosette of spring lamb in meat juice sabayon and tomato coulis with crispy potato straws; and grilled lobster from the tank flamed in whiskey.

74 Dame St., Dublin 2. © **01/679-4555.** Reservations recommended. Set-price lunch £15 (€19, $19); set-price dinner £25 (€32, $31). A la carte also available. AE, DC, MC, V. Mon–Fri 12:30–2:30pm and 7:30–11pm; Sat 7–11pm. Bus: 50, 50A, 54, 56, or 77.

Lord Edward ☆ SEAFOOD   Established in 1890, this cozy upstairs dining room claims to be Dublin's oldest seafood restaurant. A dozen different preparations of sole (including au gratin and Véronique) are served, as are seven variations of prawns (from Thermidor to Provençal), and fresh lobster is prepared au naturel or in sauces. There's also fresh fish from salmon and sea trout to plaice and turbot—grilled, fried, or poached. Vegetarian dishes are also available. At lunchtime light snacks and simpler fare are served in the bar (Monday to Friday noon to 2:30pm).

23 Christ Church Place, Dublin 8. © **01/454-2420.** Reservations required. Main courses £10–£17 (€13–€22, $13–$21); set-price dinner £20 (€25, $25). AE, DC, MC, V. Mon–Fri noon–10:45pm; Sat 6–10:45pm. Bus: 50, 54A, 56A, 65, 65A, 77, 77A, 123, or 150.

Moderate
bruno's FRENCH/MEDITERRANEAN   This is a sure-fire spot for a flawlessly prepared, interesting lunch or dinner without serious damage to the budget. The atmosphere is light and modern, with the focus on food that is consistently excellent without flourish or pretense. The spinach and goat cheese tart; salad of prawns with honey, lime, sesame seeds, and jalapeño peppers; and the bruschetta of chicken are all worthy of mention. The new Millennium Bridge makes bruno's all the more convenient as it crosses the Liffey at Eustace Street which is directly opposite the restaurant. You can also find a bruno's at 21 Kildare St., Dublin 2 © **01/662-4724.**

30 E. Essex St., Dublin 2. © **01/670-6767.** www.brunos.ie. Reservations recommended. Dinner main courses £13.50–£23 (€17–€29, $17–$29). Service charge 10% on tables over 4. AE, DC, MC, V. Mon–Fri 12:30–3pm; Mon–Sat 6:30–10:30pm. DART: Tara St. Station. Bus: 21A, 46A, 46B, 51B, 51C, 68, 69, or 86.

Chameleon ☆☆ INDONESIAN   Only a dim, candlelit window and an orange sign signal Chameleon, well camouflaged on a small side street off Temple Bar Square. The Chameleon offers a variety of menus featuring samplings of seven different dishes and an assortment of condiments. The staff are quick in explaining how to best complement chicken sate with roasted peanuts. Sambalbadjak, a red curry paste, gives the rice a robust, pleasantly spicy flavor. Finally, a small morsel of pickled vegetable is suggested as a "palate cleanser"—good advice to swallow if you want to take advantage of the abundance of delicately flavored dishes that Chameleon has to offer.

No.1 Fownes St. Lower, Temple Bar, Dublin 2. ℃ **01/671-0362.** Main courses £10.50–£14.50 (€13–€18, $13–$18); set menus £16.50 (€21, $21), £18.50 (€24, $23), and £21.50 (€27, $27). MC, V. Tues–Sat 6–11pm; Sun 5:30–10pm. Bus: Any city-center bus.

Dish NOUVEAU INTERNATIONAL   Dish offers a relaxed, tasteful atmosphere. The menu is eclectic and enticing, with an emphasis on fresh grilled seafood and Mediterranean flavors that are complex without being confusing. The grilled salmon with avocado, papaya, and tequila-lime dressing, the baked hake, and the char-grilled tiger prawns are particularly outstanding. The desserts we tried—caramelized lemon tart with cassis sauce and the amaretti chocolate cheesecake—were superior. Dish promises to be one of Temple Bar's finest venues, and at a modest price.

2 Crow St., Dublin 2. [tel]01/671-1248. Reservations recommended. Main courses £10–£18 (€13–€23, $13–$23). Service charge 10% on tables over 5. AE, DC, MC, V. Daily noon–11:30pm. DART: Tara St. Station. Bus: 21A, 46A, 46B, 51B, 51C, 68, 69, or 86.

Juice VEGETARIAN   Juice tempts carnivorous, vegan, macrobiotic, celiac, and yeast-free diners alike, using organic produce to create delicious dressings and entrees among its largely conventional but well-prepared offerings. The avocado filet of blue cheese and broccoli wrapped in filo was superb, and I also highly recommend the spinach-and-ricotta cannelloni. The latter is included in the early-bird dinner—a great deal. Coffees, fresh-squeezed juices, organic wines, and late weekend hours add to the lure of this casual modern place frequented by mature diners who know their food.

Castle House, 73 S. Great Georges St., Dublin 2. ℃ **01/475-7856.** Reservations recommended Fri–Sat. Main courses £9–£12 (€12–€15, $11–$15); early bird fixed-price dinner £8.95 (€11, $11) Mon–Thurs 6:30–7pm. MC, V. Daily 11am–11pm. Bus: 50, 50A, 54, 56, or 77.

Inexpensive

Govinda's *Value* VEGETARIAN   Govinda's serves healthy square meals on square plates for very good prices. The meals are generous, belly-warming concoctions of vegetables, cheese, rice, and pasta. Two main courses are offered cafeteria-style: one East Indian and the other a simple, plainly flavored staple like lasagna or macaroni and cheese. Veggie burgers are also prepared to order. All are accompanied by a choice of two salads. Desserts are healthy and huge, like the rich wedge of carob cake with a dollop of cream or homemade ice cream (each £1.40/€1.78/$1.96). The restaurant is no-smoking throughout.

4 Aungier St., Dublin 2. ℃ **01/475-0309.** Main courses £5.10 (€6.50, $6.40); soup and freshly baked bread £2 (€2.55, $2.50). MC, V. Mon–Sat noon–9pm. Bus: 16, 16A, 19, or 22.

Leo Burdock's FISH-AND-CHIPS   For three generations, Brian Burdock's family has been serving up the country's best fish-and-chips. Cabinet ministers, university students, and almost every other type can be found in the queue, waiting for fish bought fresh that morning and those good Irish potatoes, both cooked in "drippings" (none of that modern vegetable oil!). Service is take-out only, but you can sit on a nearby bench or stroll down to the park at St. Patrick's Cathedral. It's located across from Christchurch, around the corner from Jury's Inn.

2 Werburgh St., Dublin 8. ℃ **01/454-0306.** Main courses £2.50–£4.70 (€3.20–€6, $3.15–$6). No credit cards. Mon–Sat noon–midnight; Sun 4pm–midnight. Bus: 21A, 50, 50A, 78, 78A, or 78B

ST. STEPHEN'S GREEN/GRAFTON STREET AREA

Very Expensive

The Commons ✹ MODERN EUROPEAN   Nestled on the south side of St. Stephen's Green, the Commons occupies the basement level of Newman House, the historic seat of Ireland's major university. For an aperitif in fine weather, there is a lovely stone courtyard terrace surrounded by a "secret garden" of lush plants and trees. The inventive menu changes daily, but you'll often see dishes such as confit of duck leg on a beetroot boxty, grilled shark with peppered carrot, and loin of rabbit with a stuffing of marinated prune.

85–86 St. Stephen's Green, Dublin 2. ✆ **01/478-0530.** Reservations required. Set-price lunch £18 (€23, $23) and £25 (€32, $31); dinner main courses £23–£30 (€29–€38, $29–$38). AE, DC, MC, V. Mon–Fri 12:30–2:15pm and 7–10:15pm. DART: Pearse Station. Bus: 10, 11, 13, or 46A.

Moderate

Fitzers Cafe ✹ INTERNATIONAL   In the middle of a busy shopping street, this airy Irish-style bistro has a multi-windowed shopfront facade and a modern Irish decor of light woods. The food is excellent and reasonably priced, contemporary and quickly served, with choices ranging from penne with chorizo, tomato, basil, and feta or roasted salmon or cod to chargrilled venison with grain mustard mash.

Fitzers has three other locations, each with a different menu and character: in the Royal Dublin Society (RDS), Ballsbridge, Dublin 4 (✆ **01/667-1302**); in Temple Bar Square, Dublin 2 (✆ **01/679-0440**); and in the new Millennium Wing of the National Gallery, Merrion Sq. West, Dublin 2. Consistency is the operative word here: You can count on Fitzers not to disappoint.

51 Dawson St., Dublin 2. ✆ **01/677-1155.** Reservations recommended. Lunch main courses £7.50–£12.50 (€9.55–€16, $9.40–$16); dinner main courses £10–£17 (€13–€22, $13–$21). AE, DC, MC, V. Daily 11:30am–11pm. DART: Pearse. Bus: 10, 11A, 11B, 13, or 20B.

Il Primo ✹ MODERN ITALIAN   Word of mouth is what brought me to Il Primo—little else would have, so obscurely is it tucked away off Harcourt Street. From the street all you see are several tables, a bar, an assembly of wooden stools, and a staircase, which happens to lead to some of the most distinguished, innovative Italian cuisine you'll ever meet up with outside Rome or Tuscany. Awaken your palate with a glass of sparkling Venetian prosecco; open with a plate of Parma ham, avocado, and balsamic vinaigrette; and then go for broke with the ravioli Il Primo, an open handkerchief of pasta over chicken, Parma ham, and mushrooms in a light tarragon cream sauce.

16 Montague St., Dublin 2 (off Harcourt St., 50 yards down from St. Stephen's Green). ✆ **01/478-3373.** Reservations required on weekends. Dinner main courses £10–£23 (€13–€29, $13–$29). 10% service charge. AE, DC, MC, V. Mon–Fri 12:30–3pm and 6–11pm; Sat 6–11pm. DART: Pearse Station. Bus: 10, 11, 13, or 46A.

Inexpensive

Bewley's Café TRADITIONAL/PASTRIES   This is Dublin's old reliable, a chain with a 150-year history. The interior is a subdued, mellow mix of dark wood, amber glass, and deep red velvet. Bewley's bustles with the clink of teapots and the satisfied hum of customers sated on scones, almond buns, and baked goods. Less appealing but equally filling are warm suppers of lasagna, sausages and chips, or a variety of casseroles. Most Bewley's are self-service cafeterias, but Bewley's of Grafton Street also has several full-service tearooms. Other locations are at 11 Westmoreland St., Dublin 2; 40 Mary St., Dublin 1 (near the ILAC shopping center north of the Liffey); shopping centers in Dundrum, Stillorgan, and Tallaght; and Dublin Airport.

78 Grafton St. (between Nassau St. and St. Stephen's Green). ℂ 01/677-6761. Cafeteria main courses
£3–£6.50 (€3.80–€8.30, $3.75–$8); lunch specials from £5 (€6.35, $6). AE, DC, MC, V. Daily 7:30am–11pm
(continuous service for breakfast, hot food, and snacks). Bus: Any city-center bus.

Café Bell IRISH/SELF-SERVICE   In the cobbled courtyard of early 19th-
century St. Teresa's Church, this serene little place is one of a handful of dining
options springing up in historic or ecclesiastical surroundings. With high ceilings
and an old-world decor, Café Bell is a welcome contrast to the bustle of Grafton
Street a block away and Powerscourt Town House Centre across the street. The
menu changes daily but usually includes homemade soups, sandwiches, salads,
quiches, lasagna, sausage rolls, hot scones, and other baked goods.

St. Teresa's Courtyard, Clarendon St., Dublin 2. ℂ 01/677-7645. All items £2–£5 (€2.55–€6.35,
$2.50–$6.25). No credit cards. Mon–Sat 9am–5:30pm. Bus: 16, 16A, 19, 19A, 22A, 55, or 83.

FITZWILLIAM/MERRION SQUARE AREA
Very Expensive
Restaurant Patrick Guilbaud ⭐⭐ FRENCH NOUVELLE   After being
tucked away for many years on James Place, this distinguished restaurant has
transferred to new quarters but kept its glowing reputation for fine food and art-
ful service. The menu features such dishes as casserole of black sole and prawns,
steamed salmon with orange and grapefruit sauce, filet of spring lamb with parsley sauce and herb salad, roast duck with honey, and breast of guinea fowl with
Madeira sauce and potato crust.

21 Upper Merrion St., Dublin 2. ℂ 01/676-4192. Reservations required. Set-price lunch £22 (€28, $28);
main courses around £30 (€38, $38). AE, DC, MC, V. Jan–Nov Tues–Sat 12:30–2:15pm and 7:30–10:15pm;
Dec 1–Dec 24 Mon–Sat 12:30–2:15pm and 7:30–10:15pm. DART: Westland Row. Bus: 5, 7A, or 8.

Expensive
L'Ecrivain ⭐ FRENCH/IRISH   This is one of Dublin's truly fine restaurants,
from start to finish. The atmosphere is relaxed and welcoming, without the
bother of pretense. You can dine on the garden terrace, weather permitting. Each
course seems to receive the same devoted attention, and most consist of traditional "best of Irish" ingredients. The seared sea trout with sweet potato puree
and the entrecôte steak with caramelized onion were perfectly prepared for me.
A final note: The desserts are not an afterthought, but the creations of a talented
pastry chef. The crème brûlée here is the best I've tasted north of the Chunnel.

109 Lower Baggot St., Dublin 2. ℂ 01/661-1919. Reservations recommended. Fixed-price 3-course lunch
£20 (€25, $25). Fixed-price 3-course dinner £35 (€45, $44). Dinner main courses £23–£26 (€29–€33,
$29–$33). 10% service charge on food only. AE, DC, MC, V. Mon–Fri 12:30–2pm and 7–11pm; Sat 7–11pm.
Bus: 10. 5-minute walk from St. Stephen's Green. Ample street parking on nearby Merrion Sq.

Moderate
Lloyds Brasserie FRENCH NOUVELLE   This is famed chef Conrad
Gallagher's latest venture. The decor is minimalist and contemporary, with hints
of Art Deco—clear, bright, and simple. The food is another matter—bold, often
intense, and in presentation nothing less than architectural. The menu certainly
commands attention, although the essential ingredients are often in danger of
being taken for granted, even overlooked. A meal here is an adventure, well
worth the relatively moderate price, and where else will you find "bubble and
squeak" (corned beef, ground lamb, and cabbage), a surprisingly subtle dish?

20 Upper Merrion St., Dublin 2. ℂ01/662-7240. Reservations recommended. Set-price lunch £15 (€19,
$19); main courses £10–£20 (€13–€25, $13–$25). No service charge. AE, DC, MC, V. Daily 10am for coffee;
lunch Mon–Fri noon–2:30pm; brunch Sat–Sun 1–4pm; dinner daily 6pm–2am. DART: Westland Row. Bus: 10,
11A, 11B, 13, or 20B.

Inexpensive
The Steps of Rome ⚔ *Finds* ITALIAN/PIZZA   Word is out that this restaurant just off the busy shopping thoroughfare of Grafton Street offers some of the best simple Italian fare in Dublin. Large, succulent pizza slices available for takeout are one way to enjoy the wonders of this authentic Italian kitchen when the dining room is full—the seven tables huddled within this tiny restaurant seem to be perennially occupied. The potato, mozzarella and rosemary pizza, with a thick crust resembling focaccia, is unusual and exceptionally delicious. Although the pasta dishes are also quite good, it's that pizza that remains unforgettable.

Chatham Court, off Chatham St., Dublin 2. ℂ 01/670-5630. Main courses £6–£8 (€7.60–€10, $7.60–$10); pizza slices £1.90 (€2.40, $2.40). No credit cards. Mon–Sat 10am–midnght; Sun 1–11pm.

O'CONNELL STREET AREA
Moderate
101 Talbot ⚔ INTERNATIONAL/VEGETARIAN   Opened in 1991, this restaurant features light and healthy foods, with a strong emphasis on vegetarian dishes, including choices for vegans. The setting is bright and casual, with big windows, yellow rag-rolled walls, ash-topped tables, and newspapers for browsing. Main courses include jambalaya of lamb, smoked sausage, and black-eyed peas; vegetable satay with rice; and tandoori chicken with mango. The menu changes weekly. Espresso and cappuccino are always available for sipping, and there's a full bar. It's located at Talbot Lane near Marlborough Street, convenient to the Abbey Theatre.

100 Talbot St., Dublin 1. ℂ01/874-5011. Reservations recommended. Dinner main courses £10–£18 (€13–€23, $13–$23). AE, MC, V. Tues–Sat 5–11pm. DART: Connolly Station. Bus: 27A, 31A, 311B, 32A, 32B, 42B, 42C, 43, or 44A.

Inexpensive
Winding Stair CAFETERIA/TEASHOP   Those who resist reading the texts that paper the walls of this cafe's three-storied 18th-century winding stair will soon find themselves in a comforting enclave overlooking the Ha'penny bridge and the River Liffey. Solicitous staff are quick to serve bookish clientele. Thick sandwiches heaped with fresh vegetables and a choice of cheeses and salamis are made to order. Salads include the exotic and the local, with both a hearty tabouli and an "Irish Brie and cranberry" gracing the chalkboard menu. A banana and honey sandwich as well as carrot cake and lemon-poppyseed loaf make up the "sweet" menu. Evening events include poetry readings and recitals.

40 Lower Ormond Quay, Dublin 1. ℂ 01/873-3292. All items £1.50–£5 (€1.90–€6.35, $1.90–$6.25). MC, V. Mon–Sat 10am–6pm; Sun 1–6pm. Bus: 70 or 80.

BALLSBRIDGE/EMBASSY ROW AREA
Expensive
Le Coq Hardi ⚔ FRENCH   Newly redecorated and offering a new cocktail bar, this plush 50-seat restaurant draws a well-heeled local and international business clientele. Chef John Howard has garnered many an award by offering such specialties as Dover sole stuffed with prawns, Irish wild salmon on fresh spinach leaves, filet of hake roasted on green cabbage and bacon with Pernod butter sauce, and filet of prime beef flamed in Irish whiskey. The 700-bin wine cellar boasts a complete collection of Château Mouton Rothschild, dating from 1945 to the present. Le Coq Hardi's latest trophy was the Year 2000 "Restaurant of the Year" award from Bord Bia.

35 Pembroke Rd., Ballsbridge, Dublin 4. ℂ **01/668-9070.** Reservations required. Set-price lunch £24.50 (€31, $31) for full menu; dinner main courses from £20 (€25, $25). AE, MC, V. Mon–Fri 12–2:30pm and 7–10:30pm; Sat 7–10:30pm. DART: Lansdowne Rd. Station. Bus: 18, 46, 63, or 84.

Moderate

Rolys Bistro ✦ IRISH/INTERNATIONAL   Opened in 1992, this restaurant quickly skyrocketed to success, thanks to its genial and astute host Roly Saul and its master chef Colin O'Daly. What you get is excellent and imaginatively prepared food at mostly moderate prices. The main dining rooms can be noisy when the house is full, but the no-smoking section has a quiet enclave of booths laid out in an Orient Express style for those who prefer a quiet tête-à-tête. Main courses include roasted venison, pan-fried Dublin Bay prawns, game pie with chestnuts, and wild mushroom risotto. An excellent array of international wines is offered, starting at £10.95 (€13.90, $15) a bottle.

7 Ballsbridge Terrace, Dublin 4. ℂ **01/668-2611.** Reservations required. Main courses £10–£20 (€13–€25, $13–$25); set-price lunch £14 (€18, $18). AE, DC, MC, V. Daily noon–3pm and 6–10pm. DART: Lansdowne Rd. Station. Bus: 5, 6, 7, 8, 18, or 45.

Inexpensive

Da Vincenzo ✦ ITALIAN   A block from the Hotel Burlington, this informal and friendly owner-run bistro offers ground level and upstairs seating. The casual decor consists of glowing brick fireplaces, pine walls, and a busy open kitchen. Pizza with a light, pita-style dough, cooked in a wood-burning oven, is a specialty here. Other main courses range from pastas to veal and beef dishes, including an organically produced filet steak.

133 Upper Leeson St., Dublin 4. ℂ **01/660-9906.** Reservations recommended. Main courses £7–£15 (€8.90–€19, $8.75–$19). AE, DC, MC, V. Mon–Fri 12:30–11pm; Sat 1–11pm; Sun 3–10pm. Bus: 10, 11A, 11B, 46A, or 46B.

SEEING THE SIGHTS
SIGHTSEEING SUGGESTIONS FOR FIRST-TIME VISITORS

If You Have 1 Day Start at the beginning—Dublin's medieval quarter, the area around **Christ Church** and **St. Patrick's Cathedral.** Tour these great churches and then walk the cobblestoned streets and inspect the nearby old city walls at **High Street.** From Old Dublin, take a turn eastward and see **Dublin Castle** and then **Trinity College** with the famous Book of Kells. Cross over the River Liffey to **O'Connell Street,** Dublin's main thoroughfare. Walk up this wide street, passing the landmark General Post Office (GPO), to Parnell Square and the picturesque Garden of Remembrance. If time permits, visit the **Dublin Writers Museum,** and then hop on a double-decker bus heading to the south bank of the Liffey for a visit to **St. Stephen's Green** for a relaxing stroll amid the greenery. Cap the day with a show at the **Abbey Theatre** and maybe a drink or two at a nearby pub.

If You Have 2 Days On your second day, take a **Dublin Bus city sightseeing tour** to give you an overview of the city—you'll see all the local downtown landmarks, plus some of the leading sites on the edge of the city, such as the **Guinness Brewery,** the **Royal Hospital,** and **Phoenix Park.** In the afternoon, head for **Grafton Street** for some shopping. If time allows, stroll around **Merrion** or

Fitzwilliam squares to give you a sampling of the best of Dublin's Georgian architecture.

If You Have 3 Days Make day 3 a day for Dublin's artistic and cultural attractions—visit the **National Museum** and **National Gallery,** the **Guinness Hop Store,** or a special-interest museum, such as the **Writers Museum.** Save time for a walk around **Temple Bar,** the city's Left Bank district, lined with art galleries and film studios, interesting secondhand shops, and casual eateries.

If You Have 4 Days On day 4, take a ride aboard DART to the suburbs, either southward to **Dun Laoghaire** or **Dalkey,** or northward to **Howth.** DART follows the rim of Dublin Bay in both directions, so you'll enjoy a scenic ride and get to spend some time in an Irish coastal village. Or take a trip to the **Boyne Valley** and the north coast to visit the burial mounds at Newgrange, the site of the Battle of the Boyne, King William's Glen, and other sites. This trip is also worthwhile for the glimpses of Irish countryside it affords.

DUBLIN'S TOP ATTRACTIONS

Trinity College and The Book of Kells ☆☆☆   The oldest university in Ireland, Trinity was founded in 1592 by Queen Elizabeth I. It sits in the heart of the city on a beautiful 16-hectare (40-acre) site just south of the River Liffey, with cobbled squares, gardens, a picturesque quadrangle, and buildings dating from the 17th to the 20th centuries. The college is home to the Book of Kells, an 8th-century version of the four Gospels with elaborate scripting and illumination. This famous treasure and other early Christian manuscripts are on permanent public view in the Colonnades, an exhibition area on the ground floor of the Old Library. Also housed in the Old Library is the Dublin Experience (© **01/608-1177**), an excellent multimedia introduction to the history and people of Dublin.

College Green, Dublin 2. © **01/608-2320.** www.tcd.ie. Admission to the college grounds is free; admission to Old Library/Book of Kells £4.50 (€5.70, $6) adults, £4 (€5.10, $5) students and seniors, £9 (€11, $11) families, free for children under 12; Dublin Experience, £3.25 (€4.15, $4) adults, £2.75 (€3.50, $4.70) seniors/students. Combination tickets also available. Credit cards accepted for shop purchases only. Oct–May Mon–Sat 9:30am–5pm, Sun noon–4:30pm; June–Sept Sun 9:30am–4:30pm. Dublin Experience May–Sept daily 10am–5pm, closed Oct–Apr. DART: Pearse St. Station. Bus: All city center buses.

Archaeology and History ☆☆   This important museum reflects Ireland's heritage from 2000 B.C. to the present. It's the home of many of the country's greatest historical finds, including the Ardagh Chalice, Tara Brooch, and Cross of Cong. Other highlights range from the artifacts from the Wood Quay excavations of the Old Dublin Settlements to an extensive exhibition of Irish gold ornaments from the Bronze Age.

Kildare St., Dublin 2. © **01/677-7444.** Free admission. Tues–Sat 10am–5pm; Sun 2–5pm. DART: Pearse Station. Bus: 7, 7A, 8, 10, 11, or 13.

Collins Barracks ☆   This is the latest venue of the National Museum, which has already occupied 2 of the 4 blocks available here. Even if it were empty, Collins Barracks—the oldest military barracks in Europe—would be well worth a visit; the structure itself is a splendidly restored early 18th-century masterwork by Colonel Thomas Burgh, Ireland's Chief Engineer and Surveyor General under Queen Anne. The collection housed here focuses on the decorative arts and weaponry. Most notable is the extraordinary display of Irish silver and furniture. Collins Barracks also houses a cafe and gift shop.

Tips **National Museum**

The National Museum of Ireland currently comprises three separate venues and plans to add a fourth. A special MuseumLink shuttle bus (Route 172) runs daily between these museums; shuttle schedules are available at any of the three museums below.

Benburb St., Dublin 7. ℭ **01/677-7444.** Free admission. Tours at varying hours, depending on groups, £1 (€1.30, $1.25). Tues–Sat 10am–5pm; Sun 2–5pm. Bus: 25, 66, 67, or 90.

Natural History Museum A division of the National Museum, the recently renovated Natural History Museum is considered one of the finest traditional museums in the world. In addition to presenting the zoological history of Ireland, it offers examples of major animal groups from around the world, including many rare or extinct groups. The Blaschka glass models of marine animals are quite famous.

Merrion St., Dublin 2. ℭ **01/677-7444.** Free admission. Tues–Sat 10am–5pm; Sun 2–5pm. Bus: 7, 7A, or 8.

Dublin Castle ℛℛ Built between 1208 and 1220, this complex represents some of the oldest surviving architecture in the city and was the center of British power in Ireland for more than 7 centuries until it was taken over by the new Irish government in 1922. Highlights include the 13th-century Record Tower; the State Apartments, once the residence of English viceroys; and the Chapel Royal. The newest developments are the Undercroft, an excavated site on the grounds where an early Viking fortress stood, and the Treasury, built between 1712 and 1715 and believed to be the oldest surviving office building in Ireland. At hand, as well, are a craft shop, heritage center, and restaurant.

Palace St. (off Dame St.), Dublin 2. ℭ **01/677-7129.** Admission £3.15 (€4, $3.95) adults, £2.40 (€3.05, $3) students and seniors, £1.20 (€1.50, $1.50) children. Tours given every 20–25 minutes Mon–Fri 10am–5pm, Sat–Sun and bank holidays 2–5pm. The State Apartments are sometimes closed to the public due to official state functions. Bus: 50, 50A, 54, 56A, 77, 77A, or 77B.

Dublin Writers Museum Housed in a stunning 18th-century Georgian mansion with splendid plasterwork and stained glass, the museum is itself an impressive reminder of the grandeur of the Irish literary tradition. Yeats, Joyce, Beckett, Shaw, Wilde, Swift, and Sheridan are among those whose lives and works are celebrated here. One of the museum's rooms is devoted to children's literature.

18–19 Parnell Sq. N., Dublin 1. ℭ **01/872-2077.** Fax 01/872-2231. Admission £4 (€5.10, $5) adults, £3 (€3.80, $3.75) seniors/students, £2 (€2.55, $2.50) ages 3–11, £11 (€14, $14) families (2 adults and up to 4 children). AE, DC, MC, V. Mon–Sat 10am–5pm (6pm June–Aug); Sun and holidays 11am–5pm. DART: Connolly Station. Bus: 11, 13, 16, 16A, 22, or 22A.

Christ Church Cathedral Standing on a ridge above the site of the original Norse town, the cathedral was founded in 1038, although the present building dates from around 1172, with substantial renovations from 1871 to 1878. Inside you'll find a monument to Strongbow, the ruler who had the cathedral built. Make sure to look back from the altar and note the leaning wall of Dublin, which has been out of perpendicular by some 18 inches since 1562. The newly restored crypt, intact since the 13th century, is one of the largest medieval crypts in either Britain or Ireland.

Christ Church Place. © **01/677-8099**. Admission: suggested donation £2 (€2.55, $2.50) adults, £1 (€1.30, $1.30) children, £5 (€6.35, $6.25) family. Daily 10am–5:30pm. Closed Dec 26. Bus: 21A, 50, 50A, 78, 78A, or 78B.

St. Patrick's Cathedral   It is said that St. Patrick baptized converts on this site and consequently a church has stood here since A.D. 450, making it the oldest Christian site in Dublin. The present cathedral dates from 1190, but because of a fire and subsequent rebuilding in the 14th century, not much remains from the cathedral's foundation days. It's mainly early English in style, with a square medieval tower that houses the largest ringing peal bells in Ireland, an 18th-century spire, and a 90-meter- (300-foot-) long interior, making it the longest church in the country. St. Patrick's is closely associated with Jonathan Swift, who was dean here from 1713 to 1745 and whose tomb lies in the south aisle. St. Patrick's is the national cathedral of the Church of Ireland.

21–50 Patrick's Close, Patrick St., Dublin 8. © **01/475-4817**. www.stpatrickscathedral.ie. Admission £2.70 (€3.45, $3.40) adults, £2 (€2.55, $2.50) students and seniors, £6.50 (€8.30, $8.15) family. MC, V. Mon–Fri 9am–6pm year-round; Mar–Oct Sat 9am–6pm; Sun 9–11am, 12:45–3pm, and 4:15–6pm. Nov–Feb Sat 9am–5pm; Sun 10–11am and 12:45–3pm. Closed except for services Dec 24–26 and Jan 1. Bus: 65, 65B, 50, 50A, 54, 54A, 56A, or 77.

MORE ATTRACTIONS
Dvblinia   What was Dublin like in medieval times? Here is a historically accurate presentation of the Old City from 1170 to 1540, re-created through a series of theme exhibits, spectacles, and experiences. Highlights include an illuminated Medieval Maze complete with visual effects, background sounds, and aromas that lead you on a journey through time from the first arrival of the Anglo-Normans in 1170 to the closure of the monasteries in the 1530s. The next segment depicts everyday life in medieval Dublin with a diorama, as well as a prototype of a 13th-century quay along the banks of the Liffey. The finale takes you to The Great Hall for a 360-degree wrap-up portrait of medieval Dublin via a 12-minute cyclorama-style audiovisual.

St. Michael's Hill, Christ Church, Dublin 8. © **01/679-4611**. Admission (Dublinia and the cathedral) £4 (€5.10, $5) adults, £3 (€3.80, $3.75) seniors/students/children, £10 (€12.75, $15) families. AE, MC, V. Apr–Sept daily 10am–5pm; Oct–Mar Mon–Sat 11am–4pm, Sun 10am–4:30pm. Bus: 50, 78A, or 123.

GAA Museum   On the grounds of Croke Park, principal stadium of the Gaelic Athletic Association, this museum dramatically presents the athletic heritage of Ireland. The Gaelic Games (Gaelic football, hurling, handball, and camogie) have long been contested on an annual basis between teams representing the various regions of Ireland. Test your skills with interactive exhibits, and peruse the extensive video archive of football finals dating back to 1931. The 12-minute film "A Sunday in September" captures admirably the hysteria of a final match. Note that on match days the museum is open only to new stand ticket holders.

Croke Park, Dublin 3. © **01/855-8176**. Admission £3 (€3.80, $3.75) adults, £2 (€2.55, $2.50) students, £1.50 (€1.90, $1.90) children, £6 (€7.60, $7.50) families. May–Sept daily 9:30am–4:30pm; Oct–Apr Tues–Sat 10am–4:30pm, Sun 12–4:30pm. Bus: 3, 11,11A, 16, 16A, 51A, or 123.

Guinness Brewery Hop Store Visitor Center   Founded in 1759, this is one of the world's largest breweries. Part industrial icon and part shopping mall, the new visitor center relies on sensory overload to convey the story of the famous brew. Exhibits presenting everything you ever wanted to know about Guinness are organized around a high atrium in the shape of a pint glass: history, the brewing process, and even the companies' advertising campaigns are on display. On the top floor you can sample a pint in the "Gravity Bar," a glass-walled room on the top floor offering a truly panoramic view of Dublin. The complex also includes a conference center, a restaurant, and an additional bar/lounge.

James's Gate, Dublin 8. ✆ 01/408-4800. www.guinness.ie. Admission £9 (€12, $11) adults, £6 (€7.60, $8) students over 18, £4 (€5.10, $5) students under 18 and seniors, £20 (€25, $25) family. Apr–Sept daily 9:30am–7pm; Oct–Mar daily 9:30am–5pm. Bus: 51B and 78A from Aston Quay, or 123 from O'Connell Street.

Irish Traditional Music Centre (Ceol) and Jameson Chimney ☞
Ceol offers a good introduction to Irish traditional music for the uninitiated, and a few items which may be of interest to experienced listeners and performers. The center consists of several interactive audiovisual displays that present the basic components of Irish traditional music—song, dance, and instruments. Videos demonstrating set dancing are projected onto 6-foot screens, and audio recordings of early Irish radio broadcasts are continuously played in a small circular chamber at the center of the museum. A 30-minute film intersperses brief interviews with performers, clips from live sessions, and spectacular views of the Irish countryside. Adjacent to the center is the **Jameson Chimney,** a 46-meter (150-ft.) industrial tower with a recently constructed observation deck that provides unparalleled views of the city.

Smithfield Village, off Arran Quay, Dublin 1. ✆ 01/817-3820. www.ceol.ie. Ceol Admission (Ceol or the tower) £5 (€6.35, $6.25) adults, £4 (€5.10, $5) students, £3.50 (€4.45, $4.40) children, £15 (€19, $19) families. Mon–Sat 10am–6pm; Sun 12–7pm (last film 45 minutes before closing). Bus: 67, 67A, 68, 69, 79, or 90.

James Joyce Centre ☞
Located near Parnell Square and the Dublin Writers Museum, this newly restored Georgian town house, built in 1784, gives literary enthusiasts one more reason to visit Dublin's north side. The house itself was once the home of Denis J. Maginni, a dancing instructor who appears briefly in *Ulysses.* The Ulysses Portrait Gallery on the second floor has a fascinating collection of photographs and drawings of characters from *Ulysses* who had a life outside the novel. Another room holds the writing table used by Joyce in Paris when he was working on *Finnegans Wake,* as well as Joyce's beloved piano. Talks and audiovisual presentations are offered daily, as are the pastries and teas in the coffee shop. Guided walking tours are offered through the neighboring streets of "Joyce Country" in Dublin's northern inner city.

35 N. Great George's St., Dublin 1. ✆ 01/878-8547. Fax 01/878-8488. www.jamesjoyce.ie. Admission £3 (€3.80, $3.75) adult, £2 (€2.55, $2.50) student/senior, 75p (€0.95E, 95¢) child, £6 (€7.60, $7.50) family; walking tours £6.50 (€8.30, $8.20) adult, £5 (€6.35, $6.25) student/senior, £12 (€15, $15) family; tour of house with Ken Monaghan £4.50 (€5.70, $5.65) adult, £4 (€5.10, $5) student/senior. AE, MC, V. Mon–Sat 9:30am–5pm; Sun 12:30–5pm. Closed Dec 24–26. DART: Connolly Station. Bus: 1, 40A, 40B, or 40C.

The Joyce Tower Museum ☞
No James Joyce fan should miss this small museum housed in the Sandycove Martello Tower where Joyce lived for a while in 1904—it's described in the first chapter of *Ulysses.* The museum contains exhibits on Joyce and Dublin at the time *Ulysses* was written. If you pick up a copy of the "Ulysses Map of Dublin," you can make this the starting point of a Joyce tour of the city. Robert Nicholson, the museum's curator, is a great source of information on all topics relating to Joyce, and has published *The Ulysses Guide,* the best guide to *Ulysses* sites in Dublin.

Sandycove, County Dublin. ✆01/280-9265. Admission £2.70 (€3.45, $3.40) adults, £2.20 (2.80, $2.75) seniors and students, £1.40 (€1.80, $1.75) children, and £7.95 (€10, $9.95) family. Apr–Oct Mon–Sat 10am–1pm and 2–5pm; Sun 2–6pm; open Nov–Mar by appointment only (call ✆ 01/872-2077). DART: Sandycove Station. Bus: 8.

Kilmainham Gaol Historical Museum ∉   Within these walls political prisoners were incarcerated, tortured, and killed from 1796 until 1924, when Eamon de Valera left as its final prisoner. To walk along these corridors, through the exercise yard, or into the Main Compound is a moving experience that lingers hauntingly in the memory.

Note: The **War Memorial Gardens** (© 01/677-0236), located along the banks of the Liffey, are a 5-minute walk from nearby Kilmainham Gaol. The gardens were designed by the famous British architect Sir Edwin Lutyens (1869–1944), who completed a number of commissions for houses and gardens in Ireland. Thankfully, the gardens are fairly well maintained and continue to present a moving testimony to Ireland's war dead. This is one of the finest small gardens in Ireland. The opening times are from Monday to Friday 8am to dark and Saturday 10am to dark.

Kilmainham. © **01/453-5984.** Admission £3.50 (€4.45, $4.40) adults, £2.50 (€3.20, $3.15) seniors, £1.50 (€1.90, $1.90) children, £8 (€10, $10) families. Tours given Apr–Sept daily 9:30am–4:45pm; Oct–Mar Mon–Fri 9:30am–4pm, Sun 10am–4:45pm. Bus: 21, 78, 78A, 78B, or 79 at O'Connell Bridge.

Hugh Lane Municipal Gallery of Modern Art   Housed in a finely restored 18th-century building known as Charlemont House, this gallery is situated next to the Dublin Writers Museum. It is named after Hugh Lane, an Irish art connoisseur who died in the sinking of the *Lusitania* in 1915 and who willed his collection (including works by Courbet, Manet, Monet, and Corot) to be shared between the government of Ireland and the National Gallery of London. With the Lane collection as its nucleus, this gallery also contains Impressionist and post-Impressionist paintings, Rodin sculptures, stained glass, and works by modern Irish artists. The museum also houses the studio of Irish painter Francis Bacon.

Parnell Sq. N., Dublin 1. © **01/874-1903.** Free admission but donations accepted. Tues–Thurs 9:30am–6pm; Fri–Sat 9:30am–5pm; Sun 11am–5pm. DART: Connolly or Tara stations. Bus: 10, 11, 11A, 11B, 13, 16, 16A, 19, 19A, 22, 22A, or 36.

National Gallery ∉   Established by an act of Parliament in 1854, this gallery first opened its doors in 1864, with just over 100 paintings. Today the collection of paintings, drawings, watercolors, miniatures, prints, sculpture, and objets d'art is considered one of Europe's finest. Every major European school of painting is represented, including an extensive assemblage of Irish work. Of special note is the new Yeats Museum, dedicated to Jack B. Yeats (1871–1957). The museum features a fine gallery shop. All public areas are wheelchair-accessible.

Merrion Sq. West, Dublin 2. © **01/661-5133.** www.nationalgallery.ie. Free admission. Mon–Wed and Fri–Sat 9:30am–5:30pm; Thurs 9:30am–8:30pm; Sun noon–5:30pm. Free public tours: Sat 3pm; Sun 2:15, 3, and 4pm. DART: Pearse Station. Bus: 5, 6, 7, 7A, 8, 10, 44, 47, 47B, 48A, or 62.

The Irish Museum of Modern Art   One of the city's newest museums is located in its oldest classical building, the stately Kilmainham Hospital. Modeled on Les Invalides in Paris, the old hospital is a quadrangle with chapel and majestic dining hall in the north wing and a row of stables to the south, now converted to artists' studios. Situated in an expansive parkland setting, the building has an elaborate formal garden on its north side and a long, tree-lined ceremonial entrance to the west, extending all the way to the Kilmainham Gaol. The high entrance hall on the south side is adjoined by a fine bookshop and tea house, serving light meals under £5 (€6.35, $6.25). The galleries contain the work of Irish and international artists from the small but impressive permanent collection, with numerous temporary exhibitions at any given time.

Royal Hospital, Military Rd., Kilmainham, Dublin 8. © **01/612-9900**. Fax 01/612-9999. www.modernart.ie. Admission free. Tues–Sat 10am–5:30pm; Sun noon–5:30pm. Unlimited parking. DART: Feeder bus from Connolly and Tara St. stations to Heuston. Bus: 68A, 69, 78A, 79, 90, or 123.

Waterways Visitor Centre This intriguing modern building is home to a fascinating exhibit describing the history of Ireland's inland waterways, a network of canals connecting Dublin westward and northward to the Shannon watershed. The center's shiny white exterior gives way inside to the subdued tones of Irish oak wall panels and a hardwood ship's floor—a series of exhibits describe aspects of canal design, and several interactive models attempt to demonstrate dynamically the daily operations of the canals. No longer used for transporting goods, the canals of Ireland are now popular with boaters and hikers, and there's some information here for those interested in these activities.

Grand Canal Quay, Ringsend Rd., Dublin 2. © **01/677-7510**. www.heritageireland.ie. Admission £2 (€2.55, $2.50) adults, £1.50 (€1.90, $1.90) seniors, £1 (€1.30, $1.25) children or students, £5 (€6.35, $6) families. June–Sept daily 9:30am–6:30pm; Oct–May Wed–Sun 12:30–5pm. DART: Pearse (5-minute walk). Bus: 1 or 3.

PARKS & ZOOS

St. Stephen's Green ⚐, in the heart of Dublin 2, has been preserved as an open space for Dubliners since 1690. A short walk from most city center locations, this large park is popular for picnics, reading, a quiet stroll, and summertime concerts. The hours are from Monday to Saturday 8am to dark and Sunday 10am to dark. While you're here, be sure to visit the **Iveagh Gardens** ⚐, a small garden hidden behind the National Concert Hall. Largely neglected by visitors, this is something of a hidden treasure within the city center. The main entrance is from Clonmel Street, off Harcourt Street, less than 5 minutes from Stephen's Green. The hours are the same as those for St. Stephen's Green.

The Phoenix Park ⚐ Dublin's 712-hectare (1,760-acre) playground (Europe's largest enclosed urban park) opened in 1747. Situated 3 kilometers (2 miles) west of the city center, it is traversed by a network of roads and quiet pedestrian walkways, and informally landscaped with ornamental gardens, nature trails, and broad expanses of grassland separated by avenues of trees, including oak, beech, pine, chestnut, and lime. The homes of the Irish president (see below) and the U.S. ambassador are on its grounds. Livestock graze peacefully on pasturelands, deer roam the forested areas, and horses romp on polo fields. The new Phoenix Park Visitor Centre, adjacent to Ashtown Castle, has exhibitions and an audiovisual presentation on the history of the Phoenix Park, and houses its own restaurant. Tickets are issued at the Phoenix Park Visitor Centre every Saturday (except December 24 to 26) from 9:40am to 4:20pm for tours of **Áras an Uachtaráin (The Irish White House)**. Admission is free. No advance booking is possible. The entire tour lasts 1 hour. As only 525 tickets are given out, first come first served, every Saturday, it is advisable, especially in the summer months, to arrive before 1:30pm. The **Dublin Zoo** (© **01/677-1425**), also located here in the Phoenix Park, was established in 1830 and is the third-oldest zoo in the world (after London and Paris).

Parkgate St., Dublin 7. © **01/677-0095**. www.heritageireland.ie. Free admission. Daily 24 hours. Visitor Centre: Admission £2 (€2.55, $2.50) adults, £1.50 (€1.90, $1.90) seniors, £1 (€1.30, $1.25) students and children, £5 (€6.35, $6.25) families. June–Sept 10am–6pm (call for off-season hours). Bus: 37, 38, or 39.

National Botanic Gardens Established by the Royal Dublin Society in 1795 on a rolling 18-hectare (50-acre) expanse of land north of the city center, this is Dublin's horticultural showcase. The attractions include more than 20,000 different plants and cultivars, a Great Yew Walk, a bog garden, a water garden, a rose garden, and an herb garden. There are also a variety of Victorian-style glass houses filled with tropical plants and exotic species. Parking is currently £1 (€1.30, $1.25).

Botanic Rd., Glasnevin, Dublin 9. ©01/837-4388. Free admission; parking. Gardens: Summer Mon–Sat 9am–6pm, Sun 11am–6pm; winter Mon–Sat 10am–4:30pm, Sun 11am–4:30pm. Glasshouses: Summer Mon–Wed and Fri–Sat 9am–5:15pm, Thurs 9am–3:15pm, Sun 2–5:45pm; winter Mon–Wed and Fri–Sat 10am–4:15pm, Thurs 10am–3:15pm, Sun 2–4:15pm. Bus: 13, 19, or 134.

ORGANIZED TOURS

BUS TOURS   For the standard see-it-all-in-under-3-hours tour, climb aboard the **Dublin Bus** open-deck sightseeing coach. Tours leave from the Dublin Bus office, 59 Upper O'Connell St. © 01/873-4222), at 10:15am and 2:15pm. You can purchase your ticket at the office or on the bus: £10 (€13, $13) adults, £5 (€6.35, $6) under age 14. This tour takes in most of the important sights but doesn't stop at any.

For more flexible touring, there's the **Dublin City Tour,** a continuous guided bus service connecting 10 major points: museums, art galleries, churches and cathedrals, libraries, and historic sites. For £7 (€8.90, $9) adults, £3.50 (€4.45, $4.40) under age 14, you can ride the bus for a full day, getting off and on as often as you wish; included is a small discount in admission charges. The bus operates daily from 9:30am to 4:30pm.

WALKING TOURS   You can set out on your own with a map, but the best way to avoid any hassles or missed sights is to follow one of the four signposted and themed **"tourist trails":** Old City Trail for historic sights; Georgian Trail for the landmark buildings, streets, squares, terraces, and parks; and Cultural Heritage Trail for a circuit of the top literary sites, museums, galleries, theaters, and churches. Each trail is mapped out in a handy booklet, available for £2.50 (€3.20, $3.15) from Dublin Tourism.

A number of firms offer tours led by knowledgeable local guides. Tour times and charges vary, but most last about 2 hours and cost between £5 and £7 (€6.35, $6.25 and €8.90, $9). Discover Dublin Tours (© 01/478-0193) offers a **Traditional Music Pub Crawl** led by two professional musicians. The **Jameson Dublin Literary Pub Crawl** (© 01/454-0228) departs each evening from the Duke Pub, 9 Duke St.; your guides will recount the stories connecting these pubs with Dublin's literary greats. Information/booking for these and other theme tours can be had at most Dublin Tourism offices. **Historical Walking Tours of Dublin** (© 01/878-0227) depart from the front gate of Trinity College. Many guides are history graduates of Trinity College, and participants are encouraged to ask questions. From May to October **Trinity College Walking Tours** depart every 40 minutes (approximately) from Trinity's front gate.

HORSE-DRAWN CARRIAGE TOURS   If you don't mind being conspicuous, you can tour Dublin in style in a handsomely outfitted horse-drawn carriage while your driver points out the sights. To arrange a ride, consult with one of the drivers stationed with carriages on the Grafton Street side of St. Stephen's Green. Rides range from a short swing around the Green to an extensive half-hour Georgian tour or an hour-long Old City tour. Rides are available on a first-come, first-served basis and cost anywhere from £10 to £35 (€13 to €44, $13 to $44) for two to five passengers, depending on the duration of the ride. They run from April to October, daily and nightly, depending on the weather.

MORE TOURS   This is something new to Dublin's friendly skies: **First Flight Aviation Ltd,** Dublin, Helicopter Centre NSC, Cloghran, County Dublin

(© **01/890-0222;** www.firstflight.ie), now offers 20-minute **helicopter tours** of the center city, with more distant views of Dublin Bay and the north and south coastlines. The cost is £65 (€83, $81) per person, for the standard tour. Also new to the Dublin scene is **Viking Splash Tours** (© **01/855-3000;** www.vikingsplashtours.com), a different way to see the town, especially its Viking-related sights. Aboard a reconditioned World War II amphibious landing craft or "duck," this tour starts on land (from Bull Alley Street beside St. Patrick's Cathedral) and eventually splashes into the Grand Canal. Tours depart roughly every half hour from Monday to Saturday 10am to 5pm and Sunday 10:30am to 5pm and last an hour and 15 minutes. It costs £9.95 (€13, $13) adults and £5.50 (€7, $6.90) children under 12; tickets can be purchased at the Suffolk Street or O'Connell Street office of Dublin Tourism.

SPORTS & OUTDOOR ACTIVITIES

SPECTATOR SPORTS   Ireland's national games, **hurling** and **Gaelic football,** are played every weekend throughout the summer at various local fields, culminating in September with the All-Ireland Finals, an Irish version of the Super Bowl. For schedules and admission charges, contact the **Gaelic Athletic Association,** Croke Park, Jones Road, Dublin 3 (© **01/836-3222**).

GOLF   Leading 18-hole courses in the Dublin area are the **Elm Park Golf Club,** Nutley Lane (© **01/269-3438**); the **Portmarnock Golf Club,** Portmarnock, County Dublin (© **01/846-2968**); and the **Royal Dublin Golf Club,** Bull Island, Dollymount (© **01/833-6346**), a top course that has often been compared to St. Andrews in layout, and has hosted several Irish Open tournaments.

WALKING   The walk from **Bray to Greystones** along the rocky promontory of Bray Head is a great excursion, with beautiful views back toward Killiney Bay, Dalkey Island, and Howth. Bray, the southern terminus of the DART line, is readily accessible from Dublin. In Bray, follow the beachside promenade south through town; at the outskirts of town the promenade turns left and up, beginning the ascent of Bray Head. Shortly after the beginning of this ascent, a trail branches to the left—this is the cliffside walk, which continues another 3½ miles along the coast to Greystones. From the center of Greystones, there's a train that takes you back to Bray. This is an easy walk, about 2 hours one-way.

THE SHOPPING SCENE

In general, Dublin shops are open from Monday to Saturday 9 or 9:30am to 5:30 or 6pm, with late hours Thursday to 8pm. In tourist season, many shops also post Sunday hours. **Grafton Street,** a pedestrians-only zone near Trinity College, is a chic shopping district where trendy boutiques, department stores, and specialty shops proliferate. **Powerscourt Townhouse Centre** and **St. Stephen's Green Centre** are two of this area's focal points and prime examples of Dublin's ongoing renovation and gentrification. In the **Temple Bar area** are unusual shops selling Asian and Latin American imports, secondhand clothes, and hard-to-find records. North of the Liffey, shopping is best on and just off **O'Connell Street** and on **Henry Street.**

BOOKS   This city of literary legends has quite a few fine bookstores. For new books, try **Eason Hanna's,** 27–29 Nassau St., Dublin 2 (© **01/677-1255**); or **Waterstones Bookshop,** 7 Dawson St., Dublin 2 (© **01/679-1415**). For fine used books, including first editions of works by famous Irish authors, try **Cathach Books,** 10 Duke St., Dublin 2 (© **01/671-8676;** fax 01/671-5120;

www.rarebooks.ie.); more affordable used books can be found at **Greene's Bookshop,** 16 Clare St., Dublin 2 (✆ **01/676-2554;** fax 01/678-9091; greenes@iol.ie); or **The Winding Stair,** 40 Lower Ormond Quay, Dublin 1 (✆ **01/873-3292**).

CHINA & CRYSTAL   China Showrooms, 32/33 Abbey St. (✆ **01/878-6211**), is a one-stop source of fine china such as Belleek, Aynsley, Royal Doulton, and hand-cut crystal from Waterford, Tipperary, and Tyrone. The **Dublin Crystal Glass Company,** Brookfield Terrace, Carysfort Avenue, Blackrock (✆ **01/288-7932**), is Dublin's own distinctive hand-cut crystal business, founded in 1764 and revived in 1968. Dublin Crystal is a 15-minute walk from the Blackrock DART station.

CRAFTS & GIFTS   The Powerscourt Townhouse Centre, 59 S. William St. (✆ **01/679-4144**), is a four-story complex with more than 60 boutiques, crafts shops, art galleries, snackeries, wine bars, and restaurants. The wares include all kinds of crafts, antiques, paintings, prints, and hand-dipped chocolates and farmhouse cheeses.

If you're searching for contemporary Irish design, head to **The Kilkenny Shop,** 6–10 Nassau St. (✆ **01/677-7066**), a modern multilevel showplace for original Irish designs and quality products including pottery, glass, candles, woolens, pipes, knitwear, jewelry, books, and prints; and **DESIGNyard,** 12 E. Essex St. (✆ **01/677-8453**), a nonprofit gallery for the finest contemporary Irish and European jewelry, furniture, ceramics, glass, lighting, and textiles. Also, the **House of Ireland,** 37–38 Nassau St. (✆ **01/677-7473**), is a happy blend of European and Irish products, from Waterford and Belleek to Wedgwood and Lladro, as well as tweeds, linens, knitwear, Celtic jewelry, mohair capes, shawls, kilts, blankets, and dolls. For quality ceramics, the creations of **Louis Mulcahey,** a noted Kerry potter, now have a Dublin home at 17 Kildare St. (✆ **01/662-8787**).

FASHIONS   Cleo, 18 Kildare St. (✆ **01/676-1421**), is the shop for the Joyce family's designer ready-to-wear clothing in a rainbow of vibrant tweed colors. **Pat Crowley,** 3 Molesworth Place (✆ **01/661-5580**), is known for her exclusive line of tweeds and couture evening wear. Men shouldn't miss **Kevin and Howlin,** 31 Nassau St. (✆ **01/677-0257**), a shop that has specialized in men's tweed garments for more than 50 years. There's also a selection of sweaters, scarves, vests, and hats. **Louis Copeland,** 39–41 Capel St. (✆ **01/872-1600**), is known for high-quality work in made-to-measure and ready-to-wear men's suits, coats, and shirts. There are also branches at 30 Pembroke St. and 18 Wicklow St.

HERALDRY   Heraldic Artists, 3 Nassau St. (✆ **01/679-7020**), has been known for helping visitors celebrate their family roots for over 20 years. In addition to tracing surnames, it also sells all the usual heraldic items, from parchments and mahogany wall plaques to crests, scrolls, and books on researching ancestry.

KNITWEAR   The Blarney Woolen Mills, 21–23 Nassau St. (✆ **01/671-0068**), known for its competitive prices, stocks a wide range of woolen knitwear made at its home base in Blarney, as well as crystal, china, pottery, and souvenirs. The **Dublin Woolen Mills,** 41 Lower Ormond Quay (✆ **01/677-0301**), is on the north side of the River Liffey next to the Ha'penny Bridge, a leading source of Aran hand-knit sweaters as well as vests, hats, jackets, and tweeds. If you want a cashmere sweater, go to **Monaghan's,** 15–17 Grafton Arcade, Grafton Street

(© **01/677-0823**), which has the best selection of colors, sizes, and styles for both men and women anywhere in Ireland. It's also located at 4–5 Royal Hibernian Way, off Dawson Street (© **01/679-4451**).

MARKETS   For a walk into the past, don't miss the **Moore Street Market,** Moore Street, full of streetside barrow vendors plus plenty of local color and chatter. It's the principal open-air fruit, flower, fish, and vegetable market of the city. Up and running from Monday to Saturday 9am to 6pm—or until supplies run out.

At the **Blackrock Market,** 19a Main St., Blackrock (© **01/283-3522**), more than 60 vendors sell a wide variety of old and new goods at great prices in this indoor/outdoor setting; it's open Saturday 11am to 5:30pm and Sunday noon to 5:30pm.

The **Mother Red Caps Market,** Back Lane, off High Street (© **01/454-4655**), is one of Dublin's best, an enclosed market in the heart of Old Dublin. The stalls offer everything from antiques and used books and coins to silver, handcrafts, music tapes, furniture, and even a fortune-teller! It's worth a trip here just to sample the farm-made cheeses, baked goods, and jams at the Ryefield Foods stall. Open Friday to Sunday, 10am to 5:30pm.

DUBLIN AFTER DARK

The best way to find out what's going on is to consult *In Dublin,* the leading magazine for upcoming events and happenings. The *Event Guide* (www. eventguide.ie) also contains a useful and up-to-date listing of events throughout Ireland, with a focus on Dublin.

THE PERFORMING ARTS
Concert & Performance Halls

National Concert Hall, Earlsfort Terrace, Dublin 2 (© **01/475-1572;** www.nch.ie), Dublin's main venue for classical music, was originally part of University College, Dublin. The hall stays busy with performances several nights a week for much of the year and is home to the National Symphony Orchestra. The box office is open Monday through Saturday 11am to 7pm. Tickets are £6 to £32 (€7.60 to €41, $8 to $40). Lunchtime concerts are £4 (€5.10, $5).

For more than 90 years, the **Abbey Theatre**, Lower Abbey St., Dublin 1 (© **01/878-7222;** www.abbeytheatre.ie), has been the national theater of Ireland. The original theater, destroyed by fire in 1951, was replaced in 1966. The Abbey's artistic reputation within Ireland has risen and fallen many times and is at present reasonably strong. The box office is open from Monday to Saturday 10:30am to 7pm; performances begin at 8 or 8:15pm. Tickets are £8 to £17.50 (€10 to €22, $10 to $22).

The Gate, 1 Cavendish Row, Dublin 1 (© **01/874-4368;** fax 01/874-5373), just north of O'Connell Street off Parnell Square, was founded in 1928 by Hilton Edwards and Michael MacLiammoir to provide a showing for a broad range of plays. This policy prevails today, with a program that includes a blend of modern works and the classics. Although less well known by visitors, the Gate is easily as distinguished as the Abbey. The box office is open from Monday to Saturday 10am to 7pm. Tickets are £13 to £15 (€17 to €19, $16 to $19). With its Victorian jewel-box facade and garish red lobby, the **Olympia Theatre,** 72 Dame St., Dublin 2 (© **01/677-7744**), looks as though it should be home to high-stepping cancan girls. However, it's one of Dublin's busier old theaters, hosting everything from contemporary Irish plays to rock concerts. The box office is open from Monday to Saturday 10:30am to 6:30pm. Tickets are £10 to £20 (€13 to €25, $13 to $25).

The relatively new **Andrews Lane Theatre,** 12–16 Andrews Lane, Dublin 2 (✆ **01/679-5720**), has an ascending reputation for fine theater. It consists of a main theater where contemporary works from home and abroad are presented, and a studio geared for experimental productions. The box office is open from Monday to Saturday 10:30am to 7pm. Tickets are £8 to £15 (€10 to €19, $10 to $19). With a seating capacity of 3,000, **The Point,** East Link Bridge, North Wall Quay (✆ **01/836-3633**), is Ireland's newest large theater/concert venue, attracting top Broadway-caliber shows and international stars. The box office is open from Monday to Saturday 10am to 6pm. Tickets are £20 to £50 (€25 to €64, $25 to $63).

The **City Arts Centre,** 23–25 Moss St., at City Quay (✆ **01/677-0643**), is an affiliate of Trans Europe Halles, the European network of independent arts centers. It presents a varied program, from dramatic productions, theatrical discussions, and readings by local writers to shows by touring companies from abroad. Tickets are £5 to £8 (€6.35 to €10, $6.25 to $10).

DINNER & A SONG

There are several venues in Dublin where you can have dinner and listen to traditional music. At the **Abbey Tavern,** Abbey Road, Howth, County Dublin (✆ **01/839 0307**), dinner is accompanied by authentic Irish ballad music, with its blend of fiddles, pipes, tin whistles, and spoons. The cover is usually £4 (€5.10, $5). Traditional music is performed daily from March to October; from November to February it's best to call ahead to find out on which nights music will be offered.

THE PUB SCENE
Pubs for Conversation & Atmosphere

The brass-filled and lantern-lit **Brazen Head,** 20 Lower Bridge St. (✆ **01/679-5186**), claims to be the city's oldest—and with good reason, considering that it was licensed in 1661 and occupies the site of an earlier tavern dating from 1198. On the south bank of the River Liffey, it's at the end of a cobblestoned courtyard and was once the meeting place of Irish freedom fighters, such as Robert Emmet and Wolfe Tone.

The recently rejuvenated **Castle Inn,** Christchurch Place, Dublin 8 (✆ **01/475-1122**), situated between Dublin Castle and Christ Church Cathedral, exudes an "old city" atmosphere, with stone walls, flagstone steps, knightly suits of armor, big stone fireplaces, beamed ceilings, and lots of early Dublin memorabilia. It is also the setting for an Irish Ceili and Banquet (May to September) featuring Irish traditional musicians and set dancers. Referred to as a "moral pub" by James Joyce in *Ulysses,* **Davy Byrnes,** 21 Duke St., just off Grafton St. (✆ **01/677-5217**), has drawn poets, writers, and lovers of literature ever since. Davy Byrnes first opened the doors in 1873; he presided here for more than 50 years and visitors today can still see his likeness on one of the turn-of-the-twentieth-century murals hanging over the bar.

Flannery's Temple Bar, 47–48 Temple Bar (✆ **01/497-4766**), in the heart of the trendy Temple Bar district on the corner of Temple Lane, was established in 1840. The decor is an interesting mix of crackling fireplaces, globe ceiling lights, old pictures on the walls, and shelves filled with local memorabilia. Tucked into a busy commercial street, **The Long Hall,** 51 S. Great George's St. (✆ **01/475-1590**), is one of the city's most photographed pubs, with a beautiful

Victorian decor of filigree-edged mirrors, polished dark woods, and traditional snugs. The hand-carved bar is said to be the longest counter in the city.

Adjacent to the back door of the Gaiety Theatre, **Neary's,** 1 Chatham St., Dublin 2 (ⓒ 01/677-7371), is a favorite with stage folk and theater-goers. Trademarks here are the pink-and-gray marble bar and the brass hands that support the globe lanterns adorning the entrance. Three generations of the Ryan family have contributed to the success of **W. Ryan,** 28 Parkgate St. (ⓒ 01/677-6097), located on the north side of the Liffey near Phoenix Park. The pub has such fine features as a metal ceiling and domed skylight, beveled mirrors, etched glass, brass lamp holders, a mahogany bar, and four old-style snugs.

Pubs with Traditional/Folk Music
For fans of traditional Irish music, **O'Donoghue's,** 15 Merrion Row, Dublin 2 (ⓒ 01/660-7194), is a must. The Dubliners, one of Ireland's favorite traditional bands, got their start here, and impromptu music sessions are held almost every night. Situated in the heart of Temple Bar and named for one of Ireland's liter-ary greats, **Oliver St. John Gogarty,** 57–58 Fleet St. (ⓒ 01/671-1822), has an inviting old-world atmosphere, with shelves of empty bottles, stacks of dusty books, a horseshoe-shaped bar, and old barrels for seats. There are traditional music sessions every night from 9 to 11pm. A Saturday session is at 4:30pm, and a Sunday session from noon to 2pm.

THE CLUB & MUSIC SCENE
The club and music scene in Dublin is confoundingly complex and changeable. Jazz, blues, folk, country, traditional, rock, and comedy move from venue to venue, night by night. The same club could be a gay fetish scene one night and a traditional music hotspot the next, so you have to stay on your toes to find what you want. The first rule is to get the very latest listings and see what's on and where.

CHAPTER 10 · IRELAND

Dozens of clubs and pubs all over town feature rock, folk, jazz, and traditional Irish music. This includes the so-called "late-night pubs"—pubs with an exemption allowing them to remain open past the usual closing time, mandated by law (11pm in winter, 11:30pm in summer). Check *In Dublin* magazine or the *Event Guide* for club schedules. One of the most popular rock clubs is **Whelan's,** 25 Wexford St., Dublin 2 (✆ **01/478-0766**); you should also visit the new **Hot Press Irish Music Hall of Fame,** 57 Middle Abbey Street, Dublin 1 (✆ **01/ 878-3345**), with music from Celtic to rock most nights; and the second-oldest pub in Dublin, **Bleeding Horse,** 24–25 Camden St., Dublin 2 (✆ **01/475-2705**). Other venues especially popular with the over-30 late crowd include: **Break for the Border,** Lower Steven's Street, Dublin 2 (✆ **01/478-0300**); **Bad Bob's Backstage Bar,** East Essex Street, Dublin 2 (✆ **01/677-5482**); **Major Tom's,** South King Street, Dublin 2 (✆ **01/478-3266**); the **Baggot Inn,** Baggot Street, Dublin 4 (✆ **01/676-1430**); and **Sinnotts,** South King Street, Dublin 2 (✆ **01/478-4698**). All are open daily, with live music most nights. Where there is a cover charge, it's usually £3 to £7 (€3.80 to €8.90, $3.75 to $9). The center of Irish social life, the pub is the place where Dubliners gather for conversation, music, and foaming pints of local brews. Day and night, the pub is for Dubliners an extension of the household, both dining room and parlor. Though pub meals are rarely exciting, they're always filling and offer budgeters an inexpensive alternative to the city's restaurants.

GAY & LESBIAN BARS

A great pub to check out is **The George,** 89 S. Great George's St., Dublin 2 (✆ **01/478-2983**). Upstairs at The George is a club called **The Block** (✆ **01/ 478-2983**), open from Wednesday to Saturday 11pm to 2am; it's a comfortable mixed-age venue with something for everyone. **Stonewallz,** Molloy's Bar, High St., Christchurch, Dublin 8, is a women-only club night on Saturdays 8:30pm to 2am; the cover is £4 (€5.10, $5) before 10pm, £6 (€7.60, $7.50) thereafter. **Out on the Liffey,** 27 Upper Ormond Quay, Dublin 1 (✆ **01/872-2480**), is a relaxed, friendly pub catering to a balance of men and women that serves up pub food with good conversation. In 1998, "Out" expanded to include a new and happening late-night venue called Oscar's, where you can dance (or drink) until you drop. The cover charge at all the above venues is £3 to £6 (€3.80 to €7.60, $3.75 to $8).

DANCE CLUBS

Here are the most established cutting-edge clubs (with correspondingly strict door policies): **The Kitchen,** in the Clarence Hotel, 6–8 Wellington Quay, Dublin 2 (✆ **01/677-6178**), open from Wednesday to Sunday 11pm to 2am; **POD** ("Place of Dance"), Harcourt Street, Dublin 2 (✆ **01/478-0166**), open from Wednesday to Saturday 11pm to 2am or later; and **Lillie's Bordello,** 45 Nassau St., Dublin 2 (✆ **01/679-9204**), open daily from 10pm to 1am or later.

There are also a few kinder, gentler clubs with less strict door policies and a mixed-age crowd: **Club M,** in Blooms Hotel, Anglesea Street, Dublin 2 (✆ **01/671-5622**), open from Tuesday to Sunday 11pm to 2am; **Ri-Ra,** 1 Exchequer St., Dublin 2 (✆ **01/677-4835**), open daily from 11:30pm until 4am or later; and **Annabel's,** in the Burlington Hotel, Leeson Street Upper, Dublin 4 (✆ **01/660-5222**), open from Tuesday to Saturday 10pm to 2am. Admission charges for these clubs range from £4 to £12 (€5.10 to €15, $5 to $15).

SIDE TRIPS FROM DUBLIN

Malahide Castle ✦ About 13 kilometers (8 miles) north of Dublin, Malahide is one of Ireland's most historic castles, founded in the 12th century by Richard Talbot and occupied by his descendants until 1973. The fully restored interior of the building is the setting for a comprehensive collection of Irish furniture dating from the 17th through the 19th centuries, and the walls are lined with one-of-a-kind Irish historical portraits and tableaux on loan from the National Gallery. The furnishings and art reflect life in and near the house over the past 8 centuries.

After touring the house, you can explore the 100-hectare (250-acre) estate, which includes prized gardens with more than 5,000 species of plants and flowers. The Malahide grounds also contain the Fry Model Railway Museum, an exhibit of rare handmade models of more than 300 Irish trains, from the introduction of rail to the present.

Malahide, County Dublin. ℭ **01/846-2184.** Admission to castle £3.15 (€4, $3.95) adults, £2.65 (€3.40, $3.30) students and seniors, £1.75 (€2.25, $2.20) children under 12, £8.75 (€11, $11) family. AE, DC, MC, V. Combination tickets available with Fry Model Railway and Newbridge House. Apr–Oct Mon–Sat 10am–5pm, Sun 11am–6pm; Nov–Mar Mon–Fri 10am–5pm, Sat–Sun 2–5pm; gardens May–Sept daily 2–5pm. Closed for tours 12:45–2pm (restaurant remains open). Bus: 42.

Newgrange ✦✦✦ Newgrange is Ireland's best-known prehistoric monument and one of the archaeological wonders of Western Europe. Built as a burial mound more than 5,000 years ago—long before the Great Pyramids and Stonehenge—it sits atop a hill near the Boyne, massive and impressive. The huge mound—11 meters (36 ft.) tall and approximately 80 meters (260 ft.) in diameter—consists of 200,000 tons of stone, a 6-ton capstone, and other stones weighing up to 16 tons each, many of which were hauled from as far away as County Wicklow and the Mountains of Mourne. Each stone fits perfectly in the overall pattern and the result is a watertight structure, an amazing feat of engineering. Carved into the stones are myriad spirals, diamonds, and concentric circles. Inside, a passage 18 meters (60 ft.) long leads to a central burial chamber with a 6-meter (19-ft.) ceiling.

Fascination with Newgrange reaches a peak each winter solstice, when at 8:58am, as the sun rises to the southeast, sunlight pierces the inner chamber with an orange-toned glow for about 17 minutes. This occurrence is so remarkable that, as of this writing, the waiting list for viewing extends through the year 2004. Admission to Newgrange is by guided tour only. It's located 3 kilometers (2 miles) east of Slane, off N51.

All tickets are issued at the new visitor center. Combined tickets with Knowth, another nearby megalithic passage tomb, are available at the center. Because of the great numbers of visitors to Newgrange, especially in the summer, delays are to be expected and access is not guaranteed.

Off N51, Slane, County Meath. ℭ **041/988-0300.** Admission to Newgrange and Brugh na Boinne Centre £4 (€5.10, $5) adults, £3 (€3.80, $3.75) seniors, £2 (€2.55, $2.50) students and children over 6, £10 (€13, $13) family. No credit cards accepted. Open daily Nov–Feb 9:30am–5pm; Mar–Apr 9:30am–5:30pm; May 9am–6:30pm; June to mid-Sept 9am–7pm; mid- to end Sept 9am–6:30pm; Oct 9:30am–5:30pm.

Knowth ✦✦✦ Dating from the Stone Age and under seemingly perpetual excavation, this great mound is believed to have been a burial site for the high kings of Ireland. Archaeological evidence points to occupation from 3000 B.C. to A.D. 1200. Located 1.5 kilometer (1 mile) northwest of Newgrange (see listing above), between Drogheda and Slane, Knowth is more complex than

Newgrange, with two passage tombs surrounded by another 17 smaller satellite tombs. The site has the greatest collection of passage tomb art ever uncovered in Western Europe. All tickets are issued at the new visitor center. Combined tickets with Newgrange are available at the center.

Off N51, Slane, County Meath. ℂ 041/988-0300. Admission to Knowth and Brugh na Boinne Centre £3 (€3.80, $3.75) adults, £2 (€2.55, $2.50) seniors, £1.25 (€1.60, $1.60) students and children over 6, £7.50 (€9.55, $9) family. No credit cards accepted. Open daily Nov–Feb 9:30am–5pm; Mar–Apr 9:30am–5:30pm; May 9am–6:30pm; June to mid-Sept 9am–7pm; mid- to end Sept 9am–6:30pm; Oct 9:30am–5:30pm.

2 Kerry & the Dingle Peninsula

Kerry is a place of disorienting contrasts, where the tackiest tourist attractions coexist with some of Ireland's most spectacular scenic wonders. It's a rugged place for the most part, some of it so rugged that it's seldom visited and remains quite pristine; Ireland's two highest mountains, Carrantuohill and Mount Brandon, are two examples. You could be driving along—say, on the famous and popular Ring of Kerry, which traces the shores of the Iveragh Peninsula—make one little detour from the main road, and be in wild and unfrequented territory. The transition can be startling.

Thanks to its remoteness, County Kerry has always been an outpost of Gaelic culture. Poetry and music are intrinsic to Kerry lifestyle, as is a love of the outdoors and sports. Gaelic football is an obsession in this county, and Kerry wins most of the national championships. You'll also find some of Ireland's best golf courses here, and the fishing for salmon and trout is equally hard to resist.

GETTING TO COUNTY KERRY   By Plane   Aer Arann (ℂ **890/462726** within Ireland, or ℂ **01/814-1058**) offers daily direct flights from Dublin into **Kerry County Airport,** Farranfore, County Kerry (ℂ **066/64644**), about 16 kilometers (10 miles) north of Killarney and 24 kilometers (15 miles) south of Tralee. Travel time is 1 hour.

By Car   Roads leading into Kerry include N-21 and N-23 from Limerick, N-22 from Cork, N-72 from Mallow, and N-70 from West Cork.

KILLARNEY TOWN

Killarney is a relatively small town with a population of around 7,000 people. The town is very walkable, although the streets are usually crowded with tourists, especially in summer. The busiest section of town is at the southern tip of Main Street, where it meets East Avenue Road. Here the road curves and heads southward out to Muckross Road and the entrance to Killarney National Park.

It's important to remember that the reason Killarney draws millions of visitors a year has nothing to do with Killarney town. Rather, it's all about the lakes and mountains of quite enchanting beauty just beyond the town's reach; and it's ever so easy to enter these wonders. Just walk from the town car park towards the cathedral and turn left into the National Park. In a matter of minutes you'll see for yourself why there's all the fuss. During the summer, the evenings are long, the light is often indescribable, and you needn't share the lanes with jaunting cars. Apart from deer and locals, the park is all yours till dark.

ESSENTIALS
GETTING THERE   By Train   Irish Rail offers daily service from most major Irish cities, arriving at **Killarney Railway Station,** Railway Road, off East Avenue Road (ℂ **064/31067**).

County Kerry

Blennerville Windmill **3**	Gap of Dunloe **13**	Kerry the Kingdom **1**
Crag Cave **14**	Ionad An Bhlascaoid	Skellig Experience **8**
Derrynane House	(The Blasket Centre) **5**	Skellig Islands **9**
National Historic Park **11**	Kenmare Heritage Town	Staigue Fort **10**
Dingle Oceanworld **6**	Exhibition Centre **12**	Tralee Steam Railway **2**
Gallarus Oratory **4**	Kerry Bog Village Museum **7**	

By Bus **Bus Eireann** operates regularly scheduled bus service from all parts of Ireland. The **bus station** is adjacent to the train station at Railway Road, off East Avenue Road, Killarney (✆ **064/34777**).

VISITOR INFORMATION The **Killarney Tourist Office,** Aras Fáilte, is located at the Town Centre Car Park, Beech Road, Killarney (✆ **064/31633**). It's open from January to April, Monday to Saturday 9:15am to 1pm and 2:15 to 5:30pm; May, Monday to Saturday 9:15am to 5:30pm; June, Monday to Saturday 9am to 6pm, Sunday 10am to 1pm and 2:15 to 6pm; July to August, Monday to Saturday 9am to 8pm, Sunday 10am to 1pm and 2:15 to 6pm; September, Monday to Saturday 9am to 6pm, Sunday 10am to 1pm and 2:15 to 6pm; October to December, Monday to Saturday 9:15am to 1pm and 2:15 to 5:30pm. It offers many helpful booklets, including the Tourist Trail walking-tour guide and the Killarney Area Guide with maps.

Useful local publications include *Where: Killarney,* a quarterly magazine distributed free at hotels and guesthouses. It's packed with all types of current information on tours, activities, events, and entertainment.

GETTING AROUND The town is so small and compact that it's best traversed on foot. **Taxis** line up at the rank on College Square (✆ **064/31331**). You can also phone for a taxi from **John Burke** (✆ **064/32448**), or **Dero's Taxi Service** (✆ **064/31251**).

You can drive to Killarney National Park, or go by **jaunting car.** The horse-drawn jaunting cars line up at Kenmare Place, offering rides to Killarney National Park sites and other scenic areas.

KILLARNEY NATIONAL PARK 🏵🏵

This is Killarney's centerpiece: a 10,000-hectare (25,000-acre) area of natural beauty. You'll find three storied lakes—the Lower Lake (or Lough Leane), the Middle Lake (or Muckross Lake), and the Upper Lake—myriad waterfalls, rivers, islands, valleys, mountains, bogs, and woodlands, and lush foliage and trees, including oak, arbutus, holly, and mountain ash. There's also a large variety of wildlife, including a rare herd of red deer. No automobiles are allowed within the park, so touring is best done on foot, bicycle, or horse-drawn jaunting car. The park offers four signposted walking and nature trails along the lakeshore.

Access is available from several points along the Kenmare road (N71), with the main entrance being at Muckross House, where there is a new visitor center featuring background exhibits on the park and a 20-minute film titled *Mountain, Wood, Water.* Admission is free, and the park is open year-round during daylight hours.

VIEWS & VISTAS The journey through the **Gap of Dunloe** 🏵 is a must. The winding and rocky Gap of Dunloe is situated amid mountains and lakelands about 10 kilometers (6 miles) west of Killarney. The route through the gap passes a kaleidoscope of craggy rocks, massive cliffs, meandering streams, and deep valleys. The road through the gap ends at Upper Lake. One of the best ways to explore the gap is by bicycle. Horse fanciers may want to take one of the horseback excursions offered by **Castlelough Tours,** 7 High St. (☎ 064/ 31115); **Corcoran's Tours,** Kilcummin (☎ 064/36666; www.kerry-insight. com/corcorans); and **Dero's Tours,** 22 Main St. (☎ 064/31251).

Aghadoe Heights, on Tralee Road (off N-22) is a spectacular viewing point over the lakes and town. To your left is the ruin of the 13th-century Castle of Parkvonear, erected by Norman invaders and well worth a visit. In the nearby churchyard are the remains of a stone church and round tower dating from 1027.

MORE ATTRACTIONS

Muckross House and Gardens 🏵 The Muckross Estate is the focal point of the Middle Lake. The gracious ivy-covered, Elizabethan-style residence with its colorful and well-tended gardens was built by Henry Arthur Herbert in 1843 and visited by Queen Victoria in 1861. The house is now a folk museum, and the cellars have been converted into crafts shops where local artisans demonstrate the traditional trades of bookbinding, weaving, and pottery making. The adjacent gardens are known for their fine collection of rhododendrons and azaleas.

Just across from Muckross House is an attraction you might overlook but which is really quite fascinating, especially for families with children. **Muckross Traditional Farms,** a 28-hectare (70-acre) park, is home to displays of traditional farm life and artisans' shops. The farmhouses and buildings are so authentically detailed that visitors feel they are dropping in on working farms and lived-in houses. The animals and household environments are equally fascinating for children and adults. Combined tickets are available with Muckross House.

Kenmare Rd. (N-71), Killarney. ☎ **064/31440.** www.muckross-house.ie. Admission to house £4 (€5.10, $5) adults, £3 (€3.80, $3.75) seniors, £1.60 (€2.05, $2) students and children, £10 (€13, $13) family. Daily mid-Mar to June and Sept–Oct 9am–6pm; July–Aug 9am–7pm; Nov to mid-Mar 9am–5:30pm. The gardens are open year-round without admission fee.

Ross Castle   Newly restored, this 15th-century fortress sits on the edge of the Lower Lake, 3 kilometers (2 miles) outside Killarney Town. Built by the O'Donoghue chieftains, this castle distinguished itself in 1652 as the last stronghold in Munster to surrender to Cromwell's forces. All that remains today is a tower house, surrounded by a fortified bawn with rounded turrets. The tower has been furnished in the style of the late 16th and early 17th centuries and offers a magnificent view of the lakes and islands from its top. Access is by guided tour only. A lovely lakeshore walk stretches for 1.5 kilometers (2 miles) between Killarney and the castle.

Ross Rd., off Kenmare road (N71), Killarney. (℗ 064/35851. www.heritageireland.ie. Admission £3 (€3.80, $3.75) adults, £2 (€2.55, $2.50) seniors, £1.25 (€1.60, $1.60) students and children, and £7.50 (€9.50, $9) family. Apr daily 10am–5pm; May and Sept daily 10am–6pm; June–Aug daily 9am–6:30pm; Oct Tues–Sun 10am–5pm.

SIGHTSEEING TOURS
BUS TOURS   Dero's Tours, 7 Main St., Killarney (℗ **064/31251** or 064/31567; www.derostours.com), offers "Killarney Highlights." Besides showing off Killarney's lakes from the best vantage points, the 3-hour tour takes you to Aghadoe, the Gap of Dunloe, Ross Castle, Muckross House and Gardens, and Torc Waterfall. The tour is offered May to September daily at 10:30am, but schedules vary, so check in advance. It costs £9 (€11.40, $11). Frommer's readers who book directly with the Deros office may receive a 5% discount.

   Castlelough Tours, 7 High St., Killarney (℗ **064/31115**), offers "Gap of Dunloe" through the spectacularly scenic Gap of Dunloe and includes a boat tour of the Killarney lakes for £17 (€22, $21). It's offered from May to September; call for current hours and bookings.

   In addition to Killarney's main sights, some bus tours also venture into the two prime scenic areas nearby: the Ring of Kerry and Dingle Peninsula. In the May-to-September period, tours are offered daily; prices average £17 (€22, $21) per person. Check the following companies if that's the kind of tour for you: **Bus Eireann,** Bus Depot, Railway Road, off East Avenue Road (℗ **064/34777**); **Castlelough Tours,** 7 High St. (℗ **064/31115**); **Corcoran's Tours,** 10 College St. (℗ **064/36666**); and **Dero's Tours,** 22 Main St. (℗ **064/31251** or 064/31567).

JAUNTING-CAR TOURS   If you enjoy walking or bicycling, just say no to the numerous drivers who will inevitably offer their services as you make your way around the Killarney lakes. These quaint horse-driven buggies are one of the main features of the landscape here, and if at some point you decide to give them a try, keep in mind that jaunting-car rates are set and carefully monitored by the Killarney Urban District Council. Current rates, all based on four persons to a jaunting car, run roughly from £5 to £12 (€6.35 to €15, $6 to $15) per person round-trip, depending on destinations which include Ross Castle, Muckross House and Gardens, Torc Waterfall, Muckross Abbey, Dinis Island, and Kate Kearney's Cottage, gateway to the Gap of Dunloe. To arrange a tour in advance, contact **Tangney Tours,** Kinvara House, Muckross Road, Killarney (℗ **064/33358**).

BOAT TOURS   There is nothing quite like seeing the sights from a boat on the Lakes of Killarney. Two companies operate regular boating excursions, with full commentary. **M.V. Pride of the Lakes Tours,** Scotts Gardens, Killarney (℗ **064/32638**), sails daily in an enclosed boat from the pier at Ross Castle from April to October at 11am, 12:30pm, 2:30pm, 4pm, and 5:15pm. The trip lasts just over an hour, and reservations are suggested. Cost is £6 (€7.60, $8) adults, £3.50 (€4.45, $4.40) students, £3 (€3.80, $3.75) children. **M.V. Lily of Killarney Tours,** 3 High St., Killarney (© **064/31068**), sails from April to October at 10:30am, noon, 1:45pm, 3:15pm, and 4:30pm for £6 (€7.60, $8) adults.

ENJOYING THE GREAT OUTDOORS

BICYCLING   The **Killarney National Park** is a paradise for bikers. Various types of bikes, from 21-speed touring bikes and mountain bikes to tandems, are available. Rental charges average £7 (€8.90, $8.75) per day or £35 (€45, $44) per week. Try one of the following shops: **Killarney Rent-a-Bike,** High Street (© **064/32578**); **O'Neills Cycle Shop,** 6 Plunkett St., Killarney (© **064/ 31970**); and D. O'Sullivan's **The Bike Shop,** High Street, Killarney (© **064/ 31282**). Most shops are open year-round from 9am to 6pm daily, with extended hours until 7 or 8pm in the summer months.

One great ride beginning in Killarney takes you through the Gap of Dunloe along a dirt forest road, where you'll see some of the best mountain scenery in the area; it can be made into a 56-kilometer (35-mile) loop if you return on N71.

FISHING   Fishing for salmon and brown trout in Killarney's unpolluted lakes and rivers is a big attraction. Brown trout fishing is free on the lakes, but a permit is necessary for the rivers Flesk and Laune. A trout permit costs £3 to £10 (€3.80 to €13, $3.75 to $13) per day.

Salmon fishing anywhere in Ireland requires a license; the cost is £3 (€3.80, $3.75) per day or £10 (€13, $13) for 21 days. In addition, some rivers also require a salmon permit, which costs £8 to £10 (€10 to €13, $10 to $13) per day. Permits and licenses can be obtained at the Fishery Office at the **Knockreer Estate Office,** New Street, Killarney (© **064/31246**).

For fishing tackle, bait, rod rental, and other fishing gear, as well as permits and licenses, try **O'Neill's,** 6 Plunkett St., Killarney (© **064/31970**). This shop also arranges the hire of boats and ghillies (fishing guides) on the Killarney Lakes, leaving from Ross Castle.

GOLF   Visitors are always welcome at the twin 18-hole championship courses of the **Killarney Golf & Fishing Club,** Killorglin Road, Fossa, Killarney (© **064/31034**), located 5 kilometers (3 miles) west of the town center. Widely praised as one of the most scenic golf settings in the world, these courses, known as "Killeen" and "Mahony's Point," are surrounded by lake and mountain vistas. Greens fees are £50 (€64, $63) on either course.

HORSEBACK RIDING   Many trails in the Killarney area are suitable for horseback riding. The cost of hiring a horse ranges from £10 to £15 (€13 to €19, $13 to $19) per hour at the following establishments: **Killarney Riding Stables,** R562, Ballydowney, Killarney (© **064/31686**); **O'Donovan's Farm,** Mangerton Road, Muckross, Killarney (© **064/32238**); and **Rocklands Stables,** Rockfield, Tralee Road, Killarney (© **064/32592**). Lessons and week-long trail rides can also be arranged.

WALKING   Killarney is ideal for walking enthusiasts. On the outskirts of town, the **Killarney National Park** offers four signposted nature trails. Leaflets with maps of these four trails are available at the park's visitor center. For long-distance walkers, there is the 200-kilometer (125-mile) "Kerry Way," a signposted walking route that extends from Killarney around the Ring of Kerry.

THE SHOPPING SCENE: KERRY GLASS & MORE

Shopping hours are normally from Monday to Saturday 9am to 6pm, but May to September most shops stay open to 9 or 10pm. Although there are more souvenir and crafts shops in Killarney than you can shake a stick (or shillelagh) at, here are a few of the best.

Christys Irish Stores, 10 Main St. (© **064/33222;** www.shamrockshop.com), until recently known as Blarney Woolen Mills, has everything from hand-knit or hand-loomed Irish-made sweaters to tweeds, crystal, china, pottery, and souvenirs. **Quill's Woolen Market,** 1 High St. (© **064/32277**), is one of the best shops in town for hand-knit sweaters of all kinds, as well as tweeds, mohair, and sheepskins.

The **Frank Lewis Gallery,** 6 Bridewell Lane (© **064/31108**), shows and sells a wide variety of contemporary and traditional paintings, sculptures, and photographs by some of Ireland's most acclaimed emerging artists.

WHERE TO STAY
Expensive
Killarney Park Hotel ♠   With a striking yellow neo-Georgian facade, this new four-story property is located on its own grounds on the eastern edge of town. Public areas are posh and spacious, with open fireplaces and a sunlit conservatory-style lounge overlooking the gardens. Among the hotel's recent plaudits are the 1997/98 AA "Irish Hotel of the Year" award as well as several RAC dining awards for 1999/2000.

Kenmare Place, Killarney, County Kerry. © 064/35555. Fax 064/35266. www.killarneyparkhotel.ie. 75 units. £250 (€318, $313) double; f350–£500 (€445–635, $438–$625) suite. No service charge. Rates include full breakfast. AE, DC, MC, V. Closed Dec 24–31. **Amenities:** Restaurant; bar; indoor heated pool; health club; Jacuzzi; sauna; library; all rooms no-smoking. *In room:* A/C, TV, tea/coffeemaker, hair dryer, trouser press.

Moderate
Castlerosse   Set on its own parklands between the Lower Lake and surrounding mountains, this modern, rambling, ranch-style inn is 3 kilometers (2 miles) from the heart of town and next to Killarney's two golf courses; the hotel also has its own 9-hole course. The recently refurbished rooms offer views of the lake. Rooms specially fitted for guests with disabilities are available on request. New self-catering minisuites, sleeping up to five persons, are also available.

Killorglin Rd., Killarney, County Kerry. © 800/528-1234 from the U.S., or 064/31114. Fax 064/31031. castler@iol.ie. 121 units. £124 (€158, $155) double. Rates include full Irish breakfast. No service charge. AE, DC, MC, V. Closed Dec–Feb. **Amenities:** Golf course (9 holes with putting green); tennis courts; health club; walking paths and jogging trails. *In room:* TV.

Earls Court Guesthouse   Earls Court is among Killarney's newest and most attractive quality guesthouses. The spacious and immaculately clean rooms are furnished with exceptional style and taste. Some have sitting areas, and nearly all have balconies. The second-floor rooms, in particular, have clear views of the mountains. All rooms have firm beds. In 1998 Earls Court won the "RAC Small Hotel of the Year" award for Ireland, and in 2000 the "RAC Little Gem" award.

Woodlawn Junction, Muckross Rd., Killarney, County Kerry. © 064/34009. Fax 064/34366. www.killarney-earlscourt.ie. 11 units (1 single with shower only). £60–£96 (€76–€122, $75–$120) double. Rates include full Irish breakfast and service charge. MC, V. Closed Nov 6 to Feb. Follow the sign off N-71; it's a 5-minute walk from Killarney center. **Amenities:** Room service; laundry; all rooms no-smoking. *In room:* TV, hair dryer.

Kathleen's Country House ♠   Of the many guesthouses in this area, this one stands out. Located about a mile north of town on its own 1.5 hectares (3 acres) of gardens next to a dairy farm, it is a two-story contemporary house with a modern mansard-style roof and many picture windows. Enthusiastic and efficient hostess Kathleen O'Regan-Sheppard quite recently refurbished all the rooms in antique pine furniture and orthopedic beds, complemented by Kathleen's collection of contemporary pastels and paintings. A cozy new library/drawing room has been added. Smoking is permitted only in the enclosed front foyer of the house.

Madam's Height, Tralee road (N22), Killarney, County Kerry. ℂ **064/32810**. Fax 064/32340. www. kathleens.net. 17 units. £95 (€121, $119) double. No service charge. Rates include full breakfast. AE, MC, V. Closed mid-Nov to early Mar. **Amenities:** All rooms no-smoking. *In room:* TV, tea/coffeemaker, hair dryer, trouser press.

Inexpensive
Gleann Fia Country House 𝒢   Although only a mile from town, this modern guesthouse feels pleasantly secluded, tucked away as it is in 10 hectares (26 acres) of lawns and woodlands. Amenities include an airy conservatory with tea-making facilities, a guest lounge, a drying room for golfers, and an unusually extensive breakfast menu. There is a nature walk along the stream that runs by one side of the house. Bicycles can be rented on the premises. The rooms in the most recent addition are slightly larger and more elegantly furnished than those in the main house, and are correspondingly pricier. There's also a spacious family room on the ground floor of the main house with a double bed, single bed, and couch.

Deerpark, Killarney, County Kerry. ℂ **064/35035**. Fax 064/35000. gleanfia@iol.ie. 17 units. £50–£70 (€64–€89, $63–$88) double. No service charge. Rates include full breakfast. AE, MC, V. Closed Dec–Feb. **Amenities:** All rooms no-smoking. *In room:* TV.

WHERE TO DINE
Expensive
Gaby's Seafood Restaurant 𝒢 SEAFOOD   One of Killarney's longest established restaurants, this nautically themed place is a mecca for lovers of fresh seafood. It's known for its succulent lobster, served grilled or in a house sauce of cognac, wine, cream, and spices. Other choices include turbot, haddock in wine, local salmon, and a giant Kerry shellfish platter, a veritable feast of prawns, scallops, mussels, lobster, and oysters.

27 High St., Killarney. ℂ **064/32519**. Reservations recommended. Main courses £14–£29 (€18–€37, $18–$36). AE, DC, MC, V. Mon–Sat 6–10pm. Closed mid-Feb to mid-Mar.

Moderate
Bricín 𝒢 IRISH   Traditional Kerry *boxty* dishes (potato pancakes with various fillings, such as chicken, seafood, curried lamb, or vegetables) are the trademark of this upstairs restaurant. The menu also offers a variety of fresh seafood, pastas, Irish stew, and specials. Housed in one of Killarney's oldest buildings, Bricín sports original stone walls, turf fireplaces, and, something very rare in Ireland—a completely no-smoking room seating 40.

26 High St., Killarney. ℂ **064/34902**. Reservations recommended for dinner. Main courses £8.50–£15 (€11–€19, $11–$19); snacks £2–£5 (€2.55–€6.35, $2.50–$6.25). AE, DC, MC, V. Year-round Tues–Sat 10am–4:30pm; Easter–Oct Mon–Sat 6–9:30pm.

THE RING OF KERRY
Undoubtedly Ireland's most popular scenic drive, the Ring of Kerry is a 177-kilometer (110-mile) panorama of seacoast, mountain, and lakeland vistas. Bicyclists usually avoid this route, since the scores of tour buses that thunder through here every day in the summer aren't always generous about sharing the road.

ESSENTIALS

MAKING THE DRIVE   By Bus   Bus Eireann (© 064/34777) provides limited daily service from Killarney to Caherciveen, Waterville, Kenmare, and other towns on the Ring of Kerry.

By Car   This is by far the best way to get around the Ring. For the most part, the route follows N-70.

VISITOR INFORMATION   For year-round information, stop in at the **Killarney Tourist Office,** Town Centre Car Park, Beech Road, Killarney (© 064/31633), before you begin your drive. From June to September, **The Barracks Tourist Office,** Caherciveen (© 066/947-2589), is open; from Easter through September, the **Kenmare Tourist Office,** Market Square, Kenmare (© 064/41233), is open. Most telephone numbers on the Ring of Kerry use the **064** or **066** code.

EXPLORING THE RING

The drive can be undertaken in either direction, but we strongly recommend a counterclockwise route for the most spectacular views. It's worth noting that the farther you get along the road, the more the signs tend to be in Gaelic only. Since the maps are all in English, this can be somewhat confusing. Careful study of the maps is suggested when exploring away from N-20. You can buy an Ordnance Survey map (sheet 83) from the tourist office, which gives names in both English and Gaelic.

Leave Killarney and follow the signs for **Killorglin.** Be sure to make the detour to visit **Ballymalis Castle.** Probably built by the Ferris family at the end of the 16th century, this ruin is typical of the tower houses built by wealthy landlords to protect their households from unwelcome intruders. Climbing the narrow, winding staircase, you're rewarded with splendid views over mountains, rivers, and fields. Backtrack to the main road and continue.

When you arrive in **Killorglin,** you might want to stop and walk around this spot, known far and wide for its annual mid-August horse, sheep, and cattle fair. Its official name is Puck Fair. The locals capture a wild goat from the mountains and enthrone it in the center of town as a sign to begin unrestricted merrymaking—although not necessarily for the goat.

Continuing on N-70, follow the signs for **Glenbeigh,** with views of Ireland's tallest mountain, **Carrantuohill** (1,040m/3,414 ft.), to your left. Open bogland is a constant companion on this stretch, and locals dig peat, or turf, to burn in their fireplaces. On your right just before you reach Glenbeigh is the **Kerry Bog Village Museum** (© 066/976-9184), where a cluster of thatched cottages illustrates Kerry life in the early 1800s. As you explore the blacksmith's forge, the turf cutter's house, and the laborer's cottage, the smell of burning peat hangs heavy in the air. The village is also home to the Kerry Bog pony, a breed that has been saved from extinction and is now unique to this museum.

The next town on the Ring is **Glenbeigh,** a palm tree–lined fishing resort with a lovely duney beach called Rossbeigh Strand. You may want to stop here, or continue on the Ring, with the first sightings of the Atlantic appearing away to your right. The views on the next section of the Ring are breathtaking, although the drive can be a bit hair-raising since the road twists and winds around the cliffs. There's a gorgeous view down over **Kells Bay,** best viewed from the road, instead of making the drive down to it. The route then moves inland with mountains to your right and a patchwork of fields in many shades of green to your left.

When you reach **Cahersiveen,** follow the signs right for the two forts, reached along a scenic though narrow road. You need to park a little way past the first fort, **Cahergeal,** and walk back along a rough track. The fort is made from gray stones and boulders piled one on top of the other. Staircases and walkways snake their way up and around ramparts, and the view across the bay is magical. The second fort can be reached along a narrow road to the right a little farther along. This is **Leacanabuaile Fort,** one of the few stone forts to have been excavated. The objects found suggest that the fort was in use until the 9th or 10th century. The castle that can be seen from both forts is Ballycarbery, but isn't really worth a visit, being best viewed from the distance.

Return to Cahersiveen and rejoin N-70, and then follow the signs right marked VALENTIA VIA FERRY. **Valentia** (also spelled Valencia) can also be reached by road, following the signs for Port Magee farther along N-70, but the ferry crossing saves a good deal of time and costs £3 (€3.80, $3.75) per car. Valentia Island, 11 kilometers (7 miles) long, is one of the most westerly points in Europe. It has the distinction of being the place from which the first telegraph cable was laid across the Atlantic, in 1866.

Once ashore at Knightstown, follow the signs for **Glanleam Gardens,** Glanleam House (© 066/947-6176). Created over 150 years ago by the Knights of Kerry, the gardens are justly famous for a unique collection of southern hemisphere plants. Broad walks weave through junglelike plantings of South American palms, Australian tree ferns, bananas, giant groves of bamboo, and rust-colored myrtles from Chile.

Leaving the gardens, follow the signs for **Portmagee,** stopping on the outskirts to visit the **Skellig Experience,** Skellig Heritage Centre (© 066/947-6306). This attraction blends right in with the terrain, with a stark stone facade framed by grassy mounds. The center gives you a detailed look at the bird and plant life of the Valentia area. In particular it tells the story of the **Skellig rocks**—Skellig Michael and Little Skellig—two rocky islands sitting off the coast in the Atlantic. In the 6th century, Skellig Michael, the larger of the two, became home to a group of monks who founded a monastery that survived for more than 600 years. Today, the other Skellig is one of the largest breeding grounds for the gannet in Western Europe. Admission to the Skellig Experience, for the exhibition and audiovisual, is £3 (€3.80, $3.75) adults, £2.70 (€3.45, $3.40) seniors and students, £1.50 (€1.90, $1.90) children under 12, and £7 (€8.90, $9) family of two adults and up to four children; for the exhibition, audiovisual, and sea cruise circuiting the Skelligs the fee is £17 (€22, $21) per person. The Skellig Experience is open from 10am to 7pm daily April to September, and 10am to 5:30pm Sunday to Thursday October to mid-November.

It's well worth making the 13-kilometer (8-mile) sea journey to the **Skelligs** 🎇🎇🎇, if only to climb the "stairway to Heaven" leading to the remains of the monastic settlement, where you can marvel at the lifestyle of the monks who once lived here. Thanks to the degree to which the place has been preserved, little imagination is needed to picture those early years of Irish Christianity. Ferries leave daily from May to September from Ballinskelligs, usually 9am to noon; call **Joe Roddy** (© 066/947-4268) or **Sean Feehan** (© 066/947-9182) to make a reservation. Ferries departing from Portmagee are run by **Murphy's** (© 066/947-7156). Depending on the boat, the cost ranges from £25 to £35 (€32 to €44, $31 to $44) per person. Reservations should be made 2 days in advance to assure a place and to confirm weather conditions: Boats are frequently unable to sail due to rough seas.

In the 18th century Valentia harbor was famous as a refuge for smugglers and privateers; tradition has it that John Paul Jones, the Scottish-born American naval officer in the War of Independence, anchored here frequently.

The route now continues into **Portmagee** and on through the **Coomanaspig Pass,** with dramatic views across St. Finan's Bay. This remote Irish-speaking area is an outpost of Gaelic culture and has an Irish college to which children come in the summer months to learn their native language. Continue through the glen, passing miles of golden, sandy beaches. When you reach Ballinskelligs, follow the road around the bay to **Waterville.** An overnight at this idyllic spot is highly recommended. There are many excellent restaurants, and from 9pm on, almost every bar on the seafront comes alive with the singing of traditional Irish songs.

Leaving Waterville, continue along N-70. If time allows (you'll need a good 50 minutes), take the first left turn, signposted CLUB MED (yes, you'll pass their only branch in Ireland) and enjoy a spectacular drive along the shores of **Lough Currane.** This is a very narrow and little-used road, but the dramatic views are well worth the effort. To your left, the dark waters of the lough and the towering ruggedness of the purple mountains suddenly give way to a patchwork of green fields. Take your time and take it all in. The road ends at a cottage, where you'll need to turn around and backtrack to N-70.

Continuing on N-70 through the Coomakista Pass, you arrive at another viewpoint at the crest of the road, where there's a statue of the Virgin Mary looking down onto the mouth of the Kenmare River and back along the pass to Waterville.

The next village is **Caherdaniel,** where a right turn leads to **Derrynane House** (© **066/75113**), the home, for most of his life, of Daniel O'Connell, the liberator. The house is now a museum dedicated to his struggle, with documents, maps, and memorabilia. Nature trails twist and turn through the 130-hectare (320-acre) grounds, and an explanatory booklet is available.

Return to N-70 and continue on until you reach signs to the left for the **Staigue Fort,** which possibly dates from around 1000 B.C. Forts such as this, with massive stone walls, were built as centers for communal refuge. The fort is nestled between the hills and mountains, and the views down over the tree tops across the bay and estuary are magnificent.

Back on N-70, you'll arrive at the pretty, colorful village of **Sneem,** its houses painted in vibrant shades of blue, pink, yellow, and purple. There's a memorial commemorating General de Gaulle's visit in 1969, and don't miss, to the right of the Catholic church, *The Way the Fairies Went,* a creation by James Scanlon, with four pyramid-shaped natural-stone structures with stained-glass panels.

Once through Sneem, you have a choice. You can continue on the Ring to Kenmare, a route that's pretty but at times tedious and uneventful. Or for a truly awe-inspiring scenic drive, follow the signs left to **Killarney,** on a route that takes you through the mountains. At every twist and turn of the road, a spectacular new vista opens out before you—myriad shades of green, surrounded on all sides by the moody, purple mountains, and babbling brooks that trickle into dark roadside lakes. When you reach Molls Gap, turn right for a visit to **Kenmare,** an enchanting place originally called Neidin, meaning "Little Nest." Well laid out and immaculately maintained by its proud residents (population 1,200), Kenmare more than rivals Killarney as a base for County Kerry sightseeing.

However, our last section of the Ring and the grand finale beckons. Backtrack to Molls Gap and then follow the signs for **Killarney.** Soon you're crossing the boundary of the national park, and every viewpoint is well worth the time it takes to stop and gaze across the Lakes of Killarney. Most popular is **Ladies View,** so called because of the pleasure expressed by Queen Victoria's ladies in waiting when they visited this picturesque spot in 1861. Farther on, don't miss the **Torc Waterfall,** signposted from the road and located in a peaceful woodland setting. From here it's a short distance to Muckross House and then back to Killarney.

WHERE TO STAY AROUND THE RING
Very Expensive
Park Hotel Kenmare 🏨🏨   Ensconced amid palm tree–lined gardens beside Kenmare Bay, this 1897 Victorian-style château is a haven of impeccable service and luxurious living. The interior is rich with high-ceilinged sitting rooms and lounges, fireplaces, plush furnishings, and antiques. The individually decorated rooms are decked out in a mix of Georgian and Victorian styles, many with four-poster or canopy beds. Most have views of the river and mountains. All rooms are wheelchair accessible. The dining room is one of the more highly acclaimed hotel restaurants in Ireland. In 1998, the Park Hotel was named the Condé Nast "Best Hotel in Ireland."

Kenmare, County Kerry. [tel **800/525-4800** from the U.S., or 064/41200. Fax 064/41402. www.parkkenmare. com. 48 units. £300–£500 (€381–€635, $375–$625) double. No service charge. Rates include full breakfast. AE, DC, MC, V. Closed Nov to Dec 23 and Jan 2 to mid-Apr. **Amenities:** Restaurant; 18-hole golf course; tennis court; croquet lawn; salmon fishing (ghillies are available); no-smoking rooms. *In room:* TV, CD player, fax, hair dryer.

Expensive
Parknasilla Great Southern Hotel 🏨   Facing one of the loveliest seascape settings in Ireland, this château-style hotel is set amid 120 hectares (300 acres) of lush, subtropical palm trees and flowering shrubs. George Bernard Shaw stayed here and was inspired to write much of his play *Saint Joan.* The hotel has a private 12-hole golf course and offers riding, fishing, boating, and guided walks on trails through the hotel grounds and neighboring woodlands. Rooms are individually furnished, and most look out onto broad vistas of the Kenmare River and the Atlantic.

Ring of Kerry Rd. (N-70), Parknasilla, County Kerry. ℭ **064/45122.** Fax 064/45323. www.gsh.ie. 84 units. £186–£220 (€236–€279, $233–$275) double. Service charge 12.5%. AE, DC, MC, V. Open year-round. **Amenities:** Heated indoor saltwater pool; 12-hole golf course; tennis courts; sauna. *In room:* TV, tea/coffeemaker, hair dryer, trouser press.

Moderate
Towers   If you'd like to be right in the heart of one of the Ring of Kerry's most delightful towns, then this vintage brick-faced country inn is for you. Shaded by ancient palms, it sits in the middle of a small fishing village, yet is within a mile of the sandy Rossbeigh Strand. Recently refurbished and updated, most of the rooms are in a contemporary-style new wing with lovely views of the nearby waters.

Ring of Kerry Rd. (N-70), Glenbeigh, County Kerry. ℭ **066/976-8212.** Fax 066/976-8260. 28 units. £76–£94 (€97–€119, $95–$118) double. Service charge 12.5%. Rates include full breakfast. AE, MC, V. Closed Nov–Mar. **Amenities:** Restaurant (seafood), pub. *In-room:* TV, hair dryer.

WHERE TO DINE AROUND THE RING
The Huntsman 🍴   INTERNATIONAL   It's worth a trip to Waterville just to dine at this contemporary beachfront restaurant on the shore of Ballinskelligs Bay. Owner/chef Raymond Hunt takes the time to circulate and chat with diners, offering suggestions as to the extensive menu, specializing in seafood and

featuring only the freshest local catch and produce. Skellig lobster fresh from the tank, swordfish, and Kenmare Bay scampi are among the seafood dishes; meat dishes include rack of lamb, venison, seasonal pheasant, rabbit, duck, and Irish stew. All this is assisted by an extensive award-winning wine list. In addition, there's a complimentary feast comprised of spectacular views.

The Strand, Waterville. ℭ 066/947-4560. Reservations recommended. Main courses £12–£20 (€15–€25, $15–$25). AE, DC, MC, V. Mar–Oct daily 10am–10pm; Nov–Feb Sat–Sun noon–9pm.

Lime Tree ℛ IRISH   Innovative cuisine is the focus at this restaurant in an 1821 landmark renovated schoolhouse next to the grounds of the Park Hotel. The decor includes a skylit gallery and stone walls lined with paintings by local artists, and the menu offers such dishes as goat's cheese potato cake with balsamic glaze, oak planked wild salmon, filet of Irish beef with colcannon, and oven-roasted Kerry lamb.

Shelbourne Rd., Kenmare. ℭ 064/41225. Reservations recommended. Main courses £11–£17 (€14–€22, $14–$22). MC, V. Apr–Oct daily 6:30–10pm.

Packie's IRISH   With window boxes full of colorful seasonal plantings, this informal, bistro-style restaurant in the middle of town exudes a welcoming atmosphere. The interior has a slate floor, stone walls, and dark oak tables and chairs. On the walls is a collection of wonderful contemporary Irish art, and on the menu are tried-and-true favorites: Irish stew and rack of lamb. Also offered are creative combinations, such as gratin of crab and prawns, beef braised in Guinness with mushrooms, and blackboard fish specials. Chef-owner Maura Foley uses herbs from her own garden to enhance each dish.

Henry St., Kenmare, County Kerry. ℭ 064/41508. Reservations recommended. Main courses £10–£20 (€13–€25, $13–$25). MC, V. Easter to mid-Nov Tues–Sat 5:30–10pm.

SHOPPING IN KENMARE

Cleo, 2 Shelbourne Rd. (ℭ 064/41410), is a branch of the long-established Dublin store of the same name. This trendy women's wear shop is known for its colorful tweed and linen fashions, as well as specialty items like Kinsale cloaks. **The Green Note,** 18 Henry St. (ℭ 064/41212), is a traditional Irish-music store selling banjos, harps, and tin whistles. You can also purchase a bodhran, the Irish hand drum, at an attractive price. The **Kenmare Bookshop,** Shelbourne Street (ℭ 064/41578), specializes in books on Ireland, particularly Irish biographies and books by Irish writers, as well as maps and guides to the surrounding area, including ordinance survey maps, walking and specialist guides, and marine charts. **Nostalgia Linen and Lace,** 27 Henry St. (ℭ 064/41669), specializes in Irish linens and sells lace by the meter. Finally, you can't miss stumbling into **Quills Woolen Market,** Market Square and Main Street (ℭ 064/41078), one of the many Quills branch stores known for Aran handknits, Donegal tweed jackets, Irish linen, Celtic jewelry, and colorful hand-loomed knitwear.

TRALEE

Tralee, with its population of 22,000, is County Kerry's chief town and the gateway to the Dingle Peninsula. A busy, bustling, and not particularly attractive place, its greatest claim to fame is that it was the inspiration for the song "The Rose of Tralee," composed by local resident William Mulninock more than 100 years ago. Consequently, Tralee is now the setting for the Rose of Tralee festival, the country's largest annual festival, held in August. It's also the permanent home of the National Folk Theatre of Ireland, Siamsa Tíre.

ESSENTIALS

GETTING THERE   By Air   Aer Arann (© **890/462726** within Ireland, or
© **01/814-1058**) offers daily direct flights from Dublin into **Kerry County
Airport,** Farranfore, County Kerry (© **066/ 64644**), about 15 miles south of
Tralee. Flying time is 1 hour.

By Train   Trains from major cities arrive at the **Tralee Railway Station** on
John Jo Sheehy Road (© **066/712-3522**).

By Bus   Buses from all parts of Ireland arrive daily at the **Bus Eierann Depot**
on John Jo Sheehy Road, near the train station (© **066/712-3566**).

VISITOR INFORMATION   The **Tralee Tourist Office,** in Ashe Memorial
Hall, Denny Street, Tralee (© **066/712-1288**), is open year-round from Monday to Friday 9am to 1pm and 2 to 5pm, with extended hours in the summer
season. There is also a first-rate cafe on the premises.

SEEING THE SIGHTS

One of Ireland's largest indoor heritage centers, **Kerry the Kingdom,** Ashe
Memorial Hall, Denny Street, Tralee (© **066/712-7777**), offers three separate
attractions that give an in-depth look at 7,000 years of life in County Kerry. A
10-minute video, "Kerry in Colour," presents the seascapes and landscapes of
Kerry; the **Kerry County Museum** chronologically examines the county's
music, history, legends, and archaeology through interactive and hands-on
exhibits; and the exhibit on Gaelic football is unique. Many items of local origin that were previously on view at the National Museum in Dublin are now
here. Complete with lighting effects and aromas, a theme park–style ride called
"Geraldine Tralee" takes you through a re-creation of Tralee's streets, houses, and
abbeys during the Middle Ages. Admission is £5.50 (€7, $7) adults, £4.75
(€6.05, $6) students, £3 (€3.80, $3.75) children, £17 (€22, $21) family. Open
daily from mid-March to July 10am to 6pm, August 10am to 7pm, from
September to October 10am to 6pm, and from November to December 22
noon to 5pm.

The restored **Tralee Steam Railway** (© **066/712-8888**) offers 3-kilometer
(2-mile) narrated scenic trips from Tralee's Ballyard Station to Blennerville. It uses
equipment that was once part of the Tralee & Dingle Light Railway, one of the
world's most famous narrow-gauge railways. Trains run on the hour, and the trip
costs £2.75 (€3.50, $3.45) adults, £2.25 (€2.90, $2.80) seniors and students,
£1.50 (€1.90, $1.90) children, £7 (€8.90, $8.75) family. It operates daily from
May to September; closed on the second Monday and Tuesday of each month for
maintenance.

WHERE TO STAY

Abbey Gate Hotel   This modern hotel is located in the center of Tralee.
Rooms are spacious and tastefully decorated, and public areas are modern and
functional. All beds are orthopedic. The hotel's pub, the Old Market Place, is a
lively night spot.

Maine St., Tralee, County Kerry. © **066/712-9888**. Fax 066/712-9821. 100 units. £50–£98 (€64–€125,
$63–$123) double. No service charge. AE, DC, MC, V. **Amenities:** 2 restaurants; pub; no-smoking rooms. *In
room:* TV, coffeemaker.

Ballyseede Castle Hotel   This turreted four-story castle was once the chief
garrison of the legendary Fitzgeralds, the earls of Desmond. The two drawing
rooms are warmed by marble fireplaces. Residents can feel like royalty in the

elegant bedrooms, a feeling that's reiterated in the newly refurbished Regency restaurant. It goes without saying that the castle is haunted.

Tralee-Killarney Rd., Tralee, County Kerry. © **066/712-5799.** Fax 066/712-5287. 12 units. £140–£200 (€178–€254, $175–$250) double. Full breakfast £8.50 (€11, $11). Service charge 12.5%. DC, MC, V. **Amenities:** Restaurant; no-smoking rooms. *In room:* TV.

The Shores The Shores, a modern house on the south side of Brandon Bay, commands good views of Tralee Bay and Mount Brandon. Annette O'Mahoney is an avid interior decorator, and she has done a great job of giving each room a unique ambience. Furnishings are lavish, with a canopy bed in one of the upstairs rooms and writing desks in three of the rooms. The downstairs room has a private entrance and a fireplace. Breakfast options are particularly extensive, with smoked salmon and waffles given as alternatives to the standard fry.

Cappatigue, Castlegregory, County Kerry. © and fax **066/713-9196.** theshores@eircom.net. 6 units (4 with bathtub). £46 (€58, $58) double. Rates include full breakfast. AE, DC, MC, V. Closed Dec–Jan. [1/2 mile west of Stradbally on the Conor Pass Rd. **Amenities:** No-smoking rooms. *In room:* TV, tea/coffeemaker, hair dryer, trouser press.

WHERE TO DINE

In addition to the recommendation below, you can get excellent pub grub, especially steaks, at **Kirby's Olde Brogue Inn,** Rock Street, Tralee (© **066/712-3357**). This pub has a barnlike layout, with an interior that incorporates farming memorabilia and rush-work tables and chairs. Sometimes traditional music and folk ballads are served up, too.

Larkins (*Value* IRISH/SEAFOOD/VEGETARIAN This bright, welcoming Irish-country restaurant is widely acclaimed for its catch of the day and its roast rack of Irish lamb. Modestly priced and immodestly tasty, Larkins' offerings are well worth a stop.

Princes St., Tralee. © **066/712-1300.** Main courses £9–£18 (€11–€23, $11–$23). May–Sept. DC, MC, V. Mon–Fri 12:30– 2pm and 6:30–9:30pm; Sat 6:30–9:30pm (Sun hours June–Sept).

The Tankard SEAFOOD/IRISH Ten kilometers (6 miles) northwest of Tralee, this is one of the few restaurants in the area that capitalizes on sweeping views of Tralee Bay. Situated right on the water's edge, it is outfitted with wide picture windows and a sleek contemporary decor. The straightforward and extensive menu primarily features local shellfish and seafood such as lobster, scallops, prawns, and black sole, but also includes rack of lamb, duck, quail, and a variety of steaks, as well as a range of vegetarian options. Bar food is available all day, but this restaurant is at its best in the early evening, especially at sunset.

Kilfenora, Fenit. © **066/713-6164.** Reservations recommended. Main courses £10–£20 (€13–€25, $13–$25). AE, DC, MC, V. Daily 12:30–2pm and 6–10pm.

TRALEE AFTER DARK

Siamsa Tire, the National Folk Theatre of Ireland, is located at Town Park, Tralee (© **066/712-3055;** fax 066/712-7276). Founded in 1974, Siamsa (pronounced Sheem-sha) offers a mixture of music, dance, and mime. The scenes depict old folk tales and farmyard activities such as thatching a cottage roof, flailing sheaves of corn, and twisting a sugan (straw) rope.

In addition to these folk theater entertainments, Siamsa presents a full program of drama and musical concerts (from traditional to classical) performed by visiting amateur and professional companies. Admission is £12 (€15, $15) adults; £9 (€11, $11) seniors, students, and children. The schedule is from Monday to Saturday April to mid-October; curtain time is 8:30pm.

PUBS   Tralee pubs can be a little crowded and impersonal. **Olde Macs,** The Mall (© **066/712-1572**), is an exception. From the delightful flowers in the hanging baskets outside to the dark-wood interior, the pub exudes atmosphere. Conversation is lighthearted, and the regulars are extremely friendly.

THE DINGLE PENINSULA

While the Dingle Peninsula is an ideal drive, it also makes a fine bicycling tour. Dingle village is a delightful place to stay (see below) while exploring the peninsula.

The best route to the Dingle Peninsula is to follow the camp road (N-86) from Tralee. To the west 5 kilometers (3 miles) you'll pass the **Blennerville Windmill** (© **066/712-1064**). This is the largest working windmill in Ireland and was built in 1850. After years of neglect, it was recently restored and now produces 5 tons of whole-meal flour per week. The visitors' complex has an emigration exhibition center, crafts workshops, and a cafe. Admission is £2.75 (€3.50, $3.45) adults, £2.25 (€2.90, $2.80) seniors and students, £1.50 (€1.90, $1.90) children over 5, and £7 (€8.90, $8.75) family; it's open daily from March to October, 10am to 6pm.

The route continues with delightful vistas over Tralee Bay, passing through the town of **Camp.** From here on the road hugs the shore with vistas of **Brandon Mountain,** Ireland's second highest. Follow the signs for the **Conor Pass,** a spectacular drive through the mountains that reaches a height of 460 meters (1,500 ft.). Rising steeply, the often very narrow road passes through a landscape of rocky mountain slopes, dark lakes, and cliffs. On a clear day, the views of Tralee and Brandon Bay are superb. Be sure to stop at the viewpoint when you reach the top of the pass. The final descent offers views over Dingle Bay and an enticing glimpse of Dingle itself (see below).

From **Dingle,** follow the signs for **Slea Head Drive,** a route that takes you on a spectacular, often rugged trip, returning eventually to Dingle. The **Beehive Huts** that stand to the right of the road past **Ventry** are worth a stop. These unmortared, prehistoric cells or huts owe their shape to the ancient method of construction known as drystone corbelling, in which the circular walls are constructed of overlapping stones and curve gradually inward until they can be covered with a capstone at the top.

Also worth a visit is the **Dunbeg Fort,** situated on an oceanside site with beautiful sea views. A viewpoint at **Slea Head** overlooks a mountainous curve at the end of the peninsula; it's been the setting for many a picture postcard and sea-splashed landscape painting. You also have a view of the seven **Blasket Islands,** sitting out in the Atlantic. Until 1953 the largest of these, Great Blasket, was still inhabited. Great Blasket was once an outpost of Irish civilization and nurtured a small band of Irish-language writers. The quite splendid **Blasket Centre,** on the westerly tip of the Dingle Peninsula near Dunquin (© **066/915-6371**), has a series of displays, exhibits, and a video presentation that celebrate the cultural and literary traditions of the Blaskets. Admission is £2.50 (€3.20, $3.15) adults, £1.75 (€2.25, $2.20) seniors, £1 (€1.30, $1.25) children and students, and £6 (€7.60, $7.50) families; it's open from Easter to June and September to October daily 10am to 6pm; from July to August daily 10am to 7pm.

The route now continues to **Ballyferriter,** a largely Gaelic-speaking village. From here you head east and follow the signs to the **Gallarus Oratory,** one of the best-preserved early Christian church buildings in Ireland. Constructed of unmortared stone and shaped like an upturned boat, it's still watertight even after a thousand years.

Continue following the signs marked SLEA HEAD DRIVE until you arrive at the **Kilmalkedar Church,** dating from the 12th century. Inside the ruined church is an abecedarian stone, with the Latin alphabet crudely carved, a relic of a 7th-century school and probably the oldest-surviving Irish relic of Roman script. Don't miss the 15th-century ruins of **St. Brendan's House,** hidden among the bushes a little way past the church, once a substantial priests' dwelling.

Continue on the road and turn right, following the signs to **Brandon Creek.** It was from here, in the 6th century, that St. Brendan reputedly set out for the Islands of Paradise in the Western Ocean, a 7-year voyage that led him, it has been claimed, to discover America. The life of the saint and the story of his voyage, Navigation Sancti Brendai Abbatis, was written in the 9th century. The Latin narrative was popular reading in medieval Europe and the inspiration for many voyagers and explorers, including Christopher Columbus.

Backtrack to Slea Head Drive and follow it on a picturesque route back to Dingle. From here take R-561 eastward along Dingle Bay, through the villages of Lispole and Annascaul to **Inch,** one of Dingle's most beautiful seascapes, a 6.5-kilometer (4-mile) stretch of sandy beach, with distant views of the Ring of Kerry and Killarney. From here you can return to Camp or Tralee or continue to Castlemaine (where the Wild Colonial Boy was born) and onward to Limerick or other parts of Kerry and Cork.

DINGLE TOWN

With a charter dating back many centuries, Dingle was Kerry's principal harbor in medieval times. Even though it's just a small town (pop. 1,500), Dingle has more fine restaurants than many of Ireland's major cities, and is known for the traditional Irish music in its pubs.

EXPLORING THE TOWN

The new gem in Dingle town is **Dingle Oceanworld** *ℛ*, Dingle Harbour, Dingle (𝒞 **066/915-2111;** fax 066/52155; www.dingle-oceanworld.ie). Admission is £5 (€6.35, $6) adults, £4 (€5.10, $5) seniors and students, £3 (€3.80, $3.75) children, and £12 (€15, $15) family. It's open September, May, and June daily from 9:30am to 6pm, from July to August daily 9:30am to 8:30pm, and from October to April daily 9:30am to 5pm. This new harborside aquarium, which is dedicated to the exploration and understanding of the nearby ocean's depths and its critters, is already a main family attraction. All but the sharks are indigenous to local waters. In addition, there are exhibits on Brendan the Navigator and the Spanish Armada, as well as a cafe and gift shop.

In 1984 Fungie, an adult male bottle-nosed dolphin, swam solo into the waters of Dingle harbor. Since then a whole industry has grown up around him. **The Dingle Boatmen's Association** (𝒞 **066/915-1163**) will ferry you out to find him (if there's no sighting, you don't pay). Fungie happily swims alongside the boats, although his enthusiasm has abated slightly in recent years. Fares for the 1-hour boat trip are £7 (€8.90, $9) adults and £3 (€3.80, $3.75) children under 12. More adventurous visitors can swim with him on a dolphin encounter, arranged by Bridgit Flannery (𝒞 **066/915-1967** or 066/915-1163) most any day from 8am to 8pm. The procedure is to book a swim the day before, when you rent your gear (semi-dry suit, mask, snorkel, boots, and fins—all in one duffel). The full outfitting cost is £14 (€18, $18) per person. Then you show up in your gear early the next morning to be brought out by boat to your aquatic rendezvous. The 2-hour escorted swim period costs an additional £10 (€13, $13). If you prefer, you can use your rented outfit and swim out on your own. Fungie also welcomes drop-ins. This outing is for teenagers on up, although smaller children will certainly enjoy watching.

Also departing from Dingle Harbor is the new boat tour to the Blasket Islands, run by **Dingle Marine Ecotours,** The Pier, Dingle (✆ **086-285-8802;** www.dinglemarine.com). Guided tours depart daily from April to October and include information on the recent history, archaeology, geology, and wildlife of the Blasket Islands; the frequency of tours during the day is based on demand, and tours last for 2½ hours. The cost is £15 (€19, $19) adults, £5 (€6.35, $6) children 10 to 14, and £3 (€3.80, $3.75) children under 10.

ENJOYING THE GREAT OUTDOORS

BICYCLING   Rentals average £6 (€7.60, $7.50) per day or £30 (€38, $38) per week. Contact **Foxy John's Hardware Store,** Main Street (✆ **066/915-1316**). Mountain bikes can be rented at **The Mountain Man,** Strand Street, Dingle (✆ **066/915-2400** or 066/915-1868).

HORSEBACK RIDING   At **Dingle Horse Riding,** Ballinaboula House, Dingle (✆ **066/915-2018**), rides are available along nearby beaches or through the mountains; the cost is £15 (€19, $19) for a 1-hour ride. Half-day, full-day, and 3- to 5-day packages including accommodation, meals, and riding can be arranged.

SAILING   The **Dingle Sailing Club,** c/o Brenda Farrell, The Marina, Dingle Town (✆ **066/915-1984;** lfarrell@eircom.net), offers an array of sailing courses taught by experienced, certified instructors. To charter a yacht, contact **Dingle Sea Ventures,** Dingle (✆ **066/915-2244;** www.charterireland.com). Yachts, sleeping from six to 10 persons, are available, ranging in price from £910 to £2,200 (€1,156 to €2,794, $1,138 to $2,750) per week, depending on boat and season. Skipper's fees are £50 (€64, $63) per day.

SEA ANGLING   For sea angling packages and day trips, contact Nicholas O'Connor at **Angler's Rest,** Ventry (✆ **066/915-9947;** avalon@iol.ie); or Seán O'Conchúir (✆ **066/915-5429**), representing the **Kerry Angling Association.**

WALKING   The **Dingle Way** begins in Tralee and circles the peninsula, covering 153 kilometers (95 miles) of gorgeous mountain and coastal landscape. The most rugged section is along Brandon Head, where the trail passes between Mount Brandon and the ocean; the views are tremendous, but the walk is long (about 24km/15 miles or 9 hours) and strenuous, and should be attempted only when the sky is clear. The section between Dunquin and Ballyferriter (24km/15 miles) follows an especially lovely stretch of coast. For more information see The Dingle Way Map Guide, available in local tourist offices and shops.

WHERE TO STAY

Doyle's Townhouse   This old-world guesthouse is just a few minutes' walk away from Dingle's main street. It has a lovely Victorian fireplace in the main sitting room area, and many of the antique furnishings date back 250 years or more. Period pieces and country pine predominate in the rooms, although the fixtures and fittings are modern and include semi-orthopedic beds. Some back rooms face a garden with mountain vistas in the background.

5 John St., Dingle, County Kerry. ✆ **800/223-6510** from the U.S., or 066/915-1174. Fax 066/915-1816. www.doylesofdingle.com. 16 units. £72–£80 (€91–€102, $90–$100) double. Service charge 10%. Rates include full breakfast. MC, V. Closed mid-Nov to mid-Mar. *In-room:* TV.

Greenmount House ✿   Perched on a hill overlooking Dingle Bay and town, this modern bungalow-style bed-and-breakfast home is a standout in its category. It has all the comforts of a hotel at bargain prices, including rooms decorated with contemporary furnishings and orthopedic beds, a public sitting room with an open fireplace, and a sunlit conservatory filled with plants. No smoking is allowed in the bedrooms or breakfast room.

John St., Dingle, County Kerry. ⓒ **066/915-1414.** Fax 066/915-1974. www.greenmounthouse.com. 12 units. £50–£90 (€64–€114, $63–$113) double. No service charge. Rates include full breakfast. MC, V. Closed Dec 20–26. **Amenities:** All rooms no-smoking. *In room:* TV, fridge, tea/coffeemaker, hair dryer.

Milltown House ★ You couldn't wish for a more picturesque Dingle setting than this bay-side haven. A narrow road leads to it and, once inside, you'll see why much of their business is repeat. Rooms are tastefully and individually furnished, several offering bay windows that gaze out onto a bay and harbor panorama. The public areas include a peaceful lounge with an open fire and a bright, airy conservatory. The Kerry family have recently renovated the house, converting three bedrooms with sea views into suites. A four-course evening meal is offered with a full wine list. There are also on-site stables for riding and trekking.

Dingle, County Kerry. ⓒ **066/915-1372.** Fax 066/915-1095. http://indigo.ie/~milltown/. 10 units (all with bathtub). £60–£95 (€76–€121, $75–$119) double. Rates include full breakfast. AE, MC, V. **Amenities:** Restaurant; riding stable. *In room:* TV, tea/coffeemaker, hair dryer.

WHERE TO DINE

Beginish Restaurant ★★ SEAFOOD If you're looking for the best seafood in Dingle, this is the place. Mrs. Pat Moore runs this delightful small restaurant, and she's managed to achieve an atmosphere of quiet elegance, unassuming and comfortable. There's a lovely conservatory overlooking the garden in back, with room for outdoor tables in summer. Although there are lamb and beef dishes, and a vegetarian special each night, the emphasis is on fish—the cooking is simple, traditional, and always delightful. Among the starters, the smoked salmon with shallots, capers, and horseradish cream is exquisite—nothing fancy, just excellent ingredients combined in the perfect proportions. You can't go wrong with any of the fish courses.

Green St., Dingle, County Kerry. ⓒ **066/915-1588.** Reservations recommended. Lunch £7–£16 (€8.90–€20, $8.75–$20); dinner main courses £13–£22 (€17–€28, $16–$28). AE, DC, MC, V. Tues–Sun 12:30–2:15pm and 6–10pm.

Doyle's Seafood Bar SEAFOOD This cozy old pub has rock walls, a flagstone floor, and a blackboard menu showing a selection of seafood from local fishing boats' same-day catch. In addition to lobster (a specialty of the house), salmon, oysters, and other shellfish, there's good homemade soup. If you haven't booked in advance you can expect a wait for a seat in this small dining room. There's a separate no-smoking room.

John St., Dingle, County Kerry. ⓒ **066/915-1174.** Reservations recommended. Main courses £12–£25 (€15–€32, $15–$31). 10% service charge. DC, MC, V. Mid-Feb to Dec Mon–Sat 5:30–9:30pm.

Waterside Café INTERNATIONAL For a daytime snack with a Dingle ambience, this restaurant offers a setting opposite the busy town marina. It's a bright and airy place with a decor of blue and white, enhanced by seasonal flowers and plants. There is seating in a sunlit conservatory-style room as well as on an outdoor patio. It operates as a cafe by day and as a full-service restaurant on summer nights. The choices include oysters on the half-shell, cockle and mussel sandwiches, prawn and crab seafood salads, and soups, as well as quiches, omelets, crêpes, and pastries. The evening menu concentrates on local seafood and steaks.

Strand St., Dingle. ℂ **066/915-1458.** Reservations recommended for dinner. Cafe items £2–£10 (€2.55–€13, $2.50–$13); restaurant main courses £10–£16 (€13–€20, $13–$20). MC, V. Easter–Sept cafe daily 10am–6pm; restaurant daily 7–10pm.

THE SHOPPING SCENE

Brian De Staic, The Wood (ℂ **066/915-1298;** www.brian-de-staic.ie), is considered by many to be Ireland's leading goldsmith. His workshop is just west of the Dingle Pier. He specializes in unusual Irish jewelry, handcrafted and engraved with the letters of the Ogham alphabet, an ancient Irish form of writing dating back to the 3rd century.

At **Holden Dingle,** Main Street (ℂ **066/915-1796;** holdenj@iol.ie), Jackie and Conor Holden offer beautiful handcrafted leather handbags lined with suede and silk pockets as well as duffle and travel bags and briefcases.

At **The Weavers Shop,** Green Street (ℂ **066/915-1688**), Lisbeth Mulcahy, one of Ireland's leading weavers, creates fabrics and tapestries inspired by seasonal changes in the Irish land- and seascapes. Pure Irish wool, linen/cotton, and alpaca are used in weaving wall hangings and tapestries, as well as scarves, shawls, and knee rugs.

DINGLE AFTER DARK

At night virtually every pub in Dingle offers live music from 9pm on. **An Droichead Beag/The Small Bridge,** Lower Main St. (ℂ **066/915-1723**), is one of Dingle's most atmospheric pubs. It has a dark, cavernous interior that's filled with banter and laughter. Traditional Irish music takes place every night at 9pm. But be warned: It's popular, so get there early if you want a seat.

Although Richard "Dick" Mack died a few years ago, his family keeps up the traditions at **Dick Mack's "Haberdashery,"** Green Street (ℂ **066/915-1070**), where Dick handcrafted leather boots, belts, and other items in between pub chores. Corridors lined with old pictures and mugs lead into tiny snug bars where locals and visitors stand around sipping stout and exchanging jokes and gossip. It's been a favorite pub with celebrities such as Robert Mitchum, Timothy Dalton, and Paul Simon, whose names are now commemorated with stars on the sidewalk just outside.

11

Italy

by Darwin Porter & Danforth Prince

Italy is a feast for the senses and the intellect. Any mention of Italy calls up visions of Pompeii, the Renaissance, and Italy's rich treasury of art and architecture. But some of the country's best experiences can involve the simple act of living in the Italian style, eating the regional cuisines, and enjoying the countryside.

1 Rome

The city of Rome is simultaneously strident, romantic, and sensual. And although the romantic poets would probably be horrified at today's traffic, pollution, overcrowding, crime, political discontent, and the barely controlled chaos of modern Rome, the city endures and thrives in a way that is called "eternal."

It would take a lifetime to know a city filled with 27 centuries of artistic achievement. A cradle of Western civilization, Rome is timeless with its ancient history, art, and architecture, containing more treasures per square foot than any other city in the world. Caesar was assassinated here, Charlemagne crowned, and the list of the major events goes on and on.

In between all that absorption of culture and history, take time to relax and meet the Romans. Savor their succulent pastas while enjoying a fine glass of wine on one of the city's splendid squares where one of the reigning Caesars might have gone before you, or perhaps Michelangelo or Raphael.

ESSENTIALS

GETTING THERE By Plane Chances are that you'll arrive in Italy at Rome's **Leonardo da Vinci International Airport** (© **06-65951** or 06-65953640 for information), popularly known as Fiumicino, 30 kilometers (18½ miles) from the city center. Domestic flights arrive at one terminal, international ones at the other. If you're flying by charter, you might arrive at Ciampino Airport.

To get into the city, there's a **shuttle service** known as the Leonardo Express which takes you directly from Fiumicino to Stazione Termini, the main train station. Upon leaving Customs, follow the signs marked TRENI. Trains go back and forth between the airport and the rail station daily from 7:37am to 10:37pm. A one-way ticket costs 17,000L (€8.85, $9).

Taxis from Fiumicino to city center are expensive—75,000L (€39, $38k) and up.

Should you arrive on a charter flight at **Ciampino Airport** (© **06-794941**), take a COTRAL bus, departing every 20 minutes or so, which will deliver you to the Anagnina stop of Metropolitana (subway) line A. At Anagnina you can take line A to Stazione Termini, where your final connections can be made. The trip takes about 45 minutes and costs 1,500L (€0.83, 75¢).

By Train   Trains arrive in the center of old Rome at **Stazione Termini,** Piazza dei Cinquecento (✆ **1478-88088**), the train and subway transportation hub for the city. Many hotels lie near the station, and you can walk to your hotel if you don't have too much luggage. Otherwise, an array of taxi, bus, and subway lines awaits you.

If you're taking the **Metropolitana** (subway), follow the illuminated M sign in red that points the way. To catch a bus, go straight through the outer hall of the Termini and enter the sprawling bus lot of Piazza dei Cinquecento. Taxis are also found here.

By Bus   Arrivals are at the **Stazione Termini** (see "By Train," above).

By Car   From the north the main access route is **A-1 (Autostrada del Sole),** cutting through Milan and Florence, or you can take the coastal route, SSI Aurelia, from Genoa. If you're driving north from Naples, you take the southern lap of the **Autostrada del Sole (A-2).** All these autostrade join with the **Grande Raccordo Anulare,** a ring road that encircles Rome, channeling traffic into the congested city.

VISITOR INFORMATION   Tourist Offices   Information is available at three locations maintained by the Azienda Provinciale di Turismo (APT). They include kiosks at **Leonardo da Vinci Airport** (✆ **06-6595-6074**) and their headquarters at Via Parigi 5 (✆ **06-4889-9253**). Via Parigi 5 is open from Monday to Friday 8:15am to 7:15pm, Saturday to 3:45pm. The airport and Stazione Termini kiosk is open daily from 8:15am to 7:15pm. However, don't expect much from this office.

More helpful, stocking maps and brochures, are the offices maintained by the **Comune di Roma** at half a dozen sights around the city. You can identify them by their red-and-orange or yellow-and-black signs saying COMUNE DI ROMA— PUNTI DI INFORMAZIONE TURISTICA. The City Hall also offers an information service by phone at ✆ **06-36004399** where both English- and Italian-speaking representatives will be able to assist you. They're staffed daily from 9am to 6pm, and can be found in Piazza Pia, near the Castello Sant'Angelo (✆ **06-6880-9707**); in Piazza San Giovanni in Laterano (✆ **06-7720-3598**); along Largo Carlo Goldoni, near the intersection of Via del Corso and Via Condotti (✆ **06-6813-6061**); on Via Nazionale, near the Palazzo delle Esposizioni (✆ **06-4782-4525**); on Largo Corrado Ricci, near the Colosseum (✆ **06-6992-4307**); and in Trastevere on Piazza Sonnino (✆ **06-5833-3457**). The Stazione Termini office (✆ **06-4890-6300**) is open daily from 8am to 9pm. Other offices have also opened, including Piazza 5 Lune, near Piazza Navona (✆ **06-6880-9240**); Piazza Santa Maria Maggiore (✆ **06-4788-0294**); and Piazza dei 500, outside Stazione Termini (✆ **06-4782-5194**).

Websites   It takes a while to load, but **www.commune.roma.it**, Rome's official site, has a fair amount of info on most aspects of the Rome experience. It appears to be only in Italian, but click on the "Roma Review" box on the welcome page and then on the English phrases of interest—what's on, what to hear, what to see. Maintained by a private company, **www.enjoyrome.com** fills you in on useful information for visiting the city (they, after all, pen the official tourist office's "Info for Tourists" pamphlet) while promoting its walking tours in Rome, Florence, and Venice as well as guided trips to Pompeii.

The extensive **www.initaly.com** helps you find all sorts of accommodations (country villas, historic residences, convents, and farmhouses) and includes tips on shopping, dining, driving, and viewing works of art. Check out

www.italytour.com for coverage of the arts, culture, business, tours, entertainment, restaurants, lodging, media, shopping, sports, and major Italian cities. To stay up to date on trends in modern Italian culture, go to **www.dolcevita.com**, the self-proclaimed "insider's guide to Italy." It's all about style—as it pertains to fashion, cuisine, design, and travel.

CITY LAYOUT   The drive into the city from the airport is rather uneventful until you pass through the still remarkably intact **Great Aurelian Wall,** begun in A.D. 271 to calm Rome's barbarian jitters. Suddenly, ruins of imperial baths loom on one side and great monuments can be seen in the middle of blocks.

Stazione Termini, the modern railroad station, faces the huge **Piazza dei Cinquecento,** named after 500 Italians who died heroically in a 19th-century battle in Africa.

The bulk of ancient, Renaissance, and baroque Rome lies on the east side of the **Fiume Tevere (Tiber River),** which meanders between 19th-century stone embankments. However, several important monuments are on the other side: **St. Peter's Basilica** and the **Vatican,** the **Castel Sant' Angelo** (formerly the tomb of the emperor Hadrian), and the colorful section known as **Trastevere.** The city's various quarters are linked by boulevards that have mostly been laid out since the late 19th century.

Major streets fan out from **Piazza Venezia** in front of the **Vittorio Emmanuele monument,** a highly controversial pile of snow-white Brescian marble. Running north to **Piazza del Popolo** and the city wall is **Via del Corso,** one of Rome's main streets. Called simply "Il Corso," it's noisy, congested, and always crowded with buses and shoppers. Going west across the Tiber toward St. Peter's is **Corso Vittorio Emanuele.** Running toward the Colosseum is **Via dei Fori Imperiali,** named for the excavated ruins of the imperial forums that flank this avenue. **Via Quattro Novembre** runs east and becomes **Via Nazionale** before terminating at **Piazza della Repubblica.**

GETTING AROUND

Much of the inner core of Rome is traffic-free—so you'll need to walk whether you like it or not. However, walking in many parts of the city is hazardous and uncomfortable because of overcrowding, heavy traffic, and very narrow and uneven sidewalks.

By Subway   The **Metropolitana,** or **Metro** for short, is the fastest means of transportation in Rome. It has two underground lines: **A** and **B.** A big red letter M indicates the subway entrance. The fare is 1,500L (€0.83, 75¢). Tickets are available from vending machines at all stations. Ticket booklets are available at *tabacchi* (tobacco) shops and in some terminals. *Tip:* Avoid riding the trains when the Romans are going to or from work or you'll be mashed flatter than fettuccine.

By Bus/Tram   Roman buses are operated by **ATAC (Azienda Tramvie e Autobus del Comune di Roma),** Via Volturno 65 (© **06-46951** for information). The service is quite good and you can ride to most parts of Rome for only 1,500L (€0.83, 75¢). The ticket is valid for 1¼ hours, and you can get on as many buses during that time period as you want, using the same ticket; you can also transfer free between the metro and the bus within the 75 minutes of validity. Bus service runs from 5:30am to midnight and the night service is from 12:10am to 5:30am; an N after the line number defines buses running at night. There is also a 2-hour bus tour of the city offered by bus 110, leaving from Stazione Termini daily at 2:30pm.

> ### *Tips* Traveler's Tip
>
> At the Stazione Termini, you can purchase a special **tourist bus and subway pass,** which costs 6,000L (€3.10, $3) for 1 day or 24,000L (€12.53, $12) for a week.

By Taxi   Don't count on hailing a taxi on the street or even getting one at a stand. If you're going out, have your hotel call one. At a restaurant, ask the waiter or cashier to dial for you. If you want to call yourself, try one of these numbers: © **06-6645,** 06-3570, or 06-4994. The meter begins at 4,500L (€2.35, $2.25) for the first 3 kilometers, then 1,300L (€0.73, 65¢) per kilometer. On Sunday, a 2,000L (€1.05, $1) supplement is assessed, plus another 5,000L (€2.60, $2.50) supplement from 10pm to 7am. There's yet another 2,000L (€1.05, $1) supplement for every suitcase. The driver will expect a 10% tip.

By Car   You can rent a car from **Hertz,** near the parking lot of the Villa Borghese, Via Veneto 156 (© **06-3216831**); **Italy by Car,** via Ludovisi 60 (© **06-4820966**); the local Italian company **Maggiore,** Via di Tor Cervara 225 (© **06-229351**); or **Avis** at Stazione Termini (© **06-4814373**).

By Bicycle   You can rent bicycles at many places throughout Rome. Ask at your hotel for the nearest rental location, or else go to **I Bike Rome,** Via Veneto 156 (© **06-322-5240**), which rents bicycles from the underground parking garage at the Villa Borghese. Most bikes cost 5,000L (€2.60, $2.50) per hour or 15,000L (€7.80, $7.50) per day. It's open daily from 9am to 7pm. Bring an ID card with you.

Ⓕ FAST FACTS: Rome

American Express   The offices are at Piazza di Spagna 38 (© **06-67641**; Metro: Spagna). The travel service and tour desk are open from Monday to Saturday 9am to 6:30pm. Hours for financial and mail services are from Monday to Friday 9am to 5pm and Saturday 9am to noon.

Business Hours   In general, **banks** are open from Monday to Friday 8:30am to 1:30pm and 3 to 4pm. Most **stores** are open generally Monday from 3:30 to 7:30pm and from Tuesday to Saturday 9:30 or 10am to 1pm and from 3:30 to 7 or 7:30pm. Some shops are open on Monday mornings, however, and some shops don't close for the afternoon break.

Currency   The Italian unit of currency is the lira, almost always used in the plural form, lire (abbreviated "L"). The rate of exchange used in this chapter was $1 = 2,000L, or 100L = 0.05¢. At press time, €1 = 1,936L (or 100L = €0.052) and £1 = approximately 3,000L (or 100L = .03p). From January 1, 2002, the monetary unit in Italy is the euro, though the lire will still be legal tender until March 1.

Currency Exchange   American Express (see above) can fill most banking needs. For the best exchange rate, cash your traveler's checks at banks or foreign-exchange offices, not at shops and hotels.

Dentist   For an English-speaking dentist, call the U.S. Embassy (© **06-46741**). There's also the 24-hour **G. Eastman Dental Hospital,** Viale Regina Elena 287 (© **06-844831**; Metro: Policlinico).

Rome Metropolitana

Doctor The U.S. Embassy (℗ **06-46741**) will provide a list of English-speaking doctors. All big hospitals in Rome have a 24-hour first-aid service (go to the emergency room or "pronto soccorso"). You'll find English-speaking doctors at the **Rome American Hospital,** Via Emilio Longoni 69 (℗ **06-22551;** bus: 112).

Drugstores A reliable pharmacy is **Farmacia Internazionale,** Piazza Barberini 49 (℗ **06-4871195;** Metro: Barberini), open day and night. Most pharmacies are open from 8:30am to 1pm and 4 to 7:30pm. In general, they follow a rotation system so that several are always open on Sunday.

Embassies/Consulates The Embassy of the **United States,** Via Vittorio Veneto 119A (℗ **06-46741;** Metro: Barberini), is open from Monday to Friday 8:30am to 5:30pm. Consular and passport services for **Canada,** Via Zara 30 (℗ **06-445981;** bus: 36; Metro: Policlinico), are open from Monday to Friday 10am to 12:30pm; the Canadian Embassy is at Via G. B. De Rossi 27 (℗ **06-445-981;** bus: 36 or 60). The office of the **United Kingdom,** Via XX Settembre 80A (℗ **06-42200001;** Metro: Barberini), is open from Monday to Friday 9:15am to 1:30pm. The Embassy of **Australia,** Via Alessandria 215 (℗ **06-852721;** bus: 36 or 60; Metro: Policlinico), is open from Monday to Thursday 9am to noon and 1:30 to 5pm and Friday 9am to noon; the Australian Consulate is at Corso Trieste 25 (℗ **06-852-721;** bus: 36 or 60). The

New Zealand office, Via Zara 28 (🕾 **06-441-71-71;** bus: 36 or 60; Metro: Policlinico), is open from Monday to Friday 8:30am to 12:45pm and 1:45 to 5pm. The Embassy of **Ireland** is at Piazza di Campitelli 3 (🕾 **06-697-912;** bus: 46; Metro: Circo Massimo); for consular queries call 🕾 **06-697-91211.** In case of emergency, embassies have a 24-hour referral service.

Emergencies Dial 🕾 **113** for an ambulance, police, or fire. In case of a breakdown on an Italian road, dial 🕾 **116** at the nearest telephone box; the nearest Automobile Club of Italy (ACI) will be notified to come to your aid.

Internet Access You can log onto the Web in central Rome at **Thenetgate,** Piazza Firenze 25 (🕾 **06-689-3445;** bus: 116). Hours are from Monday to Saturday 10am to 9pm and Sunday 2pm to 9pm. A 20-minute visit costs 5,000L (€2.60, $2.50), with 1 hour (including mailbox) at 10,000L (€5.20, $5). Access is free Saturdays 10:30 to 11am and 2 to 2:30pm. You can kill two birds with one stone just north of Stazione Termini at **Splash,** Via Varese 33 (🕾 **06-4938-2073;** Metro: Termini), a do-it-yourself Laundromat (13,000L/€6.75/$6.50 per load, including soap) with a satellite TV and four computers hooked up to the Net (4,000L/€2.13/$2 per half hour).

Post Office The **central post office,** Piazza San Silvestro 19, behind the Rinascente department store on Piazza Colonna (🕾 **06-6771;** bus: 52, 53, 58, 61, or 160), is open from Monday to Friday 9am to 6pm and Saturday 9am to 2pm.

Safety Purse snatching is commonplace in Rome. Young men on Vespas ride through the city looking for victims. To avoid trouble, stay away from the curb and hold on tightly to your purse. Don't lay anything valuable on tables or chairs where it can be grabbed up easily. Gypsy children are a particular menace. You'll often virtually have to flee, if they completely surround you. They'll often approach you with pieces of cardboard hiding their hands.

Telephone The **country code** for Italy is **39.** The **city code** for Rome is **06,** which is the code you'll use every time you dial a party located within Rome, regardless of whether you're within the city limits or not. To call **from one city code to another** within Italy, dial the city code, complete with the initial zero, then the local number. To **dial direct internationally,** dial **00,** then the country code for the country you are calling, then the area or city code and then the local number. Direct-dial calls from the United States to Italy are usually cheaper than calls placed from an Italian hotel to most phones in North America, so if possible, try to arrange for friends and acquaintances to call you at your hotel at prearranged times.

To ring national **telephone information** (in Italian) in Italy dial **12.** International information is available at **176,** but costs 1,200L (€0.60, 60¢) per request.

To make a **collect or calling-card call** from a public phone, drop in 200L (€0.10, 10¢) or insert a prepaid phone card (available from most *tabacchi*) and dial one of the following access numbers to reach an American operator or an English-language voice prompt: **AT&T** 🕾 **172-10-11** (if calling a country other than the United States, after access code dial 01, the country code of country you are calling, city code, and local number); **MCI** 🕾 **172-1022;** and **Sprint** 🕾 **172-1877.**

WHERE TO STAY
NEAR STAZIONE TERMINI
Expensive
Hotel Artemide ✪   A refined four-star hotel, this establishment was transformed from a 19th-century palazzetto into an elegant hotel named for Artemis, the Greek goddess. Close to the Opera, it combines stylish simplicity with modern comforts against an Art Nouveau backdrop. The original stained-glass skylight dome was retained in the lobby. Rooms have good furnishings along with spacious bathrooms.

Via Nazionale 22, 00184 Roma. ℂ 06-489911. Fax 06-48991700. www.spacehotels.it or www.travel.it. 85 units. 540,000–560,000L (€280.80–€291.20, $270–$280) double; 640,000L (€332.80, $320) suite. Rates include breakfast. AE, MC, DC, V. Parking 30,000L (€15.60, $15). Metro: Repubblica. **Amenities:** Restaurant, bar; room service; laundry/dry cleaning; no-smoking rooms. *In room:* A/C, TV, minibar.

Hotel Diana ✪   The Diana has recaptured the flavor of its heyday a century ago when both the aristocracy and the bourgeoisie dropped in for a drink after the Opera. In the heart of 19th-century Rome, Diana offers an elegant yet comfortable atmosphere. Rooms are tastefully furnished. Bathrooms offer heated towel racks, and a choice of tub or shower.

Via Principe Amedeo 4, 00185 Roma. ℂ 06-4827541. Fax 06-486998. www.hoteldianaroma.com. 186 units. 410,000L (€213.20, $205) double; 610,000L (€317.20, $305) junior suite. Rates include breakfast. AE, DC, MC, V. Parking 35,000L (€18.20, $18). Metro: Termini. **Amenities:** Restaurant, bar; panoramic rooftop terrace; no-smoking rooms. *In room:* A/C, TV, minibar, hair dryer.

Moderate
Aberdeen Hotel   This completely renovated hotel near the Opera is centrally located for most landmarks and for rail and bus connections. It lies in front of the Ministry of Defense, a rather quiet and fairly safe area of Rome. The recently renovated rooms are furnished with modern styling and firm, frequently renewed mattresses.

Via Firenze 48, 00184 Roma. ℂ 06-4823920. Fax 06-4821092. www.travel.it/roma/aberdeen. 27 units. 300,000L (€156, $150) double. Rates include buffet breakfast. AE, DC, MC, V. Parking 40,000L (€20.80, $20). Metro: Repubblica. Bus: 64 or 170. *In-room:* A/C, TV, minibar, hair dryer, safe.

Hotel Ranieri   Ranieri is a winning three-star hotel in a 19th-century freshly restored building. From the hotel you can stroll to the Opera, Piazza Della Repubblica, and Via Veneto. Rooms feature double-panel windows and rejuvenated bathrooms. Units have a minimalist decor, almost Scandinavian in design, with built-in furniture.

Via XX Settembre 43, 00187 Roma. ℂ 06-481-4467. Fax 06-481-8834. www.hotelranieri.com. 47 units. 298,000L (€154.95, $149) double. Rates include breakfast. AE, MC, V. Parking 30,000–45,000L (€15.60–€23.40, $15–$23). Metro: Repubblica. **Amenities:** Restaurant, bar; 24-hour room service. *In room:* A/C, TV, minibar, hair dryer, safe.

Medici   The Medici, built in 1906, is a substantial hotel that has easy access to the shops along Via XX Settembre. Many of its better rooms overlook an inner patio garden. Rooms are a generous size and were renovated in 1997 in a classic Roman style. The cheapest rooms are called standard; superior units offer air-conditioning, more antiques, and better furnishings. Breakfast is the only meal served.

Via Flavia 96, 00187 Roma. ℂ 06-482-7319. Fax 06-474-0767. www.hotelmedici.com. 69 units. 350,000L (€182, $175) double. Rates include breakfast. AE, DC, MC, V. Parking 35,000–40,000L (€18.20–€20.80, $18–$20). Metro: Repubblica. **Amenities:** Bar; room service. *In room:* A/C, TV, minibar, hair dryer.

Rome Accommodations

Aberdeen Hotel **18**
Alexandra **14**
Colosseum Hotel **21**
Hassler **12**
Hotel Artemide **19**
Hotel Atlante Star **4**
Hotel Columbus **3**

Hotel delle Muse **9**
Hotel de Russie **8**
Hotel Diana **20**
Hotel Eden **13**
Hotel Gregoriana **11**
Hotel Locarno **6**
Hotel Margutta **7**

Hotel Pavia **17**
Hotel Ranieri **16**
Marcus **5**
Medici **15**
Scalinata di Spagna **10**
Teatro di Pompeo **2**
Trastevere Manara **1**

Inexpensive

Hotel Pavia   This is a popular choice on this quiet street near the gardens of the Baths of Diocletian. Established in the 1980s, it occupies a much-renovated century-old building. The front rooms tend to be noisy, but that's the curse of all Termini hotels. Nevertheless, the rooms are comfortable and fairly attractive, and were last renovated in 1998. Each comes with a neatly tiled shower bathroom.

Via Gaeta 83, 00185 Roma. ℂ **06-483-801**. Fax 06-481-9090. www.travel.it/roma/hotelpavia. 25 units. 285,000L (€148.20, $143) double. Rates include breakfast. AE, DC, MC, V. Parking 25,000L (€13, $13). Metro: Termini. **Amenities:** Bar; room service. *In room:* A/C, TV, minibar, hair dryer, safe.

NEAR VIA VENETO & PIAZZA BARBERINI
Very Expensive

Hotel Eden ✦✦✦   During the heyday of this ornate hotel, all the big names—Hemingway, Maria Callas, Ingrid Bergman, Fellini—checked in here. In 1994, it reopened after a 2-year (and $20 million) radical renovation that enhanced its original fin de siècle grandeur and added the modern amenities its five-star status calls for. Its hilltop position guarantees a panoramic city view from most rooms. Understated elegance is the rule.

Via Ludovisi 49, 00187 Roma. ℂ **800/225-5843** in the U.S., or 06-478121. Fax 06-4821584. www. hotel-eden.it. 119 units. 1,210,000–1,408,000L (€629.20–€732.15, $605–$704) double; from 3,190,000L (€1,658.80, $1,595) suite. AE, DC, MC, V. Parking 45,000L (€23.40, $23). Metro: Barberini. **Amenities:** Restaurant, bar; gym; health spa. *In room:* A/C, TV, minibar, hair dryer, safe.

Moderate

Alexandra ✦ *Finds*   Here's where you can stay on Via Veneto without going broke. Set in what was originally a 19th-century private mansion, this hotel offers well kept, comfortable accommodations filled with antique furniture and modern conveniences. Rooms facing front are exposed to roaring traffic and animated street life; those in back are quieter but have less of a view. Breakfast is the only meal served. The garden-inspired breakfast room designed by Paolo Portoghesi is especially appealing.

Via Veneto 18, 00187 Roma. ℂ **06-4881943**. Fax 06-4871804. www.venere.it/roma/alexandra. 46 units. 410,000L (€213.20, $205) double; 600,000L (€312, $300) suite for 2. Rates include a continental breakfast. AE, DC, MC, V. Parking 50,000L (€26, $25). Metro: Barberini. **Amenities:** Laundry/dry cleaning. *In room:* A/C, TV, hair dryer.

IN PARIOLI
Inexpensive

Hotel delle Muse   A classic, family run three-star establishment, this hotel is 1 kilometer (½ mile) north of the Villa Borghese, a winning but unheralded choice. Most rooms have been renovated but remain rather spartan.

Via Tommaso Salvini 18, 00197 Roma. ℂ **06-8088333**. Fax 06-8085749. www.venere.it/roma/muse. 61 units. 260,000L (€135.20, $130) double; 290,000L (€150.80, $145) triple. Rates include buffet breakfast. AE, DC, MC, V. Bus: 360. Tram: 19. **Amenities:** Restaurant (summer only), bar. *In room:* TV, hair dryer.

AROUND THE SPANISH STEPS & PIAZZA DEL POPOLO
Very Expensive

Hassler ✦✦✦   The only deluxe hotel in this old part of Rome, it uses the Spanish Steps as its grand entrance. The crown worn by the Hassler is still in place after all these years; the hostelry has such a mystique that it prospers and endures in spite of high prices. Rooms, some of which are small, have a personalized look, with French windows, comfortable beds, and—the nicest touch of all—bowls of fresh flowers. Some have balconies with views of the city.

Piazza Trinità d. Monti 6, 00187 Roma. ℂ 800/223-6800 in the U.S., or 06-699-340. Fax 06-678-9991. www.hotelhasslerroma.com. 100 units. 790,000–960,000L (€410.80–€499.20, $395 $480) double; from 1,200,000L (€624, $600) suite. AE, DC, MC, V. Parking 45,000L (€23.40, $23). Metro: Spagna. **Amenities:** Restaurant, bar; baby-sitting; laundry/dry cleaning. *In room:* A/C, TV, minibar, hair dryer, safe.

Hotel de Russie ✪✪✪ This five-star deluxe hotel lies just off the Piazza del Popolo. Lovers of *luxe* are deserting such traditional favorites as the Hassler to stay here. In one of the choicest platinum locations in Rome, it is lavishly furnished. It was once a favorite of Russian dignitaries (hence, its name) and of such artists as Jean Cocteau, Picasso, and Stravinsky. In World War II, it was the spy center for Italy. About 30% of the spacious rooms are traditionally furnished, the others more minimalist with a strikingly contemporary motif. Bathrooms are elegantly tiled.

Via del Bahuino, 00187 Roma. ℂ 800/323-7500 In the U.S. and Canada, or 06-328-881. Fax 06-328-8888. www.rfhotels.com. 129 units. 950,000–1,160,000L (€494–€603.20, $475–$580) double; from 1,250,000L (€650, $625) suite. AE, DC, MC, V. Metro: Flaminia. **Amenities:** Restaurant, bar; health club; 24-hour room service; laundry/dry cleaning. *In room:* A/C, TV, minibar, hair dryer, safe.

Expensive
Hotel Locarno ✪ This little charmer is near Piazza del Popolo, said to be haunted by the imperial ghost of Nero, although that isn't expected to disturb your night's sleep. You can count on Rome's heavy traffic to do that. The hotel's most winning feature is its large roof terrace where you can take your breakfast while enjoying some of the major sights of Rome's skyline. If you'd like to go exploring, the Locarno will provide you with a bike. A 1920s aura pervades the hotel, as evoked by the wrought-iron elevator cage or the marble-topped walnut bar with its Tiffany-style lamp. Rooms and bathrooms are completely up to date.

Via della Penna 22, 00186 Roma. ℂ 06-3610841. Fax 06-3215249. www.hotellocarno.com. 52 units. 396,000L (€205.90, $198) double; 800,000L (€416, $400) suite. Rates include buffet breakfast. AE, DC, MC, V. Metro: Flaminio. **Amenities:** Restaurant, bar; roof terrace; garden. *In room:* A/C, TV, minibar, safe.

Scalinata di Spagna ✪✪ This upscale B&B near the Spanish Steps has always been one of the most sought-after in Rome. It's right at the top of the steps, directly across the small piazza from the deluxe Hassler. Decor varies radically from one room to the next; some have low beamed ceilings and ancient-looking wood furniture, others offer loftier ceilings and more average appointments. All rooms were renovated and upgraded in 1998, bathrooms receiving special attention. In season, breakfast is served on the rooftop garden terrace with its sweeping view of the dome of St. Peter's across the Tiber.

Piazze. Trinità dei Monti 17, 00187 Roma. ℂ 06-6793006. Fax 06-69940598. www.italyhotel.com/home/roma/scalinata. 16 units. 400,000–600,000L (€208–€312, $200–$300) double; from 900,000L (€468, $450) suite. Rates include breakfast. AE, MC, V. Parking 45,000L (€23.40, $23). Metro: Spagna. **Amenities:** Roof terrace; baby-sitting; laundry/dry cleaning. *In room:* A/C, TV, minibar, hair dryer, safe.

Moderate
Hotel Gregoriana ✪ Although surrounded by much more expensive neighbors like the pricey Hassler, the small Gregoriana in a former 17th-century convent has its own fans—mainly members of the Italian fashion industry. Rooms are small but comfortable. The elevator cage is a black-and-gold Art Deco fantasy, and the door to each room has a reproduction of an Erté print whose fanciful characters indicate the letter designating that room.

Via Gregoriana 18, 00187 Roma. ℂ 06-6794269. Fax 06-6784258. 20 units. 400,000L (€208, $200) double. Rates include breakfast. AE, DC, V. Parking 45,000L (€23.40, $23). Metro: Spagna. *In-room:* A/C, TV, hair dryer.

Inexpensive
Hotel Margutta   Located on a cobblestone street near Piazza del Popolo, this hotel offers attractively decorated but exceedingly small rooms and cramped shower-only bathrooms. Its helpful staff makes it an enduring favorite, nonetheless. The best rooms are on the top floor; two of these share a terrace, and another larger room has a private terrace.

Via Laurina 34, 00187 Roma. ℰ **06-3223674.** Fax 06-3200395. 24 units. 190,000–260,000L (€98.80–€135.20, $95–$130) double; 250,000L (€130, $125) triple. Rates include breakfast. AE, DC, MC, V. Metro: Flaminio. **Amenities:** Breakfast room. *In room:* Hair dryer.

Marcus *(Kids)*   This family-run hotel is near the Spanish Steps, right in the historical and shopping center of Rome. It is housed in a 16th-century palace that offers all modern comforts with reasonable prices. Rooms, in a variety of sizes, are tastefully furnished and the windows are double-glazed. Bathrooms are simple with shower stalls. Breakfast is the only meal served. The helpful Salvatore de Caro and his family will be glad to make you feel at home in this charming two-star hotel.

Via del Clementino 94 (corner of Via Ripetta and Via della Scrofa), 00186 Roma. ℰ **06-6830-0320.** Fax 06-6830-0312. www.venere.it/roma/marcus. 18 units, 17 with bathroom. 190,000–250,000L (€98.80–€130, $95–$125) double. Rates include breakfast. AE, MC, V. Metro: Spagna. **Amenities:** Room service. *In room:* A/C, TV, hair dryer, safe.

NEAR CAMPO DE' FIORI
Moderate
Teatro di Pompeo *(★)(Finds)*   Built on the top of the ruins of the Theater of Pompey, which dates from about 55 B.C., this small charmer lies near the spot where Julius Caesar met his fate. Intimate and refined, it's on a quiet piazzetta near the Palazzo Farnese and Campo de' Fiori. Rooms, all doubles, are decorated in an old-fashioned Italian style with hand-painted tiles, and the beamed ceilings date from the days of Michelangelo. There's no restaurant, but breakfast is served.

Largo del Pallaro 8, 00186 Roma. ℰ **06-68300170.** Fax 06-68805531. 13 units. 350,000L (€182, $175) double. Rates include breakfast. AE, DC, MC, V. Bus: 46, 62, or 64. **Amenities:** Room service; baby-sitting; laundry/dry cleaning. *In room:* A/C, TV, minibar, hair dryer, safe.

NEAR VATICAN CITY
Very Expensive
Hotel Atlante Star *(★★★)*   This is a first-class hotel a short distance from St. Peter's. The upper floors give the impression of being inside a luxuriously appointed ocean liner. Rooms are small but posh, outfitted with all the modern comforts. A royal suite features a Jacuzzi. The views of St. Peter's are the most striking of any hotel in Rome.

Via Vitelleschi 34, 00193 Roma. ℰ **06-6873233.** Fax 06-6872300. www.atlantehotels.com. 90 units. 580,000L (€301.60, $290) double; from 700,000L (€364, $350) suite. Rates include buffet breakfast. AE, MC, V. Parking 40,000L (€20.80, $20). Metro: Ottaviano. Tram: 19 or 30. **Amenities:** Restaurant, rooftop cafe; room service; baby-sitting; laundry/dry cleaning. *In room:* A/C, TV, minibar, hair dryer.

Expensive
Hotel Columbus *(★)*   In an impressive 15th-century palace, Hotel Columbus lies a few minutes' walk from St. Peter's. It was once the private home of a wealthy cardinal who later became Pope Julius II and had Michelangelo paint the Sistine Chapel. The building looks much as it must have those long centuries ago. Rooms are considerably simpler than the tiled and tapestried salons. All are

spacious; a few are enormous and still have such original details as decorated wood ceilings and frescoed walls.

Via della Conciliazione 33, 00193 Roma. © 06-6865435. Fax 06-6864874. 92 units. 570,000L (€296.40, $285) double; 660,000L (€343.20, $330) suite. Rates include buffet breakfast. AE, DC, MC, V. Hotel has a few free parking spaces. Bus: 62 or 64. Amenities: Restaurant; room service; laundry/dry cleaning. In room: A/C, TV, minibar, hair dryer.

NEAR ANCIENT ROME
Inexpensive
Colosseum Hotel ★ *Finds*   Not far from the Santa Maria Maggiore, the Colosseum offers baronial living on a miniature scale. The tasteful hotel reflects the best of Italy's design heritage. Rooms are furnished with well-conceived antique reproductions. The drawing room, with its long refectory table, white walls, red tiles, and provincial armchairs, invites lingering.

Via Sforza 10, 00184 Roma. © 06-4827228. Fax 06-4827285. www.venere.it/home/roma/colosseum/colosseum.html. 47 units 246,000L (€127.90, $123) double. Rates include breakfast. AE, DC, MC, V. Parking 40,000L (€20.80, $20). Metro: Cavour. Amenities: Bar; room service. In room: A/C, TV, hair dryer, safe.

IN TRASVETERE
Trastevere Manara ★ *Finds*   Deep in the heart of Trastevere, which tourists used to avoid in the '50s and '60s, there's today a demand for suitable lodgings. Time was, you'd stay here only if you were writing a book called *Down and Out in Roma*. But those cobweb memories have been chased away, and this little gem has emerged with freshly decorated rooms and a price that's hard to beat for those who want to stay in one of the most atmospheric sections of Rome. Most rooms open onto Piazza San Cisimato, and all have comfortable albeit functional furnishings. Shower-only bathrooms are quite small. Breakfast is the only meal served, but many good restaurants lie just minutes outside the door.

Via L. Manara 24–25, 00153 Roma. © 06-581-4713. Fax 06-588-1016. 9 units. 150,000L (€78, $75) double. Continental breakfast included. AE, MC, V. Free parking on street. Bus: H. Tram: 8. In room: TV.

WHERE TO DINE
NEAR STAZIONE TERMINI
Expensive
Agata e Romeo ★ ROMAN   Named after the husband-wife team Romeo and Agata Caraccio, this is a small-scale and charming enclave of culinary creativity in the shadow of Santa Maria Maggiore. Menu examples include a puree of eggplant capped with slices of rabbit filet; or a deceptively simple version of white beans capped with fried cuttlefish. Spaghetti is often prepared with shellfish, especially clams. Breast of duck with porcini and herb sauce, or rack of lamb with rosemary sauce, are perennial favorites. One of their most enduring dessert specialties is their own version of *millefoglie*—chantilly cream laced with liqueur and served in puff pastry.

Via Carlo Alberto 45. © 06-4466115. Reservations recommended. Main courses 30,000–42,000L (€15.60–€21.85, $15–$21). AE, DC, MC, V. Mon–Sat 12:30–2:30pm and 7:30–10:30pm. Metro: Vittorio Emanuele.

Moderate
Scoglio di Frisio ★ NEAPOLITAN/PIZZA   South of the Stazione Termini, Scoglio di Frisio is the choice *suprême* to introduce yourself to the Neapolitan kitchen. While here, you should get reacquainted with pizza—this is the genuine article. At night, you can begin with a plate-size Neapolitan pizza (crunchy,

oozy, and excellent) with clams and mussels. After a medley of stuffed vegetables and antipasti, you may settle for chicken cacciatore or veal scaloppini. Scoglio di Frisio also presents Neapolitan songs, so it makes for an inexpensive night on the town.

Via Merulana 256. ⓒ **06-4872765**. Reservations recommended. Main courses 15,000–32,000L (€7.80–€16.65, $7.50–$16). AE, DC, MC, V. Mon–Fri 12:30–3pm and 7:30–11pm; Sat–Sun 7:30–11pm. Bus: 714 from Stazione Termini.

Inexpensive
Il Dito e La Luna SICILIAN/ITALIAN   At this charming, small restaurant, the menu is equally divided between traditional Sicilian recipes and more creative up-to-date recipes prepared with gusto and flair. The setting emulates an unpretentious bistro. Menu items include fresh orange-infused anchovies served on orange segments; a creamy flan of mild onions and mountain cheese; seafood couscous loaded with shellfish; and such succulent pastas as square-cut spaghetti (*tonnarelli*) prepared with mussels, bacon, and tomatoes, and exotic mushrooms.

Via dei Sabelli 49–51, San Lorenzo. ⓒ **06-4940726**. Reservations recommended. Main courses 20,000–25,000L (€10.40–€13, $10–$12.50). No credit cards. Mon–Sat 8pm–midnight. Metro: Vittorio Emanuele.

NEAR VIA VENETO & PIAZZA BARBERINI
Very Expensive
Sans Souci ✦✦✦ FRENCH/ITALIAN   Sans Souci, which was getting a little tired, has now bounced back, and Michelin has restored its coveted star. It is now the market leader for glitz, glamour, and nostalgia for *la dolce vita*. This is a major stop on the see-and-be-seen circuit, and might be your best bet for spotting a movie star, albeit a faded one. The menu is ever changing, as "new creations" are devised. You might begin with a terrine of goose liver with truffles, a special creation of the chef. The fish soup, according to one Rome restaurant critic, is "a legend to experience." The soufflés are also deservedly popular; artichoke, asparagus, and spinach are our favorites.

Via Sicilia 20. ⓒ **06-4821814**. Reservations recommended. Main courses 35,000–68,000L (€18.20–€35.35, $18–$34). AE, DC, MC, V. Tues–Sun 8pm–1am. Closed Aug 10–30. Metro: Barberini.

Expensive
Colline Emiliane ✦ EMILIANA-ROMAGNOLA   This small restaurant right off Piazza Barberini serves *classica cucina bolognese*. It's a family-run place where everybody helps out. The owner is the cook and his wife makes the pasta, which, incidentally, is about the best you'll encounter in Rome. The house specialty is an inspired *tortellini alla panna* (cream sauce) with truffles. An excellent main course is *braciola di maiale*—boneless rolled pork cutlets that have been stuffed with ham and cheese, breaded, and sautéed. *Bollito misto* (mixed boiled meats) is another specialty.

Via Avignonesi 22. ⓒ **06-4817538**. Reservations required. Main courses 30,000–60,000L (€15.60–€31.20, $15–$30). MC, V. Sat–Thurs 12:45–2:45pm and 7:45–10:45pm. Closed Aug. Metro: Barberini.

Moderate
Césarina EMILIANA-ROMAGNOLA/ROMAN   This restaurant perpetuates the culinary traditions of the late Cesarina Masi in a newer manifestation of the original hole-in-the-wall. Today, with three dining rooms and more than 200 seats, the restaurant serves excellent versions of *bollito misto* (an array of well-seasoned boiled meats), rolled from table to table on a cart; and *misto Cesarina*—three kinds of pasta, each handmade and served with a different

ⓒ The Cafe Scene

Caffè de Paris, Via Vittorio Veneto 90 (© **06-4885284;** Metro: Barberini), rises and falls in popularity depending on the decade. In the 1950s, it was a haven for the fashionable and now it's a popular restaurant in summer where the tables spill out onto the sidewalk filled with patrons. Open from Wednesday to Monday 8am to 1:30am. **Canova Café,** Piazza del Popolo 16 (© **06-3612231;** Metro: Flaminio), has a sidewalk terrace for people-watching, plus a snack bar, a restaurant, and a wine shop inside. In summer you'll have access to a courtyard with ivy-covered walls. Meals cost 25,000L (€13, $13) and up. Open daily from 8am to midnight or later depending on the crowd.

Since 1760, **Antico Caffè Greco,** Via Condotti 84 (© **06-6791700;** Metro: Spagna), has been Rome's most posh and fashionable coffee bar. It has for years enjoyed a reputation as the gathering place of the literati. In the front is a wooden bar, and beyond that a series of small salons, decorated in a 19th-century style. Open from Monday to Saturday 8am to 9pm. **Caffè Sant'Eustachio,** Piazza Sant'Eustachio 82 (© **06-6861309;** bus: 116), is one of the city's most celebrated espresso shops, on a small square near the Pantheon. The water supply comes from a source outside Rome, which the emperor Augustus funneled into the city with an aqueduct in 19 B.C. Rome's most experienced espresso judges claim that the water plays an important part in the coffee's flavor. Open from Tuesday to Friday and Sunday 8:30am to 1am, Saturday 8:30am to 1:30am.

sauce. Equally appealing is *saltimbocca* (veal with ham) and *cotoletta alla bolognese* (veal cutlet baked with ham and cheese).

Via Piemonte 109. © **06-4880828.** Reservations recommended. Main courses 18,000–28,000L (€9.35–€14.55, $9–$14). AE, DC, MC, V. Mon–Sat 12:30–3pm and 7:30–11pm. Bus: 52, 53, 56, or 910 from Stazione Termini.

Girarrosto Toscano ℛ *(Value* TUSCAN   You may have to wait for a table at this popular place facing the walls of the Borghese Gardens. Under vaulted ceilings in a cellar setting, fine Tuscan specialties are served. Begin with an enormous selection of antipasti. You're then given a choice of pasta. *Bistecca alla fiorentina* (grilled steak seasoned with oil, salt, and pepper) is the best item to order, although it's expensive. Oysters and fresh fish from the Adriatic are also served every day. Meat and fish dishes are priced according to weight and costs can run considerably higher than the prices quoted above.

Via Campania 29. © **06-4823835.** Reservations required. Main courses 25,000–45,000L (€13–€23.40, $13–$23). AE DC, MC, V. Thurs–Tues 12:30–2:30pm and 7:30–11pm. Bus: 90B, 95, 490, or 495. Metro: Barberini, then a long stroll.

NEAR VILLA BORGHESE
Moderate

Testa Food & Wine ℛ *(Finds* ITALIAN   Near Villa Borghese, this recently renovated restaurant draws discerning palates seeking food and wine at a reasonable price. Its *orecchiette* (ear-shaped pasta) gratinée with broccoli and sautéed clams is one of the city's finest pasta dishes. Another excellent home-made pasta dish is *cacio e pepe* made with crunchy artichokes. The tuna steak with sun-dried tomatoes is a delight, as is the duck breast stuffed with foie gras, sprinkled with roasted almonds, and served with plums marinated in port. The bar features live jazz on Tuesday nights and has become one of the best places to be in Rome.

Via Tirso 30. ✆ 06-8530-0692. Main courses 25,000–35,000L (€13–€18.20, $13–$18). Mon–Sat noon–3pm and 8pm–midnight (bar open until 3am). Closed Aug. Bus: 19.

IN PARIOLI
Very Expensive
Relais Le Jardin ₳₳₳ ITALIAN/INTERNATIONAL   For a traditional and creative cuisine in an elegantly romantic and classic setting, Relais Le Jardin is the place to go. A chichi crowd with demanding palates patronizes it nightly. The pasta and soups are among the best in town—the tonnarelli pasta with asparagus and smoked ham served with concassé tomatoes is delectable, as is the pasta with ricotta sauce, black olives, corn, and oregano. For your main course you face such selections as roast loin of lamb with artichoke romana, pork filet stuffed with crab, or grilled beef sirloin with hot chicory and sautéed potatoes.

In the Hotel Lord Byron, Via G. de Notaris 5. ✆ 06-3613041. Reservations required. Main courses 45,000–55,000L (€23.40–€28.60, $23–$28). AE, DC, MC, V. Mon–Sat 12:30–2:30pm and 8–10:30pm. Bus: 26 or 52.

Moderate
Al Ceppo ₳ *Finds* ROMAN   This restaurant's somewhat hidden location (although it's only 2 blocks from the Villa Borghese, near Piazza Ungheria) means that the clientele is likely to be Roman rather than foreign. At this longtime and enduring favorite, the cuisine is as good as it ever was in its heyday. "The Log" fea-tures an open fireplace where the chef prepares lamb chops, liver, and bacon to charcoal perfection. The beefsteak, which hails from Tuscany, is also succulent. Other dishes include *tagliolini monteconero* (made with clams and fresh tomatoes), and a savory version of spaghetti with pepperoni, fresh basil, and pecorino cheese.

Via Panama 2. ✆ 06-8419696. Reservations recommended. Main courses 23,000–38,000L (€11.95–€19.75, $12–$19). AE, DC, MC, V. Tues–Sun 12:30–3pm and 8–11pm. Closed the last 3 weeks of Aug. Bus: 4, 52, or 53.

NEAR THE SPANISH STEPS & PIAZZA DEL POPOLO
Expensive
El Toulà ₳ ROMAN/VENETIAN   This *luxe* restaurant offers quintessential Roman haute cuisine with a creative flair in an elegant setting of vaulted ceilings and large archways. One menu section is devoted exclusively to culinary spe-cialties of Venice, including Venice's classic dish, *fegato* (liver) *alla Veneziana;* calamari stuffed with vegetables; *baccalà* mousse (codfish) with polenta, and another Venetian classic, *broetto* (fish soup made with monkfish and clams). There's a charming bar. El Toulà usually isn't crowded at lunchtime.

Via della Lupa 29B. ✆ 06-6873498. Reservations required for dinner. Main courses 40,000–50,000L (€20.80–€26, $20–$25); 5-course menu *degustazione* 120,000L (€62.40, $60); 4-course menu veneto 100,000L (€52, $50). AE, DC, MC, V. Tues–Fri noon–3pm and Mon–Sat 7:30–11pm. Closed Aug. Bus: 81, 90, 90b, 628, or 913.

Moderate
Dal Bolognese ₳ BOLOGNESE   If *La Dolce Vita* were being filmed now, this restaurant would be used as a backdrop, its patrons photographed in their latest Fendi drag. It's one of those rare dining spots that's not only chic, but

noted for its food as well. To begin your meal, we suggest *misto di pasta*—four pastas, each flavored with a different sauce, arranged on the same plate. For your main course, specialties include *lasagne verdi, tagliatelle alla bolognese,* and a most recommendable *cotoletta alla bolognese* (veal cutlet topped with cheese). Although almond cake is the house specialty, it's hard to resist the fresh strawberry tart.

Piazza del Popolo 1–2. © 06-3611426. Reservations required. Main courses 18,000–35,000L (€9.35–€18.20, $9–$18). AE, DC, MC, V. Tues–Sun 12:30–3pm and 8:15pm–1am. Closed 20 days in Aug. Metro: Flaminio.

Otello alla Concordia ROMAN   On a side street amid the glamorous boutiques near the northern edge of the Spanish Steps, this is a popular and consistently reliable restaurant. Diners choose a table (space permitting) in either an arbor-covered courtyard or in a cramped but convivial series of inner dining rooms. The *spaghetti alle vongole veraci* (spaghetti with clams) and the pasta with chickpeas are excellent, as are Roman-style *abbacchio arrosto* (roasted baby lamb), a selection of grilled or sautéed fish dishes, and classic eggplant parmigiana.

Via della Croce 81. © 06-6791178. Reservation recommended. Main courses 15,000–25,000L (€7.80–€13, $8–$13); fixed-price menu 38,000L (€19.75, $19). AE, DC, MC, V. Mon–Sat 12:30–3pm and 7:30–11pm. Closed 2 weeks in Feb. Metro: Spagna.

Ristorante Nino dal 1934 TUSCAN   Ristorante Nino, off Via Condotti a short walk from the Spanish Steps, is a tavern mecca for writers, artists, and international models from one of the nearby high-fashion houses. The Guarnacci brothers, the owners, deserve acclaim for their Tuscan dishes, such as pappardelle with hare sauce or bean soup from the Tuscan hills. The hearty cooking is completely unpretentious. The restaurant is particularly known for its steaks, shipped in from Florence and charcoal broiled (priced according to weight). Cannelloni Nino is one of the chef's specialties, as are *ravioli di tartufo* (dumplings stuffed with truffles) or *baccalà* (dried cod fish, usually on Friday).

Via Borgognona 11. © 06-6795676. Reservations recommended. Main courses 20,000–45,000L (€10.40–€23.40, $10–$23). AE, DC, MC, V. Mon–Sat 12:30–3pm and 7:30–11pm. Closed Aug. Metro: Spagna.

NEAR CAMPO DE' FIORI & THE JEWISH GHETTO
Moderate

Da Giggetto ROMAN   Da Giggetto, in the old ghetto, is a short walk from the Theater of Marcellus. Romans flock to this bustling trattoria for their special traditional dishes. None are more typical than *carciofi alla giudea,* baby-tender fried artichokes. This is a true delicacy! The cheese concoction, mozzarella in carrozza, is another good choice, as are the zucchini flowers stuffed with mozzarella and anchovies, even the dried salted cod filet. Also sample *fettuccine al 'Amatriciana,* with shrimp sautéed in garlic and olive oil.

Via del Portico d'Ottavia 21–22. © 06-6861105. Reservations recommended. Main courses 20,000–30,000L (€10.40–€15.60, $10–$15). AE, DC, MC, V. Tues–Sun 12:30–3pm and 7:30–11pm. Closed Aug 1–15. Bus: 62, 64, 75, 90, or 170.

Il Drappo 🔎 *Finds* SARDINIAN   Il Drappo, on a hard-to-find, narrow street off a square near the Tiber, is operated by a woman known to her habitués only as "Valentina." Fixed-price dinners may include a wafer-thin appetizer called *carte di musica* (sheet-music paper), topped with tomatoes, green peppers, parsley, and olive oil, followed by fresh spring lamb in season, or a changing selection of strongly flavored regional specialties. Among these is roast suckling Sardinian pig with an herb sauce, and casserole of rabbit with black olives and capers. For dessert, try a Sardinian sweet known as *sebadas,* like a little crepe stuffed with cheese and honey and served very hot. Only Sardinian wines are served, one of the best being a red wine known as Cannolau di Erzo.

Vicolo del Malpasso 9. ✆ **06-6877365.** Reservations required. Main courses 20,000–45,000L (€10.40–€23.40, $10–$23); fixed-price menus 70,000L (€36.40, $35). AE, MC, V. Mon–Sat 7pm–midnight. Closed Aug 15–31. Bus: 46, 62, or 64.

Vecchia Roma ITALIAN/ROMAN   This charming, moderately priced trattoria is in the heart of the Jewish ghetto (a short walk from the Campidoglio). The owners are known for their selection of fresh seafood, and the minestrone of the day is made with fresh vegetables. An interesting selection of antipasti is always presented, including salmon and a vegetable antipasto. The pastas and risottos are also excellent; the "green" risotto with porcini mushrooms is invariably good. Lamb is a specialty of the chef.

Via della Tribuna di Campitelli 18. ✆ **06-6864604.** Reservations recommended. Main courses 24,000–40,000L (€12.53–20.80, $12–$20). AE, DC. Thurs–Tues 1–3:30pm and 8–11pm. Closed 10 days in Aug. Bus: 64, 90, 90b, 97, or 774.

NEAR PIAZZA NAVONA & THE PANTHEON
Very Expensive
Quinzi & Gabrieli 🏠🏠🏠 SEAFOOD   We've never found better, or fresher, seafood than that served here. Don't be put off by the rough and ready service, but be prepared to pay for the privilege, as fresh seafood is extremely expensive in Rome. Everything tastes natural and fresh, and heavy sauces aren't used to disguise old fish as they are in many restaurants. In fact, the restaurant is known for its raw seafood, such as a delicate carpaccio of swordfish, sea bass, and deep-sea shrimp. The house specialty is spaghetti with lobster, but all sorts of fish are served, including sea urchins, octopus, sole, and red mullet. Check out what's available in a special display on ice at the entrance. In summer French doors lead to a small dining terrace.

Via delle Coppelle 5/6, 00185 Roma. ✆ **06-6879389.** Reservation required as far in advance as possible. Main courses 50,000–80,000L (€26–€41.60, $25–$40). AE, DC, MC, V. Mon–Sat 7:30–11:30pm. Closed Aug. Bus: 44, 46, 55, 60, 61, 62, 64, or 65.

Expensive
Il Convivio 🏠🏠🏠 ROMAN/INTERNATIONAL   This is one of the most acclaimed restaurants in Rome, and one of the very few to be granted a coveted Michelin star. The Troiano brothers turn out an inspired cuisine based on shopping for the best and freshest ingredients at the market. To launch yourself, order their giant shrimp tossed with fresh greens. Among the pasta selections their gnocchi stuffed with zucchini and dribbled with a well-seasoned seafood sauce delights, as does one of the chef's specialties—*petto di faraona*, stuffed chicken spiced up with fresh olives.

Vicolo dei Soldati 31. ✆ **06-686-9432.** Reservations required. Main courses 46,000L (€23.90, $23) each. AE, DC, MC, V. Mon 8–11pm; Tues–Sat 1–2:30pm and 8–11pm. Bus: 40 and 64.

Troiani 🏠 ITALIAN   Chef Angelo Troiana is on the A-list of Roman chefs. Since 1989, Angelo and his two brothers have excited discriminating palates with seasonal Italian cooking and creative culinary innovation. Launch yourself into the excitement with a warm seafood salad made with clams, mussels, white fish, and a giant prawn with al dente vegetables and a "mayonnaise of the sea," a fragrant lemony sauce. Worthy main courses include saddle of rabbit that might be stuffed with porcini mushrooms and served with an onion marmalade, or boned rack of lamb cooked in an herb and vegetable crust. For dessert, consider a slice of almond and bitter chocolate cake accented with fresh currants.

Via dei Soldati 28. ✆ **06-688805950**. Reservations recommended. Main courses 45,000L (€23.40, $23). AE, DC, MC, V. Tues–Sat 1–2:30pm and Tues–Sun 8–10:30pm. Bus: 70, 87, or 90.

Moderate

Bramante ROMAN On a cobblestone street in back of the Piazza Navona, this cafe-restaurant opens onto a delightful small square of vine-draped taverns. Behind the ivy-covered facade the interior is completely hand painted, as white candles illuminate the marble bar, making for a cozy, inviting atmosphere. The owner, Mr. Giuseppe, tries to make visitors appreciate Italian food and traditions, and succeeds admirably. Recipes are simple but rich in Mediterranean flavor. You can taste wonderful pastas made just with fresh tomato sauce, garlic, and pasta, or else something heavier such as braised beef or tender grilled steak flavored with herbs and served with potatoes. They don't serve fish, however.

Via della Pace 25. ✆ **06-68803916**. Reservations recommended. Main courses 20,000–30,000L (€10.40–€15.60, $10–$15). AE, DC, MC, V. Mon–Sat 5pm–1am; Sun noon–1am. Closed Dec 24. Bus: 44, 46, 55, 60, 61, 62, 64, or 65.

Il Chicco d'Uva ✿ ITALIAN/INTERNATIONAL Among fashionable Romans, this is a current hot dining ticket lying just off Piazza Navona. You can see members of Roman society laughing, drinking, and eating in elegant surroundings softly lit by candles. The food is secondary here as this place is on the see-and-be-seen circuit. But the cuisine has been greatly improved. Our party recently delighted in such dishes as the fresh fish of the day cooked with chopped tomatoes and perfect seasonings. Among the pastas, we went for the wide noodle, pappardelle, which was served with fresh artichokes and calamari, a winning combination. One of the chef's specialties is *embuttiti di vitello*, a lamb sausage. Try it.

Corso Rinascimento 70. ✆ **06-686-7983**. Reservations required. Main courses 23,000–35,000L (€11.95–€18.20, $12–$18). AE, MC, V. Mon–Sat 7:30pm–midnight. Closed 2 weeks in Aug (dates vary). Bus: 87.

La Carbonara ROMAN In a palazzetto at the edge of the market square, this amicable trattoria claims to be the home of the original spaghetti carbonara. The current chef still prepares the dish as his predecessor did, as well as succulent antipasti, grilled meats, and fresh seasonal vegetables. A dish that is truly *divino* is the sautéed artichokes with pumpkin flowers. The chef also specializes in a wide selection of risottos, flavored with asparagus, porcini mushrooms, zucchini, or fresh artichokes—whatever is in season. In summer, some sidewalk tables are available for people-watchers.

Piazza Campo de' Fiori 23. ✆ **06-6864783**. Reservations recommended. Main courses 18,000–25,000L (€9.35–€13, $9–$12.50). AE, MC, V. Wed–Mon noon–2:30pm and 6:30–10:30pm. Closed 3 weeks in Aug. Bus: 64.

L'Eau Vive ✿ *Finds* FRENCH/INTERNATIONAL This discovery is run by lay missionaries who wear the dress of their native countries. The restaurant occupies the cellar and the ground floor of a 17th-century palace. In this formal atmosphere, at 10pm nightly, the waitresses sing religious hymns and "Ave Marias." Your gratuity for service will be turned over for religious purposes. Pope John Paul II used to dine here when he was still archbishop of Kraków. Specialties include hors d'oeuvres and frogs' legs. Main dishes range from guinea hen with onions and grapes in a wine sauce to couscous. Other selections include salad Niçoise, several kinds of homemade pâté, and beefsteak in wine sauce. A smooth finish is the chocolate mousse.

Fun Fact The Origin of Spaghetti Carbonara

A much-disputed legend claims that the dish was invented at La Carbonara when American GIs donated their K-rations of powdered eggs and salted bacon to the chef—the result was that tempting concoction of egg, cheese, and bacon-enriched pasta that has become well-loved throughout the world. Actually the name comes from the Carbonari, men who delivered coal for heating, who were served meals here. The owner's father was a carbonaro, so he dedicated the restaurant to his memory.

Via Monterone 85. ✆ **06-68801095**. Reservations recommended. Main courses 15,000–38,000L (€7.80–€19.75, $8–$19); fixed-price menus 22,000L (€11.45, $11), 30,000L (€15.60, $15), and 50,000L (€26, $25). AE, MC, V. Mon–Sat 12:30–2:30pm and 8–10:30pm. Closed Aug 1–20. Bus: 46, 62, 64, 70, or 115.

Osteria dell'Antiquario INTERNATIONAL/ROMAN Virtually undiscovered, this little Roman osteria lies a few blocks down the Via dei Coronari as you leave the Piazza Navona and head toward St. Peter's. It has three dining rooms and a terrace for fair-weather dining. We prefer to begin with a delectable appetizer of sautéed shellfish (usually mussels and clams), although you might opt for the risotto with porcini mushrooms. For a main course, you can go experimental with the filet of ostrich covered by a slice of ham and grated Parmesan, or else opt for shellfish flavored with saffron. The fish soup with fried bread is excellent, as is an array of freshly made soups and pastas. Veal rolls Roman style and turbot flavored with fresh tomatoes and basil are other excellent choices. This is dining in the classic Roman style.

Piazzetta di S. Simeone 26/27, Via dei Coronari. ✆ **06-6879694**. Reservations recommended. Main courses 16,000–48,000L (€8.30–€24.95, $8–$24). AE, DC, MC, V. Tues–Sat 12:30–2:30pm and 8–11pm; Mon 8–11pm. Closed 15 days in mid-Aug, Christmas, Jan 1–15. Bus: 70, 87, or 90.

Inexpensive

Pizzeria Baffetto 🍷 *Kids* PIZZA Our Roman friends always take out-of-towners here when they request the best pizza in Rome. Arguably, Pizzeria Baffetto fills the bill and has done so admirably for the past 80 years. Pizzas are sold as *piccolo* (small), *media* (medium), or *grande* (large). Most pizza aficionados order the margherita, the simplest version with mozzarella and a delectable tomato sauce, but a wide range of toppings is served. The chef is preening proud of his pizza Baffetto, the house specialty. It comes with a topping of tomato sauce, mozzarella, mushrooms, onions, sausages, roasted peppers, and eggs. The pizza crusts are delightfully thin, and the pies are served piping hot from the intense heat of the ancient ovens.

Via del Governo Vecchio 114. ✆ **06-686-1617**. Reservations not accepted. Pizza 6,000–15,000L (€3.10–€7.80, $3–$8). No credit cards. Daily 6:30pm–1am. Closed Aug. Bus: 46, 62, or 64.

Tre Scalini 🍷 ROMAN/ITALIAN Established in 1882, this is the most famous and respected restaurant on Piazza Navona—a landmark for ice cream as well as more substantial meals. Yes, it's literally crawling with tourists, but its waiters are friendly and helpful. Although there's a cozy bar on the upper floor with a view over the piazza, most visitors opt for a seat either in the ground-floor cafe or at tables on the piazza. House specialties include risotto with porcini mushrooms, spaghetti with clams, roast duck with prosciutto, a carpaccio of sea bass, and roast lamb in the Roman style. No one will object if you order just a pasta and salad, unlike at other restaurants nearby. Their famous *tartufi* (ice cream disguised with a coating of bittersweet chocolate, cherries, and whipped cream) and other ice creams cost 12,000L (€6.25, $6) each.

Piazza Navona 30. ☎ **06-6879148.** Reservations recommended. Main courses 20,000–35,000L (€10.40–€18.20, $10–$18). AE, DC, MC, V. Thurs–Tues noon–3pm and 7–11pm. Closed Dec–Feb. Bus: 70, 87, or 90.

NEAR VATICAN CITY
Very Expensive
Les Etoiles ★★★ MEDITERRANEAN   Les Etoiles deserves all the stars it receives—both for its cuisine and for its panoramic view of Rome. At this garden in the sky you'll have an open window over the rooftops of Rome. In summer everyone wants a table outside, but in winter almost the same view can be seen through the picture windows. Refined Mediterranean cuisine, with perfectly balanced flavors, is served here. Dishes include quail cooked either with radicchio or in a casserole with mushrooms and herbs, artichokes stuffed with ricotta and pecorino cheese, Venetian-style risotto with squid ink, and roast suckling lamb with mint.

In the Hotel Atlante Star, Via dei Bastioni 1. ☎ **06-689-9494.** Reservations required. Main courses 45,000–80,000L (€23.40–€41.60, $23–$40). AE, DC, MC, V. Daily 12:30–2:30pm and 7:30–11pm. Metro: Ottaviano.

Moderate
Ristorante Il Matriciano ROMAN   Il Matriciano is a family restaurant with a devoted following among many actors from the Italian stage. The food is good country fare—nothing fancy. In summer, try to sit at a sidewalk table behind a green hedge under a shady canopy. For openers, we suggest *tagliolini con tartufi* (truffles). For a main course, we recommend *abbacchio al forno* (oven-roasted lamb) and *trippa alla romana* (tripe). The house specialty is based on that Roman favorite, Amatriciana sauce. Here, it's prepared with bucatini pasta and richly flavored with bacon, tomatoes, and basil. Another specialty is *bucatini alla matriciana,* served with a tomato sauce enriched with fried bacon, onion, and hot pepper powder, covered with a topping of pecorino cheese.

Via dei Gracchi 55. ☎ **06-3212327.** Reservations required. Main courses 18,000–28,000L (€9.35–€14.55, $9–$14). AE, DC, MC, V. Daily 12:30–3pm and 8pm–midnight. Closed Aug 5–25. Metro: Ottaviano.

Inexpensive
Ristorante Giardinaccio ITALIAN/MOLISIAN/ROMAN   This popular restaurant is only 200 yards from St. Peter's. Unusual for Rome, it offers specialties from the provincial Molise region in southeast Italy, and is appropriately decorated in rustic country-tavern style. Flaming grills provide succulent versions of perfectly done quail, goat, and other dishes, but you might want to be adventurous and try the mutton goulash. Many pastas are featured, including *taconelle,* a homemade pasta with lamb sauce. Vegetarians and others will like the large self-service selection of antipasti.

Via Aurelia 53. ☎ **06-631367.** Reservations recommended, especially on weekends. Main courses 18,000–40,000L (€9.35–€20.80, $9–$20); fixed-price menus 20,000–60,000L (€10.40–€31.20, $10–$30). AE, DC, MC, V. Daily 12:15–3:15pm and 7:15–11:15pm. Bus: 46, 62, or 98.

IN ANCIENT ROME
Moderate
Trattoria San Teodoro ★ *Finds* ROMAN   At last there's a good place to eat in the former gastronomic wasteland near the Roman Forum and Palatine Hill. The helpful staff welcomes you to a shady terrace or to a dimly lit dining room.

The chef specializes in seafood, and does such exceedingly well, as reflected by his minisized baby squid sautéed with Roman artichokes. His signature dish is seafood carpaccio made with tuna, turbot, or sea bass. Succulent meats such as medallions of veal in a nutmeg-enhanced cream sauce round out the menu at this family friendly place. All the pastas are homemade.

Via dei Fienili 49-51. ℭ 06-678-0933. Reservations recommended. Main courses 35,000–50,000L (€18.20–€26, $18–$25). MC, V. Mon–Sat 1–3:30pm and 7:45pm–midnight. Closed Jan 15–Feb 7. Metro: Circo Massimo.

Inexpensive

Abruzzi *Value* ABRUZZESE   Abruzzi takes its name from a little-explored region east of Rome known for its haunting beauty and curious superstitions. The restaurant is located at one side of piazza SS. Apostoli, just a short walk from piazza Venezia. Good food at reasonable prices makes it enduringly popular among students. The chef is justly praised for his satisfying assortment of cold antipasti. For a starter, you'll find good *stracciatella* (an egg-and-Parmesan cheese soup). A typical main dish is *vitello tonnato con capperi* (veal in tuna fish sauce with capers).

Via del Vaccaro 1. ℭ **06-6793897**. Reservations recommended. Main courses 15,000–25,000L (€7.80–€13, $8–$13). AE, DC, MC, V. Sun–Fri 12:30–3pm and 7–10:30pm. Closed 2 weeks in Aug (dates vary). Bus: 57, 64, 70, or 17.

Alvaro al Circo Massimo *R* *Finds* ITALIAN   Alvaro al Circo Massimo, at the edge of the Circus Maximus, is the closest thing in Rome to a genuine provincial inn. The antipasti and pasta dishes are fine, the meat courses well prepared, and there's an array of fresh fish—never overcooked. Other specialties include tagliolini with mushrooms and truffles, and roasted turbot with potatoes. They're especially well stocked with exotic seasonal mushrooms, including black truffles so good you'd have to go directly to Spoleto to find better.

Via dei Cerchi 53. ℭ **06-6786112**. Reservations required. Main courses 18,000–35,000L (€9.35–€18.20, $9–$18). AE, MC, V. Tues–Sat 12:30–3:30pm and 7:30–11pm; Sun 12:30–3:30pm. Closed Aug. Metro: Circo Massimo.

IN TRASTEVERE
Expensive

Alberto Ciarla *RR* SEAFOOD   Alberto Ciarla is the best and most expensive restaurant in Trastevere, although it's not as chic as it was in the 1980s. It serves some of the most elegant fish dishes in the city. Specialties include a handful of ancient recipes subtly improved by Signor Ciarla, such as soup of pasta and beans with seafood. Original dishes include a delectable salmon Marcel Trompier with lobster sauce, as well as well-flavored sushi, a full array of shellfish, and filet of sea bass prepared in at least three different ways, including an award-winning version with almonds.

Piazza San Cosimato 40. ℭ **06-5818668**. Reservations required. Main courses 32,000–48,000L (€16.65–€24.95, $16–$24); fixed-price menus 80,000–120,000L (€41.60–€62.40, $40–$60). AE, DC, MC, V. Mon–Sat 8:30pm–12:30am. Closed 1 week in Jan and 1 week in Aug. Bus: 44, 75, 170, 280, or 718.

Moderate

La Cisterna ROMAN   This trattoria lies deep in the heart of Trastevere. For more than half a century it has been run by the Simmi family, who are genuinely interested in serving only the best as well as providing a good time for all guests. If you like traditional cookery based on the best of regional produce, come here. In summer you can inspect the antipasti—a mixed selection of hors d'oeuvres—right out on the street before going in. House specialties include Roman-style suckling lamb *(abbacchio)*, *rigatoni a l'Amatriciana* (with diced bacon, olive oil, garlic, tomatoes, red peppers, and onions), and fresh fish—especially sea bass baked with herbs.

Via della Cisterna 13. ℂ 06-5812543. Reservations recommended. Main courses 18,000–30,000L (€9.35–€15.60, $9–$15). AE, DC, MC, V. Mon–Sat 7pm–1:30am. Bus: 44, 75, 170, 280, or 710.

EXPLORING THE ETERNAL CITY

Rome is studded with ancient monuments that silently evoke its history as one of the greatest centers of Western civilization—once all roads led to Rome, with good reason. It was the first cosmopolitan city in Europe, importing everything from slaves and gladiators to great art from the far corners of the empire. With all its carnage and mismanagement, it left a legacy of law and order and an uncanny lesson in how to conquer enemies by absorbing their cultures. But ancient Rome is only part of the spectacle. The Vatican also made the city a center of the world in art as well as religion. And although Vatican architects rifled much of the glory of the past for their projects, they also created the great Renaissance treasures we come to see today.

SIGHTSEEING SUGGESTIONS FOR FIRST-TIME VISITORS

If You Have 1 Day Rome wasn't built in a day and you aren't likely to see it in a day either, but make the most of your limited time. You'll basically have to decide on the legacy of **imperial Rome**—the Roman Forum, the Imperial Forum, and the Colosseum—or else St. Peter's and the **Vatican.** Walk along the **Spanish Steps** at sunset. At night go to **Piazza del Campidoglio** for a fantastic view of the Forum below. Have a nightcap on **Via Veneto,** which, although past its prime, is still appealing. Toss a coin in the **Trevi fountain** and promise yourself you'll return.

If You Have 2 Days If you elected to see the Roman Forum and the Colosseum on your first day, then spend the second day exploring St. Peter's and the **Vatican Museums** (or vice versa). Have dinner in a restaurant in **Trastevere.**

If You Have 3 Days In the morning go to the **Pantheon** in the heart of Old Rome; then, after lunch, explore the **Castel Sant'Angelo** and the **Etruscan Museum.** Have dinner at a restaurant in or around **Piazza Navona.**

If You Have 4 or 5 Days On day 4 head for the environs, notably **Tivoli,** where you can see the Villa d'Este and Hadrian's Villa. On Day 5 explore the ruins of **Ostia Antica,** return to Rome for lunch, and visit the **Capitoline Museum** and **Basilica di San Giovanni in Laterano** in the afternoon.

ST. PETER'S & THE VATICAN

Basilica di San Pietro (St. Peter's Basilica) ✸✸✸   As you stand in Bernini's **Piazza San Pietro** (St. Peter's Square), you'll be in the arms of an ellipse; like a loving parent, the Doric-pillared colonnade reaches out to embrace the faithful. Holding 300,000 is no problem for this square. Inside, the size of this famous church is awe-inspiring—though its dimensions (about two football fields long) are not apparent at first. St. Peter's is said to have been built over the tomb of the crucified saint. The original church was erected on the order of Constantine, but the present structure is Renaissance and baroque; it showcases the talents of some of Italy's greatest artists.

Rome Attractions

Tips   A St. Peter's Warning

St. Peter's has a strict dress code: no shorts, no skirts above the knee, and no bare shoulders. They will not let you in if you don't come dressed appropriately. In a pinch, men and women alike can buy a big cheap scarf from a nearby souvenir stand and wrap it around their legs as a long skirt or throw it over their shoulders as a shawl.

In such a grand church, don't expect subtlety. But the basilica is rich in art. Under Michelangelo's dome is the celebrated **baldacchino** ✫✫✫ by Bernini. In the nave on the right (the first chapel) is the best-known piece of sculpture, the *Pietà* ✫✫✫ that Michelangelo sculpted while still in his early twenties. You can visit the **treasury** ✫, filled with jewel-studded chalices, reliquaries, and copes. One robe worn by Pius XII strikes a simple note in these halls of elegance. The sacristy now contains a **Historical Museum (Museo Storico)** displaying Vatican treasures, including the large 1400s bronze tomb of Pope Sixtus V by Antonio Pollaiuolo and several antique chalices. In addition you can visit the **Vatican grottoes** ✫✫, with their tombs, both ancient and modern (Pope John XXII gets the most adulation).

The grandest sight is yet to come: the climb to **Michelangelo's dome** ✫✫✫, which towers about 115 meters (375 ft.) high. Although you can walk up the steps, we recommend the elevator as far as it'll carry you. You can walk along the roof, for which you'll be rewarded with a panoramic view of Rome and the Vatican.

To tour the area around **St. Peter's tomb,** you must apply several days in advance to the excavations office (✆ **06-69885318**), open from Monday to Saturday 9am to noon and 2 to 5pm. Pass under the arch to the left of the facade of St. Peter's to find it.

Piazza San Pietro. ✆ **06-6988-4466** (for information on celebrations). Basilica (including grottoes), free; guided tour of excavations around St. Peter's tomb, 15,000L (€7.80, $7.50) (children younger than 15 are not admitted); stairs to the dome 7,000L (€3.65, $3.50); elevator to the dome 8,000L (€4.15, $4); Sacristy (with Historical Museum) 9,000L (€4.73, $4.50). Basilica (including the sacristy and treasury), Oct–Mar daily 7am–6pm; Apr–Sept daily 7am–7pm. Grottoes daily 8am–5pm. Dome, Oct–Mar daily 8am–5pm; Apr–Sept 8am–6pm. Bus: 46. Metro: Ottaviano then a long stroll.

Vatican Museums and the Sistine Chapel ✫✫✫   The Vatican Museums contain a gigantic repository of treasures. You can follow one of four itineraries— A, B, C, or D—according to the time you have (from 1½ to 5 hours) and your special interests. You can choose from the picture gallery, which houses paintings from the 11th to the 19th century, the Egyptian collection, the Etruscan museum, Greek and Roman sculpture, and, of course, the **Sistine Chapel.** Consult the large panels at the entrance, then follow the letter and color of the itinerary chosen. Facilities for persons with disabilities are available.

Michelangelo labored for 4 years (1508–12) over the epic Sistine Chapel, now restored, although not without controversy, to its original glory. The work was so physically taxing that it permanently damaged his eyesight. Glorifying the human body as only a sculptor could, Michelangelo painted nine panels taken from the pages of Genesis, and surrounded them with prophets and sibyls. To get the best view of the Sistine Chapel's frescoes, bring binoculars. Also, visit the Stanze di Raphael, rooms decorated by Raphael when still a young man.

> ⌒ *Tips* **A Vatican Tip**
>
> On the left side of Piazza San Pietro is the **Vatican Tourist Office**
> (ⓒ **06-6988-4866;** www.vatican.va), open from Monday to Saturday
> 8:30am to 7pm with maps and guides and reservations for Vatican Gar-
> dens tours.

Viale Vaticano, Vatican City. ⓒ **06-69883333.** Admission 18,000L (€9.35, $9), free for everyone the last Sun of each month (be ready for a crowd). Mar 16–Oct 30 Mon–Fri 8:45am–3:30pm; Sat and the final Sun of the month 8:45am–12:30pm. Off-season Mon–Sat and the final Sun of the month 8:45am–12:35pm. Closed religious holidays (except Easter week), and Aug 15–16. Metro: Ottaviano. The museum entrance is a long walk around the Vatican walls north from St. Peter's Square.

THE FORUM, THE COLOSSEUM & THE HIGHLIGHTS OF ANCIENT ROME

Foro Romano (Roman Forum) 🦊🦊🦊   The Roman Forum was built in the marshy land between the Palatine and the Capitoline Hills. It flourished as the center of Roman life in the days of the Republic, before it gradually lost prestige to the Imperial Forum. By day the columns of now-vanished temples and the stones from which long-forgotten orators spoke are mere shells. But at night, when the Forum is silent in the moonlight, it isn't difficult to imagine that Vestal Virgins still guard the sacred temple fire.

If you want the stones to have some meaning, you'll have to purchase a detailed plan, as the temples can be hard to locate. The best of the lot is the handsomely adorned **Temple of Castor and Pollux** 🦊🦊🦊, erected in the 5th century B.C. in honor of a battle triumph. The **Temple of Faustina** 🦊🦊, with its lovely columns and frieze (griffins and candelabra), was converted into the San Lorenzo in Miranda Church. The **Temple of the Vestal Virgins** 🦊🦊🦊 is a popular attraction; some of the statuary, mostly headless, remains.

A long walk up from the Roman Forum leads to the **Palatine Hill** 🦊🦊🦊, one of the seven hills of Rome; your ticket from the Forum will admit you to this attraction (it's open the same hours). The Palatine, tradition tells us, was the spot on which the first settlers built their huts, under the direction of Romulus. In later years, the hill became a patrician residential district that attracted citizens like Cicero. It's worth the climb for the panoramic, sweeping view of both the Roman and Imperial forums, as well as the Capitoline Hill and the Colosseum. Of the ruins that remain, none is finer than the so-called **House of Livia** 🦊🦊 (the "abominable grandmother" of Robert Graves's *I, Claudius*).

When the glory that was Rome has completely overwhelmed you, you can enjoy a respite in the cooling **Farnese Gardens** 🦊, laid out in the 16th century, which incorporate some of Michelangelo's designs.

Via dei Fori Imperiali. ⓒ **06-6990110.** Foro Romano free; Palatine Hill 12,000L (€6.25, $6). Apr–Sept daily 9am–8pm; Oct–Mar daily 9am–3:30pm; last admission 1 hour before closing. Closed Dec 25, Jan 1, and May 1. Metro: Colosseo.

Colosseo (Colosseum) 🦊🦊🦊   In spite of the fact that it's a mere shell, the Colosseum remains the greatest architectural inheritance from ancient Rome. It was inaugurated by Titus in A.D. 80 with a weeks-long bloody combat between gladiators and wild beasts. At its peak, the Colosseum could seat 50,000 spectators, and exotic animals—humans also—were shipped in from the far corners of the empire to satisfy jaded tastes. Many historians now believe that one of the

Moments **Death in the Ring**

Good news for fans of the Oscar®-winning film, *Gladiator*. You can now get the same center-stage view of the Colosseum the fighters had before they met a bloody death or glory in the ring. Roman cultural authorities, following an 8-year restoration, are now allowing visitors to wander spaces under the Colosseum where elephants, lions, and other wild animals from North Africa once waited to be hoisted up in cages to take on the gladiators.

most enduring legends linked to the Colosseum—that Christians were fed to the lions here—is unfounded.

Next to the Colosseum is the **Arch of Constantine** ☆☆☆, erected in honor of Constantine's defeat of the pagan Maxentius (A.D. 306).

Piazzale del Colosseo, Via dei Fori Imperiali. ℭ **06-7004261**. Admission 10,000L (€5.20, $5) all levels. Oct–Jan 15 daily 9am–3pm; Jan 16–Feb 15 daily 9am–4pm; Feb 16–Mar 17 daily 9am–4:30pm; Mar 18–Apr 16 daily 9am–5pm; Apr 17 to Sept daily 9am–6pm. Metro: Colosseo.

Domus Aurea (Golden House of Nero) ☆ Nero's fabulous Golden House reopened in 1999 after a 15-year restoration. In A.D. 64, Rome was swept by a disastrous fire—contrary to gossip it has never been proven that Nero set the fire. The emperor did, however, seize more than 80 hectares (200 acres) of the burned-out historic core to create one of the most sumptuous palaces in history. Subsequent emperors, seeking to distance themselves from their unpopular predecessor, destroyed much of the place by using its vast network of rooms and walls as a foundation for new construction. Out of its original 250 rooms, 30 are now open to the public, decorated with some of the sculptures, mosaics, and frescoes that have survived the past 2,000 years. When Nero moved in, he shouted, "At last I can start living like a human being!"

Via della Domus Aurea, on the Esquiline Hill. ℭ **06-3996-7700**. Admission 10,000L (€5.20, $5), plus 2,000L (€1.05, $1) for advance reservation (highly recommended). Audio tour 3,000L (€1.55, $1.50); guided tour 6,000L (€3.10, $3), plus additional 1,000L (€0.5, 50¢) reservation. Daily 9am–7pm. Metro: Colosseo.

Campidoglio (Capitoline Hill) ☆☆☆ Of the Seven Hills of Rome, the Campidoglio is the most sacred—its origins stretch way back into antiquity (an Etruscan temple to Jupiter once stood on this spot). The approach to the Capitoline Hill is dramatic—climbing the long, sloping steps designed by Michelangelo. At the top is a perfectly proportioned square, Piazza del Campidoglio, also laid out by the Florentine artist.

One side of the piazza is open; the others are bounded by the **Senatorium** ☆☆ (Town Council), the statuary-filled **Palazzo dei Conservatori** ☆☆☆, and the **Museo Capitolino** ☆☆ (Capitoline Museum; see "More Attractions," below). The Campidoglio is dramatic at night (walk around to the back for a regal view of the floodlit Roman Forum).

Piazza del Campidoglio. Bus: 44, 89, 92, 94, or 716.

Castel Sant'Angelo ☆☆☆ This overpowering structure, in a landmark position on the Tiber just east of Vatican City, was originally built in the 2nd century A.D. as a tomb for the emperor Hadrian; it continued as an imperial

Ancient Rome & Attractions Nearby

Antiquarium Comunale **42**
Arch of Constantine **32**
Arch of Septimius Severus **19**
Arch of Titus **33**
Basilica of Constantine &
  Maxentius **26**
Basilica di San Clemente **30**
Basilica di San Giovanni
  in Laterno **30**
Basilica Julia **17**
Baths of Caracalla **43**
Capitoline Museum **10**
Circus Maximus **41**
Colosseum **31**
Curia **20**
Farnese Gardens **36**
Forum of Augustus **6**

Forum of Julius Caesar **8**
Forum of Nerva **7**
Forum of Trajan **4**
Golden House of Nero **29**
Hippodrome **34**
House of Livia **35**
House of the Vestal Virgins **24**
National Museum
  of Palazzo Venezia **1**
Palazzo dei Conservatori **11**
Palazzo Senatorio **14**
San Pietro in Vincoli **28**
Santa Maria in Aracoeli **9**
Santa Maria in Cosmedin **39**
Tabularium **13**
Temple of Antoninus
  & Faustina **25**

Temple of the Dioscuri **22**
Temple of Fortuna Virile
  (Temple of Portunus) **37**
Temple of Hercules **38**
Temple of Romulus **27**
Temple of Saturn **16**
Temple of Vespasian
  & Titus **15**
Temple of Vesta **23**
Theater of Pompey **12**
Trajan's Column **3**
Trajan's Market **5**
Umbilicus Urbus/
  Imperial Rostra **18**
Via Sacra **21**
Vittorio Emanuele
  Monument **2**

mausoleum until the time of Caracalla. It's an imposing and grim castle with thick walls and cylindrical shape. If it looks like a fortress, it should, as that was its function in the Middle Ages. In the 14th century it became a papal residence. Its legend rests largely on its link with Pope Alexander VI, whose mistress bore him two children—Cesare and Lucrezia Borgia. Today the highlight of the castle is a trip through the Renaissance apartments with their coffered ceilings and lush decoration. Their walls have witnessed plots and intrigues that make up some of the arch-treachery of the High Renaissance. You can climb to the top terrace for another one of those dazzling views of the Eternal City.

Lungotevere Castello 50. ℭ 06-681-91-11. Admission 10,000L (€5.20, $5). Tues–Sun 9am–7pm. Metro: Ottaviano. Bus: 23, 46, 49, 62, 64, 87, 98, 280, or 910.

Pantheon ✰✰✰   Of all the great buildings of ancient Rome, only the Pantheon ("All the Gods") remains intact today. It was built in 27 B.C. by Marcus Agrippa, and later reconstructed by the emperor Hadrian in the first part of the 2nd century A.D. This remarkable building is among the architectural wonders of the world because of its dome and its concept of space. The Pantheon was once ringed with white marble statues of Roman gods in its niches. Animals were sacrificed and burned in the center, and the smoke escaped through the only means of light, an opening at the top 8 meters (27 ft.) in diameter. Michelangelo came here to study the dome before designing the cupola of St. Peter's, whose dome is only 0.5 meters (2 ft.) smaller than the Pantheon's.

Piazza della Rotonda. ℭ 06-68300230. Free admission. Mon–Sat 9am–6:30pm; Sun 9am–1pm. Bus: 46, 62, 64, 170, or 492 to Lgo. di Torre Argentina.

THE CATACOMBS OF THE APPIAN WAY

Of all the roads that led to Rome, Via Appia Antica—built in 312 B.C.—was the leader. It eventually stretched all the way from Rome to the seaport of Brindisi, through which trade with the colonies in Greece and the East was funneled.

Along the Appian Way the patrician Romans built great monuments above the ground, whereas Christians met in the catacombs beneath. The remains of both can be visited today. In some dank, dark grottoes (never stray too far from either your party or one of the exposed light-bulbs), you can still discover traces of early Christian art.

Of the catacombs open to the public, those of St. Callixtus and of St. Sebastian are the most important. Both can be reached by bus 118, which leaves from near the Colosseo metro station.

Catacombe di San Sebastiano ✰✰✰ are at Via Appia Antica 136 (ℭ 06-7887035; bus: 118). Today the tomb of the martyr is in the basilica, but it was originally in the catacomb under the building. From the reign of Valerian to that of Constantine, the bodies of Sts. Peter and Paul were hidden in these catacombs. The tunnels, if stretched out, would reach a length of 11 kilometers (7 miles). Admission is 8,000L (€4.15, $4) adults, 4,000L (€2.13, $2) children 6 to 15, free for children 5 and under. Open from April to October Monday to Saturday 9am to noon and 2:30 to 5:30pm; from January to March Monday to Saturday 8:30am to noon and 2:30 to 5pm. Closed from November 13 to December 11.

The **Catacombe di San Callisto** ✰✰✰, Via Appia Antica 110 (ℭ 06-51301580; bus: 118), are the first cemetery of the Christian community of Rome, burial place of 16 popes in the 3rd century. They bear the name of St. Callixtus, the deacon whom the pope St. Zephyrinus put in charge of them. Callixtus himself was later elected pope (217–22). The cemeterial complex is made up of a network of galleries stretching for nearly 19 kilometers (12 miles), structured in five different levels, reaching a depth of about 20 meters (65 ft.). Admission is 8,000L (€4.15, $4) adults, 4,000L (€2.13, $2) children 6 to 15, free for children 5 and under. Hours are from April to October Thursday to Tuesday 8:30am to noon and 2:30 to 5:30pm; from November to January Thursday to Tuesday 8:30am to noon and 2:30 to 5pm. Closed February.

MORE ATTRACTIONS

Spanish Steps (Scalinata di Spagna) ✿✿✿   The steps—filled in spring with azaleas and other flowers, flower vendors, jewelry dealers, and photographers snapping pictures of visitors—and the square take their names from the Spanish Embassy, which used to be headquartered here. Designed by Italian architect Francesco de Sanctis and built from 1723 to 1725, they were funded almost entirely by the French as a preface to Trinità dei Monti at the top. At the foot of the steps is a boat-shaped fountain designed by Pietro Bernini (not to be confused with his son, Giovanni Lorenzo Bernini, a far greater sculptor). The steps and the piazza below are always packed with a crowd: strolling, reading in the sun, browsing the vendors' carts, and people-watching.

Piazza di Spagna. Metro: Spagna.

Terme di Caracalla (Baths of Caracalla) ✿✿✿   Named for the emperor Caracalla, the baths were completed in the early part of the 3rd century. The richness of decoration has faded and the lushness can only be judged from the shell of brick ruins that remain.

Via delle Terme di Caracalla 52. ✆ 06-5758626. Admission 8,000L (€4.15, $4). Jan 16–Feb 15 daily 9am–4pm; Feb 16–Mar 15 daily 9am–4:30pm; Mar 16 to Oct daily 9am–5pm; Nov to Jan 15 daily 9am–3:30pm. Last admission 1 hour before closing. Closed holidays. Bus: 628.

Basilica di San Clemente ✿✿   From the Colosseum, head up Via di San Giovanni in Laterano, which leads to the Basilica of Saint Clement. In this church-upon-a-church, centuries of history peel away: A 4th-century church was built over a secular house from the 1st century A.D., beside which stood a pagan temple dedicated to Mithras; Normans destroyed the lower church, and a new one was built in the 12th century. Down in the eerie grottoes (which you can explore on your own—unlike the catacombs on the Appian Way), you'll discover well-preserved frescoes from the 1st to the 3rd centuries.

Via San Giovanni in Laterano at Piazza San Clemente, Via Labicana 95. ✆ 06-7045-1018. Church, free; excavations, 4,000L (€2.08, $2). Mon–Sat 9am–12:30pm and 3–6pm; Sun 10am–12:30pm and 3–6pm. Metro: Colosseo.

Basilica di San Giovanni in Laterano ✿✿✿   This church—not St. Peter's—is the cathedral of the diocese of Rome. Catholics all over the world refer to it as their "mother church." Originally built in A.D. 314 by Constantine, the cathedral has suffered many vicissitudes and was forced to rebuild many times. The present structure is characterized by its 18th-century facade by Alessandro Galilei (statues of Christ and the Apostles ring the top). Borromini gets the credit—some say blame—for the interior, built for Innocent X.

The most unusual sight is across the street at the "Palace of the Holy Steps," called the **Santuario della Scala Sancta** ✿, Piazza San Giovanni in Laterano (✆ 06-70494619). It's alleged that these were the actual steps that Christ climbed when he was brought before Pilate. These steps are supposed to be climbed only on your knees, which you're likely to see the faithful doing throughout the day. Visiting hours are daily 6:15am to noon and 3:30 to 6:30pm. Admission is free.

Piazza San Giovanni in Laterano 4. ✆ 06-69886433. Basilica, free; cloisters, 4,000L (€2.13, $2). Summer daily 7am–6:45pm (off-season to 6pm). Metro: San Giovanni.

Basilica di Santa Maria Maggiore (Saint Mary the Great) 🎟🎟🎟   This great church was originally founded by Pope Liberius in A.D. 358 but was rebuilt by Pope Sixtus III from 432 to 440. Its campanile, erected in the 14th century, is the loftiest in the city. Much doctored in the 18th century, the facade is not an accurate reflection of the treasures inside. The basilica is especially noted for the 5th-century Roman mosaics in its nave, as well as for its coffered ceiling, said to have been gilded with gold brought from the New World. In the 16th century Domenico Fontana built a now-restored "Sistine Chapel." The church contains the tomb of Bernini, Italy's most important architect during the flowering of the baroque in the 17th century.

Piazza Santa Maria Maggiore. ✆ 06-4881094. Free admission. Daily 7am–7pm. Metro: Termini.

Museo Capitolino 🎟🎟 and **Palazzo dei Conservatori** 🎟🎟🎟   The Capitoline Museum was built in the 17th century, based on an architectural sketch by Michelangelo. In the first room is *The Dying Gaul,* a work of majestic skill; in a special gallery all her own is *The Capitoline Venus,* who demurely covers herself—this statue (a Roman copy of the Greek original) has been a symbol of feminine beauty and charm down through the centuries. The famous statue of *Marcus Aurelius* is the only bronze equestrian statue to have survived from ancient Rome. It was retrieved from the Tiber where it had been tossed by marauding barbarians. For centuries it was thought to be a statue of Constantine the Great; this mistake protected it further, since papal Rome respected the memory of the first Christian emperor.

The **Palazzo dei Conservatori,** across the way, is rich in classical sculpture and paintings. In the courtyard are fragments of a colossal statue of Constantine. One of the most notable bronzes is the *Spinario* (little boy picking a thorn from his foot), a Greek classic from the 1st century B.C. In addition, you'll find *Lupa Capitolina* (Capitoline She-Wolf), a rare Etruscan bronze possibly from the 5th century B.C. (Romulus and Remus, the legendary twins that the she-wolf suckled, were added at a later date.)

Piazza del Campidoglio. ✆ 06-67102071. Admission to both museum and palace 10,000L (€5.20, $5) adults, 5,000L (€2.60, $2.50) children 18 and under and seniors 60 and over. Tues–Sun 9am–7pm. Bus: 44, 81, 95, 160, 170, 715, or 780.

Galleria Borghese 🎟🎟🎟   Closed for 14 years, this jewel box collection of masterworks is finally back. The masterpieces are displayed in what was once the Borghese's summer residence. However, in spring 1997, after a complete restoration, it was back in all its fabulous glory. The bad news is that it may be hard to get in because of limited access (see below). This treasure trove of art includes such masterpieces as Bernini's *David, The Rape of Persephone,* and his *Apollo and Daphne;* Titian's *Sacred and Profane Love;* Raphael's *Deposition;* even Caravaggio's *Jerome.* One of the most viewed pieces of sculpture in today's gallery is Canova's life-size sculpture of Napoléon's sister, Pauline, in the pose of "Venus Victorious." When Pauline was asked if she felt uncomfortable about posing in the nude, she replied, "Why should I? The studio was heated."

Piazza Scipione Borghese, off Via Pinciano. ✆ 06-32010 for reservations, or 06-8417645 for information. Admission 12,000L (€6.25, $6). Nov–Apr Tues–Sat 9am–7:30pm, Sun 9am–7pm; May–Oct Tues–Fri

9am–8pm, Sat–Sun 9am–9pm. Bus: 56 or 910. *Note:* No more than 300 visitors at a time are allowed on the ground floor, no more than 90 on the upper floor. Reservations are essential (call Mon–Fri 9am–6pm).

Galleria Nazionale d'Arte Antica ☆☆   Palazzo Barberini, right off piazza

Barberini, is one of Rome's most magnificent baroque palaces. It was begun by Carlo Maderno in 1627 and completed in 1633 by Bernini, whose lavishly decorated rococo apartments are on view. The palace houses the Galleria Nazionale. On the first floor, a splendid array of paintings includes works that date from the 13th and 14th centuries, notably the *Mother and Child* by Simone Martini. Art from the 15th and 16th centuries include works by Filippo Lippi, Andrea Solario, Francesco Francia, Il Sodoma, and Raphael. Since 1998, you can visit a newly restored 18th-century apartment decorated with frescoes from the school of Barberini. Admission is 2,000L (€1.05, $1), and hours are Tuesday to Sunday 9am to 7pm.

Via delle Quattro Fontane 13. ✆ 06-4814430. Admission to both museum and apartment 12,000L (€6.25, $6). Tues–Sun 9am–7pm. Metro: Piazza Barberini.

Museo Nazionale di Villa Giulia (Etruscan) ☆☆☆   A 16th-century papal

palace in the Villa Borghese shelters this priceless collection of art and artifacts of the mysterious Etruscans, who predated the Romans, and of whom little is known except for their sophisticated art and design. If you have time only for the masterpieces, head for Sala 7, which has a remarkable *Apollo* from Veio from the end of the 6th century B.C. (clothed, for a change). Two other widely acclaimed pieces of statuary in this gallery are *Dea con Bambino* (goddess with a baby) and a greatly mutilated, but still powerful, *Hercules* with a stag. In the adjoining Sala 8, you'll see the lions' sarcophagus from the mid-6th century B.C., which was excavated at Cerveteri, north of Rome. Finally, in Sala 9, is one of the world's most important Etruscan art treasures, the bride and bridegroom coffin from the 6th century B.C., also from Cerveteri.

Piazzale di Villa Giulia 9. ✆ 06-3201951. Admission 8,000L (€4.15, $4). Tues–Sat 8:30am–7pm; Sun 9am–2pm. Metro: Flaminio. Tram: 225.

MUSEO NAZIONALE ROMANO

Originally the museum occupied only the Diocletian Baths; today it's divided into four sections: Palazzo Massimo alle Terme; Terme di Diocleziano (Diocletian Baths) with the annex Octagonal Hall; and Palazzo Altemps. A ticket including the entry into any of the four sections is 15,000L (€7.80, $7.50).

Palazzo Massimo alle Terme ☆   If you'd like to go wandering in a virtual

garden of classical statues, head for this 19th-century palazzo built to resemble the patrician palaces from the baroque period. If you ever wanted to know what emperors looked like, this museum will make them live again, togas and all. In the central hall are works representing the political and social life of Rome at the time of Augustus. Other works include an altar from Ostia Antica, the ancient port of Rome, plus a statue of a wounded Niobid from 440 B.C. that is a masterwork of expression and character. Upstairs stand in awe at frescoes, stuccoes, and mosaics from the 1st century B.C. to the Imperial Age. The most celebrated mosaic is of the Four Charioteers. In the basement are a rare numismatic collection and an extensive collection of Roman jewelry.

Largo di Villa Peretti 67. ✆ 06-489-035-00. Admission 10,000L (€5.20, $5) (ticket includes Diocletian Baths). Tues–Sun 9am–8pm. Last admission 1 hour before closing. Metro: Termini.

Palazzo Altemps ☆   This other branch of the National Roman Museum is

housed in a 15th-century palace only a few steps from the Piazza Navona. It is home to the fabled Ludovisi Collection of Greek and Roman sculpture. Among the masterpieces of the Roman Renaissance, you'll find the *Ares Ludovisi*, a Roman copy of the original dated 330 B.C. and restored by Bernini. In the *Sala delle Storie di Mosè* is the *Ludovisi's Throne* representing the birth of Venus. The *Sala delle Feste* (The Celebrations Hall) is dominated by *Grande Ludovisi*, a sarcophagus depicting the Romans fighting against the Ostrogoth Barbarians from the 2nd century A.D. Other outstanding art includes a 1st-century B.C. copy of Phidias's celebrated Athena that once stood in the Parthenon.

Piazza San Apollinare 44. ☎ 06-489-035-00. Admission 10,000L (€5.20, $5). Tues–Fri 9am–9pm; Sat 9am–midnight; Sun 9am–8pm. Last admission 1 hour before closing. Metro: Termini.

Terme di Diocleziano (Diocletian Bath) and the Aula Ottagona (Octagonal Hall) ⚶

This museum occupies part of the 3rd-century A.D. baths of Diocletian and part of a convent that may have been designed by Michelangelo. The Diocletian baths were the biggest thermal baths in the world. Nowadays they host a marvelous collection of funereal art and decorations from the Aurelian period. The Octagonal Hall occupies the southwest corner of the central building. Here you can see the *Lyceum Apollo*. This statue was found in the area surrounding the Trajan Baths. Worthy of a note is the *Aphrodite of Cyrene*, discovered in Cyrene, Libya.

Viale E. di Nicola 79. ☎ 06-489-035-00. Admission to the Baths 8,000L (€4.15, $4) (ticket includes Palazzo Massimo alle Terme), Octagonal Hall, free. Tues–Fri 9am–2pm; Sat–Sun 9am–1pm. Last admission 1 hour before closing. Metro: Termini.

ORGANIZED TOURS

One of the leading tour operators (among the zillions of possibilities) is **American Express,** Piazza di Spagna 38 (☎ **06-67641;** Metro: Spagna), open from Monday to Friday 9am to 5:30pm and Saturday 9am to 12:30pm. One popular tour is a 4-hour orientation tour of Rome and the Vatican, which departs most mornings at 9:30am and costs 70,000L (€36.40, $35) per person. Another 4-hour tour, which focuses on ancient Rome (including visits to the Colosseum, the Roman Forum, the Imperial Palace, and the Church of San Pietro in Vincoli), costs 60,000L (€31.20, $30). Outside Rome, a popular excursion from April to October is a 5-hour bus tour to Tivoli, where visits are conducted of the Villa d'Este and its spectacular gardens and the ruins of the Villa Adriana, all for the price of 70,000L (€36.40, $35) per person.

If your time in Italy is rigidly limited, you might opt for 1-day excursions to points farther afield on tours that are marketed (but not conducted) by American Express. A series of 1-day tours is offered to Pompeii, Naples, and Sorrento for 170,000L (€88.40, $85) per person; to Florence for 200,000L (€104, $100); and to Capri and Sorrento for 230,000L (€119.60, $115). These trips, which include lunch, depart from Rome around 7am and return to your hotel sometime after 9 or 10pm.

THE SHOPPING SCENE

The posh shopping streets **Via Borgognona** and **Via Condotti** begin near Piazza di Spagna. For the most part, the merchandise on both is chic and very, very expensive. **Via Frattina** runs parallel to Via Condotti, its more famous sibling. **Via del Corso** doesn't have the image or the high prices of Via Condotti or Via Borgognona; the styles here are aimed at younger consumers. There're, however, some gems scattered amid the shops selling jeans and sporting equipment. The most interesting shops are on the section of the street nearest the fashionable cafes of Piazza del Popolo.

Beginning at the top of the Spanish Steps, **Via Sistina** runs to Piazza Barberini. The shops are small, stylish, and based on the personalities of their owners. The pedestrian traffic is less dense than on other major streets. Most shoppers reach **Via Francesco Crispi** by following Via Sistina 1 long block from the top of the Spanish Steps. Near the intersection of these streets are several shops full of unusual and less expensive gifts. Evocative of *La Dolce Vita,* **Via Veneto** is filled these days with expensive hotels and cafes and an array of relatively expensive stores selling shoes, gloves, and leather goods.

Traffic-clogged **Via Nazionale**—just crossing the street is no small feat—begins at piazza della Repubblica and runs down almost to Piazza Venezia. Here you'll find an abundance of leather stores—more reasonable in price than those in many other parts of Rome—and a welcome handful of stylish boutiques.

Via dei Coronari, a good street for antiques, is buried in a colorful section of the Campus Martius, and is an antiquer's dream, literally lined with magnificent vases, urns, chandeliers, breakfronts, chaises, refectory tables, and candelabra. To find the entrance to the street, turn left out of the north end of Piazza Navona, pass the excavated ruins of Domitian's Stadium, and the street will be just ahead of you. There are more than 40 antique stores in the next 4 blocks.

SOME SHOPS WORTH SEEKING OUT

Anatriello del Regalo, Via Frattina 123 (© **06-6789601;** Metro: Spagna), stocks new and antique silver, some of it quite unusual. New items are made by Italian silversmiths in designs ranging from the whimsical to the severely formal. **E. Fiore,** Via Ludovisi 31 (© **06-4819296;** Metro: Spagna), sells a wide assortment of charms, bracelets, necklaces, rings, brooches, and cameos. The store also carries elegant watches, silverware, and gold ware.

La Rinascente, Via del Corso 189 (© **06-6797691** at the Piazza Colonna; Metro: Barberini or Spagna), is Rome's most famous department store. Rather upscale, it has a little bit of everything: clothing, hosiery, perfume, cosmetics, housewares, and even furniture, plus its own line of clothing (Ellerre) for men, women, and children. At **Farnese,** Piazza Farnese 52 (© **06-6896109;** bus: 64), you'll find Rome's most evocative collection of patterned tiles, which can be used on walls or floors. Motifs depict everything from the scenes of ancient Roman mosaics to the glazed tiles of Capodimonte in Naples.

Head to **Salvatore Ferragamo,** Via Condotti 73 (© **06-6798402;** Metro: Spagna), for elegant footwear, women's clothing and accessories, and ties, in an atmosphere full of Italian style. Figure on a 30-minute wait outside. Ferragamo's male collection is a few steps away at Via Condotti 66 (© **06-678-1130**). At **Emporio Armani,** Via del Babuino 140 (© **06-3600-2197;** Metro: Spagna), you'll find moderately priced men's wear crafted by the couturier who has dressed more stage and screen stars than any other designer in Italy. The designer's more expensive line—sold at prices that are sometimes 30% less than what you'd pay in the United States—lies a short walk away, at **Giorgio Armani,** Via Condotti 77 (© **06-6991460;** Metro: Spagna). **Saddlers Union,** Via Condotti 26 (© **06-6798050;** Metro: Spagna), is a great place to look for well-crafted leather accessories—handbags, belts, wallets, shoes, briefcases, and other high-quality items.

TO MARKET, TO MARKET

At the sprawling **Porta Portese** open-air flea market, held every Sunday morning, every peddler from Trastevere and the surrounding Castelli Romani sets up a temporary shop. Vendors sell merchandise ranging from secondhand paintings of Madonnas to pseudo-Etruscan hairpins. The flea market is near the end of Viale Trastevere (bus 75 to Porta Portese), then a short walk to Via Portuense. By 10:30am, the market is full of people. As you would at any street market, beware of pickpockets. Open Sunday from 7am to 1pm.

ROME AFTER DARK

There're few evening diversions quite as pleasurable as a stroll past the solemn pillars of old temples or the cascading torrents of Renaissance fountains glowing under the blue-black sky. Of the **fountains,** the Naiads (Piazza della Repubblica), the Tortoises (Piazza Mattei), and, of course, the Trevi are particularly beautiful at night. The **Capitoline Hill** is magnificently lit after dark, with its Renaissance facades glowing like jewel boxes. Behind the Senatorial Palace is a fine view of the **Roman Forum.** If you're staying across the Tiber, **Piazza San Pietro,** in front of St. Peter's Basilica, is impressive at night without tour buses and crowds. And a combination of illuminated architecture, Renaissance fountains, and, frequently, sidewalk shows and art expositions is at **Piazza Navona.** If you're ambitious and have a good sense of direction, try exploring the streets to the west of Piazza Navona, which look like a stage set when lit at night.

The minimagazines *Metropolitan* and *Wanted in Rome* have listings of jazz, rock, and such and give an interesting look at expatriate Rome. The daily *Il Messaggero* lists current cultural news, especially in its Thursday magazine supplement, *Metro.* And *Un Ospite a Roma,* available free from the concierge desks of top hotels, is full of details on what's happening. Even if you don't speak Italian, you can generally follow the listings featured in *TrovaRoma,* a special weekly entertainment supplement published in the newspaper *La Repubblica* on Thursday.

THE PERFORMING ARTS

If you're in the capital for the opera season, usually from December to June, you can attend a performance at the historic **Teatro dell'Opera (Rome Opera House),** located off Via Nazionale, at Piazza Beniamino Gigli 1 (© **06-481601;** Metro: Repubblica). In the summer the venue switches to Piazza di Siena. The **Rome Opera Ballet** also performs at the Teatro dell'Opera. Look for announcements of classical concerts that take place in churches and other venues.

THE CLUB & MUSIC SCENE

Clubs are generally open from Monday to Saturday 9 or 10pm to 2 to 4am.

NIGHTCLUBS   Arciliuto, Piazza Monte Vecchio 5 (© **06-6879419;** bus: 70, 81, or 87), reputedly the former studio of Raphael, is one of the most romantic candlelit spots in Rome. From 10pm to 2am, Monday to Saturday guests enjoy a musical salon ambience, listening to a guitarist, a pianist, and a violinist. The evening's presentation also includes live Neapolitan songs, and new Italian madrigals, even current hits from Broadway or London's West End. Cover (including one drink) is 35,000L (€18.20, $18). Closed from July 20 to September 6.

JAZZ, SOUL & FUNK   Every night but Sunday **Alexanderplatz,** Via Ostia 9 (© **06-39742171;** tram: 907 or 991), features live jazz. There's also a good restaurant here that serves everything from gnocchi alla romana to Japanese cuisine. A 2-month membership costs 15,000L (€7.80, $7.50). **Big Mama,** Vicolo San Francesco a Ripa 18 (© **06-5812551;** bus: 75, or 170), is a hangout for jazz and blues musicians; you're likely to meet the up-and-coming jazz stars of tomorrow. Sometimes the big names appear as well. Closed from June to September.

Moments   A Meal & a Song

Roman rusticity is combined with theatrical flair at **Fantasie di Traste-vere,** Via di Santa Dorotea 6 (© **06-5881671;** tram: 8, 20, 170, or 280), the "people's theater" where the famous actor Petrolini made his debut. Waiters dressed in regional garb serve with drama. The cuisine isn't subtle but is bountiful, and expect to pay 91,000 to 120,000L (€47.30 to €62.40, $46 to $60) for a full meal; your first drink will cost 35,000L (€18.20, $18). Some two-dozen folk singers and musicians in regional costumes perform, making it a festive affair. Meals are served daily beginning at 8pm, and piano bar music is offered from 8:30 to 9:30pm, followed by the show, lasting until 10:30pm.

No cover for minor shows, 20,000 to 30,000L (€10.40 to €15.60, $10 to $15) for big acts, plus 20,000L (€10.40, $10) for a seasonal membership.

Gilda, Via Mario dei Fiori 97 (© **06-6784838;** Metro: Spagna), is an adventurous combination of nightclub, disco, and restaurant known for the glamorous acts it books. The artistic direction assures first-class shows, a well-run restaurant, and disco music played between the live musical acts. The restaurant and pizzeria open at 9:30pm and occasionally present shows. International cuisine is featured as well with meals beginning at 45,000L (€23.40, $23). The nightclub, opening at midnight, presents music of the 1960s as well as modern recordings. Cover (including one drink) is 40,000L (€20.80, $20).

GAY & LESBIAN CLUBS

The Hangar, Via in Selci 69 (© **06-48813971;** Metro: Cavour), is the premier gay bar in Rome, on one of the city's oldest streets, adjacent to the Roman Forum. Women are welcome any night except Monday, when videos and entertainment for gay men are featured. The busiest nights are Saturday, Sunday, and Monday, when as many as 500 patrons cram inside. The Hangar is closed for 3 weeks in August. Open from Wednesday to Monday 10:30pm to 2:30am. No cover, but there's a card membership of 5,000L (€2.60, $2.50). **L'Alibi,** Via Monte Testaccio 44 (© **06-574-3448;** bus: 95), is a year-round venue on many a gay man's agenda, and is one of the hottest clubs in Rome. The crowd, however, tends to be mixed, both Roman and international, straight and gay, male and female. Music ranges from garage to '70s disco. One room is devoted to dancing. Open from Thursday to Sunday 11pm to 4am. Cover is 25,000L (€13, $12.50).

Angelo Azzuro, Via Cardinal Merry del Val 13 (© **06-5800472;** bus: 44, 75, or 170), a gay "hot spot" deep in the heart of Trastevere, is open from Friday to Sunday 11pm to 4am. No food is served, nor is there live music. Friday is for women only. Cover (including one drink) is 10,000L (€5.20, $5) Friday and Sunday, 20,000L (€10.40, $10) Saturday. **New Joli Coeur,** Via Sirte 5 (© **06-8621-6240;** bus: 38 or 58), in a seedy neighborhood, caters mainly to lesbians and is open on Saturday and Sunday from 11pm to 5am only. Saturday night is reserved for women only, although Sunday the crowd can be mixed. Cover (including one drink) is 25,000L (€13, $12.50).

Moments **A Chic Bar**

A former favorite haunt in the historic district of Rome, Hemingway's Pub, has been recently transformed into the sleek **Riccioli Café,** Piazza delle Coppelle 10A (© **066821-0313;** bus: 64), a new and fast-rising oyster and champagne bar. In elegant yet informal surroundings, you can order drinks, of course, but also oysters on the half shell. Many come here to see and be seen. But you can find ample and good-tasting food as well, including sea bass with mango and roast beef with green apples. The loft-like wine cellar competes with the deluxe restaurants of Rome.

SIDE TRIPS FROM ROME

TIVOLI   Tivoli, known as Tibur to the ancient Romans, was the playground of emperors. Today its reputation continues unabated: It's the most popular half-day jaunt from Rome.

While the **Villa d'Este,** Piazza Trento, Viale delle Cento Fontane (© **0774/ 312070**), is just a dank Renaissance palace with second-rate paintings that's hardly worth the trek from Rome, its **gardens** ★★★—designed by Pirro Ligorio—dim the luster of Versailles. Visitors descend a cypress-studded slope, and on their way are rewarded with everything from lilies to gargoyles spouting water, torrential streams, and waterfalls. The loveliest fountain—on this there's some agreement—is the **Fontana dell'Ovato,** designed by Ligorio. But nearby is the most spectacular achievement, the **hydraulic organ fountain,** dazzling visitors with its water jets in front of a baroque chapel, with four maidens who look tipsy. The best walk is along the promenade, which has 100 spraying fountains. Admission is 8,000L (€4.15, $4). The villa opens from Tuesday to Sunday at 9am; closing times vary according to the season (1 hour before the sunset). From November to January it closes at 4pm; closing times may be as late as 6:45pm in high season.

Whereas the Villa d'Este dazzles with artificial glamour, **Villa Gregoriana** ★, Largo Sant'Angelo (© **0774/334522**), relies more on nature. The gardens were built by Pope Gregory XVI in the 19th century. At one point on the circuitous walk carved along a slope, visitors stand and look out onto Tivoli's most panoramic waterfall (Aniene). The trek to the bottom on the banks of the Anio is studded with grottoes and balconies that open onto the chasm. From one belvedere, there's a panoramic view of the Temple of Vesta on the hill. Admission is 4,000L (€2.13, $2). It's open from May to August daily 10am to 7:30pm; September daily 9:30am to 6:30pm; from October to March daily 9:30am to 4:30pm; April daily from 9:30am to 6pm.

Of all the Roman emperors dedicated to *la dolce vita,* the globetrotting Hadrian spent the last 3 years of his life in the grandest style. Less than 6.5 kilometers (4 miles) from Tivoli he built his great estate—the **Villa Adriana (Hadrian's Villa)** ★★★, Via di Villa Adriana (© **0774/530203**)—and filled acre after acre with some of the architectural wonders he'd seen on his many trips. Hadrian directed the construction of much more than a villa—it's a self-contained world for a vast royal entourage, the guards required to protect them, and the hundreds of servants needed to bathe them, feed them, and satisfy their libidos. On the estate were theaters, baths, temples, fountains, gardens, and canals bordered with statuary. For a glimpse of what the villa once was, see the plastic reconstruction at the entrance. Admission is 12,000L (€6.25, $6). Open daily from 9am to sunset (about 7:30pm in summer, 4pm from November to March).

Getting There The town of Tivoli is 32 kilometers (20 miles) east of Rome on Via Tiburtina—about an hour's drive with traffic. You can also take public transportation: A bus marked TIVOLI leaves every 15 to 20 minutes during the day from Via Gaeta (west of Via Volturno), near the Stazione Termini. Buses also leave from the Rebibbia metro station.

OSTIA ANTICA ★★ This major attraction is particularly interesting to those who can't make it to Pompeii. At the mouth of the Tiber, it was the port of ancient Rome. Through it were funneled riches from the far corners of the empire. It was founded in the 4th century B.C., and became a major port and naval base primarily under the emperors Claudius and Trajan. A thriving, prosperous city developed, full of temples, bathrooms, theaters, and patrician homes. Ostia Antica flourished for about 8 centuries before it began eventually to wither and the wholesale business of carting off its art treasures began.

Although a papal-sponsored commission launched a series of digs in the 19th century, the major work of unearthing was carried out under Mussolini's orders from 1938 to 1942. The city is only partially dug out today, but it's believed that all the chief monuments have been uncovered.

All the principal monuments are clearly labeled. The most important spot in all the ruins is **Piazzale delle Corporazioni,** an early version of Wall Street. Near the theater, this square contained nearly 75 corporations; the nature of their businesses was identified by the patterns of preserved mosaics.

Ostia Antica is entered on Viale dei Romagnoli 717 (© **06-56358099**). Admission is 8,000L (€4.15, $4). Open from Tuesday to Sunday 9am to 6pm.

Getting There   Take the Metro to the Magliana stop, then change for the Lido train to Ostia Antica, about 26 kilometers (16 miles) from Rome. Departures are about every half hour, and the trip takes only 20 minutes. The train lets you off across the highway that connects Rome with the coast. It's just a short walk to the excavations.

HERCULANEUM & POMPEII   Both these ancient sights are more easily visited from Naples; however, many organized tours go here from Rome. **American Express,** Piazza di Spagna (© **06-67641;** Metro: Spagna), offers day tours to Pompeii, leaving Rome around 7am and returning between 9 and 10pm. You can also explore one—but rarely both—attractions on a day's drive here and back from Rome. Naples is about 2½ hours from Rome by frequent trains. For directions from Naples, see below.

The builders of **Herculaneum** ☆☆ (Ercolano in Italian) were still working to repair the damage caused by an A.D. 62 earthquake when Vesuvius erupted on that fateful August day in A.D. 79. Herculaneum, about one-fourth the size of Pompeii, didn't start to come to light again until 1709, when Prince Elbeuf launched the unfortunate fashion of tunneling through it for treasures. The prince was more intent on profiting from the sale of objets d'art than in uncovering a dead Roman town. Subsequent excavations at the site, **Ufficio Scavi di Ercolano,** Corso Resina, Ercolano (© **081/739-3327**), have been slow. Herculaneum is not completely dug out today.

All the streets and buildings of Herculaneum hold interest, especially the baths (*terme*), divided between those at the forum and those on the outskirts (Terme Suburbane, near the more elegant villas). The municipal baths, which segregated the sexes, are larger, but the ones at the edge of town are more lavishly adorned. Important private homes to see include the **House of the Bicentenary** ☆, the **House of the Wooden Cabinet** ☆☆, and the **House of Poseidon (Neptune) and Amphitrite** ☆☆, the last containing what is the best-known mosaic discovered in the ruins. The finest example of how the aristocracy lived is provided by a visit to the **Casa dei Cervi** ☆☆, named the House of the Stags because of sculpture found inside.

The ruins may be visited daily from 9am to 1 hour before sunset. Admission is 12,000L (€6.25, $6). To reach them, take the Circumvesuviana train from Stazione Centrale in Naples leaving about every half hour from Corso Garibaldi 387 for the 20-minute ride; or take bus 255 from Piazza Municipio. The excavations are a short walk from the train station. Otherwise, it's a 7-kilometer (4½-mile) drive on the autostrada to Salerno (turn off at Ercolano).

When Vesuvius erupted in A.D. 79, Pliny the Younger, who later recorded the event, thought the end of the world had come. Lying 24 kilometers (15 miles) south of Naples, the ruined Roman city of **Pompeii** ☆☆☆ (Pompei in Italian) has been dug out from the inundation of volcanic ash and pumice stone. At the excavations, the life of 19 centuries ago is vividly experienced.

The **Ufficio Scavi di Pompei** is entered at Piazza Esedra (© **081/8610744**). The most elegant of the patrician villas, the **House of Vettii** ☆☆☆ has a courtyard, statuary (such as a two-faced Janus), paintings, and a black-and-red

Pompeiian dining room frescoed with cupids. The second important villa, the **House of Mysteries (Villa dei Misteri)** ✪✪✪ near the Herculaneum Gate (Porto Ercolano), lies outside the walls. What makes the villa exceptional are its remarkable frescoes. The **House of the Faun (Casa del Fauno)** ✪✪, so called because of a bronze statue of a dancing faun found there, takes up a city block and has four different dining rooms and two spacious peristyle gardens. In the center of town is the **Forum** ✪✪✪—although rather small, it was the heart of Pompeiian life.

Pompeii's ruins may be visited daily from 9am to 1 hour before sunset. Admission is 12,000L (€6.25, $6). From Stazione Centrale in Naples, take the Sorrento-bound Circumvesuviana train leaving about every half hour and get off at the Pompei Scavi station; the excavations are across from the station. *Note:* Make sure your train is going to "Pompei Scavi," not "Pompei." Trains bound for Pompei stop at the modern town, not at the ruins.

2 Florence

No other city in Europe, with the exception of Venice, lives off its past in the way Florence does. The Renaissance began here. Florence is a bit foreboding and architecturally severe; many of its palazzi (palaces), as was the Medici style, look like fortresses. But you must remember that when these structures were built the aim was to keep foreign enemies at bay. And these facades guard treasures within, as the thousands of visitors who overrun the narrow streets know and appreciate.

Since the 19th century, Florence has been visited by seemingly half the world—the city has impressed some hard-to-impress people, including Mark Twain, who found it overwhelmed with "tides of color that make all the sharp lines dim and faint and turn the old city to a city of dreams."

It may appear that Florence is caught in a time warp—a Medici returning to the city from the past would have no trouble finding his way around. But Florence virtually pulsates with modern life. Students racing to and from the university quarter add vibrancy to the city, and it's amusing to watch the way many local businesspeople avoid the city's impossible traffic today, whizzing by on Vespas past cars stalled in traffic.

Florentines like to present *una bella figura* (a good appearance) to the rest of the world and are incredibly upset when that appearance is attacked, as in the case of the May 1993 bombing of the Uffizi. The entire city rallied to reopen this treasure trove of Renaissance art.

Try to visit this city, even on the most rushed of European itineraries. There's nothing like it anywhere else. Venice and Rome are too different from Florence to invite meaningful comparisons. Florence is also an ideal base from which to explore Tuscany. Though increasingly built up, Tuscany has enough old hill towns and rolling hills studded with olives and grapevines to attract the romantic. Florence and Siena are the chief drawing cards, but Fiesole and Pisa also have their allure.

ESSENTIALS
GETTING THERE By Plane If you're flying from New York, a much flown route is Rome, where you can board a domestic flight to the **Galileo Galilei Airport** at Pisa (② 050-500707), 93 kilometers (58 miles) west of Florence. **Alitalia** (② 050-20062 for the airport office; www.alitalia.it) also offers two flights a day from New York to Pisa with one stop in Rome. You can

Florence

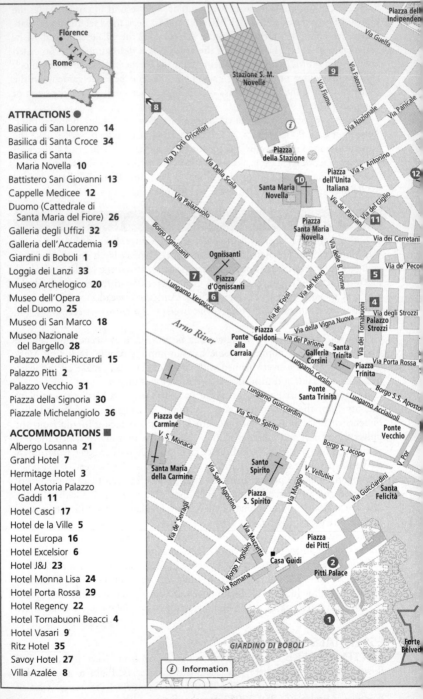

Florence
ITALY
Rome

Piazza dell
Indipenden
Via Guelfa
Stazione S. M.
Novelle
Via Fiume
Via Faenza
Via Nazionale
Via Panicale
Piazza
della Stazione
Piazza
dell'Unita
Italiana
Via S. Antonino
Via de' Panzani
Via del Giglio
Santa Maria
Novella
Piazza
Santa Maria
Novella
Via dei Cerretani
Via D. Orti Oricellari
Via Della Scala
Via Palazzuolo
Via delle B. Donne
Via de' Peco
Borgo Ognissanti
Ognissanti
Piazza
d'Ognissanti
Lungarno Vespucci
Via de' Rossi
Via del Moro
Via degli Strozzi
Palazzo
Strozzi
Via dei Tornabuoni
Arno River
Piazza
Goldoni
Ponte
alla
Carraia
Via della Vigna Nuova
Via del Parione
Galleria
Corsini
Santa
Trinita
Piazza
Trinita
Via Porta Rossa
Borgo S.S. Aposto
Lungarno Corsini
Ponte
Santa Trinita
Lungarno Acciaiuoli
Lungarno Guicciardini
Via Santo Spirito
Piazza del
Carmine
V. S. Monaca
Santa Maria
della Carmine
Via Sant'Agostino
Santo
Spirito
Piazza
S. Spirito
V. Vellutini
Via Maggio
Borgo S. Jacopo
Ponte
Vecchio
Via Guicciardini
Santa
Felicità
V. Po
Via de' Serragli
Via Mazzetta
Casa Guidi
Piazza
dei Pitti
Pitti Palace
Borgo Tegolaio
Via Romana
GIARDINO DI BOBOLI
Forte
Belved
(i) Information

Via XXVII Aprile

Via S. Zanobi

San Marco **18**

GIARDINO
DEI SEMPLICI

P. le
Donatello

Piazza San Marco

Via Guelfa

Via San Gallo

Via Cavour

Accademia **19**

Santissimi Annunziata

zza del
ercato
entrale

Via de' Ginori

17 (i)
Via Cavour **16**

Piazza della
S.S. Annunziata

Via Laura

21

20

Ospedale degli
Innocenti

Borgo Pinti

Piazza
n Lorenzo **15**

Via Ricasoli

Via degli Alfani

22

San
enzo
4

V. de' Martelli

Via dei Pucci

Via dei Servi

Via della Pergola

Via della Colonna

Santa Maria
Maddalena
del Pazzi

Piazza
d'Azeglio

Piazza
13 →
n Giovanni

Duomo
26 ✚

25

Piazza
S. M. Nuova

24

Via L. C. Farini

Sinagoga di
Firenze

Via Roma

Piazza del Duomo

Via di Proconsolo

Via dell'Oriuolo

Borgo Pinti

Via Fiesolana

Via di Mezzo

23

Sant'Ambrogio

zza
la
bblica

Via del Corso
27 Casa di
Dante

Borgo degli Albizi

Via Pietrapiana

anmichele Via D. Alighieri

Via de' Pandolfini

Badia ✚

V. d. Cimatori

28 Via Ghibellina

Via d. Stinche

29

V. d. Vigna Vecchia

Via G. Verdi

Via de' Pepi

V. M. Buonarroti

Borgo Allegri

Via de' Macci

V. dei Calzaiuoli

V. Calimala

Piazza della
Signoria **30**

Borgo de'
Greci

Via de'
Bentaccordi

Piazza
Santa Croce

31 Palazzo
Vecchio

32

Via de' Benci

34

33 Uffizi

Via del Neri

Via Magliabechi

Santa Croce

Via di San Giuseppe

Piazza
Mentana

Ponte
alle
Grazie

Lungarno delle Grazie

Piazza dei
Cavalleggeri

35

Lungarno Torrigiani

Via de' Bardi

Lungarno della Zecca Vecchia

Lungarno Serristori

Via di S. Niccolo

Via di S. Niccolo

Costa di S. Giorgio

Via di Belvedere

Via del Monte alle Croci

Viale G. Poggi

36 Piazzale
Michelangiolo

take an express train for the hour-long trip to Florence. There's also a small domestic airport, **Amerigo Vespucci,** on Via del Termine, near A-11 (**✆ 055-373498**), 6 kilometers (3½ miles northwest of Florence), a 15-minute drive. This airport can be reached by ATAF bus 62, departing from the main Santa Maria Novella rail terminal. Domestic air service is provided by **Alitalia,** with offices in Florence at Lungarno degli Acciaiuoli 10–12R (**✆ 055-27881**).

By Train If you're coming north from Rome, count on a 2- to 3-hour trip, depending on your connection. **Santa Maria Novella rail station,** in Piazza della Stazione, adjoins Piazza di Santa Maria Novella. For railway information, call **✆ 055-288185.** Some trains into Florence stop at the **Stazione Campo di Marte,** on the eastern side of Florence. A 24-hour bus service (91) runs between the two rail terminals.

By Bus Long-distance buses service Florence, run by **SITA,** Viale Cadorna 105 (**✆ 055-47821**), and **Lazzi Eurolines,** Piazza Stazione 3R (**✆ 055-215155**). Both SITA and Lazzi Eurolines offer transfer from Florence to Arezzo, Pisa, and San Giminiano. A one-way ticket from Florence to Pisa, for example, costs 11,200L (€5.80, $6). If you're traveling on SITA, and you want to go to Arezzo, the one-way fare is 3,400L (€1.75, $1.70).

By Car Autostrada A-1 connects Florence with both the north and the south of Italy. It takes about an hour to reach Florence from Bologna and about 3 hours from Rome. The Tyrrhenian coast is only an hour from Florence on **A-11** heading west. Florence lies 277 kilometers (172 miles) north of Rome, 105 kilometers (65 miles) west of Bologna, and 298 kilometers (185 miles) south of Milan. Use a car only to get to Florence. Don't even contemplate its use once here.

VISITOR INFORMATION   Tourist Offices Contact the **Azienda Promozione Turistica,** Via A. Manzoni 16 (**✆ 055-23220**), open from Monday to Saturday 8:30am to 1:30pm. Another helpful office, handling data about both Florence and Tuscany, is **APT** at Via Cavour 1R (**✆ 055-290832**). Hours here are from March to November Monday to Saturday 8:15am to 7:15pm, Sunday 8:15am to 1:45pm; from November to February Monday to Saturday 8:15am to 1:45pm.

Websites Updated weekly for news and notices about concerts and dance recitals, **www.mega.it/florence** also lets you explore the art scene by clicking on the museum map, then switch to the monument version for both the city and surrounding regions, including Chianti.

CITY LAYOUT The city is split by the **Arno River,** which usually looks serene and peaceful but can turn ferocious with floodwaters on rare occasions. The major monumental and historical core lies on the north ("right") side of the river. But the "left" side—called the **Oltrarno**—is not devoid of attractions. Many long-time visitors frequent the Oltrarno for its tantalizing trattoria meals; they also maintain that the shopping here is less expensive. Even the most hurried visitor will want to cross over the Arno to see the Pitti Palace with its many art treasures and walk through the Giardini di Boboli, a series of formal gardens.

The Arno is spanned by eight bridges, of which the **Ponte Vecchio,** lined with jewelry stores, is the most celebrated. **Ponte S. Trinità** is the second-most important bridge spanning the Arno. After crossing it you can continue along **Via dei Tornabuoni,** the most important right-bank shopping street. At the Ponte Vecchio you can walk, again on the right bank, along **Via Por Santa Maria,** which will become Calimala. This will lead you into **Piazza della Repubblica,** a commercial district known for its cafes.

From here, you can take **Via Roma,** which leads directly into **Piazza di San Giovanni.** Here you'll find the baptistery and its neighboring sibling, the larger **Piazza del Duomo,** with the world-famous cathedral and bell tower by Giotto. From the far western edge of Piazza del Duomo, **Via del Proconsolo** heads south to **Piazza della Signoria,** sight of the landmark Palazzo Vecchio and its sculpture-filled Loggia dei Lanzi.

GETTING AROUND   On Foot   Because Florence is so compact, the ideal way to get around town is on foot—at times it's the only way, because there're so many pedestrian zones. In theory at least, pedestrians have the right of way at uncontrolled zebra crossings, but don't count on that should you encounter a speeding Vespa.

By Bus   You must purchase your bus ticket before boarding one of the public vehicles. For 1,500L (€0.83, 75¢), you can ride on any public bus in the city for a total of 60 minutes. A 3-hour pass costs 2,500L (€1.30, $1.25), a 4-hour ticket is 5,800L (€3, $2.90), and a 24-hour pass costs 7,500L (€3.90, $3.75). Bus tickets can be purchased from *tabacchi* (tobacconists' shops, marked by a white T) and news vendors. The local bus station (which serves as the terminal for ATAF city buses) is at Piazza della Stazione (✆ **055-56501**). Bus routes are posted at bus stops.

By Taxi   Taxis can be found at stands at nearly all the major squares in Florence. If you need a radio taxi, call ✆ **055-4390** or 055-4798.

By Car   You'll need a car to explore the countryside of Tuscany in any depth, and these are available at **Avis,** Borgo Ognissanti 128R (✆ **055-213629**); **Italy by Car,** Borgo Ognissanti 134R (✆ **055-287161**); and **Hertz,** Via del Termine 1 (✆ **055-307370**).

By Bicycle or Motor Scooter   **Alinari** is near the rail station at Via Guelfa 85R (✆ **055-280500**). Depending on the model of bike you rent, it will cost 4,000 to 5,000L (€2.13 to €2.60, $2 to $2.50) per hour or 20,000 to 30,000L (€10.40 to €15.60, $10 to $15) per day. If you want to rent a scooter, it costs 15,000L (€7.80, $7.50) per hour, 50,000L (€26, $25) for 5 hours, or 80,000L (€41.60, $40) per day. Open from Monday to Saturday 9:30am to 1pm and 3pm to 7:30pm, Sunday 10am to 1pm and 3pm to 7pm.

✆ *FAST FACTS:* Florence

American Express Amex is at Via Dante Alighieri 22R (✆ **055-50981**), open from Monday to Friday 9am to 5:30pm and Saturday 9am to 12:30pm.

Business Hours Most **banks** are open from Monday to Friday 8:30am to 1:30pm and 2:45 to 3:45pm. **Shops** are generally open Monday from 4 to 7:30pm and Tuesday to Saturday from 9 or 10am to 1pm and 3:30 or 4 to 7:30pm. During the summer some shops are open Monday mornings. However, don't be surprised if shops close for several weeks in August, if not for the entire month.

Consulates The Consulate of the **United States** is at Lungarno Amerigo Vespucci 38 (✆ **055-2398276**), open from Monday to Friday 9am to 12:30pm and 2 to 3:30pm. The Consulate of the **United Kingdom** is at Lungarno Corsini 2 (✆ **055-284133**), near Piazza Santa Trinità, open from

Monday to Friday 9:30am to 12:30pm and 2:30 to 4:30pm. Citizens of Australia, Canada, and New Zealand should consult their missions in Rome (see"Fast Facts: Rome," earlier in this chapter).

Currency Exchange Local banks in Florence grant the best rates. Most banks are open from Monday to Friday 8:30am to 1:30pm and 2:45 to 3:45pm. The tourist office (see "Orientation," above) exchanges money at official rates when banks are closed and on holidays, but a commission is often charged. You can also go to the Ufficio Informazione booth at the rail station, open daily from 7:30am to 7:40pm.

Dentists/Doctors For a list of English-speaking dentists, consult your consulate if possible or contact **Tourist Medical Service,** Via Lorenzo il Magnifico 59 (© **055-475411**). Visits without an appointment are possible from Monday to Friday 11am to noon and 5 to 6pm. After hours, an answering service gives names and phone numbers of dentists and doctors on duty.

Emergencies For fire, call © **115**; for an ambulance, call © **118**; for the police, © **113**; and for road service, © **116.**

Hospitals Call the **General Hospital of Santa Maria Nuova,** Piazza Santa Maria Nuova 1 (© **055-27581**).

Internet Access You can check your messages or send e-mail at **Internet Train,** Via dell'Orvio 25R (© **055-263-8968**; www.internettrain.it).

Police Dial © **113** in an emergency. Foreigners who want to see and talk to the police should go to the Ufficio Stranieri station at Via Zara 2 (© **055-49771**), where English-speaking personnel are available daily 9am to 2pm.

Post Office The Central Post Office is at Via Pellicceria 3, off Piazza della Repubblica (© **055-2774539**; 055-2774322 for English-speaking operators). It's open from Monday to Saturday 8:15am to 7pm. Stamps are purchased in the main post office at windows 21–22. If you want your mail sent to Italy general delivery (*fermo posta*), have it sent in care of this post office (use the 50100 Firenze postal code). Mail can be picked up at windows 23–24.

Safety Crime consists mainly of pickpockets who frequent crowded tourist centers, such as the corridors of the Uffizi Galleries. Members of group tours who cluster together are often singled out as victims. Car thefts are relatively common: Don't leave your luggage in an unguarded car, even if it's locked in the trunk. Women should be especially careful in avoiding purse-snatchers, some of whom grab a purse while whizzing by on a Vespa, often knocking the woman down. Documents such as passports and extra money are better stored in the safe at your hotel.

Telephones The **country code** for Italy is **39.** The **city code** for Florence is **055,** which is the code you'll use every time you dial a party located within Florence, regardless of whether you're within the city limits or not. We emphasize that newly imposed technologies will require the use of the "0" and then "55" for calls to parties in Florence, regardless of whether you're within the city limits or not. For additional information, see "Fast Facts: Rome," earlier in this chapter.

WHERE TO STAY
NEAR THE DUOMO
Very Expensive

Savoy Hotel ⚜⚜⚜ Everything is fresh and new again at Florence's most legendary hotel, which opened in 1896. Completely restored, it now takes its place just under the Excelsior and Grand in luxury. Refined Italian elegance is the hallmark of this landmark monument, which experienced years of decline after World War II. Rooms are decorated sumptuously. Bathrooms are beautifully tiled (some with shower only).

Piazza della Repubblica 7, 50123 Firenze. ℂ **055-27-351.** Fax 055-2735-888. www.rfhotels.com/savoy. 107 units. 750,000L (€390, $375) double. AE, DC, MC, V. Bus: 22, 36, or 37**Amenities:** Restaurant, bar; room service; laundry/dry cleaning. *In room:* A/C, TV, minibar, hair dryer, safe.

Expensive

Hotel J and J ⚜ This charming hotel was built in the 16th century as a monastery. It's 5-minute walk from the church of Santa Croce. You'll find a flagstone-covered courtyard and a salon with vaulted ceilings and several preserved ceiling frescoes. Rooms combine an unusual mixture of modern furniture with the monastery's original beamed ceilings. Suites usually contain sleeping lofts and, in some cases, rooftop balconies overlooking the historic core.

Via di Mezzo 20, 50121 Firenze. ℂ **055-263121.** Fax 055-240282. www.jandjhotel.com. 20 units. 490,000L (€254.80, $245) double; 650,000L (€338, $325) junior suite; 800,000L (€416, $400) suite. Rates include buffet breakfast. AE, DC, MC, V. Parking 50,000L (€26, $25). Bus: A. **Amenities:** Room service; laundry/dry cleaning. *In room:* A/C, TV, minibar.

Hotel Monna Lisa ⚜ This privately owned Renaissance palazzo is 4 blocks east of the Duomo. Most of the great old rooms overlook either an inner patio or a modest rear garden. Each of the salons is handsomely furnished. Rooms vary greatly—some are quite large, though no two are alike.

Borgo Pinti 27, 50121 Firenze. ℂ **055-2479751.** Fax 055-2479755. www.monnalisa.it. 30 units. 500,000L (€260, $250) double; 650,000L (€338, $325) triple. Rates include breakfast. AE, DC, MC, V. Parking 20,000L (€10.40, $10). Bus: A, 6, 31, or 32. **Amenities:** Baby-sitting; laundry/dry cleaning. *In room:* A/C, TV, minibar.

Hotel Porta Rossa ⚜ Reportedly, this is the second oldest hotel in Italy, dating from 1386. The place is a bit dark, but on a hot Tuscan summer day you welcome that in lieu of air-conditioning. Since it isn't as well known or publicized as some of its competitors such as the Hermitage or Tornabuoni, you stand a better chance of getting a reservation. In spite of its antiquity, the hotel has kept abreast of the times, installing modern conveniences, good beds, and ample bathrooms. The managers have resisted making two new rooms out of one of the old spacious ones from centuries ago. Breakfast is the only meal served, and a little terrace offers a panoramic view.

Via Porta Rossa 19, 50123 Firenze. ℂ **055-287551.** Fax 055-282179. 79 units. 260,000L (€135.20, $130) double; 305,000L (€158.60, $152.50) suite for 3 or 4. Rates include breakfast. AE, DC, MC, V. Parking 40,000–65,000L (€20.80–€33.80, $20–$33). Bus: A. **Amenities:** Bar; roof terrace; baby-sitting; laundry/dry cleaning. *In room:* A/C, TV, minibar, hair dryer, safe.

NEAR THE PONTE VECCHIO
Moderate

Hermitage Hotel ⚜ The offbeat, intimate Hermitage is a charming place, with a sun terrace on the roof providing a view. You can take your breakfast under a leafy arbor surrounded by potted roses and geraniums. The small rooms are pleasantly furnished. Bathrooms are superb and contain lots of gadgets.

Some recently restored ones have hydro massage tubs. Those rooms overlooking the Arno offer the most scenic view, and they've been fitted with double-glazed windows.

Vicolo Marzio 1, Piazza del Pesce I, 50122 Firenze. ℭ **055-287216.** Fax 055-212208. www.venere.it/ firenze/hermitage/hermitage_it.html. 29 units. 410,000L (€213.20, $205) double; 470,000L (€244.40, $235) triple; 530,000L (€275.60, $265) family room. Rates include breakfast. MC, V. Parking 35,000–45,000L (€18.20–€23.40, $18–$23). Bus: B. **Amenities:** Bar; roof terrace; room service. *In room:* A/C, TV, hair dryer.

NEAR PIAZZA SANTA TRINITÀ
Moderate
Hotel Tornabuoni Beacci   Near the Arno and Piazza S. Trinità, on the principal shopping street, this pensione occupies the top three floors of a 14th-century palazzo. The hotel was completely renovated recently, but it still bears an air of old-fashioned gentility. The rooms are moderately well furnished. The roof terrace is for breakfast or late-afternoon drinks. The view of the nearby churches, towers, and rooftops is worth experiencing.

Via Tornabuoni 3, 50123 Firenze. ℭ **055-212645.** Fax 055-283594. www.italyhotel.com. 30 units. 400,000L (€208, $200) double. Rates include buffet breakfast. AE, DC, MC, V. Parking 45,000L (€23.40, $23). Bus: B, 6, 11, or 36. **Amenities:** Restaurant, bar; roof terrace; room service. *In room:* A/C, TV, minibar, hair dryer.

NEAR PIAZZA SAN LORENZO & THE MERCATO CENTRALE
Inexpensive
Hotel Casci   Casci is a well-run little hotel, near the Piazza del Duomo and the main rail station. The building dates from the 14th century, and some of the public rooms feature frescoes. The hotel is both traditional and modern, and the English-speaking reception staff is attentive. Rooms are comfortably furnished, and each year four or five are upgraded and renovated.

Via Cavour 13, 50129 Firenze. ℭ **055-211686.** Fax 055-2396461. www.emmeti.it/casci.html. 25 units. 220,000L (€114.40, $110) double; 290,000L (€150.80, $145) triple; 360,000L (€187.20, $180) quad. Rates include buffet breakfast. AE, DC, MC, V. Parking 35,000–45,000L (€18.20–€23.40, $18–$23). Bus: 1, 7, 25, or 33. **Amenities:** Bar; laundry/dry cleaning. *In room:* A/C, TV, minibar, hair dryer, safe.

Hotel Europa   Two long blocks north of the Duomo, this hotel in a 16th-century building has functioned as a family-run hotel since 1925. Homey touches remind newcomers of its ongoing administration by members of the Gassim family. All but four rooms overlook the back and usually open onto a view of the campanile and dome of the Duomo. Those that face the street are noisier but benefit from double-glazing.

Via Cavour 14, 50129 Firenze. ℭ **055-2396715.** Fax 055-210361. 13 units. 250,000L (€130, $125) double; 335,000L (€174.20, $168) triple. Rates include buffet breakfast. AE, MC, V. Parking 35,000–40,000L (€18.20–€20.80, $17.50–$20) in nearby garage. Bus: 1, 7, 25, or 33. **Amenities:** Laundry/dry cleaning. *In room:* A/C, TV, hair dryer, safe.

NEAR PIAZZA SANTA MARIA NOVELLA & THE TRAIN STATION
Expensive
Hotel Astoria Palazzo Gaddi 𝕽𝕽𝕽   In spite of its location in a setting of cheap railroad station hotels, this is an impressive Renaissance palace containing 16th-century frescoes by Luca Giordano. In the 17th century, John Milton wrote parts of *Paradise Lost* in one of the rooms. The Astoria has been renovated and turned into a serviceable and enduring choice, with a helpful staff. From the rooms on the upper floors, you'll have a view over the rooftops. Rooms have stylish traditional furnishings for the most part; some are decorated in more

modern style. In summer on the roof garden, you can order drinks and a wide choice of cold dishes, salads, and sandwiches while taking in a panoramic view.

Via del Giglio 9, 50123 Firenze. © **055-2398095**. Fax 055-214632. 106 units. 500,000–540,000L (€260–€280.80, $250–$270) double; from 720,000L (€374.40, $360) suite. Rates include buffet breakfast. AE, DC, MC, V. Parking 40,000L (€20.80, $20) nearby. Bus: 4. **Amenities:** Restaurant, bar; roof terrace; currency exchange; car rental desk; room service; baby-sitting. *In room:* A/C TV, minibar, safe.

Hotel de la Ville ★ On the most elegant street of the historic center, close to the Arno and the rail station, this recently refurbished hotel draws a loyal following among Italian business travelers. It has a conservatively contemporary appearance. Rooms are soundproof and have a quaint style to them.

Piazza Antinori 1, 50123 Firenze. © **055-2381805**. Fax 055-2381809. www.hoteld.aville.it. 79 units. 900,000L (€468, $450) double; 1,800,000L (€936, $900) suite. Rates include buffet breakfast. AE, DC, MC, V. Parking 45,000–50,000L (€23.40–€26, $23–$25). Bus: 80. **Amenities:** Bar; swimming pool; baby-sitting; laundry/dry cleaning. *In room:* A/C, TV, minibar.

Moderate

Villa Azalée Villa Azalée, set on a street corner with a big garden, is a private home built in the 1860s and transformed into a hotel in 1964 with an annex added. The decorating is tasteful. Rooms have distinction (one boasts a flouncy canopy bed). The hotel is a 5-minute walk from the rail station.

Viale Fratelli Rosselli 44, 50123 Firenze. © **055-214242**. Fax 055-268264. villaazalee@fi.flashnet.it. 25 units. 298,000L (€154.95, $149) double; 400,000L (€208, $200) triple. Rates include buffet breakfast. AE, DC, MC, V. Parking from 35,000L (€18.20, $18) nearby. Bus: 80. **Amenities:** Laundry/dry cleaning. *In room:* A/C, TV.

Inexpensive

Hotel Vasari Built in the 1840s as a private home, this was a run-down two-star hotel until 1993, when its owners upgraded it to one of the most fairly priced three-star hotels in town. Rooms are comfortable, albeit a bit spartan. The beds are firm, the linen crisp, and the bathrooms small but immaculate, containing showers.

Via B. Cennini 9–11, 50123 Firenze. © **055-212753**. Fax 055-294246. 27 units. 290,000L (€150.80, $145) double. Rates include breakfast. AE, DC, MC, V. Parking 20,000L (€10.40, $10). Bus: 4, 7, 10, 13, 14, 23, or 71. **Amenities:** Room service; baby-sitting. *In room:* A/C, TV, minibar, hair dryer.

ON PIAZZA OGNISSANTI

Piazza Ognissanti is a fashionable but car-clogged Renaissance square opening onto the Arno. It's home to two of the most legendary hotels in the city.

Very Expensive

Grand Hotel ★★★ The Grand is a bastion of luxury, although neither it nor the Excelsior are as exclusive as the Regency. A hotel of history and tradition, the Grand is known for its halls and salons. Rooms and suites have a refined elegance, and the most desirable overlook the Arno. A highlight of the hotel is the Winter Garden, an enclosed court lined with arches where regional and international dishes are served.

Piazza Ognissanti 1, 50123 Firenze. © **800/325-3589** in the U.S. and Canada, or 055-288781. Fax 055-217400. www.firenzealbergo.it/home/grandhotel. 107 units. 900,000–1,190,000L (€468–€618.80, $450–$595) double; from 1,900,000L (€988, $950) suite. AE, DC, MC, V. Parking from 60,000L (€31.20, $30). Bus: 6 or 17. **Amenities:** Restaurant, bar; valet; room service; laundry/dry cleaning. *In room:* A/C, TV, minibar, hair dryer.

Hotel Excelsior ★★★ The Excelsior, a former patrician mansion, is the ultimate in luxury. Cosmopolitan and sophisticated, it has the best-trained staff in town. If you like glamour and glitz, stay here. The opulent rooms have

19th-century Florentine antiques and sumptuous fabrics. Some of the more desirable rooms open onto views of the Arno. In these old palaces, expect the accommodations to come in a variety of configurations.

Piazza Ognissanti 3, 50123 Firenze. ℰ 800/325-3535 in the U.S. and Canada, or 055-264201. Fax 055-210278. www.firenzealbergo.it/home/excelsior. 191 units. 900,000–1,190,000L (€468–€618.80, $450–$595) double; from 1,900,000L (€988, $950) junior suite. AE, DC, MC, V. Parking 60,000L (€31.20, $30). Bus: 6 or 17. **Amenities:** Restaurant, bar; valet; room service; laundry/dry cleaning. *In room:* A/C, TV, minibar, hair dryer.

ON OR NEAR PIAZZA MASSIMO D'AZEGLIO

Piazza Massimo d'Azeglio is a 12-minute walk northeast of the historic core of Florence.

Very Expensive

Hotel Regency ⭐⭐⭐   The Regency is an intimate villa of taste and exclusivity. This well-built old-style villa, a member of Relais & Châteaux, has its own garden across from a park in a residential area. It's a luxurious hideaway, and offers exquisitely furnished rooms. The dining room, Relais le Jardin, is renowned for its *alta cucina.*

Piazza Massimo d'Azeglio 3, 50121 Firenze. ℰ 055-245247. Fax 055-2346735. www.regency-hotel.com. 34 units. 700,000–740,000L (€364–€384.80, $350–$370) double; from 1,000,000L (€520, $500) suite. Rates include buffet breakfast. AE, DC, MC, V. Parking 50,000L (€26, $25). Bus: 6, 31, or 32. **Amenities:** Restaurant, bar; garden; room service; baby-sitting; laundry/dry cleaning. *In room:* A/C, TV, minibar, hair dryer.

Inexpensive

Albergo Losanna   A good choice, Albergo Losanna is a tiny family-run place off Viale Antonio Gramsci, between Piazzale Donatello and Piazza Massimo d'Azeglio. It offers utter simplicity and cleanliness. Rooms are homey and well kept, but the furnishings are simple and a bit tired.

Via Vittorio Alfieri 9, 50121 Firenze. ℰ and fax 055-245840. 8 units (3 with bathroom). 95,000L (€49.40, $48) double without bathroom; 130,000L (€67.60, $65) double with bathroom. Rates include breakfast. AE, MC, V. Parking 30,000–35,000L (€15.60–€18.20, $15–$18). Bus: 6. **Amenities:** Breakfast room.

ALONG THE ARNO
Moderate

Ritz Hotel ⭐ *(Finds)*   Don't be misled by the name "Ritz" and grab to hold onto your wallet. The Ritz of Florence has nothing to do with the *luxe* palaces of London, Paris, or Madrid. The local Ritz is a family-run hotel whose youthful owners have upgraded it and turned it into a reasonably priced alternative in a lethally priced city. They offer well-furnished, medium-size rooms. A visit here is like a call on your favorite Florentine aunt back in 1870 but with more modern amenities than she had. Breakfast is the only meal served.

Lugarno Zeccia Vecchia 24, 50122 Firenze. ℰ 055-234-0650. Fax 055-240-863. www.tiac.net/pendini/ritz. 32 units. 200,000–320,000L (€104–€166.40, $100–$160) double; 320,000–520,000L (€166.40–€270.40, $160–$260) suite. Rates include breakfast. AE, DC, MC, V. Bus: 23. **Amenities:** Bar. *In room:* A/C, TV, minibar, hair dryer, safe.

WHERE TO DINE
NEAR THE DUOMO
Moderate

Il Cavallino TUSCAN/ITALIAN   A local favorite since the 1930s, Il Cavallino is the kind of discreetly famous restaurant where Florentines invariably go to be with one another. It's on a tiny street (which probably won't even be on your map) that leads off Piazza della Signoria at its northern end, not far from the equestrian statue. Menu items are typical hearty Tuscan fare, including an assortment of boiled meats in green herb sauce, grilled filet of steak, breast of chicken Medici style, and the inevitable Florentine spinach.

Piazza della Signoria, Via della Farine 6R. ℂ **055-215818**. Reservations recommended. Main courses 18,000–30,000L (€9.35–€15.60, $9–$15); fixed-price menu 35,000L (€18.20, $18). AE, DC, MC, V. Mar–Oct daily noon–3pm and 7–10:30pm; off-season Thurs–Tues noon–3pm and Thurs–Mon 7–10:30pm. Bus: A or B.

Paoli ⭐ TUSCAN/ITALIAN Paoli, between the Duomo and Piazza della Signoria, is one of Florence's finest restaurants. It turns out a host of specialties, but could be recommended almost solely for its medieval-tavern atmosphere. All pastas are homemade, and the fettuccine alla Paoli is served piping hot and full of flavor. The chef also does a superb *rognoncino trifolato* (thinly sliced kidney cooked with oil, garlic, and parsley) and sole meunière. A recommendable side dish is *piselli* (garden peas) in the Florentine style.

Via dei Tavolini 12R. ℂ **055-216215**. Reservations required. Main courses 16,000–40,000L (€8.30–€20.80, $8–$20). AE, DC, MC, V. Wed–Mon noon–2:30pm and 7–10:30pm. Closed 3 weeks in Aug. Bus: A.

NEAR THE PONTE VECCHIO
Inexpensive
Buca dell'Orafo ⭐ *Finds* FLORENTINE This little dive is one of many cellars or *buca*-type establishments beloved by Florentines. The trattoria is usually stuffed with regulars so if you want a seat, go early. Over the years the chef has made little concession to the foreign palate, turning out genuine Florentine specialties, like tripe and mixed boiled meats with a green sauce, and *stracotto e fagioli* (beef braised in a sauce of chopped vegetables and red wine), served with beans in a tomato sauce.

Via Volta dei Girolami 28R. ℂ **055-213619**. Reservations recommended. Main courses 15,000–35,000L (€7.80–€18.20, $8–$18). No credit cards. Tues–Sat 12:30–2:30pm and 7:30–10:30pm. Closed Aug and 2 weeks in Dec. Bus: A.

NEAR PIAZZA SAN LORENZO & THE MERCATO CENTRALE
Inexpensive
Le Fonticine TUSCAN/BOLOGNESE Owner Silvano Bruci took this former convent and its adjoining garden and turned it into one of the most hospitable restaurants in Florence. He and his wife use recipes she collected from her childhood in Bologna. The food, served in copious portions, is both traditional and delectable. Begin with a platter of fresh antipasti, then enjoy samplings of three of the most excellent pasta dishes of the day. This might be followed by veal scaloppini, or stewed wild boar.

Via Nazionale 79R. ℂ **055-282106**. Reservations recommended for dinner. Main courses 17,000–35,000L (€8.85–€18.20, $9–$18). AE, DC, MC, V. Tues–Sat noon–2:30pm and 7–10pm. Closed Jan 1–15 and Aug. Bus: 7, 10, 11, 12, 25, 31, 33, or 70.

Trattoria Antellesi ⭐ *Finds* TUSCAN On the ground floor of a 15th-century historic monument, a few steps from the Medici Chapel, this restaurant is devoted almost exclusively to Tuscan recipes that have stood the test of time. The restaurant prepares at least seven *piatti del giorno* that change according to the availability of the ingredients. Menu items may include tagliatelle with porcini mushrooms or with braised arugula, *crespelle alla fiorentina* (a Tuscan Renaissance cheesy spinach crepe), market-fresh fish (generally on Friday), and delicious Valdostana chicken.

Via Faenza 9R. ℂ **055-216990**. Reservations recommended. Main courses 18,000–30,000L (€9.35–€15.60, $9–$15). AE, DC, MC, V. Nov–Aug Mon–Sat noon–3pm and 7–10:30pm; Sept–Oct daily noon–3pm and 7–10:30pm. Bus: 7, 10, 11, 12, 25, 31, 33, or 70.

The Cafe Scene

Café Rivoire, Piazza della Signoria 4R (© **055-214412**; bus: B), offers a classy and amusing old-world ambience with a direct view of the statues of one of our favorite squares. Try the hot chocolate. Behind three Tuscan arches on a fashionable shopping street in the center of the old city, **Giacosa,** V. Tornabuoni 83R (© **055-2396226**; bus: B, 6, 11, 36, 37, or 68), has a warmly paneled interior, a lavish display of pastries and sandwiches, and a reputation as the birthplace of the Negroni, a drink that's a combination of gin, Campari, and sweet vermouth.

A few minutes' walk from the Duomo, **Gilli,** Piazza della Repubblica 39R (© **055-213896**; bus: A), is the oldest and most beautiful cafe in Florence, founded in 1733. The interior is all wood and brass, and tables are placed outside in summer. **Giubbe Rosse,** Piazza della Repubblica 13R (© **055-212-280**; bus: A), has always been known as a literary cafe, where intellectuals and writers met each other to discuss the Italian politics and literature. You can enjoy coffee, drinks, and also salads and sandwiches surrounded by early 1900s chandeliers and polished granite floors.

NEAR PIAZZA SANTA MARIA NOVELLA & THE TRAIN STATION

Expensive

I Quattro Amici ✿ SEAFOOD   Opened in 1990 by four Tuscan entrepreneurs, this restaurant occupies the street level of a modern building near the rail station. The place serves endless quantities of fish. Specialties include such dishes as pasta with fish sauce and sausage; fish soup; fried shrimp and squid in the style of Livorno; and grilled, stewed, or baked versions of all the bounty of the Mediterranean. The roast sea bass and roast snapper, flavored with Mediterranean herbs, are among the finest dishes, as is the fresh lobster with mixed vegetables.

Via degli Orti Oricellari 29. © 055-215413. Reservations recommended. Main courses 30,000–50,000L (€15.60–€26, $15–$25). AE, DC, MC, V. Daily noon–2:30pm and 7–10:30pm. Bus: D, 26, 27, or 35.

Moderate

Buca Lapi ✿ TUSCAN   Buca Lapi, a cellar restaurant under the Palazzo Antinori, is big on glamour, good food, and the enthusiasm of fellow diners. Its decor alone makes it fun: Vaulted ceilings are covered with travel posters from all over the world. The cooks know how to turn out the most classic dishes of the Tuscan kitchen with superb finesse. Specialties include pâté, cannelloni, *scampi giganti alla griglia* (a supersize shrimp), and *bistecca alla fiorentina* (local beefsteak), still cooked over coals in the old-fashioned way. In season, the *fagioli toscani all'olio* (Tuscan beans in the native olive oil) are a delicacy. Owner and chef Luciano Ghinasi's cookbook, available in English, reveals some of his secrets in preparing succulent Tuscan dishes.

Via del Trebbio 1R. © 055-213768. Reservations required for dinner. Main courses 25,000–45,000L (€13–€23.40, $13–$23). AE, DC, MC, V. Tues–Sat 12:30–2:30pm; Mon–Sat 7:30–10:30pm. Closed 2 weeks in Aug. Bus: 6, 11, 36, or 37.

Don Chisciotte ☆ ITALIAN/SEAFOOD   This restaurant is known for its creative cuisine and changing array of very fresh fish. Creative menu items are produced with a flourish from the kitchens. Examples include red taglierini with clams, pesto, and cheese; risotto of broccoli and baby squid; and black ravioli colored with squid ink and stuffed with a puree of shrimp and crayfish. Chefs also prepare one of the city's most flavor-filled Florentine steaks along with a succulent medley of boiled meats with fresh herb seasonings.

Via Ridolfi 4R. ☎ 055-475430. Reservations recommended. Main courses 28,000–40,000L (€14.55–€20.80, $14–$20); *menu degustazione* 95,000L (€49.40, $48). AE, DC, MC, V. Mon 8–10:30pm; Tues–Sat 1–2:30pm and 8–10:30pm. Bus: 20.

Sabatini ☆ FLORENTINE   Despite its location near the rail station, Sabatini has long been extolled by Florentines and visitors alike as the finest of the restaurants characteristic of the city. To celebrate our return visit every year, we order the same main course—boiled Valdarno chicken with savory green sauce. Other main courses are also delicious, especially the veal scaloppini with artichokes. Of course, you can always order a good sole meunière and the classic beefsteak Florentine.

Via de'Panzani 9A. ☎ 055-211559. Reservations recommended. Main courses 25,000–48,000L (€13–€24.95, $12.50–$24). AE, DC, MC, V. Tues–Sun 12:30–2:30pm and 7:30–10:30pm. Bus: 1, 6, 14, 17, or 22.

Inexpensive
Ristorante Otello FLORENTINE   Beside the train station, Ristorante Otello is a long-established comfortable Florentine dining room. Its antipasto Toscano is one of the best in town, an array of appetizing hors d'oeuvres that practically becomes a meal in itself. The waiter urges you to "*Mangi, mangi, mangi!*" ("Eat, eat, eat!"). Order one of the succulent pasta dishes, such as spaghetti with baby clams or pappardelle with garlic sauce. The meat and poultry dishes are equally delectable, including sole meunière and veal pizzaiola with lots of garlic.

Via degli Orti Oricellari 36R. ☎ 055-216517. Reservations recommended. Main courses 18,000–35,000L (€9.35–€18.20, $9–$18). AE, DC, MC, V. Daily noon–2:30pm and 7:30–10:30pm. Bus: D, 26, 27, or 35.

Trattoria Sostanza ☆ *Finds* FLORENTINE   Sostanza is a tucked-away little trattoria where working people have gone since 1869 to get excellent, reasonably priced food. It's the city's oldest and most revered trattoria. The small dining room has crowded family tables. The rear kitchen is open, its secrets exposed to diners. Specialties include breaded chicken breast and a succulent T-bone steak. You might also want to try tripe the Florentine way—cut into strips and baked in a casserole with tomatoes, onions, and Parmesan.

Via del Porcellana 25R. ☎ 055-212691. Reservations recommended. Main courses 15,000–30,000L (€7.80–€15.60, $7.50–$15). No credit cards. Mon–Fri noon–3pm and 7:30–10:30pm. Closed Aug and 2 weeks at Christmas. Bus: 12.

NEAR PIAZZA GOLDONI
Moderate
Harry's Bar ☆ INTERNATIONAL/ITALIAN   Harry's Bar, in a prime position on the Arno, is an enclave of expatriate and well-heeled visiting Yankees that deserves its reputation. A specialty is risotto or tagliatelle with ham, onions, and cheese. Harry has created his own tortellini (stuffed pasta), but Harry's hamburger and his club sandwich are the most popular items. The chef also prepares

about a dozen specialties every day, like breast of chicken "our way," grilled giant-size scampi, and lean broiled sirloin.

Lungarno Vespucci 22R. ℂ 055-2396700. Reservations required. Main courses 20,000–38,000L (€10.40–€19.75, $10–$19). AE, MC, V. Mon–Sat noon–3pm and 7–11pm. Closed 1 week in Aug and Dec 18–Jan 8. Bus: B.

Trattoria Coco Lezzone FLORENTINE   In Florentine dialect, the establishment's name refers to the sauce-stained apron of the extroverted chef who established this place more than a century ago. Today, this remains a good place to sample the nearby food of the Tuscan countryside. Go before the rush begins if you want a seat in this bustling trattoria. The rib-sticking fare includes generous portions of boiled meats with a green sauce, *pasta fagiole* (beans), *osso buco* (beef or veal knuckle braised in wine, butter, garlic, and lemon), tripe, and beefsteak Florentine, which is super-expensive, although most dishes are very moderate in price.

Via del Parioncino 26R. ℂ 055-287178. Reservations accepted only for groups of 10 or more. Main courses 18,000–45,000L (€9.35–€23.40, $9–$23). No credit cards. Mon–Sat noon–2:30pm and 7–10pm. Closed last week of July–Aug and Dec 25–Jan 6. Bus: 27 or 31.

NEAR PIAZZA SANTA CROCE
Expensive
Alle Murate 🏵 TUSCAN/SOUTHERN ITALIAN   This sophisticated eatery with a softly lit uncluttered dining room prepares some of the most creative and classic Tuscan (as well as classic southern) dishes in town. The chefs make the best lasagna in town with mozzarella and fresh tomatoes. Several soufflés are prepared with seasonal vegetables such as leeks or artichokes. Handmade tortelli (a kind of ravioli) is stuffed with small eggplants and served with a butter and thyme sauce. *Brasato di chianina* is veal braised with Brunello di Montalcino red wine. In an adjacent smaller room, Vineria, the menu is different, the service not as good, but the food is slightly cheaper.

You may also want to check out the same owner's **Osteria del Caffè Italiano,** Via Isola delle Stinche 11–13R, 2 blocks west of Piazza Santa Croce (ℂ **055-28-93-68;** bus: A or 14); and **Caffè Italiano,** V. Condotta 56R, off Via dei Calzaiuoli (ℂ **055-29-1082;** bus: 14, 23, or 71).

Via Ghibellina, 52R. ℂ 055-240618. Reservations recommended. Main courses 35,000–70,000L (€18.20–€36.40, $18–$35). AE, DC, MC, V. Tues–Sun 7:30–11:30pm. Closed 15 days at Christmas. Bus: 14.

Moderate
Cibreo 🏵 *Finds* MEDITERRANEAN   Cibreo is one of the largest eateries in the neighborhood. *The New York Times* called the chef and owner, Fabio Picchi, a poet for how he talks and a magician for how he cooks. The kitchens are noteworthy for not containing a grill and not serving pastas. They specialize in foodstuffs cooked in a wood-burning oven and cold marinated dishes, especially vegetables. Menu items include *sformato* (soufflé made from potatoes and ricotta, served with Parmesan and tomato sauce) and flan of Parmesan, veal tongue, and artichokes. A favorite dish of the chef is roast pigeon flavored with a fruity mustard. Among his classic recipes are *zuppa di cavolo* (cabbage soup), *polenta alle erbe* (polenta flavored with seasonal herbs), and *insalata di fave* (fava bean salad with parmigiano flakes).

Via dei Macci 118R. ℂ 055-2341100. Reservations recommended in the restaurant, not accepted in the trattoria. Main courses 30,000–45,000L (€15.60–€23.40, $15–$23) in the restaurant, 15,000–30,000L (€7.80–€15.60, $8–$15) in the trattoria. AE, DC, MC, V (restaurant only). Tues–Sat 12:30–2:30pm and 7:30–11pm. Closed late July to early Sept. Bus: A.

ACROSS THE ARNO
Moderate
Mamma Gina ⭐ *(Finds)* TUSCAN   This exceptional trattoria, well worth the trek across the Ponte Vecchio, is a center for hearty Tuscan fare. The menu items are rich, savory, and tied to the seasons and include such dishes as cannelloni Mamma Gina (stuffed with a puree of minced meats, spices, and vegetables); tagliolini with artichoke hearts or mushrooms and whatever else is in season at the time; and chicken breast Mamma Gina, baked in the northern Italian style with prosciutto and Emmenthaler cheese. Trust Mamma Gina's recipes and try the *panzerotti,* savory turnovers made with pizza dough and stuffed with several different types of cheese.

Borgo San'Jacopo 37R. ✆ 055-2396009. Reservations required for dinner. Main courses 20,000–35,000L (€10.40–€18.20, $10–$18). AE, DC, MC, V. Mon–Sat noon–2:30pm and 7–10:30pm. Closed Aug 9–23. Bus: B or D.

Inexpensive
Fuori Porta ⭐ *(Finds)* TUSCAN   This is the city's best enoteca or wine tavern. As the name translates, it means "outside the gates," yet it's only a 15-minute taxi or bus ride from the Piazza della Signoria. The wine list ranks at the top in Florence, yet the prices are reasonable, far cheaper than at the *luxe* restaurants. Discerning palates appreciate the Tuscan fare served here, a kind of soul food to the Florentine. We recently launched an elegant repast with carpaccio of swordfish that was perfectly cooked, as was the sautéed calf's liver to follow. We especially like the loaves of bread that arrive at table freshly baked in the oven, and most often served with mozzarella and vine-ripened tomatoes.

Via del Monte alle Croce 10R. ✆ 055-234-2483. Reservations recommended. Main courses 10,000–20,000L (€5.20–€10.40, $5–$10). AE, MC, V. Mon–Sat 12:30–3:30pm and 7pm–midnight. Closed Aug 10–20. Bus: 13 or 23.

EXPLORING THE RENAISSANCE CITY
Florence was the fountainhead of the Renaissance, the city of Dante and Boccaccio. Florentines are noted for their cunning, as represented by Machiavelli; however, they're not noted for their religious zeal, as evoked by Savonarola, who might've found a better reception in Geneva. For 3 centuries, Florence was dominated by the Medici family, patrons of the arts and masters of assassination. But it's chiefly through its artists that we know of the apogee of the Renaissance: Ghiberti, Fra Angelico, Donatello, Brunelleschi, Botticelli, and the incomparable Leonardo da Vinci and Michelangelo.

Piazza della Signoria ⭐⭐⭐, though never completed, is one of the most beautiful in Italy. On the square is the Fountain of Neptune. Nearby is the spot where Savonarola walked his last mile. This zealous monk was a fire-and-brimstone reformer who rivaled Dante in conjuring up the punishment hell would inflict on sinners. For centuries Michelangelo's *David* stood in this piazza before it was moved to the Accademia. The work you see here today is a copy.

On the piazza, the 14th-century **Loggia dei Lanzi** ⭐⭐ (sometimes called the Loggia della Signoria) is a gallery of sculpture that often depicts fierce, violent scenes. The best piece is a rare work by Benvenuto Cellini, the goldsmith and tell-all autobiographer. Critics have said that his exquisite *Perseus,* who holds the severed head of Medusa, is the most significant Florentine sculpture since Michelangelo's *Night* and *Day.*

For a view of the wonders of Florence below and Fiesole above, climb aboard bus 13 from the central station and head for **Piazzale Michelangelo** ⭐, a

19th-century belvedere with a view seen in many a Renaissance painting. It's best at dusk, when the purple-fringed Tuscan hills form a frame for Giotto's bell tower, Brunelleschi's dome, and the towering stones sticking up from the Palazzo Vecchio. Another copy of Michelangelo's *David* dominates the square.

SIGHTSEEING SUGGESTIONS FOR FIRST-TIME VISITORS

If You Have 1 Day You'll have to accept the inevitable—you can only visit a small fraction of Florence's stellar attractions. Go to the **Uffizi Galleries** as soon as they open and concentrate only on some of the masterpieces or your favorite artists. Have lunch on **Piazza della Signoria,** dominated by the Palazzo Vecchio, and admire the statues in the Loggia dei Lanzi. After lunch, visit the **Duomo** and **Baptistry,** before continuing north to see Michelangelo's *David* at the **Accademia.** Next, head back south toward the Arno and the Ponte Vecchio. On the way do a little shopping at the fabled **Straw Market** (Mercato Nuovo). Sunset should find you at the landmark **Ponte Vecchio.** Finish your very busy day with a hearty Tuscan dinner in one of Florence's many *bucas* (cellar restaurants).

If You Have 2 Days On day 2, you can spend the morning visiting the **Bargello** to see some of the Renaissance, including another version of Michelangelo's *David.* A short walk will take you to the **Palazzo Vecchio,** where you can explore the Hall of the 500 to see the Vasari Renaissance frescoes. Then in the afternoon visit the **Pitti Palace,** on the other side of the Arno, and wander through the Galleria Palatina, with its 16th- and 17th-century masterpieces, including 11 works by Raphael alone. After a visit, stroll through the adjoining **Boboli Gardens.** At sunset, go again to the Duomo and the Baptistry for a much better look.

If You Have 3 Days In the morning of day 3, head for the **Medici Chapels** adjacent to the Basilica of San Lorenzo. Look especially for Michelangelo's figures of *Dawn* and *Dusk.* Later in the morning you can go to the **Museo di San Marco,** a small museum that's a monument to the work of Fra Angelico. After lunch, visit the **Museo dell'Opera del Duomo,** with its sculptural masterpieces from the Duomo, including Donatello's *Mary Magdalene.*

If You Have 4 Days or More On day 4, begin with a morning visit to the **Palazzo Medici-Riccardi,** near the Duomo, to view the mid-15th-century frescoes by Benozzo Gozzoli in the Medici Chapel. Later that morning pop into **Santa Maria Novella,** one of Florence's most distinguished churches, with its Gondi Chapel containing Brunelleschi's wooden Christ on the Cross. Before it closes at 6:30pm, call at the **Basilica di Santa Croce,** with its two restored chapels by Giotto. On day 5, leave Florence, as fascinating as it is, and head south to yet another fascinating art city, **Siena,** the most important of the Tuscan hill towns.

THE TOP MUSEUMS

Galleria degli Uffizi ✦✦✦   This is one of the world's outstanding museums and Italy's finest collection of art. The Uffizi is nicely grouped into periods or schools to show the progress of Italian and European art. The Botticelli rooms contain his finest works, including *The Birth of Venus.* In another room you'll see

---

Tips **Reserving Tickets for the Uffizi & Other Museums**

Finally, you can bypass the hours-long ticket line at the **Uffizi Galleries** by reserving a ticket and an entry time in advance for a 2,000L (€1.05, $1) fee by calling © **055-294883** or going to **www.arca.net/uffizi.** By March, entry times can already be booked up over a week in advance. You can also reserve for the **Accademia Gallery** (another interminable line), as well as the **Galleria Palatina** in the Pitti Palace and the **Bargello** (you don't really need it for those last two) and several others. There's a nominal fee (worth every penny), and you can pay by credit card.

Leonardo da Vinci's unfinished but brilliant *Adoration of the Magi* and Verrocchio's *Baptism of Christ*, not a very important painting but noted because Leonardo painted one of the angels when he was 14. Also in this salon hangs Leonardo's *Annunciation.* In the rooms that follow are works by Perugino, Dürer, Mantegna, Bellini, Giorgione, and Correggio. Finally, you can view Michelangelo's *Holy Family,* as well as Raphael's *Madonna of the Goldfinch.*

Piazzale degli Uffizi 6. © **055-23885.** www.uffizi.firenze.it. Admission 2,000L (€6.25, $6). Tues–Sun 8:15am–7pm (last entrance 45 minutes before closing).

Galleria dell'Accademia 🏛🏛 This museum boasts many paintings and sculptures, but they're completely overshadowed by one work: Michelangelo's colossal *David* 🏛🏛🏛, unveiled in 1504. It first stood in Piazza della Signoria but was moved to the Accademia in 1873 and placed beneath the rotunda of a room built exclusively for its display. When he began work, Michelangelo was just 29. In the connecting picture gallery is a collection of Tuscan masters, such as Botticelli, and Umbrian works by Perugino (teacher of Raphael).

Via Ricasoli 60. © **055-2388609.** Admission 15,000L (€7.80, $7.50). Tues–Sun 8:15am–6:50pm. Bus: 1, 6, 11, or 17.

Palazzo Pitti and the Giardini di Boboli (Boboli Gardens) 🏛🏛 The Pitti, built in the mid-15th century (Brunelleschi was the original architect), was once the residence of the powerful Medici family. Today it contains several museums, the most important of which is the **Galleria Palatina** 🏛🏛, a repository of old masters. This gallery houses one of Europe's great art collections, with masterpieces hung one on top of the other, as in the days of the Enlightenment. In the **Sala di Saturno,** look for Raphael's *Madonna of the Canopy* and *Madonna of the Chair,* his best-known interpretation of the Virgin.

Other museums are the **Appartamenti Reali,** which the Medici family once called home; the **Museo degli Argenti** (© 055-2388-709), 16 rooms devoted to displays of the "loot" acquired by the Medici dukes; the **Coach and Carriage Museum;** the **Galleria d'Arte Moderna** (© 055-2388-601); the **Museo delle Porcellane** (porcelain); and the **Galleria del Costume.**

Behind the Pitti Palace are the **Boboli Gardens** 🏛, Piazza de'Pitti 1 (© 055-265-1838), through which the Medici romped. The gardens were laid out in the 16th century by the great landscape artist, Triboli. The Boboli is ever popular for a promenade or an idyllic interlude in a pleasant setting. The gardens are filled with fountains and statuary, such as a Giambologna *Venus* in the "Grotto" of Buontalenti. You can climb to the top of the Fortezza di Belvedere for a dazzling city view.

Piazza de'Pitti. ℂ 055-238-8611. Palatina, 12,000L (€6.25, $6); Modern Art Gallery, 8,000L (€4.15, $4); Argenti, 4,000L (€2.13, $2); Boboli Gardens, 4,000L (€2.13, $2). Galleria Palatina and Appartamenti Reali, Tues–Fri 8am–9pm; Sat 8am–midnight; Sun 8am–8pm. Museo degli Argenti and Modern Art Gallery daily 8:30am–1:30pm, closed the first, third, and fifth Mon and the second and fourth Sun of each month. Boboli Gardens, June–Sept daily 8:30am–7:45pm; Apr–May and Oct daily 8:30am–6:45pm; Nov–Mar daily 9am–5:45pm; closed the first and the last Mon of each month. Ticket office closes 1 hour before the gardens. Bus: D.

Cappelle Medicee (Medici Chapels) ★★ The Medici tombs are adjacent
to the Basilica of San Lorenzo (see "Other Churches," below). Working from 1521 to 1534, Michelangelo created the Medici tomb in a style that foreshadowed the baroque. Lorenzo the Magnificent was buried near Michelangelo's uncompleted *Madonna and Child* group. Ironically, the finest groups of sculpture were reserved for two Medici "clan" members, who (in the words of Mary McCarthy) "would better have been forgotten." They're represented as armored, idealized princes. The other two figures on Lorenzo's tomb are most often called *Dawn* (represented as woman) and *Dusk* (as man). The best-known figures are *Night* (chiseled as a woman in troubled sleep) and *Day* (a man of strength awakening to a foreboding world) at the feet of Giuliano, the duke of Nemours.

Piazza Madonna degli Aldobrandini 6. ℂ 055-238-8602. Admission 11,000L (€5.70, $5.50). Mon–Sat 8:15am–5pm; Sun 8:30am–1:50pm. Closed 2nd and 4th Sun, and 1st, 3rd, 5th Mon of each month.

Museo Nazionale del Bargello ★★★ The National Museum, a short walk
from Piazza della Signoria, is a 13th-century fortress palace whose dark underground chambers once resounded with the cries of the tortured. Today it's a vast repository of some of the most important Renaissance sculpture, including works by Michelangelo and Donatello. Here you'll see another Michelangelo *David* (formerly referred to as *Apollo*), chiseled perhaps 25 to 30 years after the figure in the Accademia. The Bargello *David* is totally different—even effete when compared to its stronger brother. Among the more significant sculptures is Giambologna's *Winged Mercury.* The Bargello displays two versions of Donatello's *John the Baptist.* Look for two more *Davids*—Donatello's and Verrocchio's. The Bargello contains a large number of terra-cottas by the della Robbia clan.

Via del Proconsolo 4. ℂ 055-2388606. Admission 8,000L (€4.15, $4). Daily 8:30am–1:50pm. Closed 1st, 3rd, 5th Sun and 2nd and 4th Mon of each month.

Museo di San Marco ★★★ This state museum is a handsome Renaissance
palace whose cell walls are decorated with 15th-century frescoes by the mystical Fra Angelico. In the days of Cosimo dei Medici, San Marco was built as a Dominican convent. It originally contained bleak, bare cells, which Angelico and his students then brightened considerably. One of his better-known paintings here is *The Last Judgment,* which depicts people with angels on the left dancing in a circle and lordly saints towering overhead. On the second floor—at the top of the hall—is Angelico's masterpiece, *The Annunciation.*

Piazza San Marco 1. ℂ 055-2388608. Admission 8,000L (€4.15, $4). Mon–Fri 8:30am–1:50pm; Sat 8:30am–7pm. Closed 1st, 3rd, and 5th Sun of the month, and 2nd and 4th Mon of the month. Bus: 1, 7, 25, or 33.

THE DUOMO, CAMPANILE & BAPTISTRY
Cattedrale di Santa Maria del Fiore (Duomo) ★★★ The Duomo, graced
by Brunelleschi's dome, is the crowning glory of Florence. But don't rush inside too quickly, as the view of the exterior, with its geometrically patterned bands of

white, pink, and green marble, is, along with the dome, the best feature. One of the world's largest churches, the Duomo represents the flowering of the "Florentine Gothic" style. Begun in 1296, it was finally consecrated in 1436, yet finishing touches on the facade were applied as late as the 19th century.

Inside, the overall effect is bleak, except when you stand under the cupola, frescoed in part by Vasari. Some of the stained-glass windows in the dome were based on designs by Donatello (Brunelleschi's friend) and Ghiberti (Brunelleschi's rival). If you resist scaling Giotto's bell tower (below), you may want to climb Brunelleschi's ribbed dome. The view is well worth the trek.

Piazza del Duomo. © 055-2302885. Cathedral, free; excavations, 5,000L (€2.60, $2.50); cupola, 10,000L (€5.20, $5). Mar–Oct Mon–Sat 8:30am–6:30pm; off-season Mon–Sat 8:30am–5:30pm.

Campanile (Giotto's Bell Tower) ★★★   Giotto left to posterity the most beautiful campanile (bell tower) in Europe, rhythmic in line and form. The 84-meter (274-ft.) tower, a "Tuscanized" Gothic, with bands of colored marble, can be scaled for a panorama of the sienna-colored city. The view will surely rank among your most memorable—it encompasses the enveloping hills and Medici villas.

Piazza del Duomo. © 055-2302885. Admission 10,000L (€5.20, $5). Daily 8:30am–6:50pm.

Battistero San Giovanni (Baptistry) ★★★   Named after the city's patron saint, Giovanni (John the Baptist), the present octagonal Battistero dates from the 11th and 12th centuries. The oldest structure in Florence, the baptistery is a highly original interpretation of the Romanesque style, with its bands of pink, white, and green marble. Visitors from all over the world come to gape at its three sets of bronze doors. The east door is a copy; the other two are originals. In his work on two sets of doors, Lorenzo Ghiberti reached the pinnacle of his artistry in *quattrocento* Florence. The gilt panels—representing scenes from the New Testament, including the *Annunciation,* the *Adoration,* and Christ debating the elders in the temple—make up a flowing, rhythmic narration in bronze.

Piazza S. Giovanni. © 055-2302885. Admission 5,000L (€2.60, $2.50). Oct–June daily 8:30am–7pm; July–Sept daily 12:30–7pm.

OTHER CHURCHES

Basilica di San Lorenzo ★★★   This is Brunelleschi's 15th-century Renaissance church, where the Medici used to attend services from their nearby palace on Via Larga, now Via Camillo Cavour. Most visitors flock to see Michelangelo's Medici Chapels (see "The Top Museums," above), but Brunelleschi's handiwork deserves some time, too. Built in the style of a Latin cross, the church is distinguished by harmonious grays and rows of Corinthian columns.

Biblioteca Medicea Laurenziana ★★ (© 055-210760) is entered separately at Piazza San Lorenzo 9 and was designed by Michelangelo to shelter the expanding library of the Medici. Beautiful in design and concept, and approached by exquisite stairs, the library is filled with some of Italy's greatest manuscripts—many of which are handsomely illustrated. Hours are from Monday to Saturday 9am to 1pm. Admission is free; the only time you'll be charged is if there's a special exhibition.

Piazza San Lorenzo. © 055-214443. Free admission or 5,000–15,000L (€2.60–€7.80, $2.50–$7.50) for special exhibitions. Library, Mon–Sat 7:30am–noon and 3:30–6pm. Bus: 1, 6, 14, or 23.

Basilica di Santa Croce ★★   The Pantheon of Florence, this church shelters tombs or monuments of everyone from Michelangelo to Machiavelli, from

Dante to Galileo. Santa Croce was the church of the Franciscans. In the right nave (first tomb) is the Vasari-executed monument to Michelangelo, whose body was smuggled back to his native Florence from its original burial place in Rome. The Trecento frescoes are reason enough for visiting Santa Croce—especially those by Giotto to the right of the main chapel.

Piazza Santa Croce 16. ✆ 055-244619. Church, free; cloisters and church museum, 8,000L (€4.15, $4). Church, Mon–Sat 9:30am–5:45pm; Sun 3–5:45pm. Museum and cloisters, Thurs–Tues 10am–7pm. Bus: 23 or 71.

Basilica di Santa Maria Novella 🎭🎭   Near the railway station is one of Florence's most distinguished churches, begun in 1278 for the Dominicans. Its geometric facade, with bands of white and green marble, was designed in the late 15th century by Leon Battista Alberti, an aristocrat and true Renaissance man. The church borrows from and harmonizes the Romanesque, Gothic, and Renaissance styles. In the left nave as you enter, (the third large painting) is Masaccio's *Trinity*, a curious work that has the architectural form of a Renaissance stage setting, but whose figures—in perfect perspective—are like actors in a Greek tragedy. Head straight up the left nave to the Gondi Chapel for a look at Brunelleschi's wooden *Christ on the Cross,* said to have been carved to compete with Donatello's same subject in Santa Croce.

Piazza Santa Maria Novella. ✆ 055-282187. Church, free; Spanish Chapel and cloisters, 5,000L (€2.60, $2.50). Church, Mon–Fri 7am–noon and 3–6pm; Sat–Sun 3–5pm. Spanish Chapel and cloisters, Sat–Thurs 8am–2pm. Bus: A, 6, 11, 12, 36, 37, or 68.

PALACES

Palazzo Vecchio 🎭🎭🎭   The secular "Old Palace" is without doubt the most famous and imposing palace in Florence. It dates from the closing years of the 13th century. Its remarkable architectural feature is its 94-meter (308-ft.) tower. Once home to the Medici, the Palazzo Vecchio is occupied today by city employees, but much of it is open to the public. The 16th-century "Hall of the 500" (Dei Cinquecento), the most outstanding part of the palace, is filled with Vasari & Co. frescoes as well as sculpture. As you enter the hall, look for Michelangelo's *Victory.* Later you can stroll through the apartments and main halls. You can also visit the private apartments of Eleanor of Toledo, wife of Cosimo I, and a chapel that was begun in 1540 and frescoed by Bronzino.

Piazza della Signoria. ✆ 055-2768325. Admission 11,000L (€5.70, $5.50). Mon–Wed and Fri–Sat 9am–7pm; Thurs and Sun 9am–2pm. July 15–Sept 15 Mon and Fri 9am–11pm. Ticket office closes 1 hour before palace.

Palazzo Medici-Riccardi 🎭🎭   A short walk from the Duomo, this 15th-century palace was the home of Cosimo dei Medici before he took his household to the Palazzo Vecchio. The brown stone building was also the scene, at times, of the court of Lorenzo the Magnificent. Art lovers visit today chiefly to see the Chapel of the Magi with its mid-15th-century frescoes by Benozzo Gozzoli, which depict the *Journey of the Magi.*

Via Camillo Cavour 1. ✆ 055-2760340. Admission 8,000L (€4.15, $4). Mon–Sat 9am–1pm and 3–6pm; Sun 9am–1pm; summer daily 9am–1pm and 3–6pm.

OTHER MUSEUMS

Museo Archeologico 🎭🎭   The Archaeological Museum, a short walk from Piazza della Santissima Annunziata, houses one of Europe's most outstanding Egyptian and Etruscan collections. Egyptian mummies and sarcophagi are on the first floor, along with Etruscan works. Pause to look at the lid of the coffin

of a fat Etruscan. Look for the bronze Chimera, a lion with a goat sticking out of its back, a masterpiece of Etruscan art.

Via della Colonna 38. © **055-23575**. Admission 8,000L (€4.15, $4). Nov–Aug Mon 2–7pm, Tues–Fri 9am–7pm, Sat and Sun 9am–2pm; Sept also Sat 9–midnight; Oct also Sun 9am–8pm. Bus: 6, 31, or 32.

Museo dell'Opera del Duomo ☆☆   Museo dell'Opera del Duomo, behind the cathedral, is beloved by connoisseurs of Renaissance sculptural works. It shelters the sculpture removed from the campanile and the Duomo. A major attraction of this museum is Michelangelo's unfinished *Pietà*, carved between 1548 and 1555 when the artist was in his seventies. Also look for the marble choirs (*cantorie*) of Donatello and Luca della Robbia. The Luca della Robbia choir is more restrained, but it still "praises the Lord" in marble—with clashing cymbals and sounding brass that constitute a reaffirmation of life.

Piazza del Duomo 9. © **055-2302885**. Admission 10,000L (€5.20, $5). Mon–Sat 9:30am–6:30pm; Sun 8am–2pm.

THE SHOPPING SCENE

Skilled craftsmanship and traditional design unchanged since the days of the Medici have made Florence a destination for serious shoppers. Florence is noted for its hand-tooled **leather goods** and its **straw merchandise,** as well as superbly crafted **gold jewelry.** Its reputation for fashionable custom-made clothes is no longer what it was, having lost its position of supremacy to Milan.

Florence is not a city for bargain shopping. Most visitors interested in gold or silver jewelry head for the **Ponte Vecchio** and its tiny shops. It's difficult to tell one from the other, but you really don't need to since the merchandise is similar. If you're looking for a charm or souvenir, these shops are fine. But the heyday of finding gold jewelry bargains on the Ponte Vecchio is long gone.

The street for antiques in Florence is **Via Maggio;** some of the furnishings and objets d'art here are from the 16th century. Another major area for antiques shopping is **Borgo Ognissanti.**

Florence's Fifth Avenue is **Via dei Tornabuoni.** This is the place to head for the best-quality leather goods, the best clothing boutiques, and stylish but costly shoes. Here you'll find everyone from Armani to Ferragamo. You'll find better shops on **Via Vigna Nuova, Via Porta Rossa,** and **Via degli Strozzi,** too. You might also stroll on the Lungarno along the Arno. For some of the best buys in leather, check out **Via del Parione,** a short narrow street of Tornabuoni.

FLORENCE'S FAMOUS MARKETS

After checking into their hotels, the most intrepid shoppers head for **Piazza del Mercato Nuovo (Straw Market),** called "Il Porcellino" by the Italians because of the bronze statue of a reclining wild boar here. Tourists pet its snout (which is well worn) for good luck. The market stands in the monumental heart of Florence, an easy stroll from the Palazzo Vecchio. It sells not only straw items but leather goods as well, along with an array of typically Florentine merchandise— frames, trays, hand embroidery, table linens, and hand-sprayed and painted boxes in traditional designs. Open from Monday to Saturday 9am to 7pm.

However, even better bargains await those who make their way through push-carts to the stalls of the open-air **Mercato Centrale** (also called the Mercato San Lorenzo), in and around Borgo San Lorenzo, near the train station. If you don't mind bargaining, which is imperative here, you'll find an array of merchandise, including raffia bags, Florentine leather purses, salt-and-pepper shakers, straw handbags, and art reproductions.

SOME SHOPS WORTH A LOOK

In front of the palazzo Vecchio, **Befani E Tai,** Via Vacchereccia 13R (✆ **055-287825**), is one of the most unusual jewelry stores in Florence—some of its pieces date back to the 19th century. The store was established right after World War II by expert goldsmiths who were childhood friends. Some of their clients design their own jewelry and have the store's artisans handcraft their creations.

Beltrami, Via del Tornabuoni 48 (✆ **055-287779**), sells well-known leather goods as well as expensive evening clothes, heavyweight silk scarves, and fashions of the best quality. This is one of several Beltrami shops in the area. High fashion, high prices, and high quality are what you'll find here, but prices are significantly lower than what you'll pay for Beltrami in the States. The **Beltrami Spa,** Via del Panzani 1 (✆ **055-212661**), offers last season's fashions at discounts of 20% to 50%. There are further discounts for multiple purchases, and since the original prices are still on the items, you can tell how much you're saving.

Sergio Bojola, a leading name in leather, has distinguished himself in Florence by the variety of his selections, in both synthetic materials and beautiful leathers. At **Bojola,** Via dei Rondinelli 25R (✆ **055-211155**), you'll find first-class quality and craftsmanship. You might be especially interested in their beautiful leather suitcases.

Galleria Masini, Piazza Goldoni 6R (✆ **055-294000**), is the oldest art gallery in Florence. The selection of modern and contemporary paintings by top artists is extensive, representing the work of more than 700 Italian painters. Even if you're not a collector, this is a good place to select a picture that will be a lasting reminder of your visit to Italy—you can take it home duty-free.

The wide inventory at **Menegatti,** Piazza del Pesce, Ponte Vecchio 2R (✆ **055-215202**), includes pottery from Florence, Faenza, and Deruta. There're also della Robbia reproductions made in red clay like the originals. Items can be sent home if you arrange it at the time of your purchase.

Officina Profumo Farmaceutica di Santa Maria Novella, Via della Scala 16N (✆ **055-216276**), is the most fascinating pharmacy in Italy. Located northwest of the Church of Santa Maria Novella, it opened its doors to the public in 1612, offering a selection of herbal remedies that were created by friars of the Dominican order. Those closely guarded secrets have been retained, and many of the same elixirs are still sold today. A wide selection of perfumes, scented soaps, shampoos, and of course potpourris, along with creams and lotions, is also sold. The shop is closed on Saturday afternoon in July and August.

FLORENCE AFTER DARK

For theatrical and concert listings, pick up a free copy of *Welcome to Florence,* available at the tourist office. This helpful publication contains information on recitals, concerts, theatrical productions, and other cultural presentations.

Many cultural presentations are performed in churches. These might include open-air concerts in the cloisters of the Badia Fiesolana in Fiesole (the hill town above Florence) or at the Ospedale degli Innocenti, the foundling "hospital of the innocents" (on summer evenings only).

THE PERFORMING ARTS

Teatro Comunale di Firenze, Corso Italia 16 (✆ **055-211158;** bus: B), is the main theater in Florence, with an opera and ballet season presented from September to December, and a concert season from January until April. This is also the venue for the **Maggio Musicale Fiorentino** (www.maggiofiorentino.com), Italy's oldest and most prestigious festival. It takes place from May to July and offers opera, ballet, concerts, recitals, and cinema productions. The box office is open from Tuesday to Friday 10am to 4:30pm, Saturday 10am to 1pm, and 1 hour before curtain. Tickets are 40,000 to 160,000L (€20.80 to €83.20, $20 to $80). During the Maggio Musicale, tickets usually range from 45,000 to 200,000L (€23.40 to €104, $23 to $100).

You'll have to understand Italian to appreciate most of the plays presented at **Teatro della Pergola,** Via della Pergola 18 (© **055-2479651;** bus: 6, 14, or 23). Plays are performed year-round except during the Maggio Musicale, when the theater becomes the setting for the many musical presentations of the festival. Performances are from Tuesday to Saturday at 8:45pm and Sunday at 3:45pm. The box office is open from Tuesday to Friday 10am to 1pm and 4 to 7pm and Saturday 10am to noon. Tickets are 24,000 to 46,000L (€12.53 to €23.90, $12 to $23); 14,500 to 29,000L (€7.55 to €15.13, $7 to $15) ages 24 and under.

MUSIC & DANCE CLUBS

Contained in the cellar of an antique building in the historic heart of town, the well-known **Full-Up,** Via della Vigna Vecchia 23–25R (© **055-293006;** bus: A or 14), attracts college students from the city's many universities, although older clients usually feel at ease, too. One section contains a smallish dance floor and recorded dance music; another is devoted to the somewhat more restrained ambience of a piano bar. Open from Wednesday to Monday 9pm to 3am. Cover (including one drink) is 15,000 to 25,000L (€7.80 to €13, $8 to $13).

Set within a 20-minute bus ride from Piazza Duomo, near the Parco della Cascine, **Meccanò,** Viale degli Olmi 1 (© **055-331371;** bus: P), is one of the few discos in Italy to offer an indoor-outdoor setting that includes century-old trees, a terrace, and three dance floors on two different levels. Gays mix with mostly straight people with ease, and the average age of patrons is 18 to around 32. Dancing reigns supreme every night except Sunday, Monday, and Wednesday, 11:30pm to 4am. There's also a restaurant offering modern Italian cuisine. It's open same days as the disco 9 to 11:30pm. Cover (including 1 drink) is 30,000L (€15.60, $15). The popular dance club **Yab,** Via Sassetti 5R (© **055-215160;** bus: A), is located in the heart of Florence's historic core. Owned and operated by the same entrepreneurs who maintain the larger, more fun, and less inhibited Meccanò, it offers much the same kind of scene, albeit in a smaller and more cramped setting. It's open from Monday to Saturday 8pm to 3am and is closed from May to October. Cover (including one drink) is 20,000 to 30,000L (€10.40 to €15.60, $10 to $15).

PUBS & BARS

La Dolce Vita, a name more evocative of Rome's Via Veneto, has recently emerged as the hot new bar of Florence. At Piazza del Carmine (© **055-284-595;** bus D or 6), the beautiful people of Florence, invariably young, show up here in their latest fashions and styles, which give even the most fashionable and hip Romans serious competition. It's a see-and-be-seen type of place, lying south of the Arno and west of the historic core. You come here to drink, gossip, and look beautiful and ever so chic. To see how you're doing, the owners have wisely covered the walls in mirrors.

If you ask whether **Dublin Pub,** Via Faenza 27R (© **055-293049;** bus: 7, 10, 11, 12, 25, 31, or 70), is an Italian pub, the all-Italian staff will respond rather grandly that such a concept doesn't exist, and that pubs are by definition Irish. And once you get beyond the fact that virtually no one on the staff here has ever been outside of Tuscany, and that there's very little to do here except drink and perhaps practice your Italian, you might settle down and have a rollicking old (very Latin) time. Beers, at least, are appropriately Celtic, and include Harp, Guinness, Kilkenny, and Strong's on tap. It's near the Santa Maria Novella train station and is open daily from 5pm to 2am. After an initial success in Rome, **Fiddler's Elbow,** Piazza Santa Maria Novella 7R (© **055-215056;** bus: A), also located near the train station, has now invaded the city of Donatello and Michelangelo. It has quickly become one of the most popular bars in Florence. It's open from Monday to Friday 5pm to 1am, Saturday and Sunday 5pm to 2am.

GAY & LESBIAN BARS

ArciGay/Lesbica (aka Azione Gay e Lesbica), Italy's largest and oldest gay organization, has a center in Florence at Via San Zanobi 54r (© and fax **055-476-557;** www.agora.stm.it/gaylesbica.fi). It's open for visits from Monday to Saturday 4 to 8pm.

Tabasco, Piazza Santa Cecilia 3 (© **055-213-000**), is Florence's (and Italy's) oldest gay dance club, open from Thursday to Tuesday 10pm to 3am, with a 15,000 to 30,000L (€7.80 to €15.60, $8 to $15) cover. The crowd is mostly men in their 20s and 30s. Florence's leading gay bar, **Crisco,** Via San Egidio 43r (© **055-248-0580**), is for men only, open Sunday, Monday, Wednesday, and Thursday from 10:30pm to 3:30am and Friday and Saturday 10:30pm to 5 or 6am. Cover is 15,000 to 20,000L (€7.80 to €10.40, $8 to $10). In summer at **Flamingo Bar,** Via del Pandolfini 26 (© **055-243-356**), the crowd is international. from Thursday to Saturday it's a mixed gay/lesbian party; the rest of the week, men only. It's open from Sunday to Thursday 10pm to 4am and Friday and Saturday from 10pm to 6am. The bar is open year-round; the disco only from September to June. Cover (including first drink) is 12,000L (€6.25, $6) from Sunday to Thursday and 15,000 to 20,000L (€7.80 to €10.40, $8 to $10) from Friday and Saturday.

A SIDE TRIP TO FIESOLE ⟨⟨

This town, once an Etruscan settlement, is the most popular outing from Florence. Bus 7, which leaves from Piazza San Marco, brings you here in 25 minutes and gives you a panoramic view along the way. You'll pass fountains, statuary, and gardens strung out over the hills like a scrambled jigsaw puzzle.

You won't find anything as dazzling here as the Renaissance treasures of Florence—the charms of Fiesole are more subtle. Fortunately, all major sights branch out within walking distance of the main piazza, beginning with the **Cattedrale di San Romolo** ⟨⟨. Dating from 1000, it was much altered during the Renaissance. In the Salutati Chapel are important sculptural works by Mino da Fiesole. It's open daily from 7:30am to noon and 4 to 7pm.

The ecclesiastical **Bandini Museum,** Via Dupre 1 (© **055-59477**), around to the side of the Duomo, belongs to the Fiesole Cathedral Chapter. On the ground floor are della Robbia terra-cotta works, as well as art by Michelangelo and Nino Pisano. From March to October hours are daily 10am to 6pm; from November to February daily 10am to 5pm. It's always closed the first Tuesday of every month. Admission is 12,000L (€6.25, $6). The ticket is valid 24 hours and also includes admission to the Teatro Romano e Museo Civico (see below).

The hardest task you'll have in Fiesole is to take the steep goat-climb up to the **Museo Missionario Francescano Fiesole,** Via San Francesco 13 (© **055-59175**). The church was consecrated in 1516. Inside are many paintings by well-known Florentine artists. In the basement is the ethnological museum. Begun in 1906, the collection has a large section of Chinese artifacts, including ancient bronzes, as well as Etruscan, Roman, and Egyptian objects. Admission is free (donation expected). It's open from Monday to Friday 9:30am to noon and 3 to 5:30pm, Saturday and Sunday 3 to 7pm in summer (closes at 6pm off-season).

On the site of the **Teatro Romano e Museo Civico,** Via Portigiani 1 (© **055-59477**), is the major surviving evidence that Fiesole was an Etruscan city 6 centuries before Christ, then later a Roman town. In the 1st century B.C., a theater was built, the restored remains of which you can see today. Near the theater are the skeleton-like ruins of the baths, which may have been built at the same time. The Etruscan-Roman museum contains many interesting finds that date from the days when Fiesole, not Florence, was supreme (a guide is on hand to show you through). For admission and hours, see the Bandini Museum above.

3 Highlights of the Tuscan & Umbrian Countryside

Rome may rule Italy, but **Tuscany** presides over its heart. The Tuscan landscapes, little changed since the days of the Medicis, look just like Renaissance paintings, with cypress trees, olive groves, evocative hill towns, and those fabled Chianti vineyards.

Tuscany was the place where the Etruscans first appeared in Italy. The Romans followed, absorbing and conquering them, and by the 11th century, the region had evolved into a collection of independent city-states, such as Florence and Siena, each trying to dominate the other. Although the Renaissance was immensely popular in Florence, it was slow to spread into the surrounding region.

When the Renaissance did arrive, however, with its titans of art, like Giotto, Michelangelo, and Leonardo, critics claim that Western civilization was "rediscovered" in Tuscany. According to D. H. Lawrence, Tuscany became "the perfect center of man's universe." Art flourished under the patronage of the powerful Medicis, and the legacy remains of Masaccio, della Francesca, Signorelli, Raphael, Donatello, Botticelli, and countless others. Tuscany also became known for its men of letters, like Dante, Petrarch, and Boccaccio (who wrote in the vernacular rather than in Latin).

Umbria, a small region at the heart of the Italian peninsula, is associated mainly with saints, like St. Francis of Assisi, founder of the Franciscan order, but Umbrian painters (such as Il Perugino) also contributed to the glory of the

---

Tips Tuscan Tours

If you love to walk or bike, **I Bike Italy** (© **055-2342371** Monday to Friday, or 0368/459123 weekends) books guided bike rides through the countryside from March to November. **Country Walks in Italy** can be booked with the same outfit year-round. If you want to see Italy as did the Romans and the Renaissance *condottieri,* you can book a horseback trek through **Equitour** (© **800/545-0019** in the U.S.).

Tuscany & Umbria

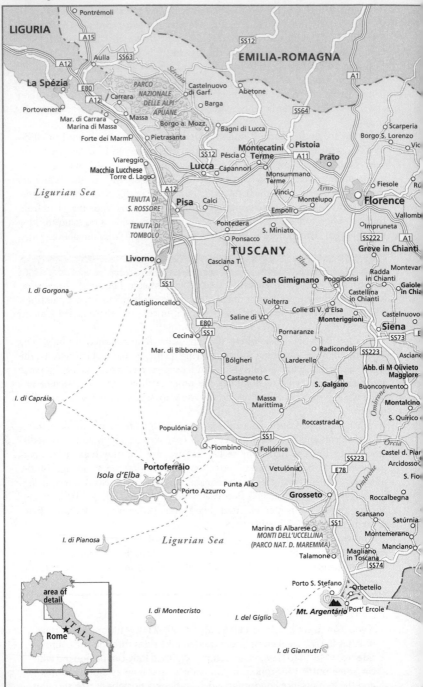

LIGURIA

Pontrémoli

A15

SS12

EMILIA-ROMAGNA

Aulla SS63

A12

A1

La Spézia

E80

Carrara

Castelnuovo di Garf.

Abetone

Scarperia

Portovenere

A12

Massa

Barga

SS64

Borgo S. Lorenzo

Mar. di Carrara

Borgo a. Mozz.

Bagni di Lucca

Vic

Marina di Massa

Pietrasanta

Montecatini

Pistoia

Forte dei Marm?

SS12 Péscia **Terme**

A11 **Prato**

Viareggio

Lucca Cápannori

Monsummano

Fiesole

Rù

Macchia Lucchese

Terme

Torre d. Lago

Vinci

Montelupo

Florence

Ligurian Sea

A12

Arno

TENUTA DI

Pisa Calci

Empoli

Vallomb

S. ROSSORE

Pontedera

Impruneta

A1

TENUTA DI

S. Miniato

SS222

TOMBOLO

Ponsacco

TUSCANY

Greve in Chianti

Livorno

Casciana T.

SS1

Elsa

Radda Montevar

San Gimignano Poggibonsi in Chianti

I. di Gorgona

San Gimignano

Gaiole

Castellina **in Chia**

Castiglioncello

Volterra

in Chianti

Colle di V. d'Elsa

Castelnuovo

E80

Saline di V?

Monteriggioni

Siena

Cecina SS1

Pornaranze

SS73 E

Mar. di Bibbona

Radicondoli

SS223 Ascian?

Bólgheri

Larderello

Abb. di M Olivieto

I. di Capráia

Castagneto C.

Maggiore

■ **S. Galgano**

Buonconvento

Massa

Montalcino

Marittima

Roccastrada

S. Quirico

Populónia

SS1

Orcia

Piombino

Folónica

Castel d. Piar

SS223

Arcidosso

Vetulónia

E78

S. Fio

Portoferráio

Punta Ala

Roccalbegna

Isola d'Elba

Porto Azzurro

Ombrone

Scansano

Satúrnia

Grosseto

I. di Pianosa

SS1

Montemerano

Manciano

Ligurian Sea

Marina di Albarese

MONTI DELL'UCCELLINA

Magliano

(PARCO NAT. D. MAREMMA)

in Toscana

Talamone

SS74

Porto S. Stefano

Orbetello

I. di Montecristo

ITALY

Port' Ercole

★ **Rome**

I. del Gíglio

▲▲ **Mt. Argentário**

area of detail

I. di Giannutri

734

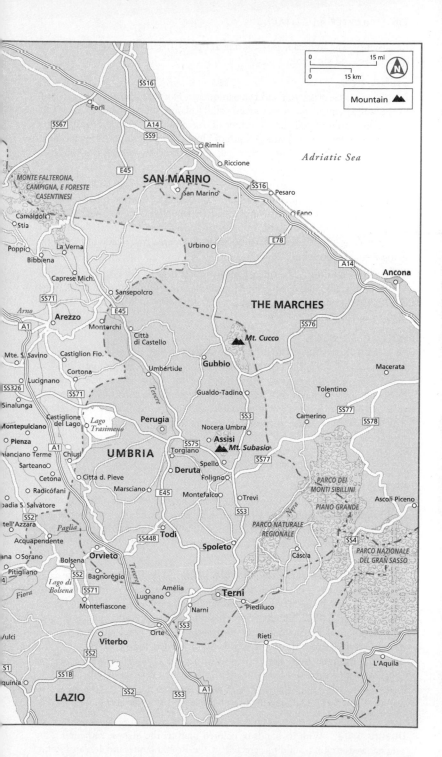

735

Renaissance. The landscape is as alluring as that of Tuscany, with fertile plains of olive groves and vineyards.

SIENA ✫✫✫

In Rome you see classicism and the baroque; in Florence, the Renaissance; but in the walled city of Siena you stand solidly planted in the Middle Ages. On three sienna-colored hills in the center of Tuscany, Sena Vetus lies in Chianti country, 34 kilometers (21 miles) south of Florence. Preserving its original character more markedly than any other Italian city, it's even today a showplace of the Italian Gothic.

Getting There   Trains arrive hourly from both Florence and Pisa, and **TRA-IN,** Piazza San Domenico 1 (✆ **0577-204245**), in Siena, offers bus service to all of Tuscany, with air-conditioned coaches. The one-way fare between Florence and Siena is 11,000L (€5.70, $6). Motorists can head south from Florence along the Firenze-Siena autostrada, a superhighway linking the cities, going through Poggibonsi.

Visitor Information   The **tourist information office** is at Piazza del Campo 56 (✆ **0577-280551**), open from Monday to Friday 8:30am to 7:30pm, Sunday 8:30am to noon. From November to March hours are Monday to Saturday 8:30am to 1pm and 3 to 7pm.

WHERE TO DINE

Al Marsili (Ristorante Enoteca Gallo Nero) ✫ SIENESE/ITALIAN   The beautiful Al Marsili is the best in Siena, standing between the Duomo and Via della Città. You dine beneath crisscrossed ceiling vaults whose russet-colored brickwork was designed centuries ago. Specialties include roast boar with tomatoes and herbs, *ribollita* (savory vegetable soup in the Sienese style), spaghetti with a sauce of seasonal mushrooms, and veal scaloppini with tarragon and tomato sauce.

Via del Castoro 3. ✆ **0577-47154.** Reservations recommended. Main courses 18,000–30,000L (€9.35–€15.60, $9–$15). AE, DC, MC, V. Tues–Sun 12:15–2:45pm and 7:15–10:15pm.

EXPLORING SIENA

Start in the heart of Siena, the shell-shaped **Piazza del Campo (Il Campo)** ✫✫✫, described by Montaigne as "the finest of any city in the world." Pause to enjoy the Fonte Gaia, with embellishments by Jacopo della Quercia (the present sculptured works are reproductions; the badly beaten original ones are found in the town hall).

Museo Civico and Torre del Mangia ✫✫✫   The Palazzo Pubblico dates from 1288 to 1309 and is filled with important art works by some of the leaders in the Sienese school of painting and sculpture. Upstairs in the Museo Civico is the **Sala della Pace,** painted from 1337 to 1339 by Ambrogio Lorenzetti, whose allegorical frescoes show the idealized effects of good and bad government. Accessible from the courtyard of the palazzo is the 102-meter (335-ft.) **Torre del Mangia,** from the 14th century. If you climb the tower, you'll be rewarded with a drop-dead view of the city skyline and Tuscan landscape.

In the Palazzo Pubblico, Piazza del Campo. ✆ **0577-292263.** Admission 18,000L (€9.35, $9). July–Sept 16 daily 10am–11pm; Mar 16–Oct 31 daily 10am–7pm; Nov 1–Mar 15 Museo daily 10am–6:30pm, Torre daily 10am–4pm. Bus: A, B, or N.

Duomo ✫✫✫   With its bands of colored marble, the Sienese cathedral is an original and exciting building, erected in the Romanesque and Italian Gothic styles during the 12th century. The dramatic facade—designed in part by Giovanni Pisano—dates from the 13th century, as does the Romanesque bell tower. The zebralike interior, with its black-and-white stripes, is equally stunning. The floor consists of various embedded works of art, many of which are roped off to preserve the richness in design, depicting both biblical and mythological subjects. The octagonal 13th-century pulpit is by Nicola Pisano (Giovanni's father), who was one of the most significant Italian sculptors before the dawn of the Renaissance (see his pulpit in the Baptistery at Pisa). The Siena pulpit is his masterpiece; it reveals in relief such scenes as the slaughter of the innocents and the Crucifixion.

Piazza del Duomo, southeast of Piazza del Campo. © 0577-283048. Free admission. Cathedral, Mar 17–Oct daily 7:30am–7:30pm; the rest of the year, closes at sunset and 1:30–2:30pm.

Battistero The Gothic facade of the Baptistry, left unfinished by Domenico di Agostino, dates from the 14th century. But you don't come to see that—you come to see the lavish frescoes inside. In the center of the interior is the star of the place, a baptismal font by Jacopo della Quercia that contains some bas-reliefs by Donatello and Ghiberti.

Piazza San Giovanni (behind the Duomo). (C) 0577-283048. Admission 4,000L (€2.13, $2). Mar 16 to Sept daily 9am–7:30pm; Oct daily 9am–6pm; Nov–Mar 15 daily 10am–1pm and 2:30–5pm. Closed Jan 1 and Dec 25.

Pinacoteca Nazionale (Picture Gallery) *★★*   Housed in the 14th-century Palazzo Buonsignori, the Pinacoteca contains a collection of the Sienese school of painting, which once rivaled that of Florence. Displayed are some of the giants of the pre-Renaissance. The principal treasures are on the second floor, where you'll contemplate the artistry of Duccio. The gallery is rich in the art of the 14th-century Lorenzetti brothers, Ambrogio and Pietro. Ambrogio is represented by an *Annunciation* and a *Crucifix,* but one of his most celebrated works is an almond-eyed *Madonna and Bambino* surrounded by saints and angels. Pietro's most important entry is an altarpiece—*The Madonna of the Carmine*— made for a church in Siena in 1329. Simone Martini's *Madonna and Child* is damaged but still one of the best-known paintings here.

Via San Pietro 29, near Pz. d. Campo. (C) 0577-281161. Admission 8,000L (€4.15, $4). Tues–Sat 8:30am–1:30pm (in the afternoon 3 guided visits only: 2:30, 4, and 5:30pm); Mon 8:30am–1:30pm; Sun 8am–1pm.

PISA *★★★*

Few buildings in the world have captured imaginations as much as the **Leaning Tower of Pisa,** one of the most instantly recognizable buildings in the world. The Leaning Tower is a landmark powerful enough to entice visitors to call at Pisa, and once here, they find many other sights to explore as well.

Getting There   Trains link Pisa and Florence every hour (trip time: 1 hour); one-way fare is 8,000L (€4.15, $4). From Florence, motorists take the autostrada west (A-11) to the intersection (A-12) going south to Pisa.

Visitor Information   The **tourist information office** is at Via Carlo Cammeo 2 ((C) **050-560464**), open from March to October Monday to Saturday 8:30am to 7:30pm; off-season, from Monday to Saturday 9:30am to 1pm and 2:30 to 5:30pm. There's also another office at Piazza della Stazione.

WHERE TO DINE
Al Ristoro dei Vecchi Macelli *★*   INTERNATIONAL/PISAN   Near Piazzetta di Vecchi Macelli is the best restaurant in Pisa. After selecting from a choice of two dozen varieties of seafood antipasti, you can enjoy a homemade pasta with scallops and zucchini or fish-stuffed ravioli in shrimp sauce. Other dishes are gnocchi with pesto and shrimp and roast veal with a velvety truffle-flavored cream sauce.

Via Volturno 49. (C) 050-20424. Reservations required. Main courses 18,000–36,000L (€9.35–€18.70, $9–$18). Mon–Tues and Thurs–Sat 1–3pm and 8–10:30pm; Sun 8–10:30pm. AE, DC. Closed 2 weeks in Aug.

SEEING THE SIGHTS
In the Middle Ages, Pisa reached the apex of its power as a maritime republic before it eventually fell to its rivals, Florence and Genoa. Its greatest legacy remains at **Piazza del Duomo** *★★★*, which D'Annunzio labeled Piazza dei Miracoli (miracles). Here you'll find an ensemble of the top three attractions— original "Pisan-Romanesque" buildings, including the Duomo, the Baptistery, and the Leaning Tower itself.

Leaning Tower (Campanile) ⭐⭐⭐   Construction of this eight-story campanile began in 1174 by Bonanno, and a persistent legend is that the architect deliberately intended the bell tower to lean (that claim is undocumented). Another legend is that Galileo let objects of different weights fall from the tower, then timed their descent to prove his theories on bodies in motion.

Alas, the tower is in serious danger of collapse. The government is taking various measures to keep it from falling, including clamping five rings of half-inch steel cable around its lower stones and pouring tons of lead around its base to keep it stabilized. The tower floats on a sandy base of water-soaked clay; it leans at least 4 meters (14 ft.) from perpendicular. If it stood up straight, the tower would measure about 55 meters (180 ft.) tall. In 1990, the government suspended visits inside.

Piazza del Duomo. Bus: 1.

Il Duomo ⭐⭐   Dating from 1063, the Duomo was designed by Buschetto, though Rainaldo in the 13th century erected the unusual facade with its four layers of open-air arches that diminish in size as they ascend. The cathedral is marked by three bronze doors—rhythmic in line—that replaced those destroyed in a fire in 1596. In the restored interior, the chief art treasure is the pulpit by Giovanni Pisano, finished in 1310. There are other treasures, too: Galileo's lamp (according to unreliable tradition, the Pisa-born astronomer used the chandelier to formulate his laws of the pendulum); mosaics in the apse said to have been designed by Cimabue; the tomb of Henry VII of Luxembourg; *St. Agnes* by Andrea del Sarto; *Descent from the Cross* by Il Sodoma; and a Crucifix by Giambologna.

Piazza del Duomo 17. ☎ 050-560547. Admission Mar–Oct 3,000L (€1.55, $1.50); Nov–Feb free. Cumulative ticket including admission into the Battistero 10,000L (€5.20, $5). May–Oct daily 10am–7:30pm; Nov–Apr 10am–1pm and 3–5pm.

Battistero (Baptistry) ⭐⭐⭐   Begun in 1153, the Baptistry is like a Romanesque crown. Although it's most beautiful on the exterior, with its arches and columns, venture inside to see the hexagonal pulpit made by Nicola Pisano in 1260. Supported by pillars resting on the backs of three marble lions, the pulpit contains bas-reliefs of the Crucifixion, the Adoration of the Magi, the Presentation of the Christ Child at the Temple, and the Last Judgment (many angels have lost their heads over the years).

Piazza del Duomo. ☎ 050-560547. Admission (including Duomo) 10,000L (€5.20, $5). June–Aug daily 9am–4:45pm, closes 1 to 2 hours earlier rest of the year. Closed Dec 31 and Jan 1.

Museo Nazionale di San Matteo ⭐⭐   Near Piazza Mazzini, the National Museum contains a good assortment of paintings and sculpture, many dating from the 13th to the 16th century. In the museum are statues by Giovanni Pisano; Simone Martini's *Madonna and Child with Saints,* a polyptych; Nino Pisano's *Madonna de Latte,* a marble sculpture; Masaccio's *St. Paul,* painted in 1426; Domenico Ghirlandaio's two *Madonna and Saints* depictions; works by Strozzi and Alessandro Magnasco; and old copies of works by Jan and Pieter Bruegel. You enter from Piazza San Matteo.

Piazzetta San Matteo 1. ☎ 050-541865. Admission 8,000L (€4.15, $4). Tues–Sat 9am–7pm and Sun 9am–1:30pm.

SAN GIMIGNANO ⭐⭐⭐

The golden lily of the Middle Ages is called the Manhattan of Tuscany since it preserves 13 of its noble towers, giving it a skyscraper skyline. It lies 42 kilometers

(26 miles) northwest of Siena and 55 kilometers (34 miles) southwest of Florence. Since you'll want to spend as much time here as possible, an overnight stay is recommended.

Getting There   Poggibonsi, serviced by regular trains from Florence and Siena, is the **rail** station nearest to San Gimignano. At Poggibonsi, buses depart from in front of the station at frequent intervals to the center of San Gimignano. For information, call **0577-204-111. Buses** operated by **TRA-IN** (© **0577-204-111**) service San Gimignano from Florence with a change at Poggibonsi (trip time: 75 minutes). The same company also operates service from Siena, with a change at Poggibonsi (50 minutes). In San Gimignano, buses stop at Piazzale Montemaggio, outside Porta San Giovanni, the southern gate. You'll have to walk into the center, as vehicles aren't allowed in most of the town's core.

If you've got a **car,** leave Florence (trip time: 1½ hours) or Siena (1¼ hours) by the Firenze-Siena autostrada and drive to Poggibonsi, where you'll need to cut west along a secondary route (S324) to San Gimignano.

Visitor Information   For tourist information, go to **Associazione Pro Loco,** Piazza del Duomo 1 (© **0577-940-008**), open from November to February daily 9am to 1pm and 3 to 6pm (from March to October to 7pm).

WHERE TO STAY
Hotel Bel Soggiorno   This hotel, though no longer the town's best, is still a good affordable alternative. The Gigli family has run it since 1886 (there's not as much antique charm as you'd think, though). The rear guest rooms and dining room open onto the lower pastureland and the bottom of the village. The medium-size rooms have functional furniture and beds verging on the over-soft, but the management is quite friendly. The best 10 rooms are those with private balconies. In summer you'll be asked to have your meals at the hotel (the cuisine is excellent). Medieval style, the dining room boasts murals depicting a wild boar hunt (see "Where to Dine," below).

Via San Giovanni 91, 53037 San Gimignano. © 0577-940-375. Fax 0577-90-7521. www.hotelbelsoggiorno. it. 22 units. 180,000–220,000L (€93.60–€114.40, $90–$110) double; 240,000–300,000L (€124.80–€156, $120–$150) suite. AE, DC, MC, V. Closed Jan–Feb. Parking: 20,000L (€10.40, $10). **Amenities:** Restaurant, bar. *In room:* A/C, TV.

Relais Santa Chiara 👡   This solid comfortable hotel lies in a residential neighborhood about a 10-minute walk south of the medieval ramparts. It's the most prestigious place to stay. It's surrounded with elegant gardens and a pool, and its spacious public rooms contain Florentine terra-cotta floors and mosaics. Though the hotel is relatively new, the furnishings and ambience blend in harmoniously with the Tuscan countryside.

Via Matteotti 15, 53037 San Gimignano. © 0577-940-701. Fax 0577-942-096. www.rsc.it. 41 units. 490,000L (€254.80, $245) double; 490,000L (€254.80, $245) suite. Rates include buffet breakfast. AE, DC, MC, V. Closed Dec–Mar. **Amenities:** Bar; swimming pool; room service. *In room:* A/C, TV, minibar, radio, hair dryer.

WHERE TO DINE
Ristorante Bel Soggiorno TUSCAN   Thanks to windows overlooking the countryside and a devoted use of fresh ingredients from nearby farms, you'll get a strong sense of Tuscany's agrarian bounty here. Two of the most appealing specialties (available only late summer to late winter) are roasted wild boar with red wine and mixed vegetables, and pappardelle pasta garnished with a savory ragout of pheasant. Other pastas are pappardelle with roasted hare, and risotto with herbs and seasonal vegetables.

In the Hotel Bel Soggiorno, Via San Giovanni 91. ⓒ 0577-940-375. Reservations recommended. Main courses 20,000–35,000L (€10.40–€18.20, $10–$18); fixed-price menu 50,000L (€26, $25). AE, DC, MC, V. Thurs–Tues 12:30–2:30pm and 7:30–10pm. Closed Jan 7 to Feb.

Ristorante Le Terrazze TUSCAN   The newer of this restaurant's two dining rooms has large windows overlooking the old town and the Val d'Elsa. The setting is one of a country inn, and the food features an assortment of produce from the surrounding farms. Soups and pastas make fine beginnings, and specialties of the house include delectable items like sliced filet of wild boar with polenta and Chianti, breast of goose with walnut sauce, vitello (veal) alla Cisterna with buttered beans, and Florence-style steaks.

In La Cisterna, Piazza della Cisterna 24 ⓒ 0577-940-328. Reservations required. Main courses 25,000–38,000L (€13–€19.75, $13–$19). AE, DC, MC, V. Wed 7:30–10pm; Thurs–Mon 12:30–2:30pm and 7:30–10pm. Closed Jan 7–Mar 10.

EXPLORING THE TOWN

In the town center is the palazzo-flanked **Piazza della Cisterna** ✶✶, so named because of the 13th-century cistern in its heart. Connected with the irregularly shaped square is its satellite, **Piazza del Duomo** ✶✶, whose medieval architecture—towers and palaces—is almost unchanged. It's the most beautiful spot in town. On the square, the **Palazzo del Popolo's Torre Grossa** ✶, at 54 meters (178 ft.), is believed to have been the tallest "skyscraper" in town.

Note: A combination ticket, available at any of the sites below, allows admission to all of them for 18,000L (€9.35, $9).

Duomo Collegiata o Basilica di Santa Maria Assunta ✶   Residents of San Gimignano still call this a Duomo (cathedral), even though it was demoted to a "Collegiata" once the town lost its bishop. Plain and austere on the outside, it's richly decorated inside. Retreat inside to a world of tiger-striped arches and a galaxy of gold stars. Head for the north aisle, where in the 1360s Bartolo di Fredi depicted scenes from the Old Testament. Two memorable ones are *The Trials of Job* and *Noah with the Animals*. In the right aisle, panels trace scenes from the life of Christ—the kiss of Judas, the Last Supper, the Flagellation, and the Crucifixion. The chief attraction is the **Chapel of Santa Fina,** designed by Giuliano and Benedetto da Maiano. Michelangelo's fresco teacher, Domenico Ghirlandaio, frescoed it with scenes from the life of a local girl, Fina, who became the town's patron saint.

Piazza del Duomo. ⓒ 0577-940-316. Church, free; chapel, 6,000L (€3.10, $3). Summer daily 9:30am–7pm. Winter 9:30am–5pm.

Civic Museum (Museo Civico) ✶   This museum is installed upstairs in the Palazzo del Popolo (town hall). Most notable is the **Sala di Dante,** where the White Guelph–supporting poet spoke out for his cause in 1300. Look for one of the masterpieces of San Gimignano—the *Maestà* (Madonna enthroned) by Lippo Memmi (later touched up by Gozzoli). The first large room upstairs contains another masterpiece: a *Madonna in Glory,* with Sts. Gregory and Benedict, painted by Pinturicchio. On the other side of it are two depictions of the *Annunciation* by Filippino Lippi.

Passing through the Museo Civico, you can scale the **Torre Grossa** and be rewarded with a bird's-eye view of this most remarkable town. The tower, the only one in town you can climb, is open from March to October daily 9:30am to 7:30pm; off-season, from Tuesday to Saturday 9:30am to 1:30pm and 2:30 to 4:30pm. Admission is 8,000L (€4.15, $4).

In the Palazzo del Popolo, Piazza del Duomo 1. *①* **0577-940-340.** Admission 7,000L (€3.65, $3.50). Apr–Oct daily 9:30am–7pm; Nov–Mar Tues–Sun 9:30am–1pm and 2:30–4:30pm.

LUCCA ✦✦✦

In 56 B.C., Caesar, Crassus, and Pompey met in **Lucca** and agreed to rule Rome as a triumvirate. By the time of the Roman Empire's collapse, it was virtually the capital of Tuscany. Periodically in its valiant, ever-bloody history, Lucca was an independent principality, similar to Genoa. This autonomy attests to the fame and prestige it enjoyed. Now, however, Lucca is largely bypassed by time and travelers, rewarding the discriminating few.

By the late 1600s, Lucca had gained its third and final set of city walls. This girdle of ramparts is largely intact and is one of the major reasons to visit the town, with its medley of architecture ranging from Roman to Liberty (the Italian term for Art Nouveau).

Today, Lucca is best known for its *olio d'oliva lucchese,* quality olive oil produced in the region outside the town's walls. Lucca is a sort of Switzerland of the south: the banks have latticed Gothic windows, the shops look like well-stocked linen cupboards, children play in landscaped gardens, and geraniums bloom from the roofs of medieval tower houses. Since Lucca will absorb so much of your time, consider it as an overnight stopover from Florence.

Getting There   At least 20 **trains** travel daily between Florence and Lucca (trip time: 1¼ hours). The rail station lies south of Lucca's historic core, a short walk from the city's ramparts. For rail information in Lucca, call *①* **1478-188-088.** The **Lazzi bus** company (*①* **0583-584-877**) operates buses traveling between Florence and Lucca (1 hour). If you've got a **car,** leave Florence and take A11 through Prato, Pistoia, and Montecatini before reaching the outskirts of Lucca. If you're in Pisa, take SS12.

Visitor Information   The Lucca **tourist office** is on Piazzale Verdi (*①* **0583-419-689**), open daily from 9:30am to 6:30pm April to October (off-season to 3:30pm). They also have a 24-hour answering machine service (in both English and Italian), giving information on events and monuments.

WHERE TO STAY

Locanda l'Elisa ✦✦✦   This Relais & Châteaux hotel is the region's most elegant, 3 kilometers (2 miles) south of the city walls. During the early 18th century, it was the home of an army officer who was the preferred escort and intimate companion of Napoléon's sister Elisa. Behind a dignified neoclassical facade, this locanda (inn) has verdant gardens, discreet and charming service, and large and plushly decorated rooms. All but two are skillfully decorated junior suites with views of either gardens or a park.

Strada Statale del Brennero 1952, 55050 Mass Pisana (Lucca). *①* **0583-379-737.** Fax 0583-379-019. www.lunet.it/aziende/locandaelisa. 10 units. 450,000L (€234, $225) double; 600,000L (€312, $300) junior suite for 2. AE, DC, MC, V. Free parking. Bus: 2 from center of Lucca. **Amenities:** Restaurant; bar; room service; baby-sitting; laundry/dry cleaning. *In room:* A/C, TV, minibar, hair dryer.

Piccolo Hotel Puccini   Your best bet in the center is this 15th-century palace across from the Puccini birthplace. The classical music played in the lobby area (often Puccini) commemorates the long-ago association. Right off Piazza San Michele, one of the most enchanting in Lucca, this little hotel is better than ever now that an energetic couple, Raffaella and Paolo, has taken it over, breathing new life into the property. Intimate and comfortable rooms are beautifully maintained with good beds. Some windows open onto the small square in front with a bronze statue of Puccini.

Via di Poggio 9, 55100 Lucca. © 0583-55-421. Fax 0583-53-487. www.hotelpuccini.com. 14 units. 130,000L (€67.60, $65) double. Rates include breakfast. AE, MC, V. Free parking nearby. *In room:* A/C, TV, hair dryer, safe.

WHERE TO DINE

Buca di Sant'Antonio ✴ TUSCAN   On a difficult-to-find alleyway near Piazza san Michele, this is Lucca's finest restaurant. The cuisine is refined and inspired, respecting the traditional ways but also daring to be innovative. Menu items include homemade ravioli stuffed with ricotta and pulverized zucchini, grilled meat and fish dishes, and roast Tuscan goat with roast potatoes and braised greens.

Via della Cervia 1. © 0583-55-881. Reservations recommended. Main courses 22,000–30,000L (€11.45–€15.60, $11–$15). AE, DC, MC, V. Tues–Sun noon–3pm; Tues–Sat 7:30–10:30pm. Closed 2 weeks in July.

Giglio REGIONAL/TUSCAN   In regional appeal and popularity, this place is rivaled only by the Buca di Sant'Antonio. The secret to its appeal might be its rustic decor, its attentive staff, and its fine interpretations of time-honored Tuscan and regional recipes. Menu items usually include steaming bowls of *minestre di farro,* homemade tortellini with meat sauce, roasted codfish with virgin olive oil, a savory stewed rabbit with olives, and *tortes* made from vegetables like carrots or with a base of cream and chocolate.

Piazza del Giglio 2. © 0583-494-058. Reservations recommended. Main courses 15,000–30,000L (€7.80–€15.60, $7.50–$15). AE, DC, MC, V. Thurs–Tues noon–3pm; Thurs–Mon 7:30–10:30pm. Closed Feb 1–15 and July 15–30.

EXPLORING THE TOWN

Le Mura ✴ enclose the old town. The Lucchesi are fiercely proud of these city walls, the best-preserved Renaissance defense ramparts in Europe. The present walls, measuring 35 meters (115 ft.) at the base and soaring 12 meters (40 ft.) high, replaced crumbling ramparts built during the Middle Ages. If you'd like to join in one of the grand promenades of Tuscany, you can gain access to the ramparts from one of 10 bastions, the most frequently used of which is in back of the tourist office at **Piazzale Verdi.** For orientation, you may want to walk completely around the city on the tree-shaded ramparts, a distance of 4 kilometers (2½ miles).

Cattedrale di San Martino (Duomo) ✴✴   On Piazza San Martino, the Duomo is the town's most visible monument. The facade is exceptional, evoking the Pisan-Romanesque style but with enough originality and idiosyncrasies to distinguish it from the Duomo at Pisa. Designed mostly by Guidetto da Como in the early 13th century, the west front contains three wide ground-level arches, surmounted by three scalloped galleries with taffy-like twisting columns tapering in size. The main relic inside—in some ways the religious symbol of Lucca itself—is the *Volto Santo,* a crucifix carved by Nicodemus (so tradition has it) from a cedar of Lebanon. The face of Christ was supposedly chiseled onto the statuary.

Piazza San Martino. © 0583-494-726. Admission: Cathedral, free; sacristy and inner sanctum, 4,000L (€2.13, $2). Church and sacristy, Apr–Oct daily 10am–6pm; Nov–Mar Mon–Fri 10am–2pm, Sat–Sun 10am–5pm.

Chiesa San Frediano ☆   Romanesque in style, this is one of Lucca's most important and famous churches, built in the 12th and 13th centuries when the town enjoyed its greatest glory. A mosaic of the Ascension relieves the severe white facade, and the campanile or bell tower rises majestically. Inside, the bas-reliefs on the Romanesque font add a note of comic relief: Supposedly depicting the story of Moses, among other themes, they show Egyptians in medieval armor chasing after the Israelites.

Piazza San Frediano. ☏ **0583-493-627.** Free admission. Mon–Sat 7:30am–noon and 3–6pm; Sun 9am–1pm and 3–6pm.

National Picture Gallery and Palazzo Mansi Museum (Pinacoteca Nazionale e Museo di Palazzo Mansi)   The Lucchesi horde their art treasures in this palace built for the powerful Mansi family. Though Tuscany has far greater preserves of art, there're some treasures here, notably a portrait of Princess Elisa by Marie Benoist. Elisa Bonaparte (1777–1820), who married into a local wealthy family, the Bacceocchis, was "given" the town by her brother Napoléon in 1805 when he made her princess of Lucca and Piombino. The collection is enriched by works from Lanfranco, Luca Giordano, and Tintoretto, among others, though not their greatest works.

Via Galli Tassi 43. ☏ **0593-55-570.** Admission 8,000L (€4.15, $4). Tues–Sat 9am–7pm; Sun 9am–2pm.

ASSISI ☆☆☆
Ideally placed on the rise to Mt. Subasio, watched over by the medieval **Rocca Maggiore,** this purple-fringed Umbrian hill town retains a mystical air. The site of many a pilgrimage, Assisi is forever linked in legend with its native son, St. Francis. The gentle saint founded the Franciscan order and shares honors with St. Catherine of Siena as the patron saint of Italy. But he's remembered by many, even non-Christians, as a lover of nature (his preaching to an audience of birds is one of the legends of his life). Dante compared him to John the Baptist. St. Francis put Assisi on the map, and making a pilgrimage here is one of the highlights of a visit to Umbria.

Getting There   Although there's no rail station in Assisi, the town, which lies 177 kilometers (110 miles) north of Rome and 24 kilometers (15 miles) southeast of Perugia, is but a 30-minute bus or taxi ride from the nearby Santa Maria degli Angeli rail station. Buses depart at 30-minute intervals for Piazza Matteotti, in the heart of Assisi. **Trains** between Florence and Assisi usually require a transfer at Terontola. Frequent **buses** connect Perugia with Assisi (trip time: 1 hour). One bus a day arrives from Rome. Two buses pull in from Florence (2½ hours).

If you have a **car,** you can be in Assisi in 30 minutes from Perugia by taking S3 southwest. At the junction of Route 147, just follow the signs toward Assisi. But you'll have to park outside the town's core, as it's usually closed to traffic.

Visitor Information   The **tourist office** is at Piazza del Comune 12 (☏ **075-812-534**), open from Monday to Friday 8am to 2pm and 3:30 to 6:30pm, Saturday 9am to 1pm and 3:30 to 6:30pm, and Sunday 9am to 1pm. Closed from December 25 and January 1.

WHERE TO STAY
Space in Assisi tends to be tight, so reservations are vital. For such a small town, however, it has a good number of accommodations.

Albergo Ristorante del Viaggiatore *Value*   This ancient town house is among the tops for value. It's been totally renovated, though the stone walls and

Assisi

Information

Basilica di San Francesco 1
Basilica di Santa Chiara 5
Duomo di San Rufino 4
Prisons' Hermitage 6
Rocca Maggiore 2
Temple of Minerva 3

arched entryways of the lobby hint at its age. The high-ceilinged rooms are spacious and very contemporary, with shower-only bathrooms.

Via San Antonio 14, 06081 Assisi. ☎ **075-816-297** or 075-812-424. Fax 075-813-051. 16 units. 130,000L (€67.60, $65) double. Rates include breakfast. Half board 80,000L (€41.60, $40) per person extra. DC, MC, V. **Amenities:** Restaurant, bar. *In room:* A/C, TV, safe.

Hotel del Priori   Opened in 1923, this hotel keeps up with the times. It occupies one of the town's most historic buildings, the 17th-century Palazzo Nepis. A homelike, somewhat old-fashioned Umbrian atmosphere prevails. Marble staircases and floors, terra-cotta, vaulted ceilings, and stone-arched doorways remain from its seigniorial palazzo heyday. Many of the rooms are a bit small, however.

Corso Mazzini 15, 06081 Assisi. ☎ **075-812-237.** Fax 075-816-804. www.assind.perugia.it/hotel/dpriori. 34 units. 150,000–240,000L (€78–€124.80, $75–$120) double; 250,000–320,000L (€130–€166.40, $125–$160) suite. Rates include breakfast. AE, DC, MC, V. Parking 15,000–20,000L (€7.80–€10.40, $8–$10). **Amenities:** Restaurant, bar; room service; laundry/dry cleaning. *In room:* A/C, TV, minibar, safe.

Hotel Sole   For Umbrian hospitality and a general down-home feeling, the Sole is a winner in the heart of medieval Assisi—comfortable but traditional, a bit tattered but affordable. Rooms are rather basic and feature aging bathrooms. We prefer the rooms in the 15th century palazzo as opposed to those in the more sterile and nondescript annex, although the latter is serviced by an elevator.

Corso Mazzini 35, 06081 Assisi. ☎ **075-812-373** or 075-812-922. Fax 075-813-706. www.umbria.org/Hotel/sole. 36 units. 130,000L (€67.60, $65) double, 160,000L (€83.20, $80) triple. Rates include breakfast. Half board (Apr–Nov only) 90,000L (€46.80, $45) extra. AE, DC, MC, V. **Amenities:** Restaurant, bar; room service. *In room:* TV, safe.

WHERE TO DINE

Il Medioevo ✵ UMBRIAN/INTERNATIONAL   Assisi's best restaurant is an authentic medieval gem. Alberto Falsinotti and his family prepare superb versions of Umbrian recipes whose origins are as old as Assisi itself. Specialties are tortelloni (a kind of dumpling) stuffed with minced turkey, veal, and beef and served with butter and Parmigiano Reggiano; gnocchi stuffed with ricotta and spinach and sprinkled with Parmigiano Reggiano; roasted rabbit with red-wine sauce and truffles; roast lamb with rosemary, potatoes, and herbs; homemade pasta stuffed with black truffles; and grilled filet of veal with herb sauce.

Via Arco dei Priori 4B. ☎ **075-813-068.** Reservations recommended. Main courses 15,000–28,000L (€7.80–€14.55, $8–$14). AE, DC, MC, V. Thurs–Tues noon–2:30pm and 7:30–10pm. Closed Jan 7–Feb 7 and July 1–20.

Ristorante Buca di San Francesco UMBRIAN/ITALIAN   Hospitable and evocative of the Middle Ages, this restaurant occupies a cave near the foundation of a 12th-century palace. There're about 100 seats in the dining room and another 60 in the garden, overlooking Assisi's historic center. Menu items change frequently, but what you're likely to find are *spaghetti alla buca,* with exotic mushrooms and meat sauce; *umbricelli* (big noodles) with asparagus sauce; *cannelloni* (stuffed pasta tubes baked in the oven) with ricotta, spinach, and tomatoes; *carlacca* (baked crepes stuffed with cheese, prosciutto, and roasted veal); and *piccione alla sisana* (roasted pigeon with olive oil, capers, and aromatic herbs).

Via Brizi 1. ☎ **075-812-204.** Reservations recommended. Main courses 28,000–40,000L (€14.55–€20.80, $14–$20). AE, DC, MC, V. Tues–Sun noon–2:30pm and 7:30–10pm. Closed July 1–15.

EXPLORING THE TOWN

In the heart of Assisi, **Piazza del Comune** ✵ is a dream for a lover of architecture from the 12th to the 14th century. On the square is a pagan structure, with six Corinthian columns, called the **Temple of Minerva (Tempio di Minerva)** ★, from the 1st century B.C. With Minerva-like wisdom, the people of Assisi turned it into a baroque church inside so as not to offend the devout. Adjoining the temple is the 13th-century **Tower (Torre)**, built by Ghibelline supporters. The site is open daily from 7am to noon and 2:30pm to dusk. In the wake of the earthquakes, the tower can no longer be visited.

Basilica di San Francesco ★★★　This great basilica, with both an upper and a lower church, houses some of the most important cycles of frescoes in Italy, including works by such pre-Renaissance giants as Cimabue and Giotto. The basilica and its paintings form the most significant monument to St. Francis. Disaster struck in 1997 when a series of devastating earthquakes hit Umbria, causing much damage. After a major restoration effort, involving some of Europe's greatest restorers, the basilica reopened to the public late in 1999.

Giotto's most celebrated frescoes, St. Francis preaching to the birds, can be seen on the entrance wall. In the nave are the cycle of 27 frescoes, some by Giotto, though the authorship of the entire cycle is a subject of controversy. Many frescoes are almost surrealistic, like stage sets that allow you to see the actors inside. In the cycle, you can see pictorial evidence of the rise of humanism that led to Giotto's and Italy's split from the rigidity of Byzantium.

The upper church also contains the damaged masterpiece by Cimabue, his *Crucifixion*. Time and quakes have robbed the fresco of its former radiance, but its power and ghostlike drama remain at least on video. The cycle of badly damaged frescoes in the transept and apse are other works by Cimabue and his helpers. Rather tragically, art experts spend hours daily sorting through boxes of rubble, trying to piece together the jigsaw puzzle caused by the quakes. There's a debate about whether the Cimabue and Giotto frescoes will ever be in good-enough condition to be restored to their historic place.

From the transept of the upper church, proceed down the stairs through the two-tiered cloisters to the lower church. In the south transept, look for Cimabue's faded but masterly *Virgin and Child* with four angels and St. Francis looking on from the far right; it's often reproduced in detail as one of Cimabue's greatest works. You'll also find works here by Giotto, Pietro Lorenzetti, and Simone Martini.

Piazza. San Francesco. ℂ **075-819-001.** Free admission. Daily 7am–5:30pm.

Prisons' Hermitage (Eremo delle Carceri) ★★　Eremo delle Carceri dates from the 14th and 15th centuries. The "prison" isn't a penal institution but rather a spiritual retreat. It's believed that St. Francis retired to this spot for meditation and prayer. Out back is a moss-covered gnarled ilex (live oak) more than 1,000 years old, where St. Francis is believed to have blessed the birds, after which they flew in the four major compass directions to symbolize that Franciscans, in coming centuries, would spread from Assisi all over the world. The friary contains some faded frescoes. One of the handful of friars who still inhabit the retreat will show you through.

Via Eremo delle Carceri. ℂ **075-812-301.** Free admission (donations accepted). Apr–Oct daily 7am–7pm; Nov–Mar daily 7am–5pm. About 4km (2½ miles) east of Assisi (out V. Eremo d. Carceri).

Basilica di Santa Chiara (Clare) ★★　The basilica is dedicated to "the little plant of Blessed Francis," as St. Clare liked to describe herself. Born in 1193 into one of the noblest families of Assisi, Clare gave all her wealth to the poor and founded, together with St. Francis, the Order of the Poor Clares. She was canonized by Pope Alexander IV in 1255. Pope Pius XII declared her Patroness of

Television in 1958. It was decided to entrust to her this new means of social communication based on a vision she had on Christmas Eve 1252 while bedridden in the Monastery of San Damiano: She saw the manger and heard the friars sing in the Basilica of St. Francis. Though many of the frescoes that once adorned the basilica have been completely or partially destroyed, much remains that's worthy of note. The basilica also houses the remains of St. Clare as well as the crucifix under which St. Francis received his command from above.

Piazza di Santa Chiara. (℃ 075-812-282. Basilica, free; however, the custodian turns away visitors in shorts, miniskirts, plunging necklines, and backless or shoulderless attire. Nov–Mar daily 8:30am–noon and 3–5pm; Apr–Oct daily 8:30am–12:05pm and 2–6:55pm.

4 Venice

Venice is a preposterous monument to both the folly and the obstinacy of humankind. It shouldn't exist, but it does, much to the delight of thousands of tourists, gondoliers, lace makers, hoteliers, restaurateurs, and glassblowers.

Fleeing the barbarians centuries ago, Venetians left dry-dock and drifted out to a flotilla of "uninhabitable" islands in the lagoon. Survival was difficult enough, but no Venetian has ever settled for mere survival. The remote ancestors of today's inhabitants created the world's most beautiful and unusual city.

However, it's sinking at a rate of about 6 centimeters (2½ inches) per decade, and it's estimated that one-third of the city's art will have deteriorated hopelessly within the next few decades if action isn't taken to save it. Clearly, Venice is in peril, under assault by uncontrolled tides, pollution, atmospheric acid, and old age.

This is one of the most enchantingly evocative cities on earth, but you must pay a price for all this beauty. In the sultry heat of the Adriatic in summer, the canals become a smelly stew. Steamy, overcrowded July and August are the worst times to visit; May and June or September and October are much more ideal.

ESSENTIALS

GETTING THERE   All roads lead not necessarily to Rome but, in this case, to the docks of mainland Venice. The arrival scene at the unattractive Piazzale Roma is filled with nervous expectation, and even the most veteran traveler can become confused. Whether you arrive by train, bus, car, or airport limousine, there's one common denominator—everyone walks to the nearby docks to select a method of transport to his or her hotel. The cheapest way is by vaporetto, the more expensive by gondola or motor launch.

By Plane   You'll land at Mestre, with its **Marco Polo Aeroporto** (℃ 041-2606111). **Boats** depart every 30 minutes directly from the airport, taking you to a terminal near Piazza San Marco. The fare is 17,000L (€8.85, $8.50).

It's less expensive to take a **bus** from the airport to Piazzale Roma (℃ 041-5287-886), a trip of less than 8 kilometers (5 miles); a one-way fare is 5,000L (€2.60, $2.50). Departures are usually every 30 minutes (trip time: 30 minutes). Once at Piazzale Roma, you can make transportation connections to most parts of Venice, including the Lido.

By Train   Trains pull into the **Stazione di Santa Lucia,** at Piazzale Roma, from Rome (trip time: 5¼ hours), Milan (3½ hours), Florence (4 hours), and Bologna (2 hours). For information about rail connections, call ℃ 1478-88088. The best and least expensive way to get from the station to the rest of town is to take a vaporetto, which departs near the main entrance to the station.

By Bus   Buses arrive from points on the mainland of Italy at **Piazzale Roma.** For information about schedules, call the office of **ACTV** at Piazzale Roma (© **041-5287886**). If you're coming from a distant city in Italy, it's better to take the train.

By Car   Venice has autostrada links with the rest of Italy, with direct routes from such cities as Trieste (driving time: 1½ hours), Milan (3 hours), and Bologna (2 hours). Bologna is 151 kilometers (94 miles) southwest of Venice; Milan, 265 kilometers (165 miles) west of Venice; and Trieste, 156 kilometers (97 miles) east. Rome is 526 kilometers (327 miles) to the southwest.

If you arrive by car, there're several multi-tiered parking areas at the terminus where the roads end and the canals begin. One of the most visible is the **Garage San Marco,** Piazzale Roma (© **041-5235101**), near the vaporetto, gondola, and motor-launch docks. You'll be charged 40,000 to 50,000L (€20.80 to €26, $20 to $25) per day, maybe more, depending on the size of your car.

VISITOR INFORMATION   You can get information at the **Azienda di Promozione Turistica,** Calle Ascensione, San Marco 71F (© **041-5208964**). Another office is at Santa Lucia railway station. Both are open daily from 9am to 1pm and from 1:30 to 5pm.

CITY LAYOUT   Venice, 4 kilometers (2½ miles) from the Italian mainland and 2 kilometers (1¼ miles) from the Adriatic, is an archipelago of some 117 islands. Most visitors, however, concern themselves only with **Piazza San Marco** and its vicinity. In fact, the entire city has only one piazza: San Marco. Venice is divided into six quarters that locals call *sestieri.* These include the most frequented, San Marco, but also Santa Croce, San Polo, Castello, Cannaregio, and Dorsoduro, the last of which has been compared to New York's Greenwich Village.

Many of the so-called streets of Venice are actually **canals,** some 150 in all. A canal is called a *rio,* and a total of 400 bridges span these canals. If Venice has a main street, it's the **Grand Canal,** which is spanned by three bridges: the Rialto, the Academy Bridge, and the stone Railway Bridge. The canal splits Venice into two unequal parts.

South of the section called Dorsoduro, which is south of the Grand Canal, is the **Canale della Giudecca,** a major channel separating Dorsoduro from the large island of La Giudecca. At the point where the Canale della Giudecca meets the Canale di San Marco, you'll spot the little **Isola di San Giorgio Maggiore,** with a church by Palladio. The most visited islands in the lagoon, aside from the **Lido,** are **Murano, Burano,** and **Torcello.**

Once you land and explore Piazza San Marco and its satellite, Piazzetta San Marco, you can head down **Riva degli Schiavoni,** with its deluxe and first-class hotels, or follow the signs along the **Mercerie,** the major shopping artery, which leads to the Rialto, site of the market area.

⟮Tips⟯ Finding an Address

The system of addresses in Venice is so confusing it's probably known only to the postman, if that. The best thing to do is to arm yourself with a good map, such as the **Falk** map of Venice, which is pocket size and available in many kiosks and bookstores.

Venice

Tips   Getting Around by Gondola

When riding in a gondola, two major agreements have to be reached: the price of the ride and the length of the trip. The official rate is 100,000L (€52, $50), but virtually no one pays that amount; prices really start at about 150,000L (€78, $75) for up to 50 minutes. Two major stations at which you can hire gondolas are Piazza San Marco (© 041-5200685) and the Ponte Rialto (© 041-5224904). Both organize gondola tours, lasting about 50 minutes and costing from 120,000 to 150,000L (€62.40 to €78, $60 to $75) per person.

GETTING AROUND

Walking is the only way to explore Venice unless you plan to see it from a boat on the Grand Canal. Everybody walks in Venice—there's no other way.

BY VAPORETTO   The motorboats, or *vaporetti,* of Venice provide inexpensive and frequent, if not always fast, transportation in this canal-riddled city. An *accelerato* is a vessel that makes every stop and a *diretto* makes only express stops. The average fare is 6,000L (€3.10, $3). In summer, the vaporetti are often fiercely crowded. Pick up a map of the system from the tourist office. There's frequent service daily 7am to midnight, then hourly midnight to 7am.

Visitors to Venice may avail themselves of a 10-tickets carnet costing 50,000L (€26, $25), which must be validated before use and shown together with the matrix (the last ticket of the booklet).

BY WATER TAXI/MOTOR LAUNCH   The city's many private motor launches are called *taxi acquei.* You may or may not have the cabin of one of these sleek vessels to yourself, since the captains fill their boats with as many passengers as the law allows before taking off. The price of a transit by water taxi from Piazzale Roma (the road and rail terminus) to Piazza San Marco begins at 80,000L (€41.60, $40) for one to six passengers. You can also call for a taxi acquei—try **Cooperativa San Marco** at © **041-5222303.**

FAST FACTS: Venice

American Express   Amex is at San Moisè 1471 (© **041-5200844;** vaporetto: San Marco), in San Marco. City tours and mail handling can be obtained here. The office is open from May to October, Monday to Saturday 8am to 8pm for currency exchange and 9am to 5:30pm for all other transactions. From November to April, Saturday hours are 9am to 12:30pm; weekday hours are 9am to 5:30pm.

Consulates   There's no U.S. consulate in Venice; the closest is in Milan, at Via Principe Amedeo 2 (© **02-290351**). The British consulate is at Dorsoduro 1051 (© **041-5227207**), open from Monday to Friday 10am to noon and 2 to 3pm.

Currency   See "Fast Facts: Rome," earlier in this chapter.

Currency Exchange   There're many banks in Venice where you can exchange money. Try the **Deutsch Bank SPA,** San Marco 2216 (© **041-5207024;** vaporetto: San Marco). Hours are from Monday to Friday 8:30am to 1:30pm and 2:45 to 4pm. Many travelers find that **Guetta Viaggi,** San Marco 1261 (© **041-5285101;** vaporetto: San Marco), offers the best rates in Venice. Hours are from Monday to Friday 9am to 12:30pm and 3 to 6:30pm. From April to October also Saturday 9am to noon.

Dentist/Doctor Your best bet is to have your hotel call and set up an appointment with an English-speaking dentist or doctor. The American Express office and the British Consulate also have a list.

Drugstores If you need a drugstore in the middle of the night, call © **192** for information about which one is open. Pharmacies take turns staying open late. A well-recommended, centrally located one is the **International Pharmacy,** Via XXII Marzo 2067 (© 041-5222311; vaporetto: San Marco).

Emergencies Emergency phone numbers are © **113** for the police, © **118** for an ambulance, and © **115** to report a fire.

Hospitals Get in touch with the **Ospedale Civile Santi Giovanni e Paolo,** Campo Santi Giovanni e Paolo in Castello (© **041-52394517).**

Post Office The main post office is at Fondaco dei Tedeschi (© **041-2717111;** vaporetto: Rialto), near the Rialto Bridge. It's open from Monday to Saturday 8:15am to 5pm. For information call © **160.**

Safety The curse of Venice is the pickpocket. Violent crime is rare, but because of the overcrowding on vaporetti and even on the small, narrow streets, it's easy to pick pockets. Purse snatchings are commonplace as well. Secure your valuables, and if your hotel has safes, keep them locked there when not needed.

Telephones The **country code** for Italy is **39.** The **city code** for Venice is **041,** which is the code you'll use every time you dial a party located within Venice, regardless of whether you're within the city limits or not. We emphasize that newly imposed technologies will require the use of the "0" and then "41" for calls to parties in Venice, regardless of whether you're within the city limits of Venice or not. For additional information, see "Fast Facts: Rome," earlier in this chapter.

WHERE TO STAY
NEAR PIAZZA SAN MARCO
Very Expensive

Gritti Palace ⋆⋆⋆   In a stately setting on the Grand Canal, Gritti Palace is the renovated palazzo of the 15th-century doge Andrea Gritti. It's a bit starchy but is topped only by the Cipriani in terms of prestige. "Our home in Venice" to Ernest Hemingway, it has for years drawn a clientele of theatrical, literary, political, and royal figures. The range and variety of the rooms seem almost limitless, from elaborate suites to relatively small singles. But in every case the stamp of glamour is evident. For a splurge, ask for Hemingway's old suite or the Doge Suite, once occupied by Somerset Maugham.

Campo Santa Maria del Giglio, San Marco 2467, 30124 Venezia. © **800/325-3535** in the U.S., 416/947-4864 in Canada, or 041-794611. Fax 041/5200942. www.sheraton.com. 93 units. 1,100,000–1,400,000L (€572–€728, $550–$700) double; from 2,400,000L (€1,248, $1,200) suite. Rates include buffet breakfast. AE, DC, MC, V. Vaporetto: Santa Maria del Giglio. **Amenities:** Restaurant, bar; room service; laundry/dry cleaning; valet. *In room:* A/C, TV, minibar, hair dryer.

Expensive
Hotel Concordia ⭐   The Concordia is the only hotel in Venice that has rooms overlooking St. Mark's Square. A series of gold-plated marble steps takes you to the lobby, where you'll find a comfortable bar area. All rooms are decorated in a Venetian antique style and contain hand-painted furnishings and small Murano chandeliers.

Calle Larga, San Marco 367, 30124 Venezia. ℂ **041-5206866.** Fax 041-5206775. www.venere.it/home/venezia/concordia. 57 units. 350,000–690,000L (€182–€358.80, $175–$345) double; 500,000–760,000L (€260–€395.20, $250–$380) suite. Rates include buffet breakfast. AE, DC, MC, V. Vaporetto: San Marco. **Amenities:** Bar; room service; baby-sitting; laundry/dry cleaning. *In room:* A/C, TV, minibar, hair dryer, safe.

Hotel la Fenice et des Artistes ⭐   This hotel offers widely varying accommodations in two connected buildings. One building is rather romantic yet time worn, with overly decorated rooms. Your satin-lined room may have an inlaid desk and a wardrobe painted in the Venetian manner to match a baroque bed frame. The carpets might be thin, however, and the fabrics aging. Bathrooms, still a little cramped, were renewed in 1999. Chambers in the other building are far less glamorous. The older of the two has no elevator.

Campiello de la Fenice, San Marco 1936, 30124 Venezia. ℂ **041-5232333.** Fax 041-5203721. 69 units. 300,000–400,000L (€156–€208, $150–$200) double; 390,000–520,000L (€202.80–€270.40, $195–$260) suite. Rates include breakfast. AE, DC, MC, V. Vaporetto: Rialto. **Amenities:** Bar; room service; baby-sitting; laundry/dry cleaning. *In room:* A/C, TV, hair dryer.

Moderate
Boston Hotel   A whisper away from St. Mark's, this hotel was named after an uncle who left to seek his fortune in Boston and never returned. The little living rooms contain many antiques and Venetian ceilings. For the skinny guest, there's a tiny self-operated elevator and a postage-stamp–size street entrance. Most rooms have built-in features, snugly designed beds, chests, and wardrobes. Several have tiny balconies opening onto canals.

Ponte dei Dai, San Marco 848, 30124 Venezia. ℂ **041-5287665.** Fax 041-5226628. 42 units. 280,000–330,000L (€145.60–€171.60, $140–$165) double. Rates include breakfast. AE, DC, MC, V. Closed Nov–Feb. Vaporetto: San Marco. **Amenities:** Bar; room service; baby-sitting; laundry/dry cleaning. *In room:* A/C, TV, hair dryer, safe.

Hotel Do Pozzi   Small, modernized, and centrally located just a short stroll from the Grand Canal and Piazza San Marco, this place is more like a country tavern than a hotel. Its original structure is 200 years old, and it opens onto a paved front courtyard with potted greenery. The sitting and dining rooms are furnished with antiques (and near antiques) mixed with utilitarian modern decor. A major refurbishing has given everything a fresh touch.

Corte do Pozzi, San Marco 2373, 30124 Venezia. ℂ **041-5207855.** Fax 041-5229413. 35 units. 350,000L (€182, $175) double. Rates include breakfast. AE, DC, MC, V. Vaporetto: Santa Maria del Giglio. **Amenities:** Bar; baby-sitting; laundry/dry cleaning. *In room:* TV, minibar, hair dryer.

IN THE DORSODURO
Moderate
American Hotel ⭐ *Value*   Set on a small waterway, the American Hotel (there's nothing American about it) is one of your best budget bets. The modest lobby is filled with murals, warm colors, and antiques, and the location is perfect for anyone wanting to avoid the crowds that descend in summer. The rooms are comfortably furnished in a Venetian style, but vary in size; some of the smaller ones are a bit cramped. Many rooms with a private terrace face the canal. On the second floor is a beautiful terrace where guests relax over drinks.

Campo San Vio, Dorsoduro 628, 30123 Venezia. ℂ **041-5204733.** Fax 041-5204048. www.hotelamerican. com. 29 units. 370,000–410,000L (€192.40–€213.20, $185–$205) double; 425,000–455,000L (€221–€236.60, $213–$228) triple. Rates include breakfast. AE, MC, V. Vaporetto: Accademia. **Amenities:** Room service; baby-sitting. *In room:* A/C, TV, hair dryer, safe.

Pensione Accademia 🟊 *Value*   This is the most patrician of the pensioni, in a villa whose garden extends into the angle created by the junction of two canals. Iron fences, twisting vines, and neoclassical sculpture are a part of the setting. There's an upstairs sitting room and a formal rose garden that's visible from the breakfast room. The recently renovated rooms are spacious and decorated with 19th-century furniture.

Fondamenta Bollani, Dorsoduro 1058, 30123 Venezia. ℂ **041-5237846.** Fax 041-5239152. pensione. accademia@flashnet.it. 27 units. 310,000–400,000L (€161.20–€208, $155–$200) double. Rates include breakfast. AE, DC, MC, V. Vaporetto: Accademia. **Amenities:** Lounge; private garden. *In room:* A/C, TV, hair dryer.

Inexpensive

Locanda Montin 🟊 *Finds*   The well-recommended Locanda Montin is an old-fashioned Venetian inn whose adjoining restaurant is one of the most loved in the area. The hotel is officially listed as a fourth-class hotel because of its lack of in-room amenities aside from a phone, but the accommodations are considerably larger and better than that rating suggests. Reservations are virtually mandatory, because of the reputation of this locanda. Marked only by a small carriage lamp etched with the name of the establishment, the inn is a little difficult to locate but worth the search.

Fondamenta di Borgo, Dorsoduro 1147, 31000 Venezia. ℂ **041-5227151.** Fax 041-5200255. 10 units (5 with bathroom). 160,000L (€83.20, $80) double without bathroom; 210,000L (€109.20, $105) double with bathroom. AE, DC, MC, V. Vaporetto: Accademia. **Amenities:** Restaurant, bar; laundry/dry cleaning.

IN SANTA CROCE
Moderate

Hotel San Cassiano Ca'Favretto 🟊   San Cassiano Ca'Favretto was once the studio of 19th-century painter Giacomo Favretto. The views from the hotel's gondola pier and from the dining room's porch encompass the lacy facade of the Ca' d'Oro, considered the most beautiful building in Venice. The hotel was constructed in the 14th century as a palace. The present owner has worked closely with Venetian authorities to preserve the original details. Fifteen of the conservatively decorated rooms overlook one of two canals.

Calle della Rosa, Santa Croce 2232, 30135 Venezia. ℂ **041-5241768.** Fax 041-721033. www.sancassiano.it. 35 units. 200,000–450,000L (€104–€234, $100–$225) double. Rates include breakfast. AE, DC, MC, V. Vaporetto: San Stae. **Amenities:** Room service; baby-sitting. *In room:* A/C, TV, hair dryer, safe.

IN CANNAREGIO
Expensive

Locanda ai Santi Apostoli 🟊   If you can't afford the Gritti Palace (and few can), but still fantasize about living in a palazzo overlooking the Grande Canal, near the Rialto, here is a possibility. The locanda knows the advantage of its location, however, and doesn't come cheap. But it's a lot less expensive than the grand palaces nearby. It's situated on the top floor of a 15th-century building, and the rooms, although simple, are rather inviting. Naturally, the two rooms actually opening onto the Grand Canal are the most requested. Even if you don't have one of these, there's a view from the main salon. Breakfast is the only meal served.

Strada Nuova, Canaregio 4391, 30123 Venezia. ℂ 041-5212612. Fax 041-5212611. 11 units. 390,000L (€202.80, $195) double; 490,000L (€254.80, $245) double with view on the Canal Grande; 690,000L (€358.80, $345) suite. Rates include breakfast. AE, DC, MC, V. Vaporetto: Ca d'Oro. **Amenities:** Lounge; laundry/dry cleaning. *In room:* A/C, TV, minibar, hair dryer.

ON ISOLA DELLA GIUDECCA
Very Expensive
Cipriani 🐾🐾🐾 Isolated, security-conscious, and elegant, the Cipriani occupies a 16th-century cloister on the residential island of Giudecca. This refined, tranquil, and sybaritic resort hotel was established in 1958 by the late Giuseppe Cipriani, the founder of Harry's Bar and the one real-life character in Hemingway's Venetian novel. Rooms have different decors—ranging from tasteful contemporary to antique—but all have splendid views. The hotel also runs a 24-hour motorboat shuttle to and from San Marco.

Isola della Giudecca 10, 30133 Venezia. ℂ 800/992-5055 in the U.S., or 041-5207744. Fax 041-5207745. www.orient-expresshotels.com. 110 units. 1,450,000–2,500,000L (€754–€1,300, $725–$1,250) double; from 2,850,000L (€1,482, $1,425) suite. Rates include buffet breakfast. AE, DC, MC, V. Closed Nov–Mar. Vaporetto: Zitelle. **Amenities:** 2 restaurants, bar; pool; tennis courts; gym; sauna; room service; baby-sitting; laundry/dry cleaning. *In room:* A/C, TV, minibar, hair dryer, private boat shuttle.

WHERE TO DINE
NEAR PIAZZA SAN MARCO
Very Expensive
Harry's Bar 🐾🐾🐾 VENETIAN   Harry's Bar serves the best food in Venice, though Quadri and the Antico Martini (see below) have more elegant atmospheres. Its fame was spread by Ernest Hemingway. A. E. Hotchner, in *Papa Hemingway,* quoted the writer as saying, "We can't eat straight hamburger in a Renaissance palazzo on the Grand Canal." So he ordered a 5-pound "tin of beluga caviar" to, as he said, "take the curse off it." Hemingway would skip the place today, fleeing from the foreign visitors, and the prices would come as a shock even to him. You can have your choice of dining in the bar downstairs or the room with a view upstairs. We recommend the Venetian fish soup, followed by scampi Thermidor with rice pilaf or seafood ravioli.

Calle Vallaresso, San Marco 1323. ℂ 041-5285777. Reservations required. Main courses 80,000–95,000L (€41.60–€49.40, $40–$48). AE, DC, MC, V. Daily 10:30am–11pm. Vaporetto: San Marco.

Expensive
Antico Martini 🐾🐾🐾 VENETIAN/INTERNATIONAL   As the city's leading traditional restaurant, Antico Martini, located near La Fenice, elevates Venetian cuisine to its highest level. The courtyard is favored in summer. An excellent beginning to your meal is the *risotto di frutti di mare,* creamy Venetian style with plenty of fresh seafood. For a main dish, try the *fegato alla veneziana,* which is tender liver fried with onions and served with polenta, a yellow cornmeal mush. The chefs are better at regional dishes than they are with those of the international kitchen.

Campo San Fantin, San Marco 1983. ℂ 041-5224121. Reservations required. Main courses 36,000–55,000L (€18.70–€28.60, $18–$28); 4-course fixed-price menus 80,000–100,000L (€41.60–52, $40–$50); 6-course *menu degustazione* 140,000L (€72.80, $70). AE, DC, MC, V. Wed 7–11:30pm; Thurs–Mon noon–2:30pm and 7–11:30pm. Vaporetto: San Marco or Santa Maria del Giglio.

Da Ivo 🐾 TUSCAN/VENETIAN   Da Ivo has such a faithful clientele that you'll think at first you're in a semiprivate club. The rustic atmosphere is both cozy and relaxing, with candles on the well-set tables. Homesick Florentines go here for fine Tuscan cookery; regional Venetian dishes are also served. In season, game, according to an ancient tradition, is cooked over an open charcoal grill. On one cold day, our hearts and plates were warmed when we ordered home-made tagliatelle. It came topped with slivers of tartufi bianchi, the pungent white truffle from the Piedmont district that's unforgettable to the palate. You'll also find such a delicacy as giant scampi with cherry tomatoes and black pepper, or a beef carpaccio covered by arugula and parmigiana flakes.

Calle dei Fuseri, San Marco 1809. ℭ 041-5285004. Reservations required. Main courses 50,000–70,000L (€26–€36.40, $25–$35). AE, DC, MC, V. Mon–Sat noon–2:30pm and 7pm–midnight. Closed Jan 6–31. Vaporetto: San Marco.

Quadri 🀄🀄🀄 VENETIAN/INTERNATIONAL   One of Europe's famous restaurants, the deluxe Quadri evokes the world of its former patrons, Marcel Proust and Stendhal. Many diners come here just for the setting and are often surprised when they're treated to high-quality cuisine and impeccable service. You pay for all this nostalgia, however. The Venetian cuisine has been acclaimed—at least by one food critic—as "befitting a doge," though we doubt if those old doges ate as well. The chef is likely to tempt you with such dishes as octopus in fresh tomato sauce, salt codfish with polenta, or sea bass with crab sauce. Try the "baked" ice cream for dessert.

Piazza San Marco, San Marco 120–124. ℭ 041-5289299. Reservations required. Main courses 55,000–75,000L (€28.60–€39, $28–$38). AE, DC, MC, V. Tues–Sun noon–2:30pm and 7–10:30pm; July–Aug Tues–Sun 7–10:30pm. Vaporetto: San Marco.

Moderate

Ristorante da Raffaele 🀄 Value ITALIAN/VENETIAN   This place is a 5-minute walk from Piazza San Marco and a minute from the Grand Canal. It has long been a favorite canal-side stop. It's often overrun with tourists, but the veteran kitchen staff holds up well. The food is excellent, beginning with a choice of tasty antipasti or well-prepared pastas. Seafood specialties include scampi, squid, or a platter of deep-fried fish from the Adriatic. The grilled meats are also succulent and can be followed by rich, tempting desserts.

The Cafe Scene

Venice's most famous cafe is the **Florian,** Piazza San Marco, San Marco 56–59 (ℭ 041-5285338; vaporetto: San Marco). It was built in 1720 and remains romantically and elegantly decorated—pure Venetian salons with red plush banquettes, elaborate murals under glass, and Art Nouveau lighting and lamps. It's open from Thursday to Tuesday 9:30am to midnight. Closed the first week in December and the first week in January.

   Quadri, Piazza San Marco, San Marco 120–124 (ℭ 041-5222105; vaporetto: San Marco), stands opposite the Florian. Founded in 1638, it's elegantly decorated in an antique style. Wagner used to drop in for a drink when he was working on *Tristan und Isolde*. The restaurant on the second floor offers refined Venetian cuisine. It's open from April to October daily 9am to midnight; off-season, Tuesday to Sunday 9am to midnight.

Calle Larga XXII Marzo (Fond. delle Ostriche), San Marco 2347. ✆ **041-5232317**. Reservations recommended Sat–Sun. Main courses 25,000–45,000L (€13–€23.40, $13–$23). AE, DC, MC, V. Fri–Wed noon–3pm and 7–10:30pm. Closed Dec 10 to mid-Feb. Vaporetto: San Marco or Santa Maria del Giglio.

Taverna la Fenice ✿✿ ITALIAN/VENETIAN   Opened in 1907, when Venetians were flocking in record numbers to hear the *bel canto* performances in the opera house nearby, this restaurant is one of Venice's most romantic dining spots. The interior is suitably elegant, but the preferred spot in clement weather is out beneath a canopy, a few steps from the burned Teatro La Fenice. The service is smooth and efficient. You might enjoy risotto with scampi and arugula, or freshly made tagliatelle with cream and exotic mushrooms. Among the wide selection of fresh fish, you may be tempted by the exquisite simplicity of the sea bream garnished with seasonal herbs. For pasta lovers the choice ranges from traditional black tagliolini with squid ink and crabmeat, to the more creative tagliatelle with a combination of scampi and artichokes.

Campiello de la Fenice, San Marco 1938. ✆ **041-5223856**. Reservations required. Main courses 25,000–40,000L (€13–€20.80, $13–$20). AE, DC, MC, V. Mon–Sat noon–3pm and 7–11pm. Vaporetto: San Marco.

Trattoria La Colomba ✿ VENETIAN/INTERNATIONAL   This is one of the most distinctive and popular trattorie in town, with a history going back at least a century. Menu items are likely to include at least five daily specials based exclusively on the time-honored cuisine of Venice. Otherwise, you can order *risotto di funghi del Montello* (risotto with mushrooms from the local hills of Montello) or *baccalà alla vicentina* (milk-simmered dry cod seasoned with onions, anchovies, and cinnamon, then served with polenta). If you're a meat fan, try the chateaubriand accompanied by steamed vegetables and almost a dozen different sauces.

Piscina Frezzeria, San Marco 1665. ✆ **041-5221175**. Reservations recommended. Main courses 35,000–65,000L (€18.20–€33.80, $18–$33). AE, DC, MC, V. Daily noon–2:30pm and 7–11pm. Closed Wed Nov–Apr. Vaporetto: San Marco or Rialto.

Vini da Arturo ✿ *Finds* VENETIAN   Vini da Arturo attracts many devoted regulars, including artists and writers. Here you get some of the most delectable local cooking—and not just the standard cliché Venetian dishes, and not seafood, which may be unique for a Venetian restaurant. Instead of ordering plain pasta, try a tantalizing dish called *spaghetti alla gorgonzola.* The beef is also good, especially when prepared with a cream sauce flavored with mustard and freshly ground pepper. The salads are made with crisp, fresh ingredients, often in unusual combinations. The place is small and contains only seven tables; it's between the Fenice Opera House and St. Mark's Square.

Calle degli Assassini, San Marco 3656. ✆ **041-5286974**. Reservations recommended. Main courses 30,000–45,000L (€15.60–€23.40, $15–$23). No credit cards. Mon–Sat noon–2:30pm and 7:30–10:30pm. Closed Aug. Vaporetto: San Marco or Rialto.

Inexpensive

Da Bruno VENETIAN   Da Bruno is like a country tavern in the center of Venice. On a narrow street about halfway between the Rialto Bridge and Piazza San Marco, this restaurant attracts its crowds by grilling meats on an open-hearth fire. Get your antipasti at the counter and watch your prosciutto being prepared—paper-thin slices of spicy flavored ham wrapped around breadsticks (*grissini*). In the right season, da Bruno does some of the finest game specialty dishes in Venice. If it's featured, try *capriolo* (roebuck) or *fagiano* (pheasant).

Another great dish is veal scaloppini with wild mushrooms. If you feel more in a pasta mood, try the "black spaghetti" with tomato sauce.

Calle del Paradiso, Castello 5731. ✆ **041-5221480.** Main courses 20,000–40,000L (€10.40–€20.80, $10–$20). AE, DC, MC, V. Daily noon–3pm and 7–11pm. Vaporetto: San Marco or Rialto.

Sempione VENETIAN   This century-old restaurant does an admirable job of feeding local residents and visitors. Set adjacent to a canal near St. Marks Square, it contains three dining rooms outfitted in a soothingly traditional style, a well-trained staff, and a kitchen that focuses on preparations of traditional Venetian cuisine. Examples include grilled fish, spaghetti with crabmeat, risotto with fish, fish soup, and a timeless and delectable version of Venetian calves' liver. If you like surprises, try spaghetti with crabmeat flavored with a mysterious sauce whose ingredients the chef doesn't want to reveal. Try for a table by the window so you can watch the gondolas slide by.

Ponte dei Beretteri, San Marco 578. ✆ **041-5226022.** Reservations recommended. Main courses 25,000–40,000L (€13–€20.80, $13–$20). AE, DC, MC, V. Daily noon–3pm and 6:30–10pm. Closed Thurs Nov–Dec. Vaporetto: Rialto.

Trattoria alla Madonna VENETIAN   This restaurant, opened in 1954 and named after *another* famous Madonna, is one of the most popular and characteristic trattorie of Venice, specializing in traditional recipes and an array of grilled fresh fish. A suitable beginning may be the antipasto *frutti di mare*. Pastas, polentas, risottos, meats (including *fegato alla veneziana,* liver with onions), and many kinds of irreproachably fresh fish are widely available.

Calle de la Madonna, San Pollo 594. ✆ **041-5223824.** Reservations recommended but not always accepted. Main courses 20,000–40,000L (€10.40–€20.80, $10–$20). AE, MC, V. Thurs–Tues noon–3pm and 7:15–10pm. Closed Dec 24–Jan and Aug 4–17. Vaporetto: Rialto.

EAST OF PIAZZA SAN MARCO
Moderate
Ristorante Corte Sconta SEAFOOD   This restaurant lies on a narrow alley, whose name is shared by at least three other streets in Venice (this particular one is near Campo Bandiere Moro and San Giovanni in Bragora). The modest restaurant has become well known as a sophisticated gathering place for artists, writers, and filmmakers. It serves a variety of flawlessly grilled fish (much of the "catch" is largely unknown in North America). It's also flawlessly fresh—the gamberi, for example, is placed live on the grill. Begin with marinated salmon with arugula and pomegranate seeds in rich olive oil. If you don't like fish, a tender filet of beef is available.

Calle del Pestrin, Castello 3886. ✆ **041-5227024.** Reservations required. Main courses 25,000–40,000L (€13–€20.80, $13–$20); fixed-price menu 70,000–90,000L (€36.40–€46.80, $35–$45). AE, DC, MC, V. Tues–Sat 12:30–2:30pm and 7:30–9:30pm. Closed Jan 7–Feb 7 and July 15–Aug 15. Vaporetto: Arsenale.

Inexpensive
Nuova Rivetta *(Value* SEAFOOD   Nuova Rivetta is an old-fashioned Venetian trattoria where you eat well without having to pay a lot. The restaurant stands in the monumental heart of the old city. Many find it best for lunch during a stroll around Venice. The most representative dish to order is *frittura di pesce,* a mixed fish fry from the Adriatic, which includes squid or various other "sea creatures" that turned up at the market that day. Other specialties are gnocchi stuffed with Adriatic spider crab, pasticcio of fish (a main course), and spaghetti flavored with squid ink.

Campo San Filippo, Castello 4625. ✆ **041/5287302.** Reservations required. Main courses 18,000–35,000L (€9.35–€18.20, $9–$18). AE, MC, V. Tues–Sun noon–10pm. Closed July 23–Aug 20. Vaporetto: San Zaccaria.

NEAR THE PONTE DI RIALTO
Moderate
"Al Graspo de Ua" ✯ SEAFOOD/VENETIAN   This is one bunch of grapes you'll want to pluck. For that special meal, it's a winner. Decorated in the old tavern style, it offers several air-conditioned dining rooms. Among the best fish restaurants in Venice, this place has been patronized by such celebs as Elizabeth Taylor, Jeanne Moreau, and even Giorgio de Chirico. You can help yourself to all the hors d'oeuvres you want—known on the menu as "self-service mammoth." The wonderful *gran fritto dell'Adriatico* is a mixed treat of deep-fried fish from the Adriatic.

Calle dei Bombaseri, San Marco 5094. ✆ 041-5200150. Reservations required. Main courses 26,000–40,000L (€13.50–€20.80, $13–$20). AE, DC, MC, V. Tues–Sun noon–3pm and 8–11pm. Closed Aug 5–20. Vaporetto: Rialto.

Poste Vechie ✯ SEAFOOD   This is one of Venice's most charming restaurants near the Rialto fish market and connected to the rest of the city by a small, privately owned bridge. It was established in the early 1500s as the local post office—food was served to the mail carriers to fortify them for their deliveries. Today, it's one of the oldest restaurants in town. Menu items include a super fresh array of fish from the nearby markets; a salad of shellfish and exotic mushrooms; a spicy soup of Adriatic fish; tagliolini flavored with squid ink, crabmeat, and fish sauce; and the restaurant's pièce de résistance, *seppie* (cuttlefish) *alla veneziana* with polenta. If you don't like fish, calves' liver or veal shank with ham and cheese are also well prepared. The desserts come rolling to your table on a trolley and are usually sumptuous.

Pescheria Rialto, San Polo 1608. ✆ 041-721822. Reservations recommended. Main courses 25,000–45,000L (€13–€23.40, $13–$23). AE, DC, MC, V. Wed–Mon noon–3:30pm and 7–10:30pm. Vaporetto: Rialto.

Ristorante à la Vecia Cavana ✯ *(Finds* SEAFOOD   This restaurant is off the tourist circuit and well worth the trek through winding streets to find it. The menu specializes in seafood, including a mixed grill from the Adriatic, fresh sole, three types of risotto (each prepared with seafood), and spicy *zuppa di pesce* (fish soup). Another specialty is *antipasti di pesce Cavana*, which includes just about every sea creature. It's worth the trek across Venice if you wish to sample the chef's special linguine with lobster and a velvety cream sauce enriched with freshly ground black pepper.

Rio Terà SS. Apostoli, Cannaregio 4624. ✆ 041-5287106. Reservations recommended. Main courses 40,000–60,000L (€20.80–€31.20, $20–$30); fixed-price menu 60,000L (€31.20, $30). AE, DC, MC, V. Tues–Sun noon–3pm and 7:30–10:30pm. Vaporetto: Ca' d'Oro.

IN SAN POLO
Moderate
Osteria da Fiore ✯ *(Finds* SEAFOOD   This restaurant serves only fish, and has done so since 1910. You'll find everything from scampi (a sweet Adriatic prawn, cooked in as many different ways as there are chefs) to granzeola, a type of spider crab. Try such dishes as *capelunghe alla griglio* (razor clams opened on the grill), *masenette* (tiny green crabs that you eat shell and all), and *canoce* (mantis shrimp). For your wine, we suggest Prosecco, which has a distinctive golden-yellow color and a bouquet that's refreshing and fruity.

Calle del Scaletèr, San Polo 2202. ✆ 041-72-13-08. Reservations required. Main courses 32,000–50,000L (€16.65–€26, $16–$25). AE, DC, MC, V. Tues–Sat 12:30–2:30pm and 8–10:30pm. Closed 3 weeks in Aug and Dec 25–Jan 14. Vaporetto: San Tomà.

IN THE DORSODURO
Moderate

La Furatola SEAFOOD   La Furatola (an old Venetian word meaning "restaurant") is very much a Dorsoduro neighborhood hangout, but it has captured the imagination of local foodies. You'll need a good map and a lot of patience to find it. The specialty is fish brought to your table in a wicker basket so you can judge its size and freshness by its bright eyes and red gills. A display of seafood antipasti is set out near the entrance. A standout is the baby octopus boiled and eaten with a drop of red-wine vinegar.

Calle Lunga San Barnaba, Dorsoduro 2870A. (℃) **041-5208594.** Reservations required. Main courses 26,000–45,000L (€13.50–€23.40, $13–$23). AE, DC, MC, V. Mon 7:30–10:30pm; Fri–Sun and Tues 12:30–2:30pm and 7:30–10:30pm. Vaporetto: Ca' Rezzonico.

Inexpensive

Locanda Montin ⭐ INTERNATIONAL/ITALIAN   Since this restaurant opened just after World War II, its famous patrons have included Ezra Pound, Jackson Pollock, Mark Rothko, and Peggy Guggenheim's artist friends. The inn is owned and run by the Carretins. Today the arbor-covered garden courtyard of this 17th-century building is filled with regulars. The menu includes a variety of salads, grilled meats, and fish caught in the Adriatic. Specialties include fresh crab with virgin olive oil and lemon, tortelloni (a kind of dumpling) stuffed with artichokes and covered in a scampi cream sauce, and seasonal fish often served in a Barolo red wine sauce.

Fondamenta di Borgo, Dorsoduro 1147. (℃) **041-5227151.** Reservations recommended. Main courses 20,000–38,000L (€10.40–€19.75, $10–$19). AE, DC, MC, V. Tues 12:30–2:30pm, Thurs–Mon 12:30–2:30pm and 7:30–10pm. Closed 10 days in mid-Aug and 20 days in Jan. Vaporetto: Accademia.

SEEING THE SIGHTS IN VENICE

Unlike Florence, Venice would reward you with treasures even if you never ducked inside a museum or church. In the city on the islands, the frame eternally competes with the picture inside.

SIGHTSEEING SUGGESTIONS FOR FIRST-TIME VISITORS

If You Have 1 Day Get up early and watch the sun rise over **Piazza San Marco,** as the city wakes up. The pigeons will already be here to greet you. Have an early morning cappuccino on the square, then visit the **Basilica of San Marco** and the **Palazzo Ducale.** We recommend a lunch stop at **Poste Vecchie,** at Pescheria Rialto, San Polo 1608 (℃ **041-721-822;** vaporetto: Rialto). This restaurant near the fish market is the oldest in Venice, open from Wednesday to Monday noon to 3pm and 7:30 to 10:30pm. Ride the **Grand Canal** in a gondola 2 hours before sunset and spend the rest of the evening wandering the narrow streets of this strangely unreal and most fascinating city. Apologize to yourself for such a short visit and promise to return.

If You Have 2 Days On day 2 it's time for more concentrated sightseeing. Begin at Piazza San Marco (viewing it should be a daily ritual, regardless of how many days you have in Venice), then head for the major museum, the **Accademia,** in the morning. In the afternoon, visit the **Collezione Peggy Guggenheim** (modern art) and perhaps the **Ca' d'Oro** and **Ca' Rezzonico.**

If You Have 3 Days Begin day 3 by having a cappuccino on Piazza San Marco, then inspect the **Campanile di San Marco.** Later in the morning visit the **Museo Correr.** In the afternoon, go to the **Scuola Grande di San Rocco** to see the works of Tintoretto. Spend the rest of the day strolling the streets of Venice and ducking into shops that capture your imagination. Even if you get lost, you'll eventually return to a familiar landmark, and you can't help but see the signs pointing you back to Piazza San Marco. Have dinner in one of the most typical of Venetian trattorias, such as **Locanda Montin.**

If You Have 4 or 5 Days On day 4 plan to visit the islands of the lagoon, including **Murano, Burano,** and **Torcello.** All three can be covered, at least briefly, on 1 busy day. On day 5, relax, wander around the streets, and take in some of the many attractions you may have missed.

THE GRAND CANAL ⚜⚜⚜

Peoria may have its Main Street, Paris its Champs-Elysées—but Venice, for uniqueness, tops them all with its **Canal Grande (Grand Canal).** Lined with *palazzi* (palaces)—many in elegant Venetian-Gothic style—this great road of water is today filled with vaporetti, motorboats, and gondolas. Along the canal, the boat moorings are like peppermint sticks. It begins at Piazzetta San Marco on one side and Longhena's Salute Church on the opposite bank. At midpoint it's spanned by the Rialto Bridge. Eventually the canal winds its serpentine course to the railway station. We can guarantee that there's not a dull sight en route.

THE BASILICA, DOGES' PALACE & CAMPANILE

Piazza San Marco (St. Mark's Square) ⚜⚜⚜ was the heartbeat of La Serenissima (the Serene Republic) in the heyday of its glory as a seafaring state, the crystallization of its dreams and aspirations. If you have only 1 day for Venice, you need not leave the square, as the city's major attractions, such as the Basilica of St. Mark and the Doges' Palace, are centered here or nearby. Thanks to Napoléon, the square was unified architecturally. The emperor added the Fabbrica Nuova, thus bridging the Old and New Procuratie. Flanked with medieval-looking palaces, Sansovino's Library, elegant shops, and colonnades, the square is now finished—unlike Piazza della Signoria in Florence.

If Piazza San Marco is the drawing room of Europe, then its satellite, **Piazzetta San Marco** ⚜⚜, is the antechamber. Hedged in by the Doges' Palace, Sansovino's Library, and a side of St. Mark's Basilica, the tiny square faces the Grand Canal. One of the two tall granite columns in the piazzetta is surmounted by a winged lion, which represents St. Mark. The other is topped by a statue of a man taming a dragon, supposedly the dethroned patron saint Theodore. Both columns came from the East in the 12th century.

Basilica di San Marco ⚜⚜⚜   This so-called "Church of Gold" dominates Piazza San Marco, and is one of the world's greatest and most richly embellished churches—in fact, it looks as if it had been moved intact from Istanbul. The basilica is a conglomeration of styles, yet it's particularly indebted to Byzantium. It incorporates other schools of design, such as Romanesque and Gothic, with freewheeling abandon. Like Venice itself, it's adorned with booty from every corner of the city's once far-flung mercantile empire—capitals from Sicily, columns from Alexandria, porphyry from Syria, sculpture from Constantinople. The basilica is capped by a dome that, like a spider plant, sends off shoots, in this case, a quartet of smaller-scale cupolas. Spanning the facade is a loggia,

---

Tips **A St. Mark's Warning**

St. Mark's has a strict **dress code:** no shorts, no skirts above the knee, and no bare shoulders. *They will not let you in if you don't come dressed appropriately.* You also must remain silent and cannot take photographs.

---

surmounted by replicas of the four famous St. Mark's horses—the *Triumphal Quadriga.*

If you look back at the aperture over the entryway, you can see a mosaic, the dance of Salome in front of Herod and his court. Wearing a star-studded russet-red dress and three white fox tails, Salome dances under a platter holding John's head. Her glassy face is that of a Madonna, not an enchantress. Proceed up the right nave to the doorway to the **treasury** (*tesoro*). The entrance to the **presbytery** is nearby. On the high altar, the alleged sarcophagus of St. Mark rests under a green marble blanket and is held up by four sculptured alabaster Corinthian columns. The Byzantine-style **Pala d'Oro,** from Constantinople, is the rarest treasure at St. Mark's—made of gold and studded with precious stones.

On leaving the basilica, head up the stairs in the atrium for the **Marciano Museum** and the Loggia dei Cavalli. The star attraction of the museum is the world-famous *Quadriga,* four horses looted from Constantinople by Venetian crusaders in the sack of that city in 1204. This is the only quadriga (a quartet of horses yoked together) to have survived from the classical era.

Piazza San Marco. ✆ **041-5225205.** Basilica, free; treasury, 4,000L (€2.13, $2); presbytery, 3,000L (€1.55, $1.50); Marciano Museum, 3,000L (€1.55, $1.50). Basilica and presbytery, Apr–Sept Mon–Sat 9:30am–5:30pm, Sun 2–5:30pm; Oct–Mar Mon–Sat 10am–4:30pm, Sun 2–4:30pm. Treasury, Mon–Sat 9:30am–5pm; Sun 2–5pm. Marciano Museum, Apr–Sept Mon–Sat 10am–5:30pm, Sun 2–4:30pm; Oct–Mar Mon–Sat 10am–4:45pm, Sun 2–4:30pm. Vaporetto: San Marco.

Palazzo Ducale ✶✶✶   You enter the Palace of the Doges through the magnificent 15th-century Porta della Carta on the piazzetta. It's somewhat like a frosty birthday cake in pinkish red marble and white Istrian stone. The Venetian-Gothic palazzo—with all the architectural intricacies of a doily—gleams in the tremulous Venetian light. The grandest civic structure in Italy, it dates back to 1309, though a fire in 1577 destroyed much of the original.

After climbing the Sansovino stairway of gold, proceed to the Anti-Collegio salon, which houses the palace's greatest artworks—notably Veronese's *Rape of Europa,* to the far left on the right wall. Tintoretto is well represented with his *Three Graces* and *Bacchus and Ariadne.* Some critics consider the latter his supreme achievement.

Now trek downstairs through the once-private apartments of the doges to the grand Maggior Consiglio, with its allegorical *Triumph of Venice* on the ceiling, painted by Veronese. What makes the room outstanding, however, is Tintoretto's *Paradise,* over the Grand Council chamber—said to be the largest oil painting in the world.

Reenter the Maggior Consiglio and follow the arrows on their trail across the **Bridge of Sighs** ✶, linking the Doges' Palace with the Palazzo delle Prigioni, where the cellblocks are found, the ones that lodged the prisoners who felt the quick justice of the Terrible Ten. The "sighs" in the bridge's name stemmed from the sad laments of the numerous victims led across it to certain torture and possible death.

Piazzetta San Marco. ✆ **041-5224951.** Admission 18,000L (€9.35, $9) adults; 10,000L (€5.20, $5) students. Apr–Oct daily 9am–7pm; off-season daily 9am–5pm. Vaporetto: San Marco.

Campanile di San Marco ⭐⭐ One summer night back in 1902, the bell tower of the Basilica of St. Mark on Piazza San Marco, which was suffering from years of rheumatism in the damp Venetian climate, gave out a warning sound that sent the fashionable crowd scurrying from the Florian Caffè in a dash for their lives. But the campanile gracefully waited until the next morning, July 14, before it tumbled into the piazza. The Venetians rebuilt their belfry, and it's now safe to ascend. A modern elevator takes you up for a pigeon's view of the city. It's a particularly good vantage point for viewing the cupolas of St. Mark's Basilica.

Piazza San Marco. ✆ **041-5224064.** Admission 10,000L (€5.20, $5). Oct–Feb daily 9:30am–4pm; Mar–June daily 9am–7pm; July–Sept daily 9am–9pm. Closed Jan 7–31. Vaporetto: San Marco.

MUSEUMS & GALLERIES
Galleria dell'Accademia ⭐⭐⭐ The pomp and circumstance, the glory that was Venice, lives on in this remarkable collection of paintings spanning the 14th to the 18th century. The hallmark of the Venetian school is color and more color. From Giorgione to Veronese, from Titian to Tintoretto, with a Carpaccio cycle thrown in, the Accademia has samples—often their best—of its most famous sons.

You'll first see works by such 14th-century artists as Paolo and Lorenzo Veneziano, who bridged the gap from Byzantine art to Gothic (see the latter's *Annunciation*). Next, you'll view Giovanni Bellini's *Madonna and Saint* (poor Sebastian, not another arrow), and Carpaccio's fascinating yet gruesome work of mass crucifixion. Two of the most important works with secular themes are Mantegna's armored *St. George,* with the dragon slain at his feet, and Hans Memling's 15th-century portrait of a young man. Giorgione's *Tempest* is the most famous painting at the Accademia.

Campo della Carità, Dorsoduro. ✆ **041-5222247.** Admission 12,000L (€6.25, $6). Mar–Oct Tues–Fri 9am–9pm, Sat 9am–11pm, Sun 9am–8pm; Nov–Feb Tues–Sat 9am–6:30pm, Sun 9am–1:30pm. Vaporetto: Accademia.

Collezione Peggy Guggenheim ⭐⭐⭐ This is one of the most comprehensive and brilliant modern-art collections in the Western world, and it reveals the foresight and critical judgment of its founder. The collection is housed in an unfinished palazzo, the former home of Peggy Guggenheim. In the tradition of her family, Guggenheim was a lifelong patron of contemporary painters and sculptors. As her private collection increased, she decided to find a larger showcase and selected Venice. Displayed here are works not only by Pollock and Ernst but also by Picasso (see his cubist *The Poet* of 1911), Duchamp, Chagall, Mondrian, Brancusi, Delvaux, and Dalí, plus a garden of modern sculpture that includes works by Giacometti.

Ca' Venier dei Leoni, Dorsoduro 701. ✆ **041-5206288.** Admission 12,000L (€6.25, $6) adults, 8,000L (€4.15, $4) students, free children 9 and under. Sun–Fri except Tues 10am–6pm; Sat 10am–10pm. Vaporetto: Accademia.

Ca' d'Oro ⭐⭐⭐ This is one of the most handsomely embellished palaces along the Grand Canal. Although it contains the important **Galleria Giorgio Franchetti,** the House of Gold (so named because its facade was once gilded) competes with its own paintings. Built in the first part of the 15th century in the ogival style, it has a lacy look. Baron Franchetti, who restored the palace and filled it with his collection of paintings, sculpture, and furniture, presented it to

Italy during World War I. In a special niche reserved for the masterpiece of the Franchetti collection is Andrea Mantegna's icy-cold *St. Sebastian,* the central figure of which is riddled with what must be a record number of arrows.

Cannaregio 3931–3932. © **041-5238790.** Admission 6,000L (€3.10, $3). Tues–Sun 8:15am–7:15pm; Mon 8am–2pm. Closed Jan 1, May 1, and Dec 25. Vaporetto: Ca' d'Oro.

Museo Civico Correr ⭐⭐

This museum traces the development of Venetian painting from the 14th to the 16th century. On the second floor are the red and maroon robes once worn by the doges, plus some fabulous street lanterns. There's also an illustrated copy of *Marco Polo in Tartaria.* You can see Cosmé Tura's *La Pietà,* a miniature of renown from the genius in the Ferrara School. This is one of his more gruesome works, depicting a bony, gnarled Christ sprawled on the lap of the Madonna. Farther on, search out a Schiavone *Madonna and Child* (no. 545), our candidate for ugliest bambino ever depicted on canvas (no wonder the mother looks askance). One of the most important rooms at the Correr is filled with three masterpieces: Antonello da Messina's *Pietà,* Hugo van der Goes's *Crucifixion,* and Dieric Bouts's *Madonna and Child.* The star attraction of the Correr is the Bellini salon, which includes works by founding padre Jacopo and his son, Gentile. But the real master of the household was the other son, Giovanni.

In the Procuratie Nuove, Piazza San Marco. © **041-5225625.** Admission 18,000L (€9.35, $9) adults, 10,000L (€5.20, $5) ages 14–29, 6,000L (€3.10, $3) children 6–14, free for children 6 and under. Mar–Oct daily 9am–7pm; Nov–Mar daily 9am–5pm. Vaporetto: San Marco. (The admission ticket includes entrance to Palazzo Ducale, Marciana Library, Archaeological Museum, and Glass Museum in Murano.)

Ca' Rezzonico ⭐⭐

This 17th- and 18th-century palace along the Grand Canal is where Robert Browning set up his bachelor headquarters. Pope Clement XIII also stayed here. It's a virtual treasure house, known for its baroque paintings and furniture. You first enter the Grand Ballroom with its allegorical ceiling, then proceed through lavishly embellished rooms with Venetian chandeliers, brocaded walls, portraits of patricians, tapestries, gilded furnishings, and touches of chinoiserie. At the end of the first walk is the Throne Room, with its allegorical ceilings by Giovanni Battista Tiepolo.

Upstairs you'll find a survey of 18th-century Venetian art. Head for the first salon on your right (facing the canal) that contains paintings from the brush of Pietro Longhi. His most famous work, *The Lady and the Hairdresser,* is the first canvas to the right on the entrance wall.

Fondamenta Rezzonico, Dorsoduro 3136. © **041-2410100.** Admission 14,000L (€7.33, $7) adults. Oct–Apr Sat–Thurs 10am–4pm; May–Sept daily 10am–5pm. Vaporetto: Ca' Rezzonico.

THE SCUOLE

Scuola di San Rocco ⭐⭐⭐

Of Venice's *scuole* (in the Renaissance, scuole were centers used by social and religious organizations affiliated with the local parish), none are as richly embellished as the Scuola di San Rocco, filled with epic canvases by Tintoretto. By clever trick, he won the competition to decorate the darkly illuminated early 16th-century building. He began painting in 1564 and the work stretched on till his powers as an artist waned. The paintings sweep across the upper and lower halls, mesmerizing the viewer with a kind of passion play. In the grand hallway, they depict New Testament scenes, devoted largely to episodes in the life of Mary (*Flight into Egypt* is among the best). In the top gallery are works illustrating the Old and New Testaments, the most renowned devoted to the life of Christ. In a separate room is Tintoretto's masterpiece—a mammoth *Crucifixion,* one of the world's most celebrated paintings.

Campo San Rocco, San Polo. ✆ **041-5234864.** Admission 9,000L (€4.73, $4.50) adults, 6,000L (€3.10, $3) students. Mar 28–Nov 2 daily 9am–5:30pm; Nov 3–30 and Mar 1–27 daily 10am–4pm; Dec–Feb Mon–Fri 10am–1pm, Sat–Sun 10am–4pm. Ticket office closes 30 minutes before last entrance. Closed Easter and Dec 25–Jan 1. Vaporetto: San Tomà; from the station, walk straight onto Ramo Mondoler, which becomes Larga Prima; then take Salizzada San Rocco, which opens into Campo San Rocco.

Scuola di San Giorgio degli Schiavoni 🐦🐦

At the St. Antonino Bridge (Fondamenta dei Furlani) is the second important scuola to visit in Venice. Between 1502 and 1509, Vittore Carpaccio painted a pictorial cycle here of exceptional merit and interest. Of enduring fame are his works of St. George and the dragon—these are our favorite pieces of art in all of Venice and certainly the most delightful. In one frame, St. George charges the dragon on a field littered with half-eaten bodies and skulls. Gruesome? Not at all. Any moment you expect the director to call "Cut!"

Calle dei Furiani, Castello. ✆ **041-5228828.** Admission 5,000L (€2.60, $2.50). Nov–Mar Tues–Sat 10am–12:30pm and 3–6pm; Sun 10am–12:30pm. Apr–Oct Tues–Sat 9:30am–12:30pm and 3:30–6:30pm; Sun 9:30am–12:30pm. Last entrance 30 minutes before closing. Vaporetto: San Zaccaria.

ORGANIZED TOURS

Daily at 9:10am, **American Express,** San Marco 1471 (✆ **041-5200844;** vaporetto: San Marco), offers a 2-hour guided tour of the city, costing 40,000L (€20.80, $20). Sights include St. Mark's Square, the basilica, the Doges' Palace, the prison, the bell tower, and in some cases a demonstration of the art of Venetian glassblowing. from Monday to Saturday at 3pm, a 2-hour guided tour incorporates visits to the exteriors of several palaces along Campo San Benetto and other sights of the city. The tour eventually crosses the Grand Canal to visit the Church of Santa Maria dei Frari, which contains an *Assumption* by Titian. The tour continues by gondola down the canal to visit the Ca' d'Oro and ends at the Rialto Bridge. The cost of the afternoon tour is 50,000L (€26, $25).

The **Evening Serenade Tour,** at 60,000L (€31.20, $30) per person, allows a nocturnal view of Venice accompanied by the sound of singing musicians in gondolas. From April to October there're two daily departures, at 7:30 and 9:30pm, leaving from Campo Santa Maria del Giglio, but from November to March there's just one departure at 3:30pm. Five to six occupants fit in each gondola as a singer and a handful of musicians perform throughout the Venetian evening. The experience lasts 50 minutes.

The **Islands Tour** is a 3-hour tour of Murano, Burano, and Torcello available for 30,000L (€15.60, $15) per person. Departures are at 2:30pm year-round and also at 9:30am from March 15 to October.

THE SHOPPING SCENE

Venetian **glass** and **lace** are known throughout the world. However, selecting quality products in either craft requires a shrewd eye, as there's much that is tawdry and shoddily crafted. Some of the glassware hawked isn't worth the cost of shipping it home. Yet other pieces represent some of the world's finest artistic and ornamental glass. Murano is famous for its handmade glass. However, you can find little glass animal souvenirs in shops all over Venice.

For lace, head out to Burano, where the last of a long line of women put in painstaking hours to produce some of the finest lace in the world.

SHOPPING STROLLS   All the main shopping streets of Venice, even the side streets, are touristy and overrun. The greatest concentration of shops is around Piazza San Marco and around the Rialto Bridge. Prices are much higher at San Marco, but the quality of merchandise is better. There're two major

> ## (Tips) Shopping for Venetian Glass & Lace
>
> Venice is literally crammed with **glass** shops. It's estimated that
> there're at least 1,000 of them in the sestiere of San Marco alone.
> Unless you go to an absolutely top-quality and reliable dealer, such as
> those we recommend, most stores sell both shoddy and high-quality
> glassware. Sometimes, only the most trained eye can tell the differ-
> ence. The big secret (which is becoming less a secret all the time) is that
> a lot of so-called Venetian glass isn't Venetian at all, but comes from
> eastern Europe, including the Czech Republic. Of course, the Czech
> Republic has some of the finest glassmakers in Europe, so that may not
> be bad either. If you're looking for an heirloom, stick to such award-
> winning houses as **Pauly & Co.** or **Venini** (see below).
>   Most of the **lace** vendors are centered around Piazza San Marco.
> Although high, prices of Venetian lace are still reasonable considering
> the painstaking work that goes into it. Much of the lace is shoddy, and
> some of it—a lot of it, really—isn't Venetian lace but machine made in
> who knows what country. *The* name in Venetian lace is **Jesurum** (see
> below), which has stood for quality since the last century.

shopping strolls in Venice. First, from Piazza San Marco you can stroll through
Venice toward the spacious square of **Campo Morosini.** You just follow one
shop-lined street all the way to its end (although the name will change several
times along the way). You begin at Salizzada San Moisè, which becomes Via 22
Marzo, and then Calle delle Ostreghe, before it opens onto Campo Santa Maria
Zobenigo. The street then narrows again and changes its name to Calle Zaguri
before widening once more into Campo San Maurizio, finally becoming Calle
Piovan before it reaches Campo Morosini. The only deviation from this tour is
a detour down Calle Vallaressa, between San Moisè and the Grand Canal, which
is one of the major shopping arteries with some of the biggest designer names in
the business.

   The other great shopping stroll in Venice wanders from Piazza San Marco to
the Rialto in a succession of streets collectively known as **The Mercerie.** It's virtually impossible to get lost because each street name is preceded by the word
merceria, such as Merceria dell'Orologio, which begins near the clock tower in
Piazza San Marco. Many commercial establishments, mainly shops, line the
Mercerie before it reaches the Rialto, which then explodes into one vast shopping emporium.

SOME SHOPS WORTH A LOOK

At **Pauly & Co.,** Ponte Consorzi, San Marco (© **041-5209899;** vaporetto: San
Zaccaria), you can wander through 21 salons, enjoy an exhibition of artistic
glassware, and later see a furnace in full action. Pauly's production, which is
mainly made-to-order, consists of continually renewed patterns, subject to
change and alteration based on customer desire. The Venetian glass of **Venini,**
Piazzetta Leoncini, San Marco 314 (© **041-5224045;** vaporetto: San Zaccaria),
has won collector fans all over the globe. The store sells lamps, bottles, and vases,
but not ordinary ones. Many are works of art, representing the best of Venetian

craftsmanship in design and manufacture. Their best-known glass has a distinctive swirl pattern in several colors, which is called a *venature*.

The elegant **Jesurum,** Mercerie del Capitello, San Marco 4857 (© 041-5206177; vaporetto: San Zaccaria or Rialto), the best place in Venice for serious lace purchases, has been in a 12th-century church since 1868. You'll find Venetian hand- or machine-made lace and embroidery on table, bed, and bath linens; and hand-printed bathing suits. **Laboratorio Artigiano Maschere,** Barbaria delle Tole, Castello 6657 (© 041-5223110; vaporetto: Rialto), is one of the best places to purchase carnival masks handcrafted in papier-mâché or leather. The masks carry names and symbols, the best known being the birdlike luck bringer, called *Buonaventura* in Italian.

Il Papiro, Calle del Piovan, San Marco 2764 (© 041-5223055; vaporetto: Accademia), is mainly noted for its stationery supplies, but it also carries and sells many textures and colors of writing paper and cards. In addition to hand-printed paper, the store stocks any number of easy-to-pack gift items.

VENICE AFTER DARK

The tourist office distributes a free pamphlet (part in English, part in Italian), called *Un Ospite di Venezia.* A section of this useful publication lists events, including any music and opera or theatrical presentations, along with art exhibitions and local special events.

In addition, classical concerts are often at various churches, such as the Chiesa di Vivaldi. To see if any **church concerts** are being presented at the time of your visit, call **Kele and Teo Travel Agency** (© 041/5208722) for information.

THE PERFORMING ARTS

The city's main venue for performing arts, the fabled **La Fenice** at Campo San Fantin, has been a blackened shell since 1996. However, you can still see performances of the Orchestra and Caro della Fenice in a temporary venue, **PalaFenice,** in the Tronchetto parking facilities near Piazzale Roma (© 041-786500 for information; vaporetto: Tronchetto). Tickets for most events range from 30,000 to 200,000L (€15.60 to €104, $15 to $100), but this could vary. The **box office** is open from Monday to Friday 8:30am to 1:30pm and 1 hour before performance (© 041-521-0161).

Teatro Goldoni, Calle Goldoni, near Campo San Luca (© 041-5205422; vaporetto Rialto), close to the Ponte Rialto in the San Marco district, honors Carlo Goldoni (1707–93), the most prolific—critics say the best—Italian playwright. The theater presents a changing repertoire of productions, often plays in Italian, but musical presentations as well. The box office is open from Monday to Saturday 10am to 1pm and 4:30 to 7pm. Tickets are 25,000 to 50,000L (€13 to €26, $13 to $25).

PIANO BARS & DANCE CLUBS

The pub **Il Piccolo Mondo,** Calle Contarini Corfu 1056A (© 041-520-0371; vaporetto: Accademia), near the Accademia, is open during the day, and at night features disco dancing and organized parties. The crowd is often young, and dance music prevails. It's open from Thursday to Tuesday 10pm to 4am, but the action actually doesn't begin until after midnight. Cover (including the first drink) is 15,000L (€7.80, $7.50) Thursday and Friday, 25,000L (€13, $12.50) Saturday, otherwise free.

Martini Scala Club, Campo San Fantin, San Marco 1980 (© 041-5224121; vaporetto: San Marco or Santa Maria del Giglio), is an elegant restaurant with a piano bar that has functioned as some kind of an inn since 1724. You can enjoy

> ### ⟨Moments⟩ **Sipping a Bellini at Harry's Bar**
>
> The single most famous of all the watering holes of Ernest Hemingway, **Harry's Bar,** Calle Vallaresso, San Marco 1323 (© **041-5285777;** vaporetto: San Marco), is known for inventing its own drinks and exporting them around the world. It's also said that *carpaccio,* the delicate raw-beef dish, was invented here. Devotees say that Harry's makes the best Bellini of any bar in the world. In Venice, this bar is a tradition and landmark, not quite as famous as the Basilica di San Marco, but almost.

its food and wine until 2am—it's the only kitchen in Venice that stays open late. After 10pm, you can come here to enjoy the piano bar. The restaurant is open from March to November, Wednesday to Monday 7pm to 11:30pm; from December to February, Wednesday to Monday noon to 2:30pm and from 7 to 11:30pm. The bar, which offers a piano bar and food, is open every day but Tuesday from 10pm to 3am, and closed in July and August.

CASINOS
If you want to risk your luck and your lire, you can take a vaporetto ride on the Casino Express, which leaves from the stops at the rail station, Piazzale Roma, and Piazzetta San Marco and delivers you to the landing dock of the **Casino Municipale,** Lungomare G. Marconi 4, Lido (© **041-5297111**). Admission is 15,000L (€7.80, $8), and bring your passport to get in. The building itself is foreboding, almost as if it could've been inspired by Mussolini-era architects. However, the action gets hotter once you step inside. At the casino, you can play blackjack, roulette, baccarat, or whatever. You can also dine, drink at the bar, or enjoy a floor show. It's open from July to September daily from 3pm to 2:30am.

October to June, the casino action moves to the **Vendramin-Calergi Palace,** Strada Nuova, Cannaregio 2040 (© **041-5297111;** vaporetto: San Marcuola). Incidentally, in 1883 Wagner died in this house, which opens onto the Grand Canal. The casino is open daily from 3pm to 2:30am. Admission is 15,000L (€7.80, $8), and bring your passport.

DAY TRIPS FROM VENICE
MURANO 𝄐𝄐   On this island, **glassblowers** have for centuries performed oral gymnastics to turn out those fantastic chandeliers that Victorian ladies used to prize so highly. They also produce heavily ornamented glasses so ruby red or so indigo blue you can't tell if you're drinking blackberry juice or pure wood grain. Happily, the glassblowers are still plying their trade, though increasing competition, notably from Sweden, has compelled a greater degree of sophistication in design. You can combine a tour of Murano with a trip along the lagoon. To reach it, take vaporetto 5 at Riva degli Schiavoni, a short walk from Piazzetta San Marco. The boat docks at the landing platform at Murano where the first furnace conveniently awaits. It's best to go from Monday to Friday 10am to noon if you want to see glassblowing action.

BURANO 𝄐𝄐   Burano became world famous as a center of **lace making,** a craft that reached its pinnacle in the 18th century. If you can spare a morning to visit this island you'll be rewarded with a charming little fishing village far removed in spirit from the grandeur of Venice, but lying only half an hour away by ferry. Boats leave from Fondamente Nuove, overlooking the Venetian grave-yard (which is well worth the trip all on its own). Take vaporetto 12 or 52 from Riva degli Schiavoni, get off at Fondamente Nuove, and catch boat 12, marked Burano.

Once at Burano, you'll discover that the houses of the islanders come in var-ied colors—sienna, robin's-egg or cobalt blue, barn-red, butterscotch, grass green. **Scuola Merietti** stands in the center of the fishing village on Piazza Baldassare Galuppi. The Burano School of Lace was founded in 1872 as part of a resurgence movement aimed at restoring the age-old craft that had earlier declined, giving way to such other lace-making centers as Chantilly and Bruges. By going up to the second floor you can see the lace makers, mostly young women, at painstaking work and can purchase hand-embroidered or handmade lace items.

After visiting the lace school, you can walk across the square to the **Duomo** and its leaning campanile (inside, look for a *Crucifixion* by Tiepolo). However, walk quickly; the bell tower is leaning so precariously it looks as if it may topple at any moment.

TORCELLO 🏛🏛   Of all the islands of the lagoon, Torcello—the so-called Mother of Venice—offers the most charm. If Burano is behind the times, Tor-cello is positively antediluvian. You can follow in the footsteps of Hemingway and stroll across a grassy meadow, traverse an ancient stone bridge, and step back into that time when the Venetians first fled from invading barbarians to create a city of Neptune in the lagoon. To reach Torcello, take vaporetto 12 from Fondamenta Nuova on Murano. The trip takes about 45 minutes.

Cattedrale di Torcello , also called the Church of Santa Maria Assunta Isola di Torcello (© 041-730084), was founded in A.D. 639 and was subsequently rebuilt. It stands in a lonely, grassy meadow beside a campanile dating from the 11th century. It's visited chiefly because of its Byzantine mosaics. Clutching her child, the weeping Madonna in the apse is a magnificent sight, whereas on the opposite wall is a powerful *Last Judgment*. It's open daily from April to October 10am to 12:30pm and 2:30 to 6:30pm; from November to March 10am to 12:30pm and 2:30 to 5pm. Admission is 2,000L (€1.05, $1).

While on the island, you can dine in Venice's most idyllic luncheon stopover, **Locanda Cipriani** 🏛🏛, Piazza San Fosca 29 (© 041-730150), operated by Bonifacio Brass, nephew of Harry Cipriani of Hotel Cipriani and Harry's Bar fame. This low-key, deliberately rustic locanda serves an authentic Venetian cui-sine, everything from a succulent risotto made from fresh vegetables and herbs from the family garden to filet of John Dory in the style of Carla, a late and much-revered matriarch here (the fish is flavored with tomatoes and capers). Main courses run from 30,000 to 45,000L (€15.60 to €23.40, $15 to $23), and hours are from Wednesday to Monday noon to 3pm and Friday and Saturday 7 to 10pm. Closed from January 15 to February 15. American Express, Diners Club, MasterCard, and Visa are accepted.

THE LIDO 🏛🏛   Nearly a century ago the Lido began to blossom into a fash-ionable beachfront resort, complete with deluxe hotels and its Casino Municipale.

The Lido today is past its heyday. The fashionable and chic of the world still patronize the **Excelsior Palace** and the **Hotel des Bains,** but the beach strip is over-touristed and opens onto polluted waters. It's not just the beaches around Venice that are polluted—the entire Adriatic is reputedly polluted. For swim-ming, guests use the pools of their hotels. They can, however, still enjoy the sands along the Lido. Try the **Lungomare G. d'Annunzio Public Bathing Beach** at the end of the Gran Viale (Piazzale Ettore Sorger), a long stroll from the vaporetto stop. You can book cabins—called *cabine*—and enjoy the sand. Rates change seasonally.

To reach the Lido, take vaporetto 6 from Riva Schiavoni, a landing stage near the Doges' Palace (the ride takes about 15 minutes).

Where to Stay   The **Excelsior Palace** ☆☆☆, Lungomare Marconi 41, 30126 Venezia Lido (© **888/625-5144** in the U.S. and Canada, or 041-5260201; fax 041-5267276; www.starwood.com; vaporetto: Lido, then bus A, B, or C), is a monument to *la dolce vita* and did much to make the Lido fashionable. Today it is the Lido's most luxurious hotel. Rooms range in style and amenities from cozy singles to suites. Most of the social life takes place around the angular pool or on the flowered terraces leading up to the cabanas on the sandy beach. All 196 guest rooms—some big enough for tennis games—have been modernized, often with vivid colors. Rates, including breakfast, are 837,000 to 1,073,000L (€435.25 to €557.95, $419 to $537) for a double and from 2,300,000L (€1,196, $1,150) for a suite. American Express, Diners Club, MasterCard, and Visa are accepted. The hotel is closed November to March 15. Amenities include restaurant, bar, room service, laundry/dry cleaning, baby-sitting, pool, tennis courts, boat rental; in room: A/C, TV, minibar, hair dryer.

Hotel des Bains ☆☆, Lungomare Marconi 17, 30126 Venezia Lido (© **888/ 625-5144** in the U.S. and Canada, or 041-5265921; fax 041-5260113; www.starwood.com; vaporetto: Lido, then bus A, B, or C), was built in the grand era of European resort hotels. It has its own wooded park and private beach with individual cabanas along with a kind of confectionery facade from the turn of the century. Thomas Mann stayed here several times before making it the setting for *Death in Venice,* and later it was used as a set for the film of the same name. The hotel has fairly large, well-furnished rooms, 191 in all. Rates are 695,000 to 975,000L (€361.40 to €507, $348 to $488) for a double; suites begin at 1,500,000L (€780, $750). American Express, Diners Club, MasterCard, and Visa are accepted. It's closed November to March. Amenities include restaurant, room service, laundry/dry cleaning, tennis courts, pool, beauty salon, motorboat shuttle; in room: A/C, TV, minibar, hair dryer.

12

The Netherlands

by George McDonald

Easygoing, prosperous Amsterdam, full of canals, bridges, and world-class museums, and enveloped in the afterglow of its 17th-century golden age, is the natural focus of a visit to the Netherlands. From here you can make leisurely day trips to historic Haarlem; the brash North Sea resort Zandvoort; the traditional IJsselmeer lakeside villages Volendam and Marken; Delft, famous for its royal connections and blue-and-white earthenware; and along the tulip trail.

1 Amsterdam

The Dutch capital has never entirely shed its twofold reputation as a hippie haven and a tulips-and-windmills landmark, even with an economy that has moved far beyond these cliches. Powered more by business than the combustion of semi-legal exotic plants, prosperity has surged like a North Sea tide through the graceful cityscape of canals and 17th-century town houses. The historic center recalls Amsterdam's golden age as the command post of a vast trading network and colonial empire, when wealthy merchants constructed gabled residences along neatly laid-out canals. Now a new generation of entrepreneurs is revitalizing old neighborhoods such as the Jordaan, turning some of the distinctive houses into offbeat stores, and bustling cafes, hotels, and restaurants.

A delicious irony is that the placid 17th-century structures also host brothels, smoke shops, and some extravagant nightlife. The city's inhabitants are proud of their live-and-let-live attitude, based on pragmatism as much as a long history of tolerance. Deciding to control what they cannot effectively outlaw, they permit licensed prostitution in the red light district and the sale of hashish and marijuana in designated "coffee shops."

But don't think Amsterdammers drift around town in a drug-induced haze. They are too busy whizzing around on bicycles, jogging through Vondelpark, feasting on arrays of ethnic dishes, or simply watching the parade of street life from the terrace of an outdoor cafe. Their zest for living is infectious. Between dips into Amsterdam's trove of artistic and historical treasures, take time out to absorb the freewheeling spirit of Europe's most vibrant city.

ESSENTIALS

GETTING THERE By Plane Amsterdam Airport Schiphol (© 0900/ 0141 for flight information; www.schiphol.nl), 18 kilometers (11 miles) south of the city, has a single terminal. You exit from Customs into Schiphol Plaza, a combined arrivals hall, train station, and shopping mall.

The **KLM hotel shuttle bus** operates between the airport and city center on a circular route directly connecting 16 top hotels, with stops close to many others. The one-way fare is 17.50Dfl (€7.95, $8); no reservations are needed, and buses leave from in front of Schiphol Plaza every 20 minutes from 7am to 6pm and every 30 minutes from 6 to 9:30pm.

Trains depart from Schiphol Station, a floor below Schiphol Plaza, for Centraal Station. The fare is 6.25Dfl (€2.85, $2.70) one-way, and the trip takes about 20 minutes.

A **taxi** from the airport to the city center costs around 60Dfl (€27.25, $26).

By Ship   Car ferry companies operate three routes to the Netherlands from England: Newcastle to **IJmuiden,** west of Amsterdam; Hull to **Rotterdam (Europoort);** and Harwich to **Hoek van Holland,** close to Rotterdam. All have train service to Amsterdam (from Europoort you can take the ferry company's bus to Rotterdam Centraal Station).

By Train   Trains arrive at Amsterdam Centraal Station (most stop at other points within the city on the way there). For information on trains (and all other public transportation) in the Netherlands, call ℭ **0900/9292;** for international trains, call ℭ **0900/9296.** To get you to your hotel, trams, buses, and taxis depart from in front of the station, and metro trains from a subway station downstairs.

By Car   European expressways E19, E35, E231, and E22 converge on Amsterdam from France and Belgium to the south and from Germany to the north and east. These roads also have Dutch designations; as you approach the city they are, respectively: A4, A2, A1, and A7. Amsterdam's ring road is A10.

VISITOR INFORMATION   Tourist Offices   Holland Tourist Information (ℭ **0900/400-4040**) has an office in Schiphol Plaza at Schiphol Airport. Amsterdam's tourist information organization, **VVV Amsterdam** (ℭ **0900/ 400-4040;** fax 020/625-2869; www.visitamsterdam.nl), has offices inside Centraal Station beside platform 1; outside the station on Stationsplein, at Leidseplein 1; and on Stadionplein. VVV Amsterdam can supply brochures and maps, and reserve hotel rooms.

Websites   The official site from the Netherlands Board of Tourism (**www. visitholland.com**) is awkwardly designed (expanding your browser to its full size helps), but it does have useful advice for upcoming events, cycling, and culture—and it even lets you know when the tulips bloom. The site **www. visitamsterdam.nl** lays out the details on sightseeing, walking routes, wining and dining, shopping for antiques, and current events. There's even a page warning you about streets that can be dangerous at night. The cleanly designed **www.go-amsterdam.org** includes an extensive "A–Z Index" with listings for museums, hotels, transportation, and other categories. One of the best virtual tours on the Net is **www.channels.nl**—the images are clear, you can direct your own tour, and you can chat with others about Amsterdam. Visitors offer their impressions of restaurants, hotels, museums, and hash houses. At **www. amsterdamhotspots.nl**, they mean "hot." Here are *the* places to fill your nights, from eating and drinking to where to toke, what the top gay bars are, and where to see those famous working girls on display behind picture windows.

CITY LAYOUT   Amsterdam center is small enough that its residents think of it as a village. However, as villages go, it can be confusing until you get the hang of it. The concentric rings of major canals are its defining characteristic, along with several important squares that act as focal points. It's easy to think you're headed in one direction along the canal ring, only to find out you're going in exactly the opposite direction. A map is essential. VVV offices have maps and

Amsterdam

guides, including the small but detailed VVV Amsterdam map, which sells for 4Dfl (€1.80, $1.75).

The city can be divided into six major touristic neighborhoods: **Center,** the oldest part of the city, around the Dam and Centraal Station; **Canal Zone,** the semicircular "necklace" of waterways that curves through the Center; **Jordaan,** a nest of small streets and canals west of the Center; **Museumplein,** a gracious residential area around the Rijksmuseum, Van Gogh Museum, and Stedelijk Museum, and including Vondelpark; **Amsterdam South,** the most prestigious modern residential area; and **Amsterdam East,** a residential area beyond the Amstel, with a multiethnic population.

There are six major squares. The Dam is the heart of the city, encircled by the Royal Palace, Nieuwe Kerk, department stores, hotels, and restaurants. Leidseplein, and the streets around it, is Amsterdam's Times Square, glittering with restaurants, cafes, nightclubs, discos, performance centers, and movie theaters. Rembrandtplein is another entertainment center, bustling with restaurants, cafes, and a casino. Museumplein and Waterlooplein are the cultural hubs, with the Rijksmuseum, Concertgebouw, Van Gogh Museum, and Stedelijk Museum of Modern Art all in and around the former, and the Muziektheater (plus a great flea market) at the latter. Muntplein is a transportation hub, identified by the Munt Tower, dating from 1620.

GETTING AROUND The public transportation system, GVB/Amsterdam Municipal Transport, runs daily from 6am to around midnight (trams start at 7:30am on Sunday). Night buses run on a limited service, usually one per hour.

A **single-journey ticket** (*enkeltje*) costs from 3 to 7.50Dfl (€1.35 to €3.40, $1.30 to $3.25) depending on how many zones you travel through, though tourists rarely travel beyond the city center zone. You can buy a **day ticket** (*dagkaart*), valid for the day of purchase and the night following, from any tram or bus driver, conductor, or ticket dispenser for 12Dfl (€5.45, $5.20). Also available are tickets valid for from 2 to 9 days, priced from 16 to 42.25Dfl (€7.25 to €19.20, $7 to $18); you purchase them from the GVB/Amsterdam Municipal Transport ticket booths outside Centraal Station. Bear in mind that you need to take a lot of trams for day and multiday cards to be worthwhile.

If you plan to do a lot of walking and only occasionally take trams around the city center, you're probably better off with a *strippenkaart* (strip card) that you can use throughout your stay. You can buy an eight-strip card for 12Dfl (€5.45, $5) from drivers and conductors, or a more cost-effective 15-strip card (12Dfl/€5.45/$5) and 45-strip card (35.25Dfl/€16/$15) from train and metro stations, GVB/Amsterdam Municipal Transport ticket booths, post offices, and many news vendors. The card is easy to use: Fold at the line and punch it in the validating machine aboard the tram and at metro platforms. On some trams a conductor at the rear validates the card; on buses, the driver does it.

Validated cards can be used for any number of transfers between lines and modes of transportation, within 1 hour of the time stamped on them at validation and within the paid-for number of zones.

Most tram/bus shelters and all metro stations have maps showing the entire system. A detailed map is available from VVV tourist offices and GVB/Amsterdam Municipal Transport ticket booths on Stationsplein in front of Centraal Station, or call transportation information (© **0900/9292**), Monday to Saturday from 7am to 10pm and Sunday from 8am to 10pm.

BY TRAM & BUS Riding the distinctive yellow trams is easily the best way of getting around; it's fast, cheap, and fun, and provides a great view of the sights. Of 17 tram routes in the city, 11 begin and end at Centraal Station. An extensive bus network complements the trams, and reaches to many points that the trams don't cover.

BY METRO   Amsterdam has four metro lines that run partly underground and are primarily used to get people to and from suburbs and new business districts.

BY TAXI   Officially, you can't simply hail a cab, but often they stop if you do. Otherwise, call **Taxi Centrale** (✆ **020/677-7777**) or find one of the taxi stands sprinkled around town, generally close to the luxury hotels, at major squares such as the Dam, Rembrandtplein, and Leidseplein, and outside train stations. Taxis are metered and fares—which include a service charge—begin at 5.80Dfl (€2.65, $2.50) when you get in and run up at the rate of 2.85Dfl (€1.30, $1.25) per kilometer, or about 4.60Dfl (€2.10, $2) per mile. For a water taxi, call ✆ **020/622-2181.**

BY BICYCLE   Follow the Dutch example and cycle. Sunday, when the city is quiet, is a good day to pedal through the parks and to practice riding on cobblestones and dealing with trams before venturing into the rush-hour fray. Bike-rental rates average 12.50Dfl (€5.70, $5) per day or 60Dfl (€27.25, $26) per week, with a deposit required. You can rent bikes from **MacBike,** Mr. Visserplein 2 (✆ **020/620-0985**); **MacBike Too,** Marnixstraat 220 (✆ **020/626-6964**); and **Bike City,** Bloemgracht 70 (✆ **020/626-3721**).

BY CAR   Don't rent a car to get around Amsterdam—you'll regret the expense and hassle. The city is a jumble of one-way streets, narrow bridges, cyclists darting every which way, vigorously enforced no-parking zones, and ruinously high charges where you are allowed to park. In addition, car break-ins are common, particularly at night.

Outside the city, driving is another story; you may want to rent a car for a trip into the country. Call **Avis,** Hogehilweg 7 (✆ **020/430-9611**); **Budget,** Overtoom 121 (✆ **020/612-6066**); or **Hertz,** Overtoom 333 (✆ **020/612-2441**).

BY WATER BUS   The **Canal Bus** (✆ **020/623-9886**) runs daily from 10am to 5pm and has three routes—Green, Red, and Blue—that connect important museums, and shopping and entertainment districts. There are two buses an hour at peak times. A day pass, valid until noon next day and including a discount on museum admissions, costs 29.50Dfl (€13.40, $13) adults and 17.50Dfl (€7.95, $8) children age 13 and under.

C FAST FACTS: Amsterdam

American Express   Offices are at Damrak 66 (✆ **020/504-8777;** tram: 4, 9, 16, 20, 24, or 25) and Van Baerlestraat 39 (✆ **020/673-8550;** tram: 2, 3, 5, 12, or 20). Both are open from Monday to Friday 9am to 5pm and Saturday 9am to noon. The Damrak office books tours and excursions and offers a full range of services, including currency exchange. The Van Baerlestraat office only books tours and excursions.

Business Hours   **Banks** are open from Monday to Friday from 9am to 4 or 5pm (some until 7pm on Thursday). Regular **shopping** hours are Monday 10 or 11am to 6pm; Tuesday, Wednesday, and Friday 9am to 6pm; Thursday 9am to 9pm; Saturday 9am to 5pm; and Sunday (some stores only) noon to 5pm.

Currency From January 1, 2002 the monetary unit in the Netherlands is the new European currency, the euro. During a transition period of some months, the old Dutch **guilder** will still be legal tender, though gradually being withdrawn from circulation. You often see it written as **Dutch florins** (abbreviated ƒ, fl, Hfl, or **Dfl**); since this is a holdover from the past, ignore the written symbol and read all prices as guilders. There are 100 Dutch cents to a guilder. The exchange rate used in this chapter is $1 = 2.30Dfl or 1Dfl = 45¢. Also, €1 = 2.2Dfl and £1 = 3.50Dfl.

Currency Exchange Change your money at **VVV tourist offices,** or if you carry American Express traveler's checks, at **American Express,** Damrak 66 (see above), where there's no commission charge. Other fair-dealing options are the **GWK exchanges** at Schiphol Airport and Centraal Station, which also handle money transfers via Western Union.

Doctors & Dentists Contact the Central Medical Service at ℂ **020/592-3434.**

Drugstores In Holland a pharmacy is called an *apotheek.* Try **Dam Apotheek,** Damstraat 2 (ℂ **020/624-4331;** tram: 4, 9, 14, 16, 20, 24, or 25). All pharmacies have the name of an all-night pharmacy posted on the door.

Embassies & Consulates The **U.S. Consulate** is at Museumplein 19 (ℂ **020/ 575-5309;** tram: 3, 5, 12, 16, or 20); the U.S. Embassy is at Lange Voorhout 102, The Hague (ℂ **070/310-9209**). The **U.K. Consulate-General** is at Koningslaan 44 (ℂ **020/676-4343;** tram: 2); the British Embassy is at Lange Voorhout 10, The Hague (ℂ **070/364-5800**).

Citizens of other English-speaking countries should contact their embassies in The Hague: **Australia,** Carnegielaan 14, Den Haag (ℂ **070/ 310-8200**); **Canada,** Sophialaan 7, Den Haag (ℂ **070/311-1600**); **Ireland,** Dr. Kuyperstraat 9, Den Haag (ℂ **070/363-0993**); **New Zealand,** Mauritskade 25, Den Haag (ℂ **070/346-9324**); and **South Africa,** Wassenaarseweg 40, Den Haag (ℂ **070/392-4501**).

Emergencies In an emergency, dial ℂ **112** to call the police, report a fire, or summon an ambulance.

Internet Access If you don't mind surfing and e-mailing in an Internet "factory," head for one of the two city stores run by **easyEverything** (www.easyeverything.com), which between them have 800 PCs: Damrak 33 (ℂ **020/320-8082;** tram: 1, 2, 4, 5, 9, 13, 16, 17, 20, 24, or 25); and Reguliersbreestraat 22 (ℂ **020/320-6291;** tram: 4, 9, 14, or 20); both are open 24 hours a day and access begins at 2.50Dfl (€1.15, $1.10). A less crowded choice is **The Internet Café,** Martelaarsgracht 11 (ℂ **020/627-1052;** info@internetcafe.nl; tram: 1, 2, 5, 13, 17, 20). It's open Sunday to Thursday 9am to 1am, Friday to Saturday 9am to 3am; access is 6Dfl (€2.75, $2.60) an hour.

Post Office The main post office is at Singel 250–256 (ℂ **020/556-3311;** tram: 13, 14, 17, or 20), at the corner of Radhuisstraat. It's open from Monday to Friday 9am to 6pm and Saturday 9am to 3pm.

Telephone The country code for the Netherlands is **31.** The city code for Amsterdam is **20** from outside the Netherlands, **020** inside the country (no code at all if you're in the city).

A local call in Amsterdam costs 0.50Dfl (€0.25, 20¢) for 3 minutes. Most pay phones in the Netherlands accept only phone cards, which are sold at newsstands, post offices, tobacconists, and railway stations for 10Dfl (€4.55, $4.35), 25Dfl (€11.35, $11), and 50Dfl (€22.70, $22). On both coin and card phones, watch the digital reading, which tracks your decreasing deposit so you know when to add more coins or another card. For information inside the country, call © **0900/8008;** for international information, dial © **0900/8418.**

To charge a call to your calling card, call **AT&T** (© **0800/022-9111); MCI** (© **0800/022-9122); Sprint** (© **0800/022-9119); Canada Direct** (© **0800/ 022-9116); or British Telecom** (© **0800/022-9944).**

WHERE TO STAY

Most Amsterdam hotels, whatever their cost, are clean and tidily furnished, and in many cases they've been recently renovated or redecorated. Booking ahead is always advised. The Dutch hotel industry runs a free hotel-booking service: the **NRC/Netherlands Reservations Center,** P.O. Box 404, 2260 AK Leidschendam (© **070/419-5500;** fax 070/419-5519).

If you arrive in Amsterdam without a reservation, the **VVV tourist offices** inside and outside Centraal Station will help you for the modest charge of 5Dfl (€2.25, $2.15) per person. Or call the VVV's **Amsterdam Reservation Center** at © **0777/000-888.**

If you need to stay close to the airport, try the **Sheraton Amsterdam Airport,** Schiphol Boulevard 101, 1118 BG Schiphol Airport (© **800/325-3535** in the U.S. and Canada, or 020/316-4300; fax 020/316-4399; www.sheraton.com/ amsterdam). You have all the comfort you would expect of a top-flight Sheraton. Doubles cost 710 to 870Dfl (€322.70 to €395.45, $309 to $379). For a cheaper option, try the **Dorint Schiphol Amsterdam,** Sloterweg 299, 1171 VB Badhoevedorp (© **020/658-8111;** fax 020/658-8100; www.dorint.de). Doubles cost 380 to 440Dfl (€172.70 to €200, $165 to $191).

VERY EXPENSIVE

American Hotel ⋩⋩   The location is hard to beat if you want to be right where the action is. Some rooms overlook kaleidoscopic Leidseplein, others the tranquil Singelgracht canal. A melding of neo-Gothic and *Jugendstil* (Art Nouveau) architecture, the American has been a city landmark and meeting place since the early 1900s. Rooms are decorated in Art Deco style, with clean lines and subtle lighting. Dine in the magnificent Art Deco Café Américain (see "Where to Dine," later in this chapter), and watch the street life from the Nightwatch Bar's glassed-in sidewalk terrace.

Leidsekade 97 (facing Leidseplein), 1017 PN Amsterdam. © 020/624-5322. Fax 020/625-3236. www. interconti.com. 188 units. 550–650Dfl (€250–€295.45, $239–$283) double; 750Dfl (€340.90, $326) suite; add 5% city tax. AE, DC, MC, V. Limited street parking. Tram: 1, 2, 5, 6, 7, 10, or 20 to Leidseplein. **Amenities:** Restaurant (international), bar; health club; sauna; concierge; 24-hour room service; laundry service; dry cleaning. *In room:* A/C, TV w/ pay movies, minibar, hair dryer, safe.

Golden Tulip Grand Hotel Krasnapolsky ⋩   One of the city's landmarks, the "Kras," as it's known locally, began life in 1866 as the Wintertuin (Winter Garden) restaurant, which still dominates the hotel's ground floor. The size and shape of the rooms vary, with 36 converted into mini-apartments. Recent

> **Tips** **A Canal-House Warning**
>
> Be prepared to climb hard-to-navigate stairways if you want to save money on lodging in Amsterdam. Narrow and steep as ladders, these stairways were designed to conserve space in the narrow houses along the canals. Today they're an anomaly that'll make your stay even more memorable. If you have difficulty climbing stairs, and your hotel has no elevator, ask for a room on a lower floor.

enhancements include a new wing with a Japanese garden and Dutch roof garden. The Winter Garden is complemented by the French Brasserie Reflet, the Japanese Edo and Kyo restaurants, and the Bedouin Shibli.

Dam 9 (facing the Royal Palace), 1012 JS Amsterdam. ℭ **020/554-9111.** Fax 020/622-8607. www. krasnapolsky.nl. 469 units. 650–690Dfl (€295.45–313.65, $283–$300) double; 980–1,495Dfl (€445.45–€679.55, $426–$650) suite; add 5% city tax. Children under 2 stay free in parents' room; children 2–12 charged half price. AE, DC, MC, V. Valet and self-parking 45Dfl (€20.45, $20). Tram: 4, 9, 14, 16, 20, 24, or 25 to the Dam. **Amenities:** 5 restaurants (continental, French, Japanese, Arabic), 2 bars; health club; sauna; concierge; salon; 24-hour room service; laundry service; dry cleaning. *In room:* A/C, TV w/ pay movies, minibar, coffeemaker, hair dryer, safe.

Hôtel de l'Europe 🏰🏰🏰   Built in 1896, the De l'Europe has a grand style and sense of ease. Its pastel-red-and-white facade overlooks the Amstel where it runs into the city's canal network. Rooms and bathrooms are spacious and bright, furnished with classic good taste. Some have minibalconies on the river. About 20 units are updated each year. Dine in the highly regarded Excelsior or in the less formal Le Relais restaurants. Le Bar and La Terrasse (summer only) serve drinks and hors d'oeuvres daily. There's a waterside cafe terrace in summer.

Nieuwe Doelenstraat 2–8 (facing Muntplein), 1012 CP Amsterdam. ℭ **800/223-6800** in the U.S. and Canada, or 020/531-1777. Fax 020/531-1778. www.leurope.nl. 100 units. 670–770Dfl (€304.55–€350, $291–$335) double; suites from 900Dfl (€409, $391); add 5% city tax. AE, DC, MC, V. Valet parking 6Dfl (€2.70, $2.60) per hour. Tram: 4, 9, 14, 16, 20, 24, or 25 to De Munt. **Amenities:** 2 restaurants (French), 2 bars; heated indoor pool; health club; sauna; concierge; 24-hour room service; massage; laundry service; dry cleaning. *In room:* A/C, TV w/ pay movies, minibar, hair dryer, safe.

EXPENSIVE

Dikker & Thijs Fenice 🏰🏰   Small and homey, this hotel reveals a cozy character behind its stylish facade. Spacious rooms, tastefully styled in a modern version of Art Deco, are clustered in groups of two or four around small lobbies, which makes the hotel feel more like an apartment building. Double-glazed windows eliminate the noise from Leidsestraat. Rooms at the front have a great view of Prinsengracht.

Prinsengracht 444 (at Leidsestraat), 1017 KE Amsterdam. ℭ **020/626-7721.** Fax 020/625-8986. www. dikkerenthijsfenice.nl. 26 units. 450–495Dfl (€204.55–€225, $195.65–$215.20) double. Rates include continental breakfast. Children 12 and under stay free in parents' room. AE, DC, MC, V. Limited street parking. Tram: 1, 2, or 5 to Prinsengracht. **Amenities:** Restaurant (French/Italian); bar; concierge; room service; laundry service; dry cleaning. *In room:* TV w/ pay movies, minibar, hair dryer, safe.

Estheréa 🏰   Family-owned and occupying neighboring 17th-century canal houses, the Estheréa has the intimacy and personality of a much smaller establishment. Most rooms and bathrooms are good size; several have extra beds, making them ideal for families. There's a comfortable lounge and bar. As an added touch, the hotel offers guests free coffee and tea. The Greek Traîterie Grekas restaurant next door delivers room-service meals.

Singel 303–309 (close to Spui), 1012 WJ Amsterdam. (C) **020/624-5146.** Fax 020/623-9001. www. estherea.nl. 70 units. 395–475Dfl (€179.55–€215.90, $172–$207) double; add 5% city tax. One child 12 and under may stay free in parents' room. AE, DC, MC, V. Limited street parking. Tram: 1, 2, or 5 to Spui. **Amenities:** Lounge; concierge; limited room service; laundry service; dry cleaning. *In room:* TV, minibar, hair dryer, safe.

Golden Tulip Schiller ☆☆   A blend of Jugendstil (Art Nouveau) and Art Deco, whose sculpted facade, wrought-iron balconies and stained-glass windows stand out on brash Rembrandtplein, the Schiller was constructed by painter/hotelier Frits Schiller during the 1890s, and no fewer than 600 of his works are on view inside. Rooms are tastefully decorated in modern style. You can dine in the oak-paneled Brasserie Schiller, and join the in crowd for a drink in the Art Deco Café Schiller next door.

Rembrandtplein 26–36, 1017 CV Amsterdam. (C) **020/554-0777.** Fax 020/626-6831. www.goldentulip.com. 92 units. 420–530Dfl (€190.90–€240.90, $182.60–$230.45) double; 750Dfl (€340.90, $326.10) suite. AE, DC, MC, V. Limited street parking. Tram: 4, 9, 14, or 20 to Rembrandtplein. **Amenities:** Restaurant (Dutch), bar; 24-hour room service; laundry service; dry cleaning. *In room:* TV, minibar (some rooms), coffeemaker.

Jan Luyken ☆   In a residential neighborhood 1 block from the P.C. Hooftstraat's classy stores, this is best described as a small hotel with many of the amenities and facilities of a big one. Rooms are classically furnished; bathrooms modern. The owners are proud of the setting they've created and are constantly improving the hotel's facilities.

Jan Luykenstraat 54–58 (close to Van Gogh Museum), 1071 CS Amsterdam. (C) **020/573-0730.** Fax 020/ 676-3841. www.janluyken.nl. 62 units. 370–540Dfl (€168.20–€245.45, $161–$235) double. Children under 4 stay free in parents' room; extra person 85Dfl (€38.65, $37). Rates include buffet breakfast. AE, DC, MC, V. Limited street parking. Tram: 2, 5, or 20 to Van Baerlestraat; 3 or 12 to Eerste Constantijn Huygensstraat. **Amenities:** Lounge; health club; Jacuzzi; sauna; limited room service. *In room:* A/C, TV, safe.

MODERATE

Amsterdam Wiechmann ☆   It takes only a moment to feel at home in the antique-adorned lobby. Owned for years by American T. Boddy and his Dutch wife, Nicky, the Wiechmann is comfortable and casual. Like a good wine, it gets better with age, and the location is one of the best you'll find in this or any price range. Most rooms are standard, with twin or double beds, some have big bay windows. Higher-priced doubles have antique furnishings, and many have a canal view.

Prinsengracht 328–332 (at Looiersgracht), 1016 HX Amsterdam. (C) **020/626-3321.** Fax 020/626-8962. www.hotelwiechmann.nl. 40 units. 250–300Dfl (€113.65–€136.35, $109–$130) double. Rates include continental breakfast. No credit cards. Limited street parking. Tram: 1, 2, or 5 to Prinsengracht. **Amenities:** Lounge; breakfast room. *In room:* TV, safe.

Apollofirst ☆   Intimate and elegant, this family-owned hotel, set amid the Amsterdam School architecture on Apollolaan, advertises itself as the "best quarters in town in the town's best quarter." That boast may be debatable, but all rooms are quiet, spacious, and grandly furnished. Those at the back overlook well-kept gardens as well as the summer terrace where guests can have a snack or a cocktail. There's an elegant French restaurant, the Chambertin.

Apollolaan 123 (off Minervalaan), 1077 AP Amsterdam. (C) **020/673-0333.** Fax 020/675-0348. apolfi@xs4all.nl. 38 units. 325Dfl (€147.70, $141) double; 495Dfl (€225, $215) suite. Rates include buffet breakfast. AE, DC, MC, V. Limited street parking. Tram: 5 or 24 to Beethovenstraat. **Amenities:** Restaurant (French), bar; 24-hour room service; laundry service; dry cleaning. *In room:* TV.

Canal House ☆☆   A contemporary approach to reestablishing the elegant canal-house atmosphere has been taken by the owner of this small hotel in an effort to create a home away from home. Three adjoining houses dating from

1630 were rebuilt to provide private bathrooms, and then filled with antiques, quilts, and Chinese rugs. Room 26 has a panoramic view of the canal. The elegant breakfast room, seemingly unchanged since the 17th century, overlooks the back garden, and there's a cozy Victorian-style saloon.

Keizersgracht 148 (close to Leliegracht), 1015 CX Amsterdam. ℂ 020/622-5182. Fax 020/624-1317. www. canalhouse.nl. 26 units. 265–365Dfl (€120.45–€165.90, $115–$159) double. Rates include continental breakfast. DC, MC, V. Limited street parking. Tram: 13, 14, 17, or 20 to Westermarkt. **Amenities:** Lounge; breakfast room; limited room service. *In room:* hair dryer.

De Filosoof ⚘   On a quiet street close to Vondelpark, one of the owners, a philosophy professor, has chosen posters, painted ceilings, framed quotes, and used unusual objects to represent philosophical and cultural themes. Rooms are dedicated to Goethe, Wittgenstein, Nietzsche, Marx, and Einstein or based on motifs like Eros, the Renaissance, astrology, and women. Rooms in an annex across the street are larger; some open onto a private terrace. All-round improvements in services and facilities raised the hotel's local rating from two to three stars in 2000.

Anna van den Vondelstraat 6, 1054 GZ Amsterdam. ℂ 020/683-3013. Fax 020/685-3750. www.xs4all. nl/~filosoof. 28 units. 215–245Dfl (€97.70–€111.35, $94–$107) double. Rates include buffet breakfast. AE, MC, V. Limited street parking. Tram: 1 or 6 to Overtoom. **Amenities:** Lounge. *In room:* TV.

Die Port van Cleve ⚘⚘   Oozing history and class, one of the city's oldest hotels began its life in 1864 as the first Heineken brewery. Behind the ornamental facade, complete with turrets and alcoves, rooms, though on the small side, are comfortably furnished in modern yet cozy style. You won't eat better Dutch food than in the Brasserie de Poort, and you can drink in the Bodega de Blauwe Parade watched over by Delft Blue tiles.

Nieuwezijds Voorburgwal 176–180 (behind the Royal Palace), 1012 SJ Amsterdam. ℂ 020/624-4860. Fax 020/622-0240. www.dieportvancleve.com. 120 units. 365–445Dfl (€165.90–€202.25, $158.70–$193.50) double; 650–780Dfl (€295.45–€354.55, $283–$339) suite; extra person 95Dfl (€43.20, $41). Rates include buffet breakfast. AE, DC, MC, V. Limited street parking. Tram: 1, 2, 5, 13, 14, 17, or 20 to the Dam. **Amenities:** Restaurant (Dutch); bar; limited room service; dry cleaning. *In room:* TV w/ pay movies, minibar (some rooms), hair dryer.

Seven Bridges ⚘   Owners Pierre Keulers and Gunter Glaner have made this one of the city's gems, and it has recently been virtually rebuilt inside, to provide every room with a bathroom. Some attic rooms have sloped ceilings and exposed wood beams. Big, bright basement rooms are done almost entirely in white. Decor includes handmade Italian drapes, hand-painted tiles, and wood-tiled floors.

Reguliersgracht 31, 1017 LK Amsterdam. ℂ 020/623-1329. 10 units. 250–400Dfl (€113.65–€181.80, $109–$174) double. Rates include full breakfast. AE, MC, V. Limited street parking. Tram: 16, 24, or 25 to Keizersgracht. **Amenities:** Lounge. *In room:* TV.

INEXPENSIVE

Acacia   Fronting a canal in the Jordaan, this well-kept hotel is run by Hans and Marlene van Vliet, who've worked hard to make it welcoming. Rooms, recently furnished with new beds, tables, and chairs, are simple but comfortable, and all have writing tables. Breakfast is served in a triangular breakfast room, with windows on both sides giving a nice view of the canal. A houseboat for guests on nearby Lijnbaansgracht adds an authentic local touch.

Lindengracht 251 (off Prinsengracht and Brouwersgracht), 1015 KH Amsterdam. ℂ 020/622-1460. Fax 020/638-0748. www.hotelnel.nl. 18 units. 155Dfl (€70.45, $67) double; 235Dfl (€106.80, $102) houseboat double. Rates include full breakfast. MC, V. Parking 25Dfl (€11.35, $11). Tram: 3 to Nieuwe Willemstraat. **Amenities:** Breakfast room. *In room:* TV.

Amstel Botel ⟨⟩   Where better to experience a city built on water than on a boat-hotel? Launched in 1993, the boat has become very popular because of its location, adventurous quality, and comfort at reasonable rates. Turn left out of Centraal Station, pass the bike rental, and you see it floating in front of you. Four decks accommodate the modernly furnished cabins. Be sure to ask for a room with a view on the water side, not on the uninspiring quay side.

Oosterdokskade 2–4 (beside Centraal Station), 1011 AE Amsterdam. ℂ 020/626-4247. Fax 020/639-1952. 176 units. 159Dfl (€72.25, $69) double. AE, DC, MC, V. Limited parking on quay. Tram: 1, 2, 4, 5, 9, 13, 16, 17, 20, 24, or 25 to Centraal Station. **Amenities:** Lounge; concierge; dry cleaning. *In room:* TV w/ pay movies.

Piet Hein ⟨⟩   Occupying a villa close to the city's most important museums, the Piet Hein is named after a Dutch folk hero, a 17th-century admiral who captured a Spanish silver shipment. Rooms are spacious and well furnished, and the staff friendly and professional. Half the rooms overlook the park; two second-floor doubles have semicircular balconies; and there is a honeymoon suite with waterbed. Lower-priced rooms are in an annex.

Vossiusstraat 52–53 (facing Vondelpark), 1071 AK Amsterdam. ℂ 020/662-7205. Fax 020/662-1526. www. hotelpiethein.com. 36 units. 165–225Dfl (€75–€102.25, $72–$98) double. Rates include continental breakfast. AE, DC, MC, V. Limited street parking. Tram: 2 or 5 to Paulus Potterstraat. **Amenities:** Concierge; limited room service; baby-sitting; laundry service; dry cleaning. *In room:* TV w/ pay movies, hair dryer (on request).

Prinsenhof   Owners Rik and André van Houten take pride in their hotel, a modernized canal house close to the Amstel River, and make you feel welcome. Most rooms are large, with basic yet reasonably comfortable beds. The hotel has recently been redecorated, and new showers and carpets installed. Front rooms look out onto the Prinsengracht, where colorful houseboats are moored. Breakfast is served in an attractive dining room. There's no elevator, but a pulley hauls your luggage up and down the stairs.

Prinsengracht 810 (at Utrechtsestraat), 1017 JL Amsterdam. ℂ 020/623-1772. Fax 020/638-3368. www. hotelprinsenhof.com. 10 units, 2 with bathroom. 125Dfl (€56.80, $54) double without bathroom; 165Dfl (€75, $72) double with bathroom. Rates include continental breakfast. AE, MC, V. Limited street parking. Tram: 4 to Prinsengracht. *In room:* TV.

Van Ostade Bicycle Hotel ⟨⟩   The young owners have hit on an interesting idea: They cater to visitors who wish to explore Amsterdam on bikes and they are helpful in planning biking routes through and around the city. You can rent bikes for only 10Dfl (€4.55, $4.35) daily, no deposit, and stable your trusty steed indoors. The recently renovated rooms have new carpets and plain but comfortable modern furnishings; some have kitchenettes and small balconies, and there are large rooms for families. The hotel is a few blocks from the popular Albert Cuyp street market, in the somewhat raggedy De Pijp neighborhood. An old bike hangs on the hotel's facade, and there are always bikes parked in front.

Van Ostadestraat 123 (off Ferdinand Bolstraat), Amsterdam 1072 SV. ℂ 020/679-3452. Fax 020/671-5213. www.bicyclehotel.com. 16 units, 8 with bathroom. 125–140Dfl (€56.80–63.65, $54–$61) double without bathroom; 185Dfl (€84.10, $80) double with bathroom. Rates include continental breakfast. No credit cards. Parking 30Dfl (€13.65, $13). Tram: 24 or 25 to Ceintuurbaan. *In room:* TV.

WHERE TO DINE

As a trading and gateway city that positively revels in its status as a melting pot, Amsterdam has absorbed culinary influences from far and wide. Just about any international cuisine can be found on the city's restaurant roster. In general, with the exception of late-night restaurants, kitchens in Amsterdam take their last dinner orders at 10 or 11pm. Restaurants with outside terraces are always in big demand on pleasant summer evenings, and few take reservations. One way to

---

Moments   A True Amsterdam Dining Experience

You haven't really eaten in Amsterdam until you've had an **Indonesian** *rijsttafel* **dinner**, a traditional "rice table" banquet of as many as 20 succulent and spicy foods served in tiny bowls. Pick and choose from among the bowls and add your choice to the pile of rice on your plate. It's almost impossible to eat all the food set on your table, but give it a shot—it's delicious. For an abbreviated version served on one plate, try *nasi rames*. At lunch, the standard Indonesian fare is *nasi goreng* (fried rice with meat and vegetables) or *bami goreng* (fried noodles prepared in the same way). My suggestion of where to have your first *rijsttafel* is **Kantjil en de Tijger** (see below).

---

combat escalating dinner tabs is to take advantage of the low-cost *dagschotel* (plate of the day) offered by many restaurants. Good eating out info is available from **www.dinner-in-amsterdam.nl**.

VERY EXPENSIVE

La Rive 🌟🌟 CLASSICAL FRENCH   Chef Robert Kranenborg has created a menu combining the finesse of classical French cuisine with the modern trend toward lighter, healthier eating. Luxury isn't forgotten either. The freshest seasonal fish and game is enhanced by sauces of truffles, cèpes, and foie gras. The setting is intimate but formal (a jacket is required for men), and several tables are next to the tall French windows that overlook the Amstel.

In the Amstel Intercontinental Hotel, Professor Tulpplein 1 (off Weesperstraat). ℭ 020/520-3273. Main courses 50–130Dfl (€22.70–€59.10, $22–$57); fixed-price menus 135–195Dfl (€61.35–€88.65, $59–$85). AE, DC, MC, V. Mon–Fri noon–2pm; Mon–Sat 6:30–10:30pm. Tram: 6, 7, 10, or 20 to Sarphatistraat.

EXPENSIVE

De Silveren Spiegel 🌟🌟🌟 TRADITIONAL DUTCH/ CLASSICAL FRENCH   The two houses forming the premises were constructed in 1614 for wealthy soapmaker Laurens Jansz Spieghel. It's typically Old Dutch inside, with the bar downstairs and more dining rooms where the bedrooms used to be. There's a garden in back, and the whole place emanates a traditionally Dutch tidiness that's very welcoming. The updated menu features finely prepared seafood and meat dishes, such as baked sole filets with wild spinach, and Texel lamb with ratatouille; traditional Zaanse mustard is always available.

Kattengat 4–6 (off Singel). ℭ 020/624-6589. Main courses 47.50–55Dfl (€21.60–€25, $21–$24); set-price menus 75–85Dfl (€34.10–€38.65, $33–$37). AE, MC, V. Daily 6–11pm (open for lunch on reservation). Tram: 1, 2, 5, 13, 17, or 20 to Martelaarsgracht.

D'Vijff Vlieghen 🌟 MODERN DUTCH   Occupying five canal houses, the restaurant is a kind of Dutch theme park with seven dining rooms decorated with artifacts from Holland's golden age. Don't miss the four original Rembrandt etchings and the collection of handmade glass. Yes, it's touristy, but at the "Five Flies," the food is authentic stick-to-the-ribs Dutch fare. The chef is passionate about an updated form of Dutch cuisine he calls "the new Dutch kitchen." The menu offers a selection of seasonal fish and game often marinated with fresh herbs and served with unusual vegetables such as chard, wild spinach, and brussels sprouts. If you're feeling adventurous, try the wild boar with sweet chestnuts and gin sauce.

Spuistraat 294–302 (entrances on Singel and Spuistraat). ℂ 020/624-8369. Main courses 47–58Dfl (€21.35–€26.35, $20–$25); set-price menus 75–97.50Dfl (€34.10–€44.30, $33–$42). AE, DC, MC, V. Daily 5:30–10.30pm. Tram 1, 2, or 5 to Spui.

Gare de l'Est ☆ *Value* TRADITIONAL FRENCH/MEDITERRANEAN The detached, distinctive house, with a recently added conservatory and a large sidewalk terrace, was originally a coffeehouse for workers at the docks. Service is both relaxed and knowledgeable, and as the fixed-price menu is excellent value for money, any surprises appear on your plate rather than on the check. The strict five-course formula (starter, salad, main course of meat or fish, cheese, and dessert) leaves no room for choice—except for the main course. How does this sound . . . *pulpo stofado* with *risotto nero* (inkfish stew with black risotto) as a starter, and roast lamb with gazpacho sauce and farfalle pasta as a main course? Cruquiusweg 9 (at the East Harbor). 020/463-0620. Reservations recommended. Fixed-price menu 52Dfl (€23.65, $23). No credit cards. Daily 6–11pm. Tram: 7 or 10 to Zeeburgerdijk; bus: 39 or 59 to Cruquiusweg.

Mangerie de Kersentuin ☆☆ INTERNATIONAL All cherry red and gleaming brass, the "Cherry Orchard" has floor-to-ceiling windows overlooking a residential street and semi-screened interior windows looking into the glimmering kitchen. It follows its own unique culinary concept, based on regional recipes from around the world, using fresh ingredients from Dutch waters and farmlands. The menu changes every 2 months, but you might find such dishes as lamb filet prepared in goose fat with creamy salsifies and coriander-scented vanilla sauce; or sea bass sautéed with peppers, garlic, sea salt, and sesame seeds, served on stir-fried bok-choy and tofu, with lemongrass butter. In the Bilderberg Garden Hotel, Dijsselhofplantsoen 7 (off Apollolaan). ℂ 020/664-2121. Reservations recommended on weekends. Main courses 42.50–49Dfl (€19.30–€22.25, $19–$21); set-price menus 52.50–72.50Dfl (€23.85–€32.95, $23–$32). AE, DC, MC, V. Mon–Fri noon–2pm; Mon–Sat 6–11pm. Tram: 5 or 24 to Apollolaan; 16 to De Lairessestraat.

't Swarte Schaep ☆ TRADITIONAL DUTCH In a house from 1687, the "Black Sheep" still seems like an Old Dutch home. You climb a steep flight of tiled steps to reach the second-floor dining room, where the beams and ceiling panels are dark with age. It's a cozy, almost crowded place made both fragrant and inviting by the fresh flowers on every table and those that spill from the polished brass buckets hanging from the ceiling beams. The "Black Sheep" is well known for its wine list and its crepes Suzette. Other menu items might include sole meunière with asparagus or grilled salmon with fresh thyme. Korte Leidsedwarsstraat 24 (at Leidseplein). ℂ 020/622-3021. Main courses 45–55Dfl (€20.45–€25, $20–$24); fixed-price menu 77.50Dfl (€35.20, $34). AE, DC, MC, V. Daily noon–11pm. Tram: 1, 2, 5, 6, 7, or 10 to Leidseplein.

MODERATE

Amsterdam ☆☆ *Finds* CONTINENTAL This restaurant in a century-old water-pumping station was an instant hit when it opened in the redeveloping Westerpark district. It's a little bit out of the way, but easily worth the tram ride. You dine amid a buzz of conviviality in the big, brightly lit former pumping hall. Service is breezy, the food is good, and the menu long. The emphasis is on seafood, but lots of meat and vegetarian dishes are offered too. If you're feeling flush, you could spring for a double starter of a half lobster with six Zeeland oysters. Watertorenplein 6 (off Haarlemmerweg). ℂ 020/682-2666. Reservations recommended on weekends. Main courses 17.50–40Dfl (€7.95–€18.20, $8–$17). AE, DC, MC, V. Daily 11:30am–1am. Tram: 10 to Van Halstraat.

Bodega Keyser ⊛ TRADITIONAL DUTCH   Whether or not you attend a concert at the Concertgebouw, you may want to plan a visit to its next-door neighbor. An Amsterdam landmark since 1903, the Keyser has enjoyed a colorful joint heritage with the world-famous concert hall. There's an elegance here that combines traditional dark-and-dusky decor and highly starched pink linens. The menu leans heavily toward local fish and, in season, game specialties, such as hare and venison.

Van Baerlestraat 96 (beside the Concertgebouw). ✆ **020/671-1441**. Main courses 39.50–67.50Dfl (€17.95–€30.70, $17–$29); fixed-price menu 65Dfl (€29.55, $28). AE, DC, MC, V. Mon–Sat 9am–midnight; Sun 11am–midnight. Tram: 2 to Willemsparkweg; 3, 5, 12, or 20 to Van Baerlestraat; 16 to De Lairessestraat.

Bolhoed ⊛⊛ VEGETARIAN   Forget the wholesome, dull, corn-sheaf-and-brown-rice image of vegetarian dining—Bolhoed adds a touch of spice to its health food formula with its Latin style, world music background, candlelight in the evenings, and fine view of the canal from its twin rooms beside the Prinsengracht. Service is zestful and friendly. Try such veggie delights as the *ragoût croissant* (pastry filled with leeks, tofu, seaweed, and curry sauce), or *zarzuela*. If you want to go whole hog, so to speak, and eat vegan, most of Bolhoed's dishes can be so prepared on request, and in any case most are made with organically grown produce.

Prinsengracht 60–62 (near Noordermarkt). ✆ **020/626-1803**. Main courses 22.50–27.50Dfl (€10.25–€12.50, $10–$12). No credit cards. Sun–Fri noon–11pm; Sat 11am–11pm. Tram: 13, 14, 17, or 20 to Westermarkt.

Café Américain ⊛ INTERNATIONAL   Café Américain is a national monument of Dutch Jugendstil and Art Deco. Mata Hari held her wedding reception here in her pre-espionage days, and since its 1900 opening, the place has been a haven for Dutch and international artists, writers, dancers, and actors. Leaded windows, newspaper-littered reading tables, bargello-patterned velvet upholstery, frosted-glass chandeliers from the 1920s, and tall, carved columns are all part of the dusky sit-and-chat setting. Menu dishes include monkfish, perch, rack of Irish lamb, and rosé breast of duck with creamed potatoes. Jazz lovers can stock up on good music at a Sunday jazz brunch.

In the American Hotel, Leidsekade 97 (at Leidseplein). ✆ **020/556-3232**. Main courses 35–52Dfl (€15.90–€23.65, $15–$23). AE, DC, MC, V. Daily 7am–12:30am. Tram: 1, 2, 5, 6, 7, or 10 to Leidseplein.

De Belhamel ⊛⊛ CONTINENTAL   Classical music complements Art Nouveau in a graceful setting overlooking the Herengracht and Brouwersgracht canals. The menu changes seasonally, and game is a specialty. You can expect such menu dishes as puffed pastries layered with salmon, shellfish, crayfish tails, and chervil beurre-blanc to start; and beef tenderloin in Madeira sauce with zucchini rösti and puffed garlic for a main course. They serve vegetarian dishes, too.

Brouwersgracht 60 (at Herengracht). ✆ **020/622-1095**. Reservations recommended. Main courses 28.50–39.50Dfl (€12.95–€17.95, $12–$17); specials 32.50Dfl (€14.75, $14). AE, MC, V. Daily 6pm–midnight. Tram: 1, 2, 5, 13, 17, or 20 to Martelaarsgracht.

Haesje Claes TRADITIONAL DUTCH   If you're yearning for a cozy Old Dutch environment and hearty Dutch food at moderate prices, go to Haesje Claes. It's an inviting, intimate place with lots of nooks and crannies and with brocaded benches and traditional Dutch hanging lamps. The menu covers a lot of ground, ranging from canapés to caviar, but you'll be happiest with such Dutch stalwarts as omelets, tournedos, *hutspot* (stew), *stampot* (mashed potatoes and cabbage), or various fish stews, including those with IJsselmeer paling (eel).

Spuistraat 275 (beside Spui). ℂ 020/624-9998. Main courses 24.50–34.50Dfl (€11.15–€15.70, $11–$16). AE, DC, MC, V. Daily noon–midnight. Tram: 1, 2, or 5 to Spui.

Kantjil en de Tijger 𝒦 INDONESIAN   Unlike Indonesian restaurants that wear their ethnic origins on their sleeve, the "Antelope and the Tiger" is modern and cool. Two best-sellers are *nasi goreng Kantjil* (fried rice with pork kebabs, stewed beef, pickled cucumbers, and mixed vegetables) and the 20-item *rijsttafel* (rice with meat, seafood, and vegetables) for two. Other choices are stewed chicken in soja sauce, tofu omelet, shrimp with coconut dressing, Indonesian pumpkin, and mixed steamed vegetables with peanut-butter sauce. Finish with the multilayered cinnamon cake or the coffee with ginger liqueur and whipped cream.

Spuistraat 291–293 (beside Spui). ℂ 020/620-0994. Main courses 22.50–30.50Dfl (€10.25–€13.85, $10–$13); rijsttafel 77.50–97.50Dfl (€35.25–€44.30, $34–$42). AE, DC, MC, V. Daily 4:30–11pm. Tram: 1, 2, or 5 to Spui.

Kort 𝒦𝒦 CONTINENTAL   This is one of the few restaurants that takes reservations for evening dining outdoors in good weather. On the edge of a canal and a wide, open square, the tree-shaded terrace is far enough away from traffic to be unaffected by noise. Service is friendly, and menu dishes include excellent vegetarian choices, such as grilled goat's cheese with spinach and salad. Look also for the Eastern spiced fish, a house specialty. Dining indoors in the restored 17th-century Amstelkerk is recommended too, with fancier table sets than outside.

Amstelveld 12 (at Prinsengracht). ℂ 020/626-1199. Reservations required for sidewalk terrace. Main courses 35–45Dfl (€15.90–€20.45, $15–$20); menus 50–70Dfl (€22.75–€31.80, $22–$30). AE, DC, MC, V. Summer daily 11:30am–midnight; winter Wed–Mon 11:30am–midnight. Tram: 4 to Prinsengracht.

Tempo Doeloe INDONESIAN   For authentic Indonesian cuisine this place is hard to beat, though its local reputation seems to go up and down with the tide. The attractive decor, fresh linen tablecloths, and fine china are unexpected pluses: You eat in an ambience that is Indonesian, of course, but not to the extent of being kitsch. If anything, this restaurant errs on the side of elegance and restraint. Try the *rijsttafel*, the *nasi koening*, or any of the vegetarian dishes. Finish with the *spekkoek*, a layered spice cake. Beware that when a dish is described on the menu as *pedis*, or hot, that's exactly what it is.

Utrechtsestraat 75 (between Herengracht and Keizersgracht). ℂ 020/625-6718. Main courses 25.50–62.50Dfl (€11.60–€28.40, $11–$27); rijsttafel 49.50Dfl (€22.50, $22) and 59.50Dfl (€27.25, $26). AE, DC, MC, V. Daily 6–11:30pm. Tram: 4 to Utrechtsestraat.

INEXPENSIVE

De Jaren CONTINENTAL   This big cafe has 300 seats inside and 150 more on a terrace beside the Amstel River. Students from the nearby campus often lunch here, contributing to its informality. Originally a bank, the renovated building has unusually high ceilings and a tiled mosaic floor. You can enjoy everything from a cup of coffee or a glass of *jenever* (potent Dutch gin) to spaghetti bolognese and rib-eye steak.

Nieuwe Doelenstraat 20–22 (close to Muntplein). ℂ 020/625-5771. Main courses 18–30Dfl (€8.20–€13.65, $7.85–$13.05); fixed-price menus 38–45Dfl (€17.25–€20.45, $17–$20). No credit cards. Daily 10am–1am; Fri–Sat until 2am. Tram: 4, 9, 16, 20, 24, or 25 to the Munt.

De Prins 𝒦𝒦 MODERN DUTCH/CONTINENTAL   This companionable, brown cafe (bar) and restaurant opposite the Anne Frankhuis serves the kind of food you'd expect from a much more expensive place. The clientele is loyal, so the relatively few tables fill up quickly. It's a quiet neighborhood restaurant—nothing fancy or trendy, but quite appealing, housed in a 17th-century canal house, with the bar on a slightly lower level than the restaurant, and a sidewalk terrace for drinks in summer.

Prinsengracht 124 (at Leliegracht). ℂ 020/624-9382. Reservations not accepted. Main courses 12–25Dfl (€5.45–€11.35, $5–$11); plate of the day 20.50Dfl (€9.30, $9); specials 23.50–28.50Dfl (€10.70–€12.95, $10–$12). AE, DC, MC, V. Daily 10am–1 or 2am. Tram: 13, 14, 17, or 20 to Westermarkt.

Keuken van 1870 TRADITIONAL DUTCH   This is one of the cheapest and plainest places to eat in Amsterdam. Opened in 1870 as a public soup kitchen, it serves meals cafeteria-style. Tables are bare, and menu dishes are basic, but the food is good. Pork chops, fish, and chicken—all accompanied by vegetables and potatoes—are some of the main courses on the menu. It's a good place to go if you're on a tight budget.

Spuistraat 4 (at Martelaarsgracht). ℂ 020/624-8965. Reservations not accepted. Main courses 9–18.50Dfl (€4.10–€8.40, $4–$8). AE, DC, MC, V. Mon–Fri 12:30–8pm; Sat–Sun 4–9pm. Tram: 1, 2, 5, 13, 17, or 20 to Martelaarsgracht.

La Place LIGHT SNACKS/CONTINENTAL   This vast, multilevel food depot has something for everyone. The ground floor offers thick slabs of quiche, an assortment of pizzas, and deliciously flavored fresh breads—the cheese-onion loaf is a meal in itself. An airy, glass-topped cafeteria covers the three upstairs floors. Menu dishes include a meat or fish of the day, often with an Indonesian touch, along with vegetables and potatoes. Vegetarians love the soup and salad selection, and there's an assortment of freshly squeezed fruit juices.

Rokin 160 (close to Muntplein). ℂ 020/622-0171. Main courses 7.50–17.50Dfl (€3.40–€7.95, $3.25–$8). MC, V. Mon–Sat 9:30am–8pm; Sun 11am–8pm. Tram: 4, 9, 14, 16, 20, 24, or 25 to Muntplein.

Pancake Bakery ⭐ *Kids* PANCAKES   This two-story canal-house restaurant serves almost nothing but pancakes—an appropriate choice for any meal. The satisfyingly large pancakes come adorned with all sorts of toppings, both sweet and spicy, including Cajun chicken (on the spicy end of the taste spectrum), ice cream and liqueur (on the sweet end), and curried turkey with pineapple and raisins (for a little bit of both). The windows provide a pretty view out over the Prinsengracht. In the summertime you can dine outside at long wooden tables, but beware: All the syrup, honey, and sugar being passed around tends to attract bees and hornets. Nonetheless, the Pancake Bakery remains a firm local favorite, especially among children.

Prinsengracht 191 (near Westermarkt, a block from the Anne Frankhuis). ℂ **020/625-1333**. Reservations required for large groups. Pancakes 8–20Dfl (€3.65–€9.10, $3.50–$9). AE, MC, V. Daily noon–9:30pm. Tram: 13, 14, 17, or 20 to Westermarkt.

SEEING THE SIGHTS
SIGHTSEEING SUGGESTIONS FOR FIRST-TIME VISITORS

If You Have 1 Day   For the perfect introduction to the city, take a **canal cruise** and admire the many gabled merchants' houses and almost 1,200 bridges. In the afternoon, visit the **Rijksmuseum** to view Rembrandts and works by other golden age masters. In the evening, dine at a traditional restaurant or opt for an Indonesian *rijsttafel*, and end your day by dropping into a brown cafe (a traditional Amsterdam bar, see later in this chapter).

If You Have 2 Days On day 2, visit the **Anne Frank house** in the morning. In the afternoon, explore the historic center on foot, visiting the **Dam** and the **Royal Palace** and other major squares. In the evening attend a concert at the Concertgebouw, or opera or dance at the Muziektheater (book ahead).

If You Have 3 or More Days On day 3, take in the **Van Gogh Museum** in the morning. Relax over coffee at the Café Américain, with its stunning Art Nouveau interior. Look into some **street markets,** either the Albert Cuyp market, the floating Flower Market, or the Waterlooplein flea market. In the evening, take a walk in the Red Light District. (If this isn't your idea of an edifying experience, consider the alternative dining option from day 1.)

THREE KEY MUSEUMS

Anne Frankhuis 🏮🏮 Anne Frank kept her famous diary here, while she and seven other Jewish refugees hid during World War II in a secret annex at the back of this large canal house. The cramped, gloomy hiding place, where they maintained nearly total silence, kept them safe for more than 2 years until they were betrayed and pro-Nazi Dutch police raided their refuge, tragically close to the war's end. Anne, age 15, and six of the other *onderduikers* (divers or hiders) died in concentration camps. The rooms are as bare as they were when Anne's father, Otto, the only survivor, returned. This lack of distraction allows you to project yourself into Anne's claustrophobic, fear-filled world. A new wing next door mounts temporary exhibits on themes such as intolerance and racism. *Note:* Lines here can be very long, especially in summer—try going on a weekday morning; once inside, an hour should do it, though many people linger.

Prinsengracht 263 (beside Westermarkt). ℂ 020/556-7100. Admission 12.50Dfl (€5.70, $5.45) adults, 5Dfl (€2.25, $2.15) children 10–17; free for children under 10. Apr–Aug daily 9am–9pm; Sept–Mar daily 9am–5pm. Tram: 13, 14, 17, or 20 to Westermarkt.

Rijksmuseum 🏮🏮🏮 The architectural legacy of Holland's 17th-century golden age is all around you in Amsterdam. For the artistic lowdown, head to the neo-Gothic Rijksmuseum, opened in 1885. It holds the world's largest collection of paintings by the Dutch masters. You won't want to miss Rembrandt's famous *The Night Watch* 🏮🏮 (1642)—but neither do all other visitors, so your viewing experience is likely to be a jostled one. The space is more tranquil in front of equally masterful works by Rembrandt, Jan Vermeer, Frans Hals, Jacob van Ruysdael, Maerten van Heemskerck, Paulus Potter, Jan Steen, Pieter de Hooch, Gerard Terborch, Gerard Dou, and many more. Fra Angelico, Tiepolo, Goya, Rubens, Van Dyck, and later artists of the Hague School and the Amsterdam Impressionist movement are also represented. You also find prints and sculpture, furniture, Asian and Islamic art, china and porcelain, trinkets and glassware, armaments and ship models, 17th-century dollhouses, costumes,

---

Value **Passport to Amsterdam**

The **Amsterdam Culture & Leisure Pass** is a sound investment if you plan to do a lot of sightseeing. Around 30 coupons allow free entry into top museums, a free canal cruise and diamond factory tour, and discounts on many other attractions and purchases. The pass costs 41.50Dfl (€18.85, $18) and is available from any of the city's VVV tourist offices or from Holland Tourist Information at Schiphol Plaza.

screens, badges, and laces. You could easily spend all day in the Rijksmuseum; 4 hours will suffice for a quick dip.

Stadhouderskade 42 (behind Museumplein). © **020/673-2121** or 020/674-7047 for taped information in English. Admission 17.50Dfl (€7.95, $8) adults, 7.50Dfl (€3.40, $3.25) children 6–18; free for children under 6. Daily 10am–5pm. Tram: 2, 5, or 20 to Hobbemastraat; 6, 7, or 10 to Spiegelgracht.

Van Gogh Museum ᴀᴀᴀ   Step through the portals and you enter into the imagination of Vincent van Gogh, arguably the world's best-known and best-loved artist—though he was neither of these during his short life. The largest van Gogh collection has more than 200 paintings that proceed chronologically through the seven distinct periods of his career. Look out for the famous *Sunflowers,* and van Gogh's last painting, *Cornfield with Crows,* whose mood seems to presage his suicide in 1890, age 37. Van Gogh drawings, and paintings by contemporaries such as Toulouse-Lautrec, Gauguin, Monet, Sisley, and others, complete the picture. *Note:* Lines here can be very long, especially in summer—try going on a weekday morning; allow 2 to 4 hours.

Paulus Potterstraat 7 (at Museumplein). © **020/570-5200.** Admission 15.50Dfl (€7.05, $7) adults, 5Dfl (€2.25, $2.15) children 13–17, free for children under 13. Daily 10am–6pm. Tram: 2, 5, or 20 to Van Baerlestraat; 3, 12, or 16 to Museumplein.

HISTORIC BUILDINGS & MONUMENTS

Begijnhof   Formerly an almshouse for *begijns,* pious laywomen involved in religious and charitable work, this beautiful cloister of small homes around a 14th-century garden courtyard makes for a perfect escape from the city's bustle. In the southwest corner stands one of two surviving timber houses in Amsterdam, from the 15th century. (The city authorities banned construction of timber houses in 1452 after a series of disastrous fires.) Most of the tiny 17th- and 18th-century buildings still house the city's elderly poor, and you should respect their privacy, especially after sunset. Allow an hour.

Gedempte Begijnensloot (at Spui). No telephone. Free admission. Daily until sunset. Tram: 1, 2, or 5 to Spui.

Koninklijk Paleis (Royal Palace)   The 17th-century neoclassical Royal Palace was Amsterdam's town hall for 153 years. It was first used as a palace during the 5-year rule of Louis Bonaparte (Napoleon's brother) in the early 19th century. You can visit its high-ceilinged Citizens' Hall, Burgomasters' Chambers, and Council Room, as well as the Vierschaar—a marble tribunal where death sentences were pronounced during the 17th century. Although this is the monarch's official palace, Queen Beatrix rarely uses it for more than occasional receptions or official ceremonies.

Dam. © **020/620-4060.** Admission 8Dfl (€3.65, $3.50) adults, 6Dfl (€2.75, $2.60) seniors and children 13–18, 2.50Dfl (€1.15, $1.10) children 5–12, free for children under 5. Easter and June–July daily 10am–5:30pm; Aug–Oct daily 12:30–5pm; otherwise, generally Tues–Thurs 12:30–5pm; closed mid-Dec to mid Feb. (Opening days and hours are highly variable, and it's best to check before going.) Tram: 1, 2, 4, 5, 9, 13, 14, 16, 17, 20, 24, or 25 to the Dam.

MUSEUMS & GALLERIES

Amsterdams Historisch Museum ᴀ   In a huge 17th-century former city orphanage that has been beautifully redesigned, this fascinating museum gives you a better understanding of everything you see as you explore the city. Gallery by gallery, century by century, you learn how a small fishing village became a major world trading center. You can also view many famous paintings by Dutch masters in the context of their time and place. Next to the museum is the **Schuttersgalerij** (Civic Guard Gallery), a narrow, two-story skylit chamber bedecked

---

(*Finds*) The World's Smallest Art Museum

Amsterdam boasts the world's smallest art museum, **Reflex**, Weteringchans 79A, opposite the Rijksmuseum (© **020/627-2832; tram: 6, 7, or 10**). It's only 13.2 square meters (140 sq. ft.) large and displays 1,500 miniature paintings, graphics, sculptures, and pictures, including works by Picasso, Lichtenstein, Oldenburg, and Christo. Admission is free, and it's open from Tuesday to Saturday 10am to 6pm.

---

with a dozen large 17th-century group portraits of militiamen. The hours are the same as for the museum, and admission is free.

Kalverstraat 92 and Nieuwezijds Voorburgwal 359 (next to the Begijnhof). © 020/523-1822. Admission 12Dfl (€5.45, $5) adults, 6Dfl (€2.75, $2.60) children 6–15, free for children under 6. Mon–Fri 10am–5pm; Sat–Sun 11am–5pm. Tram: 1, 2, 4, 5, 9, 14, 16, 20, 24, or 25 to Spui.

Joods Historisch Museum (Jewish Historical Museum)   In the restored Ashkenazi Synagogue complex, this museum tells the intertwining stories of Jewish identity, religion, culture, and history in the Netherlands through objects, photographs, artworks, and interactive displays. Take time to appreciate the beauty of the buildings, which include Europe's oldest public synagogue.

Jonas Daniel Meijerplein 2–4 (facing Waterlooplein). © 020/626-9945. Admission 10Dfl (€4.55, $4.35) adults, 4.50Dfl (€2.05, $1.95) children 13–18, 2.50Dfl (€1.15, $1.10) children 6–12, free for children under 6. Daily 11am–5pm. Tram: 9, 14, or 20 to Waterlooplein.

Museum Het Rembrandthuis   Rembrandt had to leave his home of 19 years in 1658 because of bankruptcy. Restoration has returned it to the way it looked when Rembrandt lived and worked here. About 120 of the museum's 250 Rembrandt etchings, including self-portraits and landscapes, hang on the walls at any one time and you can see the artist's printing press. Temporary exhibitions are mounted in an adjacent house that belonged to Rembrandt's wife, Saskia. *Note:* To avoid the crowds, try going early on a weekday morning.

Jodenbreestraat 4–6 (at Waterlooplein). © 020/520-0400. Admission 12.50Dfl (€5.70, $5.45) adults, 2.50Dfl (€1.15, $1.10) children 6–15, free for children under 6. Mon–Sat 10am–5pm; Sun and holidays 1–5pm. Tram: 9, 14, or 20 to Waterlooplein.

Nederlands Scheepvaartmuseum (Netherlands Maritime Museum)   A former Amsterdam Admiralty arsenal overlooking Amsterdam harbor provides the backdrop for rooms of ships, ship models, and seascapes. Old maps include a 15th-century Ptolemaic atlas and a sumptuously bound edition of the *Great Atlas* by Jan Blaeu, master cartographer of Holland's golden age. Among the historic papers on display are several pertaining to Nieuwe Amsterdam (New York City) and Nieuwe Nederland (New York State). A full-size replica of the Dutch East India Company sailing ship *Amsterdam*, which foundered in 1749 off Hastings, England, is moored at the wharf.

Kattenburgerplein 1 (in the Eastern Dock). © 020/523-2222. Admission 12.50Dfl (€5.70, $5) adults, 8Dfl (€3.65, $3.50) children 17 and under. Tues–Sat 10am–5pm (also Mon mid-June to mid-Sept); Sun noon–5pm. Bus: 22 or 32 to Kattenburgerplein.

Stedelijk Museum   The city's modern art museum centers its collection around De Stijl, CoBrA (an expressive, abstract style from the 1950s) and post-CoBrA painting, nouveau réalisme, pop art, color-field painting, zero and minimalist art, and conceptual art. On display are works by such Dutch painters as

Karel Appel, Willem de Kooning, and Piet Mondrian; French artists Chagall, Cézanne, Picasso, Renoir, Monet, and Manet; and Americans Calder, Oldenburg, Rosenquist, and Warhol. The museum houses the largest collection outside Russia of abstract painter Kasimir Malevich.

Paulus Potterstraat 13 (at Museumplein). ℂ 020/573-2737. Admission 10Dfl (€4.55, $4.35) adults, 4.50Dfl (€2.05, $1.95) children 7–16, free for children under 7. Daily 11am–5pm. Tram: 2, 5, or 20 to Van Baerlestraat; 3, 12, or 16 to Museumplein.

Tropenmuseum (Tropical Museum)   Built by the Royal Tropical Institute in the 19th century, as a monument to the nation's empire, this museum is now devoted to contemporary culture and problems in tropical areas. Its most interesting exhibits are walk-through model villages that capture daily life (minus the inhabitants) in such places as India and Indonesia; tools and techniques used to produce batik, the distinctively dyed Indonesian fabric; and instruments and ornaments you would find in a tropical residence. A new permanent exhibition covers West Asia and North Africa. A section of the museum, **Kindermuseum TM Junior** (ℂ 020/568-8300), is open only to children 6 to 12 (one adult per child is allowed).

Linnaeusstraat 2 (at Mauritskade). ℂ 020/568-8215. Admission 15Dfl (€6.80, $7) adults, 12.50Dfl (€5.70, $5) children 6–17, free for children under 6. Mon–Fri 10am–5pm; Sat–Sun and holidays noon–5pm. Tram: 7, 9, 10, or 14 to Mauritskade.

CHURCHES & A SYNAGOGUE
The most important places of worship in Amsterdam are the 14th-century **Nieuwe Kerk,** Dam (ℂ **020/638-6909;** tram: 1, 2, 4, 5, 9, 13, 14, 16, 17, 20, 24, or 25), Holland's coronation church; 17th-century **Westerkerk** ⟨, Westermarkt (ℂ **020/624-7766;** tram: 13, 14, 17, or 20), which has the tallest, most beautiful tower in Amsterdam (take the elevator to the top for a great view) and is the burial place of Rembrandt; 14th-century **Oude Kerk,** Oudekerksplein (ℂ **020/625-8284;** metro: Nieuwmarkt), in the Red Light District, surrounded by almshouses turned into prostitutes' rooms; and the ornate 17th-century **Portuguese Synagogue,** Mr. Visserplein (ℂ **020/624-5351;** tram: 9, 14, or 13), facing the Jewish Historical Museum.

OTHER SIGHTS & ATTRACTIONS
Homomonument   Dedicated to the gays and lesbians who were killed during World War II, this sculpture group of pink marble triangles also is a place of remembrance for those who've died of AIDS.

Westermarkt. Tram: 13, 14, 17, or 20 to Westermarkt.

Holland Experience   A multidimensional film and theater show takes you through the landscapes and culture of Holland at different historical periods up to the present. Exhibitions include farming and fishing scenes. A simulated dike collapse, during which 80,000 liters of water pour toward you, gives a taste of what would happen if the sea should ever break through the coastal defenses. The toilets (I can vouch only for the men's) look like the deck of a ship passing along the Dutch coast, and even sport marine sound effects and a salty breeze.

Waterlooplein 17. ℂ 020/422-2233. Admission 19.50Dfl (€8.85, $9) adults, 16Dfl (€7.25, $7) seniors and children under 13. Daily 10am–10pm. Tram: 9, 14, or 20 to Waterlooplein.

PARKS & GARDENS
Though not obviously green, the city has plenty of parks, including the famous **Vondelpark** ⟨ (tram: 1, 2, 3, 5, 6, 7, 10, 12, 20), formerly a Hippy happy

Diamond-Cutting Demonstrations

Though a diamond-cutting demonstration will probably consist of a lone polisher working at a small wheel in the back of a jewelry store or in the lobby of a factory building, it will still give you an idea of how a diamond is cut and polished.

The main diamond factories and showrooms are the five members of the Diamond Foundation Amsterdam: **Amsterdam Diamond Center,** Rokin 1, off the Dam (© **020/624-5787;** tram: 4, 9, 14, 16, 20, 24, or 25); **Coster Diamonds,** Paulus Potterstraat 2–6, close to the Rijksmuseum (© **020/676-2222;** tram: 2, 5, or 20); **Gassan Diamonds,** Nieuwe Uilenburgerstraat 173–175 (© **020/622-5333;** tram: 9, 14, or 20), **Stoeltie Diamonds,** Wagenstraat 13–17 (© **020/623-7601;** tram: 4, 9, 14, or 20); and **Van Moppes Diamonds,** Albert Cuypstraat 2–6, at the street market (© **020/676-1242;** tram: 16, 24, or 25).

camping-ground, and now home to skateboarding, Frisbee-flipping, in-line skating, model-boat sailing, soccer, softball, basketball, open-air concerts and theater, smooching in the undergrowth, parties, picnics, craft stalls, topless sunbathing—you name it. Vondelpark lies generally southwest of Leidseplein, and has entrances all around; the most popular is adjacent to Leidseplein, on Stadhouderskade. Watch out for the tasty-looking "gateau" they sell there, or you may find yourself floating above the trees: Drug-laced space-cake is an acquired taste.

Established in 1682, **Hortus Botanicus (Botanical Garden)** ✿, Plantage Middenlaan 2a (© **020/625-9021;** tram: 9, 14, or 20), near Artis Zoo, is a medley of color and scent, containing 250,000 flowers and 115,000 plants and trees from 8,000 different varieties. It owes its origins to the treasure trove of tropical plants the Dutch found in their colonies Indonesia, Surinam, and the Antilles, and its popularity to the Dutch love affair with flowers. Among highlights are the **Semicircle,** which reconstructs part of the original design from 1682; the **Mexico–California Desert House; Palm House,** with one of the world's oldest palm trees; and the **Tri-Climate House,** which displays tropical, subtropical, and desert plants. Hortus is open from April to September Monday to Friday 9am to 5pm, Saturday and Sunday 11am to 5pm; from October to March Monday to Friday 9am to 4pm, Saturday and Sunday 11am to 4pm. Admission is 10Dfl (€4.55, $4.35) adults, 6Dfl (€2.75, $2.60) children 5 to 14, free for children under 5.

Artis Zoo ✿ *Kids*   The oldest zoo in the Netherlands, established in 1838, houses more than 6,000 animals. Also on the extensive property are a planetarium, aquarium, geological and zoological museum, and children's farm. The aquarium, constructed in 1882 and recently renovated, is well presented, particularly the exhibits on the Amazon River, coral reefs, and Amsterdam's canals, with their fish and garbage.

Plantage Kerklaan 38–40. © **020/523-3400.** Admission 25Dfl (€11.35, $11) adults, 17.50Dfl (€7.95, $8) children 4–11, free for children under 4. Daily 9am–5pm. Tram: 9 or 14 to Plantage Middenlaan.

ROSSE BUURT (RED LIGHT DISTRICT)

Examine the quaint gabled architecture along the narrow canals of this district—oh, yes, and you might also notice certain ladies watching the world go by through their red-fringed windows. The warren of streets around Oudezijds

Achterburgwal and Oudezijds Voorburgwal by the Oude Kerk, also known as De Wallen (The Walls), is one of Amsterdam's most famous destinations. It's extraordinary to see women of all nationalities dressed in exotic underwear and perched in windows, knitting, brushing their hair, or just slinking, enticingly, into their seats, waiting for customers. The district has become a major tourist attraction, not only for customers of storefront sex but for sightseers. If you choose to go there, you need to exercise caution. Stick to the busy streets, particularly at night, and be wary of pickpockets at all times. *Warning:* In a neighborhood where anything seems permissible, the one no-no is taking pictures. Violate this rule and your camera could be removed from you and broken. To get there, take tram 4, 9, 14, 16, 20, 24, or 25 to the Dam, and then pass behind the Grand Hotel Krasnapolsky.

ORGANIZED TOURS

A **canal-boat cruise** ⚓ is the best way to see old Amsterdam and its large and busy harbor. A typical itinerary includes Centraal Station; the Harlemmersluis floodgates; the Cat Boat (a houseboat—one of 2,400 in the city—with a permanent population of more than 100 wayward felines); and both the narrowest building in the city and one of its largest houses still in use as a single-family residence. You may also see the burgomaster's (mayor's) official residence; the "Golden Bend" on Herengracht, traditionally the best address in town; picturesque bridges, including the famous Magere Brug (Skinny Bridge) over the Amstel; and Amsterdam Drydocks.

Trips depart at regular intervals from *rondvaart* (canal circuit) piers in key locations around town and last approximately 1 hour. The majority of launches are docked along Damrak and Prins Hendrikkade close to Centraal Station, on Rokin close to Muntplein, and close to Leidseplein. They leave every 15 to 30 minutes during summer from 9am to 9:30pm; every 45 minutes in winter from 10am to 4pm. Average fare is 12 to 18Dfl (€5.45 to €8.20, $5 to $8) adults, 10 to 12Dfl (€4.55 to €5.45, $4.35 to $5) children 4 to 13. Numerous canal-boat cruise operators offer comparable prices and trips.

A 3-hour bus tour costs 35 to 40Dfl (€15.90 to €18.20, $15 to $17) and includes tickets for a canal cruise. Children 4 to 13 are usually charged half-price. Companies offering tours include **The Best of Holland,** Damrak 34 (© 020/623-1539); **Holland International Excursions,** Dam 6 (© 020/551-2800); **Holland Keytours,** Dam 19 (© 020/624-7304); and **Lindbergh Excursions,** Damrak 26 (© 020/622-2766).

A clever way of putting all that water to use, and a great time-saver for anyone in a hurry, the **Museum Boat,** Stationsplein 8 (© 020/622-2181), motors between major museums close to the canals and harbor and offers as good a view as a regular canal-boat cruise. Stops are made every 30 minutes at seven key spots, providing access to 16 museums. The fare for the whole day, including a discount on museum admissions, is 25Dfl (€11.35, $11) adults, 20Dfl (€9.10, $9) children 13 and under. Half-day tours after 1pm cost 15Dfl (€6.80, $7), no reduction for children; single round-trip tours cost 20Dfl (€9.10, $90) adults, 15Dfl (€6.80, $7) children 13 and under.

Rent a pedal boat from **Canal Bike** (© 020/626-5574) and pedal yourself along the canals. (Amsterdammers scoff at these water bikes, but let them!) They seat two or four; the hourly rate is 15Dfl (€6.80, $7) per person for one or two people, 12.50Dfl (€5.70, $5) per person for three or four. Moorings are at Leidseplein; at Westerkerk, close to the Anne Frankhuis; at Stadhouderskade, between the Rijksmuseum and Heineken Reception Center; and at Toronto

Bridge on Keizersgracht, close to Leidsestraat. You can rent a pedal boat at one mooring and leave it at another.

THE SHOPPING SCENE

Best buys include special items the Dutch produce to perfection, or produced to perfection in the past and now retail as antiques—Delftware, pewter, crystal, and old-fashioned clocks—or commodities in which they have significantly cornered a market, like diamonds. If cost is an important consideration, remember the Dutch also have inexpensive specialties, such as cheese, flower bulbs, and chocolate.

For jewelry, trendy clothing, and athletic gear, try the department stores around the Dam and shops on Kalverstraat and Leidsestraat. For fashion, antiques, and art, shop on Van Baerlestraat, P.C. Hooftstraat, and Nieuwe Spiegelstraat. For fashion boutiques and funky little specialty shops, or a good browse through a flea market or secondhand store, the Jordaan district, Reestraat, Hartenstraat, Wolvenstraat, and Runstraat are particularly good choices.

MARKETS

All types of foods, clothing, flowers, plants, and textiles adorn the stalls at the **Albert Cuyp Markt,** Albert Cuypstraat (tram: 4, 16, 24, or 25), open 6 days a week. Every Friday there's a secondhand book market on Spui (tram: 1, 2, or 5), with around 25 booths.

The **Floating Flower Market,** a row of barges permanently moored on the Singel at Muntplein (tram: 4, 9, 14, 16, 20, 24, or 25), sells fresh-cut flowers, plants, ready-to-travel packets of tulip bulbs, and home gardening accessories. Buying flowers here is an Amsterdam ritual. The **Sunday Art Market,** at Thorbeckeplein (tram: 4, 9, 14, or 20), runs from March to December, with sculptures, paintings, jewelry, and mixed-media pieces by local artists.

You find everything and anything at the **Waterlooplein Flea Market,** Waterlooplein (metro: Waterlooplein; tram: 9, 14, or 20). On Sunday during summer (late May to September), the junk is replaced by antiques and books. **Kunst & Antiekcentrum de Looier,** Elandsgracht 109 (✆ 020/624-9038; tram: 7, 10, or 20), is a big indoor antiques market that spreads through several old warehouses along the Jordaan canals. Individual dealers rent booths and corners to show their best wares: antique jewelry, prints, and engravings.

STORES WORTH A VISIT

The city's top department store, with the best selection of goods and a great cafe, is **De Bijenkorf,** Dam 1 (✆ 020/621-8080; tram: 4, 9, 14, 16, 20, 24, or 25).

Focke & Meltzer, P.C. Hooftstraat 65–67 (✆ 020/664-2311; tram: 2, 5, or 20), is the best one-stop shop for authentic Delft Blue and Makkumware porcelain, Hummel figurines, Leerdam crystal, and a world of other fine china, porcelain, silver, glass, and crystal. Unless you simply must have brand-name articles, you can save considerably on hand-painted pottery at **Heinen,** Prinsengracht 440, off Leidsestraat (✆ 020/627-8299; tram: 1, 2, or 5), and even watch the product being made.

A landmark amid P.C. Hooftstraat's fashionable stores, **A. van der Meer,** P.C. Hooftstraat 112 (✆ 020/662-1936; tram: 2, 5, or 20), is a quiet place to enjoy antique maps, prints, and engravings, including 17th- and 18th-century Dutch world maps. The crafts and curios on sale at **Blue Gold Fish,** Rozengracht 17 (✆ 020/623-3134; tram: 13, 14, 17, or 20), cover a wide range of ceramics, jewelry, household items (including colorful lamps), and textiles, running the gamut from chic to kitsch.

Opened in 1743, **Jacob Hooy & Co.,** Kloveniersburgwal 10–12 (© **020/ 624-3041;** metro: Nieuwmarkt), is a wonderland of fragrant smells offering more than 500 different herbs and spices, along with 30 different teas, sold loose by weight. Everything is stored in wooden drawers and barrels with the name hand-scripted in gold. Lining the counter are fishbowl jars with 30 different types of *dropjes* (drops or lozenges). **H. P. de Vreng en Zonen,** Nieuwendijk 75 (© **020/624-4581;** tram: 1, 2, 5, 13, 17, or 20), creates Dutch liqueurs and gins using old-fashioned methods. Try Old Amsterdam *jenever* or some of the more flamboyantly colored brews, like the brilliant green Pruimpje *prik in.*

P. G. C. Hajenius, Rokin 92–96 (© **020/623-7494;** tram: 4, 9, 14, 16, 20, 24, or 25), has been the city's leading purveyor of cigars and smoking articles since 1826. Cigars are the house specialty, and there's a room full of Havanas. They also sell long, handmade clay pipes of the kind you see in Old Dutch paintings, and ceramic pipes. A big array of best-sellers, paperbacks, hardcover editions, and magazines is available at **American Book Center,** Kalverstraat 185 (© **020/625-5537;** tram: 4, 9, 14, 16, 20, 24, or 25).

AMSTERDAM AFTER DARK

Amsterdam has highly regarded orchestras, ballet, and opera companies, a strong jazz tradition, and a thriving club and dance-bar scene. Its brown cafes—typical Amsterdam bars (see "Brown Cafes," below)—are a highlight of any visit. Cabarets and theaters can be counted on for English-language shows on a regular basis.

Your best source of information on nightlife and culture is the VVV tourist office's monthly *What's On in Amsterdam.* Many hotels have copies for guests, and you can pick up one at VVV offices for 4Dfl (€1.80, $1.75). *De Uitkrant,* a free monthly magazine in Dutch, has an even more thorough listing of events and is available in performance venues, clubs, and VVV offices.

For tickets to theatrical and musical events (including rock concerts), contact **Amsterdam Uit Buro (AUB) Ticketshop,** Leidseplein 26 (© **020/621-1211**), which can book tickets for almost every venue in town. VVV Amsterdam also books tickets, for a 5Dfl (€2.25, $2.15) fee.

THE PERFORMING ARTS

MUSIC & BALLET Classical music in Amsterdam centers on the world-famous **Royal Concertgebouw Orchestra,** based in the superb Concertgebouw, Concertgebouwplein 2–6 (© **020/671-8345;** www.concertgebouworkest.nl; tram: 3, 5, 12, 16, or 20). Throughout the musical season (September to May) and annual Holland Festival (June to July), the world's greatest orchestras, ensembles, conductors, and soloists travel to Amsterdam to perform here. There are free concerts on Wednesdays at 12:30pm. The box office is open daily from 10am to 7pm, with tickets at 25Dfl to 200Dfl (€11.35 to €90.90, $11 to $87). **The Netherlands Philharmonic Orchestra** and the **Netherlands Chamber Orchestra** both perform at the Beurs van Berlage, Damrak 243 (© **020/ 627-0466;** tram: 4, 9, 14, 16, 20, 24, or 25). The box office is open from Tuesday to Friday 12:30 to 6pm and Saturday noon to 5pm, with tickets at 15Dfl to 55Dfl (€6.80 to €25, $7 to $24).

From September to March, the **Netherlands Opera** produces classics at the Muziektheater, Waterlooplein 22 (© **020/625-5455;** tram: 9, 14, or 20). Also performing at the Muziektheater are two dance companies: The **Dutch National Ballet** and The Hague–based **Nederlands Dans Theater,** whose artistic director/choreographer, Jiří Kylián, has enjoyed great success. The box office is open from Monday to Saturday 10am to 8pm and Sunday 11:30am to 6pm, with tickets at 30 to 125Dfl (€13.65 to €56.80, $13 to $54). Dance performances are occasionally held at the **Felix Meritis Theater,** Keizersgracht 324 (© **020/626-2321;** tram: 1, 2, or 5); the box office opens an hour before performances and tickets are 7.50 to 125Dfl (€3.40 to €56.80, $3.25 to $54).

THEATER   Amsterdammers speak English so well that Broadway road shows and English-language touring companies often make the city a stop on their European itineraries. Broadway and London musicals also come to Amsterdam.

Look for touring shows at **Koninklijke Theater Carré,** Amstel 115–125 (© **020/622-5225;** metro: Wesserplein), but get tickets as far in advance as possible—hot shows sell out fast. The **Stadsschouwburg,** Leidseplein 26 (© 020/624-2311; tram: 1, 2, 5, 6, 7, 10, or 20), is the city's main venue for Dutch theater as well as Dutch and, occasionally, English versions of international plays.

COMEDY THEATER   Compared by *Time* to Chicago's famous Second City troupe, **Boom Chicago Theater,** Leidspleintheater, Leidseplein 12 (© 020/530-7300; tram: 1, 2, 5, 6, 7, 10, or 20), puts on great improvisational comedy, and Dutch audiences have no problem with the English sketches. You can have dinner and a drink while enjoying the show at a candlelit table. It's open daily in summer, closed Sunday in winter. Tickets are 32.50Dfl (€14.75, $14); the restaurant opens at 7pm, and meals cost 20 to 25Dfl (€9.10 to €11.35, $9 to $11).

LIVE-MUSIC CLUBS

Most big-name touring rock and pop acts perform at Ajax soccer club's **Amsterdam Arena,** Arena Boulevard, Amsterdam Zuid-Oost (© **020/311-1313;** metro: Amsterdam Arena). **De IJsbreker,** Weesperzijde 23 (© **020/693-9093;** tram: 3), offers the latest in electronic music and anything else that goes out on a musical limb. It has a good cafe with a terrace beside the Amstel; music usually begins around 8pm. Cover is 15 to 25Dfl (€6.80 to €11.35, $7 to $11).

Bimhuis, Oudeschans 73–77 (© **020/623-1361;** metro: Nieuwmarkt), is relaxed, but serious about jazz. Top musicians, including European and American stars, often perform here. Closed Tuesdays for jazz workshops. Cover from Thursday to Sunday is 15 to 25Dfl (€6.80 to €11.35, $7 to $11). At the small, comfortable **Alto Jazz Café,** Korte Leidsedwarsstraat 115 (© **020/626-3249;** tram: 1, 2, 5, 6, 7, 10, or 20), there's a regular crowd and regular and guest combos in this cafe.

GAY & LESBIAN CLUBS

Amsterdam is the gay capital of Europe, proud of its open and tolerant attitude toward homosexuality. There are lots of bars and dance clubs for gay men all over the city, but fewer lesbian nightspots. Generally the trendier spots are on Reguliersdwarsstraat. You'll find a more casual atmosphere on Kerkstraat close to Leidseplein and leather bars on Warmoesstraat.

Some of the more popular places for men are **Cockring,** Warmoesstraat 96 (© **020/623-9604;** tram: 4, 9, 14, 16, 20, 24, or 25), a gay music-cafe where the music tends toward raunchy; **Café April,** Reguliersdwarsstraat 37 (© 020/623-4254; tram: 1, 2, or 5), and associated **April's Exit,** Reguliersdwarsstraat 42 (© **020/625-8788;** tram: 1, 2, or 5), a disco that attracts a young crowd; **iT,** Amstelstraat 24 (© **020/625-0111;** tram: 9, 14, or 20), a flashy disco with a mixed gay and straight crowd; and **Argos,** Warmoesstraat 95 (© 020/622-6572; tram: 4, 9, 14, 16, 20, 24, or 25), Europe's oldest leather bar. **Saarein,** Elandstraat 119 (© **020/623-4901;** tram: 7, 10, 17, or 20), is a women-only bar; and **Vive la Vie,** Amstelstraat 7 (© **020/624-0114;** tram: 4, 9, 14, or 20), is a lively lesbian bar that hosts occasional parties.

DANCE CLUBS

As long as your attire and behavior suit the management's sensibilities, you should have no problem getting past the bouncer in these clubs. Drinks can be expensive—a beer or Coke averages 10Dfl (€4.55, $4.35), and a whiskey or cocktail 15Dfl (€6.80, $7).

Escape, Rembrandtplein 11 (© **020/622-1111;** tram: 4, 9, 14, or 20), is big and popular, with several dance floors and a capacity of 2,000. Cover is 10 to 20Dfl (€4.55 to €9.10, $4.35 to $9), students free on Thursday. **Melkweg,** Lijnbaansgracht 234a (© **020/624-1777;** tram: 1, 2, 5, 6, 7, 10, or 20), is a former hippie hangout turned multipurpose venue that includes a dance club. Temporary membership (required) is 5Dfl (€2.25, $2.15) for a month; cover is 12 to 35Dfl (€5.45 to €15.90, $5 to $15).

Paradiso, Weteringschans 6–8 (© **020/626-4521;** tram: 1, 2, 5, 6, 7, 10, or 20), presents an eclectic variety of music in a former church. Theme nights range from jazz to raves to disco. Cover is 5 to 35Dfl (€2.25 to €15.90, $2.15 to $15). At **Odeon,** Singel 460 (© **020/624-9711;** tram: 1, 2, or 5), you dance to jazz, funk, house, techno, R&B, or classic disco amid graceful surroundings in a 17th-century canal house. Cover is 7.50 to 12.50Dfl (€3.40 to €5.70, $3.25 to $5). Step on the gas for hip-hop and Latin dance at **West Pacific,** Haarlemmerweg 8–10 (© **020/488-7778;** tram: 10), in the unlikely setting of the Westergasfabriek, a disused gas plant in the Westerpark district that's now a cultural center, restaurant, and bar (open longer hours than the dance club). This place was born hip and has stayed that way, so it's often crowded and hard to get in. It's open from Thursday to Sunday 10pm to 2am (3am on Friday and Saturday). Cover is 5Dfl (€2.25, $2.15) Friday and Saturday.

BROWN CAFES

You haven't tasted Dutch beer until you've tasted it in a traditional *bruine kroeg,* or brown cafe (what Americans would call a bar). Even if you're not a beer lover, brown cafes afford you a peek into the city's everyday life. You find them on almost every corner in old neighborhoods. There is no mistaking them: The smoky, mustard brownness inside comes from centuries of thick smoke and heated conversation. Some have been around since Rembrandt's time. The best are on Prinsengracht, below Westermarkt; at the Dam; on Leidseplein; on Spui; and, with a bit of looking, on tiny streets between canals.

Said to be where the builders of the Westerkerk were paid, **Café Chris,** Bloemstraat 42 (© **020/624-5942;** tram: 13, 14, 17, or 20), opened in 1624 and has some curious old features, including a toilet that flushes from outside the bathroom door. In a medieval alley, wood-paneled **In de Wildeman,** Kolksteeg 3 (© **020/638-2348;** tram: 1, 2, 5, 13, 17, or 20), serves more than 200 kinds of beer. The tile floor and rows of bottles and jars behind the counters are remnants from its early days as a distillery's retail shop. **Hoppe,** Spui 18–20 (© **020/420-4420;** tram: 1, 2, or 5), dating from 1670, has become a tourist attraction, but locals love it too, often stopping for a drink on their way home. It's usually standing-room only, and the crowds overflow onto the street.

At **De Vergulde Gaper,** Prinsenstraat 30 (© **020/624-8975;** tram: 1, 2, 5, 13, 17, or 20), you can retreat into the cozy interior in bad weather, and in good you can sit on a terrace beside the Prinsengracht—in the unlikely event you get a seat. Opened by Pieter Hoppe in 1786 as a liquor distillery/tasting house, **'t Smalle,** Egelantiersgracht 12 (© **020/623-9617;** tram: 13, 14, 17, or 20), is wonderfully cozy, though you probably won't find a seat or even be able to see one. In good weather, a balcony over the canal serves as a terrace.

MODERN CAFES

The Grand Cafe concept, combining drinks and fine food in elegant surroundings, has won plenty of devotees, tired of cramped and crowded brown cafes. Among the best are **Café Luxembourg,** Spuistraat 24 (© **020/620-6264;** tram 1, 2, or 5), a chic rendezvous that takes some of its menu dishes from top eateries around town; and **Royal Cafe De Kroon,** Rembrandtplein 15 (© **020/ 625-2011;** tram: 4, 9, 14, or 20), a mix of Louis XVI and tropical decor, over looking the square. Other chic cafes are **Café Dante,** Spuistraat 320 (© **020/ 638 8839;** tram 1, 2, or 5), whose owners' love of modern art shows itself in a different exhibition every month; and **Café Schiller,** Rembrandtplein 26 (© **020/624-9846;** tram: 4, 9, 14, or 20), whose bright glassed-in terrace on the square and finely carved Art Deco interior make it popular with both artists and writers.

Another notable hangout is **Café Schuim,** Spuistraat 189 (© **020/638-9357;** tram 1, 2, or 5), attracting an assortment of creative types. On summer evenings trendies head to the terrace of **Café Vertigo,** Vondelpark 3 (© **020/612-3021;** tram: 1, 3, 6, or 12), on the edge of the park, for the liveliest scene in town. Inside, low arched ceilings, subtle lighting, and unobtrusive music set a mood of casual sophistication.

2 Side Trips from Amsterdam

HAARLEM

Haarlem, a city of music and art just 20 kilometers (12 miles) west of Amsterdam, is traditionally considered the capital's little sister city.

ESSENTIALS

GETTING THERE   From Amsterdam, Haarlem is 20 minutes by train from Centraal Station; the trains leave about every half hour, and the fare is 10.50Dfl (€4.75, $4.55) round-trip. It can also be reached by frequent bus from outside Centraal Station, costing 6 strips of a strippenkart, about 4.80Dfl (€2.20, $2.10). By car, take A5 and then N5 west.

VISITOR INFORMATION   VVV **Haarlem** is at Stationsplein 1 (© **0900/ 616-1600;** fax 023/534-0537), outside the train station.

EXPLORING HAARLEM

Haarlem is where Frans Hals, Jacob van Ruysdael, and Pieter Saenredam lived and painted portraits, landscapes, and church interiors while Rembrandt was living and working in Amsterdam. Handel and Mozart made special visits to the city to play the magnificent organ of **St. Bavokerk** (St. Bavo's Church), also known as the **Grote Kerk** (Great Church), Oude Groenmarkt 23 (© **023/ 532-4399**). Look for Frans Hals's tombstone, and for a cannonball imbedded in the wall during the Spanish siege (1572–73). Don't miss the 1738 Christian Müller Organ, which has 5,068 pipes and is nearly 30 meters (98 ft.) tall; you can hear it at free concerts on Tuesdays and Thursdays, from April to October. The church is open from Monday to Saturday 10am to 4pm. Admission is 2.50Dfl (€1.15, $1.10) adults, 1.50Dfl (€0.70, 65¢) children under 14.

From St. Bavo's, it's a short walk to the oldest and perhaps most unusual museum in the Netherlands, the **Teylers Museum,** Spaarne 16 (© 023/ 531-9010). It houses drawings by Michelangelo, Raphael, and Rembrandt; fossils, minerals, and skeletons; and an odd assortment of inventions, including the world's biggest electrostatic generator, dating from 1784, and a 19th-century radarscope. The museum is open from Tuesday to Saturday 10am to 5pm and Sunday 1 to 5pm. Admission is 8Dfl (€3.65, $3.50) adults; 4Dfl (€1.80, $1.75) students, seniors, and children 5 to 15; free for children under 5.

Be sure to visit the **Frans Halsmuseum,** Groot Heiligland 62 (© 023/ 516-4200), whose galleries are halls and chambers of a former seniors' home. Famous paintings by Haarlem School masters hang in settings that look like the 17th-century homes they were originally intended to adorn. Open from Monday to Saturday 11am to 5pm, Sunday 1 to 5pm. Admission is 8Dfl (€3.65, $3.50) adults, 4Dfl (€1.80, $1.75) children 10 to 17, free for children under 10.

An ideal way to view the city is by hourly **canal boat cruise,** operated by Woltheus Cruises from their River Spaarne jetty at Gravensteenbrug (© 023/ 535-7723). Cruises are from April to October at 10:30am, noon, 1:30, 3, and 4:30pm.

ZANDVOORT

If you feel like a breath of sea air, do what Amsterdammers do: Head for Zandvoort, 26 kilometers (16 miles) west of Amsterdam, on the North Sea.

ESSENTIALS

GETTING THERE   Trains leave Amsterdam Centraal Station every hour; transfer at Haarlem. During summer, extra trains go direct from Centraal Station. Journey time is 30 minutes, and the fare is 13.50Dfl (€6.15, $6) roundtrip. Buses leave every 30 minutes from outside Centraal Station. You can go by car via Haarlem on A5 and N5, but during summer, there are frequent traffic jams.

VISITOR INFORMATION   VVV Zandvoort is at Schoolplein 1 (© 023/ 571-7947; fax 023/571-7003), opposite the bus station.

EXPLORING ZANDVOORT

There's not much more than a beach, but what a beach. Seemingly endless sands are lined in summertime with beach cafes and discos, and the conditions are good for sail-boarding. Down from the mainstream beaches are gay and nudist beaches.

Holland Casino Zandvoort, Badhuisplein 7 (© 023/571-8044), is one of 10 legal casinos in Holland, with roulette, blackjack, and more. Dress code is "correct" (collar and tie for men), the minimum age is 18, and you need your passport. It's open daily from 1:30pm to 2am. Admission is 6Dfl (€2.75, $2.60).

You find tranquility in the **Kennemer Duinen** and **Amsterdamse Waterleiding Duinen,** protected zones of sand dune and vegetation that play an important role in sea defense. Stroll along paths through woods on the eastern side and across dunes leading west toward the sea.

In town, there's beachy shopping and plenty of eating and drinking possibilities.

DELFT

Delft, 54 kilometers (34 miles) southwest of Amsterdam, is the home of the famous blue-and-white porcelain, but don't let Delftware be your only reason to visit. The small, handsome city is quiet and intimate, with flowers in its flower boxes and linden trees bending over gracious canals. The cradle of the Dutch Republic, Delft is still the burial place of the royal family, and the birthplace and inspiration of artist Jan Vermeer, the 17th-century master of light and subtle emotion.

ESSENTIALS

GETTING THERE   There are trains at least hourly from Amsterdam; the 1-hour trip costs 32Dfl (€14.55, $14) round-trip. By car, Delft is off A13, the main The Hague–Rotterdam expressway.

VISITOR INFORMATION   VVV Delft is at Markt 83–85 (© 015/ 212-6100; fax 015/215-8695).

EXPLORING DELFT

Vermeer's house is long gone from Delft, as are his paintings. But you can visit the **Oude Kerk,** Roland Holstlaan 753 (© 015/212-3015), where he's buried, open from April to October, Monday to Saturday 10am to 5pm. You can also visit the **Nieuwe Kerk,** Markt (© 015/212-3025), where Prince William of Orange (Willem van Oranje) and the other members of the House of Oranje-Nassau are buried. Open from April to October, Monday to Saturday 9am to 6pm; from November to March, Monday to Saturday 11am to 4pm.

The **Prinsenhof Museum,** Sint-Agathaplein 1 (© 015/260-2358), on Oude Delft canal, is where William I of Orange (William the Silent) lived and had his headquarters when he helped found the Dutch Republic. He was assassinated here in 1584, and you can see the musket-ball holes in the stairwell. The Prinsenhof is now a museum of paintings, tapestries, silverware, and pottery. It's open from Tuesday to Saturday 10am to 5pm and Sunday 1 to 5pm (also Monday from 1 to 5pm June to August). Admission is 5Dfl (€2.25, $2.15).

A fine collection of Delft tiles graces the wood-paneled setting of the 19th-century mansion that's now the **Lambert van Meerten Museum,** Oude Delft 199 (© 015/260-2358). It's open from Tuesday to Saturday 10am to 5pm, Sunday 1 to 5pm (closed Sunday from November to March). Admission is 3.50Dfl (€1.60, $1.50).

To view brand-new **Delftware** and see how it's hand painted, visit the factory showroom of **De Porceleyne Fles,** Rotterdamseweg 196 (© 015/256-0234). It's open from April to October, Monday to Saturday 9am to 5pm and Sunday 9:30am to 4pm; from November to March, Monday to Saturday 9am to 5pm. Admission is free.

VOLENDAM & MARKEN

One of these neighboring villages on the IJsselmeer lake is on the mainland, the other on a former island; one is Catholic, the other Protestant; in one, women wear white caps with wings, and in the other, caps with ribbons—but they are often combined on bus-tour itineraries.

ESSENTIALS

GETTING THERE   There are separate, hourly buses to Volendam and Marken from outside Amsterdam's Centraal Station. The fare is 8Dfl (€3.65, $3.50) round-trip; the trip is 35 minutes to Volendam and 45 minutes to Marken.

VISITOR INFORMATION   VVV Volendam is at Zeestraat 37 (© 0299/ 363-747; fax 0299/368-484). Marken has no VVV office.

EXPLORING VOLENDAM & MARKEN

Volendam, 18 kilometers (11 miles) northeast of Amsterdam, is geared for tourism, with souvenir shops, boutiques, and restaurants. Its boat-filled harbor, tiny streets, and traditional houses have an undeniable charm. If you want a snapshot of yourself surrounded by fishermen wearing little caps and balloon-legged pants, Volendammers will gladly pose. They understand that the traditional costume is worth preserving, as is the economy of a small town that lost most of its fishing industry when the Zuiderzee enclosure dam cut it off from the North Sea. You can see such attractions as the fish auction, diamond cutter, clog maker, and house with a room entirely wallpapered in cigar bands.

Marken ☆☆, 16 kilometers (10 miles) northeast of Amsterdam, was an island until a causeway connected it with the mainland, and it remains as insular as ever. Quieter than Volendam, with a village of green-painted houses on stilts around a tiny harbor, it is also more rural. Clusters of farmhouses dot the polders (the reclaimed land from the sea that makes up two-thirds of Holland), and a candy-striped lighthouse stands on the IJsselmeer shore. Marken does not gush over tourists, but it will feed and water them, and let them wander around its pretty streets. Villagers wear traditional costume, as much to preserve the custom as to appease the tourists who pour in daily. The **Marken Historisch Museum,** Kerkbuurt 44 (© **0299/601-904**), is a typical house open as a museum from Good Friday to the end of October, Monday to Saturday 10am to 5pm and Sunday noon to 4pm. Admission is 4Dfl (€1.80, $1.75) adults and 2Dfl (€0.90, 85¢) children. A clog maker works in the parking lot during the summer.

THE FLOWER CENTERS

Flowers at **Keukenhof Gardens** ☆☆, Lisse (© **025/465-555**), have a short but glorious season. You'll never forget a visit to this meandering 28-hectare (70-acre) wooded park in the heart of the bulb-producing region, planted each fall by major Dutch growers. Each spring the bulbs burst forth and produce almost eight million tulips, narcissi, daffodils, hyacinths, bluebells, crocuses, lilies, amaryllis, and more. A blaze of color is everywhere in the park and greenhouses, beside brooks and shady ponds, along paths and in neighboring fields, in neat little plots and helter-skelter on lawns. By its own report, it's the greatest flower

---

✐ The IJsselmeer

Only in Holland could you say, "This used to be a sea." The IJsselmeer, the big lake on Amsterdam's doorstep, actually was once a sea, called the Zuiderzee (as in the words of the song, "by the side of the Zuiderzee . . ."), until the Dutch decided they didn't want it to be one any longer, because it was always threatening to flood Amsterdam (and Amsterdammers don't like water in their *jenever*).

So in the 1930s, workers blocked off the mouth of the Zuiderzee with a massive dike, the Enclosing Dike (Afsluitdijk), running from Noord-Holland to Friesland, and that was that. Nowadays, in the sea's place, there is a well-behaved freshwater lake called the IJsselmeer (pronounced "*Eye*-sselmeer"). You'll find the lake's long shoreline, the "Golden Circle," to be a scenic escape from Amsterdam.

show on earth. The park is open from late March to late May only, daily 8am to 7:30pm. There are special train and bus connections via Haarlem and the nearby town of Leiden. Admission is 20Dfl (€9.10, $9) adults and 10Dfl (€4.55, $4.35) children 4 to 12.

Flowers are a billion-guilder-per-year business at **Aalsmeer Flower Auction** (✆ **0297/393-939**), held in lakeside Aalsmeer close to Schiphol Airport. Every year, three billion flowers and 400 million plants from 8,000 nurseries are auctioned off. Get there early to see the biggest array of flowers and to have as much time as possible to watch the computerized auctioning. As flower lots go by on carts, the first bid to stop the auction "clock" as it works down from 100 to 1 wins the posies. The auction is held from Monday to Friday 7:30 to 11am. Bus 172 takes you there from Amsterdam's Centraal Station. Admission is 5Dfl (€2.25, $2.15) adults, free for children 12 and under.

TEXEL ISLAND

Texel, 66 kilometers (41 miles) north of Amsterdam, is the biggest, most populated of the Wadden Islands and the only one that can be reached directly from Noord-Holland Province (though a tourist ferry between Texel and Vlieland island operates from May to September). It has the serenity intrinsic to islands, even allowing for the many visitors who pour in during the summer months. Beaches, boating, cycling, and bird-watching are the big attractions, yet eating, drinking, and partying have their place too.

ESSENTIALS

GETTING THERE   **Trains** depart at least every half hour from Amsterdam Centraal Station to Den Helder, the ferry port for Texel (trip time: 1½ hours). By **car,** take A9, and then N9 north.

A bus runs every hour between Den Helder train station and the ferry terminal. When buying your ferry ticket, if you need a ride to get to your destination on Texel, purchase a TelekomTaxi ticket as well. For 10Dfl (€4.55, $4.35) each way, a minibus will drop you wherever you want and pick you up in time for the ferry for your return.

The **TESO** company (✆ **0222/369-600**) runs two car ferries on the half-hour trip between Den Helder and 't Horntje on Texel. Ships sail every hour in both directions from 6:35am (8:35am on Sunday and public holidays) to 9:35pm; the last return from Texel is at 9:05pm. Reservations are not accepted. Fares are 12Dfl (€5.45, $5) adults, 6Dfl (€2.75, $2.60) children, and 60Dfl (€27.25, $26.10) for a standard-size car.

VISITOR INFORMATION   VVV **Texel,** Emmalaan 66, Den Burg (✆ **0222/ 312-847;** fax 0222/314-129; www.texel.net), just off N501, the main road into the town, is open from Monday to Friday 9am to 6pm, Saturday 9am to 5:30pm.

EXPLORING TEXEL

Unlike on some of the Wadden Islands, cars are allowed on Texel, but there's no doubt that the best way to get around and to keep faith with the island's environmental spirit is to go by bicycle. You can bring bikes over on the ferry for 7Dfl (€3.20, $3.05), or rented from dozens of outlets, either at the ferry port, in the island's centrally located "capital" **Den Burg,** or in the other villages dotted around the coast.

The island's varied landscape, with tidal gullies, sand dunes, and rolling meadows, offers a temporary home to some 300 bird species, around 100 of which breed here. The cream of this avian crop includes oystercatchers, Bewick swans, spoonbills, Brent geese, avocets, marsh harriers, snow buntings, ringed plovers, kestrels, short-eared owls, and bar-tailed godwits. They can be seen in three **nature reserves** that are open to the public: the **Schorren, Bol,** and **Dijkmanshuizen** reserves. You can only enter on guided tours organized by the **Natuurmonumenten,** Polderweg 2, De Waal (© **022/318-757;** call evenings only).

Nature trails through areas belonging to the **State Forest Authority** (Staatsbosbeheer) abound in the dunes and wooded areas, and can be freely visited so long as you stick to the marked paths. **EcoMare,** Ruyslaan 92, De Koog (© **0222/317-741**), does guided tours of some areas, and its visitor center is one of the best places to start a nature tour of the island. The center's seal rehabilitation facility is working to restore seal numbers in the waters around Texel, which were greatly reduced by a 1988 virus, by caring for weak and injured seals until they can be returned to the sea. From an underwater observation gallery you can watch the seals swimming happily and can view some of the rich variety of life that lives in the Waddenzee tidal mud flats. There's a bird rehabilitation program, also.

13

Norway

by Darwin Porter & Danforth Prince

Norway is a land of tradition, as exemplified by its rustic stave churches—look for these mysterious dark structures with steep gables surmounted by dragon heads and pointed steeples—and folk dances stepped to the airs of a fiddler. But Norway is also modern, a technologically advanced nation that's rich in petroleum and hydroelectric energy. One of the world's last great natural frontiers, Norway is a land of astonishing beauty; its steep and jagged fjords, salmon-teeming rivers, glaciers, mountains, and meadows invite exploration. In winter, the shimmering Northern Lights beckon; in summer, the midnight sun shines late and warm.

1 Oslo

After World War II, Oslo grew to 450 square kilometers (175 sq. miles), making it one of the 10 largest capitals in the world in sheer area, if not in urban buildup. The city is one of the most heavily forested on earth, and fewer than half a million Norwegians live and work here.

One of the oldest Scandinavian capital cities, founded in the mid-11th century, Oslo has never been a mainstream tourist site. But the city is culturally rich with many diversions—enough to fill at least 3 or 4 busy days. It's also the center for many easy excursions along the Oslofjord or to towns and villages in its environs, both north and south.

In recent years Oslo has grown from what even the Scandinavians viewed as a Nordic backwater to one of Europe's happening cities. Restaurants, nightclubs, cafes, shopping complexes, and other venues keep on opening. A kind of Nordic joie de vivre permeates the city; the only drawback is that all this fun is going to cost you—Oslo ranks as one of Europe's most expensive cities.

ESSENTIALS

GETTING THERE **By Plane** **Oslo Airport** in Gardermoen (© 67-59-70-00; www.osl.no) is about 50 kilometers (31 miles) east of downtown Oslo, a 45-minute drive from the center. Major carriers include SAS, British Airways, and Icelandair.

There's frequent bus service, departing every 15 to 30 minutes throughout the day, into downtown Oslo. It's maintained by both SAS (whose buses deliver passengers to the Central Railway station and to most of the SAS hotels within Oslo) and the **Norwegian Bus Express** (© 81-54-44-44), whose buses head for the main railway station. Both companies charge 95NOK ($11) per person, each way. There's also 20-minute high-speed railway service between Gardermoen and Oslo's main railway station, priced at 120NOK ($13) per person each way. If you want to take a taxi, be prepared for a lethally high charge of around 500NOK ($56) for up to four passengers plus their luggage. If you need a

Oslo

BYGDØY PENINSULA

Frognerkilen

← **To Bygdøy Peninsula (see inset above)**

Frognerkilen

ACCOMMODATIONS ■

Bristol **12**
First Hotel Millennium **16**
Grand Hotel **13**
Golden Tulip Rainbow Hotel Stefan **11**
Munch **10**
White House **8**

† Church
ⓘ Information
✉ Post Office
— Ⓜ Metro
—— Railway

"maxi-taxi," a minivan that's suitable for between five and 15 passengers, plus their luggage, you'll be assessed 800NOK ($89).

By Train Trains pull into **Oslo Sentralstasjon (Central Station),** Jernbanetorget 1 at the beginning of Karl Johans Gate (© **81-50-08-88** for information), in the city center. It's open daily from 7am to 11pm. From there, you can catch trains heading for Bergen and all other rail links in Norway. From the station, you can also take trams to all major parts of Oslo.

By Car If you're driving from mainland Europe, the fastest way to reach Oslo is to take the car-ferry from Frederikshavn, Denmark (see below). You can also take a car-ferry from Copenhagen (see below) or drive from Copenhagen by crossing over to Helsingborg, Sweden, from Helsingør, Denmark. Once at Helsingborg, take E-6 north all the way to Stockholm. If you're driving from Stockholm to Oslo, follow E-18 west all the way (trip time: 7 hours). Once you near the outskirts of Oslo from any direction, follow the signs into the SENTRUM, or city center.

By Ferry Ferries from Europe arrive at Oslo port, a 15-minute walk or a short taxi ride from the city center. From Denmark, car-ferries depart for Oslo from Copenhagen (trip time: 12 hours), Hirtshals (9 hours), and Frederikshavn (8½ hours). Trips start at 415NOK ($46) per person round-trip. From Strømstad, Sweden, there's a daily crossing in summer to Sandefjord, Norway (2½ hours); from Sandefjord, it's an easy drive or train ride north to Oslo. Call © **22-41-90-90** or 22-33-50-00 for schedules and information. Reservations are required.

VISITOR INFORMATION **Tourist Offices** Assistance and information for visitors are available at the **Tourist Information Office,** Vestbaneplassen 1, N-0250 Oslo (© **22-83-00-50;** bus: 27). Free maps, brochures, sightseeing tickets, and guide services are available. The office is open in June, daily from 9am to 6pm; from July and August, daily 9am to 7pm; from May and September, Monday to Saturday 9am to 4pm; from January to April and October to December, Monday to Friday 9am to 4pm.

There's also an Oslo-only **information office** at the Oslo Sentralstasjon (Central Station), Jernbanetorget 1, at the beginning of Karl Johans Gate (no phone), open daily 8am to 11pm.

Websites For information online, try the Norwegian Tourist Board (**www.visitnorway.com**) or Virtual Oslo (**www.oslorightnow.com**).

CITY LAYOUT Oslo is at the mouth of the 95-kilometer (60-mile) Oslofjord. Opening onto the harbor is **Rådhusplassen** (City Hall Square), dominated by the modern City Hall, a major attraction. Guided bus tours leave from this square, and the launches that cruise the fjords depart from the pier facing the municipal building. (You can catch ferries to the Bygdøy Peninsula from the quay at Rådhusplassen.)

Out on a promontory to the east is the **Akershus Castle.** At **Bygdøy,** the much larger peninsula that juts out to the west, are four of Oslo's major attractions: the Viking ships, the Polar Ship *Fram* Museum, the *Kon-Tiki* Museum, and the Folk Museum.

Karl Johans Gate, Oslo's main street (especially for shopping and strolling) is north of City Hall Square. This boulevard begins at Oslo **Sentralstasjon** (Central Station) and stretches all the way to the 19th-century **Royal Palace** at the western end. A short walk from the palace is the famed **Student's Grove** (the University of Oslo is nearby), where everybody gathers on a summer day to socialize. Dominating this area is the **National Theater.** South of the theater and near the harbor is **Stortingsgaten,** another shopping street.

The main city square is **Stortorvet,** although it's no longer the center of city life, which has now shifted to Karl Johans Gate.

At a subway stop near the National Theater you can catch an electric train to **Tryvannstårnet,** the loftiest lookout in Scandinavia, and to the **Holmenkollen Ski Jump.**

GETTING AROUND   A 24-hour **Tourist Ticket (Turistkort)** lets you travel anywhere in Oslo whenever you wish, by bus, tram, subway, local railway, or boat, including the Bygdøy ferries in summer. The Tourist Ticket costs 45NOK ($5) adults, half price for children 4 to 15; children 3 and under travel free. The ticket will be stamped when it's used for the first time and will then be good for the next 24 hours.

An even better deal, especially for short-term visitors, might be the **Oslo-Card,** which allows unlimited travel by public transportation, free parking validation, and free admission to all museums and major tourist attractions. A 1-day pass costs 180NOK ($20) adults and 60NOK ($7) children up to 15; a 2-day pass costs 290NOK ($32) adults and 80NOK ($9) children; and a 3-day pass costs 410NOK ($46) adults and 110NOK ($12) children.

By Bus, Tram & Subway   Jernbanetorget, in front of the Central Station, is the major bus and tram terminal in Oslo. Most buses and trams passing through the heart of town stop at Wessels Plass, next to the Parliament (Stortinget), or at Stortorvet, the main marketplace. Many also stop at the National Theater or University Square on Karl Johans Gate.

The **T-banen (subway)** has four main lines running to the east of Oslo and four lines running to the west. The most heavily traveled routes by tourists are the eastern lines. The western lines take in Holmenkollen and residential and recreational areas west and north of the city.

Single-journey tickets cost 20NOK ($2.20) for adults; children travel for half fare. You can buy tickets from bus and tram drivers, or you can purchase them in advance at Trafikanten in front of Sentralstasjon (✆ 22-17-70-30). You must cancel your ticket in the automated machines located in subway stations and on buses and trams. An eight-coupon "Maxi" card costs 120NOK ($13), half price for children. Maxi cards can be used for unlimited transfers within 1 hour of the time the ticket is stamped. For information about timetables and fares, call **Trafikanten** (✆ 22-17-70-30).

By Taxi   The cheapest and most spontaneous way to get a taxi involves hailing one on the street or waiting at a taxi stand. If you hail a taxi, the initial meter reading begins at 48NOK ($5) or else 68NOK ($8) if you call one. After that you pay from 17 to 22NOK ($1.90 to $2.45) per kilometer, depending on the time of day. You can only call a cab from a hotel—not from a cell phone or a random street corner. For service 24 hours a day, call a special number: ✆ 02323.

By Ferry   In warmer months, usually mid-April to late September, ferries depart for Bygdøy from Pier 3 in front of the Oslo Rådhuset. Call **Båtservice** (✆ 22-20-07-15) for schedule information. We recommend using a ferry or bus to Bygdøy since parking conditions are crowded. Other ferries leave for various parts of the Oslofjord; ask at the **Tourist Information Office** at Vestbaneplassen 1 (✆ 22-83-00-50). One-way fare to Bygdøy or any destination in Oslo is 25NOK ($2.80).

By Bicycle   Den Rustne Eike, Vestbaneplassen 2 (© **22-83-52-08;** T-banen: Stortinget), rents bikes at moderate rates, complete with free maps of interesting routes in Oslo and its environs. The cost is 85 to 145NOK ($9 to $16) for 24 hours, or 465 to 835NOK ($52 to $93) per week, with a 1,000NOK ($111) deposit or valid picture ID required. Helmets are included at no charge and a child's seat is available for 50NOK ($6) per day. It's open from May to October, daily 10am to 6:30pm; off-season, from Monday to Friday 10am to 6pm.

FAST FACTS: Oslo

American Express American Express Reisebyrå, Karl Johans Gate (© **22-98-37-00**), is open from Monday to Friday 9am to 6pm and Saturday 10am to 3pm.

Business Hours Most **banks** are open from Monday to Friday 8:15am to 3:30pm (Thursday to 5pm). Most **businesses** are open from Monday to Friday 9am to 4pm. **Stores** are generally open from Monday to Friday 9am to 5pm (many stay open late on Thursday to 6 or 7pm) and Saturday 9am to 1 or 2pm. Sunday closings are observed.

Currency You'll pay your way in Norway in Norwegian **kroner (NOK)**, as it is not a member of the euro zone. There are 100 øre in 1 krone. The exchange rate used in this chapter was $1 = 9NOK, or 1NOK = 11 U.S. cents. The ratio for the British pound to the krone fluctuates constantly. At press time, £1 = approximately 13NOK (or 1NOK = £0.076). For the euro the rate was currently fixed at 8.1085NOK (or 1NOK = €0.123).

Currency Exchange In addition to banks, the **Fellesbanken's Exchange** at the Oslo Central Railway Station (© **22-41-26-11**) is open from Monday to Friday 8am to 11pm, Saturday from 8am to 7pm, and Sunday from 8am to noon.

Dentists In an emergency, contact the **Tøyen Senter,** Kolstadgate 18 (© **22-67-78-00;** T-banen: Groønen), open daily from 11am to 2pm and 7 to 10pm. For private dentists, look under *Tannleger* ("tooth doctors") in volume 1B of the telephone directory; there's rarely a language barrier.

Doctors Oslo's most prominent emergency clinic is the 24-hour **Oslo Municipal Casualty Clinic (Legavakten)** at Storgata 40 (© **22-11-70-70** or 22-00-81-60; T-banen: Groønland). For more routine medical assistance, contact Oslo's biggest hospital, **Ullavel,** Kirkeveien 166 (© **22-11-80-80;** T-banen: Brattikollen). To consult a private doctor (nearly all of whom speak English), check the telephone directory or ask at your hotel for a recommendation.

Drugstores A 24-hour pharmacy is **Jernbanetorvets Apotek,** Jernbanetorget 4A (© **22-41-24-82;** T-banen: Jernbanetorget).

Embassies & Consulates The Embassy of the **United States** is at Drammensveien 18, N-0255 Oslo 2 (© **22-44-85-50;** T-banen: Nationaltheatret); **United Kingdom,** at Thomas Heftyes Gate 8, N-0264 Oslo 2 (© **23-13-27-00;** T-banen: Nationaltheatret); **Canada,** at Oscarsgate 20, N-0244 Oslo 3 (© **22-99-53-00;** T-banen: Nationaltheatret); and **South Africa,** at Drammensveien 88C, N-0255 (© **22-44-79-10;** T-banen: Nationaltheatret).

Visitors from Ireland and New Zealand should contact the British Embassy. Australians should contact the Canadian Embassy.

Emergencies Dial the Oslo **police** at © **112**; report a **fire** at © **110**; call an **ambulance** at © **113**.

Internet Access You can tap in free at the Rådhuset, the City Hall on Rådhusplassen (© **22-86-16-00**). Hours are from May to September, Monday to Saturday 9am to 5pm, Sunday noon to 5pm; from October to April, Monday to Saturday 9am to 4pm, Sunday noon to 4pm.

Post Office The **Oslo General Post Office** is at Dronningensgate 15 (© **23-14-78-02**; T-banen: Jernbanetorget), though the entrance is at the corner of Prinsensgate. It's open from Monday to Friday 8am to 6pm, Saturday 9am to 3pm; it's closed Sunday and public holidays.

Telephone The country code for Norway is **47**, and the city code for Oslo is **22**. For operator assistance in English, dial © **115**.

International calls can be made from **Telenor's Telecommunications Office**, Kongensgate 21 (© **22-40-55-09**; T-banen: Stortinget), open from Monday to Friday 9am to 8pm, Saturday 10am to 5pm, and Sunday noon to 6pm. The entrance is on Prinsensgate. Toll-free international access codes are: **AT&T** (© **800/19011**), **MCI** (© **800/19912**), or **Sprint** (© **800/19877**).

WHERE TO STAY
EXPENSIVE

Bristol ⚜⚜   In the heart of the city, on a side street north of Karl Johans Gate, this 1920s hotel is warm, inviting, and luxurious, although in spite of great efforts, it has never achieved the supremacy of the Grand (see below). The Moorish-inspired lobby, with its Winter Garden and Library Bar, sets the elegant tone. Rooms range from medium to spacious and are especially comfortable, with excellent, firm mattresses. Although the plumbing in some of the bathrooms is a bit antiquated, you'll find deluxe toiletries and adequate shelf space. Some units are no-smoking.

Kristian IV's Gate 7, N-0164 Oslo 1. © **22-82-60-00**. Fax 22-82-60-01. www.bristol.no. 252 units. 1,000–1,750NOK ($111–$194) double; from 2,800NOK ($311) suite. Children 14 and under stay free in parents' room. Rates include breakfast. AE, DC, MC, V. Parking 130NOK ($14). T-banen: Stortinget. **Amenities:** 3 restaurants (Grill the best), 3 bars; fitness center with sauna, solarium, and Jacuzzi; night club; room service; laundry/dry cleaning. *In room:* A/C, TV, minibar, hair dryer.

Grand Hotel ⚜⚜⚜   Norway's leading hotel, on the wide boulevard that leads to the Royal Palace, is a completely renovated 1874 building. Rooms have good beds with firm mattresses and double-glazed windows. An eight-story extension contains larger, brighter doubles, but many guests prefer the old-fashioned accommodations in the older section.

Karl Johans Gate 31, N-0159 Oslo 1. © **800/223-5652** in the U.S., or 22-42-93-90. Fax 47-23-21-00. E-mail: reservation@grand-hotel.no. 327 units. Summer, 1,190NOK ($132) double; 2,050–10,000NOK ($228–$1,110) suite. Fall, winter, spring, 1,875NOK ($208) double; 2,675–10,000NOK ($296–$1,110) suite. Rates include buffet breakfast. AE, DC, MC, V. Parking 145NOK ($16). T-banen: Stortinget. **Amenities:** 3 restaurants (the Grand Cafe is the most famous in Norway), hot night club in the cellar; sauna; solarium; room service; laundry/dry cleaning,. *In room:* A/C (some), TV, minibar, hair dryer, trouser press.

MODERATE

First Hotel Millennium ☆ *Finds*   One of Oslo's newest large-scale hotels lies within what was originally a 1930s Art Deco office building. It's within walking distance of virtually everything in central Oslo. This is one of the "personality" hotels of Oslo, known for its atmosphere and character, and noted for a stylish kind of minimalism. Rooms are among the most spacious in town, with many Art Deco touches. Extras include two phones and large bathrooms with both tub and shower. Some accommodations are suitable for persons with disabilities, and others are rented only to nonsmokers.

Tollbugate 25, N-0157 Oslo. ☎ **23-00-30-00.** Fax 23-00-30-30. www.firsthotels.com. 114 units. Mon–Thurs 1,349–1,749NOK ($150–$195) double; Fri–Sun 799–1,409NOK ($89–$156) double. AE, DC, MC, V. Tram: 30, 42. **Amenities:** Restaurant Primo Ciaou-Ciaou, one of Oslo's best, bar; room service; baby-sitting; laundry/ dry cleaning. *In room:* TV, minibar, hair dryer, trouser press.

Golden Tulip Rainbow Hotel Stefan   In an excellent location in the center of the city, this hotel is comfortable and unpretentious. Built in 1952, it has been modernized and much improved, with a partial renovation in 1996. Rooms are traditional in style and well furnished and maintained, with firm mattresses, and small but adequate bathrooms with showers. Two offer facilities for people with disabilities. May to September 1, weekend rates are granted only to those who make reservations less than 48 hours before arrival.

Rosenkrantzgate 1, N-0189 Oslo 1. ☎ **23-31-55-00.** Fax 23-31-55-55. www.rainbow-hotels.no. 139 units. Mon–Thurs 1,015NOK ($113) double; Fri–Sat 775NOK ($86) double. Rates include breakfast. AE, DC, MC, V. Parking 110NOK ($12). Tram: 10, 11, 17, or 18. **Amenities:** Restaurant, known for Norwegian buffets. *In room:* A/C, TV, minibar.

INEXPENSIVE

Munch *Value*   Built in 1983, this hotel offers good-value accommodations (by Oslo standards), each floor reached by elevator. Although not overly large, rooms are cozy and well heated, with firm and frequently renewed mattresses and reproductions of Edvard Munch's paintings. Bathrooms tend to be tiny, with showers or shower/tub combinations.

Munchsgaten 5, N-0130 Oslo 1. ☎ **23-21-96-00.** Fax 23-21-96-01. www.rainbow-hotels.no. 180 units. 870NOK Mon–Thurs ($97) double; Fri–Sun 690NOK ($77) double. Rates include breakfast. AE, DC, MC, V. Parking 100NOK ($11). T-banen: Stortinget. Tram: 7 or 11. Bus: 37. *In-room:* TV, minibar.

White House ☆   This hotel lies in the forested residential district of Breskeby, a short walk from the rear of the Royal Palace. Set on a steeply sloping lot, and greatly modernized since its original construction around 1900 as a private home, it attracts a loyal clientele that appreciates the hotel's small scale and sense of intimacy. Rooms have a cozy Norwegian charm, almost like something encountered in the countryside. They range from small to medium, but have good beds and firm mattresses, and snug but adequate bathrooms (mostly with showers).

President Harbitzgate 18, N-0259 Oslo 2. ☎ **22-44-19-60.** Fax 22-55-04-30. www.hotel-whitehouse.com. 21 units. Mon–Thurs 1,095NOK ($122) double; Fri–Sun 795NOK ($88) double. Rates include breakfast. AE, DC, MC, V. Free parking. Tram: 1. **Amenities:** Restaurant. *In room:* TV, minibar.

WHERE TO DINE

Norwegians are as fond of *smørbrød* (smorgasbord) as the Danes (you'll see it offered everywhere for lunch, except they spell it differently). Basically, this is an open-faced sandwich that can be stacked with virtually anything, including ham with a slice of peach resting on top or perhaps a mound of dill-flavored shrimp.

EXPENSIVE

D'Artagnan 🦅🦅 FRENCH   This restaurant is one of Oslo's most elegant and upscale. Its French food rivals that of Statholdergaarden below, which has a slight edge. Amid flickering candles and bouquets of flowers, you'll enjoy menu items that might include a salad of king crab from Finnmark with avocado and grapefruit segments, yogurt-marinated reindeer with a boysenberry sauce, wild duck served with roasted mixed nuts and a port wine sauce, and one of the most unusual dishes of all: wild lamb served with an herb-flavored mustard sauce. Always featured in various salads and main dishes is salmon, smoked on the premises using various types of wood and tea leaves.

Øvre Slottsgate 16. 📞 **22-41-50-62.** Reservations required. Main courses 250–285NOK ($28–$32); 5-course fixed-price menu 645NOK ($72). AE, DC, MC, V. Mon–Fri (and Sat Oct to Dec 21) 6–11pm. Closed July 8–Aug 8 and Dec 22–Jan 3. Bus: 27, 29, 30, 41, or 61.

Statholdergaarden 🦅🦅🦅 NOUVELLE NORWEGIAN/FRENCH   The most richly historic restaurant setting in Oslo is directed by one of the capital's most feted and successful chefs, Bent Stiansen. The setting, beneath stucco-covered and frescoed ceilings, was built in 1640 as the governor's headquarters. Dishes are crafted with a genuine personal touch, and you get the finest quality of ingredients of any restaurant in Oslo. Menu items might include grilled cray-fish served with a scallop and salmon tartare, and thyme-infused codfish with a crabmeat mousse and two sauces. One of the most appealing and all-time favorites we've enjoyed was a lightly fried Arctic char with sautéed Savoy cabbage, deep-fried black roots, and a lime beurre blanc. Don't confuse this upscale and prestigious site with the less expensive bistro, Statholderstueakroen, in the building's vaulted cellar.

Rådhusgata 11. 📞 **22-41-88-00.** Reservations recommended. Main courses 260–330NOK ($29–$37); 650NOK ($72) for 4 courses, 760NOK ($84) for 6 courses. Mon–Sat 6–10pm. Tram: 11, 15, or 18.

MODERATE

Grand Café 🦅 NORWEGIAN   This is the grand old cafe of Oslo, steeped in legend and tradition—in fact, atmosphere and tradition are more compelling than the cuisine. Ibsen once enjoyed whale steaks here. The menu relies on the best of Norwegian country traditions (after all, how many places still serve elk stew?). Choices range from a Napoleon with coffee to a full meal; you'll find fried stingray, standard veal and beef dishes, and reindeer steaks. Sandwiches are also available. This is tasty, unpretentious cooking that will win you over if you like solid, honest, and earthy flavors.

In the Grand Hotel, Karl Johans Gate 31. 📞 **22-42-93-90.** Reservations recommended. Main courses 175–275NOK ($19–$31). AE, DC, MC, V. Mon–Sat 11am–midnight; Sun noon–11pm. T-banen: Stortinget.

Lipp INTERNATIONAL   Stylish and lighthearted, this restored brasserie is the Oslovian version of Paris in the 1920s. Each day a special dish is offered. The kitchen changes the menu about every 5 weeks. You might face a delectable salmon in a white wine sauce, or else reindeer in a mushroom sauce. Lighter fare is also offered as well for those watching their weight—perhaps an array of freshly made salads or grilled fish dishes. Succulent pastas are also a regular feature of the menu.

In the Hotel Continental, Stortingsgaten 24. 📞 **22-82-40-60.** Reservations recommended. Main courses 158–245NOK ($18–$27). AE, DC, MC, V. Daily 12:30pm–3am. T-banen: Stortinget.

INEXPENSIVE

Det Gamla Rådhus (Old Town Hall) 𝕔 NORWEGIAN   The oldest restaurant in Oslo, Gamla Rådhus is located in what in 1641 was Oslo's Town Hall. At noon you can sit in the spacious dining room and choose from an array of open-face sandwiches (*smørbrød*). Dinner selections include fresh fish, game, and Norwegian specialties. Ingredients are fresh, and the service accommodating. Come here if you want to sample some of the dishes Ibsen might have enjoyed.

Nedre Slottsgate 1. 𝕔 **22-42-01-07.** Reservations recommended. Main courses 120–220NOK ($13–$24); open-faced sandwiches 48–65NOK ($5–$7). AE, DC, MC, V. Mon–Fri 11am–3pm; Mon–Sat 4–11pm. Kroen Bar, Mon–Sat 4pm–midnight. Bus: 27, 29, 30, 41, or 61.

Engebret Café NORWEGIAN   An enduring Oslovian favorite since 1857, this restaurant, directly north of Akershus Castle, has an old-fashioned atmosphere and good food. During lunch, a tempting selection of open-face sandwiches is available. The menu grows more elaborate in the evening when you might begin with a terrine of game with blackberry/port-wine sauce or fish soup. You can then order such traditional dishes as trout in sour cream with boiled potatoes and pickled cucumber, red wild boar with whortleberry sauce, or smoked or roasted reindeer filets served in a port wine cream sauce with seasonal vegetables. It's the type of food Ms. Claus cooks for Santa.

Bankplassen 1. 𝕔 **22-33-66-94.** Reservations recommended. Main courses 205–295NOK ($23–$33); smørbrød 55–95NOK ($6–$11). AE, DC, MC, V. Mon–Sat noon–11pm. Bus: 27, 29, or 30.

Mamma Rosa ITALIAN   Established by two brothers from Tuscany, this Italian-style trattoria enjoys popularity that's a good indication of Norwegians' changing tastes. You can order 15 kinds of pizza, fried scampi and squid, rigatoni, pasta Mamma Rosa (three kinds of pasta with three sauces), grilled steaks, and *gelato* (ice cream). Frankly, some of the dishes have lost a bit of flavor on the trip this far north, but Mamma Rosa is nonetheless a marvelous change of taste and texture.

Øvre Slottsgate 12. 𝕔 **22-42-01-30.** Main courses 86–210NOK ($10–$23); pizzas from 97NOK ($11). DC, MC, V. Mon–Sat noon–11:30pm; Sun 1–10:30pm. T-banen: Stortinget.

SEEING THE SIGHTS
IN THE BYGDØY PENINSULA

Vikingskiphuset (Viking Ship Museum) 𝕔𝕔𝕔   Displayed here are three Viking burial vessels that were excavated on the shores of the Oslofjord and preserved in clay. The most spectacular find is the 9th-century *Oseberg*, discovered near Norway's oldest town. This 20-meter (64-ft.) dragon ship features a wealth of ornaments and is the burial chamber of a Viking queen and her slave. The *Gokstad* find is an outstanding example of Viking vessels because it's so well preserved. The smaller *Tune* ship was never restored. Look for the *Oseberg* animal-head post, the elegantly carved sleigh used by Viking royalty, and the *Oseberg* four-wheeled cart.

Huk Aveny 35, Bygdøy. 𝕔 **22-43-83-79.** Admission 30NOK ($3.35) adults, 10NOK ($1.10) children. Apr, daily 11am–4pm; May–Aug, daily 9am–6pm; Sept, daily 11am–5pm; Oct, daily 11am–6pm; Nov–Mar, daily 11am–3pm. Ferry: From Pier 3 facing the Rådhuset (summer only). Bus: 30 from the National Theater.

Frammuseet (Polar Ship Fram)   A long walk from the Viking ships, the Frammuseet contains the sturdy polar exploration ship *Fram*, which Fridtjof Nansen sailed across the Arctic (1893–96). The vessel was later used by Norwegian explorer Roald Amundsen, the first man to reach the South Pole (1911).

Bygdøynesveien. ☎ **22-43-83-70**. Admission 25NOK ($2.80) adults; 15NOK ($1.65) children. May 1–15 and Sept, daily 10am–4:45pm; May 16–Aug, daily 9am–5:45pm; Mar–Apr, Mon Fri 11am–3:45pm, Sat–Sun 11am–3:45pm; Oct–Nov, Mon–Fri 11am–2:45pm, Sat–Sun 11am–3:45pm; Dec–Feb, Sat–Sun 11am–3:45pm. Ferry: From Pier 3 facing the Rådhuset (summer only). Bus: 30 from the National Theater.

Kon-Tiki Museum ⛵ *Kon-Tiki* is the world-famed balsa-log raft that the young Norwegian scientist Thor Heyerdahl and his five comrades sailed in for 7,000 kilometers (4,300 miles) in 1947—all the way from Callao, Peru, to Raroia, Polynesia. Besides the raft, there're other exhibits from Heyerdahl's subsequent visit to Easter Island, including an Easter Island family cave, with a collection of sacred lava figurines.

Bygdøynesveien 36. ☎ **23-08-67-67**. Admission 30NOK ($3.35) adults, 15NOK ($1.65) children, 70NOK ($7.75) family ticket. June–Aug, daily 9:30am–5:45pm; Apr–May and Sept, daily 10:30am–5pm; Oct–Mar, daily 10:30am–4pm. Ferry: From Pier 3 facing the Rådhuset (summer only). Bus: 30 from the National Theater.

Norsk Sjøfartsmuseum (Norwegian Maritime Museum) ⛵ This museum, which contains a complete ship's deck with helm and chart house, and a three-deck-high section of the passenger steamer *Sandnaes*, chronicles the maritime history and culture of Norway. The Boat Hall features a fine collection of original small craft. The fully restored polar vessel *Gjoa*, used by Roald Amundsen in his search for America's Northwest Passage, is also on display. The three-masted schooner *Svanen* (Swan) is moored at the museum.

Bygdøynesveien 37. ☎ **22-43-82-40**. Admission to museum and boat hall 30NOK ($3.35) adults; 20NOK ($2.20) children. May–Sept, daily 10am–7pm; Oct–Apr, Mon and Fri–Sat 10:30am–4pm, Tues–Thurs 10:30am–7pm. Ferry: From Pier 3 facing the Rådhuset (summer only). Bus: 30 from the National Theater.

Norsk Folkemuseum (Norwegian Folk Museum) ⛵ From all over Norway, 140 original buildings have been transported and reassembled on 14 hectares (35 acres) on the Bygdøy Peninsula. This open-air folk museum includes a number of medieval buildings, such as the Raulandstua, one of the oldest wooden dwellings still standing in Norway, and a stave church from about 1200. The rural buildings are grouped together by region of origin, while the urban houses have been laid out in the form of an old town.

Museumsveien 10. ☎ **22-12-37-00**. Admission 70NOK ($8) adults; 20NOK ($2.20) children under 17. Jan 1–May 14 and Sept 15–Dec 31, Fri–Sat 11am–3pm, Sun 11am–4pm; May 15–June 14 and Sept 1–Sept 14, daily 10am–5pm; June 15–Aug 31, daily 10am–6pm. Ferry: From Pier 3 facing the Rådhuset (summer only). Bus: 30 from the National Theater.

IN WESTERN OLSO

Vigelandsparken ⛵ The lifetime work of Gustav Vigeland, Norway's greatest sculptor, is displayed inside the museum as well as throughout the nearby 30-hectare (75-acre) Frogner Park in western Oslo. Nearly 211 sculptures in granite, bronze, and iron can be admired. See in particular his four granite columns, symbolizing the fight between humanity and evil (a dragon, the embodiment of evil, embraces a woman). The angry boy is the most photographed statue in the park, but the really celebrated work is the 16-meter (52-ft.) monolith, composed of 121 figures of colossal size—all carved into one piece of stone.

Frogner Park, Nobelsgate 32. ☎ **22-54-25-30**. Park, free; museum, 30NOK ($3.35) adults, 15NOK ($1.65) children. Park, daily 24 hours. Museum, May–Sept Tues–Sat 10am–6pm, Sun noon–7pm; Oct–Apr Tues–Sat noon–4pm, Sun noon–6pm. Tram: 12 or 15. Bus: 20, 45, or 81.

IN EASTERN OSLO

Edvard Munch Museum ⛵⛵⛵ Devoted exclusively to the works of Edvard Munch (1863–1944), Scandinavia's leading painter, this exhibit (Munch's gift to the city), traces his work from early realism to his latter-day expressionism. The collection comprises 1,100 paintings, some 4,500 drawings, around 18,000 prints, numerous graphic plates, six sculptures, and important documentary material.

Tøyengate 53. ℭ 23-24-14-00. Admission 50NOK ($6) adults, 20NOK ($2.20) children. June to mid-Sept, daily 10am–6pm; mid-Sept to May, Tues–Wed and Fri–Sat 10am–4pm, Thurs and Sun 10am–6pm. T-banen: Tøyen. Bus: 20.

IN THE CITY CENTER

Akershus Castle   One of the oldest historical monuments in Oslo, Akershus Castle was built in 1300 by King Haakon V Magnusson. It was a fortress and a royal residence for several centuries. A fire in 1527 devastated the northern wing, and the castle was rebuilt and transformed into a Renaissance palace under the Danish-Norwegian king Christian IV. Now it's used for state occasions. A few rooms, including the chapel, are open to the public. In the rectangular court, markings show where the massive medieval keep used to stand. You can wander through two large halls (Olav's and Christian IV's), which occupy the top floor of the north and south wings, respectively. For many, the most interesting part is the dungeon, which includes an "escape-proof room" built for a prisoner, Ole Pedersewn Hoyland. After he was placed in the chamber and realized there was no way he could ever escape, he killed himself.

Festnings-Plassen. ℭ 22-41-25-21. Admission 20NOK ($2.20) adults, 10NOK ($1.10) children. May to Sept 15, Mon–Sat 10am–4pm, Sun 12:30–4pm; Apr 15–30 and Sept 16 to Oct, Sun 12:30–4pm. Closed Nov to Apr 14. Tram: 10 or 12. Bus: 60.

ATTRACTIONS NEARBY

Tryvannstårnet (Lookout Tower)   This is the loftiest lookout tower in Scandinavia—the gallery is approximately 580 meters (1,900 ft.) above sea level and offers a view of the Oslofjord with Sweden to the east. A walk down the hill takes you to the famous restaurant Frognerseteren. You can take another 20-minute walk down the hill to the Holmenkollen ski jump, the site of the 1952 Olympic competitions as well as the Holmenkollen Ski Festival, when skiers compete in downhill, slalom, giant slalom, cross-country ski races, and jumping.

Voksenkollen. ℭ 22-14-67-11. Admission 30NOK ($3.35) adults, 20NOK ($2.20) children. May and Sept, daily 10am–5pm; June, daily 10am–7pm; July, daily 9am–10pm; Aug, daily 9am–8pm; Oct–Apr, Mon–Fri 10am–3pm, Sat–Sun 11am–4pm. T-banen: Holmenkollen SST Line 15 from near the National Theater to Voksenkollen (30-minute ride), then an uphill 15-minute walk.

Henie-Onstad Kunstsenter (Henie-Onstad Art Center) 🎯🎯   On a site beside the Oslofjord 11 kilometers (7 miles) west of Oslo, ex-movie star and skating champion Sonja Henie and her husband, Niels Onstad, a shipping tycoon, opened a museum to display their art collection. This especially good 20th-century collection includes some 1,800 works by Munch, Picasso, Matisse, Léger, Bonnard, and Miró. Henie's Trophy Room is impressive, with 600 trophies and medals, including three Olympic gold medals—she was the star at the 1936 competition—and 10 world skating championships.

Høkvikodden, Baerum. ℭ 67-80-48-80. Admission 60NOK ($7) adults, 30NOK ($3.35) ages 15–25. Free 14 and under. June–Aug Mon 11am–5pm, Tues–Fri 9am–9pm, Sat–Sun 11am–7pm; Sept–May Tues 9am–9pm, Sat–Mon 11am–5pm. Bus: 151, 152, 251, or 261.

ORGANIZED TOURS

H. M. Kristiansens Automobilbyrå, Hegdehaugsveien 4 (ℭ 22-20-82-06), known as H.M.K. tours, has been showing visitors around Oslo for more than

Exploring the Fjords from Oslo

The scenery around Bergen is more spectacular, but if the Oslo area is your only chance to see Norwegian fjord country, then go for it. The eastern side is sunny and preferable for touring. Along the way you'll pass old Viking ruins, once fortified towns, woodlands, and endless blue waters. Quaint cottages pose on rolling hills that suddenly plunge downward to the deeply blue, narrow depths that dramatically snake their way inland.

Oslofjord links the capital with the open sea. It is studded with islets and sheltered waters. Regrettably, industry has blighted some the shoreline, but there's much that is still pristine, beautiful, and unspoiled, a perfect combination of mountain scenery and fjord waters.

Departing from Pier 3 in front of the Oslo Rådhuset (City Hall), **Båtservice Sightseeing,** Rådhusbrygge 3, Rådhusplassen (© 22-20-07-15; bus: 27), offers a 50-minute minicruise boat tour, with a view of the harbor and the city, including the ancient fortress of Akershus and the islands in the inner part of the Oslofjord. Cruises depart from mid-May to late August, on the hour daily from 11am to 8pm (limited sailing at the season's beginning and end). Adults pay 85NOK ($9); children, 40NOK ($4.45).

An evening fjord cruise, including a maritime buffet at the Norwegian restaurant Lanternen, leaves late from June through August, daily at 3:30 and 5:45pm. The 3½-hour cruise costs 310NOK ($34) adults and 155NOK ($17) children.

If you have more time, take the 2-hour fjord cruise through the maze of islands and narrow sounds in the Oslofjord. Departures are May to September, daily at 10:30am and 1, 3:30, and 5:45pm; the cost is 155NOK ($17) adults, 75NOK ($8) children. Refreshments are available on board. There are variants of this cruise, such as the fjord cruise with lunch, also 2 hours, leaving from May to mid-September, daily at 10:30am, and costing 310NOK ($34) adults, 155NOK ($17) children. After the cruise, the boat anchors so the passengers can go ashore for lunch at Lanternen Restaurant.

a century. Year-round the agency offers a 3- to 4-hour Oslo sightseeing tour, leaving daily at 10am and 1:30pm. It costs 235NOK ($26) adults and 120NOK ($13) children—not including lunch. The tour passes through the city center and makes stops at the Vigeland Sculpture Park, the Holmenkollen ski jump, the Viking Ship Museum, the *Kon-Tiki* Museum, and the Vikingland theme park. A shorter 2-hour tour departs daily at 10am and 5:30pm, costing 150NOK ($19) adults and 80NOK ($10) children. Tours leave from the Norway information center, Vestbaneplassen 1 (bus: 27); you should arrive 15 minutes before departure. Authorized guides speak English.

THE SHOPPING SCENE

Near the marketplace and the cathedral (Oslo Domkirche), **Den Norske Husfliden,** Møllergata 4 (© 22-42-10-75; T-banen: Stortinget; bus: 17)—or

Husfliden, as it's called—is the display and retail center for the Norwegian Association of Home Arts and Crafts, founded in 1891. Today it's almost eight times larger than any of its competitors, with two floors displaying the very finest of Norwegian design in ceramics, glassware, furniture, and woodworking. You can also purchase souvenirs, gifts, textiles, rugs, knotted Rya rugs, embroidery, wrought iron, and fabrics by the yard. Goods are shipped all over the world.

Norway's largest department store, **Steen & Strøm,** Kongensgate 23 (© **22-00-40-00;** T-banen: Stortinget), is a treasure house with hundreds of Nordic items spread through 58 individual departments. Look for hand-knit sweaters and caps, hand-painted wooden dishes reflecting traditional Norwegian art, and pewter dinner plates made from old molds. **Heimen Husflid,** Rosenkrantzgate 8 (© **22-41-40-50;** T-banen: Nationaltheatret), about a block from Karl Johans Gate, carries folk costumes, antiques, and reproductions. Hand-knit sweaters in traditional Norwegian patterns are a special item, as are pewter and brass items.

William Schmidt, Karl Johans Gate 41 (© **22-42-02-88;** T-banen: Stortinget), established in 1853, is a leading purveyor of unique souvenirs, including pewter items (everything from Viking ships to beer goblets), Norwegian dolls in national costumes, wood carvings (the troll collection is the most outstanding in Oslo), and sealskin moccasins. The shop specializes in hand-knit cardigans, pullovers, gloves, and caps; sweaters are made from mothproofed 100% Norwegian wool.

OSLO AFTER DARK

To find out what's happening when you're visiting, pick up *What's On in Oslo,* which details concerts and theaters and other useful information.

Theater, ballet, and opera tickets are sold at various box offices and also at **Billettsentralen,** Karl Johans Gate 35 (© **81-53-31-33;** T-banen: Stortinget)—although this service costs quite a bit more than your typical box office. Tickets to sports and cultural events can now be purchased easily and more cheaply via computer linkup at any post office in the city, so when you buy a stamp you can also buy a voucher for a ticket to the ballet, theater, or hockey game.

THE PERFORMING ARTS

Home to the National Theater Company, the **National Theater,** Johans Eidvolls Plass 1 (© **22-00-14-00;** T-banen: Nationaltheatret), stages dramatic performances 6 nights a week (Monday to Saturday) every month except June to August. Ticket prices range from 110 to 190NOK ($12 to $21).

Two blocks from the National Theater, **Oslo Konserthus,** Munkedamsveien 14 (© **23-11-31-00;** T-banen: Nationaltheatret), is the home of the widely acclaimed Oslo Philharmonic. Performances are given on Thursday and Friday evenings except in June and July, and ticket prices range from 200 to 700NOK ($22 to $78). Big-name jazz and pop acts show up regularly; ticket prices depend on the act.

The 1931 building, originally a movie theater, at Storgaten 23, was adapted for better acoustics and dedicated in 1959 to the **Den Norske Opera (Norwegian National Opera)** (© **22-42-94-75;** T-banen: Jernbanetorget). It's also the venue for the National Ballet. Productions of both companies are staged from September to mid-June. Between the two companies, there're generally three performances a week, with the only set performance night being Saturday. Tickets range from 170 to 320NOK ($19 to $36).

The **Norwegian Folk Museum,** on Bygdøy (ferry: Pier 3 near the Rådhuset), often presents folk-dance performances by its own ensemble on summer Sunday afternoons at the museum's open-air theater. Admission is free, as the performance is included in the museum's entrance price.

THE CLUB & MUSIC SCENE

Smuget, Rosenkrantzgate 22 (© **22-42-52-62;** T-banen: Nationaltheatret), is the most talked-about nightlife joint in the city, and has the long lines (especially on weekends) to prove it. It's in a 19th-century building in back of the City Hall and has a restaurant, an active dance floor, and a stage where live bands perform. It's open from Monday to Saturday 8pm to 3am; the cover is 50NOK ($6) on weekdays and 70NOK ($8) on Saturday.

With a capacity of 1,200 patrons, the **Rockefeller Music Hall,** Torggata 16 (© **22-20-32-32;** T-banen: Stortinget), a combination concert hall and nightclub, is one of the largest establishments of its kind in Oslo. There're live concerts every night, everything from reggae to rock to jazz. Cover runs from 60 to 300NOK ($7 to $33). It's usually open from Sunday to Thursday 8pm to 2:30am and Friday to Saturday 9pm to 3:30am. Show time is about an hour after the doors open.

One of the most all-encompassing restaurant and nightlife complexes in Oslo is **Restaurant Huset,** Universitatsgata 26 (© **22-41-36-33;** tram: 5, 6, or 7), a warehouse-like building with a labyrinth of hallways, dance areas, and bars. In the cellar, you'll find the **New Orleans Restaurant** (© **22-42-44-20**), devoted to the gumbos and filés you'd expect in Louisiana. It's open daily from 5 to 11pm. Upstairs, and under the same management, is **Barock Disco** (© **22-42-44-20**). Three bars encircle a common dance floor with a 20-something clientele. Open from Thursday to Sunday 10pm to 3:30am. Cover on disco nights costs 60 to 100NOK ($7 to $11). In the same complex, with a somewhat more sedate clientele, is **John's Bar** (© **22-11-37-09**), open from Wednesday to Sunday 10pm till 3am.

Club Spartacus, Pilestredet 9 (© **22-41-52-04;** T-banen: Nationaltheatret), is a lively, hot place, and young men predominate, although there's also a fair share of older and wealthier guys hoping to make contact with that mythical Viking god. The place is primarily for drinking, talking, and flirting. Open from Tuesday to Sunday 10pm to 3:30am; cover 50NOK ($6).

DAY TRIPS FROM OSLO

The best 1-day excursion from Oslo includes visits to Fredrikstad and Tønsberg, which gives you a chance to explore the scenic highlights of the Oslofjord. A trip to Fredrikstad, in Østfold on the east bank of the Oslofjord, can easily be combined in 1 day with a visit to the port of Tønsberg on the west bank, by crossing over on the ferry from Moss to Horten, then heading south.

Getting There   To reach the first stop, Fredrikstad, take E-6 south from Oslo toward Moss. Continue past Moss until you reach the junction of Route 110, which is signposted south of Fredrikstad. About six buses per day depart for the town from the Central Station in Oslo. Trains from Oslo's Central Station depart from Fredrikstad about every 2 hours during the day (trip time: 30 minutes).

FREDRIKSTAD   In recent years Fredrikstad, 95 kilometers (60 miles) south of Oslo, has become a major tourist center, thanks to its Old Town and 17th-century fortress. Across the river on the west is a modern industrial section, and although a bridge links the two sections, the best way to reach Old Town is by ferry, which costs 5NOK (55¢). The departure point is about 4 blocks from the Fredrikstad railroad station—simply follow the crowd out the main door of the station, make an obvious left turn, and continue down to the shore of the river. It's also possible to travel between the two areas by bus 360 or 362, although most pedestrians opt for the ferry.

Visitor Information   **Fredrikstad Turistkontor** is on Turistsenteret, Østre Brohode in Gamle Fredrikstad (© **69-32-03-30**). From June to September, it's open Monday to Friday 8am to 7pm and Saturday 10am to 7pm; from October to May, Monday to Friday 8am to 4pm.

Fredrikstad was founded in 1567 as a marketplace at the mouth of the River Glomma. **Gamlebyen** (Old Town) became a fortress in 1663 and continued in that role until 1903, boasting some 200 guns in its heyday. It still serves as a military camp. The main guardroom and old convict prison are now the **Fredrikstad Museum,** Gamleslaveri (© **69-32-09-01**), open from May to September, Monday to Friday 11am to 5pm, Saturday and Sunday noon to 5pm. Admission is 30NOK ($3.35) adults and 10NOK ($1.10) children.

Outside the gates of Old Town is **Kongsten Fort,** on what was first called Gallows Hill, an execution site. When Fredrikstad Fortress was built, it was pro-visionally fortified in 1677, becoming known as Svenskeskremme (Swede Scarer). Present-day Kongsten Fort with its 20 cannons, underground chambers, passages, and countermines, eventually replaced it.

Since Fredrikstad's heyday as a trading port and merchant base, Old Town has attracted craftspeople and artisans, many of whom create their products in the Old Town's historic houses and barns. Many of these glassblowers, ceramic artists, and silversmiths choose not to display or sell their products at their studios, preferring instead to leave the sales aspect to local shops.

En Route to Tønsberg   You can drive back north from Fredrikstad to the town of Moss, where you can take a ferry to Horten. Once at Horten, signs will point the way south for the short drive to Tønsberg. Tønsberg is about 1½ hours from Oslo, with some 20 trains arriving daily.

TØNSBERG ⚓   Bordering the western bank of the Oslofjord, Tønsberg, 100 kilometers (64 miles) south of Oslo, is Norway's oldest town. It's divided into a historic area, filled with old clapboard-sided houses, and the commercial center, where the marketplace is located.

Visitor Information   In Tønsberg, **Tourist Information** is at Nedre Langgate 36B, N-3100 Tønsberg (© **33-31-02-20**). From June and August, it's open Monday to Saturday 10am to 5pm; July hours are daily from 10am to 8pm; and from September to May, it's open Monday to Friday 10am to 3:30pm.

Tønsberg was founded a year before King Harald Fairhair united parts of the country in 872, and this Viking town became a royal coronation site. Svend Foyn, who invented modern whaling and seal hunting, was born here.

Slottsfjellet, a huge hill fortress directly ahead of the train station, is touted as "the Acropolis of Norway." But it has only some meager ruins, and people mostly come here for the view from the lookout tower. Built in 1888, the **Slottsfjelltårnet** (© **33-31-18-72**) is open from May 18 to June 23, Monday to Friday 10am to 3pm; from June 24 to August 18, daily 11am to 6pm; from August 19 to September 15, Saturday and Sunday noon to 5pm; and from September 16 to 29, Saturday and Sunday noon to 3pm. Admission is 10NOK ($1.10) adults and 5NOK (55¢) children.

Nordbyen is the old and scenic part of town, with well-preserved houses. **Haugar** cemetery, at Møllebakken, is right in the town center, with the Viking graves of King Harald's sons, Olav and Sigrød.

Sem Church, Hageveien 32 (℗ **33-36-93-99**), the oldest in Vestfold, was built of stone in the Romanesque style around 1100. It's open from Tuesday to Friday 9am to 2pm; ask at the vestry. Admission is free.

You should also see **Fjerdingen,** a street of charming restored houses. Tønsberg was also a Hanseatic town during the Middle Ages, and some houses have been redone in typical Hanseatic style.

In the **Vestfold Folk Museum** ✿, Frammannsveien 30 (℗ **33-31-29-19**), there're many Viking and whaling treasures. One of the biggest (literally) thrills is the skeleton of a blue whale. There's also a real Viking ship displayed, the *Klastad* from Tjolling, built about A.D. 800. Admission is 30NOK ($3.35) adults, 20NOK ($2.20) seniors and students, and 10NOK ($1.10) children. It's open from mid-May to mid-September, Monday to Saturday 10am to 5pm, Sunday and holidays noon to 5pm; from mid-September to mid-May, Monday to Friday 10am to 2pm.

2 Bergen & the Fjords

In western Norway the landscape takes on an awesome beauty, with iridescent glaciers, deep fjords that slash into rugged, snowcapped mountains, roaring waterfalls, and secluded valleys that lie at the end of corkscrew-twisting roads. From Bergen the most beautiful fjords to visit are the **Hardanger** (best at blossom time, May and early June), to the south; the **Sogne,** Norway's longest fjord, immediately to the north; and the **Nordfjord,** north of that. A popular excursion on the Nordfjord takes visitors from Loen to Olden along rivers and lakes to the Brixdal Glacier.

If you have time, on the Hardangerfjord you can stop over at one of the fjord resorts, such as Ulvik or Lofthus. From many vantage points it's possible to see the Folgefonn Glacier, Norway's second-largest ice field, which spans more than 250 square kilometers (100 sq. miles).

Bergen, with its many sightseeing attractions, good hotels and restaurants, and its excellent boat, rail, and coach connections, is the best center for touring the fjord district. This ancient city looms large in Viking sagas. Until the 14th century, it was the seat of the medieval kingdom of Norway. The Hanseatic merchants established a major trading post here, holding sway until the 18th century.

BERGEN: GATEWAY TO THE FJORDS
ESSENTIALS
GETTING THERE   By Plane   The **Bergen Airport** at Flesland, 19 kilometers (12 miles) south of the city, offers frequent flights to Copenhagen and London, through which most international flights are routed.

Frequent airport bus service circles from the airport to the SAS Royal Hotel, Braathens SAFE's office at the Hotel Norge, and the city bus station. Buses depart every 20 minutes from Monday to Friday and every 30 minutes Saturday and Sunday. The one-way fare is 40NOK ($4.45). Taxis are readily available at the airport, or call ℗ **55-99-70-00.** A ride to the center costs 235NOK ($26).

By Train   Day and night trains arrive from Oslo (trip time: 6 to 8½ hours). For information, call the Bergen train station at ℗ **55-96-69-00.**

By Bus   Express buses travel to Bergen from Oslo in 11 hours. For long-distance bus information, call ℂ **55-32-14-80.**

By Car   A toll is charged on all vehicles driven into the city center Monday to Friday 6am to 10pm. A single ticket costs 10NOK ($1.10), a book of 20 tickets, 90NOK ($10).

To cross from Oslo to Bergen is a mountain drive filled with dramatic scenery. Since the country is split by mountains, there's no direct road. You can take the southern route, E76, going through mountain passes until the junction with Route 47; then head north to the ferry crossing at Kinsarvik that goes across the fjords to E16 leading west to Bergen. The northern route is via Highway 7, going through the resort of Geilo, to the junction with Route 47; then head south to Kinsarvik. After crossing on the ferry, you arrive at E16 and head west to reach Bergen.

VISITOR INFORMATION   Tourist Information, Bryggen 7 (ℂ **55-32-14-80**), is open from June to August, daily 8:30am to 10pm; from May and September, daily 9am to 8pm; from October to April, Monday to Saturday 9am to 4pm. They'll help you find accommodations, exchange foreign currency, and cash traveler's checks when banks are closed. You can also purchase tickets for city sightseeing or for tours of the fjords.

SPECIAL EVENTS   The annual **Bergen Festival,** held for 12 days in late May, features performances by regional, national, and international orchestras, dance ensembles, and theater groups. The complete festival schedule is usually available by February of each year. For festival and ticket information, contact the **Bergen Festival office** (ℂ **50-31-38-60**).

GETTING AROUND   By Bus   The **Central Bus Station** (Bystasjonen), Strømgaten 8 (ℂ **55-55-90-70**), is the terminal for all buses serving the Bergen and the Hardanger area, as well as the airport bus. Gaia Traffic runs a network of yellow-sided **city buses** (ℂ **55-59-32-00**) that serve the city center.

By Taxi   Sightseeing by taxi costs about 325NOK ($36) per hour.

WHERE TO STAY
Expensive
Clarion Admiral Hotel ✪   When it was originally built in 1906, this building was one of the largest warehouses in Bergen. In 1987, it was transformed into a comfortable, tastefully appointed hotel, and in 1998, it was enlarged and renovated into the bustling establishment you'll see today. Most rooms and bathrooms are a bit small but comfortable. However, the front rooms overlooking the harbor are not only more spacious but have dramatic nighttime vistas of

---

Value The Bergen Card

To cut costs, purchase a **Bergen Card,** which gives you free bus transport and usually free museum entrance throughout Bergen, plus discounts on car rentals, parking, and some cultural and leisure activities. Ask at Tourist Information. A 24-hour card costs 150NOK ($17) adults and 60NOK ($7) children 3 to 15. A 48-hour card sells for 230NOK ($26) adults and 100NOK ($11) children. Children 2 and under generally travel or enter free.

the Bergen harbor. The most desirable units open onto flower-bedecked balconies with the best harbor views in town.

Christian Sundts Gate 9, N-5004 Bergen. © **55-23-64-00.** Fax 55-23-64-64. 205 units. Mon–Thurs 1,545NOK ($172) double, from 2,500NOK ($278) suite; Fri–Sun 910NOK ($101) double, from 1,800NOK ($200) suite. AE, DC, MC, V. Bus: 2, 4, or 11. **Amenities:** Restaurant, bar; room service (noon–11pm). *In room:* TV, minibar, hair dryer.

First Hotel Marin 🏵🏵 In the heart of Bergen, this first-class hotel is new and elegant, catering almost equally to both business and leisure clients. Rooms are moderate to spacious in size, with bathrooms that are immaculately kept. For Bergen, the hotel offers a large number of suites, 34 deluxe ones in all. Many accommodations are reserved for nonsmokers, and the finest units are in front, overlooking the harbor. The best suites are a trio of penthouse units with a view so panoramic it encompasses all seven mountains surrounding Bergen.

Rosenkrantzgaten 8, N-5003 Bergen. © **53-05-15-00.** Fax 53-05-15-01. 122 units. 1,348–1,548NOK ($150–$172) double, 2,045NOK ($227) suite. AE, DC, MC, V. Bus: 1, 5, or 9. **Amenities:** Coffee shop, restaurant, bar; fitness center; Turkish bath; sauna; solarium; room service; laundry. *In room:* TV, minibar, hair dryer, trouser press.

Moderate

Augustin Hotel ☆ *Finds*   One of the best located hotels in Bergen, Augustin stands right in the shopping area along the harbor. Its best rooms open onto harbor views. One of the oldest family-run hotels of Bergen, Augustin was constructed in 1909 in the Jugendstil or Art Nouveau style. It has been in the same family for four generations. The more traditional rooms are in the old section, whereas the units in the new wing are better equipped and more modern. Rooms are available for allergy sufferers and wheelchair users, and many units are rented only to nonsmokers. Bathrooms have both showers and tubs.

Carl Sundts Gate 24, N-5004 Bergen. © **55-30-40-40.** Fax 55-30-40-10. www.scantours.com/augustin-hotel. htm. 87 units. 750–1,490NOK ($83–$165) double. AE, DC, MC, V. Bus: 1, 5, or 9. **Amenities:** Restaurant, wine cellar, bar; room service; baby-sitting. *In room:* TV, minibar, hair dryer, trouser press.

Inexpensive

Romantik Hotel Park ☆   This converted 1890 town house is in an attractive university area near Grieghall and Nygård Park. Rooms are traditionally furnished, often with antiques, and vary in size; all have good beds and adequate bathrooms with shower stalls. In summer, a neighboring building accommodates overflow guests, but these units, although comfortable, have less character. In the summer, reserve well in advance. The Romantik is a 10-minute walk from the train and bus stations.

Harald Hårfagresgaten 35 and Parkveien 22, N-5000 Bergen. © **55-54-44-60.** Fax 55-54-44-44. 40 units. 900NOK ($100) double. Rates include breakfast. AE, V. Free parking. Bus: 11. **Amenities:** Dining room serves big Norwegian breakfast, and later sandwiches and hot dishes as well as beer. *In room:* TV.

Steens Hotel *Value*   This is a stylish 1890 house that has been successfully converted to receive guests. The house has been owned and run by the same family since 1950. Rooms are moderate in size and most comfortable, and the bathrooms, though small, are beautifully maintained, containing shower stalls. The most ideal units are the front accommodations because they open onto a park. Within a short walk are the bus and railway stations. All doubles have private bathrooms; a few singles are rented without bathrooms for 620NOK ($69) per night.

22 Parkveien, N-5007 Bergen. © and fax **55-31-40-50.** 20 units, 16 with bathroom. 650–840NOK ($72–$93) double. Extra bed 150NOK ($17). Rates include Norwegian breakfast. AE, MC, V. Bus: 11. **Amenities:** Coffee and light meals served throughout the day. *In room:* TV.

Victoria Hotel   Between the harbor and the railway station, this hotel, constructed around 1912 and completely rebuilt in 1985, is a longtime favorite. It offers comfort and tradition. Rooms are medium-size and well furnished; half are reserved for nonsmokers, all come with shower units.

Kong Oscars Gate 29, N-5017 Bergen. © **800/528-1234** in the U.S., or 55-31-50-30. Fax 55-32-81-78. 43 units. Mid-May to mid-Sept, 1,290NOK ($143) double; mid-Sept to mid-May, 1,050NOK ($117) double Mon–Thurs, 750NOK ($83) double Fri–Sun. Rates include breakfast. AE, DC, MC, V. Parking 80NOK ($9). Bus: 2 or 4. **Amenities:** One of only two Japanese restaurants in Bergen; breakfast room and lounge with open fireplace. *In room:* TV, minibar.

WHERE TO DINE

Bryggeloftet/Stuen NORWEGIAN   This is the best-established restaurant along the harborfront. At street level the Stuen has low ceiling beams, carved banquettes, and 19th century murals of old Bergen, along with dozens of clipper-ship models. For a more formal meal, head upstairs to the Bryggeloftet, with its high ceilings and wood paneling. A dinner in either section might include fried porbeagle (a form of whitefish) served with shrimp, mussels, and a white-wine sauce; roast reindeer with cream sauce; or pepper steak with a salad. Several dif-ferent preparations of salmon and herring are featured, along with roast pork with Norwegian sour cabbage. This is a quintessential Norwegian type of place; come here if you're seeking authentic flavors, the type sea captains might have enjoyed a long time ago when they sailed into Bergen harbor.

Bryggen 11. © **55-31-06-30.** Reservations recommended. Main courses 130–159NOK ($14–$18); lunch smørbrød 65–79NOK ($7–$9). AE, DC, MC, V. Mon–Sat 11am–11:30pm; Sun 1–11:30pm. Bus: 1, 5, or 9.

Finnegaardstuene *Finds* NORWEGIAN/FRENCH At this restaurant, you'll find a richly timbered, partially paneled environment where four small-scale dining rooms create a cozy atmosphere of welcome intimacy. Cuisine revolves around Norwegian ingredients, especially very fresh fish, and classical French methods of preparation. Menus are likely to include platters of crayfish served with filets of French foie gras in a cider and foie gras sauce; a gratin of monkfish with sea scallops; filets of venison with juniper-berry sauce; and breast of duck with lime and fig sauce. We really like the way the chefs have created some culinary magic in sleepy Bergen. The menu is well thought out with care-fully prepared dishes.

Rosenkrantzgate 6. © **55-55-03-00.** Reservations recommended. Main courses 220–275NOK ($24–$31); set-price menu 520NOK ($58). AE, DC, MC, V. Mon–Sat 4:30–11pm. Closed 1 week at Easter, Dec 22–Jan 8. Bus: 5, 21.

To Kokker FRENCH Favored by celebrities, this restaurant occupies a building reconstructed in 1703 after a fire. Menu items include such time-tested favorites as lobster soup; whitebait roe with chopped onions, sour cream, and fresh-baked bread; and a filet of lamb with mustard sauce and pommes Provençal. Savvy local foodies are increasingly gravitating to this restaurant because of the competence of its cuisine and the use of first-rate ingredients.

Enhjørninggården. © **55-32-28-16.** Reservations required. Main courses 210–275NOK ($23–$31). AE, DC, MC, V. Mon–Sat 5–10pm. Bus: 1, 5, or 9.

SEEING THE SIGHTS

In addition to the sights below, take a stroll around **Bryggen (the Quay)**. This row of Hanseatic timbered houses, rebuilt along the waterfront after the disastrous fire of 1702, is what remains of medieval Bergen. The northern half burned to the ground as recently as 1955. Bryggen is on UNESCO's World Heritage List as one of the world's most significant cultural and historical re-creations of a medieval settlement. It's a center for arts and crafts, where painters, weavers, and craftspeople have their workshops.

Det Hanseatiske Museum In one of the best-preserved wooden build-ings at Bryggen, this museum illustrates Bergen's commercial life on the wharf centuries ago. German merchants, representatives of the Hanseatic League cen-tered in Lübeck, lived in these medieval houses built in long rows up from the harbor. The museum is furnished with authentic articles dating from 1704.

Finnegårdsgaten 1A, Bryggen. © **55-31-41-89.** Admission May–Sept 35NOK ($3.90) adults; Oct–Apr 20NOK ($2.20) adults; free for children. June–Aug daily 9am–5pm; Sept–May daily 11am–2pm. Bus: 1, 5, or 9.

Mariakirke (St. Mary's Church) The oldest building in Bergen (its exact date is unknown, but perhaps from the mid-12th century) is this Romanesque church, one of the most beautiful in Norway. Its altar is the oldest ornament in the church, and there's a baroque pulpit, donated by Hanseatic merchants, with carved figures depicting everything from Chastity to Naked Truth. Church-music concerts are given from May to August several nights a week.

Dreggen. ☎ **55-31-59-60.** Admission 10NOK ($1.10) adults, free for children. May 18–Sept 10 Mon–Fri 11am–4pm; Sept 11–May 17 Tues–Fri noon–1:30pm. Bus: 1, 5, or 9.

Fløybanen   A short walk from the fish market is the station where the funicular heads up to Fløien, the most famous of Bergen's seven hills. At 320 meters (1,050 ft.), the view of the city, the neighboring hills, and the harbor is worth every øre.

Vetrlidsalm 23A. ☎ **55-31-48-00.** Round-trip 40NOK ($4.45) adults, 20NOK ($2.20) children. May 25–Aug, Mon–Fri 7:30am–midnight, Sat 8am–midnight, Sun 9am–midnight; Sept to May 24, Mon–Thurs 8am–11pm, Fri 8am–11:30pm, Sat 8am–11:30pm, Sun 9am–11pm. Bus: 6.

Gamle Bergen ⋇   At Elsesro and Sandviken is a collection of houses from the 18th and 19th centuries set in a park. Old Town is complete with streets, an open square, and narrow alleyways. Some of the interiors are exceptional, including a merchant's living room in the typical style of the 1870s—padded sofas, heavy curtains, potted plants—a perfect setting for Ibsen's *A Doll's House.*

Elsesro and Sandviken. ☎ **55-25-78-50.** Admission 40NOK ($4.45) adults, 20NOK ($2.20) children and students. Houses, mid-May to Aug only, guided tours daily on the hour 10am–4pm. Park and restaurant, daily noon–6pm. Bus: 1 or 9 from the city center (every 10 minutes).

Troldhaugen (Troll's Hill) ⋇   This Victorian house, in beautiful rural surroundings at Hop, near Bergen, was the summer villa of composer Edvard Grieg. The house contains Grieg's own furniture, paintings, and other mementos. His Steinway grand piano is frequently used at concerts given in the house during the annual Bergen festival, as well as at Troldhaugen's own summer concerts. Grieg and his wife, Nina, are buried in a cliff grotto on the estate.

Troldhaugveien 65, Hop. ☎ **55-91-17-91.** Admission 50NOK ($6) adults, free for children. Apr 21–Sept, daily 9am–6pm; Oct–Nov, Mon–Fri 10am–2pm, Sat–Sun 10am–4pm; Jan–Apr 20, Mon–Fri 10am–2pm. Closed Dec. Bus: To Hop from the Bergen bus station (Platforms 18–20); exit, turn right, walk about 200 yards, turn left at Hopsvegen, and follow signs (15-minute walk).

ORGANIZED TOURS

A 1-hour **tram tour** uses the city tram lines and specially designed red-sided streetcars equipped with multilingual headsets. The tour departs every hour on the hour from Bryggen and costs 75NOK ($8) for adults and 40NOK ($4.45) for children. It operates from May to September daily 10am to 7pm.

The most popular and most highly recommended **bus tour** of Bergen is the 3-hour city tour, which departs daily at 10am and covers all major sightseeing attractions. These include Troldhaugen and Old Bergen. It also runs from May to September and costs 230NOK ($26) adults and 100NOK ($11) children. For information and tickets for either tour, contact the tourist office at Bryggen 7 (☎ **55-32-14-80**).

THE SHOPPING SCENE

Bergen's pedestrian shopping area includes the streets **Gamle Strandgaten, Torgalmenningen,** and **Marken.** Shops are open weekdays 9am to 4:30pm (Thursdays to 7pm). Saturday hours are from 9am to 3pm. Shopping centers are open weekdays from 9am to 8pm, and close at 4pm on Saturday. When cruise ships are anchored in the harbor, most shops extend their hours to take advantage of the tourist trade. You'll find the widest selection of national handcrafts in and around **Bryggen Brukskunst,** the restored Old Town near the wharf, where many craftspeople have taken over old houses and ply ancient Norwegian trades. Crafts boutiques often display Bergen souvenirs, many based on designs 300 to 1,500 years old. For example, we purchased a reproduction of a Romanesque-style cruciform pilgrim's badge. Other attractive items are likely to include sheepskin-lined booties and exquisitely styled handwoven wool dresses. The leading outlet for glassware and ceramics, **Prydkunst-Hjertholm,** Olav Kyrres Gate 7 (© **55-31-70-27**), purchases much of its merchandise directly from the studios of Norwegian and other Scandinavian artisans who turn out quality goods not only in glass and ceramics, but also in pewter, brass, wood, and textiles.

BERGEN AFTER DARK

Opened in mid-1978, the modern **Grieg Hall (Grieghallen),** Lars Hillesgate 3A (© **55-21-61-50**), is Bergen's monumental showcase for music, drama, and a host of other cultural events. The Bergen Symphony Orchestra, founded in 1765, performs here from August to May on Thursday and some Fridays.

Norway's oldest theater performs from September to June at **Den National Scene,** Engen 1 (© **55-54-97-10**). Its repertoire consists of classical Norwegian and international drama and contemporary plays, as well as visiting productions of opera and ballet in conjunction with the annual Bergen Festival. Performances are held from Monday to Saturday.

In summer, the **Bergen Folklore dancing troupe** (© **55-31-67-10**) arranges a 1-hour folklore program at the Bryggens Museum on Tuesday and Thursday at 9pm. Tickets, which cost 95NOK ($11), are on sale at the tourist information center or at the door. **Ulriken Mountain Concerts** offers free folk and classical concerts weekdays at 7pm from June to August. A round-trip ticket to reach this mountaintop show costs 70NOK ($8) adults and 35NOK ($3.90) children, which includes rides on a shuttle bus from the Bergen tourist office (leaving at a quarter past the hour from 9:15am to 8:15pm) and the Ulriken cable car.

The most-frequented pub in the city center, the **Kontoret Pub,** Ole Bulls Plass 8–10 (© **55-90-07-60**), is in the Hotel Norge next to the Dickens restaurant/pub. Drinkers can wander freely between the two places, since they're connected. In the Kontoret you can order the same food served at Dickens, though most people seem to come here to drink. It's open from Sunday to Thursday 4pm to 1am and Friday and Saturday 4pm to 3am.

Wednesday to Friday, **Engelen,** in the Radisson SAS Royal Hotel (© **55-54-30-00**), is one of Bergen's more elegant discos. On these nights an older, sedate crowd gathers to enjoy the music and ambience. On Saturday, however, beware—the atmosphere changes drastically with the arrival of 20-somethings intent on having fun. It's open from Wednesday to Saturday 9pm to 3am, with a cover of 50NOK ($6); hotel guests enter free.

EXPLORING THE FJORDS

Norway's fjords can be explored from both Oslo and Bergen by ship and car or by a scenic train ride. Here are the details.

BY CAR FROM BERGEN

Bergen is the best departure point for trips to the fjords: To the south lies the famous **Hardangerfjord** ✶✶ and to the north the **Sognefjord** ✶✶✶, cutting 180 kilometers (111 miles) inland. We've outlined a driving tour of the fjords, starting in Bergen and heading east on Route 7 to Ulvik, a distance of 150 kilometers (93 miles).

ULVIK   Ulvik is that rarity: an unspoiled resort. It lies like a fist at the end of an arm of the Hardangerfjord that's surrounded in summer by misty peaks and fruit farms. The village's 1858 church is attractively decorated in the style of the region. It's open from June to August, daily 9am to 5pm, and presents concerts.

From Ulvik, you can explore the **Eidfjord** district, which is the northern tip of the Hardangerfjord, home to some 1,000 people and a paradise for hikers. Anglers are attracted to the area because of its mountain trout.

The district contains nearly one-quarter of **Hardangervidda National Park** (*, which is on Europe's largest high-mountain plateau. It's home to 20,000 wild reindeer, and well-marked hiking trails connect a series of 15 tourist huts.

Several canyons, including the renowned **Måbø Valley,** lead down from the plateau to the fjords. Here, you'll see the famous 170-meter (550-ft.) **Voringfoss** (* waterfall; the Valurefoss in Hjømo Valley has a free fall of almost 245 meters (800 ft.).

Part of the 1,000-year-old road across Norway, traversing the Måbø Valley, has been restored for hardy hikers.

En Route to Voss   From Ulvik, take Highway 20 to Route 13. Follow Route 13 to Voss, 40 kilometers (25 miles) west of Ulvik and 100 kilometers (63 miles) east of Bergen.

VOSS   Between the Sogne and Hardanger fjords, Voss is a famous year-round resort, also known for its folklore and as the birthplace of football hero Knute Rockne. Maybe the trolls don't strike fear into the hearts of farm children anymore, but they're still called out of hiding to give visitors a little fun.

Voss is a natural base for exploring the two largest fjords in Norway, the Sognefjord to the north and the Hardangerfjord to the south. In and around Voss are glaciers, mountains, fjords, waterfalls, orchards, rivers, and lakes.

A ride on the **Hangursbanen cable car** (✆ **56-51-12-12**) offers panoramic views of Voss and the environs. The hardy take the cable car up, then spend the rest of the afternoon strolling down the mountain. A round-trip ride costs 50NOK ($6) adults, 25NOK ($2.80) children 8 to 16, and it's free for children 7 and under. The cable-car entrance is on a hillside that's a 10-minute walk north of the town center. It's open in summer and winter, but is closed May and from September to November.

Built in 1277, the **Vangskyrkje,** Vangsgata 3 (✆ **56-51-22-78**), with a timbered tower, contains a striking Renaissance pulpit, a stone altar and triptych, fine wood carvings, and a painted ceiling. It's a 5-minute walk east of the railroad station. We recommend that you call in advance to reserve an English-speaking guide. Admission is 15NOK ($1.65) adults, 5NOK (55¢) children, and free for children 6 and under. The church is open only June to August daily 10am to 4pm.

Voss Folkemuseum, Mølster (✆ **56-51-15-11**), is a collection of authentically furnished houses that shows what early farm life was like. Lying just north of Voss on a hillside overlooking the town, the museum consists of more than a dozen farmhouses and other buildings, ranging in age from the 1500s to around 1870. Admission is 30NOK ($3.35) adults, and it's free for children. It's open from May and September daily 10am to 5pm; from June to August daily 10am to 7pm; and from October to April Monday to Friday 10am to 3pm and Sunday noon to 3pm.

A little west of Voss in Finne, **Finnesloftet** (© **56-51-11-00**) is one of Norway's oldest timbered houses, dating from the mid-13th century. It's a 15-minute walk west of the railway station. Admission is 30NOK ($3.35) adults and 15NOK ($1.65) children. It's open from June 15 to August 15 daily 10:30am to 4:30pm.

An Excursion to the Sognefjord   If you have time, you may want to visit the Sognefjord district, the largest of all Norwegian fjords. From Voss continue north on Route 13 to **Vik.** The scenery is beautiful and the road goes along for miles across a desolate tableland at 900 meters (3,000 ft.) above sea level. The lakes on a summer day appear green, and on the distant slopes is snow.

In Vik, see the stave church, one of the most attractive in Norway; then take the road to **Vangsnes,** where you can make the short car-ferry connection across the Sognefjord to Balestrand or Dragsvik. Once across, take Route 5 north. The highway is steep, bringing you through rolling countryside with waterfalls until you reach **Viksdalen,** about 65 kilometers (40 miles) from Dragsvik.

BALESTRAND   Long known for its arts and crafts, Balestrand lies on the northern rim of the Sognefjord, at the junction of the Vetlefjord, the Esefjord, and the Fjaerlandsfjord.

Kaiser Wilhelm II, a frequent visitor to Balestrand, presented the district with two statues of old Norse heroes, King Bele and Fridtjof the Bold, which stand in the town center.

You can explore by setting out in nearly any direction, on scenic country lanes with little traffic, or a wide choice of marked trails and upland farm tracks. A touring map may be purchased at the **tourist office** in the town center (© **57-69-16-17**). There's good sea fishing, as well as lake and river trout fishing. Fishing tackle, rowboats, and bicycles can all be rented in the area.

En Route to Flåm   From Balestrand, follow Route 55 east along the Sognefjord, crossing the fjord via ferry at Dragsvik and by bridge at Sogndal. At Sogndal, drive east to Kaupanger, where you'll cross the Ardalsfjord by ferry, south to Revsnes. In Revsnes, pick up Route 11 heading southeast. Drive east until you connect with a secondary road heading southwest through Kvigno and Aurland. When you arrive in Aurland, take Route 601 southwest to the town of Flåm, 95 kilometers (60 miles) southeast of Balestrand and 165 kilometers (103 miles) east of Bergen.

FLÅM ⚓   Flåm (pronounced *Flawm*) lies on the Aurlandsfjord, a tip of the more famous Sognefjord. In the village you can visit the old church dating from 1667, with painted walls done in typical Norwegian country style.

Flåm is an excellent starting point for excursions by car or boat to other well-known centers on the Sognefjord, Europe's longest and deepest fjord. Worth exploring are two of the wildest and most beautiful fingers of the Sognefjord: Nærøyfjord and Aurlandfjord. Ask at the **tourist office,** near the rail station (© **57-63-21-06**), about a summer-only cruise from Flåm, where you can experience the dramatic scenery of both of these fjords. From Flåm by boat, you can disembark either in Gudvangen or Aurland and continue the tour by coach. Alternatively, you can return to Flåm by train.

There're also a number of easy walks in the Flåm district. The tourist office has a map detailing these walks.

BY SHIP/TOUR FROM BERGEN

There're several ways to visit Sognefjord, Norway's longest fjord, from Bergen. One way is to cross the fjord on an express steamer that travels from Bergen to

What a Ride: Exploring the Fjords by Scenic Train

One of the great train rides of Europe is the **Bergensbanen** 🚂🚂🚂 (© **55-96-69-00** for information), with five daily departures from Oslo, plus an additional train on Sunday. The most popular routing is Oslo to Bergen, although you can also take the train from Bergen to Oslo, depending on where you land in Norway. We think this is the most scenic and beautiful train ride in the world. Departures are from Oslo Central Station, and the trip takes 7½ to 8½ hours to cut across some of the most panoramic fjord and mountain scenery in Europe. The cost of a one-way ticket is 550NOK ($61), but a 30NOK ($3.35) seat reservation is required.

If your time is more limited, you can take a brief train ride from Bergen that will cover the most panoramic part of the journey.

The most exciting rail journey in Norway is a 12-hour tour from Bergen, encompassing two arms of the Sognefjord. The main feature of this journey—and the reason most passengers take the ride—is the 19-kilometer (12-mile) route from Myrdal to Flåm (see above). An electric train "drops" 880 meters (2,900 ft.), past seemingly endless waterfalls. In summer, the tour leaves from the Bergen railroad station daily at 8:05am and 8:30am, and from Monday to Friday at 11:48am. Guests may have lunch at Flåm, then board a river steamer for Gudvangen, where they hop on a bus to Voss, then a train back to Bergen. The round-trip fare, excluding meals, is 560NOK ($62) adults and 280NOK ($31) children under 12. Holders of Eurail or Scandinavian Rail Passes get a reduced fare. For more information, contact the Bergen tourist office (© **55-32-14-80**).

Gudvangen. From Gudvangen, passengers go to Voss (see above), and from Voss a train runs back to Bergen. You can go by boat, bus, and then train for 550NOK ($61) round-trip. Details about this and other tours are available from the **Tourist Information** office in Bergen, Bryggen 7 (© **55-32-14-80**).

If you have more than a day to see the fjords in the environs of Bergen, you can take the grandest fjord cruise in the world, a **coastal steamer** going all the way to the North Cape and beyond. The coastal steamers are elegantly appointed ships that travel along the western coast of Norway from Bergen to Kirkenes, carrying passengers and cargo to 34 ports along the Norwegian coast. Eleven ships in all make the journey year-round. The ships sail through Norway's more obscure fjords, providing panoramic scenery and numerous opportunities for adventure. Along the way, sightseeing excursions to the surrounding mountains and glaciers are offered, as well as sails on smaller vessels through some of the more obscure fjords.

The chief operator of these coastal cruises is the **Norwegian Coastal Voyage/Bergen Line,** 405 Park Ave., New York, NY 10022 (© **800/323-7436** or 212/319-1300 in the U.S.). Tours may be booked heading north from Bergen, or south from Kirkenes. The 7-day northbound journey costs $636 to $2,865 per person, including meals and taxes. Visitors opting for the southbound trip from Kirkenes pay $643 to $2,370.

14

Portugal

by Darwin Porter & Danforth Prince

Lisbon presides over a country that has one of Europe's fastest-growing economies, much of it fueled by investments that have poured in since Portugal joined the European Union. About 260 kilometers (160 miles) south of Lisbon, the maritime province of the Algarve, often called the "garden of Portugal," is the southwestern most part of Europe. Its coastline stretches 160 kilometers (100 miles) and is dotted with hundreds of beaches—the finest in Portugal.

1 Lisbon & Environs

Lisbon has blossomed into a cosmopolitan city—Europe's smallest capital is no longer a backwater at the far corner of Iberia. Sections along Avenida da Liberdade, the main street, at times evoke Paris in miniature. Sidewalk portrait painters beg to sketch your likeness, artisans offer you jewelry claiming it's gold (you both know it isn't), and vendors peddle handcrafts from embroidery to leather work. Some of the formerly clogged streets of the Baixa have been closed to traffic, and cobblestone pedestrian malls have been created.

Today, after a long slumber, there's excitement again in this city of seven hills. The world dropped in on Lisbon as it celebrated EXPO '98, marking the 500th anniversary of Vasco da Gama's journey to India. Many of the attractions and facilities remain, including the Oceanarium, the largest aquarium in Europe. The Utopia Pavilion—an indoor stadium with advanced theatrical equipment—becomes Lisbon's first multimedia arena for concerts, sporting events, theatrical shows, and international congresses. The Lisbon Exhibition Center today holds dozens of international affairs every year, and the recreational harbor now has a capacity for between 700 to 900 moorings for leisure craft.

Some 1.6 million people now call Lisbon home, and many Lisboetas (Lisboans), having drifted in from the far corners of the world, don't even speak Portuguese.

Consider an off-season visit, especially in spring or fall, when the city is at its most glorious, before the hot and humid days of July and August. Lisbon isn't infested with visitors then, and you can wander about without fear of being trampled underfoot.

ESSENTIALS

GETTING THERE By Plane Both foreign and domestic flights land at Lisbon's **Aeroporto de Lisboa** (© **21-841-35-00** or 21-849-4323; www.ana-aeroportos.pt), located about 6 kilometers (4 miles) from the heart of the city. An AERO-BUS costing 500$ (€$2.80) goes between the airport and the Cais do Sodre train station every 20 minutes, from 7am to 9am. It makes 10 intermediate stops, including Praça dos Restauradores and Praça do Comercio. You can also go by taxi. Passengers line up, British style, in a usually well-organized line at the sidewalk in front of the airport. The average fare to central Lisbon is 2,000$ to 3,000$ (€10 to €15, $10 to $14). Luggage is 340$ (€1.70, $1.65) extra per piece.

For ticket sales, flight reservations, and information about the city and the country, you can get in touch with the Lisbon personnel of TAP Air Portugal at Praça do Marquês de Pombal 3A (© 21-841-69-90 for reservations).

By Train   Most international rail passengers from Madrid and Paris arrive at the **Santa Apolonia Rail Station,** the major terminal, by the Tagus near the Alfama district. Two daily trains make the 10-hour run from Madrid to Lisbon. Rail lines from northern and eastern Portugal also arrive at this station. **Gare de Oriente** at Expo Urbe opened in 1998 and is the hub for some long-distance and suburban trains, including such destinations as Porto, Sintra, the Beiras, Minho, and the Douro. Other rail terminals are **Estaçaodo Rossio,** where you can get trains to Sintra, and the **Cais do Sodré,** with trains to Cascais and Estoril on the Costa do Sol. At **Sul e Sueste,** you can board trains to the Algarve. For **rail information** at any of the terminals, call © **21-888-40-25.**

By Bus   Buses from all over Portugal arrive at the Rodoviaria da Estremadura, av. Casal Ribeiro 18B (© 21-357-77-15), which lies near Praça Saldanha, about a 30-minute walk from the Praça dos Restauradores. Buses 1, 21, and 32 will deliver you to the Rossio, and bus 1 goes on to the Cais do Sodré, if you're checked into a hotel at Estoril or Cascais. At least 10 buses a day leave for Lagos, a gateway to the Algarve, and 15 buses head north every day to Porto. There are eight daily buses leaving from here for Coimbra, the university city in the north.

By Car   International motorists must arrive through Spain, the only nation connected to Portugal via road. You'll have to cross Spanish border points, which usually poses no great difficulty. The roads are moderately well maintained. From Madrid, if you head west, the main road (N-620) from Tordesillas goes southwest by way of Salamanca and Ciudad Rodrigo to reach the Portuguese frontier at Fuentes de Onoro.

If you have a rented car, make sure that your insurance covers Portugal. Drive on the right side of the road; international signs and symbols are used. There are 15 border crossings, most of which are open daily from 7am to midnight.

VISITOR INFORMATION   **Tourist offices**   The main tourist office in Lisbon is at the **Palácio da Foz,** Praça dos Restauradores, at the Baixa end of Avenida da Liberdade (© **21-346-63-07;** www.portugalinside.pt; metro: Restauradores), open from Monday to Saturday 9am to 8pm, Sunday 10am to 6pm.

Lisboa Turismo, Rua do Praça dos Restauradores (© **21-346-3314;** metro: Restauradores), dispenses information about the city itself. It is open from 9am to 6pm. It sells the Lisbon Card, an open sesame for visitors, and an inexpensive and convenient way to see the town. The card provides free city transportation and entrance fees to museums and other attractions, plus discounts to see events. For adults, a 1-day pass costs 2,100$ (€10.50, $10); 2 days 3,500$ (€17.50, $17); 3 days 4,500$ (€22.50, $22). Children 5 to 11 pay 850$ (€4.25, $4.13) for 1 day, 1,200$ (€6, $6) for 2 days, and 1,700$ (€8.50, $8) for 3 days.

Websites   In addition to the tourist office's Web site, **www.portugalvirtual.pt** offers an extensive collection of Web links for exploring Portugal in depth. Main categories include "Tourism," "Shopping," "Accommodations," and "Restaurants."

Lisbon

ATTRACTIONS ●
Alfama 24
Bairro Alto 21
Belém 28
Castelo São Jorge 25
Mosteiro dos Jerónimos 30
Museu Antóniano 22
Museu da Marinha 29
Museu de Arte Popular 31
Museu de Fundação Calouste Gulbenkian 12
Museu Nacional de Arte Antiga 1
Oceanário de Lisboa 13
Padrão dos Descobrimentos 32
Sé Cathedral 23
Torre de Belém 27

ACCOMMODATIONS ■
Avenida Palace 20
Británia 15
Casa de São Mamede 5
Da Lapa 4
Dom Carlos 11
Four Seasons The Ritz Lisbon 8
Hotel Albergaria da Senhora do Monte 26
Hotel Dom Pedro 6
Hotel Lisboa Plaza 17
Hotel Tivoli 14
Hotel Veneza 16
Janelas Verdes Inn 2
Jorge V Hotel 7
Lisboa Sheraton Hotel & Towers 10
Orion Lisboa 19
Principe Real 18
Residência Nazreth 9
York House 3

CITY LAYOUT   Lisbon is best approached through its gateway, **Praça do Comércio** (Commerce Square or Black Horse Square), bordering the Tagus. This is one of Europe's most perfectly planned squares, and it's the site of the Stock Exchange and various government ministries. Directly west stands the late 19th-century City Hall, fronting Praça do Município. Heading north from Commerce Square, you enter the bustling **Praça Dom Pedro IV,** popularly known as the Rossio. The "drunken" undulation of the sidewalks, with their arabesques of black and white, have led to the appellation "the dizzy praça." Opening onto the Rossio is the Teatro Nacional Dona Maria II. If you arrive by train, you'll enter the **Estação do Rossio,** whose exuberant Manueline architecture is worth seeing. Separating the Rossio from Avenida da Liberdade is **Praça dos Restauradores,** named in honor of the Restoration, when the Portuguese chose their own king and freed themselves from 60 years of Spanish rule. The event is marked by an obelisk.

Lisbon's main street is handsomely laid out **Avenida da Liberdade (Avenue of Liberty),** dating from 1880 and once called the "antechamber of Lisbon." Avenida da Liberdade is like a mile-long park, with shade trees, gardens, and center walks for the promenading crowds. Flanking it are fine shops, headquarters for many major airlines, travel agents, coffeehouses with sidewalk tables, and hotels, including the Tivoli. At the top of the avenue is **Praça Marquês de Pombal,** with a statue erected in honor of Pombal, the 18th-century prime minister credited with Lisbon's reconstruction in the aftermath of the 1755 earthquake. Proceeding north, you'll enter **Parque Eduardo VII,** named in honor of Queen Victoria's son, who paid a state visit to Lisbon. In the park is the Estufa Fria, a greenhouse well worth a visit.

GETTING AROUND   CARRIS (℃ 21-363-20-44) operates the network of funiculars, trains, subways, and buses in Lisbon. They sell a *"bihete de assinatura turistico"* good for 4 days of unlimited travel, costing 1,660$ (€8.30, $8). You can also purchase a 1-day pass for 460$ (€2.30, $2.20) or a 7-day pass for 2,490$ (€12.45, $12). Passes are sold in CARRIS booths, open from 8am to 8pm daily, in most Metro stations and network train stations. You must show a passport to purchase one of these passes.

By Metro   Metro stations are designated by large M signs. The subway runs daily from 6:30am to 1am. A single ticket costs 80$ (€0.40, 43¢) per ride. You can buy 10 tickets at one time for 660$ (€3.30, $3.15). For more information, call ℃ **21-355-84-57.**

By Bus & Tram   These are among the cheapest in Europe. Electric trams (**electricos**) make the steep run up to the Bairro Alto and are usually painted a rich Roman gold. You pay a flat fare of 160$ (€0.80, 75¢) on a bus if you buy the ticket from the driver. The transportation system within the city limits is divided into zones ranging from one to five, and your fare depends on how many zones you traverse. Buses and electricos run daily from 6am to 1am.

By Electric Train   Lisbon is connected to all the towns and villages along the Portuguese Riviera by a smooth-running modern electric train system. You can board at the waterfront **Cais do Sodre Station** in Lisbon and head up the coast all the way to Cascais. Only one class of seat is offered, and the rides are cheap and generally comfortable. Sintra can't be reached by the electric train. You must go to the **Estação do Rossio,** opening onto Praça Dom Pedro IV, where frequent connections can be made. On the Lisbon-Cascais, Lisbon-Estoril, and Lisbon-Sintra run, the one-way fare is 195$ (€1.03, 95¢).

By Taxi   Taxis usually are diesel-engine Mercedes, charging a basic fare of 310$ (€1.55, $1.54) for the first 440 meters (480 yd). Most fares in the city average 900$ (€4.50, $4.30), with 20% extra from 10pm to 6am. The driver is allowed by law to tack on another 50% if your luggage weighs more than 30 kilograms (66 lbs). Portuguese tip about 20% of an already modest fare. It is important to verify that the meter has indeed been activated the moment you step into a cab. For a **radio taxi,** call ✆ **21-811-90-00** or 21-793-27-56.

By Car   Car-rental kiosks at the airport and in the city center include **Avis,** Avenida Praia da Vitoria 12C (✆ **21-351-45-60**); **Hertz,** Qto. Frangelha Baixio (✆ **21-849-27-22**); and **Budget,** Qto. Pasereinha 2685 (✆ **21-994-04-43**). *Warning:* Driving in congested Lisbon is extremely difficult and potentially dangerous; the city has an alarmingly high accident rate and parking is impossible. It's best to wait and rent a car for excursions from the capital.

ⓒ *FAST FACTS:* Lisbon

American Express Amex is represented by Top Tours, av. Duque de Loule 108 (✆ **21-317-02-40**; metro: Restauradores), open from Monday to Friday 9:30am to 1pm and 2:30 to 6:30pm.

Business Hours Typically, **shops** are open from Monday to Friday 9am to 1pm and 3 to 7pm (some stay open through lunch) and Saturday 9am to 1pm; some are also open Saturday afternoon. **Banks** are open from Monday to Friday 8:30am to 3pm; some offer a foreign-exchange service from Monday to Saturday 6 to 11pm.

Currency The Portuguese currency unit is the **escudo,** written **1$00.** Fractions of an escudo (**centavos**) follow the "$"; for example, 100 escudos is written "100$00." The exchange rate used in this chapter was $1 = 210 escudos, or 1 escudo = 4.8¢. At press time, £1 = approximately 310 escudos. The euro rate is currently fixed at €1 = 200.48 escudos (or 1 escudo =€.005).

Dentists/Doctors Contact **Clinica Medical Espanha,** Rua Dom Luis de Noroha 32 (✆ **21-796-74-57**; metro: Plaça Espanha), where some dentists speak English. Virtually every hotel maintains a list of doctors and dentists who can be called upon in emergencies.

Drugstores A central and well-stocked one is **Farmácia Vall,** Av. Visconde Valmor 60A (✆ **21-797-30-43**; metro: Saldanha). Pharmacies that are closed post a notice indicating the nearest one that's open.

Embassies/Consulates If you lose your passport or have some other pressing problem, you'll need to get in touch with the **U.S. Embassy,** Avenida das Forcas Armadas (Sete Rios), 1600 Lisboa (✆ **21-727-33-00**; metro: Entre Campos). Hours are from Monday to Friday 8am to 12:30pm and 1:30 to 5pm. If you've lost a passport, the embassy can take photos for you and help you obtain the proof of citizenship needed to get a replacement. The **Canadian Embassy** is at Av. da Liberdade 144, 4th floor, 1250 Lisboa (✆ **21-347-48-92**; metro: Avenida); hours are from Monday to Friday 9:30am to 12:30pm and 1:30 to 5pm (in July and August, the embassy closes at 1pm on Fridays). The **British Embassy,** Rua São Bernardo 33, 1200 Lisboa (✆ **21-392-40-00**; metro: Avenida), is open from Monday to Friday 9:30am to 12:30pm and 3 to 4:30pm. **Australians and New Zealanders** can refer to the British Embassy. The **Republic of Ireland Embassy,** Rua de Imprensa à Estrêla 1, 1200 Lisboa (☏ **21-396-15-69;** metro: Rossio), is open from Monday through Friday from 9:30am to noon and 2:30 to 4:30pm.

Emergencies   To call the police or an ambulance in Lisbon, telephone ☏ **112.** In case of fire, call ☏ **21-342-22-22.**

Hospitals In case of a medical emergency, inquire at your hotel or call your embassy and ask the staff there to recommend an English-speaking physician; or try the **British Hospital,** Rua Saraiva de Carvalho 49 (☏ **21-395-50-67;** bus: 7, 40, 49, or 60), where the telephone operator, staff, and doctors all speak English.

Post Office The general post office is on Praça do Comércio (☏ **21-346-32-31;** metro: Rossio), open from Monday to Friday 7am to 7pm.

Telephone The **country code** for Portugal is **351.** The **city code** for Lisbon was changed in November 1999 from 01 to **21;** use this code when calling from anywhere outside or inside Portugal—you must add it even within Lisbon itself.

You can make a **local call** in Lisbon in one of the many telephone booths. For most **long-distance calls,** particularly transatlantic calls, go to the central post office (see above). Give an assistant there the number you wish, and he or she will make the call, billing you at the end. Some phones are equipped for using calling cards, including American Express and Visa. You can also purchase phone cards from the post office in denominations of 50 units for 555$ (€2.83, $2.65), 100 units for 1,011$ (€5.05, $4.85), or 150 units for 1,624$ (€8.10, $8). Phone cards can be used at any public phone in Portugal. Phone debit cards are used only in public phones in public places. These cards bear one of two different names; T.L.P. or Cred-iFone. Both are sold at the cashier's desk of most hotels as well as at post offices.

To make an international call using your calling card, and thereby bypassing many of the add-on charges imposed by your hotel, dial the appropriate access number to reach a North American operator or an English-language voice prompt. For **AT&T,** call ☏ **05-017-1288;** for **MCI,** call ☏ **05-017-1234;** for **Sprint,** call ☏ **05-017-1877.**

WHERE TO STAY
IN THE CENTER
Very Expensive

Da Lapa 🕭🕭🕭   We never thought we'd see a hotel replace the Ritz as the premier address, but Da Lapa does it. Its lushly manicured gardens (huge by urban standards) lie close to the Tagus, south of the city center. All but about 20 of the units are in a six-story modern wing. The public areas have multicolored ceiling frescoes and patterned marble floors in sometimes startling geometric patterns.

Rua do Pau de Bandeira 4, 1200 Lisboa. ☏ **21-395-00-05.** Fax 21-395-06-65. www.orient-expresshotels. com. 102 units. 60,000$–80,000$ (€300–€400, $288–$384) double; from 110,000$ (€550, $528) suite. Rates include breakfast. AE, DC, MC, V. Free parking. Bus: 13 or 27. **Amenties:** 2 restaurants; bar; pool; room service; laundry/dry cleaning. *In room:* A/C, TV, minibar, hair dryer.

Four Seasons Hotel The Ritz Lisbon 🕭🕭🕭   One of the most famous and legendary hotels in Lisbon, this was built by dictator Antonio Salazar in the late

1950s. In 1998, its management contract was taken over by the Four Seasons group, which immediately embarked on a sweeping upgrade from the English Victorian-themed lobby to the supremely comfortable rooms. Each has its own terrace, about half of them overlooking Edward VII Park. Bathrooms have double basins and lots of electronic extras. Service, especially among the concierge staff, is superb.

Rua Rodrigo Fonseca 88, 1200 Lisboa. ℂ **800/332-3442** in the U.S., or 21-383-20-20. Fax 21-383-17-83. www.fourseasons.com. 284 units. 45,000$–63,000$ (€225–€315, $216–$302) double; from 115,000$ (€575, $552) suite. AE, DC, MC, V. Free parking. Metro: Rotunda. Bus: 1, 2, 9, or 32. **Amenities:** 2 restaurants, bar, cafe; fitness center; salon; room service; baby-sitting; laundry/dry cleaning. *In room:* A/C, TV, minibar, hair dryer, safe.

Hotel Dom Pedro ⟨R⟩⟨R⟩   One of Lisbon's newest hotels, rated five stars by the Portuguese government and associated with some of the most glamorous hotels of the Algarve and Madeira, the Dom Pedro is set within the very central Amoreiras district, across from one of the city's biggest shopping centers. The interior is as conservative and rich-looking as the exterior is futuristic. Rooms are richly furnished.

Av. Engenheiro, Duarte Pacheco, 1070 Lisboa. ℂ **21-389-6600.** Fax 21-389-6601. www.dompedro-hotels.com. 262 units. 55,000$–80,000$ (€275–€400, $264–$384) double; from 110,000$ (€550, $528) suite. Rates include breakfast. AE, DC, MC, V. Free parking. Metro: Marqués de Pombal. **Amenities:** 2 restaurants, bar; room service; laundry/dry cleaning; valet. *In room:* A/C, TV, minibar, hair dryer.

Expensive

Avenida Palace ⟨R⟩   Built in 1892 and long closed for a massive overhaul, Avenida Palace is the grandest old-fashioned hotel in Lisbon, a link to the past, a world etched in crystal and antiques. Its location right at the Rossio is terribly convenient and terribly noisy, but once inside it is another world entirely. Still "The Grande Dame of Lisbon hotels," it retains its Belle Époque aura and elegance, while offering all the modern comforts. Rooms are soundproof against the busy street and supplied with elegant, antique-style furnishings and deluxe mattresses.

Rua ler Dezembro 123, 1200 Lisboa. ℂ **21-346-01-55.** Fax 21-342-28-84. www.hotel-avenida-palace.pt 96 units. 36,000$–45,000$ (€180–€225, $173–$216) double; 55,000$ (€275, $264) junior suite; 75,000$ (€375, $360) suite. Rates include breakfast. AE, DC, MC, V. Free parking. Metro: Restaurador. Tram: 35. **Amenities:** Bar; room service; laundry/dry cleaning; valet. *In room:* A/C, TV, minibar, hair dryer.

Hotel Lisboa Plaza ⟨R⟩   This family owned and operated hotel in the heart of the city is a charmer, with many appealing Art Nouveau touches. Rooms—boasting well-stocked bathrooms and in-house videos—are well styled and comfortable. Try for a room in the rear, overlooking the botanical gardens.

Travessa do Salitre 7, av. da Liberdade, 1269 Lisboa. ℂ **21-321-82-18.** Fax 21-347-16-30. www.heritage.pt 112 units. 27,000$–35,000$ (€135–€175, $130–$168) double; 34,000$–45,000$ (€170–€225, $163–$216) suite. Rates include buffet breakfast. Children 12 and under stay free in parents' room. AE, DC, MC, V. Parking 2,500$ (€12.50, $12) nearby. Metro: Avenida. Bus: 1, 2, 36, or 44. **Amenities:** Restaurant, bar; car rental desk; room service; baby-sitting; laundry/dry cleaning. *In room:* A/C, TV, minibar, hair dryer.

Hotel Tivoli ⟨R⟩⟨R⟩⟨R⟩   The Tivoli offers enticing features, including the only hotel pool in central Lisbon. After a much-needed 1998 renovation, it sparkles again, and it boasts extensive facilities. Best of all, its prices aren't extravagant, considering the amenities. The largest and best rooms face the front, though those in the rear are quieter. Some are better appointed and more spacious than others. Facilities include access to the Tivoli Club, surrounded by a lovely garden, and views of Lisbon.

Av. da Liberdade 185, 1298 Lisboa Codex. ☎ **21-319-89-00.** Fax 21-319-89-50. www.srs.hotel.com 357 units. 29,000$–36,000$ (€145–€180, $139–$173) double; from 60,000$ (€300, $288) suite. Rates include continental breakfast. AE, DC, MC, V. Parking 2,000$ (€10, $9.60). Metro: Avenida. Bus: 1, 2, 9, or 32. **Amenities:** 2 restaurants, bar; pool; tennis courts; boutiques; room service; baby-sitting; laundry/dry cleaning. *In room:* A/C, TV, minibar, hair dryer.

Lisboa Sheraton Hotel & Towers 🐶🐶
This skyscraper lies at a traffic-clogged intersection a bit removed from the center, a few blocks north of Praça Marquês de Pombal. Rooms don't match the grandeur of the public areas, but they're generally spacious, and each was renovated in the late '90s. The most desirable are in the tower, opening onto views of the longest bridge in Europe.

Rua Latino Coelho 1, 1097 Lisboa. ☎ **800/325-3535** in the U.S., or 21-357-57-57. Fax 21-314-22-92. www.sheraton.com/lisboa. 388 units. 46,000$ (€230, $221) double; from 95,000$ (€475, $456) suite. AE, DC, MC, V. Parking 2,000$ (€10, $10). Bus: 1, 2, 9, or 32. **Amenities:** 2 restaurants, bar; pool; health spa; car rental facilities; salon; room service; baby-sitting; laundry/dry cleaning. *In room:* A/C, TV, minibar, hair dryer.

Moderate

Britânia 🐶
In its own way, the Britânia is one of Lisbon's most traditional and refreshingly conservative hotels, designed by well-known Portuguese architect Cassiano Branco in 1944. About a block from Avenida da Liberdade, it boasts a distinguished clientele that returns repeatedly, and an old-fashioned, almost courtly, staff. The only meal served is breakfast, but the facilities of the much larger Lisboa Plaza Hotel (with which the Britânia is affiliated) lie just across the busy avenue.

Rua Rodrigues Sampaio 17, 1150 Lisboa. ☎ **21-315-50-16.** Fax 21-315-50-21. www.heritage.pt. 30 units. 22,400$–30,600$ (€112–€153, $108–$147) double. Rates include buffet breakfast. AE, DC, MC, V. Metro: Avenida. Bus: 1, 2, 11, or 21. **Amenities:** Bar; room service; baby-sitting. *In room:* A/C, TV, minibar, hair dryer.

Dom Carlos
Just off Praça Marquês de Pombal, the Dom Carlos faces its own triangular park dedicated to the partially blind Camilo Castelo Branco, a 19th-century "eternity poet." The curvy facade is all glass, giving guests an outdoorsy feeling reinforced by green trees and beds of orange and red canna. In a neighborhood of similar competitors, this is the best three-star hotel of the lot because its rooms are more spacious and maintenance is high.

Av. Duque de Loulé 121, 1050 Lisboa. ☎ **21-351-25-90.** Fax 21-352-07-28. www.maisturismo.pt/htcarlos. 76 units. 20,800$ (€104, $100) double; 24,000$ (€120, $115) triple. Rates include buffet breakfast. AE, DC, MC, V. Metro: Marquês de Pombal. Bus: 7, 36, 44, or 45. **Amenities:** Restaurant, bar; room service; baby-sitting; laundry/dry cleaning. *In room:* A/C, TV, minibar, hair dryer.

Hotel Veneza
The Veneza, which opened in 1990, occupies one of the few remaining century-old palaces that once lined Avenida da Liberdade. Inside, a grand staircase leads to the three upper floors. The well-appointed midsize rooms are furnished in a soothing modern style, each with a firm mattress. The staff is extremely pleasant. Its position adjacent to the better-equipped Hotel Tivoli (see above) ensures its clients access to all the facilities they might need.

Av. da Liberdade 189, 1200 Lisboa. ☎ **21-352-26-18.** Fax 21-352-66-78. 36 units. 26,000$ (€130, $125) double. Rates include continental breakfast. AE, DC, MC, V. Parking 1,400$ (€7, $6.70). Metro: Avenida. **Amenities:** Bar; room service; laundry/dry cleaning. *In room:* A/C, TV, minibar, hair dryer.

Janelas Verdes Inn 🐶 *Finds*
Owned by the proprietors of the Lisboa Plaza (see above), this is an aristocratic 18th-century mansion, the former home of Portuguese novelist Eça de Queiros. Near the Museum of Ancient Art, its large, luxurious, and marvelously restored rooms have abundant closet space and generous bathrooms. Breakfast is brought on a tray to your room, to the lounge, or to the rear walled-in terrace.

Rua das Janelas Verdes 47, 1200 Lisboa. ℰ **21-396-81-43**. Fax 21 396-81-44. www.heritage.com. 17 units. 23,500$–37,000$ (€117.50–€185, $113–$178) double; 29,900$–47,700$ (€149.50–€238.50, $144–$229) triple. Rates include continental breakfast. AE, DC, MC, V. Bus: 27, 40, 49, or 60. **Amenities:** Bar, room service; baby-sitting; laundry/dry cleaning; library. In room: A/C, TV, minibar, hair dryer, safe.

Orion Lisboa 🍴 This is a contemporary hotel installed in what used to be the Eden Theatre standing in the bull's-eye center of the capital. Behind an Art Deco facade, its owners have created a series of small studios or more spacious apartments, all with kitchenettes, dishwashers and refrigerators. Overnight bookings are accepted, although it's much better for those who plan to settle into Lisbon for a few days, at which time it can become your home away from home. Apartments are well furnished and neatly maintained.

24 Praça dos Restauradores, 1200 Lisboa. ℰ **21-321-6600**. Fax 21-321-6666. www.citadines.com. 134 units. 23,500$ (€117.50, $113) double; 30,700$ (€153.50, $147) suite. AE, DC, MC, V. **Amenities:** Bar; pool; baby-sitting; laundry/dry cleaning. In room: A/C, TV, kitchenette, coffeemaker, hair dryer, iron, safe.

Príncipe Real 🍴 _Finds_ This modern hotel, built in the 1960s and renovated several times since, is reached after a long, steep climb from Avenida da Liber-dade. Selectivity and care are shown in the small but tasteful individualized rooms. Beds, reproductions of fine antiques, have excellent mattresses. The hotel is a short stroll from the nearby botanical gardens.

Rua de Alegria 53, 1200 Lisboa. ℰ **21-346-01-16**. Fax 21-342-21-04. hbelver@mail.telepac.pt. 24 units. 17,500$–20,000$ (€87.50–€100, $84–$96) double. Rates include buffet breakfast. AE, DC, MC, V. Metro: Avenida. Bus: 2. **Amenities:** Restaurant, bar; room service; laundry/dry cleaning. In room: A/C, TV, minibar, hair dryer, safe.

York House 🍴 York House mixes the drama of the past with modern con-venience. Once a 16th-century convent, it's outside the center of traffic-filled Lisbon, almost opposite the National Art Gallery. York House was tastefully fur-nished by one of the most distinguished Lisbon designers. The various-sized rooms have antique beds and good mattresses. On-street parking might be free but is rarely available. Book well in advance.

Rua das Janelas Verdes 32, 1200 Lisboa. ℰ **21-396-24-35**. Fax 21-397-27-93. www.yorkhouselisboa.com. 34 units. 22,900$–34,000$ (€114.50–170, $109.90–$163.20) double. Rates include buffet breakfast. AE, DC, MC, V. Bus: 27, 40, 49, 54, or 60. **Amenities:** Restaurant (French/Portuguese), bar; room service; laundry/dry cleaning; private garage. In room: TV, hair dryer.

Inexpensive
Casa de São Mamede Constructed in the 1800s as a villa for the count of Coruche, this building, behind the Botanical Gardens about midpoint between Avenida da Liberdade and the Amoreiras shopping center, dates from 1945. It's managed by the Marquês family. Breakfast is served in a sunny second-floor dining room. Though renovated, rooms retain an aura of their original high-ceilinged, somewhat frayed charm.

Rua da Escola Politécnica 159, 125 Lisboa. ℰ **21-396-31-66**. Fax 21-395-1896. 28 units. 13,000$ (€65, $62) double, 16,000$ (€80, $77) triple. Rates include continental breakfast. No credit cards. Tram: 24. Bus: 22, 49, or 58. **Amenities:** Dining area; lounge. In room: hair dryer.

Jorge V Hotel Jorge V, a neat little hotel with a 1960s design, boasts a choice location a block off noisy Avenida da Liberdade. Its facade contains rows of cellular balconies, roomy enough for guests to have breakfast or afternoon "coolers." A tiny elevator takes guests to a variety of aging rooms, which aren't generous in size but are comfortable in a compact way; all have small shower-only bathrooms.

Rua Mouzinho da Silveira 3, 1200 Lisboa. ℂ **21-356-25-25.** Fax 21-315-03-19. 49 units. 14,500$ (€72.50, $70) double; 18,500$ (€92.50, $89) suite. Rates include continental breakfast. AE, DC, MC, V. Parking 1,500$ (€7.50, $7.20). Metro: Avenida or Marquês de Pombal. **Amenities:** Bar; room service; laundry/dry cleaning. *In room:* A/C, TV, minibar, hair dryer, safe.

Residência Nazareth   You'll recognize this place by its dusty-pink facade and windows, some of which are surrounded with decorative arches in low relief. Take an elevator to the fourth-floor landing, where, far from the beauticians, hair stylists, and offices below, there's a medieval vaulting you might find in a romanticized Portuguese fortress. Even the spacious bar/TV lounge looks like a vaulted cellar. Some rooms, which are very basic, contain platforms, requiring guests to step up or down to the bathroom or to the comfortable bed. A little refurbishing is in order here.

Av. António Augusto de Aguiar 25, 1000 Lisboa. ℂ **21-354-20-16.** Fax 21-356-08-36. 32 units. 8,800$ (€44, $42) double. Rates include continental breakfast. AE, DC, MC, V. Metro: São Sebastião or Park. Bus: 31, 41, or 46. **Amenities:** Bar. *In room:* A/C, TV, minibar, hair dryer.

IN THE GRAÇA DISTRICT
Moderate
Hotel Albergaria da Senhora do Monte 🏛   This little hilltop hotel from 1969 is imbued with a unique character. It's perched near a belvedere, the Miradouro Senhora do Monte, with a memorable nighttime view of the city, St. George's Castle, and the Tagus. Multilevel corridors lead to the excellent rooms, all with verandas. There's a panoramic bar on site, but other than breakfast, no meals are served.

Calçada do Monte 39, 1100 Lisboa. ℂ **21-886-60-02.** Fax 21-887-77-83. 32 units. 21,000$ (€105, $101) double; 28,000$ (€140, $134) suite. Rates include continental breakfast. AE, DC, MC, V. Metro: Socorro. Tram: 28. Bus: 12, 17, or 35. **Amenities:** Bar; room service; laundry/dry cleaning. *In room:* A/C, TV.

WHERE TO DINE
IN THE CENTER
Very Expensive
Gambrinus 🏛🏛 SEAFOOD   One of Lisbon's premier restaurants since 1936, Gambrinus is the finest choice for fish and shellfish. Have your meal in the severely macho dining room with leather chairs under a cathedral-beamed ceiling or select a little table beside a fireplace on the raised end of the room. The soups are good, especially the shellfish bisque. The most expensive items, logically, are shrimp and lobster dishes. However, you might try conch with shellfish Thermidor or sea bass minhota. If you don't fancy fish but do like your dishes hot, ask for chicken piri-piri. The restaurant also offers elaborate desserts. Coffee with a 30-year-old brandy is the perfect end to a sumptuous meal here.

Rua das Portas de Santo Antão 25. ℂ **21-342-14-66.** Reservations required. Main courses 5,800$–14,000$ (€29–€70, $28–$67). AE, MC, V. Daily noon–1:30am. Metro: Rossio.

Expensive
António Clara 🏛🏛 PORTUGUESE/INTERNATIONAL   This Art Nouveau villa is famous as the former home of one of Portugal's most revered architects. Although it is no longer as chic and glamorous as it was in the early '90s, it still offers a first-rate cuisine in romantic surroundings. Meals include specialties like smoked swordfish, paella for two, chateaubriand béarnaise, monkfish rice, codfish Margarida da Praça, and beef Wellington. These dishes may be familiar, but only the highest-quality ingredients go into them.

Av. da República 38. ℂ **21-799-42-80.** Reservations required. Main courses 2,500$–3,500$ (€12.50–€17.50, $12–$17). AE, DC, MC, V. Mon–Sat noon–3pm and 7–10:30pm. Metro: Saldainha.

Casa da Comida ⭐⭐⭐ PORTUGUESE/FRENCH Casa da Comida, off Rua Alexandre Herculano, is touted by local gourmets as having some of the finest food in Lisbon. You'll find the cuisine good and the atmosphere pleasant. Specialties include roast kid with herbs, a medley of shellfish Casa da Comida, and lobster with vegetables. One specialty is stewed pheasant that has been marinated in port, a recipe dating from the Middle Ages. An excellent selection of wines is available. The food is often more imaginative here than at some of the other top-rated choices.

Travessa de Amoireiras 1 (off Rua Alexandre Herculano). ℂ **21-388-53-76.** Reservations required. Main courses 3,200$–5,000$ (€16–€25, $15–$24). AE, DC, MC, V. Mon–Fri 1–3pm and 8pm–midnight; Sat 8pm–midnight. Metro: Rato.

Cipriani ⭐ ITALIAN/MEDITERRANIAN This dignified dining room, with flowered curtains and a view of one of the most lavish gardens in this exclusive neighborhood, is a favorite with diplomats from the foreign embassies and consulates nearby. The a la carte items are available at lunch and dinner and include, depending on the season, fresh salmon fried with sage, lamb chops with mint sauce, and a succulent version of tortellini stuffed with seafood. While you may not run to phone *Gourmet* magazine, you'll be amply rewarded with deluxe ingredients perfectly handled by the staff.

In the Da Lapa, Rua do Pau de Bandeira 4. ℂ **21-395-00-05.** Reservations recommended. Main courses 2,700$–6,000$ (€13.50–€30, $13–$29); fixed-price lunch buffet 5,500$ (€27.50, $26) per person; *menu dégustation* 6,550$ (€32.75, $31). AE, DC, MC, V. Daily 12:30–3:30pm and 7:30–10:30pm. Bus: 13 or 27. Tram: 25 or 28.

Clara ⭐⭐ PORTUGUESE/INTERNATIONAL In a hillside location amid decaying villas and city squares, this green tile house contains an elegant restaurant. During lunch, you may prefer to sit near the garden terrace's plants and fountain. At night, an indoor seat—perhaps near the large marble fireplace—is more appealing. Specialties include tournedos Clara, stuffed rabbit with red-wine sauce, Valencian paella, filet of sole with orange, and pheasant with grapes. Shellfish dishes are often lethal in price, ranging from 5,600$ (€28, $27) for a shrimp platter to 9,000$ (€45, $43) for a lobster. As in many top Lisbon restaurants, these dishes aren't creative or innovative, but they're often prepared flawlessly. The wine list is very selective, containing mostly Portuguese wines from small scale and prestigious wineries throughout the country's best districts.

Campo dos Mártires da Pátria 49. ℂ **21-885-30-53.** Reservations required. Main courses 2,900$–4,000$ (€14.50–€20, $14–$19). AE, DC, MC, V. Mon–Fri noon–3:30pm and Mon–Sat 7pm–midnight. Closed Aug 1–15. Metro: Avenida.

Escorial ⭐ INTERNATIONAL Near Praça dos Restauradores, this place combines classic Spanish dishes with an inviting rosewood-paneled dining room. A menu is printed in English. For an appetizer, you may enjoy Portuguese oysters or squid on a skewer. The chef's specialties are barbecued baby goat, beef Stroganoff, or partridge casserole. In spite of its neighborhood, which grows increasingly sleazy at night, Escorial has stood the test of time and remained an enduring though not incredibly innovative favorite.

Rua das Portas de Santo Antão 47. ℂ **21-346-44-29.** Reservations recommended. Main courses 3,500$–8,000$ (€17.50–€40, $17–$38). AE, DC, MC, V. Daily 12:30–midnight. Metro: Rossio or Restauradores.

Il Gatto Pardo ⭐ ITALIAN The most appealing and stylish Italian restaurant in Lisbon is distinctly different from the pasta and pizza joints that until now have passed for Italian within the Portuguese capital. The staff prepare ultrafresh versions of pasta with clams; risotto with cuttlefish; pappardelle with zucchini and saffron; sea wolf coated in breadcrumbs; grilled swordfish steak in parsley sauce; roasted veal cooked in heady Barolo wine; and duck breast flavored with honey and vinegar sauce. During clement weather, an outdoor terrace that's ringed with potted shrubs and vines provides sweeping views out over the surrounding neighborhood.

In the Hotel Dom Pedro, av. Engenheiro, Duarte Pacheco. © 21-389-6600. Reservations recommended. Main courses 2,500$–3,500$ (€12.50–€17.50, $12–$17). Set-price menus 7,000$–10,000$ (€35–€50, $34–$48). AE, DC, MC, V. Daily 12:30–3:30pm and 8–11pm. Metro: Marquês de Pombal.

Restaurante Tavares ★★ PORTUGUESE/CONTINENTAL   Lisbon's oldest restaurant, Tavares is a nostalgic favorite, still serving competently prepared food with flawless service. It may be one of the capital's more glittering settings, but it's beginning to show a little wear. Your meal may begin with crepes de marisco prepared with shellfish. A main-course selection may be sole in champagne, stuffed crab Tavares style, or tournedos Grand Duc. Many continental dishes are on the menu, including the classic scallops of veal Viennoise.

Rua da Misericórdia 37. © 21-342-11-12. Reservations required. Main courses 4,500$–7,800$ (€22.50–€39, $22–$37); fixed-price lunch or dinner 8,500$–10,500$ (€42.50–€52.50, $41–$50). AE, DC, MC, V. Mon–Fri 12:30–3pm and 8–10:30pm; Sun 8–10:30pm. Bus: 15.

Sua Excelência ★★ *Finds* PORTUGUESE   The restaurant is just a block up the hill from the entrance to the National Art Gallery. Some dishes are uncommon in Portugal, including Angolan chicken cooked in palm oil with a medley of vegetables. Specialties include prawns piri-piri (not unreasonably hot), *lulas a moda da casa* (squid stewed in white wine, crème fraîche, and cognac), what Queiroz proclaims the "best smoked swordfish in Portugal," and clams cooked at least five ways. One unusual specialty is "little jacks," a small fish eaten whole, served with a well-flavored "paste" made from 2-day-old bread.

Rua do Conde 34. © 21-390-36-14. Reservations required. Main courses 2,500$–3,500$ (€12.50–€17.50, $12–$17). AE, MC, V. Mon–Tues and Thurs–Fri 1–3pm; Thurs–Tues 8–10:30pm. Closed Sept. Bus: 27 or 49. Tram: 25.

Moderate

Alemontes ★ *Finds* PORTUGUESE   Owners of inexpensive hotels in Lisbon often send their guests to this little bistro. The place offers excellent food with good, well-chosen ingredients—all served at a fair price. "We don't get movie stars around here," said one of the waiters, "just people wanting an honest and decent meal." *Fadistas* entertain nightly, and the place has a real cozy atmosphere. Many of the dishes are based on recipes from the Portuguese provinces of Trá-os-Montes. Try such delights as tender loin of veal grilled perfectly and served with fresh potatoes and vegetables. Other excellent prepared regional dishes include hare with white beans and roasted suckling pig on the spit.

Traversa da Santa Marta 4B. © 21-315-77-93. Reservations recommended. Main courses 2,500$–4,000$ (€12.50–\€20, $12–$19). AE, MC, V. Daily 12:30–5pm and 7:30pm–midnight. Metro: Marquês de Pombal.

Bachus ★ INTERNATIONAL   The ambience is a mix of a salon in a Russian palace, an English club (ca. 1900), and a stylized Manhattan bistro. Full meals might include mixed grill Bachus, chateaubriand with béarnaise, mountain goat, beef Stroganoff, shrimp Bachus, or other daily specials. The chef has a conservative approach to his cuisine and reportedly rarely gets any complaints. The wine list is extensive.

Largo da Trindade 8–9. © 21-342-28-28. Reservations recommended. Main courses 1,700$–3,800$ (€8.50–€19, $8.15–$18). AE, DC, MC, V. Mon–Fri noon–3pm; Sat 7pm–midnight. Metro: Chiado. Bus: 58.

Bonjardim *(Kids* PORTUGUESE   Bonjardim caters mostly to families, providing wholesome meals that fit most budgets. The restaurant, one of the most popular in Lisbon, is just east of Avenida da Liberdade near the grimy Praça dos Restauradores. During your dinner, the aroma of plump chickens roasting to a golden brown on the charcoal spit is likely to prompt you to try one. An order of this house specialty, called *frango no espeto,* is adequate for two, with a side dish of french fries. The cook also bakes hake in the Portuguese style; an alternative dish is pork fried with clams.

Travessa de Santo Antão 10–12. *©* **21-342-74-24.** Main courses 1,100$–2,900$ (€5.50–€14.50, $5–$14). AE, DC, MC, V. Daily noon–4pm and 7–12:30am. Metro: Restauradores.

Conventual *♣* PORTUGUESE   In many ways this is one of our favorite Lisbon restaurants. The owner, Dina Marquês, invented a few of the delectably flavored recipes, including creamy coriander soup, stewed partridge in port, duck in champagne sauce, grilled monkfish in herb-flavored cream sauce, and stewed clams in a sauce of red peppers, onions, and cream.

Praça das Flores 45. *©* **21-390-91-96.** Reservations required. Main courses 2,500$–4,000$ (€12.50–€20, $12–$19). AE, DC, MC, V. Mon–Fri 12:30–3pm and 7:30–11pm; Sat–Sun 7:30–11:30pm. Metro: Avenida. Bus: 100.

Restaurant 33 PORTUGUESE/INTERNATIONAL   Restaurant 33 is a treasure. Decorated like an English hunting lodge, it lies near many recommended hotels, including the Ritz. Specialties include shellfish rice served in a crab shell, smoked salmon or lobster tour d'Argent, and pepper steak. Large portions, tasty stews, and strong-flavored ingredients characterize the food. You can order a glass of port in the small bar. A pianist performs during dinner.

Rua Alexandre Herculano 33A. *©* **21-354-60-79.** Reservations recommended. Main courses 2,300$–3,800$ (€11.50–€19, $11–$18). AE, DC, MC, V. Mon–Fri noon–3:30pm and 8–10:30pm; Sat 8–10pm. Metro: Rotunda. Bus: 6 or 9.

Inexpensive

António Oliveira PORTUGUESE/INTERNATIONAL   This place caters to Portuguese businesspeople who want a relaxing ambience and good food. Just a bit away from the din of central traffic, it's a refreshing oasis. Fish dishes, garnished with vegetables, include filets with tomato sauce and baked sole. *Polvo á lagareira* (octopus with broiled potatoes, olive oil, and garlic) is a specialty. From among the fowl and meat dishes, try the *frango na prata* (chicken broiled in foil with potatoes) or pork with clams Alentejana style. The owner/manager recommends his *açorda de marisco,* a stewlike breaded shellfish-and-egg dish that's a treat.

Rua Tomá Ribiero 63. *©* **21-353/87-80.** Main courses 800$–2,500$ (€4–€12.50, $4–$12). MC, V. Mon–Sat noon–10:30pm. Metro: Picoas. Bus: 44 or 55.

Casa Nostra ITALIAN   Maria Paola Porru, a movie sound engineer whose travels have exposed her to cinematic circles across Europe, runs this postmodern and very hip hideaway in the Bairro Alto. All pastas are homemade on the premises. Accomplished menu items include fettuccine al mascarpone, lasagna, spaghetti with Portuguese clams, and several versions of grilled meat. The preferred dessert of many repeat clients is the Sicilian-style tiramisu, a rich dessert made with ladyfingers, coffee, and mascarpone cream. Despite the fact that this restaurant's official address is on Rua de Rosa, its entrance lies around the corner, at Travessa de Poco da Cidade 60.

Rua de Rosa 84–90. *©* **21-342-59-31.** Reservations recommended. Regular main courses 1,000$–2,600$ (€5–€13, $5–$13); seafood main courses 1,500$–3,000$ (€7.50–€15, $7–$14). AE, MC, V. Tues–Fri 12:30–2:30pm and 8–11pm; Sat 8–11pm; Sun 1–2:30pm. Metro: Chiado. Tram: 28 or 28B.

Cervejaria Brilhante SEAFOOD/PORTUGUESE   Lisboans from every walk of life stop here for a stein of beer and *mariscos* (seafood). You can dine either at the bar or at marble tables. The front window is packed with an appetizing array of king crabs, oysters, lobsters, baby clams, shrimp, and even barnacles. Prices change every day, depending on the market; you pay by the kilo. This is hearty, robust eating. It's a challenge to attract a waiter's attention.

Rua das Portas de Santo Antão 105. ℂ 21-346-14-07. Main courses 1,600$–3,400$ (€8–€17, $8–$16); tourist menu 2,000$ (€10, $10). AE, DC, MC, V. Daily noon–midnight. Metro: Rossio. Bus: 1, 2, 36, 44, or 45.

Cervejaria Ribadoura SEAFOOD   Cervejaria Ribadoura is one of central Lisbon's typical shellfish-and-beer places, midway along the major boulevard at the corner of Rua do Salitre. The decor is simple; the emphasis is on fish. The classic *bacalhau* (codfish) *a Bras* is a good choice; for a lighter bite, try the shrimp omelet. Many diners follow fish with a meat dish. Beware the sautéed pork cutlets with piri-piri, made with red-hot peppers from Angola—only those who've been trained for many years on the most mouth-wilting Indian curries should order this blazing dish.

Av. da Liberdade 155. ℂ 21-354-94-11. Main courses 1,400$–4,000$ (€7–€20, $7–$19). AE, DC, MC, V. Daily noon–1:30am. Metro: Avenida. Bus: 1, 2, 44, or 45.

Cervejaria Trindade PORTUGUESE   Cervejaria Trindade is a German beer hall/Portuguese tavern. In operation since 1836, it's the oldest tavern in Lisbon. You can order tasty little steaks and heaps of crisp french-fried potatoes. Many Portuguese prefer *bife na frigideira*—steak with mustard sauce and a fried egg, served in a clay frying pan. The tavern features shellfish, which come from private fish ponds, and the house specialties are *ameijoas* (clams) *à Trindade* and giant prawns.

Rua Nova de Trindade 20C. ℂ 21-342-35-06. Main courses 1,500$–3,000$ (€7.50–€15, $7–$14). AE, DC, MC, V. Daily 10am–1:30am. Metro: Rossio or Chiado. Bus: 15, 20, 51, or 100.

Pastelaria Sala de Cha Versailles SANDWICHES/PASTRIES   This is Lisbon's most famous teahouse, and has been declared part of the "national patrimony." In older days, the specialty was Licungo, Mozambique's famed black tea; you can still order it, but nowadays many drinkers enjoy English brands. The Portuguese claim they (not the English) introduced the custom of tea drinking to the English court, after Catherine of Bragança married Charles II in 1662. You can also order milk shakes, mineral water, and fresh orange juice, along with beer and liquor. Snacks come in many varieties, including codfish balls and toasted ham-and-cheese sandwiches. They now serve a limited array of Portuguese fare that's simple but wholesome.

Av. da República 15A. ℂ 21-354-63-40. Sandwiches 250$–350$ (€1.25–€1.75, $1.20–$1.73); pastries 130$–200$ (€0.65–€1, 60¢–95¢); plats du jour 1,200$–2,550$ (€6–€12.75, $6–$12). AE, MC, V. Daily 7:30am–10pm. Metro: Salvanhe.

IN THE CHIADO DISTRICT
Expensive

Tágide ✦✦✦ PORTUGUESE/INTERNATIONAL   Tágide reigns as one of Portugal's leading restaurants. It's up from the docks, atop a steep hill overlooking the old part of Lisbon and the Tagus. The Louis XIV dining room's windows look down on the ships moored in the port. Specialties include suprême of halibut with coriander, pork with clams and coriander, and grilled baby goat with herbs. Habitués from the world of Lisbon finance and government, including Portugal's president, are given preferential seating and treatment.

Largo da Académia Nacional de Belas Artes 18–20. ℭ **21-342-07-20.** Reservations required. Main courses 2,200$–3,800$ (€11–€19, $11–$18). AE, DC, MC, V. Mon–Fri 12:30–2:30pm and 7:30–10:30pm. Metro: Chiado. Tram: 20. Bus: 15.

Moderate

A Brasileira SANDWICHES/PASTRIES One of Lisbon's oldest coffeehouses, A Brasileira was once a gathering place of Lisbon literati. Guests sit at small tables on chairs made of tooled leather, amid mirrored walls and marble pilasters. The restaurant here serves basic fare like omelets, steaks, and fish. Note that you'll pay more for sandwiches and pastries in the restaurant than in the coffee bar.

Rua Garrett 120. ℭ **21-346-95-41.** Sandwiches 260$–550$ (€1.30–€2.75, $1.25–$2.65); pastries 120$–360$ (€0.60–€1.80, 63¢–$1.75); meals in restaurant 1,200$–5,500$ (€6–€27.50, $6–$26). AE, MC, V (restaurant only). Daily 7am 11pm. Metro: Russio.

IN THE ALCÂNTARA
Expensive

Café Alcântara ☟ FRENCH/PORTUGUESE One of Lisbon's most fun and hip dining-and-entertainment complexes, it attracts an international crowd. Menu items include filet of salmon with lemon sauce, fresh fish, steak tartare, three different preparations of duck, and a Portuguese platter of the day, which might include fried *bacalhau* (codfish) or a hearty *feijoada* (bean-and-meat stew).

Rua Maria Luisa Holstein 15. ℭ **21-363-71-76.** Reservations recommended. Main courses 2,800$–6,800$ (€14–€34, $13–$33). AE, DC, MC, V. Daily 8pm–1am. Bar daily 9pm–3am. Bus: 57.

AT MARINA EXPO
Expensive

Notre ☟ PORTUGUESE/CONTINENTAL This is a successful reincarnation of a landmark Portuguese restaurant. The chefs prepare finely honed dishes such as sea bass meunière flavored with country butter and freshly chopped herbs. We suggest one of our favorite dishes, a local white fish called robina, which is perfectly seasoned and baked in the oven. The aromatically flavored duck breast is yet another delightful dish, as are two kinds of fish cooked with champagne. Service is first rate. Reaching it by public transport is difficult—a taxi is recommended.

Edificio Nau, Marina Expo '98. ℭ **21-893-1604.** Reservations required. Main courses 4,000$–6,000$ (€20–€30, $19–$29). AE, DC, MC, V. Mon–Sat 12:30–3:30pm and 7:30–11:30pm.

SEEING THE SIGHTS
SIGHTSEEING SUGGESTIONS FOR FIRST-TIME VISITORS

If You Have 1 Day This is just enough time to take a walking tour of the **Alfama,** Lisbon's most interesting district. Visit the 12th-century **Sé** (cathedral) and take in a view of the city and the river Tagus from the **Santa Luzia Belvedere.** Climb up to the **Castelo São Jorge (St. George's Castle).** Take a taxi or bus to **Belém** to see the **Mosteiro dos Jerónimos (Jerónimos Monastery)** and the **Torre de**

Belém. While at Belém, end your day at a **fado cafe.**

If You Have 2 Days Spend the morning of day 2 at the **Museu Calouste Gulbenkian,** one of Europe's artistic treasure troves. Have lunch at a *típico* restaurant in the Bairro Alto. In the afternoon see the **Fundção Ricardo Esprito Santo (Museum of Decorative Art)** and the **Museu Nacional**

de Art Antiga (National Museum of Ancient Art). At the day's end, wander through Parque Eduardo VII.

If You Have 3 Days On day 3, head for Sintra, the single most visited sight in the environs—Byron called it "glorious Eden." You can spend the day here, exploring the castle and other palaces in the panoramic area. Try at least to visit the Palácio Nacional de Sintra and the Palácio Nacional da Pena. Return to Lisbon for a night at a fado cafe.

If You Have 4 or 5 Days On day 4, take an excursion from Lisbon (perhaps an organized tour) to visit the fishing village of Nazaré and the walled city of Óbidos. Those interested in Roman Catholic sights might also want to go to the shrine at Fátima, though it would be hectic to see this on the same day. On the final day, slow your pace a bit with a morning at the beach at Estoril on Portugal's Costa do Sol. Then continue along the coast to Cascais for lunch. After lunch, wander around this old fishing village now turned into a major resort. Go to Guincho, 6 kilometers (4 miles) along the coast from Cascais, which is near the westernmost point on the European continent and has panoramic views.

THE ALFAMA ✹✹✹

Old Lisbon lives on in the Alfama district. The wall built by the Visigoths and incorporated into some of the houses is testimony to its ancient past. The Alfama was the Saracen sector centuries before its conquest by the Christians. Some of the buildings were spared from the devastating 1755 earthquake, and the Alfama has retained much of its original charm—narrow cobblestone streets, cages of canaries chirping in the afternoon sun, strings of garlic and pepper inviting you inside *típico* taverns, old street markets, and charming balconies.

One of the best views is from the belvedere of Largo das Portas do Sol, near the Museum of Decorative Art. It's a balcony opening onto the sea, overlooking the typical houses as they sweep down to the Tagus. One of the oldest churches is Santo Estevão (St. Stephen), at Largo de Santo Estevão. It was first built in the 13th century; the present marble structure dates from the 18th. Also of medieval origin is the Church of São Miguel (St. Michael), at Largo de São Miguel, deep in the Alfama on a palm tree–shaded square. Rua da Judiaria (Street of the Jews) is another reminder of the past. It was settled largely by Jewish refugees fleeing Spain to escape the Inquisition.

Castelo São Jorge ✹✹   Believed to have predated the Romans, the hilltop was used as a fortress to guard the Tagus and its settlement below. Beginning in the 5th century A.D., the site was a Visigothic fortification; it fell in the early 8th century to the Saracens. Many of the walls still standing were erected during the centuries of Moorish domination. The Moors were in control until 1147, when Afonso Henríques, the country's first king, chased them out and extended his

---

Tips **Traveler's Tip**

If your time is limited, explore the National Coach Museum, the Jerónimos Monastery, and the Alfama with St. George's Castle. At least two art museums merit attention: the Museu Nacional de Art Antiga and the Museu Calouste Gulbenkian.

The Alfama

SANTA CRUZ

† Igreja e
■ Mosteiro de
São Vicente

Rua São Vicente

Campo de Santa Engrácia

Castelo
São Jorge

Rua da Costa do Castelo

Rua das Escolas Gerais

Museu
Militar

Largo das
Portas del Sol

Rua dos
Corvos

Museu-Escola de
Artes Decorativas
Portuguesas

Beco do Carniero

† Santo
Estavão

Rua da Regueira

Rua dos Remedios

Mercado

Rua Milagres

Rua Loios

Rua São Tiago

Santa
Luzia
Belvedere

Beco de
Cardosa

Rua Jardim Tabaco

Rua de São Mamede

Rua João Evangelisto

Rua da Madalena

Rua do Limoeiro

Rua de São Pedro

Terreiro do Trigo

Doca do Trigo

BAIXA

Rua A. Rosa

Sé
(Cathedral)

Rua des
Judiara

Rua Cais de Santarem

Museu
Antóniano

Rua da Prata

Rua da Alfândega

Campo das
Cebolas

Praça da
Ribeira

Praça do Comércio
(Terreiro do Paço)

Av. Infante D. Henrique

Doca da Marinha

Rio Tejo

Estação do
Sul e Sueste

Embarcadouro

† ■ Church

0 ——— 1 mi
0 ——— 1 km

---

kingdom south. Even before Lisbon was made the capital of the newly emerging nation, the site was used as a royal palace. For what is the finest view of the Tagus and the Alfama, walk the esplanades and climb the ramparts of the old castle, named in commemoration of an Anglo-Portuguese pact dating from as early as 1371. On the grounds you can stroll through a setting of olive, pine, and cork trees, all graced by swans and rare white peacocks.

Rua da Costa do Castelo. (✆ 21-887-7244. Free admission. Apr–Sept daily 9am–9pm; Oct–Mar daily 9am–6pm. Bus: 37. Tram: 12 or 28.

Sé Cathedral ⦿   Characterized by twin towers flanking its entrance, the Sé represents an architectural wedding of Romanesque and Gothic. The facade is severe enough to resemble a medieval fortress. When the city was captured early in the 12th century by Christian Crusaders, led by Portugal's first king, Afonso Henríques, the Sé became the first church in Lisbon. It was damaged in the earthquakes of 1344 and 1755. Inside the rough exterior are many treasures, including the font where St. Anthony of Padua is said to have been christened in 1195. The cloister, built in the 14th century by King Dinis, is of ogival construction, with garlands, a Romanesque wrought-iron grille, and tombs with inscription stones. In the sacristy or Treasury Museum are marbles, relics, valuable images, and ecclesiastical treasures from the 15th and 16th centuries.

Largo da Sé. (✆ 21-886-67-52. Admission: Cathedral, free; cloister, 100$ (€0.50, 53¢). Mon–Sat 10am–6pm. Tram: 28 (Graça). Bus: 37.

Museu Antóniano   St. Anthony of Padua, an itinerant Franciscan monk who became Portugal's patron saint, was born in 1195 in a house that once stood here. The original church was destroyed by the 1755 earthquake, and the present building was designed by Mateus Vicente in the 18th century. In the crypt, a guide will show you the spot where the saint was allegedly born (he's buried in Padua, Italy). The devout come to this little church to light candles under his picture. He's known as a protector of young brides and also has a special connection with the children of Lisbon.

Largo de Santo António de Sé. ℭ **21-886-91-45**. Free admission. Daily 7:30am–7:30pm. Métro: Rossio. Bus: 37.

THE BAIRRO ALTO ✿

Like the Alfama, the Bairro Alto (Upper City) preserves the characteristics of an older Lisbon. It once was called the heart of the city, probably for both its location and its inhabitants. Many of its buildings survived the 1755 earthquake. Today it's the home of some of the finest fado cafes, making it a center of nightlife. The Bairro Alto is also a fascinating place to visit during the day, when its charming narrow cobblestone streets and alleys, lined with ancient buildings, can be appreciated in the warm light coming off the sea.

From the windows and balconies, streamers of laundry hang out to dry, and there are cages of canaries, parrots, parakeets, and other birds. In the morning, the street scene is made up of housewives emerging from their homes to shop, following the cries of the *varinas* (fishmongers) and other food vendors. At night, the area comes alive with fado clubs, discos, and small bars; Victorian lanterns light the streets; and people stroll along leisurely.

Belém ✿✿   At Belém, the most southwestern district of Lisbon, the Tagus meets the sea. From here the caravels that charted the unknown were launched on their missions: Vasco da Gama to India, Ferdinand Magellan to circumnavigate the globe, and Bartolomeu Dias to round the Cape of Good Hope. Belém emerged from the Restelo, the point of land from which the ships set sail across the so-called Sea of Darkness. From these explorations, wealth flowed into Belém, especially from the spice trade with the Far East. In time, the royal family established a summer palace here. Wealthy Lisboans began moving out of the city center and building town houses here, establishing the character of the district. For many years Belém was a separate municipality but is now incorporated into Lisbon as a parish.

Largo de Santo António de Sé. ℭ **21-886-91-45**. Free admission. Daily 7:30am–7:30pm. Métro: Rossio. Bus: 37.

Torre de Belém   The quadrangular Tower of Belém is a monument to Portugal's Age of Discovery. Erected between 1515 and 1520 in Manueline style, the tower is Portugal's classic landmark. It stands on or near the spot where the caravels once set out to sea. Its architect, Francisco de Arruda, blended Gothic and Moorish elements, using such architectural details as twisting ropes carved of stone. The coat-of-arms of Manuel I rests above the loggia, and balconies grace three sides. Along the balustrade of the loggias, stone crosses symbolize the Portuguese crusaders.

Praça do Imperio. ℭ **21-362-00-34**. Admission 600$ (€3, $2.93) adults, free for children under 12 and seniors. Tues–Sun 10am–5pm. Bus: 27, 28, 43, 49, or 51.

Padrão dos Descobrimentos (Memorial to the Discoveries) ✿   Like the prow of a caravel from the Age of Discovery, this memorial stands on the Tagus, looking as if it's ready at any moment to strike out across the Sea of Darkness. Memorable explorers, chiefly Vasco da Gama, are immortalized in stone along the ramps. At the point where the two ramps meet is a representation of Henry the Navigator, whose genius opened up new worlds. One of the stone figures is that of a kneeling Philippa of Lancaster, Henry's English mother; other figures symbolize Crusaders, navigators, monks, cartographers, and cosmographers. Beneath the heroic representations of figures crucial to the country's history, it contains a permanent exhibition on the role of the Portuguese in exploring the world, as well as a temporary exhibition related to the Portuguese experience.

Praça da Boa Esperança. ℂ **21-303-19-50**. Admission 350$ (€1.75, $1.73). Tues–Sun 9:30am–6:30pm. Bus: 27, 28, 43, or 49.

Mosteiro dos Jerónimos (Jerónimos Monastery) ✪✪✪   In an expansive mood of celebration, Manuel I, the Fortunate, ordered this monastery built in 1502 to commemorate Vasco da Gama's voyage to India and to give thanks to the Virgin Mary for its success. Manueline, the style of architecture to which the king contributed his name, combines flamboyant Gothic and Moorish influences with elements of the nascent Renaissance in Portugal. The 1755 earthquake damaged the monastery, and extensive restoration, some ill conceived, was carried out. The church interior is divided into a trio of naves, noted for their fragile-looking pillars. Some of the ceilings, like those in the monks' refectory, have a ribbed barrel vault. The "palm tree" in the sacristy is exceptional.

Praça do Império. ℂ **21-362-00-34**. Church, free. Cloisters, 500$ (€2.50, $2.40); free for children and seniors. Tues–Sun 10am–5pm. Bus: 27, 28, 29, 43, or 49; tram: 15.

Museu de Marinha (Maritime Museum) ✪✪   The pageant and the glory that characterized Portugal's domination of the high seas is evoked for posterity in the Maritime Museum, one of the most important in Europe. Appropriately, it's installed in the west wing of the Mosteiro dos Jerónimos. These royal galleys re-create an age of opulence that never feared excess, as exemplified by dragons' heads dripping with gilt and sea monsters coiling with abandon. The museum contains hundreds of models, from 15th-century sailing ships to 20th-century warships. In a special room is a model of the queen's stateroom on the royal yacht of Carlos I, the Bragança king who was assassinated at Praça do Comércio in 1908.

Praça do Império. ℂ **21-362-00-19**. Admission 500$ (€2.50, $2.40) adults, 200$ (€1, 95¢) students; free for children under 9 and seniors. Tues–Sun 10am–6pm (to 5pm off-season). Bus: 27, 28, 29, 43, 49, or 51.

Museu de Arte Popular (Folk Art Museum) ✪   This is the most dramatic exhibition of the folk arts and customs of the Portuguese. The walls of the building are painted by contemporary artists, including Carlos Botelho, Eduardo Anahory, Estréla Faria, Manuel Lapa, Paulo Ferreira, and Tomás de Melo. The 1948 opening of the Folk Art Museum was a result of a campaign for ethnic revival directed by António Ferro. The collections—including ceramics, furniture, wickerwork, clothes, farm implements, and paintings—are displayed in five rooms that correspond more or less to the provinces, each of which maintains its own distinct personality.

Av. de Brasília. ℂ **21-301-16-75**. 350$ (€1.75, $1.73) adults; free for children 12 and under. Tues–Sun 10am–12:30pm and 2–5pm. Closed holidays. Bus: 27, 28, 29, 43, 49, or 51. Tram: 15.

ELSEWHERE IN LISBON
Museu Nacional de Arte Antiga (National Museum of Ancient Art) ✪✪
This museum has many notable paintings, including the 15th-century famous polyptych from St. Vincent's monastery attributed to Nuno Gonçalves.

Outstanding works are Hieronymus Bosch's triptych *The Temptation of St. Anthony;* Hans Memling's *Mother and Child;* Albrecht Dürer's *St. Jerome;* and paintings by Velázquez, Zurbarán, Poussin, and Courbet. Paintings from the 15th through the 19th century trace the development of Portuguese art, and the museum also exhibits a remarkable collection of gold- and silversmiths' work.

Rua das Janelas Verdes 9. ☎ **21-396-41-51.** Admission 600$ (€3, $2.93) adults, 300$ (€1.50, $1.45) students; free for children 13 and under. Tues 2–6pm; Wed–Sun 10am–6pm. Bus: 27, 40, 49, or 60. Tram: 15 or 18.

Museu de Fundação Calouste Gulbenkian ☆☆☆   Opened in 1969, this museum houses the collection of Armenian oil tycoon Calouste Gulbenkian— called by one critic "one of the world's finest private art collections." It covers Egyptian, Greek, and Roman antiquities; remarkable Islamic art; and vases, prints, and lacquerwork from China and Japan. European works include medieval illuminated manuscripts and ivories, 15th- to 19th-century painting and sculpture, 18th-century French decorative works, French Impressionist painting, and Lalique jewelry and glassware. Notable are two Rembrandts, Rubens's *Portrait of Hélène Fourment,* and Renoir's *Portrait of Madame Claude Monet.*

Av. de Berna 45. ☎ **21-795-02-36.** Admission 700$ (€3.50, $3.35) adults; free for children under 10 and seniors. Free for everyone on Sun. Wed–Sun 10am–6pm; Tues 2–6pm. Metro: Sebastião; bus: 16, 26, 31, 46, or 56.

Oceanario de Lisboa ☆☆ *Kids*   This world-class aquarium remains the most enduring, and impressive, achievement of EXPO '98, which was meant to propel Portugal into the consciousness of Europe and the world. Defined as the second-biggest aquarium in the world, exceeded in size only by an equivalent facility in Osaka, Japan, it's contained within a stone and glass building whose centerpiece is a 5 million-liter (1.3 million-gallon) holding tank. Its waters are divided into four distinct ecosystems replicating the Atlantic, Pacific, Indian, and Antarctic Oceans. Each is supplemented with land portions on which birds, amphibians, and reptiles flourish. Look for otters in the Pacific, penguins in the Antarctic, Polynesian trees and flowers in the Indian, and puffins, terns, and seagulls in the Atlantic.

Parque das Nações. ☎ **21-891-7002.** Admission 2,000$ (€10, $10) adults, 900$ (€4.50, $4.30) students and children under 13. Daily 10am–7pm. Metro: Estação do Oriente.

ORGANIZED TOURS

Offering seven different year-round tours of Lisbon and its environs, **Star Travel,** Travessa Escola Arauio 31 (☎ **21-330-12-00**), is popular with visitors who want to see the sights or get their bearings in and around the city. A daily half-day tour, "Touristic Lisbon," starts with a drive down Avenida da Liberdade to Rossio, the heart of the city, and on every day but Monday and holidays the tour concludes at the Coach Museum, which houses the nation's largest collection of coaches. The price of the tour is 5,500$ (€27.50, $26).

Offered on Tuesday and Thursday, **"Lisbon and the Blue Coast"** is a full-day tour that includes the same sites as "Touristic Lisbon" but which also crosses the Tagus in the afternoon for a drive along the Blue Coast through the "Three Castles" region of Sesimbra, Setubal, and Palmela. Included in the sightseeing is a stop for coffee at the Pousada do Castelo, and a visit to a wine cellar and handcrafts center at Azeitão. The cost is 13,500$ (€67.50, $65). A similar half-day tour, offered daily, is **"Arrábida/Sesimbra,"** which includes the same stop as the afternoon of the "Blue Coast" tour, with an additional stop in the nature preserve on Arrábida Mountain. The cost is 8,900$ (€44.50, $43).

For a different view, take the **"Lisbon by Night"** tour, offered on Monday, Wednesday, and Friday evenings year-round. The night tour includes the same city stops as the other tours and then delves into the old quarter of Alcântara. The evening concludes with dinner and drinks at a restaurant featuring entertainment by a *fadista.* The price of the tour is 11,000$ (€55, $53) with two drinks at the restaurant, and 13,000$ (€65, $62) for dinner and drinks. A nighttime offering on Tuesday, Thursday, or Saturday, the **"Casino Estoril"** tour has the same itinerary as "Lisbon by Night," but concludes with dinner and an international show at the casino located in the coastal resort of Estoril. The cost is 13,000$ (€65, $62) with two drinks at the casino and 14,500$ (€72.50, $70) with dinner.

THE SHOPPING SCENE

Baixa, between the Rossio and the Tagus, is a major shopping area. **Rua do Ouro (Street of Gold), Rua da Prata,** and **Rua Augusta** are the principal shopping streets. Another major upscale shopping artery is **Rua Garrett,** in the Chiado; to reach the area, you can take the Santa Justa elevator near the Rossio.

At the **Feira da Ladra,** you can experience the fun of haggling for bargains at an open-air street market. The vendors peddle their wares on Tuesday and Saturday. About a 5-minute walk from the waterfront in the Alfama, the market sits behind the Maritime Museum, adjoining the Pantheon of São Vicente. Start your browsing at Campo de Santa Clara in the Alfama. Portable stalls and individual displays are lined up on this hilly street with its tree-lined center.

AZULEJOS & PORCELAIN   The most unusual buys in Lisbon are *azulejos,* the decorated glazed tiles that are sought by collectors, and pottery from all over Portugal. Pottery with brightly colored roosters from Barcelos is legendary and blue-and-white pottery is made in Coimbra. Our favorites come from Caldas da Rainha, including yellow-and-green dishes in the shape of vegetables, fruit, and animals. Vila Real is known for its black pottery, and polychrome pottery comes from Aceiro. The red-clay pots from the Alentejo region are based on designs that go back to the Etruscans.

Founded in 1741 in the Chiado, **Sant'Anna,** rua do Alecrim 95–97 (© 21-342-25-37; metro: Estação do Cais do Sodré), is Portugal's leading ceramic center, famous for its azulejos (glazed tiles). The showroom is on Rua do Alecrim, but you can also visit the factory at Calçada da Boa Hora 96; however, you make an appointment by calling © 21-363-31-17). **Vista Alegre,** Largo do Chiado 18 (© 21-347-54-81; metro: Chiado), turns out some of the finest porcelain dinner services in the country, along with objets d'art and limited editions for collectors and a range of practical day-to-day tableware.

GOLD   One of the very best buys in Portugal is gold. Gold is strictly regulated by the government, which requires jewelers to put a minimum of 19¼ karats in the jewelry they sell. Filigree jewelry, made of fine gold or silver wire, is an art that dates from ancient times. **W. A. Sarmento,** Rua Áurea 251 (© 21-347-07-83; metro: Rossio or Chiado), is the most distinguished silver- and goldsmith in Portugal, specializing in lacy filigree jewelry, including charm bracelets. Well on its way to being a century old, the **Joalharia do Carmo,** Rua do Carmo 87B (© 21-342-42-00; metro: Rossio), is one of the best shops in Lisbon for gold filigree work.

ART & ANTIQUES   Along both sides of narrow **Rua de S. José** are treasure troves of shops packed with antiques from all over the world. **Rua Dom Pedro V** is another street of antique shops. Near the Ritz Hotel, the **Galleria Sesimbra,**

rua Castilho 77 (℮ **21-387-02-91;** metro: Marquês de Pombal), is a top art gallery, mainly displaying Portuguese artists. It was established in the 1970s by an expatriate Scotsman. Open from Monday to Friday 10am to 6pm and Saturday 10am to 1pm.

OTHER SELECT SHOPS   Casa Quintão, Rua Serpa Pinto 12A (℮ **21-346-58-37;** metro: Chiado), is the showcase for Arraiolos carpets. Rugs sold here are priced by the square foot, according to the density of the stitching. Casa Quintão can reproduce intricate Oriental or medieval designs in rugs or tapestries as well as create any customized pattern. The shop, dating from 1880, also sells materials and gives instructions on how to make your own carpets and tapestry-covered pillows.

In the same building as the Hotel Avenida Palace, **Casa Bordados da Madeira,** Rua 1 de Dezembro 137 (℮ **21-342-14-47;** metro: Restauradores), offers handmade embroideries from Madeira and Viana. If you wish to place an order, the staff will mail it to you. **Casa Regional da Ilha Verde,** Rua Paiva de Andrade 4 (℮ **21-342-59-74;** metro: Chiado), sells handmade items, especially embroideries from the Azores—that's why it's called the "Regional House of the Green Island." You can get some good buys here. **Madeira House,** Rua Augusta 131–135 (℮ **21-342-68-13;** metro: Chiado), specializes in high-quality regional cottons, linens, and gift items.

For something typically Portuguese, try **Casa das Cortiças,** Rua da Escola Politécnica 4–6 (℮ **21-342-58-58;** metro: Rato). "Mr. Cork," the original owner, became somewhat of a legend in Lisbon for offering "everything conceivable" that could be made of cork, of which Portugal controls a hefty part of the world market. He's long gone, but the store carries on.

Adelia Almeida has created a sensation with the shop she's recently opened in the Alfama–**Lavandaria,** 11–13 Rua Augusto Rosa (℮ **21-887-5691;** tram 12 or 28). In Portuguese, her shop simply means "laundry," which hardly suggests she has a collection of the finest linens in Lisbon. Many of her treasures come from the city in Guimarães in northern Portugal where hand weavers still work at home. Other linens are copies of 18th-century designs, including tablecloths. Look for the green-and-yellow embroidery of mimosa flowers on many of the linens.

LISBON AFTER DARK

Consult *What's On in Lisbon,* available at most newsstands, for the latest listings. The local newspaper, *Diário de Notícias,* also carries cultural listings, but in Portuguese. No special discount tickets are offered, except that students get 50% off on tickets purchased for the national theater. Also of interest is *Agenda Cultural,* an English-and Portuguese-language seasonal periodical that's available without charge at cafes, at hotels, and at the Lisbon branch of the Portuguese tourist office. Inside, you'll find an abbreviated listing of musical, theatrical, and cultural choices available throughout the city.

THE PERFORMING ARTS

Teatro Nacional de São Carlos, Rua Serpa Pinto 9 (℮ **21-346-59-14;** tram: 24, 28, or 28B; bus: 15 or 100), attracts opera and ballet aficionados from all over Europe. Top companies from around the world perform at this 18th-century theater; the season begins in mid-September and extends through July. The box office is open daily from 1 to 7pm. There are no special discounts. Tickets are 3,000$ to 13,500$ (€15 to €67.50, $14 to $65).

Chamber-music and symphony concerts and ballet are presented at the **Teatro Municipal de São Luís,** Rua António Maria Cardoso 40 (*©* **21-325-08-00;** metro: Estação Cais do Sodré; tram: 10, 28, or 28B). Check locally to see if anything is featured when you are in Lisbon. Tickets are 1,200$ to 3,500$ (€6 to €17.50, $6 to $17).

Originally built in the 1840s, and restored after a disastrous fire in 1964, the **Teatro Nacional Doña Maria II,** Plaza Dom Piedro IV (Rossio) (*©* **21-342-22-10;** metro: Rossio), ranks along with the Teatro San Carlos and the Teatro San Luis as the most important cultural venue in Lisbon. Despite its funding by the Ministry of Culture, it does not limit its repertoire to just Portuguese-language productions, although those are the most common. Tickets are 3,500$ (€17.50, $17). Students with a valid ID get a 50% discount.

From October to June, concerts, recitals, and occasionally ballet are performed at the **Museu da Fundação Calouste Gulbenkian,** av. de Berna 45 (*©* **21-793-51-31;** metro: Sebastião; bus: 16, 18, 26, 31, 42, 46, or 56). Sometimes there are also jazz concerts. You'll have to inquire locally about what is happening at the time of your visit.

BARS

Bachus, Largo da Trindade 9 (*©* **21-342-28-28;** bus: 58 or 100), is a restaurant and a convivial watering spot. Amid Oriental carpets, fine hardwoods, bronze statues, and intimate lighting, you can hobnob with some of the most glamorous people in Lisbon. Late-night candlelit suppers are served in the bar. The array of drinks is international, costing from 600$ (€3, $3). Open daily from noon to midnight. There's no cover.

A longtime favorite of journalists, politicians, and foreign actors, the once-innovative **Procópio Bar,** Alto de San Francisco 21A (*©* **21-385-28-51;** bus: 9), has become a tried-and-true staple. It might easily become your favorite bar—if you can find it. It lies just off Rua de João Penha, which itself lies off the landmark Praça das Amoreiras. It's open from Monday to Saturday from 6pm to 3am. A mixed drink costs from 850$ (€4.25, $4), whereas the price of beer begins at 600$ (€3, $3). There's no cover. It's open Monday to Friday 6pm to 3am, Saturday 9pm to 3am; closed August 1 to 15.

Panorama Bar, in the Lisboa Sheraton Hotel, Rua Latino Coelho 1 (*©* **21-357-57-57;** metro: Picos; bus: 1, 2, 9, or 32), occupies the top floor of the Lisboa Sheraton. The view features the old and new cities, the mighty Tagus, and many towns on the river's far bank. Amid a decor of chiseled stone and stained glass, a polite uniformed staff serves you. You'll pay 1,400$ to 2,000$ (€7 to €10, $7 to $10) for a whiskey and soda. The bar is open daily from 6pm to 2am. There's no cover.

Though the sophisticated restaurant draws many visitors, many people come to **The Bar of the Café Alcântara,** Rua Maria Luisa Holstein 15 (*©* **21-363-71-76;** bus: 12 or 18), for its bar. The bar is long and curvy, with accessories you might've expected in a railway car pulling into Paris (ca. 1900). The bar is open nightly from 8pm to 3am. There's no cover.

PORT WINE TASTING   A bar devoted exclusively to the drinking and enjoyment of port in all its known types, **Solar do Vinho do Porto,** rua de São Pedro de Alcântara 45 (*©* **21-347-57-07;** bus: 58 or 100), lies near the Bairro Alto and its fado clubs. Owned and sponsored by the Port Wine Institute, Solar displays many artifacts related to the industry. But the real reason for dropping in during the day is for its *lista de vinhos*—there are more than 200 wines from which to choose. Solar is not far from the upper terminus of the Gloria

Moments The Quintessential Lisbon Experience: Fado

Fado is Portugal's most vivid art form; no visit to Lisbon is complete without at least 1 night in one of the taverns where this traditional music is heard. Fado is typically sung by women, called *fadistas*, accompanied by guitar and viola. The songs express romantic longing and sadness, *saudade*, the country's sense of nostalgia for the past.

Adega Machado, Rua do Norte 91 (*℃* **21-347-05-50;** bus: 58 or 100), has passed the test of time, and is still one of Portugal's favored fado clubs. Alternating with the fadistas are folk dancers whirling, clapping, and singing their native songs in colorful costumes. Dinner is a la carte, and the cuisine is mostly Portuguese, with a number of regional dishes. Expect to spend 6,000$ to 7,000$ (€30 to €35, $29 to $34) for a complete meal. Dining starts at 8:30pm, and the doors don't close until 3am. The first show starts at 9:15pm. Cover (including two drinks) is 2,800$ (€14, $13). It's open from Tuesday to Sunday.

Every night at **A Severa,** Rua das Gaveas 51 (*℃* **21-346-40-06;** bus: 20 or 24), top fadistas sing, both male and female, alternating with folk dancers. In a niche you'll spot a statue honoring the club's namesake, Maria Severa, the legendary 19th-century Gypsy fadista who made fado famous. The kitchen turns out regional dishes based on recipes from the north of Portugal. Expect to spend from 6,000$ (€30, $29) per person for a meal with wine. Cover (including two drinks) is 3,500$ (€17.50, $17) and the club is open from Friday to Wednesday 8pm to 3:30am.

Try to catch the tempestuous Fernanda Maria, the owner of **Lisboa a Noite,** Rua das Gaveas 69 (*℃* **21-346-85-57;** bus: 58 or 100), when she's about to make her first appearance of the evening. The 17th-century-style setting is rustic yet luxurious (this Bairro Alto club was once a stable). In the rear is an open kitchen and charcoal grill. The price of an average meal is around 6,000$ to 7,500$ (€30 to €37.50, $29 to $36). Cover (including two drinks) is 3,000$ (€15, $14), and hours are from Monday to Saturday 8pm to 3am; shows begin at 9:30pm.

Seemingly every fadista worth her shawl has sung at the old-time **Parreirinha da Alfama,** Beco do Espirito Santo 1 (*℃* **21-886-82-09;** bus: 39 or 46), just a minute's walk from the docks of the Alfama. It's fado and fado only here, and it's open daily from 8:30pm to 2:30am; music begins at 9:30pm. In the first part of the program, fadistas get all the popular songs out of the way, then settle in to their more classic favorites. You can order a good regional dinner for around 5,000$ (€25, $24) as part of the experience, although many visitors opt to come here just for a drink. Cover (credited toward drinks) is 2,000$ (€10, $10).

funicular. It's open from Monday to Saturday 2pm to midnight. A glass of wine costs 300$ to 4,500$ (€1.50 to €22.50, $1.45 to $22).

GAY & LESBIAN BARS

Since the collapse of Salazar and the new openness of Lisbon nightlife, at least eight gay bars have sprung up in the district known as **Príncipe Real.** The dark pink **Agua No Bico Bar,** Rua de São Marçal 170 (*C* **21-347-28-30;** bus: 15, 58, or 100; tram: 24), is lined with movie posters and filled mainly with young men and the hottest bartenders in Lisbon. You won't see any sign out in front, but there's a discreet brass plaque set on a steeply sloping street lined with dignified 18th-century villas. Recorded music plays in an atmosphere that might remind you of an English pub—but with Iberian art work. Beer costs from 500$ (€2.50, $2.40); whiskey and soda begins at 650$ (€3.25, $3). It's open nightly from 9pm to 2am. There's no cover.

In the narrow streets of the Bairro Alto, **Memorial Bar,** Rua Gustavo de Matos Sequeira 42A (*C* **21-396-88-91;** bus: 58 or 100), is a "household word" for dozens of lesbians, who consider it one of the premier networking sites in Portugal. This small and rather cramped disco with ample bar space welcomes newcomers. There's an occasional round of live entertainment; otherwise, the place is low-key and unpretentious. A beer costs 600$ (€3, $3). It's open from Tuesday to Saturday 10pm to 4am, but disco music begins at midnight. On Sunday it's open 4 to 8pm. Cover is 1,000$ (€5, $5).

Queens, Rua de Cintura do Porto de Lisboa, Armazém 8, Naves A&B, Doca de Alcântara Norte (*C* **21-395-58-70;** tram: 15), is one of the most frequented gay nightclubs in Lisbon, larger than any of its competitors, and outfitted with an enormous dance floor that's flooded with late-breaking music from a sophisticated sound system. Most of the hip crowd is gay, male, and under 35, although today, in spite of its name, the club also attracts straights. It's open from Tuesday to Saturday 11pm to 5am or sometimes later, depending on the energy level of the dance floor. Cover is 1,000$ (€5, $5).

Some 20 years old, **Frágil,** Rua da Atalia 126–128 (*C* **21-346-95-78;** metro: Baixa Chiado), is a dance bar and music joint featuring DJs who play the latest in underground music. The chic crowd includes many professional and attractive gay men: Lisbon's core of gay journalists, designers, painters, and financiers. There's a large dance floor. The owner changes the decor every 6 months, and often throws a dance party for the occasion. You'll pay 700$ (€3.50, $3.35) for a beer; a whiskey starts at 1,000$ (€5, $5). Open from Monday to Saturday 11:30pm to 4am.

DANCE CLUBS

As its name implies, **Docks,** Avenida 24 de Julio, at Centro Mare (*C* **21-395-08-56;** tram 15), is adjacent to the Tagus in Alcântara and has windows overlooking the river. Sophisticated and stylish, with a decor that's one of the most beautiful in the neighborhood, it has a 30-ish crowd. It's open from Tuesday to Saturday 11pm to 6am. Cover is 1,000$ (€5, $5) if full, otherwise free.

Kremlin, Escadinhas da Praia 5 (*C* **21-390-87-60;** bus: 32 or 37), the most energetic and iconoclastic of Lisbon's dance clubs, welcomes a very hip crowd of techno and garage music lovers into an angular and metallic-looking environment that's an artfully surreal takeoff on pomposity of what used to be known as the Soviet dictatorship. Some of that dictatorship lives on in the doorman who evaluates each patron, as they did in the heyday of New York's Studio 54, letting in what he perceives as the young and trendy. It's open from Tuesday and Sunday from 11pm to 5am. Cover is 1,000$ (€5, $5).

Plateau, Escadinhas da Praia 7 (*C* **21-396-51-16;** tram: 15), near the Kremlin club (see above), is a one-story nightclub with a confetti-colored decor and a mixed clientele. The elite mingle with everyday folk who are just looking for love and good music. What you see is what you get: comfortable seating, cooperative bartenders skilled at mixing anything you can think of, and an appealing mixture of rock 'n' roll, garage, hip-hop, and, on rare occasions, even reggae. Surprisingly, the place is less dance oriented than you might think; many patrons come to watch and listen, not to boogie. Cover is 1,000$ (€5, $5); open from Tuesday to Saturday midnight to 4:30am.

The club of the hour is **Lux,** Rua Gustavo Matos Sequeria 42 (© **21-882-08-90**), by the Santa Apolonia Train Station. Under a disco ball, you can dance the night away or else retreat upstairs for R&R (or whatever). House and techno music fill the space, and it's Lisbon club culture at its best. Guests are in a wide age group (22 to 55), and many of the younger ones stick around until sunrise. The bar upstairs is open from Wednesday to Saturday 6pm to 3am, and the downstairs disco is open from Thursday to Saturday 11pm to 6am. There's no cover but a minimum drink order of 2,000$ (€10, $10).

LIVE MUSIC CLUBS

Fusion jazz and mainstream is the feature at the appropriately named **Hot Club de Portugal,** Praça da Alegria 39 (© **21-346-7369;** metro: Avenida), a smoky subterranean dive. This is one of the city's best jazz clubs, attracting a wide age group from 18 to 50. A beer costs 500$ (€2.50, $2.40), and the cover is 1,000$ to 1,500$ (€5 to €7.50, $5 to $7).

Havana, Doca de Santo Amaro, Armazem 5 (© **21-397-98-93;** metro: Alcântara), brings the Cuban music craze sweeping Europe to Lisbon. Decorated in a motif of "Havana heat," it is both a bar and a restaurant. Of course it plays salsa but also pop and dance tunes. Palm trees and ceiling fans evoke the Havana of Hemingway days. Most of the patrons are in the 25 to 40 age range. The cuisine is quite good if you'd like to have a meal here. Open daily from noon to 2am (bar daily midnight to 4am). There's no cover.

Salsa Latina, Gare Maritima de Alcântara, Docas (© **21-395-0550;** bus: 12 and 20), rocks with Latino rhythms, everything from namesake salsa to the tango and mambo that evokes '40s movies starring Carmen Miranda. Some nights the music is recorded; at other times the club vibrates to the sound of live acts. On-site is a good restaurant serving Mexican cuisine with south of the border decor. The cover for the bar is 2,500$ (€12.50, $12), with a beer costing 650$ (€3.25, $3). The restaurant is open from Tuesday to Saturday 8 to 11:30pm, the bar the same days 10:30pm to 6:30am.

A DAY TRIP TO THE COSTA DO SOL: THE PORTUGUESE RIVIERA

Lisbon's environs are so intriguing that many fail to see the capital itself, lured by Guincho (near the westernmost point in continental Europe), the Mouth of Hell, and Lord Byron's "glorious Eden" at Sintra. You could spend a day drinking in the wonders of the pretty pink rococo palace at Queluz or enjoying seafood at the Atlantic beach resort of Cascais.

The **Costa do Sol** ⨞⨞⨞ is the string of beach resorts forming the Portuguese Riviera on the northern bank of the mouth of the Tagus. If you arrive in Lisbon when the sun is shining and the air balmy, consider heading for this cabana-studded shoreline. So near to Lisbon is Estoril that it's easy to dart in and out of the capital to see the sights or visit the fado clubs, while you spend your nights in a hotel by the sea. An inexpensive electric train leaving from the Cais do Sodré in Lisbon makes the trip frequently throughout the day and evening, ending its run in Cascais.

The Riviera is a microcosm of Portugal. Ride out on the train, even if you don't plan to stay there. Along the way you'll pass pastel-washed houses with red-tile roofs and façades of antique blue-and-white tiles; miles of modern apartment dwellings; rows of canna, pines, mimosa, and eucalyptus; swimming pools; and in the background, green hills studded with villas, chalets, and new homes. The sun coast is sometimes known as the Costa dos Reis, the "coast of kings," because of all the deposed royalty who have settled there—everybody from exiled kings to pretenders, marquesses from Italy, princesses from Russia, and baronesses from Germany.

ESTORIL 🏵 The first stop is 24 kilometers (15 miles) west of Lisbon. This chic resort has long basked in its reputation as a playground of monarchs. The **Parque Estoril,** in the town center, is a well-manicured piece of landscaping, a subtropical setting with plants swaying in the breeze. At night, when it's floodlit, you can go for a stroll. The palm trees studding the grounds have prompted many to call it "a corner of Africa." At the top of the park sits the **casino,** offering not only gambling but also international floor shows, dancing, and movies.

Across the railroad tracks is the **beach,** where some of Europe's most fashionable women sun themselves on the peppermint-striped canvas chairs along the Tamariz Esplanade. The atmosphere is cosmopolitan and the beach sandy, unlike the pebbly strand at Nice. If you don't want to swim in the polluted ocean, you can check in at an oceanfront pool for a plunge.

CASCAIS🏵 Just 6 kilometers (4 miles) west of Estoril and 30 kilometers (19 miles) west of Lisbon, Cascais has more of a Portuguese atmosphere than Estoril, even though it has been increasingly overbuilt. That Cascais is growing is an understatement: It's leapfrogging! Apartment houses, new hotels, and the finest restaurants along the Costa do Sol draw a never-ending stream of visitors every year.

However, the life of the simple fisher folk still goes on. Auctions, called *lotas,* at which the latest catch is sold, still take place on the main square, though a modern hotel has sprouted up in the background. In the small harbor, rainbow-colored fishing boats share space with pleasure craft owned by an international set that flocks to Cascais from early spring until autumn.

The most popular excursion outside Cascais is to the **Boca de Inferno (Mouth of Hell)** 🏵. Reached by heading out the highway to Guincho, then turning left toward the sea, the Boca deserves its ferocious reputation. At their peak, thundering waves sweep in with such power and fury they long ago carved a wide hole (*boca*) in the cliffs. However, if you should arrive when the sea is calm, you'll wonder why it's called a cauldron. The Mouth of Hell can be a windswept roar if you don't stumble over too many souvenir hawkers.

The three sandy **beaches** at Cascais are almost as overcrowded as those at Estoril, and the waters here are less polluted but contaminated nonetheless. Hotel pools remain the safer choice. Though there's a dangerous undertow, the best beach—at least from the standpoint of lying on the sand—is Praia do Guincho, around Cabo da Roca, right outside Cascais. The beach has dunes and is mostly uncrowded and relatively pollution free. The continental winds make it a favorite for surfers.

QUELUZ 🏵🏵 At the Estação Rossio in Lisbon, take the Sintra line train 15 kilometers (9 miles) northwest to Queluz. Trains depart every 15 minutes (trip time: 30 minutes). After leaving the train station in Queluz, take a left turn and follow the signs to the **Palácio de Queluz** 🏵, Largo do Palácio (✆ **21-435-00-39**), a brilliant example of the rococo in Portugal. Pedro III ordered its construction in 1747, and the work dragged on until 1787. What you see now isn't exactly what it was in the 18th century. Queluz suffered a lot during the French invasions, and almost all its belongings were transported to Brazil with the royal family. A 1934 fire destroyed a great deal of Queluz, but tasteful reconstruction has restored the lighthearted aura of the 18th century. Inside, you can wander through the queen's dressing room, lined with painted panels depicting a children's romp; the Don Quixote Chamber (Dom Pedro was born here and returned from Brazil to die in the same bed); the Music Room, complete with a French grande pianoforte and an 18th-century English harpsichord; and the mirrored throne room adorned with crystal chandeliers. The palace is open from Wednesday to Monday (except holidays) from 10am to 5pm. Admission is 600$ (€3, $3). It's always free for anyone under 12, and free for general admission every Sunday morning.

SINTRA ⭐⭐⭐   Sintra, 29 kilometers (18 miles) northwest of Lisbon, is a 45-minute train ride from the Estação Rossio in Lisbon. Lord Byron called it a "glorious Eden," and so it remains. Visitors flock here not only to absorb the town's beauty and scenic setting but also to visit two major sights.

Opening onto the central town square, the **Palácio Nacional de Sintra** ⭐⭐, Largo da Rainha D. Amélia (© **21-910-68-40**), was a royal palace until 1910. Much of it was constructed in the days of the first Manuel, the Fortunate. Two conical chimney towers form the most distinctive landmark on the Sintra skyline. The Swan Room was a favorite of João I, one of the founding kings, father of Henry the Navigator and husband of Philippa of Lancaster. The Room of the Sirens or Mermaids is one of the most elegant in the palace. In the Heraldic or Stag Room, coats-of-arms of aristocratic Portuguese families and hunting scenes are depicted. The palace is rich in paintings and Iberian and Flemish tapestries. But it's at its best when you wander into a tree- and plant-shaded patio and listen to the fountain. Admission is 600$ (€3, $3) adults, half-price for children 6 to 16, free for children under 6. The palace is open from Thursday to Tuesday 10am to 1 and 2 to 5pm.

Towering over Sintra, the **Palácio Nacional da Pena** ⭐⭐, Estrada de Pena (© **21-910-53-54**), sits on a plateau about 450 meters (1,500 ft.) above sea level. At the top the castle is a soaring agglomeration of towers, cupolas, and battlemented walls. Crossing over a drawbridge, you'll enter the palace proper, whose last royal occupant was Queen Amélia in 1910. Pena has remained much as Amélia left it, which is part of its fascination; it emerges as a rare record of European royal life in the halcyon days preceding World War I. Admission is 600$ (€3, $3), free for children under 15. The palace is open from October to May Tuesday to Sunday 10am to 5:30pm (last admittance at 5pm); from June to September Tuesday to Sunday 10am to 6:30pm (last admittance 6pm).

2 The Algarve

The maritime province of the Algarve, often called the "garden of Portugal," is the southwesternmost part of Europe. Its coastline stretches 160 kilometers (100 miles)—all the way from Henry the Navigator's Cape St. Vincent to the border town of Vila Real de Santo António. The varied coastline contains sluggish estuaries, sheltered lagoons, low-lying areas where the cluck of the marsh hen can be heard, long sandy spits, and promontories jutting out into the white-capped aquamarine foam. Called Al-Gharb by the Moors, the land south of the *serras* (hills) of Monchique and Caldeirão remains a spectacular anomaly that seems more like a transplanted section of the North African coastline. The countryside abounds in vegetation: almonds, lemons, oranges, carobs, pomegranates, and figs.

The Algarve

SPAIN

Rio Guadiana

Vila Real de Santo António

Monte Gordo

Castro Marim

Mertola

N122

N124

Rio de Foupana

Rio de Odeleite

N337

Ribeira de Alportel

Rio Vascão

Ribeira de Carreiras

N267

Barronca Velho

São Brás de Alportel

Tavira

Ilha de Armona

Olhão

Cabo de Santa Maria

N2

Estói

Faro

Ilha da Barreta

Loulé

Almancil

N125

Serra do Caldeirão

N124

Vale do Lobo

Quinta do Lago

IP1

Albufeira

N262

São Bartolomeu de Messines

Armação de Pêra

IP1

E01

N264

Silves

Lagoa

ATLANTIC OCEAN

São Marcos da Serra

N266

Portimão

Praia da Rocha

Rio Mira

Caldas de Monchique

Alvor

Lagos

Ponta da Piedade

Serra de Monchique

Odemira

N120

Aljezur

N120

N125

Odeceixe

Carrapateira

N268

Vila do Bispo

Sagres

Ponta de Sagres

Cabo de São Vicente

PORTUGAL

SPAIN

area of detail

5 mi

5 km

0

0

859

Many Moorish and even Roman ruins remain. In the character of its fret-cut chimneys, mosquelike cupolas, and cubist houses, a distinct Oriental flavor prevails. Phoenicians, Greeks, Romans, Visigoths, Moors, and Christians all touched this land. However, much of the historic flavor is gone forever, swallowed by a sea of dreary high-rise apartment blocks surrounding most towns. Many former fishing villages, now summer resorts, dot the Algarvian coast: Carvoeiro, Albufeira, Olhão, Portimão. The sea is still the source of life, as it always has been. The marketplaces in the villages sell esparto mats, copperwork, pottery, and almond and fig sweets that are sometimes shaped like birds and fish.

Our tour stretches along the coast, beginning at Lagos, 264 kilometers (164 miles) south of Lisbon. From Lagos the road 34 kilometers (21 miles) west to Sagres (N-125) generally has minor traffic, unlike in the rest of the Algarve.

LAGOS ⋆

Lagos, known to the Lusitanians and Romans as Locobriga and to the Moors as Zawaia, became an experimental shipyard of caravels during the time of Henry the Navigator. Edged by the Costa do Ouro (Golden Coast), the Bay of Sagres at one point in its epic history was big enough to allow 407 warships to maneuver with ease. An ancient port city (one historian traced its origins back to the Carthaginians 3 centuries before the birth of Christ), Lagos was well known by the sailors of Admiral Nelson's fleet.

Actually, not that much has changed since Nelson's day. The reasons to go to Lagos are to enjoy the pleasures of table and beach. In winter, the almond blossoms match the whitecaps on the water and the climate is often warm enough for sunbathing. In town, the flea market sprawls through narrow streets, the vendors selling rattan baskets, earthenware pottery, fruits, vegetables, crude furniture, cutlery, knitted shawls, and leather boots.

Just down the coast, the hustle and bustle of market day is forgotten as the rocky headland of the Ponta da Piedade (Point of Piety) appears. This spot is the most beautiful on the entire coast. Amid the colorful cliffs and secret grottoes carved by the waves are the most flamboyant examples of Manueline architecture.

ESSENTIALS

GETTING THERE   By Ferry & Train   From Lisbon's Praça do Comércio, take the ferry across the Tagus to Barreiro. From there, make connections with the Southern Line Railway on its run to Lagos (℡ **21-888-40-25** for information). Three trains per day depart from Lisbon (trip time: 6½ hours). Tickets cost from 2,000$ (€10, $10) one-way.

By Bus   Eight **Rodoviária** buses (℡ **21-357-77-15**) a day make the run between Lisbon and Lagos (trip time: 5 hours) and cost 2,800$ (€14, $13) one-way.

By Car   Take N-120 south of Lisbon to Lagos.

VISITOR INFORMATION   The **Lagos Tourist Office** is at Largo Marquês de Pombal (℡ **282-76-30-31**).

WHERE TO STAY

Hotel de Lagos ⋆   This is a 20th-century castle of Moorish and Portuguese design, with its own ramparts and moats. Standing at the eastern side of the old town, far removed from the beach, this first-class hotel is spread over a hilltop overlooking Lagos; no matter which room you get, you'll have a view, even if it's a courtyard with semitropical greenery. Some rooms have ground-level patios, but most are on the upper six floors; you have a choice of standard or deluxe rooms. The hotel has its own beach club a mile away.

Rua Nova da Aldeia 1, 8600 Lagos. © 282-76-99-67. Fax 282-76-99-20. www.hotel.lagos@mail.telepac.pt. 315 units. 16,750$–27,550$ (€83.75–€137.75, $80–$132) double; 24,600$–32,550$ (€123–€162.75, $118–$156) suite. Rates include breakfast. AE, DC, MC, V. Free parking outside, 750$ (€3.75, $3.60) garage. Closed Nov 25–Dec 15. **Amenities:** 2 restaurants, 2 bars, cafe; pool; tennis courts; health spa; game rooms; horseback riding; room service; laundry/dry cleaning. *In room:* A/C, TV, hair dryer.

Hotel de Meia Praia This first-class hotel, 4 kilometers (2½ miles) northeast of Lagos, is for those who want sand, sun, and good food rather than exciting decor. The hotel stands at a point where a hill begins its rise from the sea. Surrounded by private gardens, it regrettably fronts railway tracks, but also a 6.5-kilometer- (4-mile-) long, wide, sandy beach. The ocean-side midsize rooms have balconies with partitions for sunbathing; they were recently renovated. The furnishings are uncluttered and functional, and frankly, have known better times. Still, the place is comfortable, and the beds are firm. The best units have sea views.

Meia Praia, 8600 Lagos. © 282/76-20-01. Fax 282/76-20-08. 66 units. 15,000$–18,000$ (€75–€90, $72–$86) double. Rates include breakfast. AE, DC, MC, V. **Amenities:** Restaurant, bar; pool; tennis court; minigolf. *In room:* TV, hair dryer.

WHERE TO DINE

Alpendre ℛ PORTUGUESE Alpendre offers one of the most elaborate and sophisticated menus along the Algarve, but, considering the lackluster competition, that's not saying too much. The food is tasty, but the portions aren't large. Service tends to be slow, so don't come here if you're rushed. House specialties include shellfish rice, steak Diane, and filet of sole sautéed in butter, flambéed with cognac, and served with a sauce of cream, orange and lemon juices, vermouth, and seasonings known only to the chef. For dessert you can opt for the mixed fruits flambé or crepes flambés with coffee, both for two.

Rua António Barbosa Viana 17. © 282-76-27-05. Reservations recommended. Main courses 1,500$–4,000$ (€7.50–20, $7.20–$19.20). AE, DC, MC, V. Daily noon–11pm.

SEEING THE SIGHTS

Igreja de Santo António (Church of St. Anthony) ℛ Just off the waterfront sits this 18th-century church. Decorating the altar are some of Portugal's most notable rococo gilt carvings. They were damaged in the 1755 earthquake but subsequently restored. What you see represents the work of many artisans— at times, each apparently pursuing a different theme.

Rua General Alberto Silveira. © 282-76-23-01. Admission 360$ (€1.80, $1.75). Tues–Sun 9:30am–12:30pm and 2–5pm.

Museu Municipal Dr. José Formosinho (Municipal Museum) This museum contains replicas of the fret-cut chimneys of the Algarve, three-dimensional cork carvings, 16th-century vestments, ceramics, 17th-century embroidery, ecclesiastical sculpture, a painting gallery, weapons, minerals, and a numismatic collection. In the archaeological wing are Neolithic artifacts, along with Roman mosaics found at Boca do Rio near Budens, fragments of statuary and columns, and other remains of antiquity from excavations along the Algarve.

Rua General Alberto Silveira. © 282-76-23-01. Admission 360$ (€1.80, $1.75). Tues–Sun 9:30am–12:30pm and 2–5pm. Closed holidays.

Antigo Mercado de Escravos (Old Customs House) The Old Customs House, now in ruins, stands as a painful reminder of the age of exploration. The arcaded slave market, the only one of its kind in Europe, looks peaceful today, but under its four Romanesque arches captives taken from their homelands were sold to the highest bidders. The house opens onto a peaceful square dominated by a statue of Henry the Navigator.

Praça Infante Dom Henríques. No phone. Free admission. Open for viewing any time.

PLAYING GOLF
Parque da Floresta, Budens, Vale do Poco, 8650 Vila do Bispo (© **282-69-00-54**), lies 16 kilometers (10 miles) west of Lagos, just inland from the fishing hamlet of Salema. Designed by Spanish architect Pepe Gancedo and built as the centerpiece of a complex of holiday villas, it offers sweeping views. Some shots must be driven over vineyards and others over ravines, creeks, and gardens. Critics of the course have cited its rough grading and rocky terrain. Greens fees are 7,000$ (€35, $34) for 9 holes and 11,500$ (€57.50, $55) for 18 holes.

Some 4 kilometers (2½ miles) west of Lagos is the par-71 **Palmares** course (© **282-76-29-61**), designed by Frank Pennink with many differences in altitude. Some fairways require driving a ball across railroad tracks, over small ravines, or around groves of palms. Its landscaping is more evocative of North Africa than of Europe, partly because of its hundreds of palm, fig, and almond trees. The view from the 17th green is among the most dramatic of any golf course on the Algarve. Greens fees for 18 holes are 7,000$ to 12,000$ (€35 to €60, $34 to $58), depending on the season.

SAGRES: "THE END OF THE WORLD" 𝓡𝓡
At the extreme southwestern corner of Europe—once called *o fim do mundo* (the end of the world)—Sagres is a rocky escarpment jutting into the Atlantic Ocean. It was from here that Henry the Navigator, the Infante of Sagres, launched Portugal and the rest of Europe on the seas of exploration. Here he established his school of navigation, where Magellan, Diaz, Cabral, and even Vasco da Gama apprenticed. Henry died in 1460, before the great discoveries of Columbus and Vasco da Gama, but the later explorers owed a debt to him. A virtual ascetic, he brought together the best navigators, cartographers, geographers, scholars, sailors, and builders, infused them with his rigorous devotion, and methodically set Portuguese caravels upon the Sea of Darkness.

ESSENTIALS
GETTING THERE   By Bus   Some 10 **Rodoviária** buses (© **282-76-29-44**) per day head west from Lagos to Sagres (trip time: 1 hour). A one-way ticket costs 470$ (€2.35, $2.25).

By Car   From Lagos, drive west on N-125 to Vila do Bispo, where you head south along N-268 to Sagres.

VISITOR INFORMATION   Until Sagres gets a full-time tourist office, these functions will be performed by a privately run travel agency: **Turifo,** Praça da República (© **282-62-00-03**), open daily from 10am to 7pm.

WHERE TO STAY
Hotel da Baleeira   In a ship's-bow position, Hotel da Baleeira is a first-class whaleboat (*baleeira* in Portuguese) spread out above the fishing port with vessels tied up in the harbor. The largest hotel on this land projection, it offers rooms with sea-view balconies. The hotel has nearly doubled the number of its rooms in recent years; the older ones are quite small and some have linoleum floors. Bathrooms are also tiny.

If you're exploring the Algarve and are in Sagres just for the day, you can stop and order lunch or dinner in a dining room cantilevered toward the sea, where every seat has a view.

Sítio da Baleeira, Vila do Bispo, 8650 Sagres. © **282-624-212**. Fax 282-624-425. www.sagres.net/baleeira. 118 units. 7,500$ (€37.50, $36) double. Rates include breakfast. AE, DC, MC, V. Free parking. **Amenities:** Restaurant, bar; room service; laundry/dry cleaning. *In room:* TV, hair dryer.

Pousada do Infante ⚲   Built in 1960, the glistening white-painted govern-ment-owned tourist inn is spread along the edge of a cliff projecting rather dar-ingly over the sea. It boasts a long colonnade of arches with an extended stone terrace set with garden furniture. The public areas are generously proportioned, gleaming with marble and decorated with fine tapestries depicting the exploits of Henry the Navigator. On the second floor are midsize, rather sterile rooms with private balconies. Rooms 1 to 12 are the most desirable. An official annex of the pousada, the Fortaleza do Belixe (see "Where to Dine," below), offers less luxurious rooms.

Ponta da Atalaia, 8650 Sagres. © **282-624-222**. Fax 282-624-225. www.pousadas.pt. 39 units. 18,000$–25,100$ (€90–€125.50, $86–$121) double; 22,000$–32,000$ (€110–€160, $106–$154) suite. Rates include breakfast. AE, DC, MC, V. Free parking. **Amenities:** Restaurant, bar; pool; tennis courts; room service; laundry. *In room:* A/C, TV, minibar.

WHERE TO DINE

Fortaleza do Belixe PORTUGUESE/INTERNATIONAL   Set on a sandy and rocky stretch of the coastal road stretching between Sagres and the south-westernmost tip of Portugal, Cabo de São Vicente, this establishment occupies the much-restored remnants of a medieval fortress built around the heyday of Henry the Navigator. The menu offerings are simple, straightforward, and fla-vorful, and include such items as caldo verde; a tasty fish soup; fried or grilled squid; grilled swordfish; well-prepared but uncomplicated versions of veal, pork, and beef; and whatever fresh fish happens to be available from the local market.

In addition to its restaurant, the establishment maintains a quartet of rooms, each with TV. With breakfast included, doubles cost 16,000$ (€80, $77).

Fortaleza do Belixe, Vila do Bispo, 8650 Sagres. © **282-62-41-24**. Main courses 1,000$–4,200$ (€5–€21, $4.80–$20); fixed-price menu 3,500$ (€17.50, $17). AE, MC, V. Daily 1–3pm and 7:30–9:30pm. Closed Nov 15–Feb 15. From Sagres, drive west for 5km (3 miles) along the coastal road, following the signs to Cabo de São Vicente.

EXPLORING THE AREA

Both the cape and Sagres (especially from the terrace of the pousada) offer a view of the sunset. To the ancient world, the cape was the last explored point, although in time the Phoenicians pushed beyond it. Many mariners thought that when the sun sank beyond the cape, it plunged over the edge of the world, and thus to ven-ture around the promontory was to face the demons of the unknown.

Today, at the reconstructed site of Henry's windswept fortress on Europe's Land's End (named after the narrowing westernmost tip of Cornwall, England), you can see a huge stone compass dial, Venta de Rosa, that Henry is alleged to have used in the naval studies pursued at Sagres. Housed in the fortress is a small museum of minor interest that documents some of the area's history. Admission is 300$ (€1.50, $1.45), and it's open Tuesday to Sunday 10am to noon and 2 to 6pm. At a simple chapel, restored in 1960, sailors are said to have prayed for help before setting out into unchartered waters. The chapel is closed to the public.

The promontory of **Cabo de São Vicente** ⚲⚲ is 5 kilometers (3 miles) away. The cape is so named because, according to legend, the body of St. Vincent arrived mysteriously here on a boat guided by ravens. Others claim that the body of the patron saint, murdered at Valencia, Spain, washed up on Lisbon's shore. A lighthouse, the second most powerful in Europe, beams light 100 kilometers (60 miles) across the ocean. It's generally open daily from 8am to noon and 2 to 9pm, but you must get permission from the gatekeeper to climb it. Here, seagulls glide on the air currents, and on the approach, a few goats graze on a hill where even the trees are bent from the gusty winds.

No buses connect the cape with Sagres. You must go by car.

OUTDOOR ACTIVITIES
BEACHES Many beaches fringe the peninsula—some attracting nude bathers. **Mareta,** at the bottom of the road leading from the center of town toward the water, is not only the best but the most popular. Rock formations can be seen jutting far out into the Atlantic. East of town is **Tonel,** also a good sandy beach. The beaches west of town, **Praia de Baleeira** and **Praia de Martinhal,** are better for windsurfing than for swimming.

EXPLORING If you'd like to rent a **bike** to explore the cape, go to **Turinfo,** Praça da República in Sagres (© **282-62-00-03**). The charge is 1,200$ (€6, $6) per half day. It also offers **Jeep tours** of the natural preserve of the cape, including lunch, at a cost of 7,000$ (€35, $34).

PRAIA DA ROCHA
En route to Praia da Rocha, off N-125 between Lagos and Portimão, 18 kilometers (11 miles) away, you'll find several good beaches and rocky coves, particularly at **Praia dos Três Irmãos** and **Alvor.** But the most popular seaside resort on the Algarve is the creamy yellow beach of Praia da Rocha. At the outbreak of World War II there were only two small hotels on the Red Coast, but nowadays Praia da Rocha is booming, as many have been enchanted by the spell cast by its shoreline and climate.

It's named the Beach of the Rock because of its beautiful sculptural rock formations. At the end of the mussel-encrusted cliff, where the Arcade flows into the sea, are the ruins of the **Fort of St. Catarina,** whose location offers many views of Portimão's satellite, Ferragudo, and of the bay.

To reach Praia da Rocha from Portimão, you can catch a bus for the 2.5-kilometer (1½-mile) trip south. Service is frequent. Algarve buses aren't numbered but are marked by their final destination, such as PRAIA DA ROCHA.

WHERE TO STAY
Bela Vista An artfully rustic Moorish-style mansion built during the last century by a wealthy family as a summer home, Bela Vista is set atop its own palisade, with access to a sandy cove where you can swim. The villa is ideal for those who respond to the architecture of the past and those who make a reservation way in advance. The entry hall has an Art Nouveau bronze torchère and a winding staircase. Rooms facing the sea, the former master bedrooms, are the most desirable, though all rooms have character. Decorations vary from an inset tile shrine to the Virgin Mary to crystal sconces.

Av. Tómas Cabreira, Praia da Rocha, 8500 Portimão. © **282-450-480.** Fax 282-41-53-69. 14 units. 10,000$–20,000$ (€50–€100, $48–$96) double; 15,000$–31,000$ (€75–€155, $72–$149) suite. Rates include breakfast. AE, DC, MC, V. Free parking. **Amenities:** Bar; room service; laundry. *In room:* TV, minibar, hair dryer.

Residencial Sol The painted concrete facade of this hotel appears somewhat bleak. Appearances can be deceiving. Once you go inside, you find a neat and attractive hotel, with good-size rooms, each furnished with a comfortable bed and a tidily maintained shower-only bathroom. Units in the rear are quieter, but also darker. The front units are more spacious and open onto a lush town park studded with bougainvillea. The breakfast lounge doubles as a TV room.

Av. Tomás Cabreira 10, Praia da Rocha, 8500 Portimão. (℃ 282-42-40-71. Fax 282-41-71-99. 22 units. 8,000$–9,000$ (€40–€45, $38–$43) double; 9,500$ (€47.50, $46) suite. Rates include breakfast. AE, DC, MC, V. Free parking. Closed Nov–Mar. **Amenities:** Dining area; lounge; room service; laundry. *In room:* hair dryer.

WHERE TO DINE

Titanic INTERNATIONAL   Complete with gilt and crystal, the air-conditioned Titanic is the most elegant restaurant in town. From its open-view kitchen, it serves the best food, including shellfish and flambé dishes. You can dine very well here on such appealing dishes as the fish of the day, pork filet with mushrooms, prawns *à la plancha* (grilled), Chinese fondue, and sole Algarve. Service is among the best at the resort.

Edifício Colúmbia, Rua Engenheiro Francisco Bivar. (℃ 282-42-23-71. Reservations recommended, especially in summer. Main courses 1,600$–2,800$ (€8–€14, $8–$13). AE, DC, MC, V. Daily 7–midnight. Closed Nov 27–Dec 27.

PLAYING GOLF

Vale de Pinta (Pestana Golf), Praia do Carvoeiro (℃ 282-34-09-00), are twin par-72 courses, sharing a clubhouse and staff. They're set amid a landscape of tawny rocks and arid hillocks. Both of them route their players through groves of twisted olive, almond, carob, and fig trees. Views from the fairways, designed in 1992 by Californian Ronald Fream, sweep over the low masses of the Monchique mountains, close to the beach resort of Carvoeiro. Experts cite the layout of these two courses as one of the most varied set of challenges in the competitive world of Portuguese golf. Clusters of bunkers, barrier walls, and abrupt changes in elevation make the course complicated. Greens fees are 10,000$ to 14,000$ (€50 to €70, $48 to $67) per person.

PRAIA DOS TRÊS IRMÃOS & ALVOR 🐟🐟

You can also visit **Praia dos Três Irmãos (the Beach of the Three Brothers)** for its beach, even if you prefer not to stay here. It's just a 5-kilometer (3-mile) drive southwest of Portimão, or you can reach it or the tourist development at Alvor by bus. Service is frequent throughout the day. At Praia dos Três Irmãos, you get 14 kilometers (9 miles) of burnished golden sand, broken only by an occasional crag riddled with arched passages. This beach has been discovered by skin divers who explore its undersea grottoes and shoreside cave.

Its neighbor is the whitewashed fishing village of **Alvor,** where Portuguese and Moorish arts and traditions have mingled since the Arabs gave up their 500 years of occupation. Alvor was a favorite coastal haunt of João II. The summer hordes descend on the long strip of sandy beach here. It's not the best in the area, but at least you have space.

WHERE TO STAY

Carlton Alvor Hotel 🐟🐟   This citadel of hedonism is so self-contained you may never stray from the premises. On a landscaped crest, the luxury hotel has many rooms exposed to the ocean view and garden. Rooms are decorated in a classically modern style; most contain oversize beds. Many have private balconies where you can eat breakfast with a view of the Bay of Lagos. Those to avoid are in the rear with so-so views, small balconies, and Murphy beds. The bi-level main dining room boasts three glass walls so every guest has an ocean view.

Praia dos Três Irmãos, Alvor, 8500 Portimão. © **282-40-09-15.** Fax 282-40-09-99. www.pestana.com. 216 units. 16,600$–25,350$ (€83–€126.75, $80–$122) double; from 24,800$–41,850$ (€124–€209.25, $119–$201) suite. Rates include buffet breakfast. AE, DC, MC, V. Free parking. **Amenities:** 3 restaurants, bar; pool; tennis courts; health spa; horseback riding; waterskiing; room service; baby-sitting; laundry/dry cleaning. *In room:* A/C, TV, minibar, hair dryer.

Le Meridien Penina Golf Hotel ⭐⭐⭐   The first deluxe hotel on the Algarve between Portimão and Lagos continues as a major sporting mecca. Most rooms contain picture windows and honeycomb balconies, with views of the course and pool or vistas of the Monchique hills. Standard rooms are spacious and contain good-size Portuguese provincial spool beds; the so-called attic rooms have the most charm, with French doors opening onto terraces. Facilities include three championship golf courses (one 18 hole and two 9 hole), and a private beach.

Montes de Alvor, 8502 Portimão. © **800/225-5843** in the U.S., or 282/420-200. 213 units. 23,500$–35,500$ (€117.50–€177.50, $113–$170) double; 48,000$–58,000$ (€240–€290, $230–$278) suite. Children 3–11 stay free in parents' room. Rates include breakfast. AE, DC, MC, V. Free parking. **Amenities:** 5 restaurants, bar, cafe; pool; 3 golf courses; tennis courts; private beach; water-skiing; horseback riding; salon; room service; baby-sitting; laundry/dry cleaning. *In room:* A/C, TV, minibar, hair dryer.

WHERE TO DINE

Restaurante O Búzio INTERNATIONAL   This restaurant stands at the end of a road encircling a resort development dotted with exotic shrubbery. Lunch and dinner are served in separate locations. Your dinner might include fish soup, gazpacho, *carre de borrego Serra da Estrela* (gratinée of roast lamb with garlic, butter, and mustard), Italian pasta dishes, or lamb kebabs with saffron-flavored rice. The wine cellar is extensive.

Aldeamento da Prainha, Praia dos Três Irmãos. © **282-45-87-72.** Reservations recommended. Main courses 2,500$–4,500$ (€12.50–€22.50, $12–$22). AE, DC, MC, V. Daily 7–10:30pm. Closed Nov–Dec.

PLAYING GOLF

Penina, Apartado 146 (© **282-42-02-00**), lies 5 kilometers (3 miles) west of Portimão, farther west than many of the other great golf courses of the Algarve. Completed in 1966, it was one of the first courses here and the universally acknowledged masterpiece of British designer Sir Henry Cotton. It occupies what was once a network of marshy rice paddies, on level terrain that critics said was unsuited for anything except wetlands. The solution involved planting groves of eucalyptus (350,000 trees in all), which grew quickly in the muddy soil, eventually drying it out enough to bulldoze dozens of water traps and a labyrinth of fairways and greens. The course wraps itself around a luxury hotel (the Meridien Penina). Greens fees are 17,000$ (€85, $82) for 18 holes, whereas greens fees for each of the two 9-hole courses are 5,000$ to 7,000$ (€25 to €35, $24 to $34).

ALBUFEIRA ⭐

The cliff-side town of Albufeira, formerly a fishing village, is the St-Tropez of the Algarve. The lazy life, sunshine, and beaches make it a haven for young people and artists, though the old-timers still regard the invasion that began in the late 1960s with some ambivalence. Some residents open the doors of their cottages to those seeking a place to stay. Travelers without the money often sleep in tents on the cliff or under the sky.

The big, bustling resort retains characteristics more closely associated with a North African seaside community. Its streets are steep, and the villas are staggered up and down the hillside. Albufeira rises above a sickle-shaped **beach** that

Silves: Ghosts of Crusaders & Moors

When you pass through the Moorish-inspired entrance of this hillside town, you'll quickly realize that Silves is unlike other Algarve towns and villages. It lives in the past, recalling its heyday when it was known as Xelb, the seat of Muslim culture in the south before it fell to the crusaders. Christian warriors and earthquakes have been rough on the town.

To reach Silves from Portimão, drive on N-125 east for 8 kilometers (5 miles) to Lagoa, a market town that is the junction with N-124 leading 7 kilometers (4½ miles) north to Silves. There is bus service to Silves 8 times a day.

The red-sandstone **Castle of Silves** ✦, crowning the hilltop, may date from the 9th century. From its ramparts you can look down on the saffron-mossed tile roofs of the village houses and the narrow cobbled streets where roosters strut and scrappy dogs sleep peacefully in the doorways. Once, the blood of the Muslims, staging their last stand in Silves, "flowed like red wine," as one Portuguese historian wrote, and the cries and screams of women and children resounded over the walls. Inside the walls, the government has planted a flower garden, adorning it with golden chrysanthemums and scarlet poinsettias. In the fortress, water rushes through a huge cistern and a deep well made of sandstone. Below are dungeon chambers and labyrinthine tunnels where the last of the Moors hid out before the crusaders found them and sent them to their deaths.

The 13th-century former **cathedral of Silves** ✦ (now a church), down below, was built in the Gothic style. You can wander through its aisles and nave, noting the beauty in their simplicity. Both the chancel and the transept date from a later period, having been built in the flamboyant Gothic style. The Christian architects who originally constructed it may have torn down an old mosque. Many of the tombs contained here are believed to have been the graves of crusaders who took the town in 1244. The structure is one of the most outstanding religious monuments in the Algarve.

Stop for lunch or dinner at **Ladeira,** Ladeira de São Pedro 1 (℗ **282-44-28-70**). This rustic restaurant is known to virtually everyone in its neighborhood on the western outskirts of Silves. It features grilled fish, home cooking, and regional specialties. Steak Ladeira and mixed-fish *cataplana* (a local stew) are especially good. In season, game like partridge or rabbit is often served. Main courses run 1,400$ to 2,500$ (€7 to €12.50, $7 to $12). It's open from Monday to Saturday, noon to 3pm and 7 to 10pm. American Express, MasterCard, and Visa are accepted.

shines in the bright sunlight. A rocky grottoed bluff separates the strip used by the sunbathers from the working beach, where brightly painted fishing boats are drawn up on the sand. Beach access is through a passageway tunneled through the rock.

ESSENTIALS

GETTING THERE By Train Trains connect Albufeira with Faro (see below), which has good connections to and from Lisbon. The train station is 6 kilometers (4 miles) north of the center, but buses run back and forth to the resort every 30 minutes. The fare is 183$ (€0.90, 93¢) one-way. Call ℂ **289-80-17-26** for information and schedules.

By Bus Buses run between Albufeira and Faro every hour (trip time: 1 hour) and cost 600$ (€3, $3) one-way. Seven buses per day link Portimão with Albufeira (1 hour) and cost 730$ (€3.65, $3.50). Call ℂ **289-58-97-55** for information and schedules.

By Car From Portimão, take N-125 east; from Faro, take N-125 west.

VISITOR INFORMATION The **Tourist Information Office** is on Rua 5 de Outubro (ℂ **289-58-52-79**).

WHERE TO STAY

Estalagem do Cerro This inn captures Algarvian charm yet doesn't neglect modern amenities. This "Inn of the Craggy Hill" is just east of the center at the top of a hill overlooking Albufeira's bay, about a 10-minute walk down to the beach. The older regional-style building has been renovated, but its character has been maintained; it's joined to a modern structure in a similar Moorish style. The tasteful rooms have verandas overlooking the sea or garden. On most nights, guests can dance to disco music and be provided with some kind of entertainment from Monday to Friday.

Rua Samora Barros, 8200 Albufeira. ℂ and fax **289-58-61-91**. 95 units. 10,000$–17,000$ (€50–€85, $48–$82) double. AE, DC, MC, V. Free parking on street if available. **Amenities:** Restaurant, bar; pool; health spa; room service; baby-sitting; laundry/dry cleaning. *In room:* A/C, TV, hair dryer, safe.

Hotel Montechoro 🏵🏵 This is the largest hotel in and around Albufeira, a four-star resort set in the vacation-oriented suburb of Montechoro, about a mile northeast of Albufeira's center. Rooms are done in a modern and somewhat streamlined style, opening onto views of the sunbaked countryside. The hotel's only drawback is its lack of a beach adjacent to its grounds, though management supplies frequent minivans to both Oura Beach, about a mile away, and the bar-packed center of Albufeira.

Rua Alexandre O'Neill, (Apartado 928), 8200 Albufeira. ℂ **289-58-94-23**. Fax 289-58-99-47. www.grupomontechoro.com. 362 units. 17,300$–28,000$ (€86.50–€140, $83–$134) double, 26,000$–42,000$ (€130–€210, $125–$202) suite. Rates include buffet breakfast. AE, V. Parking 350$ (€1.75, $1.73). **Amenities:** 2 restaurants, bar; 2 pools; tennis courts; gymnasium; room service; laundry/dry cleaning. *In room:* A/C, TV, hair dryer.

WHERE TO DINE

O Cabaz da Praia FRENCH/PORTUGUESE The 3-decade-old "Beach Basket" sits on a colorful little square near the Church of São Sebastião, now a museum. In a former fisher's cottage, the restaurant has an inviting ambience and good food. With its large sheltered terrace, it offers diners a view over the main Albufeira beach. Main courses, including favorites like cassoulet of seafood, salade océane, and monkfish with mango sauce, are served with fresh vegetables. The restaurant is renowned for its lemon meringue pie and for its soufflés. If you're visiting in winter, call first.

Praça Miguel Bombarda 7. ℂ **289-51-21-37**. Reservations recommended. Main courses 2,500$–6,000$ (€12.50–€30, $12–$29). AE, MC, V. Fri–Wed noon–2:30pm and 7–10:30pm. Closed Nov 10–Dec 15.

VALE DO LOBO☆

Almancil, 13 kilometers (8 miles) west of Faro and 24 kilometers (15 miles) east along N-125 from Albufeira, is a small market town of little interest, yet it's a center for two of the most exclusive tourist developments along the Algarve: **Vale do Lobo,** 6 kilometers (4 miles) southeast of Almancil, and **Quinta do Lago,** 10 kilometers (6 miles) southeast of town. Both are a golfer's paradise.

WHERE TO STAY

Le Meridien Dona Filipa ☆☆☆   Dona Filipa is a deluxe golf hotel with impressive grounds embracing 210 hectares (450 acres) of rugged coastline. The exterior is somewhat uninspired, but a greater dimension was brought to the interior with green-silk banquettes, marble fireplaces, Portuguese ceramic lamps, and old prints over baroque-style love seats. The well-furnished rooms have balconies.

Vale do Lobo, 8136 Almancil ✆ **289-39-41-41.** Fax 289/39-42-88. www.fortehotel.com. 162 units. 25,000$–45,000$ (€125–€225, $120–$216) double; 47,000$–65,000$ (€235–€325, $226–$312) junior suite; 70,000$–98,000$ (€350–€490, $336–$470) deluxe suite. Rates include breakfast. AE, DC, MC, V. Free parking. **Amenities:** 2 restaurants, bar, cafe; pool; tennis courts; salon; room service; baby-sitting laundry/dry cleaning. *In room:* A/C, TV, minibar, hair dryer.

Quinta do Lago ☆☆☆   This hotel is associated with the massive Quinta do Lago resort development, a sprawling, 750-hectare (1,600-acre) estate that incorporates private villas, golf courses, beachfront, swimming pools, and a host of resort-oriented amenities. Rooms are generally spacious, with balconies that open onto views of the estuary. Riding facilities and golf courses are among some of the best in all of Europe.

Quinta do Lago, 8135 Almancil. ✆ **800/223-6800** in the U.S., or 289-35-03-50. Fax 289-39-49-05. www.quintadolagohotel.com. 141 units. 36,000$–44,000$ (€180–€220, $173–$211) double; from 95,000$ (€475, $456) suite. Rates include breakfast. AE, DC, MC, V. Free parking. **Amenities:** 2 restaurants, bar, disco; 2 pools; golf course; tennis courts; health spa; horseback riding; room service; baby-sitting; laundry. *In room:* A/C, TV, minibar, hair dryer.

WHERE TO DINE

Casa Velha ☆☆☆ FRENCH   Casa Velha is an excellent choice. It's not part of the Quinta do Lago resort but overlooks the resort's lake from a century-old farmhouse. The menu is French, with a scattering of Portuguese and international dishes as well. Specialties include a salad of chicken livers and gizzards with leeks and vinaigrette and roasted duck en service (the staff presents different parts of the bird throughout the meal, beginning with the thighs en confit and ending with the breast en magret). Other choices are carefully flavored sea bass, délices of sole, and lobster salad flavored with an infusion of vanilla.

Quinta do Lago. ✆ **289-39-49-83.** Reservations recommended. Main courses 3,800$–4,600$ (€19–€23, $18–$22); fixed-price menu 8,100$ (€40.50, $39). AE, MC, V. Mon–Sat 7:30–10:30pm.

Restaurant Ermitage ☆ *(Finds* ITALIAN/SWISS/INTERNATIONAL   Our favorite restaurant in the region occupies an 18th-century farmhouse. Surrounded by gardens and flowering vines, its focal point is a cozy dining room whose fireplaces add warmth in winter and whose outdoor terrace adds beauty in summer. Starters include goose-liver terrine with blackberry sauce and a "symphony of homemade pastas" surrounding a portion of shrimp and spinach-stuffed ravioli with four other pastas and sauces. Main courses include grilled fish of the day with herb-flavored hollandaise sauce and filet of monkfish with prawn-and-curry sauce. A favorite dessert is a walnut-flavored parfait with freshly made ice cream and mocha sauce.

Estrada Almancil-Vale de Lobo. © **289-39-43-29.** Reservations recommended. Main courses 3,000$–5,000$ (€15–€25, $14–$24); set menu 12,500$ (€62.50, $60). AE, MC, V. Tues–Sat 7–10:30pm. Closed Dec–Jan and 10 days in June. From Almancil, drive 3km (2 miles) south, following the signs to Vale do Lobo.

PLAYING GOLF

Vale do Lobo, Vale do Lobo, 8135 Almancil (© **289-39-39-39**), has played an important role in establishing Portugal's image as a golfer's mecca. Its name, which means valley of the wolf, suggests some forlorn spot set amid bleak terrain—this course is hardly that. It was designed by British golfer Henry Cotton as three 9-hole courses; the courses have been reconfigured into the 18-hole Oceanfront Course and the 18-hole Royal Course. Some of the long shots along both of these courses require driving the ball over ravines, where variable winds make a straight shot difficult. Greens fees, depending on the day of the week, range from 10,000$ to 12,000$ (€50 to €60, $48 to $58) for nine holes and 18,000$ to 22,000$ (€90 to €110, $86.40 to $106) for 18 holes.

Since its opening in 1991, **Vila Sol,** Alto do Semino (© **289-30-05-05**), has been judged as having the best fairways and the boldest and most inventive contours of any course in the Algarve. Designed by English architect Donald Steel, it's part of a 170-hectare (362-acre) residential estate. Great care was taken in allowing the terrain's natural contours to determine the layout of the fairways and greens. Golfers especially praise the configuration of holes 6, 8, and 14, which collectively manage to funnel golf balls around and over ponds, creek beds, and pine groves in nerve-racking order. Par is 72, and greens fees for 18 holes are 15,000$ to 18,000$ (€75 to 90, $72 to $86).

The most famous and sought-after of this complex's trio of golf courses is the **Vilamoura Old Course,** sometimes called Vilamoura I (© **289-31-03-41**), laid out in 1969 by noted English architect Frank Pennink. Its design, texture, and conception are the most English of south Portugal's golf courses, and it's invariably cited for its beauty, its lushness, and the maturity of its trees and shrubberies. Though some of its holes are almost annoyingly difficult (four of them have pars of 5), the course is among the most consistently crowded on the Algarve. Its par is 73, and greens fees are 12,500$ to 20,000$ (€62.50 to €100, $60 to $96) for 18 holes.

Adjacent to the Old Course are a pair of newer, less sought-after courses. They include the **Pinhal Golf Course,** formerly known as Vilamoura II (© **289-32-15-62**), noted for the challenging placement of its many copses of pines. Greens fees are 7,000$ to 12,000$ (€35 to €60, $34 to $58), depending on the season and the time of day. Nearby is the newest of the three, **Laguna Golf Course,** Vilamoura III (© **289-31-01-80**), known for its labyrinth of water traps and lakes. Greens fees are 8,500$ to 11,400$ (€42.50 to €57, $41 to $55) depending on the season and the time of day. Tee-offs in the heat of noon are less expensive than the more sought-after early mornings. Pars for both Pinhal and Laguna are 72.

Quinta do Lago also has superb facilities and is one of the most elegant "tourist estates" on the Algarve. This pine-covered beachfront property has been the retreat of everybody from movie stars to European presidents. The resort's 27 superb holes of golf are also a potent lure.

Of the four golf courses that undulate across the massive Quinta do Lago development, the par-72 **São Lourenço** (© **289-39-65-22**) is the most interesting, challenging, and prestigious. Set amid the grassy wetlands of the Rio Formosa Nature Reserve, home to millions of waterfowl, its contours were crafted by American golf designers William (Rocky) Roquemore and Joe Lee. In 1997,

Golf World magazine voted it the second most-desirable course in continental Europe as part of its annually revised rating systems. Ironically, although the hotel lies within the confines of Quinta do Logo, it's closely associated with the Meridien Doa Felipa Hotel in Vale do Lobo, 7 kilometers (4½ miles) to the west. The most panoramic hole on this course is the sixth; the most frustrating are the 8th and 18th. Many long drives, especially those aimed at the 17th and 18th holes, soar over the waters of a saltwater lagoon. Greens fees are 12,500$ (€62.50, $60) for nine holes and 24,500$ to 25,500$ (€122.50 to 127.50, $117.60 to $122.40) for 18 holes.

Quinta do Lago (℡ **289-39-07-00**), the namesake course of the massive development, is actually composed of two 18-hole golf courses: Quinta do Lago and Rio Formosa. Together they comprise more than 280 hectares (600 acres) of sandy terrain abutting the Rio Formosa Wildlife Sanctuary. Very few long drives here are over open water; instead, the fairways undulate through cork forests, groves of pine trees, and terrain with sometimes abrupt changes in elevation. Greens fees run 8,500$ to 10,000$ (€42.50 to €50, $41 to $48) for nine holes and 17,000$ to 20,000$ (€85 to €100, $82 to $96) for 18 holes.

Pinheiros Altos, Quinta do Lago (℡ **289-39-43-40**), is one of the most deceptive golf courses on the Algarve, with contours that even professional golfers cite as being far more difficult than they appear at first glance. Abutting the wetland refuge of the Rio Formosa National Park, its 120 hectares (250 acres) of terrain, designed by U.S. architect Ronald Fream, are dotted with umbrella pines and with dozens of small lakes at nine of the course's 18 holes. Carts navigate their way around the terrain on cobble-covered paths. The par is 73. Greens fees are 8,500$ to 11,500$ (€42.50 to €57.50, $41 to $55) for nine holes and 17,000$ to 21,000$ (€85 to €105, $82 to $101) for 18 holes.

FARO ⊛

Once loved by the Romans and later by the Moors, Faro is the main city of the Algarve. Since Afonso III drove out the Moors for the last time in 1266, Faro has been Portuguese. On its outskirts an international jet airport brings in thousands of visitors every summer. The airport has done more than anything else to speed tourism not only to Faro but also to the entire Algarve.

ESSENTIALS
GETTING THERE   By Plane   You can fly to Faro from Lisbon in 45 minutes. For **flight information,** call ℡ **289-80-08-01.** You can take bus 14 or 16 to the railway station in Faro. The bus operates daily from 7:10am to 9:45pm, leaving every 45 minutes. The one-way fare is 183$ (€0.90, 93¢).

By Train   Trains arrive in Faro from Lisbon six times a day (trip time: 4 to 7 hours). One-way fares cost 2,280$ (€11.40, $11). For rail information in Faro, call the **railway station** at Largo Estação (℡ **289-80-17-26**). For information in Lisbon, dial ℡ **21-888-40-25.**

By Bus   Buses arrive every hour from Lisbon (trip time: 4½ hours). The **bus station** is on Avenida da República (℡ **289-89-97-60**), adjacent to the railway station. A one-way ticket costs 2,600$ (€13, $13).

By Car   After leaving Vale do Lobo, continue east along N-125 directly into Faro.

VISITOR INFORMATION   The **Tourist Office** is at Rua da Misericórdia 8–12 (℡ **289-80-36-04**). At the tourist office, you can pick up a copy of the Algarve Guide to Walks, which will direct you on nature trails in the area.

WHERE TO STAY

Eva ⚅ Eva dominates the harbor like a fortress, and is the best choice within town. This modern hotel occupies an entire side of the yacht-clogged harbor. It was beginning to look worn and tired, but a recent rejuvenation has perked it up. There are direct sea views from most rooms, which are furnished in a restrained, even austere, style. The better rooms open onto the water with large balconies.

Av. da República, 8000 Faro. ⓒ **289-80-33-54.** Fax 289-80-23-04. 148 units. 17,200$–25,500$ (€86–€127.50, $83–$122) double; 25,180$–34,800$ (€125.90–€174, $121–$167) suite. Rates include breakfast. AE, DC, MC, V. Free parking on street if available. **Amenities:** 2 restaurants, 3 bars; salon; room service; baby-sitting; laundry/dry cleaning. *In room:* A/C, TV, minibar, hair dryer.

WHERE TO DINE

Dois Irmãos *(Value* PORTUGUESE This popular Portuguese bistro, founded in 1925, provides a no-nonsense atmosphere, yet it has its devotees. The menu is as modest as the place and its prices, but you get a good choice of fresh fish and shellfish. Ignore the paper napkins and concentrate on the fine kettle of fish placed before you. Clams in savory sauce is a favorite, and sole is regularly featured—of course, everything depends on the catch of the day. Service is slow but amiable.

Largo do Terreiro do Bispo 13–15. ⓒ **289-82-33-37.** Reservations recommended. Main courses 1,100$–3,700$ (€5.50–18.50, $5–$18); set price menu 2,000$ (€10, $10). AE, MC, V. Daily noon–11pm.

Restaurant Griséus ⚅ INTERNATIONAL/PORTUGUESE Even though Faro is the capital of the Algarve, it is a bit of a gastronomic wasteland. With one or two exceptions, it offers little more than some taverns with questionable sanitation. However, the Griséus, located on the ground level of the town's best hotel, provides an elegant setting for some good-tasting dishes. Start with the smoked salmon, and most definitely try the *assorda de mariscos,* which is a kettle of mixed seafood with some enticing spicing. The chefs also prepare an excellent beef *à la pimienta* (beef with peppers).

Av. da República 1. ⓒ **282/80-33-54.** Reservations required. Main courses 1,900$–4,500$ (€9.50–€22.50, $9–$22). AE, DC, MC, V. Daily 9am–11pm.

SEEING THE SIGHTS

The most bizarre attraction in Faro is the **Capela d'Ossos (Chapel of Bones)** ⚅, entered via a courtyard from the rear of the Igreja (Church) de Nossa Senhora do Monte do Carmo do Faro, on Largo do Carmo. Erected in the 19th century, this chapel is completely lined with the skulls and bones of human skeletons, an extraordinarily ossicular rococo. In all, it's estimated that there are 1,245 skulls. The chapel is open from Monday to Friday 10am to 1pm and 2:30 to 5pm, Saturday 10am to 1pm. Entrance is free to the church but 270$ (€1.35, $1.30) to the chapel.

Other religious monuments include the old **Sé (cathedral),** Largo da Sé, built in the Gothic and Renaissance styles (originally a Muslim mosque stood on this site); and the **Igreja de São Francisco,** Largo de São Francisco, with panels of glazed earthenware tiles in milk white and Dutch blue depicting the life of the patron saint. The church is open from Monday to Friday 10am to 5pm, Saturday 10am to 1:30pm. Entrance to the church is 270$ (€1.35, $1.30). Yes, they charge admission to enter the church, somewhat of a rarity in Portugal. Sunday masses are conducted Sunday at 10am and 11am (no charge then, of course).

But most visitors don't come to Faro to look at churches. Rather, they take the harbor ferry to the wide white-sand beaches called the **Praia de Faro,** on an islet.

The ride is available only in summer. The beach is also connected to the mainland by bridge, a distance of 6 kilometers (4 miles) from the town center. Once here, you can water ski and fish or just rent a deck chair and umbrella and lounge in the sun.

DAY TRIPS FROM FARO

OLHÃO 🏛 Olhão, described as the living re-creation of a Georges Braque collage, is the famous cubist town of the Algarve, so long beloved by painters. In its heart, white blocks stacked one on the other, with flat red-tile roofs and exterior stairs on the stark walls, evoke the aura of the Casbahs of North African cities. But let us not paint too romantic a portrait. Many readers have found it disappointing—dirty, dusty, and too commercial.

If you do go here, try to attend the **fish market** near the waterfront when a *lota* (auction) is underway. Olhão is also known for its bullfights of the sea, in which fishermen wrestle with struggling tuna trapped in nets and headed for the smelly warehouses along the harbor.

For the best view, climb **Cabeça Hill,** its grottos punctured with stalagmites and stalactites, or **St. Michael's Mount,** offering a panorama of the Casbah-like Barreta. Finally, for what is one of the most idyllic beaches on the Algarve, take a 10-minute motorboat ride to the **Ilha de Armona,** a nautical mile away. Olhão is 10 kilometers (6½ miles) west of Faro and is reached by going east on N-125.

SÃO BRAS DE ALPORTEL Traveling north from Faro for 20 kilometers (12½ miles), you'll pass through groves of figs, almonds, and oranges, through pinewoods where resin collects in wooden cups on the tree trunks. At the end of the run, you'll come on isolated São Bras de Alportel, one of the Algarve's most charming and least-known spots.

Far from the crowded beaches, it attracts those wanting pure air, peace, and quiet—a bucolic setting filled with flowers pushing through nutmeg-colored soil. Northeast of Loulé, this whitewashed, tile-roofed town rarely gets lively except on **market days.** Like its neighbor, Faro, it's noted for its perforated plaster chimneys. Lying at the foot of the Serra do Caldeirão, the whole area has been called one vast garden.

A change of pace from the seaside accommodations is offered at **Pousada de São Bras,** Estrada de Lisboa, N2, 8150 São Brás de Alportel (ⓒ **289-84-23-05**). The government-owned inn built in 1942 is a hilltop villa, with fret-cut limestone chimneys and a crow's-view of the surrounding serras. Many visitors arrive just for lunch or dinner (daily 12:30 to 3pm and 7:30 to 10pm). The cuisine is plain but good. The pousada, the third one built in Portugal, also offers 22 well-furnished rooms, each with air-conditioning, minibar, TV, and telephone. The cost is 25,100$ (€125.50, $121) a day with breakfast included. American Express, MasterCard, and Visa are accepted.

VILA REAL DE SANT ANTÓNIO/MONTE GORDO

Twenty years after the marquês de Pombal rebuilt Lisbon, which had been destroyed in the 1755 earthquake, he sent architects and builders to Vila Real de Santo António, where they reestablished the frontier town on the bank opposite Spain. It took only 5 months. Pombal's motivation was jealousy of Spain. Much has changed, of course, though Praça de Pombal remains. An obelisk stands in the center of the square, which is paved with inlays of black-and-white tiles radiating like rays of the sun. Separated from its Iberian neighbor by the Guadiana River, Vila Real de Santo António offers a car-ferry between Portugal and Ayamonte, Spain.

Today, Vila Real is a mostly residential and industrial community that prides itself on its royal and antique associations as a border town. It's supplemented today by Monte Gordo, a town whose buildings mostly date from the 1920s and later. Set 3 kilometers (2 miles) to the east, it's the site of most of the region's tourist facilities and hotels, with easier access to the sandy beaches that attract tourists every summer from as far away as northern Europe.

ESSENTIALS

GETTING THERE   By Train   The railway facilities in Vila Real are bigger, better accessorized, and more convenient than those in Monte Gordo, which is the site of a railway stopping point but not a bona-fide station. In Vila Real, however, 11 trains per day arrive from Faro (trip time: 2½ hours). Tickets are 550$ (€2.75, $2.65) each way. Four direct trains arrive from Lagos (4½ hours) and cost 920$ (€4.60, $4.40) each way. For railway information and schedules, call ℂ **21-888-40-25.**

By Bus   It's faster to take the bus from Faro to Vila Real. Five *espressos* per day arrive from Faro (trip time: 1 hour). The cost is 750$ (€3.75, $3.60). Eight buses arrive from Lagos (4 hours). Call ℂ **289-89-96-61** for information. Buses pull into Vila Real at the bus station on the Avenida Da República.

By Car   From Faro, take N-125 85 kilometers (53 miles) east to reach our final destination, at the Spanish frontier.

VISITOR INFORMATION   The **tourist office** on Avenida Infante Henrique in Monte Gordo (ℂ **281-54-44-95**) is open daily from 9:30am to 5:30pm.

WHERE TO STAY
In Vila Real
Hotel Apolo   Built in the mid-1980s, this hotel lies on the western edge of town as you enter from Monte Gordo or Faro. Near the beach and the river, it attracts vacationers as well as travelers who don't want to cross the Spanish border at night. The hotel is a marginal choice, with a spacious lobby leading into a large bar and flooded with sunlight. Each of the simply furnished rooms has a balcony.

Av. dos Bombeiros Portugueses, 8900 Vila Real de Santo António. ℂ **281-51-24-48.** Fax 281-51-24-49. 42 units. 9,000$–15,000$ (€45–€75, $43–$72) double. Rates include breakfast. AE, DC, MC, V. Free parking. **Amenities:** Bar; pool; bike rental; baby-sitting; laundry. *In room:* A/C, TV, hair dryer.

Hotel Guadiana ⓕ   This is the best hotel in town (which isn't saying a lot), housed in a mansion classified as a historic national monument. Close to the river and the Spanish border, it's ideally located for exploring the town, not far from Santo António beach and near the beach attractions of Monte Gordo. *Azulejos* (decorated tiles) line some of the walls. Rooms are traditional and old-fashioned but have modern amenities. Breakfast is the only meal served.

Av. da República 94, 8900 Vila Real de Santo António. ℂ **281-51-14-82.** Fax 281-51-14-78. 39 units. 10,000$–13,000$ (€50–€65, $48–$62) double; from 14,000$–16,500$ (€70–€82.50, $67–$79) suite. Rates include breakfast. AE, DC, MC, V. Free parking. **Amenities:** Bar; room service; laundry. *In room:* A/C, TV, minibar.

In Monte Gordo
Hotel Alcázar   Hotel Alcázar is the best at the resort but was last renovated in 1994. A free-form pool is built on terraces into the retaining walls that shelter it from the wind and extend the hot-weather season late into autumn. The interior

is a vaguely Arab-style series of repetitive arches and vaults of distressed concrete. Each rather austere unit contains its own sun terrace. The basement disco is open in summer.

Rua de Ceuta, Monte Gordo, 8900 Vila Real de Santo António. ℂ 281-51-01-84. Fax 281-51-01-49. 97 units. 20,500$–22,500$ (€102.50–€112.50, $98–$108) double; 21,000$–26,000$ (€105–€130, $101–$125) suite. Rates include breakfast. AE, DC, MC, V. **Amenities:** Restaurant, bar, disco; room service; baby-sitting; laundry. *In room:* A/C, TV, minibar, hair dryer.

Hotel dos Navegadores *(Kids)* This hotel is popular with vacationing Portuguese and British families, who congregate under the dome covering the atrium's pool. The public areas are clean and functional, and about three-fourths of the standardized rooms have balconies. The beach is only a 5-minute walk away. There are dull boutiques in a corridor along the grounds.

Monte Gordo, 8900 Vila Real de Santo António. ℂ 281-51-08-60. Fax 281-51-08-79. 431 units. 11,000$–18,500$ (€55–€92.50, $53–$89) double; 15,000$–25,000$ (€75–€125, $72–$120) suite. Rates include breakfast. AE, DC, MC, V. Free parking. **Amenities:** Restaurant, bar; children's center; salon; laundry/dry cleaning. *In room:* A/C, hair dryer.

Hotel Vasco da Gama The entrepreneurs here know what their guests seek—lots of sunbathing and swimming. Though this hotel enjoys a position on a long, sandy beach, it also offers nearly an acre of flagstoned sun terrace. All the Spartan rooms are furnished conservatively, and glass doors open onto balconies.

Av. Infante Dom Henrique, Monte Gordo, 8900 Vila Real de Santo António. ℂ 281-51-09-00. Fax 281-51-09-01. vagamahotel@mail.telepac.pt. 172 units. 12,000$–14,500$ (€60–€72.50, $58–$70) double; 15,000$–17,500$ (€75–€87.50, $72–$84) suite. Rates include breakfast. AE, DC, MC, V. Free parking. **Amenities:** Restaurant, 2 bars; lounge; room service; baby-sitting; laundry/dry cleaning. *In room:* A/C, TV, hair dryer.

WHERE TO DINE

Edmundo PORTUGUESE Long known in the Algarve, this restaurant attracts Spaniards who often visit just for the day. It overlooks the river and Spain across the water—try to get a sidewalk table. The people who run this place are friendly and proud of their repertoire of local cuisine, especially fresh fish. You might begin with shrimp cocktail, then follow with fried sole, crayfish, or sautéed red mullet. You can also order such meat dishes as lamb cutlets and veal filet.

Av. da República 55. ℂ 281-54-46-89. Reservations recommended. Main courses 1,500$–3,200$ (€7.50–€16, $7–$15). AE, DC, MC, V. Mon–Sat noon–3pm and 7–10pm; Sun 7–10pm.

EXPLORING VILA REAL

A long esplanade, **Avenida da República,** lines the river, and from its northern extremity you can view the Spanish town across the way. Gaily painted **horse-drawn carriages** take you sightseeing past the shipyards and the lighthouse.

A short drive north on the road to Mertola will take you to the gull-gray castle-fortress of **Castro Marim.** This formidable structure is a legacy of the old border wars between Spain and Portugal. The ramparts and walls watch Spain across the river. Afonso III, who expelled the Moors from this region, founded the original fortress, which was razed by the 1755 earthquake. Inside the walls are the ruins of the **Church of São Tiago,** dedicated to St. James.

Directly southwest of Vila Real is the emerging resort of **Monte Gordo,** which has the greatest concentration of hotels in the eastern Algarve after Faro. Monte Gordo is the last in a long line of Algarvian resorts; it's 3 kilometers

(2 miles) southwest of the frontier town of Vila Real de Santo António at the mouth of the Guadiana River. Its wide beach, one of the finest along the southern coast of Portugal, is backed by pine-studded lowlands.

Sadly, this was once a sleepy little fishing village. Now young men tend to work in the hotels instead of on the sea, fishing for tips instead of tunny. Monte Gordo has succumbed to high-rises; it often attracts Spaniards from across the border. It has many good hotels, and a number of Europeans use it as their place in the Algarvian sun.

15

Scotland

by Darwin Porter & Danforth Prince

Whether you go to Scotland to seek out your ancestral roots, explore ancient castles, drive the Malt Whisky Trail, or partake in the internationally acclaimed Edinburgh Festival, you'll find a country rich in history, legend, and romance. If it's the outdoors you love, Scotland offers great salmon fishing, peaceful walks in heather-covered Highland hills, and some of the best (and oldest) golf courses.

1 Edinburgh & Environs

Called one of Europe's fairest cities, the "Athens of the North," Edinburgh is the second most visited city in Britain after London. It's a white-collar city in contrast to industrialized bastions like Aberdeen and Glasgow. Home of the Royal Mile, Princes Street, and the ever-growing Edinburgh Festival with its action-packed list of cultural events, Edinburgh is both hip and historic. John Knox, Mary Queen of Scots, Robert Louis Stevenson, Sir Arthur Conan Doyle, Alexander Graham Bell, Sir Walter Scott, Bonnie Prince Charlie, and Deacon Brodie are all part of the city's past; you can walk in their footsteps and explore sights associated with them.

ESSENTIALS

GETTING THERE   By Plane   Edinburgh is 632 kilometers (393 miles) north of London, about an hour's flying time. **Edinburgh Airport** (✆ **0131/333-1000** for flight info; www.edinburgh-airport.com) lies 10 kilometers (6 miles) west of the city's center. Flights from within the British Isles and Europe land here; most transatlantic flights go to Glasgow's airport. A double-decker Airlink bus makes the trip between the airport and the city center every 10 minutes, letting you off near Waverley Bridge, between Old Town and New Town; the one-way fare is £3.30 ($5). A taxi suitable for up to 4 passengers into the city costs £14 ($21) or more, depending on traffic.

By Train   Fast air-conditioned InterCity trains with restaurant and bar service link London with Edinburgh. Trains from London's King's Cross or Euston stations arrive in Edinburgh at **Waverley Station,** at the east end of Princes Street (✆ **0345/484-950** in London for information). Trains depart London every hour or so (trip time: 4½ to 5 hours). An overnight sleeper requires reservations. Taxis and buses are found right outside the station in Edinburgh.

By Bus   The least expensive way to go from London to Edinburgh is by bus, but it's an 8-hour journey. The fare is £20 ($30) one way or £30 ($45) round-trip. National Express coaches depart from London's Victoria Coach Station, delivering you to Edinburgh's **St. Andrew Square Bus Station,** St. Andrew Square (✆ **0990/808-080** in Edinburgh).

Edinburgh

By Car   Edinburgh lies 74 kilometers (46 miles) east of Glasgow and 169 kilometers (105 miles) north of Newcastle upon Tyne in England. There's no express motorway linking London and Edinburgh. The M-1 from London takes you part of the way north, but you'll have to come into Edinburgh along secondary roads: A-68 or A-7 from the southeast, A-1 from the east, or A-702 from the north. A-71 or A-8 comes in from the west, A-8 connecting with M-8 just west of Edinburgh; A-90 comes down from the north over the Forth Road Bridge.

VISITOR INFORMATION   Tourist offices   The **Edinburgh & Scotland Information Centre,** Waverley Shopping Plaza, 3 Princes St. (© **0131/ 473-3800**), can give you sightseeing information and can help with accommodations. The center sells bus tours, theater tickets, and souvenirs. It's open May, June, and September from Monday to Saturday 9am to 7pm and Sunday 10am to 7pm; July and August from Monday to Saturday 9am to 8pm and Sunday 10am to 8pm; from October to April Monday to Saturday 9am to 6pm and Sunday 10am to 6pm. There's also an **information and accommodation desk** at Edinburgh Airport (© **0131/473-3800**), which is open April to October daily 6:30am to 10:30pm and November to March 7:30am to 9:30pm.

Websites   The official site of the Scottish Tourist Board (**www.holiday. scotland.net**) is an excellent source for events, lodging, getting around, and outdoor activities. However, the "Special Offers" section requires a lot of clicks for little payoff. The Edinburgh and Lothians Tourist Board (**www.edinburgh.org**) discusses what's new, travel tips, and events and festivals for city, coast, and country; they also include a page about what to do with kids, written *by* kids.

Scotland Holiday Net (**www.aboutscotland.co.uk**) combines information on dining, lodging, and sightseeing with some personal accounts. Curious about Scotland's top 20 free attractions? Interested in restaurant reviews from other diners? Try **www.travelscotland.co.uk**. The *Daily Record* and *Sunday Mail* site (**www-discover-scotland.com**) combines news headlines with travel advice ranging from fine dining to golf. Listing locations and greens fees, **www. uk-golf.com/courses/scotland/index.shtml** will help you find a course wherever you plan to be.

CITY LAYOUT   Edinburgh is divided into an **Old Town** and a **New Town.** Chances are, you'll find lodgings in New Town and visit Old Town for dining, drinking, shopping, or sightseeing.

New Town, with its world-famous **Princes Street,** came about in the 18th century in the "Golden Age" of Edinburgh. The first building went up in New Town in 1767, and by the end of the century, classical squares, streets, and town houses had been added. Princes Street runs straight for about a mile; it's known for its shopping and for its beauty, as it opens onto the **Princes Street Gardens** with stunning views of Old Town.

North of Princes Street, and running parallel to it, is the second great street of New Town, **George Street.** It begins at Charlotte Square and runs east to St. Andrew Square. Directly north of George Street is another impressive thoroughfare, **Queen Street,** opening onto Queen Street Gardens on its north side.

You'll also hear a lot about **Rose Street,** directly north of Princes Street. It has more pubs per square block than any other place in Scotland, and is also filled with shops and restaurants.

Everyone seems to have heard of **the Royal Mile,** the main thoroughfare of Old Town, beginning at Edinburgh Castle and running all the way to the Palace of Holyroodhouse. A famous street to the south of the castle (you have to descend to it) is **Grassmarket,** where convicted criminals were hanged on the dreaded gallows that once stood here.

GETTING AROUND   Walking is the best way to explore Edinburgh, particularly Old Town with its narrow lanes, wynds, and closes. Most attractions are along the Royal Mile, along Princes Street, or in one of the major streets of New Town.

By Bus   This will probably be your chief method of transport within the Scottish capital. The fare you pay depends on the distance you ride, based on a confusing system that derives from "stages" that usually incorporate between two and five bus stops and a distance of about a half-mile. The minimum fare depends on the distance you travel, based on what you tell the driver, who will determine the fare, sell you your ticket, and even make change. Minimum fare is £80p ($1.20) for three stages or less, going up to a maximum of £1.60 ($2.40) for travel between 44 or more stages. Children 5 to 15 pay a flat rate of £50p (75¢), regardless of how many stages they traverse, and children 4 and under ride free and must be accompanied by an adult. There's a family ticket for two adults and four children for £6 ($9) a day and another for £1.60 ($2.40) which operates 6:30pm onward.

The **Edinburgh Day Saver Ticket** allows 1 day of unlimited travel on city buses at a cost of £1.50 to £2.20 ($2.25 to $3.30) adults and £1.50 ($2.25) children ages 5 to 15. For daily commuters or for die-hard Scottish enthusiasts, a **RideCard** season ticket allows unlimited travel on all buses at £10.50 ($16) for adults for 1 week and £30.50 ($46) for 4 weeks. Travel must begin on Sunday. Prices for children are £6.50 ($10) for 1 week, £18 ($27) for 4 weeks.

These tickets and further information may be obtained in the city center at the **Waverley Bridge Transport Office,** Waverley Bridge (© **0131/554-4494;** bus: 3, 31), open daily from 6:30am to 10:30pm; or at the Hanover Street office, which operates from 9am to 7pm daily. For information on timetables call © **0131/555-6363.**

By Taxi   Cabs can be hailed on the street or met at any of several taxi stands, each of which lie at prominent intersections throughout the city. Some of the more important of these are at Hanover Street, North St. Andrew Street, Waverley Station, Princes Street (at the Caledonian Hotel), Haymarket Station, Frederick Street, Castle Street, and Lauriston Place. Fares are prominently displayed in the front of each taxi. The meter begins ticking at £1.80 ($2.70). Regardless of the time of day, you'll be charged 20p (30¢) per 300 yards of distance your cab covers. If you phone for a cab to come to a point you specify to them, you'll pay a surcharge of 60p (90¢) at any time of the day or night. To call a taxi, dial **City Cabs** (© **0131/228-1211**) or **Central Radio Taxi** (© **0131/229-2468**).

By Car   Car rentals are relatively expensive, and driving in Edinburgh is a tricky business. It's a warren of one-way streets, with parking spots at a premium. However, a car is convenient, and sometimes a must, for touring the countryside. Most companies will accept your U.S. or Canadian driver's license, provided you have held it for more than a year and are over 21. At the Edinburgh airport, try **Avis** (© **0131/333-1866**), **Hertz** (© **0131/344-3260**), or **Europcar** (© **0131/333-2588**).

By Bicycle   You can rent bikes by the day or by the week from a number of outfits. Nevertheless, bicycling is not a good idea for most visitors because the city is constructed on a series of high ridges and terraces.

You may, however, want to rent a bike for exploring the flatter countryside. Try **Central Cycle Hire,** 13 Lochrin Place (© **0131/228-6333;** bus: 10), off Home Street in Tollcross, near the Cameo Cinema. Depending on the type of bike, rates range from £10 to £15 ($15 to $23) per day. A deposit of £50 to £100 ($75 to $150) is imposed. The shop is open from Monday to Saturday 10am to 5:30pm; June to September it also opens Sunday noon to 7pm.

C *FAST FACTS:* Edinburgh

American Express The office at 139 Princes St. (© **0131/225-7881;** bus: 3, 39, 69), 5 blocks from Waverley Station, is open from Monday to Wednesday and Friday 9am to 5:30pm and Thursday 9:30am to 5:30pm.

Business Hours In Edinburgh, **banks** are usually open from Monday to Wednesday 9:30am to 3:45pm, and Thursday and Friday 9:30am to 5 or 5:30pm. **Shops** are generally open from Monday to Saturday 10am to 5:30 or 6pm; on Thursday stores are open until 8pm. **Offices,** in the main, are open Monday to Friday 9am to 5pm.

Currency The basic unit of currency is the **pound sterling** (£), which is divided into 100 **pence** (p). The exchange rate at the time we wrote this chapter was £1 = $1.50. Note that though the United Kingdom is part of the EU, it does not plan to switch to the euro at this time.

Currency Exchange There's a **Bureau de Change** of the Clydesdale Bank at 5 Waverley Bridge and at Waverley Market.

Dentists For a dental emergency, go to the **Edinburgh Dental Institute,** 39 Lauriston Place (© **0131/536-4900;** bus: 23, 41), open from Monday to Friday 9am to 3pm.

Doctors In a medical emergency, you can seek help from the **Edinburgh Royal Infirmary,** 1 Lauriston Place (© **0131/536-1000;** bus: 23, 41). Medical attention is available 24 hours.

Drugstores There're no 24-hour drugstores ("chemists" or "pharmacies") in Edinburgh. The major drugstore is **Boots,** 48 Shandwick Place (© **0131/225-6757;** bus: 3, 31), open from Monday to Wednesday and Friday 8am to 6pm, Thursday from 8am to 7:30pm, Saturday from 8am to 7pm, and Sunday from 10am to 5pm.

Embassies/Consulates The Consulate of the **United States** is at 3 Regent Terrace (© **0131/556-8315;** bus: 26, 85, or 86), which is an extension of Princes Street beyond Nelson's Monument. All the other embassies are in London.

Emergencies Call © **999** in an emergency to summon the police, an ambulance, or firefighters.

Hospital The best and most convenient is the **Edinburgh Royal Infirmary,** 1 Lauriston Place (© **0131/536-1000;** bus: 23, 41).

Internet Access You can check your e-mail or send messages at the **International Telecom Centre,** 52 High St (© **0131/559-7114;** bus: 1 or 6), along the Royal Mile. Rates are £1 ($1.50) for 15 minutes. Open daily from 9am to 10pm.

Post Office The Edinburgh Branch **Post Office,** St. James's Centre (✆ **0131/5508232;** bus: 23 or 41), is open from Monday to Friday 9am to 5:30pm and Saturday 9am to noon.

Telephones The United Kingdom's **country code** is **44.** The city code for **Edinburgh** is **0131.** If you're calling from inside the United Kingdom but outside the city code area, dial the complete area code; if you're calling from outside the United Kingdom, drop the zero. As in the United States, if you're calling from inside the code area, dial just the seven-digit number.

Public phones cost 10p (15¢) for the first 3 minutes and accept coins of various denominations. You can also buy a phone card for use in special phones at post offices and newsstands. You can receive U.S. rates for collect or credit card calls by dialing toll free **AT&T** (✆ **0800/890011**), **MCI** (✆ **0800/890222**), or **Sprint** (✆ **0800/890877** or 0500/890877).

WHERE TO STAY
IN THE CENTER
Very Expensive
Balmoral Hotel ✦✦✦   This legendary establishment was opened in 1902 as the largest, grandest, and most impressive hotel in the north of Britain. Its soaring clock tower is a city landmark. Rooms are distinguished, conservative, and rather large, a graceful reminder of Edwardian sprawl with a contemporary twist. Many benefit from rounded or oversize windows and the many Victorian/ Edwardian quirks that were originally designed as part of its charm.

Princes St., Edinburgh, Lothian EH2 2EQ. ✆ **800/225-5843** in the U.S., or 0131/556-2414. Fax 0131/ 557-3747. www.rfhotels.com. 188 units. Apr–Oct £260 ($390) double; from £430 ($645) suite. Off-season £230 ($345) double; from £430 ($645) suite. AE, DC, MC, V. Parking £15 ($23). Bus: 50. **Amenities:** No. 1 Princes St. restaurant (see "Where to Dine," below), bar; pool; heath club; room service. *In room:* A/C, TV, minibar, hair dryer.

Caledonian Hilton Hotel ✦✦✦   "The Caley" is Edinburgh's most visible hotel, with commanding views over Edinburgh Castle and the Princes Street Gardens. The pastel-colored public areas are reminiscent of Edwardian splendor. Rooms are conservatively but individually styled, and are often exceptionally spacious. Fifth-floor rooms are the smallest. Although the accommodations are comparable to other first-class hotels in Edinburgh, the Caledonian lacks the leisure facilities of its major competitor, the Balmoral.

Princes St., Edinburgh EH1 2AB. ✆ **0131/459-9988.** Fax 0131/225-6632. www.hilton.com. 249 units. £235–£315 ($353–$473) double; from £350 ($525) suite. Children 15 and under stay free in parents' room. AE, DC, MC, V. Parking £7.50 ($11). Bus: 33. **Amenities:** 2 restaurants, bar; pool; gym; room service; laundry/dry cleaning. *In room:* TV, minibar, hair dryer, safe.

Expensive
The Bonham ✦✦   One of Edinburgh's newest and most stylish hotels occupies a trio of regency town houses. Rooms are outfitted in an urban and very hip blend of old and new. The decor combines ancient vases, Art Nouveau objects, marble busts, contemporary art—an eclectic but tasteful mix. Each accommodation has a TV with a keyboard hooked up to a barrage of facilities on the Internet, the first setup of its kind in Scotland.

35 Drumsheugh Gardens, Edinburgh EH3 7RN. ℂ **0131/226-6050.** Fax 0131/226-6080. www.thebonham. com. 48 units. £165–£235 ($248–$353) double; £295 ($442) suite. Rates include a continental breakfast. AE, DC, MC, V. Bus: 23, 27. **Amenities:** Restaurant; 24-hour room service. *In room:* A/C, TV, minibar, coffeemaker, hair dryer.

Carlton Highland Hotel 𝄞𝄞

The Victorian turrets, Flemish gables, and severe gray stonework rise imposingly from a street corner on the Royal Mile, a few steps from Waverley Station. The former department store has been converted into a bright and airy milieu full of modern conveniences. Rooms have a kind of Scandinavian simplicity. Bathrooms tend to be small. To relax, enjoy the sounds of a pianist in the lounge area, or stop by the cafe "Central Perk" based on the same coffee bar as the TV show *Friends*. Although it doesn't have the style and grandeur of the Caledonian, it has more facilities.

19 North Bridge, Edinburgh, Lothian EH1 1SD. ℂ **0131/556-7277.** Fax 0131/556-2691. 197 units. £225 ($338) executive double. Rates include breakfast. Children 14 and under stay free in parents' room. AE, DC, MC, V. Parking £6 ($10). Bus: 55 and 80. **Amenities:** Restaurant, bar; pool; gym; aerobics studio; solarium; 2 squash courts; whirlpool. *In room:* TV, coffeemaker, hair dryer.

Channings Hotel 𝄞𝄞

Five Edwardian terrace houses were combined to create this hotel 7 blocks north of Dean Village in a tranquil residential area. It maintains the atmosphere of a Scottish country house. Rooms are outfitted in a modern yet elegant style. Front units have views of a cobblestoned street. Back units are quieter, and standard rooms are a bit cheaper but are much smaller. The most desirable rooms are labeled "Executive," and often have bay windows and wingback chairs.

South Learmonth Gardens 15, Edinburgh EH4 1EZ. ℂ **0131/315-2226.** Fax 0131/332-9631. www. channings.co.uk. 48 units. £175–£205 ($263–$308) double; £240 ($360) suite. Rates include breakfast. Children 14 and under stay free in parents' room. AE, DC, MC, V. Bus: 18, 19, 41, or 81. **Amenities:** Restaurant, bar; room service; laundry/dry cleaning; shoeshine. *In room:* TV, coffeemaker, hair dryer.

Roxburghe Hotel 𝄞

Originally a stately Robert Adam town house, the hotel stands on a tree-filled square a short walk from Princes Street. In 1999, it opened a new wing, more than doubling the original size of the hotel. The old wing maintains a traditional atmosphere with ornate ceilings and woodwork, antique furnishings, and tall arched windows. The new wing offers four-star hotel comfort, completely contemporary styling, and up-to-date furnishings.

38 Charlotte Sq., Edinburgh EH2 4HG. ℂ **0131/225-3921.** Fax 0131/220-2518. www.macdonaldhotels.co. uk. 197 units. £145–£195 ($218–$293) double; from £250 ($375) suite. Children 13 and under stay free in parents' room. AE, DC, MC, V. Parking £4.50 ($7) Bus: 100. **Amenities:** 2 restaurants, 2 bars; pool; gym; sauna; 24-hour room service; baby-sitting; laundry/dry cleaning. *In room:* TV, minibar, coffeemaker, hair dryer.

Sheraton Grand Hotel 𝄞𝄞

This elegant hotel, in a postmodern complex on a former railway siding, a short walk from Princes Street, is the most appealing modern hotel in the capital. If you seek Victorian grandeur, make it the Caledonian. But if you'd like to be in the "new Edinburgh" (a financial center called The Exchange), then make it the Sheraton Grand. The hotel has more of international flavor than its rival, the Balmoral. Rooms may lack character but they are exceedingly comfortable. The best units are called "Castle View," and they are on the top three floors.

1 Festival Sq., Edinburgh, Lothian EH3 9SR. ℂ **800/325-3535** in the U.S. and Canada, or 0131/229-9131. Fax 0131/228-4510. www.sheraton.com. 260 units. June–Sept £220–£250 ($330–$375) double; from £350 ($525) suite. Off-season, £145 ($218) double, £215 ($323) suite. Children 16 and under stay free in parents' room. AE, DC, MC, V. Bus: 4, 15, or 44. **Amenities:** 2 restaurants, 2 bars; pool; gym; room service; laundry/dry cleaning. *In room:* A/C, TV, minibar, hair dryer, safe, trouser press.

Moderate

Nova Hotel The Nova, an 1875 Victorian, is on a quiet cul-de-sac a 10-minute ride from the center, with a view over Brunsfield Links in front and the Pentland Hills in back. It's within walking distance of the Royal Mile and Princes Street. You'll find its rooms large and well appointed, with shower-only bathrooms. On the ground floors, guests enjoy the lounge that also operates as a cocktail bar. There's street parking.

5 Brunsfield Crescent, Edinburgh EH10 4EZ. © **0131/447-6437.** Fax 0131/452-8126. www.novahotel.com. uk. 12 units. £90–£100 ($135–$150) double; £110–£140 ($165–$210) family room for up to 6. AE, MC, V. Bus: 42 or 46. **Amenities:** Bar; lounge. *In room:* TV, coffeemaker, hair dryer.

17 Abercromby Place ⚡ Eirlys Lloyd runs this fine B&B, a 5-minute walk north of Princes Street. The gray stone terrace house was home in the 1820s to William Playfair, who designed many of Edinburgh's most visible landmarks, including the Royal Scottish Academy and Surgeon Hall of the Royal College of Surgeons. Rooms vary in size, but all are acceptable with king- to queen-size beds. Two rooms are in what was originally conceived as a mews house (living quarters adapted from stables).

17 Abercromby Place, Edinburgh EH3 6LB. © **0131/557-8036.** Fax 0131/558-3453. www.abercrombyhouse. com. 10 units. £90–£120 ($135–$180) double. Rates include breakfast. MC, V. Free parking. Bus: 15 or 100. **Amenities:** Meals arranged. *In room:* TV, hair dryer.

Inexpensive

A Haven This semidetached 1862 Victorian house is a 15-minute walk or 5-minute bus ride north of the rail station. Rooms are of various sizes (the biggest on the second floor). Some in back overlook the Firth of Forth, and those in the front open onto views of Arthur's Seat. Moira and Ronnie Murdock extend a Scottish welcome in this family-type place, and often advise guests about sightseeing.

180 Ferry Rd., Edinburgh EH6 4NS. © **0131/554-6559.** Fax 0131/554-5252. www.a-haven.co.uk. 12 units. £60–£99 ($90–$149) double. Rates include breakfast. AE, MC, V. Free parking. Bus: 1, 6, 7, 25, C3, 17, 14A, or 25A. **Amenities:** Bar; baby-sitting; laundry/dry cleaning. *In room:* TV, coffeemaker, hair dryer.

Greenside Hotel This 1786 Georgian house is furnished with antiques to give it the right spirit. There are singles, doubles, twins, and three family rooms, all centrally heated and all with private bathrooms with showers. Rooms, refurbished in 1998, open onto views of a private garden or the Firth of Forth and are so large that 10 of them contain a double bed and two singles.

9 Royal Terrace, Edinburgh EH7 5AB. © and fax **0131/557-0022.** www.townhouisehotels.co.uk. 15 units. £45–£90 ($68–$135) double. Rates include breakfast. AE, DC, MC, V. Bus: 4, 15, or 44. **Amenities:** Meals arranged; bar; lounge. *In room:* TV, coffeemaker, hair dryer.

7 Danube Street ⚡ This B&B is in Stockbridge, a quiet, stylish residential neighborhood a 10-minute walk north of the center. It's the 1825 home of Fiona Mitchell-Rose and her husband, Colin. The establishment is proud of its charmingly decorated rooms that reflect Fiona's experience as a decorator in London. Rooms look out onto the sloping garden. The most desirable has a four-poster bed and direct garden access. Bathrooms are shower-only. You're likely to meet your hosts and other guests in the formal dining room in the morning, where the lavish breakfast is inspired by Scotland's old-fashioned agrarian tradition.

7 Danube St., Edinburgh EH4 1NN. © **0131/332-2755.** Fax 0131/343-3648. www.aboutedinburgh.com/ danube. 5 units. £95 ($143) double. Rates include breakfast. MC, V. Free parking nearby. Bus: 28. **Amenities:** Baby-sitting; laundry; complimentary whisky. *In room:* TV, coffeemaker, hair dryer.

WEST OF THE CENTER
Jarvis Ellersly Country House Hotel ⚜   Standing in walled gardens, this three-story Edwardian country house offers the privacy of a home. It's in a dignified west-end residential section near the Murrayfield rugby grounds, about a 5-minute ride from the center, and is one of Edinburgh's best moderately priced hotels. The well-equipped rooms vary in size and are in either the main house or a less desirable annex. After recent refurbishments, the hotel is better than ever, and service is first class.

4 Ellersly Rd., Edinburgh EH12 6HZ. [tel]**0131/337-6888.** Fax 0131/313-2543. 57 units. £139 ($209) double; £154 ($231) suite. AE, DC, MC, V. Free parking. Take A-8 4km (2½ miles) west of the city center. Bus: 2, 2A, 21, 26, 31, 36, 36A. **Amenities:** Restaurant, wine cellar; room service; laundry; valet. *In room:* TV, hair dryer.

SOUTH OF THE CENTER
Teviotdale House ⚜ *Value*   Some visitors rate this 1848 house, 10 minutes by bus from Princes Street, Waverley Station, and Edinburgh Castle, as the finest B&B in Edinburgh. Elizabeth and Willy Thiebaud's attention to detail has earned them an enviable reputation. The house is completely no-smoking, and is furnished with antiques. The three largest can accommodate up to four beds. The home-cooked breakfast may be the highlight of your day's dining, and can include smoked salmon, kippers, and home-baked bread and scones.

Grange Loan, Edinburgh EH9 2ER. © and fax **0131/667-4763.** 7 units. £56–£90 ($84–$135). AE, MC, V. Bus: 42. **In-room Amenities:** TV, coffeemaker, hair dryer.

WHERE TO DINE
IN THE CENTER—NEW TOWN
Expensive
The Atrium ⚜ MODERN SCOTTISH/INTERNATIONAL   Since 1993, this is one of the most emulated restaurants in Edinburgh. The "deliberately moody" atmosphere is a fusion of Argentine hacienda and stylish Beverly Hills bistro. Flickering oil lamps create shadows on the dark-colored walls while patrons enjoy dishes prepared by chef Alan Metheison. Our favorites include grilled salmon or roasted sea bass. Whether it's game or lamb from the Scottish Highlands, dishes have taste, style, and flair. The desserts are equally superb, especially the lemon tart with berry coulis and crème fraîche.

10 Cambridge St. (beneath Saltire Court). © **0131/228-8882.** Reservations recommended. Fixed-price meal £14–£18 ($21–$27) at lunch, main courses £13.50–£18.50 ($20–$28) at dinner. AE, DC, MC, V. Mon–Fri noon–2pm and 6:30–10pm; Sat 6:30–10pm. Closed for 1 week at Christmas.

No. 1 Princes Street ⚜ SCOTTISH/CONTINENTAL   This intimate, crimson-colored enclave is the premier restaurant in the Balmoral Hotel. The walls are studded with Scottish memorabilia in formal, yet sporting patterns. You can sample the likes of pan-seared Isle of Skye monkfish with saffron mussel broth; roulade of Dover sole with langoustine, oyster, and scallop garnish; or grilled filet of Scottish beef served with bourguignonne sauce. For dessert you can have a variety of sorbets, British cheeses, or something more exotic such as mulled wine parfait with a cinnamon sauce. There's a separate vegetarian menu and a wide-ranging wine list with celestial tariffs.

In the Balmoral Hotel, 1 Princes St. © **0131/556-2414.** Reservations recommended. Main courses £20–£35 ($30–$53); fixed-price 2-course lunch £18.50 ($28); fixed-price 3-course dinner £37.50 ($56); fixed-price 6-course dinner £50 ($75). AE, DC, MC, V. Mon–Fri noon–2pm; daily 7–10pm (10:30pm on Fri).

Moderate
Café Saint-Honoré FRENCH/SCOTTISH. Between Frederick and Hanover Streets, this is a French-inspired bistro with a dinner format that's much more formal and expensive than its deliberately rapid lunchtime venue. An upbeat and usually enthusiastic staff serves a combination of Scottish and French cuisine that includes venison with juniper berries and wild mushrooms; local pheasant in wine and garlic sauce; or lamb kidneys with broad beans inspired by the cuisine of the region around Toulouse. Fish is very fresh.

34 NW Thistle St. Lane. © **0131/226-2211.** Reservations recommended. Main courses £7.50–£12.50 ($11–$19) at lunch; pre-theater fixed-price meal £13.50–£18 ($20–$27); £13.75–£17.25 ($21–$26) at dinner. AE, DC, MC, V. Mon–Fri noon–2:15pm; Mon–Fri (pre-theater meal) 5:30–7pm; Mon–Sat 7–10pm and sometimes 11pm. Bus: 3, 16, 17, 23, 27, or 31.

Duck's at Le Marché Noir SCOTTISH/FRENCH The cuisine here is more stylish, and more tuned to the culinary sophistication of London, than the cuisine at many other restaurants in Edinburgh. Set within a wood house whose outside and inside are both decorated in shades of dark green, its handful of dishes honor the traditions of Scotland. (An example is their baked haggis in phyllo pastry on a bed of turnip puree and red wine sauce.) More modern dishes include a boudin of chicken and foie gras served with wilted spinach and applesauce; seared salmon with leeks, asparagus, zucchini, and a pickled ginger and sesame salad; roasted rack of lamb with thyme juice and roasted vegetables; and grilled red snapper with wild rice and lime-marinated sweet potato pickles.

2/4 Eyre Place. © **0131/558-1608.** Reservations recommended. Lunch set price menu £15 ($23); dinner main courses £12–£17 ($18–$26). AE, DC, MC, V. Mon–Sat noon–2pm and 7–9:30pm. Bus: 23 or 27.

Haldanes Restaurant SCOTTISH Set in the cellar of the Albany Hotel building, within a pair of royal blue and gold-tinted dining rooms, Haldanes features the cuisine of George Kelso. During clement weather, the venue moves out to the building's verdant garden. Menu items include a traditional haggis in phyllo pastry with tatties (roasted turnips) and whisky sauce; pan-fried crab cakes with a tomato and spring onion salsa; a panaché of West Coast scallops, monkfish, and salmon with saffron-flavored risotto and roasted asparagus; and a pavé of lamb with mint-flavored herb crust, wild mushrooms, and zucchini. For dessert, try the caramelized lemon tarte with crème fraîche.

39A Albany St. © **0131/556-8407.** Reservations recommended. Set-price lunch £10.50–£15 ($16–$23); dinner main courses £15–£22 ($23–$33). AE, DC, MC, V. Daily noon–1:30pm and 6–9:30pm. Bus: 15.

The Tower SEAFOOD/MODERN BRITISH This is the town's hot new dining ticket set at the top of the Museum of Scotland. The inventive kitchen will regale you with hearty portions of some of the finest steak and roast beef dishes along with excellent and freshly caught seafood. Dig into an array of oysters, lobsters, and platters with a mixed seafood medley. We still remember fondly the smoked haddock risotto with a poached egg and shavings of Parmesan cheese. A sea bass was perfectly seasoned and grilled, and there's even sushi on the menu. Scottish loin of lamb is given a modern twist with a side dish of minted couscous.

In the Museum of Scotland, Chambers St. © **0131/225-3003.** Reservations required. Lunch main courses £10–£14 ($15–$21). Dinner main courses £13–£25 ($20–$38). AE, DC, MC, V. Daily noon–11pm. Bus: 3, 7, 21, 30, 31, 53, 69, or 80.

Inexpensive
Far Pavilions INDIAN/CONTINENTAL Established in 1987, this Indian restaurant offers finely tuned service. Highly recommended is the house specialty,

Murgi Massala, concocted with tandoori chicken that falls off the bone thanks to slow cooking in a garlic-based butter sauce. Menu items include curry dishes influenced by British tastes, as well as authentic platters whose composition is faithful to their original Indian tradition. Most items are suitably pungent, and concocted from lamb, seafood, vegetables, and beef, and the staff is always able to combine the garnishes and side dishes that form a worthy Indian meal.

10 Craighleith Rd., Comely Bank. ✆ 0131/332-3362. Reservations recommended. Lunch main courses £8–£17 ($12–$26), lunch buffet £6.95 ($10) per person, dinner main courses £7–£13 ($11–$20). AE, MC, V. Mon–Fri noon–2pm; Mon–Sat 5:30–11:30pm. Bus: 19, 39, 55, 81, or X91.

Henderson's Salad Table ⓖ ⓥⓐⓛⓤⓔ VEGETARIAN   This is a Shangri-la for health-food lovers. Hot dishes such as peppers stuffed with rice and pimiento are served on request, and a vegetarian twist on the national dish of Scotland, haggis, is usually available. Other well-prepared dishes filled with flavor include cheese and onion potato croquet, vegetable lasagna, and a broccoli and cheese crumble. The homemade desserts include a fresh fruit salad or a cake with double-whipped cream and chocolate sauce. The wine cellar offers 30 wines. Live music, ranging from classical to jazz to folk, is played every evening.

94 Hanover St. ✆ 0131/225-2131. Main courses £3.50–£4.75 ($6–$8); fixed-price meal at lunch £4.95 ($7); fixed-price meal at dinner £10.95 ($16). AE, MC, V. Mon–Sat 7:30am–10:45pm. Bus: 23 or 27.

Valvona & Crolla INTERNATIONAL   In 1872, a recent arrival from Italy opened this restaurant, and it's still going strong. It shares space with a delicatessen and food emporium. A few steps down from the main shopping area, a cafe and luncheon restaurant serves very fresh food at refreshingly low prices. Here, you can order three kinds of breakfasts (continental, Scottish, or vegetarian) for a fixed price of £3.95 ($6); or platters of pasta, mixed sausages, and cold cuts; crostini, risottos, and omelets. Don't expect leisurely dining, as the place caters to office workers and shoppers who appreciate the informality, low prices, and freshness of the food.

19 Elm Row. ✆ 0131/556-6066. Breakfast £4.95 ($7); pizzas, pastas, or platters £3–£10 ($4.50–$15). AE, DC, MC, V. Cafe with limited food service Mon–Sat 8:30am–5pm; full lunch service Mon–Sat noon–3pm. Bus: 7, 10, 11, 12, or 14.

IN THE CENTER—OLD TOWN
Moderate
Dubh Prais SCOTTISH   Dub Prais (Gaelic for "The Black Pot") conjures up an image of old-fashioned Scottish recipes bubbling away in a stewpot above a fireplace. Menu items are time-tested and not at all experimental, but flavorful nonetheless. Examples include smoked salmon; ragout of wild mushrooms and Ayrshire bacon served with garlic sauce; saddle of venison with juniper sauce; and a supreme of salmon with grapefruit-flavored butter sauce.

123B High St., Royal Mile. ✆ 0131/557-5732. Reservations recommended. Lunch main courses £6.50 ($10); dinner main courses £11.90–£16.50 ($18–$25). AE, MC, V. Tues–Fri noon–2pm; Tues–Sat 6–10:30pm. Bus: 11.

Inexpensive
Baked Potato Shop ⓥⓐⓛⓤⓔ VEGETARIAN/WHOLE FOOD   This is the least expensive restaurant in a very glamorous neighborhood, and it attracts mobs of office workers every day. Many carry their food away. Only free-range eggs, whole foods, and vegetarian cheeses are used. Vegetarian cakes are a specialty.

56 Cockburn St. ✆ 0131/225-7572. Reservations not accepted. Food items 60p–£3.20 (90¢–$4.80). No credit cards. Daily 9am–9pm (to 10pm in summer). Bus: 5.

Pierre Victoire FRENCH   This was the original model for a series of franchises that have sprouted up in recent years in six other areas of Edinburgh. Many residents still prefer the original to the newer versions. It's an ideal, if chaotic, stopover if you're antiques shopping and climbing Victoria Street. It's also one of the most popular evening gathering places as it keeps long hours. In a bistro setting with crowded tables, you can order grilled mussels in garlic with Pernod butter, salmon with ginger, or roast pheasant with Cassis. Vegetarians will also find selections to suit their taste.

10–14 Victoria St. 🕐 0131/225-1721. Reservations recommended. Main courses £6.40–£10 ($10–$15); fixed-price lunch £4.90 ($7)and £6.90 ($10) Sun. MC, V. Daily noon–3pm and 6–11pm. Bus: 1, 34, or 35.

SOUTH OF THE CENTER

Kelly's 🏖 MODERN SCOTTISH/MODERN FRENCH   Catering to a crowd of barristers, artists, financiers, and employees of the nearby university, this stylish restaurant is a 20-minute walk south of the center in a residential neighborhood. The menu includes such dishes as asado of lamb in olive and herb crust with spicy couscous, roast breast of Barbary duck with black pepper and blueberries, or ravioli of lobster with asparagus. Dessert might include a caramelized lemon tart.

46 W. Richmond St. 🕐 0131/668-3847. Reservations recommended. Main courses £13–£15 ($20–$22.50); fixed-price 3-course dinner £27 ($41); 3-course lunch £11 ($17). DC, MC, V. Mon–Sat noon–2pm and 6–10pm. Bus: 11, 12, or 14.

LEITH

In the northern regions of Edinburgh, Leith is the old port town, opening onto the Firth of Forth. Once it was a city in its own right until it was slowly absorbed into Edinburgh.

Expensive

Martin Wishart 🏖🏖🏖 MODERN FRENCH   Several gourmet associations claim this is the "Scottish restaurant of the year." The chef/owner Martin Wishart takes it all in stride and continues to improve the quality of his cuisine in a fashionable part of the Leith docklands. With white walls and modern art, the decor is minimalist. The menu is short but sweet and ever changing. Many dishes are simply prepared, the natural flavors coming through. Others show a touch of elegance and fantasy, including partridge breast with black truffle and foie gras or the lobster ravioli with an oyster velouté. After eating the glazed lemon tart with praline ice cream on which white raspberry coulis has been dribbled, the day is yours.

54 The Shore, Leith. 🕐 0131/553-35571. Reservations required. Main courses £15.50–£20 ($23–$30). Set lunch £13.50–£15.50 ($20–$23). Tues–Fri noon–2pm; Tues–Thurs 6:30–10pm; Fri–Sat 6:30–10:30pm. Bus: 7 or 10.

Moderate

Vintner's Room FRENCH/SCOTTISH   Join locals and visitors down by the waterfront in Leith. Chances are they are heading to this restaurant. Near the entrance, beneath a venerable ceiling of oaken beams, a wine bar serves platters and drinks beside a large stone fireplace. Most diners, however, head for the small but elegant dining room, illuminated by flickering candles. A robust cuisine includes seafood salad with mango mayonnaise, a terrine of pigeon and duck, loin of pork with mustard sauce, and venison in a bitter chocolate sauce.

The Vaults, 87 Giles St., Leith. 🕐 0131/554-6767. Reservations recommended. Table d'hôte meal £11.50–£15 ($17–$23) at lunch; dinner main courses £15–£32 ($23–$48). AE, MC, V. Mon–Sat noon–2pm and 7–10:30pm. Closed 2 weeks at Christmas. Bus: 7 or 10.

SEEING THE SIGHTS

SIGHTSEEING SUGGESTIONS FOR FIRST-TIME VISITORS

If You Have 1 Day Visit **Edinburgh Castle** as soon as it opens in the morning, then walk the **Royal Mile** to the Palace of **Holyroodhouse,** former abode of Mary, Queen of Scots. Look out over the city from the vantage point of **Arthur's Seat,** and stroll through **Princes Street Gardens,** capping your day with a walk along the major shopping thoroughfare, **Princes Street.**

If You Have 2 Days In the morning of your second day, head for Old Town again, but this time explore its narrow streets, wynds, and closes, and visit the **John Knox House,** the **High Kirk of St. Giles,** and the small museums. After lunch, climb the **Scott Monument** for a good view of Old Town and the Princes Street Gardens. Spend the rest of the afternoon exploring the **National Gallery of Scotland.**

If You Have 3 Days Spend day 3 getting acquainted with the major attractions of New Town, including the **National Museum of Scotland, National Portrait Gallery, Georgian House,** and **Royal Botanic Garden.**

If You Have 4 or 5 Days On the fourth day, take a trip west to **Stirling Castle** and see some of the dramatic scenery of the **Trossachs.** On the fifth day you'll feel like a native, so seek out some of the city's minor but interesting attractions, such as the **Camera Obscura,** the **Scotch Whisky Heritage Centre,** and **Dean Village.**

THE ROYAL MILE ⚔⚔

The Royal Mile (bus: 1, 6, 23, 27, 30, 34, or 36) stretches from Edinburgh Castle all the way to the Palace of Holyroodhouse. Walking along, you'll see some of the most interesting old structures in Edinburgh, with their turrets, gables, and towering chimneys.

High Kirk of St. Giles   Built in 1120, a short walk downhill from Edinburgh Castle, this church is one of the most important architectural landmarks along the Royal Mile. It combines a dark and brooding stone exterior with surprisingly graceful and delicate flying buttresses. One of its outstanding features is its **Thistle Chapel,** housing beautiful stalls and notable heraldic stained-glass windows. A group of cathedral guides is available at all times to conduct tours.

High St. ✆ **0131/225-9442.** Free admission, but £1 ($1.50) donation suggested. Easter–Sept Mon–Fri 9am–7pm, Sat 9am–5pm, Sun 1–5pm; Oct–Easter Mon–Sat 9am–5pm, Sun 1–5pm. Sun services at 8, 10 and 11:30am and 6 and 8pm.

Writers' Museum   This 1622 house takes its name from a former owner, Elizabeth, the dowager countess of Stair. Today it's a treasure trove of portraits, relics, and manuscripts relating to three of Scotland's greatest men of letters. The Robert Burns collection includes his writing desk, rare manuscripts, portraits, and many other items. Also on display are some of Sir Walter Scott's possessions, including his pipe, chess set, and original manuscripts. The museum holds one of the most significant Robert Louis Stevenson collections anywhere, including personal belongings, paintings, photographs, and early editions.

In Lady Stair's House, off Lawnmarket. ✆ **0131/529-4901.** Free admission. Mon–Sat 10am–5pm.

Museum of Childhood *Kids*   The world's first museum devoted solely to the history of childhood stands just opposite John Knox's House. Contents of its four floors range from antique toys to games to exhibits on health, education, and costumes, plus video presentations and an activity area. Because of the youthful crowd it naturally attracts, it ranks as the noisiest museum in town.

42 High St. ℭ **0131/529-4142.** Free admission. Mon–Sat 10am–5pm; during the Edinburgh Festival, also Sun 2–5pm.

John Knox's House   Even if you're not interested in the reformer who founded the Scottish Presbyterian Church, you may want to visit his house, as it's characteristic of the "lands" that used to flank the Royal Mile. All of them are gone now, except Knox's house, with its timbered gallery. Inside, you'll see the tempera ceiling in the Oak Room, along with exhibitions of Knox memorabilia.

43–45 High St. ℭ **0131/556-9579.** Admission £2.25 ($3.40) adults, £1.75 ($2.65) seniors/students, 75p ($1.15) children. Mon–Sat 10am–4:30pm.

The People's Story   If you continue walking downhill along Canongate toward Holyroodhouse, you'll see one of the handsomest buildings on the Royal Mile. Built in 1591, the **Canongate Tolbooth** was once the courthouse, prison, and center of municipal affairs for the burgh of Canongate. Now it contains a museum celebrating the social history of the inhabitants of Edinburgh from the late 18th century to the present, with lots of emphasis on the cultural displacements of the Industrial Revolution.

163 Canongate. ℭ **0131/529-4057.** Free admission. Mon–Sat 10am–5pm (Aug also Sun 2–5pm). Bus 1.

Huntly House   Across from the Canongate Tolbooth is this fine example of a restored 16th-century mansion. Today it functions as Edinburgh's principal museum of local history. The interior contains faithfully crafted reproductions of rooms inspired by the city's traditional industries, including exhibits devoted to glassmaking, pottery, wool processing, and cabinetry, always with a focus on the stamina and struggles of the workers who labored within.

142 Canongate. ℭ **0131/529-4143.** Free admission. Mon–Sat 10am–5pm; during the Edinburgh Festival, also Sun 2–5pm. Bus: 1.

Scotch Whisky Heritage Centre   This center is privately funded by a conglomeration of Scotland's biggest distillers. It highlights the economic effect of whisky on both Scotland and the world and illuminates the centuries-old traditions associated with whisky making, showing the science and art of distilling. There's a 7-minute audiovisual show and an electric car ride past 13 sets showing historic moments in the whisky industry. A tour entitling you to sample five whiskies and take away a miniature bottle is £11.95 ($18) per person.

354 Castlehill. ℭ **0131/220-0441.** Admission £6.50 ($10) adults, £4.25 ($6) seniors, £4.50 ($7) students with ID, £3.25 ($5) ages 5 to 17; free for children 4 and under. Daily 10am–5pm.

HISTORIC SITES

Edinburgh Castle ⋆⋆   Although its early history is vague, it's believed that Edinburgh was built on the dead volcano, Castle Rock. It's known that in the 11th century Malcolm III (Canmore) and his Saxon queen, later venerated as St. Margaret, founded a castle on this same spot. The only fragment left of their original castle—in fact the oldest structure in Edinburgh—is **St. Margaret's Chapel.** Built in the Norman style, the oblong structure dates principally from the 12th century.

Inside the castle you can visit the **State Apartments,** particularly Queen Mary's bedroom, where Mary, Queen of Scots gave birth to James VI of Scotland (later James I of England). The highlight is the Crown Chamber, which

> **Moments For Mr. Hyde Fans**
>
> Near Gladstone's Land is **Brodie's Close,** a stone-floored alleyway. You can wander into the alley for a view of old stone houses that'll make you think you've stepped into a scene from a BBC production of a Dickens novel. It was named in honor of the notorious Deacon Brodie, a respectable councilor by day and a thief by night (he was the inspiration for Robert Louis Stevenson's *The Strange Case of Dr. Jekyll and Mr. Hyde,* though Stevenson set his story in foggy London town, not in Edinburgh). Brodie was hanged in 1788, and the mechanism used for the hangman's scaffolding had previously been improved by Brodie himself—for use on others, of course. Across the street is the most famous pub along the Royal Mile: **Deacon Brodie's Tavern** (see later in this chapter).

houses the Honours of Scotland (Scottish Crown Jewels), used at the coronation of James VI, along with the scepter and the sword of state of Scotland.

You can also view the Stone of Scone or "Stone of Destiny," on which Scottish kings had been crowned since time immemorial. Edward I of England carried the stone off to Westminster Abbey in 1296, where it rested under the British coronation chair. It was finally returned to its rightful home in Scotland in November 1996, where it was welcomed with much pomp and circumstance.

Castlehill. ℰ **0131/225-9846.** Admission £7.50 ($11) adults, £2 ($3) children 15 and under. Apr–Sept daily 9:30am–5:15pm; Oct–Mar daily 9:30am–4:15pm. Bus: 1 or 6.

Palace of Holyroodhouse 🐾🐾   This palace was built adjacent to an Augustinian abbey established by David I in the 12th century. The nave, now in ruins, remains today. James IV founded the palace nearby in the early part of the 16th century, but only the north tower is left. Much of what you see today was ordered built by Charles II.

The most dramatic incident in the history of Holyroodhouse occurred in the old wing when Mary, Queen of Scots was in residence. Her Italian secretary, David Rizzio, was murdered (with 56 stab wounds) in the audience chamber by Mary's husband, Lord Darnley, and his accomplices. The palace suffered long periods of neglect, although it basked in glory at the ball thrown by Bonnie Prince Charlie in the mid-18th century. The present queen and Prince Philip live at Holyroodhouse whenever they visit Edinburgh. When they're not in residence, the palace is open to visitors.

Canongate, at the eastern end of the Royal Mile. ℰ **0131/556-7371.** Admission £6.50 ($10), £5 ($8) seniors, £3.30 ($5) children 15 and under; £16.50 ($25) family pass for 2 adults and 2 children. Daily 9:30am–4:45pm. Closed 2 weeks in May and 3 weeks in late June and early July (dates vary). Bus: 1 or 6.

MORE ATTRACTIONS

Scott Monument 🐾   Completed in the mid-19th century, the Gothic-inspired Scott Monument is the most famous landmark of Edinburgh. Sir Walter Scott's heroes are carved as small figures in the monument, and you can climb to the top. You can also see the first-ever **floral clock,** which was constructed in 1904, in the West Princes Street Gardens.

In the East Princes St. Gardens. ℰ **0131/529-4068.** Admission £2.50 ($3.75). Mar–May and Oct, Mon–Sat 9am–6pm, Sun 10am–6pm; June–Sept, Mon–Sat 9am–8pm, Sun 10am–6pm; Nov–Feb, Mon–Sat 9am–4pm, Sun 10am–4pm. Bus: 1 or 6.

National Gallery of Scotland ⭐⭐⭐   This museum is located in the center of Princes Street Gardens. The gallery is rather small, but the collection was chosen with great care. The duke of Sutherland has lent the museum some paintings, including two Raphaels, Titian's two Diana canvases, his *Venus Rising from the Sea*, and the *Seven Sacraments*, a work of the great 17th-century Frenchman Nicolas Poussin. The Spanish masters are represented as well. You can also see excellent examples of English painting: Gainsborough's *The Hon. Mrs. Graham* and Constable's *Dedham Vale*, along with works by Turner, Reynolds, and Hogarth. Naturally, the work of Scottish painters is prominent, including Alexander Naysmith and Henry Raeburn, whose most famous work, *The Reverend Walker*, can be seen.

2 The Mound. ℂ 0131/624-6200. Free admission. Mon–Sat 10am–5pm; Sun noon–5pm (during the festival, Mon–Sat 10am–6pm, Sun 11am–6pm). Bus: 3, 21, or 26.

Our Dynamic Earth ⭐ *(Kids*   The Millennium Dome at Greenwich outside London may have been a bust, but the new millennium museum for Scotland is packing in the crowds. Not far from the Palace of Holyroodhouse, Dynamic Earth tells the story of Earth itself in all its diversity. You can push buttons to simulate earthquakes, meteor showers, and views of outer space. You can see replicas of the slimy green primordial soup where life began. Time capsules wind their way back through the aeons, and a series of specialized aquariums re-create primordial life forms; and that's not all. There is so much more, ranging from simulated terrains of polar Ice Caps to tropical rain forests with plenty of creepy crawlies. All 11 galleries have stunning special effects.

Holyrood Rd. ℂ 0131/550-7800. Easter–Oct daily 10am–6pm. Nov–Easter Wed–Sun 10am–5pm. Admission £6.95 ($10) adults, £4.95 ($7) students, £3.95 ($6) seniors and ages 14 and under. Family ticket £8.50 ($13).

Outlook Tower & Camera Obscura   The 1853 periscope is at the top of the Outlook Tower, from which you can view a panorama of the surrounding city. Trained guides point out the landmarks and talk about Edinburgh's fascinating history. In addition, there're several entertaining exhibits, all with an optical theme, and a well-stocked shop selling books, crafts, and compact discs.

Castlehill. ℂ 0131/226-3709. Admission £4.25 ($6) adults, £2.70 ($4) seniors, and £2.10 ($3.15) children. Open Apr–Oct Mon–Fri 9:30am–6pm, Sat–Sun 10am–6pm, until 7:30pm in July and 7pm in Aug; Nov–Mar daily 10am–5pm. Bus: 1 or 6.

Royal Observatory Visitor Centre   On display here are the works of the Scottish National Observatory at home and abroad, featuring the finest images of astronomical objects, Scotland's largest telescope, and antique instruments. There's also a panoramic view of the city from the balcony. An exhibit, *The Universe*, uses photographs, videos, computers, and models to take you on a cosmic whirlwind tour from the beginning of time to the farthest depths of space in a couple of hours.

Blackford Hill. ℂ 0131/668-8405. Admission £3.50 ($5) adults; £2.50 ($3.75) students, seniors, and children 5–16; free for children 4 and under. Mon–Sat 10am–5pm; Sun noon–5pm. Bus: 40 or 41.

National Museum of Scotland (NMS) ⭐⭐⭐   In 1998, two long-established museums, the Royal Museum of Scotland and the National Museum of Antiquities, were united into this single institution 2 blocks south of the Royal Mile. The museum showcases exhibits in the decorative arts, ethnography, natural history, geology, archaeology, technology, and science. Six modern galleries distill billions of years of Scottish history, a total of 12,000 items ranging from rocks found on the island of South Uist dating back 2.9 billion years to a

Britannia: The People's Yacht

In case the queen never invited you to sail aboard her 125-meter (412-foot) yacht, there's still a chance to go aboard this world famous vessel. Launched on April 16, 1953, the luxury yacht was decommissioned December 11, 1997. Today, the yacht—technically a Royal Navy ship—which has sailed more than a million miles, rests at anchor in the port of Leith, 3 kilometers (2 miles) from the center of Edinburgh. The gangplank is now lowered for the public, whereas it once was lowered for such world leaders as Mahatma Gandhi, Tony Blair, and Nelson Mandela.

British taxpayers spent £160 million maintaining the yacht throughout most of the '90s. Even a major refit would have prolonged the vessel's life for only a few more years. Because of budgetary constraints, a decision was made to put it in dry dock. The public reaches the vessel by going through a visitor center designed by Sir Terence Conran. At its centerpiece is the yacht's 12-meter (41-ft.) tender floating in a pool.

Once on board, you're guided around all five decks by an audio tour. You can also visit the drawing room and the Royal Apartments, once occupied by the likes of not only the queen, but Prince Philip and princes William, Harry, Edward, and Andrew, as well as princesses Anne and Margaret. Even the engine room, the galleys, and the captain's cabin can be visited.

All tickets should be booked as far in advance as possible by calling ℂ **0131/555-5566.** The yacht is open daily except Christmas, with the first tour beginning at 10:30am, the last tour at 3:50pm. Lasting 90 to 120 minutes, each tour is self-guided with the use of a headset lent to participants. Adults pay £7.75 ($12), seniors £5.95 ($9), and ages 5 to 17 £3.75 ($6); those 4 and under visit free. A family ticket, good for two adults and up to two children, is £5.95 ($9). From Waverley Bridge, take either city bus (Lothian Transport) X50, or else the Guide Friday tour bus marked BRITANNIA.

Hillman Imp, one of the last 500 cars manufactured at the Linwood plant near Glasgow before it closed in 1981. One gallery is devoted to Scotland's role as an independent nation before it merged with the United Kingdom in 1707. Another gallery, devoted to industry and empire from 1707 to 1914, includes exhibits on shipbuilding, whisky distilling, the railways, and such textiles as the tartan and paisley.

Chambers St. ℂ **0131/225-7534.** Admission £3 ($4.50) adults, £1.50 ($2.25) seniors and students, family ticket £15 ($23), and free for children under 18; supplement for some temporary exhibitions. Mon and Wed–Sat 10am–5pm; Tues 10am–8pm; Sun noon–5pm. Walk south from Waverley Station for 10 minutes to reach Chambers St., or take bus no. 3, 7, 21, 30, 31, 53, 69, or 80.

Scottish National Gallery of Modern Art 🅐🅐 Scotland's national collection of 20th-century art is set on 5.5 hectares (12 acres) of grounds, just a 15-minute walk from the west end of Princes Street. The collection is international in scope and high in quality despite its modest size. Major sculptures outside the building include pieces by Henry Moore and Barbara Hepworth. Inside, the collection ranges from a fauve Derain and cubist Braque and Picasso to recent works by Paolozzi. There's a strong representation of English and Scottish artists—William Turner, John Constable, Henry Raeburn, and David Wilkie to name a few. Works by Matisse, Miró, Kirchner, Kokoschka, Ernst, Ben Nicholson, Nevelson, Balthus, Lichtenstein, Kitaj, and Hockney are also on view.

Belford Rd. (℗ 0131/556-8921. Free admission, except for some temporary exhibits. Mon–Sat 10am–5pm; Sun noon–5pm. Bus: 13, or take 18, 20, or 41; ask the driver for the stop closest to the museum and then take the 5-minute walk up Queensferry Terrace and Belford Rd. to the gallery.

Scottish National Portrait Gallery   Housed in a red stone Victorian Gothic building by Rowand Anderson, this portrait gallery gives you a chance to see what the famous people of Scottish history looked like. The portraits, several by Ramsay and Raeburn, include everybody from Mary, Queen of Scots to Sean Connery, from Flora Macdonald to Irvine Welsh.

1 Queen St. (℗ 0131/624-6200. Free admission, except for some temporary exhibits. Mon–Sat 10am–5pm; Sun noon–5pm. Bus: 18, 20, or 41.

A GARDEN

Gardeners and nature lovers will be attracted to the **Royal Botanic Garden,** Inverleith Row (℗ **0131/552-7171**). Main areas of interest are Exhibition Hall, Alpine House, the Demonstration Garden, annual and herbaceous borders (summer only), the copse, the Woodland Garden, Wild Garden, Arboretum, Peat Garden, Rock Garden, Heath Garden, and the Pond. Admission is by voluntary donation, and it's open from April to August 9:30am to 7pm, March and September from 9:30am to 6pm, from February and October 9:30am to 5pm, and from November to January 9:30am to 4pm.

ORGANIZED TOURS

If you want a quick introduction to the principal attractions in and around Edinburgh, consider one or more of the tours offered by **Lothian Region Transport,** 14 Queen St. (℗ 0131/555-6363). You won't find a cheaper way to hit the highlights. The buses leave from Waverley Bridge, near the Scott Monument. The tours are given from April to late October; a curtailed winter program is also offered.

You can see most of the major sights of Edinburgh, including the Royal Mile, the Palace of Holyroodhouse, Princes Street, and Edinburgh Castle, by

---

⌒Moments A Step Back in Time at Historic Dean Village

The village is one of the most photographed sights in the city. Set in a valley about 30 meters (100 ft.) below the level of the rest of Edinburgh, it's full of nostalgic charm. The settlement dates from the 12th century, and for many centuries it was a grain-milling center. The current residents worked hard to restore the old buildings—many of which were converted into flats and houses—and managed to maintain all of the original Brigadoon-like charm. A few minutes from the West End, it's located at the end of Bell's Brae, off Queensferry Street, on the Water of Leith. You can enjoy a celebrated view by looking downstream under the high arches of Dean Bridge, designed by Telford in 1833. The most scenic walk is along the water in the direction of St. Bernard's Well.

double-deck motor coach for £7.50 ($11) adults, £6 ($9) seniors and students, and £2.50 ($3.75) children. This ticket is valid all day on any LRT Edinburgh Classic Tour bus, which allows passengers to get on and off at any of the 15 stops along its routes. Buses start from Waverley Bridge every day beginning at 9:15am, departing every 15 minutes in summer and about every 30 minutes in winter, then embark on a circuit of Edinburgh, which if you remain on the bus without ever getting off will take about 2 hours. Commentary is offered along the way.

Tickets for any of these tours can be bought at LRT offices at Waverley Bridge, or at 14 Queen St., or at the tourist information center in Waverley Market. Advance reservations are a good idea. For more information, call © **0131/ 555-6363,** 24 hours a day.

THE SHOPPING SCENE

The best buys are in tartans and woolens, along with bone china and Scottish crystal. Princes Street, George Street, and the Royal Mile are the major shopping arteries. Here are a few suggestions.

Looking for a knitted memento? Moira-Anne Leask, owner of the **Shetland Connection,** 491 Lawnmarket (© **0131/225-3525;** bus: 1), promotes the skills of the Shetland knitter, and her shop is packed with sweaters, hats, and gloves in colorful Fair Isle designs. She also offers hand-knitted mohair, Aran, and Icelandic sweaters. Her oldest knitter is 90 years old! Items range from fine-ply cobweb shawls to chunky ski sweaters handcrafted by skilled knitters in top-quality wool.

If you've ever suspected that you might be Scottish, **Tartan Gift Shops,** 54 High St. (© **0131/558-3187;** bus: 1), has a chart indicating the place of origin, in Scotland, of your family name. You'll then be faced with a bewildering array of hunt-and-dress tartans. The high-quality wool is sold by the yard as well as in the form of kilts for both men and women.

Clan Tartan Centre, 70–74 Bangor Rd., Leith (© **0131/553-5100;** bus: 7 or 10), is one of the leading specialists in Edinburgh, regardless of which clan you claim as your own. If you want help in identifying a particular tartan, the staff at this shop will assist you. There's also the **James Pringle Woollen Mill,** 70–74 Bangor Rd., Leith (© **0131/553-5161;** bus: 7 or 10), which produces a large variety of top-quality wool items, including a range of Scottish knitwear—cashmere sweaters, tartan and tweed ties, travel rugs, tweed hats, and tam o'shanters. In addition, the mill has the only Clan Tartan Centre in Scotland, where more than 2,500 sets and trade designs are accessible through their research facilities.

Along the Royal Mile, **Ness Scotland,** 367 High St. (© **0131/226-5227**), is filled with whimsical tartan accessories searched out by Gordon MacAulay and Adrienne Wells. They have scoured the country from the Orkney Islands to the Borders for that unique item. Displayed are hand-loomed cardigans, tasteful scarves, and an array of other items, including charming Dinky bags made during the long winters on the Isle of Lewis. **Schuh,** 6 Frederick St. (© **0131/ 220-0290;** bus: 30 or 34), has the latest in unique footwear, specializing in the yellow, red, and blue plaid boots made famous by the local rugby team. The footwear here has been called "fierce." At **Anta,** 32 High St. (© **0131/ 557-8300;** bus: 35), you meet Anne and Lachian Stewart, the designers behind Ralph Lauren Home Tartan Fabrics.

The wooden blankets with hand-purled fringe are made on old-fashioned looms but in such contemporary motifs that Robbie Burns would surely turn over in his grave. The designers also produce pottery decorated in old-style ancestral Scottish plaids. Scottish fashion has become completely updated at the new and trendy **Corniche,** 2 Jeffrey St. (© **0131/556-3707;** bus: 3). Nina Grant is the guiding light, selling everything from fur-trimmed Harris tweed jackets (they're real foxy) to Vivienne Westwood's "Anglomania kilts" that have earned the designer the appellation of "queen of punk design."

Edinburgh Crystal factory, Eastfield, Penicuik (© **01968/675128;** bus: 62, 64, 65, 81, or 87), lies about 16 kilometers (10 miles) south of Edinburgh, just off A-701 to Peebles. It's devoted entirely to handmade crystal glassware, and you can take tours to watch glassmakers at work from Monday to Friday 9am to 3:30pm. There's a free minibus link from Waverley Station, which leaves on the hour and runs from Monday to Friday 10am to 4pm and on the weekend 11am to 2pm. from April to September, weekend tours are also given between 11am and 2:30pm. At the Visitor Centre is a factory shop where the world's largest collection of Edinburgh crystal is on view and for sale. You can find inexpensively priced factory seconds.

For beautiful wall hangings, you can make your own brass rubbings or buy them ready-made from the **Scottish Stone and Brass Rubbing Centre,** Trinity Apse, Chalmers Close, near the Royal Mile (© **0131/556-4364;** bus: 1). You can visit the center's collection of replicas molded from ancient Pictish stones, rare Scottish brasses, and medieval church brasses.

The two best department stores in Edinburgh are **Debenham's,** 109–112 Princes St. (© **0131/2251320;** bus: 3, 31, or 69), and **Jenners,** 48 Princes St. (© **0131/2252442;** bus: 3, 31, or 69). Both stock Scottish and international merchandise.

Other Scottish shopping venues worth checking out include **Old Town Weaving Company,** 555 Castlehill (© **0131/226-1555;** bus: 1), where you can converse with various craftspeople and purchase some of their work. If you're interested in old-fashioned Scottish crafts, this is the place. Established in 1866, **Hamilton & Inches,** 87 George St. (© **0131/225-4898;** bus: 41 or 42), is a gold and silversmith with both modern and antique designs. It has a stunning late Georgian interior as well.

EDINBURGH AFTER DARK

For a thorough list of entertainment options during your stay, pick up a copy of *The List,* a biweekly entertainment paper available at the Tourist Information Office for £1.90 ($2.85).

FESTIVALS

The highlight of Edinburgh's year—some would say the only time when the real Edinburgh emerges—comes in the last weeks of August during the **Edinburgh International Festival.** Since 1947, the festival has attracted artists and companies of the highest international standard in all fields of the arts, including music, opera, dance, theater, exhibition, poetry, and prose, and "Auld Reekie" takes on a cosmopolitan air.

During the festival, one of the most exciting spectacles is the Military Tattoo on the floodlit esplanade in front of Edinburgh Castle, high on its rock above the city. Vast audiences watch the precision marching of Scottish regiments and military units from all parts of the world, and of course the stirring skirl of the bagpipes and the swirl of the kilt.

Less predictable in quality but greater in quantity is the **Edinburgh Festival Fringe,** an opportunity for anybody—professional or nonprofessional, an individual, a group of friends, or a whole company of performers—to put on a show wherever they can find an empty stage or street corner. Late-night reviews, outrageous and irreverent contemporary drama, university theater presentations, maybe even a full-length opera—Edinburgh gives them all free rein. A **Film Festival,** a **Jazz Festival,** a **Television Festival,** and a **Book Festival** (every second year) all overlap at varying times during August.

Ticket prices vary from £5 ($8) up to about £50 ($75) a seat. Information can be obtained at **Edinburgh International Festival,** The Hub, Castle Hill, Edinburgh EH1 7ND (✆ **0131/473-2000;** fax 0131/473-2003; www.go-edinburgh. co.uk). The office is open from Monday to Friday 9:30am to 5:30pm.

Other sources of event information include **Edinburgh Festival Fringe,** 180 High St., Edinburgh EH1 1BW (✆ **131/226-5257**); **Edinburgh Book Festival,** 137 Dundee St., Edinburgh EH11 1BG (✆ **0131/228-5444**); **Edinburgh Film Festival,** 88 Lothian Rd., Edinburgh EH3 9BZ (✆ **0131/228-4051**); and **Edinburgh Military Tattoo,** 32 Market St., Edinburgh EH1 1QB (✆ **0131/ 225-1188**).

THEATER

Edinburgh has a lively theater scene. In 1994, the **Festival Theatre,** 13–29 Nicolson St. (✆ **0131/662-1112** for administration, 0131/529-6000 for tickets during non-festival times, or 0131/225-5756 for tickets during the festival; bus: 3, 31, or 33), opened in time for some aspects of the Edinburgh Festival. Set on the eastern edge of Edinburgh, near the old campus of the University of Edinburgh, it has since been called "Britain's de facto Dance House" because of its sprung floor, its enormous stage (the largest in Britain), and its suitability for opera presentations of all kinds. Tickets are £5.50 to £45.50 ($8 to $68).

Another major theater is the **King's Theatre,** 2 Leven St. (✆ **0131/ 529-6000;** bus: 10 or 11), a Victorian venue offering a wide repertoire of classical entertainment, including ballet, opera, and West End productions. The **Netherbow Arts Centre,** 43 High St. (✆ **0131/556-9579;** bus: 1), has been called "informal," and productions here are often experimental and delightful— new Scottish theater at its best. Ask about lunchtime performances.

The resident company of **Royal Lyceum Theatre,** Grindlay Street (✆ **0131/ 248-4848;** bus: 11 or 15), also has an enviable reputation; its presentations range from the works of Shakespeare to new Scottish playwrights. The **Traverse Theatre,** Cambridge Street (✆ **0131/228-1404;** bus: 11 or 15), is one of the few theaters in Britain funded solely to present new plays by British writers and first translations into English of international works.

BALLET, OPERA & CLASSICAL MUSIC

The **Scottish Ballet** and the **Scottish Opera** perform at the **Playhouse Theatre,** 18–22 Greenside Place (✆ **0131/557-0540;** bus: 7 or 14), which, with 3,100 seats, is the town's largest theater. The **Scottish Chamber Orchestra** makes its home at the **Queen's Hall,** Clerk Street (✆ **0131/668-2019;** bus: 3, 33, or 31), also a major venue for the Edinburgh International Festival.

FOLK MUSIC & CEILIDHS

Folk music is presented in many clubs and pubs in Edinburgh, but these strolling players tend to be somewhat erratic or irregular in their appearances. It's best to read notices in pubs and talk to the tourist office to see where the ceilidh will be on the night of your visit.

Some hotels regularly feature traditional Scottish music in the evenings. You might check with the **George Hotel** 19–21 George St. (✆ **0131/225-1251;**

Moments A Wee Dram for Fans of Malt Whisky

It requires a bit of an effort to reach it (take bus 10A, 16, or 17 from Princes Street to Leith), but for fans of malt whisky, the **Scotch Malt Whisky Society** has been called "The Top of the Whisky Pyramid" by distillery-industry magazines in Britain. It's on the second floor of a 16th-century warehouse at 87 Giles St., Leith (✆ **0131/554-3451**), and was originally designed to store Bordeaux and port wines from France and Portugal. All you can order are single-malt whiskies, served neat, usually in a dram (unless you want yours watered down with branch water) and selected from a staggering choice of whiskies from more than 100 distilleries throughout Scotland. Hours are from Monday to Wednesday 8:30am to 5:30pm, from Thursday to Saturday 10am to 11pm.

---

bus: 3, 31, 33). **Jamie's Scottish Evening** is presented daily at the King James Hotel on Leith Street (✆ **0131/556-0111;** bus: 7 or 14) from Tuesday through Sunday at 7pm, costing £41 ($62) for a four-course dinner, wine, and show.

DANCE & ROCK CLUBS

The Cavendish, 3 West Tollcross (✆ **0131/228-3252;** bus: 11, 15, or 23), isn't necessarily where you go to hear the next Oasis or Blur, but who knows? A rock-and-roll legend might be born here every Friday or Saturday night when the doors open at 10pm and close at 2am. There's a dress code—that is, no tennis shoes or jeans. The bar is open from Thursday to Saturday 10pm to 3am, with a £6 ($9) cover Friday and Saturday.

The glamorous **Club Mercado,** 36–39 Market St. (✆ **0131/226-4224;** bus: 1), attracts an 18- to 35-year-old crowd. Once the headquarters of the British Rail's Scottish branch, it hangs suspended over the tracks behind the city's main station. On Friday, the action kicks off with free-admission TFIS, which stands for a somewhat saltier version of "Thank God It's Friday"; it runs from 5 to 10pm and caters to youngish workers who indulge in the cut-price drinks while tapping to the kitsch music. Other special nights are alternate-Saturday Viva (a night of eclectic music attracting all sorts from toughs to drag queens) and The Colours of Love (basically a rave featuring the latest house music); both charge £8 to £10 ($12 to $15). Sunday's Bubbalicious is student night, charging £3 to £4 ($4.50 to $6), and the first Sunday of the month is gay night, charging £5 ($8). Generally, cover runs £3 to £10 ($4.50 to $15), and it's open daily from 10pm to 3am.

Po Na Na, 43B Frederick St. (✆ **0131/226-2224;** bus: 80), is a branch of Britain's most successful nightclub chain. The theme is a Moroccan Casbah, thanks to wall mosaics, brass lanterns, and artifacts shipped in from Marrakech. You'll dance in the cellar of a transformed 19th-century building, beneath a tented ceiling illuminated with strobes. Expect 25- to 40-year-olds and a highly danceable mix of house and funk. Po Na Na isn't specifically gay but does draw a strong gay following. It's open daily from 8pm to 3am, with a cover running £2 to £3 ($3 to $4.50). **Revolution,** 31 Lothian Rd. (✆**0131/229-7670;** bus: 11 or 15), is Edinburgh's largest nightclub, popular with an under-25 crowd and with a capacity for 1,500. Mainstream contemporary dance music (plus five bars) attracts the crowds, and there are theme and student nights. Cover is £3 to £7 ($4.50 to $11), and it's open from Wednesday to Sunday 10pm to 2am.

In the basement of the Dome Bar & Grill, **Whynot,** 14 George St. (© 0131/ 624-8633; bus: 41 or 42), is a hot new entertainment complex that opened in the former Bank of Scotland building across from the George Inter-Continental Hotel. It has low ceilings with veil-like curtains above the dance floor and lots of seating coves tucked away for privacy. The club swings from Thursday to Sunday 10pm to 3am. On Thursday, there's a £3 ($4.50) cover for dancing to the music of the '60s, '70s, and '80s. Friday features mainstream pop, with a £5 ($8) cover, and Saturday features contemporary dance music, with a £7.50 ($11) cover.

Behind the main Post Office and Waverley Station is **The Venue,** 15 Calton Rd. (© 0131/557-3073; bus: 26), the principal stage for live music. Some of the biggest bands in the United Kingdom perform here, and other entertainment is by Scottish wannabes. Posters and flyers around town will let you know what's on at any given time. This large hall isn't open unless there's a concert, and admission fees and times are on a per-show basis, so call for details.

PUBS & BARS

Edinburgh's most famous pub, **Café Royal Circle Bar,** 17 W. Register St. (© 0131/556-1884; bus: 3, 31, or 33), is a long-enduring favorite. One part is now occupied by the Oyster Bar of the Café Royal, but life in the Circle Bar continues at its old pace. The opulent trappings of the Victorian era are still to be seen. Go up to the serving counter, which stands like an island in a sea of drinkers, and place your order.

The Abbotsford, 3 Rose St. (© 0131/225-5276; bus: 3, 31, or 33), is near the eastern end of Rose Street, a short walk from Princes Street. This pub has served stiff drinks and oceans of beer since it was founded in 1887. Inside, the gaslight era is alive and thriving, thanks to a careful preservation of the original dark paneling, long, battered tables, and an ornate plaster ceiling. The inventories of beer on tap change about once a week, supplementing a roster of single-malt scotches. Platters of food, priced at from £2.20 to £7 ($3.30 to $11), are dispensed from the bar. Established in 1806, **Deacon Brodie's Tavern,** 435 Lawnmarket (© 0131/225-6531; bus: 1), is the neighborhood pub along the Royal Mile. It perpetuates the memory of Deacon Brodie, good citizen by day, robber by night (see earlier in this chapter). The tavern and wine cellars contain a restaurant and lounge bar.

GAY BARS & CLUBS

C. C. Bloom's, 23–24 Greenside Place (© 0131/556-9331; bus: 7 or 14), is one of the most popular gay bars in Edinburgh. The upstairs bar offers drinks and same-sex camaraderie. The downstairs club features dancing to a wide range of music, and one night a week is set aside for karaoke. Attracting a larger female clientele than most other gay bars in Edinburgh is **Planet Out,** 6 Baxters Place (© 0131/524-0061; bus: 8, 9, or 19). It's mainly a place to sit and enjoy a drink, but once a month there's a theme night with drink specials and activities. Another gay venue is **Habana,** 22 Greenside Place (© 0131/556-4349; bus: 7 or 14). This pub answers the eternal question of what's under the kilt. Gays enjoy the cafe downstairs or the disco upstairs on Friday and Saturday nights.

DAY TRIPS FROM EDINBURGH

LINLITHGOW   In this royal burgh, a county town in West Lothian, 29 kilometers (18 miles) west of Edinburgh, Mary, Queen of Scots was born in 1542. Her birthplace, the roofless **Linlithgow Palace** (© 01506/842-896), can still be explored today, even if it's but a shell of its former self. The queen's suite was in the north quarter, but was rebuilt for the homecoming of James VI (James I of England) in 1620. The palace burned to the ground in 1746. The Great Hall is on the first floor, and a small display shows some of the more interesting architectural relics. The ruined palace is 1 kilometer (half a mile) from Linlithgow Station. Admission is £2.80 ($4.20) adults, £2 ($3) seniors, £1 ($1.50) children. Hours are from April to October 9:30am to 6:30pm, from November to March Monday to Saturday 8:30am to 4:30pm, Sunday 2 to 4:30pm.

South of the palace stands the medieval kirk of **St. Michael's Parish Church** (*C* **01506/842188**), open only from May to September 10am to 4:30pm. It's been where many a Scottish monarch has worshipped since its consecration in 1242. Despite being ravaged by the disciples of John Knox and transformed into a stable by Cromwell, it's one of Scotland's best examples of a parish church.

In the midst of beautifully landscaped grounds, laid out along the lines of Versailles, sits **Hopetoun House** (*C* **0131/331-2451**), 16 kilometers (10 miles) from Edinburgh. This is Scotland's greatest Adam mansion, and a fine example of 18th-century architecture. The splendid reception rooms are filled with 18th-century furniture, paintings, statuary, and other artworks. From a rooftop platform you see a panoramic view of the Firth of Forth. You can take the nature trail, explore the deer parks, investigate the Stables Museum, or stroll through the formal gardens, all on the grounds. The house is 3 kilometers (2 miles) from the Forth Road Bridge near South Queensferry, off A-904. If you don't have a car, take a cab from the rail station in Linlithgow for about £7 to £9 ($11 to $14). Admission is £5.30 ($8) adults, £4.70 ($7) seniors, £2.70 ($4) children; family ticket (for up to six) £15 ($26). Open daily May to September, Easter weekend, and weekends in October, from 10am to 5:30pm (last admission 4:30pm).

Getting There   From Edinburgh direct trains (*C* **0345/484950**) run every 15 minutes during the day to Linlithgow (trip time: 20 minutes). Round-trip fare is £5 to £6 ($8 to $9) adults, £2.50 to £3 ($3.75 to $4.50) children. Buses also leave from St. Andrew's Square in Edinburgh (*C* **01324/613-777** for schedules), every 20 minutes (1 hour). Round-trip fare is £4.50 ($7) adults, £2.30 ($3.45) children. Motorists can take A902 to Corstorphine, then A8 to M9, getting off at the signposted junction (no. 3) to Linlithgow.

NORTH BERWICK   This royal burgh, created in the 14th century, was once an important Scottish port. In East Lothian, 39 kilometers (24 miles) east from Edinburgh, it's today a holiday resort popular with the Scots. Visitors are drawn to its golf courses, beaches, and harbor life on the Firth of Forth. You can climb the rocky shoreline or enjoy the heated outdoor swimming pool in July and August.

At the **information center,** Quality Street (*C* **01620/892-197**), you can pick up information on boat trips to the offshore islands, including **Bass Rock,** a volcanic island that is a breeding ground for about 10,000 gannets (a type of seabird). Hours are from Monday to Saturday 9am to 1:30pm and 2:30 to 5pm.

Some 3 kilometers (2 miles) east of North Berwick, and 40 kilometers (25 miles) east of Edinburgh on A-198, stand the ruins of the 14th-century diked and rose-colored **Tantallon Castle** (*C* **01620/892-727**). This was the ancient stronghold of the Douglases until their defeat by Cromwell's forces in 1650. Overlooking the Firth of Forth, the castle ruins are still formidable, with a square, five-story central tower and a dovecote, plus the shell of its east tower, a D-shaped structure with a wall from the central tower. The best way to get to the castle is by car; there're buses that run every 2 hours from North Berwick. The castle can be visited from April to September, daily 9:30am to 6:30pm; the rest of the year it's open Monday to Wednesday and Saturday 9:30am to 4pm,

Thursday 9:30am to 4:30pm, and Sunday 2 to 4:30pm. Admission is £2.80 ($4.20) adults, £2 ($3) seniors, and £1 ($1.50) children.

Getting There   Trains (© 0345/484950) leave from Edinburgh about every half hour for the 30-minute trip, round-trip costing £4.50 to £7 ($7 to $11) adults or £2.25 to £3.50 ($3.40 to $5) children. **Buses** (© 0131/366-39233) also leave from Charlotte Square in Edinburgh at 33 minutes past the hour daily from 8:03am to 5:33pm, taking 1¼ hours and costing £4.50 ($7) round-trip adults or £2.25 ($3.40) children. **Motorists** follow A198 from Edinburgh to North Berwick (it's signposted all the way).

DIRLETON   This little town, a preservation village, vies for the title of "prettiest village in Scotland." The town plan, drafted in the early 16th century, is essentially unchanged today. Dirleton has two greens shaped like triangles, with a pub opposite Dirleton Castle, placed at right angles to a group of cottages.

A rose-tinted 13th-century castle with surrounding gardens, once the seat of the wealthy Anglo-Norman de Vaux family, **Dirleton Castle** (© 01620/ 850330) looks like a fairy-tale fortification, with its towers, arched entries, and oak ramp. Ruins of the Great Hall and kitchen can be seen, as well as what's left of the lord's chamber where the de Vaux family lived. The 16th-century main gate has a hole through which boiling tar or water could be poured to discourage unwanted visitors. The castle's country garden and bowling green are still in use. Admission is £2.80 ($4.20) adults, £2 ($3) seniors, £1 ($1.50) children. You can tour the castle from April to September, Monday to Saturday 9:30am to 6pm, Sunday 10am to 6pm; from October to March, Monday to Saturday 9:30am to 4pm, Sunday 2 to 4pm.

Getting There   Dirleton is on the Edinburgh–North Berwick road (A-198), 8 kilometers (5 miles) west of North Berwick and 3 kilometers (19 miles) east of Edinburgh. Buses (© 0131/663-9233) leave from St. Andrew's Square station in Edinburgh at 10 past and 20 to the hour (trip time: 1 hour). The last bus departs at 5:10pm. One-way fare is £1.60 ($2.40) adults or 85p ($1.30) children.

2 Tayside & Grampian

Tayside and Grampian, two history-rich sections in northeast Scotland, offer a vast array of sightseeing, even though they're relatively small areas. Tayside, for example, is about 137 kilometers (85 miles) east to west, and some 97 kilometers (60 miles) south to north. The two regions share the North Sea coast between the Firth of Tay in the south and the Firth of Moray farther north. The so-called Highland Line separating the Lowlands in the south from the Highlands in the north crosses both regions. The Grampians, the highest mountain range in Scotland, are to the west of this line.

Carved out of the old counties of Perth and Angus, **Tayside** is named for its major river, the 190-kilometer (119-mile) Tay. The region is easy to explore, and its tributaries and dozens of lochs and Highland streams are among the best salmon and trout waters in Europe. One of the loveliest regions of Scotland, Tayside is filled with heather-clad Highland hills, long blue lochs under tree-lined banks, and miles and miles of walking trails. Perth and Dundee are among the six leading cities of Scotland. Tayside provided the backdrop for many novels by Sir Walter Scott, including *The Fair Maid of Perth, Waverley,* and *The Abbot.* Its golf courses are world famous, ranging from the trio of 18-hole courses at Gleneagles to the open championship links at Carnoustie.

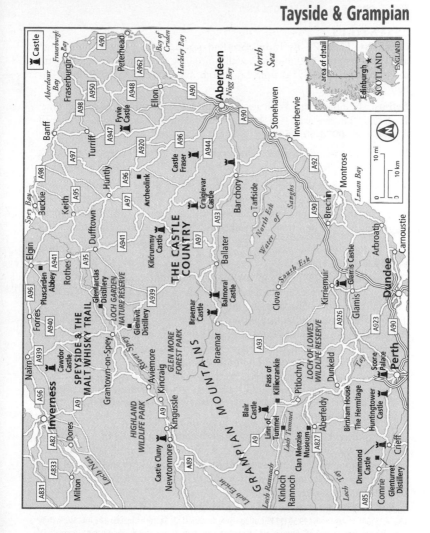

The **Grampian region** has Aberdeen, Scotland's third-largest city, and Braemar, site of the most famous of the Highland gatherings. The queen herself comes here to holiday at Balmoral Castle, her private residence, a tradition dating back to the days of Queen Victoria and her consort, Prince Albert. As you journey on the scenic roads of Scotland's northeast, you'll pass heather-covered moorland and peaty lochs, wood glens and salmon-filled rivers, granite-stone villages and ancient castles, and fishing harbors as well as North Sea beach resorts.

After exploring Edinburgh, you can tour Tayside and Grampian. Perth, 70 kilometers (44 miles) north of Edinburgh, makes the best "gateway" to the region.

PERTH 🏵

From its majestic position on the Tay, the ancient city of Perth was the capital of Scotland until the middle of the 15th century. It's here that the Highlands meet the Lowlands. Perth itself has few historic buildings. The main attraction, Scone Place, lies on the outskirts.

ESSENTIALS

GETTING THERE   By Train   ScotRail provides service between Edinburgh and Perth (trip time: 90 minutes), with continuing service to Dundee. The trip to Perth costs £9.40 ($14) from Edinburgh; phone ✆ **0345/484950** for 24-hour information.

By Bus   Edinburgh and Perth are connected by frequent bus service (trip time: 1½ hours). The fare is £5 ($8). For more information and schedules, check with CityLink (✆ **0990/505050**).

By Car   To reach Perth from Edinburgh, take A-90 northwest and go across the Forth Road Bridge, continuing north along M-90 (trip time: 1½ hours).

VISITOR INFORMATION   The **tourist information center** is at Lower City Mills, West Mill St. (✆ **01738/450600**), and is open from April to June daily 9am to 6pm, from July to September daily 9am to 7pm, October daily from 9am to 6pm, and from November to March, Monday to Saturday 10am to 5pm.

WHERE TO STAY

Dupplin Castle 🏰🏰   This modern, severely dignified mansion was built in 1968 by well-known architect Schomber Scott to replace the last of the three castles that had once risen proudly from the site. Surrounded by 14 hectares (30 acres) of forest and spectacular gardens (some of its specimens are 250 years old), the site is one of the most beautiful near Perth. Rooms are rented in a spirit of elegance and good manners. Views from many overlook the valley of the River Earn. Meals must be booked 24 hours in advance.

Near Aberdalgie, Perth PH2 0PY. ✆ 01738/623224. Fax 01738/444140. www.dupplin.co.uk. 7 units. £110–£130 ($165–$195) double. Rates include breakfast. MC, V. From Perth, follow the main highway to Glasgow, turning left onto B-9112 toward Aberdalgie and Forteviot. **Amenities:** Dining room; clay shooting. *In room:* coffeemaker, hair dryer.

Hunting Tower 🏰   This late-Victorian country house, about a 10-minute drive from the city center, is set in 1.5 hectares (3½ acres) of well-manicured gardens, with a modern wing of rooms added in 1998. Taste and concern went into the interior decoration. Rooms, which vary wildly in size, each has its specific charm. Seven offer spa baths.

Crieff Rd., Perth PH1 3JT. ✆ 01738/583771. Fax 01738/583777. www.huntingtowerhotel.co.uk. 34 units. £89.50 ($134) double; from £99.50 ($149) cottage suite. Rates include Scottish breakfast. AE, DC, MC, V. Drive 6km (3½ miles) west on A-85. **Amenities:** Restaurant, bar; room service; laundry/dry cleaning. *In room:* TV, radio, minibar, coffeemaker, hair dryer.

Parklands Hotel 🏰   Luxuriously overhauled, this is a country-house hotel in the middle of the city. The beautifully decorated rooms overlook the South Inch Park. All are spacious and well furnished. Light traditional fare is served in country-house style.

2 St. Leonard's Bank, Perth PH2 8EB. ✆ 01738/622451. Fax 01738/622046. centuryhousehotel@compuserve.com. 14 units. £89–£105 ($134–$158) double. Rates include breakfast. AE, DC, MC, V. Free parking. **Amenities:** Restaurant, bar; room service; laundry/dry cleaning. *In room:* TV, coffeemaker, hair dryer.

WHERE TO DINE

Let's Eat 🏰 BRITISH/INTERNATIONAL   The most visually striking, and most appealing, restaurant in Perth occupies the premises of an 1822 theater and intersperses its tables amid its soaring white columns. There's a particularly cozy lounge, site of a log-burning iron stove and comfortable sofas, where you might want a drink or aperitif before your meal. Menu items might include a gratin of goat's cheese studded with roasted peppers; filet of roasted venison with port wine sauce; marinated tuna on a bed of couscous; and grilled brochettes of monkfish with king prawns, rice, and salad. Dessert might be any of several "puddings" including an apple strudel that are headlined on the menu as "glorious" and that usually live up to their billing. Be careful not to confuse this restaurant with its less grand, less expensive sibling, Let's Eat Again (see below).

77–79 Kinnoul St. ℂ 01738/643377. Reservations recommended. Lunch main courses £6.50–£11 ($10–$17); dinner main courses £8–£15 ($12–$23). AE, MC, V. Tues–Sat noon–2pm and 6:30–9:45pm.

Let's Eat Again BRITISH/INTERNATIONAL   This upbeat bistro caters to the young-at-heart with well-prepared but relatively inexpensive versions of Mediterranean and international cuisine like what you might have expected in a trendy eatery in London. Your meal might begin with charcoal-grilled Mediterranean vegetables with mozzarella; smoked haddock and chive-laced risotto; smoked local venison with spicy pears; salmon and codfish cakes with lemon-flavored butter sauce; roasted salmon with sun-dried tomatoes and pesto; and Thai-style chicken curry with noodles. Don't confuse this restaurant with the more upscale Let's Eat, under the same management (see above).

33 George St. ℂ 1738/633771. Reservations recommended. Main courses £7–£12 ($11–$18). AE, MC, V. Tues–Sat noon–2pm and 6–9:30pm.

Littlejohn's INTERNATIONAL   On one of Perth's busiest commercial streets, this restaurant has one large dining room with old-fashioned wood paneling, antique signs, and lots of Scottish charm. Despite the conservative nature of the setting, the food offerings are eclectic and include pizzas, pastas, Mexican tortillas, burgers, steaks, and an occasional lobster dish.

24 St. John's St. ℂ 01738/639888. Main courses £3.95–£12.85 ($6–$19). AE, DC, MC, V. Daily 10am–11pm.

SEEING THE SIGHTS

Kirk of St. John the Baptist   This is the main sightseeing attraction of "the fair city." It's believed that the original foundation is from Pictish times. The present choir dates from 1440 and the nave from 1490. In 1559 John Knox preached his famous sermon here attacking idolatry, which caused a turbulent wave of iconoclasm to sweep across the land. In its wake, religious artifacts, stained glass, and organs were destroyed all over Scotland. The church was restored as a World War I memorial in the mid-1920s.

31 St. John Place. ℂ 01738/622241. Free admission. Mon–Fri 10am–noon and 2–4pm.

Branklyn Garden   Once the finest hectare (2 acres) of private garden in Scotland, the garden now belongs to the National Trust for Scotland. It has a superb collection of rhododendrons, alpines, and herbaceous and peat-garden plants from all over the world.

116 Dundee Rd. (A-85), in Branklyn. ℂ 01738/625535. Admission £3.50 ($5) adults; £1 ($1.50) children, students, and seniors; £6.40 ($11) family ticket. Mar–Oct daily 9:30am–sunset; closed in winter.

A DAY TRIP TO SCONE

Old Scone, 3 kilometers (2 miles) from Perth on the River Tay, was the ancient capital of the Picts. On a lump of sandstone called the "Stone of Destiny," the early Scottish monarchs were enthroned. In 1296 Edward I, the "Hammer of the Scots," moved the stone to Westminster Abbey, and for hundreds of years it rested under the chair on which British monarchs were crowned. The Scots have always bitterly resented this theft, and at last it has been returned to Scotland, to find a permanent home in Edinburgh Castle, where it can be viewed by the public.

The seat of the earls of Mansfield and birthplace of David Douglas of fir-tree fame, **Scone Palace** 🏰🏰, along A-93 (© **01738/552300**), was largely rebuilt in 1802, incorporating the old palace of 1580. Inside is an impressive collection of French furniture, china, ivories, and 16th-century needlework, including bed hangings executed by Mary, Queen of Scots. A fine collection of rare conifers is found on the grounds in the Pinetum. Rhododendrons and azaleas grow profusely in the gardens and woodlands around the palace. To reach the palace, head northeast of Perth on A-93. The site is open from Good Friday to mid-October only, daily 9:30am to 5pm. Admission is £5.90 ($9) adults, £5.10 ($8) seniors, £3.40 ($5) children under 17, including entrance to both house and grounds. Admission to the grounds only is £2.90 ($4.35) adults and £1.70 ($2.55) children.

Where to Stay & Dine

The Murrayshall 🏰🏰🏰   This elegant country-house hotel is set in 120 hectares (300 acres) of parkland. It was completely refurbished in 1987 and reopened as one of the showpieces of Perthshire. Because of the excellence of its challenging courses, this hotel is frequented by golfers and their families. Rooms come in a wide range of styles and space. Suites and executive rooms have the best amenities and views. The less-desired standard rooms are also comfortable but lack the character of the others. Memory note: On a windy night in Scotland there is no better place to be than the well-stocked bar with its log fire.

New Scone, Perthshire PH2 7PH. © **01738/551171.** Fax 01738/552595. 27 units. £130–£140 ($195–$210) double; from £160–£170 ($240–$255) suite; £160 ($240) lodge. Rates include Scottish breakfast. AE, DC, MC, V. Take A-94 2.5km (1½ miles) east of New Scone. **Amenities:** 2 restaurants, 2 bars; 2 golf courses; tennis courts; gym; room service; baby-sitting; laundry/dry cleaning. *In room:* TV, hair dryer.

GLENEAGLES

This famous golfing center and sports complex is on a moor between Strathearn and Strath Allan. Gleneagles has four **18-hole golf courses:** King's Course, the longest one; Queen's Course, next in length; Prince's Course, shortest of all; and Glendevon, the newest of the quartet, built in 1980. They're among the best in Scotland, and the sports complex is one of the best-equipped in Europe.

ESSENTIALS

GETTING THERE   By Train   The 15-minute ride from Perth costs £3.90 ($6). The trip takes 1 hour and 40 minutes from Edinburgh and costs £8.40 ($13). For information call © **0345/484950.**

By Bus   The only service departs from Glasgow. The trip takes slightly more than an hour and costs £6 ($9). For information and schedules, call © **01738/ 26847.**

By Car   Gleneagles is on A-9, about halfway between Perth and Stirling, a short distance from the village of Auchterarder. It lies 88 kilometers (55 miles) from Edinburgh and 72 kilometers (45 miles) from Glasgow.

VISITOR INFORMATION   The year-round **tourist center** is at 90 High St., Auchterarder (© **01764/663450**). Open from November to March Monday to Friday 9:30am to 5pm, Saturday 11am to 3pm; from April to June Monday to Saturday 9:30am to 5:30pm, Sunday 11am to 4pm; July and August from Monday to Saturday 9am to 7pm, Sunday 11am to 6pm; and September and October from Monday to Saturday 9:30am to 5:30pm, Sunday 11am to 4pm.

WHERE TO STAY & DINE

Auchterarder House *★★★*   Auchterarder House, 1.5 kilometers (1 mile) from Gleneagles, sits on its own grounds off B-8062 between Auchterarder and Crieff. A fine example of 1830s architecture and construction in the Scots Jacobean style, the mansion house has been completely restored and the interior refurbished to a high standard of luxury by its present owners in a mix of Victorian and modern. The house has elegant public areas and comfortable rooms, with a well-mannered staff whose aim is to please.

Auchterarder PH3 1DZ. ℂ **01764/663646.** Fax 01764/662939. www.wrensgroup.com. 15 units. £170–£295 ($255–$443) double. Rates include Scottish breakfast. AE, DC, MC, V. Free parking. **Amenities:** Restaurant; room service; baby-sitting; laundry/dry cleaning; croquet. *In room:* TV, hair dryer.

Gleneagles Hotel *★★★*   Britain's greatest golf hotel stands on its own 390-hectare (830 acre) estate. When it was built in isolated grandeur in 1924, it was Scotland's only five-star hotel. It's a true resort and has tried to keep ahead of the times by offering spa treatments. Rooms vary greatly in size. The best and most spacious choices are in the 60 to 90 block series. They have recently been refurbished. The less desirable rooms are called courtyard units, a bit small and equipped with shower-only bathrooms. As for cuisine, the golfers rarely complain, but no one dines here to collect recipes.

Auchterarder PH3 1NF. ℂ **01764/662231.** Fax 01764/662134. www.gleneagles.com. 229 units. £290–£410 ($435–$615) double; from £555 ($833) suite. Rates include Scottish breakfast. AE, DC, MC, V. Free parking. Take A-9 1½ miles southwest of Auchterarder. **Amenities:** 3 restaurants, 2 bars; pool; health spa; hunting excursions; room service; baby-sitting laundry/dry cleaning. *In room:* TV, minibar, hair dryer, safe.

CRIEFF

From Perth, head west on A-85 for 29 kilometers (18 miles) to Crieff . At the edge of the Perthshire Highlands, with good fishing and golf, Crieff makes a pleasant stopover. This small burgh was the seat of the court of the earls of Strathearn until 1747, and the gallows in its marketplace was once used to execute Highland cattle rustlers.

You can take a "day trail" into **Strathearn,** the valley of the River Earn, the very center of Scotland. Here highland mountains meet gentle Lowland slopes, and moorland mingles with rich green pastures. North of Crieff, the road to Aberfeldy passes through the narrow pass of the **Sma' Glen,** a famous spot of beauty, with hills rising on either side to 600 meters (2,000 ft.).

ESSENTIALS

GETTING THERE   By Train   There's no direct service. The nearest rail stations are at Gleneagles, 14 kilometers (9 miles) away, and at Perth, 29 kilometers (18 miles) away. Call ℂ **0345/484950** for information and schedules.

By Bus   Once you arrive in Perth, you'll find regular connecting bus service hourly during the day. For information and schedules, call **Stagecoach** at ℂ **01738/629339.** The bus service from Gleneagles is too poor to recommend.

By Taxi   From Gleneagles a taxi will cost from £20 to £30 ($30 to $45).

VISITOR INFORMATION   The year-round **tourist information office** is in the Town Hall on High Street (ℂ **01764/652578**). Open from November to March, Monday to Friday 9:30am to 5pm, Saturday 10am to 2pm; from April to June, Monday to Saturday 9:30am to 5:30pm, Sunday 11am to 4pm; July and August, from Monday to Saturday 9am to 7pm, Sunday 11am to 6pm; and September and October, from Monday to Saturday 9:30am to 5:30pm, Sunday 11am to 4pm.

WHERE TO STAY & DINE

Murraypark Hotel   This stone-fronted house lies in a residential neighborhood about a 10-minute walk from Crieff's center and close to a golf course. In 1993, a new wing was opened, enlarging the public areas and the number of well-furnished rooms. The property has been considerably upgraded. Rooms in this former 19th-century sea captain's house vary in size and shape, but most open onto views. Although those in the new wing are more comfortable, they're hardly as evocative and we still prefer the older wing's traditional Victorian aura.

Connaught Terrace, Crieff PH7 3DJ. © **01764/653731.** Fax 01764/655311. www.scotland.hotels.com. 19 units. £60–£75 ($90–$113) double or suite. Rates include Scottish breakfast. AE, DC, MC, V. Free parking. **Amenities:** Dining room, bar; room service; baby-sitting. *In room:* TV, coffeemaker, hair dryer.

SEEING THE SIGHTS

Glenturret Distillery Ltd   Scotland's oldest distillery, Glenturret was established in 1775 on the banks of the River Turret. Visitors can see the milling of malt, mashing, fermentation, distillation, and cask filling, followed by a free "wee dram" dispensed at the end of the tour. Guided tours take about 25 minutes and leave at frequent intervals—sometimes as often as every 10 minutes when there's a demand for it. This can be followed or preceded by a 20-minute video, *The Water of Life,* that's presented adjacent to a small museum devoted to the implements of the whisky trade.

Hwy. A-85, Glenturret. © **01764/656565.** Guided tours £3.50 ($5) adults, £3 ($4.50)) seniors, £2.30 ($3.45) persons 12–17, family ticket £9 ($14), free for children 11 and under. Mar–Dec Mon–Sat 9:30am–6pm, Sun noon–6pm; Feb Mon–Fri 11:30am–4:30pm, Sun noon–4pm. Closed Jan and Dec 25–26. Take A-85 toward Comrie; 1.5km (³⁄₄ mile) from Crieff, turn right at the crossroads; the distillery is 0.5km (¹⁄₄ mile) up the road.

Drummond Castle Gardens 🔊   The gardens of Drummond Castle, first laid out in the early 17th century by John Drummond, second earl of Perth, are among the finest formal gardens in Europe. There's a panoramic view from the upper terrace, overlooking an example of an early Victorian parterre in the form of St. Andrew's Cross. The multifaceted sundial by John Mylne, master mason to Charles I, has been the centerpiece since 1630.

Grimsthorpe, Crieff. © **01764/681257.** Admission £3.50 ($5) adults, £2.50 ($3.75) seniors, £1.50 ($2.25) children. May–Oct daily 2–6pm; Easter weekend 2–6pm. Closed Nov–Apr. Take A-822 for 5km (3 miles) south of Crieff.

PLAYING GOLF

Crieff Golf Club (© **01764/652909**) has two courses—both with panoramic views and excellent facilities. The most challenging is the 18-hole Fern Tower, a par-71 course with three par-5 holes. The Dornock is a 64-par, 9-hole course with three par-3 holes. It's not quite as difficult as the Fern Tower, but a test nonetheless. Greens fees for the Fern Tower are £25 ($38) per round from Monday to Friday, and £33 ($50) on weekends. Greens fees for the Dornock are £8 ($12) for 9 holes and £12 ($18) for 18 holes. Carts cost £14 ($21) per round. From April to October, the golf club is open 8am to 11pm; from November to March, Friday 9am to 7pm and Saturday and Sunday 8am to 7:30pm.

ABERFELDY 🔊

The "Birks o' Aberfeldy" are among the beauty spots made famous by the poet Robert Burns. Once a Pictish center, this small town makes a fine base for touring Perthshire's glens and lochs. Loch Tay lies 10 kilometers (6 miles) to the west; Glen Lyon, 24 kilometers (15 miles) west; and Kinloch Rannoch, 29 kilometers

(18 miles) northwest. The town's shops offer good buys in tweeds and tartans, plus other items of Highland dress.

ESSENTIALS

GETTING THERE   By Train   There's no direct service into Aberfeldy. You can take a train to either Perth or Pitlochry, then continue the rest of the way by bus. Call ✆ **0345/484950** for schedules.

By Bus   Connecting buses at either Perth or Pitlochry make the final journey to Aberfeldy. The private bus line **Stagecoach** (✆ **01738/629339**) handles much of the bus travel to the smaller towns and villages in the area.

By Car   From Crieff, take A-822 on a winding road north to Aberfeldy. The 48-kilometer (30-mile) drive from Perth takes 30 to 45 minutes.

VISITOR INFORMATION   The **tourist office** is at The Square (✆ **01887/820276**). Hours are July and August, daily from 9:30am to 5pm; from April to June, September, and October, daily 9am to 5:30pm; and from October to March, Monday to Saturday 9am to 5:30pm.

WHERE TO STAY & DINE

Farleyer House Hotel ✦   A tranquil oasis, this hotel of character stands on 33 hectares (70 acres) of grounds in the Tay Valley. Although restored and altered over the years, the building dates back to the 1500s. The staff entertains guests as if they were in a private home. The public areas are immaculate and beautifully furnished, and the rooms are well maintained and comfortable.

Hwy. B-846, Aberfeldy PH15 2JE. ✆ **01887/820332.** Fax 01887/829430. www.farleyer.com. 19 units. £120–£140 ($180–$210) double; £120–£150 ($180–$225) family suite. Rates include breakfast. AE, DC, MC, V. Take B-846 for 2 miles west of Aberfeldy. **Amenities:** 2 restaurants, 2 bars; room service; baby-sitting; laundry/dry cleaning. *In room:* TV, coffeemaker.

PLAYING GOLF

Aberfeldy Golf Club, at Aberfeldy (✆**01887/820535**), is a flatland course located on the banks of the River Tay. It's an 18-hole par 68 that is viewed as a "challenge" by the local pro. The River Tay comes into play on several holes, and if you're not careful, you'll be making trips back to the Pro Shop for more balls. Greens fees are £15 ($23) for 18 holes (or £20 ($30) on weekends), and cart fees are £2 ($3) per round (pull carts). From April to October the club is open daily 8am to 11pm. During other months, call first to see if they're open: It depends on the weather.

DUNKELD ✦

A cathedral town, Dunkeld lies in a thickly wooded valley of the Tay River at the edge of the Perthshire Highlands. Once a major ecclesiastical center, it's one of the seats of ancient Scottish history and an important center of the Celtic church.

ESSENTIALS

GETTING THERE   By Train   Trains from Perth arrive every 2 hours and cost £5 ($8) (trip time: 1½ hours). Call ✆ **0345/484950** for information and schedules.

By Bus   Pitlochry-bound buses leaving from Perth make a stopover in Dunkeld, letting you off at the Dunkeld Car Park, which is at the train station (trip time: 50 minutes). The cost is £3.10 ($4.65). Contact **Stagecoach** at ✆ **01738/629339.**

By Car   From Aberfeldy, take A-827 east until you reach the junction of A-9 heading south to Dunkeld.

VISITOR INFORMATION   A **tourist information office** is at The Cross (© **01350/727688**). It's open from April to June, Monday to Saturday 9:30am to 5:30pm and Sunday 11am to 4pm; from July 1 to September 8, Monday to Saturday 9am to 7:30pm and Sunday 11am to 7pm; from September 9 to October 27, Monday to Saturday 9:30am to 5:30pm and Sunday 11am to 4pm; from October 28 to December, Monday to Saturday 9:30am to 1:30pm (closed January to March).

WHERE TO STAY & DINE

Hilton Dunkeld House 🏛🏛   The hotel, offering the quiet dignity of life in a Scottish country house, is ranked as one of the leading leisure and sports hotels in the area. On the banks of the Tay, the surrounding grounds—132 hectares (280 acres) in all—make for a parklike setting. The house is beautifully kept, and rooms come in a wide range of styles, space, and furnishings. In 1999, an annex was converted into an extra wing offering another nine rooms. Its salmon and trout fishing are possible right on the grounds, as well as an array of other outdoor activities.

Dunkeld PH8 0HX. © **01350/727771.** Fax 01350/728924. www.hilton.com. 97 units. £149 ($224) double; £199–£219 ($299–$329) suite. Rates include Scottish breakfast. AE, DC, MC, V. **Amenities:** Restaurant; pool; tennis courts; fishing; room service; baby-sitting; laundry/dry cleaning. *In room:* TV, minibar, hair dryer.

Kinnaird 🏛🏛🏛   On a 4,200-hectare (9,000-acre) private estate, this is a small hotel of great warmth, charm, and comfort. Built in 1770 as a hunting lodge, the house has been restored to its previous grandeur. All the beautifully furnished rooms have king-size beds, full private bathrooms, and views. Some rooms overlook the valley of the River Tay; others open onto gardens and woodlands. There are eight cottages on the estate, two of which sleep eight and the others four.

Kinnaird, Kinnaird Estate, Dunkeld PH8 0LB. © **01796/482440.** Fax 01796/482289. www.kinnairdestate. com. 9 units and 8 estate cottages. £275–£345 ($413–$518) double; £440 ($660) suite; £375–£1,000 ($563–$1,500) estate cottages. Rates include dinner and Scottish breakfast. MC, V. Free parking. No children under 12 accepted in the hotel. **Amenities:** Restaurant; bar; tennis courts; fishing and hunting excursions; room service; baby-sitting; laundry/dry cleaning. *In room:* TV, hair dryer.

SEEING THE SIGHTS

Founded in A.D. 815, the **Cathedral of Dunkeld** 🏛 was converted from a church to a cathedral in 1127 by David I. It stands on Cathedral Street in a scenic setting along the River Tay. The cathedral was first restored in 1815, and traces of the 12th-century structure remain today. Admission is free, and the cathedral is open from May to September, Monday to Saturday 9:30am to 6:30pm, Sunday 2 to 6:30pm; from October to April, Monday to Saturday 9:30am to 4pm.

The National Trust for Scotland has restored many of the old houses and shops around the marketplace and cathedral. The trust owns 20 houses on High Street and Cathedral Street as well. Many of these houses were constructed in the closing years of the 17th century after the rebuilding of the town following the Battle of Dunkeld. The Trust runs the **Ell Shop,** The Cross (© **01350/ 727460**), which specializes in Scottish handcrafts. From Easter weekend to December 24, it's open Monday to Saturday 10am to 5:30pm.

The **Scottish Horse Museum,** The Cross (no phone), has exhibits tracing the history of the Scottish Horse Yeomanry, a cavalry force first raised in 1900. The museum is open from Easter to October only, Saturday to Wednesday 10am to noon and 1:50 to 5pm. Admission is free.

Shakespeare fans may want to seek out the oak and sycamore in front of the destroyed Birnam House, a mile to the south. This was believed to be a remnant of the **Birnam Wood** in *Macbeth;* you may recall, "Macbeth shall never vanquished be until great Birnam Wood to high Dunsinane Hill shall come against him."

The Hermitage, lying off A-9 about 3 kilometers (2 miles) west of Dunkeld, was called a "folly" when it was constructed in 1758 above the wooded gorge of the River Braan. Today it makes for one of the most scenic woodland walks in the area.

PLAYING GOLF

Dunkeld & Birnam, at Dunkeld (© **01350/727524**), is touted as the best in the area. The 18-hole course is not too long, but can be quite difficult. It's edged in many areas with bracken, and many a golfer has had to take a drop instead of searching for the errant ball. There are sweeping views of the surrounding environs. Greens fees: from Monday through Friday £18 ($27) for 18 holes; Saturday and Sunday £21 ($32) for 18 holes. There are no electric carts; pull carts are available for £2 ($3) per round. Hours are daily from 7am to 11pm April to September. From October to March greens fees are reduced to £9 to £10 ($14 to $15) and hours are daily from 8am to 4pm. There's no official dress code, although if the starter feels you are not dressed "appropriately" you will be asked to "smarten up" the next time you play the course.

DUNDEE & GLAMIS CASTLE 🏯🏯

This royal burgh and old seaport is an industrial city on the north shore of the Firth of Tay. When steamers took over the whaling industry from sailing vessels, Dundee became the leading home port for the ships from the 1860s until World War I. Long known for its jute and flax operations, we think today of the Dundee fruitcakes, marmalades, and jams. This was also the home of the man who invented stick-on postage stamps, James Chalmers. Dundee has a raffish charm and serves well as a base for a trip to Glamis Castle .

Spanning the Firth of Tay is the **Tay Railway Bridge,** opened in 1888. Constructed over the tidal estuary, the bridge is some 3 kilometers (2 miles) long, one of the longest in Europe. There's also a road bridge 2 kilometers (1¼ miles) long, with four traffic lanes and a walkway in the center.

ESSENTIALS

GETTING THERE   By Train   ScotRail offers frequent service between Perth, Dundee, and Aberdeen. One-way fare from Perth to Dundee is £4.60 ($7), from Aberdeen, £17.40 ($26). Phone © **0345/484950** for schedules and departure times.

By Bus   CityLink buses offer frequent bus service from Edinburgh and Glasgow. Call © **0990/505050** for information.

By Car   The fastest way to reach Dundee is to cut south back to Perth along A-9 and link up with A-972 going east.

VISITOR INFORMATION   The **tourist information office** is at 21 Castle St. (© **01382/527-527.** Hours are from April to September, Monday to Saturday 9am to 6pm, Sunday 10am to 4pm; from October to March, Monday to Saturday 9am to 5pm.

WHERE TO STAY

Hilton Dundee ℛ   This chain hotel helps to rejuvenate the once-seedy water-front of Dundee. Built in a severe modern style, the five-story block takes its name from a famous English tea, which most often accompanies marmalade and Dundee fruitcakes, the city's two most famous products. Some of the well-furnished rooms overlook the Firth, the river, or the Tay Bridge. Both the business and the leisure traveler will find solace here in rooms with bright floral uphol-stery and draperies, blond wood furnishings, and small bathrooms.

Earl Grey Place, Dundee DD1 4DE. ℂ **01382/229271.** Fax 01382/200072. www.hilton.com. 129 units. £120–£140 ($180–$210) double; from £220 ($330) suite. AE, DC, MC, V. Free parking. Bus: 1A, 1B, or 20. **Amenities:** Restaurant; pool; health spa; room service; baby-sitting; laundry/dry cleaning. *In room:* TV, cof-feemaker, hair dryer, safe, trouser press.

Invercarse Hotel   In landscaped gardens overlooking the River Tay, this pri-vately owned hotel lies 5 kilometers (3 miles) west of the heart of Dundee. Many prefer it for its fresh air, tranquil location, and Victorian country-house aura. Well-maintained rooms come in a variety of sizes and open onto views across the Tay to the hills of the Kingdom of Fife.

371 Perth Rd., Dundee DD2 1PG. ℂ **01382/669231.** Fax 01382/644112. 44 units. £90 ($135) double; £100 ($150) suite. Rates include Scottish breakfast. AE, DC, MC, V. Free parking. **Amenities:** Restaurant, bar; room service; laundry/dry cleaning. *In room:* TV, coffeemaker, hair dryer.

WHERE TO DINE

Jahangir Tandoori INDIAN   Built around an indoor fishpond in a dining room draped with the soft folds of an embroidered tent, this is one of the most exotic restaurants in the region. Meals are prepared with fresh ingredients and cover the gamut of recipes from both north and south India. Some preparations are slow-cooked in clay pots (tandoori) and seasoned to the degree of spiciness you prefer. Both meat and meatless dishes are available.

1 Sessions St. (at the corner of Hawk Hill). ℂ **01382/202022.** Reservations recommended. Main courses £6.50–£15 ($10–$23). AE, MC, V. Daily 5pm–midnight.

SEEING THE SIGHTS

For a panoramic view of Dundee, the Tay bridges across to Fife, and mountains to the north, go to **Dundee Law,** a 175-meter (572-ft.) hill just north of the city. The hill is an ancient volcanic plug.

HMS Unicorn ℛ *Kids*   This 46-gun wooden ship of war commissioned in 1824 by the Royal Navy, now the oldest British-built ship afloat, has been restored and visitors can explore all four decks: the quarterdeck with 32-pound cannonades, the gun deck with its battery of 18-pound cannons and the cap-tain's quarters, the berth deck with officers' cabins and crews' hammocks, and the orlop deck and hold. Various displays portraying life in the sailing navy and the history of the *Unicorn* make this a rewarding visit.

Victoria Dock. ℂ **01382/200900.** Admission £3.50 ($5) adults, £2.50 ($3.75) seniors and children; £7.50–£9.50 ($11–$14) family ticket. Easter–Oct daily 10am–5pm; Nov–Easter Wed–Sun 10am–4pm. Bus: 6, 23, or 78.

Broughty Castle   This 15th-century estuary fort lies about 6 kilometers (4 miles) east of the city center on the seafront, at Broughty Ferry, a little fishing hamlet and once the terminus for ferries crossing the Firth of Tay before the bridges were built. Besieged by the English in the 16th century, and attacked by Cromwell's army under General Monk in the 17th century, it was eventually restored as part of Britain's coastal defenses in 1861. Its gun battery was dismantled in 1956, and it's now a museum with displays on local history, arms and armor, and Dundee's whaling story. The observation area at the top of the castle provides fine views of the Tay estuary and northeast Fife.

Castle Green, Broughty Ferry. © **01382/436916.** Free admission. July–Sept Mon 11am–5pm, Tues–Thurs 10am–1pm and 2–5pm, Sun 2–5pm; Oct–June Mon 11am–5pm, Tues–Thurs 10am–1pm and 2–5pm. Bus: 75 or 76.

PLAYING GOLF

Caird Park, at Dundee (© **01382/453606**), is an 18-hole, par-72 course that presents most golfers with an average challenge. The course is quite flat, but there're more than a few bunkers to navigate. There's also a restaurant and bar on the premises. Greens fees are £15 ($23) for 18 holes, or £25 ($38) for a day ticket. No carts of any sort are allowed on the course, and there's no particular dress code. The park is open from April to October daily 7am to 8pm.

A DAY TRIP TO GLAMIS

The little village of Glamis (pronounced without the "i") grew up around **Glamis Castle** , Castle Office, Glamis (© **01307/840393**). Next to Balmoral Castle, visitors to Scotland most want to see Glamis Castle for its link with the crown. For 6 centuries it has been connected to members of the British royal family. The Queen Mother was brought up here; and Princess Margaret was born here, becoming the first royal princess born in Scotland in 3 centuries. The present owner is the queen's great-nephew. The castle contains Duncan's Hall—the Victorians claimed this was where Macbeth murdered King Duncan, but in the play, the murder takes place at Macbeth's castle near Inverness. In fact, Shakespeare was erroneous, as well—he had Macbeth named Thane of Glamis, but Glamis wasn't made a thaneship (a sphere of influence in medieval Scotland) until years after the play takes place.

The present Glamis Castle dates from the early 15th century, but there're records of a castle having been in existence in the 11th century. Glamis Castle has been in the possession of the Lyon family since 1372, and it contains some fine plaster ceilings, furniture, and paintings.

The castle is open to the public, with access to the Royal Apartments and many other rooms, as well as the fine gardens, from the end of March to the end of October only, daily 10:30am to 5:30pm. Admission to the castle and gardens is £6 ($9) adults, £3 ($4.50) children, family ticket £16.50 ($25). If you wish to visit the grounds only, the charge is £3 ($4.50) adults, £1.50 ($2.25) children. Buses run between Dundee and Glamis. The 35-minute ride costs £3.70 ($6) one way. *Note:* Buses don't run on Sunday, and they don't stop in front of the castle, which lies 1.5 kilometers (1 mile) from the bus stop.

Where to Stay

Castleton House This Victorian hotel is run with love and care by its owners, Anthony and Sheila Lilly. In cool weather you're greeted by welcoming coal fires in the public lounge; the youthful staff is the most considerate we've encountered in the area. Rooms of various sizes are furnished with reproductions of antiques.

Eassie by Glamis, Forfar, Tayside DD8 1SJ. © **01307/840340.** Fax 01307/840506. www.dundeechamber. co.uk/castleton. 6 units. £110 ($165) double. Children 10 and under stay free in parents' room. Rates include Scottish breakfast. MC, V. Drive 5km (3 miles) west of Glamis on A-94. **Amenities:** 2 restaurants; bar; room service; baby-sitting; laundry/dry cleaning. *In room:* TV, coffeemaker, hair dryer.

C Playing the World's Oldest Course

At **St. Andrew's,** 23 kilometers (14 miles) southeast of Dundee and 82 kilometers (51 miles) northeast of Edinburgh, the rules of golf in Britain and the world were codified and arbitrated. Golf was played for the first time in the 1400s, probably on the site of St. Andrew's Old Course, and enjoyed by Mary, Queen of Scots, here in 1567. All six of St. Andrew's golf courses are open to the public on a more-or-less democratic basis—ballots are polled one day in advance. To participate in the balloting, you first must be staying in St. Andrews for a minimum of 2 days, and you must be able to present a current handicap certificate issued by the governing golf body of your home country. If you meet those requirements, you can enter the ballot in person at the golf course, or by phone at *C* **01334/466666,** before 1:45pm on the day before the one on which you wish to play. At 2pm each day, the balloting is drawn, and the following day's players are announced at 4pm. Bear in mind that your wait to play will most likely be from 4 to 6 days; however, some lucky players get on the course the next day. Players who call the golf course several weeks in advance to make reservations can often circumvent the balloting system, depending on demand.

The **Old Course,** St. Andrews, Golf Place, St. Andrew's, Fife (*C* **01334/466666),** is a 6,000-meter (6,566-yd.) 18-hole course billed as "the Home of Golf." Greens fees are £85 ($128) per round from April to September or £34 ($51) otherwise. A caddy will cost £27 ($41) plus tip. Golf clubs rent for £15 ($23) per round. Electric carts are not allowed, and you can rent a cart only on afternoons from May to September for £3 ($4.50). The course is a par 72.

To reach St. Andrews from Edinburgh, travel along the A90 north to Dunfermline. From there, continue northeast along A910, which becomes A915 at Leven. From Leven, drive northeast on A915 directly to St. Andrews (trip time: 1 hour).

Where to Dine

Strathomore Arms CONTINENTAL/SCOTTISH Try this place near the castle for one of the best lunches in the area. You might begin with freshly made soup of the day or the fresh prawns. Some of the dishes regularly featured might include steak pie or venison. For something a little more exotic there's the Indian chicken breast, marinated in yogurt and spices; and for vegetarians phyllo parcels stuffed with asparagus and cauliflower.

The Square Glamis. *C* 01307/840248. Reservations recommended. Main courses £5.50–£15 ($8–$23). AE, MC, V. Daily noon–2pm and 6:30–9pm.

BRAEMAR

In the heart of some of Grampian's most beautiful scenery, Braemar is not only known for its own castle, but it also makes a good center from which to explore Balmoral Castle (see "Ballater & Balmoral Castle," below). In this Highland village, set against a massive backdrop of hills covered with heather in summer,

Clunie Water joins the River Dee. The massive **Cairn Toul** towers over Braemar, reaching a height of 1,293 meters (4,241 ft.).

ESSENTIALS

GETTING THERE   By Train   Take the train to Aberdeen, then continue the rest of the way by bus. For information and schedules, call © **0345/484950.**

By Bus   Buses run daily from Aberdeen to Braemar at the rate of 6 per day (trip time: 2 hours). One-way fare is £6 ($9). The bus and train stations in Aberdeen are next to each other on Guild Street (© **01224/212266** for information about schedules).

By Car   To reach Braemar from Dundee, return west toward Perth, then head north along A-93, following the signs into Braemar. The 113-kilometer (70-mile) drive will take 70 to 90 minutes.

VISITOR INFORMATION   The year-round **Braemar Tourist Office** is in The Mews, Mar Road (© **013397/42208**). In June, hours are daily from 10am to 6pm; July and August, daily from 9am to 7pm; and September, daily from 10am to 1pm and 2 to 6pm. In off-season, hours are from Monday to Saturday 10am to 1pm and 2 to 5pm, Sunday noon to 5pm.

SPECIAL EVENTS   The spectacular **Royal Highland Gathering** takes place annually in late August or early September in the Princess Royal and Duke of Fife Memorial Park. The queen herself often attends the gathering. These ancient games are thought to have been originated by King Malcolm Canmore, a chieftain who ruled much of Scotland at the time of the Norman conquest of England. He selected his hardiest warriors from all the clans for a "keen and fair contest."

Call the tourist office (see "Visitor Information," above) for more information. Braemar is overrun with visitors during the gathering—anyone thinking of attending would be wise to reserve accommodations anywhere within a 32-kilometer (20-mile) radius of Braemar no later than early April.

WHERE TO STAY & DINE

Braemar Lodge Hotel *(Kids)*   This hotel, popular with skiers who frequent the nearby Glenshee slopes, is set on 1 hectare (2 acres) of grounds at the head of Glen Clunie. Rooms vary in shape and size, but each is comfortable and well equipped, containing well-maintained bathrooms with tubs and showers. Rooms are bright and airy, with soothing color schemes. Two rooms are large enough for families. On cool evenings, you're greeted with log fires. The hotel is on the road to the Glenshee ski slopes near the cottage where Robert Louis Stevenson wrote *Treasure Island.* On the grounds three log cabins have been recently built. Fully equipped with all modern conveniences, they can sleep up to six persons.

6 Glenshee Rd., Braemar AB35 5YQ. © and fax 013397/41627. 7 units. TV. £70 ($105) double; £200–£500 ($300–$750) log cabin. Rates include Scottish breakfast. MC, V. Free parking. Closed Nov. **Amenities:** Restaurant; laundry/dry cleaning. *In room:* TV, hair dryer.

Invercauld Arms Thistle Hotel *(R)*   This is the leading inn of town, with superior amenities and greater comfort than Braemar Lodge. The oldest part of this old granite building dates from the 18th century. In cool weather there's a roaring log fire on the hearth. You can go hill walking and see deer, golden eagles, and other wildlife. Fishing and, in winter, skiing are other pursuits in the nearby area. Rooms are comfortably furnished. Although they lack any style or glamour, they serve their purpose well, but come in a wide range of sizes. In the pub close by, you'll meet the "ghilles" and "stalkers" (hunting and fishing guides).

Braemar AB35 5YR. ℂ 013397/41605. Fax 013397/41428. 68 units. £109 ($164) double. Rates include Scottish breakfast. AE, DC, MC, V. Free parking. Bus: 201. **Amenities:** Restaurant (Scottish/international), bar; room service; baby-sitting; laundry/dry cleaning. *In room:* TV, coffeemaker, hair dryer.

SEEING THE SIGHTS

If you're a royal family watcher, you might be able to spot members of the family, even the queen, at **Crathie Church,** 14 kilometers (9 miles) east of Braemar on A-93 (ℂ 013397/42208), where they attend Sunday services when in residence. Services are at 11:30am; otherwise, the church is open to view from April to October, Monday to Saturday 9:30am to 5:30pm and Sunday 2 to 5:30pm.

Nature lovers may want to drive to the **Linn of Dee,** 10 kilometers (6 miles) west of Braemar, a narrow chasm on the River Dee, which is a local beauty spot. Other beauty spots include Glen Muick, Loch Muick, and Lochnagar. A **Scottish Wildlife Trust Visitor Centre,** reached by a minor road, is located in this Highland glen, off the South Deeside road. An access road joins B-976 at a point 26 kilometers (16 miles) east of Braemar. The tourist office (see above) will give you a map pinpointing these beauty spots.

Braemar Castle 𝒢 This romantic 17th-century castle is a fully furnished private residence with architectural grace, scenic charm, and historical interest. The castle has barrel-vaulted ceilings and an underground prison and is known for its remarkable star-shaped defensive curtain wall.

On the Aberdeen-Ballater-Perth Rd. (A-93). ℂ 013397/41219. Admission £3 ($4.50) adults, £2.50 ($3.75) seniors and students, £1 ($1.50) ages 5–15; free for age 4 and under. Mon after Easter to Oct, Sat–Thurs 10am–6pm. Closed Nov–Easter. Take A93 0.8km (½ mile) northeast of Braemar.

PLAYING GOLF

Braemar Golf Course, at Braemar (ℂ 013397/41618), is the highest golf course in the country. The green of the second hole is 380 meters (1,250 ft.) above sea level—this is the trickiest hole on the course. Pro golf commentator Peter Alliss has deemed it "the hardest par 4 in all of Scotland." Set on a plateau, the hole is bordered on the right by the River Clunie and lined on the left by rough. Greens fees are as follows: from Monday to Friday £15 ($23) for 18 holes and £18 ($27) for a day ticket; Saturday and Sunday £15 ($23) for 18 holes and £23 ($35) for a day ticket. Pull carts can be rented for £2 ($3.40) per day and sets of clubs can be borrowed for £5 ($8) per day. The only dress code is "be reasonable." The course is open only from April to October daily (call in advance as hours can vary).

BALLATER & BALMORAL CASTLE 𝒢𝒢

Ballater is a vacation resort center on the Dee River, with the Grampian Mountains in the background. The town still centers around its Station Square, where the royal family used to be photographed as they arrived to spend vacations. The railway is now closed.

ESSENTIALS

GETTING THERE   By Train   Go to Aberdeen and continue the rest of the way by connecting bus. For rail schedules and information, call ℂ **0345/484950.**

By Bus   Buses run hourly from Aberdeen to Ballater. The bus and train stations in Aberdeen are next to each other on Guild Street (ℂ **01224/212266** for information). Bus 201 from Braemar runs to Ballater (trip time: 1¼ hours). The fare is £3 ($4.50).

By Car From Braemar, go east along A-93.

VISITOR INFORMATION The **tourist information office** is at Station Square (© **013397/55306**). Hours are July and August, daily from 10am to 1pm and 2 to 6pm; September and October and May and June, from Monday to Saturday 10am to 1pm and 2 to 5pm, Sunday 1 to 5pm. Closed November through April.

WHERE TO STAY
Hilton Craigendarroch Hotel ⚡ This hotel, built in the Scottish baronial style, is set amid old trees on a 13-hectare (28-acre) estate. Modern comforts have been added, but the owners have tried to maintain a 19th-century aura. The public rooms include a regal oaken staircase and a large sitting room. The fair-size rooms open onto views of the village of Ballater and the River Dee. Each is furnished in individual style, with private bathrooms (showers only). Public facilities are luxurious, especially the study with oak paneling, a log fire, and book-lined shelves.

Braemar Rd., Ballater AB35 5XA. © **013397/55858**. Fax 013397/55447. www.hilton.com. 45 units. £169 ($254) double; £244 ($366) suite. Rates include Scottish breakfast. Half board £15 ($23) extra per person. AE, DC, MC, V. **Amenities:** 2 restaurants, bar; tennis courts; solarium; salon; 24-hour room service; baby-sitting; laundry/dry cleaning. *In room:* TV, fridge, hair dryer, trouser press.

Monaltrie Hotel *Kids* This 1835 hotel, the first in the region, is built of Aberdeen granite to accommodate the clients of a now-defunct spa. Today it bustles with a clientele who come for the live music in its pub and for the savory food served, the most unusual of which is a Thai cuisine. Each of the fair-size rooms has comfortable beds along with neatly maintained bathrooms with shower stalls. The hotel lies a 3-minute walk east of the center of town.

5 Bridge Sq., Ballater AB35 5QJ. © **013397/55417**. Fax 013397/55180. www.andersonhotel.com. 24 units. £60–£70 ($90–$105) double. Rates include Scottish breakfast. AE, DC, MC, V. Free parking. **Amenities:** 2 restaurants, bar; children's play area. *In room:* TV, radio, coffeemaker, hair dryer.

WHERE TO DINE
Green Inn SCOTTISH In the heart of town, what was once a temperance hotel is now one of the finest dining rooms in town, especially for traditional Scottish dishes. The chef places emphasis on local produce, including home-grown vegetables when available. In season, loin of venison is served with a bramble sauce, and you can always count on fresh salmon and the best of Angus beef. Three very simply furnished double rooms are rented here, all with private bathrooms (with showers) and TV. Half board costs £55 ($83) per person.

9 Victoria Rd., Ballater AB35 5QQ. © and fax **013397/55701**. Reservations required. Fixed-price menu £25 ($38) for 2 courses, £29.50 ($44) for 3 courses. AE, DC, MC, V. Mar–Oct daily 7–9pm; Nov–Feb Tues–Sat 7–9pm.

Oaks Restaurant BRITISH The most glamorous restaurant in the region, the Oaks is in the century-old mansion that was originally built by the "marmalade kings" of Britain, the Keiller family. (The company's marmalade is still a household word throughout the United Kingdom.) This is the most upscale of the three restaurants in a resort complex that includes hotel rooms, time-share villas, and access to a nearby golf course. To start, try the venison and duck terrine flavored with orange and brandy and served with a warm black conch vinaigrette. Other main courses include roast rack of lamb, breast of Grampian chicken, loin of venison, or filet of Aberdeen Angus beef.

In the Hilton Craigendarroch Hotel, Braemar Rd. ℂ 013397/55858. Reservations strongly recommended. Fixed-price 4-course dinner £29 ($44). AE, DC, MC, V. Daily 7–10:30pm.

THE CASTLE

Balmoral Castle   "This dear paradise" is how Queen Victoria described Balmoral Castle, rebuilt in the Scottish baronial style by her "beloved" Albert and completed in 1855. Today Balmoral, 13 kilometers (8 miles) west of Ballater, is still a private residence of the British sovereign, and its principal feature is a 30-meter (100-ft.) tower. On the grounds are many memorials to the royal family. In addition to the gardens there're country walks, pony trekking, souvenir shops, and a refreshment room. Of the actual castle, only the ballroom is open to the public; it houses an exhibition of pictures, porcelain, and works of art.

Balmoral, Ballater. ℂ 013397/42334. Admission £4 ($6) adults, £3 ($4.50) seniors, £1 ($1.50) for children 5–16, free 4 and under. Apr 10–May 3, Mon–Sat 10am–5pm; June 1–Aug 2, daily 10am–5pm. Closed Aug 3–Apr 9. Crathie bus from Aberdeen to the Crathie station; Balmoral Castle is signposted from there (a short walk).

PLAYING GOLF

Ballater Golf Club, at Ballater (ℂ 013397/55567), is one of the more scenic courses in the area. Set in a bowl of mountains and situated on the banks of the River Dee, this is a 5,155-meter (5,638-yd), par-67 course. Greens fees are as follows: from Monday through Friday, £19 ($29) for 18 holes or £28 ($42) for a day ticket; Saturday and Sunday, £22 ($33) for 18 holes or £32 ($48) for a day ticket. There're no electric carts for hire; pull-carts rent for £2 ($3) per day. Dress should be smart but casual. The course is open daily from April to September 7:30am to sunset. From October to March hours are daily 9am to sunset but only if the weather permits.

ABERDEEN✫ & THE CASTLE COUNTRY✫✫

The city of **Aberdeen,** Scotland's "third city," is bordered by fine sandy beaches (if you're a polar bear) and is one of the largest fishing ports in the country. However, far more interesting to visitors with limited time is the array of 40 inhabited castles on the city's periphery, which has earned the area the title of "castle country." Since time is limited for most motorists, we've spotlighted only the most intriguing.

ESSENTIALS

GETTING THERE   By Train   Scotrail runs trains from Edinburgh to Aberdeen at the rate of nine per day from Monday to Saturday and 10 per day on Sunday, costing £28 ($42) for a one-way ticket. For information, call ℂ 0345/484950.

By Bus   Scottish CityLink (ℂ 08705/505050) arrives in Aberdeen from Edinburgh at the rate of at least one bus per hour during the day, costing £14.50 ($22) one-way.

WHERE TO STAY

Mannofield Hotel   Built of silver granite around 1880, this hotel is a Victorian fantasy, with step gables, turrets, spires, bay windows, and a sweeping mahogany-and-teakwood staircase. Owners Bruce and Dorothy Cryle offer a warm Scottish welcome. The nicely sized rooms, refurbished in 1998, are equipped with well-maintained shower-only bathrooms.

447 Great Western Rd., Aberdeen AB10 6NL. © **01224/315-888.** Fax 01224/208-971. 9 units. £64 ($96) double. Rates include Scottish breakfast. AE, DC, MC, V. Free parking. Bus: 18 or 24. **Amenities:** Restaurant; lounge area; room service; baby-sitting; laundry/dry cleaning. *In room:* TV, coffeemaker, hair dryer.

Marcliffe at Pitfodels ✿✿✿   It's the best in Aberdeen, dwarfing the competition. On Aberdeen's western edge, this traditional manor house was built around a courtyard and stands on 26 hectares (8 acres) of landscaped grounds. The spacious rooms are furnished in Chippendale and reproduction pieces. We liked the big mirrored closets and the green marble bathrooms. Even though less expensive, many patrons prefer the ground floor rooms which open onto patios.

N. Deeside Rd., Aberdeen AB1 9YA. © **01224/861-000.** Fax 01224/868-860. www.marcliffe.com. 42 units. £165–£185 ($248–$278) double. AE, DC, MC, V. Free parking. Drive about a mile off A90 at the Aberdeen ring road, A93. **Amenities:** 2 restaurants; lounge area; room service laundry/dry cleaning. *In room:* TV, minibar, hair dryer, iron/ironing board.

WHERE TO DINE
Elrond's Cafe Bar INTERNATIONAL   White marble floors, a long oak-capped bar, evening candlelight, and a garden-inspired decor create the ambience. No one will mind if you show up just for a drink, a pot of tea, a midday salad or snack, or a full-blown feast. Specialties are burgers, steaks, pastas, fresh fish, lemon chicken supreme, chicken Kiev, and vegetarian dishes. This isn't the world's greatest food, but it's popular nevertheless. Though it's in one of Aberdeen's well-known hotels, the restaurant has a separate entrance onto Union Terrace.

In the Caledonian Thistle Hotel, 10–14 Union Terrace. © **01224/640-233.** Main courses £5.95–£12.50 ($9–$19); pot of tea with pastry £2 ($3). AE, DC, MC, V. Mon–Sat 10am–midnight; Sun 10am–11pm. Bus: 16 or 17.

Ferryhill House INTERNATIONAL   In its own park and garden on Aberdeen's southern outskirts, Ferryhill House dates back 250 years. It was built by the region's most successful brick maker/quarry master. It has Georgian detailing, but recent refurbishment has removed many of the original panels and all the ceiling beams. The restaurant boasts one of the region's largest collections of single-malt whiskies—more than 140 brands. There's a fireplace for chilly afternoons and a beer garden for midsummer, as well as a conservatory. Food items include steak or vegetable tempura, chicken dishes like chicken fajita, fried haddock filet, pastas, and chili. Ferryhill House also rents nine standard rooms, with TVs and hair dryers. Breakfast included, the double rate is £79 ($119) from Sunday to Thursday and £50 ($75) Friday and Saturday.

Bon Accord St., Aberdeen AB11 6UA. © **01224/590-867.** Fax 01224/586-947. Reservations recommended Sat–Sun. Main courses £6–£12 ($9–$18). AE, DC, MC, V. Free parking. Bus: 16.

SEEING THE CASTLES
Castle Fraser ✿   One of the most impressive of the fortresslike castles of Mar, Castle Fraser stands in a 12-hectare (25-acre) parkland setting. The sixth laird, Michael Fraser, began the structure in 1575, and his son finished it in 1636. Its Great Hall is spectacular, and you can wander around the grounds, which include an 18th-century walled garden.

Sauchen, Inverurie. © **01330/833463.** Admission £5 ($8) adults, £3.50 ($5) seniors, £1.30 ($1.95) children, free for age 4 and under. Easter weekend and Oct, Sat–Sun 2–4:45pm; May–June, daily 1:30–5pm; July–Aug, daily 11am–4:45pm; Sept, daily 1:30–5:30pm. Closed Nov–Mar. Head 5km (3 miles) south of Kemnay, 26km (16 miles) west of Aberdeen, off A944.

Kildrummy Castle ⚔ This is the most extensive example of a 13th-century castle in Scotland. Once the ancient seat of the earls of Mar, you can still see the four round towers, the hall, and the chapel from the original structure. The great gatehouse and other remains date from the 16th century. The castle played a major role in Scottish history up to 1715, when it was dismantled.

Hwy. A-97, Kildrummy. ✆ 019755/71331. Admission £2 ($3) adults, £1.50 ($2.25) seniors, 75p ($1.15) children. Easter–Sept daily 9:30am–6:30pm; Oct–Nov daily 9:30am–4pm. Closed Oct–Easter. Take A-97 for 56km (35 miles) west of Aberdeen; it's signposted off A-97, 16km (10 miles) west of Alford.

Fyvie Castle ⚔ The National Trust for Scotland opened this castle to the public in 1986. The oldest part, dating from the 13th century, is the grandest existing example of Scottish baronial architecture. There're five towers, named after Fyvie's five families—the Prestons, Melddrums, Setons, Gordons, and Leiths—who lived here over 5 centuries. Originally built in a royal hunting forest, Fyvie means "deer hill" in Gaelic. The interior, created by the first Lord Leith of Fyvie, a steel magnate, reflects the opulence of the Edwardian era. His collections contain arms and armor, 16th-century tapestries, and important artworks by Raeburn, Gainsborough, and Romney. The castle is rich in ghosts, curses, and legends.

Turriff, on the Aberdeen-Banff road. ✆ 01651/891266. Admission £4.40 ($7) adults, £2.90 ($4.35) seniors and children. Easter–June and Sept daily 1:30–4:45pm; July–Aug daily 11am–4:45pm; Oct Sat–Sun 1:30–4:45pm. Closed Nov–Mar. Take A947 for 37km (23 miles) northwest of Aberdeen.

Craigievar Castle ⚔ Structurally unchanged since its completion in 1626, Craigievar Castle is an exceptional tower house where Scottish baronial architecture reached its pinnacle of achievement. It has contemporary plaster ceilings in nearly all its rooms. The castle had been continuously lived in by the descendants of the builder, William Forbes, until it came under the care of the National Trust for Scotland in 1963. The family collection of furnishings is complete. Some 6 kilometers (4 miles) south of the castle, clearly signposted on a small road leading off A980, near Lumphanan, is **Macbeth's Cairn,** where the historical Macbeth is supposed to have fought his last battle. Built of timber in a rounded format known by historians as "motte and bailey," it's now nothing more than a steep-sided rounded hillock marked with a sign and a flag.

Hwy. A980, 10km (6 miles) south of Alford. ✆ 013398/83635. Admission £6 ($9) adults, £4 ($6) seniors/children. Castle May–Sept daily 1:30–4:45pm. Grounds year-round daily 9:30am–sunset. Head west on A96 to Alford, then south on A980.

SPEYSIDE ⚔ & THE MALT WHISKY TRAIL ⚔

Much of the Speyside region covered in this section is in the Moray district, on the southern shore of the Moray Firth, a great inlet cutting into the northeastern coast of Scotland. The district stretches in a triangular shape south from the coast to the wild heart of the Cairngorm Mountains near Aviemore. It's a land steeped in history, as its many castles, battle sites, and ancient monuments testify. It's also a good place to fish and, of course, play golf. Golfers can purchase a 5-day ticket from tourist information centers that will allow them to play at more than 11 courses in the area.

One of the best of these courses is **Boat of Garten,** Speyside (✆ 01479/831282). Relatively difficult, the almost 5,500-meter (6,000-yd.) course is dotted with many bunkers and wooded areas. April to October, greens fees are £23 ($35) Monday to Friday and hours are 7:30am to 11pm. Saturday greens fees are £28 ($42), and hours are 10am to 4pm. In winter, call to see if the course is open. Greens fees are then reduced to £12 ($18). Pull-carts can be rented for

£2 ($3.40) and electric carts are available for £5 ($8). Dress reasonably; blue jeans are not acceptable.

The valley of the second-largest river in Scotland, the Spey, lies north and south of Aviemore. It's a land of great natural beauty. The Spey is born in the Highlands above Loch Laggan, which lies 64 kilometers (40 miles) south of Inverness. Little more than a creek at its inception, it gains in force, fed by the many "burns" that drain water from the surrounding hills. It's one of Scotland's great rivers for salmon fishing, and it runs between the towering Cairngorms on the east and the Monadhliath Mountains on the west. Its major center is Grantown-on-Spey.

The major tourist attraction in the area is the **Malt Whisky Trail,** 113 kilometers (70 miles) long, running through the glens of Speyside. Here distilleries, many of which can be visited, are known for their production of *uisge beatha* or "water of life." "Whisky" is its more familiar name.

Half the malt distilleries in the country lie along the River Spey and its tributaries. Here peat smoke and Highland water are used to turn out single-malt (unblended) whisky. There're five malt distilleries in the area: **Glenlivet, Glenfiddich, Glenfarclas, Strathisla,** and **Tamdhu.** Allow about an hour each to visit them.

The best way to reach Speyside from Aberdeen is to take A-96 northwest, signposted Elgin. If you're traveling north on the A-9 road from Perth and Pitlochry, your first stop might be at Dalwhinnie, which has the highest whisky distillery in the world at 575 meters (1,888 ft.). It's not in the Spey Valley but is at the northeastern end of Loch Ericht, with views of lochs and forests.

KEITH

Keith, 18 kilometers (11 miles) northwest of Huntly, grew up because of its strategic location, where the main road and rail routes between Inverness and Aberdeen cross the River Isla. It has an ancient history, but owes its present look to the "town planning" of the late 18th and early 19th centuries. Today it's a major stopover along the Malt Whisky Trail.

The oldest operating distillery in the Scottish Highlands, the **Strathisla Distillery,** on Seafield Avenue (© **01542/783044**), was established in 1786. Hours are from February to mid-March, Monday to Friday 9:30am to 4pm; mid-March to November 30, Monday to Saturday 9:30am to 4pm, Sunday 12:30 to 4pm; closed December and January. Admission is £4 ($7) adults, free for ages 8 to 18, children under 8 not admitted. The admission fee includes a £2 ($3) voucher redeemable in the distillery shop against a 70cl bottle of whisky. Be warned that tours of this distillery are self-guided.

Where to Stay

Grange House 🏵 This dignified-looking stone house dates from 1815 when it was the manse (home of a minister) for the nearby Church of Scotland, which is still the most prominent building in this tiny hamlet. Doreen Blanche, assisted by her husband Bill, rents two well-decorated and comfortable rooms within her private home. The venue is upscale, charming, and comfortable, with a calm and quiet that's enhanced by the 4 hectares (8 acres) of park and garden that surround this isolated place. Ask the owners to point out the late Victorian addition here, completed in 1898, that greatly enlarged the size of the original house. Smoking is not permitted inside.

Grange, near Keith AB55 6RY. © and fax **01542/870206.** www.aboutscotland.com/banff/grangehouse.html. 2 units. £50–£55 ($75–$53) double. Rate includes breakfast. No credit cards. From Keith, drive 5km (3 miles) east of town, following the signs to Banff, into the hamlet of Grange. **Amenities:** Dining area; baby-sitting; laundry/dry cleaning. *In room:* coffeemaker, hair dryer.

DUFFTOWN

James Duff, the fourth earl of Fife, founded this town in 1817. The four main streets of town converge at the battlemented **clock tower,** which is also the tourist information center. A center of the whisky-distilling industry, Dufftown is surrounded by seven malt distilleries. The family-owned **Glenfiddich Distillery** is on A-941, just north of Dufftown (© **01340/820373**). It's open from Monday to Friday 9:30am to 4:30pm; from Easter to mid-October it's also open on Saturday 9:30am to 4:30pm and on Sunday noon to 4:30pm. Guides in kilts show visitors around the plant and explain the process of distilling. A film of the history of distilling is also shown. At the finish of the tour, you're given a dram of malt whisky to sample. The tour is free, but there's a souvenir shop where the owners hope you'll spend a few pounds.

Other sights include **Balvenie Castle,** along A-941 (© **01340/820121**), the ruins of a moated stronghold from the 14th century on the south side of the Glenfiddich Distillery. During her northern campaign against the earl of Huntly, Mary, Queen of Scots spent 2 nights here. It's open from April to September, daily 9:30am to 6:30pm. Admission is £1.50 ($2.25) adults, £1.10 ($1.65) seniors, and 50p (75¢) children under 16.

Mortlach Parish Church in Dufftown is one of the oldest places of Christian worship in the country. It's reputed to have been founded in 566 by St. Moluag. A Pictish cross stands in the graveyard. The present church was reconstructed in 1931 and incorporates portions of an older building.

Where to Dine
Taste of Speyside 🍴 SCOTTISH   True to its name, this restaurant in the town center, just off the main square, avidly promotes a Speyside cuisine as well as malt whiskies, and in the bar you can buy the product of each of Speyside's 46 distilleries. A platter including a slice of smoked salmon, smoked venison, smoked trout, pâté flavored with malt whisky, locally made cheese (cow or goat), salads, and homemade oat cakes is offered at noon and at night. Nourishing soup is made fresh daily and is served with homemade bread. There's also a choice of meat pies, including venison with red wine and herbs or rabbit. For dessert, try Scotch Mist, which contains fresh cream, malt whisky, and crumbled meringue.

10 Balvenie St. © **01340/820860.** Reservations recommended in the evening. Main courses £9.50–£12.50 ($14–$19); Speyside platter £10 ($15) at lunch, £13 ($20) at dinner. MC, V. Mon–Sat noon–9pm. Closed Nov–Feb.

ROTHES

A Speyside town with five distilleries, Rothes is just to the south of the Glen of Rothes, 100 kilometers (62 miles) northwest of Aberdeen. Founded in 1766, the town lies between Ben Aigan and Conerock Hill. The original settlement grew up around **Rothes Castle,** ancient stronghold of the Leslie family, who lived here until 1622. Only a single massive wall of the castle remains.

Among the several distilleries launched by the Grant family is the **Glen Grant Distillery** (© **01542/783318**), opened in the mid-19th century. It's located right outside town (signposted from the center). Admission is £2.50 ($3.75) adults, free for children ages 8 to 18, children under 8 not allowed. The visit includes a tour of both the gardens and distillery, a taste of whisky, plus a £2 ($3) voucher applied against one of the large bottles of whisky on sale here. Hours are from March to November Monday to Saturday 9:30am to 4pm, Sunday 12:30pm to 4pm.

GRANTOWN-ON-SPEY

This vacation resort, with its gray granite buildings, is 55 kilometers (34 miles) southeast of Inverness, in a wooded valley from which it commands views of the Cairngorm Mountains. It's a key center of winter sports in Scotland. Fishers are also attracted to this setting, because the Spey is renowned for its salmon. One of Scotland's many 18th-century planned towns, it was founded on a heather-covered moor in 1765 by Sir James Grant of Grant and became the seat of that ancient family. The town was famous in the 19th century as a Highland tourist center.

From a base here, you can explore the valleys of the Don and Dee, the Cairngorms, and Culloden Moor, scene of the historic battle in 1746, when Bonnie Prince Charlie and his army were defeated.

A year-round **tourist information office** is on High Street (© **01479/ 872773**). Hours from April to October are daily 9am to 7pm, Sunday 10am to 5pm; from November to March, Monday to Friday 9am to 5pm, Saturday 10am to 5pm.

Where to Stay

Garth Hotel   The elegant, comfortable Garth stands on 2 hectares (4 acres) of ground beside the town square. Guests enjoy the use of a spacious upstairs lounge, whose high ceilings, wood-burning stove, and vine-covered veranda make it an attractive place for morning coffee or afternoon tea. The comfortable and handsomely furnished rooms have all the necessary amenities. Extensive and selective meals with a French slant favor "Taste of Scotland" dishes, with emphasis on fresh local produce.

The Square, Castle Rd., Grantown-on-Spey, Morayshire PH26 3HN. © **01479/872836**. Fax 01479/872116. 17 units. £59–£69 ($89–$104) double. Rates include Scottish breakfast. MC, V. Free parking. **Amenities:** Restaurant, bar; room service; laundry/dry cleaning. *In room:* TV, coffeemaker, hair dryer.

Tulchan Lodge ⭐⭐   Built in 1906 to serve as the 10,800-hectare (23,000-acre) Tulchan Estate's fishing and shooting lodge, this is a place for both sports-oriented visitors and travelers who want to experience a place designed with the elegance required by Edward VII, who came here for sports. The lodge has panoramic views of the Spey Valley, and each room is different in size and furnishings. In the two elegant dining rooms, Scottish and international dishes are served, with only full board residents accepted.

Advie, Grantown-on-Spey PH26 3PW. © **01807/510200**. Fax 01807/510234. www.tulchan.com. 13 units. £350–£500 ($525–$750) double. Rates include full board. MC, V. Closed Feb–Mar. Drive 14km (9 miles) northeast of Grantown on B-9102. **Amenities:** 2 dining areas; lounge; tennis court; shooting; room service; babysitting; laundry/dry cleaning. *In room:* hair dryer.

Where to Dine

Craggan Mill BRITISH/ITALIAN   This licensed restaurant and lounge bar, a 10-minute walk south of the town center, is housed in a restored ruined granite mill whose waterwheel is still visible. The owners offer British or Italian cuisine at attractive prices. Main courses might be breast of chicken with cream or chicken cacciatore, followed by a dessert of rum-raisin ice cream or peach Melba. You've probably had better versions of all the dishes offered here, but what you get isn't bad. A good selection of Italian wines is also offered.

Spotting Nessie

Sir Peter Scott's *Nessitera rhombopteryx* continues to elude her pursuers. "Nessie," as she's more familiarly known, has captured the imagination of the world, drawing thousands of visitors yearly to Loch Ness. The Loch Ness monster has been described as one of the world's greatest mysteries. Half a century ago A82 was built alongside the banks of the loch's western shores. Since that time many more sightings have been recorded.

All types of high-tech underwater contraptions have searched for the Loch Ness monster, but no one can find her. Dr. Robert Rines and his associates at the Academy of Applied Science in Massachusetts maintain a year-round watch with sonar-triggered cameras and strobe lights suspended from a raft in Urquhart Bay.

The loch is 39 kilometers (24 miles) long, 1.5 kilometers (1 mile) wide, and some 230 meters (755 feet) deep. Even if the monster doesn't put in an appearance, you can enjoy the loch seascape. In summer, you can take boat cruises across Loch Ness from both Fort Augustus and Inverness.

Buses from either Fort Augustus or Inverness traverse A82, taking you to Drumnadrochit. Call ✆ **0990/808080** for schedules and more information. The bucolic hamlet of Drumnadrochit lies a mile from Loch Ness at the entrance to Glen Urquhart. It's the nearest village to the part of the loch from which sightings of the monster have been reported most frequently.

From Grantown-on-Spey, take A938 west until you merge with northwest-bound E15/A9, which leads to Inverness, on the north tip of Loch Ness. From Inverness, travel on the A82 south, which runs the length of the western shoreline. The eastern shoreline can be traveled by following signposted rural roads from Inverness.

Hwy. A-95 1km (³/₄ mile) south of Grantown-on-Spey. ✆ 01479/872288. Reservations recommended. Main courses £3.95–£12.50 ($6–$19). MC, V. May–Sept daily noon–2pm and 6–10pm; Oct–Apr Tues–Sun 7–10pm. Closed the first 2 weeks in Nov.

GLENLIVET

As you leave Grantown-on-Spey and head east along A-95, drive to the junction with B-9008; go south and you won't miss the **Glenlivet Distillery.** The location of the **Glenlivet Reception Centre** (✆ 01542/783220) is 16 kilometers (10 miles) north of the nearest town, Tomintoul. Near the River Livet, a Spey tributary, this distillery is one of the most famous in Scotland. It's open from mid-March to October Monday to Saturday 10am to 4pm, and Sunday 12:30 to 4pm. from July and August, it's open Monday to Saturday 10am to 6pm and Sunday 12:30pm to 6pm. The £2.50 ($3.75) admission fee for visitors over 18 includes a £2 ($3) voucher off the purchase of a bottle of whisky.

Back on A-95, you can visit the **Glenfarclas Distillery** at Ballindalloch (✆ 01807/500245), one of the few malt whisky distilleries that's still independent of the giants. Founded in 1836, Glenfarclas is managed by the fifth generation of the Grant family. It's open year-round, Monday to Friday 9am to

5pm; June to September, it's also open Saturday 10am to 4pm and Sunday 12:30 to 4:30pm. There's a small craft shop, and each visitor is offered a dram of Glenfarclas Malt Whisky. The admission of £2.50 ($3.75) is for visitors over 18 and there's a discount of £7 ($11) on any purchase of £10 ($15) or more.

Where to Stay

Minmore House Hotel 🏨   Standing on 2 hectares (5 acres) of private grounds adjacent to the Glenlivet Distillery, this is an impressive country house. It was the home of the distillery owners before becoming a hotel. The drawing room opens onto views of the plush Ladder Hills. Well-furnished rooms have vital amenities, and the oak-paneled lounge bar has an open log fire on chilly nights.

Glenlivet, Ballindalloch AB37 9DB. (© **01807/590378.** Fax 01807/590472. www.smoothhound.co.uk/hotels/minmore.html. 10 units. £150–£160 ($225–$240) double. Rates include breakfast, afternoon tea, and 4-course dinner. MC, V. Closed mid-Oct to mid-Apr. **Amenities:** Dining room, bar; pool. *In room:* coffeemaker, hair dryer.

KINCRAIG *Kids*

Kincraig enjoys a scenic spot at the northern end of Loch Insh, overlooking the Spey Valley to the west and the Cairngorm Mountains to the east. Near Kincraig, the most notable sight is the **Highland Wildlife Park** 🏨 (© **01540/651270**), a natural area of parkland with a collection of wildlife, some of which is extinct elsewhere in Scotland. Herds of European bison, red deer, shaggy Highland cattle, wild horses, St. Kilda Soay sheep, and roe deer range the park. In enclosures are wolves, polecats, wildcats, beavers, badgers, and pine martens. Protected birds to see are golden eagles and several species of grouse—of special interest is the capercaillie ("horse of the woods"), a large Eurasian grouse native to Scotland's pine forests. There's a visitor center with a gift shop, cafe, and exhibition areas. Ample parking and a picnic site are also available.

You need a car to go through the park; walkers are discouraged and are picked up by park rangers. The park is open daily at 10am. April and October, the last entrance is at 4pm, except during July and August, when the last entrance is at 5pm. November to March, the last entrance is at 2pm. All people and vehicles are expected to vacate the park within 2 hours of the day's last admission. Admission to the park is £6.50 ($10) adults, £5.40 ($8) seniors, and £4.35 ($7) children. A family ticket costs £21.70 ($33).

KINGUSSIE

Your next stop along the Spey might be at the little summer vacation resort and winter ski center of Kingussie (it's pronounced King-*you*-see), just off A-9, the capital of Badenoch, a district known as "the drowned land" because the Spey can flood the valley when the snows of a severe winter melt in the spring.

Kingussie, 188 kilometers (117 miles) northwest of Edinburgh, 66 kilometers (41 miles) south of Inverness, and 18 kilometers (11 miles) southwest of Aviemore, practically adjoins Newtonmore (see below), directly northeast along A-86.

Highland Folk Museum 🏨, Duke St. (© **01540/661307**), is the first folk museum established in Scotland (1934), and its collections are based on the life of the Highlanders. You'll see domestic, agricultural, and industrial items. Open-air exhibits are a turf kailyard (kitchen garden), a Lewis "black house," and old vehicles and carts. Traditional events such as spinning, music making, and handcraft fairs are held throughout the summer. Admission is £5 ($8) adults,

£3 ($4.50) children and seniors, £15 ($23) family ticket. Hours are from April to October Monday to Friday 10:30am to 4pm, Saturday and Sunday 1 to 4pm.

A summer-only **tourist center** is on King Street (© **01540/661297**). It's open only from May 22 to September 22, Monday to Saturday 10am to 1pm and 2 to 6pm, and on Sunday 10am to 1pm and 2 to 5pm.

Where to Stay

Homewood Lodge ⭐ *Kids*   One of the best B&Bs in the area, this small Highland house offers large, simply furnished rooms for either two travelers or families. In a garden and woodland setting, the house has a sitting room with an open fire. Good traditional local fare is served in the evening (reservations recommended). Summer barbecues are also offered, and children are welcome.

Newtonmore Rd., Kingussie PH21 1HD. © **01540/661507**. www.bigfoot.com/tildahomeward-lodge. 4 units. £40 ($60) double. Rates include Scottish breakfast. No credit cards. Free parking. **Amenities:** Dining area; laundry/dry cleaning. *In room:* TV, radio, coffeemaker, hair dryer.

Osprey Hotel   This 1895 Victorian structure, 275 meters (300 yd.) from the rail station, is a convenient place to stay, with comfortable although very plain rooms, all with hot and cold running water, central heating, electric blankets, and electric fires. The hotel has a residents' lounge, and TV lounge. The place is known for its pure, fresh, 100% homemade food. Prime Scottish meats are served; in summer, salmon and trout from local rivers are offered either fresh or peat-smoked.

Ruthven Rd. (at High St.), Kingussie PH21 1EN. © and fax **01540/661510**. www.ospreyhotel.freeserve. co.uk. 8 units. £85–£98 ($128–$147) double. Rates include half board. AE, DC, MC, V. Free parking. **Amenities:** Restaurant, bar; baby-sitting. *In room:* TV, coffeemaker, hair dryer.

Where to Dine

The Cross ⭐⭐ SCOTTISH   This chic restaurant comes as a surprise: In an out-of-the-way setting in a remote Highland village, it serves superlative meals that involve theater as much as fine food. The restaurant has an open-beam ceiling and French doors leading out onto a terrace over the water's edge where alfresco dinners are served. Specialties might include venison Francatelli, wild pigeon with grapes, or Highland lamb with sorrel.

Nine rooms are rented in a new building. Each room is different in size and style—for example, two rooms have canopied beds, and another has a balcony overlooking the mill pond. Doubles, including half board, cost from £190 ($285). Personal service and attention to detail go into the running of this place, operated by Ruth and Tony Hadley, and Ruth's cooking has put it on the gastronomic map of Scotland.

Tweed Mill Brae, off the Ardbroilach road, Kingussie PH21 1TC. © **01540/661166**. Fax 01540/661080. Reservations recommended. Fixed-price 5-course dinner £37.50 ($56). MC, V. Wed–Mon 7–9pm. Closed Dec–Feb.

NEWTONMORE

This Highland resort in Speyside is a good center for the Grampian and Monadhliath mountains, and it offers excellent fishing, golf, pony trekking, and hill walking. A track from the village climbs past the Calder River to Loch Dubh and the massive 940-meter (3,087-ft.) **Carn Ban,** where eagles fly. **Castle Cluny,** ancient seat of the MacPherson chiefs, is 10 kilometers (6 miles) west of Newtonmore.

You may want to stop and have a look at **Clan Macpherson House & Museum,** Main Street (© **01540/673332**). Displayed are clan relics and memorials, including the Black Chanter and Green Banner as well as a "charmed sword," and the broken fiddle of the freebooter, James MacPherson—a Scottish Robin Hood. Relics associated with Bonnie Prince Charlie are also here. An annual clan rally is held in August. Admission is free, but donations are accepted. It's open Monday to Saturday 10am to 5pm, Sunday 2:30 to 5pm, from April to October only.

Where to Stay

Pines Hotel   Built in 1903, this somber-looking house sits on a hill overlooking the Spey Valley, and lies just west of the hamlet's center. Your hosts are Colin and Pamela Walker, who charge the bargain price of £25 ($38) for a double if it's taken by one person. All rooms have pleasant views of the Highland countryside and each comes with a small but neat shower-only bathroom. The food is wholesome, straightforward Scottish cuisine, made from fresh ingredients such as salmon, lamb, venison, and Aberdeen Angus beef. Pamela is an expert on desserts and has a particular interest in creating treats for diabetics.

Station Rd., Newtonmore PH20 1AR. ℂ 01540/673271. 5 units. £47–£50 ($71–$75) double. Rates include Scottish breakfast. MC, V. Free parking. Closed Dec 28–Jan 15. **In-room Amenities:** TV, coffeemaker, hair dryer.

16

Spain

by Darwin Porter & Danforth Prince

The fascinating history of Spain is perceptible in towns small and large, but this country of 40 million is no relic mired in the past. Spain today is a vital and exciting place. This land of sun-drenched beaches, terraced vineyards, sleepy villages, and jeweled Moorish palaces is undergoing a remarkable cultural renaissance. Spain's rebirth is tied to both the death of Franco and the nation's 1986 entry into the European Union. Contemporary art, literature, cinema, and fashion are the tools of new and original expression, and cafes and bars hum with animated discussion about politics, society, and Spain's newfound prosperity.

1 Madrid

Landlocked Madrid lies on a windswept and often arid plain, beneath a sky that has been described as Velázquez blue. Certain poets have even labeled Madrid the "gateway to the skies": *de Madrid al cielo.* The city is populated by adopted sons and daughters from virtually every region of Spain, adding to its cosmopolitan gloss. Despite its influence as the cultural beacon of the Spanish-speaking world and its quintessentially Spanish nature, Madrid lacks features that for many bespeak Spain: a beach, an ancient castle or cathedral, an archbishop. Madrileños long ago learned how to compensate: They substituted long strolls through the city's verdant parks and along its *paseos,* and they built an elegant palace and erected countless churches, many with baroque ornamentation and gilt.

Artists and writers gravitate to the newly revitalized Madrid and its fertile artistic climate. This is the city, after all, that is itself a central character in Pedro Almodóvar's films, such as *All About My Mother.* Spaniards—and particularly Madrileños—pursue nightlife with passion; they stay awake till the wee hours and top off the night by congregating, as late as 6am, over hot chocolate and *churros* (fried fingerlike doughnuts). But despite the city's many pleasures, Madrileños recognize that their city is also a place for work, evidenced by the spate of emerging local industries, services, and products.

ESSENTIALS

GETTING THERE   By Plane   Aeropuerto Madrid/Barajas (© 91-305-83-43; www.aena.es), 14 kilometers (9 miles) east of the city center, Madrid's international airport, has two terminals—one international, the other domestic. Air-conditioned yellow airport buses take you from the arrivals terminal to the bus depot under Plaza de Colón, a central point. You can also get off at stops along the way, provided that your baggage isn't stored in the hold. The fare is 385Pts (€2.30, $2.25), and the buses leave every 15 minutes, either to or from the airport. You can also take the Metro to the city center, but this involves at least one change and takes longer than the airport bus.

C Bilbao & the Guggenheim

The world is flocking to Bilbao, that "ugly, gray, decaying smokestack" city, 395 kilometers (246 miles) north of Madrid. The capital of the Basque country, and Spain's sixth largest city, Bilbao is the home of the new $100 million **Guggenheim Museum** *𝕽𝕽𝕽*, designed by American architect Frank Gehry. If this new art mecca is on your Spain or Europe itinerary, here are some details:

The easiest way to get to Bilbao is to fly to the **Aeropuerto de Bilbao** (*C* **94-486-93-00;** www.aena.es), 8 kilometers (5 miles) north of the city. From the airport, yellow bus A-3247 runs into the city center. Flights on Iberia arrive frequently from Barcelona and Madrid, plus other key cities in Spain, as well as from London, Paris, Milan, and Zurich. Two trains arrive daily from both Barcelona (trip time: 11 hours) and Madrid (6 or 7 hours); phone *C* **94-423-86-23** for rail information.

Once in Bilbao, you can pick up information and a city map at the **Bilbao Tourist Office**, Plaza Arriaga (*C* **94-416-00-22**), open from Monday to Friday 9am to 1:30pm and 4 to 7:30pm, Saturday 9am to 2pm, and Sunday 10am to 2pm.

Inaugurated in October 1997, the **Guggenheim Museum**, Muella Abando Ibarrad 2 (*C* **94-423-27-99**), stands at the intersection of the Puente de la Salve bridge and the Nervión River. The museum is devoted to American and European art of the 20th century, including works by Kandinsky, Mondrian, Picasso, Ernst, Pollock, Lichtenstein, Oldenburg, Serra, and others. It's open from Tuesday to Sunday 10am to 8pm.

While in Bilbao, also visit the **Museum de Bellas Artes,** Plaza del Museo 2 (*C* **94-439-60-60**), one of Spain's most important art museums, containing both medieval and modern works, including paintings by Velásquez, Goya, Zurbarán, and El Greco. It's open from Tuesday to Saturday 10am to 8pm, Sunday 10am to 2pm.

Since Bilbao up to now has mainly attracted business travelers, its hotels lack the charm of those found in art cities such as Barcelona and Seville. We consider the **Hotel López de Haro,** Obispo Orueta 2 (*C* **94-423-55-00;** www.hotellopezdeharo.com), the finest in town. Although sterile looking, it has the most efficient staff and polished service. Its major competitor is the also-sterile **Gran Hotel Ercilla,** Ercilla 37–39 (*C* **94-410-20-00**). A good, moderately priced choice is **Hotel Avenida,** Zumalacárregui 40 (*C* **94-412-43-00**). For a bargain, head for **Roquefer,** Lotería 2–4 (*C* **94-415-07-55**).

Basque cuisine is the finest in Spain, featuring *pintxos* (pronounced *peen*-chohz), or tapas. The best place for tapas bars is Calle Licenciado Poza, between Alameda del Doctor Areilza and Calle Iparraguirre. The most enticing bar, however, is **Victor,** Plaza Nueva 2 (*C* **94-415-16-78**), which specializes in seafood tapas. Other favorites include **Atlanta,** Calle Rodríguez 28 (*C* **94-427-64-72**), famous for their prosciutto sandwiches, and **Busterri,** calle Licenciado Poza 43 (*C* **94-441-50-67**), known for their grilled anchovies.

Madrid

**Legend (map):**
- † Church
- ⓘ Information
- Ⓜ Metro
- ⊠ Post Office
- — Railway

If you go into town by taxi, expect to pay 4,000Pts (€24, $23)and up, plus surcharges for the trip to/from the airport and for baggage handling. If you take an unmetered limousine, negotiate the price in advance.

By Train   Madrid has three major railway stations: **Atocha,** Avenida Ciudad de Barcelona (Metro: Atocha RENFE), for trains to Lisbon, Toledo, Andalusia, and Extremadura; **Chamartín,** in the northern suburbs at Augustín de Foxá (Metro: Chamartín), for trains to Barcelona, Asturias, Cantabria, Castilla y León, the Basque country, Aragón, Catalonia, Levante (Valencia), Murcia, and the French border; and **Estación Príncipe Pío** or Norte, Po. del Rey 30 (Metro: Norte), for trains to northwest Spain (Salamanca and Galicia). For information about connections from any of these stations, contact **RENFE,** Spanish State Railways (℡ **90-224-02-02** daily 7am to 11pm; www.renfe.es). For tickets, go to the principal office of RENFE, Alcalá 44 (Metro: Banco de España), open from Monday to Friday 9:30am to 8pm.

By Bus   Madrid has at least eight major bus terminals, including the large **Estación Sur de Autobuses,** Calle Méndez Alvaro (℡ **91-468-42-00;** Metro: Alvaro). Most buses pass through this station.

By Car   The following are the major highways into Madrid, with information on driving distances to the city: Route NI from Irún, 507 kilometers (315 miles); NII from Barcelona, 626 kilometers (389 miles); NIII from Valencia, 349 kilometers (217 miles); NIV from Cádiz, 624 kilometers (388 miles); NV from Badajoz, 409 kilometers (254 miles); and NVI from Galicia, 602 kilometers (374 miles).

VISITOR INFORMATION   Tourist Office   The most convenient **tourist office** is on Calle Duque de Medinad (℡ **91-429-31-77;** www.comadrid.es; Metro: Banco de España); it's open from Monday to Friday 9am to 7pm and Saturday 9:30am to 1pm. Ask for a street map of the next town on your itinerary, especially if you're driving.

Websites   The Tourist Office of Spain (**www.okspain.org**) can help plan your trip with listings of lodging options, attractions, tour operators and packages, and handy tips on getting around. Guilty of almost too much information, **www.cyberspain.com** has the basics on lodging and dining but much more, like background on Spanish traditions like La Tuna and an extensive section on artists such as Goya. On the Web for years, Madrid Man's Yankee Home Page (**www.madridman.com**) hides a surprising amount of info; the museum descriptions, for example, are both long and insightful, with nuts-and-bolts details that surpass most other sources.

CITY LAYOUT   In modern Spain, all roads and rail and phone lines lead to Madrid. The capital has outgrown all previous boundaries and is branching out in all directions.

Every new arrival ought to find the **Gran Vía,** which cuts a winding path across the city beginning at **Plaza de España,** where you'll find one of Europe's tallest skyscrapers, Edificio España. On this principal avenue is the largest concentration of shops, hotels, restaurants, and movie houses. **Calle de Serrano,** in the Salamanca neighborhood, is a runner-up in terms of importance.

South of the avenue lies the **Puerta del Sol.** All road distances in Spain are measured from this square. However, its significance has declined, and today it's prime hunting ground for pickpockets and purse-snatchers. Here **Calle de Alcalá** begins and runs for 4 kilometers (2½ miles).

Plaza Mayor is the heart of Old Madrid, an attraction in itself with its mix of French and Georgian architecture. (Again, be wary, especially late at night.) Pedestrians pass under the arches of the huge square onto the narrow streets of the old town, where you can find some of the capital's most intriguing restaurants and tascas.

The area south of Plaza Mayor—known as **barrios bajos**—merits exploration. The narrow cobblestone streets are lined with 16th- and 17th-century architecture. Directly south of the plaza is the **Arco de Cuchilleros,** a street packed with markets, restaurants, flamenco clubs, and taverns.

Gran Vía ends at Calle de Alcalá, and at this juncture lies **Plaza de la Cibeles,** with its fountain to Cybele, "the mother of the gods," and what has become known as "the cathedral of post offices." From Cibeles, the wide **Paseo de Recoletos** begins a short run to **Plaza de Colón.** From this latter square rolls the serpentine **Paseo de la Castellana,** flanked by expensive shops, apartment buildings, luxury hotels, and foreign embassies.

Back at Cibeles again: Heading south is **Paseo del Prado,** where you'll find Spain's major attraction, the **Museo del Prado,** as well as the **Jardín Botánica** (Botanical Garden). The paseo also leads to the Atocha Station. To the west of the garden lies the **Parque del Retiro,** once reserved for royalty, with restaurants, nightclubs, a rose garden, and two lakes.

GETTING AROUND

Getting around Madrid isn't easy, because everything is spread out. Even many Madrileño taxi drivers, often new arrivals from outside the city or a foreign country, are unfamiliar with their own city once they're off the main boulevards.

ON FOOT   This is the perfect way to see Madrid, especially the narrow streets of the old town. If you're going to another district (and chances are that your hotel will be outside the old town), you can take the bus or Metro. For such a large city, Madrid can be covered amazingly well on foot, because so much of what will interest a visitor lies in various clusters.

BY METRO (SUBWAY)   The Metro (© **91-429-31-77**) is easy to learn and convenient. The central converging point is the Puerta del Sol, and the fare is 135Pts (€0.80, 83¢). The Metro operates daily from 6am to 1:30am; avoid rush hours if possible. You can save money on public transportation by purchasing a 10-trip ticket known as a *bonos*—for the Metro it costs 705Pts (€4.25, $4).

BY BUS   A bus network also services the city and suburbs, with routes clearly shown at each stop on a schematic diagram. Buses are fast and efficient because they travel along special lanes. Both red and yellow buses charge 130Pts (€0.83, 75¢). For 705Pts (€4.25, $4) you can purchase a 10-trip ticket (but without transfers) for Madrid's bus system. It's sold at **Empresa Municipal de Transportes,** Plaza de Cibeles (© **91-406-88-00**), where you can also purchase a guide to the bus routes. The office is open daily from 8am to 4pm.

The hop-off, hop-on **Madrid Vision Bus** lets you set your own pace and itinerary. A scheduled panoramic tour lasts a half hour, provided that you don't get off the bus. Otherwise, you can opt for an unlimited number of stops, exploring at your leisure. The Madrid Vision makes four complete tours daily, two in the morning and two in the afternoon; on Sunday and Monday buses depart only in the morning. Check with **Trapsa Tours** (© **91-767-17-43**) for departure times, which are variable. The full-day tour with unlimited stops costs 3,000Pts (€18, $17). You can board the bus at the Madrid tourist office.

Madrid Metro

Monncloa — Metro Terminal
○ Metro Station
● Transfer Station

Pitis 7

9 Herrera Oria

10 Fuencarral

Begoña

Lacoma

Barrio
del Pilar

Chamartín

Avda. Ilustración

Ventilla

Duque c
Pastrar

Peñagrande

Valdeacederas

1

Antonio Machado

Tetuán

Plaza de
Castilla

Estrecho

Cuzco

Valdezarza

Alvarado

Santiago
Bernabéu

Francos Rodríguez

Guzmán
el Bueno

Cuatro
Caminos

República
Argentina

Metropolitano

6

Nuevos
Ministerios

Ciudad
Universitaria

2

Ríos
Rosas

Alonso
Cano

Gregorio
Marañón

Islas
Filipinas

Canal

Monncloa 3

Quevedo

Iglesia

Rubén
Darío

4

San
Bernardo

Bilbao

Argüelles

Ventura
Rodríguez

Noviciado

Alonso
Martínez

Serranc

Plaza de España

Tribunal

Colón

Príncipe Pío

Santo
Domingo

Chueca

Lago

R

Callao

Gran Vía

Reti

Puerta
del Angel

Sevilla

Banco de
España

Batán

Opera

Sol

Tirso de Molina

Alto de
Extremadura

La Latina

Antón Martír

Lucero

Puerta de
Toledo

Lavapiés

Atocha

Laguna

Acacias

Embajadores

Atocha
Renfe

Campamento

Pirámides

Palos de
la Frontera

6

Carpetana

Marqués de
Vadillo

Delicias

Empalme

Urgel

Méndez
Alvaro

10

Eugenia de
Montijo

Oporto

Aluche 5

Vista
Alegre

Opañel

Plaza
Elíptica

3

Usera

Legazpi

Carabanchel

Abrantes

5

Pan Bendito

Parque de Santa María **4**

San Lorenzo

Barajas **8**

Mar de Cristal **8**

Aeropuerto

Campo de las Naciones

Pío XII

Canillas

Colombia

Esperanza

Concha Espina

Arturo Soria

Cruz del Rayo

Avda. de la Paz

5 Canillejas

Alfonso XIII

Prosperidad

TorreArias

Avda. de América

Cartagena

Parque de las Avenidas

Suanzes

Barrio de la Concepción

Ciudad Lineal

úñez de Balboa

Diego de León

Ventas

Pueblo Nuevo

7 Las Musas

Lista

2

Manuel Becerra

El Carmen

Quintana

Ascao

lázquez

Goya

García Noblejas

Simancas

San Blas

Príncipe de Vergara

O'Donnell

Ibiza

Sáinz de Baranda

Estrella

VInateros

6

Artilleros

Conde de Casal

Pavones

enéndez Pelayo

Vicálvaro

San Cipriano

Valdebernardo

Puerta de Arganda

Pacifico

Puente de Vallecas

Nueva Numancia

Portazgo

Buenos Aires

Rivas Urbanizaciones

Alto del Arenal

Miguel Hernández

Rivas Vaciamadrid

Sierra de Guadalupe

La Poveda

Villa de Vallecas

1
Congosto

ZONA B1

ZONA B2

ZONA B3

9

Arganda del Rey

935

BY TAXI   Even though cab fares have risen recently, they're still reasonable. When you flag down a taxi, the meter should register 190Pts (€1.15, $1.10); for every kilometer thereafter, the fare increases by 95Pts (€0.55, 55¢). A supplement is charged for trips to the rail station or the bullring, as well as on Sundays and holidays. The ride to Barajas Airport carries a 400Pts (€2.40, $2.30) surcharge, and there's a 180Pts (€1.13, $1) supplement for trips from the rail stations. In addition, there's a 210Pts (€1.25, $1.20) supplement on Sundays and holidays, plus a 150Pts (€0.90, 85¢) supplement at night. It's customary to tip about 10% of the fare. To call a taxi, dial ℭ **91-447-51-80.**

BY CAR   Driving is nightmarish and potentially dangerous in very congested Madrid—it always feels like rush hour. It's not a good idea to maintain a rental car while staying in the city. It's nearly impossible to park, and rental cars are the frequent targets of thieves. Should you want to rent a car to tour the environs, however, you'll have several choices. In addition to its office at Barajas Airport (ℭ **91-393-72-22**), **Avis** has a main office downtown at Gran Vía 60 (ℭ **91-548-42-05**). **Hertz,** too, has an office at Barajas Airport (ℭ **91-393-72-28**), and another in the heart of Madrid in the Edificio España, Gran Vía 88 (ℭ **91- 541-99-24**). **Budget Rent-a-Car** maintains an office at Barajas Airport (ℭ **91- 393-72-16**).

BY BICYCLE   Ever wonder why you see so few people riding bicycles in Madrid? Those who tried were overcome by the traffic pollution. Plus, the traffic would be very difficult to contend with. It's better to walk.

ℭ FAST FACTS: Madrid

American Express   For your mail or banking needs, you can go to the Amex office at the corner of Marqués de Cubas and Plaza de las Cortes 2, across the street from the Palace Hotel (ℭ **91-322-55-00**; Metro: Banco de España). Open from Monday to Friday 9am to 5:30pm and Saturday 9am to 2pm.

Currency   The unit of currency is the Spanish **peseta (Pts)**. The rate of exchange used in this chapter is $1 = 170Pts, or 100Pts = 58¢. At press time, £1 = 245Pts (or 100Pts = 41p). The euro rate was currently fixed at €1 = 166.386Pts (or 100Pts = €0.60). From January 1, 2002, the monetary unit in Spain is the euro, though the peseta will still be legal tender until March 1.

Dentist/Doctor   For an English-speaking dentist or doctor, contact the U.S. Embassy, Calle Serrano 75 (ℭ **91-587-22-00**); it maintains a list of dentists and doctors who have offered their services to Americans abroad. For dental services, consult also **Unidad Médica Anglo-Americana,** Conde de Arandá 1 (ℭ **91-435-18-23**; Metro: Retiro), near Plaza de Independencia; office hours are from Monday to Friday 9am to 8pm, Saturday 10am to 1pm; there's a 24-hour answering service.

Drugstores   For a late-night pharmacy, dial ℭ **098** or look in the daily newspaper under "Farmacias de Guardia" to learn what drugstores are open after 8pm. Another way to find out is to go to any pharmacy, even if it's closed—it will have posted a list of nearby pharmacies that are open late on that date.

Embassies/Consulates The Embassy of the **United States,** Calle Serrano 75 (☎ **91-587-22-00;** Metro: Núñez de Balboa), is open Monday to Friday 9:30am to noon and 3 to 5pm. The Embassy of **Canada,** Núñez de Balboa 35 (☎ **91-423-32-50;** Metro: Velázquez), is open from Monday to Friday 9am to 5:15pm. The **United Kingdom** Embassy, Calle Fernando el Santo 16 (☎ **91-319-02-00;** Metro: Colón), is open from Monday to Friday from 9am to 1:30pm and 3 to 5:30pm. The Republic of **Ireland** embassy, Paseo de La Castellana 46 (☎ **91-576-35-00;** Metro: Serrano), is open from Monday to Friday from 10am to 2pm. The **Australian** Embassy, Paseo de la Castellana 143 (☎ **91-579-04-28;** Metro: Cuzco), is open from Monday to Thursday 8:30am to 1:30pm and 2:30 to 5pm, Friday 8:30am to 2pm. The **New Zealand** embassy, Plaza de la Lealtad 2 (☎ **91-523-02-26;** Metro: Banco de España), is open from Monday to Friday 9am to 1:30pm and 2:30 to 5:30pm.

Emergencies In an emergency, call ☎ **080** to report a **fire,** ☎ **091** to reach the **police,** or ☎ **734-25-54** to request an **ambulance.**

Hospitals/Clinics Unidad Médica Anglo-Americana, Conde de Arandá 1 (☎ **91-435-18-23;** Metro: Retiro), isn't a hospital but a private outpatient clinic where someone on staff is always available. It's open daily from 9am to 8pm. For a real medical emergency, call ☎ **734-25-54** for an ambulance.

Police In an emergency, dial **091.**

Post Office If you don't want to receive your mail at your hotel or the American Express office, direct it to *Lista de Correos* at the central post office in Madrid. To pick up mail, go to the window marked LISTA, where you'll be asked to show your passport. Madrid's central office is the **Palacio de Comunicaciones** at Plaza de Cibeles (☎ **902/197-197**).

Safety Because of an increasing crime rate in Madrid, the U.S. Embassy has warned visitors to leave their valuables in a hotel safe or other secure place when going out. Your passport may be needed, however, as the police may stop foreigners for identification checks. The embassy advises that you carry only enough cash for the day's needs. Purse snatching is common, and criminals often work in pairs, grabbing purses from pedestrians, cyclists, and even cars. Several scams to divert one's attention are well known. Even a friendly, "Do you know the time?" can be used to establish that you are a foreigner and distract you.

Telephone The country code for Spain is **34** and the city code for Madrid is **91.** For **long-distance calls,** especially transatlantic ones, it may be best to go to the main phone exchange, Locutorio Gran Vía, at Gran Vía 30, or Locutorio Recoletos, at Paseo de Recoletos 37–41. You may not be lucky enough to find an English-speaking operator, but you can fill out a simple form that will facilitate the placement of a call. For **AT&T,** call ☎ **900/ 99-0011;** for **MCI,** call ☎ **900/99-0014;** for **Sprint,** call ☎ **800/877-4646.**

WHERE TO STAY
NEAR PLAZA DE LAS CORTES
Very Expensive

Palace 𝕣𝕣𝕣   The Palace, an ornate Victorian "wedding cake" that captures the elegant pre–World War I grand hotel style, faces the Prado and Neptune

Fountain. When it first opened in 1912, it was the largest hotel in Europe.
Everyone from Dalí to Picasso, from Sarah Bernhardt to Sophia Loren, has spent
the night. Nevertheless, it doesn't achieve the snob appeal of its sibling, the Ritz
(under the same management). Rooms are conservative and traditional, boasting plenty of space and large, full bathrooms with lots of amenities.

Plaza de las Cortes 7, 28014 Madrid. (C) 800/325-3535 in the U.S., 800/325-3589 in Canada, or
91-360-80-00. Fax 91-360-81-00. 465 units. 65,000Pts (€390, $377) double; from 150,000Pts (€900, $870)
suite. AE, DC, MC, V. Metro: Banco de España. **Amenities:** 2 restaurants, bar; currency exchange; room service; baby-sitting; laundry/dry cleaning. *In room:* A/C, TV, minibar, hair dryer.

Inexpensive
Hostal Cervantes   This is one of Madrid's most pleasant family-run hotels.
The much-restored Cervantes (ca. 1940s) has been widely appreciated by our
readers for years. You'll take a tiny birdcage-style elevator to the immaculately
maintained second floor of this stone-and-brick building. Rooms contain a bed
and spartan furniture. No breakfast is served, but the owners, the Alfonsos, will
direct you to one of several nearby cafes. The hotel is convenient to the Prado,
Retiro Park, and the older sections of Madrid.

Cervantes 34, 28014 Madrid. (C) and fax **91-429-27-45.** 12 units. 6,500Pts (€39, $38) double. MC, V. Metro:
Banco de España or Anton Martin. *In room:* TV, hair dryer, safe.

NEAR PLAZA DE ESPAÑA
Expensive
Holiday Inn Crowne Plaza 𝒦   The Plaza, built in 1953, is the Waldorf-Astoria of Spain. One of the tallest skyscrapers in Europe, it's a landmark visible for
miles around. Once one of the best hotels in Spain, the Plaza no longer enjoys
such a lofty position, having fallen way down the list in the wake of all the new
deluxe hotels built in Madrid. Accommodations include both conventional doubles and luxurious suites; the latter have sitting rooms and abundant amenities.
The quieter rooms are on the upper floors.

Plaza de España 8, 28013 Madrid. (C) 800/465-4329 in the U.S., or 91-547-12-00. Fax 91-548-23-89.
www.holidayinn.com. 306 units. 36,605Pts (€219.65, $212) double; from 45,890Pts (€275.35, $266) suite.
AE, DC, MC, V. Free parking. Metro: Plaza de España. **Amenities:** Restaurant, bar; gym; whirlpool; salon; room
service; laundry/dry cleaning . *In room:* A/C, TV, minibar, hair dryer.

Moderate
Hotel Opera 𝒦 *Finds*   Set close to the royal palace and the opera house, the
hotel isn't regal, but offers first-rate comfort and a warm welcome from the
English-speaking staff. Rooms range from medium to surprisingly spacious,
each fitted with first-rate twin or double beds with quality mattresses. Bathrooms are also excellent. The Opera remains one of Madrid's relatively undiscovered boutique hotels.

Cuesta de Santo Domingo 2, 28013 Madrid. (C) **91-541-2800.** Fax 91-541-6923. hotelopera@sinix.net. 79
units. 14,600Pts (€87.60, $85) double. AE, DC, MC, V. Metro: Opera. **Amenities:** Restaurant, bar; room serv-
ice; baby-sitting; laundry/dry cleaning. *In room:* A/C, TV, minibar, hair dryer.

Inexpensive
Casón del Tormes   The attractive three-star Casón del Tormes is around the
corner from the Royal Palace and Plaza de España. The long, narrow lobby contains wood paneling and marble floors. The individually styled rooms aren't
spectacular, but they are generally roomy and comfortable.

Calle del Río 7, 28013 Madrid. (C) **91-541-97-46.** Fax 91-541-18-52. 63 units. 15,000Pts (€90, $87) double;
18,300Pts (€109.80, $106) triple. MC, AE, V. Parking 1,800Pts (€10.80, $10). Metro: Plaza de España.

Amenities: Restaurant, bar; currency exchange; room service; baby-sitting; laundry/dry cleaning. *In room:* A/C, TV, hair dryer.

ON OR NEAR THE GRAN VÍA
Expensive
Hotel Gaudí ✦   This hotel is located in a beautifully restored landmark Modernist building constructed in 1898 by Emilio Salas y Cortes, one of the teachers of the great Barcelona architect, Gaudí. It was completely overhauled and expanded in 1998. Some of the most important attractions of Madrid are within an easy walk, including the Prado, the Thyssen Museum, and the Plaza Mayor with its rustic taverns. Rooms come in a number of sizes, but each is comfortably furnished and beautifully maintained.

Gran Vía 9, 28013 Madrid. ✆ **91-531-22-22.** Fax 91-531-54-69. www.hoteles-catalonia.es. 88 units. 27,900Pts (€167.40, $162) double; 41,000Pts (€246, $238) suite. AE, DC, MC, V. Metro: Gran Vía. **Amenities:** Restaurant, bar; fitness center; Jacuzzi; room service; laundry/dry cleaning. *In room:* A/C, TV, minibar, hair dryer, safe.

Moderate
Carlos V *Value*   Once the featured hotel in the pioneering *Spain on $5 a Day*, this establishment is still going strong and still offering good value, even though its prices are no longer $2.50 a night. Renovations have much improved this hotel, directly north of Puerta del Sol. The medium-size rooms are sparkling clean and comfortable, with excellent beds. Try for one of the top-floor rooms with little balconies overlooking the central city.

Maestro Vitoria 5, 28013 Madrid. ✆ **91-531-41-00.** Fax 91-531-37-61. 67 units. 15,583Pts (€93.50, $90). AE. Parking 1,250Pts (€7.50, $7). Metro: Puerta del Sol. **Amenities:** Bar; courtesy car; room service; laundry. *In room:* A/C, TV, minibar, hair dryer, safe.

Residencia Liabeny   This hotel, named after the original owner, is in a prime location midway between the tourist highlights of the Gran Vía and the Puerta del Sol. The comfortable, contemporary rooms, though newly redecorated, are a bit too pristine for our tastes. Personalized attention from the staff adds to the allure during your stay.

Salud 3, 28013 Madrid. ✆ **91-531-90-00.** Fax 91-532-74-21. 222 units. 20,250Pts (€121.50, $117) double; 24,000Pts (€144, $139) triple. AE, MC, V. Parking 1,500Pts (€9, $9) . Metro: Puerta del Sol, Callao, or Gran Vía. **Amenities:** Restaurant, 2 bars; room service; baby-sitting; laundry/dry cleaning. *In room:* A/C, TV, minibar, hair dryer, safe.

Inexpensive
Anaco   Modest yet modern, with a simple boxy design from 1963, Anaco is just off the Gran Vía. Opening onto a tree-shaded plaza, it attracts those seeking a resting place that features contemporary appurtenances and cleanliness. Rooms are compact, with built-in headboards, reading lamps, and lounge chairs. Ask for one of the five terraced rooms on the top floor, which rent at no extra charge.

Tres Cruces 3, 28013 Madrid. ✆ **91-522-46-04.** Fax 91-531-64-84. 40 units. 11,880Pts (€71.33, $69) double; 16,035Pts (€96.20, $93) triple. AE, DC, MC, V. Parking 1,600Pts (€9.60, $9). Metro: Gran Vía, Callao, or Puerta del Sol. **Amenities:** Restaurants, bar; room service; baby-sitting; laundry. *In room:* A/C, TV, hair dryer.

NEAR THE PUERTA DEL SOL
Expensive
Gran Hotel Reina Victoria ✦   Since a renovation and upgrading by Spain's Tryp Hotel Group, this hotel is less staid and more impressive than ever. Though

it's in a congested and noisy neighborhood in the center of town, Reina Victoria opens onto a sloping plaza, rich in tradition as a meeting place of intellectuals during the 17th century. Rooms contain sound-resistant insulation, and bathrooms with many amenities.

Plaza de Santa Ana 14, 28012 Madrid. © **91-531-45-00.** Fax 91-522-03-07. 201 units. 30,000Pts (€180, $174) double; 36,000–60,000Pts (€216–€360, $209–$348) suite (includes breakfast). AE, DC, MC, V. Parking 1,750Pts (€10.50, $10). Metro: Tirso de Molina or Puerta del Sol. **Amenities:** Restaurant, bar; room service; baby-sitting. *In room:* A/C, TV, minibar, hair dryer.

Inexpensive
Hostal la Macarena *(Value)*   Known for its reasonable prices and praised by readers for the warmth of its reception, this unpretentious, clean hostel is run by the Ricardo González family. One of the hostel's assets is its location on a street (an admittedly noisy one) immediately behind Plaza Mayor, near one of the best clusters of tascas in Madrid. Windows facing the street are double glazed. No breakfast is served, but there's an array of neighborhood cafes.

Cava de San Miguel 8, 28005 Madrid. © **91-365-92-21.** Fax 91-364-27-57. 25 units. 8,500Pts (€51, $49) double; 12,000Pts (€72, $70) triple; 13,500Pts (€81, $78) quad. MC, V. Metro: Puerta del Sol, Opera, or La Latina. **Amenities:** Bar. *In room:* TV, hair dryer.

Hostal la Perla Asturiana   Ideal for those who want to stay in the heart of Old Madrid (1 block off Plaza Mayor and 2 blocks from the Puerta del Sol), this is a small family-run establishment. It has a courteous staff member at the desk 24 hours a day for security and convenience. You can socialize in the small, comfortable lobby. Rooms are clean but simple and often cramped. Many inexpensive restaurants and tapas bars are nearby; no breakfast is served.

Plaza de Santa Cruz 3, 28012 Madrid. © **91-366-46-00.** Fax 91-366-46-08. perlaasturiana@mundivia.es. 30 units. 6,206Pts (€37.25, $36) double; 8,025Pts (€48.15, $47) triple. AE, MC, V. Metro: Puerta del Sol. **Amenities:** Laundry/dry cleaning. *In room:* TV.

Hostal-Residencia Principado *(Finds)*   The two-star Principado is a real find. Located one floor above street level in a well-kept century-old town house, it's run by a gracious owner who keeps everything clean and inviting. New tiles, attractive bedspreads, and curtains give the rooms a fresh look. No meals are served, but most guests retreat to a nearby cafe for breakfast.

Zorrilla 7, 28014 Madrid. © and fax **91-429-81-87.** www.hr.principado.turincon.com. 15 units. 6,000Pts (€36, $35) double. AE, MC, V. Metro: Sevilla or Banco de España. Bus: 5, 9, or 53. *In room:* TV, safe.

Hotel Inglés   On a central street lined with lively tascas, this hotel is still going strong even though it opened its doors in 1853. It's more modern and impersonal than it was when Virginia Woolf made it her address in Madrid. The lobby is air-conditioned, though the rooms aren't. Rooms are unpretentious and contemporary, all well maintained. Guests who open their windows at night are likely to hear noise from the enclosed courtyard, so light sleepers beware.

Calle Echegaray 8, 28014 Madrid. © **91-429-65-51.** Fax 91-420-24-23. 58 units. 12,000Pts (€72, $70) double; 16,000Pts (€96, $93) suite. AE, DC, MC, V. Parking 1,300Pts (€7.80, $8). Metro: Puerta del Sol or Sevilla. **Amenities:** Cafeteria; bar; gym; currency exchange; room service. *In room:* TV, hair dryer, safe.

NEAR ATOCHA STATION
Moderate
Hotel Mercátor   Only a 3-minute walk from the Prado, Reina Sofía, and Thyssen-Bornemisza museums, the Mercátor (ca. 1953) draws a clientele seeking a good hotel—orderly, well run, and clean, with enough comforts and

conveniences to please the weary traveler. The public areas are simple and minimalistic. Some rooms are more inviting than others.

Calle Atocha 123, 28012 Madrid. 📞 **91-429-05-00.** Fax 91-369-12-52. 87 units. 12,700Pts (€76.20, $74) double; 14,000Pts (€84, $81) suite. AE, DC, MC, V. Parking 1,600Pts (€9.60, $9). Metro: Atocha or Antón Martín. **Amenities:** Restaurant, bar; currency exchange; car rental; room service; baby-sitting; laundry/dry cleaning. *In room:* A/C, TV, minibar, hair dryer.

NEAR RETIRO & SALAMANCA
Very Expensive
Hotel Ritz 🟆🟆🟆   Spain's most famous hotel, encased in a shell of soaring ceilings and graceful columns, is Madrid's most prestigious address and a bastion of glamour. The Ritz was built at the command of Alfonso XIII, with the aid of César Ritz, in 1908. Rooms are spacious and elegantly furnished, each filled with fresh flowers, well-accessorized bathrooms, and beds that are the epitome of comfort.

Plaza de la Lealtad 5, 28014 Madrid. 📞 **800/225-5843** in the U.S. and Canada, or 91 521-28-57. Fax 91-532-87-76. www.ritz.es. 156 units. 64,000–72,000Pts (€384–€432, $371–$418) double; 150,000–250,000Pts (€900–€1,500, $870–$1,450) suite. AE, DC, MC, V. Parking 4,000Pts (€24, $23) ($25). Metro: Banco de España. **Amenities:** 2 restaurants, bar; fitness center; currency exchange; room service; baby-sitting; laundry/dry cleaning. *In room:* A/C, TV, minibar, coffeemaker, hair dryer.

Park Hyatt Villa Magna 🟆🟆🟆   One of Europe's finest hotels is set behind a bank of pines and laurels on the city's most fashionable boulevard. Today it's an even finer choice than the Palace and is matched in luxury, ambience, and tranquillity only by the Ritz. This luxury palace offers plush but dignified rooms decorated in Louis XVI, English Regency, or Italian provincial style. The hotel is known for its summer terraces, set in gardens.

Paseo de la Castellana 22, 28046 Madrid. 📞 **800/223-1234** in the U.S. and Canada, or 91-587-12-34. Fax 91-431-22-86. www.madrid.hyatt.com. 182 units. 72,000Pts (€432, $418) double; from 112,000Pts (€672, $650) suite. AE, DC, MC, V. Parking 3,000Pts (€18, $17) . Metro: Rubén Darío. **Amenities:** 3 restaurants, 2 bars; car rental; salon; room service; baby-sitting; laundry/dry cleaning. *In room:* A/C, TV, minibar, coffeemaker, hair dryer.

Expensive
Emperatriz 🟆   This eight-story hotel is just off the wide Paseo de Castellana, only a short walk from some of Madrid's most deluxe hotels, but it charges relatively reasonable rates. Rooms (classically styled and comfortable, with both traditional and modern furniture) remain much finer than the somewhat unimaginative public areas. Ask for a 7th-floor room, where you'll get a private terrace at no extra charge.

López de Hoyos 4, 28006 Madrid. 📞 **91-563-80-88.** Fax 91-563-98-04. www.hotel-emperatriz.com. 158 units. 28,000Pts (€168, $162) double; 53,000–64,000Pts (€318–€384, $307–$371) suite. AE, DC, MC, V. Metro: Rubén Darío. **Amenities:** Restaurant, bar; currency exchange; salon; room service; baby-sitting; laundry/dry cleaning. *In room:* A/C, TV, minibar, hair dryer.

Grand Hotel Velázquez 🟆   On an affluent residential street near the center of town, this hotel sits behind an art deco facade and a 1940s interior. Be advised that this is a very Spanish hotel with less international exposure than some of its more cosmopolitan competitors. As in many hotels of its era, the rooms vary; some are large enough for entertaining, with a small but separate sitting area. This is one of the most attractive medium-size hotels in Madrid, with plenty of comfort and convenience.

Calle de Velázquez 62, 28001 Madrid. 📞 **91-575-28-00.** Fax 91-575-28-09. 146 units. 45,000Pts (€270, $261) double; from 75,000Pts (€450, $435) suite. AE, DC, MC, V. Parking 2,300Pts (€13.80, $13). Metro:

Retiro. **Amenities:** Restaurant, bar; salon; room service; baby-sitting; laundry/dry cleaning. *In room:* A/C, TV, minibar, hair dryer.

Moderate
Gran Hotel Colón   East of Retiro Park, Gran Hotel Colón lies a few minutes from the city center by Metro. It offers comfortable yet moderately priced rooms. More than half have private balconies, and all contain comfortably traditional furniture, much of it built-in.

Pez Volador 11, 28007 Madrid. (C) 91-573-59-00. Fax 91-573-08-09. 380 units. 12,000–15,000Pts (€72–€90, $70–$87) double. AE, DC, MC, V. Parking 2,000Pts (€12, $12). Metro: Sainz de Baranda. **Amenities:** Restaurant, bar; gym; salon; room service; laundry/dry cleaning. *In room:* A/C, TV, minibar, hair dryer, safe.

WHERE TO DINE
NEAR PLAZA DE LAS CORTÉS
Moderate
El Espejo ✸ INTERNATIONAL   Here you'll find good-tasting food and one of the most perfectly crafted Art Nouveau decors in Madrid. If the weather is good, you can choose one of the outdoor tables. There's also a charming cafe/bar. Menu items include grouper ragout with clams, steak tartare, guinea fowl with Armagnac, and lean duck meat with pineapple.

Paseo de Recoletos 31. (C) 91-308-23-47. Reservations required. Menú del día 3,200Pts (€19.20, $19). AE, DC, MC, V. Sun–Fri 1–4pm and 9pm–midnight; Sat 9pm–1am. Metro: Banco de España or Colón. Bus: 27.

Errota-Zar ✸ BASQUE   Next to the House of Deputies and the Zarzuela Theater, Errota-Zar, means "old mill," a nostalgic reference to the Basque country, home of Spain's most refined cuisine. The deliciously prepared food is an array of sun-kissed bounty from the fields and rivers of Spain. Many Basques begin their meal with a *tortilla de bacalao* or salt cod omelet. For main dishes, sample the delights of *chuleton de buey* or oxtail, along with grilled vegetables, or *kokotxas de merluza en aceite,* the latter the cheeks of the hake fish cooked in the finest virgin oil.

Jovellanos 3. (C) 91-531-25-64. Reservations recommended. Main courses 2,800–3,000Pts (€16.80–€18, $16–$17). AE, DC, MC, V. Mon–Sat 1–4pm and 9pm–midnight. Closed Aug 15–30. Metro: Banco España and Sevilla.

ON OR NEAR THE GRAN VÍA
Expensive
La Barraca ✸ VALENCIAN   This longtime local favorite right off the Gran Vía is like a country inn. The four dining rooms are colorfully cluttered with ceramics, paintings, photographs, Spanish lanterns, flowers, and local artifacts. The house specialty, paella à la Barraca, is made with pork and chicken. Specialties in the appetizer category include *desgarrat* (a salad of codfish and red peppers), mussels in a white-wine sauce, and shrimp sautéed with garlic. In addition to the recommended paella, you can select at least 16 rice dishes, including black rice and queen paella. Main-dish specialties include brochette of anglerfish and prawns and rabbit with fines herbs.

Reina 29–31. (C) 91-532-71-54. Reservations recommended. Main courses 3,000–7,000Pts (€18–€42, $17–$41); fixed-price menu 3,800–4,900Pts (€22.80–€29.40, $22–$28). AE, DC, MC, V. Daily 1–4pm and 8:30pm–midnight. Metro: Gran Vía or Bancode España. Bus: 1, 2, or 74.

Moderate
El Mentidero de la Villa *(finds)* SPANISH/FRENCH   This "Gossip Shop" is certainly a multicultural experience. The owner describes the cuisine as "modern

✐ Our Favorite Tascas

Don't starve waiting around for Madrid's fashionable 9:30 or 10pm dinner hour. Throughout the city you'll find *tascas,* bars that serve wine and platters of tempting hot and cold hors d'oeuvres known as tapas: mushrooms, salads, baby eels, shrimp, lobster, mussels, sausage, ham, and, in one establishment at least, bull testicles. Below we've listed our favorite tapas bars. Keep in mind you can often save pesetas by ordering at the bar rather than occupying a table.

Casa Mingo, Paseo de la Florida 2 (© **91-547-79-18;** Metro: Norte), has been known for decades for its cider, both still and bubbly. The perfect accompanying tidbit is a piece of Asturian cabrales (goat cheese), but the roast chicken is the specialty of the house. There's no formality here, since customers share big tables under the vaulted ceiling in the dining room; in summer, the staff sets up tables and wooden chairs out on the sidewalk. This isn't so much a restaurant as it is a bodega/taverna that serves food daily from 11am to midnight. Hemingway and celebrated bullfighter Luís Miguel Dominguín used to frequent the casual **Cervecería Alemania,** Plaza de Santa Ana 6 (© **91-429-70-33;** Metro: Alonso Martín or Tirso de Molina)—ask the waiter to point out Hemingway's table. However, it earned its name because of its long-ago German clients. Opening onto one of the liveliest little plazas in Madrid, it clings to its early-1900s traditions, and you can sit at one of the tables, leisurely sipping beer or wine, since the waiters make no attempt to hurry you along. To accompany your beverage, try the fried sardines or a Spanish omelet. It's open from Sunday to Thursday 11am to 12:30am and Friday and Saturday 11am to 2am.

Unique in Madrid, the **Cervecería Santa Bárbara,** Plaza de Santa Bárbara 8 (© **91-319-04-049;** Metro: Alonzo Martínez; bus: 3, 7, or 21), is an outlet for a beer factory, and the management has spent a lot to make it modern and inviting. Hanging globe lights and spinning ceiling fans create an attractive ambience, as does the black-and-white marble floor. You go here for beer, of course: *cerveza negra* (black beer) or *cerveza dorada* (golden beer). The local brew is best accompanied by homemade potato chips or by fresh shrimp, lobster, crabmeat, or barnacles. You can either stand at the counter or go to one of the wooden tables for waiter service. It's open daily 11:30am to midnight. Many Madrileños begin their nightly tasca crawl at the **Taberna Toscana,** Manuel Fernandez y Gonzales 10 (© **91-429-60-31;** Metro: Puerta del Sol or Sevilla). The ambience is that of a village inn far removed from 21st-century Madrid. You sit on crude country stools, under sausages, peppers, and sheaves of golden wheat that hang from the age-darkened beams. The long tiled bar is loaded with tasty tidbits, including the house specialties: *lacón y cecina* (boiled ham), *habas* (broad beans) with Spanish ham, and *chorizo* (a sausage of red peppers and pork)—almost meals in themselves. Especially delectable are the kidneys in sherry sauce and the snails in hot sauce. It's open from Tuesday to Saturday noon to 4pm and 8pm to midnight (closed August).

Spanish with Japanese influence; the cooking technique is French." The kitchen prepares such adventuresome dishes as black spaghetti, flavored with squid ink, served with lobster sauce, mussels, and medallions of crayfish; an avocado/crabmeat/watercress and bacon salad; rack of lamb stuffed with minced leg of lamb that's been enhanced with a pepper/white wine/and potato sauce. Despite many newer desserts, the most popular remains a sherry trifle that British visitors usually applaud.

Santo Tomé 6. ℭ 91-308-12-85. Reservations required. Main courses 3,500–5,500Pts (€21–€33, $20–$32); menú del día 2,700Pts (€16.20, $16). AE, DC, MC, V. Mon–Fri 1:30–4pm and 9pm–midnight; Sat 9pm–midnight. Closed last 2 weeks of Aug. Metro: Alonso Martínez, Chueca. Bus: 37.

Mad Cafe Club INTERNATIONAL   This restaurant/bar in the very center of Madrid is a fine representative of the new Spain and is a popular night-time haunt for the fashionable. There's a garden where diners and drinkers can languish on the hot summer nights. Staples include starters such as goat cheese on caramelized onions and corral salad (wild chicken marinated in vinegar and cream in four types of lettuce). Other dishes to savor are marinated salmon with dill and golden caviar from an inland sea in the dry southern province of Murcia. Desserts include an apple tart, not too sweet and topped with egg yolk.

Calle Virgin de los Peligros 4. ℭ 91-532-62-28. Reservations recommended. Main courses 1,700–2,200Pts (€10.20–€13.20, $11–$14); fixed-price menu (at lunch only) 1,700Pts (€10.20, $10). AE, DC, MC, V. Mon–Wed 1–4pm and 9:30pm–3am; Thurs–Sat 1–4pm and 9:30pm–4am. Dinner served until 12:30am. Metro: Sevilla, Gran Vía.

NEAR THE PUERTA DEL SOL
Expensive
Casa Paco ⚜ STEAK   Madrileños know that here you can get the thickest, juiciest steaks in Spain, priced according to weight. Señor Paco was the first in Madrid to sear steaks in boiling oil before serving them on plates so hot that the almost-raw meat continues to cook, preserving the natural juices. Reservations are imperative—otherwise, you face a long wait. Casa Paco isn't just a steak house. You can start with fish soup and proceed to a dish such as grilled sole, lamb, or Casa Paco *cocido,* the famous chickpea/meat soup of Madrid.

Plaza de la Puerta Cerrada 11. ℭ 91-366-31-66. Reservations required. Main courses 3,000–6,000Pts (€18–€36, $17–$35). MC, DC, V. Mon–Sat 1:30–4pm and 8:30pm–midnight. Closed Aug. Metro: Puerta del Sol, Tirso, or La Latina. Bus: 3, 21, or 65.

Lhardy ⚜ SPANISH/INTERNATIONAL   A Madrileño legend since it opened in 1839, this is a gathering place for the city's literati and political leaders. Its street level contains what might be the most elegant snack bar in Spain, where cups of steaming consommé are dispensed from silver samovars into delicate porcelain cups. The real culinary skill of the place, however, is visible on the second floor, where you'll find a formal restaurant. Specialties include many preparations of fresh fish; tripe in a garlicky tomato-and-onion/wine sauce; and cocido, the chickpea stew of Madrid, made with sausage, pork, and vegetables. *Soufflé sorpresa* (baked Alaska) is the dessert specialty.

Carrera de San Jerónimo 8. ℭ 91-521-33-85. Reservations recommended in the upstairs dining room. Main courses 4,000–8,000Pts (€24–€48, $23–$46). AE, DC, MC, V. Daily 1–3:30pm and 8:30–11:30pm. Closed Aug. Metro: Puerta del Sol or Sevilla.

Platerías Comedor ⚜ SPANISH   Despite the busy socializing on the plaza outside, this serene oasis makes few concessions to the new generation in its food, decor, or formally attired waiters. Specialties are beans with clams, stuffed partridge with cabbage and sausage, hake prepared in several variations, magret of duckling with orange sauce or pomegranates, duck liver with white grapes, veal stew with snails and mushrooms, and guinea hen with figs and plums. You might finish with passion fruit sorbet.

Plaza de Santa Ana 11. (*C*) **91-429-70-48.** Reservations recommended. Main courses 2,800–5,500Pts (€16.80–€33, $16–$32). AE, DC, MC, V. Tues–Sat 1:30–4pm and 9pm–midnight. Metro: Puerta del Sol.

Moderate
Café de Oriente FRENCH/SPANISH   With the allure of a setting on one of Madrid's most historic and regal-looking squares, the Oriente manages both bistro-style informality and some very grand dining. Expect lots of high-powered corporate groups that dine in the private dining rooms nestled off to the side of the central room. On the street level, you'll find a less intense, more workaday crowd of cafe patrons who appreciate the rich array of tapas, the dozens of small tables, coffee, wine, and foaming mugs of beer, and a set-price menu that's one of the bargains of this gilt-edged neighborhood.

Plaza de Oriente 2. (*C*) **91-541-39-74.** Reservations recommended (in formal restaurant only). In cafe, tapas 850Pts (€5.10, $5), coffee 550Pts (€3.30, $3.24). In restaurant, main courses 7,000–7,500Pts (€42–€45, $41–$44). AE, DC, MC, V. Cafe daily 8:30am–1:30am. Restaurant daily 1–4pm and 9pm–midnight. Metro: Opera.

Inexpensive
Casa Alberto CASTILIAN   One of the oldest tascas in the neighborhood, Casa Alberto is on the street level of the house where Miguel de Cervantes lived briefly in 1614 and contains an appealing mixture of bullfighting memorabilia, engravings, and reproductions of old master paintings. Tapas are continually replenished from platters on the bar top, but there's also a sit-down dining area in the back for more substantial meals. Specialties include fried squid, shellfish in green sauce, *chorizo* (sausage) in cider sauce, and several versions of baked or roasted lamb.

Huertas 18. (*C*) **91-429-93-56.** Reservations recommended. Main courses 1,800–3,500Pts (€10.80–€21, $10–$20); fixed-price lunch 2,000Pts (€12, $12). AE, DC, MC, V. Tues–Sat 1:30am–4pm. Metro: Antón Martín.

Hylogui SPANISH   Hylogui, a local legend since the 1930s, is one of the largest dining rooms along Ventura de la Vega, but there're many arches and nooks for privacy. One globe-trotting American wrote enthusiastically that he took all his Madrid meals here, finding the soup pleasant and rich, the flan soothing, the regional wine dry, and the prices affordable. The food is old-fashioned Spanish home-style cooking.

Ventura de la Vega 3. (*C*) **91-429-73-57.** Reservations recommended. Main courses 2,000–4,000Pts (€12–€24, $12–$23); fixed-price menu 2,500Pts (€15, $15). AE, MC, V. Mon–Sat 1–4:30pm and 9pm–midnight; Sun 1–4:30pm. Metro: Sevilla.

NEAR RETIRO & SALAMANCA
Very Expensive
Alkalde ☆☆☆ BASQUE/INTERNATIONAL   Alkalde serves top-quality Spanish food in a setting decorated like a Basque inn. Upstairs is a large *típico* tavern; downstairs is a maze of stone-sided cellars that are pleasantly cool in summer. Basque cookery is the best in Spain, and Alkalde honors that tradition nobly. You might begin with the cream-of-crabmeat soup, followed by *gambas a la plancha* (grilled shrimp), chicken cutlets, or *cigalas* (crayfish). Other

well-recommended dishes are *mero en salsa verde* (brill in a green sauce), trout Alkalde, stuffed peppers, and chicken steak.

Jorge Juan 10. ⓒ **91-576-33-59.** Reservations required. Main courses 4,500–6,500Pts (€27–€39, $26–$38); fixed-price menu from 6,000Pts (€36, $35). AE, DC, MC, V. Daily 1:15–4:30pm and 8:30pm–midnight. Closed Sat–Sun July–Aug. Metro: Serrano. Bus: 8, 21, 29, or 53.

Horcher ✸✸ GERMAN/INTERNATIONAL   This deluxe restaurant still dazzles, having first opened in 1904 in Berlin. Prompted by a tip from a high-ranking German officer that Germany was losing the war, Herr Horcher moved his restaurant to Madrid in 1943. The restaurant has continued its grand European traditions, including excellent service, ever since. You might try the skate or shrimp tartare or the distinctive warm hake salad. The venison stew in green pepper with orange peel and the crayfish with parsley and cucumber are the type of elegant fare served with impeccable style; you can sample game dishes like wild boar or roast wild duck in autumn.

Alfonso XII 6. ⓒ **91-532-35-96.** Reservations required. Jackets and ties required for men. Main courses 6,000–10,000Pts (€36–€60, $35–$58). AE, DC, MC, V. Mon–Fri 1:30–4pm and 8:30pm–midnight; Sat 8:30pm–midnight. Metro: Retiro.

Viridiana ✸✸ INTERNATIONAL   Praised as one of Madrid's top restaurants, Viridiana is known for the creative imagination of chef and part-owner Abraham García, who named his restaurant after the Luís Buñuel 1961 classic. Menu specialties are usually contemporary adaptations of traditional recipes and change frequently. Examples are tartare of tuna, a salad of exotic lettuces with smoked salmon, filet steak with truffles, guinea fowl stuffed with herbs and wild mushrooms, baby squid with curry served on a bed of lentils, and roast lamb in puff pastry with fresh basil. A delectable dish is vineyard snails cooked in vine leaves, rosemary, tomato sauce, and pimientos.

Juan de Mena 14. ⓒ **91-523-44-78.** Reservations recommended. Main courses 8,000–12,000Pts (€48–€72, $46–$70). AE, MC, V. Mon–Sat 1:30–4pm and 9pm–midnight. Closed Aug and 1 week at Easter. Metro: Retiro Bancode España.

Expensive

El Amparo ✸ BASQUE   This is one of Madrid's most elegant gastronomic enclaves, a pioneer of a new type of cuisine. It introduced (some 16 years ago) cod cheeks in a smooth puree of red peppers. You are served innovative food, including, for example, ravioli with crayfish dressed in balsamic vinegar and a vanilla-scented oil. A battalion of polite uniformed waiters serves well-prepared nouvelle-cuisine versions of cold marinated salmon with tomato sorbet, delectable fish salads, bisque of shellfish with Armagnac, ravioli stuffed with seafood, and a platter of steamed fish of the day.

Callejón de Puígcerdá 8 (at the corner of Jorge Juan). ⓒ **91-431-64-56.** Reservations required. Main courses 11,500–13,500Pts (€69–€81, $67–$78). AE, MC, V. Mon–Fri 1:30–3:30pm and 9–11:30pm; Sat 9:30–11:30pm. Closed the week before Easter and 1 week in Aug. Metro: Goya. Bus: 21 or 53.

La Gamella ✸✸ CALIFORNIAN/CASTILIAN   In 1988, La Gamella's Illinois-born owner, former choreographer Dick Stephens, moved his restaurant into this 19th-century building. Low-key, glamorous, and soothing, the restaurant serves a roster of ongoing staples, plus some newfangled cuisine that in North America might be referred to as fusion. Examples include what has been called "the only edible hamburger in Madrid" and steak tartare spiked with Jack Daniels, as well as more upscale food such as sliced duck liver in truffle sauce, duck breast with sweet-and-sour sauce, spicy Thai chicken, and a perennial favorite of quiche made with Spanish sausage and red peppers. Also look for creative dishes such as their fish of the day with a poblano sauce.

Alfonso XII 4. © **91-532-45-09.** Reservations required. Main courses 5,000–7,500Pts (€30–€45, $29–$44). AE, DC, MC, V. Mon–Fri 1:30–4pm and 9pm–midnight; Sat 9pm–midnight. Closed 2 weeks around Easter and 2 weeks in Aug. Metro: Retiro. Bus: 19.

Inexpensive
Gran Café de Gijón SPANISH   Each European capital has a coffeehouse that traditionally attracts the literati. In Madrid it's the Gijón, which opened in 1888. Artists and writers still patronize this venerated cafe; many spend hours over one cup of coffee. Hemingway made the place famous for Americans. Gijón has open windows looking out onto the wide paseo, as well as a large terrace for sun worshipers and bird-watchers. Along one side is a stand-up bar and on the lower level is a restaurant. The cookery is the "way it used to be" in Madrid.

Paseo de Recoletos 21. © **91-521-54-25.** Reservations required for restaurant. Main courses 3,000–5,900Pts (€18–€35.40, $17–$34); fixed-price menu 1,500–3,500Pts (€9–€21, $9–$20). MC, V. Daily 8am–2am. Metro: Banco de España, Colón.

CHAMBERÍ
Very Expensive
Jockey 🕸🕸🕸 INTERNATIONAL   Since its opening in 1945, it was Madrid's premier restaurant during the long, dark Franco era. Still strong, it takes number two position to Zalacain today (see below). At any rate, it's still a favorite of international celebrities. The chef prides himself on coming up with new and creative dishes. Try his fatted duck with ginger and citrus sauce, or slices of Jabugo ham. His cold melon soup with shrimp is soothing on a hot day, especially when followed by grill-roasted young pigeon from Talavera cooked in its own juice or monkfish en papillote with Mantua sauce. Stuffed small chicken Jockey style is a specialty.

Amador de los Ríos 6. © **91-319-24-35.** Reservations required. Main courses 10,000–12,500Pts (€60–€75, $58–$73). AE, DC, MC, V. 1–3:30pm and 9pm–midnight. Closed Aug. Metro: Colón or Serrano.

Las Cuatro Estaciones 🕸🕸🕸 MEDITERRANEAN   Praised by gastronomes and horticulturists, Las Cuatro Estaciones rivals the prestigious Jockey. Each person involved in food preparation spends a prolonged apprenticeship at one of the great restaurants of France. Representative specialties are petite marmite of fish and shellfish, imaginative preparations of salmon, a salad of eels, black rice with squid ink and squid, hake with a tomato and garlic butter sauce, and a three-fish platter with *fines herbes*.

General Ibañez Ibero 5. © **91-553-63-05.** Reservations required. Main courses 7,000–9,000Pts (€42–€54, $41–$52); fixed-price dinner 8,500Pts (€51, $49). AE, DC, MC, V. Mon–Fri 1:30–4pm and 9pm–midnight; Sat 9–11:30pm. Closed Aug. Metro: Guzmán el Bueno.

Inexpensive
La Bola MADRILEÑA   Just north of the Teatro Real, La Bola hangs on to tradition like a tenacious bull. Time has passed, but not inside this restaurant: Ava Gardner, with her entourage of bullfighters, used to patronize this establishment, but that was long before La Bola became so well known to tourists. Grilled sole, filet of veal, and roast veal are regularly featured. Basque-style hake

and grilled salmon also are well recommended. A host of refreshing dishes to begin your meal includes grilled shrimp, red-pepper salad, and lobster cocktail.

Calle de la Bola, 5. ℂ **91-547-69-30.** Reservations required. Main courses 2,500–5,000Pts (€15–€30, $15–$29). No credit cards. Daily 1–4pm; Mon–Sat 8:30pm–midnight. Metro: Plaza de España or Opera. Bus: 1 or 2.

OFF PLAZA MAYOR
Moderate
Sobrino de Botín ✿ SPANISH   Ernest Hemingway made Sobrino de Botín famous. In the final pages of *The Sun Also Rises,* Jake invites Lady Brett there for the Segovian specialty, roast suckling pig, washed down with Rioja Alta. You'll see an open kitchen with a charcoal hearth, hanging copper pots, an 18th-century tile oven for roasting the suckling pig, and a big pot of regional soup whose aroma wafts across the room. The other house specialty is roast Segovian lamb. But if you're not in the mood for those, you can order an excellent and robust filet steak. You can accompany your meal with Valdepeñas or Aragón wine, or even sangría.

Calle de Cuchilleros 17. ℂ **91-366-42-17.** Reservations required. Main courses 3,000–6,000Pts (€18–€36, $17–$35); fixed-price menu 4,500Pts (€27, $26). AE, DC, MC, V. Daily 1–4pm and 8pm–midnight. Closed Christmas. Metro: Puerta del Sol or Tirso de Molina.

CHAMARTIN
Expensive
Zalacaín ✿✿✿ INTERNATIONAL   Outstanding in both food and decor, Zalacaín reigns as the gastronomic citadel of Madrid. When it opened in 1973, it introduced nouvelle cuisine to Madrid. The menu features many Basque and French specialties, often with nouvelle cuisine touches. It might offer a superb sole in a green sauce, but it also knows the glory of grilled pigs' feet. Among the most recommendable main dishes are oysters with caviar and sherry jelly; crêpes stuffed with smoked fish; ravioli stuffed with mushrooms, foie gras, and truffles; and Spanish bouillabaisse. For dessert, we'd suggest one of the custards, perhaps raspberry or chocolate. Men should wear jackets and ties.

Alvarez de Baena 4. ℂ **91-561-48-40.** Reservations required. Main courses 10,000–15,000Pts (€60–€90, $58–$87). AE, DC, MC, V. Mon–Fri 1:30–4pm; Mon–Sat 9pm–midnight. Closed week before Easter and Aug. Metro: Rubén Darío.

Moderate
El Olivo Restaurant ✿ MEDITERRANEAN   Locals praise the success of French-born Jean Pierre Vandelle in recognizing the international appeal of two of Spain's most valuable culinary resources, olive oil and sherry. Menu specialties include grilled filet of monkfish marinated in herbs and olive oil, then served with black-olive sauce over a compote of fresh tomatoes, and four preparations of codfish arranged on a single platter and served with a pil-pil sauce. Desserts might be one of several different chocolate pastries. A wide array of reasonably priced Bordeaux and Spanish wines can accompany your meal.

General Gallegos 1. ℂ **91-359-15-35.** Reservations recommended. Main courses 3,000–7,000Pts (€18–€42, $17–$41); fixed-price meals 3,950–5,950Pts (€23.70–€35.70, $23–$35). AE, MC, V. Tues–Sat 1–4pm and 9pm–midnight. Closed Aug 15–31 and 4 days around Easter. Metro: Plaza de Castilla.

SEEING THE SIGHTS
Madrid has changed drastically in recent years. It is no longer fair to say that this lively European capital has only the Prado, and after you see that, you should head for Toledo or El Escorial. As you'll discover, Madrid has something to amuse and delight everyone.

SIGHTSEEING SUGGESTIONS FOR FIRST-TIME VISITORS

If You Have 1 Day Spend the morning seeing a few of the masterpieces at the **Prado,** one of the world's great art museums. It's best to arrive when it opens at 9am (remember, it's closed Monday). Have lunch and then visit the **Palacio Real (Royal Palace).** Have an early dinner near Plaza Mayor.

If You Have 2 Days On day 2 visit the **Thyssen-Bornemisza Museum** in the morning, stroll around Madrid's medieval area, and visit the **Museo Nacional Centro de Arte Reina Sofía** in the late afternoon or early evening (it closes at 9pm most nights). Here you can see Picasso's *Guernica* plus other great art of the 20th century. Have dinner once again at one of the many restaurants off Plaza Mayor.

If You Have 3 Days On your third day take a trip to **Toledo,** where you can visit the Cathedral, the Santa Cruz Museum, and the Alcázar. Return to Madrid in the evening.

If You Have 4 or 5 Days On day 4 take a 1-hour train ride to the Monastery of San Lorenzo de **El Escorial,** in the foothills of the Sierra de Guadarrama. Return to Madrid in the evening. On day 5 you could take a trip to **Segovia.**

THE TOP MUSEUMS

Museo del Prado 🌟🌟🌟   With more than 7,000 paintings, the Prado is one of the most important repositories of art in the world. In paintings of the Spanish school the Prado has no equal, so on your first visit, concentrate on the Spanish masters. You'll find a treasure trove of works by El Greco, the Crete-born artist who lived much of his life in Toledo. Look for *Las Meninas,* the museum's most famous painting, and other works by the incomparable Diego Velázquez. The Francisco de Goya collection includes his unflattering portraits of his patron, Charles IV, and his family, as well as the *Clothed Maja* and the *Naked Maja* and pictures from his black period. Look also for paintings by Zurbarán and Murillo, and be sure to search out Flemish genius Hieronymus Bosch's best-known work, *The Garden of Earthly Delights.*

Paseo del Prado. ✆ **91-330-28-00.** http://museoprado.mcu.es. Admission 500Pts (€3, $2.90) adults, 250Pts (€1.50, $1.45) students, free for children 11 and under and seniors. Tues–Sat 9am–7pm; Sun and holidays 9am–2pm. Closed Jan 1, Good Friday, May 1, and Dec 25. Metro: Cibeles or Atocha. Bus: 10, 14, 27, 34, 37, 45, or M6.

Museo Thyssen-Bornemisza 🌟🌟🌟   The Thyssen-Bornemisza family's unrivaled private collection was amassed over a period of about 60 years. Baron von Thyssen is married to a Spaniard, who desperately wanted to see the collection permanently reside in her native Spain. When it went on the market, Spain acquired it for $350 million. To house the collection, an 18th-century Villahermosa Palace, adjacent to the Prado, was retrofitted so that by following the order of the various rooms a logical sequence of European and American painting can be traced from the 13th through the 20th century. The nucleus of the collection consists of 700 world-class paintings. They include works by El Greco, Velázquez, Dürer, Rembrandt, Watteau, Canaletto, Caravaggio, Frans Hals, Hans Memling, and Goya, among many others.

Palacio de Villahermosa, Paseo del Prado 8. ✆ **91-369-01-51.** www.museothyssen.org. Admission 700Pts (€4.20, $4) adults, 450Pts (€2.70, $2.60) seniors and students, free for children 12 and under. Tues–Sun 10am–7pm. Metro: Banco de España. Bus: 1, 2, 5, 9, 10, 14, 15, 20, 27, 34, 45, 51, 52, 53, 74, 146, or 150.

> **(Value** Three Museums, One Price
>
> If you plan on visiting the Prado, Thyssen-Bornemisza, and Reina Sofía
> museums, you should buy a **Paseo del Arte,** priced at 1,275Pts (€7.65, $7),
> which grants admission to all three. You can buy the pass at any of the
> three museums.

Museo Nacional Centro de Arte Reina Sofía ☞ Madrid's greatest repository of 20th-century art is here, in a high-ceilinged showplace named after the
Greek-born wife of Spain's present king. One of Europe's largest museums, it
was designated "the ugliest building in Spain" by the Catalán architect Oriol
Bohigas, though many are thrilled with the huge glass-enclosed elevators on the
outside. Special emphasis inside is paid to the great 20th-century artists of
Spain: Juan Gris, Dalí, and Miró. Picasso's masterpiece, *Guernica,* now rests here
after a long and troubling nomadic history. This antiwar piece immortalizes the
blanket bombing by the German Luftwaffe for Franco during the Spanish Civil
War of the village of Guernica, cradle of the Basque nation.

Santa Isabel 52. ✆ **91-467-50-62.** http://museoreinasofia.mcu.es. Admission 500Pts (€3, $2.90) adults,
250Pts (€1.50, $1.45) students and children 11 and under. Mon and Wed–Sat 10am–9pm, Sun
10am–2:30pm. Sat after 12:30pm and Sun morning admission is free. Metro: Atocha. Bus: 6, 14, 26, 27, 32,
45, 57, or C.

Palacio Real (Royal Palace) ☞☞ This huge palace was begun in 1738 on
the site of the Madrid Alcázar, which burned in 1734. Some of its 2,000 rooms
are open to the public, though others are still used for state business. The guided
tour includes the Reception Room, the State Apartments, the Armory, and the
Royal Pharmacy. The rooms are literally stuffed with art treasures and
antiques—salon after salon of monumental grandeur, with no apologies for the
damask, mosaics, stucco, Tiepolo ceilings, gilt and bronze, chandeliers, and
paintings. In the Armory you'll see a fine collection of weaponry.

Plaza de Oriente, Calle de Bailén 2. ✆ **91-542-00-59.** Admission 900Pts (€5.40, $5) adults, 450Pts (€2.70,
$2.60) seniors, students, and children 11 and under; guided tour 1,000Pts (€6, $6). Mon–Sat 9am–6pm; Sun
9am–3pm. Metro: Opera or Plaza de España.

MORE ATTRACTIONS

**Real Academia de Bellas Artes de San Fernando (San Fernando Royal
Fine Arts Academy)** ☞ An easy stroll from the Puerta del Sol, this museum
is located in the restored and remodeled 17th-century baroque palace of Juan de
Goyeneche. The collection—more than 1,500 paintings and 570 sculptures,
ranging from the 16th century to the present—was started in 1752 during the
reign of Fernando VI (1746–59). It emphasizes works by Spanish, Flemish, and
Italian artists. Masterpieces by El Greco, Rubens, Velázquez, Zurbarán, Ribera,
Cano, Coello, Murillo, and Sorolla are here. The Goya collection in itself is
worth a visit. Goya was a member of the academy from 1780, and the museum
houses two of his self-portraits, along with a full-size portrait of the actress, La
Tirana, and the royal "favorite" Manuel Godoy, plus the carnival scene, *Burial
of the Sardine,* and eight more oils.

Alcalá 13. ✆ **91-522-14-91.** 400Pts (€2.40, $2.30) adults, 200Pts (€1.20, $1.15) students, free for children
and seniors 60 and over; Sat–Sun free for everyone. Tues–Fri 9am–7pm; Sat–Mon 9am–2pm. Metro: Puerta
del Sol or Sevilla. Bus: 15, 20, 51, 52, or M12.

Panteón de Goya (Goya's Tomb) 🕀   Several blocks beyond the North Station lies Goya's tomb, containing one of his masterpieces: an elaborately beautiful fresco depicting the miracles of St. Anthony on the dome and cupola of the little hermitage of San António de la Florida. This has been called Goya's Sistine Chapel. Already deaf when he began the painting, Goya labored from dawn to dusk for 16 weeks, painting with sponges rather than brushes. By depicting common street life—stone masons, prostitutes, and beggars—Goya raised the ire of the nobility. However, when Carlos IV viewed it and approved, the formerly "outrageous" painting was deemed acceptable.

Glorieta de San António de la Florida. ℭ **91-542-07-22.** Admission 300Pts (€1.80, $1.75) adults, 150Pts (€0.90, 85¢) seniors and children 17 and under. Tues–Fri 10am–2pm and 4–8pm; Sat–Sun 10am–2pm. Metro: Principe Pio. Bus: 41, 46, 75, or C.

Museo Lázaro Galdiano 🕀🕀   This well-preserved 19th-century mansion bulges with artworks of all kinds. Take the elevator to the top floor and work your way down; there are 15th-century hand-woven vestments, swords and daggers, royal seals, 16th-century crystal from Limoges, Byzantine jewelry, Italian bronzes from ancient times to the Renaissance, and medieval armor. There are also works by the Old Masters El Greco, Velázquez, Zurbarán, Ribera, Murillo, and Valdés-Leal, and Tiepolo and Guardi, and a section is devoted to works by the English artists Reynolds, Gainsborough, and Constable.

Serrano 122. ℭ **91-561-60-84.** Admission 500Pts (€3, $2.90) adults, 250Pts (€1.50, $1.45) students, free for seniors and children 11 and under. Tues–Sun 10am–2pm. Closed holidays and Aug. Metro: Gregorio Marámon. Bus: 9, 16, 19, 51, or 89.

Monasterio de las Descalzas Reales 🕀🕀   In the mid-16th century, aristocratic women came to this convent to take the veil. Each of them brought a dowry, making this one of the richest convents in the land. But by the mid-20th century the convent sheltered mostly poor women. Although it contained a priceless collection of art treasures, the sisters were forbidden to auction anything. The state intervened, and the pope granted special dispensation to open the convent as a museum. In the Reliquary are the noblewomen's dowries, one of which is said to include bits of wood from the True Cross; another, some bones of St. Sebastian. The most valuable painting is Titian's *Caesar's Money.* The Flemish Hall shelters other fine works, including paintings by Hans de Beken and Breugel the Elder, and tapestries based on Rubens's cartoons.

Plaza de las Descalzas Reales. ℭ **91-454-87-00.** Admission 700Pts (€4.20, $4) adults, 350Pts (€$2.20) seniors and children 11 and under. Tues–Thurs and Sat 10:30am–12:45pm and 3–5:45pm; Fri 10:30am–12:30pm; Sun 11am–1:15pm. Bus: 1, 2, 5, 20, 46, 52, 53, 74, M1, M2, M3, or M5. From Plaza del Callao, off Gran Vía, walk down Postigo de San Martín to Plaza de las Descalzas Reales; the convent is on the left.

PARKS & GARDENS

Casa de Campo (Metro: Lago or Batán), the former royal hunting grounds, is composed of miles of parkland lying south of the Royal Palace across the Manzanares River. You can see the gate through which the kings rode out of the palace grounds—either on horseback or in carriages—on their way to the park. Casa de Campo has a variety of trees and a lake, usually filled with rowers. You can have drinks and light refreshments around the water or go swimming in a municipally operated pool. The park can be visited daily from 8am to 9pm.

   Retiro Park 🕀🕀 (Metro: Retiro), originally a playground for the Spanish monarchs and their guests, extends over 165 hectares (350 acres). The huge palaces that once stood here were destroyed in the early 19th century, and only the former dance hall, Casón del Buen Retiro (housing the Prado's modern works), and the building containing the Army Museum remain. The park boasts numerous fountains and statues, plus a large lake. There're also two exposition centers, the Velásquez and Crystal Palaces (built to honor the Philippines in 1887) and a lakeside monument, erected in 1922 in honor of Alfonso XII. In summer, the rose gardens are worth a visit, and you'll find several places where you can have inexpensive snacks and drinks. The park is open daily 24 hours, but it's safest, like most public parks, during the day (7am to 8:30pm).

Across Calle de Alfonso XII, at the southwest corner of Retiro Park, is the **Real Jardín Botánico (Royal Botanical Garden),** Plaza de Murillo 2 (✆ **91-420-30-17;** Metro: Atocha; bus: 10, 14, 19, 32, or 45). Founded in the 18th century, the garden contains more than 100 species of trees and 3,000 types of plants. Also on the premises are an exhibition hall and a library specializing in botany. The park is open daily from 10am to 9pm; admission is 250Pts (€1.50, $1.45) for adults and 125Pts (€0.75, 75¢) for children, free for 10years old and under.

ORGANIZED TOURS

One of Spain's largest tour operators is **Pullmantours,** Plaza de Oriente 8 (✆ **91-541-18-07;** Metro: Opera). Regardless of its destination or duration, virtually every tour departs from the Pullmantour terminal at that address. Half-day tours of Madrid include an artistic tour at 4,900Pts (€29.40, $28) per person, which provides entrance to a selection of the city's museums, and a panoramic half-day tour for 2,800Pts (€16.80, $16).

Southward treks to **Toledo** are the most popular full-day excursions. They cost 8,700Pts (€52.20, $50). These tours, including lunch, depart daily at 9:30am from the above-mentioned departure point, last all day, and include ample opportunities for wandering at will through the city's narrow streets. You can take an abbreviated half-day tour of Toledo, without stopping for lunch, for 5,650Pts (€33.90, $33). From May to September, these half-day visits to Toledo are conducted in both the morning and afternoon; the rest of the year, they depart only in the afternoon.

Another popular tour stops briefly in Toledo and continues on to visit both the monastery at **El Escorial** and **Valle de los Caídos** (the Valley of the Fallen) before returning the same day to Madrid. With lunch included, this all-day excursion costs 12,000Pts (€72, $70).

A final touring option involves Pullmantour's full-day excursions from Madrid that incorporate **Segovia** and **Ávila**—both focal points of Spanish culture and history—on the same day. Departing every day at 8:45am, and returning the same day at 6:30pm, they cost 7,000Pts (€42, $41)for participants who don't want lunch included in their experience, and from 9,200 to 10,700Pts (€55.20 to €64.20, $53 to $62) for those who opt for lunch.

THE SHOPPING SCENE

Tirso de Molina, the 17th-century playwright, called Madrid "a shop stocked with every kind of merchandise." It's estimated that 50,000 stores sell everything from high-fashion clothing to flamenco guitars to art and ceramics.

THE MAIN SHOPPING AREAS

The sheer diversity of shops in Madrid's **center** is staggering. Their densest concentration lies immediately north of Puerta del Sol, radiating out from Calle del Carmen, Calle Montera, and Calle Preciados.

> ### *C* Spain's Biggest Flea Market
>
> Foremost among Madrid flea markets is **El Rastro,** Plaza Cascorro and Ribera de Curtidores (Metro: La Latina; bus: 3 or 17), which occupies a roughly triangular district of streets and plazas a few minutes' walk south of Plaza Mayor. This market will delight anyone attracted to a mishmash of fascinating junk interspersed with bric-a-brac and paintings. But thieves are rampant here (hustling more than just antiques), so secure your wallet carefully, be alert, and proceed with caution. Open Saturday and Sunday only, from 9:30am to 1:30pm and to a lesser extent from 5 to 8pm.

Conceived, designed, and built in the 1910s and 1920s as a showcase for the city's best shops, hotels, and restaurants, the **Gran Vía** has since been eclipsed by other shopping districts, although its Art Nouveau and Art Deco glamour still survives. The bookshops here are among the best in the city, as are outlets for fashion, shoes, jewelry, and handcrafts from all regions of Spain. Under the arcades of the **Plaza Mayor** are exhibitions of lithographs and oil paintings, and within 3 or 4 blocks in every direction you'll find tons of souvenir shops.

The **Salamanca** district is known throughout Spain as the quintessential upper-bourgeois neighborhood. Here you'll find exclusive furniture, fur, and jewelry shops as well as several department stores. The main streets are calle de Serrano and calle de Velázquez. The district lies northeast of the center of Madrid, a few blocks north of Retiro Park. Its most central Metro stops are Serrano and Velázquez.

SOME NOTEWORTHY SHOPS

Established in 1904 as the "first house of Spanish ceramics," **Antigua Casa Talavera,** Isabel la Católica 2 (*C* **91-547-34-17;** Metro: Santo Domingo; bus: 1, 2, 46, 70, 75, or 148), has wares that include a sampling of regional styles from every major area of Spain. Sangría pitchers, dinnerware, tea sets, plates, and vases are all handmade. Inside one of the showrooms is an interesting selection of tiles painted with scenes from bullfights, dances, and folklore. One series of tiles depicts famous paintings at the Prado.

El Arco de los Cuchilleros Artesanía de Hoy, Plaza Mayor 9 (basement level) (*C* **91-365-26-80;** Metro: Puerta del Sol or Opera), is devoted to unusual craft items from throughout Spain. The merchandise is one-of-a-kind, Spanish, and in most cases contemporary, and includes a changing array of pottery, leather, textiles, wood carvings, glassware, wickerwork, papier-mâché, and silver jewelry.

El Corte Inglés, Preciados 3 (*C* **91-379-80-00;** Metro: Puerta del Sol), is the mother of all Spanish department stores, and this is the flagship store in Madrid. It sells Spanish handcrafts and also glamorous fashion articles, such as Pierre Balmain designs, for about a third less than in most European capitals. **Lasarte,** Gran Vía 44 (*C* **91-521-49-22;** Metro: Callao), is Madrid's, and Spain's, largest outlet for Lladró porcelain—the most characteristic and memorable form of fine porcelain made in Spain. You'll find at least 1,500 styles of figurines here, priced from 3,000Pts (€18, $17) for a small plate. Since Lladró introduces and recalls about 50 new models every year, the establishment's inventory is constantly rotating. Anything you buy here can be shipped.

Since 1846, **Loewe,** Gran Vía 8 (© **91-522-68-15;** Metro: Gran Vía), has been Spain's most elegant leather store. Its designers have always kept abreast of changing tastes and styles, but the inventory still retains a timeless chic. The store sells luggage, handbags, and jackets for men and women (in leather or suede). At **Casa de Diego,** Puerta del Sol 12 (© **91-522-66-43;** Metro: Puerta del Sol), you'll find a wide inventory of fans, ranging from plain to fancy, from plastic to exotic hardwood, from cost-conscious to lavish.

MADRID AFTER DARK

In summer, Madrid sponsors a series of plays, concerts, and films, and the city takes on the air of a virtual free festival. Pick up a copy of *Guía del Ocio* (available at most newsstands) for listings of these events. This guide also provides information about occasional discounts for commercial events, such as the concerts given in Madrid's parks. Also check the program of the Fundación Juan March, Calle Castello 77 (© **91-435-42-40;** Metro: Núñez de Balboa), which frequently stages free classical and chamber music concerts.

Flamenco in Madrid is geared mainly to tourists with fat wallets, and nightclubs are expensive. But since Madrid is preeminently a city of song and dance, you can often be entertained at very little cost—in fact, for the price of a glass of wine or beer, if you sit at a bar with live entertainment.

Tickets to dramatic and musical events usually range from 850 to 19,000Pts (€5.10 to €114, $5 to $110), with discounts of up to 50% granted on certain days (usually Wednesday and early performances on Sunday). In the event your choice is sold out, you may be able to get tickets (with a reasonable markup) at **Localidades Galicia,** Plaza del Carmen 1 (© **91-531-27-32;** Metro: Puerta del Sol). This agency, however, mainly markets tickets to bullfights and sports events. It's open from Tuesday to Sunday 9:30am to 1pm and 4:30 to 7pm.

THE PERFORMING ARTS

For those who speak Spanish, **Compañía Nacional de Nuevas Tendencias Escénicas** is an avant-garde troupe that performs new—and often controversial—works by undiscovered writers. **Compañía Nacional de Teatro Clásico,** as its name suggests, is devoted to the Spanish classics, including works by the ever-popular Lope de Vega or Tirso de Molina.

Among dance companies, **Ballet Nacional de España** is devoted exclusively to Spanish dance; its performances are always well attended. The national ballet company of the country is the **Ballet Lírico Nacional.** Also look for performances by choreographer Nacho Duato's **Compañía Nacional de Danza.**

World-renowned flamenco sensation António Canales and his troupe, **Ballet Flamenco António Canales** (© **91-531-27-32**), offer high-energy, spirited performances. Productions are centered around Canales's impassioned *Torero*—his interpretation of a bullfighter and the physical and emotional struggles within the man.

CLASSICAL MUSIC

Madrid's opera company is the **Teatro de la Opera,** and its symphony orchestra is the outstanding **Orquesta Sinfónica de Madrid** (at Teatro Real, see below).

Reopened in 1997 after a massive $157 million renovation, the **Teatro Real,** Plaza Isabel II (© **91-516-06-60;** Metro: Opera), is one of the world's finest stage and acoustic settings for opera. Its extensive state-of-the-art equipment affords elaborate stage designs and special effects. Today, the building is the home of the Compañía del Teatro Real and is the major venue for classical music and opera. On November 19, 1850, under the reign of Queen Isabel II, the Royal Opera house opened its doors with Donizett's *La Favorita*. Tickets are 2,000 to 17,000Pts (€12 to €102, $12 to $99).

Auditorio Nacional de Música, Príncipe de Vergara 146 (© **91-337-01-00;** Metro: Cruz del Rayo), is the ultramodern home of both the **National Orchestra of Spain,** which pays particular attention to the music of Spanish composers, and the **National Chorus of Spain.** Just north of Madrid's Salamanca district, it ranks as a major addition to the competitive circles of classical music in Europe. Tickets are 1,500 to 10,000Pts (€9 to €60, $9 to $58)

FLAMENCO

One of the best flamenco clubs in town, **Café de Chinitas,** Torija 7 (© **91-559-51-35;** Metro: Santo Domingo; bus: 1 or 2), features an array of (usually) Gypsy-born flamenco artists from Madrid, Barcelona, and Andalusia, whose acts and performers change about once a month. You can arrange for dinner before the show. It's open from Monday to Saturday, with dinner served from 9 to 11pm and the show lasting from 10:30pm to 3am. Reservations are recommended. Dinner and show cost from 10,250Pts (€61.50, $59), show and one drink 4,450Pts (€26.70, $26) after 12:15am.

Following an upswing in interest in flamenco after a period of declining interest in the 1980s, **Casa Patas,** Calle Cañizares 10 (© **91-369-04-96;** Metro: Tirso de Molina), is now one of the best places to see "true" flamenco as opposed to the more tourist-oriented version. It's also a bar/restaurant, with space reserved in the rear for flamenco. Shows are presented from Monday to Thursday at 10:30pm, Friday to Saturday from 9pm and midnight, and during Madrid's major fiesta month of May. The club itself is open daily from 9pm to 5am. Admission is 3,000Pts (€$18, $17).

CABARET

Since the mid-1990s, **Café de Foro,** Calle San Andres 38 (© **91-445-37-52;** Metro: Bilbao; bus: 40, 147, 149, or N19), in the Malasaña district, has been one of the most fashionable places in Madrid to hang out after dark. Patronizing the club are members of the literati along with a large student clientele. You never know exactly what the program for the evening will be, though live music such as pop, rock, merengue, salsa, or flamenco generally starts at 11pm. Cabaret is often featured, along with live merengue and salsa. It's open daily from 8pm to 3am. Admission is free, but cover might be imposed for a specially booked act.

Scala Melía Castilla, Calle Capitán Haya 43 (entrance at Rosario Pino 7) (© **91-571-44-11;** Metro: Cuzco), Madrid's most famous dinner show, is a major Las Vegas-style spectacle. The program is varied—you might see international or Spanish ballet, magic acts, ice skaters, whatever. Most definitely, you'll be entertained by a live orchestra. It's open from Tuesday to Saturday 8:30pm to 3am. Dinner is served beginning at 9pm; the show is presented at 10:30pm. Reservations are needed for the 90-minute show, which is changed annually. It's been running successfully since 1981. Dinner and show are 10,500Pts (€63, $61). Show and one drink are 5,500Pts (€33, $32).

LIVE MUSIC

Off Plaza de Santa Ana, **Café Central,** Plaza del Angel 10 (© **91-369-41-43;** Metro: Antón Martín), has a vaguely Art Deco interior, with an unusual series of stained-glass windows. Many of the patrons read newspapers and talk at the marble-top tables during the day, but the ambience is far more animated during the nightly jazz sessions. It's open from Sunday to Thursday 1:30pm to 2:30am and Friday and Saturday from 1:30pm to 3:30am; live jazz is offered daily from 10pm to 2am. Cover is 1,500Pts (€9, $9).

Madrid's ever-changing nightlife trendies flock to **Café La Palma** 62 (© **91-522-50-31**), Metro: San Bernardo), where live Cuban groups often dominate the agenda. As in Paris, anything Cuban is chic in Madrid. The setting is laid-back, and you can hang out in the lounge in a comfortable room filled with pillows. Mixed drinks cost from 750Pts (€4.50, $4.35). Open daily from 4pm to 3:30am. A young crowd in their early 20s and 30s flock here but don't even start to show up until after 10pm.

With dozens of small tables and a huge bar in its dark and smoky interior, **Clamores,** Albuquerque 14 (© **91-445-79-38;** Metro: Bilbao), is the largest and one of the most popular jazz clubs in Madrid. It has thrived because of the American and Spanish jazz bands that appear here. The place is open daily from 6pm to 3am or so, but jazz is presented only from Tuesday to Saturday. Tuesday to Thursday, performances are at 11pm and 1am; Saturday at 11:30pm and 1:30am. There are no live performances Sunday or Monday. Cover from Tuesday to Saturday is 800 to 1,200Pts (€4.80 to €7.20, $5 to $7), depending on the act.

DANCE CLUBS

Kapital, Atocha 125 (© **91-420-29-06;** Metro: Antón Martín), is the most sprawling, labyrinthine, and multicultural dance club in Madrid. In what was formerly a theater, it contains seven levels, each with at least one bar, and a sometimes radically different ambience and musical theme in each. If you grow tired of the sometimes frenetic dancing on the lower levels, keep climbing: Things get calmer and more laid-back as you rise. In warm weather, the seventh floor opens onto an outdoor terrace. It's open from Thursday to Sunday from 11:30pm to 5:30am. Cover, with first drink included, is 2,000Pts (€12, $12).

Set near the Puerta del Sol in the very center of Madrid, **Joy Eslava,** Arenal 11 (© **91-366-37-33;** Metro: Puerta de Sol), has survived fashions and styles and remains popular even though some of its former competitors have gone belly-up. This club attracts a wide range of professions and age groups, including members of the Madrileño *movida.* You've got a choice of three bars and a dance floor. Expect videos and some laser shows. Admission from Sunday to Wednesday is 2,000Pts (€12, $12),going up to 2,500 pesetas from Thursday to Saturday. Open from Thursday to Saturday 11:30pm to 6am, and from Sunday to Wednesday 11:30pm to 5:30am.

PUBS & BARS

Bar Cock, De la Reina 16 (© **91-532-28-26;** Metro: Gran Vía), attracts some of the most visible artists, actors, models, and filmmakers in Madrid, among them the award-winning Spanish director Pedro Almódovar. The name comes from the word *cocktail,* or so they say. The decoration is elaborately unique, in contrast to the hip clientele. It's open daily from 7pm to 3am; closed December 24 to 31.

Beloved by Hemingway, who had quite a few drinks here, **Chicote,** Gran Vía 12 (© **91-532-67-37;** Metro: Gran Vía), is Madrid's most famous cocktail bar. It's a classic, with the same 1930s decor it had when the foreign press sat out the Civil War here. Even the seats are original. Long a favorite of artists and writers, the bar became a haven for prostitutes in the late Franco era. No more. It's back in the limelight again, a sophisticated and much frequented rendezvous. It's open daily from 7:30am to 3am.

One of the best located bars in town, the fashionable **El Aljibe,** 4 Plaza de Oriente (℡ 91-548-46-20; Metro: Opera), at the majestic Plaza de Oriente, lies in a historic section in the very heart of the city. Velázquez lived at no. 4 on the square where he painted *Las Meninas.* Fancy coffees and elegant drinks are served here in a setting that reveals the remains of Madrid's medieval stone wall. Arabic tapestries form a part of the decor. Open daily from 7pm to 3am.

The 1847 construction of the **Palacio Gaviria,** Calle del Arenal 9 (℡ 91-526-60-69; Metro: Puerta del Sol or Opera), was heralded as the architectural triumph of one of the era's most flamboyant aristocrats, the marqués de Gaviria. Famous as one of the paramours of Isabel II, he outfitted his palace with the ornate jumble of neoclassical and baroque styles that later became known as Isabelino. In 1993, after extensive renovations, the building was opened to the public as a concert hall for the occasional presentation of classical music and as a late-night cocktail bar. Ten high-ceilinged rooms now function as richly decorated multipurpose areas for guests to wander and dance in what is the most kitschy and rococo disco in Madrid. Open from Monday to Friday 10pm to 3am, Saturday and Sunday 11pm to 5am. Cover is 1,200 to 2,500Pts (€7.20 to €15, $7 to $15) including your first drink.

GAY & LESBIAN CLUBS & CAFES

Plaza de Chueca (Metro: Chueca) has no fewer than four gay cafes lining the square's edges and something approaching a gay living room (with a healthy number of lesbians as well) is created every evening from 8pm to early the next morning. Open daily from 4pm to midnight, both **Café Figueroa,** Calle Augusto Figueroa 17 (℡ 91-521-16-73), and **Café Aquarella,** Calle Gravina 10 (℡ 91-522-21-43), have elevated gay table-hopping to a fine art. A diverse clientele includes both gay men and lesbians.

Leading the way as one of the various lesbian bars now established in Plaza de Chueca, the **Sutileza,** Plaza de Chueca (no phone), is the perfect starting point for the discerning lesbian on the prowl. The crowd is predominately women with a few gay men thrown in for good measure. from May to September there's an outside terrazza that competes with the other lesbian bars in the square, namely Escape and **Truco,** a *bar de copas* at Gravina 10 (℡ 91-532-89-21). The atmosphere at all the bars is friendly and frequently quite cruisey, and they're all open from Tuesday to Thursday and Sunday 7pm to 2:30am, and Friday and Saturday 7pm to 3:30am.

One of the predominant gay bars of Madrid, a center for gay consciousness-raising and gay cruising (though they say the name refers to automobile driving), **Cruising,** Perez Galdos 5 (℡ 91-521-51-43; Metro: Chueca), has probably been visited at least once by virtually every gay male in Castile. There're virtually no women inside, but always a hustler looking for a tourist john. It doesn't get crowded or lively until late at night. Open daily from 7pm to 3:30am. Beer costs from 400 to 600Pts (€2.40 to €3.60, $2.30 to $3.50).

CAVE CRAWLING

To capture a glimpse of the unique Madrid joie de vivre, visit some *mesones* and *cuevas,* many found in the *barrios bajos.* From Plaza Mayor, walk down Arco de Cuchilleros until you find a Gypsy-like cave that fits your fancy.

The bartenders at the **Mesón del Champiñón,** Cava de San Miguel 17 (no phone; Metro: Puerta del Sol or Opera), keep a brimming bucket of sangría behind the long stand-up bar as a thirst quencher for the crowd. The name of the establishment means mushroom, and that's exactly what you'll see depicted in various sizes along sections of the vaulted ceilings. A more appetizing way to experience a champiñón is to order a *ración* (serving) of grilled, stuffed, and salted mushrooms, served with toothpicks. Open daily from 7pm to 1:30am. Our favorite cueva in the area, the **Mesón de la Guitarra,** Cava de San Miguel 13 (© **91-559-95-31;** Metro: Puerta del Sol or Opera), is loud and exciting any night of the week, and it's as warmly earthy as anything you'll find in Madrid. The decor combines terra-cotta floors, antique brick walls, hundreds of sangría pitchers clustered above the bar, murals of gluttons, old rifles, and faded bull-fighting posters. Like most things in Madrid, the place doesn't get rolling until around 10:30pm. Open daily from 7pm to 2am.

DAY TRIPS FROM MADRID

TOLEDO ✪✪✪   If you have only 1 day for an excursion outside Madrid, go to Toledo, 66 kilometers (42 miles) to the southwest, a place made special by its blending of Arab, Jewish, Christian, and even Roman and Visigothic elements. Declared a national landmark, the city that inspired El Greco in the 16th century has remained relatively unchanged in parts of its central core. You can still stroll through streets barely wide enough for a man and his donkey.

Getting There   Daily **RENFE trains** run here frequently (© **902/240-202;** www.renfe.es). Those departing Madrid's Atocha Station run daily from 7:05am to 8:40pm; those leaving Toledo for Madrid run daily from 6:30am to 8:55pm (trip time: approximately 1 hour 15 minutes). One-way fare costs 760Pts (€4.55, $4.40).

Bus transit between Madrid and Toledo is faster and more convenient than travel by train. Buses, operated by several companies, the largest of which include Continental and Galiano, depart from Madrid's South Bus Station (Estacíon Sur de Autobuses), calle Méndez Alvaro (© **91-527-29-61** for tickets and information). Buses depart at 30-minute intervals every day from 6:30am to 10pm, and a one-way ticket costs 590Pts (€3.55E,$3.40).

Motorists exit Madrid via Cibeles (Paseo del Prado) and take N-401 south.

Visitor Information   The **tourist office** is at Puerta de Bisagra (© **925-22-08-43**), open from Monday to Saturday 9am to 7pm, and Sunday 9am to 3pm.

Exploring Toledo   Ranked among the greatest of Gothic structures, the **Cathedral** ✪✪✪, Arcos de Palacio (© **925-22-22-41;** bus: 5 or 6), actually reflects a variety of styles because of the more than 2½ centuries that went into its construction, from 1226 to 1493. The portals have witnessed many historic events, including the proclamation of Joanna the Mad and her husband, Philip the Handsome, as heirs to the throne of Spain. Among its art treasures, the *transparente* stands out—a wall of marble and florid baroque alabaster sculpture overlooked for years because of the cathedral's poor lighting. The sculptor Narcisco Tomé cut a hole in the ceiling, much to the consternation of Toledans, and now light touches the high-rising angels, a *Last Supper* in alabaster, and a Virgin in ascension. The 16th-century Capilla Mozárabe, containing works by Juan de Borgona, is another curiosity of the cathedral. The Treasure Room has a 500-pound 15th-century gilded monstrance—allegedly made with gold brought back from the New World by Columbus—that's still carried through the streets of Toledo during the feast of Corpus Christi. Admission to the cathedral is free;

admission to the Treasure Room is 700Pts (€4.20, $4). Open from Monday to Saturday 10am to 6pm, Sunday 2pm to 6:30pm.

The **Alcázar** ✸, Calle General Moscardó 4, near Plaza de Zocodover (© **925-22-30-38;** bus: 5 or 6), at the eastern edge of the old city, dominates the Toledo skyline. It became famous at the beginning of the Spanish Civil War when it underwent a 72-day siege that almost destroyed it. Today it has been rebuilt and turned into an army museum, housing such exhibits as a plastic model of what the fortress looked like after the Civil War, electronic equipment used during the siege, and photographs taken during the height of the battle. A walking tour gives a realistic simulation of the siege. Admission is 200Pts (€1.20, $1.15). Entrance is free on Wednesday and always free for children 10 and under. It's open from Tuesday to Sunday 9:30am to 2pm (6:30pm July to September).

Today a museum of art and sculpture, the **Museo de Santa Cruz** ✸✸, Miguel de Cervantes 3 (© **925-22-10-36;** bus: 5 or 6), was originally a 16th-century Spanish Renaissance hospice, founded by Cardinal Mendoza—"the third king of Spain"—who helped Ferdinand and Isabella gain the throne. The facade is almost more spectacular than any of the exhibits inside. It's a stunning architectural achievement in the classical plateresque style. The major artistic treasure inside is El Greco's *The Assumption of the Virgin,* his last known work. Paintings by Goya and Ribera are also on display. Admission is 1,000Pts (€6, $5.80). Open from Tuesday to Saturday 10am to 6:30pm, Sunday 10am to 2pm. To get here, pass beneath the granite archway on the eastern edge of Plaza de Zocodover and walk about 1 block.

SAN LORENZO DE EL ESCORIAL ✸✸✸

The second most important excursion from Madrid is the austere Royal Monastery of San Lorenzo de El Escorial, 48km (30 miles) to the west. Philip II ordered the construction of this rectangular granite-and-slate monster in 1563, 2 years after he moved his capital to Madrid. Once the haunt of aristocratic Spaniards, El Escorial is now a resort where hotels and restaurants flourish in summer, as hundreds flock here to escape the heat of the capital.

Getting There   More than two dozen **trains** depart daily from Madrid's Atocha, Nuevos Ministerios, and Chamartín stations (trip time: 1¼ hours). During summer extra coaches are added. For schedules and information, call © **902/240-202.**

The Office of Empresa Herranz, Calle del Rey 27 in El Escorial (© **91-890-41-22**), runs some 40 **buses** per day back and forth between Madrid's Moncloa Station and El Escorial; on Sunday service is curtailed to 10 buses. Trip time is 1 hour, and a round-trip fare is 870Pts (€5.20, $5).

Motorists can follow NVI (marked on some maps as A-6) from the northwest perimeter of Madrid toward Lugo, La Coruña, and El Escorial. After about half an hour, fork left onto C-505 toward San Lorenzo. Driving time from Madrid is about an hour.

Visitor Information   The **tourist information office** is at Floridablanca 10 (© **91-890-15-54**), open from Monday to Friday 10am to 2pm and 3 to 5pm and Saturday 10am to 2pm.

Exploring the Monastery   The huge granite fortress of the **Real Monasterio de San Lorenzo de El Escorial** ✸✸✸, Calle San Lorenzo de El Escorial 1 (© **91-890-59-03**), houses a wealth of paintings and tapestries and serves as a burial place for Spanish kings. Foreboding both inside and out because of its sheer size and institutional look, El Escorial took 21 years to complete. Philip II, who collected many of the paintings exhibited here in the New Museums, didn't appreciate El Greco and favored Titian. But you'll still find El Greco's *The Martyrdom of St. Maurice,* rescued from storage, and his *St. Peter.* Other superb works are Titian's *Last Supper* and Velázquez's *The Tunic of Joseph.* The Royal Library houses a priceless collection of 60,000 volumes—one of the most significant in the world. The displays range from the handwriting of St. Teresa of Avila to medieval instructions on playing chess.

You can also visit the Philip II Apartments; these are strictly monastic, and Philip called them the "cell for my humble self" in this "palace for God." The Apartments of the Bourbon Kings are lavishly decorated, in contrast to Philip's preference for the ascetic.

A comprehensive ticket costs 900Pts (€5.40, $5) adults and 400Pts (€2.40, $2.30) children. The monastery is open from Tuesday to Sunday: April to August 10am to 7pm, September 10am to 6pm, and October to March 10pm to 5pm.

SEGOVIA 𝒜𝒜𝒜   Less commercial than Toledo, Segovia, 87 kilometers (54 miles) northwest of Madrid, typifies the glory of Old Castile. Wherever you look, you'll see reminders of a golden era—whether it's the most spectacular Alcázar on the Iberian Peninsula or the well-preserved and still-functioning Roman aqueduct. Segovia lies on the slope of the Guadarrama Mountains, where the Eresma and Clamores rivers converge. This ancient city stands in the center of the most castle-rich part of Castile. Isabella was proclaimed queen of Castile here in 1474.

Getting There   Fifteen **trains** leave Madrid's Chamartín and Atocha stations every day (trip time: 2 hours). A one-way rail fare from Madrid costs 775Pts (€4.65, $4.50). Segovia's station, **Paseo Obispo Quesada** (✆ 902-24-02-02), is a 20-minute walk from the town center. Bus 3 departs every quarter hour for Plaza Mayor.

Buses arrive and depart from the **Estacionamiento Municipal de Autobuses,** Paseo de Ezequile González 10 (✆ 921-42-77-25), near the corner of Avenida Fernández Ladreda and the steeply sloping Paseo Conde de Sepúlveda. There are 10 to 15 buses a day to and from Madrid (which depart from Paseo de la Florida 11; Metro: Norte). A one-way bus fare from Madrid to Segovia sells for 765Pts (€$4.80).

Motorists can take NVI (on some maps it's known as A-6) or the Autopista del Nordeste northwest from Madrid, toward León and Lugo. At the junction with Route 110 (signposted Segovia), turn northeast.

Visitor Information   The **tourist office** is at Plaza Mayor 10 (✆ 921-46-03-34), open daily from 10am to 2pm and 5 to 7pm.

Exploring Segovia   You'll view the **Alcázar** 𝒜, Plaza de la Reina Victoria Eugenia (✆ 921-46-07-59; bus: 3), first from below, at the junction of the Clamores and Eresma Rivers. It's on the west side of Segovia, and you may not spot it when you first enter the city. But that's part of the surprise. The castle dates back to the 12th century, and royal romance is inextricably associated with it. Isabella first met Ferdinand here, and today you can see a facsimile of her dank bedroom. Walk the battlements of this once-impregnable castle, from which its occupants hurled down boiling oil onto the enemy below. Brave the hazardous stairs of the tower, built by Isabella's father as a prison, for a panoramic view of Segovia. Admission is 400Pts (€2.40, $2.30) adults, 200Pts

(€1.20, $1.15) children 8 to 12, and free for children under 8. The castle is open daily, from April to September 10am to 7pm, and from October to March 10am to 6pm. Take either Calle Vallejo, Calle de Velarde, Calle de Daoiz, or Paseo de Ronda.

The **Roman aqueduct** ⭐⭐⭐, Plaza del Azoguejo, is an architectural marvel built by the Romans more than 2,000 years ago. Until recent times, it was still used to carry water. Constructed of mortarless granite, it consists of 118 arches, and in one two-tiered section it soars 30 meters (95 ft.) to its highest point. The Spanish call it simply El Puente. It spans Plaza del Azoguejo, the old market square, stretching nearly 730 meters (800 yd). When the Moors took Segovia in 1072, they destroyed 36 arches, which were rebuilt under Ferdinand and Isabella in 1484.

Constructed between 1515 and 1558, the **Cabildo Catedral de Segovia** ⭐⭐, Plaza de la Catedral, Marqués del Arco (📞 **921-46-22-05**), is the last Gothic cathedral built in Spain. Fronting historic Plaza Mayor, it stands on the spot where Isabella I was proclaimed queen of Castile. Affectionately called La Dama de las Catedrales ("the Lady of Cathedrals"), it contains numerous treasures, such as the Blessed Sacrament Chapel (created by the flamboyant Churriguera); stained-glass windows; elaborately carved choir stalls; and 16th- and 17th-century paintings, including a reredos portraying the deposition of Christ from the cross by Juan de Juni. Admission to the cathedral is free; admission to the cloisters, museum, and chapel room is 300Pts (€1.80, $1.75) adults and 150Pts (€0.90, 85¢) children. Open daily spring and summer from 9am to 7pm and off-season from 9am to 6pm.

2 Barcelona

Hardworking Barcelona enjoys the most diversified and prosperous economy of any region in Spain. And culturally, it is as rich as any. Its roster of natives and longtime residents—the *modernista* architect Antoni Gaudí, artists Pablo Picasso, Salvador Dalí, and Joan Miró, as well as the opera star Montserrat Caballé—have been instrumental in defining Catalan culture.

As one local newspaper critic put it, "If there were an award for the city that has done the most in the last few years to rebuild, reclaim, and expand while maintaining its elegance and charm, Barcelona would win hands down." The years that led up to and immediately following the 1992 Olympics made a huge difference to the city. Residual benefits from the games have included a roster of impressive new hotels, top-notch sporting facilities, the refurbishing of an airport capable of funneling 18 million annual visitors into Catalonia, and new ring roads that have alleviated some crucial traffic problems. And Barcelona, despite its dearly protected Catalán cultural and linguistic identity, continues a proud role as Spain's literary and publishing headquarters.

With a reputation as the savviest business center in Spain, Barcelona boasts buildings by I. M. Pei, Arata Isozaki, Richard Meier, Norman Foster, Victorio Gregotti, and native son Ricardo Bofill. Miles of grimy industrial waterfronts have been returned to clean and sandy beaches. In fact, the entire city has been reoriented toward the Mediterranean, whereas it once almost seemed to turn its back on the sea. Flower stalls, bird cages, and decorative pavements along the gorgeous pedestrian boulevard Les Rambles have been rejuvenated, and a state-of-the-art transportation network carries visitors past monuments that look better than when they were first erected. Unlike either of its landlocked

Barcelona

Plaça de
Francesc Macia

Carrer de Buenos Aires

Carrer de Londres

Carrer de Paris

Travessara de Gràcia

Avinguda Diagonal

Carrer de Còrsega

Gran de Gràcia

Travessara de Gràcia

Av. de Sant Antoni Maria Claret

Carrer de la Industria

EIXAMPLE

Carrer de Provença

Carrer Enric Granados

Carrer de Balmes

Rambla de Catalunya

Passeig de Gràcia

Carrer de Pau Claris

Carrer de Rosselló

Avinguda Diagonal

Carrer de Mallorca

Carrer de València

Carrer d'Aragó

Carrer de R. de Flor

Plaça de la
Sagrada
Família

Carrer del Comte d'Urgel

Carrer de Villaroel

Carrer de Casanova

Carrer de Muntaner

Carrer d'Aribau

Carrer del Consell de Cent

Carrer de la Diputació

Gran Via de les Corts Catalanes

Carrer de R. de Uria

Carrer del Bruc

Carrer de Girona

Carrer de Bailén

Passeig de Sant-Joan

Carrer de Napols

Carrer de Sicilia

Plaça de la
Universitat

Ronda Universitat

Carrer de Pelai

Plaça
Catalunya

Plaça de
Tetuan

Ronda de Sant Antoni

RAVAL

Plaça
Urquinaona

Ronda de Sant Pere

Carrer   de Casp

Carrer   d'Auslas Marc

Carrer   d'Ali Bei

Carrer de Ribes

Carrer de Sardenya

Av. Portal de l'Àngel

La Rambla

Via Laietana

BARRI GÒTIC

Carrer de Hospital

Carrer de Sant Pau

C. de

Ferran   C. de la Princesa

Passeig de Lluís Companys

Passeig de Pujades

Carrer de la Marina

Carrer Nou de la Rambla

Avda. de les Drassanes

La Rambla

LA RIBERA

Carrer del Comerç

Passeig de Picasso

PARC DE LA
CIUTADELLA

Carrer de Wellington

Carrer Ample

Passeig de Colom

Moll de la Fusta

Pg. Isabel II

Plaça Portal
de la Pau

Moll d'Espanya

Avinguda d'Icaria

PARC
ZOOLÒGIC

Villa
Olímpica →

Port
Vell

BARCELONETA

Passeig   Marítim

0   1/4 mi

0   0.25 km

(i) Information

(i) EIXAMPLE

(i)

competitors, Seville or Madrid, Barcelona welcomes the newest phenomenon in tourism, the cruise-ship industry.

Despite the city's burgeoning population (and the regrettable growth in both drug addiction and street crime), people are flocking to the newly revived Barcelona. Nearly 40% of tourists to Spain go to Catalonia, and many are repeat visitors.

ESSENTIALS

GETTING THERE   By Plane   The **Aeropuerto de Barcelona,** 08820 Prat de Llobregat (© **93-298-38-38;** www.aena.es), lies 12 kilometers (7½ miles) southwest of the city. Even post-Olympics, most transatlantic passengers are obliged to change aircraft in Madrid before continuing on to Barcelona. The only exception is **TWA** (© **800/892-4141**), which maintains nonstop transatlantic service to Barcelona from New York. A train runs at 30-minute intervals between the airport and Barcelona's Estació Central de Barcelona-Sants daily from 6:14am to 10:44pm (10:14pm is the last city departure, 6:14am the first airport departure). The 21-minute trip costs 400Pts (€2.40, $2.30). If your hotel lies near Plaça de Catalunya, you might opt for an Aerobús that runs daily every 15 minutes from 5:30am to 10pm. The fare is 500Pts (€3, $2.90). A taxi from the airport into central Barcelona will cost about 3,000Pts (€18, $17.40).

By Train   The *Barcelona Talgo* train provides rail service between Paris and Barcelona in 11½ hours. For many other connections from the mainland of Europe, it'll be necessary to change trains at Port Bou. Most trains issue seat and sleeper reservations.

Trains departing from the **Estació de Franca,** Avenida Marqués de l'Argentera, cover long distances in Spain as well as international routes. There are express night trains to Paris, Zurich, Milan, and Geneva. All the international routes served by the state-owned RENFE rail company use the Estació de Franca, including some of its most luxurious express trains, such as the *Pau Casals* and *Talgo Catalán*. From this station, you can book tickets to the major cities: Madrid (five *talgos,* 7 hours; three *rápidos,* 10 hours), Seville (two per day, 10½ hours), and Valencia (11 per day, 4 hours). For general **RENFE information,** call © **902/240-202.**

By Bus   Bus travel to Barcelona is cheaper than the train, faster than all but the *talgos,* and very popular among Spaniards who travel frequently between the two main cities. **Enatcar,** Estació del Nord (© **902/422-242**), operates five buses per day to Madrid (trip time: 8 hours) and 10 buses per day to Valencia (trip time: 4½ hours). A one-way ticket to Madrid costs 3,465Pts (€20.84, $20); a one-way ticket to Valencia is 3,115Pts (€18.74, $18).

By Car   From France (the usual road approach to Barcelona), the major access route is at the eastern end of the Pyrenees. You have a choice of the express highway (E-15) or the more scenic coastal road. From France, it's possible to approach Barcelona via Toulouse. Cross the border into Spain at Puigcerdá (frontier stations are there), near the principality of Andorra. From here, take N-152 to Barcelona. From Madrid, take N-2 to Zaragoza, then A-2 to El Vendrell, followed by A-7 to Barcelona.

VISITOR INFORMATION   Tourist Office   A conveniently located tourist office is the **Oficina de Informacio de Turisme de Barcelona,** Plaça de Catalunya, 17-S (© **93-304-32-32;** Metro: Plaça de Catalunya). It's open daily from 9am to 9pm.

Websites   A good place to start is **www.barcelona-on-line.es**, where you can find up-to-date information and book hotels, restaurants, and tours. See Madrid "Visitor Information," earlier in this chapter, for additional websites.

CITY LAYOUT   **Plaça de Catalunya** (Plaza de Cataluña in Spanish) is the city's heart; the world-famous Rambles (Ramblas) and the grand boulevard Paseo de Gracia, its arteries. Les Rambles begin at Plaça Portal de la Pau, with its 50-meter (164-ft.) monument to Columbus and a panoramic view of the port, and stretch north to Plaça de Catalunya, with its fountains and trees.

At the end of Les Rambles is the **Barri Xinés** (Barrio Chino, the "Chinese Quarter"), which in the past was notorious as a haven of prostitution and drugs. It is being cleaned up, but is still not a terribly safe district; it's best viewed during the day. Off Les Rambles is **Plaça Reial** (Plaza Real in Spanish), Barcelona's most harmoniously proportioned square.

The major wide boulevards are **Avinguda Diagonal** and **Passeig de Colom** and the elegant shopping street **Passeig de Gràcia** (Paseo de Gracia). A short walk from Les Rambles will take you to **Passeig del Moll de la Fusta,** a waterfront promenade developed for the Olympic renewal with some of the finest (but not the cheapest) restaurants in Barcelona. To the east is the old port of the city, **La Barceloneta,** from the 18th century.

Barri Gótic (Barrio Gótico, the Gothic Quarter) lies to the east of Les Rambles. This is the site of the city's oldest buildings, including the cathedral and many gorgeous palaces with central courtyards. North of Plaça de Catalunya, the **Eixample** unfolds. An area of wide boulevards, in contrast to the Gothic Quarter, it contains two major roads leading out of Barcelona, Avinguda Diagonal and Gran Vía de les Corts Catalánes. Another major area, **Gràcia,** lies north of the Eixample. **Montjuïc,** one of the mountains of Barcelona, begins at Plaça d'Espanya, a traffic rotary. This was the setting for the 1992 Summer Olympic Games and is today the site of Vila Olimpica. The other mountain is **Tibidabo,** in the northwest, offering fine views of the city and the Mediterranean and boasting an amusement park.

GETTING AROUND

To save money on public transport, buy one of the transportation cards, each valid for 10 trips: **Tarjeta T-1,** for 825Pts (€4.95, $5), is good for the Metro, bus, Montjuïc funicular, and Tramvía Blau, which runs from Passeig de Sant Gervasi/Avinguda del Tibidabo to the bottom part of the funicular to Tibidabo.

Passes (*abonos temporales*) are available at any Metro station or at the office of **Transports Metropolita de Barcelona,** Calle Go 2123 (© **93-298-70-00** for information), open from Monday to Friday 8am to 5pm.

Tips Traveler's Tip

To save money on sightseeing tours during summer, take a ride on **Bus Turistic,** which passes by a dozen of the most popular sights. You can get on and off the bus as you please and ride the Tibidabo funicular and the Montjuïc cable car and funicular for the price of a single ticket. Tickets, which may be purchased on the bus or at the transportation booth at Plaça de Catalunya, cost 2,000Pts (€12, $12) for 1 day or 2,500Pts (€15, $15) for 2 days.

BY METRO (SUBWAY)   Barcelona's Metro consists of five main lines. Two commuter trains also service the city, fanning out to the suburbs. A one-way fare is 150Pts (€0.90, 85¢), and the major station for all subway lines is Plaça de Catalunya.

BY BUS   Some 50 bus lines traverse the city, and the driver issues a ticket as you board at the front. Most buses operate daily from 6:30am to 10pm; some night buses go along the principal arteries from 10pm to 4am. Buses are color-coded— red ones cut through the city center during the day, and blue ones do the job at night. A one-way fare is 150Pts (€0.90, 85¢).

The **Barcelona "Moon Express"** is a tourist train that runs through the city from 10pm to 2am and costs 900Pts (€5.40, $5) for a ride. It takes in the city's most scenic highlights at night, including floodlit Gothic buildings. Tickets can be purchased on the train. For more information, phone ℂ **906-30-12-82.**

BY TAXI   Each yellow-and-black taxi bears the letters *sp* (*servicio público*) on both its front and its rear. The basic rate begins at 300Pts (€$1.90). For each additional kilometer in the slow-moving traffic, you're assessed a charge of 110 to 118Pts (€0.65 to €0.70, 65¢ to 73¢). For a taxi, call ℂ **93-330-08-04.**

BY CAR   Driving is a headache in congested Barcelona, and it's potentially dangerous. However, a car would be ideal to tour the environs. All three of the major U.S.-based car-rental firms are represented in Barcelona, both at the airport and at downtown offices. Check with **Budget,** at Barcelona Airport 71 (ℂ **93-298-35-00**); **Avis,** at Carrer de Casanova 209 (ℂ **93-209-95-33**); or **Hertz,** at Carrer Tuset 10 (ℂ **93-217-80-76**).

BY FUNICULAR & TELEFÉRICO   Two of Barcelona's high-altitude vantage points, Montjuïc and Tibidabo, accessible by funicular, are visited for a panoramic overview of the city. The departure point for Tibidabo lies on the northern outskirts of Barcelona's central core, on the *Avinguda del Tibidabo.* To reach the funicular's departure point, you can take either a taxi (by far the easiest and least confusing way), a conventional bus (it's marked "Tibidabo") or, on weekends, the **Tramvía Blau (blue streetcar),** a trolleycar that operates only during limited hours on Saturday and Sunday, and which charges 450Pts (€2.70, $2.60) to hop aboard. The core of the Tibidabo experience, however, concerns the funicular itself, which operates at 20- to 30-minute intervals every day from 7:15am to 9:45pm. A one-way ride costs 600Pts (€3.60, $3.53).

Tibidabo's counterpart is the panoramic eyrie of Montjuïc, a gentle rise southeast of Barcelona's central core. Site of some of the sporting activities during the 1992 Olympic games, it can be reached by the Montjuïc funicular, whose point of origin begins at the Parallel Metro station. The funicular operates in summer daily from 11am to 8pm, and in winter only on Saturday, Sunday, and holidays from 10:45am to 2pm. It charges a round-trip fare of 420Pts (€2.50, $2.45).

You can always get off the funicular at Montjuïc, exploring the attractions here, but for high-altitude freaks, it's sometimes worthwhile to continue from Montjuïc on yet another cable-operated conveyance, the Montjuïc teleférico. Its destination is yet another panoramic hilltop and the Castell de Montjuïc. Operating daily in summer from 11am to 10pm, and in winter daily from 10:45am to 8pm, it charges a one-way fare of 400Pts (€2.40, $2.30) and a round-trip fare of 650Pts (€3.90, $3.75).

For another spectacular aerial view of Barcelona—definitely not for the acrophobic—book a ride aboard the **Transbordador Aeri del Puerto.** This

Barcelona Metro

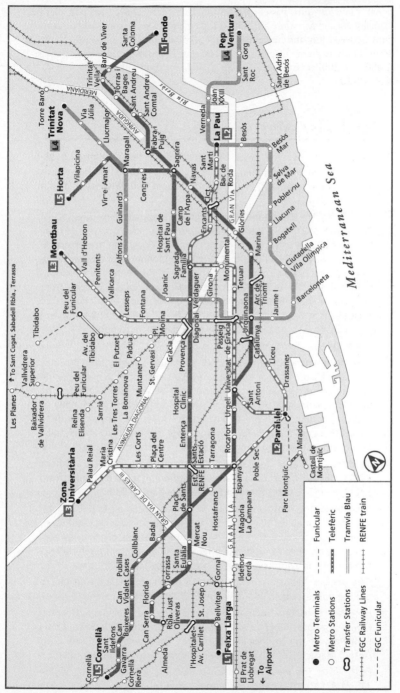

aerial cable car lifts passengers hundreds of feet above the port between Barceloneta and Montjuïc hill. The ride's a bit scary, so be warned. The cable car runs between July and September daily 10:30am to 7pm; off-season hours are from 11am to 5pm. Departures are every 15 minutes; a one-way passage is 1,000 to 1,200Pts (€6 to €7.20, $6 to $7). For more information, call ℂ **93-441-48-20.**

✐ *FAST FACTS:* Barcelona

American Express The Amex office at Passeig de Gràcia 101 (ℂ **93-217-00-70;** Metro: Diagonal), near the corner of Carrer del Rosselló, is open from Monday to Friday 9:30am to 6pm and Saturday 10am to noon.

Consulates The Consulate of the **United States,** at Reina Elisenda 23 (ℂ **93-280-22-27;** train: Reina Elisenda), is open from Monday to Friday 9am to 12:30pm and 3 to 5pm. The **Canadian Consulate,** Travessera de les Corts 265 (ℂ **93-215-07-04;** Metro: Plaça Molina), is open from Monday to Friday 10am to noon. The Consulate of the **United Kingdom,** Av. Diagonal 477 (ℂ **93-366-62-00;** Metro: Hospital Clínic), is open from Monday to Friday 9:30am to 1:30pm and 4 to 5pm. The Consulate of **Australia** is at Gran Vía Carlos III 98, 9th floor (ℂ **93-330-94-96;** Metro: María Cristina), open from Monday to Friday 10am to noon.

Currency See "Fast Facts: Madrid."

Currency Exchange Most banks will exchange currency from Monday to Friday 8:30am to 2pm and Saturday 8:30am to 1pm. A major *oficina de cambio* (exchange office) is operated at the Estació Central de Barcelona-Sants, the principal rail station; it's open from Monday to Saturday 8:30am to 10pm and Sunday 8:30am to 2pm and 4:30 to 10pm. There are three major banks at Plaça de Catalunya, including La Caixa, with currency exchange windows frequented by tourists.

Dentists Call **Clinica Dental Beonadex,** Paseo Bona Nova 69, 3rd floor (ℂ **93-418-44-33;** bus: 22), for an appointment. It is open Monday from 3 to 9pm and Tuesday through Friday from 8am to 3pm.

Drugstores The most central one is **Farmacia Manuel Nadal i Casas,** Rambla de Canaletes 121 (ℂ **93-317-49-42;** Metro: Plaça de Catalunya), open daily from 9am to 10pm. After hours, various pharmacies take turns staying open at night. All pharmacies that are not open do post the names and addresses of after-hours pharmacies in the area.

Emergencies In an emergency, phone ℂ **080** to report a **fire,** ℂ **092** to call the **police,** and ℂ **061** to request an **ambulance.**

Hospitals Barcelona has many hospitals and clinics, including **Hospital Clínic,** Casanova 143 (ℂ **93-227-54-00**), and **Hospital de la Santa Creu i Sant Pau,** at the intersection of Carrer Cartagena and Carrer Sant Antoni Maria Claret (ℂ **93-291-90-00;** Metro: Hospital de Sant Pau).

Post Office The main post office is at Plaça d'Antoni López (ℂ **93-219-71-97;** Metro: Jaume I). It's open from Monday to Friday 8am to 9pm and Saturday 9am to 1pm.

Safety Be particularly careful with cameras, purses, and wallets, all favorite targets of thieves and pickpockets in Barcelona—particularly on the world-famous Les Rambles. The southern part of Les Rambles, near the waterfront, is the most dangerous section, especially at night. Proceed with caution.

Telephone The **country code** for Spain is **34**. The **city code** for Barcelona is **93**. To make an **international call,** dial **07,** wait for the tone, and dial the country code, the area code, and the number. Note that an international call from a public phone booth requires stacks and stacks of 100 peseta coins. As an alternative, purchase a **phone card** from a tobacco shop (*estanco*), the post office, or other authorized dealer.

WHERE TO STAY
CIUTAT VELLA (OLD CITY)
Expensive

Hotel Colón 🏨🏨   This postwar hotel is blessed with one of the most dramatic locations in Barcelona, opposite the cathedral's main entrance. Inside you'll find conservative and slightly old-fashioned public areas and a helpful staff. Rooms are filled with comfortable furniture and (despite recent renovations) an appealingly dowdy kind of charm. Though lacking views, those in back are quieter. Sixth-floor rooms with balconies overlooking the square are the most desirable. Some lower rooms are dark.

Av. de la Catedral 7, 08002 Barcelona. 📞 800/845-0636 in the U.S., or 93-301-14-04. Fax 93-317-29-15. www.hotelcolon.es. 147 units. 26,300–39,850Pts (€157.80–€239.10, $153–$231) double; from 46,350Pts (€278.10, $269) suite. AE, DC, MC, V. Bus: 16, 17, 19, or 45. **Amenities:** 2 restaurants, bar; room service; baby-sitting; laundry/dry cleaning. *In room:* A/C, TV, minibar, hair dryer.

Le Meridien Barcelona 🏨🏨🏨   This is the finest hotel in the old town, thanks in large part to a major refurbishment in 1997. It's superior in both amenities and comfort to its closest rival, the Colón. Rooms are spacious and comfortable, with double-glazed windows, extra-large beds, and bathrooms with heated floors.

Rambles 111, 08002 Barcelona. 📞 800/543-4300 in the U.S., or 93-318-62-00. Fax 93-301-77-76. www.meridienbarcelona.com. 206 units. 42,000–52,000Pts (€252–€312, $244–$302) double; from 65,000Pts (€390, $377) suite. AE, DC, MC, V. Parking 2,000Pts (€12, $12). Metro: Liceu or Plaça de Catalunya. **Amenities:** Restaurant, bar; gym; room service; baby-sitting; laundry/dry cleaning. *In room:* A/C, TV, minibar, hair dryer.

Moderate

Duques de Bergara 🏨   Barcelona's newest upscale hotel occupies what was originally the private 1899 town house of the Duke of Bergara (look for his coat of arms in the stained-glass panels of the reception area). Public areas artfully contain stained glass and decorative accessories originally installed by modernist architect Emilio Salas I Cortes. In 1998, a new tower was added. Rooms are outfitted with conservatively traditional comforts.

Bergara 11. 📞 93-301-51-51. Fax 93-317-34-42. www.duqueshoteles-catalonia.es. 150 units. 34,900Pts (€209.40, $202) double; 37,900Pts (€227.40, $220) triple. AE, DC, MC, V. Metro: Catalunya. **Amenities:** restaurant, bar, cafe; pool; room service; laundry. *In room:* A/C, TV, minibar, hairdryer.

Granvía 🏨   A grand hotel on one of the most fashionable boulevards in Barcelona, the Granvía offers public areas that reflect the opulence of the 1860s.

It's your best choice if you want to feel like royalty. The traditional rooms are comfortable rather than luxurious. Rooms come in a variety of shapes and sizes. The courtyard, graced with a fountain and palm trees, is set with tables for alfresco drinks; in the garden room off the courtyard, continental breakfast is served. Centrally heated in the winter, the hotel has one drawback: street noise, which might disturb the light sleeper.

Gran Vía de les Cortes Catalanes 642, 08007 Barcelona. © 93-318-19-00. Fax 93-318-99-97. 50 units. 14,000Pts (€84, $81) double. AE, DC, MC, V. Metro: Plaça de Catalunya. **Amenities:** restaurant; laundry/dry cleaning. *In room:* A/C, TV, minibar.

Hotel Regencia Colón *Value*   This stately stone hotel stands behind the more prestigious, superior, and expensive Hotel Colón in the shadow of the cathedral. The formal lobby seems a bit dour, but the well-maintained rooms are comfortable and often roomy, albeit worn. Rooms are insulated against sound, and 40 of them have full-tub bathrooms, the remainder have showers only. The hotel is a good value for Barcelona.

Carrer Sagristans 13–17, 08002 Barcelona. © 93-318-98-58. Fax 93-317-28-22. www.hotelregenciacolon. com. 55 units. 20,000Pts (€120, $116) double; 25,750Pts (€154.50, $149) triple. AE, DC, MC, V. Metro: Jaume 1 or Urquinaona. **Amenities:** Restaurant, bar; baby-sitting; laundry/dry cleaning. *In room:* A/C, TV, minibar, hair dryer, safe.

Mesón Castilla   This two-star hotel, originally established in 1952, occupies a former apartment building. Owned and operated by the Spanish hotel chain HUSA, the Castilla is clean, charming, and well maintained. Its nearest rival is the Regencia Colón, to which it is comparable in atmosphere. Rooms, which benefited from a renovation in 1997, are comfortable—beds have ornate headboards—and some open onto large terraces.

Carrer Valldoncella 5, 08002 Barcelona. © 93-318-21-82. Fax 93-412-40-20. Hmesoncastilla@teleline.es. 56 units. 14,800Pts (€88.80, $86) double. V. Parking 2,500Pts (€15, $15). Metro: Plaça de la Universitat. **Amenities:** Dining area; laundry. *In room:* A/C, TV, minibar, hair dryer, safe.

Montecarlo   This hotel stands beside the wide and sloping promenade of Les Rambles, and was built around 200 years ago as an opulent private home. In the 1930s it was transformed into the comfortably unpretentious hotel you'll find today. Rooms are efficiently decorated. Double-glazed windows help keep out some of the noise. The public areas include some of the building's original accessories, with carved doors, a baronial fireplace, and crystal chandeliers.

Ramble dels Estudis 124, 08002 Barcelona. © 93-412-04-04. Fax 93-318-73-23. montecarlobcn@ abaforum.es. 60 units. 20,100Pts (€120.60, $117) double. AE, DC, MC, V. Parking 2,100Pts (€12.60, $12). Metro: Plaça de Catalunya. **Amenities:** room service; baby-sitting laundry/dry cleaning. *In room:* A/C, TV, minibar, hair dryer, safe.

Inexpensive

Hostal Levante   The small and very simple rooms here are scattered over two floors of a 200-year-old building connected by a cramped and creaking elevator. Drawbacks are that you're likely to be confronted with lots of screaming children, relatives of the family that owns the place. Benefits include a position in the heart of the historic Barri Gòtic, near the Plaça de Sant Jaume, and clean, utterly unpretentious rooms. No meals are served, and the place is strictly laissez-faire, but a worthy choice for its location and rock-bottom prices.

Baïxada de Sant Miguel 2, 08002 Barcelona. © 93-317-95-65. Fax 93-317-05-26. 27 units (7 with bathroom). 5,500Pts (€33, $32) double without bathroom; 6,500Pts (€39, $38) double with bathroom. AE, MC, V. Metro: Liceu or Jaume 1. **Amenities:** TV lounge. *In room:* No phone.

Hostal Neutral   If you're looking for a modest, inexpensive pension, this is a decent choice. The name, Hostal Neutral, may seem odd to many present-day guests, but it reflected the owner's neutrality during the armed conflicts of World War I that had by then engulfed all of Europe. Today, it functions as an older but highly recommendable pension; the affordable rooms are "neutral" in decor, but clean and comfortable nonetheless. Breakfast, the only meal available, is served in a salon with a coffered ceiling.

Rambla de Catalunya 42, 08007 Barcelona. ✆ **93-487-63-90.** 35 units (28 with full bathroom, 7 with shower only [no toilet]). 5,460Pts (€32.75, $32) double with shower only (no toilet); 6,530Pts (€39.23, $38) double with bathroom. MC, V. Metro: Paseo de Gracia. **Amenities:** Dining area; TV lounge.

SUR DIAGONAL
Very Expensive

Barcelona Hilton ⭐⭐⭐   This five-star property, opposite the gates to the fairgrounds (beyond that, to the Olympic Stadium), is part of a huge commercial complex. Most rooms are rather large and finely equipped. Furnishings are Hilton-standardized, but filled with thick carpeting, rich wood furnishings, and some of the best combination bathrooms in the city, with all the extras. Some units are reserved exclusively for women.

Av. Diagonal 589–591, 08014 Barcelona. ✆ **800/445-8667** in the U.S. and Canada, or 93-495-77-77. Fax 93-495-77-00. www.hilton.com. 286 units. 44,000–52,000Pts (€264–€312, $255–$302) double; from 54,000–120,000Pts (€324–€720, $313–$696) suite. AE, DC, MC, V. Parking 3,000Pts (€18, $17). Metro: María Cristina. **Amenities:** Restaurant, bar; fitness center; room service; laundry/dry cleaning; no-smoking rooms. *In room:* A/C, TV, minibar, hair dryer, safe, robes.

Claris ⭐⭐   One of the most unusual hotels in Barcelona, the postmodern Claris is one of only two five-star grand luxe hotels in the city center. It opened in 1992, in time for the Olympics, and includes a pool and garden on its roof, and a minimuseum of Egyptian antiquities on its second floor. Rooms are painted an iconoclastic blue-violet and incorporate copies of ancient Egyptian art with state-of-the-art electronic accessories.

Carrer de Pau Claris 150, 08009 Barcelona. ✆ **800/888-4747** in the U.S., or 93-487-62-62. Fax 93-215-79-70. www.derbyhotels.es. 120 units. 42,900–46,800Pts (€257.40–€280.80, $249–$271) double; 55,000–65,000Pts (€330–€390, $319–$377) suite. AE, DC, MC, V. Parking 2,250Pts (€13.50, $14). Metro: Passeig de Gràcia. **Amenities:** 2 restaurants, bar; pool; fitness center; private museum; room service; baby-sitting; laundry/dry cleaning. *In room:* A/C, TV, minibar, hair dryer, safe.

Hotel Ritz ⭐⭐⭐   The finest, most prestigious, and most architecturally distinguished hotel in Barcelona, the Art Deco Ritz dates from 1919. It has welcomed more millionaires, celebrities, and aristocrats than any other hotel in northeastern Spain. One of the finest features is its cream-and-gilt neoclassical lobby, featuring marble floors and potted palms. Rooms are formal and richly furnished, sometimes with Regency furniture; bathrooms are accented with mosaics and tubs inspired by those in ancient Rome.

Gran Vía de les Corts Catalanes 668, 08010 Barcelona. ✆ **93-318-52-00.** Fax 93-318-01-48. www. ritzbcn.com. 122 units. 38,000–45,000Pts (€228–€270, $220–$261) double; 140,000Pts (€840, $812) suite. AE, DC, MC, V. Parking 3,500Pts (€21, $22). Metro: Passeig de Gràcia. **Amenities:** Restaurant, bar; fitness center; boutiques; room service; baby-sitting; laundry/dry cleaning. *In room:* A/C, TV, minibar, hair dryer, safe.

Rey Juan Carlos I/Conrad International Barcelona ⭐⭐⭐   Named for the Spanish king, who attended its opening and who has visited it several times since, this is the only five-star choice that competes effectively against the Ritz and Claris. Rooms contain many electronic extras, conservatively comfortable furnishings, and in many cases, views out over Barcelona to the sea.

Av. Diagonal 661, 08028 Barcelona. © **800/445-8355** in the U.S., or 93/364/4040. Fax 93-364-42-64. www.lhw.com. 432 units. 35,000–48,000Pts (€210–€288, $203–$278) double; from 80,000Pts (€480, $464) suite. AE, DC, MC, V. Free parking for guests. Metro: Zona Universitaria. **Amenities:** 2 restaurants, bar; 2 pools; fitness center; car rental; salon; room service; laundry/dry cleaning. *In room:* A/C, TV, minibar, hair dryer, safe.

Expensive

Hotel Condes de Barcelona ✿   There is a bit of charm here, and its public areas contain more references to medieval Barcelona than any other hotel in town. Business was so good that it opened a 74-room extension, which regrettably lacks the élan of the original. Some of the comfortable rooms are beginning to show wear and tear, but all have soundproof windows. The handsome marble bathrooms are well equipped with such extras as makeup mirrors. In spite of its allure, the Claris still outdazzles it.

Passeig de Gràcia 73–75, 08008 Barcelona. © **93-488-22-00.** Fax 93-488-06-14. www.condesdebarcelona. com. 183 units. 31,000Pts (€186, $180) double; 50,000–70,000Pts (€300–€420, $290–$406) suite. AE, DC, MC, V. Parking 2,000Pts (€12, $13). Metro: Passeig de Gràcia. **Amenities:** Restaurant, bar, cafe; pool; fitness center; boutiques; room service; laundry/dry cleaning. *In room:* A/C, minibar, hair dryer, safe.

Moderate

Hotel Derby/Hotel Gran Derby   These twin hotels are in a tranquil neighborhood about 2 blocks south of the busy intersection of Avinguda Diagonal and Avinguda Sarría. The Derby offers conventional rooms and the Gran Derby (across the street) contains suites, many of which have small balconies overlooking a flowered courtyard. (All drinking, dining, and entertainment facilities are in the Derby.) Rooms and suites are outfitted with simple furniture in a variety of styles, each comfortable and quiet.

Loreto 21–25, and Loreto 28, 08029 Barcelona. © **93-322-32-15.** Fax 93-419-68-20. www.derbyhotels.es. 141 units. 19,800–24,400Pts (€118.80–€146.40, $115–$142) double; 35,000Pts (€210, $203) suite. AE, DC, MC, V. Parking 2,200Pts (€13.20, $14). Metro: Hospital Clínic. **Amenities:** Restaurant, bar; pool; currency exchange; room service; laundry/dry cleaning. *In room:* A/C, TV, minibar, hair dryer.

Inexpensive

Hotel Astoria *Value*   One of our favorites, the 1954 Astoria features an Art Deco facade that makes it appear older than it is. The high ceilings, geometric designs, and brass-studded detailings in the public areas could be Moorish or Andalusian. The comfortable rooms are soundproofed. The more old-fashioned ones have warm textures of exposed cedar and elegant modern accessories.

París 203, 08036 Barcelona. © **93-209-83-11.** Fax 93-202-30-08. www.derbyhotels.es. 117 units. 22,200Pts (€133.20, $129) double; 35,000Pts (€210, $203) suite. AE, DC, MC, V. Metro: Diagonal. **Amenities:** Bar; room service; laundry/dry cleaning. *In room:* A/C, TV, minibar, hair dryer, safe.

NORTE DIAGONAL
Moderate

Hotel Hesperia   Built in the late 1980s, this hotel, on the northern edge of the city, a 12-minute taxi ride from the center, sits in one of Barcelona's most pleasant residential neighborhoods. Sunlight floods the monochromatic interiors of the rooms. The uniformed staff offers fine service.

Los Vergós 20, 08017 Barcelona. © **93-204-55-51.** Fax 93-204-43-92. www.hoteles-hesperia.es. 134 units. 25,000–27,000Pts (€150–€162, $145–$157). AE, DC, MC, V. Parking 1,750Pts (€10.50, $10). Metro: Tres Torres. **Amenities:** Restaurant, bar; room service; baby-sitting; laundry/dry cleaning. *In room:* A/C, TV, minibar, hair dryer, safe.

VILA OLÍMPICA
Expensive
Hotel Arts ⋒⋒⋒   This hotel, managed by the luxury-conscious Ritz-Carlton chain, occupies part of a 44-floor postmodern tower. It is the only hotel in Barcelona to give the Ritz serious competition. The location is about 2.5 kilometers (1½ miles) southwest of Barcelona's historic core, adjacent to the sea and the Olympic Village. Its decor is contemporary and elegant. Views from the rooms sweep out over the skyline and the Mediterranean.

Carrer de la Marina 19–21, 08005 Barcelona. ⓒ **800/241-3333** in the U.S., or 93-221-10-00. Fax 93-221-10-70. www.ritzcarlton.com. 453 units. 55,000Pts (€330, $319) double; 75,000Pts (€450, $435) suite. Fri–Sun 30,000Pts (€180, $174) double; 40,000Pts (€240, $232) suite. AE, DC, MC, V. Parking 3,200Pts (€19.20, $19). Metro: Ciudadela-Vila Olímpica. **Amenities:** 2 restaurants, bar, cafe; pool; fitness center; room service; laundry/dry cleaning. In room. A/C, TV, minibar, hair dryer, safe.

WHERE TO DINE
CIUTAT VELLA (OLD CITY)
Expensive
Agut d'Avignon ⋒ CATALÁN   One of our favorite restaurants in Barcelona is near Plaça Reial, in a tiny alleyway (the cross street is calle d'Avinyó 8). The restaurant explosion here has toppled Agut d'Avignon from its once stellar position, but partly because of its nostalgic charm, it's still going strong. Specialties range from the strictly traditional to the culinary avant-garde and are likely to include local shrimp with *aioli* (garlicky mayonnaise), acorn-squash soup served in its shell, fisher's soup with garlic toast, duck with figs, and haddock stuffed with shellfish, the latter a dish that's forever associated with Catalonia.

Carrer Trinitat 3. ⓒ **93-302-60-34.** Reservations required. Main courses 4,500–8,000Pts (€27–€48, $26–$46). AE, MC, V. Daily 1–3:30pm and 9pm–11:30am. Metro: Jaume I or Liceu.

Casa Leopoldo ⋒ *Finds* SEAFOOD   This warm and surprisingly sophisticated restaurant has thrived here since 1929. It offers some of the freshest seafood in town, and caters to a loyal clientele. There's a popular stand-up tapas bar in front, then two dining rooms, one slightly more formal than the other. Specialties include oxtail stew; fried sea bass with chives, lemon, olive oil, and garlic; shellfish soup; and deep-fried eels. An enduring specialty, prepared only for two, is an enormous platter of fish and shellfish that's configured entirely as a meal unto itself.

Carrer Sant Rafael 24. ⓒ **93-441-30-14.** Reservations required. Main courses 3,500–10,500Pts (€21–€63, $20–$61); fixed-price menu 5,500Pts (€33, $32). AE, DC, MC, V. Tues–Sun 1–4pm; Tues–Sat 9–11pm. Closed 1 week in Aug and at Easter. Metro: Liceu.

Moderate
Brasserie Flo FRENCH/INTERNATIONAL   The Art Deco dining room here is spacious, palm-filled, comfortable, and air-conditioned. It's as close as Barcelona gets to a brasserie you might find in Alsace. Menu items are equally divided between specialties from the bistro traditions of France and Catalonia. French-derived items include fresh foie gras and large platters of *choucroute* (sauerkraut) served with sausages, pork chops, and a steamed ham hock. Catalan specialties include *mariscado* (shellfish stew), *parillada de mariscos* (mixed grilled shellfish), *caldereta* of lobster, and fresh seasonal oysters.

Jonqueras 10. ⓒ **93-319-31-02.** Reservations recommended. Main courses 3,000–6,000Pts (€18–€36, $17–$35); fixed-price menu 3,180Pts (€19.13, $18) AE, DC, MC, V. Mon–Thurs 1–4pm and 8:30pm–midnight; Fri–Sun 1–4pm and 8:30pm–1am. Metro: Urquinaona.

Can Culleretes CATALÁN   Founded in 1786 as a *pastelería* (pastry shop) in the Barri Gótic, Barcelona's oldest restaurant still retains many architectural features. The well-prepared food, mostly seafood, features authentic dishes of northeastern Spain, including sole Roman style, *zarzuela à la marinara* (shellfish medley), *canalones* (cannelloni), filet of sole with clams, and paella. From October to January special game dishes are available, including *perdiz* (partridge).

Quintana 5. ℂ **93-317-64-85.** Reservations recommended. Main courses 2,500–3,500Pts (€15–€21, $15–$20). DC, V. Tues–Sun 1:30–4pm; Tues–Sat 9–11:30pm. Closed 3 weeks in July. Metro: Liceu. Bus: 14 or 59.

Egipte *(Value* CATALÁN/SPANISH   A favorite among locals, this tiny place, set amid narrow medieval streets, behind the central marketplace, is lively day and night. The excellent menu includes spinach vol-au-vent (traditionally served with an egg on top), *lengua de ternera* (tongue), and *berengeras* (stuffed eggplant), a chef's specialty. The local favorite is codfish prepared several ways, including one savory version in cream sauce. A savory beginning to your meal is baked bread layered with ham and a salty Catalán cheese. Expect hearty market-fresh food and a total lack of pretension.

La Rambla 79. ℂ **93-317-74-80.** Reservations recommended. Main courses 1,500–4,000Pts (€9–€24, $9–$23); fixed-price menu (Mon–Sat) 1,990–2,790Pts (€11.95–€16.75, $12–$16). AE, DC, MC, V. Mon–Sat 1–4pm and 8pm–midnight. Metro: Liceu.

Els Quatre Gats CATALÁN   This is a Barcelona legend since 1897. The "Four Cats" was the favorite of Picasso and other artists. In their heyday, their works decorated the walls of this cafe on a narrow cobblestone street near the cathedral. Today a *tertulia* (clublike) bar in the heart of the Barri Gótic, it was restored but retains its fine old look. The good food is prepared in an unpretentious style of Catalán cooking called *cuina de mercat* (based on whatever looked fresh at the market that day).

Montsió 3. ℂ **93-302-41-40.** Reservations required Sat–Sun. Main courses 2,000–3,500Pts (€12–€21, $12–$20); fixed-price lunch 1,500Pts (€9, $9). AE, MC, V. Restaurant, Mon–Sat 1–4pm and 9pm–midnight; cafe, daily 8am–2am. Metro: Plaça de Catalunya.

Los Caracoles *(Overrated* CATALÁN/SPANISH   This is still the most famous restaurant in Barcelona, and it appears in every guidebook ever written on Spain. It still serves the dishes it always did, but competition has buried it. It's been around since 1835, serving spit-roasted chicken, roast suckling pig, roast suckling lamb, and its namesake, snails. In summer tables overflow onto the sidewalk. A combination Spanish and Catalán cuisine is featured, including a mixed grill of seafood or a medley of fried fish in rich sauces. It remains a number one tourist spot, or is that tourist trap?

Escudellers 14. ℂ **93-302-31-85.** Reservations required. Main courses 1,500–5,000Pts (€8.70–€29, $9–$30). AE, DC, MC, V. Daily 1pm–midnight. Metro: Drassanes.

Restaurant Hoffman ✦ CATALÁN/FRENCH/INTERNATIONAL   This restaurant's creative cuisine continues to make it one of the most famous in Barcelona. During clement weather, tables are also set up outside. Menu items change every 2 months. The best examples include a superb version of *fine tarte* with deboned sardines; foie gras wrapped in puff pastry; a ragout of crayfish with green risotto; and a succulent version of pigs' feet with eggplant. Especially flavorful is a filet steak cooked in Rioja wine and served with a confit of shallots and a gratin of potatoes. Fondant of chocolate makes a worthy dessert.

Argenteria 74–78. ℂ **93-319-58-89.** Reservations required. Main courses 1,500–3,500Pts (€9–€21, $9–$20); set lunch (wine and coffee included) 5,000Pts (€30, $29). AE, DC, MC, V. Mon–Fri 1:30–4pm and 9pm–midnight. Metro: Jaume I.

Inexpensive

Biocenter VEGETARIAN   This is Barcelona's largest and best-known vegetarian restaurant, a funky, counterculture sort of place. Meals are served in two ground-floor dining rooms. There's a salad bar, an array of vegetarian casseroles, such soups as gazpacho and lentil, and a changing selection of seasonal vegetables.

Pintor Fortuny 25. ℂ **93-301-45-83.** Fixed-price menu 1,150Pts (€6.90, $6.65). Main courses 800–2,000Pts (€4.80–€12, $4.65–$12). No credit cards. Mon–Sat 1–5pm. (Bar, Mon–Sat 9am–11pm.) Metro: Plaça de Catalunya.

Garduña *(Finds* CATALÁN   Battered and somewhat ramshackle, this famous restaurant in La Boquería, the covered food market, enjoys a fashionable reputation among actors, sculptors, writers, and painters who appreciate a blue-collar atmosphere. Because of its position near the back of the market, you'll pass endless rows of fresh produce, cheese, and meats that whet your appetite before you reach it. You can dine downstairs, near a crowded bar, or a bit more formally upstairs. The food is ultra-fresh and might include "hors d'oeuvres of the sea," *canalones* (cannelloni) Rossini, grilled hake with herbs, seafood rice, filet steak with green peppercorns, or zarzuela of fresh fish.

Mercado La Boquería. Morera 17–19. ℂ **93-302-43-23.** Reservations recommended. Main courses 1,500–4,500Pts (€9–€27, $9–$28); fixed-price menu 1,000Pts (€6, $6). AE, MC, V. Daily 1–4pm and 8pm–midnight. Metro: Liceu.

Pitarra CATALÁN   This restaurant in the Barri Gòtic is named after the 19th-century Catalán playwright who lived and wrote his plays and poetry in the back room. Menu items read like a roster of traditional Catalán specialties. Examples include mushroom crêpes layered with strips of duck meat; pork chops smothered with morel mushrooms; and an ultratraditional version of sea bass baked with tomatoes, peppers, onions, and garlic. There're also two forms of paella served here: the Valencian version with fish, shellfish, and assorted meats, and an all-seafood version beloved by Catalonians.

Avinyó 56. ℂ **93-301-16-47.** Reservations required. Main courses 2,500–4,000Pts (€15–€24, $15–$23). AE, DC, MC, V. Mon–Sat 1–4pm and 8:30–11pm. Metro: Liceu.

SUR DIAGONAL
Very Expensive

Beltxenea *(finds* BASQUE/INTERNATIONAL   In a late 19th-century modernist apartment building, this restaurant celebrates the nuances and subtleties of Basque cuisine. The restaurant is one of the most elegantly and comfortably furnished in Barcelona. Save a visit for that special night—it's worth the money. Menu examples are hake either fried with garlic or garnished with clams and served with fish broth. Roast lamb, grilled rabbit, and pheasant are well prepared and succulent, as are the desserts. Summer dining is possible out in the formal garden.

Mallorca 275. ℂ **93-215-30-24.** Reservations recommended. Main courses 3,000–6,900Pts (€18–€41.40, $17–$40); menú degustación 7,000Pts (€42, $41). AE, DC, MC, V. Mon–Fri 1:30–3:30pm; Mon–Sat 9–11:30pm. Closed 2 weeks in Aug. Metro: Passeig de Gràcia.

La Dama *(finds* CATALÁN/INTERNATIONAL   This stylish and well-managed place is one of the few Barcelona restaurants that deserves and gets a

Michelin star. La Dama serves a clientele of local residents and civic dignitaries with impeccable taste. Specialties may include warm scampi salad with orange zest; house-style pigs' trotters with mushrooms and truffles; tenderloin of beef layered with foie gras; salmon steak served with vinegar derived from cava and onions; an abundant seasonal platter of autumn mushrooms; and succulent preparations of lamb, fish and shellfish, beef, and veal.

Av. Diagonal 423. ✆ 93-202-06-86. Reservations required. Main courses 6,000–12,000Pts (€36–€72, $35–$70); fixed-price menu 4,000–10,000Pts (€24–€60, $23–$58). AE, DC, MC, V. Daily 1–4pm and 8:30–11:30pm. Metro: Provença.

Inexpensive
Ca La María CATALÁN   This small, family-operated, good-natured, and charming restaurant accommodates only 36 guests, who dine in cozy intimacy on a quiet square opposite a Byzantine-style church near Plaça de la Universitat. With some recent exceptions, menu items are endearingly homelike—provided you grew up in a family of Catalán cooks. Examples include anglerfish with brown garlic sauce, filet of sole with mushrooms and prawns, tournedos with cèpe mushrooms, and a veal filet "Café de Paris."

Tallers 76 bis. ✆ 93-318-89-93. Reservations recommended. Main courses 2,000–3,500Pts (€12–€21, $12–$20). AE, DC, MC, V. Mon–Sat 1:30–3:30pm and 8:30–11pm. Metro: Plaça de la Universida.

NORTE DIAGONAL
Very Expensive
Botafumiero 𝕉𝕉𝕉 SEAFOOD   Although the competition is severe, this well-managed *restaurante marisquería* (seafood restaurant) consistently serves Barcelona's finest seafood. Much of the allure comes from the attention to detail paid by the white-jacketed staff. Menu items include grilled sea bass with a paprika, garlic, olive oil, and lemon sauce; braised grouper with cider and cava sauce; and baked hake with a tomato-herb sauce. The establishment prides itself on its fresh- and saltwater fish, clams, mussels, lobster, crayfish, scallops, and several varieties of crustaceans that you may never have seen before.

Gran de Gràcia 81. ✆ 93-218-42-30. Reservations recommended for dining rooms, not necessary for meals at the bar. Main courses 3,500–10,000Pts (€21–€60, $20–$58). AE, DC, MC, V. Mon–Sat 1pm–1am; Sun 1–5pm. Metro: Fontana.

Neichel 𝕉𝕉𝕉 MEDITERRANEAN   Alsatian-born Jean Louis Neichel has been called "the most brilliant ambassador French cuisine has ever had in Spain." Focusing on a light-textured culinary display that uses olive oil instead of butter and cream, Neichel prepares dishes that include fresh foie gras with a confit of figs; crayfish salad with a truffle-studded vinaigrette; a salad of wild mushrooms with a carpaccio of wild duck; John Dory with pulverized shellfish suspended in an emulsion of olive oil; and filet of beef stuffed with foie gras and served with a sauce made from a heady Spanish red wine known as *merlap*. In 1996, the dessert cart at this glamorous restaurant won an award as the most appealing roster of desserts in Spain.

Pedralbes 16. ✆ 93-334-06-99. Reservations required. Main courses 4,000–10,000Pts (€24–€60, $23–$58). AE, DC, MC, V. Tues–Sat 1:30–3:30pm and 8:30–11pm. Closed Aug and holidays. Metro: María Christina.

MOLL DE LA FUSTA & BARCELONETA
Expensive
Can Costa 𝕉 SEAFOOD   One of the most long-lived seafood restaurants in this seafaring town is Can Costa, whose big windows overlook the water.

Established in the late 1930s, it contains two busy dining rooms and an outdoor terrace. Fresh seafood rules the menu here. This includes the best baby squid in town—it's sautéed in a flash so that it has an almost grilled flavor, and is almost never overcooked or too rubbery. A chef's specialty that has endured through many a season is *fideuá de piex*, which is equivalent to a classic Valencian shellfish paella, except in this case, noodles are used in lieu of rice. All the desserts are homemade by the kitchen staff daily.

Passeig Don Juan de Borbo 70. ⓒ **93-221-59-03.** Reservations recommended. Main courses 3,000–7,000Pts (€18–€42, $17–$41). AE, MC, V. Daily 1:30–4pm; Mon–Sat 8–11:30pm. Metro: Barceloneta.

Can Solé CATALÁN   In Barceloneta at the harbor, Can Solé still honors the traditions of this former fishing village. Many of the seafood joints here are too touristy for our tastes, but this one is authentic and delivers good value. Begin with the sweet tiny clams or the codfish cakes, perhaps some bouillabaisse. Little langoustines are an eternal but expensive favorite, and everything is aromatically perfumed with fresh garlic. You might also sample one of the seafood rice dishes. Desserts are so good they're worth saving room for, especially the orange pudding or the praline ice cream.

4 Carrer Sant Carles. ⓒ **93-221-50-12.** Reservations required. Main courses 4,500–7,000Pts (€27–€42, $26–$41). AE, DC, MC, V. Tues–Sun 1–4pm; Tues–Sat 8:30–11:30pm. Metro: Barceloneta.

Moderate
Siete Puertas (aka 7 Portes) SEAFOOD   This is a lunchtime favorite for businesspeople (the Stock Exchange is across the way) and an evening favorite for in-the-know clients who have made it their preferred restaurant in Catalonia. It's been going since 1836. Regional dishes—the portions are enormous—include fresh herring with onions and potatoes, a different paella daily (sometimes with shellfish, or with rabbit), and a wide array of fresh fish, succulent oysters, and an herb-laden stew of black beans with pork.

Passeig d'Isabel II 14. ⓒ **93-319-30-33.** Reservations required. Main courses 3,500–7,500Pts (€21–€45, $20–$44). AE, DC, MC, V. Daily 1pm–1am. Metro: Barceloneta.

Inexpensive
Cal Pep *(Finds* CATALÁN   Cal Pep lies close to the Picasso Museum and is a slice of local life. It's generally packed, and the food is some of the tastiest in the old town. In the rear is a small dining room but most patrons like to occupy one of the counter seats up front. Try the fried artichokes or the mixed medley of seafood that includes small sardines. Tiny clams come swimming in a well-seasoned broth given extra spice by a sprinkling of hot peppers. A delectable tuna dish comes with a sesame sauce, and fresh salmon is flavored with such herbs as basil—sublime.

8 Plaça de les Olles. ⓒ **93-310-79-61.** Reservations needed. Main courses 1,600–3,000Pts (€9.60–€18, $9–$17). AE, MC, V. Mon 8:30–11:30pm; Tues–Sat 1–4:30pm and 8:30–11:30pm. Closed Aug. Metro: Barceloneta.

SEEING THE SIGHTS
Spain's second-largest city is also its most cosmopolitan and avant-garde. Barcelona is filled with landmark buildings and world-class museums offering many sightseeing opportunities. These include Antoni Gaudí's Sagrada Familia, Museu Picasso, Barcelona's Gothic cathedral, and Les Rambles, the famous tree-lined promenade cutting through the heart of the old quarter.

SIGHTSEEING SUGGESTIONS FOR FIRST-TIME VISITORS

If You Have 1 Day Spend the morning exploring the **Barri Gótic.** In the afternoon visit Antoni Gaudí's unfinished masterpiece, **La Sagrada Família,** before returning to the heart of the city for a walk down **Les Rambles.** To cap your day, take the funicular to the fountains at **Montjuïc** or go to the top of **Tibidabo** for a panoramic view of Barcelona and its harbor.

If You Have 2 Days On day 2, visit the **Museu Picasso** in the Gothic Quarter. Then stroll through the surrounding district, the **Barri de la Ribera,** which is filled with Renaissance mansions and is the site of the gorgeous church Santa María del Mar. Follow this with a ride to the top of the **Columbus Monument** for a panoramic view of the harborfront. Have a seafood lunch at **La Barceloneta** and in the afternoon, stroll up Les Rambles again. Explore **Montjuïc** and visit the **Museu d'Art de Catalunya** if time remains. End the day with a meal at

Los Caracoles, a famous restaurant in the old city, just off Les Rambles.

If You Have 3 Days On day 3, make a pilgrimage to the monastery of **Montserrat,** about 45 minutes outside of Barcelona, to see the venerated Black Virgin and a host of artistic and scenic attractions. Try to time your visit to hear the 50-member boys' choir.

If You Have 4 or 5 Days On day 4, take a morning walk along the **harborfront,** or in the modernist **Eixample** district of Barcelona, the planned urban expansion area from 1860. Have lunch on the pier. In the afternoon visit Montjuïc again to tour the **Fundació Joan Miró** and walk through the **Poble Espanyol,** a miniature village with reproductions of representative regional architecture, created for the 1929 World's Fair. On Day 5, take another excursion from the city. If you're interested in history, visit the former Roman city of **Tarragona** to the south. If you want to unwind on a beach, head south to **Sitges.**

THE TOP ATTRACTIONS

Catedral de Barcelona 🖈🖈   Barcelona's cathedral is a celebrated example of Catalonian Gothic. Except for the 19th-century west facade, the basilica was begun at the end of the 13th century and completed in the mid-15th century. The three naves, cleaned and illuminated, have splendid Gothic details. With its large bell towers, blending of medieval and Renaissance styles, beautiful cloister, high altar, side chapels, sculptured choir, and Gothic arches, it ranks as one of Spain's most impressive cathedrals. The cloister, illuminated on Saturday and fiesta days, contains a museum of medieval art.

Plaça de la Seu. ✆ **93-315-15-54.** Cathedral, free; museum, 200Pts (€1.20, $1.15); cloisters, 100Pts (€0.60, 63¢). Daily 8am–1:30pm and 4–7:30pm. Metro: Jaume I.

Fundació Joan Miró 🖈   Born in 1893, Joan Miró went on to become one of Spain's greatest painters, known for his whimsical abstract forms and brilliant colors. Some 10,000 works by this Catalán surrealist, including paintings, graphics, and sculptures, have been collected here. The building has been greatly expanded in recent years, following the design of the Catalán architect Josep Lluís Sert, a close friend of Miró's. An exhibition in a modern wing charts Miró's complete artistic evolution, from his first drawings to his last works.

> **Tips   An Ancient Neighborhood to Explore**
>
> The **Barri Gòtic** ✹✹ is Barcelona's old aristocratic quarter, parts of which have survived from the Middle Ages. Spend at least 2 or 3 hours exploring the Gothic Quarter's narrow streets and squares. Start by walking up Carrer del Carme, east of Les Rambles. A nighttime stroll takes on added drama, but exercise extreme caution. The buildings, for the most part, are austere and sober, the cathedral being the crowning achievement. Roman ruins and the vestiges of 3rd-century walls add further interest. This area is intricately detailed and filled with many attractions that are easy to miss.

Plaça de Neptú, Parc de Montjuïc. ✆ **93-329-19-08.** Admission 800Pts (€4.80, $4.65) adults, 450Pts (€2.70, $2.60) students, free for children under 15. Tues–Wed and Fri–Sat 10am–8pm (July–Sept) or 10am–7pm (Oct–June); Thurs 10am–9:30pm; Sun 10am–2:30pm. Bus: 61 from Plaza d'España.

La Sagrada Família ✹✹   Gaudí's masterpiece is one of the most idiosyncratic works of architecture in the world. If you have time to see only one Catalán landmark, make it this one. Begun in 1882 and still incomplete at Gaudí's death in 1926, this incredible church—the Temple of the Holy Family—is a bizarre wonder. The languid, amorphous structure embodies the essence of Gaudí's style, which some have described as Art Nouveau run rampant. The spires—Gaudí planned to construct a total of 12 to reflect the 12 disciples—look a bit like dripping candles. Work continues on the structure but without any sure idea of what Gaudí intended, so disagreements are constant. The newest sculptures have provoked outrage among many art critics.

Mallorca 401. ✆ **93-207-30-31.** Church, 800Pts (€4.80, $4.65), including a 12-minute video about Gaudí's religious and secular works; elevator to the tower, 200Pts (€1.20, $1.15). Apr–Aug daily 9am–8pm; Mar and Oct daily 9am–7pm; Nov–Feb daily 9am–6pm. Metro: Sagrada Família.

Museu Picasso ✹   Five converted palaces on a medieval street have been turned into a museum housing works by Pablo Picasso, who donated some 2,500 of his paintings, engravings, and drawings to the museum in 1970. Picasso was particularly fond of Barcelona, where he spent much of his formative youth. Many of the works, especially the early paintings, show the artist's debt to van Gogh, El Greco, and Rembrandt; a famous series, *Las Meninas* (1957), is said to "impersonate" the work of Velázquez. From his Blue Period, the *La Vie* drawings are perhaps the most interesting. Some of the museum is devoted to temporary exhibitions, often showcasing Picasso works on loan from other museums such as the Picasso Museum in Paris as well as private collections.

Montcada 15–19. ✆ **93-319-63-10.** Admission 725Pts (€4.35, $4.20) adults, 400Pts (€2.40, $2.30) students, free for children under 13. Tues–Sat 10am–7:30pm; Sun 10am–2:30pm. Metro: Jaume I.

Parc Güell ✹✹   This fanciful park on the northern tier of Barcelona's inner core is much more than green space. It was begun by Antoni Gaudí as a real-estate venture for a wealthy friend, Count Eusebi Güell, a well-known Catalán industrialist, but never completed. Only two houses were constructed, but Gaudí's whimsical creativity, seen in soaring columns that impersonate trees and splendid winding benches of broken mosaics, is on abundant display. The city took over the property in 1926 and turned it into a public park. The panoramic views are excellent.

Ⓒ **93-424-38-09.** Free admission. May–Sept daily 10am–9pm; Oct–Apr daily 10am–6pm. Bus: 27, 60, 85, or 73.

MORE ATTRACTIONS

Monument à Colom (Columbus Monument)   This monument to Christopher Columbus was erected at Barcelona's harbor front for the Universal Exhibition of 1888. It's divided into a plinth with bronze bas-reliefs depicting the principal feats of Columbus; an eight-sided polygonal base; the column itself, rising 50 meters (167 ft.); and finally an 8-meter (25-ft.) bronze statue of Columbus by Rafael Ataché. Inside the iron column, an elevator ascends to the mirador, where a panoramic view of Barcelona and its harbor unfolds.

Portal de la Pau. Ⓒ **93-302-52-24.** Admission 250Pts (€1.50, $1.45) adults, 150Pts (€0.90, 85¢) children 4–12, free for children under 4. Sept 25–May 31, Mon–Fri 10am–1:30pm and 3:30–6:30pm, Sat–Sun and holidays 10am–6:30pm; June 1–Sept 24, daily 9am–8pm. Closed Jan 1, Jan 6, and Dec 25–26. Metro: Drassanes. Bus: 14, 18, 36, 57, 59,or 64.

Museu d'Art Contemporáreo de Barcelona (MACBA) 🎟   A soaring, glistening edifice in Barcelona's Raval district, the Museum of Contemporary Art is to Barcelona what the Pompidou Center is to Paris. Designed by American architect Richard Meier, the building itself is a work of art, manipulating sunlight to offer brilliant natural interior lighting. On display in the 6,875 square meters (74,000 sq. ft.) of exhibit space is the work of such modern luminaries as Tápies, Klee, Miró, and many others. The museum contains a library, bookshop, and cafeteria.

Plaça de los Angels. Ⓒ **93-412-08-10.** www.macba.es. Admission 550Pts (€3.30, $3.20) adults, 500Pts (€3, $2.90) seniors and students, free for children under 13. Mon and Wed–Fri 11am–7:30pm; Sat 11am–8pm; Sun 10am–3pm. Closed Tues. Metro: Plaça de Catalunya.

Poble Espanyol 🎟   In this re-created Spanish village, built for the 1929 World's Fair, various regional architectural styles are reproduced. The infrastructure is crumbling a bit and the format has grown stale and a bit corny, but it remains an enduring attraction nonetheless. There're 115 life-size reproductions of buildings and monuments, ranging from the 10th to the 20th century. The center of the village has an outdoor cafe. Shops sell crafts from all the provinces, and in some of them you can see artists at work, printing fabric or blowing glass. The village has 14 restaurants of varying styles, a dance club, and eight musical bars. The whole attraction is a lot more appealing at night.

Marqués de Comilias, Parc de Montjuïc. Ⓒ **93-325-78-66.** Village, 975Pts (€5.85, $5.65) adults, 775Pts (€4.65, $4.50) seniors, students, and children 7–11, free for children under 7; audiovisual hall, free. Mon 9am–8pm; Tues–Thurs 9am–2am; Fri–Sat 9am–4am; Sun 9am–midnight. Bus: 13 or 50.

ADDITIONAL MUSEUMS

Fundació Antoni Tàpies 🎟   When it opened in 1990, this became Barcelona's third museum devoted to the work of a single artist. Antoni Tàpies probably has the greatest international renown of any living artist in Spain. In 1984 Tàpies set up the foundation bearing his name, and the city of Barcelona donated an ideal site near the Passeig de Gràcia in Eixample. One of Barcelona's landmark buildings, the splendid brick-and-iron structure was built between 1881 and 1884 by the Gaudí contemporary exponent of Catalán modernism, Lluís Domènech i Montaner. The core of the museum is a collection of works by Tàpies (most contributed by the artist), covering the stages of his career as it evolved into abstract expressionism.

Aragó 255. ℭ **93-487-03-15**. Admission 700Pts (€4.20, $4) adults, 350Pts (€2.10, $2) students and children 10–18, free for children under 10. Tues–Sun 10am–8pm. Metro: Passeig de Gràcia.

Museu Barbier-Mueller Art Precolombí ⚜

Opened by Queen Sofia in the spring of 1997, this is one of the most prominent collections of pre-Columbian art in the world. The collection contains almost 6,000 pieces of tribal or ancient art. Pre-Columbian cultures created religious, funerary, and ornamental objects of great stylistic variety with relatively simple means. They were especially outstanding in stone sculpture and ceramic objects. For example, the Olmecs, who settled on the coast of the Gulf of Mexico at the beginning of the first millennium B.C., executed notable monumental sculpture in stone and magnificent figures in jade. Rich in exhibits is the Mayan culture, the most homogenous and widespread of its time, its origins going back to 1000 B.C.

Carrer de Montcada 14. ℭ **93-319-76-03**. Admission 500Pts (€3, $2.90) adults, 200Pts (€1.20, $1.15) students, free for children under 12. Free admission on the first Sat of every month. Tues–Sat 10am–6m; Sun and holidays 10am–3pm. Metro: Jaume. Bus: 14, 17, 19, 39, 40, 45, or 51.

Museu de la Ciència (Science Museum) ⚜ Kids

The science museum's modern design and hands-on activities have made it a major cultural attraction. You can touch, listen, watch, and participate in a variety of exhibits designed to convey a sense of wonder about science and technology. From the beauty of life in the sea to the magic of holograms, the museum offers a world of science to discover. Watch the world turn beneath the Foucault pendulum, ride on a human gyroscope, hear a friend whisper from 18 meters (20 yd.) away, feel an earthquake, or use the tools of a scientist to examine intricate life forms with microscopes and video cameras.

Teodoro Roviralta 55. ℭ **93-212-60-50**. Museum 500Pts (€3, $2.90) adults, 250Pts (€1.50, $1.45) children. Planetarium only 250Pts (€1.50, $1.45). Daily 10am–8pm. Bus: 17, 22, 58, or 73.

Museu Frederic Marés/Museu Sentimental ⚜⚜

One of the biggest repositories of medieval sculpture in the region is the Frederic Marés Museum, just behind the cathedral. It's housed in an ancient palace whose interior courtyards, chiseled stone, and soaring ceilings are impressive in their own right, an ideal setting for the hundreds of polychrome sculptures. The sculpture section dates from pre-Roman times to the 20th century. Also housed here is the Museu Sentimental, a collection of everyday items that help to illustrate life in Barcelona during the past 2 centuries.

Plaça de Santa Iú 5–6. ℭ **93-310-58-00**. Admission (to both museums) 500Pts (€3, $2.90) adults, 300Pts (€1.80, $1.75) students, free for children under 13. Tues–Thurs 10am–5pm; Fri–Sat 10am–7pm; Sun 10am–3pm. Metro: Jaume I. Bus: 17, 19, or 45.

Museu Marítim ⚜⚜

In the formal Royal Shipyards of the Drassanes Reials, this 13th-century civil Gothic complex was used for the construction of ships for the Catalán-Aragonese rulers. The most outstanding exhibition here is a reconstruction of *La Galería Real* of Don Juan of Austria, a lavish royal galley. Another special exhibit features a map by Gabriel de Vallseca that was owned by explorer Amerigo Vespucci.

Av. de las Drassanes. ℭ **93-318-32-45**. Admission 800Pts (€4.80, $4.65) adults, 400Pts (€2.40, $2.30) seniors and ages 15–25, free for children under 15. Apr–Oct daily 10am–7pm; winter Tues–Sat 10am–6pm, Sun 10am–2pm. Closed holidays. Metro: Drassanes. Bus: 14, 18, 36, 38, or 57.

Museu Nacional d'Art de Catalunya ⚜⚜⚜

This recently reopened and redesigned museum is the world's major depository of Gothic and Romanesque

Catalán art, a treasure trove of this important region of the world. More than 100 pieces, including sculptures, icons, and frescoes, are on display. The highlight of the museum is the collection of murals from various Romanesque churches throughout Catalonia.

Palau Nacional, Parc de Montjuïc. © **93-622-03-60.** Admission 900Pts (€5.40, $5.20) adults, 700Pts (€4.20, $4.05) ages 7–20, free for children under 7. Tues–Sat 10am–7pm; Sun 10am–2:30pm. Metro: Espanya.

Museu d'Art Modern   This museum shares a wing of the Palau de la Ciutadella with the Catalonian Parliament. Constructed in the 1700s, it once formed part of Barcelona's defenses as an arsenal. Its collection of art focuses on the early 20th century and features the work of Catalán artists, including Martí Alsina, Vayreda, Casas, Fortuny, and Rusiñol. The collection also encompasses modernist furniture, including designs by architect Puig i Cadafalch.

Plaça do Armaj, Parque de la Ciudadella. © **93-319-57-28.** Admission 500Pts (€3, $2.90) adults, 350Pts (€2.10, $2) students and seniors 65 and over, free for children under 7. Tues–Sat 10am–7pm; Sun 10am–2:30pm. Closed Jan 1 and Dec 25. Metro: Arc de Triomf or Barceloneta. Bus: 14, 16, 17, 39, or 40.

PARKS & GARDENS

While Barcelona is not a city of abundant green space, most people head to the hills for a respite from the density and activity of the city below. The mountain park of **Montjuïc** ✦ has splashing fountains, gardens, outdoor restaurants, and museums. This is where the principal Olympic stadiums are located. The re-created village, the Poble Espanyol, and the Joan Miró Foundation are also in the park. There are many walks and vantage points for viewing the Barcelona skyline.

Another attraction, **Tibidabo Mountain** ✦, offers the finest panoramic view of Barcelona. A funicular takes you up 490 meters (1,600 ft.) to the summit. The funicular runs daily from 7:15am to 9:45pm and costs 450Pts (€2.70, $2.60) each way. A slightly kitschy amusement park—with Ferris wheels that spin over Barcelona—has been here for years. There's also a church in this carnival-like setting called Santa Creu (Sacred Heart), plus restaurants and mountaintop hotels. From Plaça John Kennedy take the funicular uphill, or catch any of the buses from central Barcelona labeled TIBIDABO.

ORGANIZED TOURS

Pullmantur, Gran Vía de les Corts Catalánes 635 (© **93-317-12-97**), offers a morning tour departing from the terminal at the above address at 9:30am, taking in the cathedral, the Gothic Quarter, the Rambles, the monument to Columbus, and the Spanish Village and the Olympic Stadium. It costs 4,895Pts (€29.35, $28). An afternoon tour leaves at 3:30pm, with visits to some of the most outstanding buildings in the Eixample, including Gaudí's Sagrada Família, Parc Güell, and a stop at the Picasso Museum. This tour costs 4,895Pts (€29.35, $28). Pullmantur also offers several excursions into the environs. The daily tour of the monastery of Montserrat departs at 9:30am and returns to the city at 2:30pm. Tours include a visit to the Royal Basilica to view the famous sculpture of the Black Virgin. The tour returns to Barcelona to the harbor, where passengers have the option to remain for the afternoon. Tours cost 6,185Pts (€37.10, $36).

Another company that offers tours of Barcelona and the surrounding countryside is **Juliatours,** Ronda Universitat 5 (© **93-317-64-54;** Metro: Universitat). Itineraries are similar to those above, with similar prices. One, the Visita

> **Moments Sunset at Tibidabo**
>
> The ideal time to visit the summit of Tibidabo Mountain north of the port (the culmination of the Sierra de Collcerola) is at sunset, as the city lights begin to flicker.

Ciudad Artistica, offers a tour of Barcelona focusing on the city's artistic significance. Tours pass many of Gaudí's brilliant buildings, including La Sagrada Família. Also included are visits to the Museu Picasso or Museu d'Art Modern, depending on the day of your tour. Tours cost 4,800Pts (€28.80, $28) and leave at 3:30pm.

THE SHOPPING SCENE
THE BEST SHOPPING STREETS

The main shopping street in Barcelona is **Passeig de Gràcia.** Stroll this street from the Avinguda Diagonal to the Plaça de Catalunya, and you'll pass some of Barcelona's most elegant boutiques.

In the **old quarter,** the principal shopping streets are the Ramblas, Carrer del Pi, Carrer de la Palla, and Avenguda Portal de l'Angel. Moving north in the Eixample are Passeig de Catalunya, Passeig de Gràcia, and Rambla de Catalunya. Going even farther north, Avinguda Diagonal is a major shopping boulevard. Vía Augusta is another prominent street.

Another shopping expedition is to the **Mercat de la Boquería,** Rambla 101, near Carrer del Carme. Here you'll see a wide array of straw bags and regional products, along with handsome displays of fruits, vegetables, cheeses, meats, and fish.

THE BEST BUYS

Barcelona, a city of design and fashion, offers a wealth of shopping opportunities. In addition to modern, attractively designed, and stylish clothing, shoes and decorative objects are often good buys. Designs for both women and men are sold at **Groc,** Ramble de Catalunya 100 (℗ **93-215-74-74;** Metro: Plaça de Catalunya). One of the most stylish shops in Barcelona, the Catalán designer Antonio Miró's shop is expensive but filled with high-quality apparel made from the finest of natural fibers. The men's store is downstairs, the women's store one flight up. Miró has a newer, fancier, and bigger store a few blocks down the Ramble, Consejo de Ciento 349 (℗ **93-487-06-70**).

Adolfo Dominguez, 32 Passeig de Gracia (℗ **93-487-41-70**), has been called "the Spanish Armani." Suits in earth tones for both men and women have a rather austere but very stylish look. One of the best showcases for Catalán fashion designers for women is **On Land,** 273 Carrer Valencia (℗ **93-215-56-25**). For designer housewares and the best in Spanish contemporary furnishings, your best bet is **Vincón,** Passeig de Gràcia, 96 (℗ **93-215-60-50**), housed in the former home of artist Ramón Casas.

In the city of Miró, Tàpies, and Picasso, **art** is a major business. You'll find dozens of galleries, especially in the Barri Gótic and around the Picasso Museum. In business since 1840, **Sala Parés,** Petritxol 5 (℗ **93-318-70-20;** Metro: Plaça de Catalunya), is one of the city's finest art galleries. Paintings are displayed in a two-story amphitheater; exhibitions change about once a month. Petritxol is one of the nicest shopping and strolling streets in the Gothic Quarter. At **Art Picasso,** Tapineria 10 (℗ **93-310-49-57;** Metro: Jaume I), you can get good lithographs of works by Picasso, Miró, and Dalí, as well as T-shirts with the designs of these masters and books. Tiles sold here often carry their provocatively painted scenes.

Unless you're seeking some specialty item, one of your best bets for **antiques** is **El Bulevard des Antiquarius,** Passeig de Gràcia 55. This 70-unit complex, just off one of the city's most aristocratic avenues, has a huge collection of art and antiques assembled in a series of boutiques, and there's also a cafe-bar on the upper level. Most shoppers from abroad settle happily for **handcrafts,** and the city is rich in offerings, ranging from simple pottery to handmade furniture. Named after the Victorian English illustrator, **Beardsley,** Petritxol 12 (© **93-301-05-76;** Metro: Plaça de Catalunya), is on the same street where the works of Picasso and Dalí were exhibited before they became world famous. The wide array of gifts includes a little bit of everything from everywhere—dried flowers, writing supplies, silver dishes, unusual bags and purchases, and lots more.

Six Catalán architects showcase the city's most stunning collection of modern furniture. Their wares are on display at **Bd Ediciones de Diseño,** Calle Mallorca 291 (© **934-58-69-09;** Metro: Verdaguer), installed in a former 19th-century print shop. The variety and scope of furnishings here is astonishing, from reproductions of works by such grand old masters as Aalto and Hoffman, to the very latest designers. About 30% of the collection is imported, the rest made locally. An enormous warehouse, **Otranto,** Paseo de San Juan (© **932-07-26-97;** Metro: Verdaguer), has been converted into a sales floor of architectural objects rescued from demolished buildings in Barcelona. Most of the collection is a century old, ranging from marble mantels and columns to wrought-iron balustrades, and some stunning hard-carved modernist doors.

At **Itaca,** Carrer Ferran 26 (© **93-301-30-44;** Metro: Liceu), you'll find a wide array of handmade pottery, not only from Catalonia but also from Spain, Portugal, Mexico, and Morocco. The merchandise has been selected for its basic purity, integrity, and simplicity. If your time and budget are limited, you may want to patronize Barcelona's major department store, **El Corte Inglés,** Plaça de Catalunya (© **93-302-12-12;** Metro: Plaça de Catalunya). The store sells everything from Spanish handcrafts to high-fashion items to Catalán records and food. The store also has restaurants and cafes and offers a number of consumer-related services, such as a travel agent. It will arrange for the mailing of purchases back home.

BARCELONA AFTER DARK

Your best source of information about the cornucopia known as Barcelona nightlife appears within either of two magazines, *Guía del Ocio,* and its less comprehensive counterpart, *La Semana de Barcelona.* The price of both publications is 150Pts (€0.90, 85¢). Both are in Spanish, but the listings seem to be worded in ways that even nonnative speakers can benefit a lot from referring to them. Both publications are available at virtually every news kiosk along Les Rambles.

Culture and the arts are deeply ingrained in the Catalán soul. The performing arts are strong here—this is the city, after all, that produced the opera legends Plácido Domingo, José Carreras, and Montserrat Caballé. Other, more popular arts take place on the street, especially along Les Rambles, where crowds often gather around a singer or mime.

The explosion of bars and restaurants is not equaled anywhere else in Spain. You might launch your evening at the **Bar Hivernacle,** Parc de la Ciutadella (© **932-95-40-17;** Metro: Arco del Triunfo), a wine tavern luring a young, hip crowd to a setting of towering palms in a 19th-century greenhouse, just inside the gates of the city's most centrally located park. A fashionable crowd likes to come here to "graze" upon the tapas. A restaurant adjoins. Open from Monday to Saturday 10am to midnight and Sunday 10am to 4pm.

THE PERFORMING ARTS

Founded in 1847, **Gran Teatre del Liceu,** Rambla de Caputxins 61 (© 93-485-99-13; Metro: Liceu), was once one of the world's leading opera stages until it was destroyed by fire on January 31, 1997. When it burned, distraught crowds gathered outside on the Ramblas, and the singer Montserrat Caballé wept. Following a complete restoration, the theater reopened in 1999. The auditorium's appearance and its capacity of 2,320 seats is much the same as before. But many technical improvements have been made, including a modernized stage. It focuses on Opera, dance performances, concerts, and recitals. Box offices open 1 hour before the presentation. Tickets cost 2,000 to 28,000Pts (€12 to €168, $12 to $162).

Mercat de Les Flors, Lleida 59 (© 93-426-18-75; Metro: Plaça de Espanya), the other major Catalán theater, is housed in a building constructed for the 1929 International Exhibition at Montjuïc. Peter Brook used it for a 1983 presentation of *Carmen.* Innovators in drama, dance, and music are showcased here, as are modern dance companies from Europe, including troupes from Italy and France. The 999-seat house also contains a restaurant overlooking the rooftops of the city. Tickets are 1,500 to 4,000Pts (€9 to €24, $9 to $23).

In a city of architectural highlights, **Palau de la Música Catalán,** Sant Francesc de Paula 2 (© 93-295-72-00; Metro: Urquinaona), recently named to the roster of UNESCO World Heritage sites, stands out. In 1908, Lluís Doménech i Montaner, a Catalán architect, designed this fantastical modernist structure, including stained glass, ceramics, statuary, and ornate lamps. It stands today, restored, as a classic example of modernism. Classical concerts, leading recitals, and the occasional jazz and pop performance are presented here. The box office is open from Monday to Friday 10am to 9pm and Saturday 3 to 9pm. Ticket prices are 1,200 to 8,000Pts (€7.20 to €48, $7 to $46).

FLAMENCO

El Tablao de Carmen, Poble Espanyol de Montjuïc (© 93-325-68-95; Metro: Plaça de Espanya, then a 10-minute walk), is the most durable of Barcelona's flamenco shows, with a reputation for authenticity and dancers who derive from Andalusia. It's set on the panoramic highlands of Montjuïc, within the Poble Espanyol compound. You can either eat dinner—traditional Catalán specialties— at tables set up in front of the stage, or dine elsewhere and opt just for a drink or two as the dancers clap and stamp. The club is open Tuesday to Sunday 8pm to midnight or later. During the week, they sometimes close around 1am, often staying open until 2 or 3am on weekends (everything depends on business). The first show is always at 9:30pm, and second show from Tuesday through Thursday and Sunday is at 11:30pm and on Friday and Saturday at midnight. Reservations are encouraged. Dinner and show are 8,150Pts (€48.90, $47); show and one drink, 4,325Pts (€25.95, $25).

At the southern end of Les Rambles, you'll hear the strum of the guitar, the sound of rhythmic hand clapping punctuated by staccato heels, and the haunting sound of the flamenco, a tradition since 1968 at **Tablao Flamenco Cordobés,** Les Rambles 35 (© 93-317-66-53; Metro: Drassanes or Liceu). Head upstairs to an Andalusian-style room where performances take place with the traditional *cuadro flamenco*—singers, dancers, and guitarist. Cordobés is said to be the best showcase for flamenco in Barcelona. From November 1 to March 15 (except for 1 week in December), the show begins at 10pm. From March 15 to October shows are offered nightly at 8:15 and 11:30, with meals beginning about an hour before show time. Reservations are required. Dinner and show is 8,000Pts (€48, $46); show and one drink, 4,500Pts (€27, $26).

A CABARET

The **Bodega Bohemia,** Lancaster 2 (© **93-302-50-61;** Metro: Liceu), off Les Rambles, is a Barcelona institution. This cabaret extraordinaire rates as high camp—a talent showcase for theatrical personalities whose joints aren't so flexible but who perform with bracing dignity. Curiously, most audiences fill up with young people, who cheer, boo, catcall, and scream with laughter—and the old-timers on stage love it. In all, it's an incredible entertainment bargain if your tastes lean slightly to the bizarre. The street outside is none too safe; take a taxi right to the door. Open daily from 11pm to 4am.

DANCE CLUBS

In the basement of a commercial-looking shopping center, **Bikini,** Deu I Mata 105 (© **093-322-00-05;** Metro: Les Corts), is one of the most comprehensive and wide-ranging nightlife compounds in the city, with at least two venues for dancing in every conceivable genre (including funky, rock-and-roll, and golden-oldie music). There's a separate room for Puerto Rican salsa (the owners refer to it as a "salsoteca") and a very large area where fans of emerging musical groups applaud wildly to the music of their favorite band of the minute. The venue changes every night of the week, and has even been known to include sophisticated adaptations of conventional tango music. Open from Tuesday to Thursday 7pm to 4:30am, Friday and Saturday 7pm to 6am. Cover is 1,200 to 2,600Pts (€7.20 to €15.60, $7 to $15).

The chic atmosphere of **Up and Down,** Numancia Diagonal 179 (© **93-205-51-94;** Metro: María Cristina), attracts the elite of Barcelona, spanning a generation gap. The more mature patrons, specifically the black-tie, post-opera crowd, head for the upstairs section, leaving the downstairs to the loud music and "flaming youth." Up and Down is the most cosmopolitan disco in Barcelona, with a carefully planned ambience, impeccable service, and a welcoming atmosphere. Technically, this is a private club and you can be turned away at the door. The disco is open from Tuesday to Saturday from midnight to anytime between 5am and 6:30am, depending on business. Cover is 1,500 to 2,500Pts (€9 to €15, $9 to $15), including first drink.

JAZZ & BLUES

Long beloved by jazz aficionados, **Barcelona Pipa Club,** Plaça Reial 3 (© **93-302-47-32;** Metro: Liceu), is for pure devotees. Ring the buzzer and you'll be admitted (at least we hope you will) to a club reached after a climb of two flights up a seedy run-down building. A series of five rooms are decorated with displays or photographs of pipes—naturally Sherlock Holmes gets in on the act. Depending on the performer, music ranges from New Orleans jazz to Brazilian rhythms. Jazz is featured from Thursday to Sunday 10pm to 5am, although the club with its comfortable bar is open daily during the same hours. Cover is 1,030Pts (€6.23, $6).

In the heart of the Barric Gótic, **Jamboree,** Plaça Reial 17 (© **93-301-75-64;** Metro: Liceu), has long been one of the city's premier venues for good blues and jazz. However, it varies its musical performances and doesn't feature jazz every night, perhaps a Latin dance band. Sometimes a world-class performer will appear here, but most likely it'll be a younger group. Shows are at midnight, and the club is open daily from 11pm to 5am. Cover is 1,800Pts (€10.80, $10).

CHAMPAGNE BARS

The Cataláns call their own version of champagne *cava*. In Spanish, champagne bars are called *champanerías*, and in Catalán the name is *xampanyerías*. These Spanish wines are often excellent, said by some to be better than their French counterparts.

Someone had to fashion a champagne bar after the Bogart-Bergman film, and **Xampanyería Casablanca,** Bonavista, 6 (© 93-237-63-99; Metro: Passeig de Gràcia), is it. Four kinds of house *cava* are served by the glass. The staff also serves a good selection of tapas, especially pàtés. The Casablanca is close to the Passeig de Gràcia. It's open from Sunday to Thursday 7pm to 2:30am and Friday and Saturday 7pm to 3am.

GAY & LESBIAN CLUBS

Gay residents of Barcelona refer to **Chaps,** Av. Diagonal 365 (© 93-215-53-65; Metro: Diagonal), a saloon-style watering hole, as Catalonia's premier leather bar. However, the dress code usually steers more toward boots and jeans than leather and chains. Set behind a pair of swinging doors evocative of the old American West, Chaps contains two bar areas and is open from Monday to Saturday 9pm to 3am, Sunday 7pm to 3am.

Behind a pair of unmarked doors, in a neighborhood of Art Nouveau buildings, **Martin's Disco,** Passeig de Gràcia 130 (© 93-218-71-67; Metro: Passeig de Gràcia), is one of the more popular gay dance clubs in Barcelona. In a series of all-black rooms, you'll wander through a landscape of men's erotic art, upended oil drums (used as cocktail tables), and the disembodied front-end chassis of yellow cars set amid the angular surfaces of the drinking and dancing areas. Another bar supplies drinks to a large room where films are shown. Open daily from midnight to 5am. Cover, including the first drink, is 1,000Pts (€6, $6).

Santanassa, Carrer Aribau 27 (no phone; Metro: Universidad), is a regular staple on Barcelona's gay circuit, with a bar and dance floor along with provocative art, plus a clientele whose percentage of gay women has greatly increased in the past several years. However, gay males are still the dominant sex. Open nightly from 11pm to 3am. Cover is 1,000Pts (€6, $6), including your first drink, only on Friday and Saturday.

DAY TRIPS FROM BARCELONA

PENEDÉS WINERIES From the Penedés wineries comes the famous *cava* (Catalán champagne), which you can sample in Barcelona's champagne bars. You can see where this wine originates by driving 40 kilometers (25 miles) from Barcelona via highway A-2, Exit 27. There're also daily trains from Barcelona-Sants to Sant Sadurní d'Anoia, home to 66 cava firms.

The winery best equipped to receive visitors is **Codorníu** (© 93-818-32-32), the largest producer of cava—some 40 million bottles a year. Your best bet is to visit Codorníu by car because public transportation is unreliable. Tours, conducted from Monday to Friday 9am to 5pm, Saturday to Sunday 9am to 1pm, are presented in English and take 1½ hours; they visit some of the 16 kilometers (10 miles) of underground cellars by electric cart. Take a sweater, even on a hot day. The tour ends with a cava tasting.

SITGES ✦   One of the most frequented resorts of southern Europe, Sitges, 40 kilometers (25 miles) south of Barcelona, is the brightest spot on the Costa Dorada. It's crowded in summer, mostly with affluent young northern Europeans, many of them gay. For years the resort was patronized largely by prosperous middle-class industrialists from Barcelona, but those rather staid days have gone; Sitges is as lively today as Benidorm and Torremolinos down the coast, but it's nowhere near as tacky. It has earned a reputation as a gay resort, but the attitude is hardly in-your-face.

Sitges has long been known as a city of culture thanks in part to resident artist/playwright/Bohemian mystic Santiago Rusiñol. The 19th-century modernist movement largely began at Sitges, and the town remained the scene of artistic encounters and demonstrations long after modernism waned. Sitges continued as a resort of artists, attracting such giants as Salvador Dalí and the poet Federico García Lorca. Then the Spanish Civil War (1936–39) erased what has come to be called the "golden age" of Sitges.

Getting There   RENFE (✆ **902/240-202;** www.renfe.es) runs trains from Barcelona-Sants or Passeig de Gràcia to Sitges. From 5:45am to 10pm daily, there's a train at the rate of one every 10 to 15 minutes (trip time: 40 minutes). A one-way ticket costs 305Pts (€1.85, $1.75).

Sitges is a 45-minute drive from Barcelona along C-246, a coastal road. An express highway, A-7, opened in 1991. The coastal road is more scenic, but it can be extremely slow on weekends because of the heavy traffic, as all of Barcelona seemingly heads for the beaches.

Visitor Information   The **tourist information office** is at Carrer Sínis Morera 1 (✆ **93-894-42-51;** www.sitgestur.com). It's open from June to September 15, daily 9am to 9pm; from September 16 to May, Monday to Friday 9am to 2pm and 4 to 6:30pm, Saturday 10am to 1pm.

Exploring Sitges   It's the **beaches** that attract most visitors. They have showers, bathing cabins, and stalls. Kiosks rent such items as motorboats and air cushions for fun on the water. Beaches on the eastern end and those inside the town center are the most peaceful, including **Aiguadoiç** and **Els Balomins. Playa San Sebastián, Fragata Beach,** and **"Beach of the Boats"** (under the church and next to the yacht club) are the area's family beaches. Most young people go to the **Playa de la Ribera,** in the west.

Beaches aside, Sitges has a handful of interesting museums. The Catalán artist Santiago Rusiñol combined two 16th-century cottages to make the house that contains the **Museu Cau Ferrat,** Carrer del Fonollar (✆ **93-894-03-64**). He lived and worked here and upon his death in 1931 he willed it to Sitges along with his art collection. The museum collection includes two paintings by El Greco and several small Picassos, including *The Bullfight.* A number of Rusiñol's works are displayed. Admission is 500Pts (€3, $2.90) adults, 250Pts (€1.50, $1.45) students, and free for children under 16. A combination ticket to this museum and the two below is 900Pts (€5.40, $5) adults or 500Pts (€3, $2.90) students and children. All three museums keep the same hours: June 22 to September 10, from Tuesday to Saturday 10am to 2pm and 5 to 9pm, Sunday 9:30am to 3pm. The rest of the year, hours are from Tuesday to Friday 10am to 1:30pm and 3 to 6:30pm, Saturday 10am to 7pm, and Sunday 10am to 3pm.

Opened by the king and queen of Spain, the **Museu Maricel,** Carrer del Fonallar (✆ **93-894-03-64**), contains art donated by Dr. Jesús Pérez Rosales. The palace, owned by American Charles Deering when it was built right after World War I, is in two parts connected by a small bridge. The museum has a good collection of Gothic and Romantic paintings and sculptures, as well as many fine Catalán ceramics. There are also three noteworthy works by Rebull and an allegorical painting of World War I by Sert. Admission is 500Pts (€3, $2.90) adults, 250Pts (€1.50, $1.45) students, and free for children under 16. See Museu Cau Ferrat above for combination ticket and hours.

Museu Romàntic ("Can Llopis"), Sant Gaudenci 1 (© **93-894-29-69**), recreates the daily life of a Sitges landowning family in the 18th and 19th centuries. The family rooms, furniture, and household objects are most interesting. You'll also find wine cellars and an important collection of antique dolls (upstairs). Admission is 500Pts (€3, $2.90) adults, 250Pts (€1.50, $1.45) students, and free for children under 16. See Museu Cau Ferrat above for combination ticket and hours.

MONTSERRAT ★★   Lying 56 kilometers (35 miles) northwest of Barcelona, Montserrat ("the serrated mountain") is the most popular day excursion, though it's too crowded for Sunday visits. The winds blow cold at Montserrat, even in summer, so take along warm sweaters, jackets, or coats; in winter, thermal underwear might not be a bad idea.

Getting There   The best and most exciting way to go is via the Catalán railway—Ferrocarrils de la Generalitat de Catalunya (Manresa line), with five trains a day leaving from Plaça de Espanya in Barcelona. The central office is at Plaça de Catalunya 1 (© **93-205-15-15**). The train connects with an aerial cableway (Aeri de Montserrat), included in the rail passage. Expect to spend 1,905Pts (€11.45, $11), including the funicular.

Motorists can take N-2 southwest of Barcelona toward Tarragona, turning west at the junction with N-11. The signposts and exit to Montserrat will be on your right. From the main road, it's 14 kilometers (9 miles) to the monastery through dramatic scenery, with eerie rock formations.

Visitor Information   The **tourist office** is at Plaça de la Creu (© **93-877-77-77**), open from daily 10am to 6pm.

Exploring Montserrat   Sitting atop a 1,210-meter (4,000-ft.) mountain 11 kilometers (7 miles) long and 6 kilometers (3½ miles) wide, Montserrat is one of the most important pilgrimage spots in Spain. Thousands travel here every year to see and touch the 12th-century statue of **La Moreneta** (The Black Virgin), the patron saint of Catalonia. The 50-member **Escolanía** (boys' choir) is one of Europe's oldest and most renowned, dating from the 13th century. At 1pm daily, you can hear them singing "Salve Regina" and the "Virolai" (hymn of Montserrat) in the Nostra Senyora de Montserrat. The basilica is open daily from 8 to 10:30am and noon to 6:30pm. Admission is free. To view the Black Virgin statue, enter the church through a side door to the right. At Plaça de Santa María you can also visit the **Museu de Montserrat** (© **93-877-77-77**), known for its collection of ecclesiastical paintings, including works by Caravaggio and El Greco. The museum is open from Monday to Friday 9:30am to 6pm, Saturday and Sunday 9:30am to 6:30pm, charging 600Pts (€3.60, $3.50) adults or 300Pts (€1.80, $1.75) children and students.

3 Andalusia & the Costa del Sol

This once-great stronghold of Muslim Spain is incredibly rich in history and tradition, containing some of the country's most celebrated sightseeing treasures: the Mezquita (mosque) in Córdoba, the Alhambra in Granada, and the great Gothic cathedral in Seville. This is also the land of the famed *pueblos blancos* ("white villages") and interminable, undulating olive groves. Give Andalusia a week and you'll still have only skimmed the surface of its many offerings.

This dry, mountainous region also embraces the Costa del Sol (Málaga, Marbella, and Torremolinos are covered here), a popular beach strip of Spain. Go to the Costa del Sol for resorts, after-dark fun, and relaxation; visit Andalusia for its architectural wonders, beauty, and relaxed way of life.

The mild winter climate and almost-guaranteed sunshine in summer have made the razzle-dazzle Costa del Sol shoreline a year-round attraction. It begins at the western frontier harbor city of Algeciras and stretches east to the port city of Almería. Sandwiched between these points is a steep, rugged coastline, with poor-to-fair beaches, set against the Sierra Nevada. You'll find sandy coves, whitewashed houses, olive trees, lots of new apartment houses, fishing boats, golf courses, souvenir stands, fast-food outlets, and widely varied flora—both human and vegetable. From June to October the coast is mobbed, so make sure that you've nailed down a reservation.

A driving tour of Andalusia and the Costa del Sol can begin at the "gateway" city of Córdoba, 418 kilometers (260 miles) southwest of Madrid. The city lies astride NIV (E-5) connecting Madrid with Seville.

CÓRDOBA ✮✮✮

Ten centuries ago Córdoba was one of the world's greatest cities. The capital of Muslim Spain, it was Europe's largest city (with a population of 900,000) and a cultural and intellectual center. This seat of the Western Caliphate flourished, constructing public baths, mosques, a great library, and palaces. But greedy hordes descended on the city, sacking ancient buildings and carting off art treasures. Despite these assaults, Córdoba retains traces of its former glory—enough to rival Seville and Granada as the most fascinating city in Andalusia.

Today this provincial capital is known chiefly for its mosque, but it abounds in other artistic and architectural riches, especially its domestic dwellings. The old Arab and Jewish quarters are famous for their narrow streets lined with whitewashed homes and flower-filled patios and balconies; it's perfectly acceptable to walk along gazing into the courtyards.

ESSENTIALS

GETTING THERE Córdoba is a railway junction for routes to the rest of Andalusia and the rest of Spain. The main rail station is on the town's northern periphery, at Av. de América 130, near the corner of Avenida de Cervantes. For information about services in Córdoba, contact **RENFE** (© **957/40-02-02;** www.renfe.es). There're about 22 *talgo* and AVE trains daily between Córdoba and Madrid (trip time: 1½ to 2 hours). Other trains (*tranvías*) take 5 to 8 hours for the same trip. There're also 25 trains from Seville every day (1½ hours).

There're several different bus companies, each of which maintains a separate terminal. The town's most important bus terminal is at Calle Torrito 10, 1 block south of Av. Medina Azahara 29 (© **957-40-40-40**), on the western outskirts of town (just west of the gardens beside Paseo de la Victoria). From the bus terminal operated by Empresa Bacoma, Av. de Cervantes 22 (© **957-40-40-40**), a short walk south of the railway station, there're three buses per day to Seville (trip time: 2 hours) and five daily buses to Jaén (3 hours). Buses arrive here from Madrid (5½ hours).

VISITOR INFORMATION Córdoba's **tourist information office** is at Calle Torrijos 10 (© **957-47-12-35;** www.andalucia.org). Open from Monday to Saturday 9:30am to 7pm and Sunday 10am to 2pm.

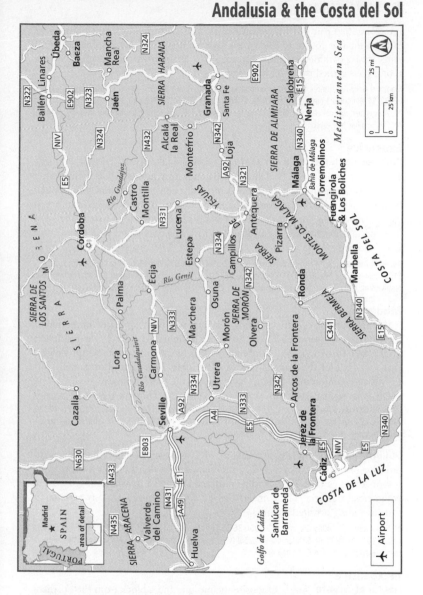

Andalusia & the Costa del Sol

DEPARTING BY CAR Take NIV toward Seville but try to stop over in Carmona, 105 kilometers (65 miles) to the southwest. Partially surrounded by its Roman walls, this is one of the most scenic towns in all of Andalusia. You can lunch here at the parador. After lunch, continue on NIV for another 39 kilometers (24 miles) into Seville.

WHERE TO STAY
Very Expensive
El Conquistador Hotel ☾ Benefiting from one of the most evocative locations in Córdoba, this hotel lies just across a narrow street from one side of the Mezquita. It opened in 1986 within the much renovated premises of an

interconnected pair of 19th-century villas. The marble-and-granite lobby opens onto an interior courtyard filled with seasonal flowers, a pair of splashing fountains, and a symmetrical stone arcade. The quality, size, and comfort of the rooms have earned the hotel four stars.

Magistral González Francés 15, 14003 Córdoba. © 957-48-11-02. Fax 957-47-46-77. 102 units. 22,000Pts (€132, $128) double; from 30,000Pts (€180, $174) suite. AE, DC, MC, V. Parking 1,950Pts (€11.70, $11). Bus: 12. **Amenities:** Bar, coffee shop; sauna; car rental; room service; baby-sitting; laundry/dry cleaning. *In room:* A/C, TV, minibar, hair dryer.

Expensive
Parador Nacional de la Arruzafa ⓡ   Lying 4 kilometers (2½ miles) outside town in the suburb of El Brillante, this parador from around 1960 (named after an Arab word meaning "palm grove") offers the conveniences and facilities of a luxurious resort hotel at reasonable rates. Built atop the foundations of a former caliphate palace, it's one of the finest paradors in Spain, with a panoramic view. The spacious rooms have been furnished with fine dark-wood pieces, and some have balconies.

Av. de la Arruzafa 33, 14012 Córdoba. © **957-27-59-00.** Fax 957-28-04-09. 96 units. 19,500Pts (€117, $113) double; 28,000Pts (€168, $162) suite. AE, DC, MC, V. Free parking. **Amenities:** Restaurant, bar; pool; tennis court; room service; baby-sitting; laundry/dry cleaning. *In room:* A/C, TV, minibar, hair dryer.

Moderate
Hotel González   Within walking distance of Córdoba's major monuments, the González is clean and decent but not a lot more. The hotel's the result of a radical reconstruction of a crumbling antique house that was so comprehensive that very little of the original core is still visible. Rooms are functionally furnished and comfortable. Readers have praised the staff's attitude.

Manríquez 3, 14003 Córdoba. © **957-47-98-19.** Fax 957-48-61-87. 17 units. 5,900–9,800Pts (€35.40–€58.80, $34–$57) double; 7,500–11,900Pts (€45–€71.40, $44–$69) triple; 20,000Pts (€120, $116) quad. Rates include breakfast. AE, DC, MC, V. Parking 1,600Pts (€9.60, $9). **Amenities:** Restaurant, bar; laundry/dry cleaning. *In room:* A/C, TV, hair dryer.

Sol Inn Gallos   Half a block from a wide, tree-shaded boulevard on the western edge of town, this aging 1977 hotel stands eight floors high, crowned by an informal roof garden. The blandly international hotel is a favorite of groups and commercial travelers. The comfortable but small rooms have many extra comforts including private balconies.

Medina Azahara 7, 14005 Córdoba. © **800/336-3542** in the U.S., or 957-23-55-00. Fax 957-23-16-36. 114 units. 12,250Pts (€73.50, $71) double; 15,250Pts (€91.50, $88) triple. AE, DC, MC, V. **Amenities:** Restaurant, bar; pool. *In room:* A/C, TV, hair dryer.

Inexpensive
Hostal el Triunfo *(Finds)*   Opposite the mosque and a block from the northern bank of the Guadalquivir River is a real find—a simple hotel with a formal entrance; a pleasant, white-walled lounge; and comfortable, well-furnished rooms. El Triunfo offers polite and efficient service. The three-floor hotel has no elevator; its only other drawback is that the bells of the Mezquita cathedral may make it difficult for one to sleep.

Corregidor Luís de la Cerda 79, 14003 Córdoba. © **957-47-55-00.** Fax 957-48-68-50. 50 units. 8,000Pts (€48, $46) double; 9,600Pts (€57.60, $56) triple. AE, DC, MC, V. Parking 2,000Pts (€12, $12). Bus: 12. **Amenities:** Restaurant, bar; baby-sitting; laundry/dry cleaning. *In room:* A/C, TV, hair dryer.

Hotel Riviera   The genial owner of this 1978 hotel is likely to be behind the reception desk when you arrive. His establishment—on a triangular plaza in a commercial section of town a short walk south of the train station—offers very clean "no-frills" accommodations. No meals are served, but many cafes are within walking distance.

Plaza de Aladreros 5, 14001 Córdoba. ⓒ 957-47-30-00. Fax 957-47-60-18. 30 units. 5,600–7,500Pts (€33.60–€45, $33–$44) double; 8,500–10,000Pts (€51–€60, $49–$58) triple. AE, DC, V. Parking 1,000Pts (€6, $6). **Amenities:** Laundry/dry cleaning. *In room:* A/C, TV, hair dryer.

WHERE TO DINE
Moderate
El Caballo Rojo ⓖ SPANISH   This restaurant is the most popular in Andalusia, and except for La Almudaina, it's Córdoba's best, though often overrun by tourists. The place has a noise level matched by no other restaurant in town, but the skilled waiters seem to cope with all demands. Try a variation on the usual gazpacho—almond-flavored broth with apple pieces. In addition to Andalusian dishes, the chef offers Sephardic and Mozarabic specialties, an example of the latter being monkfish with pine nuts, currants, carrots, and cream. Real aficionados come for the *rabo de toro* (stew made with the tail of an ox or a bull).

Cardinal Herrero 28, Plaza de la Hoguera. ⓒ 957-47-53-75. Reservations required. Main courses 1,300–5,000Pts (€7.80–€30, $8–$29). AE, DC, MC, V. Daily 1–4:30pm and 8pm–midnight. Bus: 12.

La Almudaina ⓖⓖ SPANISH/FRENCH   Fronting the river in what used to be the Jewish Quarter, La Almudaina is one of the most attractive restaurants in Andalusia, where you can dine in one of the lace-curtained salons or in a glass-roofed central courtyard. Specialties include salmon crêpes; a wide array of fish, such as hake with shrimp sauce; and meats, such as pork loin in wine sauce. For dessert, try the not-too-sweet chocolate crepe. The cuisine's success is in its use of very fresh ingredients that are deftly handled by the kitchen.

Plaza de los Santos Mártires 1. ⓒ 957-47-43-42. Reservations required. Main courses 2,500–7,000Pts (€15–€42, $15–$41); fixed-price menu 3,000Pts (€18, $17). AE, DC, MC, V. Mon–Sat noon–4pm and 8:30pm–midnight; Sun noon–5pm. Closed Sun July–Aug. Bus: 12.

Inexpensive
Restaurante Da Vinci ⓥ*alue* ITALIAN/INTERNATIONAL   This ranks as one of the leading restaurants in town. Although it's not as highly rated as those above, for value it has both of them beat. Both the cuisine and the decor are a blend of Andalusian, international, and Italian influences. Menu items include a choice of roast meats (veal, pork, beefsteak, and lamb), a selection of pastas and salads, and many kinds of fish and seafood, especially hake, monkfish, squid, and salmon. This is standard Andalusian fare, with no innovation and little flair, but it's still good.

Plaza de los Chirinos 6. ⓒ 957-47-75-17. Reservations required. Main courses 1,500–2,300Pts (€9–€13.80, $9–$13); menú del día 1,100Pts (€6.60, $6). V. Daily 1:30–4:30pm and 8pm–midnight.

EXPLORING CÓRDOBA
Alcázar de los Reyes Cristianos ⓖⓖ   Commissioned in 1328 by Alfonso XI (the "Just"), the Alcázar de los Reyes Cristianos (Alcázar of the Christian Kings) is a fine example of military architecture. Ferdinand and Isabella governed Castile from this fortress on the river as they prepared to reconquer Granada, the last Moorish stronghold in Spain. Columbus journeyed here to fill Isabella's ears with his plans for discovery. Two blocks southwest of the mosque, the quadrangular building is notable for powerful walls and a trio of towers: the Tower of the Lions, the Tower of Allegiance, and the Tower of the River. The Tower of the Lions contains intricately decorated ogival ceilings that are the

most notable example of Gothic architecture in Andalusia. The beautiful gardens (illuminated from May to September, Tuesday to Saturday 10pm to 1am) and the Moorish bathrooms are celebrated attractions. The Patio Morisco is a lovely spot, its pavement decorated with the arms of León and Castile.

Amador de los Ríos. ℂ 957-42-01-51. Admission 500Pts (€3, $2.90) adults, 250Pts (€1.50, $1.45) children. May–Sept Tues–Sat 10am–2pm and 6–8pm, Sun 10am–3pm; Oct–Apr Tues–Sat 9:30am–3pm and 4:30–6:30pm, Sun 9:30am–3pm. Bus: 3 or 12.

Mezquita-Catedral de Córdoba ✿✿✿ Dating from the 8th century, this mosque was the crowning Muslim architectural achievement in the West, rivaled only by the one at Mecca. Córdoba's is a fantastic labyrinth of red-and-white-striped pillars. To the astonishment of visitors, a cathedral sits awkwardly in the middle of the mosque, disturbing the purity of the lines. The 16th-century cathedral, a blend of many styles, is impressive in its own right, with an intricately carved ceiling and baroque choir stalls. Additional ill-conceived annexes later turned the mezquita into an architectural oddity. Its most interesting feature is the mihrab, a domed shrine of Byzantine mosaics that once housed *The Koran*. After exploring the interior, stroll through the Courtyard of the Orange Trees, which has a beautiful fountain.

Calle Cardenal Herrero. ℂ 957-47-05-12. Admission 900Pts (€5.40, $5) adults, 450Pts (€2.70, $2.60) children under 13. May–Sept daily 10am–7pm; Oct–Apr daily 10am–6pm. Bus: 3 or 12.

Museo de Bellas Artes de Córdoba Housed in an old hospital, the Fine Arts Museum contains medieval Andalusian paintings, examples of Spanish baroque art, and works by many of Spain's important 19th- and 20th-century painters, including Goya. The museum is east of the Mezquita, about a block south of the Church of St. Francis (San Francisco).

Plazuela del Potro 1. ℂ 957-47-33-45. Admission 250Pts (€$1.60), free for children under 12. June 15–Sept 15, Tues–Sat 10am–2pm and 5–7pm, Sun 10am–1:30pm; Sept 16–June 14, Tues–Fri 3–8pm, Sat 9am–8pm, Sun 9am–3pm. Bus: 3 or 4.

Museo Municipal de Arte Taurino Memorabilia of great bullfights are housed in this museum, a 16th-century building in the Jewish Quarter, inaugurated in 1983. Its ample galleries recall Córdoba's great bullfighters with "suits of light," pictures, trophies, posters, even stuffed bulls' heads. You'll see Manolete in repose and the blood-smeared uniform of El Cordobés—both of these famous matadors came from Córdoba.

Plaza de las Bulas (also called Plaza Maimónides). ℂ 957-20-10-56. Admission 450Pts (€2.70, $2.60), free for children under 18. May–Sept Tues–Sat 10am–2pm and 5:30–7:30pm, Sun 9:30am–2:30pm; Oct–Apr Mon–Sat 10am–2pm and 4:30–6:30pm, Sun 9:30am–2:30pm. Bus: 3 or 12.

THE SHOPPING SCENE

The largest and most comprehensive association of craftspeople in Córdoba is **Arte Zoco,** Calle de los Júdios (no phone). Opened in the Jewish quarter as a business cooperative in the mid-1980s, it assembles the creative output of about a half dozen artisans, whose media include leather, wood, silver, crystal, terracotta, and iron. Some of the artisans maintain on-premises studios, which you can visit to check out the techniques and tools they use to pursue their crafts. The center is open from Monday to Friday 9:30am to 7pm and Saturday and Sunday 9:30am to 2pm. The workshops and studios of the various artisans open and close according to the whims of their occupants but are usually open from Monday to Friday 10am to 2pm and 5:30 to 8pm.

At **Meryan,** Calleja de las Flores 2 (© **957-47-59-02**), you can see artisans plying their ancient craft of leather-making in a 250-year-old building. Most items must be custom ordered, but there're some ready-made pieces for sale, including cigarette boxes, jewel cases, attaché cases, book and folio covers, and ottoman covers. Meryan is open Monday to Friday 9am to 8pm and Saturday 9am to 2pm.

SEVILLE ☆☆☆

Seville, the capital of Andalusia, is justly famous for its beauty and romance. It lies 550 kilometers (341 miles) southwest of Madrid and 217 kilometers (135 miles) northwest of Málaga. In spite of the sultry (some would say oppressive) heat in summer and its many problems, such as rising unemployment and street crime, it remains one of the most charming Spanish cities. Don Juan, Carmen, and that wily barber, Figaro—aided by Mozart, Bizet, and Rossini—have given Seville a romantic reputation it seems unable to live down. If a visitor can see only two Spanish cities in a lifetime, they ought to be Seville and Toledo.

Unlike most Spanish cities, Seville has fared well under most of its conquerors—the Romans, Arabs, and Christians. When Spain entered its 16th-century golden age, Seville funneled gold from the New World into the rest of the country. Columbus docked here after his journey to America.

ESSENTIALS

GETTING THERE By Plane From the **Aeropuerto de Sevilla,** Calle Almirante Lobo (© **95-467-29-81;** www.aena.es), 10 kilometers (6 miles) north of the center of Seville, Iberia flies several times a day to and from Madrid and Barcelona. A bus, identified by the sign AE (*Aeropuerto*), runs at frequent intervals between the airport, the bus station, and strategic points within the city center.

By Train Train service into Sevilla is now centralized into the **Estación Santa Justa,** Avenida Kansas City (© **902/240-02-02** for information and reservations). Buses C1 and C2 travel between the railway station and the town's bus station at Prado de San Sebastian. The high-speed AVE train between Madrid and Seville charges 9,900 to 17,400Pts (€59.40 to €104.40, $57 to $101) each way, depending on when you travel (trip time: 2½ hours). It makes 14 cross-country runs a day, with a stop in Córdoba. Between Seville and Córdoba, the AVE train takes 50 minutes, the *talgo* train 1½ hours, and conventional trains, which charge 1,500Pts (€9, $9) each way, about 2 hours, with many stops en route.

By Bus Most buses arrive and depart from the city's largest **bus terminal,** on the southeast edge of the old city, at Prado de San Sebastián, Calle José María Osborne 11 (© **95-441-71-11**). Many lines also converge on Plaza de la Encarnación, on Plaza Nueva, in front of the cathedral on Avenida Constitución, and at Plaza de Armas (across the street from the old train station, Estación de Córdoba). From here, buses from several companies make frequent runs to and from Córdoba (trip time: 2½ hours). For information and prices, call **Alsina Graells** at © **95/490-8040.**

VISITOR INFORMATION The tourist office, **Oficina de Información del Turismo,** at Av. de la Constitución 21B (© **95-422-14-04**), is open from Monday to Saturday 9am to 7pm and Sunday and holidays 10am to 2pm.

DEPARTING BY CAR After Seville, the next major city of interest in Andalusia is Granada. To get there, you can drive along one of Europe's most fabled beach strips, the Costa del Sol, beginning at Marbella, the chicest enclave. Take A-4 (E-5) south toward Cádiz, bypassing the city by going along NIV, where you connect with N340 heading southeast. This coastal road will take you past Algeciras and Gibraltar and through the resort of Estepona until you reach Marbella.

WHERE TO STAY
Very Expensive
Hotel Alfonso XIII 👑👑👑   At the southwestern corner of the gardens fronting Seville's famous Alcázar, this is a legendary hotel and Seville's premier address. Now under the management of Westin Hotels, it reigns supreme in Seville as a bastion of glamour. Built in the Mudéjar/Andalusian Revival style, it contains halls that glitter with hand-painted tiles, acres of marble and mahogany, antique furniture embellished with intricately embossed leather, and a spacious floor plan that are nothing short of majestic.

San Fernando 2, 41004 Sevilla. ℭ 800/221-2340 in the U.S. and Canada, or 95-422-28-50. Fax 95-421-60-33. www.westin.com. 146 units. 55,000–70,000Pts (€330–€420, $319–$406) double; from 109,000–200,000Pts (€654–€1,200, $632–$1,160) suite. AE, DC, MC, V. Parking 3,000Pts (€18, $17). **Amenities:** Restaurant, bar; pool; tennis courts; car rental boutiques; room service; baby-sitting; laundry/dry cleaning. *In room:* A/C, TV, minibar, hair dryer.

Expensive
Hotel Inglaterra 👑   Opened in 1857 and since modernized, this eminently respectable and rather staid hotel lies a 5-minute walk southwest of the cathedral. Rooms still have old-fashioned touches of Iberian gentility; the best are on the fifth floor.

Plaza Nueva 7, 41001 Sevilla. ℭ 95-422-49-70. Fax 95-456-13-36. www.hotelinglaterra.es. 116 units. May–Mar, 19,000Pts (€114, $110) double. Apr, 30,000Pts (€180, $174) double. AE, DC, MC, V. Parking 1,500Pts (€9, $8.70). **Amenities:** 2 restaurants, bar; room service; baby-sitting; laundry/dry cleaning. *In room:* A/C, TV, minibar, hair dryer, safe.

Moderate
Bécquer   A short walk from the action of the Seville bullring (Maestranza) and only 2 blocks from the river, the Bécquer lies on a street of cafes. The Museo de Bellas Artes also is nearby. The hotel occupies the site of a mansion and retains many *objets d'art* rescued before that building was demolished. Rooms are functionally furnished, well kept, and reasonably comfortable.

Calle de los Reyes Católicos 4, 41001 Sevilla. ℭ 95-422-89-00. Fax 95-421-44-00. www.hotelbecquer.com. 118 units. 15,000Pts (€90, $87) double. AE, DC, MC, V. Parking 1,500Pts (€9, $9). Bus: 21, 31, 32, or 33. **Amenities:** Restaurant, bar; room service; laundry/dry cleaning. *In room:* A/C, TV, minibar, hair dryer, safe.

Hotel Doña María 👑   Its location a few steps from the cathedral creates a dramatic view from the rooftop terrace. Originally built in 1969, this well-conceived four-star four-story hotel has since been radically upgraded. Each of the one-of-a-kind rooms is well furnished and comfortable, though some are rather small. A few have four-poster beds.

Don Remondo 19, 41004 Sevilla. ℭ 95-422-49-90. Fax 95-421-95-46. 69 units. Mar–June and Sept–Dec 19,000–27,000Pts (€114–€162, $110–$157) double; Jan–Feb and July–Aug 15,000Pts (€90, $87) double. AE, DC, MC, V. Parking 2,000Pts (€12, $11.60). **Amenities:** Restaurant, bar; pool; room service; baby-sitting; laundry/dry cleaning. *In room:* A/C, TV, minibar, hair dryer, safe.

Inexpensive
Hostal Goya   The location of this 1960s-era hotel is one of the Goya's strongest virtues. Rooms, though extremely simple and spartan, can be cozy

Seville

To Isla de
←la Cartuja

Calle Baños
Calle J. Rañalán
Calle San Vicente
Calle Santa Clara
Calle Marqués de Paradas
Calle de Alfonso XII
Calle de Jesús del Gran Poder
Calle de Trajano
Calle Amor de Dios
Calle Gerona
Calle Santiago
Calle Tavera
Calle Castellar
Convento de Santa Paula
Calle Arroyo
Calle Salesianos
Calle Sol

Plaza de Armas

1 Plaza Gavidia

Calle San Eloy

Calle Canalejas

Plaza Duque

Calle Tetuán

Calle Laraña

Plaza de la Encarnación

Plaza Salvador

Plaza Cristo de Burgos

Calle Trastámara

Calle Arjona

Calle de San Pablo
2

Calle Méndez Núñez

Calle Sierpes

Paseo Galindo

Calle de los Reyes Católicos

Calle Zaragoza
Calle Pastor y Landero
3

Plaza de San Francisco

Plaza des Pilatos
Calle de Luis Montoto

Puente de Isabel II

Calle Adriano

Plaza de Toros

Calle Condé
de Ibarra
Calle de Recaredo

Guadalquivir

Paseo de Colón
Calle de Dos de Mayo

Calle Vinuesa
Avenida de la Constitución

Plaza de la Virgen de los Reyes
5 † **6** **7**

Plaza de los Venerables
4

8 Plaza Santa Cruz

Barrio de Santa Cruz
Calle Domercio Ríos

Avenida de Eduardo Dato

Calle Beatis
Calle de Rodrigo de Triana
Pagés del Corro
Genova

Hospital de la Santa Caridad ✉

ⓘ

Torre del Oro ■

Almirante Lobo

Puerta de Jerez

9

10 Alcázar

JARDINES DE MURILLO

Calle de Menéndez Pelayo

Puente de San Telmo

11

Calle de San Fernando

Avenida de la República Argentina

Calle de Sebastián Elcano

San Telmo Palace

Real Fábrica de Tabacos

Main Bus Station

Avenida de Carlos V

Paseo de las Delicias

Glorieta San Diego

Avenida Portugal

Gta. des los Marinerios Voluntarios

Avenida María Luisa

12
PARQUE MARÍA LUISA

Avenida de Isabel la Católica

Plaza de España

† Church
ⓘ Information
✉ Post Office

Glorieta Buenos Aires
↓

Puente del Generalísimo

Glorieta Covadonga
↓

0 ——— 1/4 mi
0 ——— 0.25 km
Ⓝ

PORTUGAL
SPAIN
★ Madrid
● Seville

ATTRACTIONS ●

Alcázar **9**
Barrio de Santa Cruz **4**
Catedral **6**
La Giralda **5**
Museo Provincial de Bellas Artes de Sevilla **1**
Parque María Luisa **12**

ACCOMMODATIONS ■

Béquer **2**
Hostal Goya **8**
Hotel Alfonso XIII **11**
Hotel Doña María **7**
Hotel Inglaterra **3**
Residencia Murillo **10**

nonetheless. Guests congregate in the marble-floored salon, where a skylight floods the slightly battered couches and chairs with sunlight. There's no restaurant, but lots of cafes nearby serve morning coffee.

Mateus Gago 31, 41004 Sevilla. ☎ 95-421-11-70. Fax 95-456-02-88. 20 units (10 with bathrooms). Jan–Mar and May–Dec 6,400Pts (€38.40, $37) double without bathroom, 7,300Pts (€43.80, $42) double with bathroom. Apr 7,600Pts (€45.60, $44) double without bathroom, 8,600Pts (€51.60, $49.93) double with bathroom. No credit cards. **Amenities:** Lounge. *In room:* No phone.

Residencia Murillo   Tucked away on a narrow street in the heart of Santa Cruz, the old quarter, the 1950s style Murillo (named after the artist who used to live in this district) is almost next to the Alcázar's gardens. Inside, the lounges have some fine architectural characteristics and antique reproductions; behind a grilled screen is a retreat for drinks. Many of the rooms we inspected were cheerless and gloomy, so have a look before checking in. Like all of Seville's hotels, the Murillo is in a noisy area.

Calle Lope de Rueda 7–9, 41004 Sevilla. ☎ **95-421-60-95.** Fax 95-421-96-16. murillo@nexo.es. 57 units. 8,300Pts (€49.80, $48.15) double; 10,500Pts (€63, $60.90) triple. AE, DC, MC, V. Parking 2,000Pts (€$13) nearby. **Amenities:** Room service; laundry/dry cleaning. *In room:* A/C, hair dryer.

WHERE TO DINE
Very Expensive
Egaña Oriza ✦✦ BASQUE/INTERNATIONAL   Seville's best restaurant lies in a mansion built as a showplace for the city's 1929 international exposition. The restaurant is one of the few that specializes in game in Andalusia—a province that's otherwise devoted to seafood. Many of the raw ingredients that go into the dishes were trapped or shot in Andalusia. Try the salad of wild partridge, casserole of wild boar with cherries and raisins, quenelles of duck in a potato nest with apple puree, rice with stewed thrush, hake cooked in a salt crust, or even woodcock flamed in Spanish brandy.

San Fernando 41. ☎ **95-422-72-11.** Reservations required. Main courses 4,000–8,000Pts (€24–€48, $23–$46). AE, DC, MC, V. Mon–Fri 1:30–4pm and 9pm–midnight; Sat 9–11:30pm. (Bar, daily 9am–midnight.) Closed Aug.

Expensive
Casa Robles ✦ ANDALUSIAN   This restaurant has developed into a courteous but bustling dining hall. You can enjoy some surprisingly complicated dishes, most of them full of flavor and well prepared, in a setting that retains touches of old-fashioned formality. Menu items include fish soup in the Andalusian style; *lubina con naranjas* (sea bass with Sevillana oranges); a suprême of hake garnished with clams, shrimp, and strips of Serrano ham; and filet of beef layered with foie gras.

Calle Alvarez Quintero 58. ☎ **95-421-31-50.** Reservations recommended. Main courses 2,500–5,000Pts (€15–€30, $15–$29); fixed-price menus 4,200Pts (€25.20, $24). AE, DC, MC, V. Daily 1–4:30pm and 8pm–1am.

Moderate
Enrique Becerra ✦ *Value* ANDALUSIAN   Off Plaza Nueva near the cathedral, this restaurant has flourished since 1979 and might provide one of your best meals in Seville. A popular tapas bar and Andalusian dining spot, it offers an intimate setting and a hearty welcome. The gazpacho is among the city's best, and the sangría is served ice cold. Specialties include hake real, sea bream Bilbaon style, rockfish cooked in Amontillada sherry, and oxtail braised in red wine. Many vegetarian dishes are also featured.

Gamazo 2. ☎ **95-421-30-49.** Reservations recommended. Main courses 2,000–4,500Pts (€12–€27, $12–$26). AE, DC, MC, V. Mon–Sat 1–4pm and 8:30–11:30pm.

Inexpensive
Hostería del Laurel ANDALUSIAN This eatery, one of the oldest in the city, lies in one of the most charming buildings on tiny, difficult-to-find Plaza de los Venerables in the labyrinthine Barrio de Santa Cruz. Many diners delay their entrance into the plant-filled dining room until after a round of drinks—preferably sherry—at the beamed and smoke-stained tapas bar. Fish and grilled meats are typical of the region, and served in generous portions.

Plaza de los Venerables 5, 41001 Sevilla. ☎ **95-422-02-95.** Reservations recommended. Main courses 1,200–3,500Pts (€7.20–€21, $7–$20). AE, DC, MC, V. Daily 11am–4pm and 8pm–midnight.

EXPLORING SEVILLE
Alcázar ✿✿✿ A magnificent 14th-century Mudéjar palace, the Alcázar, the oldest royal residence in Europe still in use, was built by Pedro the Cruel. From the Dolls' Court to the Maidens' Court through the domed Ambassadors' Room, it contains some of the finest work of Sevillian artisans. In many ways it evokes the Alhambra at Granada. Ferdinand and Isabella, who at one time lived in the Alcázar, welcomed Columbus here on his return from America. On the top floor, the Oratory of the Catholic Monarchs has a fine altar in polychrome tiles made by Pisano in 1504.

Plaza del Triunfo. ☎ **95-450-23-23.** Entrance is north of the cathedral. Admission 700Pts (€4.20, $4). Free for seniors, students, and children under 16. Apr–Sept Tues–Sat 9:30am–7pm, Sun 9:30am–5pm. Oct–Mar Tues–Sat 9:30am–5pm, Sun 9:30am–2:30pm.

Catedral ✿✿✿ The largest Gothic building in the world, Seville's cathedral was designed by builders with a stated goal—that "those who come after us will take us for madmen." Construction began in the late 1400s and took centuries to complete. Built on the site of an ancient mosque, the cathedral claims to contain the remains of Columbus, with his tomb mounted on four statues. Works of art abound, many of them architectural, such as the 15th-century stained-glass windows, the iron screens (*rejas*) closing off the chapels, the elaborate 15th-century choir stalls, and the Gothic reredos above the main altar. Emerge into the sunlight in the Patio of Orange Trees, with its fresh citrus scents and chirping birds.

Plaza del Triunfo, Av. de la Constitución. ☎ **95-421-49-71.** Admission, including Giralda Tower, 700Pts (€4.20, $4), 200Pts (€1.20, $1.15) children and students, free for children under 13. Mon–Sat 11–5pm; Sun 2–6pm.

La Giralda ✿✿✿ Just as Big Ben symbolizes London, La Giralda conjures up Seville. This Moorish tower, next to the cathedral, is the city's most famous monument. Erected as a minaret in the 12th century, it has seen later additions, such as 16th-century bells. To climb it is to take the walk of a lifetime. There're no steps—you ascend an endless ramp. If you make it to the top, you'll have a dazzling view of Seville.

Plaza del Triunfo. Entrance through the cathedral (admission is included with cathedral).

Museo Provincial de Bellas Artes de Sevilla ✿✿✿ A lovely old convent off Calle de Alfonso XII, this museum houses an important Spanish art collection. Some art experts claim that after the two leading art museums of Madrid, this is the most valuable and significant repository of art in Spain. A whole gallery is devoted to two paintings by El Greco, and works by Zurbarán are

---

Moments **Don't Miss Strolls**

What was once a ghetto for Spanish Jews, who were forced out of Spain in the 15th century in the wake of the Inquisition, the **Barrio de Santa Cruz** 🎿🎿🎿 today is Seville's most colorful district. Near the old walls of the Alcázar, winding medieval streets with names like Vida (Life) and Muerte (Death) open onto pocket-size plazas. Balconies with draping bougainvillea and potted geraniums jut out over this labyrinth, and through numerous wrought-iron gates you can glimpse patios filled with fountains and plants. To enter the Barrio Santa Cruz, turn right after leaving the Patio de Banderas exit of the Alcázar. Turn right again at Plaza de la Alianza and go down Calle Rodrigo Caro to Plaza de Doña Elvira. Use caution when strolling through the area, particularly at night; many robberies have occurred here.

About a 7-minute walk northeast of the cathedral on the northern edge of the Barrio de Santa Cruz is the **Casa de Pilatos** 🎿, Plaza Pilatos 1 (📞 **954/225-298**). This 16th-century palace of the dukes of Medinaceli recaptures the splendors of the past, combining Gothic, Mudéjar, and plateresque styles in its courtyards, fountains, and salons. Don't miss the two old carriages or the rooms filled with Greek and Roman statues. Admission to the museum is 1,000Pts (€6, $6); to the the patios and gardens only 500Pts (€3, $2.90). The museum and gardens are open daily from 9am to 7pm.

Parque María Luisa 🎿🎿, dedicated to María Luisa, sister of Isabella II, was once the grounds of the Palacio de San Telmo, Avenida de Roma. The former private royal park was later the site of the 1929 Ibero-Americana exposition, for which the vast Plaza de España was created. Running south along the Guadalquivir River, the park attracts those who want to take boat rides, walk along paths bordered by flowers, jog, or go bicycling. The most romantic way to traverse it is by rented horse and carriage, but this can be expensive, depending on your negotiation with the driver. Exercise caution while walking through this otherwise delightful park, as many muggings have been reported.

---

exhibited; however, the devoutly religious paintings of the Seville-born Murillo are the highlights. An entire wing is given over to macabre paintings by the 17th-century artist Valdés-Leál. The top floor, which displays modern paintings, is less interesting.

Plaza del Museo 9. 📞 **95-422-18-29**. Admission 250Pts (€1.50, $1.45) adults, free for students. Tues 3–8pm; Wed–Sat 9am–8pm; Sun 9am–2pm. Bus: 21, 24, 30, or 31.

SHOPPING

Close to Seville's town hall, **Ceramics Martian,** Calle Sierpes 74 (📞 **95-421-34-13**), sells a wide array of painted tiles and ceramics, all made in or near Seville. Many of the pieces exhibit ancient geometric patterns of Andalusia. Near the cathedral, **El Postigo,** Calle Arfe (📞 **95-456-00-13**), contains one of the biggest selections in town of the ceramics for which Andalusia is famous. Some of the pieces are much, much too big to fit into your suitcase; others—especially the hand-painted tiles—make charming souvenirs that can be packed with your luggage.

Carmen fluttered her fan and broke hearts in ways that Andalusian maidens have done for centuries. **Casa Rubio,** Calle Sierpes 56 (© **95-422-68-72**), stocks a large collection of fans and castanets that range from the austere or dramatic to some of the most florid and fanciful aids to coquetry available in Spain.

SEVILLE AFTER DARK
In the 1990s Seville finally got its own opera house, **Teatro de la Maestranza,** Núñez de Balboa (© **95-422-65-73**), which quickly became a premier venue for world-class operatic performances. Jazz, classical music, and even the quintessentially Spanish *zarzuelas* (operettas) are also performed here. The opera house can't be visited except during performances. The box office is open daily from 11am to 2pm and 5 to 8pm. Tickets vary in cost depending on the attraction.

In central Seville on the riverbank between two historic bridges, **El Patio Sevillano,** Paseo de Cristóbal Colón 11 (© **95-421-41-20**), is a showcase for Spanish folk song and dance, performed by exotically costumed dancers. The presentation includes a wide variety of Andalusian flamenco and songs, as well as classical pieces by composers like Falla, Albéniz, Granados, and Chueca. Three shows are presented nightly at 7:30, 10, and 11:45pm. From November to February there're only two shows nightly at 7:30 and 10pm. Admission, including one drink, is 4,000Pts (€24, $23).

MARBELLA ⚐
Though it's packed with tourists, ranking just behind Torremolinos in popularity, Marbella is still the most exclusive resort along the Costa del Sol—with such bastions of posh as the Marbella Club. Despite the hordes, Marbella remains a pleasant Andalusian town at the foot of the Sierra Blanca, 80 kilometers (50 miles) east of Gibraltar and 76 kilometers (47 miles) east of Algeciras, or 600 kilometers (373 miles) south of Madrid.

Traces of the past are found in its palatial town hall, its medieval ruins, and its ancient Moorish walls. Marbella's most charming area is the **old quarter,** with narrow cobblestone streets and Arab houses, centering around Plaza de los Naranjos.

The biggest attractions in Marbella, however, are **El Fuerte** and **La Fontanilla,** the two main beaches. There are other, more secluded beaches, but you need your own transportation to get to them.

ESSENTIALS
GETTING THERE   Twenty buses run between Málaga and Marbella daily, plus three buses that come in from Madrid and another three from Barcelona.

VISITOR INFORMATION   The **tourist office,** on Glorieta de la Fontanilla (© **95-277-14-42;** www.pgb.es/marbella), is open from April to October, Monday to Friday 9:30am to 9pm and Saturday 10am to 2pm. Another **tourist office** is on Plaza Naranjos (© **95-282-35-50**), keeping the same hours.

DEPARTING BY CAR   From Marbella, it's just a short drive east along E-15 to Fuengirola, though traffic tends to be heavy.

WHERE TO STAY
Hostal El Castillo   This small 1960s hotel is at the foot of the castle in the narrow streets of the old town. The spartan rooms are scrubbed clean and look

out onto a small, covered courtyard. No meals are served, but many cafes, suitable for breakfast, lie nearby.

Plaza San Bernabé 2, 29600 Marbella. © **95-277-17-39**. 26 units. 5,600–7,000Pts (€33.60–€42, $33–$41) double. MC, V. **In-room Amenities:** No phone.

Hotel El Fuerte ⚐
This is the largest and most recommendable hotel in the center of Marbella. An underground tunnel leads beneath an all-pedestrian traffic-free promenade to the sands of the beach. Built in 1957, it was last renovated in 1994. It caters to a sedate clientele of conservative northern Europeans. There's a palm-fringed pool across the street from a sheltered lagoon and a wide-open beach. The hotel offers a handful of terraces, some shaded by flowering arbors.

Av. del Fuerte, 29600 Marbella. © **800/448-8355** in the U.S., or 95-286-15-00. Fax 95-282-44-11. www. fuertehoteles.com. 263 units. 20,100–23,100Pts (€120.60–€138.60, $117–$134) double; from 37,100Pts (€222.60, $215) suite. AE, DC, MC, V. Parking 850Pts (€5.10, $5). **Amenities:** Restaurant, coffee shop; pool; tennis courts. *In room:* A/C, TV, minibar, hair dryer.

Los Monteros ⚐
Los Monteros, 365 meters (400 yd.) from a beach and 4 kilometers (2½ miles) east of Marbella, is one of the most tasteful resort complexes along the Costa del Sol, attracting those seeking intimacy and luxury. It reopened in 1998 after a radical upgrade. The hotel offers various salons, Andalusian/Japanese in concept, with open fireplaces, a library, and terraces. Rooms are brightly decorated and have terraces. The hotel has drinking and dining on different levels that open onto flower-filled patios, gardens, and fountains.

Carretera de Cádiz, km 187, 29600 Marbella. © **95-277-17-00**. Fax 95-282-37-21. www.monteros.com. 180 units. 32,400–37,060Pts (€194.40–€222.35, $188–$215) double; 40,000–80,000Pts (€240–€480, $232–$464) suite. Rates include breakfast. AE, DC, MC, V. Free parking. **Amenities:** 4 restaurants, bar; 2 pools; tennis courts; gym; health spa; room service; baby-sitting; laundry/dry cleaning. *In room:* A/C, TV, mini-bar, hair dryer, safe.

Marbella Club ⚐⚐⚐
This exclusive enclave was established in 1954, sprawling over a landscaped property that slopes from its roadside reception area down to the beach. It's composed of small, ecologically conscious clusters of garden pavilions, bungalows, and small-scale annexes. Elegantly furnished rooms have private balconies or terraces. Golf can be arranged nearby, and tennis courts are within a 2-minute walk.

Bulevar Príncipe Alfonso von Hohenlohe, 29600 Marbella. © **800/448-8355** in the U.S., or 95-282-22-11. Fax 95-282-98-84. www.marbellaclub.com. 136 units. 44,500–70,000Pts (€267–€420, $258–$406) double; 68,000–90,500Pts (€408–€543, $394–$525) suite; 199,000–219,000Pts (€1,194–€1,314, $1,154–$1,270) bungalow. AE, DC, MC, V. Free parking. **Amenities:** Restaurant, bar; 2 pools; private beach; room service; baby-sitting; laundry/dry cleaning. *In room:* A/C, TV, minibar, hair dryer.

WHERE TO DINE
Balcón de la Virgen SPANISH   Set in the historic core of old Marbella, this restaurant is named after a 200-year-old statue of the Virgin that adorns a wall niche—the focal point of the antique house that contains it. You'll find it within a short walk of the Plaza de los Naranjos, and regardless of when you arrive, it's likely to be well patronized because of its floral charm, good food, attentive service, and reasonable prices. The menu—derived mostly from Andalusia and, to a lesser degree, the rest of Spain—features Málaga-style meat stew, baked hake with olive oil and herbs, marinated swordfish, roasted pork, and grilled filets of beef.

Remedios 2. © **95-277-60-92**. Reservations recommended. Main courses 1,500–3,500Pts (€9–€21, $9–$20). AE, MC, V. Daily 7pm–midnight. Closed Tues Nov–May.

La Hacienda *&* INTERNATIONAL La Hacienda, a tranquil choice 13 kilometers (8 miles) east of Marbella, enjoys a deserved reputation for serving some of the best food along the Costa del Sol. In cooler months, you can dine in the rustic tavern before an open fireplace; in fair weather, meals are served on a patio. The chef is likely to offer foie gras with lentils, lobster croquettes (as an appetizer), and roast guinea hen with cream, minced raisins, and port. The food has a great deal of flavor, is presented with style, and is prepared with the freshest ingredients available. Although the food is admirable, the service is sometimes lacking.

Urbanización Hacienda Las Chapas, Carretera de Cádiz, km 193. *&* **95-283-12-67.** Reservations recommended. Main courses 2,300–7,000Pts (€13.80–€42, $13–$41); fixed-price menu 6,800Pts (€40.80, $39). AE, DC, C, V. Summer daily 8:30–11:30pm. Winter Wed–Sun 1–3:30pm and 8:30–11:30pm. Closed Nov 15 Dec 20.

MARBELLA AFTER DARK

Near Puerto Banús, **Casino Nueva Andalucía Marbella,** Urbanización Nueva Andalucía (*&* **95-281-40-00**), is on the lobby level of the Andalucía Plaza Hotel. It lies in an upscale development surrounded by foreign-owned condos and verdant golf courses, 7 kilometers (4½ miles) from Marbella's center beside the road leading to Cádiz. Gambling includes individual games such as French and American roulette, blackjack, punto y banco, craps, and chemin de fer. Entrance to the casino is 600Pts (€3.60, $3.50) and you'll have to present a valid passport. You can dine before or after gambling in the Casino Restaurant. The casino is open daily from 6pm to 4 or 5am. La Caseta Bar offers flamenco shows at 11pm Friday to Saturday. Entrance is free but drinks cost 1,800Pts (€10.80, $10) and up.

TORREMOLINOS

This is the most famous Mediterranean beach resort in Spain. It's a gathering place for international visitors, a melting pot of Europeans and Americans. Many relax here after a whirlwind tour of Europe—the living's easy, the people are fun, and there're no historic monuments to visit. Thus the sleepy fishing village of Torremolinos has been engulfed in a cluster of concrete-walled resort hotels. Prices are on the rise, but it nevertheless remains one of Europe's vacation bargains. The sands along the beachfront tend to be gritlike and grayish. The best beaches are **El Bajondillo** and **La Carihuela,** the latter bordering an old fishing village. All beaches here are public, but don't expect changing facilities. Although it's technically not allowed, many women go topless on the beaches.

ESSENTIALS

GETTING THERE Torremolinos is served by the nearby Málaga airport, 14 kilometers (9 miles) west. There're also frequent rail departures from the terminal at Málaga; for information, call *&* **902/240-202.** Buses run frequently between Málaga and Torremolinos; for information, call *&* **95-235-00-61.**

VISITOR INFORMATION The **tourist information office** is at Plaza de las Comunidades Autonomas (*&* **952-213-445**). Open daily from 8am to 3pm.

DEPARTING BY CAR From Torremolinos, continue east along E-15 for 11 kilometers (7 miles) into Málaga.

WHERE TO STAY

Hotel Las Palomas Built during Torremolinos's construction boom (1968), this well-managed low-rise hotel is one of the town's most attractive, surrounded by gardens. A 1-minute walk from the beach and a 10-minute walk south of the town center, it has an Andalusian decor that extends into the rooms, a formal entrance, and a clientele of repeat visitors. Rooms have private balconies. None are air-conditioned, though guests can open windows and balcony doors to catch the sea breezes.

Carmen Montes 1, 29620 Torremolinos. ℂ **95-238-50-00.** Fax 95-238-64-66. 303 units. 7,750–9,900Pts (€46.50–€59.40, $45–$57) double. AE, DC, MC, V. **Amenities:** Restaurant, bar; 3 pools; baby-sitting; laundry/dry cleaning. *In room:* A/C, TV, hair dryer.

Sol Don Pablo 🕊 One of the most desirable hotels in Torremolinos is housed in a modern building located a minute from the beach and surrounded by its own garden and playground. The surprise is the glamorous interior, which borrows heavily from Moorish palaces and medieval castles. Splashing fountains are found in the arched-tile arcades, and niches with life-size stone statues of nude figures line the grand staircase. The comfortably furnished rooms have sea-view terraces and private bathrooms. The full day and night entertainment program includes fitness classes, dancing to a live band, and a disco.

Paseo Marítimo, s/n, 29620 Torremolinos. ℂ **95-238-38-88.** Fax 95-238-37-83. www.solmelina.com. 443 units. 14,872–21,300Pts (€89.25–€127.80, $86–$124) double. Rates include buffet breakfast. Free parking. AE, DC, MC, V. **Amenities:** Restaurant, bar; lounge; pool; room service; baby-sitting; laundry/dry cleaning. *In room:* A/C, TV, minibar, hair dryer.

Sol Élite Aloha Puerto Heralded as one of the most modern hotels along the Costa del Sol when it was built in 1972, this now-aging hotel stands on the seashore in the residential suburb of El Saltillo, on the southwestern edge of Torremolinos. Away from the noise of the town center, it offers spacious rooms, all defined by the hotel as minisuites. Each faces the sea, the Benalmádena marina, or the beach, and each contains a separate sitting area. The most popular lunchtime option is a poolside buffet that includes an all-you-can-eat medley.

Calle Salvador Allende 45, 29620 Torremolinos. ℂ **800/336-3542** in the U.S., or 95-238-70-66. Fax 95-238-57-01. 430 units. 17,900–21,828Pts (€107.40–€130.95, $104–$127) double. Rates include buffet breakfast. AE, DC, MC, V. **Amenities:** 2 restaurants, 4 bars; pool; room service; laundry/dry cleaning. *In room:* A/C, TV, minibar, hair dryer.

WHERE TO DINE

Casa Juan SEAFOOD This seafood restaurant west of Torremolinos center is set within a modern-looking building in the old-fashioned satellite hamlet of La Carihuela. Menu items include selections from a lavish display of fish and shellfish prominently positioned near the entrance. Dishes include a fried platter of mixed fish; several different versions of codfish; meat or fish kebabs; and paella. Of special note is *lubina a la sal*—sea bass that's packed in layers of roughly textured salt, which is then broken open at your table and deboned in front of you. Whenever it gets busy (which is frequently), the staff is likely to rush around hysterically and, at times, even brusquely, although many of the restaurant's local fans think this only adds to its charm.

Calle Mar 14, La Carihuela. ℂ **95-238-4106.** Reservations recommended. Main courses 1,500–3,500Pts (€9–€21, $9–$20). AE, DC, MC, V. Tues–Sun 12:30–4:30pm and 7:30pm–midnight. Closed Dec.

El Gato Viudo SPANISH Simple and amiable, this old-fashioned tavern with sidewalk seating occupies the street level and cellar of a building off Calle San Miguel. The menu includes tasty dishes such as platters of grilled fish; marinated hake; roasted pork, steak, and veal; calamari with spicy tomato sauce; grilled shrimp; and shellfish or fish soup.

La Nogalera 8. © **95-238-51-29**. Main courses 1,200–2,800Pts (€7.20–€16.80, $7–$16). AE, DC, MC, V. Nov–Apr Thurs–Tues 1–4pm and 6–11:30pm. May–Oct daily 1–4pm and 6–11:30pm.

TORREMOLINOS AFTER DARK

One of the major casinos along the Costa del Sol, **Casino Torrequebrada,** Carretera de Cádiz 220, Benalmádena Costa (© **95/244-60-00**), is on the lobby level of the Hotel Torrequebrada. The Torrequebrada combines a nightclub/cabaret, a restaurant, and an array of tables devoted to blackjack, chemin de fer, punto y banco, and two kinds of roulette. The nightclub presents a flamenco show from Tuesday to Saturday at 10:30pm. Many visitors prefer to attend just the show, paying 600Pts (€3.60, $3.50), including the first drink. Dinner is served from Wednesday to Saturday at 9pm and costs 8,800Pts (€52.80, $51), which includes admission to the show. The casino is especially lively in midsummer. The casino, its facilities, and its gaming tables are open daily from 9pm to 4am. The entrance fee to the gaming rooms is 600Pts (€3.60, $3.50). You need a passport to enter.

MÁLAGA ⊛

Málaga is a bustling commercial and residential center whose economy doesn't depend exclusively on tourism. Its chief attraction is the mild off-season climate—summer can be sticky. Málaga's most famous native son is Pablo Picasso, born in 1881 at Plaza de la Merced, in the center of the city.

ESSENTIALS

GETTING THERE Iberia (© **800/772-4642** in the United States) has flights every 2 hours into Málaga from Madrid. There're at least five trains a day from Madrid (trip time: 4½ hours). For rail information in Málaga, call **RENFE** at © **902/240-202.** Buses from all over Spain arrive at the terminal on Paseo de los Tilos, behind the RENFE office. Málaga is linked by bus to all the major cities of Spain, including eight buses per day from Madrid (7 hours) and seven per day from Seville (13 hours). Call © **95-235-00-61** in Málaga for **bus information.**

VISITOR INFORMATION The **tourist information office** at Pasaje de Chinitas 4 (© **95-221-34-45**) is open from Monday to Friday 9am to 7pm and Saturday and Sunday 9am to 2pm. Keeping longer hours is **Municipal,** Av. Cervantes 1 (© **95-260-44-10**), open Monday to Friday 8:15am to 2:45pm and 4:30 to 7pm, Saturday 9:30am to 1:30pm.

DEPARTING BY CAR From Málaga, N-340, a curving, winding road, heads east to Nerja.

WHERE TO STAY

Parador de Málaga-Gibralfaro ⊛ Originally established in 1948, and renovated in the 1990s, this parador is located immediately adjacent to the foundations of a medieval castle. Although the feeling inside is modern-day and streamlined, it enjoys a scenic position overlooking the city and the Mediterranean, with views of the bullring, mountains, and beaches. Rooms, with private entrances, have living-room areas and wide glass doors opening onto sun terraces with garden furniture. They're tastefully decorated with modern furnishings and reproductions of Spanish antiques.

Monte Gibralfaro, 29016 Málaga. © **95-222-19-02**. Fax 95-222-19-04. gibralfaro@parado.es. 38 units. 19,000Pts (€114, $110) double. AE, DC, MC, V. Free parking. **Amenities:** Restaurant; bar; pool; currency exchange; room service; laundry/dry cleaning. *In room:* A/C, TV, minibar, hair dryer.

Parador Nacional del Golf 𝒢 A resort hotel created by the Spanish government, this hacienda-style parador is flanked by a golf course on one side and the Mediterranean on another. It's 3 kilometers (2 miles) from the airport, 10 kilometers (6½ miles) from Málaga, and 4 kilometers (2½ miles) from Torremolinos. Rooms have balconies with a view of the golfing greens, the circular pool, or the water; some are equipped with Jacuzzis. Long tile corridors lead to the air-conditioned public areas and graciously furnished lounges.

Carretera de Málaga, Torremolinos, 29080 Apartado 324, Málaga. 𝒞 **95-238-12-55.** Fax 95/238-89-63. Malaga@parador.es. 60 units. 17,500Pts (€105, $102) double. AE, DC, MC, V. Free parking. **Amenities:** Restaurant, bar; pool; golf course tennis courts; room service; baby-sitting; laundry. *In room:* A/C, TV, minibar, hair dryer.

WHERE TO DINE

Café de Paris 𝒢 FRENCH/SPANISH Málaga's best restaurant is in La Malagueta, the district surrounding the Plaza de Toros (bullring). Much of the Cortés's cuisine has been adapted from classic French dishes to please the Andalusian palate. You might be served crepes gratinées (filled with baby eels) or local white fish baked in salt (it doesn't sound good but is excellent). Meat Stroganoff is made here, not with the usual cuts of beef, but with ox meat. Other specialties include artichokes Café de Paris stuffed with foie gras and a succulent version of hake that's stuffed with pulverized shellfish and served with a fish-based tomato sauce.

Vélez Málaga 8. 𝒞 **95-222-50-43.** Reservations required. Main courses 2,200–5,000Pts (€13.20–€30, $13–$29); menú del día 2,600Pts (€15.60, $15). AE, DC, MC, V. Mon–Sat 1–4pm and 8:30pm–midnight. Closed July 1–15. Bus: 13.

EXPLORING MÁLAGA

The remains of the ancient Moorish **Alcazaba** 𝒢, Plaza de la Aduana, Alcazabilla (𝒞 **95-221-60-05;** bus: 4, 18, 19, or 24), are within easy walking distance of the city center, off Paseo del Parque (plenty of signs point the way up the hill). The fortress was erected in the 9th or 10th century, though there have been later additions and reconstructions. Ferdinand and Isabella stayed here when they reconquered the city. The Alcazaba now houses an archaeological museum, with exhibits of cultures ranging from Greek to Phoenician to Carthaginian. Admission to the museum is 100Pts (€0.60, 63¢).

The 16th-century Renaissance **cathedral,** Plaza Obispo (𝒞 **95-221-59-17;** bus: 14, 18, 19, or 24), in Málaga's center, was built on the site of a great mosque and suffered damage during the Civil War. But it remains vast and impressive, reflecting changing styles of interior architecture. Its most notable attributes are the richly ornamented choir stalls by Ortiz, Mena, and Michael. Admission is 300Pts (€1.80, $1.75). It's open daily from 10am to 12:45pm and 4 to 6:30pm; closed holidays.

NERJA 𝒢

Nerja, 51 kilometers (32 miles) east of Málaga, is known for its good beaches and small coves, its seclusion, its narrow streets and courtyards, and its whitewashed, flat-roofed houses. Nearby is one of Spain's greatest attractions, the Cave of Nerja.

At the mouth of the Chillar River, Nerja gets its name from an Arabic word, *narixa,* meaning "bountiful spring." Its most dramatic spot is the **Balcón de Europa** 𝒢, a palm-shaded promenade that juts out into the Mediterranean. The sea-bordering walkway was built in 1885 in honor of a visit from king

Alfonso XIII in the wake of an earthquake that had shattered part of nearby Málaga. The phrase "Balcón de Europa" is said to have been coined by the king during one of the speeches he made in Nerja praising the beauty of the panoramas around him. To reach the best beaches, head west from the Balcón and follow the shoreline.

ESSENTIALS

GETTING THERE   There's no railway station in Nerja, so railway passengers get off in Málaga and then go by bus. Nerja is well serviced by buses from Málaga—at least 10 per day make the 90-minute run. Buses depart from a point immediately adjacent to the railway station. For bus information in both Málaga and Nerja, call © **95-235-00-61.**

VISITOR INFORMATION   The tourist information office is at Puerta del Mar 2 (© **95-252-15-31;** www.nerja.net). Open from Monday to Friday 10am to 2pm and 5:30 to 8:30pm and Saturday 10am to 1pm.

DEPARTING BY CAR   From Nerja, N-340 continues east to Salobreña, where you can connect with E-902 heading north to Granada.

WHERE TO STAY

Parador Nacional de Nerja 🐾   A 5-minute walk from the center of town, this government-owned hotel takes the best of modern motel designs and blends them with a classic Spanish ambience of beamed ceilings, tile floors, and hand-loomed draperies. It was built in the 1960s on the edge of a cliff, around a flower-filled courtyard with a splashing fountain. There's a sandy beach below, reached by an elevator, plus lawns and gardens. Rooms are spacious and furnished in an understated but tasteful style.

Calle Almuñecar 8, Playa de Burriana-Tablazo, 29780 Nerja. © **95-252-00-50.** Fax 95-252-19-97. nerja@ paradox.es. 80 units. 19,000Pts (€114, $110) double. AE, DC, MC, V. Free parking. **Amenities:** Restaurant, bar; pool; tennis courts; room service. *In room:* A/C, TV, minibar, hair dryer.

WHERE TO DINE

Restaurante Rey Alfonso SPANISH/INTERNATIONAL   Few visitors to the Balcón de Europa realize they're standing directly above one of the most unusual restaurants in town. You enter from the bottom of a flight of stairs that skirts the rocky base of what was designed in the late 19th century as a *miradore* (viewing station), which juts seaward as an extension of the town's main square. The restaurant's menu and interior decor don't hold many surprises, but the close-up view of the crashing waves makes dining here worthwhile. Specialties include a well-prepared paella Valenciana, tournedos Nerja (flambéed with mushrooms) and entrecôte Rey Alfonso with a red wine and cream sauce, five preparations of sole (from grilled to meunière), and crayfish in whiskey sauce.

Paseo Balcón de Europa. © **95-252-09-58.** Reservations recommended. Main courses 1,300–3,000Pts (€7.80–€18, $8–$17). AE, DC, MC, V. Thurs–Tues 11am–4pm and 7–11pm. Closed Nov.

EXPLORING A CAVE

The most popular outing from either Málaga or Nerja is to the **Cueva de Nerja** 🐾🐾 (Cave of Nerja), Carretera de Maro (© **95-252-96-35**), which scientists believe was inhabited from 25,000 to 2,000 B.C. This prehistoric stalactite and stalagmite cave lay undiscovered until 1959, when it was found by chance by a handful of boys. When fully opened, it revealed a wealth of treasures left from the days of the cave dwellers, including Paleolithic paintings. These depict horses and deer, but as of this writing they're not open to public viewing. The archaeological museum in the cave contains a number of prehistoric artifacts. You can walk through its stupendous galleries, where the ceiling soars to a height of 60 meters (200 ft.).

The cave is open daily from 10am to 2pm and 4 to 6:30pm (to 8pm July and August). Admission is 800Pts (€4.80, $4.65) adults, 400Pts (€2.40, $2.30) children 6 to 12, free for children under 6. If you want to visit the Nerja caves directly from Málaga, buses depart from Málaga's railway station, then stop en route at Málaga's Muelle de Heredia, at intervals of between 60 and 90 minutes every day between 7am and 8:15pm. The trip takes about an hour.

GRANADA ✿✿

Granada, 122 kilometers (76 miles) northeast of Málaga, is 670 meters (2,200 ft.) above sea level. It sprawls over two main hills, the Alhambra and the Albaicín, and it's crossed by two rivers, the Genil and the Darro. The **Cuesta de Gomérez** is one of the most important streets in Granada, climbing uphill from Plaza Nueva, the center of the modern city, to the Alhambra, Spain's major tourist attraction. This former stronghold of Moorish Spain, in the foothills of the snow-capped Sierra Nevada range, is replete with romance and folklore. In his *Tales of the Alhambra,* Washington Irving used the symbol of the city, the pomegranate (*granada*), to conjure up a spirit of romance.

ESSENTIALS

GETTING THERE   By Plane   Iberia flies to Granada once or twice daily from both Barcelona and Madrid. Granada's airport (© **958/245-223**) is 16 kilometers (10 miles) west of the city center. Airline ticketing problems and airline information are more easily handled at the **Iberia** ticketing office in the city center, at Plaza Isabel la Católica 2 (© **958-22-75-92**). A shuttle bus makes runs several times a day between the airport and the city center, at hours that are timed to coincide with the arrival and departures of flights. The buses meander through the city center before heading out to the airport, but the most convenient and central place to catch one is on the Gran Vía de Colón, immediately in front of the city's cathedral. Passage costs 510Pts (€3.05, $2.95) each way.

By Train   Two **trains** daily connect Granada with Madrid's Atocha Station (trip time: 6 to 8 hours). Granada's railway station is on Calle Dr. Jaime García Royo (© **902/240-202**), at the end of Avenida Andaluces.

By Bus   Most buses pull into the station on the fringe of Granada at Carretera de Madrid. **Alsina Graells** (© **958-18-50-10**) is the most useful company here, offering six buses per day to Córdoba (3 hours), 12 per day from Jaen (1½ hours), nine per day from Madrid (5 hours), 15 from Málaga (2 hours), and six from Sevilla (3 hours).

VISITOR INFORMATION   The **tourist information office** is at Plaza de Mariana Pineda 10 (© **958/22-10-22**), open from Monday to Saturday 9am to 7pm and Sunday 10am to 2pm.

WHERE TO STAY

Hotel América *Value*   Located within the ancient Alhambra walls, this is one of Granada's small hotels built during the 19th-century administration of Napoléon's brother. Walk through the covered entry of this former villa into the shady patio that's lively yet intimate, with large trees, potted plants, and ferns. Other plants cascade down the white plaster walls and entwine with the ornate grillwork. Garden chairs and tables are set out for home-cooked Spanish meals.

The living room of this homey retreat is graced with a collection of regional decorative objects; some of the rooms have Andalusian reproductions.

Real de la Alhambra 53, 18009 Granada. ℂ **958-22-74-71.** Fax 958-22-74-70. 14 units. 16,600Pts (€99.60, $96) double; 19,200Pts (€115.20, $111) suite. AE, DC, MC, V. Parking 1,400Pts (€8.40, $8). Closed Dec–Feb. Bus: 2. **Amenities:** Dining area. *In room:* A/C, hair dryer.

Hotel Granada Center 🦊   One of the most recommendable modern hotels in Granada lies adjacent to the university. Rooms are comfortable, with ample use of postmodern furniture and slabs of polished stone, especially in the bathrooms.

Av. Fuentenueva, s/n, 18002 Granada. ℂ **958-20-50-00.** Fax 958-28-96-96. 172 units. 20,500Pts (€123, $119) double; 60,000Pts (€360, $348) suite. AE, DC, MC, V. Parking 2,000Pts (€12, $11.60). **Amenities:** Restaurant, bar; currency exchange; room service; baby-sitting; laundry/dry cleaning. *In room:* A/C, TV, minibar, hair dryer.

Hotel Rallye *Value*   This is one of the best hotels in town, and it's a relatively good value for the price. Built as a three-star hotel in 1964, it was thoroughly upgraded into a four-star format in 1990. It's a 15-minute walk from the cathedral, on the northern perimeter of Granada's urban center. Rooms are comfortable and well maintained.

Camino de Ronda 107, 18003 Granada. ℂ **958-27-28-00.** Fax 958-27-28-62. 79 units. 16,800Pts (€100.80, $97) double. AE, DC, MC, V. Parking 1,400Pts (€8.40, $8). Bus: 1 or 5. **Amenities:** Restaurant, bar, cafe; room service; baby-sitting. *In room:* A/C, TV, minibar, hair dryer.

Hotel Residencia Cóndor   The attractive 1987 design of this hotel helps make it one of Granada's best in its price range. In 1997, following renovations, it was upgraded to four-star status. It's in the center of town, a 5-minute walk from the cathedral. Many of the pleasant rooms have terraces, and all have light-grained contemporary furniture.

Constitución 6, 18012 Granada. ℂ **958-28-37-11.** Fax 958-28-38-50. condor@maeiahotelas.com. 104 units. 10,000–16,500Pts (€60–€99, $58–$96) double. AE, DC, MC, V. Parking 1,500Pts (€9, $8.70). Bus: 6, 8, 9, or 10. **Amenities:** Restaurant, bar; room service; baby-sitting; laundry/dry cleaning. *In room:* A/C, TV, hair dryer, safe.

Parador Nacional de San Francisco 🦊🦊   Spain's most famous parador—and the hardest to get a room at—is housed in an old brick building with a new annex, set on the grounds of the Alhambra. The decor is tasteful, and the place evokes a lot of history and a rich Andalusian ambience. The parador itself is a former convent founded by the Catholic monarchs immediately after they conquered the city in 1492. One side opens onto its own lovely gardens and the other fronts the Alhambra. From its terrace, you'll have views of the Generalife gardens and the Sacromonte caves. Rooms are generally spacious and comfortable.

Alhambra, 18009 Granada. ℂ **800/343-0020** in the U.S., or 958-22-14-40. Fax 958-22-22-64. Granada@parador.es. 36 units. 33,000Pts (€198, $191) double. AE, DC, MC, V. Free parking. Bus: 13. **Amenities:** Restaurant, bar; currency exchange; room service; laundry/dry cleaning. *In room:* A/C, TV, minibar, hair dryer.

WHERE TO DINE

Cunini SEAFOOD   The array of seafood specialties offered here, perhaps a hundred selections, extends even to the tapas served at the long, stand-up bar. After a drink or two, patrons move on to the paneled ground-floor restaurant, where the cuisine reflects the whole of Spain. Meals often begin with soup, such as *sopa Sevillana* (with ham, shrimp, and whitefish). Also popular is a deep fry of small fish called a *fritura Cunini;* other specialties are rice with seafood, *zarzuela* (fish stew), smoked salmon, and grilled shrimp. Plaza de la Pescadería is adjacent to the Gran Vía de Colón, just below the cathedral.

Plaza de la Pescadería 14. (📞) **958-25-07-77.** Reservations recommended. Main courses 2,200–5,500Pts (€13.20–€33, $13–$32); fixed-price menu 5,000Pts (€30, $29). AE, DC, MC, V. Tues–Sun noon–4pm and 8pm–midnight.

Restaurante Sevilla SPANISH/ANDALUSIAN   Attracting a mixed crowd of all ages, the Sevilla was the favorite restaurant of such hometown boys as García Lorca and Manuel de Falla. Our most recent meal included gazpacho, Andalusian veal, and dessert (selections included caramel custard and fresh fruit). To break the gazpacho monotony, try *sopa virule*, made with pine nuts and chicken breasts. For a main course, we recommend the *cordero à la pastoril* (lamb with herbs and paprika). The best dessert is bananas flambé. You can dine inside, where it's pleasantly decorated, or on the terrace.

Calle Oficios 12. (📞) **958-22-12-23.** Reservations recommended. Main courses 1,500–4,000Pts (€9–€24, $9–$23); fixed-price menu 2,200Pts (€13.20, $13). AE, DC, MC, V. Mon–Sat 1–4pm and 8–11pm; Sun 1–4pm.

Ruta del Valleta �貨 ANDALUSIAN/INTERNATIONAL   Despite its origins in 1976 as an unpretentious roadhouse restaurant, this place rapidly evolved into what's acclaimed as the best restaurant in or around Granada. It's in Cenés de la Vega, about 6 kilometers (3½ miles) northwest of Granada's center. Menu items change with the seasons but are likely to include roast suckling pig, breast of duck in a sweet-and-sour sauce, roasted game birds such as pheasant and partridge (often served with Rioja wine sauce), and preparations of fish and shellfish.

Carretera de la Sierra Nevada, km 5.5, Cenés de la Vega. (📞) **958-48-61-34.** Reservations recommended. Main courses 2,500–5,500Pts (€15–€33, $15–$32); fixed-price menus 6,000–6,500Pts (€36–€39, $35–$38). AE, DC, MC, V. Mon–Sat 1–4:30pm and 8pm–midnight; Sun 1–4:30pm.

EXPLORING GRANADA

Alhambra �貨�货�货   The last remaining fortress-palace in Spain, built for the conquering caliphs of old, the Alhambra is a once-royal city surrounded by walls. The most famous part of the Alhambra, the **Palacios Nazaríes** (Masrid Palaces), is a series of three palaces leading from one to the other as if part of a whole. You'll enter a world of the *Arabian Nights,* where sultans of old conducted state business, raised their families, and were entertained by their harems.

You may be surprised by its somewhat somber exterior. You have to walk across the threshold to discover the true delights of this Moorish palace. The most-photographed part is the Court of Lions, named after its highly stylized fountain. This was the heart of the palace, the most private section. Opening onto the court are the Hall of the Two Sisters, where the "favorite" of the moment was kept, and the Gossip Room, a factory of intrigue. In the dancing room in the Hall of Kings, entertainment was provided nightly to amuse the sultan's party. You can see the room where Washington Irving lived (in the chambers of Charles V) while he was compiling his *Tales of the Alhambra.*

Charles V may have been horrified when he saw the cathedral placed in the middle of the great mosque at Córdoba, but he's responsible for his own architectural meddling here, building a Renaissance palace at the Alhambra—though it's quite beautiful, it's terribly out of place. Today, it houses the **Museo de la Bellas Artes en la Alhambra** ((📞) **958/22-48-83**), a site devoted to painting and sculpture from the 16th to the 19th centuries, and the **Museo de la Alhambra** ((📞) **958/22-62-79**), which focuses more intensely on the region's breathtaking traditions of Hispanic-Muslim art and architecture. Both museums are open from Monday to Saturday 9am to 2pm.

Palacio de Carlos V. (📞) **958/22-83-59.** Comprehensive ticket, including Alhambra and Generalife (below), 1,125Pts (€6.75, $7); Museo Bellas Artes, 250Pts (€1.50, $1.45); Museo de la Alhambra, 250Pts (€1.50,

$1.45); illuminated visits, 1,127Pts (€6.75 ,$7). Mar–Oct, daily 8am–8pm, floodlit visits daily 10pm–midnight; Nov–Feb, daily 9am–5:45pm, floodlit visits daily 8–10pm. Bus: 2. *Note:* Crowds can be overwhelming at the Alhambra. Though you can visit the vast grounds at almost any time, visits to the Nasrid Palaces are timed; some visitors arriving after 10am might not be admitted to the palaces until 1:30pm or later, and if you arrive after 4pm, there's a chance you won't get in at all.

Generalife 🏵🏵   The sultans used to spend their summers in this palace (pronounced hay-nay-rahl-*ee*-fay), safely locked away with their harems. Built in the 13th century to overlook the Alhambra, the Generalife depends for its glory on its gardens and courtyards. Don't expect an Alhambra in miniature: The Generalife was always meant to be a retreat, even from the splendors of the Alhambra.

Alhambra, Cerro de Sol. ⓒ **91/374-54-20** or 958/228-359. Comprehensive ticket, including Alhambra and Generalife, 1,125Pts (€6.75, $7). For hours, see the Alhambra above.

Catedral & Capilla Real 🏵🏵   The richly ornate Spanish Renaissance cathedral, with its spectacular altar, is one of the country's great architectural highlights, acclaimed for its beautiful facade and gold-and-white decor. It was begun in 1521 and completed in 1714. Behind the cathedral (entered separately) is the flamboyant Gothic **Royal Chapel** where lie the remains of Isabella and Ferdinand. It was their wish to be buried in recaptured Granada, not Castile or Aragón. The coffins are remarkably tiny—a reminder of how short they must have been. Accenting the tombs is a wrought-iron grill, a masterpiece. Occupying much larger tombs are the remains of their daughter, Joanna the Mad, and her husband, Philip the Handsome. The Capilla Real abuts the cathedral's eastern edge.

Plaza de la Lonja, Gran Vía de Colón 5. ⓒ **958-22-29-59.** Admission to cathedral, 700Pts (€4.20, $4) chapel, 350Pts (€2.10, $2). Cathedral open daily 10am–8pm; chapel Mon–Sat 10am–1pm and 4–7pm; Sun 2:30–7pm (closes at 6:30pm in winter).

ALBAICÍN 🏵

This old Arab quarter, on one of the two main hills of Granada, doesn't belong to the city of 19th-century buildings and wide boulevards. It, and the surrounding Gypsy caves of Sacromonte, are holdovers from the past. The Albaicín once flourished as the residential section of the Moors, even after the city's reconquest, but it fell into decline when the Christians drove them out. This narrow labyrinth of crooked streets escaped the fate of much of Granada, which was torn down in the name of progress. Fortunately, it has been preserved, as have its plazas, whitewashed houses, villas, and the decaying remnants of the old city gate. Here and there, you can catch a glimpse of a private patio filled with fountains and plants, a traditional and graceful-appearing way of life that flourishes today. To reach the Albaicín from the medieval and 19th-century center of Granada, take bus 7 to Calle de Pagés. Alternatively, you can hop aboard any of the small red-and-white buses marked "ALBAICÍN" that make runs at 15-minute intervals from the Plaza Isabel la Católica. The buses operate daily from 7am to 11pm; the fare is 130Pts (€0.83, 75¢).

THE GYPSY CAVES OF SACROMONTE *Overrated*

The Gypsy Caves of Sacromonte are a tourist trap, one of the most obviously commercial and shadowy rackets in Spain. Yet visitors seem to flock to them in spite of the warnings. It's safer to go on an organized tour. A visit to the caves is almost always included as part of the morning and (more frequently) afternoon city tours offered every day by such companies as **Grana Vision** (ⓒ **958-13-58-04**). A tour of Granada, including not only the caves but the cathedral, the monastery, the royal chapel, and the Albaicín, costs 9,000Pts (€54, $52) per person. Tours depart daily at 9am, ending at 7pm. Night tours of the caves (when they're at their most eerie, evocative, and, unfortunately, larcenous) are usually offered only to those who can assemble 10 or more people into a group. Before agreeing to a tour, negotiate the price carefully.

THE SHOPPING SCENE

The **Alcaicería,** once the Moorish silk market, is next to the cathedral in the lower city. The narrow streets of this rebuilt village of shops are filled with vendors selling the arts and crafts of the province. The Alcaicería offers you one of Spain's most splendid assortments of tiles, castanets, and wire figures of Don Quixote chasing windmills. The jewelry found here compares favorably with the finest Toledan work. For the window shopper, in particular, it makes a pleasant stroll.

GRANADA AFTER DARK

The best **flamenco** show in Granada is staged at the **Jardines Neptuno,** Calle Arabial (© **958-25-11-12**), nightly at 10:15pm. The acts are a bit racy, though they've been toned down. In addition to flamenco, performers attired in regional garb perform folk dances and present guitar concerts. The show takes place in a garden setting. There's a high cover charge of 3,800Pts (€22.80, $22), including your first drink. It's best to take a taxi here to the location about a mile south of the center.

17

Sweden

by Darwin Porter & Danforth Prince

Although it was founded 7 centuries ago, Stockholm didn't become Sweden's capital until the mid-17th century. Today it's the capital of a modern welfare state with a strong focus on leisure activities and access to nature only a few minutes away.

1 Stockholm & Environs

Stockholm is built on 14 islands in Lake Mälaren, marking the beginning of an archipelago of 24,000 islands, skerries, and islets that stretches all the way to the Baltic Sea. It's a city of bridges and islands, towers and steeples, cobblestone squares and broad boulevards, Renaissance splendor and steel-and-glass skyscrapers. The medieval walls of Gamla Stan (the Old Town) no longer stand, but the winding streets have been preserved. You can even go fishing in downtown waterways, thanks to a long-ago decree from Queen Christina.

Once an ethnically homogeneous society, Stockholm has experienced a vast wave of immigration in the past several years. More than 10% of Sweden's residents are immigrants or children of immigrant parents, with most coming from other Scandinavian countries. Because of Sweden's strong stance on human rights, the country has also become a major destination for political and social refugees from Africa and the Middle East and the former Yugoslavia as well.

An important aspect of Stockholm today is a growing interest in cultural activities. Over the past quarter of a century, attendance at live concerts has grown, book sales are up, and more and more people are visiting museums.

ESSENTIALS

GETTING THERE **By Plane** You'll arrive at **Stockholm Arlanda Airport** (© 08/797-61-00; www.lfv.se), about 45 kilometers (28 miles) north of Stockholm on the E-4 highway. **SAS** (© 800/221-2350) is the most common carrier. A **bus** (© 08/600-10-00) outside the terminal building goes to the City Terminal, Klarabergsviadukten, in the city center every 10 to 15 minutes (trip time: 35 minutes), for 70SEK ($8). Alternatively, you can take the **Flight Taxi limousine service** (© 08/686-10-10). Go to the desk in the arrivals hall at Arlanda; the limousine will take you to central Stockholm for 350SEK ($39). A taxi to or from the airport will cost 435SEK ($48).

By Train Trains arrive at Stockholm's **Centralstationen (Central Station)** on Vasagatan, in the city center (© 020/75-75-75), where connections can be made to Stockholm's subway, the T-bana. Follow the sign marked TUNNELBANA.

By Bus Buses arrive at the **Centralstationen** on Vasagatan, and from here you can catch the T-bana to your final Stockholm destination. For bus information or reservations in the Stockholm area, call © 08/440-85-70. Ticket office hours are from Monday to Friday and Sunday 9am to 6pm; Saturday 9am to 4pm.

Stockholm

ACCOMMODATIONS ■

Berns' Hotel **27**

Clas på Hörnet **2**

Elite Stockholm Plaza **14**

Esplanade Hotel **19**

Grand Hotel **26**

Hotel Örnsköld **16**

Hotel Tegnérlunden **3**

Lady Hamilton Hotel **11**

Långholmen Hotel **7**

Lydmar Hotel **15**

Mälardrottningen **8**

Scandic Sergel Plaza **13**

Victory Hotel **10**

By Car Getting into Stockholm by car is relatively easy because the major national expressway from the south, E-4, joins with the national express highway E-3 coming in from the west and leads right into the heart of the city. Stay on the highway until you see the turnoff for Central Stockholm or Centrum.

VISITOR INFORMATION **Tourist Offices** After getting settled in your room, your first stop in Stockholm should be **Sverige Huset (Sweden House),** Hamnagatan 27 (T-bana: Kungsträdgården). On the ground floor is the **Stockholm Information Service** (✆ 08/789-24-90). Even if you desire no other information, get a free copy of *Stockholm This Week* for its lists of special and free events and good map. You can buy the Stockholm Card (see box below) here, as well as city tour and archipelago-excursion tickets. This office will reserve a hotel room for a 60SEK ($7) service charge, plus a 10% deposit, or a youth hostel room for a 20SEK ($2.20) service charge. The reservations desk can also book summer cottages and overnight packages and sell tickets to concerts and soccer games. It's open from June to August, Monday to Friday 8am to 7pm, Saturday and Sunday 9am to 5pm; from September to May, Monday to Friday 9am to 6pm and Saturday and Sunday 10am to 3pm. Maps and other free material are available.

Hotell Centralen, Vasagatan in the main hall of Central Station (✆ 08/789-24-25; T-bana: Centralen), is an authorized tourist information office that will also book accommodations for free if you contact them in advance by mail, telephone, or fax. Booking requests made in person at the office cost 50SEK ($6). It's open from June to August daily 7am to 9pm; from May and September daily 8am to 7pm; and from October to April 9am to 6pm. Credit and charge cards are accepted.

The **SL Center** is on the lower level of Sergels Torg in Norrmalm (✆ 08/686-11-97; if it's busy, or if you need only info about times for buses, subways, and local trains, call ✆ 08/600-10-00; T-bana: Centralen). The SL Center offers information about local subway and bus transportation and sells a good transport map, as well as tickets for the system. Open from Monday to Friday 7am to 6:30pm, and Saturday and Sunday 10am to 5pm.

Websites Check **www.stockholmtown.com** just before you go for updated event listings; advice for dining, lodging, and museums; and links to media outlets. Go to **www.cityguide.se** for hotel reservations, upcoming events, entertainment, and places of tourist interest in Stockholm.

CITY LAYOUT On the island of Norrmalm north of the Old Town are Stockholm's major streets, such as **Kungsgatan** (the main shopping street), **Birger Jarlsgatan,** and **Strandvägen** (leading to the Djurgården—home of many of the city's top sights). **Stureplan,** at the junction of the major avenues Kungsgatan and Birger Jarlsgatan, is the city's commercial hub.

About 4 blocks west of the Stureplan rises **Hötorget City,** a landmark of modern urban planning. Its main traffic-free artery is the **Sergelgatan,** a 3-block shopper's promenade that eventually leads to the modern sculptures in the center of the **Sergels Torg.** About 9 blocks south of the Stureplan, at **Gustav Adolfs Torg,** are the Royal Dramatic Theater and the Royal Opera House. A block east of the flaming torches of the Royal Opera House is the verdant north-south stretch of **Kungsträdgården,** part avenue, part public park, which serves as a popular gathering place for students and as a resting perch for shoppers. Three blocks southeast, on a famous promontory, lie the landmark Grand Hotel and the National Museum.

Value The Stockholm Card

Costing just 199SEK ($22) for 1 day, 398SEK ($44) for 2 days, or 498SEK ($55) for 3 days, the **Stockholmskortet (Stockholm Card)** is a personal discount card that includes unlimited travel on Stockholm's public transport network (except airport buses), admission to most museums, and a guidebook to the city. You can also take a free sightseeing tour with City Sightseeing, which allows you to get on and off as often as you choose, looking at the sights according to your own schedule. You also get boat sightseeing at half price, plus a one-way ticket to Drottningholm Palace. Cards are sold at the tourist information counter at Sweden House and at Hotell Centralen at Central Station, and each is valid for one adult and two children 17 and under.

Kungsholmen, King's Island, is across a narrow canal from the rest of the city, a short walk west of the Central Station. It's visited chiefly by those wanting to tour Stockholm's elegant Stadshuset (City Hall). South of the island where **Gamla Stan** (Old Town) is located and separated from it by a narrow but much-navigated stretch of water is **Södermalm,** the southern district of Stockholm. Quieter than its northern counterpart, it's an important residential area with a distinctive flavor of its own.

To the east of Gamla Stan, on a large and forested island completely surrounded by the complicated waterways of Stockholm, is **Djurgården** (Deer Park). The rustically unpopulated summer pleasure ground of Stockholm, it's the site of many of the city's most popular attractions: the open-air museums of Skansen, the *Vasa* man-of-war, Gröna Lund's Tivoli, the Waldemarsudde estate of the "painting prince" Eugen, and the Nordic Museum.

GETTING AROUND
Walking is the best way to get to know the city. In any case, you have to explore Gamla Stan on foot, as cars are banned from most of the streets. Djurgården and Skeppsholmen are other popular haunts for strolling.

BY SUBWAY Subways (called Tunnelbana or T-bana) and buses are operated by **SL** (© **08/600-10-00),** the city transportation network, and charge according to a zone system—the price increases the farther you go. The subway system is fast, efficient, and far-reaching. Color-coded maps are on station walls and printed in most tourist publications. Timetables for each train are also posted. Subway entrances are marked with a blue T on a white background.

One ticket costs 16SEK ($1.75) and is good for 1 hour (use it as often as you want), or you can get a strip of 20 coupons for 110SEK ($12). Your best transportation bet is to purchase a **tourist season ticket.** A 1-day card costs 70SEK ($8) and is valid for 24 hours of unlimited travel by T-bana, bus, and commuter train in Stockholm. It also includes passage on the ferry to Djurgården. Most visitors will probably want the 3-day card for 135SEK ($15), valid for 72 hours in both Stockholm and the adjacent county. The 3-day card is also valid for admission to Skansen, Kaknästornet, and Gröna Lund. Children under 18 pay 40SEK ($4.40) for a 1-day card or 60SEK ($7) for a 3-day card, but children up to age 7 can travel free with an adult. Tickets are sold at tourist-information offices, in subway stations, and at most news vendors. You can buy day passes at the SL center (see "Visitor Information," above).

If you're paying with cash or using a strip ticket, pass through the gate and tell the person in the ticket booth where you're going. He or she will either ask for your fare or stamp your ticket. If you have a Stockholm Card, just flash it. Sometimes the ticket collector is absent; in these instances, few commuters wait for the collector to return—they just walk through.

BY BUS A bus will fill the need when the T-bana isn't convenient. The two systems have been coordinated to complement each other. Many visitors use a bus to reach Djurgården (though you can walk there), since the T-bana doesn't go there. Enter through the front door and pay the driver, show your Stockholm Card, or have your strip ticket stamped. For a list of bus routes, purchase the *SL Stockholmskartan,* available for 35SEK ($3.85) at the Stockholm Information Service in the Sweden House or the SL Center (see "Visitor Information," above). Many buses depart from Normalmstorg, catercorner to Kungsträdgården and 2 blocks from Sweden House.

BY FERRY Ferries run between Gamla Stan (near the bridge to Södermalm) and Djurgården year-round, providing the best link between these two. In summer, boats depart every 15 minutes from 9am to midnight (to 10:40pm Sunday); in winter, daily every 20 minutes from 9am to 6pm. The ride costs 20SEK ($2.20) adults, half price for seniors and children 7 to 18, free for children 6 and under. Ferries also run between Nybroplan and Djurgården (summer only) and between Slussen and Djurgården (year-round). Contact the Stockholm information service for more information.

Large ships, including those of the **Silja Line,** Kungsgatan 2 (✆ 08/22-21-40), and the **Viking Line,** Centralstationen (✆ 08/452-40-00), arrive at berths near the junction of Södermalm and the entrance to Gamla Stan. This neighborhood is Stadsgården, and the avenue that runs along the adjacent waterfront is Stadsgårdshamnen. The Slussen T-bana stop, right at the berths, is a 3-minute walk from the Old Town. Holders of a valid Eurailpass receive discounts on Silja ferries to Helsinki and Turku.

Ferries from Gotland (whose capital is Visby) dock at Nynäshamn, south of Stockholm. Take a Nynäshamn-bound bus from the Central Station in Stockholm or the SL commuter train to reach the ferry terminal at Nynäshamn.

BY TAXI Taxis are expensive in Stockholm—in fact, they're among the most expensive in the world, with a double-tiered charge that applies both for the distance you travel, and for the time your ride takes. The meter begins at 28SEK ($3.10), and mounts quickly, with an average ride costing at least 100SEK ($11). If you're heading from anywhere in downtown Stockholm to Arlanda airport, there's a set-price charge of 435SEK ($48) that's valid for up to four passengers and their luggage. Taxis whose dome lights display the word LEDIG aren't otherwise engaged, and can be hailed on the street. If you want to call for a taxi, the most reputable taxi companies include **Taxi Stockholm** (✆ 08/15-00-00 or 08/15-04-00), and **Taxi Kurir** (✆ 08/30-00-00). *Note:* there're some occasional independent, unmetered taxis within Stockholm, which tend to be frowned upon by local authorities. If you opt to travel within one of these, negotiate a reasonable fare with the driver before leaving the curb.

BY CAR **Avis** (✆ 08/797-9970) and **Hertz** (✆ 08/797-9900) maintain offices at Arlanda Airport. Hertz's downtown office is at Vasagatan 26 (✆ 08/240-720); Avis's downtown office is at Vasagatan 10B (✆ 08/20-20-60). Rentals at both organizations are usually cheaper if you reserve them by phone before leaving North America.

BY BICYCLE The best place to go cycling is on Djurgården. You can rent bicycles from **Skepp o Hoj,** Djurgårdsbron (© **08/660-57-57**), for about 150SEK ($17) per day. A valid credit-card number is held on deposit on any bicycle rental. The shop is open from May to August, daily 9am to 9pm.

C *FAST FACTS:* Stockholm

American Express Amex, Norrlandsgatan 21 (© **08/411-05-40**; T-Bana: Mariatorget), is open from Monday to Friday 9am to 6pm (until 5pm in winter) and Saturday 10am to 3pm (until 1pm in winter).

Currency You'll pay your way in Stockholm in SwedishKr or crowns (singular, **krona**), internationally abbreviated **SEK**, which are divided into 100 öre. The exchange rate used in this chapter was $1 = 9SEK, or 1KR = 11¢. At press time, £1 = 12.60SEK (or 1SEK = 8p). The euro rate was currently fixed at €1 = 8.1SEK (or 1SEK = €0.12). Note that though Sweden is part of the EU, it does not plan to switch to the euro at this time.

Dentists Emergency dental treatment is offered at **St. Eriks Hospital, Fleminggatan 22** (© **08/654-11-17**; T-bana: Fridhemsplan), open daily from 8am to 8:30pm.

Doctors If you need emergency medical care, check with **Medical Care Information** (© **08/672-10-00**). There's also a private clinic, **City Akuten,** at Holländargartan 3 (© **08/412-29-61**; T-bana: Skanstull).

Drugstores One 24-hour pharmacy is **C. W. Scheele,** Klarabergsgatan 64 (© **08/454-81-00**; T-bana: Centralen).

Embassies/Consulates The **U.S. Embassy** is at Strandvägen 101, S-115 89 Stockholm (© **08/783-53-00**; T-bana: Östermalmstorg); the **British Embassy** (© **08/671-90-00**) is at Skarpögatan 6–8 (mailing address: P.O. Box 27819, S-115 93 Stockholm); the **Canadian Embassy** is at Tegelbacken 4, S-103 23 Stockholm (© **08/453-30-00**; T-bana: Centralen); the **Irish Embassy** (© **08/661-80-05**; T-bana: Östermalmstorg) is at Östermalmsgatan 97 (mailing address: P.O. Box 10326, S-100 55 Stockholm); the **Australian Embassy** (© **08/613-29-00**; T-bana: Hötorget) is at Sergels Torg 12 (mailing address: P.O. Box 7003, S-103 86 Stockholm); and the **South Africa Embassy** is at Linnég 76, S-115 00 Stockholm (© **08/24-39-50**; T-bana: Östermalmstorg). **New Zealand** doesn't maintain an embassy in Sweden. Inquiries should be made through the embassy of New Zealand in The Hague (© **31-70/346-93-24**).

Emergencies Call © **90-000** anywhere in Sweden if you need an ambulance, the police, or fire department.

Hospitals Call **Medical Care Information** at © **08/672-10-00** and an English-speaking operator will inform you of the hospital closest to you.

Internet Cafe One of the most central places for receiving e-mail or checking messages is **Café Nine,** Odengatan 44 (© **08/673-67-97**; info@ninestudios.com; T-Bana: Odenplan). It charges only 1 krone (10¢) per minute, and is open from Monday to Friday 10am to 1am and Saturday and Sunday 11am to 1am.

Post Office The main post office is at Vasagatan 28–34 (© **08/781-20-00**), open from Monday to Friday from 8am to 7am and Saturday 10am to 2pm. Mail can be sent c/o general delivery as follows: Post Restante, c/o Postens Huyudkontor (Main Post Office), Vasagatan 28–34, S-10 430 Stockholm, Sweden.

Telephone The **country code** for Sweden is **46**. The **city code** for Stockholm is **8**; use this code when you're calling from outside Sweden. If you're within Sweden but not in Stockholm, use **08**. If you're calling within Stockholm, simply leave off the code and dial the regular phone number.

Instructions in English are posted in **public phone boxes,** which can be found on street corners. Very few phones in Sweden are coin operated; most require the purchase of a phone card (called a **Telekort**). You can obtain phone cards at most newspaper stands and tobacco shops.

You can make international calls from the **TeleCenter Office** on the Central Station's ground floor (© **08/456-74-94**), open daily from 8am to 9pm, except major holidays. Long-distance rates are posted. To make a collect or calling card call, dial one of the following access numbers to reach an American operator or an English-language voice prompt: **AT&T** © **020/795-611; MCI** © **020/795-9222;** and **Sprint** © **020/799-011.**

For directory listings or other information for Stockholm or other parts of Sweden only, dial © **118118;** for other parts of Europe, dial © **118119.**

WHERE TO STAY

If you want to stay in a hotel convenient to your flight, there's nothing closer than the **Radisson SAS SkyCity Hotel**, Stockholm/Arlanda Airport, 190 45 Stockholm/Arlanda (© **08/590-77300;** fax 08/50-67-40-01). With 230 modernized and tastefully styled rooms, it's right in the airport complex. Doubles cost 2,179 to 2,419SEK ($240 to $266). There's also a bar, fitness center, and international restaurant.

Nearby, accessible from the main airport terminals via airport bus 14, but not accessible via covered walkway, is the SkyCity Hotel's twin, the nearly identical, 300-room **SAS Arlandia Hotel,** Bernstocksvägen 1, 190 45 Stockholm/Arlanda (© **08/59361-800;** fax 08/59361-970), charging comparable rates. *Note:* The hotel has a slightly different spelling from the name of the airport.

A shuttle bus runs between the hotels and Stockholm's main railway station, and charges 60SEK ($7) per person each way. It's marked **Flygbus** and it's silver.

IN THE CITY CENTER
Very Expensive
Grand Hotel 🏵🏵🏵 Opposite the Royal Palace, this hotel is grand indeed, the only five-star hotel in Sweden. Built in 1874, it has been continuously renovated, but its old-world style has been maintained. Rooms come in all shapes and sizes, but each is elegant. The mattresses and level of comfort are the finest in town. The spacious bathrooms have heated floors; the most expensive—and best—accommodations overlook the harbor.

Södra Blasieholmshamnen 8, S-103 27 Stockholm. © **800/223-5652** in the U.S. and Canada, or 08/ 679-35-00. Fax 08/611-86-86. www.grandhotel.se. 320 units. 3,195–3,995SEK ($351–$439) double; from 4,895SEK ($538) suite. Rates include breakfast. AE, DC, MC, V. Parking 340SEK ($37). T-bana: Kungsträdgården. Bus: 46, 55, 62, or 76. **Amenities:** Best hotel restaurant in Stockholm, informal buffet dining room, elegant bar; fitness center; 24-hour room service; laundry/dry cleaning. *In room:* A/C (some rooms), TV, minibar, hair dryer.

Expensive

Berns' Hotel ★★★   In its 19th-century heyday, this was Sweden's most elegant hotel. With its lush gilded age interior, it still surfaces near the top, surpassed only by the Grand (see above). Rooms range from medium to spacious; each is soundproof and has a good-size bathroom containing such amenities as a phone and a makeup mirror. The open-air terrace on the hotel's rooftop offers views over the city's historic core.

Näckströmsgatan 8, S-111 47 Stockholm. ℂ **08/614-07-00.** Fax 08/566-32-201. www.beans.se. 65 units. 2,495–2,995SEK ($274–$329) double; from 3,790SEK ($417) suite. Rates include breakfast. AE, DC, MC, V. Parking 295SEK ($32). T-bana: Östermalmstorg. **Amenities:** Restaurant, bar; room service; baby-sitting; dry cleaning/laundry; no-smoking rooms. *In room:* A/C, TV, CD player, minibar, hair dryer.

Lydmar Hotel ★   This is a "hotel secret" of Stockholm and needs to be better known. Opposite the garden of the King's Library, in what looks like an office building, the Lydmar opened in 1930. The exceptionally well-maintained rooms are traditionally furnished and range from small singles to medium-size doubles. Mattresses are firm and frequently renewed, and bathrooms are state of the art.

Sturegatan 10, S-114 36 Stockholm. ℂ **98/566-11-300.** Fax 08/566-11-301. www.lydmar.se. 63 units. 2,200–3,750SEK ($242–$413) double; 7,500SEK ($825) junior suite. Rates include buffet breakfast. AE, DC, MC, V. Parking 250SEK ($28). T-bana: Östermalmstorg. Bus: 41, 46, 56, or 91. **Amenities:** Restaurant, lobby bar with live jazz; room service; baby-sitting; laundry/dry cleaning. *In room:* TV, minibar, hair dryer.

Scandic Sergel Plaza ★★   This hotel at the entrance to Drottninggatan, the main shopping street, is one of the city's best. The elegant decor includes 18th-century artwork and antiques. It's a bastion of comfort and good taste, as reflected by the beautifully decorated, generally spacious rooms. All contain firm mattresses, have good double-glazed windows, and have average-size, immaculately maintained bathrooms with plenty of soft towels. Some units are wheelchair accessible.

Brunkebergstorg 9, S-103 27 Stockholm. ℂ **800/THE-OMNI** in the U.S., or 08/22-66-00. Fax 08/21-50-70. www.provobis.se. 418 units. 2,200–3,200SEK ($242–$352) double; from 7,000SEK ($770) suite. Rates include breakfast. AE, DC, MC, V. Parking 210SEK ($23). T-bana: Centralen. Bus: 47, 52, or 69. **Amenities:** Anna Rella gourmet restaurant, bar; sauna; solarium; Jacuzzi; 24-hour room service; baby-sitting; laundry; no-smoking rooms. *In room:* A/C, TV, hair dryer.

Moderate

Clas på Hörnet ★★   Small and choice, this is an upscale, very charming 1739 inn that occupies what was built in the 1730s as a private house, about a half mile north of the commercial heart of Stockholm. Its attention to period detail—whose installation was supervised by the curators of the Stockholm City Museum—gives a distinctive country-inn ambience that's enhanced with bedrooms outfitted in the

---

Tips Traveler's Tip

Most European capitals experience high season in summer, when hordes of visitors arrive. But the situation is different in Stockholm. Although most tourists arrive in summer, the city's hotels are more dependent on business travelers than tourists. Consequently, hotels sometimes *lower* their prices in summer. Even during the busier winter season, hotels will often lower prices on Friday, Saturday, and possibly Sunday nights. It always pays to ask if any discounts are available.

late 18th-century style of Gustavus III. Ranging from midsize to spacious, accommodations come with wide floorboards, excellent beds, generous bathrooms, and, in some cases, four-poster beds.

Surbrunnsgatan 20, S-113 48 Stockholm. © 08/16-51-36. Fax 08/612-53-15. 10 units. Mon–Thurs 1,545SEK ($170) double, 1,445SEK ($159) suite. Fri–Sun 1,345SEK ($148) double, 1,445SEK ($159) suite. Rates include breakfast. Parking: 200SEK ($22). Bus: 46, 53. **Amenities:** Restaurant, bar; room service. *In room:* TV, minibar.

Elite Stockholm Plaza This is an inviting choice in the city center. Directly east of the center, it was built in 1920 as a private apartment building before its late 1980s conversion to a hotel. The small to medium-size rooms have light, fresh interiors with firm beds. The medium-size bathrooms are kept immaculately and provided with adequate shelf space.

Birger Jarlsgatan 29, S103 95 Stockholm. © **08/566-22-000.** Fax 08/566-22-020. www.elite.se. 151 units. 1,290–2,095SEK ($142–$230) double; 2,495–3,495SEK ($274–$384) suite. Rates include breakfast. AE, DC, MC, V. Parking 220SEK ($24). T-bana: Hötorget or Östermalmstorg. **Amenities:** Restaurant, bar. *In room:* TV.

Esplanade Hotel This informal hotel attracts diplomats from the nearby embassies and others who like its traditional atmosphere. Originally constructed in 1910, it was transformed into a hotel in 1954 and has enjoyed a devoted following ever since. Single rooms are minuscule, but doubles, for the most part, are more spacious, with double-glazed windows, extra-long beds with comfortable mattresses, and medium-size bathrooms. Four rooms open onto a water view. The English lounge has a balcony with a view of the Djurgården.

Strandvägen 7A, S-114 56 Stockholm. © **08/663-07-40.** Fax 08/662-59-92. hotelesplanade.se. 34 units. 1,495–1,995SEK ($164–$219) double. Rates include breakfast. AE, DC, MC, V. Parking: 200SEK ($22). T-bana: Östermalmstorg. Bus: 47 or 69. **Amenities:** Breakfast room. *In room:* TV, minibar (some rooms), trouser press.

Inexpensive

Hotel Örnsköld ⚘ This hidden jewel is secretly secluded in back of the Royal Dramatic Theater. Picture this as your own private town house in the heart of Stockholm. Large and high-ceilinged public areas set the tone of the place. Rooms range from small to midsize, and are furnished with tasteful contemporary pieces. Some of the more spacious units are large enough for extra beds for traveling families. Bathrooms are small with shower stalls.

Nybrogatan 6, S-11434 Stockholm. © **08/667-02-85.** Fax 08/667-69-91. 27 units. 1,175–1,275SEK ($129–$140) double; 300SEK ($33) discount on selected weekends (Fri–Sat). Rates include breakfast. AE, MC, V. Parking 100SEK ($11) in a nearby public garage. T-bana: Östermalmstorg. *In-room:* TV, minibar.

Hotel Tegnérlunden In a 19th-century building at the edge of a park, this hotel's best feature is its tasteful rooms, each blissfully quiet, opening onto the rear. They come in a variety of sizes and shapes, with most on the small to medium side. Each is well maintained but furnished in a somewhat functional Scandinavian style evocative of a good motel. Nonetheless, you'll be comfortable here, (especially on the excellent Swedish mattresses). Bathrooms, although tidy, are small with shower stalls.

Tegnérlunden 8, S-113 59 Stockholm. © **08/5454-5550.** Fax 08/5454-5551. 103 units. 990–1,460SEK ($109–$161) double. Rates include breakfast. AE, DC, MC, V. Parking 140SEK ($15) at a nearby garage. Bus: 47, 53, or 69. **Amenities:** Sauna. *In room:* TV.

Långholmen Hotel *Finds* This is an offbeat choice, and a lot of fun. In 1724 it was a state penitentiary on the little island of Lang Holmen detaining women charged with "loose living." Today it's a newly restored and reasonably priced accommodation which, in addition to comfortable but small rooms, also houses a museum of Sweden's prison history and a fine restaurant. "Cells" have been transformed into cramped but serviceable rooms equipped with modern amenities such as private bathrooms with small showers. Some rooms are suitable for persons with disabilities. This is one of the best hotels in Stockholm for the single visitor on a budget, as many rooms are rented only to solo travelers.

Kronohåktet, S-101 72 Stockholm. ⓒ 08/668-05-00. Fax 08/720-85-75. www.langholmen.com/hotellang. html. 102 units. Sun–Thurs 1,255SEK ($138) double; Fri–Sat 925SEK ($102) double. Extra bed 205SEK ($23) per person. AE, MC, V. Rates include breakfast. T-bana: Hornstul. Bus: 4, 40, and 66. **Amenities:** Restaurant, snack bar; no-smoking rooms. *In room:* TV.

Mälardrottningen 🏨 Once the world's most famous yacht, this is now Stockholm's most unusual hotel. It was built in 1924 by millionaire C. K. G. Billings as the largest (240 feet long) motor yacht in the world, and was later acquired by the Woolworth heiress, Barbara Hutton. Its below deck space originally contained only seven suites, but after its transformation in the early 1980s into a hotel, it was permanently moored beside a satellite island of Stockholm's Old Town, and subdivided into cramped and somewhat claustrophobic cabins. Space within the cabins is definitely limited, and most have bunk-style twin beds, which you may or may not find enchanting. Bathrooms aren't really rooms but extremely small cubicles with showers. Of course, this was typical of many cabins on ships back then.

Riddarholmen, S-11128 Stockholm. ⓒ 08/545-187-80. Fax 08/24-36-76. www.malardrottningen.se. 60 units. Fri–Sun 860–1,360SEK ($95–$150) double; Mon–Thurs 1,020–1,460SEK ($112–$161) double. Rates include breakfast. AE, DC, MC, V. Parking 15SEK ($1.65) per hour. T-bana: Gamla Stan. **Amenities:** Sweden's most upscale floating restaurant, bar; sauna. *In room:* A/C, TV.

IN GAMLA STAN (OLD TOWN)

Lady Hamilton 🏨🏨🏨 It's a Mexican stand-off between this hotel and its sibling, Victory. Both are equally good and atmospheric. Consider yourself lucky if you get a booking in either one of them. The major difference is that the Victory offers one of Stockholm's best restaurants, but it's only a short walk over from the Lady Hamilton. This historic hotel on a quiet street scatters dozens of antiques in its medium-size rooms. Top-floor units have skylights and memorable views. Beds have firm, frequently renewed mattresses. Bathrooms come in a variety of sizes, from spacious to cramped. All have heated racks and heated floors, although only some have tubs (the rest offer showers only).

Storkyrkobrinken 5, S-111 28 Stockholm. ⓒ 08/23-46-80. Fax 08/411-11-48. www.lady-hamilton.se. 34 units. 1,590–2,570SEK ($175–$283) double. Rates include breakfast. AE, DC, MC, V. Parking: 250SEK ($28). T-bana: Gamla Stan. Bus: 48. **Amenities:** Snacks throughout the day in the breakfast room; sauna; no-smoking rooms. *In room:* TV, minibar.

Victory Hotel 🏨🏨🏨 This small and stylish hotel runs a neck-in-neck race with Lady Hamilton (see above) as the most charming and atmospheric overnight in the Old Town. Built on the foundation of a 1382 fortified tower, it opened as a chic hotel in 1980. The warm and inviting midsize rooms have a pleasing combination of exposed wood, carpeting, antiques, and 19th-century memorabilia. Beds are comfortable with firm mattresses. The average-size bathrooms come with heated floors and phones, but only the suites offer tub baths (the rest have showers).

Lilla Nygatan 3–5, S-111 28 Stockholm. ⓒ 08/506-400-00. Fax 08/20-21-77. www.victory-hotel.se. 48 units. 1,750–2,750SEK ($193–$303) double; 3,590–4,890SEK ($395–$538) suite. Rates include breakfast. AE, DC, MC, V. T-bana: Gamla Stan. Bus: 48. **Amenities:** Restaurant Leijontornet (one of Stockholm's best); saunas; room service (7am–11pm); laundry/dry cleaning; no-smoking rooms. *In room:* A/C, TV, minibar, hair dryer, robes.

WHERE TO DINE
IN THE CITY CENTER
Very Expensive

Operakällaren ✿✿ FRENCH/SWEDISH   Opposite the Royal Palace is Sweden's most famous and luxurious restaurant. Dress formally (the dress code isn't strictly enforced, but men are encouraged to wear jackets and ties) to enjoy its impeccable service and house specialties, including the platter of northern delicacies, with everything from smoked eel to smoked reindeer along with Swedish red caviar. This place became a grande dame institution because of its cuisine, a repertoire of original dishes and traditional Swedish favorites. A glass-enclosed outer room has a lofty ceiling and is brightly sunlit during the day. After midnight, the cafe turns into a popular disco (see "Stockholm After Dark," later in this chapter).

Operahuset, Kungsträdgården. ✆ 08/676-58-00. Reservations required. Main courses 300–400SEK ($33–$44); 3-course fixed-price menu 480SEK ($53); 4-course set menu 800SEK ($88); 7-course menu dégustation 1,250SEK ($138). AE, DC, MC, V. Daily 5–10pm. Closed July. T-bana: Kungsträdgarden.

Paul & Norbert ✿✿✿ CONTINENTAL   In a patrician residence dating from 1873, this is Stockholm's most innovative restaurant. Come here to sample a cutting-edge culinary technique, or go to Operakällaren (see above) for tradition. The chef's foie gras is the finest in town. Main courses, which change seasonally, tend to favor game and game birds; perfectly prepared examples include juniper-marinated noisettes of reindeer with cheese, and escargot-filled breast of guinea fowl in rosemary sauce with garlic and onion. The seafood menu offers sole and salmon dishes along with a daily catch.

Strandvägen 9. ✆ 08/663-81-83. Reservations required. Main courses 150–296SEK ($17–$33); 8-course grand menu de frivolité 1,300SEK ($143). AE, DC, MC, V. Tues–Fri noon–3pm; Mon–Sat 5:30–10:30pm. July to mid-Aug Mon–Sat 5:30–10:30pm (no lunch). Closed July and Dec 24–Jan 6. T-bana: Östermalmstorg.

Wedholms Fisk ✿✿ SWEDISH/FRENCH   This classic restaurant is one of the best in Stockholm. You might begin with marinated herring with garlic and bleak roe, or tartare of salmon with salmon roe. The chef has reason to be proud of such dishes as perch poached with clams and saffron sauce; prawns marinated in herbs and served with Dijon hollandaise; and grilled filet of sole with a Beaujolais sauce. For dessert, try the homemade vanilla ice cream with cloudberries. The cuisine is both innovative and traditional. How many places today would prepare a chàvre mousse to accompany a simple tomato salad?

Nybrokajen 17. ✆ 08/611-78-74. Reservations required. Main courses 255–450SEK ($28–$50) at dinner, 110–260SEK ($12–$29) at lunch. AE, DC, MC, V. Mon–Sat 5–11pm.Closed July. T-bana: Östermalmstorg.

Moderate

Akvarium CONTINENTAL   Don't expect bubbling fish tanks. This hip and stylish restaurant's name derives from its former incarnation as a seafood restaurant. Our favorite delicacy on the menu is the amusingly named "duck expresso," prepared with breast of duck with port wine sauce and plums. Items on the menu are fabulously fresh and handled faultlessly in the kitchen, the chefs of whom know about delicate seasoning. Veal saltimbocca (with ham) lives up to its Roman meaning—literally "jump in your mouth," and a savory tagliatelle is prepared with mussels, clams, and squid ink. Few dishes equal the grilled butterfish with pesto sauce, and vegetarians take delight in the ravioli stuffed with porcini mushrooms.

Kungsträdgården. ✆ **08/100-626**. Reservations recommended. Main courses 150–175SEK ($17–$19); set-price lunches 55–110SEK ($6–$12). AE, DC, MC, V. Mon–Fri 11:30am–2:30pm and 5pm–midnight; Sat–Sun 11:30am–midnight. T-bana: Kungsträdgården.

Eriks Bakfica 🐟 *Value* SWEDISH Though there are other restaurants here bearing the name Eriks, this one is relatively moderate and offers particularly good value. It features a small, bustling bistro with a bar, and a quieter main dining room. The menu features a handful of Swedish dishes from the tradition of *husmanskost* (wholesome home cooking). There's a daily choice of herring appetizers. We suggest you try the "archipelago stew," a ragout of fish flavored with tomatoes and served with garlic mayonnaise. If none of these strike your fancy, you might delight in grilled char with lobster sauce or else grilled veal schnitzel with mushrooms and a delicate red wine sauce.

Fredrikshovsgatan 4. ✆ **08/660-15-99**. Reservations recommended. Main courses 145–245SEK ($16–$27); 5-course entrecôte dinner 345SEK ($38). AE, DC, MC, V. Mon–Fri 11:30am–11pm; Sat 4–10pm; Sun 5–11pm. Bus: 47.

KB Restaurant SWEDISH/CONTINENTAL Artists and the literati still flock to this old-time favorite, and have been gathering here ever since it opened on New Year's Eve back in 1931. Located in the center of town, KB offers good Swedish cookery as well as continental dishes. The fish dishes are especially recommended. You might begin with any of a number of herring starters followed by baked North Sea cod with broad beans and lobster in lemon sauce, or perhaps enjoy a dish cooked with a personal touch, fried pigeon with onion marmalade, potato terrine, and currant pepper sauce.

Smålandsgatan 7. ✆ **08/679-60-32**. Reservations recommended. Main courses 195–310SEK ($21–$34); fixed-price menu 265–325SEK ($29–$36) at lunch, 365–470SEK ($40–$52) at dinner. AE, DC, MC, V. Mon–Fri 11:30am–11:30pm; Sat 5–11:30pm. Closed June 23–Aug 7. T-bana: Östermalmstorg.

Inexpensive

Bakfickan 🐟 SWEDISH Tucked away in the back of the swanky Operakällaren restaurant (see above), the "Hip Pocket" is a chic place to get a reasonably priced meal. It's a small Art Nouveau room, meticulously maintained since 1904. Although it's within the Operakällaren, it has its own kitchen and a separate menu. On a recent visit we fell in love with the grilled marinated filet of cod served with a perfect mustard sabayon that added just the right zest. For a taste of Granny Sweden's repertoire, opt for the sautéed roulades of pork stuffed with Swedish cheese in a cider sauce and served with mashed vegetables and lingonberries. One dish that never fails is the salmon butterfly with béarnaise sauce and fried parsley.

Jakobs Torg 12. ✆ **08/676-58-09**. Reservations not accepted. Main courses 87–169SEK ($10–$19). AE, DC, MC, V. July Mon–Fri 5–11:30pm; Aug–June Mon–Sat 11:30am–11:30pm. T-bana: Kungsträdgården.

Lisa Elmquist *Value* SEAFOOD Under the soaring roof and amid the food stalls of Stockholm's produce market (the Östermalms Saluhall), sits this likable cafe/oyster bar. The only thing better than the value here is the people-watching. The menu varies daily according to the catch, but might include fried monkfish with scampi and mixed vegetables, and boiled lemon sole with tarragon sauce and trout roe. Some people just order a portion of shrimp with bread and butter. On Saturday, when only the bar is open, only cold and raw seafood items are available. Except for expensive lobster and shellfish, most dishes are at the bottom of the price scale.

Östermalms Saluhall, Nybrogatan 31. ℭ **08/660-92-32**. Reservations recommended. Main courses 100–350SEK ($11–$39). AE, DC, MC, V. Mon–Thurs 10am–6pm; Fri 10am–6:30pm; Sat 9am–4pm. T-bana: Östermalmstorg.

Prinsens SWEDISH　A 2-minute walk from the Stureplan, this is a favorite haunt of artists and has been feeding people since 1897. The cuisine is fresh and full of flavor and includes daily dishes and traditional Swedish menu items such as veal patty with homemade lingonberry preserves, sautéed fjord salmon, and roulades of beef. The most popular item on the menu is a filet of beef, served with fried potatoes and onions, marinated cucumbers, and egg yolk and mayonnaise on the side. For dessert, try the homemade vanilla ice cream.

Mäster Samuelsgatan 4. ℭ **08/611-13-31**. Reservations recommended. Main courses 169–245SEK ($19–$27); fixed-price lunch 99–250SEK ($11–$28). AE, DC, MC, V. Mon–Fri 11:30am–10:30pm, Sat 1–10:30pm, Sun 5–9:30pm. T-bana: Östermalmstorg.

IN GAMLA STAN (OLD TOWN)
Very Expensive
Pontus in the Green House 🟊🟊🟊 FRENCH/SWEDISH/ASIAN　This is a well-orchestrated and elegant restaurant that has attracted some of the most powerful figures in modern Stockholm. Dishes include garlic-sautéed turbot with sweetbreads; tender veal tongue with Jerusalem artichokes; steamed turbot with horseradish, prawns, and brown butter; and a divine citrus-glazed Challonais duck breast that's served with foie gras, shiitake mushrooms, spring onions, and teriyaki sauce. In our view, his herring with a vinegar and onion marmalade is the old town's tastiest. It's worth the trek across town to sample the creamy Roquefort made from the first milk the nursing cows produce.

Österlånggatan 17. ℭ **08/23-85-00**. Reservations recommended. Main courses 350–500SEK ($39–$55); 8-course set-price menu 985SEK ($108). AE, DC, MC, V. Mon–Fri 11:30am–3pm and 6–11pm; Sat noon–4pm and 5:30–11pm. T-bana: Gamla Stan.

Expensive
Den Gyldene Freden 🟊 SWEDISH　The "Golden Peace" is Stockholm's oldest tavern, opened in 1722. The cozy dining rooms, named for Swedish historic figures, are divided between the traditional 18th-century pub and the medieval cellar vaults. You get good traditional Swedish cooking here, and the chefs are especially fond of fresh Baltic fish and game from the forests of Sweden. If you plan never to go to the north of Sweden, bring the land above the Arctic to your plate by ordering roast reindeer in a juniper-berry sauce with a timbale of black grouse. Less exotic, but very tasty, is the breast of pigeon and leg of guinea hen stuffed with duck liver and asparagus in a sherry sauce. Not so daring? Opt for a very good sautéed sole with lemon, horseradish, and butter—no need to gild the lily with this dish.

Österlånggatan 51. ℭ **08/24-97-60**. Reservations recommended. Main courses 110–265SEK ($12–$29). AE, DC, MC, V. Mon–Fri 6–11pm; Sat 1–11pm. Closed July 2–Aug 2. T-bana: Gamla Stan.

Moderate
Cattelin Restaurant 🟊 (Value) SWEDISH　Don't expect genteel service at this boisterous restaurant where the clattering of china can be almost deafening at times. Nonetheless, it's an old Gamla Stan favorite that has endured wars and changing food tastes. It delivers a series of tasty dishes that are hearty, filling, and authentically Swedish items such as fried brill with mushrooms and sliced beef with fried potatoes and, of course Swedish meatballs. If you want something

more elegant, the swordfish in lobster sauce is excellent, as is a perfectly prepared filet mignon in a pepper sauce.

Storkyrkobrinken 9. © 08/20-18-18. Reservations recommended. Main courses 95–195SEK ($10–$21); *dagens menu* 65SEK ($7). AE, DC, MC, V. Mon–Fri 11am–10pm; Sat–Sun noon–10pm. T-bana: Gamla Stan.

ON DJURGÅRDEN
Moderate
Djurgårdsbrunns Wärdshus ✿ SWEDISH   This establishment occupies a cluster of antique and modern buildings in the Royal Deer Park, about 3 kilometers (2 miles) east of Stockholm's center. Although there's a simple cafeteria on the premises, most diners prefer the more formal restaurant. You don't come here to be trendy but to get good honest cooking with flavor. Ingredients are well chosen, and the recipes have stood the test of time. The prices are also quite fair. Among the time tested favorite dishes we've enjoyed, a grilled salmon in a morel butter sauce was memorable, as were the noisettes of venison with fresh vegetables. The chefs don't mind keeping old-fashioned dishes on the menu if they're still good: roast beef with horseradish and fried trout with almonds.

Djurgårdsbrunnsvägen 68. © 08/667 90-95. Main courses 166–200SEK ($18–$22). AE, DC, MC, V. Summer daily 11:30am–9pm. Off-season Mon–Fri 11:30am–3pm; Sat–Sun 11:30am–5pm. Bus: 69.

EXPLORING STOCKHOLM
Everything from the *Vasa* Ship Museum to the changing of the guard at the Royal Palace to the Gröna Tivoli amusement park will keep you intrigued. Even just window shopping for well-designed Swedish crafts can be a great way to spend an afternoon.

SIGHTSEEING SUGGESTIONS FOR FIRST-TIME VISITORS

If You Have 1 Day Take a ferry to Djurgården to visit the **Royal Warship Vasa,** Stockholm's most famous attraction, and to explore the open-air **Skansen** folk museum. In the afternoon, walk through **Gamla Stan (Old Town)** and have dinner at one of its restaurants.

If You Have 2 Days On day 2, get up early and visit the **Kaknästornet** TV tower for a panoramic view of Stockholm, its many islands, and the archipelago. Go to the **Nordic Museum** for insight into 5 centuries of life in Sweden. After lunch, visit the **Millesgården** of Lidingö, the sculpture garden and former home of Carl Milles.

If You Have 3 Days Spend your third morning walking through the center of Stockholm and doing

some shopping. At noon (1pm on Sunday), return to Gamla Stan to see the **changing of the guard at the Royal Palace.** View this French-inspired building that has been the residence of Swedish kings for more than 700 years. In the afternoon, see the attractions at the **National Museum.**

If You Have 4 or 5 Days On day 4, take one of the many tours of the **Stockholm archipelago.** Return to Stockholm and spend the evening at the **Gröna Tivoli** amusement park on Djurgården. On your last day, visit **Drottningholm Palace** and its 18th-century theater. In the afternoon, explore the university town of **Uppsala,** north of Stockholm, easily reached by public transportation.

THE TOP ATTRACTIONS
At Djurgården

Royal Warship Vasa 𝓚𝓚𝓚   This 17th-century man-of-war is the number-one attraction in Scandinavia—and for good reason. Housed in a museum specially constructed for it at Djurgården near Skansen, the *Vasa* is the world's oldest identified and complete ship. In 1628, on its maiden voyage and in front of thousands of horrified onlookers, the ship capsized and sank to the bottom of Stockholm harbor. When it was salvaged in 1961, more than 4,000 coins, carpenters' tools, and other items of archaeological interest were found on board. Best of all, 97% of the 700 original sculptures were retrieved. Carefully restored and preserved, they're back aboard the ship, which looks stunning now that it once again carries grotesque faces, lion masks, fish-shaped bodies, and other carvings, some with their original paint and gilt.

Galärvarvsvägen, Djurgården. 𝒞 **08/666-48-00.** www.vasamuseet.se. Admission 60SEK ($7) adults, 40SEK ($4.40) seniors and students, 10SEK ($1.10) children 7–15, free for children under 7. June 10–Aug 20, daily 9:30am–7pm; Aug 21–June 9, Wed 10am–8pm, Thurs–Tues 10am–5pm. Closed Jan 1, May 1, Dec 24–26 and 31. Bus: 44 or 47. Ferry from Slussen year-round, from Nybroplan in summer only.

Skansen 𝓚𝓚𝓚   Often called "Old Sweden in a Nutshell," this 35-hectare (75-acre) open-air museum, near Gröna Lund's Tivoli, contains more than 150 dwellings, most from the 18th and 19th centuries. Exhibits range from a windmill to a manor house to a complete town quarter. Browsers can explore the old workshops and see where the early book publishers, silversmiths, and pharmacists plied their trade. Handcrafts (glassblowing, for example) are demonstrated here, along with peasant crafts like weaving and churning. Folk dancing and open-air symphonic concerts are also featured (see "Special Events with a Local Flavor at Skansen," later in this chapter).

Djurgården 49–51. 𝒞 **08/442-80-00.** www.skansen.se. Admission 30–60SEK ($3.30–$7) adults (depending on time of day, day of the week, and season), 10SEK ($1.10) children 6–15, free for children 5 and under. Historic buildings, May–Aug, daily 11am–5pm; Sept–Apr, daily 11am–3pm. Bus: 47 from central Stockholm. Ferry from Slussen.

Nordiska Museet 𝓚𝓚   This museum houses an impressive collection of implements, costumes, and furnishings of Swedish life from the 1500s to the present. Highlights are period costumes ranging from matching garters and ties for men to purple flowerpot hats from the 1890s. In the basement is an extensive exhibit of the tools of the Swedish fishing trade, plus relics from nomadic Lapps.

Djurgårdsvägen 6–16, Djurgården. 𝒞 **08/5195-6000.** www.nordm.se. Admission 60SEK ($7) adults, 50SEK ($6) seniors, 30SEK ($3.30) students, 20SEK ($2.20) ages 7–12, free for children under 7. Tues–Sun 2–5pm (until 8pm Tues and Thurs). Bus: 44, 47, or 69.

Prins Eugens Waldemarsudde 𝓚𝓚   This once-royal residence is today an art gallery and a memorial to one of the most famous royal artists in recent history, Prince Eugen (1865–1947). The youngest of King Oscar II's four children, he was credited with making innovative contributions to the techniques of Swedish landscape paintings, specializing in depictions of his favorite regions in central Sweden. Among his most visible works are the murals on the inner walls of the Stadshuset.

Prins Eugens Väg 6. 𝒞 **08/545-837-00.** Admission 60SEK ($7) adults, 40SEK ($4.40) seniors and students, free for children under 17. June–Aug, Tues and Thurs 11am–8pm, Wed and Fri–Sun 11am–5pm; Sept–May, Tues–Sun 11am–4pm. Bus: 47 to the end of the line.

Moments **The Changing of the Royal Guard**

It may not have the pomp of a similar show in London, but the **Changing of the Royal Guard** in Stockholm at least provides a photo opt. You can watch the parade of the military guard daily in summer and on Wednesday and Sunday in winter (on all other days you can see only the changing of the guard). The parade route on weekdays begins at Sergels Torg and proceeds along Hamngatan, Kungsträdgårdsgatan, Strömgatan, Gustav Adolfs Torg, Norrbro, Skeppsbron, and Slottsbacken. On Sunday the guard departs from the Army Museum, going along Riddargatan, Artillerigaten, Strandvägen, Hamngatan, Kungstradgårdsgatan, Strömgatan, Gustav Adolfs Torg, Norrbro, Skeppsbron, and Slottsbacken. For information on the time of the march, ask at the Information Service in the Sweden House (see "Visitor Information," earlier in this chapter). The actual changing of the guard takes place at noon Monday to Saturday (at 1pm on Sunday) in front of the Royal Palace in Gamla Stan.

On Gamla Stan & Neighboring Islands

Kungliga Slottet (Royal Palace) & Museum ⊛⊛   Severely dignified, even cold looking on the outside, this palace has a lavish interior designed in the Italian baroque style. Kungliga Slotta is one of the few official residences of a European monarch that's open to the public. Although the Swedish king and queen prefer to live at Drottningholm, this massive 608-room showcase, built between 1691 and 1754, remains their official address. The most popular rooms include the **State Apartments** ⊛⊛; look for at least three magnificent baroque ceiling frescoes and fine tapestries. In the building's cellar is the **Stattkammaren (Treasury)** ⊛⊛, the repository for Sweden's crown jewels. Most intriguing to any student of war and warfare is the **Royal Armoury,** whose entrance is on the castle's rear side, at Slottsbacken 3. Gustavas III's collection of sculpture from the days of the Roman Empire can be viewed in the **Antikmuseum** (Museum of Antiquities).

Kungliga Husgerådskammaren. ⓒ **08/402-61-32** for Royal Apartments & Treasury; ⓒ 08/402-61-34 for the Skattkammaren; ⓒ 08/666-44-75 for Royal Armory; ⓒ 08/402-61-30 for Museum of Antiquities. www.royalcourt.se. Royal Apartments, 50SEK ($6) adults, 25SEK ($2.75) students, free for children under 7. Royal Armory, 50SEK ($6) adults, 30SEK ($3.30) seniors and students, 15SEK ($1.65) children, free for children under 7. Museum of Antiquities, 50SEK ($6) adults, 25SEK ($2.75) seniors and students, free for children under 7. Treasury, 50SEK ($6) adults, 25SEK ($2.75) seniors and students, free for children under 7. Combination ticket to all parts of palace: 100SEK ($11) adults, 70SEK ($8) students and children. Apartments and Treasury Sept–June Tues–Sun noon–3pm; July–Aug daily 10am–4pm; closed during government receptions. Royal Armory, Sept–Apr Tues–Sun 11am–4pm; May–Aug daily 11am–4pm. Museum of Antiquities, May–Aug daily 10am–4pm; Sept–Apr daily noon–3pm. T-bana: Gamla Stan. Bus: 43, 46, 59, or 76.

Riddarholm Church ⊛   The second-oldest church in Stockholm is on the tiny island of Riddarholmen, next to Gamla Stan. It was founded in the 13th century as a Franciscan monastery. Almost all the royal heads of state are entombed here, except for Christina, who is buried in Rome. There're three principal royal chapels, including one, the Bernadotte wing, that belongs to the present ruling family.

Riddarholmen. ✆ 08/402-61-30. Admission 20SEK ($2.20) adults, 10SEK ($1.10) students and children. June–Aug daily 11am–4pm; May and Sept Wed and Sat–Sun noon–3pm. Closed Oct–Apr. T-bana: Gamla Stan.

In the City Center

Historiska Museet (Museum of National Antiquities) ⭐⭐   If you're interested in Swedish history, especially the Viking era, here you'll find the nation's finest repository of relics left by those legendary conquerors who once terrorized Europe. Many relics have been unearthed from ancient burial sites. The collection of artifacts ranges from prehistoric to medieval times, including Viking stone inscriptions and 10th-century coins, silver and gold jewelry, large ornate charms, elaborate bracelet designs found nowhere else in the world, and a unique neck collar from Färjestaden.

Narvavägen 13–17. ✆ 08/519-556-00. www.historiska.se. Admission 60SEK ($7) adults, 50SEK ($6) seniors and students, 35SEK ($3.85) children 7–15, free for children under 7. Family ticket 140SEK ($15). Apr–Sept Tues–Sun 11am–5pm; Oct–Mar Tues–Wed and Fri–Sun 11am–5pm, Thurs 11am–8pm. T-bana: Karlaplan or Östermalmstorg. Bus: 44, 47, or 54.

Nationalmuseum (National Museum of Art) ⭐⭐   At the tip of a peninsula, a short walk from the Royal Opera House and the Grand Hotel, is Sweden's state treasure house of paintings and sculpture, one of the oldest museums in the world. The first floor is devoted to applied arts (silverware, handcrafts, porcelain, furnishings), but first-time visitors may want to head directly to the second floor to the painting collection with works by Rembrandt and Rubens, Lucas Cranach's most amusing *Venus and Cupid,* and a rare collection of mid-16th century Russian icons. The most important room in the gallery has one whole wall devoted to Rembrandt—*Portrait of an Old Man, Portrait of an Old Woman,* and *Kitchen Maid.*

Södra Blasieholmshamnen. ✆ 08/519-54-300. www.nationalmuseum.se. Admission 75SEK ($8) adults, 60SEK ($7) seniors and students, free for children under 16. Tues 11am–8pm; Wed–Sun 11am–5pm. T-bana: Kungsträdgården. Bus: 46, 62, 65, or 76.

Moderna Museet (Museum of Modern Art)   This museum focuses on contemporary works by Swedish and international artists, including kinetic sculptures. Highlights are a small but good collection of Cubist art by Picasso, Braque, and Léger; Matisse's *Apollo* découpage; the famous *Enigma of William Tell* by Salvador Dalí; and works by Brancusi, Max Ernst, Giacometti, and Arp, among others.

Skeppsholmen. ✆ 08/519-55-200. www.modernamuseet.se. Admission 60SEK ($7) adults, 40SEK ($4.40) seniors and students, free for children under 17. Tues–Thurs 11am–10pm; Fri–Sun 11am–6pm. T-bana: Kungsträdgården. Bus: 65.

Stadshuset (Stockholm City Hall) ⭐⭐   Built in what is called the "National Romantic Style," the Stockholm City Hall, on the island of Kungsholmen, is one of Europe's finest examples of modern architecture. Designed by Ragnar Ostberg, the redbrick structure is dominated by a lofty square tower, topped by three gilt crowns and the national coat-of-arms. The Nobel Prize banquet takes place here in the Blue Hall. About 18 million pieces of gold and colored mosaics made of special glass cover the walls, and the southern gallery contains murals by Prince Eugen, the painter prince.

Hantverksgatan 1. ✆ 08/508-290-59. Admission 50SEK ($6)adults, free for children under 12. Tower, May–Sept, daily 10am–4pm. City Hall tours (subject to change), June–Sept, daily at 10am, 11am, noon, and 2pm; Oct–Apr, daily at 10am and noon. T-bana: Centralen or Rådhuset. Bus: 3 or 62.

Just Outside Stockholm

Drottningholm Palace and Theater ★★★ Originally conceived as the centerpiece of Sweden's royal court, this regal complex of stately buildings sits on an island in Lake Mälaren. Dubbed the Versailles of Sweden, Drottningholm, or Queen's Island, is about 11 kilometers (7 miles) west of Stockholm. The palace—loaded with courtly art and furnishings—is surrounded by fountains and parks, and still functions as one of the official residences of the country's royal family. On the grounds is one of the most perfectly preserved 18th-century theaters in the world, **Drottningholm Court Theater** (© 08/759-04-06; www.drottningholmteatern.dtm.se), with 30 annual performances (mostly 18th-century operas) from May to September. The theater only seats 450, and performances often sell out long in advance. (For ticket information, see "Stockholm After Dark," below.)

Ekerö, Drottningholm. © 08/402-62-80. Palace, 50SEK ($6) adults, 25SEK ($2.75) students and persons under 26; theater, guided tour 50SEK ($6) adults, 20SEK ($2.20) students and persons under 26; Chinese Pavilion, 50SEK ($6) adults, 25SEK ($2.75) students and persons under 26, free for children under 16. Palace, Oct–Apr Sat–Sun noon–3:30pm; May–Aug daily 10am–4:30pm; Sept daily noon–3:30pm. Theater, guided tours in English, May daily 12:30pm, 1:30pm, 2:30pm, 3:30pm, and 4:15pm; June–Aug daily 11:30am, 12:30pm, 1:30pm, 2:30pm, 3:30pm, and 4:15pm; Sept daily 1:30pm, 2:30pm, and 3:30pm. Chinese Pavilion, Apr and Oct daily 1–3:30pm; May–Aug daily 11am–4:30pm; Sept daily noon–3:30pm. T-bana: Brommaplan, then bus no. 301 or 323 to Drottningholm. Ferry from the dock near City Hall.

Millesgården ★★ On the island of Lidingö, northeast of Stockholm, is Carl Milles's former villa and sculpture garden beside the sea, now a museum. Many of his best-known works are displayed here (some are copies), as are works of other artists. Milles (1875–1955), who relied heavily on mythological themes, was Sweden's most famous sculptor.

Carl Milles Väg 2, Lidingö. © 08/446-75-90. www.millesgarden.se. Admission 70SEK ($8) adults, 50SEK ($6) seniors and students, 20SEK ($2.20) children 7–16, free for children under 7. May–Sept daily 10am–5pm; Oct–Apr Tues–Sun noon–4pm. T-bana: Ropsten, then bus to Torsviks Torg or train to Norsvik.

A VIEW ON HIGH

Kaknästornet (Kaknäs Television Tower) (Moments Situated in the northern district of Djurgården is the tallest constructed structure in Scandinavia—a radio and television tower that stands 155 meters (508 ft.) high. Two elevators take visitors to an observation platform, where you can see everything from the cobblestone streets of Gamla Stan (Old Town) to the city's modern concrete-and-glass structures and the archipelago beyond.

Mörkakroken. © 08/789-24-35. Admission 25SEK ($2.75) adults, 15SEK ($1.65) children 7–15, free for children under 7. May–Aug daily 9am–10pm; Sept–Apr daily 10am–9pm. Closed Dec 24–25. Bus: 69.

AN AMUSEMENT PARK

Gröna Lunds Tivoli (Kids Unlike its Copenhagen namesake, this is an amusement park, not a fantasyland. For those who like Coney Island–type thrills, it's a good nighttime adventure.

Djurgården. © 08/587-501-00. Admission 45SEK ($5) adults, free for children under 13. Bus: 44 or 47. Djurgården ferry from Nybroplan.

ORGANIZED TOURS

Stockholm City Sightseeing (© 08/587-140-20; www.citysightseeing.com) operates the best tours. From early June to early August, 1½-hour tours leave from the Opera House at 10 and 1pm; the cost is 130SEK ($14) adults, half

> ⌒*Tips* **Traveler's Tip**
>
> Many stores offer tax rebates to visitors spending over 200SEK ($22). When you make your purchase, ask the retailer for a Tax Free Check (valid for 1 month) and leave your purchase sealed until you leave the country. At any border crossing on your way out of Sweden (or at repayment centers in Denmark, Finland, or Norway), show both the check (to which you've added your name, address, and passport number) and the purchase to an official at the tax-free desk. You'll get a cash refund of about 16% to 18% in U.S. dollars (or seven other currencies) after the service charge has been deducted (remember not to check the purchase in your luggage until after you receive the refund). For more information, call ✆ **0410/613-01.**

price for children 6 to 11. Ask about the combination excursions that include walking, touring by bus, and/or taking a boat.

Also offered are **boat tours** of the city, departing from Strömkajen, in front of the Grand Hotel. (Locals insist that the best way to explore their city is by boat.) Get tickets at the kiosk topped with yellow flags with a red S on them. The company's "Under the Bridges of Stockholm" tour takes 2 hours and costs 140SEK ($15) adults, half price for children 6 to 15; it's offered from mid-April to mid-December. The hour-long "Royal Canal Tour" runs from mid-May to early September for 90SEK ($10).

THE SHOPPING SCENE

A whopping 25% goods tax makes shopping in Sweden expensive, and you can get most items at home for less money. On the positive side, Swedish stores usually stock items of the highest quality. Favorite buys include crystal, clothing, and Scandinavian-design furniture.

For the best shopping and window-shopping, stroll along the streets of **Gamla Stan** (especially **Västerlånggatan**), filled with boutiques, art galleries, and jewelry stores. Attractive shops and galleries can also be found along the **Hornsgats-Puckeln** (the Hornsgatan-Hunchback, a reference to the shape of the street), on **Södermalm.** Other good browsing streets are **Hamngatan, Birger Jarlsgatan, Biblioteksgatan,** and **Kungsgatan,** all in **Norrmalm.**

Blås & Knåda, Hornsgatan 26 (✆ **08/642-77-67;** T-bana: Slussen), sells the products of a cooperative of 50 Swedish ceramic artists and glassmakers. Prices begin at 160SEK ($18) for small functional pieces, and go way up for museum-quality works of art. Bone china, stoneware dinner services, and other fine table and decorative ware are made at **Keramiskt Centrum Gustavsberg** (Gustavsberg Ceramics Center) (✆ **08/570-356-58;** bus: 422 or 24400), on Värmdö Island, about 21 kilometers (13 miles) east of Stockholm.

In the center of Stockholm, the largest department store in Sweden is **Åhlesns City,** Klarabergsgatan 50 (✆ **08/676-60-00;** T-bana: T-Centralen), with a gift shop, a restaurant, and a famous food department. Also seek out the fine collection of home textiles and Orrefors and Kosta crystal ware. **Nordiska Kompanient (NK),** Hamngatan 18–20 (✆ **08/762-80-00;** T-bana: Kungsträdgården), is another high-quality department store. Most of the big names in Swedish glass are displayed at NK, including Orrefors (see the Nordic Light collection) and Kosta. Swedish handcrafted items are in the basement. Stainless steel is also a good buy in Sweden. Greta Garbo got her start in the millinery department at **PUB,** Hötorget 13 (© **08/239-915;** T-bana: Hötorget), a popular department store that sells middle-bracket clothing and good-quality housewares.

At **Loppmarknaden I Skärholmen (Skärholmen Shopping Center),** Skärholmen (© **08/710-00-60;** T-bana: 13 or 23 to Skärholmen), the biggest flea market in northern Europe, you might find *anything.* Try to go on Saturday or Sunday (the earlier the better) when the market is at its peak. Weekend admission is 10SEK ($1.10), but weekdays are free. **Geocity,** Tysta Marigången 5, Tegélbacken (© **08/411-11-40;** T-bana: T-Centralen), offers exotic mineral crystals, jewelry, Scandinavian gems, Baltic amber, and lapidary equipment. Its staff includes two certified gemologists who'll cut and set any gem you select, as well as appraise jewelry you already own. Its inventory includes stones from Scandinavia and around the world, including Greenland, Madagascar, Siberia, and South America.

An unusual outlet, **Slottsbodarna (Royal Gift Shop),** in the south wing of the Royal Palace, Slottsbacken (© **08/402-61-48;** T-bana: Gamla Stan), sells items related to or copied from the collections in the Royal Palace, re-created in silver, gold, brass, pewter, textiles, and glass. Every item is made in **Sweden. Svensk Hemslojd (Society for Swedish Handcrafts),** Sveavägen 44 (© **08/ 23-21-15;** T-bana: Hötorget), has a wide selection of glass, pottery, gifts, and wooden and metal handcrafts, the work of some of Sweden's best artisans. You'll also see a display of hand-woven carpets, upholstery fabrics, tapestries, lace, and embroidered items; and you can even find beautiful yarns for your own weaving and embroidery.

STOCKHOLM AFTER DARK
Pick up a copy of *Stockholm This Week,* distributed at the Stockholm Information Service in the Sweden House (see "Visitor Information," earlier in this chapter), to see what's on.

THE PERFORMING ARTS
All the major opera, theater, and concert performances begin in autumn, except for special summer festival performances. Fortunately, most of the major opera and theatrical performances are funded by the state, which keeps the ticket price reasonable.

Founded by King Gustavus III in 1766, the **Drottningholm Slottsteater,** Drottningholm (© **08/660-82-25;** www.drottningholmteatern.dtm.se; T-bana: Brommaplan), stands on an island in Lake Mälaren, 11 kilometers (7 miles) from Stockholm. It stages operas and ballets with full 18th-century regalia, complete with period costumes and wigs. The theater, a short walk from the royal residence, seats only 450 patrons, which makes tickets hard to come by. Eighteenth-century music performed on antique instruments is a perennial favorite. The season is from May to September and most performances begin at 7:30pm, lasting 2½ to 4 hours. Tickets are 150 to 545SEK ($17 to $60) and should be ordered at least 2 months in advance by phoning the number above; only American Express is accepted.

Filharmonikerna I Konserthuset (Concert Hall), Hötorget 8 (© **08/ 8-786-02-00;** T-bana: Hötorget), home of the **Stockholm Philharmonic Orchestra,** is the principal place to hear classical music in Sweden. (The Nobel Prizes are also awarded here.) Box office hours are from Monday through Friday noon to 6pm, Saturday 11am to 3pm. Tickets are 100 to 200SEK ($11 to $22).

Special Events with a Local Flavor at Skansen

The open-air museum **Skansen** (see "The Top Attractions," earlier in this chapter) arranges traditional seasonal festivities like autumn market days and a Christmas Fair as well as summer concerts, sing-alongs, and guest performances. Folk dancing is staged from June to August, Monday to Saturday at 7pm and Sunday at 2:30 and 4pm. Live music accompanies outdoor dancing from June to August, Monday to Friday 8:30 to 11:30pm. Admission is 30 to 60SEK ($3.30 to $7) adults and 10SEK ($1.10) children 7 to 14; free for children under 7.

Founded in 1773 by King Gustavus III, who was assassinated here at a masked ball, the **Operan (Royal Opera House),** Gustav Adolfs Torg (© 08/ 24-82-40; T-bana: Kungsträdgården), is the home of the **Royal Swedish Opera** and the **Royal Swedish Ballet.** Performances are usually from Monday to Saturday at 7:30pm (closed mid-June to August). The box office is open from Monday to Friday noon to 7:30pm (to 6pm if no performance is scheduled) and Saturday noon to 3pm. Tickets are 150 to 545SEK ($17 to $60); many are discounted 10% to 20% for seniors and students.

NIGHTCLUBS

Café Opera, Operahuset, Kungsträdgården (© 08/676-58-07; T-bana: Kungsträdgården)—Swedish beaux arts at its best—functions as a bistro, brasserie, and tearoom during the day and as one of the most popular nightclubs in Stockholm at night. (Don't confuse this spot with the opera's main dining room, the Operakällaren, whose entrance is through a different door.) Near the entrance of the cafe is a stairway leading to one of the Opera House's most beautiful corners, the clublike Operabaren (Opera Bar). It's open from Monday to Saturday 11:30am to 3am and Sunday 1pm to 3am. There's no cover before 10pm, 80SEK ($9) after.

Göta Källare, in the Medborgplatsen subway station, Södermalm (© 08/ 642-08-28; T-bana: Medborgplatsen), is the largest and most successful supperclub-style dance hall in Stockholm, with a long list of clients who have met here, and subsequently fallen in love and gotten married. Large, echoing, and paneled with lots of wood in a *faux-español* style, it has a large terrace that surrounds an enormous tree, and a restaurant. Expect a crowd aged 45 and older, and music from a live orchestra (performing "Strangers in the Night" a bit too frequently). The place is open every night from 8:30pm. Cover is 70SEK ($8) before 9:30pm, 95SEK ($10) after.

ROCK & JAZZ CLUBS

Some of Sweden's and the world's best known jazz musicians regularly play **Fasching,** Kungsgatan 63 (© 08/21-62-67; T-bana: T-Centralen). It's so small, you almost feel like you're in the band. Weekend late nights are for dancing, and after midnight on Friday there's salsa; Saturday late is dedicated to soul. Hours can be irregular, so it's best to call in advance, but it's usually open nightly from 7pm to at least 2am. Cover is 90 to 200SEK ($10 to $22).

The Swedish branch of **Hard Rock Cafe,** Sveavägen 75 (© 08/16-03-50; T-bana: Hötorget), is fun and gregarious. Sometimes an American, British, or

Scandinavian band gives a live concert; otherwise, it's the sound system. Club sandwiches, hamburgers, T-bone steaks, and barbecued spareribs are available. Open in summer, from Sunday to Thursday 11am to 1am and Friday and Saturday 11am to 3am; in winter, from Sunday to Thursday 11am to midnight and Friday and Saturday 11am to 1am. There's no cover.

   Pub Engelen/Nightclub Kolingen, Kornhamnstorg 59B (© **08/20-10-92;** T-bana: Gamla Stan), is a three-in-one combination consisting of the Engelen Pub, the Restaurant Engelen, and the Nightclub Kolingen in the cellar. The restaurant, which serves some of the best steaks in town, is open from Sunday to Thursday 5 to 11:30pm and Friday to Saturday 5pm to 1:30am. Swedish groups (mostly) perform live in the pub daily from 8:30pm to midnight—usually soul, funk, and rock. The pub is open from Tuesday to Thursday 4pm to 1am, Friday and Saturday 4pm to 2am, and Sunday 5pm to 1am. In the cellar (which dates from the 15th century), the Nightclub Kolingen is a disco nightly from 10pm to about 3am. Pub and nightclub cover is 40 to 60SEK ($4.40 to $7) from Monday to Friday after 9pm. You must be 23 or over to enter.

BARS

One of the hippest and most talked-about bars in Stockholm, **Tiger Bar/ Havana Bar,** 18 Kungsgatan (© **08-244-700;** T-bana: Östermalmstorg), attracts a bevy of supermodels and TV actors. It's divided into a street-level site (the Tiger Bar) that's outfitted in black leather upholstery and a postmodern kind of cool, and a basement-level re-creation of pre-Castro Cuba (the Havana Bar) that's outfitted with plastic palms and the deliberately garish colors associated with Old Havana's most raunchy 1950s-era excesses. You're likely to hear anything from recorded disco (every Friday and Saturday beginning at midnight), and live salsa and merengue (every Wednesday 9pm to 5am). The place is open Wednesday and Thursday from 7pm to 3am, and Friday and Saturday from 7pm to 4am.

   Named after the builder of the deluxe Grand Hotel, the **Cadier Bar,** Södra Blasieholmshamnen 8 (© **08/679-35-00;** T-bana: Kungsträdgården), enjoys a view of the harbor and Royal Palace. It's one of the most sophisticated places for a rendezvous in Stockholm. You can also enjoy light meals at any time of day in the extension overlooking the waterfront. Open from Monday to Saturday noon to 2am and Sunday noon to 12:30am; a piano player performs from Monday to Saturday 9:30pm to 1:30am.

A GAY BAR

If you're gay, consider slugging back a round or two at **Sidetrack,** Wollmar Yxkullsgatan 7 (© **08/641-1688;** T-bana: Mariatorget). Small, and committed to shunning any semblance of trendiness, it was named after its founder's favorite gay bar in Chicago. It's open every night from 6pm to 1am. Tuesdays here seem to be something of an institution in gay Stockholm. Other nights, however, it's fine too—something like a Swedish version of a bar and lounge at your local bowling alley where everyone happens to be into same-sex encounters.

DAY TRIPS FROM STOCKHOLM

SKOKLOSTER CASTLE ♣ **Skokloster,** S-746 96 Skokloster (© **018/ 38-60-77),** is a splendid 17th-century castle and one of the most interesting baroque museums in Europe. It's next to Lake Mälaren, 64 kilometers (40 miles) west of Stockholm and 40 kilometers (31 miles) south of Uppsala. Original interiors aside, the castle is noted for its rich collections of paintings, furniture, applied art, tapestries, arms, and books. Admission is 65SEK ($7) adults, 50SEK ($6) seniors, 30SEK ($3.30) students and children. Guided tours are conducted from May to August daily every hour at 11am to 4pm; in September daily at noon; and in April and October on Saturday and Sunday only at 1, 2, and 3pm. The site is closed from November to March.

Skokloster Motor Museum (© 018/38-61-06), on the palace grounds, contains the largest collection of vintage automobiles and motorcycles in the country. One of the most notable cars is a 1905 8-horsepower De Dion Bouton. Unlike the castle, the museum is open year-round. It costs 40SEK ($4.40) adults, 10SEK ($1.10) children 7 to 14, free for children under 7. It's open only from May to September, daily 11am to 5pm; and from October to April, every Saturday and Sunday 11am to 5pm.

Getting There   From Stockholm take a **train** to the hamlet of Bålsta, which lies 19 kilometers (12 miles) from the castle. At the village train station, you can either take **bus** 894 directly to Skokloster, or call for a taxi from a direct telephone line that's prominently positioned just outside the railway station.

UPPSALA ⧕⧕   The major university city of Sweden, Uppsala, 68 kilometers (42 miles) northwest of Stockholm, is the most popular destination for daytrippers from Stockholm, and for good reason. Uppsala not only has a great university, but also a celebrated 15th-century cathedral. Even in the time of the Vikings, this was a religious center, the scene of animal and human sacrifices in honor of the old Norse gods, and was once the center of royalty as well. Queen Christina occasionally held court here. The church is still the seat of the archbishop, and the first Swedish university was founded here in 1477.

Getting There   The town is easily reached by **train** from Stockholm's Central Station. Trains leave about every hour during peak daylight hours (trip time: 45 minutes). **Boats** from Stockholm to Uppsala (or vice versa) also stop at Skokloster and Sigtuna. Check with the tourist office in Stockholm or Uppsala for details.

Visitor Information   The **tourist office** is at Fyris Torg 8 (© 018/27-48-00), open from Monday to Friday 10am to 6pm and Saturday 10am to 3pm.

Exploring Uppsala   At the end of Drottninggatan is the **Carolina Rediviva (University Library)** ⧕ (© 018/471-00-00; bus: 6, 7, or 22), with its more than five million volumes and 40,000 manuscripts, among them many rare works from the Middle Ages. But the manuscript that really draws visitors is the *Codex Argenteus* (Silver Bible), translated into the old Gothic language in the middle of the 3rd century and copied in about A.D. 525. It's the only book extant in the old Gothic script. Also worth seeing is *Carta Marina,* the earliest map (1539), a fairly accurate map of Sweden and its neighboring countries. Admission is 20SEK ($2.20); free for children under 12. The Library's exhibition room is open from Monday to Friday 9am to noon.

Linnaeus Garden and Museum, Svartbäcksgatan 27 (© 018/13-65-40 for the museum, or 018/10-94-90 for the garden; walk straight from the rail station to Kungsgatan, and go for about 10 minutes to Svartbäcksgatan), is the former home of Swedish botanist Carl von Linné, known as Carolus Linnaeus, who developed a classification system for the world's plants and flowers. This museum is on the spot where he restored Uppsala University's botanical garden, which resembles a miniature baroque garden. His detailed sketches and descriptions of the garden have been faithfully followed. Admission to the museum is

25SEK ($2.75) adults, free for children. A donation is suggested for admission to the gardens. The gardens are open from May to August daily 9am to 9pm and September daily from 9am to 7pm. The museum is open from June to mid-September, Tuesday to Sunday noon to 4pm. Closed otherwise.

The largest cathedral in Scandinavia at nearly 120 meters (400 ft.) tall, the twin-spired Gothic **Uppsala Domkyrka** ⚛, Domkyrkoplan 5 (℃ 018/18-72-01; bus: 1 or 2), was founded in the 13th century. It was severely damaged in 1702 in a disastrous fire that swept over Uppsala, then was restored near the turn of the last century. Among the regal figures buried in the crypt is Gustavus Vasa. The remains of St. Erik, patron saint of Sweden, are entombed in a silver shrine. Botanist Linnaeus and philosopher-theologian Emanuel Swedenborg are also buried here. A small museum displays ecclesiastical relics of Uppsala. Admission to the cathedral is free; museum admission is 20SEK ($2.20) adults and 15SEK ($1.65) children 7 to 15, free for children under 7. The cathedral is open daily from 8am to 6pm.

GRIPSHOLM CASTLE ⚛   On an island in Lake Mälaren, Gripsholm Castle (Gripsholm Slottsfervaltning), P.O. Box 14, 64721 Mariefred (℃ 0159/101-94)—the fortress built by Gustavus Vasa in the late 1530s—is one of the best-preserved castles in Sweden. It lies near Mariefred, an idyllic small town known for its vintage narrow-gauge railroad.

Even though Gripsholm was last occupied by royalty (Charles XV) in 1864, it's still a royal castle. Its outstanding features include a large collection of portrait paintings depicting obscure branches of the Swedish monarchy, its brooding architecture, and its 18th-century theater built for the amusement of the 18th-century actor-king Gustavus III. It's open from May to August daily 10am to 4pm; in September, Tuesday to Friday from 10am to 3pm; from October to March, Saturday and Sunday only, noon to 3pm. Admission is 50SEK ($6) adults and 25SEK ($2.75) children under 12.

Getting There   The castle is 68 kilometers (42 miles) southwest of Stockholm, easily reached either by the E-20 south or by taking the fast X-2000 **train** from Stockholm's main railway station (trip time: 35 minutes). In summertime, you might also opt to take a **ferryboat** from Stockholm's Klara Malarstrand Pier, near Stadshuset. Your best bet is to take one of the ferries that departs every Monday to Friday at 10am for an arrival at Mariefred at 1:30pm. It's a 5-minute stroll from the Mariefred pier to the castle.

18

Switzerland

by Darwin Porter & Danforth Prince

Switzerland evokes images of towering peaks, mountain lakes, lofty pastures, and alpine villages, but it also offers a rich cultural life in cities such as sophisticated Geneva and perfectly preserved medieval Bern.

1 Geneva

Geneva is in the Rhône Valley at the southwestern corner of Lake Geneva (Lac Léman in French), between the Jura Mountains and the Alps. It's the capital of the canton of Geneva, the second-smallest canton in the Swiss confederation.

Switzerland's second-largest city is truly cosmopolitan. The setting is idyllic, on one of the biggest alpine lakes and within view of the glorious pinnacle of Mont Blanc. Filled with parks and promenades, the city becomes a virtual garden in summer. It's also one of the world's healthiest cities because the prevailing north wind blows away any pollution.

The yachts bobbing in the harbor and the Rolls-Royces cruising the promenades testify that Geneva is home to some of the richest people in the world. Its state religion is said to be banking—half of Switzerland's banks are located here.

Geneva has long held a position as a center of enlightenment and humane tolerance. Over the years it has offered a refuge to such controversial figures as Voltaire, Lenin, and native son Jean-Jacques Rousseau. Geneva also hosted religious reformers Knox and Calvin, and provided a safe haven for many artists. Today the headquarters of the International Red Cross and the World Health Organization are here, and it attracts many other international organizations.

ESSENTIALS

GETTING THERE By Plane Geneva International Airport (© 022/ 717-71-11; www.gva.ch), though busy, is compact and easily negotiated. **Swissair** (© 800/221-4750 in the U.S.) has the most frequent flights from North America.

To get into the center of Geneva, there's a train station linked to the air terminal with trains leaving about every 8 to 20 minutes from 5:39am to 11:36pm (trip time: 7 minutes); the one-way fare is 8.50SF ($5) first class and 5SF ($3.15) second class. A taxi into town costs 45SF ($28) and up, or you can take bus 10 for 2.50SF ($1.55).

By Train Geneva's busiest, most central, and most visible CFF (Chemins de fer fédéraux) rail station is **Gare Cornavin** (sometimes referred to as Genève-Cornavin), place Cornavin (© 0900/300-300). Don't confuse it with **Gare Genève-Cointrin,** near the airport, which handles some of the spillover from its larger sibling.

By Car   From Lausanne, head southwest on N1 to the very "end of south-western Switzerland."

By Lake Steamer   From late May to late September there are frequent daily arrivals by Swiss lake steamer from Montreaux, Vevey, and Lausanne (you can use your Eurailpass). If you're staying in the Left Bank (Old Town), get off at the Jardin Anglais stop in Geneva; Mont Blanc and Pâquis are the Right Bank stops. For more information, call ✆ **022/312-52-23.**

VISITOR INFORMATION   Tourist Office   The **Office du Tourisme de Genève,** 3 rue du Mont-Blanc (✆ **022/909-70-00;** www.geneve-tourisme.ch), is at Gare Cornavin. The staff provides information and can arrange hotel reservations (in Geneva and throughout Switzerland) and excursion bookings, and can refer you to car-rental agencies. The office is open from June to September, Monday to Friday 8am to 6pm and Saturday to Sunday 8am to 5pm; the rest of the year, it's open from Monday to Saturday 9am to 6pm.

Websites   After visiting the Geneva Tourist Office site noted above, check the following. Not so much a destination in itself as a good launching pad to other websites, **www.switzerland.com** can point the way to museums, hotels, restaurants, and other attractions. Although awkwardly designed, **www.myswitzerland. com** does have useful travel advice on hotels and travel packages and throws in current snow reports.

CITY LAYOUT   Geneva is divided by **Lake Geneva (Lac Léman)** and the **Rhône River** into two sections: the Right Bank and Left Bank. You may rent an audio-guided tour in English from the tourist office (see above) for 10SF ($6). This tour covers more than two dozen highlights in Old Town and comes with a cassette player and map. A 50SF ($31) deposit is required.

Rive Gauche (Left Bank)   This compact and colorful area is the oldest section. Here you'll find Old Town, some major shopping streets, the famous Flower Clock, the university, and several important museums. **Grand' Rue** is Old Town's well-preserved main street, flanked by many houses from the 15th and 18th centuries. The street winds uphill from the ponts de l'Ile; at place Bel-Air it becomes rue de la Cité, then Grand' Rue, and finally rue Hôtel-de-Ville. Eventually it reaches **place du Bourg-de-Four**—one of Geneva's most historic squares (Rousseau was born in no. 40).

South of this street is **promenade des Bastions,** a greenbelt area with a monument to the Reformation; it overlooks the Arve River. Directly to the west, in the northern corner of promenade des Bastions, is **place Neuve,** Geneva's finest square. From place Neuve, you can take **rue de la Corraterie,** once surrounded by the city wall, to the Rhône and the **ponts de l'Ile.** On this bridge is the Tour de l'Ile, what's left of the 13th-century bishop's castle.

On the shore of Lake Geneva is the **Jardin Anglais (English Garden)** with its Flower Clock, and farther out are the **Parc La Grange** and **Parc des Eaux-Vives.**

Rive Droite (Right Bank)   You can cross to the other side of the Rhône on any of several bridges, including **pont du Mont-Blanc, pont de la Machine, pont des Bergues,** and **ponts de l'Ile.** The Right Bank is home to **Gare Cornavin** (the train station), the major international organizations, and several attractive parks. **Place St-Gervais** is in the St-Gervais district; since the 18th century this has been an area for jewelers and watchmakers. Along the northern shore of Lake Geneva is **quai du Président-Wilson,** named for the U.S. president who helped found the League of Nations.

Geneva

The Right Bank is surrounded by parks, from the tree-shaded promenades along the Rhône to the **Parc de la Perle du Lac, Parc Barton,** and **Parc Mon-Repos** on the outskirts.

GETTING AROUND   By Public Transportation   For the most part, all of Geneva's bus and tram lines begin at place Cornavin, in front of the rail station—running roughly from 5:30am to midnight daily. From here, you can take bus F or 8 to the Palais des Nations. Tickets for Zone 10, the urban area, are sold from automatic vending machines at each stop, operated by coins or magnetic cards (free cards are available from Geneva public transport agencies). Tickets for other zones, including Geneva's suburbs and France, are sold by drivers on the corresponding buses.

Four **basic tickets** are provided: free transfers for 1 hour in Zone 10, with as many changes as you wish on any vehicle, for 2.20SF ($1.40); a trip limited to three stops, valid for half an hour, allowing a return trip, at 1.50SF (95¢); unlimited transportation for 1½ hours in all zones of the network of Geneva, at 4SF ($2.50); and a ride for 1 hour in Zone 10 for children 6 to 12 as well as seniors (women over 62 and men over 65), at 1.50SF (95¢); children 5 and under ride free.

You can buy **multiuse tickets** and **daily cards** from agents whose addresses are listed on posts at the various stops. A wide range of these is available, and often you can adapt the system to your needs. For example, a daily ticket for unlimited transportation in Zone 10 is 5SF ($3.15) for as many trips and changes as you need; it's valid from the time you stamp it up to the termination of the day's service, around midnight. There's also a daily ticket at 8.50SF ($5) including transportation not only in Zone 10, but in Zones 21, 31, and 41, taking in practically the whole network of greater Geneva. Many worthy attractions and restaurants are in the suburbs.

These tickets and many other kinds, including combined bus/cable-car tickets to climb to the top of Mont Salève, are available from the Geneva public transport systems agencies or from official dealers. For customer service and more information, call ℂ **022/308-34-34.**

By Taxi   Cab fares start at 6.50SF ($4.05), plus 2.85 to 3.30SF ($1.80 to $2.05) for each kilometer in the city. No tipping is required; for a taxi, call ℂ **022/ 331-41-33** or 022/320-20-20.

By Car   Driving isn't recommended—parking is too difficult and the many one-way streets make navigation complicated. However, should you wish to rent a car and tour Lake Geneva, you'll find many rental companies at the airport or in the city center. Major offices include **Avis,** 44 rue de Lausanne (ℂ **022/ 731-90-00,** or 022/929-03-30 at the airport); **Budget,** 36 rue de Zurich (ℂ **022/900-24-00,** or 022/798-22-52 at the airport); **Hertz,** 60 rue de Berne (ℂ **022/731-12-00,** or 022/798-11-02 at the airport); and **Europcar** (ℂ **022/ 909-69-90** at the airport).

By Bicycle Or Motor Scooter   Touring the city by bicycle isn't practical because of the steep cobblestone streets and general congestion. However, you might want to rent a bike to visit the nearby countryside. The major rental outlet is at the *bagages* desk at **Gare Cornavin** (ℂ **022/715-2111**), where city bikes are 27SF ($17) per day and mountain bikes 35SF ($22) per day.

If you're interested in renting a motor scooter, try **Horizon Motos,** 51 rue de Lausanne (ℂ **022/732-29-90**), where rentals begin at 50SF ($31) per day.

ⓒ FAST FACTS: Geneva

American Express The office at 7 rue du Mont-Blanc (☎ 022/731-76-00; bus: 1) is open from Monday to Friday 8:30am to 5:30pm and Saturday 9am to noon.

Business Hours Most **banks** are open from Monday to Friday 8:30am to 4:30pm (to 5:30pm on Wednesday). Most **offices** are open from Monday to Friday 8am to noon and 2 to 6pm, though this can vary. It's always best to call first.

Consulates If you lose your passport or have other business with your home government, go to your nation's consulate: **United States,** World Trade Center Building no. 2 (☎ 022/798-16-15; tram to Gare Genè-Cointrin [airport]); **Australia,** 56–58 rue Moillebeau (☎ 022/79-991-00; bus: 3); **Canada,** 1 chemin du Pré-de-la-Bichette (☎ 022/919-92-00; bus: 5, 8, or 18); **New Zealand,** 28A chemin du Petit-Saconnex (☎ 022/929-03-50; bus: 3); the **United Kingdom,** 37–39 rue de Vermont (☎ 022/918-24-00; bus: 3); or **South Africa,** rue de Rhône 65 (☎ 022/849-54-54; bus: 2, 9, or 22).

Currency The basic unit of currency is the **Swiss franc (SF),** made up of 100 centimes. At press time, the rate of exchange, and the one used throughout this chapter, was $1 = 1.60SF, or 1SF = 63¢; £1 = approximately 2SF. The rate for the euro was €1 = 1.50SF. *Note:* Switzerland is not part of the euro zone.

Currency Exchange The exchange at **Gare Cornavin,** 10 place Cornavin (☎ 022/375-33-60; tram to Gare Cornavin), is open daily from 8:30am to 8:30pm. For other financial transactions, the **Société de Banque Suisse** (Swiss Bank Corporation) is at 2 rue de la Confédération (☎ 022/375-75-75; bus: 12).

Dentists English-speaking dentists are available at one of the *cliniques dentaires* at 5 rue Malombré (☎ 022/346-64-44; tram: 12), from Monday to Friday 7:30am to 8pm and Saturday to Sunday 8am to 6pm.

Doctors In a medical emergency, call ☎ 022/322-20-20; or arrange an appointment with an English-speaking doctor at the **Hôpital Cantonal,** 24 rue Micheli-du-Crest (☎ 022/372-3311; tram: 12).

Drugstores One of the world's biggest drugstores, **Pharmacie Principale,** Confédération-Centre, rue de la Confédération (☎ 022/318-66-60; bus: 12), offers everything from medicine to clothing, perfumes, optical equipment, cameras, and photo supplies. It's open from Monday to Friday 9am to 7pm and Saturday 9am to 5pm.

Emergencies In an emergency, dial ☎ 117 for the police, ☎ 144 for an ambulance, and ☎ 118 to report a fire.

Hospitals You can go to the **Hôpital Cantonal,** 24 rue Micheli-du-Crest (☎ 022/372-3311).

Internet Access Try **Pont Six,** rue de Vieux-Billard, 7A (☎ 022/800-2600), lying off rue des Bains. Charges are 45SF ($28) per half hour or 65SF ($41) per hour. Open Monday, Tuesday, and Thursday from noon to midnight, Wednesday 10am to midnight, Friday noon to 2am, Saturday 10am to 2am, and Sunday 10am to 10pm.

Post Office The city's main post office, **Bureau de Poste Montbrillant,** rue de Gares (℡ **022/739-21-11;** tram to Gare Cornavin), offers a full range of telephone, telegraph, and mail-related services from Monday to Friday 7:30am to 10:45pm, Saturday 8am to 10pm, and Sunday noon to 8pm. There's a branch, which offers less extensive services, at **Gare Cornavin,** 16 rue de Gares (℡ **022/739-24-61),** open from Monday to Friday 6am to 10:45pm, Saturday 6am to 8pm, and Sunday noon to 8pm.

Telephones/Telex/Fax The **country code** for Switzerland is **41.** The **city code** for Geneva is **22;** use this code when you're calling from outside Switzerland. If you're within Switzerland but not in Geneva, use **022.** If you're calling within Geneva, simply leave off the code and dial the regular phone number.

There's a big, 24-hour **long-distance phone center** at the main train station, Gare Cornavin, place Cornavin. It's much cheaper to make your calls here than at your hotel—some Geneva hotels add a 40% surcharge to long-distance calls. Telegrams and faxes can be sent at the post office at 16 rue des Gares (℡ **022/739-24-61),** 2 blocks from the train station. For **AT&T,** call ℡ **888/288-4685;** for **Sprint,** call ℡ **800/877-4646;** for **MCI,** call ℡ **800/444-4141.**

WHERE TO STAY
ON THE RIGHT BANK
Very Expensive

Hôtel Beau-Rivage 🟦🟦🟦 This landmark 1865 hotel receives our highest recommendation for its traditional Victorian charm and impeccable service. However, you pay dearly for them. The "romantic" rooms are bigger than the "classical." Double-glazing cuts down on street noise, and each unit has a roomy bathroom, with robes and a tub and shower combo. Units in front open onto views of the Right Bank.

13 quai du Mont-Blanc, CH-1201 Genève. ℡ 022/716-66-66. Fax 022/716-60-60. www.beau-rivage.ch. 97 units. 540–750SF ($338–$469) double; from 2,490SF ($1,556) suite. AE, DC, MC, V. Parking 50SF ($31). Bus: 1. **Amenities:** 2 restaurants (see "La Chat-Botté" under "Where to Dine," below), piano bar; 24-hour room service; laundry. *In room:* A/C (some), TV, minibar, hair dryer, safe, robes.

Hôtel des Bergues 🟦🟦🟦 Even more dazzling than the Beau-Rivage, this is one of the world's grand hotels, the choice of any visiting monarch. It's grandly memorable from its central position at the edge of the Rhône. The staff is the most hospitable in Geneva. Rooms have Directoire and Louis-Philippe furnishings. Those ranked superior on the Bel Etage floor are the finest choices, although lake view rooms are more expensive. Bathrooms have tub/shower combinations, phones, and full-length mirrors.

33 quai des Bergues, CH-1211 Genève. ℡ 022/908-70-00. Fax 022/908-70-90. www.hoteldesbergues.com. 120 units. 465–795SF ($291–$497) double; from 1,560SF ($975) suite. AE, DC, MC, V. Parking 50SF ($31) per night. Bus: 7. **Amenities:** 2 restaurants, bar; 24-hour room service; laundry. *In room:* A/C, TV, minibar, hair dryer, safe.

Le Richemond 🟦🟦🟦 This regal palace is Geneva's greatest hotel and counts some of the world's most prominent people among its guests. Erected in 1875, the neoclassical building is near the lake. Nearly half of the units are suites. A large number are renovated every year but even those between rehabs look as good as new. This is true Grand Hotel living, with luxurious beds and spacious bathrooms with tub and shower combos. Some rooms are reserved for non-smokers.

Jardin Brunswick, CH-1211 Genève. © **022/715-70-00.** Fax 022/715-70-01. www.richemond.ch. 91 units. 640–740SF ($400–$463) double; from 1,200SF ($750) suite. AE, DC, MC, V. Parking 50SF ($31). Bus: 1. **Amenities:** Gentilhomme is among the finest dining rooms in Geneva, and Le Jardin is the city's most fashionable cafe, elegant piano bar; health club; 24-hour room service; laundry. *In room:* A/C, TV, minibar, hair dryer, safe, robes.

Moderate

Hôtel du Midi On a tree-lined square near the center of Geneva, this hotel resembles an apartment building. Midsize rooms, though not spectacular, are well maintained and comfortable, with double-glazed windows to keep out traffic noise. Bathrooms are a bit cramped but have adequate shelf space and warming racks for towels.

4 place Chevelu, CH-1211 Genève. © **022/544-1500.** Fax 022/731-00-20. midihotel@prolink.ch. 90 units. 240–260SF ($150–$163) double. Rates include continental breakfast. AE, DC, MC, V. Bus: 7. **Amenities:** Small weekday-only restaurant; bar; room service; laundry. *In room:* A/C, TV, minibar, safe.

Hôtel Moderne This hotel is near the rail station and the lake. Public areas are modern. Rooms, with soundproof windows, are modern, clean and sunny, though predictably furnished and a bit sterile. Some are reserved for nonsmokers. You'll probably wish the bathrooms had more room to spread out your stuff. The nearest parking is at the Cornavin rail station's underground garage nearby.

1 rue de Berne, CH-1211 Genève. © **022/732-81-00.** Fax 022/738-26-58. www.hotelmoderne.ch. 54 units. 125SF ($78) double with shower; 190SF ($119) double with complete bathroom. Rates include buffet breakfast. AE, DC, MC, V. Bus: 10. **Amenities:** Breakfast only, but an Italian restaurant under separate management in the same building; room service; baby-sitting; laundry. *In room:* TV.

Strasbourg-Geneva It may have been constructed at the beginning of this past century, but 1999 renovations mean it's up to date and better than ever. For decades it has offered a safe haven for those arriving at the Geneva train station. The most spacious rooms tend to be those on the lower floors. The compact bathrooms are minimally equipped, each with a shower unit.

10 rue J.-J.-Pradier, CH-1201 Genève. © Best Western, **800/528-1234** in the U.S., or 022/906-58-00. Fax 022/738-42-08. www.strasbourg-geneva.ch. 53 units. 240–270SF ($150–$169) double; 350–530SF ($219–$331) suite. Rates include continental breakfast. AE, DC, MC, V. Bus: 1, 2, 3, 4, 8, 12, 13, or 44. **Amenities:** Breakfast only. *In room:* TV, minibar.

Inexpensive

Bal-Esperance ⭐ (Value) This is an accommodation oddity, and a bit of a discovery. Once it was known as a *foyer pour dames* or boardinghouse for women. Right near the Old Town's place du Bourg-de-Four, it's owned by the Salvation Army, but don't fear that this is a rawbone joint. This little hotel of charm and grace has a panoramic terrace and bright midsize rooms with shower baths. It's also a choice for families, as some rooms are large enough for four beds. Try to get one with a balcony with a view of the Cathedrale St-Pierre.

1 rue de la Vallée, CH-1204 Geneva. © **022/818-3737.** Fax 022/818-3773. www.hotel-bal-esperance. ch/an_tariff.htm. 40 units. 120–130SF ($75–$81) double; 150–180SF ($94–$113) triple. AE, DC, MC, V. Bus: 8. Tram: 12. **Amenities:** Non-alcoholic restaurant. *In room:* TV.

Hôtel de la Cloche (Value) This small hotel, one of Geneva's best deals, occupies the second floor of a 19th-century apartment building on a narrow street behind the Noga Hilton. It's unpretentious despite a glamorous location. Rooms are spacious, well cared for, and designed with an eye to old-fashioned comfort. Some have views over a quiet inner courtyard and others open onto views over the lake. Private bathrooms have rather cramped shower stalls; corridor bathrooms are well maintained, and there's rarely a wait.

6 rue de la Cloche, CH-1211 Genève. (© 022/732-94-81. Fax 022/738-16-12. 8 units, 3 with bathroom (shower only). 90SF ($56) double without bathroom, 120SF ($75) double with bathroom; 100SF ($63) triple without bathroom; 140SF ($88) quad without bathroom. AE, MC, V. Bus: 1. **Amenities:** Breakfast only. *In room:* TV.

Hôtel International & Terminus   This hotel lies across from the main entrance of Geneva's railway station and has been run by three generations of the Cottier family. Built around 1900, it was radically upgraded in 2000, with pairs of smaller rooms reconfigured into larger units. Don't expect grand style; the allure of this place is its exceedingly good value. Bathrooms seem to have been added as an afterthought in areas not designed for them, and are a bit cramped, each with a shower stall.

20 rue des Alpes, CH-1201 Genève. (© **022/732-80-95.** Fax 022/732-18-43. international-terminus@ swissonline.ch. 53 units. 160–220SF ($100–$138) double. Rates include continental breakfast. AE, DC, MC, V. Bus: 6, 10, or 33. **Amenities:** Restaurant and bar (pizza a feature). *In room:* TV, minibar, safe.

Hôtel St-Gervais ⋦ ⟨Value⟩   This good-value hotel lies in an old-fashioned, vaguely nondescript building within Geneva's medieval core, a 3-minute walk from Gare Cornavin. This old inn has the kind of quirky idiosyncrasies that appeal to architects and historic renovators. If you don't mind the lack of a bathroom, you'll find the midsize bedrooms tidily kept, tastefully furnished, and most comfortable. Most rooms have a sink, but the hall bathrooms are frequently tidied for the next guest's use.

20 rue des Corps-Saints, CH1201 Genève. (© and fax **022/732-45-72.** 26 units, 2 with shower or bathroom. 78SF ($49) double without bathroom; 105SF ($66) double with shower or bathroom. AE, MC, V. Tram: 1, 3, 4, 5, or 6. **Amenities:** Convivial pub; breakfast only. *In room:* No phone.

ON THE LEFT BANK
Moderate
Hotel Tiffany ⋦ ⟨Value⟩   This little charmer of a Belle Époque boutique hotel lies on a Left Bank street 3 blocks south of the river and about a 12-minute stroll from the center and the lake. Although it can hardly match the style and glamour of the lakeside palaces, it is attractive in its modest way. In its category, it offers some of the most reasonable prices in Geneva. Rooms are midsize with lots of extras, including soundproofing and spacious bathrooms with tub and shower combos. We prefer the rooms in the "attic," with their beams, rooftop vistas, and sloping walls.

1 rue des Marbriers, CH-1204 Genève. (© **022/708-1616.** Fax 022/708-1617. www.hotel-tiffany.ch/ Hotel_GB1.htm. 43 units. 300–320SF ($188–$200) double; from 390SF ($244) suite. Buffet breakfast included. AE, DC, MC, V. Bus: 1 or 4. **Amenities:** Restaurant, English bar, sidewalk cafe (summer). *In room:* A/C, TV, minibar, hair dryer, safe.

Hôtel Touring-Balance   Previously two hotels across the street from each other, the Touring-Balance is in the heart of the Left Bank's shopping district. A major renovation in 1999 transformed the lobby with a theme like that of an Italian garden, complete with *jardinières* and potted plants. Rooms in both sections are comparable in style and amenities. Upper floors are more modern than the traditional lower floors. Some units are air-conditioned. Bathrooms are compact, neat, and well kept.

13 place Longemalle, CH-1204 Genève. (© **022/818-62-62.** Fax 022/818-62-61. 58 units. 250SF ($156) double; 350–500SF ($219–$313) suite. Rates include buffet breakfast. AE, DC, MC, V. Parking 28SF ($18). Bus: 6, 8, or 9. **Amenities:** Coffee shop. *In room:* TV, minibar.

Inexpensive

Hotel Central 🍸 (Value)   This is a Left Bank bargain that has been completely rejuvenated. Since its reopening, it's been a success as word of its good value has spread to budget-minded travelers. On a shopping street, it has a warm and inviting Bali-inspired decor. The location is at the foot of the Old Town and only a 3-minute walk to the lake. The Gansted family is on hand to welcome you, and each of their rooms is personalized, containing comfortable beds and small but neat bathrooms with shower stalls. A few rooms have bunk beds suitable for families or friends traveling together. Some rooms are very large with 2 separate bathrooms.

2 rue de la Rôtisserie, CH-1204 Genève. © 022/818-8100. Fax 022/818-8101. www.hotelcentral.ch/hotelcentral/en/plan/htm. 28 units. 95–120SF ($59–$75) double; 195SF ($122) junior suite, 75SF ($47) per person bunk bed. Rates include breakfast. AE, DC, MC, V. Tram: 12. **Amenities:** Lounge. *In room:* TV.

WHERE TO DINE
ON THE RIGHT BANK
Very Expensive

Le Chat-Botté 🍸🍸🍸 FRENCH   "Puss in Boots" is in one of Geneva's grandest hotels. It's a close race between this deluxe dining room and the Hilton's Le Cygne (see below) as to which serves the best cuisine in Geneva. We'd give the honors to Le Chat Botté for French dishes, with Le Cygne winning for fresh seafood. Decorated with tapestries, sculpture, and rich upholstery, and graced by a polite staff, it serves delectable food. In nice weather you can dine on the flower-decked terrace, overlooking the Jet d'Eau. The cuisine, though inspired by French classics, is definitely contemporary. The large selection includes filets of red mullet vinaigrette, a divine lobster salad with eggplant "caviar," and breast of chicken stuffed with vegetables. Highly recommended is delicate perch filet from Lake Geneva, sautéed until it's golden and sometimes served with fava beans. In the autumn, gourmets flock here for the roast saddle of roebuck, prepared only for two or more diners.

In the Hôtel Beau-Rivage, 13 quai du Mont-Blanc. © 022/716-66-66. Reservations required. Main courses 40–60SF ($25–$38); set-price menu 60–145SF ($38–$91) at lunch. AE, DC, MC, V. Daily noon–2pm and 7–10pm. Bus: 6 or 33.

Le Cygne 🍸🍸🍸 FRENCH   This swank restaurant overlooks the harbor with the famous Jet d'Eau and, in the distance, the Alps. A refined cuisine is offered, with impeccable service. The menu may present such stellar choices as terrine of blackened chicken in crayfish- and anise-flavored aspic. Also worthy of an award are the smoked filet of sea bass with truffle-flavored vinaigrette and the roasted lamb with coriander and tomatoes stuffed with moussaka. Five elaborate carts make one of the most spectacular arrays of desserts in Switzerland.

In the Noga Hilton International, 19 quai du Mont-Blanc. © 022/908-90-85. Reservations required. Main courses 38–70SF ($24–$44); fixed-price meal 59–80SF ($37–$50) at lunch, 75–155SF ($47–$97) at dinner. AE, DC, MC, V. Daily noon–2pm and 7–10pm. Closed 1 week in Jan, 11 days at Easter, and 3 weeks in July. Bus: 1.

Le Neptune 🍸🍸🍸 SEAFOOD   This is Geneva's finest seafood restaurant. The decor is intimate, intensely floral, and graced with an enormous fresco displaying an inside view of Neptune's kingdom. Though the menu changes, you're likely to be offered such dishes as herbed vichyssoise with hazelnut oil and a dollop of foie gras; a perfect cassolette of oysters seasoned with algae-flavored butter sauce; or a memorable Atlantic sea bass roasted in a salt crust with thyme. If you're not in the mood for fish, try rack of Scottish lamb in puff pastry with spices or partridge roasted en casserole with autumn herbs.

In the Hôtel du Rhône, 1 quai Turrettini. ℂ 022/731-98-31. Reservations required. Main courses 45–70SF ($28–$44). AE, DC, MC, V. Mon–Fri noon–2pm and 7:30–10pm. Bus: 6, 8, 10, or 15.

Moderate

Chez Jacky ✪ SWISS   This French provincial bistro is a delightful place for dining, attracting everyone from staid grandmothers to young skiers en route to Verbier. It's the domain of Jacky Gruber, an exceptional chef from Valais. You might begin with Chinese cabbage and mussels and continue with filet of turbot roasted with thyme or beautifully prepared pink duck on spinach with onion confit. Be prepared to wait for each course, as everything is prepared to order.

9–11 rue Necker. ℂ 022/732-86-80. Reservations recommended. Main courses 38–42SF ($24–$264); 3-course business lunch 45SF ($284). AE, DC, MC, V. Mon–Fri 11am–2pm and 6:30–11pm. Closed first week of Jan and 3 weeks in Aug. Bus: 5, 10, or 44.

Jeck's Place ✪ PAN ASIAN   Near the Cornavin rail station, this delightful place is like taking a culinary trip to southeast Asia, with stopovers in such places as China, Malaysia, Thailand, and India. The cuisine of Asian specialties provides temptation with every order. The specialties of the day will be seasoned with delicate blends of spices, notably lemon grass and curry but also chile and ganlaga (from the ginger family). We often make a meal of the appetizers alone, including homemade steamed dumplings stuffed with a blend of pork and vegetables flavored with coriander. The house specialty, and our favorite dish, is Jeck's chicken in green curry. Another exotic treat is a delicate whiting spread with spicy lemon grass sauce and grilled on banana leaves.

14 rue de Neuchâtel. ℂ 022/731-3303. Reservations recommended. Main courses 18–30SF ($114–$19). Special lunch platter 13SF ($84). Mon–Fri 11:30am–2pm and 6:30–10pm. AE, DC, MC, V. Bus: 4, 5, or 9.

La Mère Royaume ✪ FRENCH   Opened around the turn of the century, this is one of the oldest restaurants in town. It's named after a heroine who in 1602 poured boiling stew over a Savoyard soldier's head and cracked his skull with the kettle. With an antecedent like that, you'd expect some of the heartiest fare in Geneva, but instead the kitchen offers perfectly cooked French specialties such as *omble chevalier*, a delicate Lake Geneva whitefish known as "the world's most divine trout." Less expensive meals are served in the brasserie.

9 rue des Corps-Saints. ℂ 022/732-70-08. Reservations required. Brasserie, main courses 17–30SF ($11–$19); fixed-price menu 36–50SF ($23–$31). Restaurant, main courses 30–50SF ($19–$31); fixed-price menus 50–98SF ($31–$61). AE, DC, MC, V. Mon–Fri noon–2pm and 7–10:30pm; Sat 7–10:30pm. Bus: 4, 6, or 7.

Le Boeuf Rouge ✪ LYONNAIS   This brasserie serves Geneva's best cookery in the style of Lyons, the gastronomic capital of France. As such, you'll find authentic versions of such dishes as Lyonnais sausage with scalloped potatoes; chateaubriand in red wine sauce; blood sausage; and quenelles of pike-perch, any of which might be preceded by a delectable version of onion soup or green salad with croutons and bacon. The decor is appealingly kitschy, complete with lots of Art Nouveau posters and late 19th-century ceramics. The staff here is brusque but kindly.

17 rue Alfred-Vincent (at the corner of rue Paquis). ℂ 022/732-75-37. Reservations recommended. Main courses 29–50SF ($18–$31); set-price lunches 18–35SF ($11–$22); set-price dinners 45–50SF ($28–$31). AE, DC, MC, V. Mon–Fri noon–2pm and 7–10:30pm. Bus: 1.

ON THE LEFT BANK
Expensive

Le Béarn ✪✪✪ FRENCH   This is the only deluxe restaurant on the Left Bank that matches the previously recommended three-star choices on the Right

Bank. Jean-Paul Goddard and his excellent staff have created the best restaurant in Geneva's business center. With only 10 tables, everything is on a small scale, and the service is personal. The chef prepares dishes that appeal to the Rothschild palates, including such spectacular delights as tender morels stuffed with fresh asparagus tips. One of the world's most expensive birds, roasted Scottish thrush, might rest on your platter, or our all-time favorite concoction here, a platter called "three terrines of autumn" (rabbit, partridge, and thrush).

4 quai de la Poste. ☎ 022/321-00-28. Reservations required. Main courses 30–65SF ($19–$41); fixed-price meal 55–90SF ($34–$56) at lunch, 90–160SF ($56–$100) at dinner. AE, DC, MC, V. Mon–Fri noon–2pm; Mon–Sat 7:30–10pm. Closed mid-July to mid-Aug and Sat June–Sept. Bus: 2, 10, or 22.

Moderate

Au Pied de Cochon LYONNAISE/SWISS   Come here for hearty Lyonnaise fare if you don't mind smoke and noise. A lot of young people are attracted to this place, as well as lawyers from the Palais de Justice across the way, artists, and local workers. The cooking is like grandma's—provided she came from Lyon. Naturally, the namesake *pieds de cochon* (pigs' feet) is included on the menu, along with *petit salé* (lamb), tripe, and some of the best grilled andouillettes (sausages made of chitterlings) in Geneva.

4 place du Bourg-de-Four. ☎ 022/310-47-97. Reservations recommended. Main courses 25–40SF ($16–$25). AE, DC, MC, V. Daily 11:30am–2:30pm and 7–11pm (closed Sun June–Aug). Bus: 2 or 22. Tram: 12.

Brasserie de l'Hôtel de Ville SWISS   This is one of the most deliberately archaic-looking restaurants in Geneva, with a reputation that goes back to 1764 and a clientele that prefers its old-fashioned decor and its choice of menu items absolutely not change. The menu is stylish and fashionable, offering such time-tested Swiss dishes as fondue, *tafelspitz* (boiled beef), Wiener schnitzel, glazed ham with béarnaise sauce; and, best of all, filets of perch and fera from the nearby lake.

19 Grand Rue. ☎ 022/311-70-30. Reservations recommended. Main courses 30–50SF ($19–$31); set-price menu 59SF ($37). AE, DC, MC, V. Daily 11am–11:30pm. Bus: 17.

Brasserie Lipp SWISS   This bustling place is named after the famous Parisian brasserie, and when you enter (especially at lunch), you'll think you've been transported to France. The impossibly long menu contains a sampling of the repertoire of bistro dishes, but like its namesake, the Geneva Lipp specializes in several versions of charcuterie. You can also order three kinds of pot-au-feu and such classics as Toulousian cassoulet with *confit de canard* (duckling), available in autumn and winter. The fresh oysters are among the best in the city, and tables are placed outside in summer.

Confédération-Centre, 8 rue de la Confédération. ☎ 022/311-10-11. Reservations recommended. Main courses 23–45SF ($14–$28); fixed-price menus 50–70SF ($31–$44). AE, DC, MC, V. Daily 9am–1am. Bus: 12.

La Coupole SWISS/FRENCH   This is a true brasserie, and far more elegant than its Parisian namesake. The place is most popular at noon, especially with shoppers and office workers. The menu is limited but well selected; the *cuisine du marché* (cooking based on market-fresh ingredients) is some of the finest in this part of town. Chefs search the market in the early morning for the freshest and best of ingredients.

116 rue du Rhône. ☎ 022/787-50-10. Main courses 30–45SF ($19–$28); fixed-price menus 50–70SF ($31–$44). AE, DC, MC, V. Mon–Sat 11:30am–2:30pm; Tues–Sat 7–10:30pm. Bus: 2, 9, or 22. Tram: 12.

L'Aïoli PROVENÇAL   This popular neighborhood restaurant stands opposite Le Corbusier's Maison de Verre. Something of a local secret, it offers personalized service and the finest Provençal cooking in town. We recommend frogs' legs Provençal, simmered in a savory tomato, onion and garlic sauce; and also lamb *gigot*, in which the meat is infused with fresh herbs and garlic and baked to a tender perfection. The chefs also prepare a delectable lamb stew called *gardiane camarguaise*.

6 rue Adrien-Lachenal. ℂ 022/736-79-71. Reservations not necessary. Main courses 22–35SF ($14–$22); *menu dégustation* 70SF ($44). AE, DC, MC, V. Mon–Fri 11:30am–2:30pm and 7–10:30pm. Closed Aug. Bus: 1 or 6. Tram: 12.

La Favola ⋇ TUSCAN/ITALIAN   This is the best Italian dining spot in Geneva, and its most devoted habitués go even further, hailing it as the best restaurant in Geneva. The menu is small and short but choice, varying with the availability of ingredients and the season. Look for such well-crafted dishes as carpaccio of beef; *vitello tonnato* (paper-thin veal with a tuna sauce); lobster salad; potato salad with cèpe mushrooms; and a highly pleasing ravioli made with either eggplant or mushrooms.

15 rue Jean-Calvin. ℂ 022/311-74-37. Reservations required. Main courses 39–49SF ($24–$31). AE, MC, V. Mon–Fri noon–2pm and 7:15–10pm. Closed 1 week at Christmas, 2 weeks between July–Aug. Tram: 12.

Le Lyrique ⋇ SWISS   This is the best place for a pre-theater dinner, with both a formal restaurant and a brasserie. The restaurant bustles with urban vitality and is very tuned to the arts, music, and business lives of Geneva. The brasserie, which has a terrace, is open all day but serves hot meals only during the hours mentioned below. When there's a performance at the nearby Grand Théâtre de Genève on Saturday or Sunday, the restaurant is also open. In the restaurant, you can try such carefully prepared dishes as filet of sea wolf with grapefruit segments, a roulade of rabbit with pasta maison, and tagliatelle with scampi. In the brasserie, menu items include chicken suprême with ravioli and leeks, and an *assiette Lyrique,* a meal in itself that combines four vegetarian and fish dishes—tartare of salmon, tartare of vegetables, terrine of vegetables, and eggplant "caviar."

12 bd. du Théâtre. ℂ **022/328-00-95.** Reservations recommended. Restaurant, main courses 27–48SF ($17–$30); fixed-price menu 48–60SF ($30–$38). Brasserie, main courses 20–30SF ($13–$20); fixed-price menu (lunch or dinner) 39–50SF ($24–$31). AE, MC, V. Mon–Fri noon–2pm and 6:30–10pm. Bus: 2 or 22.

Restaurant du Palais de Justice SWISS/ITALIAN/FRENCH   An inviting place with lots of atmosphere, this restaurant is in the old town on a colorful square, across from the Palais de Justice. It was established in the late 1950s in a medieval building complete with a cellar with a vaulted ceiling, and has thrived ever since. Small pizzas, fondues, and *plats du jour,* including an array of beef dishes, draw the crowds. The food is in the usual brasserie style, nothing special but nothing really bad either.

8, place du Bourg-de-Four. ℂ 022/318-37-37. Main courses 20–45SF ($13–$28); fondues 21–39SF ($13–$24). AE, DC, MC, V. Mon–Sat noon–2:30pm and 6:30–10pm. Bus: 2 or 22.

Inexpensive

Pizzeria da Paolo *Value* ITALIAN/PIZZA   Bustling, convivial, and completely unpretentious, this simple pizzeria offers a cozy, wood-sheathed setting from a position very close to the Jet d'Eau. There are more than 20 kinds of pizza offered—the house specialty is a Pizza Paolo, made from fresh spinach and cheese. But if pizzas aren't your thing, there's also a full complement of chicken parmigiana; stuffed and roasted turkey; fresh salads; ham dishes; and fresh fish. Don't expect glamour or too much cosseting from the overworked staff—instead, you'll get a dose of reality, everyday grittiness, good value, and some filling and very tasty Italian food.

3 rue du Lac. © 022/736-3049. Reservations recommended. Pizza 15–25SF ($9–$16). Main platters 25–45SF ($16–$28). AE, DC, MC, V. Daily 11:45am–2pm and 6:45–11pm. Tram 12.

Taverne de la Madeleine SWISS   This very good restaurant is set against the old city wall beside the Eglise de la Madeleine. The brusquely efficient staff caters to a lunchtime business crowd, and the place is operated by a philanthropic organization that forbids the consumption of alcohol (alcohol-free beer is available). You can order a variety of well-prepared dishes or specials like four types of pasta, vegetarian sandwiches, and a big plate of *osso buco* (braised veal shank) with *pommes frites*. The kitchen prides itself on its filet of lake perch meunière style (in butter sauce) or Vevey style with exotic mushrooms. Most dishes are at the lower end of the price scale.

20 rue Toutes-Ames. © 022/310-60-70. Reservations recommended. Main courses 12–25SF ($8–$16); *plat du jour* 14SF ($9). MC, V. Sept–June Mon–Fri 7:30am–6pm (last food order at 4pm), Sat 9am–4:30pm (last food order at 2:30pm). July–Aug Tues–Sat 7:30am–9pm. Bus: 2. Tram: 12.

SEEING THE SIGHTS

You can see most of Geneva on foot, which is the best way to familiarize yourself with the city.

SIGHTSEEING SUGGESTIONS FOR FIRST-TIME VISITORS

If You Have 1 Day Begin the day by viewing the spectacular water fountain, **Jet d'Eau,** and the **Flower Clock** in the Jardin Anglais. Then take a **steamer cruise** of Lake Geneva. Return in the early afternoon and explore the Left Bank's **Old Town.** Have dinner at a restaurant on or around place du Bourg-de-Four.

If You Have 2 Days On day 2, visit some of the most important museums, each completely different. It'll take a full day of sightseeing to absorb the **Musée d'Art et d'Histoire,** the **Musée International de la Croix-Rouge et du Croissant-Rouge (Red Cross Museum),** and the **Palais des Nations.**

If You Have 3 Days On day 3, take a stroll along the **quays** of Geneva in the morning, and in the afternoon go on an organized excursion to the Alps, including **Mont Blanc,** for a panoramic view.

If You Have 4 or 5 Days On day 4, take a lake steamer to **Lausanne.** You'll have time to explore its old town and walk its lakeside quays at Ouchy before returning to Geneva in the evening. On day 5, take another lake steamer, this time to **Montreux;** after visiting this lakeside resort, take a trip outside the town to see the **Château de Chillon,** immortalized by Lord Byron.

THE TOP ATTRACTIONS

In addition to the sights below, Geneva's top attractions are the **Jet d'Eau,** the famous fountain that has virtually become the city's symbol; the **Flower Clock,** in the Jardin Anglais; and the **Old Town,** the oldest part of the city.

Baur Collections ⚓   The collections, housed in a 19th-century mansion with a garden, constitute a private exhibit of artworks from 7th- to 20th-century China and 17th- to 20th-century Japan . The choice ceramics here are from the T'ang dynasty (618–908). On display are jade, ceramics, lacquer, ivories, and delicate sword fittings.

8 rue Munier-Romilly. ℂ **022/346-17-29.** Admission 5SF ($3.15) adults, free for children. Tues–Sun 2–6pm. Bus: 1 or 8.

Cathédrale St-Pierre ℛ̄ The old town, **Vieille Ville,** on the Left Bank, is dominated by the cathedral, built in the 12th and 13th centuries and partially reconstructed in the 15th century. In 1536, the people of Geneva gathered in the cloister of St-Pierre's and voted to make the cathedral Protestant. The church has a modern organ with 6,000 pipes. The northern tower was reconstructed at the end of the 19th century. If you don't mind the 145 steps, you can climb to the top of the north tower for a panoramic view.

To enter the St-Pierre archaeological site, called **Site Archéologique de St-Pierre,** go through the entrance in the Cour St-Pierre, at the right corner of the cathedral steps. The underground passage extends under the present cathedral and the High Gothic (early 15th-century) **Chapelle des Macchabées,** which adjoins the church's southwestern corner. The chapel was restored during World War II, after having been used as a storage room following the Reformation. Excavations have revealed baptisteries, a crypt, the foundations of several cathedrals, the bishop's palace, 4th-century mosaics, and sculptures and geological strata.

Cour St-Pierre. ℂ **022/311-75-75.** Admission 3SF ($1.90). Cathedral, tower, and excavations open Jun–Sept daily 9am–7pm; Oct–May Mon–Sat 10am–noon and 2–5pm, Sun 11:30am–12:30pm and 1:30–5pm.

Maison Tavel ℛ̄ Built in 1303 and partially reconstructed after a fire in 1334, this is the city's oldest house and one of its newest museums. The museum exhibits historical collections from Geneva dating from the Middle Ages to the mid-19th century. The Magnin relief in the attic is outstanding, as is the copper-and-zinc model of 1850s Geneva. Objects of daily use are displayed in the old living quarters.

6 rue du Puits-St-Pierre. ℂ **022/310-29-00.** Free admission. Tues–Sun 10am–5pm. Bus: 3, 5 or 17.

Musée Ariana ℛ̄ℛ̄ This is one of the top porcelain, glass, and pottery museums of Europe. To the west of the Palais des Nations, this Italian Renaissance building was constructed by Gustave Revilliod, the 19th-century Genevese patron who began the collection. Here you'll see Sèvres, Delft faïence, and Meissen porcelain, as well as pieces from Japan and China. It's also the headquarters of the International Academy of Ceramics.

10 av. de la Paix. ℂ **022/418-54-50.** Free admission, but 5SF ($3.15) for special exhibits. Wed–Mon 10am–5pm. Bus: 8 or F.

Musée d'Art et d'Histoire (Museum of Art and History) ℛ̄ℛ̄ Geneva's most important museum is between boulevard Jacques-Dalcroze and boulevard Helvétique. It virtually presents the story of civilization from prehistoric times up to the present. Displays include prehistoric relics, Greek vases, medieval stained glass, 12th-century armor, Swiss timepieces, and Flemish and Italian paintings. The Etruscan pottery and medieval furniture are quite impressive. A 1444 altarpiece by Konrad Witz depicts the "miraculous" draught of fishes. Many galleries also contain works by such artists as Rodin, Renoir, Le Corbusier, Picasso, Chagall, Corot, Monet, and Pissarro.

2 rue Charles-Galland. ℂ **022/418-26-00.** Free admission. Tues–Sun 10am–5pm. Bus: 2, 3, 5, 7, 12, or 16.

Musée de l'Horlogerie (Watch Museum) This town house chronicles the history of watches and clocks from the 16th century. It displays everything from sand timers to sundials, though most of the exhibits are concerned with Geneva's

> **Fun Fact The Red Cross Flag**
>
> When Henry Dunant founded the Red Cross in Geneva in 1863, he needed a recognizable symbol to suggest neutrality. The Swiss flag (a white cross on a red field), with the colors reversed, ended up providing the perfect symbol for one of the world's greatest humanitarian movements.

watches, usually from the 17th and 18th centuries. The enameled watches of the 19th century are particularly intriguing (many play chimes when you open them).

15 route de Malagnou. ℂ 022/418-64-70. Free admission. Wed–Mon 10am–5pm. Bus: 6 or C. Tram: 12.

Musée International de la Croix Rouge et du Croissant-Rouge (International Red Cross and Red Crescent Museum) ⋆ Here you can experience the legendary past of the Red Cross in the city where it started; it's across from the visitors' entrance to the European headquarters of the United Nations. The dramatic story from 1863 to the present is revealed through displays of rare documents and photographs, films, multiscreen slide shows, and cycloramas. You're taken from the battlefields of Europe to the plains of Africa to see the Red Cross in action.

17 av. de la Paix. ℂ 022/748-95-11. Admission 10SF ($6) adults, 5SF ($3.15) seniors, students, and children. Wed–Mon 10am–5pm. Bus: 18, F, V, or Z.

Palais des Nations ⋆ Surrounded by ancient trees and modern monuments, these buildings comprise the second-largest complex in Europe after Versailles. Until 1936, the League of Nations met at the Palais Wilson, when the League's headquarters were transferred to the Palais des Nations. The international organization continued minor activities through the war years until it was dissolved in 1946, just as the newly created United Nations met in San Francisco. Today the Palais des Nations is the headquarters of the United Nations in Europe, with a modern wing added in 1973.

Inside are a **philatelic museum** and the **League of Nations Museum,** though the building itself is the most interesting attraction. Daily tours leave from the visitors' entrance at 14 av. de la Paix, opposite the Red Cross building. For information, contact the **Visitors' Service,** United Nations Office, 14 av. de la Paix (ℂ **022/907-45-60**).

Parc de l'Ariana, 14 av. de la Paix. ℂ 022/907-48-96. Admission 8.50SF ($5) adults, 6.50SF ($4.05) students, 4SF ($2.50) children under 6. June–Aug daily 9am–6pm; Sept–Oct daily 10am–noon and 2–4pm; Nov–May Mon–Fri 10am–noon and 2–4pm. Bus: 5, 8, 18, F, V, or 2.

ORGANIZED TOURS

A 2-hour city tour is operated daily by **Key Tours S.A.,** 7 rue des Alpes, square du Mont-Blanc (ℂ **022/731-41-40**). The tour starts from the Gare Routière, the bus station at place Dorcière, near the Key Tours office. From November to March, a tour is offered only once a day at 2pm; the rest of the year, two tours leave daily, at 10am and 2pm. A bus will drive you through the city to see the monuments, landmarks, and lake promenades. In the Old Town, you can take a walk down to the Bastions Park to the Reformation Wall. After an English-language tour through the International Center—where you'll be shown the headquarters of the International Red Cross—the bus returns to its starting place. Adults pay 35SF ($22), children 4 to 12 accompanied by an adult are 18SF ($11), and children 3 and under go free.

(*Moments*) **Exploring Geneva's Parks & Gardens**

If you walk along the quays, heading north as if to Lausanne, you'll come to some of the lushest parks in Geneva. **Parc Mon-Repos** is off avenue de France and **La Perle du Lac** lies off rue de Lausanne. Directly to the right is the **Jardin Botanique (Botanical Garden),** opened in 1902. It has an alpine garden, a little zoo, greenhouses, and exhibitions; you can visit it free daily from October to April 9:30am to 5pm and from May to September 8am to 7:30pm.

Back at lakeside, you can take a boat to the other bank, getting off at quai Gustave-Ador. From here you can explore two more lakeside parks—**Parc la Grange,** which has the most extravagant rose garden in Switzerland (especially in June), and, next to it, **Parc des Eaux-Vives.**

When you leave the Botanical Garden on the Left Bank, you can head west, along avenue de la Paix, about a mile north from pont du Mont-Blanc, to the Palais des Nations in **Parc de l'Ariana.**

THE SHOPPING SCENE

As one might suspect, watches, knives, cheese, and chocolate are among Geneva's best buys. Check prices carefully; many Swiss watches are currently cheaper in the United States than in Switzerland. Swiss army knives are still a good deal, and as for chocolate, well, it's incomparable and just not the same when you buy it in another country.

Geneva's Left Bank shopping area is along the exclusive **rue du Rhône** and adjacent streets. Here you'll find shop after shop of designer fashions and expensive watches. Along the winding streets of the **Old City** you can explore antiques stores and galleries. For Swiss army knives and watches, stroll along the pedestrians-only **rue du Mont-Blanc** on the Right Bank. You'll find an endless assortment of watches, knives, and other souvenirs, all priced similarly.

Colorful **outdoor markets,** overflowing with flowers and fruit, take place several times a week at places Rive, Coutance, Carouge, and others. A **flea market** is held every Wednesday and Saturday on the Plaine de Plainpalais; markets for books take place on place de la Madeleine on most days during summer.

SELECT SHOPS   Virtually all the inventory at **Antiquorum,** 2 rue du Mont-Blanc (© **022/738-02-22;** bus: 1), consists of antique jewelry and antique watches—a sure attraction for a city that derives so much of its income from selling timepieces. The array includes some of the world's most historically important watches.

The aroma of chocolate from the **Confiserie Rohr,** 3 place du Molard (© **022/311-63-03;** bus: 9, 10, or 12), practically pulls you in off the street. You'll find chocolate-covered truffles, "gold" bars with hazelnuts, and *poubelles au chocolat* (chocolate "garbage pails"). There's another branch at 42 rue du Rhône (© **022/311-68-76;** bus: 2, 9, or 22).

On place du Molard, **Bon Genie,** 34 rue du Marché (© **022/818-11-11;** tram: 12), is a department store selling high-fashion women's clothing and a limited selection of men's. Its windows display art objects from local museums alongside designer clothes. Geneva's largest department store, **Globus & Grand Passage,** 48 rue du Rhône (© **022/319-50-50;** bus: 2, 9, or 22), has just about everything: a travel bureau, an agency selling theater tickets, a hairdresser, a newsstand, a handful of boutiques, a restaurant, and a sandwich shop. **Bruno Magli,** 47 rue du Rhône ((C) **022/311-53-77;** bus: 2, 9, or 22), is one of Geneva's best-stocked shoe stores, with an elegant variety of Italian shoes (mainly women's), purses, and accessories.

Opposite pont du Mont-Blanc, the chrome-and-crystal **Bucherer,** 45 rue du Rhône ((C) **022/319-62-66;** bus: 2, 9, or 22), sells expensive watches and diamonds. The store offers such name brands as Rolex, Piaget, Baume & Mercier, Tissot, Rado, and Swatch. The third floor is filled with relatively inexpensive watches, cuckoo clocks, music boxes, embroideries, souvenirs, porcelain pillboxes, and other gift items.

Established over a century ago, **Leinen Langenthal,** 13 rue du Rhône ((C) **022/310-65-10;** bus: 2, 9, or 22), boasts an enviable reputation for good-quality merchandise and a showroom on the city's most prestigious shopping street, across from the Union des Banques Suisses. The merchandise includes napery, towels, bed linens, and "table suites," some of it embroidered by hand in the Swiss lace center of St-Gallen.

At the corner of rue de la Fontaine, **Jouets Weber,** 12 rue de la Croix-d'Or ((C) **022/310-42-55;** bus: 2 or 12), is the best toy store in the city. It has all kinds of children's toys, from slide shows to cartoon characters, as well as dolls and sports equipment.

GENEVA AFTER DARK

For a preview of events at the time of your visit, pick up a copy of the monthly "List of Events" issued by the tourist office.

THE PERFORMING ARTS

Modeled on Paris's Opéra Garnier, the **Grand Théâtre de Genève,** Place Neuve ((C) **022/418-31-30;** bus: 12), was opened in 1879, and is often included in lists of the world's ten best opera houses. It burned down in 1951 and was subsequently rebuilt in the same style, except for the modern auditorium. From September to July, it presents operas, ballets, recitals, and chamber music concerts. Tickets are 25 to 150SF ($16 to $94) for opera, 20 to 85SF ($13 to $53) for ballet.

The 1,866-seat **Victoria Hall,** 14 rue du Général-Dufour, is home to the celebrated **Orchestre de la Suisse Romande** ((C) **022/32881-21;** bus: 12). Tickets are 16 to 70SF ($10 to $44).

THE CLUB & MUSIC SCENE

In the suburb of Carouges, **Au Chat Noir,** 13 rue Vautier, Carouges ((C) **022/ 343-49-93;** tram: 12 from Place Bel-Air), is the current hot spot in town, a venue for funk, rock, salsa, jazz, and some good old New Orleans blues. It's crowded on weekends but the club will take reservations. Concerts are presented nightly at either 9 or 10pm. The club itself is open from Tuesday to Thursday 6pm to 4am, Friday 6pm to 5am, Saturday 9pm to 5am, and Sunday 9am to 4am. After a few drinks, you begin to fear that the car suspended from the ceiling might fall in on you. Cover is 10 to 15SF ($6 to $9).

The fun, unpretentious **Arthur's Club,** Centre I.C.C., Rte. des Près-Bois 20 ((C) **022/791-77-00;** tram to Gare Genève-Cointrin), near the Geneva airport, is committed to preserving a healthy balance of clients between the ages of 18 and 45. Inside, each of the 10 different bars manages to attract a mini-subculture all its own, so regardless of your age or preferences, you'll eventually find something or someone that appeals to you. On busy nights, expect as many as 2,500 patrons, many of whom dance, dance, dance, crammed inside. It's open Friday and Saturday 10pm to 5am. Cover is 20 to 25SF ($13 to $16) and includes the first drink.

Griffin's Club, 36 bd. Helvétique (© 022/735-12-18; bus 26), is the choicest club in Geneva. Technically, it's private—you may or may not get in, depending on the mood of the management at the time of your visit. On Friday and Saturday, precedence is usually given to members. Jackets are required for men. The restaurant serves main courses priced at 35 to 60SF ($22 to $38) nightly from 8pm till 3:30am. The disco opens at 11pm and closes between 5 and 6am, depending on the night of the week. There's no cover.

The private **Club 58,** 15 Glacis de Rive (© 022/735-15-15; bus: 26), allows nonmembers to enter, although men are required to wear jackets. It's mainly a disco, but there's an attached restaurant. Occasionally the club presents some top names in show business. It opens daily at 10pm; the restaurant opens at 8pm. Drinks in the club cost 25SF ($17). Cover is 15 to 20SF ($9 to $13). **L'Interdit,** Quai du Seujet 18 (© 022/738-90-91; bus: 12), isn't as difficult to get into as other clubs in Geneva. It's hip, heterosexual, and worthy of a visit if you want to meet attractive strangers of the opposite sex. There's also a restaurant here, but the main appeal is the dancing, which starts every night at 10pm and lasts until around 5am. Cover is 20SF ($13), including first drink.

Within its genre, **Velvet,** 7 rue de Jeu-de-l'Arc (© 022/735-00-00; bus: 26), is a safe and well-recommended nightclub, but it isn't for the timid, and unless you're an unusually brazen woman, or firmly attached to an attentive male escort, it's more appropriate as a nighttime venue for (temporarily) unattached men. It's very heterosexual, very permissive, and loaded with working women waiting for a male visitor to buy them a drink of, perhaps, champagne. In most instances, its tawdrier aspects are rather artfully concealed, although that's a tall order for a venue where, beginning around 11pm, as many as 32 international beauties, many of them topless, begin strutting their stuff in a nonstop, informally choreographed *spectacle* that continues, on and off, till around 5am. There's a restaurant and a disco on the premises. It's open nightly from 9pm to 5am. On Sunday, the restaurant is closed, but not the cabaret and bar. Drinks begin at 19SF ($12), but usually average around 24SF ($15) each. There's no cover from Sunday to Thursday; cover is 10SF ($6) Friday and Saturday.

BARS

Sheathed in mahogany, brass, and dark-green upholstery, the fashionable **Bar des Bergues,** in the Hôtel des Bergues, 33 quai des Bergues (© 022/908-70-00; bus: 7), is decorated with a series of late 19th-century menus from the Cercle des Arts et des Lettres. Though most people come just for a drink or two, the place also serves lunches and platters from the hotel's top-notch kitchen. Ask the barman for the list of daily specials. Beginning in the early evening, there's an international array of pianists.

Though this is technically the aperitif bar for the elegant Restaurant Le Gentilhomme, many visitors consider Le Jardin, in the Hôtel Richemond, Jardin Brunswick (© 022/715-77-20; bus: 1 or 9), an attractive and stylish option in its own right. It attracts a chic crowd, ranging from U.S.-based beneficiaries of corporate mergers to Zurich bankers to glamorous women in $50,000 furs.

GAY GENEVA

Many lesbian groups meet at the **Centre Femmes Nathalie Barney (Le Maison),** 30 av. Peshier (© 022/797-27-14; tram: 12), in the Champel district.

It's the best-organized outlet for gay women in French-speaking Switzerland and is named for Nathalie Barney, a well-known lesbian liberationist (from Dayton, Ohio) who ran a salon in Paris at the turn of the 19th century. Different social and political gatherings take place several nights a week. The center maintains a restaurant open for group dinners only on designated nights of the week and a women's bar open only Friday and Saturday nights.

In the district of Servette, **Dialogai,** 57 av. de Wendt (© 022/906-40-40; bus: 12), provides multilingual information and advice. On the basement-level premises are a library, a cafe and bar, and meeting rooms for Wednesday-night dinners and Saturday-night dancing parties. The organization publishes a list—free to anyone who asks—of the gay bars of Geneva and French-speaking Switzerland, and is the best conduit to Geneva's male homosexual network.

Le Loft and **Le Night Fever,** 20 quai du Seujet (© 022/738-28-28; bus: 12), are set within the same building and managed by the same team. These two gay bars offer a convivial venue for drinking and dancing. Shows begin every night at 11pm. The place functions as a cafe throughout the day, serving croissants and café au lait to office workers as early as 6am, but its most amusing times are nightly beginning around 10pm and lasting till around 3am.

DAY TRIPS FROM GENEVA

MONT SALÈVE 🏔 The limestone ridge of Mont Salève (House Mountain) is 6 kilometers (4 miles) south of Geneva in France, so you'll need your passport. Its peak is at 1,200 meters (4,000 ft.). If you have a car, you can take a road that goes up the mountain; it's also popular with rock climbers. Bus 8 will take you to Veyrier, on the French border, where there's a passport and Customs control. A 6-minute cable-car ride will carry you to a height of 1,140 meters (3,750 ft.) on Mont Salève. From the top you'll have a panoramic sweep of the Valley of the Arve, with Geneva and Mont Blanc in the background.

MONT BLANC & CHAMONIX 🏔🏔🏔 We highly recommend a Mont Blanc excursion; an all-day trip to Chamonix, France, by bus; and a cable-car ride to the 3,850-meter (12,610-ft.) summit of the Aiguille du Midi. The tour leaves Geneva at 8am and returns at 6pm daily. Buses leave from Gare Routière, and you must take your passport.

Other climbs on this tour are Vallée Blanche by télécabin, an extension of the Aiguille du Midi climb, from April to October; to Mer de Glâce via electric rack railway to the edge of the glacier, from which you may descend to the ice grotto (the climb isn't available in winter); and to Le Brevent, an ascent by cable car to a rocky belvedere at 2,400 meters (7,900 ft.), facing the Mont Blanc range.

An English-speaking guide will accompany your bus tour. **Key Tours S.A.,** 7 rue des Alpes (place du Mont-Blanc), Case Postale 1745, CH-1211 Genève (© 022/731-41-40), require a minimum of eight people per trip. Tours begin at 199SF ($124) adults and 99SF ($62) children.

LAKE GENEVA CRUISES 🏔🏔🏔 Two companies offer cruises on Lac Léman. The smaller one, **Mouettes Genevoises Navigation,** 8 quai du Mont-Blanc (© 022/732-29-44), specializes in small-scale boats carrying only about 100 passengers. Each features some kind of guided (pre-recorded) commentary, in French and English. An easy promenade that surveys the landscapes and bird life along the uppermost regions of the Rhône draining the lake is the company's "Tour du Rhône" (Rhône River Tour). The trip originates at a point adjacent to Geneva's pont de l'Ile and travels downstream for about 15 kilometers (9 miles) to the Barrage de Verbois (Verbois Dam) and back. From April to October, departures are daily at 2:15pm and Wednesday, Thursday, Saturday, and Sunday at 10am. It costs 22SF ($14) adults and 15SF ($9) children 4 to 12; free for children under 4. The same company also offers 1¼-hour tours (four times a day) and 2-hour tours (twice a day) out onto the lake. The longer tour includes a prerecorded commentary on the celebrity residences and ecology of the lake. It's 12SF ($8) for the shorter tour and 20SF ($13) for the longer tour; no stops are made en route.

Bateaux de la Mouette's largest competitor, **CGN (Compagnie General de Navigation),** quai du Mont-Blanc (© **022/312-52-23**), offers roughly equivalent tours, from May to September, that last an hour and depart four to six times a day from the company's piers along the quai du Mont-Blanc. Known as "Les Belles Rives Genevoises," they charge 12SF ($8) adults and 6SF ($3.75) children 6 to 16 (free for children under 6). Tours include pre-recorded commentaries and are about as long in duration as many short-term visitors to the city really want.

2 Bern & the Berner Oberland

Dating from the 12th century, Bern is one of the loveliest and oldest cities in Europe. Since much of its medieval architecture has remained untouched, the United Nations declared it a world landmark in 1983. As the capital of Switzerland, it's also a city of diplomats and the site of many international organizations and meetings.

Bern is a convenient center for exploring the lakes and peaks of the Berner Oberland—a vast recreation area only minutes from the capital, sprawling between the Reuss River and Lake Geneva. It's an important center for winter sports, one of the best-equipped areas for downhill skiers, and a challenging place for hikers and mountain climbers. The 4,158-meter (13,642-ft.) Jungfrau and the 4,274-meter (14,022-ft.) Finsteraarhorn are the highest alpine peaks. The canton of Bern, encompassing most of the area, is Switzerland's second largest, and contains 260 square kilometers (100 sq. miles) of glaciers.

The best center for exploring the Berner Oberland is Interlaken, a popular summer resort. Summer and winter playgrounds are at Gstaad, Grindelwald, Kandersteg, and Mürren. You can ski in the mountains in winter, and surf, sail, and water-ski on Lake Thun in summer.

BERN

The modern mingles harmoniously with the old in this charming city. Contemporary buildings are discreetly designed to blend in with the historic environment. The city stands on a thumb of land that's bordered on three sides by the Aare River, and several bridges connect the old part of the city with the newer sections.

Market days in Bern are Tuesday and Saturday, when people from the outlying areas come to town to sell their produce and wares. If you're fortunate enough to arrive on the fourth Monday of November, you'll witness the centuries-old Zwiebelmarkt (Onion Market). This is the city's last big event before the onset of winter, as residents traditionally stock up on onions in anticipation of the first snows.

ESSENTIALS

GETTING THERE By Plane The **Bern-Belp Airport** (© **031/960-21-11**) is 10 kilometers (6 miles) south of the city in Belpmoos. International flights arrive from London, Paris, and Nice, but transatlantic jets are not able to land here. Fortunately, it's a short hop to Bern from the international airports in Zurich and Geneva.

Taxis are about 45SF ($28) to the city center, so it's better to take the shuttle bus that runs between the airport and the Bahnhof (train station), costing 14SF ($9) one way.

By Train   Bern has direct connections to France, Italy, Germany, and the Benelux countries, even Scandinavia and Spain. The superfast TGV train connects Paris with Bern (trip time: 4½ hours). Bern also lies on major Swiss rail links, particularly those connecting Geneva and Zurich (90 minutes).

The **Bahnhof,** on Bahnhofplatz, is in the center of town near all the major hotels. If your luggage is light, you can walk to your hotel; otherwise, take one of the taxis waiting outside the station. For **information** about tickets and train schedules for the Swiss Federal Railways, call ℂ **0900/300-300.**

VISITOR INFORMATION   Tourist Office   The **Bern Tourist Office,** in the Bahnhof, on Bahnhofplatz (ℂ **031/328-12-12;** www.berntourism.ch), is open from June to September, daily 9am to 8:30pm; from October to May, Monday to Saturday 9am to 6:30pm and Sunday 10am to 5pm. If you need help finding a hotel room, the tourist office can make a reservation for you.

Websites   Besides the Bern Tourist Office noted above, check under Geneva "Visitor Information" for other Swiss sites. Get the lowdown on skiing the high country at **www.goski.com/switz.htm.** This site will help you find a resort, tell you the best time to go, and keep you posted about conditions.

GETTING AROUND   By Bus & Tram   The public transportation system, the **Stadtische Verkehrs-betriebe (SVB),** is a reliable 77-kilometer (48-mile) network of buses and trams. Before you board, purchase a ticket from the self-service automatic machines at each stop (conductors don't sell tickets). If you're caught traveling without one, you'll be fined 50SF ($31). A short-range ticket (six stations) costs 1.50SF (95¢); a regular ticket, valid for 45 minutes one-way only, is 2.40SF ($1.50).

By Taxi   You can catch a taxi at the public cab stands, or you can call a dispatcher. Try **Nova Taxi** at ℂ **031/301-11-11.** The meter registers as 6.50SF ($4.05) when you get in, then goes up to 3.10SF ($1.95) per kilometer. After 8pm and until 6am daily, the per kilometer rate rises to 3.50SF ($2.20).

By Car   Don't try to drive in the city; use your car for exploring the environs. Car-rental companies in Bern include **Hertz,** Casinoplatz at Kochergasse 1 (ℂ **031/318-21-60**), and **Avis,** Wabernstrasse 41 (ℂ **031/372-13-13**).

By Bicycle   The Altstadt is compressed into such a small area that it's better to cover it on foot rather than on a bike. Bicycles aren't allowed on the many pedestrians-only streets anyway. However, in Greater Bern and its environs there

---

⸤Value⸥ One-day Tickets

To save time, and possibly money, you can purchase a **1-day ticket** for 7.50SF ($4.70), entitling you to unlimited travel on the SVB network. Just get the ticket stamped at the automatic machine before you begin your first trip. One-day tickets are available at the ticket offices at Bubenbergplatz 5 and in the underpass of the Bahnhof, as well as at other outlets in the city.

are 400 kilometers (248 miles) of cycling paths. These are marked on a special cycling map available at the tourist office (see above). Bicycle lanes are indicated by yellow on parts of the road network. The point of departure for most official cycling routes is Bundesplatz (Parliament Square). Special red signs will guide you through a wide variety of landscapes. For 26SF ($16) per day, you can rent bicycles at the SBB Railway Station, Bahnhofplatz (© 0900/300-300). Call the day before for a reservation.

WHERE TO STAY
Very Expensive
Hotel Schweizerhof 🏩🏩🏩   Built in 1859, this central hotel managed by the Gauer family is popular with diplomats and remains the grandest hotel in the Swiss capital. It contains many antiques and some of the best decorative art in Bern. Some rooms are quite contemporary, others more antique; some are air-conditioned. The bathrooms are luxurious.

Bahnhofplatz 11, CH-3001 Bern. © **031/326-80-80.** Fax 031/326-80-90. www.schweizerhof-bern.ch. 84 units. 290–385SF ($181–$241) double; from 600SF ($375) suite. AE, DC, MC, V. Parking 26SF ($16). Tram: 3, 9, or 12. **Amenities:** 2 elegant restaurants (see Jack's Brasserie, "Where to Dine," below), formal bar. *In room:* A/C, TV, minibar, hair dryer, robes.

Expensive
Belle Epoque 🏩🏩   Though not as swanky as the Schweizerhof, this reno-vated medieval home in Bern's historic core is a delight. One of the highlights is a bar outfitted like an art and antiques gallery, lined with late 19th- and early 20th-century oil paintings and filled with Jugendstil (German Art Nouveau) furnishings and comfortable settees. Many bathrooms have both tubs and show-ers, and one floor is reserved for nonsmokers. A tiny restaurant is used mainly for breakfast, although it's often possible to order light meals at other times.

Gerechtigkeitsgasse 18, CH-3001 Bern. © **031/311-43-36.** Fax 031/311-39-36. www.belle-epoque.ch. 17 units. 220–285SF ($138–$178) double; 300–350SF ($188–$219) suite. AE, DC, MC, V. Bus: 12. **Amenities:** Breakfast-only restaurant, charming bar dedicated to Toulouse-Lautrec. *In room:* TV, minibar.

Innere Enge 🏩   When you tire of impersonal bandboxes, head for this small, choice hotel just outside the city center. The light, spacious, and airy rooms have style and character, with traditional (if not antique) beds and roomy bath-rooms, sometimes with a tub/shower combination. Many have a view of the Bernese Alps.

Engestrasse 54, CH-3012 Bern. © **031/309-61-11.** Fax 301/309-61-12. www.zghotel.ch. 26 units. 260–390SF ($163–$244) double; from 410SF ($256) suite. Rates include continental breakfast. AE, DC, MC, V. Free parking. Bus: 21 from the rail station. **Amenities:** Restaurant (Swiss regional and international), Louis Arm-strong Bar (jazz acts). *In room:* TV, minibar.

Moderate
Hotel Ambassador   This nine-story hotel in a neighborhood of older houses with red-tile roofs is not far from the train station and easily reached by tram. Rooms tend to be smallish and furnished somewhat impersonally, but they're well maintained, each with a tidy bathroom containing a shower stall. Many have a view of the Bundeshaus.

Seftigenstrasse 99, CH-3007 Bern. © **031/371-41-11.** Fax 031/371-41-17. 97 units. 178–198SF ($111–$124) double. AE, DC, MC, V. Free parking. Tram: 9. **Amenities:** Restaurant Pavilion Café, Japanese Teppan Restaurant; 24-hour indoor pool; sauna; solarium. *In room:* TV, minibar.

Hotel Krebs   This winning three-star hotel near the train station shares its ground floor with a store. Rooms are rather spartan but occasionally sunny, and

Bern

SWITZERLAND
★ Bern

ATTRACTIONS ●

Bärengraben (Bear Pits) **14**
Cathedral of St. Vincent **12**
Church of the Holy Ghost **4**
Kunstmuseum **8**
Parliament **5**
Prison Gate **6**
Zytgloggeturm **11**

ACCOMMODATIONS ■

Belle Epoque **13**
Goldener Schlüssel **10**
Hotel Ambassador **2**
Hotel Krebs **7**
Hotel Schweizerhof **3**
Innere Enge **1**
Jardin **9**

✝ Church
ⓘ Information
— Railway

wood paneling adds more warmth. Some rooms can be converted for families. The singles, without bathroom, are among the more reasonably priced in the area. Private bathrooms are small and a little short of shelf space; those in the hall are tidily kept.

Genfergasse 8, CH-3011 Bern. ℂ **031/311-49-42.** Fax 031/311-10-35. hotelkrebs@thenet.ch. 46 units, 41 with bathroom (shower only). 130SF ($81) double without bathroom, 163–178SF ($102–$111) double with bathroom. Rates include buffet breakfast. AE, DC, MC, V. Tram: 3 or 9. **Amenities:** Breakfast room, cafe; laundry. *In room:* TV, Internet access.

Inexpensive
Goldener Schlüssel   In the heart of Altstadt, opening onto Rathausgasse, this little inn dates from the 13th century, when it was used as a stable. Rooms are beautifully maintained, and they're comfortably furnished but a little shopworn. The bathrooms are extremely small. There's more atmosphere here than luxury. As it's fairly busy on the street outside, ask for a rear room if you want less noise. If you're a bargain hunter, request a room without bathroom—the hallway plumbing is adequate.

Rathausgasse 72, CH-3011 Bern. ℂ **031/311-02-16.** Fax 031/311-56-88. www.goldener-schluessel.ch. 29 units, 21 with bathroom. 114SF ($71) double without bathroom, 145SF ($91) double with bathroom; 150SF ($94) triple without bathroom, 185SF ($116) triple with bathroom. Rates include continental breakfast. AE, MC, V. Free parking. Bus: 12. Tram: 9. **Amenities:** Restaurant (see "Where to Dine," below), beer tavern. *In room:* TV.

Jardin   Set above the Old Town, this is a good choice for those who want a clean, well-maintained room at a decent price for the night, but can do without a lot of frills. In 1985, this building just north of the city center was converted from a restaurant and apartment building into a modern and warmly appealing hotel. Rooms are larger than virtually any others in their price range. The hotel is run by identical twins Andy and Daniel Balz, whose similarities may confuse you; one or the other is almost always available to help guests. Joggers and nature lovers appreciate the verdant areas across the street; they're part of the land surrounding Bern's largest military academy.

Militarstrasse 38, CH-3014 Bern. ℂ **031/333-01-17.** Fax 031/333-09-43. 17 units. 135SF ($84) double; 205SF ($128) triple. Rates include breakfast. AE, DC, MC, V. Free parking. Tram: 9 to Breitenrainplatz. **Amenities:** Restaurant (see "Where to Dine," below). *In room:* TV.

WHERE TO DINE
Expensive
Della Casa 🏵 CONTINENTAL   From under an arcade, you enter a low-ceilinged paneled room that's often crowded with chattering diners. For those eager to follow the latest political trends and opinions, an inner room has all the day's newspapers—indeed, the place has been called Switzerland's "unofficial Parliament headquarters." Upstairs is a quieter, somewhat more formal dining room. The menu features continental and Italian dishes. Two of our favorites are the ravioli maison and the fried zucchini; a justifiably popular meat specialty is filet mignon à la bordelaise with Creole rice. More typical, however, is the calf's heart with onions, tomatoes, and potatoes with an herbed vinaigrette.

Schauplatzgasse 16. ℂ **031/311-21-42.** Reservations recommended. Main courses 25–40SF ($16–$25). Mon–Fri 11am–2pm and 6–9:30pm; Sat 9:30am–3pm. Upstairs level closed in July (downstairs dining room remains open). Tram: 3, 5, or 9.

Jack's Brasserie (Stadt Restaurant) 🏵 FRENCH/CONTINENTAL   Although this restaurant is the less formal eatery within the Schweizerhof, it's perfectly acceptable as the site for an important meal or even a celebratory dinner. Nostalgically outfitted in a style that evokes a Lyonnais bistro, it bustles in a way that's chic, convivial, and matter-of-fact, all at the same time. The best dishes on the menu include the kind of Wiener schnitzels that hang over the sides of the plate, a succulent version of sole meunière and sea bass, veal head vinaigrette for real regional flavor, tender pepper steaks, and smaller platters piled high with salads, risottos, and succulent pastas.

In the Hotel Schweizerhof, Bahnhofplatz 11. ℭ 031/311-45-01. Reservations recommended. Main courses 25–60SF ($16–$38); set-price menu 70SF ($44). AE, DC, MC, V. Daily 11:30am–2pm and 6:30–10:30pm. Limited menu daily 1:45–6:15pm. Tram: 3, 9, or 12.

Räblus 🍸 FRENCH/SWISS REGIONAL   A popular haunt, this 2-century-old restaurant lies near the landmark Clock Tower. It has a ground-floor bar where you can stop for an aperitif before proceeding up to the dining room. The kitchen prepares a French cuisine with a definite Swiss/German influence. Try our favorites such as saffron-flavored sole, a splendid potpourri of seafood flavored with Pernod, or citrus-flavored veal.

Zeughausgasse 3. ℭ 031/311-59-08. Reservations required. Main courses 16–40SF ($10–$25); 3-course fixed-price menus 30–50SF ($19–$31). AE, DC, MC, V. Mon–Wed 6pm–1:30am; Thurs 6pm–2:30am; Fri–Sat 6pm–3:30am. Tram: 3 or 9.

Moderate

Goldener Schlüssel 🍸 SWISS   You'll relish both the food and the bustling atmosphere at this very Swiss restaurant. Serving wholesome food in ample portions, the restaurant is on the street level of a budget-priced hotel of the same name. Specialties include a well-flavored *mignon d'agneau au poivre vert* (tenderloin of lamb with green-pepper sauce and corn croquettes), *schweinbratwurst mit zwiebelsauce* (butter-fried sausage with onion sauce), and rösti.

Rathausgasse 72. ℭ 031/311-02-16. Reservations recommended. Main courses 25–35SF ($16–$22); fixed-price lunch 16.80–21.80SF ($11–$14). AE, MC, V. Sun–Thurs 7am–11:30pm; Fri–Sat 7am–12:30am. Bus: 12. Tram: 9.

Restaurant Harmonie 🍸 SWISS/BERNESE   Located at the corner of Münstergasse a few blocks from Parliament, this Art Nouveau local favorite evokes 1890s Paris with its grimy overlay. It has been in the hands of the Gyger family since 1915. Service is efficient, and tables are spaced far enough apart to allow a feeling of privacy. There are two dining rooms and a handful of sidewalk tables set beneath ivy-clad trellises. You get the same regional specialties that Grandmother Gyger might have served between the wars: pork sausage with rösti, tripe with tomatoes, and cheese fondues. In the unlikely event that you're not ravenously hungry, the simple platter of cooked ham might be consumed with pickles, pickled onions, and sliced bread.

Hotelgasse 3. ℭ 031/313-11-41. Reservations recommended. Main courses 18–40SF ($11–$25). MC, V. Mon–Sat 11am–3pm and 6–11:30pm. Closed mid-July to mid-Aug. Tram: 9.

Inexpensive

Jardin *Value* INTERNATIONAL   This stately looking restaurant is set in the hotel of the same name. The restaurant flourished long before the hotel was established in 1985. Part of its appeal derives from its ability to be as formal or informal as you want; consequently, it serves snacks such as cheese croquettes to accompany your foaming mugfuls of beer, as well as more substantial grilled steaks, minced Zürich-style veal with rösti potatoes, and schnitzels of pork with braised cabbage. Most dishes are inexpensively priced, and set menus are good deals in dining.

Militärstrasse 38. ⓒ 031/333-01-17. Reservations recommended. Main courses 12–45SF ($8–$28); set price menu 15SF ($9). AE, DC, MC, V. Mon–Sat 11am–2pm and 5–10pm. Tram: 9 to Breitenrainplatz.

Ratskeller SWISS   There is no more typical Bernese restaurant than this local favorite, serving ample portions of good, rib-sticking food. Specialties include rack of lamb à la diable for two, an omelet soufflé aux fruits, veal kidneys Robert, and côte de beau in butter sauce. Your best bet is the *egli* (tiny filet of perch) with white sauce on a bed of spinach. Prized by gourmets, this tiny fish is native to the lakes around Bern. Most dishes are priced at the lower end of the scale.

Gerechtigkeitsgasse 81. ⓒ 031/311-17-71. Reservations recommended. Main courses 15–45SF ($9–$28); fixed-price lunch 18SF ($11). AE, DC, MC, V. Daily 11:30am–2pm and 6–10pm. Tram: 9.

SEEING THE SIGHTS

The **Zutgloggeturm (Clock Tower)** 𝒢, on Kramgasse, was built in the 12th century and restored in the 16th. Four minutes before every hour, crowds gather for the world's oldest (since 1530) and biggest horological puppet show: Mechanical bears, jesters, and emperors put on an animated performance. The tower marked the west gate of Bern until 1250.

The **Bärengraben (Bear Pits)** 𝒢, on the opposite side of the river, is a deep moon-shaped den where bears, Bern's mascots, have been kept since 1480. According to legend, when the duke of Zähringen established the town in 1191, he sent his hunters into the encircling woods, which were full of wild game. The duke promised to name the city after the first animal slain, which was a Bär (bear). Since then the town has been known as Bärn or Bern. Today, the bears are beloved, pampered, and fed by residents and visitors (carrots are most appreciated). The **Nydegg Bridge (Nydeggbrücke)** was built over one of the gorges of the Aare River; its central stone arch has a span of 55 meters (180 ft.) and affords a sweeping view of the city from its center. Below the Bear Pits, you can visit the **Rosengarten (Rose Gardens),** from which there's a much-photographed view of the medieval sector and the river.

Cathedral of St. Vincent 𝒢   The Münster is one of Switzerland's newer Gothic churches; although dating from 1421, the belfry was completed only in 1893. The most exceptional feature of this three-aisle pillared basilica is the tympanum over the main portal, depicting the Last Judgment with more than 200 figures, some painted. Mammoth 15th-century stained-glass windows line the chancel. The 1523 choir stalls brought the Renaissance to Bern. In the Matter Chapel is a remarkable stained-glass window, the *Dance of Death,* created in the last year of World War I, but based on a much older design. The 90-meter (300-ft.) belfry offers a panoramic sweep, though you must climb 270 steps to get to the viewing platform. Outside the basilica on Münsterplatz is the 1545 Moses Fountain.

Münsterplatz. ⓒ 031/312-04-62. Cathedral, free; viewing platform, 3SF ($1.90) adults, 1SF (65¢) children. Easter Sun–Oct Tues–Sat 10am–5pm, Sun 11:30am–5pm; off-season Tues–Fri 10am–noon and 2–4pm, Sat 10am–noon and 2–5pm, Sun 11:30am–2pm. Viewing platform closes half an hour before cathedral. Bus: 12.

Kunstmuseum (Fine Arts Museum) 𝒢𝒢   The world's largest collection of Swiss-born Paul Klee's works is the star attraction here. The Klee collection includes 40 oils and 2,000 drawings, gouaches, and watercolors. Other works emphasize the 19th and 20th centuries. The important 20th-century collection has works by Kandinsky, Modigliani, Matisse, Soutine, and Picasso, and by the Surrealist and Constructivist schools as well as contemporary Swiss artists.

Moments   Taking a Cable Train to Mont Gurten

The most panoramic attraction in the immediate vicinity is the **belvedere atop Mont Gurten** 𝒢𝒢, where there's also a children's fairy-land and a walking area. The belvedere is connected to Bern by the Gurtenbahn cable-train, one of the fastest in all Europe. The train departs from a station beside the Monbijoustrasse, about 2.5 kilometers (1½ miles) from Bern's center. Round-trip passage on the cable-train is 7SF ($4.40). The train operates year-round, daily 7:30am to sunset. For details, contact **Gurtenbahn Bern,** Eigerplatz 3 (⑦ 031/961-23-23). To reach the departure platform, take tram 9 to the Gurtenbahn station for 2SF ($1.50) each way. If you're driving, follow the road signs to Thun. There's a parking lot in the hamlet of Wabern, a short walk from the cable-train station.

There's also a collection of Italian 14th-century primitives, notably Fra Angelico's *Virgin and Child,* and Swiss primitives, including the *Masters of the Carnation.*

Hodlerstrasse 12. ⑦ 031/328-09-44. Permanent collection, 7SF ($4.40) adults, 5SF ($3.15) seniors; special exhibit, 12–18SF ($8–$11) extra. Tues 10am–9pm; Wed–Sun 10am–5pm. Bus: 20.

ORGANIZED TOURS

Highly recommended is the **2-hour bus tour** leaving from the tourist office at the Bahnhof, at Bahnhofplatz. An English-speaking guide will take you through the city's residential quarters, past museums, and down to the Aare River, which flows below the houses of Parliament. You'll see the Rose Gardens and the Late Gothic cathedral and stroll under the arcades to the Clock Tower. After visiting the Bear Pits, you'll be led through medieval streets and back to the railroad station. Tours are offered from June to September daily at 2pm; from November to March, Saturday only at 2pm; and April, May and October, from Monday to Saturday at 2pm. The cost is 23SF ($14) adults, and 11.50SF ($7) children 6 to 16; free for children 5 and under.

The tourist office also conducts 2-hour **walking tours** of Bern from May to September. Tours leave daily at 11am from the tourist office and at 11:15am from Zytglogge. The cost is 12SF ($8) adults and 6SF ($3.75) children 6 to 16; free for children 5 and under.

BERN AFTER DARK

This Week in Bern, distributed free by the tourist office, has a list of cultural events.

PERFORMING ARTS   The **Bern Symphony Orchestra,** one of Switzerland's finest, is directed by the widely acclaimed Russian-born Dmitrij Kitajenko; famous guest conductors also frequently appear. Performances are usually at the concert facilities in the **Bern Casino,** Herrengasse 25 (⑦ 031/311-42-42).

Major opera and ballet performances are usually staged in the century-old **Stadttheater,** Kornhausplatz 20 (⑦ 031/329-51-51). Plays and dance programs are presented in the **Theater am Käfigturm,** Spitalgasse 4 (⑦ 031/311-61-00).

Plays are usually in German, and to a lesser degree, French. Contemporary German-language theater is featured in the **Kleintheater,** Kramgasse 6 (© 031/320-26-26).

WINE CELLARS & TRADITIONAL MUSIC **Klötzlikeller,** 62 Gerechtigkeitsgasse (© 031/311-74-56), the oldest wine tavern in Bern, is near the Gerechtigkeitsbrunnen (Fountain of Justice), the first fountain you see on your walk from the Bear Pits to the Clock Tower. Watch for the lantern outside an angled cellar door. The tavern, dating from 1635, is owned by the city and leased to an independent operator (by tradition, an unmarried woman). Some 20 wines are sold by the glass, with prices ranging from 8SF ($5). The traditional kitchen serves various dinner plates from 25 to 42SF ($16 to $26) that reflect regional specialties and prices. The bar is open from Tuesday to Saturday 4pm to 12:30am.

Kornhaus Keller, Kornhausplatz 18 (© 031/311-11-33), a former grain warehouse in the Altstadt, is the city's best-known wine cellar. The symmetrical stone building, with an arcade on the ground floor, seats 462 diners in a baronial atmosphere; musical acts are often performed in the evening. Main courses—go for the classic, a plate of smoked meats and sauerkraut—are 20 to 45SF ($13 to $28); the tagesteller (a meal itself) costs 20SF ($13), but is served only at lunch. Food is served daily from 11:30am to 1:45pm and 6 to 9:45pm, but guests usually linger over their drinks till around midnight.

A JAZZ CLUB The Louis Armstrong Bar, site of **Marians' Jazzroom** in the Innere Enge Hotel, Engerstrasse 54 (© 031/309-61-11), has its own separate entrance from the hotel. Unique in Bern, it's a setting for not only food and drink, but the finest traditional jazz performed live by top artists from around the world. It's open from Tuesday to Thursday 7pm to 1am, Friday and Saturday 7:30pm to 2am. On Saturday, there is a Concert Apéro from 4 to 6:30pm. Cover is 25 to 35SF ($16 to $22), depending on the act. Closed from June 6 to September 6.

A GAY BAR **Samurai Club,** Aarbergergasse 35 (© 031/311-88-03), draws many people who work in the local embassies, Bern locals, and young men from the Bernese Oberland in for a night on the town. Women are also welcome. The club is open from Sunday to Thursday 8pm to 2:30am; Friday and Saturday 8pm to 3:30am. On weekdays from 5 to 8pm, beer is 4SF ($2.50); at other times, 5SF ($3.15).

A CASINO Across the river from the oldest section of Bern, the **Kursaal, Schanzlistrasse** 71–77 (© 031/333-10-10 or 031/333-18-55), is the only place in town to gamble. Indeed, it's a great spot for novices to learn gambling, because serious money rarely changes hands here. Betting is limited to 1 to 5SF ($3.15), as required by Swiss law. It's open daily from noon to 2am, and admission is free. Drinks cost 10 to 15SF ($6 to $9). There's also a restaurant, serving nightly from 5:30 to 10pm. In addition, a dance hall, called Insight, charges an admission of 15SF ($9). It's open Thursday from 9pm to 2am, Friday and Saturday 9pm to 3:30am. You'll need your passport.

THE BERNER OBERLAND

The Berner Oberland is Valhalla for walkers, hikers, and skiers. Here nature's scenery satisfies both the most ambitious adventurer and the slowest stroller. It's one of the world's best-equipped regions for winter sports, and walking trails branch out from almost every junction. Most of these are paved and signposted, with distances posted and estimated walking times given. Most tourist offices, including those at Interlaken (see below), will provide guidance and suggested itineraries.

EXPLORING THE AREA BY TRAIN & BICYCLE If you're not driving, you'll find that public transport is quite adequate for exploring the area. You can buy a **transportation pass** for the Bernese Oberland from the Swiss Rail System (℡ 051/220-1111). The train ticket is valid for 7 days, and costs 165SF ($103) in second class and 202SF ($126) in first class. Another pass, valid for 15 days, costs 205SF ($128) in second class and 251SF ($157) in first class. With the 7-day pass, you'll travel free for 3 days and pay a reduced fare for the final 4. With a 15-day pass, you'll travel free for 5 days and pay reduced fares for the rest of the time. Children travel at half price. The pass is valid on most railroads; all mountain trains, cable cars, chairlifts, steamers on Lakes Thun and Brienz; and most postal-bus lines in the area. The ticket also qualifies you for a 25% reduction on the Kleine Scheidegg-Eigergletscher-Jungfraujoch railway, the Mürren-Schilthorn aerial cable line, and the bus to Grosse Scheidegg and Bussalp.

Cycling tours through the Berner Oberland often begin at Interlaken. Hundreds of miles of cycling paths cover the area. Separate from the network of hiking paths, the bicycle routes are signposted and marked on rental maps

---

Tips **Buying the Bernese Oberland Pass**

You must purchase the pass at least 1 week before you arrive. For information, call ℂ **212/757-5944** in New York City, ℂ **310/640-8900** in Los Angeles, ℂ **312/332-9900** in Chicago, or ℂ **416/695-2090** in Toronto.

---

distributed at bike rental agencies. Some 13 rail stations in the Berner Oberland offer bike rental services, and rates are reasonable. For example, families can rent four bikes (two for adults, two for children 15 and under) for an all-inclusive price of 54SF ($34) per day or 260SF ($163) per week. Individual rentals cost 27SF ($17) per day or 130SF ($81) per week. You must make reservations at least the evening before the tour at any of the rail stations providing the service. Call ℂ **033/828-73-19** or 033/826-47-50 for reservations.

INTERLAKEN 𝆄𝆄𝆄

Interlaken is the Berner Oberland's tourist capital. Cableways and cog railways designed for steeply inclined hills and mountains connect it with most of the region's villages. A dazzling sight is the snowy heights of the Jungfrau, which rises a short distance to the south.

The "town between the lakes" (Thun and Brienz) has been a holiday resort for more than 300 years. Though it was once a summer resort, it has developed into a year-round playground. Interlaken charges low-season prices in January and February, when smaller resorts at higher altitudes charge their highest rates. The most expensive time to visit is midsummer, when high-altitude ski resorts often charge their lowest rates.

ESSENTIALS

GETTING THERE   By Train   There are several trains daily between Zurich and Interlaken (trip time: 2 hours) and between Bern and Interlaken (40 minutes). Frequent train service also connects Geneva and Interlaken (2½ hours). Though the town has two rail stations, about 3 kilometers (2 miles) apart, **Interlaken East** and **Interlaken West,** most of the city center lies near or around Interlaken West. Call ℂ **051/220-111** for schedules and fares.

By Car   To reach Interlaken from Bern, drive south on N6 to Spiez, then continue west on N8 to Interlaken.

VISITOR INFORMATION   The **Tourism Organization Interlaken** is at Höheweg 37 (ℂ **033/822-21-21**), in the Hotel Metropole, and will provide itineraries for hikers. It's open July and August, from Monday to Friday 8am to noon and 1:30 to 6:30pm, Saturday 8am to 5pm, and Sunday 5 to 7pm; the rest of the year, hours are from Monday to Friday 8am to noon and 1:30 to 6pm and Saturday 9am to noon.

WHERE TO STAY

Hotel Beau-Site   A short walk from the Interlaken West train station, this hotel is surrounded by spacious gardens with parasol-shaded card tables and chaise longues in summer, and provides a pleasant, relaxing oasis. Rooms are modern; some open onto mountain views. Rooms on upper floors are a bit small and often rented as singles. The spotless bathrooms are a bit small.

Seestrasee 16, CH-3800 Interlaken. ℂ **033/826-75-75.** Fax 033/826-75-85. www.beausite.ch. 50 units, 43 with bathroom (showers only). 110SF ($69) double without bathroom, 200–260SF ($125–$163) double with bathroom. Rates include continental breakfast. AF, DC, MC, V. Free parking outside, 20SF ($13) in garage. Closed Nov–Dec 15. **Amenities:** 2 restaurants, bar; room service; laundry. *In room:* TV and minibar (most units).

Hotel Bellevue

Hotel Bellevue   In a central spot opening directly on the Aare, this hotel retains something of its original 1789 design as a mock fortified castle and is surrounded by an English-style garden. The modernized rooms, in a variety of shapes and sizes, often have balconies with a view of the river and the distant mountains. All contain a mixture of modern and traditional furniture. Bathrooms are compact, often with a tub and shower. Breakfast and dinner are served in the formal dining room, and guests relax in a nicely furnished salon facing the garden and a view of the Alps.

Marktgasse 59, CH-3800 Interlaken. (C) **033/822-44-31.** Fax 033/822-92-50. www.interlakentourism.ch./ alplodge. 38 units. 170–280SF ($106–$175) double. Half-price reduction for children up to 12 sharing parents' room. Half board 35SF ($22) per person. Rates include buffet breakfast. AE, DC, MC, V. Free parking. **Amenities:** Restaurant; room service; laundry. *In room:* TV, minibar.

Hotel de la Paix   This family-run hotel is a block from the Interlaken West train station. You'll recognize it by its ornate roofline, which is gabled and tiled like a house in a Brothers Grimm fairy tale. Gillian and Georges Etterli offer a pleasant, relaxed atmosphere. Rooms are simply but comfortably furnished. Those downstairs are quite spacious. Bathrooms are small.

Bernastrasse 24, CH-3800 Interlaken. (C) **033/822-70-44.** Fax 033/822-87-28. 22 units. 126–150SF ($79–$94) double. Rates include buffet breakfast. AE, DC, MC, V. Free parking. Closed mid-Oct to mid-Mar. **Amenities:** Restaurant; room service; laundry. *In room:* TV, no phone.

Park-Hotel Mattenhof   This old-fashioned hotel is in a secluded area at the edge of a forest 1.5 kilometers (1 mile) south of the center; you can reach it by heading away from the center toward Wilderswil. Originally a simple 19th-century pension, it adopted a mock-medieval look after a massive 1908 enlargement. The Bühler family offers a calm retreat, with terraces, manicured lawns, and panoramic views of the Alps. Rooms come in a variety of sizes and bathrooms are compact.

Hauptstrasse, Matten, CH-3800 Interlaken. (C) **033/821-61-21.** Fax 033/822-28-88. www.parkmattenhof.ch. 76 units. June–Sept and Dec 26–Jan 1, 230–260SF ($144–$163) double; off-season, 190SF ($119) double. Rates include buffet breakfast. AE, DC, MC, V. Free parking. Bus: 5. **Amenities:** Restaurant, bar; pool; tennis court play areas; terraces. *In room:* TV.

Swiss Inn   This is a small-scale Edwardian-era inn with a sense of economy. Mrs. Vreny Müller Lohner offers conventional doubles that are simply decorated and a bit spare. Bathrooms are very small and have shower stalls. There are also some self-contained apartments with kitchens that receive clean-up service only once a week. Guests have access to a lounge, a sitting area with a fireplace, a laundry, and within the garden, a barbecue grill.

Général-Guisan-Strasse 23, CH-3800 Interlaken. (C) **033/822-36-26.** Fax 033/823-23-03. www.swiss-inn. com. 10 units. 130–140SF ($81–$88) double; 180SF ($113) apt for 2; 200SF ($125) apt for 4. Rates in double include buffet breakfast. AE, MC, V. Free parking. *In room:* TV.

Victoria-Jungfrau Grand Hotel & Spa 🌟🌟   This is one of Switzerland's grandest resort properties, a position held since 1986. Were Mark Twain to return today, he would surely sing his praises as he did during his stay here. In richly ornate Victorian styling, it sits in the town center at the foot of rigidly symmetrical gardens. The hotel boasts one of the best-trained staffs in the country. Deluxe rooms open onto views of the Jungfrau. Nearly all are spacious. Bathrooms have tub/shower combinations.

Höheweg 41, CH-3800 Interlaken. (© **800/223-6800** in the U.S., or 033/828-28-28. Fax 033/828-28-80. www.victoria-jungfrau.ch. 216 units. Summer 560–640SF ($350–$400) double. Winter 420–480SF ($263–$300) double. Year-round from 650SF ($406) junior suite; from 1,150SF ($719) suite. Half board 95SF ($59) per person extra. AE, DC, MC, V. Parking free outside, 18SF ($11) in garage. **Amenities:** 3 restaurants, 2 bars; indoor and outdoor pools; 7 tennis courts; sauna; solarium; whirlpools; steam baths; one of Switzerland's best spas. *In room:* TV, minibar, hair dryer, iron/ironing board.

WHERE TO DINE

Gasthof Hirschen *(Value* SWISS   This hotel restaurant offers some of the best and most reasonably priced meals in town, and the menu is varied, with most dishes at the lower price on the menu. The potato soup with mountain cheese is the finest we've ever tasted. Other appetizers include salmon-filled ravioli. For a main dish, try such standard but well-prepared fare as sautéed calves' liver, filet of beef bordelaise, broiled trout, or the resort's best chateaubriand. Many of the

---

Moments   Glaciers in the Sky: A Trip to Jungfraujoch

A trip to **Jungfraujoch** *★★★*, at 3,454 meters (11,333 ft.), can be the highlight of your visit. Since the 1860s it's been the highest rail station in Europe. It's also one of the most expensive: A round-trip tour is 184.50SF ($115) first class or 161.60SF ($101) second. However, families can fill out a Family Card form, available at the rail station; it allows children 16 and under to ride free. There are departures from Interlaken's East Railway Station (**Bahnhof Interlaken Ost**) every hour in winter, and every half hour in summer, but for true aficionados of the experience, the area is at its panoramic best if you depart at 8:05am and return to Bahnhof Interlaken Ost at 4pm. You'll get to see the mountain when it is most dazzlingly lit, and will have enough time for a leisurely lunch. To check times, contact the sales office of **Jungfrau Bahnen** (Jungfrau Railways), Höheweg 37 ((© **033/828-71-11**).

Once at the Jungfraujoch terminus, you may feel a little giddy until you get used to the air. You'll find much to do in this eerie world high up, Jungfrau. But take it slowly—your metabolism will be affected and you may tire quickly.

Within a 5-minute, well-marked walk from the Jungfraujoch railway terminus is an elevator that leads to the famed **Eispalast (Ice Palace)** *★*. Here you'll be walking within what's called "eternal ice"—caverns hewn out of the slowest-moving section of the glacier. Cut 20 meters (65 ft.) below the glacier's surface, they were begun in 1934 by a Swiss guide and subsequently enlarged and embellished with additional sculptures. The cost of entrance to the Ice Palace is included in the price of a railway ticket to the Jungfraujoch. Hours of the Ice Palace coincide with the arrival of the first and the departure of the last train.

After returning to the station, you can take the **Sphinx Tunnel** to another elevator. This one takes you up 108 meters (356 ft.) to an observation deck called the **Sphinx Terraces,** overlooking the saddle between the Mönch and Jungfrau peaks. You can also see the **Aletsch Glacier,** a 23-kilometer (14-mile) river of ice—the longest in Europe. The snow melts into Lake Geneva and eventually flows into the Mediterranean.

items it features are home-grown, including Bio-Angus beef, veal, cheese, and fresh vegetables and herbs.

Hauptstrasse 11, Matten. ℂ **033/822-15-45.** Reservations recommended. Main courses 20–70SF ($13–$44). AE, DC, MC, V. Wed–Mon 11:30am–2pm and 6–10pm.

Il Bellini 𝕽 ITALIAN This is the finest Italian restaurant in the area, with food that evokes some of the best trattorie south of the border. An assortment of antipasti from the buffet or a homemade minestrone is followed by such main courses as beefsteak Florentine, saltimbocca (veal with ham), or chicken breast grilled with tomatoes and mozzarella. The fish selections are limited but well chosen, and can be grilled on request.

In the Hotel Metropole, Höheweg 37. ℂ **033/828-66-66.** Reservations recommended Fri–Sun. Main courses 27–36SF ($17–$23); pastas 14–20SF ($9–$13). AE, DC, MC, V. Daily 11:30am–2pm and 6:30–10pm.

Schuh SWISS/CONTINENTAL This attractive restaurant and tearoom in the center of town offers a sunny terrace with a view of the Jungfrau. The calves' liver is excellent, perfectly grilled and seasoned, and their daily soups are pure homemade goodness. Salads rely on market fresh ingredients, and the desserts often incorporate locally grown berries and fruits. Their pastries are justifiably acclaimed as the finest in the area. A pianist provides music.

Höheweg 56. ℂ **033/822-94-41.** Main courses 20–52SF ($13–$33); set price menu 37–41SF ($23–$26). AE, DC, MC, V. Tues–Sun 8am–10:30pm. Closed Oct 25–Dec 9.

EXPLORING INTERLAKEN

What you do in Interlaken is walk. You can walk at random, as there are panoramic views in virtually all directions, or, if you'd like some guidance, go to the tourist office for a copy of "What to Do in Interlaken"; it maps out walks of all levels of difficulty.

The **Höheweg** 𝕽𝕽 covers 16 hectares (35 acres) in the middle of town, between the west and east train stations. Once the property of Augustinian monks, it was acquired in the mid-19th century by Interlaken's hotel keepers, who turned it into a park. As you stroll along **Höhenpromenade,** admire the famous view of the Jungfrau. Another beautiful sight is the **flower clock** at the Kursaal (casino), and you'll also see **fiacres** (horse-drawn cabs). The promenade is lined with hotels, cafes, and gardens.

Cross over the Aare River to **Unterseen,** built in 1280 by Berthold von Eschenbach. Here you can visit the **parish church,** with its Late Gothic tower from 1471. This is one of the most photographed sights in the Berner Oberland. The Mönch mountain appears on the left of the tower, the Jungfrau on the right.

Back in Interlaken, visit the **Touristik-Museum der Jungfrau-Region,** am Stadthausplatz, Obere Gasse 26 (ℂ **033/822-98-39**), the country's first regional museum of tourism, showing development over the past 2 centuries. It's open from May to mid-October, Tuesday to Sunday 2 to 5pm. Admission is 5SF ($3.15), or 3SF ($1.90) with a Visitor's Card. Children 12 and under pay 2SF ($1.25).

For a sightseeing fiacre ride, go to the Westbahnhof. The half-hour round-trip is 35SF ($22) for one or two, plus 10SF ($6) for each extra person; children 7 to 16 are charged half fare, and those 6 and under ride free.

Other attractions include animal parks, afternoon concerts, and the luscious pastries sold in cafes. During summer, you can sit in covered grandstands and watch Schiller's version of the William Tell story. Steamers carry passengers across Lakes Brienz and Thun.

MÜRREN 🏔🏔

At 1,650 meters (5,414 ft.) above the Lauterbrunnen Valley, Mürren is the highest permanently inhabited village in the Berner Oberland. It's an exciting excursion from Interlaken in summer and a major ski resort in winter. Downhill skiing was developed and the slalom invented here in the 1920s, and Mürren is also the birthplace of modern alpine racing.

ESSENTIALS

GETTING THERE   By Train   Trains from Interlaken to Mürren's train station require a change of equipment in both Lauterbrunen and Grutschalp. The combined trip takes an hour from Interlaken, and round-trip fare costs 18.40SF ($12).

By Bus & Car   A regular postal-bus service departs once an hour from Lauterbrunnen to the hamlet of Stechelberg, the last town along the Lauterbrunnen Valley road, the end of the line for cars and buses, and the departure point for a cable car which runs uphill to Mürren. The cable car that continues from Stechelberg on to Mürren departs at 30-minute intervals, costs 34.20SF ($21) round-trip, and takes about 10 minutes each way.

VISITOR INFORMATION   The **Mürren Tourist Information Bureau** is at the Sportzentrum (☎ **033/856-86-86**), and is open from November to April, Monday to Friday 9am to noon and 2 to 5pm. From May to October, it's open Monday, Wednesday, and Friday 9am to noon and 2 to 7:30pm, Thursday 9am to noon and 2 to 8pm, and Saturday 2 to 7pm.

WHERE TO STAY

Hotel Alpenruh   In the most congested, yet still charming, section of the village, the Alpenruh offers a plusher interior than its chalet-style facade implies. The old building was upgraded to three-star status without sacrificing any of its small-scale charm. Rooms have pine paneling and a mix of antique and contemporary furniture; most have a view of the Jungfrau. The tidy bathrooms are small, compact, and efficiently organized, each with a shower stall.

CH-3825 Mürren. ☎ **033/856-88-00.** Fax 033/856-88-88. 26 units. www.schilthorn.ch. 180–250SF ($113–$156) double. 50% discount for children 12 and under sharing parents' room. Half board 30SF ($19) per person. Rates include breakfast. AE, DC, MC, V. **Amenities:** Restaurant, bar; private sauna. *In room:* TV, minibar.

Hotel Blumental   Centrally located and redecorated and remodeled, this is a small chalet-type hotel, with stone masonry and wood-paneled public areas. Run by the von Allmen family, it offers a cozy atmosphere inspired by the nearby mountains. Several rooms have private balconies, and the small bathrooms have shower stalls.

CH-3825 Mürren. ☎ **033/855-18-26.** Fax 033/855-36-86. www.muerren-ch/blumental. 16 units. 140–195SF ($88–$122) double. Half board 25SF ($16) per person. Rates include buffet breakfast. AE, DC, V. **Amenities:** Restaurant (French), bar; room service. *In room:* TV, minibar.

Hotel Eiger 🏔   Founded in the 1920s and last renovated in 1994, this chalet is the longest-established hotel in Mürren. The public areas are warmly decorated, and many of the windows have panoramic views. Rooms are small, cozy, comfortable, and decorated in a typical alpine style. The hotel, managed by Annelis Stähli-von Allmen and family, lies across the street from the terminus of the cable car from Lauterbrunne.

CH-3825 Mürren. ☎ **033/856-54-54.** Fax 033/856-54-56. www.muerren.ch./eiger. 44 units. Summer 220–280SF ($138–$175) double; 460–480SF ($288–$300) suite. Winter 260–340SF ($163–$213) double; 520–680SF ($325–$425) suite. Rates include breakfast. AE, DC, MC, V. Closed Easter to mid-June and mid-

Sept to Dec 19. **Amenities:** Restaurant (see "Where to Dine," below), popular après-ski bar; room service; laundry. *In room:* TV.

WHERE TO DINE

Eigerstübli ⭐ SWISS   Here you'll find Mürren's best food, served in a festive ambience. The cuisine includes fondue as well as an international range of hearty specialties well suited to the alpine heights and chill. Try, for example, roast lamb shoulder with lentils, roast breast of duck with orange sauce, or—our favorite—poached filet of trout with a sauce flavored with alpine herbs. All main dishes may be ordered with rösti.

In the Hotel Eiger. © **033/856-54-64.** Reservations recommended. Main courses 22–49SF ($14–$31). AE, DC, MC, V. Daily 11:30am–2pm and 6–9pm. Closed Easter to mid-June and mid-Sept to mid-Dec.

HITTING THE SLOPES & OTHER ACTIVE ENDEAVORS

There are 48 kilometers (30 miles) of prepared ski runs, including 16 downhills; the longest run measures 12 kilometers (7½ miles). For cross-country skiers there's a 12-kilometer (7½ mile) track in the Lauterbrunnen Valley, 10 minutes by railway from Mürren.

The alpine **Sportzentrum (Sports Center)** (© **033/856-86-86**), in the middle of Mürren, is one of the finest in the Berner Oberland. The modern building has an indoor pool, a lounge, a snack bar, an outdoor skating rink, a tourist information office, and a children's playroom and library. There are facilities for playing squash, outdoor tennis, and curling. Hotel owners subsidize the operation, tacking the charges onto your hotel bill. Supplemental charges include 16 to 30SF ($10 to $19) per hour for tennis or per 45-minute session for squash, and 13 to 16SF ($8 to $10) per hour for use of the sauna. The facility is usually open year-round from Monday to Friday 9am to noon and 2 to 6pm; and from Christmas to April and July to mid-September, also on Saturday 1 to 6:30pm and Sunday 1 to 5:30pm; but check locally as these times can vary.

NEARBY EXCURSIONS

The famous **Mürren-Allmendhubel Cableway** leaves from the northwestern edge of Mürren. From the high destination, there's a panoramic view of the Lauterbrunnen Valley as far as Wengen and Kleine Scheidegg, and from mid-June to late August, the alpine meadows are covered with wildflowers. A hill walk in this region might be a highlight of your trip. The cable car operates daily from 8am to 5pm. However, there are annual closings for maintenance in May and November. It costs 14SF ($9) per person round-trip.

The most popular excursion from Mürren is a cable-car ride to the **Schilthorn** ⭐⭐⭐, famous for its 360° view. The panorama extends from the Jura to the Black Forest and includes the Eiger, Mönch, and Jungfrau. The Schilthorn is also called "Piz Gloria" after the James Bond film *On Her Majesty's Secret Service,* partly filmed at this dramatic location. Today Piz Gloria is the name of the revolving restaurant here, and the summit is the start of the world's longest downhill ski race. The cable car to Schilthorn leaves every 30 minutes. A round-trip ticket is 66SF ($41), and the journey to the top takes 20 minutes. For details, call © **033/823-14-44.**

WENGEN ⭐⭐⭐

The Mönch, Jungfrau, and Eiger loom above this sunny resort, built on a sheltered terrace high above the Lauterbrunnen Valley, at about 1,270 meters (4,160 ft.). Wengen (pronounced *Ven*-ghen) is one of the more chic and better-equipped ski and mountain resorts in the Berner Oberland. It has 30 hotels in all price categories, as well as 500 apartments and chalets for rent.

In the 1830s, the International Lauberhorn Ski Race was established here. At that time, Wengen was a farm community, but the Brits popularized the resort after World War I. Parts of the area retain their rural charm, but the main street is filled with cafes, shops, and restaurants. No cars are allowed in Wengen, but the streets still bustle with service vehicles and electric luggage carts.

ESSENTIALS

GETTING THERE **By Train** Take the train (frequent service) from Interlaken East to Lauterbrunnen. For information, call © **033/828-7333.** From here, the journey to Wengen is by cog railway, a 15-minute trip. A one-way fare is 11.50SF ($7).

By Car Unlike Mürren, Wengen, 26 kilometers (16 miles) south of Interlaken, can be reached by car—at least for part of the trip. From Interlaken, head south in the direction of Wilderswil, following the minor signposted road to Lauterbrunnen, where there are garages or open-air spaces for parking. After that, it's cog railway the rest of the way to Wengen.

VISITOR INFORMATION The **Wengen Tourist Information Office** (© **033/855-14-14;** www.wengen-muerren.ch), in the center of the resort, is open from Monday to Friday 8am to noon and 2 to 6pm, Saturday 8:30 to 11:30am only.

WHERE TO STAY

Hotel Eden You'll feel comfortable and at home in this economy oasis that stands among guesthouses and private chalets above the commercial center of town. Kerstin Bucher directs a cooperative staff. There's a small TV lounge and a tiny Jägerstübli, where guests mix with locals over Swiss wine and specialties. Although the rooms are a bit spartan, the beds are comfortable. Only a few units have private bathrooms, and these are quite small without much room for your stuff.

CH-3823 Wengen. © **033/855-16-34.** Fax 033/855-39-50. 30 units, 6 with bathroom. Summer 145SF ($91) double without bathroom, 160SF ($100) double with bathroom. Winter 168SF ($105) double without bathroom, 185SF ($116) double with bathroom. Half board 35SF ($22) per person. Rates include breakfast. AE, DC, MC, V. Closed Nov–Dec 20. **Amenities:** Restaurant, beer tavern. *In room:* No phone.

Hotel Eiger Rustic timbers cover the walls and ceilings of this attractive hotel behind the cog-railway station. Karl Fuchs and his family offer spacious attractive rooms with balconies. A modern dining room has views of the Jungfrau massif and the Lauterbrunnen Valley. Rooms have cozy, alpine styling, but bathrooms are small and cramped, each with a shower stall. In the lobby is an inviting sitting area with a fireplace.

CH-3823 Wengen. © **800/528-1234** in the U.S. and Canada, or 033/855-11-31. Fax 033/855-10-30. www. wengen.com./hotel/eiger. 33 units. Summer 184–206SF ($115–$129) double. Winter 204–228SF ($128–$143) double. Suite for two, 240–342SF ($150–$214). Half board 30SF ($19) per person. Rates include breakfast. AE, DC, MC, V. Closed mid-Apr to June 1 and Nov to Dec. 10. **Amenities:** Restaurant, bar. *In room:* TV.

WHERE TO DINE

Hotel Hirschen Restaurant SWISS An alpine flavor permeates this tranquil retreat at the foot of the slopes. The rear dining room is decorated with hunting trophies, pewter, and wine racks. Johannes Abplanalp and his family offer a dinner special called Galgenspiess—filet of beef, veal, and pork flambéed at your table. Other dishes include filet of breaded pork, rump steak Café de Paris, and fondue Bacchus (in white-wine sauce), bourguignonne (hot oil), or chinoise (hot bouillon). A hearty lunch is *winzerrösti*, consisting of country ham, cheese, and a fried egg with homemade rösti.

In the Hotel Hirschen. ℂ **033/855-15-44.** Reservations recommended. Main courses 14.50–44.50SF ($9–$28); set price menu 40–69SF ($25–$43). DC, MC, V. Mon–Fri 5–11pm; Sat–Sun 11:30am–2:30pm and 5–11pm (closed Wed over the summer and Tues over the winter). Closed mid-Apr to May and Nov–Dec 15.

EXPLORING THE AREA

The ski area around Wengen is highly developed, with both straight and serpentine trails carved into the sides of such sloping geological formations as Männlichen, Kleine Scheidegg, Lauberhorn, and Eigergletscher. A triumph of alpine engineering, the town and its region contain three mountain railways, two aerial cableways, one gondola, five chairlifts, nine ski lifts, and three practice lifts. You'll also find a branch of the Swiss ski school, more than 12 kilometers (7 miles) of trails for cross-country skiing, an indoor and outdoor skating rink, a curling hall, an indoor pool, and a day nursery.

In summer, the district attracts hill climbers from all over Europe. Hiking trails are well maintained and carefully marked, with dozens of unusual detours to hidden lakes and panoramas.

NEARBY ATTRACTIONS

In winter, skiers take the cableway to **Männlichen** ✦, at 2,236 meters (7,335 ft.), which opens onto a panoramic vista of the treacherous Eiger. From here, there's no direct run back to Wengen; however, skiers can enjoy an uninterrupted ski trail stretching 7 kilometers (4½ miles) to Grindelwald.

There are many sights you can visit up and down the Lauterbrunnen Valley from either Wengen or Grindelwald. **Trümmelbach Falls** ✦✦✦ plunges in five powerful cascades through a gorge. An elevator built through the rock leads to a series of galleries; the last stop is at a wall where the upper fall descends (bring a raincoat). You can visit the falls daily from May to June and September to October 9am to 5pm and from July to August 8:30am to 6pm. Admission is 10SF ($6) adults, 4SF ($2.50) children 6 to 16, and free for children 5 and under. It takes about 45 minutes to reach the falls on foot. For information, call ℂ **033/855-32-32.** The postal bus from Lauterbrunnen departs once an hour and stops at Trëmmelbach Falls; fares are 4SF ($2.50) adults, 2SF ($1.25) children.

You might also want to visit the base of the **Staubbach Waterfall** ✦✦, which plunges nearly 300 meters (1,000 ft.) in a sheer drop over a rock wall in the valley above Lauterbrunnen. Lord Byron compared this waterfall to the "tail of the pale horse ridden by Death in the Apocalypse."

GRINDELWALD ✦✦✦

The "glacier village" of Grindelwald, both a summer and a winter resort, is set against a backdrop of the Wetterhorn and the towering north face of the Eiger. Grindelwald is surrounded with folkloric hamlets, swift streams, and as much alpine beauty as you're likely to find anywhere in Switzerland. It's also easier to reach from Interlaken than either Wengen or Mürren. Though at first, the hiking options and cable car networks might seem baffling, the tourist office can provide helpful maps.

ESSENTIALS

GETTING THERE   By Train   The Berner Oberland Railway (BOB) leaves from the Interlaken East station (trip time: 35 minutes). Call ✆ **033/828-7333** for information.

VISITOR INFORMATION   Grindelwald's **tourist office,** Sportszentrum, Hauptstrasse, CH-3818 Grindelwald (✆ **033/854-12-12;** www.grindelwald.ch), is open from mid-June to late September Monday to Friday 8am to 7pm, Saturday 8am to 5pm, Sunday 9 to 11am and 3 to 5pm. Otherwise, hours are from Monday to Friday 8am to noon and 2 to 6pm, Saturday 8am to noon, and Sunday 10am to noon and 3 to 5pm.

WHERE TO STAY

Grand Hotel Regina 🏵🏵   Across from the Grindelwald train station, this turn-of-the-19th-century hotel is part rustic, part urban slick. The facade of the oldest part has an imposing set of turrets with red-tile roofs. Antiques blend with modern furnishings into a harmonious whole, and the beds are exceedingly comfortable. Bathrooms are well maintained, with tub and shower combo.

CH-3818 Grindelwald. ✆ **800/223-6800** in the U.S. or 033/854-86-00. Fax 033/853-47-17. 98 units. 420SF ($263) double; from 1,000SF ($625) suite. AE, DC, MC, V. Parking free outside, 15SF ($9) in garage. Closed mid-Oct to Dec 18. **Amenities:** Restaurant, disco; indoor and outdoor pools; 2 tennis courts; sauna; solarium; salon; room service; massages; laundry. *In room:* TV, minibar, hair dryer, robes.

Hotel Eiger   This hotel appears to be a collection of interconnected balconies, each on a different plane, angled toward the alpine sunshine and built of contrasting shades of white stucco and natural wood. The interior is attractive and unpretentious, with lots of warmly tinted wood, hanging lamps, and contrasting lights. Rooms range from small to medium; each has a soft, snug bed, and a compact bathroom with adequate shelf space and a shower stall.

CH-3818 Grindelwald. ✆ **033/853-31-31.** Fax 033/853-31-30. www.eiger-grindelwald.ch. 50 units. Summer 196–276SF ($123–$173) double. Winter 266–296SF ($166–$185) double. Half board 35SF ($22) per person. Rates include buffet breakfast. AE, DC, MC, V. Free parking outdoors; 6–12SF ($3.75–$8) in garage. Closed mid-Oct to mid-Dec. **Amenities:** Restaurant (steakhouse), Gepsi-Bar (live music); sauna; steam room; children's playroom. *In room:* TV, minibar.

Hotel Hirschen *(Value)*   In the three-star Hirschen, the Bleuer family offers one of the resort's best values. Rooms are a bit small but each is cozy, warm, and a great place to retreat to on a cold winter's night. Bathrooms are tiny but tidy, each with a shower stall.

CH-3818 Grindelwald. ✆ **033/854-84-84.** Fax 033/854-84-80. www.grindelwald.ch. 28 units. 156–195SF ($98–$122) double. Half board 28SF ($18) per person. Rates include continental breakfast. AE, DC, MC, V. Free parking outside; 8SF ($5) garage. Closed Nov to Dec 19. **Amenities:** Restaurant; bowling alley. *In room:* TV.

WHERE TO DINE

Il Mercato ITALIAN/SWISS   The dining room's centerpiece is a large window with a sweeping view over the mountains; during warm weather, tables are set on the terrace. Menu items include virtually everything Italian, with an emphasis on cold-weather dishes from the Val d'Aosta (northern Italy's milk and cheese district). Especially good are the risottos, simmered rice dishes that come in infinite varieties. The chefs also specialize in grilled meats and homemade salads. Their pizzas are the best in town. Daily pastas are featured, each with a succulent sauce.

In the Hotel Spinne. ✆ **033/854-88-88.** Reservations recommended. Main courses 15–20SF ($9–$13). AE, DC, MC, V. Daily noon–2pm and 6–10pm. Closed Nov to mid-Dec.

Restaurant Français 🌟 INTERNATIONAL Special buffets feature at Grindelwald's best restaurant. After you study the ever-changing menu to the soothing sounds of a live pianist, you may decide on an appetizer of game terrine, Grindewald air-dried meat, or thinly sliced lamb carpaccio. On recent visits, the best dishes have included poached turbot filet on zucchini, a superb peppercorn-coated lamb entrecôte, and breast of guinea fowl with red wine and prunes.

In the Hotel Belvedere. ℂ **033/854-54-54.** Reservations recommended. Main courses 30–45SF ($19–$28); set price menu 52–65SF ($33–$41). AE, DC, MC, V. Daily noon–2pm and 6:30–9pm.

SEEING THE GLACIERS

Adjacent to the base of the **Lower Grindelwald Glacier (Untere Gletscher)** 🌟🌟 is a sheltered observation gallery offering a look at the rock-strewn ravine formed by the glacier and its annual snowmelt. The half-mile gallery stretches past deeply striated rocks, which include formations of colored marble worn smooth by the glacier's erosion. Don't expect a view of the glacier from this point, as you'll have go to a higher altitude, at least in summer, to see the actual ice. The gallery is easy to reach on foot or by car from the center of Grindelwald. Yellow-sided buses labeled GLETSCHERSCHLUCHT depart from a point in front of Grindelwald's rail station at least four times a day, year-round, for the lower glacier and points beyond. Passage to the lower glacier costs 11.50SF ($7) each way, but since the distance from the center of Grindelwald is about 4 kilometers (2½ miles), in nice weather, many hardy souls opt to trek across well-marked hiking trails instead.

A more exotic destination farther afield is the **Blue Ice Grotto** 🌟, whose frozen mass is part of the Upper Grindelwald Glacier (Obere Gletscher). Popular with hill climbers, it's a 3-hour hike (which includes navigating up an 890-step alpine staircase) or a 15-minute bus ride from the Lower Grindelwald Glacier. The upper and lower glaciers are separated by rocky cliffs and flow in different valleys. At midday, the 45-meter (150-ft.) -thick ice walls of the grotto take on an eerie blue tinge. Local guides assure you that though the grotto—and the glacier containing it—are moving slowly downhill, you're perfectly safe. The grotto is open daily from mid-June to October 9am to 6pm. If you don't want to make the uphill trek on foot from Grindelwald, a yellow-sided bus marked GROSSE SCHEIDEGG departs at approximately 1-hour intervals, year-round, during daylight hours. Round-trip fares from Grindelwald to the Obere Gletscher and its grotto cost 11.60SF ($7). *Note:* Once you get off the bus, you'll still have to climb 900 steps to reach the grotto.

HIKING & MOUNTAIN CLIMBING

Grindelwald and environs offer dozens of challenging paths and mountain trails that are well marked and maintained. Outdoor adventures range from an exhilarating ramble across the gentle incline of an alpine valley to a dangerous trek with ropes and pitons along the north face of Mount Eiger. The choice depends on your inclination, degree of experience, and mountaineering skills. Maps showing the paths, trails, and their various elevations are available at the town's tourist office.

From Grindelwald, you can reach the high-altitude plateau known as **First Mountain** 🌟🌟 at 2,168 meters (7,113 ft.) after a 30-minute ride on a six-passenger gondola ("bubble car"). The round-trip transport is 45SF ($28). You can stop at such intermediate stations as Bort and Grindel (a site that some locals refer to as Scheckfeld) on your way to **First Mountain terminal and sun terrace.** From First, where there are dining facilities, you'll have many hiking possibilities into the neighboring Bussalp or Grosse Scheidegg area. Also, from First, an hour's brisk hike will take you to the still high-altitude waters of **Bachalpsee** (Lake Bachalp). Buses depart from Gindelwald from both Bussalp and Grosse Scheidegg if you opt not to walk all the way back.

Faulhorn ⋒⋒⋒, at 2,681 meters (8,796 ft.), is a historic vantage point with a panorama of untouched alpine beauty. Near the summit is the Faulhorn Hotel (© **033/853-27-13**), which has been here for more than 150 years. Faulhorn is a 7-hour hike from Grindelwald. For a shorter climb, take either the bus to Bussalp, the cable car to First, or the train to Schynige Platte. From any of these intermediate points, climbers can continue their treks on to Faulhorn. Hikes from Bussalp take 2¾ hours; from First, 2½ hours; and from Schynige Platte, 4 hours.

Grosse Scheidegg ⋒, at 1,961 meters (6,434 ft.), is a famous pass between the Grindelwald and Rosenlaui valleys. You can hike here in 3 hours from Grindelwald or can take a 40-minute bus ride from Grindelwald to Grosse Scheidegg and begin hill walking at a point that's far from the village traffic and crowds. Round-trip bus passage from Grindelwald to Grosse Scheidegg is 32SF ($20).

KANDERSTEG ⋒

Between Grindelwald and Gstaad, Kandersteg is a popular resort at one of the southern points of the Berner Oberland. It's a tranquil and lovely mountain village with rust- and orange-colored rooftops and green Swiss meadows. The summer and winter resort is spread over 4 kilometers (2½ miles), so nothing is crowded. The village itself is at the foot of the 3,660-meter (12,000-ft.) Blumlisalp chain and provides access to six remote alpine hamlets.

Kandersteg developed as a resting point on the road to the Gemmi Pass, which long ago linked the Valais with the Berner Oberland. The village still has many old farmhouses and a tiny church from the 16th century.

ESSENTIALS

GETTING THERE **By Train** Kandersteg is at the northern terminus of the 14-kilometer (9-mile) Lotschberg Tunnel, which, ever since the beginning of World War I, has linked Bern with the Rhône Valley. The railroad that runs through the tunnel can transport cars. Trains leave every 30 minutes; no reservations are necessary. The resort is also served by the Bern-Lotschberg-Simplon railway. Call © **033/828-7333** for information. The station is in the center of town.

By Car Kandersteg is 43 kilometers (27 miles) southwest of Interlaken. Take N8 east to where the Kandersteg road then heads south into the mountains. The journey from Spiez to Kandersteg along a well-built road takes only 20 minutes.

VISITOR INFORMATION The **Kandersteg Tourist Office,** Hauptstrasse CH-3718 Kandersteg (© **033/675-80-80;** www.kandersteg.ch), is open from Monday to Friday 8am to noon and 2 to 6pm.

WHERE TO STAY & DINE

Hotel Adler An open fire crackling in the foyer sets the tone at this cozy inn, a wood-sided chalet on the main street near the town center. The fourth-generation owner, Andreas Fetzer, and his Finnish-born wife, Eija, offer comfortable pinewood-paneled rooms, some with Jacuzzis. Almost all open onto a private balcony. The small, neat bathrooms are inviting and have adequate shelf space and shower stalls.

CH-3718 Kandersteg. ⓒ **033/675-80-10**, Fax 033/675-80-11. www.kandersteg.ch./adler. 24 unlts. Feb–Mar and July–Sept 170–210SF ($106–$131) double. Off-season, 160SF ($100) double. Rates include breakfast. Half-board 25SF ($16). AE, DC, MC, V. Closed Nov 22–Dec 26. Free parking. **Amenities:** Restaurant, brasserie, Adler-Bar (popular après-ski hangout). *In room:* TV, minibar.

OUTDOOR ACTIVITIES

Around Kandersteg is an extensive network of level footpaths and strategically located benches; these paths are open year-round. In summer, qualified riders in proper clothes can rent horses at the local riding school. In winter, the resort attracts cross-country skiers and downhill novices (top-speed skiers go elsewhere). It has a cable car, two chairlifts, and four ski tows; the National Nordic Ski Center offers a ski-jumping station. The 2.5-kilometer (1½-mile) cross-country ski trail is floodlit in the evening, and other facilities include an indoor and outdoor ice rink.

EXCURSIONS NEARBY

The most popular excursion from Kandersteg is to **Oeschinensee (Lake Oeschinen)** 𝔸𝔸𝔸, high above the village. The lake is surrounded by the snow-covered peaks of the Blumlisalp, towering 1,830 meters (6,000 ft.) above the extremely clear water. You can walk to it from the Victoria Hotel or take a chairlift, costing 16.20SF ($10), to the Oeschinen station and walk down from that point. If you opt to walk, allow about 1½ hours, or 2 hours if you'd like to stroll. Many visitors who take the chairlift decide to hike back to Kandersteg. Be aware, however, of the steep downhill grade.

Another popular excursion is to **Klus Gorge** 𝔸𝔸. Park your car at the cable station's lower platform at Stock and walk 3 kilometers (2 miles) to the gorge, which was formed by the abrasive action of the Kander River. The rushing water creates a romantic, even primeval, setting. There's a tunnel over the gorge, but in winter, the access route is dangerous and icebound.

GSTAAD 𝔸𝔸

Against a backdrop of glaciers and mountain lakes, Gstaad is a haven for the rich and famous. Built at the junction of four quiet valleys near the southern tip of the Berner Oberland, Gstaad was once only a place to change horses on the grueling trip by carriage through the Berner Oberland. As the rail lines developed, it grew into a resort for the wealthy who flocked to the Palace Hotel, which promised the ultimate in luxury.

The town retains much of its late 19th-century charm. Some first-time visitors, however, say that the resort is a bore if you can't afford to stay at the Gstaad Palace or mingle with the stars in their private chalets. Yet the town has many moderately priced hotels, taverns, and guesthouses, with an allure of their own.

ESSENTIALS

GETTING THERE   By Train   About a dozen trains come into Gstaad every day from Interlaken (trip time: 30 minutes) and Montreux (1⅓ hours). Call ⓒ **051/220-111** for information.

By Car   From Spiez, follow Route 11 southwest to Gstaad.

VISITOR INFORMATION   The **Gstaad-Saanenland Tourist Association,** CH-3780 Gstaad (ⓒ **033/748-81-81;** www.gstaad.ch), can help you find hotels, restaurants, and attractions if the signposts don't point you in the right direction. It's open from Monday to Friday 8am to noon and 1:30 to 6pm, and Saturday 9am to noon only.

WHERE TO STAY

Hostellerie Alpenrose ⟨⟨⟨ For those who like the charm of a small inn, this is the preferred choice, the only Relais & Châteaux listing within 50 kilometers (30 miles). Its owner, Michel von Siebenthal, is a memorable host, setting the fashionable tone of the chalet, which is famous for its cuisine. The pine-paneled public areas are exquisitely decorated with rustic furnishings. Rooms are tastefully appointed and have mountain views, and bathrooms have showers, but no tubs. Although the original house has more character, accommodations in the contemporary annex are more spacious and luxurious—some are fireplace suites, quite romantic on a wintry night.

Hauptstrasse, CH-3778 Schönried Gstaad. ⟨⟨ **033/744-67-67.** Fax 033/744-67-12. www.integrafr-relaischateau.ch/alpenrose. 19 units. Summer 320–480SF ($200–$300) double. Winter 360–730SF ($225–$456) double. Half board 45SF ($28) per person extra. AE, DC, MC, V. Free parking. Closed Nov–Dec 10. **Amenities:** Restaurant, bar; sauna; whirlpool; solarium. *In room:* TV, minibar.

Hotel Olden ⟨⟨ This is a low-key and gracefully unpretentious hotel, a sort of Victorian country inn set amid a sometimes chillingly glamorous landscape. The facade is painted with regional floral designs and pithy bits of folk wisdom. The folkloric alpine-style rooms are very cozy. The small bathrooms don't have a lot of extras, but maintenance is spotless, and each comes with a shower stall. Rooms in the chalet wing are generally roomier and more up to date.

Hauptstrasse, CH-3780 Gstaad. ⟨⟨ **033/744-34-44.** Fax 033/744-61-64. 15 units. 220–300SF ($138–$188) double. Rates include continental breakfast. AE, DC, MC, V. Free parking. Closed Nov–Dec 5 and late Apr to late May. **Amenities:** Restaurant (see "Where to Dine," below), bar; summer terrace; room service; laundry. *In room:* TV, minibar.

Palace Hotel Gstaad ⟨⟨⟨ This landmark hotel is on a wooded hill overlooking the center of Gstaad. It's one of the most sought-after luxury hideaways in the world, attracting corporation heads, film stars, jet-setters, and the titled. The nerve center of this chic citadel is an elegantly paneled main salon, with an eternal flame burning in the baronial stone fireplace. Rooms (some large enough for Elizabeth Taylor and all her husbands) are country deluxe with regional artifacts, cheerful print wallpaper, and rustic pine furnishings. Bathrooms are exceedingly luxurious with tub and shower combos.

CH-3780 Gstaad. ⟨⟨ **800/223-6800** in the U.S., or 033/748-50-50. Fax 033/748-5000. www.palace.ch. 124 units. Summer 580–840SF ($363–$525) double; from 1,700SF ($1,063) suite. Winter 890–1,160SF ($556–$725) double; from 2,190SF ($1,369) suite. Rates include breakfast. Half board 80SF ($50) per person extra. AE, DC, MC, V. Parking free outside, 18SF ($11) in garage. Closed end of Mar to mid-June and Nov–Dec 16. **Amenities:** 4 restaurants, piano bar; night club; indoor and outdoor pools; 4 tennis courts; health club; steam room; 2 saunas. *In room:* TV, minibar, hair dryer, robes.

WHERE TO DINE

Olden Restaurant ⟨⟨ MEDITERRANEAN/SWISS Although there are grander restaurants in Gstaad, and dining rooms serving a more haute cuisine, the Olden remains our most satisfying choice year after year after countless visits. The service is formal and refined, the food as good as, or better than, anything in the area. The always tempting menu might include smoked salmon, fresh goose-liver terrine, shrimp bisque with green peppercorns, house-style tagliatelle, raclette, Scottish lamb, and a truly memorable sea bass with olives, potatoes, tomatoes, and onions.

In the Hotel Olden, Hauptstrasse. ⟨⟨ **033/744-34-44.** Reservations recommended. Main courses 28–75SF ($18–$47). AE, DC, MC, V. Daily noon–2:30pm and 6:30–10:30pm. Closed mid-Apr to mid-May and Nov.

Restaurant Chesery ★★★ FRENCH/SWISS   One of Switzerland's 10 best restaurants perches at an elevation of 1,100 meters (3,600 ft.). Natural stone floors and polished pine walls pair naturally with a menu that changes daily, but is always based on the freshest of ingredients—grouse from Scotland, Charolais beef from France, truffles from Umbria. Taste the salt-crusted sea bass with wild rice or chicken Houban (a special breed from France), each a sensation. In the basement bar, Casino, a piano player entertains nightly; the bar is open from 6pm to around 3am.

Lauenenstrasse. ✆ 033/744-24-51. Reservations required. Main courses 45–65SF ($28–$41); set-price lunch 49–64SF ($31–$40); set-price dinner 95–148SF ($59–$93). AE, DC, MC, V. Tues–Sun 11:30am–2:30pm and 7pm–midnight. Closed mid-Oct to mid-Dec and in winter (Tues–Fri) for lunch. Closed after Easter to June 10.

SKIING & HIKING

The resort is rich in **sports facilities.** Many skiers stay in Gstaad and go to one of the nearby ski resorts in the daytime. Cable cars take passengers to altitudes of 1,500 meters and 3,000 meters (5,000 and 10,000 ft.)—at the higher altitude there's skiing even in summer. Other facilities include tennis courts, heated indoor and outdoor pools, and some 320 kilometers (200 miles) of hiking trails. Many of these scenic trails are possible to walk or hike year-round (the tourist office will advise). The Gstaad International Tennis Tournament, held the second week in July, is the most important tennis event in Switzerland.

Skiers setting off from Gstaad have access to 70 lifts, mountain railroads, and gondolas. The altitude of Gstaad's highest skiable mountain is 2,000 meters (6,550 ft.), with a vertical drop of 1,084 meters (3,555 ft.). Most beginner and intermediate runs are east of the village in **Eggli,** a sunny, south-facing ski area that's reached by cable car.

Wispellan-Sanetch is good for afternoon skiing, and has lots of runs down to the village. At the summit is the Glacier des Diablerets, at 3,000 meters (9,900 ft.). **Wasserngrat,** prized by skilled skiers for its powder skiing on steep slopes, is reached from the south side of the resort.

Appendix

A Average Travel Times by Rail

AMSTERDAM TO
Berlin   8½ hr.
Cologne   3 hr.
Copenhagen   11½ hr.
Frankfurt   6 hr.
Munich   8½ hr.
Paris   4¼ hr.
Zurich   10 hr.

ATHENS TO
Munich   42½ hr.
Vienna   43 hr.

AVIGNON TO
Barcelona   6½ hr.
Paris   3½ hr.

BARCELONA TO
Madrid   7 hr.
Paris   11½ hr.

BATH TO
London   1¼ hr.

BERLIN TO
Frankfurt   6 hr.
Munich   7 hr.
Paris   11 hr.
Prague   6½ hr.

BERN TO
Interlaken   1 hr.
Milan   4½ hr.
Paris   4½ hr.
Zurich   1½ hr.

BORDEAUX TO
Paris   3 hr.

BRUSSELS TO
Frankfurt   5½ hr.
London   2¾ hr.
Paris   1½ hr.

BUDAPEST TO
Frankfurt   15½ hr.
Prague   9½ hr.
Vienna   4 hr.

CANNES TO
Paris   6 hr.

COPENHAGEN TO
Oslo   10½ hr.
Paris   15 hr.
Stockholm   8 hr.

EDINBURGH TO
London   4 hr.

FLORENCE TO
Geneva   8 hr.
Milan   3 hr.
Paris   12½ hr.
Rome   1½ hr.
Venice   3 hr.
Zurich   8 hr.

FRANKFURT TO
Munich   3½ hr.
Paris   6¼ hr.
Prague   8 hr.
Salzburg   5 hr.
Vienna   8 hr.
Zurich   5 hr.

GENEVA TO
Milan   4¼ hr.
Paris   3½ hr.
Venice   8 hr.

GLASGOW TO
London   5 hr.

GRANADA TO
Madrid   6½ hr.

HELSINKI TO
Stockholm   10 hr.

INNSBRUCK TO
Munich   3 hr.
Vienna   8 hr.
Zurich   5 hr.

LAUSANNE TO
Milan   4½ hr.
Paris   3¾ hr.

LILLEHAMMER TO
Oslo   2½ hr.

LISBON TO
Madrid   10 hr.

LONDON TO
Paris   3 hr.

LUXEMBOURG TO
Paris   4 hr.

LUZERNE TO
Paris   7½ hr.
Venice   8 hr.

LYON TO
Nice   5 hr.
Paris   2 hr.

MADRID TO
Malaga   7 hr.

MARSEILLE TO
Paris   4¼ hr.

MILAN TO
Nice   5 hr.
Paris (day)   6¾ hr.
Rome   5 hr.
Venice   3 hr.
Zurich   4½ hr.

MUNICH TO
Paris   8½ hr.
Prague   7½ hr.
Rome   11 hr.
Salzburg   2 hr.
Venice   9 hr.
Vienna   4¾ hr.
Zurich   5 hr.

NANTES TO
Paris   2 hr.

NAPLES TO
Rome   2 hr.

NICE TO
Paris   6½ hr.
Rome   10 hr.
Venice   10 hr.

OSLO TO
Stockholm   6½ hr.

PARIS TO
Rome   15 hr.
Salzburg   10 hr.
Strasbourg   4 hr.
Toulouse   5 hr.
Tours   1 hr.
Venice   12¼ hr.
Vienna   13½ hr.
Zurich   6 hr.

PISA TO
Rome   4 hr.

PRAGUE TO
Vienna   5 hr.

ROME TO
Siena   3 hr.
Venice   4½ hr.
Zurich   8½ hr.

SALZBURG TO
Vienna   4 hr.

VENICE TO
Vienna   8 hr.

VIENNA TO
Zurich   12 hr.

B Metric Conversions

LIQUID VOLUME

To convert	multiply by
U.S. gallons to liters	3.8
Liters to U.S. gallons	.26
U.S. gallons to imperial gallons	.83
Imperial gallons to U.S. gallons	1.20
Imperial gallons to liters	4.55
1 liter = .26 gal.	1 gal = 3.8 liters

DISTANCE

To convert	multiply by
Inches to centimeters	2.54
Centimeters to inches	.39
Feet to meters	.30
Meters to feet	3.28
Yards to meters	.91
Meters to yards	1.09
Miles to kilometers	1.61
Kilometers to miles	.62

1 mile = 1.6km   1km = .62 mile   1 ft.= .30m   1m = 3.3 ft.

WEIGHT

To convert	multiply by
Ounces to grams	28.35
Grams to ounces	.35
Pounds to kilograms	.45
Kilograms to pounds	2.20

1 oz. =28g   1g =.04 oz.   1 lb. =.4555kg   1kg =2.2 lb.

TEMPERATURE

°C	−18°	−10		0	10	20	30	40
°F	0°	10	20	32	40	50	60	70	80	90	100

To **convert °F to °C**, subtract 32 and multiply by ⅝ (.555).
To **convert °C to °F**, multiply by 1.8 and add 32.
32°F = 0°C

C Clothing Size Conversions

WOMEN'S CLOTHING

American	6	8	10	12	14	16
Continental	36	38	40	42	44	46
British	8	10	12	14	16	18

WOMEN'S SHOES

American	5	6	7	8	9	10
Continental	36	37	38	39	40	41
British	4	5	6	7	8	9

CHILDREN'S CLOTHING

American	3	4	5	6	6X
Continental	98	104	110	116	122
British	18	20	22	24	26

CHILDREN'S SHOES

American	8	9	10	11	12	13	1	2	3
Continental	24	25	27	28	29	30	32	33	34
British	7	8	9	10	11	12	13	1	2

MEN'S SUITS

American	34	36	38	40	42	44	46	48
Continental	44	46	48	50	52	54	56	58
British	34	36	38	40	42	44	46	48

MEN'S SHIRTS

American	$14\frac{1}{2}$	15	$15\frac{1}{2}$	16	$16\frac{1}{2}$	17	$17\frac{1}{2}$	18
Continental	37	38	39	41	42	43	44	45
British	$14\frac{1}{2}$	15	$15\frac{1}{2}$	16	$16\frac{1}{2}$	17	$17\frac{1}{2}$	18

MEN'S SHOES

American	7	8	9	10	11	12	13
Continental	$39\frac{1}{2}$	41	42	43	$44\frac{1}{2}$	46	47
British	6	7	8	9	10	11	12

Index

FROMMER'S® COMPLETE TRAVEL GUIDES

Alaska
Amsterdam
Argentina & Chile
Arizona
Atlanta
Australia
Austria
Bahamas
Barcelona, Madrid & Seville
Beijing
Belgium, Holland & Luxembourg
Bermuda
Boston
British Columbia & the Canadian Rockies
Budapest & the Best of Hungary
California
Canada
Cancún, Cozumel & the Yucatán
Cape Cod, Nantucket & Martha's Vineyard
Caribbean
Caribbean Cruises & Ports of Call
Caribbean Ports of Call
Carolinas & Georgia
Chicago
China
Colorado
Costa Rica
Denmark
Denver, Boulder & Colorado Springs
England
Europe

European Cruises & Ports of Call
Florida
France
Germany
Greece
Greek Islands
Hawaii
Hong Kong
Honolulu, Waikiki & Oahu
Ireland
Israel
Italy
Jamaica
Japan
Las Vegas
London
Los Angeles
Maryland & Delaware
Maui
Mexico
Montana & Wyoming
Montréal & Québec City
Munich & the Bavarian Alps
Nashville & Memphis
Nepal
New England
New Mexico
New Orleans
New York City
New Zealand
Nova Scotia, New Brunswick & Prince Edward Island
Oregon
Paris
Philadelphia & the Amish Country
Portugal

Prague & the Best of the Czech Republic
Provence & the Riviera
Puerto Rico
Rome
San Antonio & Austin
San Diego
San Francisco
Santa Fe, Taos & Albuquerque
Scandinavia
Scotland
Seattle & Portland
Shanghai
Singapore & Malaysia
South Africa
Southeast Asia
South Florida
South Pacific
Spain
Sweden
Switzerland
Texas
Thailand
Tokyo
Toronto
Tuscany & Umbria
USA
Utah
Vancouver & Victoria
Vermont, New Hampshire & Maine
Vienna & the Danube Valley
Virgin Islands
Virginia
Walt Disney World & Orlando
Washington, D.C.
Washington State

FROMMER'S® DOLLAR-A-DAY GUIDES

Australia from $50 a Day
California from $70 a Day
Caribbean from $70 a Day
England from $70 a Day
Europe from $70 a Day

Florida from $70 a Day
Hawaii from $70 a Day
Ireland from $60 a Day
Italy from $70 a Day
London from $85 a Day

New York from $80 a Day
Paris from $80 a Day
San Francisco from $60 a Day
Washington, D.C., from $70 a Day

FROMMER'S® PORTABLE GUIDES

Acapulco, Ixtapa & Zihuatanejo
Alaska Cruises & Ports of Call
Amsterdam
Australia's Great Barrier Reef
Bahamas
Baja & Los Cabos
Berlin
Boston
California Wine Country
Charleston & Savannah
Chicago

Dublin
Hawaii: The Big Island
Hong Kong
Houston
Las Vegas
London
Los Angeles
Maine Coast
Maui
Miami
New Orleans
New York City
Paris

Phoenix & Scottsdale
Portland
Puerto Rico
Puerto Vallarta, Manzanillo & Guadalajara
San Diego
San Francisco
Seattle
Sydney
Tampa & St. Petersburg
Vancouver
Venice
Washington, D.C.

FROMMER'S® NATIONAL PARK GUIDES

Family Vacations in the National Parks
Grand Canyon

National Parks of the American West
Rocky Mountain
Yellowstone & Grand Teton

Yosemite & Sequoia/ Kings Canyon
Zion & Bryce Canyon

FROMMER'S® MEMORABLE WALKS

Chicago	New York	San Francisco
London	Paris	Washington, D.C.

FROMMER'S® GREAT OUTDOOR GUIDES

Arizona & New Mexico	Northern California	Southern New England
New England	Southern California & Baja	Vermont & New Hampshire

FROMMER'S® BORN TO SHOP GUIDES

Born to Shop: France	Born to Shop: Italy	Born to Shop: New York
Born to Shop: Hong Kong, Shanghai & Beijing	Born to Shop: London	Born to Shop: Paris

FROMMER'S® IRREVERENT GUIDES

Amsterdam	Los Angeles	Seattle & Portland
Boston	Manhattan	Vancouver
Chicago	New Orleans	Walt Disney World
Las Vegas	Paris	Washington, D.C.
London	San Francisco	

FROMMER'S® BEST-LOVED DRIVING TOURS

America	France	New England
Britain	Germany	Scotland
California	Ireland	Spain
Florida	Italy	Western Europe

THE UNOFFICIAL GUIDES®

Bed & Breakfasts in California	Golf Vacations in the Eastern U.S.	New Orleans
Bed & Breakfasts in New England	The Great Smokey & Blue Ridge Mountains	New York City
Bed & Breakfasts in the Northwest	Inside Disney	Paris
Bed & Breakfasts in Southeast	Hawaii	San Francisco
Beyond Disney	Las Vegas	Skiing in the West
Branson, Missouri	London	Southeast with Kids
California with Kids	Mid-Atlantic with Kids	Walt Disney World
Chicago	Mini Las Vegas	Walt Disney World for Grown-ups
Cruises	Mini-Mickey	Walt Disney World for Kids
Disneyland	New England with Kids	Washington, D.C.
Florida with Kids		World's Best Diving Vacations

SPECIAL-INTEREST TITLES

Frommer's Britain's Best Bed & Breakfasts and Country Inns	Hanging Out in Europe
Frommer's France's Best Bed & Breakfasts and Country Inns	Hanging Out in France
	Hanging Out in Ireland
Frommer's Italy's Best Bed & Breakfasts and Country Inns	Hanging Out in Italy
	Hanging Out in Spain
Frommer's Caribbean Hideaways	Israel Past & Present
Frommer's Adventure Guide to Australia & New Zealand	Frommer's The Moon
	Frommer's New York City with Kids
Frommer's Adventure Guide to Central America	The New York Times' Guide to Unforgettable Weekends
Frommer's Adventure Guide to India & Pakistan	Places Rated Almanac
Frommer's Adventure Guide to South America	Retirement Places Rated
Frommer's Adventure Guide to Southeast Asia	Frommer's Road Atlas Britain
Frommer's Adventure Guide to Southern Africa	Frommer's Road Atlas Europe
Frommer's Gay & Lesbian Europe	Frommer's Washington, D.C., with Kids
Frommer's Exploring America by RV	Frommer's What the Airlines Never Tell You
Hanging Out in England	

Let Us Hear From You!

Dear Frommer's Reader,

You are our greatest resource in keeping our guides relevant, timely, and lively. We'd love to hear from you about your travel experiences—good or bad. Want to recommend a great restaurant or a hotel off the beaten path—or register a complaint? Any thoughts on how to improve the guide itself?

Please use this page to share your thoughts with me and mail it to the address below. Or if you like, send a FAX or e-mail me at frommersfeedback@hungryminds.com. And so that we can thank you—and keep you up on the latest developments in travel—we invite you to sign up for a free daily Frommer's e-mail travel update. Just write your e-mail address on the back of this page. Also, if you'd like to take a moment to answer a few questions about yourself to help us improve our guides, please complete the following quick survey. (We'll keep that information confidential.)

Thanks for your insights.

Yours sincerely,

Michael Spring, *Publisher*

Name (Optional) _____

Address _____

_____

City_____ State_____ ZIP _____

Name of Frommer's Travel Guide _____

Comments _____

_____

_____

_____

_____

_____

_____

_____

_____

_____

_____

_____

Please tell us a little about yourself so that we can serve you and the Frommer's community better. We will keep this information confidential.

Age: ( )18-24; ( )25-39; ( )40-49; ( )50-55; ( )Over 55

Income: ( )Under $25,000; ( )$25,000-$50,000; ( )$50,000-$100,000; ( )Over $100,000

I am: ( )Single, never married; ( )Married, with children; ( )Married, without children; ( )Divorced; ( )Widowed

Number of people in my household: ( )1; ( )2; ( )3; ( )4; ( )5 or more

Number of people in my household under 18: ( )1; ( )2; ( )3; ( )4; ( )5 or more

I am ( )a student; ( )employed full-time; ( )employed part-time; ( )not employed at this time; ( )retired; ( )other

I took ( )0; ( )1; ( )2; ( )3; ( )4 or more leisure trips in the past 12 months

My last vacation was ( )a weekend; ( )1 week; ( )2 weeks; ( )3 or more weeks

My last vacation was to ( )the U.S.; ( )Canada; ( )Mexico; ( )Europe; ( )Asia; ( )South America; ( )Central America; ( )The Caribbean; ( )Africa; ( )Middle East; ( )Australia/New Zealand

( )I would; ( )would not buy a Frommer's Travel Guide for business travel

I access the Internet ( )at home; ( )at work; ( )both; ( )I do not use the Internet

I used the Internet to do research for my last trip. ( )Yes; ( )No

I used the Internet to book accommodations or air travel on my last trip. ( )Yes; ( )No

My favorite travel site is ( )frommers.com; ( )travelocity.com; ( )expedia.com;

other_____

I use Frommer's Travel Guides ( )always; ( )sometimes; ( )seldom

I usually buy ( )1; ( )2; ( )more than 2 guides when I travel

Other guides I use include _____

What's the most important thing we could do to improve Frommer's Travel Guides?

_____

_____

_____

_____

Yes, please send me a daily e-mail travel update. My e-mail address is

_____